AGE, WEIGHT & DISTANCE TABLE

Timeform's scale of weight-for-age for the flat

Dist	Age	Jan 1-16	17-31	Feb 1-16	17-28	Mar 1-16	17-31	Apr 1-16	17-30	May 1-16	17-31	June 1-16	17-30
5f	4	10-0	10-0	10-0	10-0	10-0	10-0	10-0	10-0	10-0	10-0	10-0	10-0
	3	9—5	9—5	9—6	9—7	9—7	9—8	9—8	9—9	9—9	9-10	9-10	9—11
	2						8—0	8—1	8—3	8—4	8—5	8—6	8—7
6f	4	10-0	10-0	10-0	10-0	10-0	10-0	10-0	10-0	10-0	10-0	10-0	10-0
	3	9—2	9—3	9—4	9—5	9—5	9—6	9—7	9—7	9—8	9—8	9—9	9—9
	2									8—0	8—2	8—3	8—4
7f	4	9-13	9-13	10-0	10-0	10-0	10-0	10-0	10-0	10-0	10-0	10-0	10-0
	3	9—0	9—1	9—2	9—3	9—4	9—4	9—5	9—6	9—6	9—7	9—8	9—8
	2											7-13	8—1
1m	4	9-13	9-13	9-13	9-13	10-0	10-0	10-0	10-0	10-0	10-0	10-0	10-0
	3	8-12	8-13	9—0	9—1	9—2	9—2	9—3	9—4	9—5	9—5	9—6	9—7
	2												
9f	4	9-12	9-12	9-12	9-13	9-13	9-13	9-13	10-0	10-0	10-0	10-0	10-0
	3	8-10	8-11	8-12	8-13	9—0	9—1	9—2	9—2	9—3	9—4	9—5	9—5
	2												
1¼m	4	9-11	9-12	9-12	9-12	9-13	9-13	9-13	9-13	9-13	10-0	10-0	10-0
	3	8—8	8—9	8-10	8-11	8-12	8-13	9—0	9—1	9—2	9—2	9—3	9—4
	2												
11f	4	9-10	9-11	9-11	9-12	9-12	9-12	9-13	9-13	9-13	9-13	9-13	10-0
	3	8—6	8—7	8—8	8—9	8-10	8-11	8-12	8-13	9—0	9—1	9—2	9—2
1½m	4	9-10	9-10	9-10	9-11	9-11	9-12	9-12	9-12	9-13	9-13	9-13	9-13
	3	8—4	8—5	8—6	8—7	8—8	8—9	8-10	8-11	8-12	8-13	9—0	9—1
13f	4	9—9	9—9	9-10	9-10	9-11	9-11	9-11	9-12	9-12	9-12	9-13	9-13
	3	8—2	8—3	8—4	8—5	8—7	8—8	8—9	8-10	8-11	8-12	8-13	9—0
1¾m	4	9—8	9—8	9—9	9—9	9-10	9-10	9-11	9-11	9-12	9-12	9-12	9-13
	3	8—0	8—2	8—3	8—4	8—5	8—6	8—7	8—8	8—9	8-10	8-11	8-12
15f	4	9—7	9—8	9—8	9—9	9—9	9-10	9-10	9-11	9-11	9-11	9-12	9-12
	3	7-13	8—0	8—1	8—2	8—4	8—5	8—6	8—7	8—8	8—9	8-10	8-11
2m	4	9—6	9—7	9—7	9—8	9—9	9—9	9-10	9-10	9-11	9-11	9-11	9-12
	3	7-11	7-12	7-13	8—1	8—2	8—3	8—4	8—5	8—6	8—7	8—8	8—9
2¼m	4	9—5	9—5	9—6	9—7	9—7	9—8	9—9	9—9	9-10	9-10	9-10	9-11
	3	7—8	7—9	7-11	7-12	7-13	8—0	8—2	8—3	8—4	8—5	8—6	8—7
2½m	4	9—3	9—4	9—5	9—6	9—6	9—7	9—7	9—8	9—9	9—9	9-10	9-10
	3	7—5	7—7	7—8	7—9	7-11	7-12	7-13	8—1	8—2	8—3	8—4	8—5

For 5-y-o's and older, use 10-0 in all cases
Race distances in the above tables are shown only at 1 furlong intervals.
For races over odd distances, the nearest distance shown in the table should be used:
thus for races of 1m to 1m 109 yards, use the table weights for 1m;
for 1m 110 yards to 1m 219 yards use the 9f table

**The age, weight and distance table covering July to December
appears on the end paper at the back of the book**

RACEHORSES
OF 2007

Price £75.00

A TIMEFORM PUBLICATION

CONTENTS

The age, weight and distance tables, for use in applying the ratings in races involving horses of different ages, appear on the end papers at the front and back of the book

Compiled and produced by

G. Greetham (Publishing Editor), C. S. Williams (Managing Editor & Handicapper), J. Ingles (Essays & 'Top Horses Abroad'), E. K. Wilkinson (Essays & Editor), A. J. Mealor (Handicapper & Editor), S. T. Heath (Essays & Editor for pedigrees), D. W. Johnson, S. Molyneux (Handicappers), J. Early, D. P. Cleary, H. W. J. Bowles (Essays), P. Jupp, J. M. Lynch, J. A. Todd, M. R. Dixon (Short Commentaries), S. Wright (pedigrees, database updates), G. Crowther, G. Johnstone (proof checking), H. Brewer, M. Hall, D. Holdsworth, W. Muncaster, A-M. Stevens, R. Todd, C. Wright (Production)

© **Portway Press Limited 2008**   ISBN 978 1 901570 68 7

Racehorses of 2007

Introduction

The works of Banksy, the celebrated British street artist, have appeared as far afield as New York and the Israeli West Bank (where he left images, on the Palestinian side of the wall, of a ladder and of children making a hole). In April, a graffiti removal team painted over Banksy's iconic image, near Old Street tube station, of a scene from the film *Pulp Fiction*, a work estimated to be worth more than £300,000. A Transport for London spokesman acknowledged that there were some who viewed Banksy's work as legitimate art, but that its graffiti removal teams were 'staffed by professional cleaners, not professional art critics.' Zeal, it is said, is fit only for wise men, but is found mostly in fools, something which arguably applied not only to graffiti removers employed by Transport for London, but also to some of the team which conducted the long-running City of London police investigations into so-called 'race fixing' in horse racing. The graffiti painting in question portrayed the mob characters, played by Samuel L. Jackson and John Travolta, clutching bananas instead of guns. The City of London police and the Crown Prosecution Service believed they were armed to the teeth—the trial began with 40,000 pages of evidence including 1,300 statements—to secure the conviction of jockeys Kieren Fallon, Fergal Lynch and Darren Williams, together with other defendants Miles Rodgers, Phillip Sherkle and Shaun Lynch, on charges of conspiracy to defraud (all of which were denied). In the end, the primed guns turned out to have all the firepower of bananas as the biggest criminal investigation in the history of British sport—estimated to have cost the public purse £10m—collapsed when Mr Justice Forbes called an end to proceedings early in December in a trial that had started in Court 12 at the Central Criminal Court, Old Bailey, two months earlier.

The defences were not even called upon to present their respective cases as the jury was directed to acquit the defendants who 'had no case to answer' once the prosecution case had been heard. Judge Forbes said that the prosecution's expert witness, an Australian racing steward Ray Murrihy, had fallen 'far, far short' of proving its case. Murrihy's admission that he lacked knowledge of British racing and its rules was described by the judge as

Racing's attention was fixed on the Central Criminal Court, Old Bailey, from early-October

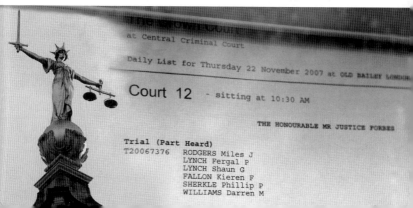

'extraordinary ... given that he was purporting to give evidence about twenty-seven races run in the UK according to UK racing rules ... it is tantamount to Mr Murrihy disqualifying himself in giving evidence in relation to the suspect races.' The rest of the evidence—such as records of telephone contact and text messages, the evidence of covert surveillance, and documentation showing allegedly suspicious betting patterns—was nowhere near strong enough to prove a criminal conspiracy and was, said the judge, 'almost entirely consistent with normal social intercourse or the innocent transmission of racing tips or information by the jockeys.' Businessman Miles Rodgers (whom the court heard was a compulsive heavy gambler and also bet massive sums on the outcome of reality TV events such as *The X-Factor*) was said to have staked over £2m with Betfair, some of it using pseudonyms, on horses to lose in the races concerned. The information provided by Betfair's 'audit trail' had been an important factor in the Jockey Club's deciding to hand over the case to the police in March 2004, at the same time as Rodgers was warned off (and therefore no longer bound by the rules of racing) for two years for laying horses owned by his racing club on the exchanges, a practice against Jockey Club rules (the Horseracing Regulatory Authority took over the regulatory functions of the Jockey Club in April 2006 and was merged in July 2007 with the body responsible for promoting the interests of racing, the British Horseracing Board, forming the British Horseracing Authority).

That the three jockeys involved were found innocent of the criminal charges brought against them came as no surprise, judged purely on the evidence of the races themselves, which took place between December 2002 and September 2004. The prosecution had to prove that the jockeys had 'agreed not to permit horses to run on their merits in that riding practices would, if necessary, be used which would interfere with the running of those horses and thereby affect the results of those races.' In effect, the jockeys had to be shown to have contravened rule 157 of the *Rules of Racing*, the most serious of the four so-called 'non-triers' rules, which deals with deliberately preventing a horse from winning. Without proof of the active involvement of the jockeys in 'stopping' horses, there was no conspiracy. In the twenty-seven races about which the prosecution presented evidence, only two of the rides under question had been the subject of a stewards' inquiry at the time, those involving Cd Europe in February 2003 at Southwell and Ballinger Ridge (on whom Rodgers had a liability of more than £72,000) in March 2004 at Lingfield. The notorious Ballinger Ridge case, in which Fallon eased up believing he had done enough to win, had been dealt with under a less serious rule, Fallon found to have been negligent in dropping his hands and receiving a twenty-one-day ban. Further investigations into claims that Fallon had accepted money or benefit in kind for tips, as alleged by a Sunday newspaper, came to nothing.

The witness Murrihy said he would have ordered an inquiry into thirteen of the twenty-seven races, but the defence was ready to call experts to challenge Murrihy's opinion. The prosecution's own witnesses included the trainers of some of the horses involved, Sir Michael Stoute, John Dunlop, Luca Cumani, Michael Bell and Alan Jarvis, but, far from criticising the rides and agreeing the horses were 'non-triers', or the rides were consistent with such a possibility, they presented very different evidence. Timeform's managing director Jim McGrath, a British Horseracing Authority director, had also been interviewed by the City of London police to obtain his views on all twenty-seven races, including the thirteen over which Murrihy had concerns. McGrath's views were mostly completely at variance with Murrihy's interpretation and the prosecution never called him. In relation to McGrath's evidence, the City of London officer in charge of the investigation, acting detective inspector Mark

Manning, was accused in court by Fergal Lynch's QC of failing to disclose correctly to the defence 'material which might undermine the prosecution case or support the defence case.' Manning agreed it would be 'unfortunate' to suppress or hide such evidence, and also described as 'an oversight' the failure of the police to ask for a copy of the notes McGrath had made in advance of their meeting, though the defence suggested this might have been because the opinions did not fit the prosecution case. The lack of detailed knowledge of racing and betting matters shown by investigating officers was exposed in cross-examination (Manning also maintained in court that he was unsure of Jim McGrath's 'expert status'). The defence for Fallon, who had ridden in seventeen of the alleged 'fixed' races, pointed out the absurdity of Fallon's being involved in a plot in which he won five of the races he had allegedly been trying to 'throw', a considerably higher percentage of winners to rides (29.4%) than that he had achieved in all races between 2002 and 2004 (19%); the prosecution claimed Fallon had cost Rodgers and his syndicate backers—there was talk of unknown, shadowy conspirators in Spain—£338,000 in the five races he won, which included the 2004 Lockinge Stakes on Russian Rhythm.

There was speculation, after the court case ended, that admissions and evidence presented might give rise to separate charges against some of the accused under the rules of racing (associating with a disqualified person, use of unregistered mobile phones etc), but the British Horseracing Authority went no further at the time than saying it was 'reviewing all available evidence presented.' Its statement also stressed that the investigation had been 'wholly' out of its hands once the case had been taken over by the police (though the security department had assisted with information and intelligence when requested). Lynch and Williams were given leave to reapply for their licences (which had been withdrawn automatically once charges had been brought), and Fallon, who was licenced by the Irish Turf Club, was told that the ban on his riding in Britain was lifted with immediate effect. Fallon's ban had applied to Britain only (though some other jurisdictions had decided independently that he could not ride) and he had taken the regulatory authority to the High Court after his appeal against the ban had been dismissed. Fallon's High Court

Kieren Fallon was backed publicly by the Coolmore triumvirate of Michael Tabor (left), Derrick Smith (centre) and John Magnier (right), but he was unable to ride their runners in Britain (the trio are pictured after their 1,2,3 in the St James's Palace Stakes)

action also failed. Lynch and Williams received compensation while banned, based on previous earnings, but Fallon received none, as he had no 'contractual relationship' with the Horseracing Regulatory Authority. Fallon's legal team raised the possibility of action for damages after his acquittal, but there were two periods during the ban when Fallon would have been unable to ride in Britain, the first when he was serving a worldwide ban between December 2006 and June 2007 after failing a drugs test in France, and the second while on trial. Fallon continued to earn substantial sums from riding—principally in Ireland and France—in the other periods between July 2006 (when he was charged) and October 2007.

The acquittal of Fallon, Lynch and Williams (and the dropping of the Hillside Girl case, stemming from the same investigations, and involving trainer Alan Berry) lifted a dark cloud that had cast a shadow over racing and brought unwelcome media coverage before and during the trial, portraying racing as corrupt. The extensive TV and media coverage at the conclusion of the trial, it must be said, went only some way to repairing the damage, suspicions about the integrity of racing certain to linger with the public at large. An independent review led by Ben Gunn (a former Chief Constable of Cambridgeshire) which reported in 2003 found no evidence of institutional or widespread corruption in racing and it is important to stress that the majority of the other jockeys banned or suspended after a so-called 'corruption crackdown' by the Horse-racing Regulatory Authority in 2006 were not found guilty of stopping horses from winning, most of them involving offences such as the passing of informa-tion for reward. Two more jockeys, Tony Culhane (a year) and Dean Mernagh (nine months), were suspended in another case heard some time after *Racehorses of 2006* had gone to print after admitting aiding and abetting former jump jockey and PA race reporter Gary Lyons (warned off for two years) and Culhane's father-in-law Dave Watkins (five years) by passing information.

The understandable outrage of those who bore the brunt of criminal invest-igations and suffered 'ill-founded vilification' inevitably focussed attention on the credibility of the sport's security arrangements and raised the issue of whether the evidence presented (much of it inferential) and the judgements arrived at in some of the internal disciplinary cases (which have to be held in private) were beyond question. How many would have been investigated had it not been for unusual betting patterns noticed in the monitoring of accounts of people with whom the accused jockeys, in some cases, denied ever having

Continuing to ride in Ireland and on the Continent, Fallon won Europe's richest race, the Prix de l'Arc de Triomphe, on Dylan Thomas; the horse survived a lengthy stewards' inquiry after drifting right in the closing stages (stable-companion Soldier of Fortune, rail, was one of those who suffered interference)

personal contact? Is there reason to believe that, collectively, jockeys are any more opportunistic than other groups involved in racing? It might be argued that they make convenient scapegoats. That said, things have certainly moved on since the days when 'a little honest fiddling within the Rules' was tolerated —the new Gambling Act makes it an offence to cheat—and owners, trainers, jockeys, stable employees and others need to be fully aware of their obligations under the code of conduct belatedly issued in 2007 by the British Horseracing Authority which purports to outline acceptable and unacceptable uses of inside information. There are grey areas and some of the restrictions appear to require powers of extrasensory perception, in being able to tell, for example, whether a person might use information imparted in casual conversation for 'a corrupt betting purpose'. Mum's the word seems the best advice under the circumstances, unless information is being put into the public domain.

For Kieren Fallon, any feeling of relief at being cleared in the Old Bailey case must have been short lived. He walked out of court into new revelations that he was facing the prospect of another worldwide suspension after failing a drugs test in France in August on the day he won the Prix Morny on **Myboycharlie**. Tests revealed traces of a banned substance, reportedly cocaine. Fallon's ban was confirmed at eighteen months by the French racing authorities after the turn of the year and one of its first consequences was a decision by Coolmore to end Fallon's position as its retained rider (the job has gone to Johnny Murtagh for 2008). There was a widespread feeling throughout in Ireland that Fallon had been treated unfairly in being banned by the British racing authorities and he was received warmly during the year at Irish racecourses, getting a tumultuous welcome from the Tipperary crowd on his return in June from his first drugs ban, and an even bigger one when he made his first ride back—on The Bogberry—a winning one. The Coolmore partners put their faith in Fallon's innocence of the criminal charges brought against him by putting him up on the Ballydoyle stable's horses whenever and wherever he was able to ride them. The day before the Old Bailey proceedings were due to get under way (the trial was delayed when a court room was flooded by a burst pipe), Fallon rode **Dylan Thomas** to victory in the Prix de l'Arc de Triomphe.

The Arc win crowned a fine campaign for Dylan Thomas who became only the sixth horse to win both the Arc and Britain's midsummer championship the King George VI and Queen Elizabeth Stakes in the same season. The Arc, with a new sponsor, is set to become the world's richest race on turf in 2008, while the King George, in sixtieth place on the world list in 2007, remains in need of a boost (the essay on Dylan Thomas examines the status of the King George). With **Youmzain** filling second behind Dylan Thomas at Ascot and Longchamp, it was the first time the winner and runner-up in the King George had gone on to fill the same places in the Arc. Youmzain's place money in the Arc and in the Dubai Sheema Classic (the joint richest turf race in the world in 2007), along with placed efforts in other Group 1s overseas, helped his trainer Mick Channon to top the list of British trainers by earnings on foreign soil in 2007, just ahead of Sir Michael Stoute whose big-race winners overseas included **Notnowcato**, **Mountain High** and **Echelon**. It was, however, a relatively unexceptional year overall for British-trained winners abroad with prize-money earnings of £9,147,233, according to the annual figures produced by the International Racing Bureau. Ireland (£3,605,329), France (£2,158,224) and the Dubai International Carnival (£1,479,582) were the three most lucrative sources of foreign prize money, the last-named series providing a focus for international competition in the first part of the year. **Invasor** won the Dubai World Cup, the world's richest race, and German middle-distance performer

Quijano first made his mark on the international stage by winning three races over the course of the Carnival (stretching an unbeaten sequence to ten). At the opposite end of the year, European-trained challengers drew a rare blank at the Breeders' Cup, where **George Washington** (whose essay discusses the growing international mistrust of American racing) broke down in the Classic and had to be put down. There was, however, success for Europe at Sha Tin in December when the well-travelled **Doctor Dino** won the Hong Kong Vase and **Ramonti** took the Hong Kong Cup.

Godolphin's private purchases of prominent horses in training are reported regularly each autumn, but the purchase of Ramonti from Italy at the end of 2006 could easily have gone unnoticed. No-one could have failed to notice him in 2007, though, when he had a superb run in the top mile races, winning four Group 1s including the Sussex Stakes and the Queen Elizabeth II Stakes and accounting for a third of the total prize money won in Britain by Godolphin (leading owner in Britain for the seventh time). Ramonti's successful season owed much to the tactical awareness and strength of Frankie Dettori, whose victory in the Derby on **Authorized**, after fourteen losing rides in the race, brought racing much needed publicity that showed the sport in a good light. Dettori also won the Prix du Jockey Club the next day on **Lawman** and the Prix de Diane the following weekend on the Sheikh Mohammed-owned **West Wind**. The wide-ranging essay on Authorized, who reasserted his status (after defeat by Notnowcato in the Eclipse) by beating Dylan Thomas and Notnowcato in the International at York, examines the unprecedented spending on horses in training in the second half of 2007 by Sheikh Mohammed's Darley operation (which acquired Authorized as a future stallion in June).

The TV audience for the Derby of 3m (34% share of the terrestrial audience watching at the time) was the first fall after a steady growth in recent years, but that was attributed partly to the fine, warm weather on the day. The summer, though, was one of the wettest since records began, with widespread flooding in June and July bringing misery to many parts of the country (some victims were still in temporary homes as the year came to an end). For racing, the unrelenting wet weather resulted in the loss of thirty-five meetings in June, July and August because of waterlogging (in some cases, flooding of the whole racecourse). Haydock lost its three-day meeting in July and Timeform Charity Day at York in June was also a washout (despite the abandonment of the raceday, £196,033 was still raised from a record-breaking eve-of-the-meeting dinner, the last organised by Reg Griffin, who retired as chairman of Timeform in November after fifty years with the company).

Despite the unseasonable summer weather, racecourse attendances overall showed only a small drop on 2006, reaching a total of 5,802,698 for the year. No sooner had the weather finally settled down in September than racing was reminded of 2001, with foot and mouth restrictions in force after an outbreak—thankfully fairly short-lived—in Surrey. Horseboxes and cars had to be disinfected at meetings at Kempton and Sandown in mid-September, and with Ascot only just outside the designated protection zone any further spread would have threatened its three-day September meeting. The crowds were down on four of the five days of the Royal meeting (most noticeably on the first two days), but the £10m alterations carried out to remedy complaints the previous year about viewing from the new grandstand and about the unfinished silver ring were generally well received. Overall, the Royal Ascot crowds fell 12%, from 312,700 in 2006 to 274,970.

The racing at the Royal meeting was superb, as usual. Ramonti's triumph in a blanket finish to the Queen Anne Stakes and a one, two, three for Aidan O'Brien-trained runners **Excellent Art**, **Duke of Marmalade** and **Astronomer**

Royal in the St James's Palace Stakes were first-day highlights, but they were just topped by the victory of **Miss Andretti** in the King's Stand Stakes. She became the third Australian sprinter to win at Royal Ascot since 2003, following Choisir (King's Stand and Golden Jubilee) and Takeover Target (King's Stand), their presence a result partly of the dramatic changes to world sprinting brought about by the creation of the Global Sprint Challenge. Takeover Target, fourth in the latest King's Stand, went down by a head to **Soldier's Tale** in the Golden Jubilee later in the week. The Prince of Wales's Stakes on Wednesday has arguably become Royal Ascot's premier race and it produced the best performance of the year in Europe as **Manduro**, described by his trainer Andre Fabre as the best he has trained, beat Dylan Thomas and Notnowcato. Manduro won Group 1s at a mile, nine furlongs and a mile and a quarter in a five-race unbeaten sequence before his career was ended by injury in his preparatory race for the Prix de l'Arc de Triomphe, for which he would have started a warm favourite. Gold Cup day, the only one of the five for which attendances were up (74,172, compared to 72,947 in 2006), saw **Yeats** beat a thoroughly representative field to win the Gold Cup for the second time. Only Sagaro has landed a hat-trick of victories and Yeats, who was beaten afterwards at odds on by the Gold Cup third **Le Miracle** in the Prix du Cadran, will be back in 2008 to try to emulate Sagaro.

The best performance by a Cup horse in the latest season, however, came from Yeats's stablemate **Septimus** in the Doncaster Cup, the day before the stable's top three-year-old stayer **Honolulu**, who had put up the best performance in any handicap in Britain since 1999 when going down to **Purple Moon** in the Ebor, was third behind **Lucarno** in the St Leger. The St Leger attracted a record crowd for recent times of 31,000 on its return to a redeveloped Doncaster. On the same day, Yeats won the Irish St Leger (from another stablemate, the Coronation Cup winner **Scorpion**) to complete a full set of British and Irish classics for Aidan O'Brien. O'Brien was champion trainer in both Britain (for the third time) and Ireland (for the tenth) in the latest season when his horses won fifteen Group 1s. There is plenty about O'Brien's career achievements in the essays on Yeats and Irish Derby winner **Soldier of Fortune**.

Ballydoyle also housed Europe's top middle-distance filly **Peeping Fawn**, who turned the tables on the Oaks winner **Light Shift** in both the Irish Oaks and the Nassau Stakes. Light Shift's Oaks victory over Peeping Fawn provided one of the human interest stories of the racing year, Henry Cecil enjoying his first classic victory for seven years. Neither Peeping Fawn nor Light Shift ran against the colts in the top open races—a subject touched on in the extended entry on Peeping Fawn—but the top three-year-old filly at a mile **Darjina** put up her best performance when beating Ramonti and George Washington in the Prix du Moulin. Back in the spring, Darjina foiled an ambitious tilt by **Finsceal**

Manduro put up the best performance of the year in Europe
when winning the Prince of Wales's Stakes at Royal Ascot from Dylan Thomas

Beo at a European Guineas treble, Darjina collaring the impressive Newmarket winner in the last strides in the Poule d'Essai des Pouliches. Finsceal Beo went on to add the Irish One Thousand Guineas but, like **Cockney Rebel** who landed the Anglo-Irish Two Thousand Guineas double, she didn't win again after the Curragh. The first three in the Two Thousand Guineas—**Vital Equine** and **Dutch Art** filled the places—were all sold relatively cheaply as yearlings, while Authorized and **Eagle Mountain**, first and second in the Derby, were also purchased at public auction. Dutch Art, who reverted to sprinting later in the season, was the Guineas runner with the best two-year-old form after the defection of winter favourites Teofilo (injured) and Holy Roman Emperor (pressed into stud duty when George Washington experienced fertility problems).

The lack of suitable opportunities for good three-year-old sprinters early in the year is highlighted in the essay on the Group 1-winning two-year-old **Dark Angel**, who has been sent to stud without racing at three. The excessive generosity of the BHA's weight-for-age scale did produce a victory for a two-year-old against older sprinters, **Kingsgate Native** becoming only the second of his age to win the Nunthorpe in half a century. The 2006 Prix de l'Abbaye winner **Desert Lord** found the concession of 24 lb to Kingsgate Native beyond him but, in finishing second, he put up one of the best performances of the year over five furlongs in Europe before managing only third (beaten by Kingsgate Native again) when trying to repeat his Abbaye victory. The latest Prix de l'Abbaye winner was British-trained **Benbaun** whose best form in a long career has been shown outside Britain. The year's best sprinter, however, was **Sakhee's Secret**, winner of the six-furlong July Cup from Dutch Art and **Red Clubs**. The last-named earned Group 1 success in the Sprint Cup at Haydock, but his win was overshadowed somewhat by controversy over the state of the going (a subject dealt with in the entry on beaten favourite Sakhee's Secret, and also touched on under Peeping Fawn).

The two-year-old list was headed by Irish-trained **New Approach**, whose unbeaten campaign mirrored that of Teofilo (who didn't race at three), his victories including the National Stakes at the Curragh and the Dewhurst. New

Henry Cecil and Aidan O'Brien (who won the trainers' championship in Britain for the third time) exchange pleasantries in the winner's enclosure after Light Shift and Peeping Fawn had fought out the finish of the Oaks

Approach will be racing in the colours of Princess Haya as a three-year-old, Sheikh Mohammed having purchased him, as well as taking a major share in **Raven's Pass** before he finished third in the Dewhurst. With the Jean-Luc Lagardere winner **Rio de La Plata**, the Racing Post winner **Ibn Khaldun** and Dewhurst runner-up **Fast Company** (transferred from Brian Meehan) all with Godolphin, the Maktoum family owns or has a sizeable interest in the first five in the betting on the Two Thousand Guineas. The two-year-old colts from Ballydoyle had a substandard season by their usual very high standards, something discussed in the essays on **Henrythenavigator** and on the stable's top filly **Listen**. Coolmore bolstered its team by purchasing a majority share in Peeping Fawn's half-brother **Thewayyouare** as a future stallion after he had won the Criterium International at Saint-Cloud. Andre Fabre will continue to train Thewayyouare as a three-year-old, with the Irish Derby on the agenda. Fabre, who was champion trainer in France for the twenty-first successive year, also has a good classic prospect among his fillies in **Proviso**, second to Listen in the Fillies' Mile at Ascot. A French stable won the Cheveley Park, Pascal Bary saddling **Natagora**. Bary has been at the top of his profession for fifteen years in France but, for most of that time, has not paid much attention to Britain.

Fabre's closest pursuers in the latest season in the trainers' table in France were the Provincial trainers Jean-Claude Rouget (whose record-breaking career is discussed in the write-up on Champion Stakes winner **Literato**) and Henri-Alex Pantall who had his first Group 1 winner in thirty years of training with West Wind (in whose essay more details can be found). Another trainer in the Provinces, Francois Rohaut, saddled the Prix Vermeille winner **Mrs Lindsay**. The strength of the market for top fillies and racemares was illustrated when the French five-year-old **Satwa Queen** made a European record for a filly or mare in training of 3,400,000 guineas at the December Sales. Satwa Queen won the Prix de l'Opera on the Arc day programme which has been staging six Group 1s and been shaping up more and more into a 'European Breeders' Cup'. The six Group 1s featured winners from France, Britain, Ireland and Germany in the latest season (more details in Satwa Queen's essay).

As in France, where Deauville is staging more listed events on its relatively new all-weather track, there has been an increase in the number of listed races on the all-weather in Britain, which also now has several Group 3 events, the improvement in quality reflected by more pictures in this Annual of races on the all-weather. There were a number of smart performances in the latest season, including those of Areyoutalkingtome, under top weight in a handicap at Lingfield in February, Gentleman's Deal, in the Winter Derby, and Dansant, in two listed races at Kempton at the end of the year. One of Dansant's listed races was inside the turf season, but none of the others counted for the Jockeys' Association's version of the jockeys' championship which is decided over the turf season and resulted in a dead heat between Jamie Spencer and Seb Sanders on one hundred and ninety winners each. The media attention on the closing stages of a see-sawing 'title race' was created by the most exciting run-in since Cauthen pipped Eddery by two in 1987 (before the arrival of the all-weather and all-the-year-round Flat racing).

While Spencer confessed to being 'glad it was all over' after riding the winner of the final race Inchnadamph to draw level at Doncaster on November Handicap day, Sanders went on to Wolverhampton's evening fixture (outside the period chosen for the championship) where he won a maiden for his retaining stable. Sanders was one of the riders who objected to the restriction, imposed by the BHB at the request of the Jockeys' Association, that jockeys can ride at only nine meetings a week [though not including meetings outside

Britain] from mid-April to the end of the evening racing period in August. Sanders (213) and Spencer (207) both rode over two hundred winners in Britain in the calendar year, only the second time that has happened in British racing. Frankie Dettori (233) and Jason Weaver (200) both made a flying start on the all-weather in 1994 (the Jockeys' Association's turf season title was not inaugurated until 1997) and Dettori had an astonishing 1,317 rides (still a British record), Weaver having 1,085. Sanders had 1,244 rides in Britain in 2007, Spencer 1,040 (Chris Catlin had 1,292). Although all-weather meetings are poorly attended (the average at the 306 fixtures in 2007 was 1,084, compared to 6,113 for the 539 Flat turf fixtures), they have become an integral part of the sport. Winners at all-weather meetings that take place within the period defined as the turf season have counted towards the Jockeys' Association's championship up to now, but, within minutes of the razzamatazz that attended the crowning of Flat racing's champions at Doncaster, it was revealed that changes to the way the jockeys' title is determined were being considered, with run-of-the-mill races possibly counting for less than pattern events and other big races from 2009. Meanwhile, the trainers, who supported a 2007 championship which was also officially decided over the turf season, now have some among their number who are campaigning for a return to a championship based on prize money throughout the year.

At one time, until Dubai Holding signed up in September to a two-year deal to take over sponsorship of the production costs for eighty days' racing on Channel 4, it looked as if terrestrial coverage of the sport was under serious threat (BBC TV shows only around twenty days' racing nowadays and has also scaled down its Ceefax racing service). Much of racing's income is dependent on an agreement linked to the profits made on the sport by bookmakers. Betting increases significantly when racing is on terrestrial TV which also makes individual race sponsorship more attractive. With racing's contribution to bookmakers' turnover now below 50%, the sport needs to improve its relations with the bookmakers to tackle the marketing of racing to the betting public. Research shows that racing is regarded as 'too complicated' by most young people who are much more likely nowadays to have their first bet on football or even on the fixed odds betting terminals that feature so prominently in betting shops. Ladbrokes chief executive Chris Bell hit the nail

Frankie Dettori, pictured with his Derby trophy, earned the most prize money, while Seb Sanders and Jamie Spencer dead-heated for the Jockeys' Association title decided by number of winners in the turf season

Greg Fairley (left), attached to Mark Johnston's stable, was champion apprentice with seventy-six winners; Kevin Darley, who had a long association with the Johnston stable, announced his retirement at the end of the season

on the head when he said 'If we poured as much energy into working together as we do into damaging each other, the results would be amazing.'

Meanwhile, the income from the VAT-free levy on betting on British horseracing (three quarters of which comes from Ladbrokes, Hills and Coral) has dropped further (from a peak of £102m in 2003/4) to £85.5m for 2007/8 from £90m in 2006/7. A row over the 'unreasonable new costs' of TurfTV, which has broken the twenty-year monopoly of SIS over the provision of pictures for betting shops, resulted in failure to agree a levy scheme for 2008/9 which had to be referred to the Government (which decided to repeat the 2007/8 scheme). The extension of the levy (its planned abolition was announced as far back as 2000) was agreed while the future funding of racing was being examined. The emergence of Turf TV, set up by the Racing UK-aligned courses (which include nearly all the top ones), in a joint venture with Alphameric, perhaps points the way to a long-term commercial solution. The leading bookmakers now want the levy ditched, having supported its extension.

The chief executive of the Levy Board, Sir Tristram Ricketts, who died in November aged sixty-one, was among those mourned by racing in 2007. The *Racehorses* annual suffered the loss of one of its most perceptive and entertaining writers, Paul Morrell, who died in tragic circumstances in July at the age of only forty-six. Retirements included Cockney Rebel's trainer Geoff Huffer, the former trainer of Excellent Art, Neville Callaghan, who handed over to his son Simon, and the former champion jockey Kevin Darley, who won the title in 2000 and included the classic winners Attraction, Bollin Eric and Celtic Swing among around 2,500 winners he rode in a thirty-year career. As usual, the horses highlighted in bold in this introduction are among those dealt with in essay-form. Ireland still has a section in 'Top Horses Abroad', but there is also a separate Irish Supplement, including ratings and commentaries for all horses that ran on the Flat in Ireland in 2007 but are not included in *Racehorses*. Together, *Racehorses* and its Irish Supplement deal individually with more than 14,000 horses, providing a fully comprehensive, accurate and authoritative record of the achievements on the Flat of all the thoroughbreds in the two countries.

February 2008

13

2007 STATISTICS

The following tables show the leading owners, trainers, jockeys, sires of winners and horses on the Flat in Britain during 2007 (Jan 1–Dec 31). The prize money statistics, compiled by *Timeform*, relate to first-three prize money and win money. Win money was traditionally used to decide the trainers' championship until, in 1994, the BHB and the National Trainers' Federation established a championship decided by total prize money as determined by *Racing Post*. In 2007, the trainers' and owners' championships were decided over the turf season (March 31st-November 11th). The jockeys' championship has traditionally been decided by the number of winners ridden during the year, though since 1997 the Jockeys' Association has recognised a championship that runs for the turf season.

OWNERS (1,2,3 earnings)	Horses	Indiv'l Wnrs	Races Won	Runs	%	Stakes £
1 Godolphin	115	55	73	285	25.6	1,561,810
2 Mr Hamdan Al Maktoum	166	73	101	557	18.1	1,548,259
3 Saleh Al Homeizi & Imad Al Sagar	17	6	10	35	28.5	1,368,997
4 Cheveley Park Stud	49	29	46	195	23.5	1,185,880
5 Mrs John Magnier & Mr M. Tabor	7	3	3	21	14.2	907,088
6 Mr D. Smith, Mrs J. Magnier, Mr M. Tabor	13	2	3	24	12.5	845,873
7 Sheikh Mohammed	101	38	58	329	17.6	697,730
8 Mr K. Abdulla	104	46	67	308	21.7	689,171
9 Mr Jaber Abdullah	44	16	24	175	13.7	604,957
10 Mr George Strawbridge	17	11	15	61	24.5	507,972
11 Mr Raymond Tooth	16	8	14	93	15.0	473,378
12 Mr J. C. Smith	29	11	14	137	10.2	418,273

Note: Godolphin was also leading owner in the turf season

OWNERS (win money, £½m+)	Horses	Indiv'l Wnrs	Races Won	Runs	%	Stakes £
1 Saleh Al Homeizi & Imad Al Sagar	17	6	10	35	28.5	1,263,872
2 Godolphin	115	55	73	285	25.6	1,234,542
3 Mr Hamdan Al Maktoum	166	73	101	557	18.1	988,403
4 Cheveley Park Stud	49	29	46	195	23.5	891,124
5 Mrs John Magnier & Mr M. Tabor	7	3	3	21	14.2	590,512
6 Sheikh Mohammed	101	38	58	329	17.6	539,669

TRAINERS (1,2,3 earnings)	Horses	Indiv'l Wnrs	Races Won	Runs	%	Stakes £
1 A. P. O'Brien, Ireland	53	16	18	112	16.0	3,267,317
2 Sir Michael Stoute	144	80	113	498	22.6	2,400,234
3 R. Hannon	190	102	148	1075	13.7	1,867,496
4 P. W. Chapple-Hyam	77	22	33	235	14.0	1,830,729
5 B. W. Hills	150	68	91	659	13.8	1,641,157
6 Saeed bin Suroor	115	55	73	285	25.6	1,561,810
7 M. Johnston	247	107	161	998	16.1	1,552,001
8 M. R. Channon	162	73	109	1086	10.0	1,525,332
9 J. H. M. Gosden	125	47	67	401	16.7	1,486,640
10 R. A. Fahey	145	64	85	926	9.1	1,041,983
11 K. A. Ryan	167	76	107	931	11.4	1,011,477
12 J. Noseda	75	39	56	258	21.7	1,004,046

Note: Aidan O'Brien was also leading trainer in the turf season

TRAINERS (win money, £1m+)	Horses	Indiv'l Wnrs	Races Won	Runs	%	Stakes £
1 Sir Michael Stoute	144	80	113	498	22.6	1,691,394
2 A. P. O'Brien, Ireland	53	16	18	112	16.0	1,666,718
3 P. W. Chapple-Hyam	77	22	33	235	14.0	1,463,802
4 Saeed bin Suroor	115	55	73	285	25.6	1,234,542
5 B. W. Hills	150	68	91	659	13.8	1,213,024
6 R. Hannon	190	102	148	1075	13.7	1,192,362
7 M. Johnston	247	107	161	998	16.1	1,188,803
8 J. H. M. Gosden	125	47	67	401	16.7	1,046,066

TRAINERS (with 100+ winners)	Horses	Indiv'l Wnrs	Races Won	2nd	3rd	Runs	%
1 M. Johnston	247	107	161	125	117	998	16.1
2 R. Hannon	190	102	148	140	103	1075	13.7
3 Sir Michael Stoute	144	80	113	79	59	498	22.6
4 M. R. Channon	162	73	109	116	119	1086	10.0
5 K. A. Ryan	167	76	107	108	89	931	11.4

JOCKEYS (by winners)	1st	2nd	3rd	Unpl	Mts	%
1 Seb Sanders	213	167	147	717	1244	17.1
2 Jamie Spencer	207	151	119	563	1040	19.9
3 N. Callan	170	155	132	679	1136	14.9
4 Richard Hughes	139	115	108	506	868	16.0
5 Ryan Moore	128	100	72	375	675	19.0
6 Chris Catlin	112	119	114	947	1292	8.7
7 Jimmy Fortune	109	83	92	435	719	15.1
8 Steve Drowne	106	104	91	669	970	10.9
9 Ted Durcan	96	96	74	527	793	12.1
10 Dane O'Neill	92	92	107	648	939	9.8
11 Kerrin McEvoy	93	66	56	310	525	17.7
12 Jim Crowley	92	93	95	662	942	9.7

Note: Jamie Spencer and Seb Sanders were joint leading jockeys in the turf season with 190 winners

JOCKEYS (1,2,3 earnings)	Races Won	Rides	%	Stakes £
1 L. Dettori	77	376	20.4	2,890,272
2 J. Murtagh	21	131	16.0	2,808,588
3 Jamie Spencer	207	1040	19.9	2,730,436
4 Ryan Moore	128	675	19.0	2,334,283
5 Jimmy Fortune	109	719	15.1	2,240,797
6 Richard Hughes	139	868	16.0	1,752,144
7 Seb Sanders	213	1244	17.1	1,415,231
8 Kerrin McEvoy	93	525	17.7	1,372,797
9 R. Hills	73	420	17.3	1,306,083
10 Michael Hills	50	455	10.9	1,262,909
11 Ted Durcan	96	793	12.1	1,257,644
12 Steve Drowne	106	970	10.9	1,165,787

JOCKEYS (win money, £1m+)	Races Won	Rides	%	Stakes £
1 L. Dettori	77	376	20.4	2,359,492
2 Jamie Spencer	207	1040	19.9	2,106,933
3 J. Murtagh	21	131	16.0	1,793,197
4 Ryan Moore	128	675	19.0	1,646,909
5 Jimmy Fortune	109	719	15.1	1,477,761
6 Richard Hughes	139	868	16.0	1,015,711

APPRENTICES (by winners)	1st	2nd	3rd	Unpl	Mts	%
1 Greg Fairley	76	52	43	408	579	13.1
2 William Buick	67	57	58	358	540	12.4
3 Liam Jones	65	51	70	436	622	10.4
4 Adam Kirby	56	69	53	541	719	7.7

Note: Greg Fairley was also leading apprentice in the turf season

SIRES OF WINNERS (1,2,3 earnings)	Races Won	Runs	%	Stakes £
1 Montjeu (by Sadler's Wells)	47	372	12.6	2,011,030
2 Danehill (by Danzig)	44	355	12.3	1,889,748
3 Pivotal (by Polar Falcon)	89	643	13.8	1,145,898
4 Galileo (by Sadler's Wells)	57	287	19.8	1,144,090
5 Sadler's Wells (by Northern Dancer)	55	318	17.2	1,134,212
6 Danehill Dancer (by Danehill)	75	649	11.5	1,128,703
7 Royal Applause (by Waajib)	86	868	9.9	869,726
8 Rock of Gibraltar (by Danehill)	35	270	12.9	835,329
9 Dansili (by Danehill)	78	644	12.1	811,993
10 Acclamation (by Royal Applause)	35	243	14.4	766,558
11 In The Wings (by Sadler's Wells)	51	397	12.8	684,392
12 Green Desert (by Danzig)	71	566	12.5	667,027

SIRES OF WINNERS (win money)	Horses	Indiv'l Wnrs	Races Won	Stakes £
1 Montjeu (by Sadler's Wells)	105	34	47	1,571,996
2 Danehill (by Danzig)	78	31	44	1,294,499
3 Galileo (by Sadler's Wells)	78	37	57	856,036
4 Sadler's Wells (by Northern Dancer)	102	36	55	791,652
5 Danehill Dancer (by Danehill)	134	51	75	692,257
6 Pivotal (by Polar Falcon)	130	57	89	688,024
7 Royal Applause (by Waajib)	137	58	86	678,786
8 Acclamation (by Royal Applause)	43	22	35	671,075
9 Dansili (by Danehill)	101	51	78	554,414
10 Night Shift (by Northern Dancer)	73	36	59	540,187
11 Kyllachy (by Pivotal)	96	34	50	512,158
12 In The Wings (by Sadler's Wells)	68	29	51	488,409

LEADING HORSES (1,2,3 earnings)	Races Won	Runs	Stakes £
1 Authorized 3 b.c Montjeu – Funsie	3	4	1,191,296
2 Dylan Thomas 4 b.c Danehill – Lagrion	1	3	618,879
3 Ramonti 5 b.h Martino Alonso – Fosca	3	4	489,333
4 Lucarno 3 b.c Dynaformer – Vignette	4	8	444,947
5 Eagle Mountain 3 b.c Rock of Gibraltar – Masskana	0	4	374,792
6 Peeping Fawn 3 b.f Danehill – Maryinsky	2	3	362,494
7 Notnowcato 5 ch.h Inchinor – Rambling Rose	1	5	355,919
8 Dark Angel 2 gr.c Acclamation – Midnight Angel	4	9	337,547
9 Light Shift 3 b.f Kingmambo – Lingerie	3	4	274,080
10 Sakhee's Secret 3 ch.c Sakhee – Palace Street	4	5	256,381
11 Excellent Art 3 b.c Pivotal – Obsessive	1	3	253,425
12 Maraahel 6 b.h Alzao – Nasanice	3	6	251,353

HORSE OF THE YEAR
BEST OLDER MALE
BEST MIDDLE-DISTANCE HORSE RATED AT 135
MANDURO

BEST TWO-YEAR-OLD FILLIES RATED AT 117p
LISTEN
ZARKAVA

BEST TWO-YEAR-OLD COLT RATED AT 127
NEW APPROACH

BEST THREE-YEAR-OLD FILLY
BEST MILER RATED AT 128
DARJINA

BEST THREE-YEAR-OLD COLT RATED AT 133
AUTHORIZED

BEST OLDER FEMALE RATED AT 127
MISS ANDRETTI

BEST SPRINTER RATED AT 128
SAKHEE'S SECRET

BEST STAYER RATED AT 128
SEPTIMUS

BEST PERFORMANCE IN A HANDICAP IN BRITAIN
HONOLULU
ran to 124
when second in totesport Ebor at York

BEST PERFORMANCE ON ALL-WEATHER IN BRITAIN
AREYOUTALKINGTOME
ran to 121
when winning Bonusprint.com Handicap at Lingfield

THE TIMEFORM 'TOP HUNDRED'

Here are listed the 'Top 100' two-year-olds, three-year-olds and older horses in the annual. Fillies and mares are denoted by (f).

2 YEAR OLDS

127	New Approach
126	Fast Company
125p	Raven's Pass
122	Kingsgate Native
120+	Rio de La Plata
119+	Ibn Khaldun
118	Myboycharlie
117p	Listen (f)
117p	Thewayyouare
117p	Winker Watson
117p	Zarkava (f)
116p	Confront
116p	Nahoodh (f)
116p	Proviso (f)
116	Hello Morning
116	McCartney
116	Natagora (f)
115	Fleeting Spirit (f)
115	Henrythenavigator
114	Laureldean Gale (f)
114	Lizard Island
113p	Stimulation
113	Curtain Call
113	Dark Angel
112+	Sir Gerry
111p	Gothenburg
111p	Precious Boy
111	Blue Chagall
111	City Leader
111	Feared In Flight
111	River Proud
111	Strike The Deal
110p	Screen Star (f)
110+	Visit (f)
110	Achill Island
110	Alexandros
110	Captain Gerrard
110	Great Barrier Reef
110	Pomellato
110	Tajdeef
110	Young Pretender
109p	Full of Gold
109p	Modern Look (f)
109	Scintillo
108P	Sense of Joy (f)
108p	Alexander Castle
108p	High Rock
108p	One Great Cat
108p	Savethisdanceforme (f)
108	Centennial
108	Declaration of War
108	Gladiatorus
108	Luck Money
108	Saoirse Abu (f)
107p	Beacon Lodge

107p	Exclamation
107	Fat Boy
106p	Floristry (f)
106p	Iguazu Falls
106p	Kandahar Run
106p	Spacious (f)
106	Art Master
106	Bruges
106	Red Alert Day
106	Swiss Franc
105p	Jupiter Pluvius
105p	Storm Force
105	Dubai Time
105	Eastern Romance (f)
105	Hatta Fort
105	Redolent
105	Ridge Dance
105	Sharp Nephew
105	Spirit of Sharjah
104P	Twice Over
104p	Alfathaa
104p	Moynahan
104p	Muthabara (f)
104p	Nijoom Dubai (f)
104	Domestic Fund
104	Dream Eater
104	New Zealand
104	Philario
104	Starlit Sands (f)
104	Yahrab
104	Yankadi
104§	Maze
103P	Lush Lashes (f)
103p	Famous Name
103p	Kotsi (f)
103p	You'resothrilling (f)
103	Coasting
103	Latin Lad
103	Mad About You (f)
103	Pencil Hill
103	Siberian Tiger
103	Unilateral (f)
102p	Exhibition
102p	Kitty Matcham (f)
102p	Max One Two Three (f)
102p	Newly Elected
102	Albabilia (f)
102	Celtic Slipper (f)
102	Don't Forget Faith (f)
102	Emmrooz
102	Festoso (f)
102	Gaspar van Wittel
102	Lady Deauville (f)
102	Let Us Prey
102	Rock of Rochelle

3 YEAR OLDS

133	Authorized
131	Curlin
131	Soldier of Fortune
128	Darjina (f)
128	Sakhee's Secret
127	Cockney Rebel
127	Literato
126	Creachadoir
126	Dutch Art
126	Eagle Mountain
126	Peeping Fawn (f)
125	Excellent Art
124	Duke of Marmalade
124	Honolulu
124	Sagara
124	Tariq
123	Finsceal Beo (f)
123	US Ranger
122	Indian Ink (f)
122	Majestic Roi (f)
121p	Kirklees
121	Aqaleem
121	Astronomer Royal
121	Daytona
121	Lawman
121	Light Shift (f)
121	Lucarno
121	Vital Equine
120p	Pipedreamer
120p	Poet Laureate
120+	Arabian Gleam
120	Adlerflug
120	Golden Titus
120	Zaham
119	Confuchias
119	Mahler
119	Miss Lucifer (f)
119	Yellowstone
118+	Dansant
118	Ea
118	Hellvelyn
118	Hoh Mike
118	Mi Emma (f)
118	Shamdinan
118	West Wind (f)
118	Wi Dud
117p	Coastal Path
117+	Zambezi Sun
117	Admiralofthefleet
117	Evening Time (f)
117	Ezima (f)
117	Haatef
117	Halicarnassus
117	MacArthur
117	Mrs Lindsay (f)

117	Promising Lead (f)	
117	Red Moloney	
117	Regal Flush	
117	Veracity	
116	Arabian Gulf	
116	Arch Swing (f)	
116	Eddie Jock	
116	Honoured Guest	
116	Legerete (f)	
116	Lion Sands	
116	Major Cadeaux	
116	Medici Code	
116	Missvinski (f)	
116	Mores Wells	
116	Royal And Regal	
116	Salford Mill	
116	Silkwood (f)	
116	Simply Perfect (f)	
116	Turfrose (f)	
116	Vadapolina (f)	
115+	Utmost Respect	
115+	Ventura (f)	
115	Alexander of Hales	
115	Boscobel	
115	Cartimandua (f)	
115	Celestial Halo	
115	Finicius	
115	Harland	
115	Hearthstead Maison	
115	Lovelace	
115	Passage of Time (f)	
115	Prime Defender	
115	Raincoat	
115	Regime	
115d	Adagio	
114p	Hi Calypso (f)	
114p	Malt Or Mash	
114p	Speed Gifted	
114	Acapulco	
114	Alexander Tango (f)	
114	Al Shemali	
114	Archipenko	
114	Beauty Is Truth (f)	
114	Folk (f)	
114	He's A Decoy	
114	Sonny Red	
114	Summit Surge	
114	Tranquil Tiger	

OLDER HORSES

135	Manduro	
132	Dylan Thomas	
132	Invasor	
131	Sacred Kingdom	
128	Notnowcato	
128	Septimus	
127	Admire Moon	
127	Benbaun	
127	Miss Andretti (f)	
127	Youmzain	
126	Ask	
126	Ramonti	

126	Soldier's Tale	
126	Takeover Target	
126	Yeats	
125	Red Clubs	
125	Scorpion	
125	Sixties Icon	
124	George Washington	
124	Getaway	
124	Linngari	
124	Red Rocks	
124	Saddex	
124	Toylsome	
123	Asset	
123	Cesare	
123	Dandy Man	
123	Desert Lord	
123	Doctor Dino	
123	Echo of Light	
123	Greek Renaissance	
123	Marchand d'Or	
123	Mountain High	
122	Amadeus Wolf	
122	Asiatic Boy	
122	Bentley Biscuit	
122	Garnica	
122	Irish Wells	
122	Jeremy	
122	Magnus	
122	Mandesha (f)	
122	Oracle West	
122	Quijano	
122	Sir Percy	
122	Spirito del Vento	
121	Al Qasi	
121	Areyoutalkingtome	
121	Balthazaar's Gift	
121	Maraahel	
121	Moorhouse Lad	
121	Mutawaajid	
121	Nannina (f)	
121	Soldier Hollow	
121	Turtle Bowl	
121§	Papal Bull	
120	Borderlescott	
120	Boris de Deauville	
120	Candidato Roy	
120	Duff	
120	Echelon (f)	
120	Galactic Star	
120	Laverock	
120	Pressing	
120	Prince Flori	
120	Schiaparelli	
120	Sergeant Cecil	
119	Advanced	
119	Distant Way	
119	Formal Decree	
119	Galeota	
119	Irridescence (f)	
119	Kandidate	
119	Lord du Sud	
119	Racinger	

119	Rowe Park	
119	Stage Gift	
119	Stormy River	
119§	Geordieland	
119§	Munsef	
118p	Multidimensional	
118	Allegretto (f)	
118	Appalachian Trail	
118	Atlantic Air	
118	Bygone Days	
118	Championship Point	
118	Danak	
118	Fairmile	
118	Great Britain	
118	Purple Moon	
118	Racer Forever	
118	Tungsten Strike	
118	Vison Celebre	
118	Windsor Knot	
118d	Gravitas	
117	Army of Angels	
117	Best Name	
117	Blythe Knight	
117	Bussoni	
117	Champs Elysees	
117	Kapil	
117	Le Miracle	
117	Mashaahed	
117	Mighty	
117	Moss Vale	
117	Munaddam	
117	Passager	
117	Peace Offering	
117	Pinpoint	
117	Red Evie (f)	
117	Royal Oath	
117	Soapy Danger	
117	Steppe Dancer	
117	Sudan	
117	Take A Bow	
117	Tax Free	
117	Tiza	
117	Wake Up Maggie (f)	
117	Wiesenpfad	
117§	Olympian Odyssey	
117§	Tam Lin	
117d	New Seeker	

EXPLANATORY NOTES

'Racehorses of 2007' deals individually, in alphabetical sequence, with every horse that ran on the Flat in Britain in 2007, plus numerous overseas-trained horses not seen in Britain. For each of these horses is given (1) its age, colour and sex, (2) its breeding, and for most horses, where this information has not been given in a previous Racehorses Annual, a family outline, (3) a form summary giving its Timeform rating at the end of the previous year, followed by the details of all its performances during the past year, (4) a Timeform rating, or ratings, of its merit in 2007 (which appears in the margin), (5) a Timeform commentary on its racing or general characteristics as a racehorse, with some suggestions, perhaps, regarding its prospects for 2008, and (6) the name of the trainer in whose charge it was on the last occasion it ran. For each two-year-old the foaling date is also given.

TIMEFORM RATINGS

The Timeform Rating of a horse is a measure of the *best* form it displayed in the season under review, expressed in pounds and arrived at by the use of handicapping techniques which include careful examination of a horse's running against other horses. Without going into complexities, the scale used for Timeform ratings represents around 3 lb a length at five furlongs, 2 lb a length at a mile and a quarter and 1 lb at two miles. Timeform maintains a 'running' handicap of all horses in training throughout the season, the in-season ratings usually reflecting Timeform's interpretation of a horse's *current* form, as opposed to its *best* form, where the two may be different.

THE LEVEL OF THE RATINGS

The attention of buyers of British bloodstock and others who may be concerned with Timeform ratings as a measure of absolute racing merit is drawn to the fact that at the close of each season the ratings of all the horses that have raced are re-examined. If necessary, the general level of the handicap is adjusted so that all the ratings are kept at the same standard level from year to year. Some of the ratings may, therefore, be different from those in the final issue of the 2007 Timeform Black Book series. The 'Racehorses Annual' figure is the definitive Timeform Rating.

RATINGS AND WEIGHT-FOR-AGE

The reader has, in the ratings in this book, a universal handicap embracing all the horses in training it is possible to weigh up, ranging from tip-top performers, with ratings from 130 to 145, through categories such as high-class, very smart, smart, useful, fairly useful, fair and modest, down to the poorest, rated around the 20 mark. All the ratings are at weight-for-age, so that equal ratings mean horses of equal merit: perhaps it would be clearer if we said that the universal rating handicap is really not a single handicap, but four handicaps side by side: one for two-year-olds, one for three-year-olds, one for four-year-olds and one for older horses. Thus, a three-year-old rated, for argument's sake, at 117 is deemed to be identical in point of 'merit' with a four-year-old also rated at 117: but for them to have equal chances in, say, a mile race in May, the three-year-old would need to be receiving 9 lb from the four-year-old, which is the weight difference specified by the Age, Weight and Distance Tables on the end papers at the front and back of the book.

USING THE RATINGS

A. Horses of the Same Age

If the horses all carry the same weight there are no adjustments to be made, and the horses with the highest ratings have the best chances. If the horses carry different weights, jot down their ratings, and to the rating of each horse add one point for every pound the horse is set to carry less than 10 st, or subtract one point for every pound it has to carry more than 10 st.

B. Horses of Different Ages

Consult the Age, Weight and Distance Tables printed on the end papers at the front and back of the book. Treat each horse separately, and compare the weight it has to carry with the weight prescribed for it in the tables, according to the age of the horse, the distance of the race and the time of the year. Then, add one point to the rating for each pound the horse has to carry less than the weight given in the tables: or, subtract one point from the rating for every pound it has to carry more than the weight prescribed by the tables.

Example (1½ miles on June 30th)

(Table Weights: 5-y-o+ 10-0; 4-y-o 9-13; 3-y-o 9-1)

6 Bay Pearl (10-2)	....	Rating 115	....	subtract 2	113
4 Elshabeeba (9-9)	....	Rating 114	....	add 4	118
5 Regal Charge (9-5)	....	Rating 115	....	add 9	124
3 Inclination (9-2)	....	Rating 120	....	subtract 1	119

Regal Charge (124) has the best chance at the weights,
with 5 lb in hand of Inclination

TURF AND ARTIFICIAL-SURFACE RATINGS

When a horse has raced on turf and on an artificial surface and its form on one is significantly different from the other, the two ratings are given, the one for artificial surfaces set out below the turf preceded by 'a'. Where there is only one rating, that is to be used for races on both turf and artificial surfaces.

NOTE ON RIDERS' ALLOWANCES

For the purposes of rating calculations it should, in general, be assumed that the allowance a rider is able to claim is nullified by his or her inexperience. Therefore, the weight adjustments to the ratings should be calculated on the weight allotted by the handicapper, or determined by the race conditions.

WEIGHING UP A RACE

The ratings tell you which horses in a race are most favoured by the weights; but complete analysis demands that the racing character of each horse, as set out in its commentary, is also studied carefully to see if there is any reason why the horse might be expected not to run up to its rating or indeed, with a lightly raced or inexperienced horse, might improve on it. It counts for little that a horse is thrown in at the weights if it has no pretensions to staying the distance, is unable to act on the prevailing going, or to accommodate itself to the conformation of the track.

There are other factors to consider too. For example, the matter of pace versus stamina: as between two stayers of equal merit, racing over a distance suitable to both. Firm going, or a small field with the prospect of a slowly-run race, would favour the one with the better pace and acceleration, whereas good to soft or softer going, or a big field with the prospect of a strong gallop, would favour the sounder stayer. There is also the matter of the horse's temperament; nobody should be in a hurry to take a short price about a horse which might not put its best foot forward. The quality of jockeyship is also an important factor when deciding between horses with similar chances.

Incidentally, in setting out the various characteristics, requirements and peculiarities of each horse in its commentary, we have expressed ourselves in as critical a manner as possible, endeavouring to say just as much, and no more, than the facts seem to warrant. Where there are clear indications, and conclusions can be drawn with fair certainty, we have drawn them; if it is a matter of probability or possibility we have put it that way, being careful not to say the one when we mean the other; and where real conclusions are not to be drawn, we have been content to state the facts. Furthermore, when we say that a horse *may* not be suited by firm going, we do not expect it to be treated as though we had said the horse *is not* suited by firm going. In short, both in our thinking and in the setting out of our views we have aimed at precision.

THE FORM SUMMARIES

The form summary enclosed in the brackets lists each horse's performances on the Flat during the past year in chronological sequence, showing, for each race, the distance, the state of the going and the horse's placing at the finish.

The distance of each race is given in furlongs, fractional distances being expressed in the decimal notation to the nearest tenth of a furlong. The prefix 'a' signifies a race on an artificial surface (except for 'f' for fibresand at Southwell, and 'p' for polytrack at Kempton, Lingfield, Wolverhampton, Dundalk and some US tracks).

The going is symbolised as follows: f=firm (turf) or fast (artificial surface); m=good to firm, or standard to fast (artificial surface); g=good (turf) or standard (artificial surface); d=good to soft/dead, or standard to slow (artificial surface); s=soft (turf) or slow, sloppy, muddy or wet (artificial surface); v=heavy.

Placings are indicated, up to sixth place, by the use of superior figures, an asterisk being used to denote a win.

Thus [2007 81: 10s* 12f³ 11.7g f11g² Sep 7] signifies that the horse was rated 81 the previous year (if there is no rating it indicates that the horse did not appear in 'Racehorses' for that year). In 2007 it ran four times, winning over 10 furlongs on soft going first time out, then finishing third over 12 furlongs on firm going, then out of the first six over 11.7 furlongs on good going, then second over 11 furlongs on standard going on a fibresand track. The date of its last run was September 7.

Included in the pedigree details are the highest Timeform Annual ratings during their racing careers of the sires, dams and sires of dams of all horses, where the information is available.

Where sale prices are considered relevant F denotes the price as a foal, Y the price as a yearling, 2-y-o as a two-year-old, and so on. These are given in guineas unless prefixed by $ (American dollars) or € (euros). Other currencies are converted approximately into guineas or pounds sterling at the prevailing exchange rate. Significant sales after the horse's final outing are mentioned at the end of the commentaries.

THE RATING SYMBOLS

The following may be attached to, or appear instead of, a rating:-

p   likely to improve.

P   capable of *much* better form.

+   the horse may be better than we have rated it.

d   the horse appears to have deteriorated, and might no longer be capable of running to the rating given.

§   unreliable (for temperamental or other reasons).

§§   so temperamentally unsatisfactory as not to be worth a rating.

?   the horse's rating is suspect. If used without a rating the symbol implies that the horse can't be assessed with confidence, or, if used in the in-season Timeform publications, that the horse is out of form.

RACEHORSES OF 2007

Horse	Commentary	Rating

AAHAYSON 3 b.c. Noverre (USA) 125 – See You Later 98 (Emarati (USA) 74) [2007 **112** 99: p7g 6m² 7m⁵ 6g* 6d* 6m⁵ 6s* 6v⁴ 5.5d Oct 8] small, sturdy colt: improved into a smart performer, winning minor event and handicap at Hamilton in May, and handicap at Windsor (beat Phantom Whisper by ½ length) in June: below form last 2 starts, including when fourth to Al Qasi in Phoenix Sprint Stakes at the Curragh: stays 6f: has won on good to firm going, best efforts on good or softer: game front runner. *K. R. Burke*

AAIM FOR APPLAUSE 2 b.c. (Jan 16) Royal Applause 124 – Picot 76 (Piccolo 121) **82 §** [2007 5.7g² 6g² 5.7g³ 6m³ 6m³ 6m² 5d² 6m⁵ 6g 5.7d⁶ Oct 1] 35,000F, 65,000Y: leggy colt: second foal: half-brother to 4-y-o Colton: dam, 2-y-o 6f winner, half-sister to useful 6f to 1m performer Hoh Chi Min: fairly useful maiden: placed first 5 starts: likely to stay 7f: unraced on extremes of going: once visored: temperamental: sold 17,000 gns. *M. R. Channon*

AAIM TO STORM (USA) 2 ch.g. (Jan 27) Storm Boot (USA) – Lenient (USA) (Mt **84** Livermore (USA)) [2007 5m⁴ 5g* 6m² 6m 6m⁴ 6m² 7g⁴ 7g 8d³ Sep 20] $25,000F, €205,000Y: tall, useful-looking gelding: has a fluent action: second foal: dam, ran 3 times in USA, half-sister to US Grade 2 1m winner Conserve: fairly useful performer: won maiden at Musselburgh in May: well beaten both tries in pattern company, but in frame all other starts, gelded prior to final one: probably stays 1m: acts on good to firm and good to soft going: nervy sort: sold 20,000 gns. *M. R. Channon*

AAIM TO SUCCEED (IRE) 2 b.f. (Mar 16) Montjeu (IRE) 137 – Dicharachera 91 **68** (Mark of Esteem (IRE) 137) [2007 7.1d⁶ p8g 8m⁶ Sep 21] €70,000F, €65,000Y: leggy filly: first foal: dam, 1m winner, out of half-sister to high-class performer up to 1½m Legal Case and to dam of Oaks winner Love Divine: fair maiden: will be suited by 1¼m/ 1½m: sold 11,000 gns. *M. R. Channon*

AAJEL (USA) 3 gr.c. Aljabr (USA) 125 – Awtaan (USA) 77 (Arazi (USA) 135) [2007 **104 p** p10g* p10g⁶ 11g³ 12f³ 14.1g* Sep 20] big colt: second foal: brother to 7f winner Baleegh: dam, 1¾m winner, out of close relative to Nayef and half-sister to Nashwan and Unfuwain: useful form: won maiden at Lingfield in February and handicap at Yarmouth (by ½ length from Irish Quest, making all) in September: also ran well when third to Ajaan in similar event at Pontefract penultimate start: stays 1¾m: acts on polytrack, raced only on good ground or firmer on turf: likely to do better still. *M. P. Tregoning*

AALIYAH (IRE) 4 b.f. Fasliyev (USA) 120 – Rosie (FR) 76 (Bering 136) [2007 p8g – 5.7m Aug 9] first foal: dam, Irish maiden who stayed 1¾m, out of useful miler Scarlet Plume: well-held seventh of 8 on only outing in Spain in January 2006: tailed off both starts in Britain, tongue tied in latter. *E. J. Creighton*

AARON'S WAY 3 b. or gr.f. Act One 124 – Always On My Mind 91 (Distant Relative **63** 128) [2007 67: 8.2m 6m 6d⁵ 5.7g 6.1v³ Jul 20] leggy, lengthy filly: modest maiden: free-going sort, will prove best at 5f/6f: acts on good to soft going: sold 800 gns in December. *A. W. Carroll*

ABADIA 3 b.f. Bahamian Bounty 116 – Shafaq (USA) 90 (Dayjur (USA) 137) [2007 6m **44** p7.1g 7m 6d⁶ 6s 8.5s f7d Dec 12] leggy filly: second foal: dam 2-y-o 6f winner: poor maiden: form only at 6f: tried in cheekpieces. *J. G. Given*

ABANDON (USA) 4 ch.f. Rahy (USA) 115 – Caerless (IRE) 77 (Caerleon (USA) 132) **94** [2007 90p: 10f* May 2] fairly useful form: has won 3 of 4 starts, including when beating Flying Clarets by short head in handicap at Pontefract in May, making most and showing good attitude: should stay 1¾m: raced only on all-weather and firm ground. *W. J. Haggas*

ABBEY EXPRESS 2 b.g. (Apr 23) Bahamian Bounty 116 – Glimpse 77 (Night Shift – (USA)) [2007 6g 6d⁶ 5f⁶ 6g 7g Oct 19] signs of a little ability: tried blinkered. *M. Dods*

ABBEYGATE 6 b.g. Unfuwain (USA) 131 – Ayunli 81 (Chief Singer 131) [2007 –, – a57: p9.5g⁴ p9.5g⁶ p10g p10g⁴ p9.5g p10g³ p9.5g Dec 13] strong gelding: modest **a55** performer: stays easy 1½m: acts on all-weather, little form on turf: tried blinkered/in cheekpieces/tongue tied. *T. Keddy*

ABBONDANZA (IRE) 4 b.g. Cape Cross (IRE) 129 – Ninth Wonder (USA) (Forty **97**
Niner (USA)) [2007 82: 9.1d⁶ 10.1v 8g* p9.5g⁶ p9.5g⁴ p8.6g* p8.6g* p8.6d* p10g
Dec 16] lengthy, good-topped gelding: useful handicapper: left J. Howard Johnson after
second start: won at Ayr in August, and Wolverhampton in November (2) and December:
stays 1¼m: acts on polytrack, best efforts on turf on good going: wears cheekpieces
nowadays: often races prominently. *I. Semple*

ABBOTTS ACCOUNT (USA) 3 b.g. Mr Greeley (USA) 122 – Agenda (USA) **54**
(Private Account (USA)) [2007 55: 12.6m 14.1m 12m Jul 12] rangy gelding: modest
maiden: acts on good to firm ground: blinkered final outing (ran as if amiss):
sold 1,700 gns in August. *Mrs A. J. Perrett*

ABBY ROAD (IRE) 3 b.f. Danehill (USA) 126 – Bells Are Ringing (USA) 92 **88**
(Sadler's Wells (USA) 132) [2007 99: 6g⁴ May 18] good-topped filly: useful performer at
2 yrs: best form behind Sakhee's Secret in listed race at Newbury sole start in 2007:
best at 5f: best efforts on good ground: tends to hang left: forces pace: stud in USA.
B. J. Meehan

ABERAVON 2 b.f. (Apr 19) Cadeaux Genereux 131 – Dodo (IRE) 90 (Alzao (USA) **60 ?**
117) [2007 6g 6m 6m 7g 6d p8.6g Nov 30] good-topped filly: sixth foal: sister to smart
6f/7f winner Tarjman, and half-sister to 5-y-o Nota Bene and fairly useful 1m winner
Porthcawl (by Singspiel): dam, 6f winner, out of very smart but temperamental sprinter
Dead Certain: seemingly modest maiden: left D. Elsworth after fifth outing: raced mainly
at 6f: tried blinkered/in cheekpieces. *P. D. Evans*

ABERLADY BAY (IRE) 4 ch.f. Selkirk (USA) 129 – Desert Serenade (USA) (Green **–**
Desert (USA) 127) [2007 62d: 8m 8f Jun 8] leggy filly: little solid form: tried visored/
blinkered. *T. T. Clement*

ABERLADY LAD 2 br.c. (May 8) Millkom 124 – Lady El Ee 51 (Komaite (USA)) **–**
[2007 6g 6s Sep 24] no sign of ability. *B. Mactaggart*

ABEYANCE (IRE) 2 ch.c. (Apr 11) Dubai Destination (USA) 127 – Peneia (USA) **–**
(Nureyev (USA) 131) [2007 7m 7m Sep 21] €200,000Y: sturdy colt: well held in
maidens: sold 5,000 gns. *J. Noseda*

ABFABFONG (IRE) 2 b.c. (Apr 5) Dr Fong (USA) 128 – Flatter (IRE) (Barathea **54**
(IRE) 127) [2007 5m p5g⁵ 6m p7.1g⁵ 8m p8g Oct 14] useful-looking colt: modest maid-
en: stays 7f: sold 7,000 gns. *P. F. I. Cole*

ABHISHEKA (IRE) 4 b.f. Sadler's Wells (USA) 132 – Snow Bride (USA) 121 **104**
(Blushing Groom (FR) 131) [2007 108: 9g² 9m⁴ 10.9d⁵ Jun 18] smallish, well-made,
attractive filly: useful performer: creditable 2¼ lengths second to Royal Alchemist in
listed event at Nad Al Sheba on reappearance: below best in Dahlia Stakes at Newmarket
(fourth to Echelon) and listed race at Warwick after: will stay 1½m, but not lacking in
speed: has won on good to firm ground, best efforts on good or softer: left Godolphin, and
sent to USA. *Saeed bin Suroor*

ABIENTOT (IRE) 5 b.g. Danetime (IRE) 121 – Clandolly (IRE) 89 (Burslem 123) **68**
[2007 f5g³ 5d⁶ Jun 27] leggy gelding: fair performer nowadays: best at 5f/6f: acts on
polytrack, good to firm and good to soft going: sold £750 in November. *D. W. Barker*

A BIG SKY BREWING (USA) 3 b.g. Arch (USA) 127 – Runalpharun (USA) **59**
(Thunder Rumble (USA) 116) [2007 53p: 7.1g 6m⁵ 6m⁵ 8m⁴ 11.1f⁶ 7m Aug 1] big,
strong gelding: modest performer: won maiden at Pontefract in April: gelded prior to
final outing: stays 1m: acts on good to firm going: races lazily. *T. D. Barron*

ABITOFAFATH (IRE) 2 b.g. (Apr 2) Fath (USA) 116 – Queen's Victory 93 (Mujadil **–**
(USA) 119) [2007 p6g Sep 13] last in maiden at Wolverhampton (gelded after).
J. G. Given

ABLAAN (USA) 2 ch.c. (Feb 1) Sunday Break (JPN) 121 – La Danzadora (ARG) (El **75**
Sembrador (ARG)) [2007 7g 8m p8g² a7f* Dec 13] $1,200Y, resold $21,000Y, £70,000
2-y-o: big, strong, lengthy colt: first foal: dam, 1m winner, half-sister to 5-y-o Candy
Critic: fair form: ½-length second to King Columbo in maiden at Kempton (finished well)
prior to winning similar event at Nad Al Sheba in December by ¼ length from Jasmines
Hero: will stay 1¼m: acts on dirt/polytrack. *M. F. de Kock, South Africa*

ABLE MIND 7 b.g. Mind Games 121 – Chlo-Jo 65 (Belmez (USA) 131) [2007 68: 7.9f **–**
Aug 6] rather leggy, lengthy gelding: fair handicapper on turf, modest on all-weather:

below form sole start in 2007: stays 1¼m: acts on polytrack, soft and good to firm going: tried in cheekpieces: carries head awkwardly. *D. W. Thompson*

ABOLITION (USA) 2 b.c. (Mar 4) Harlan's Holiday (USA) 124 – Open House (USA) **84** (Deputy Minister (CAN)) [2007 6d² 6m⁴ 6.3v⁵ p8.6g* 8m⁵ p8m Oct 6] $42,000Y: lengthy colt: sixth foal: half-brother to 3 winners in US: dam unraced: fairly useful performer: won minor event at Wolverhampton in September: stays 8.6f: acts on polytrack, heavy and good to firm ground: races prominently: sold 30,000 gns. *M. Johnston*

ABORIGINIE (USA) 2 ch.c. (Apr 14) Street Cry (IRE) 130 – Native Roots (IRE) **80** (Indian Ridge 123) [2007 p8g³ p8g² 8.1g⁵ 8d Oct 3] $310,000Y: good-topped colt: third living foal: half-brother to Breeders' Cup Juvenile winner Wilko (stays 1¼m, by Awesome Again): dam US 6.5f winner: fairly useful maiden: placed both starts on polytrack: will stay 1¼m. *J. H. M. Gosden*

ABOUNDING 3 b.f. Generous (IRE) 139 – Ecstasy 81 (Pursuit of Love 124) [2007 54: **77** p12.2g* p12.2g⁴ 12m³ 12g³ 14g p13.9g⁴ p12.2g³ p12.2s* Dec 20] neat filly: fair handicapper: won at Wolverhampton in June and, having left R. Beckett, December: stays 1¾m: acts on polytrack and good to firm ground: very slowly away fifth outing: held up. *M. J. Attwater*

ABOUSTAR 7 b.g. Abou Zouz (USA) 109 – Three Star Rated (IRE) 79 (Pips Pride 117) **44** [2007 56: f6g f6g⁵ Jan 25] tall, leggy gelding: just poor performer in 2007: stays 6f: acts on fibresand: sometimes wears headgear. *M. Brittain*

ABOVE AND BELOW (IRE) 3 b.f. Key of Luck (USA) 126 – Saramacca (IRE) 54 **44 +** (Kahyasi 130) [2007 –: p8g⁴ p7.1g 8s 8d Jun 29] good-bodied, workmanlike filly: seemingly best effort on reappearance. *M. Quinn*

ABOYNE (IRE) 4 b.g. Mull of Kintyre (USA) 114 – Never End 74 (Alzao (USA) 117) **–** [2007 58d: 6m 10.1g Sep 19] small, sturdy gelding: of little account nowadays. *K. F. Clutterbuck*

ABRAHAM LINCOLN (IRE) 3 b.c. Danehill (USA) 126 – Moon Drop 103 **109** (Dominion 123) [2007 98p: 6v⁴ 6m* 6g p6g* Oct 12] strong, useful-looking colt: useful performer: won minor events at the Curragh (by 1¾ lengths from Inourthoughts) and Dundalk (beat Mist And Stone comfortably by length) in October: respectable ninth (second home stand side) to Haatef in Diadem Stakes at Ascot in between: will stay 7f: acts on polytrack, soft and good to firm going. *A. P. O'Brien, Ireland*

ABSOLUTELYTHEBEST (IRE) 6 b.g. Anabaa (USA) 130 – Recherchee (Rain- **–** bow Quest (USA) 134) [2007 –: 14.1m Aug 31] good-topped gelding: little impact both starts on Flat since 2005: tried visored. *J. G. M. O'Shea*

ABSTRACT ART (USA) 4 ch.g. Distorted Humor (USA) 117 – Code From Heaven **83** (USA) (Lost Code (USA)) [2007 81: 10.5g 12g May 16] well-made gelding: fairly useful handicapper: much better effort in 2007 when seventh at Haydock on reappearance: stays 1½m: acts on polytrack and good to firm going: tried visored (ran as if amiss). *Miss Venetia Williams*

ABSTRACT FOLLY (IRE) 5 b.g. Rossini (USA) 118 – Cochiti 35 (Kris 135) [2007 **75** 67: p12.2g 12m⁵ 14.1m* 16g³ 16.4m³ 16.2g⁶ Oct 2] leggy gelding: good mover: fair handicapper: won at Redcar in August: stays 2m: acts on polytrack, firm and good to soft going: tried blinkered: held up. *J. D. Bethell*

ABTAK (IRE) 7 b.m. Royal Abjar (USA) 121 – Takhiyra (Vayrann 133) [2007 6m p8g **–** 7m Sep 11] big, workmanlike mare: little form, left D. Kelly in Ireland and off nearly 2 years prior to return. *P. Burgoyne*

ABUNAI 3 ch.f. Pivotal 124 – Ingozi 91 (Warning 136) [2007 88: 6g 6g 7m³ 7m³ p7m² **100** p6g² Nov 16] small, workmanlike filly: useful handicapper: placed last 4 starts, further improvement when short-head second to Curtail at Wolverhampton final one: stays 7f: acts on polytrack and firm going. *R. Charlton*

ABWAAB 4 b.g. Agnes World (USA) 123 – Flitteriss Park 62§ (Beldale Flutter (USA) **88** 130) [2007 88: 8.3f 6m* 6m 6g⁴ 6m³ 6g 6d 6d p6m Oct 11] lengthy gelding: fairly useful handicapper: won at Windsor in May: well below form last 3 starts: effective at 6f to 8.3f: acts on good to firm ground: tongue tied early in career: blinkered/visored after reappearance: sold 5,000 gns, sent to France. *Eve Johnson Houghton*

ABYDOS 3 b.c. King's Best (USA) 132 – Polska (USA) 103 (Danzig (USA)) [2007 **92** 8.3m³ 8d⁵ 10m² p10m² 10d* Oct 18] angular, quite attractive colt: half-brother to several winners, including useful 2-y-o 7f winners White Hawk (by Silver Hawk) and Queen of Poland (by Halling): dam, 2-y-o 6f winner, closely related to useful 5f performer Millstream: fairly useful form: in cheekpieces, won maiden at Nottingham (comfortably by 2½ lengths from Eco Centrism) in October: stays 1¼m: acts on polytrack, good to firm and good to soft going: sold 65,000 gns. *Saeed bin Suroor*

ABYLA 3 b.f. Rock of Gibraltar (IRE) 133 – Animatrice (USA) 115 (Alleged (USA) **71** 138) [2007 65p: p10g³ 10.2g² 10f p12g Sep 18] fair maiden: placed first 2 starts in 2007: should stay 1½m: acts on polytrack: sold 125,000 gns. *M. P. Tregoning*

ACAPULCO BAY 3 b.g. Pursuit of Love 124 – Lapu-Lapu 62 (Prince Sabo 123) [2007 **53** f7g² f7g⁵ 10.1d⁶ 7g⁶ 7g 9.1s⁴ Oct 26] modest maiden: effective at 7f to 9f: acts on fibre-sand and soft ground: refused to enter stall intended debut at 2 yrs. *Miss J. A. Camacho*

ACAPULCO (IRE) 3 b.c. Galileo (IRE) 134 – Harasava (FR) (Darshaan 133) [2007 **114** 10s* 10m² 12g 12d⁴ 14.6m 12g⁶ Sep 30] 180,000F, 180,000Y: tall colt: fifth foal: half-brother to German 7f/1m winner Haraplata (by Platini) and German 1¼m winner Harasar (by Alwuhush): dam unraced out of half-sister to Derby Italiano winner Houmayoun: smart performer: won minor event at Navan (by 9 lengths) in April: best efforts when 2¾ lengths fourth to Lucarno in Great Voltigeur Stakes at York and 4¼ lengths eighth to same rival in St Leger at Doncaster fourth/fifth outings: acted as pacemaker in Cumberland Lodge Stakes at Ascot final outing: stays 14.6f: acts on soft and good to firm going: has run well sweating: sold 95,000 gns. *A. P. O'Brien, Ireland*

ACCELERATION (IRE) 7 b.g. Groom Dancer (USA) 128 – Overdrive 99 (Shirley **– §** Heights 130) [2007 –§, a56§: f16g⁶ Jan 1] big gelding: just modest handicapper in 2006: tailed off only 7-y-o start: best at 2m+: acts on fibresand, heavy and good to firm ground: usually wears headgear: tried tongue tied: ungenuine. *Karen McLintock*

ACCENT (IRE) 4 b.g. Beckett (IRE) 116 – Umlaut (Zafonic (USA) 130) [2007 –: p7g **–** May 23] leggy, lengthy gelding: lightly-raced maiden on Flat: should be suited by at least 1m. *Miss Tor Sturgis*

ACCOLATION 3 b.g. Royal Applause 124 – Jasmine Breeze 61 (Saddlers' Hall (IRE) **50** 126) [2007 8.3d p7g³ p7.1g⁴ p6g⁶ Dec 29] 42,000F: lengthy gelding: first foal: dam, ran twice, half-sister to dam of smart US sprinter Friendly Island: modest maiden: bred to prove best at 5f/6f. *Pat Eddery*

ACCORDELLO (IRE) 6 b.m. Accordion – Marello (Supreme Leader 123) [2007 66: **–** 15.8m Apr 4] fair maiden on Flat in 2006 (fairly useful hurdler): below form in handicap at Catterick sole start at 6 yrs (looked awkward): should be suited by 2m+: acts on good to soft ground. *K. G. Reveley*

ACCORDING TO PETE 6 b.g. Accordion – Magic Bloom (Full of Hope 125) [2007 **81** 72: 12d³ 14.6g Oct 26] good-topped gelding: fairly useful maiden on Flat, lightly raced: much better effort at 6 yrs when third in handicap at York on return: stays 1½m: acts on good to soft going. *J. M. Jefferson*

ACCUMULUS 7 b.g. Cloudings (IRE) 112 – Norstock 52 (Norwick (USA) 125) [2007 **58** –: 11.7g⁵ Jun 27] rangy gelding: better effort in maidens 10 months apart when fifth at Bath: fair hurdler. *Noel T. Chance*

ACCUSATION (IRE) 3 b.f. Barathea (IRE) 127 – Uncertain Affair (IRE) 79 (Dar- **72** shaan 133) [2007 9.2s⁴ 9.9s² p12g⁵ p9.5g Dec 8] 310,000Y: sister to fairly useful winner around 11f Subtle Affair and half-sister to several winners, notably smart 1½m/1¾m winner Lochbuie (by Definite Article): dam Irish 1¾m winner: fair maiden: easily best effort when second at Goodwood: bred to be suited by 1½m+: raced only on polytrack and soft going. *L. M. Cumani*

ACCUSED (IRE) 2 b.g. (Mar 28) Xaar 132 – Danedrop (IRE) (Danehill (USA) 126) **73** [2007 6m³ 7m 7m Oct 5] €75,000Y, €360,000Y: big, deep-girthed gelding: third foal: half-brother to 3-y-o Valdan: dam unraced out of half-sister to dam of Groom Dancer: fair maiden: highly tried second start, gelded after final one: should be suited by 1m. *J. Noseda*

ACE BABY 4 b.g. First Trump 118 – Mise En Scene 85 (Lugana Beach 116) [2007 –: **–** f8g Feb 22] neat gelding: fair performer at 2 yrs: little impact since: stays 6f: acts on soft going: tried in cheekpieces: blinkered/tongue tied. *K. J. Burke*

ACECE 3 b.c. Muthahb (IRE) – Berry Brook 37 (Magic Ring (IRE) 115) [2007 56: f8g **–** p12.2g f11g 10f⁵ 8m p12g p7g⁶ p5.1g Dec 4] little form since debut. *D. K. Ivory*

ACE CLUB 6 ch.g. Indian Rocket 115 – Presently 48 (Cadeaux Genereux 131) [2007   **– §**
–§, a54§: f6g f6g* p6g f6g⁵ f5g p5.1g* Dec 31] angular gelding: modest performer: left   **a64 §**
M. Attwater after reappearance: won handicaps at Southwell in February and Wolverhampton in December: effective at 5f to 7f: acts on all-weather, firm and soft ground:
usually wears headgear: inconsistent. *S. Parr*

ACELA (IRE) 2 ch.f. (Apr 20) Hawk Wing (USA) 136 – Altishaan (Darshaan 133)   **–**
[2007 f8d Dec 12] €15,000Y, 10,000 2-y-o: third foal: half-sister to 2003 2-y-o 6f winner
Easily Averted (by Averti): dam unraced: 40/1, tailed off in maiden at Southwell.
R. A. Fahey

ACE OF HEARTS 8 b.g. Magic Ring (IRE) 115 – Lonely Heart 101 (Midyan (USA)   **106**
124) [2007 110: 8m 9m⁵ 8.1d⁶ 8m 9m* 8m² 8g³ 9m⁶ 9m Oct 6] short-backed gelding:
useful handicapper nowadays: won apprentice event at Goodwood (by 1¼ lengths from
Pagan Sword, making all) in August: creditable efforts when placed at Ascot and Ripon
(third to Bolodenka) next 2 starts: well below form in Cambridgeshire at Newmarket final
outing: best at 1m/1¼m: acts on fibresand, firm and soft going: free-going sort. *C. F. Wall*

ACE OF SPIES (IRE) 2 b.c. (Jan 15) Machiavellian (USA) 123 – Nadia 116 (Nash-   **79 p**
wan (USA) 135) [2007 p8m p8.6g³ Dec 14] second foal: dam French 1¼m (including
Prix Saint-Alary) winner: better effort when 1½ lengths third of 6 to Hilbre Court in
minor event at Wolverhampton, still looking green: stays 8.6f: likely to do better still.
M. Johnston

ACHEEKYONE (IRE) 4 b.g. Indian Ridge 123 – Tafrah (IRE) 71 (Sadler's Wells   **93**
(USA) 132) [2007 101: 8m⁶ p8g⁶ 8g 8.3m⁵ Jun 9] well-made gelding: fairly useful
handicapper nowadays: shaped better than bare result first 2 starts in 2007: best around
1m: acts on polytrack, soft and good to firm ground: often takes good hold: reportedly
finished distressed third start. *B. J. Meehan*

ACHILLES OF TROY (IRE) 2 b.c. (Mar 3) Danehill Dancer (IRE) 117 – Twice The   **101**
Ease 46 (Green Desert (USA) 127) [2007 5g³ 5m* 5m⁴ 5m 6.5m² 6m⁵ Oct 5] 115,000Y:
strong, lengthy, heavy-bodied colt: has a quick action: fourth foal: half-brother to 5-y-o
Oranmore Castle: dam, ran twice in Ireland, half-sister to smart Irish performer up to
1¼m Two-Twenty-Two: useful performer: won maiden at Newmarket in May: off 3
months, ran well last 2 starts, 1¼ lengths second of 22 to Dream Eater in St Leger 2-y-o
Stakes at Doncaster and 3½ lengths fifth of 9 to Dark Angel in Middle Park Stakes at
Newmarket: will probably stay 1m: raced only on good/good to firm going: sent to Hong
Kong. *A. P. O'Brien, Ireland*

ACHILL ISLAND (IRE) 2 b.c. (May 5) Sadler's Wells (USA) 132 – Prawn Cocktail   **110**
(USA) (Artichoke (USA)) [2007 8s² 7.5s² 7.5m* 8d² 8d² Oct 26] good-bodied colt:
closely related to fairly useful Irish 1997 2-y-o 5f winner Marigot Bay (by Fairy King)
and half-brother to several winners, notably 2000 2-y-o 5f Group 2 winner Langoustine
and 5f (at 2 yrs)/6f (Group 3) winner One World, both in Australia and by Danehill: dam
unraced half-sister to Royal Academy and dam of Storm Cat: smart performer: won
maiden at Tipperary in August: much improved after, second in Royal Lodge Stakes at
Ascot (¾ length behind City Leader) and Breeders' Cup Juvenile Turf at Monmouth
(beaten ½ length by Nownownow, leading briefly final 1f): will stay 1¼m/1½m: acts on
soft and good to firm ground: held up last 2 starts. *A. P. O'Brien, Ireland*

ACKNOWLEDGEMENT 5 b.g. Josr Algarhoud (IRE) 118 – On Request (IRE) 53   **61 +**
(Be My Guest (USA) 126) [2007 79: p16g May 7] well-made gelding: fair maiden:
travelled strongly for long way in handicap at Kempton only Flat outing in 2007: stays
1¾m: acts on polytrack, soft and good to firm going: blinkered last 4 starts: joined
G. Bridgwater. *Carl Llewellyn*

ACOSTA 3 b.c. Foxhound (USA) 103 – Dancing Heights (IRE) 80 (High Estate 127)   **–**
[2007 56: 7m 12.1g⁶ 12m⁶ 7.6s⁶ 9g⁶ p12g⁶ Sep 11] workmanlike colt: maiden: little form
in 2007: tried blinkered/visored. *Dr J. R. J. Naylor*

ACQUIFER 2 b.f. (Apr 28) Oasis Dream 129 – Llyn Gwynant 115 (Persian Bold 123)   **75**
[2007 6d⁶ 6d 6f⁵ p6g³ p7g⁴ Nov 17] close-coupled filly: half-sister to several winners,
including useful stayer Lady of The Lake (by Caerleon) and 4-y-o Guest Connections:
dam 7f/1m winner: fair maiden: stays 7f: acts on polytrack, firm and good to soft going.
J. L. Dunlop

ACROPOLIS (IRE) 6 b.g. Sadler's Wells (USA) 132 – Dedicated Lady (IRE) 101   **98**
(Pennine Walk 120) [2007 –: 9.8g⁵ 12.1d³ 14m⁴ 12s 12g 12m³ 12d Aug 21] strong, sturdy

gelding: good walker, but has a short, unimpressive action in faster paces: very smart performer in his prime, useful nowadays: creditable efforts last 3 starts: stays 13.4f: acts on soft and good to firm going: tried in cheekpieces/tongue tied (successful), visored last 3 outings: has run in snatches/wandered. *I. Semple*

ACTABOU 2 b.c. (Apr 2) Tobougg (IRE) 125 – Carreamia 62 (Weldnaas (USA) 112) **71**
[2007 7m 6m² 6.1d Oct 18] workmanlike colt: fifth foal: half-brother to a winner in Greece by Warningford: dam sprint maiden: fair maiden: second at Thirsk, standout effort: should stay 7f/1m: acts on good to firm going. *M. Dods*

ACTILIUS (IRE) 3 gr.c. Medicean 128 – Afto (USA) (Relaunch (USA)) [2007 p9.5g⁵ **70**
8s⁵ 10.5m⁴ Aug 9] big colt: half-brother to fairly useful 1½m winner Ardea Brave (by Chester House) and 3 winners in USA: dam US Grade 2 7f winner: easily best effort in maidens when fifth at Wolverhampton on debut, fading: should stay 1m. *M. Botti*

ACTIVE ASSET (IRE) 5 ch.g. Sinndar (IRE) 134 – Sacristy 54 (Godswalk (USA) **94**
130) [2007 92: p11g³ p12g* p11g 10m⁶ 11.6m² 12m³ 12m⁴ 12m 10m 12.3m⁶ 10m⁴ 12g⁴ p13g 10m⁵ 10.1g p12.2g⁴ p12.2g⁵ Oct 21] good-topped gelding: fairly useful handicapper: won minor event at Lingfield in March: not at best after sixth start: stays 1½m: acts on polytrack, firm and good to soft ground: usually held up. *M. Quinn*

ACTIVIST 9 ch.g. Diesis 133 – Shicklah (USA) 106 (The Minstrel (CAN) 135) [2007 **51**
67: p16.5g p16.5g f12g⁵ p12.2g f14g p12.2g⁴ f11g² p13.9g⁵ May 14] leggy, lengthy gelding: modest performer, on downgrade: stays 16.5f: acts on all-weather, firm and good to soft going: often wears cheekpieces/visor. *D. Carroll*

ACTIVITY (IRE) 8 gr.g. Pennekamp (USA) 130 – Actoris (USA) (Diesis 133) [2007 **76**
p7.1g* p8.6g² f8g⁵ p7.1g p8.6g³ p8.6g³ Mar 24] quite good-topped gelding: fair handicapper: won apprentice event at Wolverhampton in January: stays easy 8.6f: acts on all-weather, raced only on good/good to firm going on turf: sold £1,300 in November. *M. J. Gingell*

ACTIVO (FR) 6 b.g. Trempolino (USA) 135 – Acerbis (GER) (Rainbow Quest (USA) **82**
134) [2007 93: p10g p12g Mar 1] good-bodied gelding: fairly useful handicapper: below form both starts in 2007: stays 11f: acts on polytrack, seems best on good/good to soft ground on turf. *S. Dow*

ACTODOS (IRE) 3 gr.g. Act One 124 – Really Gifted (IRE) (Cadeaux Genereux 131) **88**
[2007 80: f12g* 12.3m³ 14g³ 16d Jun 22] big, angular gelding: fairly useful performer: landed odds in maiden at Southwell in April: good third in handicaps next 2 starts: finished lame in Queen's Vase at Royal Ascot final outing (misses 2008): stays 1¾m: acts on fibresand, good to firm and good to soft going: front runner. *B. R. Millman*

ACT SIRIUS (IRE) 3 ch.g. Grand Lodge (USA) 125 – Folgore (USA) 83 (Irish River **–**
(FR) 131) [2007 81: 12g 12s⁵ Jul 9] fairly useful winner at 2 yrs: well held in handicaps in 2007: should be suited by 1½m: raced only on good going or softer. *J. Howard Johnson*

ACT THREE 3 b.f. Beat Hollow 126 – Rada's Daughter 107 (Robellino (USA) 127) **60**
[2007 12m⁵ 11.5s⁶ 10.2g Oct 24] 13,500Y: second foal: half-sister to 1¼m winner Theatre Royal (by Royal Applause): dam 1¼m/1½m winner (stayed 2m): modest form in maidens: should stay 1¾m+ if settling better. *Mouse Hamilton-Fairley*

ACUZIO 6 b.g. Mon Tresor 113 – Veni Vici (IRE) (Namaqualand (USA)) [2007 66: **66**
12.3f² 12d² 15.9d⁴ 14m⁴ 12.3m⁴ 12g³ 12.3m³ 12.3m⁵ Aug 31] sturdy, compact gelding: fair handicapper: in frame first 7 starts in 2007: effective at 1½m, barely stays 2m: acts on polytrack, firm and good to soft going: tried blinkered/in cheekpieces/tongue tied: sometimes hangs left. *W. M. Brisbourne*

ADABI 3 b.g. Soviet Star (USA) 128 – Clincher Club 77 (Polish Patriot (USA) 128) **56**
[2007 p7g p8g 7m⁶ May 11] big, strong gelding: best effort in maidens when seventh at Lingfield second start: sold 6,500 gns, sent to Qatar. *M. P. Tregoning*

ADAB (IRE) 2 b.c. (Feb 12) Invincible Spirit (IRE) 121 – Acate (IRE) (Classic Music **68**
(USA)) [2007 5m² May 11] €19,000F, 70,000Y: strong, sturdy colt: sixth foal: half-brother to 3 winners in Italy: dam Italian maiden: 11/4, encouraging second to Barraland in maiden at Lingfield in spring. *J. H. M. Gosden*

ADAGE 4 b.f. Vettori (IRE) 119 – Aymara 85 (Darshaan 133) [2007 64: 12m p12g⁵ **69**
p13.9g* 11.9s² 12s⁶ p13.9g* p16g p13.9g* p13.9g⁶ p16g⁶ Oct 17] lengthy, quite good-topped filly: fair handicapper: better than ever in 2007, winning at Wolverhampton in May, July and September: best form at 1¾m: acts on polytrack, soft and good to firm going: tongue tied. *David Pinder*

ADAGIO 3 br.c. Grand Lodge (USA) 125 – Lalindi (IRE) 80 (Cadeaux Genereux 131) **115 d**
[2007 109p: 8m* 8m 10.4g⁴ 9f 8f³ 8f Dec 26] strong, lengthy colt: good walker: fluent
mover with a smooth action: smart performer: won banshahousestables.com Craven
Stakes at Newmarket in April convincingly by 1½ lengths from Sonny Red: below form
after in 2000 Guineas on same course (favourite, met trouble when twelfth behind
Cockney Rebel), Dante Stakes at York (7½ lengths fourth to Authorized, reportedly sold
privately and left Sir Michael Stoute after) and varied company in US, including when
third in non-graded stakes at Aqueduct (only outing for J. Rodriguez): should stay 1¼m+:
acts on good to firm and good to soft going: bandaged hind joints second/third outings:
wore special bridle in Craven. *R. E. Dutrow, jnr, USA*

ADAM ETERNO (IRE) 2 ch.g. (Feb 20) Spartacus (IRE) 107 – Mermaid Melody **53 §**
(Machiavellian (USA) 123) [2007 6g 6f 7.1g p7.1g p6g⁶ 7m 8g* 8.3d p8g p10g p8m⁴
p8.6d⁶ Dec 10] compact gelding: modest performer: left B. Meehan after fourth outing:
won selling nursery at Yarmouth in September: sold £4,000 from T. Dascombe after next
start: stays 1m: acts on polytrack: sometimes blinkered/tongue tied: unreliable.
A. B. Haynes

ADANTINO 8 b.g. Glory of Dancer 121 – Sweet Whisper 63 (Petong 126) [2007 88: **90**
p6g⁴ p6f p7g⁴ 6f³ 6m³ 6m² 6g⁴ 6m* 6s 6m 6g⁵ 6m p6g p7g p6g 6d⁴ Oct 1] compact **a83**
gelding: fairly useful handicapper, better on turf than all-weather: won at Windsor in
June: effective at 6f/7f: acts on all-weather, firm and good to soft going (well held both
starts on soft): blinkered. *B. R. Millman*

ADAPTATION 3 b.f. Spectrum (IRE) 126 – Key Academy 103 (Royal Academy **83**
(USA) 130) [2007 88: 6g⁴ 8.2g 8m 6.9f⁴ Aug 6] good-bodied filly: fairly useful handicapper: stays 1m: acts on firm going: sold 4,000 gns in December. *M. Johnston*

ADARE (GER) 4 b.g. Saddlers' Hall (IRE) 126 – Aughamore Beauty (IRE) (Dara **63**
Monarch 128) [2007 10g⁶ May 29] half-brother to several winners, including useful
performer up to 1½m Albany Hall (by Turtle Island): dam unraced from family of
high-class French middle-distance filly Saraca: fairly useful form in bumpers: 20/1, never
dangerous in maiden at Redcar. *T. P. Tate*

ADA RIVER 2 b.f. (Apr 3) Dansili 127 – Miss Meltemi (IRE) 100 (Miswaki Tern **70 p**
(USA) 120) [2007 7g⁶ Nov 3] strong filly: third foal: sister to 4-y-o Dont Dili Dali: dam
Italian 2-y-o 1m winner (third in Oaks d'Italia): 40/1, sixth of 20 to Infallible in maiden at
Newmarket, plenty to do: will do better at 1m/1¼m. *A. M. Balding*

ADDICTIVE 3 b.f. Averti (IRE) 117 – Shadow Bird 70 (Martinmas 128) [2007 69: 8d **–**
8.3g 11.5m Aug 9] tall, quite good-topped filly: well held in 2007. *S. C. Williams*

ADDIKT (IRE) 2 b.c. (Feb 11) Diktat 126 – Frond 85 (Alzao (USA) 117) [2007 6d **75 +**
8.1m⁶ 7s⁵ p7g³ p7g⁴ Nov 30] 2,500F, €10,000Y, resold €45,000Y: sixth foal: half-brother
to several winners, including useful 2006 2-y-o 1m winner Streets Ahead (by Beat
Hollow): dam 2-y-o 7f winner in only season to race: fair maiden: in frame in nurseries at
Lingfield last 2 starts, finishing strongly: should stay 1m: acts on polytrack, soft and good
to firm ground. *S. Kirk*

ADDWAITYA 2 b.c. (Apr 11) Xaar 132 – Three White Sox 73 (Most Welcome 131) **69 ?**
[2007 6d p7m 7g⁶ Oct 26] leggy colt: third foal: dam 1½m winner: seemingly best effort
in maidens when sixth at Doncaster: will stay at least 1m. *C. F. Wall*

ADEJE (IRE) 2 b.c. (Feb 21) Mull of Kintyre (USA) 114 – Comet Dust (Ezzoud (IRE) **–**
126) [2007 6d Oct 15] 7,500F, €46,000Y: lengthy, useful-looking colt: second foal:
brother to useful Italian 7f/1m winner Kintyre Comet: dam twice-raced half-sister to very
smart middle-distance performer Zimzalabim: green and behind in maiden at Windsor:
sold 800 gns. *C. G. Cox*

ADENIUM (IRE) 3 b.g. Desert Style (IRE) 121 – Kelsey Rose 97 (Most Welcome **68**
131) [2007 p8.6g p8.6g³ p7.1g⁴ May 21] 30,000Y: first foal: dam 5f winner (including at
2 yrs): fair maiden: stays 8.6f: slowly away on debut. *W. R. Swinburn*

ADJAMI (IRE) 6 b.g. Entrepreneur 123 – Adjriyna 82 (Top Ville 129) [2007 14.1d **–**
11.8s⁵ 12.1g Aug 15] fair winning hurdler: lightly-raced maiden on Flat: has worn
blinkers. *John A. Harris*

ADLERFLUG (GER) 3 ch.c. In The Wings 128 – Aiyana (GER) (Last Tycoon 131) **120**
[2007 11g⁸ 11g⁶ 11s* 12s* 12g² Sep 2] fourth foal: half-brother to 3 winners in Germany,
including useful miler Anthyllis (by Lycius), 6f winner at 2 yrs: dam, German 6f (at
2 yrs)/7f winner, out of sister to dam of Urban Sea and King's Best: very smart performer:
trained by P. Schiergen only 2-y-o start: won maiden at Bremen in April, listed race at
Hanover (by 5 lengths) in May and BMW Deutsches Derby at Hamburg (drew clear to

BMW Deutsches Derby, Hamburg—Adlerflug is a wide-margin winner from Antek (left) and Anton Chekhov (third right) providing Jens Hirschberger with a second classic success in his first year of training

beat Antek 7 lengths) in July: good keeping-on neck second to Quijano in Grosser Preis von Baden at Baden-Baden final start: stays 1½m: acts on soft ground, yet to race on firmer than good. *J. Hirschberger, Germany*

ADMIRALCOLLINGWOOD 2 b.g. (Apr 25) Reel Buddy (USA) 118 – Chocolate (IRE) 77 (Brief Truce (USA) 126) [2007 5m⁶ 5g 6f 6s⁵ Oct 26] modest maiden: bred to stay 7f/1m. *J. J. Quinn* **59**

ADMIRAL COMPTON 6 ch.g. Compton Place 125 – Sunfleet 59 (Red Sunset 120) [2007 69, a77d: 9.1g Jun 22] lengthy gelding: one-time fair handicapper: well held only Flat outing in 2007: sometimes wears headgear. *B. Storey* **–**

ADMIRAL DUNDAS (IRE) 2 b.c. (Mar 5) Noverre (USA) 125 – Brandish (Warning 136) [2007 p7g⁵ Dec 19] 36,000Y: second living foal: half-brother to Irish 1m winner Sans Reserve (by Foxhound): dam, second at 1m in France, out of smart performer up to 10.5f Ala Mahlik: 33/1 and green, encouraging 1½ lengths fifth of 13 to Parisian Gift in maiden at Lingfield, never nearer: sure to do better. *W. Jarvis* **71 p**

ADMIRAL (IRE) 6 b.g. Alhaarth (IRE) 126 – Coast Is Clear (IRE) 60 (Rainbow Quest (USA) 134) [2007 95: 18.7m May 9] rangy, good sort: fluent mover: useful handicapper: won Chester Cup in 2006 heavily bandaged, said to have finished lame in same race on only start in 2007: effective at 1¼m to 2¼m: acts on firm and good to soft going. *T. J. Pitt* **–**

ADMIRALOFTHEFLEET (USA) 3 b.c. Danehill (USA) 126 – Rafina (USA) (Mr Prospector (USA)) [2007 116p: 8g 10.3m* 12g 10g⁵ 10d⁴ Aug 11] rather leggy, quite good-topped colt: has a quick action: smart performer: won Aktiv Kapital UK Ltd Dee Stakes at Chester in May by 2 lengths from Desert Dew: below form after in Derby at Epsom (tenth to Authorized), Eclipse Stakes at Sandown (7 lengths fifth behind Notnow-cato) and Secretariat Stakes at Arlington (blinkered, 7¾ lengths fourth to Shamdinan): stays 10.3f: acts on good to firm and good to soft going: joined M. de Kock in UAE. *A. P. O'Brien, Ireland* **117**

ADMIRAL SAVANNAH (IRE) 3 b.g. Dilshaan 119 – Valmarana (USA) 51 (Danzig Connection (USA)) [2007 –: 12.1m⁵ 12s⁴ 16.2s 12m² 14.1m⁴ Aug 25] modest maiden handicapper: stays easy 1¾m, not 2m: acts on good to firm going: tried visored/blinkered: looked ungenuine third start. *T. D. Easterby* **57**

ADMIRAL'S CRUISE (USA) 5 b.h. A P Indy (USA) 131 – Ladies Cruise (USA) (Fappiano (USA)) [2007 119: 12m⁵ 12m² 12d⁴ 12m 11m⁵ Sep 21] big, strong, close-coupled horse: smart performer: creditable efforts first 3 starts, in frame in Jockey Club Stakes at Newmarket (3 lengths second to Sixties Icon) and Hardwicke Stakes at Royal Ascot (fourth to Maraahel, finding little): below form after: stays 13f: acts on firm and soft going: blinkered in 2007 bar fourth start: sent to USA. *B. J. Meehan* **115**

Aktiv Kapital UK Ltd Dee Stakes, Chester—Admiralofthefleet shows his Derby credentials in seeing off Desert Dew, Habalwatan (hidden by runner-up) and Monzante (right)

ADMIRALS WAY 2 ch.g. (Mar 30) Observatory (USA) 131 – Dockage (CAN) – (Riverman (USA) 131) [2007 p6g 6d Oct 23] well beaten in maidens (then gelded): bred to stay 1m+. *C. N. Kellett*

ADMIRE MOON (JPN) 4 b.c. End Sweep (USA) – My Katies (JPN) (Sunday **127** Silence (USA)) [2007 124: 11g* 8.9g* 10m³ 11g* 10g⁶ 12f* Nov 25] high-class performer: won 3 times in pattern company in 2006, including Group 2 events at Nakayama and Sapporo: finished strongly and beaten nose by Pride in Hong Kong Cup at Sha Tin final 3-y-o start: successful in 2007 in Group 2 Kyoto Kinen at Kyoto (by neck from Pop Rock) in February, Takarazuka Kinen at Hanshin (by ½ length from Meisho Samson) in June and Japan Cup at Tokyo (led over 1f out, held on by head and neck from Pop Rock and Meisho Samson) in November: was effective at 9f to 1½m: raced only on good ground or firmer: had had tongue tied: to stand at Darley Japan Farm. *H. Matsuda, Japan*

ADOBE 12 b.g. Green Desert (USA) 127 – Shamshir 116 (Kris 135) [2007 64, a53: **56** 8.1m⁵ 9g 10.2f 8.1d 8m 8m Sep 25] small, stocky gelding: modest handicapper: stays 9.5f: acts on all-weather, firm and good to soft going: tongue tied earlier in career: often claimer ridden: usually held up. *W. M. Brisbourne*

ADOPTED HERO (IRE) 7 b.g. Sadler's Wells (USA) 132 – Lady Liberty (NZ) – (Noble Bijou) [2007 –: 12g 20m Jun 19] strong, good-bodied gelding: well held in handicaps in 2007: tried blinkered/in cheekpieces: fairly useful hurdler/maiden chaser. *G. L. Moore*

ADORABELLA (IRE) 4 b.f. Revoque (IRE) 122 – Febrile (USA) (Trempolino **73** (USA) 135) [2007 p10g 10.2g⁴ 11.7d² 11.7f⁴ 11d⁴ Oct 11] first foal: dam unraced half-sister to Ribblesdale winner Spanish Sun: fair maiden: will be suited by 1½m+: acts on good to soft going. *A. King*

ADORE MOI 5 b.m. Keen 116 – Dominuet 95 (Dominion 123) [2007 8d 9.7s Aug 22] – second foal: dam 5f/6f winner: well held in maidens. *R. W. Price*

A DREAM COME TRUE 2 b.f. (Mar 6) Where Or When (IRE) 124 – Katy Ivory **59** (IRE) 68 (Night Shift (USA)) [2007 p7g p7g⁴ p7g⁵ p7g Sep 4] good-topped filly: fourth foal: half-sister to Italian 6f/7f winner Gloria Day (by Pivotal): dam maiden (stayed 1m): modest maiden: will stay 1m: raced only on polytrack. *D. K. Ivory*

ADVANCED 4 b.c. Night Shift (USA) – Wonderful World (GER) (Dashing Blade 117) **119** [2007 116: 6f⁵ 6m 6v 7g² 6g 6d* 7g⁴ 6d⁵ 6d² 6m Nov 10] good-topped, attractive colt: very smart performer: won totesport.com Ayr Gold Cup in September by neck from Benwilt Breeze, edging right: creditable neck second to Duff in listed race at York fourth start: below form last 4 outings, including when 3 lengths second to Tiza in Prix de

31

totesport.com Ayr Gold Cup (Handicap), Ayr—Advanced defies 9-9 and improves on his third in the race in 2006, beating Benwilt Breeze, Patavellian and Beaver Patrol (stand side)

Seine-et-Oise at Maisons-Laffitte: effective at 6f/7f: acts on polytrack, firm and good to soft going: twice tongue tied at 2 yrs. *K. A. Ryan*

ADVANCEMENT 4 b.g. Second Empire (IRE) 124 – Lambast 70 (Relkino 131) [2007 **74** 74: f8g 7.5m 8.1s⁶ 9.9v² 12v⁴ 12.3m 11.1m Aug 31] tall gelding: fair handicapper: stays 1¼m: acts on fibresand, heavy and good to firm going: sometimes races freely: sold 3,000 gns. *R. A. Fahey*

ADVENTURESS 4 b.f. Singspiel (IRE) 133 – Arriving 105 (Most Welcome 131) **92** [2007 94: p10g 8.1g⁵ 8d³ 8.1d 8d Jun 23] lengthy filly: fairly useful performer: stays 1¼m: acts on polytrack, good to firm and good to soft going: tried blinkered: wandered third start: sometimes races freely: reportedly in foal to Dr Fong. *B. J. Meehan*

ADVERSANE 3 ch.c. Alhaarth (IRE) 126 – Cragreen (Green Desert (USA) 127) [2007 **74** 65p: p10g² 11g⁶ 14g³ 15g 14.1s Jul 28] rangy colt: has a quick action: fair maiden handicapper: stays 1¾m: acts on polytrack: tried visored: not straightforward: sold £2,200. *J. L. Dunlop*

ADVERSITY 2 b.c. (Apr 7) Oasis Dream 129 – Tuxford Hideaway 102 (Cawston's **89 p** Clown 113) [2007 p7g² p7g* Oct 29] 88,000F, 140,000Y: half-brother to numerous winners, notably very smart 1m/1¼m winner Desert Deer (by Cadeaux Genereux) and smart 5f (including at 2 yrs) to 7f winner Branston Abby (by Risk Me): dam 5f winner (including at 2 yrs): plenty of promise both starts, winning maiden at Kempton by 1½ lengths (value extra) from Mafioso: may prove best up to 1m: useful prospect. *Sir Michael Stoute*

ADVERTISEMENT 2 b.g. (Feb 18) Averti (IRE) 117 – Adhaaba (USA) 76 (Dayjur **73** (USA) 137) [2007 5m³ 5s² 6m⁶ 5.1g 5.5m 5g Sep 19] €26,000Y: sturdy gelding: first foal: dam, ran once, out of sister to useful dam of Dewhurst Stakes winner Mujahid: fair maiden: failed to confirm early promise: should prove best at 5f/6f: best run on soft ground: suspect attitude (tried blinkered): sold only 2,000 gns. *C. G. Cox*

AEGEAN DANCER 5 b.g. Piccolo 121 – Aegean Flame 86 (Anshan 119) [2007 87: **109** 5f* 5g³ 5m 5g* 5m 6m² 5g⁴ 5g² 6m p5.1g* Nov 19] close-coupled, quite good-topped gelding: improved into a useful performer, winning handicaps at Thirsk in April, Musselburgh (GNER Scottish Sprint Cup, beat Celtic Mill by length) in June and Wolverhampton (by neck from Ebraam) in November: good seventh to Galeota in listed race at Doncaster penultimate outing: best at 5f/easy 6f: acts on all-weather and firm going: reliable. *B. Smart*

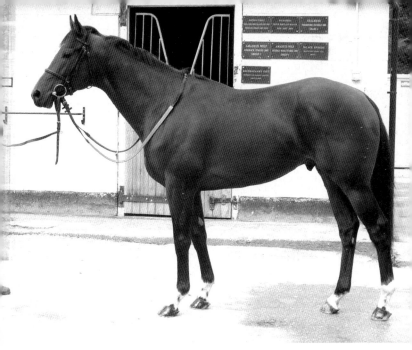

T. Doherty and McHeen's "Advanced"

AEGEAN PRINCE 3 b.c. Dr Fong (USA) 128 – Dizzydaisy 57 (Sharpo 132) [2007 **88** 80p: 8.1g² 9g 8s 9.9g 9d³ p9.5g⁶ 10.5s⁵ 10d Oct 10] compact colt: fairly useful handicapper: placed at Sandown (2): stays 10.5f: acts on polytrack and soft ground: in cheekpieces/blinkers last 4 starts. *W. R. Muir*

AEGIS (IRE) 3 b.g. Beckett (IRE) 116 – Silver Spoon (IRE) (College Chapel 122) **77** [2007 79: p8.6g⁶ f8g* 10s⁶ 8.1m⁵ 10.3m 10g 10g 10m⁵ 10d⁵ Oct 1] unfurnished gelding: fair performer: won maiden at Southwell in May: best around 1m: acts on all-weather, good to firm and good to soft going: tried blinkered: hung right third outing: sold 11,000 gns. *B. W. Hills*

AERIALIST 2 b.f. (Feb 2) Mind Games 121 – Polar Fair 62 (Polar Falcon (USA) 126) **53** [2007 5d 6m⁵ 6g Oct 30] 800Y: fourth foal: dam 8.5f winner: modest maiden: dead. *A. Berry*

AEROPLANE 4 b.c. Danehill Dancer (IRE) 117 – Anita At Dawn (IRE) 77 (Anita's **–** Prince 126) [2007 111: 6m Sep 15] medium-sized colt: smart performer: reportedly cracked pelvis on only 2-y-o outing: well below form in listed race at Goodwood (carried head awkwardly and flashed tail), only outing in 2007: should stay 1m: acts on soft and good to firm going. *P. W. Chapple-Hyam*

AFFILIATION (IRE) 3 b.f. Danehill Dancer (IRE) 117 – Latin Beauty (IRE) (Sad- **59** ler's Wells (USA) 132) [2007 –: 7m⁶ 8.3d⁵ p8g² May 31] smallish filly: modest maiden: stays 1m: acts on polytrack and good to firm going: early reminders final start. *R. Hannon*

AFFIRMATIVELY 2 b.f. (Jan 23) Diktat 126 – Circlet 74 (Lion Cavern (USA) 117) **71** [2007 5m 5m* 5g⁴ 6g p7g Nov 30] leggy, useful-looking filly: third foal: dam 1m winner: fair form: won maiden at Windsor in April: absent 5 months after tailed off in Albany Stakes at Royal Ascot and below form in nursery at Lingfield final outing: should stay 7f/1m: raced only on polytrack and good ground or firmer. *D. R. C. Elsworth*

AFFRETTANDO (IRE) 3 b.g. Danetime (IRE) 121 – Trading Aces 71 (Be My Chief **68**
(USA) 122) [2007 p7g³ p6g³ 7.1m⁵ p7g* p7g Dec 28] 33,000Y: leggy gelding: fifth living
foal: half-brother to fairly useful 2m winner Spring Breeze (by Dr Fong) and useful 8.6f
(at 2 yrs) to 2m winner Sirce (by Josr Algarhoud): dam, 6f (at 2 yrs)/7f winner, half-sister
to useful 1997 2-y-o 6f winner Crazee Mental: fair form: won maiden at Kempton in
December: will stay at least 1m: acts on polytrack. *J. A. R. Toller*

A FOOT IN FRONT 3 b.g. Sugarfoot 118 – Scoffera 63 (Scottish Reel 123) [2007 –: **–**
5m May 22] no sign of ability: tried visored. *N. Tinkler*

AFRAD (FR) 6 gr.g. Linamix (FR) 127 – Afragha (IRE) 88 (Darshaan 133) [2007 –: **98 §**
18.7m 20m⁶ 21g² 18d Oct 20] smallish, leggy gelding: useful handicapper: best effort in
2007 when 1¼ lengths second to Secret Ploy at Goodwood: respectable ninth in Cesarewitch at Newmarket next time: stays 21f: acts on soft going: useful hurdler/winning
chaser: temperamental. *N. J. Henderson*

AFRAM BLUE 2 b.g. (Apr 2) Fraam 114 – Tup Tim (Emperor Jones (USA) 119) [2007 **80**
6g⁴ p6g* p7g⁴ p8g³ p8g³ Dec 22] 18,000Y: first foal: dam French 7.5f (at 2 yrs) to 10.5f
winner: fairly useful form: won maiden at Lingfield (quickened well) in July: further
improvement when in frame in nurseries on same course next 2 starts: stays 1m: raced
only on polytrack and good ground. *W. J. Knight*

AFRICAN CONCERTO (IRE) 4 b.g. Mozart (IRE) 131 – Out of Africa (IRE) 98 **–**
(Common Grounds 118) [2007 67d: p5.1g 6m p7g Jun 5] leggy gelding: disappointing
maiden. *S. Kirk*

AFRICAN FLIGHT 2 b.f. (Feb 23) Hawk Wing (USA) 136 – Valiantly 103 (Anabaa **64**
(USA) 130) [2007 7d⁴ 8g 8.2g⁶ Nov 7] 65,000Y: leggy filly: first foal: dam, 6f winner,
out of half-sister to dam of very smart sprinter Continent: modest form in maidens: will
prove best up to 1m. *M. L. W. Bell*

AFRICAN PURSUITS (USA) 3 b.g. Johannesburg (USA) 127 – Woodland Orchid **71**
(IRE) 64 (Woodman (USA) 126) [2007 p8g 8.1m² 8.2g⁶ p10g Dec 22] 50,000Y:
good-topped gelding: sixth foal: half-brother to 3 winners, including useful Cd
Europe (by Royal Academy): dam, Irish maiden, half-sister to smart 7f/1m performer
D'Anjou: fair maiden: stays 1m: acts on good to firm going. *H. Morrison*

AFRICAN STORM (IRE) 5 b.g. Fasliyev (USA) 120 – Out of Africa (IRE) 98 **57**
(Common Grounds 118) [2007 5g⁴ p6g f5g³ Dec 27] maiden: off over 2 years, just modest
form in Britain in 2007: best efforts at 5f: acts on good to firm going, probably not on soft.
T. McLaughlin, Ireland

AFRIC STAR 3 b.f. Woodborough (USA) 112 – America Star (Norwick (USA) 125) **–**
[2007 46: 5m 6d p5.1g 5m 8.5g Aug 15] close-coupled filly: no longer of any account.
John A. Harris

AFTER NINE 3 b.f. Classic Cliche (IRE) 128 – Eponine 70 (Sharpo 132) [2007 12m **–**
13.8m Jul 11] first foal: dam 13f and hurdles winner: last in maidens. *F. Watson*

AFTER THE SHOW 6 b.g. Royal Applause 124 – Tango Teaser (Shareef Dancer **75**
(USA) 135) [2007 84: f5g p5g⁶ 5s³ 5.1d⁴ 6d p6g⁵ 6.1d³ 6.1s⁴ p6g p5g³ Dec 22] useful-
looking gelding: just fair handicapper in 2007: effective at 5f/6f: acts on all-weather, soft
and good to firm going: tends to hang left: held up. *Rae Guest*

AFTON VIEW (IRE) 2 gr.g. (Apr 25) Clodovil (IRE) 116 – Moonlight Partner (IRE) **65**
81 (Red Sunset 120) [2007 6.1m⁶ 7m⁵ 5g⁶ 6f f8d⁴ p7.1d³ Dec 27] fluent mover: fair
maiden: gelded, in frame in nurseries last 2 starts: stays 1m: raced on all-weather and
good ground or firmer. *D. J. Murphy*

AGENT ELEVEN (IRE) 4 b.g. Desert Story (IRE) 115 – Elizabethan Air 55 (Elegant **–**
Air 119) [2007 –: p12g p12g⁶ Jun 16] well held in 3 maidens. *A. J. Lidderdale*

AGENTE ROMANO (USA) 2 b. or br.c. (Feb 3) Street Cry (IRE) 130 – Dixie Bay **74 p**
(USA) (Dixieland Band (USA)) [2007 p8m² p8m⁶ Dec 7] $70,000Y: third foal: half-
brother to winning US sprinter by Yankee Victor: dam US 1m/8.5f winner: similar form
in maidens at Lingfield, poorly positioned and not clear run in latter: worth another
chance to progress. *G. A. Butler*

AGE OF REASON (UAE) 2 b.g. (Feb 27) Halling (USA) 133 – Time Changes (USA) **90 p**
(Danzig) [2007 p8g* Dec 28] 200,000Y: fourth foal: half-brother to 3-y-o Deadline: dam, useful French miler, out of multiple US Grade 1 runner-up (9f to 1½m) Make
Change: 9/2, won maiden at Lingfield by 3½ lengths from McConnell, leading entering
straight and soon in command: useful prospect. *M. Johnston*

AGGBAG 3 b.g. Fath (USA) 116 – Emaura 61 (Dominion 123) [2007 57: p6g³ p6g **57**
p7.1g⁵ 7g p6g p6g p7m² p6g Dec 8] strong gelding: modest performer: stays easy 7f: acts
on all-weather and good to firm going: tried in cheekpieces. *B. P. J. Baugh*

AGGLESTONE ROCK 2 b.g. (Apr 8) Josr Algarhoud (IRE) 118 – Royalty (IRE) **62**
(Fairy King (USA)) [2007 p7.1g 7d p7m³ p7g⁶ Oct 23] big, workmanlike gelding: modest
maiden: likely to stay 1m: form only on polytrack. *W. G. M. Turner*

AGGRAVATION 5 b.g. Sure Blade (USA) 130 – Confection (Formidable (USA) 125) **79**
[2007 78: p8g⁶ p8g 7m 8m* 8.3m* 8.3g⁴ 8m 8.3m⁵ 8g⁶ 8m³ 8.1g⁴ 8.3g³ p8g⁶ p8g³
Nov 15] compact, deep-girthed gelding: fair handicapper: won at Newmarket in May and
Windsor in June: at least respectable efforts when in frame after: best at 1m/9f: acts on
polytrack, firm and good to soft ground: tried visored: effective tongue tied or not: waited
with. *D. R. C. Elsworth*

AGILETE 5 b.g. Piccolo 121 – Ingerence (FR) (Akarad (FR) 130) [2007 68: f12g⁵ **64**
p13.9g³ p9.5g⁵ 9g⁴ 8.1d 12.6d³ 11.6f³ 12.3m⁴ Aug 31] workmanlike gelding: modest
performer: effective at 9f to 12.6f: acts on all-weather, firm and good to soft going: tried
in cheekpieces/blinkered: tongue tied once: sometimes slowly away. *J. Pearce*

AGITATOR 3 b.g. Lujain (USA) 119 – Forum Girl (Sheikh Albadou 128) **62**
[2007 54p: p7.1g⁴ p7.1g Aug 30] modest maiden: stays 7f: sold 6,500 gns. *Mrs G. S. Rees*

AGNES GIFT 4 b.f. Agnes World (USA) 123 – Evocatrice 91 (Persepolis (FR) 127) **43**
[2007 –: f6g f7g⁶ p8g Apr 20] poor form on all-weather. *Rae Guest*

AGON EYES (USA) 2 b.f. (May 14) Stravinsky (USA) 133 – Dixie Eyes Blazing **49**
(USA) 56 (Gone West (USA)) [2007 6m p7.1g 5.7m 8f p8m Nov 11] 13,000Y: eighth
foal: half-sister to several winners, including 3-y-o Greyt Big Stuff: dam, ran twice, out
of sister to dam of Zafonic: poor maiden: best short of 1m (raced freely last 2 starts).
D. J. Coakley

AHAZ 5 b.g. Zaha (CAN) 106 – Classic Faster (IRE) (Running Steps (USA) 79) [2007 –: **–**
f8g f7g f12g Mar 22] quite good-topped gelding: maiden: little form since 2005: tried in
blinkers/cheekpieces at 2 yrs. *J. F. Coupland*

AHLAWY (IRE) 4 gr.g. Green Desert (USA) 127 – On Call 103 (Alleged (USA) 138) **90**
[2007 83: 8m f8g 10.5g 9.8g⁴ 14.1m⁴ 10.5s⁶ 10.1v⁵ 10.1f² 9.8m* 10m* 9.9m⁴ 8.9d² 10d
9.1v Nov 3] close-coupled gelding: fairly useful handicapper: won at Ripon and Redcar
(ladies event) in August: should stay beyond 1¼m: acts on firm and good to soft going
(well below form on soft/heavy): held up. *M. W. Easterby*

AIDE MEMOIR (IRE) 2 gr.f. (Mar 1) Lend A Hand 124 – Secret Justice (USA) (Lit **89**
de Justice (USA) 125) [2007 5m⁴ 5.1d⁶ 5.7f* 6g⁴ 6m 5g 6d⁴ p6g³ Oct 17] €6,500F: leggy,
close-coupled filly: first foal: dam, French maiden, out of Prix de l'Opera winner Secret
Form: fairly useful performer: won maiden at Bath in June: in frame after in Albany
Stakes at Royal Ascot (best effort, fourth of 20 to Nijoom Dubai), and minor events at
Salisbury and Lingfield last 2 starts: will stay 7f: acts on polytrack, firm and good to soft
ground: sold 13,500 gns, sent to Bahrain. *S. Kirk*

AI HAWA (IRE) 4 b.f. Indian Danehill (IRE) 124 – Arabian Princess (Taufan (USA) **57**
119) [2007 65: 8s 8.1d p9.5g p8g* p8.6d⁶ Dec 17] good-topped filly: modest performer:
won minor event at Kempton in December: stays 1m: acts on polytrack, firm and good to
soft ground: tried blinkered/in cheekpieces. *E. Tyrrell, Ireland*

AIM 2 b.c. (Apr 14) Weetman's Weigh (IRE) 104 – Ballet On Ice (FR) 46 (Fijar Tango **53**
(FR) 127) [2007 7d 8g⁵ 7s p7g p7g Dec 19] close-coupled colt: modest form in maidens/
nurseries, flattered second start: stays 7f. *J. R. Jenkins*

AINAMA (IRE) 3 b.g. Desert Prince (IRE) 130 – Gilah (IRE) (Saddlers' Hall (IRE) **88**
126) [2007 63: p6g p7g p12g² 11.5g* 10m* 13.4g* 14m⁵ 14.6g⁵ Oct 25] €72,000Y:
strong gelding: third foal: half-brother to fairly useful 2-y-o 1m winners Night of Joy (by
King's Best) and Congressional (by Grand Lodge): dam unraced half-sister to smart 1¼m
winner Cocotte, herself dam of Pilsudski: left K. Prendergast in Ireland after sole 2-y-o
outing: much improved when winning handicaps at Lingfield in June, Yarmouth and
Newmarket in July, and Chester in September: ran well final outing: stays 1¾m: acts on
polytrack and good to firm going. *M. Wigham*

AIRBOUND (USA) 4 ch.g. Fusaichi Pegasus (USA) 130 – Secrettame (USA) **–**
(Secretariat (USA)) [2007 77: p13g⁶ Jan 31] only start in 2007: fair winner at 3 yrs for
M. Johnston, well held only start in 2007: stays 1½m: acts on all-weather. *H. J. L. Dunlop*

AIR CHIEF 2 ch.g. (Apr 13) Dr Fong (USA) 128 – Fly For Fame (Shaadi (USA) 126) **59**
[2007 7g 7m⁶ 7.1g p8g Sep 5] tall gelding: modest maiden: gelded after final start: bred
to be suited by 1¼m/1½m. *H. J. L. Dunlop*

AIREDALE LAD (IRE) 6 b.g. Charnwood Forest (IRE) 125 – Tamarsiya (USA) **–**
(Shahrastani (USA) 135) [2007 52: 8.5m p13.9g Dec 1] leggy gelding: modest maiden at
5 yrs: below form on Flat in 2007: stays 10.5f: acts on fibresand, firm and soft ground:
tried in cheekpieces: poor hurdler, won in October. *R. M. Whitaker*

AIR GUITAR (IRE) 7 b.g. Blues Traveller (IRE) 119 – Money Talks (IRE) (Lord **–**
Chancellor (USA)) [2007 10d⁴ 5g Jul 20] big, workmanlike gelding: fair hurdler (tends to
find little): visored, last both starts on Flat. *J. Ryan*

AIRMAN (IRE) 4 b.g. Danehill (USA) 126 – Jiving 69 (Generous (IRE) 139) [2007 **73**
10.3d 10f⁶ 7.1m⁶ 7.1m² p7.1g⁶ p8.6g³ p9.5g³ Nov 1] 2,200 3-y-o: sturdy gelding: third
foal: brother to winner in USA and half-brother to 5-y-o Excusez Moi: dam, ran twice,
half-sister to outstanding broodmare Hasili: modest form in bumpers: fair maiden handicapper on Flat: stays 9.5f: acts on polytrack and good to firm going: tried in cheekpieces.
W. M. Brisbourne

AIZEN MYOO (IRE) 9 b.g. Balla Cove 119 – Fly In Amber (IRE) (Doubletour **–**
(USA)) [2007 73: p12.2g Feb 16] lightly-raced maiden: well held in seller only start in
2007: tried blinkered/visored. *Seamus Fahey, Ireland*

AJAAN 3 br.c. Machiavellian (USA) 123 – Alakananda 92 (Hernando (FR) 127) [2007 **100**
87p: 10d 10g⁴ 12g³ 12f* 14.8s* 14.1g⁴ Sep 20] smallish colt: useful handicapper: won at
Pontefract (best effort, by neck from Bauer) and Newmarket (beat Newnham ¾ length),
both in August: stays 14.8f: acts on firm and soft going: blinkered last 3 starts: held up.
H. R. A. Cecil

AJHAR (USA) 3 b.g. Diesis 133 – Min Alhawa (USA) 108 (Riverman (USA) 131) **103**
[2007 85: 10g* 10d² 10d² Oct 27] strong, compact gelding: type to carry condition:
useful performer, lightly raced: won maiden at Newbury in May by ½ length from Jalil:
runner-up all other starts, good 1¼ lengths second to Heaven Knows in handicap on same
course final outing: gelded after: will stay 1½m: acts on soft and good to firm ground.
M. P. Tregoning

AJIGOLO 4 ch.c. Piccolo 121 – Ajig Dancer 86 (Niniski (USA) 125) [2007 101: p6g⁵ **101**
p5g⁴ p7f p6g* p6g² 6m⁶ 5g 5m 6m⁶ 6g 5m 6g⁴ 6m⁵ p6g* p6g* p6g p5.1g⁴ p6m Dec **a107**
7] tall, good-topped colt: useful handicapper: won at Wolverhampton in March, and
Lingfield and Wolverhampton (beat Sir Nod by 1¼ lengths, edging right) in October: best
at 5f/6f: acts on polytrack and good to firm going: tried visored: has got on edge: usually
held up. *M. R. Channon*

AJZAL (IRE) 3 b.g. Alhaarth (IRE) 126 – Alkaffeyeh (IRE) (Sadler's Wells (USA) **–**
132) [2007 12d Jun 24] half-brother to several at least useful winners, including 7f
(at 2 yrs) and 1¾m winner Tholjanah (by Darshaan) and 1½m/1¾m winner Ta-Lim
(by Ela Mana-Mou): dam unraced half-sister to Ardross: 9/4 from 6/1, well
held in maiden at Pontefract (said to have had breathing problem): sold 21,000 gns.
M. P. Tregoning

AKAREM 6 b.h. Kingmambo (USA) 125 – Spirit of Tara (IRE) 106 (Sadler's Wells **108**
(USA) 132) [2007 117: 11d⁶ 12m 12s² 12.1d⁴ 12g 12m³ 12d 14s⁵ 12d 12g 12s 12g³ 12m
p12g⁴ Dec 1] strong, angular horse: smart performer, largely disappointing after third
start in 2007, when 4 lengths second to Mountain High in listed event at Ascot: stays
1¾m: acts on heavy and good to firm going (all wins on softer than good): tried tongue
tied/visored: has won when sweating. *K. R. Burke*

AKASH (IRE) 7 b.g. Dr Devious (IRE) 127 – Akilara (IRE) 87 (Kahyasi 130) [2007 –: **–**
f11g Mar 15] well-made gelding: one-time useful performer: little form since 2004: tried
blinkered/tongue tied. *Miss J. Feilden*

AKIYAMA (IRE) 3 b.g. Traditionally (USA) 117 – Dark Albatross (USA) 89 (Sheikh **70**
Albadou 128) [2007 74: 10m 7d⁴ 8g Jul 9] fair maiden: stays 7f: acts on soft ground.
J. Howard Johnson

AKRAM (IRE) 5 b.g. Night Shift (USA) – Akdariya (IRE) 103 (Shirley Heights 130) **80 d**
[2007 93: 8m 8.1m 8.1m⁶ 7s 8.2v⁴ 8.2g 7.6m Aug 23] neat gelding: useful in 2005 when
trained by J. Oxx in Ireland: on the downgrade, and said to have finished lame final start:
tried tongue tied. *Jonjo O'Neill*

ALABAMA MAMA (IRE) 2 b.f. (Mar 24) Fath (USA) 116 – Radiance (IRE) 54 **55**
(Thatching 131) [2007 7d p6g⁶ Oct 23] 6,000Y: compact filly: eighth foal: sister to 3-y-o
Chjimes, closely related to 7f/1¼m winner Freecom Net (by Zieten) and half-sister to
fairly useful Irish 2001 2-y-o 5f/7f winner Barriance (by Charnwood Forest): dam, sprint

maiden, half-sister to smart 1m to 1½m performer Bustan: better effort in maidens when sixth at Lingfield: sold 1,500 gns. *H. J. L. Dunlop*

ALABAMA SPIRIT (USA) 2 b. or br.f. (May 8) Dixie Union (USA) 121 – Appealing **67** Spirit (USA) (Valid Appeal (USA)) [2007 5m⁶ 5d² 5.2f² 6m⁴ p6g p7.1g p5.1g⁵ p6g⁵ p6g⁶ p6g p6d³ p7g² Dec 19] $25,000Y: neat filly: half-sister to several minor US sprint winners: dam unraced half-sister to Canadian triple crown winner Izvestia: fair maiden: left K. Burke after fourth start: stays easy 7f: acts on polytrack, firm and good to soft going: edgy sort. *D. Shaw*

ALADDINS CAVE 3 b.c. Rainbow Quest (USA) 134 – Flight of Fancy 114 (Sadler's – Wells (USA) 132) [2007 10d⁶ Oct 18] big, strong, lengthy colt: second foal: half-brother to fairly useful 1¼m winner Fleeting Memory (by Danehill): dam, 2-y-o 7f winner and runner-up in Oaks, out of smart winner up to 13f Phantom Gold: 9/2 and green, 16½ lengths sixth to Abydos in maiden at Nottingham: sold 35,000 gns. *Sir Michael Stoute*

ALAGHIRAAR (IRE) 3 b.g. Act One 124 – Tarsheeh (USA) 53 (Mr Prospector **88** (USA)) [2007 67p: 10d* 12g 14s⁵ 14d Oct 13] rangy gelding: has scope: fairly useful performer, lightly raced: won maiden at Leicester in July: ran creditably after only when fifth in handicap at Haydock (wandered): stays 1¾m: raced only on good ground or softer: blinkered (well held) final start: sold 35,000 gns, then gelded. *J. L. Dunlop*

ALAGON (IRE) 7 b.g. Alzao (USA) 117 – Forest Lair (Habitat 134) [2007 p16.5g³ **62** f14g* p16g⁶ Jan 24] modest performer, lightly raced in Britain: won handicap at Southwell in January: stays 2m: acts on all-weather: tried visored, blinkered last 2 starts: sold 14,000 gns in May. *Ian Williams*

ALAMBIC 4 gr.f. Cozzene (USA) – Alexandrine (IRE) 78 (Nashwan (USA) 135) [2007 **99** 88: 17.1m2 16.4g² 13d⁵ 14g 14g Aug 29] big, strong filly: useful performer: won 6 handicaps at 3 yrs: best effort when ½-length second of 4 to Balkan Knight in listed race at Sandown on second start: well below form after: stayed 17f: acted on firm going: tried blinkered: sometimes took keen hold: tended to wander/idle in front: to visit Galileo. *Sir Mark Prescott*

ALAN DEVONSHIRE 2 b.c. (Feb 27) Mtoto 134 – Missed Again 84 (High Top 131) **98** [2007 7v³ 7m⁶ 7g* 7m² 7m² 8m³ Oct 22] 47,000Y: rather leggy, close-coupled colt: brother to useful 9f and 1½m winner (including in Norway) Miss The Boat and half-brother to 3 winners, including useful sprinter Canterloupe (by Wolfhound): dam 1¼m winner: useful performer: won maiden at Newcastle in August: more progress after, placed in nurseries at Chester and listed race at Pontefract (2 lengths third of 6 to Siberian Tiger): will stay 1¼m: acts on good to firm ground. *M. H. Tompkins*

ALANNAH (IRE) 2 b.f. (Apr 30) Alhaarth (USA) 126 – Aljeeza (Halling (USA) 133) **40** [2007 6g 8.3d p7g p8m⁶ Nov 24] third foal: half-sister to 11f to 2m winner Diamond Key (by Key of Luck): dam unraced: poor maiden. *Mrs P. N. Dutfield*

AL AQABAH (IRE) 2 ch.f. (Apr 27) Nayef 134 – Snow Eagle (IRE) 57 (Polar **76** Falcon (USA) 126) [2007 p6g⁵ p7g²* Nov 4] €30,000Y, £50,000 2-y-o: sixth foal: half-sister to fairly useful 2000 2-y-o 5f winner Elsie Plunkett (by Mind Games): dam maiden (stayed 8.5f at 2 yrs, only season to race): fair form: improved from debut to win maiden at Lingfield, finishing strongly: likely to stay 1m. *B. Gubby*

ALASIL (USA) 7 b.g. Swain (IRE) 134 – Asl (USA) 114 (Caro 133) [2007 72: p11g **58** 10m 8.5g⁵ 8d³ 8.1m p9.5g² p12.2g p8.6g⁶ Oct 26] good-topped gelding: modest handicapper nowadays: stays 1½m: acts on polytrack, firm and good to soft going: sometimes races freely. *R. J. Price*

ALAVANA (IRE) 3 b.f. Kyllachy 129 – Grey Galava 64 (Generous (IRE) 139) [2007 **58** 53: 9m 7m⁶ 8.2m 8m⁶ 7m⁶ 6.9g⁶ 7s⁵ 5.9f 6.9g⁵ 11.1m Aug 31] rather leggy filly: modest performer: won maiden at Catterick in April: stays 7f: acts on good to firm ground. *D. W. Barker*

AL AZY (IRE) 2 b.c. (Jan 20) Nayef (USA) 129 – Nasheed (USA) 113 (Riverman **74** (USA) 131) [2007 7.1d⁶ 8.1d⁵ 8m⁶ 10.2d⁴ Oct 1] sturdy colt: fourth foal: half-brother to useful 7f/1m winner Tamazug and fairly useful 7f to 1¼m winner Mutaderek (both in Ireland and by Machiavellian): dam, 7f (at 2 yrs) and 1¼m winner, closely related to Sakhee: fair maiden: will stay 1½m. *J. L. Dunlop*

ALBABILIA (IRE) 2 b.f. (Jan 29) King's Best (USA) 132 – Sonachan (IRE) 73 **102** (Darshaan 133) [2007 6m⁴ 6d⁴ 7m* 7g⁴ 7m Sep 14] €45,000Y: big, strong filly: has plenty of scope: second foal: half-sister to fairly useful 1m (at 2 yrs)/8.5f (in US) winner Brainy Benny (by Barathea): dam Irish 1¾m winner: useful performer: won maiden at Ascot in July and 7-runner skybet.com Sweet Solera Stakes at Newmarket (beat Don't Forget Faith by ½ length) in August: creditable 3 lengths fourth of 9 to Saoirse Abu in Moyglare Stud Stakes at the Curragh, but tailed off (reportedly clinically abnormal) in valuable sales race there final start: will stay at least 1m: acts on good to firm and good to soft ground: races prominently. *C. E. Brittain*

AL BADEYA (IRE) 3 ch.f. Pivotal 124 – Out of Africa (IRE) 98 (Common Grounds   **68**
118) [2007 8m⁴ 8m⁵ 7.1d² 7m p7.1g³ 6g⁴ p5.1g³ Oct 20] 380,000Y: quite attractive filly: third foal: half-sister to 4-y-o African Concerto: dam, 2-y-o 6f/7f winner, half-sister to very smart sprinter Pipalong: fair maiden: effective at 6f to 1m: acts on polytrack, good to firm and good to soft ground: visored (well below form) final start: races prominently. *Sir Michael Stoute*

ALBANY BECKY (IRE) 2 br.f. (Apr 30) Namid 128 – Alchi (USA) 112 (Alleged   **–**
(USA) 138) [2007 p7g p6g⁶ p6g p6g Sep 13] compact filly: half-sister to several winners, including fairly useful 11f to 2m winner Pickens (by Theatrical): dam French 2-y-o 1m winner: no form in maidens. *M. G. Quinlan*

ALBAQAA 2 ch.g. (Apr 11) Medicean 128 – Basbousate Nadia 92 (Wolfhound (USA)   **81**
126) [2007 6g 7s² 7m 7g⁵ 6d⁶ 7g⁶ Oct 25] 50,000Y: leggy, close-coupled gelding: second foal: dam, 2-y-o 5f winner, out of half-sister to smart 7f/1m performer Gothenberg: fairly useful maiden: mid-field in nurseries, visored final start: stays 7f: acts on soft and good to firm going: sold 18,000 gns, then gelded. *E. A. L. Dunlop*

ALBARAARI 2 b.f. (Jan 21) Green Desert (USA) 127 – Brigitta (IRE) (Sadler's Wells   **79 p**
(USA) 132) [2007 6d p7g* Sep 24] 200,000Y: deep-girthed filly: third foal: dam, French 9.5f/10.5f winner, sister to Racing Post Trophy winner Commander Collins and closely related to Breeders' Cup Sprint winner Lit de Justice and 2000 Guineas/Derby third Colonel Collins: needed debut at Newbury, then won maiden at Kempton (by length from Miss Jolyon) more impressively than bare result, showing good turn of foot: should prove best up to 1m: will continue progressing. *Sir Michael Stoute*

ALBERTS STORY (USA) 3 b.g. Tale of The Cat (USA) 113 – Hazino (USA)   **64**
(Hazaam (USA) 113) [2007 52: 8m⁵ 10.3f 7.9m* 8.1m 8.3m² 9.9d⁴ p9.5g⁵ p12m⁵ Oct 13] lengthy, rather leggy gelding: modest handicapper: won at Carlisle in July: stays easy 1½m: acts on polytrack, soft and good to firm going. *R. A. Fahey*

ALCHARINGA (IRE) 5 b.g. Ashkalani (IRE) 128 – Bird In Blue (IRE) 57 (Bluebird   **–**
(USA) 125) [2007 –: p7.1g Jan 15] strong gelding: maiden: well held both outings since 2005: tried blinkered. *T. J. Etherington*

ALCIMEDES 2 b.g. (Apr 2) Domedriver (IRE) 128 – Allegra 73 (Niniski (USA) 125)   **73**
[2007 7m 7g p8m² p8g Dec 28] lengthy gelding: half-brother to several winners, including 6f winners All Is Fair (at 2 yrs in 1996, by Selkirk) and Alconbury (by Green Desert): dam, 1½m winner, half-sister to very smart 1¼m performer Last Second (dam of very smart miler Aussie Rules) and to dams of Alborada/Albanova and Quarter Moon/ Yesterday: gelded and off 4 months, easily best effort in maidens when second at Lingfield: should stay 1¼m. *P. W. Chapple-Hyam*

AL COBRA (IRE) 2 b.f. (Apr 27) Sadler's Wells (USA) 132 – Marienbad (FR) (Dar-   **70 P**
shaan 133) [2007 7.1g⁵ Nov 9] 170,000Y: closely related to 1½m winner Marine City (by Carnegie) and half-sister to several winners, notably high-class 1½m (including Prix de l'Arc de Triomphe)/1¾m winner Marienbard (by Caerleon): dam, French 1m winner (including at 2 yrs), out of half-sister to very smart winner up to 1m Sakuro Reiko: 11/4, needed experience when fifth in maiden at Musselburgh, but made eye-catching late headway: will do much better at 1¼m/1½m. *M. A. Jarvis*

ALDBURY GREY (IRE) 4 gr.f. Alhaarth (IRE) 126 – Alphilda 83 (Ezzoud (IRE)   **–**
126) [2007 p8g p11g Nov 14] leggy filly: modest maiden in 2005: missed 3 yrs, and no form in 2007. *A. B. Haynes*

ALDERNEY (USA) 3 b.f. Elusive Quality (USA) – Adonesque (IRE) 106 (Sadler's   **102**
Wells (USA) 132) [2007 93: 6m⁵ 6m⁴ 8m Jun 20] big, well-made filly: useful performer: best effort when 4¾ lengths fifth to Lipocco in handicap at Salisbury: reportedly finished distressed when tailed off in listed handicap at Royal Ascot final start: headstrong, but should have stayed 7f: had worn crossed noseband/been early to post: stud. *M. A. Jarvis*

ALEATRICIS 2 br. or gr.g. (Apr 16) Kingmambo (USA) 125 – Alba Stella 92 (Nash-   **– p**
wan (USA) 135) [2007 p7.1g p7g p7.1g Nov 9] first foal: dam, 1½m winner, half-sister to very smart dual Champion Stakes winner Alborada, an excellent family: behind in maidens on polytrack (within 3 weeks): likely to prove different proposition over middle distances at 3 yrs. *Sir Mark Prescott*

ALECIA (IRE) 3 gr.f. Keltos (FR) 132 – Ahliyat (USA) 55 (Irish River (FR) 131)   **74**
[2007 71: 8.3d³ p9.5g⁶ 8d³ 8g p8m³ p8.6g² p8.6d³ Dec 27] good-bodied filly: fair maiden   **a55 +**
on turf, modest on all-weather: should stay 1¼m: acts on polytrack, good to firm and good to soft ground. *A. M. Balding*

AL EILE (IRE) 7 b.g. Alzao (USA) 117 – Kilcsem Eile (IRE) (Commanche Run 133) **108**
[2007 103: 16.1v⁴ 18d⁴ Oct 20] tall gelding: useful handicapper, lightly raced nowadays:
fourth in Northumberland Plate at Newcastle and Cesarewitch at Newmarket (best effort,
beaten 5½ lengths by Leg Spinner) in 2007: stays 2¾m: acts on any going: blinkered
(well held) once: very smart hurdler, won Grade 1 in December. *John Queally, Ireland*

ALEKHINE (IRE) 6 b.g. Soviet Star (USA) 128 – Alriyaah 73 (Shareef Dancer (USA) **68**
135) [2007 81, a75: 11g 11.6f p9.5g⁶ 10g Oct 31] strong, lengthy gelding: just fair
handicapper in 2007 (left J. Boyle after second outing): stays 1¼m: acts on polytrack and
firm ground: sometimes wears cheekpieces. *J. W. Unett*

ALERON (IRE) 9 b.g. Sadler's Wells (USA) 132 – High Hawk 124 (Shirley Heights **71**
130) [2007 77: 13.8m³ 12.4m May 7] tall gelding: fair handicapper on Flat (fairly useful
hurdler/chaser): barely stays 2m: acts on dirt/fibresand, soft and good to firm going: tried
in tongue tie/visor, usually wears cheekpieces: has hung/found little. *J. J. Quinn*

ALESSANDRO VOLTA 2 b.c. (Feb 11) Montjeu (IRE) 137 – Ventura Highway **101 p**
(Machiavellian (USA) 123) [2007 7s 8m³ 9m* Nov 4] 300,000Y: tall, quite attractive
colt: first foal: dam unraced daughter of smart miler Hyabella, herself half-sister to high-
class 1¼m performer Stagecraft: useful form: developed well, and not fully extended
when winning listed race at Leopardstown by 2 lengths from The Fist of God: will be
suited by 1¼m/1½m: smart performer in the making. *A. P. O'Brien, Ireland*

ALESSANO 5 ch.g. Hernando (FR) 127 – Alessandra 101 (Generous (IRE) 139) [2007 **94**
102: p13g⁵ Mar 17] workmanlike gelding: useful handicapper at 4 yrs: respectable fifth
at Lingfield only outing in 2007: will stay 2m: acts on polytrack, firm and good to soft
going, probably on soft: tried in cheekpieces, usually blinkered. *G. L. Moore*

ALEXANDER CASTLE (USA) 2 b.c. (Apr 5) Lemon Drop Kid (USA) 131 – **108 p**
Palapa (USA) (Storm Cat (USA)) [2007 7m* 7m² Sep 15] 90,000 2-y-o: lengthy colt,

Mr Noel O'Callaghan's "Alexander Castle"

unfurnished at 2 yrs: second living foal: half-brother to US 1m winner by Wild Again: dam unraced sister to US Grade 3 9f winner Batique out of US Grade 1 7f winner Serape: won maiden at Newcastle in August by 3½ lengths: on toes, much improved when 2½ lengths second of 10 to McCartney in Champagne Stakes at Doncaster, still rather green and one of first off bridle, but responding well: will stay 1m: smart prospect. *K. A. Ryan*

ALEXANDER GURU 3 ch.g. Ishiguru (USA) 114 – Superspring (Superlative 118) **71** [2007 p11g² 10d p12g p8.6g² p8.6g⁴ p8.6g³ p7g Dec 5] €19,000F, 18,000Y: workmanlike gelding: seventh foal: half-brother to 3 winners, including fairly useful 1m (at 2 yrs) and 10.5f winner The Composer (by Royal Applause): dam unraced sister to smart sprinter Superpower: fair maiden: may prove best around 1m. *M. Blanshard*

ALEXANDER MONARCHY (IRE) 2 b.f. (Mar 14) Royal Applause 124 – Alex- **55** ander Confranc (IRE) 73 (Magical Wonder (USA) 125) [2007 5m p5.1g* 6s⁵ 5m² 7m⁴ 6.1d 7g⁴ p6g 7d Oct 9] unfurnished filly: fourth foal: half-sister to 5-y-o Capable Guest and fairly useful sprinter Petardias Magic (by Petardia): dam Irish 2-y-o 7f winner: modest performer: won claimer at Wolverhampton in May: left K. Ryan after seventh start: stays 7f: acts on polytrack and good to firm going: sold 9,000 gns. *D. W. Barker*

ALEXANDER NEPOTISM (IRE) 2 b.f. (Mar 7) Fasliyev (USA) 120 – Willow- **72** bridge (IRE) (Entrepreneur 123) [2007 5m⁵ 5.1f² 5m⁵ Jun 4] 50,000F: unfurnished filly: second foal: dam unraced close relation to Breeders' Cup Turf winner Northern Spur: fair maiden: runner-up at Bath: should prove best at 5f/6f: sold 17,000 gns in July, sent to Greece. *B. J. Meehan*

ALEXANDER OF HALES (USA) 3 b.c. Danehill (USA) 126 – Legend Maker **115** (IRE) 111 (Sadler's Wells (USA) 132) [2007 79: 10d* 10g* 10.5g 12s² Jul 1] smallish, useful-looking colt: sixth foal: brother to smart Irish 2002 2-y-o 1m winner Chevalier and half-brother to 1000 Guineas winner Virginia Waters (by Kingmambo): dam, French 10.5f and 1½m (Prix de Royaumont) winner: smart performer: won maiden at Naas and Gallinule Stakes at the Curragh (by ½ length from Spanish Harlem), both in May: well held in Prix du Jockey Club at Chantilly next time, then best effort when 9 lengths second to stable-companion Soldier of Fortune in Irish Derby at the Curragh, under pressure early in straight and taking second final strides: will stay 1¾m: raced only on good going or softer. *A. P. O'Brien, Ireland*

Airlie Stud Gallinule Stakes, the Curragh—Alexander of Hales readily picks off Spanish Harlem

Sheikh Mohammed's "Alexandros"

ALEXANDER TANGO (IRE) 3 ch.f. Danehill Dancer (IRE) 117 – House In Wood **114**
(FR) (Woodman (USA) 126) [2007 101: 7m² 7m⁴ 8m* 8g⁴ 9v* 10v² 9f* 10f Sep 29]
strong, well-made filly: smart performer: won Derrinstown Stud 1000 Guineas Trial at
Leopardstown in May, listed race at the Curragh in July and Garden City Stakes at
Belmont (by ¾ length from Bit of Whimsy) in September: good efforts at the Curragh
when 2¼ lengths fourth to Finsceal Beo in Irish 1000 Guineas on fourth start and 2½
lengths second of 4 to Eagle Mountain in Royal Whip Stakes on sixth outing: just
respectable seventh to Lahudood in Flower Bowl Invitational at Belmont final start: was
effective at 1m, barely at testing 1¼m: acted on any turf going: fatally injured in paddock
accident while in quarantine in US in November. *T. Stack, Ireland*

ALEXANDROS 2 ch.c. Kingmambo (USA) 125 – Arlette (IRE) (King of Kings (IRE) **110**
125) [2007 6d² 7g* 7g* 6d* 6d³ Aug 19] first foal: dam, French 8.5f (at 2 yrs) to 9.5f
winner, closely related to In The Wings: smart performer: won minor event at Saint-
Cloud in June, and listed race at Longchamp (by 2 lengths from Salut L'Africain) and
Prix de Cabourg at Deauville (shade comfortably by 1½ lengths from Stern Opinion) in
July: ran well when keeping-on 2½ lengths third to Myboycharlie in Prix Morny at
Deauville final start: will be well suited by 1m: raced only on good/good to soft ground:
has joined Godolphin. *A. Fabre, France*

ALEXIAN 4 b.g. Almushtarak (IRE) 122 – Rough Guess (IRE) 52 (Believe It (USA)) **72**
[2007 75, a72: p12.2g⁵ 8m 12d⁶ 10m p12.2g² Jun 25] neat gelding: fair performer:
claimed to join G. L. Moore £6,000 after final outing: stayed easy 1¾m: acted on
polytrack and good to firm gong: sometimes raced freely: dead. *D. W. P. Arbuthnot*

41

ALEXIA ROSE (IRE) 5 b.m. Mujadil (USA) 119 – Meursault (IRE) (Salt Dome **46**
(USA)) [2007 –, a69: 6m 5g p5.1g 5g⁵ 6d⁶ 5v 5g 5d 6d 5d 5g 5m⁶ 5m 5s 5g p6g f6d Dec
11] leggy, lengthy mare: poor performer nowadays: effective at 5f/6f: acts on all-weather,
firm and soft going: sometimes blinkered: often tongue tied: tends to wander/flash tail:
often slowly away. *A. Berry*

ALFATHAA 2 b.c. (Mar 22) Nayef (USA) 129 – Arctic Char 102 (Polar Falcon (USA) **104 p**
126) [2007 7d³ 8m* 8d⁵ Sep 29] 115,000F, 100,000 2-y-o: rangy, good-topped colt:
second foal: dam, 6f/7f winner, half-sister to German sprinter Barrow Creek and 7f
performer Last Resort, both smart: third to Spacious in maiden at Leicester prior to
winning similar event at Newbury (beat Slam by 5 lengths) in September: another
promising effort when 1½ lengths fifth of 11 to City Leader in Royal Lodge Stakes at
Ascot, still somewhat green and tight for room in sprint finish: stays 1m: has plenty of
scope, and will progress further. *W. J. Haggas*

ALFIE FLITS 5 b.g. Machiavellian (USA) 123 – Elhilmeya (IRE) 94 (Unfuwain **114**
(USA) 131) [2007 122: p10g 12g⁵ 14m² 12d⁶ 14s³ Jun 30] tall, good-topped gelding:
smart performer: creditable effort in 2007 only when head second to Balkan Knight in
listed race at Musselburgh third start: stays easy 1¾m: acts on soft and good to firm going,
below form sole start on polytrack: raced freely/found little fourth outing. *G. A. Swinbank*

ALFIE LEE (IRE) 10 ch.g. Case Law 113 – Nordic Living (IRE) 53 (Nordico (USA)) **–**
[2007 –: 5g 5m 5m 5g 5d 5s⁵ 5s 5d Sep 17] compact, well-made gelding: little solid form
since 2005. *D. A. Nolan*

ALFIE TUPPER (IRE) 4 ch.g. Soviet Star (USA) 128 – Walnut Lady 91 (Forzando **78**
122) [2007 88: 6m 7s p7g 6m 7.1f⁶ p9.5g* p10g³ p9.5g² p10g⁴ p10m³ p12m² p9.5g*
p9.5s⁴ Dec 21] leggy, attractive gelding: fair performer nowadays: won minor event at
Wolverhampton in September and, having left S. Kirk, handicap there in December: stays
1½m: acts on polytrack and good to firm ground, below form on soft: free-going sort,
usually held up. *J. R. Boyle*

ALFONSO 6 ch.g. Efisio 120 – Winnebago 63 (Kris 135) [2007 78, a87: 12.4m 13.1g* **75**
14g⁴ 13.1g³ Jun 22] good-bodied gelding: has a round action: fair handicapper: won at
Ayr in May: stays 13f: acts on fibresand, soft and good to firm going: often blinkered in
2006: none too consistent: sold 10,000 gns in August. *P. Monteith*

ALFREDIAN PARK 3 ch.g. Bertolini (USA) 126 – Ulysses Daughter (IRE) 88 **–**
(College Chapel 122) [2007 77p: p8.6g 9g 8.3s⁶ 8s 7g p7.1g Sep 8] sturdy, lengthy gelding: fair winner of only race at 2 yrs: very disappointing in 2007: blinkered final outing
(raced too freely). *S. Kirk*

ALFREDTHEORDINARY 2 b.g. (Apr 22) Hunting Lion (IRE) 115 – Solmorin **70**
(Fraam 114) [2007 5.1f 5.1f⁴ 6g⁶ 7g⁴ 7f 7.5g 7g⁵ 8f 8.2g³ p8m* Nov 11] 2,000Y:
close-coupled gelding: first foal: dam ran once: fair performer: improved to win
nursery at Kempton (all-weather debut): stays 1m: acts on polytrack and firm ground.
M. R. Channon

ALFRESCO 3 b.g. Mtoto 134 – Maureena (IRE) (Grand Lodge (USA) 125) [2007 59p: **74**
p7g⁶ p7g² p8g* p8g* 8.3m 8.1m p8g⁶ p10g p8g³ 8m p8g p7g* p7m⁴ p8m⁴ p8.6d² p8g* **a94**
Dec 30] useful-looking gelding: fairly useful handicapper on all-weather, fair on turf:
won at Lingfield in March and April, Kempton in September and, having left P. Eddery
32,000 gns after thirteenth start, Lingfield in December: effective at 7f to 8.6f: acts on
polytrack: blinkered nowadays: sometimes slowly away: held up. *I. A. Wood*

ALGARADE 3 b.f. Green Desert (USA) 127 – Alexandrine (IRE) 78 (Nashwan (USA) **79**
135) [2007 77p: 10m² 12d⁵ 10.3m⁵ Aug 23] tall filly: fair performer: stays 1¼m: tongue
tied second start: pulled much too hard final outing. *Sir Mark Prescott*

ALGHAAZY (IRE) 6 b.g. Mark of Esteem (IRE) 137 – Kentmere (FR) (Galetto (FR) **–**
118) [2007 15.8m 16.1m 16.1m Aug 8] strong, close-coupled gelding: maiden: missed
2006: no form in 2007. *Micky Hammond*

ALI BRUCE 7 b.g. Cadeaux Genereux 131 – Actualite (Polish Precedent (USA) 131)
[2007 83: f8g³ p8g² Feb 3] big gelding: just modest form in sellers in 2007: effective at 6f **a57**
to 1m: acts on all-weather, good to firm and good to soft going: sometimes wears
cheekpieces. *P. A. Blockley*

ALICE HOWE 3 b.f. Vettori (IRE) 119 – Peacock Alley (IRE) 98 (Salse (USA) 128) **–**
[2007 –: 8.3s⁴ 10f Aug 12] little form. *W. R. Muir*

ALI D 9 b.g. Alhijaz 122 – Doppio 62 (Dublin Taxi) [2007 69: 8s 8m 8f Aug 12] sturdy **–**
gelding: fair handicapper at best: well held in 2007: has worn cheekpieces. *G. Woodward*

ALIMACDEE 3 ch.f. Compton Place 125 – Howards Heroine (IRE) 70§ (Danehill –
Dancer (IRE) 117) [2007 6.9m 8m Sep 1] first foal: dam 7f to 9.4f winner: well held in
maidens. *I. Semple*

ALISAR (IRE) 7 b.g. Entrepreneur 123 – Aliya (IRE) 105 (Darshaan 133) [2007 p10g –
p9.5g p16g p11g f11g p9.5g p12.2g Oct 18] first foal: dam, Irish 1½m winner, sister to
disqualified Oaks winner Aliysa: fairly useful form in 3 starts for J. Oxx in Ireland in
2003: ran in Spain subsequently for current trainer, winning twice at Madrid in 2005:
tongue tied, well held in Britain in 2007. *E. J. Creighton*

ALISDANZA 5 b.m. Namaqualand (USA) – Enchanting Eve 67 (Risk Me (FR) 127) –
[2007 57: f12g 8m p8.6g 8m 10g May 29] quite lightly-made mare: modest maiden at
3/4 yrs: little form in 2007: signs of temperament. *N. Wilson*

ALISTAIR JOHN 4 b.g. Komaite (USA) – Young Rosein 74 (Distant Relative 128) **51**
[2007 59: p5.1g p6g f5g² f6g⁵ p5.1g p7.1g Apr 30] modest performer: stays 6f: acts on
all-weather: tried tongue tied. *Mrs G. S. Rees*

A LITTLE MORE (IRE) 3 b.c. Princely Heir (IRE) 111 – A Little While (Millfon- **70**
taine 114) [2007 10f⁶ 10m 9g⁶ 11.7g p8.6g Oct 30] seventh foal: half-brother to French
1997 2-y-o 6f winner Small But Sharp (by Conquering Hero): dam unraced: fair form
first 2 starts: sold 4,000 gns. *P. A. Blockley*

ALIZADORA 2 b.f. (Feb 15) Zilzal (USA) 137 – Ballymac Girl 63 (Niniski (USA) **76**
125) [2007 5.1g* 6m² 6g Jun 22] quite good-topped filly: sixth foal: half-sister to useful
1¼m and 13f winner Coat of Honour (by Mark of Esteem): dam, 1½m to 15f winner,
closely related to smart stayer Alleluia, and half-sister to Last Second and to dams of
Alborada/Albanova and Quarter Moon/Yesterday: fair form: 33/1, winning debut in
maiden at Nottingham in May: 6 lengths second to Drawnfromthepast in minor event at
Brighton next start, but then well held in Albany Stakes at Royal Ascot (blinkered):
fractured pastern on gallops in July: will stay at least 1m: stays in training. *Sir Mark
Prescott*

AL KHALEEJ (IRE) 3 b.g. Sakhee (USA) 136 – Mood Swings (IRE) 77 (Shirley **108**
Heights 130) [2007 85p: 9g² 8m* 8g³ p8g Oct 12] lengthy, good-bodied gelding: type to
carry condition: improved into a useful handicapper in 2007, winning at Newmarket (by
2 lengths from Annemasse) in July: very good 2¾ lengths third to The Illies in quite
valuable event at Ascot 7 days later: off 2½ months, below form at Lingfield final outing:
gelded after: stays 9f: acts on polytrack and good to firm going. *E. A. L. Dunlop*

ALL ABOUT HIM (USA) 4 ch.g. Mt Livermore (USA) – Inscrutable Dancer (USA) –
(Green Dancer (USA) 132) [2007 –: p5.1g Jan 21] no form. *N. I. M. Rossiter*

ALLAHOR 2 b.g. (Mar 8) Rock City 120 – Miss Puci 66 (Puissance 110) [2007 6m 5m **67**
6s* 7.1g³ 7s⁴ 7m 7.5g Aug 16] 3,500Y: leggy, close-coupled gelding: first foal: dam 2-y-o
5f winner: fair performer: won maiden at Newcastle in June: lost his way (looked hard
ride): should prove best up to 7f: acts on soft ground: gelded after final start. *A. Berry*

ALLAIRE 3 b.f. Keltos (FR) 132 – Allegra 73 (Niniski (USA) 125) [2007 p10g⁴ 9.2g **55**
9.8m⁴ 8.1m p9.5g Oct 6] tall filly: half-sister to several winners, including 6f winners All
Is Fair (at 2 yrs, by Selkirk) and Alconbury (by Green Desert): dam, 1½m winner, half-
sister to very smart 1¼m performer Last Second, an excellent family: modest maiden:
probably stays 1¼m: unruly in stall second outing. *M. Johnston*

ALL BEGAN (IRE) 3 b.f. Fasliyev (USA) 120 – Sea Mistress (Habitat 134) [2007 7m **63**
8.2m May 2] 82,000Y: close-coupled filly: sister to Irish 2004 2-y-o 6f winner Intriguing
and half-sister to several winners, notably smart Irish 6f to 1m winner Nautical Pet (by
Petorius): dam unraced: better effort in maidens when 6½ lengths seventh of 10 to
Arabian Treasure at Nottingham second outing, though never a threat. *G. Wragg*

ALLEGRETTO (IRE) 4 ch.f. Galileo (IRE) 134 – Alleluia 117 (Caerleon (USA) **118**
132) [2007 115: 14g⁵ 16.4d* 20g 16g* 12d² 18m³ 15.5m* Oct 28]

Opportunities for above-average fillies and mares suited by a test of stamina
have never been that extensive and even with the increase in restricted stakes races
over the last five years there is still something of a void. Of the fifty European
pattern and listed races over a mile and three quarters, only the Group 2
Park Hill Stakes and Group 3 Lillie Langtry Stakes—the latter was elevated in
status from listed in 2004—are solely for fillies and mares. Both contests are
around a mile and three quarters, and there are no races over two miles or more. The
number of good fillies at home over extreme distances has never been large, as
much because of relatively early retirement which the extension of the pattern for

ABN Amro Goodwood Cup, Goodwood—
Allegretto responds well against the three-year-old Veracity (centre) and Finalmente (rail)

fillies and mares set out to address. Certainly, few have tried their luck in recent seasons, unlike in the early nineteenth century, when seven won the Gold Cup between 1809 and 1833. It may, therefore, be damning Allegretto with faint praise to say her victories in the Henry II Stakes, Goodwood Cup and Prix Royal-Oak established her as one of the better staying fillies of the last fifty years. To put her achievements in context, in the period since Indian Queen won the Gold Cup in 1991—she had dead-heated for first in the Prix Royal-Oak the year before—only ten fillies or mares have contested the Gold Cup with none placed. Just seven have run in the Goodwood Cup and ten in the Doncaster Cup, with the high point in the last-named a victory for Allegretto's dam Alleluia in 2001. The situation has been rather better in France, where fifteen fillies and mares have contested the Prix du Cadran since 1990, with Victoire Bleu, Sought Out and Molesnes winning and Sought Out, Shamdala and Varevees, beaten a short head by Le Miracle in October, finishing second. Sought Out was the highest rated of these on 119, and Allegretto is almost on a par with that, just ahead of her dam. Going back a bit further, the best filly to win over two miles or more in the 'seventies was Attica Meli, an easy winner of the Doncaster Cup in 1973 when rated 125. Attica Meli's half-sister Royal Hive was rated 123 and finished second in the Gold Cup of 1978. In the 'eighties, Gold River won the Prix du Cadran before running to a rating of 132 in landing the Prix de l'Arc de Triomphe.

Allegretto shaped like a stayer as a three-year-old, notably when winning the Lancashire Oaks and coming third in the Yorkshire Oaks, though, oddly, she appeared not to be suited by a longer trip when third in the Park Hill Stakes on her final start. On her reappearance, too, there was no firm suggestion that a test of stamina would ultimately suit her. She finished fifth of nine to Sergeant Cecil in the Yorkshire Cup, at no stage looking likely to play a major part. As a result, Allegretto started at 12/1 when visored for the first time in the wbx.com Henry II Stakes at Sandown at the end of May. The favourite, in what looked a fairly weak renewal, was Tungsten Strike, winner of the race in 2006 and recently successful in the Sagaro Stakes. Allegretto sweated up and raced freely early on but the longer trip proved just the job as she challenged two furlongs out and battled on to get the better of Balkan Knight by three quarters of a length. The form was not up to Gold Cup standard but, understandably, Allegretto took her chance at Royal Ascot. Visored again, she got herself very worked up in the preliminaries, raced much too freely under restraint and was a spent force by the home turn, trailing in ninth of fourteen behind Yeats, beaten more than twenty lengths.

This was the low point of Allegretto's season, if not of her career, and she looked to have her work cut out in the ABN Amro Goodwood Cup at the start of August against the warm favourite Geordieland, runner-up in the Gold Cup, and the Gold Cup fourth Finalmente. The twelve other runners, five of whom started at 33/1 or longer, included Distinction making his seasonal debut, Balkan Knight and Queen's Vase second Veracity. The visor was left off Allegretto this time and, after being still last entering the straight, she made ground relentlessly under vigorous

44

driving to hit the front in the last thirty yards and win going away by half a length from Veracity, with Finalmente three quarters of a length back in third. Not for the first time, Geordieland failed to go through with his effort in fifth. A good performance, but some way behind the best form shown by the last two mares to land the Goodwood Cup, Gladness and Brulette. The former was rated 131 in 1958, when she also won the Gold Cup and the Ebor Handicap in a canter under top weight of 9-7. Brulette, winner of the Oaks the previous year, won the Prix du Cadran before triumphing at Goodwood in 1932. Almost certainly the best of the twenty-two fillies and mares to have won the Goodwood Cup since it started in 1812 was Kincsem in 1878; she was unbeaten in fifty-four starts.

Allegretto's chances of landing a Group 1 prize still looked questionable, a view that her next two appearances seemed to reinforce, though she ran creditably both times. At the height of the summer no filly in training could hold a candle to Peeping Fawn over middle distances but Allegretto beat everything else in the Yorkshire Oaks when visored again. She was ridden much more positively but had no answer when Peeping Fawn came through, and was beaten four lengths, finishing five lengths clear of the rest. Allegretto carried a penalty in the Doncaster Cup three weeks later and put up marginally the best performance of her career up to that time. However, she was no match for another Aidan O'Brien-trained runner, Septimus, who won by five lengths from Geordieland, the latter finishing half a length in front of Allegretto at level weights. Without the visor, Allegretto looked a more amenable ride at Doncaster and she was also more tractable in the Prix Royal-Oak - Principaute de Monaco at Longchamp at the end of October. Counter-attractions to this race now include the Melbourne Cup, as well as more prestigious prizes over shorter trips, and there were no three-year-olds among the eleven runners. The pick of the six colts and geldings were the German six-year-old Le Miracle, successful in the Prix du Cadran, the 2006 Queen's Vase winner Soapy Danger, Prix Vicomtesse Vigier winner Lord du Sud and listed scorers Brisant, also from Germany, and Latin Mood. The fillies and mares, trying to add to Montare's success for their sex in 2006, looked the stronger group. Varevees, who had won the Prix Gladiateur before her good run in the Prix du Cadran, started favourite, backed up by Allegretto, Prix de Pomone winner Macleya, Prix Vicomtesse Vigier runner-up Ponte Tresa and, also from Britain, Prix de Royallieu winner Anna Pavlova. Held up again, Allegretto began a forward move from three furlongs out and stayed on gamely to catch Macleya near the finish, Ponte Tresa giving the so-called 'weaker sex' a clean sweep of the first three places. The time was a record for a race often contested on softer going. This was the twelfth Prix Royal-Oak victory since 1980 for a British- or Irish-trained runner (two dead-heated). The list includes Gold Cup winners Ardross and Mr Dinos. In a policy applied consistently, and to great effect, by her owners with their fillies, Allegretto stays in training

Prix Royal-Oak - Principaute de Monaco, Longchamp—no three-year-olds as Allegretto lands her third big prize of the year; Macleya (left) is second, ahead of the grey Ponte Tresa and Le Miracle (second right)

at five. With Yeats and Septimus also still around, and such as Mahler coming through, she will not find life easy in any of the Cup races, and she is reportedly to be kept to races between fifteen and eighteen furlongs, the Gold Cup not on her agenda.

Allegretto (IRE) (ch.f. 2003)	Galileo (IRE) (b 1998)	Sadler's Wells (b 1981)	Northern Dancer Fairy Bridge
		Urban Sea (ch 1989)	Miswaki Allegretta
	Alleluia (b 1998)	Caerleon (b 1980)	Nijinsky Foreseer
		Alruccaba (gr 1983)	Crystal Palace Alara

The bulk of the Cheveley Park Stud's fillies in training are homebreds but its owners are also active at the sales. Russian Rhythm, a 440,000-guinea yearling and successful in four Group 1 races, is the best example but Allegretto and another four-year-old, Queen's Best, who won the Winter Hill Stakes and finished a close second in the Blandford Stakes and the Princess Royal Stakes, are others purchased as yearlings. Allegretto cost 415,000 guineas. Her dam Alleluia won six of her eleven starts, improving after being given a test of stamina and winning two handicaps at around two miles before her Doncaster Cup victory. She fractured a sesamoid when sixth of thirty-one in the Cesarewitch, starting favourite, on her final appearance. Allegretto is her first foal. The second, Alleviate, is by the sprinter Indian Ridge but she proved well suited by a mile and three quarters when winning handicaps at Haydock and Sandown in August. The unraced two-year-old Alvee, a 900,000-guinea yearling, is by Key of Luck and there is a yearling colt by Indian Ridge who sold for €600,000 at Goffs in October, plus a filly foal by Dalakhani. Alleluia then returned to Allegretto's sire Galileo. The grandam Alruccaba should be familiar to readers of *Racehorses*. A winner over six furlongs as a two-year-old, she bred seven other winners, notably Last Second (Nassau Stakes and Sun Chariot Stakes). Her daughters have surpassed themselves at stud: Last Second foaling Aussie Rules (Poule d'Essai des Poulains); Jude foaling Quarter Moon (Moyglare Stud Stakes), Yesterday (Irish One Thousand Guineas) and All My Loving, all placed in the Oaks; Alouette producing Alborada (two Champion Stakes) and German Horse of the Year Albanova, a triple Group 1 winner; another of Alouette's daughters, Alakananda, is the dam of Derby runner-up Dragon Dancer. Other high-priced yearlings from the family include Albarouche, a full sister to Dragon Dancer, who cost €2,000,000 in 2006, and a Sadler's Wells filly out of Albanova bought on behalf of Coolmore by Demi O'Byrne for €2,400,000 at Goffs in October. A strong filly who, as noted, on occasions spoils her appearance by sweating, Allegretto is much more imposing than her dam, who was smallish and close-coupled with little scope. Although effective at a mile and a half, Allegretto is better over further, and she acts on good to firm and good to soft going. *Sir Michael Stoute*

ALLEVIATE (IRE) 3 br.f. Indian Ridge 123 – Alleluia 117 (Caerleon (USA) 132) **84 +** [2007 64p: 11.5m 12.1s² p12g 14m* 14g* 13.1f³ Aug 24] tall filly: improved into a fairly useful handicapper, winning at Haydock and Sandown in August: respectable third at Bath final outing: will stay 2m: acts on polytrack, firm and soft ground: front runner. *Sir Mark Prescott*

ALLEZ MOUSSON 9 b.g. Hernando (FR) 127 – Rynechra 102 (Blakeney 126) [2007 **–** 15d May 23] tall, leggy gelding: little form on Flat and over hurdles (ungenuine) since 2003: tried in headgear. *A. Bailey*

ALLIED POWERS (IRE) 2 b.c. (Mar 23) Invincible Spirit (IRE) 121 – Always **– p** Friendly 111 (High Line 125) [2007 8.3g Oct 16] 62,000Y: lengthy colt: half-brother to several winners, including smart 1¼m winner Arabie (by Polish Precedent) and useful Italian 1m winner Dane Friendly (by Danehill): dam, 1½m winner (including Princess Royal Stakes), also second in Prix Royal-Oak: backward when well held in maiden at Leicester: type to do better. *M. L. W. Bell*

ALL IN THE RED (IRE) 2 ch.c. (Mar 10) Redback 116 – Light-Flight (IRE) (Brief **66** Truce (USA) 126) [2007 6.1m⁵ 5m³ Sep 2] 13,000Y, 7,000 2-y-o: third foal: dam, Swedish 6f winner, half-sister to smart stayer Jardines Lookout: fair form in maidens at Chester and Folkestone: will be suited by 7f/1m. *Miss Gay Kelleway*

*Irish Stallion Farms EBF Fillies Maiden, Leopardstown—All My Loving overcomes Akua'ba
and Aqraan (rail) before collecting plenty of place money in much better company*

ALL LIT UP 2 b.g. (Apr 7) Fantastic Light (USA) 134 – Maiden Aunt (IRE) 60§ **54 p**
(Distant Relative 128) [2007 p8g p8g 8.3m Oct 8] 21,000Y: lengthy, useful-looking
gelding: third foal: dam, maiden who stayed 1½m, half-sister to useful 7f to (in Hong
Kong) 9f winner Noon Gun: modest form in maidens, then gelded: type to progress at
1¼m/1½m. *A. King*

ALL MY LOVING (IRE) 3 b.f. Sadler's Wells (USA) 132 – Jude 53 (Darshaan 133) **113**
[2007 10g* 11.4m² 12d³ 12g² 12v³ 14.6m² 12d² 12.5d 12d³ 11s⁵ Oct 27] big, rangy filly:
has scope: sixth foal: sister to 3 winners (all at least useful), including smart Irish 1000
Guineas winner Yesterday, also 7f and 9f winner at 2 yrs, and very smart 2001 Moyglare
Stud Stakes winner Quarter Moon, both second in Oaks: dam, lightly-raced maiden, sister
to dam of Alborada/Albanova and half-sister to very smart 1¼m performer Last Second:
smart performer: won maiden at Leopardstown in April: much better form after in Oaks
at Epsom (4½ lengths third to Light Shift), Irish Oaks at the Curragh (5½ lengths third to
Peeping Fawn), Park Hill Stakes at Doncaster (neck second to Hi Calypso), listed race at
Ascot (½-length second to Brisk Breeze) and Breeders' Cup Filly & Mare Turf at
Monmouth (2½ lengths fifth behind Lahudood) on third/fifth/sixth/seventh and final
starts: stayed 14.6f: acted on heavy and good to firm ground: twice visored, including at
Monmouth: often made running: visits Dansili. *A. P. O'Brien, Ireland*

ALL NATIVE (IRE) 8 b.g. Revoque (IRE) 122 – Psyche (IRE) (Nashaama 113) [2007 **53**
49: p16.5g³ p13.9g⁶ Dec 31] modest maiden: good third in handicap at Wolverhampton
on reappearance: stays 16.5f: acts on polytrack: usually tongue tied. *C. P. Donoghue,
Ireland*

ALL OF ME (IRE) 3 b.g. Xaar 132 – Silk Point (IRE) (Barathea (IRE) 127) [2007 80: **86 d**
p7.1g* p8.6g⁶ 8.3s 7.1d 8g Sep 18] good-topped, quite attractive gelding: fairly useful
performer: won handicap at Wolverhampton in April: well below form after: stays 7f: acts
on polytrack: tried blinkered: has hung left/carried head high: sold 2,500 gns. *T. G. Mills*

ALLORO 3 ch.g. Auction House (USA) 120 – Minette 55 (Bishop of Cashel 122) [2007 **50**
63: 7m⁵ 8.1g⁴ 8m 8m 10v 7s⁵ 8.1m 13.8g 6g Oct 30] compact gelding: modest maiden:
left D. ffrench Davis £1,500 after seventh start: stays 1m: probably acts on soft and good
to firm going: tried in cheekpieces. *D. W. Thompson*

ALLS FAIR 2 br.c. (Feb 8) Bertolini (USA) 125 – Comme Ca (Cyrano de Bergerac 120) **72**
[2007 6m⁶ 6f p6g³ Aug 30] 50,000Y: big, strong colt: has scope: fourth foal: half-brother
to 2003 2-y-o 6f winner Even Easier (by Petong) and 5-y-o Grand Place: fair maiden:
third at Lingfield, hanging and headed home turn: may prove best at 5f/6f:
sold 8,000 gns. *R. Hannon*

ALL TALK 3 b.f. Muhtarram (USA) 125 – Bron Hilda (IRE) 50 (Namaqualand (USA)) **–**
[2007 46: p7g 8.1m 7m 8d⁶ 11.6m 10.1g 8m 12g Aug 29] medium-sized filly: maiden:
little form at 3 yrs, leaving Mrs C. Dunnett after reappearance. *M. J. Gingell*

ALL THAT BRASS 2 ch.c. (Feb 8) Compton Place 125 – Ebba 88 (Elmaamul (USA) **–**
125) [2007 6g⁵ Jun 17] 36,000Y: well held in maiden at Folkestone: sold 800 gns, sent to
Spain. *E. J. O'Neill*

ALL THE ACES (IRE) 2 b.c. (Apr 24) Spartacus (IRE) 107 – Lili Cup (FR) (Fab- **86 p**
ulous Dancer (USA) 124) [2007 7.1g³ 8.1s² p10g* Oct 31] 95,000 2-y-o: good-topped
colt: half-brother to several winners, notably useful Italian sprinter Uruk (by Efisio): dam

47

unraced: progressive form in maidens, won at Lingfield by neck from Howdigo (pair clear): stays 1¼m: capable of further improvement. *M. A. Jarvis*

ALL THE GOOD (IRE) 4 ch.c. Diesis 133 – Zarara (USA) (Manila (USA)) [2007 **107** 101: p11g⁶ 12g 14m⁴ 14s⁴ 14g 11.9m⁵ 14d p10.7g² 10.3m⁴ 12g* Sep 30] close-coupled colt: useful handicapper: won at Musselburgh in June and Ascot (beat Ladies Best impressively by neck) in September: stays 2m: acts on polytrack, good to firm and good to soft going: tried blinkered (raced freely): hung right sixth/seventh starts: usually held up: has joined Godolphin. *G. A. Butler*

ALL TIED UP (IRE) 3 ch.f. Desert Prince (IRE) 130 – Half-Hitch (USA) 88 (Diesis **69** 133) [2007 6p1: 8d⁶ 6g 8m 10m 10d 8.5g 12g² p10.7g³ p10.7g p12.2g⁵ Dec 15] €52,000Y: fifth foal: half-sister to a winner in Spain by Hector Protector: dam, 2-y-o 6f winner, out of very smart miler Marling: fair maiden handicapper: left D. Weld (Ireland) 4,000 gns after fourth start: below best last 2 outings, at Wolverhampton on latter: stays 1½m: acts on polytrack, yet to race on extremes of going on turf. *T. Hogan, Ireland*

ALL WOMAN 5 ch.m. Groom Dancer (USA) 128 – Flight Soundly (IRE) 78 (Caerleon **–** (USA) 132) [2007 f8g⁶ Jan 11] half-sister to several winners, including useful German 5f/6f (at 2 yrs) winner Elli (by Polar Falcon): dam, 2-y-o 6f winner, out of Queen Mary winner Night of Wind: fair performer: successful in 2005 in maiden at Naas (final start for C. Swan) and 2 minor events at Mijas: missed 2006: well held only outing at 5 yrs: stays 10.5f: acts on heavy ground and sand: tried in cheekpieces. *E. J. Creighton*

ALLY MAKBUL 7 b.m. Makbul 104 – Clarice Orsini (Common Grounds 118) [2007 **–** –: f11g May 8] tailed off both outings since 2004. *Ian Emmerson*

ALL YOU NEED (IRE) 3 b.g. Iron Mask (USA) 117 – Choice Pickings (IRE) **76** (Among Men (USA) 124) [2007 80: 5g 6m p6g* 6m p6g⁶ p7.1g² p6g p7.1g³ 6.1s Oct 18] rather leggy gelding: fair performer: won maiden at Wolverhampton in July: stays 7f: acts on polytrack and firm going, below form both outings on softer than good: tried in cheekpieces. *R. Hollinshead*

ALMAHAZA (IRE) 3 b.c. Alzao (USA) 117 – Morna's Moment (USA) 59 (Timeless **63** Moment (USA)) [2007 10d 10d 10m 12g p11g 16g p10g² 10g* p8g² p9.5g³ Dec 3] rangy colt: modest performer: won seller at Windsor (left Mrs A. Perrett £5,000) in October: effective at 1m to 1¼m (refused to settle at 2m): acts on polytrack, unraced on extremes of going on turf: wears blinkers/cheekpieces nowadays: quirky. *A. J. Chamberlain*

ALMAJD (IRE) 2 b.c. (Mar 21) Marju (IRE) 127 – Irish Valley (USA) (Irish River **99 p** (FR) 131) [2007 7m* 7d⁵ Oct 27] half-brother to several winners, notably very smart 7f (when champion 2-y-o) to 9.8f winner Alhaarth (by Unfuwain): dam maiden half-sister to Green Dancer: useful form: made good impression in winning 15-runner maiden at Newmarket (beat Virtual by 1¼ lengths) in October: 15/8 favourite, showed inexperience when 3 lengths fifth of 11 to Beacon Lodge in Horris Hill Stakes at Newbury later in month, rallying in finish: will be suited by 1m: sure to progress further. *Sir Michael Stoute*

ALMA MATER 4 b.f. Sadler's Wells (USA) 132 – Alouette 105 (Darshaan 133) [2007 **102 p** p10g³ p12.2g³ 12g* 12.5s* Nov 26] seventh foal: half-sister to several winners, including very smart 7f (at 2 yrs) and 1¼m (dual Champion Stakes) winner Alborada and smart winner up to 1½m Albanova (both by Alzao): dam, Irish 1m (at 2 yrs) and 1½m winner, sister to dam of Quarter Moon and Yesterday (both by Sadler's Wells) and half-sister to very smart 1¼m winner Last Second and smart stayer Alleluia: unraced prior to 2007 (reportedly sustained tendon injury as a yearling): progressed well after 4-month break, winning maiden at Musselburgh and 17-runner listed race at Fontainebleau (useful form, made all to beat Sworn Mum shade comfortably by 4 lengths) in November: will stay beyond 12.5f: sure to improve further. *Sir Mark Prescott*

ALMAMIA 2 b.f. (Mar 10) Hernando (FR) 127 – Alborada 122 (Alzao (USA) 117) **78 p** [2007 8.2m³ 8s³ p8.6g³ Nov 8] leggy filly: fourth foal: half-sister to useful 1m/10.5f winner Alvarita (by Selkirk): dam, dual Champion Stakes winner (also 7f winner at 2 yrs), sister to smart 1¼m/1½m performer Albanova, an excellent family: fair maiden: third at all starts, much better form on turf than polytrack: will be well suited by 1¼m/1½m. *Sir Mark Prescott*

ALMANSHOOD (USA) 5 b.g. Bahri (USA) 125 – Lahan 117 (Unfuwain (USA) 131) **65** [2007 81: p13.9g⁵ p13.9g 12.7d 14d⁶ 8s⁶ 16m f14d⁶ Dec 15] big, good sort: fluent mover: just fair nowadays: left P. Gilligan after second outing: stays 1¾m: acts on polytrack and good to firm going, probably on soft: tried tongue tied/in headgear. *T. Hogan, Ireland*

ALMATY EXPRESS 5 b.g. Almaty (USA) – Express Girl 75 (Sylvan Express **–** 117) [2007 66, a72: p5.1g* p5.1g* p5.1g² p5.1g* p5.1g p5.1g 5m 5g p5.1g⁵ p5.1g **a85** p5.1d⁶ p5.1s⁴ Dec 21] smallish gelding: fairly useful handicapper on all-weather, lightly raced on turf nowadays: better than ever in 2007, winning 3 times at Wolverhampton in January/February: best at 5f: acts on polytrack: wears blinkers/cheekpieces: usually makes running. *J. R. Weymes*

ALMAVARA (USA) 5 b. or br.g. Fusaichi Pegasus (USA) 130 – Name of Love (IRE) 105 (Petardia 113) [2007 12g⁵ p12g⁵ Jun 23] fair performer at 3 yrs: well held on return to Flat in 2007: tried visored/blinkered: signs of temperament. *C. P. Morlock* –

ALMIZAN (IRE) 7 b.g. Darshaan 133 – Bint Albaadiya (USA) 108 (Woodman (USA) 126) [2007 69: p16g 16.4m Jul 12] leggy, angular gelding: just modest handicapper nowadays: stays 21f: acts on polytrack, firm and soft going: tried visored, blinkered nowadays: fairly useful hurdler. *G. L. Moore* **61**

AL MOGEER (IRE) 2 b.g. (Mar 24) Montjeu (IRE) 137 – Jumbo Delight (IRE) (Don't Forget Me 127) [2007 8g f8d Dec 15] good-bodied gelding: last in maidens. *K. A. Ryan* –

ALMONDILLO (IRE) 3 b.g. Tagula (IRE) 116 – Almond Flower (IRE) (Alzao (USA) 117) [2007 –: 7.1m p7.1g p6g p6g⁵ p7g⁴ Nov 6] strong, stocky gelding: modest maiden: stays easy 7f: raced only on polytrack and good to firm going: blinkered final outing. *C. F. Wall* **56**

ALMORA GURU 3 b.f. Ishiguru (USA) 114 – Princess Almora 88 (Pivotal 124) [2007 58: 6g³ 6m 6m* 6.1m 6g² 5g⁵ 6d 6m 6m p6g p6g⁶ p7.1g⁵ p8.6g³ p8.6d Dec 17] close-coupled filly: modest performer: won handicap at Yarmouth in April: stays easy 8.6f: acts on polytrack and firm going, probably on soft. *W. M. Brisbourne* **58**

ALMOST MARRIED (IRE) 3 b.g. Indian Ridge 123 – Shining Hour (USA) 104 (Red Ransom (USA)) [2007 f8g⁴ p6g Jun 29] 35,000Y: third foal: half-brother to useful 6f winner Clear Impression (by Danehill): dam 2-y-o 5f (Queen Mary Stakes)/5.7f winner (only season to race): better effort in maidens when fourth to Aegis at Southwell: sold 6,800 gns in October. *J. D. Bethell* **59**

AL MOULATHAM 8 b.g. Rainbow Quest (USA) 134 – High Standard 83 (Kris 135) [2007 f16g³ p13.9g f12g⁶ f14g* f16g² 18g f14g³ 13d 15.9d p16g⁵ p16.5g Oct 20] rather leggy, attractive gelding: fair performer nowadays: won claimer at Southwell in March: stays 2m: acts on fibresand and dirt, no recent form on turf: wears headgear/tongue strap: front runner. *R. Ford* **a67**

ALMOUTAZ (USA) 2 b. or br.c. (Jan 29) Kingmambo (USA) 125 – Dessert (USA) 109 (Storm Cat (USA)) [2007 6m⁴ 6g⁵ 6g* Nov 2] strong, good-topped colt: first foal: dam, US Grade 1 9f winner, half-sister to Breeders' Cup Turf winner Johar, out of very smart US performer up to 1¾m Windsharp: fairly useful form: off 2 months, improved to win maiden at Newmarket by length from The Gatekeeper, travelling strongly: bred to stay at least 1m, but has plenty of speed: looks highly strung, has given trouble at stalls. *B. W. Hills* **84**

ALMOUTEZAH (USA) 2 br.f. (Apr 15) Storm Cat (USA) – Probable Colony (USA) (Pleasant Colony (USA)) [2007 7g Nov 3] $2,300,000Y: rangy filly: has fluent action: sixth foal: closely related to very smart US performer up 1¼m Summer Colony (by Summer Squall) and half-sister to winner in US by Saint Ballado: dam unraced out of Kentucky Oaks runner-up Withallprobability: 11/4 favourite but better for race, 3 lengths eighth of 19 to La Coveta in maiden at Newmarket, going well long way: will do better. *M. A. Jarvis* **65 p**

ALMOWJ 4 b.g. Fasliyev (USA) 120 – Tiriana (Common Grounds 118) [2007 61: p8g² f8g p7g⁵ Feb 25] sturdy gelding: modest maiden: stays 8.6f: acts on all-weather and good to firm ground: tried blinkered/in cheekpieces: has hung left. *C. E. Brittain* **53**

AL MUHEER (IRE) 2 b.c. (Mar 22) Diktat 126 – Dominion Rose (USA) 65 (Spinning World (USA) 130) [2007 5.1m³ 5g³ 7d³ 7m² 7.6f* 6m⁵ p8m² Oct 6] 35,000Y: close-coupled, quite good-topped colt: second foal: half-brother to 3-y-o Suki Bear: dam, 7f winner, closely related to smart Irish/US winner up to 9f Castledale: useful performer: won maiden at Lingfield in August: placed 5 of 6 other starts, 2 lengths second to Art Master in minor event at Lingfield final one (tongue tied): stays 1m: acts on polytrack and firm going. *C. E. Brittain* **97**

AL NAAHADTH (USA) 3 b. or br.g. Storm Cat (USA) – Ajina (USA) 125 (Strawberry Road (AUS) 128) [2007 8.3m 10m⁴ Sep 14] $3,000,000Y: lengthy gelding: fourth foal: half-brother to minor winners in USA by Deputy Minister and A P Indy: dam winner up to 1¼m in USA, including 3 Grade 1s (also successful in Grade 2 at 2 yrs): visored, much better effort in maidens when fourth to Kaateb at Sandown, tiring: gelded after: may prove best at 1m: has left Godolphin. *Saeed bin Suroor* **73**

ALNWICK 3 b.g. Kylian (USA) – Cebwob 85 (Rock City 120) [2007 57: p10g^4 p12g^2 **65** p12g^6 p13g^2 p16g^6 14g^5 16g^3 Aug 25] tall, close-coupled gelding: fair maiden: stays 2m: acts on polytrack, unraced on going softer than good on turf: consistent. *P. D. Cundell*

ALONE IT STANDS (IRE) 4 b.g. King Charlemagne (USA) 120 – Golden Concorde – (Super Concorde (USA) 128) [2007 –: 6g 6g p5.1g Jun 1] compact gelding: little solid form: tried visored. *D. Nicholls*

ALONG THE NILE 5 b.g. Desert Prince (IRE) 130 – Golden Fortune 102 (Forzando **89** 122) [2007 93: 10.1s 10g^2 10m 9.9g 10.3m 10m^5 Sep 27] strong, lengthy gelding: fairly useful handicapper: stays 1¼m: best form on good/good to firm ground: often tongue tied, in cheekpieces final start: none too consistent: won both starts over hurdles late in year. *K. G. Reveley*

ALONSO DE GUZMAN (IRE) 3 b.g. Docksider (USA) 124 – Addaya (IRE) **70** (Persian Bold 123) [2007 –: p9.5g* p12.2g* f11d^4 p12.2d^4 Dec 27] €5,000Y: seventh foal: brother to 1½m winner Night Cruise and half-brother to several winners, including smart 7f (including at 2 yrs)/1m winner Priors Lodge (by Grand Lodge): dam ran once: fair performer: well-backed winner of handicaps at Wolverhampton in October and November: ran well final start: stays 1½m: acts on polytrack. *J. R. Boyle*

ALO PURA 3 b.f. Anabaa (USA) 130 – Rubies From Burma (USA) 104 (Forty Niner **85** (USA)) [2007 8g^2 8d^3 a5f^3 Dec 21] 210,000Y: strong, lengthy filly: third foal: half-sister to 4-y-o Ivory Gala: dam, Irish 5f/6f winner, half-sister to smart miler Culture Vulture: won maiden at Ascot in July by head from Safwa, still green and hanging left: left M. Jarvis and off nearly 5 months, inadequate trip when third to Secret Place in handicap at Jebel Ali final outing: stays 1m: acts on good to soft going. *D. J. Selvaratnam, UAE*

ALOVERA (IRE) 3 ch.f. King's Best (USA) 132 – Angelic Sounds (IRE) (The Noble – Player (USA) 126) [2007 93: 8m^5 7.1d Jun 24] leggy filly: fairly useful form at 2 yrs: well below form in minor event at Ascot and listed race at Warwick in 2007: stays 1m: sold €150,000 in November. *M. R. Channon*

ALPEN ADVENTURE (IRE) 2 b.g. (Mar 12) Shinko Forest (IRE) – Alpina (USA) **67** 69 (El Prado (IRE) 119) [2007 5d 5g^4 6d^4 6g^5 6g^2 7.5v Jul 7] 2,000Y: strong, good-bodied gelding: fifth foal: half-brother to 2 winners, including 3-y-o Lapina: dam lightly-raced half-sister to dam of Rodrigo de Triano: fair maiden: should have stayed 1m: tried in cheekpieces: dead. *Mrs L. Stubbs*

ALPES MARITIMES 3 b.g. Danehill Dancer (IRE) 117 – Miss Riviera 103 (Kris **94** 135) [2007 82: 10m^3 11.9g 8d^5 8d^3 10m^3 10.3m^3 8m^4 7v^4 p7g^2 p10g* p10g* Dec 4] big, strong gelding: fairly useful performer: sold from G. Wragg 77,000 gns, won maiden in November (despite drifting right) and handicap in December, both at Lingfield: stays 1¼m: acts on polytrack, good to firm and good to soft going: ran poorly in cheekpieces seventh outing. *G. L. Moore*

ALPHUN (IRE) 5 b.g. Orpen (USA) 116 – Fakhira (IRE) 83 (Jareer (USA) 115) [2007 – § –: p12.2g May 14] ungenuine maiden: refused to race only outing on Flat in 2007. *N. B. King*

ALQAAYID 6 b.g. Machiavellian (USA) 123 – One So Wonderful 121 (Nashwan **63 §** (USA) 135) [2007 66§, a56§: 14.1m 10.5d 10s* 11g^5 10g 12g p10g p10g 10.5s Nov 23] **a– §** sturdy gelding: modest performer: first win in handicap at Brighton in May: stays 11f: acts on polytrack, soft and good to firm going: tried blinkered: ungenuine. *P. W. Hiatt*

AL QASI (IRE) 4 b.c. Elnadim (USA) 128 – Delisha (Salse (USA) 128) [2007 117p: **121** 6g^6 6d 6d^2 6v* 6g^5 7d^2 8g Dec 9] good-topped, attractive colt: very smart performer: won Patrick P. O'Leary Memorial Phoenix Sprint Stakes at the Curragh in August by 1¼ lengths from Evening Time: better than bare result next 2 starts, good 1¼ lengths second of 15 to Miss Lucifer in Challenge Stakes at Newmarket on second, crossed by winner final 1f: stays 7f (behind throughout in Hong Kong Mile final start): acts on polytrack and any turf going: sometimes bandaged fore joints: held up. *P. W. Chapple-Hyam*

AL QUDRA (IRE) 5 b.h. Cape Cross (IRE) 129 – Alvilda (IRE) (Caerleon (USA) – 132) [2007 6g Jul 9] leggy horse: no form since 2004 (missed 2006): tried blinkered. *J. R. Jenkins*

AL RAYANAH 4 b.f. Almushtarak (IRE) 122 – Desert Bloom (FR) (Last Tycoon 131) **56** [2007 70: 8m 8d 8d^6 p7.1g^2 7d 8g^6 p8g 8m 7m 7g^3 8d^2 8d^3 p8g^5 Nov 12] modest performer: stays 1¼m: acts on all-weather, firm and soft going: has hung. *G. Prodromou*

ALRIDA (IRE) 8 b.g. Ali-Royal (IRE) 127 – Ride Bold (USA) (J O Tobin (USA) 130) **78** [2007 p13.9g^5 14g^2 18g 14m^5 Jun 2] leggy gelding: fair handicapper: unraced in 2005/06: stayed 2¼f: acted on polytrack and any turf going: tried in cheekpieces: held up: dead. *R. A. Fahey*

ALSADAA (USA) 4 b.g. Kingmambo (USA) 125 – Aljawza (USA) 86 (Riverman **72** (USA) 131) [2007 79: 8.2g 8m f7g* f7g f7g 7m 10.5m³ 12s 10.1d⁵ 10s 10m³ Aug 10] close-coupled, quite attractive gelding: fair handicapper: won at Southwell in April: left M. Easterby 16,000 gns prior to final start: stays 10.5f: acts on fibresand and good to firm ground: tongue tied at 3 yrs: held up: useful hurdler, successful 3 times in 2007. *Mrs L. J. Mongan*

ALSADEEK (IRE) 2 b.c. (Apr 9) Fasliyev (USA) 120 – Khulan (USA) 103 (Bahri **79** (USA) 125) [2007 6g² 6m³ 6.1m Oct 3] lengthy, unfurnished colt: third foal: half-brother to 4-y-o Miswadah and to a 1m winner in Qatar by King's Best: dam, 2-y-o 6f winner, out of close relative to high-class sprinter Elnadim and half-sister to Irish 1000 Guineas winner Mehthaaf: fair maiden: placed at Goodwood and Newbury (third to Stimulation), over 3 months apart: seemed amiss final start: may prove best at 5f/6f. *J. L. Dunlop*

ALSERAAJ (USA) 2 ch.f. (Mar 21) El Prado (IRE) 119 – Barzah (IRE) 98 (Darshaan **58 p** 133) [2007 7d⁶ Oct 9] lengthy, good-bodied filly: second foal: dam, 2-y-o 6f winner (stayed 1½m), out of half-sister to high-class 1½m to 2m performer Glacial Storm: 7/1 and green, best of those that raced towards far side when sixth of 14 to stable-companion Laughter in maiden at Leicester: likely to stay 1¼m: will improve. *Sir Michael Stoute*

AL SHEMALI 3 ch.c. Medicean 128 – Bathilde (IRE) 102 (Generous (IRE) 139) [2007 **114** 97p: 9m⁴ 8m 10.4g³ 10g² 12s Jul 1] good-bodied colt: has a quick, unimpressive action: smart performer: good efforts in 2007 when placed in Dante Stakes at York (5 lengths third to Authorized) and listed event at Royal Ascot (head second to Zaham, finishing strongly): tongue tied, only seventh behind Soldier of Fortune in Irish Derby at the Curragh final start: should stay 1½m: acts on soft going, probably on good to firm: sold privately, and joined Godolphin. *Sir Michael Stoute*

ALTAR (IRE) 3 b.c. Cape Cross (IRE) 129 – Sophrana (IRE) (Polar Falcon (USA) 126) **81** [2007 77: 9.9g 8m* Jun 14] good-topped colt: fairly useful performer: won handicap at Newbury in June: should stay 1¼m: acts on good to firm going: sold 33,000 gns, sent to Bahrain. *R. Hannon*

ALTENBURG (FR) 5 b.g. Sadler's Wells (USA) 132 – Anna of Saxony 111 (Ela- **74** Mana-Mou 132) [2007 88: 11.7d 14s 16g⁴ Nov 2] good-topped gelding: good walker: just fair maiden in 2007: stays 2m: acts on good to firm and good to soft going: signs of temperament. *Mrs N. Smith*

ALTERCATION 2 ch.f. (May 9) Polish Precedent (USA) 131 – Show Off 56 (Efisio **51** 120) [2007 5.1g 5.1f⁵ 5.1g 5.3f⁶ 7f Sep 10] small, leggy filly: fifth foal: half-sister to 3 winners, including fairly useful 2005 2-y-o 6f winner Bling (by Mark of Esteem) and 7f winner Bluff (by Bluebird): dam sprint maiden (ran only at 2 yrs): modest maiden: will prove best at 5f/6f: acts on firm ground: sold 3,000 gns. *W. Jarvis*

Patrick P. O'Leary Memorial Phoenix Sprint Stakes, the Curragh—Al Qasi (right) improves again and is well on top at the finish; Evening Time and Grecian Dancer are placed

AL THARIB (USA) 3 b.c. Silver Hawk (USA) 123 – Ameriflora (USA) (Danzig **113**
(USA)) [2007 87p: 10g⁵ 10.3m* 12d p11g* p12g² 9d Oct 19] strong, well-made colt: has
powerful, round action: smart performer: won maiden at Chester in May and 4-runner
minor event at Kempton (beat Marzelline by 4 lengths) in August: best effort when 1½
lengths second to Steppe Dancer in September Stakes at Kempton: gone in coat, well
below form in Darley Stakes at Newmarket final start (said to have finished lame): stays
1½m: acts on polytrack and good to firm going: front runner. *Sir Michael Stoute*

ALTILHAR (USA) 4 b.g. Dynaformer (USA) – Al Desima 93 (Emperor Jones (USA) **89**
119) [2007 86: p12g⁵ p12g 14.6g Oct 26] robust gelding: fairly useful handicapper: stays
11.5f: acts on polytrack and good to firm going: sometimes blinkered: useful hurdler.
G. L. Moore

ALTITUDE 2 gr.f. (Mar 28) Green Desert (USA) 127 – Alouette 105 (Darshaan 133) **83**
[2007 p6g⁶ p7g² 7g⁴ p8.6g² p8.6g⁵ 10m² Oct 3] unfurnished filly: half-sister to several
winners, including very smart 7f (at 2 yrs) and 1¼m (dual Champion Stakes) winner
Alborada, smart winner up to 1½m Albanova (both by Alzao) and 4-y-o Alma Mater:
dam, Irish 1m (at 2 yrs) and 1½m winner, sister to dam of Oaks-placed trio Quarter Moon,
Yesterday and All My Loving, also half-sister to very smart 1¼m winner Last Second:
fairly useful maiden: second 3 times, including in nursery at Nottingham final start: will
be suited by 1½m+: acts on polytrack and good to firm going. *Sir Mark Prescott*

ALTO SINGER (IRE) 2 b.f. (Jan 19) Alhaarth (IRE) 126 – Sonatina 103 (Distant **–**
Relative 128) [2007 5m Apr 9] 18,000Y: compact filly: first foal: dam 2-y-o 6f winner
(stayed 1m): last in maiden at Warwick. *B. R. Millman*

ALTOS REALES 3 b.f. Mark of Esteem (IRE) 137 – Karsiyaka (IRE) (Kahyasi 130) **66**
[2007 p7.1g p9.5g p6g 7m 8d⁶ 9.9m p8.6g p9.5g⁴ p11g* p11g⁴ p12g³ p12.2d³ p12.2d²
Dec 27] 6,000Y: fourth foal: half-sister to useful 7f winner (including at 2 yrs) Contractor
(by Spectrum) and fairly useful 1m winner Pearl's Girl (by King's Best): dam unraced:
fair performer: won handicap at Kempton in November: suited by 11f/1½m: acts on
polytrack: often slowly away: held up: signs of temperament. *D. Shaw*

ALTO VERTIGO 4 b.g. Averti (IRE) 117 – Singer On The Roof 62 (Chief Singer **74**
131) [2007 5m² 6g² 6m p6g³ p7.1g* f7d² Dec 11] strong gelding: fair performer: won on
handicap debut at Wolverhampton (by 6 lengths) in December, dictating: stays 7f: raced
only on all-weather and good/good to firm ground. *P. C. Haslam*

ALUCICA 4 b.f. Celtic Swing 138 – Acicula (IRE) 96 (Night Shift (USA)) [2007 –: **55**
p7.1g p6g p7.1g f5g f6g p6g² p6g p6g⁴ 5g 6g³ p7g* 7.1d Jun 25] modest performer: won
handicap at Lingfield in June: stays easy 7f: acts on polytrack: often slowly away: usually
visored. *D. Shaw*

ALUGAT (IRE) 4 b.g. Tagula (IRE) 116 – Notley Park 71 (Wolfhound (USA) 126) **–**
[2007 78: 6m 5g 6m Aug 7] sturdy gelding: fair handicapper in 2006: last all starts at
4 yrs: tried visored, usually wears cheekpieces. *Mrs A. Duffield*

ALUJAWILL (IRE) 4 b.g. Erhaab (USA) 127 – El-Libaab 84 (Unfuwain (USA) 131) **–**
[2007 –: 8.2s May 12] small gelding: little sign of ability. *Evan Williams*

ALWAABEL 2 b.c. (Jan 27) Green Desert (USA) 127 – Etizaaz (USA) 117 (Diesis 133) **85**
[2007 6m⁶ 6m² 6d² 6m⁴ Nov 10] tall, lengthy colt: has plenty of scope: fourth foal: half-
brother to 5-y-o Munaddam: dam, 7f (at 2 yrs)/1m winner who was second in Prix
Vermeille, out of half-sister to Swain: fairly useful maiden: runner-up at Newbury and
Leicester (absent 4 months in between), and better than bare result (hampered) final start:
will probably stay 7f/1m. *J. L. Dunlop*

ALWARIAH 4 b.f. Xaar 132 – Signs And Wonders 75§ (Danehill (USA) 126) [2007 63: **53**
f8g⁶ p10g 8.1m 8d p7g 7g p7g⁶ Jun 14] smallish, lengthy filly: modest maiden: left
C. Brittain 3,500 gns after reappearance: stays 7f: acts on all-weather, firm and good to
soft going. *Ms J. S. Doyle*

ALWAYS A STORY 5 b.g. Lake Coniston (IRE) 131 – Silk St James (Pas de Seul 133) **44**
[2007 43: p8g⁶ p8g⁵ p8g f8g 10.1d 10.1d p10m Oct 13] poor maiden: stays easy 1m: tried
blinkered/in cheekpieces. *Miss D. Mountain*

ALWAYS ATTRACTIVE (IRE) 2 ch.f. (Apr 26) King's Best (USA) 132 – Fife **– p**
(IRE) 95 (Lomond (USA) 128) [2007 7.1g Oct 2] €46,000F, 15,000Y: half-sister to
several winners, including useful 1m and 9.8f winner in UAE Hudood (by Gone West) and
fairly useful 1995 2-y-o 6f/7f winner Witch of Fife (by Lear Fan), herself dam of
smart sprinter Ho Choi: dam 1m winner: 14/1, drawn wide and needed experience in
maiden at Warwick: should do better. *M. Johnston*

ALWAYS BAILEYS (IRE) 4 ch.g. Mister Baileys 123 – Dubiously (USA) (Jolie Jo **69 d** (USA)) [2007 73: p12.2g⁵ p13.9g⁵ p13.9g 12.6s⁴ 12.1s 14m p13.9g Nov 12] tall gelding: fair handicapper: below form after reappearance in 2007: stays 1½m: acts on polytrack, firm and good to soft ground: tried blinkered: often looks hard ride. *T. Wall*

ALWAYS BEST 3 b.g. Best of The Bests (IRE) 122 – Come To The Point (Pursuit of **64** Love 124) [2007 70: 12m* 12m⁵ 12.6m 9.9m⁵ p12.2g 10.9d² 12.1s⁵ 12s⁴ p12.2g⁵ 14m 12.4m⁵ p13.9g p13.9g 11.9g⁴ p10g² Oct 31] tall gelding: modest handicapper: won 3-runner event at Catterick in April: stays 1½m: acts on polytrack, firm and soft going: tried in headgear: races prominently: none too consistent: sold 9,000 gns. *M. Johnston*

ALWAYS BRAVE 2 ch.g. (Mar 4) Danehill Dancer (IRE) 117 – Digge Park (USA) **75** (Capote (USA)) [2007 7m 7f⁴ 8g⁴ 6m⁶ p8.6g Oct 5] 2,000F, 9,000Y: tall gelding, on weak side as 2-y-o: first foal: dam, a 2-y-o 9f winner in Italy, half-sister to US Grade 1 9f winner Famous Digger: fair maiden: fourth at Goodwood third start (standout effort), gelded after final one: should stay 1¼m. *M. Johnston*

ALWAYS CERTAIN (USA) 2 ch.g. (Apr 9) Giant's Causeway (USA) 132 – Mining **71 p** Missharriet (USA) (Mining (USA)) [2007 7.1m⁶ 6d⁶ Oct 12] $170,000F, $40,000Y: good-topped gelding: second foal: half-brother to winner in US by Crafty Prospector: dam US 2-y-o 5f/6f (minor stakes) winner: encouraging sixth in maidens at Chepstow and York (behind Calming Influence): gelded after: will stay 1m: capable of better. *M. Johnston*

ALWAYS ESTEEMED (IRE) 7 b.g. Mark of Esteem (IRE) 137 – Always Far (USA) **– §** (Alydar (USA)) [2007 103d: 8m Aug 1] big, lengthy gelding: unreliable performer, useful in 2006: well held in claimer only start at 7 yrs: best around 1m: acts on polytrack, firm and good to soft ground: wears blinkers/cheekpieces: tends to hang. *J. O'Reilly*

ALWAYS FRUITFUL 3 b.c. Fruits of Love (USA) 127 – Jerre Jo Glanville (USA) **94** (Skywalker (USA)) [2007 90: 8m 8g 10m⁵ 12g³ 12f 11.8d⁴ Oct 9] angular, quite good-topped colt: fairly useful handicapper: good efforts in frame 2 of last 3 starts: stays 1½m: acts on good to firm and good to soft going: sold 18,000 gns. *M. Johnston*

ALWAYS READY 2 ch.c. (Mar 12) Best of The Bests (IRE) 122 – Tahara (IRE) **83** (Caerleon (USA) 132) [2007 6d 6s³ 7m 7m² 8s⁴ 7.1m² 8g² p8m Oct 11] 21,000F, 23,000Y: good-topped colt: sixth foal: half-brother to several winners, including 4-y-o Godfrey Street and 7f winner Tamora (by Dr Fong): dam ran twice: fairly useful maiden: runner-up 4 times, twice in nurseries: stays 1m: acts on soft and good to firm going, below form on polytrack final start: races prominently: consistent. *C. E. Brittain*

ALWAYS SPARKLE (CAN) 3 ch.c. Grand Slam (USA) 120 – Dancing All Night **65** (USA) (Nijinsky (CAN) 138) [2007 60: 10.2g p12.2g⁶ p12g p10g⁴ Dec 12] fair maiden: stays 1½m: acts on polytrack, unraced on extremes of going on turf. *B. Palling*

AMADEUS WOLF 4 b.c. Mozart (IRE) 131 – Rachelle (IRE) (Mark of Esteem (IRE) **122** 137) [2007 120: 6g* 6d 6m 5g 6g 6g Sep 8] good-topped, attractive colt: impresses in appearance: very smart performer: better than ever when winning Duke of York Hearth-stead Homes Stakes at York in May, beating Red Clubs by 1¼ lengths: below form after in Golden Jubilee Stakes at Royal Ascot (said to have had inflamed throat), July Cup at Newmarket, Nunthorpe Stakes at York (seventh to Kingsgate Native) and Sprint Cup at

Duke of York Hearthstead Homes Stakes, York—in a strong renewal, Amadeus Wolf wins from Red Clubs (right), Soldier's Tale (third left), Rising Shadow (far left) and Assertive (second left)

Haydock: was effective at 5f/6f: acted on soft and good to firm going: had had 2 handlers: to stand at Irish National Stud, fee €10,000. *K. A. Ryan*

AMANDA CARTER 3 b.f. Tobougg (IRE) 125 – Al Guswa 98 (Shernazar 131) [2007 **73** –: 7.1g 9.3m* 10m² 12.1s⁶ 10.1d* 9.1s 10.3m⁶ Aug 31] leggy filly: fair handicapper: improved to win at Carlisle in June and Newcastle in July: should stay 1½m: acts on good to firm and good to soft going, seemingly not on soft. *R. A. Fahey*

AMANDALINI 2 b.f. (Feb 9) Bertolini (USA) 125 – Luxurious (USA) (Lyphard **–** (USA) 132) [2007 p8g 8g Oct 26] 27,000F, 70,000Y: tall, lengthy filly: half-sister to numerous winners, notably smart French/US performer up to 1¾m Luberon: dam, French maiden, out of Prix Marcel Boussac winner Tropicaro: no impact in maidens: sold 5,000 gns. *B. J. Meehan*

AMANDA'S LAD (IRE) 7 b.g. Danetime (IRE) 121 – Art Duo 86 (Artaius (USA) **48** 129) [2007 52, a63: f6g⁶ f5g f5g f5g⁶ 5g 5f Apr 20] tall gelding: modest performer: effective at 5f to 7f: acts on all-weather, firm and good to soft going: tried blinkered. *M. C. Chapman*

AMANJENA 2 b.f. (Apr 24) Beat Hollow 126 – Placement (Kris 135) [2007 8d⁶ 8.2g³ **76 p** Nov 7] lengthy, unfurnished filly: sixth foal: half-sister to useful 5f (at 2 yrs)/7f winner Presto Vento (by Air Express): dam unraced close relative of smart French sprinter Pole Position/half-sister to Sun Chariot Stakes winner Danceabout: fair form in maidens at Newmarket and Nottingham (still green/awkward, third to Wintercast): likely to stay 1¼m: open to further improvement. *A. M. Balding*

AMARNA (USA) 3 b.c. Danzig (USA) – Mysterial (USA) (Alleged (USA) 138) [2007 **105 p** 8.1d⁴ p8g* p8g* 8.1m* p8m² 8d* Oct 12] good-topped, attractive colt: sixth foal: brother to very smart miler (7f winner at 2 yrs) Librettist and half-brother to high-class 7f (at 2 yrs)/1m winner Dubai Destination and useful 1¼m winner Destination Dubai (both by Kingmambo): dam, ran twice, half-sister to very smart Japanese sprinters Agnes World (by Danzig) and Hishi Akebono: useful form: won maiden and handicap at Kempton in August, and handicaps at Sandown in September and York (beat Prince of Thebes ½ length, racing wide before strong pressure to get up) in October: stays 1m: acts on polytrack, good to firm and good to soft ground: waited with: smart performer in the making. *Saeed bin Suroor*

AMARYLLIS (GER) 5 br.m. Law Society (USA) 130 – Alyeska (GER) (Northjet **64** 136) [2007 12s 11d⁵ 12d 12m 12d⁵ 12m 12.5m⁵ 12g³ 13.8g⁴ Oct 20] first foal: dam German 10.5f/1½m winner: trained by M. Trybuhl in Germany in 2006, winning maiden at Cologne and handicaps at Cologne and Hamburg: modest handicapper: creditable fourth at Catterick final start: stays 1¾m: acts on heavy going: tongue tied: tried in cheekpieces. *T. Hogan, Ireland*

AMAZING DAY 2 b.g. (Mar 31) Averti (IRE) 117 – Daynabee 61 (Common Grounds **61** 118) [2007 5m⁴ 5m⁵ p5.1g³ 6g* 6m 6f Jul 30] sturdy gelding: modest performer: won seller at Ripon (left W. Turner £6,000) in May: raced at 5f/6f. *John A. Harris*

AMAZING KING (IRE) 3 b.g. King Charlemagne (USA) 120 – Kraemer (USA) **62** (Lyphard (USA) 132) [2007 63: p8g 7g³ 7d p7g⁴ p8g⁵ Aug 18] rather leggy gelding: modest maiden on Flat: should stay 1m: acts on polytrack and good to soft going: won juvenile hurdle in November: sold 9,500 gns following month, then gelded. *W. G. M. Turner*

AMAZING REQUEST 3 b.c. Rainbow Quest (USA) 134 – Maze Garden (USA) **87** (Riverman (USA) 131) [2007 85: 10m⁶ 12.3m 11.6m⁵ 12d 13.3m Aug 17] good-topped colt: fairly useful handicapper: stays 1½m: raced only on good to firm/good to soft going: pulled up and dismounted inside final 1f second start: sold 8,000 gns. *R. Charlton*

AMAZING SPIRIT 2 ch.f. (Mar 30) Hawk Wing (USA) 136 – Free Spirit (IRE) **–** (Caerleon (USA) 132) [2007 5m 6m 7v 6.5m Sep 12] 12,000F, 12,000Y: tall, leggy filly: sixth foal: half-sister to 1m winner (including at 2 yrs) Arkholme (by Robellino) and 6f winner Perfect Love (by Pursuit of Love), both fairly useful: dam unraced half-sister to smart 1m/1¼m performer Gold Academy: no form. *Miss V. Haigh*

AMAZING STAR (IRE) 2 b.c. (Apr 5) Soviet Star (USA) 128 – Sadika (IRE) 55 **81** (Bahhare (USA) 122) [2007 7g p7g* p7g³ Dec 7] €29,000Y, £110,000 2-y-o: first foal: dam, little form, half-sister to several useful performers, including dam of very smart 1¼m performer Best of The Bests: fairly useful form: won minor event at Lingfield in November by neck from Regal Bird, quickening well: creditable third to Reformist in minor event at Dundalk next time: will probably stay 1m. *M. Halford, Ireland*

AMBER BAMBER 2 b.f. (Apr 18) Piccolo 121 – Martha P Perkins (IRE) 51 (Fayruz **–** 116) [2007 5.7f Sep 16] third foal: dam sprint maiden: last in maiden. *D. Burchell*

AMBER GLORY 4 b.f. Foxhound (USA) 103 – Compton Amber 78 (Puissance 110) – [2007 65: f6g Jan 9] close-coupled filly: modest performer: well held only start in 2007: stays 6f: acts on all-weather and heavy going: usually wears cheekpieces/blinkers: races up with pace: sent to Israel. *K. A. Ryan*

AMBER ISLE 3 b.g. Weet-A-Minute (IRE) 106 – Cloudy Reef 57 (Cragador 110) 57 [2007 66: p6g⁵ p7.1g 5.9f p7.1g⁶ 7g p6m Nov 11] modest maiden: raced only around 6f/7f: acts on polytrack. *D. Carroll*

AMBER RIDGE 2 b.g. (Feb 4) Tumbleweed Ridge 117 – Amber Brown 67 (Thowra 57 (FR)) [2007 p5.1g p6g 5.7s⁶ 6.1d⁵ 6s⁴ Sep 24] modest maiden: claimed from D. Ivory £6,000 after debut: bred to stay 7f: acts on soft ground. *B. P. J. Baugh*

AMBROSE PRINCESS (IRE) 2 b.f. (Apr 27) Chevalier (IRE) 115 – Mark One 85 58 (Mark of Esteem (IRE) 137) [2007 6m 6m⁶ 7m 6g* p8g⁴ p7.1g* p8.6g p7.1g⁶ p6g⁵ p8.6g f6d³ p7g Dec 19] €6,500Y: close-coupled, angular filly: third foal: dam, 1¼m/1½m winner, out of half-sister to very smart stayer Arctic Owl: modest performer: won sellers at Ripon in August and Wolverhampton (left J. S. Moore 6,000 gns) in October: creditable third in nursery at Southwell: will stay 1¼m: acts on polytrack and good to firm going: below form in cheekpieces. *R. A. Harris*

AMBROSIANO 3 b.g. Averti (IRE) 117 – Secret Circle (Magic Ring (IRE) 115) [2007 77 68: p8g* 8.2g* 8.2m 7m⁴ 8.1g⁴ 7g⁶ Jul 20] big gelding: fair performer: won maiden at Lingfield in March and handicap at Nottingham in April: stays 1m: acts on polytrack, raced only on good/good to firm going on turf: sometimes races freely. *C. G. Cox*

AMEEQ (USA) 5 b. or br.g. Silver Hawk (USA) 123 – Haniya (IRE) 92 (Caerleon 90 (USA) 132) [2007 88: p12g² 12m⁶ Jul 13] quite good-topped gelding: fairly useful handicapper (also over hurdles): good second to Polish Power at Lingfield on reappearance: should stay 1¾m: acts on polytrack, good to firm and good to soft going: tried tongue tied. *G. L. Moore*

AMERICAN ART (IRE) 2 b.g. (Mar 4) Statue of Liberty (USA) 115 – Peshawar 79 (Persian Bold 123) [2007 5m⁶ 6g⁴ 6s 6f* 7m³ Aug 31] €35,000F, 58,000Y: rangy, useful-looking gelding: has a fluent action: half-brother to several winners abroad, including useful German 7.5f to 9.5f winner Pure Pleasure (by Platini): dam unraced half-sister to dam of very smart German 1m to 11f winner Arcadio: fair performer: won maiden at Pontefract in August: again soon off bridle when third in nursery at Chester (gelded after): will stay 1m: acts on firm going: tongue tied last 2 starts: difficult ride. *B. W. Hills*

AMERICAN WELCOME (IRE) 2 b.c. (May 10) Statue of Liberty (USA) 115 – 57 Double Opus (IRE) (Petorius 117) [2007 6m 6m 6g 8g 8.3d Oct 1] tall, attractive colt: signs of ability in maidens, but well beaten in nursery and seller (blinkered): may prove best short of 1m. *B. J. Meehan*

AMERIGO (IRE) 2 gr.g. (Jan 25) Daylami (IRE) 138 – Geminiani (IRE) 106 (King of 68 p Kings (IRE) 125) [2007 8.2g Nov 7] well-made gelding: first foal: dam, 2-y-o 7f winner (stayed 1¼m), closely related to Queen Mary/Phoenix Stakes winner Damson: 9/1 and green (troublesome at stalls), never-nearer seventh to Wintercast in maiden at Nottingham: will benefit from experience. *M. A. Jarvis*

AMES SOUER (IRE) 4 b.f. Fayruz 116 – Taispeain (IRE) 86 (Petorius 117) [2007 48: 43 p5.1g⁵ f6g⁶ Jan 23] leggy filly: poor maiden: best efforts at 5f: raced on all-weather and good to soft ground. *P. D. Evans*

AMHOOJ 2 b.f. (Feb 12) Green Desert (USA) 127 – Harayir (USA) 119 (Gulch (USA)) 68 [2007 7g p7g³ Oct 12] compact filly: seventh foal: half-sister to 3 winners, including smart 1¼m winner Izdiham and useful 1½m winner (stayed 1¾m) Moonjaz (both by Nashwan): dam 6f (at 2 yrs) to 1m (1000 Guineas) winner: better effort in maidens when third to The Which Doctor at Lingfield: will be suited by at least 1m. *M. P. Tregoning*

AMICABLE TERMS 2 b.f. (Apr 18) Royal Applause 124 – Friendly Finance 52 (Auction Ring (USA) 123) [2007 6g Nov 2] half-sister to several winners, including useful Irish 7f winner who stayed 1½m Leonor Fini (by Peintre Celebre): dam unraced half-sister to Riverman: 50/1, ninth of 11 in maiden at Newmarket. *Rae Guest*

AMICAL RISKS (FR) 3 bl.g. Take Risks (FR) 116 – Miss High (FR) (Concorde Jr 52 (USA)) [2007 9.5g⁵ 9.5g³ p11g⁵ Dec 19] third foal: brother to smart Irish 1m (at 2 yrs)/1¼m winner/smart hurdler Mister Hight: dam French maiden: third in maiden at Lisieux in April (left S. Wattel in France after): modest form in similar event at Kempton on British debut when next seen out: stays 11f: raced only on good/good to soft ground on turf. *W. J. Musson*

AMICHI 3 b.f. Averti (IRE) 117 – Friend For Life 64 (Lahib (USA) 129) [2007 8g 8.3m –
p8g Sep 18] fourth foal: sister to 3 winners, including fairly useful 6f (at 2 yrs) to 8.5f
winner Amica and 1m winner Miss Maguire: dam, fourth at 1m, out of useful half-sister
to Shirley Heights: well held in maidens. *G. L. Moore*

AMICUS 2 br.f. (Feb 9) Xaar 132 – Kartuzy (JPN) 82 (Polish Precedent (USA) 131) –
[2007 p8g p7g p8m Nov 11] €20,000Y: first foal: dam, 11.5f winner, half-sister to Prix de
l'Arc de Triomphe winner Marienbard: little impact in maidens at Kempton. *D. K. Ivory*

AMIE MAGNIFICENT (IRE) 2 b.f. (Feb 13) Mujahid (USA) 125 – Darbela (IRE) **54**
102 (Doyoun 124) [2007 7m p8g⁵ p8g Oct 4] €30,000F, 24,000Y: fifth foal: dam, Irish
1½m, 2m and hurdles winner, half-sister to Prix de Diane/Vermeille winner Daryaba:
modest form in maidens: will stay 1¼m+. *P. Winkworth*

AMMEYRR 3 b.g. Mark of Esteem (IRE) 137 – Walimu (IRE) 82 (Top Ville 129) [2007 **74 d**
p12.2g f7g² f8g 7.5m⁴ 8v⁴ 9.2d 12m 12g⁴ 10.1m⁶ 8.5g Sep 19] lengthy gelding: fair
maiden: well below form after leaving M. Johnston 12,500 gns following second start:
stays 7f: acts on fibresand: tried blinkered/visored. *A. Crook*

AMNESTY 8 ch.g. Salse (USA) 128 – Amaranthus (Shirley Heights 130) [2007 62, –
a55: p12g 12.6s⁵ 12g Aug 16] lengthy gelding: modest performer, better on turf than
all-weather: below form in 2007: usually wears blinkers: of suspect temperament: won
over hurdles in September/October. *G. L. Moore*

AMORIST (IRE) 5 b.g. Anabaa (USA) 130 – Moivouloirtoi (USA) 106 (Bering 136) **54**
[2007 –, a86: f7g⁵ 8s p7.1g⁴ f8d Dec 20] fairly useful handicapper at best: only modest in
2007, reportedly finished lame on reappearance (left J. Howard Johnson after): stays
1¼m: acts on all-weather and heavy going. *D. W. Chapman*

A MOTHERS LOVE 3 gr.f. Act One 124 – Oiselina (FR) (Linamix (FR) 127) [2007 **63**
p8g p9.5g p8g p10g² f11g⁹ 10g⁶ 9.9g 10.1g² 12.1s⁴ 10.1d p11g⁵ Aug 1] leggy filly: fifth
foal: half-sister to fairly useful 2005 2-y-o 1m winner Salute The General (by Mark of
Esteem) and winner in Japan by Diktat: dam, French 10.5f winner, half-sister to smart
French performer up to 12.5f Oiseau Rare: modest performer: won minor event at Southwell in April: barely stays 1½m: acts on all-weather and soft ground: patiently ridden.
P. J. McBride

AMOURETTA 2 b.f. (Jan 13) Daylami (IRE) 138 – Allumette (Rainbow Quest (USA) –
134) [2007 p7g 10d 8d Oct 19] quite good-topped filly: second foal: dam unraced out of
smart 1¼m winner Flame Valley: no form: unseated leaving stall second outing, visored
final one. *T. T. Clement*

AMPHIBALUS (IRE) 2 gr.g. (Apr 10) Daylami (IRE) 138 – Dramatically (USA) –
(Theatrical 128) [2007 p8g Sep 24] tall gelding: last in maiden at Kempton (gelded after):
bred for middle distances. *D. K. Ivory*

AMWAAL (USA) 4 b.c. Seeking The Gold (USA) – Wasnah (USA) 96 (Nijinsky **?**
(CAN) 138) [2007 93: 8m 8m 7g 10f a9f⁴ 8.5f³ Dec 20] strong, rangy colt: fairly
useful performer in 2006: well held first 3 starts at 4 yrs, then left J. Dunlop: blinkered,
ran respectably final outing: stays 8.5f: acts on firm and good to soft ground.
K. P. McLaughlin, USA

AMWELL BRAVE 6 b.g. Pyramus (USA) 78 – Passage Creeping (IRE) 75 (Persian **63**
Bold 123) [2007 57, a72: p12g* p16g⁴ f12g⁴ 14.1g⁵ p12g⁴ 12g⁶ 11.5d⁴ 12d 12s p12g⁴ **a72**
p13g⁴ 12m⁶ p12g² p12g p12g⁵ p12g Oct 10] rather leggy gelding: fair handicapper on
all-weather, modest on turf: won at Kempton in January: effective at 1½m to easy 2m:
acts on all-weather, firm and soft ground: tried visored/tongue tied: held up. *J. R. Jenkins*

AMWELL HOUSE 2 gr.g. (Apr 6) Auction House (USA) 120 – Amwell Star (USA) –
46 (Silver Buck (USA)) [2007 5m⁵ 5m 6m 7m 7m 8d Oct 18] close-coupled gelding: no
form. *J. R. Jenkins*

AMYANN (IRE) 2 b.f. (Feb 5) Indian Lodge (IRE) 127 – Moral Certainty (USA) **59 ?**
(Seeking The Gold (USA)) [2007 p7.1g f7d³ Dec 20] 6,000F, 8,000Y: first foal: dam
unraced close relative of very smart 1¼m/1½m performer Notable Guest: seemingly
better effort in maidens (very slowly away on debut) when third of 6 at Southwell: will
stay 1m+. *J. R. Holt*

AMYLEE (IRE) 2 b.f. (May 2) Danehill Dancer (IRE) 117 – Igreja (ARG) 101 **87**
(Southern Halo (USA)) [2007 5d³ 6d 6d² 7m⁶ Sep 14] €90,000Y: neat filly: sixth foal:
half-sister to fairly useful 9.5f winner Blue Train (by Sadler's Wells): dam South African
Group 1 1m winner: fairly useful maiden: second to Rinterval at Newbury: more progress
when 4 lengths sixth of 22 to Lush Lashes in valuable sales race at the Curragh, always
handy: will stay 1m. *C. G. Cox*

AMY LIONHEART 2 b.f. (Jan 7) Makbul 104 – So Generous (Young Generation 129) –
[2007 5m 5m⁴ 6d⁵ 7d⁶ 7g⁴ 7m Aug 24] 1,200Y: small filly: fifth foal: half-sister to 1989
2-y-o 5f winner Dalston (by Dalsaan) and winner in Hong Kong by Nishapour: dam
unraced: of little account. *N. Tinkler*

AMY LOUISE (IRE) 4 ch.f. Swain (IRE) 134 – Mur Taasha (USA) 108 (Riverman **87**
(USA) 131) [2007 87: 6g⁶ 8d* 7d⁵ 7d³ 7g Aug 17] close-coupled filly: fairly useful
handicapper: won at Thirsk in June: stays 1m: acts on heavy and good to firm ground.
T. D. Barron

ANABAA'S SECRET (IRE) 2 b. or br.g. (Mar 23) Anabaa Blue 122 – Rizo Amoro **53**
(USA) (Fit To Fight (USA)) [2007 7.1g p6g 6.1v p8g p10g p8m Nov 11] well-grown
gelding: modest maiden: no impact in nurseries (blinkered once): should stay at least 1m.
J. A. Osborne

ANAMARKA 2 b.f. (Mar 30) Mark of Esteem (IRE) 137 – Anna of Brunswick 78 **57**
(Rainbow Quest (USA) 134) [2007 8.1f 8.3m Sep 11] close-coupled filly: eighth foal:
half-sister to several winners, including fairly useful 1½m winner who stayed 1¾m
Goslar (by In The Wings) and 2004 2-y-o 6f winner Annals (by Lujain): dam, 1¼m
winner (stayed 1¾m), half-sister to dams of very smart performers up to 1½m Annaba
and Annus Mirabilis: modest maiden: better effort at Leicester latter start: will be suited
by 1¼m/1½m: sold 3,500 gns, sent to Czech Republic. *H. Candy*

ANATOLIAN PRINCE 3 b.g. Almutawakel 126 – Flight Soundly (IRE) 78 (Caerleon **60 d**
(USA) 132) [2007 67: 8.2g⁵ 8.3m 8d 7g 10.1m² 10g p10g Sep 18] strong, good-topped
gelding, type to carry condition: has a quick action: modest maiden at best: probably stays
1¼m: acts on good to firm ground: tongue tied last 3 starts: reportedly had breathing
problem third/sixth outings: gelded after final start. *J. M. P. Eustace*

ANCIEN REGIME (IRE) 2 b.c. (Feb 3) King's Best (USA) 132 – Sadalsud (IRE) **98 p**
(Shaadi (USA) 126) [2007 6d⁵ 6m⁴ 5g² Oct 8] 38,000F, 60,000Y: tall colt: sixth foal:
half-brother to 2 winners in Italy: dam 5f (at 2 yrs)/1m winner: impressive winning debut
in maiden at Yarmouth (made all to beat Street Star 1¾ lengths, Ibn Khaldun fourth) in
August: better form after when fourth in minor event at Doncaster (did best of front
runners) and second in nursery at Windsor (failed to settle held up): should prove best at
5f/6f: already useful, and will go on improving. *M. A. Jarvis*

ANCIENT CROSS 3 b.c. Machiavellian (USA) 123 – Magna Graecia (IRE) 112 –
(Warning 136) [2007 9.2d Jun 28] second foal: brother to 2005 2-y-o 1m/9f winner
Taranto (later smart up to 13f): dam, French 9f to 15.5f winner, out of useful half-sister to
Dubai World Cup winner Street Cry (by Machiavellian): 6/1 and better for run, seemed to
need experience when well-held eighth of 9 to Gone Gold in maiden at Hamilton, slowly
away: should stay at least 1¼m: sold 11,500 gns in July. *M. Johnston*

ANCIENT CULTURE 3 b.c. Sadler's Wells (USA) 132 – Wemyss Bight 121 **89 §**
(Dancing Brave (USA) 140) [2007 10m⁶ 10g⁴ 11.8s⁶ 12g³ 12m² 12m* 14g 14m Oct 4]
well-made colt: brother to high-class 1m (at 2 yrs)/1¼m winner Beat Hollow (also third
in Derby) and half-brother to useful 1m/1¼m winner (including in USA) Yaralino (by
Caerleon): dam won Irish Oaks: fairly useful performer: won maiden at Newmarket in
August: stays 1¾m: acts on good to firm ground: visored/blinkered last 4 starts:
sometimes tongue tied: has run well when sweating: irresolute: sold 57,000 gns, sent to
USA. *Sir Michael Stoute*

ANCIENT PRIDE (IRE) 3 br.g. Inchinor 119 – Carrie Pooter 95 (Tragic Role (USA)) **53**
[2007 8m⁶ 6g³ 8m⁵ Sep 10] modest form in maidens: stays 1m. *Miss L. A. Perratt*

ANCIENT SITE (USA) 3 ch.c. Distant View (USA) 126 – Victorian Style 88 –
(Nashwan (USA) 135) [2007 –: p7.1g 6d 7m Aug 12] little form. *B. P. J. Baugh*

AND AGAIN (USA) 4 b.f. In The Wings 128 – Garah 107 (Ajdal (USA) 130) [2007 **65**
83: 9.7m⁵ 12d⁶ 11.6m 11.9d⁴ p13g 10d² p10g³ 9.7m³ p10g 8g p10g³ p10m Nov 26] sturdy
filly: fair handicapper nowadays: stays easy 1½m: acts on polytrack, firm and soft going:
often wears cheekpieces nowadays. *R. A. Teal*

ANDAMAN SUNSET 2 b.c. (Feb 20) Red Ransom (USA) – Miss Amanpuri 92 **85**
(Alzao (USA) 117) [2007 6m 6g 6m² 7s⁴ 8d² Oct 22] sturdy colt: fourth foal: half-brother
to 2003 2-y-o 6f winner (stayed 1½m) Miss Langkawi (by Daylami): dam, 2-y-o 7f
winner who stayed 1¼m, half-sister to middle-distance performers Asian Heights (very
smart) and St Expedit (smart): fairly useful maiden: steadily progressive, second to
Whistledownwind at Newbury final start: will be suited by 1¼m/1½m: acts on soft and
good to firm ground. *G. Wragg*

AND I 4 b.f. Inchinor 119 – Fur Will Fly 66 (Petong 126) [2007 73: 11g 7m p8g Jul 3] tall –
filly: fair maiden at 2/3 yrs: no form in 2007: tried in cheekpieces. *C. A. Horgan*

ANDMOREAGAIN (USA) 3 b.f. Distorted Humor (USA) 117 – It's Personal (USA) **74**
(Personal Flag (USA)) [2007 8d³ 7g⁵ p8g³ 7m* p9f⁴ 8.5d⁶ Oct 26] $125,000Y, $350,000
2-y-o: attractive filly: fifth foal: sister to US Grade 2 1¼m winner It's No Joke and
half-sister to 2 winners abroad: dam US 5f (at 2 yrs) to 8.5f (including 2 Grade 3s) winner:
fair form in maidens in Britain, winning at Newbury in August: left J. Noseda after and
trained by P. Biancone, USA for next start only: stays easy 1m. *F. Parisel, USA*

ANDORRAN (GER) 4 b.g. Lando (GER) 128 – Adora (GER) (Danehill (USA) 126) **56**
[2007 –: 7m⁴ 7m⁴ 8.3g 7.1m⁴ 8m⁶ 8g⁴ 11.1g² 10.1d⁶ 13g⁶ p12.2g⁴ 17.5s p12g⁴ Oct 17]
close-coupled gelding: modest maiden: left A. Dickman £6,000 after sixth start: stays
13f: acts on polytrack, good to firm and good to soft going: tried in cheekpieces/blinkers/
tongue strap: often slowly away/held up. *A. Bailey*

ANDRASTA 2 b.f. (Mar 17) Bertolini (USA) 125 – Real Popcorn (IRE) 52 (Jareer **68**
(USA) 115) [2007 5m⁴ p5g⁵ 5.1d 5.5m p6g 6s³ 6d* 6.1d 7g 6v⁵ p6g² p6d f6d³ f5g³
Dec 27] 14,000Y: good-topped filly: half-sister to several winners, including fairly useful
7f (at 2 yrs) to 1½m winner Winners Delight (by First Trump): dam 1½m winner: fair
performer: left B. Meehan after fifth start (in cheekpieces): won nursery at Catterick in
October: effective at 5f/6f: acts on all-weather and soft going, probably good to firm:
suspect temperament. *A. Berry*

ANDRE CHENIER (IRE) 6 b.g. Perugino (USA) 84 – Almada (GER) (Lombard **60**
(GER) 126) [2007 64: 12.4m 9.1d Jul 23] modest performer nowadays: stays 1½m: acts
on soft going: sold 10,000 gns. *P. Monteith*

ANDRONIKOS 5 ch.h. Dr Fong (USA) 128 – Arctic Air 79 (Polar Falcon (USA) 126) **96 §**
[2007 114§: 6g 6d p6g⁵ p6g p7m³ p6m⁴ p7g p7g⁵ Dec 28] lengthy horse: just useful
performer in 2007: made frame in handicaps fifth/sixth starts: free-going sort, best at
6f/7f: acts on polytrack, firm and soft going: usually tongue tied: has run well when
sweating: sometimes looks none too keen, and is inconsistent. *P. F. I. Cole*

ANDURIL 6 ch.g. Kris 135 – Attribute 69 (Warning 136) [2007 80§: f8g³ f8g⁵ p10g **64 §**
9.1g 8s p8.6g 9.1s p10g⁶ Dec 19] workmanlike gelding: modest handicapper nowadays:
stays 1¼m: acts on all-weather, firm and soft ground: usually wears headgear: races
freely: sometimes slowly away: tends to find little. *Miss M. E. Rowland*

AND YOUR POINT IS (USA) 3 b.g. Point Given (USA) 134 – Ascend (USA) **62**
(Risen Star (USA)) [2007 7.1s 8m⁵ 8.3m Aug 13] big, strong gelding: easily best effort in
maidens (modest form) when 10½ lengths eighth to Noisy Silence at Windsor final start,
hanging left: bred to stay 1¼m. *C. R. Egerton*

ANEEBEE (IRE) 2 b.f. (Feb 4) Fraam 114 – Emilia Romagna (GER) (Acatenango **57**
(GER) 127) [2007 p7g 7.6f 8.1f 8.3d² p8g p10g Oct 24] 20,000Y: rather leggy filly: third
foal: half-sister to 4-y-o Rehearsed and a winner in Italy by Java Gold: dam, German
maiden who stayed 15f, sister to smart German winner up to 10.5f Elacata: modest
maiden: second in seller at Windsor: should stay 1¼m: acts on good to soft going: sold
3,000 gns, sent to Sweden. *R. Hannon*

ANFIELD DREAM 5 b.g. Lujain (USA) 119 – Fifth Emerald 54 (Formidable (USA) –
125) [2007 71, a88: f5g p7g p6g f5g f5g p6g 5.5d p6g* p6g p6g 6d p6g³ p6m⁴ p6g Dec 4] **a67**
close-coupled gelding: fair handicapper: won at Kempton in September: effective at 5f/
6f: acts on all-weather, lightly raced on turf nowadays: tried visored/tongue tied: none too
reliable. *J. R. Jenkins*

ANGARIC (IRE) 4 ch.g. Pivotal 124 – Grannys Reluctance (IRE) 63 (Anita's Prince **83**
126) [2007 86: 7.1g² 7f² 7.1g⁶ 6g 6m³ p7g³ 7g³ 7g p7.1d³ p7.1g⁴ Dec 31] neat gelding:
fairly useful handicapper: placed several times in 2007: stays 8.3f: acts on polytrack, firm
and good to soft ground: races prominently. *B. Smart*

ANGEL KATE (IRE) 3 b.f. Invincible Spirit (IRE) 121 – Lake Nyasa (IRE) 67 (Lake **81**
Coniston (IRE) 131) [2007 7m⁵ 8.2m² 8m⁴ 8.3g³ 8.1m* Aug 31] neat filly: third foal:
half-sister to useful Irish 2005 2-y-o 6f winner Mrs Snaffles (stayed 9.5f, by Indian Danehill): dam, Irish maiden (stayed 1¼m), half-sister to Ascot Gold Cup winner Mr Dinos:
fairly useful form: won maiden at Sandown in August by short head from Meynell: raced
only around 7f/1m on good/good to firm ground: races prominently. *H. R. A. Cecil*

ANGELOFTHENORTH 5 b.m. Tomba 119 – Dark Kristal (IRE) 66 (Gorytus (USA) –
132) [2007 67: 5.9g Aug 22] leggy mare: fair handicapper in 2006: well held only start
at 5 yrs: best at 5f: acts on heavy and good to firm going: tried blinkered: none too
consistent. *C. J. Teague*

ANGEL PIE 2 b.f. (Mar 20) Diesis 133 – Name of Love (IRE) 105 (Petardia 113) [2007 –
p7g 7m Aug 11] angular filly: sixth foal: half-sister to 5-y-o Almavara and winner in US
by Lemon Drop Kid: dam, 7f winner (including Rockfel Stakes), ran only at 2 yrs: behind
in maidens. *R. Charlton*

ANGEL ROCK (IRE) 2 b.c. (Feb 2) Rock of Gibraltar (IRE) 133 – Nomothetis (IRE) **66 p**
(Law Society (USA) 130) [2007 8m⁶ Sep 12] rangy, quite attractive colt: fifth foal:
half-brother to smart Italian miler Spirit of Desert (by Desert Prince): dam once-raced
half-sister to very smart 1½m performer Posidonas: 14/1, in need of experience when
sixth to Kandahar Run in maiden at Doncaster: sure to improve. *P. W. Chapple-Hyam*

ANGEL SPRINTS 5 b.m. Piccolo 121 – Runs In The Family 69 (Distant Relative 128) **84**
[2007 89: 6g⁶ 7g³ 6s⁴ 7m² 7.1g³ 7d⁴ 7s⁴ 6f* 6d 6d⁶ Sep 26] sturdy mare: fairly useful
handicapper: won at Lingfield in August: effective at 6f/7f: acts on firm and soft going:
consistent. *C. J. Down*

ANGEL VOICES (IRE) 4 b.f. Tagula (IRE) 116 – Lithe Spirit (IRE) 74 (Dancing **64**
Dissident (USA) 119) [2007 74: f8g⁵ 7s³ 6.9d⁵ 7.1g⁵ 6m² 7d⁴ 6s⁵ p8.6g p6g* Dec 12]
good-bodied filly: has a moderate, quick action: just modest performer nowadays: in
cheekpieces, won minor event at Kempton in December: effective at 6f to 1m: acts on
polytrack, soft and good to firm ground: races prominently. *K. R. Burke*

ANGLE OF ATTACK (IRE) 2 b.g. (Mar 31) Acclamation 118 – Travel Spot Girl **76**
(Primo Dominie 121) [2007 5g⁵ 5m⁴ 5g⁴ 6s⁶ 6g² 6m p6g⁵ 6s³ p5g* 5g³ p5.1g⁶ Nov 16]
€40,000F, €52,000Y: lengthy gelding: second foal: dam unraced half-sister to useful
performers Fast Eddy (stayed 1m) and Stone Mill (stayed 1¼m): fair performer: won
nursery at Lingfield in October: best at 5f: acts on polytrack, soft and good to firm
ground: usually makes running: looked none too keen final start. *R. A. Fahey*

ANGUS NEWZ 4 ch.f. Compton Place 125 – Hickleton Lady (IRE) 64 (Kala Shikari **102**
125) [2007 103: p6f⁶ 6d 5m 6.1s 6g* 5g⁶ 6s 4s 5m 6g⁵ 5.2g² 6m* 6d³ Oct 19] lengthy,
plain filly: useful performer: won handicaps at Ripon in May and Newmarket (beat
Plucky by 1¼ lengths) in October: creditable third to Lady Grace in listed event at Newmarket final start: raced only at 5f/6f: acts on soft and good to firm going: usually visored:
looks ungainly, tends to hang/carry head high: front runner: inconsistent. *M. Quinn*

ANIMATED 3 b.g. Averti (IRE) 117 – Anita Marie (IRE) (Anita's Prince 126) [2007 –
65: f5g Jan 25] well-grown, close-coupled gelding: maiden: blinkered, well held only
outing at 3 yrs. *A. J. McCabe*

ANIMATOR 2 b.c. (Apr 11) Act One 124 – Robsart (IRE) 91 (Robellino (USA) 127) **73 +**
[2007 7g p8g⁵ p8.6g⁴ p8.6g* Nov 30] 13,000Y: sturdy colt: fifth foal: half-brother to
useful 2004 2-y-o 7f winner (stayed 1¼m) Fu Manchu (by Desert Style) and fairly useful
2002 2-y-o 5f winner (stayed 1m) Tourmalet (by Night Shift): dam, 7f and 1¼m winner,
out of smart French 1¼m winner Sharp Girl: fair form: improved to win nursery at
Wolverhampton in November: will be suited by 1¼m/1½m. *P. F. I. Cole*

ANKARA 3 ch.f. Elusive Quality (USA) – Maeander (FR) 101 (Nashwan (USA) 135) –
[2007 f8g Feb 13] second foal: dam, French 1½m winner, out of sister to Miesque: 5/1
and green, 11½ lengths eighth to Rich Lord in maiden at Southwell, soon niggled: sold
32,000 gns in July (reportedly in foal to Bertolini), sent to South Africa. *M. Johnston*

ANKO (POL) 8 b.g. Saphir (GER) – Arietta (GER) (Kings Lake (USA) 133) [2007 –
11.6d Jul 23] rather leggy gelding: successful 5 times from 6f to 1¼m in Poland: well held
in seller at Windsor on British Flat debut. *J. D. Frost*

ANNALIESSE (IRE) 2 ch.f. (Apr 15) Rock of Gibraltar (IRE) 133 – Oh So Well (IRE) **75**
(Sadler's Wells (USA) 132) [2007 6s⁴ 7d* 8m 8s⁴ Sep 22] smallish, close-coupled filly:
half-sister to several winners, including very smart 7f (at 2 yrs) to 12.5f winner Dark
Moondancer (by Anshan) and useful 1996 2-y-o 6f winner (stayed 1m) Dances With
Dreams (by Be My Chief): dam unraced out of high-class sprinter Soba: fair performer:
won maiden at Redcar in July: good fourth in nursery at Ayr final start: will stay 1¼m:
acts on soft going. *R. A. Fahey*

ANNAMBO 7 ch.g. In The Wings 128 – Anna Matrushka (Mill Reef (USA) 141) [2007 **86**
82: 14.1m⁴ 14m⁴ 13.3m* 13.9g² p12.3g* 16g p12g⁶ p12g² Nov 30] smallish, lengthy
gelding: unimpressive mover: fairly useful performer: won handicap at Newbury in June
and, having left D. Morris, seller at Wolverhampton (left S. Williams after) in August:
effective at 1½m to 16.5f: acts on polytrack, firm and good to soft going: formerly
visored: signs of temperament: joined A. Reid £6,000. *P. J. McBride*

Prix de Royallieu Hotel Hermitage Barriere de La Baule, Longchamp—Anna Pavlova is given a confident ride by Frankie Dettori to gain her biggest prize; Princesse Dansante is second

ANNA PAVLOVA 4 b.f. Danehill Dancer (IRE) 117 – Wheeler's Wonder (IRE) 43 **114** (Sure Blade (USA) 130) [2007 114: 10s* 10.4g² 16.4d³ 10s* 12.5d* 15.5m⁶ Oct 28] tall, leggy, quite good-topped filly: smart performer: better than ever in 2007, winning listed events at Navan (by 5 lengths from Bon Nuit) in April and Ayr (beat Dunaskin by 1¾ lengths) in September and Prix de Royallieu Hotel Hermitage Barriere de La Baule at Longchamp (beat Princesse Dansante decisively by 2½ lengths) in October: creditable 2 lengths sixth to Allegretto in Prix Royal-Oak at Longchamp final start: also ran well when 2 lengths third to Septimus in Lonsdale Cup at York third start: effective at 1¼m to 16.4f: acts on soft and good to firm ground: held up: quirky (tends to hang), but tough and reliable: a credit to connections. *R. A. Fahey*

ANNA TOWKASKA 3 b.f. Polish Precedent (USA) 131 – Eliza Acton 70 (Shirley **60** Heights 130) [2007 9m⁴ 10m 9.9m 10m Sep 25] lengthy filly: fourth foal: half-sister to 4-y-o Stotsfold and fairly useful 8.6f (at 2 yrs) and 1¾m winner Maggie Tulliver (by Spectrum): dam, 1m winner who should have stayed at least 1½m, sister to useful stayer Top Cees and half-sister to smart 1¼m performer Supreme Sound: easily best effort when fourth in maiden at Lingfield: tongue tied final start. *W. R. Swinburn*

ANNA WALHAAN (IRE) 8 b.g. Green Desert (USA) 127 – Queen's Music (USA) **–** 66 (Dixieland Band (USA)) [2007 p9.5g Sep 27] close-coupled, deep-bodied gelding: one-time useful performer: no form since 2004: sometimes visored. *Ian Williams*

ANNE BONNEY 3 b.f. Jade Robbery (USA) 121 – Sanchez 77 (Wolfhound (USA) **55** 126) [2007 58p: p9.5g³ f8g 8m⁵ 11.5m p6g Sep 14] modest maiden: stays 9.5f: acts on polytrack and good to firm going: tried tongue tied. *E. J. O'Neill*

ANNE BRONTE 3 ro.f. Act One 124 – Anka Britannia (USA) (Irish River (FR) 131) **71** [2007 p12g⁴ p12g² 10.1m 10m³ p12.2g³ 14.1s Jun 14] fourth foal: half-sister to useful French winners Cool Britannia (1¼m/10.5f) and Britannic (1½m), both by Rainbow Quest: dam, French maiden, half-sister to US Grade 1 1¼m winner Deputy Commander: fair maiden: stays 1½m: acts on polytrack and good to firm going: front runner: has looked awkward under pressure: sold 10,000 gns in July. *M. Johnston*

ANNEMASSE 3 b.g. Anabaa (USA) 130 – Statua (IRE) 98 (Statoblest 120) [2007 f6g* **106** p7g* p7g³ 7.6m* 8.1m² 7d⁵ 8m⁶ 6m 8m² 8g⁵ 8.1m* 8g 8g⁴ 9m Oct 6] 19,000Y: big, strong gelding: fourth foal: half-brother to fairly useful 2004 2-y-o 5f winner Dance Anthem (by Royal Academy) and 7f (at 2 yrs) and 2m winner Dream Mountain (by Mozart): dam, US 1m winner (third in Rockfel Stakes at 2 yrs), half-sister to useful 7f to 9f performer Bluegrass Prince: progressed into a useful performer, winning maiden at Southwell in February and handicaps at Kempton in March, Chester in May and Haydock (beat Electric Warrior by 2½ lengths) in August: respectable tenth to Pipedreamer in Cambridgeshire at Newmarket final outing: should stay 9f: acts on all-weather and good to firm going: races prominently: sold 45,000 gns, joined R. Fahey. *M. Johnston*

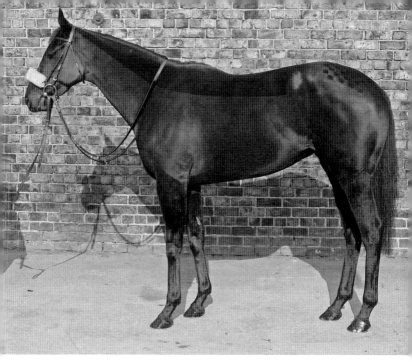

Galaxy Racing's "Anna Pavlova"

ANNE OF KIEV (IRE) 2 b.f. (Mar 10) Oasis Dream 129 – Top Flight Queen 82 **80** (Mark of Esteem (IRE) 137) [2007 6g⁴ p7m² Nov 1] 250,000Y: well-made filly: third foal: half-sister to 3-y-o Big Robert and French 8.5f winner Ellazaria (by Vettori): dam, 1¼m winner, half-sister to smart performer up to 1¾m Sacrament: in frame in maidens at Redcar and Lingfield (fairly useful form, short-head second to Debonnaire): likely to stay 1m. *J. H. M. Gosden*

ANNES ROCKET (IRE) 2 b.c. (Feb 18) Fasliyev (USA) 120 – Aguilas Perla (IRE) **70** (Indian Ridge 123) [2007 5m 6.5d⁵ p6g⁵ p5.1g⁴ p6g* Dec 26] lengthy, unfurnished colt: third foal: half-brother to fairly useful Irish 5f and 6.5f winner Spirit of Pearl (by Invincible Spirit): dam unraced sister to useful Irish 7f winner Cool Clarity: fair performer: trained by K. Prendergast in Ireland on debut: won maiden at Wolverhampton: should stay 7f. *J. C. Fox*

ANNIA FAUSTINA (IRE) 3 ch.f. Docksider (USA) 124 – Benguela (USA) 76 (Little **–** Current (USA)) [2007 60: p8.6g⁵ f7g Feb 13] close-coupled filly: maiden: well beaten in handicaps in 2007: should be suited by 1m+: blinkered final start. *J. L. Spearing*

ANNIBALE CARO 5 b.g. Mtoto 134 – Isabella Gonzaga 75 (Rock Hopper 124) [2007 **53** –: 12v 12m⁵ 13.8g 12g Oct 30] good-topped gelding: fairly useful handicapper in 2005: lightly raced and on downgrade since. *Grant Tuer*

ANNIE SKATES (USA) 2 ch.f. (Mar 25) Mr Greeley (USA) 122 – Vivalita (USA) **95** (Deputy Minister (CAN)) [2007 7s² p7g* 7m³ 8d² Oct 26] $62,000Y: close-coupled, angular filly: has a round action: seventh foal: closely related to winning US sprinter by Grand Slam and half-sister to 3 US sprint winners: dam unraced: useful performer: second to Kotsi in maiden at Newmarket prior to winning minor event at Lingfield

61

in September: much improved subsequently when placed in Oh So Sharp Stakes at Newmarket (½-length third to Raymi Coya) and non-graded event at Monmouth (strong-finishing ¾-length second to Sea Chanter): stays 1m: acts on polytrack, soft and good to firm going. *Jane Chapple-Hyam*

ANNUNZIO 4 b.g. Big Shuffle (USA) 122 – Abrakadabra (GER) (Aratikos (GER) 112) **71** [2007 9m⁵ 12m 7g⁶ 7g³ 8s 8.5g⁶ 9m p9.5g Nov 30] quite good-topped gelding: fair performer: below form last 2 starts, in handicap at Wolverhampton in latter: stays 8.5f: acts on soft going: in cheekpieces last 3 starts: tried tongue tied. *T. G. McCourt, Ireland*

A NOD AND A WINK (IRE) 3 b.f. Raise A Grand (IRE) 114 – Earth Charter 60 **53** (Slip Anchor 136) [2007 53: p7g⁴ p8g² p8g p8g p8.6g⁶ p10g³ 10m p12.2g 8m Sep 25] modest maiden: stays 1¼m: acts on polytrack: usually held up: has been awkward leaving stall/looked temperamental. *J. C. Fox*

ANOSTI 2 b.f. (Mar 26) Act One 124 – Apennina (USA) (Gulch (USA)) [2007 5d* 6m² **92** 6g² 6.5m 6.5d⁵ 6m² Oct 5] good-topped filly: fourth foal: half-sister to 2 winners by Diktat, including 4-y-o Dictatrix: dam unraced half-sister to smart sprinter Blue Goblin: fairly useful form: won maiden at Hamilton in July: second 3 times, including in listed event at Ripon (3 lengths behind Fat Boy) and valuable sales race at Newmarket (beaten a neck by Exclamation, 28 ran) third/final starts: should prove best at 5f/6f: acts on good to soft and good to firm going: races prominently: usually hangs right. *K. A. Ryan*

ANOTHER CHOICE (IRE) 6 ch.g. Be My Guest (USA) 126 – Gipsy Rose Lee **–** (IRE) 100 (Marju (IRE) 127) [2007 p12.2g 10.5m May 25] big, workmanlike gelding: fairly useful handicapper in 2005: missed 2006, and no form at 6 yrs: usually tongue tied. *N. P. Littmoden*

ANOTHER DECREE 2 b.c. (Mar 29) Diktat 126 – Akhira 90 (Emperor Jones (USA) **80** 119) [2007 6d⁴ 6s⁴ 6m Oct 5] 34,000Y: good-topped colt: third foal: half-brother to 4-y-o Empress Jain: dam, 7f winner, out of half-sister to smart 6f/7f performer Danehill Dancer: fairly useful maiden: twice fourth at Ayr, then mid-field in 28-runner valuable sales race at Newmarket: will prove best at 5f/6f. *M. Dods*

ANOTHER GENEPI (USA) 4 br.f. Stravinsky (USA) 133 – Dawn Aurora (USA) **71** (Night Shift (USA)) [2007 73: p8g p8g p7g⁴ p6g p7g² 7.1m³ p7.1g* p6g⁶ 7.1m² 7m⁴ 6m³ **a79** p7.1g³ 7.2g⁶ 6m p7.1g* p7.1g p6g p7.1g Dec 26] angular filly: fair handicapper: left J. Hills after third start: won at Wolverhampton in April and October: stays 1m: raced only on polytrack/good going or firmer: tried in cheekpieces, blinkered nowadays: races prominently: has shown signs of temperament. *K. A. Ryan*

ANOTHER GLADIATOR (USA) 4 br.c. Danzig (USA) – Scarab Bracelet (USA) **68** (Riverman (USA) 131) [2007 63: p7g f6g⁶ p7g* Feb 7] big, strong colt: fair performer: best effort when winning handicap at Lingfield in February: likely to prove best at 7f/1m: acts on all-weather: in cheekpieces/blinkers last 3 starts: sold 13,500 gns later in February. *K. A. Ryan*

ANOTHER SOCKET 2 b.f. (May 5) Overbury (IRE) 116 – Elsocko 76 (Swing Easy **75 p** (USA) 126) [2007 5.1d⁶ p5.1g² p5.1g* Nov 5] sturdy filly: half-sister to several winners, including fairly useful 1997 2-y-o 5f/6f winner Socket Set (by Tragic Role): dam maiden (stayed 7f): progressive form in maidens, won in smooth style at Wolverhampton: will be best at 5f/6f: capable of better still. *E. S. McMahon*

ANOTHER TOY 4 b.f. Sugarfoot 118 – Nampara Bay 50 (Emarati (USA) 74) [2007 f6g p6g Feb 26] second foal: half-sister to 6-y-o Estoille: dam sprint maiden: well held in maidens. *A. D. Brown*

AN SCARIBH 2 br.c. (Feb 3) Where Or When (IRE) 124 – Wadenhoe (IRE) 69 (Persian **60** Bold 123) [2007 5m 6s² 6g 6d Sep 28] leggy, angular colt: modest maiden: will stay 7f/1m. *P. D. Evans*

ANSELLS PRIDE (IRE) 4 b.g. King Charlemagne (USA) 120 – Accounting (Sillery **83** (USA) 122) [2007 p9.5g² f8g² p8g* 9.1v 8g* Nov 9] 19,500F, 26,000Y: second foal: half-brother to 5-y-o Berkhamsted: dam, maiden in France/Britain (stayed 12.5f), out of half-sister to very smart US 8.5f/9f winner Joyeux Danseur and dam of Arazi/Noverre: fairly useful performer: won maiden at Kempton in February and handicap at Mussel-burgh (much improved, beat Esoterica by length) in November: stays easy 9.5f: acts on all-weather, possibly not on heavy going. *B. Smart*

ANTHEA 3 b.f. Tobougg (IRE) 125 – Blue Indigo (FR) (Pistolet Bleu (IRE) 133) [2007 **65** 66: 8.2g p8.6g 12.1g⁴ 10s² 9m 11.7d⁵ 10.2d² 10.2g p8m⁵ p10g Nov 19] leggy filly: fair maiden: stays 1¼m: acts on polytrack, soft and good to firm going: blinkered (raced freely) final start: races prominently: tends to wander. *B. R. Millman*

APA

ANTHEMION (IRE) 10 ch.g. Night Shift (USA) – New Sensitive (Wattlefield 117) **63**
[2007 67: 8.3m⁵ 9.2g 8.3f³ 7.1g⁴ 8g 8m³ 9.2m 7.9g 8m⁴ 8.3m 8m⁵ 7.1d p8.6g⁴ p8.6g⁵
Oct 26] good-topped gelding: modest handicapper: stays 9f: acts on fibresand, firm and
good to soft going: usually makes running. *Mrs J. C. McGregor*

ANTHILL 3 b.f. Slickly (FR) 128 – Baddi Heights (FR) (Shirley Heights 130) [2007 –: **70**
8.2m⁶ 7g 8m 7s² p7.1g Oct 25] leggy filly: fair maiden: stays 1m: acts on soft going:
probably wayward. *I. A. Wood*

ANTIGONI (IRE) 4 ch.f. Grand Lodge (USA) 125 – Butter Knife (IRE) (Sure Blade **70**
(USA) 130) [2007 74: 7m p7.1g² p7g p7.1g Jul 10] quite good-topped filly: fair maiden
handicapper: stays 1m: acts on polytrack and firm going: tried visored: often slowly
away. *A. M. Balding*

ANTON CHEKHOV 3 b.c. Montjeu (IRE) 137 – By Charter 104 (Shirley Heights **108**
130) [2007 98p: 10m⁵ 11g* 12g 12s³ 12.5d⁶ Aug 26] medium-sized, quite attractive colt:
useful performer: made all in Prix Hocquart Mitsubishi Motors at Longchamp (beat
Royal And Regal by head) in May: towards rear in Derby at Epsom next time before
creditable staying-on 8 lengths third of 15 to Adlerflug in Deutsches Derby at Hamburg,
final start for A. O'Brien: below form in Grand Prix de Deauville final start: will stay
1¾m: acts on soft ground. *U. Ostmann, Germany*

ANTRIM ROSE 3 b.f. Giant's Causeway (USA) 132 – Aunty Rose (IRE) 103 (Caer- **68**
leon (USA) 132) [2007 58: 9.7m p10g³ p9.5g⁶ p7.1g⁶ Oct 18] fair maiden handicapper:
stays 1¼m: raced mainly on polytrack: in cheekpieces final start: sold 6,000 gns.
E. F. Vaughan

ANYBODY'S GUESS (IRE) 3 b.g. Iron Mask (USA) 117 – Credibility 65 (Komaite **–**
(USA)) [2007 –: 5.9m 7.1g Jun 22] little form. *J. S. Wainwright*

ANY GIVEN DAY (IRE) 2 gr.c. (Apr 28) Clodovil (IRE) 116 – Five of Wands 71 **67 p**
(Caerleon (USA) 132) [2007 7.1g 7d 7g p10g* Oct 24] €20,000F, 25,000Y: strong colt:
has round action: third foal: half-brother to fairly useful Italian 2004 2-y-o 8.5f winner
Lujana Boy (by Lujain) and 3-y-o Patavian: dam maiden (would have stayed 2m): fair
form: improved to win nursery at Kempton, off bridle long way out: should do better as
stamina is tested more (will stay 1½m+). *D. M. Simcock*

ANYTHING ONCE (USA) 4 b.g. Elusive Quality (USA) – Bushy's Pride (USA) **60**
(Hagley's Reward (USA)) [2007 70: p9.5g 8f 9.8m 8.5g⁴ 10m 10s³ 10g⁶ 11.8g³ p12g
f11d⁴ p12.2s Dec 21] workmanlike gelding: modest maiden: trained by B. Smart on
reappearance: stays 13f: acts on soft and good to firm ground, probably on polytrack:
visored/blinkered nowadays: held up. *D. Carroll*

A ONE (IRE) 8 b.g. Alzao (USA) 117 – Anita's Contessa (IRE) 68 (Anita's Prince 126) **–**
[2007 –: 10m 6v 8.1m 11.6f 8.3m Aug 12] rather leggy gelding: fair performer in 2005:
lightly raced and little form since. *H. J. Manners*

APACHE CHANT (USA) 3 b. or br.g. War Chant (USA) 126 – Sterling Pound (USA) **61**
(Seeking The Gold (USA)) [2007 –: 12.1g3 11.9m⁵ 9.9s 16.2f³ 12.1m⁴ Sep 13] tall, rather
leggy gelding: has a moderate, quick action: modest maiden: stays 2m: acts on firm
going: tried blinkered. *A. W. Carroll*

APACHE DAWN 3 ch.g. Pursuit of Love 124 – Taza (Persian Bold 123) [2007 83p: **93**
9.2d⁵ 7m⁴ 7s* 8s 7.5s⁶ 8m p8g² Dec 16] big, good-topped gelding: has scope: fairly useful
handicapper: won at Newcastle in June by 11 lengths from Chjimes, making all: left
K. Ryan, good second at Kempton final start: stays 1m: acts on polytrack and soft going:
reared leaving stall sixth outing: sometimes finds little/hangs. *G. L. Moore*

APACHE FORT 4 b.g. Desert Prince (IRE) 130 – Apogee 113 (Shirley Heights 130) **73**
[2007 –: p12.2g³ᵈ p12.2g* p10g* p12.2g³ 12.4m³ 10g⁴ 11.8s⁴ 13.3m² 14.8d³ p12g²
p16g³ 16m p12g* 9.9m³ 12d² 14d⁶ p12g² Nov 21] good-topped gelding: fair performer:
won minor event at Wolverhampton and handicap at Lingfield in January, and handicap
at latter track in September: stays 2m: acts on polytrack, soft and good to firm going:
reliable. *T. Keddy*

APACHE NATION (IRE) 4 b.g. Fruits of Love (USA) 127 – Rachel Green (IRE) 46 **71**
(Case Law 113) [2007 69: 6g 6m 7m 9.1d 7.9m 8s* 8.1d⁶ 8s³ 8.1v² 8v³ 8.5s 8g² 10.1d
9.1v Nov 3] good-bodied gelding: fair handicapper: won at Ripon in June: stays 9f: acts
on heavy and good to firm going. *M. Dods*

APACHE POINT (IRE) 10 ch.g. Indian Ridge 123 – Ausherra (USA) 106 (Diesis **59**
133) [2007 67, a–: 9.9m 8.5m 9.1g⁶ 10d² 8s² 8d 8m⁵ 9m⁴ 10.1g² 8.5g 9m⁶ 10m Oct 22]

63

rather leggy gelding: modest performer: stays 1¼m: acts on any turf going: sometimes races freely: usually waited with. *N. Tinkler*

A PEACEFUL MAN 3 b.g. Tipsy Creek (USA) 115 – My Hearts Desire (Deploy 131) [2007 58p: p7g 7m p11g 15.4m Aug 9] sturdy gelding: little form, leaving B. Hills after reappearance: tried in cheekpieces. *Mrs L. C. Jewell* —

APERITIF 6 ch.g. Pivotal 124 – Art Deco Lady 51 (Master Willie 129) [2007 77: p8.6g f7g p8.6g f7g f7g² 7g⁴ p8.6g Apr 16] strong, good sort: fair performer, better on turf than all-weather: effective at 7f/1m: acts on all-weather, soft and good to firm going. *D. Nicholls* **72 a66**

APEX 6 ch.g. Efisio 120 – Royal Loft 105 (Homing 130) [2007 72d: p7.1g p7.1g⁶ p7.1g³ f7g⁵ f6g⁴ 10.9m* p8g* f11g² 8d* 8m* 8d⁴ 8m⁵ 10m p8.6g⁵ p8.6g³ 8.2g² Oct 31] leggy, angular gelding: has a short, round action: fairly useful handicapper: left N. Tinkler after fifth start: first past post at Warwick and Kempton (made all) in April and Southwell (demoted after causing interference) and Bath (twice) in May: has form up to 11f, though best efforts at 1m: acts on all-weather, soft and good to firm going: tried blinkered/in cheekpieces: has been slowly away: has found little. *M. Hill* **90**

APHORISM 4 b.f. Halling (USA) 133 – Applecross 117 (Glint of Gold 128) [2007 74: 14.1d³ 15.9m³ 16.2g* 16s³ Oct 18] smallish, leggy filly: fairly useful handicapper: progressive in 2007, winning at Warwick (idled) in October: likely to stay beyond 2m: acts on fibresand, soft and good to firm going: raced freely final outing. *J. R. Fanshawe* **83**

APHRODELTA 5 b.m. Delta Dancer – Mouton (IRE) 70 (Dolphin Street (FR) 125) [2007 p6g⁶ p7g² p7.1g Apr 30] modest maiden: stays 7f: raced mainly on polytrack. *P. D. Cundell* **53**

APHRODISIA 3 b.f. Sakhee (USA) 136 – Aegean Dream (IRE) 97 (Royal Academy (USA) 130) [2007 –p: 8.3g 7.1d 12f² p12g² Sep 19] good-topped filly: fair maiden: stays 1½m: acts on polytrack and firm ground. *S. C. Williams* **69**

APOCALYPTO (IRE) 3 b.c. Auction House (USA) 120 – Scared (Royal Academy (USA) 130) [2007 p7g May 9] 40/1, tailed-off last in maiden at Kempton. *E. J. Creighton* —

APOLINA 3 b.f. Pursuit of Love 124 – Caerosa 70 (Caerleon (USA) 132) [2007 7d 6g⁵ 6s 8g 9.7m Aug 9] 1,000F, 1,500Y: second foal: half-sister to 4-y-o Tous Les Deux: dam, 11f/1½m winner, half-sister to useful miler Brave Kris: little form in maidens/handicaps, leaving P. McEntee after third outing: blinkered last 2 starts. *Miss K. B. Boutflower* —

APOLLO FIVE 3 ch.g. Auction House (USA) 120 – Dazzling Quintet 73 (Superlative 118) [2007 84: 7m 7.1g 8s 10m 8f³ 8.3m 8d p7g Oct 31] compact gelding: just modest performer nowadays: probably stays 1m: acts on firm going: tried visored. *D. J. Coakley* **71 d**

APOLLO SHARK (IRE) 2 ch.g. (Apr 3) Spartacus (IRE) 107 – Shot of Redemption (Shirley Heights 130) [2007 6g⁴ 7d* 7.1g* 6g Aug 23] €20,000F, 52,000Y: rather leggy, lengthy gelding: sixth foal: closely related to 5-y-o Danzare and half-brother to 3 winners abroad, notably useful French 6f to 1m (including at 2 yrs) winner Lykios (by Night Shift): dam ran 3 times in US: fairly useful form: won maiden at Thirsk in June and nursery at Musselburgh (by 4 lengths) in July: unsuited by drop back in trip in sales race at York: will stay 1m: raced only on good/good to soft ground. *J. Howard Johnson* **80**

APPALACHIAN TRAIL (IRE) 6 b.g. Indian Ridge 123 – Karinski (USA) (Palace Music (USA) 129) [2007 113: 7.5g⁴ 6.5g* 6.5g⁵ 6d⁴ 7.1g 6d 6v² 6d 8.1g⁵ 6d 7g* 7g* p8g⁵ Nov 28] sturdy gelding: smart performer: won handicap at Nad Al Sheba (by 3 lengths from Tiza) in February and listed event at Redcar (beat Rahiyah by neck) and minor event at Doncaster (better than ever, beat Dijeerr by ½ length) in October: denied clear run in listed race at Kempton final outing: effective at 6f to 8.6f: acts on polytrack, heavy and good to firm ground: tried visored, usually blinkered: usually waited with, and has found little. *I. Semple* **118**

APPLAUDED (IRE) 2 b.f. (Feb 15) Royal Applause 124 – Frappe (IRE) 93 (Inchinor 119) [2007 6d³ 6g² 7d p7.1d* Dec 7] sturdy filly: fifth foal: half-sister to useful 7f (at 2 yrs) to 1½m (Ribblesdale Stakes) winner Thakafaat (by Unfuwain) and 1¼m winner Quantum (by Alhaarth): dam, 2-y-o 6f winner, half-sister to 2000 Guineas winner Footstepsinthesand: fairly useful form: blinkered, won maiden at Wolverhampton in December: better form previously when placed in similar company at Newbury and Yarmouth (short-head second to Street Star) and last of 10 in Rockfel Stakes at Newmarket (stiff task): should stay 1m. *B. J. Meehan* **83**

APPLE BLOSSOM (IRE) 3 b.f. Danehill Dancer (IRE) 117 – Silk (IRE) (Machiavellian (USA) 123) [2007 –: 8m² 7m 8m² 7m* 7g Aug 26] workmanlike filly: fairly useful performer: won maiden at Thirsk in August: better form when runner-up in similar events: should stay 1¼m: raced only on good/good to firm going. *G. Wragg* **81**

APPLEBY 3 b.f. Anabaa (USA) 130 – May Ball 115 (Cadeaux Genereux 131) [2007 **72 d** p7g 7g³ 7g⁵ 7s 6g⁴ 6d Oct 9] lengthy filly: first foal: dam 6.5f (Prix Maurice de Gheest) to 1m winner: fair maiden: below form after second start, twice finishing lame: will stay 1m: often hangs left. *J. H. M. Gosden*

APPLE PIE ORDER (IRE) 2 b.f. (Apr 23) Namid 128 – Apple Sauce 70 (Prince – Sabo 123) [2007 7g Sep 6] tall filly: fifth foal: half-sister to 3 winning sprinters, including 3-y-o Steelcut: dam, 5f winner, half-sister to smart sprinter Sizzling Melody: tailed off in maiden at Salisbury. *R. J. Hodges*

APPLY DAPPLY 4 b.f. Pursuit of Love 124 – Daring Destiny 113 (Daring March 116) **89** [2007 81: 7g* 8d² 8.5d 8d³ 8.3m⁵ 8.1m⁵ 10d² 8d 10d³ 12g⁶ Nov 2] tall, useful-looking filly: fairly useful handicapper: won at Folkestone in April: good efforts at Newmarket and Newbury seventh/ninth starts: stays 1¼m: acts on heavy and good to firm going. *H. Morrison*

APPOINTMENT 2 ch.f. (Feb 21) Where Or When (IRE) 124 – Shoshone (Be My **65 +** Chief (USA) 122) [2007 8m p8g p8g⁴ Oct 17] 16,000F, €105,000Y: workmanlike filly: half-sister to 2 winners by Wyoming, including useful 2001 2-y-o 6f winner (stayed 1m) Asheer: dam, maiden (stayed as a stayer), half-sister to very smart 7f to 1¼m performer Lockton: fair maiden: advancing form, close fourth at Kempton: not sure to stay much beyond 1m. *Mrs A. J. Perrett*

APRIL FOOL 3 ch.g. Pivotal 124 – Palace Affair 113 (Pursuit of Love 124) [2007 61: **65** 8.3g⁵ 8.3d 9m³ Jul 11] close-coupled, compact gelding: fair maiden: stays 9f: acts on good to firm and good to soft ground: visored (ran well) final start. *J. A. Geake*

APRIL REIGNS 2 ch.f. (Mar 24) Ballet Master (USA) 92 – Princess Oberon (IRE) 91 – (Fairy King (USA)) [2007 5.1f 7m p6g Oct 12] sparely-made filly: seventh foal: half-sister to 2-y-o 5f winners Midnight Arrow (fairly useful in 2000, by Robellino) and Withering Lady (in 2004, by Tagula): dam 5f winner, including at 2 yrs: no form. *D. Burchell*

APRIL'S QUEST (IRE) 2 ch.f. (Feb 15) Spectrum (IRE) 126 – Coastal Jewel (IRE) – (Kris 135) [2007 p7g 6d p7.1g 5.1f p6g Sep 21] €13,000F: well-grown filly: half-sister to several winners, including fairly useful 5f (at 2 yrs) to 1m (in Hong Kong) winner Barrier King (by Sovereign Dancer): dam unraced: no show in maidens. *David Pinder*

APRIL THE SECOND 3 b.g. Tomba 119 – Little Kenny 50 (Warning 136) [2007 f8g – f11g 10g Jun 7] workmanlike gelding: well held in maidens. *R. J. Price*

APSARA 6 br.m. Groom Dancer (USA) 128 – Ayodhya (IRE) (Astronef 116) [2007 75: **67** 8f 8m⁴ 9.8m 8s 8v⁶ 8m⁵ 10s Sep 26] compact mare: fair handicapper: effective at 1m/ 1¼m: acts on firm and soft going: tried visored/in cheekpieces. *G. M. Moore*

AQALEEM 3 b.c. Sinndar (IRE) 134 – Dalayil (IRE) (Sadler's Wells (USA) 132) **121** [2007 86: 11.5g* 12g³ 12g² Jul 31]
    Marcus Tregoning virtually had to shut up shop for a couple of months in the spring when his stable's horses began coughing. Sir Percy, out of harm's way in Dubai, was the yard's only runner during that period, the 2006 Derby winner finishing fourth in the Sheema Classic. Tregoning's fortunes soon took a turn for the better once normal service was resumed. His second runner back was a winner, and no ordinary one at that, Aqaleem's victory in the Derby Trial at Lingfield raising hopes that Tregoning might have another good enough to win the Derby itself. Aqaleem, very different to Sir Percy, had achieved nothing like so much as his stablemate by this stage, but his performance at Lingfield promised better to come, and he certainly looked well worth his place in the line-up at Epsom.
    Sir Percy was a leading juvenile who finished second in the Two Thousand Guineas on his reappearance, whereas Aqaleem was still a maiden when he lined up at Lingfield in May. Aqaleem had run twice as a juvenile, following a third in a maiden at Newbury with an even more encouraging effort when second to Teslin, one place ahead of Authorized, in a minor event at the same venue. The leggy, rather lengthy Aqaleem, who had been one of the first in the stable to get the cough, still looked rather unfurnished before the totesport Derby Trial, by no means the finished article physically. Yet in the race itself he showed just how much he had improved over the winter. Benefiting greatly, as his pedigree suggested strongly he would, from the step up to just short of a mile and a half, Aqaleem was well on top at the line, four lengths clear of Hearthstead Maison and Kid Mambo who battled it

totesport Derby Trial Stakes, Lingfield—Aqaleem books his Derby place, showing significant improvement on his two-year-old form to win from Hearthstead Maison (left), Kid Mambo and Many Volumes (right)

out for second. The form of the Lingfield race had taken a few knocks by the time the Derby came round, but Aqaleem, a 9/1-shot with only three ahead of him in the betting, produced a fine run at Epsom despite sweating up during the preliminaries. In touch more or less from the off, Aqaleem was easily outpaced by Authorized approaching the final furlong and then overhauled by Eagle Mountain, but he kept on well to come off best in the battle for third with Lucarno and Soldier of Fortune, Aqaleem seven and a half lengths behind the winner at the line. He looked an ideal type for the St Leger, and he ran next in the Gordon Stakes at Goodwood, where once again he became increasingly on edge as the preliminaries unfolded. Aqaleem ran a sound Leger trial in finishing a neck second to Yellowstone, surprisingly waited with this time in contrast to the tactics employed at Epsom. Short of room as the pace increased in the straight, and losing momentum when tightened up at one stage, Aqaleem stayed on dourly once in the clear, giving the impression he might well have won under different circumstances. The St Leger was to be Aqaleem's next race, and he was one of just fourteen declared at a forfeit stage less than three weeks before the race. However, on the following day, he pulled some muscles in his hindquarters on the gallops and missed not only the Leger but also the remainder of the season. With Lucarno coming out on top at Doncaster, Aqaleem's connections were left to ponder what might have been. At least Aqaleem will have the chance to make good at four when he should have plenty of good opportunities to add to his single victory so far.

Aqaleem (b.c. 2004)	Sinndar (IRE) (b 1997)	Grand Lodge (ch 1991)	Chief's Crown / La Papagena
		Sinntara (b 1989)	Lashkari / Sidama
	Dalayil (IRE) (b 1995)	Sadler's Wells (b 1981)	Northern Dancer / Fairy Bridge
		Irish Valley (ch 1982)	Irish River / Green Valley

Aqaleem is the fifth foal of the unraced Dalayil who is closely related to Alhaarth, the champion two-year-old of 1995 and subsequently a very smart performer up to a mile and a quarter. Dalayil and Alhaarth are out of Irish Valley, a disappointing mare on the racecourse—she failed to reach a place in six outings, on the last of them wearing blinkers—but a very different proposition at stud. The Prix du Calvados winner Green Pola is one of many other winners produced by Irish Valley, the promising two-year-old Almajd the most recent. Aqaleem's great grandam, the unraced Green Valley, was another prolific winner-producer, her most notable offspring the triple Group 1 winner Green Dancer who has also made a name for himself at stud. There is more about the family in the essay on Authorized who shares his great grandam Green Valley with Aqaleem. Aqaleem himself is a half-brother to a couple of winners, Maghazi (by Fasliyev), a fairly useful seven-furlong winner, and Maal (by Mozart), successful in a bumper in Ireland in May. Aqaleem will stay at least a mile and three quarters. He raced on good to soft going on his debut but has encountered only good ground since. *M. P. Tregoning*

AQLAAM 2 b.c. (Jan 18) Oasis Dream 129 – Bourbonella (Rainbow Quest (USA) 134) **93 p**
[2007 6d³ Jul 29] 260,000Y: lengthy colt: second foal: dam unraced half-sister to several
at least useful stayers, notably very smart Persian Punch: 5/1, shaped well when length
third of 13 to Atlantic Sport in newcomers event at Ascot, travelling strongly: good
prospect, sure to win races. *W. J. Haggas*

AQMAAR 3 b.c. Green Desert (USA) 127 – Hureya (USA) 82 (Woodman (USA) 126) **97**
[2007 91: 7m⁴ 8m* 8.1m 8m 8g a7f⁵ Dec 7] neat, quite attractive colt: useful performer:
won handicap at Newmarket in May by ½ length from We'll Come: well held next 3
starts, then left J. Dunlop: ran well final start: edgy/free-going sort, but stays 1m: acts on
dirt, yet to race on extremes of going on turf. *E. Charpy, UAE*

AQUAMARINE BEAUTY (FR) 3 b.f. Daliapour (IRE) 122 – Dix Huit Brumaire **59**
(FR) (General Assembly (USA)) [2007 11.5s 11.7f⁵ 12g⁶ 10g a12g Dec 18] fifth foal:
dam unraced: modest maiden: left Sir Michael Stoute after second start: bred to be suited
by 1½m+: blinkered final outing. *Rupert Pritchard-Gordon, France*

AQUARIAN DANCER 2 b.f. (Jan 19) Mujahid (USA) 125 – Admonish 57 (Warning **60 ?**
136) [2007 5m 6m 6m 7m 7.5d⁵ Sep 25] 3,500F, 5,000Y: close-coupled, workmanlike
filly: sixth foal: sister to 2005 2-y-o 5f winner Conciliate and half-sister to 2001 2-y-o 5f/
6f winner Villa Del Sol (by Tagula): dam ran twice at 2 yrs: no threat in maidens and
nursery, seemingly modest form final start: stays 7.5f. *Jedd O'Keeffe*

AQUILEGIA (IRE) 3 b.f. Desert Style (IRE) 121 – Pyatshaw (Common Grounds 118) **76**
[2007 72: 5.1g² 5.7d⁴ 5.1g⁴ Jun 1] leggy filly: fair performer: best efforts at 5f: acted on
soft and good to firm going: tended to start slowly: dead. *E. S. McMahon*

ARABELLAS HOMER 3 b.f. Mark of Esteem (IRE) 137 – Rush Hour (IRE) (Night **49**
Shift (USA)) [2007 49: f6g⁵ f8g p7.1g p8.6g 12.1g² 10d³ 10.1f 10f 9.8m 10g⁵ 8.2m p9.5g
p13.9s⁵ Dec 20] short-backed filly: poor maiden: left Mrs N. Macauley prior to final
outing: stays 1½m: acts on all-weather and good to soft going. *Mrs N. S. Evans*

ARABESQUE DANCER 2 b.f. (Apr 15) Dubai Destination (USA) 127 – Seven of **58**
Nine (IRE) 66 (Alzao (USA) 117) [2007 p8.6g p8.6d⁵ p8.6d⁴ Dec 28] 23,000Y: third foal:
half-sister to winner in Greece by Hernando: dam, ran 3 times (should have stayed 1¼m),
sister to smart performer up to 1¼m Rabi: modest maiden: all 3 runs at Wolverhampton,
easily best effort when fifth in claimer. *M. Botti*

ARABIAN ART (USA) 2 br.f. (May 24) E Dubai (USA) 124 – Slamya (USA) (Seattle **70**
Slew (USA)) [2007 7g p7g⁵ Nov 17] $95,000Y: lengthy filly, unfurnished at 2 yrs:
sixth foal: closely related to winner in Japan and half-sister to 3 winners abroad: dam,
US maiden, half-sister to very smart French stayers Agent Double and Air de Cour:
better effort in maidens when fifth of 11 to Fantasy Princess at Lingfield, dictating.
H. R. A. Cecil

ARABIAN FERN 2 b.f. (Feb 25) Tobougg (IRE) 125 – Cryptogam 73 (Zamindar **–**
(USA) 116) [2007 6d⁴ 7d⁵ 7.5v⁵ 6v 7.5g Sep 19] small, compact filly: first foal:
dam, maiden (stayed 1½m), out of half-sister to St Leger winner Toulon: no form.
M. E. Sowersby

ARABIAN GLEAM 3 b.c. Kyllachy 129 – Gleam of Light (IRE) 81 (Danehill **120 +**
(USA) 126) [2007 p7g² p6g* 7m³ 7g⁵ 7m* 7d⁶ Oct 20]
The *Racing Post*'s misprinted headline 'Arabian Gloom confirmed for
Hungerford' turned out to be prophetic. Arabian Gleam wasn't declared for the race
the following day. In the event, there was nothing untoward with Arabian Gleam
and he soon had another good opportunity to gain a first pattern-race success. The
race was the Group 2 GNER Park Stakes at Doncaster in September, and in winning
it, on what was only his fifth start, Arabian Gleam underlined just how far he had
come in a short time, having made his debut just over four months earlier.
A promising second in a maiden over seven furlongs on the polytrack at
Lingfield first time up, Arabian Gleam went one better in a similar event over six
on the same course later in May. All his subsequent races were at seven, and all at
pattern level, the Jersey Stakes at Royal Ascot the first of them. It was a huge step
up for Arabian Gleam, but he coped admirably with it, and with the switch to turf,
held up after missing the break and running on well to take third behind Tariq and
US Ranger. There was further improvement next time too, in the Lennox Stakes at
Goodwood, only fifth to Tariq this time but reducing the deficit between the pair
from three and three quarter lengths to two and a half despite having anything but a
clear run. More still was required from Arabian Gleam in the Park Stakes, even

GNER Park Stakes, Doncaster—very smart performances from the first two, Arabian Gleam and Duff (rail); Wake Up Maggie, King Jock (right) and Mac Love are next

though it wasn't a strong renewal, Arabian Gleam being the least experienced in a six-runner field. The betting suggested it lay between Hungerford fourth Wake Up Maggie, the 2/1 favourite, 5/2-shot Arabian Gleam and Duff, successful in a listed race at York on his previous start who started at 11/4. The market leaders took the first three places, Arabian Gleam responding well to pressure to collar Duff well inside the last furlong and win a shade cosily by a neck, with a gap of two and a half lengths back to Wake Up Maggie. Arabian Gleam was some way below that form on his only subsequent start, in the Challenge Stakes at Newmarket, the ground a possible reason as it was his first run on softer than good. More likely, though, an explanation was to be found in the way the race was run, with those dropped out in the early stages probably at a disadvantage, Arabian Gleam in particular. He was last when the pace was stepped up significantly three furlongs out and, soon off the bit, never looked like getting into contention, drifting left after two furlongs out before being switched back towards the outer. To his credit, Arabian Gleam ran on fairly well to finish sixth of fifteen, six lengths behind Miss Lucifer, not disgraced under the circumstances.

			Pivotal		Polar Falcon
	Kyllachy		(ch 1993)		Fearless Revival
	(b 1998)		Pretty Poppy		Song
Arabian Gleam			(b 1988)		Moonlight Serenade
(b.c. 2004)			Danehill		Danzig
	Gleam of Light (IRE)		(b 1986)		Razyana
	(b 1991)		Gold Runner		Runnett
			(b 1985)		African Doll

Arabian Gleam has shaped on occasions as if well worth a try over a mile, though a glance at his pedigree offers no encouragement. His sire Kyllachy was a sprinter purely and simply, raced only at five furlongs, while his dam Gleam of Light's two wins were both gained over Chester's sharp seven and a half furlongs. The grandam Gold Runner also had stamina limitations, her sole placing when third over six furlongs at two, but Arabian Gleam's great grandam African Doll did win at a mile and a half in Ireland. African Doll is better known as the dam of the 1987 Two Thousand Guineas winner Don't Forget Me. Arabian Gleam, a 26,000-guinea foal and 50,000-guinea yearling, is a half-brother to four winners all of whom stay at least a mile, though they are by stallions who are much more of an influence for stamina than Kyllachy. Gleaming Blade (by Diesis) was useful, while Bumptious (by Mister Baileys) and Opening Ceremony and Light Quest (both by Quest For Fame) have shown fairly useful form, the last-named in France. Gleam of Light's latest produce to reach the racecourse is the two-year-old filly Cute (by Diktat), a fairly useful maiden. Arabian Gleam, a small, good-bodied colt, acts on polytrack and good to firm ground. With only six runs under his belt, it would be no great surprise were Arabian Gleam to improve a bit more in the next season, though he's still capable of winning another good race or two even if he doesn't. *J. Noseda*

ARABIAN GULF 3 b.c. Sadler's Wells (USA) 132 – Wince 117 (Selkirk (USA) 129) **116**
[2007 73p: 10m* 12.3m² May 10] sturdy, well-made colt, type to carry condition: smart
form: won maiden at Newmarket in April by neck from Putra Square: much improved
when short-head second of 4 to Soldier of Fortune (who gave 4 lb) in Chester Vase next
time, putting up good fight: will stay 1¾m: reported in August to have suffered a tendon
injury, and isn't expected to return until the summer at the earliest. *Sir Michael Stoute*

ARABIAN SPIRIT 2 b.c. (Feb 10) Oasis Dream 129 – Royal Flame (IRE) 72 (Royal **75 p**
Academy (USA) 130) [2007 7m 7g⁴ p7g³ Oct 29] 38,000Y: close-coupled, quite
good-topped colt: has fluent, quick action: third foal: dam 1¼m winner: fair maiden:
in frame at Leicester and Kempton (third to Adversity): will stay 1m: should do better.
E. A. L. Dunlop

ARABIAN SUN 3 b.g. Singspiel (IRE) 133 – Bright Halo (IRE) (Bigstone (IRE) 126) **71**
[2007 p10g 12g⁵ 12g 11.5s⁶ 15.4m p16g⁴ p16g p16g⁴ p16.5g² p16g⁵ p16.5g Nov 12]
170,000Y, 5,500 3-y-o: compact gelding: third foal: half-brother to useful 6f (at 2 yrs)
and 1m winner Nantyglo (by Mark of Esteem): dam, French 1¼m winner, from excellent
family: fair maiden handicapper: stays 16.5f: acts on polytrack: visored last 4 starts: not
straightfoward. *M. J. Attwater*

ARABIAN TREASURE (USA) 3 br.f. Danzig (USA) – Very Confidential (USA) **78**
(Fappiano (USA)) [2007 64p: 7m⁶ 8.2m* 8.2m⁴ 8.3m⁶ 10m⁵ Sep 7] strong, good-bodied
filly: type to carry condition: has a quick action: fair performer: made all in maiden at
Nottingham in May: stays 1¼m: acts on good to firm going. *Sir Michael Stoute*

ARABIYAH 3 b.f. Halling (USA) 133 – Jumaireyah 91 (Fairy King (USA)) [2007 **62**
10.2m 8.1g⁴ 8.2g³ 10.1d³ 11.7m⁵ 14.1m p12.2g p9.5g Oct 19] lengthy, attractive filly:
second foal: half-sister to useful 8.6f and 10.4f winner Reem Three (by Mark of Esteem):
dam, 1m (at 2 yrs)/1¼m winner, half-sister to smart stayer Lost Soldier Three: modest
maiden: should stay 1½m: sold €6,000. *L. M. Cumani*

ARAB LEAGUE (IRE) 2 b.g. (Feb 28) Dubai Destination (USA) 127 – Johnny And –
Clyde (USA) (Sky Classic (CAN)) [2007 5m 7m Sep 25] rather leggy, unfurnished
gelding: good mover: well held in maidens, 4 months apart: sold 3,000 gns. *M. Johnston*

ARAFAN (IRE) 5 b.g. Barathea (IRE) 127 – Asmara (USA) 109 (Lear Fan (USA) 130) **74**
[2007 72: f12g³ 15d f14g⁵ May 15] fair maiden: stays 12.5f: acts on fibresand, raced only
on good ground or softer on turf: tried blinkered. *Dr R. D. P. Newland*

ARAGLIN 8 b.g. Sadler's Wells (USA) 132 – River Cara (USA) 86 (Irish River (FR) –
131) [2007 p16.5g 17.1d Aug 19] useful-looking gelding: little form since 2001: often
blinkered. *J. T. Stimpson*

ARCANGELA 4 b.f. Galileo (IRE) 134 – Crafty Buzz (USA) (Crafty Prospector **40**
(USA)) [2007 –: f14g³ 15.8m 16m⁴ 16.1m 16g 12g Jul 10] lengthy filly: poor maiden:
stays easy 1¾m: acts on all-weather and good to firm going. *Miss Tracy Waggott*

ARCETRI (IRE) 2 b.f. (May 25) Galileo (IRE) 134 – Shewillifshewants (IRE) (Alzao **63 p**
(USA) 117) [2007 7g 6m⁵ 6m Oct 4] €44,000Y, 70,000 2-y-o: strong filly: has quick
action: seventh foal: half-sister to 3 winners, including 6f winner Billy Bling (by Enrique)
and 5-y-o Formidable Will: dam unraced half-sister to very smart 1½m performer
Acropolis: modest form in maidens, fading: bred to be suited by 1m+: should progress.
K. A. Ryan

ARCHDUKE FERDINAND (FR) 9 ch.g. Dernier Empereur (USA) 125 – Lady –
Norcliffe (USA) (Norcliffe (CAN)) [2007 90: p16g Jan 20] strong, close-coupled gelding: fairly useful handicapper in 2006: well held only Flat start at 9 yrs: best at 2m+: acts
on polytrack, firm and soft ground: has worn cheekpieces: often races freely: none too
consistent: fair hurdler. *A. King*

ARCH FOLLY 5 b.g. Silver Patriarch (IRE) 125 – Folly Fox (Alhijaz 122) [2007 67: –
12.1g 14.1m Aug 31] close-coupled gelding: fair performer at 4 yrs: well below form in
2007: stays 2¼m: acts on polytrack and firm going: tried in cheekpieces. *R. J. Price*

ARCHIESTOWN (USA) 4 b.g. Arch (USA) 127 – Second Chorus (IRE) (Scenic **82**
128) [2007 81: 10d 8g* 10m 10d 8s Oct 14] tall, angular, quite attractive gelding: fairly
useful handicapper: won at Newmarket in July: below form after: best form at 1m on
good ground: sold 16,000 gns. *J. L. Dunlop*

ARCHILINI 2 b.c. (Mar 7) Bertolini (USA) 125 – Dizzy Knight 64 (Distant Relative **62**
128) [2007 p5g⁴ p5.1g p7g Dec 19] modest form in maidens: bred to prove best at 5f/6f.
K. A. Morgan

Derrinstown Stud Derby Trial Stakes, Leopardstown—Archipenko beats Yellowstone (left) and Macarthur in a race in which Aidan O'Brien was responsible for four of the five runners

ARCHIMAGE (USA) 3 b. or br.g. Arch (USA) 127 – Powerful Package (USA) (Star **44** de Naskra (USA)) [2007 6m 7d 6d 5m Sep 10] quite good-topped gelding: poor form in maidens: sold 2,800 gns. *T. D. Barron*

ARCHIMBOLDO (USA) 4 ch.g. Woodman (USA) 126 – Awesome Strike (USA) 84 **68 §** (Theatrical 128) [2007 77§: 14m Aug 10] strong gelding: fair handicapper: stays easy 2m: acts on polytrack and firm ground: tried blinkered: tends to carry head high: ungenuine. *T. Wall*

ARCHIPENKO (USA) 3 b.c. Kingmambo (USA) 125 – Bound (USA) (Nijinsky **114** (CAN) 138) [2007 97p: 10m* 12g 10g 8g⁵ 8g⁵ Sep 9] neat, quite attractive colt: smart performer: won Derrinstown Stud Derby Trial Stakes at Leopardstown (by ¾ length from Yellowstone, quickening well) in May: well below form in Derby at Epsom (last of 17) and Eclipse Stakes at Sandown next 2 starts: creditable 6½ lengths fifth to Darjina in Prix du Moulin at Longchamp final outing: stays 1¼m: acts on soft and good to firm ground: joined M. de Kock in UAE. *A. P. O'Brien, Ireland*

ARCHIVED (IRE) 2 b.c. (Feb 2) Millkom 124 – La Fija (USA) 49 (Dixieland Band **91** (USA)) [2007 6g² 6g* 6m⁴ 7m⁵ 6m² 6m 7d Oct 27] 8,500Ỹ: good-topped colt: fifth foal: half-brother to 5-y-o Time For You: dam ran 3 times: fairly useful performer: won maiden at Folkestone in June: ran well all other starts, particularly when seventh of 11 to Beacon Lodge in Horris Hill Stakes at Newbury final one: likely to stay 1m: yet to race on extremes of going: sold 36,000 gns, sent to Norway. *M. G. Quinlan*

ARCH OF TITUS (IRE) 3 ch.c. Titus Livius (FR) 115 – Cap And Gown (IRE) 81 **83** (Royal Academy (USA) 130) [2007 77: p7.1g² p7.1g³ f8g³ f7g* p7.1g* 7.5m⁶ 6m⁶ 7d⁶ 7g Jul 28] lengthy colt: fairly useful performer: won maiden at Southwell in March and handicap at Wolverhampton in April: tailed off in ladies handicap at Ascot final outing: likely to prove best short of 1m: acts on all-weather, good to firm and good to soft going: usually tongue tied: often slowly away: tends to take strong hold: sold 11,000 gns in October, sent to UAE. *M. L. W. Bell*

ARCH REBEL (USA) 6 b.g. Arch (USA) 127 – Sheba's Step (USA) (Alysheba **116** (USA)) [2007 114: 10.5g 10m³ 11.3s³ 12v³ 10s⁵ 12d³ 10m² 10g* 12g² 12g⁴ Dec 9] well-made gelding: smart performer: several creditable placed efforts before winning listed race at Fairyhouse in September by 1¼ lengths from Fracas, racing lazily early on: good efforts last 2 starts when beaten nose by Montare in Prix du Conseil de Paris at

70

Longchamp (again off bridle long way in rear) and 2¾ lengths fourth to Doctor Dino in Hong Kong Vase at Sha Tin (stayed on well): effective at 1¼m/1½m: acts on soft and good to firm ground: often in blinkers/cheekpieces: tongue tied (respectable effort) fifth start: often slowly away: held up: consistent. *N. Meade, Ireland*

ARCH SWING (USA) 3 b.f. Arch (USA) 127 – Gold Pattern (USA) (Slew O' Gold (USA)) [2007 104p: 7g* 8m2 8g 8d4 8m3 8m3 Sep 8] well-made filly: smart performer: won Dimitrova 1000 Guineas Trial at Leopardstown in April by short head from Four Sins: good efforts when placed after in 1000 Guineas (2½ lengths second to Finsceal Beo) and Falmouth Stakes (1¼ lengths third to Simply Perfect), both at Newmarket, and Matron Stakes at Leopardstown (2 lengths fourth, promoted to third, behind Echelon, again forced to switch): stays 1m: acts on good to firm going, probably on good to soft: reportedly pulled muscles in hindquarters when last in Irish 1000 Guineas at the Curragh third outing. *John M. Oxx, Ireland* **116**

ARCTIC CAPE 2 b.c. (May 6) Cape Cross (IRE) 129 – Arctic Air 79 (Polar Falcon (USA) 126) [2007 6d6 6s* 7.1m4 Sep 1] unfurnished colt: fifth living foal: half-brother to 5-y-o Andronikos and 3-y-o Selkirk Sky: dam, 2-y-o 7f winner, half-sister to smart performers Barrow Creek (6f to 1m) and Last Resort (7f): fairly useful form: sixth in strong newcomers event at Ascot, then won maiden at Ayr (beat Quest For Success by ¾ length) in August: favourite, still looked to be learning when fourth in nursery at Sandown: will probably stay 1m: likely to do better. *M. Johnston* **89 p**

ARCTIC DESERT 7 b.g. Desert Prince (IRE) 130 – Thamud (IRE) (Lahib (USA) 129) [2007 83§: f8g p8g3 p7g p8g4 p8g4 p7g2 p8g 8g 7f 8m5 8m4 10.1d5 7m2 7f p8.6g* p9.5g3 p8.6g4 Dec 13] big, good-topped gelding: impresses in appearance: fairly useful performer on all-weather, fair on turf: left Gay Kelleway prior to fourteenth start (only one for R. Harris): won seller at Wolverhampton in December: free-going sort, but stays easy 9.5f: acts on polytrack, firm and good to soft going: tried visored: tongue tied: sometimes slowly away/looks none too keen. *Miss Gay Kelleway* **71 a83**

ARCTIC WINGS (IRE) 3 b.c. In The Wings 128 – Arctic Hunt (IRE) (Bering 136) [2007 75: 10.5g4 11.6d* 11.8s6 12m p11g4 12.6m4 10.9m3 p12g p10g Oct 12] rather leggy, dipped-backed colt: fair handicapper: won at Windsor in May: likely to stay 1¾m: acts on polytrack, good to firm and good to soft going: blinkered (raced too freely) final outing: sold 32,000 gns. *W. R. Muir* **76**

ARCTIZ (USA) 3 b. or br.c. Tiznow (USA) 133 – Perfect Arc (USA) 120 (Brown Arc (USA)) [2007 12g4 p9.5g 10.9g Jul 12] big, strong colt: easily best effort in maidens when fourth at Folkestone on debut: well beaten after: sent to USA. *P. F. I. Cole* **62**

ARDENNES (IRE) 3 b.g. Jade Robbery (USA) 121 – Ribbon Glade (UAE) (Zafonic (USA) 130) [2007 –p: 6d4 p6g4 7g5 Sep 18] modest maiden on all-weather, poor on turf: wore cheekpieces final outing, tongue tied first 3. *M. Botti* **45 a59**

Dimitrova 1000 Guineas Trial Stakes, Leopardstown—
Arch Swing (rail) keeps her unbeaten record by beating stablemate Four Sins

ARDENT NUMBER 7 b.g. Alderbrook 120 – Pretty Average 40 (Skyliner 117) [2007 –
9.2d May 18] third foal: half-brother to 2 winners, including 7f to 8.6f winner Cherished
Number (by King's Signet): dam disqualified 6f winner: no show in bumpers: 200/1,
tailed off in maiden at Hamilton. *D. A. Nolan*

ARDENT PRINCE 4 b.g. Polar Prince (IRE) 117 – Anthem Flight (USA) (Fly So Free 64
(USA) 122) [2007 53: 8.1s 8.1m p13.9g² p16g p13.9g p12g Oct 17] tall gelding: modest
maiden: free-going sort, though stays 1¾m: acts on polytrack. *Heather Dalton*

ARDMADDY (IRE) 3 b.g. Generous (IRE) 139 – Yazmin (IRE) 94 (Green Desert 64
(USA) 127) [2007 63: p8g 8d p9.5g² p10m² p12.2g² p12g Oct 29] workmanlike gelding:
modest maiden: stays 1½m: acts on polytrack: hung left fifth start: sold 16,000 gns.
J. A. R. Toller

ARENA'S DREAM (USA) 3 gr. or ro.g. Aljabr (USA) 125 – Witching Well (IRE) 75
(Night Shift (USA)) [2007 81: p9.5g⁵ p8.6g⁴ 8.2m⁴ 8.5g³ 8m² 10m⁴ 9g² 9.2d³ 8m²
10f⁵ 9.2m* p8m⁶ f8d³ p10g³ Dec 28] rather leggy, angular gelding: fair performer: won
maiden at Hamilton in August (left R. Fahey 5,000 gns after): stays 1¼m: acts on
polytrack, firm and good to soft going: has twice worn cheekpieces, including for win:
sometimes looks awkward under pressure. *J. R. Boyle*

AREWEPLAYINGOUT (IRE) 2 b.f. (Apr 22) Namid 128 – Bobbydazzle 81 (Rock 50
Hopper 124) [2007 p5g⁵ 5g 5m 5m³ p5.1g* p5g² Jul 10] 11,000Y: lengthy filly: fourth
foal: half-sister to 3-y-o Distiller and Irish 5f winner Shinko Dancer (by Shinko Forest),
both fairly useful: dam, 1m (including at 2 yrs) winner, half-sister to smart 7f performer
Tumbleweed Ridge: modest performer: won seller at Wolverhampton in June (blinkered): raced only at 5f: acts on polytrack and good to firm going. *Peter Grayson*

AREYAAM (USA) 3 b.f. Elusive Quality (USA) – Yanaseeni (USA) (Trempolino 75
(USA) 135) [2007 8m³ 8.1s³ p8g³ 9g p8.6g⁵ Sep 13] strong filly: second foal: half-sister
to French 1m winner Falcon Dive (by Diesis): dam, won in USA, sister to very smart
German 1¼m/1½m performer Germany: fair maiden: stays 8.6f: acts on polytrack and
good to firm going. *L. M. Cumani*

AREYOUTALKINGTOME 4 b.c. Singspiel (IRE) 133 – Shot At Love (IRE) 79 111
(Last Tycoon 131) [2007 118: p8.6g⁴ p6g* p5g* p6f⁵ a6f 8.1g 7g 7m⁶ 6m⁴ 7d Sep 29] **a121**

*Bonusprint.com Handicap, Lingfield—Areyoutalkingtome puts up the best performance of the
year on the all-weather as he gives Maltese Falcon (far side) 12 lb and a short-head beating*

rather leggy, quite good-topped colt: very smart performer on all-weather, smart on turf: much improved on all-weather over winter 2006/7, winning 6 times, including minor event in January and handicap (best effort, beat Maltese Falcon by short head under top weight) in February, both at Lingfield: best effort on turf when sixth to Lovelace in Supreme Stakes at Goodwood eighth outing: well held in handicap at Ascot final appearance: has won at 1¼m, best form at 5f to 7f: acts on polytrack and firm going: reportedly returned jarred up sixth start: sold 90,000 gns, sent to Saudi Arabia. *C. A. Cyzer*

ARFINNIT (IRE) 6 b.g. College Chapel 122 – Tidal Reach (USA) 68 (Kris S (USA)) **62** [2007 45: p6g³ p7f p7g p6g⁶ p6g³ 6m 6g p5g* 5.3m p5g⁵ 6m p6g* p5.1g⁴ p6g⁶ 5m⁴ p5.1g p6g p6g² p6g Dec 29] good-topped gelding: has a quick action: modest performer: won minor event at Lingfield in May and handicap at Wolverhampton in August: stays 6f: acts on polytrack, firm and soft going: wears headgear: held up. *Mrs A. L. M. King*

ARGANIL (USA) 2 ch.c. (Feb 5) Langfuhr (CAN) 124 – Sherona (USA) (Mr Greeley **– p** (USA) 122) [2007 7.2s Sep 21] $50,000Y: smallish, strong colt: second foal: dam US 2-y-o 6f winner: 9/1 and burly, no impression in maiden at Ayr: should do better. *K. A. Ryan*

ARGENTINE (IRE) 3 b.g. Fasliyev (USA) 120 – Teller (ARG) (Southern Halo **83** (USA)) [2007 84: 5m 5g⁵ 5g⁴ 5d 6g⁴ 7.1g⁶ Nov 8] strong, lengthy gelding: fairly useful handicapper: likely to prove best at 5f/6f: acts on polytrack, firm and good to soft going. *L. Lungo*

ARIEGE (USA) 2 b. or br.f. (Mar 27) Doneraile Court (USA) – Kostroma 116 (Caer- **93** leon (USA) 132) [2007 8.5d* 7v⁴ 8m 8f³ Dec 30] $75,000Y: big, useful-looking filly: has a quick, moderate action: half-sister to several winners, including useful 7f to 1¼m (in France) winner Ballet Pacifica (by Minardi): dam, US Grade 1 9.5f winner, half-sister to high-class 1m to 1¼m winner Grise Mine: fairly useful form: won maiden at Killarney (by 7 lengths) in July: dam 2½ lengths fourth to Campfire Glow in Debutante Stakes at the Curragh, then disappointed in May Hill Stakes at Doncaster: left T. Stack, Ireland, creditable 2¾ lengths third to Gorgeous Goose in non-graded stakes at Santa Anita final start: stays 8.5f: acts on any going. *R. J. Frankel, USA*

ARIES MAGIC 2 b.f. (Apr 5) High Tension (USA) 86 – Mountain Magic 58 (Magic **–** Ring (IRE) 115) [2007 5.1g 7m 8g⁵ Sep 6] neat filly: fourth foal: dam 7f winner: no form. *S. C. Burrough*

ARIODANTE (USA) 5 b.g. Groom Dancer (USA) 128 – Maestrale (Top Ville 129) [2007 75: **71 d** p13g² p12g 10g 12.3f 11.9d 11.9f p12g Aug 28] smallish gelding: fair performer: below form after reappearance in 2007: often slowly away: stays 13f: acts on polytrack and firm ground: blinkered final outing: said to have had breathing problems: sold £1,600 in October. *J. M. P. Eustace*

ARISTI (IRE) 6 b.m. Dr Fong (USA) 128 – Edessa (IRE) 104 (Tirol 127) [2007 61d: **48** p16.5g⁶ Apr 24] angular mare: poor performer: stays 2¼m: acts on polytrack and heavy going: tried blinkered, usually wears cheekpieces: joined E. Williams, successful over hurdles in September. *R. M. Stronge*

ARITHMATIX (USA) 3 b.c. Arch (USA) 127 – Startarette (USA) (Dixieland Band **64** (USA)) [2007 6.1m 8.3m⁶ 7.1d p8.6g Aug 12] $100,000Y, 115,000 2-y-o: strong colt: first foal: dam, US maiden, half-sister to useful dam of Dewhurst Stakes winner Mujahid: modest maiden: stays 8.6f: sold 12,000 gns in November. *G. A. Butler*

ARKANDO (IRE) 2 b.f. (Mar 12) Mull of Kintyre (USA) 114 – Arjan (IRE) 88 (Paris **– p** House 123) [2007 6m Aug 1] third foal: half-sister to 5f seller (including at 2 yrs) winner Little Biscuit (by Indian Lodge): dam 5f winner (including at 2 yrs): 20/1, green (slowly away) in maiden at Redcar: open to improvement. *K. R. Burke*

ARMADA 4 b.g. Anabaa (USA) 130 – Trevillari (USA) (Riverman (USA) 131) [2007 **73** 78: p8g p10g p8.6g 9.5g* 9.5g* 9.5m 9.5g⁶ Jul 1] leggy, quite good-topped gelding: fair performer: little impact in handicaps for W. Haggas first 3 starts before sold 10,000 gns: won minor event and handicap at Mannheim in April: stays 9.5f: acts on polytrack: blinkered (looked moody) third start: has twice refused to enter stall. *C. von der Recke, Germany*

ARMURE 2 gr.f. (Apr 27) Dalakhani (IRE) 133 – Bombazine (IRE) 97 (Generous (IRE) **79** 139) [2007 7g 7.5m⁴ 8.1s³ Sep 29] big, rangy filly: closely related to 4-y-o Gravitas and half-sister to several winners, including useful French 1½m and 15.5f winner Affirmative Action (by Rainbow Quest), later successful in US at 8.5f: dam, 1¼m winner who stayed 1½m, half-sister to Barathea and Gossamer: fair form in maidens, in frame at Beverley and Haydock (awkward under pressure): will be suited by 1¼m/1½m. *M. A. Jarvis*

ARMY OF ANGELS (IRE) 5 ch.g. King's Best (USA) 132 – Angelic Sounds (IRE) **117**
(The Noble Player (USA) 126) [2007 117: 8g⁶ 8.3d* 8m² Jun 9] strong gelding: smart
performer, lightly raced: won listed event at Windsor (by neck from Take A Bow, idling)
in May: below-form 4 lengths second to eased Dunelight in similar event at Goodwood
(hung right) final outing (sustained ankle injury and underwent surgery): stays 1m: acts
on soft and good to firm going: tongue tied first 5 starts. *Saeed bin Suroor*

ARNIECOCO 2 b.c. (Feb 14) Dr Fong (USA) 128 – Groovy 87 (Shareef Dancer (USA) **–**
135) [2007 p7g Jul 25] second foal: dam, 1m winner, out of smart miler Only Yours: 12/1,
green and not knocked about in maiden at Lingfield. *B. J. Meehan*

ARNIE'S JOINT (IRE) 3 b.g. Golan (IRE) 129 – Green Green Grass 56 (Green **63**
Desert (USA) 127) [2007 68: p6g⁶ p5g⁵ p5.1g⁵ p5g⁶ 7.1m³ 6g p6g² a6g a6g Nov 6]
close-coupled gelding: modest performer: mostly creditable efforts in handicaps before
sold from N. Littmoden 7,500 gns after seventh outing: may prove best at 6f: acts on
polytrack, good to firm and good to soft ground: blinkered/visored last 4 starts in Britain.
B. Hallencreutz, Sweden

AROMATHERAPY 2 b.f. (Apr 30) Oasis Dream 129 – Fragrant View (USA) 99 **78 p**
(Distant View (USA) 126) [2007 7m³ 7g⁴ Oct 6] strong, useful-looking filly: second
foal: half-sister to 3-y-o Venerable: dam, 1¼m winner, above-form high-class performer up
to 1¼m Distant Music (Dewhurst Stakes winner at 2 yrs): in frame in maidens at
Newmarket (third to Fr Dominic) and Redcar (odds on), 2 weeks apart: will stay 1m:
remains capable of better. *H. R. A. Cecil*

ARONDO (GER) 4 ch.g. Areion (GER) 115 – Arrancada (GER) (Riboprince (USA) **62**
118) [2007 10m 7s p10.7g² p8g³ p12.2g⁴ Dec 15] rather leggy gelding: modest performer:
won 3 races in Germany in 2006, when trained by C. Von der Recke: in frame in handicaps last 3 starts in 2007, including at Wolverhampton: barely stays 10.7f: acts on
polytrack, sand and soft going. *Mervyn Torrens, Ireland*

ARQAAM 3 b.c. Machiavellian (USA) 123 – Khams-Alhawas (IRE) 93 (Marju (IRE) **110**
127) [2007 9m* 10.4d⁴ Oct 12] good-bodied colt: first foal: dam, 1¼m winner who
stayed 1½m, out of useful daughter of 1000 Guineas winner Shadayid: 7/4-on, created
good impression when winning maiden at Redcar (by 5 lengths from Ashmal) in
September: gone in coat, smart form when 4¼ lengths fourth to Fairmile in minor event
at York next time, tiring: stays 1¼m: joined D. Watson in UAE. *Saeed bin Suroor*

ARRABIATA 2 b.f. (Apr 2) Piccolo 121 – Paperweight 77 (In The Wings 128) [2007 **–**
p6g Dec 28] second foal: dam, 9f winner (stayed 1½m), out of close relative to 1000
Guineas third Crystal Gazing: 20/1, well held in maiden at Wolverhampton, very slowly
away. *C. N. Kellett*

ARREWIG LISSOME (USA) 2 b.c. (Mar 25) Black Tie Affair 128 – Lissome **–**
(USA) (Lear Fan (USA) 130) [2007 8m p8g Dec 28] strong colt: behind in maidens at
Newmarket (backward) and Lingfield 3 months apart. *A. M. Balding*

ARRIVEE (FR) 4 bl.f. Anabaa (USA) 130 – Quiet Dream (USA) (Seattle Slew (USA)) **–**
[2007 93: 9m 7g p7g Jun 13] strong, good-topped filly: fairly useful performer at 3 yrs for
A. Fabre in France: tailed off in pattern races/handicap in 2007: stays 7f: acts on good to
soft ground: wore cheekpieces final outing: sold 75,000 gns in December. *Mrs P. Sly*

ARSAD (IRE) 4 b.f. Cape Cross (IRE) 129 – Astuti (IRE) 84 (Waajib 121) [2007 62, **–**
a69: f14g* f14g² p16g f14g² f14g² 12m p12.2g⁵ Oct 2] good-topped filly: fairly useful **a80**
handicapper on all-weather: won at Southwell (by 5 lengths) in January: creditable
efforts when runner-up after: stays 1¾m: acts on all-weather: blinkered 2 of last 3 starts.
C. E. Brittain

ART ADVISOR (IRE) 2 b.c. (Apr 14) Noverre (USA) 125 – Monarchy (IRE) **98**
(Common Grounds 118) [2007 5g² 5m* 5m² 5.5m⁵ 6g 6g Oct 6] €38,000F, 50,000Y:
strong, close-coupled colt: sixth foal: half-brother to 3 winners, including Italian 9f
winner Mr Positano (by Foxhound): dam, ran twice, out of half-sister to top-class miler
Second Set: useful performer: won maiden at Carlisle in May: best efforts next 2 starts,
1¼ lengths second of 11 to Winker Watson in Norfolk Stakes at Royal Ascot then 4¼
lengths fifth of 7 to Natagora in Prix Robert Papin at Maisons-Laffitte: well below form
after: should prove best at 5f/6f: raced only on good/good to firm going: blinkered final
start: sold 95,000 gns, sent to Qatar. *J. Howard Johnson*

ART COLLECTOR (USA) 2 ch.c. (May 14) Mr Greeley (USA) 122 – Fellwaati **–**
(USA) (Alydar (USA)) [2007 7.1m Aug 31] very green when tailed off in maiden at
Sandown. *G. L. Moore*

ART CURRENCY (USA) 2 b. or br.c. (Apr 1) Street Cry (IRE) 130 – Lady In Silver **74**
(USA) 127 (Silver Hawk (USA) 123) [2007 p8g⁶ 7d² 7m⁶ Sep 15] 42,000 2-y-o: half-
brother to several winners, including US 5.5f to 7f winner Solid Silver Star (by Silver
Deputy): dam won Prix de Diane: fair maiden: short-head second to Mr Keppel at
Brighton: seemed amiss final start: should stay 1m. *M. J. Wallace*

ARTDEAL 2 b.g. (Feb 8) Fasliyev (USA) 120 – Eternal Beauty (USA) 63 (Zafonic **73**
(USA) 130) [2007 p5g² 5m* 5.1m 5m³ 5m* 6d* Jul 3] 20,000Y: lengthy, good-topped
gelding: first foal: dam, ran 3 times, out of smart Irish 1m/9f winner (including at 2 yrs)
Strawberry Roan, herself sister to Oaks winner Imagine and half-sister to Generous: fair
performer: won maiden at Beverley in April and claimers there in June and Brighton in
July: will prove best kept to 5f/6f: acts on polytrack, good to firm and good to soft ground:
in cheekpieces after third start: sold 20,000 gns. *M. J. Wallace*

ART DECO (IRE) 4 ch.c. Peintre Celebre (USA) 137 – Sometime (IRE) (Royal –
Academy (USA) 130) [2007 116: 10g⁶ Apr 27] rather leggy, close-coupled colt: smart
performer at 3 yrs: met with minor setbacks after final outing that year: ran poorly in
Gordon Richards Stakes at Sandown (said to have bled) sole outing in 2007: stays 1½m:
acts on soft and good to firm going. *C. R. Egerton*

ART ELEGANT 5 b.g. Desert Prince (IRE) 130 – Elegant (IRE) (Marju (IRE) 127 **57**
[2007 76§: 9.5g 7m 8m 7.5m⁴ 9d⁴ 8.5d⁶ 7s 8g³ 5m³ 5m 5g⁵ p8.6g⁶ Nov 30] useful-
looking gelding: modest handicapper: below form both starts in Britain at 5 yrs: effective
at 5f to 9f: acts on polytrack, firm and good to soft going: usually in cheekpieces/blinkers:
tried tongue tied: none too genuine. *T. G. McCourt, Ireland*

ART EXHIBITION (IRE) 2 ch.c. (Mar 20) Captain Rio 122 – Miss Dilletante (Primo **55 p**
Dominie 121) [2007 p5g Nov 15] €20,000F, 60,000Y: third foal: dam thrice-raced half-
sister to useful winner up to 1¾m Misbelief: 7/2, eighth of 10 in maiden at Lingfield:
should be capable of better. *J. Noseda*

ART GALLERY 3 ch.g. Indian Ridge 123 – Party Doll 108 (Be My Guest (USA) 126) –
[2007 55p: p8g⁶ 8m p10m p8g Nov 14] rangy gelding: maiden: little form in 2007: tried
blinkered. *G. L. Moore*

ART GAMBLE (IRE) 3 b.g. Shinko Forest (IRE) – Kiva (Indian Ridge 123) [2007 –
6m 6g 5.1m⁶ Jun 6] €25,000Y, 48,000 2-y-o: big, good-topped gelding: second foal: dam
unraced out of half-sister to high-class 1m to 11f performer Sarafan: always behind in
maidens: bred to need further. *N. A. Callaghan*

ARTHUR PARKER 6 b.g. Cloudings (IRE) 112 – Black H'Penny (Town And –
Country 124) [2007 p12.2g 10g 10s Jun 4] strong gelding: modest form in maidens: last
in maidens/claimer on Flat, looking ungenuine second start: tongue tied. *J. A. B. Old*

ARTHURS DREAM (IRE) 5 b.g. Desert Prince (IRE) 130 – Blueprint (USA) –
(Shadeed (USA) 135) [2007 51: f11g p12.2g Apr 30] modest maiden: below form both
starts in 2007: stays 11.6f: acts on good to soft ground: tried visored/in cheekpieces:
sometimes slowly away: has looked none too genuine. *A. W. Carroll*

ARTHUR'S EDGE 3 b.g. Diktat 126 – Bright Edge 102 (Danehill Dancer (IRE) 117) **67**
[2007 –: 7d 8.2g⁴ p10g² p9.5g³ p8.6g* Nov 30] lengthy gelding: fair performer: won
handicap at Wolverhampton in November: stays 1¼m: acts on polytrack. *B. Palling*

ARTHUR'S GIRL 2 b.f. (Feb 12) Hernando (FR) 127 – Maid of Camelot 102 (Caer- **72 p**
leon (USA) 132) [2007 p6g⁵ Oct 15] fifth foal: half-sister to 3-y-o Messiah Garvey: dam
1¼m winner: 16/1, encouraging never-nearer fifth in maiden at Lingfield, inadequate
test: will be well suited by at least 1m: sure to progress. *G. Wragg*

ARTIC BLISS 5 ch.m. Fraam 114 – Eskimo Nel (IRE) 75 (Shy Groom (USA)) [2007 –
p11g p13g Mar 5] leggy mare: little form: joined C. Longsdon, won over hurdles in
September. *G. F. Bridgwater*

ARTIE 8 b.g. Whittingham (IRE) 104 – Calamanco 71 (Clantime 101) [2007 –: 5d 5v 5s –
Jul 13] big, good-topped gelding: fairly useful handicapper in 2005: lightly raced and
little impact since: tried blinkered. *T. D. Easterby*

ARTIMINO 3 b.c. Medicean 128 – Palatial 101 (Green Desert (USA) 127) [2007 90p: **104**
7.5m⁴ 8m* 8m⁴ 8m² 7m⁴ 7d Oct 19] sturdy, lengthy colt: useful maiden: won at
Newmarket (by length from Bid For Glory) in May: best efforts when 1¾ lengths second
to Tybalt and 1¼ lengths fourth to Giganticus there fourth/fifth outings: below form on
same course final start: effective at 7f/1m: unraced on extremes of going: tongue tied last
5 starts. *J. R. Fanshawe*

ART INVESTOR 4 b.g. Sinndar (IRE) 134 – Maid For Romance 71 (Pursuit of Love **70 §**
124) [2007 75: p10g³ p12g³ p13g 14.1g 9.9g⁴ 10d 10.1d² 12d 10g 12m Sep 22] strong,
stocky gelding: fair maiden: stays 1½m: acts on all-weather, good to firm and good
to soft going: blinkered last 6 outings: has raced freely: ungenuine: sold 10,500 gns.
D. R. C. Elsworth

ARTISTIC LIASON 3 ch.f. Auction House (USA) 120 – Hometheclassics 48 (Tate –
Gallery (USA) 117) [2007 55: 8m⁴ p7.1g Sep 28] maiden: modest form only start at
2 yrs: tailed off in 2007: gave trouble at start and withdrawn on intended reappearance.
G. C. H. Chung

ARTISTIC LICENSE (IRE) 2 b.f. (Jan 10) Chevalier (IRE) 115 – Alexander Eliott **73 p**
(IRE) 73 (Night Shift (USA)) [2007 5m* 6.5d 6d Oct 12] 22,000Y: attractive filly:
unfurnished at 2 yrs: third foal: closely related to 4-y-o Brandywell Boy: dam, Irish
maiden, stayed 1¼m: fair form: won maiden at Folkestone in September: shaped well
from unfavourable draw when seventh of 22 to Lady Rangali in sales race at Ascot later
in month: again isolated wide in nursery at York final start: likely to stay 1m: should
improve. *M. R. Channon*

ARTISTIC LIGHT 2 ch.f. (Mar 2) Fantastic Light (USA) 134 – Artisia (IRE) (Peintre **65 +**
Celebre (USA) 137) [2007 7m p7.1g⁴ p7.1g² p8.6g² p8g Dec 12] unfurnished filly:
first foal: dam, maiden, half-sister to smart sprinter Almaty: fair maiden: best effort when
second in nursery at Wolverhampton penultimate start: stays 8.6f: raced only on polytrack
after debut. *W. R. Muir*

ARTISTIC STYLE 7 b.g. Anabaa (USA) 130 – Fine Detail (IRE) 93 (Shirley Heights – §
130) [2007 92§: 10.9s⁵ 10g Jul 9] rather leggy gelding: one-time useful but unreliable
handicapper: little form in 2007: reluctant both starts in visor. *B. G. Powell*

ARTIST'S MUSE (USA) 4 b.f. Royal Academy (USA) 130 – Atelier (Warning 136) –
[2007 68: p12.2g Feb 12] good-topped filly: fair maiden at 3 yrs: tailed off only start in
2007. *M. S. Saunders*

ARTLESS (USA) 4 b.f. Aptitude (USA) 128 – Eternity 77 (Suave Dancer (USA) 136) **90**
[2007 f8g³ f11g² 11.9m⁴ 14g* 13.1d* 16d⁴ Aug 10] fourth foal: half-sister to 1½m to 2m
winner Etching (by Groom Dancer): dam, 11f/1½m winner, half-sister to Fillies' Mile
winner Tessla: fairly useful performer: won handicaps at Musselburgh and Ayr in July:
upped in trip: below form in amateur race at Wexford final outing: stays 1¾m: acts on
good to soft going: usually up with pace: joined J. Howard Johnson, won over hurdles in
October. *Sir Mark Prescott*

ART MAN 4 b.g. Dansili 127 – Persuasion 79 (Batshoof 122) [2007 77: 9.9d⁶ p10g⁴ **84 +**
p10m⁵ Nov 1] big gelding: fairly useful maiden: better than bare result all starts in 2007:
stays 1¼m: acts on polytrack and firm going. *G. L. Moore*

ART MARKET (CAN) 4 ch.g. Giant's Causeway (USA) 132 – Fantasy Lake (USA) **70**
(Salt Lake (USA)) [2007 90: 6g 5m 7d 8.3f p9.5g⁶ Oct 18] rangy gelding: just fair
performer nowadays: best form at 6f/7f: acts on good to firm going: tried blinkered/
tongue tied: sold 6,000 gns, joined Jo Crowley. *G. L. Moore*

ART MASTER 2 b.c. (Feb 12) Peintre Celebre (USA) 137 – Eurolinka (IRE) (Tirol **106**
127) [2007 7.1g² 7s* 8m⁶ 8m* p8m* 8g⁴ Oct 27] 22,000Y: quite attractive colt: sixth foal:
half-brother to fairly useful 17f winner Faraway Lady (by Alzao): dam unraced half-sister
to useful 1½m performer Duke of Eurolink: won maiden at Leicester
in July and minor event at Kempton (beat Al Muheer by 2 lengths) in October: good 5
lengths fourth of 12 to Ibn Khaldun in Racing Post Trophy at Doncaster final outing,
patiently ridden and finishing well: will stay 1¼m/1½m: acts on polytrack, soft and good
to firm going. *S. Kirk*

ART MODERN (IRE) 5 ch.g. Giant's Causeway (USA) 132 – Sinead (USA) (Irish **89**
River (FR) 131) [2007 84: p10g p12g³ p10g* p12g* 10m⁴ 10.1g 12m 10d 9d 9.9m⁴
p10m³ Oct 13] lengthy gelding: fairly useful performer: won handicaps at Lingfield in
March and April: below best last 6 starts, including in claimer final outing: stays 1½m:
acts on polytrack, good to firm and good to soft going: wore cheekpieces second outing,
often blinkered (including for all 3 wins). *G. L. Moore*

ART PROFESSOR (IRE) 3 b.g. In The Wings 128 – Itab (USA) 71 (Dayjur (USA) **77**
137) [2007 p7g⁶ p8.6g⁴ 7g 9.9g² p12.2g³ 11.9s³ Sep 28] good-bodied gelding: fourth
foal: half-brother to fairly useful 1½m winner Permanent Way (by Fantastic Light): dam,
7f winner, half-sister to Poule d'Essai des Pouliches winner Ta Rib: fair maiden on Flat:
placed last 3 outings: stays 1½m: acts on polytrack and soft ground: joined Venetia
Williams, fairly useful winner over hurdles. *J. W. Hills*

ART SALE 2 b.c. (Mar 20) Compton Place 125 – Bandanna 98 (Bandmaster (USA) 97) **101** [2007 6g⁶ 5.1g³ 5m³ 5.3f* 5m³ 6g² 6m² Sep 15] 38,000F, €75,000Y, 75,000 2-y-o: small, strong colt: moderate mover: second foal: dam, 5f/6f (latter at 2 yrs) winner, half-sister to July Stakes winner Rich Ground: useful performer: won nursery at Brighton in August: best form last 2 starts, second to Mr Keppel in nursery at Haydock and to Spitfire in minor event at Doncaster: should prove best kept to 5f/6f: acts on firm going: sent to Hong Kong, where renamed Ever Beauty. *G. L. Moore*

ARTSU 2 b.g. (Apr 27) Bahamian Bounty 116 – War Shanty 66 (Warrshan (USA) 117) **85** [2007 6m⁴ 6d* 6m 6s² 6m¹ 6d⁶ Sep 28] 42,000Y: tall, useful-looking gelding: sixth foal: half-brother to 3 winners, including fairly useful 7f/1m winner All Quiet (by Piccolo): dam lightly-raced half-sister to very smart sprinter Bold Edge: fairly useful performer: won maiden at Yarmouth in June: below form in nurseries either side of excellent second of 17 to Edge of Gold in sales race at Newmarket: will prove as effective at 5f as 6f: acts on soft going: possibly ungenuine. *M. L. W. Bell*

ART VALUE 2 ch.c. (Apr 10) Barathea (IRE) 127 – Empty Purse (Pennine Walk 120) **79** [2007 8.3g 8d³ p8m Dec 7] 36,000Y: compact colt: brother to 8-y-o Barathea Blazer and 1¼m winner (stayed 1¾m) Barathea Blue, and half-brother to several winners, including fairly useful 1m winner Zilcash (by Mujahid): dam unraced: fair maiden: best efforts at Leicester and Yarmouth (third to First Avenue): inadequate test at Lingfield final start: will be well suited by 1¼m/1½m. *P. W. Chapple-Hyam*

ARTZOLA (IRE) 7 b.m. Alzao (USA) 117 – Polistatic 53 (Free State 125) [2007 60: – p10g Feb 19] good-bodied mare: modest performer: below form sole outing in 2007: stays easy 1½m: acts on polytrack and good to firm going. *C. A. Horgan*

ASBURY PARK 4 b.g. Primo Valentino (IRE) 116 – Ocean Grove (IRE) 84 (Fairy – King (USA)) [2007 68: f12g⁶ May 1] good-topped gelding: maiden: tongue tied, well held in seller only 4-y-o outing: stays easy 11f: best efforts on good going. *M. R. Bosley*

ASCALON 3 ch.c. Galileo (IRE) 134 – Leaping Flame (USA) (Trempolino (USA) 135) **87** [2007 8m⁵ 8g* 10g 11m 10.3g Oct 26] big, strong colt: fourth foal: half-brother to fairly useful 9f winner Firesong (by Dansili) and 1½m/1¾m winner Zaffeu (by Zafonic): dam, French 7f winner, half-sister to smart performers up to/around 1m Apple of Kent and War Zone: fairly useful form: won maiden at Newmarket in May: little impact in handicaps last 2 starts, though not knocked about at Doncaster in latter: will stay 1½m: raced only on good/good to firm ground. *Pat Eddery*

ASCOT LIME 2 ch.c. (Jan 25) Pivotal 124 – Hector's Girl 99 (Hector Protector (USA) **77 P** 124) [2007 7m⁶ Sep 12] strong, well-made, attractive colt: first foal: dam, 2-y-o 6f winner (stayed 7f), out of half-sister to very smart sprinter College Chapel: 15/8 favourite but burly and lethargic, shaped encouragingly under the circumstances in minor event at Doncaster (3½ lengths sixth of 7 to Newly Elected), hampered at start and unsuited by steady pace, not knocked about: may prove best up to 1m: type to improve considerably. *Sir Michael Stoute*

ASFURAH'S DREAM (IRE) 2 b.f. (Feb 27) Nayef (USA) 129 – Asfurah (USA) 108 **73 p** (Dayjur (USA) 137) [2007 p7g⁴ Oct 12] leggy, attractive filly: sixth foal: half-sister to 3 winners, including fairly useful 1¼m winner Ijtihad (by Darshaan): dam, 2-y-o 5f/6f (including Cherry Hinton) winner, half-sister to smart US 6f/7f performer Istintaj: 15/2 and steadily to post, pulled very hard when fourth to Storm Force in maiden at Lingfield: will progress if settling down. *M. P. Tregoning*

ASHDOWN EXPRESS (IRE) 8 ch.g. Ashkalani (IRE) 128 – Indian Express 61 **111** (Indian Ridge 123) [2007 122: 6.5g³ 6.5g² 6g⁶ 6g⁴ 6m⁵ 6m⁵ 6d 6d Jul 27] sturdy, lengthy gelding: smart performer nowadays: several creditable efforts in 2007, including third to Appalachian Trail in handicap at Nad Al Sheba and fourth to Sierra Vista in minor event at Haydock on reappearance/fourth outing: best at 5f/6f: acts on firm and good to soft going, well held on soft/heavy: blinkered once, visored final outing: often sweats: often wears crossed noseband/goes early to post: held up. *C. F. Wall*

ASHES (IRE) 5 b.m. General Monash (USA) 107 – Wakayi 87 (Persian Bold 123) **69** [2007 77: 5m³ p5.1g* 5m³ 5m⁴ 5d 5m² 5d 5d⁶ 5m³ 5g 5d 5g⁶ 5g⁴ p5.1g 5g p5.1s **a72** p6g⁶ Dec 30] good-topped mare: fair performer: won handicap at Wolverhampton in April: best at 5f/6f: acts on polytrack, heavy and good to firm going: tried blinkered/in cheekpieces. *K. R. Burke*

ASHES REGAINED 4 b.c. Galileo (IRE) 134 – Hasty Words (IRE) 103 (Polish **98** Patriot (USA) 128) [2007 ?: p8.6g³ p8.6g* 8m⁵ 8m² Jul 11] useful handicapper, lightly raced: won at Wolverhampton in May: good second at Newmarket final outing: stays easy 8.6f: raced only on polytrack and good/good to firm going: saddle slipped and pulled hard on reappearance: sold 4,500 gns in October. *B. W. Hills*

ASHKAZAR (FR) 3 b.g. Sadler's Wells (USA) 132 – Asharna (IRE) (Darshaan 133) **105** [2007 11m² 12g* 12v² 12d⁶ 12g⁵ Jul 14] good-topped gelding: first foal: dam, French 1m winner, half-sister to high-class French miler Ashkalani: useful performer: won minor event at Saint-Cloud in May: beaten short neck by Royal And Regal in listed race at Longchamp next time and ran creditably when 5¾ lengths sixth to Boscobel in King Edward VII Stakes at Royal Ascot and 7½ lengths fifth to Zambezi Sun in Grand Prix de Paris at Longchamp: should be suited by further than 1½m: acts on heavy ground: gelded, joined D. Pipe and fairly useful winner over hurdles. *A. de Royer Dupre, France*

ASHLEIGH ANDERSON (FR) 3 b.f. Black Minnaloushe (USA) 123 – Miswakette **66** (USA) (Miswaki (USA) 124) [2007 70: 7m³ 10.5g⁶ p11g p7.1g Nov 19] €3,000Y: half-sister to several minor US sprint winners: dam sprint winner in USA (including at 2 yrs): fair maiden: well held in handicaps in Britain last 2 starts: stays 7f: acts on good to firm ground. *E. Tyrrell, Ireland*

ASHMAL (USA) 3 b.f. Machiavellian (USA) 123 – Alabaq (USA) 111 (Riverman **71** (USA) 131) [2007 –: 10m 9.9d³ 12.1s³ 10d⁶ 9m² 9m² 10.2d⁴ 10.2g² Oct 24] angular filly: fair maiden: placed 5 times in 2007: stays 1¼m: acts on soft and good to firm ground: blinkered last 4 starts: sold 38,000 gns. *J. L. Dunlop*

ASHMOLIAN (IRE) 4 b.g. Grand Lodge (USA) 125 – Animatrice (USA) 115 **51** (Alleged (USA) 138) [2007 11.9m 11s⁴ 12.1s⁴ 12.1s p12g p10g Nov 19] workmanlike gelding: modest maiden: stays 1½m: acts on soft ground. *Miss Z. C. Davison*

ASHWELL ROSE 5 b.m. Anabaa (USA) 130 – Finicia (USA) (Miswaki (USA) 124) **63** [2007 47: 7d 11.5g 12m² 12g 16g⁶ 10.3g 12g⁴ 12g* Nov 6] close-coupled mare: modest performer: won maiden at Catterick in November: effective at 1½m, probably stays 2m: yet to race on extremes of going on turf: tried blinkered, visored last 6 starts. *J. R. Jenkins*

ASIAN ALLIANCE (IRE) 6 ch.m. Soviet Star 128 – Indian Express 61 **51** (Indian Ridge 123) [2007 57: p12.2g⁶ Jan 8] modest maiden on Flat, lightly raced: barely stays easy 1½m: acts on polytrack and soft going: in cheekpieces last 2 starts. *K. A. Ryan*

ASIAN CLASSIC (IRE) 2 b.g. (Mar 14) Montjeu (IRE) 137 – Yafoul (USA) 95 (Tor- **56 p** rential (USA) 117) [2007 8.2g Oct 31] 90,000Y: medium-sized gelding: first foal: dam, 2-y-o 6f winner, half-sister to smart 7f/1m performer Ramooz: 9/1, made only brief effort when ninth of 11 in maiden at Nottingham, shaping as though in need of race: gelded after: open to improvement. *R. Charlton*

ASIAN LADY 2 br.f. (Mar 3) Kyllachy 129 – Prancing 98 (Prince Sabo 123) [2007 **–** 6m Nov 10] 80,000Y: useful-looking filly: seventh foal: half-sister to several winners, including 4-y-o Levera: dam, 2-y-o 5f winner (stayed 1m), half-sister to Middle Park winner First Trump: 8/1, eighth of 9 (beaten 5 lengths) in steadily-run maiden at Don- caster. *R. Charlton*

ASIAN POWER (IRE) 2 ch.g. (Feb 14) Bertolini (USA) 125 – Cynara 65 (Imp **72** Society (USA)) [2007 6m 6d 7m 7m⁵ 7.5g 8s p6g* 7m⁴ p6g Oct 27] €24,000F, 28,000Y: good-topped gelding: first foal: dam 2-y-o 7f/1m and hurdles winner: fair performer: won nursery at Kempton in September: reportedly lost action final start: best up to 7f: acts on polytrack and good to firm going. *P. J. O'Gorman*

ASIATIC BOY (ARG) 4 b.c. Not For Sale (ARG) – S S Asiatic (USA) (Polish Navy **122** (USA)) [2007 a7f* a8f* a9f* a9f* 8g⁴ 10.4d⁵ Aug 21] robust colt: type to carry plenty of condition: fluent mover: third known foal: half-brother to winner in US by Roar: dam US

UAE Derby Sponsored by S. & M. Al Naboodah Group, Nad Al Sheba—
Asiatic Boy has no trouble in becoming the first to complete the so-called 'UAE triple crown';
Jack Junior is runner-up ahead of the grey Adil

8.5f winner: very smart performer: won once from 3 starts in Argentina in 2006, when also second in Grade 1 Gran Criterium at San Isidro: unbeaten in first 4 starts for new connections (all at Nad Al Sheba), namely minor event in January, UAE 2000 Guineas (by 4½ lengths from Traffic Guard) in February, and minor event and UAE Derby (beat Jack Junior 9½ lengths, leading over 2f out and soon clear), in March: off 4 months, creditable 2 lengths fourth to Ramonti in Sussex Stakes at Goodwood before just respectable fifth to Authorized in Juddmonte International Stakes at York final outing: may prove best short of 1¼m: acts on dirt and any turf going. *M. F. de Kock, South Africa*

ASK 4 b.c. Sadler's Wells (USA) 132 – Request 87 (Rainbow Quest (USA) 134) **126**
[2007 116: 13.4m* 12g* 12f² Oct 21]

When Ask was sold privately at the end of his first season it was for what one of his former part owners, the Duke of Devonshire, referred to as 'a good price'. In view of the colt's performances since, Ask's new owner Patrick Fahey will surely be of the same opinion. Ask remained in Sir Michael Stoute's yard and continued the improvement he had made as a three-year-old, developing into a high-class performer in 2007, winning two Group 3 events and just failing to land a first prize of over £600,000 in the Canadian International at Woodbine on his only other start.

Ask was unraced at two and got off the mark on his third start, winning a maiden at Chepstow. He failed to add to it as a three-year-old though he did leave that form well behind at York on his last two appearances, finishing a short-head second to Trick Or Treat in the Melrose Handicap then three and three quarter lengths fourth to Sixties Icon in the St Leger. The 2005 St Leger winner Scorpion was in opposition when Ask reappeared in the Blue Square Ormonde Stakes at Chester. In a six-runner field, Scorpion started the even-money favourite with Ask next in the betting at 5/2, and the pair dominated the race pulling clear of the rest off the final bend, Ask holding a narrow advantage at this stage and winning by two lengths. Unfortunately, Ask picked up a foot injury shortly afterwards and didn't return to action until the last day of September, in the Grosvenor Casinos Cumberland Lodge Stakes at Ascot. Ask again started second favourite behind an Aidan O'Brien-trained runner, this time Honolulu, who earlier in the month had finished third in the St Leger. Looking to have done well physically during his lay-off and in outstanding condition, Ask was the only one of the eight runners with a penalty, in this case 3 lb, in what looked a good renewal of the Cumberland Lodge. Ask showed further improvement to win in good style, showing himself at least as effective at a mile and a half as at a mile and three quarters. Ridden more patiently than at Chester, Ask still had all but one of his rivals ahead of him when Honolulu struck for home early in the straight. Yet so well did Ask respond to pressure that he was in front approaching the final furlong and ran on strongly to win by two lengths from Zaham, with Honolulu a further three quarters of a length back in third. Ask's owner, whose heart is really in jump racing, had considered the possibility of Stoute training Ask for the Champion Hurdle, as he'd done successfully with Kribensis in 1990. He was more realistic after the Cumberland Lodge, though. 'I suspect the horse may be too valuable to take that route now,' he said. Ask's performance in the Canadian International at Woodbine three weeks later would have strengthened that

Blue Square Ormonde Stakes, Chester—Ask sees off Scorpion; Steppe Dancer is third

Grosvenor Casinos Cumberland Lodge Stakes, Ascot—after missing four months,
Ask returns with another high-class performance; second is Zaham and then come Honolulu (rail),
Hattan (right), Laverock and Acapulco

view. Waiting tactics were again employed on Ask, but this time they worked against him as the pace was just steady. Cloudy's Knight, trained in the States, was handily ridden and got first run on Ask, who finished strongly but just failed to peg him back. In front a stride after the line, Ask should have have won.

Ask (b.c. 2003)	Sadler's Wells (USA) (b 1981)	Northern Dancer (b 1961)	Nearctic
			Natalma
		Fairy Bridge (b 1975)	Bold Reason
			Special
	Request (b 1997)	Rainbow Quest (b 1981)	Blushing Groom
			I Will Follow
		Highbrow (b 1985)	Shirley Heights
			Highclere

Ask, who was bred by the Duke of Devonshire, is the first foal of Request, a mare who was bred by the Queen and ran twice for her. Both runs were at a mile and a quarter, Request showing fairly useful form when second in a maiden at Sandown and fourth in a listed event at Newbury. The royal colours have been carried with distinction by many representatives of this family over the years, among them Request's very smart half-brother Blueprint and smart half-sister Fairy Godmother. The next dam Highbrow, runner-up in the Ribblesdale Stakes, is a daughter of Highclere who won the One Thousand Guineas and Prix de Diane for the Queen in 1974. Highclere is also responsible for Height of Fashion, the dam of Nashwan, Nayef and Unfuwain and for Burghclere, the grandam of the top-class Japanese horse Deep Impact. The mares on the bottom line of Ask's pedigree did have their quirks. Request and Highbrow were both tail swishers, the latter looking ungenerous at times, and, while Highclere was genuine, she did wear blinkers on all of her starts at three to correct a tendency to look about her. Ask is also genuine but he hasn't always kept a straight course in the closing stages of his races, edging continually left in the straight at Woodbine on the firmest ground he has encountered to date. He had run well under very different conditions as a three-year-old, winning on good to soft and finishing second on soft in the Melrose. The good-topped Ask was fitted with a tongue strap on his last two outings at three. Incidentally, Ask's former owners had his two-year-old full brother in training with Stoute. Named Kensington Oval, he has yet to race. *Sir Michael Stoute*

ASKAR TAU (FR) 2 b.c. (Mar 14) Montjeu (IRE) 137 – Autriche (IRE) 104 (Acatenango (GER) 127) [2007 8m 8d Oct 27] 145,000Y: compact colt: fifth foal: half-brother to 2 winners in Germany: dam German 6f (at 2 yrs) to 1¼m winner: probably needed experience (not knocked about) in minor event and maiden at Newbury: should do better over middle distances at 3 yrs. *M. P. Tregoning* – p

ASK JENNY (IRE) 5 b.m. Marju (IRE) 127 – Waltzing Matilda (Mujtahid (USA) 118) [2007 49: p5g Jan 6] modest maiden at 3 yrs: little form since, including at Kempton sole start in 2007: tried in cheekpieces. *Patrick Morris, Ireland* –

ASK NO MORE 4 b.g. Pyramus (USA) 78 – Nordesta (IRE) 72 (Nordico (USA)) [2007 76: p8g p7g p8g⁴ f6g⁴ f5g³ p6g f6g⁵ f6g⁴ p7.1d Dec 27] modest performer: effective at 6f to 8.6f: acts on all-weather: blinkered. *J. Ryan* 55

ASK THE BUTLER 3 b.g. Dansili 127 – Heronetta 78 (Halling (USA) 133) [2007 78: 7m 9.9m⁴ 12g² 16d Jun 22] €46,000Y: leggy gelding: first foal: dam 1½m winner: fairly useful maiden: left D. Gillespie in Ireland after 2 yrs: creditable efforts when in frame in handicaps: well held in Queen's Vase at Royal Ascot final outing: stays 1½m: acts on good to firm going. *A. W. Carroll* 84

ASK THE CLERK (IRE) 6 b.g. Turtle Island (IRE) 123 – Some Fun (Wolverlife 115) [2007 80: 7g² 8.5g⁶ 8.5g⁵ 7g² 9g⁴ 8.5g⁵ 7g 8.5g p7.1g² a8g⁴ 8g a7.5g⁶ a4.8g a6.5g Dec 12] close-coupled gelding: modest performer nowadays: second twice in Jersey, and in claimer at Wolverhampton ninth start, final one for Mrs J. Le Brocq, Jersey: stays 1m: acts on polytrack and any turf going: tried in cheekpieces/blinkers earlier in career. *L. Braem, Belgium* 62

ASK YER DAD 3 b.g. Diktat 126 – Heuston Station (IRE) 72 (Fairy King (USA)) [2007 64: 8.2g⁴ 8.3d⁶ 7s³ 7d⁵ p7g³ p7g p7g 7s⁵ Aug 24] strong, lengthy gelding: fair maiden: stays 1m: acts on polytrack, soft and good to firm ground: usually wears blinkers/cheekpieces. *Mrs P. Sly* 68

ASLAN 3 b.c. Averti (IRE) 117 – Opopmil (IRE) 68 (Pips Pride 117) [2007 6m 7f 5m⁶ May 26] sturdy colt: poor form in maidens: dead. *T. D. Easterby* 44

ASLEEP AT THE BACK (IRE) 4 b.g. Halling (USA) 133 – Molomo 104 (Barathea (IRE) 127) [2007 59: p16g³ f14g⁴ Jan 25] modest maiden: stays 2m: acts on all-weather: reportedly had breathing problem on debut, and tongue tied next 2 outings. *J. G. Given* 51

ASMODEA 2 b.f. (Feb 3) Dr Fong (USA) 128 – Latina (IRE) (King's Theatre (IRE) 128) [2007 p7.1d⁶ Dec 28] 8,000Y: third foal: dam French 6f winner (stayed 1m): 12/1, never dangerous in maiden at Wolverhampton, slowly away. *D. J. Coakley* –

ASPERITY (USA) 3 b.c. War Chant (USA) 126 – Another Storm (USA) (Gone West (USA)) [2007 104P: 10g³ 8m* 8s⁶ 10g⁵ 9f Oct 13] close-coupled, quite attractive colt: has a markedly round action: smart performer: won Prix Paul de Moussac at Chantilly (by a nose from Stoneside, rallying) in June: best effort after when creditable 2 lengths fifth to Harland in Prix Eugene Adam at Maisons-Laffitte: last in Oak Tree Derby at Santa Anita final outing: barely stays 1¼m, will prove best at shorter: acts on good to firm ground: usually makes running. *J. H. M. Gosden* 112

ASRAR 5 b.m. King's Theatre (IRE) 128 – Zandaka (FR) (Doyoun 124) [2007 11.1m 9.2d May 18] 7,500 2-y-o: third foal: sister to 1m and 11f winner Critical Stage: dam unraced half-sister to Poule d'Essai des Pouliches winner Zalaiyka: in frame in bumpers, little impact over hurdles: much better effort in maidens at Hamilton when seventh on debut. *Miss Lucinda V. Russell* 49

ASSERTIVE 4 ch.c. Bold Edge 123 – Tart And A Half 83 (Distant Relative 128) [2007 111: 6m² 6g⁵ 6m* 6d 6d⁴ 7g 6v⁵ 7m 7.1m³ 6g³ 6d Oct 20] angular, good-topped colt: smart performer: won listed event at Windsor (by ½ length from Borderlescott) in June: creditable efforts when in frame after, notably listed race at Sandown (third to Eisteddfod) and Diadem Stakes at Ascot (third to Haatef) ninth/tenth outings: poorly drawn at Newmarket final appearance: best form at 6f: acts on soft and good to firm ground: tried blinkered: changed hands 280,000 gns later in October. *R. Hannon* 116

ASSET (IRE) 4 b.g. Marju (IRE) 127 – Snow Peak (Arazi (USA) 135) [2007 110: 6m* 6d³ 6m⁶ 7g² 6g⁶ 7m² 7d⁵ Oct 20] tall, rather leggy, good-topped gelding: very smart performer: significant improvement first 2 starts in 2007, winning listed race at Newmarket (impressively by 2½ lengths from Assertive) in April before good ¾-length third to Soldier's Tale in Golden Jubilee Stakes at Royal Ascot: respectable efforts in July Cup at Newmarket (sixth to Sakhee's Secret) and Lennox Stakes at Goodwood (1¼ lengths 123

Highclere Thoroughbred Racing XXVI's "Asset"

second to Tariq) next 2 outings: blinkered, below form after: has won over 1m, but will prove best at 6f/7f: acts on polytrack, good to firm and good to soft going: sold 180,000 gns, joined Godolphin. *R. Hannon*

ASSISTACAT (IRE) 3 br.f. Lend A Hand 124 – Cattiva (ITY) (Lomond (USA) 128) – [2007 p7g Mar 16] €10,000Y, resold 16,000Y: fifth foal: half-sister to 3 winners in Italy: dam Italian maiden, half-sister to Prix Morny/Middle Park Stakes winner Bahamian Bounty: 25/1, well held in maiden at Lingfield. *A. P. Jarvis*

ASTANIA 2 b.f. (May 4) Shahrastani (USA) 135 – So Ambitious (Teenoso (USA) 135) **73** [2007 6d⁵ p7g⁵ 8.2m⁴ Oct 3] rather leggy filly: third foal: half-sister to 4-y-o High Ambition: dam unraced: fair maiden: benefited from stiffer test when close fourth at Nottingham: will be suited by 1¼m/1½m. *P. W. D'Arcy*

ASTARTE 3 b.f. Slip Anchor 136 – Nanouche (Dayjur (USA) 137) [2007 –: 12g 7g – p10g Jun 20] neat filly: well held in maidens. *P. R. Chamings*

ASTON BOY 2 ch.c. (Feb 14) Dr Fong (USA) 128 – Hectic Tina 85 (Hector Protector – (USA) 124) [2007 7.1g Aug 15] quite attractive colt: very green in rear in maiden at Sandown: bred to stay at least 1m. *M. Blanshard*

ASTON LAD 6 b.g. Bijou d'Inde 127 – Fishki 36 (Niniski (USA) 125) [2007 55: 16.1d⁶ **59 +** 12.4d³ Oct 16] modest performer, lightly raced on Flat nowadays: stays 2m: acts on soft ground: fairly useful hurdler. *Micky Hammond*

ASTORYGOESWITHIT 4 b.g. Foxhound (USA) 103 – La Belle Mystere 48 (Lycius – (USA) 124) [2007 47: p6g f6g² f6g* f7g² f6g f6g f7g⁶ f7g³ 7.1d 7f p8g f7d³ Dec 15] **a54** close-coupled gelding: modest performer: won minor event at Southwell in February

82

(only start for J. Ryan): rejoined P. McEntee until ninth start: effective at 6f/7f: acts on all-weather: usually wears headgear: has hung/found little. *G. C. Bravery*

ASTRAL CHARMER 3 b.g. Tobougg (IRE) 125 – Blushing Sunrise (USA) (Cox's – Ridge (USA)) [2007 62: 11.6d 11.8s 11.5m Aug 9] modest form at 2 yrs: last in handicaps all starts in 2007: should stay 1½m: tried blinkered. *M. H. Tompkins*

ASTROANGEL 3 b.f. Groom Dancer (USA) 128 – Nutmeg (IRE) 70 (Lake Coniston **68 §** (IRE) 131) [2007 73§: 6g⁴ 7.5m² 8.5g 8s⁵ 8g² p8g 8g⁴ 8m³ 8d 8g p8g³ p7.1g⁴ f8d⁵ Dec 12] neat, leggy filly: fair maiden handicapper: stays 1m: acts on polytrack, firm and good to soft going: tried in blinkers/visor: has found little, and not one to trust. *M. H. Tompkins*

ASTROBELLA 4 ch.f. Medicean 128 – Optimistic 90 (Reprimand 122) [2007 84: 12m – 10m 16.2g Oct 2] neat filly: fairly useful handicapper at 3 yrs: well below form in 2007: stays 11f: acts on good to firm and good to soft going. *M. H. Tompkins*

ASTRODODOME 2 b.g. (Mar 9) Domedriver (IRE) 128 – Alexandrine (IRE) 78 – **p** (Nashwan (USA) 135) [2007 7d p7.1g⁶ p8g Nov 14] 85,000Y: third foal: half-brother to 4-y-o Alambic and 3-y-o Algarade: dam, 1¼m to 13f winner, half-sister to very smart 1¼m performer Last Second and to dams of Alborada/Albanova and Yesterday/Quarter Moon: behind in maidens (within 16 days): sure to improve at 1½m+. *Sir Mark Prescott*

ASTRODONNA 2 ch.f. (Apr 24) Carnival Dancer 123 – Mega (IRE) 66 (Petardia 113) **70 p** [2007 7.1g⁶ p8.6g* Nov 2] second foal: half-sister to 2006 2-y-o 7f winner Marvo (by Bahamian Bounty): dam maiden who should have stayed 1½m: better for debut, won maiden at Wolverhampton by 3½ lengths: will go on improving, especially at 1¼m/1½m. *M. H. Tompkins*

ASTROL 2 b.f. (May 3) Diktat 126 – Magic Myth (IRE) 81 (Revoque (IRE) 122) [2007 – 6m 7d 6s⁶ 7g 5.4m Sep 9] leggy filly: first foal: dam, unreliable 2-y-o 5f/6f winner, half-sister to smart 5f winner Flanders: well beaten in maidens (once blinkered). *T. D. Easterby*

ASTROLIBRA 3 b.f. Sakhee (USA) 136 – Optimistic 90 (Reprimand 122) [2007 50: **59** 7g⁴ 9.7m⁴ 12.1m 11.5s 10m³ p10m³ p12m⁴ p10g Oct 29] good-topped filly: modest maiden: barely stays 1½m: acts on polytrack and good to firm ground. *M. H. Tompkins*

ASTRONOMER ROYAL (USA) 3 b.c. Danzig (USA) – Sheepscot (USA) (Easy **121** Goer (USA)) [2007 90p: 8g⁶ 8g* 8m³ 8s⁴ 8g 8f⁶ Oct 6]

Aidan O'Brien trained the winners of three major European classics in the latest season—or four counting Yeats' Irish St Leger success—but how many could immediately name them all? Soldier of Fortune made a big impression with his runaway win in the Irish Derby. Peeping Fawn dominated the fillies' middle-distance division, her Irish Oaks win almost certainly readily springing to mind. But, by the end of the season, how many would instantly recall Astronomer Royal's success in the Poule d'Essai des Poulains?

For the second year in succession, O'Brien targeted a team of four at the fourteen-runner Poulains. The quartet were bracketed in France for betting purposes, but there was a marked difference in the industry prices that were available in Britain, with Astronomer Royal, the winner of a maiden at Newbury on the second of two starts as a juvenile, returned the longest of them at 33/1, behind Honoured Guest (9/2), Excellent Art (6/1) and Brave Tin Soldier (25/1). What's more, with stable-jockey Kieren Fallon suspended until the following month, high profile jockeys Gerald Mosse, Jamie Spencer and Thierry Thulliez had been booked, respectively, for the stable's three other representatives, whilst Colm O'Donoghue—who failed to ride a winner in Britain or Ireland for the stable all season from thirty-eight mounts—was entrusted with the ride on Astronomer Royal, having partnered the colt for both his two-year-old successes and in the Prix de Fontainebleau run over the same course and distance a month previously, when he finished only sixth behind Chichi Creasy. Defeat in the Fontainebleau hadn't been a barrier to O'Brien's two previous Poulains winners, Landseer and Aussie Rules, however, and Astronomer Royal proceeded to show marked improvement. In a race run at a slightly slower gallop than the earlier Poule d'Essai des Pouliches, Astronomer Royal had only two rivals behind him turning into the straight, but quickened well down the outside as his stablemate Excellent Art found trouble attempting to come from a similar position through the pack. Though edging right

Poule d'Essai des Poulains, Longchamp—Anglo-Irish runners take the first six places; Astronomer Royal gets home from Creachadoir (rail), Honoured Guest (No.8), the unlucky Excellent Art (No.12), Thousand Words (No.1) and Followmyfootsteps (on Honoured Guest's right)

to join Creachadoir in the final furlong, Astronomer Royal asserted in the last hundred yards to win by half a length. His stable had dominated the race the previous season with a one, two, and only the Jim Bolger-trained runner-up prevented an O'Brien-trained first three this time, with Honoured Guest and the strong-finishing Excellent Art, the likely winner with a clear passage, a further length and a half and three quarters of a length back respectively.

The St James's Palace Stakes at Royal Ascot provided Astronomer Royal with the chance to tackle the Two Thousand Guineas winner at Newmarket and the Curragh, Cockney Rebel. It wasn't billed as a high-profile clash of the classic winners though, Cockney Rebel sent off at evens whilst Astronomer Royal, with O'Donoghue retaining the ride, was again neglected at 14/1, seventh choice of the eight runners, also behind Creachadoir and Excellent Art, and another stable companion in Duke of Marmalade, who had finished fourth at Newmarket. Market predictions weren't altogether accurate, and a reproduction of his Longchamp form saw Astronomer Royal finishing a good third, beaten a neck and a length and a quarter, as Excellent Art made the most of a clear run this time in leading home an O'Brien one, two, three.

By the middle of the summer, Astronomer Royal's best performances were behind him. The first of his three subsequent appearances brought a meeting with the winner of France's other colts' classic—the Prix du Jockey Club winner Lawman—in the Prix Jean Prat at Chantilly, though Astronomer Royal appeared unsuited to the testing conditions as he trailed in only fourth of the seven, beaten eight and a half lengths. By the time of the Prix du Moulin back at Longchamp, Astronomer Royal had had a two-month break but was passed over again by the betting public, starting the outsider of nine, and made little impact. For his final outing, he followed the path trodden by stablemates Landseer and Aussie Rules to America for the Shadwell Turf Mile at Keeneland. Running on lasix for the first time, Astronomer Royal was sent off as 3/1 favourite only to give the impression of putting up little fight after looking dangerous turning in.

		Danzig (USA) (b 1977)	Northern Dancer (b 1961)	Nearctic
				Natalma
			Pas de Nom (b or br 1968)	Admiral's Voyage
Astronomer Royal (USA) (b.c. 2004)				Petitioner
		Sheepscot (USA) (ch 1994)	Easy Goer (ch 1986)	Alydar
				Relaxing
			Escrow Agent (ch 1986)	El Gran Senor
				Viva Sec

Sheepscot, the dam of Astronomer Royal, won five of her ten starts on dirt in the States at six furlongs to a mile, the highlight being a minor stakes event in her second and final season as a four-year-old. Retired to stud at the end of that campaign, she produced three winners from as many foals before Astronomer

Royal, two of them by A P Indy, and a colt by Unbridled in between, named Nave-sink River, who won the Grade 2 Pan American Handicap over a mile and a half at Gulfstream on turf, as well as winning two non-graded stakes over an extra furlong on dirt. Subsequently, she produced an unraced two-year-old filly by Unbridled's Song, now named Magnificent Melody, a colt yearling by Fusaichi Pegasus, and, after being sold for 950,000 dollars in 2006, a colt foal by Giant's Causeway. Sheepscot is due to visit Mr Greeley in 2008. Sheepscot is a well-bred mare herself, a half-sister to Florida Derby and Fountain of Youth Stakes winner Vicar. Escrow Agent, Astronomer Royal's grandam, won a seven-furlong maiden in Ireland at two, before being stakes-placed at three in America over an extended mile. The quite good topped and attractive Astronomer Royal stays in training. However he fares from now on, Astronomer Royal, from the final crop of Danzig, has main-tained his sire's record of producing a Group or Grade 1 winner in each year at stud. He is unlikely to stay beyond a mile and is effective on good to firm going. *A. P. O'Brien, Ireland*

ASTRONOMIC 7 b.g. Zafonic (USA) 130 – Sky Love (USA) 93 (Nijinsky (CAN) – 138) [2007 14m⁶ 18d Jun 24] useful performer when with A. Fabre in 2003: little impact in 3 Flat starts since (fairly useful but unreliable hurdler). *J. Howard Johnson*

ASTRONOMICAL ODDS (USA) 4 b.g. Miswaki (USA) 124 – Perfectly Polish   65
(USA) (Polish Numbers (USA)) [2007 73: f8g³ p7g f7g p10g f7g³ p8g Dec 7] fair handi-capper: sold from T. D. Barron 7,000 gns after fifth start: stays 1m: acts on fibresand. *J. J. Lambe, Ireland*

ASTURIAS 3 b.f. Anabaa (USA) 130 – Halcyon Daze 82 (Halling (USA) 133) [2007   68
63: 8.3g³ 9f⁴ 8f⁵ 9f⁵ Nov 4] sturdy filly: fair maiden: left J. Hills after reappearance: stays 9f. *H. L. Bacorn, USA*

ATABAAS PRIDE 2 b.c. (Mar 5) Pivotal 124 – Atabaa (FR) (Anabaa (USA) 130)   85
[2007 5f⁴ 6g² 6d² 6m² 6m* Sep 10] close-coupled, good-topped colt: has a quick, fluent action: third foal: dam, 1m and 9.5f winner, out of smart French performer up to 12.5f Alma Ata: fairly useful from: steady progress, runner-up 3 times (including in nursery) prior to winning maiden at Newcastle by 2½ lengths from Andaman Sunset: will stay 7f. *M. Johnston*

ATACAMA KING (USA) 3 b.g. Chester House (USA) 123 – Santona (CHI) (Win-   –
ning (USA)) [2007 10m Apr 23] 50/1, well held in maiden at Windsor, very slowly away: sold 9,000 gns after. *J. H. M. Gosden*

ATACAMA STAR 5 ch.g. Desert King (IRE) 129 – Aunty (FR) 114 (Riverman (USA)   –
131) [2007 10g Oct 31] close-coupled, workmanlike gelding: fair performer in 2005: well beaten only outing on Flat since: stays 11.7f: acts on firm ground: often front runner. *B. G. Powell*

ATAENSIC 2 b.f. (Apr 1) Warningford 119 – Enchanting Eve 67 (Risk Me (FR) 127)   –
[2007 p6g 5.2g Jul 24] 2,500Y: half-sister to 2 winners by Case Law, including 6-y-o Red Romeo: dam 5f (at 2 yrs) to 1m winner who stayed 1¼m: blinkered in maidens at Lingfield (wayward) and Yarmouth (lame/dismounted). *C. N. Allen*

ATAYEB (USA) 3 ch.f. Rahy (USA) 115 – Sarayir (USA) 104 (Mr Prospector (USA))   81
[2007 8g 8g⁴ 7g⁴ p11g² p12g* 14g Sep 12] useful-looking filly: fifth foal: half-sister to 1¼m winner Sundus (by Sadler's Wells) and 1m winner Itqaan (by Danzig), both fairly useful: dam, 7f (at 2 yrs) and 1¼m winner, closely related to Nayef and half-sister to Nashwan and Unfuwain: reportedly had splints and a pelvic problem at 2 yrs: fairly useful performer: best effort when winning maiden at Lingfield in August: said to have been in season next time: stayed 1½m: acted on polytrack: visits Oasis Dream. *M. P. Tregoning*

A TEEN 9 ch.g. Presidium 124 – Very Good (Noalto 120) [2007 54§: p6g³ p6g p7g* p8g   54 §
f7g p7g⁶ f7g² f8g⁶ p7.1g⁵ 6m⁴ f7g 6v³ p6g³ p6g f7d p7g⁶ Dec 30] sturdy gelding: modest performer: won minor event at Kempton in January: effective at 5f to 7f: acts on all-weather and any turf going: tried blinkered (not since 2001): often races prominently: unreliable. *P. Howling*

ATEPHOBIA 2 b. or br.c. (Feb 24) Auction House (USA) 120 – Seren Teg 80 (Timeless   65
Times (USA) 99) [2007 5m⁶ 5m⁴ 6g⁵ p6g⁶ 6m⁴ 6m 6g² 5d⁶ 6g⁶ p6g* p5.1g p6g² p6d³ Dec 27] 17,500Y: smallish colt: second foal: half-brother to 4-y-o Triskaidekaphobia: dam 5f/6f (latter at 2 yrs) winner: fair performer: won seller at Lingfield in November: effective at 5f/6f: acts on polytrack and good to firm going: races up with pace. *K. R. Burke*

ATH

ATHBOY AUCTION 2 b.f. (May 1) Auction House (USA) 120 – Thabeh 57 (Shareef **66** Dancer (USA) 135) [2007 6f 5m⁶ 5m⁵ 7.1g p6g p7g⁵ p8g Dec 12] smallish filly: half-sister to 7f/1m winners Jamestown and Melody Queen (both by Merdon Melody), latter subsequently useful up to 11f in North America: dam irresolute maiden (stayed 1m): fair maiden: caught the eye when fifth at Sandown, but failed to progress in nurseries: may prove best at 5f/6f: raced on polytrack and good ground or firmer. *H. J. Collingridge*

ATHEA LAD (IRE) 3 b.g. Indian Danehill (IRE) 124 – Persian Empress (IRE) 51 **–** (Persian Bold 123) [2007 55d: p6g⁶ Jan 5] little form since first 2 starts at 2 yrs: tried blinkered. *W. K. Goldsworthy*

ATHEER DUBAI (IRE) 2 b.c. (Jan 31) Dubai Destination (USA) 127 – Atheer **85** (USA) 74 (Lear Fan (USA) 130) [2007 6g² 6m 6m 6g⁴ 7m⁵ 7g⁴ 7g⁴ Oct 20] sturdy colt: first foal: dam, 1m winner, out of sister to smart French 2-y-o Fotitieng: fairly useful maiden: highly tried second/third (badly struck into) starts: creditable efforts on form in nurseries, but looked none too keen (blinkered once): stays 7f: raced on good/good to firm ground. *C. E. Brittain*

ATHENIAN WAY (IRE) 3 b.f. Barathea (IRE) 127 – Grecian Bride (IRE) (Groom **104** Dancer (USA) 128) [2007 57p: 8s⁶ 8m* 9.5m⁴ 12g² 11.3s² 12v 10.1g 12s Oct 13] good-bodied filly: fifth foal: sister to smart 7.5f (at 2 yrs) to 1½m winner Allexina and half-sister to fairly useful 7f to 9.4f winner Champain Sands (by Green Desert): dam unraced half-sister to very smart 11f to 13f winner Gamut out of half-sister to smart dam of North Light: useful performer: won maiden at the Curragh in April: good efforts when runner-up in Noblesse Stakes at Cork (beaten length by Nick's Nikita) and listed event at Limerick (1½ lengths behind Honolulu): left J. Oxx in Ireland, well below form last 2 starts: stays 1½m: acts on soft and good to firm going. *J. R. Fanshawe*

ATLANTIC AIR (FR) 5 gr.h. Kaldounevees (FR) 118 – Beg Meil (FR) (Tel Quel (FR) **118** 125) [2007 108: 9g⁵ 10g 10g³ 10d* 10g² 10g⁴ 10g⁴ 7g³ Dec 27] second foal: half-brother to French 2002 2-y-o 7.5f winner Westmount (by Wolfhound): dam, French maiden, half-sister to very smart Hong Kong performer up to 1½m Precision: smart performer: won twice in 2006, notably Prix Gontaut-Biron at Deauville: trained by E. Charpy in UAE first 2 starts on return, then returned to former trainer: won Grand Prix de Vichy in July by ½ length from dead-heaters Balius and Kentucky Dynamite: giving winner 6 lb when excellent short-head second to Echo of Light in Prix Gontaut-Biron at Deauville next time: sold from Y. de Nicolay €140,000 before last 2 starts: stays 1¼m: acts on soft going: has been tongue tied: held up. *A. de Mieulle, Qatar*

ATLANTIC CITY 6 ch.g. First Trump 118 – Pleasuring 68 (Good Times (ITY)) [2007 **–** –: p12g Jan 10] quite good-topped, attractive gelding: fair performer in 2005: lightly raced and below form since: has worn cheekpieces. *Mrs L. Richards*

ATLANTIC COAST (IRE) 3 b.g. In The Wings 128 – Reasonably Devout (CAN) **87 §** (St Jovite (USA) 135) [2007 –: p12g 13d* 12v³ 16.1m² 16m* 15.8g* 16.4m⁵ 16g* 16.2g³ 18d⁴ Oct 13] good-topped gelding: fairly useful handicapper: much improved in 2007, winning at Hamilton in July, Newbury and Catterick in August and Yarmouth in September: stays 2m (seemed stretched by 2¼m final start): acts on good to firm and good to soft ground: usually blinkered/visored (not final outing): wayward. *M. Johnston*

ATLANTIC DAME (USA) 3 ch.f. Lemon Drop Kid (USA) 131 – While Rome Burns **–** (USA) (Overskate (CAN)) [2007 –: 9.9d 12.1s Jun 21] little form: sold 32,000 gns, sent to USA. *Mrs A. J. Perrett*

ATLANTIC GAMBLE (IRE) 7 b.g. Darnay 117 – Full Traceability (IRE) 53 (Ron's **71** Victory (USA) 129) [2007 55: p12.2g* p12.2g* p12.2g* p12.2g* p12.2g⁴ p12g⁶ 12s⁴ p12.2g⁵ 11.8d* 13m⁵ 12m p11g* p11g⁵ p12g p12.2g Dec 22] lengthy gelding: fair performer: won 2 handicaps in January and February, all at Wolverhampton, and claimers at Leicester in July and Kempton in September: stays 1¾m: acts on all-weather and good to soft ground: in cheekpieces nowadays: reportedly bled final start at 6 yrs. *K. R. Burke*

ATLANTIC LIGHT 3 gr.f. Linamix (FR) 127 – Atlantic Destiny (IRE) 99 (Royal **79** Academy (USA) 130) [2007 95: 6g 8.2g 8m⁴ 9.2d⁵ Aug 15] leggy, close-coupled filly: fairly useful performer at 2 yrs: below best in handicaps in 2007: should stay 1m+: acts on heavy going. *M. Johnston*

ATLANTIC QUEST (USA) 8 b. or br.g. Woodman (USA) 126 – Pleasant Pat (USA) **–** (Pleasant Colony (USA)) [2007 90: p10g³ p8.6g³ p8.6g⁴ p10g⁵ p12g⁵ p12.2g p10g p8.6g **a90** 12m Jul 19] rather leggy, close-coupled gelding: fairly useful handicapper on all-weather, fair on turf: effective at 1m to easy 1½m: acts on polytrack, firm and good to soft going:

86

has been visored/in cheekpieces: tends to wander/carry head high: effective held up or racing prominently. *Miss Venetia Williams*

ATLANTIC RHAPSODY (FR) 10 b.g. Machiavellian (USA) 123 – First Waltz (FR) 117 (Green Dancer (USA) 132) [2007 81: 14.1d Jul 12] tall gelding: one-time useful performer: left T. Walsh in Ireland 6,200 gns, well below form only Flat start in 2007: stays 1½m: acts on fibresand and any turf going: has worn blinkers/cheekpieces: has looked difficult ride. *B. J. Llewellyn* — **–**

ATLANTIC SPORT (USA) 2 b.c. (Feb 12) Machiavellian (USA) 123 – Shy Lady (FR) 91 (Kaldoun (FR) 122) [2007 6d* 7m⁶ Sep 15] $500,000Y: tall, well-made colt: fifth foal: closely related to useful 2001 2-y-o 6f/7f (Prix du Calvados) winner Ya Hajar (by Lycius) and half-brother to very smart 6f (at 2 yrs)/1m (St James's Palace Stakes) winner Zafeen (by Zafonic): dam German 2-y-o 5f/6f (listed) winner: useful form: impressive debut to win newcomers event at Ascot (beat Skadrak by short head) in July, showing his inexperience and not all out: 5/2, below expectations in Champagne Stakes at Doncaster (sixth of 10 to McCartney) 2 months later: will stay 1m: should still make a smart 3-y-o. *M. R. Channon* — **98 p**

ATLANTIC STORY (USA) 5 b. or br.g. Stormy Atlantic (USA) – Story Book Girl (USA) (Siberian Express (USA) 125) [2007 81+: p8.6g* p8g* 8m⁶ p8g p8g⁴ p8g* p8g* p8g* Dec 29] angular, good-topped gelding: has a short, quick action: useful handicapper: won at Wolverhampton in January, Kempton in February, and Lingfield, Kempton and Lingfield again (beat Orchard Supreme by ¾ length, idling) in December: stays 8.6f: acts on all-weather, firm and good to soft going: blinkered last 2 starts: usually tongue tied: has worn crossed noseband: has carried head high: strong traveller. *M. W. Easterby* — **101 +**

ATLANTIC VIKING (IRE) 12 b.g. Danehill (USA) 126 – Hi Bettina 96 (Henbit (USA) 130) [2007 71, a58: p7.1g⁶ Jan 15] well-made gelding: fair handicapper in 2006: below form sole outing at 12 yrs: best at 5f/easy 6f: acts on sand, polytrack, firm and soft going: often wears headgear: sometimes wanders: none too consistent. *P. D. Evans* — **–**

ATRAAS (IRE) 3 b.g. King's Best (USA) 132 – Sundus (USA) 80 (Sadler's Wells (USA) 132) [2007 83: 8.1g* 8m p8g Oct 17] leggy gelding: won maiden at Chepstow (hung badly right before jinking that way close home) in May: reportedly had breathing problem when tailed off in handicaps after: likely to stay 1¼m. *M. P. Tregoning* — **78**

ATTACCA 6 b.g. Piccolo 121 – Jubilee Place (IRE) 76 (Prince Sabo 123) [2007 63: p7.1g³ 7.1m⁶ p7.1g⁵ 7.1m f7g⁵ 5.9g 7.1g³ 8.1d 7.1g* 7.1v p7.1g² 7g 8m⁶ 7.1m³ p7.1g 7.1d³ 7.1m 7.1g p7g Oct 29] tall, quite good-topped gelding: modest handicapper: won at Musselburgh in July: stays easy 1m: acts on polytrack and any turf going: tried in headgear: none too consistent. *J. R. Weymes* — **62**

AT THE MONEY 4 b.g. Robellino (USA) 127 – Coh Sho No 59 (Old Vic 136) [2007 77: 18g⁵ May 17] close-coupled gelding: fair handicapper: stays 2¼m: acts on fibresand, heavy and good to firm going. *J. M. P. Eustace* — **77**

ATTICUS TROPHIES (IRE) 4 b.g. Mujadil (USA) 119 – Nezool Almatar (IRE) (Last Tycoon 131) [2007 64: p10g p8g p6g p6g p8g p12g p12g 11.6m 10.2d 11s⁶ 10m Jul 11] sturdy gelding: poor maiden: stays 1¼m: acts on polytrack, best turf efforts on good going: usually wears headgear: tried towards rear. *Ms J. S. Doyle* — **47**

ATTILA'S PEINTRE 3 b.g. Peintre Celebre (USA) 137 – Atabaa (FR) (Anabaa (USA) 130) [2007 –: 10g⁶ 11.1g² 16.2s 15.8m⁴ Aug 7] big, useful-looking gelding: modest maiden: probably stays 2m: blinkered final outing. *P. C. Haslam* — **64**

ATTRIBUTION 2 b.c. (Mar 29) Royal Applause 124 – Thrilling Day 112 (Groom Dancer (USA) 128) [2007 5d 5.1g* 5.3f⁵ p5g² 5.5m⁴ 5m p6g³ p5g Oct 15] neat colt: fair performer: won seller at Bath (left K. R. Burke 10,000 gns) in July: in frame 3 times in nurseries: should prove best kept to 5f/6f: acts on polytrack and firm going. *A. B. Haynes* — **65**

AUBURNDALE 5 b.g. Mind Games 121 – Primitive Gift 38 (Primitive Rising (USA) 113) [2007 –: 7.9m Jun 4] no form. *A. Crook* — **–**

AUCTION OASIS 3 b.f. Auction House (USA) 120 – Shining Oasis (IRE) 73 (Mujtahid (USA) 118) [2007 68: 6g 6.1m 5.7d 5.1s 5.7m p6g Dec 12] modest performer: no form after reappearance: best at 5f/6f: acts on good to firm ground: once withdrawn (unruly stall). *B. Palling* — **50 d**

AUDIENCE 7 b.g. Zilzal (USA) 137 – Only Yours 113 (Aragon 118) [2007 98: 8s⁶ 8m 8g⁸ 8m² Jun 9] big, good-topped gelding: useful handicapper: best effort in 2007 when short-head second to King of Argos at Goodwood final start: probably stays 9f: acts on — **101**

firm and soft going: tried blinkered, effective with/without cheekpieces: has sweated: usually held up. *J. Akehurst*

AUDIT (IRE) 3 b.g. Fusaichi Pegasus (USA) 130 – Amethyst (IRE) 111 (Sadler's Wells (USA) 132) [2007 75§: 11.8g⁶ f8g² f11g* p12g* p12g Dec 5] big, rangy gelding: has a quick action: fairly useful performer: won maiden at Southwell in May and handicap at Kempton in June: left Sir Michael Stoute 65,000 gns and off 6 months before final outing: stays 1½m: acts on all-weather and good to soft going: often visored/blinkered, latter for both wins: carries head high. *Seamus Lynch, Ireland* **86**

AUDLEY 3 b.f. Averti (IRE) 117 – Midnight Break 78 (Night Shift (USA)) [2007 8.3d 7.1m⁴ Aug 27] strong, rangy filly: half-sister to several winners, including useful 13.3f winner Mac (by Fleetwood): dam 5f/6f winner: green, 3¼ lengths fourth to Musaalem at Warwick on completed start in maidens: tongue tied, refused to race on debut: one to treat with caution. *M. P. Tregoning* **43 §**

AUENTRAUM (GER) 7 br.g. Big Shuffle (USA) 122 – Auenglocke (GER) (Surumu (GER)) [2007 66: p5g p7.1g p6g p6g p6g p6g p5g⁵ p6g⁶ 7g Jun 12] modest performer: best short of 1m: acts on all-weather and good to soft going: often wears headgear: has found little. *Ms J. S. Doyle* **54 §**

AUGMENTATION 2 br.c. (Mar 13) Dansili 127 – Moulin Rouge 77 (Shareef Dancer (USA) 135) [2007 8m 8.2d Oct 18] 31,000Y: big, heavy-topped colt: third foal: brother to 1m winner Parisette: dam raced 4 times at 1¼m: not fully wound up in maidens, showing ability at Nottingham second start: capable of better still. *P. W. D'Arcy* **52 p**

AUGUSTINE 6 b.g. Machiavellian (USA) 123 – Crown of Light 112 (Mtoto 134) [2007 86: p9.5g p12.2g² p12g⁶ p12.2g⁶ p10g f12g⁴ p12g⁴ p10g³ 12g⁴ 9.9m⁵ 10m³ 9.9m² 10s² 10.2s² 11s³ 9.9v⁴ 10d⁴ 12.1g³ Jul 31] close-coupled gelding: fair handicapper: in frame 13 times in 2007: stays 1½m: acts on all-weather and any turf going: tried blinkered: races prominently: tough and consistent: sold 30,000 gns and joined Lucinda Russell, won over hurdles in November/December. *P. W. Hiatt* **81**

AUGUSTUS CAESER (IRE) 3 b.g. Beckett (IRE) 116 – Miss Sabre (Sabrehill (USA) 120) [2007 p10g p12g 10.9s⁶ Jul 6] little form in maiden/sellers. *E. J. Creighton* –

AUGUSTUS JOHN (IRE) 4 gr.g. Danehill (USA) 126 – Rizerie (FR) 98 (Highest Honor (FR) 124) [2007 –: p10g² p9.5g² p10g² 12.3g² May 11] strong, useful-looking gelding: fairly useful maiden, lightly raced: runner-up all starts in 2007: stays 1½m: raced only on polytrack and good/good to firm ground: tried visored: gelded after final start. *T. J. Pitt* **83**

AUGUSTUS LIVIUS (IRE) 4 b.g. Titus Livius (FR) 115 – Regal Fanfare (IRE) 94 (Taufan (USA) 119) [2007 48, a35: f8g⁴ f12g Jan 30] workmanlike gelding: poor maiden: barely stays 9.8f: acts on fibresand, good to firm and good to soft going: tried in cheekpieces: blinkered both outings in 2007. *W. Storey* –

AUNTIE MAME 3 b.f. Diktat 126 – Mother Molly (USA) 78 (Irish River (FR) 131) [2007 51: 8.3g⁶ 7g⁴ p9.5g² p9.5g⁵ p11g² p11g* Dec 19] modest performer: won maiden at Kempton in December: stays 11f: raced only on polytrack and good going. *D. J. Coakley* **62**

AU PAIR (IRE) 2 ch.f. (Feb 23) Domedriver (IRE) 128 – Noble Dane (IRE) 79 (Danehill (USA) 126) [2007 6d⁵ 6d 5.1g Oct 24] €65,000Y, 19,000 2-y-o: leggy, quite attractive filly: fifth foal: half-sister to 6-y-o Let It Be: dam, 2-y-o 1m winner (stayed 1½m), sister to smart but ungenuine performer up to 1¼m Amrak Ajeeb: fair maiden: failed to progress from debut (fifth at Newbury), hinting at temperament: should stay 1m: tail flasher: sold 5,500 gns. *P. W. Chapple-Hyam* **75**

AURA 2 b.f. (Apr 20) Barathea (IRE) 127 – Finger of Light 89 (Green Desert (USA) 127) [2007 7g Nov 3] 115,000Y: leggy filly: eighth foal: sister to 2 winners abroad, including fairly useful Italian 5f (at 2 yrs) to 7f winner Far Hope, and half-sister to 2002 2-y-o 7f winner The Local (by Selkirk) and 3-y-o Lawyers Choice: dam 2-y-o 6f winner out of Lowther winner Circus Ring: 5/1 favourite, faded to finish eighteenth of 20 in maiden at Newmarket: bound to improve. *Sir Michael Stoute* **53 p**

AUREATE 3 ch.g. Jade Robbery (USA) 121 – Anne d'Autriche (IRE) 75 (Rainbow Quest (USA) 134) [2007 81p: 12m³ 9.9m⁶ 12.3d* 14d⁵ 12g Aug 1] big, rangy gelding: fairly useful handicapper: won 4-runner event at Chester (by 19 lengths) in June: left M. Johnston 75,000 gns, always behind final outing: gelded after: stays 1¾m: acts on polytrack, soft and good to firm going: usually races up with pace. *B. Ellison* **94**

AUSONE 5 b.m. Singspiel (IRE) 133 – Aristocratique 71 (Cadeaux Genereux 131) [2007 63: p12g² f16s p16.5g Mar 14] tall, good-topped mare: modest maiden on Flat: stays 1½m: acts on polytrack: sold 15,500 gns in May. *Miss J. R. Gibney* **62**

AUSSIE BATTLER (IRE) 2 b.c. (May 1) Noverre (USA) 125 – Dancerette (Groom **64** Dancer (USA) 128) [2007 7m⁵ 8d Sep 29] compact colt: modest form: fifth to Fifteen Love in maiden at Newmarket: out of depth in Royal Lodge Stakes at Ascot (tongue tied, reported breathing problem): should stay 1m/1¼m. *B. W. Duke*

AUSSIE BLUE (IRE) 3 b.g. Bahamian Bounty 116 – Luanshya 78 (First Trump 118) **71** [2007 –: 6m⁶ 7g⁶ 6d² 6d⁶ 7m³ 8.1m⁵ 7m 7m³ 7g³ 8g² Nov 2] strong gelding: good mover: fair maiden handicapper: stays 1m: acts on firm and good to soft ground: tried blinkered/visored: has looked wayward. *R. M. Whitaker*

AUSSIE CRICKET (FR) 3 gr.f. Verglas (IRE) 118 – Coup de Colere (FR) (Pistolet **69** Bleu (IRE) 133) [2007 71: p11g³ p8.6g³ 8g³ 10s 8m Jul 14] fair maiden: free-going sort, but stays 9.5f: acts on polytrack and firm going: not straightforward. *D. J. Coakley*

AUSTINTATIOUS (USA) 2 ch.c. (Apr 30) Distorted Humor (USA) 117 – Fancy **96** Ruler (USA) (Half A Year (USA) 130) [2007 6d⁴ 8m² Oct 4] $140,000Y, $150,000 2-y-o: strong, useful-looking colt: sixth foal: brother to 5-y-o Shrine Mountain, and half-brother to 3 winners, including smart 7f (at 2 yrs) to miler Sohaib (by Kingmambo) and 3-y-o Faithful Ruler: dam, ran twice in US, out of half-sister to Breeders' Cup Juvenile winner Success Express: in frame in maidens at Lingfield and Newmarket, useful form (despite pulling hard to post) when 2 lengths second of 17 to Twice Over in latter: not sure to stay much beyond 1m. *B. J. Meehan*

AUTHORIZED (IRE) 3 b.c. Montjeu (IRE) 137 – Funsie (FR) (Saumarez 132) **133** [2007 118p: 10.4g* 12g* 10g² 10.4d* 12g Oct 7]

The Derby may not be so significant as it once was, given racing's broader global horizons, but it continues to provide publicity for British racing on a scale unsurpassed by the coverage for any other race apart from the Grand National. Like the National, the Derby comes in for criticism in some quarters from time to time, but the fact that it provides entertainment on a scale approached by no other event on the Flat far outweighs any other considerations. The latest Derby provided racing with the right type of headlines, a welcome antidote to the clouds of suspicion hanging over the sport because of a series of betting and so-called race-fixing cases which received wide coverage. The victory of the charismatic Frankie Dettori on the short-priced favourite Authorized showed racing in a good light on the front pages and at the top of the television news bulletins.

Dettori has transcended his sport in a way few other jockeys have managed and Authorized provided him with his first win in the Derby after fourteen losing rides in the race, a saga that was becoming part of the annual Derby ritual. Dettori's seven wins on the Queen Elizabeth II Stakes card at Ascot in September 1996 were a once-in-a-lifetime occurrence and made headlines around the world, ensuring that the Dettori name would enter racing folklore. Frequent TV appearances over the years have also helped Dettori to become instantly recognisable to a much wider audience. So much so, that straight after his Derby win his odds for the BBC Sports Personality of the Year award were cut to 5/1. Dettori finished third in the year of his 'Magnificent Seven', a notable achievement for a racing personality. Lester Piggott, whose long and distinguished career included a record nine Derby victories, never managed higher than fourth, though he was given a special trophy by the programme in 1995. The peerless Tony McCoy's achievements over jumps —which include surpassing Flat champion Sir Gordon Richards' enduring British record of 269 winners in a season (McCoy set the new mark of 289 in 2001/2)— earned him third in 2003, and Bob Champion and Aldaniti received the team award after the 1981 Grand National.

Racing is a minority sport, however, and the fame of even its top names has its boundaries. By December, Dettori didn't even figure on the final short-list of ten drawn up by a panel of newspaper and magazine sports editors for the BBC's annual award. The worthy winner was the undefeated super-middleweight boxer Joe Calzaghe who made a twenty-first successful defence of his WBO title in 2007. The short-list contained a number of contenders who had narrowly missed out on their sport's major titles (including rugby players Jonny Wilkinson and Jason Robinson and racing driver Lewis Hamilton), but it also included the tennis player Andy Murray in a year when he missed Wimbledon and failed to reach a Grand Slam quarter-final. The top ten also included 400 metres world champion Christine Ohuruogu, who had served a ban for a drugs offence (she received less than one per cent of the popular vote), though at least there was no place for footballers in a year when England were knocked out in the qualifying stages for Euro 2008.

Calzaghe's triumph in the BBC Sports Personality award was achieved despite most of his fights over the years being shown on satellite channels or pay-per-view programmes. Exposure on the terrestrial TV channels, with their swathe of casual viewers, is usually essential in building up the celebrity status often needed to carry off an award for which achievement alone is seldom the deciding factor. The absence of Dettori from the short-list was not the only indicator of what, it must be hoped, is a temporary decline in racing's public appeal. Until long-running sponsor Vodafone agreed an extension for 2008, the Derby itself looked likely to be run without a sponsor as Epsom failed to secure a suitable blue-chip backer to replace Vodafone, which had announced an end to its relationship with the race after thirteen years.

The latest Derby had all the ingredients to be a TV spectacular—Dettori even helped by calling his own press conference a week before the race—but the viewing figures were still arguably disappointing. The 2006 Derby viewing peaked at 4.1m at the time of the race (an audience share of 43%) but the corresponding figure for the latest edition was 3m (34% share), despite the added interest. It was the first drop after a steady growth (2.7m in 2002, 3m in 2003, 3.1m in 2004, 3.2m in 2005), though the latest viewing figure was still comfortably ahead of the 2.4m in 2000, the last Derby before the race was transferred from Channel 4 to the BBC. As with the 2007 Grand National (7.6m, audience share 66.5%), the fall in the Derby viewing figures could partly be attributed to the fine, warm weather on the day while, with the Derby, there was also the fact that in 2006 the race followed hot on the heels of an England football match shown live on *Grandstand* and achieved a 43% audience share, its highest since 1994. Like the Grand National, the Derby would attract an even bigger audience if its starting time was changed to 5.00—'a time that has become a key slot for live TV sport on a Saturday,' according to the BBC. A tea-time Derby was suggested in *Racehorses of 2003* and dismissed.

The racing landscape has altered dramatically since the days when the Derby was in its prime and its status as 'the greatest race in the world' could be justified. The growing internationalisation of racing has gradually eroded its importance. The significance of all-aged championship races such as the Prix de l'Arc de Triomphe (dating from 1949 when it had its prize money raised substantially) and the King George VI and Queen Elizabeth Stakes (founded in 1951) and the elevation in 1962 of the Irish Derby to a race of international importance—and a rival to the Derby—were among the first critical developments. The Derby still clung for a time to its reputation as the world's premier Flat race but its prestige—and the prestige of its winners—has been further eroded by the growth in the number of high-value international races, starting with the inauguration of the Japan Cup and the Breeders' Cup in the 'eighties, those occasions joined since by others, notably the World Cup meeting in Dubai and the richly-endowed international meeting each December in Hong Kong. The Prix de l'Arc and the Derby were the two most valuable races in Europe in 2007, in eleventh and thirteenth place respectively on the world list (though the Arc's prize money is set to double

totesport.com Dante Stakes, York—Authorized strengthens his position at the head of the Derby betting; Raincoat finishes second ahead of Al Shemali (right) and Adagio

Vodafone Derby Stakes, Epsom—
Kid Mambo leads Anton Chekhov and Acapulco (rail) round Tattenham Corner;
Authorized (stars on sleeve) sits in ninth while Eagle Mountain (striped sleeves) has only two behind him

in 2008 to make it the world's richest race on turf). The world's most valuable races in 2007 were headed by the Dubai World Cup, the Dubai Duty Free and the Dubai Sheema Classic, with the Breeders' Cup Classic and the Japan Cup in fourth and fifth (the Breeders' Cup Turf and the Hong Kong Cup were among the other races more valuable than the Derby).

The prospect of a longer season at three, given the lucrative international targets which are mostly concentrated in the autumn, has led to a change in approach by some trainers to the domestic classics. Lighter two-year-old campaigns, reflecting a more patient policy, are more commonplace for horses with pretensions to becoming top three-year-olds, making it harder sometimes to spot modern-day Derby winners as juveniles. Of the dozen Derby winners immediately preceding Authorized, only five had run in a pattern race at two and, of those five, only Dewhurst winner Sir Percy had won in pattern company over a distance shorter than a mile. Like the 2002 Derby winner High Chaparral and 2005 winner Motivator, Authorized won the Racing Post Trophy at two. While High Chaparral won the Racing Post Trophy on his third start, Authorized emulated Motivator by winning it on only his second, though, unlike Motivator, Authorized was successful as a maiden, the first to achieve the feat in the now-lengthy history of a race founded in 1961 as the Timeform Gold Cup. As with Motivator, there was talk of Authorized being trained for the Two Thousand Guineas before a tilt at the Derby (like High Chaparral and Motivator, he was bred to stay a mile and a half as a three-year-old). However, Authorized bypassed Newmarket and went on to follow in the footsteps of Motivator by taking in the most important of the spring trials for the Derby staged over middle distances, the totesport.com Dante at York in May. Taking the dozen Derby winners before Authorized as a sample again, two of them, Lammtarra and Shaamit, were successful at Epsom without a preparatory run as a three-year-old. Sir Percy contested the Derby after finishing second in the Two Thousand Guineas but the nine others all won one of the major spring trials, Benny The Dip, North Light and Motivator successful in the Dante, Oath and Kris Kin in the Dee Stakes at Chester, High-Rise in the Lingfield Derby Trial and Sinndar, Galileo and High Chaparral in the Derrinstown Stud Derby Trial at Leopardstown.

Dettori rode Authorized in the Racing Post Trophy, staged at Newbury because of redevelopment at its traditional home at Doncaster, but it was announced at first that Jimmy Fortune would partner Authorized during his three-year-old career. Godolphin retain Dettori but they had no runner in the Dante and were looking increasingly unlikely to have a leading Derby contender. Authorized's owners replaced Fortune with Dettori for the Dante and the partnership landed the odds in emphatic style, Authorized taking control soon after moving smoothly into contention two furlongs out and going clear to beat Raincoat by four lengths. The performance cemented Authorized's position in the Derby ante-post market—he had been among the favourites ever since winning the Racing Post Trophy—and he stood out on form among those who had contested the spring trials. Regime (Sandown Classic Trial), Salford Mill (Newmarket Stakes), Anton Chekhov (Prix Hocquart), Soldier of Fortune (Chester Vase), Admiralofthefleet (Dee Stakes), Aqaleem (Lingfield Derby Trial) and Archipenko (Derrinstown Stud Derby Trial) all lined up against Authorized at Epsom. Anton Chekhov, Soldier of Fortune, Admiralofthefleet and Archipenko were among eight saddled by Aidan O'Brien, the others being Two Thousand Guineas fifth Eagle Mountain—the highest-placed runner in that race to go on to the Derby—the Derrinstown runner-up Yellowstone, Newmarket Stakes runner-up Acapulco and Mahler, odds-on winner of an uncompetitive affair staged under the banner of the Gowran Classic Trial. There was a deal of confusion about the pecking order among the 'Ballydoyle eight' (the stable had run four in the race in each of the two previous years and also saddled four in 2003), though Michael Kinane, who had won the trials on Soldier of Fortune, Admiralofthefleet and Archipenko and had ridden Eagle Mountain when he was beaten at odds on in the Racing Post Trophy, was on board Archipenko. The most significant absentee from the Derby field was the previous year's leading two-year-old, Irish-trained Teofilo, who had yet to reappear because of injury (he was eventually retired without racing at three). Godolphin's only declared runner, outsider Eastern Anthem, was one of two defectors after the final declaration stage, leaving a field of seventeen. Dettori had been released by Godolphin to ride Authorized at Epsom soon after his victory in the Dante, his owners taking out a full page advertisement in the *Racing Post* to thank 'a true sportsman' Sheikh Mohammed 'for giving us the opportunity to dream'. Dettori injured a knee when unseated at Goodwood eight days before the Derby and, although winning on his next ride, he missed four days racing in the run-up to the two-day Epsom meeting. His six rides at Epsom before Authorized included last of seven on the Coronation Cup favourite Sixties Icon and thirteenth of fourteen on Godolphin's Oaks runner Measured Tempo.

There was some speculation that Dettori might face a tactical headache on Authorized, particularly being faced by an octet of Ballydoyle runners (there had been allegations of 'team tactics' when Dettori's mount Librettist suffered interference from a Ballydoyle runner in the previous year's Queen Elizabeth II Stakes), but, in the event, his Derby ride couldn't have been more straightforward. Dettori described it as being 'smooth like an oil painting'. 'This is the first year I haven't been knocked over in the race—it maybe helps being on the best horse,' he added after bringing home 5/4 favourite Authorized a five-length winner. In an almost trouble-free Derby, run at a good gallop, Dettori settled Authorized off the pace after a sluggish start and, after rounding Tattenham Corner in ninth, quickly improved his position before setting his mount alight inside the two-furlong marker. Authorized was soon in front and kept on strongly—Dettori administering a couple of unnecessary cracks of the whip in the closing stages—with none of his rivals able to live with him. Eagle Mountain, backed from 9/1 to 6/1 second favourite, half a point shorter than Archipenko, came out of the pack, after being in the last pair for a long way, to chase home Authorized, with 9/1-shot Aqaleem two and a half lengths away third, a head in front of the relatively inexperienced Lucarno, who justified his connections' late decision to run after winning a listed event at Newmarket in good style the previous Saturday. Soldier of Fortune and Salford Mill came fifth and sixth, ahead of the front-running Kid Mambo, who was not reeled in until inside the last two furlongs. The big disappointment of the race was Archipenko who was held up and never looked likely to take a hand, trailing home last. But all eyes afterwards were on the ecstatic Dettori, who broke with tradition and took Authorized past the photographers for a victory parade in front of the stands, turning back only after going halfway to the furlong marker. The trademark flying dismount was executed in the winner's circle as Authorized and Dettori received a tumultuous reception.

Vodafone Derby Stakes, Epsom—Authorized has made ground smoothly and is beginning to draw clear

Not since Gordon Richards ended his so-called Derby 'hoodoo' on Pinza back in 1953 had there been a Derby which, in the public mind, was so much about the winning jockey. Richards was champion twenty-six times and eventually retired with a then-world record 4,870 winners, but he didn't land the Derby until his twenty-eighth attempt (shortly after being knighted). Leicester's final Flat meeting at the end of October staged the Sir Gordon Richards Stakes to commemorate the sixtieth anniversary of the day when Richards broke his own record, that had stood since 1933, of 259 winners in a season (he ended 1947 with 269). The self-effacing Richards was greeted with scenes of tremendous enthusiasm when he won the final race that day at Leicester to pass the record, but his attempts to slip away unnoticed by climbing through a window in the weighing room were foiled when he was spotted as he neared his car! He reportedly signed over a hundred race cards before driving away. Neither his wife nor any of his family saw him ride that day but he told the crowd 'I know they will all be listening to the six o'clock news to hear how I got on.' Richards excelled on all types of horses and was a jockey of unimpeachable integrity whose knighthood in 1953 was universally popular, as was his Derby win on Pinza. His overall Derby record has been used by some, however, to cast doubt on his big-race temperament, a harsh judgement on the greatest jockey of his time, with whom only Fred Archer and Lester Piggott are worthy of comparison among British jockeys on the Flat. Another fine champion, Scobie Breasley, had to wait a long time to win the Derby, which he did at the thirteenth time of asking, while Lester Piggott didn't win the Prix de l'Arc de Triomphe until his seventeenth attempt. Two of the greatest owner-breeders of the first half of the twentieth century, Lord Derby and Lord Rosebery, also had a long wait for a Derby triumph. 'I've won all the other classics,' said Dettori, 'but this is the one I've always wanted. My dad [Gianfranco] was in tears after finishing fifth on the favourite Wollow in 1976, and my mum says it was the only time she ever saw him cry.'

With all the attention given to Frankie Dettori, it was easy to overlook the contribution of Authorized's trainer Peter Chapple-Hyam who has put his somewhat chequered career firmly back on course since returning to Britain in 2004 after an unsuccessful four-year stint in Hong Kong. Chapple-Hyam had won the Derby before, with Dr Devious in 1992, that success coming only a little over a

Vodafone Derby Stakes, Epsom—Authorized gives Frankie Dettori his first success in the Derby;
Eagle Mountain (striped sleeves) runs on strongly for second with Aqaleem (striped cap),
Lucarno (light colours), Soldier of Fortune (dark colours) and Salford Mill (hooped sleeves) next

year after taking out a licence (he won the Two Thousand Guineas at Newmarket and the Curragh in the same year with Rodrigo de Triano). Chapple-Hyam pointed out after Authorized's win that Dettori might have ridden Dr Devious in different circumstances, Chapple-Hyam about to sign him as stable jockey before Godolphin came along at the same time and snapped him up. Dettori has been champion three times but riding winners in the big races is what matters most to him now. His flow of big-race winners has been affected in recent seasons by the lull in Godolphin's fortunes, but he won the Prix du Jockey Club the day after the Derby on Lawman and the Prix de Diane on the Sheikh Mohammed-owned West Wind the following weekend, both for French stables. It was, however, rather puzzling to see him snub the latest Racing Post Trophy winner Ibn Khaldun to take rides for outside stables at the Breeders' Cup the same weekend. Ibn Khaldun's owners Godolphin reputedly pay Dettori the world's largest jockey's retainer but they had to recall their second string Kerrin McEvoy from Australia. After an emphatic victory at Doncaster, McEvoy will no doubt be delighted to take the mount on Ibn Khaldun in the Two Thousand Guineas should Dettori choose to look elsewhere. Dettori, by the way, missed an opportunity to ride the Sheikh Mohammed-owned Boscobel in the Irish Derby (keeping alive the dream of a Derby treble) after a slip-up resulted in his missing the deadline to defer a two-day suspension incurred for a whip ban at Sandown in mid-June (he would also have been able to ride West Wind in the Pretty Polly).

As part of the celebrations for its sixtieth year, Timeform published the ratings recorded in the Derby by all the winners since 1947. The best Derby-winning performances (different from the highest Annual ratings) were recorded by Shergar (140), Pinza, Grundy and Troy (all 137). Authorized ran to a rating of 132 in the Derby which put him joint-fifteenth on the extensive list, alongside the 2001 winner Galileo, among others. Authorized's timefigure in the Derby was 1.24 fast, equivalent to a timerating of 131, the fastest recorded in any race in Britain in 2007. It provided confirmation of the merit of his performance on Derby day, which, along with that of Galileo, was the finest seen in the race since Generous in 1991. The Derby form was upheld by results at Royal Ascot where Lucarno and eighth-placed Yellowstone were placed in the King Edward VII Stakes, Kid Mambo finished a close fourth in the Hampton Court Stakes and the Derby eleventh Mahler won the Queen's Vase. The 2005 Derby winner Motivator had been rated 134 for a time after the Derby but his Epsom form didn't look so good by the end of the season, by which time Motivator's rating had fallen to 131. Authorized emulated Motivator when winning the Derby by five lengths—only Shergar (ten lengths), Troy, Slip Anchor (both seven) and Arctic Prince and Relko (both six) won the race by further in the first sixty years of Timeform—but Authorized's followers must have been hoping that the parallels with Motivator's career would end with Epsom. Motivator had looked set for a fine summer after turning the Derby into a one-horse race, but he failed to win again, beaten in the Eclipse, the Irish Champion and the Arc, the best of him, in hindsight, seen on Derby Day.

Dettori's firm preference for Authorized's next race was reportedly the Irish Derby but the owners and the trainer stepping back to a mile and a quarter for the Coral-Eclipse at Sandown, partly to give Authorized a week longer to recover from his exertions at Epsom, though they were almost certainly also conscious of the modern perception that a Group 1 victory at a mile and a quarter has the potential to make a Derby winner a more valuable stallion property. The plan was that Authorized would revert to a mile and a half for the King George VI and Queen Elizabeth Stakes at Ascot, a logical step for the Derby winner which has stood the test of time. Thirteen Derby winners have gone on to success in the King George in the same season and only two of them—Pinza and Lammtarra—weren't seen out in between. Tulyar, Mill Reef and Nashwan won the Eclipse, while Nijinsky, Grundy, The Minstrel, Troy, Shergar, Generous and Galileo were all successful in the Irish Derby. The odd one out, Reference Point, landed the King George after being beaten in the Eclipse, a race in which no Derby winner has been successful since Nashwan in 1989, two years after Reference Point's defeat. Authorized followed in the footsteps of Erhaab, Benny The Dip and Motivator, the first two placed behind older horses and the last-named beaten by fellow three-year-old Oratorio who beat him again over the same trip in the Irish Champion. By coincidence, the last Derby winner successful after Epsom over a mile and a quarter as a three-year-old had been Dr Devious in the Irish Champion Stakes (a race won by High Chaparral as a four-year-old).

With Dettori able to postpone a hearing at Shaftesbury Avenue, after being referred for transgressing the whip guidelines on Ramonti in the Queen Anne, his so-far unbeaten partnership with Authorized remained intact for Sandown, which was one of the few remaining meetings that week not under threat from a sustained period of very wet weather. The going at Sandown was good but Authorized was beaten at 7/4-on, victory going to the five-year-old Notnowcato whose rider made an audacious switch to the stands' side shortly after turning for home. With the other runners remaining on the far side, Notnowcato continued on in splendid isolation and won by a length and a half, with Authorized holding off George Washington by a head for second. Notnowcato's jockey Ryan Moore, who walked the course beforehand, claimed that there was a firmer strip of ground on the stands' side in the straight, alongside the hedge that marks the outside of the course. In all probability, however, it wasn't so much where Notnowcato's jockey made his bid for victory that was decisive, but when he made it. The pacemaker provided for Authorized was rendered largely ineffective after being harried early on and then left marooned by two of George Washington's stable-companions. With the gallop in the main pack no stronger than fair, Notnowcato was the first to be sent up to join the pacemaker, his jockey making first run on Authorized and George Washington. Dettori was outmanoeuvred, seemingly keeping more of an eye on George Washington than Notnowcato and, as he himself put it afterwards, 'once he had pinched three lengths it was going to be very hard for us to make it up.' The Eclipse was a muddling race and Authorized didn't run anywhere near his Derby form (the close fourth Yellowstone had finished eleven lengths behind Authorized at Epsom). Despite his defeat, Authorized remained the 6/4 ante-post favourite for the King George VI and Queen Elizabeth Stakes, although Soldier of Fortune had improved out of all recognition when recording a nine-length success in the Irish Derby and had put Authorized's position as the season's top middle-distance three-year-old under threat. It was reportedly Authorized's owners who eventually made the surprising decision not to run him in the King George, their racing manager saying that 'after three hard races this season, the horse will benefit from a longer break with the Arc in mind.'

A rematch with Notnowcato came on Authorized's next appearance, in the Juddmonte International at York in August, a race Notnowcato had won the previous year. Notnowcato had not run since the Eclipse, and nor had Ballydoyle's presumed main challenger for the International, George Washington. George Washington was ruled out, however, and replaced by his stable-companion Dylan Thomas, the winner of the King George VI and Queen Elizabeth Stakes which failed to attract a single representative of the classic crop. In a vintage renewal of the International, Authorized reaffirmed his status as a top-class performer, narrowly bettering his excellent Derby form in beating Dylan Thomas and Notnowcato by a length and three lengths, with Ballydoyle's second string Duke of Marmalade, runner-up in the St James's Palace and in the frame in the Two Thousand Guineas at Newmarket and the Curragh, back in fourth in a field of seven. Authorized was the first Derby winner successful in the International since Troy and the first three-year-old to win since Giant's Causeway. Tactics played some part in Authorized's victory, Dettori holding in Dylan Thomas against the rail for a time in the home straight until sending Authorized ahead over a furlong out, the King George winner closing but never able to mount a serious challenge after his rider extricated him.

Authorized reversed the Eclipse form with Notnowcato, who was again sent ahead early in the straight, to the tune of five and a half lengths. Authorized's victory at York made him the first Derby winner since High Chaparral to win again after Epsom and he looked to hold strong claims in the Prix de l'Arc de Triomphe, even allowing for the fact that Dylan Thomas's Prince of Wales's Stakes conqueror Manduro and Soldier of Fortune were likely to be in the line-up. Manduro missed the Arc after suffering a career-ending injury in the Prix Foy (Soldier of Fortune won the Prix Niel on the same day) and Authorized started 11/8 favourite in a field of twelve at Longchamp. The Arc was run to suit Authorized—the Ballydoyle pacemakers ensured a strong gallop which favoured those held up—but Authorized was in trouble the moment Dettori called on him to improve. There was virtually no response and Authorized eventually beat only the two pacemakers, finishing around eleven lengths behind the winner Dylan Thomas (who had won the Irish Champion since his run in the International). Third-placed Sagara and fifth-placed Soldier of Fortune (a good way below his Irish Derby form) were among three three-year-olds who finished ahead of Authorized, the fifth Derby winner beaten in the Arc since Sinndar completed that particular double in 2000. Sinndar and 1995 Arc winner Lammtarra are, incidentally, the only Derby winners to remain unbeaten for the rest of their three-year-old career in the last twenty years or so. Both were kept at a mile and a half after Epsom. As for Authorized's lamentable performance in the Arc, no ready explanation came to light, although his trainer, who reported beforehand that Authorized was 'in great form and everything is spot-on', reflected afterwards that 'he has had a few hard races and maybe I had done too much with him.' For the record, Authorized had five races during the season, half as many as the year-older Dylan Thomas, who won the Arc on his eighth start of the season.

Juddmonte International Stakes, York—Authorized becomes the first Derby victor since 2002 to win again after Epsom; Dylan Thomas finishes second, ahead of Notnowcato (rail) and Duke of Marmalade

Authorized was acquired in June by Darley as a future stallion and was leased back to his former owners Saleh Al Homaizi and Imad Al Sagar to complete his racing career. Darley had not stood a Derby winner since Lammtarra, although a Darley stallion Mark of Esteem had sired the 2006 Derby winner Sir Percy. The record of Derby winners at stud has been nothing to write home about in recent times. If and when Galileo tops the list of leading sires in Britain—he finished third behind the now-deceased Danehill and Authorized's sire Montjeu in 2007 and second in the combined British and Irish table—he will be only the seventh Derby winner to do so in the now-extensive era covered by Timeform. For the record, the six so far are Hyperion, Never Say Die, Psidium, Mill Reef, Nijinsky and Nashwan. Mill Reef was champion sire twice and since the year of his first success—1978—twenty different sires have been champion in Britain. They include Kentucky Derby and Preakness winner Northern Dancer, Poule d'Essai des Poulains winner Blushing Groom, Prix du Jockey Club winner Caerleon, Two Thousand Guineas and Irish Derby winner El Gran Senor, Irish Two Thousand Guineas winner Sadler's Wells, triple crown winner Nijinsky (sire of Lammtarra), Two Thousand Guineas and Derby winner Nashwan and Prix du Jockey Club and Irish Derby winner Montjeu. None of the twelve others won a classic. Of course, classic winners are among the best horses to breed from, but only around one in ten new stallions makes the grade and the most successful ones are by no means predictable from their racing records, or, indeed, from their early years at stud. *A Century of Champions*, published to mark the millennium, nominated Sea-Bird as Horse of the Century, Secretariat as American Horse of the Century, Ribot as Italian Horse of the Century and Brigadier Gerard as British Horse of the Century. Of those paragons, only Ribot went on to be an outstanding success at stud.

In his racing days, the high-class Danehill was best as a sprinter and Judd-monte let him go at the end of his three-year-old campaign (sold to a partnership between Coolmore and Australian stud Arrowfield). Danehill took his time to rise up the pecking order at Coolmore and didn't become fully recognised as a major sire in Europe for several years. On the same theme, how many would have forecast that the Queen Anne winner Cape Cross (who was the longest-priced of Godol-phin's three runners in that race) would turn out to be clearly the best of the crop of stallions that stood their first season in 2000? The outstanding racehorse Daylami (Timeform 138) and the July Cup and Nunthorpe winner Stravinsky were the two with easily the best track records and both were retired at two and a half times the fee commanded by Cape Cross. Daylami's first crop included Irish Derby winner Grey Swallow but that success proved something of a flash in the pan and Daylami was sold to South Africa in 2006; Stravinsky departed at the same time to Japan and is now shuttled between there and Australasia. Cape Cross has become firmly established as a top-ten sire in Britain and Ireland. For the record, Docksider, Dr Fong, Fasliyev (Japan in 2008), Indian Rocket, Princely Heir, Second Empire (now in South Africa) and Silver Patriarch were others retired to stud at the same time as Cape Cross, Daylami and Stravinsky. None looks like making a lasting impression as a stallion. Darley boss Sheikh Mohammed has first-hand experience of the fact that ability on the racecourse doesn't necessarily translate to success at stud. Lammtarra (by Nijinsky out of an Oaks winner) had the pedigree as well as the racing record to do well as a sire and started his career at Dalham Hall at a fee of £30,000. He was sold after only one season to Japan where he did not live up to expectations and was repatriated in 2006 and is now retired at Dalham Hall. Sheikh Mohammed also acquired a half share in the outstanding two-year-old of 1991 Arazi. His career at stud, however, has taken him from Dalham Hall to Japan, Australia and Switzerland, a journey that tells its own story.

A stand-off between Darley and arch rivals Coolmore, whose stallions dominated the sires' tables again in 2007, led to a much publicised decision by the Maktoum family in 2005 not to purchase yearlings by, or send mares to, stallions under the Coolmore banner (the family had been reducing its Coolmore yearling purchases and sending fewer mares to Coolmore stallions in the years before 2005). Concentrating on their own sires has not proved conspicuously successful, however, so the Maktoums set off on an unprecedented spending spree on horses in training in the latest season. Though no prices were divulged for any of the deals (Authorized was rumoured to have cost £15m), Darley purchased the first two in the Kentucky Derby, Street Sense and Hard Spun, at around the same time as a deal was struck for Authorized, and then proceeded to add, among others, the leading older horse in Japan Admire Moon, the champion two-year-old of 2006 Teofilo, the world's top-ranked racehorse of 2007 Manduro, another top American three-year-old Any Given Saturday, the leading European two-year-old of 2007 New Approach, the Champion Stakes winner Literato, the four-time Group 1 winner Schiaparelli, the Dewhurst runner-up Fast Company, the Arc third Sagara and the very smart Asset, not to mention taking stakes in other top prospects and also some established stallions. Having set its stall out to collect the most attractive prospective stallions that money could buy, Darley spared no expense on new mares either, spending 15,825,000 guineas at the December Sales, close to a quarter of the aggregate spent on mares during the week. A story doing the rounds at the end of the year may well be apocryphal, but it illustrates the apparent determination of Darley to disprove the old adage that you can't cure a problem by throwing money at it. Darley is said to have asked its agent to enquire about an American two-year-old after it had won a prestigious late-season race. The agent asked the owners how much they wanted for the colt, the owners said they would prefer it if Darley made an offer. Pressed a few days later for a price, the owners sent a message asking for a staggering sixty million dollars (£30m)! The agent ignored the message but, in the meantime, Coolmore stepped in to buy the colt. On hearing this, Sheikh Mohammed is said to have enquired 'Why didn't we buy that colt?' When the agent replied that the owners had wanted sixty million, the Sheikh—so the story goes—fired back 'So, why didn't we buy it?' Think Big is Darley's current advertising slogan, but it will be five or six years before the success or otherwise of the latest purchasing strategy by racing's biggest spenders can properly be judged.

		Sadler's Wells	Northern Dancer
	Montjeu (IRE)	(b 1981)	Fairy Bridge
	(b 1996)	Floripedes	Top Ville
Authorized (IRE)		(b 1985)	Toute Cy
(b.c. 2004)		Saumarez	Rainbow Quest
	Funsie (FR)	(b or br 1987)	Fiesta Fun
	(b 1999)	Vallee Dansante	Lyphard
		(b 1981)	Green Valley

Authorized's sire Montjeu, who stands at Coolmore, has now sired two winners of the Derby from his first three crops, Motivator being from his first, as also were Irish Derby and Arc winner Hurricane Run and St Leger winner Scorpion, among others. Montjeu was a tip-top racehorse, winner of the Prix du Jockey Club, the Irish Derby and the Arc, and, as a four-year-old, one of the easiest winners of the King George (Hurricane Run also won a King George at four). But Montjeu, with his stamina-laden pedigree, wasn't everyone's idea of a top stallion prospect at first. He started out at a fee of IR 30,000 guineas, a fraction of that commanded by his admirable contemporary Giant's Causeway, for example. Coolmore's own support of Montjeu was nowhere near so strong as that given to Giant's Causeway but he has overcome the prejudice against staying types at stud in spectacular style and looks set to continue to be prominent in the sires' lists, provided he overcomes what Coolmore believes to be a temporary setback experienced in the 2007 breeding season caused by a back problem. According to the *Return of Mares*, Montjeu covered just a hundred mares (compared to 185 in 2005 and 139 in 2006).

Authorized is the first foal out of Funsie, who was unraced but comes from one of the Wertheimer families (the Wertheimer brothers sold her privately, out of training, and she is part-owned by jockey Michael Kinane, who rode Montjeu to several of his major victories). Authorized's grandam, the winning Lyphard mare Vallee Dansante, produced eight winners and three of her daughters have now produced pattern winners. The seven-furlong winner Krissante (who made 500,000 guineas in 2006 in foal to Montjeu) and the smart performer over middle distances Brooklyn's Dance produced the 2000 Grand Criterium winner Okawango and the 2004 Prix du Jockey Club runner-up Prospect Park respectively. Another daughter of Vallee Dansante, Quest of Fire, is grandam of the latest season's Grosser Preis von Baden winner Quijano. Quest of Fire, Krissante, Brooklyn's Dance and Okawango were all trained by Criquette Head, as was Vallee Dansante, who is a

Saleh Al Homeizi & Imad Al Sagar's "Authorized"

close relative of Green Dancer, successful in the Observer Gold Cup (a previous incarnation of the Racing Post Trophy) and the Poule d'Essai des Poulains and Prix Lupin when trained by Criquette's father Alec and ridden by her brother Freddie. Authorized's great grandam Green Valley was unraced but she too had a prolific career at stud, producing thirteen winners, her only runner not to win being Irish Valley who became the dam of champion two-year-old Alhaarth. An unraced daughter of Irish Valley, Dalayil, is the dam of Derby third Aqaleem, who was ante-post favourite for the St Leger before his campaign was interrupted by injury. Further back, Green Valley's dam Sly Pola won the Prix de l'Abbaye and was a half-sister to another speedy mare in Polamia, the dam of a champion French two-year-old in Grey Dawn, and also to the very smart sprinter Takawalk II. Authorized, the third successive Derby winner to go through the Tattersalls sale-ring, was bought on behalf of his Kuwaiti owners (who also enjoyed classic success in 2006 with Araafa) for 95,000 guineas as a foal. Authorized was sent up to the sales again as a yearling and was knocked down to his trainer for 400,000 guineas, which was evidently quite a way short of the reserve put on him. Funsie's second foal, a colt by Fasliyev, made 110,000 guineas as a yearling just before Authorized's Racing Post Trophy victory. Purchased by Authorized's trainer and now owned by Cheveley Park Stud, the Fasliyev colt Empowered has yet to race. Funsie also has a yearling full-brother to Authorized who did not come up at the latest round of yearling sales, having been sold privately. He will be trained by Aidan O'Brien. The strong, good-topped Authorized was a fluent mover and travelled strongly in his races. He was effective at around a mile and a quarter to a mile and a half and raced only on good going or softer. A fair proportion of Montjeu's offspring display touches of temperament but Authorized generally seemed a relaxed and tractable sort, though he became restless in the Eclipse preliminaries when he had two handlers. He starts his stallion career at Dalham Hall, Newmarket, at £25,000 with the October 1st special live foal concession. *P. W. Chapple-Hyam*

AUTOCUE 2 b.c. (Jan 16) Dansili 127 – Sing For Fame (USA) 90 (Quest For Fame 127) [2007 7m* 8d⁵ Oct 19] smallish, compact colt: second foal: half-brother to 3-y-o Secret Tune: dam, 9f winner (stayed 11.6f), out of half-sister to Prince of Wales's Stakes winner Two Timing: fairly useful form: won maiden at Newmarket (dead-heated with Menadha) in July: off 3 months, possibly didn't handle softer ground (never travelling) when only fifth to Kandahar Run in minor event there (Rowley Mile): will stay 1¼m/1½m: worth another chance to progress. *Sir Michael Stoute*   **90 p**

AUTOGRAPH HUNTER 3 b.g. Tobougg (IRE) 125 – Kalindi 102 (Efisio 120) [2007 80: p7g⁸* 8.2m 8m p7g p6g p7.1g³ p9.5g p12g⁵ p12g⁵ p12.2g⁵ Nov 24] good-bodied gelding: fairly useful performer: won handicap at Lingfield in April: well below form after, leaving M. Johnston 6,000 gns after fourth start: probably stays 1½m: acts on all-weather: tried blinkered: temperamental. *Peter Grayson*   **83 d**

AUTUMN BLADES (IRE) 2 ch.c. (Apr 25) Daggers Drawn (USA) 114 – September Tide (IRE) 58 (Thatching 131) [2007 p7g⁴ 7.1g⁴ p7m Nov 1] compact colt: eighth foal: half-brother to 4-y-o Gallery Girl: dam Irish sprint maiden: fair maiden: fourth at Kempton and Warwick: raced only at 7f, may prove best at 5f/6f. *J. W. Hills*   **72**

AUTUMN CHARM 2 ch.f. (Feb 22) Reel Buddy (USA) 118 – Eurolink Cafe (Grand Lodge (USA) 125) [2007 6d⁴ p7g⁵ p8m f7d* Dec 18] 5,500Y: fourth foal: half-sister to a winner in Greece by Averti: dam unraced out of half-sister to high-class 1¼m performer Fanmore and very smart miler Labeeb: modest form: won seller at Southwell in December (sold 4,100 gns after): stays 7f, should prove at least as effective at 1m+. *W. Jarvis*   **58**

AUTUMN STAR (IRE) 2 b.f. (Mar 15) Mujadil (USA) 119 – Second Omen (Rainbow Quest (USA) 134) [2007 5.1f Aug 24] €100,000Y: third foal: sister to 2005 2-y-o 5.5f to 7f winner Soothsay (later useful up to 9f in US): dam unraced: 14/1, ruined chance when swerving right at start in maiden at Bath. *M. R. Channon*   **–**

AUTUMN STORM 3 b.f. Auction House (USA) 120 – Cozette (IRE) 49 (Danehill Dancer (IRE) 117) [2007 58: 5m⁶ 5m Jun 9] modest performer at 2 yrs: well below form in 2007: tried blinkered. *R. Ingram*   **–**

AVA GEE 2 br.f. (Mar 2) Averti (IRE) 117 – Spring Sunrise 59 (Robellino (USA) 127) [2007 5.1m⁶ 5g 6m 5m 6s Oct 4] sturdy filly: sister to 2003 2-y-o 6f winner Averlline: dam 2-y-o 6f/7f winner: modest maiden on balance: raced only at 5f/6f. *B. De Haan*   **55**

AVANTI 11 gr.g. Reprimand 122 – Dolly Bevan 53 (Another Realm 118) [2007 52: p13.9g⁴ p12g⁴ p12g Feb 10] smallish, well-made gelding: modest performer: stays 7f: acts on polytrack and good to firm going: tried blinkered, often visored. *Dr J. R. J. Naylor*   **52**

AVA'S WORLD (IRE) 3 b.f. Desert Prince (IRE) 130 – Taibhseach (USA) 94 (Secreto (USA) 128) [2007 79: 6.9d p5.1g p5.1g p5.1g Dec 31] small filly: fair performer at 2 yrs: little impact in handicaps in 2007, leaving M. Johnston after reappearance: has looked difficult ride. *Peter Grayson*   **–**

AVENING 7 br.g. Averti (IRE) 117 – Dependable (Formidable (USA) 125) [2007 89: 5.2f 5d 5m 6d Sep 26] useful-looking gelding: fairly useful handicapper for J. Hammond in France at 6 yrs: regressive form in 2007: best at 5f/6f: acts on firm and soft going: usually blinkered/tongue tied (not final outing). *Eve Johnson Houghton*   **76 d**

AVENTURA (IRE) 7 b.g. Sri Pekan (USA) 117 – La Belle Katherine (USA) (Lyphard (USA) 132) [2007 61: p8.6g p7.1g p7.1g p8.6g Feb 23] sturdy, close-coupled gelding: modest performer: stayed 8.6f: acted on all-weather, good to firm and good to soft going: tried blinkered: raced prominently: dead. *S. R. Bowring*   **50**

AVEROO 2 br.g. (Feb 1) Averti (IRE) 117 – Roo 97 (Rudimentary (USA) 118) [2007 p8g p8g⁵ 8m 7g² Oct 20] 110,000Y: useful-looking gelding: third foal: half-brother to useful 5f (at 2 yrs) and 7f winner Roodeye (by Inchinor) and 3-y-o Roodolph: dam 2-y-o 5f/6f winner: fair form in maidens, improved when second at Catterick, again travelling strongly: will prove at least as effective at 6f as 7f: sold 30,000 gns. *E. A. L. Dunlop*   **78**

AVERTICUS 3 b.g. Averti (IRE) 117 – Santa Vida (USA) 64 (St Jovite (USA) 135) **83**
[2007 83: 6m⁶ p6g 6.1d³ 6m⁵ 7m 7m⁶ 7v Oct 9] leggy, quite attractive gelding: fairly
useful handicapper: stays 7f: acts on good to firm and good to soft going: tried in cheekpieces, blinkered last 2 starts: inconsistent: sold 7,500 gns. *B. W. Hills*

AVERTIS 2 b.c. (Feb 25) Averti (IRE) 117 – Double Stake (USA) (Kokand (USA)) **73**
[2007 p7m* Oct 3] fifth foal: dam US 6f to 9f minor stakes winner: 6/1, won maiden at
Kempton by a neck from Locum, weaving through: likely to stay 1m. *M. Botti*

AVERTI STAR 3 b.g. Averti (IRE) 117 – Zinzi (Song 132) [2007 49: 8m 7s 7s 12g **49**
Aug 29] leggy gelding: poor maiden: stays 1m. *Mrs A. Duffield*

AVERTITOP 2 b.c. (Apr 24) Averti (IRE) 117 – Lucayan Belle (Cadeaux Genereux **73**
131) [2007 5m⁶ 5m² 5.1f⁵ p5g⁴ 7m⁵ Jul 13] 25,000Y: close-coupled colt: first foal: dam
once-raced half-sister to smart sprinter Ringmoor Down: fair maiden: fifth in nursery at
Newmarket following first start (moved poorly to post): stays 7f: acts on good to firm going,
probably polytrack. *R. Hannon*

AVERTUOSO 3 b.g. Averti (IRE) 117 – First Musical 107 (First Trump 118) [2007 93: **91**
5f⁵ 5g³ 5m⁵ 5.6m 6g² 6m 5m 5g² p6g p5.1g Dec 8] big, strong gelding: type to carry **a89**
condition: fairly useful handicapper: in-and-out form in 2007, placed at York, Ripon
and Musselburgh: effective at 5f/6f: acts on firm and good to soft going: tried visored.
B. Smart

AVERY 3 gr.c. Averti (IRE) 117 – Bandanna 98 (Bandmaster (USA) 97) [2007 63: **48**
p5.1g⁶ p7g 7g⁵ 5.1f p7.1g Apr 21] maiden: just poor form in 2007: should prove best at
5f/6f: raced only on good ground or firmer on turf: tried blinkered. *R. J. Hodges*

AVIAN FLEW 2 b.f. (Mar 20) Averti (IRE) 117 – Ice Bird (Polar Falcon (USA) 126) **53 d**
[2007 5d⁵ 5s⁵ p6g 5g p6g Oct 2] 3,500Y: close-coupled filly: first foal: dam unraced
daughter of useful 2-y-o 5f winner Absaloute Service: showed a little ability first 2 starts.
J. A. Pickering

AVOCA DANCER (IRE) 4 ch.f. Compton Place 125 – Kashra (IRE) 95 (Dancing **58**
Dissident (USA) 119) [2007 82: 5.5d 5.7m 5m p5.1m p5.1g⁶ p5.1g Nov 9] sturdy, lengthy
filly: fairly useful maiden handicapper when trained by Edward Lynam in Ireland at
3 yrs: well below form in 2007: stays 7f: acts on good to firm ground (well held on ground
softer than good): tried in cheekpieces. *M. Wigham*

AVONCREEK 3 b.g. Tipsy Creek (USA) 115 – Avondale Girl (IRE) 73 (Case Law 113) **48**
[2007 53: p7.1g⁶ p6g 6.1g⁶ 5.9m 6.1v⁶ p6g⁶ 6m Aug 9] close-coupled, quite attractive
gelding: poor maiden: likely to prove best at 5f/6f: tried in cheekpieces. *B. P. J. Baugh*

AVONTUUR (FR) 5 ch.g. Kabool 119 – Ipoh (FR) (Funambule (USA) 118) [2007 8m⁴ **50**
6s 7.1s 6m⁶ p6g* p8.6g p6g Oct 8] lengthy gelding: modest performer: won minor event
at Wolverhampton in September: stays 1m: acts on polytrack, good to soft and good to
firm going: usually blinkered: often slowly away. *D. W. Chapman*

AVORIAZ (IRE) 4 gr.g. Desert Prince (IRE) 130 – Abbatiale (FR) 117 (Kaldoun (FR) **97 §**
122) [2007 88: 9.1g* 8.9s Jul 14] tall, close-coupled, good-topped gelding: useful handicapper, lightly raced: reluctant to post, won at Ayr (by 1¾ lengths from Shy Glance) in
June: refused to race in valuable maiden at York final outing: gelded after: stays 1¼m: acts
on good to firm going: one to treat with caution: sold 14,000 gns in October, sent to UAE.
R. A. Fahey

AVRIL VALLEY 2 b.f. (Mar 3) Averti (IRE) 117 – Shamrock Fair (IRE) 77 (Shavian **–**
125) [2007 7.1m p8g p8g p7g⁶ Nov 12] 2,500Y: fifth foal: half-sister to 7-y-o Fair Shake
and 4-y-o Fairdonna: dam 2-y-o 7f winner: of no account. *D. J. S. ffrench Davis*

AWAKEN 6 b.m. Zafonic (USA) 130 – Dawna 106 (Polish Precedent (USA) 131) [2007 **62**
65: 9.1g 12m⁴ 9m* 9.9m⁵ 10.1m⁵ Sep 10] modest performer: won claimer at Redcar in
August: stays 11f: acts on firm and good to soft going: held up: reportedly had breathing
problem final 5-y-o start. *Miss Tracy Waggott*

AWATUKI (IRE) 4 b.g. Distant Music (USA) 126 – Itkan (IRE) (Marju (IRE) 127) **91**
[2007 85: p11g* p12g p11g² 10.1d p11g⁵ p10g³ Dec 16] strong, workmanlike gelding:
fairly useful handicapper: won at Kempton in February: creditable efforts last 2 starts:
stays 11f: acts on polytrack, firm and good to soft ground. *A. P. Jarvis*

AWELMARDUK (IRE) 3 b.c. Almutawakel 126 – Claba di San Jore (IRE) (Barathea **109**
(IRE) 127) [2007 10m* 10m³ 12m* May 20] first foal: dam, Italian 1¼m winner, half-
sister to Italian Listed winner up to 1½m Clasem di San Jore: useful performer: won
maiden at Milan at 2 yrs, minor event there in April and Derby Italiano Antonveneta ABN
AMRO at Rome (stayed on from rear to lead inside final 1f, beat Shrek ½ length) in May:

stays 1½m: acts on good to firm ground: has been blinkered/tongue tied: joined M. Botti. *A. & G. Botti, Italy*

A WISH FOR YOU 2 ch.f. (Feb 24) Tumbleweed Ridge 117 – Peperonata (IRE) 91 **75** (Cyrano de Bergerac 120) [2007 p5g 5m 5m³ 5d³ p5g 5.5m p5.1g³ p5.1g² p5.1g⁵ p5m⁴ f5d² p5.1g* Dec 29] sturdy, lengthy filly: seventh foal: half-sister to 3 winners, including 5-y-o Bens Georgie: dam unreliable 2-y-o 5f winner: fair performer: in cheekpieces, won maiden at Wolverhampton in December: best at bare 5f: acts on all-weather, good to firm and good to soft going. *D. K. Ivory*

AWWAL MALIKA (USA) 3 b.f. Kingmambo (USA) 125 – First Night (IRE) 102 **73 +** (Sadler's Wells (USA) 132) [2007 73p: 5g p7g 8s p7g⁴ 8m² 8m² 7g² 6s* 7m 7d Sep 29] good-bodied filly: fair performer: won 4-runner handicap at Folkestone in August: probably flattered in final start of stiff tasks in listed races after: should stay beyond 1m: acts on soft and good to firm ground. *C. E. Brittain*

AXIOM 3 ch.c. Pivotal 124 – Exhibitor (USA) 68 (Royal Academy (USA) 130) [2007 **87** 8g⁴ 8s³ p8g p8g² 8.3d² 7d* Oct 9] useful-looking colt: first foal: dam 1¼m winner: fairly useful form: odds on, won maiden at Leicester (smoothly by 3½ lengths) in October: stays 8.3f: acts on polytrack and good to soft going: sold 34,000 gns. *E. A. L. Dunlop*

AXIS MUNDI (IRE) 3 b.f. Titus Livius (FR) 115 – Inventive 84 (Sheikh Albadou 128) **44 ?** [2007 –: 7v p7.1g⁶ p8g⁵ p8g Oct 17] good-topped filly: poor maiden. *T. J. Etherington*

AXIS SHIELD (IRE) 4 b.f. Shinko Forest (IRE) – La Doyenne (IRE) 65 (Masterclass **63** (USA) 116) [2007 52: f6g f5g f5g⁵ f7g 5g 5.1d⁴ 5s f5g* Dec 27] sturdy, lengthy filly: modest performer: won claimer at Southwell in December: was effective at 5f to 7f: acted on all-weather and firm ground, probably on good to soft: dead. *M. C. Chapman*

AYE AYE DEFINITELY (IRE) 3 b.f. Danetime (IRE) 121 – Taispeain (IRE) 86 **74** (Petorius 117) [2007 76: 6m 8m 6g 6.5g 6g² 5m⁴ 6s⁶ 6d 5m 5s³ p6g 6s Oct 4] smallish filly: fifth foal: sister to useful Irish 5f (including at 2 yrs) to 1m winner Chained Emotion and half-sister to fairly useful 2004 2-y-o 7f winner Keep Bacckinhit (by Raise A Grand): dam Irish 6f winner: fair handicapper: left P. Prendergast in Ireland after fourth outing: pulled up (said to have finished lame) final appearance: stays 6f: acts on heavy and good to firm ground: sold 2,000 gns. *R. A. Fahey*

AYE AYE DIGBY (IRE) 2 b.c. (Apr 28) Captain Rio 122 – Jane Digby (IRE) 84 **90** (Magical Strike (USA) 114) [2007 6m⁶ 7m 7d* 7.1g³ 6d⁵ Oct 12] €6,000, resold €17,000, 20,000 2-y-o: strong, quite attractive colt: has a quick action: seventh foal: dam, Irish 2-y-o 7f and hurdles winner: fairly useful form: won maiden at Salisbury (beat Dauberval by ¾ length) in August: sound efforts after in minor event at Sandown (third to Billion Dollar Kid) and nursery at York (gone in coat, inadequate test): likely to stay 1m: acts on good to soft going: tends to hang. *H. Candy*

AYPEEYES (IRE) 3 b.g. King Charlemagne (USA) 120 – Habaza (IRE) 68 (Shernazar **79** 131) [2007 78: 10d 9.9g p10g³ 10d² 11.7m² 9.9g 11.9d⁵ p12.2g* Sep 21] rather leggy gelding: fair handicapper: won at Wolverhampton in September: stays 1½m: acts on polytrack, good to firm and good to soft ground: joined A. King. *S. Kirk*

AZAROLE (IRE) 6 b.g. Alzao (USA) 117 – Cashew 80 (Sharrood (USA) 124) [2007 **105** 112: 7.5g 8m⁵ 8g⁵ 7.5g⁶ 8g 7g⁵ 8.1g Sep 8] strong gelding: one-time smart performer, just useful nowadays: mostly creditable efforts in 2007, including in valuable handicap at Goodwood (seventh to Third Set) and listed race at York (fifth to Duff) fifth/penultimate outings: stays 1m: acts on polytrack, heavy and good to firm going: tongue tied first 2 starts at 4 yrs: not straightforward. *J. S. Moore*

AZEEMA (IRE) 3 b.f. Averti (IRE) 117 – Kazeem 73 (Darshaan 133) [2007 7m⁶ 7m* **82** 7g 8d Sep 28] lengthy filly: has a quick action: second foal: dam, maiden, out of smart performer up to 1½m Kanz: fairly useful form: won maiden at Chester (by 1¼ lengths from Medicea Sidera) in May: well below form in handicaps after: should stay 1m: acts on good to firm ground. *B. W. Hills*

AZEER (USA) 2 ch.c. (Jan 6) Giant's Causeway (USA) 132 – Touch of Love (USA) **87** (Alydar (USA)) [2007 6m⁴ 7g 6m Jun 23] $130,000: strong, close-coupled colt: closely related to winner in Japan by Storm Cat and half-brother to several winners, including smart French/US 1m (including at 2 yrs)/11f winner Alyzig (by Danzig): dam US 6f to 8.5f winner, including 7f at 2 yrs: fairly useful form: raced only in June, fourth in maiden at Windsor (green) then never-dangerous eighth of 12 to Maze in listed event at Royal Ascot: jarred up after: will stay 1m. *P. W. Chapple-Hyam*

AZREME 7 ch.g. Unfuwain (USA) 131 – Mariette 35 (Blushing Scribe (USA) 107) **80** [2007 76, a54: p9.5g 8.1g² 10.2d 8.1g 8s³ 8g³ 8.3v* 8s* 8.1v⁴ 8.1d⁵ p8g⁵ p8m 8g Oct 24] **a61** well-made gelding: fairly useful handicapper on turf, modest on all-weather: won at Windsor and Ripon within 8 days in July: stays 8.3f: acts on polytrack and heavy ground: sometimes wears headgear (not in 2007): usually waited with. *P. Howling*

AZURE MIST 2 ch.f. (Mar 27) Bahamian Bounty 116 – Inquirendo (USA) 81 (Roberto **68** (USA) 131) [2007 7f² 7.2s⁶ 8g³ Nov 9] 9,000Y: sparely-made filly: half-sister to 3 winners abroad: dam, 7f winner, half-sister to US Grade 1 1¼m winner Bequest: fair maiden: placed at Yarmouth and Musselburgh (testing conditions in between): barely stays 1m: acts on firm going. *M. H. Tompkins*

AZYGOUS 4 ch.g. Foxhound (USA) 103 – Flag (Selkirk (USA) 129) [2007 88: p5f p6g **80** 6m 5m² 5m⁴ 5m 5m 5.3d 5m p5g³ 5g 5m 5d⁵ p5.1g⁶ 5.1g p5g p5g² p5g⁵ Dec 12] neat gelding: fairly useful handicapper: below form after fifth outing: best at 5f: acts on all-weather, firm and good to soft going: races prominently. *J. Akehurst*

B

BAAHER (USA) 3 b.c. War Chant (USA) 126 – Raajiya (USA) 83 (Gulch (USA)) **72** [2007 p8g³ Feb 17] second foal: half-brother to fairly useful 2005 2-y-o 7f winner Dahaaleez (by Red Ransom): dam, 7f winner, half-sister to Dewhurst Stakes winner Mujahid: 5/4 favourite, 2½ lengths third of 12 to Zar Solitario in maiden at Lingfield, edging left and not knocked about: sold 35,000 gns in October. *M. P. Tregoning*

BAAN (USA) 4 ch.g. Diesis 133 – Madaen (USA) (Nureyev (USA) 131) [2007 102, **85** a96: 9s⁵ 10g⁶ 10.1d 9.8m³ 10d⁴ᵈ 12.1m 11.9g⁴ p12g 16d⁵ p8.6g⁶ p9.5g³ p8.6g² p9.5g³ **a77** p8.6d² p10g⁶ Dec 19] small, good-topped gelding: fairly useful handicapper on turf, fair on all-weather: effective at 9.5f, probably stays 2m: acts on all-weather, soft and good to firm going: blinkered/visored 7 of last 8 starts. *M. Johnston*

BAARRIJ 3 ch.f. Tobougg (IRE) 125 – Bint Albaadiya (USA) 108 (Woodman (USA) **51** 126) [2007 49: 6.1m 8g 9.7m 10.1m⁵ p8g Sep 4] modest maiden: stays 9.7f. *G. A. Huffer*

BABA GANOUGE (IRE) 3 ch.f. Desert Prince (IRE) 130 – Le Montrachet (Nashwan **82** (USA) 135) [2007 50: 10m³ 12.1s* 12.3d⁴ 13m Jul 12] good-topped filly: fairly useful form: won maiden at Chepstow (by 11 lengths) in June: tailed-off last after in handicap at Chester (reportedly lost shoe) and listed race at Newmarket (stirred up beforehand): stays 1½m: acts on soft ground, probably on good to firm. *B. J. Meehan*

BABA GHANOUSH 5 ch.m. Zaha (CAN) 106 – Vrennan 74 (Suave Dancer (USA) **64** 136) [2007 61: p7g p7g p8g p7g p8g⁶ Dec 5] fair at 3 yrs, only modest form since: left W. Jarvis after third start in 2007: should stay 1m+: acts on polytrack. *J. Akehurst*

BABILU 2 ch.f. (Mar 3) Lomitas 129 – Creeking 65 (Persian Bold 123) [2007 6g 6d Sep **–** 28] 18,000Y: big, close-coupled, good-topped filly: seventh foal: half-sister to 3 winners, including useful 6f winner Coconut Squeak (by Bahamian Bounty): dam, maiden (stayed 1¼m), half-sister to useful performers Fast Eddy (up to 1m) and Stone Mill (up to 1¼m): well beaten in maidens. *J. G. Given*

BABODANA 7 ch.h. Bahamian Bounty 116 – Daanat Nawal (Machiavellian (USA) **107** 123) [2007 115, a99: 8.1g⁶ 8g 8m³ 8.3s² 8g 8g 9m 7d² p8g⁶ p8g Nov 28] good-topped horse: useful performer nowadays: creditable efforts when placed in 2007, including in listed race at Windsor (4 lengths second to Winged Cupid) and minor event at Leicester (beaten ¾ length by Welsh Emperor) fourth/eighth outings: best form at 1m: acts on polytrack, heavy and good to firm going: tried in blinkers/visor. *M. H. Tompkins*

BABY BARRY 10 b.g. Komaite (USA) – Malcesine (IRE) 46 (Auction Ring (USA) **57** 123) [2007 61: f7g 8.5m³ 10.2f p8.6g 10m 8g⁵ 8m Sep 18] good-topped gelding: modest performer: left K. Burke after second start: stays 1¼m: acts on all-weather, firm and good to soft going: effective with or without headgear. *S. Parr*

BABY DORDAN (IRE) 3 b.f. Desert Prince (IRE) 130 – Three Owls (IRE) 79 **69** (Warning 136) [2007 70: 8.2g⁵ 7.1m⁴ 7s⁴ 8s⁴ 7d p7m² Aug 10] leggy filly: fair maiden: should be suited by 1m: acts on polytrack, soft and good to firm going: sold 8,500 gns. *H. J. L. Dunlop*

BABY JACK 2 b.c. (Mar 6) Josr Algarhoud (IRE) 118 – Mashmoon (USA) 80 (Habitat **53** 134) [2007 5m⁴ 5.9d 5m 5g⁵ 7m 5g Sep 19] sturdy colt: modest maiden: bred to stay 1m: blinkered (came loose) final start. *D. Nicholls*

BACHNAGAIRN 3 b.g. In The Wings 128 – Purple Heather (USA) 93 (Rahy (USA) **71** 115) [2007 70: 10.2f² 10.2f² 12.1g³ p12.2g Jul 2] good-topped gelding: fair maiden handicapper: stays 1½m: acts on firm and good to soft going: blinkered (below form) final outing. *R. Charlton*

BACK IN THE RED (IRE) 3 ch.g. Redback 116 – Fureur de Vivre (IRE) (Bluebird **82** (USA) 125) [2007 62: 5m⁶ p5g⁴ p6g⁵ 5d* 5.1f* p6g⁴ 5m⁴ 5m p6m p5g p5.1g* p5g p5.1d p6d⁵ Dec 28] strong gelding: fairly useful handicapper: won at Leicester and Bath in August and Wolverhampton in November: effective at 5f/6f: acts on polytrack, firm and good to soft going: tried in cheekpieces. *R. A. Harris*

BACKLASH 6 b.m. Fraam 114 – Mezza Luna (Distant Relative 128) [2007 10.2f p9.5g **–** 10f³ May 7] poor performer in 2005: little form on return: tried tongue tied/visored: won over hurdles in October. *A. W. Carroll*

BADALONA 2 b.f. (Mar 12) Cape Cross (IRE) 129 – Badawi (USA) 103 (Diesis 133) **82** [2007 7g² 7g² 7.5m² 8.1s* Sep 29] lengthy, good-bodied filly, type to carry plenty of condition: closely related to 3 winners, notably useful 6f/7f winner Cala (by Desert Prince), and half-sister to several useful winners, including 6f (at 2 yrs)/7f winner Badminton (by Zieten): dam 1m/9f winner: fairly useful form: runner-up all 3 starts (including behind Celtic Slipper at Goodwood) prior to winning maiden at Haydock: will probably stay 1¼m: acts on soft and good to firm going. *M. L. W. Bell*

BADDAM 5 b.g. Mujahid (USA) 125 – Aude La Belle (FR) 81 (Ela-Mana-Mou 132) **114 d** [2007 114: 16m² 20g 21.7s² 16g 18m 16g⁵ 18m³ 18d Oct 20] rather leggy, quite good-topped gelding: smart performer: as good as ever when second to Tungsten Strike in Sagaro Stakes at Ascot on reappearance: below form after, tailed off in Cesarewitch at Newmarket final outing: gelded after: stays 2¾m: acts on firm and good to soft going. *M. R. Channon*

BAD MOON RISING 2 ch.c. (Feb 9) Piccolo 121 – Janette Parkes 39 (Pursuit of Love **58** 124) [2007 6d⁴ p7g p7g Dec 19] strong colt: modest form in maidens: bred to be best at 5f/6f. *J. Akehurst*

BADOURA 2 ch.f. (Mar 21) Dr Fong (USA) 128 – Kalindi 102 (Efisio 120) [2007 5m **61** 6.5d p7m⁵ Nov 1] 50,000Y: sturdy filly: fourth foal: half-sister to useful Irish 2005 2-y-o 6f/7f winner Abigail Pett (by Medicean), 5-y-o Mambazo and 3-y-o Autograph Hunter: dam 5f (at 2 yrs) and 7f winner: modest maiden: stiff task (sales race) second start, stirred up before final one: will stay 1m. *G. A. Butler*

BA DREAMFLIGHT 2 b.g. (Mar 24) Noverre (USA) 125 – Aunt Tate (Tate Gallery **– p** (USA) 117) [2007 p7m p8g p8g Oct 29] 20,000Y: rather leggy gelding: half-brother to several winners, including useful 7f winner Doctorate (by Dr Fong), later successful in USA, and useful performer up to 1½m in Bahrain Lodge Keeper (by Grand Lodge), 7f winner at 2 yrs: dam ran twice: well held in maidens, all on polytrack in October: bred to stay 1m/1¼m: gelded after final start: type to do better at 3 yrs. *H. Morrison*

BAFFLED (USA) 2 b. or br.f. (Mar 14) Distorted Humor (USA) 117 – Surf Club **89** (USA) (Ocean Crest (USA)) [2007 p6g* 6g³ 7m⁶ 7m Aug 11] $350,000Y: good-topped filly: has scope: second foal: dam US 5.5f (at 2 yrs) to 8.5f winner, half-sister to US 2-y-o Grade 1 7f winner Awesome Humor (by Distorted Humor): fairly useful form: won maiden at Lingfield in May: much improved when 3¼ lengths third of 20 to Nijoom Dubai in Albany Stakes at Royal Ascot: disappointing after (firmer ground) in minor event at Ascot and Sweet Solera Stakes at Newmarket: should stay 7f: edgy type: sent to USA. *J. Noseda*

BAGENALSTOWN (IRE) 2 b.c. (Apr 6) Fath (USA) 116 – Rhapsani (IRE) 24 **–** (Persian Bold 123) [2007 5g 7.6f p8.6g Nov 17] tailed off in maidens. *M. Wellings*

BAHAMA BAILEYS 2 ch.g. (Mar 30) Bahamian Bounty 116 – Baileys Silver (USA) **78** (Marlin (USA) 124) [2007 5g⁴ 5m⁴ 5g⁴ 5m³ 6g 6m⁴ 6g 7m⁶ 6g⁴ Sep 23] 22,000Y: tall gelding: second foal: dam unraced half-sister to useful miler Zaheemah: fair performer: won maiden at Newcastle in May: twice in frame in nurseries: best at 5f/6f: acts on good to firm going: raced prominently, but often awkward under pressure (tried in blinkers): gelded after final start. *M. Johnston*

BAHAMA GOLD 3 b.f. Bahamian Bounty 116 – Pictina (Petong 126) [2007 p8g³ p7g **52 d** p8.6g 6m 8f 7d May 17] leggy filly: fourth foal: half-sister to 7f winner Dispol Isle (by Trans Island) and 2005 2-y-o 5f winner Mytton's Pride (by Tagula): dam unraced out of sister to very smart miler Dominion: modest form in claimer on debut: left A. Balding £8,000, no impact after: wore cheekpieces final outing. *D. G. Bridgwater*

BAHAMARAMA (IRE) 2 ch.f. (Apr 14) Bahamian Bounty 116 – Cole Slaw (Absa- **64** lom 128) [2007 6m p5g³ 5v³ p6g p5.1g* p5.1g⁴ p7.1g p6g p6g p6d⁵ Dec 17] 8,000Y, resold 2,000Y, 13,000 2-y-o: rather leggy filly: half-sister to 3 winners, including 1999 2-y-o 6f winner Coley (by Pursuit of Love): dam unraced out of useful miler Collide: modest performer: won seller at Wolverhampton (left J. Boyle 12,000 gns) in August: best form at 5f on polytrack. *R. A. Harris*

BAHAMA REEF (IRE) 6 b.g. Sri Pekan (USA) 117 – Caribbean Dancer 71 (Shareef **–** Dancer (USA) 135) [2007 –: p10g Jan 29] angular gelding: one-time fair performer: lightly raced and little impact since 2005: tried visored/in cheekpieces. *B. Gubby*

BAHAMIAN BALLAD 2 ch.f. (Feb 21) Bahamian Bounty 116 – Record Time 69 **69** (Clantime 101) [2007 5d 6m 5.4m³ 6g Sep 24] 18,000Y: medium-sized, good-topped filly: fourth foal: half-sister to 3 winners, including 4-y-o Moorhouse Lad and 3-y-o Off The Record: dam 5f winner: maiden: only form when never-nearer third to Excitement at York: should prove best at 5f/6f. *J. D. Bethell*

BAHAMIAN BALLET 5 ch.g. Bahamian Bounty 116 – Plie 75 (Superlative 118) **91** [2007 79: 5g 5m³ 5m* 5d* 5d⁴ 5.1m⁶ 5m p5.1g 5m³ Oct 22] workmanlike gelding: fairly useful handicapper: won at Windsor in June and Catterick in July: best at 5f: acts on polytrack, good to firm and good to soft ground. *E. S. McMahon*

BAHAMIAN BAY 5 b.m. Bahamian Bounty 116 – Moly 64 (Inchinor 119) [2007 61: **39** f6g f6g 5s p6g p5.1g⁵ Oct 30] quite good-topped mare: just poor form in 2007: stays 6f: acts on fibresand, best effort on turf on good ground. *M. Brittain*

BAHAMIAN BLUE (IRE) 2 ch.g. (Apr 19) Touch of The Blues (FR) 125 – Cattiva **55** (ITY) (Lomond (USA) 128) [2007 6s 7m⁶ 8.1m p6g p7g Sep 26] modest maiden: gelded after final start: best up to 7f. *H. J. L. Dunlop*

BAHAMIAN DUKE 4 ch.g. Bahamian Bounty 116 – Madame Sisu 47 (Emarati **69** (USA) 74) [2007 69: 6m³ 5.9m 5.1d³ 5g 6m p6g p6g p6g Dec 19] big, workmanlike **a–** gelding: fair handicapper: best at 5f/6f: acts on firm and good to soft ground: tried visored: has shown signs of temperament. *K. R. Burke*

BAHAMIAN GIFT 2 ch.f. (Jan 17) Bahamian Bounty 116 – Desert Nomad 56 (Green **67** Desert (USA) 127) [2007 6g* Jun 22] 1,500Y: half-sister to several winners, including useful Italian sprinter Desert Vert (by Distant Relative) and 4-y-o Bowl of Cherries: dam 7f winner: 16/1 and inexperienced (gave trouble at start), won maiden at Ayr despite carrying head awkwardly, leading final furlong. *M. Brittain*

BAHAMIAN LAD 2 b.c. (Mar 20) Bahamian Bounty 116 – Danehill Princess (IRE) **74** 62 (Danehill (USA) 126) [2007 6m² 6g 6d 5.1m p6g⁴ p5.1g² Dec 29] 34,000Y: lengthy colt: fourth foal: dam maiden (stayed 7f): fair maiden: in frame at Wolverhampton (including nursery) last 3 starts: may prove best kept to 5f/6f: acts on polytrack and good to firm going. *R. Hollinshead*

BAHAMIAN LOVE 3 br.f. Bahamian Bounty 116 – Asian Love (Petong 126) [2007 **63** 68: f6g p6g 5.1g⁵ p6g³ f5g p6g Jun 2] compact filly: just modest performer in 2007: stays 6f: acts on all-weather and good to firm going: tried tongue tied: has wandered under pressure: sold 6,000 gns, sent to Greece. *B. W. Hills*

BAHAMIAN PIRATE (USA) 12 ch.g. Housebuster (USA) – Shining Through **102** (USA) (Deputy Minister (CAN)) [2007 109: f6g⁴ f7s⁵ f6g* p6g⁵ 6d 6s² 6m² 6g³ 7g 6.3s⁴ 6d⁵ 6s 6m Aug 18] sturdy gelding: won 2004 Nunthorpe: useful handicapper nowadays: won at Southwell (by ¾ length from Saviours Spirit) in February: creditable efforts when placed at Ascot (2½ lengths second to Zidane) and Thirsk sixth/seventh outings: largely below form after: best at 5f/6f: acts on fibresand and any turf going: held up (sometimes slowly away), and takes time to warm up. *D. Nicholls*

BAHAMIAN PRINCESS 2 ch.f. (May 1) Bahamian Bounty 116 – Cutlass Princess **–** (USA) 41 (Cutlass (USA)) [2007 p6g Sep 21] 10,000Y: eighth foal: half-sister to useful 1997 2-y-o 5f/6f winner Jimmy Too (by Nomination) and 5f to 7f winner Princess Efisio (by Efisio): dam maiden: 20/1, very green in maiden at Wolverhampton. *E. S. McMahon*

BAHARAH (USA) 3 b.f. Elusive Quality (USA) – Bahr 119 (Generous (IRE) 139) **113** [2007 6g³ p7g² p7g* Dec 1] 30,000 3-y-o: fifth foal: half-sister to useful 7f (in UAE)/7.5f (at 2 yrs) winner Naaddey (by Seeking The Gold) and fairly useful 2005 2-y-o 1m winner In Dubai (by Giant's Causeway): dam 7f (at 2 yrs) to 1½m (Ribblesdale Stakes) winner: smart form: still green, much improved when winning minor event at Kempton in

December by 2 lengths from Orchard Supreme, bursting clear: likely to stay 1m: acts on polytrack. *G. A. Butler*

BAHAR SHUMAAL (IRE) 5 b.h. Dubai Millennium 140 – High Spirited 80 (Shirley Heights 130) [2007 106: p10g p10g⁵ p12g⁵ 8.1m⁴ 9m Sep 15] big, good-topped horse: useful performer on all-weather, lightly raced on turf in 2007: best effort in 2007 when fifth to Very Wise in handicap at Lingfield second outing: well below form after: effective at 9.5f to 1½m: acts on polytrack and good to firm going: usually wears blinkers: tried tongue tied: none too reliable. *C. E. Brittain* **80 + a103**

BAHHMIRAGE (IRE) 4 ch.f. Bahhare (USA) 122 – Border Mirage (Selkirk (USA) 129) [2007 60: f7g 8.1d* 8g 8.1m p9.5g Dec 26] leggy filly: modest performer: won (first success) amateur handicap at Warwick in June: stays 1m: acts on all-weather, good to firm and good to soft going: often wears headgear: tongue tied on reappearance: often slowly away. *C. N. Kellett* **59**

BAHIA BREEZE 5 b.m. Mister Baileys 123 – Ring of Love 77 (Magic Ring (IRE) 115) [2007 106: 8.1g² 8.5d² 7s⁵ 8m⁶ 10d² 10m⁵ 9d Oct 19] small, well-made mare: useful performer: runner-up in Betfred Mile at Sandown (beaten 1¼ lengths by Jeremy), Princess Elizabeth Stakes at Epsom (beaten ¾ length by Echelon) and Prix Jean Romanet at Deauville (short-headed by Satwa Queen, hanging late on) in 2007: well held in Darley Stakes at Newmarket final start: effective at 7f to 1¼m: acts on firm and soft going. *Rae Guest* **109**

BAHIANO (IRE) 6 ch.g. Barathea (IRE) 127 – Trystero (Shareef Dancer (USA) 135) [2007 109: p6g³ 7.5g a7f 6m⁵ 6s 7.1d 7g 6m 7m 7m 7g² 7m² p6m p7g⁴ Dec 19] compact gelding: useful performer: good efforts when in frame in handicaps in 2007, and when fourth to Bonus in listed event at Kempton final outing: has form up to 8.5f, but best at 6f/7f: acts on polytrack and firm going: often held up. *C. E. Brittain* **95**

BAHIA PALACE 2 b.f. (Apr 30) Zamindar (USA) 116 – Inya Lake 101 (Whittingham (IRE) 104) [2007 p5.1g⁶ p6g p7.1g 5.1g Nov 7] 5,000Y: leggy filly: fifth foal: half-sister to 3-y-o Jimmy Styles, 4-y-o Lake Hero and 5f winner Special Gold (by Josr Algarhoud): dam 5f (including Molecomb Stakes at 2 yrs) winner: no form. *M. D. I. Usher* **–**

BAHRAIN GOLD (IRE) 7 b.g. Great Commotion (USA) 123 – Hassosi (IRE) (High Estate 127) [2007 53, a61: f7g f6g Jan 23] modest performer at 6 yrs: no form in 2007: stays 7f: acts on all-weather: tried in cheekpieces, often blinkered. *N. P. McCormack* **–**

BAHRALL 4 b.g. Bahri (USA) 125 – Navajo Love Song (IRE) 43 (Dancing Brave (USA) 140) [2007 10.1m f8g 7g Jun 12] leggy gelding: no form: tried visored. *A. P. Jarvis* **–**

BAILEY (IRE) 2 ch.g. (Feb 21) Captain Rio 122 – Baileys Cream 79 (Mister Baileys 123) [2007 p6g² p6g² p7g² 8s⁵ 8m³ 7s² Oct 4] €72,000F, 97,000Y: rangy gelding: has scope: third foal: half-brother to Italian 9f winner Rich of Promises (by Imperial Ballet): dam 2-y-o 7f winner: fairly useful maiden: placed 4 times, including close third in nursery at Goodwood penultimate start: stays 1m: act on polytrack, soft and good to firm going: gelded after final start. *B. J. Meehan* **84**

BAILEYS BEST 5 b.g. Mister Baileys 123 – Miss Rimex (IRE) 84 (Ezzoud (IRE) 126) [2007 10.2f Apr 11] fair performer at 3 yrs: well held on sole Flat start since: stays 1¼m: acts on soft and good to firm going: tried blinkered. *J. G. M. O'Shea* **–**

BAILEYS OUTSHINE 3 ch.f. Inchinor 119 – Red Ryding Hood 83 (Wolfhound (USA) 126) [2007 73: 5g² p5.1g⁶ 6f³ f5g² 5g* 5m 5m³ 5d⁴ 5g⁵ 5g p5.1g⁶ p5g³ p5.1s⁶ Dec 21] small filly: fair handicapper: won at Ayr in May: best at 5f/6f: acts on all-weather, good to firm and good to soft ground: often races prominently. *J. G. Given* **79**

BAILIEBOROUGH (IRE) 8 b.g. Charnwood Forest (IRE) 125 – Sherannda (USA) (Trempolino (USA) 135) [2007 97: 8s 8m³ 8.1g⁵ 9.1g² 10.4g³ 10m³ 8d² p8.6g⁵ 8.9s 10.4d 7m p9.5g⁵ f11d⁵ Dec 18] quite good-topped gelding: fairly useful handicapper: placed 5 times in first half of 2007: left B. Ellison after ninth outing, claimed £15,000 after final one: stays 10.4f: acts on polytrack, firm and good to soft going: tried visored/blinkered. *N. Wilson* **94 a85**

BAINISTEOIR 2 b.g. (Apr 22) Tobougg (IRE) 125 – Peruvian Jade 76 (Petong 126) [2007 7s 6.5d⁶ p8.6g⁴ Nov 4] 11,000F, 23,000Y: tall, close-coupled gelding: third foal: half-brother to 3-y-o Mac Gille Eoin: dam 2-y-o 6f winner: fair maiden: sixth to Fateh Field at Newbury, only form (didn't handle turn at Wolverhampton final start): should stay 1m. *S. Kirk* **67**

BAIRAG (USA) 2 b.c. (Feb 24) Grand Slam (USA) 120 – Brilliance (FR) 117 (Priolo (USA) 127) [2007 6g 6.5d Oct 11] $57,000Y, 65,000 2-y-o: attractive colt: fourth foal: **64**

106

half-brother to French 1½m winner Aljiwaar (by Bahri): dam French 1¼m winner (including Prix Saint-Alary) who stayed 1½m: ninth in maidens at Yarmouth (travelled well) and Newbury (found little on softer ground). *Mrs C. A. Dunnett*

BAIZICALLY (IRE) 4 ch.g. Galileo (IRE) 134 – Baize 95 (Efisio 120) [2007 89: f8g³ **96** p10g⁶ 11.7f² 14m 16g 12m² Sep 22] strong gelding: useful performer, lightly raced: good second in handicap at Bath third start: below form after (acted as pacemaker penultimate start): should stay beyond 11.7f: acts on all-weather and firm ground: sold 33,000 gns, joined George Baker. *J. A. Osborne*

BAJAN PARKES 4 b. or br.g. Zafonic (USA) 130 – My Melody Parkes 102 (Teenoso **89** (USA) 135) [2007 84: 6m 8m⁵ 7.9d⁶ 9.1g³ 10.3d⁴ 9.8v³ 10.1d⁴ 9.1s² 10.9m³ 11.9g* 14g 13s⁵ Sep 24] good-topped gelding: fairly useful handicapper: won at Haydock in September: stamina stretched both starts after: stays 1½m: acts on any turf going: effective held up or making running: consistent. *E. J. Alston*

BAJAN PRIDE 3 b.g. Selkirk (USA) 129 – Spry 84 (Suave Dancer (USA) 136) [2007 **87** 78p: 9.9m³ 12m⁵ 11g 9.9g 10d⁵ p8g* 8m* 8g² 8.3m 8.1m⁵ 8d 8s Oct 14] well-made gelding: fairly useful handicapper: won at Kempton and Newmarket in July: well below form last 2 starts: best form at 1m: acts on polytrack, soft and good to firm going: sold 30,000 gns. *R. Hannon*

BAJEEL (IRE) 3 b.c. Traditionally (USA) 117 – Calypso Grant (IRE) 98 (Danehill **76** (USA) 126) [2007 53: p6g⁴ 7m⁶ p7.1g⁵ 5d⁶ Jul 14] strong, lengthy colt: fair maiden: probably stays 7f: acts on polytrack: tried tongue tied, blinkered final outing: sent to Saudi Arabia. *G. A. Butler*

BAKER OF OZ 6 b.g. Pursuit of Love 124 – Moorish Idol 90 (Aragon 118) [2007 **–** p16.5g p16.5g Feb 2] strong, close-coupled gelding: on downgrade: unraced on Flat at 5 yrs, and well held both starts in 2007: tried in cheekpieces/blinkers. *M. A. Doyle*

BAKERS BOY 3 ch.g. Tipsy Creek (USA) 115 – Unparalleled 64 (Primo Dominie 121) **–** [2007 p8m p7g Dec 5] well held in maidens at Kempton. *J. E. Long*

BAKHOOR (IRE) 4 b.f. Royal Applause 124 – First Waltz (FR) 117 (Green Dancer **88** (USA) 132) [2007 74p: 7s* 6g² 7d⁶ Jun 22] angular filly: fairly useful handicapper: won at Leicester in May: raced too freely when below form at Newmarket final outing: stays 7f: acts on firm and soft going: tried tongue tied: reportedly in foal to Green Desert. *W. Jarvis*

BALAIS FOLLY (FR) 2 ch.g. (Apr 30) Act One 124 – Bhima (Polar Falcon (USA) **49** 126) [2007 7d 8.1m 10.2d p10g p8.6g p8.6g⁶ Dec 3] poor maiden on balance: bred to stay 1¼m: tried in cheekpieces. *B. Palling*

BALAKAR (IRE) 11 b.g. Doyoun 124 – Balaniya (USA) (Diesis 133) [2007 13d² 16g⁶ **68** 15s³ 16.1m² 17.5s* Sep 21] fair handicapper: won at Ayr in September: stays 17.5f: acts on soft and good to firm ground: wears cheekpieces: held up: fair hurdler. *J. J. Lambe, Ireland*

BALAKIREF 8 b.g. Royal Applause 124 – Pluck 80 (Never So Bold 135) [2007 85: 5g **89** 6s* 6d⁵ 6g⁵ 6d⁶ 6v* 7d* 7g 6d⁶ 7.2s⁴ 7g 7m Nov 10] quite attractive gelding: fairly useful handicapper: won at Leicester in May and Haydock and Newcastle in July: effective at 5f to 7f: acts on all-weather and any turf going: tried visored (not since 2003): usually held up (often misses break). *M. Dods*

BALANCHINE MOON 3 ch.f. Zilzal (USA) 137 – Crescent Moon (Mr Prospector **51** (USA)) [2007 57: 7.1m p8.6g p5g Oct 19] small filly: modest maiden: left M. Tregoning after second start: bred to stay 1m+. *G. A. Kingston, Ireland*

BALATA 2 b.f. Averti (IRE) 117 – Manila Selection (USA) (Manila (USA)) **71** [2007 5m⁵ 6m² 6d³ 5.1g⁵ Oct 24] 18,000Y: close-coupled gelding: fifth foal: half-brother to 3 winners, including 4-y-o Danski: dam unraced: fair maiden: off 5 months (and gelded) after debut: placed at Leicester and Windsor: should prove best kept to 5f/6f. *B. R. Millman*

BALDEMAR 2 b.g. (Apr 12) Namid 128 – Keen Melody (USA) 60 (Sharpen Up 127) **86** [2007 5g 6m* 6s 5d² 5.1g³ Sep 29] 21,000F, 26,000Y: leggy, quite good-topped gelding: has moderate, quick action: half-brother to several winners, including fairly useful 2003 2-y-o 6f winner Embassy Lord (by Mind Games): dam maiden (stayed 1m): fairly useful form: won maiden at Ripon in August: placed in minor event at Beverley (best effort, second to In Uniform) and nursery at Chester, then gelded: won at 6f, may prove best at 5f: acts on good to firm and good to soft going: has hung under pressure. *K. R. Burke*

Weatherbys VAT Services Stakes (Esher), Sandown—
Balkan Knight lands his second listed win of the season; Alambic (hoops) puts up her best effort in second,
ahead of Finalmente (left) and The Geezer (right)

BALDOVINA 3 b.f. Tale of The Cat (USA) 113 – Baldwina (FR) 111 (Pistolet Bleu **66**
(IRE) 133) [2007 73: p8g p8g³ 9.7g⁵ 11.7g p10g Jul 21] neat filly: fair maiden: left
M. Botti after second start: stays easy 1m: raced only on polytrack and good ground or
firmer on turf: tried blinkered: joined D. Pipe. *Tom Dascombe*

BALERNO 8 b.g. Machiavellian (USA) 123 – Balabina (USA) 110 (Nijinsky (CAN) **63**
138) [2007 62: p6g p7.1g² p8g p6g* p6g² 7m⁵ p6g p6g⁶ p8g 6m 6f p6g Dec 19] close-
coupled gelding: modest handicapper: won at Lingfield in March: effective at 6f, barely
at 1¼m: acts on all-weather, firm and soft going: tried in headgear/tongue tie earlier in
career: held up. *Mrs L. J. Mongan*

BALFOUR HOUSE 4 b.g. Wizard King 122 – Tymeera 62 (Timeless Times (USA) **–**
99) [2007 –: 10.2m p12m Oct 3] no form: tried blinkered. *C. Roberts*

BALIAN 4 b.g. Mujahid (USA) 125 – Imperial Jade 105 (Lochnager 132) [2007 71§, **53 §**
a61§: f5g p6g³ p6g f6g Apr 26] modest maiden: should stay 7f: acts on firm going: wears
blinkers/cheekpieces nowadays: one to be wary of. *Mrs P. Sly*

BALI BELONY 3 b.f. Erhaab (USA) 127 – Daarat Alayaam (IRE) (Reference Point **–**
139) [2007 –: p8g p9.5g 10s 9g 10.1m p12g Nov 28] stocky filly: little form: tried
visored. *J. R. Jenkins*

BALKAN KNIGHT 7 b.g. Selkirk (USA) 129 – Crown of Light 112 (Mtoto 134) **115**
[2007 115: 12s³ 16.4d² 14m* 16.4g* 16g⁴ 16.4d² 18m⁶ 20g⁴ 16d² Oct 20] strong, well-
made gelding: smart performer: won listed events in small fields at Musselburgh
(beat Alfie Flits a head) in June and Sandown (beat Alambic by ½ length) in July: also
second in Henry II Stakes at Sandown (beaten ¾ length by Allegretto), Lonsdale Cup
at York (length behind Septimus) and Jockey Club Cup at Newmarket (went down by
1¼ lengths to Royal And Regal): stays 2½m: acts on soft and good to firm going: has
been bandaged behind: formerly visored: held up: consistent, and a credit to connections.
D. R. C. Elsworth

BALLAD MAKER (IRE) 3 b.g. Marju (IRE) 127 – Cappella (IRE) 75 (College **78**
Chapel 122) [2007 8.2m p8g³ p8.6g³ Oct 29] €37,000F, €310,000Y: sturdy, lengthy
gelding: fourth foal: half-brother to 3 winners, including useful 6f (at 2 yrs)/7f winner
Dickensian (by Xaar): dam 2-y-o 5f winner: third in maidens at Kempton and Wolverhampton (odds on): sold 21,000 gns. *J. H. M. Gosden*

BALLET BOY (IRE) 3 b.g. Sadler's Wells (USA) 132 – Happy Landing (FR) **88**
(Homing 130) [2007 54p: 10g* p12g³ 12s⁶ 12s* p13.9g² Oct 15] big, strong gelding:
fairly useful handicapper: won at Windsor in June and Catterick in October: stays 1¾m:
acts on polytrack and soft going: races prominently: sold 95,000 gns. *Sir Mark Prescott*

BALLETIC (IRE) 2 b.f. (Jan 17) Noverre (USA) 125 – Feminine Touch (IRE) **54**
(Sadler's Wells (USA) 132) [2007 7g p7g p7g Oct 29] €30,000F: big, strong filly: first
foal: dam unraced daughter of smart performer up to 1¼m Feminine Wiles: modest form
in maidens: needs to settle to stay 1m: sold 1,500 gns, sent to Serbia. *S. Kirk*

108

BALLIASTA (IRE) 3 b.f. Grand Lodge (USA) 125 – Obeah 112 (Cure The Blues **66** (USA)) [2007 57p: 8m⁴ 8m 8f⁶ 10.3g Sep 29] medium-sized, good-bodied filly: fair maiden: stays 1m: acts on soft and good to firm ground: sold 40,000 gns. *B. W. Hills*

BALLINSKELLIGS BOY 2 b.c. (Apr 30) Compton Place 125 – Autumn Affair 100 **65** (Lugana Beach 116) [2007 5m 5m3 6g2 6d5 Jun 26] strong colt: fair maiden: placed at Lingfield and Salisbury: will stay 7f: acts on good to firm going. *R. Hannon*

BALLINTENI 5 b.h. Machiavellian (USA) 123 – Silabteni (USA) (Nureyev (USA) **100** 131) [2007 85: 8m⁶ 10m* 12g 10d³ 10d² 12g⁶ 10m⁴ 10d⁵ 9m 10d⁵ Oct 27] leggy horse: useful performer: won handicap at Windsor in May: good efforts after in handicap at Sandown and listed race at Goodwood fifth/sixth starts: left D. Simcock after next outing, below form subsequently: stays 1½m: acts on polytrack, soft and good to firm going: tried tongue tied: has been bandaged all round. *Miss Gay Kelleway*

BALLISODARE 2 b.c. (Apr 20) Elusive Quality (USA) – River Jig (USA) 98 (Irish **68 p** River (FR) 131) [2007 8d Oct 27] closely related to 2 winners by Gone West, including useful 5f (Queen Mary Stakes) to 1m (US Grade 2 event) winner Dance Parade, and half-brother to 2 winners, including US Grade 3 9f winner Ocean Queen (by Zilzal): dam 9f (at 2 yrs) winner: 17/2, seventh of 15 to Trianon in maiden at Newbury, getting hang of things late on: likely to stay 1¼m: will benefit from experience. *P. W. Chapple-Hyam*

BALLOCHROY (IRE) 2 b.c. (Apr 22) Mull of Kintyre (USA) 114 – Shonara's Way **79** 99 (Slip Anchor 136) [2007 6m 7g⁴ 7.1g² 8.1s* 8g Oct 26] 26,000Y: sturdy colt: fourth foal: closely related to winner in Italy by Foxhound and half-brother to Irish 1½m winner Don't Be Bitin (by Turtle Island): dam ½m/15f and hurdles winner: fair form: progressed when upped in trip, won maiden at Haydock in September: not disgraced in nursery final start: will be suited by 1¼m/1½m: acts on soft going. *B. W. Hills*

BALLORA (FR) 2 ro.f. (Feb 12) Kendor (FR) 122 – Vodka (FR) (Ali-Royal (IRE) 127) **84 p** [2007 6d 8.1f² p8g* Sep 26] €50,000Y: first foal: dam, French 10.5f/11f winner, half-sister to useful French 1½m winner Masalarian: fairly useful form: clear second to Spell Caster in maiden at Chepstow then readily won similar event at Kempton: free-going sort, but should stay 1¼m: will improve further. *S. Kirk*

BALLROOM DANCER (IRE) 3 b.f. Danehill Dancer (IRE) 117 – Dwell (USA) 96 **91** (Habitat 134) [2007 7pp: p7g² 8m* 8.1g² 8.1m⁶ Aug 9] good-topped, quite attractive filly: fairly useful performer: won maiden at Goodwood (mulish at stall) in June by head from Medicea Sidera: good second in handicap at Sandown next time: not sure to stay beyond 1m: acts on good to firm ground. *J. Noseda*

BALLYBUNION (IRE) 8 ch.g. Entrepreneur 123 – Clarentia 111 (Ballad Rock 122) **58** [2007 65: 5.3m 5.7d p5.1g 5.1g p5g² 5.2d 5m 5.7m p6g 5.1m Sep 13] strong gelding: modest performer: effective at 5f to easy 7f: acts on polytrack and firm going: tried tongue tied/in headgear. *R. A. Harris*

BALLYCROY BOY (IRE) 2 b.g. (Mar 13) Captain Rio 122 – Royal Baldini (USA) **53** (Green Dancer (USA) 132) [2007 f5g² 5g f5g* 5g p7.1g 6.1m f7d³ Dec 18] lengthy **a65** gelding: has scope: fair performer: best efforts at Southwell, won maiden in May: stays 7f: acts on fibresand: tried blinkered. *A. Bailey*

BALLYHEALY LADY 2 b.f. (May 5) Tobougg (IRE) 125 – Amal (Top Ville 129) **–** [2007 p5g p6g 5m 5.1f Aug 24] 5,000Y: quite attractive filly: half-sister to several winners in France, including 5.5f (at 2 yrs) to 1¼m winner Fait Divers (by Highest Honor): dam French 1¼m/1½m winner: no form. *D. K. Ivory*

BALLYHURRY (USA) 10 b.g. Rubiano (USA) – Balakhna (FR) (Tyrant (USA)) **74** [2007 76, a54: 8.3g* 9g* 7.9d 9.1d² 7.1m² Jul 24] angular gelding: fair performer: won seller at Hamilton and claimer at Musselburgh (sixth course win), both in June: effective at 7f to 9.5f: acts on polytrack, firm and good to soft ground (seemingly not on soft): successful in blinkers earlier in career: held up. *J. S. Goldie*

BALLYSHANE SPIRIT (IRE) 3 b.c. Distant Music (USA) 126 – Nationalartgallery **62** (IRE) (Tate Gallery (USA) 117) [2007 50: p9.5g⁶ p10g⁴ f8g* p8.6g² p8g² 8.2g Apr 21] tall colt: modest handicapper: won at Southwell in February: stays 8.6f: acts on all-weather and good to soft going: takes strong hold: sold 16,000 gns in July. *N. A. Callaghan*

BALNAGORE 3 b. or br.c. Tobougg (IRE) 125 – Bogus Mix (IRE) 52 (Linamix (FR) **83** 127) [2007 74+: 8g⁵ Aug 18] tall, quite good-topped colt: fairly useful maiden: best effort when fifth to Lap of Honour in handicap at Newmarket only start in 2007, finishing well: will be suited by 1¼m/1½m. *J. L. Dunlop*

BALTHAZAAR'S GIFT (IRE) 4 b.c. Xaar 132 – Thats Your Opinion 48 (Last **121** Tycoon 131) [2007 123: 7g⁴ 7.1g 6m⁵ 6m 6d* 6m⁶ 6d² 6g 7d⁴ Oct 20] tall, good-topped colt: not a good walker: very smart performer: sweating, won H.B.L.B. Hackwood Stakes at Ascot in July by 1½ lengths from Al Qasi: also ran well in 2007 when 1¾ lengths third to Dark Missile in Wokingham (Handicap) at Royal Ascot, close sixth to Zidane in Stewards' Cup (Handicap) at Goodwood (not well drawn) and 1¼ lengths third to Red Clubs in Sprint Cup at Haydock (slowly away before finishing strongly): best at 6f: acts on good to firm and good to soft going (below form only start on soft): held up: has had foot problems and worn stick-on shoes. *L. M. Cumani*

BALTIC BELLE (IRE) 3 b.f. Redback 116 – Skerries Bell 71 (Taufan (USA) 119) **86** [2007 82: p8g⁵ p7g³ 8.5g⁴ p8.6g⁵ 8.3m* 7s* 7.1g³ 9g 8.3d³ p8g Oct 14] smallish, close- **a67** coupled filly: fairly useful handicapper on turf, fair on all-weather: won at Windsor and Lingfield in June: good efforts when third after: stays 8.3f: acts on polytrack, soft and good to firm going: has looked none too straightforward: sold 11,500 gns. *R. Hannon*

BALTIC KING 7 b.h. Danetime (IRE) 121 – Lindfield Belle (IRE) 78 (Fairy King **111** (USA)) [2007 120: 6m⁴ 6m 6d 6d⁵ 6.1m² 5m 6g 6d Oct 20] strong, lengthy horse: very smart performer in 2006 (won Wokingham at Royal Ascot under 9-10): just smart in 2007, unlucky when short-head second to Green Manalishi in listed event at Chester: was effective at 5f/6f: acted on firm and good to soft going (all wins on good or firmer): tongue tied: had been bandaged behind: usually held up: to stand at Tally-Ho Stud, Co Westmeath, Ireland, fee €4,000. *H. Morrison*

BALTIC PRINCESS (FR) 4 ch.f. Peintre Celebre (USA) 137 – Snow House (IRE) **–** (Vacarme (USA) 121) [2007 81: 13.8m Apr 4] leggy filly: fairly useful handicapper at 3 yrs: seemed amiss only start in 2007: stays 1½m (not 15f): acts on firm and good to soft going: sold 30,000 gns in July. *M. Johnston*

BALTIMORE JACK (IRE) 3 b.g. Night Shift (USA) – Itsibitsi (IRE) (Brief Truce **85** (USA) 126) [2007 85: 6g* 6.1d⁴ 7m³ 6g* 6g 6f⁶ 6g⁴ 6m p6g 6v Nov 3] good-topped gelding: fairly useful handicapper: won at Ripon in April and Ayr in June: effective at 6f/ 7f: acts on soft and good to firm going. *M. W. Easterby*

BALWEARIE (IRE) 6 b.g. Sesaro (USA) 81 – Eight Mile Rock 76 (Dominion 123) **62** [2007 66: 12.4m³ Apr 14] sturdy gelding: fair handicapper in 2006: creditable effort only start in 2007: stays 13f: unraced on heavy going, acts on any other: often wears cheek- pieces. *Miss L. A. Perratt*

BALYAN (IRE) 6 b.g. Bahhare (USA) 122 – Balaniya (USA) (Diesis 133) [2007 85: **83** 13.8m⁵ 13m² 13.8m⁴ 16.1s⁴ Jun 28] quite good-topped gelding: fairly useful handi- capper: likely to prove best at 1½m to 2m: acts on firm and soft going: ran poorly only start in cheekpieces: fair form over hurdles. *J. Howard Johnson*

BAMBOO BANKS (IRE) 4 b.g. Indian Lodge (IRE) 127 – Emma's Star (ITY) **55** (Darshaan 133) [2007 73d: 10m⁵ 11.8g Oct 16] regressive maiden. *J. L. Dunlop*

BANANA BELLE 3 b.f. Josr Algarhoud (IRE) 118 – Scurrilous 56 (Sharpo 132) [2007 **48** –: 6v 5.3g³ 5.2m 5g 6g 5m 5.3d 5.7d⁶ Oct 1] leggy, angular filly: poor maiden: raced only at 5f/6f: tried in cheekpieces. *J. Ryan*

BAND 7 b.g. Band On The Run 102 – Little Tich (Great Nephew 126) [2007 65: 8.1d **61** p8.6g p8.6g⁵ 8.1d p10g p9.5g p8.6g Nov 2] strong, close-coupled gelding: modest per- former: effective at 1m to 10.5f: acts on all-weather and any turf going. *E. S. McMahon*

BANDAMA (IRE) 4 b.c. Green Desert (USA) 127 – Orinoco (IRE) 53 (Darshaan 133) **104** [2007 104: 12m⁴ p10g² 12s 9.9g 12m 10m⁴ 10m 12m³ 12g² 12m Nov 10] big, lengthy, good sort: useful handicapper: placed at Kempton, Newmarket (not clear run) and Doncaster (3 lengths second to Night Hour) in 2007: effective at 1¼m/1½m, should stay 1¾m: acts on polytrack, good to firm and good to soft going (tailed off both starts on soft): visored (failed to impress with finishing effort) seventh start. *Mrs A. J. Perrett*

BANDOS 7 ch.g. Cayman Kai (IRE) 114 – Lekuti (Le Coq d'Or 101) [2007 61: p7.1g **51 d** f7g⁴ f7g⁵ 7.1d 8g 6m 6g Sep 3] lengthy gelding: modest performer: left I. Semple after third start, below form subsequently: stays 1m: acts on polytrack, firm and soft going: has been tongue tied, tried in cheekpieces/blinkers. *M. Smith*

BANJO BANDIT (IRE) 2 b.c. (Mar 10) Mujadil (USA) 119 – Common Cause 87 **52** (Polish Patriot (USA) 128) [2007 7m 7d p7g³ Nov 12] stocky colt: maiden: off 3 months, first form when 10 lengths third to Roaring Forte at Lingfield: will stay 1m. *J. S. Moore*

BANKABLE (IRE) 3 b.c. Medicean 128 – Dance To The Top 107 (Sadler's Wells **97 p** (USA) 132) [2007 8d 8m* 8d* Sep 28] 40,000F, 160,000Y: big, close-coupled, good-topped colt: ninth foal: closely related to 1m winner Dress Rehearsal and 1¼m winner Audition (both fairly useful by Machiavellian), and half-brother to 2 winners, including smart French 1m to 10.5f winner Cheshire (by Warning): dam 2-y-o 7f winner (second in Fillies' Mile) who stayed 10.4f: highly progressive form: won maiden at Newcastle and handicap at Ascot (favourite, beat Oceana Gold by a length, confidently ridden and hanging left when leading 1f out, still green), both in September: will stay beyond 1m: already useful, will continue improving. *L. M. Cumani*

BANKNOTE 5 b.h. Zafonic (USA) 130 – Brand (Shareef Dancer (USA) 135) [2007 **112** 100: p8g* 8g* 8.8g² 8m⁶ 8d⁵ p10m Nov 24] smallish, quite good-topped horse: smart performer: improved in 2007, winning listed race at Lingfield in March and Badener Meile at Baden-Baden (by length from Aspectus) in May: creditable efforts after when length second to Soldier Hollow in Grosser Preis der Wirtschaft at Dortmund and 2 lengths fifth to Sabirli in Topkapi Trophy at Veliefendi: stays 8.8f: acts on polytrack, good to firm and good to soft going: took strong hold fourth/final starts: genuine. *A. M. Balding*

BANK ON BENNY 5 b.g. Benny The Dip (USA) 127 – Green Danube (USA) 92 (Irish **82** River (FR) 131) [2007 74: p10g² p12.2g* p13.9g⁶ Nov 8] big, strong gelding: fairly useful handicapper: further improvement when winning at Wolverhampton in October: placed around 2m, best form at shorter: acts on all-weather and good to soft going: sold 20,000 gns in December. *P. W. D'Arcy*

BANK ON BERTIE 2 b.g. (Apr 28) Bertolini (USA) 125 – Piggy Bank 71 (Emarati **–** (USA) 74) [2007 f5g 5m 5m 5f⁵ Apr 20] deep-girthed gelding: no form: dead. *M. W. Easterby*

BANQUET (IRE) 2 ch.c. (Feb 22) Dr Fong (USA) 128 – Barbera 54 (Barathea (IRE) **–** 127) [2007 8d 8d Oct 27] well-made colt: behind in maidens: sold 10,000 gns. *M. R. Channon*

BANTHAM BAY 2 ch.f. (Feb 11) Reel Buddy (USA) 118 – Florentynna Bay 61 (Ara- **–** gon 118) [2007 5m p5.1g 5.7f 7m 7g 7m 8g Sep 20] 10,000Y: sturdy filly: half-sister to numerous winners, including useful miler Sunstreak (by Primo Dominie): dam, 2-y-o 5f winner, half-sister to smart sprinter Superpower: no form: tried blinkered. *B. J. Meehan*

BANTRY BERE (IRE) 3 b.g. Distant Music (USA) 126 – Tirana (IRE) (Fappiano **65** (USA)) [2007 67: 11m p12.2g⁶ Oct 27] tall, strong gelding: fair maiden handicapper on Flat: bred to be suited by 1¼m+: acts on polytrack: sold 20,000 gns, joined N. Twiston-Davies and fair winner over hurdles. *J. R. Best*

BANUS FLYER (IRE) 2 gr.g. (Apr 19) Distant Music (USA) 126 – Gracious Gretclo **–** 54 (Common Grounds 118) [2007 6g 5m Jun 5] smallish, compact gelding: well beaten in maidens: bred to stay 1m. *N. Tinkler*

BARAARI (USA) 2 b. or br.f. (Feb 25) Nayef (USA) 129 – Reem Al Barari (USA) 69 **76** (Storm Cat (USA)) [2007 6m 7g 8.3m² 8.1s Sep 29] leggy, sparely-made filly: first foal: dam once-raced half-sister to Derby winner Erhaab: fair maiden: upped in trip, short-head second to Nowaira at Leicester: will be suited by 1¼m/1½m: acts on good to firm going (below form on soft final start). *J. L. Dunlop*

BARASHI 2 b.g. (Mar 20) King's Best (USA) 132 – Maid To Dance 62 (Pyramus (USA) **–** 78) [2007 7d Jul 22] 25/1, took strong hold and weakened in maiden at Redcar. *J. Howard Johnson*

BARATARIA 5 ch.g. Barathea (IRE) 127 – Aethra (USA) 89 (Trempolino (USA) 135) **66** [2007 59: 9.1d 7g*⁷ 7.9g 7.1g³ 7f 7g 8m Aug 30] quite good-topped gelding: fair performer: won maiden at Catterick in June: stays 7f: acts on heavy going, possibly not firmer than good. *R. Bastiman*

BARATHEA BLAZER 8 b.g. Barathea (IRE) 127 – Empty Purse (Pennine Walk 120) **85** [2007 92: p10g⁵ Apr 1] sturdy, good-bodied gelding: just fairly useful handicapper nowadays: stays 15f: acts on soft and good to firm ground, probably on polytrack: usually races prominently. *K. McAuliffe*

BARATHEA DREAMS (IRE) 6 b.g. Barathea (IRE) 127 – Deyaajeer (USA) 64 **66** (Dayjur (USA) 137) [2007 84, a74: p8g⁵ 10g 9.9g 10m Jun 9] strong, lengthy gelding: handicapper: form in 2007 only on reappearance: best around 1m: acts on polytrack, firm and soft going: tried in cheekpieces. *J. S. Moore*

BARATI (IRE) 6 b.g. Sadler's Wells (USA) 132 – Oriane 109 (Nashwan (USA) 135) **–** [2007 71: 21.7s Jun 23] stocky, good-bodied gelding: useful performer for J. Oxx in Ireland in 2004: well below that form both starts on Flat since: will stay 1¾m: acts on soft and good to firm going: tried blinkered. *B. N. Pollock*

BARAWIN (IRE) 2 ch.f. (Jan 24) Hawk Wing (USA) 136 – Cosabawn (IRE) 57 **83 p** (Barathea (IRE) 127) [2007 6m 8.1s* 8g Oct 26] big, lengthy filly: first foal: dam, maiden, half-sister to useful 1½m winner Ridaiyma out of half-sister to smart Irish performer up to 1¾m Rayseka: fairly useful form: won maiden at Haydock in September, getting up close home: better than bare result when mid-division in nursery at Doncaster: will benefit from 1¼m/1½m: acts on soft ground: will do better. *K. R. Burke*

BARBAR 4 b.g. Anabaa (USA) 130 – Prends Ca (IRE) 98 (Reprimand 122) [2007 7.1m **61** 7m 6g⁵ p6g Oct 31] workmanlike gelding: modest maiden, lightly raced: best effort on third start. *Eve Johnson Houghton*

BARBAROSSA 2 b.c. (Apr 14) Beat All (USA) 120 – Gagajulu 75 (Al Hareb (USA) **75** 123) [2007 6g⁵ 6g³ 5.7g* 6m⁶ 6.1d⁵ 6m p8m Oct 11] 25,000F, 57,000Y: good-bodied colt: eighth foal: half-brother to several winners, including 5-y-o Obe Gold and Irish 7f (at 2 yrs)/1m winner Ardbrae Lady (by Overbury), both useful: dam 2-y-o 5f winner: fair performer: won maiden at Bath in June: little impact (but mostly ran creditably) in nurseries: should stay 7f: yet to race on extremes of going on turf: sold 5,000 gns, sent to Sweden. *R. Hannon*

BARBARY BOY (FR) 2 b.c. (Apr 25) Rock of Gibraltar (IRE) 133 – Don't Worry **79 p** Me (IRE) 113 (Dancing Dissident (USA) 119) [2007 5m⁶ 6d² 6d² Oct 23] €90,000Y: medium-sized, strong-quartered colt: fifth foal: closely related to fairly useful Irish 6f winner Rol'over Beethoven (by Mozart) and half-brother to 2 winners in France, including useful 1m winner Bits of Paradise (by Desert Prince): dam, French sprinter, won King's Stand Stakes: progressive form in maidens, travelled strongly long way when second at Haydock and Yarmouth (to Wingbeat, pair clear): should prove at least as effective at 5f as 6f: remains capable of better. *M. L. W. Bell*

BARBIROLLI 5 b.g. Machiavellian (USA) 123 – Blushing Barada (USA) 53 **75 d** (Blushing Groom (FR) 131) [2007 76: p9.5g⁴ 10.3d² 10m⁶ 9.2m⁶ 10.1g 9.2s³ 10m⁶ 10.2m 12g p9.5g Nov 16] leggy gelding: fair handicapper: below form after third outing: effective at 9f to easy 1½m: acts on polytrack, firm and soft going: tried visored/tongue tied: waited with. *W. M. Brisbourne*

BARBOSSA 2 ch.g. (Apr 14) Bahamian Bounty 116 – Marjurita (IRE) 85 (Marju (IRE) **–** 127) [2007 6.1s p5.1g Jul 30] well held in maidens. *A. J. McCabe*

BARBS PINK DIAMOND (USA) 3 b.f. Johannesburg (USA) 127 – Unsaddled **62** (USA) (Pancho Villa (USA)) [2007 60: 8m 10s⁵ p8g 9.7m⁵ 12g³ 12m² p12g⁶ 11.9m⁴ Sep 25] lengthy, unfurnished filly: modest maiden handicapper: barely stays 1½m: acts on polytrack and good to firm ground: tried blinkered: races prominently. *Mrs A. J. Perrett*

BARILOCHE 4 b.c. Benny The Dip (USA) 127 – Bella Lambada 87 (Lammtarra **– §** (USA) 134) [2007 78: f11g⁴ f14g Apr 3] fair performer at 3 yrs: well below form in 2007: wears headgear: temperamental. *J. R. Boyle*

BARKASS (UAE) 3 b.g. Halling (USA) 133 – Areydha 99 (Cadeaux Genereux 131) **83** [2007 65p: p8g⁴ p8g⁴ 6d² 7m³ 7.5m⁵ 7g 7m Nov 10] fairly useful maiden handicapper: left M. Tregoning after second start: should stay 1m: acts on polytrack, good to firm and good to soft ground. *B. Ellison*

BARLEY MOON 3 b.f. Vettori (IRE) 119 – Trojan Desert 97 (Troy 137) [2007 67?: **–** 8.2m 8g 8m 11.5m Aug 9] workmanlike filly: maiden: little form in 2007. *T. Keddy*

BARLIFFEY (IRE) 2 b.c. (Feb 5) Bahri (USA) 125 – Kildare Lady (IRE) (Indian **74** Ridge 123) [2007 7m⁶ 7f² 7.1m⁴ Sep 13] €38,000F, 25,000Y: good-topped colt: first foal: dam unraced half-sister to useful miler Shaard: fair maiden: runner-up at Brighton and Warwick: will stay 1m: acts on firm going: slow starter. *D. J. Coakley*

BARNABY RUDGE (IRE) 2 b.c. (Apr 30) Danetime (IRE) 121 – Gild (IRE) 80 **81** (Caerleon (USA) 132) [2007 6d² p6g³ a6.5g* a7.5g⁴ Dec 4] €9,500Y, €20,000 2-y-o: good-topped colt: fifth foal: dam, Irish 1½m winner, sister to smart stayer Capal Garmon: fairly useful form: made all in minor event at Deauville in November, beating El Puerto by 1½ lengths: creditable fourth to Traphalgar in similar event there next time: stays 7.5f: has been bandaged near hind: sent to Germany. *Jane Chapple-Hyam*

BARNEY MCGREW (IRE) 4 b.g. Mark of Esteem (IRE) 137 – Success Story 60 **97** (Sharrood (USA) 124) [2007 84p: p8g³ p7g² p7g² 7m⁵ p8.6g⁵ 7m* 6d² 6s 6g* 6m⁶ p6g* 6g Oct 26] rather leggy gelding: useful handicapper: won at Goodwood in June, Newmarket (by neck from Curtail) in August and Lingfield (beat Capricorn Run by ½ length) in October: best at 6f/7f: acts on polytrack, good to firm and good to soft going: edgy sort, has been early to post and given trouble at start: sold 87,000 gns. *J. A. R. Toller*

BARNEY'S DANCER 3 b.f. Iron Mask (USA) 117 – Alcalali (USA) 96 (Septieme **46** Ciel (USA) 123) [2007 49: f8g f7s⁴ p8.6g p12g³ Jun 9] poor maiden: left J. Balding after third start: stays 1½m: withdrawn after bolting intended final outing. *C. L. Popham*

BARODINE 4 ch.g. Barathea (IRE) 127 – Granted (FR) 100 (Cadeaux Genereux 131) – [2007 92: p9.5g Feb 12] leggy, close-coupled gelding: has a round action: well held only Flat start in 2007: stays easy 1½m: acts on firm and good to soft going. *R. J. Hodges*

BARONESS RICHTER (IRE) 3 b.f. Montjeu (IRE) 137 – Principium (USA) **103** (Hansel (USA)) [2007 88p: 10.5s³ 10.5d* 12g⁴ 12.5g⁵ Aug 16] big, lengthy filly: has scope: useful performer: trained by R. Hannon at 2 yrs: won listed race at Toulouse (by length from Misk) in April: ran well last 2 starts when 7 lengths fourth to Silkwood in Ribblesdale Stakes at Royal Ascot and 2½ lengths fifth to Synopsis in Prix Minerve at Deauville, staying on both times: will stay 1¾m: acts on soft and good to firm ground: has been bandaged in front: sent to USA. *J-C. Rouget, France*

BARONOVICI (IRE) 2 b.c. (Feb 26) Namid 128 – Allegrina (IRE) 70 (Barathea **76** (IRE) 127) [2007 6m² 6.1s² 6m* 6s Aug 24] €9,000F, 20,000Y: strong, lengthy colt: first foal: dam 7f winner: fair form: won maiden at Windsor (race worked out well) in July: only seventh in sales race at Newmarket final start: should prove best at 5f/6f: best efforts on good to firm going: sold 14,500 gns. *R. Hannon*

BARON'S COURT 2 ch.c. (Apr 7) Pivotal 124 – Grafin (USA) 113 (Miswaki (USA) **72** 124) [2007 f7d⁴ p7.1s⁴ Dec 21] half-brother to smart US 2003 2-y-o 5f to 1m (Grade 3 event) winner Zosima (by Capote) and French 11f winner Violin Time (by Theatrical): dam, French/US 1m/1¼m winner, half-sister to dam of very smart middle-distance stayer Mamool: fair form when fourth in maidens at Southwell and Wolverhampton, making running in latter. *M. Johnston*

BARON'S PIT 7 gr.g. Night Shift (USA) – Incendio (Siberian Express (USA) 125) **107** [2007 5.2m⁵ 6g 5m² p5g⁶ 6d 5g⁶ 6m 7m 6m³ Sep 16] big, well-made gelding: type to carry condition: just useful in 2007, best efforts on first/third starts, second to Pivotal's Princess in minor event at Beverley latter occasion: probably best at 5f (given test)/6f: acts on firm ground: tried blinkered/visored: tends to swish tail in paddock: often bandaged in front. *E. F. Vaughan*

BARONS SPY (IRE) 6 b.g. Danzero (AUS) – Princess Accord (USA) 115 (D'Accord **84** (USA)) [2007 80: 8d² 8.1m² 8m 7.1s⁵ 8.3m 7d² 6m* 6m³ p7.1g 8.3d 7g Nov 3] lengthy gelding: fairly useful handicapper: won at Warwick in September: effective at 6f to 1m: acts on polytrack, firm and good to soft going: tongue tied at 2 yrs: has flashed tail: often travels well. *R. J. Price*

BARRALAND 2 b.g. (Mar 19) Compton Place 125 – Dance Land (IRE) (Nordance **74** (USA)) [2007 5f⁴ 5f³ 5m* 5m 6g 6v² 5.1s² 6m 6g 5m⁴ 5g⁴ 5.1g 5g⁴ 5.1m⁵ Oct 14] 44,000F, €105,000Y: neat gelding: brother to a 5f winner in Italy and half-brother to several winners, including 2001 2-y-o 5f winner My Dancer (by Alhaarth) and 1m winner Grouville (by Groom Dancer): dam unraced: fair performer: won maiden at Lingfield in May: held form well through busy campaign, mostly in nurseries: best at 5f: probably acts on any going: races prominently: tough. *M. R. Channon*

BARRICADO (FR) 2 b.c. (Apr 11) Anabaa (USA) 130 – Aube d'Irlande (FR) (Selkirk **78 p** (USA) 129) [2007 7g³ Oct 16] €60,000Y: strong colt: fourth foal: half-brother to 3 winners in France, including fairly useful 1m winner Spring Is Here (by King's Best): dam French 1m winner: 9/1 and in need of run, encouraging third to Port Quin in maiden at Leicester, finishing well not knocked about: will stay 1m: sure to improve and win races. *R. Charlton*

BARRY ISLAND 8 b.g. Turtle Island (IRE) 123 – Pine Ridge 80 (High Top 131) [2007 **70** 84d: p10g³ p10g⁵ p10g 11.5g 10.2m⁵ p11g³ p10m p10g⁵ p10g² Dec 30] good-topped gelding: type to carry condition: fair performer: best at 1¼m/1½m: acts on polytrack and firm going: held up (sometimes slowly away). *D. R. C. Elsworth*

BARRY THE BRAVE 5 b.g. Mujadil (USA) 119 – Rakli 84 (Warning 136) [2007 60: **46** p7.1g⁶ f8g Jan 25] just poor performer nowadays: stays 1m: acts on all-weather/dirt and firm ground. *Micky Hammond*

BARSHIBA (IRE) 3 ch.f. Barathea (IRE) 127 – Dashiba 102 (Dashing Blade 117) **110** [2007 73P: p8g* 7m⁵ 8m 8m* 8.1g² 8d⁴ 9.9g 8m 8m⁶ Oct 6] big, lengthy filly: smart performer: won maiden at Lingfield in February and listed handicap at Royal Ascot (beat Selinka by 1¼ lengths) in June: further progress after, best efforts when 2½ lengths fourth to Darjina in Prix d'Astarte at Deauville (saddle slipped leaving stall) and 4½ lengths

Sandringham Handicap, Royal Ascot—Barshiba sweeps through to get the better of Selinka (right); top weight Costume (centre) is third and Italian Girl (striped cap) fourth

sixth to Majestic Roi in Sun Chariot Stakes at Newmarket: should stay 1¼m: acts on polytrack, good to firm and good to soft ground: held up: reportedly has problems with her vision, and has carried head awkwardly/hung left. *D. R. C. Elsworth*

BARTON BELLE 5 b.m. Barathea (IRE) 127 – Veronica (Persian Bold 123) [2007 74:   **53** p12g f11g⁵ 16.2m May 26] fairly useful bumper winner: fair form only Flat outing at 4 yrs for G. A. Swinbank: modest at best in 2007. *C. N. Kellett*

BARTON SANDS (IRE) 10 b.g. Tenby 125 – Hetty Green (Bay Express 132) [2007   **63** –, a68: p10g² p12m* p10g⁴ Dec 22] neat gelding: modest performer nowadays: won minor event at Lingfield in December: stays easy 1½m: acts on polytrack, firm and good to soft going, well beaten on soft/heavy: tried blinkered/visored: tongue tied. *Andrew Reid*

BARZAK (IRE) 7 b.g. Barathea (IRE) 127 – Zakuska 96 (Zafonic (USA) 130) [2007   **51** 57: p8.6g f6g f7g⁵ f7g f8g⁵ f8g p12.2g Jul 6] sturdy gelding: modest performer: effective at 6f to easy 9.5f: acts on all-weather and good to soft ground: usually in headgear/tongue tied: reportedly lame sixth start. *S. R. Bowring*

BASAATA (USA) 3 b.f. Dixieland Band (USA) – Asareer (USA) 71 (Gone West   **108** (USA)) [2007 85p: 10m⁵ 8m⁴ 8d 8.1m³ 9.9m⁴ Sep 16] big, good-topped filly: useful performer: reportedly suffered from a cough in the spring: in frame in listed races at Goodwood and Sandown (¾-length third to Sweet Lilly) and Select Stakes at Goodwood (excellent 1½ lengths fourth to Stotsfold): stayed 1¼m: acted on polytrack and good to firm ground (below form on softer than good): visits Haafhd. *M. P. Tregoning*

BASANTI (USA) 2 ch.f. (Feb 13) Galileo (IRE) 134 – Ozone Friendly (USA) 107   **68 p** (Green Forest (USA) 134) [2007 7g Nov 3] 260,000Y: sparely-made filly: closely related to several winners by Sadler's Wells, including smart 1m winner (including at 2 yrs) Musalsal and useful 1¼m winner Amusing Time, and half-sister to useful French 2000 2-y-o 5f/5.5f winner Ozone Layer (by Zafonic): dam won Prix Robert Papin: 14/1, seventh of 20 to Infallible in maiden at Newmarket, slowly away before staying on well: will be suited by 1m: should do better. *B. W. Hills*

BA SPEEDBIRD (IRE) 2 b.f. (Apr 30) Spartacus (IRE) 107 – Missing Slate (IRE) – (Dolphin Street (FR) 125) [2007 5m 6m p8.6g⁴ Sep 8] 18,000Y: close-coupled filly: second foal: dam unraced: little sign of ability: sold £400. *M. R. Channon*

BASQUE BEAUTY 2 b.f. (Mar 5) Nayef (USA) 129 – River Cara (USA) 86 (Irish **77 p** River (FR) 131) [2007 7s³ Aug 24] 60,000Y: big, rangy filly: has plenty of scope: good walker/mover: sixth foal: closely related to 11.7f winner Rill (by Unfuwain) and half-sister to 3 winners, including 3-y-o Beck: dam French 2-y-o 1m winner: 33/1, promising third of 17 to Kotsi in maiden at Newmarket, doing well to come from off pace: will be suited by 1¼m/1½m: useful prospect. *W. J. Haggas*

BASRA (IRE) 4 b.g. Soviet Star (USA) 128 – Azra (IRE) 102 (Danehill (USA) 126) **93** [2007 95: 8v 8.7g⁵ 12m⁴ 10m 10m² 12s p8g⁶ p10g p8g² p8g² Dec 30] sturdy gelding: fairly useful handicapper: left J. Bolger in Ireland after sixth start: effective at 1m, seemingly at 1½m: acts on polytrack, good to firm and good to soft going: tried in cheekpieces/blinkers/tongue tie. *Miss Jo Crowley*

BASTAKIYA (IRE) 2 ch.f. (Apr 8) Dubai Destination (USA) 127 – Ting A Folie **81** (ARG) (Careafolie 109) [2007 p6g² f6g* 5m Jun 20] €70,000Y: tall, quite good-topped filly: has a quick action: second foal: dam, Group 2 winner in Argentina, half-sister to Argentinian Group 1 winner Campesino: fairly useful form: won maiden at Southwell (by 11 lengths) in June: probably insufficient test when mid-field in 21-runner Queen Mary Stakes at Royal Ascot, and not seen after: will stay 7f. *J. H. M. Gosden*

BATCHWORTH BLAISE 4 b.g. Little Jim – Batchworth Dancer 67 (Ballacashtal **54** (CAN)) [2007 49: p8g 6m 6d 6m 7.1m² 8m⁴ 8.1m p8g⁵ p7g p8g³ Dec 16] angular gelding: modest maiden: stays 1m: acts on polytrack and good to firm ground: tried blinkered. *E. A. Wheeler*

BATCHWORTH FLEUR 4 b.f. Little Jim – Batchworth Belle 100 (Interrex (CAN)) **52** [2007 48: p6g 6g 6s² 6g 6f⁴ 6g 6m 6g p7g³ p6g Nov 28] leggy filly: modest maiden: probably stays 7f: acts on firm and soft going, probably on polytrack: tried blinkered: said to have bled on several occasions, including on final outing. *E. A. Wheeler*

BATELEUR 3 b.g. Fraam 114 – Search Party 78 (Rainbow Quest (USA) 134) [2007 **81** 85p: 6g⁶ p6g 6g⁶ 6m³ 6f³ 5m⁶ 7.1m⁴ 8d Sep 28] good-topped gelding: fairly useful handicapper: stays 6f: acts on firm ground: failed to settle last 2 starts. *M. R. Channon*

BATHWICK BREEZE 3 ch.g. Sugarfoot 118 – She's A Breeze 35 (Crofthall 110) **67** [2007 67: p8g p9.5g 12.6m⁴ 12.1m 11.7d* 11.5g 13.1f⁵ 10m⁶ Sep 25] close-coupled gelding: fair handicapper: left B. R. Millman after second start: won at Bath in June: barely stays 12.6f: acts on good to firm and good to soft ground, probably on polytrack: joined D. Pipe, fair winner over hurdles. *A. B. Haynes*

BATHWICK EMMA (IRE) 4 ch.f. Raise A Grand (IRE) 114 – Lindas Delight 54 **62** (Batshoof 122) [2007 69, a62: p8.6g* p9.5g⁴ p7.1g p8.6g⁵ p9.5g p8.6g⁴ p9.5g⁶ f8g p8.6g p8.6g 10.5m Jun 8] leggy filly: modest performer: won seller at Wolverhampton in January: left P. D. Evans after second start: stays 8.6f: acts on polytrack, heavy and good to firm going: often wears cheekpieces, tried blinkered. *M. A. Doyle*

BATHWICK FANCY (IRE) 3 b.f. Desert Sun 120 – Fleetwood Fancy (Taufan **56** (USA) 119) [2007 63: p8g² p8g 7m 7g 11.6m p8g 9m⁶ 11.9m Aug 8] lengthy filly: modest maiden: stays easy 1m: acts on polytrack, soft and good to firm going: often tongue tied (said to have had breathing problem fourth outing): tried blinkered. *J. G. Portman*

BATHWICK ICON (IRE) 2 b.f. (Feb 3) Xaar 132 – Greek Icon 87 (Thatching 131) **54** [2007 5.7m 7.1m 5.1f⁶ 6d Oct 9] €12,000Y: workmanlike filly: sixth foal: half-sister to 3 winners abroad, including Italian 7.5f/1m winner Icon Painting (by Spectrum): dam 2-y-o 6f winner: modest maiden: should stay 7f/1m: acts on firm ground. *A. B. Haynes*

BATHWICK LETI (IRE) 3 b.f. Trans Island 119 – Brandon Princess (Waajib 121) – [2007 –: p6m Sep 6] well held in maidens 14 months apart: sold £900. *A. M. Balding*

BATHWICK MAN 2 b.g. (Apr 20) Mark of Esteem (IRE) 137 – Local Abbey (IRE) **62 ?** (Primo Dominie 121) [2007 7d 7m³ 7m Sep 22] close-coupled gelding: modest maiden: third at Lingfield after final start: gelded: likely to stay 1m. *B. R. Millman*

BATHWICK ROX (IRE) 4 b.g. Carrowkeel (IRE) 106 – Byproxy (IRE) (Mujtahid – (USA) 118) [2007 –: p8.6g Mar 2] lengthy gelding: modest maiden at 2 yrs: lightly raced and well held since: usually wears headgear. *P. D. Evans*

BATTLECRUISER (IRE) 2 b.c. (Mar 2) Red Ransom (USA) – First Fleet (USA) –
106 (Woodman (USA) 126) [2007 5m 6v 6g 7m p6g Oct 17] strong colt, type to carry
condition: no form in maidens/nurseries: tried blinkered: sold 3,800 gns. *M. Johnston*

BAUER (IRE) 4 gr.c. Halling (USA) 133 – Dali's Grey (Linamix (FR) 127) [2007 98p: **108**
12g 12f² 13.4m* 11m⁶ Sep 21] strong colt: useful performer: further improvement in
2007 (unlucky neck second to Ajaan in handicap at Pontefract second start), winning
listed handicap at Chester in September by 2 lengths from Lundy's Lane: more positively
ridden when well held in Arc Trial at Newbury final outing: should stay 2m: acts on firm
going, probably on soft: can take time to pick up. *L. M. Cumani*

BAUHAUS BOURBON (USA) 2 gr.f. (Feb 19) Behrens (USA) 130 – Southern **72 p**
Tradition (Family Doctor (USA)) [2007 p6g⁶ p8m* Dec 10] sixth living foal:
half-sister to 3-y-o Malt Or Mash and 3 minor winners in US: dam US Grade 3 8.5f/9f
winner: upped in trip, much better effort in maidens 5 months apart when winning at
Lingfield by 1¾ lengths from Nice Wee Girl, running on strongly to lead final 1f: will be
suited by 9f+: tongue tied on debut: open to further improvement. *P. F. I. Cole*

BAUHAUS (IRE) 6 b.g. Second Empire (IRE) 124 – Hi Bettina 96 (Henbit (USA) 130) **73**
[2007 71: 21g 16m Aug 17] lengthy gelding: lightly raced and only fair on Flat nowadays:
stays 21f: acts on good to soft going: tried in cheekpieces/blinkers: fair hurdler/chaser.
R. T. Phillips

BAUNAGAIN (IRE) 2 b.g. (Mar 14) No Excuse Needed 123 – Manuka Honey **55 p**
(Mystiko (USA) 124) [2007 6d Aug 26] €20,000F, 8,000Y: second foal: half-brother to
Irish 7f winner Cornfield Road (by Pursuit of Love): dam unraced half-sister to smart
French 1m/9f performer Lethals Lady: 66/1, mid-division behind Ancien Regime in
maiden at Yarmouth: will improve. *M. J. Wallace*

BAVARIAN NORDIC (USA) 2 b.c. (Feb 21) Barathea (IRE) 127 – Dubai Diamond **81**
(Octagonal (NZ) 126) [2007 7m 7.5g⁵ 7.5g⁸ 8.3d² 8d² Oct 23] 23,000Y: good-bodied
colt: has round action: first foal: dam, French maiden, half-sister to Canadian Grade 1 1m
winner Riviera: fairly useful maiden: second in nurseries at Windsor and Yarmouth: stays
8.3f: sold 65,000 gns, joined Mrs A. Duffield. *E. A. L. Dunlop*

BAVARICA 5 b.m. Dansili 127 – Blue Gentian 96 (Known Fact (USA) 135) **82**
[2007 81: p12.2g⁶ p9.5g² p8g² 9.9m f11g⁵ 10m² 10m³ 10m* 8d⁴ 8s⁵ 10f² 12.3m 10.5g
Sep 7] rather leggy mare: fairly useful handicapper: won amateur event at Newbury
in June: effective at 1m/1¼m: acts on all-weather and firm ground: claimer ridden.
Miss J. Feilden

BAYBERRY KING (USA) 4 b.g. Lear Fan (USA) 130 – Myrtle 96 (Batshoof 122) –
[2007 51: 8.3m 5.9g 8v⁵ 7.1g Jul 9] robust gelding: maiden handicapper: little impact in
2007. *J. S. Goldie*

BAY BOY 5 b.g. Tomba 119 – Gay Reign (Lord Gayle (USA) 124) [2007 89: p8g⁶ p10g³ **80**
p10g⁵ p12.2g² p12g⁴ f12g³ p13.9g 8m 9.1d² 10s* 7.5v² 7g⁵ 8.5g 9.6d⁶ 9.1v 7v Oct 28] **a83**
fairly useful performer: won claimer at Leicester (left M. Johnston, rejoined former
trainer) in June: stays 1½m: acts on polytrack, heavy and good to firm going: effective
blinkered or not. *Andrew Oliver, Ireland*

BAYBSHAMBLES (IRE) 3 b.g. Compton Admiral 121 – Payvashooz 78 (Balla- **69**
cashtal (CAN)) [2007 –: 5f⁶ 7m 6m³ 5d⁴ 6g⁶ 5d⁶ 6f⁵ 5m⁴ 5f³ 6s 5s* 5g⁶ Oct 30] fair
handicapper: won at Redcar in June and Catterick (apprentices) in October: effective at
5f/6f: acts on firm and soft going: sometimes slowly away. *R. E. Barr*

BAY CITY STROLLER (IRE) 3 ch.f. City On A Hill (USA) 114 – Baywood (Ema- **46**
rati (USA) 74) [2007 f6g⁶ Apr 22] €28,000Y: third foal: half-sister to 4-y-o Left Nostril:
dam unraced: 16/1 and green, 10½ lengths sixth to Gold Digger Miss in maiden at
Southwell, outpaced. *A. J. McCabe*

BAY HAWK 5 b.g. Alhaarth (IRE) 126 – Fleeting Vision (IRE) 79 (Vision (USA)) **72**
[2007 79: p10g Nov 17] fair handicapper: should stay 1¾m+: acts on polytrack and good
to soft ground. *B. G. Powell*

BAYLAW STAR 6 b.g. Case Law 113 – Caisson 67 (Shaadi (USA) 126) [2007 83: **80 d**
p7.1g 7.1m 7.1m⁶ 8.3m³ 7.1m* 7.1m² 8.5v 7.1m 6.9m⁶ 7.1s⁵ 8m⁶ Aug 27] sturdy, close-
coupled gelding: fairly useful performer: won claimer at Musselburgh in May: well
below form after next start: effective at 7f to 9f: acts on all-weather, firm and soft going:
tried in headgear earlier in career: front runner. *I. W. McInnes*

BAYLINI 3 gr.f. Bertolini (USA) 125 – Bay of Plenty (FR) (Octagonal (NZ) 126) [2007 **91**
87: 8d³ 7m 7m 8.1g⁵ 8d⁵ 7g⁵ p10g³ p10g* Nov 15] tall, angular filly: fairly useful handi-

capper: won at Lingfield in November: stays 1¼m: acts on polytrack and good to soft going. *Ms J. S. Doyle*

BAY OF LIGHT 3 b.f. Fantastic Light (USA) 134 – Lady Bankes (IRE) 69 (Alzao **63** (USA) 117) [2007 78: 8m 10g⁶ 8m p9.5g Oct 5] small filly: disappointing maiden: sold 2,000 gns. *P. W. Chapple-Hyam*

BAYONYX (IRE) 3 b.g. Montjeu (IRE) 137 – Dafariyna (IRE) 71 (Nashwan (USA) **79** 135) [2007 74p: 12.1g² 12s⁴ Jun 21] strong gelding: fair performer, lightly raced: stays 1½m: acts on heavy ground: gelded after final start. *J. Howard Johnson*

BAY STORY (USA) 5 b.g. Kris S (USA) – Sweeping Story (USA) (End Sweep (USA)) **110** [2007 110: 16g² 12.7d 14g Nov 6] tall gelding: smart performer: trained by M. Johnston in 2005: ran only in Australia subsequently, in frame 4 times, including in Group 2 Perth Cup at Ascot (game ½-length second to Respect) in January: off 9 months after: running a good race in handicap at Flemington in November when breaking near-hind inside final 1f and put down: stayed 2m: acted on good to firm and good to soft going: blinkered last 6 starts in 2005: tended to hang/carry head awkwardly. *B. Ellison*

BAYTOWN BLAZE 2 ch.f. (Apr 3) Zaha (CAN) 106 – Lightning Blaze 58 (Cosmo- **75** naut) [2007 p5g f5g* 5m³ 5.1m⁶ 5g² 5g⁶ 6g 5g p5.1g⁵ Sep 13] tall, plain filly: fourth foal: dam 2-y-o 5f winner: won maiden at Southwell in April: left P. McEntee after seventh start, J. Ryan after eighth: best at 5f: acts on all-weather and good to firm going: front runner: has joined G. Bravery. *Miss K. B. Boutflower*

BAYTOWN PAIKEA 2 b.f. Primo Valentino (IRE) 116 – Mystical Song 68 (Mystiko **47** (USA) 124) [2007 58: p5g⁵ p6g p5.1g⁶ Jan 22] small filly: just poor form in 2007: best at 5f: acts on polytrack, firm and good to soft going: races up with pace. *P. S. McEntee*

BAYTOWN ROSIE (IRE) 3 ch.f. Intikhab (USA) 135 – Masaniya (IRE) (Kris 135) **37** [2007 –: f7g⁴ Jan 11] poor maiden: raced only on all-weather and good to soft ground. *P. S. McEntee*

BAYTOWN VALENTINA 4 b.f. Lugana Beach 116 – Baytown Rhapsody 62 (Emp- **38** eror Jones (USA) 119) [2007 44: 6s 7d⁵ Aug 21] workmanlike filly: poor performer: stays 7f: acts on firm going: often in headgear. *R. Brotherton*

BAZART 5 b.g. Highest Honor (FR) 124 – Summer Exhibition (Royal Academy (USA) **100 d** 130) [2007 10.3m 10.1d 9m 12g 12m Nov 10] rangy gelding: useful performer: left P. Bary in France 70,000 gns and gelded before 5-y-o reappearance: creditable effort in handicaps in 2007 on reappearance only: stays 10.5f: acts on soft and good to firm ground. *K. R. Burke*

BAZERGAN (IRE) 2 b.c. (Mar 12) Machiavellian (USA) 123 – Lunda (IRE) 60 **101** (Soviet Star (USA) 128) [2007 7s 7m³ 7m⁴ 8m⁵ Oct 22] €260,000Y: strong, deep-girthed colt: eighth foal: brother to 7f winner Jakarta and half-brother to several winners, notably very smart 1m (at 2 yrs) to 11f winner Blue Monday and 7-y-o Lundy's Lane (both by Darshaan): dam, maiden, half-sister to Luso and Warrsan: useful maiden: soon stepped up in grade, and improved markedly when 2 lengths fourth of 8 to River Proud in Somerville Tattersall Stakes at Newmarket in October: sweating, only fifth in listed race at Pontefract final start: should be suited by 1m/1¼m: acts on good to firm going. *C. E. Brittain*

BAZGUY 2 b.g. (Jan 27) Josr Algarhoud (IRE) 118 – Ewenny 71 (Warrshan (USA) 117) **77** [2007 p5g 5m⁵ 6m³ 6.1s⁶ p6g 6s 5.5m⁵ p7g p7g p6g* p6g³ p5m² p6g Dec 30] 26,000Y: close-coupled gelding: fourth foal: half-brother to 2 winners, including useful 2005 2-y-o 6f/7f winner Johnny The Fish (by Most Welcome): dam 2-y-o 5f winner: fair performer: won nursery at Kempton in November: best at 5f/6f: acts on polytrack and good to firm going: tried tongue tied, best form in blinkers. *P. D. Evans*

BAZROY (IRE) 3 b.g. Soviet Star (USA) 128 – Kunucu (IRE) 94 (Bluebird (USA) **91** 125) [2007 94: p6g 6m 6m 6m 6s 8m 5g 6m³ 6m⁴ 5m⁵ 6m⁶ p6m² Dec 9] good-topped gelding: fairly useful handicapper: best at 5f/6f: acts on polytrack and good to firm going: effective blinkered/visored or not: none too consistent, and quirky. *P. D. Evans*

BEACON LODGE (IRE) 2 b.c. (Jan 31) Clodovil (IRE) 116 – Royal House (FR) 104 **107 p** (Royal Academy (USA) 130) [2007 6g² 6.5d* 7d* Oct 27] 58,000F, 150,000Y: big, strong, good sort: type to carry plenty of condition: fifth foal: half-brother to several winners, including 5f (at 2 yrs) to 1m winner Royal Island (by Trans Island), Irish 7f/1m winner Sugarhoneybaby (by Docksider) and Italian 2002 2-y-o 7.5f winner Lips Plane (by Ashkalani), all useful: dam, Irish 6f (at 2 yrs)/1m winner, half-sister to smart French/US 9f/1¼m performer Ranger: useful form: progressed fast after debut (very nervy), successful at Newbury in October in maiden and Mountgrange Stud Stakes (Horris Hill,

Mountgrange Stud Stakes (Horris Hill), Newbury—Beacon Lodge looks a smart prospect as he narrowly holds off the strong-finishing Stimulation (checked cap) and Iguazu Falls (centre); Dark Prospector (rail) is fourth

11 ran), in latter beating Stimulation (who met trouble) by head, getting first run over 1f out and holding on well: has plenty of speed, but should stay 1m: raced only on good/ good to soft ground: type to make an even better 3-y-o. *C. G. Cox*

BEAMISH PRINCE 8 ch.g. Bijou d'Inde 127 – Unconditional Love (IRE) 104 – § (Polish Patriot (USA) 128) [2007 15.8s Oct 9] close-coupled gelding: one-time fair performer: tailed off only Flat outing in 2007: tried blinkered: ungenuine. *Mrs S. A. Watt*

BEAMSLEY BEACON 6 ch.g. Wolfhound (USA) 126 – Petindia 65 (Petong 126) 56 [2007 51: p5.1g³ f6g 5g⁴ p5.1g² p5.1g⁴ 5m 5g p5.1g⁵ 8m⁵ 9m³ 8g³ p9.5m³ 8.5g p8.6g p8.6g Nov 2] sturdy gelding: modest performer: stays easy 9.5f: acts on all-weather, probably on firm going: sometimes wears headgear/tongue tie: races prominently. *S. T. Mason*

BEAR BOTTOM 3 b.g. Imperial Ballet (IRE) 110 – Pigeon Hole (Green Desert (USA) 58 127) [2007 p7g p6g³ p7g p8g Dec 16] modest maiden: refused to enter stall prior to intended debut. *W. J. Musson*

BEAR ESSENTIAL 3 ch.g. Rambling Bear 115 – Adar Jane (Ardar 87) [2007 –: f5g 54 p7g⁶ f8g p6g Apr 4] modest maiden at best: stays 7f: acts on polytrack. *Mrs P. N. Dutfield*

BEARNA BHUI (IRE) 4 b.f. Daggers Drawn (USA) 114 – Beechwood Quest (IRE) – 65 (River Falls 113) [2007 46: p10g Apr 30] poor maiden at 3 yrs: well held only start in 2007: should stay 1m. *S. Dow*

BEAT THE BULLY 3 b.g. Ishiguru (USA) 114 – Edgeaway 70 (Ajdal (USA) 130) 65 § [2007 54§: 6.1s³ 7m² 6g 7g⁵ 6f p7.1g Nov 22] unfurnished gelding: fair maiden handicapper: left I. Wood before final start: stays 7f: acts on good to firm going: sometimes blinkered: inconsistent. *D. J. Wintle*

BEAT THE RAIN 2 b.f. (Mar 20) Beat Hollow 126 – Love The Rain (Rainbow Quest 65 (USA) 134) [2007 7g 7m p8.6g³ Sep 3] workmanlike filly: fifth foal: closely related to 3-y-o Raincoat and half-sister to useful 1¼m/1½m winner Quenched (by Dansili): dam, French 11f winner, from excellent family: fair form in maidens, third at Wolverhampton: will be well suited by 1¼m/1½m: sold 32,000 gns in December. *J. H. M. Gosden*

BEAU BRAMBLE 3 b.g. Gorse 116 – Belle de Jour 54 (Exit To Nowhere (USA) 122) – [2007 7.1m p8g p7m p6g Oct 29] good-topped gelding: little form. *C. F. Wall*

BEAUCHAMP TWIST 5 b.m. Pharly (FR) 130 – Beauchamp Cactus 86 (Niniski – (USA) 125) [2007 –: p13g Mar 5] sparely-made mare: modest maiden in 2005: lightly raced and well held since: often blinkered/visored: tried tongue tied. *M. R. Hoad*

BEAUCHAMP VICEROY 3 ch.g. Compton Admiral 121 – Compton Astoria (USA) 97 (Lion Cavern (USA) 117) [2007 92+: p7g⁵ 7.6m 8g Sep 30] tall, close-coupled, good-topped gelding: useful performer: good 2 lengths fifth to Hinton Admiral in listed race at Lingfield on reappearance in March: possibly needed next start 5 months later, shaped like non-stayer final outing: gelded after: stays 7f: acts on polytrack, soft and good to firm going. *G. A. Butler*

118

BEAUCHAMP VIKING 3 b.g. Compton Admiral 121 – Beauchamp Jade 105 (Kala- –
glow 132) [2007 10g p12g⁵ Jun 16] raw-boned gelding: well held in maidens at Newbury
(raced freely) and Lingfield (tongue tied): sold £2,100 in July. *G. A. Butler*

BEAUCHAMP WARRIOR 2 b.c. (Mar 27) Compton Admiral 121 – Beauchamp **62 p**
Buzz 85 (High Top 131) [2007 8g⁵ p8m p10g Dec 12] half-brother to useful 1½m winner
who stayed 14.6f Beauchamp Jade (by Kalaglow) and 1½m to 2m winner Beauchamp
Magic (by Northern Park): dam, maiden (stayed 1m), half-sister to very smart 1½m
winner Beauchamp Hero: modest form in maidens (nearest finish final outing): should be
suited by 1¼m/1½m: open to further improvement. *G. A. Butler*

BEAUCHAMP WIZARD 2 b.c. (Jan 31) Compton Admiral 121 – Compton Astoria **73 p**
(USA) (Lion Cavern (USA) 117) [2007 6m³ p7g⁴ Dec 19] big, strong colt: fifth foal:
brother to 3-y-o Beauchamp Viceroy: dam unraced out of half-sister to Culture Vulture:
better effort in maidens when length fourth to Parisian Gift at Lingfield, still green and
nearest finish: open to further improvement. *G. A. Butler*

BEAUFORT 5 b.g. Yaheeb (USA) 95§ – Royal Blaze (Scallywag 127) [2007 –: p16g –
May 2] tall, good-topped gelding: maiden, little form since 2005: unseated leaving stall
only outing in 2007: refused to enter stall once in 2006: modest hurdler. *Mike Murphy*

BEAU JAZZ 6 br.g. Merdon Melody 98 – Ichor 52 (Primo Dominie 121) [2007 45: 5.2f –
Aug 5] strong gelding: poor maiden: best at 5f/6f: tried in cheekpieces. *W. de Best-Turner*

BEAU MICHAEL 3 b.g. Medicean 128 – Tender Moment (IRE) 78 (Caerleon (USA) **78**
132) [2007 p8g 8m⁶ 10g 9.9s⁶ 12m* p10.7g Dec 5] good-topped gelding: half-brother to
several winners, including 5-y-o Tucker and fairly useful 6f (at 2 yrs)/7f winner Marlo
(by Hector Protector): dam 7f winner: fair performer: blinkered, improved when winning
handicap at Folkestone in July: sold from W. Swinburn 27,000 gns and gelded before
final start: stays 1½m: acts on good to firm going, well held both starts on polytrack: has
flashed tail. *Adrian McGuinness, Ireland*

BEAUMONT BOY 3 b.g. Foxhound (USA) 103 – Play The Game 70 (Mummy's **58**
Game 120) [2007 62: 7.5m 8.3m⁴ 8m 6d² 7s³ 5.9f 9.1s⁵ 9.1v Nov 3] leggy, close-coupled
gelding: modest maiden: left G. A. Swinbank after sixth start: stays 7f: acts on soft
ground. *A. G. Foster*

BEAU SANCY 3 b.g. Tobougg (IRE) 125 – Bride's Answer 81 (Anshan 119) [2007 **86**
64§: p10g³ p7.1g⁶ p10g² p10g⁶ p9.5g* p10g⁴ p11g⁴ f12g³ p9.5g² 10f⁵ 9.7m* 10.2f⁴ 10d
11.7d⁴ 10g⁴ 8.1v* 11.5s³ 8.1g 9g p9.5g 10.3g Oct 26] workmanlike gelding: improved
into a fairly useful handicapper, winning at Wolverhampton in February, Folkestone in
April, and Brighton and Haydock in July: stays 1½m: acts on any going: tried in cheek-
pieces/blinkers: often hangs: sold 30,000 gns. *R. A. Harris*

BEAUTIFUL DANCER (IRE) 3 b.f. Danehill Dancer (IRE) 117 – Beautiful France **50**
(IRE) (Sadler's Wells (USA) 132) [2007 p8g⁵ 8.2m Oct 3] 45,000F, €240,000Y: good-
topped filly: closely related to Irish 2003 2-y-o 9f winner Beautiful Hill (by Danehill) and
half-sister to several winners, including useful Irish 1996 2-y-o 7f winner Beautiful Fire
(by Selkirk), later successful in Hong Kong: dam Irish 9f winner: better effort in maidens
when fifth to Rhyming Slang at Lingfield: sold 16,000 gns. *L. M. Cumani*

BEAUTIFUL MADNESS (IRE) 3 ch.f. Shinko Forest (IRE) – Dosha 47 (Touching **72**
Wood (USA) 127) [2007 68: 7d⁴ 6d⁵ 6m² 6m* 5g⁴ 6f⁵ Sep 17] workmanlike filly: fair
performer: won maiden at Yarmouth in August: stays 6f: acts on firm and good to soft
ground. *M. G. Quinlan*

BEAUTIFUL MOVER (USA) 5 ch.m. Spinning World (USA) 130 – Dancer's **52**
Glamour (USA) (Danzig Connection (USA)) [2007 48: p8g p10g⁶ p10g p10g Jul 3]
sturdy mare: modest maiden: stays 1¼m: acts on polytrack and firm going: tried in cheekpieces. *J. E. Long*

BEAUTIFUL REWARD (FR) 3 ch.f. Diesis 133 – Toujours Elle (USA) (Lyphard –
(USA) 132) [2007 79p: 10m 8.1s⁶ Jun 23] big filly: fair form only start at 2 yrs: disap-
pointing in 2007, found to have irregular heartbeat on reappearance: sold 36,000 gns in
December. *J. R. Fanshawe*

BEAUTIFUL SUMMER (IRE) 4 br.f. Zafonic (USA) 130 – Sadler's Song 54 **60**
(Saddlers' Hall (IRE) 126) [2007 59: p8.6g 8.3g May 11] modest maiden: probably stays
1¼m: acts on polytrack, firm and soft going. *R. A. Fahey*

BEAU TORERO (FR) 9 gr.g. True Brave (USA) – Brave Lola (FR) (Dom Pasquini **64**
(FR) 122) [2007 p12.2g³ p12.2g³ p12.2g p16.5g⁵ p12.2g p12.2g May 21] modest maiden
on Flat: seems to stay 16.5f: raced only on polytrack. *B. N. Pollock*

Prix du Gros-Chene Mitsubishi Motors, Chantilly—
a commentator's nightmare with similar-looking colours for the first four; Beauty Is Truth accounts for
the Lady O'Reilly-owned pair Peace Offering and Moss Vale (left); New Girlfriend is fourth

BEAUTY IS TRUTH (IRE) 3 b.f. Pivotal 124 – Zelding (IRE) 108 (Warning 136) **114**
[2007 105: 7g³ 5m² 5g* 5m 5g 5g Oct 7] angular filly: smart performer: ½-length second
to Peace Offering in Prix de Saint-Georges at Longchamp before beating same rival 2½
lengths in Prix du Gros-Chene Mitsubishi Motors at Chantilly in June: not discredited
after when seventh to Miss Andretti in King's Stand Stakes at Royal Ascot and tenth to
Kingsgate Native in Nunthorpe Stakes at York: stumbled leaving stall and always behind
in Prix de l'Abbaye at Longchamp final outing: speedy, and best around 5f: acts on soft
and good to firm ground: hung right third 2-y-o start, blinkered (off side only) since.
R. Collet, France

BEAUTY SHINE 3 ch.f. Selkirk (USA) 129 – Lines of Beauty (USA) (Line In The **–**
Sand (USA)) [2007 11.1d⁵ 12m Aug 6] third foal: sister to smart 8.5f (at 2 yrs) to 2m
winner Linas Selection: dam US Grade 3 9f winner: well held in maidens at Hamilton and
Ripon (looked ungenuine): sold 20,000 gns. *M. Johnston*

BEAVER (AUS) 8 b.g. Bite The Bullet (USA) – Mahenge (AUS) (Twig Moss (FR)) **65**
[2007 8s 10g⁵ 11.1s⁵ 16s Oct 14] won 3 times up to around 1¼m in Australia in 2002:
fair form in Britain, including over hurdles: stays 11f, not 2m: acts on soft going.
J. G. M. O'Shea

BEAVER PATROL (IRE) 5 ch.g. Tagula (IRE) 116 – Erne Project (IRE) 80 (Project **111**
Manager 111) [2007 101: 6m* 7s⁵ 6g⁶ 6d 6s⁵ 6m⁵ 6m² 6m* 6d⁴ p6m² Oct 6] strong,
well-made gelding: smart handicapper: won at Newmarket in May and Newbury (beat
Genki by 1¾ lengths) in September: good ½-length second to Bonus at Kempton final
outing: stays easy 7f: acts on polytrack, firm and soft going: blinkered sixth start, visored
last 3: tough and consistent. *Eve Johnson Houghton*

BECHARM 3 b.f. Singspiel (IRE) 133 – Zuleika Dobson 106 (Cadeaux Genereux 131) **66**
[2007 68: p9.5g⁶ 10m 7m 8d 7g⁶ Jul 26] good-topped filly: fair maiden: left M. Jarvis
after reappearance: probably stays 1¼m: acts on polytrack and good to firm ground.
A. G. Newcombe

BECK 3 ch.g. Cadeaux Genereux 131 – River Cara (USA) 86 (Irish River (FR) 131) **61**
[2007 58: f8g f8g⁶ p7g 7.9m 8f⁵ 8m⁶ 8.3g⁴ 7g⁶ p8.6g p8.6g p8.6g⁵ p7.1g³ p8.6d* p8.6s²
p7.1d³ p8.6g⁴ Dec 29] good-bodied gelding: modest handicapper: left M. Bell after
second start: won at Wolverhampton in December: stays 8.6f: acts on polytrack and firm
ground: tried in visor/cheekpieces. *W. M. Brisbourne*

BECKENHAM'S SECRET 3 b.g. Foxhound (USA) 103 – Berliese (IRE) (High **61**
Estate 127) [2007 73: p7g 8.2g⁶ 8.3d 7g⁴ 9.9s p8g 7m 8f p10g⁵ 12.1m² p12.2g 11.9g⁶
Oct 25] smallish, close-coupled gelding: modest performer nowadays: left B. R. Millman

120

after tenth start: stays 1½m: acts on polytrack, firm and good to soft going: tried blinkered: has shown signs of temperament. *A. W. Carroll*

BECKERMET (IRE) 5 b.g. Second Empire (IRE) 124 – Razida (IRE) 106 (Last **116** Tycoon 131) [2007 114: 6.5g 6.5g a6f 6f⁶ 7.6m² 6g³ 7m³ 7.1m² 6d 6m 6.1m 7d 6d* 7m⁵ 6m* 7m⁵ 6g⁶ 6d² Oct 20] rather leggy, close-coupled gelding: smart performer: better than ever when winning listed events at Newmarket (by 5 lengths from Balthazaar's Gift) in August and Goodwood (by length from Galeota) in September: creditable 2 lengths second to Greek Renaissance in Bentinck Stakes at former course final outing: stays 7.6f: acts on firm and good to soft going (ran poorly on dirt third start): often front runner. *R. F. Fisher*

BECKY QUICK (IRE) 2 b.f. (Mar 13) Fantastic Light (USA) 134 – Private Bluff **–** (USA) (Pine Bluff (USA)) [2007 6s⁶ Sep 24] €32,000F, 8,500 2-y-o: third foal: dam useful French 10.5f winner: tailed off in maiden at Hamilton. *Garry Moss*

BED FELLOW (IRE) 3 b.g. Trans Island 119 – Moonlight Partner (IRE) 81 (Red **83** Sunset 120) [2007 83: p8g⁴ p8g³ 10.4g 10.1g 8m p8g 8g 8g³ 10.3g Oct 26] sturdy gelding: fairly useful performer: stays 1m: acts on polytrack and firm ground: tried visored: not straightforward. *A. P. Jarvis*

BEDIZEN 4 b.g. Fantastic Light (USA) 134 – Barboukh 95 (Night Shift (USA)) [2007 **87** –: 10m² 8.5m 10d⁴ 10d Oct 1] strong, useful-looking gelding: fairly useful maiden: unlucky at Leicester on reappearance: left Sir Michael Stoute 33,000 gns after third start, poor effort subsequent outing: should stay 1½m: unraced on extremes of ground. *Mrs P. Sly*

BEDOUIN BEAUTY (IRE) 3 gr.f. King's Best (USA) 132 – Manchaca (FR) (High- **47** est Honor (FR) 124) [2007 p8g p9.5g Feb 16] 70,000Y: fifth foal: half-sister to useful 5f to 1¼m winner Strawberry Dale (by Bering) and French 1¼m winner Marguerita (by Sillery): dam, French 9f winner, half-sister to useful French miler Marethea: better effort in maidens when eighth to Silkwood at Wolverhampton second start: sold 10,000 gns in May. *E. A. L. Dunlop*

BEDOUIN BLUE (IRE) 4 b.g. Desert Style (IRE) 121 – Society Fair (FR) (Always **77** Fair (USA) 121) [2007 77: p12m⁶ f11d² Dec 15] strong gelding: fair performer: stays 1½m: acts on all-weather and soft ground: tried blinkered (hung right). *P. C. Haslam*

BEECH GAMES 3 b.g. Mind Games 121 – Dane Dancing (IRE) 68 (Danehill (USA) **63 §** 126) [2007 79: p8.6g⁶ 8.3d⁴ p7.1g⁵ p8.6g⁶ 10d p11g⁴ Dec 19] maiden: just modest form in 2007, leaving E. O'Neill after reappearance: stays 11f: best efforts on polytrack and good going on turf: tried blinkered/in cheekpieces: temperamental. *F. Jordan*

StanJamesUK.com Stakes (Handicap), Newmarket—one of the first winners for Eve Johnson Houghton after taking over her father's stable; Beaver Patrol battles on well from Mutamared (spotted cap) as Grantley Adams leads home Dark Missile on the other side

BEECHSIDE (IRE) 3 b.f. Orpen (USA) 116 – Tokurama (IRE) (Mtoto 134) [2007 –: **57** 5m³ 5m 5m⁶ 5d⁴ 5s⁴ 5g⁴ 5m* 5m 5s 5v³ 5.1g f5d Dec 14] big, workmanlike filly: modest performer: won maiden at Newcastle in September: should stay 6f: acts on heavy and good to firm ground: tried tongue tied: often slowly away. *W. A. Murphy, Ireland*

BEE EATER (IRE) 3 b.f. Green Desert (USA) 127 – Littlefeather (IRE) 107 (Indian **105** Ridge 123) [2007 6m* 6s³ 6s* 6m* 6m* 6d³ Aug 19] good-bodied filly: second foal: closely related to 2004 2-y-o 5f winner Rock Dove (by Danehill): dam, 5f/6f winner (including at 2 yrs), half-sister to very smart miler Marling out of top-class sprinter Marwell: useful performer: progressed quickly to win maiden at Haydock and handicaps at Warwick and Newmarket (2) between June/August, beating Come Out Fighting by 1½ lengths for last success: favourite, only third to Ripples Maid in listed race at Pontefract final outing: reportedly fractured a pastern on gallops in September: raced only at 6f: acted on soft and good to firm ground: tail flasher: looked ungainly: stud. *Sir Mark Prescott*

BEE MAGIC 4 ch.g. Magic Ring (IRE) 115 – Miss Bananas 63 (Risk Me (FR) 127) – [2007 –: f6g² f6g f6g⁶ f5g 6f 6s p5.1g* 5m p6g p5.1g Aug 30] close-coupled gelding: **a51** modest performer on all-weather, little form on turf: won seller at Wolverhampton (edged left) in July: will prove best at 5f/6f: acts on all-weather: blinkered last 5 starts. *C. N. Kellett*

BEE STING 3 b.g. Selkirk (USA) 129 – Desert Lynx (IRE) 79 (Green Desert (USA) **89 p** 127) [2007 8g 10g⁵ 10.3d* Jun 30] 55,000Y: lengthy gelding: fifth foal: half-brother to several winners, including smart 5f (at 2 yrs) to 7f winner Nufoos (by Zafonic) and 6-y-o Neon Blue: dam, 6f winner, half-sister to smart sprinter Watching: progressive form in maidens, winning at Chester by 4 lengths from Soul Mountain, making all and eased: suffered setback after: will probably stay 1½m: should continue to improve all being well. *W. R. Swinburn*

BEE STINGER 5 b.g. Almaty (IRE) 113§ – Nest Egg (Prince Sabo 123) [2007 92: 8m **91** 8g³ 7m p8g⁴ 8.3f p8.6d⁵ p8g⁴ Dec 30] workmanlike gelding: fairly useful handicapper: **a88** stays 1m: acts on polytrack and firm going: tried blinkered/visored. *I. A. Wood*

BEETUNA (IRE) 2 b.c. (Mar 17) Statue of Liberty (USA) 115 – High Atlas 65 (Shirley **80** Heights 130) [2007 7g 7f² 7m⁴ Sep 18] €42,000F, €58,000Y, 40,000 2-y-o: medium-sized, quite good-topped colt: seventh foal: half-brother to fairly useful 7f (at 2 yrs) to 1¾m winner Red Forest (by Charnwood Forest) and 7f to 9.5f winner Tokewanna (by Danehill): dam, ran once, granddaughter of Ribblesdale Stakes winner Ballinderry: fairly useful maiden: neck second to Giant Love at York, standout effort: will be suited by 1m/1¼m: joined E. Charpy in UAE. *B. Smart*

BEFORE YOU GO (IRE) 4 b.g. Sadler's Wells (USA) 132 – Here On Earth (USA) **105** (Mr Prospector (USA)) [2007 107: 10d⁶ 12d³ 12m* 12g Sep 30] rather leggy gelding: useful performer: won 4-runner minor event at Newmarket in August by 4 lengths from Camrose: creditable efforts in handicaps otherwise in 2007, seventh to All The Good at Ascot final start: stays 1½m: acts on polytrack, soft and good to firm ground: below form in visor: has looked tricky ride: has joined Godolphin. *T. G. Mills*

BEFORTYFOUR 2 b.g. (Feb 19) Kyllachy 129 – Ivania 81 (First Trump 118) [2007 **82** 5m² 5m Jun 19] 43,000F, €110,000Y: strong, close-coupled gelding: first foal: dam 2-y-o 5f winner: placed both starts (in June), second in maiden at Ripon then mid-field in 20-runner listed race at Royal Ascot: suffered injury after, then gelded: looks all speed, will prove best at 5f. *M. A. Jarvis*

BEGGARS END (USA) 2 gr. or ro.g. (Feb 23) Mizzen Mast (USA) 121 – Hasardeuse **76 p** (USA) (Distant View (USA) 126) [2007 7g⁶ Nov 2] $16,000Y: first foal: dam unraced out of US Grade 3 7f winner Harpia, herself sister to Danehill: 10/1, gave trouble at start but prominent long way when sixth to Classic Descent in maiden at Newmarket: subsequently gelded: will progress. *E. F. Vaughan*

BEL CANTOR 4 b.c. Largesse 112 – Palmstead Belle (IRE) 79 (Wolfhound (USA) **90** 126) [2007 90: 5f 7f f6g⁵ 6g 6g³ 6d 5s⁶ 6d² 6d* 6s⁶ 6m³ 6d⁵ 5m 7g* 6v⁶ f6d³ Dec 12] **a78 +** leggy colt: fairly useful handicapper on turf, fair on all-weather: won at Pontefract in July and Catterick in October: stays 7f: acts on all-weather and firm going, but suited by good or softer: effective with/without cheekpieces: front runner. *W. J. H. Ratcliffe*

BELDON HILL (USA) 4 b.f. Rahy (USA) 115 – Bevel (USA) (Mr Prospector (USA)) **80** [2007 69: p12.2g² f12g* p12.2g* p13.9g³ f14g* f12g⁵ 13.1m 12.6s Jul 5] quite good-topped filly: fairly useful handicapper: won at Southwell (apprentices) and Wolverhampton in January, and again at Southwell in February: should stay 2m: acts on all-weather and good to firm ground: tried in cheekpieces: sometimes wanders. *R. A. Fahey*

BELGRAVE SQUARE (USA) 2 ch.c. (Feb 2) Hennessy (USA) 122 – Dream Profit **99** (USA) (Deputy Minister (CAN)) [2007 6s⁵ 7m² 7.1m⁴ Sep 1] $320,000F, $400,000Y: good-topped colt: has a quick action: first foal: dam unraced half-sister to US Grade 3 7f winner Final Round: useful maiden: progressive form, second to Latin Lad at Goodwood prior to 7¾ lengths fourth of 9 to Raven's Pass in Solario Stakes at Sandown (left with plenty to do): will be suited by 1m: sent to USA. *A. P. O'Brien, Ireland*

BELIAR (GER) 4 ch.c. Tertullian (USA) 115 – Brighella (GER) (Lomitas 129) [2007 **69** –: 7g 9.5g 13m² 14g 12g 12v³ 16m 12.5m p12g p12g⁴ Nov 19] fair performer: won maiden at Bremen in 2006 (final start for A. Wohler in Germany): creditable fourth in handicap at Kempton final 4-y-o outing: stays 1¾m: acts on heavy and good to firm ground: in blinkers/cheekpieces nowadays. *Eoin Doyle, Ireland*

BELINDA ROSE (IRE) 3 b.f. Namid 128 – Barathiki 81 (Barathea (IRE) 127) [2007 **61** p8g 10d⁶ p10g p6g p6g² Dec 13] tall, unfurnished filly: first foal: dam, 2-y-o 6f winner, half-sister to useful 7f winner Peacock Alley: modest maiden: left B. Meehan after third start: best effort at 1¼m (bred for sprinting): acts on good to soft ground: has looked difficult ride. *E. J. Alston*

BELLA GRANDE 3 ch.f. Primo Valentino (IRE) 116 – Florie Nightingale 60 (Tragic **–** Role (USA)) [2007 6d 6g 7g 6g p7.1g Dec 15] 2,200Y: second foal: dam, 2-y-o 7f seller winner, half-sister to smart 7f/1m performer Sunstreak: no form. *Garry Moss*

BELLALATINO (IRE) 2 b.f. (Mar 18) Modigliani (USA) 106 – Quaver (USA) 74 **50** (The Minstrel (CAN) 135) [2007 p5g⁶ 6g 7g³ 7g 7.6f 5.5m Aug 27] 3,000Y: small, close-coupled filly: half-sister to several winners, including 6f (at 2 yrs) to 8.3f winner Dove Tree (by Charnwood Forest) and 2000 2-y-o 1m winner Steel Band (later stayed 1½m, by Kris), both fairly useful: dam, 7f winner, out of useful sprinter Que Sympatica: modest maiden: sometimes highly tried: will stay 1m. *Mrs Norma Pook*

BELLALINI 4 b.f. Bertolini (USA) 125 – Primum Tempus 49 (Primo Dominie 121) **–** [2007 6g Oct 19] little sign of ability. *E. J. Alston*

BELLA MARIE 4 b.f. Kasakov – Onemoretime (Timeless Times (USA) 99) [2007 49: **–** 5m 8m Aug 4] close-coupled filly: little form. *L. R. James*

BELLAMY CAY 5 b.g. Kris 135 – Trellis Bay 100 (Sadler's Wells (USA) 132) [2007 **116** 118: 10s⁶ 12g 14m 10g Sep 22] smart performer: best effort in 2007 when eighth in Dubai Sheema Classic at Nad Al Sheba on second start: left A. Fabre, France and gelded, last in Irish St Leger at the Curragh and listed race at Fairyhouse last 2 starts: stays 15.5f: acts on soft and good to firm ground. *D. K. Weld, Ireland*

BELLA NATASHA (IRE) 2 b.f. (Apr 19) Intikhab (USA) 135 – Baldemara (FR) **59** (Sanglamore (USA) 126) [2007 p5g⁴ 5g Apr 28] €32,000Y: lengthy filly: seventh foal: half-sister to 3 winners, including useful 5f (at 2 yrs) to 7f winner Tesary (by Danehill): dam unraced half-sister to dam of top-class sprinter Anabaa: better run in maidens in April when fourth to Fat Boy at Kempton. *K. A. Ryan*

BELLAPAIS BOY 3 b.g. Spectrum (IRE) 126 – Denice 106 (Night Shift (USA)) [2007 **–** 49: 11g 9.9g May 9] sturdy gelding: poor maiden: tried blinkered. *T. D. Easterby*

BELLAS CHICAS (IRE) 2 ch.f. (Apr 28) Captain Rio 122 – Persian Light (IRE) 52 **44** (Persian Heights 129) [2007 5g⁴ 5m 6g Oct 3] €3,200F, €10,000Y: tall, close-coupled filly: half-sister to several winners, including fairly useful 7f/1m winner Inch Island (by Turtle Island): dam, Irish maiden (stayed 1m), half-sister to useful miler Bronzewing: poor maiden: best effort (debut) at 5f. *P. T. Midgley*

BELLE BELLINO (FR) 2 b.f. (Apr 22) Robellino (USA) 127 – Hoh Chi Min 103 **62** (Efisio 120) [2007 6s 6d 7d Aug 16] 36,000Y: smallish filly: third foal: half-sister to 1m winner Khe Sanh (by Mtoto): dam 5f (at 2 yrs) to 1m (in US) winner: modest form when mid-field in maidens: will stay 1m. *B. R. Millman*

BELLINI STAR 4 b.g. Fraam 114 – Rewardia (IRE) 66 (Petardia 113) [2007 61?: 10.2f **–** p8.6g Jul 10] leggy gelding: modest performer at best: no form in 2007: often blinkered/ visored: has looked awkward ride. *G. A. Ham*

BELLOMI (IRE) 2 br. or gr.g. (Feb 25) Lemon Drop Kid (USA) 131 – Reina Blanca **88** 102 (Darshaan 133) [2007 6d² 6d² 7m² 7m* 7m Oct 5] 42,000F, 110,000Y: unfurnished gelding: first foal: dam Irish/US 1m/9f winner: fairly useful form: second all 3 starts before winning maiden at Chester in September: stiff task, seventh of 8 behind River Proud in Somerville Tattersall Stakes at Newmarket (pulled hard) final start: will stay 1m: sold 20,000 gns. *M. R. Channon*

Sodexho Prestige Shergar Cup Mile (Handicap), Ascot—Benandonner (nearer camera), under Hugh Bowman, edges ahead of Ace of Hearts to give the Rest of The World victory in the Shergar Cup in front of a crowd of over 27,000, more than on King George day; Bowman also won the individual prize as the Rest of The World scored 86 points, with Ireland on 66, Britain 58 and the Rest of Europe 42

BELOTTO (IRE) 2 b.f. (Mar 12) Peintre Celebre (USA) 137 – Bel 83 (Darshaan 133) **67 p** [2007 p7g⁴ Nov 17] €15,000F: second foal: dam, 1½m winner, out of half-sister to top-class Japanese 1m/1¼m performer Agnes Digital: 12/1, 1¾ lengths fourth of 9 to Mafasina in maiden at Lingfield, keeping on: bred to be suited by 1¼m+: sure to progress. *R. Charlton*

BELSHAZZAR (USA) 6 b.g. King of Kings (IRE) 125 – Bayou Bidder (USA) **–** (Premiership (USA)) [2007 p8g p11g May 9] good-bodied gelding: fair maiden in 2004: well held on return to Flat in 2007. *D. C. O'Brien*

BELVEDERE VIXEN 3 b.f. Foxhound (USA) 103 – Aunt Susan (Distant Relative **58** 128) [2007 p6g⁵ p6g p5.1g* Mar 10] modest performer: won claimer at Wolverhampton in March: effective at 5f to 7f: raced only on all-weather and ground firmer than good: wore visor/cheekpieces last 3 starts: sometimes finds little: sold 5,500 gns in July, resold €22,000 in November (in foal to Diktat). *M. J. Wallace*

BEN 2 b.c. (Mar 4) Bertolini (USA) 125 – Bold Byzantium (Bold Arrangement 127) **73** [2007 p5g⁴ 5.1f⁴ 5g² 5.5d³ 5m³ 6m⁵ p5g³ 5m² p6g⁶ 5m⁶ 5m³ p5g³ 6g Oct 6] sturdy colt: fair maiden: in frame 9 times: best at 5f: acts on polytrack and firm going: visored last 2 starts. *P. G. Murphy*

BENANDONNER (USA) 4 ch.g. Giant's Causeway (USA) 132 – Cape Verdi (IRE) **100** 126 (Caerleon (USA) 132) [2007 88: 8m² 10.1g³ 10m 8.9s³ 8m³ 8m* 8g⁶ 10.3m⁵ 10m⁹m Oct 6] sturdy gelding: useful handicapper: improved form in 2007, won at Ascot (by ½ length from Ace of Hearts) in August: good sixth to The Illies at York next time: below form in Cambridgeshire at Newmarket final outing: effective at 1m/1¼m: acts on polytrack, soft and good to firm going: races up with pace. *R. A. Fahey*

BENBAUN (IRE) 6 b.g. Stravinsky (USA) 133 – Escape To Victory (Salse (USA) **127** 128) [2007 121: 6m* 5m 5g* 6m* 5g* 6g Dec 9]
    Benbaun is some way from fulfilling the role of the proverbial prophet, who was not without honour save in his own country, but virtually all his best form has been shown outside Britain. The first eleven of his thirty-six starts were in Britain,

but the twelfth was at Naas and, since then, eighteen of his twenty-four appearances have been abroad. Only one of the six in that period on home turf has resulted in victory, a minor event at Sandown in 2004, though there have been two second places, notably when going down by a short head to Takeover Target in the King's Stand as a five-year-old. In contrast, Benbaun's nineteen runs on foreign soil include seven wins, six of them at the Curragh, and seven places. The shame of it for British racegoers is that at six he was better than ever, only just behind Sakhee's Secret as the top British-trained sprinter of the year, with four pattern wins to his name culminating in a decisive victory in the Prix de l'Abbaye de Longchamp. Not bad for a horse whose first two successes came in nurseries off marks of 56 and 62.

Given the likelihood of a long season, not ending until Hong Kong in December, Benbaun commenced his latest campaign in one of the Irish pattern events he had not previously contested—the Weatherbys Ireland Greenlands Stakes at the Curragh towards the end of May. Evidence that he had retained his ability came as he forged clear in the final furlong to beat Moss Vale (gave 2 lb) by two and a half lengths. An attempt to go one better than the previous year in the King's Stand Stakes came to nought when Benbaun managed only twelfth of twenty behind Miss Andretti, though a shoe was pulled off during the race, something that had happened to him in the same contest two years previously. With the going at the Curragh regarded as too soft for Benbaun, connections bypassed the Phoenix Sprint there in August. His next stop was supposed to be Japan for a Group 2 then the Group 1 Sprinters Stakes in which he had run respectably when fifth to Takeover Target in 2006. Benbaun did not make it to Japan, with results that may encourage some to believe the old phrase 'It's an ill wind that blows nobody any good'. In mid-August, Japan suffered from its first outbreak of equine influenza for more than thirty years. Thoroughbreds are vaccinated against the illness in Japan but

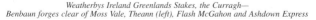

Weatherbys Ireland Greenlands Stakes, the Curragh—
Benbaun forges clear of Moss Vale, Theann (left), Flash McGahon and Ashdown Express

Nolan & Brophy Auctioneers Flying Five Stakes, the Curragh—
Benbaun (left) beats Dandy Man in a downpour to win this race for the third year in a row

racing was still curtailed, with no meetings for a week, and there were no Japanese-trained runners in the Melbourne Cup—Australia was also suffering from an outbreak. While the problem was nothing like so severe as that of 1971, when there was no racing in Japan for nine weeks, any prospect of Benbaun's travelling there and competing, then being returned to Britain, was virtually eliminated. In the event, the Sprinters Stakes was run on soft going, so Benbaun might not even have taken part. As a result of all this, Benbaun took the next best option and lined up for the nine-runner Noland & Brophy Auctioneers Flying Five at the Curragh at the start of September. This was a severe task, in so far as Benbaun was giving 3 lb to the short-priced favourite Dandy Man, runner-up in the King's Stand Stakes; Moss Vale, also in receipt of weight, tried his luck again. Benbaun rose to the occasion, taking over in front from Dandy Man a furlong out and battling on to hold the latter's renewed challenge by a head to record his third successive victory in the race. It would have been four had Benbaun managed to beat Ringmoor Down in the race in 2004 when he lost by a head. Rallying was also the name of the game in the St Jovite Renaissance Stakes on the same course later in the month. A warm order in the market, although giving Moss Vale 5 lb this time, Benbaun led, lost the lead two furlongs out but came again to beat his old rival by three quarters of a length.

With the Diadem Stakes at Ascot ruled out because the ground was perceived to be too soft—it was in fact good—Benbaun took his chance in the Prix de l'Abbaye de Longchamp Majestic Barriere de Cannes, but only after his connections had agonised over the going again. Trainer Mark Wallace explained: 'I was very concerned, but Pat (Smullen) and the boys walked the track and said it wasn't that soft, so we took the chance.' In the event the going was good, so it would have been most unfortunate to have missed this race as well. Although the top sprints, like all others, are gone in sixty seconds or slightly longer, there tends to be a fair bit of continuity in the top contests, which can only be beneficial—in racing familiarity tends to breed enthusiasm not contempt. The Prix de l'Abbaye typified this trait. Seven-year-old Les Arcs and six-year-old Reverence, neither in the form they had shown in 2006, were missing from the seventeen-runner field but, overall, the rest were mostly familiar to the audience. Nine-year-old Patavellian and seven-year-old Desert Lord were previous winners, in 2003 and 2006 respectively. Prix de Saint-Georges winner Peace Offering was also seven, while second favourite Benbaun and his old rival Moss Vale were both six. Five-year-old Tiza had been one of the top sprinters in South Africa before joining Alain de Royer-Dupre, for whom he had landed the Prix de Ris-Orangis in July. Four-year-old Dandy Man was also prominent in the market, which was headed by the two-year-old Kingsgate Native, successful in the Nunthorpe Stakes, and the three three-year-olds—a pretty sorry tally—included Beauty Is Truth (Prix du Gros-Chene) and Hoh Mike (Laurent-Perrier Champagne Sprint Stakes). Ten of the runners were trained in Britain and Robert Collet was responsible for four of the five home-trained contenders, confirming the habitual lack of strength in depth in sprint racing in France. Benbaun led home four other raiders to give Britain its sixth Prix de l'Abbaye in a row and thirteenth since 1990. He won in good style, too. After Beauty Is Truth lost all chance when stumbling at the start, Benbaun chased the pace set by Dandy Man, Desert Lord, Strike Up The Band and Moss Vale, travelling strongly. Taking it up over a furlong out, Benbaun never looked like surrendering his advantage and, although Kingsgate Native tried to reduce the deficit, Benbaun had two lengths in hand at the line, with Desert Lord third, Moss Vale fourth and Patavellian fifth. Kingsgate Native did not quite run to the form he had shown at York—receiving less weight-for-age from the older horses than he had in the Nunthorpe—but Benbaun's was still the best performance by a winner of the Abbaye since Namid in 2000.

The shape of world sprinting underwent a dramatic and beneficial change with the creation of the Global Sprint Challenge, and the levels of prize-money now available in the Far East in particular suggest some of the best European races may suffer because of relatively low prize money. News that the Singapore Turf Club aims to make the Lion City Cup in May an international event with a purse of a million dollars, and the creation of a Breeders' Cup Sprint on turf worth the same amount, perhaps should cause some alarm in Europe, where the money available remains way behind that which can be garnered abroad. The Sprinters Stakes and

Prix de l'Abbaye de Longchamp Majestic Barriere de Cannes, Longchamp—Benbaun gains his first Group 1 win and prevents the two-year-old Kingsgate Native (rail) from gaining an historic double; behind them are the 2006 winner and third Desert Lord (rail) and Moss Vale

Hong Kong Sprint are both worth more than twice the amount earned by Sakhee's Secret in Europe's most valuable sprint, the July Cup, and the absence of a Group 1 event in Europe before Royal Ascot, alluded to in the essay on Dark Angel, is hardly encouraging to anyone with a top sprinter of any age, not just a three-year-old. Mark Wallace mentioned the Breeders' Cup Sprint as a possible target after Longchamp, but Benbaun missed that and it was Sha Tin again for the Hong Kong Sprint, in which Benbaun had finished sixth in 2005 and third in 2006. Unfortunately, starting at 40/1, remarkable odds for a runner of his ability, Benbaun ran no sort of race, finishing over sixteen lengths last of thirteen to odds-on Sacred Kingdom. Prominent to halfway, Benbaun came under pressure over a furlong out and soon dropped back after being squeezed.

	Stravinsky (USA) (b 1996)	Nureyev (b 1977)	Northern Dancer Special
		Fire The Groom (b 1987)	Blushing Groom Prospector's Fire
Benbaun (IRE) (b.g. 2001)		Salse (b 1985)	Topsider Carnival Princess
	Escape To Victory (b 1995)	Gaijin (b 1986)	Caerleon Resooka

Benbaun's sire Stravinsky was also affected by the equine influenza outbreak. He has been shuttling between Japan and the Cambridge Stud in New Zealand but, with the latter country having escaped any sign of the illness, the decision was made to stand him at Coolmore's Hunter Valley stud in Australia for a season, before returning to Cambridge Stud in 2009. Benbaun has now overtaken Soldier's Tale, winner of the Golden Jubilee Stakes, as Stravinsky's best runner in the northern hemisphere. The dam Escape To Victory and her family were covered in detail in *Racehorses of 2006*. To update the story, Escape To Victory's three-year-old Fairy Festival (by Montjeu), a 200,000-guinea yearling, has shown only a modicum of ability in seven races and her two-year-old Woody's Dream (by Hawk Wing) beat only three of her twenty-six rivals in two maiden events at Leopards-town in June. Escape To Victory's yearling filly by Dubai Destination was knocked down to David Wachman for €200,000 at the Goffs Million Sale. Benbaun, a useful-looking gelding who acts on firm and good to soft going, is equally effective at five and six furlongs and is usually ridden prominently. He invariably wears a visor, but those who see these aids as a rogue's badge will be disappointed to learn that Benbaun is as tough and reliable as they come. He is also a credit to his enter-prising connections, and if he maintains his form as a seven-year-old he will once again brighten the season—with luck in Britain as well as overseas. *M. J. Wallace*

BEN CHORLEY 3 gr.g. Inchinor 119 – Arantxa 77§ (Sharpo 132) [2007 79p: f7g May 24] fair form at 2 yrs: ran as if amiss in handicap sole start in 2007: stays 7f. *P. W. Chapple-Hyam*

BENCOOLEN (IRE) 2 b.c. (Mar 17) Daylami (IRE) 138 – Jakarta (IRE) 79 (Machia-vellian (USA) 123) [2007 7d⁵ 8.1f* 8s Sep 22] 110,000Y: good-topped colt: second foal: half-brother to 3-y-o Puggy: dam, 7f winner, half-sister to very smart performer up to 11f Blue Monday: fairly useful form: followed promising debut (fifth to City Leader at Ascot) with a win in maiden at Chepstow in August: possibly unsuited by testing condi-tions in nursery final start: will stay 1¼m: acts on firm going: worth a chance to progress. *R. Charlton* **88 p**

BENCORR (USA) 2 ch.c. (Apr 6) Proud Citizen (USA) 122 – Exquisite Mistress (USA) (Nasty And Bold (USA)) [2007 p6g⁶ p7g⁶ 6s p6g² 8m p7.1g³ p8g⁵ Oct 14] $100,000Y: close-coupled colt: half-brother to several winners in North America, includ-ing smart Canadian Grade 2 9f winner Ready's Gal (by More Than Ready): dam USA 7f minor stakes winner: fair maiden: twice placed in nurseries at Wolverhampton: effective at 6f/7f: acts on polytrack, well held both turf starts: sold 14,000 gns. *M. J. Wallace* **– a73**

BENEATH THE TREES (USA) 2 b.c. (Feb 24) Forestry (USA) 121 – Arabis (USA) (Deputy Minister (CAN)) [2007 7m Sep 3] first foal: dam, US 7f to 9f (minor stakes) winner, sister to very smart US Grade 2 winner Atelier and half-sister to US Grade 1 9f winner Aldiza: 20/1, started slowly and ran green when last of 9 in maiden at Lingfield. *J. A. Osborne* **–**

BENEDETTO 2 b.c. (Mar 25) Fasliyev (USA) 120 – Inchyre 102 (Shirley Heights 130) [2007 p7g 6g⁵ 6m Nov 10] rather leggy, useful-looking colt: fifth foal: half-brother to **68**

1¼m/1½m winner Inchiri (by Sadler's Wells) and 9.5f to 11f winner Whirly Bird (by Nashwan), both useful: dam, 1m winner who stayed 1½m, half-sister to smart 7f/1m performer Inchinor: fair maiden: had 3 runs in quite quick succession, staying on: should be suited by 1m. *Mrs A. J. Perrett*

BENEDICT BAY 5 b.g. In The Wings 128 – Persia (IRE) (Persian Bold 123) [2007 – p12.2g⁶ May 14] sturdy gelding: modest maiden: unraced on Flat at 4 yrs: well beaten only start in 2007: barely stays 2m: acts on soft ground: visored. *J. A. Geake*

BENEDICT SPIRIT (IRE) 2 b.c. (May 3) Invincible Spirit (IRE) 121 – Kathy Caerleon (IRE) (Caerleon (USA) 132) [2007 7s p7.1s³ Dec 21] €82,000Y, 85,000 2-y-o: sturdy colt: fifth foal: half-brother to 4-y-o Khun John and 2 winners in Italy: dam unraced half-sister to smart 1m to 1½m winner High Baroque out of half-sister to Irish 2000 Guineas winner Nikoli: much better effort in maidens when third of 6 to Fadhb Ar Bith at Wolverhampton: will be suited by 1m+. *M. H. Tompkins*   **72**

BENEKING 7 b. or br.g. Wizard King 122 – Gagajulu 75 (Al Hareb (USA) 123) [2007 63: p6g* p7g⁴ p7g⁴ p7f p7g⁶ p6g p8g⁶ p6g* p7g⁴ 7m² 10.2d p8g² p7g³ p7g p7.1s Dec 20] rather leggy gelding: fair handicapper: won at Kempton in January: effective at 6f to 1m: acts on polytrack and good to firm going: tried blinkered, usually wears cheekpieces. *D. Burchell*   **65**

BENELLINO 4 b.g. Robellino (USA) 127 – Benjarong 50 (Sharpo 132) [2007 8d³ 10.2g 8f⁵ p12g Sep 12] little form. *R. M. Stronge*   **–**

BENHAVIS 2 b.c. (Mar 19) Lomitas 129 – Northern Goddess 111 (Night Shift (USA)) [2007 6g 7.1g³ 7f³ 8g⁵ 9d² 8g* Oct 19] 32,000Y: smallish, compact colt: half-brother to several winners, including smart performer in France/US up to 1½m Northern Quest (by Rainbow Quest): dam sprinter: fairly useful form: generally progressive, won maiden at Redcar (made all): will stay 1¼m/1½m: acts on firm and good to soft going: said to have had breathing problem fourth start, and tongue tied after. *J. L. Dunlop*   **82**

BENITEZ BOND 2 ch.c. (Apr 15) Bahamian Bounty 116 – Triple Tricks (IRE) 70 (Royal Academy (USA) 130) [2007 6m Sep 10] detached in maiden at Newcastle: bred to prove best up to 1m. *G. R. Oldroyd*   **–**

BENLLECH 3 b.g. Lujain (USA) 119 – Four Legs Good (IRE) 58 (Be My Guest (USA) 126) [2007 87: 6d 7.1g⁶ p8g⁴ p8g p7m p7.1g⁴ p6g* Dec 30] close-coupled gelding: has a round action: fair performer: won claimer at Lingfield (joined M. Wigham) in December: best up to 7f: acts on polytrack, good to firm and good to soft going: once tongue tied. *S. Kirk*   **76**

BENNY THE BAT 3 gr.g. Victory Note (USA) 120 – Little Emily 48 (Zafonic (USA) 130) [2007 77: p8g⁴ 8.5g p10g 11.9m 14.1s 14.1d Aug 16] good-topped gelding: fair handicapper: left H. Morrison after fourth start: best form around 1m: acts on polytrack: tried blinkered: twice unruly in stall: often pulls hard, and is one to treat with caution: sold £850. *K. O. Cunningham-Brown*   **73 §**

BENNY THE BUS 5 b.g. Komaite (USA) – Amy Leigh (IRE) 78 (Imperial Frontier (USA) 112) [2007 68: p6g f7g p7.1g² p7.1g p7.1g 8.2s p7.1g⁴ p7.1g* p7.1g³ p7.1g⁴ 8.1g p7.1g p7.1g Oct 12] strong gelding: fair handicapper: won at Wolverhampton in June: stays 7f: acts on all-weather and good to firm ground: has worn cheekpieces: races prominently: sold 6,000 gns. *Mrs G. S. Rees*   **65**

BENNY THE RASCAL (IRE) 5 b.g. Benny The Dip (USA) 127 – Bolshoi Star 65§ (Soviet Star (USA) 128) [2007 –: f11g³ Mar 6] maiden, lightly raced: third in seller sole start in 2007: stays 11f. *J. Pearce*   **62**

BENS GEORGIE (IRE) 5 ch.m. Opening Verse (USA) 126 – Peperonata (IRE) 91 (Cyrano de Bergerac 120) [2007 77: p7.1g³ p6g⁴ p7.1g³ 6m p6g⁵ 6s³ 6v² 7.6g p7.1g² p6m 6d³ p7g p7.1s* Dec 20] good-quartered mare: fair handicapper: won at Wolverhampton in December: effective at 6f/7f: acts on polytrack, heavy and good to firm going: tried visored: sometimes awkwardly away. *D. K. Ivory*   **65**

BENTLEY 3 b.g. Piccolo 121 – April Lee 70 (Superpower 113) [2007 50: p6g³ f5g² p6g* p6g⁴ f5g* p5.1g* p5g⁶ 5m⁶ p6g² p6g⁴ 5d⁴ p6g 5.7g⁵ 6m⁵ 5d 6d p6g f6d³ p5.1g² Dec 31] sturdy gelding: fair handicapper: won at Wolverhampton in January, and Southwell and Wolverhampton in February: effective at 5f, should stay 7f: acts on all-weather and good to soft going: visored: sometimes races prominently: takes plenty of driving: quirky and one to treat with caution. *D. Shaw*   **67 §**

BENTLEY BISCUIT (AUS) 6 ch.g. Peintre Celebre (USA) 137 – Tycoon Joy (AUS) (Last Tycoon 131) [2007 5.5d⁴ 6v* 7d* 6g* 5m 6m 6.5m Aug 5] tall, strong gelding: **122**

developed into a very smart performer: unbeaten in his first 8 starts, in 2005 and early-2006: continued progress in first half of 2007, winning 3 Group 1s, namely T. J. Smith Stakes and All-Aged Stakes, both at Randwick in April, and BTC Cup at Doomben (by short neck from Takeover Target, despite slow start and being squeezed out early) in May: well below best on good to firm ground all 3 starts in Europe, in King's Stand Stakes at Royal Ascot (reportedly jarred up), July Cup at Newmarket (tenth behind Sakhee's Secret) and Prix Maurice de Gheest at Deauville (seventh to Marchand d'Or): effective at 5.5f to 1m: acts on heavy going. *Gai Waterhouse, Australia*

BENTLEY BROOK (IRE) 5 ch.g. Singspiel (IRE) 133 – Gay Bentley (USA) (River- **73** man (USA) 131) [2007 73d: f14g5 p9.5g5 9.7m p12.2g4 p12.2g5 f12d* f12g* Dec 27] workmanlike gelding: fair handicapper: won twice at Southwell in December: stays 1½m: acts on all-weather, good to firm and good to soft going: tried blinkered/tongue tied: waited with. *P. A. Blockley*

BENTONG (IRE) 4 b.g. Anabaa (USA) 130 – Miss Party Line (USA) (Phone Trick **107** (USA)) [2007 110: 6m 6m2 6d 7m 6m Aug 4] tall, good-bodied gelding: useful handicapper: creditable effort in 2007 only when head second to Dingaan at Goodwood second outing: has won at 7f, best form at 6f: acts on firm going: tongue tied: free-going sort. *P. F. I. Cole*

BENWILT BREEZE (IRE) 5 b.g. Mujadil (USA) 119 – Image of Truce (IRE) (Brief **109** Truce (USA) 126) [2007 103: 5g5 5m 5.8d5 5d* 6.3s 5s2 p6g2 5m 6d2 6d3 5g3 6d Oct 21] quite good-topped gelding: useful performer: won handicap at Navan in June: several creditable placed efforts after, including when runner-up in handicaps at Tipperary and Dundalk (beaten short head by Rainbow Rising) and Ayr Gold Cup (neck behind Advanced, hanging right): respectable third in listed races at the Curragh and Tipperary after, but well below form back in handicap company final start: effective at 5f/6f: acts on polytrack, firm and soft ground (below form on heavy): in cheekpieces third outing: usually tongue tied. *G. M. Lyons, Ireland*

BERBATOV 3 b.g. Alhaarth (IRE) 126 – Neptunalia 70 (Slip Anchor 136) [2007 60: **52** p7.1g 8.1v 7.9m 10.3m6 8.5g3 Aug 16] big, strong gelding: modest maiden handicapper: bred to stay 1¼m: acts on fibresand: held up (has taken strong hold). *Paul Green*

BERBICE (IRE) 2 gr.c. (Mar 13) Acclamation 118 – Pearl Bright (FR) 80 (Kaldoun **99** (FR) 122) [2007 6g3 6g4 6g* 6g4 6m3 6d2 Oct 3] 70,000F, 43,000Y: tall, close-coupled colt: second foal: dam 7f winner: useful performer: won maiden at Goodwood in June: in frame all other starts, length third of 6 to Dark Angel in Mill Reef Stakes at Newbury penultimate one: raced at 6f: acts on good to firm and good to soft going: tends to look awkward under pressure. *R. Hannon*

BERE DAVIS (FR) 2 gr.g. (Jan 28) Verglas (IRE) 118 – Zerelda (Exhibitioner 111) **80** [2007 6m* 6m 6s5 Jul 2] 28,000F, €90,000Y: sturdy, close-coupled gelding: has a round action: half-brother to several winners abroad: dam French 7f/1m winner: fairly useful form: 25/1, winning debut in maiden at Haydock (hung left) in June: stiff tasks after, and further signs of temperament: will stay 7f. *P. D. Evans*

BERESFORD LADY 3 b.f. Presidium 124 – Coney Hills 35 (Beverley Boy 99) [2007 **53** 7.5g 8.5s4 7g 8d5 p8g6 p9.5g6 p12g Nov 16] leggy filly: fourth foal: sister to 2003 2-y-o 5f winner Fitzwarren: dam maiden (stayed 7f): modest maiden: stays 9.5f: acts on polytrack and soft ground: tried in cheekpieces. *A. D. Brown*

BERGONZI (IRE) 3 ch.g. Indian Ridge 123 – Lady Windley (Baillamont (USA) 124) **93** [2007 80p: 10m* 10g2 12.3m2 11.6g* 10.1g6 12d 12m3 11d2 Sep 26] rangy gelding: fairly useful performer: won maiden at Leicester in April and handicap at Windsor in May: good efforts when placed in handicaps last 2 starts (visored final one): stays easy 1½m: acts on polytrack, good to firm and good to soft going: consistent: sold 140,000 gns, then gelded. *J. H. M. Gosden*

BERINGOER (FR) 4 ch.g. Bering 136 – Charmgoer (USA) (Nureyev (USA) 131) **–** [2007 9g a8f 8g 8m Jun 20] lengthy gelding: first foal: dam, French 13f winner, half-sister to high-class US Grade 1 1¼m winner Dare And Go: useful performer in France at 2/3 yrs for A. Fabre: no form in handicaps in 2007: bred to stay 1¼m: acts on good to firm and good to soft going: tried tongue tied: sold 12,500 gns in July, sent to Greece. *A. M. Balding*

BERKHAMSTED (IRE) 5 b.g. Desert Sun 120 – Accounting (Sillery (USA) 122) **79** [2007 83: p10g2 p10g p10g6 Jan 27] strong, good-topped gelding: good mover: one-time useful performer, fair in 2007: stayed 1½m: acted on polytrack and heavy ground, probably on firm: tried visored/blinkered/tongue tied: joined Evan Williams 12,000 gns, placed over fences in April: dead. *Tom Dascombe*

BERLIN BUNKER (IRE) 6 b.g. Right Win (IRE) 119 – Venture To Heaven (IRE) **52** (The Parson 119) [2007 p12.2g⁶ Apr 27] fair winning hurdler/winning pointer: 8/1, sixth in apprentice seller at Wolverhampton on Flat debut (claimed £6,400, and joined L. Dace): broke down over hurdles following month: dead. *B. Ellison*

BERMACHA 2 ch.f. (Mar 5) Bertolini (USA) 125 – Machaera (Machiavellian (USA) **81** 123) [2007 6g⁵ p6g 6f⁶ p6g⁴ p8g³ p8m² p8.6g² p8.6g* Oct 25] 23,000Y: rather unfurnished filly: seventh foal: half-sister to 4 winners, including 3-y-o Squadron and Irish 7f winner Megec Bliss (by Soviet Star): dam unraced half-sister to smart sprinters Russian Bond and Snaadee: fairly useful performer: placed 3 times (including in nurseries) prior to winning weak maiden at Wolverhampton by 7 lengths: stays 8.6f: raced mainly on polytrack. *W. R. Muir*

BERMUDA BEAUTY (IRE) 4 b.f. Elnadim (USA) 128 – Believing 74 (Belmez **–** (USA) 131) [2007 45: p5.1g p6g Feb 12] leggy filly: poor performer at 3 yrs: well held in sellers in 2007: stays 7f: acts on polytrack, firm and good to soft going: blinkered final outing. *J. M. Bradley*

BERNABEU (IRE) 5 b.g. Mark of Esteem (IRE) 137 – Snow Ballet (IRE) (Sadler's **63** Wells (USA) 132) [2007 –: p12g³ p7.1g p10g* p12.2d* p12g² Dec 12] modest performer: left C. O'Brien in Ireland and gelded prior to reappearance: won minor event at Lingfield in November and handicap at Wolverhampton in December: stays 1½m: acts on polytrack and soft ground: blinkered final start at 4 yrs. *S. Curran*

BERNASCONI (USA) 3 b.g. Rahy (USA) 115 – Argentina (USA) (Storm Cat (USA)) **99** [2007 p7.1g⁴ f6g⁴ 8f³ 8f⁶ a9f* 8f³ a8f³ Aug 20] 11,500 2-y-o: first foal: dam, US 2-y-o 6f winner, out of US Grade 3 2-y-o 8.5f winner Gold Sunrise: useful form: won maiden at Southwell in February (gelded after, then left G. A. Swinbank) and allowance race at Hollywood in June: third after in non-graded stakes and allowance optional claimer, both at Del Mar: stays 9f: acts on fibresand/dirt and firm going. *P. Gallagher, USA*

BERNIX 5 gr.g. Linamix (FR) 127 – Bernique (USA) (Affirmed (USA)) [2007 10.1m⁶ **70** 8.5m³ 12f² 12m⁵ 12g Jun 1] modest maiden hurdler: fair form on Flat: should stay 1¾m: acts on firm ground: first tongue tied. *T. D. Easterby*

BERRY BABY (IRE) 2 b.f. (Mar 4) Rainbow Quest (USA) 134 – Inchberry 110 **61 p** (Barathea (IRE) 127) [2007 7.1g 7.1g⁶ p8m⁵ Nov 26] first foal: dam, disqualified 2-y-o 1m winner (fourth in Oaks), out of useful half-sister to smart 7f/1m performer Inchinor: easily best effort in maidens when fifth (behind Jaser) at Lingfield: will be suited by 1¼m/ 1½m: open to further improvement. *G. A. Butler*

BERRY HILL LASS (IRE) 3 b.f. Alhaarth (IRE) 126 – Gold Mist 85 (Darshaan 133) **66** [2007 10m⁵ 12.1s⁴ 10d³ 10g 12.1m Sep 13] €15,000Y: leggy filly: fifth foal: dam, 1¼m and 1¾m winner, sister to useful Irish/French 1½m performer Shandon Lake: fair maiden: stays 1½m: acts on soft and good to firm going. *J. G. M. O'Shea*

BERRYMEAD 2 br.f. (Mar 29) Killer Instinct 111 – Mill End Quest 65 (King's Signet **61** (USA) 110) [2007 5m⁴ f5g⁴ 6m⁵ 6g⁶ p6g⁶ 7d Oct 29] 3,000Y: neat filly: fourth foal: dam 5f (at 2 yrs)/6f winner: modest maiden: should stay 7f: acts on good to firm going. *M. W. Easterby*

BERRYNARBOR 2 b.f. (Feb 16) Tobougg (IRE) 125 – River Art (USA) (Irish River **59** (FR) 131) [2007 6s⁶ 7g 8g p7.1g* Nov 20] smallish, sturdy filly: third foal: half-sister to Italian 1¼m (including at 2 yrs) winner Sinart (by Singspiel): dam, ran once in France, half-sister to useful stayer Allegan: modest form: won claimer at Wolverhampton: will stay 1¼m. *A. G. Newcombe*

BERS TREASURE (IRE) 4 b.f. Tagula (IRE) 116 – City Imp (IRE) 74 (Mac's Imp **45** (USA) 116) [2007 11.9s 9d 6.5d⁶ 5m p6g Nov 19] €900 3-y-o: sturdy filly: fourth foal: half-sister to Irish 10.5f to 1½m winner Peak Fare (Sri Pekan) and Irish 6f winner Vicky Lane (by Victory Note): dam Irish 9f winner: poor maiden: ran respectably at Wolverhampton final start: tried tongue tied. *Seamus Fahey, Ireland*

BERTBRAND 2 b.c. (Feb 6) Bertolini (USA) 125 – Mi Amor (IRE) 47 (Alzao (USA) **65** 117) [2007 8g p7g p7g⁴ p6g⁴ p6d⁶ Dec 28] fair maiden: debut at Milan for A. & G. Botti: should prove best up to 7f: acts on polytrack. *M. Botti*

BERTI BERTOLINI 4 b.g. Bertolini (USA) 125 – Cosmic Countess (IRE) 74 (Lahib **64** (USA) 129) [2007 –: f6g p6g² p6g⁴ p6g Sep 28] sturdy gelding: modest maiden: raced mainly at 6f: acts on polytrack. *Rae Guest*

BERTIE BEAR 4 b.c. Bertolini (USA) 125 – Philarmonique (FR) (Trempolino (USA) **–** 135) [2007 42: 6g May 31] poor maiden: stays 7f: acts on polytrack and good to firm ground: blinkered/visored in 2006: tried tongue tied. *G. G. Margarson*

BERTIES BROTHER 4 ch.g. Forzando 122 – Sweets (IRE) (Persian Heights 129) – [2007 –, a45: p8g p8g Jan 14] lengthy gelding: poor performer: no form in 2007: stays 7f: acts on polytrack. *D. G. Bridgwater*

BERTIES GOODENOUGH 2 b.g. (May 10) Bertolini (USA) 125 – Goodenough **48 §** Girl (Mac's Imp (USA) 116) [2007 5.1g 5.7g 6f 6d 5.1g p6g⁵ p5.1g Nov 30] rather leggy gelding: poor maiden, none too keen. *Andrew Turnell*

BERTIE SOUTHSTREET 4 b. or br.g. Bertolini (USA) 125 – Salvezza (IRE) 97 **83** (Superpower 113) [2007 83: p6g⁵ 7f p6g² p6g p6g⁶ p7g Dec 28] leggy gelding: fairly useful handicapper: should stay 7f: acts on polytrack and firm going. *J. R. Best*

BERTIE SWIFT 3 b.g. Bertolini (USA) 125 – Hollybell 87§ (Beveled (USA)) [2007 – 70: p6g² p6g² p6g² p7g 6.1m 6g Jun 23] sturdy gelding: fair maiden: should stay 7f: acts **a68** on polytrack and good to firm going. *J. Gallagher*

BERTIE VISTA 2 b.g. (Apr 12) Bertolini (USA) 125 – Off Camera (Efisio 120) [2007 **63** 6s 6m⁶ Sep 1] good-bodied gelding: better run in maidens when sixth to Crystany at Ripon, then gelded: will stay 7f. *T. D. Easterby*

BERTOLIVER 3 b.g. Bertolini (USA) 125 – Calcavella 75 (Pursuit of Love 124) [2007 **96** 81: 6g⁶ 5g* 5m* 5d 6m⁵ 5.2m p5.1g⁶ p6g³ 5g⁶ Oct 27] good-topped gelding: useful handicapper: made all at Windsor in May and Sandown in June: good efforts last 3 starts: stays easy 6f: acts on polytrack and good to firm going: gelded after final start. *D. K. Ivory*

BERTRADA (IRE) 3 b.f. King Charlemagne (USA) 120 – Goldenfort Queen (IRE) – (Distinctly North (USA) 115) [2007 51: p6g⁴ f8g² f8g² p8.6g f8g p10g⁴ 9.7g p10g 10g **a54** Oct 8] angular filly: modest maiden: left H. Morrison after sixth outing: probably stays 1¼m: acts on all-weather: tried blinkered/visored. *G. P. Enright*

BERT'S MEMORY 3 b.f. Bertolini (USA) 125 – Meg's Memory (IRE) 59 (Super- **62** lative 118) [2007 69: p8.6g 7.1s 9.1s 7g* 9.1s 7d⁶ p7.1g p8.6g⁶ f8d⁵ Dec 20] workmanlike filly: modest performer: won selling handicap at Leicester in October: stays 1m: acts on fibresand and any turf going: usually wears cheekpieces: has sweated up. *K. A. Ryan*

BESEECH (IRE) 3 b.f. Danehill (USA) 126 – Francfurter 89 (Legend of France (USA) – 124) [2007 10.5g May 12] big, strong, angular filly: half-sister to several winners, not- ably smart 7f (at 2 yrs) to 1¼m (E. P. Taylor Stakes) winner Fraulein (by Acatenango): dam 1¼m winner: 20/1, well held in maiden at Haydock: sold privately after. *B. J. Meehan*

BESHAIRT 3 b.f. Silver Wizard (USA) 117 – Irja (Minshaanshu Amad (USA) 91§) **46** [2007 –: 8d 8g p12.2g Jul 16] poor maiden: seems to stay 1½m. *D. Burchell*

BESI 5 b.g. Lavirco (GER) 125 – Brangane (IRE) (Anita's Prince 126) [2007 a7.5g³ **66** a8.5g a7.5g* a7.5g* 8d² 8d² 8.5g⁴ 9.2g 10.1m Jun 2] won 3 times in Germany, including in handicaps at Neuss in February and April: left U. Stoltefuss, tailed off in similar events in Britain: has form up to 9.4f, raced mainly around 1m: acts on sand, raced mainly on good going or softer. *P. Monteith*

BESPOKE BOY 2 b.c. (Jan 30) Acclamation 118 – Milly Fleur 67 (Primo Dominie **96 d** 121) [2007 6g* 6g² 5m 5g 5d⁶ Sep 17] 34,000F, 45,000Y: small, sturdy colt: first foal: dam, 6f winner, out of close relative to very smart sprinter Prince Sabo: useful performer: won maiden at Ripon in May: fine length second to Declaration of War in listed race at Epsom next time, but not so good after: speedy, raced at 5f/6f. *P. C. Haslam*

BESSEMER (JPN) 6 b.g. Carnegie (IRE) 129 – Chalna (Darshaan 133) **66** [2007 84: p7.1g p7.1g* p7g³ 7m 9.9m³ 9.1g p7.1g Jun 25] rangy gelding: just fair per- former in 2007: won seller at Wolverhampton in January (sold from D. Carroll 7,000 gns): effective at 7f to 1¼m: acts on all-weather, firm and soft ground: usually visored/in cheekpieces (not final start): effective tongue tied or not: waited with. *I. W. McInnes*

BEST ALIBI (IRE) 4 b.c. King's Best (USA) 132 – Chauncy Lane (IRE) 90 (Sadler's **113** Wells (USA) 132) [2007 117: 12g⁶ 12g 10.4d³ Oct 12] big, good-topped colt: has a fluent, round action: smart performer: not discredited when sixth to Quijano in Dubai City of Gold Stakes and tenth to Vengeance of Rain in Dubai Sheema Classic at Nad Al Sheba first 2 starts in 2007: below form when third to Fairmile in minor event at York final outing: stays 1½m: acts on firm and soft going. *Saeed bin Suroor*

BEST LEAD 8 b.g. Distant Relative 128 – Bestemor 60 (Selkirk (USA) 129) [2007 –: **60** f5g⁴ f6g* f6g³ f6g f6g f6g May 15] leggy gelding: modest performer: won handicap at Southwell in February: best at 5f/6f: acts on all-weather, unraced on turf in 2006/7: tried visored, blinkered nowadays. *Ian Emmerson*

BEST NAME 4 b.c. King's Best (USA) 132 – Flawly 106 (Old Vic 136) [2007 123: 9g⁴ **117**
8.9g Mar 31] strong, lengthy colt: very smart performer for R. Collet at 3 yrs: easily
better effort in 2007 when 1¼ lengths fourth to Seihali in Jebel Hatta at Nad Al Sheba on
reappearance: ran poorly in Dubai Duty Free next time: suffered arthritis and given time
off after: suited by further than 9f and stays 1½m: acts on good to firm and good to soft
going. *Saeed bin Suroor*

BEST OF GOLD (IRE) 3 b.c. Montjeu (IRE) 137 – Penny Fan 58 (Nomination 125) **56**
[2007 8.1m 10.2g 12.1g⁴ May 28] good-topped colt: modest maiden: stays 1½m: blinkered
final outing: sold 5,500 gns in July. *B. J. Meehan*

BEST OF THE LOT (USA) 5 b.g. Lear Fan (USA) 130 – Aerosilver (USA) (Re- **71**
launch (USA)) [2007 77: 13m 15d 10.1m* 10.1v⁶ 9.2m 10.1g 12m³ 12f 9.2s Sep 24] fair
handicapper: won at Newcastle in June: effective at 1¼m to 1¾m: acts on good to firm
going: tried blinkered at 3 yrs: sometimes races freely. *R. A. Fahey*

BEST ONE 3 ch.g. Best of The Bests (IRE) 122 – Nasaieb (IRE) 89 (Fairy King (USA)) **80**
[2007 10.1d 8g 7g³ 6f³ 8d⁴ 6m³ 7v³ p6m⁶ Dec 9] sturdy, quite attractive gelding: third
foal: closely related to useful 2004 2-y-o 5f winner Kissing Lights (by Machiavellian)
and half-brother to French 2005 2-y-o 9f winner Nilassiba (by Dalyami): dam, 2-y-o 5f
winner, half-sister to smart 7f/1m performer Raise A Grand: fairly useful maiden: best
effort in handicap final start: stays 7f: acts on polytrack and probably any turf going:
tongue tied last 3 starts. *C. E. Brittain*

BEST OPTION 3 b.f. Best of The Bests (IRE) 122 – B'Elanna Torres 66 (Entrepreneur **55**
123) [2007 –: p6g³ p7g p7.1g 7g⁶ Apr 3] modest maiden: will be suited by 1m+: acts on
polytrack. *W. R. Muir*

BEST PROSPECT (IRE) 5 b.g. Orpen (USA) 116 – Bright Prospect (USA) **97 §**
(Miswaki (USA) 124) [2007 103: 10g p10g 10.4g 8s⁶ 12m 9.9g 10s² 10.5s* 10.4d³ 10d
Oct 27] big, lengthy gelding: useful handicapper: won at Haydock (by length from Folio)
in September: better effort after when third at York next time: stays 1½m: acts on soft
and good to firm going: often tongue tied: weak finisher, and best treated with caution.
M. Dods

BEST SELECTION 3 ch.f. Inchinor 119 – Manila Selection (USA) (Manila (USA)) **73**
[2007 65: p10g⁴ 9.7g² 10.5g 11m³ p11g⁵ p11g⁶ p12g⁵ 9.9d² p10m² p10g Dec 22] lengthy
filly: fair maiden: left A. Jarvis after penultimate start: stays 1½m: acts on polytrack,
good to firm and good to soft going. *Mrs L. J. Mongan*

BEST SUITED 2 b.f. (Apr 8) Averti (IRE) 117 – Scarlett Holly 81 (Red Sunset 120) **55**
[2007 5d 5s² 5g⁴ 6m 6g⁵ 5g² Sep 19] 4,500F, 6,000Y: good-bodied filly: half-sister to
several winners, including useful 6f (at 2 yrs)/7f winner Scarlett Ribbon (by Most
Welcome): dam 6f (at 2 yrs)/7f winner: modest maiden: twice runner-up, in selling
nursery latterly: best efforts at 5f: acts on soft and good to firm going. *J. J. Quinn*

BEST WARNING 3 br.f. Best of The Bests (IRE) 122 – Just Warning (Warning 136) **–**
[2007 –: f11g 10.1g 14.1s 12m Aug 4] little sign of ability: tried visored. *J. Ryan*

BEST WOMAN 3 b.f. Best of The Bests (IRE) 122 – Business Woman (Primo Dominie **51**
121) [2007 49: p8g⁴ p8.6g⁶ p8.6g p10g² p12g⁴ Jun 9] modest performer: stays 1½m: acts
on polytrack and good to soft going. *P. Howling*

BE SUPERIOR 2 b.f. (Feb 7) Superior Premium 122 – Miss Tun (Komaite (USA)) **–**
[2007 6m Nov 10] heavy-bodied filly: first foal: dam unraced half-sister to useful
sprinters Matty Tun and Tom Tun: tailed off in maiden at Doncaster. *J. Balding*

BETHANYS BOY (IRE) 6 ch.g. Docksider (USA) 124 – Daymoon (USA) (Dayjur **67**
(USA) 137) [2007 –, a84: p12.2g² p13.9g f16g p12.2g f12g* f14g p12.2g³ 10.2f⁴ p12.2g⁴
p12.2g² 9.7g* p8.6g* p9.5g 8m Oct 14] close-coupled gelding: fair performer: left
A. Hales after reappearance: won seller at Southwell in March and, having been claimed
from P. Blockley £7,000 after tenth outing, handicaps at Folkestone in August and
Wolverhampton in September: left D. Daly after thirteenth start: stays 1¾m, effective at
much shorter: acts on all-weather, soft and good to firm going. *M. Wigham*

BETHS CHOICE 6 b.g. Midnight Legend 118 – Clare's Choice (Pragmatic 115) [2007 **–**
10.9g 11.7d p12g Aug 29] compact gelding: well held in maidens on Flat: won selling
hurdle in September. *J. M. Bradley*

BET NOIR (IRE) 2 b.f. (Mar 30) King's Best (USA) 132 – Ivowen (USA) 104 (Theat- **61 p**
rical 128) [2007 8g Oct 26] €32,000Y: leggy, useful-looking filly: first foal: dam Irish 9f
to 1½m winner: 66/1, green when tenth of 17 behind Cruel Sea in maiden at Doncaster:
will do better. *W. R. Swinburn*

BETTERAS BERTIE 4 gr.g. Paris House 123 – Suffolk Girl (Statoblest 120) [2007 **47** f8g 8.5m 6d⁵ 8d p8.6g 10s Sep 26] never dangerous in bumper: poor maiden: stays 8.5f: acts on good to firm going: often slowly away. *M. Brittain*

BETTER HAND (IRE) 2 b.c. (Jan 17) Montjeu (IRE) 137 – Silly Game (IRE) (Big- **94 p** stone (IRE) 126) [2007 7.1d² 7.1d* 7g Aug 18] €75,000F, 100,000Y: compact colt: first foal: dam Italian 2-y-o 7.5f winner (also won over jumps): fairly useful form: shaped well in maidens at Sandown, second to Scintillo prior to winning later in July by 2½ lengths from Jedediah (McCartney third): 7/2, possibly did too much too soon when only eighth in listed race at Newbury: likely to stay 1¼m/1½m: should progress. *M. R. Channon*

BETTER IN HEAVEN 2 b.c. (Feb 15) Zamindar (USA) 116 – Peace 85 (Sadler's **–** Wells (USA) 132) [2007 7.1g p7g Oct 12] close-coupled colt: well held in maidens: bred to stay 1m. *H. J. L. Dunlop*

BETTERLATETHANEVER (IRE) 3 ch.g. Titus Livius (FR) 115 – First Nadia **–** (Auction Ring (USA) 123) [2007 7s 8g⁵ 9.8m⁶ 8m f11d Dec 12] strong gelding: well held in maidens: tried in cheekpieces. *C. J. Teague*

BETTER OFF RED (USA) 3 b. or br.f. Red Ransom (USA) – Unending Love (USA) **–** (Dixieland Band (USA)) [2007 –: 10.1g 9s⁵ Jul 2] sturdy filly: little form. *D. M. Simcock*

BETT'S SPIRIT (IRE) 2 b.f. (Mar 13) Invincible Spirit (IRE) 121 – Hi Bettina 96 **97** (Henbit (USA) 130) [2007 5m³ 6m³ p5g* 6g³ Nov 2] medium-sized filly: half-sister to numerous winners, including useful sprinters Atlantic Viking and Fred Bongusto (in Italy), both by Danehill: dam Irish sprinter: useful performer: won maiden at Dundalk in September: third in listed races either side, beaten ½ length by Forthefirstime at the Curragh and 1½ lengths by Spinning Lucy at Newmarket: should prove best at 5f/6f. *M. J. Grassick, Ireland*

BETTY BURKE 2 b.f. (Feb 17) Choisir (AUS) 126 – Island Lover (IRE) (Turtle Island **63** (IRE) 123) [2007 5m p6g⁵ 5.1m² 5.1f³ 5m⁵ p7.1g⁵ p6g Oct 10] 6,500F, 10,000Y: good-topped filly: fifth foal: half-sister to winners in Italy by Indian Ridge and Alzao: dam unraced half-sister to Nassau/Musidora Stakes winner Optimistic Lass, herself dam of high-class sprinter/miler Golden Opinion: modest maiden: trained by W. M. Brisbourne on debut: stays 7f: raced only on polytrack and going firmer than good. *H. J. L. Dunlop*

BETTY OXO 3 b.f. Mind Games 121 – Kildine (IRE) (Common Grounds 118) [2007 –: **–** p7.1g f5g a8g Oct 7] of no account: left B. Baugh after second start. *R. Verheye, Belgium*

BETTYS TOUCH 2 b.f. (Apr 17) Lujain (USA) 119 – Fadaki Hawaki (USA) 60 (Vice **48** Regent (CAN)) [2007 5d 6d² 6d 6m⁶ Aug 13] 2,500Y: close-coupled filly: half-sister to 3 winners, including unreliable 7.5f winner Sutton Common (by Common Grounds) and French 1¼m winner Premiership (by Zinaad): dam, maiden (stayed 1m), closely related to Mujadil and half-sister to Fruits of Love: poor maiden: second in seller (left P. McBride £5,000) at Yarmouth: stays 6f. *W. J. Musson*

BEVERLEY BEAU 5 b.g. Inchinor 119 – Oriel Girl 65 (Beveled (USA)) [2007 61, **47** a55: p6g² p5.1g p6g p7g 5g 5g⁴ p6g 5g 6m⁴ p6g⁴ 6f Sep 10] leggy gelding: poor performer: stays 6f: acts on polytrack and firm going: tried in cheekpieces: has sweated: ridden by 7-lb claimer Kristin Stubbs: none too consistent. *Mrs L. Stubbs*

BEVERLY HILL BILLY 3 b.g. Primo Valentino (IRE) 116 – Miss Beverley (Beveled **84** (USA)) [2007 82: 8.1m³ 10v² 11.6m Jul 16] leggy gelding: fairly useful handicapper: placed first 2 starts in 2007: stays 1¼m (failed to settle over 11.6f): acts on polytrack, heavy and good to firm going. *A. King*

BEWDLEY 2 b.f. (May 4) Best of The Bests (IRE) 122 – Garota de Ipanema (FR) (Al **55** Nasr (FR) 126) [2007 7g⁵ p7.1g p8.6g⁶ Nov 1] fourth foal: dam French 1¼m winner: modest maiden: should stay 1m. *P. D. Evans*

BEWILDERING (IRE) 3 b.c. Tagula (IRE) 116 – Mystic Belle (IRE) 88 (Thatching **68** 131) [2007 55p: p9.5g³ p8g 10.5g 10d⁴ May 14] fair maiden: stays 1¼m: visored final start: virtually pulled up third outing: sold 5,000 gns in October. *E. J. O'Neill*

BE WISE GIRL 6 ch.m. Fleetwood (IRE) 107 – Zabelina (USA) 57 (Diesis 133) [2007 **–** –: 10.9m p9.5g f12g⁶ 11.9s p12.2g Jun 11] workmanlike mare: modest performer in 2005: lightly raced and little form since: flashes tail. *A. W. Carroll*

BEYABI 2 br.f. (Apr 25) Tumbleweed Ridge 117 – Sifat 77 (Marju (IRE) 127) [2007 5g **–** 5.1m 6d p6m 5m Aug 25] sturdy filly: second foal: dam 1m/1¼m winner: no form: tried visored. *J. R. Jenkins*

BEYOND BELIEF (IRE) 4 b.f. Sadler's Wells (USA) 132 – Adjriyna 82 (Top Ville –
129) [2007 –: p9.5g Jan 27] little worthwhile form. *M. J. Wallace*

BIANCA CAPELLO 2 b.f. (Mar 5) Medicean 128 – Totom 81 (Mtoto 134) [2007 **60 p**
7g⁶ 7.1g Oct 2] leggy filly: third foal: dam 1¼m/11.5f winner: mid-field in maidens, not
knocked about: will be suited by 1m/1¼m: will do better. *J. R. Fanshawe*

BIARRITZ 6 b.m. Prince Daniel (USA) – Sweet Fun (Meadowbrook 83) [2007 8.3d 8m –
Aug 27] first foal: dam well beaten both starts over hurdles: tailed off in bumper/claimers.
Mrs J. C. McGregor

BIASED OPINION (IRE) 2 b.c. (Jan 22) Fasliyev (USA) 120 – Atnab (USA) 64 **61**
(Riverman (USA) 131) [2007 6m 6.1g p6g⁶ p6g⁵ p6g⁶ p5.1g 5f⁵ p5g⁶ Oct 24]
small, sturdy colt: modest maiden: raced at 5f/6f: acts on polytrack and firm going.
H. J. L. Dunlop

BICOASTAL (USA) 3 ch.f. Gone West (USA) – Ocean Queen (USA) (Zilzal (USA) **101**
137) [2007 101: p8g⁴ 8g 9.9g⁵ 8.1m⁴ 8d 8.5g* 9f Nov 17] big, strong filly: useful performer: creditable efforts in Europe in 2007 only when seventh to Darjina in Poule
d'Essai des Pouliches at Longchamp second start and ¾-length fourth to Sweet Lilly in
listed race at Sandown: left B. Meehan, won allowance race at Keeneland in October: last
in Grade 1 Cardinal Handicap at Churchill Downs final outing: stays 8.5f: acts on good to
firm and good to soft going: usually blinkered/in cheekpieces: sweating, well below form
fifth start. *A. McKeever, USA*

BIDABLE 3 b.f. Auction House (USA) 120 – Dubitable 59 (Formidable (USA) 125) **70**
[2007 61: 8.2g 8.2m³ 8.1g⁵ 8.1s³ 8.3d³ 8.3d² 8.1m* 8f⁴ 10.2m 8d Oct 1] leggy filly: fair
handicapper: won at Chepstow in August: stays 8.3f: acts on polytrack, soft and good to
firm ground. *B. Palling*

BID ART (IRE) 2 b.g. (Feb 25) Hawk Wing (USA) 136 – Crystal Theatre (IRE) 72 **68**
(King's Theatre (IRE) 128) [2007 5.1g 6m 6d³ 7m 7m⁵ p8g³ Nov 7] 22,000Y: smallish,
sturdy gelding: first foal: dam, maiden (stayed 1½m), out of smart May Hill Stakes
winner Solar Crystal: fair maiden: third at Brighton and Kempton (nursery): gelded after:
free-going sort, stays 1m: acts on polytrack and good to soft going. *A. M. Balding*

BIDDERS ITCH 3 b.f. Auction House (USA) 120 – Sharp Ego (USA) (Sharpen Up –
127) [2007 –: 5m 6g 6m Sep 1] close-coupled filly: of no account. *A. Berry*

BIDDING TIME 3 b.f. Rock of Gibraltar (IRE) 133 – Bianca Nera 107 (Salse (USA) –
128) [2007 7m 6s Jun 14] fifth foal: half-sister to Irish 2001 2-y-o 7f winner Pietra Dura
(by Cadeaux Genereux) and 5f to 7f winner Glencairn Star (by Selkirk), both fairly
useful: dam, 2-y-o 5f to 7f (including Lowther and Moyglare Stud Stakes) winner: well
held in maidens at Newbury and Yarmouth. *M. L. W. Bell*

BID FOR FAME (USA) 10 b. or br.g. Quest For Fame 127 – Shroud (USA) (Vaguely –
Noble 140) [2007 73: p13.9g 12g Apr 2] leggy, lengthy gelding: fair handicapper at 9 yrs:
well held in 2007: effective at 1½m to 16.5f: acts on all-weather and firm going. *J. Pearce*

BID FOR GLORY 3 ch.c. Auction House (USA) 120 – Woodland Steps 86 (Bold Owl **101**
101) [2007 90: 8m² 8.2g* 10m 8d 8g⁵ p11g* p10g⁴ Dec 16] close-coupled, good-topped
colt: has a quick action: useful handicapper: won at Nottingham in June and Kempton
(by neck from Pinch of Salt) in December: in cheekpieces, creditable fourth to Evident
Pride on same course after: stays 11f: acts on polytrack, soft and good to firm going.
H. J. Collingridge

BID FOR GOLD 3 b.g. Auction House (USA) 120 – Gold And Blue (IRE) (Bluebird **84**
(USA) 125) [2007 78: 6m³ 6m* 7s³ 7s⁶ 6s* 6d⁴ 7g³ 8.1g 7m Nov 10] compact gelding:
fairly useful performer: won maiden at Redcar in May and handicap at Pontefract in July:
barely stays 7f: acts on firm and soft going. *Jedd O'Keeffe*

BID TO THE BEAT 2 b.c. (Mar 2) Auction House (USA) 120 – Sophies Symphony **52 +**
78 (Merdon Melody 98) [2007 7m p8g 8.2g Nov 7] deep-girthed colt: not fully wound
up, well held in maidens, showing a little ability second start. *H. J. Collingridge*

BIENHEUREUX 6 b.g. Bien Bien (USA) 125 – Rochea 67 (Rock City 120) [2007 71: **71**
f16g² f14g³ f14g³ p16g⁵ f16g⁶ f14g³ f12g 11.9m* 11.9d⁴ 12d p12g³ p12g⁵ p12g⁴ 11.9d*
11.9f³ 12.1d² 12s² 11.5g⁵ 11.9m⁵ 11.9d⁵ Oct 18] workmanlike gelding: fair handicapper:
won at Brighton in April and July: effective at 1½m to easy 2m: acts on all-weather, firm
and soft going: tried in headgear: tongue tied: held up. *Miss Gay Kelleway*

BIGALOS BANDIT 5 ch.g. Compton Place 125 – Move Darling (Rock City 120) **91**
[2007 p6g⁵ 5m⁶ 5.1m⁶ 5g 5g Jun 2] big, useful-looking gelding: good walker: useful
performer at best: unraced in 2006: left J. Quinn 34,000 gns and gelded, just fairly useful

form in 2007: best at 5f: acts on polytrack, soft and good to firm ground: has been early to post. *D. Nicholls*

BIGALO'S MAGIC (UAE) 2 ch.c. (Jan 26) Halling (USA) 133 – Roseate (USA) **70** (Mt Livermore (USA)) [2007 7m p7g⁴ 8f⁴ 7g Oct 27] 4,000Y, 30,000 2-y-o: strong colt: second foal: dam, ran twice in France, out of sister to dual US champion turf mare Flawlessly: fair maiden: fourth at Lingfield (minor event) and Pontefract: stays 1m. *E. J. O'Neill*

BIGFANOFTHAT (IRE) 2 b.c. (Feb 8) Rock of Gibraltar (IRE) 133 – Miss Salsa **87** (USA) (Unbridled (USA) 128) [2007 6g* May 31] €70,000Y: first foal: dam unraced half-sister to smart performer up to 1m Mutakddim: 12/1, fairly useful form when winning maiden at Ayr (beat Atabaas Pride by ½ length): suffered accident after: will stay 1m. *K. R. Burke*

BIG NOISE 3 b.c. Lake Coniston (IRE) 131 – Mitsubishi Video (IRE) (Doulab (USA) **100** 115) [2007 6g* p6g² 6s* 7m* 7m² Sep 22] strong, good-topped colt: third foal: dam Irish 1m winner: useful and progressive form: won maiden at Yarmouth in May and handicaps at Newmarket in June and August (beat Spriggan by 2½ lengths): best effort when 1¾ lengths second to Premio Loco in similar event at Newbury final outing: stays 7f: acts on soft and good to firm ground: has worn crossed noseband. *Dr J. D. Scargill*

BIG RALPH 4 ch.g. Mark of Esteem (IRE) 137 – Wish Me Luck (IRE) 100 (Lycius **53** (USA) 124) [2007 52: p7g⁵ p7g⁵ p10g⁵ f11g p8g p12g p12m⁵ p11g⁴ Dec 19] modest maiden: left M. Wigham after fifth start: effective at 7f to 1½m: raced on all-weather: tried blinkered. *D. K. Ivory*

BIG ROBERT 3 b.c.h. Medicean 128 – Top Flight Queen 82 (Mark of Esteem (IRE) 137) **106 +** [2007 106p: 8m⁶ 10g⁴ 10g 10d³ 10d* 12g⁶ 14g 10.3m⁶ Sep 13] well-made, medium-sized colt: useful performer: won 3-runner minor event at Leicester (by length from Rallying Cry) in July: probably flattered when sixth to Yellowstone in Gordon Stakes at Goodwood sixth outing: creditable sixth to Kirklees in minor event at Doncaster final start: stays 1½m: acts on good to firm and good to soft going: usually tongue tied: said to have finished distressed seventh outing. *W. R. Muir*

BIG SLICK (IRE) 2 ch.c. (Jan 17) Rossini (USA) 118 – Why Worry Now (IRE) 75 **–** (College Chapel 122) [2007 6g 6s 6s 6d 7g Oct 3] strong colt: no form. *M. Brittain*

BIG TIMER (USA) 3 ch.g. Street Cry (IRE) 130 – Moonflute (USA) 82 (The Minstrel **90** (CAN) 135) [2007 104: p7g 6d⁵ p7g Dec 19] tall, close-coupled, good-topped gelding: just fairly useful form at 3 yrs: bred to stay 1m, but free-going sort: acts on firm and good to soft going. *I. Semple*

BIJOU DAN 6 ch.g. Bijou d'Inde 127 – Cal Norma's Lady (IRE) 87 (Lyphard's Special **72** (USA) 122) [2007 64, a77: p9.5g⁵ f8g⁶ 9.1d* 9.1g* 9.1g³ 9.1g 10.1d⁵ 10.5m 12.4d 9.1v⁵ p9.5g Dec 14] angular, close-coupled gelding: fair handicapper: won twice at Ayr in May: stays 1¼m: acts on all-weather, heavy and good to firm ground: wears headgear: usually held up. *D. W. Thompson*

BIJOUTERIE 3 ch.f. Tobougg (IRE) 125 – Branston Gem 59 (So Factual (USA) 120) **–** [2007 64: f6g Feb 28] lengthy filly: modest maiden at 2 yrs: well held at Southwell only start in 2007. *T. J. Pitt*

BIKINI 2 b.f. (Feb 21) Trans Island 119 – Chimere (FR) (Soviet Lad (USA)) [2007 6s **72 p** 7.1g³ Oct 2] 3,500F: seventh foal: half-sister to French 4.5f (at 2 yrs) and 7f winner Tambour Battant (by Tagula): dam French 2-y-o 1m winner: better effort in maidens over 3 months apart when third to Love of Dubai at Warwick: should progress further. *H. Candy*

BILBOA 2 b.g. (Mar 17) Averti (IRE) 117 – Anita Marie (IRE) (Anita's Prince 126) **44 +** [2007 5.7g 6s Jun 25] compact gelding: poor form (and difficult ride) in maidens. *B. R. Millman*

BILKIE (IRE) 5 ch.g. Polish Precedent (USA) 131 – Lesgor (USA) 106 (Irish River **50** (FR) 131) [2007 f11g⁵ Feb 20] modest maiden: stays 11f: acts on fibresand. *John Berry*

BILL BENNETT (FR) 6 b.g. Bishop of Cashel 122 – Concert (Polar Falcon (USA) **– §** 126) [2007 70§, a58§: p12.2g² p12g Apr 25] small, stocky gelding: modest performer: **a56 §** effective at 1½m to 2m: acts on all-weather, earlier had form on firm and soft going: blinkered/tongue tied over 2 yrs: inconsistent. *J. Jay*

BILLBERRY 2 gr.g. (Apr 29) Diktat 126 – Elderberry (Bin Ajwaad (IRE) 119) [2007 **52 p** 6d⁶ Oct 29] 13,000Y: big gelding: fourth foal: half-brother to 3-y-o The Grey Berry and 5-y-o Fisberry: dam, last on only start, half-sister to smart sprinter Argentum: 14/1, needed experience when sixth in maiden at Leicester: subsequently gelded: should do better. *S. C. Williams*

BILLICH 4 ch.c. Observatory (USA) 131 – Pomponette (USA) (Rahy (USA) 115) **91**
[2007 90: p16g² p13.9g 16.2m p13.9g 16g* Aug 24] good-topped colt: fairly useful
handicapper: left E. O'Neill, won handicap at Thirsk in August: stays 16.5f: acts on
polytrack and firm ground. *D. E. Cantillon*

BILLION DOLLAR KID 2 br.c. (Jan 28) Averti (IRE) 117 – Fredora 93 (Inchinor **98**
119) [2007 6m² 7.1s² 7f* 7.1g* Sep 19] 11,000F, 75,000Y: big, strong colt: third foal:
closely related to German 7f to 9f winner Gold Dragon (by Piccolo) and half-brother to
3-y-o Dora Explora: dam 7f to 1¼m winner: useful form: improved to win maiden at
Folkestone and minor event at Sandown (beat Hobby by 1½ lengths) in September: stays
7f: acts on firm going: has awkward head carriage: sold 100,000 gns. *R. Hannon*

BILLY DANE (IRE) 3 b.g. Fayruz 116 – Lomalou (IRE) (Lightning Dealer 103) [2007 **88 §**
92: 7g⁵ 8.1m³ 10.1g 8m 8d Aug 19] tall, lengthy gelding: fairly useful handicapper:
good efforts first 2 starts in 2007: well below form after: stays 1m: acts on polytrack and
firm going: suspect temperament. *R. A. Fahey*

BILLY HOT ROCKS (IRE) 2 b.c. (Apr 4) Intikhab (USA) 135 – Rock Abbey (IRE) **–**
(College Chapel 122) [2007 6m Jul 14] well held in minor event at Salisbury: bred to stay
1m. *R. M. Beckett*

BILLY ONE PUNCH 5 b.g. Mark of Esteem (IRE) 137 – Polytess (IRE) (Polish **73**
Patriot (USA) 128) [2007 76: 10g 10m 9.8m 7m⁶ 10.1f⁴ 10.1m² 10.1m² 9.7f² 11.5g³
p9.5g Oct 5] strong, good-bodied gelding: fair handicapper: barely stays 11.5f: acts on
firm and soft going. *G. G. Margarson*

BILLY RED 3 ch.g. Dr Fong (USA) 128 – Liberty Bound 85 (Primo Dominie 121) **71 §**
[2007 72: 6m⁶ 6m⁵ f5g⁴ p6g⁶ 5.3g⁴ 5d* 5d 5m⁴ 5.1s 7d Oct 23] lengthy gelding: fair
handicapper: won at Sandown in July: probably best at 5f: acts on polytrack (probably on
fibresand), good to firm and good to soft going: usually visored/blinkered: ungenuine.
J. R. Jenkins

BILLY RUFFIAN 3 ch.g. Kyllachy 129 – Antonia's Folly 64 (Music Boy 124) [2007 **63**
69: p5.1g³ 6f⁵ 6.1m 5d⁶ 5d 6m Aug 9] big, strong gelding: just modest performer in 2007:
effective at 5f/easy 6f: tried blinkered/in cheekpieces: sold 1,200 gns
in October, sent to Sweden. *T. D. Easterby*

BINANTI 7 b.g. Bin Ajwaad (IRE) 119 – Princess Rosananti (IRE) (Shareef Dancer **103**
(USA) 135) [2007 95: 8m⁶ 7m² 7.1d² 7g* 7g³ 7g⁴ 7g 7d p7g p6g Nov 17] smallish,
useful-looking gelding: useful handicapper: won Buckingham Palace Stakes at Royal
Ascot (by length from Fajr, edging left) in June: creditable efforts in frame in International Stakes at Ascot (third to Third Set) and minor event at Goodwood (fourth to Laa
Rayb) next 2 starts (4 days apart): below form after: stays 8.6f: acts on all-weather, firm
and soft going: effective blinkered/visored or not. *P. R. Chamings*

BINARIO UNO 2 b.g. (Mar 31) Bertolini (USA) 125 – Madame Curie (Polish Pre- **69**
cedent (USA) 131) [2007 6g³ 6g³ Jun 20] 1,000F, €11,000Y: sixth foal: dam ran once:
third in maidens at Hamilton, showing good speed: subsequently gelded: may prove best
at 5f/6f. *D. Nicholls*

Buckingham Palace Stakes (Handicap), Royal Ascot—
Binanti holds on for his only success of the campaign; Fajr is second with Dabbers Ridge (left) third

BINFIELD (IRE) 2 b.f. (Apr 30) Officer (USA) 120 – Identify (IRE) 105 (Persian Bold **62** 123) [2007 5g 6s² p7g⁴ 7m 7d Oct 30] €45,000F, €48,000Y, 55,000 2-y-o: tall, unfurnished filly: fifth foal: half-sister to 3 winners, including useful French/US performer up to 1½m Oh So Awesome (by Awesome Again): dam Irish 7f (at 2 yrs) to 1¼m winner: modest maiden: runner-up at Newbury (flattered in testing conditions): well held in nurseries: should stay 7f/1m. *B. G. Powell*

BINHAM BOY 3 ch.g. Pebble Powder – Northwold Star (USA) 71 (Monteverdi 129) **–** [2007 p10g f7g p10g p12f Feb 24] well held in maidens/seller (reportedly finished lame final start): tried in cheekpieces/visor. *M. J. Gingell*

BINIOU (IRE) 4 b.c. Mozart (IRE) 131 – Cap Coz (IRE) 110 (Indian Ridge 123) [2007 **106** 118: 5m 5m p5g 5g 5g 5.1d² 6d³ 5.5d⁴ 6d 6s* Nov 26] leggy ex-French colt: smart performer for R. Collet in 2006: just useful in 2007, though won listed race at Fontainebleau in November by 1½ lengths from Kourka: best effort in Britain when 1¼ lengths second of 4 to Galeota in minor event at Nottingham: effective at 5f/6f: acts on soft and good to firm going. *R. M. H. Cowell*

BINNION BAY (IRE) 6 b.g. Fasliyev (USA) 120 – Literary 79 (Woodman (USA) **82** 126) [2007 61: p7g⁶ p6g p7g* p8g⁴ p7f⁴ p7g² p8g² p8g³ p8g* p8g⁴ p8g* p7g p8g* 7g* 6g p8g⁵ 7g⁶ p8g 7m 8d p8g p7g p8g⁵ p8m Dec 10] tall, useful-looking gelding: fairly useful handicapper: won at Lingfield in February, Kempton in March and Lingfield again in April and May (2): best at 7f/1m nowadays: acts on all-weather and good to firm ground: wears headgear: sometimes slowly away. *J. J. Bridger*

BINOCULAR 3 ch.c. Observatory (USA) 131 – Well Beyond (IRE) 101 (Don't Forget **71** Me 127) [2007 72p: 8f³ 10f³ 10.2g⁵ Jul 9] smallish, sturdy colt: fair maiden: stays 1¼m: raced only on good ground or firmer: sold 17,000 gns. *B. W. Hills*

BINYAMINA 2 b.f. (Feb 11) Elmaamul (USA) 125 – Latour 79 (Sri Pekan (USA) 117) **–** [2007 7g Nov 3] good-topped filly: third foal: dam, maiden (stayed 1m), half-sister to useful sprinter Watch Me, out of smart performer up to 9f Fenny Rough: 66/1 and edgy, behind in maiden at Newmarket. *E. F. Vaughan*

BIRBALINI 4 b.f. Bertolini (USA) 125 – La Birba (IRE) 44 (Prince of Birds (USA) **–** 121) [2007 –: 5m Jun 9] little form. *J. R. Best*

BIRDIE BIRDIE 3 b.f. Superior Premium 122 – Cautious Joe 73 (First Trump 118) **41** [2007 51: p7.1g⁶ p6g⁵ f7g⁶ p7.1g⁵ f8g³ 7s⁴ 7.1g Jun 22] strong filly: just poor maiden in 2007: should stay 1m: acts on all-weather and good ground: visored nowadays. *R. A. Fahey*

BIRDSVILLE 2 b.f. (Mar 2) Tobougg (IRE) 125 – Fred's Dream 67 (Cadeaux **–** Genereux 131) [2007 7s 6g⁴ p7.1g Jul 27] second foal: dam maiden (stayed 1m): no form. *Rae Guest*

BIRKINTASTIC 2 ch.g. (Feb 8) Dr Fong (USA) 128 – Sharpe's Lady (Prince Des **74** Coeurs (USA)) [2007 6m⁴ 6s 6g³ 6m 8g Oct 26] 60,000Y: sturdy gelding: fluent mover: second foal: dam maiden on Flat (hurdles winner): fair maiden: third at Haydock: below form in nurseries: should stay 1m: sold 9,500 gns. *B. J. Meehan*

BIRKSIDE 4 ch.g. Spinning World (USA) 130 – Bright Hope (IRE) 84 (Danehill (USA) **92** 126) [2007 86: p8g p10g⁶ 15.4m⁵ 10.2f³ 10.2m³ 8d⁵ 10s* p10g* 9.7s 10m 10g⁵ p10g* 10g* 10g* p11g* p10m* p9.5g² p12.2d* p12.2g² p12.2g* Dec 26] lengthy, well-made gelding: fairly useful performer: claimed from B. Powell £6,000 after fourth outing: won seller at Brighton in May, handicap at Lingfield in June, seller at Lingfield and claimer at Leicester (claimed from S. Dow £10,000) in September, seller at Redcar and claimer at Kempton in October, claimer at Kempton in November and handicaps (2) at Wolverhampton in December: stays 1½m: acts on polytrack, firm and soft ground: tried tongue tied: found little fourth/fifth starts: held up. *D. Carroll*

BIRKSPIEL (GER) 6 b.g. Singspiel (IRE) 133 – Beaute (GER) (Lord Udo (GER)) **–** [2007 112: p10f 11d Apr 1] angular ex-German gelding: smart performer at 5 yrs: well below form in 2007: stays 1½m: acts on heavy going: has worn crossed noseband. *S. Dow*

BIRTHDAY STAR (IRE) 5 b.g. Desert King (IRE) 129 – White Paper (IRE) (Marignan (USA) 117) [2007 57, a68: p12g p10g p10g p12.2g⁴ p12.2g p13.9g² p12.2g* p12.2g **a65** p13.9g⁴ p12.2g⁵ p13.9d⁶ Dec 17] close-coupled gelding: fair performer on all-weather: left W. Musson £6,000, won claimer at Wolverhampton in July: stays easy 1¾m: acts on polytrack, good to firm and good to soft ground: tried blinkered (raced freely)/in cheekpieces: held up. *A. G. Juckes*

BISHOP AUCKLAND (IRE) 3 b.g. Docksider (USA) 124 – Chancel (USA) 60 (Al **–** Nasr (FR) 126) [2007 –: 7.5m 13.8m⁵ 10.1g 11.5g Jul 24] little form. *Mrs A. Duffield*

BISHOPBRIGGS (USA) 2 ch.g. (Jan 21) Victory Gallop (CAN) 130 – Inny River **69**
(USA) (Seattle Slew (USA)) [2007 6.1m 8g³ 6g³ 7.2v 6m Nov 10] $15,000Y, 38,000
2-y-o: lengthy, unfurnished gelding: sixth foal: half-brother to 3 winners, including smart
6f/7f (including at 2 yrs) winner Montgomery's Arch (by Arch): dam, US sprint maiden,
half-sister to very smart US performer up to 1¼m Golden Larch: fair maiden: third at
Redcar and Catterick: free-going sort, should prove best up to 1m. *D. J. Murphy*

BITE THE BOSS 2 b.c. (Apr 2) Mujahid (USA) 125 – Clashfern (Smackover 107) **73**
[2007 7.1m⁵ 9f³ 10m⁴ Oct 8] 30,000Y: good-bodied colt: half-brother to 3 winners,
including 5f (at 2 yrs) to 6.5f (US Grade 3 event) winner Shuffling Kid (by Rock City):
dam unraced: fair form in maidens: in frame at Redcar and Pontefract (fourth to Planetarium), but seeming lazy: stays 1¼m. *E. J. O'Neill*

BIT OF A MONKEY 3 b.g. Superior Premium 122 – Rita's Rock Ape 87 (Mon Tresor
113) [2007 7.1d 7g Sep 24] no form in maiden at Chepstow (slowly away) and seller at
Leicester. *L. P. Grassick*

BITOOH 2 b.f. (Mar 20) Diktat 126 – Sitara 74 (Salse (USA) 128) [2007 p8g Sep 26] –
26,000F, 340,000Y: second foal: dam, 1½m winner, half-sister to very smart stayer
Golden Quest and to dam of Oaks winner Alexandrova and Cheveley Park Stakes winner
Magical Romance: 9/2 and tongue tied, behind in maiden at Kempton: joined
H-A. Pantall in France. *Saeed bin Suroor*

BIVOUAC (UAE) 3 b.g. Jade Robbery (USA) 121 – Tentpole (USA) 85 (Rainbow **59**
Quest (USA) 134) [2007 f7g³ 10.1m f8g 10m³ 8.3s² 9.1d Jul 16] modest maiden: should
stay 1½m: acts on soft and good to firm ground. *G. A. Swinbank*

BLACKAT BLACKITTEN (IRE) 3 ch.c. Inchinor 119 – Tara's Girl (IRE) 95 (Fay- **107 p**
ruz 116) [2007 p6g⁵ 6.9m* 6m³ p7g² p8g* 8m* Oct 4] 260,000Y: lengthy, unfurnished
colt: third foal: half-brother to fairly useful 6f/7f (latter including at 2 yrs) winner Triple
Two (by Pivotal): dam 2-y-o 5f winner: quickly progressed into useful performer,
winning maiden at Carlisle in July and handicaps at Kempton in September and Newmarket (beat Heroes by 4 lengths) in October: stays 1m: raced only on polytrack and good
to firm ground: often held up: has joined Godolphin: will improve further. *G. A. Butler*

BLACKBERRY PIE (USA) 3 b.f. Gulch (USA) – Name of Love (IRE) 105 (Petardia **74**
113) [2007 8.2m³ 8m⁶ 8.1m 8.3m⁶ p10g Oct 4] good-topped filly: fifth foal: closely
related to 9.5f winner Almavara (by Fusaichi Pegasus) and half-sister to a winner in USA
by Lemon Drop Kid: dam, 7f winner (including Rockfel Stakes), ran only at 2 yrs: fair
maiden: best effort on debut: should stay 1¼m: raced only on polytrack and good to firm
going: hinted at temperament second/third outings: sold 6,000 gns. *R. Charlton*

BLACKBURY 5 b.m. Overbury (IRE) 116 – Fenian Court (IRE) (John French 123) **49**
[2007 p8.6g³ p9.5d p8.6g Dec 29] poor maiden, lightly raced on Flat (no form in bumper/
over hurdles): stays 8.6f: raced only on polytrack: tried tongue tied. *W. M. Brisbourne*

BLACK CHARMER (IRE) 4 b.g. Black Minnaloushe (USA) 123 – Abla (Robellino **106 d**
(USA) 127) [2007 –: 8g⁵ 8m 7.1d* 7g 7v 7s Jul 14] good-bodied gelding: useful handicapper: easily best effort in 2007 when winning at Sandown (by 3 lengths from Binanti)
in June: way out later: makes running: acts on firm and soft going: makes running:
sold only 2,000 gns in October. *M. Johnston*

BLACK DAHLIA 2 br.f. (Feb 16) Dansili 127 – South Rock 102 (Rock City 120) **71**
[2007 7m³ 7.1m⁴ 8.3m⁶ 8g p7g Nov 4] 5,000Y: sturdy filly: seventh foal: half-sister to
7-y-o Cold Turkey and Italian winner up to 9.5f Halling Rock (by Halling): dam, 7f/1m
winner, out of half-sister to very smart miler Soviet Line: fair maiden: may prove best up
to 7f: acts on good to firm going. *A. J. McCabe*

BLACK DUKE 2 br.c. (Jan 30) Diktat 126 – Cool Question 99 (Polar Falcon (USA) **56**
126) [2007 5m 6d³ p6g 7.5m 5f p6g Oct 24] lengthy colt: modest maiden: best at 5f/6f:
sold 3,500 gns, sent to Sweden. *M. G. Quinlan*

BLACK FALCON (IRE) 7 ch.g. In The Wings 128 – Muwasim (USA) (Meadowlake **78 §**
(USA)) [2007 80§: f12g² f11g² 14g 11.6m⁵ Jun 11] rather leggy, quite attractive gelding:
fair handicapper nowadays: stays 1½m: acts on all-weather and firm going: tried visored/
in cheekpieces: sometimes slowly away: ungenuine. *M. A. Peill*

BLACK HEART 2 b.c. (Feb 24) Diktat 126 – Blodwen (USA) 52 (Mister Baileys 123) **60**
[2007 p8.6g⁶ p10g f8d⁶ Dec 21] modest form in maidens, green on debut. *M. Botti*

BLACKHEATH (IRE) 11 ch.g. Common Grounds 118 – Queen Caroline (USA) 67 **63**
(Chief's Crown (USA)) [2007 83: p6g² f5g⁵ p5g³ p6g⁵ p5.1g² 6m² p5.1g* 5m⁴ p6g² 6g
5g 5d⁵ 6s⁶ 5m⁴ 5g² p6g³ 5g² p5.1g p6g³ Dec 8] round-barrelled gelding: type to carry

condition: fluent mover: modest performer nowadays: won claimer at Wolverhampton in May: left D. Nicholls after seventeenth start: best at 5f/6f: acts on polytrack, firm and soft going: tried blinkered/tongue tied: usually travels strongly: hung eighth outing. *S. T. Mason*

BLACK JACARI (IRE) 2 b.g. (Mar 14) Black Sam Bellamy (IRE) 121 – Amalia (IRE) 111 (Danehill (USA) 126) [2007 7m 8.1f^5 8.1m* 8m^5 Oct 14] €34,000Y, 31,000 2-y-o: third foal: dam 7.5f to 1¼m winner: fairly useful form: won maiden at Chepstow in September: creditable fifth to Meer Kat in minor event at Bath final start (gelded after): will be suited by 1¼m/1½m: raced only on ground firmer than good. *A. King* **82**

BLACKMAIL (USA) 9 b.g. Twining (USA) 120 – Black Penny (USA) (Private Account (USA)) [2007 69: p10g^4 p12g p10g^2 p10g^2 p10g p10g p9.5g p12g p12g* p12g 11.9d^6 p10g^3 11.9f^6 p12g^4 p12g p12g 11.9m Sep 25] sturdy gelding: fair handicapper on all-weather, modest on turf: won at Lingfield in June: stays easy 1¾m: acts on polytrack, firm and good to soft going: tried tongue tied/visored, usually blinkered. *P. Mitchell* **54 + a68**

BLACKMALKIN (USA) 3 b.f. Forest Wildcat (USA) 120 – Farrfesheena (USA) 89 (Rahy (USA) 115) [2007 6m^3 6m* p6g^3 6d^6 p7g^8 Nov 7] unfurnished filly: second foal: dam second at 1m from 3 starts: fair form: won maiden at Yarmouth in April and handicap at Kempton in November: stays 7f: acts on polytrack and good to firm ground: sold €15,000. *C. E. Brittain* **75**

BLACK MEYEDEN (FR) 3 b.f. Black Minnaloushe (USA) 123 – Eye Witness (IRE) 72 (Don't Forget Me 127) [2007 p7g^5 7g Jul 24] €15,000Y, resold 6,000Y: half-sister to 3 winners, including useful Irish 7f (at 2 yrs) and 9f winner Hasanat (by Night Shift): dam, maiden, best effort at 8.5f: better effort in maidens when fifth at Lingfield on debut: sold 2,200 gns. *S. W. Hall* **45**

BLACK MOGUL 3 b.g. Robellino (USA) 127 – Brilliance 74 (Cadeaux Genereux 131) [2007 –: p8g 10.1g^6 p10g p12g 10m 10.1m^2 11.9d^3 12g 12.6m^3 p12.2g^4 p13.9g^5 p11g^6 p16.5g^4 f11d^5 Dec 21] modest maiden: stays 12.6f (stamina stretched at 16.5f): acts on polytrack and good to firm going: tried blinkered/in cheekpieces: usually races prominently. *R. Hollinshead* **59**

BLACK MOMA (IRE) 3 b.f. Averti (IRE) 117 – Sareb (FR) (Indian Ridge 123) [2007 76: p6g^3 p5g^3 6m 5m^4 5g^3 5s* 5m^3 5.2f 5d 5d p5g^6 p5.1g p5g 5g Dec 22] attractive, close-coupled filly: fairly useful handicapper: won at Lingfield in June: left R. Hannon 16,000 gns after eleventh outing: speedy, and best at 5f: acts on polytrack, firm and soft going: races prominently. *A. B. Haynes* **80**

BLACK OR RED (IRE) 2 b.c. (Apr 25) Cape Cross (IRE) 129 – Gentle Thoughts 73 (Darshaan 133) [2007 p7.1g p7g p7.1g^3 Nov 30] 15,000Y: fifth foal: half-brother to 5-y-o Blue Bajan and 4-y-o Picacho: dam, Irish maiden (should have been suited by 1¼m+), half-sister to smart stayer Anak Pekan: fair maiden: only form when third at Wolverhampton: bred to be suited by 1¼m+. *I. A. Wood* **71**

BLACK OVAL 6 b.m. Royal Applause 124 – Corniche Quest (IRE) 74 (Salt Dome (USA)) [2007 63§: p7.1g^3 p7.1g^4 p6g^2 p6g^2 p6g^6 p6g 6d p6g^6 6m 6m 8g 7.6s Aug 18] quite good-topped mare: modest performer, on long losing run: caught the eye on reappearance (jockey banned for 28 days, trainer fined £5,000 and horse suspended from running for 40 days, appeal still pending): effective at 5f to 7f: acts on polytrack, firm and good to soft ground: tried visored: held up: ungenuine. *S. Parr* **– § a58 §**

BLACK RAIN 2 b.g. (Feb 16) Desert Prince (IRE) 130 – Antigua (Selkirk (USA) 129) [2007 8m 8d^3 7g* Nov 2] 15,000Y: workmanlike gelding: fourth foal: half-brother to fairly useful 7f/1m (including at 2 yrs) winner Zingari (by Groom Dancer) and German 1½m to 15f winner Phantastic Wings (by In The Wings): dam unraced: fairly useful form: carried left near finish when short-head second to Classic Descent in maiden at Newmarket final start, subsequently awarded race: stays 1m: tongue tied. *P. J. McBride* **86**

BLACK ROCK (IRE) 3 ch.c. Rock of Gibraltar (IRE) 133 – Biraya (Valiyar 129) [2007 91p: 8m^3 10d^3 10d* 10m 12g* 13.1s* Sep 22] strong, good-topped colt: powerful galloper with a long stride: useful form: progressed well to win maiden at Sandown in June, and handicaps at Ripon in August and Ayr (beat Sphinx by 1¼ lengths) in September: will stay at least 1¾m: acts on polytrack, soft and good to firm ground: should progress further. *M. A. Jarvis* **102 p**

BLACK SEA PEARL 4 b. or br.f. Diktat 126 – Made of Pearl (USA) 107 (Nureyev (USA) 131) [2007 72: f7g^8 f6g^2 f6g^2 f7g p8g^5 8.3m 7.6g^5 p8g 8m^4 Aug 3] lengthy filly: fair handicapper: won at Southwell in January: stayed 1m: acted on all-weather, good to firm and good to soft going: in foal to Indian Haven. *P. W. D'Arcy* **71**

BLACKTOFT (USA) 4 b. or br.g. Theatrical 128 – Black Truffle (USA) (Mt Liver- **83** more (USA)) [2007 78: p10g* f11g² f11g 10m² 9m 9.9g⁵ 8.3m² 7.9d 10g⁵ p8.6g p8g Dec 1] big, leggy gelding: fairly useful handicapper: won at Lingfield in January: in-and-out form after: stays 11f: acts on all-weather and good to firm going: free-going sort. *S. C. Williams*

BLACK TOR FIGARRO (IRE) 2 b.c. (Apr 22) Rock of Gibraltar (IRE) 133 – Will **65 ?** Be Blue (IRE) (Darshaan 133) [2007 8.3g 8d p8m Nov 26] close-coupled colt: seemingly best effort in maidens when mid-division at Leicester on debut: bred to stay 1¼m. *B. W. Duke*

BLACK WADI 5 br.m. Desert King (IRE) 129 – Tamelia (USA) (Caerleon (USA) 132) **–** [2007 11.9m 10.1d 11.8d⁶ Oct 29] big mare: lightly raced and little sign of ability: tongue tied. *T. Keddy*

BLADES GIRL 4 ch.f. Bertolini (USA) 125 – Banningham Blade 94 (Sure Blade **81** (USA) 130) [2007 100: 6m 8g 7m 7g 8ep 29] big, leggy filly: has a fluent action: useful handicapper at 3 yrs: well below form in 2007 (brought down second start): stays 7f: acts on firm and good to soft going: wears cheekpieces: once refused to enter stall. *K. A. Ryan*

BLAKESHALL BOY 9 b.g. Piccolo 121 – Giggleswick Girl 67 (Full Extent (USA) **–** 113) [2007 –: p7.1g Jan 13] rather leggy, quite attractive gelding: handicapper: lightly raced and little form after 2003: tried visored: dead. *A. J. Chamberlain*

BLAKESHALL DIAMOND 2 gr.f. (Mar 19) Piccolo 121 – Hi Hoh (IRE) (Fayruz **64** 116) [2007 p5.1g 5.1g p5g* Nov 15] sixth foal: half-sister to 3 winners by Fraam, including 1m/8.6f winner Wrenlane and 8-y-o Zinging: dam seemed of little account: modest form: improved to win maiden at Lingfield (33/1, made all): should be best kept to 5f. *A. J. Chamberlain*

BLAKESHALL HOPE 5 ch.g. Piccolo 121 – Elite Hope (USA) 84 (Moment of Hope **45** (USA)) [2007 49: p8g p8.6g p8.6d³ p8.6s p9.5g Dec 29] smallish, workmanlike gelding: poor maiden handicapper: stays 8.6f: acts on polytrack and good to firm going: tried visored. *A. J. Chamberlain*

BLAKESHALL QUEST 7 b.m. Piccolo 121 – Corniche Quest (IRE) 74 (Salt Dome **63** (USA)) [2007 61: f6g³ p6g⁴ f6g⁶ f6g p6g f6g p6g f6g.6d² Dec 11] compact mare: modest handicapper: effective at 5f to easy 7f: acts on all-weather and good to soft going: visored/blinkered. *R. Brotherton*

BLAKESHALL ROSE 3 b.f. Tobougg (IRE) 125 – Giggleswick Girl 67 (Full Extent **– §** (USA) 113) [2007 38: 5m p5.1g Apr 21] angular filly: poor maiden: sometimes slowly away: refused to race final outing (wore cheekpieces). *A. J. Chamberlain*

BLANDYS WOOD 2 ch.f. (Apr 13) Fleetwood (IRE) 107 – Blandys (IRE) 53 (Dolp- **66** hin Street (FR) 125) [2007 6g 6m⁴ 7g p7.1g 8f⁶ p8g 8g³ 8.3d* 8m Oct 22] rather leggy filly: first foal: dam 6f winner: fair performer: won seller at Windsor in October: shapes as though will stay 1¼m: acts on firm and good to soft going: visored (below form) once. *M. R. Channon*

BLAZE TRAILER (IRE) 4 b.g. Indian Danehill (IRE) 124 – Moonlight Melody 60 **54** (Merdon Melody 98) [2007 58: p8.6g 7.2g³ 7.5g 9d Jul 23] modest maiden handicapper, lightly raced: well held at Wolverhampton (visored) on reappearance: stays 1¼m: best efforts on good going. *T. G. McCourt, Ireland*

BLAZING BULLET (IRE) 2 b.g. (Feb 4) Tagula (IRE) 116 – Shao (FR) (Alzao **–** (USA) 117) [2007 5d 5m 5m 5m⁶ p5.1g 5m⁶ Jul 11] small, stocky gelding: no form, including in blinkers. *N. Wilson*

BLAZING HEIGHTS 4 b.g. Compton Place 125 – Harrken Heights (IRE) (Belmez **90** (USA) 131) [2007 87: 5g⁶ 5d³ 5m 5g² 5m⁵ 5.1d⁵ 5s² 5d 5m 5g 5d⁵ 6d 5d 5g* p5.1g Nov 19] dipped-backed gelding: fairly useful handicapper: won at Musselburgh in November: well beaten on all-weather debut final start: has won at 6f, best at 5f: acts on firm and soft going: sometimes slowly away. *J. S. Goldie*

BLAZING MASK (IRE) 2 b.f. (Apr 18) Barathea (IRE) 127 – Alphilda 83 (Ezzoud **–** (IRE) 126) [2007 6m 7m⁶ 8.5m 8f Sep 27] 14,500 2-y-o: small, strong filly: third foal: dam 2-y-o 6f winner: no form: tried in cheekpieces. *Mrs A. Duffield*

BLENDON BOY (IRE) 5 b.g. Brave Act 119 – Negria (IRE) (Al Hareb (USA) 123) **–** [2007 p12.2g Feb 5] close-coupled gelding: little form. *D. W. Thompson*

BLESSED PLACE 7 ch.g. Compton Place 125 – Cathedra (So Blessed 130) [2007 77, **73** a69: p6g p6g 5m 5.7d 6d² 5.2s* 6g 5m⁶ 5m 5d⁴ 5.1g² 6m⁵ 5g 5.7d⁶ 5.1m* p5.1m p5m **a60**

5.3d p6g³ 5.1g p6g p5m Nov 11] leggy gelding: fair handicapper on turf, modest on all-weather: won at Newbury in June and Chester in August: effective at 5f/easy 6f: acts on all-weather, firm and soft going: tried in cheekpieces/blinkers (raced too freely): usually tongue tied: front runner. *D. J. S. ffrench Davis*

BLIMEY O'RILEY (IRE) 2 b.c. (Mar 13) Kalanisi (IRE) 132 – Kafayef (USA) 46 **67** (Secreto (USA) 128) [2007 8d 8d Oct 30] 20,000Y: big, strong colt: half-brother to several winners, including useful French 2004 2-y-o 5.5f/7f winner Ascot Dream (by Pennekamp): dam, ran 3 times, half-sister to smart stayer Melrose Avenue: mid-field in maidens at York (seemingly fair form) and Yarmouth: will probably stay 1¼m/1½m. *M. H. Tompkins*

BLINDSPIN 2 b.c. (Jan 27) Intikhab (USA) 135 – Blinding (IRE) (High Top 131) [2007 **68** 6m 7.1g⁴ Sep 12] 36,000Y: good-topped colt: half-brother to several winners, including 1995 2-y-o 5f winner High Priority (by Marju) and 1m winner Doc Watson (by Dr Devious), both fairly useful: dam ran twice: better run in maidens at Haydock when fourth to Maryqueenofscots: will stay 1m. *M. Dods*

BLISSFULLY 3 b.f. Kyllachy 129 – Bliss (IRE) 75 (Statoblest 120) [2007 –: f6g f6g **–** Mar 13] sturdy filly: little form: tried blinkered. *S. Parr*

BLISSPHILLY 5 b.m. Primo Dominie 121 – Majalis 79 (Mujadil (USA) 119) [2007 –: **–** f6g Jan 2] leggy, quite good-topped mare: little form: tried blinkered/visored. *M. Mullineaux*

BLITZEN (IRE) 2 b. or br.c. (Mar 8) Indian Danehill (IRE) 124 – Notable Dear (ITY) **66** (Last Tycoon 131) [2007 5g⁵ 6m⁵ p6g⁴ 7d⁴ Oct 30] €12,500F, €15,000Y: fourth foal: half-brother to fairly useful Irish 2005 2-y-o 7f winner (stays 1½m) Celtic Warrior (by Celtic Swing): dam Italian 7f to 8.5f winner: fair maiden: best effort when fourth in nursery at Yarmouth final start: likely to stay 1m: sold 10,000 gns. *E. S. McMahon*

BLOCKLEY (USA) 3 b.g. Johannesburg (USA) 127 – Saintly Manner (USA) (St **64** Jovite (USA) 135) [2007 52²: p9.5g 10.1g³ 11.5s 10.5v⁵ 12s² 10.1g 14.5m Aug 15] modest maiden: stays 1½m: acts on heavy going: tried tongue tied: visored last 3 starts: travels with little fluency. *Ian Williams*

BLUE ADMIRAL 2 ch.g. (May 2) Fleetwood (IRE) 107 – Poly Blue (IRE) 82 (That- **70** ching 131) [2007 7m⁶ 7m Oct 5] 24,000Y: compact gelding: fifth foal: half-brother to 3 winners, including useful 2005 2-y-o 5f/6f winner Pickett (by Piccolo): dam, 2-y-o 6f winner, out of half-sister to Gold Cup winner Sadeem: fair form (but no threat) in maidens at Newmarket, gelded in between. *M. H. Tompkins*

BLUE AURA (IRE) 4 b.g. Elnadim (USA) 128 – Absent Beauty (IRE) 74 (Dancing **78** Dissident (USA) 119) [2007 80: 6m 5m⁶ 6d³ 5d² 5.1g⁶ 5d⁶ 6d Oct 1] strong gelding: fair handicapper: raced at 5f/6f: acts on good to firm and good to soft going: tried in cheek-pieces, usually blinkered. *R. M. Beckett*

BLUE BAJAN (IRE) 5 b.g. Montjeu (IRE) 137 – Gentle Thoughts 73 (Darshaan 133) **114** [2007 110: p10f² p10g⁵ 10.1g* 10.3m² 12d⁵ 10d³ 10.4s Jul 28] tall, quite good-topped gelding: smart performer: further progress in 2007, winning handicap at Epsom in April by 1¼ lengths from Charlie Tokyo: good efforts next 3 starts, behind Maraahel in Huxley Stakes at Chester (head second) and Hardwicke Stakes at Royal Ascot (fifth, racing freely), before 2 lengths third to Harland in listed race at Sandown: seemingly amiss when tailed off in York Stakes at York final outing: effective at 9f to 1½m: acts on polytrack, soft and good to firm going: blinkered once: often sweats up/edgy: held up: reliable: fairly useful winner over hurdles. *Andrew Turnell*

BLUE BAMBOO 3 b.f. Green Desert (USA) 127 – Silver Bandana (USA) (Silver Buck **70** (USA)) [2007 67: p7g* 7g p7g⁵ 7m p7g⁵ Oct 29] strong, close-coupled filly: fair handi-capper: won at Lingfield in April: stays 7f: acts on polytrack, raced only on good/good to firm going on turf. *Mrs A. J. Perrett*

BLUEBELLE DANCER (IRE) 3 b.f. Danehill Dancer (IRE) 117 – Spring To Light **67** (USA) 93 (Blushing Groom (FR) 131) [2007 70: 8g⁵ 7s 7f³ 8d² 7g p6g⁶ p6g 8d⁶ Oct 18] rangy filly: has scope: fair maiden handicapper: probably stays easy 1m: acts on poly-track, firm and good to soft going: tried in cheekpieces: often slowly away. *W. R. Muir*

BLUEBELL RIDGE (IRE) 2 b.f. (Apr 13) Distant Music (USA) 126 – Miss Indigo **60** 62 (Indian Ridge 123) [2007 p8g⁵ p8g⁶ Oct 17] 4,500Y: third foal: half-sister to 3-y-o Mickleberry: dam maiden half-sister to useful performer up to 1½m Musetta: modest form when mid-division in maidens at Kempton: hung/flashed tail second start. *D. W. P. Arbuthnot*

BLUE BIRD'S DREAM 4 b.g. Lake Coniston (IRE) 131 – Bedtime Model (Double **62**
Bed (FR) 121) [2007 p9.5g⁶ 10m 6m 8.1v 8s 7.1m⁶ p8.6g p7.1g² p6g⁴ 7g Oct 16] big,
lengthy gelding: modest maiden: stays 7f: acts on polytrack and good to firm ground:
races prominently: sold 3,000 gns. *E. J. Alston*

BLUEBOK 6 ch.g. Indian Ridge 123 – Blue Sirocco (Bluebird (USA) 125) [2007 90: **90**
5m⁴ 5g⁵ 5m² 5g 5g 5.2f 5.1m² 5f 5g⁶ p5g³ p5g⁴ p5g p5g⁴ Nov 12] compact gelding: fairly **a83**
useful handicapper: best at 5f: acts on polytrack and firm going (well below form on soft):
tongue tied: effective held up or ridden prominently. *J. M. Bradley*

BLUE CHAGALL (FR) 2 br.c. (Mar 2) Testa Rossa (AUS) – Eloisey 70 (Pitskelly **111**
122) [2007 7d* 8m² 8g* 8s⁵ Nov 1] half-brother to numerous winners in France: dam 5f
(at 2 yrs) and 11.5f (in France) winner: smart form: won maiden at Vichy (by 6 lengths)
in July and Prix des Chenes at Longchamp (prominent, led over 1f out when beating
Dubai Time 2½ lengths) in September: below form when fifth to Thewayyouare in
Criterium International at Saint-Cloud final start: will stay 1¼m. *H-A. Pantall, France*

BLUE CHARM 3 b.g. Averti (IRE) 117 – Exotic Forest 66 (Dominion 123) [2007 84: **80**
p6g³ Apr 2] fairly useful performer, lightly raced: should stay 7f: raced only on polytrack.
S. Kirk

BLUE CITADEL (USA) 2 ch.c. (Feb 16) Dubai Destination (USA) 127 – Cloud **81**
Castle 119 (In The Wings 128) [2007 8.1m 7.2s³ 8.1s⁶ 9s³ 8d⁴ Oct 23] 75,000Y:
smallish, sturdy colt: good walker: sixth foal: closely related to 4-y-o Queen's Best and
half-brother to 2 winners, including smart French 1½m winner Reverie Solitaire (by
Nashwan): dam, won Nell Gwyn Stakes and second in Prix Vermeille, half-sister to Luso,
Warrsan and Needle Gun: fairly useful maiden: in frame 3 times, including nursery
at Yarmouth final start: will stay 1¼m/1½m: acts on soft going: sold 50,000 gns.
J. H. M. Gosden

BLUECROP BOY 3 b.g. Zaha (CAN) 106 – Pearl Dawn (IRE) 91 (Jareer (USA) 115) **48**
[2007 p10g⁶ p10g p12g⁶ p10g 11g 10s 15.4g³ Aug 16] poor maiden: tried blinkered
(looked ungenuine)/in cheekpieces. *D. J. S. ffrench Davis*

BLUE CROSS BOY (USA) 2 gr. or ro.c. (Feb 9) Sunday Break (JPN) 121 – Intro- **77**
ducer (USA) (Cozzene (USA)) [2007 5m 6m* 7m Aug 25] $42,000F, $37,000Y, 43,000
2-y-o: first foal: dam, US 7f to 9f winner, out of sister to US Grade 1 2-y-o 8.5f winner
Qualify: fair form: won maiden at Redcar in August: stamina stretched in minor event
there later in month: will prove best at 5f/6f: sold 16,000 gns. *J. Howard Johnson*

BLUE DENIM 3 b.f. Singspiel (IRE) 133 – Velvet Lady 102 (Nashwan (USA) 135) **–**
[2007 f11g 12g⁶ May 18] rangy filly: third foal: sister to German 1¼m winner Velveteen
Rabbit: dam, 1m winner, half-sister to Dubai World Cup winner Moon Ballad (by Singspiel) out of half-sister to very smart 1¼m to 2m performer Central Park: well held in
maidens: sold 8,000 gns in July. *M. A. Jarvis*

BLUE ECHO 3 b.f. Kyllachy 129 – Mazarine Blue 65 (Bellypha 130) [2007 96: 6.1s³ **97**
5g 6s⁴ 5g⁵ 6.1m* 5g Sep 23] strong, deep-girthed filly: good walker: useful performer:
won listed race at Chester in September by 3 lengths from Diamond Diva: will prove best
at 5f/6f: acts on soft and good to firm going: races prominently. *M. A. Jarvis*

BLUE EMPIRE (IRE) 6 b.g. Second Empire (IRE) 124 – Paleria (USA) 77 (Zilzal **66**
(USA) 137) [2007 71: f8g⁶ p10g f8g 7.5m⁵ 8.1m 8.5m⁵ 7m⁴ 8d 8m² 8g* p7.1g 7d² p8g
f8g⁶ Dec 27] leggy gelding: fair handicapper: won at Thirsk in August: stays 8.6f: acts on
all-weather and firm going: sometimes wears cheekpieces/visor. *C. R. Dore*

BLUE EYED ELOISE 5 b.m. Overbury (IRE) 116 – Galix (FR) (Sissoo) [2007 p12g³ **48**
p12g⁵ Jul 17] 3,000 4-y-o: second foal: dam French chase winner: some ability on
bumper debut: poor form in claimer (visored)/maiden (reluctant to enter stall) on Flat,
leaving B. Johnson in between. *J. M. Bradley*

BLUE EYED MISS (IRE) 2 b.f. (Apr 16) Statue of Liberty (USA) 115 – Classic **89**
Jenny (IRE) 69 (Green Desert (USA) 127) [2007 p6g² 5m* 6d 5g² Nov 9] €5,000Y:
good-topped filly: half-sister to 3 winners, including Irish 1¼m winner Majestic Jenny
(by Zamindar): dam, lightly-raced 1¼m winner, out of smart performer up to 1½m Eileen
Jenny: fairly useful form: won maiden at Sandown in September: resumed progress when
second in nursery at Newmarket, best at 5f. *P. A. Blockley*

BLUE HEDGES 5 b.h. Polish Precedent (USA) 131 – Palagene (Generous (IRE) 139) **69**
[2007 63, a71: p16.5g p12.2g⁵ 12g⁵ p13.9g 12d⁴ 10.1f⁵ p12.2g p12g* f12d p13g⁶ Dec
28] big, workmanlike horse: fair handicapper: won at Lingfield (amateurs) in November:
stays easy 1¾m: acts on polytrack, firm and good to soft going: tried in cheekpieces.
H. J. Collingridge

143

BLUE HILLS 6 br.g. Vettori (IRE) 119 – Slow Jazz (USA) 106 (Chief's Crown (USA)) **63** [2007 67: f14g⁵ f16g⁴ f16g* p16.5g³ f14g² p13.9g* f14g² p16g f14g* 18g 14.1m⁵ 15d **a75** 17.2m 14.1m³ p13.9g³ p13.9g⁴ 16f p13.9g p13.9g³ p13.9g* p13.9g f14d³ Dec 15] tall gelding: fair handicapper on all-weather, modest on turf: won at Southwell (amateurs) in January and Wolverhampton (amateurs) and Southwell in March and again at Wolverhampton in November: stays 2m: acts on all-weather, firm and good to soft going: usually in headgear: has wandered. *P. W. Hiatt*

BLUE JACK 2 b.c. (Mar 19) Cadeaux Genereux 131 – Fairy Flight (IRE) 86 (Fairy **76** King (USA)) [2007 5.1d* p6g³ p6m⁴ Dec 7] 27,000F, 30,000 2-y-o, resold 28,000 2-y-o: sturdy colt: sixth foal: half-brother to 8-y-o Just James: dam Irish 2-y-o 6f winner: fair performer: won maiden at Nottingham in October on debut: similar form in nurseries at Lingfield: likely to prove best at 5f/6f. *W. R. Muir*

BLUEJAIN 2 b.c. (Mar 14) Lujain (USA) 119 – Belle of The Blues (IRE) (Blues **60 p** Traveller (IRE) 119) [2007 6f 6.1d Oct 18] 8,000Y: tall, useful-looking colt: second foal: half-brother to 4-y-o Soto: dam twice-raced half-sister to smart sprinter Croft Pool: modest form in maidens at York and Nottingham (drawn wide/still green, better effort): should continue to progress. *Miss Gay Kelleway*

BLUE JAVA 6 ch.g. Bluegrass Prince (IRE) 110 – Java Bay (Statoblest 120) [2007 84: **81** 7g² 7g² 7s² 7g⁶ 8m⁵ 7d³ 7m 7f* 8s 7g⁵ Nov 3] smallish gelding: fairly useful handicapper: won at Folkestone in September: stays 1m, all wins at 7f: acts on polytrack, firm and soft going: tried visored/blinkered: sometimes tongue tied: races prominently. *H. Morrison*

BLUE JET (USA) 3 b.g. Black Minnaloushe (USA) 123 – Clickety Click (USA) **65** (Sovereign Dancer (USA)) [2007 –: 9.8g 10.1d 13.8m* 12d 14f⁵ 16.1g³ 13.8g Oct 20] leggy, close-coupled gelding: fair performer: won maiden at Catterick in July: stays 2m: acts on good to firm ground. *R. M. Whitaker*

BLUE KNIGHT (IRE) 8 ch.g. Bluebird (USA) 125 – Fer de Lance (IRE) (Diesis 133) **56** [2007 74d: p7g p7.1g⁴ p7.1g⁶ f7g p8g p7.1g⁴ p6g* p7.1g³ 6g 6m⁶ 6f 6m³ 7d 6m p7g Sep 12] big, lengthy gelding: modest performer: won seller at Lingfield in April: effective at 5f to 7f: acts on all-weather, soft and good to firm going: has been visored/tongue tied, usually in cheekpieces nowadays: sometimes looks none too keen. *P. Howling*

BLUE KSAR (FR) 4 b.c. Anabaa (USA) 130 – Delicieuse Lady (Trempolino (USA) **116** 135) [2007 116: 10g* 8.5g² 8d* 8g³ 9.9m⁶ 8d⁶ 9d³ Oct 19] big, close-coupled colt: smart performer: won minor event at Lingfield (beat Hard Top by 1¼ lengths) in May and listed race at Pontefract (beat Contentious by 2½ lengths, taking strong hold) in July: good efforts after when third in Celebration Mile at Goodwood (beaten 2¾ lengths by Echelon) and in Darley Stakes at Newmarket (beaten ¾ length by Windsor Knot, not finding much off bridle and losing second on line, jockey banned 7 days for dropping hands): best at 1m/1¼m: acts on good to firm and good to soft going: tongue tied: sometimes slowly away: usually races prominently. *Saeed bin Suroor*

BLUE LAW (IRE) 2 ch.g. (Apr 16) Fath (USA) 116 – Mica Male (ITY) (Law Society **70** (USA) 130) [2007 p8g⁵ f8d² Dec 12] €8,000F: eighth foal: half-brother to 3 winners, notably useful 6f (including at 2 yrs) winner Moyenne (by Trans Island): dam Italian 7f to 11f winner: fair form in maidens at Dundalk and Southwell. *Andrew Oliver, Ireland*

Pomfret Stakes, Pontefract—Blue Ksar puts daylight between himself and Contentious (USA) (left); fourth-placed Flying Clarets is the other horse in the picture

BLUE LINE 5 gr.m. Bluegrass Prince (IRE) 110 – Out Line 98 (Beveled (USA)) [2007 **58**
58, a65: p8g⁴ p8g* p10g³ 8d⁴ p8g 8m p7g 8m⁴ 8d⁵ Oct 3] lengthy mare: fair handicapper **a65**
on all-weather, modest on turf: won at Lingfield in May: barely stays 1¼m: acts on polytrack, firm and good to soft ground: has been visored. *M. Madgwick*

BLUE MADEIRA 3 b.g. Auction House (USA) 120 – Queen of Scotland (IRE) 75 **72 d**
(Mujadil (USA) 119) [2007 81: 8m 8.1s⁵ 10g 8.3m⁶ 9g Oct 5] fairly useful at 2 yrs:
regressed in 2007: probably stays 1m: yet to race on firm going, acts on any other turf and
polytrack: in cheekpieces last 2 starts. *Mrs L. Stubbs*

BLUE MISTRAL (IRE) 3 ch.f. Spinning World (USA) 130 – Blue Sirocco (Bluebird **69 §**
(USA) 125) [2007 67: 6m⁵ p8g 8g* 8d 8m 8f⁵ 10.2m 10m* p10g p12g Oct 29] well-made,
medium-sized filly: fair handicapper: won at Brighton in July and September: stays
1¼m: acts on firm ground: usually in visor/blinkers: tongue tied: often slowly away: not
straightforward, and not one to rely on. *W. J. Knight*

BLUE MONKEY (IRE) 3 b.c. Orpen (USA) 116 – Resurgence (Polar Falcon (USA) **88**
126) [2007 69: p8g³ p8g² p8.6g³ p8g⁴ f7g* 7m⁵ 8.1s* 8s² 8.2d² 8.1s⁶ Sep 28]
useful-looking colt: fairly useful performer: won maiden at Southwell in April, and
handicaps at Haydock in June and Sandown in July: stays 8.6f: acts on all-weather and
soft going: sold 34,000 gns, sent to Bahrain. *M. L. W. Bell*

BLUE OPAL 5 b.m. Bold Edge 123 – Second Affair (IRE) 85 (Pursuit of Love 124) **–**
[2007 –, a57: p12.2g Apr 30] modest performer at best: lightly raced and little form
since 2006: barely stays 1¾m: acts on fibresand: effective with/without cheekpieces.
Miss S. E. Hall

BLUE PATRICK 7 gr.g. Wizard King 122 – Great Intent (Aragon 118) [2007 83d: f8g **–**
Jan 30] rather leggy gelding: fluent mover: fairly useful early in 2006: has lost way since:
has worn cheekpieces. *P. A. Blockley*

BLUE QUIVER (IRE) 7 b.g. Bluebird (USA) 125 – Paradise Forum 78 (Prince Sabo **–**
123) [2007 –, a65: p12g p12.2g³ p12g p7g* p8g⁵ p8g* p7m³ p8.6g⁵ Oct 19] fair **a67**
performer: won seller in June and handicap in September, both at Lingfield: stays 8.6f:
acts on polytrack: sometimes slowly away. *C. A. Horgan*

BLUE RHAPSODY 2 b.f. (Feb 5) Cape Cross (IRE) 129 – Blue Symphony 73 **79**
(Darshaan 133) [2007 7m 6d p7g* 7m⁵ 8d Oct 23] sturdy, lengthy filly: type to carry
condition: first foal: dam, 1¼m winner, out of Cheveley Park Stakes winner Blue Duster:
fair performer: won maiden at Lingfield in September: should stay 1m: acts on polytrack
and good to firm going: tried tongue tied: sold 60,000 gns, sent to USA. *L. M. Cumani*

BLUE ROCKET (IRE) 3 ch.f. Rock of Gibraltar (IRE) 133 – Champagne Girl 67 **97**
(Robellino (USA) 127) [2007 92: 7m³ 8m 5g³ 6d 6g 8g⁶ 8.2g³ 10.3m p6g* p7g⁵ f6d p6g
Dec 28] close-coupled filly: useful performer: trained by T. Pitt first 2 outings: good third
in Nell Gwyn Stakes at Newmarket (to Scarlet Runner) and listed race at Hamilton (to
Loch Verdi) first/third starts: mostly below that form after, including when winning minor
event at Dundalk (blinkered) in November: probably stays 1m: acts on polytrack and
good to firm ground. *D. J. Murphy*

BLUES IN THE NIGHT (IRE) 4 ch.g. Bluebird (USA) 125 – Always True (USA) **82**
67 (Geiger Counter (USA)) [2007 88: 7g 6g p7g⁶ p8g 7m 8.1g⁵ Sep 12] strong gelding:
fairly useful handicapper: stays 1m: acts on polytrack and good to firm going: tried
tongue tied (below form): sold 10,000 gns in October. *P. J. Makin*

BLUE SKY BASIN 2 b.g. (Feb 18) Desert Prince (IRE) 130 – Kimba (USA) (Kris S **81 +**
(USA)) [2007 7.1g⁴ p7g* 8m 7s³ Oct 14] close-coupled gelding: third foal: half-brother
to 4-y-o Gordonville: dam, ran once in France, half-sister to Breeders' Cup Turf winner
Tikkanen and very smart stayer Turgeon: fairly useful form: won maiden at Kempton in
August: good third to Unbreak My Heart in nursery at Goodwood, again taking strong
hold: best short of 1m: acts on polytrack and soft going. *A. M. Balding*

BLUE SKY THINKING (IRE) 8 b.g. Danehill Dancer (IRE) 117 – Lauretta Blue **84**
(IRE) (Bluebird (USA) 125) [2007 92: p10g⁶ p9.5g² p9.5g* p8.6g* p8.6g* 8d* 7.9m⁶
Jun 4] tall, rather leggy gelding: fairly useful performer nowadays: has reportedly had
joints pin fired: won claimers at Wolverhampton in March (2) and April and Newcastle in
May: stays easy 1¼m: acts on polytrack, good to firm and good to soft going: has been
bandaged in front: often hangs left: sometimes races freely. *K. R. Burke*

BLUES MINOR (IRE) 2 b.c. (Mar 23) Acclamation 118 – Narbayda (IRE) 68 (Kah- **84**
yasi 130) [2007 5g⁴ 7d² 6d⁵ 6m 7s* Oct 14] 34,000Y: quite attractive colt: has a moderate
quick action: second foal: half-brother to 3-y-o Goose Green: dam, ran twice, half-sister
to very smart 1¼m/1½m winner Narwala: fairly useful performer: won maiden at

Goodwood (made most, beat Bailey by short head) final start: likely to stay 1m: acts on soft going: sold 18,000 gns. *R. Hannon*

BLUE SPACE 3 b.f. Mtoto 134 – La Tour de Blay (USA) (Irish River (FR) 131) [2007 8m 9m³ p10g⁴ p10g* 12m Sep 2] tall, unfurnished filly: second foal: dam, ran twice in France, out of half-sister to high-class filly up to 1½m Mrs Penny: fair performer: won handicap at Lingfield in August: should stay 1½m (pulled hard and said to have returned jarred up when tried): raced only on polytrack and good to firm ground. *P. J. Makin* **72**

BLUE SPINNAKER (IRE) 8 b.g. Bluebird (USA) 125 – Suedoise (Kris 135) [2007 105: 8s 10.3m 10.4g 10m⁴ 10d² 8.9s 8.5m³ 8m 8g 10.3m 10.5s 8.9d 9.1v 9.1v⁵ Nov 3] sturdy gelding: just fairly useful performer at best in 2007: placed at Pontefract and Beverley in summer: well below form after: worth a try at 1½m: probably acts on any going: tried blinkered/in cheekpieces: held up. *M. W. Easterby* **93 d**

BLUE TOMATO 6 b.g. Orpen (USA) 116 – Ocean Grove (IRE) 84 (Fairy King (USA)) [2007 98: 5m 7.1m 6m⁶ 6g³ 7.1g Jun 9] lengthy, useful-looking gelding: impresses in appearance: fairly useful handicapper: creditable effort in 2007 only when third at Salisbury: has form at 1m, but races mostly at shorter nowadays: acts on polytrack and firm going: tried tongue tied: often wore cheekpieces in 2005. *J. M. Bradley* **92**

BLUE TROJAN (IRE) 7 b.g. Inzar (USA) 112 – Roman Heights (IRE) (Head For Heights 125) [2007 93: 8.1g Jul 7] lengthy gelding: fairly useful handicapper: ran poorly only start in 2007: best at 7f/1m: acts on all-weather, firm and good to soft going: blinkered (below form) once: quirky (sometimes edges left) and dropped out nowadays. *S. Kirk* **–**

BLUE ZENITH (IRE) 2 ch.f. (Feb 17) Daggers Drawn (USA) 114 – Secret Combe (IRE) 81 (Mujadil (USA) 119) [2007 5.1f 6m⁶ 5.1d² 5.1f² 5m⁵ 6m⁴ 6d p5.1g⁴ p5g* 6m Nov 10] tall, leggy filly: second foal: dam 2-y-o 6f winner: fair performer: won maiden at Kempton in October: should be best at 5f/6f: acts on polytrack, firm and good to soft going. *J. S. Moore* **69**

BLU MANRUNA 4 ch.g. Zaha (CAN) 106 – Vrennan 74 (Suave Dancer (USA) 136) [2007 66: p10g⁴ p12g³ p10g² 9g⁶ 9.7f* 9.9m 10m⁵ 10.2m³ p10g⁶ p10g³ p12g⁴ p10m² p10g Dec 28] leggy gelding: fair handicapper: won at Folkestone (made all) in September: stays easy 1½m: acts on polytrack, firm and good to soft going: wears headgear: none too consistent. *J. Akehurst* **74**

BLUSHING HILARY (IRE) 4 ch.f. City On A Hill (USA) 114 – Trinida (Jaazeiro (USA) 127) [2007 78: 12s⁵ 12.1g⁴ 14d³ 16m p13.9g Sep 13] strong filly: fair maiden handicapper: stays 1¾m: acts on polytrack, good to firm and good to soft ground: has been visored/in cheekpieces: has found little. *Miss J. A. Camacho* **70**

BLUSHING LIGHT (USA) 4 b. or br.g. Mt Livermore (USA) – Swan River (USA) (Hennessy (USA) 122) [2007 66: p8g p10g⁵ p9.5g Aug 13] fair maiden, lightly raced: likely to stay 1½m: acts on polytrack: tongue tied (well held) final outing: sold £500 in October. *M. A. Magnusson* **65**

BLUSHING PRINCE (IRE) 9 b.g. Priolo (USA) 127 – Eliade (IRE) 82 (Flash of Steel 120) [2007 47§: f8g³ f8g* p9.5g⁶ 10m⁵ 8s 10m 10.1g⁴ 11.1s Sep 24] sturdy gelding: modest handicapper: won apprentice event at Southwell in February: stays 1¼m: acts on all-weather, heavy and good to firm ground: tried in cheekpieces: tongue tied: one to treat with caution. *R. C. Guest* **55 §**

BLUSHING RUSSIAN (IRE) 5 b.g. Fasliyev (USA) 120 – Ange Rouge (Priolo (USA) 127) [2007 55: p8g p5.1g⁵ p5.1g* p6g f6g⁶ p6g⁶ p5.1g f6g p5.1g⁶ 6m p5.1g p6g⁵ Dec 19] useful-looking gelding: poor performer: won handicap at Wolverhampton in January: effective at 5f to 1m: acts on all-weather: wears cheekpieces: has looked wayward. *J. M. Bradley* **49**

BLUSH ON CUE (USA) 3 b.f. Theatrical 128 – Goldminess (USA) (Mr Prospector (USA)) [2007 p11g 12m⁶ Aug 11] $70,000Y, $105,000 2-y-o: rather leggy filly: sixth foal: half-sister to winning US sprinter by Holy Bull: dam, unraced, half-sister to smart French miler Smolensk, from excellent family: 50/1 and green, ninth at Kempton on debut, much better effort in maidens: sent to USA. *J. H. M. Gosden* **54**

BLUTO 3 b.g. Mtoto 134 – Low Line 66 (High Line 125) [2007 11.1g Jun 13] 20/1, well held in claimer at Hamilton (trotted round at start as if amiss). *P. C. Haslam* **–**

BLYTHE KNIGHT (IRE) 7 ch.g. Selkirk (USA) 129 – Blushing Barada (USA) 53 (Blushing Groom (FR) 131) [2007 107: p8.6g² 8s 10.3m³ 8g* 8.5g* 8g 10s⁴ 8d³ 9d Oct 19] quite good-topped gelding: has a round action: smart hurdler: smart performer on **117**

Vodafone Diomed Stakes, Epsom—the versatile Blythe Knight sees off the challenge of Blue Ksar; Welsh Emperor and King Jock are next in the five-runner field

Flat: won listed handicap at York in May and Vodafone Diomed Stakes at Epsom (better than ever when beating Blue Ksar by length, taking while to settle) in June: best effort after when respectable third to Spirito del Vento in Prix Daniel Wildenstein at Longchamp eighth start: barely stays 1¼m: acts on polytrack, firm and soft going: has worn headgear: races more in touch nowadays. *J. J. Quinn*

BLYTHE SPIRIT 8 b.g. Bahamian Bounty 116 – Lithe Spirit (IRE) 74 (Dancing Dissident (USA) 119) [2007 57: p5.1g³ f6g⁴ f6g⁴ f6g⁵ f6g* f6g* p6g p6g⁴ 7g f6g⁶ 6g p7.1g 7.6d 6d p6g p6g p7.1g³ p8.6g p8.6g f7d Dec 15] lengthy gelding: modest on all-weather, poor on turf: won handicaps at Southwell in February and March: left R. Fahey after eleventh outing: stays easy 7f: acts on all-weather, firm and soft ground: usually wears headgear: tried tongue tied. *Mrs L. Williamson* — **46 a59**

BOANERGES (IRE) 10 br.g. Caerleon (USA) 132 – Sea Siren 68 (Slip Anchor 136) [2007 66: p6g p5.1g Jan 15] smallish, strong gelding: fair performer: well below form in handicaps in 2007: tried in headgear: dead. *J. M. Bradley* — **–**

BOBAL GIRL 2 ch.f. (Mar 16) Tobougg (IRE) 125 – Al Guswa 98 (Shernazar 131) [2007 8.5m 7.1g p6m² Oct 13] 2,000Y: sister to 9.3f/1¼m winner Amanda Carter and half-sister to several winners, including useful 7f (at 2 yrs) to 1½m winner Tough Leader (by Lead On Time): dam Irish 1m (at 2 yrs) and 1¼m winner: modest form in maidens, possibly flattered (held up off strong pace) when 5 lengths second at Kempton: should be suited by 1m+. *E. F. Vaughan* — **59 ?**

BOBANSHEIL (IRE) 3 b.f. Dushyantor (USA) 123 – Bobanlyn (IRE) 76 (Dance of Life (USA)) [2007 66: 10.4g⁵ 8.5g 12.1m Jun 13] strong, lengthy filly: maiden: little form in 2007: bred to stay 1½m+. *J. S. Wainwright* — **–**

BOB BAILEYS 5 b.g. Mister Baileys 123 – Bob's Princess 69 (Bob's Return (IRE) 123) [2007 59: f7g³ f8g² f8g⁶ p11g May 9] modest performer: stays 8.6f, probably not 1¼m: acts on all-weather: tried in cheekpieces, blinkered nowadays. *P. R. Chamings* — **55**

BOBBY CHARLES 6 ch.g. Polish Precedent (USA) 131 – Dina Line (USA) 60 (Diesis 133) [2007 88: p10g⁵ p10g 10d⁵ Jun 29] good-topped gelding: fairly useful handicapper: has won at 1½m, best at 1¼m: acts on all-weather, firm and soft going: sold 17,000 gns in August. *Dr J. D. Scargill* — **84**

BOBBY DARLING (IRE) 2 b.f. (Apr 29) Montjeu (IRE) 137 – Karinski (USA) (Palace Music (USA) 129) [2007 7g 9d 9s⁶ Oct 14] 42,000Y: good-bodied filly: seventh foal: half-sister to several winners, notably 6-y-o Appalachian Trail: dam unraced: form in maidens only when well-held sixth at Goodwood. *M. R. Channon* — **51**

BOBBY ROSE 4 b.g. Sanglamore (USA) 126 – Grown At Rowan 75 (Gabitat 119) [2007 72: p6g f6g p6g* 6g 6m⁶ p6g 6s⁵ 6g³ 5.1g³ 5.1d⁶ 5.3d 6g² p6g* 6.1m* p6g⁵ 6d Oct 30] good-topped gelding: fairly useful handicapper: won at Kempton in March and — **82**

September and apprentice event at Nottingham in October: best at 5f/6f: acts on poly-track, good to firm and good to soft going: tried in cheekpieces/blinkers: sometimes finds little. *D. K. Ivory*

BOBERING 7 b.g. Bob's Return (IRE) 123 – Ring The Rafters (Batshoof 122) [2007 **64** 55: p8.6g⁶ p9.5g* p9.5g⁴ 10.9m p8.6g p8.6g p9.5m² p9.5g⁴ p12.2g⁶ p9.5g³ p9.5g Nov 22] strong gelding: modest handicapper: won at Wolverhampton in January: effective at 8.6f to 1½m: acts on all-weather: held up: usually apprentice ridden. *B. P. J. Baugh*

BOBSKI (IRE) 5 b.g. Victory Note (USA) 120 – Vivid Impression (Cure The Blues **84** (USA)) [2007 90: p8g* p7g⁶ 7g 7d 8m p8g 7.6m⁴ 8.1g⁶ p7g² p8g³ Oct 24] good-topped **a94** gelding: fairly useful handicapper: won at Lingfield in January: effective at 6f to 1m: acts on polytrack and good to firm going: tried blinkered: ran creditably in cheekpieces last 2 starts, though seemed to hang fire final one: often slowly away: held up. *G. A. Huffer*

BOBSLEIGH 8 b.g. Robellino (USA) 127 – Do Run Run 75 (Commanche Run 133) **54** [2007 66: p16g p16g⁶ 16m⁴ 16m⁶ p13g Jul 10] leggy, useful-looking gelding: modest handicapper: stays 21f: acts on polytrack, firm and good to soft going: tried blinkered/in cheekpieces: has run well when edgy: usually makes running: signs of temperament. *H. S. Howe*

BOBS SURPRISE 2 ch.c. (Apr 22) Bertolini (USA) 125 – Flourish (Selkirk (USA) **99** 129) [2007 6g* 6m 6m⁵ 6g Aug 3] 60,000Y: rangy colt: fifth foal: closely related to fairly useful 2003 2-y-o 5f/6f winner Baltic Wave (later winner at 1m in Hong Kong, by Polish Precedent) and half-brother to 3-y-o Non Compliant and 4-y-o Rondo: dam unraced half-sister to useful 1¼m performer Forthwith: useful form: won maiden at Goodwood in June: contested pattern races after, namely Coventry Stakes at Royal Ascot, July Stakes at Newmarket (best effort, 3½ lengths fifth of 13 to Winker Watson) and Richmond Stakes at Goodwood: will prove at least as effective at 5f as 6f: highly strung, and gets stirred up in preliminaries. *B. W. Hills*

BOB'S YOUR UNCLE 4 br.g. Zilzal (USA) 137 – Bob's Princess 69 (Bob's Return **63** (IRE) 123) [2007 73: 10.9m 11g³ p12g² p12g* p16g² p13g³ p16g⁵ 16m⁵ 14.1m⁶ p16g **a70** 11.9g² Oct 25] leggy gelding: fair handicapper: won at Lingfield in June: stays 2m: acts on polytrack, good to firm and good to soft going: patiently ridden: sometimes hangs. *J. G. Portman*

BOCHINCHE (USA) 3 b.f. Kingmambo (USA) 125 – Hatoof (USA) 124 (Irish River **59** (FR) 131) [2007 p8g⁵ 10.2d Oct 1] closely related to useful USA/UAE winner around 1m Dubai Edition and fairly useful 1½m winner Prospects of Glory (both by Mr Prospector) and half-sister to French 10.5f winner Mighty Isis (by Pleasant Colony): dam 1m to 1½m performer (won 1000 Guineas and Champion Stakes): much better effort in maidens when fifth to stable-companion Gold Sovereign at Lingfield: folded tamely next time: should be suited by 1¼m: has left Godolphin. *Saeed bin Suroor*

BODDEN BAY 5 b.g. Cayman Kai (IRE) 114 – Badger Bay (IRE) 67 (Salt Dome **66** (USA)) [2007 68: p6g f6g⁵ p6g² 6g² p7.1g f6g⁶ p6g 7g Sep 19] fair performer: left Gay Kelleway after third start: stays 7f: acts on all-weather, good to firm and good to soft going: tried in cheekpieces/visor/tongue tie: races prominently: has run well when sweating. *I. W. McInnes*

BOEKENHOUTSKLOOF (IRE) 3 b.f. Selkirk (USA) 129 – Labrusca 58 (Grand – Lodge (USA) 125) [2007 12.1s p11g 12m Jul 27] 7,500F, 32,000Y: workmanlike filly: first foal: dam, once-raced maiden, half-sister to very smart Yorkshire Oaks winner Catchascatchcan (later dam of very smart miler Antonius Pius): well held in maidens: sold £4,000 in August. *E. F. Vaughan*

BOGAZ (IRE) 5 b.g. Rossini (USA) 118 – Fastnet (Forzando 122) [2007 48: 7m⁶ 8m⁵ **30** Jun 13] smallish, robust gelding: only poor nowadays: stays 1m: acts on fibresand and firm going: tried in visor/cheekpieces: none too consistent. *Mrs H. Sweeting*

BOGSIDE KATIE 3 b.f. Hunting Lion (IRE) 115 – Enchanting Eve 67 (Risk Me (FR) – 127) [2007 48: p6g⁵ f7g Jan 11] maiden: well held in 2007. *G. M. Moore*

BOGSIDE THEATRE (IRE) 3 b.f. Fruits of Love (USA) 127 – Royal Jubilee (IRE) **96** 81 (King's Theatre (IRE) 128) [2007 10.1m* 10m⁶ 13d* 12f⁴ 14g 14s² Sep 29] €8,500Y: close-coupled, quite good-topped filly: second foal: dam, Irish 9f winner (stayed 1½m), half-sister to useful performer up to 1¼m Postage Stampe, out of half-sister to Kooyonga: useful performer: won maiden at Newcastle (100/1) in June and handicap at Hamilton (by 6 lengths from Charlotte Vale) in July: good efforts in frame in similar events 2 of 3 starts after: stays 1¾m: acts on firm and soft ground (unraced on heavy). *G. M. Moore*

BOHOBE (IRE) 2 b.f. (Jan 28) Noverre (USA) 125 – Green Life 63 (Green Desert **71** (USA) 127) [2007 f6g⁴ 6g⁶ 5d* 6m³ 6.5m 6.1d Oct 18] 8,000Y: quite good-topped filly: half-sister to 3 winners, including fairly useful 2002 2-y-o 7f/1m winner Agilis (by Titus Livius): dam, Irish maiden (stayed 7f), half-sister to Molecomb Stakes winner Classic Ruler: fair performer: won maiden at Catterick in July: third at Redcar, only form in nurseries: should stay 7f: acts on good to firm and good to soft going. *J. G. Given*

BOISDALE (IRE) 9 b.g. Common Grounds 118 – Alstomeria 61 (Petoski 135) [2007 **49** 44: f6g f5g p6g³ p7g⁶ p6g³ 5s p6g⁵ p6g Dec 29] workmanlike gelding: poor performer: effective at 6f/7f: acts on all-weather, soft and good to firm going: tried tongue tied. *P. S. Felgate*

BOLCKOW 4 b.g. Marju (IRE) 127 – Stamatina (Warning 136) [2007 63: f12g* f12g⁵ **72** f11g² f12g² f11g f11g⁴ p12g f11d³ f12d Dec 20] tall gelding: fair handicapper: won at Southwell in January: stays 1½m: acts on all-weather and firm going. *J. T. Stimpson*

BOLD ABBOTT (USA) 3 b.c. Mizzen Mast (USA) 121 – Ms Isadora (USA) (Mis- **83** waki (USA) 124) [2007 85: 7m* 7g⁴ 7.1d³ 7m⁵ 8.1g⁶ 7f⁶ Sep 25] lengthy, good-topped colt: has a quick action: fairly useful performer: won maiden at Goodwood in May: generally creditable efforts in handicaps after: stays 1m: acts on good to firm and good to soft going: blinkered/visored last 3 starts: sent to USA. *Mrs A. J. Perrett*

BOLD ADVENTURE 3 ch.g. Arkadian Hero (USA) 123 – Impatiente (USA) **76** (Vaguely Noble 140) [2007 47p: 10.1g 10d 10.1g⁴ 11.5m p12.2g³ p16g* p13.9g* p13.9g* p13.9g Nov 8] good-bodied gelding: fair handicapper: much improved when winning at Kempton and Wolverhampton in September and Wolverhampton in October: stays 2m: acts on polytrack. *W. J. Musson*

BOLD ARGUMENT (IRE) 4 ch.g. Shinko Forest (IRE) – Ivory Bride 86 (Domyn- **68** sky 110) [2007 76: p6g 7d⁴ 6g⁴ p5g 5.1g 6d p6g⁴ p7g⁵ Oct 31] big, lengthy gelding: fair handicapper: best form at 6f: acts on polytrack, firm and good to soft going: tried tongue tied. *Mrs P. N. Dutfield*

BOLD BOBBY 3 b.f. Pivotal 124 – Mrs P 96 (First Trump 118) [2007 6s⁵ 6d³ p6g Jul **54** 10] 150,000Y: second foal: dam, 2-y-o 5f winner (including Flying Childers), half-sister to smart sprinter Sarcita: modest maiden: worth a try at 5f: edged left second start. *J. M. P. Eustace*

BOLD CHOICE (IRE) 2 b.c. (Apr 7) Dubai Destination (USA) 127 – Sheer Spirit **97** (IRE) 86 (Caerleon (USA) 132) [2007 7d² 7.1m² 7m 8m⁴ Oct 22] €220,000Y: small, heavy-bodied colt: fourth foal: half-brother to 3 winners, including 4-y-o River Bravo and 3-y-o Solid Rock: dam, 1½m winner, half-sister to Derby winner Oath and high-class 1m/1¼m performer Pelder: useful maiden: stiff task and well held third start (valuable sales race at the Curragh), but progressive form otherwise: second at Ascot (to City Leader) and Sandown, and fourth to Siberian Tiger in listed event at Pontefract (dictated): stays 1m. *M. A. Jarvis*

BOLD CROSS (IRE) 4 b.g. Cape Cross (IRE) 129 – Machikane Akaiito (IRE) **71** (Persian Bold 123) [2007 67: p10g⁵ p10g 8m⁴ 8.1g⁵ 10.9d p8g 10d p7.1g* 7.1m² 7.1m* p8.6g⁶ p7.1g³ p7g³ Oct 29] leggy gelding: fair performer: won minor event at Wolver-hampton and handicap at Warwick, both in September: effective at 7f to 1¼m: acts on polytrack, soft and good to firm ground: pulled too hard fifth outing (said to have finished distressed): sometimes slowly away. *E. G. Bevan*

BOLD DIKTATOR 5 b.g. Diktat 126 – Madam Bold (Never So Bold 135) [2007 85: **85** p8g* p8.6g* p10g p8g⁶ 8.1g* 8.1g 8m⁶ p8.6g 8.1m p8.6g⁶ p8.6g⁴ Oct 6] strong gelding: fairly useful handicapper: won at Lingfield in January, Wolverhampton in February and Sandown in April: stays 8.6f: acts on polytrack and firm going: effective with or without blinkers: usually races prominently: sold 27,000 gns. *Tom Dascombe*

BOLD DIVA 2 ch.f. (Apr 15) Bold Edge 123 – Trina's Pet 65 (Efisio 120) [2007 5m 5m **40** 5.7f 6g⁴ 6d 6m 8.1f 8f 6.1d Oct 18] 1,500Y: rather leggy filly: fifth foal: half-sister to a winner in Italy by Bahamian Bounty: dam 2-y-o 5f seller winner: poor maiden: tried blinkered. *A. W. Carroll*

BOLD FINCH (FR) 5 b.g. Valanour (IRE) 125 – Eagle's Nest (FR) 62 (King of Mace- **49** don 126) [2007 –: 11.8s 9g Jun 1] poor maiden handicapper: stays easy 9f: said to have finished lame final outing. *J. M. Bradley*

BOLD GLANCE 3 gr.c. Kingmambo (USA) 125 – Last Second (IRE) 121 (Alzao **93** (USA) 117) [2007 10m* 12m Oct 6] 1,250,000Y: useful-looking colt: has scope: sixth foal: half-brother to very smart miler Aussie Rules (by Danehill), 7.5f and 1¼m winner Approach (stayed 1½m) and 2004 2-y-o 8.5f winner Intrigued (both useful and by Darshaan): dam, won Nassau and Sun Chariot Stakes, half-sister to dams of Alborada/ Albanova and Quarter Moon/Yesterday: fairly useful form when winning maiden at Pontefract in September by ½ length from stable-companion Abydos: ran poorly in handicap at Newmarket only subsequent outing, then left Godolphin. *Saeed bin Suroor*

BOLD HAZE 5 ch.g. Bold Edge 123 – Melody Park 104 (Music Boy 124) [2007 64: 6s⁵ **71 d** 5.9g* 7.1g⁶ 6d 6f 6m 7.1g Oct 5] big, good-bodied gelding: fair handicapper at best: won at Carlisle in June: below form after: stays 7f: acts on soft and good to firm going: visored: tends to edge left: has been slowly away. *Miss S. E. Hall*

BOLD INDIAN (IRE) 3 b.g. Indian Danehill (IRE) 124 – Desert Gift 69 (Green **71** Desert (USA) 127) [2007 73: 9m³ 9.9m⁵ 8m 7m 7g* 7d 7m 8.3m* 8.3m 8s⁵ p8.6g³ p8.6g⁵ p7.1g Nov 1] sturdy gelding: fair performer: won claimers at Catterick in June and Hamilton in August: seems to stay 9.9f: acts on polytrack, soft and good to firm going: well below form in cheekpieces: not straightforward, but is consistent. *I. Semple*

BOLD JOSR 3 b.g. Josr Algarhoud (IRE) 118 – Skiddaw Bird (Bold Owl 101) [2007 **–** p12g Aug 29] 66/1, well beaten in maiden at Kempton. *D. J. S. ffrench Davis*

BOLD LOVE 4 ch.f. Bold Edge 123 – Noor El Houdah (IRE) 61 (Fayruz 116) [2007 **42** 47: f7g⁵ p7.1g⁵ f6g⁵ May 14] workmanlike filly: poor performer: stays 7f: acts on all-weather, probably good to firm going: tried in cheekpieces/blinkered/tongue tied: sold 5,500 gns in December (in foal to Superior Premium). *J. Balding*

BOLD MARC (IRE) 5 b.g. Bold Fact (USA) 116 – Zara's Birthday (IRE) 71 (Waajib **89** 121) [2007 88: 8.1g⁴ 7f⁵ 8.1m* 8m 8.1m 7.9d* 8.1g 7g 8.3m 8s Sep 21] leggy, good-topped gelding: fairly useful handicapper: won at Haydock in May and Carlisle in June: stays 1m: acts on all-weather and any turf going: tried visored/in cheekpieces. *K. R. Burke*

BOLD MINSTREL (IRE) 5 br.g. Bold Fact (USA) 116 – Ponda Rosa (IRE) 66 (Case **82** Law 113) [2007 87: p5f f5g 5m 5m² 5.2g* 5m 5s⁶ 5g 5d p5g p5.1d Dec 7] good-bodied gelding: fairly useful handicapper: won at Yarmouth in May: barely stays 5.7f: acts on polytrack, good to firm and good to soft going: tried visored: none too consistent. *M. Quinn*

BOLD NEVISON (IRE) 3 b.g. Danehill Dancer (IRE) 117 – La Pieta (IRE) 96 **51** (Spectrum (IRE) 126) [2007 62: p7.1g 8m 8.5m 9g p7.1g f6d⁶ Dec 21] modest maiden: stays 7f: acts on all-weather: has raced freely. *B. Smart*

BOLD PHOENIX (IRE) 6 b.g. Dr Fong (USA) 128 – Subya 107 (Night Shift (USA)) **57** [2007 66: f12g p9.5g 10.1m p8.6g² May 3] sturdy gelding: modest nowadays: stays 9.5f: acts on all-weather, soft and good to firm going: effective blinkered or not: has hung. *B. J. Curley*

BOLD SAXON (IRE) 3 ch.g. Desert Sun 120 – Sirdhana 79 (Selkirk (USA) 129) **66** [2007 70: p9.5g⁵ p8.6g f7g³ 7s⁶ 8.3m p7g⁶ p8.6g⁶ p8g p9.5g⁴ p9.5g⁵ p8.6g p10g Oct 31] strong, lengthy gelding: fair maiden: stays 9.5f: acts on polytrack and soft going: tried visored: sold 7,000 gns. *M. D. I. Usher*

BOLD TIGER (IRE) 4 b.g. Bold Fact (USA) 116 – Heart of The Ocean (IRE) 73 **–** (Soviet Lad (USA)) [2007 48: 7g 7m 7m 8d May 15] poor maiden: stays 7f: acts on firm going: tried blinkered/in cheekpieces/tongue tied. *Miss Tracy Waggott*

BOLD TRUMP 6 b.g. First Trump 118 – Blue Nile (IRE) 70 (Bluebird (USA) 125) **–** [2007 57: f14g⁴ f14g Jan 25] leggy gelding: modest performer at 5 yrs: well below form in 2007 (reportedly bled final start): stays 1½m: acts on all-weather: tried in visor/ cheekpieces/tongue tie: modest hurdler, successful in June. *Mrs N. S. Evans*

BOLEYNA (USA) 3 b.f. Officer (USA) 120 – Cassation (USA) (Lear Fan (USA) 130) **53** [2007 f6g⁵ 6f 6m Aug 15] $20,000Y, 40,000 2-y-o: lengthy filly: third live foal: half-sister to winner in USA by Stravinsky: dam unraced sister to very smart 1m/1¼m performer Ryafan: form in maidens only when fifth at Southwell. *Rae Guest*

BOLLIN DEREK 4 gr.c. Silver Patriarch (IRE) 125 – Bollin Magdalene 55 (Teenoso **95** (USA) 135) [2007 83: f11g⁶ 16g⁵ 14g* May 17] big, strong colt: has a moderate, quick action: useful handicapper: better than ever when winning at York final start by 5 lengths from Sphinx: suffered leg injury after: stays 2m: has won on good to firm going, better form on good or softer (acts on heavy): has raced in snatches/made running. *T. D. Easterby*

BOLLIN DOLLY 4 ch.f. Bien Bien (USA) 125 – Bollin Roberta 75 (Bob's Return **73** (IRE) 123) [2007 72: 10.5m 9.8g⁵ 9.9m⁴ 12.1m Sep 11] good-topped filly: fair maiden handicapper: stays 1½m: acts on firm and good to soft ground: has been troublesome at stall: usually makes running. *T. D. Easterby*

BOLLIN FELIX 3 br.c. Generous (IRE) 139 – Bollin Magdalene 55 (Teenoso (USA) **88**
135) [2007 49p: 11g⁴ 14.1g* 12.1m³ 12s* 12s* 14.6m³ 14g 13.1s³ 16m⁶ Oct 3] leggy,
close-coupled colt: fairly useful handicapper: much improved in 2007, winning at
Nottingham in May, and Pontefract and Ripon (beat Music Review by 7 lengths) in July:
stays 2m: acts on good to firm going, may prove ideally suited by more testing conditions
(acts on soft): blinkered nowadays. *T. D. Easterby*

BOLLIN FERGUS 3 br.c. Vettori (IRE) 119 – Bollin Harriet (Lochnager 132) [2007 ?: **58**
8.2g 7m³ 7.1g⁶ 7s 9.8g⁵ Aug 27] modest maiden handicapper: probably stays 1¼m: acts
on soft and good to firm ground: sold 4,500 gns. *T. D. Easterby*

BOLLIN FRANNY 3 br.c. Bertolini (USA) 125 – Bollin Ann 72 (Anshan 119) [2007 **70**
72d: 5g 5m² 5v⁶ 6m 5d⁵ 5g 5f⁶ Sep 5] good-topped colt: fair handicapper: ran creditably
in 2007 only on second start: best at 5f: acts on firm going: tried blinkered: sold 5,000
gns. *T. D. Easterby*

BOLLIN FREDDIE 3 ch.g. Golden Snake (USA) 127 – Bollin Roberta 75 (Bob's **51**
Return (IRE) 123) [2007 –: 8.5g 12.1m 12.1s⁶ 12g⁶ Aug 29] good-topped gelding:
modest maiden handicapper: stays 1½m: acts on soft and good to firm ground: reportedly
finished lame second start. *A. J. Lockwood*

BOLLIN GRETA 2 b.f. (Jun 16) Mtoto 134 – Bollin Zola 90 (Alzao (USA) 117) [2007 **– p**
7.5g Sep 19] closely related to St Leger winner Bollin Eric (by Shaamit) and half-sister to
several winners, including Duke of York Stakes winner Bollin Joanne (by Damister): dam
5f (at 2 yrs) and 7f winner: 20/1, not recover from very slow start in maiden at Beverley:
sure to do better. *T. D. Easterby*

BOLLIN GUIL 2 b.c. (Apr 1) Helissio (FR) 136 – Bollin Ann 72 (Anshan 119) [2007 **52 ?**
6g 7d 7.5g Jul 31] stocky colt: seemingly best effort in maidens when eighth at Beverley
final start. *T. D. Easterby*

BOLLIN THOMAS 9 b.g. Alhijaz 122 – Bollin Magdalene 55 (Teenoso (USA) 135) **–**
[2007 72: 13d 13d Jul 13] strong gelding: fair handicapper at best: no form in 2007:
effective at 1½m to 2m: acts on heavy and good to firm going: has worn blinkers/cheek-
pieces: usually races prominently: sometimes hangs. *R. Allan*

BOLLYWOOD (IRE) 4 ch.g. Indian Rocket 115 – La Fille de Cirque 49 (Cadeaux **52**
Genereux 131) [2007 56, a70d: p10g 6m⁴ p7g 7d⁶ 7s⁵ 7m⁴ 8s⁵ p7g 10d 8m⁵ 7.6s² 8m
p10g p7g p8g p7g⁴ Dec 30] modest performer: stays easy 1¼m: acts on polytrack, soft
and good to firm going: tried in blinkers/cheekpieces: inconsistent. *J. J. Bridger*

BOLLYWOOD STYLE 2 b.f. (Mar 1) Josr Algarhoud (IRE) 118 – Dane Dancing **54**
(IRE) 68 (Danehill (USA) 126) [2007 p6m² p6g² p8g⁴ p10g³ p7g p10g⁴ Nov 19] 3,000Y:
fourth foal: half-sister to 5-y-o Viking Spirit: dam, 9.4f winner, sister to useful performer
up to 1¼m Sundari: modest maiden: raced only in sellers/claimers (left P. Winkworth
£6,000 second start), in frame 5 times: stays 1¼m: raced on polytrack. *J. R. Best*

BOLODENKA (IRE) 5 b.g. Soviet Star (USA) 128 – My-Lorraine (IRE) 77 (Mac's **104**
Imp (USA) 116) [2007 107: p8.6g³ 8g⁴ 8g⁵ 8s 8m 8d⁵ 8.5g 7s 8g* 7m 10m⁴ Sep 22]
leggy, useful-looking gelding: useful handicapper: won at Ripon in August by head from
Ragheed: better effort after when creditable 3 lengths fourth to Monte Alto in John
Smith's Stakes at Newbury: effective at 7f to 1¼m: acts on polytrack, soft and good to
firm going: patiently ridden. *R. A. Fahey*

BOLTON HALL (IRE) 5 b.g. Imperial Ballet (IRE) 110 – Muneera (USA) 67 (Green **70 §**
Dancer (USA) 132) [2007 74: 8m⁶ 8m 7.9m 10s 9.1m³ 8m² p8g³ 8.5g* 7.5m² 8g³ 10.5g
p8.6g p8.6g³ p8g Dec 1] strong, angular gelding: fair handicapper: won amateur event at
Beverley in August: stays 9f: acts on polytrack and firm going: tried in cheekpieces: edgy
sort, sometimes races freely: often slowly away (virtually refused to race twelfth/
penultimate starts): one to treat with caution. *R. A. Fahey*

BOMBARDIER WELLS 2 b.c. (Mar 11) Red Ransom (USA) – Bow River Gold **61**
(Rainbow Quest (USA) 134) [2007 6m⁵ 6.5d Oct 11] good-topped colt: raced in maidens
at Newbury, promising fifth to Paco Boy on debut, then possibly didn't handle softer
ground: will stay 7f/1m. *Eve Johnson Houghton*

BOMBER COMMAND (USA) 4 b.g. Stravinsky (USA) 133 – Parish Manor (USA) **85**
(Waquoit (USA)) [2007 71+, a104: p7f² p8.6g² p8g⁵ 8.1g 7g 7m* 7g² 6g⁶ p6g⁵ p7g⁶ **a102**
p8g p7m Nov 1] big, workmanlike gelding: useful handicapper on all-weather, fairly
useful on turf: won at Ascot (by ½ length from Moonlight Man) in July: stays 8.6f: acts on
polytrack and good to firm going: tends to idle: sometimes wears headgear. *J. W. Hills*

BO MCGINTY (IRE) 6 ch.g. Fayruz 116 – Georges Park Lady (IRE) (Tirol 127) **93**
[2007 92: 5g 7g 5g² f5g⁴ 5m⁴ 5m³ 5m 5d⁴ 5v⁴ 6s³ 5s 5.4v² 6m⁵ 5g 5g* 5g² 5d³ 5d³ 5g⁴ 5g **a74 +**
Oct 27] good-topped gelding: fairly useful handicapper on all-weather, fair on turf: won
at Haydock in September: best at 5f/6f: acts on any turf going: usually wears headgear:
races prominently. *R. A. Fahey*

BONA FIDELIS (IRE) 2 b.f. (Mar 8) Namid 128 – Sacred Love (IRE) 69 (Barathea —
(IRE) 127) [2007 p7g Sep 24] 10,000Y: compact filly: first foal: dam, maiden (should
have stayed at least 1¼m), out of sister to very smart French 1½m performer De Quest:
burly, well beaten in maiden at Kempton. *A. J. McCabe*

BONCHESTER BRIDGE 6 b.m. Shambo 113 – Cabriole Legs (Handsome Sailor —
125) [2007 12s⁴ Jun 26] first foal: dam unraced half-sister to useful 2m hurdler Indian
Quest: won bumper in 2005: also fair winner over hurdles (has carried head high/found
little): 10/3, well held in maiden at Newbury on Flat debut. *N. J. Henderson*

BOND ANGEL EYES 4 b.f. Dr Fong (USA) 128 – Speedybird (IRE) 71 (Danehill **46**
(USA) 126) [2007 57: p7.1g p8.6g⁶ 7m May 3] just poor maiden nowadays: likely to
prove best at 7f/1m: acts on firm and good to soft going: tried in cheekpieces/visor.
G. R. Oldroyd

BOND BECKS (IRE) 7 ch.g. Tagula (IRE) 116 – At Amal (IRE) (Astronef 116) [2007 **64**
63: 5m 5m⁶ 5m 5m⁵ 5m⁴ 5g 5m p6g* p6g* p6g Dec 22] big, lengthy gelding: reportedly
tubed: modest handicapper nowadays: won at Wolverhampton in November and Lingfield in December: stays 6f: acts on polytrack and firm going: headstrong. *G. R. Oldroyd*

BOND BOY 10 b.g. Piccolo 121 – Arabellajill 97 (Aragon 118) [2007 95: 5f³ 5g f5g 6d **84**
5s² 5v² 5s⁴ 5s 5g 5s⁵ 5d 5s Sep 26] sturdy gelding: useful handicapper at his best: fairly
useful when placed in 2007, below form otherwise: stayed 6f: acted on fibresand and any
turf going: usually wore headgear: usually held up: reportedly retired. *G. R. Oldroyd*

BOND CASINO 3 b.f. Kyllachy 129 – Songsheet 74 (Dominion 123) [2007 54: 6m **69**
6m³ 6d 6v 7m 10.1m⁴ 12g² p12.2g² p12.2g* p12.2g³ p12.2g⁴ p13.9g³ p16.5g Dec 8]
good-bodied filly: fair handicapper: won at Wolverhampton in September (awarded race
outright after dead-heating): stays 1¾m: acts on polytrack and good to firm ground: tried
in cheekpieces. *G. R. Oldroyd*

BOND CITY (IRE) 5 b.g. Trans Island 119 – Where's Charlotte 53 (Sure Blade (USA) **112**
130) [2007 114: 5.1g² 6f² 5m³ 6g 5g 5g³ 5g³ 5.1d³ 5g 6m 5m⁴ 5d² 5m 5g Oct 20] strong
gelding: smart performer: placed 7 times in 2007, including when third in Palace House
Stakes at Newmarket (to Tax Free) and Sprint Stakes at Sandown (to Hoh Mike) third/
seventh starts: ran respectably after only when second to Philharmonic in minor event at
Beverley in September: effective at 5f/easy 6f: acts on polytrack, firm and soft going: in
cheekpieces last 4 starts. *G. R. Oldroyd*

BOND CRUZ 4 b.g. King's Best (USA) 132 – Arabis 88 (Arazi (USA) 135) [2007 –: —
10m May 25] sturdy gelding: modest maiden at 2 yrs: little form since: tried in headgear.
D. Burchell

BOND DIAMOND 10 gr.g. Prince Sabo 123 – Alsiba 68 (Northfields (USA)) [2007 **54**
72: p8.6g⁶ 8.5m⁴ 8m p8.6g⁵ 8m³ 8f Aug 12] strong, lengthy gelding: just modest nowadays: won seller at Beverley in April: effective at 7f to easy 1¼m: acts on all-weather,
firm and good to soft going: tried in cheekpieces: tends to carry head awkwardly:
sometimes races freely: held up. *P. T. Midgley*

BOND FREE SPIRIT (IRE) 4 br.f. Shinko Forest (IRE) – Sawaki 71 (Song 132) —
[2007 54: p7.1g 6f f8g May 15] rather leggy filly: maiden: no form in 2007. *G. R. Oldroyd*

BOND PLAYBOY 7 b.g. Piccolo 121 – Highest Ever (FR) (Highest Honor (FR) 124) **68**
[2007 74: p6g³ p5.1g⁶ p5.1g⁵ p7.1g 5s 5d 6m 6d⁵ 5.9g p6g⁶ p6g⁴ p6g* p6g² Oct 12] good-
bodied gelding: fair handicapper won apprentice event at Wolverhampton in October:
best up to 7f: acts on all-weather, good to firm and good to soft going: wears headgear:
often slowly away. *G. R. Oldroyd*

BOND SCISSORSISTER (IRE) 2 b.f. (Jan 29) Xaar 132 – Musical Refrain (IRE) **51**
(Dancing Dissident (USA) 119) [2007 6m 6m⁶ 6.5d Sep 28] 3,000Y: lengthy filly: fourth
foal: half-sister to fairly useful Irish 5f/6f winner Ms Victoria (by Fasliyev): dam unraced
half-sister to very smart 6f/7f performer Monsieur Bond: modest maiden: stiff task (sales
race at Ascot) final start. *G. R. Oldroyd*

BOND SEA BREEZE (IRE) 4 b.f. Namid 128 – Gold Prospector (IRE) 78 (Spec- —
trum (IRE) 126) [2007 –: p5.1g p8.6g⁶ Jan 19] well-made filly: no form. *G. R. Oldroyd*

BONJOUR ALLURE (IRE) 2 b.f. (Apr 22) Hawk Wing (USA) 136 – Exact Replica **85**
(Darshaan 133) [2007 7g^2 7.5g* 8m Sep 13] €66,000Y: tall filly: fifth foal: half-sister to
7f winner Authenticate (by Dansili) and French 1m winner Greenfly (by Green Desert):
dam unraced sister to smart 1m to 1¼m performer Darnay: fairly useful form: won
maiden at Beverley by short head from Dubai Time (Floristry third) in August: seemed
amiss in nursery at Doncaster: should be suited by 1m. *Mrs A. Duffield*

BONNE D'ARGENT (IRE) 3 b.f. Almutawakel 126 – Petite-D-Argent 91 (Noalto **73**
120) [2007 76: 6g 8g p7g p8g^3 7d p10g Nov 30] small, sturdy filly: fair maiden: stays 1m:
acts on polytrack and good to soft going. *J. R. Boyle*

BONNET O'BONNIE 3 br.f. Makbul 104 – Parkside Prospect 65 (Piccolo 121) [2007 **54**
–: f6g^4 p7.1g^4 6.1g^6 p6g^4 p6g^5 p6g p6g p8g Dec 5] modest maiden: stays 7f: acts on
all-weather. *J. Mackie*

BONNIE BELLE 4 b.f. Imperial Ballet (IRE) 110 – Reel Foyle (USA) 77 (Irish River **–**
(FR) 131) [2007 64: p7g May 22] modest maiden, lightly raced: tailed off only outing in
2007: best effort at 1m on good ground. *J. R. Boyle*

BONNIE PRINCE BLUE 4 ch.g. Tipsy Creek (USA) 115 – Heart So Blue (Dilum **88**
(USA) 115) [2007 95: 8.3f^6 p7g* 7g 7g p7g^3 p7g 7s^4 7.1s^6 7.1d^3 p7g^6 p7g^4 p7.1g^3 p8g 7m
p6g^2 Nov 30] quite attractive gelding: fairly useful handicapper: won at Kempton in May:
good second at Lingfield final outing: effective at 6f to 1m: acts on polytrack, good to
firm and good to soft going: tried blinkered. *B. W. Hills*

BONNY ROSE 2 ch.f. (Mar 6) Zaha (CAN) 106 – Marina Park 112 (Local Suitor **73**
(USA) 128) [2007 6m^2 7.1g^2 6s^2 7.1g* 7g Oct 27] good-topped filly: fifth foal: half-sister
to 3 winners, including useful 6f (at 2 yrs) to 1¼m winner Marinas Charm (by Zafonic):
dam 5f/6f winner (including at 2 yrs): fair performer: second 3 times prior to winning
maiden at Musselburgh in October: ran as though something amiss in nursery at
Doncaster: stays 7f: acts on soft and good to firm going. *M. Johnston*

BONNY'S BABE 2 b.f. (Feb 9) City On A Hill (USA) 114 – Ashtree Belle 87 (Up And **55**
At 'em 109) [2007 f6g 6m* 6m 6.1d p6g p7.1g 7g^2 Oct 19] 5,000Y: leggy filly: first foal:
dam 6f (at 2 yrs)/7f winner: modest performer: won seller at Redcar in June: second in
claimer final start (tongue tied): effective at 6f/7f. *B. Smart*

BONNY SCOTLAND (IRE) 3 b.f. Redback 116 – Muckross Park 41 (Nomination **–**
125) [2007 47: f5g f5g f7g f5g^5 Feb 20] workmanlike filly: maiden: little form in 2007:
often slowly away. *I. W. McInnes*

BON TON ROULET 2 ch.f. (Jan 29) Hawk Wing (USA) 136 – Evangeline (Sadler's **56**
Wells (USA) 132) [2007 p7g Nov 17] second foal: dam unraced half-sister to useful 2003
2-y-o 7f/1m winner Sgt Pepper: 10/1, never a threat in maiden at Lingfield. *R. Hannon*

BONUS (IRE) 7 b.g. Cadeaux Genereux 131 – Khamseh 85 (Thatching 131) [2007 106: **95 +**
p6g^3 6.5g p5g^2 5m 6d 7g p6g^6 p6m^4 p6m^4 p7g* Dec 19] big, strong, angular gelding: **a112**
smart performer on all-weather, useful on turf: won handicap in October (by ½ length
from Beaver Patrol) and listed race in December (by neck from Carcinetto), both at
Kempton: creditable fourth to Maltese Falcon in listed race at Lingfield in between:
effective at 5f to easy 7f: acts on polytrack and firm going, not softer than good: tried
tongue tied/in headgear: often lethargic in preliminaries: reportedly bled fourth outing:
held up. *G. A. Butler*

BOO 5 b.g. Namaqualand (USA) – Violet (IRE) 77 (Mukaddamah (USA) 125) [2007 **83 +**
100, a103: a9f 10g 12g p10g p10g^6 8s 8.9s 10g^5 p10.7g 10.3g Oct 26] quite good-topped **a88 +**
gelding: useful at best, though hasn't won since 2005: only fairly useful and none too
consistent in 2007: stays 1¼m: acts on polytrack and firm going: sometimes wears
headgear: sold 30,000 gns. *K. R. Burke*

BOOGIE BOARD 3 b.f. Tobougg (IRE) 125 – Royal Gift (Cadeaux Genereux 131) **51**
[2007 52: 10.2f^4 8.2g p7g^5 p7.1g p8.6g Jul 10] lengthy, workmanlike filly: modest
maiden: seems to stay 8.6f: acts on polytrack. *S. Parr*

BOOGIE DANCER 3 b.f. Tobougg (IRE) 125 – Bolero (Rainbow Quest (USA) 134) **71**
[2007 68: 9g^3 9.7g^4 p8.6g p7g Dec 28] good-topped filly: fair maiden handicapper: will
stay 1¼m: acts on polytrack and good to firm going. *H. S. Howe*

BOOGIE MAGIC 7 b.m. Wizard King 122 – Dalby Dancer 71 (Bustiki) [2007 55: f8d **–**
Dec 21] good-topped mare: modest performer: well held in handicap at Southwell only
start in 2007: effective at 7f, barely stays 11.6f: acts on polytrack, soft and good to firm
going: tried in cheekpieces: held up. *R. W. Price*

BOOKIEBASHER BABE (IRE) 2 b.f. (Apr 13) Orpen (USA) 116 – Jay Gee (IRE) **56**
93 (Second Set (IRE) 127) [2007 f6g 5.2d⁶ p7.1g p10g² Oct 24] €7,000Y: fifth foal: sister
to 4-y-o Collateral Damage: dam unreliable 2-y-o 6f winner: modest maiden: improved
when runner-up in claimer at Lingfield: stays 1¼m. *M. Quinn*

BOOKIEBASHER DUDE 2 b.c. (Feb 7) Elnadim (USA) 128 – Masaader (USA) 96 **70**
(Wild Again (USA)) [2007 p5g³ 5.1m⁵ 5m p6g² p6g³ 5.3f³ 5.7f² p6g³ Sep 3] €25,000Y:
first foal: dam, 6f winner (including at 2 yrs), half-sister to Middle Park winner Hayil and
smart performer up to 1¼m (in UAE) Tamhid: fair maiden: placed 6 times, including both
starts in nurseries: should prove best kept to 5f/6f: acts on polytrack and firm going: front
runner: sold 17,000 gns. *M. Quinn*

BOOKIESINDEX BOY 3 b.g. Piccolo 121 – United Passion 74 (Emarati (USA) 74) **75 §**
[2007 73§: 5.2m³ f5g² 5g² 5m 5d p5g² p5g 5g 5.1d² 5m⁴ 5f 5s⁵ Oct 4] strong, good-topped
gelding: fair handicapper: best at 5f: acts on all-weather and good to soft going: often
blinkered/visored: gelded after final start. *J. R. Jenkins*

BOOKISH 2 b.f. (Feb 23) Dubai Destination (USA) 127 – Daybook (IRE) (Daylami **68**
(IRE) 138) [2007 p7g⁴ 8.1s⁵ 8d⁶ p7g⁵ p7g* Dec 5] lengthy filly: first foal: dam unraced
out of sister to Miesque: fair performer: improved to win at Kempton in December on
nursery debut: stays 1m: acts on polytrack. *M. Johnston*

BOOK OF DAYS (IRE) 4 b.f. Barathea (IRE) 127 – Beeper The Great (USA) (Whad- **–**
jathink (USA)) [2007 –: p12g 12s Jun 29] little form. *Evan Williams*

BOOK OF FACTS (FR) 3 ch.g. Machiavellian (USA) 123 – Historian (IRE) (Penne- **–**
kamp (USA) 130) [2007 84: 8m 7s⁶ p8.6g 10.1g Jul 24] strong gelding: fairly useful
at 2 yrs for M. Johnston: well held on Flat in 2007, including in seller: tried blinkered.
J. McAuley

BOOK OF MUSIC (IRE) 4 b.c. Sadler's Wells (USA) 132 – Novelette (Darshaan **116**
133) [2007 107: 12g⁶ 10g² 12g* 12g 12.3m⁵ 12m⁶ Oct 5] strong, close-coupled colt:
smart performer: best effort when winning handicap at Nad Al Sheba in February by 3¾
lengths from Leitmotiv: left I. Mohammed in UAE after next start and off 6 months:
below form in listed events at Chester and Newmarket last 2 outings: stays 1½m: acts on
soft and good to firm going: visored 4 of last 5 starts. *Saeed bin Suroor*

BOOM OR BUST (IRE) 8 ch.g. Entrepreneur 123 – Classic Affair (USA) 66 (Trem- **–**
polino (USA) 135) [2007 –: p12.2g Jan 19] lightly raced and little form on Flat since
2003: wears headgear. *Karen George*

BOOMTOWN 2 b.c. (Apr 14) Fantastic Light (USA) 134 – Ville d'Amore (USA) (Irish **71**
River (FR) 131) [2007 6m² 6s⁶ 7m 7.5g³ 8m⁵ 10m p8.6g p8.6d Dec 10] lengthy, good-
topped colt: fair maiden: third in nursery at Beverley, best effort: should stay 1¼m: acts
on good to firm going. *M. Johnston*

BOOT 'N TOOT 6 b.m. Mtoto 134 – Raspberry Sauce 65 (Niniski (USA) 125) [2007 **71**
84: p10g⁴ p12g⁵ 11.7f³ 14.8m⁵ 11.9f p13g* p11g² p11g² Sep 15] workmanlike mare: **a87**
fairly useful on all-weather, fair on turf: won handicap at Lingfield in August: stays 13f:
acts on polytrack and firm going, below form both outings on soft: joined M. Sheppard.
C. A. Cyzer

BOOT STRAP BILL 2 ch.g. (Apr 3) Timeless Times (USA) 99 – Nuthatch (IRE) 36 **63 d**
(Thatching 131) [2007 7.1m³ 7m 6.1d p7.1g p6g Dec 4] sturdy gelding: maiden:
regressive after debut (third at Warwick): will stay 1m: tried in cheekpieces/blinkered.
Miss J. R. Tooth

BOPPYS DANCER 4 b.g. Clan of Roses – Dancing Mary 59 (Sri Pekan (USA) 117) **59**
[2007 58: f12g⁶ f11g⁶ f11g* f11g⁵ 12.4m⁵ 12.1v⁶ 12m 10.5m 12.1m p12.2g f11d Dec 11]
close-coupled gelding: modest handicapper: won at Southwell in March: stays 12.4f: acts
on fibresand and good to firm ground: blinkered/in cheekpieces: not straightforward.
P. T. Midgley

BOPPYS DIAMOND 3 b.f. Clan of Roses – Dancing Mary 59 (Sri Pekan (USA) 117) **–**
[2007 6g 8.2g Oct 31] 800Y: leggy filly: second foal: sister to 4-y-o Boppys Dancer: dam
maiden (stayed 1¾m): well held in maidens. *P. T. Midgley*

BOPPYS DREAM 5 ch.m. Clan of Roses – Laurel Queen (IRE) 76 (Viking (USA)) **42**
[2007 42: f6g³ f7g f6g⁴ 6m 5d 6g 6d 5g 5m 6m³ 7f⁵ 6g p5.1g Dec 4] small, strong mare:
poor maiden: stays 1m: acts on all-weather, good to firm and good to soft going: usually
in cheekpieces/blinkers. *P. T. Midgley*

BOPPYS PRIDE 4 ch.c. Clan of Roses – Joara (FR) (Radetzky 123) [2007 65: p12g **64**
10.1m 10m² 10m² 10.1d 12g p10g⁵ p12.2d Dec 7] modest handicapper: stays 1½m: acts
on polytrack, heavy and good to firm going: in cheekpieces last 2 starts. *R. A. Fahey*

BORASCO (USA) 2 ch.f. (Jan 19) Stormy Atlantic (USA) – Seek (USA) (Devil's Bag **74** (USA)) [2007 6m³ 6m⁶ 7d* 6m 6m³ p6g³ Aug 20] $60,000Y: lengthy filly: has scope: first foal: dam, US maiden, half-sister to US Grade 3 8.5f/9f winner Discover: fair form: won maiden at Redcar in June: third in nurseries at Haydock (to Lady Rangali) and Wolverhampton last 2 starts, travelling strongly: should prove best up to 7f: acts on poly-track, good to firm and good to soft going. *T. D. Barron*

BORA SHAAMIT (IRE) 5 b.m. Shaamit (IRE) 127 – Bora Bora (Bairn (USA) 126) **–** [2007 p10g Sep 29] angular mare: no sign of ability, Flat or jumps. *M. Scudamore*

BORDELLO 4 b.g. Blow Me A Kiss 72 (Kris 135) [2007 74: 8.1g p9.5g **–** 8.1m 6.9g Aug 22] tall, close-coupled gelding: lightly-raced maiden: well held in handicaps in 2007: stays 1m: acts on good to soft going. *K. A. Ryan*

BORDER ARTIST 8 ch.g. Selkirk (USA) 129 – Aunt Tate (Tate Gallery (USA) 117) **67** [2007 72, a68: p7g⁴ p7.1g⁵ p7f² 6g 7m⁶ p8.6g⁶ p8g 7d³ 7f 7g⁶ 7.1f 7g* 7.1g⁶ p7m 7d p7m p7g p8.6g Nov 27] well-made gelding: fair handicapper: won at Yarmouth in September: stays 8.5f: acts on all-weather, firm and good to soft going: tried in headgear: usually held up. *J. Pearce*

BORDER DEFENCE (IRE) 2 b. or br.g. (Mar 14) Princely Heir (IRE) 111 – Dakhira **52** 65 (Emperor Jones (USA) 119) [2007 f5g 5.1f 6m p6g⁵ 6d p6g Oct 22] rather leggy gelding: modest maiden: will stay 7f/1m: tried blinkered/visored. *P. A. Blockley*

BORDER EDGE 9 b.g. Beveled (USA) – Seymour Ann (Krayyan 117) [2007 74: 8m **70 §** 10m p8g⁴ 7.6g⁴ 7s 7g 10d p8g 10m* 9m 10g 8g p11m 7d⁴ 8g⁴ p8g⁶ p10g p10m⁵ p8g⁵ **a66 §** Dec29] sturdy, close-coupled gelding: fair handicapper: won at Lingfield in August: effective at 7f to 11f: acts on all-weather, firm and soft going: usually visored/blinkered: races prominently: not one to trust. *J. J. Bridger*

BORDERLESCOTT 5 b.g. Compton Place 125 – Jeewan 82 (Touching Wood (USA) **120** 127) [2007 120: 6g² 6m² 6d 6m 6m² 5m² 6d 6d⁴ 6m² p6m² Nov 24] strong, close-coupled gelding: very smart performer: runner-up 6 times in 2007, including when beaten short head in latest renewal of Stewards' Cup at Goodwood (by Zidane), and listed events at Beverley (by Hellvelyn) and Doncaster (by Galeota) fifth/sixth/ninth outings, caught near line all 3 occasions: effective at 5f/6f: acts on polytrack, firm and soft going: often races up with pace: genuine and consistent. *R. Bastiman*

BORDER MUSIC 6 b.g. Selkirk (USA) 129 – Mara River 86 (Efisio 120) [2007 91, **98** a115: p7.1g* p5g p6g⁴ 6g p5g⁴ 5m* 6g 6m⁴ 5g⁶ p6m⁶ Oct 6] big gelding: smart on **a111** all-weather, useful on turf: won listed race at Wolverhampton (by 1¾ lengths from Jack Sullivan) in March and handicap at Ascot (coaxed home to beat Hoh Hoh Hoh by ¾ length) in July: at least respectable efforts last 3 starts: effective at 5f to 7f: acts on polytrack, firm and good to soft going: blinkered: travels strongly, but often finds little. *A. M. Balding*

BORDER OWL (IRE) 2 b.g. (May 9) Selkirk (USA) 129 – Nightbird (IRE) 108 **78 p** (Night Shift (USA)) [2007 9s 8d⁵ p7g² Nov 7] €31,000Y, resold 17,000Y: sixth foal: half-brother to fairly useful 1¼m winner Silent Hawk (by Halling) and winners abroad by Cadeaux Genereux and Cape Cross: dam, 5f to 7f (latter at 2 yrs) winner, out of half-sister to dam of 2000 Guineas winner Footstepsinthesand: progressive form in maidens, short-head second to Southpaw Lad at Kempton, held up well: should be suited by 1m: capable of better still. *R. Hannon*

BORDER TALE 7 b.g. Selkirk (USA) 129 – Likely Story (IRE) 94 (Night Shift (USA)) **–** [2007 75d: 12g³ 12.4m May 7] strong gelding: one-time fairly useful handicapper: little Flat form in 2007: stays 1¾m: acts on all-weather, soft and good to firm going: tried visored/tongue tied/in cheekpieces: has had breathing problems: fair hurdler, successful in September/October. *James Moffatt*

BOREANA 4 ch.f. Nashwan (USA) 135 – Aliena (IRE) (Grand Lodge (USA) 125) **64** [2007 73: 8f 6g p7.1g² p8.6g⁴ p7.1g⁴ p7.1g p7.1g³ p6g² p7.1g p6g p6g Nov 27] modest maiden handicapper: effective at 6f to 8.6f: acts on polytrack and good to firm going: sold 2,400 gns. *Jedd O'Keeffe*

BORIS DE DEAUVILLE (IRE) 4 b.c. Soviet Star (USA) 128 – Logjam (IRE) **120** (Royal Academy (USA) 130) [2007 114: 10s⁴ 10s* 10.5m⁴ 9.8d³ 10d³ Nov 4] first foal: dam French 9.5f winner out of useful French performer up to 1½m Loophole: very smart performer: improved again at 4 yrs, winning Prix d'Harcourt at Longchamp (beat Pearl Sky 1½ lengths) in April: in frame after in Prix Ganay on same course (3 lengths fourth to Dylan Thomas, off 5 months after), Prix Dollar there (promoted third to Musical Way) and Premio Roma at Rome (third to Pressing): stays 10.5f: acts on soft and good to firm ground. *S. Wattel, France*

BORITA (IRE) 4 ch.f. Lahib (USA) 129 – Bora Bora (Bairn (USA) 126) [2007 10d 10f 11.7d 10.2m Sep 13] lengthy, rather sparely-made filly: second foal: dam bumper/hurdle winner: little form, including in bumpers. *M. Scudamore* –

BORN FOR DIAMONDS (IRE) 5 b.m. Night Shift (USA) – Kirri (IRE) (Lycius (USA) 124) [2007 36: 6s Jun 21] well-made mare: poor maiden: tried visored. *R. E. Barr* –

BORN WEST (USA) 3 b. or br.g. Gone West (USA) – Admirer (USA) (Private Terms (USA)) [2007 70: 10.1g³ 11.5m⁴ 15.8g² p16g⁴ p13.9g³ Dec 3] stocky gelding: fair maiden handicapper: stays 2m: raced only on polytrack and good/good to firm going: gelded, then sold 20,000 gns. *P. W. Chapple-Hyam* **74**

BORODINSKY 6 b.g. Magic Ring (IRE) 115 – Valldemosa 81 (Music Boy 124) [2007 57: f8g f8g⁶ 8.5m 7m⁵ 6f³ 7d³ 8g⁶ 8d⁶ 6d³ 7.1m⁴ 7m* 8f² 8m 8g Oct 6] heavy-topped gelding: fair handicapper: won at Catterick in August: effective at 6f to 9f: acts on firm and soft going: tried visored. *R. E. Barr* **72**

BORORA 8 gr.g. Shareef Dancer (USA) 135 – Bustling Nelly 94 (Bustino 136) [2007 14m 14.1m Aug 31] modest maiden handicapper on Flat: stays 12.4f: raced only on polytrack and good/good to firm going: fairly useful chaser, won in September. *R. Lee* **64**

BORSCH (IRE) 5 b.g. Soviet Star (USA) 128 – Cheese Soup (USA) (Spectacular Bid (USA)) [2007 –: 16m⁵ 16.1m 13g 16g 13.1d 15.8m⁶ 14d⁵ 12m 16.1m 12m Sep 30] poor maiden: seems to stay 2m: acts on good to firm and good to soft ground: tried blinkered/visored. *Miss L. A. Perratt* **48**

BORZOI MAESTRO 6 ch.g. Wolfhound (USA) 126 – Ashkernazy (IRE) 60 (Salt Dome (USA)) [2007 64: p5.1g⁵ f6g² p5.1g* p6g p5.1g 5.7d p5g p5.1g p5.1g Oct 30] small gelding: modest performer nowadays: left R. Harris £800 after reappearance: won seller at Wolverhampton in April: well held after: effective at 5f/6f: acts on all-weather and firm going: wears headgear: races prominently. *G. F. Bridgwater* **61 d**

BOSAMCLIFF (IRE) 2 b.f. (Mar 1) Daylami (IRE) 138 – L'Animee (Green Tune (USA) 125) [2007 p7g p10g⁶ Oct 31] 18,000Y: fourth foal: half-sister to fairly useful French 1m winner Miguel do Brazil (by Spectrum): dam, French 9f winner, half-sister to smart French 1¼m performer Bailador: better run in maidens at Lingfield when never-nearer sixth to All The Aces: likely to stay 1½m. *A. B. Haynes* **62**

BOSCOBEL 3 ch.c. Halling (USA) 133 – Dunnes River (USA) 84 (Danzig (USA)) [2007 91p: p7g* p8.6g* 10m² 11.1d* 12d* 12s⁴ 12d Aug 21] lengthy, workmanlike colt: improved into a smart performer, winning handicaps at Lingfield in January and Wolverhampton (dead-heated) in February, listed race at Hamilton (by 6 lengths from Dansant) in May and King Edward VII Stakes at Royal Ascot (best effort, beat Lucarno by length, dictating) in June: just respectable fourth to Soldier of Fortune in Irish Derby at the Curragh next time: tailed-off last in Great Voltigeur Stakes at York final outing: stays 1½m: acts on polytrack, good to firm and good to soft going: carries head awkwardly, but is genuine: has joined Godolphin. *M. Johnston* **115**

BOSUN BREESE 2 b.g. (Jan 27) Bahamian Bounty 116 – Nellie Melba 82 (Hurricane Sky (AUS)) [2007 5m³ 6g⁴ 5g* 6m³ 6g 6m 5.1m² Oct 14] 9,000F, 15,000Y: lengthy, rather hollow-backed gelding: first foal: dam 7f/1m winner: fairly useful performer: won maiden at Sandown in June: ran well last 2 starts when ninth of 28 (beaten 3½ lengths) to Exclamation in sales race at Newmarket and second in nursery at Bath: should prove best at 5f/easy 6f: acts on good to firm going. *P. W. D'Arcy* **88**

King Edward VII Stakes, Royal Ascot—an impressive front-running display from Boscobel (left), who beats the Derby fourth Lucarno and eighth Yellowstone; Lion Sands (dark colours, third right) is fourth

BOTHAM (USA) 3 b. or br.g. Cryptoclearance (USA) – Oval (USA) (Kris S (USA)) **62**
[2007 49: 6m 7.1m p10m⁵ p9.5g⁵ p9.5g p8.6g⁴ p9.5g f14d² p12.2d⁵ Dec 28] good-topped
gelding: modest maiden: effective at 8.6f, seems to stay 1¾m: acts on all-weather,
probably on good to firm and good to soft ground: often blinkered: tried tongue tied.
D. J. Murphy

BOTHAR BRUGHA (IRE) 3 b.g. Alexius (IRE) 120 – Denise's Stride (IRE) (Fumo **–**
di Londra (IRE) 108) [2007 57: p10g⁶ p12g⁶ p12g Nov 28] smallish gelding: trained by
K. Condon in Ireland only 2-y-o start: little impact in Britain. *J. G. M. O'Shea*

BOTTOMLESS WALLET 6 ch.m. Titus Livius (FR) 115 – Furry Dance (USA) **–**
(Nureyev (USA) 131) [2007 –: 8d 10.1m Jun 2] big mare: maiden: little form since 2005:
tried in cheekpieces/visor. *F. Watson*

BOUCHEEN 4 b.g. Foxhound (USA) 103 – Anytime Baby 56 (Bairn (USA) 126) [2007 **49**
51: p9.5g p7.1g⁵ 9.8m Aug 28] tall, angular gelding: poor maiden: left Ms Deborah Evans
after reappearance: stays 9.5f: acts on all-weather, firm and good to soft going. *J. W. Unett*

BOUGGLER 2 b.g. (Mar 8) Tobougg (IRE) 125 – Rush Hour (IRE) (Night Shift **50**
(USA)) [2007 7.5g 8g⁶ 8g⁶ Oct 19] good-topped gelding: modest form at best in maidens:
stays 1m. *Miss J. A. Camacho*

BOUGUEREAU 2 b.c. (Feb 21) Alhaarth (IRE) 126 – Blessed Honour 77 (Ahonoora **86 +**
122) [2007 7m 8m⁴ 8m³ Sep 15] 25,000F, 65,000Y: good-topped colt: has a moderate,
quick action: seventh foal: half-brother to several winners, including 1999 2-y-o 6f/7f
(Prestige Stakes) winner Icicle (by Polar Falcon): dam, 2-y-o 7f winner on only start,
half-sister to smart performer up to 1¾m Sacrament: fairly useful form: possibly flattered
when 3½ lengths fourth to Gipson Dessert in listed race at Deauville: favourite, 1½
lengths third to Emmrooz back in maiden company at Goodwood: will probably stay
1¼m. *P. W. Chapple-Hyam*

BOULEVIN (IRE) 7 b. or br.g. Perugino (USA) 84 – Samika (IRE) (Bikala 134) [2007 **46**
54: p12.2g p16.5g Feb 2] good-topped gelding: poor performer: stays 1½m: acts on polytrack and good to soft ground: wore cheekpieces final outing: sometimes races freely.
R. J. Price

BOUNDLESS PROSPECT (USA) 8 b.g. Boundary (USA) 117 – Cape (USA) (Mr **88**
Prospector (USA)) [2007 92, a78: f8g⁴ f8g⁴ 8d⁶ 8.1d 8.3d³ p8g p8g³ 8g⁴ 8s* 8g⁵ 8d* **a76**
8.2g³ 9.1v⁴ 8g p8g⁴ f8d⁴ f8d⁵ Dec 21] lengthy gelding: fairly useful performer on turf,
fair on all-weather: won claimers at Redcar in September and Yarmouth in October: stays
1¼m: acts on all-weather, firm and soft going: tried in headgear: sometimes slowly away:
free-going sort, held up. *Miss Gay Kelleway*

BOUNTY QUEST 5 b.h. Fasliyev (USA) 120 – Just Dreams 85 (Salse (USA) 128) **102**
[2007 a6f* a6f² a5f² a6f² a6f 5g⁵ 6f³ 5m⁶ 5.6m Sep 15] sturdy horse: useful performer: **a107**
won handicap at Nad Al Sheba in January: good second to Terrific Challenge in Mahab
Al Shimaal there fourth outing: left D. Watson in UAE after next start: creditable efforts
when third to Presto Shinko in minor event at Windsor and sixth to Hellvelyn in listed
event at Beverley seventh/eighth starts: ran poorly in Portland Handicap at Doncaster
final outing: effective at 5f to 7f: acts on dirt and firm going: visored once. *K. A. Ryan*

BOURBON BALISTIC 2 ch.c. (Apr 25) Piccolo 121 – Last Ambition (IRE) 29 **61**
(Cadeaux Genereux 131) [2007 5m⁴ 5d⁵ 6m Oct 22] modest maiden: standout effort at 5f
on good to soft going. *Mrs A. Duffield*

BOURBON HIGHBALL (IRE) 2 b.g. (May 4) Catcher In The Rye (IRE) 115 – Be **65**
Exciting (IRE) 88 (Be My Guest (USA) 126) [2007 6d 6s⁵ 6s³ 7.5g 8s Sep 26] good-
topped gelding: fair maiden: third at York: well held in nurseries: should stay 1m: raced
only on good ground or softer: sold 5,000 gns. *P. C. Haslam*

BOURNONVILLE 4 b.g. Machiavellian (USA) 123 – Amellnaa (IRE) 86 (Sadler's **–**
Wells (USA) 132) [2007 43: p9.5g p11g f11g² f8s⁶ p12g f11g 10.1m f11g⁶ f12g 16g **a50**
12.6d Jun 28] rather leggy gelding: modest maiden: stays 1½m: acts on fibresand: tried
tongue tied/in cheekpieces/blinkered: none too reliable. *M. Wigham*

BOURSE (IRE) 2 b.g. (Feb 16) Dubai Destination (USA) 127 – Quarter Note (USA) **55**
109 (Danehill (USA) 126) [2007 6m 6g Jun 8] compact gelding: third foal: half-
brother to French 2005 2-y-o 1¼m winner Demi Voix (by Halling): dam, French 7.5f/
1m winner, half-sister to very smart 6f/7f performer Quito: modest form in maidens at
Newmarket and Goodwood (subsequently gelded): will be suited by 7f/1m: sold 1,500
gns in December. *J. H. M. Gosden*

BOUZOUKI (USA) 4 b. or br.g. Distant Music (USA) 126 – Pamina (IRE) (Perugino **61 §**
(USA) 84) [2007 61: 8d 12g p10g³ p12.2g Jul 6] rather leggy gelding: modest maiden,
lightly raced: stays easy 1¼m: acts on polytrack: raced freely second start: refused to race
final outing, and is one to treat with caution. *Karen George*

BOVERED (IRE) 3 b.f. Fayruz 116 – Lucky Pick 69 (Auction Ring (USA) 123) [2007 **–**
6g⁶ 5g⁵ 6g 7g Sep 22] €6,500Y: sturdy filly: half-sister to 2 winners abroad: dam, maiden
(stayed 1¼m) sister to very smart 7f/1m performer Lucky Ring: no form. *A. Berry*

BOWDER STONE (IRE) 3 b.c. (Apr 17) Rock of Gibraltar (IRE) 133 – Ghita (IRE) **– p**
69 (Zilzal (USA) 137) [2007 6m Aug 3] 90,000F, 15,000Y: fourth foal: dam, 1m/9f
winner in France, half-sister to high-class miler Landseer and very smart 1¼m performer
Ikhtyar: 10/1, outpaced in maiden at Haydock: should do better at 1m+. *M. H. Tompkins*

BOWL OF CHERRIES 4 b.g. Vettori (IRE) 119 – Desert Nomad 56 (Green Desert **43**
(USA) 127) [2007 67: 8m 8d p10g p10g² p8g p8.6g p8g⁶ p10g 10.1m⁶ p10g⁴ **a62**
p11g⁵ p12.2g p10g* p10g⁴ p9.5g p10m⁶ p10g Dec 12] compact gelding: modest
handicapper on all-weather, poor on turf: won at Kempton in October: stays 1¼m: acts on
all-weather and good to firm going: wears headgear. *I. A. Wood*

BOWNESS 5 b.m. Efisio 120 – Dominio (IRE) 99 (Dominion 123) [2007 81: 6.1s⁶ 6g **80**
5g 8d Jul 27] strong, compact mare: fairly useful performer: effective at 5f/6f: acts on
polytrack, firm and good to soft ground. *J. G. Given*

BOXHALL (IRE) 5 b.g. Grand Lodge (USA) 125 – March Hare 60 (Groom Dancer **74**
(USA) 128) [2007 80: f12g⁴ 16m² 16.2m³ 14m³ 16m 14m² 14m 18m⁵ 13.8g Nov 6] rangy
gelding: fair handicapper: stays 2m: acts on firm going: effective tongue tied or not: often
makes running. *N. Wilson*

BOY BLUE 2 b.c. (Feb 8) Observatory (USA) 131 – Rowan Flower (IRE) 67 (Ashka- **86**
lani (IRE) 128) [2007 7g⁵ 7.1g² 7.2s* Sep 21] 27,000 2-y-o: sturdy colt: second foal:
dam, 7f winner, half-sister to 1¼m winner Muakaad and 1½m winner Suhaad,
both smart: fairly useful form: developed well, making all to win maiden at Ayr by ½
length from Lady Sorcerer (pair well clear): will stay 1m: raced only on good and soft
ground. *D. Nicholls*

BOY DANCER (IRE) 4 ch.g. Danehill Dancer (IRE) 117 – Mary Gabry (IRE) (Kris **65**
135) [2007 70: f8g⁵ f8g p7g³ p7.1g⁶ 7m⁵ 8f 8.3m 8m² 7.9m Jun 4] strong, stocky gelding: **a61**
fair handicapper on turf, modest on all-weather: stays 1m: acts on polytrack and good to
firm going: wore cheekpieces last 3 starts: has run well when sweating: often slowly
away: reportedly struck into on final start. *D. W. Barker*

BOZ 3 gr.c. Grand Lodge (USA) 125 – Dali's Grey (Linamix (FR) 127) [2007 7.1m p8.6g **92 p**
p8g 11.5g 11.5m 9.7g³ 12.4m³ p10g* p12.2g* p12.2g* p12.2g* p13.9g* Nov 8] good-
bodied colt: third foal: half-brother to useful 1¼m to 1¾m winner Bauer (by Halling) and
fairly useful 1¼m/1½m winner Batik (by Peintre Celebre): dam, French 11f winner, sister
to smart French 10.5f winner Diamonixa and half-sister to very smart 1m/1¼m performer
Diamond Green: fairly useful handicapper, really progressive: won at Kempton and
Wolverhampton (4 times) between September and November, beating Heathyards Pride
by ½ length for final success: stays 1¾m: acts on polytrack: blinkered sixth/seventh
starts: open to further improvement. *L. M. Cumani*

BOZEMAN TRAIL 2 b.c. (Mar 17) Averti (IRE) 117 – Crystal Power (USA) **62**
(Pleasant Colony (USA)) [2007 p7.1g⁶ 7.6f⁵ 8.1m⁴ 10m p8g Nov 7] close-coupled colt:
modest maiden: left M. Channon after second start: no impact in nurseries: stays 1m: acts
on polytrack and firm going. *P. F. I. Cole*

BRABAZON (IRE) 4 b.g. In The Wings 128 – Azure Lake (USA) (Lac Ouimet **62**
(USA)) [2007 81: 12m 9.5g 13.1g⁴ 13g 13m Aug 2] quite good-topped, attractive
gelding: fair maiden handicapper for R. Charlton at 3 yrs: just modest form in 2007,
including in Britain last 3 starts: should stay 1¾m: acts on good to firm ground: tried
visored/blinkered. *Barry Potts, Ireland*

BRACE OF DOVES 5 b.g. Bahamian Bounty 116 – Overcome (Belmez (USA) 131) **56**
[2007 61: 8m 7m 7.9g 6.9m 8s 8m 8m 9m Sep 30] quite good-topped gelding: modest
performer: stays 1m: acts on fibresand, firm and soft going: tried in cheekpieces.
D. W. Whillans

BRACKENRIDGE 3 b.g. Tumbleweed Ridge 117 – I Have A Dream (SWE) (Mango **–**
Express 106) [2007 6.1g 7s⁵ 6m Jun 9] lengthy gelding: well held in maidens.
Miss E. C. Lavelle

BRADDOCK (IRE) 4 b.c. Pivotal 124 – Sedna (FR) (Bering 136) [2007 75: 7d⁸ 6.1s⁶ **85**
p7.1g⁵ p7.1g Oct 22] close-coupled colt: fairly useful performer, very lightly raced:

reportedly suffered a fracture after final 3-y-o start: won handicap at Newcastle in May: ran as if amiss second/final outings: stays 1m, likely to be effective at 6f: raced on poly-track and going softer than good (acts on heavy): sold 13,000 gns. *T. D. Barron*

BRAMCOTE LORNE 4 b.g. Josr Algarhoud (IRE) 118 – Dreamtime Quest **59** (Blakeney 126) [2007 67, a59: f12g⁴ p11g⁵ p12g³ f11d Dec 11] stocky gelding: modest maiden: left John Harris after second start: acts on all-weather and firm going: tried in cheekpieces: has raced prominently. *R. C. Guest*

BRANDANE (IRE) 2 br.g. (May 8) Danehill Dancer (IRE) 117 – Oumaldaaya (USA) **60** 111 (Nureyev (USA) 131) [2007 6f⁶ 6g Aug 24] modest maiden: some promise when sixth at Pontefract (got loose in paddock): well beaten in visor next time (reportedly scoped dirty after), then gelded: will stay at least 1m. *Mrs A. Duffield*

BRANDYWELL BOY (IRE) 4 b.g. Danetime (IRE) 121 – Alexander Eliott (IRE) **80** 73 (Night Shift (USA)) [2007 81, a88: p6g 5.1f 5m 5.7m 6g p6g³ p6g 6f 6g² 5m p6g 5m³ 6g² 5.1s 5.1g² p6g* p6m² p6g² p6g⁶ Dec 15] close-coupled gelding: fairly useful handicapper: won at Kempton in November: best at 5f/6f: acts on polytrack and firm going: tried in headgear: often held up. *D. J. S. ffrench Davis*

BRANSTON TIGER 8 b.g. Mark of Esteem (IRE) 137 – Tuxford Hideaway 102 **73** (Cawston's Clown 113) [2007 –: f6g⁴ f6g* f6g f6s³ f7g³ f7g⁵ May 15] rangy gelding: fair performer, lightly raced in recent years: won claimer at Southwell in January: effective at 6f/7f: acts on all-weather, firm and soft going: blinkered/visored. *Ian Emmerson*

BRASINGAMAN HIFIVE 2 b.f. (Apr 22) High Estate 127 – Our Miss Florence **76** (Carlitin 50) [2007 7.1g* 7g⁶ Oct 20] leggy filly: first foal: dam unraced: fair form: 100/1, won maiden at Haydock in September: sixth in nursery at Catterick: likely to stay 1m. *Mrs G. S. Rees*

BRASSINI 2 gr.g. (Apr 28) Bertolini (USA) 125 – Silver Spell 54 (Aragon 118) [2007 **82** 5.1g⁴ 5m³ 5m³ 5.1f* 5.1s* 6.1m⁶ 5g³ 5m 6m Sep 22] 16,000Y: close-coupled gelding: sixth foal: brother to 4-y-o Don Pietro and half-brother to 9-y-o Warden Warren: dam, 2-y-o 5f winner, sister to smart sprinter Argentum: fairly useful performer: won maiden at Chester in June and minor event at Chepstow in July: gelded after final start: best efforts at 5f: acts on firm and soft ground. *B. R. Millman*

BRASTAR JELOIS (FR) 4 b.f. True Brave (USA) – Star Angels (FR) (Ski Chief **66** (USA) 115) [2007 10.9m p12.2g² f11g² p10g p12.2g⁴ p12.2g³ p12.2g³ 10d 9.9m³ p12.2g* 10d² 10.5s⁵ Sep 28] ex-French filly: fair performer: claimed from D. Pipe £6,400 after second start: won seller at Wolverhampton in September: stays easy 1½m: acts on all-weather, soft and good to firm ground: visored second outing, in cheekpieces last 4 starts: held up: consistent. *R. Hollinshead*

BRAVE DANE (IRE) 9 b.g. Danehill (USA) 126 – Nuriva (USA) 100 (Woodman **– §** (USA) 126) [2007 73: p8.6g Feb 26] lengthy, angular gelding: fair performer at 8 yrs: stays 1¼m: acts on polytrack and any turf going: tried blinkered: often slowly away (reluctant to race sole start in 2007): held up: one to treat with caution. *K. J. Burke*

BRAVE FALCON (IRE) 3 b.g. Fasliyev (USA) 120 – Don't Care (IRE) 93 (Nordico **71** (USA)) [2007 74: 5s 5m 6.7g 5f⁴ 5d 5g 5v⁴ 7s p5.1g⁴ Oct 20] fair maiden: trained by D. Weld at 2 yrs: below form at Wolverhampton final outing in 2007: effective at 5f to 7f: acts on any turf going: tried in cheekpieces/blinkered: often tongue tied. *Leo J. Temple, Ireland*

BRAVE HIAWATHA (FR) 5 b.g. Dansili 127 – Alexandrie (USA) 114 (Val de **–** L'Orne (FR) 133) [2007 –: p13.9g Jul 16] no form on Flat in Britain. *G. J. Smith*

BRAVE JACK (IRE) 3 b.g. Royal Applause 124 – Zaynah (IRE) (Kahyasi 130) [2007 **53** p6g⁶ p6g p5g p7g⁴ p8g⁴ p8g⁴ 10g 8f³ 10g 10m p8g 7m 6f³ 7g² p7g³ p7g⁴ p8g⁵ Oct 17] **a58** sturdy gelding: modest maiden: should stay beyond 1m: acts on polytrack and firm ground: tried visored: has missed break/raced freely: sold 6,000 gns, sent to Sweden. *J. R. Best*

BRAVE MAVE 2 gr.f. (Mar 26) Daylami (IRE) 138 – Baalbek 76 (Barathea (IRE) 127) **78** [2007 6m 7s⁵ 7d* Oct 9] 22,000Y: leggy filly: fourth foal: half-sister to 3 winners, including 5-y-o Cross The Line and 3-y-o Silca Key: dam, 1m winner, granddaughter of Irish 1000 Guineas winner Front Row: fair form: much improved to win maiden at Leicester by neck from Siyabona, rallying: will be suited by 1m. *W. Jarvis*

BRAVE PROSPECTOR 2 b.c. (Mar 4) Oasis Dream 129 – Simply Times (USA) 64 **100** (Dodge (USA)) [2007 6d² 6d⁴ 7d⁴ Oct 27] 140,000Y: medium-sized, well-made colt: sixth foal: half-brother to several winners, notably 8-y-o Welsh Emperor and 7-y-o

Majestic Times: dam ran twice: useful form: in frame in maidens at Windsor and Newmarket, then marked progress when 2½ lengths fourth of 11 to Beacon Lodge in Horris Hill Stakes at Newbury (quickened to lead briefly): stays 7f, should prove just as effective at 6f: raced only on good to soft going. *P. W. Chapple-Hyam*

BRAVE QUEST (IRE) 3 b.g. Indian Danehill (IRE) 124 – Mill Rainbow (FR) **69**
(Rainbow Quest (USA) 134) [2007 56: p10g³ 9.7g* p10g 8g Nov 2] big gelding: fair performer: won handicap at Folkestone in April: stays easy 1¼m: acts on polytrack, unraced on extremes of going on turf. *Mrs L. J. Mongan*

BRAVE VISION 11 b.g. Clantime 101 – Kinlet Vision (IRE) 56 (Vision (USA)) [2007 **46**
15d⁵ 16.1m⁵ Jun 2] poor maiden nowadays, lightly raced on Flat: stays 2m: acts on soft and good to firm going: tried blinkered. *A. C. Whillans*

BRAVO BOLIVAR (IRE) 2 b.c. (Mar 31) Red Ransom (USA) – Fantasy Girl (IRE) **51**
55 (Marju (IRE) 127) [2007 7m 7d 8d Oct 3] good-bodied colt: seventh foal: closely related to smart 7f (at 2 yrs) to 10.5f winner Big Bad Bob (by Bob Back) and half-brother to fairly useful Irish 7f winner Woodland Dream (by Charnwood Forest): dam, maiden who stayed 1½m, half-sister to smart 1¼m/1½m performer Persian Lightning: behind in maidens, modest form at Salisbury final start: sold 5,500 gns, sent to Holland. *J. L. Dunlop*

BRAZILIAN BRUSH (IRE) 2 ch.c. (Mar 14) Captain Rio 122 – Ejder (IRE) (Indian **73**
Ridge 123) [2007 6.5d³ p6g⁴ p6g⁴ Dec 29] €16,000F, €44,000Y: well-made colt: second foal: dam, no form, out of half-sister to Oaks runner-up Bourbon Girl: fair maiden: in frame all starts, tongue tied final one (trapped wide): stays 6.5f. *H. Morrison*

BREAKER MORANT (IRE) 5 b.h. Montjeu (IRE) 137 – Arcade (Rousillon (USA) **67**
133) [2007 79: 8.2g 8m 7f 7.5m 7s 8s p9.5s³ Dec 21] good-topped gelding: fair handicapper: left E. Tyrrell after fifth outing: barely stays 9.5f: acts on polytrack, firm and good to soft going: usually blinkered. *James G. Burns, Ireland*

BREAKING SHADOW (IRE) 5 br.g. Danehill Dancer (IRE) 117 – Crimbourne 83 **71**
(Mummy's Pet 125) [2007 87: 8m 8m f6g 6m 7d⁴ 6v⁵ 7.1v⁵ 6s⁴ 6d p9.5g⁵ p7.1g Nov 10] close-coupled gelding: just fair handicapper in 2007: was effective at stiff 6f to 9f: acted on polytrack, soft and good to firm going: sometimes blinkered/in cheekpieces: inconsistent: won twice over hurdles in December: dead. *M. A. Peill*

BREAK 'N' DISH 3 b.g. Montjoy (USA) 122 – Ship of Gold 78 (Glint of Gold 128) **–**
[2007 –: 10g Oct 8] leggy gelding: tailed off all starts. *B. R. Johnson*

BREAK OUT 3 b.c. Kayf Tara 130 – Clifton Girl (Van Der Linden (FR)) [2007 8g 8.2g⁵ **–**
p10g 10.1g 9.7g Aug 16] lengthy colt: third foal: dam no form in 3 starts: signs of a little ability. *J. M. Bradley*

BREAN DOT COM (IRE) 3 b.g. Desert Sun 120 – Anna Elise (IRE) 106 (Nucleon **57**
(USA) 94) [2007 62: f8g⁶ f6g⁶ p7g p10g⁶ f8g³ p10g⁶ 8.1d p8g 9.9g p10g Aug 23] sturdy gelding: modest maiden handicapper: stays 1¼m: acts on all-weather. *Mrs P. N. Dutfield*

BREEDER'S FOLLY 5 b.m. Mujahid (USA) 125 – Wynona (IRE) 89 (Cyrano de **–**
Bergerac 120) [2007 –: f8d p12.2d Dec 28] maiden: very lightly raced and no form on Flat since 2005: tried tongue tied. *E. J. Creighton*

BREEZE IN (IRE) 4 b.g. Houmayoun (FR) 114 – Breeze Up 66 (Coquelin (USA) 121) **–**
[2007 51: f7g Jan 16] modest maiden: well beaten only 4-y-o start. *R. A. Fahey*

BREIZ DREAM'S (FR) 5 ch.g. East of Heaven (IRE) 112 – Impish (FR) (Epervier **63 ?**
Bleu 131) [2007 10.5v 15.5s⁵ 12v 12.5m 12.1g Aug 22] form on Flat in 2007 only when fifth in handicap at Saint-Cloud second start: left Y. Fouin, France, well held in similar event at Hamilton on British debut: stays 15.5f: raced mainly on good ground or softer. *Heather Dalton*

BRET MAVERICK (IRE) 3 b.g. Josr Algarhoud (IRE) 118 – Shady Street (USA) **60**
(Shadeed (USA) 135) [2007 60: 12.1g 9.2g⁴ 9.8s² 10.1g⁵ 12.1g³ 10.3m³ 10m p12.2g⁴ p13.9g Nov 16] tall, workmanlike gelding: modest maiden: claimed from J. Weymes after fifth start: stays 1½m: acts on polytrack, soft and good to firm going: tried in cheekpieces. *B. P. J. Baugh*

BRETTON 6 b.g. Polar Prince (IRE) 117 – Understudy 60 (In The Wings 128) [2007 **–**
p12g Apr 25] stocky, close-coupled gelding: modest performer at best: missed 2006: well held only outing in 2007: tried in blinkers, usually wore cheekpieces: dead. *J. E. Long*

BRETWALDA (IRE) 4 b.g. Imperial Ballet (IRE) 110 – Prime Time Girl 73 (Primo **69 ?**
Dominie 121) [2007 7f³ Sep 17] €32,000Y: second foal: half-brother to winner in Italy by Revoque: dam, ran twice at 6f, half-sister to Flying Childers Stakes winner Poker Chip: 66/1, 2¾ lengths third to Step In Line in maiden at Redcar. *P. T. Midgley*

BREXCA (IRE) 2 b.g. (Feb 17) Diktat 126 – Hemaca (Distinctly North (USA) 115) **79 p**
[2007 7.1m 8.1g⁴ 8d² Oct 11] 20,000F, 40,000Y: good-topped, quite attractive gelding:
third foal: closely related to 3-y-o Ficoma and half-brother to fairly useful 5f (at 2 yrs) to
7f winner Premier Fantasy (by Pivotal): dam unraced out of useful half-sister to smart
miler Kahir Almaydan: promise in maidens, in frame at Sandown and Newbury (second
to Robby Bobby), then gelded: stays 1m: should make a useful 3-y-o. *C. G. Cox*

BRIANNSTA (IRE) 5 b.g. Bluebird (USA) 125 – Nacote (IRE) (Mtoto 134) [2007 87: **82**
p6g⁴ p6g 6g 6m² 6g 5.7g⁵ 6m p7.1g p6g⁶ Oct 29] lengthy, quite attractive gelding: fairly
useful handicapper: left C. Cox after seventh start: has won at 7f, best form at 6f: acts
on polytrack, good to firm and good to soft ground: tried visored: effective ridden
prominently or held up. *B. Smart*

BRIARWOOD BEAR 3 ch.g. Woodborough (USA) 112 – Bramble Bear 72 (Beveled **59**
(USA)) [2007 59: p8g f8g² f11s⁴ p10f⁵ Feb 27] modest maiden: stays at least 1m: acts on
all-weather. *M. Blanshard*

BRICK (IRE) 2 b.f. (Feb 6) Averti (IRE) 117 – Wicked 40 (Common Grounds 118) **45**
[2007 p7.1g⁵ 7g Sep 29] €26,000Y: third foal: half-sister to two 2-y-o sprint winners,
including 2006 5f winner Wicked Wilma (by Tagula): dam, maiden, half-sister to useful
performer up to 10.5f Serious: poor maiden: fifth in seller (left J. Osborne £6,000) on
debut. *M. Mullineaux*

BRIDGE IT JO 3 gr.f. Josr Algarhoud (IRE) 118 – T G'S Girl 57 (Selkirk (USA) 129) **79**
[2007 91: 5.1f 6s⁶ 5d 6g⁴ 6g 5f⁶ 5m⁵ 5m p6m Oct 11] good-topped filly: just fair
performer in 2007: left Miss J. Feilden after second start: best at 5f/6f: acts on firm
going, probably on soft: edgy sort: very slowly away third outing: sold 9,000 gns, sent to
Malaysia. *G. G. Margarson*

BRIDGE OF FERMOY (IRE) 2 b.c. (Jan 22) Danetime (IRE) 121 – Banco Solo **66**
(Distant Relative 128) [2007 7v⁶ 6m 7m² 8s p7g⁴ p8g* Sep 15] 28,000Y: tall, lengthy
colt: fourth foal: brother to useful Italian sprinter Golden Danetime, and half-brother to
useful 1m/1¼m winner Internationalguest (by Petardia) and fairly useful 1m winner Bold
Act (by Brave Act): dam unraced sister to smart performer up to 1m My Branch, herself
dam of Sprint Cup winner Tante Rose: fair performer: left N. Callaghan after third start:
steady progress subsequently (tongue tied), won nursery at Kempton: stays 1m: acts on
polytrack, soft and good to firm going. *Miss Gay Kelleway*

BRIDGET'S TEAM 3 b.f. Elnadim (USA) 128 – Overcome (Belmez (USA) 131) **47**
[2007 58: f7g p6g⁶ p5g f6g Apr 13] just poor form in 2007: stays 6f: acts on all-weather:
tried tongue tied/blinkered. *D. G. Bridgwater*

BRIDGEWATER BOYS 6 b.g. Atraf 116 – Dunloe (IRE) 54 (Shaadi (USA) 126) **74**
[2007 74: f8g³ p9.5g³ p12.2g p9.5g p8.6g⁴ f11g* p9.5g⁶ f11g⁴ p10g² p12.2g⁴ 12s² 12m²
p12.2g⁴ 11.6d* p12g² p12g² 10g* p10m² Nov 11] lengthy gelding: fair performer: won
sellers at Southwell in March, Windsor (left K. Ryan £6,000) in August and selling
handicap at Brighton in October: stays 1½m: acts on all-weather, firm and soft ground:
usually blinkered/in cheekpieces: tried tongue tied. *G. L. Moore*

BRIEF ENGAGEMENT (IRE) 4 br.f. Namid 128 – Brief Fairy (IRE) (Brief Truce **–**
(USA) 126) [2007 –: p6g p7g 5s 6f Aug 4] sparely-made filly: no sign of ability.
T. D. McCarthy

BRIEF GOODBYE 7 b.g. Slip Anchor 136 – Queen of Silk (IRE) 93 (Brief Truce **89**
(USA) 126) [2007 89: 10m⁶ 10m 10m 10g² 10d⁶ 10f 10m 10m⁴ 10g 14.1d⁶ Oct 3] quite
good-topped gelding: fairly useful handicapper: below best after fourth start: should stay
1½m: seems best on good going or firmer: held up: sometimes slowly away/finds little.
John Berry

BRIERLEY LIL 3 ch.f. Intikhab (USA) 135 – Pooka 65 (Dominion 123) [2007 46: **52**
p9.5g p9.5g p8.6g⁴ 10.1d⁴ 10.1g⁴ Sep 19] modest maiden: stays 1¼m: acts on polytrack
and good to soft going: has worn blinkers/cheekpieces. *J. L. Spearing*

BRIERY BLAZE 4 b.f. Dansili 127 – Sabonis (USA) 68 (The Minstrel (CAN) 135) **58**
[2007 60: 6m 7.9m 8d⁶ 12d 6.9m 7.6m² p8g⁵ 8f p7g⁴ 7g p7.1g⁴ p6g* p6g⁶ p7.1g⁴
p7.1g Dec 4] plain filly: modest performer: left Mrs K. Walton 1,500 gns prior to fifth
outing (only start for G. Bridgwater): won apprentice handicap at Wolverhampton in
October: effective at 6f to 1m: acts on polytrack and firm going: blinkered last 4 starts:
inconsistent. *J. W. Unett*

BRIERY LANE (IRE) 6 ch.g. Tagula (IRE) 116 – Branston Berry (IRE) 86 (Mukad- **67**
damah (USA) 125) [2007 71: 6m⁴ 6.1g⁴ 6.1g 5.2d² 6f 5.1d* 5m² 5g 5.3d 5.1s⁴ 5.7g³ p5.1g
Nov 9] lengthy gelding: fair handicapper: won at Bath in August: effective at 5f to easy
7f: acts on polytrack, firm and soft going: tried in cheekpieces: inconsistent. *J. M. Bradley*

EBF Pricewaterhousecoopers Harvest Stakes, Ascot—Brisk Breeze (centre)
reverses Park Hill Stakes form with All My Loving (left); Under The Rainbow is third

BRIGADORE 8 b.g. Magic Ring (IRE) 115 – Music Mistress (IRE) 55 (Classic Music **74**
(USA)) [2007 71: 6g* 6m⁴ 5.7m⁴ 5m 5.9m⁴ 6m³ 6m³ 6g⁶ 6g 6s 5.9m 6m 6m⁶ 6g³ 6v
Oct 26] small, good-quartered gelding: fair handicapper: won at Pontefract in April: stays
6f: acts on any turf going: often slowly away: usually held up. *J. G. Given*

BRIGADORE (USA) 4 gr. or ro.g. Sandpit (BRZ) 129 – Mersey 123 (Crystal Palace **73**
(FR) 132) [2007 83: 14g 10.5g 13.1g⁵ 14d Jul 6] angular, unfurnished gelding: just fair
handicapper in 2007: stays 1¾m: acts on firm going: tried in cheekpieces: has joined Ian
Williams. *E. J. Alston*

BRIGHT 4 ch.g. Mister Baileys 123 – Razzle Dazzle (IRE) (Caerleon (USA) 132) [2007 **–**
–: f14g 7.1d 11.6d⁶ p8g Oct 10] little form: tried in cheekpieces/visor. *W. K. Goldsworthy*

BRIGHT FALCON 2 ch.c. (Jan 15) Hawk Wing (USA) 136 – Cream Tease 99 (Pursuit **88 p**
of Love 124) [2007 8d* Oct 13] 50,000F, 54,000Y: good-topped colt: third foal: half-
brother to 3-y-o Treat: dam, 7f winner (including at 2 yrs), half-sister to smart miler En-
harmonic: 11/1 and better for race, won maiden at York by 3 lengths from No To Trident,
dictating and soon in control when shaken up 2f out: useful prospect. *D. J. Murphy*

BRIGHT MIND 3 b.c. Zamindar (USA) 116 – Bright Spells (USA) (Alleged (USA) **91**
138) [2007 10.3m² 9.9m² Aug 31] tall, quite good-topped, attractive colt: sixth foal:
closely related to 7f winners (including at 2 yrs) Clearing (smart, also second in Poule
d'Essai des Poulains) and Blazing Thunder (useful), both by Zafonic: dam, fairly useful
French 1½m winner, sister to smart French stayer Non Partisan: runner-up in maidens at
Doncaster (clearly better effort when 3 lengths second to Broomielaw) and Salisbury
(length second to Demolition): sold 55,000 gns. *J. H. M. Gosden*

BRIGHT SUN (IRE) 6 b.g. Desert Sun 120 – Kealbra Lady (Petong 126) [2007 77: **72**
12f 12.3g 9g³ 9.8m⁴ 9.1g 10g Jul 20] good-topped gelding: fair handicapper: stays easy
1½m: acts on firm and good to soft going: usually tongue tied: free-going sort, often
makes running. *N. Tinkler*

BRILLIANTSENSATION (IRE) 2 b.g. (Mar 4) Danetime (IRE) 121 – Looks Sen- **49**
sational (USA) (Majestic Light (USA)) [2007 6m 7d 7m⁵ 6m 6g Aug 27] close-coupled

gelding: poor maiden: bred to stay 1m: wayward second start, wore cheekpieces/blinkers after. *J. G. Given*

BRING IT ON HOME 3 b.g. Beat Hollow 126 – Dernier Cri 63 (Slip Anchor 136) **72**
[2007 –: 8g⁶ 10g p11g 12m 13.1f⁶ Sep 10] fair maiden: stays 1¼m: best efforts on good ground: has shown signs of temperament. *G. L. Moore*

BRISK BREEZE (GER) 3 ch.f. Monsun (GER) 124 – Bela-M (IRE) 106 (Ela-Mana- **112**
Mou 132) [2007 76p: 10m² 11.5g² 12.1g* 16d 12m⁴ 14g⁴ 12g² 14.6m³ 12d* 12s⁴ Oct 13] close-coupled filly: has a fluent action: smart performer: won maiden (odds on) at Chepstow in May and listed event at Ascot (best effort, beat All My Loving by ½ length) in September: also ran well when length third to Hi Calypso in Park Hill Stakes at Doncaster eighth start: should stay 2m: acts on good to firm and good to soft going, probably on soft: often races prominently. *H. R. A. Cecil*

BRITANNIC 4 ch.g. Rainbow Quest (USA) 134 – Anka Britannia (USA) (Irish River **85**
(FR) 131) [2007 105: 12m 10.4d 11v* Nov 10] big, rangy gelding: useful performer in 2006, winning minor event at Longchamp and third in listed race and Prix du Lys at same course: sold from A. Fabre 43,000 gns after final 3-y-o start: tailed off both starts in Britain, then sold from T. Tate 9,000 gns before winning amateur minor event at Mulheim in November: should stay further than 1½m: acts on heavy ground. *C. von der Recke, Germany*

BRIXWORTH SCRIBE 2 b.g. (Jan 25) Forzando 122 – Segretezza (IRE) 48 (Peru- **72**
gino (USA) 84) [2007 5m 5s³ 6g² 5d* 6.1d 6g p6g⁴ p6g Oct 27] 7,000Y: good-topped gelding: first foal: dam maiden (stayed 1m): fair performer: won maiden at Carlisle in June: well beaten in nurseries: will stay 7f: acts on polytrack and soft going: starts slowly. *B. Smart*

BROAD TOWN GIRL 4 b.f. Woodborough (USA) 112 – Fortunes Course (IRE) 55 **–**
(Crash Course 128) [2007 p8g p8.6g p10g⁵ p7g p8.6g p7.1g Dec 15] smallish filly: second foal: dam, 2¼m winner, also successful over jumps: no form. *Mrs H. Sweeting*

BROGHILL 3 ch.c. Selkirk (USA) 129 – Mystify 104 (Batshoof 122) [2007 93p: 8m **96**
10m⁴ 11g³ May 24] angular, useful-looking colt: useful performer: stiffish tasks in 2007, creditable efforts in listed races at Newmarket (blinkered, fourth to Salford Mill) and Goodwood (last of 3 to Halicarnassus) last 2 starts: may prove best at short of 11f: unraced on extremes of going: sold 50,000 gns in July. *J. H. M. Gosden*

BROGUE LANTERNS (IRE) 5 ch.m. Dr Devious (IRE) 127 – Landrail (USA) 63 **–**
(Storm Bird (CAN) 134) [2007 –: p8g 10d Jul 17] fairly useful performer at 2/3 yrs for T. Hogan in Ireland: well held since in varied events, including in Spain: tried visored. *E. J. Creighton*

BROKEN APPLAUSE (IRE) 2 br.f. (Mar 22) Acclamation 118 – Pink Cashmere **94**
(IRE) (Polar Falcon (USA) 126) [2007 5s* 5.1s² 6m⁴ 6.5m⁴ 6d² 6g Oct 6] €25,000Y, 27,000 2-y-o: smallish filly: half-sister to several winners, including 2005 2-y-o 5f winner Pike Bishop (by Namid) and German sprinter Medina (by Pennekamp), both useful: dam unraced half-sister to very smart sprinter Owington: fairly useful performer: won maiden at Haydock in June: ran well in frame next 4 starts, particularly when ¾-length second of 11 to Unilateral in Firth of Clyde Stakes at Ayr (finished strongly): will stay 7f: acts on soft and good to firm going: blinkered (found little) final outing. *R. A. Fahey*

BROKEN MOON 2 gr.f. (Apr 8) Galileo (IRE) 134 – Bedazzling (IRE) 105 (Darshaan **72 p**
133) [2007 7s 7.1g³ Oct 2] useful-looking filly: fluent mover: fourth foal: closely related to a winner in Italy by Barathea and half-sister to 5-y-o Don Pasquale: dam, 7f winner, sister to smart 1¼m/1½m performer Bustan: encouragement in maidens at Newmarket (needed race) and Warwick (third to Swanky Lady), not knocked about: will be suited by 1m+: bound to go on improving. *J. R. Fanshawe*

BRONCO'S FILLY (IRE) 3 b. or br.f. Val Royal (FR) 127 – Lady Esther (IRE) 75 **–**
(Darnay 117) [2007 –: 8g 10g p9.5g⁶ Nov 16] sparely-made filly: little form. *J. G. M. O'Shea*

BRONTE'S HOPE 3 ch.f. Gorse 116 – General Jane (Be My Chief (USA) 122) [2007 **70**
67p: p6g* p6g⁴ Jan 29] fair form: confirmed debut promise when winning maiden at Lingfield in January: shaped better than bare result on handicap debut there next start: likely to prove best at 5f/6f. *M. P. Tregoning*

BRONZE CANNON (USA) 2 b. or br.c. (Mar 1) Lemon Drop Kid (USA) 131 – **93 p**
Victoria Cross (IRE) 101 (Mark of Esteem (IRE) 137) [2007 p7g p8g* p8m* Oct 11] medium-sized colt: second foal: half-brother to 3-y-o Valiance: dam, 7f winner, out of smart performer up to 1¾m Glowing With Pride: fairly useful form: progressed well in 3

starts at Kempton (within a month), winning maiden and nursery, in latter quickening from rear to beat Palm Court by head: will be suited by 1¼m/1½m: should do better still. *J. H. M. Gosden*

BRONZE DANCER (IRE) 5 b.g. Entrepreneur 123 – Scrimshaw (Selkirk (USA) 129) [2007 81: 12m² 16m³ 14g 13f* 13g⁵ 11.9s 12g² Oct 20] lengthy gelding: fair performer: won handicap at Hamilton in June: effective at 1½m to easy 2m: acts on firm and soft going: has shown signs of temperament: sold 5,000 gns. *G. A. Swinbank* **79**

BRONZE STAR 4 b.f. Mark of Esteem (IRE) 137 – White House 84 (Pursuit of Love 124) [2007 73: 9.9m 11.7d⁴ 11.5d² 12d³ 10.1m* Jul 17] good-topped filly: fair performer: won claimer at Yarmouth (claimed by B. Palling £15,000) in July: stays 1½m: acts on polytrack, good to soft and good to firm going. *J. R. Fanshawe* **76**

BRONZO DI RIACE (IRE) 3 b.c. Montjeu (IRE) 137 – Afreeta (USA) (Afleet (CAN)) [2007 –: p9.5g 11.3m⁴ 11m⁵ 8g 10m 11s 8.5g Nov 4] little form: left M. Quinlan after reappearance. *S. Billeri, Italy* **–**

BROOKBY (NZ) 7 b.g. Groom Dancer (USA) 128 – Kappadios (NZ) (Great Charmer (USA)) [2007 p8g⁵ p8g⁵ Jan 31] New Zealand-bred gelding: successful twice up to 1m from 20 starts in New Zealand for S. Curtis: no show on hurdling debut: better effort on Flat in Britain when fifth to Rebellious Spirit in handicap at Kempton on reappearance: should stay beyond 1m: tongue tied last 2 starts. *Miss S. West* **76**

BROOK LASS (IRE) 3 b.f. Dilshaan 119 – Polish Widow 74 (Polish Precedent (USA) 131) [2007 –: 10s 8d 9d 12s 10m 12m Sep 30] €1,400Y: quite good-topped filly: fifth foal: half-sister to 1m seller winner Polish Paddy (by Priolo): dam maiden: poor maiden: blinkered, well held in seller at Musselburgh final outing: seems to stays 1½m: tried in cheekpieces. *T. G. McCourt, Ireland* **39**

BROOMIELAW 3 ch.c. Rock of Gibraltar (IRE) 133 – Peony 108 (Lion Cavern (USA) 117) [2007 86p: 10m⁴ 10.3m* Aug 17] tall, close-coupled, good-topped colt: progressive form in maidens: reportedly injured on reappearance: useful form when winning at Doncaster (by 3 lengths from Bright Mind, responding well after initially idling) in August: likely to stay 1½m: raced only on firm ground: remains open to improvement. *E. A. L. Dunlop* **98 p**

BROTHER BARRY (USA) 2 b. or br.g. (Apr 9) Forestry (USA) 121 – Saratoga Sugar (USA) (Gone West (USA)) [2007 6g⁶ Nov 2] $80,000Y: first foal: dam, US maiden, sister to US Grade 1 9f winner Link River: 66/1, shaped well when sixth to Almoutaz in maiden at Newmarket, green once shaken up: subsequently gelded: sure to improve. *W. J. Musson* **65 p**

BROUGH (IRE) 2 b.c. (Apr 1) Fasliyev (USA) 120 – Metaphor (USA) (Woodman (USA) 126) [2007 5m 7.5g 5m p5.1g p7.1g p8.6g Nov 14] compact, good-bodied colt: no form: tongue tied once. *J. O'Reilly* **–**

BROUGHTONS FLIGHT (IRE) 2 ch.f. (Feb 15) Hawk Wing (USA) 136 – Aldburgh (Bluebird (USA) 125) [2007 7d 8d p7.1d⁵ p7.1d² Dec 27] 46,000 2-y-o: strong, lengthy filly: fourth foal: closely related to a winner in Japan by Timber Country and half-sister to fairly useful 2005 2-y-o 1m winner Montreux (by Jade Robbery): dam once-raced half-sister to dam of Attraction: modest maiden: best effort when second in nursery at Wolverhampton: should be suited by 1m+: capable of better still. *W. J. Musson* **64 p**

BROUGHTONS FOLLY 4 b.f. Groom Dancer (USA) 128 – Cressida (Polish Precedent (USA) 131) [2007 76: p10g p10g⁴ f11g 11.6m⁶ p12.2g* 16g 14d Sep 23] lengthy filly: fair performer: won at Wolverhampton in July, then left W. Musson 14,000 gns: refused to race final outing: stays 1½m, not 2m: acts on polytrack and good to firm going: reportedly lame third outing. *Seamus Lynch, Ireland* **71 § a78 §**

BROUGHTONS REVIVAL 5 b.m. Pivotal 124 – Ella Lamees 61 (Statoblest 120) [2007 55: p12.2g⁵ p9.5g³ p10g³ 11.5d* p10g³ 12.6s⁴ 11.8s* 14s* Sep 29] long-backed mare: fairly useful handicapper: improved to win at Yarmouth in May, Leicester in July and Haydock in September: stays 1¾m: raced only on polytrack and good to soft/soft going on turf. *W. J. Musson* **88 +**

BROUHAHA 3 b.g. Bahhare (USA) 122 – Top of The Morning 56 (Keen 116) [2007 65: p8g 7m 10.9d 8m⁵ 8d p8g² Oct 4] big, well-made gelding: modest maiden: free-going sort, stays 1m: acts on polytrack: in cheekpieces final outing: tongue tied last 4 starts. *Miss Diana Weeden* **61**

BRUGES (IRE) 2 b.c. (Jan 18) Marju (IRE) 127 – Liege (IRE) (Night Shift (USA)) [2007 6g²* 7s* Jul 4] lengthy, useful-looking colt: fifth foal: brother to French 7.5f/1m winner Moore's Melody and Hong Kong 5f/6f winner Sounds Better: dam, unraced, out of useful close relative to Generous and half-sister to Imagine: tongue tied, won maiden **106**

at the Curragh in June and listed race at Leopardstown in July, latter impressively by 2 lengths from Going Public, first off bridle in race that wasn't truly-run, leading final 1f: sustained stone bruise and changed hands after: will stay 1m: looked a smart prospect. *D. Myerscough, Ireland*

BRUKI (IRE) 2 b.f. (Apr 15) Captain Rio 122 – Coup de Coeur (IRE) (Kahyasi 130) **61** [2007 p10g p10g³ Dec 12] 36,000F: second foal: dam unraced half-sister to smart French middle-distance performers Premier Amour and Fleur d'Oranger: modest form in maidens at Lingfield and Kempton: tongue tied. *M. Botti*

BRUNELLESCHI 4 ch.g. Bertolini (USA) 125 – Petrovna (IRE) 78 (Petardia 113) **85** [2007 78: 5.1m² 6.1g* 6g* 6d² 6m 6d⁶ 6m⁶ 6d 5d² 6d Oct 30] strong, compact gelding: has a quick action: fairly useful handicapper: won at Nottingham (apprentices), Newmarket and Yarmouth, all in May: left P. Gilligan after sixth start: below form final outing: stays 6f: acts on polytrack, firm and soft going: tried visored, blinkered nowadays: has hung left: sometimes slowly away. *M. G. Quinlan*

BRUNTON BLUE 2 b.f. (Mar 30) Compton Place 125 – Persian Blue 64 (Persian Bold **54** 123) [2007 p6g Dec 29] fifth foal: half-sister to 3 winners, including 5f/6f winner Maluti (by Piccolo) and 5-y-o Hits Only Cash: dam maiden who stayed 1½m: 14/1, eighth of 11 in maiden at Lingfield. *W. Jarvis*

BRUNTON (IRE) 5 b.g. Charnwood Forest (IRE) 125 – Lady Nathalie (IRE) **48** (Bigstone (IRE) 126) [2007 61: 8d 6g 7g⁵ 9m 8s 6s⁴ 6.3d 5g f6d f6g Dec 27] lengthy gelding: poor maiden handicapper: left D. Barry in Ireland after eighth start: effective at testing 6f to 1m: acts on soft going: tried tongue tied: often blinkered. *A. Berry*

BRUT 5 b.g. Mind Games 121 – Champenoise 64 (Forzando 122) [2007 73: f6g² f6g⁴ **79** f5g 6g⁵ 5g 5.1m⁶ 5m* 5m 5f² 6g* 6g* 5d⁵ 5s³ 6d 6g 5d⁴ 5d* 5g 5g* Nov 6] lengthy, **a60** good-topped gelding: fair performer on turf, modest on all-weather: won handicaps in May, June (2) and September, all at Hamilton, and claimer at Catterick in November: stays easy 7f, races mostly at 5f/6f: acts on fibresand, firm and soft going: tried visored, wears cheekpieces nowadays: front runner. *D. W. Barker*

BRYNRIS 3 gr.g. Perryston View 114 – Isle of Mull (Elmaamul (USA) 125) [2007 35: **–** p7.1g⁵ f8g p7.1g p6g 6s Jun 4] little form in 2007. *Mrs G. S. Rees*

BUACHAILL DONA (IRE) 4 b.g. Namid 128 – Serious Contender (IRE) (Tenby **109** 125) [2007 101p: 6g⁴ 5m⁶ 5d 5g³ 5m* 5.6m 6d Sep 22] quite good-topped gelding: useful handicapper: won at Musselburgh (by ½ length from Harry Up) in September: better than result in Portland behind Fullandby at Doncaster next time, third home far side: well below form in Ayr Gold Cup final outing: effective at 5f/6f: acts on firm and good to soft going. *D. Nicholls*

BUBBLY GIRL 3 b.f. Tamayaz (CAN) 121 – Alexander Star (IRE) 68 (Inzar (USA) **53** 112) [2007 10m p8.6g 8g 10g p8g⁴ 10.1g 8m⁵ Aug 9] leggy filly: first foal: dam 5f winner: modest maiden: stays 8.6f: acts on polytrack: held up. *P. J. McBride*

BUCCELLATI 3 ch.c. Soviet Star (USA) 128 – Susi Wong (IRE) (Selkirk (USA) 129) **108** [2007 86: 8.1g⁴ 10g⁵ 10.1g⁴ 8m 10m⁵ 9.9g⁶ 10.3m* 10.3g* 12s* Oct 13] close-coupled, quite attractive colt: useful performer: much improved when winning minor event at Doncaster and handicap at Chester in September and ladbrokes.com Stakes (Handicap) at Ascot (beat St Savarin by short head) in October: stays 1½m: acts on soft and good to firm going: visored last 4 starts: sometimes races freely/carries head awkwardly: waited with. *A. M. Balding*

ladbrokes.com Stakes (Handicap), Ascot—
the visored Buccellati is about to get up close home and win his third race of the autumn;
second is St Savarin (No.7) with Players Please (left) and Dubai Twilight next

BUCHAREST 4 b.g. Barathea (IRE) 127 – Zorleni (Zafonic (USA) 130) [2007 70: 7m* **77**
p8g* p7g² 7m⁶ p7g p6g² p6g² p6g Oct 23] workmanlike gelding: fair handicapper:
won at Brighton in June and Kempton in July: effective at 6f to 1m: acts on polytrack
and firm going: tends to wander: front runner: sold 11,000 gns, sent to Saudi Arabia.
M. Wigham

BUCKIE MASSA 3 ch.g. Best of The Bests (IRE) 122 – Up On Points 97 (Royal **82**
Academy (USA) 130) [2007 77: 6g 5g⁶ 7m⁶ 6f² 7m³ 6m⁴ 5g 6m* 6m 7m⁴ p6g 8d p8.6g⁴
Oct 27] good-topped gelding: fairly useful handicapper: won at Brighton in August: ran
creditably when fourth after: stays 8.6f: acts on polytrack and firm ground: sold 25,000
gns. *S. Kirk*

BUCKLE AND HYDE 4 ch.f. Foxhound (USA) 103 – Step On Degas 69 (Super- **44**
power 113) [2007 56: p6g 7m⁴ p8.6g 8f⁶ p10g Sep 18] lengthy filly: poor maiden nowadays: stays 7f: acts on polytrack: tried in cheekpieces. *Mrs A. L. M. King*

BUCKS 10 b.g. Slip Anchor 136 – Alligram (USA) 61 (Alysheba (USA)) [2007 73: **66**
p12g³ Nov 30] quite good-topped gelding: fairly useful performer in 2005: lightly raced
and just fair since, ran in seller sole start at 10 yrs: effective at 1¼m to easy 2m: acts on
all-weather, firm and soft going: waited with. *Mike Murphy*

BUCKTHORN 3 ch.c. Lomitas 129 – Emma Peel 113 (Emarati (USA) 74) [2007 56: **73**
10m 10m 10d⁵ p10g Jul 12] strong, sturdy colt: fair maiden: stays 1¼m: acts on good to
firm and good to soft ground: won 7,000 gns in October. *G. Wragg*

BUDDY HOLLY 2 b.c. (Jan 23) Reel Buddy (USA) 118 – Night Symphonie (Cloud- **–**
ings (IRE) 112) [2007 6m 7d Oct 16] good-topped colt: no show (green) in maidens. *Pat
Eddery*

BUDS DILEMMA 3 b.f. Anabaa (USA) 130 – Lady Thynn (FR) (Crystal Glitters **45**
(USA) 127) [2007 –: 6m 7d⁵ 7.9m 7.1s 9.9m 10.3g⁶ p9.5g Oct 6] workmanlike filly: poor
maiden: left I. McInnes after fifth outing. *W. M. Brisbourne*

BUFFY BOO 4 b. or br.f. Agnes World (USA) 123 – Bunty Boo 110 (Noalto 120) [2007 **–**
6s Jun 14] 40,000Y: fifth foal: half-sister to 3 winners, including 2002 2-y-o 5f/6f winner
Silca Boo (by Efisio) and 6f (including at 2 yrs)/7f winner Zilch (by Zilzal), both useful:
dam 5f/6f winner: 50/1 and green, signs of ability when tenth to Vainglory in maiden at
Yarmouth. *C. R. Egerton*

BUGAKU 2 ch.c. (Mar 18) Montjeu (IRE) 137 – Bryony Brind (IRE) 105 (Kris 135) **56 p**
[2007 8d Oct 27] third foal: dam 1m to 12.5f winner: 5/1, green and considerably handled
down the field in maiden at Newbury: will benefit from 1¼m/1½m: certain to improve.
Sir Michael Stoute

BUGSY'S BOY 3 b.g. Double Trigger (IRE) 123 – Bugsy's Sister (Aragon 118) [2007 **72**
p8.6g f8g⁶ p8g p12m⁴ p12m p13.9g² p16.5g* Dec 8] fourth foal: half-brother to 1½m
seller winner Phase Eight Girl (by Warrshan): dam unraced: fair performer: won handicap
at Wolverhampton in December: stays 16.5f: raced on all-weather. *P. W. D'Arcy*

BUJU 2 b.g. (Feb 13) Sugarfoot 118 – Edge of Darkness 62 (Vaigly Great 127) [2007 6s **52**
7m 7m³ 7.5m 8g⁵ 7g Oct 19] close-coupled, workmanlike gelding: modest maiden: bred
to stay 1½m: sold 3,000 gns, sent to Sweden. *N. Tinkler*

BUKIT TINGGI (IRE) 3 b.g. Peintre Celebre (USA) 137 – Puteri Wentworth 88 **82 +**
(Sadler's Wells (USA) 132) [2007 10.3m⁶ p12g⁴ p12g⁶ 14s² 14.1g³ 16g⁴ Nov 8] good-
bodied gelding: fourth foal: half-brother to useful 1m (at 2 yrs)/8.6f winner Putra Sas (by
Sri Pekan): dam, 1½m to 2½m winner, half-sister to smart sprinter Watching: fairly useful
maiden: in frame in handicaps last 2 starts: will prove best at 2m+: acts on polytrack and
soft ground: reportedly suffered breathing problem third outing: gelded after final start.
M. A. Jarvis

BULAS BOY 2 ch.g. (Mar 23) Exit To Nowhere (USA) 122 – Bula Rose (IRE) 57 **–**
(Alphabatim (USA) 126) [2007 10m Oct 8] compact gelding: well beaten in maiden at
Pontefract. *E. W. Tuer*

BULBERRY HILL 6 b.g. Makbul 104 – Hurtleberry (IRE) 87 (Tirol 127) [2007 56: **62**
f14g⁴ f16g² f16s² 16.1m p16g p13.9g p12.2g f12d⁴ Dec 12] modest handicapper: stays
2m: acts on all-weather, probably on firm ground: tried tongue tied. *R. W. Price*

BULLET MAN (USA) 2 b. or br.c. (May 18) Mr Greeley (USA) 122 – Silk Tapestry **82 p**
(USA) 77 (Tank's Prospect (USA)) [2007 7m² p7.1g³ Sep 28] $80,000Y, 88,000 2-y-o:
seventh foal: half-brother to 3 winners in US, including sprinter Forest Hunter (by Forest
Wildcat): dam, 1m winner, half-sister to US Grade 1 1¼m winner Tactile out of US 2-y-o
Grade 1 9f winner Only Queens: placed in maidens at Lingfield (promising second to
Mujaadel) and Wolverhampton (odds on, still green): will be suited by 1m: should still
progress. *L. M. Cumani*

BULL MARKET (IRE) 4 b.g. Danehill (USA) 126 – Paper Moon (IRE) 92 (Lake **86** Coniston (IRE) 131) [2007 12m³ 14.8m 10f⁶ 12g p12.2g⁵ Aug 30] big, strong gelding: fairly useful handicapper: in-and-out form in 2007: stays 1½m: raced only on all-weather and good ground or firmer: free-going sort: joined C. Morlock. *J. A. Osborne*

BULWARK (IRE) 5 b.g. Montjeu (IRE) 137 – Bulaxie 110 (Bustino 136) [2007 109§: **113 d** 12m 14g³ 16.4d³ 20g 16g 14.1g⁵ 14.6m 16.5m⁵ Nov 10] good-bodied gelding: smart performer: good efforts when third in 2007, to Sergeant Cecil in Yorkshire Cup at York and to Allegretto in Henry II Stakes at Sandown: below form after, leaving Mrs A. Perrett 36,000 gns prior to final outing (gelded after): stays easy 2¼m: acts on polytrack, firm and soft going: usually blinkered nowadays (not last 2 starts): patiently ridden: tends to carry head awkwardly/wander under pressure: one to treat with caution. *Ian Williams*

BUNDEROS (IRE) 3 b.f. Areion (GER) 115 – Bundheimerin (GER) (Ordos (GER)) **50** [2007 –: 6m 7d 6.9m⁵ 8.3m³ 7.5m Aug 26] leggy filly: modest maiden: left Mrs A. Duffield after second start: stays 8.3f: acts on good to firm ground. *R. A. Fahey*

BUNDLE UP 4 b.f. Diktat 126 – Bundle (Cadeaux Genereux 131) [2007 8g p12g⁴ 8.3g **66** Jul 9] 24,000Y: second foal: half-sister to fairly useful 1¼m winner Top Gear (by Robellino): dam unraced out of half-sister to Japan Cup winner Jupiter Island and high-class 2-y-o sprinter Precocious: easily best effort in maidens when seventh to Passing at Goodwood on debut, slowly away. *Mrs L. J. Mongan*

BUNGIE 3 gr.g. Forzando 122 – Sweet Whisper 63 (Petong 126) [2007 64: p5g⁴ 5.1s **58** p6g p7.1g p5.1s Dec 20] leggy, useful-looking gelding: modest handicapper: left Ms Deborah Evans after reappearance: may prove best at 5f: acts on all-weather and good to soft ground: tried visored. *Paul Green*

BUNNY HUG 2 b.f. (Mar 29) Royal Applause 124 – White Rabbit 99 (Zilzal (USA) **–** 137) [2007 6m⁶ 7m Aug 17] big, leggy, useful-looking filly: second foal: half-sister to 3-y-o Magic Show: dam 2-y-o 6f winner who stayed 1m: well beaten in minor event/maiden. *T. D. Easterby*

BUNTY MALENOIR 2 b.f. (Apr 5) Silver Patriarch (IRE) 125 – Captivating (IRE) **–** 63 (Wolfhound (USA) 126) [2007 6m⁴ 6m p7g Jul 4] 5,000Y: fourth foal: half-sister to 3 winners, including 5-y-o 1m Spartacus: dam maiden (stayed 17f): no form. *I. A. Wood*

BURFORD LASS (IRE) 4 b.f. Quws 116 – Dancing Willma (IRE) (Dancing Dissi- **62** dent (USA) 119) [2007 5.1f p7g² 7m p7g⁶ p8.6g⁵ p8g⁴ 6g* p7.1g⁶ p6g² p6g p6g⁶ Oct 5] modest performer: won seller at Folkestone in July: effective at 6f to 8.6f: acts on polytrack and firm going: tended to hang left third appearance. *D. K. Ivory*

BURGUNDY 10 b.g. Lycius (USA) 124 – Decant 68 (Rousillon (USA) 133) [2007 80: **80** p12g⁵ p12g p12g p10g⁴ 11.9d² 10g² p11g³ 10d* 10g⁶ 11.9d⁴ p10g Nov 17] smallish gelding: fairly useful handicapper: won apprentice event at Sandown in July: trained by P. Mitchell prior to final start: stays 1½m: acts on polytrack, firm and soft going: wears headgear: sometimes slowly away: held up: reliable. *R. A. Teal*

BURHAAN (IRE) 5 b.h. Green Desert (USA) 127 – Arjuzah (IRE) 110 (Ahonoora **66** 122) [2007 –, a63: p7g³ p6g* p6g⁶ p7g* p7g³ 5s a6g 6g 6s 11m⁶ Dec 5] sturdy horse: fair handicapper: won at Lingfield in January and February: left J. Boyle after fifth start and J. F. O'Shea in Ireland before final one: effective at 6f to 8.6f: acts on polytrack and good to firm ground: tried visored/tongue tied earlier in career: sometimes finds little. *Maria R. Salvioni, Italy*

BURLEY FLAME 6 b.g. Marju (IRE) 127 – Tarsa 81 (Ballad Rock 122) [2007 –: 8.1g³ **85** 7.9d⁶ Jun 27] sturdy, angular gelding: fairly useful handicapper: suffered tendon injury after sole start in 2006: better effort at 6 yrs when close third on reappearance: stays 1m: acts on polytrack, good to firm and good to soft going: tried visored: none too consistent. *J. G. Given*

BURNBRAKE 2 b.c. (Mar 10) Mujahid (USA) 125 – Duena (Grand Lodge (USA) 125) **67** [2007 7g p7g⁴ p8m⁵ Dec 8] 11,000Y: fourth foal: half-brother to 2004 2-y-o 5f winner Music Teacher (by Piccolo): dam unraced half-sister to useful 6f/7f performer Presto Vento: fair form in maidens: stays 1m. *J. A. R. Toller*

BURNINGFOLD BABE 3 b.f. Muhtarram (USA) 125 – Laser Light Lady (Tragic **52** Role (USA)) [2007 52: p6g² Jan 20] modest maiden: best form at 6f: raced mainly on all-weather: blinkered final 2-y-o start (raced freely). *P. Winkworth*

BURNING INCENSE (IRE) 4 b.g. Namid 128 – Night Scent (IRE) 85 (Scenic 128) **106** [2007 106: 6m 6d⁶ 6s 7g⁵ 7d 6m 6d⁵ 6g⁴ Oct 14] big, strong gelding: useful handicapper: eye-catching sixth to Dark Missile in Wokingham Stakes at Royal Ascot second start (from poor draw): good efforts when seventh to Aahayson at Windsor and fifth to Third Set in International Stakes at Ascot next 2 starts: respectable efforts last 2 outings: effective at 6f/7f: acts on soft and good to firm ground: sometimes blinkered, in cheekpieces final outing: held up: sold 85,000 gns. *R. Charlton*

BURNING MOON 6 b.g. Bering 136 – Triple Green 69 (Green Desert (USA) 127) [2007 –: f8g p12.2g Feb 21] leggy, useful-looking gelding: fairly useful winner at 3 yrs: lightly raced and no form since: tried visored/in cheekpieces. *S. W. Hall* —

BURNLEY AL (IRE) 5 ch.g. Desert King (IRE) 129 – Bold Meadows 80 (Persian Bold 123) [2007 72: p8.6g p8.6g³ p7.1g³ f7g p8.6g⁶ Apr 28] close-coupled gelding: modest performer nowadays: effective at 7f to 1¼m: acts on polytrack (well held on fibresand), soft and good to firm going: usually wears headgear: pulled hard second outing: tough. *Peter Grayson* **59**

BURNLEY (IRE) 4 b.g. Distant Music (USA) 126 – Dance Ahead 81 (Shareef Dancer (USA) 135) [2007 10.2m 11.7g 10.9g Jul 12] little form in bumper/maidens: reportedly finished distressed last 2 outings. *Mrs A. L. M. King* —

BURN THE BREEZE (IRE) 2 b.f. (Apr 4) Beat Hollow 126 – Madiyla 73 (Darshaan 133) [2007 7m⁵ 8.3m⁴ 8.2m³ Oct 3] big filly: half-sister to several winners, including smart French 1m winner Lethals Lady (by Rudimentary) and useful 2005 2-y-o 7f winner Giving (by Generous): dam, 1½m winner, half-sister to National Stakes winner Manntari: shaped with promise in maidens, ½-length third to La Rosa Nostra at Nottingham final start (made running): will be suited by 1¼m/1½m: has scope, should improve further. *H. R. A. Cecil* **74 p**

BURNTOAKBOY 9 b.g. Sir Harry Lewis (USA) 127 – Sainte Martine (Martinmas 128) [2007 80: 16g 14s Oct 4] leggy gelding: unraced on Flat prior to 2006: fairly useful form: much better effort when eighth in handicap on reappearance: stays 2m: acts on soft and good to firm going: useful hurdler, won over fences in October. *Dr R. D. P. Newland* **77**

BURNWYND BOY 2 b.g. (Mar 19) Tobougg (IRE) 125 – Cadeau Speciale 54 (Cadeaux Genereux 131) [2007 6d* 6m* 6m 7m 6g³ 6d Oct 13] tall, good-topped gelding: first foal: dam, maiden (should have stayed beyond 6f), out of half-sister to St Leger/Gold Cup winner Classic Cliche: fairly useful performer: won minor events at Newcastle and Pontefract in May: ran well after in Coventry Stakes at Royal Ascot (tenth) and nurseries at Ascot and Hamilton (third to Nezami): hampered final start (visored): stays 7f: acts on good to firm and good to soft going. *I. Semple* **90**

BURRISCARRA 2 b.f. (Apr 15) Mujahid (USA) 125 – Cressida (Polish Precedent (USA) 131) [2007 7m p8m* p7g³ Nov 30] 4,500Y: fourth foal: half-sister to 7f seller winner Strathtay (by Pivotal) and 1½m winner Broughtons Folly (by Groom Dancer): dam, ran twice, out of useful performer up to 14.6f Regent's Folly: fair form: won maiden at Kempton in November by head from Girl of Pangaea: creditable third in minor event at Lingfield final start: stays 1m. *E. Tyrrell, Ireland* **72**

BURY TREASURE (IRE) 2 ch.c. (Apr 20) Choisir (AUS) 126 – Future Treasure 88 (Habitat 134) [2007 6d 5.2g⁴ 6d Aug 26] good-quartered colt: modest maiden: likely to prove best at 5f/6f. *Miss Gay Kelleway* **56**

BUSCADOR (USA) 8 ch.g. Crafty Prospector (USA) – Fairway Flag (USA) (Fairway Phantom (USA)) [2007 52, a70: p9.5g p9.5g³ p9.5g p9.5g⁴ p9.5g p9.5g³ p12.2g² p9.5g⁶ p12.2g² p12.2g p9.5g p12.2d p12.2g⁴ Dec 29] modest handicapper, better on all-weather than turf: stays 1½m: acts on all-weather, soft and good to firm ground: front runner. *W. M. Brisbourne* **64**

BUSHY DELL (IRE) 2 br.f. (Feb 9) King Charlemagne (USA) 120 – Nisibis (In The Wings 128) [2007 p7g⁵ p8.6g* Oct 5] 11,000Y: lengthy, rather unfurnished filly: fourth foal: half-sister to 6-y-o Spectested and winner in Sweden by Distant Music: dam, maiden, half-sister to smart performer up to 9f Nijo: fair form: better for debut, won maiden at Wolverhampton by short head from the wayward No To Trident: will stay 1¼m. *Miss J. Feilden* **70**

BUSSELL UP 2 b.f. (Mar 29) Danehill Dancer (IRE) 117 – Digamist Girl (IRE) (Digamist (USA) 110) [2007 5.1g³ Nov 7] 40,000Y: lengthy filly: has scope: sixth foal: half-sister to several winners, including 6f (including at 2 yrs) winner Glaramara (by Nicolotte) and 7f winner Queen's Rhapsody (by Baryshnikov), both useful: dam winning sprinter in Belgium: 40/1, eye-catching debut when ½-length third to Quaroma in maiden at Nottingham, green and detached early before storming home: will be suited by 6f/7f: sure to win races. *S. C. Williams* **77 p**

BUSSEL (USA) 3 ch.f. Royal Academy (USA) 130 – Reigning Princess (USA) (Storm **82**
Boot (USA)) [2007 76: f7g³ 7s³ 6g⁶ 7g p8m* Nov 24] strong, good-bodied filly: fairly
useful performer: left W. Haggas, much improved when winning handicap at Lingfield in
November: stays 1m: acts on polytrack, unraced on going firmer than good on turf: often
races prominently. *D. M. Simcock*

BUSSONI (GER) 6 b.h. Goofalik (USA) 118 – Blumme (CHI) (Jadar (CHI)) [2007 **117**
111: 11d³ 12g² 16g* 14g* 12d³ 12d* 12m⁴ 12g³ Dec 9] half-brother to several winners in
Germany, including smart 1m to 9.5f winner Baleno (by Heraldiste): dam, winner in
Chile, later 8.5f/9f winner in USA: smart performer: improved again in 2007, winning
Betty Barclay-Rennen at Baden-Baden (for second year running, by 1½ lengths from
Bergo) in May, Prix Maurice de Nieuil at Longchamp (held on by nose from Champs
Elysees) in July and valuable Bosphorus Cup at Veliefendi (again made all, beat Pressing
2 lengths) in September: also ran well when 1¾ lengths third to Saddex in Rheinland-
Pokal at Cologne fifth start and to Doctor Dino in Hong Kong Vase at Sha Tin final
outing: effective at 1½m to 2m: acts on soft and good to firm ground: races prominently:
has had tongue tied. *H. Blume, Germany*

BUSTAN (IRE) 8 b.g. Darshaan 133 – Dazzlingly Radiant 81 (Try My Best (USA) 130) **99**
[2007 105: 7f* 8f² 7g 8m³ 7g 8m 8.1m 8s² 8g 8.2g p8g Nov 14] strong gelding: useful
handicapper: won at Thirsk in April: good neck second to My Paris in Thirsk Hunt Cup
next time: below form after, markedly so last 2 starts: effective at 7f to 1½m: acts on polytrack, firm and soft going: blinkered (raced freely) once at 5 yrs: none too consistent.
G. C. Bravery

BUSTER HYVONEN (IRE) 5 b.g. Dansili 127 – Serotina (IRE) 73 (Mtoto 134) **79**
[2007 80: 14.1m³ Apr 26] well-made gelding: fairly useful handicapper (similar level
over hurdles): creditable third sole Flat start in 2007: stays 1¾m, worth a try at 2m: raced
on all-weather and good/good to firm going. *J. R. Fanshawe*

BUSTIN JUSTIN (USA) 4 b.c. Forestry (USA) 121 – Designatoree (USA) (Alysheba **–**
(USA)) [2007 104: a7f Feb 8] lengthy, good-topped colt: useful form: won first 3 starts at
3 yrs: below form in handicap at Nad Al Sheba sole start in 2007: should prove as
effective at 6f as 7f: raced on dirt and good/good to firm ground on turf: has worn rope
halter for stall entry: sent to USA. *J. Noseda*

BUSY MAN (IRE) 8 b.g. Darnay 117 – Make Or Mar 84 (Daring March 116) [2007 **–**
59: p10m Dec 10] tall, rather leggy gelding: modest maiden at 7 yrs: well beaten sole start
in 2007: stays 1¼m: acts on polytrack. *R. C. Guest*

BUTE STREET 2 b.g. (Apr 21) Superior Premium 122 – Hard To Follow (Dilum **–**
(USA) 115) [2007 7m 5.7d Oct 1] last in maidens. *R. J. Hodges*

BUTLERS BEST 3 b.g. Best of The Bests (IRE) 122 – Evening Charm (IRE) (Bering **–**
136) [2007 63: 11.1g Aug 22] strong gelding: maiden: stays 8.6f: acts on polytrack: has
shown signs of temperament: sold 600 gns in October. *E. J. O'Neill*

BUTTERFLY BUD (IRE) 4 b.g. Lend A Hand 124 – Rathbawn Realm (Doulab **57**
(USA) 115) [2007 69: 6.1g³ 6g⁴ 7g⁴ 6d 6m 6m Aug 25] useful-looking gelding: modest
maiden: stays 7f: acts on firm and good to soft ground. *J. O'Reilly*

BUXTON 3 b.g. Auction House (USA) 120 – Dam Certain (IRE) 61 (Damister (USA) **77**
123) [2007 –: 7m² p7.1g* 7.1g p6g³ p6m⁴ p6g³ 6m⁶ p6g⁴ p6g³ 7g p6g p8m p8m⁴ p8g **a87**
Dec 30] close-coupled gelding: fairly useful on all-weather, fair on turf (lightly raced):
won maiden at Wolverhampton in May: stays 1m: acts on polytrack and good to firm
going: tried blinkered. *R. Ingram*

BUY ON THE RED 6 b.g. Komaite (USA) – Red Rosein 97 (Red Sunset 120) [2007 **79**
81, a89: p7.1g² p6g⁴ 6d 6f* 6f⁵ 6m² 6m² p6g p7g p6g³ p6g⁶ p7.1g⁴ p7.1g Dec 31] **a97**
tall, quite good-topped gelding: useful handicapper on all-weather, fair on turf: won at
Windsor in August: stays 7f: acts on polytrack and firm going: tried blinkered, wears
cheekpieces nowadays: often races prominently. *W. R. Muir*

BUZBURY RINGS 3 b.g. Piccolo 121 – Mory Kante (USA) (Icecapade (USA)) [2007 **59**
56: p7g p6g 5.1f May 1] modest maiden: should stay 7f: tried in cheekpieces.
A. M. Balding

BUZZIN'BOYZEE (IRE) 4 ch.f. Monashee Mountain (USA) 115 – Las Bela 75 **62**
(Welsh Pageant 132) [2007 67: p6g p6g³ p7.1g³ p8g⁴ p7g⁴ p7g p8.6g⁴ p8.6g⁴ f8g⁶ 7.1m
p6g 7g⁶ p7g⁶ p7g p7g Nov 19] angular filly: modest handicapper nowadays: stays easy
8.6f: acts on polytrack and firm ground, probably on good to soft: tried visored/blinkered.
P. D. Evans

BYANITA (IRE) 3 b.f. Anita's Prince 126 – Byliny (IRE) (Archway (IRE) 115) [2007 —
—: p8.6g Jan 8] no form: tried in cheekpieces. *B. Palling*

BY COMMAND 2 b.c. (Feb 20) Red Ransom (USA) – Rafha 123 (Kris 135) [2007 **76 p**
7.1g⁴ 7m⁵ Jul 14] sturdy colt: closely related to 3-y-o Jafaru and half-brother to numerous
at least useful winners, including very smart sprinter Invincible Spirit (by Green Desert)
and smart 7.6f (at 2 yrs) to 1¾m winner Sadian (by Shirley Heights): dam, 6f (at 2 yrs) to
11.5f winner, including Prix de Diane: promise in maidens, seemingly inadequate test, at
Sandown and Salisbury (favourite, fifth to Fast Company): will be suited by 1¼m/1½m:
should do better. *J. L. Dunlop*

BYGONE DAYS 6 ch.g. Desert King (IRE) 129 – May Light 62 (Midyan (USA) 124) **118**
[2007 120: 6m⁴ 6d⁶ 6.5m 7m³ 7.1m² Sep 13] quite attractive gelding: smart performer:
best effort in 2007 when fourth to Assertive in listed race at Windsor on reappearance:
respectable efforts in Supreme Stakes at Goodwood (third to Lovelace) and listed race at
Sandown (1¼ lengths second to Eisteddfod) last 2 starts: stays 7f: acts on soft and good
to firm going. *Saeed bin Suroor*

BYRON BAY 5 b.h. My Best Valentine 122 – Candarela 41 (Damister (USA) 123) **91**
[2007 91, a95: f7g⁵ f8g² f8g⁴ 8s Mar 31] tall, leggy horse: fairly useful handicapper: in
frame at Southwell second/third outings, poorly drawn at Newcastle final start: effective
at 7f to 1¼m: acts on all-weather and any turf going: sometimes wears cheekpieces: has
made running, usually waited with more nowadays: sometimes looks awkward. *I. Semple*

BY STORM 4 b.f. Largesse 112 – Polar Storm (IRE) 76 (Law Society (USA) 130) [2007 **37**
55: 9.7m 10m p10g 10m 12d f8d⁵ Dec 20] modest performer at 3 yrs: only poor in 2007:
left J. Berry after fourth start: stays 1¼m: acts on good to firm and good to soft going.
Miss J. E. Foster

BY THE EDGE (IRE) 3 b.f. Shinko Forest (IRE) – Magic Annemarie (IRE) 75 **66**
(Dancing Dissident (USA) 119) [2007 —: 5d 6d⁴ 5d² 5m⁴ 5m² 5d³ 5g⁵ p5.1g³ 5g²
p5.1g⁵ 5v⁴ p5.1g³ p5.1s* Dec 20] strong, good-bodied filly: fair performer: left P. Deegan
in Ireland after second start: won maiden in October and handicap in December, both at
Wolverhampton: will prove best at 5f/6f: acts on polytrack, heavy and good to firm going:
effective visored or not: races prominently. *T. D. Barron*

BYTHEHOKEY (IRE) 6 b.g. Barathea (IRE) 127 – Regal Portrait (IRE) 57 (Royal **50**
Academy (USA) 130) [2007 12.6m 10.9g p12.2g Oct 30] modest maiden at 4 yrs for
A. Mullins in Ireland, unraced in 2006: left B. Baugh, little impact on Flat in 2007: stays
1½m: tried blinkered. *W. M. Brisbourne*

BY THE RIVER 3 b.g. Zamindar (USA) 116 – Baby Bunting 63 (Wolfhound (USA) **53**
126) [2007 —: 12g 12s⁶ 11.6m⁵ 16.2s⁴ Jul 27] strong, heavy-topped gelding: type to carry
condition: modest maiden: stays 1½m (not 2m): acts on soft and good to firm ground:
usually races prominently. *P. Winkworth*

C

CABINET (IRE) 3 b.c. Grand Lodge (USA) 125 – Passe Passe (USA) 78 (Lear Fan **101 +**
(USA) 130) [2007 96p: 9g⁴ 11.9m⁶ 10d⁷* 9.9m⁴ 10.3g² Sep 29] 85,000Y: lengthy, quite
good-topped colt: useful handicapper: won at Sandown (by 1¾ lengths from Weightless)
in July: further improvement next 2 starts, ½-length second to Buccellati at Chester on
final outing: may prove best around 1¼m: acts on polytrack, good to firm and good to
soft going. *Sir Michael Stoute*

CABOURG (IRE) 4 b.g. Danehill (USA) 126 – Loire Valley (IRE) (Sadler's Wells **69**
(USA) 132) [2007 65: p8.6g² p8.6g p7.1g² p7f⁴ p7.1g⁵ 7.5m⁴ 7m⁴ 6g 7m 7m⁵ 6g⁵ 7.1g²
p7g⁴ p7.1g* p8g⁶ Dec 29] close-coupled gelding: fair handicapper: won at Wolverhampton in December: stays 8.6f: acts on polytrack, firm and good to soft ground: often
blinkered: tends to find little. *R. Bastiman*

CACTUS KING 4 b.g. Green Desert (USA) 127 – Apache Star 96 (Arazi (USA) 135) **90 d**
[2007 91, a81+: p10g* 10.1g 8.1g 10m⁶ p10m Dec 8] big, strong gelding: fairly useful
handicapper: won at Lingfield in April: ran poorly after: stays 1¼m: acts on polytrack,
soft and good to firm ground: has raced freely, including in cheekpieces final outing.
P. M. Phelan

CACTUS ROSE 3 b.g. Zamindar (USA) 116 – Bolsena (USA) (Red Ransom (USA)) **98**
[2007 7g 8.3m² 8g* 8m² 8.1m* Aug 31] 55,000Y: good-bodied gelding: second foal: dam

unraced out of US Grade 1 winner up to 1½m Waya: progressive form: won maiden at Brighton in July and handicap at Sandown (useful effort when beating Lang Shining by neck) in August: likely to stay beyond 1m: raced on good/good to firm going. *R. Charlton*

CADEAUX CERISE (IRE) 3 b.f. Cadeaux Genereux 131 – Cerisette (IRE) 94 (Polar –
Falcon (USA) 126) [2007 6s 7m 8.1m Aug 31] 5,000Y: good-topped filly: fourth foal: half-sister to winners abroad by Lion Cavern and Xaar: dam, 2-y-o 7f winner on only outing, half-sister to very smart 1m/1¼m performer Crimplene: well beaten in maidens. *N. I. M. Rossiter*

CADEAUX ROUGE (IRE) 6 ch.m. Croco Rouge (IRE) 126 – Gift of Glory (FR) **48**
(Niniski (USA) 125) [2007 13.8m* 12s 12m Aug 7] leggy mare: poor performer: won seller at Catterick in June: stays easy 2m: acts on firm ground: tried in blinkers/cheek-pieces/tongue tie. *D. W. Thompson*

CADI MAY 3 b.f. Fasliyev (USA) 120 – Sound of Sleat (Primo Dominie 121) [2007 –: **54**
8.1m⁴ 7.5g p7.1g 7.9f 7m Aug 12] tall, leggy filly: maiden: form only on reappearance. *W. M. Brisbourne*

CADOGEN SQUARE 5 ch.m. Takhlid (USA) 91 – Mount Park (IRE) 73 (Colonel **57**
Collins (USA) 122) [2007 7.5v 7.6d* 8m 6g³ 6m⁴ 7m 6m 7g 8g 6v p7.1g Nov 1] smallish, strong mare: modest handicapper: won apprentice event at Chester in July: stays 7.6f: acts on polytrack, good to firm and good to soft ground: sometimes blinkered: inconsistent. *D. W. Chapman*

CADRE (IRE) 2 b.c. (Feb 1) King's Best (USA) 132 – Desert Frolic (IRE) 94 (Persian **76 p**
Bold 123) [2007 7m Oct 5] €200,000F: tall, rather leggy, close-coupled colt: has plenty of scope: seventh foal: half-brother to 2 winners by Royal Abjar, including useful Irish 1m to 1½m winner Jakarta Jade: dam, 11f and 13f winner, half-sister to high-class 1¼m/1½m performer Storming Home: 16/1, nervy and green when eighth to Fireside in maiden at Newmarket: will be suited by 1m/1¼m: sure to progress. *J. H. M. Gosden*

CADWELL 3 b.g. Pivotal 124 – Sur Les Pointes (IRE) 62 (Sadler's Wells (USA) 132) –
[2007 56p: f8g² 10.1s 6.9g p5.1g p9.5g⁵ p12.2g p9.5g² f8d³ f8d³ Dec 20] strong, good- **a64**
bodied gelding: fair maiden: left D. Nicholls after second start, D. Murphy after fourth: stays 9.5f: acts on all-weather: tried blinkered/tongue tied: often finds little. *T. J. Pitt*

CAFFARI (GER) 2 ch.f. (Apr 13) Seattle Dancer (USA) 119 – Calarca (GER) –
(Goofalik (USA) 118) [2007 8.1s 7d⁶ Oct 16] €22,000Y: fifth foal: half-sister to German 2004 2-y-o 6f winner Citaro (by Sternkonig): dam, German 1¼m/11f winner, half-sister to Deutsches St Leger winner Caballo: well held in maidens. *K. R. Burke*

CAFFE CORETTO 2 b.f. (Mar 17) Mark of Esteem (IRE) 137 – Sempre Sorriso 52 –
(Fleetwood (IRE) 107) [2007 p7g Dec 29] 2,700F: first foal: dam, maiden who should have stayed 9f, out of smart 7f/1m (including May Hill and Hungerford Stakes) winner Ever Genial: no show in maiden at Lingfield. *B. G. Powell*

CAFFREY KELLY 2 b.c. (Apr 22) Rock City 120 – Mochras 64 (Mtoto 134) [2007 –
5d 6g Aug 27] well beaten in maiden/seller. *J. J. Quinn*

CAIRNBRAE 2 ch.g. (Mar 30) Where Or When (IRE) 124 – Hill Welcome 52 (Most **60**
Welcome 131) [2007 6m⁶ 7d⁶ 7d Jul 22] lengthy gelding: modest maiden: best effort at 6f: dead. *Miss J. A. Camacho*

CAJ (IRE) 3 b.f. Tagula (IRE) 116 – Notley Park 71 (Wolfhound (USA) 126) [2007 56: **59**
p6g⁴ p8g p7g 7g Jul 28] smallish, workmanlike filly: modest maiden: form in 2007 only at Lingfield on reappearance: likely to prove best at 5f/6f: acts on polytrack and firm going: tried blinkered: flashes tail. *Luke Comer, Ireland*

CAKE (IRE) 2 b.f. (Feb 5) Acclamation 118 – Carpet Lady (IRE) 70 (Night Shift **99**
(USA)) [2007 p5g* 5m* 5g³ 5m⁵ 6s⁵ 5g 5.2m* 5g² 5m 5d³ Oct 13] 13,000Y: small, strong filly: third foal: half-sister to 2006 2-y-o 6f winner Wachiwi (by Namid) and German winner by Shinko Forest: dam, maiden (should have stayed at least 7f), out of sister to smart middle-distance stayer Shambo: useful performer: won maiden at Lingfield in April, minor event at Salisbury in May and listed event at Newbury (beat Cute Ass by neck) in August: ran well after when placed behind Captain Gerrard in listed race at York and Cornwallis Stakes at Ascot (1½ lengths third of 12, left with a fair bit to do): best at 5f: acts on polytrack, good to firm and good to soft going. *R. Hannon*

CALABASH COVE (USA) 3 ch.c. Rahy (USA) 115 – I Need A Holiday (USA) **90**
(Nureyev (USA) 131) [2007 79p: 7.5g 10g* 9.8m* 10g⁶ 10.9m⁵ Sep 15] big, lengthy, good-topped colt: good mover: has a quick action: fairly useful performer: won maiden at Lingfield in May and handicap at Ripon (by neck from Tetouan) in June: will stay 1½m:

raced only on polytrack and good/good to firm ground: ran creditably in tongue tie last 2 starts, though didn't find much final one. *Saeed bin Suroor*

CALABAZA 5 ch.g. Zaha (CAN) 106 – Mo Stopher 47 (Sharpo 132) [2007 75: 6g⁶ 6g **71** 5m⁵ 5g 5.2m 6m 5m² 5d 6g* 5d 5.3d* 6g p6m Nov 26] strong gelding: fair handicapper: left W. Jarvis after sixth start: won at Warwick and Brighton in October: effective at 5f/6f: acts on good to firm and good to soft ground: usually blinkered/in cheekpieces. *J. Akehurst*

CALATAGAN (IRE) 8 ch.g. Danzig Connection (USA) – Calachuchi 74 (Martinmas **75** 128) [2007 73: 17.5s⁶ 12g⁵ 15.8g² p16.5g Nov 12] short-backed gelding: fair handicapper: stays 2m: acts on polytrack, good to firm and good to soft going (well held on soft): races freely/prominently: useful chaser, won in December. *J. M. Jefferson*

CALCULATING (IRE) 3 b.g. Machiavellian (USA) 123 – Zaheemah (USA) 96 (El **77** Prado (IRE) 119) [2007 –p: 7m⁵ 7m⁵ 8g 10g 10d² 10.5g⁵ 10d p12g⁵ p12.2g² f12d² f12d² Dec 20] strong, attractive gelding: fair maiden handicapper: left J. Gosden 13,000 gns after fifth start: stays 1½m: acts on all-weather, good to firm and good to soft going: tongue tied on debut. *M. D. I. Usher*

CALDRA (IRE) 3 b.g. Elnadim (USA) 128 – Lady Rachel (IRE) 75 (Priolo (USA) **113** 127) [2007 114: 8d⁴ 8.1g³ 10s 7d 8g³ Nov 3] sturdy, close-coupled gelding: smart performer: suffered a condylar fracture of off-fore and off 10 months after 2 yrs: ran creditably in 2007 in Sovereign Stakes at Salisbury (fourth to Pride of Nation) and when third in listed races at Haydock and Newmarket (beaten 2 necks by Jalmira): stays 1m: acts on soft and good to firm going: bandaged in front on reappearance. *S. Kirk*

CALIBAN (IRE) 9 ch.g. Rainbows For Life (CAN) – Amour Toujours (IRE) (Law **–** Society (USA) 130) [2007 –: p12.2g p12.2g Feb 21] lengthy gelding: modest performer at best: lightly raced and little form since 2004: tried visored/blinkered. *Ian Williams*

CALIFORNIA LAWS 5 b.g. Pivotal 124 – Noor El Houdah (IRE) 61 (Fayruz 116) **–** [2007 77, a89: f7g⁴ 7g Jun 15] strong, lengthy gelding: useful handicapper on all- **a98** weather, fair on turf: further progress when winning at Southwell in January by ¾ length from Waterside, idling: left T. D. Barron, well below form at Goodwood subsequent outing: needs a test at 6f, and stays 1m: acts on all-weather, soft and good to firm going: sold 5,000 gns in October. *R. M. Beckett*

CALISTOS QUEST 2 b.c. (Mar 5) Rainbow Quest (USA) 134 – Carambola (IRE) 100 **66 p** (Danehill (USA) 126) [2007 7.1d⁵ 7m⁴ 8.1f Aug 27] 60,000Y: good-bodied colt: fourth foal: half-brother to 4-y-o Lady Stardust: dam, Irish 1m winner, half-sister to Irish 1000 Guineas winner Matiya: fair form in maidens (prominent in betting), fifth to Scintillo at Sandown on debut: should be suited by 1m/1¼m: will do better. *M. Johnston*

CALL FOR LIBERTY (IRE) 2 b.c. (Feb 6) Statue of Liberty (USA) 115 – Give A **79** Whistle (IRE) 100 (Mujadil (USA) 119) [2007 6d 6m² 6g² 6g⁵ Sep 7] €42,000F, 30,000Y: strong, medium-sized colt: second foal: dam, Irish 5f winner, out of half-sister to high-class miler Indian Lodge: fair maiden: runner-up at Haydock (neck behind Fitzroy Crossing despite slipped bit) and Thirsk: likely to stay 7f: acts on good to firm going: joined E. Charpy in UAE. *B. Smart*

CALLISTO MOON 3 b.g. Mujahid (USA) 125 – Nursling (IRE) 57 (Kahyasi 130) **73** [2007 71: p8.6g⁵ p10g 10.9m* 12.6m⁶ May 7] close-coupled gelding: fair performer: won handicap at Warwick in April: stays at least 11f: acts on polytrack and good to firm going: effective blinkered or not: fairly useful juvenile hurdler. *Ian Williams*

CALLITQUITS (IRE) 5 b.g. Desert Story (IRE) 115 – Quits (IRE) (Brief Truce **58 ?** (USA) 126) [2007 p12.2g p12.2g³ p12.2g p12.2g p16.5g Jul 27] modest maiden: unraced on Flat in 2006: stays 12.2f: acts on polytrack, soft and good to firm ground: tried in cheekpieces/tongue tie. *Jennie Candlish*

CALL ME CRAZY (IRE) 4 b.f. Key of Luck (USA) 126 – Smile Awhile (USA) **64** (Woodman (USA) 126) [2007 74: p7.1g 8.7g 12m⁴ 12d 11.9s⁵ 10s² 12d⁵ 10m Sep 5] fifth foal: half-sister to 3 winners, including useful 2003 2-y-o 5f winner Caldy Dancer (by Soviet Star): dam once-raced sister to useful performer up to 1½m Gypsy Passion: modest maiden handicapper: left E. Tyrrell after third start: effective at 1¼m/1½m: acts on soft and good to firm going, below form on polytrack at Wolverhampton on reappearance: tried blinkered: often races prominently. *Patrick Martin, Ireland*

CALL ME PUNCH 6 ch.g. Bettergeton 97 – Tradjazz (Alhijaz 122) [2007 7.1d³ 7.1m **68** 8d² Oct 3] lengthy gelding: fair maiden, lightly raced: stays 1m: acts on good to soft going. *E. S. McMahon*

CALL ME ROSY (IRE) 3 ch.f. Shinko Forest (IRE) – Fanciful (IRE) (Mujtahid **63**
(USA) 118) [2007 69: p6g³ p6g p6m⁴ p7g Oct 10] sturdy, workmanlike filly: modest
maiden handicapper: should be suited by 7f: acts on polytrack. *C. F. Wall*

CALL MY BLUFF (FR) 4 b.g. Highest Honor (FR) 124 – Baino Bluff (IRE) (Be My **74**
Guest (USA) 126) [2007 71: p10g* p9.5g³ f8g⁵ 9.8g 7.1s² 8d⁵ 8g⁵ 8g⁶ 10d⁶ p9.5g⁴ p8.6g⁴ **a82**
p9.5g⁵ Oct 18] tall gelding: fairly useful performer: won maiden at Lingfield in January:
stays 1¼m: acts on polytrack and soft ground: sold 38,000 gns, joined Seamus Braddish,
Ireland. *Rae Guest*

CALL OF DUTY (IRE) 2 br.c. (Apr 13) Storming Home 128 – Blushing Barada **81 p**
(USA) 53 (Blushing Groom (FR) 131) [2007 p8m* p8g² Dec 22] closely related to 5-y-o
Barbirolli and half-brother to several winners, including 7-y-o Blythe Knight and fairly
useful 2m winner High Topper (by Wolfhound): dam maiden half-sister to Irish St Leger
winner Authaal: fairly useful form: won maiden at Lingfield in December: still green,
neck second of 4 to Straight And Level in minor event there next time: will stay 1¼m:
open to further improvement. *M. Johnston*

CALLOFF THE SEARCH 3 b.g. Piccolo 121 – Unchain My Heart 70 (Pursuit of **61**
Love 124) [2007 63d: p7g³ p7.1g³ p7g⁶ p6g⁶ 7.1m⁵ 7d p7g p7g² 6g² 7m³ 7g² 7g⁴ 7g
p6g³ p7.1g⁵ p6g⁵ p8g p8m p6g³ p6g p7.1g Dec 26] strong gelding: modest maiden: left
W. Turner after sixteenth start: stays 7f: acts on polytrack, unraced on extremes of going
on turf: usually wears headgear: very slowly away final outing. *Stef Liddiard*

CALL OF KTULU (IRE) 2 b.g. (Apr 17) Noverre (USA) 125 – Yankee Dancer 62 **–**
(Groom Dancer (USA) 128) [2007 7g 7g Oct 19] no show in maiden and claimer (in
cheekpieces). *J. S. Wainwright*

CALMDOWNMATE (IRE) 2 b.g. (Mar 26) Danehill Dancer (IRE) 117 – Lady **91**
Digby (IRE) 96 (Petorius 117) [2007 6s⁶ 6m² 6m* 7g⁵ 7m Sep 14] 40,000 2-y-o: strong,
medium-sized gelding: first foal: dam, Irish 1m/8.5f winner (latter at 2 yrs), half-sister to
useful Irish 2-y-o 6f winner Flip The Switch: fairly useful performer: won minor event at
Ripon in August by 2 lengths from Anosti, showing good speed: stiff tasks after in Acomb
Stakes at York (6½ lengths fifth of 7 to Fast Company) and valuable sales race at the
Curragh, then gelded: stays 7f: acts on good to firm going. *K. R. Burke*

CALMING INFLUENCE (IRE) 2 b.c. (Mar 21) King's Best (USA) 132 – Idilic **100 P**
Calm (IRE) 78 (Indian Ridge 123) [2007 6d* Oct 12] €110,000Y, resold €240,000Y:
lengthy colt, unfurnished at 2 yrs: fourth foal: half-brother to smart 5f (in Ireland at 2 yrs)
to 7f (in North America) winner Steel Light (by Stravinsky) and 6f winner Marajel (by
Marju): dam, Irish 7f winner, out of half-sister to dam of Refuse To Bend and Media
Puzzle: evens favourite, made big impression when winning 14-runner maiden at York
by 5 lengths (value extra), in control from halfway and not hard ridden: will probably stay
1m: pattern performer in the making. *Saeed bin Suroor*

*IG Index EBF Maiden Stakes, York—Calming Influence makes a big impression on his debut against
the more experienced Hamish McGonagall, Harrison George (blaze) and Horatio Carter (noseband)*

CALMING WATERS 4 ch.g. Dr Fong (USA) 128 – Faraway Waters 102 (Pharly (FR) **79**
130) [2007 79: 8.1g p9.5g² Jun 11] fair maiden: stays easy 1¼m: raced on polytrack and
good going. *D. W. P. Arbuthnot*

CALTIRE (GER) 2 b.g. (Mar 25) Pentire 132 – Caluna (SWI) 102 (Lagunas) [2007 **65**
p8.6g⁶ 8.3d p8g* p8m* p8.6g⁵ p9.5s² Dec 20] €28,000Y: lengthy, angular gelding: first
foal: dam German 7f (at 2 yrs)/9f winner: fair performer: won claimer in October (left
J. Osborne) and seller in November, both at Lingfield: good second in nursery at Wolverhampton: stays 9.5f: acts on polytrack: blinkered third to fifth starts. *M. G. Quinlan*

CALUBA 3 ch.f. Daggers Drawn (USA) 114 – Canlubang (Mujtahid (USA) 118) [2007 **62**
7m 8.1m⁵ 9g⁶ 6d⁵ 8.1m 6.9g⁶ 7.1d Sep 17] workmanlike filly: sixth foal: half-sister to 2
winners, including 1m seller winner Zonnebeke (by Orpen): dam ran 3 times at 2 yrs:
modest maiden handicapper: should stay beyond 1m: acts on good to firm going: refused
to enter stall prior to intended debut. *K. R. Burke*

CALUSA LADY (IRE) 7 ch.m. Titus Livius (FR) 115 – Solas Abu (IRE) 82 (Red **–**
Sunset 120) [2007 42: p7g Jan 22] smallish, lengthy mare: poor maiden: well held only
start in 2007: effective at 6f/easy 7f: acts on polytrack, firm and soft going: tried tongue
tied/visored. *J. A. Geake*

CALYPSO CHARMS 2 b.f. (May 14) Dansili 127 – Chrysalis 66 (Soviet Star (USA) **76**
128) [2007 7m 7g⁴ 8g⁵ Oct 26] close-coupled filly: fifth foal: half-sister to 3 winners,
including smart 2004 2-y-o 6f winner Moth Ball (by Royal Applause) and 6-y-o Western
Roots: dam, maiden (stayed 1m), out of half-sister to Arc winner Saumarez: fair maiden:
progressive form, again raced freely when fifth to Cruel Sea at Doncaster: stays 1m.
M. L. W. Bell

CALYPSO KING 4 gr.g. Agnes World (USA) 123 – T G'S Girl 57 (Selkirk (USA) **72**
129) [2007 86: 5f 6m⁶ f6g⁶ p6g* p5g³ 6d⁶ 6g p5.1g p7.1g p5g³ p5g⁵ p5.1g⁴ p5.1s Dec 20]
tall, quite good-topped gelding: just fair performer nowadays: won claimer at Lingfield
(left R. Beckett) in June: best at 5f/6f: acts on polytrack and firm ground: tried blinkered:
edgy sort. *Peter Grayson*

CALZA DI SETA 2 b.f. (Mar 13) Lujain (USA) 119 – Isla Negra (IRE) (Last Tycoon **–**
131) [2007 6m Jun 11] fifth foal: dam, Italian 13f winner, out of half-sister to US Grade 1
winner up to 9f Polish Navy: 66/1, well held in maiden at Pontefract. *G. M. Moore*

CALZAGHE (IRE) 3 ch.g. Galileo (IRE) 134 – Novelette (Darshaan 133) [2007 –: **85**
12g² p12.2g² 12m⁶ 14g³ 14.6m⁵ p12.2g* Sep 14] big, good-topped gelding: fairly useful
handicapper: won at Wolverhampton in September: will probably stay 2m: visored: acts
on polytrack and good to firm ground: sold 68,000 gns, joined K. R. Burke. *A. M. Balding*

CAMBO (FR) 6 b. or br.g. Mansonnien (FR) 122 – Royal Lie (FR) (Garde Royale 120) **–**
[2007 p16g p16g 15.4g⁶ Aug 16] fair performer in 2005: poor efforts on return to Flat in
2007: stays 2m: acts on polytrack: tried blinkered/tongue tied. *Miss S. West*

CAME BACK (IRE) 4 ch.c. Bertolini (USA) 125 – Distant Decree (USA) (Distant **81**
View (USA) 126) [2007 72: p6g² f6g⁴ f6g* p6g p6g f6g² p6g* p6g* p6g⁵ f6g⁵ p6g p6g
p6g² p6g f5g² Dec 27] fairly useful handicapper: left J. Osborne after reappearance: won
at Southwell in February and Wolverhampton in March and April: effective at 5f/6f: acts
on all-weather, just one run on turf: races prominently. *J. Mackie*

CAMELLIA'S GIRL 4 b.f. Golden Snake (USA) 127 – Stormy Heights 62 (Golden **–**
Heights 82) [2007 11.6m 7s⁶ Jul 28] lengthy filly: sixth foal: half-sister to 1½m winner
Quest On Air (by Star Quest): dam sprinter: tongue tied, well held in seller/claimer.
J. J. Bridger

CAMEROONEY 4 b.g. Sugarfoot 118 – Enkindle 39 (Relkino 131) [2007 10m **–**
p12.2g⁴ 12g p12.2g Nov 1] modest form in bumpers: little form on Flat. *A. D. Brown*

CAMI COLLINS (FR) 3 ch.g. Colonel Collins (USA) 122 – Camiriva (FR) (River **61**
River (FR) 117) [2007 56: 8m 11.9g 10s⁶ 9d⁴ p10m p8g p10g Dec 28] modest maiden
handicapper: left C. Swan in Ireland after fourth start: stays 1¼m: acts on soft ground:
tried in cheekpieces. *J. R. Best*

CAMILLE PISSARRO (USA) 7 b.g. Red Ransom (USA) – Serenity 98 (Selkirk **66**
(USA) 129) [2007 f8g⁶ f7g³ 10g² 10m³ f12g³ 10.2m⁵ May 8] big, strong, lengthy gelding:
fair performer: was effective at 7f to 1¼m: acted on fibresand and good to firm ground:
occasionally blinkered: held up: said to have finished lame final start: dead. *D. J. Wintle*

CAMISSA 3 b.f. Averti (IRE) 117 – Ambitious 98 (Ardkinglass 114) [2007 74: 5.2m⁵ **63**
p5g 5m 6d⁶ p8g⁵ Jul 10] tall, quite good-topped filly: just modest form in 2007: best at 5f:
acts on good to firm ground: tried in cheekpieces. *D. K. Ivory*

CAMOLIN (IRE) 4 b.f. Fantastic Light (USA) 134 – Maritsa (IRE) 59 (Danehill **61** (USA) 126) [2007 42: 8d 11.9g 12.1g⁵ 8s³ 9d* 9.1v p9.5g Dec 14] modest handicapper: won at Ballinrobe in September: below form in Britain after: stays 9f: acts on soft ground: often blinkered. *Michael McElhone, Ireland*

CAMPANOLOGIST (USA) 2 b.c. (May 5) Kingmambo (USA) 125 – Ring of Music **93** (Sadler's Wells (USA) 132) [2007 7.1g* 7g⁴ 8.1g* 8d Sep 29] tall, rather leggy, useful-looking colt: has scope: seventh foal: brother to UAE 1¼m winner Melodic Score: dam unraced close relation to Singspiel and half-sister to Rahy, out of US Grade 1 9f winner/champion older mare Glorious Song: fairly useful performer: won maiden at Sandown in August and minor event at Haydock (by ½ length from Eileen's Violet) in September: fourth of 7 to Fast Company in Acomb Stakes at York in between: softer ground, dropped away tamely in Royal Lodge Stakes at Ascot final start: will stay 1¼m, probably 1½m. *M. Johnston*

CAMP ATTACK 4 b.g. Fleetwood (IRE) 107 – Queen of Tides (IRE) 62 (Soviet Star **–** (USA) 128) [2007 60: p10g p10g 9.7m 11.9m Apr 29] fair maiden handicapper at 3 yrs: well held in 2007. *S. Dow*

CAMPBELLS LAD 6 b.g. Mind Games 121 – T O O Mamma's (IRE) 50 (Classic **66** Secret (USA) 91) [2007 62: p12.2g⁵ p12.2g 12s* 12d⁴ 12m³ p13.9g⁵ Aug 20] big gelding: fair performer: won claimer at Catterick in July: seems to stay 1¾m: acts on all-weather, soft and good to firm going: tried in cheekpieces/blinkers. *Mrs G. S. Rees*

CAMPBELTOWN (IRE) 4 b.g. Mull of Kintyre (USA) 114 – Jallaissine (IRE) **57 d** (College Chapel 122) [2007 87: p7.1g³ p7f p5g 6m 6m 7m p6g p7m Dec 10] strong, good-bodied gelding: type to carry condition: useful performer at 2 yrs: regressed since, and only modest at best in 2007, leaving R. Harris after reappearance and M. Hoad after sixth outing: seems to stay easy 7f: acts on polytrack, good to firm and good to soft going: tried in cheekpieces/blinkers. *A. B. Haynes*

CAMP COUNSELLOR 3 b.g. Royal Applause 124 – Rash (Pursuit of Love 124) **67 d** [2007 p8g p9.5g p12f⁴ p12.2g p12g⁶ p8g⁶ 10.1m⁵ 14.1d Aug 26] fair maiden: easily best effort at Lingfield third start: left J. Osborne before final outing: stays 1½m: blinkered/in cheekpieces last 4 starts: found little penultimate outing. *M. J. Gingell*

CAMPEON (IRE) 5 b.g. Monashee Mountain (USA) 115 – Arctic Lead (USA) (Arctic **47** Tern (USA) 126) [2007 60: p5.1g 5.1g 5.3m 5.7d 6f⁵ 5.1m 6d Oct 1] good-bodied gelding: just poor nowadays: effective at 5f to easy 7f: acts on all-weather, firm and soft going: tried in headgear: sometimes races freely/wanders. *J. M. Bradley*

CAMPFIRE GLOW (IRE) 2 b. or br.f. (Mar 4) Invincible Spirit (IRE) 121 – Ski **99** Lodge (IRE) 78 (Persian Bold 123) [2007 6s⁵ 7g* 7v* 7m⁵ Sep 14] €250,000Y: neat filly: fourth foal: closely related to Italian winner around 7f Roman Castle (by Desert Prince) and half-sister to smart 7f/1m winner Serre Chevalier (by Marju): dam, 2-y-o 7f winner, half-sister to smart German miler Sinyar: useful form: won maiden at Galway in July and Ballygallon Stud Debutante Stakes at the Curragh (led final 1f to beat Listen by neck) in August: not discredited when fifth of 22 to Lush Lashes in valuable sales race at the Curragh final start: likely to stay 1m: acts on heavy going. *D. K. Weld, Ireland*

CAMPLI (IRE) 5 b.g. Zafonic (USA) 130 – Sept A Neuf (Be My Guest (USA) 126) **70** [2007 10.1m² 12m³ 10.1m 13.8m⁵ 14m³ 14m 12g³ Oct 5] fair maiden: stays 1¾m: raced on good/good to firm ground: has raced freely. *Micky Hammond*

CAMPO BUENO (FR) 5 b.g. Septieme Ciel (USA) 123 – Herba Buena (FR) (Fabu- **71 d** lous Dancer (USA) 124) [2007 99d: 7.1g 7.6m 7f 8.1s⁴ 7d³ 6g 7.1v 8v 6d 7.2s 6s 6v 8g³ p7.1g Dec 4] strong gelding: just fair nowadays: below form after fifth start in 2007: best form short of 1m: acts on heavy going: often blinkered. *A. Berry*

CAMPS BAY (USA) 3 b.c. Cozzene (USA) – Seewillo (USA) (Pleasant Colony **100** (USA)) [2007 74: 9.9g* 9.9g³ 11.6m* 12g² 14g 14.1g⁵ Sep 20] rangy colt: useful handi-capper: won at Salisbury in May and Windsor in July: better form after when second to Regal Flush in BGC Stakes at Goodwood and ninth to Speed Gifted in Melrose Stakes at York: stays 1¾m: acts on good to firm going: waited with. *Mrs A. J. Perrett*

CAMROSE 6 ch.g. Zafonic (USA) 130 – Tularosa (In The Wings 128) [2007 106: 12g³ **106 §** 12.1d² 12d 12g 12m² 12m³ Sep 15] good-bodied gelding: useful performer: best effort in 2007 when short-head second to Scriptwriter in listed handicap at Hamilton on second start: was best around 1½m: acted on soft and good to firm going: blinkered: tended to carry head high/run in snatches: was one to treat with caution: retired. *J. L. Dunlop*

CANADIAN DANEHILL (IRE) 5 b.g. Indian Danehill (IRE) 124 – San Jovita **96** (CAN) 71 (St Jovite (USA) 135) [2007 78: f5g² p5.1g* f5g* p5.1g* p6g³ f5g* f5g⁴ 6g f5g² 5d⁶ 5.1f⁵ p6g³ 5.3d⁵ 5m³ 5g 5s³ 5m* 5m³ 5.2g* 5g⁶ Oct 7] big, lengthy gelding: progressed into useful performer in 2007: won handicaps at Wolverhampton (2), Southwell (2), Sandown and Yarmouth between January and September: gelded after final start: has won at 7f, best at 5f/easy 6f: acts on all-weather, firm and soft going: wears cheekpieces: races prominently. *R. M. H. Cowell*

CANARY GIRL 4 br.f. Primo Valentino (IRE) 116 – Cumbrian Concerto 44 (Petong 126) [2007 41: 6m 6m⁵ 6v 6f 6m Aug 9] workmanlike filly: modest maiden: stays 1m: acts on polytrack and firm going: visored last 4 starts: inconsistent. *Mrs C. A. Dunnett* **51**

CAN CAN STAR 4 br.c. Lend A Hand 124 – Carrie Can Can 73 (Green Tune (USA) 125) [2007 70: p11g² p9.5g* p9.5g² 10.2f² 10g* 10m⁴ 10.2g 10g² 11.8s⁴ 10m 10.9m² 10.5s² Sep 28] rather leggy colt: fairly useful performer: won maiden at Wolverhampton in January and handicap at Leicester in April: stays 10.9f: acts on polytrack and firm going: tried blinkered: edgy sort, has sweated/raced freely: saddle slipped seventh outing. *A. W. Carroll* **82**

CANDARLI (IRE) 11 ch.g. Polish Precedent (USA) 131 – Calounia (IRE) (Pharly (FR) 130) [2007 67: p16.5g⁵ p13.9g³ Aug 20] fair maiden: stays 2m: acts on polytrack: winning hurdler. *D. R. Gandolfo* **67**

CANDELA BAY (IRE) 2 b.f. (Mar 4) Captain Rio 122 – Incendio (Siberian Express (USA) 125) [2007 5m* 6d Oct 11] €55,000F, €100,000Y, 42,000 2-y-o: eighth foal: half-sister to several winners, notably 7-y-o Baron's Pit: dam winning sprinter in Italy: readily won maiden at Pontefract in September on debut: joint favourite, well beaten in nursery at Newbury (softer going) 3 weeks later: should prove best at 5f/6f: worth another chance to progress. *W. J. Haggas* **74 p**

CANDIDA'S BEAU 2 b.g. (May 13) Bertolini (USA) 125 – Breezy Louise 60 (Dilum (USA) 115) [2007 p7m p7g³ Nov 7] 17,000Y: third foal: brother to fairly useful Irish 7f (including at 2 yrs) winner Rockie: dam 5f winner (including at 2 yrs): better effort in maidens at Kempton when third to Southpaw Lad, always prominent: may prove best up to 7f. *R. M. Beckett* **76**

CANDIDATO ROY (ARG) 6 ch.g. Roy (USA) – Candila (ARG) (Mariache (ARG)) [2007 115: 7.1m² 7d* 7d Oct 20] heavy-topped gelding: type to carry condition: very smart performer: won handicap at Nad Al Sheba early in 2006 when trained by M. de Kock: career-best effort when winning 23-runner totesport.com Challenge Cup (Heritage Handicap) at Ascot in September by ¾ length from Shevchenko, racing alone against stand rail: only seventh to Miss Lucifer in Challenge Stakes at Newmarket subsequent outing: stays 7f: acts on dirt, good to firm and good to soft ground: has worn blinkers/tongue tie (not in Britain). *W. J. Haggas* **120**

CANDLE 4 b.f. Dansili 127 – Celia Brady 62 (Last Tycoon 131) [2007 92: 12d³ 11.8s³ 13.3m³ 12s* Oct 4] close-coupled, quite attractive filly: fairly useful handicapper: won at Goodwood in October by 2 lengths from Pivotal Answer: stays 1¾m: acts on polytrack, soft and good to firm ground. *H. Candy* **94**

totesport.com Challenge Cup (Handicap), Ascot—
the ex-South African-trained Candidato Roy (right) is clear from an early stage and holds off
Shevchenko (dark colours), Docofthebay (blaze, next to runner-up) and Presumptive (behind winner)

CANDLE SAHARA (IRE) 2 b.f. (Feb 6) Noverre (USA) 125 – Staylily (IRE) (Grand **89**
Lodge (USA) 125) [2007 6s⁴ 6g³ 7f⁴ 6m⁴ Sep 4] strong, good-bodied filly: type to carry
plenty of condition: second foal: half-sister to 3-y-o Kyle: dam unraced out of half-sister
to Coronation Cup winner Be My Native: easily best effort in maidens (fairly useful form)
when ½-length third to Fashion Rocks at Goodwood: should stay 7f: reluctant at stall on
debut. *M. R. Channon*

CANDY ANCHOR (FR) 8 b.m. Slip Anchor 136 – Kandavu 87 (Safawan 118) [2007 **50**
–: p9.5g² Dec 29] lengthy mare: modest maiden, lightly raced nowadays: stays 1½m: acts
on polytrack, firm and good to soft going: tried blinkered/tongue tied. *R. E. Peacock*

CANDY CRITIC (ARG) 5 ch.m. Candy Stripes (USA) 115 – Tough Dancer (ARG) **109 §**
(Tough Critic (USA) 90) [2007 10g⁶ 12g³ 12g² 10m⁶ Aug 10] tall mare: useful performer:
won Group 2 South African Oaks at Turffontein in 2006: good 1¼ lengths second to
Crime Scene in handicap at Nad Al Sheba third start, though carried head high/flashed
tail: reluctant to post, failed to take eye and folded tamely in minor event at Newmarket
final outing: stays 1½m: raced only on good/good to firm going: blinkered/tongue tied:
one to treat with caution. *M. F. de Kock, South Africa*

CANDYLAND (IRE) 3 b.f. Bubble Gum Fellow (JPN) 120 – Capoeira (USA) (Nure- **59**
yev (USA) 131) [2007 64: p5g⁶ p5.1g⁴ p5.1g³ p7f³ 7.1m² 6m⁴ p8g 7g* Sep 18] workman- **a54**
like filly: modest performer: won seller at Yarmouth (joined Mrs C. Dunnett 9,200 gns)
in September, drifting markedly left: stays 7f: acts on polytrack, firm and good to soft
going. *M. Quinn*

CANDY MOUNTAIN 3 ch.f. Selkirk (USA) 129 – Valthea (FR) (Antheus (USA) 122 **86**
[2007 10.2m⁴ 10.1m³ 8.3s⁶ 10f² 12g 10m* p10g² 10.3g⁵ p10g³ Nov 15] big, rangy filly:
half-sister to 6.5f (at 2 yrs)/7f winner Vert Val (by Septieme Ciel, later dam of Norfolk
Stakes winner Russian Valour) and 1m winner Prospectheus (by Gone West), both useful
in France: dam French 10.5f winner: fairly useful handicapper: won apprentice event
at Newmarket in September: should stay 1½m: acts on polytrack and firm going.
L. M. Cumani

CANINA 4 b.f. Foxhound (USA) 103 – Fizzy Fiona (Efisio 120) [2007 69: p6g 10.3f **57**
p6g p6g⁴ p6g³ p6g⁴ p6g p6g² p7.1g Dec 1] tall filly: modest handicapper: left Ms Deborah Evans after reappearance: stays 7f: acts on polytrack and heavy ground. *Paul Green*

CANKARA (IRE) 4 b.f. Daggers Drawn (USA) 114 – Suddenly 86 (Puissance 110) **62**
[2007 –: p7g p8.6g* p9.5g Mar 23] modest performer: easily best effort when winning
handicap at Wolverhampton in February: stays 8.6f: acts on polytrack: has been slowly
away: said to have bled final outing. *D. Carroll*

CANONGATE 3 gr.c. Highest Honor (FR) 124 – Tremiere (FR) (Anabaa (USA) 130) **93**
[2007 8v⁵ 7s⁴ a6.5g* 8v* 8m 8g Sep 7] big colt: second foal: dam, fairly useful French
maiden (stayed 1m), sister to smart UAE/US miler Tsigane: fairly useful handicapper:
won at Deauville (all-weather) in March and Longchamp in May: not discredited when
ninth of 30 to Eddie Jock in Britannia Stakes at Royal Ascot next time: stays 1m: acts on
heavy ground. *R. Gibson, France*

CANTABILLY (IRE) 4 b.g. Distant Music (USA) 126 – Cantaloupe (Priolo (USA) **77**
127) [2007 76, a82: 17.2f² p16g⁴ 14.1d Oct 3] close-coupled gelding: fairly useful handi- **a87**
capper on all-weather, fair on turf: effective at 9.5f, and stays 17f: acts on polytrack, firm
and soft going: fairly useful hurdler, successful later in October. *R. J. Hodges*

CANTIQUE (IRE) 3 b.f. Danetime (IRE) 121 – Bethania 70 (Mark of Esteem (IRE) **54**
137) [2007 65: p6g² 7m 6.1m 7d⁵ 8g 11.5m p12g⁵ 8g⁶ 10.9s 11.6d⁶ 7.1g p8.6d p8.6s
p9.5g Dec 29] quite good-topped filly: modest maiden: left A. Newcombe after reappearance, Ms J. Doyle after eleventh start: stays 1m: acts on polytrack and firm ground: tried
in cheekpieces. *R. J. Price*

CAPABLE GUEST (IRE) 5 b. or br.g. Cape Cross (IRE) 129 – Alexander Confranc **103 §**
(IRE) 73 (Magical Wonder (USA) 125) [2007 102: p8f⁵ 8s 8m 8.1g* 7s 8m 7.6m⁶ 9m 8g
9m 7d³ 8g³ p8g⁵ Nov 17] rather leggy, attractive gelding: useful handicapper: won at
Sandown in April by 2½ lengths from Humungous: respectable efforts at best after: stays
1¼m: acts on polytrack, firm and soft going: tried blinkered, usually visored nowadays:
held up, and suited by well-run race: moody. *M. R. Channon*

CAPANIA (IRE) 3 br.f. Cape Cross (IRE) 129 – Gentle Papoose (Commanche Run **68**
133) [2007 54p: 7.1m³ 7m⁶ p8g⁴ p8.6d³ Dec 7] sturdy filly: fair maiden, lightly raced:
stays 8.6f: raced only on polytrack/good to firm going: has started slowly/raced freely.
Pat Eddery

CAPE 4 b.f. Cape Cross (IRE) 129 – Rubbiyati 56 (Cadeaux Genereux 131) [2007 101p **93**
6m⁶ 6g⁵ 6m 6d⁴ 6s 6d⁴ Oct 19] good-bodied, quite attractive filly: fairly useful performer:

left J. Fanshawe after third start: creditable effort when 1½ lengths fourth to Lady Grace in listed event at Newmarket final outing: raced only at 6f: unraced on firm/heavy going, acts on any other turf. *P. Howling*

CAPE AMBER (IRE) 2 b.f. (Mar 22) Cape Cross (IRE) 129 – Maramba 97 (Rainbow Quest (USA) 134) [2007 7m* Aug 11] rangy filly: has scope: fourth foal: half-sister to useful 2003 2-y-o 5f to 6.5f winner Nyramba (by Night Shift): dam, 1m winner, out of high-class 6f/7f winner Gayane: 10/3, created excellent impression when winning 18-runner maiden at Newmarket by 3 lengths from Fitty, soon close up and forging clear: suffered a stress fracture on gallops after: should stay 1m: will go on to better things all being well. *P. W. Chapple-Hyam* **95 p**

CAPE COBRA 3 ch.g. Inchinor 119 – Cape Merino 103 (Clantime 101) [2007 7d⁴ 7g² p7m³ 6g* Oct 19] 400,000Y: fifth foal: brother to very smart sprinter Cape of Good Hope and half-brother to 2 winners, including useful 2004 2-y-o 6f winner Cape Columbine (stays 1m, by Diktat): dam 5f/6f winner, including at 2 yrs: fair performer: best effort when winning maiden at Redcar in October by 1¾ lengths from Navene, making all: stays 7f: blinkered last 2 outings: has given trouble at start. *J. H. M. Gosden* **68**

CAPE COLONY 2 gr.c. (Mar 29) Cape Town (IRE) 119 – Lucky Princess (Bijou d'Inde 127) [2007 8m Sep 15] good-topped colt: 50/1, last of 8 behind Emmrooz in maiden at Goodwood. *R. Hannon* **53 ?**

CAPE DANCER (IRE) 3 b.f. Cape Cross (IRE) 129 – Yankee Dancer 62 (Groom Dancer (USA) 128) [2007 66: 7f⁶ 9.9m 8.5s⁶ 8.3d 8.5m 6g 7d f6d Dec 21] sturdy, workmanlike filly: fluent mover: poor maiden nowadays: probably stays 1m: acts on firm ground, probably on soft: tried in cheekpieces. *J. S. Wainwright* **45**

CAPE DIAMOND (IRE) 4 b.g. Cape Cross (IRE) 129 – Jemalina (USA) 52 (Trempolino (USA) 135) [2007 70, a83: 10m² 10d³ Aug 20] leggy, quite good-topped gelding: fairly useful handicapper on all-weather, fair on turf: stays 1¼m: acts on polytrack, firm and good to soft going: has looked lazy/quirky. *W. R. Swinburn* **77 a–**

CAPEFLY 2 b.f. (Feb 18) Cape Cross (IRE) 129 – Patacake Patacake (USA) 67 (Bahri (USA) 125) [2007 p7g 6f³ 5.1g³ 5g² Nov 8] 110,000F: neat filly: third foal: half-sister to 4-y-o Mashaahed: dam, maiden (stayed 1¼m), closely related to smart performers Bog Trotter (at 7f) and Poteen (at 1m): fair maiden: placed 3 times, doing best when third to Masada at Bath penultimate start: effective at 5f/6f: acts on firm going. *P. F. I. Cole* **71**

CAPE GREKO 5 ro. or gr.g. Loup Sauvage (USA) 125 – Oneforth1ditch (USA) 79 (With Approval (CAN)) [2007 94: p8g⁵ p8g 8.1g⁶ 10m 9.9g⁵ 12d³ Sep 28] tall, good-bodied gelding: fairly useful handicapper: left A. Balding after third start, only respectable efforts subsequently, though won over hurdles in August/September: stays 9f: acts on polytrack and firm ground: sometimes races freely: sometimes visored. *B. G. Powell* **82**

CAPE HAWK (IRE) 3 b.g. Cape Cross (IRE) 129 – Hawksbill Special (IRE) (Taufan (USA) 119) [2007 73p: p8g² 7g² p8g* 8m⁴ p8g* p8g⁴ Sep 8] strong, well-made gelding: fairly useful handicapper: won at Kempton in June and August: good fourth to Magical Music in valuable event there final start (said to have lost a shoe): stays 1m: acts on polytrack and good to firm ground. *R. Hannon* **94**

CAPE OF LUCK (IRE) 4 b.g. Cape Cross (IRE) 129 – Fledgling 76 (Efisio 120) [2007 93: 7g² 8m⁶ 8m 7d⁶ p7g 7m⁶ 7f 6d p6g⁵ p8g p7g Dec 28] smallish, well-made gelding: useful handicapper: gradual decline in 2007 (left P. Mitchell after ninth start): stays 1m: acts on polytrack, good to firm and good to soft going: tongue tied final start: tends to edge left. *P. M. Phelan* **101 d a83**

CAPE OF STORMS 4 b.g. Cape Cross (IRE) 129 – Lloc 79 (Absalom 128) [2007 70d: p7.1g⁵ p7.1g p9.5g⁵ p9.5g² 10.2f p8.6g⁶ 8.1s 8.2m p6g⁵ f6g² Dec 27] compact gelding: modest maiden: effective at 6f to 9.5f: acts on polytrack and good to firm going: tried in cheekpieces: races prominently. *R. Brotherton* **54**

CAPE PRESTO (IRE) 4 b.c. Cape Cross (IRE) 129 – Samhat Mtoto 64 (Mtoto 134) [2007 86: f5g p7.1g⁴ 6m³ 6m⁵ May 12] strong, deep-girthed colt: had a quick action: fairly useful handicapper: was effective at 6f to 1m: acted on polytrack and good to firm ground: usually visored: raced prominently: dead. *Mrs C. A. Dunnett* **80**

CAPE ROCK 2 b.g. (Mar 18) Cape Cross (IRE) 129 – Wildwood Flower 107 (Distant Relative 128) [2007 7m 8d p7g⁵ Oct 24] good-topped gelding: modest maiden: free-going sort, should prove best up to 7f: gelded after final start. *C. A. Horgan* **64 ?**

CAPE ROYAL 7 b.g. Prince Sabo 123 – Indigo 86 (Primo Dominie 121) [2007 102: 5.1g⁶ 5m² 5g* 5m⁵ 5m⁵ 5g 5d 5m² 5g 5g 5m⁵ 5g² 5.1m 5g Oct 27] good-bodied gelding, type to carry plenty of condition: useful handicapper: won at Epsom in April by short head from Kay Two: creditable efforts after only when in frame, short- **104**

headed by same horse at Leicester fifteenth start: best at 5f: acts on polytrack, firm and soft going: wears blinkers/tongue tie: usually claimer ridden: sometimes slowly away, otherwise front runner. *J. M. Bradley*

CAPE SECRET (IRE) 4 b.g. Cape Cross (IRE) 129 – Baylands Sunshine (IRE) **93** (Classic Secret (USA) 91) [2007 92: 14.1m* 12g 16.1v 14g 16.1m² 14g⁵ p12g⁶ Oct 15] leggy gelding: fairly useful handicapper: won at Salisbury in May: creditable fifth to Regal Flush in Old Borough Cup at Haydock penultimate start: stays 2m: acts on good to firm and good to soft going: front runner: sold 50,000 gns: joined G. Elliott in Ireland. *R. M. Beckett*

CAPE SYDNEY (IRE) 4 b.f. Cape Cross (IRE) 129 – Lady At War (Warning 136) **52** [2007 47: p7g f8g 7m 6m² May 3] good-topped filly: modest performer: stays 7f: unraced on extremes of going on turf: wore cheekpieces last 2 starts. *D. W. Barker*

CAPE THEA 3 b.f. Cape Cross (IRE) 129 – Pasithea (IRE) 101 (Celtic Swing 138) **59 d** [2007 71p: p8.6g 7m⁵ p7.1g p7g Dec 16] smallish filly: disappointing maiden, leaving W. Swinburn after second start: stays 7f: acts on polytrack: tried blinkered. *Mark Gillard*

CAPE VALE (IRE) 2 b.c. (Jan 23) Cape Cross (IRE) 129 – Wolf Cleugh (IRE) 65 **88 p** (Last Tycoon 131) [2007 6g⁶ 6d* Sep 21] 58,000F, 82,000Y: good-bodied, attractive colt: sixth foal: closely related to 6-y-o Moss Vale and half-brother to 2 winners, including fairly useful 2000 2-y-o 1m winner Natural Force (by King's Best): dam lightly-raced half-sister to smart sprinter King's College: won both starts, namely maiden at Thirsk in August and nursery at Ayr (all out but still rather green) in September: will prove at least as effective at 5f as 6f: should go on improving. *D. Nicholls*

CAPE VELVET (IRE) 3 b.f. Cape Cross (IRE) 129 – Material Lady (IRE) 74 (Bara- **75** thea (IRE) 127) [2007 80: 6m⁴ 7g² 7g 7d⁵ 9g 8.3m³ p8.6g² p8.6g 8m⁶ Oct 14] angular filly: fair maiden handicapper: free-going sort, but should stay 9f: acts on polytrack and good to firm going, probably on good to soft: inconsistent. *J. W. Hills*

CAPISTRANO 4 b.g. Efisio 120 – Washita (Valiyar 129) [2007 79: p11g⁶ p12g 10.9m⁶ **74 d** 7d 8.2g p8g Aug 8] close-coupled gelding: fair handicapper: form in 2007 only on reap-pearance: should stay 1½m: acts on polytrack: tried blinkered (failed to impress with attitude). *Mrs P. Sly*

CAPITALISE (IRE) 4 b.g. City On A Hill (USA) 114 – Prime Interest (IRE) (Kings **72** Lake (USA) 133) [2007 55, a61: p16f p13.9g² p16.5g³ 18g⁴ p16g³ p16g³ 18m² p13.9g³ Dec 31] workmanlike gelding: fair maiden handicapper: effective at 1¾m to 2¼m: acts on polytrack and firm going: tried blinkered/tongue tied/in cheekpieces: fair hurdler. *V. Smith*

CAPITAL LASS 4 b. or br.f. Forzando 122 – Fair Test 95 (Fair Season 120) [2007 61: **65 d** f7g* f7g³ f8g⁴ f7g p7.1g f8g f7g p8.6g⁵ f7g f7g f7g f7d⁶ Dec 12] compact filly: fair performer: won seller at Southwell (left D. Ivory) in January: regressive after: stays 7f: acts on all-weather and good to firm going: tried blinkered/in cheekpieces: often slowly away. *A. J. McCabe*

CAPITANA (GER) 6 ch.m. Lando (GER) 128 – Capitolina (FR) (Empery (USA) 128) **82** [2007 10m 12m⁶ Sep 21] leggy mare: fairly useful performer: useful and progressive form over hurdles prior to respectable efforts in handicaps at Newbury on Flat return: stays 1¼m. *N. J. Henderson*

CAPONE (IRE) 2 b.c. (Mar 8) Daggers Drawn (USA) 114 – Order of The Day (USA) **69** (Dayjur (USA) 137) [2007 6g⁶ 6.1d⁴ p6g³ Nov 10] €10,500Y: lengthy colt: third foal: half-brother to winner in Italy by Vettori: dam unraced out of half-sister to US Grade 2 1¼m winner Star de Naskra: fair maiden: fourth to Italian Art at Nottingham: will stay 7f. *S. Parr*

CAPPANRUSH (IRE) 7 gr.g. Medaaly 114 – Introvert (USA) (Exbourne (USA) 125) **–** [2007 –: p13g Feb 14] modest winning hurdler: well held both starts on Flat (12 months apart). *A. Ennis*

CAPPING (IRE) 3 ch.c. Rahy (USA) 115 – Hawksleys Jill (Mujtahid (USA) 118) **55** [2007 p7.1g p6g 7g p7.1g 6.1d Aug 16] modest maiden: should stay 7f: tongue tied last 3 starts, visored last 2. *W. R. Swinburn*

CAPRICCIOSO 2 b.f. (Feb 7) Cape Cross (IRE) 129 – Heart of India (IRE) (Try My **– p** Best (USA) 130) [2007 p7g Dec 19] 23,000Y: half-sister to 3 winners, including useful Irish 6f winner (including at 2 yrs) King of Russia (by Common Grounds) and 6-y-o Fast Heart: dam unraced half-sister to very smart sprinter Bolshoi: 20/1, travelled well much of way when last of 8 in maiden at Lingfield: should do better, especially at 5f/6f. *G. L. Moore*

Willmott Dixon Cornwallis Stakes, Ascot—Captain Gerrard concludes his first season with a fifth win; Cute Ass (left) takes second in front of Cake (partially hidden by winner) and Hammadi (noseband)

CAPRICHO (IRE) 10 gr.g. Lake Coniston (IRE) 131 – Star Spectacle (Spectacular Bid (USA)) [2007 83d: 7g⁵ p7g² p8g 7g⁴ 7g⁵ p8g 7d⁵ 7.6f 6g 6g 6d³ Oct 15] tall gelding: just fair handicapper nowadays, on long losing run: effective at 6f, and probably stays 1m: acts on polytrack, firm and soft going: tried in cheekpieces, blinkered nowadays: sometimes finds little. *J. Akehurst* **72**

CAPRICORN RED 7 ch.m. Rashik 97 – Bella Maggio (Rakaposhi King 119) [2007 p9.5d Dec 17] small, sturdy mare: no sign of ability, including over hurdles. *R. Hollinshead* **–**

CAPRICORN RUN (USA) 4 br. or b.g. Elusive Quality (USA) – Cercida (USA) (Copelan (USA)) [2007 –: f7g 8.5m 6d⁵ p6g⁴ 7m p6g* 6m 6m* 7m p6g² p7g* p7m* p8g p7m* p7g Dec 19] well-made gelding: left Saeed bin Suroor 7,000 gns after 3 yrs: progressed into smart handicapper in 2007, won at Lingfield and Newmarket in September and Lingfield in October/November (2): further improvement when beating Fajr by ½ length for final success: effective at 6f, should stay 1m: acts on all-weather and firm ground: usually visored/in cheekpieces: sometimes looks wayward (virtually refused to race seventh start). *A. J. McCabe* **113**

CAPRIMA (IRE) 2 ch.f. (Apr 26) Captain Rio 122 – Titchwell Lass 57 (Lead On Time (USA) 123) [2007 5g 5g 5d⁵ 5m 5m⁶ 5f Sep 17] €7,000Y: compact filly: half-sister to several winners, including 5-y-o Sundance and 6-y-o Louisiade: dam 1¼m winner: poor maiden: raced only at 5f. *M. Brittain* **47**

CAPRIO (IRE) 2 ch.c. (Mar 23) Captain Rio 122 – Disarm (IRE) (Bahamian Bounty 116) [2007 6d 6d⁵ 5.1g⁶ p6g* p6g* Nov 28] €25,000F, 25,000Y: useful-looking colt: first foal: dam unraced half-sister to useful 2-y-o 6f/7f winner Nominator: fair form: improved and won nurseries at Wolverhampton and Kempton in November: likely to stay easy 7f: acts on polytrack: unseated rider to post first 2 starts. *R. Charlton* **71**

CAP ST JEAN (IRE) 3 b.g. Cape Cross (IRE) 129 – Karminiya (IRE) 58 (Primo Dominie 121) [2007 f6g⁴ f6g⁴ f8g 6g 9m² 8.5s 8.3d⁵ 8.1m³ 8.5m³ p9.5g² p9.5g³ p8.6g³ Oct 30] €25,000F, 16,500Y: sturdy gelding: second foal: dam, ran once, out of sister to very smart 1¼m performer Kartajana: fair maiden handicapper: left P. Haslam after sixth outing: should stay 1¼m: acts on all-weather and good to firm ground: tried in cheekpieces: sometimes slowly away. *R. Hollinshead* **66**

CAPTAIN BOLSH 4 b.g. Tagula (IRE) 116 – Bolshoi Star 65§ (Soviet Star (USA) 128) [2007 59, a49: p11g p9.5g⁴ p11g f11g f8g³ p8g 10.1m⁴ Apr 26] strong, workmanlike gelding: modest maiden: effective at 1m to 1½m: acts on all-weather and firm ground: tried visored: inconsistent: sent to Belgium. *J. Pearce* **55**

CAPTAIN BRILLIANCE (USA) 2 ch.c. (Feb 25) Officer (USA) 120 – Bloomin Genius (USA) (Beau Genius (CAN)) [2007 6m² 6m* Aug 3] $160,000Y: big, good-topped colt: fifth foal: half-brother to 3 winners in US, including 5f (at 2 yrs) to 8.5f (including minor stakes) winner Mavoreen (by Sir Cat): dam maiden US sprinter: plenty of promise both starts, at Newmarket, second in minor event then winning maiden comfortably by 2 lengths from Polmaily: may well stay 1m: already useful, and will improve further. *J. Noseda* **96 p**

CAPTAIN CROONER (IRE) 2 ch.g. (Jan 29) Captain Rio 122 – Kurfuffle (Bluebird (USA) 125) [2007 p5.1m p6g 5.1d p5.1g 5.1g f5d* p6d Dec 28] stocky gelding: poor **47 ?**

performer: won nursery at Southwell in December, likely flattered (came from off strong pace): should stay 6f: acts on fibresand: once visored. *D. Shaw*

CAPTAIN DARLING (IRE) 7 b.g. Pennekamp (USA) 130 – Gale Warning (IRE) – (Last Tycoon 131) [2007 –, a70: p8g p7g Oct 17] big gelding: fair at best: well held both runs in 2007 (said to have finished lame final outing): effective at 7f, barely at 1¼m: acts on all-weather, firm and good to soft going: tried in headgear: has worn tongue tie: has edged left/raced freely: usually makes running: sold 600 gns. *R. W. Price*

CAPTAIN DUNNE (IRE) 2 b.g. (Jan 27) Captain Rio 122 – Queen Bodicea (IRE) 80 (Revoque (IRE) 122) [2007 6g 5m* 6s⁴ 5s³ Jul 14] €29,000F, 30,000Y: workmanlike gelding: first foal: dam, Irish maiden, half-sister to useful Italian miler Meanya: fairly useful performer: won maiden at Haydock in May: good third to Lady Rangali in nursery at York: gelded after: best form at 5f: acts on soft and good to firm going. *T. D. Easterby*

CAPTAIN ESTEEM 2 b.g. (Mar 15) Mark of Esteem (IRE) 137 – Daring Destiny 113 75 d (Daring March 116) [2007 6g⁴ 6m⁶ p6g⁴ 7m 6m⁶ Sep 25] 22,000F, 60,000Y: neat gelding: fourth foal: half-brother to 6-y-o Daring Affair and 4-y-o Apply Dapply: dam 6f/7f (latter including at 2 yrs) winner: fair maiden: gelded/off 3 months after third start, below form on return: should stay 7f: sold 4,000 gns, sent to Bahrain. *B. W. Hills*

CAPTAIN GENERAL 5 br.h. In The Wings 128 – Sea Quest (IRE) (Rainbow Quest 74 (USA) 134) [2007 78: p12g⁵ p12g p13g⁴ p12g p12g Oct 12] sturdy horse: fair handicapper: will probably stay 2m: acts on polytrack and good to firm going: sold 6,000 gns. *J. A. R. Toller*

CAPTAIN GERRARD (IRE) 2 b.c. (Feb 27) Oasis Dream 129 – Delphinus (Soviet 110 Star (USA) 128) [2007 6g⁶ 5m² 5m³ 5.1d* 5.1s* 5g³ 5g* 5m⁴ 5d* 5d* Oct 13] 85,000F, 130,000Y: smallish, strong colt: type to carry condition: fifth foal: half-brother to smart

Mr R. C. Bond's "Captain Gerrard"

2002 2-y-o 7f/1m winner Saturn (by Marju, later successful up to 1½m in Hong Kong) and useful Irish 6f/7f winners Glocca Morra (by Catrail) and Sedna (by Priolo): dam French 1¼m winner: smart performer: won minor events at Chester in June and July, listed races at York in August and Ayr in September, and Willmott Dixon Cornwallis Stakes at Ascot (beat Cute Ass by 1½ lengths) in October: will prove best at 5f: acts on soft going: front runner: tough and consistent. *B. Smart*

CAPTAIN HURRICANE 5 b.g. Desert Style (IRE) 121 – Ravine 81 (Indian Ridge **91** 123) [2007 –: p7g 6g 6m 6g 6g 6m 6m Sep 1] tall, leggy gelding: one-time smart performer: left P. Chapple-Hyam, little impact in handicaps in 2007: tried blinkered/in cheekpieces: dead. *B. J. Meehan*

CAPTAIN JACK BLACK 2 br.c. (Apr 29) Superior Premium 122 – La Volta 86 **–** (Komaite (USA)) [2007 6m 6m⁶ 5.7f Aug 24] good-quartered colt: no form: tongue tied after debut. *M. R. Bosley*

CAPTAIN JACKSPARRA (IRE) 3 b.c. Danehill (USA) 126 – Push A Venture 58 **98 +** (Shirley Heights 130) [2007 73p: f7g² f6g* p7g* p7.1g² 7.1m² 7d 8m 6g⁵ 7m* Sep 3] quite attractive, dipped-backed colt: useful performer: won maiden at Southwell and handicap at Lingfield in March and (having lost way briefly) handicap at Lingfield (beat Nadawat by 1¼ lengths with something in hand) in September: effective from 6f to 1m: acts on all-weather and good to firm going, possibly unsuited by softer than good: often races freely. *K. A. Ryan*

CAPTAIN KIR (IRE) 2 ch.c. (Apr 30) Captain Rio 122 – A Lot of Kir (IRE) (Selkirk **61** (USA) 129) [2007 p5g³ 5.1d Aug 19] better run in maidens when third at Lingfield: likely to prove best at 5f/6f. *B. De Haan*

CAPTAIN MACARRY (IRE) 2 ch.c. (Apr 14) Captain Rio 122 – Grannys Reluct- **72** ance (IRE) 63 (Anita's Prince 126) [2007 5d⁶ 6m* 6m 6g Oct 6] €37,000F, 35,000Y: strong, sturdy colt: closely related to 4-y-o Angaric and half-brother to 2 winners, includ-ing 5-y-o Inka Dancer: dam, maiden (stayed 1m), half-sister to smart Italian/French miler Sole Che Sorgi: fair form: won maiden at York in September, dominating: little form otherwise, hung badly left penultimate start: should prove best at 5f/6f: acts on firm going. *B. Smart*

CAPTAIN MAINWARING 2 b.g. (Mar 18) Auction House (USA) 120 – Shalyah **67** (IRE) 65 (Shalford (IRE) 124§) [2007 8.1m 8m 8.2d⁴ Oct 18] compact gelding: fourth foal: dam maiden (stayed 1m): maiden: form only when fourth at Nottingham, possibly flattered: stays 1m. *N. P. Littmoden*

CAPTAIN MARRYAT 6 ch.g. Inchinor 119 – Finlaggan 83 (Be My Chief (USA) 122) **–** [2007 p12g p10g p13g 15.4g Aug 16] useful-looking gelding: fair maiden in 2004: unraced in 2005/06, and little form on return (pulled up final start). *J. Akehurst*

CAPTAIN MARVELOUS (IRE) 3 b.c. Invincible Spirit (IRE) 121 – Shesasmart- **102** lady (IRE) (Dolphin Street (FR) 125) [2007 114: 7m⁶ 7m⁶ 6g 7d Oct 20] well-made, quite attractive colt: smart performer at 2 yrs: form in 2007 only when eighth to Miss Lucifer in Challenge Stakes at Newmarket final outing: stays 6f: acts on good to firm and good to soft going. *B. W. Hills*

CAPTAIN NEMO (USA) 3 b.g. Officer (USA) 120 – Macarena Macarena (CAN) **–** (Gone West (USA)) [2007 70: 7m 7.5m 10.1m 10f 13.8g Sep 22] useful-looking gelding: fair maiden at 2 yrs: no form in 2007, including in sellers: tried blinkered: very slowly away fourth outing. *T. D. Barron*

CAPTAIN OATS (IRE) 4 b.g. Bahhare (USA) 122 – Adarika (Kings Lake (USA) **63** 133) [2007 –: p9.5g 10d³ Aug 20] modest maiden: stays 1¼m: acts on firm and good to soft going: tried in cheekpieces. *Mrs P. Ford*

CAPTAIN ROYALE (IRE) 2 ch.c. (Mar 18) Captain Rio 122 – Paix Royale (Royal **76** Academy (USA) 130) [2007 p6g⁶ 6s* 6v⁶ 6g 7g Oct 27] €64,000F, 56,000Y: strong, good-topped colt: seventh foal: half-brother to several winners abroad, including useful French/US 7f and 9f winner Peacefully (by Grand Lodge): dam, French 2-y-o 1m winner (stayed 10.5f), half-sister to smart French/US performer up to 12.5f Playact: fair per-former: won maiden at Ripon in June by 5 lengths: flattered when last of 6 to Saoirse Abu in Phoenix Stakes at the Curragh next time: below form in nurseries last 2 starts (visored, said to have finished lame final one): should stay 7f: acts on soft going. *J. Noseda*

CAPTAIN TURBOT (IRE) 2 ch.g. (May 9) Captain Rio 122 – Kiriwai (ITY) (Al- **–** wasmi (USA) 115) [2007 5d 5.4m 6d 5d Oct 9] neat gelding: no form in maidens: tried in cheekpieces. *D. W. Barker*

CAPTAIN WEBB 2 br.c. (Jan 29) Storming Home 128 – Criquette 104 (Shirley **83 p** Heights 130) [2007 8d* Oct 18] closely related to fairly useful Irish 2004 2-y-o 7f winner Hestia (by Machiavellian), and half-brother to 2000 2-y-o 1m winner Candice (by Caerleon) and French 7f/1m winner Open Offer (by Cadeaux Genereux), both useful: dam, 2-y-o 7f winner and later 9f winner in UAE, half-sister to top-class miler Markofdistinction: 13/2, won maiden at Brighton by 2 lengths, gradually asserting: likely to stay 1¼m: should do better. *M. Johnston*

CAPTIVATE 4 ch.f. Hernando (FR) 127 – Catch (USA) (Blushing Groom (FR) 131) **54** [2007 55: p16g p12.2g⁴ p13.9g Jan 22] modest performer: stays 1¾m: acts on all-weather and good to firm going: wears blinkers/cheekpieces: none too consistent. *A. J. McCabe*

CARACCIOLA (GER) 10 b.g. Lando (GER) 128 – Capitolina (FR) (Empery (USA) **107** 128) [2007 –: 14s³ 16m² 17.2f* 18d² Oct 20] angular gelding: useful hurdler/chaser: useful handicapper on Flat, lightly raced: won 4-runner event at Bath in September by neck (value extra) from Colloquial: excellent ¾-length second of 33 to Leg Spinner in Cesarewitch at Newmarket next time, again travelling well: stays 2¼m: acts on firm and good to soft ground, probably soft. *N. J. Henderson*

CARADAK (IRE) 6 b.h. Desert Style (IRE) 121 – Caraiyma (IRE) 84 (Shahrastani **115** (USA) 135) [2007 121: 7d 8d⁴ 7g³ 8g⁵ Nov 3] strong, useful-looking horse: very smart performer in 2006, winning Prix de la Foret at Longchamp: just smart in 2007, best effort when length third to Appalachian Trail in listed race at Redcar: was effective at 7f/1m: acted on firm and good to soft going: had been bandaged behind: to stand at Dehesa de Milagro, Spain. *Saeed bin Suroor*

CARADOC PLACE 2 b.g. (Jan 21) Compton Place 125 – Queen Linear (USA) **68** (Polish Navy (USA)) [2007 6s 6m⁴ 6m⁴ 5m 6s⁵ 6.1d⁶ Oct 18] 17,000F, 50,000Y: quite good-topped gelding: half-brother to 1m winner Ellway Queen (by Bahri) and winner in US by Miner's Mark: dam, US 5f winner, half-sister to very smart winner up to 1¼m Hardgreen: fair maiden: mid-field in nurseries: should prove best at 5f/6f: acts on sand and good to firm going: sold 7,500 gns. *M. P. Tregoning*

CARAMAN (IRE) 9 ch.g. Grand Lodge (USA) 125 – Caraiyma (IRE) 84 (Shahrastani **68** (USA) 135) [2007 72, a76: p12.2g⁶ p13.9g 12d Jul 29] quite good-topped gelding: fair performer: stays easy 2m: acts on polytrack and good to soft ground: none too consistent: useful hurdler. *J. J. Quinn*

CARAVEL (IRE) 3 ch.g. Medicean 128 – Caraiyma (IRE) 84 (Shahrastani (USA) 135) **97 p** [2007 p6g 7.1s 7m⁶ 7.9m² 8m* 8.1m* 9g* 8m* 9d* Sep 24] €80,000Y: good-topped gelding: seventh foal: half-brother to 3 winners, notably 6-y-o Caradak and useful Irish 6f winner Carralia (by Common Grounds): dam, Irish 9f winner, sister to smart Irish middle-distance performer Cajarian: progressive performer: won last 5 starts, namely handicaps at Brighton, Haydock, and Goodwood, all in August, and handicap at Redcar and minor event at Ballinrobe (beat Princely Hero by head, not handling track particularly well) in September: will be suited by 1¼m: acts on good to firm and good to soft going: should continue to improve. *Sir Mark Prescott*

CARCINETTO (IRE) 5 b.m. Danetime (IRE) 121 – Dolphin Stamp (IRE) (Dolphin **96** Street (FR) 125) [2007 67: p6g p7g³ p7.1g⁴ p7.1g* p7.1g p7.1g⁴ p7.1g* p6g³ 7m⁶ 7.1m² 5.7g³ 7m³ 5.7d p7.1m³ p6g* p6g* p6g⁵ p6g* p7.1g³ p7g² Dec 19] angular mare: progressed into useful performer in 2007: won handicaps at Wolverhampton in February, April, September, October and November: good neck second to Bonus in listed event at Kempton final outing: effective at 6f/7f: acts on polytrack and firm ground (below form on soft): sometimes visored/in cheekpieces (not in 2007): sometimes flashes tail/wanders. *P. D. Evans*

CARDINGTON QUEEN 3 b.f. Cois Na Tine (IRE) 101 – Bold Feliciter 45 (Bold – Arrangement 127) [2007 p8.6g 8.2g 7d 6f 9.9g 10.3m Aug 31] leggy filly: second foal: dam maiden who stayed 1½m: no sign of ability. *M. Mullineaux*

CAREENYA (IRE) 2 b.f. (Mar 8) Captain Rio 122 – Carallia (IRE) 101 (Common **–** Grounds 118) [2007 5.1g⁵ 5.1m Aug 9] €16,000Y: first foal: dam, Irish 6f winner, half-sister to very smart 7f/1m winner Caradak: well held in sellers. *R. M. Beckett*

CAREFREE 3 b.f. Medicean 128 – Hertha (Hernando (FR) 127) [2007 59p: f8g* f8g **58** p7f* 7.2s Oct 26] modest performer: won seller at Southwell (left W. Haggas 11,000 gns) in January and handicap at Lingfield in February: left S. Parr/off 8 months before well held final outing: will stay 1¼m: raced mainly on all-weather. *G. A. Swinbank*

CAREFREE FLAPPER 3 ch.f. Generous (IRE) 139 – Roaring Twenties 81 (Halling **58** (USA) 133) [2007 f8g⁶ 10.1d⁵ May 15] second foal: sister to winner in Greece: dam, 1m winner, closely related to smart performer up to 14.6f Eco Friendly: better effort in maidens when fifth at Newcastle, looking awkward under pressure: sold 800 gns in July. *G. A. Swinbank*

CARELESS FREEDOM 2 ch.f. (Jan 24) Bertolini (USA) 125 – Humble Pie 92 **– p** (Known Fact (USA) 135) [2007 5.1g Oct 24] half-sister to several winners, including smart sprinter Leap For Joy (by Sharpo) and useful 7f winner (including at 2 yrs) Pie High (by Salse): dam, 2-y-o 6f winner, half-sister to very smart 6f/7f performer College Chapel: 16/1, shaped better than position suggests when eleventh in maiden at Bath, still to be asked for full effort when stumbling badly over 1f out: will improve. *B. J. Meehan*

CARIBANA 2 ch.f. (Jan 12) Hernando (FR) 127 – Carenage (IRE) 83 (Alzao (USA) **69 p** 117) [2007 p8.6g⁴ f8d³ Dec 21] first foal: dam, 1½m winner, out of Yorkshire Oaks winner Key Change: better effort in maidens when length third to Pharaohs Justice at Southwell: will be suited by 1½m+: will do better still. *M. A. Jarvis*

CARIBBEAN CORAL 8 ch.g. Brief Truce (USA) 126 – Caribbean Star 81 (Soviet **100** Star (USA) 128) [2007 98: 5m 5.1m* 5g³ 5v³ 5d 6m³ 5.6m 6d 6d 5g 5g Oct 27] strong, good sort: useful handicapper: won at Chester (beat Corridor Creeper by ½ length) in May: creditable third 3 of next 4 starts, then lost his form: effective at 5f/easy 6f: acts on any turf ground: sometimes visored/in cheekpieces before 2007: tends to carry head awkwardly: has found little: usually waited with. *J. J. Quinn*

CARIBBEAN CRUISER 2 b.g. (Feb 27) Diktat 126 – Caribbean Star 81 (Soviet Star **–** (USA) 128) [2007 6g 6g⁵ 7d 6m 7g 7g Oct 20] angular gelding: no form: tried blinkered. *Garry Moss*

CARLETON 2 b.g. (Mar 28) Hunting Lion (IRE) 115 – Canadian Capers 70 (Balla- **94** cashtal (CAN)) [2007 5d* 5g 5.1d* 5m⁶ 6m 5g 6m⁵ 5g 6.1m⁴ 6.5m 5d³ 6d⁶ 5d Oct 13] big, strong gelding: usually takes the eye: brother to 4-y-o Psycho Cat: dam 5.7f (at 2 yrs) and 7.6f winner: fairly useful performer: won maiden at Windsor in May and minor event at Bath in June: inconsistent rest of season, but often highly tried: probably best at 5f: acts on good to firm and good to soft going: tends to get behind: sold 25,000 gns, then gelded. *M. R. Channon*

CARLITOS SPIRIT (IRE) 3 ch.g. Redback 116 – Negria (IRE) (Al Hareb (USA) **75** 123) [2007 66: 8.3g 7g² 8m⁵ 7s² 8.3m p7m⁴ p7.1g⁴ p8g* f7d⁵ Dec 11] fair handicapper: improved when winning apprentice event at Kempton in December: stays 1m: acts on polytrack, firm and soft going: tried blinkered: tends to wander: has looked less than straightforward. *B. R. Millman*

CARLOWSANTANA (IRE) 4 b.g. Blue Ocean (USA) 87 – Lees First Step 61 **86** (Reprimand 122) [2007 79: 8d 7.5g 7g p8.6g² 8v* 7.5m 7s² p8g³ p10.7g⁴ 10g p10.7g p8g Nov 30] fairly useful performer: won handicap at Tralee in August: effective at 7f to 10.7f: acts on polytrack (second in handicap at Wolverhampton fourth outing) and heavy ground: usually races close up: game. *Adrian Sexton, Ireland*

CARLTON MAC 2 ch.g. (Apr 4) Timeless Times (USA) 99 – Julie's Gift (Presidium **–** 124) [2007 6g 7d 6m 6m⁶ 7m 5g 8g 7g Nov 6] no form: tried blinkered/visored. *N. Bycroft*

CARLTON SCROOP (FR) 4 ch.g. Priolo (USA) 127 – Elms Schooldays (Emarati **68** (USA) 74) [2007 66: p12.2g* 12.4m⁶ p12g² p12g⁶ p13.9g⁴ p12g p16g⁴ 16m⁴ p13.9g Nov 5] stocky gelding: fair handicapper: won at Wolverhampton in March: probably stays 2m: acts on polytrack and good to firm ground: usually blinkered: often gives trouble at stall: sometimes hangs. *J. Jay*

CARMELA MARIA 2 b.f. (Jan 20) Medicean 128 – Carmela Owen (Owington 123) **60 p** [2007 6.5d Oct 11] sturdy filly: fourth foal: half-sister to 5-y-o Zowington, 4-y-o Fins-bury and 3-y-o Little Carmela: dam unraced out of half-sister to smart middle-distance stayer Sudden Victory: 33/1, encouraging speed when seventh to Fateh Field in maiden at Newbury: should do better. *C. F. Wall*

CARMENERO (GER) 4 b.g. Barathea (IRE) 127 – Claire Fraser (USA) (Gone West **83** (USA)) [2007 84: 8f³ 8d 8m p8g* p8.6g⁶ p8g 8m p7g³ p7g⁴ p7g⁴ p7g p6g⁶ p7g³ p7.1d⁵ p7g² Dec 28] sturdy, close-coupled gelding: fairly useful handicapper: won at Lingfield in June: stays 1m: acts on polytrack and firm going: tried in cheekpieces: held up. *W. R. Muir*

CARMINE ROCK 2 ch.f. (May 12) Arkadian Hero (USA) 123 – Cloudy Reef 57 **51** (Cragador 110) [2007 5.1g p5.1g Dec 1] half-sister to several winners, including 4-y-o Ochre Bay and 7-y-o Gilded Cove: dam sprint maiden: better effort in maidens when seventh to Fast Feet at Wolverhampton second start. *R. Hollinshead*

CAR

CARNIOLAN 2 b.g. (Apr 10) Royal Applause 124 – Dancing Feather 72 (Suave **75 p**
Dancer (USA) 136) [2007 6m³ Jun 14] 80,000Y: smallish, sturdy gelding: sixth foal:
brother to useful 2-y-o 7f winner Feathers Flying and half-brother to 3 winners, including
4-y-o Wagtail: dam, 1m winner, out of Prince of Wales's Stakes winner English Spring:
7/1, promising third to River Proud in maiden at Newbury, hampered over 1f out then
finishing well: gelded after: will stay 7f: looks sure to improve. *W. R. Swinburn*

CARNIVAL DREAM 2 b.f. (Apr 18) Carnival Dancer 123 – Reach The Wind (USA) **72**
(Relaunch (USA)) [2007 6d⁵ 6m⁴ 7d⁴ 6m² 7f³ 6g⁵ 6m⁵ 6.5d f5g⁵ p5.1g⁵ Dec 29] 3,200Y:
leggy, close-coupled filly: half-sister to 3 winners, including 6f winner Thundergod (by
Torrential): dam, Irish 6f winner (including at 2 yrs), half-sister to useful sprinter Ozone
Friendly: fair maiden: left A. Berry after eighth start: stays 7f: acts on firm going: tried
blinkered. *R. A. Harris*

CARNIVAL QUEEN 2 ch.f. (Mar 17) Carnival Dancer 123 – Irish Light (USA) 91 **84**
(Irish River (FR) 131) [2007 7s⁴ 6m³ 6m⁵ 8g² 7d* 8f Nov 24] compact filly: sixth foal:
closely related to winner in Greece by Barathea and half-sister to 7-y-o Polar Force and
2001 2-y-o 1m winner Harnour (by Desert King), both useful: dam, 1m winner, out of
half-sister to smart US 6f/7f performer Gold Land: fairly useful performer: generally progressive, winning nursery at Yarmouth (despite hanging left) in October: left J. Fanshawe
42,000 gns, not discredited when tenth of 11 in Grade 3 Miesque Stakes at Hollywood
final outing: stays 1m: acts on good to firm and good to soft going: visored/blinkered last
2 starts: has looked quirky. *P. Gallagher, USA*

CARNIVORE 5 ch.g. Zafonic (USA) 130 – Ermine (IRE) 86 (Cadeaux Genereux 131) **89**
[2007 83: 7g⁶ 7g 7.1d* 7g p7g³ p8g⁶ p8g⁵ Dec 16] tall gelding: fairly useful handicapper:
won at Musselburgh in June: effective at 7f/1m: acts on polytrack (probably on fibresand), firm and good to soft going. *T. D. Barron*

CAROLE OS (IRE) 2 b.f. (Mar 26) Catcher In The Rye (IRE) 115 – Kuda Chantik **60 ?**
(IRE) 53 (Lashkari 128) [2007 6m p6g Sep 21] 8,500 2-y-o: fifth foal: half-sister to a
winner in Italy by Cape Cross: dam, Irish maiden, half-sister to smart performer up to
1½m Madiriya: mid-division in maidens, seemingly modest form on debut. *S. W. Hall*

CAROLINA BELLE (USA) 2 b. or br.f. (Jan 23) Dixie Union (USA) 121 – Stormy **73**
Reply (USA) (Storm Cat (USA)) [2007 p5g² 6m³ p5g* 5g Aug 22] $160,000Y: stocky
filly: second foal: dam unraced sister to US Grade 2 7f winner Cat Chat: fair form: won
maiden at Lingfield (by 4 lengths, making all) in August: stiff task in listed race at York
(ninth of 10 to Captain Gerrard) only subsequent start: should be best kept to 5f/6f: sent
to USA. *M. J. Wallace*

CAROLINA BLINI 2 b.f. (Feb 13) Bertolini (USA) 125 – Key 70 (Midyan (USA) **61**
124) [2007 5m⁵ 5m p5g³ 5.7f⁴ p5g² Jun 21] 19,500Y: third foal: closely related to Italian
8.5f winner Big Snake (by Golden Snake): dam 2-y-o 5f winner: modest maiden: best
efforts in blinkers (in frame) last 2 starts: speedy, raced only around 5f: acts on polytrack
and firm ground: sold 3,000 gns, sent to Sweden. *B. J. Meehan*

CARO MIO (IRE) 3 b.f. Danehill Dancer (IRE) 117 – Our Hope (Dancing Brave **–**
(USA) 140) [2007 7m Apr 20] unfurnished filly: half-sister to useful Irish 2000 2-y-o 7f
to 9f winner Derivative (by Erins Isle) and Irish 1½m winner Dochas Mor (by Project
Manager): dam unraced out of smart Irish winner up to 1¼m Calandra, herself half-sister
to Oaks winner Intrepidity: 20/1, very much in need of experience when tailed off in
maiden at Newbury: sold 21,000 gns in July. *R. Charlton*

CARR HALL (IRE) 4 b.g. Rossini (USA) 118 – Pidgeon Bay (IRE) 66 (Perugino **69**
(USA) 84) [2007 60: 12g⁴ 10g 9g³ 8.5g²* 12g² 12g² p12.2g³ Sep 22] tall gelding: fair
performer: won handicap and minor event (Jersey Derby) at Les Landes in July: good
third in handicap at Wolverhampton final start, only outing in Britain in 2007: stays 1½m:
acts on polytrack, firm and good to soft going. *Mrs J. L. Le Brocq, Jersey*

CARRICKMACROSS (IRE) 2 b.c. (Feb 7) Mull of Kintyre (USA) 114 – Lady **78**
Corduff (IRE) 78 (Titus Livius (FR) 115) [2007 f5g³ f5g² p6g⁵ 6d⁴ 5m⁵ 6m* 6s* Oct 4]
€30,000Y: chunky colt: first foal: dam Irish 2-y-o 6.5f/7f winner: fair performer: improved form (and attitude) to win nurseries at Lingfield in September and Ayr: should prove
best at 5f/6f: acts on all-weather, soft and good to firm going: once visored: sold 13,000
gns. *E. S. McMahon*

CARRIE MCCURRY (IRE) 3 b.f. Fath (USA) 116 – Simply Devious (IRE) (Dr **71**
Devious (IRE) 127) [2007 71: p7.1g⁵ 6s 6d p6g 6s⁵ Oct 22] medium-sized filly: fair
maiden handicapper: below best at Wolverhampton on reappearance: should stay 7f: acts
on polytrack and soft going. *Patrick Martin, Ireland*

185

Timeform Silver Salver (Cecil Frail), Haydock—
Cartimandua slams her rivals stepped back up in grade; Ripples Maid (left) is second

CARRY ON CLEO 2 ch.f. (Feb 23) First Trump 118 – Classy Cleo (IRE) 102 (Mujadil 55
(USA) 119) [2007 5m³ p5g p6g p6m p6g p7.1g⁶ p8.6g³ p8m³ p10g⁶ p8m p8.6d* p9.5g³
p8.6d* Dec 28] compact filly: fourth foal: half-sister to 4-y-o Princess Cleo and 3-y-o
Mick Is Back: dam 5f/6f winner (including at 2 yrs): modest performer: won 2 claimers
at Wolverhampton in December: should stay 1¼m: raced only on polytrack and good to
firm going: tried visored, both wins in blinkers. *P. D. Evans*

CARSON'S SPIRIT (USA) 3 ch.g. Carson City (USA) – Pascarina (FR) (Exit To 78
Nowhere (USA) 122) [2007 82: p9.5g⁵ 8.1m⁴ 7m May 22] good-topped gelding: fair
handicapper: stays 1m: acts on good to firm and good to soft going: blinkered final 2-y-o
outing: has raced freely/tended to hang. *W. S. Kittow*

CARTIMANDUA 3 b.f. Medicean 128 – Agrippina 99 (Timeless Times (USA) 99) 115
[2007 81p: 7m 8m 6g* 6m*] Jun 9] big, strong, good-bodied filly: smart performer, lightly
raced: dropped back to sprinting (after tried in 1000 Guineas), made all in maiden at
Salisbury in May and listed race at Haydock (much improved to beat Ripples Maid
by 4 lengths) in June: should prove best at 5f/6f: raced on good/good to firm ground: stays
in training. *E. S. McMahon*

CASABLANCA MINX (IRE) 4 b.f. Desert Story (IRE) 115 – Conspire (IRE) 81 71
(Turtle Island (IRE) 123) [2007 81: p9.5g p8g p13g² p12.2g p12g⁵ p10g⁵ p8g p8.6g⁴
8.1m 10m 8s³ p8.6g² 8g⁴ p8.6g* 8.1m p8.6g⁶ p7.1g* p8.6g² p8.6g³ p9.5g⁴ p8.6g p8.6g³
p8.6g³ 8d² p8.6g⁴ p10m⁴ p10m p8.6g³ p9.5g³ p9.5s² p9.5g³ Dec 29] lengthy filly: fair
handicapper: left N. Littmoden after eighth start: won at Wolverhampton in July and
August: effective at 7f, seems to stay easy 13f: acts on polytrack, firm and soft ground:
usually blinkered/visored: held up: no easy ride (has hung left), but is tough and consistent. *P. D. Evans*

CASA CATALINA (IRE) 2 b.f. (Mar 20) King's Best (USA) 132 – Ruacana Falls 84
(USA) 86 (Storm Bird (CAN) 134) [2007 p7g 7m* 7m Sep 14] €40,000Y: close-coupled
filly: third foal: half-sister to 7f/1¼m winner Michaels Pride (by Distant View): dam,
2-y-o 1m winner, closely related to Chester Vase winner Panama City: fairly useful form:
better for debut, won maiden at Thirsk in August: led to 2f out in valuable sales race at the
Curragh final start: will stay 1m/1¼m. *M. Johnston*

CASA MIA (IRE) 2 b.f. (May 7) Frenchmans Bay (FR) 118 – Isla Bonita (Kings Lake 46
(USA) 133) [2007 6m⁶ p7.1g Oct 15] close-coupled filly: half-sister to 2 winners,
including Italian 11f/11.5f winner Ercole Il Grande (by Persian Heights): dam unraced
half-sister to dam of very smart performer up to 10.4f Almushtarak: maiden: showed a
little ability when sixth at Thirsk: disappointing in seller. *R. A. Fahey*

CASHEL MEAD 7 b.m. Bishop of Cashel 122 – Island Mead 86 (Pharly (FR) 130) 94
[2007 94: p5.1g 5m 5m³ 5m 5.1d 5d* 5d 5g p5.1g 6s Oct 14] leggy mare: fairly
useful handicapper: won at Sandown (by neck from Golden Dixie) in July: respectable
efforts at best after: effective at 5f/6f: acts on all-weather, soft and good to firm going: has
worn blinkers (not since early-2006): sometimes fractious in stall/slowly away: tough.
J. L. Spearing

CASHEMA (IRE) 6 b.m. Cape Cross (IRE) 129 – Miss Shema (USA) 81 (Gulch –
(USA)) [2007 –: 7m⁵ 8d May 15] leggy, lengthy mare: poor maiden: tried in cheekpieces/
visor/tongue tie. *James Moffatt*

CASHMERE JACK 2 b.g. (Feb 25) Daylami (IRE) 138 – Cashmere 86 (Barathea –
(IRE) 127) [2007 7d Oct 16] tailed off in maiden at Newcastle. *K. G. Reveley*

CASH ON (IRE) 5 ch.g. Spectrum (IRE) 126 – Lady Lucre (IRE) 73 (Last Tycoon 131) – §
[2007 –§: p12g Sep 18] good-topped gelding: fair performer: lightly raced since 2005:
tried visored (reluctant to race)/in cheekpieces: one to treat with caution. *Karen George*

CASINO NIGHT 2 ch.f. (May 3) Night Shift (USA) – Come Fly With Me (Bluebird **64**
(USA) 125) [2007 6g⁴ p7.1g³ 7.1g⁵ 7m⁶ 7m* 7m 7m⁶ 7g⁵ 7.1m Sep 30] 26,000Y: strong
filly: fourth foal: half-sister to 2003 2-y-o 7f winner On The Wing (by Pivotal) and Italian
sprinter by Mind Games: dam once-raced half-sister to smart 7f/1m winner Madid:
modest performer: won claimer at Newcastle (left M. Johnston £8,000) in August:
respectable efforts in mid-field in nurseries: stays 7f: acts on polytrack and good to firm
going: races prominently. *J. R. Weymes*

CASLA BEAG (IRE) 2 b.f. (Feb 20) Acclamation 118 – Carna (IRE) 60 (Anita's **62**
Prince 126) [2007 5.1g⁴ 5.1d 5.1d⁴ Oct 10] leggy filly: first foal: dam, sprint maiden (ran
only at 2 yrs), half-sister to useful 1½m winner Libk: modest maiden: fourth at Chepstow
and Nottingham, latter after 4 months off: free-going type, will be best at 5f. *B. Palling*

CASPIAN ROSE 4 b.f. Paris House 123 – Caspian Morn 63 (Lugana Beach 116) [2007 **38**
38: f6g⁶ f7g⁶ f8g Feb 11] compact filly: poor maiden: stays 6f: acts on fibresand.
M. J. Attwater

CASSABLANCA 2 b.f. (Feb 27) Royal Applause 124 – Ravine 81 (Indian Ridge 123) **83**
[2007 7m 7d Oct 20] lengthy filly: fourth foal: half-sister to 5-y-o Captain Hurricane and
3-y-o Nelly's Glen: dam, 6f/7f winner, half-sister to 1000 Guineas second Niche: needed
debut in maiden at Newmarket, then seemingly fairly useful form when ninth of 10
behind Kitty Matcham in Rockfel Stakes there: may prove best up to 7f: sold 47,000 gns,
sent to USA. *M. L. W. Bell*

CASSIARA 3 gr.f. Diktat 126 – Heaven-Liegh-Grey 90 (Grey Desire 115) [2007 82: **84 d**
7m² p7.1g² 7g⁶ 8.2m³ 7d⁵ 7.5s² 8d⁴ 8m⁴ 8g³ 8.1m³ 7f² 7g² 8.3d⁴ Oct 1] tall, lengthy, leggy
filly: has a quick action: fairly useful maiden: usually in frame in 2007, though well
below form last 4 starts: acts on soft and good to firm going: in cheekpieces/blinkers last
7 starts: sold 18,500 gns. *J. Pearce*

CASSIE'S CHOICE (IRE) 3 b.f. Fath (USA) 116 – Esteraad (IRE) 90 (Cadeaux **70**
Genereux 131) [2007 70: 7m⁴ 6.9d 6m³ 6d³ 6g Aug 29] good-topped, close-coupled filly:
fair maiden handicapper: needs good test at 6f, should stay 1m: acts on firm and good to
soft going. *B. Smart*

CASTANO 3 br.g. Makbul 104 – Royal Orchid (IRE) 74 (Shalford (IRE) 124§) [2007 **73**
74: p5g⁵ 5.1m² 5g⁵ 5s* 5m 5f 6m 6v⁴ Oct 9] sturdy, workmanlike gelding: fair performer:
won maiden at Folkestone in June: well below form after: best form at 5f: acts on firm
and soft going: often looks away: tried visored. *B. R. Millman*

CASTARA BAY 3 b.c. Sakhee (USA) 136 – Mayaro Bay 108 (Robellino (USA) 127) **80**
[2007 85: 10m⁴ 8g² 8.3s² 8.1m 7d 10g 10m* 9.9d³ p8m Oct 11] smallish, sturdy colt:
fairly useful performer: won claimer at Leicester in September: stays 1¼m: acts on polytrack, soft and good to firm ground: said to have bled fourth outing: held up of late: sold
10,000 gns. *R. Hannon*

CAST IN GOLD (USA) 3 b.f. Elusive Quality (USA) – Crystal Crossing (IRE) 99 **92**
(Royal Academy (USA) 130) [2007 90: 7m⁴ 10g⁵ May 18] big filly: fairly useful
performer: creditable fourth to Majestic Roi in Fred Darling Stakes at Newbury on
reappearance: reportedly finished distressed when well held in listed event there next
time: will probably stay 1m: sold 200,000 gns in December, sent to USA. *B. J. Meehan*

CASTLEBURY (IRE) 2 b.g. (Mar 27) Spartacus (IRE) 107 – La Vie En Rouge (IRE) –
(College Chapel 122) [2007 6s Jul 20] strong gelding: 33/1, very green in maiden at
Pontefract. *G. A. Swinbank*

CASTLE DURROW (IRE) 3 b.f. Strike Out (IRE) – Marylin Park (IRE) (Kendor **51**
(FR) 122) [2007 f8g p7.1g⁵ p6g 6g 8.5g p8g⁴ p5g⁵ p8g⁶ Dec 7] first foal: dam Italian
5f winner, including at 2 yrs: modest maiden: best effort when fifth in claimer at
Wolverhampton on second start: acts on polytrack, no form on turf: blinkered last 2 starts.
Seamus Fahey, Ireland

CASTLE HOWARD (IRE) 5 b.g. Montjeu (IRE) 137 – Termania (IRE) (Shirley **102**
Heights 130) [2007 99: 12m² 11.6s* 14g 14d 14.6m⁶ 16d 12s Oct 13] rather leggy

gelding: useful handicapper: won at Windsor in June by 5 lengths from Dan Dare: below form after: stays 15f: has form on good to firm ground, very best efforts on soft: sometimes takes good hold: sold 16,000 gns. *W. J. Musson*

CASTLES IN THE AIR 2 b.c. (Apr 8) Oasis Dream 129 – Dance Parade (USA) 107 **75**
(Gone West (USA)) [2007 6s⁵ 6m 6f⁴ p6g² Oct 31] 52,000Y: rather leggy, quite attractive colt: second foal: half-brother to US 8.5f winner Special Jig (by Theatrical): dam 5f (Queen Mary Stakes) to 1m (US Grade 2 event) winner: fair maiden: good second in nursery at Lingfield final start, rallying: likely to stay 7f: acts on polytrack and firm going. *Pat Eddery*

CASUAL AFFAIR 4 b.g. Golden Snake (USA) 127 – Fontaine Lady 41 (Millfontaine **74**
114) [2007 71: 8.2s² 10g³ 12.1g⁴ 14m* 14.1f⁵ 14d² 14.6g Oct 26] leggy, quite attractive gelding: fair handicapper: won at York in September: stays 1¾m: acts on polytrack, soft and good to firm going: often held up. *J. D. Bethell*

CASUAL GARCIA 2 gr.g. (Apr 2) Hernando (FR) 127 – Frosty Welcome (USA) 105 **–**
(With Approval (CAN)) [2007 6m p8g 8.2d 8.2g p8m Nov 11] 27,000Y: leggy gelding: second foal: dam 9f to 1½m winner: well held in maidens/nursery: bred to be well suited by middle distances. *Sir Mark Prescott*

CAT DE MILLE (USA) 3 b. or br.c. Stormin Fever (USA) 116 – De Mille (USA) 88 **76**
(Nureyev (USA) 131) [2007 86p: 8m⁶ 8.1g 7d 8m³ 10.3m² 11d Oct 11] workmanlike colt: fair handicapper: barely stays 1¼m: acts on good to firm and good to soft going: tried blinkered (well held): sold 9,000 gns. *P. W. Chapple-Hyam*

CATEGORICAL 4 b.g. Diktat 126 – Zibet 90 (Kris 135) [2007 81: 12m⁴ 14.1f⁴ 14.1g⁶ **74**
Oct 19] leggy gelding: fair handicapper: probably stays 1¾m: acts on fibresand and soft going: fair hurdler. *K. G. Reveley*

CATERINA BALLERINA (USA) 3 b.f. Catienus (USA) 115 – La Serina (IRE) 90 **52**
(Royal Academy (USA) 130) [2007 p7g f6g³ Apr 3] second foal: dam, Irish 7f winner, half-sister to useful sprinters Atlantic Viking and (in Italy) Fred Bongusto: better effort in maidens when 3½ lengths ninth to Hatherden at Lingfield, making running to 1f out: hung right from early stage at Southwell next time. *K. A. Ryan*

CATE WASHINGTON 4 b.f. Superior Premium 122 – Willisa 67 (Polar Falcon **–**
(USA) 126) [2007 44: p6g Jan 4] leggy filly: poor maiden at 3 yrs: well held sole outing in 2007. *Mrs L. Williamson*

CATHEDRAL WALK (USA) 2 ch.c. (Apr 28) Johannesburg (USA) 127 – Hilarity **66**
(USA) (Kingmambo (USA) 125) [2007 6d³ 6g Oct 3] unfurnished colt: second foal: half-brother to US 6f winner Inside Joke (by Officer): dam, French 1¼m/10.5f winner, half-sister to smart UAE sprinter Estimraar and US Grade 1 9f winner High Fly: maiden: third to Merchant of Dubai at Ayr: weakened as if amiss 3 months later: likely to stay 1m. *K. R. Burke*

CATHERINE PALACE 3 b.f. Grand Lodge (USA) 125 – Tereshkova (USA) 113 (Mr **60**
Prospector (USA) 126) [2007 9g⁶ 10m p10g Jun 20] fifth foal: half-sister to several winners, including 7f to 11f (in UAE) winner Kriskova (by Kris S) and 8.2f (at 2 yrs) and 1½m winner Alessandria (by Sunday Silence), both useful: dam, 6f (at 2 yrs in France) to 1m (in UAE) winner, sister to Middle Park winner Lycius: modest form in maidens, best effort on debut: sent to France. *E. A. L. Dunlop*

CATHERINES CAFE (IRE) 4 b.f. Mull of Kintyre (USA) 114 – Wisecrack (IRE) **61**
(Lucky Guest 109) [2007 68d: f11g 7.9m⁴ 7.9g² 8d* 9.1g 7.2v⁵ Nov 3] good-bodied filly: modest performer: won minor event at Musselburgh in June: stays 1m: acts on good to firm and good to soft going: tried visored/in cheekpieces. *A. C. Whillans*

CATIVO CAVALLINO 4 ch.g. Bertolini (USA) 125 – Sea Isle 73 (Selkirk (USA) **89**
129) [2007 66d: p7f* p6g* p7g* 6f⁴ 6d* p7g⁵ 6d p6m* p6g⁴ Nov 4] lengthy gelding: fairly useful handicapper, improved in 2007: won at Lingfield in February, March, April and August and Kempton in October: stays 7f: acts on polytrack, firm and good to soft ground: tried in cheekpieces (tailed off) at 3 yrs. *J. E. Long*

CAT JUNIOR (USA) 2 b. or br.c. (Mar 18) Storm Cat (USA) – Luna Wells (IRE) 119 **100 P**
(Sadler's Wells (USA) 132) [2007 6f* Aug 5] $500,000Y: brother to Irish 2005 2-y-o 6f winner The Wild Swan and half-brother to winner in US by Kingmambo: dam, French 9f (at 2 yrs) to 1¼m (Prix Saint-Alary) winner, half-sister to high-class performer up to 1¼m Linamix: evens favourite, useful form when winning maiden at Newbury (beat Harlech Castle by 3½ lengths) only start, plainly green but leading over 1f out and quickening clear: will be suited by 1m: should progress to much higher level. *B. J. Meehan*

CATLIVIUS (IRE) 3 ch.f. Titus Livius (FR) 115 – Cat's Tale (IRE) (Catrail (USA) –
123) [2007 66: p6g Jan 5] quite good-topped filly: has a quick action: regressive maiden:
lost all chance with very slow start only outing in 2007: should stay 6f: in cheekpieces
last 4 outings, tried tongue tied: sometimes hangs right. *K. A. Ryan*

CAT SIX (USA) 3 b.f. Tale of The Cat (USA) 113 – Hurricane Warning (USA) (Thun- **70**
der Gulch (USA) 129) [2007 54p: 8.2g 9g⁵ 10f⁵ p12g p8g³ 8.1m⁵ 8.1m 8d 10.2m 10d
p12.2g p9.5g⁶ Nov 10] angular filly: fair maiden: left B. Meehan 13,000 gns after fifth
start: probably stays 1¼m: acts on polytrack and firm ground: blinkered final outing: has
looked wayward from stall. *T. Wall*

CATSPRADDLE (USA) 4 ch.f. High Yield (USA) 121 – Beaux Dorothy (USA) **71**
(Dehere (USA) 121) [2007 76, a70: p6f³ Feb 24] workmanlike filly: fair handicapper:
best at 5f/6f: acts on polytrack and firm going: races up with pace (pulled hard once held
up). *R. Hannon*

CAT WHISTLE 2 b.f. (Feb 7) Dansili 127 – Mighty Flyer (IRE) (Mujtahid (USA) 118) **84 p**
[2007 6m⁴ 5.9g³ 6m⁵ 6m* 6m Oct 5] 23,000Y: unfurnished filly: fifth foal: sister to 5-y-o
Lady Pilot and half-sister to winners abroad by Zilzal and Unfuwain: dam, French 9f
winner, half-sister to useful sprinter Sylva Paradise: fairly useful form: impressively won
nursery at Redcar in August: off 2 months, ran with credit in mid-field in 28-runner sales
race at Newmarket: will be suited by at least 1m: should improve further. *R. A. Fahey*

CAUCASIENNE (FR) 4 b.f. Galileo (IRE) 134 – Carousel Girl (USA) (Gulch (USA)) **79**
[2007 p13g* p16f⁶ 15.4m³ 11.9d* 13.1m³ 12.1g⁴ 12.3d 14.5d Sep 14] first foal: dam,
French 2-y-o 1m winner, out of half-sister to dam of Bosra Sham and Hector Protector:
fair performer: sold from E. Lellouche in France 14,000 gns after final 3-y-o start: won
maiden at Lingfield in February and handicap at Brighton in May: sold from J. Hills
26,000 gns after sixth start: stays 15.4f: acts on polytrack, soft and good to firm ground:
found little sixth outing. *Rodolphe Collet, France*

CAUGHT IN PARADISE (IRE) 2 b.c. (Feb 3) Catcher In The Rye (IRE) 115 – **53 §**
Paradis (Bijou d'Inde 127) [2007 6g⁵ 6m² 5m* 6d⁵ 5.2m* 6.1m 5.1m 5m Aug 25] rather
leggy colt: modest performer: won claimer at Haydock (left D. Nicholls £10,000) in
June and selling nursery at Yarmouth in July: looked temperamental after (including in
blinkers): best at 5f: acts on good to firm going: one to avoid. *A. B. Haynes*

CAUGHT YOU LOOKING 3 b.f. Observatory (USA) 131 – Corndavon (USA) 95 **56**
(Sheikh Albadou 128) [2007 70p: 6g⁵ Jun 23] lightly-raced maiden: encouraging effort at
Lingfield, not knocked about, but not seen out again: stud. *W. R. Swinburn*

CAUSTIC WIT (IRE) 9 b.g. Cadeaux Genereux 131 – Baldemosa (FR) (Lead On **73**
Time (USA) 123) [2007 79, a70: p6g² p6g⁶ f6g⁴ p6g⁶ p6g 6m 5g* p6g² 5.1g² 5m* 5m⁴
p6g³ 5.1s⁴ 6f³ 5.7d³ 6g 5g p6g⁵ 5s² 6d Oct 15] leggy, quite good-topped gelding: fair
handicapper: won at Lingfield in June and Folkestone in July: effective at 5f to 7f:
acts on all-weather, firm and soft going: effective with or without cheekpieces: tough.
M. S. Saunders

CAVALLINI (USA) 5 b. or br.g. Bianconi (USA) 123 – Taylor Park (USA) (Sir **74**
Gaylord) [2007 85: p16g p12g² 11.6m⁵ 11.6g 14d³ p11g 16s Oct 14] tall gelding: just fair
handicapper nowadays: stays 1½m: acts on polytrack, good to firm and good to
soft going: tried blinkered: none too consistent. *G. L. Moore*

CAVALLO DI FERRO (IRE) 3 b.g. Iron Mask (USA) 117 – Lacinia 107 (Groom **63**
Dancer (USA) 128) [2007 70: p8g p8g p9.5g⁶ 7m p8g* p10p⁶ p8.6g p10g Dec 30] modest
performer: won handicap at Lingfield in May: stays 1m: acts on polytrack. *M. J. Gingell*

CAVALRY GUARD (USA) 3 ch.g. Officer (USA) 120 – Leeward City (USA) **74 §**
(Carson City (USA)) [2007 83§: 8.5m⁵ 7m² 7d⁶ p7g Dec 28] good-topped gelding: fair
maiden: left H. Cecil 25,000 gns before final start: should stay 1m: acts on good to firm
ground: tried in visor/cheekpieces: temperamental. *J. R. Boyle*

CAVALRY TWILL (IRE) 3 b.g. Alhaarth (IRE) 126 – Blue Mantle (IRE) 79 (Bara- **71**
thea (IRE) 127) [2007 70: 10f 11g 14g 12m 12m⁵ 12m⁶ p11g⁵ 14m⁶ p12.2g³ Oct 26] big,
strong gelding: fair maiden handicapper: stays 1½m: acts on polytrack and good to firm
ground: blinkered last 5 starts: makes running/races prominently: has shown signs of
temperament: sold 26,000 gns, joined G. L. Moore. *P. F. I. Cole*

CAVENDISH 3 b.g. Pursuit of Love 124 – Bathwick Babe (IRE) 71 (Sri Pekan (USA) **68**
117) [2007 –: p12.2g³ p12.2g⁴ 12.1m p9.5g⁵ 10.9d* 9.9s⁴ p12g³ 12g⁶ p9.5g⁵ p12g⁶
Nov 21] fair handicapper: won at Warwick in June: barely stays 1½m: acts on polytrack
and soft ground: visored (ran well but found little) sixth start, blinkered otherwise in
2007: races prominently. *J. M. P. Eustace*

CAVIAR HEIGHTS (IRE) 3 b.g. Golan (IRE) 129 – Caviar Queen (USA) (Crafty   **56**
Prospector (USA)) [2007 50: 9.8g 11.1m⁶ 8.1m⁴ 12.1s 9.1d⁶ 10f 10g² 14m⁵ 9.1s⁵ Oct 26]
modest maiden: probably stays 11f: acts on good to firm ground: blinkered nowadays:
looks none too keen. *Miss L. A. Perratt*

CAV OKAY (IRE) 3 gr.g. Fasliyev (USA) 120 – Dane's Lane (IRE) (Danehill (USA)   **92**
126) [2007 99: p6g⁴ 6m⁶ p5g 5.1m p6g Nov 4] close-coupled, quite attractive gelding:
has a fluent, easy action: fairly useful performer: respectable fourth to Eisteddfod in
minor event at Kempton on reappearance: well held in listed event/handicaps last 3 starts:
speedy, and best at 5f/easy 6f: acts on polytrack and good to firm going: blinkered final
2-y-o outing: usually makes running: none too reliable: sold 7,000 gns. *R. Hannon*

CAVORT (IRE) 3 ch.f. Vettori (IRE) 119 – Face The Storm (IRE) 72 (Barathea (IRE)   **79**
127) [2007 75: p7g 10m p8.6g* f8g⁶ 9.7g² p10g 10f 8.3m p8g Sep 15] leggy, quite
attractive filly: fair handicapper: won at Wolverhampton in May: stays 9.7f: acts on
polytrack and soft going: inconsistent: sold 7,000 gns, sent to Saudi Arabia. *Pat Eddery*

CAYMAN BREEZE 7 b.g. Danzig (USA) – Lady Thynn (FR) (Crystal Glitters (USA)   **54**
127) [2007 63: p6g p6g p6g⁵ 6.1g 7.1m 7d p6g p6m p6g Dec 19] smallish, sturdy gelding:
modest performer: effective at 6f/7f: acts on all-weather and firm going: tried in headgear: has looked none too keen. *J. M. Bradley*

CAYMAN CALYPSO (IRE) 6 ro.g. Danehill Dancer (IRE) 117 – Warthill Whispers   **47**
59 (Grey Desire 115) [2007 55: p16g⁶ Dec 6] tall gelding: modest performer, lightly raced
on Flat nowadays: stays 2m: acts on all-weather, good to firm and good to soft going:
tried visored/blinkered: modest hurdler. *Mrs P. Sly*

CAYMAN FOX 2 ch.f. (Apr 20) Cayman Kai (IRE) 114 – Kalarram (Muhtarram   **72**
(USA) 125) [2007 5m⁴ 5g² 5m⁶ 5m⁶ 5d³ 5.1s⁵ 5m Aug 2] lengthy filly: second foal: dam
well held in 3 starts: fair maiden: placed at Haydock and Warwick: raced at 5f: front
runner. *James Moffatt*

CEALTRA STAR (IRE) 2 b.f. (May 16) Mujadil (USA) 119 – Haraabah (USA) 99   **51**
(Topsider (USA)) [2007 6.1m 6g 6d p6g Dec 1] leggy filly: sister to 3-y-o Zanida and
half-sister to several winning sprinters, including 1998 2-y-o 5f winner Speedy James (by
Fayruz): dam 5f (at 2 yrs) to 7f winner: modest maiden: form only on debut: should prove
best at 5f/6f. *K. A. Ryan*

CEARAN (CZE) 4 b.g. Rainbows For Life (CAN) – Ceara (CZE) (Corvaro (USA)   **–**
124) [2007 11.8m⁶ Aug 12] won handicap in Switzerland in 2006: fit from hurdling (no
solid form), well held on British Flat debut. *F. Jordan*

CECINA MARINA 4 b.f. Sugarfoot 118 – Chasetown Cailin 59 (Suave Dancer (USA)   **50**
136) [2007 8m 8.1m 8.5s⁵ 8g 12.1g³ 14.1m⁶ 12.1d⁴ 14.1g Oct 19] 3,000Y: lightly-made
filly: second foal: dam maiden (stayed 1¼m): modest maiden: stays 1½m: acts on good
to firm going. *C. W. Thornton*

CEDAR MOUNTAIN (IRE) 4 b.c. Galileo (IRE) 134 – Ventura (IRE) 91 (Spectrum   **98**
(IRE) 126) [2007 10g² f11g* p10g³ 12s 10m 10f² Oct 13] first foal: dam, Irish 1m winner,
out of close relative to Generous and half-sister to Oaks winner Imagine: useful
performer: landed odds in maiden at Southwell in May easily by 7 lengths from Move
Over Darling: ran creditably otherwise when placed, 1¾ lengths second to Soupy in
allowance race at Santa Anita final outing: should stay 1½m: acts on all-weather and firm
going, possibly unsuited by soft. *J. H. M. Gosden*

CEE BARGARA 2 b.g. (Mar 14) Acclamation 118 – Balsamita (FR) (Midyan (USA)   **97**
124) [2007 5g⁵ 5g² 5f* 6g p6g* 6m⁶ 6m³ 6g 6g p6g p6g 5d Sep 21] 30,000F, 54,000Y: small,
well-made gelding: half-brother to several winners abroad, including useful French
1m winner (including at 2 yrs) Lovage (by Pursuit of Love): dam French 1m winner:
useful performer: won maiden at Pontefract in May and minor event at Kempton in June:
ran well when sixth of 20 to Henrythenavigator in Coventry Stakes at Royal Ascot and
third of 6 to Fat Boy in minor event at Newmarket: lost form later in season (tried
blinkered), and subsequently gelded: effective at 5f/6f: acts on polytrack and firm going.
J. A. Osborne

CEKA DANCER (IRE) 2 ch.f. (Apr 9) Danehill Dancer (IRE) 117 – Tidal Reach   **77**
(USA) 68 (Kris S (USA)) [2007 7m⁵ p6g² 6f p7.1d² p8.6g⁴ Dec 14] €85,000Y: strong,
useful-looking filly: closely related to Irish 1m winner Miss Latina (by Mozart) and
half-sister to several winners, including useful 2000 2-y-o 5f to 1m winner Innit (by
Distinctly North), later US Grade 2 1¼m winner: dam 2-y-o 1m winner: fair maiden:
second to Dream Day at Kempton second start: below form after: has raced freely, and
may prove best up to 7f: acts on polytrack and good to firm going. *E. J. O'Neill*

CELEBERRY (IRE) 2 b.c. (Jan 20) Val Royal (FR) 127 – Caeribland (IRE) 90 (Nam- **79**
aqualand (USA)) [2007 5m² 5g⁴ 6g³ 6g⁴ 7s⁵ Jul 28] big, strong colt: first foal: dam 2-y-o
6f winner (stayed 1m): fair maiden: in frame 4 times, including at Musselburgh second
start: will stay 1m. *James G. Burns, Ireland*

CELEBRATION SONG (IRE) 4 b.g. Royal Applause 124 – Googoosh (IRE) 77 **79**
(Danehill (USA) 126) [2007 88: 8.3f⁶ Aug 6] quite good-topped gelding: fair handicapper: respectable effort only outing in 2007: stays easy 1m: acts on polytrack, firm and
soft ground (yet to race on heavy): sold 3,000 gns in October. *W. R. Swinburn*

CELEB STYLE (IRE) 3 b.f. Tagula (IRE) 116 – Lovely Me (IRE) 70 (Vision (USA)) **54**
[2007 7m 6d³ 5d⁵ f5d p5.1s Dec 20] €36,000F, €85,000Y: sturdy filly: sister to useful 5f
winner (including at 2 yrs) Red Millennium and half-sister to 5-y-o Regal Dream: dam
maiden (stayed 7f): modest maiden: left D. Nicholls after third start: likely to prove best
at 5f/6f: best efforts on good to soft going: has edged right. *Paul Green*

CELESTIAL HALO (IRE) 3 b.g. Galileo (IRE) 134 – Pay The Bank 81 (High Top **115**
131) [2007 86p: 10.1m* 10g⁶ 12.3m³ 12g 12g 14g² 14.6m Sep 15] tall, rather leggy,
useful-looking gelding: smart performer: landed odds impressively in maiden at New-
castle (by 13 lengths) in April: upped in trip, ran well last 2 outings, 2 lengths second to
Speed Gifted in Melrose Stakes (Handicap) at York then 3 lengths seventh to Lucarno in
St Leger at Doncaster: stays 14.6f: acts on good to firm ground: sold privately, joined
P. Nicholls and gelded: useful form when successful on hurdling debut in December.
B. W. Hills

CELESTIAL SPHERE (USA) 3 b.c. Dixieland Band (USA) – Skybox (USA) **–**
(Spend A Buck (USA)) [2007 8.3d Oct 15] tall colt: 8/1 and looking weak, showed little
in maiden at Windsor: sold 5,000 gns, sent to Holland. *J. H. M. Gosden*

CELT 2 b.c. (May 9) Selkirk (USA) 129 – Puce 112 (Darshaan 133) [2007 7.1m p8g⁶ **57 p**
Sep 24] stocky colt: seventh foal: half-brother to several winners, including 1¼m (at
2 yrs)/11f winner Pukka (by Sadler's Wells), 1¼m/1½m winner Pongee (by Barathea)
and 3-y-o Lion Sands, all smart: dam, 1¼m/1½m winner (stayed 14.6f), closely related
to dam of Oaks winner Alexandrova: some promise in mid-field in maidens, probably
inadequate test: will do better at 1¼m/1½m. *L. M. Cumani*

CELTIC CHANGE (IRE) 3 br.c. Celtic Swing 138 – Changi (IRE) (Lear Fan (USA) **89**
130) [2007 70: 6.1m⁵ 7m⁶ 7m² 8d² 8d* 8g² 10d Oct 10] good-topped colt: fairly useful
handicapper: won at Redcar in July, despite hanging right: should stay at least 9f: acts on
good to firm and good to soft ground. *M. Dods*

CELTIC CHARLIE (FR) 2 ch.c. (Mar 23) Until Sundown (USA) – India Regalona **71**
(USA) (Dehere (USA) 121) [2007 p7g² p8m⁶ p8g⁶ Dec 28] €18,000Y, 24,000 2-y-o: third
foal: half-brother to 11f winner Quito Bere (by Verglas) and 1¼m to 13f winner Piper
Bere (by Epistolaire), both in France: dam unraced out of Chilean Grade 1 winner India
Pomposa: fair form in maidens at Lingfield: stays 1m. *P. M. Phelan*

CELTIC DRAGON 2 b.c. (Mar 13) Fantastic Light (USA) 134 – Zanzibar (IRE) 113 **74 p**
(In The Wings 128) [2007 8g² 8.2g⁴ p8m⁴ Dec 8] 80,000Y: sturdy colt: second foal:
half-brother to 3-y-o Spice Route: dam 11f (Oaks d'Italia) and 1½m winner: fair form in
frame in maidens, short-head second to Ragamuffin Man at Bath: will be suited by 1¼m/
1½m: likely to do better. *Mrs A. J. Perrett*

CELTICELLO (IRE) 5 b. or br.g. Celtic Swing 138 – Viola Royale (IRE) 90 (Royal **60**
Academy (USA) 130) [2007 –: 10.2m⁴ May 8] leggy gelding: fairly useful at 3 yrs for
M. Jarvis: lightly raced on Flat since, fourth in claimer only start in 2007: stays 1m: acts
on soft ground: tried in cheekpieces: won over hurdles in July. *Heather Dalton*

CELTIC EMPIRE (IRE) 4 b.g. Second Empire (IRE) 124 – Celtic Guest (IRE) (Be **–**
My Guest (USA) 126) [2007 43: f14g 15d May 23] workmanlike gelding: poor maiden:
stays 1¾m: acts on fibresand. *Jedd O'Keeffe*

CELTIC MEMORIES (IRE) 3 ch.f. Selkirk (USA) 129 – Memories (IRE) 95 (Don't **55**
Forget Me 127) [2007 59p: p8.6g 8m f11g⁶ 12.1m⁵ 12.1m⁶ 12.1s 10.1d³ 8s Jul 2] angular
filly: modest maiden: stays 1½m: acts on good to firm and good to soft going: effective
blinkered or not: has hung: sometimes makes running: sold 14,000 gns later in July.
M. W. Easterby

CELTIC MILL 9 b.g. Celtic Swing 138 – Madam Millie 99 (Milford 119) [2007 113: **113**
6.5g⁴ 6g³ a5f⁶ 6g⁶ p5g 6f⁴ 5m⁵ 5g² 5d 5g* 5g 5g Aug 23] tall, leggy gelding: smart
performer: some creditable efforts in 2007 (including length second to Aegean Dancer
in Scottish Sprint Cup Handicap at Musselburgh) prior to winning minor event at Newmarket in July by short head from Tabaret: respectable twelfth to Kingsgate Native in

Nunthorpe Stakes at York final outing (hung throughout at Goodwood penultimate start): effective at 5f/6f: acts on all-weather, firm and good to soft going: usually in cheekpieces, effective without: normally front runner: good servant to connections. *D. W. Barker*

CELTIC SLIPPER (IRE) 2 b.f. (Mar 5) Anabaa (USA) 130 – Celtic Silhouette (FR) **102** (Celtic Swing 138) [2007 6m⁶ 7g* 7g² 8m³ 8g* 8m⁵ Oct 14] 40,000Y: good-topped filly: has moderate, quick action: first foal: dam, French maiden who stayed 11.5f, sister to smart performer up to 2m Celtic Silence and half-sister to smart French stayer Royal And Regal: useful performer: won maiden at Goodwood in August and Premio Dormello at Milan (beat Short Affair by 5½ lengths) in October: placed in between in Prestige Stakes at Goodwood (½-length second to Sense of Joy) and May Hill Stakes at Doncaster (¾-length third to Spacious), and respectable fifth to Scintillo in Gran Criterium at Milan final start: will stay 1¼m/1½m: raced only on good/good to firm going. *R. M. Beckett*

CELTIC SPA (IRE) 5 gr.m. Celtic Swing 138 – Allegorica (IRE) (Alzao (USA) 117) **78** [2007 75, a62: 7.1s⁶ 6.9m 8.1m² 7f⁴ 8.3m⁶ 8d² 8.1f⁵ Aug 27] small, leggy mare: fair handicapper: stays 1m: acts on polytrack, firm and soft going. *P. D. Evans*

CELTIC SPIRIT (IRE) 4 ch.g. Pivotal 124 – Cavernista 75 (Lion Cavern (USA) 117) **95** [2007 90: p11g⁴ 9.9d* Jun 27] leggy gelding: useful performer: improved when winning handicap at Salisbury in June by length from Oh Glory Be: will stay 1½m: acts on polytrack and soft going: sold 20,000 gns, joined G. L. Moore. *R. M. Beckett*

CELTIC STEP 3 br.g. Selkirk (USA) 129 – Inchiri 108 (Sadler's Wells (USA) 132) **81 d** [2007 86: p10g 8v p8m p12.2g Dec 26] big gelding: fairly useful handicapper: below form after reappearance: probably stays 1¼m: acts on polytrack, soft and good to firm going: sometimes blinkered: hung left second start. *M. Johnston*

CELTIC STRAND (IRE) 2 b.g. (Apr 15) Celtic Swing 138 – Mur Taasha (USA) **73** 108 (Riverman (USA) 131) [2007 6m⁴ 7d⁴ 7m⁶ 7.5g² 8g* p8.6g⁵ Nov 27] close-coupled gelding: eighth foal: half-brother to several winners, including smart 1998 2-y-o 7f winner Iftitah (by Gone West), useful 1m to 1¼m (including in UAE) winner Mahroos (by Kingmambo) and 4-y-o Amy Louise: dam 7f/1m winner: fair performer: won maiden at Redcar (made all) in October: will stay 1¼m. *T. P. Tate*

CELTIC SULTAN (IRE) 3 b.c. Celtic Swing 138 – Farjah (IRE) (Charnwood Forest **110** (IRE) 125) [2007 92: 6g⁴ 6m³ 6m⁴ 6m⁴ 7g³ 7m* 7g⁴ Oct 27] sturdy, useful-looking colt: smart performer: improved in 2007, winning handicap at Newmarket in October by length from Sir Xaar, soon clear against fair rail: respectable fourth to Appalachian Trail in minor event at Doncaster final outing: stays 7f: acts on good to firm going, well held on soft: front runner. *T. P. Tate*

CELTIC THUNDER 6 b.g. Mind Games 121 – Lake Mistassiu 86 (Tina's Pet 121) **70** [2007 63: p6g² p6g* p6g⁵ Feb 5] good-topped gelding: fair handicapper: won at Lingfield in January: had form at 7f, but best at 5f/6f: acted on polytrack, firm and good to soft going: was usually blinkered: dead. *T. J. Etherington*

CENTENARY (IRE) 3 b.g. Traditionally (USA) 117 – Catherinofaragon (USA) **61** (Chief's Crown (USA)) [2007 71: 8.2g 6m 8s 7.9m p8g 9.8g² p12.2g p10g p13.9g⁵ **a55 +** Nov 16] neat gelding: just modest nowadays: left J. Quinn after seventh start: should stay 1¼m: acts on good to firm ground: tried visored/in cheekpieces. *D. E. Cantillon*

CENTENEROLA (USA) 2 b.f. (Mar 5) Century City (IRE) 124 – Lady Angharad **62 p** (IRE) 95 (Tenby 125) [2007 7d 6d⁵ Oct 29] big, strong filly: second foal: dam, 6f (at 2 yrs) to 1¼m winner, half-sister to useful 1m/1¼m performer Able Baker Charlie: better run in maidens at Leicester when fifth to Minshar, still looking to be learning: will be suited by 1m: type to go on improving. *B. W. Hills*

CENTENNIAL (IRE) 2 gr.c. (Jan 28) Dalakhani (IRE) 133 – Lurina (IRE) 111 (Lure **108** (USA) 131) [2007 7m³ 8m* 8m* 8d² Oct 13] 360,000Y: angular colt: third foal: dam, 7f winner, half-sister to high-class French 1¼m/1½m performer Croco Rouge: useful and progressive form: third to stable-companion Raven's Pass at Yarmouth on debut, then won maiden at Newmarket in August and minor event at Newbury (beat North Parade by length) in September: good 2½ lengths second to Thewayyouare in Prix Thomas Bryon at Saint-Cloud final start: will stay 1¼m: acts on good to firm and good to soft going. *J. H. M. Gosden*

CENTRAL FORCE 3 ch.f. Pivotal 124 – Lady Joyce (FR) (Galetto (FR) 118) [2007 **82** p8g⁶ 10m³ 10g 9.7m² 9g² 10m* 10g⁴ 8.2g Oct 31] 100,000Y: unfurnished filly: half-sister to several winners, including fairly useful 6f (at 2 yrs) to 9f winner Command-ing (by Pennekamp) and 4-y-o Melpomene: dam unraced: fairly useful handicapper: best effort when winning at Newmarket in August: stays 1¼m: acts on good to firm ground: usually held up. *E. A. L. Dunlop*

CENTREBOARD (USA) 3 gr. or ro.f. Mizzen Mast (USA) 121 – Corsini 88 (Machiavellian (USA) 123) [2007 72: 6g 5f 5m 5m p7g Oct 31] fair maiden at 2 yrs for R. Charlton: well held in 2007. *M. W. Easterby* —

CEOL EILE (IRE) 4 b.f. Distant Music (USA) 126 – Strina (IRE) (Indian Ridge 123) [2007 63: p9.5g 10.2f 10s⁶ 11.6m⁴ 11.6d⁵ p12.2g Aug 13] angular filly: modest maiden: stays 1¼m: acts on heavy going: in cheekpieces/blinkers last 3 starts. *D. Haydn Jones* **51**

CEREBUS 5 b.m. Wolfhound (USA) 126 – Bring On The Choir 87 (Chief Singer 131) [2007 69: f7g p6g² f6g* f6g⁶ p6g f5g³ f7g* p6g 7g f7g⁵ f6g⁵ p6g⁵ p6g* Nov 10] strong, close-coupled mare: fair handicapper: won at Southwell in February and March, and Wolverhampton in November: effective at 5f to 7f: acts on all-weather, firm and soft going: usually blinkered/tongue tied: sometimes slowly away, often races up with pace otherwise. *A. J. McCabe* **76**

CEREDIG 4 b.g. Lujain (USA) 119 – Anneli Rose 56 (Superlative 118) [2007 63: p5.1g² p5g² p5.1g⁵ p5g⁵ p5g⁶ 5g⁵ 5.1f⁶ f7g 6.1g⁵ 5.7m 6g² 7s p8g⁴ 6g 6.1s p7g* p8.6g p7g 7m p7m⁴ p8.6g² Nov 27] tall gelding: modest performer: left W. Muir after fifth outing: won selling handicap at Lingfield (left P. Hiatt) in June: can be headstrong, but seems to stay 8.6f: acts on polytrack and firm ground: tried blinkered/in cheekpieces: has been tongue tied: finds little, and best treated with caution. *Mrs L. J. Mongan* **66 §**

CEREMONIAL JADE (UAE) 4 b.g. Jade Robbery (USA) 121 – Talah 87 (Danehill (USA) 126) [2007 100: p8g² p7g 7m⁴ p7g² 7g 7g 7m² 6m³ p7g³ p6g* Nov 17] good-topped gelding: useful handicapper: better than ever when winning at Lingfield in November by neck from King's Caprice: effective at 6f to 1m: acts on polytrack and firm going: usually tongue tied: in cheekpieces last 2 starts. *M. Botti* **108**

CERIS STAR (IRE) 3 b.g. Cadeaux Genereux 131 – Midsummernitedream (GER) 43 (Thatching 131) [2007 –: 9.7s⁶ 10.2m p7.1g* p9.5g⁶ p7g* p7.1g Dec 1] rangy gelding: modest performer: won apprentice minor event at Wolverhampton in October and handicap at Kempton in November: stays 7f: acts on polytrack. *B. R. Millman* **61**

CERTAIN JUSTICE (USA) 9 gr.g. Lit de Justice (USA) 125 – Pure Misk 55 (Rainbow Quest (USA) 134) [2007 79: f7g⁵ p7g² f6g⁵ p7g⁴ f7g 6g² p7g 6m 7d 7d² Oct 18] rather leggy gelding: fairly useful handicapper: effective at 6f to 1m: acts on all-weather, soft and good to firm going: tried blinkered/in cheekpieces: held up. *Stef Liddiard* **80**

CERTAIN PROMISE (USA) 2 b.f. (Apr 14) El Prado (IRE) 119 – Shining Bright 98 (Rainbow Quest (USA) 134) [2007 7g Nov 3] good-topped filly: sister to smart 7f (at 2 yrs) and 1½m (Ribblesdale Stakes) winner Spanish Sun and 3-y-o Spanish Moon, and half-sister to 3 winners: dam French 1¼m winner: 11/2, needed experience when mid-field in 19-runner maiden at Newmarket: sure to improve, particularly at 1¼m/1½m. *Sir Michael Stoute* **61 p**

CERTIFIABLE 6 b.g. Deploy 131 – Gentle Irony 65 (Mazilier (USA) 107) [2007 p13g p8g p8g p8g⁵ p7g p11g p12g p10g Dec 28] unraced on Flat in 2005/6, just modest in 2007: left G. L. Moore after reappearance: effective at 7f/1m: acts on polytrack and good to soft ground: tried in cheekpieces. *Miss Z. C. Davison* **60**

CERULEAN ROSE 8 ch.m. Bluegrass Prince (IRE) 110 – Elegant Rose 72 (Noalto 120) [2007 71: 5.7g⁶ 6d 6f 6d 5m⁶ 7.1m 5.1m* 5d 5.7d⁵ 5.7g Oct 24] workmanlike mare: modest handicapper: won at Chepstow in September: effective at 5f/6f: acts on firm and soft going: tried blinkered/tongue tied at 3 yrs. *A. W. Carroll* **64**

CESARE 6 b.g. Machiavellian 123 – Tromond 94 (Lomond (USA) 128) [2007 116: 8m* 8m⁵ 8m* 8g² 8d⁴ 7d Oct 20] deep-girthed gelding: very smart performer: further progress in 2007, winning twice at Ascot, namely listed race in May and Sony Summer Mile (by 1¼ lengths from Royal Oath) in July: also ran well in Queen Anne Stakes at Royal Ascot (close fifth to Ramonti), Celebration Mile at Goodwood (1¼ lengths second to Echelon) and Queen Elizabeth II Stakes at Ascot (length fourth to Ramonti): favourite, surely amiss when last of 15 in Challenge Stakes at Newmarket final outing: stays 1m: acts on polytrack, soft and good to firm going: held up: normally consistent. *J. R. Fanshawe* **123**

CESC 3 b.c. Compton Place 125 – Mana Pools (IRE) 76 (Brief Truce (USA) 126) [2007 95: p7g p7g² 7m 7d 8m 7g⁶ 7d 8.1m p8m⁴ p7g Oct 24] well-made colt: useful performer: in-and-out form in 2007, though ran well when in frame, including when fourth to Kay Gee Be in handicap at Kempton: stays 1m: acts on polytrack and good to firm ground, probably unsuited by softer than good. *P. J. Makin* **96**

C'EST LA VIE 5 ch.m. Bering 136 – Action de Grace (USA) (Riverman (USA) 131) – [2007 10.1g Jul 23] modest maiden in 2005: tongue tied, well held only Flat outing since. *Miss J. E. Foster*

CETSHWAYO 5 ch.g. Pursuit of Love 124 – Induna (Grand Lodge (USA) 125) [2007 – 66: p10g Jan 6] big gelding: fair performer at 4 yrs: well beaten in seller only outing in 2007: said to have bled once in 2006: sold 800 gns in February. *J. M. P. Eustace*

CHA CHA CHA 3 b.f. Efisio 120 – Shall We Dance 83 (Rambo Dancer (CAN) 107) 82 [2007 6m* 5g³ 6d² 6g 7g⁶ 7.1g*⁷ p7.1g⁵ Dec 15] leggy, lengthy filly: second foal: sister to 5-y-o Mademoiselle: dam 1m winner: fairly useful performer: won maiden at Pontefract in April and handicap at Musselburgh in November: stays 7f: acts on good to firm and good to soft ground: has raced freely: sweated (below form) fourth outing. *K. A. Ryan*

CHAENOMELES (USA) 2 b. or br.f. (Mar 9) Fusaichi Pegasus (USA) 130 – Eliza 74 (USA) 118 (Mt Livermore (USA)) [2007 7g 8.2d⁵ p7g⁴ Oct 24] $100,000Y: rather leggy, lengthy filly: sister to useful Irish 2006 2-y-o 5f and 7.5f winner Country Song and half-sister to several winners in US, including 2000 2-y-o sprint winner Miss Doolittle (second in Grade 3 6f event, by Storm Cat): dam US Grade 1 8.5f winner (including Breeders' Cup Juvenile Fillies): fair maiden: progressive form, fourth to Malibu Girl at Lingfield: should be suited by 1m. *M. Johnston*

CHAIN OF GOLD 2 ch.c. (Jan 10) Bahamian Bounty 116 – Beading 82 (Polish 71 Precedent (USA) 131) [2007 5m⁴ Jun 4] 28,000Y: third foal: half-brother to fairly useful 7f winner Cindertrack (by Singspiel) and 3-y-o Satin Braid: dam, 1m winner, half-sister to useful miler Intrepidous: 5/4 favourite, showed promise when fourth to Philario in maiden at Carlisle (started slowly), only outing. *E. S. McMahon*

CHAIRMAN BOBBY 9 ch.g. Clantime 101 – Formidable Liz 66 (Formidable (USA) 54 d 125) [2007 66: 7m³ 7.1m⁵ 6m 5m 5g 6m 5m 6g⁶ Sep 3] smallish, sturdy gelding: modest at best nowadays: best form at 5f/6f: acts on all-weather, firm and good to soft going: often wears cheekpieces. *D. W. Barker*

CHALENTINA 4 b.f. Primo Valentino (IRE) 116 – Chantilly Myth 81 (Sri Pekan 63 (USA) 117) [2007 80, a63: p7.1g p7.1g⁴ p8g p7g³ 8.1g 7g³ 7m³ p7.1g⁴ 7.1m p7.1g⁵ p6m p7g³ Oct 17] lengthy filly: just modest nowadays: best form at 7f: acts on polytrack, firm and good to soft going: tried blinkered. *P. Howling*

CHALFORD 2 ch.g. (Feb 5) Compton Place 125 – Red Head And Dotty (Risk Me (FR) – 127) [2007 f6d f7d⁶ Dec 20] small, strong gelding: blinkered, tailed off in maidens at Southwell: unseated rider to post and withdrawn prior to intended debut. *J. Balding*

CHALICE WELCOME 4 b.g. Most Welcome 131 – Blue Peru (IRE) 48 (Perugino 49 (USA) 84) [2007 46: p8g⁵ p8g⁴ p10g⁴ 10.2f Apr 24] poor maiden: stays 1¼m: acts on polytrack: tried blinkered/visored. *C. F. Wall*

CHALLIS (IRE) 3 b.c. Barathea (IRE) 127 – Chalosse (Doyoun 124) [2007 69p: 85 p9.5g² p10g* 8g 12g⁶ a9g a11g² 11g³ Dec 30] fairly useful performer: won maiden at Lingfield in February cosily by short head, final start for J. Noseda: placed in minor events at Mijas and Dos Hermanas last 2 starts: stays 1½m: acts on polytrack/sand. *J. L. Eyre, Spain*

CHALLOW HILLS (USA) 2 ch.f. (Mar 20) Woodman (USA) 126 – Cascassi (USA) 62 91 (Nijinsky (CAN) 138) [2007 p7g⁵ 7g⁶ 10g Nov 3] $55,000Y: good-topped filly: half-sister to useful French 1999 2-y-o 1m winner Checkers Speech (by Arazi) and 1¼m winner Gentle Dame (by Kris): dam, 1¼m and 12.5f (in France) winner, half-sister to Oaks winner Diminuendo: modest form in maidens/minor event: will stay at least 1½m. *B. W. Hills*

CHAMPAGNE CRACKER 6 ch.m. Up And At 'em 109 – Kiveton Komet 71 (Pre- 68 d cocious 126) [2007 71: 5m⁵ 6.1m 5m 5d* 5m 5m 5d 5d 6g Aug 17] big, strong mare: fair handicapper: won at Newcastle in May: well below form after: best at 5f: acts on firm and good to soft going: has been early to post/very slowly away. *M. Dods*

CHAMPAGNE DANCER 2 ch.g. (Apr 21) Lomitas 129 – Rosewood Belle (USA) – 70 (Woodman (USA) 126) [2007 5.7g⁶ 7.1s⁶ 6m 10.2d Oct 1] lengthy gelding: no form: bred to stay 1½m. *D. J. S. ffrench Davis*

CHAMPAGNE MINDY 3 b.f. Superior Premium 122 – Oakwell Ace 57 (Clantime – 101) [2007 5s⁴ 6g p7.1g 5g Oct 30] first foal: dam 6f winner: little sign of ability. *Garry Moss*

CHAMPAGNE ROSSINI (IRE) 5 b.g. Rossini (USA) 118 – Alpencrocus (IRE) 32 (Waajib 121) [2007 41: f6g 7g Apr 24] workmanlike gelding: poor maiden: stays 1m: acts on fibresand and good to firm going: tried blinkered. *M. C. Chapman*

CHAMPAGNE SHADOW (IRE) 6 b.g. Kahyasi 130 – Moet (IRE) 72 (Mac's Imp **68 +**
(USA) 116) [2007 86: f16g³ p12.2g 9.9m⁵ 10.5m p12g* p12.2g* p12.2g* p16g* p16g⁴ **a84**
p12g⁵ p13.9g² p13.9g⁶ p16.5g⁴ Nov 19] fairly useful performer on all-weather, fair on
turf: won 4 times in June/July, namely claimers at Lingfield (left K. Ryan) and Wolverhampton (2) and handicap at Lingfield: effective at 1½m to 16.5f: acts on polytrack and
soft going, probably on good to firm: usually wears cheekpieces/blinkers: refused to race
on 4-y-o return. *Miss Tor Sturgis*

CHAMPAGNE SUE 3 ch.f. Foxhound (USA) 103 – Pigeon 84 (Casteddu 111) [2007 **–**
5m 6g⁵ 5m Sep 10] first foal: dam 5f/6f winner (latter at 2 yrs): well held in maidens.
D. W. Barker

CHAMPAIN SANDS (IRE) 8 b.g. Green Desert (USA) 127 – Grecian Bride (IRE) **75**
(Groom Dancer (USA) 128) [2007 74: 8f⁶ 8f⁴ p7.1g³ 8m 7.9d⁵ p8g 7.1m³ 8m* 8.1m⁴ 8m⁶
8g⁴ 8m 7.1m² 7g³ Nov 6] smallish gelding: fair handicapper: won at Thirsk in August:
best at 7f/1m: acts on all-weather, firm and good to soft going: tried visored/blinkered/
tongue tied (not since 2003): held up. *E. J. Alston*

CHAMPERY (USA) 3 b.g. Bahri (USA) 125 – Ice Ballet (IRE) 103 (Nureyev (USA) **106 +**
131) [2007 97: p8g² 8g³ 8m* 10g 10g 12g⁴ 10m Aug 18] good-topped, medium-sized
gelding: smart performer: won listed race at Rome (beat Baylani de S'ena 4 lengths,
making all) in May: seemed to run well when length fourth to Yellowstone in muddling
Gordon Stakes at Goodwood, but probably flattered: only seventh to Literato in Prix
Guillaume d'Ornano at Deauville final start: gelded after: stays 1½m: raced only on
polytrack and good ground or firmer: acted as pacemaker in Eclipse Stakes at Sandown
fifth outing. *M. Johnston*

CHAMPFLEURIE 3 b.f. Efisio 120 – Blossom (Warning 136) [2007 8g* 8.1s² 8v* **91**
7m Jul 11] lengthy filly: second foal: sister to 2004 2-y-o 6f winner (stays 11f) Je Suis
Belle: dam unraced out of half-sister to very smart 1½m performer Apache: won maiden
at Newmarket in May and handicap at Newcastle (beat Wheels In Motion 4 lengths) in
June: drawn on unfavoured side and not knocked about when mid-field in handicap won
by Tarteel at Newmarket final outing: stayed 1m: acted on heavy going, probably on good
to firm: dead. *G. A. Swinbank*

CHAMPION LION (IRE) 8 b.g. Sadler's Wells (USA) 132 – Honey Bun 51 (Unfu- **–**
wain (USA) 131) [2007 60: 12.4d p12.2g Nov 1] strong, close-coupled gelding: fluent
mover: modest performer at 7 yrs: well held in 2007: barely stays 1¾m: acts on all-
weather, heavy and good to firm going: sometimes slowly away. *R. Allan*

CHAMPIONSHIP POINT (IRE) 4 b.c. Lomitas 129 – Flying Squaw 102 (Be My **118**
Chief (USA) 122) [2007 112: 10g⁶ 10g 9.8g² 10m³ 9.9g 10d* 9.9g* 10v⁴ 10m⁶ 10s 10d
Oct 20] quite good-topped colt: smart performer: won listed Wolferton Handicap at Royal

Bank of Scotland Investment Services Stakes, Goodwood—a good weight-carrying performance by Championship Point, who edges ahead of Lake Poet (left), Peruvian Prince (rail) and Snoqualmie Boy (right)

Mr John Livock's "Championship Point"

Ascot (by length from Heaven Sent) in June and quite valuable handicap at Goodwood (under 9-10, by ¾ length from Lake Poet) in July, coming with strong run from rear both times: below form in pattern/listed races after: should stay 1½m (found 1¾m too far): possibly unsuited by soft/heavy going, acts on any other: seemed to hang fire third start: best held up. *M. R. Channon*

CHAMPION'S WAY (IRE) 5 b.g. Namid 128 – Savage (IRE) 98 (Polish Patriot (USA) 128) [2007 52: p7g² f7g⁴ p5g⁴ p6g Nov 23] fair maiden: left B. R. Millman after second start: best effort at 5f: acts on all-weather. *Daniel William O'Sullivan, Ireland*   **66**

CHAMPS ELYSEES 4 b.c. Danehill (USA) 126 – Hasili (IRE) (Kahyasi 130) [2007 110: 12g* 12g⁵ 14g² 12.5d³ 12m² 12g² Dec 8] brother to Banks Hill, Cacique, Dansili and Intercontinental and closely related to Heat Haze (by Green Desert), all at least very smart performers at 1m and/or 1¼m: dam useful French 2-y-o 5f to 8.5f winner: smart performer: improved in 2007, winning Prix d'Hedouville at Longchamp in May by 1½ lengths from Mister Conway: good efforts last 4 starts, nose second to Bussoni in Prix Maurice de Nieuil at Longchamp, 3 lengths third to Irish Wells in Grand Prix de Deauville, 1¾ lengths second to Schiaparelli in Gran Premio del Jockey Club at Milan and, having left A. Fabre in France, 2¾ lengths second to Sunriver in Hollywood Turf Cup (plenty to do): stays 1¾m: acts on good to firm and good to soft ground. *R. J. Frankel, USA*   **117**

CHAMPUS (GER) 3 ch.c. Banyumanik (IRE) 119 – Cordona (GER) (Lagunas) [2007 9d* 11g⁴ 10g* 10m⁵ 8d* Oct 3] strong, rangy colt: fourth foal: half-brother to 3 winners in Germany, including 1¼m/1½m winner Casanova (by Broadway Flyer): dam German 7f (at 2 yrs) and 11f winner: fairly useful performer: won minor events at Le Croise-Laroche in May, Duindigt in July and Munich (quite valuable race by length from Wonderful Day) in October: respectable fifth to Many Volumes in similar event at Newmarket penultimate start, hanging left after racing prominently: stays 1¼m: raced mainly on good/good to soft ground: sold 60,000 gns. *C. von der Recke, Germany*   **91**

CHANCELLOR (IRE) 9 ch.h. Halling (USA) 133 – Isticanna (USA) 96 (Far North – §
(CAN) 120) [2007 103§: p10g 10.3d 10g Jul 9] strong, lengthy horse: one-time smart but
untrustworthy performer: no form in 2007: tried in cheekpieces: usually tongue tied: sold
8,000 gns in November. *D. K. Ivory*

CHANGE ALLEY (USA) 2 b.c. (Feb 9) Elusive Quality (USA) – Fortune (IRE) 80 **66**
(Night Shift (USA)) [2007 6d p7g p6g² Oct 26] strong, good-bodied colt: second foal:
dam, Irish 6f winner, sister to smart French sprinter Dyhim Diamond and US Grade 1
2-y-o 8.5f winner Creaking Board: fair maiden: second at Wolverhampton, but again
looked awkward: should stay 7f: sold 16,000 gns, sent to UAE. *M. Johnston*

CHANGE COURSE 3 b.f. Sadler's Wells (USA) 132 – Orford Ness 107 (Selkirk **67**
(USA) 129) [2007 –p: 8.1m⁵ 10.3g³ Sep 29] big, good-topped filly: fair form in 3 maidens, travelling strongly long way when third to House Maiden at Chester: stayed 1¼m:
stud. *Sir Michael Stoute*

CHANGE TACK 2 gr.f. (Jan 20) Mizzen Mast (USA) 121 – Jibe (USA) 107 **74**
(Danzig (USA)) [2007 6m² p6g³ Sep 21] third foal: dam, 7f (at 2 yrs) and 1¼m winner,
sister to Ribblesdale winner Yashmak, out of outstanding broodmare Slightly Dangerous:
placed in maidens at Lingfield (second to Festival) and Wolverhampton 3 months apart:
will be suited by 1m+: sold 78,000 gns, sent to USA. *Mrs A. J. Perrett*

CHANGING SKIES (IRE) 2 b.f. (May 4) Sadler's Wells (USA) 132 – Magnificient **79 p**
Style (USA) 107 (Silver Hawk (USA) 123) [2007 8d³ Oct 11] lightly-made filly: seventh
foal: sister to smart 7f (at 2 yrs) to 1½m (Lancashire Oaks) winner Playful Act and 6-y-o
Percussionist, and half-sister to 3 winners, notably smart 1m (Sun Chariot Stakes) to
14.6f (Park Hill Stakes) winner Echoes In Eternity (by Spinning World) and 3-y-o Petara
Bay: dam won Musidora Stakes: 11/2, always prominent when third to Strategic Mission
in maiden at Newbury: will be suited by 1¼m/1½m: open to improvement. *B. J. Meehan*

CHANTACO (USA) 5 b.g. Bahri (USA) 125 – Dominant Dancer 97 (Primo Dominie **100**
121) [2007 103: 9.8g⁴ 10m 10.3m 10d 10d* 10d Oct 27] leggy, close-coupled gelding:
useful handicapper: won at Nottingham in October by 1½ lengths from Forroger: barely
stays 1½m: acts on polytrack, firm and soft going: sold 55,000 gns. *A. M. Balding*

CHANT DE GUERRE (USA) 3 b.f. War Chant (USA) 126 – Fatwa (IRE) 95 (Lahib **73**
(USA) 129) [2007 62: 7m⁶ p8.6g⁶ p8g³ p8g p12g² 10m* 12g 10m* 12m³ 10d² 11.6d³
11.9d Oct 18] close-coupled filly: fair performer: won seller at Lingfield (left H. Dunlop)
in July and handicap at Brighton in August: stays easy 1½m: acts on polytrack, good to
firm and good to soft going. *P. Mitchell*

CHANTEUSE DE RUE (IRE) 2 b.f. (May 1) Street Cry (IRE) 130 – Mt Morna –
(USA) (Mt Livermore (USA)) [2007 6d 7.1g⁵ 8s⁶ Oct 26] 29,000F, €25,000Y: half-sister
to several winners, including minor US sprint winner Formal Event (by Formal Gold):
dam, US 1m/8.5f winner, half-sister to Kentucky Derby runner-up Casual Lies: well held
in maidens. *M. Johnston*

CHANTILLY BEAUTY (FR) 5 b.m. Josr Algarhoud (IRE) 118 – Lysabelle (FR) –
(Lesotho (USA) 118) [2007 103: 7g⁶ May 12] big mare: useful performer at best: well
below form in Chartwell Fillies' Stakes at Lingfield only outing in 2007 (good second in
same race year before): best at 7f/1m: acts on firm going: blinkered: tried in cheekpieces/
tongue tie: suspect attitude. *Rupert Pritchard-Gordon, France*

CHANTILLY TIFFANY 3 ch.f. Pivotal 124 – Gaily Royal (IRE) (Royal Academy **95**
(USA) 130) [2007 8m* 8m⁴ 8g* 8m 8.1g⁶ 7m⁶ 8.1m 7m 8.3g⁴ Oct 16] lengthy filly: fifth
foal: half-sister to untrustworthy 2m winner Turner (by El Prado): dam, Japanese 9f/1¼m
winner, half-sister to smart French stayer New Frontier: useful performer: successful at
Newmarket in newcomers event in April and minor event (beat Go On Be A Tiger by 1¼
lengths) in May: creditable efforts most outings after, including in listed races: should be
as effective at 7f as 1m: acts on good to firm ground: tried blinkered: said to have finished
distressed penultimate start: carried head high final outing. *E. A. L. Dunlop*

CHAPELIZOD (IRE) 4 b.g. Raphane (USA) 102 – Fulminus Instar (IRE) (Classic **68**
Secret (USA) 91) [2007 53: 7m* 7g² 6g* 6s 7d⁶ 6.3d³ 7.1m⁴ 6s Oct 22] good-topped
gelding: fair handicapper: won at Roscommon and Naas in June: creditable fourth at
Musselburgh penultimate outing: effective at 6f/7f: acts on polytrack and any turf going:
in blinkers/cheekpieces last 4 starts: usually up with pace. *T. G. McCourt, Ireland*

CHAPTER (IRE) 5 ch.g. Sinndar (IRE) 134 – Web of Intrigue 66 (Machiavellian **57**
(USA) 123) [2007 74d: 8.1m⁴ 9.9m 10g p10g⁶ 10m p10g 12.6m 10.9g² 12.4d Oct 16]
rather leggy gelding: just modest handicapper nowadays: stays 1¼m: acts on firm going:
wears blinkers/cheekpieces: often slowly away. *Mrs A. L. M. King*

CHARANNE 4 b.f. Diktat 126 – Mystique (Mystiko (USA) 124) [2007 –: 7g Apr 3] no – form in maidens: tried blinkered. *J. M. Bradley*

CHARIOTS OF FIRE (IRE) 3 b.c. Galileo (IRE) 134 – Tadkiyra (IRE) (Darshaan **109** 133) [2007 8.7g* 10g⁴ 7m⁶ 7d* 7m Jun 20] €950,000Y: big, good-bodied, attractive colt: eighth foal: closely related to smart 2004 2-y-o 5f/6f winner Damson (by Entrepreneur) and useful 2002 2-y-o 7f winner Geminiani (stayed 1¼m, by King of Kings) and half-brother to fairly useful 1¼m winner Motorway (by Night Shift): dam French 1¼m winner: useful performer: won maiden at Cork in April and minor event at Naas (beat She's Our Mark by ½ length) in June: on edge (missed pre-parade), well below form in Jersey Stakes at Royal Ascot final outing, bumped leaving stall: best effort at 7f on good to soft going: tongue tied last 3 starts: sent to Hong Kong. *D. Wachman, Ireland*

CHARLES DARWIN (IRE) 4 ch.g. Tagula (IRE) 116 – Seymour (IRE) 78 (Eagle **91** Eyed (USA) 111) [2007 95: 5.1g⁵ 6m 6s 6d⁴ 6m 6s 6m Sep 13] well-made gelding: fairly useful performer: effective at stiff 5f to 7f: acts on polytrack, firm and soft going: has been gelded: inconsistent. *M. Blanshard*

CHARLES PARNELL (IRE) 4 b.g. Elnadim (USA) 128 – Titania (Fairy King **83** (USA)) [2007 83: 5.1m 6m⁵ 6m 5.9m 6g 6m⁴ 7.1g⁵ 6g⁴ 6d* 6d* 6m 6s⁴ 6m⁴ 6g⁴ 5d* 5d³ 6v³ Nov 3] leggy gelding: fairly useful handicapper: won at Ayr and Catterick in July and Ayr in September: effective at 5f/6f: acts on polytrack and any turf going: tried in headgear (very slowly away twice): looked temperamental in first half of 2007. *M. Dods*

CHARLESTON 6 ch.g. Pursuit of Love 124 – Discomatic (USA) (Roberto (USA) 131) – [2007 p16g Dec 4] sturdy gelding: fair maiden at 3 yrs: lightly raced and little Flat form since: tried in blinkers. *R. Rowe*

CHARLEVOIX (IRE) 2 b.f. (Mar 7) King Charlemagne (USA) 120 – Cayman Sound **53** 72 (Turtle Island (IRE) 123) [2007 5g p6g⁶ 8d Oct 23] second foal: dam 1½m winner: modest maiden: should be suited by 1m+. *C. F. Wall*

CHARLEY FOX 3 ch.g. Lahib (USA) 129 – Bumpse A Daisy (Lord Bud 121) [2007 – p7g 9m May 22] well held in maidens at Kempton and Lingfield. *D. C. O'Brien*

CHARLIE BEAR 6 ch.h. Bahamian Bounty 116 – Abi 84 (Chief's Crown (USA)) **59** [2007 66: p8g⁴ 8.1m⁵ 7.5m² 7m 9g 8.3g p8g Sep 3] tall horse: modest handicapper: effective at 6f to 1m: acts on polytrack, firm and good to soft going: tried in cheekpieces. *Miss Z. C. Davison*

CHARLIE BE (IRE) 2 ch.g. (Feb 4) King Charlemagne (USA) 120 – Miriana (IRE) – (Bluebird (USA) 125) [2007 p5g⁶ 5d 6g 8f p7g Oct 23] no form. *Mrs P. N. Dutfield*

CHARLIE COOL 4 ch.c. Rainbow Quest (USA) 134 – Tigwa 68 (Cadeaux Genereux **113** 131) [2007 110: 9g³ 10g* 10g⁴ p10g³ 9m 9.9g⁴ 8.2m* 10d³ 8m 8g⁶ 10m⁴ Sep 16] lengthy, good-topped colt: smart performer: won handicap at Nad Al Sheba in February and minor event at Nottingham (beat Shumookh 2 lengths) in June: good third to Championship Point in listed handicap at Royal Ascot next time: respectable efforts at best after: effective at 1m/1¼m: acts on polytrack, good to firm and good to soft going: visored last 5 starts: held up: joined D. Selvaratnam in UAE. *W. J. Haggas*

CHARLIE DELTA 4 ch.g. Pennekamp (USA) 130 – Papita (IRE) 77 (Law Society **78** (USA) 130) [2007 88: f6g* p6g⁵ p6g f5g p6g p6g 6m* f7g² p6g² 6g* 7g* 7.6g 6f 6g p7.1m⁶ 7f p6g Oct 5] close-coupled gelding: just fair nowadays: won claimers at Southwell (left D. Carroll) in January, Yarmouth in April and May and Salisbury (hung right, left J. Boyle) in June: below form after: best at 6f/7f: acts on all-weather, heavy and good to firm going: wears headgear: usually held up. *J. M. Bradley*

CHARLIE FARNSBARNS (IRE) 3 b.c. Cape Cross (IRE) 129 – Lafleur (IRE) 75 **102** (Grand Lodge (USA) 125) [2007 115: 8.1d² May 29] good-topped colt: 5/2-on, just useful form when neck second of 4 to Massive in tactical listed event at Sandown only 3-y-o start: likely to stay 1¼m: acts on soft and good to firm going: tends to hang right: ran poorly only try in blinkers. *B. J. Meehan*

CHARLIE GREEN (IRE) 2 b.g. (May 5) Traditionally (USA) 117 – Saninka (IRE) – 82 (Doyoun 124) [2007 5m 5.1f 5m Jul 20] lengthy gelding: well held in maidens: raced at 5f, bred for much further (dam 12.5f winner): tried in visor/tongue tie. *Paul Green*

CHARLIE OXO 2 br.g. (Jun 4) Puissance 110 – Aegean Mist 63 (Prince Sabo 123) – [2007 5g 6d 5.1d Oct 10] workmanlike gelding: last in maidens. *B. P. J. Baugh*

CHARLIES GIRL (IRE) 3 ch.f. Trans Island 119 – Indian Charm (IRE) 70 (Indian – Ridge 123) [2007 –: f6g p8.6g p8.6g Mar 14] little form: left M. Attwater after reappearance: tried in cheekpieces last 2 outings. *K. J. Burke*

John Smith's Cup (Handicap), York—Richard Fahey saddles five of the runners and is rewarded with a 1,2 as Charlie Tokyo (blinkers) and Flying Clarets finish clear of Collateral Damage (right) and Greek Well in a race run over a shortened trip due to waterlogging in the back straight

CHARLIE TIPPLE 3 b.g. Diktat 126 – Swing of The Tide 75 (Sri Pekan (USA) 117) [2007 77p: 7.5m 7m 6d⁴ 6.1v* 6v⁴ 6f² 6g⁵ 7m⁴ 8.5d⁵ 7.1g² Nov 8] big, good-topped gelding: fairly useful handicapper: won at Nottingham in July: best effort final start: stays 8.5f: acts on any going: has carried head awkwardly: consistent. *T. D. Easterby* **83**

CHARLIE TOKYO (IRE) 4 b.g. Trans Island 119 – Ellistown Lady (IRE) (Red Sunset 120) [2007 92: p11g 10g* 10.1g² 10.3m⁴ 8.9s* 10.4s⁶ 10s 10.4d⁵ Oct 12] good-bodied gelding: good walker: useful performer: further improvement in 2007, winning handicaps at Pontefract in April and York (John Smith's Cup, beat stable-companion Flying Clarets by ½ length) in July: good 5¼ lengths sixth of 8 to Stage Gift in York Stakes at York next time: effective at 9f to 1½m: unraced on firm ground, acts on any other turf: blinkered/visored nowadays: held up: quirky but reliable. *R. A. Fahey* **108**

CHARLOTTEBUTTERFLY 7 b.m. Millkom 124 – Tee Gee Jay 63 (Northern Tempest (USA) 120) [2007 53: p7g* p6g p7g p8g p7.1g 8g 7f⁶ 7.6s⁵ p8g* p8.6g² p10g² p8m⁶ p9.5g p8.6g* p10g³ p8.6d⁶ Dec 27] good-topped mare: fair on all-weather, modest on turf: won minor events at Kempton in January and Lingfield in September, and amateur handicap at Wolverhampton in November: stays easy 1¼m: acts on all-weather and firm going: tried visored. *P. J. McBride* **52**
a65

CHARLOTTE GREY 3 gr.f. Wizard King 122 – Great Intent (Aragon 118) [2007 64: p7.1g⁴ p6g⁴ p5.1g² p6g 6m p5.1g* 5g⁶ p6g⁴ p5.1g p5.1g² p6g⁶ 5d³ p5.1g⁶ p5.1g⁴ p6g p5g p5m f6d⁵ p6g Dec 30] tall, leggy filly: fair handicapper: won at Wolverhampton in April: effective at 5f to 7f: acts on all-weather and good to soft ground. *C. N. Allen* **69**

CHARLOTTE VALE 6 ch.m. Pivotal 124 – Drying Grass Moon 66 (Be My Chief (USA) 122) [2007 84d: 13.8m² 10m⁶ 12g⁴ 12d* 13d* 13d² 12s⁶ Jul 20] leggy, plain mare: fairly useful handicapper: won at Thirsk and Hamilton (ladies) in June: stays 13.8f: acts on firm and soft going: sometimes hangs left. *Micky Hammond* **84**

CHARLOTTI CARLOTTI (IRE) 2 b.f. (Feb 10) Celtic Swing 138 – Kunucu (IRE) 94 (Bluebird (USA) 125) [2007 5m² 5g⁶ 5g* 6d⁴ 6m⁶ 5d⁵ 7m 6.1d p5.1g p6g Nov 14] €30,000Y: angular filly: half-sister to several winning sprinters, including 7-y-o Raccoon and 3-y-o Bazroy: dam 5f winner, including at 2 yrs: fairly useful performer: won maiden at Ayr in June: lost her way (left T. D. Barron after seventh start): probably best at 5f: tried in cheekpieces. *D. W. Chapman* **80 d**

CHARMATIC (IRE) 6 br.m. Charnwood Forest (IRE) 125 – Instamatic 97 (Night Shift (USA)) [2007 p10g* 13.1m⁵ 11.6m³ 11s² Jun 26] strong, lengthy mare: fairly useful handicapper: missed 2006: won at Kempton in April: good placed efforts last 2 starts: stays 12.6f: acts on polytrack and any turf going: tongue tied once at 2 yrs. *Andrew Turnell* **80**

CHARMEL'S LAD 2 ch.g. (Feb 4) Compton Place 125 – Fittonia (FR) 66 (Ashkalani (IRE) 128) [2007 7d⁵ p7g 7d⁶ Oct 16] 21,000F, 30,000Y: lengthy, useful-looking gelding: first foal: dam, 1¼m winner, out of useful French performer up to 1½m Fly For Fame: fair form: better than bare result in maidens (tongue tied final start), not knocked about: gelded after: likely to stay 1m: sort to do better in handicaps at 3 yrs. *W. R. Swinburn* **70 p**

199

CHARMING BALLET (IRE) 4 b.g. Imperial Ballet (IRE) 110 – Some Merit **64**
(Midyan (USA) 124) [2007 5m p6g 6g 6g⁴ 6m* 5g p7g 6g p5.1m 6d 6d Oct 23] strong,
lengthy gelding: has a round action: modest handicapper: unraced in 2006 (reportedly
had flake of bone removed after final 2-y-o outing): won at Lingfield in June: effective at
5f/6f: acts on polytrack and firm ground: sometimes in cheekpieces/blinkers: has given
trouble at stall. *N. P. Littmoden*

CHARMING TALE (USA) 2 b.f. (Mar 11) Kingmambo (USA) 125 – Crystal Cross- **56 p**
ing (IRE) 99 (Royal Academy (USA) 130) [2007 7g Nov 3] strong filly: sixth foal: sister
to high-class 7f (at 2 yrs) to 14.6f (St Leger) winner Rule of Law and half-sister to 3-y-o
Cast In Gold: dam, 2-y-o 6f winner, sister to smart performer up to 8.5f Circle of Gold:
16/1, very green towards rear in maiden at Newmarket: will do better. *B. J. Meehan*

CHARNWOOD STREET (IRE) 8 b.g. Charnwood Forest (IRE) 125 – La Vigie **48**
(King of Clubs 124) [2007 p16g⁶ p13.9g p16.5g Apr 24] leggy gelding: poor performer:
stays easy 2m: raced on all-weather nowadays: usually wears headgear. *D. Shaw*

CHART EXPRESS 3 b.g. Robellino (USA) 127 – Emerald Angel (IRE) (In The Wings
128) [2007 –: p6g 10d Jul 17] strong, workmanlike gelding: no form. *J. R. Best*

CHARTIST 2 ch.c. (May 10) Choisir (AUS) 126 – Sareb (FR) (Indian Ridge 123) [2007 **86 p**
6d 5.1g* Oct 31] 31,000Y: rangy colt: has scope: third foal: half-brother to 3-y-o Black
Moma: dam, ran once, out of useful sprinter Prends Ca: better for debut, won maiden at
Nottingham by 1½ lengths from Incomparable, impressing with speed making all: will
prove best at 5f: useful prospect. *R. Hannon*

CHART OAK 4 b.g. Robellino (USA) 127 – Emerald Angel (IRE) (In The Wings 128) **62**
[2007 62: p9.5g⁴ p12.2g⁴ f14g f7g f12g³ p9.5g Jun 11] modest maiden: probably stays
easy 1½m: acts on polytrack, unraced on turf. *P. Howling*

CHASING MEMORIES (IRE) 3 b.f. Pursuit of Love 124 – Resemblance (State **64**
Diplomacy (USA)) [2007 67: 8m³ 8.5g⁴ 9.2g⁶ 8.5s³ 8.5s* 8m 8g⁵ 9.1s⁴ 10g p9.5g p12.2g⁵
Dec 22] sturdy filly: modest handicapper: won at Beverley (hung markedly left) in July:
left B. Smart after ninth outing: stays 8.5f: acts on all-weather, soft and good to firm
going: blinkered (ran creditably) once at 2 yrs. *W. K. Goldsworthy*

CHASTITY (IRE) 3 b.f. Dilshaan 119 – Fanny Bay (IRE) 76 (Key of Luck (USA) **–**
126) [2007 –: f7g Jan 11] well held in minor event and seller. *N. Tinkler*

CHATEAU (IRE) 5 ch.g. Grand Lodge (USA) 125 – Miniver (IRE) (Mujtahid (USA) **48**
118) [2007 69: 7m⁵ 7.9m⁵ 10d⁴ p8.6g 12m 10f⁵ Aug 12] modest performer at 4 yrs: just
poor in 2007: tried 1m: tried in cheekpieces: tongue tied. *M. E. Sowersby*

CHATEAU NICOL 8 b.g. Distant Relative 128 – Glensara (Petoski 135) [2007 87d: **–**
6d p7g Aug 27] well-made gelding: fairly useful handicapper at best: regressing and no
form in 2007: usually visored/blinkered. *B. G. Powell*

CHATHAM ISLANDS (USA) 2 b.f. (Feb 7) Elusive Quality (USA) – Zelanda (IRE) **77**
108 (Night Shift (USA)) [2007 5m⁵ p6g⁴ 6m* 6g² 6g⁵ Sep 12] good-topped filly: fifth
foal: closely related to useful 2003 2-y-o 5f/6f winner Pearl Grey and 2005 2-y-o 5f
winner Chaski (both by Gone West), and half-sister to fairly useful 2002 2-y-o 6f winner
Silver Seeker (by Seeking The Gold): dam, 5f/6f (including at 2 yrs) winner, out of smart
Irish St Leger third Zafadola: fair performer: won maiden at Haydock in August: good
second to Harlech Castle in nursery at Newbury next time: should be as good as 5f as 6f:
acts on polytrack and good to firm going. *M. Johnston*

CHATILA (USA) 4 b.f. Red Ransom (USA) – Silvester Lady 108 (Pivotal 124) [2007 **92**
–: 8m⁵ 9.9g 10.1g p8m Nov 1] quite attractive filly: fairly useful performer, lightly raced:
missed most of 2006 with back problem: best effort in 2007 when creditable ninth to
Samira Gold in listed event at Yarmouth penultimate start, crowded most of straight: stays
1¼m: raced on polytrack and good/good to firm ground. *J. H. M. Gosden*

CHATSHOW (USA) 6 br.g. Distant View (USA) 126 – Galanty Show 76 (Danehill **75**
(USA) 126) [2007 75: 5.1f⁵ 5m² 6m² 5.7m⁶ 5.7g² 5.3f² 5.7d⁵ 6d 6d⁶ 6f⁶ p6g⁴ p6g⁶
6g⁴ p6g² p6g² p6g⁴ Nov 23] leggy gelding: fair handicapper: effective at 5f/6f: acts on
all-weather, firm and soft going: tried visored/tongue tied: held up: tough and reliable.
A. W. Carroll

CHATTAN CLAN 3 ch.g. Kyllachy 129 – Shona (USA) 60 (Lyphard (USA) 132) **81**
[2007 p5g⁵ p6g⁴ p7g* 8.3m p8g p6g² p7.1g p6g⁶ a8g* a8g* a6.8d⁵ Dec 16] 10,500Y,
25,000: fifth foal: half-brother to a winner in Italy by Tagula: dam lightly-raced
sister to useful 7f/1m winner Tregaron: fairly useful performer: won maiden at Lingfield
in April and (after leaving R. Kvisla) minor events at Taby in November and December:

stays 1m: acts on dirt/polytrack, below form only start on turf: tongue tied. *Yvonne Durant, Sweden*

CHEAP N CHIC 4 ch.f. Primo Valentino (IRE) 116 – Amber Mill 96 (Doulab (USA) –
115) [2007 79: p7g Mar 17] lengthy filly: fair performer at 3 yrs: well held sole start in
2007: stays 6.5f: raced only on polytrack and good or firmer going: tried in blinkers/
cheekpieces. *K. A. Ryan*

CHEAP STREET 3 ch.c. Compton Place 125 – Anneliina 80 (Cadeaux Genereux 131) 82
[2007 90: 6m 6g⁵ 7d 9d 7.1g 7s⁶ 6d Sep 26] smallish, compact colt: fairly useful
handicapper: best form at 6f: acts on firm and good to soft ground: blinkered last 3 starts.
J. G. Portman

CHECK UP (IRE) 6 b.g. Frimaire – Melons Lady (IRE) (The Noble Player (USA) 56
126) [2007 8.1m³ Aug 7] modest and wayward hurdler: third to Croft in seller at Chepstow on Flat debut (joined Andrew Leyshon £6,000). *B. W. Duke*

CHEEKY JACK (USA) 3 b.c. A P Indy (USA) 131 – Poetically (CAN) (Silver 66
Deputy (CAN)) [2007 8m f8g⁶ p9.5g a8.5g⁵ Nov 1] quite good-topped colt: fair maiden:
best effort when eighth to Chantilly Tiffany in newcomers event at Newmarket: sold from
B. Meehan 9,000 gns after third start. *M. Hofer, Germany*

CHEERY CAT (USA) 3 b. or br.g. Catienus (USA) 115 – Olinka (USA) (Wolfhound 69
(USA) 126) [2007 63: f8g⁶ 8g 7g² 6d⁸ 7s³ 6g⁴ 6d⁴ 7m* 7m³ 7g 7.5d⁶ Sep 25] rather leggy,
close-coupled gelding: fair handicapper: won at Pontefract in June and Redcar in August:
effective at 6f/7f: acts on polytrack, good to firm and good to soft going: wears cheekpieces nowadays: races prominently: sold 12,500 gns. *D. W. Barker*

CHELSEA BALLAD (USA) 3 b.f. Street Cry (IRE) 130 – Chelsey Dancer (USA) 52
(Affirmed (USA)) [2007 p10g Jun 9] $285,000F, $450,000Y: half-sister to several
winners in USA, notably Grade 1 1¼m winner Chelsey Flower (by His Majesty): dam
ran twice in USA: 8/1, eighth to Come April in maiden at Lingfield, well placed before
fading, not given hard time: stud in USA. *J. H. M. Gosden*

CHELSEA GIRL 2 b.f. (Mar 26) Kyllachy 129 – Ghassanah 73 (Pas de Seul 133) 50
[2007 5d May 29] 24,000Y: tall, quite attractive filly: half-sister to several winners,
including 5f/6f winner (including at 2 yrs) Alzianah (by Alzao) and 6f and (at 2 yrs) 7f
winner Return of Amin (by Salse), both useful: dam 7f winner: 4/1, looked fit but found
little when tenth of 11 in maiden at Sandown. *C. G. Cox*

CHEMISE (IRE) 2 b.f. (Feb 7) Chevalier (IRE) 115 – Louvolite (IRE) 81 (Fayruz 116) 47
[2007 5.7f 5.1m⁶ 5.1d p6g⁴ 5f p7g⁶ p6m⁴ p6d⁶ Dec 17] 12,000 2-y-o: first foal:
dam, 2-y-o 5f winner, half-sister to 3-y-o Dimenticata: poor maiden: effective at 5f/6f.
R. J. Hodges

CHEONMADO (USA) 3 ch.g. Miswaki (USA) 124 – Academie Royale (IRE) 62 67 ?
(Royal Academy (USA) 130) [2007 10f p8g 9.7m⁴ May 3] fair form at best in maidens:
has carried head awkwardly/started slowly: gelded after final start. *Simon Earle*

CHEQUE 2 b.g. (Mar 3) Mujahid (USA) 125 – Watheeqah (USA) 60 (Topsider (USA)) 75
[2007 7m⁵ 7.1m⁴ p8g* 9m⁵ Sep 21] 9,000F, 4,000Y: big, strong gelding: seventh foal:
half-brother to 5-y-o Kenmore and fairly useful 9.7f to 2m winner Nounou (by Starborough): dam, 5f winner, closely related to useful miler Abs: fair form: won maiden at
Lingfield in September: dropped away tamely in nursery final start: stays 1m: sold 20,000
gns. *J. A. Osborne*

CHERIE'S DREAM 3 b.f. Silver Wizard (USA) 117 – Last Dream (IRE) 80 (Alzao 72
(USA) 117) [2007 57p: p7g* 8m³ p8g⁶ Jul 18] good-bodied filly: fair performer, lightly
raced: won maiden at Kempton in May: better effort in handicaps after when good third
at Goodwood: free-going sort, stays 1m: sent to USA. *A. M. Balding*

CHERISHED SONG 2 b.f. (Mar 21) Mark of Esteem (IRE) 137 – Waseyla (IRE) 71 56
(Sri Pekan (USA) 117) [2007 5m 5m⁴ p8g Oct 4] €21,000Y: second foal: dam 1¼m
winner: modest form in maidens: probably stays 1m: sold 2,200 gns. *N. A. Callaghan*

CHEROKEE STAR 2 br.g. (May 12) Primo Valentino (IRE) 116 – Me Cherokee 48 –
(Persian Bold 123) [2007 p8.6g Sep 21] 150/1, well beaten in maiden at Wolverhampton.
C. C. Bealby

CHERRI FOSFATE 3 b.g. Mujahid (USA) 125 – Compradore 82 (Mujtahid (USA) 78
118) [2007 80d: p6g* f6g³ p6g f7g⁴ f6g² p7g² p7g p8.6g* p7.1g³ p10g p7.1g 8.2s⁶ 7s 7d
p8.6g 7.5m⁵ 7.1m p7.1g p8.6g⁶ 10s* 10d⁴ Oct 1] close-coupled gelding: fair performer
nowadays: won claimer at Wolverhampton (left W. Turner) in January, handicap there in

March and seller at Redcar in September: stays 1¼m: acts on all-weather and soft going: usually wears headgear, though not last 3 starts: sometimes slowly away. *D. Carroll*

CHERRY HINTON 3 b.f. Green Desert (USA) 127 – Urban Sea (USA) 126 (Miswaki **103** (USA) 124) [2007 8m³ 10g² 12d⁵ 8d 9v³ Jul 15] close-coupled, angular filly: has quick action: eighth foal: half-sister to several at least smart winners, notably Derby winner Galileo and very smart 1¼m/1½m winner Black Sam Bellamy (both by Sadler's Wells): dam, 1m (at 2 yrs) to 1½m (Prix de l'Arc de Triomphe) winner, closely related to 2000 Guineas winner King's Best: useful performer: best efforts when 2½ lengths second to Four Sins in Blue Wind Stakes at Naas and 11 lengths fifth to Light Shift in Oaks at Epsom: below form in Coronation Stakes at Royal Ascot before respectable third to Alexander Tango in listed event at the Curragh: stayed 1½m: probably acted on heavy going: has worn crossed noseband: visits Montjeu. *A. P. O'Brien, Ireland*

CHERRY MIX (FR) 6 gr.h. Linamix (FR) 127 – Cherry Moon (USA) (Quiet Ameri- **113** can (USA)) [2007 123: 10m⁴ 20g 10d⁴ Nov 4] small, quite attractive horse: very smart performer at best: successful in 2006 in Rheinland-Pokal at Cologne and Premio Roma at Rome: just smart in 2007, best effort when fourth to Pressing in latest renewal of latter race: effective at 1¼m to 12.5f (raced freely and failed to stay 2½m in Gold Cup at Royal Ascot): acts on heavy and good to firm going, below form only start on dirt: usually tongue tied: heavily bandaged on forelegs at Ascot: stud in Russia. *Saeed bin Suroor*

CHESHIRE PRINCE 3 br.g. Desert Prince (IRE) 130 – Bundle Up (USA) (Miner's **81** Mark (USA) 120) [2007 67: 7m⁵ 12.6m 8.5g³ 10.3f² 9.1d⁵ 10.3m³ 10.1m* 10.3m* Aug 23] close-coupled gelding: fairly useful handicapper: won at Newcastle (apprentices) and Chester in August: stays 10.3f: acts on firm and good to soft going. *W. M. Brisbourne*

CHESHIRE ROSE 2 ch.f. (Feb 23) Bertolini (USA) 125 – Merch Rhyd-Y-Grug **71** (Sabrehill (USA) 120) [2007 5s* 5m 5.1g 6.1d 6s Oct 26] 5,000Y: angular filly: fourth foal: half-sister to 5-y-o Peopleton Brook and 1m winner Three Welshmen (by Muhtarram): dam no form: fair form when winning maiden at Ripon in July on debut: soon regressed: should prove best at 5f: acts on soft going. *T. D. Barron*

CHESTERTON (IRE) 2 b. or br.c. (Apr 6) Namid 128 – Beguine (USA) 77 (Green **71 p** Dancer (USA) 132) [2007 p7.1g⁵ Nov 20] fifth foal: half-brother to 3 winners, including useful Irish 1¼m winner Liss Ard (by In The Wings) and fairly useful Irish 2001 2-y-o 5f/ 7f winner Master Papa (by Key of Luck): dam, maiden, half-sister to Grand Lodge: 14/1, 4¾ lengths fifth to The Gatekeeper in maiden at Wolverhampton, not unduly knocked about: should improve. *John Joseph Murphy, Ireland*

CHEVELEY FLYER 4 ch.g. Forzando 122 – Cavern Breeze (Lion Cavern (USA) **59** 117) [2007 59d: 10d* 10.1m Aug 9] modest performer on Flat (fair hurdler): won handicap at Brighton in July: should stay 1½m: acts on polytrack and heavy going: tried visored. *J. Pearce*

CHEVIOT RED 2 b.f. (Apr 15) Red Ransom (USA) – Cheviot Hills (USA) (Gulch **59** (USA)) [2007 6d 7g Sep 6] 34,000Y: sturdy filly: fourth foal: closely related to fairly useful 7f winner Enrapture (by Lear Fan): dam, French 9f/1¼m winner, out of half-sister to Derby winner Henbit: better effort in maidens when seventh of 18 to Joffe's Run at Salisbury latter start: will stay 1m. *B. J. Meehan*

CHEYENNE STAR (IRE) 4 b.f. Mujahid (USA) 125 – Charita (IRE) 103 (Lycius **114** (USA) 124) [2007 106: 8v 7m* 8m* 8g² 8g* p8g* Nov 16] good-topped filly: third foal: half-sister to 11f and 2m winner Herne Bay (by Hernando): dam Irish 7f (at 2 yrs)/1m winner: smart performer: won handicap at Gowran and Ridgewood Pearl Stakes at the Curragh (beat Heaven Sent by ¾ length) in May, and listed events at Naas in October and Dundalk (comfortably, by length from Bush Maiden) in November: effective at 7f/1m: acts on polytrack, firm and soft ground: game and consistent. *Ms F. M. Crowley, Ireland*

CHIA (IRE) 4 ch.f. Ashkalani (IRE) 128 – Motley (Rainbow Quest (USA) 134) [2007 **71** 72: p8g² p9.5g* p8.6g⁶ p8.6g² 11.7f³ p12.2g⁴ 10m² p12.2g⁴ p12g⁶ p9.5g³ p9.5g² p9.5g² **a74** p8g⁶ p9.5g² Dec 26] leggy filly: fair handicapper: won at Wolverhampton in January: effective at 8.6f to easy 1½m: acts on all-weather and firm ground: tried visored/in cheekpieces: has raced freely: consistent. *D. Haydn Jones*

CHICA GUAPA (IRE) 2 b.f. (Feb 21) Carrowkeel (IRE) 106 – Money Spinner (USA) **–** 61 (Teenoso (USA) 135) [2007 6m 6m 6m p8.6g p7.1g Nov 8] €9,000Y: big, leggy filly: eighth foal: closely related to fairly useful Italian 5f (at 2 yrs) to 9f winner Windy Day (by Waajib) and half-sister to several winners, including fairly useful Irish 2005 2-y-o 6f winner Seal Colony (by Cape Cross): dam, 1m winner, out of useful 2-y-o 6f winner Silver Dollar: no form. *Paul Green*

202

CHICAMIA 3 b.f. Kyllachy 129 – Inflation 68 (Primo Dominie 121) [2007 –: 8.1s 6d **48**
7m⁶ 7.6m³ 10.3g Sep 29] close-coupled filly: poor maiden: seems to stay easy 1¼m: acts
on good to firm and good to soft ground. *M. Mullineaux*

CHICHEROVA (IRE) 4 b.f. Soviet Star (USA) 128 – Ruby Rose 55 (Red Ransom **–**
(USA)) [2007 48: p9.5g p8.6g Mar 24] poor maiden at 3 yrs: well beaten both starts in
2007: stays 1m: acts on fibresand and good to firm ground: tried tongue tied: has been
slowly away. *W. M. Brisbourne*

CHICKEN GEORGE (IRE) 3 ch.g. Observatory (USA) 131 – Missing 57 (Sing- **82**
spiel (IRE) 133) [2007 5m 8m* 7g⁵ 7g⁴ Oct 27] 5,000Y: sturdy gelding: first foal: dam,
maiden (stayed 1¼m), out of useful winner up to 1¾m Misbelief: fairly useful form: won
maiden at Musselburgh in September: creditable efforts in handicaps after: will stay at
least 1¼m: raced only on good/good to firm ground. *D. Nicholls*

CHICKEN SOUP 5 br.g. Dansili 127 – Radiancy (IRE) 77 (Mujtahid (USA) 118) **86 +**
[2007 97: p7.1g* p7.1g⁵ p10g⁴ p8g² p10g⁵ 8.2m⁵ 6d 8g 12m p8g⁴ p7g³ p7g⁵ p8g⁴ Dec 22] **a107**
leggy gelding: useful on all-weather, fairly useful on turf: won handicap at Wolverhampton in January: very good efforts in listed races at Lingfield (½-length second to
Banknote) and Kempton (fifth to Imperial Star) fourth/fifth outings: left T.Pitt after sixth
start: best at 7f to 1¼m: acts on all-weather, firm and soft going: tried visored/blinkered:
has worn crossed noseband and been bandaged in front. *D. J. Murphy*

CHIEF COMMANDER (FR) 4 br.g. Commands (AUS) – Neeran (USA) (Fast Play **94 d**
(USA)) [2007 101: f7s⁴ p7.1g 8m 7.6m 8m Jun 9] tall, rather leggy gelding: useful
performer at 3 yrs: respectable fourth to Party Boss in handicap at Southwell on reappearance: ran as if amiss after: stays 1m: acts on all-weather and soft going: wore cheekpieces
final outing. *Jane Chapple-Hyam*

CHIEF DIPPER 5 b.g. Benny The Dip (USA) 127 – Cuban Reef 54 (Dowsing (USA) **45**
124) [2007 p9.5g p8.6g⁵ Mar 2] smallish, stocky gelding: fair performer in 2005: unraced
at 4 yrs: just poor form in sellers in 2007: stays 1¼m: acts on polytrack, no form in 2 races
on turf. *D. Morris*

CHIEF EDITOR 3 b.g. Tomba 119 – Princess Zara (Reprimand 122) [2007 87: 5d⁴ **99 +**
p5.1g* Nov 4] big, strong, well-made gelding: useful performer: improved form in 2007,
and won handicap at Wolverhampton (by short head from Turn On The Style, forced to
switch over 1f out) in November: raced only at 5f: acts on all-weather and soft going.
M. J. Wallace

*Ridgewood Pearl Stakes, the Curragh—
the improved Cheyenne Star (left) has the edge over Heaven Sent (right) and Modeeroch*

CHIEF ERIC 2 b. or gr.c. (Apr 19) Slickly (FR) 128 – Last Romance (IRE) (Last **67** Tycoon 131) [2007 7g⁵ Aug 24] workmanlike colt: third foal: dam, French maiden, out of smart French performer up to 1½m Fleur d'Oranger: 66/1, never-nearer fifth to Perfect Act in maiden at Newbury: will be suited by 1m. *B. I. Case*

CHIEF EXEC 5 b.g. Zafonic (USA) 130 – Shot At Love (IRE) 79 (Last Tycoon 131) **68** [2007 –, a91: p7.1g⁴ p8g 8d⁴ p8g² p7g² 7.1f² 8.1m 7g² p8g p7m³ p7m³ p7g⁵ Dec 28] **a76** leggy gelding: fair handicapper: left C. Cyzer 11,000 gns after third start: stays 1¼m, best over shorter: acts on polytrack and firm ground: tried in visor. *J. R. Gask*

CHIEF POWDERFACE (IRE) 2 ch.c. (Mar 30) Modigliani (USA) 106 – Better **–** Look (IRE) (College Chapel 122) [2007 5m f5g 5s 5m⁵ Jul 11] strong colt: no form: tried blinkered. *Jedd O'Keeffe*

CHIFF CHAFF 3 ch.f. Mtoto 134 – Hen Harrier 94 (Polar Falcon (USA) 126) [2007 **67** 59: p12.2g³ 12.6m² 12g⁵ p12g⁵ p12.2g² 11.5g p11g Nov 7] sturdy filly: fair maiden: claimed from M. Bell after fifth start: will be suited by 1¾m: acts on polytrack and good to firm going. *C. R. Dore*

CHILDISH THOUGHTS 3 b.f. River Falls 113 – Simmie's Special 75 (Precocious **–** 126) [2007 –: p5g p6g⁶ p6g 8.1g p7g Jun 5] little form: has looked difficult ride. *Mrs Norma Pook*

CHILSDOWN 4 b.g. Mozart (IRE) 131 – Goodwood Blizzard 97 (Inchinor 119) [2007 **–** –: 7.5m 8.5s⁶ 7g Sep 22] strong, close-coupled gelding: fair maiden at 2 yrs: little form since: stays 1m: acts on good to soft ground. *J. G. Given*

CHIMES AT MIDNIGHT (USA) 10 b.h. Danzig (USA) – Surely Georgie's (USA) **53 §** (Alleged (USA) 138) [2007 49§: p11g³ p11g p13g f14g p12g⁴ Jun 14] well-made horse: modest performer nowadays: stays 14.6f: acts on polytrack, firm and good to soft going: often blinkered: inconsistent. *Luke Comer, Ireland*

CHINA CHERUB 4 ch.f. Inchinor 119 – Ashlinn (IRE) 86 (Ashkalani (IRE) 128) **94** [2007 78: 6f⁶ 6m p6g⁵ 7m 6g* p6g⁴ 6g² 6m² 6m⁵ 6g 6d p6g p7g p7m⁵ p6g⁴ p6m Dec 9] lengthy filly: fairly useful handicapper: improved form in 2007, winning at Windsor in June and Lingfield in July: left R. Hannon before final outing: best at 6f: acts on polytrack, firm and good to soft ground: blinkered nowadays. *S. Dow*

CHINALEA (IRE) 5 b.g. Danetime (IRE) 121 – Raise-A-Secret (IRE) (Classic Secret **72** (USA) 91) [2007 81: 5m⁴ 6m 6m⁴ 6g 6m⁴ 5d⁵ 5g⁴ 5m 5d Jul 25] rather leggy gelding: fair handicapper nowadays: best at 5f/6f: acts on firm and soft going: wears blinkers/ cheekpieces: tried tongue tied: none too consistent. *C. G. Cox*

CHINA PINK 2 b.f. (Feb 27) Oasis Dream 129 – Red Bouquet (Reference Point 139) **–** [2007 p6g 7.5g 7f Aug 12] 120,000Y: lengthy, workmanlike filly: seventh foal: closely related to smart 1¼m to 1½m winner Red Fort (by Green Desert), and half-sister to several winners, including useful 1m to 1½m winners Red Carnation (by Polar Falcon) and 8-y-o Red Wine: dam, German 1½m/13f winner, half-sister to smart miler Red Camellia: no show in maidens: carried head bit high final outing. *Sir Mark Prescott*

CHINESE PROFIT 2 b.g. (Mar 26) Acclamation 118 – Tancholo (So Factual (USA) **68 ?** 120) [2007 7m 7g Nov 2] 32,000Y: plain gelding: second foal: dam once-raced half-sister to dam of Sussex Stakes winner Reel Buddy: well held in maidens at Newmarket, seemingly fair form in latter: subsequently gelded. *G. C. Bravery*

CHINESE TEMPLE (IRE) 2 b.c. (Mar 5) Choisir (AUS) 126 – Savage (IRE) 98 **75** (Polish Patriot (USA) 128) [2007 6f³ 5m* 5m p7.1g³ Dec 26] €16,500F: quite good-topped colt: half-brother to 3 winners, including useful French miler Sentinelese (by Cape Cross) and Irish 11f/1½m winner Fascinating (by Desert King): dam German 5f (at 2 yrs) and 1m winner: fair performer: won maiden at Cork in May: left Daniel O'Sullivan in Ireland 25,000 gns after third start: stays easy 7.1f: acts on polytrack and firm ground. *M. G. Quinlan*

CHINESE WHISPER (IRE) 3 b.c. Montjeu (IRE) 137 – Majinskaya (FR) 110 (Mar- **109** ignan (USA) 117) [2007 104: 10g² 9g³ 10.5g 10g⁶ 8s⁶ Jul 1] small, sturdy colt: useful performer: good efforts when ¾-length second to Literato in Prix La Force at Longchamp and 2½ lengths third to Lawman in Prix de Guiche at Chantilly (in cheekpieces): respectable sixth to Zaham in listed Hampton Court Stakes at Royal Ascot penultimate outing: should stay 1½m: raced only on good going or softer: sent to USA. *A. P. O'Brien, Ireland*

CHINESE WHITE (IRE) 2 gr.f. (Mar 12) Dalakhani (IRE) 133 – Chiang Mai (IRE) **93 p**
113 (Sadler's Wells (USA) 132) [2007 7m* Sep 8] useful-looking filly: third foal: dam,
Irish 1m (at 2 yrs) and 11f (Blandford Stakes) winner (stayed 15.5f), half-sister to Prix
de Diane winner Rafha, herself dam of very smart sprinter Invincible Spirit: 7/2 and
looking quite fit, won 15-runner maiden at Leopardstown in September by 6 lengths from
Carbonia, dictating and quickening 3f out, not extended: will stay 1m/1¼m+: looks a
very useful prospect. *D. K. Weld, Ireland*

CHINGFORD (IRE) 3 ch.f. Redback 116 – Beverley Macca 73 (Piccolo 121) [2007 **53**
64: p6g p7f 6g 6m⁶ 5.1m⁶ p6g 5g⁵ 5f Sep 25] strong filly: modest maiden: barely stays 7f:
acts on polytrack: blinkered last 3 starts. *J. G. Portman*

CHIN WAG (IRE) 3 b.g. Iron Mask (USA) 117 – Sweet Chat (IRE) (Common **64**
Grounds 118) [2007 87: 8g 8m 7.6s⁶ p8g⁴ 8m⁵ p7g* 7.1g Nov 8] workmanlike gelding: **a77**
just fair performer in 2007: in cheekpieces, won claimer at Kempton in October, leaving
K. R. Burke 5,500 gns after: may prove best at 6f/7f: acts on polytrack and good to firm
going. *J. S. Goldie*

CHIP N PIN 3 b.f. Erhaab (USA) 127 – Vallauris 94 (Faustus (USA) 118) [2007 –: 8g **56**
7m⁴ 9.9g² 8m 12.1g⁴ 12.1s 8.1v 10.1m³ 10f/1g² Aug 22] strong filly: modest maiden:
best around 1¼m: acts on firm ground. *T. D. Easterby*

CHISEL 6 ch.g. Hector Protector (USA) 124 – Not Before Time (IRE) (Polish Precedent **–**
(USA) 131) [2007 10m 16g 12.6d Jun 28] little form. *M. Wigham*

CHIVOLA (IRE) 2 b.c. (Mar 9) Invincible Spirit (IRE) 121 – Boudica (IRE) (Alhaarth **76**
(IRE) 126) [2007 5.9d⁴ 6s³ 6g⁵ 5g⁶ 6s³ 6g³ p5.1g² Dec 1] 37,000Y, 45,000 2-y-o:
medium-sized, sturdy colt: second foal: half-brother to 3-y-o Sandrey: dam, no form,
half-sister to several useful sprinters: fair maiden: third in nurseries at Ayr and Catterick:
should prove best at 5f/6f: acts on polytrack, raced only on good or softer going on turf.
B. Smart

CHJIMES (IRE) 3 b.g. Fath (USA) 116 – Radiance (IRE) 54 (Thatching 131) [2007 **93**
94d: f6g⁴ 7.6m⁶ f7g⁴ 7s² 7.1g² 6d² 7s² 6s² 7g³ Oct 27] close-coupled gelding: has a round
action: fairly useful performer: placed last 6 starts: effective at 6f/7f: acts on fibresand
and soft ground: tried visored: usually races prominently: consistent: sold 25,000 gns,
joined C. Dore. *K. R. Burke*

CHOCKDEE (FR) 7 b.g. King's Theatre (IRE) 128 – Chagrin d'Amour (IRE) (Last **–**
Tycoon 131) [2007 p13g Aug 28] ran 6 times in France in 2002/2003: in cheekpieces and
tongue tied, well beaten on sole Flat start since (fairly useful hurdler/modest chaser).
M. J. McGrath

CHOCOLATE CARAMEL (USA) 5 b.g. Storm Creek (USA) – Sandhill (BRZ) **91**
(Baynoun 128) [2007 96: 11.8s⁶ 12m⁴ 12g⁶ p13g³ 12d² p12g⁴ p12g⁴ 16.5m⁴ p12m⁵ **a94**
Dec 7] tall gelding: fairly useful handicapper: good efforts when in frame fourth to sixth
starts: stays 1¾m (possibly not 2m): acts on polytrack, soft and good to firm ground
(unraced on firm): blinkered final outing. *Mrs A. J. Perrett*

CHOCOLATE SANDS 3 ch.g. Compton Place 125 – Coffee Ice 92 (Primo Dominie **–**
121) [2007 p5.1g p6g f5g Dec 27] no form. *J. G. Given*

CHOISEAU (IRE) 2 b.c. (Mar 27) Choisir (AUS) 126 – Little Linnet 75 (Be My Guest **76**
(USA) 126) [2007 6m 6m² Aug 31] 2,000Y: good-bodied colt: second foal: dam Irish
1½m winner: fair form in maidens at Newbury and Salisbury (second to Max One Two
Three): may prove best at 5f/6f. *Pat Eddery*

CHOISETTE 2 b.f. (Feb 10) Choisir (AUS) 126 – Final Pursuit 92§ (Pursuit of Love **75**
124) [2007 5f⁴ 6s⁵ 5d⁴ 5d* 6g⁴ p5.1g² p5.1g* 5g 5g⁴ Nov 9] 40,000Y: leggy filly: third foal:
dam, untrustworthy 2-y-o 5.7f winner, half-sister to smart sprinters Double Action and
Sir Nicholas: fair performer: won nurseries at Musselburgh in August and Wolverhampton in September: best at 5f: acts on polytrack and good to soft ground: races prominently.
B. Smart

CHOISKY (IRE) 2 b.c. (Mar 3) Choisir (AUS) 126 – Vinicky (USA) (Kingmambo **66**
(USA) 125) [2007 5.1d p5g⁵ 5g p5g⁵ 5d⁵ p6g³ 7d⁵ p6g⁵ 6m³ 7g p6g Oct 31] €34,000F, **a69**
42,000Y: neat colt: fourth foal: dam, French maiden, closely related to useful UAE 9f/
1¼m performer Mackook: fair maiden: twice placed in nurseries: best at 5f/6f: acts on
polytrack and good to firm going: sold 7,000 gns. *J. Akehurst*

CHOOKIE HAMILTON 3 ch.g. Compton Place 125 – Lady of Windsor (IRE) 73§ **70**
(Woods of Windsor (USA)) [2007 73: p9.5g* p8.6g* 8.1g 8m 12m⁶ 8.3s 10g⁶ 9.1s **a81**
p12.2g⁵ p8.6d⁴ Dec 10] lengthy, angular gelding: fairly useful handicapper on all-

weather, fair on turf: won twice at Wolverhampton in January: effective at 8.6f to easy 1½m: acts on all-weather and good to firm ground, probably on soft: in headgear last 4 starts. *I. Semple*

CHOOKIE HEITON (IRE) 9 br.g. Fumo di Londra (IRE) 108 – Royal Wolff (Prince Tenderfoot (USA) 126) [2007 108: 5m⁶ 5d 6m 6g Sep 3] strong, lengthy gelding: one-time smart performer: very much on downgrade: tried in cheekpieces. *I. Semple* –

CHOOKIE WINDSOR 4 b.g. Lake Coniston (IRE) 131 – Lady of Windsor (IRE) 73§ (Woods of Windsor (USA)) [2007 61: f11g Apr 3] modest performer at 3 yrs: below form sole start in 2007: stays easy 1¼m: acts on all-weather and firm ground: tried in cheekpieces/visor. *A. G. Juckes* –

CHOOSE YOUR MOMENT 2 b.c. (Mar 30) Choisir (AUS) 126 – Time Will Show (FR) (Exit To Nowhere (USA) 122) [2007 5.9d* 6m³ 7m* Sep 9] 21,000F, £75,000 2-y-o: big, rather leggy colt: third foal: half-brother to German 9f to 1¼m winner Cavan Gael (by Dansili) and 4-y-o Maximix: dam fairly useful French maiden (best at 1m): useful form: developed well and won 2 of 3 starts, namely maiden at Carlisle in June and nursery at York (by 3 lengths, value extra) in September: will stay 1m: should go on improving. *P. C. Haslam* **99 p**

CHORD 3 ch.g. Pivotal 124 – Choirgirl 106 (Unfuwain (USA) 131) [2007 61: 10g³ p12.2g* 12d p12.2g* p11g p12g Oct 12] good-topped, angular gelding: fairly useful performer: won maiden in July and handicap in August, both at Wolverhampton: stays 1½m: acts on polytrack: visored last 5 starts: sold 25,000 gns, joined D. McCain Jnr. *Sir Michael Stoute* **92**

CHOREOGRAPHY 4 ch.g. Medicean 128 – Stark Ballet (USA) (Nureyev (USA) 131) [2007 81: p7.1g 8m 7m 5.9m 7.9d 5.9m³ 6m² 6d⁶ 6m³ 6m 7.1d⁶ 6s⁴ 6.1m² 6v² Oct 26] leggy gelding: fair handicapper: best at 6f/7f: acts on heavy and good to firm going: tried visored. *D. Nicholls* **74**

CHORISTAR 6 ch.g. Inchinor 119 – Star Tulip 99 (Night Shift (USA)) [2007 66: f11g f11g p12.2g p12.2g⁵ 10.9m² 9.9m* 10g Apr 28] smallish gelding: fair handicapper: won at Beverley in April: broke down at Leicester next time: seemed to stay easy 1½m: acted on polytrack and firm going: dead. *J. Mackie* **73**

CHOYSIA 4 b.f. Pivotal 124 – Bonica 56 (Rousillon (USA) 133) [2007 77§: 7.1m 6m² 5m 6s 7m* 7m 6m* 6d 6m³ 6.1m⁴ Sep 15] leggy, workmanlike filly: fairly useful handicapper: won at Catterick in July and August: best at 6f/7f: acts on firm and soft going: tried in cheekpieces: edgy sort: sometimes slowly away: formerly ungenuine. *D. W. Barker* **85**

CHRISTALINI 3 b.g. Bertolini (USA) 125 – Jay Tee (IRE) (Charnwood Forest (IRE) 125) [2007 82: 9.9g 8m p8g p11g p12m p10g p10m p8g Dec 16] close-coupled gelding: just modest maiden in 2007: best form around 7f: acts on good to soft ground: tried blinkered: has been slowly away. *J. C. Fox* **62**

CHRISTIAN BENDIX 5 ch.g. Presidium 124 – Very Good (Noalto 120) [2007 –, a58: p6g⁴ p6g⁵ f6g⁴ f7g⁴ f6g⁴ p6g⁴ p7.1g 7m p6g f6g⁵ p6g* f6g⁵ p6g p6m f6d Dec 11] strong gelding: modest handicapper: won at Southwell in February and Kempton in May: stays 7f: acts on all-weather, little form on turf: usually wears cheekpieces: front runner. *P. Howling* **–** **a57**

CHRISTMAS TRUCE (IRE) 8 b.g. Brief Truce (USA) 126 – Superflash (Superlative 118) [2007 71, a66: p10g p8.6g p10g³ p8g p10g 10.2f 8m³ 9g 8d⁶ 10m⁵ 8m⁴ p12g Jun 30] good-topped gelding: modest performer: left Ms J. Doyle after fifth start, J. Bridger after ninth: effective at 1m to 13f: acts on all-weather, heavy and good to firm going: usually wears headgear: sometimes slowly away: virtually refused to race sixth outing: ungenuine. *M. R. Hoad* **54 §**

CHRISTY RYAN (IRE) 3 b.g. Danetime (IRE) 121 – Esterlina (IRE) 95 (Highest Honor (FR) 124) [2007 p8.6g Jan 15] 20/1, tailed off in claimer at Wolverhampton. *M. J. Wallace* **–**

CHRYSTAL VENTURE (IRE) 2 ch.f. (Mar 13) Barathea (IRE) 127 – Ukraine Venture 96 (Slip Anchor 136) [2007 7g 7m 7.1m p7.1g 7d² p7.1g* Nov 8] 34,000Y: big, useful-looking filly: sixth foal: half-sister to several winners, including 5-y-o Russian Consort, 6f (including at 2 yrs) to 1m winner Indian Steppes (by Indian Ridge), both useful, and 3-y-o Russian Invader: dam 1¼m winner: fair performer: progress in cheekpieces last 2 starts (made running), won nursery at Wolverhampton: likely to prove best up to 7f: acts on polytrack, good to firm and good to soft going. *A. J. McCabe* **69**

CHUNKY'S CHOICE (IRE) 3 b.g. Key of Luck (USA) 126 – Indian Imp (Indian   **82**
Ridge 123) [2007 74: 8g p10g 9.9g 11.6s⁶ 14.1m⁶ 14.1m² 11.9m* p12m 11.9d* Oct 18]
close-coupled gelding: fairly useful handicapper: won at Brighton in September and October: stays 1¾m: acts on good to firm and good to soft going: sold 38,000 gns. *J. Noseda*

CHUNSA 2 b.c. (May 5) Makbul 104 – Mynador (USA) 90 (Forty Niner (USA)) [2007   **–**
p6g p6g Oct 24] well beaten in maiden/claimer. *W. Jarvis*

CHURCHTOWN 3 b.g. Kyllachy 129 – Manhattan Diamond 54 (Primo Dominie 121)   **47**
[2007 –: 6g⁴ 8d a11g⁴ 7g² 7.5m Dec 16] poor maiden: sold from K. R. Burke 3,200 gns
after second start: second in amateur minor event at Madrid penultimate outing: stays 7f.
P. Haley, Spain

CICCONE 4 ch.f. Singspiel (IRE) 133 – Untold Riches (USA) 94 (Red Ransom (USA))   **67**
[2007 67: p8.6g² p10g p10g⁵ p8.6g p10g⁴ 8g 10.1g² p10g² 10m⁴ 11.6m⁶ Aug 25] strong
filly: fair handicapper: stays easy 1½m: acts on polytrack, raced only on good ground or
firmer on turf (acts on firm): tried blinkered, often wears cheekpieces. *G. L. Moore*

CIGALAS 2 ch.g. (Apr 4) Selkirk (USA) 129 – Langoustine (AUS) 117 (Danehill   **82 p**
(USA) 126) [2007 6g 7m⁴ Sep 12] 75,000Y: tall, good-topped gelding: has fluent action:
first foal: dam, Australian 2-y-o 5f winner (including Group 2 event), out of half-sister
to Royal Academy and dam of Storm Cat: fairly useful form in maiden at Goodwood
(eye-catching seventh) and minor event at Doncaster (fourth to Newly Elected, free to
post/in race): gelded after: needs to settle to stay 1m: should progress. *B. W. Hills*

CIMYLA (IRE) 6 b.g. Lomitas 129 – Coyaima (GER) 100 (Night Shift (USA)) [2007   **100**
113: 9g⁶ 10g⁵ 10g p10g⁶ p10g a8.5f p8.5f p8f⁴ a8.5f⁵ 8.5f⁴ Nov 29] good-topped gelding: **a111**
smart on all-weather, useful on turf: creditable equal-sixth to Gentleman's Deal in Winter
Derby at Lingfield fourth start: below form after, leaving C. Wall following sixth outing:
stays 1¼m: acts on polytrack, soft and good to firm going: blinkered final appearance:
has hung left: patiently ridden. *B. D. A. Cecil, USA*

CINAMAN (IRE) 3 b.g. Key of Luck (USA) 126 – Madame Nureyev (USA) (Nureyev   **–**
(USA) 131) [2007 –: 12g Apr 8] small gelding: well held in maiden at Haydock at 2 yrs:
unseated as stall opened at Musselburgh only start in 2007. *R. F. Fisher*

CINEMATIC (IRE) 4 b.g. Bahhare (USA) 122 – Eastern Star (IRE) (Sri Pekan (USA)   **83**
117) [2007 77: p7g p8g p8g³ p7g p10g* p10g² 10.5m² 10m⁴ p11g⁵ 9d⁶ p8g p8.6g² p10m⁴
p9.5g* Nov 8] tall, leggy gelding: fairly useful handicapper: won at Lingfield in March
and Wolverhampton in November: stays 1¼m: acts on polytrack, firm and good to soft
going. *J. R. Boyle*

CINERAMA (IRE) 2 b.f. (Feb 11) Machiavellian 123 – Disco Volante 105   **62 p**
(Sadler's Wells (USA) 132) [2007 p7g Oct 24] first foal: dam, 1m winner, half-sister to
smart but irresolute 7f/1m performer Valentino: 25/1, late headway into seventh in
maiden at Lingfield: should do better. *M. P. Tregoning*

CINNAMON GIRL 4 ch.f. Erhaab (USA) 127 – Distant Cheers (USA) 77 (Distant   **–**
View (USA) 126) [2007 f12g Apr 13] 800Y, £550 3-y-o: first foal: dam 8.5f winner: 25/1,
well beaten in maiden at Southwell. *A. M. Hales*

CINNAMON HILL 3 ch.f. Compton Place 125 – Cajole (IRE) 72 (Barathea (IRE)   **72**
127) [2007 7m⁴ 7d² p7g⁵ Oct 29] lengthy, angular filly: third foal: half-sister to winner in
Greece by Josr Algarhoud: dam maiden (stayed 7f): progressive form in maidens: fifth to
Swop at Lingfield final start: worth a try at 6f. *Eve Johnson Houghton*

CIRCLE OF LOVE 3 b.f. Sakhee (USA) 136 – Claxon 110 (Caerleon (USA) 132)   **86**
[2007 86: 10m² 10s* 10.4s⁶ Jul 28] tall, leggy, close-coupled filly: fairly useful form:
landed odds in maiden at Pontefract (by 10 lengths) in July: stirred up beforehand, below
form on handicap debut at York next time: will stay 1½m: acts on soft and good to firm
going: refused to enter stall intended second outing. *J. L. Dunlop*

CIRCLE OF TRUTH 3 b.g. Makbul 104 – Jade's Girl (Emarati (USA) 74) [2007 58:   **–**
p5.1g p5.1g Jan 26] modest maiden at 2 yrs: well held in 2007. *W. G. M. Turner*

CIRCUIT DANCER (IRE) 7 b.g. Mujadil (USA) 119 – Trysinger (IRE) (Try My   **84**
Best (USA) 130) [2007 94: p6g 5g 5m 5d 5g 6m⁴ 5.1m* 5g 5.1g⁴ 5m Oct 22] tall gelding:
fairly useful handicapper: won at Chester in September: effective at 5f to easy 7f: acts on
polytrack, firm and soft going: tried in cheekpieces at 5 yrs. *D. Nicholls*

CIRCUS POLKA (USA) 3 br.c. Stravinsky (USA) 133 – Far Wiser (USA) (Private   **75**
Terms (USA)) [2007 82p: p8g⁶ p10g p10g p10m p8.6g* p7.1g⁶ Dec 26] fair performer:

won seller at Wolverhampton (left P. Cole 8,500 gns) in November: stays 1¼m: raced only on all-weather: blinkered fourth/fifth starts: usually tongue tied: has carried head awkwardly/hung. *W. M. Brisbourne*

CITRUS CHIEF (USA) 3 b.g. Lemon Drop Kid (USA) 131 – Tricky Indy (USA) (A P Indy (USA) 131) [2007 61: p10g p9.5g p10f² p10g³ 12m³ p12.2g 12.1g p8g Jul 17] modest maiden: stays 1¼m: acts on polytrack, raced only on good ground or firmer on turf: often in blinkers/cheekpieces. *R. A. Harris* **60**

CITY FOR CONQUEST (IRE) 4 b.f. City On A Hill (USA) 114 – Northern Life (IRE) (Distinctly North (USA) 115) [2007 77: f5g⁶ p6g² p5.1g² p6g p6g p5g 5.1m p5.1g² p5.1g 5m p5.1g⁴ p5g⁵ Jul 25] compact filly: just modest performer in 2007: left T. Pitt 6,000 gns after sixth start: stays 6f: acts on polytrack and firm going: visored/blinkered: sometimes slowly away: tends to find little: temperamental. *John A. Harris* **59 §**

CITY HUSTLER (USA) 2 b.c. (Apr 29) Century City (IRE) 124 – French Buster (USA) (Housebuster (USA)) [2007 7m 7d⁴ p8g² 8.5m⁵ p7g² p7g⁴ Oct 23] $15,000Y: good-topped colt: has round action: fifth foal: half-brother to winner in US by Coronado's Quest: dam US 6f (at 2 yrs) to 8.5f winner: fair maiden: twice runner-up at Lingfield: stays 8.5f: acts on polytrack, good to firm and good to soft going: joined A. Manuel in UAE. *J. S. Moore* **74**

CITY LEADER (IRE) 2 gr.c. (Apr 15) Fasliyev (USA) 120 – Kanmary (FR) 117 (Kenmare (FR) 125) [2007 7d⁴ 7.1m² 8d* 8g² Oct 27] tall, leggy colt: half-brother to several winners, notably Breeders' Cup Sprint winner Lit de Justice and 2000 Guineas/ Derby third Colonel Collins (both by El Gran Senor) and Racing Post Trophy winner Commander Collins (by Sadler's Wells), later stayed 1½m: dam, French 2-y-o 5f (Prix du Bois) winner, stayed 9f: smart performer: successful at Ascot in maiden in July and Juddmonte Royal Lodge Stakes (found plenty in front when beating Achill Island ¾ length) in September: very good 3 lengths second to Ibn Khaldun in Racing Post Trophy at Doncaster final outing, rallying: will stay at least 1¼m: unraced on extremes of ground. *B. J. Meehan* **111**

CITY MISS 4 br.f. Rock City 120 – Miss Pigalle 55 (Good Times (ITY)) [2007 –: 7.1m 5g 7.1m 8.3g 9.1g 13.1d 15s* 14m 16.1m 17.5s Sep 21] modest performer: won handicap at Ayr in August: stays 15f: acts on soft ground: withdrawn (unruly at start) once. *Miss L. A. Perratt* **55**

CITY OF DREAMS (IRE) 2 b.c. (Mar 22) Dubai Destination (USA) 127 – America Calling (USA) 81 (Quiet American (USA)) [2007 p10g Oct 24] 10/1, well beaten in claimer at Lingfield. *J. S. Moore* **–**

CITY OF THE KINGS (IRE) 2 b.c. (Mar 17) Cape Cross (IRE) 129 – Prima Volta 80 (Primo Dominie 121) [2007 6m 8m⁴ p8g* 7m* Sep 15] 80,000F: well-made colt: seventh foal: half-brother to useful 5f (at 2 yrs) to 1m winner Bouncing Bowdler (by Mujadil) and 4-y-o Our Putra: dam 6f (at 2 yrs) to 9f winner: fairly useful performer: improved to win maiden at Kempton in August and nursery at Chester in September: stays 1m: acts on polytrack and good to firm going. *R. Hannon* **89**

Juddmonte Royal Lodge Stakes, Ascot—City Leader fends off his rivals in a bunched finish; Achill Island (second left) and Scintillo (rail) are next

CITY OF TRIBES (IRE) 3 b.g. Invincible Spirit (IRE) 121 – Yellow Trumpet 75 **102** (Petong 126) [2007 94: 5m³ 5.1m* 6m³ 5d² 5s⁵ 6m 5g² Oct 7] smallish, quite attractive gelding: useful performer: won handicap at Chester in May: creditable placed efforts after in listed races at Haydock, Sandown and Tipperary (2½ lengths second to Senor Benny): ran as if amiss penultimate start: effective at 5f/easy 6f: acts on firm and good to soft ground: joined T. W. Leung in Hong Kong. *G. M. Lyons, Ireland*

CITY STABLE (IRE) 2 b.c. (Feb 10) Machiavellian (USA) 123 – Rainbow City (IRE) **79 p** 85 (Rainbow Quest (USA) 134) [2007 7g² 8.3m² 8g³ Oct 25] rather leggy colt: first foal: dam, 1¼m winner, sister to smart 10.4f/13.3f winner Multicoloured: placed in maidens at Yarmouth, Windsor and Brighton, each time held up and finishing well: will be suited by 1¼m/1½m: should make a useful 3-y-o. *Sir Michael Stoute*

CITY WIZZARD 2 ch.g. (Feb 12) Bahamian Bounty 116 – Aries (GER) 79 (Big Shuffle (USA) 122) [2007 5m 6s Jun 25] big, strong gelding: well held in maidens (said to have finished lame second outing): dead. *M. L. W. Bell*

CLARE PARK 3 ch.f. Kier Park (IRE) 114 – Shafayif 43 (Ela-Mana-Mou 132) [2007 10.9s 16.2s⁶ Jul 27] £1,000Y: sixth foal: dam, untrustworthy winning 2m selling hurdler, out of smart miler Rare Roberta: tailed off in seller and claimer. *H. J. Manners*

CLARRICIEN (IRE) 3 b.g. Key of Luck (USA) 126 – Tango Two Thousand (IRE) **78** 84 (Sri Pekan (USA) 117) [2007 80: 12m⁴ 12g May 18] compact gelding: fair performer: seems to stay 1½m: suspect temperament: sold 4,000 gns in July. *E. J. O'Neill*

CLASSICAL RHYTHM (IRE) 2 ch.c. (May 6) Traditionally (USA) 117 – Golden **64** Angel (Slew O' Gold (USA)) [2007 6m p6g⁶ 6m 7.1m 7m⁶ 8s Sep 26] tall colt: modest maiden: mid-field in nurseries: should stay 1m. *J. R. Boyle*

CLASSICAL WORLD (USA) 2 gr.c. (Mar 23) El Prado (IRE) 119 – Tethkar 75 **71** (Machiavellian (USA) 123) [2007 6m 7m* 8s 8m Sep 4] good-topped colt: fifth foal: half-brother to 3 winners, including 8.5f and 1¼m winner (including in UAE) Otranto (by Rahy): dam maiden (should have stayed beyond 1m): fair form: won maiden at Catterick in August: last in nurseries (hinted at temperament): should stay 1m/1¼m: acts on good to firm ground: sold 34,000 gns. *Sir Michael Stoute*

CLASSIC BLUE (IRE) 3 b.f. Tagula (IRE) 116 – Palace Blue (IRE) (Dara Monarch **49** 128) [2007 60: 10.2m p10m p8.6g p9.5g Oct 22] compact filly: poor maiden: stays easy 1¼m: best form on polytrack. *Ian Williams*

CLASSIC DESCENT 2 b.c. (Feb 19) Auction House (USA) 120 – Polish Descent **86** (IRE) (Danehill (USA) 126) [2007 6g⁴ p6g³ 7g² Nov 2] 65,000F: strong, lengthy colt: sixth foal: half-brother to several winners, including smart Irish 7f (at 2 yrs)/1m (Irish 1000 Guineas) winner Saoire (by Pivotal) and fairly useful 6f (at 2 yrs)/7f winner Foronlymo (by Forzando): dam unraced: fairly useful form: progressive in maidens, first past post at Newmarket by short head (edged left close home, hampered Black Rain, demoted): will stay 1m. *P. J. Makin*

CLASSIC ENCOUNTER (IRE) 4 b.g. Lujain (USA) 119 – Licence To Thrill 83 **97** (Wolfhound (USA) 126) [2007 98: p5g⁶ p5g p5g 5g⁶ 5m* 5g⁶ p5g⁵ 5g 5g Aug 2] rather leggy, quite attractive gelding: useful performer: won handicap at Goodwood in May: creditable efforts next 2 outings: well below form after: raced only at 5f: acts on polytrack and good to firm going: blinkered final outing: carries head high. *D. M. Simcock*

CLASSIC FORTUNE (IRE) 2 b.c. (Feb 1) Royal Applause 124 – Injaaz 99 (Sheikh **87 p** Albadou 128) [2007 p6g* p6g² Dec 4] 70,000Y: first foal: dam, 6f (including at 2 yrs)/7f winner, sister to useful dam of smart 2-y-o sprinter Nevisian Lad (by Royal Applause): odds on both outings, slowly away when winning maiden at Lingfield in November cosily by short head from Fast Feet: still green, better form when neck second to Haybrook in minor event at same track, again taking strong hold: a useful prospect. *D. R. C. Elsworth*

CLASSIC HALL (IRE) 4 b.f. Saddlers' Hall (IRE) 126 – Classic Mix (IRE) 72 **–** (Classic Secret (USA) 91) [2007 –: p9.5g p12g 10.1g 15.4g p12g Sep 24] sturdy filly: no form. *T. Keddy*

CLASSIC LEGEND 2 b.f. (Jan 23) Galileo (IRE) 134 – Lady Lahar 106 (Fraam 114) **92 p** [2007 8.2m* 8g* Nov 3] £140,000Y: compact filly: third foal: half-sister to 3-y-o Kilburn: dam 6f (at 2 yrs) to 8.3f winner: fairly useful form: won both starts, namely maiden at Nottingham (by 4 lengths) in October and listed race at Newmarket, in latter beating Jazz Jam by short head after quickening pace 3f out: will stay 1¼m/1½m: should continue to progress. *B. J. Meehan*

Ladbrokes Fred Archer Stakes, Newmarket—
Persian Punch's half-brother Classic Punch shows improvement on his reappearance;
Hard Top (light colours) is second ahead of Munsef (blinkers) and the grey Under The Rainbow

CLASSIC PUNCH (IRE) 4 b.g. Mozart (IRE) 131 – Rum Cay (USA) 75 (Our Native (USA)) [2007 104: 12s* 12m* 13.3d⁵ 11.6m² 12m 12g Sep 30] big, rangy gelding: smart performer: much improved when winning listed race in June (by 2½ lengths from Hard Top) and minor event in July (by ½ length from New Beginning), both at Newmarket: easily best effort after when length second to Dragon Dancer in listed event at Windsor: should stay 1¾m: acts on soft and good to firm ground: inconsistent. *D. R. C. Elsworth* **112 §**

CLASSIC ROLE 8 b.g. Tragic Role (USA) – Clare Island 108 (Connaught 130) [2007 11.6g Jul 9] sparely-made gelding: fairly useful handicapper at best: lightly raced on Flat since 2004 and ran poorly sole 8-y-o start: effective at 1¼m to 13f: acts on polytrack, soft and good to firm ground: wears visor: has carried head awkwardly/raced freely. *L. Wells* **–**

CLASSIRA (IRE) 3 b.f. Danehill (USA) 126 – Alleged Devotion (USA) (Alleged (USA) 138) [2007 8.2m² 8g² p8g* 8m³ 7m⁵ 7s⁴ p7g Sep 11] lengthy, good-topped filly: sister to useful Irish performer up to 1¼m Altius (later successful in South Africa), 7f winner at 2 yrs, and half-sister to several winners, including Irish 1¼m/1½m winner Royal Devotion (by Sadler's Wells) and 7f winner Thady Quill (by Nureyev), both useful: dam unraced half-sister to Oaks/Irish Derby winner Balanchine: fairly useful performer: won maiden at Lingfield in July: good third in handicap at Newmarket next time: likely to be suited by 1¼m: acts on polytrack and good to firm ground: wore cheekpieces final outing: sent to USA. *M. A. Jarvis* **86**

CLAWS 4 b.f. Marju (IRE) 127 – Paws (IRE) 72§ (Brief Truce (USA) 126) [2007 63: p9.5g⁶ p8.6g⁵ p8g p7.1s⁶ p7.1d² Dec 27] modest handicapper: stays 7f: acts on polytrack, firm and good to soft ground: tried tongue tied. *A. J. Lidderdale* **60**

CLEAN SHEET (USA) 2 b.f. (Apr 11) Fasliyev (USA) 120 – Starlight Night (USA) 71 (Distant View (USA) 126) [2007 6f Sep 27] $85,000F, 130,000Y: angular filly: second foal: half-sister to fairly useful Irish 2006 2-y-o 6f winner Divine Night (by Danehill): dam, maiden (raced at 1¼m), half-sister to US Grade 1 1¼m/11f winner Senure out of half-sister to Xaar: no form in maidens (injured pelvis second start): dead. *W. J. Haggas* **–**

CLEAR DAYLIGHT 2 b.c. (May 1) Daylami (IRE) 138 – Barbara Frietchie (IRE) (Try My Best (USA) 130) [2007 6m 7s p7g p8g⁵ p7g Nov 30] good-bodied colt: type to carry condition: modest maiden: bred to be suited by 1¼m+: acts on polytrack and soft ground. *J. R. Best* **63**

CLEARING SKY (IRE) 6 gr.m. Exploit (USA) 117 – Litchfield Hills (USA) (Re-launch (USA)) [2007 64: 6f 6g p6g p7g Sep 26] strong mare: modest handicapper: well held in 2007: effective at 5f to 7f: acts on polytrack and firm going: tried in cheekpieces: usually races prominently. *J. R. Boyle* **–**

CLEAR PICTURE 4 ch.f. Observatory (USA) 131 – Defined Feature (IRE) 91 (Nabeel Dancer (USA) 120) [2007 –: p7g f8g⁴ May 1] well held in maidens/claimer. *A. P. Jarvis* **–**

CLEAR REEF 3 b.c. Hernando (FR) 127 – Trinity Reef 80 (Bustino 136) [2007 8.3d p12g⁴ p12g⁶ f11d* Dec 21] tall, angular colt: fifth foal: brother to fairly useful 1½m/1¾m winner Tangible: dam, 1½m winner, sister to smart 1¼m/1½m performer Talented: fair form: easily best effort when winning handicap at Southwell: will be suited by return to 1½m+: will progress further. *Jane Chapple-Hyam* **73 p**

CLEAR SAILING 4 b.g. Selkirk (USA) 129 – Welsh Autumn 107 (Tenby 125) [2007 –
87: 10g⁵ 10d 10f Aug 4] big, strong gelding: fairly useful form at 3 yrs: well held in 2007
(shaped as if amiss on reappearance): raced around 1¼m: acts on good to soft ground:
carries head high (wears net muzzle). *Mrs A. J. Perrett*

CLEAVER 6 ch.g. Kris 135 – Much Too Risky 87 (Bustino 136) [2007 83: 10.1s⁴ p12g⁴ **89 §**
p12g³ 10g³ 10.1v² 10.9s² 12v Jul 21] leggy, quite good-topped gelding: fairly useful
handicapper: in frame first 6 starts in 2007: stays 1½m: acts on polytrack and heavy
ground: usually held up: ungenuine. *Lady Herries*

CLEIDE DA SILVA (USA) 3 gr.f. Monarchos (USA) 129 – Sage Cat (USA) (Tabasco **84**
Cat (USA) 126) [2007 73: 10g⁴ 8.3m⁵ p7.1g* p6g Jul 11] lengthy, good-topped filly: has
scope: fairly useful performer: won handicap at Wolverhampton in June: stays 8.3f: acts
on polytrack and good to firm ground: visored last 2 starts. *J. Noseda*

CLEVELAND 5 b.g. Pennekamp (USA) 130 – Clerio 108 (Soviet Star (USA) 128) **59 +**
[2007 68: f8g f6g² f7g⁵ f7g² p6g⁶ f6g³ f7g² f7g⁴ 5d⁵ 5.1g⁵ p6g Nov 14] lengthy gelding: **a73**
fair handicapper on all-weather, modest on turf: stays 7f: acts on fibresand and good to
firm going: difficult ride, has hung right. *R. Hollinshead*

CLEW BAY (IRE) 8 b.g. Nicolotte 118 – Lady Danjar (FR) (Nadjar (FR) 128) [2007 –
6g May 10] one-time fairly useful performer: lightly raced and little impact since 2004:
stays 7f: acts on heavy going: tried in blinkers/cheekpieces. *Barry Potts, Ireland*

CLEWER 3 b.f. Bahamian Bounty 116 – Polisonne (Polish Precedent (USA) 131) [2007 –
59: p10g 6g Apr 2] modest maiden at 2 yrs: well held in handicaps in 2007: form only at
5f/6f: acts on polytrack and firm going: wore cheekpieces final outing. *P. A. Blockley*

CLICHE (IRE) 3 b.f. Diktat 126 – Sweet Kristeen (USA) 69 (Candy Stripes (USA) **108**
115) [2007 92p: 8.3g* 8m 8.1g⁴ 9.9g² Aug 26] angular filly: useful performer: reported
in early-March to have suffered a bone chip: won maiden at Windsor in May: better form
in listed races after, fourth to Selinka at Sandown and ½-length second to Samira Gold in
handicap at Goodwood: stays 1¼m: acts on good to soft ground: sold 70,000 gns. *Sir
Michael Stoute*

CLIFTON DANCER 2 b.f. (Mar 17) Fraam 114 – Crofters Ceilidh 101 (Scottish Reel **78**
123) [2007 5.1m 6.1d³ 6s⁵ 7m* 6m 7d Oct 27] 38,000Y: quite good-topped filly: seventh
foal: half-sister to 3 winners, including useful 2003 2-y-o 5f/6f winner Cop Hill Lad (later
successful abroad, by Atraf) and 3-y-o Okikoki: dam, 5f winner (including at 2 yrs), half-
sister to smart sprinter Lord Kintyre: fair performer: won nursery at Lingfield in September: should prove best up to 7f: acts on soft and good to firm going. *Tom Dascombe*

CLIFTON FOUR (USA) 2 b.f. (Mar 3) Forest Wildcat (USA) 120 – Black Truffle **78**
(USA) (Mt Livermore (USA)) [2007 6d⁶ 6f³ p7g⁶ Sep 24] $60,000, $60,000 2-y-o: sturdy
filly: third foal: half-sister to 4-y-o Blacktoft and winner in US by Mr Greeley: dam,
French 10.5f winner, later won in US: fair maiden: third at Folkestone (minor event):
should stay 1m. *R. Hannon*

CLIMATE (IRE) 8 ch.g. Catrail (USA) 123 – Burishki 49 (Chilibang 120) [2007 72: **69**
p7.1g³ p9.5g* p8.6g* p8.6g* p8.6g p9.5g³ p9.5g³ p8.6g p9.5g p8.6g⁴ p7.1g p10m⁵ p8.6g⁶
p8.6g⁵ p8.6s⁴ p9.5g² Dec 29] strong, compact gelding: fair performer: won claimers at
Wolverhampton in January (2) and February: effective at 7f to easy 1¼m: acts on all-
weather and any turf going: usually wears headgear: reportedly had irregular heartbeat
fifth start: signs of temperament. *R. Hollinshead*

CLIMAXTACKLEDOTCOM 2 b.g. (Mar 3) Bahri (USA) 125 – La Danseuse 50 **72**
(Groom Dancer (USA) 128) [2007 6v⁵ 5d 6m³ Nov 10] strong, angular gelding: first
foal: dam, maiden (stayed 1¼m), half-sister to smart French 7f to 1¼m performer
Goofalik out of smart French miler Alik: fair maiden: off 3 months after debut (once
broke through stall): staying-on third to Incomparable at Doncaster: will be suited by 1m.
M. W. Easterby

CLIP CLOP (IRE) 2 b.f. (Mar 25) Minardi (USA) 119 – Vailmora (USA) (Mt Liver- **– §**
more (USA)) [2007 p6g f6d⁵ p8.6d⁵ Dec 28] second foal: dam unraced half-sister to
useful 7f winner Velvet Glade out of close relation to Selkirk: temperamental maiden,
refused to race on debut. *Miss J. Feilden*

CLIPPER HOY 5 ch.g. Bahamian Bounty 116 – Indian Flag (IRE) 39 (Indian Ridge **58**
123) [2007 70: p5.1g p5g 5g Jun 23] fair handicapper at 4 yrs: last all starts in 2007
(reportedly finished lame on reappearance). *Mrs H. Sweeting*

CLOCK FACE (IRE) 3 b.f. Danetime (IRE) 121 – Sugar River (FR) (Polish Precedent –
(USA) 131) [2007 p6g p6g f6g⁴ Apr 3] first foal: dam, French 9f winner, granddaughter

211

of US Grade 1 9f winner Fitzwilliam Place: signs of a little ability in maidens: reluctant at stall on debut. *M. D. I. Usher*

CLOSE TO PARADISE (IRE) 2 gr.f. (Feb 20) Clodovil (IRE) 116 – Tropical **77** Paradise (USA) (Manila (USA)) [2007 6d 7g⁴ 6d* 6.5m 6g 7s Oct 14] €15,000Y, 90,000 2-y-o: close-coupled filly: has quick action: fifth foal: dam-coupled half-sister to 2 winners, including US 6f winner Come For The Gold (by Distant View): dam unraced half-sister to US Grade 1 8.5f winner Antiqua out of high-class French/US performer up to 1¼m Paradise: fair performer: won maiden at Leicester in August: best effort in nursery next time: stays 7f: acts on good to firm and good to soft going: sent to South Africa. *E. A. L. Dunlop*

CLOUDED LEOPARD (USA) 3 b.f. Danehill (USA) 126 – Golden Cat (USA) 102 – (Storm Cat (USA)) [2007 81: 7m Jul 12] maiden: well held both starts since debut: raced only at 7f. *J. H. M. Gosden*

CLOVIS 2 b.c. (May 9) Kingmambo (USA) 125 – Darling Flame (USA) 101 (Capote **81** (USA)) [2007 8.3m⁵ 8.3g⁶ 8.2g⁴ p9.5g⁶ f8d² p9.5s⁵ Dec 20] tall, lengthy colt: unfurnished **a74** at 2 yrs: seventh foal: brother to 2003 2-y-o 6f winner Catherine Howard and half-brother/closely related to 3 winners, notably smart French 7f winner Bezrin (by Danzig): dam, 6f (at 2 yrs)/7f winner, out of US Grade 1 8.5f winner My Darling One: fairly useful maiden on turf, fair on all-weather: below form after third start, in nursery (blinkered) final outing: stays 1m. *M. Johnston*

CLOWANCE 2 b.f. (Feb 16) Montjeu (IRE) 137 – Freni (GER) (Sternkoenig (IRE) **78 p** 122) [2007 8d⁴ Oct 11] rangy filly: second foal: half-sister to German 1¼m to 11.5f winner Festero (by Silvano): dam, German 10.5f/11f (including Group 2) winner, half-sister to smart German 1½m performer Ferarri: 14/1, promising fourth to Strategic Mission in maiden at Newbury, finishing well from rear: will be suited by 1¼m/1½m. *R. Charlton*

CLUB CAPTAIN (USA) 4 b.g. Red Ransom (USA) – Really Fancy (USA) (In – Reality) [2007 –: 8.3d Oct 15] big gelding: little solid form. *T. D. McCarthy*

CLUELESS 5 b.g. Royal Applause 124 – Pure (Slip Anchor 136) [2007 12m² 13.1m⁴ **93 d** 12m 14g 12m⁶ 13.1s 10.3g Oct 26] big, lengthy gelding: fairly useful performer: not discredited first 2 starts at 5 yrs: lost his way after: stays 13f: acts on soft and good to firm ground: tried blinkered: has twice given trouble at stall: tends to hang: has run well when sweating. *N. G. Richards*

CLYTHA 3 ch.f. Mark of Esteem (IRE) 137 – India Atlanta (Ahonoora 122) [2007 57: – 10g 8.1m May 7] close-coupled, quite good-topped filly: has fluent action: maiden: little form at 3 yrs. *M. L. W. Bell*

C'MON YOU IRONS (IRE) 2 b.c. (Feb 11) Orpen (USA) 116 – Laissez Faire (IRE) **79** (Tagula (IRE) 116) [2007 5g⁴ 6s* 6g Oct 6] €8,000F, €21,000Y: neat colt: first foal: dam unraced out of half-sister to high-class miler Chalon: fair form: won maiden at Hamilton in September: stiff task, mid-field in 23-runner Two-Year-Old Trophy at Redcar: will stay 7f: raced only on good going or softer. *B. Smart*

CNOC MOY (IRE) 3 b.g. Mull of Kintyre (USA) 114 – Ewar Sunrise 67 (Shavian **85** 125) [2007 –: p8g p9.5g⁶ p10g² p8g* 8d 8.3g* 8.1m* 8.3f² p8.6g Oct 2] lengthy gelding: fairly useful handicapper: progressed well in 2007, winning at Lingfield in April, and Windsor and Sandown in July: good neck second at Windsor after: will prove best at 7f/1m: acts on polytrack and firm going: races prominently: sold 39,000 gns, joined O. Sherwood. *C. F. Wall*

COACHHOUSE LADY (USA) 2 b.f. (Mar 3) Rahy (USA) 115 – Secret Advice **81** (USA) (Secreto (USA) 128) [2007 5g p6g 7f² 7.5m⁵ 7g* Oct 6] $275,000Y: well-made filly: sister to US 5f (at 2 yrs) to 1m (minor stakes) winner Rahy's Secret and half-sister to several US winners: dam, US 7f/8.5f winner (also third in 8.5f Grade 3 event), out of half-sister to Champion Stakes winner Northern Baby: fairly useful form: improved to win maiden at Redcar final start, making all: will prove best up to 7f: acts on firm going. *K. A. Ryan*

COALITE (IRE) 4 b.g. Second Empire (IRE) 124 – Municipal Girl (IRE) 53 (Mac's **59** Imp (USA) 116) [2007 65: f6g 6g* 6g 8s⁶ p6g 7.1m⁶ 8m Sep 18] compact gelding: modest handicapper: won at Ayr in May: effective at 6f, barely stays 1m: acts on good to form going: often wears blinkers/cheekpieces: none too consistent. *A. D. Brown*

COASTAL BREEZE 4 b.g. Fasliyev (USA) 120 – Classic Design (Busted 134) [2007 **46** 56: p12g p8g p7m p8g⁶ Dec 16] modest maiden at 3 yrs: only poor in 2007, including in blinkers: stays 7f: raced only on polytrack. *A. J. Chamberlain*

Prix Chaudenay Casino Barriere de Menton, Longchamp—Coastal Path maintains his unbeaten record; Noble Prince (hidden by winner), Royal And Regal (left) and Friston Forest (third right) make it a 1,2,3,4 for Andre Fabre

COASTAL COMMAND 3 b.g. Sakhee (USA) 136 – Zenith 88 (Shirley Heights 130) **80** [2007 62p: 10.5g² 10g⁴ p12g⁵ Sep 24] good-topped gelding: fairly useful maiden: best effort when fourth to Walking Talking at Sandown: stays 1¼m: raced on polytrack and good ground: races freely: temperament under suspicion: sold 32,000 gns. *R. Charlton*

COASTAL PATH 3 b.c. Halling (USA) 133 – Coraline (Sadler's Wells (USA) 132) **117 p** [2007 12s* 12.5g* 15g* 15d* Oct 6] sixth foal: half-brother to smart French performers (all stayed at least 15f) Clear Thinking (by Rainbow Quest), and Martaline and Reefscape (both by Linamix): dam, French 12.5f winner, half-sister to Irish Oaks winner Wemyss Bight: smart form: unbeaten in newcomers race at Clairefontaine in July, minor event at Deauville in August, Qatar Prix de Lutece at Longchamp (ran on strongly to beat Dancing Lady 4 lengths) in September and Prix Chaudenay Casino Barriere de Menton at Longchamp (by ¾ length from Noble Prince) in October: stays 15f: type to progress further at 4 yrs. *A. Fabre, France*

COASTING 2 b.g. (Mar 23) Cape Cross (IRE) 129 – Sweeping 104 (Indian King (USA) **103** 128) [2007 5m³ 6g* 6m 7g* 7m Aug 11] 30,000F, 38,000Y: medium-sized, quite attractive gelding: good walker: has a quick action: closely related to 2 winners by Green Desert, including 6f winner Desert Lynx, and half-brother to smart 5f winner (including at 2 yrs) Watching (by Indian Ridge) and fairly useful 1½m to 2½m winner Puteri Wentworth (by Sadler's Wells): dam 2-y-o 6f winner (stayed 9f): useful performer: won maiden at Newbury in May and nursery at Goodwood (by 4 lengths) in August: well beaten both outings at Ascot, in Coventry Stakes third start and nursery final one (reportedly scoped dirty after): subsequently gelded: will stay 1m. *Mrs A. J. Perrett*

COBBOLD POINT 2 b.g. (Jan 16) Tipsy Creek (USA) 115 – Mofeyda (IRE) 70 **–** (Mtoto 134) [2007 7d 6d 7d Jul 22] no form. *M. W. Easterby*

COBO BAY 2 b.c. (May 6) Primo Valentino (IRE) 116 – Fisher Island (IRE) 59 (Sri **96** Pekan (USA) 117) [2007 6s⁴ p6g³ 7.5g⁴ p7.1g* 8s* 8m 8s* Sep 22] tall, good-topped colt: third foal: half-brother to 3-y-o Foxxy and 4-y-o Cool Isle: dam, 1¼m winner (stayed 2m), half-sister to useful Irish 1½m performer Smuggler's Song: useful performer: generally progressive, won nurseries at Wolverhampton and Newmarket in August and Ayr in September: will stay 1¼m: acts on polytrack and soft going, ran as if amiss on good to firm: front runner. *K. A. Ryan*

COCABANA 2 b.f. (Apr 13) Captain Rio 122 – Hiraeth 76 (Petong 126) [2007 5g⁶ 5.7f⁶ **69** 5d⁵ 5v⁴ 5.2f* 5.2m 5.5m 5m² 5.1m p6g⁴ p5.1g p5m Dec 8] 4,000Y: smallish filly: third foal: dam, half-sister to smart sprinter Ringmoor Down: fair performer: won maiden at Yarmouth in July: twice in frame in nurseries: best at 5f/easy 6f: acts on polytrack, firm and good to soft going. *J. G. Portman*

213

COCKATOO (USA) 4 b.g. Dynaformer (USA) – Enticed (USA) (Stage Door Johnny **71**
(USA)) [2007 64: p13.9g 16m³ Jun 8] heavy-topped gelding: fair maiden: stays 2m:
acts on polytrack and good to firm ground: tried in cheekpieces/blinkers: fair hurdler.
G. L. Moore

COCKNEY REBEL (IRE) 3 b.c. Val Royal (FR) 127 – Factice (USA) 78 **127**
(Known Fact (USA) 135) [2007 108: 8m* 8m* 8m⁵ Jun 19]
    When Speciosa, from a stable more familiar to followers of jumping, won
the One Thousand Guineas in 2006, her trainer said 'I hope this gives all the little
people hope. Don't give up. You can do it.' Multi-millionaire owners with their
multiple options dominate the big Group 1 races on the Flat and classic victories by
the likes of Speciosa, the 2006 Derby winner Sir Percy (a 16,000-guinea yearling)
and the latest Two Thousand Guineas winner, the unheralded Cockney Rebel,
provide a welcome ray of hope for the massed ranks of supposedly ordinary
owners. Cockney Rebel was sold not once, but twice, before setting foot on a
racecourse, making 15,000 guineas as a foal at the December Sales and 30,000
guineas at the Doncaster St Leger yearling sale. In fact, the first three in the Two
Thousand Guineas were all sold relatively cheaply as foals and yearlings, 70,000
guineas the combined cost of the trio as yearlings.
    The rollercoaster career of Cockney Rebel's trainer Geoff Huffer, whose
string numbered around twenty, added colour to the winner's story. A one-time pop
musician who was in his second spell with a training licence, Huffer had served
time in 2001 for VAT and duty fraud while running a transport business during the
thirteen-year break following his first spell as a trainer. The presence in the
unsaddling enclosure of veteran pop singer Steve Harley, a keen racing man and a
friend of the owner, also provided a talking point. Cockney Rebel took his name
from Harley's band with whom he topped the charts for two weeks with *Make Me
Smile (Come Up And See Me)* in February 1975. Despite three other top ten hits,
Harley and Cockney Rebel—who still perform—are considered in some quarters
to be a 'one-hit wonder' which was probably what many observers believed Cockney Rebel the horse would turn out to be. He started at 25/1 at Newmarket, the
longest-priced winner of the Two Thousand Guineas since 1978, but, in fact, he
remained at number one for three times as long as his pop group namesakes,
completing the Anglo-Irish Two Thousand Guineas double before being toppled
when managing only fifth behind a one, two, three for 'Team Ballydoyle' in the
St James's Palace Stakes at Royal Ascot.
    The absence of the two best two-year-olds of 2006, Teofilo and Bally-
doyle's Holy Roman Emperor, from the Stan James Two Thousand Guineas was
regarded at first as a big blow for the race. The pair had fought out a close finish to
the Dewhurst and they had dominated the ante-post market on the Guineas over the
winter. Holy Roman Emperor, however, was dashed off to stud at Coolmore in
March to replace the previous year's Two Thousand Guineas winner, his former
stable-companion George Washington (by the same sire, Danehill), who had
fertility problems. Cause for concern over the unbeaten Teofilo, whom his trainer

*Stan James 2000 Guineas Stakes, Newmarket—the field splits into two groups with
Cockney Rebel and Vital Equine (rail) in the right-hand bunch and third-placed Dutch Art on the far left*

had hoped could become a contender for the triple crown, surfaced in mid-April when leading bookmakers briefly suspended betting on the 5/4 ante-post favourite. Confirmation of a minor training setback, which restricted Teofilo to walking and swimming for a week, seemed to restore expectations and reassure ante-post punters, but Teofilo suffered a recurrence of soreness in a knee and was not among the runners at the final declaration stage. The Two Thousand Guineas had to find not only a new favourite, but also virtually a new identity.

The Ballydoyle/Coolmore partners, who were seeking a third successive victory in the Two Thousand Guineas following Footstepsinthesand and George Washington, might have lost their principal candidate but there were still five Two Thousand Guineas runners representing one or more of the ownership triumvirate of John Magnier, Michael Tabor and Derrick Smith. They were: the new favourite at 4/1, the Stoute-trained Craven Stakes winner Adagio; the second favourite, unbeaten French-trained US Ranger who had put up a smart performance when winning the Prix Djebel; and three—Duke of Marmalade, Eagle Mountain and Yellowstone—saddled by Aidan O'Brien, for whom Footstepsinthesand and George Washington had been among four previous winners of the race, leaving the master of Ballydoyle only one behind Sir Michael Stoute's modern-day record, the two stables having saddled seven of the ten previous Two Thousand Guineas winners between them.

The Middle Park winner Dutch Art had the best two-year-old form on offer among the twenty-four who lined up at Newmarket (the biggest field since 2000), but he looked at the time more likely to make a top sprinter than a miler and was sent off at 14/1, the same odds as Duke of Marmalade and Eagle Mountain. Among those at shorter odds were the lightly-raced Diamond Tycoon, well supported after a very impressive victory in a Newbury maiden, the Dewhurst third and fourth Strategic Prince and Haatef, and Major Cadeaux, who had beaten Dutch Art in the Greenham. Cockney Rebel hadn't been seen since finishing a close third in the Champagne Stakes at York to Vital Equine, subsequently fifth in the Dewhurst and a 33/1-shot in the Guineas. A planned preparatory outing in the Craven had been missed because Cockney Rebel developed a 'dirty throat' and—with his training including a gallop at Lingfield—he became the ninth winner in the last twelve runnings to triumph in the Two Thousand Guineas on his seasonal reappearance, a trend that seems set to continue with all-weather training grounds and racecourse gallops providing alternatives to the traditional trials for some of the leading candidates. All four of the O'Brien-trained Two Thousand Guineas winners went straight to Newmarket, as did Duke of Marmalade and Eagle Mountain in the latest edition.

Eagle Mountain's performances had included a second in the Champagne Stakes and that race, rather than the Dewhurst, turned out to provide the best background to the Two Thousand Guineas. Cockney Rebel's trainer left race tactics to jockey Olivier Peslier who brought Cockney Rebel over from a potentially awkward middle draw to race on the stand side, where Vital Equine made the running, as the field split into two groups against each rail. The stalls had been

placed in the centre of the track, the clerk of the course issuing an assurance beforehand that watering, made necessary by the lack of recent rain, had been meticulously monitored and the going would be uniform across the course. Though the spectacle was somewhat spoiled by the distinct groups racing wide apart, the result (and that of the twenty-nine-runner sprint handicap which followed), did indeed suggest there was no advantage with one side or the other. The patiently-ridden Cockney Rebel, who made up ground effortlessly to get into contention over a furlong out, hung left when ridden in earnest but got the better of Vital Equine to win by a length and a half, with Dutch Art defying doubts about his stamina and coming through from the back in the far-side group to finish third, three quarters of a length behind Vital Equine. With Duke of Marmalade and Eagle Mountain fourth and fifth, it meant that four of the first five were making their seasonal reappearances. Major Cadeaux came sixth, US Ranger (second home on the far side) seventh, Strategic Prince eighth, Diamond Tycoon ninth and Haatef tenth; Adagio managed only twelfth, while Godolphin's sole challenger, 33/1-shot Truly Royal, came nineteenth, and Drayton, a first British classic runner for South African trainer Mike de Kock, twenty-first. The starting prices of the first six—25/1, 33/1, 14/1, 14/1, 14/1 and 10/1—might have led the uninitiated to conclude that the form would turn out to be substandard for a classic. But the latest Guineas looked an up-to-standard renewal, despite its high profile absentees, and the winner's timefigure in a strongly-run race of 0.96 fast (equivalent to a timerating of 124) backed up the form rating. Cockney Rebel's performance was more or less a match for the Dewhurst performances of Teofilo and Holy Roman Emperor.

Cockney Rebel, Vital Equine and Duke of Marmalade were in a twelve-runner line-up for the Boylesports Irish Two Thousand Guineas under similar ground conditions at the Curragh three weeks after Newmarket. They were joined by Irish-trained Creachadoir, runner-up in the Poule d'Essai des Poulains to the O'Brien-trained Astronomer Royal. The quartet dominated the betting, Cockney Rebel starting favourite at 6/4, with Duke of Marmalade at 9/4, Creachadoir at 7/1 and Vital Equine at 8/1, with 12/1 bar. Though more than half the field started at 33/1 or longer, the Irish Two Thousand was up to standard and Cockney Rebel, in the lead earlier than at Newmarket after taking a good hold, ran on under pressure to win in workmanlike style by a length from Creachadoir, with the 40/1-shot He's A Decoy snatching third from Duke of Marmalade, who was just over two lengths behind the winner, fractionally closer than at Newmarket. Front-running Vital Equine managed no better than a respectable sixth, beaten around three lengths by the winner and possibly not fully over his exertions at Newmarket. Cockney Rebel was the sixth Two Thousand Guineas winner to follow up at the Curragh, following Right Tack (1969), Don't Forget Me (1987), Tirol (1990), Rodrigo de Triano (1992) and Rock of Gibraltar (2002). The double is not attempted so often as it might be, but the defeats of the six others who have tried, High Top, Nebbiolo, To-Agori-Mou, Lomond, Island Sands and George Washington (four of them at odds on), emphasise Cockney Rebel's achievement.

Stan James 2000 Guineas Stakes, Newmarket—a closer view of the stand-side group; 25/1 Cockney Rebel becomes the longest-priced winner since 1978; Vital Equine is second with Duke of Marmalade (second left) fourth, Eagle Mountain (rail) fifth and Major Cadeaux sixth

Boylesports Irish 2000 Guineas, the Curragh—Cockney Rebel completes the Guineas double; Creachadoir (checked cap) is second with He's A Decoy (stars on sleeves) third and Duke of Marmalade (left) fourth

Cockney Rebel wasn't able to emulate Right Tack and Rock of Gibraltar, though, by completing a treble in the St James's Palace Stakes, a race won by Cockney Rebel's trainer in 1988 with Persian Heights. The first four from the Curragh reopposed at Royal Ascot, where ground conditions were again on the firm side, and Ballydoyle—represented at the Curragh only by Duke of Marmalade and his presumed pacemaker—also saddled Astronomer Royal and the unlucky Poule d'Essai des Poulains fourth Excellent Art, who had been an intended runner in the Irish Two Thousand Guineas until suffering a foot injury on the eve of the race. The St James's Palace was a triumph for Ballydoyle, Aidan O'Brien responsible for a one, two, three with Excellent Art, Duke of Marmalade and Astronomer Royal, the last-named pipping Dutch Art to complete the clean sweep. The race developed into considerably more of a tactical affair than either of the Two Thousand Guineas at Newmarket and the Curragh and Cockney Rebel, the evens favourite, finished fifth, beaten a length and three quarters by the winner despite veering sharply left off a true line in the closing stages after looking dangerous when beginning his challenge. It transpired that Cockney Rebel had a stress fracture of the pelvis. The pelvis was not displaced, however, and it was expected that Cockney Rebel would be back in time for the Queen Elizabeth II Stakes at Ascot in September. Unfortunately, he struck into himself on his near-fore when spooking at something on the gallops earlier in the month. He would have needed a further three months to recover and it was decided to retire him. He will be standing alongside his sire Val Royal at the National Stud in Newmarket. Not long after Cockney Rebel's retirement, his trainer announced that he would be handing in his licence for a second time. 'It's for good, Cockney Rebel has made it a magnificent experience second time around and it makes sense to go out at the top now,' he said.

Cockney Rebel (IRE) (b.c. 2004)	Val Royal (FR) (b 1996)	Royal Academy (b 1987)	Nijinsky
			Crimson Saint
		Vadlava (br 1984)	Bikala
			Vadsa
	Factice (USA) (ch 1993)	Known Fact (b 1977)	In Reality
			Tamerett
		Wacky Princess (ch 1986)	Miswaki
			Cornish Princess

If Cockney Rebel's trainer was unfashionable, then so too was his sire Val Royal, who won in pattern company in France at three and gained easily his biggest success in the Breeders' Cup Mile as a five-year-old. His injury-interrupted racing career comprised only twelve races, one of them in Oath's Derby, and he had spells at stud in Australia, Argentina and Ireland (Cockney Rebel is from his first Irish

Mr Phil Cunningham's "Cockney Rebel"

crop) before moving on to the National Stud where his fee has gone up from £6,500 to £10,000 for 2008. Cockney Rebel's dam Factice gained her only win in a five-furlong maiden at Tipperary from two starts as a two-year-old, but Cockney Rebel is her fifth winner, including Cockney Rebel's close relative the Irish two-year-old seven-furlong winner Factice Royal, a daughter of Val Royal's sire Royal Academy, who also won the Breeders' Cup Mile. None of Factice's previous winners was a patch on Cockney Rebel, easily the best performer to come from his immediate family in recent times. His great grandam Cornish Princess is, however, out of Rare Exchange, a half-sister to Belmont Stakes winner Jaipur and to Rare Treat, who won sixteen races in a career spanning one hundred and one starts and became the dam of the champion three-year-old filly of 1965 in the States, What A Treat. What A Treat bred the high-class miler and very successful sire Be My Guest, while another daughter of Rare Treat, the unraced Exotic Treat, was the dam of Derby winner Golden Fleece. The tall Cockney Rebel stayed a mile, acted on good to firm going and also probably on soft, and had worn a crossed noseband. He will be joined at stud by both the second and third in the Two Thousand Guineas, Vital Equine and Dutch Art, the former standing at Bearstone Stud at £6,000 and the latter at Cheveley Park at £10,000. It will be interesting to follow their progress. *G. A. Huffer*

COCKTAIL SHAKER (USA) 2 b.c. (Apr 9) Gulch (USA) – Carr Shaker (USA) **63** (Carr de Naskra (USA)) [2007 7.1g 7.1g p8g 9m³ Sep 21] $50,000Y, £38,000 2-y-o: rangy colt, has scope: closely related to 2 US winners by Big Mukora, notably 6f (minor stakes at 2 yrs) to 9f (Grade 3) winner Dewars Rocks and half-brother to 3 US winners, including 7f (at 2 yrs) to 8.5f winner Northern Shaker (by Compliance): dam US sprinter: modest maiden: blinkered, third in nursery at Newmarket: stays 9f: sold 8,500 gns. *B. J. Meehan*

COCOBEAN 3 b.g. Josr Algarhoud (IRE) 118 – Aker Wood 86 (Bin Ajwaad (IRE) 119) – [2007 –: p12g⁶ 10.9s 11.5s 15.8m Aug 7] no form. *M. Appleby*

COCONUT MOON 5 b.m. Bahamian Bounty 116 – Lunar Ridge (Indian Ridge 123) **90** [2007 86: p6g p5.1g p5.1g 5m 5m² 5m² 5.1f³ 5.1d² 5g⁶ 5s⁵ 5m 5s² 5.1m* 5g 5.1m² 5.1g **a66** Sep 29] smallish mare: fairly useful handicapper on turf, fair on all-weather: won at Chester (for second successive year) in September: best at 5f: acts on polytrack, firm and soft going: usually races up with pace. *E. J. Alston*

COCONUT QUEEN (IRE) 3 b.f. Alhaarth (IRE) 126 – Royal Bounty (IRE) 80 **77** (Generous (IRE) 139) [2007 70: 8f⁴ 7m⁴ 9.9m⁶ 7m³ 6.9g⁶ 6.9d⁶ 7m 7.5s 8m 8.5d Sep 25] compact filly: fair handicapper: won at Carlisle in June: stays 1m: acts on firm and good to soft going: in cheekpieces last 6 starts: sold 30,000 gns. *Mrs A. Duffield*

CODA AGENCY 4 b.g. Agnes World (USA) 123 – The Frog Lady (IRE) 52 (Al Hareb **58** (USA) 123) [2007 67: 17.2m 16m⁵ p16g⁴ 16.2d⁶ p16g 18d Aug 16] strong gelding: modest maiden handicapper: stays 17f: acts on polytrack and good to firm ground: won over hurdles in October. *D. W. P. Arbuthnot*

CODE (IRE) 6 b.g. Danehill (USA) 126 – Hidden Meaning (USA) (Gulch (USA)) – [2007 11.9m 11.9m⁶ p16g 12.6s⁶ 15g⁶ Jul 12] big gelding: fair in bumpers, little form on Flat: wore cheekpieces last 2 starts. *Miss Z. C. Davison*

COEUR COURAGEUX (FR) 5 b.g. Xaar 132 – Linoise (FR) 108 (Caerwent 123) **85** [2007 96: p6g⁶ 6m 7s 8.1m⁶ 6g⁴ 7.1m p7.1g* p8.6g⁶ p7g p8g p10g⁴ p8.6g Oct 27] tall, rather leggy gelding: fairly useful performer nowadays: won handicap at Wolverhampton in August: left D. Nicholls after next outing: should prove best at 7f/1m: acts on polytrack, best turf form on good going: tongue tied. *G. L. Moore*

COEUR DE LIONNE (IRE) 3 b.g. Invincible Spirit (IRE) 121 – Lionne (Darshaan **108 +** 133) [2007 80: p11g* 10d⁴ 10m³ 11m² 14g p11g* p12g* Sep 24] sturdy, useful-looking gelding: useful performer: won maiden in April and handicaps (2, further improvement when beating Pivotal Answer by short head for latter success) in September, all at Kempton: likely to prove best up to 1½m (below form tried at 1¾m): acts on polytrack, unraced on extremes of going on turf: sold 350,000 gns, and joined E. Dunlop. *R. Charlton*

COFFEE CUP (IRE) 2 b.f. (Apr 28) Royal Academy (USA) 130 – Christel Flame **70** (Darshaan 133) [2007 5d⁶ 7g⁴ 7g* 7m Sep 6] 14,000Y: quite good-topped filly: first foal: dam useful 1m/1½m winner in USA/France: fair form: won seller at Thirsk in August: will stay 1m. *G. A. Swinbank*

COFFIN DODGER 4 ch.f. Dracula (AUS) 121 – Karakul (IRE) 78 (Persian Bold 123) **47 d** [2007 53: 10.1m³ f11g 11.8s 11.5d 10m³ 10.1m 11.9m⁵ Aug 14] angular filly: poor performer: below form after reappearance in 2007: stays 1½m: acts on all-weather, firm and good to soft going: tried in headgear: often visibly away. *C. N. Allen*

COLCHIUM (IRE) 3 br.f. Elnadim (USA) 128 – Dog Rose (SAF) (Fort Wood (USA) **76** 117) [2007 76: 8.2m⁵ 8g² 9g⁵ 6.9d⁴ 8m⁶ 8m⁵ p7.1g Oct 2] sturdy filly: fair handicapper: stays 9f: acts on polytrack, good to firm and good to soft going. *H. Morrison*

COLDITZ (IRE) 3 ch.g. Noverre (USA) 125 – West Escape 95 (Gone West (USA)) **64** [2007 77: f12g⁵ 12m² 12m 9g⁴ 9.8m 11.1g³ 8.3g 8.3s 9.8s⁴ 9.1d² 8d⁴ 9.1d⁴ 10.1m 10f³ Sep 17] smallish, attractive gelding: just modest performer at 3 yrs: stays easy 1½m: acts on good to firm and good to soft going: sometimes races freely: wears cheekpieces nowadays: sold 5,600 gns. *D. W. Barker*

COLD QUEST (USA) 3 b.g. Seeking The Gold (USA) – Polaire (IRE) 108 (Polish **100** Patriot (USA) 128) [2007 90: 10g³ 12g Aug 1] strong, medium-sized gelding: useful form: best effort when length third to Winter Sunrise in handicap at Newmarket on reappearance: tailed off in similar event at Goodwood next time: gelded after: stays 1¼m, worth a try at 1m. *J. H. M. Gosden*

COLD TURKEY 7 b.g. Polar Falcon (USA) 126 – South Rock 102 (Rock City 120) **95** [2007 102: p12g p12g⁶ p12m⁴ Dec 9] sturdy gelding: useful performer: best effort in 2007 when sixth to Dansant in listed race at Kempton: effective at 1½m, and stays 2¼m with emphasis on speed: acts on polytrack, firm and soft ground: free-going sort: held up. *G. L. Moore*

COLEORTON DAGGER 3 ch.f. Daggers Drawn (USA) 114 – Tayovullin (IRE) 65 – (Shalford (IRE) 124§) [2007 f5g p6g f5g⁴ f8d Dec 20] fourth foal: half-sister to useful 5f/6f winner Coleorton Dancer (by Danehill Dancer): dam 7f winner: little form: left K. Ryan after third start: tried in cheekpieces: possibly temperamental. *J. R. Holt*

COLEORTON DANCER 5 ch.g. Danehill Dancer (IRE) 117 – Tayovullin (IRE) 65 **87**
(Shalford (IRE) 124§) [2007 106: 6m 6m 7s 6d 6d p6g⁵ 7g⁵ p6g² p6m f6d³ Dec 21] leggy,
quite good-topped gelding: one-time useful handicapper, just fairly useful in 2007: stays
easy 7f: acts on all-weather, heavy and good to firm going: tried blinkered/in cheekpieces.
K. A. Ryan

COLERIDGE (AUS) 8 ch.g. Yeats (USA) – Coco Cheval (AUS) (Zephyr Bay (AUS)) **78**
[2007 81: p8g⁶ p8g 8m Oct 14] well-made gelding: fair handicapper: below form after
reappearance in 2007, reportedly bled final start: stays 1m: acts on polytrack: tried
blinkered: has raced freely. *J. C. Fox*

COLINCA'S LAD (IRE) 5 b.g. Lahib (USA) 129 – Real Flame (Cyrano de Bergerac **73**
120) [2007 71: 8m⁶ 8d⁴* 9.7s⁴ 8g p8g⁶ 8.3m p11m p8g⁴ p8.6g Nov 30] tall gelding: fair **a63**
handicapper on turf, modest on all-weather: won apprentice event at Newmarket in
June: stays 1¼m: acts on polytrack, firm and good to soft going: tends to edge right.
T. T. Clement

COLINETTE 4 b.f. Groom Dancer (USA) 128 – Collide 102 (High Line 125) [2007 **72**
57: 10.5m⁵ 11.6m² 13.4g p12.2g⁴ p12.2g⁵ Oct 26] leggy filly: fair maiden handicapper: stays 1½m: acts on polytrack and good to firm ground: blinkered final outing.
R. T. Phillips

COLLATERAL DAMAGE (IRE) 4 b.c. Orpen (USA) 116 – Jay Gee (IRE) 93 **94**
(Second Set (IRE) 127) [2007 94: p8.6g 8s 10.3m⁵ 10.4g 10m⁵ 9s³ 8.9s³ 9.9g 11.9m⁶
10.4d 10.3m Sep 12] big, strong colt: fairly useful handicapper: stays 1½m: acts on heavy
and good to firm ground: often tongue tied: held up. *T. D. Easterby*

COLLECTION (IRE) 2 b.c. (Feb 13) Peintre Celebre (USA) 137 – Lasting Chance **87 p**
(USA) (American Chance (USA) 117) [2007 7d² 7d* Oct 16] €130,000Y: good-topped,
attractive colt: third foal: half-brother to fairly useful 7f/1m winner (including in Ireland)
Dapple Dawn (by Celtic Swing): dam Canadian 6f (at 2 yrs) to 9f (Grade 3) winner:
plenty of promise both starts, 1¼ lengths second to Fifteen Love in minor event at
Salisbury prior to easily winning maiden at Newcastle: will be suited by 1m/1¼m: useful
prospect. *W. J. Haggas*

COLLEGE LAND BOY 3 b.g. Cois Na Tine (IRE) 101 – Welcome Lu 45 (Most **55**
Welcome 131) [2007 68: 5v 7g 5d 6m Sep 1] stocky, compact gelding: maiden: just
modest form in 2007: should stay 7f. *J. J. Quinn*

COLLEGE QUEEN 9 b.m. Lugana Beach 116 – Eccentric Dancer 47 (Rambo Dancer **41**
(CAN) 107) [2007 42: p8g p6g⁶ f5d⁶ Dec 14] strong mare: poor performer nowadays:
effective at 5f/6f: acts on all-weather, firm and good to soft going: tried in headgear/
tongue tied. *S. Gollings*

COLLEGE REBEL 6 b.m. Defacto (USA) – Eccentric Dancer 47 (Rambo Dancer **–**
(CAN) 107) [2007 56: f16g f14g f14g f14g 14.1m 17.1d 15.8g Aug 29] tall mare: no
longer of any account. *J. F. Coupland*

COLLEGE SCHOLAR (GER) 3 ch.c. Dr Fong (USA) 128 – Colina (GER) (Caer- **93**
leon (USA) 132) [2007 96: 6m 6m⁶ 6s⁶ 7d p6g Sep 24] lengthy, quite good-topped
colt: fairly useful performer: easily best effort in 2007 when sixth in handicap at Newmarket third outing: left M. Channon after: raced mostly at 6f, bred to stay much further:
acts on firm and soft going: tried visored/blinkered: sold 3,500 gns. *E. A. L. Dunlop*

COLLEMATTEO (IRE) 3 b.g. Alexius (IRE) 120 – Saraho'byrne (IRE) 20 (Brief **–**
Truce (USA) 126) [2007 5s⁶ Jul 25] 28/1, last in maiden at Leicester. *D. J. Wintle*

COLLEONI (IRE) 2 b.c. (May 28) Sadler's Wells (USA) 132 – Francfurter 89 (Leg- **–**
end of France (USA) 124) [2007 8g Nov 9] 140,000Y: half-brother to several winners,
notably smart 7f (at 2 yrs) to 1¼m (E. P. Taylor Stakes) winner Fraulein (by Acatenango):
dam 1¼m winner: 14/1, last in maiden at Musselburgh. *G. A. Butler*

COLLETTE'S CHOICE 4 b.f. Royal Applause 124 – Brilliance 74 (Cadeaux Gener- **70**
eux 131) [2007 67: 9.9m⁴ 9.9g 12m⁵ 12m² 12m⁶ 12g⁵ 14m* 14f⁴ 10m Sep 27] strong,
good-bodied filly: fair handicapper: won at Musselburgh in August: stays 1¾m: raced on
good going or firmer on turf (acts on firm): in cheekpieces last 6 outings. *R. A. Fahey*

COLLIOURE (USA) 3 b.f. Gulch (USA) – Saraa Ree (USA) 102 (Caro 133) [2007 **65**
f8g³ f8g⁶ 8.3g May 21] attractive filly: half-sister to several winners, notably high-class
performer up to 11f in USA Sarafan (by Lear Fan), 6f to 1m winner in Britain at 2 yrs:
dam, 7f winner, out of sister to Irish River: form in maidens only when 12 lengths third to
Idle No More at Southwell. *P. F. I. Cole*

COLLOQUIAL 6 b.g. Classic Cliche (IRE) 128 – Celia Brady 62 (Last Tycoon 131) **98**
[2007 97: 14g 16.2m* 16.1v 16m³ 17.2f² Sep 16] sparely-made gelding: useful handicapper: won at Haydock (by 2 lengths from River Alhaarth) in June: good efforts final
2 starts: stays 17f: acts on firm and good to soft ground (well beaten on heavy in
Northumberland Plate at Newcastle): usually visored nowadays. *H. Candy*

COLMAR MAGIC (IRE) 2 b.f. (Feb 28) Dixie Union (USA) 121 – On View (USA) **–**
(Distant View (USA) 126) [2007 6f 6d 7m⁶ p7g p10g Oct 24] 16,000Y: neat filly: first
foal: dam, US maiden, out of very smart performer up to 13.5f Wandesta: little form.
R. Hannon

COLONEL BILKO (IRE) 5 b.g. General Monash (USA) 107 – Mari-Ela (IRE) 60 **47 §**
(River Falls 113) [2007 –§, a58d: p8g⁴ p8g⁴ p8g p10g Mar 26] poor performer: left
J. Bridger after third start: stays 1¼m, probably not 11f: acts on all-weather, soft and good
to firm going: tried in blinkers/tongue tie/cheekpieces: has started slowly: tends to hang:
unreliable. *Ms J. S. Doyle*

COLONEL COTTON (IRE) 8 b.g. Royal Applause 124 – Cutpurse Moll 76 (Green **45**
Desert (USA) 127) [2007 79d: 5.5d 7s 8f² Jun 8] good-topped gelding: fair handicapper
at 7 yrs: just poor form in 2007: best at 5f/6f: acts on firm and soft going, little form on
all-weather: often blinkered/visored: no easy ride, sometimes slowly away. *W. J. Knight*

COLONEL FLAY 3 ch.g. Danehill Dancer (IRE) 117 – Bobbie Dee 93 (Blakeney 126) **70**
[2007 76: 9.9m³ 9.9g⁶ 11.7g 10m p12m⁵ p16g⁵ Oct 17] good-topped gelding: fair maiden
handicapper: effective at 1¼m to 2m: acts on polytrack and good to firm ground: once
refused at stall: usually held up: gelded after final start. *Mrs P. N. Dutfield*

COLONEL GUN (IRE) 7 ch.g. Catrail (USA) 123 – Return Again (IRE) 81 (Top **–**
Ville 129) [2007 p10g p12.2g Mar 2] ex-Irish gelding: poor maiden: missed 2005/6: stays
13f: acts on firm going. *C. R. Dore*

COLONY (IRE) 2 b.c. (Apr 8) Statue of Liberty (USA) 115 – Funoon (IRE) 74 (Kris **79 p**
135) [2007 7.1m 8g* Oct 24] €200,000Y: attractive colt: half-brother to 2 winners by
Grand Lodge, including 4-y-o Hopeful Purchase: dam, 1½m winner, out of sister to Try
My Best and El Gran Senor: improved from debut (2 months earlier) to win maiden at
Bath, well on top at finish: will be suited by 1¼m/1½m: type to thrive at 3 yrs. *Sir Michael
Stoute*

COLOPHONY (USA) 7 ch.g. Distant View (USA) 126 – Private Line (USA) 105 **68**
(Private Account (USA)) [2007 p13.9g⁴ Mar 23] big, strong gelding: fair performer,
lightly raced on Flat since 2004 (fair hurdler): stays 1¾m: acts on polytrack, raced only
on good going or firmer on turf: usually tongue tied. *K. A. Morgan*

COLORADO BLUE (IRE) 2 ch.g. (Mar 28) Nayef (USA) 129 – Colouring (IRE) 79 **85 p**
(Catrail (USA) 123) [2007 7g⁵ Oct 26] €40,000F, 52,000 2-y-o: smallish, lengthy, quite
attractive gelding: fourth foal: half-brother to 3-y-o Go On Green: dam Irish 8.5f winner:
33/1 and green, promising never-nearer fifth to Speedy Dollar in maiden at Doncaster:
gelded after: will stay 1m: sure to improve. *R. Charlton*

COLORADO RAPID (IRE) 3 b.c. Barathea (IRE) 127 – Rafting (IRE) 87 (Darshaan **105 p**
133) [2007 84p: 8g* 8m³ 8m* 8m 8.1g² Jul 7] tall, well-made colt: useful form: won
maiden at Ripon in April and handicap at Pontefract (overcame trouble to beat Dream
Lodge by 2½ lengths) in May: had rough race when only mid-field in Britannia Stakes
(Handicap) at Royal Ascot next time: excellent ½-length second to Ordnance Row in
totescoop6 Stakes (Handicap) at Sandown final start, finishing strongly: likely to stay
1¼m: raced only on good/good to firm going: looked awkward ride earlier in career: has
joined Godolphin: will continue to progress. *M. Johnston*

COLORADO SPRINGS 2 b.f. (Apr 1) Olden Times 121 – Engulfed (USA) 72 (Gulch **64**
(USA)) [2007 7.1g p8g² p8m Nov 26] lengthy filly: first foal: dam maiden (third at 7f):
modest form in maidens, runner-up at Lingfield: likely to stay 1¼m. *W. Jarvis*

COLORATURA (IRE) 2 b.f. (Mar 22) Cape Cross (IRE) 129 – Elauyun (IRE) (Muh- **55**
tarram (USA) 125) [2007 6m 8d 7g Nov 3] 47,000F: angular filly: third foal: dam unraced
half-sister to high-class 1¼m performer Oratorio: modest form in rear in maidens.
E. A. L. Dunlop

COLOR MAN 3 b.g. Rainbow Quest (USA) 134 – Subya 107 (Night Shift (USA)) **57**
[2007 48: p10g⁶ p9.5g p12f⁵ f11g³ p11g² 14.1m* 14.1s⁶ Jun 14] modest performer:
won handicap at Redcar in May: stays 1¾m: acts on all-weather and firm ground:
tried blinkered, in cheekpieces last 4 starts: sold 19,000 gns, sent to Czech Republic.
Mrs A. J. Perrett

COLORUS (IRE) 4 b.g. Night Shift (USA) – Duck Over 72 (Warning 136) [2007 78: **88** 5g 5g* f5g 5m* 5m 5m 5s⁶ 5s 5d 5f 5g³ 5m⁵ 5d Oct 12] stocky, good sort: fairly useful handicapper: won at Ripon in April and Thirsk in May: below form after: best form at 5f: acts on fibresand, good to firm and good to soft going (below form on soft): tried in headgear: not one to rely on. *M. W. Easterby*

COLOSO 3 ch.g. Compton Place 125 – Nashville Blues (IRE) 94 (Try My Best (USA) **57** 130) [2007 10d⁴ p7g⁶ Dec 5] strong gelding: much the better effort in maidens when sixth at Kempton, slowly away. *P. D. Cundell*

COLOURFUL LIFE (IRE) 11 ch.g. Rainbows For Life (CAN) – Rasmara 94§ (Kalaglow 132) [2007 14.1m Jun 12] big, workmanlike gelding: lightly-raced maiden on Flat, first outing since 2003 when well held in claimer at Redcar: one-time useful chaser, successful over hurdles in September. *K. G. Reveley*

COLOURFUL SCORE (USA) 3 b.c. Storm Cat (USA) – Serena's Song (USA) 126 **– §** (Rahy (USA) 115) [2007 p8g 8d Aug 19] $3,500,000Y: neat colt: brother to Coronation Stakes winner Sophisticat and 6f (including at 2 yrs) to 9f winner Grand Reward, both smart, and half-brother to 3 winners in USA: dam multiple Grade 1 winner in USA: tongue tied, showed only temperament, unseating rider leaving stall at Lingfield then virtually refusing to race at Pontefract: has left Godolphin. *Saeed bin Suroor*

COLOUR TROOPER (IRE) 2 ch.c. (Apr 12) Traditionally (USA) 117 – Viola Roy- **66** ale (IRE) 90 (Royal Academy (USA) 130) [2007 7.1m Aug 31] 20,000 2-y-o: compact colt: half-brother to 7-y-o St Andrews, 5-y-o Celticello and 3-y-o Hurricane Thomas: dam Irish 2-y-o 6f/7f winner: 50/1, weakened into twelfth behind Ridge Dance in maiden at Sandown. *P. Winkworth*

COLTON 4 b.g. Zilzal (USA) 137 – Picot 76 (Piccolo 121) [2007 78: 10f 10g 10.1d **55** 10g p12.2g Aug 31] tall, close-coupled gelding: handicapper: well below best in 2007. *J. M. P. Eustace*

COLUMBUS (IRE) 10 b.g. Sadler's Wells (USA) 132 – Northern Script (USA) 95 **–** (Arts And Letters (USA)) [2007 –: 21.6m 15.8m May 8] lengthy gelding: lightly raced and little form on Flat in recent years. *Jennie Candlish*

COLWYN BAY (IRE) 5 b.g. Sadler's Wells (USA) 132 – Stolen Tear (FR) 76 (Cade- **74** aux Genereux 131) [2007 p12.2g² p16g* 15d³ p16g* 16.4m* 14.1d* p16g Sep 19] deep-girthed gelding: fair handicapper: won at Kempton in May and June, Folkestone in July and Salisbury in August: stays 16.4f: acts on polytrack, good to firm and heavy going: wears cheekpieces: not straightforward, and tends to wander under pressure: sold 9,000 gns. *Jane Chapple-Hyam*

COME APRIL 3 b.f. Singspiel (IRE) 133 – So Admirable (Suave Dancer (USA) 136) **77** [2007 p10g* Jun 9] 52,000F: second foal: dam unraced sister to Eclipse winner Compton Admiral and half-sister to Queen Elizabeth II Stakes winner Summoner: 5/1, overcame greenness to win maiden at Lingfield by short head from Cybersnow, niggled along early and still plenty to do entering straight (lame after): bred to stay 1½m: stays in training. *Sir Mark Prescott*

COMEBACK QUEEN 2 b. or gr.f. (Mar 21) Nayef (USA) 129 – Miss Universe (IRE) **90** 99 (Warning 136) [2007 p8g* 8g⁵ Nov 3] close-coupled filly: fourth foal: half-sister to 8.6f (at 2 yrs) to 9f (including US Grade 2 event) winner Worldly (by Spinning World), 2004 2-y-o 7f winner Tasdeed (by Cadeaux Genereux) and 6-y-o Day To Remember, latter 2 useful: dam 2-y-o 6f winner: fairly useful form: won maiden at Lingfield in October: improved when close fifth of 10 to Classic Legend in listed event at Newmarket: will be suited by 1¼m/1½m. *S. Kirk*

COME BYE (IRE) 11 b.g. Star Quest 79 – Boreen Dubh (Boreen (FR) 123) [2007 **–** 14s Oct 4] fair hurdler on his day up to 2¾m: tongue tied, tailed off on Flat debut. *Miss A. M. Newton-Smith*

COMEINTOTHESPACE (IRE) 5 b.g. Tagula (IRE) 116 – Playa Del Sol (IRE) **59** (Alzao (USA) 117) [2007 54: p8g* p8g³ f8g² f7g³ p10g* f12g p9.5g 9.7m⁶ p12g* p12g* p12.2g⁴ p16.5g Jul 27] quite good-topped gelding: modest performer nowadays: won minor event at Kempton in January, handicaps at Lingfield in March and Kempton in April, and claimer at Lingfield (left R. Farrant £8,000) later in April: stays easy 1½m: acts on all-weather and any turf going: tried blinkered/in cheekpieces. *K. J. Burke*

COME ON NELLIE (IRE) 3 b.f. Diktat 126 – Bauci (IRE) (Desert King (IRE) 129) **–** [2007 7g 8.1s 10.2g 10d 10.2m p12.2g Oct 12] €40,000F, 8,500Y: small filly: first foal: dam unraced out of sister to Rainbow Quest: little form. *J. G. M. O'Shea*

COME OUT FIGHTING 4 b.c. Bertolini (USA) 125 – Ulysses Daughter (IRE) 88 **100** (College Chapel 122) [2007 100: 6s³ 6g 5d 6m² 6m 6g² 6d² p5.1g⁵ Nov 4] compact colt: useful performer: creditable efforts in 2007 when placed, and when fifth in handicap at Wolverhampton final outing: effective at 5f to 7f: acts on polytrack, soft and good to firm going: often races prominently: bled second start. *P. A. Blockley*

COME WHAT AUGUSTUS 5 b.g. Mujahid (USA) 125 – Sky Red 75 (Night Shift **58** (USA)) [2007 –: p16g³ p16g³ p16.5g⁵ p16.5g Mar 14] modest maiden: stays 16.5f: acts on polytrack and firm ground: in cheekpieces last 3 starts. *R. M. Stronge*

COME WHAT JULY (IRE) 6 b.g. Indian Rocket 115 – Persian Sally (IRE) (Persian **56** Bold 123) [2007 –, a52: f12g f12g p16.5g⁶ p16.5g² p16f⁴ p13.9g⁶ p16.5g⁴ p16g⁶ p12g p10g² p11g⁴ 12d p12g⁶ p9.5g Dec 29] compact gelding: modest handicapper: stays 2m: acts on all-weather, good to firm and good to soft going: tried in headgear. *D. Shaw*

COME WHAT MAY 3 b.f. Selkirk (USA) 129 – Portelet 91 (Night Shift (USA)) **62** [2007 67p: 5m³ 6d 6s 5d² 5d⁵ p5g 5g Oct 3] big filly: has scope: modest handicapper: won at Newmarket in June: below form after: should stay beyond 5f: acts on good to soft going: blinkered and tongue tied last 4 starts. *Rae Guest*

COMIC TALES 6 b.g. Mind Games 121 – Glorious Aragon 88 (Aragon 118) [2007 47: **41** p5.1g p5.1g p8.6g p5.1g³ Jan 28] good-topped gelding: poor maiden on balance: probably stays 7f: acts on all-weather and good to firm going: tried blinkered/in cheekpieces: often starts slowly. *M. Mullineaux*

COMMANDER CAVE (USA) 2 b. or br.c. (Mar 7) Tale of The Cat (USA) 113 – **59** Royal Shyness 104 (Royal Academy (USA) 130) [2007 p7g⁵ p7g Oct 24] $95,000Y: compact colt: modest form in maidens at Lingfield. *R. Hannon*

COMMANDER WISH 4 ch.g. Arkadian Hero (USA) 123 – Flighty Dancer (Pivotal **70** 124) [2007 –: 12g 16m p7.1g p5.1g* p5.1g* p6d⁶ p6g Dec 22] stocky gelding: fair performer: won minor event in October and handicap in November, both at Wolverhampton: may prove best at 5f: acts on polytrack: in cheekpieces last 5 starts, also tongue tied last 4. *Lucinda Featherstone*

COMMAND MARSHAL (FR) 4 b.g. Commands (AUS) – Marsakara (IRE) (Turtle **70** Island (IRE) 123) [2007 12.3s³ Jul 13] fair handicapper: won at Nantes in 2006 when trained by J. L. Guillochon: 13 lengths third at Chester sole Flat run in Britain: stays 1½m: raced on all-weather and good ground or softer. *M. Scudamore*

COMMANDMENT (IRE) 3 b.g. Titus Livius (FR) 115 – Alpine Flair (IRE) (Tirol **78** 127) [2007 10d² p9.5g³ 8d² 8m* Aug 14] €190,000Y: well-made gelding: fourth living foal: half-brother to 3 winners, including 4-y-o Road To Love: dam unraced: fair performer: won 4-runner maiden at Brighton in August: much better form when placed in similar events previously: stays 1¼m: sold 20,000 gns. *E. A. L. Dunlop*

COMMANDO SCOTT (IRE) 6 b.g. Danetime (IRE) 121 – Faye 79 (Monsanto (FR) **101** 121) [2007 99: p7g 7m 7f 6m 7.6m 6g⁶ 6d* 6g 7g⁵ 6d 7.2s* 6d² 6d³ 7d 6g² 6m Nov 10] good-topped gelding: useful handicapper: better than ever in 2007, winning at Newmarket in May and Ayr (beat Heroes by ½ length) in September: good efforts when placed after at Haydock, York and Doncaster (2 lengths second to Tamagin): probably best at 6f (given a test)/7f: acts on any turf going, though all 7 wins on good or softer: has raced freely. *I. W. McInnes*

COMMA (USA) 3 b.f. Kingmambo (USA) 125 – Flute (USA) 124 (Seattle Slew **87** (USA)) [2007 88: p8g² 8m⁴ 8m⁵ p10g² 10.2g Oct 24] well-made filly: fairly useful maiden: best effort on reappearance: probably stayed 1¼m: acted on polytrack: wasn't straightforward: stud. *Sir Michael Stoute*

COMMEMORATION DAY (IRE) 6 b.g. Daylami (IRE) 138 – Bequeath (USA) **73** (Lyphard (USA) 132) [2007 16m* 21g Aug 1] strong gelding: has a fluent, round action: successful 5 times on Flat in Germany for C. von der Recke in 2006: successful twice over hurdles in 2007, and fair form when winning handicap at Goodwood in June: well held after: stays 2m: acts on good to firm and good to soft ground: tongue tied last 2 starts, visored final one. *M. F. Harris*

COMMIT TO MEMORY 2 br.c. (Apr 18) Best of The Bests (IRE) 122 – Simonida **77** (IRE) (Royal Academy (USA) 130) [2007 7m 7d 7g⁶ p7g⁵ f8d* Dec 12] 4,000F, €13,000Y: lengthy colt: first foal: dam, German 8.5f winner, stayed 14.5f: fair performer: won maiden at Southwell in December by 6 lengths, despite hanging left: should be suited by 1¼m: acts on all-weather, best turf effort on good going. *Andrew Oliver, Ireland*

COMMON PURPOSE (USA) 3 b.g. Elusive Quality (USA) – Kithira 106 (Danehill **75**
(USA) 126) [2007 74p: 10f⁴ p8g³ 8m² Jun 8] strong gelding: fair maiden, lightly raced:
stays 1m: raced only on polytrack and firm/good to firm going on turf: sold 13,000 gns in
October. *J. H. M. Gosden*

COMPETITOR 6 b.h. Danzero (AUS) – Ceanothus (IRE) 61 (Bluebird (USA) 125) **–**
[2007 –, a69: p12g p10g* p10g p10g* p12g p10g³ 12m 10.2f 10s p12g Jun 5] fair **a68**
performer on all-weather: won seller in January and handicap in March, both at Lingfield: stays 1½m: acts on polytrack, little recent form on turf: wears headgear: sometimes
tongue tied: has suffered breathing problems/run as if amiss. *J. Akehurst*

COMPLETE FRONTLINE (GER) 2 ch.c. (Feb 19) Tertullian (USA) 115 – Carola **62**
Rouge (Arazi (USA) 135) [2007 5g 5m⁵ 6s² Jul 14] angular colt: modest but progressive
form in maidens, second in weak event at York: will stay 7f. *K. R. Burke*

COMPOSING (IRE) 3 b.f. Noverre (USA) 125 – Aqaba 65 (Lake Coniston (IRE) **68**
131) [2007 71p: 10m 10.2m⁵ 12m p12g 12m 16g⁴ p16g² p16g 17.2g⁶ p13.9g⁴ p12.2g
Nov 24] leggy, lengthy filly: fair maiden handicapper: stays 2m: acts on polytrack and
good to soft going: tried visored/blinkered: tongue tied nowadays. *H. Morrison*

COMPROMIZNOTENSION (IRE) 4 br.g. Key of Luck (USA) 126 – Music Khan **78**
(Music Boy 124) [2007 84: 10.1s Mar 31] good-topped gelding: fairly useful performer:
shaped as if stamina stretched when respectable seventh in handicap at Newcastle only
start in 2007: stays 1m: acts on heavy and good to firm ground: fractious in stall and
possibly amiss third 3-y-o start (wore cheekpieces): makes running: joined J. Howard
Johnson. *I. Semple*

COMPTON ABBESS 2 ch.f. (Mar 11) Compton Place 125 – Celt Song (IRE) (Unfu- **59**
wain (USA) 131) [2007 5d 7s⁶ 6m 5g 7.1g p6g Oct 10] unfurnished filly: half-sister to
smart 1999 2-y-o 6f/7f winner Princess Ellen (by Tirol), later second in 1000 Guineas and
successful in US: dam unraced: modest maiden: may prove best short of 7f: blinkered
(tailed off) once. *B. R. Millman*

COMPTON CHARLIE 3 b.g. Compton Place 125 – Tell Tale Fox (Tel Quel (FR) **57**
125) [2007 67: p8g 8.3d p12g 11.6m² Jul 16] leggy gelding: maiden, only modest in
2007: stays 11.6f: acts on good to firm and good to soft ground: hung badly right once at
2 yrs. *J. G. Portman*

COMPTON CLASSIC 5 b.g. Compton Place 125 – Ayr Classic 74 (Local Suitor **86**
(USA) 128) [2007 67: 5g 5g² 5m 5g5 5g* 5g* 5d² 5s 5g 5g³ 5d* 5.4v⁴ 5d⁶ 6s* 5g 5d³ 5g* **a81**
5d p6g p6g* p5.1d³ f6d⁴ f5g⁵ Dec 27] good-bodied gelding: fairly useful performer: won
handicaps at Carlisle and Musselburgh in June, Ayr in July and August and claimers at
Musselburgh (left J. Goldie £15,000) in October and Kempton in November: stays 6f:
acts on polytrack, heavy and good to firm going: sometimes in headgear: free-going type:
held up: unreliable. *J. R. Boyle*

COMPTON COMMANDER 9 ch.g. Baratéa (IRE) 127 – Triode (USA) 105 **47 §**
(Sharpen Up 127) [2007 –§: 21.6m 15.8m 16.2m⁵ 16d³ 16s 16g⁶ Aug 13] useful-looking
gelding: poor handicapper: seemingly stays 2m: acts on any turf going and polytrack:
sometimes wears headgear: ungenuine. *E. W. Tuer*

COMPTON DRAGON (USA) 8 ch.g. Woodman (USA) 126 – Vilikaia (USA) 125 **72**
(Nureyev (USA) 131) [2007 61: 16m 12.3f³ 12.1g* 13d² 12.3s⁴ 12m* 12d p12.2g p12.2g
Nov 20] compact gelding: fair handicapper: won at Hamilton (apprentices) in June and
Pontefract in October: stays 13f: acts on polytrack, firm and good to soft going: often in
headgear prior to 2007: edgy sort: usually held up. *W. M. Brisbourne*

COMPTON ECLAIRE (IRE) 7 ch.m. Lycius (USA) 124 – Baylands Sunshine **– §**
(IRE) (Classic Secret (USA) 91) [2007 66§: 16.1m 16g 16.1m Sep 10] good-topped
mare: handicapper: little form in 2007: stays 2m: acts on all-weather and firm going:
usually blinkered/visored: held up: ungenuine. *N. Wilson*

COMPTON ECLIPSE 7 ch.g. Singspiel (IRE) 121 – Fatah Flare (USA) (Alydar **54**
(USA)) [2007 72, a76: 9.5g p8.6g p8.6g p9.5g p8g Dec 7] leggy gelding: modest handicapper nowadays: ran creditably at Wolverhampton third/fourth starts: stays 9.5f: acts on
polytrack and firm ground: has been blinkered/tongue tied: sometimes carries head high.
J. J. Lambe, Ireland

COMPTON EXPRESS 4 gr.f. Compton Place 125 – Jilly Woo 60 (Environment **48**
Friend 128) [2007 49: p11g² p12g³ p13g⁵ p16g p12g⁵ 11.5m 10m p10g 8m p11g p10m **a54**
p8g Dec 16] modest maiden: stays 1½m (seemingly not 2m): acts on polytrack: tried
blinkered/visored. *Jamie Poulton*

COMPTON FALCON 3 ch.g. Peintre Celebre (USA) 137 – Lesgor (USA) 106 (Irish **75 d**
River (FR) 131) [2007 10.2f³ 11.9m 10.2g³ 11.9d⁶ 12g⁶ p12g Dec 1] 45,000Y: rangy
gelding: fifth foal: half-brother to 2 winners, including useful 2005 2-y-o 7f winner Guilia
(stays 1½m, by Galileo): dam French 1¼m winner: fair maiden: stays 10.2f: acts on firm
going: ran creditably in tongue tie third start. *G. A. Butler*

COMPTON LAD 4 b.g. Compton Place 125 – Kintara (Cyrano de Bergerac 120) [2007
51: 5g 5d 5d 6m 5m 5m 5d 5d 5s Oct 4] maiden: little form in 2007: should stay 6f: acts
on all-weather, soft and good to firm ground: tried in cheekpieces/tongue tie. *D. A. Nolan*

COMPTON MICKY 6 ch.g. Compton Place 125 – Nunthorpe 79 (Mystiko (USA) **41**
124) [2007 49: p5.1g⁶ Jan 15] strong gelding: poor performer: stays 7f: acts on all-
weather, firm and soft going: tried blinkered/in cheekpieces: somewhat wayward.
R. F. Marvin

COMPTON PLUME 7 ch.g. Compton Place 125 – Brockton Flame 72 (Emarati **66**
(USA) 74) [2007 67: f5g 6m⁴ 7m³ 7m 6m⁵ p7.1g⁶ 6s³ 6m⁵ 6f⁶ 6m Sep 10] strong, lengthy
gelding: fair handicapper: stays 7f: acts on firm ground: sometimes blinkered/visored:
sold 800 gns, sent to Spain. *M. W. Easterby*

COMPTON QUAY 5 ch.g. Compton Place 125 – Roonah Quay (IRE) (Soviet Lad –
(USA)) [2007 p12.2g Apr 27] rather leggy gelding: fair performer at best: missed 2006:
in cheekpieces, well held sole start in 2007: probably stays 1¼m: acts on polytrack. *Karen
George*

COMPTON RIDGE 2 b.c. (Mar 8) Compton Place 125 – Mana Pools (IRE) 76 (Brief **76**
Truce (USA) 126) [2007 6m⁵ 6d⁴ 7s⁴ Oct 9] good sort: fair maiden: fourth at Windsor and
Folkestone: stayed 6f: dead. *Mrs A. J. Perrett*

COMPTON ROSE 2 ch.f. (Apr 28) Compton Place 125 – Benjarong 50 (Sharpo 132) **60 p**
[2007 5m⁵ Jul 30] lengthy filly: fifth foal: half-sister to fairly useful 6f winner Ben
Lomand (by Inchinor): dam 5f (at 2 yrs) and 1m winner: 11/1, got hang of things only late
on when fifth to Wise Son in maiden at Windsor: will do better. *H. Candy*

COMPTON'S ELEVEN 6 gr.g. Compton Place 125 – Princess Tara 85 (Prince Sabo **95**
123) [2007 107: 6g⁶ 6.5g 7m⁵ 6m 6g 7g 7g² 7d⁴ 7.1s³ 7d 6g* 6m⁵ 7m⁵ 6d³ 6d 6s Oct 14]
good-topped gelding: useful handicapper: won at Newmarket (by short head from Certain
Justice) in August: needs good test at 6f nowadays and stays 7f: acts on polytrack, firm
and soft going: sometimes carries head high/edges left. *M. R. Channon*

COMPTON SPECIAL 3 ch.f. Compton Place 125 – Spectina 92 (Spectrum (IRE) **41**
126) [2007 46: 6m⁵ 6d p5.1g 8g⁵ 5.9f p6g⁵ p6m Sep 6] lengthy, workmanlike filly: poor
maiden: may prove best at 6f/7f: acts on polytrack. *J. G. Given*

COMPTONSPIRIT 3 ch.f. Compton Place 125 – Croeso Cynnes 70 (Most Welcome **75**
131) [2007 –: p7.1g p6g³ 6m⁴ p6g⁶ p7.1g⁴ 6d³ p6g⁴ 6m⁶ 5d² 5g* 5f⁴ 5.1m⁶ Sep 15]
workmanlike filly: fair handicapper: won at Ayr in August: best at 5f: acts on polytrack,
firm and good to soft ground: often wears cheekpieces: usually races prominently.
B. P. J. Baugh

COMPULSION 4 br.f. Bertolini (USA) 125 – Comme Ca (Cyrano de Bergerac 120) **62**
[2007 p6g⁵ p7g⁶ 6g p6g³ p6g Nov 28] 20,000Y: lengthy filly: third foal: half-sister to
2003 2-y-o 6f winner Even Easier (by Petong) and 2004 2-y-o 5f winner Grand Place (by
Compton Place): dam unraced: modest maiden: may prove best at 5f/6f. *Pat Eddery*

COMRADE COTTON 3 b.g. Royal Applause 124 – Cutpurse Moll 76 (Green Desert **67**
(USA) 127) [2007 51: p6g² p6g* p6g 5.3d² p5g 6.1m⁴ 6f⁵ 6s⁴ 7d 7d p7.1g⁴ Oct 25]
lengthy, unfurnished gelding: fair handicapper: won at Lingfield in January: best at 5f/6f:
acts on polytrack, soft and good to firm going: blinkered (not discredited) final outing.
N. A. Callaghan

CONBEXTRA 3 ch.g. Pivotal 124 – Muffled (USA) 67 (Mizaaya 104) [2007 p7g p6g⁴ **68**
6m Jun 9] easily best effort in maidens when fourth at Lingfield: dead. *J. S. Moore*

CONCEALMENT (IRE) 2 b.f. (Apr 6) Iron Mask (USA) 117 – Akatib (IRE) (Lahib **77**
(USA) 129) [2007 p6g⁶ p6g* Oct 6] €5,500Y 2-y-o: second foal: dam, little form, out of
close relative to smart sprinter Ya Malak: much improved from debut to win maiden
at Wolverhampton by 3 lengths, making all and eased: likely to prove best at 5f/6f: sold
15,500 gns. *R. M. Beckett*

CONCERTMASTER 2 b.c. (Mar 15) Bertolini (USA) 125 – Cumbrian Concerto 44 **76**
(Petong 126) [2007 p5g² 5.1f³ 5.3m² p5g* p5g* 5g⁶ 6m⁶ 5g⁶ Oct 8] €11,000Y, resold **a80**
€12,000Y: sturdy colt: third foal: dam, maiden, out of sister to Millkom: fairly useful on
all-weather, fair on turf: won maiden at Kempton in June and nursery at Lingfield in July:

probably best at 5f: acts on polytrack and firm going: sold 12,000 gns, sent to Bahrain. *R. M. Beckett*

CONDI (IRE) 3 b.f. Diktat 126 – Bea's Ruby (IRE) 86 (Fairy King (USA)) [2007 10d **60** 8.3g 8g Jun 1] lengthy, rather unfurnished filly: fourth foal: half-sister to 6-y-o Miss Monica and Irish winner around 1m Kilmannin (by College Chapel): dam 7f/1m winner: promising seventh in maiden at Windsor on debut: not knocked about unduly in similar events after. *A. J. Lidderdale*

CONDUIT (IRE) 2 ch.c. (Mar 23) Dalakhani (IRE) 133 – Well Head (IRE) (Sadler's **86 p** Wells (USA) 132) [2007 7m p8g³ p8.6g* Sep 22] closely related to 2 winners by Darshaan, notably 5-y-o Hard Top, and half-brother to 3 winners, including useful French performer up to 1½m Spray Gun (by Octagonal): dam unraced half-sister to Spectrum and to dam of Petrushka: shaped well in maidens, progressive form, and won at Wolverhampton (by ¾ length from Oberlin, despite still looking green) final start: will be well suited by 1¼m/1½m: should make a useful 3-y-o. *Sir Michael Stoute*

CONFIDE IN ME 3 b.g. Medicean 128 – Confidante (USA) 95 (Dayjur (USA) 137) **–** [2007 p7g May 2] 14/1, behind in maiden at Kempton: subsequently gelded. *G. A. Butler*

CONFIDENCE TRICK (USA) 2 ch.c. (Feb 15) Rahy (USA) 115 – Hiaam (USA) **90 p** 110 (Alydar (USA)) [2007 7s 7.1m* Sep 13] lengthy, good-bodied colt: has scope: has quick, fluent action: half-brother to numerous winners, notably smart French 1996 2-y-o 6f winner (stayed 1m) Sheer Reason (by Danzig): dam 6f (Princess Margaret Stakes) to 1m winner: better for debut (soft ground), impressive winner of maiden at Chepstow by 2½ lengths from Connor's Choice, not fully extended: will stay at least 1m: sure to go on and win more races. *Sir Michael Stoute*

CONFIDENTIALITY (IRE) 3 b.f. Desert Style (IRE) 121 – Confidential 60 **92 +** (Generous (IRE) 139) [2007 8s 8s⁵ 8d 11.3m⁴ p8g* p8g* p9.5g* p8.6g* p9.5g* p8.6g* Dec 13] €6,000Y: third foal: half-sister to fairly useful 7f winner Confide (by Namid): dam twice-raced half-sister to smart performers Reprimand (miler) and Wiorno (up to 1½m): fairly useful handicapper: left E. Lynam in Ireland, much improved when winning last 6 starts at Lingfield (apprentices), Kempton and Wolverhampton (4) in November/December: stays 9.5f: acts on polytrack. *M. Wigham*

CONFIDENTIAL LADY 4 b.f. Singspiel (IRE) 133 – Confidante (USA) 95 (Dayjur **–** (USA) 137) [2007 116: 10s Sep 22] good-topped filly: smart performer: won Prix de Diane at Chantilly in 2006: last in listed race at Ayr on only outing in 2007: stayed 10.5f, below form at 1½m in Irish Oaks: acted on soft and good to firm ground (below form on heavy): visits Medicean. *Sir Mark Prescott*

CONFIRM (IRE) 3 b.f. In The Wings 128 – Ashkirk (Selkirk (USA) 129) [2007 8g **62** 10g³ 9g³ 9.5d 8.5d⁵ 12m⁵ 12f 12g⁴ Oct 11] €8,000 3-y-o: good-topped filly: fifth foal: half-sister to 3 winners, including Irish 6f winner Antigone (by Cape Cross): dam French 1¼m winner: modest maiden: below form at Folkestone seventh outing: stays 1½m: acts on good to firm going: blinkered last 4 starts: sometimes slowly away. *Harry Rogers, Ireland*

CONFRONT 2 b.c. (Feb 11) Nayef (USA) 129 – Contiguous (USA) (Danzig **116 p** (USA)) [2007 7m² 7d* Oct 13]
'He had looks as well as pedigree and performance to commend him to breeders, and as he proved equally effective at ten and twelve furlongs, he went to stud hailed as one who might be expected to deliver classic middle-distances horses of the future.' That's what Tony Morris, writing in the *Timeform 2006 Stallion Statistical Review*, had to say about Nayef, whose first crop reached the racecourse in the latest season and did enough to suggest that such enthusiasm for their sire's stallion prospects is not misplaced. From relatively few runners, Nayef made quite an impression, his winners including Spacious and Kotsi, the first two home in the May Hill Stakes at Doncaster, Alfathaa, a close fifth in the Royal Lodge Stakes, and Confront. The last-named showed the best form of all Nayef's representatives when successful on the second of his two starts, and he looks a particularly good prospect for 2008.

Confront started favourite for both his races, the first of those a twelve-runner maiden at Newbury in September. He failed to justify the support, beaten by Fool's Wildcat, who already had three runs under his belt, but newcomers from the Sir Michael Stoute yard usually improve significantly for the outing and Confront did just that. Three weeks later he faced five rivals in a minor event at Ascot, all of

whom had shown at least fairly useful form, among them Stimulation who had created a most favourable impression when successful in a Newbury maiden on his only appearance. Sam's Cross, the winner of a maiden at Goodwood on his previous start, dictated the pace as Confront, who had taken the eye beforehand, raced handily. Shaken up to lead over two furlongs out, Confront found plenty when Stimulation challenged wide, showing his inexperience as he hung right but always having the upper hand as the pair pulled right away. At the line there was a length between them, with Sam's Cross nine lengths further back in third. Confront still held entries in the Racing Post Trophy and the Horris Hill Stakes, which took place on the same day, looking more likely to take up his engagement in the Racing Post Trophy for which he was clear ante-post favourite. As it turned out, Confront missed both races. 'We hope he will be a very decent horse next year so we have decided to be patient,' was the explanation given by his owner's racing manager.

		Nayef (USA) (b 1998)	Gulch (b 1984)	Mr Prospector Jameela
Confront (b.c. Feb 11, 2005)			Height of Fashion (b 1979)	Bustino Highclere
	Contiguous (USA) (b 1998)	Danzig (b 1977)	Northern Dancer Pas de Nom
		Modena (b 1983)	Roberto Mofida

Nayef, a Group 1 winner at three, four and five, was effective at a mile and a quarter to a mile and a half, and Confront is sure to stay the shorter trip and will probably be fully effective at the longer. A well-made individual, Confront is the third foal and third winner out of Contiguous, following on from Twin Town, a filly by Halling who won over seven and a half furlongs in Australia, and Nearby, a colt by King's Best who was successful at a mile and a quarter and showed useful form in France in the latest season. Contiguous is closely related to the 1997 Oaks winner Reams of Verse, and is a half-sister to the high-class mile-and-a-quarter performer Elmaamul. Their dam Modena, also unraced, is a half-sister to the smart performer at up to a mile Zaizafon, the dam of Zafonic and Zamindar. *Sir Michael Stoute*

CONFUCHIAS (IRE) 3 b.c. Cape Cross (IRE) 129 – Schust Madame (IRE) 46 **119** (Second Set (IRE) 127) [2007 96: 8g² 7m⁵ 8m 6v* 6d⁵ 6d Oct 20] rather leggy, attractive colt: smart performer: much improved to win Newcastle Brown Ale 80th Birthday Chipchase Stakes at Newcastle in June by ½ length from Appalachian Trail: off 3 months after: poorly drawn in Bentinck Stakes at Newmarket final outing: has form at 1m, best effort at 6f: acts well on heavy going: sold 110,000 gns. *Francis Ennis, Ireland*

CONFUCIUS CLASSIC (IRE) 3 ch.g. Danehill Dancer (IRE) 117 – Sublime **66 +** Beauty (USA) 93 (Caerleon (USA) 132) [2007 6m 6g p6g³ 7.1m⁴ p7g³ 7m⁴ Sep 21] lengthy gelding: fair maiden: very much flattered 2 of last 3 starts: bred to be suited by 7f/1m: acts on polytrack and good to firm going: sent to Hong Kong. *J. R. Boyle*

CONJECTURE 5 b.g. Danzig (USA) – Golden Opinion (USA) 127 (Slew O' Gold **63**
(USA)) [2007 79: 6g p6g 5m⁵ 5g² 5.2m³ 5.2d⁴ 6m² 5.9g³ 6m² 6s Sep 26] modest
handicapper nowadays: effective at 5f/6f: acts on polytrack, firm and soft ground: tried
blinkered/visored: tends to edge left: races up with pace: consistent. *R. Bastiman*

CONNECT 10 b.g. Petong 126 – Natchez Trace 52 (Commanche Run 133) [2007 101, **83**
a89+: p7.1g⁶ p6g⁶ 6m 6m 5g 6m 6d 6g³ 6m⁶ 6g 6m 6m 5g* Sep 19] strong, lengthy gelding: unimpressive mover: useful performer at best: mostly below form in 2007, though
won claimer at Sandown in September: effective at 5f/easy 6f: acts on all-weather, firm
and good to soft going: wears visor/blinkers: sometimes hangs: held up. *M. H. Tompkins*

CONNOR'S CHOICE 2 b.g. (Mar 13) Bertolini (USA) 125 – Susan's Dowry 74 **82**
(Efisio 120) [2007 p5g 5m 7.1m² 7s³ 7g2 Oct 25] neat gelding: has round action: second
foal: dam 6f (at 2 yrs) to 1½m winner: fairly useful maiden: second to Confidence Trick
at Chepstow and to Maxwil at Brighton: will stay 1m: acts on soft and good to firm going.
Andrew Turnell

CONNOTATION 5 b.m. Mujahid (USA) 125 – Seven Wonders (USA) (Rahy (USA) **60 §**
115) [2007 80d: p9.5g⁵ f8g² p10g Mar 9] leggy mare: handicapper, only modest nowadays: stays 9.5f: acts on all-weather and firm ground: sometimes wears headgear:
flashes tail under pressure: one to treat with caution. *A. G. Newcombe*

CONNY NOBEL (IRE) 3 gr.g. Marju (IRE) 127 – Beauharnaise (FR) (Linamix (FR) **62 §**
127) [2007 64: p9.5g p8g p12.2g p10g⁵ p9.5g⁵ 10f⁶ p7.1g p12.2g² 10.2f⁵ p12g 16.2s³
18d² 16.2f⁵ Aug 27] modest maiden: left R. Kvisla after second start, J. Flint after
eleventh one: stays 2¼m, effective at much shorter: acts on polytrack and soft going,
probably on firm: tried in visor/cheekpieces/tongue tie: ungenuine. *C. Roberts*

CONORVILLE (IRE) 3 b.g. Compton Place 125 – Courtenay (Vettori (IRE) 119) **43**
[2007 p6g p7f p6g Mar 14] poor form in maidens: sold 1,800 gns in July. *B. W. Hills*

CONQUEST (IRE) 3 b.g. Invincible Spirit (IRE) 121 – Aguinaga (IRE) 76 (Machia- **107 §**
vellian (USA) 123) [2007 114§: 6g 5g⁵ 5m 6d⁵ 5m³ 5m 6d Oct 13] strong, good-topped
gelding: has scope: has a quick, fluent action: just useful performer at 3 yrs, best effort
when fifth to Beauty Is Truth in Prix du Gros-Chene at Chantilly on second start (gelded
after third outing): ran respectably subsequently only when third in listed event at Doncaster: stays 6f: unraced on heavy going, acts on any other: often blinkered: tried tongue
tied: reportedly lost action/got tongue over bit final 2-y-o start: ungenuine. *W. J. Haggas*

CONQUISTO 2 ch.g. (Feb 6) Hernando (FR) 127 – Seal Indigo (IRE) 93 (Glenstal **72**
(USA) 118) [2007 6g 6d⁶ 7m Oct 5] 32,000Y: close-coupled gelding: half-brother to
several winners, including useful 2001 2-y-o 6f winner Prism (by Spectrum) and fairly
useful 1¼m winner Deep Purple (by Halling): dam, 10.5f/1½m winner, out of half-sister
to Irish Oaks winner Give Thanks: fair maiden: best effort when tenth at Newmarket
(made running) final start: gelded after: will stay 1m+. *C. G. Cox*

CONRAD 4 b.g. Royal Applause 124 – Milly-M (Cadeaux Genereux 131) [2007 77: **76 d**
f7g³ p6g⁶ p7.1g f7g⁵ f8g⁴ p8.6g Apr 5] long-backed gelding: fair performer: below form
after reappearance in 2007: stays 8.5f: acts on fibresand, soft and good to firm ground:
tried in cheekpieces/blinkers. *R. A. Fahey*

CONSERVATIVE 4 b. or br.g. Pivotal 124 – Happy Omen (Warning 136) [2007 74: **65**
p10g p12g⁶ Apr 1] fair maiden: stays 1m: acts on polytrack, good to firm and good to soft
ground. *P. G. Murphy*

CONSONANT (IRE) 10 ch.g. Barathea (IRE) 127 – Dinalina (FR) (Top Ville 129) **–**
[2007 75, a87: p9.5g p9.5g⁶ p8.6g 10.9m 8.1m May 7] sturdy, lengthy gelding: fair handi- **a69**
capper: little impact in 2007: stays 1¼m: acts on all-weather, firm and soft ground: tried
visored: tends to hang. *D. G. Bridgwater*

CONSTANT CHEERS (IRE) 4 b.g. Royal Applause 124 – Juno Marlowe (IRE) 100 **72**
(Danehill (USA) 126) [2007 64: 11.9d³ p12.2g³ 11.6m* p12g⁴ p13g⁴ Nov 4] sturdy gelding: fair handicapper: won at Windsor in August: stays 1½m: acts on polytrack and good
to firm ground: in headgear nowadays. *W. R. Swinburn*

CONSUELITA 4 b. or br.f. Singspiel (IRE) 133 – Green Rosy (USA) (Green Dancer **57 +**
(USA) 132) [2007 –: p12g Jan 10] modest maiden: barely stays easy 1½m: raced on
polytrack and good ground or firmer. *B. J. Meehan*

CONSULATE (IRE) 3 b.c. Rock of Gibraltar (IRE) 133 – Soha (USA) 58 (Dancing **106**
Brave (USA) 140) [2007 9g⁴ 13m* 16g* 16d 12g³ 12.9g* Sep 1] tall colt: half-brother
to 3 winners, notably smart 1m/9f winner Gold Academy (by Royal Academy): dam,
second at 1½m, out of Oaks d'Italia winner Paris Royal: useful performer: won maiden at

Wexford in May, handicap at Leopardstown in June and minor event at Down Royal (gamely, by a neck from Temlett) in September: failed to settle in Queen's Vase at Royal Ascot fourth start: stays 2m: unraced on extremes of going: has joined D. Weld. *D. Wachman, Ireland*

CONTEMPLATION 4 b.g. Sunday Silence (USA) – Wood Vine (USA) (Woodman (USA) 126) [2007 67: f7g⁶ 9.9g⁵ 8.5m 7s 7m⁶ 7m 10d 10f* 12s⁵ 10g⁶ Oct 19] fair performer: left J. Balding and returned to former trainer before winning seller at Redcar in September: stays 1¼m, not 1½m: acts on polytrack, firm and good to soft going, probably unsuited by soft: blinkered/tongue tied fourth outing: held up: said to have had breathing problem final outing: none too consistent. *G. A. Swinbank* **69**

CONTENDED (IRE) 5 b.g. Orpen (USA) 116 – Joyfullness (USA) (Dixieland Band (USA)) [2007 59, a66: 7.6g 6f⁶ 6g* 6m³ 5s⁶ p6g p7g² p7g⁵ p8g Dec 5] fair handicapper: won apprentice event at Goodwood in August: effective at 6f, seems to stay 1¼m: acts on all-weather and good to soft going: usually wears cheekpieces: has looked none too keen. *Mrs L. C. Jewell* **66**

CONTENTIOUS (IRE) 3 b.f. Danetime (IRE) 121 – Serious Contender (IRE) (Tenby 125) [2007 59p: 6m 5s⁴ 5.3g* p5g* Jul 25] fair performer, lightly raced: won handicaps at Brighton and Lingfield, both in July: best form at 5f: acts on polytrack. *D. M. Simcock* **67**

CONTENTIOUS (USA) 3 b.f. Giant's Causeway (USA) 132 – Illicit (USA) (Mr Prospector (USA)) [2007 77p: 8m* 8.1g⁵ 8d² 10.5g 8d³ 10d 8s² Nov 4] leggy, quite attractive filly: useful performer: won maiden at Goodwood in June: better form after, particularly when third to Perfect Star in listed handicap at Ascot and ¾-length second to Vincennes in Kolner Herbst-Stuten-Meile at Cologne: stays 1m: acts on soft and good to firm going: sent to USA. *J. L. Dunlop* **107**

CONTESSINA (IRE) 2 ch.f. (Jan 21) Medicean 128 – Queen's Music (USA) 66 (Dixieland Band (USA)) [2007 6g p7g p7g⁵ Dec 19] well-made filly: seventh foal: half-sister to useful 6f (at 2 yrs)/1m winner Anna Walhaan and 5f winner Smitten Kitten, both by Green Desert: dam, Irish 13f winner, half-sister to smart 6f to 8.5f winner Aim For The Top: modest form in maidens, not knocked about final outing: will stay 1m: probably capable of better. *P. F. I. Cole* **60 p**

CONTEST (IRE) 3 b.c. Danehill Dancer (IRE) 117 – Mala Mala (IRE) 104 (Brief Truce (USA) 126) [2007 6.7g⁴ 5f* 6g* 5d³ 5m Sep 14] lengthy, useful-looking colt: useful performer: won maiden at Navan in April and handicap at Naas in May: creditable 3¼ lengths third (despite being bumped) to Hoh Mike in listed race at Sandown in June, better effort after: will prove best at 5f/6f: acts on firm and good to soft going: in cheekpieces (stiff task) final outing. *D. Wachman, Ireland* **100**

CONTINENT 10 ch.g. Lake Coniston (IRE) 131 – Krisia (Kris 135) [2007 100§: p6g 5m 5m² 5.1f 6d* 6d⁵ 5v 6g 5g* 5g 6g⁶ 6d⁵ 6d Sep 29] angular gelding: fairly useful handicapper nowadays: won at Thirsk in June and Goodwood (beat Diane's Choice by ½ length) in August: respectable effort after only when fifth to Utmost Respect in Ayr Silver Cup: effective at 5f to 7f: acts on firm and soft ground: has worn tongue tie: visored once at 6 yrs: often slowly away: usually held up: unreliable. *D. Nicholls* **93 §**

CONTRADA 2 b.c. (Apr 1) Medicean 128 – Trounce (Barathea (IRE) 127) [2007 8d Oct 11] 160,000Y: rangy colt: fourth foal: half-brother to 3 winners, including fairly useful 6f (at 2 yrs)/7f winner Glebe Garden (by Soviet Star) and 4-y-o Pleasing: dam, French 7f winner, half-sister to smart French/US 1m to 1½m performer Bon Point: 25/1, needed experience when seventh to Strategic Mission in maiden at Newbury: will do better. *R. Charlton* **72 p**

CONTRA MUNDUM (USA) 4 ch.g. Giant's Causeway (USA) 132 – Speak Softly To Me (USA) (Ogygian (USA)) [2007 81: f11g f12g⁵ f12g p8.6g p8.6g 8.5m 12m 10s 8d May 15] quite good-topped gelding: fairly useful maiden at best on Flat, very much on downgrade: tried in cheekpieces: joined B. Powell, won over hurdles in August. *B. S. Rothwell* **–**

CONTROVENTO (IRE) 5 b.m. Midhish 109 – La Maya (IRE) 54 (Scenic 128) [2007 69: 5s* 5d 5.1g⁴ 5m 5d 5s⁴ 5f Oct 24] fair handicapper: won at Navan (all 3 wins there) in April: some creditable efforts (including in Britain) after: best at 5f: acts on heavy and good to firm ground, well held only try on polytrack: tried in cheekpieces, usually blinkered. *E. Tyrrell, Ireland* **77**

CONVALLARIA (FR) 4 b.f. Cape Cross (IRE) 129 – Scarlet Davis (FR) (Ti King (FR) 121) [2007 –: p7g⁶ 8d² 8d p8g 7d p7g⁵ p7m³ Nov 26] workmanlike filly: fair maiden: stays 1m: acts on polytrack and good to soft ground: said to have had a breathing problem third start, tongue tied last 2 outings. *G. Wragg* **67**

CONVERTI 3 b.g. Averti (IRE) 117 – Conquestadora 98 (Hernando (FR) 127) [2007 **59** 60: p10g p12g² p12g p12g⁵ 11.6m* 10m Jul 30] leggy gelding: modest performer: won seller at Windsor (left P. Cole) in July: stays 1½m: acts on polytrack and good to firm going. *H. J. Manners*

CONVINCE (USA) 6 ch.g. Mt Livermore (USA) – Conical 63 (Zafonic (USA) 130) **66 d** [2007 71: p6g⁶ 8.1m³ 8.1m⁵ 7m* 8.1g 7g 7m 7.1m 7d⁶ p7m⁶ p8m Oct 13] tall, close-coupled gelding: fair performer: won seller at Leicester in May: below form after: barely stays 1m: acts on firm ground, probably on good to soft: usually in cheekpieces, tried visored: has carried head awkwardly: none too consistent. *J. M. Bradley*

CONVIVIAL SPIRIT 3 b.g. Lake Coniston (IRE) 131 – Ruby Princess (IRE) 70 **66** (Mac's Imp (USA) 116) [2007 64: p5.1g² p6g* p5g³ p7g* p7.1g⁵ 6g 7m p6g⁴ 6f⁵ 7g 7f⁶ **a76** 8m⁵ 8g³ p8.6g⁵ p7m³ Dec 8] strong, workmanlike gelding: fair handicapper, better on all-weather than turf: won at Wolverhampton in February and Lingfield in March: stays easy 8.6f: acts on polytrack and firm going: tongue tied: sometimes races freely: usually held up nowadays. *E. F. Vaughan*

COOLAW (IRE) 4 b.f. Priolo (USA) 127 – Cool Gales 85 (Lord Gayle (USA) 124) **–** [2007 –: p10g p13g Mar 5] little form: tried in visor/blinkers. *G. G. Margarson*

COOL BOX 3 b.c. Grand Slam (USA) 120 – Frigidette (USA) (It's Freezing **86** (USA) 122) [2007 90: 7m 7.6m p7g² 8.3m p8g⁶ 10m⁶ p8m⁵ p8g⁵ Oct 24] tall, good-topped colt: fairly useful handicapper: barely stays 1m: acts on polytrack and good to firm going: blinkered final outing: consistent: sold 25,000 gns, sent to Qatar. *Mrs A. J. Perrett*

COOL EBONY 4 br.g. Erhaab (USA) 127 – Monawara (IRE) 73 (Namaqualand **82** (USA)) [2007 86: 7.1g⁵ 7f⁶ 8m 9.1g⁴ 8m⁴ 8m⁶ 9.1s³ 8m* 8m² 8.3g⁵ 8.9d Oct 13] sturdy, angular gelding: fairly useful handicapper: won at Musselburgh in September: stays 9f: acts on firm and soft going: tried in cheekpieces: sold 13,000 gns. *M. Dods*

COOLE DODGER (IRE) 2 ch.c. (Mar 5) Where Or When (IRE) 124 – Shining High **64** 90 (Shirley Heights 130) [2007 p6g p6g⁴ p8g⁴ p7g p6g³ Dec 5] modest form in maidens: stays 1m: looks difficult ride. *B. G. Powell*

COOL FASHION (IRE) 2 b.f. (Feb 5) Orpen (USA) 116 – Fun Fashion (IRE) 64 **–** (Polish Patriot (USA) 128) [2007 p7.1g f6d Dec 14] 4,000Y: sixth foal: half-sister to 2002 2-y-o 5f winner Royal Fashion (by Ali-Royal): dam Irish maiden: well held in maidens. *Ollie Pears*

COOL HUNTER 6 ch.g. Polar Falcon (USA) 126 – Seabound 65 (Prince Sabo 123) **–** [2007 90: p12g Mar 16] lengthy gelding: fairly useful handicapper: well beaten only outing in 2007: stays easy 1½m: acts on good to firm and good to soft going: inconsistent. *R. C. Guest*

COOL ISLE 4 b.f. Polar Prince (IRE) 117 – Fisher Island (IRE) 59 (Sri Pekan (USA) **48** 117) [2007 51, a59: f12g p11g 12d 11.6m p12.2g⁵ p12.2g⁴ 10.1g³ p10g p12.2g⁵ p12.2d² p12.2g⁶ Dec 22] close-coupled filly: poor performer: stays 1½m: acts on all-weather and firm ground: tried in cheekpieces, wears blinkers nowadays. *P. Howling*

COOL JUDGEMENT (IRE) 2 b.c. (Jan 29) Peintre Celebre (USA) 137 – Sadinga **81 p** (IRE) 85 (Sadler's Wells (USA) 132) [2007 7s³ 7m 9s* Oct 14] 70,000Y: strong, useful-looking colt: second foal: dam, Irish 1½m winner, half-sister to Moyglare Stud Stakes winner Priory Belle out of Phoenix Sprint Stakes winner Ingabelle: fairly useful form: brought along steadily, won maiden at Goodwood by short head from Rattan, finding plenty for pressure: will benefit from 1½m: acts on soft going: should continue to progress. *M. A. Jarvis*

COOL PANIC (IRE) 5 b.g. Brave Act 119 – Geht Schnell (Fairy King (USA)) [2007 **–** 94?: 7m⁶ 7g 6d Oct 1] close-coupled, quite good-topped gelding: one-time useful handi-capper, on downgrade: tried visored. *M. L. W. Bell*

COOL SANDS (IRE) 5 b.g. Trans Island 119 – Shalerina (USA) (Shalford (IRE) **–** 124§) [2007 59, a69: p7.1g³ p7g p6g³ f6g* f7g³ p7.1g³ p6g* p7.1g⁵ f6g⁵ p6g* f6g* f6g **a76** p6g⁶ p6g 6g p6g p6g p6m⁴ p7g Dec 28] strong gelding: fair handicapper on all-weather, lightly raced on turf nowadays: won at Southwell and Kempton in February, Kempton in March and Southwell in May: best at 6f/7f: acts on all-weather: visored. *D. Shaw*

COOL STING (IRE) 4 b.g. Bluebird (USA) 125 – Honey Bee (Alnasr Alwasheek **53** 117) [2007 74: p8g 6m Apr 24] leggy gelding: fair performer at 3 yrs: just modest form in 2007: stays 7f: acts on polytrack and good to firm ground: often wears headgear nowadays: tried tongue tied. *M. G. Quinlan*

COOL THE HEELS (IRE) 2 b.g. (Apr 19) Catcher In The Rye (IRE) 115 – Alinea **56** (USA) (Kingmambo (USA) 125) [2007 7m p8g 8.1m⁵ Sep 7] modest maiden: gelded after final start: bred to stay 1¼m. *J. S. Moore*

COOL TIGER 4 ch.g. Vettori (IRE) 119 – Juvenilia (IRE) 55 (Masterclass (USA) 116) **55** [2007 64: f6g⁵ p7g⁶ p7f f7g⁶ p6g 7m Apr 9] modest handicapper: stays 6f, probably not 7f: acts on all-weather and good to firm going: tried in cheekpieces. *P. Howling*

COOMBE CENTENARY 5 b.m. Robellino (USA) 127 – Shining Dancer 71 (Rainbow Quest (USA) 134) [2007 p12g p10g Feb 19] maiden: unraced in 2006: well held in handicaps in 2007. *L. Montague Hall*

COOPERSTOWN 4 ch.g. Dr Fong (USA) 128 – Heckle 47 (In The Wings 128) [2007 **74** 87: 9.2d² 6.9m³ 8.3g p9.5g⁶ Oct 26] good-bodied gelding: fair maiden, lightly raced: well below form after second start: should stay 1¼m: acts on good to firm and good to soft ground. *I. Semple*

COPERNICAN 3 ch.g. Hernando (FR) 127 – Wonderful World (GER) (Dashing Blade **91 +** 117) [2007 54p: 11.1f* 11.9m* 12s* p13g⁵ Jul 3] big, lengthy, good-topped gelding: fairly useful form: much improved to win handicaps at Hamilton, Brighton and Ripon (best effort, beat Honorable Love by 5 lengths, making all), all in June: well below form in similar event at Lingfield 12 days later, setting overly-strong pace: should stay 1¾m: acts on firm and soft going. *Sir Mark Prescott*

COPPERBOTTOMED (IRE) 2 ch.g. (May 1) Redback 116 – Stoneware (Bigstone **69** (IRE) 126) [2007 p6g 5g⁵ 5.7d p6g⁵ p6g⁵ 5.1g p6g⁵ p7.1g* p7.1d² p7.1g⁵ p6d² Dec 27] fair performer: won seller at Wolverhampton in November: claimed from R. Hollinshead after next start: stays 7f: acts on polytrack: tends to wander/flash tail: tried blinkered. *J. R. Boyle*

COPPER DOCK (IRE) 3 b.g. Docksider (USA) 124 – Sundown 71 (Polish Precedent **71** (USA) 131) [2007 52: 6.5d 5m* 5m 5d⁵ 5v 5s⁵ 5f⁶ 5m³ p5g Oct 19] sturdy gelding: fair handicapper: won apprentice event at Tipperary in April: good third at Musselburgh penultimate outing: best at 5f: acts on firm and good to soft ground, probably not on soft/heavy. *T. G. McCourt, Ireland*

COPPERGIRL (IRE) 3 b.f. Iron Mask (USA) 117 – Scarlet Woman (Sri Pekan (USA) **69** 117) [2007 p8.6g 10.1g* 8m⁴ 11.5g p10g Oct 17] 10,000F, 11,000Y: attractive filly: third foal: half-sister to winner in Greece by Daggers Drawn: dam, ran twice, half-sister to useful German performer up to 11f Silvester Lady: fair performer: won seller at Yarmouth in July: stays 1¼m: tried blinkered: sold 3,500 gns. *G. A. Huffer*

COPPER KING 3 ch.g. Ishiguru (USA) 114 – Dorissio (IRE) 75 (Efisio 120) [2007 78: **82 d** p7g³ p7.1g² p8.6g⁴ p10g 8.2m² 8.1m⁶ 7.6m³ 7.1m 8.1m⁴ 6.9m* p7.1g⁶ 8.1f p8g p7.1g Oct 6] good-bodied gelding: fairly useful performer: below form after seventh start, though still won claimer at Carlisle (left P. D. Evans) in July: stays 8.6f: acts on polytrack, good to firm and good to soft ground: tried in cheekpieces, effective visored or not: sold 6,000 gns. *J. W. Hills*

COPPERMALT (USA) 9 b.g. Affirmed (USA) – Poppy Carew (IRE) 110 (Danehill **–** (USA) 126) [2007 51: p10g Jan 31] maiden: lightly raced nowadays, and well held sole 9-y-o start (visored). *R. Curtis*

COPPERWOOD 2 ch.c. (Mar 16) Bahamian Bounty 116 – Sophielu 80 (Rudimentary **74** (USA) 118) [2007 7g² 7.1g⁴ 6.5d⁵ Oct 11] lengthy colt: has scope: second foal: half-brother to 3-y-o Sophie's Dream: dam 7f winner: fair maiden: in frame at Newbury and Haydock: will probably stay 1m. *M. Blanshard*

COPPINGTON MELODY (IRE) 4 b.f. Ordway (USA) 117 – Chorus (USA) (Darshaan 133) [2007 61: p12.2g p16g f14g Apr 3] maiden: little form in 2007. *B. W. Duke*

COPYWRITER 2 b.g. (Mar 2) Efisio 120 – Copy-Cat 60 (Lion Cavern (USA) 117) **100** [2007 7m⁴ p5g² p7g* p7g⁴ 6m³ Oct 5] 50,000Y: useful-looking gelding: has round action: third foal: half-brother to useful 2006 2-y-o 6f winner Chataway (by Mujahid) and fairly useful 2005 2-y-o 5f winner Gilt Linked (by Compton Place): dam, sprint maiden, half-sister to smart English sprinter Averti: useful performer: won maiden at Kempton in August: much improved after when 1½ lengths third in sales races at Doncaster (behind Dream Eater) and Newmarket (won by Exclamation): should prove best at 5f/6f: acts on polytrack and good to firm going: nervy sort: sold 180,000 gns, joined J. Moore in Hong Kong. *J. H. M. Gosden*

Ecurie des Monceaux's "Coquerelle"

COQUERELLE (IRE) 3 b.f. Zamindar (USA) 116 – Cracovie (Caerleon (USA) 132) **111**
[2007 9.8g* 10s* 10.5m 9f³ Oct 13] €70,000Y: third foal: closely related to French
2004 2-y-o 7.5f winner Winning Sequence (by Zafonic) and half-sister to 9f (at 2 yrs in
France)/11f (in Spain) winner Colosseo (by Nashwan): dam, French maiden, half-sister
to smart/very smart middle-distance performers Trampoli and Luth Dancer: smart
performer: won first 4 starts, namely newcomers race at Deauville and minor event at
Saint-Cloud at 2 yrs, minor event at Longchamp in April and Montjeu Coolmore Prix
Saint-Alary at Longchamp (made all, kept on well to beat Believe Me ½ length) in May:
reportedly bled badly when last in Prix de Diane at Chantilly next time: creditable
3¼ lengths third to Bit of Whimsy in Queen Elizabeth II Challenge Cup at Keeneland
final start: stayed 1¼m: acted on firm and soft going: bandaged in front: visits Dansili.
J-C. Rouget, France

CORAL CREEK (IRE) 3 b.f. Invincible Spirit (IRE) 121 – Antapoura (IRE) 82 **80**
(Bustino 136) [2007 73: 8m 9g³ 10m⁶ 10d³ 10s 8.5d⁴ 9d* 8.5g² 9s⁶ 8s³ 7d⁵ p10.7g⁶
9m p9.5g* p10.7g Dec 5] fairly useful handicapper: won at Ballinrobe in July and
Wolverhampton (awkward under pressure) in November: effective at 7f to 10.7f: acts on
polytrack and heavy going, probably on good to firm: blinkered (below form) fifth
outing. *M. J. Grassick, Ireland*

CORAL SHORES 2 b.f. (Apr 28) Carnival Dancer 123 – Leading Role 90 (Cadeaux **61 d**
Genereux 131) [2007 7m³ 7.1m 6m p8.6g⁶ 7d⁵ p7g p8.6g⁶ f8d Dec 12] 10,000Y: good-
topped filly: third foal: dam, 2-y-o 7f winner, half-sister to smart 7f/1m winner Unscrupulous: modest maiden: failed to progress, leaving P. Chapple-Hyam 2,500 gns after fifth
start: stays 7f: acts on good to firm going, probably polytrack. *P. W. Hiatt*

CORANGLAIS 7 ch.g. Piccolo 121 – Antonia's Folly 64 (Music Boy 124) [2007 60: – p6g p6g Dec 19] compact gelding: good walker: modest at 6 yrs: well held both starts in 2007: effective at 5f to easy 7f: acts on polytrack, firm and soft ground: wears blinkers/cheekpieces. *J. M. Bradley*

CORDELL (IRE) 2 b.c. (Feb 9) Fasliyev (USA) 120 – Urgele (FR) 102 (Zafonic **89** (USA) 130) [2007 5d⁴ 6m⁴ 6g 5g³ 6.5m p8g* 8d⁶ Oct 19] €26,000F, €50,000Y: strong, rangy colt: has scope: second foal: dam French 1m winner (including at 2 yrs): fairly useful performer (only all-weather start) when winning maiden at Kempton in September: stays 1m: acts on polytrack and good to firm going. *R. Hannon*

CORDIER 5 b.g. Desert Style (IRE) 121 – Slipper 94 (Suave Dancer (USA) 136) [2007 – –, a85: f11g² 12d 10.5m Aug 9] fairly useful handicapper: stays 1½m: acts on all-weather, **a82** no form on turf: races up with pace. *J. Mackie*

CORDON BLEU (IRE) 2 br.c. (May 10) Key of Luck (USA) 126 – Blue Note (FR) **61** 122 (Habitat 134) [2007 6s 5m³ p6g³ 7m 6d p6g Oct 17] medium-sized, useful-looking colt: modest maiden: form only at 5f/6f: acts on polytrack and good to firm going: sold 5,200 gns. *M. Johnston*

CORKING (IRE) 2 b.f. (Mar 2) Montjeu (IRE) 137 – Scanno's Choice (IRE) 54 **58** (Pennine Walk 120) [2007 p7g 7d Oct 9] 26,000F, €41,000Y: sturdy filly: half-sister to several winners, notably smart 7f (at 2 yrs) to 10.4f winner Sobriety (later successful in Hong Kong as Industrial Pioneer, by Namaqualand): dam Irish maiden: not fully wound up in maidens at Kempton and Leicester (modest form): will be suited by 1¼m/1½m. *Eve Johnson Houghton*

CORKSCREW HILL (IRE) 3 b.f. Golan (IRE) 129 – Perugia (IRE) 94 (Perugino **55** (USA) 84) [2007 10d 8d⁴ 10.1m⁶ 8m p6g p8g Oct 12] quite attractive filly: second foal: half-sister to 4-y-o Kilworth: dam 2-y-o 6f winner: modest maiden: left N. Callaghan after fourth start: stays 1m: acts on polytrack and good to soft going: sometimes slowly away. *Andrew Slattery, Ireland*

CORLOUGH MOUNTAIN 3 ch.g. Inchinor 119 – Two Step 60 (Mujtahid (USA) **78** 118) [2007 71p: 7d² 8.3v³ 8g⁵ 6v p7g⁵ p7g³ p7g* Dec 29] workmanlike gelding: fair handicapper: left N. Callaghan after fifth start: won at Lingfield in December: stays 1m: acts on polytrack and heavy going. *M. J. McGrath*

CORMORANT WHARF (IRE) 7 b.g. Alzao (USA) 117 – Mercy Bien (IRE) 63 (Be **77** My Guest (USA) 126) [2007 76: 11g 12d 10m³ 11.5m² 12g Aug 18] well-made gelding: fair handicapper: stays 1½m: yet to race on heavy going, acts on any other turf and polytrack: tried tongue tied/in headgear earlier in career. *T. E. Powell*

CORNELL PRECEDENT 3 ch.g. Polish Precedent (USA) 131 – Shamwari (USA) **46** 63 (Shahrastani (USA) 135) [2007 58: 8.5g 10m 8.3d⁴ 14m 12.4m Aug 27] smallish, shallow-girthed gelding: just poor maiden handicapper on Flat in 2007: should stay 1¼m: acts on good to soft going: hung left penultimate start: gelded, won juvenile hurdle in October. *J. J. Quinn*

CORNERSTONE 3 ch.g. Pivotal 124 – Splice 114 (Sharpo 132) [2007 p6g p8g p7f 6s⁴ **61** 6d³ 6.1v 7g* Jul 28] modest performer: easily best effort when winning handicap at Lingfield (edged left) in July: stays 7f: blinkered/visored last 4 starts: quirky. *S. C. Williams*

CORNUS 5 ch.g. Inchinor 119 – Demerger (USA) (Distant View (USA) 126) [2007 77§, **90** a87§: f6g⁶ p6g* p6g p5.1g⁵ 5f 6m⁵ 6g³ 6s² 6m⁶ 6d³ 6d 6v³ p7.1g 6d 5m 6m* 5m⁵ 5m 7.1m 6.1m⁴ 6.1d* 6.1s* 6g p6g⁴ p6g² p7.1g Nov 30] smallish, sturdy, attractive gelding: fairly useful handicapper: won at Wolverhampton in February, Thirsk in September and Nottingham (twice) in October: stays 6f: acts on polytrack (well held on fibresand), and any turf going: blinkered nowadays. *A. J. McCabe*

CORONADO'S GOLD (USA) 6 ch.g. Coronado's Quest (USA) 130 – Debit My **62** Account (USA) (Classic Account (USA)) [2007 57: 10.5m* p8.6g 10.1f⁶ 8s⁴ 8m Aug 25] modest handicapper: won ladies event at Haydock in June: stays 10.5f: acts on good to firm going, probably on soft: tried in cheekpieces. *B. Ellison*

CORONATION FLIGHT 4 b.f. Missed Flight 123 – Hand On Heart (IRE) 62 – (Taufan (USA) 119) [2007 54: 8m p9.5g 8d⁶ 11.1d⁶ 6.9m Jul 29] angular filly: modest maiden at best, little form in 2007: dead. *F. P. Murtagh*

CORREY 3 ch.f. Tobougg (IRE) 125 – Numerate 69 (Bishop of Cashel 122) [2007 p8g⁶ **51** 7d 8.1m 12.1d* p12g Oct 29] second foal: dam 6f winner (stayed 1¼m): modest performer: easily best effort when winning seller at Chepstow (left B. Palling) in August: stays 1½m: acts on good to soft ground: tried blinkered. *Miss J. S. Davis*

CORRIB ECLIPSE 8 b.g. Double Eclipse (IRE) 122 – Last Night's Fun (IRE) (Law – Society (USA) 130) [2007 101: 21.7s Jun 23] good-topped gelding: useful performer: lightly raced in recent years, including over hurdles, and well held sole 8-y-o start: stays 2¾m: acts on polytrack, firm and good to soft going. *Ian Williams*

CORRIB (IRE) 4 b.f. Lahib (USA) 129 – Montana Miss (IRE) 80 (Earl of Barking   74 (IRE) 119) [2007 78: 7g 7.1m 7d 8d³ 10.2g⁵ 8.1s 9m* 8.1m³ 8.1m² p9.5g p8.6g Dec 13] leggy filly: fair handicapper: won apprentice event at Newbury in August: stays 9f: acts on polytrack and good to firm going, probably good to soft. *B. Palling*

CORRIDOR CREEPER (FR) 10 ch.g. Polish Precedent (USA) 131 – Sonia Rose 105 d (USA) (Superbity (USA)) [2007 115: 5.2m 5.1m² 5g² 5m⁴ 5g 6d 5m³ 5d 5.6m 5g 5m 5g⁵ 5.2g⁵ 5d Oct 13] smallish gelding: handicapper, just useful nowadays: second at Chester and York in May: below form after: has form at 6f, but best at 5f: acts on firm and soft going: tried blinkered/tongue tied, wears cheekpieces: races prominently. *J. M. Bradley*

CORRIOLANUS (GER) 2 b.g. Zamindar (USA) 116 – Caesarea (GER) (Generous 104 d (IRE) 139) [2007 108: 12g⁵ 12g 12g 12m 12m⁶ 10.4m 10s Oct 13] strong, close-coupled gelding: just useful at best nowadays: fifth to Quijano in handicap at Nad Al Sheba on reappearance in 2007: below form after (left S. Seemar in UAE after third outing): stays 1½m: acts on polytrack, firm and good to soft going: tried blinkered earlier in career, wore cheekpieces final start. *A. M. Balding*

CORRYBROUGH 2 ch.c. (Mar 9) Kyllachy 129 – Calamanco 71 (Clantime 101)   94 p [2007 6d² 6d* Oct 15] 57,000Y: strong colt: eighth foal: half-brother to 8-y-o Artie and 9-y-o Kingscross: dam, 5f winner, sister to dam of very smart sprinter Cape of Good Hope: fairly useful form: looked very promising in maidens, second to Exclamation at Haydock and winning at Windsor by 3 lengths: will prove best at 5f/6f: one to follow. *H. Candy*

CORTESIA (IRE) 4 ch.f. Courteous 120 – Cecina 100 (Welsh Saint 126) [2007 90:   82 d 10m 12d⁵ 10m⁶ 10s⁴ p16g 16m 11.5g⁶ p12.2g⁵ Oct 8] good-topped filly: fairly useful handicapper: below form after second start in 2007: barely stays 1½m: acts on polytrack, good to firm and good to soft ground. *P. W. Chapple-Hyam*

CORUM (IRE) 4 b.g. Galileo (IRE) 134 – Vallee Des Reves (USA) (Kingmambo   94 (USA) 125) [2007 96: 18.7m 14m³ p13.9g* 12f 16g⁶ Aug 24] strong, good-bodied geld- ing: fairly useful handicapper: won at Wolverhampton in June: below form after: stays 1¾m: acts on polytrack and good to firm going, seemingly not softer than good: wore cheekpieces in 2007: gelded after final start. *Mrs K. Waldron*

CORVIGLIA 4 b.f. Nashwan (USA) 135 – Ski Run 112 (Petoski 135) [2007 –: 12.1s – p12g Jul 12] lightly-made filly: little form. *C. E. Longsdon*

COSEADROM (IRE) 5 b.g. Almutawakel 126 – Madam Lightfoot (USA) 85 (Vice   84 d Regent (CAN)) [2007 88: 5m² 5m⁴ 5d³ 6m 6g 5m 5m⁶ 5d p7g³ p7.1g⁵ p6g Nov 19] strong gelding: fairly useful handicapper: left P. Henley in Ireland after second start: below form after next outing: best effort at 5f/6f: acts on heavy and good to firm ground: tried blinkered/tongue tied: sent to Germany. *M. F. Harris*

COSENZA 2 b.f. (Jan 19) Bahri (USA) 125 – Dawnus (IRE) 103 (Night Shift (USA))   71 + [2007 p6g 5d⁴ 6.1g Aug 2] 42,000Y: first foal: dam, 1m/1¼m winner, out of close relative to high-class 1½m performer Wagon Master: fair maiden: shaped well when fourth to Edge of Light at Salisbury: likely to stay 1m. *H. J. L. Dunlop*

COSIMO PRIMO 3 b.g. Medicean 128 – Cugina 99 (Distant Relative 128) [2007 –: – 7g p10g Sep 3] lengthy gelding: little form: bred to stay 1¼m+. *J. A. Geake*

COSMEA 2 b.f. (Mar 26) Compton Place 125 – St James's Antigua (IRE) 79 (Law   59 Society (USA) 130) [2007 6s⁶ p6g 6m⁴ 7m 7g Oct 25] 7,000Y: sturdy filly: half-sister to several winners, including fairly useful 1m winner Magic Merlin (by Magic Ring): dam 1m winner: modest maiden: seemingly best effort at 6f on good to firm ground. *A. King*

COSMIC APOLLO 5 ch.g. Pennekamp (USA) 130 – Windmill Princess 55 (Gorytus – (USA) 132) [2007 f8g 8d May 30] well held in maidens: bred to be suited by 1¼m+. *Rae Guest*

COSMIC ART 2 b.c. (Mar 1) Bertolini (USA) 125 – Cosmic Song 58 (Cosmonaut)   94 [2007 5m⁶ p6g² p6g* p6g* 6m⁵ p6g* 6g³ Aug 23] 19,000F, 17,000Y: lengthy, good- topped colt: first foal: dam 9f/1¼m winner: fairly useful performer: won maiden and nursery in July and minor event in August, all at Wolverhampton: good 1½ lengths third of 20 to Dark Angel in sales race at York final start: will probably stay 7f: acts on poly- track and good to firm going: sent to Hong Kong, where renamed Plan B. *E. A. L. Dunlop*

COSMIC DESTINY (IRE) 5 b.m. Soviet Star (USA) 128 – Cruelle (USA) (Irish **79**
River (FR) 131) [2007 64§, a68§: p5g p5.1g p5.1g³ p6g⁶ 5.3m⁴ 5.1d 5g⁴ p5.1g⁵ 5m³
5.3m* 5.3d³ p5g² p5g² 5.1m* 5.3d* 5.1m³ 5d² 6g⁴ Oct 25] smallish mare: fair handicapper: much improved in 2007, winning at Brighton in June and Bath and Brighton in
August: free-going sort, best at 5f: acts on polytrack, good to firm and good to soft going:
has looked wayward, though not of late. *E. F. Vaughan*

COSMODROME (USA) 3 b.f. Bahri (USA) 125 – Space Time (FR) (Bering 136) **100**
[2007 p9.5g* 9.9g* 12g Jun 21] neat, attractive filly: fourth foal: half-sister to fairly useful 2003 2-y-o 1m winner Muscida (by Woodman): dam, French maiden, granddaughter
of high-class French 6f/7f performer Proskona: useful form: successful in maiden at
Wolverhampton in April and listed race at Goodwood (beat Sudoor by 1½ lengths) in
May: below-form seventh to Silkwood in Ribblesdale Stakes at Royal Ascot subsequent
outing (injured in race): stays 1¼m. *L. M. Cumani*

COSSACK PRINCE 2 b.g. (Feb 8) Dubai Destination (USA) 127 – Danemere (IRE) **84**
90 (Danehill (USA) 126) [2007 7m 8g⁴ p8.6g* Nov 24] rangy, good-topped colt: second
foal: dam 2-y-o 6f winner who stayed 1m: fairly useful form: best effort when winning at
Wolverhampton in November by length from Cosy Tiger, again making running: stays
8.6f. *B. J. Meehan*

COST ANALYSIS (IRE) 5 ch.g. Grand Lodge (USA) 125 – Flower Girl 108 (Pharly **–**
(FR) 130) [2007 p6g p6g p12.2g Nov 27] strong, lengthy gelding: maiden, no form in
2007: tried blinkered/tongue tied. *Mrs P. Ford*

COSTUME 3 b.f. Danehill (USA) 126 – Dance Dress (USA) 110 (Nureyev (USA) 131) **111**
[2007 78p: 7m³ 8g⁴ 8m* 8m³ 7g² 9f⁴ 9f⁴ 8.5f⁴ Nov 10] good-bodied filly: smart performer: simple task when winning maiden at Ripon in June: better efforts when in frame
in Poule d'Essai des Pouliches at Longchamp (4¼ lengths fourth to Darjina), listed handicap at Royal Ascot (1½ lengths third behind Barshiba), Oak Tree Stakes at Goodwood
(½-length second to Wake Up Maggie), Garden City Stakes at Belmont (¾-length fourth
to Alexander Tango, left J. Gosden after), Queen Elizabeth II Challenge Cup at Keeneland (3½ lengths fourth to Bit of Whimsy) and Grade 2 Mrs Revere Stakes at Churchill
Downs (3 lengths fourth to Bit of Whimsy) on second and last 5 starts: effective at 7f to
9f: raced only on good going or firmer. *R. J. Frankel, USA*

COTTAM BREEZE 2 b.f. (Feb 11) Diktat 126 – Flower Breeze (USA) 75 (Rahy **–**
(USA) 115) [2007 6d 7d 7.5g 7.5m p8.6g Sep 3] leggy filly: first foal: dam maiden: no
form. *M. W. Easterby*

COTTAM ECLIPSE 6 b.g. Environment Friend 128 – Che Gambe (USA) (Lyphard **55 d**
(USA) 132) [2007 9m 8.5m⁶ 8m⁶ 8.5m 7g 7.1d⁴ 8g 8m 8.5g⁶ 9.9m Aug 25] regressive
maiden: seems to stay 1m: acts on good to firm and good to soft going: often makes
running. *I. W. McInnes*

COTTAM GRANGE 7 b.g. River Falls 113 – Karminski 70 (Pitskelly 122) [2007 **–**
p12.2g 16m⁶ Apr 9] modest maiden at best on Flat: unraced in 2006 and no form in 2007.
I. W. McInnes

COTTON EYED JOE (IRE) 6 b.g. Indian Rocket 115 – Cwm Deri (IRE) (Alzao **82**
(USA) 117) [2007 80: f14g⁴ f14g⁴ 14.1g* 11.5d⁴ 14g³ 12v 14m* 14m⁴ 14m² 13s⁶ Sep 24]
lengthy, good-topped gelding: fairly useful handicapper: won at Carlisle in June and
Haydock in August: stays 1¾m: acts on fibresand, soft and good to firm going: tends to
hang left. *G. A. Swinbank*

COTTON REEL 2 b.c. (Feb 11) Cape Cross (IRE) 129 – Cotton House (IRE) 107 **79**
(Mujadil (USA) 119) [2007 6m⁴ 6d⁶ 6g³ Nov 2] 48,000Y: stocky colt: second foal: dam
5f (at 2 yrs)/6f winner: fair form in maidens, third to Almoutaz at Newmarket: will stay
7f. *P. F. I. Cole*

COUGAR BAY (IRE) 4 b.g. Daylami (IRE) 138 – Delimara (IRE) (In The Wings **110**
128) [2007 116: 8g³ 8s³ 9v² 10m³ 10m⁵ 8m² 8.5f* 8.5g² Dec 13] lengthy gelding: smart
performer: creditable efforts all starts in 2007, including when second at the Curragh in
International Stakes (beaten 2 lengths by Decado) and Solonaway Stakes (went down by
1¾ lengths to Jumbajukiba) and third in Winter Hill Stakes at Windsor (1¼ lengths
behind Queen's Best) on fourth outing: left D. Wachman in Ireland, won allowance race
at Aqueduct in November: seems best at 1m to 10.5f: acts on any going: usually blinkered
(occasionally looking tricky ride) in 2006: usually raced prominently in Ireland: consistent. *B. Tagg, USA*

COUNCELLOR (FR) 5 b.g. Gilded Time (USA) – Sudden Storm Bird (USA) (Storm **82**
Bird (CAN) 134) [2007 88: p7.1g p6g p8g³ p8.6g³ f8g* f8g² p7g p8g* f8g⁴ 8.1m⁴ 8.1g **a96**

7.1d 8m⁴ p8g 8g p7.1g² p8m³ p7.1g* p8.6g⁴ p8m* p7.1g* p8m⁴ p7g³ p7g⁶ p8g⁵ Dec 29]
big, strong gelding: useful on all-weather, fairly useful on turf: won handicaps at Southwell in February and Kempton in March, claimer at Wolverhampton in October and
handicaps at Lingfield and Wolverhampton in November: third to Bonus in listed race at
Kempton in December: stays 8.6f: acts on all-weather, good to firm and good to soft
ground: tongue tied: visored (well held) once: free-going sort: races prominently: has
awkward head carriage. *Stef Liddiard*

COUNSEL'S OPINION (IRE) 10 ch.g. Rudimentary (USA) 118 – Fairy Fortune 78 **93**
(Rainbow Quest (USA) 134) [2007 110d: p10g 10g 10.1g p10g⁶ 10d⁴ 10m 9d⁴ 10.9m⁴
10.9m⁶ Sep 15] big gelding: just fairly useful handicapper nowadays: stays 1½m: acts on
all-weather, soft and firm going: has been early to post/slowly away: takes strong hold,
and normally held up. *C. F. Wall*

COUNTBACK (FR) 8 b.g. Anabaa (USA) 130 – Count Me Out (FR) (Kaldoun (FR) **52**
122) [2007 61: p16.5g p16g⁴ p16.5g⁵ p12g⁵ p13g² p16g³ p16.5g⁵ 11.6m p12.2g⁶ Dec 29]
good-bodied gelding: modest maiden handicapper: stays 16.5f: acts on all-weather: often
wears cheekpieces, tried visored: modest hurdler, successful twice in July. *A. W. Carroll*

COUNT CEPRANO (IRE) 3 b.g. Desert Prince (IRE) 130 – Camerlata (Common **86**
Grounds 118) [2007 94p: 8.3m⁴ p8.6g³ 8.3s⁵ 8m 6g p6g Dec 30] compact gelding: fairly
useful performer: left W. Swinburn 3,000 gns after fifth start: stays 8.6f: acts on polytrack, soft and good to firm going: tried in cheekpieces. *M. D. I. Usher*

COUNT COUGAR (USA) 7 b.g. Sir Cat (USA) 118 – Gold Script (USA) (Seeking **–**
The Gold (USA)) [2007 74: f6g* f6g* f5g² f6g* f5g* f5g² f6g⁶ 5s p6g f5d* p5.1s Dec 21] **a86**
sturdy gelding: poor walker and mover: fairly useful handicapper on all-weather, modest
on turf: better than ever in 2007, winning 5 times at Southwell: effective at 5f to easy 7f:
acts on all-weather, firm and soft ground: tried blinkered/in cheekpieces earlier in career:
races prominently. *S. P. Griffiths*

COUNTDOWN 5 ch.g. Pivotal 124 – Quiz Time 90 (Efisio 120) [2007 89: 7f³ 7g⁵ 6m⁶ **91**
6g⁵ 6d⁴ 7d* 7s* 7d⁶ 7.6m⁶ 7m 7.6m 7.2s Sep 22] close-coupled gelding: fairly useful
handicapper: won at Catterick and York in July: effective at 6f to 7.6f: acts on polytrack
and any turf going: tried blinkered/visored earlier in career: held up. *T. D. Easterby*

COUNTERCLAIM 2 ch.f. (Feb 6) Pivotal 124 – Dusty Answer 97 (Zafonic (USA) **76**
130) [2007 6m 7.1g⁴ p7.1g² p8.6g² Nov 1] 250,000Y: second foal: dam, 2-y-o 7f winner,
half-sister to US Grade 2 9f winner Spotlight out of smart performer up to 1½m Dust
Dancer: fair maiden: twice runner-up at Wolverhampton: stays 8.6f: joined H-A. Pantall,
France. *Saeed bin Suroor*

COUNTERFACTUAL (IRE) 4 br.g. Key of Luck (USA) 126 – Wakayi 87 (Persian **57**
Bold 123) [2007 64: f8g p9.5g f8g⁵ 10.1m⁵ 8.5m 9.1g 10g 8m Sep 18] good-topped **a49**
gelding: modest maiden on turf, poor on all-weather: stays 1¼m: acts on good to firm
going: takes good hold. *B. Smart*

COUNTESS MAJELLA (IRE) 3 b.f. Grand Lodge (USA) 125 – Mrs Moonlight **–**
(Ajdal (USA) 130) [2007 53p: p10g Feb 7] modest form at best in 3 maidens: should stay
1¼m: tongue tied (well held) only outing in 2007: refused to enter stall next intended
appearance in July. *E. J. O'Neill*

COUNTING HOUSE (IRE) 4 ch.g. King's Best (USA) 132 – Inforapenny 111 **85**
(Deploy 131) [2007 85: 12m² f12d³ Dec 15] good-bodied gelding: fairly useful maiden:
creditable second in handicap at Newbury in September, easily better effort on Flat in
2007: will stay 1¾m: raced only on good/good to firm going on turf: successful over
hurdles in November. *J. A. B. Old*

COUNT KRISTO 5 br.g. Dr Fong (USA) 128 – Aryadne (Rainbow Quest (USA) 134) **–**
[2007 79: p8g p10g⁶ Feb 10] tall, leggy gelding: fair handicapper at 4 yrs: well beaten in
2007: tried in cheekpieces. *B. G. Powell*

COUNTRY AFFAIR (USA) 4 ch.g. Vettori (IRE) 119 – Nany's Affair (USA) 57 **74**
(Colonial Affair (USA) 126) [2007 69: p10g⁵ p12.2g Feb 26] fair maiden, lightly raced:
stays 1¼m: acts on polytrack: sold 15,000 gns, joined D. Bridgwater, gelded and successful over hurdles in August. *P. R. Webber*

COUNTRY PURSUIT (USA) 5 ch.g. Theatrical 128 – Jade Flush (USA) 117 (Jade **–**
Hunter (USA)) [2007 93: p12g 14.1m⁶ Apr 26] leggy gelding: fairly useful handicapper
at 4 yrs: well below form in 2007: tried in blinkers/cheekpieces. *C. E. Brittain*

COUNTRY SONG (USA) 3 b.c. Fusaichi Pegasus (USA) 130 – Eliza (USA) 118 (Mt **98**
Livermore (USA)) [2007 98: a7f⁴ a8f⁴ 7.5g⁴ Mar 8] close-coupled, quite attractive colt:

useful performer: raced at Nad Al Sheba in 2007, running creditably only when 8¾ lengths fourth to Asiatic Boy in UAE 2000 Guineas second start: stays 1m: acts on dirt, firm and soft going: blinkered final 2-y-o outing. *J. Noseda*

COUNTRYWIDE COMET (IRE) 2 b.g. (Jan 21) Desert Style (IRE) 121 – Darzao **68** (IRE) (Alzao (USA) 117) [2007 5m⁵ 5m⁴ f6g⁵ 7.5m⁴ 7g³ p8.6g 7g* p6g* p7.1g p6g f6d⁵ f6d⁵ Dec 21] good-topped gelding: fair performer: won claimers at Redcar and Lingfield (left K. Ryan £12,000) in October: best at 6f/7f: acts on all-weather and good to firm going: tried in cheekpieces, blinkered 5 of last 6 starts. *P. Howling*

COUNTRYWIDE STYLE (IRE) 3 b.g. Xaar 132 – Nautical Light (Slip Anchor – 136) [2007 59?: p7.1g f8g p8.6g Feb 23] quite good-topped gelding: lightly raced and little form: tried blinkered. *N. P. Littmoden*

COUNT TREVISIO (IRE) 4 b.g. Danehill (USA) 126 – Stylish (Anshan 119) [2007 **111** 104: 9f* 10g² 10g 8m 8m³ Aug 4] lengthy gelding: smart handicapper: further progress in 2007, winning at Nad Al Sheba (beat Doctor of Laws 1¾ lengths) in January: good ¾-length second to Impeller there next start: below form subsequently: stays 1¼m: acts on firm going: tends to flash tail, and probably not straightforward: sold 110,000 gns in October, left Godolphin, then gelded. *Saeed bin Suroor*

COUNTY CRYSTAL 2 b.c. (Apr 23) Mujahid (USA) 125 – Cumbrian Crystal 69 – (Mind Games 121) [2007 5g Jul 27] tall colt: 28/1, well held in maiden at Thirsk: bred for sprinting. *T. D. Easterby*

COUNTY KERRY (UAE) 3 b.f. Jade Robbery (USA) 121 – Limerick Belle (IRE) 98 – (Roi Danzig (USA)) [2007 p8g⁶ p8g⁶ p8g³ 8.3m p10g⁶ 9.9g p10m Oct 3] 6,500 2-y-o: tall **a50** filly: on weak side at present: sixth foal: closely related to 2 winners abroad, including UAE 6f to 1¼m winner Ocean Star (by Lycius), and half-sister to Irish 7f/7.5f winner Irish Verse (by Indian Ridge): dam 5f/6f (including at 2 yrs and in UAE) winner: modest maiden: probably stays 1¼m: acts on polytrack: tried tongue tied. *Jean-Rene Auvray*

COUP D'ETAT 5 b.g. Diktat 126 – Megdale (IRE) 74 (Waajib 121) [2007 92: 9.7m³ 8d **81** 8m 10.2s⁶ 7.1v² 7d⁴ 8.3m 7d* 7g 8.3g 7d³ p7.1g Oct 6] good-topped gelding: fairly useful performer: won handicap at Leicester in August: disappointing after: effective from 7f to 1¼m: acts on heavy and good to firm going: wears blinkers/cheekpieces: carried head awkwardly penultimate start: pulled hard on all-weather debut final outing. *R. A. Harris*

COURANT D'AIR (IRE) 6 b.g. Indian Rocket 115 – Red River Rose (IRE) 51 (Red – Sunset 120) [2007 15.4g 12.3m Aug 31] unraced on Flat at 5 yrs, and no form in 2007. *Lucinda Featherstone*

COURT MASTERPIECE 7 b.h. Polish Precedent (USA) 131 – Easy Option (IRE) **104** 115 (Prince Sabo 123) [2007 127: 8g a8f⁵ Mar 31] lengthy, angular horse: showed traces of stringhalt: high-class performer at 6 yrs, winning Sussex Stakes at Goodwood: left E. Dunlop, well below form in 2007 in Al Fahidi Fort (only outing for I. Mohammed) and Godolphin Mile, both at Nad Al Sheba: was effective at 7f/easy 1m: acted on polytrack, good to firm and good to soft going, probably on soft: was usually held up: to stand at Woodlands Stud, Co Galway, Ireland, fee €4,000. *Saeed bin Suroor*

COURT OF APPEAL 10 ch.g. Bering 136 – Hiawatha's Song (USA) (Chief's Crown **75** (USA)) [2007 77: 12g* 12m* 12m* 12m⁴ 11.5d³ 12.3s² 12g⁶ 15.8g⁶ Aug 29] lengthy gelding: fair performer: won amateur claimer at Southwell and seller at Musselburgh in April, and claimer at Catterick in May: stays 1¾m: acts on all-weather and any turf going: tried visored, usually wears cheekpieces/tongue strap: has looked moody and not an easy ride. *B. Ellison*

COURT ONE 9 b.g. Shareef Dancer (USA) 135 – Fairfields Cone (Celtic Cone 116) – [2007 –: 13.8m⁴ Jun 8] small, leggy gelding: shows knee action: lightly raced and little form on Flat since 2004. *R. E. Barr*

COUSTOU (IRE) 7 b.g. In Command (IRE) 114 – Carranza (IRE) (Lead On Time – (USA) 123) [2007 –: 17.2f⁶ Apr 11] lengthy, good-topped gelding: fair handicapper in 2005: lightly raced and no form on Flat since: tried blinkered, usually wears cheekpieces. *R. M. Stronge*

COVE MOUNTAIN (IRE) 5 br.m. Indian Danehill (IRE) 124 – Nordic Pride (Hor- **53** age 124) [2007 68: p8g 7m 10.2d⁵ p8.6g p10g p8.6g p12.2s⁴ Dec 21] modest maiden handicapper: left S. Kirk after fourth outing: stays 1¼m: acts on polytrack and heavy ground: tried blinkered: none too consistent. *M. G. Rimell*

COVERT MISSION 4 b.f. Overbury (IRE) 116 – Peg's Permission (Ra Nova 83) **62** [2007 9.9m⁵ 11.7f⁶ 10m 11.9s 10.2m p12.2g³ p13.9g p12.2d Dec 7] second foal: dam unraced: fairly useful bumper winner: modest maiden: stays 1½m: acts on polytrack and good to firm going. *P. D. Evans*

COW GIRL (IRE) 3 b.f. King's Best (USA) 132 – Reveuse de Jour (IRE) 79 (Sadler's **71** Wells (USA) 132) [2007 58: 7.1s⁴ 7s² 8d 7f² 8d⁵ 10.3m³ 8m⁴ 10d⁶ 7d⁵ p8.6g⁶ p7g Dec 29] compact filly: fair maiden handicapper: bred to stay 1¼m: acts on firm and soft going, probably on polytrack: none too resolute. *Miss Gay Kelleway*

COYOTE CREEK 3 b.g. Zilzal (USA) 137 – High Barn 72 (Shirley Heights 130) **83** [2007 70: 11.6m³ 10.2m³ 12m² 14d 12m³ 9.9m² Sep 4] good-bodied gelding: fairly useful maiden: creditable placed efforts 5 of 6 starts in 2007: stays 1½m: acts on good to firm and good to soft ground. *E. F. Vaughan*

COZY TIGER (USA) 2 gr.g. (Mar 6) Hold That Tiger (USA) 117 – Cozelia (USA) **82 p** (Cozzene (USA)) [2007 p8g³ p8.6g² Nov 24] 20,000 2-y-o: fourth foal: half-brother to 3 winners in US, including 2 sprinters by Elusive Quality: dam US 8.5f/9f winner: better effort in maidens when second to Cossack Prince at Wolverhampton, still looking green: will continue to progress. *W. J. Musson*

CRACKING (IRE) 2 b.c. (Apr 26) Acclamation 118 – Adieu Cherie (IRE) (Bustino **89** 136) [2007 5f 5.3m⁴ 5.1m⁴ 6g⁵ 5m 6m³ 7d 6m Oct 5] €30,000F, 30,000Y: smallish, sturdy, close-coupled colt: half-brother to several winners, including 6f winner Lord Yasmin (by Lahib): dam unraced: fairly useful performer: won maiden at Brighton in April and minor event at Chester in May: inconsistent after, best effort when equal-third to Johar Jamal in nursery at Newmarket: best at 5f/6f: acts on good to firm going: front runner: sold 25,000 gns, sent to Bahrain. *R. Hannon*

CRACKING NICK (IRE) 2 b.g. (May 5) Cape Cross (IRE) 129 – Enrich (USA) 103 **68** (Dynaformer (USA)) [2007 p6g⁵ p6g³ 6m⁵ Aug 9] sturdy gelding: fair maiden: forced pace when third at Wolverhampton: held up final start: gelded after: will stay 7f/1m. *W. R. Swinburn*

CRAFTY FOX 4 b.g. Foxhound (USA) 103 – Surrealist (ITY) (Night Shift (USA)) **60** [2007 60: p7.1g³ p8g p7g p6g p7g f6g* p7g⁴ p8g p7g³ 7.9f³ 8d p8g 7g Oct 16] well-made gelding: modest performer: won minor event at Southwell in May: left A. Jarvis 10,000 gns after tenth start: free-going sort, barely stays 1m: acts on all-weather and firm going: often visored. *John A. Harris*

CRAGGANMORE CREEK 4 b.g. Tipsy Creek (USA) 115 – Polish Abbey (Polish **–** Precedent (USA) 131) [2007 68: f12g³ f11g⁴ 11.5m p16g³ p16g f12g³ f14g 15.4g p12g² **a56** p12.2g⁵ p12.2g² p12.2g⁵ p13.9g Nov 16] tall gelding: modest performer: stays 1½m: acts on all-weather: blinkered/visored: held up. *D. Morris*

CRAGGY CAT (IRE) 2 b.c. (Feb 8) Statue of Liberty (USA) 115 – Trexana (Kaldoun **94** (FR) 122) [2007 6d³ 7m³ 6m* 6g* 6g⁶ Oct 6] €160,000Y: good-topped, quite attractive colt: third foal: half-brother to useful French 1¼m/10.5f winner Biens Nanti (by Montjeu) and Irish 7f winner Striking (by Danehill Dancer): dam, French maiden, out of half-sister to smart French performer up to 10.5f Caprarola: fairly useful form: won maiden at Redcar in August and nursery at Haydock in September: favourite, only sixth of 23 to Dubai Dynamo in Two-Year-Old Trophy at Redcar: will be suited by 1m: sold 280,000 gns to join J. Moore in Hong Kong. *L. M. Cumani*

CRAIGSTOWN 2 b.c. (Apr 8) Cape Cross (IRE) 129 – Craigmill 85 (Slip Anchor 136) **78** [2007 7m⁵ 7m⁴ 8g Oct 24] 130,000Y: lightly-made colt: fluent mover: brother to smart 1m winner Castleton and half-brother to several winners, including fairly useful 1½m to 2m winner Astyanax (by Hector Protector): dam, 7f winner, half-sister to dam of Prix du Cadran winner Invermark: fair maiden: promising fifth at Goodwood on debut, but disappointing after: should be suited by 1m+. *Saeed bin Suroor*

CRAIG Y NOS 3 ch.f. Auction House (USA) 120 – Thabeh 57 (Shareef Dancer (USA) **–** 135) [2007 –: 8.3d⁴ 7m 6g Sep 3] no form. *A. Berry*

CRANWORTH BLAZE 3 b.f. Diktat 126 – Julietta Mia (USA) 72 (Woodman (USA) **41 +** 126) [2007 –: 5g⁴ 7g p8.6g 9m⁴ 9.2m⁵ Aug 31] lengthy filly: poor maiden on balance: seems to stay 9f: unraced on extremes of going: blinkered last 2 outings. *T. J. Etherington*

CRATHORNE (IRE) 7 b.g. Alzao (USA) 117 – Shirley Blue (IRE) (Shirley Heights **69** 130) [2007 73: 13g³ 16.1m Aug 8] deep-girthed gelding: fair handicapper: stays 15.8f: acts on firm and soft going: tried in cheekpieces: fairly useful hurdler/chaser. *M. Todhunter*

CRAZY ABOUT YOU (IRE) 2 b.f. (Mar 30) Montjeu (IRE) 137 – Touch of Magic **– p** (IRE) 74 (Brief Truce (USA) 126) [2007 7s Aug 24] €135,000Y: big, good sort: fifth foal:

half-sister to winner in Japan by Danehill: dam, Irish maiden, half-sister to smart French middle-distance performers Fleur d'Oranger and Premier Amour: 33/1, burly and green in maiden at Newmarket: should do better. *B. W. Hills*

CRAZY BEAR (IRE) 4 ch.f. King Charlemagne (USA) 120 – Specifiedrisk (IRE) **70** (Turtle Island (IRE) 123) [2007 71: p12g* p12.2g⁴ Dec 13] fair performer: off 19 months, won maiden at Kempton in December: stays 1½m: acts on all-weather. *K. J. Burke*

CREACHADOIR (IRE) 3 b.c. King's Best (USA) 132 – Sadima (IRE) 103 **126** (Sadler's Wells (USA) 132) [2007 102: 8v³ 8g* 10m⁴ 7m* 8g² 8m² 8m⁶ 8m* 10d⁴ 8g² Dec 9]

A well-bred three-year-old colt with an already quite impressive CV and the physical scope for more improvement, Creachadoir not surprisingly caught the eye of the Godolphin cherry pickers; and in August it was reported that he had been bought out of Jim Bolger's stable for an undisclosed sum and was to join Saeed bin Suroor. At that stage, Godolphin's plan for Creachadoir was that he was to be prepared for the 2008 Dubai Carnival. However, he ended up running three times for his new connections before the end of the year, and his performances in those races have given Godolphin no cause to regret the purchase. Creachadoir hasn't been successful in anything more grand than a Group 3 contest so far, but there's no doubt he is well up to winning races at the highest level.

Restricted to just two outings in his first season, when reportedly troubled by sore shins, and disappointing on heavy going on his reappearance, Creachadoir was still a maiden when he lined up for the Leopardstown 2000 Guineas Trial in April. On good ground, Creachadoir showed improved form and won by three and a half lengths from Confuchias, a performance which had the effect of shortening the Guineas odds of his stablemate, the winter favourite Teofilo, still further. Apparently, Creachadoir, also in the same ownership as Teofilo at that time, had been used on occasions as the latter's lead horse! Only fourth when stepped up to a mile and a quarter in the Ballysax Stakes on the same course later in the month, Creachadoir showed himself a genuine classic contender in his own right returned to shorter. After winning the Aussie Rules EBF Tetrarch Stakes at the Curragh in May by three lengths from Mr Napper Tandy, Creachadoir finished runner-up in

Aussie Rules EBF Tetrarch Stakes, the Curragh—
Creachadoir (left) justifies favouritism ahead of Mr Napper Tandy

Countrywide Steel And Tubes Joel Stakes, Newmarket—Creachadoir makes his first appearance in Godolphin's colours a winning one; the blinkered Tell is second with Heaven Sent (blaze) next

both the Poule d'Essai des Poulains and the Irish Two Thousand Guineas. At Longchamp, Creachadoir was beaten half a length by Astronomer Royal, collared late on after taking the lead over a furlong out; and at the Curragh he went down by a length to Cockney Rebel, travelling strongly and looking like pushing the winner even closer until just inside the final furlong.

A creditable sixth behind Excellent Art in the St James's Palace Stakes at Royal Ascot on his final start for Bolger, Creachadoir then had a break and returned at a lower level, in the Countrywide Steel and Tubes Joel Stakes at Newmarket in October. If the plan was to give Creachadoir a confidence-boosting run after some hard races, then it worked a treat. Creachadoir looked in great shape and, very much a cut above the opposition, he moved smoothly to the front well over a furlong out and drew clear, hanging right as he did so but still having three lengths to spare over his nearest pursuer Tell. Stepped back up in class and also in trip, Creachadoir was returned to Newmarket two weeks later, supplemented for the Champion Stakes at a cost of £24,000. Defeat in the Ballysax Stakes might have been inconclusive about his ability to stay a mile and a quarter, but on quite testing ground the trip certainly looked too far for Creachadoir at Newmarket. He worked his way into a challenging position in the penultimate furlong then weakened into fourth behind Literato. Returned to his optimum trip, Creachadoir showed high-class form when second to Good Ba Ba in the Hong Kong Mile at Sha Tin in December. No three-year-old has won the race in its present form, but Creachadoir couldn't have come closer to doing so, beaten only a short head in a driving finish after quickening into contention approaching the final furlong.

Creachadoir (IRE) (b.c. 2004)	King's Best (USA) (b 1997)	Kingmambo (b 1990)	Mr Prospector
			Miesque
		Allegretta (ch 1978)	Lombard
			Anatevka
	Sadima (IRE) (b 1998)	Sadler's Wells (b 1981)	Northern Dancer
			Fairy Bridge
		Anima (b 1989)	Ajdal
			Cocotte

The strong and rangy Creachadoir, who fetched €83,000 as a yearling, might have been expected to stay a mile and a quarter judged on pedigree. By King's Best, he is the second foal of the useful Sadler's Wells mare Sadima who won at that distance, and whose first foal is the Prix de l'Arc de Triomphe runner-up Youmzain (by Sinndar). Sadima was lightly raced and gained that sole win in a maiden at Roscommon on her debut, which came late in her three-year-old season. There is a dual Arc runner-up further back in Creachadoir's pedigree, his grandam the twice-raced maiden Anima being a half-sister to Pilsudski. A top-class performer, Pilsudski won ten races including the Breeders' Cup Turf, Champion Stakes, Irish Champion Stakes, Eclipse Stakes and Japan Cup. Creachadoir's great grandam Cocotte, a smart mile-and-a-quarter winner, would have been deemed a successful broodmare even without Pilsudski, also being responsible for Fine Motion, the champion three-year-old filly of her year in Japan, the Group 3 winner Glowing Ardour, and for three listed winners. Such has been the start made by Sadima that she may go on to surpass Cocotte's achievements at stud. Sadima's third foal, a filly by Dalakhani, has yet to race, and she also has a yearling filly by Bahri. The tough and genuine Creachadoir has shown his best form on good and good to firm ground. *Saeed bin Suroor*

CREATIVE (IRE) 2 b.g. (Mar 30) Acclamation 118 – Pride of Pendle 80 (Grey Desire **70** 115) [2007 5d⁴ 6f² 6m⁶ 6d 7g³ 7g³ Oct 3] sturdy gelding: fair maiden: placed 3 times, including in nursery: should prove best up to 7f: acts on firm and good to soft ground: gelded after final start. *M. H. Tompkins*

CREATIVE MIND (IRE) 4 b.f. Danehill Dancer (IRE) 117 – Inventive 84 (Sheikh **95** Albadou 128) [2007 88: 7f⁴ 7g³ 6m Jun 9] close-coupled filly: fairly useful performer: possibly flattered when third to Wake Up Maggie in Chartwell Fillies' Stakes at Lingfield second start in 2007: was best up to 7.5f: unraced on heavy going and on any other turf surface and polytrack: in cheekpieces last 2 starts: front runner: game: visits Excellent Art. *E. J. O'Neill*

CREDENTIAL 5 b.h. Dansili 127 – Sabria (USA) (Miswaki (USA) 124) [2007 63: **67** f11g* f12g² f11g⁵ f12g 12.3f 10.3d 8.5g² 10.1d³ p12g p9.5g 10g Oct 31] sturdy horse: fair performer: won maiden at Southwell (by 6 lengths) in January: stays 1½m: acts on fibresand, good to firm and good to soft ground: wore cheekpieces final outing. *John A. Harris*

CREDIT (IRE) 6 b.g. Intikhab (USA) 135 – Tycooness (IRE) 80§ (Last Tycoon 131) **62** [2007 78: p12.2g³ Jan 4] big, good-topped gelding: has a quick, fluent action: useful at 3 yrs: lightly raced on Flat since, and only modest form sole run in 2007 (reportedly finished lame): worth a try over 1¾m: acts on good to firm ground, probably on polytrack. *Jennie Candlish*

CREDIT SLIP 3 b.c. Slip Anchor 136 – Credit-A-Plenty 111 (Generous (IRE) 139) **79** [2007 52p: p12.2g* 12.1g² 14.1s* Jun 14] useful-looking colt: fair performer: won handicaps at Wolverhampton (wandered) in April and Yarmouth (left 1¾m: acts on polytrack and soft ground: has shown signs of temperament. *J. L. Dunlop*

CREDIT SWAP 2 b.c. (Jan 24) Diktat 126 – Locharia 91 (Wolfhound (USA) 126) **67 p** [2007 6d⁴ Oct 23] 12,000Y: second foal: half-brother to 3-y-o Vivi Belle: dam, 2-y-o 5f winner, out of half-sister to Nunthorpe Stakes winners Lochsong and Lochangel: 25/1, prominent long way when fourth to Wingbeat in maiden at Yarmouth: will progress. *L. M. Cumani*

CREE 5 b.g. Indian Ridge 123 – Nightitude 93 (Night Shift (USA)) [2007 69: p6g⁴ p6g⁶ **63** 7s 7m Jun 13] close-coupled, quite good-topped gelding: modest performer: reportedly bled final outing: was effective at 6f/7f: acted on polytrack and any turf going: sometimes blinkered: free-going sort: dead. *W. R. Muir*

CREME BRULEE 4 b.f. College Chapel 122 – Balinsky (IRE) 55 (Skyliner 117) **50** [2007 66: p6g f6g p6g p6g p6g p6g f5d³ Dec 14] leggy filly: modest performer: left C. Egerton after third start: stays 6f: acts on all-weather: tried blinkered. *P. T. Dalton*

CRESCENTIA 4 ch.f. Vitus 82 – Another Nightmare (IRE) 59 (Treasure Kay 114) **–** [2007 p9.5g 12.6m Sep 15] second foal: dam 5f (including at 2 yrs)/6f winner: no promise in maiden/claimer. *Jane Chapple-Hyam*

CRESTA GOLD 4 b.f. Halling (USA) 133 – Fleet Hill (IRE) 99 (Warrshan (USA) 117) **–** [2007 107: 14g 11.9m⁶ 12.3m⁶ 12m Oct 6] leggy filly: useful performer at 3 yrs, but well below best in 2007 (said to have had breathing problem final outing). *A. Bailey*

CRETE (IRE) 5 b.g. Montjeu (IRE) 137 – Paesanella (Seattle Song (USA) 130) [2007 **85** 11d* p12g³ Nov 17] sturdy gelding: fairly useful handicapper: gelded and off over 2 years, won apprentice event at Newbury in October, hanging right: stays 1½m: acts on polytrack, good to firm and good to soft ground: quirky. *W. J. Haggas*

CRIME SCENE (IRE) 4 b.g. Royal Applause 124 – Crime (USA) (Gulch (USA)) **115** [2007 66: 12g⁴ 12g* 12g* 12m⁴ 12d* Oct 27] tall gelding: smart performer: further progress in 2007, winning handicaps at Nad Al Sheba in February and March (left I. Mohammed in UAE after) and Weatherbys St Simon Stakes at Newbury (beat Ivy Creek by 1¾ lengths, dictating and hanging right) in October: also ran well when fourth to Galactic Star in listed event at Newmarket penultimate start: stays 1½m: acts on good to firm and good to soft going: sometimes looks tricky ride: has run well when sweating. *Saeed bin Suroor*

CRIMSON FERN (IRE) 3 ch.f. Titus Livius (FR) 115 – Crimada (IRE) (Mukad- **59** damah (USA) 125) [2007 6g p6g³ p7.1g* p6m Nov 11] €12,000Y: lengthy, angular filly:

third foal: sister to fairly useful 5f winner Holbeck Ghyll and half-sister to winner in Greece: dam unraced: modest form: won maiden at Wolverhampton in October: stays easy 7f: acts on polytrack: sometimes slowly away. *M. S. Saunders*

CRIMSON FLAME (IRE) 4 b.g. Celtic Swing 138 – Wish List (IRE) 98 (Mujadil (USA) 119) [2007 73d: p12.2g p9.5g⁶ Jan 19] smallish, lightly-made gelding: has a quick action: fair maiden at 3 yrs: on downgrade: tried visored: sometimes looks none too keen. *A. J. Chamberlain* —

CRIMSON KING (IRE) 6 ch.g. Pivotal 124 – Always Happy 75 (Sharrood (USA) 124) [2007 93: p6g f6d* Dec 21] useful performer, successful in 3 of 5 starts including handicap at Southwell in December (beat Resplendent Alpha by 2½ lengths): stays 7f: acts on fibresand (unraced on turf). *R. W. Price* **94**

CRIMSON MITRE 2 b.c. (Apr 29) Bishop of Cashel 122 – Pink Champagne (Cosmonaut) [2007 p8.6g 8d 8d⁴ 8s Nov 26] fair form: best effort in maidens when fourth to First Avenue at Yarmouth: not discredited in minor event at Fontainebleau final start: stays 1m. *J. Jay* **73**

CRIMSON MONARCH (USA) 3 b.g. Red Ransom (USA) – Tolltally Light (USA) (Majestic Light (USA)) [2007 73§: 11.6m³ 11.6m⁴ 14.1g 14g 16.2v⁵ 14s³ 11.9d* Oct 18] sturdy gelding: fair performer: won maiden at Brighton in October: should stay 2m: acts on soft and good to firm ground: often blinkered: not one to trust: sold 32,000 gns. *Mrs A. J. Perrett* **76 §**

CRIMSON SILK 7 ch.g. Forzando 122 – Sylhall (Sharpo 132) [2007 97d: 6m⁶ Jun 4] strong, heavy-topped gelding: useful handicapper at 6 yrs, just fair form only outing in 2007: effective at 6f/7f: acts on good to firm and good to soft going: usually wears headgear. *B. Smart* **75**

CRIMSONWING (IRE) 2 b.f. (Mar 29) Vettori (IRE) 119 – Crimson Topaz 75 (Hernando (FR) 127) [2007 p7g p8g 8d⁵ p10g Oct 31] £450 2-y-o: unfurnished filly: first foal: dam, 11f winner, half-sister to smart stayer Dusky Warbler: modest maiden: will stay 1½m. *A. M. Hales* **58**

CRIPSEY BROOK 9 ch.g. Lycius (USA) 124 – Duwon (IRE) 55 (Polish Precedent (USA) 131) [2007 87: 12g* 10m* 10.5g 13m⁴ 14.1d⁴ 12m⁶ 12g⁵ 10g 12d⁶ 12g³ 15.8g⁵ Oct 30] tall gelding: fairly useful performer: won handicaps at Pontefract (apprentices) and Nottingham in April: below best after fifth outing: effective at 1¼m, probably stays 2m: acts on firm and good to soft going: tongue tied: claimer ridden nowadays: free-going sort, waited with. *K. G. Reveley* **85**

CRISPIAN (IRE) 3 b.g. Hernando (FR) 127 – Continuous (IRE) 89 (Darshaan 133) [2007 10.1s³ 10.1m⁶ 11.5d⁴ Jun 28] 105,000Y: quite attractive gelding: unfurnished at present: half-brother to 3 winners, including fairly useful but untrustworthy 6f (in UAE) to 8.5f winner Kameynn (by Green Desert): dam Irish 2-y-o 7f winner: best effort in maidens when third to Harland at Newcastle: bred to stay 1½m. *W. J. Haggas* **72**

CRISTAL CLEAR (IRE) 2 gr.f. (Apr 18) Clodovil (IRE) 116 – Spring To Light (USA) 93 (Blushing Groom (FR) 131) [2007 5g⁴ 5g³ 5g⁴ 5m 6s 6m⁶ 6g* 6g³ 6.5m³ 6d⁵ 6g Oct 6] 37,000Y: lengthy, good-topped filly: has scope: half-sister to several winners, including useful 6f (at 2 yrs in Ireland) and 7.5f (in US) winner Catch A Glimpse (by Gulch) and fairly useful 1¾m winner Stolen Light (by Grand Lodge): dam Irish 6f and (at 2 yrs) 7f winner: fairly useful performer: won maiden at Ripon in April and nursery at York (beat Oasis Wind by neck) in August: in frame 4 other times, 3 in listed races: will stay 7f: acts on good to firm going: quirky (tried in cheekpieces/blinkers), and held up. *T. D. Easterby* **92**

CRITERION 2 b.g. (Apr 6) Dr Fong (USA) 128 – Film Script 105 (Unfuwain (USA) 131) [2007 7m 8g⁴ Oct 24] good-bodied gelding: third foal: half-brother to fairly useful 1½m winner Rainbow's Edge (by Rainbow Quest): dam 1¼m/1½m winner: visored, better effort in maidens 3 months apart when fourth to Ragamuffin Man at Bath (would have gone very close with clear run): gelded after: will stay 1½m: should improve again. *Sir Michael Stoute* **69 p**

CRITICAL STAGE (IRE) 8 b.g. King's Theatre (IRE) 128 – Zandaka (FR) (Doyoun 124) [2007 70: p16g³ p16g² p16f p16g 14.1s³ p16g* p16g³ p13.9g p16g Nov 14] sturdy gelding: fair handicapper on all-weather, modest on turf: won at Kempton in September: stays 2m: acts on all-weather, good to firm and good to soft ground, probably on soft. *J. D. Frost* **63 +**
a73

CROCODILE BAY (IRE) 4 b.g. Spectrum (IRE) 126 – Shenkara (IRE) 79 (Night Shift (USA)) [2007 –: 8.1g 8d 8.1g² p8g² 8d p8g⁵ p10g 7g 8m⁵ 8.1g⁴ 7.2s² 8g* 8s² 7g² **89**

8g³ Nov 9] good-topped, attractive gelding: has a quick action: fairly useful handicapper: left B. Meehan 17,000 gns after seventh start: won at Newcastle in October: creditable placed efforts after: stays 1m: acts on polytrack, soft and good to firm going: has carried head awkwardly: waited with: consistent. *D. Nicholls*

CROESO BACH 3 b.f. Bertolini (USA) 125 – Croeso-I-Cymru 96 (Welsh Captain 113) [2007 –: 6.1g 5m⁵ 5.1m² 5.1f² 5f Sep 5] smallish filly: modest maiden: best at 5f: raced only on good going or firmer (acts on firm). *J. L. Spearing* **61**

CROESO CUSAN 2 b.f. (Apr 3) Diktat 126 – Croeso Croeso 100 (Most Welcome 131) [2007 6d⁶ Oct 15] leggy filly: first foal: dam 5f/6f winner: 11/1, early speed when sixth in maiden at Windsor: open to improvement. *J. L. Spearing* **– p**

CROFT (IRE) 4 b.g. Mull of Kintyre (USA) 114 – Home Comforts (Most Welcome 131) [2007 63: 8.1s 7s 8.1m* 8.1d 7d⁴ 8.1f 8m 8f p12.2g p12.2g⁶ Oct 18] strong, good-bodied gelding: modest performer: won seller at Chepstow in August: below form after: stays 1m: acts on good to firm going: often visored, tried in cheekpieces: inconsistent. *M. S. Saunders* **58 d**

CROIX DE GUERRE (IRE) 7 gr.g. Highest Honor (FR) 124 – Esclava (USA) (Nureyev (USA) 131) [2007 16m⁴ Jun 8] tall gelding: modest performer: creditable fourth in handicap at Goodwood sole Flat start since 2004: stays 2m: acts on firm and good to soft going: often blinkered: quirky: fairly useful hurdler/chaser. *P. J. Hobbs* **57 §**

CROIX ROUGE (USA) 5 b.h. Chester House (USA) 123 – Rougeur (USA) (Blushing Groom (FR) 131) [2007 p13.9g⁵ f11g a11g a10.5g⁴ a10.5g* a10.5g* a10.5g* a11g⁴ 14s⁵ a12g 15s Nov 25] smallish, good-topped horse: ran in Britain at 2 yrs but raced mainly in Spain since (won 2 minor events at Mijas in 2006): never dangerous in handicaps and minor event at Wolverhampton and Southwell first 2 starts in 2007: won 2 handicaps and minor event at Mijas in June/July: stays 13f: raced mainly on sand, better effort on turf when fifth in Gran Premio de San Sebastian ninth start: tried blinkered: looked none too easy ride at 2 yrs. *R. J. Smith, Spain* **?**

CROOKED THROW (IRE) 8 b. or br.g. Anshan 119 – Mary's View (IRE) (Phardante (FR) 123) [2007 100: 8v² 8s 8m⁶ 8m 8m 8s 9v³ 8.5g² 8s² 8g 9d³ 7.5g 8s⁴ Oct 22] lengthy gelding: useful performer: several creditable efforts in 2007, including in handicap at Galway (short-head second to Incline) and Concorde Stakes at Tipperary (seventh to Eastern Appeal) eighth/penultimate outings: below form in Lincoln at Newcastle and Hunt Cup at Royal Ascot on second/fifth starts: effective at 7.5f to 9f: acts on heavy and good to firm ground: tends to race freely, and is held up. *C. F. Swan, Ireland* **103**

CROON 5 b.g. Sinndar (IRE) 134 – Shy Minstrel (USA) (The Minstrel (CAN) 135) [2007 86: p12g⁴ f14g⁴ p13.9g⁴ Mar 10] close-coupled gelding: fairly useful handicapper: should stay 2m: acts on all-weather and firm ground: refused to enter stall on intended reappearance: joined Mrs Caroline Bailey, modest form over hurdles. *T. J. Pitt* **84**

CROSBY HALL 4 b.g. Compton Place 125 – Alzianah 102 (Alzao (USA) 117) [2007 –: 7.5m 7m 7.1g Jul 9] sturdy, attractive gelding: no longer of any account. *N. Tinkler* **–**

CROSBY JEMMA 3 ch.f. Lomitas 129 – Gino's Spirits 98 (Perugino (USA) 84) [2007 48: 7m² 8m 7g⁵ 7m⁵ 8m² 8.3g⁶ 8m Sep 20] unfurnished filly: modest maiden: bred to stay 1¼m: raced only on good/good to firm ground. *J. R. Weymes* **59**

CROSBY MILLIE 3 gr.f. Linamix (FR) 127 – Calling Card (Bering 136) [2007 57: 7m⁶ 9.9m 7g Jul 27] modest maiden at 2 yrs: little form in 2007. *J. R. Weymes* **–**

CROSBY VISION 4 b.g. Agnes World (USA) 123 – Aegean Blue (Warning 136) [2007 77: 7f⁴ 7d 7.1m 8m 7m⁵ 7.9g 7.2g Aug 29] quite good-topped gelding: fair handicapper: stays 1m: acts on firm going (below form all starts on softer than good): tried visored (ran poorly). *J. R. Weymes* **73**

CROSSBOW CREEK 9 b.g. Lugana Beach 116 – Roxy River 38 (Ardross 134) [2007 90: 10m⁵ p10g* 12m² 12m p11g⁵ 12s Oct 13] rangy, good-bodied gelding: useful hurdler/ smart chaser: fairly useful handicapper on Flat, lightly raced: won at Kempton in July: stays 1½m: acts on polytrack and good to firm ground: failed to settle final start. *M. G. Rimell* **94**

CROSS FELL (USA) 2 b.c. (May 12) Cherokee Run (USA) 122 – Campsie Fells (UAE) 111 (Indian Ridge 123) [2007 6m p7g 6d p7.1g* 7g* p7g³ p7.1g⁵ p7.1d* Dec 6] strong colt: first foal: dam French 1m (at 2 yrs)/9f winner: fairly useful performer: won nurseries at Wolverhampton and Catterick in October (then left M. Johnston 20,000 gns) and claimer at Wolverhampton in December: stays 7f: acts on polytrack, unraced on extremes of turf going: races up with pace. *J. R. Boyle* **80**

CROSSING BRIDGES 2 ch.f. (Apr 16) Dr Fong (USA) 128 – Pontressina (USA) (St — Jovite (USA) 135) [2007 p7.1g f8d⁵ Dec 12] fourth foal: half-sister to 4-y-o Robustian: dam German 8.5f/9f winner: well held in maidens. *T. D. Barron*

CROSSING THE LINE (IRE) 3 b.g. Cape Cross (IRE) 129 – Tropical Zone (Mach- 75 iavellian (USA) 123) [2007 63p: p12.2g² 12m Jul 12] rangy gelding: fair form: best effort when second on handicap debut on reappearance: broke down next time: stayed easy 1½m: acted on polytrack: dead. *Sir Mark Prescott*

CROSS OF LORRAINE (IRE) 4 b.g. Pivotal 124 – My-Lorraine (IRE) 77 (Mac's 75 Imp (USA) 116) [2007 75: p6g⁴ f5g³ 6m³ 6g 5.9m² 6m 6v⁴ 6d² 5.9m⁵ Jul 29] compact gelding: fair performer: left I. Semple after seventh start: stays 7f: acts on all-weather, heavy and good to firm ground: blinkered: often races prominently. *J. Wade*

CROSSTAR 2 b.c. (Jan 31) Cape Cross (IRE) 129 – Pie High 96 (Salse (USA) 128) 79 p [2007 7m³ p8m* Dec 7] 26,000F, 28,000Y: first foal: dam, 7f winner (including at 2 yrs), half-sister to smart sprinter Leap For Joy: third in maiden at Milan for A. & G. Botti: won similar event at Lingfield 3 months later by length from Seattle Storm: stays 1m: should improve further. *M. Botti*

CROSS THE LINE (IRE) 5 b.g. Cape Cross (IRE) 129 – Baalbek 76 (Barathea (IRE) 93 127) [2007 87, a95: p7g⁶ p7g² 8m⁶ 8m² 8m⁴ 7m⁴ 8g 8s 8m⁶ p7g Oct 24] big gelding: fairly useful handicapper: effective at 7f/1m: acts on polytrack, soft and good to firm ground: held up: consistent. *A. P. Jarvis*

CROWNING MOMENT (IRE) 3 b.f. Johannesburg (USA) 127 – Moment of Mad- 45 ness (USA) (Seattle Slew (USA)) [2007 –: 8m 9.7f Sep 10] €30,000F, €35,000Y: third foal: half-sister to winner in USA by Honour And Glory: dam unraced half-sister to smart performer up to 1¾m Zaajer: poor maiden. *Harry Rogers, Ireland*

CROWN OFFICE (USA) 3 ch.f. Horse Chestnut (SAF) 119 – Great Verdict (AUS) 63 + (Christmas Tree (AUS)) [2007 p8g⁴ 9.7m³ 8g 8g Oct 25] fourth foal: sister to fairly useful 1¼m winner Masterofthecourt and half-sister to very smart South African 1¼m/1½m performer Greys Inn (by Zabeel): dam Australian 5.5f to 7f winner: modest form in maidens: little impact on handicap debut final start: will be suited by 1¼m+. *H. Morrison*

CROW'S NEST LAD 3 b.g. Komaite (USA) – Miss Fit (IRE) 87 (Hamas (IRE) 125§) 70 [2007 77: f5g 6m 5v⁶ p6g 7.5d³ 7d² f8d² Dec 15] strong, workmanlike gelding: fair handicapper: left T. Easterby and gelded after seventh start: stays 1m: acts on fibresand, firm and good to soft going. *J. O'Reilly*

CROW WOOD 8 b.g. Halling (USA) 133 – Play With Me (IRE) 73 (Alzao (USA) 117) 89 [2007 94: p12g³ p12g⁵ Feb 3] strong, close-coupled gelding: fairly useful handicapper: easily better effort in 2007 when third at Lingfield on reappearance: effective at 1¼m, probably at 1¾m: acts on all-weather, firm and good to soft going: usually races handily: smart hurdler. *J. J. Quinn*

CRUEL SEA (USA) 2 gr.f. (Apr 5) Mizzen Mast (USA) 121 – Storm Dove (USA) 108 86 P (Storm Bird (CAN) 134) [2007 8g* Oct 26] big, rangy filly: half-sister to 2 winners by Distant View, including fairly useful 2000 2-y-o 7f winner Good Standing: dam, 6f (at 2 yrs) and 7f winner, out of smart French performer up to 1¼m Daeltown: 9/2 and better for race, made big impression when winning 17-runner maiden at Doncaster by 1¼ lengths from Desert Chill, quickening well from off pace: not sure to stay much beyond 1m: has plenty of scope, and looks a smart prospect. *B. W. Hills*

CRUISE DIRECTOR 7 b.g. Zilzal (USA) 137 – Briggsmaid 70 (Elegant Air 119) 88 [2007 92: 10.5g⁴ 12.3g 12g⁵ May 16] heavy-topped gelding: fairly useful handicapper: stays 1½m: acts on all-weather and soft going: held up. *Ian Williams*

CRUSH ON YOU 4 b.f. Golden Snake (USA) 127 – Mourir d'Aimer (USA) (Trempo- 53 lino (USA) 135) [2007 55: p8.6g* f8g 8.5m⁶ p7.1g 8s p8.6g³ 8g⁶ p9.5m p8.6g Sep 28] leggy, close-coupled filly: modest performer: won minor event at Wolverhampton in January: stays 8.6f: acts on all-weather and any turf going. *R. Hollinshead*

CRUSOE (IRE) 10 b.g. Turtle Island (IRE) 123 – Self Reliance 72 (Never So Bold 51 d 135) [2007 63d: p8.6g p8.6g² f12g p8.6g p8.6g f8g f8g p9.5g p8.6g p9.5g May 1] small gelding: modest performer: regressed in 2007: seems to stay 11f: acts on all-weather, lightly raced and no form on turf since 3 yrs: tried in cheekpieces/tongue tie, usually blinkered. *A. Sadik*

CRUX 5 b.g. Pivotal 124 – Penny Dip 86 (Cadeaux Genereux 131) [2007 –: f7g 6g⁶ 7m 57 7.5m⁶ 6g Jul 8] rather leggy gelding: modest maiden: stays 7.5f: acts on polytrack (below form on fibresand) and good to firm ground: reportedly bled final outing. *R. E. Barr*

CRYING ALOUD (USA) 2 b. or br.f. (Feb 17) Street Cry (IRE) 130 – Angelic Deed   **85**
(USA) (Alydeed (CAN) 120) [2007 5m p5.1g⁵ 7m² 6m 8s⁴ Oct 26] $27,000Y: big, leggy
filly: unfurnished at 2 yrs: sixth foal: half-sister to a minor sprint winner in Canada by
Service Stripe: dam US sprint winner: fairly useful maiden: head second to Dona Alba at
Folkestone (made all stand-side group), standout performance: best up to 7f: acts on good
to firm going. *P. A. Blockley*

CRY PRESTO (USA) 3 b.g. Street Cry (IRE) 130 – Sabaah Elfull 75 (Kris 135) [2007   **70 §**
85§: p8.6g p12g* 11g 14g 10g⁵ 10m p10.7g p8g Oct 5] stocky gelding: fair performer:
won maiden at Lingfield in March: left R. Hannon after fifth start: stays easy 1½m: acts
on polytrack, best turf form on good going: tried blinkered/in cheekpieces: sometimes
tongue tied: ungenuine. *D. T. Hughes, Ireland*

CRYPTIC CLUE (USA) 3 b.g. Cryptoclearance (USA) – Nidd (USA) 112 (Known   **46**
Fact (USA) 135) [2007 55: p6g f5g⁴ f7g⁵ f5g⁵ f7d Dec 15] good-topped gelding: poor
maiden: stays 1m: acts on fibresand and good to firm ground: tried blinkered/in
cheekpieces: withdrawn after unseating rider before start intended penultimate outing.
D. W. Chapman

CRYPTONITE DIAMOND (USA) 2 ch.f. (Apr 23) Hennessy (USA) 122 –   **55**
Cryptotoo (USA) (Cryptoclearance (USA)) [2007 6m 6f⁵ 7m² p8.6g Oct 12] $75,000Y:
small, sturdy filly: first foal: dam US 1m/8.5f winner: modest maiden: should stay 1m.
W. R. Swinburn

CRYSTAL ANNIE 4 b.f. Namaqualand (USA) – Crystal Canyon 59 (Efisio 120)   **–**
[2007 52: 11.1g p13.9g Sep 13] maiden: tailed off both starts in 2007. *Heather Dalton*

CRYSTAL BALL 3 b.f. Diktat 126 – First Sapphire (Simply Great (FR) 122) [2007   **48**
10.1d⁵ Jul 5] sixth foal: half-sister to 3 winners, including useful 1¼m winner Rolling
Stone (by Northern Amythest): dam, of no account, half-sister to smart sprinter Darley
Knight: 25/1, 9¼ lengths fifth of 6 to Iceman George in maiden at Yarmouth. *Rae Guest*

CRYSTAL CAPELLA 2 b.f. (Feb 21) Cape Cross (IRE) 129 – Crystal Star 100 (Mark   **79 p**
of Esteem (IRE) 137) [2007 p7g² Nov 17] first foal: dam, 2-y-o 7f winner, out of half-
sister to Poule d'Essai des Pouliches winner Rose Gypsy: 4/1 and green, shaped well
when head second to Fantasy Princess in maiden at Lingfield, running on strongly final
1f: will improve. *Sir Michael Stoute*

CRYSTAL GAZER (FR) 3 b.f. Elnadim (USA) 128 – Chrysalu 102 (Distant Relative   **90**
128) [2007 77: p6g* p7g* 7g 6d² 6m⁴ p6g* p7m Oct 6] strong, good-bodied filly: fairly
useful handicapper: won at Lingfield in April, and Kempton in May and September: ran
as if amiss final outing: stays 7f: acts on polytrack, good to firm and good to soft going:
usually held up. *R. Hannon*

CRYSTAL PLUM (IRE) 3 ch.f. Rock of Gibraltar (IRE) 133 – State Crystal (IRE)   **–**
114 (High Estate 127) [2007 67: p10g p8g Jun 16] leggy, close-coupled filly: tailed off in
handicaps in 2007. *B. W. Hills*

CRYSTAL PRINCE 3 b.g. Marju (IRE) 127 – Crystal Ring (IRE) 83 (Kris 135) [2007   **80**
–: 10g² 11.9m⁴ 12m³ Aug 6] strong, good-bodied gelding: fairly useful maiden: best
effort when runner-up on reappearance, dictating: may prove best around 1¼m. *T. P. Tate*

CRYSTAL REIGN (IRE) 2 b.g. (Mar 26) Noverre (USA) 125 – Crystal Springs   **74**
(IRE) 79 (Kahyasi 130) [2007 6m² 7s p6g⁵ Oct 29] 38,000Y: well-made gelding: third
foal: half-brother to 4-y-o Sotik Star: dam, held 1½m to 2m and hurdles winner, out of
half-sister to very smart performer up to 1¾m Lanfranco: fair maiden: second to Nacho
Libre at Windsor on debut: off 4 months (and gelded) before final start: will stay at least
1m: sold 3,500 gns. *P. W. Chapple-Hyam*

CRYSTAL ROCK (IRE) 2 br.g. (May 6) Rock of Gibraltar (IRE) 133 – State Crystal   **85**
(IRE) 114 (High Estate 127) [2007 6d 6m² 7m³ 8m Sep 13] tall, leggy gelding: half-
brother to several winners, including useful 2003 2-y-o 7f winner Crystal Curling (by
Peintre Celebre): dam, 7f (at 2 yrs) and 1½m (Lancashire Oaks) winner, half-sister to
several smart performers, including Fillies' Mile winner Crystal Music: fairly useful
maiden: placed at Windsor and Chester (third to Eastern Gift): headstrong, and possibly
best up to 7f (well held at 1m final start, then gelded). *B. W. Hills*

CRYSTANY (IRE) 2 b.f. (Apr 25) Green Desert (USA) 127 – Crystal Music (USA)   **98 p**
114 (Nureyev (USA) 131) [2007 6d⁴ 6g⁵ 6m* 6.5m² Sep 12] €520,000Y: sturdy, compact
filly: third foal: dam, 2-y-o 7f/1m winner (including Fillies' Mile), in frame in 1000
Guineas/Irish 1000 Guineas: useful form: won maiden at Ripon in September: better still
when head second of 19 to Royal Confidence in nursery at Doncaster: stays 6.5f: acts on
good to firm going: should go on progressing. *H. R. A. Cecil*

CUBAN MISSILE 2 b.g. (Jan 17) Danehill Dancer (IRE) 117 – Lady Salsa (IRE) **87 p**
(Gone West (USA)) [2007 8.3g² 8.2g* Nov 7] 48,000F, 145,000Y: strong gelding: first
foal: dam, French 1½m winner, out of Cherry Hinton winner Chicarica: plenty of promise
in maidens, second to Mountain Pride at Leicester and winning cosily at Nottingham by
¾ length from French Riviera: will stay 1¼m: useful prospect. *R. Charlton*

CUBAN RHYTHM (USA) 2 b.f. (Feb 16) Kingmambo (USA) 125 – Kournakova **71 p**
(IRE) 106 (Sadler's Wells (USA) 132) [2007 8.2d² Oct 18] $170,000Y: tall filly: second
foal: dam, Irish 1m (at 2 yrs)/1¼m winner, half-sister to very smart performers Tropical
(sprinter) and Shake The Yoke (miler): 3/1, encouraging ¾-length second to Sleepy
Hollow in maiden at Nottingham, travelling strongly long way: will stay 1¼m: sure to
improve. *R. Charlton*

CULZEAN BAY 2 b.f. (Apr 6) Mind Games 121 – Florie Nightingale 60 (Tragic Role **50**
(USA)) [2007 7s⁶ 6d 6d p5g 5.2m³ 5.1m³ 5.2m² 6m 5f² 5f p5.1g Nov 2] third foal: dam,
2-y-o 7f seller winner, half-sister to smart 7f/1m performer Sunstreak: modest maiden:
claimed from A. Bailey £5,000 seventh start: best at 5f: acts on firm going: once blinkered. *Miss Diana Weeden*

CUMAE (USA) 3 b.f. King Cugat (USA) 122 – Jubilee Walk (Generous (IRE) 139) **–**
[2007 8m p10g p12.2g⁶ p12g p12.2s Dec 21] 2,500Y: leggy filly: fifth foal: half-sister
to 3 minor sprint winners in USA: dam unraced: no form, trained by Diana Weeden on
debut: tried in cheekpieces. *J. Pearce*

CUMBERLAND ROAD 4 ch.g. Efisio 120 – Thatcher's Era (IRE) 57 (Never So Bold **53**
135) [2007 –: p8.6g p8.6g 7g 6d² 6m 6g Oct 19] workmanlike gelding: modest maiden:
should prove best around 6f: acts on polytrack, good to firm and good to soft ground: tried
in cheekpieces, visored last 4 starts. *C. A. Mulhall*

CUMBRIAN KNIGHT (IRE) 9 b.g. Presenting 120 – Crashrun (Crash Course 128) **–**
[2007 70: p16.5g* p13.9g⁴ 13m p13.9g³ p13.9g² Dec 3] fair handicapper: won amateur **a68**
event at Wolverhampton in January: stays 2m: acts on polytrack and good to firm ground:
usually amateur ridden. *J. M. Jefferson*

CUMIN (USA) 3 ch.f. Fusaichi Pegasus (USA) 130 – User Cat (USA) (Storm Cat **85**
(USA)) [2007 100: 8m⁵ 8d 9.9g Aug 26] well-grown filly: has a quick action: useful performer at 2 yrs: well below form in 2007: should stay 1m: acts on firm ground. *B. W. Hills*

CUPID'S GLORY 5 b.g. Pursuit of Love 124 – Doctor's Glory (USA) 91 (Elmaamul **89**
(USA) 125) [2007 105+: p8.6g 7.6m 7d p7m⁶ p7m p10m⁴ p10g⁵ p9.5g⁴ Dec 31] rather
lengthy, good-bodied gelding: smart performer at best, just fairly useful in 2007: left Sir
Mark Prescott 17,500 gns after reappearance: stays easy 1¼m: acts on polytrack, soft and
good to firm going: tried blinkered/in cheekpieces. *Mrs L. C. Jewell*

CUPPACOCOA 3 b.f. Bertolini (USA) 125 – Coffee Time (IRE) 88 (Efisio 120) [2007 **80**
70: 5.1g³ 5.1f* 5g 5m 5g 5.1m⁵ 5m² 5.7f⁶ 5m 5d Oct 13] small, strong filly: fairly useful
handicapper: won at Bath in May: best at 5f: acts on firm going, probably on good to soft:
has given trouble at stall: effective held up or ridden prominently. *C. G. Cox*

CURIO 2 b.f. (Apr 2) Captain Rio 122 – Luanshya 78 (First Trump 118) [2007 5g⁵ 5.1f **56**
5d 5.1g³ 5.1g⁶ p6g³ p5.1g⁶ Dec 1] good-topped filly: fourth foal: half-sister to 4-y-o Tabaret and 5f (at 2 yrs)/6f winner African Breeze (by Atraf): dam 6f winner: modest maiden:
will prove best at 5f: acts on polytrack, best turf efforts on good going. *R. M. Whitaker*

CURLIN (USA) 3 ch.c. Smart Strike (CAN) 121 – Sherrif's Deputy (USA) (Deputy **131**
Minister (CAN)) [2007 a7f* a8.5f* a9f* a10f³ a9.5f* a12f² a9f³ a10f* a10s* Oct 27]
$57,000Y: fifth foal: closely related/half-brother to winning US sprinters by Excellent
Secret and Hadif: dam unraced out of US Grade 2 8.5f winner Barbarika: unraced at
2 yrs: developed into a top-class performer (US Horse of The Year), winning maiden at
Gulfstream in February (by 12¾ lengths, sold for reported $3.5m and left Helen Pitts
after), Grade 3 Rebel Stakes in March and Grade 2 Arkansas Derby (by 10½ lengths) in
April, both at Oaklawn, Preakness Stakes at Pimlico (finished strongly to beat Street
Sense by a head) in May, Jockey Club Gold Cup at Belmont (beat Lawyer Ron by a
neck) in September and Breeders' Cup Classic - Powered By Dodge at Monmouth (by
4½ lengths from Hard Spun) in October: placed all other starts, in Kentucky Derby at
Churchill Downs (third to Street Sense), Belmont Stakes (beaten a head by filly Rags To
Riches, battling back strongly) and Haskell Invitational Handicap at Monmouth (bit
below best when 4¾ lengths third to Any Given Saturday, who rec. 4 lb): subject of an
ownership dispute late in year: stays 1½m: effective in sloppy conditions: usually held up
in mid-division: game and genuine. *S. M. Asmussen, USA*

CURRAHEE 3 b.g. Efisio 120 – Dixie Favor (USA) 82 (Dixieland Band (USA)) [2007 –
–: f7g 11g 12s 16.2s 16.1g Oct 3] good-bodied gelding: little form. *Miss J. A. Camacho*

CURRENCY 10 b.g. Sri Pekan (USA) 117 – On Tiptoes 107 (Shareef Dancer (USA) 66
135) [2007 74: 5.5d 6g² 6f² 6g* 6m² 5.7d⁴ 6g p6g 6.1m⁶ Oct 3] sturdy gelding: fair
handicapper: won at Salisbury (apprentices) in June: stays 7f: acts on polytrack (well
below form on fibresand), firm and good to soft ground: tried in cheekpieces/blinkers.
J. M. Bradley

CURRISTOWN PET (IRE) 3 b.f. Lil's Boy (USA) 109 – Moorefield (USA) 63 –
(Marquetry (USA) 121) [2007 10m 8g 8d p16.5g Dec 8] good-topped filly: third foal:
dam Irish maiden: little form: blinkered at Wolverhampton final outing. *C. P. Donoghue,
Ireland*

CURSUM PERFICIO 5 b.g. Tagula (IRE) 116 – Simply Sooty 78 (Absalom 128) –
[2007 81: p8.6g 6m Aug 11] good-bodied gelding: fairly useful handicapper at 4 yrs: little
form in 2007: stays 8.6f: acts on polytrack and firm going: tried in cheekpieces: won over
hurdles in August. *R. Lee*

CURTAIL (IRE) 4 b.g. Namid 128 – Nipitinthebud (USA) 59 (Night Shift (USA)) 101
[2007 101: p8.6g⁵ p7.1g 6m 6g 5m⁴ 5.1d⁶ 5m⁴ 5d 6g² 5s⁴ 6d p6g p6g* Nov 16] smallish,
strong gelding: useful handicapper: as good as ever when winning at Wolverhampton
(by short head from Abunai) in November: stays easy 1m, raced mainly at 5f/6f: acts on
polytrack and good to firm going (not at best on softer than good): tried visored: quirky.
I. Semple

CURTAIN CALL (FR) 2 b.c. (Jan 31) Sadler's Wells (USA) 132 – Apsara (FR) 113
(Darshaan 133) [2007 7s⁶ 8s² 7d² 8d* 8g⁵ Oct 27]
Big-race triumphs over jumps are nothing new to Jessica Harrington, many
of them having been gained by her star performer Moscow Flyer, whose twenty-
six wins over hurdles and fences included two in the Queen Mother Champion
Chase. But the County Kildare-based trainer has also had a fair amount of success
with her far smaller Flat team, and in September enjoyed a couple of pattern-race
victories. First up came Jumbajukiba, a four-year-old gelding who had been bought
for 18,000 guineas at the 2006 Newmarket Autumn Sales and shown marked
improvement for the fitting of blinkers after joining Harrington, underlining just
what a smart performer he had become when justifying favouritism in the Group 3
Solonaway Stakes at the Curragh. Then, at the same course two weeks later, Curtain
Call became his trainer's first, and what turned out to be only two-year-old winner
of the season when taking the Group 2 Juddmonte Beresford Stakes.
Aidan O'Brien had saddled the three previous winners of the Beresford
Stakes, taking his total to nine in all, and he was responsible for two of the nine
runners in the latest renewal, including the even-money favourite Lizard Island,
who on his previous start had finished fourth to New Approach in the National
Stakes. Curtain Call was next in the betting at 9/2, despite being one of two maidens
in the line-up, having already shown form bordering on smart on the most recent of
his three runs. That was in the Futurity Stakes over seven furlongs at the Curragh,
in which Curtain Call, a 40/1-shot in a five-runner field, split the two favourites
New Approach and Henrythenavigator, unable to go the early gallop before staying
on well to finish three lengths second. The step back up to a mile in the Beresford
seemed sure to suit Curtain Call who, in the event, was also to benefit from a change
in tactics, making the running this time. Increasing the tempo turning for home,
Curtain Call stayed on strongly under pressure and drew clear from over a furlong
out to win by four lengths from Domestic Fund, with the disappointing Lizard
Island only sixth. 'We're only keeping the jumpers as lead horses now!' said
Harrington after her biggest win on the Flat. Curtain Call's connections, who had
backed him at 66/1 for the Derby after the Futurity, now saw his odds cut to as low
as 20/1. A similar display in the Racing Post Trophy would have seen his odds
tumble again, but he looked past his best for the season at Doncaster. Tracking
the leaders after an awkward start, Curtain Call was off the bridle by halfway and
weakened in the final furlong to finish fifth of twelve behind Ibn Khaldun, beaten
seven and a half lengths. Harrington's involvement with Curtain Call proved
relatively short-lived however, as he has joined Luca Cumani for his three-year-old
campaign, having been syndicated at a reported £3.75m.

Mrs P. K. Cooper's "Curtain Call"

		Northern Dancer	Nearctic
	Sadler's Wells (USA)	(b 1961)	Natalma
	(b 1981)	Fairy Bridge	Bold Reason
Curtain Call (FR)		(b 1975)	Special
(b.c. Jan 31, 2005)		Darshaan	Shirley Heights
	Apsara (FR)	(br 1981)	Delsy
	(b 2000)	Whakilyric	Miswaki
		(b 1984)	Lyrism

The Derby distance won't be a problem for Curtain Call judged on pedigree. Indeed, a mile and a half should suit him very well, and he is likely to stay further. By Sadler's Wells, he is the first foal of the Darshaan mare Apsara who was placed at up to seventeen furlongs in France. Apsara was bred by the Niarchos family, a daughter of Whakilyric, who carried their colours to victory on three occasions at two and then went on to prove a goldmine at stud. Whakilyric was a smart performer on the racecourse, one of her wins coming in the seven-furlong Prix du Calvados, though on occasions she filled the role of pacemaker for her more illustrious stable-companion Miesque, including when third in the Prix de la Salamandre. Whakilyric and Miesque have produced high-class colts in Hernando and Kingmambo respectively, the Prix du Jockey Club winner Hernando one of his dam's ten winners all told to date, the very smart Johann Quatz (also by Sadler's Wells) the pick of the others. Curtain Call's great grandam Lyrism is an unraced daughter of Pass A Glance, a very useful miler for Henry Cecil who went on to show herself a smart middle-distance performer in the States. Curtain Call, a close-coupled colt who cost 60,000 guineas as a yearling (a bargain buy by Sadler's Wells' standards), has raced only on good ground or softer, his two best efforts coming on good to soft.
Mrs J. Harrington, Ireland

DAA

CURZON PRINCE (IRE) 3 b.c. Mujadil (USA) 119 – Smooth Spirit (USA) (Alydar **89** (USA)) [2007 84p: p7.1g⁴ 7m² 7.1g 8s 8d 7g² 7m p8g³ Dec 16] close-coupled colt: has a round action: fairly useful handicapper: good efforts when placed 2 of last 3 starts: stays 1m: acts on polytrack and good to firm ground. *C. F. Wall*

CUSHAT LAW (IRE) 3 b.f. Montjeu (IRE) 137 – Blush With Love (USA) (Mt Liver- **75** more (USA)) [2007 58: 10.1g⁴ 12.1m² 11.6s² 12g* 12d² 12g⁴ Aug 24] good-bodied filly: fair handicapper: won at Thirsk in July: stays 1½m: acts on soft and good to firm going. *W. Jarvis*

CUSOON 5 b.g. Dansili 127 – Charming Life 88 (Habitat 134) [2007 82, a100: p10g² **–** p10g² p10f* p10g a7.5f p8.5f p8.5f Sep 1] neat gelding: smart performer on all-weather: **a110** further improvement when winning listed race at Lingfield (beat Blue Bajan by short head) in February: not discredited when ninth to Gentlemen's Deal in Winter Derby there next time, denied clear run: left G. L. Moore, well held in USA, leaving T. West before final start: stays 1¼m: acts on polytrack and firm going: tried in cheekpieces/blinkers: held up. *S. H. Fairlie, USA*

CUTE 2 b.f. (Apr 13) Diktat 126 – Gleam of Light (IRE) 81 (Danehill (USA) 126) [2007 **87** 5.1m³ 6g⁵ 6m 7.1d⁴ Jul 26] 10,000F, 50,000Y: good-topped filly: half-sister to several winners, notably 3-y-o Arabian Gleam: dam, 7.5f winner, out of half-sister to 2000 Guineas winner Don't Forget Me: fairly useful maiden: highly tried after debut, in listed race at Sandown (fourth to Muthabara, struck into) final start: will stay 1m. *C. E. Brittain*

CUTE ASS (IRE) 2 b.f. (Apr 15) Fath (USA) 116 – John's Ballad (IRE) (Ballad Rock **99** 122) [2007 5m³ 5d² 5d⁴ 5m* 5.2m² 5m³ 5d² Oct 13] 26,000Y: small, sturdy filly: closely related to smart sprinter Peruvian Chief (by Foxhound) and half-sister to 3 winners, including fairly useful 2003 2-y-o 1m winner Cusco (later winner in US, by Titus Livius): dam unraced out of half-sister to Dewhurst Stakes winner Monteverdi: useful performer: won maiden at Musselburgh in August: continued progress, 2½ lengths third of 8 to Fleeting Spirit in Flying Childers Stakes at Doncaster and 1½ lengths second of 12 to Captain Gerrard in Cornwallis Stakes at Ascot: speedy, raced only at 5f: acts on good to firm and good to soft going: consistent. *K. R. Burke*

CUT RIDGE (IRE) 8 b.m. Indian Ridge 123 – Cutting Ground (IRE) 85 (Common **49** Grounds 118) [2007 52: 7m⁴ 7.1m⁵ 5m 6s 5v Jul 6] lengthy mare: poor performer now-adays: effective at 5f to 7.6f: acts on firm and good to soft going, well beaten on soft/heavy: often wears cheekpieces: free-going sort. *J. S. Wainwright*

CUT THE CAKE (USA) 3 b.f. Diesis 133 – Wife For Life (USA) (Dynaformer **74** (USA)) [2007 77p: 8.2m⁴ May 2] rangy filly: similar form in maidens at York and Not-tingham 7 months apart, flashing tail both times: would have been suited by 1¼m: dead. *J. Noseda*

CUTTING CREW (USA) 6 ch.g. Diesis 133 – Poppy Carew (IRE) 110 (Danehill **103** (USA) 126) [2007 13.3m⁴ 12m⁴ 12s² Oct 19] smallish, rather leggy gelding: useful handi-capper: off over 3 years prior to reappearance: as good as ever when neck second to Greek Envoy (pair clear) at Newmarket final outing: will stay at least 1¾m: acts on soft and good to firm ground: has run well when sweating: races prominently. *W. R. Swinburn*

CYBERSNOW (USA) 3 b.c. Royal Anthem (USA) 135 – Storm Dove (USA) 108 **82** (Storm Bird (CAN) 134) [2007 p10g² p10g⁵ Jun 30] half-brother to 2 winners by Distant View, including fairly useful 2000 2-y-o 7f winner Good Standing: dam, 6f (at 2 yrs) and 7f winner, out of smart French performer up to 1¼m Daeltown: better effort in maidens at Lingfield when short-head second to Come April: sold 21,000 gns in July. *Mrs A. J. Perrett*

CYFRWYS (IRE) 6 b.m. Foxhound (USA) 103 – Divine Elegance (IRE) (College **51** Chapel 122) [2007 59: 7g² 6.1g⁶ 5.7d⁶ 7m 5.7d⁴ p6g⁶ Dec 8] close-coupled mare: modest performer nowadays: effective at 5.7f to easy 7f: acts on all-weather, good to firm and good to soft ground: tried tongue tied/visored, usually wears cheekpieces: carries head high: often races prominently. *B. Palling*

CYRIL THE SQUIRREL 3 b.g. Cyrano de Bergerac 120 – All Done (Northern State **51** (USA) 91) [2007 p7g⁴ p8.6g p11g⁶ Dec 19] modest form in polytrack maidens: stays 11f: slowly away first 2 outings. *Karen George*

D

DAAWEITZA 4 ch.g. Daawe (USA) 103 – Chichen Itza (Shareef Dancer (USA) 135) **89** [2007 82: 8s 8m 8.1g³ 7.1m* 8.5m⁵ 8.1m* 7.9d³ 7v⁶ 6m 8m⁴ p8.6g Oct 8] sturdy gelding:

249

fairly useful handicapper: won at Musselburgh and Haydock in May: effective at 7f to 9f: acts on all-weather, firm and soft ground: tried blinkered/in cheekpieces. *B. Ellison*

DABAWIYAH (IRE) 3 b.f. Intikhab (USA) 135 – The Perfect Life (IRE) 106 (Try My **61** Best (USA) 130) [2007 10m 10d³ Jul 3] 260,000Y: useful-looking filly: half-sister to several winners, including smart 7f (at 2 yrs) to 1½m winner Rabah and useful 1m/1¼m winner Muhtafel (both by Nashwan): dam, French 5f (at 2 yrs) and 7f winner, sister to Last Tycoon: similar form in maidens, third to Four Miracles at Brighton, off bridle 3f out and flashing tail. *L. M. Cumani*

DABBERS RIDGE (IRE) 5 b.h. Indian Ridge 123 – Much Commended 100 (Most **112** Welcome 131) [2007 112: 7s 7g³ 7m 7g 7g 6d* 6d⁶ 7g Oct 27] rather leggy horse: smart performer: won handicap at Haydock (by 1¼ lengths from Commando Scott) in September: also ran well when third to Binanti in Buckingham Palace Stakes (Handicap) at Royal Ascot second outing: below form otherwise in 2007: best at 6f to 7.6f: acts on soft and good to firm going. *B. W. Hills*

DA BOOKIE (IRE) 7 b.g. Woods of Windsor (USA) – Hurgill Lady 62 (Emarati **53** (USA) 74) [2007 78: p8g 8.1m 8.1m⁴ p8.6g Sep 8] fair performer at 6 yrs: just modest in 2007, leaving E. Creighton and rejoining former trainer after third outing: stays 1¼m: acts on polytrack and firm going: tried tongue tied: sometimes slowly away. *P. A. Blockley*

DADDY COOL 3 b.g. Kyllachy 129 – Addicted To Love 73 (Touching Wood (USA) **80** 127) [2007 57: p5g* p5g² p5g⁴ p5g* 5f* 5.1m⁶ 5d 5g 5f Sep 10] sturdy gelding: fairly useful performer: won maiden at Kempton in January and handicaps there in March and Thirsk in April: best at 5f: acts on polytrack and firm going: wore cheekpieces final outing: makes running: gelded after final start. *W. G. M. Turner*

DADDY'S BOY 2 ch.g. (Apr 2) Selkirk (USA) 129 – Narva (Nashwan (USA) 135) **69** [2007 8m⁵ 8d Oct 3] good-topped gelding: seventh foal: half-brother to useful miler (including in US) Pretence (by Danehill): dam unraced half-sister to high-class winner up to 1½m Predappio: much better effort in maidens when fifth to Alfathaa at Newbury: will stay 1¼m. *Mrs A. J. Perrett*

DADO MUSH 4 b.g. Almushtarak (IRE) 122 – Princess of Spain (King of Spain 121) **77** [2007 62, a–: 7m 10g 7d³ p7g f8d* f8d* f8g* Dec 27] fair handicapper: improved to complete hat-trick at Southwell in December: stays 1m: acts on fibresand, good to firm and good to soft going: tried visored, wears cheekpieces nowadays. *T. T. Clement*

DAFARABAD (IRE) 5 b.g. Cape Cross (IRE) 129 – Daftara (IRE) (Caerleon (USA) **–** 132) [2007 10m 10m 10d May 18] fairly useful performer at 3 yrs: well held on return to Flat in 2007. *Jonjo O'Neill*

DAGGERMAN 2 ch.c. (Apr 22) Daggers Drawn (USA) 114 – Another Mans Cause **–** (FR) (Highest Honor (FR) 124) [2007 p7g 6m Sep 15] small colt: well beaten in maidens. *P. A. Blockley*

DAIRY MAID 3 b.f. Montjeu (IRE) 137 – Eurolink Sundance 85 (Night Shift (USA)) **45** [2007 7m May 11] 46,000Y: good-topped filly: second foal: half-sister to 4-y-o Mango Music: dam, 6f winner (including at 2 yrs), half-sister to smart 1¼m performers Bonecrusher and Mango Mischief: 25/1 and green, 11½ lengths eighth of 9 to Royal Rock in maiden at Lingfield, weakening: sold 5,000 gns in July. *W. J. Knight*

DAISY NOOK 2 b.f. (Feb 12) Domedriver (IRE) 128 – Kilbride (Selkirk (USA) 129) **48** [2007 7g 8d⁶ p8.6g Nov 1] €28,000Y, 32,000 2-y-o: unfurnished filly, weak at 2 yrs: first foal: dam unraced out of smart 1½m winner Kiliniski: poor form in maidens. *S. Kirk*

DAKOTA RAIN (IRE) 5 br.g. Indian Ridge 123 – Mill Rainbow (FR) (Rainbow **90** Quest (USA) 134) [2007 81: 10f 8.1g⁶ 7.9m² 6.1g* 6d* 6m 6m* 6m³ 6m³ Sep 18] tall, good-topped gelding: fairly useful handicapper: won at Nottingham in June, Leicester in July and Newcastle in August: creditable efforts final 2 starts, reportedly finished distressed in latter: stays 1m, best at shorter nowadays: acts on good to firm and good to soft ground: usually races prominently. *Jennie Candlish*

DALAROSSIE 2 br.g. (Mar 26) Kyllachy 129 – Damalis (IRE) 106 (Mukaddamah **66** (USA) 125) [2007 5g⁶ 5m⁴ 5.1f³ 5s⁵ p5.1g⁵ 5m⁶ Aug 4] quite attractive gelding: fair maiden: in frame at Carlisle and Chester: gelded after final start: will prove best kept to 5f: acts on firm going, probably polytrack. *E. J. Alston*

DAL CAIS (IRE) 3 b.c. Noverre (USA) 125 – Annieirwin (IRE) 94 (Perugino (USA) **101** 84) [2007 85: 10g* 8m⁵ 9.5m* 10g 10g Sep 22] good-topped colt: useful performer: won handicaps at Leopardstown in April and Gowran (by ¾ length from Ridge Boy) in May: good sixth to Alexander of Hales in Gallinule Stakes at the Curragh next start:

well below form after, including at Royal Ascot: stays 1¼m: acts on firm ground (below form on soft/heavy): often races prominently: joined P. Rothwell. *Francis Ennis, Ireland*

DALHAAN (USA) 2 b.c. (Feb 12) Fusaichi Pegasus (USA) 130 – Khazayin (USA) 74 **70 p** (Bahri (USA) 125) [2007 7m Aug 4] big, good sort: third foal: closely related to useful 2005 2-y-o 6f winner (best at 1¼m) Jaish (by Seeking The Gold) and 3-y-o Jawaaneb: dam, maiden (stayed 1¼m), sister to Arc winner Sakhee: 66/1, needed experience when ninth of 18 to Latin Lad in maiden at Goodwood: will be suited by 1¼m+: sure to improve. *J. L. Dunlop*

DALKEY GIRL (IRE) 2 ch.f. (Mar 8) Raise A Grand (IRE) 114 – Tosca (Be My **90** Guest (USA) 126) [2007 5m⁴ 5.2d* 6s⁶ 7m⁴ 7.1d 7m 6m³ 7d⁴ 8m 7m² 7m² 7d 8g⁴ Nov 3] neat, quite attractive filly: seventh foal: half-sister to 1½m/1¾m winner Tilla (by Bin Ajwaad): dam unraced: fairly useful performer: won maiden at Yarmouth in June: steady progress after, in frame 6 times, including close fourth to Classic Legend in listed race at Newmarket final start: will stay 1¼m: acts on soft and good to firm going: tough. *V. Smith*

DALLMA (IRE) 4 b.f. Daylami (IRE) 138 – Play With Fire (FR) (Priolo (USA) 127) **–** [2007 69: p9.5g p8.6g f7g Feb 22] rather leggy, close-coupled filly: fair maiden at 3 yrs: well held in 2007: tried blinkered: sold 17,000 gns in 2007. *C. E. Brittain*

DALVINA 3 ch.f. Grand Lodge (USA) 125 – Foodbroker Fancy (IRE) 113 (Halling **113** (USA) 133) [2007 90p: 10m* 12d 12g³ 12d⁵ 10m³ 12g* 12g³ Dec 15] smallish, angular, quite attractive filly: good walker: has quick action: smart performer: won StansPoker.co.uk Pretty Polly Stakes at Newmarket (by 6 lengths from Sudoor) in May and Grade 3 Long Island Handicap at Aqueduct (beat Barancella 3½ lengths) in November: below best in between, including when third in Ribblesdale Stakes at Royal Ascot (behind Silkwood) and Blandford Stakes at the Curragh (beaten 2 lengths by Four Sins): left E. Dunlop, creditable third to Redaspen in Grade 2 La Prevoyante Handicap at Calder final outing, despite meeting trouble: stays 1½m: acts on good to firm going, possibly not on good to soft. *H. G. Motion, USA*

DAMASCUS GOLD 3 b.c. Thowra (FR) – Damasquiner 56 (Casteddu 111) [2007 10g **–** Jun 18] workmanlike colt: 100/1 and in cheekpieces, tailed off in maiden at Windsor, very slowly away. *Miss Z. C. Davison*

DAMELZA (IRE) 4 b.f. Orpen (USA) 116 – Damezao (Alzao (USA) 117) [2007 78: **74** p8.6g 7m² 6.9d³ 8v⁵ 7m 8m 7.5m Aug 25] lengthy, useful-looking filly: fair handicapper: stays 1m: acts on any turf going, probably on polytrack: sometimes tongue tied. *T. D. Easterby*

DAMHSOIR (IRE) 3 b.f. Invincible Spirit (IRE) 121 – Ceide Dancer (IRE) 79 (Alzao **51** (USA) 117) [2007 55: 5.1m⁴ 5m 5f 6f 5.7f p6g⁵ p6g* p5g⁶ Oct 29] small filly: modest performer: won maiden at Wolverhampton in October: stays 6f: raced only on polytrack and ground firmer than good. *H. S. Howe*

DAMIKA (IRE) 4 ch.g. Namid 128 – Emly Express (IRE) (High Estate 127) [2007 93: **104** 6d 6v³ 6g² 7s 6d 6m* 6m 6d 7m* 7m⁶ 7d* 8g Nov 3] strong, good-topped gelding: useful handicapper: won at Ripon in September and Newmarket (best effort, beat Vitznau by ½ length in 26-runner event, racing alone on far rail) in October: gelded after final outing: stays 7f: acts on any going. *R. M. Whitaker*

DANAE 2 br.f. (May 7) Dansili 127 – Pervenche (Latest Model 115) [2007 7g⁵ Nov 3] **66 p** tall, close-coupled filly: half-sister to 3 winners, including smart sprinter Gorse (by Sharpo): dam maiden: 40/1, caught the eye when fifth of 19 to La Coveta in maiden at Newmarket, finishing strongest of all: will do better. *H. Candy*

DANAK (IRE) 4 br.c. Pivotal 124 – Daniysha (IRE) 76 (Doyoun 124) [2007 114p: 8m* **118** 8m* 10.5g⁴ 10d⁶ Aug 11] good-topped, useful-looking colt: smart performer: won listed race in April (by short head from Heliostatic) and 4-runner Amethyst Stakes (beat Lord Admiral by 2 lengths) in May, both at Leopardstown: not discredited after, in Tattersalls Gold Cup at the Curragh (5½ lengths fourth to Notnowcato) and Arlington Million (1½ lengths sixth of 7 behind Jambalaya): effective at 1m/1¼m: yet to race on extremes of going: held up: reportedly sold, and joined D. Watson in UAE. *John M. Oxx, Ireland*

DANALOVA 3 b.f. Groom Dancer (USA) 128 – Revival 86 (Sadler's Wells (USA) 132) **60** [2007 p7.1g f6g f8g f11g⁴ 10.1m⁶ f11g⁴ p12.2g⁶ 9.8s* 9.1d³ 10.1d² Jul 28] 6,000F: third foal: closely related to fairly useful Irish 8.7f winner Uva Fragola (by Nashwan): dam, 1¼m winner, half-sister to Pivotal: modest performer: won seller at Ripon in July: stays 1¼m: acts on soft going. *R. A. Fahey*

DANAMIGHT (IRE) 2 gr.f. (Apr 9) Danetime (IRE) 121 – Nuit Chaud (USA) (Wood- **67** man (USA) 126) [2007 6g 6d 7.6f p8g⁵ p8g³ 8f Sep 27] lengthy filly, weak at 2 yrs: seventh foal: half-sister to 3 winners, including useful 7f (at 2 yrs) and 1¼m winner Hallhoo (by Indian Ridge): dam, maiden, half-sister to dam of smart 6f/7f performer Danehill Dancer: fair maiden: third in nursery at Kempton: stays 1m: acts on polytrack: usually slowly away. *G. G. Margarson*

DANA MUSIC (USA) 3 b.g. Silver Hawk (USA) 123 – Inca Princess (USA) (Big **75** Spruce (USA)) [2007 64: p12g³ p12.2g⁴ 12f⁵ 9.9m² 14.1s³ 10g Jul 8] compact gelding: fair maiden: likely to prove best at 1¼m/1½m: acts on soft and good to firm ground: patiently ridden: sold 10,000 gns, sent to Qatar. *M. R. Channon*

DANAWI (IRE) 4 ch.g. Elnadim (USA) 128 – Just Rainbow (FR) (Rainbow Quest **62 §** (USA) 134) [2007 71d: 7g 8.5m² 8d² 7m⁴ 7m 8.1d² 8g⁶ 7.6g 8m 7g Oct 16] angular, good-topped gelding: modest maiden handicapper: seems to stay 8.5f: acts on polytrack, good to firm and good to soft ground: tried visored: reportedly bled fifth start: often races prominently: temperamental. *M. R. Hoad*

DAN BUOY (FR) 4 b.g. Slip Anchor 136 – Bramosia (Forzando 122) [2007 79: p8g **81** 10s⁴ 11.7g² 12.6s² 14.8m Jul 28] tall gelding: fairly useful maiden: stays 12.6f (raced too freely at 14.8f): acts on soft going: won over hurdles in August/December.

DANCE EASILY 2 b.f. (Apr 29) Dansili 127 – Crystal Flite (IRE) 76 (Darshaan 133) **–** [2007 7g 7d 8g Oct 25] 15,000Y: sturdy, close-coupled filly: third foal: half-sister to 5-y-o Kristalchen: dam 1½m winner: very green when behind in maidens, not knocked about: will be suited by 1¼m/1½m. *J. L. Dunlop*

DANCEINTHEVALLEY (IRE) 5 b.g. Imperial Ballet (IRE) 110 – Dancing Willma **53** (IRE) (Dancing Dissident (USA) 119) [2007 –: p8.6g p8.6g 14.1g p12.2g 12m³ 10m* p10g 8f Aug 9] close-coupled gelding: modest performer nowadays: left G. A. Swinbank 4,000 gns after second start: won seller at Brighton (sold from I. McInnes 9,000 gns) in June: said to have finished lame final start: stays 1½m, better at shorter: acts on good to firm and good to soft going: headstrong. *D. K. Ivory*

DANCE OF DREAMS 3 ch.g. Johannesburg (USA) 127 – Nunatak (USA) (Bering **65** 136) [2007 67: p6g p7.1g p7g* p8g⁶ 8.2g 7g⁴ 8f p7g⁴ p8g⁶ Sep 19] big, good-topped gelding: fair handicapper: won at Lingfield in March: best form at 7f: acts on polytrack and good to firm ground: tried tongue tied: wore cheekpieces (ran poorly) final outing: sold 1,000 gns, sent to Spain. *N. P. Littmoden*

DANCE OF LIGHT (USA) 3 b.f. Sadler's Wells (USA) 132 – Flamelight (IRE) 71 **102** (Seattle Slew (USA)) [2007 73P: 9.9d* 12d 10.1m³ 12g 12d⁵ p13m Nov 1] big, good-topped, attractive filly: useful performer, lightly raced: won maiden at Salisbury in May: seventh in Oaks at Epsom next time: best efforts in listed races after, 1¼ lengths third to Yaqeen at Yarmouth and fifth to Brisk Breeze at Ascot: stays 1½m: acts on good to firm and good to soft ground (well held on polytrack). *Sir Michael Stoute*

DANCER'S LEGACY 2 ch.c. (Apr 28) Nayef (USA) 129 – Blond Moment (USA) **76** (Affirmed (USA)) [2007 7g 7.1g 7.1m* 8g³ 8.3d Oct 1] 10,000Y: attractive colt: half-brother to 3 winners in US: dam US 2-y-o 5.5f to 7f winner, including minor stakes: fair performer: improved in tongue strap, won maiden at Warwick in August: third in nursery at Yarmouth next time: stays 1m: acts on good to firm going. *E. A. L. Dunlop*

DANCE SAUVAGE 4 ch.g. Groom Dancer (USA) 128 – Peace Dance (Bikala 134) **58** [2007 10s 12.4m² 14m 14d⁶ 12m² 13g² 12m 14.1g⁴ 15.8g⁶ Oct 30] tall gelding: modest maiden handicapper: stays 1¾m: acts on good to firm ground: waited with. *C. W. Thornton*

DANCE SPIRIT (IRE) 4 ch.g. Namid 128 – Phantom Act (USA) (Theatrical 128) **75 d** [2007 72: 10m p7.1m² p8g p7.1g 8d p8.6g p8.6g⁴ p8.6g Dec 1] fair maiden: trained by C. Mann on reappearance: well below form after next start: stays 1m: acts on polytrack and good to firm ground: blinkered last 2 outings. *W. R. Muir*

DANCE STEPS 3 b.f. Golan (IRE) 129 – Swift Baba (USA) (Deerhound (USA) 64) **–** [2007 p9.5g 8.3g 7g⁵ Jul 28] 2,800F: first foal: dam well beaten in 3 starts: well held in maidens, leaving P. McEntee after debut. *Miss K. B. Boutflower*

DANCE THE CLASSICS (IRE) 3 b.f. Sadler's Wells (USA) 132 – Head In The **97** Clouds (IRE) 114 (Rainbow Quest (USA) 134) [2007 10g⁵ 10.2f⁴ 12g² 12s* 12s⁵ 12g⁶ 15d⁵ 15.5v Nov 24] lengthy, unfurnished filly: second foal: dam, 1½m (Princess Royal Stakes) winner, sister to St Leger winner Millenary and half-sister to very smart middle-distance performer Let The Lion Roar (by Sadler's Wells): useful performer: landed odds in maiden at Limerick in June by 9 lengths: good efforts next 3 starts, 3 lengths fifth to Downtown in Give Thanks Stakes at Cork (final start for J. Oxx), then sixth to King Luna and fifth to Latin Mood in listed races at Chantilly: stays 15f: acts on soft going: blinkered last 5 starts: races prominently. *J. L. Dunlop*

DANCEWITHTHESTARS (USA) 3 b.f. Cryptoclearance (USA) – Sir Harry's **57 d**
Waltz (IRE) (Sir Harry Lewis (USA) 127) [2007 –p: p8g 10g 12.1m 10.1g 14.1s 10m
11.6f 10.1m⁴ Aug 15] small, angular filly: modest maiden at best: left J. Fanshawe 5,500
gns after fifth start: stays 1¼m: tongue tied last 2 starts. *Miss J. Feilden*

DANCE WORLD 7 b.g. Spectrum (IRE) 126 – Dansara (Dancing Brave (USA) 140) –
[2007 –: f11g 14d⁵ 11.5d⁵ 10m Jul 27] leggy gelding: fairly useful handicapper at best:
little form in 2007: tried in cheekpieces/blinkers. *Miss J. Feilden*

DAN CHILLINGWORTH (IRE) 2 b.c. (Apr 9) Indian Ridge 123 – Shizao (IRE) **73 p**
106 (Alzao (USA) 117) [2007 6g⁵ p7g⁵ Oct 29] 120,000Y: sturdy colt: first foal: dam
Irish 5f (at 2 yrs) to 7f winner: promising fifth in maidens at Yarmouth and Kempton,
travelling strongly before running green (considerably handled): should prove best up to
7f: sort to do well at 3 yrs. *J. R. Fanshawe*

DANCING ABBIE (USA) 2 ch.f. (Mar 7) Theatrical 128 – Sicy d'Alsace (FR) **79 p**
(Sicyos (USA) 126) [2007 8d³ Oct 23] $200,000Y: fourth foal: dam, US Grade 1 9f
winner, earlier French 2-y-o 5f to 1¼m winner: 17/2, 2¼ lengths third to Michita in
maiden at Yarmouth, only one to make much headway: will stay 1¼m: should improve.
M. L. W. Bell

DANCING BAY 10 b.g. Suave Dancer (USA) 136 – Kabayil 75 (Dancing Brave (USA) –
140) [2007 110: 18.7m May 9] sturdy gelding: smart performer at 9 yrs: ran poorly sole
Flat start in 2007: stays 2¾m: acts on any going: has been tongue tied (not since 2001):
usually held up (has found little/gone in snatches): sometimes edges left: useful hurdler/
winning chaser. *N. J. Henderson*

DANCING BEAUTY (IRE) 5 b.m. Charnwood Forest (IRE) 125 – Viennese Dancer **44**
(Prince Sabo 123) [2007 44: f6g³ f6g f6g f6g⁶ Mar 20] poor maiden on balance: stays 6f:
acts on fibresand: tried in cheekpieces. *T. T. Clement*

DANCING DEANO (IRE) 5 b.g. Second Empire (IRE) 124 – Ultimate Beat (USA) **65**
(Go And Go) [2007 71, a–: 7.5m 7d⁵ 7m p6g p7.1g* f7d* f7d⁶ Dec 15] good-topped
gelding: fair performer: won minor event at Wolverhampton in November and seller at
Southwell (hung right) in December: acts at 6f/7f: acts on all-weather, good to firm
and good to soft ground: usually visored. *R. Hollinshead*

DANCING DIK 2 b.g. (Mar 12) Diktat 126 – Maureena (IRE) (Grand Lodge (USA) **66**
125) [2007 7d 7m 8d⁶ Oct 27] big gelding: fair form in maidens: gelded/off 3 months
prior to final start, at Newbury (sixth to Whistledownwind): stays 1m. *Mrs A. J. Perrett*

DANCING DUO 3 b.f. Groom Dancer (USA) 128 – Affaire Royale (IRE) 95 (Royal **69**
Academy (USA) 130) [2007 62: p7g p8.6g p7.1g² p7.1g 6m p7g p7m³ p8m p8g Dec 29]
attractive filly: fair performer: should stay 1m: acts on polytrack: visored nowadays: has
given trouble at start, and often slowly away. *D. Shaw*

DANCING ELLIE 2 b.f. (Mar 28) Where Or When (IRE) 124 – Eleonor Sympson 50 –
(Cadeaux Genereux 131) [2007 9s Oct 14] 5,000Y: second foal: dam, maiden (only form
at 7f), half-sister to useful stayer Random Quest: tailed off in maiden at Goodwood.
P. M. Phelan

DANCING GUEST (IRE) 4 ch.f. Danehill Dancer (IRE) 117 – Saibhreas (IRE) 83 **78**
(Last Tycoon 131) [2007 86: 8m⁵ p7g⁵ May 9] leggy filly: fair handicapper nowadays:
stays 1m: acts on polytrack, good to firm and good to soft going: sold 5,000 gns in
December. *G. G. Margarson*

DANCING JEST (IRE) 3 b.f. Averti (IRE) 117 – Mezzanine (Sadler's Wells (USA) **70**
132) [2007 54: p7g 9m² 8m* 8d⁶ 8m 8m⁶ Sep 20] good-bodied, smallish filly: fair
performer: won handicap at Yarmouth in August: stays 9f: acts on good to firm going.
Rae Guest

DANCING LYRA 6 b.g. Alzao (USA) 117 – Badaayer (USA) 105 (Silver Hawk **92**
(USA) 123) [2007 90: 8s² 10m⁶ 8.9d⁶ 12g Oct 27] small, compact gelding: has a quick
action: fairly useful handicapper: effective at testing 7f to 13f: acts on polytrack, heavy
and good to firm going: tried tongue tied: patiently ridden. *R. A. Fahey*

DANCING MAITE 2 ch.c. (Apr 18) Ballet Master (USA) 92 – Ace Maite (Komaite **58 ?**
(USA)) [2007 8g p6g⁴ f6d⁴ Dec 14] seemingly modest form when fourth in claimer at
Wolverhampton and maiden at Southwell: should stay beyond 6f. *S. R. Bowring*

DANCING MARABOUT (IRE) 2 ch.g. (Feb 21) Danehill Dancer (IRE) 117 – **76**
Bluebell Wood (IRE) 87 (Bluebird (USA) 125) [2007 7.1d 5d⁵ 6m⁶ p7.1g* 8.3d p8m
Oct 11] stocky gelding: fair performer: won nursery at Wolverhampton in September:
stays 1m: best form on polytrack: gelded after final start. *C. R. Egerton*

DANCING MELODY 4 b.f. Dr Fong (USA) 128 – Spring Mood (FR) (Nashwan (USA) 135) [2007 59: 9g Jun 1] lengthy filly: modest maiden at 2/3 yrs: well held sole Flat outing in 2007 (in cheekpieces): stays 8.3f: acts on good to firm and good to soft ground. *J. A. Geake* —

DANCING MYSTERY 13 b.g. Beveled (USA) – Batchworth Dancer 67 (Balla-cashtal (CAN)) [2007 79, a100: f5g⁶ p5f f5g 6g 5m 5f 5.5d⁶ 5g³ 5m* 5.3d³ 5.3d² p5g 5.1g p5g⁴ Dec 12] close-coupled gelding: fairly useful handicapper on all-weather nowadays, fair on turf: won at Warwick in September: best at 5f: acts on all-weather and any turf going: blinkered nowadays: has spoilt chance by rearing in stall: makes running. *E. A. Wheeler* — 69 a85

DANCING STORM 4 b.f. Trans Island 119 – Stormswell 56 (Persian Bold 123) [2007 61: p7.1g⁶ 8d* 8.1m 8.1m⁵ 8d⁴ 9.5g⁴ Nov 2] lengthy filly: fair handicapper: won at Brighton in July: barely stays 9.5f: acts on polytrack, firm and good to soft ground: tried in cheekpieces (well held). *W. S. Kittow* — 65

DANCING SWORD 2 b.g. (Feb 19) Groom Dancer (USA) 128 – Kristina 92 (Kris 135) [2007 8.1m Sep 13] well held in maiden at Chepstow (gelded after): bred to be suited by middle distances (half-brother to 3-y-o Kayah). *H. J. L. Dunlop* —

DANCING WIZARD 3 ch.g. Dancing Spree (USA) – Magic Legs 54 (Reprimand 122) [2007 p7.1g² Dec 15] third foal: brother to smart 5f performer Rowe Park and half-brother to fairly useful 7f winner Magic Rush (by Almaty): dam once-raced daughter of useful 5f winner Inherent Magic: 9/1, 12 lengths second of 9 to Kirk Michael in maiden at Wolverhampton, outpaced: should do better. *C. G. Cox* — 62 p

DAN DARE (USA) 4 b.g. Dynaformer (USA) – Etheldreda (USA) 64 (Diesis 133) [2007 84: 10.1m* 10m 11.6s² 12d 10m³ 10s Sep 20] tall, good-bodied gelding: fairly useful performer, lightly raced: won maiden at Newcastle in May: good efforts when placed in handicaps after: should stay 1¾m: acts on soft and good to firm ground: visored last 4 starts. *Sir Michael Stoute* — 94

DANDY ERIN (IRE) 2 b.c. (Apr 11) Danehill Dancer (IRE) 117 – Sanctuary Line (IRE) (Lake Coniston (IRE) 131) [2007 p8g⁴ 8g³ p9.5g* Nov 17] €80,000F: tall, attractive colt: third foal: dam, unraced half-sister to smart sprinter Lugana Beach and dam of very smart sprinter The Tatling, out of half-sister to Mtoto: fairly useful form: progressive in maidens, won at Wolverhampton by 1¾ lengths from Heritage Coast (pair clear): stays 9.5f. *J. A. Osborne* — 88

DANDY MAN (IRE) 4 b.c. Mozart (IRE) 131 – Lady Alexander (IRE) 112 (Night Shift (USA)) [2007 123: 5g* 5d² 5m² 6m⁵ 5g³ 5g² 5g Oct 7] smallish, compact colt: very smart performer: won listed race at Naas in April by 4½ lengths from Flash McGahon: creditable placed efforts in King's Stand Stakes at Royal Ascot (1¾ lengths second to Miss Andretti), Nunthorpe Stakes at York (1¾ lengths third to Kingsgate Native) and — 123

Woodlands Stakes, Naas—a clear-cut success for Dandy Man in this listed race; Flash McGahon chases him home

Flying Five Stakes at the Curragh (beaten head by Benbaun, who gave 3 lb) third/fifth/
penultimate outings: not discredited when 2½ lengths fifth to Sakhee's Secret in July
Cup at Newmarket fourth start, stamina stretched: below form in Prix de l'Abbaye at
Longchamp final outing, hampered over 1f out: best at 5f: has won on good to soft going,
best efforts on good/good to firm: travels strongly up with pace: has joined Godolphin.
Miss T. A. M. Collins, Ireland

DANDYS HURRICANE 4 br.g. Diktat 126 – Bahamian Rhapsody (IRE) 76 (Fairy **49**
King (USA)) [2007 57: f8g 12g 11.8d³ Jul 19] strong gelding: poor maiden: left
D. Nicholls after reappearance: stays 1½m: acts on good to soft going: wore cheekpieces
final outing. *M. W. Easterby*

DANEBURY HILL 3 b.c. Danehill (USA) 126 – Mackie (USA) (Summer Squall **98**
(USA)) [2007 97: p8g³ 7m⁵ 8m 10g 8m Jun 21] rather leggy colt: useful performer:
creditable efforts first 3 starts in 2007, including 3 lengths third to Dubai's Touch in listed
Easter Stakes at Kempton: below form last 2 outings: stays easy 1m (probably on 1¼m):
acts on polytrack and firm going: tongue tied: sold 9,000 gns in October, sent to Serbia.
B. J. Meehan

DANEHILL FOLLY (IRE) 4 b.g. Danehill Dancer (IRE) 117 – Theorique (IRE) **–**
(Theatrical 128) [2007 p5.1g 7f 7d Oct 1] workmanlike gelding: of no account.
J. M. Bradley

DANEHILL KIKIN (IRE) 3 b.f. Danehill (USA) 126 – Miletrian (IRE) 113 (Marju **60**
(IRE) 127) [2007 58p: 7m⁵ p6g 7g 6.1d Aug 16] big, strong, long-backed filly: modest
maiden: bred to be suited by 1m+, but needs to settle better: acts on good to firm ground:
tongue tied (hung badly left) final outing. *B. W. Hills*

DANEHILL SILVER 3 b.g. Silver Patriarch (IRE) 125 – Danehill Princess (IRE) 62 **65**
(Danehill (USA) 126) [2007 71: 10.3f⁶ 12s p10g⁶ 10.2m² 10m Sep 25] strong, close-
coupled gelding: fair maiden: stumbled and unseated leaving stall final outing: stays
1¼m, may prove best at shorter: acts on firm and soft going: sold 12,000 gns. *R. Hollinshead*

DANEHILL STROLLER (IRE) 7 b.g. Danetime (IRE) 121 – Tuft Hill 92 (Grundy **60**
137) [2007 74, a66: 5.7d² 6s⁴ p5g 5.7m² Aug 9] angular gelding: modest performer
nowadays: effective at 5f/6f: acts on polytrack, good to firm and good to soft going: tried
in cheekpieces/blinkered: often held up: sold £500. *A. M. Hales*

DANEHILLSUNDANCE (IRE) 3 b.c. Danehill Dancer (IRE) 117 – Rosie's Guest **102**
(IRE) (Be My Guest (USA) 126) [2007 74: 7g² 8.2g* 7.1g* 8d 7m* 7d 8m⁴ 7d 8g Nov 3]
tall, leggy colt: useful handicapper: much improved in 2007, winning at Nottingham in
June, Sandown in July, and Doncaster (beat Miss Lucifer by short head) in September:
creditable fourth to Dream Lodge at Pontefract seventh start: below form after: stays 1m:
acts on polytrack, soft and good to firm going: versatile regarding tactics. *R. Hannon*

DANEHILL WARRIOR (IRE) 3 b.g. Indian Danehill (IRE) 124 – Karatisa (IRE) **–**
93 (Nishapour (FR) 125) [2007 f8g p8.6g f7g 8.1m 8.3m 10f 9.8m 7g Sep 24] workmanlike gelding: little form: tried blinkered/in cheekpieces. *R. C. Guest*

DANELOR (IRE) 9 b.g. Danehill (USA) 126 – Formulate 119 (Reform 132) [2007 **58**
79d: f12g p10g⁵ p9.5g f11g* f12g p10g³ f11g² p12g² p12.2g p8.6g p10m p10g Dec 12]
sturdy, good-bodied gelding: modest handicapper nowadays: won amateur event at
Southwell in February: stays 1½m: acts on all-weather, firm and good to soft going: has
been visored, in cheekpieces nowadays: free-going sort (has been early to post). *D. Shaw*

DANETHORPE (IRE) 4 b.g. Monashee Mountain (USA) 115 – Waroonga (IRE) **40**
(Brief Truce (USA) 126) [2007 53: p6g f7g³ f6g⁵ f7g⁵ f6g 5g⁵ 5d 6v Jul 21] modest **a52**
maiden on all-weather, poor on turf: stays 7f: acts on all-weather: visored. *D. Shaw*

DANETIME LORD (IRE) 4 b.g. Danetime (IRE) 121 – Seven Sisters (USA) (Sha- **64 +**
deed (USA) 135) [2007 77: f7g⁶ p7g* p7.1g³ p6g* p7g* p7g⁴ p7g³ 7f p7g² p8g p7.1g² **a90**
Dec 31] compact gelding: fairly useful handicapper on all-weather, modest on turf: won
at Lingfield in January, Wolverhampton in February and Lingfield in March: stays 7f:
acts on polytrack, heavy and good to firm going: usually wears cheekpieces: races
prominently. *K. A. Ryan*

DANETIME PANTHER (IRE) 3 b.c. Danetime (IRE) 121 – Annotate (Groom Dan- **75**
cer (USA) 128) [2007 66: 8m f8g* 10.4g May 16] tall colt: fair performer, lightly raced:
won maiden at Southwell in April: stays 1m: acts on fibresand. *P. F. I. Cole*

DANETIME ROSE (IRE) 3 b.f. Danetime (IRE) 121 – Amory (GER) (Goofalik **–**
(USA) 118) [2007 p6g Aug 1] first foal: dam winner around 9f in Germany: 66/1, well
held in maiden at Kempton. *Miss V. Haigh*

Floodlit Stakes, Kempton—the first of two listed wins on the polytrack for Dansant (right), who snatches it late on from Into The Dark

DANETTIE 6 b.m. Danzero (AUS) – Petite Heritiere 43 (Last Tycoon 131) [2007 64: **57** p7.1g p8g⁶ p7.1g⁴ p8.6g p8.6g⁵ 7.1m p10g p8.6g Jun 2] modest performer: best around 1m: acts on polytrack and good to firm going: has made running. *W. M. Brisbourne*

DANEWAY 4 ch.f. Danehill Dancer (IRE) 117 – Scylla 50 (Rock City 120) [2007 56: **45** p12.2g⁶ p12.2g⁴ f11g Mar 6] maiden: only poor form in 2007: should stay 1¾m: raced on all-weather: tried blinkered. *P. Howling*

DANGEROUS DANCER (IRE) 3 b.f. Danehill Dancer (IRE) 117 – Elite Guest **65** (IRE) (Be My Guest (USA) 126) [2007 56: 9.9d⁴ 10m 12m Aug 4] leggy filly: fair maiden: should stay 1½m: acts on good to soft going. *R. Charlton*

DANGEROUSLY GOOD 9 b.g. Shareef Dancer (USA) 135 – Ecologically Kind **64** (Alleged (USA) 138) [2007 –: f12g² Feb 20] leggy gelding: useful hurdler: lightly raced nowadays: modest form sole Flat run in 2007: stays 1¾m: acts on fibresand, good to firm and good to soft going: tried in headgear: joined G. L. Moore. *J. Howard Johnson*

DANIELLA 5 b.m. Dansili 127 – Break Point (Reference Point 139) [2007 86: 6m 6d⁴ **94** 6m 6m³ 6.1m 7m 7d 7m³ 6d p8m⁶ Nov 1] strong, deep-girthed mare: fairly useful performer: effective at 6f, barely stays 1m: acts on polytrack, unraced on extremes of going on turf: wears cheekpieces/blinkers. *Rae Guest*

DANIELLE'S LAD 11 b.g. Emarati (USA) 74 – Cactus Road (FR) (Iron Duke (FR) **43** 122) [2007 66, a55: p7g⁵ p7g⁶ p7.1g Feb 12] strong gelding: just poor form in 2007: effective at 7f to 8.6f: acts on all-weather, heavy and good to firm going: often blinkered/ in cheekpieces: races prominently: has edged right: inconsistent. *B. Palling*

DANIEL THOMAS (IRE) 5 b.g. Dansili 127 – Last Look (Rainbow Quest (USA) **86 d** 134) [2007 93: p10g⁶ 7g⁵ 7m 8d⁵ p8g 8.3m 10.5g 8.3g Oct 8] good-topped gelding: has a quick action: fairly useful handicapper: below form after second start in 2007 (left Mrs A. Perrett after fourth outing): stays 1m, not 1¼m: acts on polyrack, soft and good to firm going. *Mrs A. L. M. King*

DANISH ART (IRE) 2 b.c. (Apr 3) Danehill Dancer (IRE) 117 – Lady Ounavarra **74** (IRE) (Simply Great (FR) 122) [2007 6g³ 6d⁶ Oct 19] smallish colt: fair maiden: third to Manassas at Yarmouth and sixth to Insaaf at Newmarket: will be as effective at 5f as 6f. *J. A. R. Toller*

DANISH BLUES (IRE) 4 b.g. Danetime (IRE) 121 – Sing A Song (IRE) 82 (Blues **65 §** Traveller (IRE) 119) [2007 65: p6g⁴ f6g² p5g⁵ p6g³ 6m² 6m² 7m⁵ p7g p5.1g* p5.1g³ 5d² 6m² 5s* p5.1g 6m⁵ 5g Sep 19] fair performer: won sellers at Wolverhampton in July and, having left D. Cantillon after next start, Musselburgh in August: refused to race 2 of last 3 starts: effective at 5f to 7f: acts on all-weather, firm and soft ground: has worn cheek-pieces: pulls hard/sometimes looks wayward: one to avoid. *D. Nicholls*

DANISH REBEL (IRE) 3 b.g. Danetime (IRE) 121 – Wheatsheaf Lady (IRE) 83 **81** (Red Sunset 120) [2007 53: 12g* 12m² 12g 13d Jul 13] fairly useful performer: won maiden at Musselburgh in April, making all: stays 1½m: acts on good to firm ground: has been early to post: gelded. *G. A. Charlton*

DANJET (IRE) 4 bl.f. Danehill Dancer (IRE) 117 – Jet Lock (USA) (Crafty Prospector (USA)) [2007 82: 5m 5m 5.2g 5.2s 5s 5.1g Aug 2] quite good-topped filly: fairly useful handicapper at best: well held in 2007: tried blinkered. *J. M. Bradley* –

DANJOE 3 ch.g. Forzando 122 – Baytown Rhapsody 62 (Emperor Jones (USA) 119) [2007 –: 7s p8.6g 7.1d⁶ 6g Oct 8] workmanlike gelding: poor maiden: stays 7f: acts on good to soft going. *R. Brotherton* **43**

DANNI DI GUERRA (IRE) 3 b.g. Soviet Star (USA) 128 – Lina Bella (FR) (Linamix (FR) 127) [2007 –: 6m 7.1m 11.1f 11.1g Jun 13] workmanlike gelding: little form. *J. Barclay*

DANNY BOY BLUE 2 b.c. (Jan 31) Josr Algarhoud (IRE) 118 – Rosina May (IRE) 83 (Danehill Dancer (IRE) 117) [2007 5m 5m⁵ 6s⁶ May 28] no form. *Mrs L. J. Mongan* –

DANSANT 3 b.c. Dansili 127 – La Balagna (Kris 135) [2007 10m* 11.1d² 11.9m³ 12g 14d² 14g⁵ 14.6m* 14m⁵ p12g* p12g* Dec 1] €20,000F, 53,000Y: tall, good-topped colt: first foal: dam French 1¼m/1½m winner: progressed into a smart performer in 2007, winning maiden at Windsor in April, Ladbrokes Mallard Stakes (Handicap) at Doncaster (beat Kasthari by 1¼ lengths) in September and listed events at Kempton in November (by neck from Into The Dark) and December (best effort, beat Pivotal Answer by 5 lengths): effective at 1½m, and should stay 2m: acts on polytrack, good to firm and good to soft going. *G. A. Butler* **118 +**

DANSE THE BLUES 2 br.f. (Jan 28) Dansili 127 – Dixie d'Oats 66 (Alhijaz 122) [2007 p8g⁵ Nov 14] third foal: half-sister to 1m to 1½m winner Maritime Blues (by Fleetwood): dam, maiden, stayed 1¼m: 9/2, better for run when 4¾ lengths fifth to Howdigo in maiden at Kempton: bred to stay 1¼m: likely to improve. *E. A. L. Dunlop* **58 p**

DANSEUSE 3 b.f. Dr Fong (USA) 128 – Danemere (IRE) 90 (Danehill (USA) 126) [2007 78: 7m 7.1m May 7] smallish, strong filly: maiden: no form in 2007: sold 1,800 gns in August. *B. J. Meehan* –

DANSEUSE VOLANTE (IRE) 2 ch.f. (Apr 10) Danehill Dancer (IRE) 117 – Termania (IRE) (Shirley Heights 130) [2007 6m³ 6v* 6g Nov 2] rather unfurnished filly: fourth foal: half-sister to 2 winners, including 5-y-o Castle Howard: dam French maiden (stayed 13f): fair form: didn't need to run up to debut form (third to Paco Boy at Newbury) to win weaker maiden at Folkestone in October: stiff task in listed race final start: will be well suited by 1m+. *J. W. Hills* **73 p**

DAN'S HEIR 5 b.g. Dansili 127 – Million Heiress (Auction Ring (USA) 123) [2007 69: f14g³ f16g Jan 16] sturdy gelding: modest handicapper: stays 2m: acts on all-weather, firm and good to soft going: tried visored, usually wears cheekpieces. *P. C. Haslam* **58**

DANSILI DANCER 5 b.g. Dansili 127 – Magic Slipper 97 (Habitat 134) [2007 107: p10g⁶ 9m 8m⁵ 9.9g 11.9m* 13.4m⁵ 14g³ Sep 8] strong, close-coupled gelding: useful handicapper: won Old Newton Cup at Haydock in August by ½ length from Futun: good efforts after, particularly when 2¾ lengths third to Regal Flush in Old Borough Cup at same course final outing: stays 1¾m: acts on polytrack, good to firm and good to soft going: well beaten only start in cheekpieces. *C. G. Cox* **110**

totesport.com Old Newton Cup Stakes (Handicap), Haydock—in a race run a month later after the original fixture succumbed to waterlogging, Dansili Dancer beats the reluctant Futun (third left) with the grey Misty Dancer third and Lundy's Lane (fourth left) an unlucky fourth

DAN

DANSIL IN DISTRESS 3 b.f. Dansili 127 – Just Speculation (IRE) 86 (Ahonoora **60** 122) [2007 59: p8.6g³ p8.6g⁴ 9g 8m⁴ p8g* 8.1g 8d p8g Sep 4] rather leggy filly: fair **a75** handicapper on all-weather, modest on turf: won maiden event at Lingfield in July: stays 8.6f: acts on polytrack: sold 4,000 gns. *S. Kirk*

DANSILVER 3 b.g. Dansili 127 – Silver Gyre (IRE) 65 (Silver Hawk (USA) 123) **58** [2007 58: 16.2s² 16g⁵ Aug 25] strong gelding: modest maiden: stays 2m: acts on polytrack, soft and good to firm going. *D. J. Wintle*

DANSIMAR 3 gr.f. Daylami (IRE) 138 – Hylandra (USA) (Bering 136) [2007 73: **75** p10g⁶ 12.1m³ 11.6m 12.1g⁶ p12g² 12m³ 14.1m² 18d³ p16g 15.8g³ 16.1g⁴ p13.9g² p16.5g³ Oct 20] good-topped filly: fair maiden handicapper: in frame 10 times in 2007: stays 2¼m: acts on polytrack, good to firm and good to soft ground: often takes strong hold: sold 23,000 gns, joined Venetia Williams. *M. R. Channon*

DANSKI 4 b.c. Dansili 127 – Manila Selection (USA) (Manila (USA)) [2007 91: 8g 8s **91** p8g⁴ p8m Nov 26] leggy colt: fairly useful handicapper: easily best effort in 2007 when fourth at Lingfield in October: stays 1m: acts on polytrack and firm going: tends to wander. *P. J. Makin*

DANTE'S DIAMOND (IRE) 5 b.g. Orpen (USA) 116 – Flower From Heaven **67** (Baptism 119) [2007 65: 10.2m 7m⁴ p8.6g* p8.6g 6m⁴ p7.1g³ p8.6g Jul 27] strong, lengthy gelding: fair performer: won seller at Wolverhampton in June: left D. Burchell after sixth outing: effective at 6f to 9.5f: acts on polytrack, firm and soft going: tried in cheekpieces. *R. Lee*

DANTICAT (USA) 6 ch.g. Tale of The Cat (USA) 113 – Colonial Debut (USA) (Plea- **59 §** sant Colony (USA)) [2007 72: 7m 10g 10s 13d 14d 12.5m² 14d Sep 24] good-topped gelding: just modest handicapper nowadays: stays 13f: acts on firm and good to soft ground: often blinkered, tried in cheekpieces/tongue tied: refused to race at Musselburgh fifth outing: inconsistent. *J. Coleman, Ireland*

DAN TUCKER 3 b.g. Dansili 127 – Shapely (USA) 81 (Alleged (USA) 138) [2007 57: **77** p10g* 11g* 10.9m³ 11.6d p10g³ p12g³ p13g⁶ 14g 14g⁵ p12g⁶ 11.6d² Oct 15] close-coupled gelding: fair handicapper: won at Kempton in March and Southwell in April: barely stays 1¾m: acts on polytrack, good to firm and good to soft ground: tried blinkered: patiently ridden: consistent: sold 15,000 gns. *B. J. Meehan*

DAN TUCKET 2 b.c. (Feb 19) Dansili 127 – Fanfare 89 (Deploy 131) [2007 5g³ 5m* **90** 6d⁵ p6g 7m* 7m³ 7m⁶ 7d* 8.1g³ 7m³ 7g 7g Oct 27] 20,000Y: leggy, close-coupled colt: third foal: half-brother to 2 winners, including 4-y-o Ebert: dam 1¼m to 1¾m winner: fairly useful performer: won maiden at Folkestone in May and nurseries at Newmarket in July and August: stays 1m: acts on good to firm and good to soft going: held up: sold 38,000 gns. *M. R. Channon*

DANUM 7 b.g. Perpendicular 119 – Maid of Essex 66 (Bustino 136) [2007 52: p12.2g **54** p9.5g² p9.5g Feb 9] strong, deep-girthed gelding: modest maiden: probably stays 1½m: acts on all-weather, soft and good to firm ground: often wears cheekpieces: often front runner: unreliable. *R. Hollinshead*

DANUM DANCER 3 ch.c. Allied Forces (USA) 123 – Branston Dancer (Rudimentary **86** (USA) 118) [2007 95: 6d 6m⁵ 8m 5g⁶ 6d 6s⁵ 8m 6g 5g Sep 19] rather leggy, lengthy colt: fairly useful performer: below form after fourth outing: effective at 5f/6f: acts on firm and good to soft going: usually blinkered: often bandaged in front: carried head awkwardly second outing. *N. Bycroft*

DANUM DIVA (IRE) 3 ch.f. Danehill Dancer (IRE) 117 – Comprehension (USA) 87§ **54** (Diesis 133) [2007 –: f6g p10g⁶ f11g 9.8g 7m 10.1d⁴ 12g⁵ p8.6g p8g f11d⁴ Dec 15] angular filly: modest maiden: trained by T. Pitt until after fifth outing: seems to stay 1¼m: acts on good to soft ground: tried blinkered/tongue tied. *D. J. Murphy*

DANVERS 2 b.f. (Feb 13) Cape Cross (IRE) 129 – Tyranny 97 (Machiavellian (USA) **63** 123) [2007 p6g⁵ p6g Oct 15] small filly: first foal: dam, 7f winner, half-sister to US Grade 2 9f winner Spotlight out of smart 1¼m/1½m performer Dust Dancer: modest form in maidens at Kempton and Lingfield (too free in front): likely to stay 1m. *J. L. Dunlop*

DANZARE 5 b.m. Dansili 127 – Shot of Redemption (Shirley Heights 130) [2007 60: **64** p10g* p9.5g 10.9m 7.5m 8.5m 10.1d³ 10.2d⁶ 10.1d² 10.1d 10.1g* 10.1f³ Jul 30] leggy mare: modest handicapper: won at Kempton in January and Yarmouth (apprentices) in July: stays 1¼m: acts on polytrack, firm and good to soft ground: none too consistent. *J. L. Spearing*

258

DANZATRICE 5 b.m. Tamure (IRE) 125 – Miss Petronella (Petoski 135) [2007 65: **70**
12.4m 14m² 13.1g² 13.8m⁵ 13.1g⁵ 14g⁴ 13m* 15s⁶ 14m⁶ 14m⁵ 14m⁴ 12.4d⁶ 14.1g 16g²
Nov 8] lengthy mare: fair handicapper: won amateur event at Musselburgh in August:
effective from 13f to 17f: acts on soft and good to firm going: held up. *C. W. Thornton*

DANZIG FOX 2 b.c. (Feb 2) Foxhound (USA) 103 – Via Dolorosa (Chaddleworth **64**
(IRE) 103) [2007 6g* 8d⁶ 6d Sep 28] modest form: won maiden at Ayr (50/1) in July on
debut: no impact in minor event/nursery: should stay 7f. *M. Mullineaux*

DANZIG RIVER (IRE) 6 b.g. Green Desert (USA) 127 – Sahara Breeze 85 (Ela- **78**
Mana-Mou 132) [2007 81: p7.1g⁶ p7.1g 5f 6g* 5f⁶ 6m 5m 6m Jun 7] big, good-bodied **a69**
gelding: fair handicapper: won at Leicester in April: was best at 5f/6f: acted on firm and
soft going: left visored at 4 yrs: took good hold: often held up: had suspect temperament:
dead. *D. Nicholls*

DAPPLE DAWN (IRE) 4 b.f. Celtic Swing 138 – Lasting Chance (USA) (American **79**
Chance (USA) 117) [2007 75: f8g³ p8.6g⁴ p7.1g² p7.1g* p8g² p7.1g⁴ a7g p8g Nov 30]
fair handicapper: won at Wolverhampton in February: left D. Carroll after sixth outing:
effective at 7f to 8.6f: acts on all-weather, good to firm and good to soft ground: sometimes blinkered: tends to hang left. *Garvan Donnelly, Ireland*

DARAAHEM (IRE) 2 ch.c. (Feb 14) Act One 124 – Shamah 96 (Unfuwain (USA) **79 p**
131) [2007 7g Oct 26] big, lengthy colt: third foal: closely related to fairly useful 1m
winner Safqa (by Singspiel): dam 1m winner: 16/1, green (slowly away) when ninth to
Speedy Dollar in maiden at Doncaster: will be suited by 1m/1¼m: bound to improve.
B. W. Hills

DARCY'S PRIDE (IRE) 3 b. or br.f. Danetime (IRE) 121 – Cox's Ridge (IRE) **76**
(Indian Ridge 123) [2007 47: 5m* 5m⁴ 5m⁴ 6m 5m* 5m* 5g⁶ 5v² 5g⁶ 5s⁵ 5m² 5g 5g 5m
Sep 27] quite good-topped filly: fair handicapper: won at Catterick in April, and Newcastle and Carlisle in June: likely to prove best at 5f/easy 6f: acts on heavy and good to
firm going: races up with pace. *D. W. Barker*

DAREIOS (GER) 2 ch.g. (Jan 14) Numerous (USA) – Desert Chiara (USA) (Desert **–**
King (IRE) 129) [2007 6g 7g Aug 24] €20,000Y: second foal: dam unraced out of
half-sister to US Grade 1 9f winner Sabona: needed experience when behind in maidens
(9/2 on debut), then gelded. *G. A. Swinbank*

DAR ES SALAAM 3 ch.g. King's Best (USA) 132 – Place de L'Opera 98 (Sadler's **86**
Wells (USA) 132) [2007 10m⁵ 10d² 10g* 10g⁵ p12g 16g Nov 2] 130,000Y: well-made
gelding: sixth foal: half-brother to several at least smart winners, including high-class 6f
(at 2 yrs) to 1½m winner Imperial Stride, very smart 1½m/13f winner High Pitched (both
by Indian Ridge) and high-class 11f winner Hala Bek (by Halling): dam, 1½m winner,
half-sister to Irish 2000 Guineas winner Indian Haven out of very smart Park Hill winner
Madame Dubois: fairly useful performer: best effort when winning maiden at Pontefract
in July: well held in handicaps last 2 starts, not looking straightforward: should be suited
by 1½m: sold 20,000 gns. *E. A. L. Dunlop*

DARESTAN (IRE) 3 b.c. Sinndar (IRE) 134 – Daralbayda (IRE) 102 (Doyoun 124) **103**
[2007 12g* 12.5d² 12g* 16d 15g⁴ Aug 12] strong, lengthy colt: sixth foal: half-brother to
3 winners, including smart French 1¼m to 15f winner Darkara (by Halling) and useful
French 1½m winner Darinska (by Zilzal), latter dam of 3-y-o Darjina: dam, French 1½m
winner, half-sister to dam of Prix du Jockey Club winner Darsi: useful performer: won
maiden at Bordeaux in April and minor event at Longchamp in June: best effort when 1¾
lengths fourth to Noble Prince in listed race at Deauville final start: stays 15f (shaped as
if stamina stretched in Queen's Vase at Royal Ascot over 2m). *A. de Royer Dupre, France*

DARFOUR 3 b.g. Inchinor 119 – Gai Bulga 110 (Kris 135) [2007 76: 7m* 6g⁵ 8s³ 8g 7d **78**
8g Oct 6] lengthy, workmanlike gelding: fair handicapper: won at Newcastle in May:
below form last 3 starts: should stay 1m: acts on firm going. *J. S. Goldie*

DARGHAN (IRE) 7 b.g. Air Express (IRE) 125 – Darsannda (IRE) 86 (Kahyasi 130) **69**
[2007 70: 9m³ 10.1m* 12m⁶ 11.5g 11d 10m p11m Nov 11] strong gelding: fair handicapper: won at Yarmouth in August: stays 1¾m: acts on any going: tried tongue tied
earlier in career: held up. *W. J. Musson*

DARING AFFAIR 6 b.m. Bien Bien (USA) 125 – Daring Destiny 113 (Daring March **87 d**
116) [2007 87: p10g⁵ p9.5g* f8g f8g 10.5g⁵ 10f⁵ 8d f8g⁶ 10.4s p11g 10d⁶ p8.6g² p8.6g⁶
p8.6g⁴ p9.5g³ Dec 26] good-topped mare: fairly useful handicapper: won at Wolverhampton in January: below form after fifth start: has form at 1½m, very best efforts at
9.5f: acts on all-weather, firm and soft going: tried visored/in cheekpieces. *K. R. Burke*

DARING DREAM (GER) 2 ch.c. (Jan 22) Big Shuffle (USA) 122 – Daring Action **78**
(Arazi (USA) 135) [2007 5m⁶ 6s⁴ 6s³ 6m⁴ 6d³ 8s² 8m Oct 22] €49,000Y, 27,500 2-y-o:
leggy, workmanlike colt: brother to 2 winners in Germany, notably useful sprinter Daring
Love: dam unraced out of half-sister to Zafonic: fair maiden: in frame 5 times, including
second to Cobo Bay in nursery at Ayr: stays 1m: best form on ground softer than good.
T. D. Easterby

DARING RACER (GER) 4 ch.g. Big Shuffle (USA) 122 – Daring Action (Arazi **71**
(USA) 135) [2007 p12g 16g 11s p12g² 14m² 14d⁴ p16g Sep 7] lengthy gelding: fair
performer: successful once from 7 starts in Germany, namely maiden at Baden-Baden
final 3-y-o outing (then left U. Ostmann): creditable efforts when in frame in handicaps
in 2007: stays 1¾m: acts on polytrack, good to firm and good to soft going: sold £4,400,
joined Mrs L. Mongan. *S. Dow*

DARJINA (FR) 3 b.f. Zamindar (USA) 116 – Darinska (IRE) 105 (Zilzal (USA) **128**
137) [2007 8g* 8g* 8d³ 8d* 8g* 8d 8g³ Dec 9]
 For the second year running, the best three-year-old filly, not just in France
but in Europe, was trained by Alain de Royer-Dupre and owned by Princess Zahra
Aga Khan. In 2006, Mandesha had earned that status whilst showing a rare degree
of versatility, winning Group 1 races at a mile, a mile and a quarter, and a mile
and a half, though through the whole of her three-year-old season Mandesha was
confined to racing against other fillies and mares. Darjina also won three Group 1
races in the course of her three-year-old season but the similarities between herself
and Mandesha end there. In contrast to Mandesha's variety of distances, Darjina
has done all her racing, so far at least, at a mile, and, unlike her older stable-
companion, she put up her best effort when beating all comers, colts and older
horses included.
 Mandesha did not make her debut until the spring of her three-year-old
season and did not win her first Group 1 until the end of July. Darjina, on the other
hand, had managed to win her only outing as a two-year-old, a minor event at
Saint-Cloud in November of that year, although that still left her as the most
inexperienced member of the field in the Prix de la Grotte at Longchamp in April.
There was no shortage of confidence in her, however, and she started a short-
priced favourite, justifying the support to win by a short neck and a length from
the listed winner Missvinski and the previous season's Prix des Reservoirs winner
Chinandega.
 Looking sure to improve again, Darjina was aimed at the Poule d'Essai des
Pouliches at the same course four weeks later. On the day, though, Darjina's task
was made considerably tougher by the unexpected presence of the One Thousand
Guineas winner Finsceal Beo, who had been so impressive at Newmarket just a
week earlier. The thirteen-strong field included five fillies from Britain, among
them Sander Camillo, who had been second favourite for the Guineas when withdrawn in season on the day of the race. The betting was headed by Finsceal Beo at
5/4-on and Darjina at 4/1. The patiently-ridden Darjina was brought wide to make
her run in the straight as Finsceal Beo took the lead over a furlong out and went a
couple of lengths clear. Darjina kept on strongly to collar Finsceal Beo in the last
strides and win by a head. Two of the British fillies, Rahiyah and Costume (the
latter still a maiden), completed the frame, beaten a total of a length and a three
quarters and just over four lengths respectively.
 Darjina took her unbeaten record to Royal Ascot next for the Coronation
Stakes, where Finsceal Beo and Rahiyah, as well as Missvinski, were all in the
line-up. Darjina finished ahead of all those fillies again, but, encountering softer
conditions for the first time (she had raced only on good ground previously), she
was unable to repeat her Longchamp form, held up in touch and keeping going to
finish third, denied second by a head by the German Guineas winner Mi Emma but
six lengths behind the winner Indian Ink. The theory that the ground was to blame
for Darjina's defeat at Ascot took a knock after she kept her unbeaten record in
France in the Prix d'Astarte at Deauville, which had yielded the first of Mandesha's
Group 1 wins the year before. As at Ascot, the ground was good to soft, and the
field looked as strong as any that had contested the race since it became a Group 1
in 2004. Darjina started favourite ahead of the Falmouth Stakes winner Simply
Perfect, Mi Emma, Utrecht and All Is Vanity, the last two having won the Prix

Chloe and Prix de Sandringham respectively last time out. Once again, though, it was Missvinski (fifth at Ascot) who gave Darjina most to do. Prominent throughout, Darjina went on under two furlongs out but looked to have a fight on her hands when Missvinski challenged on her outer inside the final furlong. Headed briefly, Darjina responded gamely to win by half a length, with Simply Perfect keeping on the same distance back in third. The Coronation Stakes form was turned upside down, with Mi Emma finishing only seventh.

Thus far, Darjina had shown form no better than might be expected of an average winner of the Poule d'Essai des Pouliches. However, her next start in the Qatar Prix du Moulin back at Longchamp pitched her against colts and older horses for the first time and, in beating them all convincingly, Darjina put up the best performance at a mile in Europe in 2007. In addition, it was the best by a three-year-old filly over any distance for several years. The Prix Jacques le Marois at Deauville the previous month, although it went to a top-class horse in Manduro, had been an unusually weak renewal, but the Moulin attracted George Washington, champion miler in 2006, and Ramonti, who was looking his likely successor after wins in the Queen Anne Stakes and Sussex Stakes on his last two starts. The field also included the Poule d'Essai des Poulains winner Astronomer Royal, Darjina's stable-companion Linngari, who had been better than ever in Dubai early in the year, and the placed horses from the Jacques le Marois, Holocene and Turtle Bowl. This was the best field assembled for a mile race in Europe all year, though interestingly all the horses could have contested a similar event worth almost twice as much money the very same day. At Veliefendi in Turkey, the track's international mile event, the Topkapi Trophy, received a huge increase in prize money, making it the richest mile race in Europe with a first prize equivalent to almost £300,000; a total of five British- and French-trained horses contested the race, with the Prix d'Astarte fifth Trip To The Moon faring best of the visitors in third, just ahead of Godolphin's representative Caradak.

Back at Longchamp, Darjina was sent off third favourite in the Moulin at just under 4/1, behind Ramonti at 7/4 and George Washington at 9/4, the remaining half dozen starting at 10/1 or longer. The three principals duly took the first three places, though not in the order the betting suggested. Archipenko made the running as pacemaker for his Ballydoyle stable-companions, pursued by Ramonti, with Darjina third and George Washington held up. Ramonti took over in front two furlongs out with Darjina still tracking him, but his lead was short-lived as Darjina quickened ahead and ran on strongly for a two-length victory. Ramonti held on for second by a length from George Washington who made up a deal of ground from an unpromising position after being somewhat trapped in on the home turn and then

Poule d'Essai des Pouliches, Longchamp—
Darjina just gets the better of Newmarket Guineas winner Finsceal Beo (rail); Rahiyah is a good third

Prix d'Astarte, Deauville—three-year-olds dominate as Darjina (noseband)
gives owner and trainer a second successive win in the race; Missvinski (left) puts up her best effort
to be second ahead of Simply Perfect (rail) and Barshiba

taking time to get on to an even keel. Criticism of the ride given to George Washington (his jockey blamed his draw) got more coverage than it deserved, and Darjina's high-class performance a lot less.

With fillies having their own Group 1 programme at a mile these days, the opportunity is there for them to avoid stronger contests like the Prix du Moulin if connections choose to do so, making Darjina's win all the more praiseworthy. Marling's win in the 1992 Sussex Stakes was the last by a three-year-old filly in one of Britain's two Group 1 mile contests open to both three-year-olds and older horses. The Queen Elizabeth II Stakes last went to a three-year-old filly when Milligram won in 1987; Milligram upset the odds laid on Miesque, who had herself beaten male rivals (largely fellow three-year-olds) in both the Jacques le Marois and Moulin. France's two top mile contests have in general been happier hunting grounds for three-year-old fillies than their British counterparts. Four have won the Jacques le Marois since Miesque, most recently Six Perfections in 2003, and Darjina became the fifth three-year-old filly to win the Moulin since Miesque, after All At Sea and Ridgewood Pearl in the 'nineties, Nebraska Tornado in 2003 and Grey Lilas in 2004. In terms of form, though, Darjina achieved a higher rating in the Moulin than all the fillies who had won since Miesque. Darjina is also rated more highly than recent leading three-year-old miling fillies Attraction and Divine Proportions. Both were high-class fillies whose winning sequences earned them considerable press coverage, but neither gained a Group 1 win in open company. Like Darjina, Divine Proportions' wins included the Prix de la Grotte, Poule d'Essai des Pouliches and Prix d'Astarte (as well as the Prix de Diane over a longer trip) but she lost her unbeaten record when sustaining a career-ending injury in the Jacques le Marois. Darjina's rating of 128 was last achieved by a European-trained three-year-old filly back in 2001, by Banks Hill. She too was campaigned over a mile in Europe, finishing second to Slickly in the Prix du Moulin, before running her best race when stepped up to a mile and a quarter in the Breeders' Cup Filly & Mare Turf which she won by five and a half lengths.

Darjina herself looked in line for a step up to a mile and a quarter after the Moulin. The Prix de l'Opera, won by Mandesha the year before, had been mentioned as a possible target for her, and the way she had been finishing her races, coupled with her pedigree, suggested she would stay another two furlongs. However, in the end, Darjina was kept to a mile for her last two starts, on neither occasion running anywhere near her Moulin form. She was supplemented for the Queen Elizabeth II Stakes but again Ascot racegoers did not see the real Darjina who finished last of seven behind Ramonti, even though, as at the Royal meeting, she looked in good shape beforehand. Darjina fared better on her final start when beaten just over a length into third in the Hong Kong Mile behind the locally-trained five-year-old Good Ba Ba and the Godolphin three-year-old colt Creachadoir after lacking room for much of the straight. Another Group 1 success later on the Sha Tin card for Ramonti in the Hong Kong Cup advertised the merit of Darjina's Prix du Moulin win, and, though George Washington never got the chance to uphold the form, fourth-placed Linngari beat Golden Titus (last in the Moulin) in the Group 1 Premio Vittorio di Capua at Milan later in the autumn.

Considering that Princess Zahra is credited as the owner of just three broodmares among a band of more than two hundred and twenty in the most recent edition of the Aga Khan's stud book, it is a considerable achievement to have Europe's top filly for the second year in succession. Mandesha's dam was sold cheaply before her daughter made her mark, but there is no danger now of Darjina's dam Darinska suffering the same fate. Darjina is the first foal of Darinska who also raced in Princess Zahra's colours. Those colours—green, brown epaulets and cap—are a combination of the silks of both her father and great grandfather, taking the epaulets from the former and the colour scheme (green and chocolate hoops) from the latter. Before a review of Darjina's pedigree, her owner's own family tree is worth a mention, particularly with regard to success in the Poule d'Essai des Pouliches. Princess Zahra became the fourth generation of her family to own a winner of the race. Her father was successful with Masarika in 1984 and Zalaiyka in 1998, while, in the 'fifties, Toro's success for the current Aga Khan's grandfather in 1957, shortly before he died, was followed in consecutive years by wins for Yla and Ginetta in the ownership of Prince Aly Khan.

Darinska also ran at Ascot, like her daughter without distinction, finishing only tenth of fifteen in the 2002 Ribblesdale Stakes. Equipped with blinkers, she made a winning debut over a mile and a half at Saint-Cloud and finished third in the Prix de Royaumont at Longchamp, shaping as though she would have stayed a mile and three quarters. Darinska's three-year-old half-brother Darestan accompanied Darjina to Royal Ascot, starting second favourite for the Queen's Vase, but he too failed to improve the family's record, finishing well beaten. Darinska and Darestan were useful, but they had a better half-sister in Darkara, who was a smart listed winner in France and successful at up to fifteen furlongs. Grandam Daralbayda's only win was noteworthy on two counts. She was Princess Zahra's very first winner

Qatar Prix du Moulin de Longchamp, Longchamp—Darjina puts up the best performance by a three-year-old filly since 2001 as she leads home Ramonti (partially hidden by winner), the strong-finishing George Washington (third right), Linngari (noseband) and Archipenko (rail)

Princess Zahra Aga Khan's "Darjina"

as an owner in June 1996, and it came in the very same race, the Prix Flossie at Saint-Cloud, that Darinska won six years later. Daralbayda was one of several useful middle-distance fillies out of the smart Prix Minerve winner Daralinsha. Another of Daralinsha's daughters was Darashandeh, dam of the Aga Khan's 2006 Prix du Jockey Club winner Darsi. Darjina's dam has since produced three more fillies; the unraced two-year-old Dariena (by Highest Honor), a yearling by Highest Honor's son Verglas, and a foal by Dalakhani, the dam's first mating with an 'in-house' stallion.

Darjina (FR)	Zamindar (USA)	Gone West	Mr Prospector
(b.f. 2004)	(b 1994)	(b 1984)	Secrettame
		Zaizafon	The Minstrel
		(ch 1982)	Mofida
	Darinska (IRE)	Zilzal	Nureyev
	(b 1999)	(ch 1986)	French Charmer
		Daralbayda	Doyoun
		(b 1993)	Daralinsha

Like Mandesha before her, the close-coupled, attractive Darjina stays in training as a four-year-old. Mandesha did not recapture her best form in the latest season and ended her career wearing cheekpieces in the Arc. It will be interesting to see how Darjina fares at four as there is still plenty more to find out about her. She has raced only on good or good to soft ground so far, which makes it hard to draw any firm conclusions about the conditions which suit her best; it would certainly be wrong at this stage to put her Ascot defeats down to the ground given the way she coped with similar conditions at Deauville. It is fair to say, however, that much her best effort was on good going. Her effectiveness beyond a mile is still

264

to be proven, but she promises to stay further and is likely to be stepped up in trip in the next season, when a repeat of her Prix du Moulin form and her gameness would make her hard to beat in any company. *A. de Royer Dupre, France*

DARK ANGEL (IRE) 2 gr.c. (Apr 4) Acclamation 118 – Midnight Angel (Machiavellian (USA) 123) [2007 5m² 5.1m* 5m 6m⁴ 6g* 5m 6m* 6m* 7d Oct 20] **113**

Any novelty, by definition, can become a precedent but few manage it as swiftly as the example of Holy Roman Emperor's retirement to stud completely sound before his three-year-old campaign started. Eight months after the second-best juvenile of 2006 was plucked out of training to replace George Washington at Coolmore, another Group 1-winning two-year-old followed him straight to stud. The reaction to Dark Angel's retirement seemed much less critical than to Holy Roman Emperor's, almost certainly because he was not being trained for a classic less than two months away—Holy Roman Emperor was among the market leaders for the Two Thousand Guineas—and could not be regarded as a live candidate for the classics anyway. Dark Angel was a sprinter, with little hope of making his mark over a mile, his form in winning the Mill Reef Stakes and Middle Park Stakes putting him well short of that usually required to win the Guineas. Of more significance is the reason given by one of his owners for selling the colt: 'It was felt he would be a six-furlong specialist and it's very hard for a three-year-old who has won a Group 1, so selling him wasn't really a wrench'. The retirement of Dark Angel again puts into sharp focus the lack of suitable opportunities for good three-year-old sprinters early in the season, something commented on in *Racehorses* on a number of occasions. Dutch Art's campaign is the latest to exemplify the point. Before the Golden Jubilee Stakes there is nothing prestigious to aim at without a penalty apart from the King's Stand Stakes—to be upgraded to Group 1 in 2008—four days earlier. The two best races in Britain at this stage, the Group 2 Duke of York Stakes over six furlongs and the Temple Stakes over five, involve a Group 1 winner of any age from the previous season carrying a 7-lb penalty. Three-year-old Airwave successfully carried the impost in the Temple Stakes in 2003, as did Lochsong as a six-year-old in 1994, but one can hardly blame owners for not bothering with these races. In the interests of consistency—never a strong point in the pattern system—it would make sense to upgrade one of the Group 2 events, boosting the prize money accordingly. That way sprinters of all ages would have a full season, just as there are full seasons over longer trips, and the best three-year-olds would not be disadvantaged. The Temple Stakes—switched to Haydock with increased prize money for 2008—would be the more obvious candidate.

£300000 St Leger Yearling Stakes, York—this very valuable two-year-old race goes to Dark Angel; Gypsy Baby (left) and Cosmic Art (on runner-up's left) fight it out for some useful place money

Dark Angel did not start reaching his best until tried at six furlongs in the July Stakes at Newmarket. He had won one of his three starts, a maiden at Chester in early May when long odds on. Dark Angel made the running in the July Stakes but had no answer when challenged in the final furlong, coming home two lengths behind Winker Watson in fourth. Success, and a considerable return of £187,692, came in the £300000 St Leger Yearling Stakes at York in August, one of the most valuable sales races in Britain, just behind the St Leger Two-Year-Old Stakes at Doncaster and Tattersalls October Auction Stakes at Newmarket. The York race (run at Doncaster prior to 2006) has traditionally been well contested—Cockney Rebel finished second in 2006—but the latest renewal was a relatively weak affair with half the twenty runners at 25/1 or longer and not much in the way of stakes-race form on offer. After recovering from a sore foot caused by spreading a plate a couple of days before the race, Dark Angel started favourite ahead of three winners in maiden and/or nursery company—Johar Jamal, Berbice and Irish-trained Dedo—plus Windsor Castle Stakes winner Drawnfromthepast. The result was in no doubt from the moment Dark Angel was sent on two furlongs out after travelling strongly close up from the outset. He kept on well to beat Gypsy Baby by a length. A return to five furlongs, in the Flying Childers Stakes at Doncaster, confirmed that Dark Angel needed further, though in coming home seventh of eight to Fleeting Spirit he was some way below his best and his running could not be put down solely to the trip.

It was different in the Dubai Duty Free Mill Reef Stakes at Newbury and the Shadwell Middle Park Stakes at Newmarket. Dark Angel started favourite for the former in September, taking on two pattern winners in Philario (Sirenia Stakes) and Strike The Deal (Richmond Stakes, resulting in his carrying a 3-lb penalty). Berbice, fourth at York, tried his luck again but the race was not so strongly contested as it often has been. Dark Angel made all and battled on gamely to hold Strike The Deal by a neck. A fortnight later Dark Angel had to meet the Newbury runner-up at level weights. With Gimcrack Stakes winner Sir Gerry, Champagne Stakes fourth Tajdeef (also trained by Barry Hills) and St Leger Two-Year-Old Stakes first and second Dream Eater and Achilles of Troy in the field of nine, Dark Angel started fifth favourite. The fact that Sir Gerry ran poorly, finishing eighth, made matters a little easier for Dark Angel but he still showed improved form, lying close up from the off racing freely, regaining the lead at halfway and holding on gamely by half a length from Strike The Deal despite drifting right, his rider Michael Hills found guilty of careless riding and suspended for two days. Tajdeef was a further neck away in third. This was not a vintage Middle Park. In the last twenty runnings, Dark Angel is rated superior only to 1997 winner Hayil, who failed to win again over the next three seasons. Dark Angel was returned to the same course a fortnight later and started at 25/1 in the Dewhurst Stakes over seven

Dubai Duty Free Mill Reef Stakes, Newbury—Dark Angel has a neck to spare over Strike The Deal (right); next are the grey Berbice and Philario (second left)

Shadwell Middle Park Stakes, Newmarket—Dark Angel puts up his best performance in again beating Strike The Deal (left); Tajdeef (blaze), Red Alert Day (armlets) and Achilles of Troy (outside) are next

furlongs. This was his only run on ground softer than good, and after leading as usual he had nothing left when challenged two furlongs out, finishing last but one behind New Approach.

Dark Angel (IRE) (gr.c. Apr 4, 2005)	Acclamation (b 1999)	Royal Applause (b 1991)	Waajib / Flying Melody
		Princess Athena (b 1985)	Ahonoora / Shopping Wise
	Midnight Angel (gr 1994)	Machiavellian (b 1987)	Mr Prospector / Coup de Folie
		Night At Sea (gr 1987)	Night Shift / Into Harbour

Two of the finest sires of the post-war era, Hail To Reason and Raise A Native, were both retired to stud after their two-year-old seasons—because of injury, not for commercial reasons—and while it is scarcely likely that Dark Angel will follow their outstanding example there will be satisfaction at Morristown Lattin Stud in Ireland (where his fee will be €10,000) if he takes another leaf out of his sire Acclamation's book, he too a winner of the St Leger Yearling Stakes. The latter, a smart sprinter who gained his most important victory in the Diadem Stakes as a four-year-old, had a stunning season with his first crop, becoming champion first-season sire with earnings in excess of a million pounds. Winning sales races with Dark Angel and with Exclamation at Newmarket—the latter thirty-five minutes before the Middle Park Stakes—plus second place in the Goffs Million with Hitchens certainly helped, but there were other stakes horses too, notably listed winners Cake, Pencil Hill and Sweepstake. Six of Acclamation's yearlings fetched 100,000 guineas or more in the autumn, with one going for 350,000 guineas at Newmarket, and predictably his fee has risen markedly, from €9,000 to €30,000. It remains to be seen how successful Acclamation's progeny will be as three-year-olds and upwards. The predominant impression they give is one of possessing speed and there must be doubts about how many will be able to make a major mark at a mile, let alone further. Dark Angel's dam Midnight Angel was unraced and has produced three other winners, including Colleton River (by Croco Rouge) whose success came in a maiden over a mile and a half at Wolverhampton and who stayed two miles. For a thirteen-year-old, Midnight Angel has been through the sale-ring a

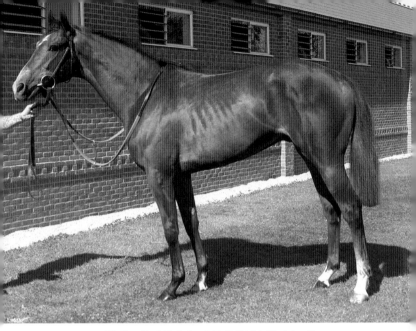

The Hon. Mrs J. M. Corbett & Mr C. Wright's "Dark Angel"

remarkable number of times, seven to be exact, starting off when bought by Darley for 50,000 guineas as a yearling. Midnight Angel was sold twice as a three-year-old, then again at four, seven, nine and twelve, knocked down to the Hong Kong Breeders Club for €34,000 at Goffs in foal to Pastoral Pursuits on the last occasion. She was back again at Goffs in November in foal to Aussie Rules but failed to reach her reserve at €340,000. Midnight Angel's foal did not reach his reserve either. Dark Angel, a good-bodied, quite attractive colt with a quick action, fetched 61,000 guineas as a yearling at Doncaster. The grandam Night At Sea was best at sprint distances, winning the listed Trafalgar House Sprint over five furlongs at Sandown, and foaled seven winners, one of them stakes-placed. She was a half-sister to the dams of winners of the seven-furlong McDonagh Boland Stakes and the five-furlong Prix de la Vallee d'Auge, illustrating that the dominant characteristic of Dark Angel's pedigree is speed. *B. W. Hills*

DARK CAMELLIA 2 b.f. (Feb 24) Olden Times 121 – Miss Mirror 77 (Magic Mirror 105) [2007 7m 7d Oct 9] tall filly: half-sister to several winners, including useful Swedish performers Magic Fact (6.5f/1½m winner, by Factual) and Tragic Love (1m/1¼m winner, by Tragic Role): dam 1m winner: modest form latter start in maidens (eighth at Leicester): will be suited by 1m/1¼m. *H. J. L. Dunlop* — **59**

DARK CHAMPION 7 b.g. Abou Zouz (USA) 109 – Hazy Kay (IRE) 77 (Treasure Kay 114) [2007 65: 7m 6m³ 5d* 5s⁵ 5g² 5f 5g Oct 6] good-topped gelding: fair handicapper: won at Catterick in July: effective at 5f to 7f: acts on fibresand and any turf going: wears headgear. *R. E. Barr* — **68**

DARK CHAPEL 4 b.g. College Chapel 122 – Possibility 59 (Robellino (USA) 127) [2007 f7g May 15] well beaten in maidens (20 months apart). *W. J. H. Ratcliffe* — –

DARK CHARM (FR) 8 b.g. Anabaa (USA) 130 – Wardara 107 (Sharpo 132) [2007 80: 8m 8.1g 8.1g 9g² 9.9m⁵ 10.5s² 9.2s⁶ 10g 8.3d² 8.3g* 11.1g⁴ 10d 9.2s Sep 24] tall, — **75**

quite good-topped gelding: fair handicapper: won at Hamilton in August: stays 10.5f: acts on polytrack, firm and soft going: effective with or without cheekpieces: inconsistent, and signs of temperament. *R. A. Fahey*

DARK DRUID (IRE) 3 b.g. Princely Heir (IRE) 111 – Super Sonic Sonia (IRE) 88 **54 d** (Tirol 127) [2007 p8g p8g⁶ 8g 8.1d 10m 11.5m p8g Aug 18] modest maiden: form only at Kempton second start. *I. A. Wood*

DARK ENERGY 3 br.g. Observatory (USA) 131 – Waterfowl Creek (IRE) 88 (Be My **81** Guest (USA) 126) [2007 76p: 8g 9.2d 10.9d⁴ 8.1v 8s² 10g 10.1d* Oct 16] small gelding: fairly useful handicapper: best effort when winning at Newcastle in October: stays 1¼m: acts on soft going, unraced on going firmer than good: has raced freely: sold 21,000 gns, joined M. Scudamore. *B. Smart*

DARK ISLANDER (IRE) 4 br.c. Singspiel (IRE) 133 – Lamanka Lass (USA) 79 **114** (Woodman (USA) 126) [2007 115: 8m 7g 7d Aug 18] rangy, angular colt: has a quick action: smart performer: creditable effort in 2007 when 3¾ lengths seventh to Tariq in Betfair Cup (Lennox) at Goodwood second start: bred to stay 1¼m, though tends to race freely: acts on polytrack and firm going, possibly not on good to soft. *J. W. Hills*

DARK MASK (IRE) 3 b.g. Iron Mask (USA) 117 – Darkness At Noon (USA) (Night – Shift (USA)) [2007 p6g 7.1s Jul 6] well held in claimer/maiden. *J. L. Spearing*

DARK MISSILE 4 b.f. Night Shift (USA) – Exorcet (FR) 78 (Selkirk (USA) 129) **114** [2007 100: 6m⁴ 6d* 6s 6m² 6g² 6f Oct 21] big, strong filly: smart performer: resumed progression in 2007, winning 26-runner Wokingham Stakes (Handicap) at Royal Ascot in June by neck from Intrepid Jack: very good second after at Ascot in handicap (to Our Faye) and Diadem Stakes (short-headed by Haatef after again travelling strongly): well below form in Grade 2 Nearctic Stakes at Woodbine final outing: best at 5f/6f: acts on polytrack, firm and good to soft going (folded tamely on soft third outing). *A. M. Balding*

DARK MOON 4 b.f. Observatory (USA) 131 – Lady Donatella 57 (Last Tycoon 131) **58** [2007 63, a48: p6g p6g³ p6g* p7.1g p6f p6g 7m p6g 6s⁶ p7g Jun 14] modest performer: won handicap at Wolverhampton in February: effective at 6f to 1m: acts on polytrack, soft and good to firm going: visored last 3 starts: often slowly away: has raced freely. *D. Shaw*

DARK PARADE (ARG) 6 b.g. Parade Marshal (USA) – Charming Dart (ARG) **73** (D'Accord (USA) [2007 61, a73: 17.2f* 14.1g² p16g⁴ 12d³ 14d p16g p16g p16g* p16.5g⁶ Nov 19] close-coupled gelding: fair handicapper: won at Bath in April (for P. D. Evans, returned to former trainer after fifth start) and Kempton in November: effective at 1½m to easy 17f: acts on sand/all-weather, firm and good to soft going: tried blinkered (including last 3 starts): not an easy ride. *G. L. Moore*

DARK PLANET 4 ch.g. Singspiel (IRE) 133 – Warning Shadows (IRE) 113 (Cadeaux **68 d** Genereux 131) [2007 68: p16.5g p12g p12g⁴ p9.5g p12g p12.2g 10g p10g⁵ Nov 19] strong gelding: fair handicapper: below form after third start in 2007: stays 1½m: acts on polytrack and firm going: in cheekpieces/visor in 2007: sold £850. *D. Burchell*

Wokingham Stakes (Handicap), Royal Ascot—Dark Missile (noseband) provides apprentice William Buick with his most valuable success; Intrepid Jack (quartered cap), Balthazaar's Gift (left) and Something (on winner's left) also make the frame

DARK PROSPECT 2 b.c. (Jan 29) Nayef (USA) 129 – Miss Mirasol 92 (Sheikh **62** Albadou 128) [2007 8.2d⁶ 8d Oct 30] good-topped colt: first foal: dam 2-y-o 6f winner who stayed 7f: green, modest form when mid-division in maidens. *M. A. Jarvis*

DARK QUEEN 2 b.f. (Mar 6) Bertolini (USA) 125 – Abstone Queen 66 (Presidium **40** 124) [2007 5m⁴ 6d 5m p5.1g⁵ Aug 31] rather leggy filly: sixth foal: half-sister to 2003 2-y-o 5f winner Amber Legend (by Fraam): dam 6f/7f winner, including at 2 yrs: poor maiden: claimed from D. Thompson £6,000 after debut: form only at 5f: tried visored. *D. Carroll*

DARK SOCIETY 9 b.g. Imp Society (USA) – No Candles Tonight 74 (Star Appeal **–** 133) [2007 –: p9.5g Nov 12] medium-sized, useful-looking gelding: lightly raced and little form nowadays: tried visored. *A. W. Carroll*

DARK TARA 2 br.f. (Apr 21) Diktat 126 – Karisal (IRE) 80 (Persian Bold 123) [2007 **75** 6d⁴ 6s* 6m⁶ 6g 6d 6m 6s⁶ Oct 26] 42,000Y: tall, quite good-topped filly: third foal: half-sister to 6f winner Karashino (by Shinko Forest): dam, 2-y-o 5f winner, half-sister to smart sprinter Palacegate Episode, herself grandam of 3-y-o Dutch Art: fair performer: won maiden at York in July: little impact in nurseries, signs of temperament (tried in blinkers/cheekpieces): raced at 6f: acts on soft and good to firm going. *R. A. Fahey*

DARLEY STAR 2 gr.f. (Mar 4) King's Best (USA) 132 – Amellnaa (IRE) 86 (Sadler's **60** Wells (USA) 132) [2007 7m⁶ 7m⁶ p7g Sep 24] rather leggy filly: fourth foal: half-sister to 1¼m winner Amerigo Vespucci (by Zafonic): dam, 1¼m winner, out of Irish Oaks winner Alydaress: modest maiden: will stay 1¼m. *C. E. Brittain*

DARLING BELINDA 3 ch.f. Silver Wizard (USA) 117 – Katyushka (IRE) 73 (Soviet **57** Star (USA) 128) [2007 66: p6g⁵ p6g⁵ 5g p6g p6m Sep 6] just modest maiden in 2007: should stay 7f: acts on polytrack and good to soft going: always wears cheekpieces: tends to hang/has carried head awkwardly. *D. K. Ivory*

DAR RE MI 2 b.f. (May 15) Singspiel (IRE) 133 – Darara 129 (Top Ville 129) [2007 **73 P** 7g² Nov 3] tall, quite attractive filly: half-sister to several winners, most at least smart, including French 1½m winner Darazari (also Group 1 1¼m winner in Australia) and 1¼m performer Diaghilev (known as River Dancer in Hong Kong), both very smart by Sadler's Wells: dam, won Prix Vermeille, half-sister to Darshaan: 10/1 and not fully wound up, shaped very well when neck second of 19 to La Coveta in maiden at Newmarket, racing in touch and running on strongly: will be suited by 1¼m/1½m: type to improve considerably. *J. H. M. Gosden*

DARRFONAH (IRE) 3 b.f. Singspiel (IRE) 133 – Avila 76 (Ajdal (USA) 130) [2007 **100** 106: a7f 7m 8m 12d 10m* 12d⁶ 10m⁶ 8m Oct 6] good-topped filly: useful performer: won listed event at Newbury in June by ¾ length from Russian Rosie (reportedly pulled muscle after): mostly stiff tasks otherwise in 2007, creditable efforts when sixth to Peeping Fawn in Yorkshire Oaks at York and to Four Sins in Blandford Stakes at the Curragh: effective at 1¼m/1½m: acts on soft and good to firm going: blinkered third start, tongue tied after: often held up. *C. E. Brittain*

DART 3 br.f. Diktat 126 – Eilean Shona 102 (Suave Dancer (USA) 136) [2007 p12g³ **72 +** p12m 12.4d² p12g³ p12.2g² f11d* Dec 12] third foal: half-sister to 9.7f winner Penny Wedding (by Pennekamp): dam 9f (at 2 yrs) to 2m winner: fair form: won maiden at Southwell in December by 7 lengths: stays 1½m: acts on all-weather and good to soft going. *J. R. Fanshawe*

DARUMA (IRE) 3 b.g. Iron Mask (USA) 117 – Mary's Way (GR) 78 (Night Shift **– §** (USA)) [2007 53§: f5g⁶ p8g Jan 22] strong, heavy-topped gelding: temperamental maiden: tried blinkered. *Peter Grayson*

DARUSSO 4 ch.g. Daylami (IRE) 138 – Rifada 103 (Ela-Mana-Mou 132) [2007 67: **66** 10m 11m 15d⁶ 17.2m 13.3m⁶ Jun 9] leggy gelding: fair maiden handicapper: should stay at least 1½m: acts on soft and good to firm going: wore cheekpieces last 2 starts *J. S. Moore*

DARYAL (IRE) 6 b.g. Night Shift (USA) – Darata (IRE) (Vayrann 133) [2007 12.3m* **87** 12f³ 14s⁴ Sep 29] good-topped gelding: fairly useful handicapper (including over hurdles): won amateur event at Chester in August: stays 1¾m: acts on firm and soft ground. *A. King*

DA SCHADENFREUDE (USA) 3 b. or br.g. Tale of The Cat (USA) 113 – Conquis- **–** tas Jessica (USA) (Boundary (USA) 117) [2007 61: p8g p7g p10g 6.1m p7g Oct 17] big gelding: little form in 2007: tried in cheekpieces. *W. G. M. Turner*

DASHEENA 4 b.f. Magic Ring (IRE) 115 – Sweet And Lucky (Lucky Wednesday 124) **76** [2007 67: p6g⁶ p6g p6g² 6m p6g² p6g p7.1g⁵ p5.1g p7.1g³ p6g²ᵈ p7m⁵ 7g* p6g 6d⁴ p7m³ p7g p6g³ p7.1g* f7d* f7d² Dec 18] angular filly: fair handicapper: won at Catterick in September and Wolverhampton and Southwell in December: stays 7f: acts on all-weather, firm and good to soft going: blinkered nowadays: tried tongue tied: usually waited with. *A. J. McCabe*

DASHING DANE 7 b.h. Danehill (USA) 126 – Baldemara (FR) (Sanglamore (USA) 126) [2007 p8.6g 8.5m p12.2g Nov 12] lightly-raced maiden: no form since 2003. *Mrs Marjorie Fife* —

DASH OF GREY (IRE) 8 gr.g. Simply Great (FR) 122 – Donna Katrina (Kings Lake (USA) 133) [2007 83: p12g 12d p12g⁴ p13g² Dec 28] fairly useful winner at best: just fair handicapper in 2007, in frame at Lingfield last 2 starts: stays 2m: acts on polytrack and firm ground: blinkered: tried tongue tied. *Ruaidhri Tierney, Ireland* **75**

DASH TO THE FRONT 4 b.f. Diktat 126 – Millennium Dash 94 (Nashwan (USA) 135) [2007 88: 9.9g⁶ 10.9d* 12m⁶ 12s⁶ 12d⁶ Oct 27] useful-looking filly: useful performer, lightly raced: upped in trip and much improved when winning listed race at Warwick (by 1¾ lengths from Queen's Best) in June: creditable effort after only when sixth to Trick Or Treat in Princess Royal Stakes at Ascot fourth start: stays 1½m: acts on polytrack, soft and good to firm ground. *J. R. Fanshawe* **105**

DAUBERVAL (IRE) 2 b.g. (Mar 15) Noverre (USA) 125 – Just In Love (FR) (Highest Honor (FR) 124) [2007 6s 7d² 8g* 8m³ Sep 15] 15,000F, €36,000Y: neat gelding: second foal: half-brother to 1m winner Nassmaan (by Alhaarth): dam unraced sister to useful French middle-distance performer Justful: fairly useful form: won maiden at Goodwood (beat Trenchtown by head, pair clear) in August: good ¾-length third to Meeriss in listed race there final start: will stay at least 1¼m. *S. Kirk* **94**

DAVAYE 3 b.f. Bold Edge 123 – Last Impression 69 (Imp Society (USA)) [2007 69: 5m 6g⁴ 6d⁵ 7.1s 7.5m⁴ 7m 7g p6g⁶ Oct 23] leggy, quite good-topped filly: fair performer: below form after second start: best at 5f/6f: probably acts on any going. *K. R. Burke* **66 d**

DAVENPORT (IRE) 5 b.g. Bold Fact (USA) 116 – Semence d'Or (FR) (Kaldoun (FR) 122) [2007 90: f8g* 10.1s⁵ f8g6 10.5g 10g 10d⁵ 10g⁵ Nov 7] leggy, close-coupled gelding: fairly useful handicapper: won at Southwell in January: stays 1¼m: acts on all-weather and soft going: usually in cheekpieces: has been slowly away: held up. *B. R. Millman* **85**

DAVIDIA (IRE) 4 b.g. Barathea (IRE) 127 – Green Life 63 (Green Desert (USA) 127) [2007 66: p6g p8g p8.6g⁶ p8.6g p12.2g⁴ p8.6g² f8d³ Dec 20] well-made gelding: modest maiden: left S. Kirk after third start, Tom Dascombe (£700) after sixth: stays easy 1¼m: acts on polytrack and good to soft ground: tried blinkered. *D. W. Thompson* **60**

DAVID'S CAVALIER 3 b.g. Beat All (USA) 120 – Foxtrot Pie 77 (Shernazar 131) [2007 p9.5g⁶ p9.5g p9.5g 11g⁵ 10g² Apr 21] modest maiden: will stay 1½m. *R. Hollinshead* **62**

DAVIDS MARK 7 b.g. Polar Prince (IRE) 117 – Star of Flanders (Puissance 110) [2007 62: p5g p6g 5.1m⁵ p5.1g³ p6g p6g² p6g⁴ p5m⁴ Nov 11] modest handicapper: best at 5f/6f: acts on all-weather, firm and soft going: tried visored/in cheekpieces/tongue tied: held up. *J. R. Jenkins* **58**

DAWEYRR (USA) 3 b.c. Kingmambo (USA) 125 – With Flair (USA) (Broad Brush (USA)) [2007 51p: 8.1d⁵ 10.5m³ Aug 9] lengthy colt: fair maiden, lightly raced: should stay 1¼m: blinkered at 3 yrs, looking hard ride latter start: sent to UAE. *M. P. Tregoning* **76**

DAWN AT SEA 5 b.m. Slip Anchor 136 – Finger of Light 88 (Green Desert (USA) 127) [2007 p13.9g p12.2g Mar 24] sturdy mare: maiden: lightly raced nowadays and well held in 2007. *Mrs K. Waldron* —

DAWN LIGHT (IRE) 2 ch.f. (Feb 10) Spartacus (IRE) 107 – Erbaluce (Be My Guest (USA) 126) [2007 5.1m⁴ 5m 5v⁵ 6f² 6m 7m⁴ Aug 24] €23,000F, €26,000Y: smallish filly: fourth foal: half-sister to winner abroad by Priolo: dam Italian 5f to 1m winner: poor maiden: in frame in seller and claimer (wore cheekpieces): stays 7f: probably acts on any going. *Mrs A. Duffield* **44**

DAWN MYSTERY 3 gr.f. Daylami (IRE) 138 – Frustration 108 (Salse (USA) 128) [2007 –: p8g 8.2g p12g Dec 16] close-coupled filly: poor form: bred to be suited by 1¼m+. *Rae Guest* **48**

DAWN SKY 3 b.c. Fantastic Light (USA) 134 – Zacheta (Polish Precedent (USA) 131) [2007 75p: 11.8s² 12g² 10.1d² 11.5s* 12g⁵ Aug 18] good-bodied colt: fairly useful performer: won maiden at Lingfield in July: stays 1½m: raced only on good going or softer (acts on soft): in cheekpieces (ran creditably) final outing. *M. A. Jarvis* **85**

DAWN STORM (IRE) 2 ch.g. (Mar 20) City On A Hill (USA) 114 – Flames (Blushing Flame (USA) 109) [2007 p6g Jul 6] 14/1, last in maiden at Wolverhampton (gelded after, joined D. Shaw): bred to stay 1m. *K. R. Burke* –

DAWN WHISPER 2 ch.f. (Mar 25) Rock City 120 – Doodle Wood (Nomination 125) [2007 6g 6f 7s Sep 26] smallish filly: first foal: dam unraced: well beaten in maidens. *M. E. Sowersby* –

DAWN WIND 2 b.f. (Apr 18) Vettori (IRE) 119 – Topper (IRE) (Priolo (USA) 127) [2007 p7g p7g p7g p8g³ Sep 5] tall, narrow filly: third living foal: dam unraced half-sister to smart performer up to 1¼m Lady Upstage: modest maiden: third in nursery: will be suited by 1¼m: raced only on polytrack. *I. A. Wood* **58**

DAWSON CREEK (IRE) 3 ch.g. Titus Livius (FR) 115 – Particular Friend 88 (Cadeaux Genereux 131) [2007 52: p7g p8g⁴ 10f 7m p10g* p9.5g² p10m p10m⁴ p7g* Dec 30] fair performer: won minor event in October and handicap in December, both at Lingfield: effective from 7f to easy 1¼m: best form on polytrack: tried in cheekpieces. *B. Gubby* **67**

DAY BY DAY 3 ch.f. Kyllachy 129 – Dayville (USA) 86 (Dayjur (USA) 137) [2007 –P: 7g 7d⁶ p8.6g p7g² p7m 6m* p6g* 5m* 5m² 5g⁵ 6d Oct 19] strong, useful-looking filly: has scope: fairly useful performer: won handicaps at Yarmouth and Lingfield in August, and Sandown in September: stiff task in listed races last 2 starts, probably flattered first occasion: effective at 5f/6f: acts on polytrack and good to firm ground: blinkered nowadays. *B. J. Meehan* **94**

DAY FLIGHT 6 b.h. Sadler's Wells (USA) 132 – Bonash 110 (Rainbow Quest (USA) 134) [2007 122: 13.3g² 12g⁶ Jun 1] good-topped horse: had a short, quick action: very smart performer at his best: just smart form in 2007: ¾-length second to Peppertree Lane in listed race at Newbury on reappearance (odds on), then reportedly sustained injury sole subsequent outing: was effective at 1¼m to 13.4f: acted on good to firm going, raced mostly on good or softer (below best only outing on heavy): carried head high/flicked tail under pressure: to stand at French National Stud, fee €1,400. *J. H. M. Gosden* **112**

DAYLAMI DREAMS 3 gr.g. Daylami (IRE) 138 – Kite Mark 58 (Mark of Esteem (IRE) 137) [2007 69: p10g* p10g³ p11g² 11.6m⁵ 14.1g⁵ 13.1f⁴ Aug 24] workmanlike gelding: fair handicapper: won at Lingfield in January: stays 13f: acts on polytrack and firm going. *J. S. Moore* **77**

DAY OF DAYS (IRE) 3 b.g. Spectrum (IRE) 126 – Private Encore (IRE) 81 (Niniski (USA) 125) [2007 10f⁵ 10d 10m May 25] leggy, lengthy gelding: fair form in maidens: will be suited by 1½m: sold 800 gns in November. *M. H. Tompkins* **65**

DAY OF DESTINY (IRE) 2 gr.c. (Apr 29) Clodovil (IRE) 116 – El Corazon (IRE) (Mujadil (USA) 119) [2007 7g⁵ Nov 2] €20,000F, €60,000Y: fourth foal: half-brother to 3-y-o Putra Laju: dam, useful up to 1½m in Scandinavia, half-sister to smart 1½m performer Sunset Boulevard: 16/1, fifth to Foolin Myself in maiden at Newmarket, green under pressure: will stay 1m+: should do better. *B. W. Hills* **73 p**

DAY SHIFT (IRE) 2 gr.f. (May 11) Night Shift (USA) – Persian Mistress (IRE) (Persian Bold 123) [2007 5m⁵ 5.2g 5.2f⁶ Jul 30] 12,000Y: half-sister to 3 winners, including 3-y-o Persian Fox and fairly useful 7f winner Belly Dancer (by Danehill Dancer): dam unraced half-sister to high-class sprinter Hallgate: well held in maidens, all over 5f (should be suited by further). *Rae Guest*

DAYS OF THUNDER (IRE) 2 b.c. (Apr 17) Choisir (AUS) 126 – Grazina (Mark of Esteem (IRE) 137) [2007 5.5d 7.1g 5g Jul 28] no form. *G. F. Bridgwater* –

DAYTONA (IRE) 3 ch.g. Indian Ridge 123 – Kyka (USA) (Blushing John (USA) 120) [2007 p7g² p6g² p7g* 6f⁴ 8.5f⁵ 8.5f* 8.5f³ p8f³ 9f* 10f* 9f* Dec 30] €360,000Y: sixth foal: brother to 6f winner Indian Sabre and half-brother to 3 winners, including fairly useful Irish 1½m and 2m winner Always The Groom (by Darshaan): dam unraced half-sister to Poule d'Essai des Pouliches winner Madeleine's Dream: very smart performer: landed odds in maiden at Lingfield in March: sold from M. Johnston 56,000 gns later in month: progressed really well in US, winning allowance optional claimer at Del Mar in July, Grade 2 Oak Tree Derby at Santa Anita in October, Hollywood Derby (by ½ length from Medici Code) in November and Grade 2 San Gabriel Handicap at Santa Anita (beat Proudinsky ¾ length) in December: stays 1¼m: acts on polytrack and firm going: races prominently: tended to hang left second outing. *D. L. Hendricks, USA* **121**

DAY TO REMEMBER 6 gr.g. Daylami (IRE) 138 – Miss Universe (IRE) 99 (Warning 136) [2007 100: 12g Oct 27] small, quite attractive gelding: useful handicapper at 5 yrs: well held only outing in 2007: stays 1½m: acts on soft and good to firm going: tried visored: tongue tied. *J. J. Quinn* –

DAZED AND AMAZED 3 b.c. Averti (IRE) 117 – Amazed 58 (Clantime 101) [2007 **103**
96: p6g³ 6m⁵ 6m⁴ p5g* 5m 5g 5g 6m⁵ 5g 5m p6m 5.1m⁶ Oct 14] compact, well-made
colt: useful performer: won listed event at Kempton in June by length from Intrepid Jack:
in-and-out form after, not discredited in handicaps last 2 starts: stays easy 6f: acts on polytrack, good to firm and good to soft going: tongue tied final 2-y-o outing: tried blinkered
(ran poorly). *R. Hannon*

DAZZLER MAC 6 b.g. Komaite (USA) – Stilvella (Camden Town 125) [2007 60: f5g **53**
7m 5.9g 8s⁵ 8s 8d 6m⁴ 5g p6g⁵ Oct 30] sturdy gelding: modest handicapper: effective at
6f to 1m: acts on polytrack, firm and soft going: tried blinkered. *N. Bycroft*

DAZZLING COLOURS 2 b.c. (Jan 16) Oasis Dream 129 – Dazzle 116 (Gone West **67 p**
(USA)) [2007 6g⁶ Sep 7] 110,000Y: sixth foal: closely related to
fairly useful 2004 2-y-o winner Regina (by Green Desert) and half-brother to 3
winners, including fairly useful 1m winner Dubois (by Sadler's Wells): dam 2-y-o 5f/6f
winner (stayed 1m): 12/1, sixth to Striking Spirit in maiden at Haydock, rallying: will
benefit from experience. *J. Noseda*

DEA CAELESTIS (FR) 2 b.f. (Feb 9) Dream Well (FR) 127 – Gwydion (USA) 118 **70**
(Raise A Cup (USA)) [2007 6g³ 6d Jun 24] smallish, quite attractive filly: closely related
to 2 winners, notably very smart 7f winner (including at 2 yrs) and 2000 Guineas runner-
up Enrique (by Barathea), and half-sister to several winners, including smart French
sprinter Piperi (by Machiavellian): dam sprinter: third at Newmarket in May on debut:
softer ground, found little at Pontefract following month, and not seen after: may prove
best at 5f/6f. *H. R. A. Cecil*

DEADLINE (UAE) 3 ch.c. Machiavellian (USA) 123 – Time Changes (USA) (Danzig **76**
(USA)) [2007 79: p8g³ p8g³ 8f³ 10.1m² 8m 10m⁶ 10m 9m* 8d⁴ 9.8m³ 8m⁵ 8.5d⁶ 10g
Oct 6] workmanlike colt: fair performer: left M. Johnston after reappearance: won maid-
en at Newcastle in August: stays 1¼m: acts on polytrack, firm and good to soft going.
P. T. Midgley

DEAL FLIPPER 2 b.f. (Apr 15) Xaar 132 – Zibet 90 (Kris 135) [2007 p5g⁴ 5g p6g⁵ **69**
6m⁵ 6m³ p7g Aug 30] €22,000Y: workmanlike filly: third foal: half-sister to 4-y-o
Categorical and 3-y-o Fragrancy: dam, 7f winner, half-sister to smart miler Zoning: fair
maiden: third in nursery at Windsor: should stay 7f/1m: acts on polytrack and good to
firm going. *P. Winkworth*

DEAR MAURICE 3 b.c. Indian Ridge 123 – Shamaiel (IRE) 113 (Lycius (USA) 124) **72 p**
[2007 8.3d⁴ Aug 20] 240,000Y: second foal: dam, 1½m to 1¾m winner, half-sister to
high-class miler Nayyir (by Indian Ridge) and very smart performer up to 1¾m Highest:
33/1 and in need of experience, encouraging 6½ lengths fourth to King's Event in maiden
at Windsor, best work at finish having started slowly: will stay 1¼m+: sure to improve.
E. A. L. Dunlop

DEAR ONE (IRE) 3 b.f. Montjeu (IRE) 137 – Siamoise (Caerleon (USA) 132) [2007 **–**
54: p7.1g Jan 8] tall, close-coupled filly: modest form in 2-y-o maidens: seemed amiss
only outing in 2007. *P. A. Blockley*

DEAR WILL 2 b. or br.g. (Feb 1) Mark of Esteem (IRE) 137 – Sweet Wilhelmina 87 **52**
(Indian Ridge 123) [2007 p8g p8m Dec 8] fourth foal: half-brother to 6-y-o Sweet Pickle:
dam 7f (at 2 yrs)/1m winner: much better effort (modest form) in maidens when seventh
to Last of The Line at Kempton on debut. *J. R. Fanshawe*

DEBDENE BANK (IRE) 4 b.f. Pivotal 124 – Nedaarah 83 (Reference Point 139) **48**
[2007 6s⁴ Jul 28] fourth foal: half-sister to fairly useful 2001 2-y-o 7f winner Night
Passion (by Night Shift): dam, won around 1¼m (including in France), half-sister to
smart French performer up to 12.5f Agog: 20/1 and better for experience, 7 lengths fourth
to Raglan Copenhagen in maiden at Salisbury. *Mrs Mary Hambro*

DEBONNAIRE 2 b.f. (Mar 23) Anabaa (USA) 130 – Ultra Finesse (USA) 107 (Rahy **80**
(USA) 115) [2007 6f⁶ 7g⁵ p7m* Nov 1] 30,000Y: well-made filly: eighth foal: closely
related to useful 6f (at 2 yrs)/7f winner Proceed With Care (by Danehill), later successful
in US, and half-sister to 2 winners, including 6f (at 2 yrs) to 1¼m winner Dramatic Quest
(by Zafonic): dam, French 8.5f and 1¼m winner who stayed 12.5f, half-sister to Suave
Dancer: fairly useful form: progressive in maidens, and won by short head from Anne of
Kiev at Lingfield: will stay 1m+. *M. Johnston*

DEBORD (FR) 4 ch.g. Sendawar (IRE) 129 – Partie de Dames (USA) (Bering 136) **67 §**
[2007 70: 10.1d 14.1m² 14d 14.1d 14.1d Oct 3] strong gelding: fair handicapper: stays
1¾m: acts on soft and good to firm going: blinkered on reappearance: unreliable. *Jamie
Poulton*

DECADO (IRE) 4 b.c. Danehill Dancer (IRE) 117 – Pirie (USA) (Green Dancer (USA) **112**
132) [2007 113: 8m³ 8m³ 9v* 8g⁶ 10v³ 8m⁶ 8d 8f⁶ Dec 26] quite attractive colt: smart
performer: won 4-runner Keeneland International Stakes at the Curragh in July by 2
lengths from Cougar Bay: below form after, including when sixth to Ramonti in Sussex
Stakes at Goodwood fourth outing: left K. Prendergast in Ireland before final outing:
stays 9f, possibly not 1¼m: acts on heavy and good to firm going. *P. Gallagher, USA*

DECCAN EXPRESS (IRE) 3 ch.g. Grand Lodge (USA) 125 – Harda Arda (USA) 66 **75**
(Nureyev (USA) 131) [2007 68: 10d 9m 10.5g* 11d⁶ 10s³ 12v⁴ 10m 10v 9.5g p12.2g⁴
Nov 19] rather leggy, quite attractive gelding: fair handicapper: won at Down Royal in
June: good fourth at Wolverhampton final start: stays easy 1½m: acts on polytrack and
soft going, probably on good to firm: patiently ridden. *Seamus Fahey, Ireland*

DECENT PROPOSAL 3 b.f. Montjeu (IRE) 137 – Markova's Dance 64 (Mark of **51**
Esteem (IRE) 137) [2007 –p: 10.1s 8m 14.1m⁶ 12.1s Jun 21] big, lengthy filly: modest
maiden: stays 1¾m: acts on good to firm ground. *T. D. Easterby*

DECHIPER (IRE) 5 b. or br.g. Almutawakel 126 – Safiya (USA) (Riverman (USA) **72**
131) [2007 58: f8g 10.1m⁴ 8.3m f8g 10.1m⁴ 10.1d* 10.1g⁵ 10.1m* 10.1m² 8g³ 10.1d⁶
Oct 15] fair handicapper: won at Newcastle in July (apprentices) and August: stays 1¼m:
acts on soft and good to firm going: tried in cheekpieces. *R. Johnson*

DECIDER (USA) 4 ch.g. High Yield (USA) 121 – Nikita Moon (USA) (Secret Hello **64**
(USA)) [2007 68: 5.1d 5.7m p5.1g 5.3d p6g p5g⁶ 5.1d⁶ 5.1m 5.1f Aug 27] rangy gelding:
modest handicapper: best at 5f/6f: acts on all-weather and firm going: gelded after final
start. *J. M. Bradley*

DECISION DAY 3 b.f. Groom Dancer (USA) 128 – Indubitable 87 (Sharpo 132) [2007 **67**
–: 7d⁶ 7m 17.2g Oct 24] lightly-raced maiden, easily best effort on reappearance: pulled
up final outing: bred to be suited by 1½m+. *J. A. Geake*

DECKGUARD 2 ch.c. (Feb 27) Bertolini (USA) 125 – Aegean Blue (Warning 136) **65**
[2007 6s 6m⁶ 6m p6g⁵ p7g p7g² p7.1g⁵ Oct 25] strong colt: has a round action: fair
maiden: second in claimer: will prove best up to 7f: acts on polytrack: tried in cheekpieces: sold 9,000 gns, sent to Denmark. *J. S. Moore*

DECLARATION OF WAR (IRE) 2 b.c. (Feb 9) Okawango (USA) 115 – Date Mate **108**
(USA) (Thorn Dance (USA) 107) [2007 6g* 6g* 6m 7m² 7g² 8g⁶ Oct 27] 10,000F,
25,000Y: rather leggy, medium-sized, attractive colt: fourth foal: half-brother to 6f to
1¼m winner (including 1m at 2 yrs) Freak Occurance (by Stravinsky): dam, US maiden,
half-sister to very smart performer up to 1¾m Lazaz: useful performer: won minor event
at Newmarket in May and listed race at Epsom in June: better form when runner-up in
Superlative Stakes at Newmarket (beaten neck by Hatta Fort) and Prix Jean-Luc
Lagardere at Longchamp (2½ lengths behind Rio de La Plata): possibly found race
coming too soon when sixth of 12 to Ibn Khaldun in Racing Post Trophy at Doncaster
final start: should stay 1m: raced only on good/good to firm ground. *P. W. Chapple-Hyam*

DEDICATE 2 b.f. (Feb 15) Beat Hollow 126 – Total Devotion 78 (Desert Prince (IRE) **66 p**
130) [2007 8g Oct 26] good-topped filly: first foal: dam, 1¼m winner, out of useful sister
to Derby winner Commander In Chief: 33/1 and burly, eighth to Cruel Sea in maiden at
Doncaster: will do better, especially at 1¼m/1½m. *R. Charlton*

DEDO (IRE) 2 b.c. (Mar 4) Modigliani (USA) 106 – Scant (FR) (Septieme Ciel (USA) **91**
123) [2007 7v² 8.5d³ 6s* 6s* 6g 6g⁶ 6g 7m⁴ Nov 4] €12,000F, 28,000Y: close-coupled
colt: first foal: dam, French maiden, half-sister to US Grade 2 7f winner Star Touch: fairly
useful performer: won maiden at Naas in July and nursery at Cork in August: ran well
next 2 starts, seventh of 20 to Dark Angel in sales race at York (did best of those towards
stand side) and sixth to Norman Invader in Round Tower Stakes at the Curragh: best at 6f/
7f: acts on soft going. *Kevin Prendergast, Ireland*

DEE BURGH 3 b.f. Zaha (CAN) 106 – Glensara (Petoski 135) [2007 56: 8d⁴ Jun 19] **–**
strong, close-coupled filly: modest maiden in 2006: well below form in seller sole 3-y-o
start: should be suited by 7f/1m. *J. Pearce*

DEE CEE ELLE 3 b.f. Groom Dancer (USA) 128 – Missouri 86 (Charnwood Forest **75**
(IRE) 125) [2007 60p: 12.1m² 11g* f11g* 14.1g⁴ 12.1g* p12g⁴ 12s 11.6m 12m⁶ 12.1m⁶
Aug 26] close-coupled filly: fair handicapper: won at Southwell (2) in April and Beverley
in May: stays 1¾m: acts on all-weather and good to firm ground: sold 10,000 gns, joined
D. Burchell. *M. Johnston*

DEE JAY WELLS 3 b.g. Ishiguru (USA) 114 – Stravaig (IRE) (Sadler's Wells (USA) **71**
132) [2007 72: 9m 9.9m⁴ 9g³ 10s⁵ 8.1d 8.5s* 8m 8m⁵ Aug 8] well-made gelding: fair

handicapper: left R. Fahey prior to winning apprentice event at Beverley in July: seems to stay 1¼m: acts on firm and soft going: tried in blinkers/visor/tongue tie. *B. Ellison*

DEEP COVER (IRE) 3 ch.c. Boundary (USA) 117 – Chibi (USA) (Dynaformer – (USA)) [2007 53: p8g p10g Mar 26] lightly-raced maiden: well held in handicaps in 2007. *R. M. Flower* —

DEEPER IN DEBT 9 ch.g. Piccolo 121 – Harold's Girl (FR) (Northfields (USA)) [2007 77, a83: 8.3m Jun 11] deep-girthed gelding: fairly useful handicapper at 8 yrs: well below form only start in 2007: stays 1¼m, races mainly around 1m: acts on all-weather, firm and soft going: tried blinkered/tongue tied earlier in career: ridden prominently. *J. Akehurst* —

DEE VALLEY BOY (IRE) 3 b.g. Val Royal (FR) 127 – Canadian Girl (IRE) 82 (Rainbows For Life (CAN)) [2007 53: p9.5g 11g⁶ 14.1m 11.1g Jun 13] poor maiden: stays 11f: visored/blinkered last 3 starts. *J. D. Bethell* **42**

DEFIES LOGIC 2 ch.g. (Mar 19) Domedriver (IRE) 128 – Khandahar (Zamindar (USA) 116) [2007 7m⁵ 8f Sep 27] workmanlike gelding: poor form in maidens (gelded after): bred to stay 1m. *J. G. Given* **48**

DEFI (IRE) 5 b.g. Rainbow Quest (USA) 134 – Danse Classique (IRE) 94 (Night Shift (USA)) [2007 81: p8.6g⁶ p8.6g⁵ p9.5g 8.3f² 8.3g 9.2d 9.2g 8g* p8.6g² p8.6d⁴ Dec 6] good-bodied gelding: has a quick, unimpressive action: fair performer: won claimer at Musselburgh in November: stays 8.3f: acts on polytrack and firm going: usually wears cheekpieces/blinkers: tried tongue tied: often races prominently. *I. Semple* **76 a68**

DEFINITE GUEST (IRE) 9 gr.g. Definite Article 121 – Nicea (IRE) 90 (Dominion 123) [2007 p8g p8.6g 8f Apr 20] leggy gelding: one-time fairly useful handicapper: little form in 2007: tried blinkered. *R. A. Fahey* —

DEFNIKOV 2 gr.g. (Mar 29) Baryshnikov (AUS) – By Definition (IRE) 54 (Definite Article 121) [2007 p5g 6.1d 5.7d Oct 1] leggy gelding: well beaten in maidens (left Miss J. Davis after debut). *A. B. Haynes* —

DEIMNE (IRE) 4 b. or br.f. Mull of Kintyre (USA) 114 – Lake Poopo (IRE) 79 (Persian Heights 129) [2007 –: p16g p12g Dec 16] maiden on Flat and over hurdles: poor form at Lingfield and Kempton in 2007: seems to stay 2m: tried blinkered. *John Joseph Murphy, Ireland* **46**

DEIRA DUBAI 2 b.f. (Jan 23) Green Desert (USA) 127 – Aspen Leaves (USA) 92 (Woodman (USA) 126) [2007 7m⁶ 7f³ 6f³ p7g² Oct 24] sturdy, lengthy filly: fifth foal: half-sister to useful Irish 1¼m winner Agenda (by Sadler's Wells): dam, Irish 7f winner, sister to Breeders' Cup Juvenile/Preakness Stakes winner Timber Country out of outstanding broodmare Fall Aspen: fair maiden: placed all starts after debut, second to Elysee Palace at Lingfield final one: likely to stay 1m: sometimes looks awkward. *B. W. Hills* **75**

DE LA GRANDERA (USA) 3 b. or br.c. Fusaichi Pegasus (USA) 130 – Torros Straits (USA) 82 (Boundary (USA) 117) [2007 49: 10g³ 9g² 8m 8.5d³ 8m* 8m⁴ p10.7g⁴ Sep 28] well-made colt: second foal: brother to winner in USA: dam, ran twice, out of half-sister to high-class American mare Heavenly Prize (best at 1¼m): fairly useful performer: won maiden at Bellewstown in August: below form in Britannia Handicap at Royal Ascot third outing: stays 1¼m: acts on good to firm going: in cheekpieces last 3 starts: sold 23,000 gns, sent to UAE. *D. Wachman, Ireland* **87**

DELLINI (IRE) 2 b.f. (Mar 26) Green Desert (USA) 127 – Belle Genius (USA) 111 (Beau Genius (CAN)) [2007 6d 6.1m¹⁸ 6.5m 6d Sep 22] useful-looking filly: fifth foal: sister to useful 6f/7f winner Birjand, closely related to Irish 8.7f winner Fereeji (by Cape Cross) and half-sister to 2 winners, including fairly useful 1m winner Bin Rahy (by Rahy) who stays 1¼m: dam won Moyglare Stud Stakes: fairly useful performer: won minor event at Chester in August, possibly flattered by run of race: well held after in sales event and Firth of Clyde Stakes at Ayr (visored): will stay 7f: acts on good to firm going. *M. R. Channon* **81**

DEL MAR SUNSET 8 b.g. Unfuwain (USA) 131 – City of Angels (Woodman (USA) 126) [2007 82, a88: 10m⁴ 10m* 10g 12m⁶ 10f 10.9m 10m³ 10m⁴ p12g² p9.5g² Nov 10] tall, rather leggy gelding: fairly useful handicapper: won at Newmarket in May: stays easy 1½m: acts on all-weather and firm going: blinkered (well held) once: has won in cheekpieces: usually held up nowadays. *W. J. Haggas* **89**

DELORAIN (IRE) 4 b.g. Kalanisi (IRE) 132 – Lady Nasrana (FR) (Al Nasr (FR) 126) [2007 54: 16m⁶ May 22] unfurnished gelding: modest maiden: stays 2m: acts on good to firm and good to soft ground: visored/blinkered nowadays. *N. B. King* **53**

DELTA DIVA (USA) 2 b.f. (Mar 4) Victory Gallop (CAN) 130 – Tjinouska (USA) 86 **78 p** (Cozzene (USA)) [2007 p7g* Aug 8] unfurnished filly: second foal: dam, 1½m winner, half-sister to useful German stayer Ocean Sea: 8/1, won maiden at Kempton by head from Bailey: will stay 1¼m/1½m: should progress. *P. F. I. Cole*

DELTA SHUTTLE (IRE) 3 b.g. Bluebird (USA) 125 – Ibtihal (IRE) 75 (Hamas **65 d** (IRE) 125§) [2007 68: 7.5m 8.2m⁵ 9g⁶ 11.8s² 11.1f⁵ 12.3d³ 11.9s 11.8g Oct 16] strong, good-bodied gelding: fair maiden: well below form last 4 starts: stays 1½m: acts on soft going: tried visored/in cheekpieces: inconsistent: sold 4,000 gns. *K. R. Burke*

DEMATRAF (IRE) 5 gr.m. Atraf 116 – Demolition Jo 89 (Petong 126) [2007 50: 5m² **69** 5m* 6d² 5.5s* 5.1g 5.1f⁴ 6.1m* 5.7f Sep 10] compact mare: fair performer: won claimer at Musselburgh (left Peter Grayson) in June and handicaps at Warwick in July and Chepstow in September: best at 5f/6f: acts on all-weather, firm and soft ground. *P. D. Evans*

DEMI SEC 4 ch.f. Bahamian Bounty 116 – Veuve (Tirol 127) [2007 –: p8g 6g 6s 7.6s **–** Aug 18] little form: tried blinkered. *Dr J. D. Scargill*

DEMISEMIQUAVER 3 b.f. Singspiel (IRE) 133 – Miss d'Ouilly (FR) (Bikala 134) **82** [2007 10.5g 10m² 12m⁴ 10.3m² 10.2g³ p9.5g² p10g² p10g* p8m* Dec 10] tall, useful-looking filly: half-sister to several winners, including useful French 10.5f winner Miss Caerleona (by Caerleon), later Grade 3 9f winner in USA: dam, French 9f winner, half-sister to Prix Jacques le Marois winner Miss Satamixa: fairly useful performer: won at Lingfield in November (maiden) and December (handicap): stays 1¼m: acts on polytrack and good to firm going: tried visored, blinkered last 2 starts. *J. Noseda*

DEMOLITION 3 ch.g. Starborough 126 – Movie Star (IRE) (Barathea (IRE) 127) **83** [2007 –: p10g 7g² 10g² 10g³ 9.9m* 10m⁶ 11d⁵ 8m⁶ Oct 8] lengthy gelding: fairly useful performer: won maiden at Salisbury in August: stays 1¼m: acts on good to firm going: sold 3,000 gns. *C. A. Cyzer*

DEMOLITION MOLLY 6 b.m. Rudimentary (USA) 118 – Persian Fortune 53 **–** (Forzando 122) [2007 5g Apr 28] compact mare: no longer of any account. *R. F. Marvin*

DEMURE PRINCESS 2 b.f. (Mar 30) Tamure (IRE) 125 – Princess Penny 46§ **56** (King's Signet (USA) 110) [2007 5m³ 6g⁴ 6s² 7d⁵ p6g 6.1m⁴ 6g Aug 24] strong filly: third foal: half-sister to 6f winners River Prince (3-y-o) and Champagner Queen (in Germany, by Tomba): dam, disqualified 2-y-o 6f seller winner, temperamental: modest maiden: best form at 6f: acts on soft and good to firm going. *W. G. M. Turner*

DENBERA DANCER (USA) 3 b.c. Danehill (USA) 126 – Monevassia (USA) (Mr **78** Prospector (USA)) [2007 60p: 10m⁴ 6.9m⁴ Jul 29] medium-sized, good-bodied colt: has round action: easily best effort in 3 maidens when fourth to Urban Spirit at Newmarket on reappearance: seems to stay 1¼m, should prove at least as effective over shorter (races freely). *M. Johnston*

DENDOR 3 b.g. Warningford 119 – Dolphin Dancer 45 (Dolphin Street (FR) 125) [2007 **63 p** 7m 7m⁵ 7m 6d³ 6d² 6s* Oct 4] big, workmanlike gelding: first foal: dam lightly-raced maiden: modest form: won handicap at Ayr in October by 2 lengths from Strabinios King, always to fore: should be as effective at 5f as 6f: acts on soft going: lightly raced, and open to further improvement. *D. W. Barker*

DENEUVE 4 ch.f. Tomba 119 – Princess Sadie 86 (Shavian 125) [2007 54: p8g⁵ p8g* **56** p8.6g Feb 21] modest performer: won minor event at Kempton in January: stays easy 1m: acts on polytrack and soft ground: has worn cheekpieces/tongue tie, blinkered last 2 starts. *M. G. Quinlan*

DEN'S BOY 2 b.c. (Feb 6) Josr Algarhoud (IRE) 118 – Den's-Joy 85 (Archway (IRE) **–** 115) [2007 6m Jul 30] compact colt: last in maiden at Windsor: bred to stay 1m. *J. R. Boyle*

DEN'S GIFT (IRE) 3 gr. or ro.g. City On A Hill (USA) 114 – Romanylei (IRE) 106 **88** (Blues Traveller (IRE) 119) [2007 74: p7g* p8g* Dec 1] sturdy gelding: second foal: dam 6f winner (including at 2 yrs): fairly useful performer, lightly raced: gelded and off 13 months, improved when winning maiden at Lingfield in November and handicap at Kempton in December: stays 1m: acts on polytrack and good to firm ground. *C. G. Cox*

DENTON HAWK 3 b.g. Mujahid (USA) 125 – Lamasat (USA) (Silver Hawk (USA) **56 d** 123) [2007 58: f7g² f8g p7.1g⁵ 8.3m³ 7m 8g 7.9f⁶ Aug 6] workmanlike gelding: modest maiden at best: stays 7f: acts on all-weather and firm going: tried in headgear. *M. Dods*

DEO VALENTE (IRE) 2 b.c. (Jan 29) Dubai Destination (USA) 127 – Pack Ice **88** (USA) (Wekiva Springs (USA) 123) [2007 7m 7m³ Oct 5] 60,000F, 48,000Y: leggy colt: first foal: dam, French maiden, from good family of Theatrical: much better

effort in maidens at Newmarket when third to Fireside, fairly useful form: will stay 1m.
B. J. Meehan

DE PORT HEIGHTS (IRE) 3 bl.g. Redback 116 – Raise-A-Secret (IRE) (Classic
Secret (USA) 91) [2007 8.3d p7g Oct 29] good-topped gelding: tailed off in maidens.
M. Madgwick —

DERRICKS DOTTY 3 br.g. Beat All (USA) 120 – Pass The Rose (IRE) (Thatching
131) [2007 8m⁴ p8.6g⁴ p8.6g⁵ 6.9m p7.1g Oct 21] compact gelding: maiden: easily best
effort when fifth at Wolverhampton: stays 8.6f: acts on polytrack. *N. J. Vaughan* **66 ?**

DESCARGO 3 ch.f. Delta Dancer – Secret Miss 55 (Beveled (USA)) [2007 49: p5.1g²
p6g 5.1g Apr 21] modest maiden: left C. Cox after second start: bred to be suited by 7f+:
acts on polytrack. *W. G. M. Turner* **53**

DESCARTES 5 b.g. Dubai Millennium 140 – Gold's Dance (FR) (Goldneyev (USA)
114) [2007 98: a10f³ 10s Sep 20] tall gelding: useful performer, lightly raced: creditable
2 lengths third to Remaadd in handicap at Nad Al Sheba on reappearance: well held in
similar event at Ayr over 7 months later: stays 1½m: raced on polytrack/dirt and soft/
heavy going: races freely: left Godolphin, then gelded. *Saeed bin Suroor* **98**

DESERT CHIEF 5 b.h. Green Desert (USA) 127 – Oriental Fashion (IRE) 110 (Marju
(IRE) 127) [2007 93: 8g³ 8m 7m Sep 15] smallish, good-bodied horse: fluent mover:
useful performer, lightly raced: creditable effort in 2007 only when 1¾ lengths third to
Sir Gerard in handicap at Nad Al Sheba: said to have finished lame at Goodwood final
start: stays 1m: yet to race on extremes of going: has left Godolphin. *Saeed bin Suroor* **96**

DESERT CHILL (USA) 2 b.f. (Feb 27) Red Ransom (USA) – Storm Song (USA)
123 (Summer Squall (USA)) [2007 7d³ 8g² Oct 26] tall, unfurnished filly: seventh foal:
half-sister to winners in US by Gone West and Coronado's Quest: dam won Breeders'
Cup Juvenile Fillies: placed in above-average maidens, third to Laughter at Leicester and
second to Cruel Sea at Doncaster: not sure to stay much beyond 1m. *Saeed bin Suroor* **83**

DESERT CLOVER (USA) 2 b. or br.c. (May 2) Mutakddim (USA) 112 – Booly
(USA) (Apalachee (USA) 137) [2007 p7.1g* Nov 22] half-brother to winners in USA by
Sheikh Albadou and Broad Brush: dam US Grade 3 2-y-o 8.5f winner: well-backed 5/4
favourite, won maiden at Wolverhampton by 1½ lengths from Molly Ann, making all
(edged right closing stages): will probably stay 1m. *P. F. I. Cole* **74**

DESERT COMMANDER (IRE) 5 b.g. Green Desert (USA) 127 – Meadow Pipit
(CAN) 113 (Meadowlake (USA)) [2007 101: 5m 6g 6m* 6.3s 5d 6m 6m p7.1g Oct 15]
robust gelding, type to carry condition: fairly useful handicapper: won at Ripon in June:
below form after: effective at 5f/6f: acts on good to firm and good to soft going: blinker-
ed/in cheekpieces last 6 outings: tried tongue tied: unreliable: sold 8,000 gns. *K. A. Ryan* **92 §**

DESERT D'ARGENT (IRE) 4 ch.f. Desert Story (IRE) 115 – Petite-D-Argent 91
(Noalto 120) [2007 p11g² 12s Oct 4] smallish, useful-looking filly: fairly useful performer: reportedly suffered fractured pedal bone and missed 2006: easily better effort in 2007
when good ¾-length second to Pivotal Answer in handicap at Kempton: should stay
1½m: raced on polytrack and going softer than good. *H. Morrison* **90**

DESERT DEW (IRE) 3 ch.c. Indian Ridge 123 – Blue Water (USA) 104 (Bering 136)
[2007 95: 8.1g* 10.3m² 10g³ Jun 21] sturdy colt: has a quick action: smart performer:
much improved in 2007, winning handicap at Sandown in April by 3 lengths from
Aegean Prince: good efforts after in Dee Stakes at Chester (2 lengths second to Admiralofthefleet, edging left) and listed Hampton Court Stakes at Royal Ascot (½-length third
to Zaham): effective at 1m/1¼m: acts on good to firm and good to soft going (below form
on soft): has joined Godolphin. *B. W. Hills* **113**

DESERT DREAMER (IRE) 6 b.g. Green Desert (USA) 127 – Follow That Dream
90 (Darshaan 133) [2007 90: p7g⁶ 6f 8.1g⁴ 8d f6g² 8.1g⁵ 6m 7d⁴ 7g* p7g* p6g² p7g⁶ 7.2s
p5.1g p7g⁶ p6g p7g⁵ p6g⁵ p7m* Dec 10] smallish, good-topped gelding: fairly useful
performer: won handicap at Brighton and claimer at Kempton (left P. Chamings), both
in July, and claimer at Lingfield in December: best at 6f/7f: acts on all-weather, firm
and good to soft ground: often starts slowly: held up: tried blinkered (below form).
G. A. Butler **88**

DESERT DUST 4 b.g. Vettori (IRE) 119 – Dust 61 (Green Desert (USA) 127) [2007
50, a62: f5g⁴ p5.1g³ p5.1g 5g Jul 8] modest performer: effective at 5f/6f: acts on all-
weather, best turf effort on good going: often wears headgear. *R. M. H. Cowell* — a54

DESERTED DANE (USA) 3 b.c. Elusive Quality (USA) – Desertion (IRE) 92
(Danehill (USA) 126) [2007 97p: a5f 7.5g 5f 5g⁴ 5g 5d* 6s⁴ 5m⁶ 5m⁶ 5m⁶ Sep 18] small, **89**

strong colt: fairly useful handicapper: won at Carlisle in June: best at 5f: acts on good to firm and good to soft ground, probably on dirt: none too consistent. *G. A. Swinbank*

DESERTER (IRE) 3 b.f. Desert Style (IRE) 121 – Tianella (GER) 74 (Acatenango (GER) 127) [2007 p8g⁴ 9.5g p10g p8g⁴ Feb 17] €17,000F, €11,000Y: first foal: dam maiden: best effort when fourth to Serpentaria in maiden at Lingfield on debut: should have stayed 1¼m: had looked less than keen: dead. *J. A. Osborne* **60**

DESERT HAWK 6 b.g. Cape Cross (IRE) 129 – Milling (IRE) 89 (In The Wings 128) [2007 59: p12.2g³ p9.5g* p9.5g p9.5g p10g p9.5g³ p9.5g p12.2g 10m⁵ 10m⁵ 10.1d* 11s³ 11.5d³ 10.1g⁴ 10.1d³ 10f p9.5g³ 10.1d* 11.1s⁴ 10.9g⁵ p9.5g p12.2g⁵ 12g³ p12.2g² Nov 24] stocky gelding: fair handicapper: won at Wolverhampton in January and apprentice events at Yarmouth in June and August: stays 1½m: acts on polytrack, firm and soft going: sometimes blinkered/visored: has refused to enter stall/looked wayward. *W. M. Brisbourne* **65**

DESERT HUNTER (IRE) 4 b.g. Desert Story (IRE) 115 – She-Wolff (IRE) 104 (Pips Pride 117) [2007 59: 7m³ 6m⁴ p7g⁴ 7m 6.9f 7g 6.9g 5m⁴ Sep 11] good-topped gelding: modest handicapper: stays 7f: acts on polytrack, good to firm and good to soft going: has raced freely. *Micky Hammond* **58**

DESERT ISLAND MISS 4 b.f. Medicean 128 – Miss Castaway (Selkirk (USA) 129) [2007 69: 8d⁴ p8g³ 10.1d p8g* 8.3g⁶ Oct 8] sturdy filly: fair handicapper: won at Kempton in September: stays 1m (pulled hard at 1¼m): acts on polytrack, unraced on extremes of going on turf: tried visored/in cheekpieces: sold 8,500 gns. *W. R. Swinburn* **76**

DESERT LARK 2 ch.c. (Mar 28) Sakhee (USA) 136 – Oyster Catcher (IRE) 105 (Bluebird (USA) 125) [2007 6m⁶ 8m Sep 8] 30,000Y: lengthy colt: fifth foal: half-brother to useful 6f winner Alderney Race (by Seeking The Gold): dam, Irish 6f winner, half-sister to Moyglare Stud Stakes winner Sequoyah (dam of 2-y-o Henrythenavigator): no show in maidens at Redcar (3/1) and Thirsk. *G. A. Swinbank* **–**

DESERT LEADER (IRE) 6 b.g. Green Desert (USA) 127 – Za Aamah (USA) (Mr Prospector (USA)) [2007 –, a84: p12.2g* p9.5g p12.2g⁴ p9.5g⁴ p8.6g p12.2g p11g p12.2g⁴ p12.2g Oct 19] good sort: fairly useful handicapper on all-weather, unraced on turf since 2005: won at Wolverhampton in January: left W. M. Brisbourne after fourth start: stays 1½m: acts on all-weather: has been slowly away. *R. W. Price* **– a81**

DESERT LIFE (IRE) 2 b.g. (Mar 29) Desert Style (IRE) 121 – Vie Privee (Hernando (FR) 127) [2007 7d 8.1f p6g⁴ p6g⁵ p7.1g⁶ p6m³ p6d⁴ p7.1g⁶ Dec 29] modest maiden: seems to stay 1m: acts on polytrack and firm going: often wears blinkers/cheekpieces. *R. A. Harris* **60**

DESERT LIGHT (IRE) 6 b.g. Desert Sun 120 – Nacote (IRE) (Mtoto 134) [2007 –, a71: p6g⁶ p6g⁴ p6g⁶ p6g p6g³ p6g³ p6g³ p6g* p6g⁴ p6g⁴ 6g p6g* p6g p5g⁵ p6g⁵ p6g⁵ p6g⁴ Dec 19] sturdy gelding: fair performer: won seller in March and amateur handicap in April, both at Wolverhampton: stays 7f: acts on all-weather, good to firm and good to soft ground: usually visored: tends to hang: held up. *D. Shaw* **66**

DESERT LIGHTNING (IRE) 5 ch.g. Desert Prince (IRE) 130 – Saibhreas (IRE) 83 (Last Tycoon 131) [2007 64: 9.1g⁵ 12m⁶ 9.1g³ 10.1m³ 10.2s⁵ 10f Aug 12] big gelding: modest performer: left K. R. Burke after fourth outing: stays easy 1¼m (seemingly not 1½m): acts on polytrack, soft and good to firm ground: tried visored/in cheekpieces/tongue tied: hangs right. *I. W. McInnes* **60**

DESERT LORD 7 b.g. Green Desert (USA) 127 – Red Carnival (USA) 109 (Mr Prospector (USA)) [2007 124: 5d³ 5m⁶ 5g 5g² 5.2m⁵ 5g³ p6m³ 6g Dec 9] **123**

While seven-year-old Desert Lord's second season for Hambleton trainer Kevin Ryan was less rewarding than his first, it is arguable that the excessive generosity of the weight-for-age scale denied him a second Group 1 success, in the Nunthorpe Stakes at York. As The Tatling and Bahamian Pirate have made an impact at an even more venerable age in recent years in the Nunthorpe it is not beyond the realms of possibility that Desert Lord will add further major successes to his name, though he is evidently dependent on very precise optimum conditions, to whit a pure test of speed over a bare five furlongs.

Desert Lord won valuable handicaps at Musselburgh and Epsom before he moved up to pattern company at six, but he had to make his way solely in listed or pattern company in 2007. His first three runs were well short of what he had shown when winning the Prix de l'Abbaye at Longchamp. He was comfortably held by Tax Free and Dandy Man in a listed event at Naas on good to soft ground, then shaped as if still running himself into form when sixth, sent off at 25/1, to Miss Andretti in the King's Stand at Royal Ascot. Neither track in any case afforded him the ideal test, but Goodwood for the King George Stakes, in which he had finished second in 2006, ought to have done and managing only eleventh, even allowing for his Group 1 penalty, was a disappointing effort.

The Nunthorpe was a much stronger affair, though, as a Group 1 race, there were no penalties, or at least no conventional penalties. Desert Lord successfully coped with the concession of 5 lb to the one three-year-old filly, 3 lb to the two older mares and 2 lb to the two three-year-old colts, and he beat the nine others who carried the same weight, but giving 24 lb to the two-year-old Kingsgate Native proved beyond him. Desert Lord went down by a length and three quarters, but, in beating the King's Stand runner-up Dandy Man into third, Desert Lord produced a performance bettered at five furlongs in Europe in 2007 only by Miss Andretti and Benbaun. Desert Lord's York display fostered renewed optimism for his prospects of a repeat win in the Prix de l'Abbaye and he was reported likely to head straight to Longchamp after York. However, connections decided instead to let him take in a seemingly straightforward opportunity in the Group 3 World Trophy at Newbury. Desert Lord was weak in the market, and showed none of his customary speed, harried by the nippy Bertoliver for the lead and eventually finishing only fifth to the progressive Rowe Park, running nearly a stone below his best.

Desert Lord's Abbaye performance was better, though easier ground wasn't in his favour and he was below his very best in finishing third to Benbaun and Kingsgate Native, the latter receiving 18 lb this time. Desert Lord ran twice more, both times over six furlongs. He went down by three quarters of a length to Maltese Falcon in the listed Golden Rose Stakes at Lingfield in November, then finished ninth in the Hong Kong Sprint in early-December. Even Lingfield's very easy six placed too much emphasis on stamina for Desert Lord, while being ridden with more restraint than usual turned out to be of no obvious benefit in top company at Sha Tin.

Desert Lord (b.g. 2000)	Green Desert (USA) (b 1983)	Danzig (b 1977)	Northern Dancer
			Pas de Nom
		Foreign Courier (b 1979)	Sir Ivor
			Courtly Dee
	Red Carnival (USA) (b 1992)	Mr Prospector (b 1970)	Raise A Native
			Gold Digger
		Seaside Attraction (b 1987)	Seattle Slew
			Kamar

Desert Lord's very smart Sadler's Wells half-brother Carnival Dancer, now at stud, had to wait until October for his initial winner but ended the campaign with three winners from just seven runners, at distances from seven furlongs to a mile and a quarter. The lengthy, good-topped Desert Lord, who is a gelding, acts on polytrack, firm and good to soft going. He wears blinkers nowadays and has been tried in cheekpieces. He has also worn bandages on his fore joints. *K. A. Ryan*

DESERT LOVER (IRE) 5 b.g. Desert Prince (IRE) 130 – Crystal Flute (Lycius (USA) 124) [2007 64, a69: p7g p8.6g⁵ p7.1g p8.6g² p8.6g² f7g* f8g³ f7g⁴ p7.1g f8g p7g p8.6g p6g⁶ p8.6g⁵ p8.6g⁴ f7d³ f7d⁵ p7.1d⁴ Dec 27] close-coupled gelding: modest handicapper: won at Southwell in March: probably best at 7f/1m: acts on all-weather and good to soft ground: has worn cheekpieces/visor/tongue tie. *R. J. Price* **58**

DESERT MASTER 4 b.g. Green Desert (USA) 127 – Khambani (IRE) 80 (Royal Academy (USA) 130) [2007 p8.6g⁵ p7g⁴ p6g³ p6g* p5.1g³ 5f 5.2g⁴ 6s⁴ p6g* Sep 27] fairly useful on all-weather, fair on turf: won maiden in February and handicap in September, both at Wolverhampton: likely to prove best at short of 7f: acts on polytrack: has taken good hold/wandered: sold 14,000 gns. *C. F. Wall* **66 a82**

DESERT OPAL 7 ch.g. Cadeaux Genereux 131 – Nullarbor (Green Desert (USA) 127) [2007 79: p5.1g p5.1g⁴ p5.1g⁶ 5.1m* p5.1g⁴ 5m* 5v³ 5m⁴ 5d⁵ 5m 5g p5.1g* p5g⁵ p6g⁵ p5.1d⁵ p5g² Dec 22] leggy, good-topped gelding: fairly useful performer: won handicaps at Nottingham in April, Beverley in May and Sandown in July, and a claimer at Wolverhampton in October: had form at 1m earlier in career, best at 5f nowadays: acts on all-weather, good to firm and heavy going: wears headgear. *C. R. Dore* **83**

DESERT PRIDE 2 b.c. (Apr 18) Desert Style (IRE) 121 – Dalu (IRE) 72 (Dancing Brave (USA) 140) [2007 p6d² p6g⁵ Dec 29] eighth foal: half-brother to 3 winners, includ- **65 p**

ing useful 1½m/1¾m winner Hambleden (by Vettori) and fairly useful 8.5f winner Princely Hero (by Royal Applause): dam 1m winner: fair form in maidens at Wolverhampton and Lingfield in December, finishing strongly: will be suited by at least 1m: capable of better. *W. S. Kittow*

DESERT SANDS (IRE) 2 b.c. (Mar 30) Dubai Destination (USA) 127 – Zvezda (USA) (Nureyev (USA) 131) [2007 p8m Nov 26] €38,000Y: second foal: dam, French maiden, sister to Dewhurst Stakes third Zentsov Street: 20/1, seventh to Jaser in maiden at Lingfield (started slowly, late headway): should improve. *John Joseph Murphy, Ireland*　**60 p**

DESERT SEA (IRE) 4 b.g. Desert Sun 120 – Sea of Time (USA) (Gilded Time (USA)) [2007 91: 16s 16.2m⁴ 14d² 16d 18m* 18d Oct 20] compact gelding: fairly useful handicapper: won at Doncaster in August by ½ length from Whispering Death: stays 2¼m: acts on polytrack, soft and good to firm going. *D. W. P. Arbuthnot*　**92**

DESERT SOUL 3 b.g. Fantastic Light (USA) 134 – Jalousie (IRE) 108 (Barathea (IRE) 127) [2007 68p: p8g 7.5m 8m² 9m 11.9d Aug 21] tall, good-topped gelding: modest maiden handicapper: left M. Johnston after fourth outing: bred to be suited by 1¼m/1½m: acts on good to firm going: has carried head high. *R. H. York*　**64**

DESERT THISTLE (IRE) 2 b.c. (Apr 20) Tamarisk (IRE) 127 – Taajreh (IRE) 89 (Mtoto 134) [2007 7f 7m 7s* Oct 9] €15,000Y, resold 13,000Y: tall colt: sixth foal: half-brother to Italian 2001 2-y-o 5f/5.5f winner Royal Rhapsody (by Ali-Royal): dam Irish 1m winner: fairly useful form: 33/1, much improved under different (testing) conditions to win maiden at Folkestone by length from Glittering Prize: likely to stay 1m. *H. J. L. Dunlop*　**80**

DESIDERIO 2 b.c. (May 11) Oasis Dream 129 – Pleasuring 68 (Good Times (ITY)) [2007 8d 8d 8d p6g² Nov 21] good-bodied colt: modest maiden: dropped in trip, second in nursery at Kempton: will prove best at 6f/7f. *R. Hannon*　**55**

DESIRABLE DANCER (IRE) 3 b.f. Fath (USA) 116 – Tender Time (Tender King 123) [2007 46: p6g Jan 15] poor maiden: tried blinkered/in cheekpieces. *R. A. Harris*　**–**

DESPERATE DAN 6 b.g. Danzero (AUS) – Alzianah 102 (Alzao (USA) 117) [2007 88, a94: f6g³ p5f³ f5g 6f 6m⁶ 5m² 5m 5m⁴ 5f p5.1g⁴* 5.7f⁵ p6g⁵ p5g² p5g* p5g³ p6g f6d Dec 12] quite good-topped gelding: fairly useful on all-weather, fair on turf: won seller at Wolverhampton (left J. Osborne) in August and handicap at Lingfield in November: best at 5f/easy 6f: acts on all-weather and firm going: usually blinkered: travels strongly, and has found little. *A. B. Haynes*　**75 a92**

DESPERATION (IRE) 5 b.g. Desert Style (IRE) 121 – Mauras Pride (IRE) (Cadeaux Genereux 131) [2007 84: p13g Jan 31] good-topped gelding: fairly useful performer at 4 yrs: well below form sole start in 2007: stays 1½m: acts on all-weather and good to firm going: tried visored/blinkered: tends to edge left: has looked none too keen. *M. R. Channon*　**–**

DESTINYS DREAM (IRE) 2 b.f. (Feb 4) Mull of Kintyre (USA) 114 – Dream of Jenny 73 (Caerleon (USA) 132) [2007 5m⁴ 5m 5s⁶ 6m 7.5g² 8.5m⁵ 7.5m* 8f³ 10m⁶ Oct 3] €5,000F, €18,000Y: sister to 4-y-o Jill Dawson and half-sister to several winners, including 10-y-o Jack Dawson: dam placed around 1m at 2 yrs (only season to race): fair performer: won nursery at Beverley in September: should be suited by 1¼m: acts on firm going, probably on soft. *Mrs A. Duffield*　**78**

DESTOUR (IRE) 3 b.c. Royal Applause 124 – Wild Missy (USA) (Wild Again (USA)) [2007 7m⁴ 7d⁵ 6m⁴ 7m³ Aug 1] 100,000F: deep-girthed, useful-looking colt: fourth foal: half-brother to 5f winners abroad by Crafty Prospector and Docksider: dam, US maiden, out of Ribblesdale Stakes winner Miss Boniface: fair maiden: stays 7f: visored (ran creditably/looked bit quirky) final outing. *J. Noseda*　**72**

DETERMIND STAND (USA) 2 b.c. (Feb 6) Elusive Quality (USA) – Sauterne 98 (Rainbow Quest (USA) 134) [2007 6m p7g³ 7m⁵ 7g⁶ p7g* 8m⁶ 8g² Oct 26] 200,000Y: good-topped colt: second foal: dam, 7.5f/1¼m winner, closely related to Cherry Hinton Stakes winner Applaud: fairly useful performer: won nursery at Lingfield in August: good second to Jack Dawkins in similar event at Doncaster final start: stays 1m: acts on polytrack and good to firm going: visored (slowly away) once: sold 100,000 gns, sent to USA. *Sir Michael Stoute*　**84**

DETONATE 5 b.g. Mind Games 121 – Bron Hilda (IRE) 50 (Namaqualand (USA)) [2007 57: p7g p7.1g p6g p6g p6g³ 7g⁶ 5.7d³ p7g 6m 5m 6g⁶ p6g p6g⁴ p5.1g⁴ p6g p5m p6g p8g⁵ f5g⁴ Dec 27] leggy, close-coupled gelding: modest maiden: left Ms J. Doyle after eighth start: stays 7f: acts on polytrack, soft and good to firm going: tried in headgear: edgy sort: sometimes slowly away. *I. A. Wood*　**57**

DETONATOR (IRE) 2 b.g. (Apr 8) Fantastic Light (USA) 134 – Narwala 120 **85 p**
(Darshaan 133) [2007 7.1g^2 p8.6g* Nov 8] half-brother to several winners, including
1¼m/1½m winner Altamura (by El Gran Senor) and French 1½m/15f winner Affidavit
(by Affirmed), both smart: dam 1¼m/1½m (latter Princess Royal Stakes) winner: fairly
useful form: confirmed promise from Warwick (second to Lord Peter Flint) when
winning maiden at Wolverhampton by 9 lengths: will be well suited by 1¼m/1½m: sure
to go on improving. *M. Johnston*

DEVILFISHPOKER COM 3 ch.g. Dr Fong (USA) 128 – Midnight Allure 85 **58**
(Aragon 118) [2007 42: p6g 9.8g^4 12.1g^3 14.1m 13.8g^6 15.8g Oct 30] close-coupled gelding: modest maiden: should stay 2m: often blinkered, tried in cheekpieces: sometimes
slowly away: temperamental winning hurdler. *R. C. Guest*

DEVILS DESIRE 3 b.f. Superior Premium 122 – Ming Blue 52 (Primo Dominie 121) **–**
[2007 8.3m Apr 23] half-sister to 2 winners, including 6f to 9f winner Wilfram (by
Fraam): dam poor maiden on Flat/over hurdles: 100/1, always behind in maiden at
Windsor. *J. M. Bradley*

DEVINE DANCER 4 ch.f. Woodborough (USA) 112 – Princess Londis 59 (Interrex **66**
(CAN)) [2007 83: 5f 6m^5 5d 5.2f Aug 5] attractive, compact filly: fairly useful at 3 yrs:
fair at best in 2007, virtually refusing to race final outing: speedy, and best at 5f: acts on
polytrack and firm ground: races prominently: none too consistent. *H. Candy*

DEVOLUTION (IRE) 9 b.g. Distinctly North (USA) 115 – Election Special 78 (Chief **–**
Singer 131) [2007 p11m Oct 11] fairly useful handicapper in 2003: well held at Kempton
only Flat start since. *Miss C. Dyson*

DEVON FLAME 8 b.g. Whittingham (IRE) 104 – Uae Flame (IRE) (Polish Precedent **67 d**
(USA) 131) [2007 88: p6g^2 p5g^2 p6g 5.1f p6g 5.1s 6f Aug 6] strong gelding: fairly useful
at best: only fair in 2007, and well held after second outing: possibly best around 6f
nowadays: acts on polytrack, firm and good to soft going. *R. J. Hodges*

DEVON HOUSE (USA) 3 b.f. Chester House (USA) 123 – Devon Heights (USA) **53**
108 (Mt Livermore (USA)) [2007 8.2g May 11] strong filly: second foal: dam, French 1m
winner, half-sister to very smart performer up to 1¼m Tinners Way and smart sprinter
Western Approach: 40/1 and backward, twelfth to In Safe Hands in maiden at Nottingham, slowly away: sold 11,000 gns in December, sent to France. *J. H. M. Gosden*

DEVONIA PLAINS (IRE) 5 ch.g. Danehill Dancer (IRE) 117 – Marlfield Lake **–**
(Cadeaux Genereux 131) [2007 68: p7g 7m p8g 7g p7g Sep 26] big gelding: maiden: little
form in 2007: tried visored/blinkered. *Mrs P. N. Dutfield*

DEXILEOS (IRE) 8 b.g. Danehill (USA) 126 – Theano (IRE) 114 (Thatching 131) **53**
[2007 57: p8g p7.1g p8g p8g^2 p8g^5 p8.6g^3 p7g^5 7.1s^3 p8.6g p10g p8.6g^3 p8g^5 p8.6g^3
p9.5g p8.6g Sep 28] close-coupled gelding: modest performer: stays 8.6f: acts on all-
weather, firm and soft ground: tried visored/blinkered/tongue tied: races up with pace.
David Pinder

DHAKA DAZZLE 2 b.g. (Feb 13) Josr Algarhoud (IRE) 118 – Magical Flute 75 (Pic- **50**
colo 121) [2007 5.1m^6 5g 6m 7.1g^4 7f 7m 8f 8g Sep 20] sturdy gelding: modest maiden:
should stay 1m: raced only on good going or firmer: tried in visor. *M. R. Channon*

DHARORI (IRE) 2 ch.c. (Mar 4) Captain Rio 122 – Sliding (Formidable (USA) 125) **63**
[2007 6d^6 p6g Oct 8] tall, quite good-topped colt: maiden: sixth at Haydock only
completed start: dead. *M. A. Jarvis*

DHAULAR DHAR (IRE) 5 b.h. Indian Ridge 123 – Pescara (IRE) 108 (Common **108**
Grounds 118) [2007 103: 7m^2 5g 5.1m 7.6m* 7m^4 6g 6v 5g^6 7m^4 7g 6.1m^4 6m 7.6m
6d 7d^5 6d 6m Nov 10] leggy, quite attractive horse: useful handicapper: won at Chester
(beat Beckermet by neck) in May: second creditable efforts after, including fourth to
Giganticus in Bunbury Cup at Newmarket ninth start: has won over 1m, better at shorter
(effective at 5f given test): acts on polytrack, soft and firm going: held up: tough.
J. S. Goldie

DHEHDAAH 6 b.g. Alhaarth (IRE) 126 – Carina Clare (Slip Anchor 136) [2007 69: **80**
p16g* 18g 14.8d* p16g^2 14s 14.6g Oct 26] compact gelding: fairly useful handicapper:
won at Kempton in April and Newmarket in June: stays 2m: acts on polytrack, firm and
soft going (unraced on heavy): blinkered once at 3 yrs: fairly useful hurdler, won in
November. *Mrs P. Sly*

DHHAMAAN (IRE) 2 b.c. (Mar 5) Dilshaan 119 – Safe Care (IRE) (Caerleon (USA) **77**
132) [2007 7m^3 p8g^2 7g 6m p7g p6g^2 p7g* p6g^3 p8.6g^2 Dec 14] 5,000Y: sturdy colt:
fourth foal: half-brother to 3-y-o Gap Princess and Irish 1¼m (stays 1½m) winner

Hazium (by In The Wings): dam unraced half-sister to smart sprinter Lugana Beach, out of half-sister to Mtoto: fair performer: won maiden at Lingfield in November: stays 8.6f: acts on polytrack and good to firm going: visored last 3 starts. *C. E. Brittain*

DHURWAH (IRE) 4 b.f. Green Desert (USA) 127 – Bintalbawadi (IRE) 67 (Diesis – 133) [2007 47: p5g 7.1m p6g Sep 14] unfurnished filly: poor at 3 yrs: no form in 2007. *T. Keddy*

DIADEMAS (USA) 2 b. or br.c. (Feb 14) Grand Slam (USA) 120 – Kona Kat (USA) **71** (Mountain Cat (USA)) [2007 5.5d² f5g* 5m⁵ 5s⁴ p5m⁵ 5.5m p5.1g p5.1g³ p5.1g⁵ p7g⁵ p6g Nov 28] tall colt: fair performer: won maiden at Southwell in May: left J. Osborne after eighth start: may prove best at 5f/6f: acts on all-weather, probably on soft ground: tried blinkered. *V. Smith*

DIAMOND DAN (IRE) 5 b.g. Foxhound (USA) 103 – Kawther (Tap On Wood 130) **63** [2007 62: p7.1g p8.6g⁴ Feb 10] smallish gelding: modest performer: stays 1¼m: acts on polytrack and firm ground: tried in cheekpieces. *P. D. Evans*

DIAMOND DIVA 3 br.f. Dansili 127 – Vivianna (Indian Ridge 123) [2007 86+: 8g³ **105** 7g⁵ p6g* 6d⁶ 7m* 7g² 6d² 6.1m² 7d² Sep 29] sturdy filly: useful performer: much improved in 2007, winning handicaps at Wolverhampton in June and Folkestone (by 1¼ lengths from Yandina) in July: runner-up after in minor event at Goodwood and in listed races at Pontefract, Chester and Ascot (beaten ¾ length by Miss Lucifer): best form at 6f/7f: acts on polytrack, soft and good to firm ground: sold 230,000 gns, sent to USA. *J. W. Hills*

DIAMOND FLUTE 2 b.f. (Jan 19) Piccolo 121 – Diamond Park (IRE) 91 (Alzao – (USA) 117) [2007 6m Jul 16] 9,600Y: compact filly: half-sister to several winners, including 1999 2-y-o 5f winner Pop Shop (by Owington) and 1½m winner Ampoule (by Zamindar): dam maiden (stayed 1¼m): always behind in maiden at Windsor: sold 1,500 gns, sent to Germany. *Mouse Hamilton-Fairley*

DIAMOND HURRICANE (IRE) 3 b.g. Mujadil (USA) 119 – Christoph's Girl 50 **49** (Efisio 120) [2007 76: 7m 6m⁵ 6m² p6g p6g p7g p6g p8g p8.6g p8.6d Dec 7] small gelding: just poor performer nowadays: left P. D. Evans after third start: effective at 5f/6f: acts on good to firm and good to soft ground: tried blinkered/in cheekpieces. *M. Wellings*

DIAMOND JOSH 5 ch.g. Primo Dominie 121 – Exit 82 (Exbourne (USA) 125) [2007 – 68: 5.9g p5.1g 5m p6g p6g 5g p6g⁶ p6d f5d p12.2g Dec 22] neat gelding: fair at best, little form in 2007: tried in visor/cheekpieces. *M. Mullineaux*

DIAMOND KATIE (IRE) 5 b.m. Night Shift (USA) – Fayrooz (USA) 74 (Gulch **53** (USA)) [2007 66: p7.1g³ f6g Jan 23] deep-girthed mare: modest handicapper nowadays: effective at stiff 5f/6f: acts on firm ground, probably on polytrack. *N. Tinkler*

DIAMOND KEY (IRE) 3 b.f. Key of Luck (USA) 126 – Aljeeza (Halling (USA) 133) **82** [2007 –: p6g f8g 12.1s 10.9s* 11.5g⁵ 10m 12.1m 10g² p13.9g* p16g* p12.2g² Oct 27] fairly useful performer: progressed well in second half of 2007, winning seller at Warwick in July and handicaps at Wolverhampton and Lingfield in October: stays 2m: acts on polytrack and soft going: blinkered nowadays: sold 30,000 gns, joined Eoin Doyle, Ireland. *M. G. Quinlan*

DIAMOND LASS (IRE) 2 b.f. (Jan 19) Rock of Gibraltar (IRE) 133 – Keralba (USA) **65** (Sheikh Albadou 128) [2007 6d⁴ 6m⁵ 7f⁶ Sep 5] €70,000Y, 75,000 2-y-o: rather leggy filly: fourth foal: half-sister to 4-y-o Orphina: dam once-raced half-sister to very smart sprinter So Factual, smart 6f/7f performer Bold Fact and dam of outstanding broodmare Hasili: fair maiden: will stay 1m. *R. A. Fahey*

DIAMOND LIGHT (USA) 3 ch.f. Fantastic Light (USA) 134 – Queen of Women **62** (USA) (Sharpen Up 127) [2007 70: p8g p9.5g² p8.6g 9.7g 9s⁶ 12g³ 10m² 10.3g² 10g* 11s 11.5g Oct 28] close-coupled, attractive filly: modest performer: left M. Botti after fourth start: won minor event at Hassloch in September: stays 1¼m: acts on polytrack, firm and good to soft going. *C. von der Recke, Germany*

DIAMOND ORCHID (IRE) 7 gr.m. Victory Note (USA) 120 – Olivia's Pride (IRE) **47 +** (Digamist (USA) 110) [2007 12.4m May 24] strong mare: modest handicapper in 2004: not knocked about on belated return: stays easy 2m: acts on all-weather, soft and good to firm ground: usually wears cheekpieces/visor. *G. A. Harker*

DIAMOND QUEST (SAF) 6 b.g. Saumarez 132 – Discover Diamonds (AUS) (Mars- **113** cay (AUS)) [2007 7.5g³ 12g⁶ 8g* 9g⁴ 10g² 12d⁶ Jun 23] rangy gelding: smart performer: won 6 of his 23 starts in South Africa, including Grade 1 Canon Gold Cup at Greyville in 2006: some good efforts in handicaps at Nad Al Sheba in 2007, winning in February by 2 lengths from Juror: left M. de Kock and off over 3½ months (looked fit), creditable sixth of 7 to Maraahel in Hardwicke Stakes at Royal Ascot final outing, racing freely (said to have returned lame on off-fore): seems to stay 2m, likely to prove best at shorter: raced mainly on good going (seems to act on good to soft): held up: returned to UAE, and joined H. Brown. *A. M. Balding*

DIAMOND ROYAL (IRE) 2 b.f. (Apr 24) Red Ransom (USA) – Gaily Royal (IRE) **74 p** (Royal Academy (USA) 130) [2007 7d⁴ Oct 9] sturdy filly: sixth foal: half-sister to 3-y-o Chantilly Tiffany and untrustworthy 2m winner Turner: dam, Japanese 9f/1¼m winner, half-sister to smart French winner up to 15f New Frontier: 20/1 and green, fourth to Laughter in maiden at Leicester, held up: will be suited by 1m: sure to progress. *E. A. L. Dunlop*

DIAMONDS AND DUST 5 b.g. Mister Baileys 123 – Dusty Shoes 72 (Shareef Dan- **84** cer (USA) 135) [2007 92: p10g* p13g* 11.5d Jun 27] smallish, close-coupled gelding: fairly useful performer: won claimers at Lingfield in January (left N. Littmoden) and February (only outing for S. Dow): tailed off (said to have finished lame) final outing: stays easy 13f: acts on polytrack, firm and good to soft going: blinkered nowadays. *F. P. Murtagh*

DIAMOND SEEKER 2 ch.f. (Apr 30) Erhaab (USA) 127 – Slavonic Dance (Muhtar- **–** ram (USA) 125) [2007 6d p8g p8g⁶ p8.6g Dec 3] workmanlike filly: second foal: half-sister to 3-y-o Slavonic Lake: dam unraced: no form in maidens/nursery. *V. Smith*

DIAMOND SOLES (IRE) 2 b.f. (Feb 12) Danetime (IRE) 121 – Villa Nova (IRE) 55 **48 §** (Petardia 113) [2007 5m⁶ 5m 5.7f p5.1g Sep 3] 30,000Y: neat filly: fifth foal: sister to useful 5f (at 2 yrs) to 8.5f (in UAE) winner Prince of Denmark, and half-sister to 4-y-o Star of Canterbury and 3-y-o Six of Diamonds: dam, Irish maiden, best at 1m/9f: poor and ungenuine maiden: tried blinkered. *B. J. Meehan*

DIAMOND TYCOON (USA) 3 b.c. Johannesburg (USA) 127 – Palacoona (FR) 105 **111** (Last Tycoon 131) [2007 84p: 8m* 8m May 5] rangy colt: fluent mover: recorded exceptional performance for a maiden race when winning at Newbury in April by 6 lengths from Lucarno, soon in front and drawing away without coming under serious pressure: 15/2, and edgy (2 handlers), respectable 5¾ lengths ninth to Cockney Rebel in 2000 Guineas at Newmarket following month, not going with same fluency: not seen out again: stays 1m: acts on good to firm going: nervy sort, tends to sweat: wears crossed noseband: stays in training. *B. J. Meehan*

DIAMOND WORLD 4 b.f. Agnes World (USA) 123 – In A Twinkling (IRE) 74 (Brief **49** Truce (USA) 126) [2007 64?: p6g p7g p8g Oct 10] quite good-topped filly: maiden: only poor in 2007: stays 6f: acts on firm going, probably polytrack. *C. A. Horgan*

DIAMOND YAS (IRE) 2 b.f. (Mar 31) Mull of Kintyre (USA) 114 – Balgren (IRE) **71 p** (Ballad Rock 122) [2007 7d³ Sep 19] €5,000Y: strong filly: half-sister to 4-y-o Steel City Boy and to 7f winners Diamond Shannon and The Block Monster (both by Petorius): dam unraced: 12/1, third to Street Star in maiden at Yarmouth, waited with: open to improvement. *H. R. A. Cecil*

DIANE'S CHOICE 4 ch.f. Komaite (USA) – Ramajana (USA) (Shadeed (USA) 135) **93** [2007 95: 6m 6g³ 6s 6m 5d 5g² 5d⁵ p6g* 6m 6m p6g⁴ p6m⁵ p6g Dec 28] rangy filly: useful handicapper: won at Kempton in August by neck from Viking Spirit: best at 5f/ easy 6f: acts on polytrack, firm and good to soft ground: usually front runner. *J. Akehurst*

DICHOH 4 b.g. Diktat 126 – Hoh Dancer 66 (Indian Ridge 123) [2007 85: p7g⁶ p8g⁵ **–** f8g* f8g* 8s f8g² p8g⁶ p8g p8.6g² p8g⁶ p8g³ Dec 30] heavy-topped gelding: fairly useful **a92** handicapper: won at Southwell in February and March: stays 8.6f: acts on all-weather, well held both attempts on turf (soft ground): blinkered (ran creditably final start). *M. A. Jarvis*

DICKIE DEANO 3 b.g. Sooty Tern 79 – Chez Bonito (IRE) 49 (Persian Bold 123) **–** [2007 –: p9.5g p9.5g p12.2g⁵ p10g Dec 19] of little account. *J. M. Bradley*

DICKIE LE DAVOIR 3 b.g. Kyllachy 129 – Downeaster Alexa (USA) (Red Ryder **93 d** (USA)) [2007 87: 6g² 6.1m⁴ 6.1d* 6m 7d 6v 6s 6d p6g³ p7.1g⁶ p7.1g* p8g⁴ Dec 28] good-topped gelding: fairly useful performer: won handicap at Nottingham in May and claimer at Wolverhampton (nowhere near best) in December: stays 7f: acts on polytrack and soft going: tried visored: edgy sort, has given trouble at stall: can take time to warm up. *K. R. Burke*

DICKIE VALENTINE 2 b.g. (Mar 23) Diktat 126 – Passionelle 56 (Nashwan (USA) **52** 135) [2007 6d 6d p7g p6g⁶ p6g⁵ Dec 26] tall, quite attractive gelding: modest maiden: should be suited by 7f+: visored last 2 starts. *M. R. Bosley*

DICTATION 5 b.m. Diktat 126 – Monaiya (Shareef Dancer (USA) 135) [2007 43: 8d⁶ **60** 8.5d 7g⁴ 9d⁵ 9m⁵ p9.5d² Dec 7] modest handicapper: easily best effort in 2007 when second at Wolverhampton: stays 9.5f: acts on polytrack, heavy and good to firm ground: wears blinkers/cheekpieces. *Mrs Valerie Keatley, Ireland*

DICTATRIX 4 gr.f. Diktat 126 – Apennina (USA) (Gulch (USA)) [2007 91?: 8m⁶ p6g⁶ **74 d** p6g 5.7d 7s⁶ 8d p11g 9.1v p9.5g p11g Nov 28] leggy filly: fairly useful at best: only fair in 2007, and little form after second outing (left J. Eustace after fifth, C. Dore after seventh): stays 7f: acts on polytrack, heavy and good to firm ground: usually blinkered/in cheekpieces nowadays. *P. D. Niven*

DIDACTIC 3 b.g. Diktat 126 – Scene (IRE) 87 (Scenic 128) [2007 51: f7g⁴ 7.5m 7.1g **51 d** 7.5v⁶ 6m⁶ 7g Sep 24] smallish, sturdy gelding: modest maiden at best: probably stays 7f: often blinkered. *A. J. McCabe*

DIDANA (IRE) 2 br.f. (Mar 21) Diktat 126 – Daanat Nawal (Machiavellian (USA) **71 p** 123) [2007 6d p7.1g⁴ f7d* Dec 20] €16,000Y: good-topped filly: seventh foal: half-sister to 3 winners, notably 7-y-o Babodana: dam unraced out of half-sister to Breeders' Cup Sprint winner Smile: fair form: won maiden at Southwell in December: will stay 1m: should improve again. *M. G. Quinlan*

DIDNTCOMEBACK 2 b.g. (Mar 27) Oasis Dream 129 – Latin Beauty (IRE) (Sad- **–** ler's Wells (USA) 132) [2007 6m p7.1g p6g Nov 12] well held in maidens: bred for speed. *M. S. Saunders*

DIDNT TELL MY WIFE 8 ch.g. Aragon 118 – Bee Dee Dancer (Ballacashtal **40** (CAN)) [2007 51: p8g p8g p8g f8g 10m 9.9s 10d⁵ 8m Aug 8] unfurnished gelding: just poor nowadays: left P. McEntee after sixth start: stays 9f: acts on all-weather, heavy and good to firm ground: usually wears headgear nowadays: sometimes edges left/races freely: reportedly has bled. *Miss K. B. Boutflower*

DIEGO CAO (IRE) 6 b.g. Cape Cross (IRE) 129 – Lady Moranbon (USA) (Trempo- **73** lino (USA) 135) [2007 90: 16g 18d Oct 20] well-made gelding: useful handicapper at his best: only fair on Flat in 2007: best efforts up to 1¼m: acted on good to soft ground: fell heavily over hurdles in November: dead. *N. J. Gifford*

DIG DEEP (IRE) 5 b.g. Entrepreneur 123 – Diamond Quest (Rainbow Quest (USA) **102** 134) [2007 88: f5g² p5.1g² 5m p5.1g* 5m 6g 5m 5m* 5d³ 5m 5.6m 5g 5.2g⁴ 5.1g 5d 5m* Oct 22] well-made gelding: useful handicapper: won at Wolverhampton (beat Financial Times by 2½ lengths) in April, Ascot in July and Pontefract (beat Westport by ¾ length) in October: has won at 7f, but best at 5f nowadays: acts on all-weather, good to firm and good to soft ground. *W. J. Haggas*

DIGGER BOY 4 b.g. King's Best (USA) 132 – Chameleon 79 (Green Desert (USA) **–** 127) [2007 70: p10g p9.5g p12.2g 10s 17.2f Jun 10] fair maiden at best for M. Jarvis: no form in 2007. *J. Gallagher*

DIG GOLD (USA) 3 ch.c. Seeking The Gold (USA) – Sheroog (USA) 77 (Shareef **88 +** Dancer (USA) 135) [2007 11.8m⁴ 11.9g⁶ 10d⁴ 10m 14m² 12.6m* Aug 27] big, strong colt: closely related to smart 9f (in UAE) to 1½m winner Sharaf Kabeer and useful 1¼m winner El Mobasherr (both by Machiavellian), and half-brother to 2 winners, notably smart performer up to 1¼m Kabool (by Groom Dancer): dam, 1m winner, sister to dam of Dubai Millennium (by Seeking The Gold): fairly useful performer: best effort when winning handicap at Warwick in August: stays 12.6f: acts on good to firm and good to soft going: often races freely: joined D. Selvaratnam in UAE. *M. A. Jarvis*

DIGGS LANE (IRE) 3 b.g. Galileo (IRE) 134 – Desert Bluebell 83 (Kalaglow 132) **–** [2007 55: 9.7g Apr 3] useful-looking gelding: maiden: well held only outing in 2007: should stay 1¼m/1½m: best effort on polytrack: tried blinkered: has looked moody. *N. A. Callaghan*

DIGITAL 10 ch.g. Safawan 118 – Heavenly Goddess (Soviet Star (USA) 128) [2007 80: **80** p7g 6g⁶ 6m⁴ 7.1m⁴ 7d³ 6g⁶ 7m⁶ 6.1g 6d⁴ 7.1g² 7.1v⁴ 6s² 6d 6f⁴ 7g⁵ 6g 5.1f² 6.1m⁶ 5.7f* 5.1m² 6g³ 5s* 5s³ 5d Oct 12] workmanlike gelding: fairly useful handicapper: won at Bath and Redcar in September: effective at 5f to 1m: acts on any turf going: visored last 8 starts: sometimes slowly away: waited with. *M. R. Channon*

DIJEERR (USA) 3 b.c. Danzig (USA) – Sharp Minister (CAN) (Deputy Minister **108** (CAN)) [2007 108: 8g 8m² 7g² Oct 27] sturdy colt: useful form: trained by M. Jarvis at 2 yrs, winning Horris Hill Stakes at Newbury: off 5 months, good efforts when runner-up in minor events at Bath (beaten 1½ lengths by Smart Enough) and Doncaster (½ length behind Appalachian Trail): stays 1m: acts on soft and good to firm going: races prominently. *Saeed bin Suroor*

DIK DIK 4 b.g. Diktat 126 – Totom 81 (Mtoto 134) [2007 65: p10g[4] p13.9g[5] p16.5g[4] **51** p13g[6] Feb 7] compact gelding: maiden: only modest nowadays: seems to stay 2m: acts on polytrack, heavy and good to firm going: usually visored/in cheekpieces. *J. S. Moore*

DIKSIE DANCER 3 br.f. Diktat 126 – Careful Dancer (Gorytus (USA) 132) [2007 **72 d** p8.6g[6] 8m[2] p7.1g[2] 6m[3] 7.5g[5] 6g 7m 6.9g p6m p6g Oct 5] leggy filly: half-sister to several winners, including 7-y-o Gift Horse and dam of smart sprinter La Cucaracha: dam ran twice: fair maiden: below form after fourth outing: stays 1m: acts on good to firm ground: blinkered final outing. *K. A. Ryan*

DIKTALEX (IRE) 4 b.f. Diktat 126 – Kingdom Royale (IRE) (Royal Academy (USA) **42** 130) [2007 66: f6g f5g[2] f5g f6g f6g[6] f6g Feb 28] big, lengthy filly: poor performer nowadays: should stay 7f: acts on all-weather and good to firm going: tried visored/in cheekpieces: tongue tied. *C. J. Teague*

DIKTATORIAL 5 br.g. Diktat 126 – Reason To Dance 96 (Damister (USA) 123) [2007 **85** 90: 10.5m 12d Aug 21] tall, leggy gelding: has a round action: fairly useful handicapper: seems to stay 1½m: acts on polytrack, good to soft and good to firm going: often tongue tied in 2006: tried blinkered earlier in career: has been blanketed/attended by expert in stall entry: little impact in 2 runs over hurdles. *J. Howard Johnson*

DIKTATORSHIP (IRE) 4 b.g. Diktat 126 – Polka Dancer 93 (Dancing Brave (USA) **66** 140) [2007 60: p12.2g[3] p12.2g[5] p12.2g* p12.2g[6] p10g p16f p10g[2] f14g[4] p12.2g[2] f11g* p12.2g[2] 12.4m p13.9g[2] p16.5g[4] p16.5g p13.9g 12.3m[6] p12.2g[3] p13.9g Nov 16] good-topped gelding: fair performer on all-weather: won minor events at Wolverhampton in January and, having left Ernst Oertel after sixth outing, Southwell in May: left G. A. Swinbank after twelfth outing: stays 1¾m: acts on all-weather and good to firm going: has worn headgear/tongue tie, effective without. *Jennie Candlish*

DILMOUN (IRE) 5 b.g. Darshaan 133 – Mannakea (USA) (Fairy King (USA)) [2007 **–** 8m Aug 3] tall gelding: always behind in maiden at Thirsk, very slowly away. *A. L. T. Moore, Ireland*

DILWIN (IRE) 3 b.g. Dilshaan 119 – Welsh Harp (Mtoto 134) [2007 67: 9m[4] 5d 8.3s **61** 7m Jul 11] strong, compact gelding: maiden: only modest in 2007: stays 7f: acts on good to firm ground. *D. Nicholls*

DIMASHQ 5 b.m. Mtoto 134 – Agwaas (IRE) (Rainbow Quest (USA) 134) [2007 50: **56** 15.8m[5] 12g[6] Oct 20] sparely-made mare: modest performer: stays 2m: acts on good to firm and good to soft ground. *J. O'Reilly*

DIMENTICATA (IRE) 3 b.f. Danetime (IRE) 121 – Non Dimenticar Me (IRE) 63 **109** (Don't Forget Me 127) [2007 98: 8v 7m[5] 9.5m[2] 8g[2] 10s 7.5m[5] 6m[3] 10g[6] 8g[4] Oct 14] €50,000Y: lengthy, angular filly: half-sister to several winners, including useful 5f (at 2 yrs) to 7f (in Hong Kong) winner Master Fay (by Fayruz) and fairly useful 6f winner Didn't We (by Mujadil): dam 5f winner (stayed 7f): useful performer: won maiden at Leopardstown at 2 yrs: second in listed race at Gowran and Irish 1000 Guineas at the Curragh (ran very well to be beaten by a neck by Finsceal Beo, finishing well) in May: best subsequent effort when unlucky 1¾ lengths third to Abraham Lincoln in minor event at the Curragh, no room near rail then finishing strongly: stays 1m, not 1¼m: acts on good to firm going. *Kevin Prendergast, Ireland*

DIMINUTO 3 b.f. Iron Mask (USA) 117 – Thicket 87 (Wolfhound (USA) 126) [2007 **80** 62: f6g[2] f5s[2] f6g f6g[4] f5g[2] 5.1g[2] 5.1g[4] f5g[3] 5.7d[3] f5g* 5.3m[5] p5.1g[4] 5.5s[3] 5.7g* 5s* 5g p6g[5] 5d p7.1g[3] p6g p5.1g[2] f6d Dec 12] small filly: fairly useful handicapper: won at Southwell in May, and Bath and Catterick in July: stays 6f: acts on all-weather, firm and soft going: has raced freely/carried head high: often forces pace. *M. D. I. Usher*

DINARIUS 2 b.c. (Feb 25) Bertolini (USA) 125 – Ambassadress (USA) (Alleged **67** (USA) 138) [2007 6m p7g[5] p8.6g[5] p8.6g[3] Dec 26] tall colt: fair maiden: left T. Tate after debut: third in nursery at Wolverhampton: stays 8.6f. *K. J. Burke*

DINGAAN (IRE) 4 b.g. Tagula (IRE) 116 – Boughtbyphone 62 (Warning 136) [2007 **91** 95: 6g 6m* 7g 6m 7g 6m[6] 7.1d 7g p6g[4] 6m[4] p6g[4] p7g[4] Oct 24] tall gelding: useful handi- **a95** capper on all-weather, fairly useful on turf: won at Goodwood (by head from Bentong) in June: good efforts at Lingfield last 2 starts: stays 7f: acts on polytrack and firm going: tried in headgear: sometimes slowly away: has shown signs of temperament. *A. M. Balding*

DINNER DATE 5 ch.g. Groom Dancer (USA) 128 – Misleading Lady (Warning 136) **69**
[2007 69: 8m³ 9m⁴ 10.1m⁵ p10g⁶ p10g² p10m Dec 9] rather leggy, quite attractive
gelding: fair handicapper: won at Kempton in November: stays easy 1½m: acts on polytrack and good to firm going. *T. Keddy*

DIPLOMATIC DAN (IRE) 4 b.g. Imperial Ballet (IRE) 110 – Yaqatha (IRE) **–**
(Sadler's Wells (USA) 132) [2007 8.5m Apr 26] 50/1, tailed off in maiden at Beverley.
E. J. Alston

DIRECTA'S DIGGER (IRE) 3 b.c. Daggers Drawn (USA) 114 – Chita Rivera 61 **68**
(Chief Singer 131) [2007 8.5s² 8.5g³ 13.4g⁵ 12.4d⁴ Oct 16] maiden: left A. Lowe in
Germany after second start, fair form in handicaps in Britain: stays 13.4f: raced only on
good going or softer. *M. Scudamore*

DIRECT DEBIT (IRE) 4 b.g. Dansili 127 – Dimple (Fairy King (USA)) [2007 95: **95**
8m p8g 8g 7d³ 8d² 8m* 7m³ Aug 3] lengthy, quite attractive gelding: useful performer:
placed in handicaps on 3 of last 4 starts and won claimer at Ascot in July on other occasion: stays easy 1¼m: acts on polytrack, good to firm and good to soft going. *M. L. W. Bell*

DIRICULOUS 3 b.g. Diktat 126 – Sheila's Secret (IRE) 97 (Bluebird (USA) 125) **70 p**
[2007 p6g⁴ p6g* Nov 28] 26,000F, 25,000Y: half-brother to several winners, including
smart sprinter Olivia Grace (by Pivotal) and useful 5f (including at 2 yrs) winner Ok Pal
(by Primo Dominie): dam 5f winner (including at 2 yrs): fair form: better effort when
winning maiden at Kempton by head from Tyrannosaurus Rex, always close up: open to
further improvement. *T. G. Mills*

DIRTY DANCING 3 b.g. Green Desert (USA) 127 – Shadow Dancing 110 (Unfuwain **63**
(USA) 131) [2007 p6g⁶ p6g 6s² 8g 8.3m Sep 17] unfurnished gelding: first foal: dam, 7f
(at 2 yrs) and 11.4f winner, out of smart performer up to 1¾m Salchow: modest maiden:
should be suited by 1¼m: acts on polytrack and soft ground. *B. W. Hills*

DISCANTI (IRE) 2 ch.g. Distant Music (USA) 126 – Gertie Laurie (Lomond **65**
(USA) 128) [2007 f5g 6m⁶ 6s³ 5s 5m⁶ Aug 13] strong, long-backed gelding: fair maiden:
gelded after final start: will stay 7f: tongue tied. *T. D. Easterby*

DISCO DAN 3 b.g. Danehill Dancer (IRE) 117 – Ghay (USA) 61 (Bahri (USA) 125) **74**
[2007 85: 6m p7g p6g 6d³ 6m Aug 8] good-topped gelding: just fair handicapper in 2007:
left D. Simcock prior to being pulled up amiss final outing: stayed 7f: acted on good to
firm and good to soft going: tried in cheekpieces: dead. *D. K. Ivory*

DISCOTHEQUE (USA) 4 ch.f. Not For Love (USA) – Disco Darlin' (USA) (Citi- **73**
dancer (USA)) [2007 68: p9.5g² p12g p9.5g* p10g³ p8.6g² p10g³ Feb 14] strong,
compact filly: fair handicapper: won at Wolverhampton in January: stays 1¼m: acts on
polytrack and firm going: tried once in blinkers. *P. Howling*

DISCREET CAT (USA) 4 b.c. Forestry (USA) 121 – Pretty Discreet (USA) 117 **110**
(Private Account (USA)) [2007 127p: a10f a6f³ a8.3s³ Oct 26] high-class performer at
his best, winning his first 6 starts (sold privately out of S. Hough's stable after only outing
at 2 yrs), including Grade 2 UAE Derby at Nad Al Sheba and Cigar Mile at Aqueduct in
2006: missed reappearance in early-March due to a slightly elevated temperature: ran no
sort of race when well-held last of 7 behind Invasor in Dubai World Cup at Nad Al Sheba
later in month, always in last 2 and failing to pick up (subsequently found to be suffering
from a throat abscess): off 6 months, below-form third on last 2 starts, in Vosburgh Stakes
at Belmont (6 lengths behind Fabulous Strike over inadequate trip) and Breeders' Cup
Dirt Mile at Monmouth (15 lengths behind Corinthian, beaten on home turn): probably
needed further than 6f, and should have stayed 1¼m: to stand at Darley's Jonabell Stud,
Kentucky, USA, fee $30,000. *Saeed bin Suroor*

DISHDASHA (IRE) 5 b.g. Desert Prince (IRE) 130 – Counterplot (IRE) 91 (Last **63**
Tycoon 131) [2007 –, a51: p12m² p12g⁵ Dec 19] strong, workmanlike gelding: fairly
useful hurdler: modest performer on Flat: stays 1½m: acts on polytrack, raced only on
good ground or firmer on turf. *Mrs A. M. Thorpe*

DISINTEGRATION (IRE) 3 b.g. Barathea (IRE) 127 – Leave Me Alone (IRE) 95 **65**
(Nashwan (USA) 135) [2007 65p: 11.6d 12g 10.9d³ 15g Jul 12] big, good-bodied gelding: fair maiden handicapper: stays 1½m: acts on good to firm and good to soft ground,
unraced on extremes: sold £800 in November. *A. King*

DISPOL ISLE (IRE) 5 gr.m. Trans Island 119 – Pictina (Petong 126) [2007 71: 7.1m* **79**
8.3m 7.1g³ 7.1m* 8d² 6.9d 7s⁴ 7.5s³ 7m 6.9g 7m 7.5d⁴ 7.1m* 7g 7g Nov 6] leggy,
workmanlike mare: fair handicapper: won at Musselburgh in April, May and September:
effective at 6f to 1m: acts on fibresand and any turf going: tried blinkered/visored at 3 yrs:
often travels strongly. *T. D. Barron*

286

DISPOL KATIE 6 ch.m. Komaite (USA) – Twilight Time (Aragon 118) [2007 81: 7m – 7m 6.1g Jun 13] tall mare: fairly useful handicapper at best: little form in 2007. *T. D. Barron*

DISPOL PETO 7 gr.g. Petong 126 – Plie 75 (Superlative 118) [2007 62: f7g f12g⁴ **55** f12g² f8g⁶ f11g² 12d⁶ 9.2d⁶ 12d* 12.4d 12g Oct 30] good-quartered gelding: modest handicapper: won apprentice event at Catterick in July: stays 1½m: acts on all-weather, soft and good to firm going: wears headgear/sometimes tongue tied: has hung right. *R. Johnson*

DISPOL TRULY (IRE) 3 b.f. Bold Fact (USA) 116 – Beautyofthepeace (IRE) (Exac- – tly Sharp (USA) 121) [2007 47: p7f 7d May 17] maiden: no form in 2007: tried in cheekpieces. *A. G. Newcombe*

DISPOL VELETA 6 b.m. Makbul 104 – Foxtrot Pie 77 (Shernazar 131) [2007 72: **69** 9.2g⁴ 9g 10s² 9.2s 8.5s⁵ 10d Aug 20] good-topped mare: fair handicapper: stays 10.3f (all wins around 1m): acts on fibresand and soft ground. *Miss T. Spearing*

DISTANT CHARM (IRE) 2 b.c. (Feb 3) Distant Music (USA) 126 – My Lucy **78** Locket (IRE) 96§ (Mujadil (USA) 119) [2007 6g⁵ 7g** 7.1s* 7g 7g 7s⁶ 8g Oct 26] quite attractive colt: fair performer: won maiden at Lingfield in June and minor event at Warwick in July: ran creditably in mid-division in nurseries (blinkered final start): stays 1m: raced only on good going or softer: sold 25,000 gns, sent to Serbia. *R. Hannon*

DISTANT DIAMOND (IRE) 2 b.c. (Mar 28) Distant Music (USA) 126 – La Belle **77 +** Katherine (USA) (Lyphard (USA) 132) [2007 p7g 7g⁶ p7g p8m* Oct 3] 15,000F: well-made colt: sixth foal: half-brother to several winners, including 7-y-o Aventura: dam ran twice in France: fair form: improved to win nursery at Kempton final start: stays 1m. *W. R. Swinburn*

DISTANT DRAMA (USA) 3 ch.f. Distant View (USA) 126 – To Act (USA) (Roberto **73** (USA) 131) [2007 6g² p6g p8g² p8.6g* Nov 22] neat filly: ninth foal: sister to smart Japanese sprinter Keeneland Swan and half-sister to several winners, including useful Irish 7f to 9.5f winner Film Festival (by Diesis): dam, US maiden, half-sister to US Grade 3 6f winner Ziggy's Act, out of US Grade 1 1¼m winner Comedy Act: fair performer: in cheekpieces, won maiden at Wolverhampton in November: stays 8.6f: acts on polytrack. *J. Noseda*

DISTANT NOBLE 2 b.g. (Mar 18) Carnival Dancer 123 – Fly In Style (Hernando (FR) **55 d** 127) [2007 6m 7s² p6g p7g 7m p8.6g p8.6d Dec 10] quite attractive gelding: modest maiden: second in seller (left M. Wallace £5,000): no form subsequently: stays 7f: blinkered final start. *R. Brotherton*

DISTANT PLEASURE 3 b.f. Diktat 126 – Our Pleasure (IRE) (Lake Coniston (IRE) **70** 131) [2007 7m⁶ 7.5m 8m* 8.1v⁴ 8m 8m Aug 30] 10,000Y: leggy filly: third foal: half-sister to 2005 2-y-o 5f winner River Kintyre (by Mull of Kintyre): dam unraced half-sister to smart Irish sprinter Lidanna: fair performer: won maiden at Redcar in June: stays 1m: acts on heavy and good to firm going. *M. Dods*

DISTANT SHORES (IRE) 4 b.f. Averti (IRE) 117 – Adeptation (USA) (Exceller – (USA) 129) [2007 p7.1g Jan 22] poor maiden at 2 yrs: well held on belated return. *Miss T. Spearing*

DISTANT SUNSET (IRE) 3 b.g. Distant Music (USA) 126 – Blushing Libra (Peru- **63** gino (USA) 84) [2007 54p: p12.2g² 12.1m⁴ p12.2g⁴ Jun 1] modest maiden handicapper: stays easy 1½m: raced only on polytrack and going firmer than good: sold 10,500 gns in July, sent to Qatar. *B. W. Hills*

DISTANT SUN (USA) 3 b.g. Distant View (USA) 126 – The Great Flora (USA) (Un- **80** accounted For (USA) 124) [2007 63p: p7.1g³ p7g² 6m 6g⁴ p7.1g 6g* 6g⁵ 6m⁵ 7m² 7.1s⁴ 6g* 6g³ 7g⁴ 6g³ 7.1g Nov 8] leggy gelding: fairly useful performer: left R. Charlton after second outing: won maiden at Ayr in May and handicap at Hamilton in August: effective at 6f to easy 8.6f: acts on polytrack and good to firm going: effective with/without cheekpieces: usually races prominently: not easiest of rides. *I. Semple*

DISTANT VISION (IRE) 4 br.f. Distant Music (USA) 126 – Najeyba 80 (Indian – Ridge 123) [2007 37: f7g p6g p6g 7.9m 9.3g⁵ Jun 18] angular filly: poor maiden: well held in 2007: tried tongue tied/visored/in cheekpieces. *A. Berry*

DISTANT WAY (USA) 6 b.h. Distant View (USA) 126 – Grey Way (USA) 109 **119** (Cozzene (USA)) [2007 119: 10m* 10m* 12m⁵ 12m 10d Nov 4] big, strong horse: smart performer: prolific winner: back to best at Rome in first half of year, winning minor event in April and Premio Presidente della Repubblica for second year running (led inside final

1f to beat Pressing ½ length) in May: lost form again in autumn, unsuitable trip in Prix Foy at Longchamp and Gran Premio del Jockey Club at Milan first 2 occasions: best at 1m/1¼m: acts on good to firm and good to soft ground. *L. Brogi, Italy*

DISTILLER (IRE) 3 b.g. Invincible Spirit (IRE) 121 – Bobbydazzle 81 (Rock Hopper **80** 124) [2007 72: p7g 8.3g² 10m 8.1g 10f* 10g 10.3m⁴ 11.9s p9.5g³ p9.5g* p8.6g Oct 27] tall gelding: fairly useful handicapper: won at Redcar in August and Wolverhampton in October: stays 1¼m: acts on polytrack, firm and good to soft going: sold 45,000 gns, joined N. Twiston-Davies. *W. R. Muir*

DISTINCTION (IRE) 8 b.g. Danehill (USA) 126 – Ivy Leaf (IRE) 76 (Nureyev **115** (USA) 131) [2007 122: 16g 16.4d⁴ 18m⁴ 16g* 16d⁴ Oct 20] big, strong, good sort: usually impresses in appearance: just smart form in 2007 (reportedly suffered leg injury and off 14 months prior to reappearance): fourth to Septimus in Doncaster Cup on third start prior to dead-heating with Solent in listed event at Ascot (briefly a length up before hanging right and joined on line) in September: visored, below par when fourth to Royal And Regal in Jockey Club Cup at Newmarket final outing: stays 2½m: acts on firm and soft going: has wandered/raced freely: stays in training. *Sir Michael Stoute*

DISTINCTIVE IMAGE (USA) 2 b.c. (Mar 27) Mineshaft (USA) 132 – Dock Leaf **66 p** (USA) (Woodman (USA) 126) [2007 p7m Nov 1] attractive colt: second foal: dam, maiden (third at 9f in US), half-sister to US Grade 1 winner Aptitude (high class up to 1½m): 11/4, very green when seventh of 9 in maiden at Lingfield: will stay at least 1¼m: sure to progress. *J. H. M. Gosden*

DISTINCTLY GAME 5 b.g. Mind Games 121 – Distinctly Blu (IRE) 70 (Distinctly **88** North (USA) 115) [2007 –: f5g⁴ p6g* p5g³ p6g p6g³ 5m 5d 6g 5.6m 6m 5m 5d⁵ 5m p6g* **a95** Nov 30] tall, quite good-topped gelding: useful handicapper on all-weather, fairly useful on turf: won at Kempton (impressively) in January and Lingfield in November: best at 5f/6f: acts on all-weather, good to firm and good to soft going: tried in cheekpieces/blinkers: none too reliable. *K. A. Ryan*

DIUM MAC 6 b.g. Presidium 124 – Efipetite 54 (Efisio 120) [2007 84: 10.1s 10.5g **84** 10.4g 12m⁶ 8m 11.5d 14.1g² 14.6g 16.5m³ Nov 10] leggy gelding: fairly useful handicapper: best efforts in 2007 when placed: stays 16.5f: acts on firm and soft going: tried blinkered. *N. Bycroft*

DIVALINI 3 ch.f. Bertolini (USA) 125 – Divine Grace (IRE) (Definite Article 121) **65** [2007 –: 6d⁶ 5.3m* 5m p5.1g⁴ p5g Oct 24] fair handicapper: won at Brighton in June: should stay 6f: acts on polytrack and good to firm going: sold 2,500 gns. *J. Akehurst*

DIVERSE FORECAST (IRE) 3 b.g. Fasliyev (USA) 120 – Motley (Rainbow Quest **–** (USA) 134) [2007 –: 11.8s Jun 4] close-coupled gelding: last in maidens. *Mrs P. Sly*

DIVERTIMENTI (IRE) 3 b.g. Green Desert (USA) 127 – Ballet Shoes (IRE) 75 **81** (Ela-Mana-Mou 132) [2007 79: p6g⁵ p6g* p8g⁵ p6g⁶ 6m* f7g³ p7.1g³ p7.1g⁴ p7g* p7g⁴ p8g² p8.6g⁴ p7.1g⁵ Dec 31] sturdy gelding: fairly useful performer: trained in Ireland at 2 yrs: won maiden at Lingfield in February, seller at Leicester (left M. Wallace) in April and handicap at Lingfield in August: stays 8.6f: acts on all-weather and good to firm ground: has worn blinkers/cheekpieces (not last 7 starts): free-going sort. *C. R. Dore*

DIVINE LOVE (IRE) 3 b.f. Barathea (IRE) 127 – Darling (Darshaan 133) [2007 78: **62 §** 10f⁶ 8m⁴ 10.2m p8g Sep 29] maiden, only modest in 2007: should stay 1¼m: raced only on polytrack and firm/good to firm ground: blinkered last 3 starts: irresolute, and one to treat with caution: sold 2,700 gns. *E. J. O'Neill*

DIVINE NIGHT (IRE) 3 b.f. Danehill (USA) 126 – Starlight Night (USA) 71 **95** (Distant View (USA) 126) [2007 78: 8m³ 8m 7.5m 8g Oct 14] lengthy filly: first foal: dam, maiden (raced at 1¼m), half-sister to useful US performer up to 11f Senure, out of half-sister to Xaar: useful performer: good 3¾ lengths third to Alexander Tango in Derrinstown Stud 1000 Guineas Trial at Leopardstown on reappearance: below form after, including at Ascot next time: will stay 1¼m: acts on good to firm ground: wore cheekpieces final start: sometimes slowly away: free-going sort. *D. Wachman, Ireland*

DIVINE POWER 2 b.f. (May 15) Kyllachy 129 – Tiriana (Common Grounds 118) **76** [2007 6.1g² 6d³ 5m⁴ p7g² Oct 24] smallish filly: sixth foal: closely related to smart 6f (at 2 yrs)/7f winner Penkenna Princess (by Pivotal) and half-sister to 3 winners, including 6-y-o Salut Saint Cloud: dam third at 1m in France: fair maiden: in frame all starts, second to Malibu Girl at Lingfield final one: stays 7f. *R. M. Beckett*

DIVINE RIGHT 3 ch.f. Observatory (USA) 131 – Grail (USA) (Quest For Fame 127) **91** [2007 84: 9d⁵ 8s 8m⁵ 9g Aug 1] sturdy, attractive filly: fairly useful handicapper: stays 9f:

acts on good to firm and good to soft ground: tended to hang right third outing: sold 22,000 gns. *B. J. Meehan*

DIVINE RIVER 4 b.f. Lujain (USA) 119 – Berliese (IRE) (High Estate 127) [2007 77: **51** 10m 10.5m 16m 10g³ p12g p12g p12g Nov 30] angular filly: only modest in 2007, leaving A. P. Jarvis after second start: stays 1½m, possibly not 1¾m: raced only on polytrack and good/good to firm going. *J. G. Portman*

DIVINE SPIRIT 6 b.g. Foxhound (USA) 103 – Vocation (IRE) 74 (Royal Academy **94** (USA) 130) [2007 76: 6g 5.1m⁶ 5.1m³ 6g⁶ 5.5d² 5f 5m³ 5g² 5g² 5s³ 5d² 5g* 5.1g* 5g 5g⁴ 5d* 5d* Sep 21] smallish, good-bodied gelding: fairly useful handicapper: won at Beverley in July, Nottingham in August, and Musselburgh and Ayr within 5 days in September: effective at 5f/6f: acts on polytrack, firm and soft going: sometimes wears cheekpieces/blinkers: versatile regards tactics. *M. Dods*

DIVINE WHITE 4 ch.f. College Chapel 122 – Snowy Mantle 54 (Siberian Express **59 d** (USA) 125) [2007 58: f7g³ 7m 8.3v⁵ 9.7m 8.1m 8.1m p7.1g Oct 19] lengthy, leggy filly: modest maiden: well below form after reappearance in 2007 (signs of temperament final outing): effective at 6f/7f: acts on all-weather and firm going, probably on heavy: tried in cheekpieces. *P. Bowen*

DIXEY 2 br.f. (Jan 26) Diktat 126 – Hoh Dancer 66 (Indian Ridge 123) [2007 p7g* 7m⁵ **98** p7.1g² Jul 30] rangy filly: fifth foal: sister to 4-y-o Dichoh: dam, maiden, half-sister to useful 2-y-o 5f winner Infanta Real: useful form: won maiden at Kempton in June: neck second to Palm Court (pair clear) in nursery at Wolverhampton: well held on turf in between: free-going sort, should prove best up to 7f: acts on polytrack. *M. A. Jarvis*

DIXIELAND BOY (IRE) 4 b.g. Inchinor 119 – Savannah Belle 84 (Green Desert **82** (USA) 127) [2007 77: f6g* f6g⁴ 5.7d² 6d² 5s⁴ Oct 4] strong, good-bodied gelding: fairly useful performer: won maiden at Southwell in January, wandering in front: better form in handicaps after: effective at 6f to 1m: acts on all-weather and good to soft going, probably on firm. *P. J. Makin*

DIYSEM (USA) 3 b.c. Johannesburg (USA) 127 – Technicolour (IRE) 79 (Rainbow **77** Quest (USA) 134) [2007 89: p8g 6m 6g⁶ a6.5f Dec 22] tall colt: just fair performer in 2007: below form after reappearance, leaving B. Meehan before final outing: may prove best around 7f: yet to race on extremes of going on turf. *R. Baffert, USA*

DIZZY DREAMER (IRE) 4 b.f. Spinning World (USA) 130 – Divine Prospect (IRE) – 75 (Namaqualand (USA)) [2007 103: 6g 5m 6d Jun 29] tall, leggy filly: useful performer at 3 yrs: well below form in 2007. *P. W. Chapple-Hyam*

DJALALABAD (FR) 3 b.f. King's Best (USA) 132 – Daraydala (IRE) 108 (Royal **66** Academy (USA) 130) [2007 9.9d³ 10m⁴ 12d 10m 8m⁶ 8d⁶ 10m² 10d 8g Oct 25] €45,000Y: leggy filly: half-sister to several winners abroad, including French 11.5f winner Darayad (by Ashkalani) and useful French 14.5f/15f winner Darayka (by Dr Fong): dam, French 1½m winner, half-sister to dam of Prix du Jockey Club winner Darsi: fair maiden: left M. Jarvis after third start: should stay 1½m: acts on good to firm and good to soft ground: inconsistent. *Mrs C. A. Dunnett*

DO AS I SAY 2 b.g. (Mar 14) Diktat 126 – Antonia's Choice 73 (Music Boy 124) [2007 **68** 5m⁶ 5g³ 5.9g⁵ Jun 18] fair maiden: third to Victorian Bounty at Musselburgh: gelded after final start: will be best at 5f/6f. *T. D. Easterby*

DOCOFTHEBAY (IRE) 3 ch.c. Docksider (USA) 124 – Baize 95 (Efisio 120) [2007 **111** 75: 8.5g² 8.3m² 8m* 8m³ 8.2g² 7m* 7g* 8g² 7d³ 9m² 9d⁶ Oct 19] sturdy, compact colt: smart and progressive in handicaps, winning at Thirsk in May, Ascot in July and Goodwood (by ½ length from Vitznau) in August: good placed efforts after at York (to The Illies), Ascot (behind Candidato Roy) and Newmarket (length second to Pipedreamer in Cambridgeshire, staying on strongly after being stopped in run): not discredited behind Windsor Knot in Darley Stakes at Newmarket final outing: effective at 7f to 9f: acts on fibresand, good to firm and good to soft going: wore cheekpieces fourth start: held up: tends to hang and has looked less than straightforward, but is tough and reliable. *J. A. Osborne*

DOCTOR DINO (FR) 5 ch.h. Muhtathir 126 – Logica (IRE) 81 (Priolo (USA) **123** 127) [2007 113: 10.5m³ 10d³ 10d³ 11f* 10d³ 12g* Dec 9]

For a horse who had spent much of his four-year-old season competing in the French Provinces—at the likes of Toulouse, Vichy, Bordeaux and Marseilles—and had never set foot outside France, Doctor Dino's horizons were broadened considerably as a five-year-old with spectacular success. In terms of form, the

Man o'War Stakes, Belmont—Doctor Dino (centre) is poised to strike as Sunriver (right) goes for home, though he is forced to display good battling qualities to prevail by a head

progress he made from four to five was not earth-shattering—he was already well established as a smart horse—but the improvement was enough to take him from a listed or Group 3 performer at best in France to one more than able to hold his own in some very big international events. Prior to the latest season, Doctor Dino's only start in Group 1 company had resulted in seventh place behind Shamardal in the Prix du Jockey Club. In contrast, his latest campaign was conducted entirely at the top level with his consistency perhaps the most striking aspect of his season, as he ran up to his new-found level of form in all six of his starts, finishing in the money each time.

The financial rewards of such a campaign were particularly lucrative. According to France-Galop, Doctor Dino's win and place earnings for the year came to the equivalent of €1,327,725 or around £950,000. A few inches another way in a couple of tight finishes, and Doctor Dino would have been a millionaire in sterling as well. What he would have earned had he stayed at home is hard to say, but it would not have been anything like the sum he earned from his world tour. Doctor Dino was not up to Arc-winning standard, though even a win in Europe's most valuable race (worth just under £800,000) would not have proved as rewarding financially. Dylan Thomas was one of Doctor Dino's rivals when he made his reappearance in the Prix Ganay at Longchamp in April. His third place to the future Arc winner, beaten two and three quarter lengths, perhaps persuaded connections that Doctor Dino had his work cut out pursuing a Group 1 campaign in Europe.

The following month Doctor Dino made his first start abroad, staying on for third behind the Japanese horses Shadow Gate and Cosmo Bulk in the Singapore Airlines International Cup at Kranji, beaten just a short head for the runner-up spot, with the Clive Brittain-trained Kandidate behind him in fifth. The Singapore race is relatively new to the international calendar, but, for his next start, Doctor Dino contested the much more established Arlington Million in August, which, when created in 1981 as the Budweiser Million, was the world's most valuable race. It has long since lost that position but still attracts an international field, and Doctor Dino was joined from Europe (in a field of just seven) by Pressing from Britain and

Danak from Ireland. A slow early pace resulted in a bunched finish, with Doctor Dino faring best of the Europeans, putting in his best work late on to be beaten three quarters of a length and a nose by the Canadian gelding Jambalaya and the previous year's winner The Tin Man.

The next big turf race in the States, the Man o'War Stakes at Belmont over eleven furlongs, may not have quite the same international profile as the Arlington Million but is nonetheless another event with a history of European success. The top-class French mare Dahlia won in 1974 and Millkom was another French-trained winner in 1995. More recently, two of Godolphin's best horses, Daylami and Fantastic Light, have been successful. Two of Doctor Dino's rivals had begun their careers in France; Grand Couturier, winner of the Sword Dancer Invitational Stakes at Saratoga on the same day as the Arlington Million, and the three-year-old Shamdinan, third in the Prix du Jockey Club and subsequently winner of the Secretariat Stakes for his new stable earlier on the Arlington Million card. The Aidan O'Brien-trained Gordon Stakes winner Yellowstone was the other European-trained runner in a field of seven for the Man o'War and was sent off favourite. From the home turn though, the race concerned only Doctor Dino and Sunriver, who had dead-heated for fourth close behind Doctor Dino at Arlington. Sunriver slipped clear off the turn and it took Doctor Dino the whole of the straight to peg him back but he showed good battling qualities to do so, responding well to gain a deserved head victory, the first two finishing over three lengths clear of Grand Couturier, with Yellowstone only sixth. Doctor Dino's win (and the injury to Manduro in France the same weekend) led connections to consider the Arc as his next race, though, when he did reappear in Europe, it was for the Champion Stakes at Newmarket. Doctor Dino's third place, three lengths behind the three-year-olds Literato and Eagle Mountain, again underlined his limitations in top company in Europe, but he emerged with plenty of credit, unlucky not to finish closer to the first two after being left with a lot of ground to make up and then not getting a smooth passage.

Doctor Dino ended the year back in the Far East in the Cathay Pacific Hong Kong Vase at Sha Tin. Of the four Group 1 contests on the card, the mile and a half event regularly attracts the strongest European challenge—the trip is too far for most of the locally-trained horses who race mainly at up to a mile and a quarter. French-trained horses have a good record in the race, with Partipral, Borgia, Ange Gabriel and Vallee Enchantee all successful since Red Bishop won the inaugural running for John Hammond in 1994. British-trained Vase winners include Luso, twice successful in the 'nineties, and the last three winners Phoenix Reach, Ouija Board and Collier Hill, all of them tough, well-travelled competitors already with worldwide successes to their names. Given his record, Doctor Dino fitted the typical profile of a Hong Kong Vase winner, though with Dylan Thomas in the field (after being denied a run in the Japan Cup), as well as the previous season's Breeders' Cup Turf winner Red Rocks, there was a distinct possibility that this

Cathay Pacific Hong Kong Vase, Sha Tin—the prize again goes to a well-travelled performer;
Doctor Dino (noseband, third left) and Quijano (black sleeves, towards right)
are about to catch Bussoni (left); Arch Rebel (noseband, far right) is fourth
while Dylan Thomas (dark colours, centre) ends his career in seventh place

particular edition would take more winning than usual. In the event, the pair ahead of Doctor Dino in the betting were nowhere near their best. Passing the post first time Doctor Dino was well placed but, turning into the short home straight at Sha Tin, he had only Dylan Thomas behind him. Clearly relishing his first attempt at a mile and a half, Doctor Dino stayed on best of all to lead in the last fifty yards. The Grosser Preis von Baden winner Quijano also stayed on strongly from behind to be beaten a length and a half, depriving another German-trained runner Bussoni of second place by a neck, while Irish challenger Arch Rebel completed the frame. European-trained horses took the first seven places in all, with Kocab for France and the other German runner Egerton next home, ahead of a disappointing Dylan Thomas. Doctor Dino is still an entire but the decision to keep him in training another year cannot have been too hard to make. His performance in Hong Kong was a career-best effort and, now proven at a mile and a half, even more valuable contests such as the Dubai Sheema Classic and Japan Cup could be on the agenda in 2008. The same could hardly have been contemplated twelve months earlier when Doctor Dino's biggest success up until then had been the Prix Andre Baboin, the Grand Prix des Provinces, at Bordeaux, the last of his three wins in 2006.

			Elmaamul	Diesis
Doctor Dino (FR)	Muhtathir		(ch 1987)	Modena
(ch.h. 2002)	(ch 1995)		Majmu	Al Nasr
			(b 1988)	Affirmative Fable
	Logica (IRE)		Priolo	Sovereign Dancer
	(b 1994)		(b 1987)	Primevere
			Salagangai	Sallust
			(ch 1982)	Malagangai

The good-topped Doctor Dino's sire Muhtathir, also represented by the Prix de l'Opera winner Satwa Queen in the latest season, was no less of an international traveller. Trained by John Gosden for his first two seasons before joining Godolphin, he had his passport stamped in France, Italy, Dubai, Japan, Hong Kong, Canada and the States, though he failed to win outside Europe, his biggest success coming in the Prix Jacques le Marois as a five-year-old. A mile proved Muhtathir's best trip after defeat in Sandown's Classic Trial on his three-year-old reappearance put paid to any ambitions over middle distances. Doctor Dino has his dam to thank for the fact that he stays a mile and a half, though he has comprehensively outshone her in terms of ability. Logica failed to win for Paul Kelleway as a two-year-old, but got off the mark when sent to France the following year for Elie Lellouche in an apprentice race at Deauville over an extended twelve furlongs. Having cost only €38,000 as a yearling at Deauville, Doctor Dino has proved a rare bargain, though he had little to recommend him on pedigree then, and even now he remains the only winner produced by his dam so far. His three-year-old half-sister Isaure (by the 2000 Hong Kong Vase winner Daliapour) was placed in a couple of minor events over a mile and a half late in the year. Doctor Dino's unraced grandam Salagangai has produced three winners in all, the best of them Millie's Choice, who was a smart and consistent Irish filly, best at seven furlongs. Great grandam Malagangai was a mile-and-a-quarter winner in France and a half-sister to the Prix de Royallieu winner Gipsy Road. *R. Gibson, France*

DOCTOR FREMANTLE 2 b.c. (Jan 29) Sadler's Wells (USA) 132 – Summer **91 p**
Breeze 101 (Rainbow Quest (USA) 134) [2007 7m² 8d² 8.2g* Oct 31] sturdy colt: fourth foal: brother to useful French 1½m/12.5f winner Summer Shower: dam, French 2-y-o 1m winner, sister to very smart stayers Sunshack and Raintrap: fairly useful form: developed well in maidens, twice runner-up then winning at Nottingham by 5 lengths, showing sharp turn of foot: will be suited by 1¼m/1½m: sure to go on and win better races. *Sir Michael Stoute*

DOCTOR NED 3 b.g. Bahamian Bounty 116 – Sangra (USA) 69 (El Gran Senor (USA) **52**
136) [2007 –p: p7g p7g⁶ 7g* 7.1g⁵ 6.1m 6g⁴ 8.1d⁵ 8d 7g 10.9g Oct 2] quite good-topped gelding: modest performer: won selling handicap at Folkestone in April (wandered, unseated jockey after line): left N. Callaghan after eighth start: probably stays 1m: acts on good to soft going: tongue tied (well held) last 2 outings. *Miss S. West*

DOCTOR ROBERT 2 b.c. (Jan 30) Sakhee (USA) 136 – Please (Kris 135) [2007 p7g **86**
7m 7g² 8m 8.3d² 8d⁴ p10g⁵ Dec 12] 40,000Y: unfurnished colt: fourth foal: half-brother

to 4-y-o Esteem: dam, ran twice, out of sister to smart middle-distance stayer Spring and close relation of Pentire: fairly useful maiden: runner-up at Newbury and Windsor (nursery): left R. Charlton 45,000 gns prior to final start: needs to settle to stay beyond 1m (bred to): acts on good to soft going. *Tom Dascombe*

DOCTOR'S CAVE 5 b.g. Night Shift (USA) – Periquitum 56 (Dilum (USA) 115) **63 +** [2007 –, a67: p5.1g p7.1g* f7g* f7g p7.1g⁴ f7g* f7g* 7.1d⁴ 8s⁶ Jul 2] sturdy, close-coupled gelding: fair handicapper on all-weather, modest on turf: won at Wolverhampton and Southwell (3) between February and May: effective at 5f to easy 8.6f: acts on all-weather, best turf efforts on good going: tried tongue tied: blinkered: races prominently: reportedly bled fourth start. *K. O. Cunningham-Brown* **a78**

DOCTOR SCOTT 4 b.g. Medicean 128 – Milly of The Vally 93 (Caerleon (USA) 132) **85** [2007 96: 12.3g 13.8m* 14m⁴ 13.1m 15.8m⁵ 21g 16.1m⁴ 16g⁵ 11.1g* 12m⁴ 13s p12g⁴ p13.9g⁴ Oct 21] good-bodied gelding: fairly useful handicapper: won at Catterick in May and Hamilton in September: effective at 11f to 2m: acts on polytrack, firm and good to soft going: sold 28,000 gns. *M. Johnston*

DODAA (USA) 4 b.g. Dayjur (USA) 137 – Ra'a (USA) 106 (Diesis 133) [2007 45: f6g³ **–** f6g³ f5g* f5g 5d 5s p6g p5.1g f6d f5d⁵ p5.1g⁵ Dec 31] workmanlike gelding: modest **a52** performer on all-weather, no form on turf: won minor event at Southwell in February: effective at 5f/6f: acts on all-weather: tried blinkered. *N. Wilson*

DOLCE DOVO 4 b.f. Medicean 128 – Dance To The Top 107 (Sadler's Wells (USA) **78 §** 132) [2007 81: p12.2g² p9.5g² 9.2d⁴ p10g⁴ 12m Aug 3] 33,000F, €40,000Y: closely related to 1m winner Dress Rehearsal and 1¼m winner Audition (both by Machiavellian), and half-brother to 2 winners, including smart French 1m to 10.5f winner Cheshire (by Warning): dam 2-y-o 7f winner (second in Fillies' Mile) who stayed 10.4f: maiden, only fair in 2007: stays 1¼m: acts on polytrack, firm and soft ground: tried in headgear: temperamental. *W. J. Haggas*

DOLLAR CHICK (IRE) 3 b.f. Dansili 127 – Dollar Bird (IRE) 103 (Kris 135) [2007 **81** 82p: 8.3g 9.8m 12g² 13.8g⁶ Nov 6] rangy filly: fairly useful handicapper, lightly raced: should stay 1¾m: unraced on going softer than good (acts on firm). *M. Johnston*

DOLLY 5 b.m. Thowra (FR) – Sweet Symphony (IRE) (Orchestra 118) [2007 45: p10g **43** p8g p8g p6g⁴ Apr 4] poor maiden: stays easy 1¼m: acts on polytrack and good to firm going: tried in cheekpieces. *Tom Dascombe*

DOLLY COUGHDROP (IRE) 3 b.f. Titus Livius (FR) 115 – Fairy Berry (IRE) **64** (Fairy King (USA)) [2007 72: p7g⁵ f7g⁵ p7g 6g⁶ 6f³ 6.9g Jun 18] fair performer at 2 yrs: regressive form in 2007: stays easy 7f: acts on polytrack, firm and soft going: sold 800 gns in July. *K. R. Burke*

DOLLY NO HAIR 2 ch.g. (Apr 30) Reel Buddy (USA) 118 – Champagne Grandy 84 **75 ?** (Vaigly Great 127) [2007 6m 6g 7g² Oct 3] tall gelding: fair maiden: 100/1, seemingly much improved effort when second at Newcastle, dictating (gelded after): stays 7f. *D. W. Barker*

DOLZAGO 7 b.g. Pursuit of Love 124 – Doctor's Glory (USA) 91 (Elmaamul (USA) **71** 125) [2007 p12g p16g p16g* p16g p16g Mar 16] good-bodied gelding: fair handicapper: won at Lingfield in January: stays 2m: acts on polytrack, no recent form on turf: usually blinkered: sold £1,200 in June. *G. L. Moore*

DOME BLONDE 2 ch.f. (Mar 4) Domedriver (IRE) 128 – Proud Titania (IRE) 103 **– §** (Fairy King (USA)) [2007 6d 8.2g p8.6g Nov 24] 4,000F: lengthy filly: seventh foal: half-sister to 3 winners, including 1½m winner Daze (by Daylami): dam Irish 7f winner (including at 2 yrs): wayward and well held in maiden/seller/claimer: in headgear last 2 starts. *W. J. Musson*

DOMENICO (IRE) 9 b.g. Sadler's Wells (USA) 132 – Russian Ballet (USA) (Nijin- **60** sky (CAN) 138) [2007 60: p16g⁴ p16g⁶ f11g⁴ p16g p16.5g 14.1m² 14.1d⁶ Aug 26] strong, close-coupled gelding: modest handicapper: probably stays 2½m: acts on all-weather, soft and good to firm going: tried blinkered: none too reliable. *J. R. Jenkins*

DOME ROCK (IRE) 2 ch.c. (Apr 29) Domedriver (IRE) 128 – My American Beauty **77** 93 (Wolfhound (USA) 126) [2007 5m⁶ p5g 5g⁵ 6g p8m p6g² Oct 24] smallish, lengthy colt: has a fluent action: fair maiden: second in claimer at Lingfield: best form at 6f: sold 24,000 gns. *L. M. Cumani*

DOMESDAY (UAE) 6 b.g. Cape Cross (IRE) 129 – Deceive 100 (Machiavellian **58** (USA) 123) [2007 –: 13d 8g 10.5m 10.1g 8m³ 8m² p9.5g⁴ p8.6g Nov 2] modest maiden: **a52** barely stays 9.5f: acts on polytrack and good to firm ground: tried visored. *W. G. Harrison*

DOMESTIC FUND (IRE) 2 b.c. (Feb 1) Sadler's Wells (USA) 132 – Market Slide **104**
(USA) 94 (Gulch (USA)) [2007 7s⁴ 7s² 7d* 8d² 8d⁵ Oct 26] lengthy, quite good-topped
colt: sixth foal: brother to 2 winners, notably high-class 7f (at 2 yrs) to 1¼m performer
Refuse To Bend and half-brother to Melbourne Cup winner Media Puzzle (by Theatrical):
dam Irish 6f winner (including at 2 yrs): useful performer: won maiden at Leopardstown
in August: much better form after, in Beresford Stakes at the Curragh (4 lengths second to
Curtain Call) and Breeders' Cup Juvenile Turf at Monmouth (visored, 3¼ lengths fifth to
Nownownow, leading briefly 1f out): stays 1m: raced only on soft/good to soft going:
usually races close to pace. *D. K. Weld, Ireland*

DOMINO DANCER (IRE) 3 b.g. Tagula (IRE) 116 – Hazarama (IRE) 91 (Kahyasi **92**
130) [2007 87: 8m⁴ 9.1m⁴ 10.1v* 12v 9.9g⁶ 14g Aug 23] quite attractive gelding: fairly
useful handicapper: left J. Howard Johnson after reappearance: won at Newcastle in June:
stays 1¼m (virtually unrideable, hanging left, when tailed off at 1¾m): acts on heavy and
good to firm going: not straightforward. *J. Wade*

DONA ALBA (IRE) 2 b.f. (Apr 14) Peintre Celebre (USA) 137 – Fantastic Fantasy **91 p**
(IRE) 85 (Lahib (USA) 129) [2007 7g⁴ 7m* 8f² Sep 27] medium-sized, workmanlike
filly: third foal: half-sister to 3-y-o Last Flight: dam, 1¼m to 1¾m winner, half-sister to
useful performers Lucky Guest (at 1m/1¼m) and Fantasy Hill (stayer): fairly useful form:
won maiden at Folkestone in September: better again when second to Jazz Jam in nursery
at Pontefract: should go on progressing at 1¼m+. *J. L. Dunlop*

DONEGAL (USA) 2 b. or br.g. (Apr 29) Menifee (USA) 124 – Vickey's Echo (CAN) **99**
(Clever Trick (USA)) [2007 7.1g² 7s* 7g³ 8m⁵ p8m⁴ 10g⁶ Nov 3] $80,000Y: close-
coupled, attractive gelding: half-brother to several winners, including 3-y-o Supersonic
Dave and smart US winner up to 1½m French Braids (by Personal Flag): dam US maiden:
useful performer: won maiden at York in July: best effort when 6 lengths third to Rio de
La Plata in Vintage Stakes at Goodwood: stays 1m: acts on polytrack and soft ground:
visored (ran creditably) once: gelded after final start. *A. M. Balding*

DON JOSE (USA) 4 b. or br.g. Dynaformer (USA) – Panthera (USA) (Storm Cat **57**
(USA)) [2007 7m 10.9d 12.1s³ p12.2g⁶ 12.1m p13.9g Dec 31] tall gelding: modest
maiden handicapper: stays 1½m: acts on soft going. *N. J. Vaughan*

DON PASQUALE 5 b.g. Zafonic (USA) 130 – Bedazzling (IRE) 105 (Darshaan 133) **62**
[2007 –: p12.2g p9.5g³ f8g⁴ f8g² f8g⁶ 10m⁴ 10g* 9.9s* 12d 12.6s 10.1g⁵ p10g 10.1m 10d
p9.5g p10g⁶ p10g⁴ p9.5g Nov 2] smallish gelding: modest handicapper: won at Nottingham and Beverley in June: stays 1¼m: acts on all-weather, soft and good to firm going:
tried blinkered/visored/tongue tied: often takes keen hold: held up. *J. T. Stimpson*

DON PELE (IRE) 5 b.g. Monashee Mountain (USA) 115 – Big Fandango (Bigstone **91**
(IRE) 126) [2007 97: 6g 6g⁶ 5m³ 6g² 5d³ 6g 6m 5d² 6d* 6d³ 5d⁶ Oct 13] good-
bodied gelding: fairly useful handicapper: left P. D. Evans after second outing: won at
Goodwood in September by short head from Dixieland Boy: effective at 5f/6f: acts on
polytrack, good to firm and good to soft going: blinkered once, in cheekpieces of late.
R. A. Harris

DON PICOLO 2 b.c. (Feb 7) Bertolini (USA) 125 – Baby Come Back (IRE) (Fayruz **–**
116) [2007 p6g 6.1v⁶ 7m 10m Oct 8] sturdy colt: well held in maidens. *P. A. Blockley*

DON PIETRO 4 b.g. Bertolini (USA) 125 – Silver Spell 54 (Aragon 118) [2007 90: 8m **85**
p8g³ 8m 10.2d² 10g⁵ p10g p10m³ Nov 11] tall gelding: fairly useful handicapper:
effective at 1m to 1¼m: acts on polytrack, soft and good to firm ground: often races
freely: joined P. Blockley. *D. J. Coakley*

DONT CALL ME DEREK 6 b.g. Sri Pekan (USA) 117 – Cultural Role 95 (Night **–**
Shift (USA)) [2007 –: 12g May 18] big, workmanlike gelding: useful handicapper in
2005: no show both starts on Flat since: wore blinkers once in 2004: sold 3,200 gns in
October, joined M. Allen. *J. J. Quinn*

DON'TCALLMEGINGER (IRE) 4 ch.g. Fruits of Love (USA) 127 – Scotia Rose **66**
(Tap On Wood 130) [2007 –: f12g 16m p16g 11.9d⁵ 10g² 12.1g* 12.1g² 12s⁴ Aug 22]
rather leggy, quite good-topped gelding: fair handicapper: won at Beverley in July: stays
1½m: acts on good to soft ground. *M. H. Tompkins*

DON'T DESERT ME (IRE) 3 b.g. Desert Style (IRE) 121 – Eye View (USA) **58**
(Distant View (USA) 126) [2007 64: p10g p10g⁵ Jan 20] modest maiden handicapper:
probably stays 1¼m: raced only on polytrack: travelled with little fluency on reappearance, blinkered next time: sold 12,000 gns in February. *R. Charlton*

DONT DILI DALI 4 b.f. Dansili 127 – Miss Meltemi (IRE) 100 (Miswaki Tern (USA) **102**
120) [2007 102: 7.5g 10g³ 10g⁴ 9g³ 12g⁶ p8g² 9m³ 10g 12m 10.1m 9.9m⁵ 10.3m 8f³ 10d

Oct 19] close-coupled, quite good-topped filly: useful performer: several good efforts in 2007, including third to Echelon in Dahlia Stakes at Newmarket and fifth to Peeping Fawn in Nassau Stakes at Goodwood, seventh/eleventh starts: below form last 3 starts: barely stays 1½m: acts on dirt, polytrack, soft and good to firm going: usually in cheek-pieces of late. *J. S. Moore*

DON'T FORGET FAITH (USA) 2 b.f. (Feb 3) Victory Gallop (CAN) 130 – Contre- **102** dance (USA) (Danzig (USA)) [2007 6d* 7m² 8m 8g⁵ Oct 7] $90,000Y: big, good-bodied filly: has scope: half-sister to 3 winners abroad: dam US Grade 1 2-y-o 7f winner: useful performer: won maiden at Newmarket (beat Visit by head) in June: good ½-length second of 7 to Albabilia in Sweet Solera there: only seventh in May Hill Stakes (free and rather isolated) at Doncaster, but respectable effort final start when 7½ lengths fifth of 10 to Zarkava in Prix Marcel Boussac at Longchamp: stays 1m: acts on good to soft and good to firm going. *C. G. Cox*

DON'T MIND ME 4 b.f. Mutamam 123 – Dynamic Dream (USA) 87 (Dynaformer **65** (USA)) [2007 58: p8g² f8g² 12g² 10g p12g* Jul 4] quite good-topped filly: fair hand- icapper: won at Kempton in July: stays easy 1½m: acts on all-weather, unraced on extremes of going on turf: sold 2,000 gns in October. *T. Keddy*

DON'T PANIC (IRE) 3 ch.g. Fath (USA) 116 – Torrmana (IRE) (Ela-Mana-Mou 132) **106** [2007 96: 9m 7m 7d⁶ 7.1d³ 8m* 7m⁵ 8s* Oct 14] strong gelding: useful handicapper: won at Goodwood in September and October, much improved when beating Crocodile Bay by 4 lengths on latter occasion: should stay 9f: acts on soft and good to firm going: has had 2 handlers. *P. W. Chapple-Hyam*

DON'T TELL ANNA (IRE) 2 b.f. (Mar 5) Choisir (AUS) 126 – Zinnia (Zilzal **61** (USA) 137) [2007 5g 5d⁶ 5m 5.1m⁴ 6m 6m p6g² p5.1g p6g Oct 17] €40,000Y: close- coupled filly: fourth foal: half-sister to useful sprinter Don't Tell Mum (by Dansili) and Irish 9f winner Fair Countenance (by Almutawakel): dam, ran once, out of useful half-sister to Danzig: modest maiden: second in nursery at Kempton: should prove best at 5f/6f: acts on polytrack, good to firm and good to soft going: sold 8,000 gns. *R. Hannon*

DON'T TELL SUE 4 ch.g. Bold Edge 123 – Opopmil (IRE) 68 (Pips Pride 117) [2007 **–** 92: 5g 5m 5s Jun 30] strong, good-topped gelding: fairly useful handicapper at 3 yrs: last all starts in 2007, unseating rider in preliminaries and rearing leaving stall final outing: sold 14,000 gns. *Miss J. R. Tooth*

DOON HAYMER (IRE) 2 b.c. (Jan 31) Barathea (IRE) 127 – Mutige (Warning 136) **79** [2007 6d³ 7.5g³ 8.3d² 7m 7.2v* Nov 3] €110,000Y: useful-looking colt: third foal: brother to fairly useful 2004 2-y-o 7f winner Lucky Red Pepper: dam, German 7f and 1¼m winner, out of sister to Prix de Diane winner Lacovia (dam of Dewhurst Stakes winner Tobougg, by Barathea): fair form: visored, won maiden at Ayr final start, making all: will stay 1¼m: acts on heavy going. *I. Semple*

DOONIGAN (IRE) 3 b.g. Val Royal (FR) 127 – Music In My Life (IRE) 59 (Law **53** Society (USA) 130) [2007 54p: p8g p7.1g 8.1d⁵ p10g 10g² Oct 8] tall gelding: modest maiden: stays 1¼m: tried visored: sometimes slowly away: sold 7,500 gns. *A. M. Balding*

DORA EXPLORA 3 br.f. Vettori (IRE) 119 – Fredora 93 (Inchinor 119) [2007 88: p8g **78 d** 10m 7.6m⁴ 7m 7.1g 7d 6s⁶ 10d 8.1m Sep 7] angular, workmanlike filly: just fair handicapper at best in 2007, leaving P. D. Evans after seventh start: best form around 7f: acts on firm and good to soft going: tried blinkered. *D. J. Wintle*

DORA'S GREEN 4 b.f. Rambling Bear 115 – Compradore 82 (Mujtahid (USA) 118) **53** [2007 57: 5.1m⁵ p7g p5.1g Sep 27] rather leggy filly: modest maiden: stays 6f: best efforts on polytrack and good to firm ground: wore cheekpieces last 4 outings. *S. W. Hall*

DORCHESTER 10 b.g. Primo Dominie 121 – Penthouse Lady (Last Tycoon 131) **63** [2007 7g p6g p6g p6g Aug 31] good-topped gelding: fair handicapper in 2005: unraced at 9 yrs, and just modest form in 2007: effective at 6f/7f: acts on all-weather, firm and soft ground: blinkered once at 3 yrs. *W. J. Musson*

DORIC DREAM 2 ch.f. (Apr 3) Ishiguru (USA) 114 – Generous Share 62 (Cadeaux **56** Genereux 131) [2007 5g⁶ 6m⁴ p6s⁵ Dec 21] 12,000Y: unfurnished filly: first foal: dam, maiden (stayed 7f), half-sister to smart miler Green Line: modest form in maidens: likely to be suited by 7f+. *B. Smart*

DORIC LADY 2 b.f. (Feb 22) Kyllachy 129 – Tanasie (Cadeaux Genereux 131) [2007 **74** 6m⁶ p6g³ 5.1g² Nov 7] 31,000Y: workmanlike filly: fifth foal: half-sister to fairly useful 8.6f winner Fiddlers Wood (by Spectrum) and German 7f winner Drax (by Mark of Esteem): dam, French 1m winner, half-sister to smart Irish 1m/1¼m performer Latino

Magic: fair maiden: placed at Lingfield and Nottingham (short-head second to Quaroma): will prove best at 5f/6f. *J. A. R. Toller*

DORIES DREAM 3 b.f. Foxhound (USA) 103 – Milliscent 49 (Primo Dominie 121) – [2007 –: p10g p12.2g Dec 8] little form in maidens. *Jane Southcombe*

DORN DANCER (IRE) 5 b.m. Danehill Dancer (IRE) 117 – Appledorn 99 (Doulab (USA) 115) [2007 71: 6g⁴ 7.1m³ 5d⁴ 6d* 5.9m 7m 6m⁴ 6v 6g⁵ 6d* 6s⁵ 6m⁶ 7m 7.2s 6s⁴ 6v³ Oct 26] good-topped mare: fair handicapper: won at Ayr in May and July: stays easy 7f: acts on heavy and good to firm going: tried blinkered/in cheekpieces: held up: not straightforward, and unreliable. *D. W. Barker* — **68 §**

DORSO ROSSO (IRE) 2 b.g. (Feb 9) Redback 116 – Baraloti (IRE) 71 (Barathea (IRE) 127) [2007 7m p7g⁶ 7g Sep 19] close-coupled gelding: no form: bred to stay 1m. *Mrs C. A. Dunnett* — –

DOT'S DELIGHT 3 b.f. Golden Snake (USA) 127 – Hotel California (IRE) 58 (Last Tycoon 131) [2007 10m 10d 9g³ 10.1m 10.1g² 10s² p9.5g⁴ p12g⁴ p9.5g Dec 3] good-topped filly: eighth foal: sister to winner in Italy and half-sister to 3 winners, including fairly useful 5.7f (at 2 yrs) and 7f winner Goldie (by Celtic Swing): dam 2-y-o 7.5f winner: modest maiden: left M. Tompkins after sixth start: raced mainly at 1¼m: acts on polytrack, soft and good to firm going: tried blinkered. *R. A. Harris* — **61**

DOTTY'S DAUGHTER 3 ch.f. Forzando 122 – Colonel's Daughter 61 (Colonel Collins (USA) 122) [2007 59: 6m⁵ 5g 5m⁵ 6m⁵ 5d⁴ 5s⁵ 5d 5g p6g Oct 22] smallish, quite attractive filly: poor nowadays: best at 5f: acts on all-weather, firm and soft going: wears headgear: tends to hang left. *Mrs A. Duffield* — **48**

DOUBLE ATTACK (FR) 2 b.f. (Jan 27) Peintre Celebre (USA) 137 – Salome's Attack 90 (Anabaa (USA) 130) [2007 6g* 7g 6s 7m 8f² 8f⁶ 10g⁴ Nov 3] €50,000Y: small, close-coupled filly: first foal: dam, French 7.5f (at 2 yrs) to 9.5f winner, half-sister to very smart stayer Double Honour: fairly useful performer: won maiden at Hamilton in June: upped in trip, best effort when fourth to Twice Over in minor event at Newmarket final start: will be suited by 1½m+: acts on firm going: once unseated/bolted to post: sold 10,000 gns. *M. Johnston* — **83**

DOUBLE BANDED (IRE) 3 b.g. Mark of Esteem (IRE) 137 – Bronzewing 103 (Beldale Flutter (USA) 130) [2007 53: 9.9s 10m 12m⁶ 12.4m* 14.1f* p13.9g³ 14.1g* 16g* 14g² Nov 9] leggy, sparely-made gelding: useful handicapper: much improved in second half of season, winning at Newcastle in August, Redcar in September and October, and Newmarket (again travelled strongly throughout when beating Dr Sharp by 5 lengths) in November: also ran well final outing: stays 2m: acts on polytrack and firm going. *J. L. Dunlop* — **95 +**

DOUBLE BAY (USA) 4 b.f. War Chant (USA) 126 – Once To Often (USA) (Raise A Native) [2007 64, a–: f8g Jan 7] rather leggy, quite good-topped filly: modest maiden: should prove best short of 1¼m: sold 8,000 gns in February, resold €85,000 in November (in foal to Singspiel). *Jane Chapple-Hyam* — **54**

DOUBLE BILL (USA) 3 b. or br.g. Mr Greeley (USA) 122 – Salty Perfume (USA) (Salt Lake (USA)) [2007 61p: 6m* p6g⁴ 7d p6g 6m Aug 17] big, strong gelding: fairly useful performer: won maiden at Leicester in May: stays 6f: acts on polytrack and good to firm going: blinkered final start: subsequently gelded. *P. F. I. Cole* — **84**

DOUBLE CARPET (IRE) 4 b.g. Lahib (USA) 129 – Cupid Miss (Anita's Prince 126) [2007 67, a55: f6g 7g³ 8m 6s* 6d f6d Dec 11] unfurnished gelding: fair handicapper on turf, modest on all-weather: won at Ayr in October: best effort at 6f: acts on fibresand and soft ground. *G. Woodward* — **67 a51**

DOUBLE DEPUTY (IRE) 6 b.g. Sadler's Wells (USA) 132 – Janaat 74 (Kris 135) [2007 –: 16.1s⁵ 16.2g⁶ Aug 15] smallish, good-bodied gelding: fairly useful performer in 2005: lightly raced and little impact on Flat since: tried tongue tied/visored/in cheekpieces: fair hurdler, successful in September: sold 8,400 gns. *J. J. Quinn* — –

DOUBLE DOORS (USA) 3 b.c. Grand Lodge (USA) 125 – Daring Miss 113 (Sadler's Wells (USA) 132) [2007 8g⁶ p8g² 8d³ 9.8m* 11.9g* p12g³ Oct 15] good-bodied colt: third foal: half-brother to useful 6.5f (in USA) and 7f (at 2 yrs) winner Quickfire (by Dubai Millennium): dam, French 1½m/14.5f winner, out of Oaks runner-up Bourbon Girl: fairly useful and progressive form: won maiden at Ripon and handicap at Haydock in September: most improved when visored, best effort when ½-length third to Eva Soneva So Fast at Lingfield final start: stays 1½m: acts on polytrack and good to firm going: sold 110,000 gns, sent to USA. *J. H. M. Gosden* — **94**

DOUBLE DUTY (IRE) 2 b.f. (Apr 27) Danehill Dancer (IRE) 117 – Taking Liberties **62 p**
(IRE) 57 (Royal Academy (USA) 130) [2007 8d⁵ Oct 11] tall, close-coupled filly: closely
related to 2 winners by Danehill, notably smart 6f (at 2 yrs in Ireland) and 1m (including
in Hong Kong) winner Troubadour, and half-sister to several winners, including fairly
useful 1m/1¼m winner Eccollo (by Spectrum): dam ran once: 14/1 and green, fifth to
Robby Bobby in maiden at Newbury, set plenty to do: will improve. *B. J. Meehan*

DOUBLE HARNESS (USA) 3 ch.c. Horse Chestnut (SAF) 119 – Lover's Lover **80**
(USA) (Woodman (USA) 126) [2007 p12g* Jun 16] $70,000Y: second foal: dam, ran
once in France, closely related to smart French miler Byzantium, out of sister to Miesque
and half-sister to dam of Six Perfections: well-backed 4/1, won maiden at Lingfield in
June by neck from Kailasha (pair well clear), gradually asserting, though broke down and
is expected to miss 2008. *H. Morrison*

DOUBLE M 10 ch.g. First Trump 118 – Girton Degree 41 (Balliol 125) [2007 –, a63: **48**
p6g⁵ p6g² p6g⁵ p6g⁴ p6g⁶ Mar 21] strong, sturdy gelding: poor performer nowadays:
stays easy 7f: acts on all-weather, firm and good to soft ground: blinkered/visored: often
waited with. *Mrs L. Richards*

DOUBLE MYSTERY (FR) 7 ch.g. Starborough 126 – Chene de Coeur (FR) (Com- **–**
rade In Arms 123) [2007 66: f12g⁶ f14g⁶ Jan 11] smallish, lengthy gelding: modest
handicapper at 6 yrs: last both outings on Flat in 2007: tried blinkered/in cheekpieces:
tongue tied. *K. J. Burke*

DOUBLE ON RED 2 b.f. (May 16) Red Ransom (USA) – Rosy Outlook (USA) 79 **77**
(Trempolino (USA) 135) [2007 6d⁵ 7m p7g 8.3d 7d² Oct 30] small, close-coupled filly:
fifth foal: closely related to useful 2001 2-y-o 6f/7f winner Rapscallion (by Robellino)
and half-sister to 6-y-o Orcadian: dam 6f winner: fair maiden: blinkered, best effort after
debut (fifth to Albabilia at Ascot) when second at Yarmouth: stays 7f: acts on good to soft
going. *J. M. P. Eustace*

DOUBLE PRECEDENT 3 b.f. Polish Precedent (USA) 131 – Jolies Eaux 73 (Shirley **–**
Heights 130) [2007 –: p12.2g 8g Jul 9] lengthy filly: little form. *M. Johnston*

DOUBLE R 2 b.f. (Feb 5) Fraam 114 – Bint Albadou (IRE) 91 (Green Desert (USA) **–**
127) [2007 p8m Dec 10] 5,500Y, resold 2,900Y: seventh foal: half-sister to several
winners, including 8.5f/1¼m winner Monduru (by Lion Cavern): dam, Irish 2-y-o 6f
winner, out of Nassau/Prix de l'Opera winner Cistus: 50/1, always behind in maiden at
Lingfield. *A. B. Haynes*

DOUBLE RAINBOW (IRE) 4 b.c. Sadler's Wells (USA) 132 – Rain Flower (IRE) **–**
(Indian Ridge 123) [2007 11.7d Aug 19] 33/1, tailed off in maiden at Bath (said to have
had breathing problem). *Jamie Poulton*

DOUBLE SPECTRE (IRE) 5 b.g. Spectrum (IRE) 126 – Phantom Ring 62 (Magic **73**
Ring (IRE) 115) [2007 74: p10g 10.2f* 10g 11g⁴ 10g 10m⁵ 11.6m⁵ 10.2f⁶ Aug 27]
smallish, close-coupled gelding: fair handicapper: won at Bath in April: effective at 1m
to 1½m: acts on firm and good to soft going: often held up: consistent: modest hurdler.
Jean-Rene Auvray

DOUBLE VALENTINE 4 ch.f. Primo Valentino (IRE) 116 – Charlottevalentina **53**
(IRE) 80 (Perugino (USA) 84) [2007 61: p7g 6.1g³ 6m p7g 7m p6g⁶ 6f 6m p6g* 6m⁶ p7g⁶
p6g⁶ p7g² p7g⁵ p8g⁴ p10m p7g Dec 30] stocky filly: modest performer: won minor event
at Lingfield in August: stays 1m: acts on polytrack and good to firm going: waited with.
R. Ingram

DOUBLOON 2 b.g. (Mar 19) Umistim 119 – Glistening Silver 58 (Puissance 110) **–**
[2007 7.1g 8.2g p6g Nov 16] angular gelding: of no account. *J. Gallagher*

DOUBLY GUEST 3 b.f. Barathea Guest 117 – Countess Guest (IRE) 59 (Spectrum **75**
(IRE) 126) [2007 74: 10.5g 10d 10g 10s⁴ 10s² 10d 10d 11.6d⁵ 17.2g²* Oct 24] workmanlike filly: has a round action: fair handicapper: upped in trip, won at Bath in October:
stays 17f: acts on firm and soft going: wore cheekpieces last 2 starts: sometimes takes
keen hold: waited with: sold 32,000 gns. *G. G. Margarson*

DOUBTFUL SOUND (USA) 3 b.c. Diesis 133 – Roam Free (USA) (Unbridled **71**
(USA) 128) [2007 71p: f6g² p6g* 6g f6d⁶ Dec 21] strong, lengthy colt: fair performer:
won maiden at Wolverhampton in March: reportedly returned jarred up third start, off 8
months after: raced only at 6f/7f: acts on all-weather. *T. D. Barron*

DOUBTLESS 2 ch.f. (Apr 3) Redoubtable (USA) 115 – Some Like It Hot 41 (Ashka- **– §**
lani (IRE) 128) [2007 5v 5m 6d 5d 7g p6g 6m Aug 28] smallish filly: first foal: dam
maiden: no form: tried blinkered: temperamental. *D. W. Chapman*

DOUGHTY 5 b.g. Bold Edge 123 – Marquante (IRE) (Brief Truce (USA) 126) [2007 –: **55** p6g p5.1g⁴ p6g³ f6g p6g Mar 5] modest maiden: stays easy 8.6f: acts on all-weather and soft ground: tried blinkered/tongue tied. *M. Mullineaux*

DOVE COTTAGE (IRE) 5 b.g. Great Commotion (USA) 123 – Pooka 65 (Dominion **77** 123) [2007 78: 10g 10.2s⁴ 11.6g³ 12.3m 10.9m⁵ 10d⁴ Oct 16] close-coupled gelding: fair handicapper: stays 11.6f: acts on polytrack, firm and soft going: below form only start in cheekpieces: front runner. *W. S. Kittow*

DOVEDALE 7 b.m. Groom Dancer (USA) 128 – Peetsie (IRE) (Fairy King (USA)) **56** [2007 65: 12.1s⁶ 14.1d Aug 16] tall, lengthy mare: fair performer in 2005: lightly raced and below form on Flat since: stays easy 1¾m: acts on polytrack, heavy and good to firm going. *Mrs S. D. Williams*

DOVEDON HERO 7 ch.g. Millkom 124 – Hot Topic (IRE) (Desse Zenny (USA)) **75** [2007 77: p13g⁴ p12g⁶ p12g² p12.2g² p13.9g⁴ Feb 21] sturdy, close-coupled gelding: fair handicapper: stays 2m: acts on all-weather and firm going: raced usually blinkered (in cheek-pieces last 2 outings): held up: races freely, and is a weak finisher. *P. J. McBride*

DOVE (IRE) 2 b.f. (Jan 25) Sadler's Wells (USA) 132 – Golden Digger (USA) 66 (Mr **83** Prospector (USA)) [2007 p8g 8d² Oct 23] smallish filly: closely related/half-sister to several winners, including smart 7f (at 2 yrs) to 1½m winner Naheef (by Marju) and useful 6f (at 2 yrs)/7f winner Golden Sahara (by Green Desert): dam, maiden, sister to dam of Irish Oaks/Nassau Stakes winner Lailani and half-sister to very smart pair Always Fair and Faithful Son: much improved from debut when second to Michita in maiden at Yarmouth, making most: will stay 1¼m/1½m. *Saeed bin Suroor*

DOWER HOUSE 12 ch.g. Groom Dancer (USA) 128 – Rose Noble (USA) 62 (Vagu- **74** ely Noble 140) [2007 74, a91: p9.5g⁴ p10g* p12g* Apr 4] lengthy, rather leggy gelding: **a83** had a fluent, round action: fairly useful handicapper on all-weather, fair on turf: won at Lingfield in March (apprentices) and April: was effective at 1m to easy 1½m: acted on all-weather, firm and soft going: tongue held: took good hold: reportedly retired. *Andrew Turnell*

DOWLLEH 3 b.g. Noverre (USA) 125 – Al Persian (IRE) (Persian Bold 123) [2007 84: **79** 6m⁶ 8.3m 6g⁵ 6f⁴ 5d⁶ 7f p7g⁵ p7m p7g Dec 16] good-topped gelding: fair handicapper: stays easy 7f: acts on polytrack, good to firm and good to soft going: in cheekpieces last 2 starts: said to have bled sixth and last 2 outings. *T. T. Clement*

DOWNHILLER (IRE) 2 ch.c. (Feb 28) Alhaarth (IRE) 126 – Ski For Gold 76 (Shir- **86** ley Heights 130) [2007 7.1g 8.1m² 8f² 8g² Oct 25] neat colt: seventh foal: half-brother to 2001 2-y-o 1m winner Ski For Me (by Barathea), 2004 2-y-o 1m winner Alpine Gold (by Montjeu) and 3-y-o Eglevski: dam, 2-y-o 7f winner (stayed 1¾m), half-sister to US Grade 1 1¼m winner Bequest: fairly useful maiden: runner-up all starts after debut, beaten short head by Yaddree at Brighton final one: will stay 1½m: acts on firm going. *J. L. Dunlop*

DOWNING STREET (IRE) 6 b.g. Sadler's Wells (USA) 132 – Photographie (USA) **83** (Trempolino (USA) 135) [2007 16m* 18m 16.1m⁴ Aug 27] big, quite good-topped gelding: fairly useful performer: first outing on Flat since 2 yrs (fairly useful hurdler) when winning handicap at Thirsk (by 13 lengths) in August: stays 2m: raced only on good to firm ground: blinkered/tongue tied at 6 yrs. *Jennie Candlish*

DOWN THE BRICK (IRE) 3 b.g. Daggers Drawn (USA) 114 – Damezao (Alzao **77** (USA) 117) [2007 64: p10g 12g 11.5m³ 11.7d⁵ 10d³ 11.6m* 12.1m* 11.6m⁴ 12m 14g 11.6d Oct 15] close-coupled gelding: fair handicapper: won at Windsor in July and Chepstow in August: stays 1½m: acts on good to firm and good to soft going: usually blinkered. *B. R. Millman*

DOWNTOWN (IRE) 3 b.f. Danehill (USA) 126 – User Friendly 128 (Slip Anchor **105** 136) [2007 53: 10.2f² 10m* 12g⁴ 12s* 12d Oct 21] lengthy filly: sister to fairly useful Irish 8.5f winner Starspangled and half-sister to several winners, including smart Irish 1½m winner (stays 2m) Two Miles West (by Sadler's Wells): dam won 5 Group 1s, including Oaks and St Leger: useful performer: won maiden at Clonmel in May and Boss Croker Centenary Give Thanks Stakes at Cork (rallied to beat Hasanka by short head) in August: also ran well when fourth to Nick's Nikita in Noblesse Stakes at Cork in between: below form in listed event at the Curragh final outing: will stay at least 1¾m: acts on soft going, promise on firm: has had 2 handlers. *D. Wachman, Ireland*

DOYLES LODGE 3 b.g. Prince Sabo 123 – True Bird (IRE) 63 (In The Wings 128) **77** [2007 71p: p7g² 7s⁴ 7m² 7.1g⁶ 7g³ 10g p8g⁶ p9.5g p12g Oct 10] lightly-made gelding: **a71** fair maiden: stays 1m: acts on polytrack, soft and good to firm going: tried visored: sold 6,000 gns. *H. Candy*

totepool August Stakes, Windsor—
2006 Derby runner-up Dragon Dancer gains his first win, beating Classic Punch and Imperial Star

DRAGON DANCER 4 b.c. Sadler's Wells (USA) 132 – Alakananda 92 (Hernando **115**
(FR) 127) [2007 119: 12g 11.6m* 12m3 12g Oct 7] tall, quite good-topped colt: smart
performer: reportedly suffered a setback in May: won listed event at Windsor (by length
from Classic Punch, first success) in August: better form when third to Manduro in Prix
Foy at Longchamp next time: stiff task, ninth to Dylan Thomas in Prix de l'Arc de
Triomphe there final outing: better suited by 1½m than 1¼m: acts on firm ground: carried
head awkwardly and hung right on reappearance. *G. Wragg*

DRAGON FLAME (IRE) 4 b.c. Tagula (IRE) 116 – Noble Rocket (Reprimand 122) **62**
[2007 63: 6g2 6s4 6s 7d Oct 29] angular colt: modest maiden: stays 6f: raced on polytrack
and good ground or softer: visored first 3 starts in 2007. *M. Quinn*

DRAGON FLOWER (USA) 3 b.f. Gulch (USA) – Rawabi (Sadler's Wells (USA) **67**
132) [2007 79: 7d 7.1d5 7.1m3 Aug 27] strong filly: fair maiden: will stay 1m: acts on
polytrack, probably on good to soft ground: withdrawn after bursting through front of
stall prior to intended final outing Sep 19: sold 34,000 gns. *B. W. Hills*

DRAGON SLAYER (IRE) 5 ch.g. Night Shift (USA) – Arandora Star (USA) (Sag- **87**
ace (FR) 135) [2007 88, a82: p9.5g* p9.5g3 a9s5 a10s 10d 10g4 p8.6g 10.3g p10g4 p10m2
p10g6 Dec 16] rather leggy gelding: fairly useful handicapper: won at Wolverhampton in
January: left Ian Williams after fifth outing: stays easy 1½m: acts on all-weather and firm
ground: tried in cheekpieces: edgy sort: usually races prominently. *P. A. Blockley*

DRAMA KID (IRE) 4 b.f. Mull of Kintyre (USA) 114 – Bold Feather (Persian Bold **46**
123) [2007 47: 9.5m 10m6 10.1m5 Aug 24] €6,500Y: half-sister to several winners,
including French 7.5f (at 2 yrs)/9.5f winner By The Face (by Orpen) and Irish 1m/1½m
winner Karramalu (by Entrepreneur): dam maiden half-sister to dam of St Leger winner
Mutafaweq: poor maiden: stays 1¼m. *D. Loughnane, Ireland*

DRAMATIC 3 ch.c. Pivotal 124 – Red Passion (USA) (Seeking The Gold (USA)) **78**
[2007 f6g6 f6g4 f6g6 p6g* p6g* 6d* p6g5 a6g* Nov 6] first foal: dam, ran once, out of
smart 7f/1m winner: fair handicapper: won at Wolverhampton (impressively
by 5 lengths), Lingfield and Yarmouth (made most to land odds both occasions) in June
and, after being sold from Sir Mark Prescott 47,000 gns, Taby in November: will stay 7f:
acts on polytrack/dirt and good to soft going. *Yvonne Durant, Sweden*

DRAMATIC REVIEW (IRE) 5 b.g. Indian Lodge (IRE) 127 – Dramatic Shift (IRE) **–**
(Night Shift (USA)) [2007 50: 12g Apr 8] close-coupled gelding: modest maiden: well
held sole start in 2007: stays 1¼m: acts on heavy and good to firm going: often wears
headgear: tongue tied nowadays. *J. Barclay*

DRAMATIC SOLO 2 ch.f. (Apr 3) Nayef (USA) 129 – Just Dreams 85 (Salse (USA) **68 p**
128) [2007 p8.6g⁴ 7m Sep 14] 15,000Y, resold €50,000Y: quite good-topped filly: fourth
foal: half-sister to useful UAE 6f/7f winner Bounty Quest (by Fasliyev): dam, 1½m
winner, sister to Classic Cliche and half-sister to Yorkshire Oaks winner My Emma: fair
maiden: fourth at Wolverhampton: stiff task other start (sales race at the Curragh): will be
suited by 1¼m/1½m: capable of better. *K. R. Burke*

DRAMATIC TOUCH 3 b.f. Royal Applause 124 – Sismique (Warning 136) [2007 **68**
49p: 8g 8m⁵ 10m Jul 18] fair maiden: best effort at 1m: sold 2,000 gns in October, sent to
Spain. *G. Wragg*

DRAMATIC TURN 3 b.f. Pivotal 124 – Eveningperformance 121 (Night Shift **70**
(USA)) [2007 87p: 5g May 21] good-topped filly: fairly useful form at 2 yrs: below form
on handicap debut at Windsor sole outing in 2007 (said to have lost a shoe): sent to Spain.
Mrs A. J. Perrett

DRASTIC MEASURE 2 ch.f. (Feb 13) Pivotal 124 – Danse Classique (IRE) 94 **73**
(Night Shift (USA)) [2007 5s² 5d 5d 7d⁶ Jul 25] fourth foal: half-sister to 5-y-o Defi and
Irish 1½m winner Dazzling Dancer (by Nashwan), both fairly useful: dam, Irish 7f
winner, closely related to Petrushka: maiden: form only on debut (second at Leicester):
should stay 1m: raced only on going softer than good: tried tongue tied. *Sir Mark Prescott*

DRAWBACK (IRE) 4 b.g. Daggers Drawn (USA) 114 – Sacred Heart (IRE) 45 **80**
(Catrail (USA) 123) [2007 64: 7m² 7s⁴ 7m* 10.2d* 10.2g* 10.5v⁶ 7.1s⁵ 10m 10d* 10.9m
9.9d⁴ 10.3g Oct 26] rather leggy gelding: fairly useful handicapper: won at Lingfield and
Bath (2) in June, and Brighton in August: effective at 7f to 1¼m: acts on fibresand and
any turf going: tried blinkered, wears cheekpieces nowadays: sometimes slowly away.
R. A. Harris

DRAWNFROMTHEPAST (IRE) 2 ch.c. (Feb 22) Tagula (IRE) 116 – Ball Cat (FR) **99**
(Cricket Ball (USA) 124) [2007 5s⁶ 6m* 5m* 6g⁵ 6g Aug 23] €25,000F, 36,000Y:
deep-girthed colt: sixth foal: brother to winner in Greece and half-brother to French 1½m
winner Aldiruos (by Bigstone): dam Belgian 7.5f winner: useful performer: successful in
June in minor event at Brighton and 20-runner listed Windsor Castle Stakes at Royal
Ascot (beat Kingsgate Native by head): good 3¾ lengths fifth of 9 to Strike The Deal in

*Windsor Castle Stakes, Royal Ascot—Drawnfromthepast just gets the better of newcomer
Kingsgate Native (nearest camera) in one of the first races not shown in betting shops due to a dispute
over the newly launched TurfTV service; Hatta Fort (No.10) is third ahead of Dream Eater (No.6)*

Richmond Stakes at Goodwood: better than bare result in sales race at York final start: may prove best kept to 5f/6f: acts on good to firm going. *J. A. Osborne*

DRAWN GOLD 3 b.g. Daggers Drawn (USA) 114 – Gold Belt (IRE) 61 (Bellypha 130) [2007 69p: 8.2m⁴ 10d⁴ 8g* Nov 2] workmanlike gelding: fair form: won apprentice handicap at Newmarket in November: probably stays 1¼m: acts on good to firm ground. *R. Hollinshead*   **75**

DRAYTON (IRE) 3 b. or br.c. Danetime (IRE) 121 – Exponent (USA) (Exbourne (USA) 125) [2007 107: 6g⁴ 8m 6d⁵ 6m 6d 6.1m⁵ 5m⁵ Sep 12] close-coupled colt: smart performer: won 2 listed races at the Curragh at 2 yrs for T. Stack: ran in Britain after reappearance, good efforts when 3¼ lengths fifth to Soldier's Tale in Golden Jubilee Stakes at Royal Ascot and eleventh behind Sakhee's Secret in July Cup at Newmarket third/fourth starts: below form after: best at 6f (failed to stay 1m in 2000 Guineas): acts on heavy and good to firm going: has worn crossed noseband/severe bridle. *M. F. de Kock, South Africa*   **113**

DR DREAM (IRE) 3 b.g. Dr Fong (USA) 128 – Only In Dreams 78 (Polar Falcon (USA) 126) [2007 p7g⁴ p8.6g⁶ p7.1g 7s⁵ 8.3s² 9g³ p12.2g 10g³ p9.5g⁵ Oct 26] lengthy gelding: modest maiden: below form after reappearance: claimed from D. Simcock £6,000 after fifth start: barely stays 1¼m: acts on polytrack and soft going: visored/blinkered last 4 starts: has carried head high. *J. G. M. O'Shea*   **63 d**

DREAM BEE 2 b.f. (Mar 8) Oasis Dream 129 – Chief Bee 89 (Chief's Crown (USA)) [2007 7m 7g 7d⁴ 7.5m 10m Oct 3] heavy-topped filly: closely related to 2003 2-y-o 7f winner Golden Grace (stayed 1¼m, by Green Desert) and half-sister to several winners, including smart 1¼m/1½m winner Beekeeper (stayed 2m, by Rainbow Quest): dam, 9f to 14.6f winner, sister to Racing Post Trophy winner Be My Chief: modest maiden: should stay 1m. *E. A. L. Dunlop*   **61**

DREAM CATCHER (SWE) 4 b.c. Songline (SWE) 110 – Queen Ida (SWE) (Diligo (FR)) [2007 95?: p11g p12g⁴ p12g p10g p11g⁶ p8.6g p9.5g Oct 5] sturdy colt: fairly useful handicapper: below form after second start in 2007: stays 1½m: acts on dirt, polytrack, and good to firm going: usually tongue tied: sold 11,500 gns. *R. A. Kvisla*   **86 d**

DREAM DAY 2 b.f. (Mar 24) Oasis Dream 129 – Capistrano Day (USA) 110 (Diesis 133) [2007 p6g⁴ 7m² 7m6 Oct 6] sturdy filly: third foal: half-sister to smart 6f (at 2 yrs) to 1m winner Sabbeeh (by Red Ransom): dam, 7f winner (including at 2 yrs) and fourth in 1000 Guineas, out of smart 1¼m performer Alcando: fairly useful form: won maiden at Kempton in September: improved after, ¾-length second to Rosa Grace in minor event at Newbury and around length sixth of 8 to Raymi Coya in Oh So Sharp Stakes at Newmarket (held up off steady pace): will stay 1m. *R. Hannon*   **94 +**

DREAM EATER (IRE) 2 gr.c. (Apr 5) Night Shift (USA) – Kapria (FR) 103 (Simon du Desert (FR) 116) [2007 6g³ p6g² 5m⁴ 6m6 6g³ 7m³ 6.5m* 6m6 Oct 3] 40,000F: lengthy, good-bodied colt: has scope: second foal: half-brother to 3-y-o Tremelo Pointe: dam French 1¼m/10.5f winner: useful form: in frame 5 times (including in listed Windsor Castle Stakes at Royal Ascot) prior to winning 22-runner sales race at Doncaster in September by 1¼ lengths from Achilles of Troy: creditable 3½ lengths sixth of 9 to Dark Angel in Middle Park Stakes at Newmarket final start: should prove best up to 7f: acts on polytrack and good to firm going. *A. M. Balding*   **104**

DREAM EXPRESS (IRE) 2 b.c. (Feb 17) Fasliyev (USA) 120 – Lothlorien (USA) 80 (Woodman (USA) 126) [2007 6d⁶ 6g⁴ 7d² 7m³ 8m 6d Sep 20] 5,000F, €40,000Y: rangy, unfurnished colt: half-brother to 7.5f winner Lorien Hill (by Danehill) and Irish 1½m to 2m winner Miss Devious (by Dr Devious): dam, 1m winner (stayed 1½m), sister to smart 1¼m/1½m winner Monsajem out of close relative to Sadler's Wells: fair maiden: placed at Redcar and Newcastle (nursery): should stay 1m: acts on good to firm and good to soft going: below form in cheekpieces/blinkers. *M. Dods*   **75**

DREAM FOREST (IRE) 4 b.g. Raise A Grand (IRE) 114 – Theresa Green (IRE) 65 (Charnwood Forest (IRE) 125) [2007 63, a70: f12g² f12g Jan 16] quite good-topped gelding: modest performer: left M. Saunders £6,000 after reappearance: stays 1½m: acts on all-weather and good to firm going. *J. Balding*   **62**

DREAM GREEN (IRE) 2 b.c. (Mar 6) Fasliyev (USA) 120 – Queen Chief (IRE) 65 (Grand Lodge (USA) 125) [2007 7m 7s Aug 24] compact colt: behind in maidens at Newmarket, modest form on debut: sold 3,200 gns. *M. R. Channon*   **50**

DREAM LODGE (IRE) 3 ch.c. Grand Lodge (USA) 125 – Secret Dream (IRE) 103 (Zafonic (USA) 130) [2007 84: p7.1g³ p8.6g² 8m² 8.2g⁵ 8s⁵ 9.1d³ p8.6g* p8.6g² 8m* p8.6g² Oct 21] good-topped colt: useful handicapper: won at Wolverhampton (despite   **103**

hanging markedly right) in August and Pontefract (beat Ella Woodcock by 1¾ lengths, dictating) in October: best effort when 1¼ lengths second to Russki at Wolverhampton final outing: stays 9f: acts on polytrack, good to firm and good to soft going: tried visored: races prominently. *J. G. Given*

DREAM MASTER (IRE) 4 b.g. Priolo (USA) 127 – Pip's Dream 52 (Glint of Gold **53** 128) [2007 –: 10s 8d 10.1d² p12g⁴ 10.9g p12.2g³ p12.2g⁴ p13.9g f11d⁶ Dec 15] very tall gelding: modest maiden: stays 1½m: acts on polytrack and good to soft going: tried blinkered. *J. Ryan*

DREAM MOUNTAIN 4 b.g. Mozart (IRE) 131 – Statua (IRE) 98 (Statoblest 120) **63** [2007 68, a57: p16g* p16g p16g p12g p12g⁶ p16g⁶ Sep 7] useful-looking gelding: modest handicapper: won at Kempton in January: stays easy 2m: acts on polytrack, good to firm and good to soft going: wore cheekpieces final outing. *Ms J. S. Doyle*

DREAM OF FORTUNE (IRE) 3 b.c. Danehill Dancer (IRE) 117 – Tootling (IRE) **78 p** (Pennine Walk 120) [2007 p8g⁵ 8g p8g⁴ p10g* Oct 17] €82,000Y: quite attractive colt: closely related to useful Irish 2000 2-y-o 6f winner Little Firefly (by Danehill) and half-brother to 2 winners, including smart Irish sprinter Antinnaz (by Thatching): dam twice-raced daughter of Prix Saint-Alary winner Tootens: fair form: improved when winning handicap at Lingfield (by ½ length from Resplendent Ace, still green) in October: stays 1¼m: raced only on polytrack and good ground: sold 35,000 gns: type to do better still. *J. Noseda*

DREAM OF PARADISE (USA) 4 ch.f. Atticus (USA) 121 – Scrumptious (USA) **–** (Slew O' Gold (USA)) [2007 67: 9.9m 9.9m p9.5g 12.3f Jun 12] leggy filly: fair handicapper at 3 yrs: little form in 2007. *Mrs L. Williamson*

DREAM ON DREAMERS (IRE) 3 b.g. Iron Mask (USA) 117 – Harifana (FR) **47** (Kahyasi 130) [2007 –: 9.8g 9.2g⁵ 8d⁶ 12d 10.1d 11.1m Aug 4] well-made gelding: poor maiden: tried blinkered/in cheekpieces. *R. C. Guest*

DREAM RIVER (USA) 6 ch.m. Irish River (FR) 131 – Pallava (USA) (Lyphard **56** (USA) 132) [2007 49: p16.5g* p12.2g³ 16g⁴ May 28] modest performer: landed gamble when winning minor event at Wolverhampton in January: stays 2m: acts on polytrack and good to firm going, probably on soft: tried tongue tied. *Patrick Martin, Ireland*

DREAM SCHEME 3 b.f. Machiavellian (USA) 123 – Dream Ticket (USA) 73 **81** (Danzig (USA)) [2007 91p: 8d 6d⁶ Jul 23] good-topped filly: has a quick action: fairly useful form: shaped as if in need of run in handicap at Newmarket on reappearance: inadequate trip at Windsor only other start in 2007: should be suited by 7f+: raced only on good/good to soft ground. *E. A. L. Dunlop*

DREAM SEA 2 b.f. (Apr 23) Barathea (IRE) 127 – Countess Sybil (IRE) 73 (Dr **75** Devious (IRE) 127) [2007 p7g³ 7m⁴ 7.5g³ Sep 19] 45,000Y: useful-looking filly: fourth foal: half-sister to an Italian winner by Mister Baileys: dam, Irish 1¾m winner, out of half-sister to smart Irish middle-distance filly Countess Tully: fair maiden: in frame all starts, including fourth to Sense of Joy at Newmarket: will be suited by 1m/1¼m. *M. R. Channon*

DREAMS JEWEL 7 b.g. Dreams End 93 – Jewel of The Nile 35 (Glenstal (USA) 118) **59** [2007 53: 10.2g 12d² 12.1m p16.5g⁴ 12m f12d⁴ Dec 20] modest hurdler: similar form on Flat, lightly raced: will stay 1¾m: acts on fibresand and good to soft going. *C. Roberts*

DREAM THEME 4 b.g. Distant Music (USA) 126 – Xaymara (USA) (Sanglamore **94** (USA) 126) [2007 105: 8.1m³ 6d Sep 22] big, good-bodied gelding: useful performer at 3 yrs: just fairly useful in 2 runs in 2007, leaving B. Hills 20,000 gns in between: stays 7f (probably not 1m): acts on polytrack, firm and good to soft going: waited with. *D. Nicholls*

DRESDEN DOLL (USA) 2 ch.f. (Mar 26) Elusive Quality (USA) – Crimson Con- **78** quest (USA) 85 (Diesis 133) [2007 6g 6m² p6g 5.1f* 6.5m Sep 12] tall filly: sister to fairly useful 2006 2-y-o 6f winner Chief Operator and half-sister to several winners, including very smart 6f (at 2 yrs) to 1¼m winner Crimplene (by Lion Cavern) and smart 1¼m/1½m winner Dutch Gold (by Lahib): dam, French 2-y-o 6f winner (stayed 1¼m): fair performer: won maiden at Bath in August: stamina stretched in nursery final start: best at 5f/easy 6f: acts on firm going. *M. L. W. Bell*

DRESSED TO DANCE (IRE) 3 b.f. Namid 128 – Costume Drama (USA) (Alleged **71** (USA) 138) [2007 67: p7.1g* p7.1g* 7m⁵ 6m⁴ p7.1g⁶ 6d² 7g* 8m⁶ 8.1g 7g⁶ 6d Oct 16] big, strong filly: fair performer: won maiden at Wolverhampton in January and, having left B. Meehan 13,000 gns later in month, claimer there in February and handicap at Folkestone in July: probably stays 1m: acts on polytrack, good to firm and good to soft ground: often blinkered/visored: free-going sort. *N. Tinkler*

DRESS TO IMPRESS (IRE) 3 b.c. Fasliyev (USA) 120 – Dress Code (IRE) 83 (Barathea (IRE) 127) [2007 79: p5.1g² p8.6g p6g Nov 16] good-topped colt: fairly useful performer: left J. Boyle before final outing: free-going sort, may prove best at 5f/6f: acts on polytrack, and any ground on turf: tried in cheekpieces. *G. A. Butler* — **82**

DR FAUSTUS (IRE) 2 gr.c. (Feb 3) Sadler's Wells (USA) 132 – Requesting (Rainbow Quest (USA) 134) [2007 7.1d⁵ 7d² 8m* Sep 8] good-topped colt: fourth foal: half-brother to 2005 2-y-o 6f winner Desert Flora (by Green Desert): dam unraced half-sister to very smart 1¼m performer Last Second (dam of Poule d'Essai des Poulains winner Aussie Rules) and to dams of Alborada, Albanova, Quarter Moon and Yesterday (last 2 by Sadler's Wells): useful form: progressive in maidens, second to Spacious at Leicester prior to winning at Thirsk by length from Funny Me, having plenty in hand: will be suited by 1¼m/1½m: one to follow. *Sir Michael Stoute* — **98 p**

DRIFT AWAY (USA) 7 b.m. Dehere (USA) 121 – Flying Blind (IRE) 87 (Silver Kite (USA) 111) [2007 60: p16.5g Jan 28] winning hurdler: modest maiden on Flat: well held only start in 2007: stays 1½m. *J. J. Lambe, Ireland* — **–**

DRIFTING GOLD 3 ch.f. Bold Edge 123 – Driftholme 27 (Safawan 118) [2007 69: p5g⁴ p6g² p5.1g* p5g² p6g² 5m* p5.1g⁵ 5m 5f* 5.1m 5m⁶ Sep 15] angular filly: fair performer: won maiden at Wolverhampton in February and handicaps at Goodwood in June and Windsor in August: best at 5f/6f: raced only on polytrack and good ground or firmer (acts on firm): wears headgear nowadays: usually races prominently. *C. G. Cox* — **79**

DRILL SERGEANT 2 br.c. (Mar 28) Rock of Gibraltar (IRE) 133 – Dolydille (IRE) 108 (Dolphin Street (FR) 125) [2007 6g³ 6.5d² 7g Oct 26] 82,000Y: tall, leggy colt: third foal: half-brother to 7f winner Elizabethan Age (by King's Best): dam, Irish 9f to 1½m winner, half-sister to dam of Irish Derby runner-up Sholokhov: fairly useful maiden: second to Beacon Lodge at Newbury: will stay at least 1m: acts on good to soft going. *M. Johnston* — **91**

DRINK TO ME ONLY 4 b.g. Pursuit of Love 124 – Champenoise 64 (Forzando 122) [2007 55: f8g p7.1g p8g p6g⁶ f7g p8g f6g 6d 8g* 8.3d 7.5g³ 8s 8.5g p9.5g p8g Oct 29] sturdy gelding: modest handicapper: won at Musselburgh in July: stays 1m: acts on polytrack, good to firm and good to soft ground: tried in cheekpieces/blinkers: tongue tied last 2 starts: waited with. *J. R. Weymes* — **55**

DRIVEN (IRE) 2 b.g. (Apr 1) Domedriver (IRE) 128 – Wonderful World (GER) (Dashing Blade 117) [2007 8d⁴ 8g 7g⁴ Nov 2] 50,000Y: useful-looking gelding: third foal: half-brother to 4-y-o Advanced and 3-y-o Copernican: dam, German 7f winner, sister to smart German 1¼m/11f performer Winning Dash: fair maiden: fourth at Salisbury and Newmarket: will stay 1¼m. *Mrs A. J. Perrett* — **78**

DRIVEN SNOW 2 ch.f. (Apr 4) Choisir (AUS) 126 – Thermal Spring 77 (Zafonic (USA) 130) [2007 6m Jul 28] rangy, attractive filly: fourth foal: half-sister to useful French 1m (at 2 yrs) and 1¼m winner Temperature (by Bering): dam, maiden (stayed 1m), half-sister to high-class miler Distant View: 14/1, very green when seventh to Francesca d'Gorgio in maiden at Newmarket: sold 14,000 gns, joined Jane Chapple-Hyam. *R. Charlton* — **63**

DRIVING MISS SUZIE 3 br.f. Diktat 126 – Santa Isobel 94 (Nashwan (USA) 135) [2007 8.3m 10.5g⁶ 11.9m² 10s⁶ 11.5m p11g³ 12g p11g³ p12m p12g⁴ Oct 24] leggy, lengthy filly: second foal: dam 1¼m winner: fair maiden: stays 1½m: acts on polytrack and good to firm going: blinkered/visored last 5 starts: one to treat with caution: joined Jonjo O'Neill. *A. M. Balding* — **69 §**

DRIZZI (IRE) 6 b.g. Night Shift (USA) – Woopi Gold (IRE) (Last Tycoon 131) [2007 10m* 10m* 10m 10d⁴ 11m² 12m² 13m² 8.8m² 8.8g* p10g² 12m* p10m 10d p12.2g³ p13.9g² f12d³ Dec 12] winner of 9 races in Italy for A. Pecoraro, including sellers at Pisa in March and Florence in April and handicap at Grosseto in August: fair form in Britain: claimed from Aldo Locatelli £6,000, won claimer at Musselburgh in September: left A. Carroll £6,000 before final outing: stays 1¾m: acts on all-weather and good to firm ground: often in cheekpieces: tried tongue tied. *P. T. Midgley* — **72**

DR LIGHT (IRE) 3 b.g. Medicean 128 – Allumette (Rainbow Quest (USA) 134) [2007 55: 10m 12g p12g Jun 30] modest maiden: should stay 1¼m: acts on polytrack. *S. Kirk* — **53**

DR LIVINGSTONE (IRE) 2 b.g. (Apr 13) Dr Fong (USA) 128 – Radhwa (FR) **77** (Shining Steel 123) [2007 7.1g 7.1m³ p7.1g⁴ Sep 28] good-topped gelding: fair maiden: in frame at Sandown (third to Ridge Dance) and Wolverhampton: gelded after: will stay 1m. *C. R. Egerton*

DR MCFAB 3 ch.g. Dr Fong (USA) 128 – Barbera 54 (Barathea (IRE) 127) [2007 63: **71** p7g⁵ p9.5g³ p8g² p9.5g² 10f⁴ Apr 16] fair maiden: stays 1¼m: raced only on polytrack and firm ground: claimed £22,000, joined Jonjo O'Neill and gelded, fair winner over hurdles. *J. A. Osborne*

DR SHARP (IRE) 7 ch.g. Dr Devious (IRE) 127 – Stoned Imaculate (IRE) 73 (Durgam **89** (USA)) [2007 95: 16g 18.7m 15g⁶ 16.1v 15.9d³ 14s³ 18d 16g² 16.5m⁶ Nov 10] heavy-topped gelding: fairly useful handicapper nowadays: creditable efforts when placed sixth/penultimate outings: stays 2½m: acts on heavy and good to firm going: usually forces pace. *T. P. Tate*

DR SYNN 6 b.g. Danzero (AUS) – Our Shirley 84 (Shirley Heights 130) [2007 71: 7m³ **71** 7d⁵ 7g⁵ 8d² p7g⁵ 7g 7g² 7g 8d 7d⁵ Oct 23] tall, good-topped gelding: fair handicapper: stays 1m: acts on polytrack, firm and soft going: tried in cheekpieces: reportedly bled eighth outing: inconsistent, and no easy ride. *J. Akehurst*

DRUMALEE LASS (IRE) 2 b.f. (Feb 28) Quws 116 – Grange Clare (IRE) 72 (Bijou **56** d'Inde 127) [2007 5v 6m 6g 5m 8d 5d* 6s Aug 5] sturdy, heavy-bodied filly: first foal: dam, 2-y-o 5f winner, half-sister to useful French miler Sao: modest performer: won seller at Leicester in July: should prove best at 5f/6f: acts on good to soft going. *Patrick Mooney, Ireland*

DRUM DANCE (IRE) 5 b.g. Namid 128 – Socialite (IRE) (Alzao (USA) 117) [2007 **62** 58: 6g 7m³ 6s* 8g p5g³ p6g p6g² p5.1g Nov 27] sturdy, close-coupled gelding: modest performer: won seller at Leicester (sold from N. Tinkler 4,500 gns) in June: stays 7f: acts on polytrack, firm and soft going: tried in cheekpieces/blinkers. *M. Hill*

DRUMFIRE (IRE) 3 b.c. Danehill Dancer (IRE) 117 – Witch of Fife (USA) 91 (Lear **109** Fan (USA) 130) [2007 106: 8m² 8g Aug 3] big, lengthy colt: useful performer: creditable 1½ lengths second to Traffic Guard in minor event at Newmarket on reappearance: still to be asked for maximum effort when clipping heels and falling over 1f out in totesport Mile (Handicap) at Goodwood next time (suffered 2 injuries, including damage to a hind fetlock): stays 1m: acts on firm and good to soft going, possibly not on soft. *M. Johnston*

DRUMHALLAGH (IRE) 2 b.g. (Apr 12) Barathea (IRE) 127 – Nashua Song (IRE) **59** (Kahyasi 130) [2007 5.7f 6m 7g Oct 16] leggy gelding: modest form in maidens, staying on: bred to be suited by 1m/1¼m. *Tom Dascombe*

DRUMMING PARTY (USA) 5 b. or br.g. War Chant (USA) 126 – Santaria (USA) **65** (Star de Naskra (USA)) [2007 69: 5.7m⁵ 5.2s⁶ p5g³ 6f⁶ p6g⁴ 5.1m Sep 13] good-topped gelding: fair handicapper: effective at 5f/6f: acts on polytrack and firm going: tongue tied: has no left eye, and tends to hang. *A. M. Balding*

DRUMOSSIE (AUS) 7 ch.g. Strategic (AUS) – Migvie (NZ) (Sir Tristram 115) [2007 **55** 14.1m⁶ 16.1m⁶ Aug 13] Australian-bred gelding: ran 5 times in Australia in 2004, winning 1m maiden at Doomben on final start: left Ian Williams, little impact both outings on Flat in Britain: tried visored/tongue tied: modest handicap chaser, successful in July, but fell fatally in October. *R. C. Guest*

DRURY LANE (IRE) 7 b. or br.g. Royal Applause 124 – Ghost Tree (IRE) 88 (Caer- **– §** leon (USA) 132) [2007 57§: p6g⁶ f16g⁶ p6g f6g f6g 6g 8m 7s 7m 6g 10.5v 8s 10g 9.2g Aug 22] tall, leggy gelding: one-time fairly useful but inconsistent handicapper: little form in 2007, leaving D. Chapman after sixth start: usually blinkered/in cheekpieces. *Miss A. Stokell*

DRYANDRA (IRE) 4 b.f. Desert Prince (IRE) 130 – Goldilocks (IRE) (Caerleon **84** (USA) 132) [2007 85: p12g³ p12g³ 13f 10m 7g p8g Sep 28] fairly useful performer: credible third to Steppe Dancer in listed race at Kempton second start: well below form after: stays easy 1½m: acts on polytrack and good to firm going: tried blinkered. *John Joseph Murphy, Ireland*

DRY SPEEDFIT (IRE) 2 b.g. (Feb 4) Desert Style (IRE) 121 – Annmary Girl **88** (Zafonic (USA) 130) [2007 6s* 7m 6m⁵ 6m Oct 5] 35,000Y: lengthy, angular gelding: has a quick action: third foal: dam Italian 6f (at 2 yrs)/6.5f winner: fairly useful performer: won maiden at Windsor in June: stiff tasks after, when also possibly unsuited by firmer ground (wears bandages): subsequently gelded: probably stays 7f: acts on soft going. *G. G. Margarson*

DUALAGI 3 b.f. Royal Applause 124 – Lady Melbourne (IRE) 76 (Indian Ridge 123) **74** [2007 55: p5g* 5g⁴ 6m³ 5.1f⁵ 6d³ 6s² 6m⁴ 5d* 5m⁶ 5m 6.1d⁵ 6d Oct 15] good-topped filly: fair performer: won maiden at Lingfield in March and handicap at Sandown in August: raced only at 5f/6f: acts on polytrack, soft and good to firm going: tried in cheek-pieces: has been early to post: signs of temperament: sold £10,500. *J. S. Moore*

DUAL FAITH (IRE) 2 b.g. (Mar 13) Almutawakel 126 – Cosa Deasa (IRE) 48 (Bara- **57** thea (IRE) 127) [2007 6g 7.1g p7m p10g⁵ Oct 24] modest maiden: best effort in blinkers (fifth in claimer): seems to stay 1¼m. *B. J. Meehan*

DUBAI ACE (USA) 6 b.g. Lear Fan (USA) 130 – Arsaan (USA) 106 (Nureyev (USA) **73** 131) [2007 72: 16g p16g p16g² p13.9g Dec 3] smallish gelding: fair maiden handicapper: stays easy 2m: acts on polytrack and good to firm going: wore cheekpieces at 6 yrs. *Miss S. West*

DUBAI DYNAMO 2 b.c. (Mar 12) Kyllachy 129 – Miss Mercy (IRE) 62 (Law Society **95** (USA) 130) [2007 5.5d⁵ 6g f6g² 6m* 6m 7g³ 6g⁵ 7m* 6g* 7d⁶ Oct 27] stocky colt: type to carry condition: brother to 3-y-o Sadeek and half-brother to several winners, including useful 2001 2-y-o 5f winner Pachara (by Mind Games), later successful in US: dam 2-y-o 6f winner: useful performer: won maiden at Goodwood in June, nursery at Doncaster in September and listed Two-Year-Old Trophy at Redcar in October: good 4¼ lengths sixth of 11 to Beacon Lodge in Horris Hill Stakes at Newbury final start: will prove best up to 7f: acts on fibresand, good to soft and good to firm going: front runner. *J. S. Moore*

DUBAI LAND 2 ch.c. (May 7) Vettori (IRE) 119 – Sundial (Cadeaux Genereux 131) **65** [2007 7g 8.1m 9f⁴ 10.2d Oct 1] neat colt: fair maiden: fourth at Redcar: should stay 1¼m: sold 11,000 gns, sent to Czech Republic. *M. R. Channon*

DUBAI MAGIC (USA) 3 ch.g. Rahy (USA) 115 – Dabaweyaa 118 (Shareef Dancer **79** (USA) 135) [2007 82: p9.5g⁴ f7g⁴ 7d⁵ 7d p6g⁶ p6m⁶ 7s⁵ Aug 22] medium-sized, attrac-tive gelding: fair handicapper: stays 9.5f: acts on polytrack and firm going (below form on softer than good): sometimes tongue tied: sold 6,500 gns. *C. E. Brittain*

DUBAI MEYDAN (IRE) 2 b.c. (May 2) High Chaparral (IRE) 132 – Miss Golden **77 p** Sands 80 (Kris 135) [2007 7.1g³ 7d Oct 20] 20,000F, 35,000 2-y-o: well-made colt: sixth foal: half-brother to 6-y-o Watamu and German 9.5f winner Lips Love (by Hernando): dam maiden (stayed 1m): promising third to Lord Peter Flint in maiden at Warwick: out of depth in Dewhurst Stakes at Newmarket: will stay at least 1m: should still do better. *Miss Gay Kelleway*

totescoop6 Two-Year-Old Trophy, Redcar—Dubai Dynamo (40/1), Vhujon (66/1, partially hidden) and Pelican Prince (50/1) make it a bookmakers' benefit

intercasino.co.uk Easter Stakes, Kempton—Dubai's Touch (left) shows improvement to beat the favourite Prime Defender; Danebury Hill (rail) is third

DUBAI PETAL (IRE) 2 b.f. (Apr 14) Dubai Destination (USA) 127 – Out of Egypt **77** (USA) (Red Ransom (USA)) [2007 5.7d 6.5d⁴ p7g 6m⁴ Nov 10] lengthy, dipped-backed filly: third foal: half-sister to fairly useful 2006 2-y-o 6f winner Johannesburg Jack (by Johannesburg): dam, ran once in US, sister to smart performer up to 1½m in Britain/US Wandering Star: fair maiden: fourth at Newbury and Doncaster (nursery, behind Generous Thought): will be suited by 7f/1m. *J. S. Moore*

DUBAI POWER 2 b.f. (Feb 5) Cadeaux Genereux 131 – Garmoucheh (USA) 99 **80** (Silver Hawk (USA) 123) [2007 5g² 6g⁴ 6.5d³ Oct 11] 150,000Y: lengthy, good-topped filly: first foal: dam, 7f (at 2 yrs) to 10.2f winner, out of smart Irish sprinter Flowing: fairly useful maiden: in frame all starts, including fourth to Fashion Rocks in listed race at Salisbury: will be suited by 7f/1m. *C. E. Brittain*

DUBAI PRINCESS (IRE) 2 b.f. (Mar 21) Dubai Destination (USA) 127 – Blue Iris **98** 105 (Petong 126) [2007 p5g* 5g⁴ 6f* 6m 5d⁶ 6g² Nov 2] €18,000Y: close-coupled, quite good-topped filly: seventh foal: half-sister to smart 5f winner (including at 2 yrs) Swiss Lake (by Indian Ridge): dam 5f/6f winner, including at 2 yrs: useful form: won maiden at Lingfield in March and (after 4-month absence due to hairline fracture of tibia) minor event at Folkestone in September: stiff task in pattern company (Cheveley Park/Cornwallis Stakes) next 2 starts, then good second to Spinning Lucy in listed race at Newmarket final one: will prove best at 5f/6f: acts on polytrack, firm and good to soft going. *J. A. Osborne*

DUBAI SAMURAI 2 b.c. (Feb 4) Dubai Destination (USA) 127 – Eishin Eleuthera **82** (IRE) (Sadler's Wells (USA) 132) [2007 7m 7d⁴ 7d⁴ 7d³ p8g Sep 24] strong colt: fifth foal: half-brother to 3 winners, including fairly useful 2005 2-y-o 7f winner Seven Samurai (by Mark of Esteem) and 1m winner Courageously (by Aljabr): dam Japanese 9f winner: fairly useful maiden: in frame at Ascot (fourth to City Leader) and Salisbury: should stay 1m: acts on good to soft going, disappointing on polytrack final start. *J. W. Hills*

DUBAI SHADOW (IRE) 3 b.f. Cape Cross (IRE) 129 – Farista (USA) (Alleged **65** (USA) 138) [2007 56: p10g 10.3d⁶ 11.5g⁴ 16g⁵ 11.5m⁵ Aug 15] fair maiden: effective at 1¼m, barely at 2m: acts on polytrack, unraced on extremes of turf going. *C. E. Brittain*

DUBAI'S TOUCH 3 b.c. Dr Fong (USA) 128 – Noble Peregrine (Lomond (USA) 128) **110** [2007 99: p8g* 7g 8m* 7d 8d 8.5s² 8m⁴ Oct 21] strong colt: smart performer: won listed races at Kempton (Easter Stakes, by ½ length from Prime Defender) in March and Goodwood (beat Traffic Guard by short head) in August: good head second to Mharadono in Grosser Preis der Landeshauptstadt Dusseldorf penultimate start: respectable fourth to Linngari in Premio Vittorio di Capua at Milan final outing: best form around 1m: acts on polytrack, firm and soft going: usually races up with pace: game. *M. Johnston*

DUBAI SUNDAY (JPN) 6 b.g. Sunday Silence (USA) – Lotta Lace (USA) (Nureyev **52** (USA) 131) [2007 58: p13g* p16g 10.1m⁵ Apr 26] leggy, close-coupled gelding: modest performer: won minor event at Lingfield in March: stays 13f: acts on all-weather and good to firm going: tried blinkered/tongue tied: hurdling in US with B. Haynes. *P. S. McEntee*

DUBAI'S WONDER (IRE) 2 b.c. (Mar 3) Galileo (IRE) 134 – Sena Desert 89 **67** (Green Desert (USA) 127) [2007 7g Nov 2] third foal: half-brother to fairly useful 7f winner Sydney Star (by Machiavellian): dam, 1¼m winner, half-sister to very smart 1¼m performer Best of The Bests: 25/1, seemingly fair form when eleventh of 12 in maiden at Newmarket: will benefit from 1¼m/1½m. *B. W. Hills*

DUBAI TIME 2 b.c. (Mar 16) Dubai Destination (USA) 127 – Time Saved 89 (Green **105** Desert (USA) 127) [2007 7.5g² 7.2g* 8.1g⁴ 8g² Sep 22] 37,000Y, 65,000 2-y-o: sturdy colt: third foal: half-brother to smart 7f (at 2 yrs) to 1½m winner Plea Bargain (by Machiavellian): dam, 1¼m winner, out of top-class 1¼m/1½m performer Time Charter: useful form: won maiden at Ayr in August: plenty of improvement when 2½ lengths second of 6 to Blue Chagall in Prix des Chenes at Longchamp, ridden more patiently: likely to stay 1¼m: sold 220,000 gns, sent to Hong Kong. *K. A. Ryan*

DUBAI TWILIGHT 3 b.c. Alhaarth (IRE) 126 – Eve 81 (Rainbow Quest (USA) 134) **97** [2007 88: p8g* 10.1g² 10g³ 8m 10m 9.9m 12g³ 12s⁴ 12s Oct 19] close-coupled, quite attractive colt: useful performer: landed odds in maiden at Lingfield in April: creditable efforts when in frame in minor event/handicaps after: free-going sort, though stays 1½m: acts on polytrack, soft and good to firm going: sent to UAE. *B. W. Hills*

DUBAI WORLD 3 b.g. Mtoto 134 – Windmill Princess 55 (Gorytus (USA) 132) [2007 **67** 10.1d³ 9g⁵ Jul 23] better effort in maidens when 1¾ lengths third to Iceman George at Yarmouth on debut: dead. *Rae Guest*

DUBONAI (IRE) 7 ch.g. Peintre Celebre (USA) 137 – Web of Intrigue 66 (Machia- **58** vellian (USA) 123) [2007 –: p12.2g² f11g Feb 6] leggy gelding: modest handicapper, lightly raced on Flat since 2004: effective at 1m to 1½m: acts on all-weather and good to firm going: often tongue tied. *G. M. Moore*

DUCAL PIP SQUEAK 3 b.f. Bertolini (USA) 125 – Creeking 65 (Persian Bold 123) **71** [2007 10.1d³ 9.2g³ 8s² 7.9m⁶ 8s³ 7.1g p7.1g p7.1g 7.2v Nov 3] 17,000Y: sixth foal: half-sister to 3 winners, including useful 6f winner Coconut Squeak (by Bahamian Bounty): dam, maiden effective from 7f to 1¼m, half-sister to useful performers Fast Eddy (up to 1m) and Stone Mill (up to 1¼m): fair maiden: stays 1m: acts on soft and good to firm going. *M. Dods*

DUCAL REGANCY RED 3 ch.f. Bertolini (USA) 125 – One For Jeannie 68 (Clan- **38** time 101) [2007 p6g 6m 6d 5m⁶ 6m Sep 8] half-sister to German 2001 2-y-o 5f winner One For Us (by Superlative): dam 5f/6f winner: poor maiden. *C. J. Teague*

DUCHESS ROYALE (IRE) 3 b.f. Danehill (USA) 126 – Fantasy Royale (USA) 96 **95 +** (Pleasant Colony (USA)) [2007 7m² 8m³ 8.3g* 8m³ 8.3d² 10d* Oct 15] long-backed, angular filly: second foal: dam, Irish 2-y-o 1m winner (stayed 1¾m), half-sister to smart French/US 6f/1m winner Naninja: useful performer: generally progressive, winning maiden in July and handicap in October, both at Windsor: likely to stay 1½m: acts on good to firm and good to soft going: effective visored or not: sent to USA. *Sir Michael Stoute*

DUDLEY DOCKER (IRE) 5 b.g. Victory Note (USA) 120 – Nordic Abu (IRE) 60 **83** (Nordico (USA)) [2007 76: f8g⁴ f8g* f7g² f8g⁶ p7.1g⁴ f8g² p8.6g* 7g* f8g 8.1m* 8.1g³ **a86** p7g² 7.1m Sep 30] leggy gelding: fairly useful performer: progressed further in 2007, winning handicap at Southwell in January, claimer at Wolverhampton (claimed from D. Carroll £12,000) in February, and handicaps at Southwell in April and Haydock in August: stays 8.6f: acts on all-weather and firm ground: effective visored/blinkered or not: tends to idle: sometimes slowly away. *C. R. Dore*

DUELING B'ANJIZ (USA) 8 b.g. Anjiz (USA) 104 – Stirling Gal (USA) (Huckster **–** (USA)) [2007 –: p16g Jan 10] little worthwhile form in 2006/7: tried blinkered/in cheekpieces/tongue tied. *E. J. Creighton*

DUELLING BANJOS 8 ch.g. Most Welcome 131 – Khadino (Relkino 131) [2007 73: **68** p10g⁴ p10g 9.9g 11s* 11d Oct 11] fair handicapper nowadays: won apprentice event at Newbury in June: stays 13f: best efforts on all-weather and going softer than good (acts on heavy): effective ridden prominently or held up. *J. Akehurst*

DUETTO (IRE) 4 b.f. Exit To Nowhere (USA) 122 – Chopins Revolution (Rakaposhi **–** King 119) [2007 8.3d Aug 20] first foal: dam hurdles winner: 80/1, well held in maiden at Leicester: sold £900 in November. *M. Scudamore*

SKF City of York Stakes, York—Irish-trained Duff steps up appreciably on previous form to win by a neck from Advanced (far side) with the blinkered Racer Forever third

DUFF (IRE) 4 b.g. Spinning World (USA) 130 – Shining Prospect (Lycius (USA) 124) **120** [2007 107: 7m² 7g⁴ 8s³ 7g* 7m² 7d Oct 20] sturdy, dipped-backed gelding: very smart performer: won listed race at York (by neck from Advanced) in August: good neck second to Arabian Gleam in Park Stakes at Doncaster next time: well below form in Challenge Stakes at Newmarket final outing, racing freely: effective at 7f/1m: acts on good to firm going (below form on going softer than good): front runner: quirky. *Edward Lynam, Ireland*

DUKE OF MARMALADE (IRE) 3 b.c. Danehill (USA) 126 – Love Me True **124** (USA) 99 (Kingmambo (USA) 125) [2007 110p: 8m⁴ 8m⁴ 8m² 10.4d⁴ 10m² 8d³ Sep 29]

If any horse deserves a pattern-race victory it is Duke of Marmalade, who returned from injury to perform consistently well at the highest level in the latest season, finishing in the frame in each of his six starts. A very smart performer at both a mile and at a mile and a quarter, Duke of Marmalade should have plenty of opportunities to put matters right in 2008.

Duke of Marmalade's only win so far came in a two-year-old maiden at the Curragh, his first season cut short when he fractured a pastern after finishing a neck second to Strategic Prince in the Vintage Stakes at Goodwood on his next outing. An operation involving the insertion of two screws proved completely successful, Duke of Marmalade finishing fourth to Cockney Rebel in both the Two Thousand Guineas at Newmarket and the Irish Two Thousand Guineas at the Curragh on his first two starts back, beaten just over two lengths each time. Duke of Marmalade got the better of Cockney Rebel when they met again in the St James's Palace Stakes at Royal Ascot, where Duke of Marmalade finished second, splitting his stable-companions Excellent Art and Astronomer Royal. Duke of Marmalade had the run of the race, allowed to dictate, but did find plenty under pressure when strongly pressed in the straight, not headed until inside the final furlong and going down by a neck. Duke of Marmalade was shaping as though well worth a try over a mile and a quarter, and two months later he tackled the trip for the first time in the International at York. He didn't improve for it but certainly didn't fail for lack of stamina either, running to a similar level of form as in the St James's Palace in finishing fourth behind Authorized, Dylan Thomas and Notnowcato, just over four lengths behind the winner. Still close up approaching the final two furlongs, Duke

308

of Marmalade was then unable to quicken and also hampered, dropping back to be last of the seven runners before rallying so well that he failed only by a neck to take third. Kept to a mile and a quarter, Duke of Marmalade didn't quite run up to the same level when second in the Irish Champion Stakes at Leopardstown, even though he finished closer to Dylan Thomas, the latter not asked for maximum effort in beating him by a length and a half. Duke of Marmalade was back to his best on his final start, though, returned to a mile at Ascot for the Queen Elizabeth II Stakes. This time he was beaten half a length by Excellent Art, the pair second and third behind the half-length winner Ramonti, again making the running but stepping up the pace significantly at halfway and rallying splendidly after the winner had gone by early in the straight. A big, strong, well-made colt, Duke of Marmalade stood out in the parade ring at Ascot, looking the sort who could well make an even better four-year-old.

Duke of Marmalade (IRE) (b.c. 2004)	Danehill (USA) (b 1986)	Danzig (b 1977)
		Northern Dancer
		Pas de Nom
	Razyana (b 1981)	His Majesty
		Spring Adieu
	Love Me True (USA) (ch 1998)	Kingmambo (b 1990)
		Mr Prospector
		Miesque
	Lassie's Lady (b 1981)	Alydar
		Lassie Dear

Duke of Marmalade is the second foal of Love Me True. Her first, also by Danehill, hasn't raced, but her third is already a winner, Soinlovewithyou, a filly by Sadler's Wells and a stable-companion of Duke of Marmalade, successful in a seven-furlong maiden at Gowran in October. Love Me True, who was also trained at Ballydoyle, made fifteen appearances but managed only one win, in a mile maiden at Naas as a three-year-old. She is from an excellent family. A sister to

Mrs John Magnier & Mr M. Tabor's "Duke of Marmalade"

winners in Japan and the States, Love Me True is a half-sister to several winners, including the very smart performer at up to a mile and three quarters Shuailaan. The next dam Lassie's Lady won over seven furlongs in the States and is a half-sister to the high-class sprinter-miler Wolfhound and to the dam of A P Indy and Summer Squall. Duke of Marmalade, unraced on extremes of ground, acts on good to firm and good to soft. *A. P. O'Brien, Ireland*

DUKE OF MILAN (IRE) 4 ch.g. Desert Prince (IRE) 130 – Abyat (USA) (Shadeed (USA) 135) [2007 75: p6g⁵ 6m p5g⁵ 6m p6g⁴ p6g⁶ 6m⁶ 6.1m⁵ p5.1g p6g p6g³ p5m⁵ Nov 11] angular gelding: fair handicapper: below form after reappearance in 2007: effective at 5f to 8.3f: acts on polytrack, good to firm and good to soft going: tried blinkered: usually held up: often finds little. *G. C. Bravery*   **71 d**

DUKE OF TOURAINE (IRE) 2 gr.g. (Apr 11) Linamix (FR) 127 – Miss Mission (IRE) (Second Empire (IRE) 124) [2007 6s 5.9d⁵ 6d³ 7m⁵ 8m 6g⁶ p8.6g⁴ Nov 9] €30,000F, 36,000 2-y-o: rather leggy, angular gelding: has powerful, round action: first foal: dam 2-y-o 6f to 1m winner: fair maiden: gelded, staying-on fourth in nursery at Wolverhampton final start: will be suited by 1¼m: acts on polytrack, good to firm and good to soft going. *P. C. Haslam*   **76**

DUKE OF TUSCANY 3 b.c. Medicean 128 – Flawless 107 (Warning 136) [2007 100: 10m⁴ 10m³ 10g² 10.1g 13m⁶ 12g p11g³ 10.3m⁵ Sep 13] strong, good-bodied colt: useful performer: mainly creditable efforts in 2007, including when placed in handicaps at Newmarket and Newbury (¾-length second to Zaham) and minor event at Kempton (4¼ lengths third of 4 to Al Tharib): stays easy 11f: acts on polytrack, good to firm and good to soft ground: wore cheekpieces final start: usually races prominently: sold 65,000 gns, sent to Bahrain. *R. Hannon*   **100**

DUKESTREET 6 ch.g. Cadeaux Genereux 131 – El Rabab (USA) 70 (Roberto (USA) 131) [2007 –: f7g p6g p5.1g 6s Jul 3] one-time fairly useful performer: poor form at best in 2007: stays 1m: acts on heavy going: tried in cheekpieces. *D. Shaw*   **44**

DULCE SUENO 4 b.f. Lahib (USA) 129 – Graceland Lady (IRE) 55 (Kafu 120) [2007 63: 7.1d² 7.1g 6d Jul 23] modest maiden handicapper: stays 7f: acts on firm and good to soft going. *I. Semple*   **56**

DUMARAN (IRE) 9 b.g. Be My Chief (USA) 122 – Pine Needle 89 (Kris 135) [2007 81: p9.5g⁵ p12g Mar 7] fair performer: stays 10.4f: acts on polytrack and any turf going: visored (below form) twice: sometimes slowly away/pulls hard: none too reliable: sold £8,000 and joined A. Bateman, modest hurdler, won in July. *W. J. Musson*   **74**

DUMAS (IRE) 3 b.g. Iron Mask (USA) 117 – Bucaramanga (IRE) (Distinctly North (USA) 115) [2007 75p: p12g Mar 7] fair maiden at 2 yrs: no form in 2007 (reportedly swallowed tongue on reappearance): tried visored/in cheekpieces. *A. P. Jarvis*   **–**

DUNASKIN (IRE) 7 b.g. Bahhare (USA) 122 – Mirwara (IRE) (Darshaan 133) [2007 103: p12.2g²⁶ p11g 10.4g⁶ 10d* 10d³ 12m 12d² 10s² 10.4d p12g Nov 3] smallish, workmanlike gelding: smart performer on turf, useful on all-weather: won handicap at Pontefract (only try in cheekpieces) in June: excellent second in similar event at York (beaten length by Galactic Star) and listed race at Ayr (1¾ lengths behind Anna Pavlova) seventh/eighth starts: ran poorly last 2 outings: stays 1½m: acts on polytrack, best turf form on good ground or softer: makes running/races up with pace. *Karen McLintock*   **112 a97 +**

DUNDRY 6 b.g. Bin Ajwaad (IRE) 119 – China's Pearl (Shirley Heights 130) [2007 83: f12g* p12g* 16m³ 14g³ 14s⁴ 14.1g p12g⁵ Oct 29] big, good-topped gelding: fairly useful handicapper: won at Southwell (drifted right) in January and Lingfield in February: creditable efforts next 2 starts: well below form after: effective at 1½m to 2m: acts on all-weather, soft and good to firm ground: wears cheekpieces. *G. L. Moore*   **88**

DUNEEN DREAM (USA) 2 ch.g. (Apr 17) Hennessy (USA) 122 – T N T Red (USA) (Explosive Red (CAN) 119) [2007 6d p7.1g p7g⁴ p8g Dec 12] 22,000 2-y-o: lengthy gelding: second foal: closely related to winner in USA by Johannesburg: dam US 6f (at 2 yrs) to 8.5f winner: modest maiden: will stay beyond 1m: steady improvement, and may do better still. *W. J. Musson*   **54 +**

DUNELIGHT (IRE) 4 ch.c. Desert Sun 120 – Badee'a (IRE) (Marju (IRE) 127) [2007 113: 9m 8m³ 8m* 8m⁵ 7g³ 8g⁴ 7m² 8m Oct 6] good sort: good walker: smart performer: won listed race at Goodwood (beat Army of Angels by 4 lengths) in June: good efforts when placed in Lennox Stakes (third to Tariq) and Supreme Stakes (neck second to Lovelace) at same course after: run best excused (raced alone and always behind) in Joel   **115**

Stakes at Newmarket final outing: free-going sort, best at 7f/1m: raced mainly on good going or firmer: visored/blinkered: front runner. *C. G. Cox*

DUNE MELODY (IRE) 4 b.f. Distant Music (USA) 126 – Desert Gift 69 (Green Desert (USA) 127) [2007 80: 8m 6m Apr 30] unfurnished filly: fairly useful performer at 3 yrs: no form in 2007: stays 7f: acts on firm and soft going: tried in cheekpieces (ran poorly): often held up. *J. S. Moore* –

DUNMORE DODGER (IRE) 2 b.c. (Feb 20) Tagula (IRE) 116 – Decrescendo (IRE) (Polish Precedent (USA) 131) [2007 p5.1g³ Dec 29] €12,000Y: eighth foal: brother to winner in Greece and half-brother to 3 winners, including fairly useful 2m winner Spitting Image (by Spectrum): dam unraced half-sister to smart 1¼m filly Calando out of Oaks winner and St Leger second Diminuendo: 16/1, third in maiden at Wolverhampton, soon off bridle: will be suited by 6f+. *R. A. Fahey* **72**

DUNN DEAL (IRE) 7 b.g. Revoque (IRE) 122 – Buddy And Soda (IRE) 75 (Imperial Frontier (USA) 112) [2007 78: 6g p6g p6g 6m⁶ 6s⁵ 6s⁶ 5d⁵ 5d³ 6g⁶ 5s⁵ p6g f6d⁶ f5d⁵ Dec 14] smallish, sturdy gelding: modest performer nowadays: left W. M. Brisbourne after firm start: effective at 5f/6f: acts on fibresand and any turf going: tried tongue tied: sometimes wanders: usually held up. *J. Balding* **55**

DUNN'O (IRE) 2 b.g. (Feb 1) Cape Cross (IRE) 129 – Indian Express 61 (Indian Ridge 123) [2007 6m³ 6.1m⁴ 5.1g² Oct 24] €55,000Y: big, good-bodied gelding: half-brother to several winners, notably 8-y-o Ashdown Express and smart 1m (including at 2 yrs) to 1¼m winner Hoh Buzzard (by Alhaarth): dam 8.5f/1¼m winner: fairly useful form in frame in maidens, second to Masada at Bath (hung left, gelded after): likely to stay 7f. *C. G. Cox* **80**

DUNTULM 2 b.c. (May 6) Sakhee (USA) 136 – Not Before Time (IRE) (Polish Precedent (USA) 131) [2007 p7g 10g 5m³ Nov 21] 90,000Y: lengthy colt: half-brother to several winners, notably 1¼m winner Time Ahead (by Spectrum) and 1m/1¼m (Musidora Stakes) winner Time Away (by Darshaan), both smart/placed in Prix de Diane: dam unraced out of top-class 1¼m/1½m performer Time Charter: better effort 3 months apart when seventh of 8 to Twice Over in minor event at Newmarket: will stay 1½m. *H. Candy* **73**

DUROVA (IRE) 3 b.f. Soviet Star (USA) 128 – Taroudannt (IRE) (Danehill (USA) 126) [2007 76: 6g f5g⁵ 5g⁴ p5.1g 5g³ 5m 5f 5m Sep 18] compact filly: fair handicapper: best at 5f: acts on firm ground: temperamental: sold 2,400 gns. *T. D. Easterby* **70**

DUSHSTORM (IRE) 6 b.g. Dushyantor (USA) 123 – Between The Winds (USA) (Diesis 133) [2007 7.5s⁶ 10s* 10s* 8.5g 8g⁵ 9g* p9.5g p8g Dec 1] won 9 races in Italy, including handicaps at Pisa in February and April and Milan (final outing for A. & G. Botti) in August: in cheekpieces, modest form in Britain: stays 1¼m: acts on soft ground. *M. Botti* **60**

DUSK 2 b.g. (Feb 6) Fantastic Light (USA) 134 – Dark Veil (USA) 96 (Gulch (USA)) [2007 7m⁵ 8m 8m 8.3d⁵ Oct 15] sturdy gelding: third foal: half-brother to Italian 1m winner Lamentation (by Singspiel): dam, Irish 1¼m winner, closely related to smart UAE sprinter Conroy out of 1000 Guineas third Crystal Gazing: fair maiden: fifth in nursery at Windsor final start (gelded after): will stay 1¼m. *J. L. Dunlop* **65**

DUSK BALLET 2 b.f. (Apr 15) Alhaarth (IRE) 126 – Curfew 102 (Marju (IRE) 127) [2007 7m p7.1g⁴ p7g p6g p7.1g⁵ Nov 20] first foal: dam 7f winner (including at 2 yrs): poor maiden: stays 7f: acts on polytrack. *S. C. Williams* **49**

DUSTOORI 3 b.c. In The Wings 128 – Elfaslah (IRE) 107 (Green Desert (USA) 127) **93** [2007 11.7d* 13s² 11s* 12g Oct 27] half-brother to several winners, including high-class 7f (at 2 yrs) to 1¼m (Dubai World Cup) winner Almutawakel, smart 1m (including UAE 1000 Guineas) winner Muwakleh and smart 1¼m/1½m (in UAE) winner Elmustanser (all by Machiavellian): dam, won around 1¼m, half-sister to high-class 1½m performer White Muzzle: fairly useful performer: won maiden at Bath in August and handicap at Goodwood in October: best effort when ½-length second to Sadler's Kingdom in handicap at Hamilton in between: stays 13f: raced only on good ground or softer: has left Godolphin. *Saeed bin Suroor*

DUSTY MOON 2 ch.f. (Apr 26) Dr Fong (USA) 128 – Dust Dancer 116 (Suave Dancer **78** (USA) 136) [2007 p7g* p7g* 7g Aug 25] leggy, attractive filly: seventh foal: sister to smart 7f (at 2 yrs) to 9f (in US) winner Spotlight and half-sister to 2001 2-y-o 7f winner Dusty Answer (by Zafonic) and 7f winner Tyranny (by Machiavellian), both useful: dam, 7f to 1½m winner, half-sister to very smart performer up to 1½m Zimzalabim: fair form: won maiden at Lingfield in July, quickening well from rear: last of 7 in Prestige Stakes at Goodwood only other start: will stay 1m. *W. J. Knight*

DUTCH ART 3 ch.c. Medicean 128 – Halland Park Lass (IRE) (Spectrum (IRE) **126** 126) [2007 124: 7m² 8m³ 8m⁴ 6m² 6.5m² 7d⁶ Oct 6]
In failing to win a race at three, Dutch Art followed the pattern of nearly all recent Middle Park winners for whom success at the Cambridgeshire meeting as a two-year-old proved the highlight of their careers. Dutch Art, though, did at least go on to show form slightly higher than his best two-year-old efforts and demonstrated his effectiveness at a mile as well as shorter. In the fairly extensive period since the 1991 Middle Park winner Rodrigo de Triano landed four Group 1 events the following year, including the Two Thousand Guineas for Dutch Art's trainer, only the 2000 Middle Park winner Minardi had made the frame in a mile classic, and only three winners—Zieten, Royal Applause and Oasis Dream (easily the most successful Middle Park winner at three since Rodrigo de Triano)—had won a race of any description the following season. Like Minardi, Zieten (winner of the Prix de Fontainebleau before finishing eighth in the Poulains) and Royal Applause (a minor winner sprinting after finishing tenth in the Guineas), Dutch Art was asked to make the transition from leading sprinting two-year-old to classic miler.
The first step towards that goal came in the Greenham at Newbury over seven furlongs. Dutch Art went into that race ante-post favourite for Newmarket, behind Teofilo, but drifted to much longer odds after defeat by Major Cadeaux seemed to suggest he had limited prospects of staying still further. Dutch Art did, though, look a stockier type than he had at two and it turned out that he was simply short of a run at Newbury, as his trainer had intimated he would be. Dutch Art reversed placings with Major Cadeaux in a wide-open Guineas, finishing third, two and a quarter lengths behind Cockney Rebel and first home of the ten that raced on the far side. It is perhaps an indication of the shortage of opportunities for three-year-old sprinters at the top level that another six in that group went on to show to better advantage at six furlongs, while only two turned out to be at their best at a mile or more. Dutch Art had one more outing at a mile, in the St James's Palace Stakes at Royal Ascot, getting the better of Cockney Rebel by a short head but failing to beat any of Aidan O'Brien's trio of runners. Dutch Art didn't progress quite as expected and left the impression his race at Newmarket might have left its mark.
As he had done after the Greenham, however, Dutch Art rather defied expectations. Dropped to six furlongs, he ran his best race of the year less than a month later when second of eighteen to Sakhee's Secret, beaten half a length, in the July Cup at Newmarket, squeezed out towards the rear in some scrimmaging three furlongs out before finishing well. Just over three weeks after that he was again runner-up, behind the July Cup fourth Marchand d'Or, in the Prix Maurice de Gheest at Deauville. Connections were inclined to blame the firmish ground for Dutch Art's running slightly below expectations in France, as indeed his rider had at Ascot—though Dutch Art had performed perfectly well on similar going in the Guineas and in the July Cup. That view of Dutch Art's going requirements, at odds with his racing record, might well have denied him his best chance of a win in 2007, as he was withdrawn from the Sprint Cup at Haydock. The ground, controversially,

turned out rather different from forecast. Sakhee's Secret ran below his July Cup form, though the third and fourth at Newmarket, Red Clubs and Marchand d'Or, boosted the July Cup form by filling the first two places. Sakhee's Secret's trainer Hughie Morrison was livid, on his own account and that of Dutch Art's trainer: 'If I were Peter Chapple-Hyam I would be furious.' Chapple-Hyam himself put things in a calmer perspective: 'It's hardly the end of the world. I don't see any point in moaning at clerks of the course, because they have a difficult enough job to do. Let's grow up and get on with life.'

Alas, Chapple-Hyam's conciliatory attitude went unrewarded, with Dutch Art at least, as the colt finished out of the frame for the first time in his career when sixth, held up further off the pace than for most of his races at three, in the Prix de la Foret at Longchamp. Zieten and Royal Applause, along with fellow Middle Park winners Primo Valentino and Amadeus Wolf, all managed wins at four but Dutch Art won't be getting the chance, retired instead to Cheveley Park Stud in Newmarket at a fee of £10,000. More's the pity, given that his sire Medicean, who raced in the Cheveley Park colours, was even better at four than three, winning the Lockinge and the Eclipse.

Dutch Art (ch.c. 2004)	Medicean (ch 1997)	Machiavellian (b 1987)	Mr Prospector
			Coup de Folie
		Mystic Goddess (ch 1990)	Storm Bird
			Rose Goddess
	Halland Park Lass (IRE) (ch 1999)	Spectrum (b 1992)	Rainbow Quest
			River Dancer
		Palacegate Episode (b 1990)	Drumalis
			Pasadena Lady

Dutch Art has a strong, sprinter's physique and is obviously likely to appeal to breeders looking for precocious stock, having himself won on his debut at two at

Mrs Susan Roy and Cheveley Park Stud's "Dutch Art"

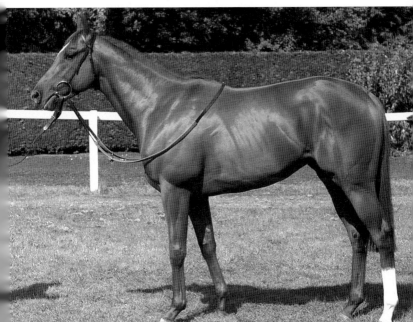

Windsor in early-June (beating a fellow dual Group 1 winner in Simply Perfect) before going on to success in the Norfolk Stakes at Royal Ascot and the Prix Morny at Deauville, as well as the Middle Park. He is the best offspring so far from three crops by his sire, ahead of the filly Nannina and the Hollywood Derby runner-up Medici Code. Dutch Art comes from a sprinting family, his grandam Palacegate Episode, who died in 2007, showing herself a smart five-furlong performer. Dutch Art's dam Halland Park Lass ran just three times and he is her first foal. Palacegate Episode has had more success with her other foals, the best the smart Scandinavian sprinter King Quantas and the latest the two-year-old Longing To Dance, a useful second in listed company at the Curragh in September. Dutch Art's successes have certainly boosted the value of his relatives. Halland Park Lass, described in *Timeform* as sparely made and as having carried her head awkwardly and raced freely, was sold for just 12,000 guineas at the Newmarket (2005) December Sales but made 710,000 guineas at the same venue a year later, following her son's two-year-old career. Halland Park Lass's 2006 filly by Kyllachy made 280,000 guineas as a foal and 480,000 guineas as a yearling. Longing To Dance herself was a 200,000-guinea yearling, while her year-younger half-brother by Kyllachy made 130,000 guineas at the same age.

Despite a presumably tongue-in-cheek remark from his trainer that Dutch Art might contest the Champion Stakes, there was not much prospect of him staying beyond a mile. He acted well on good to firm going and won the Prix Morny on soft. Bought from Matthew Green after his debut, he raced subsequently in the colours of Susan Roy, though the Cheveley Park Stud purchased him outright before the start of his three-year-old career. *P. W. Chapple-Hyam*

DUTCH KEY CARD (IRE) 6 b.g. Key of Luck (USA) 126 – Fanny Blankers (IRE) (Persian Heights 129) [2007 54: 5.1m 7g⁶ 7.5v Jul 6] just poor performer in 2007: had form up to 1m, but was probably best at 5f/6f: acted on all-weather and good to firm going: tried tongue tied: often blinkered/visored (not last 2 starts): dead. *C. Smith*   **46**

DUTY DOCTOR 2 ch.f. (Jan 24) Dr Fong (USA) 128 – Duty Paid (IRE) 99 (Barathea (IRE) 127) [2007 5.1m⁵ 7m² 6d Oct 29] attractive filly: first foal: dam, 2-y-o 5f/6f winner (stayed 1m), sister to useful performer up to 9f Lady Miletrian: fair maiden: runner-up to Harlem Shuffle at Kempton: inadequate tests on turf both other starts: will be suited by 1m. *S. Kirk*   **75**

DUTY FREE (IRE) 3 b.g. Rock of Gibraltar (IRE) 133 – Photographie (USA) (Trempolino (USA) 135) [2007 68p: p8g⁵ p12g⁴ 11.7g² p12g* 14g* 14g² 12m⁵ 14m² Oct 4] good-topped gelding: useful handicapper: won at Kempton in July and Sandown in August: further improvement when 1½ lengths second to Kahara at Newmarket final outing: stays 1¾m: raced only on polytrack and good/good to firm going: usually races prominently: sold 110,000 gns, then gelded. *H. Morrison*   **96**

DVINSKY (USA) 6 b.g. Stravinsky (USA) 133 – Festive Season (USA) (Lypheor 118) [2007 83, a78: p6g* p6g p7.1g p6g p6g³ p6g³ 7g⁴ p6g* 6m² 6s 6g p6g² p6g³ p6g⁵ 6f p6g⁵ p6g² p6m³ p6g⁴ p7.1g⁵ p6g p6m p6g* p7g⁶ Dec 16] compact gelding: fairly useful handicapper: won at Wolverhampton (dead-heat) in January and Kempton in April and December: effective at 6f, barely stays 1m: acts on polytrack, firm and soft going: tried tongue tied: has worn headgear (visored for last win): races up with pace. *P. Howling*   **83**

DYANITA 4 b.f. Singspiel (IRE) 133 – Dance Clear (IRE) 99 (Marju (IRE) 127) [2007 63, a76: p8g⁵ Feb 7] fair handicapper: stays 1¼m: acts on polytrack, yet to race on extremes of going on turf: tried blinkered: usually races prominently. *B. W. Hills*   **67**

DYLAN (IRE) 4 b.g. Mull of Kintyre (USA) 114 – Rose of Shuaib (IRE) 68 (Caerleon (USA) 132) [2007 50: p9.5g Feb 10] sturdy gelding: modest performer at 3 yrs: well held only start in 2007: stays 1m: acts on fibresand and good to firm ground. *M. A. Doyle*   **–**

DYLAN THOMAS (IRE) 4 b.c. Danehill (USA) 126 – Lagrion (USA) 68 (Diesis 133) [2007 129: 10m* 10.5m* 10.5g² 10m² 12g* 10.4d² 10m* 12g* 12s⁵ 12g Dec 9]   **132**

Dylan Thomas set the seal on a magnificent year, for himself and for his stable, when becoming his trainer's first winner of Europe's richest race, the Prix de l'Arc de Triomphe. The victory put him in illustrious company—he is only the sixth horse to win both the King George and the Arc in the same season—and provided a timely reminder that a top horse can have a full campaign and still

be at his best for Longchamp in October. Ascot's showpiece, the King George VI and Queen Elizabeth Stakes, has long been the midsummer championship of Europe for the middle-distance performers but the myth has grown up that a mid-season break, involving bypassing the King George, is a pre-requisite for any horse whose principal aim is the Arc. The Arc has understandably always been the main focus for the top French middle-distance horses—with the classic three-year-olds traditionally given a summer break—and its ever-rising status as the more important of the two principal tests of Europe's top middle-distance horses will be emphasised in 2008 when a new sponsorship deal with the Qatar Racing and Equestrian Club will make the Arc the most valuable global event on turf and the second richest race in the world, behind only the Dubai World Cup. The status of the King George looks set to come under more pressure in 2008, so Dylan Thomas's double could not have been more timely for Ascot, or for British racing generally.

It is rare for an Arc winner to run so often as Dylan Thomas. He won the race on his eighth outing of the season, having been on the go throughout, contesting top races at regular intervals, his last six before the Arc all Group 1s. Two of the Arc winners in the 'seventies, San San and Star Appeal, won the race on their tenth and ninth starts respectively. The last to complete the King George/Arc double, Lammtarra, won the Arc on only his third start of the season (after also winning the Derby). The Arc winners since—none of whom contested the same season's King George—averaged five and a half outings earlier in the season. Dylan Thomas, successful in the Irish Derby and the Irish Champion Stakes after a close third in the Derby, reappeared on April 15th, completing a straightforward task in the listed Alleged Stakes at the Curragh. He was also impressive when landing the odds in the Prix Ganay at Longchamp later in the month from Irish Wells and Doctor Dino. Two second places followed, Dylan Thomas going down narrowly to Notnowcato —the pair stretching clear—in the Tattersalls Gold Cup at the Curragh and then being beaten a length and a quarter by Manduro, with Notnowcato third, in the Prince of Wales's Stakes. Though Dylan Thomas ran well on both occasions, he raced slightly awkwardly after coming under pressure and gave the impression he might have been outbattled, hanging in behind Manduro at Royal Ascot. Dylan Thomas wasn't seen out between Royal Ascot and the King George VI and Queen Elizabeth Stakes at the end of July, the five and a half weeks between the two races the longest break he had during his campaign in Europe.

King George VI and Queen Elizabeth Stakes, Ascot—no three-year-olds
as Dylan Thomas consolidates his position at the forefront of Europe's middle-distance horses;
he has four lengths to spare over Youmzain, who is clear of Maraahel, Laverock and Scorpion

The King George VI and Queen Elizabeth Stakes lost its 'Diamond' tag, following the withdrawal of long-time sponsors De Beers, but it was not just the race name that lost the sparkle. With no representative of the classic crop and German-trained Prince Flori the only runner from outside Britain and Ireland, the field of seven—three four-year-olds, two five-year-olds, a six-year-old and an eight-year-old—struggled to catch the public imagination. For most of its history, the King George has fulfilled the objective of its architect, Sir John Crocker Bulteel, by staging a worthy championship between the best of the generations. Its roll of honour contains the names of some of the last half century's finest thoroughbreds and it has long been the most important event in the British calendar for three-year-olds and upwards. The absence of the Derby winner Authorized, withdrawn after defeat in the Eclipse and reportedly thought likely to 'benefit from a longer break with the Arc in mind' was a big blow to the King George. The race has had only two three-year-old winners in the last dozen years, the Derby winner Galileo in 2001 and the Irish Derby winner Alamshar in 2003. Alamshar's King George was the last one contested by the Epsom Derby winner. Galileo and Kris Kin, third in Alamshar's year, are the only Derby winners to have run in the King George in the last eight years, compared to nine in the eleven preceding them. Only one Oaks winner (Eswarah) has taken part in the last twenty renewals and it is twenty-one years since both the Derby and Oaks winner were in the line-up (Reference Point and Unite). The latest King George was the third in six years without a three-year-old, colt or filly, and in two of those there was only a single representative from the classic crop. Five three-year-olds, also including the Prix du Jockey Club and Derby Italiano winners, took part in Galileo's King George, the last edition that could truly be regarded as vintage, and through the 'nineties there were at least three three-year-old challengers in most years.

Ballydoyle's two likeliest prospects from the latest classic crop, runaway Irish Derby winner Soldier of Fortune and Derby runner-up Eagle Mountain, both dropped out of contention in the run up to the race and Dylan Thomas stood out on form, starting 5/4 favourite, with another stablemate the 2005 St Leger winner Scorpion next at 3/1 and the Hardwicke winner Maraahel at 6/1, the only other runner to start at single-figure odds. Scorpion made the King George a true test by trying to make all, tactics that had brought him his St Leger victory (though different to how he had been ridden since). Tackling a trip as far as a mile and a half for the first time since winning the Irish Derby, Dylan Thomas, who stood out in the paddock, produced a top-class performance, well up to standard for a King George. Although hanging over towards the rail after coming through strongly to lead over a furlong out, Dylan Thomas made short work of his rivals, driven out to win by four lengths from 12/1-shot Youmzain (third in the Tattersalls Gold Cup), with Maraahel three and a half lengths further back in third, just in front of the Godolphin challenger Laverock, and the remainder strung out (Scorpion fifth).

'Why all the public panic about the King George?' asked one leading commentator after Dylan Thomas's emphatic win. The British Horseracing Authority's racing director seemed equally unconcerned, saying: 'There is no reason why we would be sounding alarm bells. It is too early to be saying we have got a problem.' The Ascot authority was left to reflect on a big drop in the crowd, from 32,437 in 2006 to 25,177, blaming it on uncertainty over the make-up of the field—and the withdrawal of Authorized—and on bad weather in the build up to the day, as well as not having the usual 3,000 De Beers guests. New chief executive Charles Barnett has some work to do, though, and has rightly identified finding a new sponsor and raising the King George's prize money as his biggest priorities. With the autumn announcement about the massive injection of prize money for the Arc in 2008, Ascot must act quickly if the reputation and relevance of the King George is not to suffer. Except in its first eight years, when it was the most valuable race in Britain, the value of the King George has never been so high as it should have been, relative to other major races at a mile and a half. Twenty-five years ago, before the growth of international races, the King George was worth £126,472 to the winner; the Arc £165,016; the Derby £146,720, the Irish Derby £104,516 and the Prix du Jockey Club £81,008. By the latest season, the first prizes had changed to £425,850, £799,160, £709,750, £568,792 and £579,122 (the Prix du Jockey Club is now over an extended mile and a quarter), figures which speak for themselves. Among mile and a half races on turf, the King George is also well adrift of the Dubai Sheema Classic (£1,530,612), the Japan Cup (£1,121,333), the Breeders' Cup Turf (£790,244), the Canadian International (£606,060) and the Hong Kong Vase (£504,425). In the full list of the world's richest Flat races in 2007, compiled by the International Racing Bureau, the King George ranks only sixtieth.

Back in 2000, as part of a proposal for a fundamental review of the European programme which would create three-week intervals between the French, English and Irish Derbies, French racing supremo Louis Romanet suggested that the King George should become a race for four-year-olds and upwards, with the Arc staged in September instead of early-October. Since then, the Grand Prix de Paris has had its distance changed to a mile and a half and is now staged two weeks before the King George, providing competition for the top three-year-olds. Romanet's vision of the King George as a major international race for older horses, rather than a clash of the generations, has gone some way to being fulfilled, judged on recent renewals, and it seems to be a vision that the Ascot executive is also coming round to. After briefly debating whether to reduce the distance of the King George to a mile and a quarter and whether to move it to Ascot's August fixture, the executive reportedly decided that trying to attract more top-class Japanese and American horses—at which it has already had some success—represents its best

Tattersalls Millions Irish Champion Stakes, Leopardstown—
Dylan Thomas becomes the first horse to win the race twice in its twenty-four-year history;
Duke of Marmalade and Red Rock Canyon make it a 1,2,3 for Aidan O'Brien

chance of maintaining quality and interest. A considerable boost in prize money would, however, still be required to sustain the King George as a genuinely international event, and, if that could be achieved, the King George might well return to its glory days without changing its nature. The last two editions of *Racehorses* have raised the idea of the King George succeeding the St Leger and being promoted as the third leg of the triple crown in an attempt to entice the three-year-olds back. The traditional triple crown of Two Thousand Guineas, Derby and St Leger hasn't been won since Nijinsky in 1970 (Oh So Sharp landed the fillies' equivalent in 1985). Nijinsky completed the Guineas, Derby and King George treble, as did Nashwan in 1989. A Derby, Irish Derby and King George triple crown would be won more often, Nijinsky also having achieved that feat, as have six others—Grundy, The Minstrel, Troy, Shergar, Generous and Galileo. Mill Reef and Lammtarra won the Derby, King George and the Arc, the necessary big bonus probably less expensive to insure for that eventuality than for the two other suggestions (a straight Derby/King George double would be virtually uninsurable). The King George needs the Derby winner to turn up in most years to maintain the King George's original objective and any triple crown involving the Derby and King George as the first two legs would almost certainly achieve that.

Before Dylan Thomas, the fortunes of most recent King George winners had waned after Ascot. With the exceptions of Swain (in 1998) and Daylami, both of whom went on to win the same season's Irish Champion (Daylami also won the Breeders' Cup Turf), none of the winners since Lammtarra had been successful again in the same season. In that time, five of the eleven, Pentire, Swain (1997), Daylami, Montjeu and Hurricane Run, had been beaten—all unplaced—in the Arc. Dylan Thomas continued to prove his durability, maintaining his run of consistent performances in the International at York, the Tattersalls Millions Irish Champion Stakes at the Curragh and the Prix de l'Arc de Triomphe Lucien Barriere at Longchamp. The Derby winner Authorized proved just too good for Dylan Thomas (who replaced George Washington at a late stage) in the International, though tactics played some part in the victory, Authorized's rider holding in Dylan Thomas against the rail for a time in the straight. Dylan Thomas knuckled down well once in the clear to go down by a length, in the process beating Notnowcato (three lengths further back in third) for the second time since the Tattersalls Gold Cup. Johnny Murtagh rode Dylan Thomas at Ascot and York, the first time Dylan Thomas had been ridden in consecutive races by the same jockey since his two-year-old days. Murtagh was partnering him at Ascot for the first time since the Derby, Seamus Heffernan having ridden him when successful on his reappearance and in the Tattersalls Gold Cup, and Christophe Soumillon taking the mount on the Ganay and the Prince of Wales's. It was all change again for Dylan Thomas in the Irish Champion and the Prix de l'Arc in which he was reunited with Ballydoyle's number one Kieren Fallon, who had been unable to ride in Britain and had his season throughout the rest of Europe disrupted by a drugs-related ban. Fallon had ridden Dylan Thomas four times and won on him four times, including in the Irish Derby and the Irish Champion Stakes. He made it six out of six as Dylan Thomas became the first horse to win the Irish Champion for the second successive year, giving his trainer a fifth success in the race, and then won the Prix de l'Arc. Dylan Thomas started at 15/8-on for a below-par renewal of the Irish Champion, in which the One Thousand Guineas winner Finsceal Beo and the British-trained challengers Red Rocks and Maraahel all ran below form, leaving Dylan Thomas to lead home stablemates Duke of Marmalade and Red Rock Canyon, the latter sent off at 100/1. Dylan Thomas was left with a bit to do in the home straight but came through in good style once fully opened out to beat Duke of Marmalade with something in reserve by a length and a half.

While Dylan Thomas had been kept on the go, Ballydoyle's other principal Arc challenger Soldier of Fortune was given a traditional Arc preparation, put away after his nine-length Irish Derby win, a performance which, at the time, suggested there might be little between him and Authorized at the top of the rankings of the middle-distance three-year-olds. Soldier of Fortune had seemingly improved out of all recognition since coming fifth to Authorized at Epsom but, with Dylan Thomas earmarked for the King George, he wasn't given the chance to build on his Irish Derby performance and returned to action in September with a thoroughly satisfactory win in the Prix Niel, one of Longchamp's traditional Arc trials. Dylan Thomas and Soldier of Fortune, who were accompanied by stablemates Yellowstone and Song of Hiawatha (the latter supplemented at a cost of €60,000) to ensure a good gallop, were all coupled at 5/2 in a market dominated by Authorized at 11/10. The Grand Prix de Paris winner Zambezi Sun (6/1), also brought back in the Prix Niel (third) after a short summer break, and Mandesha (66/10), who had finished runner-up to Manduro in the Prix Foy on Longchamp's 'day of trials', were the only others in the Arc line-up to start at odds shorter than 20/1 in a field of twelve, in which the Prix Niel runner-up Sagara started at 32/1 and the King George runner-up Youmzain was sent off at 80/1.

With Authorized running very disappointingly and Soldier of Fortune a good way below his Irish Derby form, the latest Arc—with its off-time brought forward from recent years by an hour in a welcome move (because of the better light)—took less winning than it might have done. Dylan Thomas travelled strongly under restraint until Fallon produced him in the home straight to join issue after two furlongs out. Not for the first time, however, Dylan Thomas began to edge right under pressure, drifting across the track and, after initially hampering Zambezi Sun, also interfering with Soldier of Fortune inside the final furlong (Dylan Thomas survived a thirty-five-minute stewards' inquiry). Youmzain proved suited by the thorough test of stamina at the trip and put in a very strong challenge to Dylan Thomas before going down by a head, producing a career-best effort. It was the first time that the winner and runner-up in the King George had gone on to fill the same two places in the Arc, though Triptytch and Shahrastani had finished third and fourth respectively behind Dancing Brave in both races in 1986. Sagara was the first three-year-old to finish in the latest Arc, a length and a half behind Youmzain in third, and a short head and half a length in front of the four-year-old Getaway, a supplementary entry in the Manduro colours after originally being aimed at the Prix du Cadran, and Soldier of Fortune, the first five clear; Mandesha

Prix de l'Arc de Triomphe Lucien Barriere, Longchamp—a sixth Group 1 success for Dylan Thomas, who has only a head to spare over Youmzain this time after drifting right; Sagara (in between first two) is third as the winner's stable-companion Soldier of Fortune is forced to check slightly against the rail

and Zambezi Sun came seventh and eighth, while Authorized, in trouble as soon as he was asked for an effort, eventually beat only the two pacemakers.

Dylan Thomas was only the third older horse to win the Arc in the last fourteen runnings (Sakhee and Marienbard were the others) and the problem from a form perspective was that, apart from Sagara, the three-year-olds failed to run to form, making the Arc form look substandard. Dylan Thomas scrambled home from Youmzain, a high-class performer but by no stretch of the imagination the second best middle-distance horse in Europe (he didn't win a race as a four-year-old). Dylan Thomas was described by his trainer at the end of the year as 'probably the best we've ever had . . . to do all he did this year from a mile and a quarter to a mile and a half was amazing'; Kieren Fallon described him as having 'the best attitude, the best temperament of any horse I've ridden.' Dylan Thomas was certainly versatile so far as distance goes—there was nothing to choose between his best form at a mile and a quarter and his best at a mile and a half—and he proved himself admirably tough and consistent faced with just about as thorough a racecourse test as a middle-distance older horse can be put through in Europe. However, Authorized beat him on merit in the International, as did Manduro in the Prince of Wales's Stakes, and Dylan Thomas cannot be rated ahead of either, judged strictly on the value of the best performances of the three horses. Just one word of caution, though. The widely-held theory that Manduro, who suffered a career-ending injury in the Prix Foy, would have won the Arc had he been able to take the field can be questioned. Manduro may have been demonstrably Dylan Thomas's superior at a mile and a quarter but there is no firm evidence that he would have excelled in a strongly-run Arc. The mile-and-a-half Prix Foy was not a true test of stamina on the day and, in any event, the form of that race was some way inferior to that of the Arc. The second and third, Mandesha and Dragon Dancer, were beaten two and a half lengths and five and a half respectively by Manduro, and managed only seventh and ninth in the Arc, beaten seven lengths and eleven respectively by Dylan Thomas.

In a wider context, Timeform's reading of the form-book puts Dylan Thomas a little behind Lammtarra (rated 134) in the pecking order of those who have completed the King George/Arc double, and further adrift of the others—Ribot (142), Ballymoss (136), Mill Reef (141) and Dancing Brave (140). Top horses should not be judged solely on the prestige of the races they win, but on the quality of their performances in them. As we have said before, there may be something in the argument that the ratings of top horses who have finished their racing careers should be treated a little more flexibly, because their ratings in *Racehorses* are largely of academic, rather than practical value. It is not, however, an argument we are yet convinced by. Day-to-day handicapping could never be conducted in a way which took account of versatility, consistency, toughness and soundness. Penalising a horse further for displaying such attributes would justifiably bring protests from connections who campaign their horses openly and race them regularly, many of whom already feel the present handicapping system does them no favours. At the other end of the spectrum, 'one performance proves nothing' is sometimes the reaction when a wide-margin winner shoots to the top of the *Timeform* rankings after apparently showing significant improvement on previous efforts (Soldier of Fortune a good example in the latest season). However, any handicapper who ignored such a performance and allowed a wide margin winner another chance to repeat the form would be pilloried if it won again unpenalised. The job of handicapping and allocating ratings involves a degree of subjective judgement, more in some cases than others, but it must have a firm foundation and could never be conducted in the cavalier way some evidently imagine.

Dylan Thomas was seen out twice more after the Arc, but neither of the outings had any bearing on how he has been assessed. He managed only fifth of eight, on ground softer than any he had encountered since his juvenile days, when odds on for the Breeders' Cup Turf at Monmouth Park, and was then given an enforced spell in quarantine after being denied a run in the Japan Cup by the local authorities—they were not satisfied with the results of a routine test for equine viral arteritis. 'He was way overweight, looking as big as a bull,' according to his trainer, when only seventh of thirteen six weeks later in the Hong Kong Vase at Sha Tin, again sent off at odds on.

Mrs John Magnier & Mr M. Tabor's "Dylan Thomas"

			Danzig	Northern Dancer
	Danehill (USA)		(b 1977)	Pas de Nom
	(b 1986)		Razyana	His Majesty
Dylan Thomas (IRE)			(b 1981)	Spring Adieu
(b.c. 2003)			Diesis	Sharpen Up
	Lagrion (USA)		(ch 1980)	Doubly Sure
	(ch 1989)		Wrap It Up	Mount Hagen
			(ch 1979)	Doc Nan

Dylan Thomas was the biggest money earner for his sire for the second year running. The now-deceased Danehill topped the combined sires' list for Britain and Ireland for the third year running, and probably for the last time. His final crop were three-year-olds in 2007 and they included two fillies who won Group 1s, the redoubtable Peeping Fawn, who matched Dylan Thomas's total of four, and Falmouth winner Simply Perfect. Another of Danehill's daughters, the five-year-old Echelon, added four more wins to her record, including the Matron Stakes at Leopardstown, which set up a Group 1 double on the day for Danehill completed by Dylan Thomas in the Irish Champion two races later. Dylan Thomas's victory in the Prix de l'Arc ensured a third sires' championship for Danehill in France and he has also been champion sire nine times in Australia. where he has made a huge impact. As his sons—most notably Danehill Dancer in Europe and Redoute's Choice in Australia—have proved, Danehill is a proven sire of sires and Dylan Thomas will be joining numerous other sons of his sire at Coolmore in 2008. They include Rock of Gibraltar, seventh in the Anglo-Irish sires' table in the latest season, as well as fourth-placed Danehill Dancer. Dylan Thomas is bred on similar lines to Danehill Dancer, Dylan Thomas's dam, the middle-distance maiden Lagrion, being by a son of Sharpen Up, Diesis, while Danehill Dancer's dam was by Sharpen Up himself. Lagrion, a sister to Middle Park runner-up Pure Genius and a daughter of an unraced half-sister to the Lingfield Oaks Trial winner Gift Wrapped (dam of Royal Lodge winner Reach), has now bred two Group 1 winners. Dylan Thomas is her eighth foal and her fifth was the outstanding Cheveley Park winner Queen's Logic (by Grand Lodge). Lagrion produced two minor winners before Queen's Logic, the mile-and-a-quarter winner Tulsa (by Priolo) and Carlo Bank (by Lahib), who won at up to a mile and a half in Italy. There was another winner on the Flat between Queen's Logic and Dylan Thomas, the fairly useful miler Chatifa (by Titus Livius), and Lagrion's latest offspring to reach the race-course, the two-year-old Love To Dance (by Sadler's Wells), is with Aidan O'Brien and is probably capable of better than her tenth of eleven in a maiden at Leopardstown on her debut in November. Lagrion wasn't covered in 2005 and visited Danehill Dancer in 2006, producing a filly. The big, strong, lengthy Dylan Thomas, whose portrait was taken in mid-November, acted on good to firm and good to soft going but probably not on soft (also failed to handle dirt on his final three-year-old outing). He will start his stud career at a fee of €50,000, the highest among the crop of new stallions in Europe for 2008. *A. P. O'Brien, Ireland*

DYNAMO DAVE (USA) 2 b.c. (May 11) Distorted Humor (USA) 117 – Nothing **66** Special (CAN) (Tejabo (CAN)) [2007 p8m⁶ p7g Dec 29] $250,000Y, $375,000 2-y-o: fifth foal: half-brother to US 1m/9f winner Mercy Matters (by Cozzene) and winning US sprinter (including at 2 yrs) by Carson City: dam North American 7f (including minor stakes) to 8.5f winner: well backed in maidens at Lingfield, much better effort when sixth. *B. J. Meehan*

DYSONIC (USA) 5 b.g. Aljabr (USA) 125 – Atyab (USA) (Mr Prospector (USA)) **45** [2007 39, a63: f5g⁵ p5.1g⁴ f5g³ f7g f5g² p5.1g p5.1g⁵ p5.1g⁴ 5m 5.9g p5.1g⁴ p5m **a60** p6g⁵ Nov 20] angular gelding: modest on all-weather, poor on turf: stays easy 6f: acts on all-weather: tried in cheekpieces, usually visored: sometimes wanders: has run well when sweating: sold 3,800 gns. *J. Balding*

DZESMIN (POL) 5 b.g. Professional (IRE) 73 – Dzakarta (POL) (Aprizzo (IRE)) **92** [2007 87: p9.5g p12g p12g⁴ 12g³ 18.7m 12g⁴ 10.1v³ 12m 12s² 12d⁵ 12g* 12m Nov 10] angular gelding: fairly useful handicapper: won at Catterick (by neck from Realism) in September: well held in valuable event at Doncaster final start: stays 1½m: acts on polytrack, heavy and good to firm going: usually wears cheekpieces. *R. C. Guest*

E

EAGER DIVA (USA) 2 b. or br.f. (Feb 13) More Than Ready (USA) 120 – Divine **75** Diva (USA) (Theatrical 128) [2007 5g² 5m⁶ p6g⁵ 6m⁶ 8.5m⁶ 6d² 6m⁶ 5g⁶ p6g* Dec 1] $45,000Y: rather leggy, close-coupled filly: has a round action: second foal: half-sister to winner in US by Stormy Atlantic: dam, ran once in USA, sister to US Grade 3 8.5f winner Sing For Free: fair performer: twice runner-up, including in nursery, prior to winning maiden at Wolverhampton (blinkered) by length from Requisite: best form at 6f: acts on polytrack, good to firm and good to soft going: none too consistent: sold 10,000 gns. *K. A. Ryan*

EAGER IGOR (USA) 3 b. or br.g. Stravinsky (USA) 133 – Danube (USA) (Green **88** Desert (USA) 127) [2007 74: 8.2g³ 7.5m³ 8.3m³ 9g³ 8.1m* 9.9g p8g³ 8m 10g 10m⁵ 10g 8.1g² Oct 2] rather leggy gelding: fairly useful handicapper: won at Haydock in June: in-and-out form after: stays 1¼m: acts on polytrack, firm and good to soft going: tried blinkered: has carried head high: sold 11,000 gns. *Eve Johnson Houghton*

EAGLE MOUNTAIN 3 b.c. Rock of Gibraltar (IRE) 133 – Masskana (IRE) (Dar- **126** shaan 133) [2007 118: 8m⁵ 12g² 12s³ 12g 10.4s² 10v* 10d² Oct 20]

One distraction from all the attention showered on Frankie Dettori and Authorized in the Derby build-up was provided by Ballydoyle's declaration of no fewer than eight runners for the race. Multiple entries for big races from Aidan O'Brien are nothing new but it was unprecedented, at least in the modern era, for a single stable to be represented by such a large number in the Derby. Team tactics are not allowed under the *Rules of Racing* but there were worries that the Ballydoyle challengers might nonetheless cause a tactical headache for Dettori on the hot favourite. As one commentator put it, there was not so much a danger of Dettori taking his eye off the ball, but of not being able to see it at all! The Ballydoyle runners had arguably done enough to justify their place in the Derby field, seven of them having won or run well in Derby trials. The Ballydoyle runner who had not contested a specific Derby trial was Eagle Mountain, the most experienced in the Derby line-up. He had run in the Two Thousand Guineas on his reappearance, coming a creditable fifth of twenty-four to Cockney Rebel. Eagle Mountain's two-year-old performances—which included a seven-length win in the Beresford Stakes when stepped up to a mile and an odds-on defeat in the Racing Post Trophy behind Authorized—suggested he would not have the speed to win a Guineas. So it proved, but he finished strongly at Newmarket and, on the face of it, ran a good trial for the Derby. Judged on pedigree, however, Eagle Mountain wasn't guaranteed to get a mile and a half and there was talk at first of his being targeted at the Prix du Jockey Club over a mile and a quarter, rather than at the Derby. Perhaps concerns over Eagle Mountain's stamina dictated the exaggerated waiting tactics employed on him at Epsom. A well-backed second favourite, he was dropped out and in the last pair for much of the way before running on strongly, having no earthly chance with Authorized, to finish a five-length second, beating the rest convincingly.

Johnny Murtagh rode Eagle Mountain at Epsom, adding to his splendid Derby record which now comprises three victories (Sinndar, High Chaparral and Motivator) and three places. One of his other placed efforts came on Dylan Thomas, whom some felt had too much use made of him. Murtagh found himself criticised for coming from too far back on Eagle Mountain who, like Dylan Thomas, tackled the Irish Derby next, ridden at the Curragh, also like Dylan Thomas, by Kieren Fallon. With no Authorized to beat, Eagle Mountain started 6/4 favourite for the Irish Derby in which Ballydoyle's four runners also included the Epsom fifth Soldier of Fortune. Ballydoyle runners filled the first three places but Eagle Mountain, ridden to move up before being forced wide on the home turn, couldn't repeat his Derby form and managed only third behind the wide-margin winner Soldier of Fortune. Eagle Mountain clipped heels and unseated his rider after three furlongs in the Grand Prix de Paris on his next outing and then suffered a reverse when beaten by Stage Gift in the York Stakes (previously the Scottish Derby) before landing the odds against three rivals, led home by Alexander Tango, in the UAE Royal Whip Stakes at the Curragh in August. After being off the course

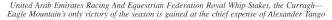

United Arab Emirates Racing And Equestrian Federation Royal Whip Stakes, the Curragh—Eagle Mountain's only victory of the season is gained at the chief expense of Alexander Tango

for over two months, Eagle Mountain met the Prix du Jockey Club runner-up Literato, among others, in an up-to-standard Champion Stakes at Newmarket on his final start for Aidan O'Brien before being sold privately and transferred to South African-based Mike de Kock. Eagle Mountain went out in style, looking much more like the horse that had chased home Authorized at Epsom and just being touched off by Literato, rallying strongly after being ridden for stamina and sent for home in earnest over two furlongs out.

Eagle Mountain (b.c. 2004)	Rock of Gibraltar (IRE) (b 1999)	Danehill (b 1986)	Danzig Razyana
		Offshore Boom (ch 1985)	Be My Guest Push A Button
	Masskana (IRE) (b 1988)	Darshaan (br 1981)	Shirley Heights Delsy
		Masarika (b 1981)	Thatch Miss Melody

The small, rather leggy, close-coupled Eagle Mountain has a quick, unimpressive action and is not the most straightforward of rides, sometimes needing to be niggled along and taking time to warm up. Like Authorized (and, incidentally, the first three in the Two Thousand Guineas), Eagle Mountain was purchased at public auction, fetching 220,000 guineas as a yearling. He is from the first crop of top-class miler Rock of Gibraltar who is making an early impact at stud and is being returned to Coolmore for 2008 after being leased to Japan and also completing another season in Australia. Eagle Mountain's dam Masskana was a product of the Aga Khan's studs—well bred by Darshaan out of Poule d'Essai des Pouliches winner Masarika—but was weeded out as a three-year-old after running only once for the Aga Khan. Masskana went on to win in minor company at up to a mile and a quarter in the French Provinces and has done very well at stud, producing five winners so far, the pick of them before Eagle Mountain being the smart miler Wallace (by Royal Academy) and the Prix Marcel Boussac winner Sulk (by Selkirk) who stayed well at three and finished second in the Prix Royal-Oak. Eagle Mountain is equally effective at a strongly-run mile and a quarter and at a mile and a half, and he acts on heavy and good to firm going. *A. P. O'Brien, Ireland*

EARL COMPTON (IRE) 3 b.g. Compton Place 125 – Noble Story 61 (Last Tycoon 131) [2007 51: p6g p5.1g p6g⁶ p5g² Dec 16] modest maiden: left P. Cole after second outing: effective at 5f/6f: acts on polytrack: blinkered (signs of temperament) final start, tongue tied last 5. *Stef Liddiard* **57 §**

EARL KRAUL (IRE) 4 b.g. Imperial Ballet (IRE) 110 – Bu Hagab (IRE) (Royal Academy (USA) 130) [2007 51: p10g* p8g² p8g³ p10g³ p10g p8g⁴ Dec 5] modest performer: won minor event at Kempton in January: first past post in similar event there (demoted after edging right and causing interference) 3 days later: stays 1¼m: acts on polytrack, good to soft and good to firm going: tried in cheekpieces, usually blinkered nowadays. *G. L. Moore* **61**

EARL MARSHAL (USA) 3 b.g. Kingmambo (USA) 125 – Fairy Godmother 113 (Fairy King (USA)) [2007 65p: 10.1d² 10d² 12m² Aug 6] good-bodied gelding: fairly useful maiden: runner-up all 3 starts in 2007, visored last 2: stays 1½m: once refused at stall: none too keen (hangs/carries head awkwardly): sold 20,000 gns in October. *Sir Michael Stoute* **87**

EARLSMEDIC 2 ch.g. (Mar 31) Dr Fong (USA) 128 – Area Girl 76 (Jareer (USA) 115) [2007 p7g⁶ Sep 12] 30,000Y: half-brother to several winners, including useful 6f (at 2 yrs)/7f winner Flying Officer (by Efisio): dam 66/1, never nearer nor knocked about when sixth to Iguazu Falls in maiden at Kempton: subsequently gelded: capable of better. *S. C. Williams* **67 p**

EARLY MARCH 5 b.h. Dansili 127 – Emplane (USA) 101 (Irish River (FR) 131) [2007 114: 7.1m⁶ Jun 7] big, strong, imposing horse: smart performer when trained in France: placed at 4 yrs in minor event at Lyon-Parilly and Prix du Chemin de Fer du Nord at Chantilly: left Mme C. Head-Maarek, fairly useful form when sixth to Mine in listed event at Haydock sole start in Britain, travelling strongly: stayed 1m: won on soft ground, probably suited by less testing conditions: tended to edge right: tended to stand at Haras du Saz, France, fee €2,300 live foal. *J. H. M. Gosden* **92**

EARLY PROMISE (IRE) 3 b.f. Abou Zouz (USA) 109 – Habla Me (IRE) (Fairy King (USA)) [2007 66: 5.1g 6m⁴ 7.1g³ 7s p7g p7.1g 6f⁶ p7m p7.1g p6g Sep 14] leggy **63 d**

filly: modest maiden at best in 2007, leaving P. Gilligan after sixth start: stays easy 7f: acts on polytrack. *Mrs A. L. M. King*

EARTHLING 6 b.g. Rainbow Quest (USA) 134 – Cruising Height 112 (Shirley   **50** Heights 130) [2007 –: f7g⁴ f8g p8.6g⁶ p16.5g p12.2g⁶ 8m Aug 2] modest maiden: stays easy 8.6f: acts on all-weather: often in cheekpieces/blinkered. *D. W. Chapman*

EASEMENT 4 b.g. Kayf Tara 130 – Raspberry Sauce 65 (Niniski (USA) 125) [2007   **57** p13.9g⁶ 18m Oct 8] sturdy gelding: fair form in bumpers: much better effort on Flat when sixth to Hareem in maiden at Wolverhampton on debut: sold 16,000 gns. *C. A. Cyzer*

EASIBET DOT NET 7 gr.g. Atraf 116 – Silvery 67 (Petong 126) [2007 71§: p13.9g⁵   **67 §** p16.5g* p16.5g⁵ p12.2g² Dec 22] tall gelding: fair handicapper: won at Wolverhampton in November: stays 16.5f: acts on all-weather, firm and good to soft going: wears head-gear: tried tongue tied: irresolute, and usually carries head high. *I. Semple*

EASTBOURNE 2 ch.c. (Apr 10) Compton Place 125 – Glascoed (Adbass (USA) 102)   **51** [2007 p6g 5m p6g 5m⁶ p7g p6g 5.1g Oct 31] sturdy colt: modest maiden: effective at 5f/ 6f: possibly temperamental (tried in blinkers). *Eve Johnson Houghton*

EAST COAST GIRL (IRE) 2 ch.f. (Mar 28) Captain Rio 122 – Toledana (IRE) (Sure   **48** Blade (USA) 130) [2007 7f 6.1m³ 7g p6g Nov 14] €18,000F, €20,000Y, 15,000 2-y-o: attractive filly: half-sister to several winners, including useful sprinter Newpark Lady (by Foxhound) and Irish 2m winner South West Nine (by Oscar): dam ran once in Ireland: maiden: form only when third at Chester (probably flattered, then left J. McAuley): may prove best at 5f/6f. *S. W. Hall*

EASTERLY BREEZE (IRE) 3 b.c. Green Desert (USA) 127 – Chiang Mai (IRE)   **79** 113 (Sadler's Wells (USA) 132) [2007 p8g² 8.5g⁵ 10g⁵ 9.8m² 12.1m³ 11m⁴ Sep 16] tall, good-topped colt: fair maiden: in frame 4 times: should stay 1½m: raced only on poly-track and good/good to firm going: sold 20,000 gns. *W. R. Muir*

EASTERN ANTHEM (IRE) 3 b.c. Singspiel (IRE) 133 – Kazzia (GER) 121 (Zinaad   **103** 114) [2007 97P: 10m³ 11g² May 24] leggy, quite good-topped colt: useful form: placed in listed races at Newmarket (2¼ lengths third to Salford Mill) and Goodwood (1¼ lengths second of 3 to Halicarnassus), both in May: will stay 1½m: acts on soft and good to firm going. *Saeed bin Suroor*

EASTERN APPEAL (IRE) 4 br.f. Shinko Forest (IRE) – Haut Volee (Top Ville 129)   **110** [2007 99: 6v⁵ 7m* 8m 7g³ 8d² 8m⁴ 7.5g* Oct 7] lengthy filly: seventh foal: half-sister to 3 winners, including useful 7f (at 2 yrs) to 8.5f winner Cat's Whiskers (by Catrail): dam German 2-y-o 6f and 1m winner: smart performer: won Oratorio EBF Athasi Stakes at the Curragh (by neck from Modeeroch) in May and Coolmore Stud Home of Champions Concorde Stakes at Tipperary (by neck from Excelerate) in October: also ran well when ½-length second to She's Our Mark in Desmond Stakes and 1¾ lengths third (demoted to fourth) behind Echelon in Matron Stakes, both at Leopardstown, fifth/sixth outings, though probably flattered in latter: effective at 7f/1m: acts on heavy and good to firm going: usually races close up. *M. Halford, Ireland*

EASTERN EMPEROR 3 ch.g. Halling (USA) 133 – B Beautiful (IRE) 57 (Be My   **75** Guest (USA) 126) [2007 10m 10m⁴ 10d⁴ p10g 8m⁵ Aug 17] lengthy, angular gelding: fair maiden: may prove best short of 1¼m: acts on polytrack and good to firm going. *W. R. Swinburn*

EASTERN GIFT 2 ch.c. (May 10) Cadeaux Genereux 131 – Dahshah 77 (Mujtahid   **95** (USA) 118) [2007 6m⁴ 7v⁵ 6g² 6m² 7m* 8m² 6m 7d⁴ p7g⁴ Nov 30] 18,500F, 65,000Y: lengthy colt: fourth foal: half-brother to winner in Spain by Cherokee Run: dam, 1m winner, half-sister to smart performer up to 1m in Britain/UAE Asaal: useful performer: won maiden at Chester in September: ran well next 2 starts, neck second to Meeriss in listed event at Goodwood and 3 lengths eighth of 28 to Exclamation in sales race at Newmarket: stays 1m: acts on good to firm going, possibly unsuited by softer than good. *R. Hannon*

EASTERN PRIDE 2 b.f. (May 5) Fraam 114 – Granuaile O'Malley (IRE) 55 (Mark of   **56** Esteem (IRE) 137) [2007 5.1f⁵ p6g Nov 8] first foal: dam, maiden, should have stayed 7f: better run in maidens when fifth at Bath: should stay 6f/7f. *P. A. Blockley*

EASTERN PRINCESS 3 b.f. Almutawakel 126 – Silvereine (FR) (Bering 136) [2007   **46** 59d: p5g³ 7.1m p5g⁶ 5.1g² p6g 5.1s⁴ 5m p6g Oct 23] leggy filly: poor maiden: claimed from J. Geake sixth outing: left J. Unett after next start: effective at 5f/6f: acts on poly-track, soft and good to firm ground: visored: suspect temperament. *G. H. Yardley*

EASTERN ROMANCE 2 b.f. (Mar 19) Oasis Dream 129 – Ocean Grove (IRE) 84 **105**
(Fairy King (USA)) [2007 5g⁶ 5g³ 5s⁴ 5d⁵ 6g³ 5g* 6.5d 6d⁴ 5m* Oct 28] 30,000Y: leggy,
close-coupled filly: seventh foal: half-sister to several winners, including 6-y-o Blue
Tomato and 5f and 7f winner Sea Hunter (by Lend A Hand), both useful: dam 2-y-o 6f
winner who stayed 1m: useful performer: won maiden at Beverley in September and
listed race at Longchamp in October, in latter much improved to make all by 5 lengths
from Garden City: in frame 4 other times, including in listed events at Beverley and York:
effective at 6f, best form at 5f: acts on good to firm and good to soft going. *K. A. Ryan*

EASTFIELDS LAD 5 b.g. Overbury (IRE) 116 – Honey Day (Lucky Wednesday 124) **–**
[2007 8m Jun 12] close-coupled gelding: little form: tried blinkered. *S. R. Bowring*

EASTWELL SMILES 3 br.g. Erhaab (USA) 127 – Miss University (USA) (Beau **78**
Genius (CAN)) [2007 p10g⁶ p10g³ p10g Aug 11] 14,000Y: fourth foal: half-brother to
US Grade 2 8.5f winner Three Degrees (by Singspiel): dam ran twice: easily best effort in
maidens at Lingfield when third to Vallemeldee: wears tongue tie. *R. T. Phillips*

EASY LAUGHTER (IRE) 6 b.g. Danehill (USA) 126 – All To Easy 91 (Alzao **64**
(USA) 117) [2007 75: p10g⁶ p13.9g Feb 21] fair handicapper at 5 yrs: modest form at
best on Flat in 2007: stays 1½m: acts on polytrack, firm and good to soft going: often
tongue tied: has been blinkered/visored: fair hurdler, won in May: sold 8,800 gns in
August. *A. King*

EASY TARGET (FR) 2 ch.c. (Feb 1) Danehill Dancer (IRE) 117 – Aiming 76 (High- **96**
est Honor (FR) 124) [2007 6.1g* 6s* 6g 6m⁵ 6g⁴ Oct 6] 60,000Y: compact colt: first foal:
dam, maiden (stayed 1m), half-sister to smart sprinter Watching: useful performer: won
maiden at Nottingham in June and minor event at Pontefract in July: sweated/hung badly
in Gimcrack Stakes at York, but creditable efforts last 2 starts (despite soon off bridle), 3
lengths fifth of 6 to Dark Angel in Mill Reef Stakes at Newbury and 1¼ lengths fourth of
23 to Dubai Dynamo in listed Two-Year-Old Trophy at Redcar: will stay 7f: acts on soft
and good to firm going. *B. Smart*

EASY WONDER (GER) 2 b.f. (Mar 7) Royal Dragon (USA) 118 – Emy Coasting **71 ?**
(USA) 78 (El Gran Senor (USA) 136) [2007 6d⁵ 5m³ 6m⁴ 7d⁴ 6v³ 7g p6g* Nov 8]
€40,000Y, 24,000 2-y-o: sixth foal: half-sister to several winners in Germany, including
7f/1m winner Exit To Luck (by Exit To Nowhere): dam German 7f/1m winner: fair
performer: won maiden at Wolverhampton: seemingly better form in frame in auction
events in Germany third to fifth starts: stays 7f: acts on polytrack, heavy and good to firm
going. *I. A. Wood*

EAT PIE (USA) 2 b. or br.f. (Mar 10) Thunder Gulch (USA) 129 – Millie's Choice **88**
(IRE) 110 (Taufan (USA) 119) [2007 p6g* 6m a8f p5.5f Dec 31] small filly: half-sister to
several winners in US, including Grade 3 8.5f winner Millie's Quest (by Quest For
Fame): dam Irish 7f/1m winner: fairly useful form: won maiden at Lingfield in July:
much better effort when 3 lengths seventh to You'resothrilling in Cherry Hinton Stakes at
Newmarket 8 days later: below form after in Grade 3 Arlington-Washington Lassie at
Arlington (left M. Wallace after) and allowance race at Turfway Park: should stay 7f/1m.
E. Kenneally, USA

EAU GOOD 3 ch.g. Cadeaux Genereux 131 – Girl's Best Friend 89 (Nicolotte 118) **89**
[2007 86: p8.6g⁵ f7g² f7g² p8g 8.3m* 7.1g 8.3s³ 10g 10g⁵ 10s 9g Aug 26] angular
gelding: fairly useful handicapper: left M. Chapman after third start: won at Windsor in
April: well below form last 2 starts: stays 1¼m: acts on all-weather, soft and good to firm
going: blinkered once at 2 yrs: held up. *B. G. Powell*

EA (USA) 3 b. or br.c. Dynaformer (USA) – Enthused (USA) 109 (Seeking The Gold **118**
(USA)) [2007 77p: 8.2m* 10.3m⁶ 8m² 8m 8g² Jul 28] close-coupled colt: smart form:
won maiden at Nottingham in April: improved form after, runner-up in 30-runner Britannia Stakes at Royal Ascot (beaten ½ length by Eddie Jock) and quite valuable handicap at
Ascot (best effort, 1½ lengths behind The Illies), coming from well off pace both times:
probably stays 1¼m: raced only on good/good to firm going: reportedly sold privately,
and has joined Godolphin. *Sir Michael Stoute*

EAU SAUVAGE 3 ch.f. Lake Coniston (IRE) 131 – Mo Stopher 47 (Sharpo 132) [2007 **–**
–: p6g p10g Dec 30] no form. *J. Akehurst*

EBERT 4 b.g. Polish Precedent (USA) 131 – Fanfare 89 (Deploy 131) [2007 86: 8g² 8m⁴ **99**
8.1m⁶ 9m³ 9.7f⁴ Sep 25] strong gelding: useful handicapper: further improvement in
2007, best effort when fourth to King of Argos at Goodwood second start: should stay
1¼m: acts on polytrack and firm ground, yet to race on going softer than good: blinkered

(very slowly away)/in cheekpieces last 2 starts: held up: nervy sort: sold 32,000 gns. *P. J. Makin*

EBN MALK (IRE) 2 ch.c. (Mar 26) King's Best (USA) 132 – Auntie Maureen (IRE) **67 p** 73 (Roi Danzig (USA)) [2007 7d Oct 30] €90,000F, 150,000Y: eighth foal: brother to 2006 2-y-o 1m winner Ommraan and half-brother to 3 winners, including 6f (at 2 yrs in Ireland) to 9f (US Grade 3 event) winner Coney Kitty (by Lycius) and 2m winner Intrum Morshaan (by Darshaan), both useful: dam Irish 9f/1¼m winner: 10/3, ran green most of way when seventh in maiden at Yarmouth, going on well at finish: will be suited by 1m/ 1¼m: bound to improve. *M. A. Jarvis*

EBN REEM 3 b.c. Mark of Esteem (IRE) 137 – Reematna 75 (Sabrehill (USA) 120) **94** [2007 90: p6g* 6g 6g⁴ 5s² Jun 16] good-topped colt: good walker: fairly useful handicapper: won at Kempton in April: in cheekpieces, back to form when runner-up at Leicester final outing: may prove best up to 7f: acts on polytrack, soft and good to firm going: races up with pace: joined D. Selvaratnam in UAE. *M. A. Jarvis*

EBN ZAHR (UAE) 3 ch.g. Halling (USA) 133 – Ginger Tree (USA) 86 (Dayjur (USA) **–** 137) [2007 f8g 12d Jun 24] well held in maidens. *Miss J. E. Foster*

EBORACUM DREAM 2 b.f. (Feb 2) Diktat 126 – Bollin Jeannie 74 (Royal Applause **54 d** 124) [2007 5g 5m 7d 6g 5g⁶ 7.1d⁵ 7g Oct 19] unfurnished filly: first foal: dam, 2-y-o 5f winner, out of smart sprinter Bollin Joanne, herself half-sister to St Leger winner Bollin Eric: modest maiden: best effort on debut: tried blinkered: sold 1,000 gns, sent to Denmark. *T. D. Easterby*

EBRAAM (USA) 4 b.g. Red Ransom (USA) – Futuh (USA) 95 (Diesis 133) [2007 72: **102** p7.1g f7g p7.1g⁶ p6g⁶ p6g⁴ p6g* p6g² p7g³ p7g³ p6g² p6g p5.1g* p6g* p5.1g² f5d⁶ p6g* Dec 28] well-made gelding: progressed into useful handicapper in 2007, winning at Wolverhampton in July and October and Lingfield in November and December: beat Turn On The Style by ½ length for last win: best at 5f/6f: acts on polytrack and firm ground: has carried head awkwardly. *D. Shaw*

ECHELON 5 b.m. Danehill (USA) 126 – Exclusive 115 (Polar Falcon (USA) 126) **120** [2007 115: 9m* 8.5d* 8m⁵ 10s⁶ 8g* 8m* 8m³ Oct 6]

Given the peculiarities of inheritance, and breeding generally, gauging the prospects of a filly on her retirement to the paddocks is a practice fraught with uncertainty. An attractive, well-bred, high-class racemare does not automatically become a high-class broodmare, while some slowcoaches with ordinary pedigrees have left an indelible mark on the breed. The only consolation about making bold predictions is that by the time they fail, if they fail, few people are likely to remember the fine words. Be that as it may, it is good to report that the forecast made about Coronation Stakes winner Exclusive in *Racehorses of 1998* on her retirement has proved entirely accurate. 'Exclusive will make an excellent addition to Cheveley Park Stud's impressive list of broodmares,' the essay noted, and with dual Celebration Mile winner Chic as her first foal and Echelon, who won the same race in August then did even better to land the Group 1 Matron Stakes, as her third she has made a dream start at stud.

totesport.com Celebration Mile, Goodwood—a 1,2 for Cheveley Park Stud as Echelon (left), carrying the second colours, holds the challenge of Cesare; the virtually obscured Blue Ksar finishes third

Coolmore Fusaichi Pegasus Matron Stakes, Leopardstown—the gamble of supplementing Echelon for this Group 1 pays off handsomely; Red Evie (left) takes second ahead of Eastern Appeal (noseband) and Arch Swing, whose placings are subsequently reversed

Echelon took rather more time to come to her best than Exclusive, who finished third in the Fillies' Mile at two and in the One Thousand Guineas before her Royal Ascot triumph. Equally, Echelon's connections were hardly entertaining an angel unawares in the way that they seemingly had with Chic, whose introduction to the big time came in a handicap at Royal Ascot as a three-year-old. Echelon ran in two of the races her dam had tried, ending up seventh when favourite for the Fillies' Mile, experiencing no luck in running, and finishing in mid-division in the Guineas. With victories in two listed races at three and in the Group 3 Chartwell Fillies Stakes and Princess Elizabeth Stakes as a four-year-old, Echelon seemed to have reached her peak, just slightly below the very top. Her first two starts at five indicated she was in good heart. Odds on for the StanJamesUK.com Dahlia Stakes at the Guineas meeting at Newmarket, her first run for nine months, she led a furlong from home and was ridden out, after idling, to beat Topatoo by a neck. After missing the Middleton Stakes at York because the ground was deemed too soft, Echelon was again favourite when attempting her second success in the ten-runner Princess Elizabeth Stakes (sponsored by Vodafone) at Epsom on Oaks day. The ground was on the easy side here as well and the pick of Echelon's opponents were Nannina, in the same ownership on her reappearance, Betfred Mile runner-up Bahia Breeze and Goodwood listed winner Harvest Queen. In a race which developed into something of a sprint in the straight, Echelon came through to lead in the final furlong, despite hanging left, and saw off Bahia Breeze by three quarters of a length with Nannina third.

Echelon's next two runs, also in June, are best forgotten. In the Windsor Forest Stakes at Royal Ascot she was clearly not herself when only fifth of nine to Nannina, who bumped her three furlongs out. In the Pretty Polly Stakes at the Curragh, a mile and a quarter on much softer going probably counted against Echelon who was pushed along turning for home and beaten over fifteen lengths into sixth behind Peeping Fawn. An eight-week break followed, and evidently did Echelon a power of good. Her three remaining runs saw her in the form of her life. Only fourth favourite of eight, she was a revelation in the totesport.com Celebration Mile at Goodwood in which she met another Cheveley Park Stud-owned contender, the penalised Summer Mile Stakes winner Cesare, and listed winners Blue Ksar for Godolphin and front runner Dunelight. Held up but never far behind, Echelon led over a furlong out and was always holding Cesare in the final hundred yards, even though he managed to get alongside. Drawing away again, Echelon won by a length and a quarter, with Blue Ksar a length and a half back in third. It was a third success in four years in the race for Cheveley Park Stud following Chic's wins in 2004 and 2005. Echelon confirmed her improved status on her last two starts. She had to be supplemented for the Coolmore Fusaichi Pegasus Matron Stakes at Leopardstown, a fortnight after Goodwood, but the principle of striking while the iron was hot paid off as she justified favouritism in a nine-runner field also containing the 2006 winner Red Evie, fresh from victory in the Hungerford Stakes, the One Thousand Guineas runner-up Arch Swing and Sweet Lilly, successful in listed company at Sandown earlier in the month. Phoenix Sprint Stakes second Evening Time and Barshiba were the only others to start at shorter than 20/1. There was only a steady pace in the early stages and, as in most muddling races, the best place proved to be close to the front. Never far behind, Echelon took over a furlong out, drifted right near the finish but was always holding the late challenge of Red Evie, who came from well back and never promised to make up the leeway. The winning margin was a length and a half, with 40/1-shot Eastern Appeal, moved down a place subsequently for interfering with fourth-placed Arch Swing, a head away third. Echelon could not add the Sun Chariot Stakes at Newmarket a month later to her Group 1 tally. She was a short-priced favourite but did not enjoy the run of the race and was beaten a length and three quarters into third behind three-year-old Majestic Roi, hampered by eventual runner-up Nannina when trying to challenge a furlong

Cheveley Park Stud's "Echelon"

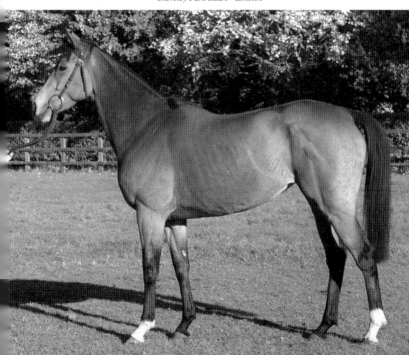

and a half out and then bumped by the winner. A good run in the circumstances, after which the announcement came that Echelon had been retired to stud.

Echelon (b.m. 2002)	Danehill (USA) (b 1986)	Danzig (b 1977)	Northern Dancer Pas de Nom
		Razyana (b 1981)	His Majesty Spring Adieu
	Exclusive (ch 1995)	Polar Falcon (b or br 1987)	Nureyev Marie d'Argonne
		Exclusive Order (ch 1979)	Exclusive Native Bonavista

Echelon's sire Danehill is the best stallion Exclusive has visited, though Chic's sire Machiavellian also has a fine record. Since Echelon, Exclusive has foaled the Grand Lodge filly Excellent, who fell a long way short of living up to her name in beating only eleven of her thirty-two rivals in two maiden races in 2005 and 2006. Exclusive has an unraced two-year-old colt named Panache (by King's Best) and the yearling filly Expressive (by Falbrav). Exclusive was barren to Machiavellian's son Medicean in 2006 then, in something of a departure from the norm, she visited a stallion who was best at a mile and a half, Montjeu. Exclusive's dam Exclusive Order, who cost Cheveley Park Stud 825,000 dollars as a brood-mare, was a smart sprinter-miler, successful in the Prix Maurice de Gheest. At stud she has produced Two Thousand Guineas winner Entrepreneur, Oaks runner-up Dance A Dream (grandam of Cambridgeshire winner Pipedreamer) and the gran-dams of Beckett, successful in the National Stakes, and another smart colt Iceman, who also raced for Cheveley Park and is now a stallion there. Echelon is a sturdy, good sort who occasionally sweated up—the accompanying portrait was taken late in the year after she had been taken out of training. A good mover who stayed nine furlongs, she acted on good to firm and good to soft going and was often waited with to make best use of her turn of foot. It may not be original to say this, but Echelon should make an excellent addition to Cheveley Park Stud's impressive list of broodmares. She visits Galileo. *Sir Michael Stoute*

ECHO OF LIGHT 5 b.h. Dubai Millennium 140 – Spirit of Tara (IRE) 106 (Sadler's **123** Wells (USA) 132) [2007 125: 8m⁴ 10g* 8.9f* 8d⁵ 8m³ Oct 21] big, well-made horse: very smart performer: won Prix Gontaut-Biron at Deauville (by short head from Atlantic Air, wandering markedly/idling) in August and TurfTV Strensall Stakes at York (for second successive year, beat Halicarnassus easily by 2½ lengths) in September: unable to dominate to same extent and below best last 2 starts, fifth to Spirito del Vento in Prix Daniel Wildenstein at Longchamp (had won race in 2006) and third to Linngari in Premio Vittorio di Capua at Milan: won at 11.5f, but best at 1m/1¼m: acted on polytrack and firm going: tongue tied early in career: wore cheekpieces last 4 starts: edgy sort, sometimes taken early to post: often hung left when pressured: front runner/raced prominently: quirky: retired, and to stand at Dalham Hall Stud, Newmarket, fee £5,000, Oct 1st, special live foal. *Saeed bin Suroor*

TurfTV Strensall Stakes, York—
Echo of Light, as in this race twelve months earlier, makes all for a two-and-a-half-length victory;
Halicarnassus (rail) is about to get the better of Kandidate in the battle for second

ECHOSTAR 2 ch.f. (Feb 9) Observatory (USA) 131 – Anqood (IRE) 82 (Elmaamul (USA) 125) [2007 5f³ 5m* 5m⁴ 6s⁴ 5.1g p6g Nov 20] sparely-made filly: first foal: dam, 7.5f winner, out of close relative to high-class miler Maroof: modest performer: won claimer at Beverley (left E. O'Neill £8,000) in April: left W. Muir after fourth start: should stay 7f/1m. *Stef Liddiard* — **51**

ECLIPSE PARK 4 ch.g. Rainbow Quest (USA) 134 – Gino's Spirits 98 (Perugino (USA) 84) [2007 –, a69: p10g a12g² a12s⁴ a12g* Jul 27] fair performer at best: on downgrade in 2006, and well beaten in seller on reappearance (sold from M. McGrath 2,500 gns before next start): won handicap at Jagersro in July: stays 1½m: acts on polytrack and dirt: tried in cheekpieces/blinkered. *Ms K. Stenefeldt, Sweden* — **?**

ECO CENTRISM 3 ch.c. Selkirk (USA) 129 – Way O'Gold (USA) (Slew O' Gold (USA)) [2007 8p1: 8.2m³ 10d² Oct 18] strong colt: fairly useful form in maidens: placed all 3 starts, again shaped with plenty of promise when 2½ lengths second to Abydos at Nottingham final outing: may prove best around 1m: tongue tied on debut: sold 45,000 gns: likely to do better. *W. J. Haggas* — **81 p**

ECONOMIC (IRE) 4 b.c. Danehill Dancer (IRE) 117 – Warusha (GER) (Shareef Dancer (USA) 135) [2007 p12g p11g 10g May 18] sturdy colt: fairly useful form in 2005: unraced at 3 yrs (left Godolphin 28,000 gns): fair form at best in 2007: stays 8.3f: acts on heavy going: tried blinkered: sold 11,000 gns in July, won at 6f and 1m in Greece after. *M. Botti* — **73**

ECO SYMPATHY 3 b.g. Dansili 127 – Tigwa 68 (Cadeaux Genereux 131) [2007 10m⁵ Sep 11] lengthy gelding: fifth foal: half-brother to 4-y-o Charlie Cool and 1998 2-y-o 7.5f winner Green Snake (by Royal Academy): dam, maiden who stayed 1m, half-sister to 1000 Guineas winner Sayyedati and high-class 1¼m/1½m performer Golden Snake: 10/1 and better for run, 6½ lengths fifth of 6 to Teodora Adivina in maiden at Leicester, taking time to settle: sold 3,200 gns in October. *M. L. W. Bell* — **53**

ECUSSON 2 b.f. (Mar 8) Singspiel (IRE) 133 – Indian Love Bird (Efisio 120) [2007 p8m Nov 26] second foal: dam unraced sister to smart 6f/7f performer Tomba and half-sister to Prix du Jockey Club winner Holding Court: 5/1, eighth in maiden at Lingfield, hampered on home turn then running on not knocked about: will do better. *M. A. Jarvis* — **52 p**

EDAARA (IRE) 4 ch.f. Pivotal 124 – Green Bonnet (IRE) (Green Desert (USA) 127) [2007 83+: 7s 8.5d⁶ 7d Jun 22] strong, good sort: fairly useful performer, lightly raced: seemingly ran well in Princess Elizabeth Stakes at Epsom second outing: well held in handicap at Newmarket final start: best up to 8.5f: raced only on good ground or softer. *W. J. Haggas* — **91**

EDAS 5 b.h. Celtic Swing 138 – Eden (IRE) 88 (Polish Precedent (USA) 131) [2007 73: 12d³ 12.1v³ 10f⁶ 12.1m³ Aug 26] good-topped horse: fair handicapper: stays 1½m: acts on polytrack and any turf going: tried in cheekpieces/visor: consistent: winning hurdler. *J. J. Quinn* — **74**

EDDIE DOWLING 2 b.c. (Apr 14) High Chaparral (IRE) 132 – Dan's Delight (Machiavellian (USA) 123) [2007 8d Oct 27] 50/1, behind in maiden at Newbury. *M. R. Channon* — **–**

EDDIE JOCK (IRE) 3 ch.g. Almutawakel 126 – Al Euro (FR) 57 (Mujtahid (USA) 118) [2007 102: 7m³ 8.3m³ 8m* 8m 8m 8m³ Sep 15] angular, rather lightly-made geld- — **116**

Britannia Stakes (Handicap), Royal Ascot—33/1-shot Eddie Jock shows smart form in defying top weight; Ea (right) and St Philip run him close

ing: smart performer: won 30-runner Britannia Stakes (Handicap) at Royal Ascot in June by ½ length from Ea (changed hands privately after): back to form when third to The Illies in similar event at Doncaster final outing: stays 1m: acts on firm and good to soft going: has joined Godolphin. *M. L. W. Bell*

EDEN ROCK (IRE) 6 b.g. Danehill (USA) 126 – Marlene-D 57 (Selkirk (USA) 129) **86 +**
[2007 102: 8m⁴ 8m Jun 20] big, good-bodied gelding: handicapper, lightly raced: useful at 5 yrs: fairly useful at best in 2007: best at 7f/1m: raced only on good going or firmer: tried tongue tied/in cheekpieces at 4 yrs. *Pat Eddery*

EDE'S 7 ch.g. Bijou d'Inde 127 – Ballagarrow Girl 66 (North Stoke 130) [2007 p12m **–**
Dec 8] lengthy gelding: maiden: only run on Flat since 2003 when well held in minor event at Lingfield. *P. M. Phelan*

EDE'S DOT COM (IRE) 3 b.g. Trans Island 119 – Kilkee Bay (IRE) 61 (Case Law **67**
113) [2007 81: p8.6g⁶ p7g⁵ 6g p8g 7g⁴ p7g p6g² p6g Oct 23] sturdy gelding: just fair handicapper in 2007: probably best at 6f: acts on polytrack and good to firm going. *P. M. Phelan*

EDGE CLOSER 3 b.c. Bold Edge 123 – Blue Goddess (IRE) 94 (Blues Traveller (IRE) **102**
119) [2007 76p: 6s² 6m* 6g* p6g* 6d Sep 28] lengthy, angular colt: progressed into a useful handicapper, winning at Ascot (2) in July and Kempton (beat Majuro by ½ length, tending to edge right and idle) in August: not discredited when seventh to Genki at Ascot final start: raced only at 6f, should prove effective at 5f: acts on polytrack, soft and good to firm ground: races prominently. *R. Hannon*

EDGE END 3 ch.g. Bold Edge 123 – Rag Time Belle 34 (Raga Navarro (ITY) 119) **64**
[2007 –: 6g⁵ 7m⁵ 6s p6g Oct 10] close-coupled gelding: modest maiden: not sure to stay much further than 7f: acts on good to firm ground. *R. A. Farrant*

EDGEFOUR (IRE) 3 b.f. King's Best (USA) 132 – Highshaan (Pistolet Bleu (IRE) **–**
133) [2007 –: 8.3g 10f 8d Aug 21] little form. *B. I. Case*

EDGE OF GOLD 2 ch.f. (Apr 19) Choisir (AUS) 126 – Beveled Edge 60 (Beveled **81**
(USA)) [2007 6s² 6d² 5.1m* 6s* 6d Oct 11] 25,000Y: good-topped filly: closely related to useful 6f winner (including at 2 yrs) Bright Edge (by Danehill Dancer) and half-sister to 2 winners, including 6-y-o Indian Edge: dam 6f winner: fairly useful form: first past post in maiden at Newbury (demoted after impeding second close home) in June: won similar event at Chepstow and 17-runner sales race at Newmarket in August: will prove best at 5f/6f: acts on soft and good to firm going: races prominently. *B. Palling*

EDGE OF LIGHT 2 b.f. (Mar 28) Xaar 132 – Bright Edge 102 (Danehill Dancer (IRE) **91 +**
117) [2007 5d* 6d⁵ 5.2m⁴ Aug 17] sparely-made filly: second foal: half-sister to 3-y-o Arthur's Edge: dam 6f winner, including at 2 yrs: fairly useful form: won maiden at Salisbury in June: improvement when fifth of 13 to Visit in Princess Margaret Stakes at Ascot (stirred up) and fourth of 10 to Cake in listed race at Newbury (outpaced): better at 6f than 5f, and likely to stay 7f. *B. Palling*

EDIE SUPERSTAR (USA) 2 b.f. (Feb 18) Forestry (USA) 121 – Just Out (USA) **76**
(Forty Niner (USA)) [2007 5g⁵ p8g³ p7g⁶ Nov 17] $260,000Y: good-topped filly: fifth foal: half-sister to several winners in US, including smart 1m/9f winner Outta Here (by Dehere): dam unraced out of half-sister to US Grade 1 9f winner Joyeux Danseur: fair maiden: third to Comeback Queen at Lingfield, only start in tongue tie: stays 1m. *M. A. Magnusson*

EDIN BURGHER (FR) 6 br.g. Hamas (IRE) 125§ – Jaljuli 107 (Jalmood (USA) 126) **53**
[2007 63: p5g p6g p6g p6g p6g p8g p7g Nov 16] modest performer: stays 1m: raced mainly on polytrack: tried in cheekpieces/visor. *T. T. Clement*

EDUCATED RISK 2 b.g. (Mar 26) Royal Applause 124 – Tantalize (Machiavellian **64 p**
(USA) 123) [2007 6d 6d³ Oct 15] 40,000F, 58,000Y: big gelding: second foal: dam unraced close relative to smart performer up to 1m Dazzle: better run in maidens when third at Windsor (still green, and open to further improvement): will stay 7f/1m: sold 35,000 gns, sent to USA. *W. J. Haggas*

EDWARD (IRE) 5 b.g. Namid 128 – Daltak (Night Shift (USA)) [2007 59: p6m p6g **–**
p8g Dec 16] lightly-raced maiden: no form in 2007. *M. Madgwick*

EFFECTIVE 7 ch.g. Bahamian Bounty 116 – Efficacy 62 (Efisio 120) [2007 82: p6g **80**
f6g² f6g p6g² p6g² p6g³ f6g⁴ 6m³ 6m³ Jun 7] lengthy gelding: fairly useful handicapper: stays 7f: acts on all-weather, firm and soft ground: tried visored: usually races prominently: tough and reliable. *A. P. Jarvis*

EFFIGY 3 b.g. Efisio 120 – Hymne d'Amour (USA) 58 (Dixieland Band (USA)) [2007 **74**
67p: 8g 8d 8.1m³ 10m⁶ p8g 11d⁵ 10m³ Oct 22] lengthy gelding: fair maiden handicapper:
stays 11f: acts on good to firm and good to soft going. *H. Candy*

EFFINGHAM (IRE) 2 b.c. (Feb 17) Celtic Swing 138 – Deemeh (IRE) 35 (Brief **75**
Truce (USA) 126) [2007 5d² 6f 6d⁴ 8.3m Oct 8] €37,000F, €75,000Y: stocky, compact
colt: second foal: dam Irish maiden (stayed 1¼m): fair maiden: in frame at Sandown and
Haydock (fourth to Exclamation): should stay 1m+: acts on good to soft going, seemingly
not good to firm/firm. *B. W. Hills*

EFIDIUM 9 b.g. Presidium 124 – Efipetite 54 (Efisio 120) [2007 75: 8f 8.1g 7d 9g⁵ 8m⁶ **76**
8d* 7s⁵ 8s⁶ 8s² 8v 8s⁵ 8m 8m⁴ 8m³ 8m³ 8s⁵ 8g Oct 6] small gelding: fair handicapper:
won at Redcar in June: stays 9f: acts on fibresand, firm and soft going: tried blinkered:
has been early to post: held up: tough. *N. Bycroft*

EFISIO PRINCESS 4 br.f. Efisio 120 – Hardiprincess (Keen 116) [2007 64: 5.7d 6d* **77**
6d² Oct 30] good-topped filly: fair handicapper, lightly raced: reportedly had infection
after reappearance: won at Windsor in October: stays 6f: acts on good to soft ground.
J. E. Long

EFISTORM 6 b.g. Efisio 120 – Abundance 62 (Cadeaux Genereux 131) [2007 82, a90: **98**
f5g p5.1g⁶ p5.1g* f5g⁵ 5f* p5.1g⁶ f5g⁶ 5m⁵ 5m³ 5d* 5.1d⁴ 5v 5g² 5g 5s* 5d² p6g⁵ 6g
Oct 26] smallish, quite good-topped gelding: improved into useful performer in 2007,
winning claimer at Wolverhampton (left J. Balding £11,000) in January and handicaps
at Windsor in April, Sandown in June and Newmarket (better than ever, beat Coconut
Moon by ½ length) in August: best at 5f/easy 6f: acts on all-weather, firm and soft ground.
C. R. Dore

EFORETTA (GER) 5 ch.m. Dr Fong (USA) 128 – Erminora (GER) (Highest Honor **69**
(FR) 124) [2007 66, a72: f11g³ f14g⁴ 16g³ p16g⁵ f14g* f14g⁶ 16.2d 14.1d Jul 12] close-
coupled mare: fair handicapper: won at Southwell in May: stays 2¼m: acts on all-weather
and firm ground: blinkered second 4-y-o start. *D. J. Wintle*

EGLEVSKI (IRE) 3 b.g. Danehill Dancer (IRE) 117 – Ski For Gold 76 (Shirley **91**
Heights 130) [2007 83: 10m⁶ 12g² 12d³ 14d⁶ 11d⁴ Sep 26] close-coupled gelding: fairly
useful performer: good efforts second to fourth starts: gelded after final outing: barely
stays 1¾m: acts on good to firm and good to soft ground. *J. L. Dunlop*

EGREGIUS MAX 3 b.c. Royal Applause 124 – Singed (Zamindar (USA) 116) [2007 **–**
p7g 7g 6g Jun 23] well held in maidens. *C. F. Wall*

EGYPTIAN LORD 4 ch.g. Bold Edge 123 – Calypso Lady (IRE) 88 (Priolo (USA) **59**
127) [2007 60, a70: f5g p5g⁵ p5.1g³ f5g²* f5g⁴ f5g²* f5g* f5g² f5g* p6g f5g⁵ 5g 5s⁴ p5g⁵ **a83 d**
5m 5.1m p5g p5g⁶ p5.1g p6g p5.1g* Dec 3] workmanlike gelding: fairly useful handicapper on all-weather, modest on turf: won at Southwell in February (2) and March (2):
mostly below form after: best at 5f: has won on polytrack, best efforts on fibresand, also
acts on soft and good to firm going: tried visored, often blinkered: sometimes slowly
away: has hung left. *Peter Grayson*

EIDSFOSS (IRE) 5 b.g. Danehill Dancer (IRE) 117 – Alca Egeria (ITY) (Shareef **–**
Dancer (USA) 135) [2007 –: p10g⁶ Jan 6] no longer of any account. *T. T. Clement*

EIGHTY TWENTY 2 b.f. (Apr 14) Diktat 126 – Stonegrave 57 (Selkirk (USA) 129) **–**
[2007 5g f6g 7m Aug 17] workmanlike filly: second foal: dam, maiden who stayed 1½m,
out of Ribblesdale Stakes winner Queen Midas: tailed off in maidens. *M. W. Easterby*

EIJAAZ (IRE) 6 b.g. Green Desert (USA) 127 – Kismah 111 (Machiavellian (USA) **62**
123) [2007 54, a66: 12m² 10.1m⁴ 12g² 10.5m² 12d 13m 10.1g 10.1m³ 9.9d⁵ 12g⁵ Oct 30]
quite attractive gelding: modest handicapper: stays 1½m: acts on polytrack and firm
going (below form on ground softer than good): tried in cheekpieces/visor. *G. A. Harker*

EILEEN'S VIOLET (IRE) 2 b.f. (Mar 28) Catcher In The Rye (IRE) 115 – Brave **93**
Cat (IRE) (Catrail (USA) 123) [2007 5.1m² 5g* 6g 6m 5.2m 7m⁴ 8.1g² Sep 8] rather
leggy, useful-looking filly: fourth foal: half-sister to Italian 5f to 9f (including at 2 yrs)
winner Revovegas (by Revoque): dam unraced: fairly useful performer: won minor event
at Windsor in May: good second to Campanologist in minor event at Haydock final start:
stays 1m: raced only on good/good to firm going: held up: sold 80,000 gns, sent to USA.
P. D. Evans

EISTEDDFOD 6 ch.g. Cadeaux Genereux 131 – Ffestiniog (IRE) 96 (Efisio 120) **113**
[2007 115: p6g* p7g³ 7s 7s* 6d 6d⁴ 7.1m* 7d Oct 20] lengthy, good-quartered gelding:
smart performer: won minor events at Kempton in March and Leicester (3 ran, by neck
from Levera) in May and listed race at Sandown (beat Bygone Days by 1¼ lengths,

dictating) in September: below form in Challenge Stakes at Newmarket final outing: effective at 6f/7f: yet to race on heavy going, acts on any other turf and polytrack: tried blinkered: tongue tied first 3 starts at 6 yrs: withdrawn after breaking through stall and running loose prior to intended third outing: reportedly finished lame fifth start. *P. F. I. Cole*

EJEED (USA) 2 b.c. (May 9) Rahy (USA) 115 – Lahan 117 (Unfuwain (USA) 131) **65 p** [2007 8.2g Nov 7] lengthy colt: second foal: half-brother to 5-y-o Almanshood: dam 7f (Rockfel Stakes)/1m (1000 Guineas) winner: 7/2, found less than looked likely (probably green) when eighth to Wintercast in maiden at Nottingham: open to improvement. *J. H. M. Gosden*

EKHTIAAR 3 b.g. Elmaamul (USA) 125 – Divina Mia 66 (Dowsing (USA) 124) [2007 **103** 89p: 10.1g⁵ 8m⁵ 10m 8m² 8m⁴ Oct 4] useful-looking gelding: useful handicapper: improved last 2 starts, in handicaps at Doncaster (neck second to Webbow) and Newmarket (fourth to Blackat Blackkitten): stays 1¼m: acts on polytrack, raced only on good/good to firm ground: joined A. Al Raihe in UAE. *J. H. M. Gosden*

EKTIMAAL 4 ch.g. Bahamian Bounty 115 – Secret Circle (Magic Ring (IRE) 115) **93** [2007 73: p7g* p7g* p7.1g* p7.1g* p7g 8m⁵ 7g 7m 7m p7g² Dec 28] tall, good-topped **a97** gelding: useful on all-weather, fairly useful on turf: much improved early in 2007, winning maiden at Kempton and handicaps there and at Wolverhampton (2) between January/March: off 3 months, good second to Vortex in handicap at Lingfield final start: best form at 7f: acts on polytrack, unraced on extremes of going on turf: tongue tied. *E. A. L. Dunlop*

ELAALA (USA) 5 ch.m. Aljabr (USA) 125 – Nufuth (USA) (Nureyev (USA) 131) **–** [2007 56: 15s Aug 11] neat mare: modest performer at 3/4 yrs: showed as if amiss only Flat start in 2007: stays 1¾m: acts on fibresand and good to soft going: fair hurdler, won 3 times between September/November. *J. T. Stimpson*

ELA FIGURA 7 ch.m. The West (USA) 107 – Chili Bouchier (USA) (Stop The Music **45** (USA)) [2007 p5l.1g⁵ p5l.1g p5l.1g f5g Feb 22] good-topped mare: poor maiden: best at 5f: acts on all-weather, firm and good to soft going: tried visored/in cheekpieces. *A. W. Carroll*

EL ALAMEIN (IRE) 4 ch.g. Nashwan (USA) 135 – El Rabab (USA) 70 (Roberto **68** (USA) 131) [2007 74: 14.1m⁶ 17.1d 14m 12m Oct 8] big, workmanlike gelding: fair handicapper: stays 2m: acts on polytrack and firm going: sold 10,000 gns. *Sir Mark Prescott*

ELAMAR 3 b.f. Rainbow High 121 – Night Transaction 59 (Tina's Pet 121) [2007 p8g **–** Feb 10] 1,400Y: half-sister to 3 winners, including sprinters Prime Recreation (by Primo Dominie) and Silca Key Silca (by Polar Falcon): dam 1m winner: 150/1, last of 12 in maiden at Lingfield, slowly away. *D. G. Bridgwater*

ELA MARIO (CYP) 3 ch.g. Ela-Aristokrati (IRE) 117 – Forgotten Times (USA) 80 **–** (Nabeel Dancer (USA) 120) [2007 p10g Nov 30] 14/1, tailed-off last in maiden at Lingfield (said to have had breathing problem). *Mrs H. Sweeting*

EL BOSQUE (IRE) 3 b.g. Elnadim (USA) 128 – In The Woods 101 (You And I (USA) **105** 118) [2007 90: p6g² 7m 6m³ p7g* 6m³ 6s* 6s 6g 7m Sep 13] leggy, attractive gelding: has a quick action: useful handicapper: improved in 2007, winning at Lingfield in May and Ripon (beat Top Bid by 7 lengths) in July: below form after: winner at 7f, but best form at 6f: acts on polytrack, soft and good to firm ground: often races prominently. *B. R. Millman*

EL CAPITAN (FR) 4 b.g. Danehill Dancer (IRE) 117 – Fille Dansante (IRE) (Dancing **53** Dissident (USA) 119) [2007 64: p9.5g 14.1m 10s p9.5g* p12g⁶ 10g p10g 12.1s 10.1f **a61** Jul 30] tall, rather leggy gelding: modest handicapper: won at Wolverhampton in May: stays easy 9.5f: acts on polytrack and good to firm ground: tried in headgear: has hung left/flashed tail. *Miss Gay Kelleway*

EL COTO 7 b.g. Forzando 122 – Thatcherella 80 (Thatching 131) [2007 97, a90: 8f⁵ 8m **92 d** 7g 9.2g* 10.4m⁴ 9d² 8s³ 9m⁵ 10d 8g⁶ p8.6g⁴ Nov 20] smallish, good-topped gelding: useful performer: regressed after reappearance in 2007, though won claimer at Hamilton in August: probably stays 10.5f: acts on polytrack, firm and soft going: tried visored/ blinkered, wears cheekpieces nowadays: has shown signs of temperament. *K. A. Ryan*

EL DECECY (USA) 3 b.g. Seeking The Gold (USA) – Ashraakat (USA) 105 (Danzig **84** (USA)) [2007 83: 10.1m³ 10f* 12g³ 10m³ 11.9m⁶ 9g 9.9m 8.5d p12.2g 10.3g⁶ Oct 26] tall, sparely-made gelding: fairly useful performer: won maiden at Pontefract (by 5 lengths) in May: well J. Dunlop 125,000 gns after fourth start: subsequently below form (gelded after final outing): barely stays 1½m: acts on firm going: blinkered last 4 starts: often races up with pace. *D. J. Murphy*

EL DEE (IRE) 4 br.g. Brave Act 119 – Go Flightline (IRE) 63 (Common Grounds 118) – [2007 48, a53: f11g⁶ 14m Aug 3] strong, close-coupled gelding: modest maiden at 3 yrs: below form both starts in 2007: stays 1½m: acts on fibresand, best effort on turf on good going. *D. Carroll*

ELDON ENDEAVOUR 3 b.g. Hunting Lion (IRE) 115 – La Noisette (Rock Hopper – 124) [2007 –: 8.3g Jun 20] little sign of ability. *B. Storey*

ELDORADO 6 b.g. Hernando (FR) 127 – Catch (USA) (Blushing Groom (FR) 131) **74** [2007 78: p16f⁵ 11m⁵ 16g 12g² 11.9d² Jul 17] workmanlike gelding: fair handicapper: probably best short of 2m: acts on polytrack and any turf going: sold £700 in November. *G. L. Moore*

EL DOTTORE 3 b.c. Dr Fong (USA) 128 – Edouna (FR) (Doyoun 124) [2007 52p: **68 d** 8.3m⁴ 13.8m⁶ 10.1d p10g Oct 17] tall, lengthy colt: maiden: easily best effort when fourth at Windsor on reappearance: stays 8.3f: sold 4,000 gns. *M. L. W. Bell*

EL DUENDE (USA) 2 b. or br.c. (Mar 5) Elusive Quality (USA) – Brianda (IRE) **63 p** (Alzao (USA) 117) [2007 7.1g⁵ 7d⁶ Oct 16] $210,000Y: well-made colt: third foal: closely related to US winner around 1m by Gone West and half-brother to useful French 1m winner Anoush (by Giant's Causeway): dam French 1¼m winner (later placed in US Grade 2 8.5f/9f events): modest form in maiden at Warwick and minor event at Leicester (seemed unsuited by softish ground): will stay 1m: capable of better. *W. Jarvis*

ELEANOR ELOISE (USA) 3 b.f. Minardi (USA) 119 – Javana (USA) (Sandpit **53** (BRZ) 129) [2007 p6g⁶ p7g⁵ Dec 5] 800 3-y-o: first foal: dam unraced out of sister to top-class miler Spinning World: better effort in maidens when fifth to Affrettando at Kempton. *J. R. Gask*

ELECTRIC BEAT 4 gr.c. Shinko Forest (IRE) – Divine Grace (IRE) (Definite Article **112** 121) [2007 113: 7g⁸ 6m 6m* Aug 26] neat, good-bodied colt: fourth foal: dam, ran twice, out of half-sister to smart miler Cape Town: smart performer: improved in 2006, winning listed race at Hanover and Lotto-Trophy at Hamburg: awarded listed race at Hanover on appeal on reappearance in June after beaten a head by Shinko's Best: stiff task in July Cup at Newmarket next time (final start for A. Lowe) before winning bestwetten.de Goldene Peitsche at Baden-Baden in August by ¾ length from Santiago Atitlan: effective at 6f/7f: acted on good to firm ground, below form on ground softer than good: to stand at Gestut Directa, Germany, fee €3,000. *C. Sprengel, Germany*

ELECTRIC WARRIOR (IRE) 4 b.g. Bold Fact (USA) 116 – Dungeon Princess **95** (IRE) 62 (Danehill (USA) 126) [2007 85: p8g² f7g⁵ 7.1d 7.1g p7g² p8g* p8g² 8.1m² p8g⁵ Sep 8] strong, lengthy gelding: useful handicapper: won at Kempton in July: good efforts after: effective at 6f to 1m: acts on all-weather and firm going: tends to race freely. *K. R. Burke*

ELECTRON PULSE 4 ch.f. Dr Fong (USA) 128 – Lost In Lucca 72§ (Inchinor 119) – [2007 59: 8.5m 6g May 29] modest maiden at 3 yrs: well held in handicaps in 2007: stays 1m: acts on firm going: tried in cheekpieces/blinkers. *M. Dods*

ELEGANS 3 b.f. Montjeu (IRE) 137 – Aymara 85 (Darshaan 133) [2007 8m p12g 10d – p8g p8.6g Nov 17] 5,000 2-y-o: lengthy filly: third foal: half-sister to 1¾m winner Adage (by Vettori): dam, 1½m winner, out of smart performer up to 1m Chipaya: no form. *Mrs C. A. Dunnett*

ELEGANT HAWK 3 b.f. Generous (IRE) 139 – Mexican Hawk (USA) 98 (Silver **98** Hawk (USA) 123) [2007 8g⁴ 9m* 10f 12g² p12g* 12d⁴ p13m⁵ Nov 1] leggy filly: first foal: dam, 1¼m winner, out of smart French sprinter Viva Zapata: useful form: won maiden in July and handicap in September, both at Lingfield: stiff task, best effort when fifth to Loulwa in listed event at same course final outing: likely to stay 1¾m: acts on polytrack, good to firm and good to soft going. *W. J. Knight*

ELEGANT STEP 2 b.f. (Jan 22) Xaar 132 – Lady's Walk (IRE) (Charnwood Forest **68** (IRE) 125) [2007 6m 6m 7m² 8g⁶ 9m⁶ 8m Oct 22] small, sturdy filly: first foal: dam unraced daughter of very smart French performer up to 1¾m Moquerie: fair maiden: second at Yarmouth: well held in nurseries: barely stays 1m: acts on good to firm going. *A. P. Jarvis*

ELEMENTAL HERO (FR) 2 ch.c. (Mar 1) Kyllachy 129 – Suerte 55 (Halling – (USA) 133) [2007 7g Oct 16] sturdy colt: 12/1, needed run when well held in maiden at Leicester. *Jane Chapple-Hyam*

EL FUSER 2 ch.c. (Feb 13) Zamindar (USA) 116 – Nimble Fan (USA) (Lear Fan (USA) **61** 130) [2007 6g 6m 6f⁵ Aug 4] sturdy colt: modest form in maidens: will stay 7f. *P. J. Makin*

ELHAMRI 3 b. or br.c. Noverre (USA) 125 – Seamstress (IRE) 72 (Barathea (IRE) 127) **98**
[2007 105: 6m⁶ p5g 5d⁵ 5d 5g 5g 7d⁶ Oct 29] small, strong colt: useful performer: not
discredited in listed races first/third outings: below form after: probably best at 5f on good
going or firmer. *S. Kirk*

ELIJAH PEPPER (USA) 2 ch.g. (Mar 8) Crafty Prospector (USA) – Dovie Dee **76**
(USA) (Housebuster (USA)) [2007 5g³ 5d⁵ 5d² 5m p6g* 6g⁵ Nov 6] $18,000Y: leggy
gelding: fifth foal: closely related/half-brother to winners in US by Numerous and Green
Dancer: dam maiden in North America: fair performer: won maiden at Wolverhampton
in October, making all: should prove best at 5f/6f: acts on polytrack and good to soft
going: gelded after final start. *T. D. Barron*

ELITE LAND 4 b.g. Namaqualand (USA) – Petite Elite 47 (Anfield 117) [2007 51: **–**
9.8g Apr 28] close-coupled gelding: modest maiden at 3 yrs: below form sole start in
2007: stays 11f: acts on firm and soft going: tried blinkered. *N. Bycroft*

ELIZABETH GARRETT 3 b.f. Dr Fong (USA) 128 – Eleonor Sympson 50 (Cade- **43**
aux Genereux 131) [2007 55: f5g⁵ p6g⁶ p8g f8g p12.2g p12.7g 10.1g⁶ 12g 10.1g⁵ Sep
19] leggy, close-coupled filly: poor maiden: left R. Cowell after second start: stays at least
1m: tried in cheekpieces/visored. *M. J. Gingell*

ELIZABETH SPIRIT (IRE) 3 b.f. Invincible Spirit (IRE) 121 – Generate 66 (Gene- **38**
rous (IRE) 139) [2007 p5.1g p6g⁶ p6g⁵ Dec 13] second foal: dam, 9.4f to 11f winner,
half-sister to useful 7f/1m performer All Ivory: poor form in maidens. *E. S. McMahon*

ELIZABETH'S QUEST 2 b.f. (Apr 3) Piccolo 121 – Reina 24 (Homeboy 114) [2007 **57**
p6g⁵ p7g 6m⁴ p7g Sep 26] angular filly: half-sister to several winners, including 2000
2-y-o 7f/1m winner Cynara (by Imp Society): dam maiden (stayed 7f): modest maiden:
should stay 7f. *R. Simpson*

ELIZABETH SWANN 2 ch.f. (Mar 24) Bahamian Bounty 116 – Last Exhibit 72 **83**
(Royal Academy (USA) 130) [2007 6m² 6d² 6m² Oct 4] 45,000Y: leggy, close-coupled
filly: second foal: dam, 6f winner, half-sister to dam of very smart 6f/7f performer
Etlaala: fairly useful maiden: runner-up all starts, beaten ½ length by Shabiba at Newmarket final one: likely to prove best at 6f/7f. *R. Hannon*

ELKHORN 5 b.g. Indian Ridge 123 – Rimba (USA) 82 (Dayjur (USA) 137) [2007 81: **91**
5g 5d² 5d* 6d⁶ 5d² 6m 5g⁴ 5g³ 5d 5m Oct 22] leggy gelding: fairly useful handicapper:
won at Hamilton in June: best at 5f/6f: acts on polytrack, firm and good to soft going:
usually wears headgear. *Miss J. A. Camacho*

ELK TRAIL (IRE) 2 ch.g. (Mar 9) Captain Rio 122 – Panpipes (USA) 69 (Woodman **71**
(USA) 126) [2007 7d⁶ 8.5m⁴ 9f² 10m⁶ Oct 8] well-made gelding: fair maiden: runner-up
at Redcar, dictating: stays 9f: acts on firm going. *T. P. Tate*

ELLABLUE 3 ch.f. Bahamian Bounty 116 – Elabella (Ela-Mana-Mou 132) [2007 62: **63**
p5.1g³ p5.1g² 6g² 5.1f⁴ p6g Sep 8] modest maiden: effective at 5f/6f: acts on polytrack
and firm ground: usually races prominently. *Rae Guest*

ELLA JUNIOR (USA) 2 ch.f. (Mar 31) Hennessy (USA) 122 – More Ribbons (USA) **66 ?**
(Dynaformer (USA)) [2007 7.1g⁵ p7g p6g Dec 1] $150,000Y, $205,000 2-y-o: unfur-
nished filly: first foal: dam US 1m/8.5f winner: easily best effort in maidens when fifth at
Warwick: will stay 1m: blinkered final start: sold only 4,000 gns. *B. J. Meehan*

ELLA WOODCOCK (IRE) 3 b.g. Daggers Drawn (USA) 114 – Hollow Haze **95**
(USA) 90 (Woodman (USA) 126) [2007 61: p7g² p8.6g³ p6g³ 7m² 7g* 8m* 8g* 9.2g*
8m² 10.3g² Oct 26] good-topped gelding: useful performer: generally progressive,
winning handicaps at Folkestone in August and Ripon in September, and claimers at
Yarmouth and Hamilton (claimed from J. Osborne £29,000) later in September: very
good second in handicaps last 2 starts: stays 10.3f: acts on polytrack and good to firm
ground: quirky. *E. J. Alston*

ELLA Y ROSSA 3 ch.f. Bertolini (USA) 125 – Meandering Rose (USA) (Irish River **67**
(FR) 131) [2007 51: p8g⁴ p7.1g* p8.6g³ p7g p7f⁵ p8.6g² p9.5g* 8f⁶ p8.6g p8.6g⁶ p8g³
p9.5g p10g⁴ p9.5g p9.5g⁵ p10m Dec 9] leggy filly: fair handicapper: won at Wolverhampton in January and March: stays easy 1¼m: acts on polytrack: held up. *P. D. Evans*

ELLCON (IRE) 4 b.f. Royal Applause 124 – Carranita (IRE) 111 (Anita's Prince 126) **71**
[2007 p6g² p6g⁵ 6.1m⁵ May 2] leggy, sparely-made filly: fair maiden: stays 6f: acts on
polytrack, good to firm and good to soft going. *J. A. Osborne*

ELLEMUJIE 2 b.g. (Feb 23) Mujahid (USA) 125 – Jennelle 97 (Nomination 125) **92**
[2007 5m p6g* 6m p6g³ 7m² 7d⁶ 8m³ 7m⁵ 6m p8.6g³ 8g⁴ Oct 26] good-topped gelding:
third foal: brother to 2005 2-y-o 7f winner Mujelle and half-brother to 5-y-o Jennverse:
dam 5f winner, including at 2 yrs: fairly useful performer: won maiden at Kempton in

June: in frame 5 times in nurseries: stays 8.6f: acts on polytrack and good to firm going: edgy sort: held up (often slowly away). *D. K. Ivory*

ELLENS ACADEMY (IRE) 12 b.g. Royal Academy (USA) 130 – Lady Ellen 67 **90** (Horage 124) [2007 88: 5f 6m³ 6g 6v 6v 5.9m 6m⁶ 6m* 6g⁴ 6g* 6m⁵ 6m* 6m Sep 22] big, useful-looking gelding: impresses in appearance: fairly useful performer: won claimer at Haydock and handicap at Ayr in August and handicap at Doncaster in September: effective at 5f/6f: acts on fibresand, firm and good to soft going: tried blinkered: sometimes slowly away/wanders: held up: reportedly resents whip, and usually ridden with hands and heels nowadays. *E. J. Alston*

ELLEN'S GIRL (IRE) 4 b.f. Desert Prince (IRE) 130 – Lady Ellen 67 (Horage 124) **82** [2007 58: p9.5g 9.7m³ 10.2f⁵ 8.1m 8d⁵ p8g 8g 7f² 8.1d* 8d* 8.3m* 8g⁵ 8d* 8g⁵ Oct 24] workmanlike filly: fairly useful handicapper: left B. Powell after seventh start: improved after, winning at Chepstow, Bath and Windsor within 10 days in August and apprentice event at Salisbury in October: stays easy 9.7f: acts on firm and good to soft going: tried visored/in cheekpieces: usually races prominently. *R. Hannon*

ELLE'S ANGEL (IRE) 3 b.f. Tobougg (IRE) 125 – Stamatina (Warning 136) [2007 **–** –: f8g May 15] compact filly: little form. *E. J. O'Neill*

ELLESAPPELLE 4 b.f. Benny The Dip (USA) 127 – Zizi (IRE) 87 (Imp Society **56** (USA)) [2007 76: p8g* p8.6g p10g f12g p10g⁶ Mar 30] leggy filly: modest performer nowadays: won seller at Lingfield (left G. L. Moore £3,600) in February: stays 1¼m: acts on polytrack, good to firm and good to soft ground: often wears headgear: has looked none too keen. *R. A. Harris*

ELLETELLE (IRE) 2 b.f. (Mar 8) Elnadim (USA) 128 – Flamanda 67 (Niniski **101** (USA) 125) [2007 6g³ 6g* 5m* 6m³ 6v³ 6m⁶ Oct 5] €26,000F: small, workmanlike filly: fifth foal: half-sister to useful German/Danish 1m/1¼m winner Freedom (by Second Empire) and French/German winner around 9f/1¼m Fitness (by Monsun): dam German 8.5f to 9.5f winner: useful performer: won maiden at Leopardstown and Queen Mary Stakes at Royal Ascot (beat Starlit Sands ½ length, weaving through) in June: held her form well, third in Cherry Hinton Stakes at Newmarket (to You'resothrilling) and Phoenix Stakes at the Curragh (2¾ lengths behind Saoirse Abu) and sixth in Cheveley Park Stakes at Newmarket: will stay 7f: acts on heavy and good to firm going: tends to start slowly. *G. M. Lyons, Ireland*

ELLIES FAITH 3 ch.f. Sugarfoot 118 – Star Dancer (Groom Dancer (USA) 128) [2007 **51** 47: 10g³ 9.8s⁵ 12s⁶ 16.2s 12.1g* 10f⁴ 12.1g 12g⁵ 10f 12.1d Sep 25] small, sturdy filly: modest performer: won selling handicap at Beverley in July: stays 1½m: acts on soft ground: usually wears blinkers nowadays: often races prominently. *N. Bycroft*

ELLIWAN 2 b.c. (Apr 4) Nayef (USA) 129 – Ashbilya (USA) (Nureyev (USA) 131) **74 p** [2007 8g 8.2g³ Oct 31] well-made colt: sixth foal: half-brother to 7f to 9.4f winner Najaaba (by Bahhare), 4-y-o Zamalik, and 6-y-o Shaaban: dam unraced: much better effort in maidens (week apart) when third at Nottingham, briefly looking likely winner: will stay 1¼m: should continue progressing. *M. Johnston*

ELLMAU 2 ch.c. (Mar 2) Dr Fong (USA) 128 – Triple Sharp 80 (Selkirk (USA) 129) **96** [2007 f6g³ 7m³ 7g⁵ 6.5m Sep 12] 10,000F, 8,000Y: close-coupled, useful-looking colt: third foal: half-brother to winner in Spain by Vettori: dam 1¼m and hurdles winner: useful performer: won maiden at Southwell in May: much improved when 2 lengths third of 10 to Hatta Fort in Superlative Stakes at Newmarket, making most: below form after in Vintage Stakes at Goodwood (set strong pace) and sales race at Doncaster (unhelpful draw): bred to stay at least 1m, but has plenty of speed. *E. J. O'Neill*

Queen Mary Stakes, Royal Ascot—Elletelle (striped sleeves) weaves through late to catch Starlit Sands (white cap), while The Loan Express (second left) also finishes well in third

ELMALEEHA 2 b.f. (Mar 22) Galileo (IRE) 134 – Winsa (USA) 80 (Riverman (USA) **76 p**
131) [2007 7g² Nov 3] unfurnished filly: fifth foal: half-sister to useful 2003 2-y-o 7f/7.5f
winner Mutahayya (by Peintre Celebre), 1½m winner Majhud (by Machiavellian) and
2005 2-y-o 5f/6f winner Qusoor (by Fasliyev): dam, 1½m winner, sister to high-class
miler Bahri: 12/1, promising second of 20 to Infallible in maiden at Newmarket, coming
from well back: will be suited by 1¼m/1½m: sure to improve. *J. L. Dunlop*

ELMASONG 3 ch.f. Elmaamul (USA) 125 – Annie's Song 69 (Farfelu 103) [2007 42: **42**
9.9d 10s⁵ 11m 8g 8g 8m² 8d p8g p7g p6g p7m p11g p10g Dec 30] workmanlike filly:
poor maiden: seems to stay 1¼m: acts on good to firm ground, probably on polytrack:
tried in cheekpieces. *J. J. Bridger*

ELMS SCHOOLBOY 5 ch.g. Komaite (USA) – Elms Schoolgirl 79 (Emarati (USA) **58**
74) [2007 55: p8.6g⁴ p11g⁶ p9.5g⁴ p10g p10g p12.2g p12.2g p10g⁶ Dec 30] smallish
gelding: modest performer: stays easy 1½m: acts on all-weather and firm ground:
blinkered: difficult ride. *P. Howling*

ELNA BRIGHT 2 b.c. (Mar 9) Elnadim (USA) 128 – Acicula (IRE) 96 (Night Shift **89**
(USA)) [2007 5.1d³ 5.1g² 6f* 7m* 7m⁶ 7d 6m² Sep 25] 9,500F, 27,000Y: quite attractive
colt: has moderate, quick action: fourth foal: half-brother to 2003 2-y-o 5f/6f seller
winner Raphoola (by Raphane) and 4-y-o Alucica: dam 2-y-o 5f/6f winner: fairly useful
performer: won maiden at Brighton in June and nursery at Newmarket in July: short-head
second to Kaldoun Kingdom in nursery at Brighton final start, detached halfway: stays
7f: acts on firm going: has joined B. Meehan. *R. Hannon*

ELOPEMENT (IRE) 5 ch.m. Machiavellian (USA) 123 – Melanzane (Arazi (USA) **83**
135) [2007 58: p9.5g p12g 10.2f 10.2d* 9.1d⁵ 10.1d⁴ 10.1m⁵ 10.9d* 11.6m 10.5m⁵ 12d*
11.1s* 12d* 12g* Oct 5] leggy mare: fairly useful handicapper: much improved in
2007, winning at Bath in May, Warwick in June, Musselburgh, Hamilton and Ascot in
September and Musselburgh in October: stays 1½m: acts on soft ground: usually races up
with pace: sold 27,000 gns. *W. M. Brisbourne*

ELOQUENT ISLE (IRE) 2 b.f. (Feb 11) Mull of Kintyre (USA) 114 – County Girl **–**
(IRE) (Prince Rupert (FR) 121) [2007 p7.1g⁵ Nov 22] €5,000F, 16,000Y: fifth foal:
half-sister to 4-y-o Moonlight Fantasy and winner up to 11.5f in Italy by Victory Note:
dam ran twice: 16/1, behind in maiden at Wolverhampton. *Mrs A. Duffield*

ELOQUENT ROSE (IRE) 3 b.f. Elnadim (USA) 128 – Quintellina 83 (Robellino **71**
(USA) 127) [2007 83: 6g 5g 5g p6g⁴ Nov 22] big, strong filly: type to carry condition:
just fair performer in 2007: effective at 5f/6f: acts on firm and soft going. *Mrs A. Duffield*

ELOUNDA (IRE) 3 b.f. Sinndar (IRE) 134 – Gaily Grecian (IRE) (Ela-Mana-Mou **58**
132) [2007 62p: 10m 11.7g 8m 10m Aug 14] sturdy, attractive filly: maiden: little impact
in 2007: tried blinkered: saddle slipped second/final outings. *H. R. A. Cecil*

EL PALMAR 6 b.g. Case Law 113 – Aybeegirl 66 (Mazilier (USA) 107) [2007 61: f8g **61**
f8g³ f7g May 8] good-topped gelding: modest performer at 5 yrs: little form in 2007: tried
in headgear. *M. J. Attwater*

EL POTRO 5 b.g. Forzando 122 – Gaelic Air 65 (Ballad Rock 122) [2007 73d: p5g **67**
p5.1g⁴ p5.1g² p5.1g⁵ f5g f5g² f5g² p6g³ 5v² 5s² 5d* 6m 5.1f⁶ 5.1s* p5.1g⁵ Nov 17] fair
handicapper: won at Pontefract in July and Nottingham in October: effective at 5f/6f: acts
on all-weather and any turf going: often races prominently. *J. R. Holt*

EL SOPRANO (IRE) 3 b.f. Noverre (USA) 125 – Lady of Kildare (IRE) 100 (Mujadil **92**
(USA) 119) [2007 85: 6s 7m 8g 6m Oct 4] €72,000Y: good-topped filly: second foal:
dam, Irish 2-y-o 6f/7f winner, out of smart Irish 1¾m/1½m winner Dancing Sunset: fairly
useful performer: trained by K. Prendergast in Ireland at 2 yrs: best effort when seventh
to Tarteel in handicap at Newmarket second start: stays 7f: acts on soft and good to firm
ground: tried blinkered. *K. A. Ryan*

EL TANGO (GER) 5 br.h. Acatenango (GER) 127 – Elea (GER) (Dschingis Khan) **109**
[2007 106: 15.5g⁵ 16g⁶ 15.5g⁴ 16v* 14d⁶ 14v* 14d⁴ 15.5v* 12v Dec 9] strong horse:
brother to useful German 7f (at 2 yrs) to 1½m winner Evil Empire and half-brother to
several winners, including useful German 7f (at 2 yrs) and 1¼m winner Enigma (by
Sharp Victor): dam German 8.5f/9f winner: useful performer: won listed race at Hamburg
in June, Grosser Preis von DSW21 - Deutsches St Leger at Dortmund (for second time,
beat Scatina ½ length) in September and listed race at Saint-Cloud (for second year
running, by short neck from Loup de Mer) in November: also creditable sixth to Purple
Moon in Ebor Handicap at York fifth start: stays 2m (inadequate trip final start): raced
mainly on good ground or softer, goes particularly well on heavy. *P. Schiergen, Germany*

ELTANIN (IRE) 3 gr.g. Linamix (FR) 127 – Housatonic (USA) 59 (Riverman (USA) – 131) [2007 68: 7f⁵ May 5] angular gelding: fair maiden at 2 yrs: in need of run sole start in 2007: stayed 1m: dead. *J. Howard Johnson*

EL TATO 2 b.c. (Mar 30) Diktat 126 – Villa Via (IRE) 71 (Night Shift (USA)) [2007 **62** 5m⁵ 5m⁵ 6m Aug 18] good-topped colt: modest maiden: dead. *T. D. Easterby*

EL TOREADOR (USA) 3 ch.f. El Corredor (USA) 123 – Marsha's Dancer (USA) **86** (Northern Dancer) [2007 74p: 7g³ 8m* p8.6g² p8g p12.2g⁴ 10.5g⁵ Sep 8] quite good-topped filly: has a fluent action: fairly useful handicapper: won maiden at Salisbury in June: creditable efforts when in frame after: effective at 1m, seems to stay easy 1½m: acts on polytrack and good to firm ground: sent to Bahrain. *G. A. Butler*

ELUSIVE DEAL (USA) 2 ch.f. (Mar 23) Elusive Quality (USA) – Peacefally (IRE) **59** (Grand Lodge (USA) 125) [2007 5.1m³ 6m 5v⁴ 6m 7m⁵ p8g⁶ p7.1g² p8.6g⁴ p8.6g p8.6g Dec 3] $30,000Y: small filly: first foal: dam useful French/US performer up to 1½m: modest maiden: will stay 1¼m/1½m: acts on polytrack and good to firm going, probably on heavy: effective with or without cheekpieces. *R. A. Fahey*

ELUSIVE DREAMS (USA) 3 ch.g. Elusive Quality (USA) – Bally Five (USA) **71** (Miswaki (USA) 124) [2007 p7.1g⁵ p8g 7d* p8g 8d Sep 28] sturdy gelding: fair performer: won maiden at Salisbury in August: may prove best at short of 1m: raced only on polytrack and good to soft ground: sold 28,000 gns, then gelded. *J. H. M. Gosden*

ELUSIVE FLASH (USA) 3 b.f. Freud (USA) 113 – Giana (USA) (Exclusive Era **98** (USA)) [2007 85: 7m³ 7.1d 7m 8.1m⁵ p8g a9.5g Dec 6] good-topped filly: useful performer: good efforts when third to Majestic Roi in Fred Darling Stakes at Newbury and fifth to Sweet Lilly in listed event at Sandown, though possibly flattered: stays easy 1m: acts on polytrack, good to firm and good to soft ground: has flashed tail under pressure. *P. F. I. Cole*

ELUSIVE HAWK (IRE) 3 b. or br.g. Noverre (USA) 125 – Two Clubs 111 (First – Trump 118) [2007 p7.1g⁵ Dec 15] 5/1, well held in maiden at Wolverhampton. *A. P. Stringer*

ELUSIVE LADY (IRE) 2 b.f. (Mar 19) Clodovil (IRE) 116 – Bella Vie (IRE) **55** (Sadler's Wells (USA) 132) [2007 6d⁴ 7s⁵ 5m⁶ 6m² 7m⁶ 6g³ 7.1d³ p7.1g² 7g⁴ p7.1g* **a72** p8.6g* Dec 26] leggy filly: third foal: closely related to 7f (including at 2 yrs) winner Sigismundus (by Mozart) and half-sister to 3-yo Snow Dancer: dam unraced close relation of useful Irish 6f winner Immovable Option: fair on all-weather, modest on turf: in cheekpieces, won maiden in November and 4-runner nursery in December, both at Wolverhampton: stays 8.6f: acts on polytrack, good to firm and good to soft going. *J. R. Weymes*

ELUSIVE WARRIOR (USA) 4 b.g. Elusive Quality (USA) – Love To Fight (CAN) **66** (Fit To Fight (USA)) [2007 74: 7g 7m 6f⁴ 7.1m p7.1g⁴ p7.1g² p7.1g² p7.1g f6d⁵ Dec 11] rangy gelding: fair handicapper: stays 7f: acts on all-weather and firm ground: wears cheekpieces. *R. A. Fahey*

ELUSORY 3 b.c. Galileo (IRE) 134 – Elude (Slip Anchor 136) [2007 –: 10m 12g⁴ 9.9m **63** 14s Oct 4] sturdy colt: modest maiden: stays 1½m: sold 7,500 gns. *J. L. Dunlop*

ELVINA 6 b.m. Mark of Esteem (IRE) 137 – Pharaoh's Joy 66 (Robellino (USA) 127) **52** [2007 55: p5.1g* f5g² p5.1g 5.1d⁵ p5.1g p5.1g⁵ Sep 20] modest performer: won minor event at Wolverhampton in January: speedy, and best at 5f: acts on all-weather and good to firm going. *A. G. Newcombe*

ELYAADI 3 b.f. Singspiel (IRE) 133 – Abyaan (IRE) 106 (Ela-Mana-Mou 132) [2007 **92** 72p: p8.6g² p8.6g² 12m* 11.5g⁵ 14d⁵ a8f³ Dec 20] strong, useful-looking filly: fairly useful performer: won minor event at Catterick in April: best effort when fifth in handicap at Sandown penultimate start: left M. Channon after: stays 1¾m: acts on polytrack, good to firm and good to soft ground. *D. J. Selvaratnam, UAE*

ELYSEE PALACE (IRE) 2 b.f. (Mar 29) King's Best (USA) 132 – Noble Rose (IRE) **80 p** 113 (Caerleon (USA) 132) [2007 p8g⁵ p7g* Oct 24] rather leggy filly: seventh foal: sister to 5-y-o Notability and half-sister to 2 winners, including fairly useful 2002 2-y-o 6f winner Illustria (by Seeking The Gold): dam 7f (at 2 yrs) to 14.6f (Park Hill Stakes) winner: fairly useful form: confirmed debut promise when winning maiden at Lingfield: should be suited by 1m/1¼m: will improve further. *M. A. Jarvis*

ELY UNE (IRE) 2 ch.f. (Apr 20) Choisir (AUS) 126 – D D's Jakette (USA) (Deputy **52** Minister (CAN)) [2007 7s p7.1g 5.1m² p6m p5g³ p6g⁶ p6g⁶ p6g Nov 16] €4,500F, 3,500Y: seventh foal: half-sister to 3 winners, including 5f (at 2 yrs) and 1¼m winner

Mizz Tee (by Orpen) and Irish 7f winner Zaraglen (by Lear Fan), both fairly useful: dam winner in US: modest maiden: left B. Duke after second start: best efforts at 5f: acts on polytrack and good to firm going: wore cheekpieces final outing. *J. S. Moore*

EMAARA 3 b.f. Fasliyev (USA) 120 – Shuruk 73 (Cadeaux Genereux 131) [2007 78: 6d³ May 15] fair maiden at 2 yrs: well below form only start in 2007: stays 6f: unraced on extremes of going: looks quirky: sold 5,500 gns in July. *J. L. Dunlop*   **60**

E MAJOR 2 ch.c. (Feb 2) Singspiel (IRE) 133 – Crystal Cavern (USA) 89 (Be My Guest (USA) 126) [2007 p7.1g³ Nov 5] seventh foal: half-brother to several winners, including 2002 2-y-o 7f winner Crystal Star (by Mark of Esteem) and Irish 7f to 8.5f winner Christavelli (by Machiavellian), both useful: dam, 2-y-o 7f winner (later won in Canada), half-sister to Poule d'Essai des Pouliches winner Rose Gypsy: 2/1, needed experience but unlucky when third in maiden at Wolverhampton, clipping heels and stumbling 1f out: will be suited by 1m/1¼m: bound to improve. *Sir Michael Stoute*   **64 p**

EMBRA (IRE) 2 b.g. (May 5) Monashee Mountain (USA) 115 – Ivory Turner (Efisio 120) [2007 p7.1g Nov 23] €25,000Y: sixth foal: brother to 5-y-o Fullandby: dam Italian 5f (at 2 yrs) to 1m winner: 16/1, hinted at ability in maiden at Wolverhampton: should do better. *T. J. Etherington*   **– p**

EMEFDREAM 3 b.g. Efisio 120 – Alkarida (FR) (Akarad (FR) 130) [2007 66: f6g⁴ p7.1g f8g f7s f7g 8f Apr 24] neat gelding: modest performer nowadays: left Mrs N. Macauley after fourth start: stays 6f: acts on fibresand and firm ground, below par all 3 starts on softer than good: often wears headgear: has gone early to post. *E. J. O'Neill*   **54 d**

EMEF PRINCESS 2 b.f. (Feb 4) Mind Games 121 – Woore Lass (IRE) 75 (Persian Bold 123) [2007 5m³ 5.7m 5g p6g 7g⁵ p7.1g⁶ p5.1g Nov 2] 8,000Y: compact filly: first foal: dam 6f (at 2 yrs) and 1m winner: modest maiden: may prove best at 5f/6f: tried in cheekpieces/blinkers. *K. A. Ryan*   **51**

EMERALD BAY (IRE) 5 b.g. King's Best (USA) 132 – Belle Etoile (FR) (Lead On Time (USA) 123) [2007 93: 8m⁵ 9m 9.1g³ 9.1d³ 7.1g⁴ 8.1s 8m 9.2d⁴ 8s⁶ 8v² 8g⁵ Nov 9] rangy gelding: fairly useful handicapper: won at Musselburgh in April: respectable efforts last 4 outings: stays 1¼m: acts on any going: races up with pace: tough and reliable. *I. Semple*   **92**

EMERALD CRYSTAL (IRE) 2 b.c. (Mar 6) Green Desert (USA) 127 – Crystal Spray 75 (Beldale Flutter (USA) 130) [2007 8d 7g⁴ Nov 2] half-brother to several winners, mostly smart, including 2000 2-y-o 7f/1m (Fillies' Mile) winner Crystal Music (by Nureyev) and 1¼m/1½m winner Dubai Success (by Sadler's Wells): dam Irish 1¾m winner: much better run in maidens when fourth to Foolin Myself at Newmarket, but again weakened: should stay 1m. *B. J. Meehan*   **79**

EMERALD ROCK (CAN) 2 b.c. (May 17) Johannesburg (USA) 127 – Classic Jones (CAN) (Regal Classic (CAN)) [2007 8.2g⁶ Nov 7] $16,000Y, 52,000 2-y-o: big, rangy colt: second foal: dam stakes-placed US winner (6f to 1m): 12/1 and stirred up, prominent long way when sixth in maiden at Nottingham: capable of better. *N. J. Vaughan*   **62 p**

EMERALD SKY 3 b.f. Diktat 126 – Dekelsmary 61 (Komaite (USA)) [2007 –: f5g 6m Apr 12] strong filly: little form. *R. Brotherton*   **–**

EMERALD TOFFEE (IRE) 2 ch.c. (Apr 12) Tagula (IRE) 116 – Spirit of Hope (IRE) (Danehill Dancer (IRE) 117) [2007 6d 8.2d Oct 18] good-topped colt: well beaten in maidens. *J. T. Stimpson*   **–**

EMERALD WILDERNESS (IRE) 3 b.g. Green Desert (USA) 127 – Simla Bibi 69 (Indian Ridge 123) [2007 79: p7g³ p8g² p8.6g² 9m² 8g² p8.6g* 10g⁴ 9.9g² 10g* 9.7m* 9.9g 8d² 9.8m³ 9m 10m³ Sep 22] tall, sparely-made gelding: improved into a useful handicapper, winning at Wolverhampton (dead-heat) in April, and having left M. Channon after eighth start, Windsor and Folkestone (by head from Tears of A Clown) in July: good efforts last 4 starts, 1¾ lengths third to Teslin at Newmarket final outing: free-going sort, but stays 1¼m: acts on polytrack, good to firm and good to soft ground: consistent: joined A. King and gelded. *E. A. L. Dunlop*   **101**

EMILIO 6 b.g. Kris 135 – Easter Moon (FR) (Easter Sun 122) [2007 89: p8g a8s⁵ a6.8g⁵ 5.8g⁶ a6g* 8g* a6.8f a6g* a8g⁵ a6g⁶ a6.8g⁵ a6g⁶ Nov 25] sturdy gelding: fair performer nowadays: not entirely discredited when eighth in handicap at Kempton on reappearance: left R. Kvisla after third start: won handicap at Jagersro and minor event at Ovrevoll in August and handicap at Jagersro in September: stays 1m: acts on dirt, good to firm and good to soft going: tongue tied in Britain. *Yvonne Durant, Sweden*   **75**

Sixty Years of Timeform Stakes (Handicap), York—
top weight Emirates Skyline makes a successful reappearance; Flying Clarets (right) finishes second

EMILION 4 ch.f. Fantastic Light (USA) 134 – Riberac 110 (Efisio 120) [2007 67: p12g **62**
p13.9g³ p13.9g Feb 5] neat filly: modest handicapper nowadays: stays 1¾m: acts on
polytrack and firm going: tried blinkered. *W. R. Muir*

EMILY'S DENS JOY (IRE) 2 b.f. (Feb 28) Daggers Drawn (USA) 114 – Cross Dall **–**
(IRE) 58§ (Blues Traveller (IRE) 119) [2007 5m 6g⁶ 6f⁶ Jul 30] 2,700Y: third foal: dam
11.6f winner: no form. *Miss D. A. McHale*

EMILY'S PLACE (IRE) 4 b.f. Mujadil (USA) 119 – Dulcinea 73 (Selkirk (USA) **75**
129) [2007 74: p10g 8d⁵ 8s* 8.1v⁵ 8.5s⁵ 8m⁶ 8.1f⁴ 8.1m p8g p9.5g² p9.5g² p9.5g² p9.5g
p9.5g⁴ p9.5g⁴ Dec 26] leggy filly: fair handicapper: won at Pontefract in July: stays
easy 9.5f: acts on polytrack and any turf going: tried in cheekpieces/visor: often held up.
J. Pearce

EMILY'S RAINBOW (IRE) 3 b.f. Rainbow Quest (USA) 134 – Showering (Dane- **58**
hill (USA) 126) [2007 10.5g p10m 8.3d⁵ p10g p8g⁶ Nov 28] angular filly: second foal:
dam once-raced half-sister to smart 7f winner Clearing: modest maiden: likely to prove
best at 1¼m+: blinkered final start. *W. J. Haggas*

EMIRATES SKYLINE (USA) 4 b.g. Sunday Silence (USA) – The Caretaker 113 **109**
(Caerleon (USA) 132) [2007 104: 10.4g* 10d⁵ 9.9g⁶ Jul 31] quite good-topped gelding:
useful handicapper, lightly raced: won at York (by ½ length from Flying Clarets) in May:
creditable efforts after at Royal Ascot (fifth to Championship Point in listed event,
carrying head awkwardly and lugging right) and Goodwood (visored, sixth to same rival,
not clear run): subsequently gelded: will stay 1½m: acts on good to firm and good to soft
going. *Saeed bin Suroor*

EMIR BAGATELLE 2 gr.g. (Apr 14) Dubai Destination (USA) 127 – Giorgia Rae **–**
(IRE) (Green Desert (USA) 127) [2007 6m 6d.5d Oct 10] 60,000F, €55,000Y, £22,000
2-y-o: lengthy gelding: first foal: dam, ran twice in France, sister to useful 1999 2-y-o
sprinter Rowaasi: no show in maidens, then gelded. *H. Morrison*

EMMA GEE 5 ch.m. Sure Blade (USA) 130 – Elusive Star 53 (Ardross 134) [2007 p8g **–**
p10g 10s May 28] second foal: dam 1½m and hurdles winner: well held in bumper, and in
claimer/sellers on Flat, leaving J. Akehurst prior to final outing. *J. Gallagher*

EMMA JEAN LAD (IRE) 3 ch.g. Intikhab (USA) 135 – Swing City (IRE) 58 (Indian **70**
Ridge 123) [2007 47: p7g² 7.1m 7g 7.1g² 6v p6g⁵ p6g⁶ p7m² p7g* p7g² Oct 29] good-
topped gelding: fair performer: won minor event at Kempton in October: will stay 1m:
acts on polytrack. *J. S. Moore*

EMMA'S SECRETS 2 b.f. (Mar 4) Fraam 114 – Hopping Higgins (IRE) 103 (Brief **– p**
Truce (USA) 126) [2007 5m 5s⁶ 7d Oct 9] 4,500F, €24,000Y, 34,000 2-y-o: fifth foal:
dam Irish 2-y-o 5f winner: bit better than bare result in maidens (gambled on when fell
debut): should prove best at 5f/6f: remains open to improvement. *Miss M. E. Rowland*

EMMROOZ 2 b.c. (Mar 23) Red Ransom (USA) – Nasmatt 96 (Danehill (USA) 126) **102**
[2007 7.1m² 8m* 8d 8d³ Oct 19] well-made, attractive colt: third foal: 2-y-o 6f
winner, closely related to Bint Allayl and Kheleyf: useful form: won maiden at Goodwood in September: improved again when 2¼ lengths seventh of 11 to City Leader in

Royal Lodge Stakes at Ascot (had looked likely to finish closer over 1f out): favourite, only third behind Kandahar Run in minor event at Newmarket: stays 1m: suspect attitude (hung first 2 starts). *Saeed bin Suroor*

EMOTIVE 4 b.g. Pursuit of Love 124 – Ruby Julie (Clantime 101) [2007 69, a63: 8.3m **54** 7.9g 15.8m³ 15.8g 15.8g Oct 30] leggy gelding: fair performer at 3 yrs: only modest in 2007: seems to stay 15.8f: acts on polytrack, good to firm and good to soft going: tried blinkered/in cheekpieces: reportedly bled second outing. *F. P. Murtagh*

EMPEROR CAT (IRE) 6 b.g. Desert Story (IRE) 115 – Catfoot Lane 50 (Batshoof **–** 122) [2007 54: 7.1s 8.1m Aug 7] close-coupled gelding: modest performer at best: no form in 2007: tried in headgear. *Mrs N. S. Evans*

EMPEROR COURT (IRE) 3 ch.c. Singspiel (IRE) 133 – Tarquina (USA) (Niniski **74** (USA) 125) [2007 7m 7g³ p8g⁴ p10m⁴ p9.5g³ p10g² Dec 30] tall colt: fair maiden: stays 1¼m: acts on polytrack. *P. J. Makin*

EMPERORS JADE 2 b.c. (Apr 30) Averti (IRE) 117 – Bliss (IRE) 75 (Statoblest 120) **71** [2007 6d 6d p6g² Nov 3] close-coupled colt: fair maiden: improved on turf form (softish ground) when second to Torch of Freedom at Kempton, dictating: should prove best at 5f/6f: acts on polytrack. *A. P. Jarvis*

EMPEROR'S WELL 8 ch.g. First Trump 118 – Catherines Well 99 (Junius (USA) **77** 124) [2007 65: 10.5m 7.9g³ 8s³ 8g² 8v* 7.5g* 8m² 8.1m 10m⁶ 10m 8g 10g Oct 31] well-made gelding: fair handicapper: won at Ripon and Beverley (ladies event, by 7 lengths) in July: stays 1¼m: acts on fibresand, heavy and good to firm going: tried visored/blinkered: usually races prominently. *M. W. Easterby*

EMPIRE DANCER (IRE) 4 b.g. Second Empire (IRE) 124 – Dance To The Beat 58 **73** (Batshoof 122) [2007 74: p6g p7.1g⁶ p8.6g⁴ 7m* 7.6m³ 8m p7g p7.1g⁶ 7d p8.6g⁴ p7.1g⁴ p8.6d⁶ Dec 10] leggy gelding: fair handicapper: won at Yarmouth in August: left C. Allen 6,000 gns after ninth start: stays 9.7f: acts on polytrack and firm going: front runner. *I. W. McInnes*

EMPIRE SEEKER (USA) 2 b.c. (Apr 7) Seeking The Gold (USA) – Lady From **67 p** Shanghai (USA) (Storm Cat (USA)) [2007 8d Oct 27] $50,000Y: second foal: dam, US maiden, half-sister to William Hill Futurity winner Bakharoff and smart miler Emperor Jones: 25/1, gradually got hang of things when eighth in maiden at Newbury: will benefit from experience. *B. J. Meehan*

EMPRESS JAIN 4 br.f. Lujain (USA) 119 – Akhira 90 (Emperor Jones (USA) 119) **88** [2007 105: 5.1f³ p5g Jun 6] leggy, sparely-made filly: useful performer at 3 yrs: just fairly useful form in listed events in 2007: speedy and best at 5f: acts on firm going: has been early to post: front runner. *M. A. Jarvis*

EMPRESS OLGA (USA) 3 br.f. Kingmambo (USA) 125 – Balistroika (USA) (Nijin- **71** sky (CAN) 138) [2007 76: p7g² f7g² 8f⁵ Apr 20] useful-looking filly: fair maiden: stays 1m: acts on all-weather: signs of temperament. *E. A. L. Dunlop*

EMULATE 3 b.f. Alhaarth (IRE) 126 – Aquarelle (Kenmare (FR) 125) [2007 81: 9m **75** p10g⁶ Jun 20] good-topped filly: fair form, lightly raced: stays 1¼m: acts on polytrack: sold 15,000 gns in December. *B. W. Hills*

ENACTMENT 2 ch.c. (Mar 21) Pivotal 124 – Live Your Dreams (USA) (Mt Livermore **85** (USA)) [2007 6s 7v⁴ 6f² 5.5m* 6m⁴ Sep 22] sturdy colt: second foal: dam, US 1m/8.5f winner (second in Grade 2 8.5f event), out of half-sister to champion US sprinter House-buster: fairly useful form: improved to win nursery at Warwick in September, quickening well: equal-fourth to Mr Keppel in similar event at Newbury final start: should prove best at 5f/6f: acts on firm going: tongue tied (ran well) once: sold 65,000 gns, sent to USA. *Sir Michael Stoute*

ENCHANTED LADY 2 b.f. (Feb 3) Dr Fong (USA) 128 – Enchanted Princess 82 **50** (Royal Applause 124) [2007 p6g 7d p6g 5.7f 5.3m⁴ p6g Oct 31] first foal: dam 1m win-ner: modest maiden: should stay 6f/7f: sold 2,500 gns, sent to Sweden. *H. J. L. Dunlop*

ENCIRCLED 3 b.f. In The Wings 128 – Ring of Esteem (Mark of Esteem (IRE) 137) **89** [2007 75: 10d 10m* 12d³ 10m Jul 17] sturdy filly: fairly useful handicapper: won at Windsor in June: good third at Newmarket next time, hanging left: stays 1½m: acts on polytrack, good to firm and good to soft ground: reportedly in season final start. *D. Haydn Jones*

ENCORES 3 b.g. Tobougg (IRE) 125 – Western Applause 76 (Royal Applause 124) **78** [2007 7g³ f8g⁴ p8.6g p10g⁵ 8d* 8.3g³ p8g p8.6g⁴ 7d² p7g* p7.1g³ Nov 9] fair handicapper: won at Newmarket in June and Kempton in October: left N. Callaghan before final start: effective at 7f/1m: acts on polytrack and good to soft ground. *M. G. Quinlan*

ENDEAVOR 2 ch.g. (Apr 13) Selkirk (USA) 129 – Midnight Mambo (USA) 53 (King-   –
mambo (USA) 125) [2007 8g Oct 3] close-coupled gelding: tailed off in maiden at Newcastle. *P. Monteith*

ENDIAMO (IRE) 3 ch.g. Indian Ridge 123 – Aldafra 91 (Spectrum (IRE) 126) [2007   **95**
91: p7g* 7.1d² 7.1g⁵ Jul 7] sturdy gelding: useful form: won maiden at Lingfield in February: good efforts in handicaps at Sandown after: stays 7f: acts on polytrack, soft and good to firm ground: joined D. Selvaratnam in UAE. *M. P. Tregoning*

ENDLESS LUCK (USA) 2 b. or br.c. (Jan 24) Giant's Causeway (USA) 132 – End-   **93 p**
less Parade (USA) (Williamstown (USA) 118) [2007 7d² 8g* Nov 9] $70,000Y, 80,000 2-y-o: strong colt: third foal: half-brother to US 7.5f to 9f (Grade 3 event) winner Drum Major (1m winner at 2 yrs, by Dynaformer): dam US 6f to 1m minor stakes winner: plenty of promise in maidens, second to Prime Exhibit at Leicester before winning at Musselburgh by 5 lengths from Tighnabruaich, quickening away final 1f: will stay 1¼m: should make a useful 3-y-o. *M. Johnston*

ENDLESS NIGHT 4 ch.g. Dracula (AUS) 121 – La Notte 88 (Factual (USA) 108)   –
[2007 68: p7g 7m p12g Aug 28] close-coupled gelding: fair maiden at 2/3 yrs: well held in 2007, leaving T. Jones after reappearance: stays 1m: acts on polytrack, soft and good to firm going: tried tongue tied/visored/in cheekpieces. *A. M. Hales*

ENDLESS POWER (IRE) 7 b.g. Perugino (USA) 84 – Charroux (IRE) 75 (Darshaan   –
133) [2007 p12.2g⁶ Feb 23] 9/2, well-held sixth in maiden at Wolverhampton on belated Flat debut: fairly useful hurdler/chaser. *J. S. Goldie*

ENDLESS SUMMER 10 b.g. Zafonic (USA) 130 – Well Away (IRE) (Sadler's Wells   **66**
(USA) 132) [2007 74: 5.5d 6m 5m⁵ 5.1d² 5.1f³ 6.1m³ 5.1m⁶ 5d⁶ 6d⁶ 5.7g² p6g Nov 1] small, sturdy gelding: had fertility problems at stud: fair handicapper: best at 5f/6f: acts on polytrack, firm and soft going: tried tongue tied: held up: sometimes carries head awkwardly: has bled. *A. W. Carroll*

END OF AN ERROR 8 b.m. Charmer 123 – Needwood Poppy 29 (Rolfe (USA) 77)   –
[2007 12.6d⁶ Jun 28] leggy, close-coupled mare: no longer of much account. *G. F. Bridgwater*

ENFLAME 3 b.f. Mtoto 134 – Eternal Flame 73 (Primo Dominie 121) [2007 f6g   –
Feb 20] 800Y: ninth foal: half-sister to fairly useful 9.4f and 1¼m winner Diamond Flame (by Suave Dancer): dam 7f/8.5f winner: 50/1, tailed off in maiden at Southwell, looking awkward. *T. T. Clement*

ENFORCE (USA) 4 b. or br.f. Kalanisi (IRE) 132 – Kinetic Force (USA) (Holy Bull   **94**
(USA) 134) [2007 9m⁶ 10.1s⁶ p8m⁵ 10.3m⁴ Nov 10] good-topped filly: second foal: half-sister to 2004 2-y-o 1m winner Sand Fairy (by Desert King), later 6f/7f winner in South Africa: dam, fairly useful French maiden who stayed 7.5f, half-sister to very smart French/US 7f to 1¼m performer Mizzen Mast: fairly useful performer: won twice in 2006 for Mme C. Head-Maarek (sold 105,000 gns after final start): winning hurdler for Mrs L. Wadham: creditable efforts in listed races last 2 starts: stays 1¼m: acts on polytrack, good to firm and good to soft ground: has had 2 handlers: sold 65,000 gns. *E. A. L. Dunlop*

ENGLISH ARCHER 4 b.g. Rock City 120 – Fire Sprite 83 (Mummy's Game 120)   **55**
[2007 50: 11.5d⁶ 10.9d⁶ 10.9d 11.1d* 11.1m⁶ 12g² 12m 12.4d 11.9g 12g Oct 30] leggy gelding: modest handicapper: won apprentice event at Hamilton in July: stays 1½m: acts on good to firm and good to soft ground: tried in cheekpieces. *W. M. Brisbourne*

ENGLISH CITY (IRE) 4 ch.c. City On A Hill (USA) 114 – Toledana (IRE) (Sure   –
Blade (USA) 130) [2007 61: 12m Jul 24] sturdy colt: modest performer at 3 yrs: well held only start in 2007: stays 10.3f: acts on firm and good to soft going (well below form both starts on polytrack): fair hurdler. *Mrs L. B. Normile*

ENJOY THE BUZZ 8 b.h. Prince of Birds (USA) 121 – Abaklea (IRE) (Doyoun 124)   **50**
[2007 61, a45: 6m 5.1m 6.1g⁶ 5.3m⁶ 5.7g 5s⁶ 5.1g⁶ 5m 6m 6d 6m 5.1m 5.7d 8m Oct 14] small, sturdy horse: modest handicapper: effective at 5f/6f: acts on all-weather, firm and soft going: wears cheekpieces nowadays: held up. *J. M. Bradley*

ENJOY THE MOMENT 4 b.g. Generous (IRE) 139 – Denial (Sadler's Wells (USA)   **108**
132) [2007 98: 12g 18.7m³ 20m 21.7s* 16d 18m⁴ 18d Oct 20] sturdy gelding: useful performer: second outing in 5 days, improved form when winning Queen Alexandra Stakes at Royal Ascot (by 3 lengths from Baddam) in June: better than result all starts

Queen Alexandra Stakes, Royal Ascot—Enjoy The Moment proves well suited by the step up in trip and shows improved form to win in good style from Baddam and Golden Quest

after, meeting plenty of trouble when fourth to Desert Sea in handicap at Doncaster: stays 2¾m: acts on soft and good to firm going: didn't seem to handle track at Epsom on reappearance. *J. A. Osborne*

ENODOC 2 b.g. (Mar 12) Efisio 120 – Raindrop 59 (Primo Dominie 121) [2007 5f 5m* 5g⁵ 5m 5g p5m⁴ 7m 5d p5m Oct 6] stocky, compact gelding: fourth foal: half-brother to 4-y-o Kasumi and 3-y-o Glencal: dam maiden: fairly useful performer: won maiden at Goodwood in May: lost form second half of season: best at 5f: acts on good to firm going: tried tongue tied: gelded after final start. *W. R. Muir* **80 d**

ENROLLER (IRE) 2 b.c. (Apr 28) Marju (IRE) 127 – Walk On Quest (FR) (Rainbow Quest (USA) 134) [2007 7m 8.1s⁵ 8d⁴ Oct 11] 37,000F, 26,000Y: leggy, close-coupled colt: fourth foal: half-brother to fairly useful Irish 1m winner Polish Odyssey (by Polish Precedent): dam French 11.5f winner: fair maiden: fourth to Robby Bobby at Newbury: will be suited by 1¼m/1½m. *W. R. Muir* **76**

ENSIGN'S TRICK 3 b.f. Cayman Kai (IRE) 114 – River Ensign 63 (River God (USA) 121) [2007 72§: 7.5m 6m³ 6.1m* 5.7d 6.1g² 6m 6d⁶ 5d⁵ 7d 6.1m 7g Sep 22] smallish, strong filly: fair handicapper: won at Chepstow in May: best form at 6f: acts on good to firm going: races prominently: unreliable. *W. M. Brisbourne* **66 §**

ENTHRALLED 4 b. or br.f. Zafonic (USA) 130 – Artifice 80 (Green Desert (USA) 127) [2007 f6g⁶ Jan 2] first foal: dam, 6f winner, sister to smart 7f/1m performer Ardkinglass: 11/2 and green, well held in maiden at Southwell: sold 16,000 gns in December (in foal to Royal Applause). *Sir Mark Prescott* **–**

ENTHUSIUS 4 b.g. Generous (IRE) 139 – Edouna (FR) (Doyoun 124) [2007 –: p12g* p10g⁴ 12m p16g³ Dec 4] lengthy gelding: modest performer, lightly raced: won handicap at Lingfield in February: ran well at same course final start (won over hurdles in June): stays 2m: acts on polytrack. *G. L. Moore* **62 +**

ENTICING (IRE) 3 b.f. Pivotal 124 – Superstar Leo (IRE) 114 (College Chapel 122) [2007 104: 5.1f* 5m⁵ 5g⁴ 5g² 5.2m² Sep 22] compact filly: smart performer: won listed race at Bath (by 5 lengths from Folga) in May: runner-up after in King George Stakes at Goodwood (beaten 2 lengths by Moorhouse Lad) and listed race at Newbury (½ length behind Rowe Park): will prove best at bare 5f: acts on polytrack, probably best on good going or firmer on turf: nervy sort, wears earplugs in preliminaries/usually early to post/has been mounted on course: reportedly in season when below form third start. *W. J. Haggas* **113**

ENTRANCED 4 b.f. Saddlers' Hall (IRE) 126 – Vent d'Aout (IRE) (Imp Society **56**
(USA)) [2007 69: 9.2g 7.1m 7.9m p8.6g Jul 2] lengthy filly: modest handicapper nowadays: races freely, and barely stays 1½m: acts on polytrack, unraced on extremes of going
on turf. *L. Lungo*

ENTRE CHAT 3 b.f. Green Desert (USA) 127 – Dance Sequence (USA) 105 (Mr **59**
Prospector (USA)) [2007 8m 8.2g 7.5g⁶ 8m⁵ p10.7g Sep 27] 65,000 2-y-o: compact filly:
sixth foal: closely related to 5-y-o Hornpipe and half-sister to 2 winners, including useful
1¼m/1½m winner Sequential (by Rainbow Quest): dam 2-y-o 6f (Lowther Stakes)
winner who stayed 1m: modest form in maidens: left M. Botti after third start: stays
10.7f: raced only on polytrack and good/good to firm ground: tongue tied first 3 outings.
P. F. Cashman, Ireland

ENVISAGE (IRE) 3 b.g. Singspiel (IRE) 133 – Truly A Dream (IRE) 116 (Darshaan **93 p**
133) [2007 10d* 12g⁶ Oct 27] 250,000Y: good-bodied gelding: half-brother to several
winners, notably smart Irish 1m winner Catcher In The Rye (by Danehill): dam, won at
1m (at 2 yrs) to 1½m in France and Canada, half-sister to smart 15f winner Wareed:
highly encouraging debut when winning maiden at Nottingham in October by 2½ lengths
from Heavenward, finishing full of running: still green, not discredited when sixth to
Night Hour in handicap at Doncaster next time, held up in tactical race: gelded after:
probably remains capable of better. *Saeed bin Suroor*

EPHESIAN (IRE) 2 b.f. (Mar 16) Efisio 120 – Maddie G (USA) (Blush Rambler **–**
(USA) 119) [2007 5m p5.1g 5d 5d p5.1g 8m⁶ Oct 14] €47,000F, €19,000Y: small,
close-coupled filly: second foal: dam, ran once in USA, half-sister to dam of high-class
7f/1m performer Le Vie dei Colori: little form: left Mrs A. Duffield after fourth start.
C. L. Popham

EPHORUS (USA) 2 b.c. (Apr 25) Galileo (IRE) 134 – No Frills (IRE) 62 (Darshaan **63 p**
133) [2007 p8.6g Nov 17] $320,000Y: third foal: half-brother to useful US 1m/9f winner
Singalong and fairly useful 1¼m/11f winner Potentiale, both by Singspiel: dam, ran
twice, sister to useful French winner up to 1¼m Bubbling Heights: 5/2, eighth in
maiden at Wolverhampton, unable to quicken and not knocked about: should improve.
Sir Michael Stoute

European Breeders' Fund Lansdown Fillies' Stakes, Bath—
Enticing is an impressive winner of this listed event from Folga (rail) and Empress Jain (second left)

EPICES 5 b.g. Mtoto 134 – French Spice 85 (Cadeaux Genereux 131) [2007 –: p7.1g – Jan 13] little form after 2 yrs: tried in cheekpieces/blinkers: dead. *R. Ingram*

EPICUREAN 5 ch.m. Pursuit of Love 124 – Arminda (Blakeney 126) [2007 71: 9.9m **52** 10.1d⁵ 10.4m Sep 9] lengthy, quite good-topped mare: fair at best, only modest nowadays: stays 1¼m: acts on soft and good to firm going: tried blinkered/in cheekpieces. *Mrs K. Walton*

EPIDAURIAN KING (IRE) 4 b.g. King's Best (USA) 132 – Thurayya (Nashwan **62** (USA) 135) [2007 –: p5.1g p6g p7.1g³ f8g p5.1g p7g p7g p8g⁴ p7g* Dec 30] modest handicapper: won at Lingfield in December: should prove best at 6f/7f: acts on polytrack: visored last 2 starts. *D. Shaw*

EPSOM SALTS 2 b.g. (Mar 20) Josr Algarhoud (IRE) 118 – Captive Heart (Conquis- **54** tador Cielo (USA)) [2007 7d p6g p5g Nov 15] sturdy gelding: modest maiden: bred to stay at least 1m. *P. M. Phelan*

EQUILIBRIA (USA) 5 b.g. Gulch (USA) – Julie La Rousse (IRE) 114 (Lomond **49** (USA) 128) [2007 59: p11g⁴ p16.5g 16.4m Jul 12] modest at best, only poor in 2007: effective at 1½m, barely stays 16.4f: acts on all-weather, firm and good to soft ground: tried visored. *G. L. Moore*

EQUULEUS PICTOR 3 br.g. Piccolo 121 – Vax Rapide 80 (Sharpo 132) [2007 64: **76** 5.7g 6d⁴ 6v 6m 6g 6.1d⁴ 6d⁴ Oct 30] tall gelding: fair handicapper: won at Ayr in July: stays 6f, should prove at least as effective at 5f: acts on good to soft ground (well held on heavy). *J. L. Spearing*

ERADICATE (IRE) 3 b.g. Montjeu (IRE) 137 – Coyote 91 (Indian Ridge 123) [2007 **105** 10.1s² 10m³ 10.2f* 10d² 11.9m* 12g⁴ 12m 12g 12d 10m⁶ 10m⁴ Oct 5] 160,000Y: sturdy, quite attractive gelding: second foal: dam, 1m winner, out of smart 1m/1¼m winner Caramba: useful performer: won maiden at Bath in May and handicap at Haydock (beat Philatelist by 2 lengths) in June: ran well under top weight when fourth to Heron Bay in King George V Stakes (Handicap) at Royal Ascot next time: stays 1½m: acts on firm and good to soft going, shaped well on soft on debut: races prominently: gelded. *M. Johnston*

ERGO (FR) 3 br.c. Grand Lodge (USA) 125 – Erhawah (Mark of Esteem (IRE) 137) **73** [2007 a10g 10.5v 10.6g³ 10.6s⁶ 13.5d⁴ 11g* 12d* 10d³ 12d² 16.1g Oct 3] second foal: closely related to winner in Spain by Erhaab: dam, French maiden, out of sister to US Grade 1 9f/1¼m winner Maplejinsky and close relation to outstanding sprinter Dayjur: won minor event at Oraison and handicap at Salon-de-Provence in May: left J-M. Capitte in France before well held in handicap on British debut at Newcastle (visored) final outing: stays 1½m: raced only on good ground or softer on turf: has been blinkered, including for both wins. *James Moffatt*

ERIDANI (IRE) 3 ch.f. Daggers Drawn (USA) 114 – Rorkes Drift (IRE) 55 (Royal – Abjar (USA) 121) [2007 –: 10g 11.5g Jul 23] little sign of ability. *M. L. W. Bell*

ERIN THOMAS (IRE) 2 ch.f. (Feb 1) High Yield (USA) 121 – Lyric Theatre (USA) **42** (Seeking The Gold (USA)) [2007 p5g⁴ 5s 5.2f p5.1g⁶ p6g p6g p6g⁶ Oct 19] sixth foal: half-sister to 1m (at 2 yrs)/1¼m winner Lyrical Girl (by Orpen) and winner in Holland by Entrepreneur: dam unraced daughter of smart sprinter Lyric Fantasy: poor maiden: raced at 5f/6f: seemed amiss third start, in cheekpieces after. *M. G. Quinlan*

ERMINE GREY 6 gr.g. Wolfhound (USA) 126 – Impulsive Decision (IRE) 71 (Nom- **65** ination 125) [2007 68, a73: 10.2g 10m⁴ 8.1d² 10.2g³ 8.1v* 10m 10d³ 10.2f p7.1g⁶ p9.5g p8.6g⁶ Oct 2] rather leggy gelding: fair handicapper: won at Haydock in July: stays 1¼m: acts on all-weather and any turf going: sometimes wears headgear/takes strong hold. *A. W. Carroll*

ERNIE OWL (USA) 2 b.c. (Apr 14) Tale of The Cat (USA) 113 – Capitol View (USA) **93** (Sports View (USA)) [2007 6m 6m* 7.1m 8m⁵ p8m⁵ p6g² 6g Oct 27] $160,000Y, $425,000 2-y-o: well-made colt: second foal: dam, US 6f (including minor stakes and at 2 yrs)/7f winner, out of half-sister to US Grade 1 winner up to 1¼m Play Fellow: fairly useful performer: won maiden at Yarmouth in August: ran well only all-weather starts, in minor events at Kempton and Lingfield (second to Kylayne): effective from 6f to easy 1m: acts on polytrack and good to firm going: below form in cheekpieces: sold 58,000 gns, sent to USA. *B. J. Meehan*

ERNMOOR 5 b.g. Young Ern 120 – Linpac North Moor 69 (Moorestyle 137) [2007 51: **51** p10g 9.7s³ 10.2m 8.3d⁶ p10g p12m Dec 8] workmanlike gelding: modest maiden: stays 1¼m: acts on polytrack, good to firm and soft going. *J. R. Jenkins*

ERRA GO ON 6 ch.g. Atraf 116 – Pastelle 52 (Tate Gallery (USA) 117) [2007 87: **80** p7.1g⁶ p7.1g 6m 7g⁴ 8g 8m 8m 7m⁴ 7g 16m Nov 4] good-topped gelding: fairly useful handicapper: ran at Wolverhampton first 2 starts in 2007, then left A. McGuinness: probably stays easy 2m: acts on polytrack, firm and good to soft going: blinkered once in 2006: usually tracks pace. *G. T. Lynch, Ireland*

ERRIGAL LAD 2 ch.g. (Feb 26) Bertolini (USA) 125 – La Belle Vie 73 (Indian King (USA) 128) [2007 6m² 6g* 6m Oct 5] 27,000F, 52,000Y: tall, good-topped gelding: half-brother to several winning sprinters, including 8-y-o Maktavish, 4-y-o Phantom Whisper and 3-y-o Ocean Blaze: dam 6f/7f winner: fairly useful form: won maiden at Haydock in September: further progress when mid-field in 28-runner sales race at Newmarket, prominent long way: gelded after: should prove best at 5f/6f: will do better still. *K. A. Ryan*
  86 p

ERTE 6 ch.g. Vettori (IRE) 119 – Cragreen (Green Desert (USA) 127) [2007 f12g 12m 16m⁵ 16g* 16m⁵ 16.1m 15.8g Sep 22] leggy, useful-looking gelding: modest handicapper: won at Thirsk in August: stays easy 2m: acts on polytrack and firm going: visored nowadays: none too consistent. *W. Storey*
  56

ESCAPE ROUTE (USA) 3 b.g. Elusive Quality (USA) – Away (USA) (Dixieland Band (USA)) [2007 87p: 7m³ p7g³ 7g⁶ 9m* 9m Oct 6] strong gelding: useful handicapper: won at Goodwood in September by length from Formax: drawn wide when below form in Cambridgeshire at Newmarket next time: stays 9f: raced only on polytrack and good/good to firm going: has twice been withdrawn after giving trouble at stall. *J. H. M. Gosden*
  105

ESCAYOLA (IRE) 7 b.g. Revoque (IRE) 122 – First Fling (IRE) 63 (Last Tycoon 131) [2007 91: 16g⁴ 16s 16.2m Jun 9] good-topped gelding: fairly useful handicapper: stayed 2¼m: acted on polytrack, firm and soft going: visored/blinkered: sometimes tongue tied: tended to hang left: held up: dead. *Grant Tuer*
  93

ESCLARMONDE (IRE) 3 b.f. In The Wings 128 – Questina (FR) (Rainbow Quest (USA) 134) [2007 9.9d 12.1s⁶ 10.2g⁴ 12m² 13.1f⁶ 16g 11.9d³ p12.2g² p12.2g³ p10g⁴ Dec 30] sister to smart French 9f (at 2 yrs) to 10.5f winner Trumbaka and half-sister to useful French 1m/1¼m winner Arctic Hunt (by Bering): dam fairly useful French 1¼m winner: fair maiden: should stay beyond 1½m: acts on polytrack, good to firm and good to soft ground: visored/blinkered end of year. *L. M. Cumani*
  79

ESCOBAR (POL) 6 b.g. Royal Court (IRE) 116 – Escola (POL) (Dixieland (POL)) [2007 54: 12d p16g Dec 4] leggy, lengthy gelding: modest performer: reportedly had breathing problem final start: probably stays 1¼m: acts on polytrack: tried tongue tied/in cheekpieces. *Mrs P. Townsley*
  51

ESCOFFIER 5 b.g. Entrepreneur 123 – Gooseberry Pie 63 (Green Desert (USA) 127) [2007 63: p12g⁴ p12.2g³ p12.2g p13.9g p12.2g Nov 14] big gelding: modest performer: left Pat Eddery after reappearance, G. Bridgwater after next outing: stays easy 1½m: acts on polytrack: tried visored/tongue tied: sold £600. *M. Appleby*
  64

ESEEJ (USA) 2 ch.g. (Feb 27) Aljabr (USA) 125 – Jinaan (USA) 72 (Mr Prospector (USA)) [2007 6g 6m⁶ Sep 11] very big, good-bodied gelding: has powerful action: second foal: dam once-raced granddaughter of Salsabil: mid-division in maidens at York and Lingfield (sixth to Missit), refusing to settle: gelded after: type to improve at 3 yrs. *B. W. Hills*
  66 p

ESOTERICA (IRE) 4 b.g. Bluebird (USA) 125 – Mysterious Plans (IRE) (Last Tycoon 131) [2007 72: 7.1m 7.1m 7.1m 9g⁴ 9.1g⁴ 8m 7.1m² 7m* 8.1m⁵ 7.2g⁴ 7m* 8m* 7.2s⁴ 7.1m 8g⁵ 7.2s⁴ 7g⁴ 8g² Nov 9] useful-looking gelding: fair handicapper: won at Thirsk in August and Redcar and Thirsk in September: seems best at 7f/1m nowadays: acts on firm and good to soft going, probably on soft: has worn cheekpieces, usually blinkered nowadays: ridden patiently. *J. S. Goldie*
  79

ESPARTANO 3 b.g. Vettori (IRE) 119 – Talighta (USA) 62 (Barathea (IRE) 127) [2007 87: 6.1m 6v 6.5v 5s 5g 7g 7d Oct 1] tall, good-topped gelding: just fair at best in 2007, leaving M. Wallace after reappearance: effective at 5f/6f: acts on polytrack and good to firm going: inconsistent. *R. McGlinchey, Ireland*
  70

ESPECIALLY (IRE) 2 b.f. (Feb 13) Fantastic Light (USA) 134 – Esperada (ARG) (Equalize (USA)) [2007 7d⁴ 7d³ p8g p7g f7d* Dec 18] rather leggy filly: fourth foal: half-sister to 3 winners, including fairly useful 7f (at 2 yrs)/7.5f (in UAE) winner Esquire (by Dubai Millennium) and French 6.8f winner Awaited (by Machiavellian): dam champion 2-y-o filly in only season to race in Argentina: fair performer: won nursery at Southwell in December: should stay 1m+: acts on fibresand and good to soft going, below form on polytrack. *M. Johnston*
  69 +

ESPEJO (IRE) 3 b.g. City On A Hill (USA) 114 – Beechwood Quest (IRE) 65 (River **61**
Falls 113) [2007 79: 8f 7.1d 7s 7g 8.3s⁶ 8.1d⁶ Aug 16] lengthy gelding: modest maiden:
left K. R. Burke after fourth outing: should prove as good at 6f as 7f: acts on good to firm
going: tried visored/in cheekpieces. *W. J. Musson*

ESPOIR DE LUMIERE 3 b.f. Mark of Esteem (IRE) 137 – Lumiere d'Espoir (FR) **–**
81 (Saumarez 132) [2007 10g May 18] lengthy filly: second foal: half-sister to 4-y-o Sahf
London: dam, 1¼m to 14.6f winner, out of sister to Alzao: 100/1 and backward, well-held
tenth to Ajhar in maiden at Newbury, soon in rear. *C. F. Wall*

ESPRIT DE CORPS 5 b.g. Hernando (FR) 127 – Entente Cordiale (USA) (Affirmed **79**
(USA)) [2007 84: 21g⁴ 16d Oct 11] rangy gelding: fairly useful handicapper for Sir Mark
Prescott at 4 yrs: better effort on Flat in 2007 when respectable fourth at Goodwood: stays
21f: acts on soft and good to firm ground, probably on polytrack: quirky: fairly useful
hurdler. *P. J. Hobbs*

ESPRIT DE NUIT (IRE) 3 b.g. Invincible Spirit (IRE) 121 – Night Spirit (IRE) 78 **–**
(Night Shift (USA)) [2007 48?: f6g 5m 6m 5d Jun 23] little form: tried visored/blinkered.
Mrs A. Duffield

ESTABLISHMENT 10 b.g. Muhtarram (USA) 125 – Uncharted Waters 68 (Celestial **72**
Storm (USA) 132) [2007 89: p16g 16m p16g 15.9d⁶ 18s³ Jul 28] smallish, workmanlike
gelding: just fair handicapper in 2007, leaving C. Cyzer after third start: seems to stay
2¾m: acts on polytrack, firm and soft going: blinkered twice: sometimes sweats/races
freely: held up. *John A. Harris*

ESTATE 5 b.g. Montjeu (IRE) 137 – Fig Tree Drive (USA) 94 (Miswaki (USA) 124) **86**
[2007 10.1g 16s* p16.5g* 14.6g 16g* p16.5g⁴ p16.5g² Nov 19] close-coupled ex-Irish
gelding: fairly useful hurdler: improved into fairly useful handicapper on Flat in 2007,
winning at Goodwood (National Hunt Jockeys event) and Wolverhampton in October
and Musselburgh in November: stays 16.5f: acts on polytrack, soft and good to firm
ground: tried blinkered/tongue tied: joined D. Pipe. *E. J. O'Neill*

ESTEEM 4 b.g. Mark of Esteem (IRE) 137 – Please (Kris 135) [2007 79: 8m p8g Jul 4] **75**
good-topped gelding: fair performer: will be suited by 1¼m: acts on polytrack: quirky:
joined D. Bridgwater. *W. Jarvis*

ESTEEMED PRINCE 3 b.g. Mark of Esteem (IRE) 137 – Princess Alaska (Northern **46**
State (USA) 91) [2007 62: f7g 6g⁶ 7m p7.1g p6m⁵ p5.1g⁶ Sep 27] poor maiden: should be
suited by 1m. *D. Shaw*

ESTEEM MACHINE (USA) 3 b.c. Mark of Esteem (IRE) 137 – Theme (IRE) **97**
(Sadler's Wells (USA) 132) [2007 p6g³ p7g⁴ p7g² 8g⁵ 7d² 7g² 7g* 6m² 6d* 6m² 6d³ 6s
Oct 14] $60,000Y: strong, lengthy colt: half-brother to 3 winners, including fairly useful
1¼m winner Drakensberg (by Bering): dam once-raced half-sister to smart performer up
to 1½m Potemkin: useful performer: left D. Elsworth after sixth start: won maiden at
Lingfield in July and handicap at Newmarket in August: good short-head second to Mac
Gille Eoin in handicap at Goodwood next time: winner at 7f, but should prove best at 5f/
6f: acts on good to firm and good to soft going. *R. A. Teal*

ESTHLOS (FR) 4 ch.g. Limnos (JPN) 124 – Cozzie 60 (Cosmonaut) [2007 79: p8.6g **93**
p8.6g* 10.1s* f8g³ 12m⁶ 12d* 12s³ Oct 19] workmanlike gelding: fairly useful handicapper: won at Wolverhampton and Newcastle in March and York (apprentice event) in
October: stays 1½m: acts on all-weather, soft and good to firm ground. *J. Jay*

ESTIMATOR 3 b.c. Auction House (USA) 120 – Fresh Look (IRE) 64 (Alzao (USA) **74**
117) [2007 79p: 6g 6g p6g⁶ p6g Oct 15] strong colt: fair performer: likely to stay 7f: acts
on polytrack: tried blinkered: sold 800 gns. *Pat Eddery*

ESTOILLE 6 b.m. Paris House 123 – Nampara Bay 50 (Emarati (USA) 74) [2007 59: **47**
f6g f6g⁶ f5g³ f5g f5g Mar 15] leggy mare: modest performer at best: only poor in 2007:
was effective at 5f/6f: acted on all-weather, firm and good to soft going: had been tongue
tied: dead. *Mrs S. Lamyman*

ETAIN (IRE) 3 b.f. Alhaarth (IRE) 126 – Brogan's Well (IRE) (Caerleon (USA) 132) **78**
[2007 p7.1g³ 8.2g 8g⁴ 10s* 10m⁶ Jul 28] 13,000F, €45,000Y: good-topped filly: fifth
foal: half-sister to 3 winners, including fairly useful 1m (at 2 yrs) to 1½m winner Liquid
Form (by Bahhare) and 1¼m winner Joint Destiny (by Desert Prince): dam unraced
half-sister to useful Irish stayer Easy To Please: fair performer: won handicap at Windsor
in June: will be suited by 1½m: best effort on soft going. *W. R. Swinburn*

ET DONA FERENTES 4 b.f. Green Desert (USA) 127 – Sister Golden Hair (IRE) **61**
(Glint of Gold 128) [2007 58: f6g⁶ p7.1g² f8s* p8.6g³ Feb 21] modest performer: won

handicap at Southwell in February: probably stays 9.5f: acts on all-weather and good to soft going: hung right final outing. *T. D. Barron*

ETERNAL LEGACY (IRE) 5 b.m. Monashee Mountain (USA) 115 – Tender Time (Tender King 123) [2007 59: 6m 6g⁴ 6g² 5.9g⁶ 7v* 6g 8d³ 6.9m⁵ 8.1m 6.9g² 7g⁴ 6v 7.2v² Nov 3] leggy, lengthy mare: fair performer: won maiden at Newcastle in June: barely stays 1m: acts on heavy and good to firm ground: usually races prominently. *E. J. Alston* **65**

ETERNAL LUCK (IRE) 2 b.c. (Jan 19) Tagula (IRE) 116 – Erne Project (IRE) 80 (Project Manager 111) [2007 6m* 6s⁷ Jun 28] 42,000Y: sturdy, attractive colt: fifth foal: brother to 5-y-o Beaver Patrol and to winner up to 1m in Italy: dam 13f winner in Ireland: fairly useful form: won maiden at Windsor in June: much improved when second to Montaquila in minor event at Newcastle: suffered injury after: likely to stay 1m. *M. A. Jarvis* **90**

ETERNALLY 5 ch.g. Timeless Times (USA) 99 – Nice Spice (IRE) (Common Grounds 118) [2007 50: f5g Jan 16] leggy gelding: modest performer: best at 5f: acts on fibresand and firm ground: wears cheekpieces/visor. *R. M. H. Cowell* **50**

ETERNAL OPTIMIST (IRE) 2 b.f. (Feb 16) Bahri (USA) 125 – Shore Lark (USA) (Storm Bird (CAN) 134) [2007 5g 5g 5m 5m 7m³ 7.1g⁶ p7.1g p8.6g⁵ p8.6g⁶ p8.6g³ Dec 3] €5,000Y: close-coupled filly: sixth foal: half-sister to 3 winners, including 5-y-o Perfect Story and fairly useful 2001 2-y-o 5f/6f winner Lake Verdi (by Lake Coniston): dam unraced half-sister to smart sprinter Tipsy Creek: modest maiden: stays 8.6f: acts on polytrack and good to firm going. *C. W. Thornton* **57**

ETERNAL PATH (USA) 3 ch.f. Theatrical 128 – Houdini's Honey (USA) 84 (Mr Prospector (USA)) [2007 83p: 10m³ 9.9d⁴ May 17] rangy, useful-looking filly: fairly useful maiden: easily better effort at 3 yrs when third at Newbury: took strong hold and hung away from whip next time: should be suited by 1¼m/1½m: sold 92,000 gns in December. *Sir Michael Stoute* **85**

ETHEREAL FLAME 2 b.f. (Jan 24) Red Ransom (USA) – Running Flame (IND) (Steinbeck (USA) 119) [2007 8.2m 8d Oct 23] rangy filly: second foal: dam Indian 1000 Guineas/Oaks winner: much better effort in maidens when seventh at Yarmouth, fading: should continue to progress. *H. R. A. Cecil* **66 p**

ETOILE D'OR (IRE) 3 ch.f. Soviet Star (USA) 128 – Christeningpresent (IRE) (Cadeaux Genereux 131) [2007 70: 10m 8d 10.1g⁶ 12.4m 12m⁶ 10d² 11.5d* Oct 23] workmanlike filly: fair performer: won seller at Yarmouth (sold 12,000 gns, joined M. Gingell) in October by 14 lengths from Ful of Grace, making all and eased: stays 11.5f: acts on soft going, probably on good to firm: has raced freely. *M. H. Tompkins* **65**

ETOILE RUSSE (IRE) 5 b.g. Soviet Star (USA) 128 – To The Skies (USA) 89 (Sky Classic (CAN)) [2007 69: 15.8m Apr 4] big, good-topped gelding: maiden handicapper: well held sole outing on Flat in 2007: stays 1¼m: acts on fibresand and good to firm ground: tongue tied: races freely: winning hurdler/chaser. *P. C. Haslam* **–**

ETON FABLE (IRE) 2 b.c. (Apr 7) Val Royal (FR) 127 – Lina Story (Linamix (FR) 127) [2007 6s⁵ 7.5g 8g⁴ 8m 8.2g⁵ Oct 31] workmanlike colt: modest maiden: dictated and probably flattered when fifth at Nottingham final start: stays 1m. *W. J. H. Ratcliffe* **63**

ETOSHA (IRE) 2 b.c. (Apr 3) Cape Cross (IRE) 129 – Zibilene 101 (Rainbow Quest (USA) 134) [2007 6d Oct 19] 340,000Y: lengthy colt: fourth foal: half-brother to smart French 6f (at 2 yrs) to 7.5f winner Mathematician (by Machiavellian) and fairly useful 1¼m winner Aryaamm (by Galileo): dam, 1½m winner, half-sister to Barathea and Gossamer: 7/1, more encouragement than bare result (seventh to Insaaf) in maiden at Newmarket, stuck well throughout and tiring: will stay at least 1m: sure to improve. *Saeed bin Suroor* **69 p**

ETRUSCAN (IRE) 2 b.g. (Feb 1) Selkirk (USA) 129 – Maddelina (IRE) 54 (Sadler's Wells (USA) 132) [2007 8.2d² 8.2g Oct 31] 190,000Y: good-topped gelding: third foal: half-brother to fairly useful 1¾m winner Merayaat (by Darshaan): dam, ran 3 times, out of useful close relative to Derby winner Generous and half-sister to Oaks winner Imagine: fair form, but signs of temperament, in maidens at Nottingham, second to Patkai on debut: will stay 1¼m: gelded after final start. *Saeed bin Suroor* **76**

ETTRBEE (IRE) 5 b. or br.m. Lujain (USA) 119 – Chief Ornament (USA) 88 (Chief's Crown (USA)) [2007 f7g f12g May 1] 5,000 2-y-o: half-sister to 3 winners abroad, including UAE 7f winner Takteek (by Machiavellian): dam 8.5f/1¼m winner: well held in bumpers, and in sellers at Southwell. *H. Alexander* **–**

ETXALAR (FR) 4 b.g. Kingsalsa (USA) 118 – Tender To Love (Old Vic 136) [2007 12.4d Oct 16] modest form in 2 claimers for E. Lellouche in France at 3 yrs: well held **–**

in maiden at Newcastle only outing on Flat in 2007: stays 1½m: tried blinkered. *Miss Lucinda V. Russell*

EUMENE (IRE) 4 ch.g. Grand Lodge (USA) 125 – Pelagic (Rainbow Quest (USA) **96** 134) [2007 p11g⁴ p12.2g² Dec 14] useful performer: trained in France by J-C. Rouget at 3 yrs, winning minor event at Tarbes: sold €125,000 after final start that year and gelded: modest form at best over hurdles prior to creditable efforts both starts on Flat in Britain, 1¾ lengths second of 4 to Invasian in handicap at Wolverhampton: stays 1½m: acts on polytrack. *C. C. Bealby*

EUROPEAN DREAM (IRE) 4 br.g. Kalanisi (IRE) 132 – Tereed Elhawa 75 (Cade- **112** aux Genereux 131) [2007 92: 8s* 8m 10.3m6* 8g* 8d* 8s 8.9s* 8g Nov 3] close-coupled gelding: progressed into smart handicapper in 2007, winning at Newcastle in March, Ripon in May, Redcar in June and York (best effort when beating Greek Envoy by neck) in July: well held in listed event at Newmarket final outing: stays 9f: acts on soft and good to firm going: has worn cheekpieces, including last 3 wins: waited with. *R. C. Guest*

EVA SONEVA SO FAST (IRE) 5 ch.g. In The Wings 128 – Azyaa 101 (Kris 135) **85** [2007 94: p12g* p12g² p12.2g² p13g⁴ p12g⁴ 14g 12s 12m 12m⁵ 13.3m 10d p12g* Oct 15] **a99** sturdy gelding: has a quick action: useful handicapper on all-weather, fairly useful on turf: won at Lingfield in January and October: should stay 1¾m: acts on polytrack and good to firm ground: sold 48,000 gns. *J. L. Dunlop*

EVA'S REQUEST (IRE) 2 ch.f. (May 6) Soviet Star (USA) 128 – Ingabelle 108 (Tau- **94 +** fan (USA) 119) [2007 5.1m p6g* p7g⁴ 7f⁵ 7g³ 7m 7d* Sep 20] €150,000Y: leggy filly: sister to Irish 2003 2-y-o 6f winner Soviet Belle and half-sister to several winners, includ- ing smart Irish 6f/7f winner Wild Bluebell (by Bluebird) and useful Irish 1995 2-y-o 6f/7f (Moyglare Stud Stakes) winner Priory Belle (by Priolo): dam won Phoenix Sprint Stakes: fairly useful form: won maiden at Kempton in June and 12-runner C. L. Weld Park Stakes at the Curragh (improved to beat Kyniska by length) in September: third to Sense of Joy in Prestige Stakes at Goodwood: will stay 1m: acts on polytrack and good to soft going, probably on firm. *M. R. Channon*

EVEN BOLDER 4 ch.g. Bold Edge 123 – Level Pegging (IRE) 48 (Common Grounds **82** 118) [2007 72: 5g⁴ 5d p5g⁴ p6g⁵ p6g* p5g² 5g² 5.7f² Sep 16] strong, workmanlike gelding: fairly useful performer: won maiden at Kempton in August: best at 5f/easy 6f: acts on polytrack and firm ground, no form on softer than good: in cheekpieces after reappearance. *R. Simpson*

EVENING AFFAIR 3 b.f. Kingmambo (USA) 125 – Neptune's Bride (USA) 110 **68** (Bering 136) [2007 8.1d³ 9.9m* Aug 26] rather leggy filly: third foal: closely related to useful French 6f and 7.5f winner Poseidon's Bride (by Seeking The Gold): dam French 1m/1¼m winner: fair form: 3/1 and still green, won maiden at Beverley in August by head from Muqadam, making most but edging left under pressure: stays easy 1¼m: left Godolphin, and sent to USA. *Saeed bin Suroor*

EVENING TIME (IRE) 3 gr.f. Keltos (FR) 132 – Shadow Casting 72 (Warning 136) **117** [2007 114p: 7v³ 6s* 6v² 8m 6d⁶ Sep 30] medium-sized, useful-looking filly: smart performer: won listed contest at Leopardstown in July by 5 lengths from Lidanski: creditable 1¼ lengths second to Al Qasi in Phoenix Sprint Stakes at the Curragh next time: below form after in Matron Stakes at Leopardstown and listed race won by US Ranger at the Curragh: likely to prove best at 5f/6f: acts well on soft/heavy going. *Kevin Prendergast, Ireland*

EVENS AND ODDS (IRE) 3 ch.c. Johannesburg (USA) 127 – Coeur de La Mer **101** (IRE) 87 (Caerleon (USA) 132) [2007 96+: p7g³ 8m 7m⁶ 7d p8g³ p7m p8m p8g³ Dec 22] lengthy, useful-looking colt: useful performer: creditable third at Lingfield in listed race (to Hinton Admiral, beaten 1¼ lengths), handicap (behind Military Cross) and minor event (to Jack Sullivan): stays 1m: acts on polytrack, firm and good to soft going: in cheekpieces/blinkers last 3 outings. *K. A. Ryan*

EVENSTORM (USA) 2 ch.f. (Mar 14) Stephen Got Even (USA) 125 – Summer Wind **60** Storm (USA) (Storm Cat (USA)) [2007 5g 6m³ 5g⁵ 5m p6g⁶ p6g 6m p5g³ 5m p6g Dec 30] $70,000Y: rather sparely-made filly: first foal: dam, US 6.5f winner, half-sister to top- class Breeders' Cup Classic winner Skip Away: modest maiden: raced at 5f/6f: acts on polytrack and good to firm going: edgy type. *B. Gubby*

EVENT MUSIC (IRE) 3 ch.f. Distant Music (USA) 126 – Evening Set (GER) 95 **65** (Second Set (IRE) 127) [2007 77: 8.3m 7.1d⁴ 7s 7g Jun 12] neat filly: fair handicapper: seems to stay 1m: acts on good to firm going, probably on good to soft: sold 4,000 gns in July. *M. R. Channon*

EVER CHEERFUL 6 b.g. Atraf 116 – Big Story 50 (Cadeaux Genereux 131) [2007 **55 +** 81: p6g p6g⁴ p6g⁴ p6g⁵ p7g² 6s³ 6m⁶ p6g 5.7m 5.3d p6g³ p7m* p7g² p6g² p6m³ p6g³ **a71** Dec 12] workmanlike mover: fluent mover: fair performer on all-weather, modest on turf: left D. Bridgwater after fourth start: won handicap at Lingfield in November: effective at 5f to easy 7f: acts on all-weather and firm going, probably on soft: tried tongue tied, has worn cheekpieces/visor of late. *A. B. Haynes*

EVER DREAMING (USA) 2 b. or br.f. (Feb 22) Dynaformer (USA) – Slept Thru It **61** (USA) (Sunny's Halo (CAN)) [2007 7m 8g p8.6g⁶ Dec 14] $60,000Y: close-coupled filly: closely related/half-sister to several minor US winners, including 1m/1¼m winner Sleeping Potion (by Kingmambo): dam US 6f (at 2 yrs) to 9f winner (third in US 2-y-o Grade 2 1m/8.5f events): modest form in maidens at Newmarket and Goodwood and minor event at Wolverhampton. *A. M. Balding*

EVEREST (IRE) 10 ch.g. Indian Ridge 123 – Reine d'Beaute 97 (Caerleon (USA) **75** 132) [2007 87, a81: p8.6g 8m 8.1g 8d 9.9m³ 9.3g² 10.1v Jun 29] strong, deep-girthed gelding: won 11 of his 72 races on the Flat, showing useful form at his peak: just fair in 2007: barely stayed 1¼m: acted on polytrack and any turf going: tried in cheekpieces: was usually held up: died on gallops in July. *B. Ellison*

EVER HOPEFUL 2 br.f. (Mar 30) Noverre (USA) 125 – Heather Mix 84 (Linamix **67** (FR) 127) [2007 6m 5.7m⁶ 5.1d³ p6g 5m² 5.1d³ 5.1g Oct 24] lightly-made filly: third foal: half-sister to 7.6f (at 2 yrs) to 1¼m (in Germany) winner Spy Glass (by Observatory): dam, 10.5f winner, half-sister to smart miler Castleton: fair maiden: placed 3 times: may prove best kept to 5f/6f: acts on good to firm and good to soft going: sold 9,000 gns, sent to Kazakhstan. *H. J. L. Dunlop*

EVER SPECIAL (IRE) 4 b.g. Fruits of Love (USA) 127 – El Corazon (IRE) (Mujadil **–** (USA) 119) [2007 43: f14g Mar 15] big, leggy gelding: poor maiden at 3 yrs: well held sole run in 2007: probably stays 9.8f: acts on good to soft and good to firm going. *J. T. Stimpson*

EVERYBODY KNOWS 2 b.c. (Mar 22) King's Best (USA) 132 – Logic 94 (Slip **61 p** Anchor 136) [2007 p8g⁶ Sep 4] sixth living foal: half-brother to several winners, including 7-y-o Logsdail and 4-y-o Rationale: dam, maiden, half-sister to useful 1½m winner Port Helene: 10/1, not clear run when sixth in maiden at Lingfield: should do better. *M. L. W. Bell*

EVERYGRAINOFSAND (IRE) 4 b.g. Desert Sun 120 – Serious Delight (Lomond **83** (USA) 128) [2007 7g⁵ p7g⁴ p7g³ 6m² p7g⁴ 5g* 7m⁴ 6g* 6m⁵ p6g⁶ Sep 4] big, strong gelding: fairly useful performer: won maiden at Folkestone in June and handicap at Yarmouth in July: effective at 5f to 7f: acts on polytrack and good to firm going: often carries head awkwardly: races prominently/makes running: sold 15,000 gns. *J. R. Best*

EVERYMAN 3 gr.g. Act One 124 – Maid To Dance 62 (Pyramus (USA) 78) [2007 56§: **60 §** 8.1g 11.7d 10.9d⁵ 10.5m 12.1d³ 10d* 11.8g⁴ p12.2g⁴ p10g⁵ f11d Dec 11] big gelding: modest performer: won seller at Leicester in October: barely stays 11.8f: acts on soft going: tried blinkered (including when successful)/visored: ungenuine. *A. W. Carroll*

EVERYMANFORHIMSELF (IRE) 3 b.c. Fasliyev (USA) 120 – Luisa Demon **96** (IRE) (Barathea (IRE) 127) [2007 95: 7m 6g 6.1d⁵ 6m⁴ 7d 6m 6g³ 6m 6m* 6d⁴ 6s³ Oct 14] big, strong, good-topped colt: has scope: has quick action: useful handicapper: won at Leicester in September by 2½ lengths from Sacre Coeur: ran creditably after: should stay 7f: acts on soft and good to firm going: often blinkered: lazy sort, tends to get behind: sold 56,000 gns. *J. G. Given*

EVERYTHING 2 bl.f. (May 18) Namid 128 – Flight Sequence 88 (Polar Falcon (USA) **71** 126) [2007 5m 5d 5m⁴ 6m⁴ 6m³ Aug 28] 4,000Y: well-grown filly: half-sister to 3-y-o Plane Painter and winner in Jersey by Piccolo: dam 1¼m winner: fair maiden: third to Sophie's Girl in nursery at Ripon: better at 6f than 5f: acts on firm going. *P. T. Midgley*

EVETTE 2 b.f. (Feb 18) Loup Solitaire (USA) 117 – La Scarlet (FR) (Highest Honor **47** (FR) 124) [2007 p8g 7g⁶ 8g p8m⁵ Nov 11] 6,000Y: leggy filly: first foal: dam, fairly useful French 12.5f winner, half-sister to smart French 1½m performer La Hernanda and useful French 10.5f winner La Sabana (by Loup Solitaire): poor maiden: bred for middle distances. *M. Johnston*

EVIDENT PRIDE (USA) 4 b.g. Chester House (USA) 123 – Proud Fact (USA) 108 **106** (Known Fact (USA) 135) [2007 93: p10g² f8g p8g* 8.3m⁴ p8g² p8g³ p10g* p10g* Dec 16] strong, lengthy gelding: useful handicapper: won at Kempton in August, Lingfield in November and Kempton (further improvement when beating Northern Spy by 1¼ lengths) in December: stays easy 1¼m: acts on polytrack and good to firm going: tends to edge left: reliable. *B. R. Johnson*

EVITA 3 b.f. Selkirk (USA) 129 – Darara 129 (Top Ville 129) [2007 –p: 10g⁵ 10.9d⁴ **76** p12.2g² p12.2g p12.2d⁴ p9.5d³ Dec 17] big, good-bodied filly: fair maiden: unlikely to stay beyond 1½m: acts on polytrack: blinkered final start: possibly quirky. *L. M. Cumani*

EVOLUTION EX (USA) 5 b. or br.g. Bahri (USA) 125 – Zoe's Gold (USA) 77 (St **–** Jovite (USA) 135) [2007 68: f12g 8.5m 10s 9.9s Jun 21] close-coupled gelding: has a short, unimpressive action: fairly useful performer at best: no form in 2007: tried visored/ tongue tied. *I. W. McInnes*

EVOLVE (USA) 4 ch.f. With Approval (CAN) – Conical 63 (Zafonic (USA) 130) **55** [2007 –: p11g* p13.9g⁶ 12g Apr 3] tall filly: modest performer, lightly raced: won maiden **a64** at Kempton in January: stays easy 1¾m: raced on polytrack and good/good to firm going: looked quirky final outing. *M. Botti*

EXCAPE (IRE) 2 b.c. (Mar 25) Cape Cross (IRE) 129 – Viscaria (IRE) 97 (Barathea **70 p** (IRE) 127) [2007 6m 7d⁴ 7m Jul 11] 65,000Y: strong, sturdy colt: fourth foal: half-brother to 3-y-o Pivotalia: dam, Irish 7.8f (at 2 yrs)/1¼m winner, half-sister to smart performers Hathrah (at 1m) and Ivan Luis (up to 1½m): fair maiden: fourth to Unnefer at Newmarket: very upset in stall final outing: will be suited by 1m: type to do better in handicaps. *D. R. C. Elsworth*

EXCELLENT ART 3 b.c. Pivotal 124 – Obsessive (USA) 102 (Seeking The Gold **125** (USA)) [2007 114: 8g⁴ 8m* 8g² 8d² 8s² 8g Dec 9]

As investments go, the record sixteen million dollars spent on The Green Monkey (rechristened by some The White Elephant) at Calder early in 2006 is looking increasingly like a write-off. His record at the end of his three-year-old career stood at a third in a maiden at Belmont in September and fourth in similar events on the same track in October and at Hollywood Park on turf in November, for earnings of 10,440 dollars, or 0.06525 per cent of his price (though he is to be given a chance at stud in 2009). On the other side of the coin, whatever Coolmore paid to take a stake in Excellent Art has turned out to be money well spent. He improved by the best part of a stone to become one of the top milers in Europe, winning one Group 1 race and looking unlucky not to add a couple more. The dividends should continue to flow, since his form, looks, antecedents and the expert marketing associated with Coolmore ought to make him a decidedly popular stallion.

Excellent Art showed no shortage of ability as a two-year-old trained by Neville Callaghan, finishing third in the Prix Morny and winning the Mill Reef Stakes on the last two of his five starts. After making the switch to Ballydoyle over the winter, he bypassed the Two Thousand Guineas and reappeared in the Poule d'Essai des Poulains at Longchamp, almost eight months after the Mill Reef. Excellent Art had not shown any signs of idling in front, there seemed no reason on breeding or style of racing why he should not stay a mile, and there was no evidence from his races that he possessed a sharp turn of foot. Whatever the thinking (the fact that he was drawn thirteen of fourteen might have been a factor), he was waited with at Longchamp, and ran into all the bad luck going before coming fourth to his stable-companion Astronomer Royal. Excellent Art was last but one on the rail turning for home, was switched left after failing to get through, then moved sharply back towards the rail when a possible gap appeared there, making some progress before being stopped in his tracks. Excellent Art finally barged his way through, resulting in Jamie Spencer receiving a ten-day suspension. Excellent Art finished just under three lengths behind Astronomer Royal in fourth. Spencer's appeal against the ban was dismissed.

Plenty can go wrong for a jockey using waiting tactics, even on a performer with an electrifying turn of foot, available on demand in an instant at any time in a race, whatever the strength of the gallop. Such a quality is manifested in only a few horses, George Washington a recent example, but Dancing Brave arguably the one who comes most readily to mind from the last few decades. Being waited with enables such runners to be produced to unanswerable effect. This doesn't necessarily have to be in the final fifty yards, dramatic and thrilling as that may be, not least for the rider. Temperamental quirks can necessitate waiting tactics, for instance if a horse habitually starts slowly or, much rarer, refuses to get involved in proceedings until the race is more than half over—Knockroe in the 'seventies a memorable example of the latter. Again, with horses that tend to idle as soon as they hit the front, such as Red Evie and Literato, a late challenge is required almost as a matter of course. Stamina doubts provide another reason for holding up a horse. In all these instances, if the jockey chooses to keep his mount at the back of the field rather than in mid-division (a less risky position which, in truth, should be adopted more often than it is), then finding a clear and uninterrupted run seriously tests the rider's skill, as well as the heart rate of connections and punters. A slow or steady pace can make life harder for a runner coming from behind, and any horse who is waited with must be adaptable, as well as possessing a decisive turn of foot. Occasionally luck is needed too.

On the evidence of Longchamp, Excellent Art did indeed have the ability to quicken, but the St James's Palace Stakes at Royal Ascot—the colt missed the Irish Two Thousand Guineas because of a foot injury on the eve of the race—confirmed that this was not instantaneous. Indeed, it became a characteristic of Excellent Art's racing style that he took a bit of time to wind up to top speed once his rider asked the question, producing a long, raking run rather than a brilliant burst of speed. There is some doubt as to whether dropping him out at the back of the field was really the most sensible way of riding him. The tactic is one of Spencer's favourite ploys though, and one which he has used to great effect in his career. Wise or not, the tactic worked like a charm at the Royal meeting, where Excellent Art started at 8/1 (Astronomer Royal was 14/1) behind hot favourite Cockney Rebel, successful in the Two Thousand Guineas and its Irish equivalent. Dutch Art, third in the Two Thousand Guineas, was second choice and the other runners in a representative field included the second, third and fourth in the Irish Guineas, Creachadoir, He's A Decoy and, also from the Aidan O'Brien stable, Duke of Marmalade. Creachadoir had also finished second to Astronomer Royal at Longchamp. Kept at the back on the inside, Excellent Art began to make ground under pressure when asked to improve two furlongs out but had to be ridden firmly, given a couple of cracks of the whip, before coming through between Duke of Marmalade and Astronomer Royal. Excellent Art won by a neck from Duke of Marmalade, with Astronomer Royal a length and a quarter away third and Dutch Art fourth. Cockney Rebel in fifth was found to have suffered a pelvic stress fracture. This was the sixth time O'Brien had saddled the first three home in a Group 1 race, following the 2001 Irish Two Thousand Guineas, Dewhurst Stakes and Criterium de Saint-Cloud, and the 2002 Irish Two Thousand Guineas and Irish Derby. Later he added a seventh and eighth race to the tally in the Irish Derby and the Irish Champion Stakes.

Spencer regarded the St James's Palace Stakes as the highlight of what turned into a remarkable season for him which will be remembered for his battle with Seb Sanders for the Jockeys' Association's jockeys' title. The eventual dead heat, on one hundred and ninety winners each, made the national news on the final day of the turf campaign after Spencer had ridden Inchnadamph to victory in the last race. It was Spencer's highest tally for a turf season—he won the title in 2005 with one hundred and sixty-three winners, riding one hundred and eighty in the year. The achievement of Spencer and Sanders *over the year as a whole* seemed to be largely overlooked. For only the second time in British racing, the two top

St James's Palace Stakes, Royal Ascot—Excellent Art arrives late to lead home a 1,2,3 for trainer Aidan O'Brien, with Duke of Marmalade and Astronomer Royal taking the minor placings

jockeys both passed the two-hundred-winner mark, Spencer ending the year on two hundred and seven and Sanders on two hundred and thirteen. The result over the year was closer than that between Frankie Dettori (233) and Jason Weaver (200) in 1994, when the Jockeys' Association title was decided over the twelve months and both made a flying start on the all-weather in January and February..

Perhaps one reason for his obvious delight at winning on Excellent Art at Royal Ascot was because Ballydoyle had been the jockey's retaining stable in 2004, an arrangement which did not work out and came to a much-publicised, abrupt end the following year. O'Brien used numerous riders as substitutes for Kieren Fallon during the year, but Excellent Art was one of only two horses Spencer rode for him (the other was Frozen Fire in the Racing Post Trophy). Excellent Art continued to prove his worth in the top mile races through the rest of the season, contesting four of them and starting favourite in the first three. First came the Sussex Stakes at Goodwood, in which he was pushed along at halfway and had to be ridden vigorously two furlongs out as Ramonti readily took it up. Jeremy nosed past Excellent Art on the outside with a furlong to go but Excellent Art kept on and got to within a head of Ramonti at the line. Perhaps the track did not suit Excellent Art but this was still a fine run, and he followed it with another in the Queen Elizabeth II Stakes at Ascot at the end of September. Last entering the straight, he had to wait for a gap on the outside as Ramonti hit the front. Under strong riding, Excellent Art made ground relentlessly once he got clear just over a furlong out and make up most of a five-length deficit to be beaten half a length. Excellent Art looked unlucky, and, in the process, also looked as if a mile and a quarter would be well worth trying. However, he was kept to a mile in his remaining starts, starting with the Breeders' Cup Mile at Monmouth Park at the end of October.

Mrs J. Magnier, M. Tabor, D. Smith & M. Green's "Excellent Art"

With four runners on the day—the others were All My Loving, Dylan Thomas and George Washington—plus Breeders' Cup Juvenile Turf runner-up Achill Island the day before, O'Brien mounted the biggest European challenge for the Breeders' Cup. Exceptionally, there were no French-trained contenders and, on balance of current form, few among the remainder (Jeremy, Red Rocks, Passage of Time, Simply Perfect and Timarwa) held much of a chance of making their presence felt. Among the various reasons for the shortfall were the tightness of the track—the turf course is only seven furlongs in circumference—and a lack of suitable runners for the races on offer, while the absence of any travelling expenses (in contrast to some other major international racedays) was also an issue that was raised widely for the first time. The configuration of the course, and the appalling weather during the week leading up to the meeting, were material to Excellent Art since he was drawn on the wide outside and had to be dropped in behind, as much through circumstance as planning. In a race which lacked the quality of many renewals, his twelve opponents included five Grade 1 winners, notably three-year-old Nobiz Like Shobiz, second favourite and winner of the Wood Memorial Stakes on dirt before being switched to turf. Host and Purim had been successful in the Shadwell Turf Mile in 2005 and 2007 and supplementary entry Kip Deville had won the Grade 1 Frank E Kilroe Handicap at Santa Anita in March. One of the best performers at a mile on turf in the States, dual Grade 1 scorer After Market, was withdrawn because of the going and another, Shakespeare, missed the race after being retired because of injury in the middle of the month. Excellent Art made ground from halfway round the outside, while Kip Deville was able to stay close to the rail and went clear halfway up the short straight. Excellent Art challenged strongly, edging left a little in the final furlong, but never looked like posing a serious threat to the leader, who beat him by a length. To claim, as Johnny Murtagh did, that Excellent Art was unlucky was at best unconvincing. Be that as it may, Excellent Art still deserves credit for a fine run in adverse conditions, although it was still a shade below his best. He was some way below form on his final appearance in the Hong Kong Mile in December, making only steady progress from the back of the field in the straight to finish eighth to Good Ba Ba, beaten four lengths.

Excellent Art (b.c. 2004)	Pivotal (ch 1993)	Polar Falcon (b or br 1987)	Nureyev
			Marie d'Argonne
		Fearless Revival (ch 1987)	Cozzene
			Stufida
	Obsessive (USA) (b or br 1993)	Seeking The Gold (b 1985)	Mr Prospector
			Con Game
		Secret Obsession (b or br 1986)	Secretariat
			Ann Stuart

Excellent Art starts his career as a stallion at a fee of €25,000. His sire Pivotal, based at Cheveley Park Stud, which bred Excellent Art and had another good year with such as Echelon and Allegretto, is still the most expensive in Britain at £85,000. Pivotal was responsible for good winners over a range of distances in 2007, including sprinter Beauty Is Truth (Prix du Gros-Chene) and middle-distance performer Windsor Knot (Darley Stakes). At the sales Pivotal had twenty-three yearlings which made 100,000 guineas or more, with a top price of 475,000 guineas. He has had twelve sell for 300,000 guineas or more in the last three years. There is no denying the commercial appeal of Excellent Art's pedigree, especially as there is enough stamina on the dam's side to suggest he will have no difficulty siring horses who stay a mile and a quarter, maybe further. The distaff side of the family was covered in detail in *Racehorses of 2006* but, as an update, the dam Obsessive, who was placed in the Musidora Stakes and is also responsible for Ascot Stakes winner Double Obsession (by Sadler's Wells), had a yearling filly by Falbrav which made 100,000 guineas at the Newmarket October Sales. The game and consistent Excellent Art is lengthy and quite attractive and showed a quick action. He acted on heavy and good to firm going. *A. P. O'Brien, Ireland*

EXCESSIVE 3 ch.f. Cadeaux Genereux 131 – Show Off 56 (Efisio 120) [2007 66p: **73** 6.1g² 5g² 6d* 6.1v⁵ 6d⁶ p7g² p7.1g* p7g Oct 15] leggy filly: fair performer: won maiden at Warwick in June and handicap at Wolverhampton in September: stays 7f: acts on polytrack and good to soft going: sold 12,000 gns, sent to Saudi Arabia. *W. Jarvis*

£250000 Tattersalls October Auction Stakes, Newmarket—
Exclamation (right) gamely edges ahead of Anosti (stars) and Copywriter (in between first two)

EXCITEMENT (IRE) 2 b.f. (Apr 5) Xaar 132 – Sunny Slope 77 (Mujtahid (USA) **88**
118) [2007 6.1m⁴ 5.4m* 6d³ 8f Nov 24]: neat filly: fourth foal: half-sister to useful 7f (at
2 yrs) to 10.7f (in Ireland) winner Lake Pontchartrain (by Invincible Spirit): dam Irish
1m/9f winner: fairly useful form: won maiden at York in September: good third to
Floristry in nursery there next time: left R. Fahey, last in Grade 3 Miesque Stakes at
Hollywood final start: free-going sort, but bred to stay 7f/1m. *B. D. A. Cecil, USA*

EXCLAMATION 2 br.c. (Feb 26) Acclamation 118 – Summer Siren (FR) (Saint **107 p**
Cyrien (FR) 128) [2007 6f⁵ 6d* 6m* Oct 5] 15,000F, 36,000Y: lengthy, useful-looking
colt: half-brother to 5-y-o Native American and 3-y-o
Kunte Kinteh: dam, ran once in France, half-sister to smart French/US 1m to 1¼m
performer Val des Bois: useful form: highly progressive, won maiden at Haydock in
September and 28-runner £250,000 Tattersalls October Auction Stakes at Newmarket,
latter by neck from Anosti after switched from middle to far side: should prove best at 6f/
7f: pattern-race performer in the making. *B. J. Meehan*

EXCLUSIONIST 3 ch.c. In The Wings 128 – Groom Order (Groom Dancer (USA) **76**
128) [2007 10g⁴ 10.1m³ Aug 24]: lengthy, well-made colt: eighth foal: closely related to
useful Irish 7f and 1m (latter at 2 yrs) winner Barring Order (by Barathea) and half-
brother to 2 winners, including smart Irish 6f (at 2 yrs) to 1m winner Beckett (by Fairy
King): dam unraced out of half-sister to 2000 Guineas winner Entrepreneur: 3¾ lengths
fourth to Fourteenth at Windsor, easily better effort in maidens: runs in snatches: sold
5,500 gns. *J. Noseda*

EXCUSEZ MOI (USA) 5 b.h. Fusaichi Pegasus (USA) 130 – Jiving 69 (Generous **109**
(IRE) 139) [2007 112: 6g a6f p5g 6m 7g² 7.1g² 5g 6v 7g Oct 27] tall, quite good-topped
horse: useful performer: good efforts in 2007 when runner-up in listed races at Leicester
(beaten 1¾ lengths by New Seeker) and Haydock (beaten 1¼ lengths by Munaddam)
fifth/sixth starts: stays 7f: acts on polytrack, dirt, soft and good to firm going: has worn
blinkers/cheekpieces/tongue tie: often troublesome at stalls, withdrawn at start of
Stewards' Cup at Goodwood intended with promise. *C. E. Brittain*

EXECUTIVE PADDY (IRE) 8 b.g. Executive Perk 120 – Illbethereforeyou (IRE) **–**
(Supreme Leader 123) [2007 67: p12g p12g p7f p10g Mar 5] winning hurdler: maiden on
Flat, little form in 2007. *I. A. Wood*

EXHIBITION (IRE) 2 b.c. (Feb 22) Invincible Spirit (IRE) 121 – Moonbi Ridge **102 p**
(IRE) 102 (Definite Article 121) [2007 7m³ 6.1v* 6g³ Aug 3] €225,000Y: strong, sturdy
colt: has a moderate, quick action: first foal: dam, Irish 1¼m/1½m winner, half-sister to
useful Irish 1m/1¼m performer Bush Maiden: useful form: third to Rio de La Plata at
Newmarket prior to winning lesser maiden at Nottingham later in July: further promise
when 2¾ lengths equal-third of 9 to Strike The Deal in Richmond Stakes at Goodwood,
always away from main action (returned slightly jarred up): likely to stay 1m: should do
better still. *N. A. Callaghan*

356

EXIT FAST (USA) 6 ch.g. Announce (USA) – Distinct Beauty (USA) (Phone Trick (USA)) [2007 f12g f11g⁶ f12g² f14g 12m 12m May 8] form only when second in seller at Southwell: stays 1½m: acts on fibresand: tried in cheekpieces. *P. T. Midgley* — a60

EXIT SMILING 5 ch.g. Dr Fong (USA) 128 – Away To Me (Exit To Nowhere (USA) 122) [2007 77: f8g f8g³ 8m* f8g² 8m² 7.9d 8s 8m 8m⁵ p8g 8m⁶ 8g Oct 6] big, good-topped gelding: fairly useful handicapper on turf, fair on all-weather: won at Newcastle in April: best form at 1m: acts on all-weather, good to firm and good to soft ground: tried visored/blinkered: sometimes races freely. *P. T. Midgley* — 85 a75

EXIT STRATEGY (IRE) 3 b.g. Cadeaux Genereux 131 – Black Belt Shopper (IRE) 82 (Desert Prince (IRE) 130) [2007 63: 8m⁵ p8.6g⁶ 7g³ 6g* 6.1v⁴ 6g⁴ 6m p7.1g p6g Nov 14] neat gelding: fair handicapper: won at Ayr in July on final start for W. Haggas: may prove as effective at 5f as 6f: best efforts on good going: blinkered nowadays. *R. A. Harris* — 69

EXIT TO LUCK (GER) 6 b.g. Exit To Nowhere (USA) 122 – Emy Coasting (USA) 78 (El Gran Senor (USA) 136) [2007 78: 10.5m f11g² 16d⁶ Jun 22] just modest handicapper nowadays: stays 11f: acts on all-weather: has worn blinkers. *S. Gollings* — 60

EXODIA 2 b.f. (Feb 8) Dr Fong (USA) 128 – Fenella's Link 92 (Linamix (FR) 127) 63 [2007 6d 7g p7g⁶ p7g⁶ Sep 11] 82,000Y: angular filly: first foal: dam, Irish 9f winner, half-sister to smart 1m/1¼m winner African Dream: modest maiden: will stay 1m: tried in cheekpieces. *Jane Chapple-Hyam*

EXOTIC VENTURE 4 b.f. Piccolo 121 – Bay Risk (Risk Me (FR) 127) [2007 6g³ 6g 60 p7.1g⁶ p8.6g⁴ p8g Sep 3] fourth foal: half-sister to 1m/1¼m winner Firewire (by Blushing Flame): dam well beaten both starts: modest maiden, lightly raced: probably stays 8.6f: acts on polytrack. *R. M. Beckett*

EXPECTED BONUS (USA) 8 b. or br.g. Kris S (USA) – Nidd (USA) 112 (Known 48 Fact (USA) 135) [2007 54: p10g³ p8g³ p10g p10g Mar 5] lengthy gelding: poor walker: poor performer: stays 1¼m: acts on polytrack, firm and good to soft going: usually in headgear nowadays: sometimes carries head awkwardly. *Jamie Poulton*

EXPEDIENCE (USA) 3 gr.f. With Approval (CAN) – Promptly (IRE) 88 (Lead On 74 Time (USA) 123) [2007 63: 8.2g⁵ p8.6g⁶ 8d* Jun 26] small, rather leggy filly: fair form in maidens, winning at Brighton by length from Commandment, dictating: stays 1m: acts on good to soft ground. *Sir Michael Stoute*

EXPEDITER 2 b.f. (Feb 26) Bahamian Bounty 116 – Iris May 87 (Brief Truce (USA) — 126) [2007 6m 6.1d Oct 18] 16,000Y: workmanlike filly: half-sister to 5-y-o Joseph Henry, 4-y-o Royal Engineer and 3-y-o Leonard Charles: dam, 5f winner (including at 2 yrs), half-sister to smart sprinter Cathedral: in rear in maidens, fading. *H. Candy*

EXPENSIVE 4 b.f. Royal Applause 124 – Vayavaig 78 (Damister (USA) 123) [2007 98 101: 7.5g³ 8g⁶ 9g⁶ p8g* 8m² 8m* 8m 7m Sep 13] strong, good-topped filly: carries plenty of condition: useful performer: won listed races at Kempton in April and Pontefract (by short head from Mont Etoile, making all) in June: ran poorly after: stays 1m, seemingly not 1¼m: acts on polytrack, raced mainly on good going or firmer on turf: sold 180,000 gns. *C. F. Wall*

EXPENSIVE ART (IRE) 3 b.f. Cape Cross (IRE) 129 – Walnut Lady 91 (Forzando 79 + 122) [2007 f6g² 6.1m³ 6d⁴ p6g* 6g² 7m⁵ p6g 6g* p5g³ p6m Nov 24] 36,000F, 57,000Y: tall filly: second foal: half-sister to 4-y-o Alfie Tupper: dam 5f to 7f winner, including at 2 yrs: fair performer: won handicaps at Lingfield in July and Catterick in October: good third in similar event at Lingfield penultimate start: probably flattered in listed event there final one: effective at 5f/6f: acts on polytrack, unraced on extremes of going on turf. *N. A. Callaghan*

EXPENSIVE DETOUR (IRE) 3 b.g. Namid 128 – Sail With The Wind 74 (Sad-76 dlers' Hall (IRE) 126) [2007 79: 6m* 6.9f 7m Sep 22] big, good-topped gelding: fair performer, lightly raced: won maiden at Thirsk in May: should be suited by 7f/1m: acts on good to firm going: sold 5,000 gns. *Mrs L. Stubbs*

EXPERIMENTAL (IRE) 13 b.g. Top of The World 103 – Brun's Toy (FR) (Bruni 58 132) [2007 58: f12g² f12g f11g⁶ p12.2g* p13.9g 10s⁴ Jun 4] modest performer: won minor event at Wolverhampton in April: stays 1½m: acts on all-weather and any turf going: none too reliable. *John A. Harris*

EXPLODE 10 b.g. Zafonic (USA) 130 – Didicoy (USA) 104 (Danzig (USA)) [2007 44 § 57§: 12d 12s³ 10.1g Aug 17] poor nowadays: stays 1½m: acts on soft and good to firm ground: blinkered: unreliable. *Miss L. C. Siddall*

EXPLOSIVE FOX (IRE) 6 ch.g. Foxhound (USA) 103 – Grise Mine (FR) 121 **50** (Crystal Palace (FR) 132) [2007 66: f12g p13.9g⁶ p16g Sep 15] handicapper, only modest nowadays: stays 1¾m: acts on polytrack, firm and good to soft going: effective with/ without headgear. *S. Curran*

EXPONENTIAL (IRE) 5 b.g. Namid 128 – Exponent (USA) (Exbourne (USA) 125) **70 d** [2007 –: 6m* 5.1m 6f⁵ 5s⁵ 5d⁵ 5f 5.1m 6g 5.7d p6g Oct 12] workmanlike gelding: fair handicapper: won apprentice event at Folkestone in April: ended year out of form: effective at 5f/6f: acts on soft and good to firm ground: tried in headgear. *J. M. Bradley*

EXPRESS PRINCESS (IRE) 2 b.f. (Mar 23) Desert Prince (IRE) 130 – Nashwan **64** Star (IRE) 68 (Nashwan (USA) 135) [2007 p8g p8.6g³ p8.6g³ p7.1g³ p7g Dec 5] 7,000F, 7,000Y: first foal: dam, maiden (stayed 1½m), half-sister to high-class miler Air Express: modest maiden: third 3 times at Wolverhampton: stays 8.6f: raced only on polytrack. *M. Botti*

EXPRESS WISH 3 b.c. Danehill Dancer (IRE) 117 – Waffle On 89 (Chief Singer 131) **99** [2007 62p: p6g² 6d* 6m* 6m 6m Sep 13] good-topped, attractive colt: useful performer: much improved in 2007, winning maiden at Brighton (by 5 lengths) in May and handicap at Haydock (beat Mac Gille Eoin by neck) in June: below form after: free-going sort, should prove as effective at 5f as 6f: acts on polytrack, good to firm and good to soft ground. *J. Noseda*

EXTRACTOR 3 b.g. Siphon (BRZ) 130 – Tri Pac (IRE) (Fairy King (USA)) [2007 61: **50** 8.2g 7m⁶ 6g⁴ May 31] quite good-topped gelding: modest maiden: blinkered (found little) final start. *J. L. Dunlop*

EXTRAVAGANCE (IRE) 3 b.f. King's Best (USA) 132 – Meritxell (IRE) (Thatching **65** 131) [2007 80: 6m³ 7m Jun 9] good-bodied filly: fair maiden, lightly raced: encouraging third in maiden at Pontefract on reappearance, best work at finish and not unduly knocked about: disappointing favourite in handicap at Newbury 2 weeks later: should be suited by 1m/1¼m. *L. M. Cumani*

EXTREME MEASURES 4 b.c. Montjeu (IRE) 137 – Fade (Persepolis (FR) 127) **–** [2007 10.4d Oct 13] lengthy, angular colt: fairly useful performer, thrice-raced: never dangerous in handicap at York only outing in 2007: bred to be suited by 1½m+: unraced on extremes of going. *Saeed bin Suroor*

EXTREME NORTH (USA) 2 b.g. (Feb 20) Stravinsky (USA) 133 – North Dream **54** (USA) (Unbridled's Song (USA) 125) [2007 p6g Dec 29] $45,000Y, 30,000Y: first foal: dam unraced half-sister to smart US performer up to 1¼m Bagshot: 20/1, ninth in maiden at Lingfield. *Miss V. Haigh*

EYE CATCHING 2 b.f. (Apr 19) Diktat 126 – Fifth Emerald 54 (Formidable (USA) **62** 125) [2007 5d 5.1m⁶ 5d⁵ 6m p6g 6d 8d Oct 23] sturdy, lengthy filly: has a scratchy action: fifth foal: half-sister to 7-y-o Goodbye Mr Bond, 5-y-o Anfield Dream and 3-y-o Five A Side: dam, 1m winner, out of close relation of smart middle-distance filly Valley of Gold: modest maiden: lost form after summer break: should stay 7f/1m. *J. R. Jenkins*

EZDEYAAD (USA) 3 b.g. Lemon Drop Kid (USA) 131 – August Storm (USA) (Storm **56** Creek (USA)) [2007 9.2m³ Aug 31] 3¾ lengths third of 5 to Arena's Dream in maiden at Hamilton. *G. A. Swinbank*

EZDIYAAD (IRE) 3 b.c. Galileo (IRE) 134 – Wijdan (USA) 101 (Mr Prospector **92 p** (USA)) [2007 7m p8g 8d* 11d³ Sep 26] big, rangy colt: sixth foal: closely related to 1¼m winner Mohafazaat (by Sadler's Wells) and half-brother to 1m winner Oriental Fashion (by Marju) and 6f to 1¼m (including Grade 2 in USA) winner Makderah (by Danehill), both smart: dam, 1m and 10.4f winner, closely related to Nayef and half-sister to Nashwan and Unfuwain: fairly useful performer: won maiden at Newmarket (by 2½ lengths from Know The Law) in August: creditable 4½ lengths third to Harry Tricker in handicap at Goodwood only subsequent outing, nowhere to go inside final 3f and again carrying head high: likely to stay 1½m: acts on good to soft going: open to further improvement. *M. P. Tregoning*

EZIMA (IRE) 3 b.f. Sadler's Wells (USA) 132 – Ezilla (IRE) (Darshaan 133) [2007 78: **117** 8s⁵ 12m² 10g p10.7g³ 12g² 12d* 10g* p10.7g² Nov 9] 87,000F: lengthy filly: fourth foal: dam unraced sister to smart Irish performer up to 1½m Ebaziya, herself dam of Gold Cup winner Enzeli and Irish Oaks/Prix Royal-Oak winner Ebadiyla (by Sadler's Wells): smart performer: won maiden at Navan in April and listed races at the Curragh (by 4 lengths from Attercliffe) and Leopardstown (by 4½ lengths from Lord Admiral) in October: below form in listed race at Dundalk final outing: effective at 1¼m/1½m: acts on soft going: usually tracks pace travelling well. *J. S. Bolger, Ireland*

EZTHEGEZZA 2 b.g. (Apr 28) Tobougg (IRE) 125 – Salvezza (IRE) 97 (Superpower **65** 113) [2007 6m 6m⁵ 6.1s³ 6m³ 6d 7g⁵ p8m⁴ 8m Oct 22] big gelding: has scope: fair maiden: in frame 3 times, twice in nurseries: stays 1m: acts on polytrack, soft and good to firm going: in cheekpieces (well beaten) once: sold 8,200 gns. *J. S. Moore*

F

FABER HALL FLYER 2 b.g. (Mar 15) Danetime (IRE) 121 – Pinini 63 (Pivotal 124) **77** [2007 5.2g⁵ 6m⁵ 6d³ 6m 5.1d² 6d³ Oct 23] close-coupled gelding: first foal: dam, maiden, best up to 1m: fair maiden: placed 3 times: free-going type, will be best kept to 5f/6f: formerly tongue tied, as good without. *Mrs C. A. Dunnett*

FABINE 3 b.f. Danehill Dancer (IRE) 117 – Waypoint 95 (Cadeaux Genereux 131) **70** [2007 70: p7g* May 4] tall filly: fair performer: won maiden at Lingfield in May by 2½ lengths from Arabian Gleam, racing freely: may prove best up to 7f: raced only on polytrack. *B. J. Meehan*

FABREZE 2 ch.c. (Feb 25) Choisir (AUS) 126 – Impulsive Decision (IRE) 71 (Nomina- **76 p** tion 125) [2007 6g⁴ Sep 7] 36,000Y: big, good sort: fifth foal: half-brother to 3 winners, including useful 6f (at 2 yrs) to 1m (in US) winner Cammies Future (by Efisio): dam 6f (at 2 yrs) and 1m winner: 50/1, burly and green, encouraging fourth to Errigal Lad in maiden at Haydock, finishing well from rear (bumped start): should prove best at 5f/6f: will do better. *P. J. Makin*

FABRIAN 9 b.g. Danehill (USA) 126 – Dockage (CAN) (Riverman (USA) 131) [2007 **80** 86: 10m 8.1g⁶ 8.1g 10s⁴ 10d 10d² 10m⁶ 8m² 8.1m 8.1m 10m Oct 3] strong gelding: fairly useful performer: stays 1¼m: acts on polytrack, firm and soft going: tends to hang right: usually races up with pace. *R. J. Price*

FABULEUX CHERIE 2 b.f. (Feb 14) Noverre (USA) 125 – Ashover Amber 81 **71** (Green Desert (USA) 127) [2007 5m⁶ 5m⁵ 5.1d 5m 5m* p5.1g* 5g³ 5f³ p5.1g² p5g² p6g* 6m p5.1g⁴ p5m³ Dec 8] good-bodied filly: fourth foal: half-sister to 7f (including at 2 yrs) and 8.5f winner (in Spain) Sir Jasper (by Sri Pekan) and winner in Greece by Celtic Swing: dam, 5f/6f winner, out of useful 7f/1m winner Zafaaf: fair performer: won seller at Windsor in August and nurseries at Wolverhampton in September and Lingfield in October: best at 5f/easy 6f: acts on polytrack and good to firm going: didn't take to blinkers. *W. R. Muir*

FABULEUX MILLIE (IRE) 3 ch.f. Noverre (USA) 125 – Flying Millie (IRE) 99 **85** (Flying Spur (AUS)) [2007 82+: 6m p6g² 6g³ p6m³ 6m p7g Nov 21] rather leggy, quite attractive filly: fairly useful performer: should stay 7f: acts on polytrack and good to firm going: sold 20,000 gns. *R. M. Beckett*

FACTUAL LAD 9 b.g. So Factual (USA) 120 – Surprise Surprise 91 (Robellino (USA) **69** 127) [2007 69: 10m³ 9.7s⁶ 10m⁶ 10.2f Aug 27] close-coupled, workmanlike gelding: fair handicapper: stays 1¼m: acts on all-weather, firm and good to soft going: tried blinkered/ in cheekpieces. *B. R. Millman*

FADANSIL 4 b.g. Dansili 127 – Fatah Flare (USA) 121 (Alydar (USA)) [2007 56: f7g **60** 10.1m 8.3d 8.5g 9.9m³ 11.1m* 12d 11.1s Sep 24] deep-girthed gelding: modest handi- capper: won at Hamilton in August: should stay 1½m: acts on good to firm going: tried blinkered. *J. Wade*

FADHB AR BITH (IRE) 2 b.g. (Feb 20) Tagula (IRE) 116 – Teodora (IRE) 93 (Fairy **80 p** King (USA)) [2007 p7.1s* Dec 21] €24,000F, 36,000Y: half-brother to 2005 2-y-o 1m winner (stays 1½m) Prince of Love (by Fruits of Love) and 3-y-o Feeling Wonderful: dam untrustworthy 2-y-o 6f winner: 40/1, tongue tied and green, won 6-runner maiden at Wolverhampton by length from Moosley, wandering: should progress. *John A. Quinn, Ireland*

FAHED 2 gr.c. (May 14) Cool Jazz 116 – Glowing Light (IRE) (Contract Law (USA) **–** 108) [2007 6d⁵ May 30] tailed off in seller at Yarmouth. *J. R. Jenkins*

FAIR ALONG (GER) 5 b.g. Alkalde (GER) – Fairy Tango (FR) (Acatenango (GER) **103** 127) [2007 92: 18.7m² 18d³ Oct 20] rather leggy, quite good-topped gelding: useful handicapper: further improvement when placed in Chester Cup and Cesarewitch at Newmarket in 2007, excellent 1½ lengths third of 33 to Leg Spinner in latter, not having so smooth a passage as first 2: stays 2¼m: acts on all-weather, good to firm and good to soft going: raced freely in cheekpieces final 3-y-o start: useful hurdler/smart chaser. *P. J. Hobbs*

FAIRDONNA 4 ch.f. Bertolini (USA) 125 – Shamrock Fair (IRE) 77 (Shavian 125) **62**
[2007 71: p7g³ p7f p7.1g* p7.1g⁵ Jun 30] leggy filly: modest performer: won handicap at
Wolverhampton in June: stays 8.3f: acts on polytrack, unraced on extremes of going on
turf. *D. J. Coakley*

FAIRFIELD PRINCESS 3 b.f. Inchinor 119 – Cool Question 99 (Polar Falcon (USA) **82 d**
126) [2007 85: p5g³ 5g 5.7f 5m 6m 6d Sep 26] leggy, quite attractive filly: has a quick
action: fairly useful handicapper: well below form after reappearance: effective at 5f/6f:
unraced on heavy going, acts on any other turf and polytrack. *M. S. Saunders*

FAIR GALE 2 b.g. (Mar 30) Storming Home 128 – Triple Green 69 (Green Desert **77**
(USA) 127) [2007 p8g p8.6g² p8m³ p8g* Dec 19] 58,000Y: fifth foal: half-brother to
3-y-o Titan Triumph and 6-y-o Burning Moon: dam, maiden (stayed 1m), half-sister to
smart 1¼m/1½m performer Talented: fair performer: further improvement when winning
maiden at Kempton: likely to stay 1¼m: raced only on polytrack. *S. Kirk*

FAIRGAME MAN 9 ch.g. Clantime 101 – Thalya (Crofthall 110) [2007 55: p6g 7m **–**
5g 5g 6g Aug 17] strong gelding: modest performer at 8 yrs: little form in 2007: sometimes wears cheekpieces/visor. *J. S. Wainwright*

FAIRLY HONEST 3 br.g. Alhaarth (IRE) 126 – Miller's Melody 86 (Chief Singer **75 d**
131) [2007 75: 10d³ 8m 8d⁵ 10.1m⁵ 10.1g⁴ 8m 9.9g p10g⁶ 10m Sep 20] leggy, close-
coupled gelding: fair maiden: below form after reappearance, leaving D. Elsworth after
fifth start: stays 1¼m: acts on good to firm and good to soft ground, probably on polytrack: tried blinkered. *P. W. Hiatt*

FAIRMILE 5 b.g. Spectrum (IRE) 126 – Juno Marlowe (IRE) 100 (Danehill (USA) **118**
126) [2007 107: 10g* 10g³ 10g³ 10.3m² 10.4d* 10g² Nov 3] tall gelding: has a quick
action: smart performer: left W. Swinburn 280,000 gns after 4 yrs: won handicap at Nad
Al Sheba in January by ¾ length from Hallhoo: left I. Mohammed in UAE and off over 6
months, better than ever when length second to Red Gala in similar event at Doncaster in
September (briefly very upset in stall) then won minor event at York in October by 3
lengths from Sunshine Kid: creditable neck second to Mashaahed in listed event at
Newmarket final outing: should stay 1½m: acts on polytrack, firm and soft going: held up
and travels well. *Saeed bin Suroor*

FAIRMONT (IRE) 2 b.f. (Feb 19) Kingmambo (USA) 125 – Fiaafy (USA) 75 (Gone **53**
West (USA)) [2007 6d⁵ Aug 26] first foal: dam, ran 3 times, sister to useful performer up
to 1m Mythical Girl, out of sister to Green Desert: 16/1, needed experience when fifth to
Ancien Regime in maiden at Yarmouth: will stay 1m. *M. Johnston*

FAIRNILEE 3 b.f. Selkirk (USA) 129 – Fantastic Belle (USA) 79 (Night Shift (USA)) **67 +**
[2007 59p: p6g* f6g⁵ Feb 22] fair performer, lightly raced: best effort when winning
maiden at Kempton in January by 1¼ lengths from Bertie Swift, making most and idling:
hung left when below form next time: should stay 7f. *Sir Mark Prescott*

FAIR SAILING (IRE) 3 ch.f. Docksider (USA) 124 – Fair of The Furze 112 (Ela- **62**
Mana-Mou 132) [2007 p8.6g⁴ p8g⁴ p8g⁴ Nov 6] half-sister to several winners, notably
high-class 1½m performer White Muzzle (by Dancing Brave), smart 7f (at 2 yrs)/1¾m
(Deutsches St Leger) winner Fair Question (by Rainbow Quest) and useful dam of Dubai
World Cup winner Almutawakel: dam 1m/1¼m winner who stayed 1½m: modest form in
maidens: will stay 1¼m. *J. W. Hills*

FAIR SHAKE (IRE) 7 b.g. Sheikh Albadou 128 – Shamrock Fair (IRE) 77 (Shavian **72**
125) [2007 75: 8m⁴ 7g 7d 9.1g 8d² 6.9m 7.2s 8g Oct 3] close-coupled gelding: fair
handicapper: stays 1m: acts on firm and soft ground: tried in cheekpieces, wears visor:
inconsistent: sold 1,500 gns. *Karen McLintock*

FAIRY FESTIVAL (IRE) 3 b.f. Montjeu (IRE) 137 – Escape To Victory (Salse **57**
(USA) 128) [2007 7.5g 7.5m 8g 7m p10m⁶ p10g⁵ p9.5g⁵ Oct 19] 200,000Y, 85,000 2-y-o:
good-topped filly: fourth foal: half-sister to 3 winners, notably 6-y-o Benbaun: dam,
Italian 7f winner, half-sister to high-class US 1m/9f performer Hawksley Hill: modest
maiden: left N. Nevin in Ireland after fourth outing: stays easy 1¼m: acts on polytrack
and good to firm ground. *J. S. Moore*

FAIRY MONARCH (IRE) 8 b.g. Ali-Royal (IRE) 127 – Cookawara (IRE) (Fairy **61 d**
King (USA)) [2007 57: 9.9m 8f⁴ p8.6g⁵ 8f 8m 7.1m⁵ 8m³ 8g 7.5m 10.4m 8m 7.1g p9.5g
p11g Oct 17] compact gelding: modest performer: effective at 1m to 1½m: yet to race on
heavy going, acts on any other turf and polytrack: wears headgear: tongue tied earlier in
career: has reportedly been difficult ride. *P. T. Midgley*

FAIRY SLIPPER 3 b.f. Singspiel (IRE) 133 – Fairlee Mixa (FR) (Linamix (FR) 127) **–**
[2007 –: 10f 9.3m⁵ Jun 4] little form in 4 starts. *Jedd O'Keeffe*

FAIRY WOOD (IRE) 2 b.f. (Apr 14) Fasliyev (USA) 120 – Fantasy Wood (IRE) – p (Charnwood Forest (IRE) 125) [2007 6d Aug 20] useful-looking filly: second foal: dam unraced half-sister to useful stayers Son of Sharp Shot and Fantasy Hill: 33/1 and very green (not knocked about) in maiden at Windsor: open to improvement. *J. L. Dunlop*

FAITH AND REASON (USA) 4 b.g. Sunday Silence (USA) – Sheer Reason (USA) **75 d** 110 (Danzig (USA)) [2007 90: 10.1s 10.9m 10g⁶ 10m 10.1d 11.6m 10g 11.5g Sep 18] good-bodied gelding: fairly useful for Saeed bin Suroor in 2005/6: form in 2007 only when sixth in handicap at Nottingham third start: stays 1¼m: acts on polytrack and good to firm going: tried visored/in cheekpieces/tongue tied: races prominently. *B. J. Curley*

FAITHFUL RULER (USA) 3 b. or br.g. Elusive Quality (USA) – Fancy Ruler (USA) **75** (Half A Year (USA) 130) [2007 p7g p7g⁵ p7.1g⁶ p6m⁴ p7g* p7g³ Dec 29] fair performer: won handicap at Kempton in November: stays 7f: raced only on polytrack: blinkered (went off hard) third outing. *M. A. Magnusson*

FAITHS PERFECTION (IRE) 4 ch.f. Docksider (USA) 124 – Wrapitraise (USA) **58** (Raise A Man (USA)) [2007 53: f8g⁶ 8d⁴ 7g⁶ 7s 6v⁵ Jul 27] strong, medium-sized filly: modest maiden: below form at Southwell on reappearance. *John Rafferty, Ireland*

FAJR (IRE) 5 b.g. Green Desert (USA) 127 – Ta Rib (USA) 116 (Mr Prospector (USA)) **115** [2007 90: p8g* p8g⁵ 8m⁵ 8m 7g² 7s³ 7m 7d⁴ 8.2g² p7m² p7g³ p8m* p8g³ Dec 29] strong, good-bodied gelding: smart performer: improved throughout 2007, winning handicaps at Lingfield in January and December: ran well most other outings, including second to Binanti in Buckingham Palace Stakes (Handicap) at Royal Ascot and third to Silver Touch in Criterion Stakes at Newmarket seventh/eighth starts, and third to Atlantic Story in handicap at Lingfield final one: stays 1m: acts on polytrack, soft and good to firm ground: held up: tends to idle: tried tongue tied (ran poorly), blinkered last 2 starts: often bandaged. *Miss Gay Kelleway*

FALCATIV 3 b.c. (Jan 20) Falbrav (IRE) 133 – Frottola 109 (Muhtarram (USA) 125) **62 p** [2007 7m Oct 5] good-bodied, attractive colt: first foal: dam, Italian 1m/9f winner, half-sister to useful Italian 1¼m performer Windy Britain: 16/1 and backward, twelfth of 14 in maiden at Newmarket won by Fireside: will be suited by 1m/1¼m: type to thrive at 3 yrs. *L. M. Cumani*

FALCOLNRY (IRE) 2 b.f. (Mar 23) Hawk Wing (USA) 136 – Fear And Greed (IRE) **81 p** 106 (Brief Truce (USA) 126) [2007 6.1g⁶ 7m* 6m Oct 5] €75,000Y: strong, lengthy filly: third foal: half-sister to Irish 5f winner Live In Fear (by Fasliyev): dam Irish 2-y-o 6f winner: fairly useful form: won maiden at Doncaster (beat Sugar Mint by length) in August: stiff task (and gone in coat), last of 14 in Cheveley Park Stakes at Newmarket: will stay 1m: refused at stall intended third start (Goffs Fillies Million): capable of better. *J. R. Fanshawe*

FALCON FLYER 3 br.f. Cape Cross (IRE) 129 – Green Danube (USA) 92 (Irish River **48** (FR) 131) [2007 –: 7.6g 9.7m⁶ p12g p7g⁴ p7g p8g⁴ Dec 16] close-coupled filly: poor maiden: seems to stay 9.7f: best efforts on polytrack and good to firm ground. *J. R. Best*

FALCON'S FIRE (IRE) 3 b.g. Orpen (USA) 116 – Tres Chic (USA) (Northern **64** Fashion (USA) 114) [2007 60: 6f² 7m* 8.1m 7.1g 7m 6.9f³ 12.4m⁴ 12.1m² 12d² Sep 17] modest performer: won maiden at Catterick in May: stays 1½m: acts on firm and good to soft ground: tried in cheekpieces: fairly useful juvenile hurdler. *Mrs A. Duffield*

FALCON SPEED 2 b.f. (Mar 1) Hunting Lion (IRE) 115 – Efficacious (IRE) 49 (Efisio – 120) [2007 5v 5d 6f⁶ 5g 6g 5g Sep 19] close-coupled filly: seventh foal: half-sister to 2 winners, including 2004 2-y-o 7.5f winner Belton (by Lujain): dam, maiden, out of half-sister to smart sprinters Hanu and Sanu: no form: tried in cheekpieces. *P. T. Midgley*

FALIMAR 3 b.f. Fasliyev (USA) 120 – Mar Blue (FR) 75 (Marju (IRE) 127) [2007 66: **68 d** p9.5g p12.2g³ 9.9m³ 9.3m² 10s 8m 9.9m 10f⁵ 9g³ Oct 5] rather leggy filly: fair maiden: free-going sort, but probably stays easy 1½m: acts on firm ground, probably on polytrack: tried in cheekpieces/visor: sold 4,500 gns. *Miss J. A. Camacho*

FALMASSIM 4 b.g. Mozart (IRE) 131 – Scostes (Cadeaux Genereux 131) [2007 77: **68 d** f6g 7g 6g 6.1g² p6g 6m 5m 5g 6m⁶ 7.1g Oct 5] sturdy gelding: fair handicapper: creditable effort in 2007 only when second at Nottingham: best efforts at 6f: acts on good to firm ground: blinkered/in cheekpieces most starts in 2007. *Miss J. A. Camacho*

FALPIASE (IRE) 5 b.g. Montjeu (IRE) 137 – Gift of The Night (USA) (Slewpy **89** (USA)) [2007 80: 15g² 15.8m² 16g 18m Aug 17] tall, angular gelding: fairly useful maiden: flattered in Goodwood Cup third start: stays 2m: acts on polytrack and good to firm going: blinkered first 2 outings at 4 yrs: temperament under suspicion. *J. Howard Johnson*

FAMILIAR AFFAIR 6 b.g. Intikhab (USA) 135 – Familiar (USA) 96 (Diesis 133) [2007 –: 8g Nov 8] leggy, close-coupled gelding: has a rather round action: fair performer at 3 yrs: lightly raced and well held since. *A. Berry* –

FAMILIAR TERRITORY 4 br.c. Cape Cross (IRE) 129 – Forever Fine (USA) (Sunshine Forever (USA)) [2007 103: p10g* 10d² 12m³ Aug 17] big, good-topped colt: smart handicapper, lightly raced: won at Kempton in June by ½ length from Bandama: probably unlucky at Ascot following month, forced to delay challenge and beaten only neck by Tears of A Clown: odds on, possibly amiss when third of 4 in minor event at Newmarket final start: should stay 1½m: acts on polytrack, firm and soft ground. *Saeed bin Suroor* **110**

FAMOUS NAME 2 b.c. (May 8) Dansili 127 – Fame At Last (USA) 98 (Quest For Fame 127) [2007 6s* 7m⁶ 7g² Oct 29] quite good-topped, useful-looking colt: fourth foal: half-brother to 3 winners, including 6f winner Anchor Date (by Zafonic) and French 1m winner Everlasting Fame (by Zamindar), both fairly useful: dam 2-y-o 7f winner (stayed 1¼m): useful form: won maiden at Naas (by 7 lengths) in July: better form after, in National Stakes at the Curragh and Killavullan Stakes at Leopardstown (¾-length second to Jupiter Pluvius, slowly away from wide draw): will stay 1m: should do better still. *D. K. Weld, Ireland* **103 p**

FANATICAL 2 b.f. (Jan 13) Mind Games 121 – Mania (IRE) (Danehill (USA) 126) [2007 6m* 5m 6d 5.2m⁵ 6.1m² 6m Oct 5] 16,000Y: small, sturdy filly: second foal: dam unraced half-sister to dam of 3-y-o Creachadoir and 4-y-o Youmzain: fairly useful performer: won maiden at Newbury in June: held her form well (often highly tried), 3 lengths seventh of 28 to Exclamation in sales race at Newmarket final start: should prove best kept to 5f/6f: yet to race on extremes of ground: sold 85,000 gns, sent to USA. *E. F. Vaughan* **89**

FAN CLUB 3 ch.g. Zamindar (USA) 116 – Starfan (USA) 101 (Lear Fan (USA) 130) [2007 8v⁵ 8m⁵ 8d⁶ a9.5g⁴ 7m 8.1s p8.6g 7.2s p8.6g Nov 14] lengthy, good-topped gelding: first foal: dam, 6f winner, half-sister to smart French/US performer up to 1m Etoile Montante: useful performer, winning maiden at Maisons-Laffite in 2006: left D. Smaga in France after fourth start, well held in handicaps subsequently: stays 1m: acts on good to firm ground: tried blinkered. *D. W. Chapman* **95 d**

FANCY (IRE) 4 b. or br.f. Key of Luck (USA) 126 – Forbidden Pleasure 82 (Pursuit of Love 124) [2007 56: p10g 10s 8.5m 7m p8.6g² p8g Sep 4] modest maiden: stayed easy 8.6f: acted on polytrack and soft ground: dead. *R. A. Farrant* **50**

FANCY WOMAN 3 b.f. Sakhee (USA) 136 – Fancy Wrap (Kris 135) [2007 –: 12g 12.1s Jun 15] compact filly: last in 3 maidens: sold 800 gns in July. *J. L. Dunlop* –

FANCY YOU (IRE) 4 b.f. Mull of Kintyre (USA) 114 – Sunset Park (IRE) 61 (Red Sunset 120) [2007 48: p7g p6g p6g p5.1g 6.1s 5.2s 6d⁶ 10g 7d p8g Nov 7] good-topped filly: poor maiden at 3 yrs: little form in 2007: tried in headgear. *A. W. Carroll* –

FANDANGERINA 2 b.f. (Mar 31) Hernando (FR) 127 – Fantastic Belle (IRE) 79 (Night Shift (USA)) [2007 6g p7g 7.1g² 7g² p8.6g* Nov 1] big, strong filly: half-sister to useful 6f (including at 2 yrs) winner Fantaisiste (by Nashwan) and 3-y-o Fairnilee: dam, 6f winner, half-sister to smart performer up to 1½m Germano: fairly useful form: improved with experience, won maiden at Wolverhampton final start: stays 8.6f: sort to make even better 3-y-o. *Sir Mark Prescott* **81 p**

FANGORN FOREST (IRE) 4 b.f. Shinko Forest (IRE) – Edge of Darkness 62 (Vaigly Great 127) [2007 77, a61: p8g⁵ f8g⁶ 7.1m 10.2d³ 9g² 10m 8d⁵ 10s⁵ 8g 9g 8.1m³ 9.9g⁶ 8d 10.2f Aug 27] lengthy, workmanlike filly: fair handicapper on turf, modest on all-weather: stays 1¼m: acts on all-weather, good to firm and good to soft ground: tried blinkered, often wears cheekpieces. *R. A. Harris* **73 a61**

FANN (USA) 4 b.f. Diesis 133 – Forest Storm (USA) (Woodman (USA) 126) [2007 83: p8g² 7m 8d⁶ 8.5d 8m⁴ 8m⁴ 10d 8d² 9.9g⁵ Aug 15] sturdy filly: useful performer: mostly highly tried in 2007, flattered when fourth to Nannina in Windsor Forest Stakes at Royal Ascot sixth start: good efforts in listed events last 2 outings, including when 6 lengths second to Whazzis on same course: stays 1¼m: acts on polytrack, good to firm and good to soft going. *C. E. Brittain* **96**

FANTADOT 2 b.g. (Feb 27) Fantastic Light (USA) 134 – Bardot (Efisio 120) [2007 p6g⁵ p6g⁴ Dec 13] modest maiden: better effort when fourth of 5 at Wolverhampton. *D. J. S. ffrench Davis* **59**

FANTASTIC CEE (IRE) 3 b.f. Noverre (USA) 125 – Tee Cee 77 (Lion Cavern (USA) 117) [2007 p8g⁶ p7f* p8.6g⁶ 6f May 5] 40,000F, 67,000Y: third foal: half-sister to 2004 2-y-o 6f winner Yajbill (by Royal Applause) and 2005 2-y-o 7f winner Bold Crus- **71**

ader (by Cape Cross), both useful: dam 7f winner: fair performer: easily best effort when winning maiden at Lingfield in February: has raced freely, but should stay at least 1m: sold 14,500 gns in October. *J. Noseda*

FANTASTIC DELIGHT 4 b.f. Fantastic Light (USA) 134 – Putout 69 (Dowsing **54** (USA) 124) [2007 –: 10.1m 10.1m 12.4m⁴ 13.1d 10f³ p9.5g⁴ p8.6g⁵ p9.5g² p10g³ p9.5g³ Oct 27] modest maiden: left G. M. Moore after fifth start: effective at 9.5f to 12.4f: acts on polytrack and good to firm ground: sometimes races freely. *B. G. Powell*

FANTASTIC LASS 2 b.f. (Mar 11) Fantastic Light (USA) 134 – Shaanara (IRE) 82 **–** (Darshaan 133) [2007 6s 7m 7f Sep 15] 11,000Y: rather leggy filly: second foal: dam, 2-y-o 7f winner, half-sister to smart winner up to 1m Cool Edge: no show in maidens. *R. A. Fahey*

FANTASTIC MORNING 3 ch.g. Fantastic Light (USA) 134 – Gombay Girl (USA) **85** 82 (Woodman (USA) 126) [2007 p8.6g⁴ 9.8m² 10.2g* Jul 9] angular, well-made gelding: first foal: dam fairly useful French 1m winner: progressive form in maidens, winning at Bath in July by 3½ lengths from Abyla, making most and not hard ridden: joined F. Jordan. *M. Johnston*

FANTASTIC VIEW (USA) 6 ch.h. Distant View (USA) 126 – Promptly (IRE) 88 **105** (Lead On Time (USA) 123) [2007 8m 7m⁶ Jul 13] small, sturdy horse: one-time smart performer (for R. Hannon), lightly raced: missed 2005 and 2006: much better effort in 2007 (bandaged behind on reappearance) when sixth to Giganticus in Bunbury Cup (Handicap) at Newmarket: stayed 1m: acted on firm going: to stand at Throckmorton Court Stud, Worcestershire, fee £1,500. *J. Noseda*

FANTASY BELIEVER 9 b.g. Sure Blade (USA) 130 – Delicious 51 (Dominion 123) **103** [2007 115: 6m 6m 7s 6g⁴ 5g 6s 5d⁵ 5d⁶ 6m 6m 5m² 5.6m 5d 6g Oct 26] sturdy gelding: just useful handicapper in 2007: some creditable efforts, including when 1¾ lengths second to Indian Trail at Sandown eleventh outing: effective at 5f to 7f: acts on any going: sometimes hangs/carries head awkwardly: waited on nowadays. *J. J. Quinn*

FANTASY CRUSADER 8 ch.g. Beveled (USA) – Cranfield Charger (Northern State **60** (USA) 91) [2007 62: p8g* p8g³ 10m 10m⁴ 10m⁵ 9g⁵ p10g* 9.7f⁶ 10m p10g Oct 10] modest handicapper: won at Kempton in June (apprentices) and August: effective at 1m/1¼m: acts on polytrack and firm going: has worn headgear: tried tongue tied. *R. M. H. Cowell*

FANTASY DEFENDER (IRE) 5 b.g. Fayruz 116 – Mrs Lucky (Royal Match 117) **50** [2007 57, a54: p8g⁴ p8.6g³ p8.6g⁴ p9.5g⁶ 7m³ 7f 8f 7d³ 7f 8m Sep 25] good-topped gelding: modest handicapper: left Ernst Oertel after fourth outing: seems to stay easy 9.5f: acts on all-weather, firm and good to soft going: tried in cheekpieces/visor. *R. M. H. Cowell*

FANTASY EXPLORER 4 b.g. Compton Place 125 – Zinzi (Song 132) [2007 96: 6m⁶ **78 +** 5g Jun 2] rather leggy, good-topped gelding: useful handicapper at 3 yrs, just fair form in 2007: best at 5f: acts on polytrack, firm and good to soft going. *J. J. Quinn*

FANTASY FIGHTER (IRE) 2 b.g. (Mar 27) Danetime (IRE) 121 – Lady Montekin **48** (Montekin 125) [2007 5m p6g⁶ Oct 6] poor form in sprint maidens (sister stayed 1¼m). *J. J. Quinn*

FANTASY LEGEND (IRE) 4 ch.g. Beckett (IRE) 116 – Sianiski (Niniski (USA) **–** 125) [2007 –: 10.1g Sep 19] little form: tried blinkered. *N. P. Littmoden*

FANTASY PARKES 3 ch.f. Fantastic Light (USA) 134 – My Melody Parkes 102 **90 d** (Teenoso (USA) 135) [2007 82p: 7m 8m 6m 6g p8m Oct 6] leggy, lengthy filly: has a fluent action: fairly useful performer: best effort when seventh to Scarlet Runner in Nell Gwyn Stakes at Newmarket on reappearance (stumbled start): well held after in 1000 Guineas and handicaps: has failed to settle, and likely to prove best short of 1m: acts on good to firm ground. *K. A. Ryan*

FANTASY PRINCESS (USA) 2 ch.f. (Feb 28) Johannesburg (USA) 127 – Fantasy **78 p** 80 (Cadeaux Genereux 131) [2007 p7g* Nov 17] €250,000Y: fourth foal: half-sister to fairly useful 2006 2-y-o 7f winner Musical Mirage (by Royal Anthem): dam twice-raced sister to smart performer up to 1m Stetchworth Prince and half-sister to smart 7f/1m winner Smirk: 12/1, promising debut when winning maiden at Lingfield by head, patiently ridden and quickening well: will stay 1m: should progress. *G. A. Butler*

FANTASY RIDE 5 b.g. Bahhare (USA) 122 – Grand Splendour 79 (Shirley Heights **64** 130) [2007 –: p9.5g⁵ p11g p11g p9.5g 10g 12d 10g⁴ p11g³ 12m⁵ 12m⁵ p12g⁵ p11g⁶ p12g² **a76** p11g Dec 19] rather leggy, quite attractive gelding: has a markedly round action: fair on all-weather, modest on turf: stays 1½m: acts on polytrack and firm and soft ground: tried blinkered. *J. Pearce*

FANTOCHE (BRZ) 5 ch.h. Roi Normand (USA) – Diet Lark (BRZ) (Roy (USA)) **94**
[2007 p8.6g⁵ p8g p12.2g p12g 10.9m² p12.2g* 12g 11.6m p12g Dec 7] good-topped
horse: shows knee action: won twice in Brazil and second in Group 1 1m event there
in 2005 (missed 2006): fairly useful handicapper: won at Wolverhampton in May: left
M. Wallace before final start: stays easy 1½m: acts on polytrack, soft and good to firm
going: tried visored/tongue tied. *Mrs J. Harrington, Ireland*

FARAAMI (IRE) 2 ch.f. (Mar 1) Fraam 114 – Maraami 83 (Selkirk (USA) 129) [2007 –
p6g 6m p8g Oct 17] 24,000Y: sturdy filly: first foal: dam, staying maiden, half-sister to
smart Irish 1m/1¼m performer Latino Magic out of close relative to 1½m performer
Most Welcome: no form. *Pat Eddery*

FARADAY (IRE) 4 b.g. Montjeu (IRE) 137 – Fureau (GER) (Ferdinand (USA)) **55**
[2007 ?: f12g p8.6g* p10g³ p12g p8.6g⁵ Nov 30] modest performer, lightly raced: landed
gamble in minor event at Wolverhampton in August: trained by B. Curley prior to final
start: stays 11f: acts on polytrack and good to soft going. *A. P. Stringer*

FARA'S KINGDOM 3 ch.g. Groom Dancer (USA) 128 – Kingdom Ruby (IRE) 70 –
(Bluebird (USA) 125) [2007 –: 10.5g Sep 12] lengthy gelding: well beaten in maidens.
Miss J. A. Camacho

FARDI (IRE) 5 b.g. Green Desert (USA) 127 – Shuruk 73 (Cadeaux Genereux 131) –
[2007 67: 12m f14g 12m Apr 25] rather leggy gelding: fair performer at best: tailed off all
starts in 2007: tried blinkered. *K. W. Hogg, Isle of Man*

FAREEHA 2 b.f. (Jan 28) King's Best (USA) 132 – Shatarah 79 (Gulch (USA)) [2007 **61**
6.1g 7m 8.3m p8g Nov 7] sturdy filly: second foal: sister to 7f winner in Greece: dam,
maiden (raced only at 7f), closely related to high-class sprinter Malhub: modest maiden:
stays easy 1m: sold 5,000 gns. *J. H. M. Gosden*

FAREFIELD LODGE (IRE) 3 b.g. Indian Lodge (IRE) 127 – Fieldfare (Selkirk **83**
(USA) 129) [2007 78: 6m² 5.1m⁶ 6s⁵ 6g 6m⁴ 6g⁴ 6.1d Oct 10] rather leggy gelding: fairly
useful handicapper: reportedly injured a knee after second outing at 2 yrs: landed odds in
maiden at Nottingham in June: blinkered, well below form final start: gelded after: stays
6f: acts on good to firm going. *C. G. Cox*

FAREHAM CREEK 3 b.g. Amrak Ajeeb (IRE) 112 – Mummy's Chick 77 (Mummy's –
Pet 125) [2007 f8g p6g p5f⁶ 6g p7.1g f8g May 15] little form: tried in cheekpieces.
D. K. Ivory

FARES (IRE) 3 b.c. Mark of Esteem (IRE) 137 – Iftitan (USA) (Southern Halo (USA)) **98**
[2007 90: p7g² p7g⁶ p8g* 8g 7m 6m 7g 7m³ 7m⁴ Sep 13] rather leggy, quite attractive
colt: useful performer: won listed race at Lingfield (by ½ length from Champery) in
April: just respectable efforts at best after: stays 1m: acts on polytrack, best turf form on
good/good to firm going: effective with or without blinkers: tends to hang: no easy ride:
joined D. Watson in UAE. *C. E. Brittain*

FAREWELL GIFT 6 b.g. Cadeaux Genereux 131 – Daring Ditty (Daring March 116) –
[2007 84: p10g Mar 9] big, good-topped gelding: fairly useful handicapper at 5 yrs: well
held only start on Flat in 2007: stays 1m: acts on polytrack, soft and good to firm going:
has been visored, usually blinkered. *Carl Llewellyn*

FAR GONE 2 b.f. (Mar 1) Diktat 126 – Fairy Jackie (IRE) (Fairy King (USA)) [2007 **70**
5m² 5.1g² 5d⁴ p6g² p6g⁴ 6.1m² p6g Sep 18] 10,000F: sturdy filly: second foal: half-sister
to French 7f winner Loupy (by Loup Solitaire): dam French maiden: fair maiden: in
frame 6 starts, twice in nurseries: speedy, raced at 5f/6f: acts on polytrack, good to firm
and good to soft going. *M. L. W. Bell*

FARLEIGH HOUSE (USA) 3 b.c. Lear Fan (USA) 130 – Verasina (USA) 83 **92**
(Woodman (USA) 126) [2007 89: 8m⁴ 8m⁴ 8.2g³ 8m 7m Oct 6] rather leggy, lengthy colt:
fairly useful handicapper: creditable efforts in frame first 3 starts in 2007: better than bare
result when tenth in Britannia Stakes at Royal Ascot next time, poorly drawn: best at 7f/
1m: acts on firm and good to soft going: sent to USA. *M. H. Tompkins*

FARLEY STAR 3 b.f. Alzao (USA) 117 – Girl of My Dreams (IRE) 51 (Marju (IRE) **84**
127) [2007 82p: p7.1g⁵ Apr 24] useful-looking filly: fairly useful form: ran creditably in
handicap sole 3-y-o outing: will stay 1m. *R. Charlton*

FARNE ISLAND 4 ch.g. Arkadian Hero (USA) 123 – Holy Island 81 (Deploy 131) **64**
[2007 66: 10.1g 11.1g² 10.1m⁶ Sep 10] sturdy gelding: modest handicapper nowadays:
stays 11f: acts on polytrack, firm and soft going. *Micky Hammond*

FARNE ISLE 8 ch.m. Midnight Legend 118 – Biloela 67 (Nicholas Bill 125) [2007 –:
13g 16s Jul 3] leggy mare: one-time fair performer: little form since 2005. *G. A. Harker*

FARNESINA (FR) 5 b.m. Anabaa (USA) 130 – Wardara 107 (Sharpo 132) [2007 **91 ?**
a7.5g* p8g⁵ p7.1g⁴ 6g a7.5g² a7.5g⁵ 7d³ 6s Nov 26] fourth foal: sister to useful 6f to 1¼m
winner Dark Charm and half-sister to very smart French sprinter Chineur (by Fasliyev):
dam 5f/6f winner: fairly useful performer: successful at Deauville in minor event in
2006 and apprentice race in January: creditable efforts in listed races at Kempton and
Wolverhampton (fourth to Border Music) next 2 starts: mainly below form afterwards:
stays easy 1m: acts on all-weather and soft going: blinkered nowadays. *E. Danel, France*

FAR NOTE (USA) 9 ch.g. Distant View (USA) 126 – Descant (USA) (Nureyev (USA) **49**
131) [2007 –, a64: f6g f7g f7g f6g f5g³ f6g f5g Mar 13] sturdy, well-made gelding: poor
performer nowadays: has form at 7f, probably best at 5f/6f: acts on fibresand, firm and
good to soft going: tried in cheekpieces, blinkered and tongue tied nowadays: none too
consistent. *S. R. Bowring*

FARPEDON 2 b.g. (Mar 1) Auction House (USA) 120 – Shining Oasis (IRE) 73 (Muj- **70**
tahid (USA) 118) [2007 p6g⁵ 6d⁴ p6g⁵ Dec 1] 58,000Y: sturdy gelding: second foal:
brother to 3-y-o Auction Oasis: dam 2-y-o 7f winner: fair form in maidens: will probably
prove best at 5f/6f: sold 9,000 gns. *H. Candy*

FAR SEEKING 3 b.c. Distant Music (USA) 126 – House Hunting (Zafonic (USA) 130) **68**
[2007 62p: 9.7m⁵ p7g⁴ p7.1g³ p7.1g p9.5d⁶ Dec 17] good-bodied colt: has a quick action:
fair maiden: left Mrs A. Perrett 6,000 gns after third start: should stay beyond 7f: acts on
polytrack: tried tongue tied. *R. A. Harris*

FARSIGHTED 2 b.f. (Mar 13) Where Or When (IRE) 124 – Classic Vision 59 (Classic **73**
Cliche (IRE) 128) [2007 6.1s⁵ 7v* 6m 7g³ 6d Oct 11] 8,000Y: small filly: first foal: dam,
6f/1m winner, closely related to smart 7f/1m performer Yeast and half-sister to smart
sprinter Orientor: fair performer: won maiden at York in July: probably flattered when
third in nursery at Yarmouth: stays 7f: acts on heavy going. *J. M. P. Eustace*

FAR SONG (IRE) 2 ch.f. (Feb 26) Distant Music (USA) 126 – Charlene Lacy (IRE) 77 **54**
(Pips Pride 117) [2007 5g p6g p6s Dec 21] 34,000Y: angular filly: fourth living foal:
half-sister to 8.6f winner Tetcott (by Definite Article) and winner in Italy by Bad As I
Wanna Be: dam 2-y-o 5f winner: best effort in maidens when ninth at Kempton second
start (off 5 months after): has been bandaged hind legs. *A. M. Balding*

FARTHERMOST (IRE) 2 ch.c. (May 14) Fath (USA) 116 – Matila (IRE) 98 (Persian **77**
Bold 123) [2007 6m⁵ 6s⁵ p6g³ p7g² 7g 7g⁴ Aug 24] sturdy colt: fair maiden: in frame 3
starts, including both on polytrack: stays 7f. *R. Hannon*

FASCINATIN RHYTHM 3 br.f. Fantastic Light (USA) 134 – Marguerite de Vine **83**
(Zilzal (USA) 137) [2007 70+: 10m⁵ 10m⁶ 12g 9.7g 11m Aug 4] leggy, sparely-made
filly: fairly useful performer: out of depth second/third starts: should stay 1½m: acts on
good to firm ground. *V. Smith*

FASHION ACCESSORY 3 b.f. Muthahb (IRE) – Queen of Fashion (IRE) 62 (Bara- **–**
thea (IRE) 127) [2007 10m⁶ 10.2d 10d Oct 9] leggy filly: first foal: dam maiden stayed
12.6f: no form. *M. Appleby*

FASHION MODEL 3 b.f. Rainbow Quest (USA) 134 – Gracious Beauty (USA) 67 **70**
(Nijinsky (CAN) 138) [2007 79p: 8.5g² Apr 25] lengthy filly: fair form in maidens: 1¼
lengths second to Shot Gun at Epsom only start in 2007: would have been suited by 1¼m/
1½m: stud. *M. A. Jarvis*

FASHION ROCKS (IRE) 2 b.f. (Apr 2) Rock of Gibraltar (IRE) 133 – La Gandilie **97**
(FR) 106 (Highest Honor (FR) 124) [2007 p6g² 6g* 6g⁶ 6g* Sep 6] 200,000Y: compact
filly: third foal: dam French 2-y-o 1m winner: useful form: won maiden at Goodwood in
August and listed race at Salisbury (improved again, beat Vive Les Rouges by neck) in
September: not clear run when sixth to Nahoodh in Lowther Stakes at York in between:
will be suited by 7f/1m: sent to USA. *B. J. Meehan*

FASHION STATEMENT 3 b.f. Rainbow Quest (USA) 134 – Shabby Chic (USA) **110**
114 (Red Ransom (USA)) [2007 89: 11.4m³ 11d* 10g Oct 28] smallish filly: smart
performer: good length third to Light Shift in listed Cheshire Oaks at Chester on reappearance before winning Oaks d'Italia at Milan (by 1¾ lengths from Moi Non Plus) in June:
well held in Premio Lydia Tesio at Rome final start: will be suited by 1½m+: acts on
heavy and good to firm going. *M. A. Jarvis*

FAST BOWLER 4 b.g. Intikhab (USA) 135 – Alegria 94 (Night Shift (USA)) [2007 **68**
87: p6g 6g May 31] small, heavy-topped gelding: just fair performer in 2007: stays
1m: acts on polytrack and good to firm ground: said to have bled on 2 occasions.
J. M. P. Eustace

FAST COMPANY (IRE) 2 b.c. (Mar 18) Danehill Dancer (IRE) 117 – Sheeza-lady (Zafonic (USA) 130) [2007 7m* 7g* 7d² Oct 20] **126**

Two-year-olds had always been the mainstay of Brian Mechan's stable before he went to Manton at the end of 2005 and nothing has changed. In 2006 seventy-one of his juveniles reached the track, winning forty-three races, while the fifty-seven three-year-olds and upwards hit the target thirty-one times. In the season under review the figures were eighty-five individual two-year-old runners for forty wins, compared with seventy three-year-olds and upwards achieving twenty-one successes between them. To provide a snapshot of this concentration of effort, in the last three months of the year Meehan saddled eighty-four runners in two-year-old races for fourteen victories; his ten runners aged three and up did not win anything. There was quality to go with the quantity through the year as five of Meehan's juvenile colts earned ratings of 100 or higher. Cat Junior (100P) was a stylish winner of his only appearance at Newbury, Sharp Nephew (105) picked up a listed event on the same course, Exclamation (107p) won twice, notably the Tattersalls October Auction Stakes, and City Leader (111) won the Royal Lodge Stakes then finished second in the Racing Post Trophy. Best of all, Fast Company proved himself one of the top colts of his generation, and one with realistic classic claims, running New Approach close in the Dewhurst Stakes on the last of his three outings. All credit to Meehan for doing the ground work with Fast Company and bringing him through to show his ability in the most hotly-contested two-year-old race of the year. However, the plaudits for the colt's achievements in future, whatever they are, will lie elsewhere since Fast Company has joined Godolphin to be trained by Saeed bin Suroor.

It was obvious from his first appearance that Fast Company was a colt with a bright future—a comment which still applies. The race was a fourteen-runner maiden at Salisbury in mid-July for which he looked fit enough to do himself justice and started third favourite. Despite running very green early on—he was niggled at after a quarter of a mile—he got the hang of things soon after halfway and breezed through to win by three lengths from Redolent. Just over a month later Fast Company was stepped up in class in the Tattersalls Millions Acomb Stakes at York, in which he started second favourite to Lucifer Sam, trained by Aidan O'Brien and winner of a maiden race at Galway. The withdrawal of promising winners Captain Brilliance and Tajdeef weakened the field somewhat but four of the five other runners had won in maiden or minor company. Fast Company slammed them. After being waited with, he made smooth headway from halfway and breezed to the front over a furlong out before quickening clear in great style despite looking a little green again, edging left. At the line he had three and a half lengths in hand over Lucifer Sam. Sometimes the way racing functions nowadays has hints of *The Godfather*, with Don Corleone's memorable line 'I'll make him an offer he can't refuse' possessing an almost comic resonance, rather than in the grim sense of

Tattersalls Millions Acomb Stakes, York—Fast Company slams his field; Lucifer Sam (right) and Without A Prayer are his nearest pursuers

author Mario Puzo's characters. Fast Company's victory at York marked him down as a colt to follow, one likely to make his mark in a higher grade, and one worth targeting for possible purchase. A week or so after the race, with Fast Company as short as 12/1 for the Two Thousand Guineas, came news that he had been bought for an undisclosed sum on behalf of one of Sheikh Mohammed's seven sons, Sheikh Hamdan bin Mohammed.

For the time being, Fast Company stayed with Meehan, but he wasn't seen out again until the Dewhurst Stakes two months later. The fact that he had been kept under wraps, and more to the point that none of the beaten colts in the Acomb had done much to advertise the race, resulted in punters giving him the cold shoulder at Newmarket. He went off 14/1 joint-fifth favourite of ten and after a couple of furlongs even those odds looked far from attractive since he was off the bridle and in last place. However, soon after halfway, Fast Company began to warm to his task and, coming widest of all, he produced a tremendous surge, making up four lengths in the space of a furlong and forcing New Approach's rider to pull out the stops. At the line Fast Company was only half a length behind, clear of the rest. Claims made in a few places that he was an unlucky loser are ill-considered, as he was being held through the last fifty yards, but coming wide, without the benefit of the rail or any company on the outside, was not ideal for such an inexperienced colt. Quotes of 9/1 for the Guineas after the race hardly did him justice in relation to New Approach's odds of 5/2, especially as, unlike the favourite, he can be expected to be trained specifically for the first classic, with the Derby ruled out on grounds of stamina. With Rio de La Plata and Ibn Khaldun also in the stable, Godolphin looks to have a strong hand for the colts' classics in the first part of the season. The stable hasn't won the Two Thousand Guineas since 1999—Snow Ridge came second in 2004, Zoning fourth in 2000 and Dubawi fifth when favourite in 2005.

		Danehill	Danzig
Fast Company (IRE)	Danehill Dancer (IRE) (b 1993)	(b 1986)	Razyana
(b.c. Mar 18, 2005)		Mira Adonde (b or br 1986)	Sharpen Up
			Lettre d'Amour
	Sheezalady (br 1997)	Zafonic (b 1990)	Gone West
			Zaizafon
		Canadian Mill (b 1984)	Mill Reef
			Par Excellance

Danehill Dancer was best at up to seven furlongs but he is siring plenty of progeny who stay a mile, notably Where Or When, Jeremy and Speciosa, or even further, such as Decado and Anna Pavlova. Neither of the unraced dam Sheezalady's two other runners showed form at a mile—Mount Klinovec (by Mujadil) was placed over six furlongs and stayed seven, while Rouen (by Noverre) was second over five and six furlongs early on as a two-year-old before breaking a leg on his fourth appearance. However, there is enough stamina in Sheezalady's pedigree to allay fears about the Guineas trip, particularly given the way Fast Company raced at Newmarket. Sheezalady is a daughter of Cheveley Park Stakes runner-up Canadian Mill whose four winners are headed by Hawajiss, successful in the May Hill Stakes and Nassau Stakes and placed in the Oaks and Irish Oaks. The next dam, Par Excellance, landed the Canadian Oaks and produced five winners, notably smart juvenile Khozaam, runner-up in the Royal Lodge Stakes. Fast Company, a close-coupled colt who has yet to race on extremes of going, cost 54,000 guineas at the Newmarket December Sales as a foal and 140,000 guineas at the same venue in October as a yearling. Incidentally, as bargains go his half-sister Mount Klinovec must be one of the best in the last few years. After fetching only €2,000 at Goffs in November 2006, she was resold a year later for 87,000 guineas at the Newmarket December Sales in foal to Royal Anthem. *B. J. Meehan*

FASTELLA (IRE) 2 b.f. (Apr 26) Fasliyev (USA) 120 – Ela Athena 119 (Ezzoud **73 p** (IRE) 126) [2007 p6g⁴ p5m² Nov 24] 35,000Y: third foal: dam 1¼m/1½m (Lancashire Oaks) winner: encouragement in frame in maidens at Lingfield, probably inadequate test: should do better at 1m+. *G. A. Butler*

FAST FEET 2 b.g. (Feb 8) Statue of Liberty (USA) 115 – Landowska (USA) (Langfuhr **84** (CAN) 124) [2007 5.1g³ 5m² 5.1m² 5m 5m 6g 5g⁴ 5.1g⁴ p6g² p5.1g* p5m⁴ p6g⁶ Dec 30] 27,000F, 70,000Y: strong, compact gelding: second foal: dam, US 6f winner, half-sister to useful French performer up to 1m Savannah's Honor: fairly useful performer: won maiden at Wolverhampton in December: below form in nurseries: will prove best at 5f/easy 6f: acts on polytrack and good to firm going: normally forces pace. *K. A. Ryan*

FAST FREDDIE 3 b.g. Agnes World (USA) 123 – Bella Chica (IRE) 95 (Bigstone (IRE) 126) [2007 75: 5f⁴ 5d p5.1m 5m p5g p6m⁶ p6g* p5.1g* p6g³ f6d Dec 11] lengthy, good-topped gelding: fair handicapper: trained by T. Pitt on reappearance: won at Wolverhampton (2) in November and Lingfield in December: stays 6f: acts on polytrack: tried blinkered. *D. J. Murphy* **71**

FAST HEART 6 b.g. Fasliyev (USA) 120 – Heart of India (IRE) (Try My Best (USA) 130) [2007 92d: p6g⁴ p5.1g p6g⁵ p5.1g² p6g p6g³ Mar 9] lengthy, good-bodied gelding: just fair performer in 2007: claimed from R. Harris £6,000 after sixth start: was effective at 5f/6f: acted on polytrack, best turf efforts on good going or firmer: blinkered once: sometimes tongue tied: sometimes started slowly: usually held up: dead. *A. Berry* **67**

FASTRAC BOY 4 b.g. Bold Edge 123 – Nesyred (IRE) 75 (Paris House 123) [2007 67: p5.1g⁶ p6g 5d p5g² p5m⁶ p5g p5m² Dec 9] lengthy gelding: modest handicapper: best form at 5f (shaped as if stamina stretched at 6f): acts on polytrack. *J. R. Best* **62**

FASUBY (IRE) 3 b.f. Fasliyev (USA) 120 – Sue's Ruby (USA) (Crafty Prospector (USA)) [2007 48: 10g⁴ 11.5d⁴ p12g Oct 31] smallish filly: poor maiden: stays 1¼m: acts on firm and soft ground: tends to wander. *P. D. Evans* **46**

FASYLITATOR (IRE) 5 b.g. Fasliyev (USA) 120 – Obsessed 80 (Storm Bird (CAN) 134) [2007 76, a85: p8g Jan 31] close-coupled gelding: fairly useful handicapper at 4 yrs: below form sole start in 2007: effective at 1m/1¼m: acts on all-weather, firm and good to soft going: visored (found little) once: gelded. *D. K. Ivory* **–**

FAT BOY (IRE) 2 ch.c. (Apr 6) Choisir (AUS) 126 – Gold Shift (USA) (Night Shift (USA)) [2007 p5g* 5m 5m⁶ 6m 6m* 6g² 6g* Aug 27] €46,000Y, 70,000 2-y-o: strong, compact colt: fifth foal: half-brother to 2 winners in Italy: dam unraced half-sister to **107**

Mr M. Sines' "Fat Boy"

smart French 2-y-o 1m winner Golden Era: useful performer: developed well, won maiden at Kempton in April, minor event at Newmarket in July and listed race at Ripon (beat Anosti by 3 lengths) in August: also ran well when 1¼ lengths second of 9 to Strike The Deal in Richmond Stakes at Goodwood: should prove best at 5f/6f: acts on polytrack and good to firm going: front runner. *R. Hannon*

FATEFUL ATTRACTION 4 b.f. Mujahid (USA) 125 – Heavens Above (FR) (Pisto- — let Bleu (IRE) 133) [2007 59, a80: p6g 5.7m 8.1d p8g³ p8g p8g⁴ 8d p7g p8g⁴ p10g⁴ p9.5g **a78** p10g* p10m Nov 26] leggy filly: fair handicapper on all-weather/little form on turf in 2007: won at Kempton in November: stays 1¼m: acts on all-weather and firm going: blinkered. *I. A. Wood*

FATEH FIELD (USA) 2 b.c. (Mar 4) Distorted Humor (USA) 117 – Too Cool To Fool **99** (USA) (Foolish Pleasure (USA)) [2007 6.5d* 6g² Oct 27] $500,000Y: leggy colt: fifth foal: half-brother to 3 winners abroad, including US 1m winner Cercatore (by Seeking The Gold): dam US 1m minor stakes winner: useful form: won maiden at Newbury on debut by 3½ lengths: much improved 2 weeks later when 1½ lengths second to Floristry in listed race at Doncaster, again impressing with speed before hanging right under pressure: may prove best up to 6.5f. *Saeed bin Suroor*

FATHOM FIVE (IRE) 3 b.g. Fath (USA) 116 – Ambria (ITY) (Final Straw 127) **105** [2007 83: 6g 5g* 5s* 5d* 5.1d² 5g Aug 22] strong, compact gelding: useful performer: won handicaps at Newmarket in May, and Leicester (by 5 lengths, making all in 4-runner event) and Newmarket (originally demoted after beating Sohraab by a head, having hung left in closing stages, but reinstated as winner on appeal), both in June: good ½-length second to Our Little Secret in listed race at Chester next time: ran poorly in handicap at York final outing: will prove best kept to 5f/6f: acts on soft and good to firm going. *B. Smart*

FATHOMING (USA) 2 ch.f. (Feb 7) Gulch (USA) – Ocean Ridge (USA) 115 (Storm — Bird (CAN) 134) [2007 7m Sep 2] fifth foal: closely related to UAE 7f winner Ocean Song (by Woodman) and half-sister to winner in South Africa by Quiet American: dam, 2-y-o 5.5f (Prix Robert Papin)/6f winner (stayed 1m), out of smart 6f performer Polar Bird: 16/1, pulled up (said to have been lame) in maiden at Folkestone: sold 35,000 gns. *E. A. L. Dunlop*

FATHSTA (IRE) 2 b.c. (May 16) Fath (USA) 116 – Kilbride Lass (IRE) (Lahib (USA) **79** 129) [2007 6g 5m⁶ 6s³ 6s² 6.1m* 6g⁶ 7.1m³ 8m 7g 6g 6m p8g⁶ p7m* p6g* Dec 30] stocky, compact colt: fair performer: won nurseries at Chester in August and Lingfield (2) in December: has form at 1m, but ideally suited by shorter: acts on polytrack, soft and good to firm going. *S. Kirk*

FAVERSHAM 4 b.g. Halling (USA) 133 – Barger (USA) (Riverman (USA) 131) [2007 **65** 80: p12g p9.5g 9.8g² 11g⁵ 10s 10g⁶ Jun 13] tall, quite good-topped gelding: fair performer nowadays: should stay 1½m: acts on good to soft going: sold 18,000 gns in July, resold £7,500 in August: joined J. Mackie. *M. Wigham*

FAVOURING (IRE) 5 ch.g. Fayruz 116 – Peace Dividend (IRE) (Alzao (USA) 117) **43** [2007 60: f7g⁵ f6g² f7g⁶ f6g² f6g³ f7g³ f5g⁴ f6g⁶ f6g² 8d 5s 7.5g⁴ 7g Sep 19] sturdy **a56** gelding: modest handicapper on all-weather, poor on turf: effective at 6f to 8.3f: acts on all-weather, firm and soft going: blinkered/visored: front runner. *M. C. Chapman*

FAYR JAG (IRE) 8 b.g. Fayruz 116 – Lominda (IRE) 80 (Lomond (USA) 128) [2007 **113** 117: 6f³ 6g 6m⁶ 6d 6v 6d 6m 6m 5m⁵ 6m Sep 9] close-coupled gelding: usually impresses in appearance: smart performer: best effort in 2007 when third to Tax Free in minor event at Thirsk on reappearance: just respectable efforts after in Duke of York Stakes at York (eighth to Amadeus Wolf), Stewards' Cup at Goodwood (seventh to Zidane) and listed event at Beverley (fifth to Hellvelyn) second/seventh/ninth outings: effective at 5f/6f: acts on firm and good to soft going, probably not on soft/heavy: reared leaving stall eighth outing. *T. D. Easterby*

FEALEVIEW LADY (USA) 3 b.f. Red Ransom (USA) – Alice White (USA) (Thun- **78** der Gulch (USA) 129) [2007 70: f7g⁶ p7.1g⁴* 7s² 7.1s⁴ 7m 8m³ p8g³ 8.5d p8.6g⁴ Oct 20] tall, good-topped filly: fair handicapper: won at Wolverhampton in May: should be suited by 1¼m: acts on all-weather, soft and good to firm going. *H. Morrison*

FEARED IN FLIGHT (IRE) 2 b.c. (Apr 5) Hawk Wing (USA) 136 – Solar Crystal **111** (IRE) 110 (Alzao (USA) 117) [2007 6g* 7g³ 7m⁶ 7m 8g³ Oct 27] €75,000Y: good-topped, attractive colt: has scope: half-brother to useful 2000 2-y-o 7f winner Lunar Crystal (by Shirley Heights) and fairly useful 1¼m winner Crystal (by Danehill): dam, 2-y-o 6f and 1m (May Hill) winner (stayed 1¼m), half-sister to Fillies' Mile winner

Crystal Music and smart middle-distance stayers Dubai Success and Tchaikovsky: smart performer: won maiden at York in May: third in listed event at Royal Ascot (unlucky) and Racing Post Trophy at Doncaster, in latter much improved when beaten 3 lengths by Ibn Khaldun (hung left under pressure): will be suited by 1¼m/1½m: raced only on good/good to firm going. *B. W. Hills*

FEARLESS WARRIOR 2 b.g. (Mar 31) Erhaab (USA) 127 – Princess Genista 108 **70 p** (Ile de Bourbon (USA) 133) [2007 7m⁴ 8m⁴ 8.2g⁶ Oct 31] short-backed gelding: brother to fairly useful 1¾m winner Queen of Iceni and half-brother to several at least useful winners, notably smart 1¾m to 2½m winner Give Notice (by Warning): dam, 1m (including at 2 yrs) winner, stayed 15f: fair form in maidens, likely insufficient test: will be well suited by 1½m+: should progress in 3-y-o handicaps. *J. L. Dunlop*

FEAR TO TREAD (USA) 4 ch.f. Peintre Celebre (USA) 137 – Pleine Lune (IRE) **85** (Alzao (USA) 117) [2007 85: p12g 11.8s² 12f p11g Sep 8] sturdy filly: fairly useful handicapper: form in 2007 only when second at Leicester: shaped as if amiss otherwise: stays 12.6f: acts on soft and good to firm going: sold 12,000 gns. *Mrs P. Sly*

FEASIBLE 2 ch.g. (Apr 28) Efisio 120 – Zoena 67 (Emarati (USA) 74) [2007 6m⁴ 7g⁵ **74** p7.1g⁵ 8f² Sep 10] good-bodied gelding: fair maiden: second in nursery at Bath: stays 1m: acts on firm going, probably polytrack. *J. G. Portman*

FEATHERLIGHT 3 b.f. Fantastic Light (USA) 134 – Feathers Flying (IRE) 100 **78** (Royal Applause 124) [2007 55: f8g⁵ p10f 11g³ p11g* p10g⁴ p12g² p11g p12g³ p16g* p16g* 16g⁶ Nov 2] rather leggy, useful-looking filly: improved into a fair performer: won claimer (claimed from J. Jay £9,000) in May and handicaps 2 weeks apart in September, all at Kempton: stays easy 2m: acts on all-weather and good to firm ground: tried visored, often blinkered (including for all 3 wins). *Jamie Poulton*

FEATHERSTONE 2 b.g. (Mar 28) Umistim 119 – Summer Passion 86 (Pennekamp **42** (USA) 130) [2007 5m⁶ 6g May 20] lengthy gelding: poor form in claimer/seller. *N. Tinkler*

FEELIN FOXY 3 b.f. Foxhound (USA) 103 – Charlie Girl 70 (Puissance 110) [2007 **76** 72§, a67§: 5.1g 5g 5.3d³ 5g⁴ 5g³ 5m³ 5m⁶ p5.1g* 5.1s⁶ 5m p5.1g² 5.1f⁴ 5f 6g* 6d⁵ 6g² Oct 30] tall filly: fair handicapper: won at Wolverhampton in June and, having left D. Shaw, Hamilton in September: stays 6f: acts on polytrack, firm and soft going: usually visored (not last 3 outings): pulled hard seventh start. *J. G. Given*

FEELING FRESH (IRE) 2 b.c. (Mar 3) Xaar 132 – Oh'cecilia (IRE) 95 (Scenic 128) **66** [2007 6m 7.1g 8.1s p7.1g p8.6g p5.1g⁵ p6d⁴ p6d⁴ Dec 28] sturdy colt: fair performer: won nursery at Wolverhampton in December: probably stays 7f: acts on polytrack and good to firm going: visored (ran respectably) once. *Paul Green*

FEELING (IRE) 3 b.g. Sadler's Wells (USA) 132 – La Pitie (USA) (Devil's Bag **77 d** (USA)) [2007 10m 10.5g 11.9m⁵ 11.9m³ 10.1d⁴ 12m 13.4g 11.6d Oct 15] useful-looking gelding: fair maiden: well below form after fourth start: may prove best at 1¼m: acts on good to firm ground: blinkered last 2 outings (hung badly final one): sold 15,000 gns and gelded. *P. W. Chapple-Hyam*

FEELING LUCKY (IRE) 2 b.c. (Mar 26) Namid 128 – Toldya 93 (Beveled (USA)) **–** [2007 6d Sep 28] good-bodied colt: 9/1, well held in maiden at Haydock won by Exclamation: bred for sprinting. *W. Jarvis*

FEELING PECKISH (USA) 3 ch.g. Point Given (USA) 134 – Sunday Bazaar **–** (USA) (Nureyev (USA) 131) [2007 f8g f11g 10g 12m⁶ 10.1d 8g 12m 8m Oct 8] sturdy gelding: no form: tried tongue tied. *M. C. Chapman*

FEELING PROUD (USA) 2 b.f. (May 1) More Than Ready (USA) 120 – Proud **72** Heart (IRE) (Caerleon (USA) 132) [2007 p5g* 5g 5g 6m p7.1g⁶ 6m Oct 5] $35,000F, 28,000Y: tall, rather leggy filly: half-sister to 3 winners abroad, including Australian 5.5f winner Melia (by Timber Country): dam unraced sister to smart 1m winner Metal Storm: fair performer: won maiden at Lingfield in May: no progress after, mostly stiff tasks: seems to stay 7f. *Jane Chapple-Hyam*

FEELING WONDERFUL (IRE) 3 b.f. Fruits of Love (USA) 127 – Teodora (IRE) **69** 93 (Fairy King (USA)) [2007 73p: 8.3g 8m p10g³ 8.1d⁴ p8.6g³ Jul 6] fair performer: bred to be suited by 1¼m+: acts on polytrack and heavy ground. *M. Johnston*

FEELIN IRIE (IRE) 4 b.g. Key of Luck (USA) 126 – Charlotte's Dancer (Kris 135) **62** [2007 65: p6g⁶ p7.1g⁶ f7g⁶ p6g f8g* f8g f8g³ p7g⁶ p8.6g⁶ 8m 7g⁶ p7g p7g Oct 31] close-coupled, workmanlike gelding: modest handicapper: won at Southwell in March: stays

1m: acts on all-weather and firm going: wears cheekpieces nowadays: tried tongue tied: free-going front runner. *J. R. Boyle*

FEELS LIKE HEAVEN 3 b.f. Mull of Kintyre (USA) 114 – Gargren (IRE) (Mujtahid — (USA) 118) [2007 f7g⁶ f7g Mar 28] 15,000Y: fourth foal: half-sister to 2002 2-y-o 5f winner Miss Twti (by Ali-Royal) and 7f/1m winner in Italy by Sri Pekan: dam unraced: well held in maidens at Southwell. *T. D. Easterby*

FEISTY ROYALE 2 b.f. (Feb 28) Royal Applause 124 – Hawait Al Barr 100 (Green **85** Desert (USA) 127) [2007 6m² 5.9d³ 6d² 6g 6g* 7m³ 6d* 7g Oct 27] €50,000Y: good-topped filly: half-sister to several winners, including 1m/9f winner Equity Princess (by Warning) and 1½m winner Blaze of Colour (by Rainbow Quest), both useful: dam 1½m to 2m winner: fairly useful performer: won nurseries at Leicester in September and Newbury in October: will stay at least 1m: acts on good to firm and good to soft going. *M. Johnston*

FELICIA 2 b.f. (Jan 28) Diktat 126 – Gracia 78 (Linamix (FR) 127) [2007 6d p6g Dec **55 p** 29] neat filly: first foal: dam 8.5f/1¼m winner: modest form in maidens, considerately handled: will be suited by 1m: should do better. *S. C. Williams*

FELLOW SHIP 7 b.g. Elmaamul (USA) 125 – Genoa 96 (Zafonic (USA) 130) [2007 — § p8g p8g Apr 2] close-coupled gelding: one-time fairly useful performer: has become ungenuine, and well held in sellers in 2007: tried tongue tied/in cheekpieces/blinkers. *P. Butler*

FELLRUNNER (IRE) 2 b.c. (Mar 16) Traditionally (USA) 117 – Via Splendida (IRE) — § 80 (Project Manager 111) [2007 7d 7g 7g Nov 6] sturdy colt: temperamental maiden, refused to race second outing. *A. Berry*

FEMINIST (IRE) 5 b.m. Alhaarth (IRE) 126 – Miss Willow Bend (USA) (Willow — Hour (USA)) [2007 –, a46: p5.1g p5.1g⁶ f5g p6g p5.1g 6m Apr 29] modest performer on **a50** all-weather, little recent form on turf: likely to prove best at 5f/6f: acts on polytrack: has worn blinkers/cheekpieces: often races prominently. *J. M. Bradley*

FENNERS (USA) 4 ch.g. Pleasant Tap (USA) – Legal Opinion (IRE) (Polish Precedent **71** (USA) 131) [2007 59: 12.4m* 12m³ 14g 12v 14m 11.1m³ 12.1m⁵ 12m³ p12g² p12g³ p12.2g* Dec 15] sturdy gelding: fair handicapper: won at Newcastle in May and Wolver-hampton in December: stays 12.4f: acts on polytrack and firm going: tongue tied at 3 yrs: tried blinkered: has looked none too keen. *M. W. Easterby*

FEOLIN 3 b.f. Dr Fong (USA) 128 – Finlaggan 83 (Be My Chief (USA) 122) [2007 75p: **75** p8g³ 10m 9g 8d* 8g³ 8d⁴ Oct 1] good-bodied filly: fair handicapper: won at Brighton (enterprisingly ridden) in August: should be suited by 1¼m/1½m: acts on polytrack, good to firm and good to soft ground. *H. Morrison*

FERNELEY (IRE) 3 b.c. Ishiguru (USA) 114 – Amber Tide (IRE) 75 (Pursuit of Love **109** 124) [2007 104: 10m² 8m 7m 10m⁴ 10g⁴ 8m Oct 6] close-coupled colt: useful performer: good efforts in frame in Ballysax Stakes at Leopardstown (½-length second to Mores Wells), Kilternan Stakes on same course (denied clear run when fourth to Hearthstead Maison) and listed race at Fairyhouse (found little when fourth to Arch Rebel): below form otherwise in Irish 2000 Guineas at the Curragh, Jersey Stakes at Royal Ascot and Joel Stakes at Newmarket (bandaged fore joints and blinkered): best at 1¼m: acts on good to firm and good to soft ground. *Francis Ennis, Ireland*

FERN HOUSE (IRE) 5 b.g. Xaar 132 – Certain Impression (USA) (Forli (ARG)) **60** [2007 46: 5g 6g 5g⁵ 5m* 5m 6g 5s 8v p6g⁵ f6d⁴ p5.1g³ Dec 31] modest handicapper: won at Catterick in August: effective at 5f/6f: acts on polytrack and good to firm going (well held on softer than good): tried blinkered: signs of temperament. *Garry Moss*

FERNLAWN HOPE (IRE) 2 b.f. (Apr 7) Danehill Dancer (IRE) 117 – Hana Marie **61** 101§ (Formidable (USA) 125) [2007 p7g 7.5m p7g p8m p8m* Nov 11] €62,000Y: compact filly: sister to fairly useful 6f winner Naughty Nell and half-sister to 2 winners, including 7-y-o Sri Diamond: dam, 2-y-o 5f/6f winner, half-sister to smart middle-distance performer Compton Bolter: modest form: won nursery at Kempton final start: will stay 1¼m: acts on polytrack. *J. A. Osborne*

FERVENT 3 b.g. Kyllachy 129 – Romancing 79 (Dr Devious (IRE) 127) [2007 7m⁵ **57** 6.1m⁶ 6m 6.1s 6.1d p7m p7g Oct 10] strong gelding: modest maiden: stays 7f: acts on good to firm ground. *J. M. Bradley*

FERVENT PRINCE 2 b.g. (Apr 4) Averti (IRE) 117 – Maria Theresa (Primo Dominie **76** 121) [2007 5g 6s 6g⁵ 5.5m³ 6m³ 6m³ 7s Oct 14] sturdy, lengthy gelding: fair maiden:

placed in 3 nurseries: should stay 7f: best form on good to firm going: hard ride, tried in blinkers/cheekpieces. *H. Morrison*

FESTIVAL DREAMS 2 ch.g. (Apr 25) Largesse 112 – Bright Spangle (IRE) 67 **52** (General Monash (USA) 107) [2007 8.1f p7g p8.6g⁵ Nov 8] modest maiden: bred to stay 1½m. *Miss J. S. Davis*

FESTIVALE (IRE) 2 b.f. (Feb 3) Invincible Spirit (IRE) 121 – Cephalonie (USA) **90 p** (Kris S (USA)) [2007 6m⁶ 6m* 6g⁵ Nov 2] close-coupled, quite good-topped filly: third foal: closely related to 4-y-o Tell: dam French 1½m winner: fairly useful form: won maiden at Lingfield in June: off 5 months, more progress when fifth to Spinning Lucy in listed race at Newmarket, held up and having to wait for gap: likely to stay 7f: should continue improving. *J. L. Dunlop*

FESTIVE CHIMES (IRE) 6 b.m. Efisio 120 – Delightful Chime (IRE) 79 (Alzao **66** (USA) 117) [2007 p12.2g³ 15.8m⁴ p16g⁶ 16f Jul 30] fair maiden on Flat (fairly useful hurdler): stays 2m: acts on polytrack and firm going: tried in cheekpieces. *N. B. King*

FESTIVE TIPPLE (IRE) 3 b.g. Tipsy Creek (USA) 115 – Gi La High 68 (Rich **45** Charlie 117) [2007 65: 6.1m 6m⁶ May 21] just poor maiden in 2007: speedy, and worth a try at 5f: acts on polytrack. *P. Winkworth*

FESTOSO (IRE) 2 b.f. (Feb 8) Diesis 133 – Garah 107 (Ajdal (USA) 130) [2007 6g* **102** 6g 6m² 6g⁴ 6m³ Oct 5] sturdy filly: half-sister to several winners, notably very smart 9f winner Olden Times (by Darshaan): dam, sprinter, out of smart sprinter Abha: useful form: won maiden at Newmarket in May: good progress in pattern events, length second of 14 to You'resothrilling in Cherry Hinton Stakes at Newmarket, 1½ lengths fifth (promoted to fourth) of 10 to Nahoodh in Lowther Stakes at York and 4¼ lengths third of 14 to Natagora in Cheveley Park Stakes (ridden more patiently than before) at Newmarket: will stay 7f: raced only on good/good to firm going. *H. J. L. Dunlop*

FEVER 3 b.g. Dr Fong (USA) 128 – Follow Flanders 92 (Pursuit of Love 124) [2007 80: **92** p10g³ 10g* 10d* 10.1g² 12g Jun 21] rather leggy, close-coupled gelding: keen walker: has a quick, unimpressive action: fairly useful performer: won maiden at Nottingham in April and handicap at Windsor (dead-heated with Maid To Believe) in May: further improvement when neck second to Zaham in handicap at Epsom, hanging left: stays 1¼m (not 1½m): acts on polytrack and good to soft ground: sold only 7,000 gns in October, and gelded. *R. Hannon*

FICOMA 3 b.f. Piccolo 121 – Hemaca (Distinctly North (USA) 115) [2007 75: 7g⁶ 7f² **81** 7g 8.1g p7g Oct 24] close-coupled filly: fairly useful performer: stays 7f: acts on firm and good to soft going: sold 3,000 gns, sent to Serbia. *C. G. Cox*

FICTIONAL 6 b.h. Fraam 114 – Manon Lescaut 56 (Then Again 126) [2007 99: 6m **–** May 5] sturdy horse: useful performer at 5 yrs: last only start in 2007: effective at 5f/ 6f: acts on good to firm ground, possibly not on softer than good: races prominently. *E. J. O'Neill*

FIDDLERS CREEK (IRE) 8 b.g. Danehill (USA) 126 – Mythical Creek (USA) **46** (Pleasant Tap (USA)) [2007 59, a75: p13.9g⁵ f11g⁶ 12s 10.1g⁶ 9.2g Aug 22] quite good- **a63** topped gelding: modest performer on all-weather, poor on turf: effective at 1m to 1½m: acts on all-weather, firm and soft going: often wears headgear: tried tongue tied: inconsistent. *R. Allan*

FIDDLERS SPIRIT (IRE) 3 b.g. Invincible Spirit (IRE) 121 – Coco Ricoh (IRE) **–** (Lycius (USA) 124) [2007 46: p7.1g 7d May 17] poor maiden at 2 yrs: well held in 2007, then gelded: tried visored/blinkered: raced freely on reappearance. *J. G. M. O'Shea*

FIDELIA (IRE) 3 b.f. Singspiel (IRE) 133 – Rosse 100 (Kris 135) [2007 78p: 10m⁴ **102** 11.4m 10m⁶ 8d³ 8.1d² 8g* 7d⁴ p8m² Nov 1] small filly: useful performer: won maiden at Ripon (by 5 lengths) in August: much improved in frame in listed races at Ascot (fourth to Miss Lucifer) and Lingfield (beaten head by Sesmen) after: effective at 7f/1m: acts on polytrack, unraced on extremes of going on turf: has been bandaged behind: sent to USA. *G. Wragg*

FIDELIAS DANCE 2 b.f. (Feb 13) Danehill Dancer (IRE) 117 – Fidelio's Miracle **72** (USA) 108 (Mountain Cat (USA)) [2007 5.1g 6g⁵ p6g³ 6m 6m⁴ 7.1m⁵ p7g³ Oct 24] 65,000Y: angular filly: first foal: dam French 7.5f to 1¼m winner: fair maiden: twice placed at Lingfield: effective at 6f/7f: acts on polytrack and good to firm going: sold 6,500 gns. *M. Johnston*

FIEFDOM (IRE) 5 br.g. Singspiel (IRE) 133 – Chiquita Linda (IRE) (Mujadil (USA) **91** 119) [2007 91: 7.1g⁴ 7g⁴ 7.1m 7m² 7.1d⁴ 7g⁶ 8m⁵ 7m² 7m⁶ 7m⁶ 7.6m³ 7m 7f⁵ 7g p7g⁵ p8g[2] p8.6g[3] p9.5g p8m p8g Dec 16] compact gelding: has a quick action: fairly useful handicapper: best efforts in 2007 when placed at Lingfield and Wolverhampton sixteenth/ seventeenth starts: stays 8.6f: acts on polytrack, firm and soft going: tried in cheekpieces/ blinkers: has hung left. *I. W. McInnes*

FIFTEEN LOVE (USA) 2 b. or br.c. (Apr 2) Point Given (USA) 134 – Nidd (USA) **101** 112 (Known Fact (USA) 135) [2007 7m[2] 7m* 7d* 7d Oct 27] strong, close-coupled colt: half-brother to several winners, including 8-y-o Expected Bonus and fairly useful 5f winner Charango (by Danzig): dam, 5.5f to 7f (at 2 yrs) winner, closely related to Breeders' Cup Classic winner Skywalker: useful form: second to Rio de La Plata in maiden at Newmarket on debut: won similar event there later in July and minor event at Salisbury (beat Collection by 1¼ lengths) in October: 11/2, seemed amiss when last in Horris Hill Stakes: will stay 1m: acts on good to firm and good to soft going. *R. Charlton*

FIFTH ZAK 3 b.g. Best of The Bests (IRE) 122 – Zakuska 96 (Zafonic (USA) 130) **–** [2007 8.3d Aug 20] 33/1, well-held seventh to Turban Heights in maiden at Leicester. *S. R. Bowring*

FIFTY CENTS 3 ch.g. Diesis 133 – Solaia (USA) 110 (Miswaki (USA) 124) [2007 **83 +** 88p: 8.1m* 8d 7.2s[5] Sep 22] good-topped gelding: has scope: fairly useful form: won maiden at Haydock in May: much better effort after when fifth in handicap at Ayr: gelded after: should be suited by 1¼m/1½m: acts on soft and good to firm ground. *R. Charlton*

FIFTY (IRE) 2 b.f. (Jan 31) Fasliyev (USA) 120 – Amethyst (IRE) 111 (Sadler's Wells **86** (USA) 132) [2007 6g[4] 7m[2] 6g 6.5d p6g[4] Oct 15] 50,000Y: angular filly: fourth foal: half-sister to 3-y-o Audit: dam, Irish 6f (at 2 yrs) and 7f winner (also second in Irish 1000 Guineas), sister to 2000 Guineas winner King of Kings: maiden: fairly useful form on debut (fourth to Fashion Rocks at Goodwood): not disgraced next start but well below best after: may prove best at 5f/6f. *R. Hannon*

FIGARO FLYER (IRE) 4 b.g. Mozart (IRE) 131 – Ellway Star (IRE) 104 (Night **89** Shift (USA)) [2007 91, a96: p5g[3] p5.1g* p6g[2] p5f[4] p6f p6g[4] f5g[2] 5f[6] p6g[3] 6m 6g f6g[3] 6m 6d 5m[5] 6g 6m 5s 5g 6g[5] p7g[4] p6g* p7g p6g p6g*] Dec 29] sturdy gelding: fair handi-capper: won at Wolverhampton in January, November and December: barely stays 7f: acts on all-weather and firm going. *P. Howling*

FIGARO'S QUEST (IRE) 5 b.g. Singspiel (IRE) 133 – Seren Quest 90 (Rainbow **53** Quest (USA) 134) [2007 70: 16d[4] 16.2v[6] p16.5g 14m[6] 14.1d p12.2g[5] p13.9g Nov 5] close-coupled gelding: only modest performer in 2007: effective at 1½m to 2m: acts on polytrack and probably any turf going: often blinkered: difficult ride. *C. N. Kellett*

FILEY BUOY 5 b.g. Factual (USA) 108 – Tugra (FR) (Baby Turk 120) [2007 49: f8g **45** 7m f8g 7m 7.1s[4] 7d 7.5v[5] 8g 8.5g Aug 15] workmanlike gelding: poor performer: best form at 7f/1m: acts on fibresand and any turf going: usually wears headgear. *R. M. Whitaker*

FILIGREE LACE (USA) 2 ch.f. (Feb 21) Seeking The Gold (USA) – Yafill (USA) **61 p** 80 (Nureyev (USA) 131) [2007 7g Nov 3] quite good-topped filly: closely related to 2 winners, including UAE 9f/1½m winner Yiflan (by Gone West), and half-sister to several winners, including French 2002 2-y-o 6f/1m winner Loving Pride (by Quiet American) and 1¼m winner Ipledgeallegiance (by Alleged), both useful: dam, 2-y-o 6f winner, out of half-sister to Zilzal: 11/1, faded into tenth (of 20) behind Infallible in maiden at Newmarket: will do better. *Sir Michael Stoute*

FILIOS (IRE) 3 b.c. Kutub (IRE) 123 – Karlinaxa (Linamix (FR) 127) [2007 79p: **107 p** 10.5g[2] 12g* 12g[2] Jun 21] leggy, angular colt: useful handicapper: won at York (comfort-ably by length from Eglevski) in May: further improvement when head second to Heron Bay in King George V Stakes at Royal Ascot next time, clear of rest: will stay 1¾m: acts on polytrack, raced only on good ground on turf: held up: sold privately, and joined Godolphin: likely to improve further. *L. M. Cumani*

FILLIEMOU (IRE) 6 gr.m. Goldmark (USA) 113 – St Louis Lady 71 (Absalom 128) **46** [2007 –: p8.6g p10g 10m 14.1g 10.2f May 1] lengthy mare: poor maiden: stays 1¼m: acts on polytrack, firm and soft ground: tried visored. *A. W. Carroll*

FILLIGREE (IRE) 2 b.f. (Mar 14) Kyllachy 129 – Clunie 84 (Inchinor 119) [2007 **65** 5.1d[3] 5.1g[5] p6g[6] Nov 21] sturdy filly: fifth foal: closely related to fairly useful 2004 2-y-o 6f winner Propellor (by Pivotal) and half-sister to 2 winners, including fairly useful 2006 2-y-o 7.6f winner Porcelain (by Peintre Celebre): dam 6f winner, including at 2 yrs: fair maiden: standout effort on debut (third to Quiet Elegance at Nottingham): should prove best at 5f/6f. *Rae Guest*

FILM MAKER (IRE) 2 b.c. (Mar 27) Danetime (IRE) 121 – Alexander Anapolis **87 p**
(IRE) 94 (Spectrum (IRE) 126) [2007 6d⁵ Oct 19] 75,000Y: good-topped colt: first foal:
dam, Irish 1½m winner, out of smart Irish 7f winner Pirouette, herself half-sister to very
smart sprinter Ballad Rock: 14/1 and green, shaped well when fifth of 14 to Insaaf in
maiden at Newmarket (started slowly, finished well): will be suited by 7f/1m: sure to win
races. *B. J. Meehan*

FILTHYGORGEOUS (IRE) 2 ch.f. (Mar 16) Bahamian Bounty 116 – Quick Flight –
72 (Polar Falcon (USA) 126) [2007 7d 5s 5s Jul 23] 12,000Y: neat filly: first foal: dam
2-y-o 5f and 7f winner: no form: dead. *J. R. Weymes*

FINAL BID (IRE) 4 b.g. Mujadil (USA) 119 – Dusky Virgin 62 (Missed Flight 123) **59**
[2007 59: 12m⁶ Apr 13] modest maiden: effective at 7f to 1½m: acts on polytrack, good
to firm and good to soft going: tried blinkered: none too consistent: fair winning hurdler.
M. G. Quinlan

FINAL DESIRE 4 b.f. Grey Desire 115 – Call Me Lucky 65 (Magic Ring (IRE) 115) –
[2007 7s⁶ 7g 6m Sep 1] big, rangy filly: third foal: sister to 7f winner Steel Grey: dam
2-y-o 6f winner: no form. *M. Brittain*

FINAL DYNASTY 3 b.f. Komaite (USA) – Malcesine (IRE) 46 (Auction Ring (USA) **104**
123) [2007 80: 5m² 5g² 5s* 6.1m⁶ 6d⁶ 5g 5g Oct 27] good-topped filly: useful performer:
much improved in 2007, winning handicap at Pontefract in July by ¾ length from Namir:
very good head second to Mecca's Mate in listed race at Ayr on second outing: just
respectable efforts at best last 4 starts: best form at 5f: acts on polytrack, firm and soft
going: races prominently. *Mrs G. S. Rees*

FINAL ESTEEM 4 ch.g. Lomitas 129 – Fame At Last (USA) 98 (Quest For Fame 127) **70 d**
[2007 67: p8.6g² p8.6g p9.5g p10g Mar 30] lengthy, angular gelding: fair performer: left
G. A. Swinbank £10,000 after reappearance, below form subsequently: should stay 1¼m
(seemingly not 1½m): acts on polytrack and firm ground. *R. A. Harris*

FINALMENTE 5 b.g. Kahyasi 130 – Sudden Spirit (FR) (Esprit du Nord (USA) 126) **114**
[2007 107: 12m³ 14g⁴ 20g⁴ 16.4g³ 16g³ 18m⁵ Sep 14] good-bodied gelding: smart
performer: further progress in 2007, including in Gold Cup at Royal Ascot (fourth to
Yeats), Goodwood Cup (third to Allegretto) and Doncaster Cup (fifth to Septimus) on
third and last 2 outings: stays 2½m: acts on polytrack, soft and good to firm ground: in
cheekpieces last 2 starts: races prominently. *N. A. Callaghan*

FINAL OVERTURE (FR) 3 b.f. Rossini (USA) 118 – Final Moment 100 (Nishapour **57**
(FR) 125) [2007 8g 9.9g³ Aug 15] half-sister to useful Irish 1998 2-y-o 5f winner Wish
List (by Mujadil) and fairly useful Irish 1m winner Kurbaan (by Woodborough): dam best
at 1m/1¼m in Ireland: better effort in maidens when 10¾ lengths eighth of 11 to Cactus
Rose at Brighton on debut: well held at Beverley next time. *H. R. A. Cecil*

FINAL TUNE (IRE) 4 ch.g. Grand Lodge (USA) 125 – Jackie's Opera (FR) (Indian **84**
Ridge 123) [2007 77: f7g³ p7.1g⁴ p8g⁶ 8.2g⁴ p7.1g² f8g³ 9.1m* 9.1g⁵ 9m Aug 4] angular
gelding: fairly useful handicapper: won at Ayr in June: effective at 7f to 9f: acts on all-
weather, firm and good to soft going: consistent. *Miss M. E. Rowland*

FINAL VERSE 4 b.g. Mark of Esteem (IRE) 137 – Tamassos 67 (Dance In Time **113**
(CAN)) [2007 113: 9m³ 8.1g⁵ 8.3d⁴ 8.3s⁴ 8m* 8d⁶ Aug 16] good-topped, attractive
gelding: has a quick action: smart performer: left Sir Michael Stoute after third start: won
minor event at Newmarket (by 2 lengths from Metropolitan Man, edging right and
flashing tail) in August: soon poorly placed when only sixth of 7 to Pride of Nation in
Sovereign Stakes at Salisbury final start: stays 9f, bred to stay 1¼m: acts on soft and good
to firm going: usually gets stirred up in preliminaries, and has raced freely (has worn
crossed noseband). *J. S. Moore*

FINANCIAL TIMES (USA) 5 b.g. Awesome Again (CAN) 133 – Investabull (USA) **89**
(Holy Bull (USA) 134) [2007 82: p5g² p5.1g² p5.1g³ p5.1g⁴ p5.1g² p5g³ p5g² p5g*
p5.1g⁶ Dec 8] strong, attractive gelding: fairly useful handicapper: won at Lingfield in
November: best at 5f: acts on polytrack and good to firm going: tongue tied: in cheek-
pieces/visor first 4 starts at 5 yrs: usually forces pace: consistent. *Stef Liddiard*

FIND IT OUT (USA) 4 b.g. Luhuk (USA) 114 – Ursula (VEN) (Phone Trick (USA)) –
[2007 –: p9.5g Oct 27] smallish, strong gelding: modest maiden at 2 yrs: little impact
since: tried tongue tied/in cheekpieces. *B. J. Llewellyn*

FINE ART WORLD (IRE) 3 br.g. Agnes World (USA) 123 – Foreign Relation (IRE) **48**
57 (Distant Relative 128) [2007 7s⁵ 7m 7s⁶ 9g⁴ Aug 30] poor maiden: stays 9f: sold 2,500
gns, sent to Spain. *N. A. Callaghan*

FINE DEED 6 b.g. Kadeed (IRE) – Kristis Girl 76 (Ballacashtal (CAN)) [2007 –: – p12.2g Jan 5] no form. *Ian Williams*

FINE EDGE 6 ch.m. Keen 116 – Cap That (Derek H 97) [2007 10.2g Jul 9] 1,100 4-y-o: – fifth foal: dam bumper winner: poor form in bumpers: 100/1, tailed off in maiden at Bath on Flat debut. *H. E. Haynes*

FINE RULER (IRE) 3 b.g. King's Best (USA) 132 – Bint Alajwaad (IRE) (Fairy King 74 (USA)) [2007 73: p8g⁶ p8g⁶ 9.7g³ p10g p8.6g⁵ p8.6g⁴ p7.1g² Dec 14] 20,000Y: tall, leggy gelding: fair maiden: left M. Channon 16,000 gns after fourth start: free-going sort, but stays 9.7f: acts on polytrack and good to firm going: often leads. *M. R. Bosley*

FINICIUS (USA) 3 b.c. Officer (USA) 120 – Glorious Linda (FR) (Le Glorieux 127) 115 [2007 96: 8s⁵ 7g⁶ 8g p6g* Dec 7] $115,000Y, resold $65,000Y: rather leggy, attractive colt: first foal: dam, 1m winner in France/USA, half-sister to very smart French 1¼m performer Execute: smart performer: claimer ridden, best effort when winning handicap at Dundalk in December readily by 1½ lengths from Johnstown Lad: not discredited when 3¾ lengths sixth to Tariq in Betfair Cup (Lennox) at Goodwood: well held in Celebration Mile there in between: should stay 1m: acts on polytrack and good to firm going. *Eoin Griffin, Ireland*

FINISHED ARTICLE (IRE) 10 b.g. Indian Ridge 123 – Summer Fashion 84 61 (Moorestyle 137) [2007 76, a64: p12.2g* p13.9g* p12.2g p12.2g³ p16f p13.9g⁶ p16g 12g⁵ Apr 2] workmanlike gelding: modest performer: won claimer and seller at Wolverhampton in January: left P. Blockley £2,200 after fourth start: stays 1¾m: acts on polytrack, firm and good to soft going: blinkered/tongue tied final outing: held up. *K. J. Burke*

FINLAY'S FOOTSTEPS 3 ch.g. Dr Fong (USA) 128 – Bay Shade (USA) 90 (Sharp- – en Up 127) [2007 –: f8g 12d⁶ Jun 24] close-coupled gelding: well held in maidens: bred to stay 1m/1¼m. *G. M. Moore*

FINMORE QUEEN (USA) 2 ch.f. (Feb 26) Grand Slam (USA) 120 – Slew City 56 p Slicker (USA) (Slew City Slew (USA)) [2007 7g Nov 3] $170,000Y, resold $260,000Y: big, strong filly: fourth foal: half-sister to 3 winners in US, notably smart Grade 1 8.5f winner Pool Land (by Silver Deputy): dam unraced half-sister to Breeders' Cup Sprint winner Very Subtle: 33/1 and in need of experience, showed ability when behind in maiden at Newmarket: will do better. *J. R. Fanshawe*

FINNEGANS RAINBOW 5 ch.g. Spectrum (IRE) 126 – Fairy Story (IRE) 80 (Per- 55 sian Bold 123) [2007 56?: 10m 10.1m 10g p12.2g⁵ Oct 30] big gelding: modest maiden: stays 1½m: acts on all-weather and good to firm ground. *M. C. Chapman*

FINSBURY 4 br. or gr.g. Observatory (USA) 131 – Carmela Owen (Owington 123) 81 [2007 89: p7g p8g⁵ 7g 8.1g⁴ 10m 8d⁵ 7m* 7g³ 6m 7v⁶ Oct 9] medium-sized gelding: fairly useful performer: won seller at Leicester (sold from Miss J. Feilden 9,500 gns) in August: stays 1m: acts on polytrack, best turf effort on good going: held up: not entirely straightforward. *J. M. Bradley*

FINSCEAL BEO (IRE) 3 ch.f. Mr Greeley (USA) 122 – Musical Treat (IRE) 98 123 (Royal Academy (USA) 130) [2007 118: 8m* 8g² 8g* 8d 10m⁶ 10g⁵ Oct 7]

Champion two-year-old filly Finsceal Beo looked an exceptional classic winner at Newmarket, recording the best performance seen in the One Thousand Guineas in the last twenty years, with the exception of Cape Verdi's in 1998, and reinforcing her claims at the time to be the outstanding filly of the generation. Finsceal Beo started 5/4 favourite in a field of twenty-one for the Stan James-sponsored classic, which did not include the second favourite in the ante-post market Sander Camillo, withdrawn on the day reportedly in season. Unlike the Guineas preparation of her stable-companion Teofilo, the winter favourite for the Derby as well as the Two Thousand, Finsceal Beo's spring had been trouble-free and she compensated her stable for Teofilo's withdrawal by triumphing just as decisively as she had in the Prix Marcel Boussac and the Rockfel Stakes on her last two juvenile starts. Finsceal Beo was never far away in a truly-run race in which most of the runners stayed stand side (joined eventually by a small group which initially raced towards the centre). Shaken up two furlongs out, Finsceal Beo was soon in command and ran on strongly to win by two and a half lengths from the winner of the Leopardstown trial Arch Swing, giving an Irish-trained one, two, with the next three to finish, Simply Perfect, Treat and Indian Ink, representing some of the best British two-year-old form. Simply Perfect (a stablemate of Sander Camillo) and Treat finished a length and a quarter and a further length and a half behind Arch Swing, reproducing almost to the pound their running when first and second in the Fillies' Mile at Ascot. Like Finsceal Beo, the pair were making their reappearance in the Guineas, while Cheveley Park winner Indian Ink, who met trouble in running and was unlucky not to make the frame, had been beaten a neck in the Fred Darling at Newbury by 25/1-shot Majestic Roi who wasn't entered at Newmarket. The promising maiden winner Yaqeen and Princess Margaret winner Scarlet Runner, who had narrowly overturned the odds laid on Sander Camillo in the Nell Gwyn, came sixth and seventh, none of the first seven—in contrast to the Two Thousand Guineas—starting at odds longer than 14/1 in a race that more or less went to form. Finsceal Beo's performance in the One Thousand Guineas was subsequently bettered among the leading fillies at a mile only by Darjina when she beat Ramonti and George Washington in the Prix du Moulin.

Finsceal Beo's stock could hardly have been higher in the immediate aftermath of the One Thousand Guineas, the headline *Finsceal Beo—'the best filly in the world'* screaming out from the front page of the *Racing Post* and the winning time, 1m 34.94sec, having statisticians scurrying to the record books to confirm that, not only was it the fastest in the history of the race (previous best 1m 36.38sec), but that it was also inside the record of 1m 35.08sec for the Two Thousand Guineas. Record times in themselves are unreliable guides to merit. The time record of 1m 34.54sec for Newmarket's Rowley Mile was set by the smart Desert Deer in the Joel Stakes in October 2002 but, on examination, the performance was no better than useful, judged on time—there was a strong following wind. Likewise, Lahan and Mister Baileys the holders at the time of the respective Guineas records, wouldn't figure highly in a list of 'Guineas greats'. However, the *time value* of Finsceal Beo's performance based on sophisticated analysis of overall times on the afternoon, taking into account weather conditions and the going, confirmed that her performance was very good. A tailwind and unseasonably firm going had a big influence on Finsceal Beo's winning time but her timefigure was 0.92 fast, equivalent to a timerating of 123. A timefigure is an expression of a *single performance only* but only a good horse is capable of producing a very fast timefigure. In the preceding fifteen years, only six fillies or mares had bettered Finsceal's Beo's timefigure. For the record, they were: Cape Verdi (1.24 fast) in the 1998 One Thousand Guineas; Lochsong (1.17 fast, 1.07 fast and 0.95 fast) in the 1994 Palace House Stakes, the 1994 Temple Stakes and the 1993 Nunthorpe respectively; the two-year-old Queen's Logic (1.05 fast) in the 2001 Cheveley Park; All At Sea (1.01 fast) when second in the 1992 International at York; Ouija Board (0.98 fast) in the 2004 Oaks; and Ridgewood Pearl (0.96 fast) in the 1995 Coronation Stakes at Royal Ascot (when, incidentally, she broke the course record). The respective Timeform ratings of those six at the end of the season were 126, 129 (twice), 125, 124, 125 and 125, and Finsceal Beo—whose name translates as 'living legend' in Gaelic—was allotted a Timeform rating immediately after the One Thousand Guineas of 123. At the time, she seemed set to carry all before her in races like the Irish One Thousand Guineas—announced as her next target after Newmarket—and the Coronation Stakes, and looked sure to play a leading role in the top open races in the second half of the season, especially with the weight-for-sex allowance.

Illustration of the maxim that 'a week is a long time in racing' was provided when Finsceal Beo was a surprise runner a week after Newmarket in the Poule d'Essai des Pouliches at Longchamp. She was said to have come out of her One

Stan James 1000 Guineas Stakes, Newmarket—Finsceal Beo has it well sewn up; Arch Swing, Simply Perfect (rail) and Treat (dark cap) are next home

Boylesports Irish 1000 Guineas, the Curragh—harder work for Finsceal Beo this time; Dimenticata stays on strongly for second, ahead of Peeping Fawn (rail)

Thousand Guineas win so well that connections had decided on an ambitious tilt at the Guineas treble, which had never been done before (Miesque and Ravinella had achieved the Newmarket/Longchamp double in the 'eighties when the two races were seventeen days apart). Finsceal Beo started odds on but was collared in the last strides by the progressive Darjina, going down by a head after taking the lead a furlong and a half out and going a couple of lengths clear. Rahiyah, the Rockfel runner-up, came third, a length and a half behind Finsceal Beo, with Costume, third in Yaqeen's Newmarket maiden, fourth and Sander Camillo a disappointing eighth. Finsceal Beo was below her Newmarket form at Longchamp and was even further below it when scrambling home at odds on from 66/1-shot Dimenticata to emulate Attraction, who was the first to land the Anglo-Irish Guineas double in 2004, in the Boylesports Irish One Thousand Guineas at the Curragh a fortnight later. The field of eleven also included the second and fourth from the One Thousand Guineas at Newmarket, both running their first race since. Treat finished sixth at the Curragh and Arch Swing last, reportedly returning with pulled muscles in her quarters. Third in a muddling race was Peeping Fawn, winner of a maiden at Naas on her last start and not yet anything like the force she was to become over longer distances. There were no portents of Finsceal Beo's performance in her appearance beforehand—she looked in magnificent shape—but flashing her tail under the whip and hanging towards the rail, after taking the lead and looking likely to win decisively, were signs in the race that three classics in three weeks might perhaps, in hindsight, have proved too tall an order. Saddled for the Coronation Stakes at Royal Ascot, where she again took the eye in the paddock, Finsceal Beo again edged right when coming under pressure, managing only eighth behind six-length winner Indian Ink, beaten also, among others, by Darjina and Arch Swing. Finsceal Beo wasn't seen again until September, missing engagements in the Prix d'Astarte (uncertainty about the going) and the Nassau (in season). Finsceal Beo trailed in last in the Irish Champion Stakes at Leopardstown, but she ran much more encouragingly, tried at a mile and a quarter again, in the Prix de l'Opera at Longchamp in October, never looking likely to win but keeping on for a fair fifth to Satwa Queen, one place in front of the Oaks winner Light Shift. Whether Finsceal Beo will ever reproduce her brilliant effort in the One Thousand Guineas remains to be seen, but at least she stays in training, so will have further opportunities to do so.

Mr M. A. Ryan's "Finsceal Beo"

Finsceal Beo (IRE) (ch.f. 2004)	Mr Greeley (USA) (ch 1992)	Gone West (b 1984)	Mr Prospector
			Secrettame
		Long Legend (ch 1978)	Reviewer
			Lianga
	Musical Treat (IRE) (ch 1996)	Royal Academy (b 1987)	Nijinsky
			Crimson Saint
		Mountain Ash (b 1989)	Dominion
			Red Berry

The pedigree of the strong, well-made, attractive Finsceal Beo, who is an excellent walker, and usually impresses in appearance, was covered fully in *Racehorses of 2006* and there is little to add. Her sire, the American sprinter-miler Mr Greeley, was also kept in the limelight by the exploits of Finsceal Beo's two-year-old stable-companion Saoirse Abu who matched her achievement of winning two Group 1 races, in her case the Phoenix Stakes and the Moyglare Stud Stakes. Mr Greeley is by Gone West, as is Darjina's sire Zamindar. Finsceal Beo is the third foal out of the Lupe Stakes runner-up Musical Treat (her first foal won in the Czech Republic) who was sold for 100,000 dollars at Keeneland in 2003 carrying Finsceal Beo who, in turn, was put through the ring at the Goffs Million Sale in 2005, making €340,000. Musical Treat's next foal, a filly by Barathea (named Musical Bar and with Barry Hills, as yet unraced) made €150,000 at the 2006 Goffs Million Sale. Musical Treat was barren to Green Desert in 2006 and visited Oasis Dream in the latest season. Musical Treat's dam Mountain Ash won ten races at up to a mile in Britain and Italy and was one of eight winners out of the Cheveley Park runner-up Red Berry. Red Berry finished seventh in the One Thousand Guineas and her dam, Big Berry, was runner-up in that race, while Big Berry's half-brother Pipe of

Peace was third in the Two Thousand Guineas and Derby. Big Berry was out of Red Briar, a three-parts sister to Red Ray, the great grandam of Mill Reef. Finsceal Beo probably stays a mile and a quarter, though her two best performances have been at a mile. She acts on good to firm and good to soft going, her trainer's opinion that she is unsuited by a soft surface not backed up by her racing record which includes a win in the Rockfel Stakes on good to soft when she produced form on a similar level to her win a fortnight earlier on good to firm in the Marcel Boussac. *J. S. Bolger, Ireland*

FIONA'S WONDER 3 b.g. Inchinor 119 – Wondrous Maid (GER) (Mondrian (GER) – 125) [2007 –: p10g p10g 7d May 17] little form: tried in cheekpieces. *R. A. Harris*

FIRE ALARM 3 b.g. Smoke Glacken (USA) 120 – Brandywine Belle (USA) (Trempo- **42** lino (USA) 135) [2007 –: p7.1g⁴ f7g p8.6g 8g May 14] poor maiden: left J. Quinn after third start: should stay 1m: tried visored. *Miss Lucinda V. Russell*

FIRE AND RAIN (FR) 4 b.g. Galileo (IRE) 134 – Quatre Saisons (FR) (Homme de – Loi (IRE) 120) [2007 107: 10g May 31] strong, good-bodied gelding: has a quick action: useful performer at 3 yrs: tailed off in Brigadier Gerard Stakes at Sandown only start in 2007: probably stays 1¾m: raced on good/good to soft ground. *Miss E. C. Lavelle*

FIRE AT WILL 5 b.g. Lugana Beach 116 – Kahyasi Moll (IRE) 35 (Brief Truce (USA) **43** 126) [2007 f11g p8.6g f11g 8f p9.5g⁴ p7g 8f³ p8.6g⁵ 10m 10.2s 7d⁴ 7d Oct 1] poor performer nowadays: barely stays 9.5f: acts on polytrack and soft going: tried visored/blinkered: often slowly away. *A. W. Carroll*

FIREBIRD ANNIE (IRE) 3 b.f. Mujadil (USA) 119 – Missing Virgin (IRE) (Mujta- **52 §** hid (USA) 118) [2007 p6g² p8.6g⁶ p7g⁶ f8g⁵ 6d 11.1g⁵ 8d² 10.1d p8g Dec 5] 5,000F, 6,200Y, 2,000 3-y-o: second foal: half-sister to Irish 7.5f/1m winner Luckyvera (by Titus Livius): dam German 1m winner: modest maiden: claimed from S. Hall £6,000 after debut: stays 11f: acts on polytrack: tried blinkered/visored: looked reluctant seventh outing, and is one to treat with caution. *A. Bailey*

FIRE IN CAIRO (IRE) 3 b.f. Barathea (IRE) 127 – Ibiza (GER) (Linamix (FR) 127) **56** [2007 59: f8g⁶ f8g³ 10s² p13.9g³ Oct 5] workmanlike filly: modest maiden handicapper: stays 1¾m: acts on polytrack (probably on fibresand) and soft going. *P. C. Haslam*

FIRENZA BOND 2 b.g. (Mar 18) Captain Rio 122 – Bond Stasia (IRE) 54 (Mukad- **80** damah (USA) 125) [2007 5m 5d⁶ 5.1d* 5m 5d⁶ 5g* Oct 20] 10,000Y: tall gelding: first foal: dam sprint maiden: fairly useful performer: won maiden at Chester in July and minor event at Catterick in October: speedy, raced at 5f: best form on good/good to soft going. *G. R. Oldroyd*

FIRENZE 6 ch.m. Efisio 120 – Juliet Bravo 61 (Glow (USA)) [2007 109: 6.1s* 5g³ 6d **109** 6s⁶ 6d Aug 25] strong, lengthy mare: useful performer: won listed event at Nottingham (readily by 2 lengths from Perfect Story) in May: creditable efforts in Temple Stakes at Sandown (third to Sierra Vista) and Golden Jubilee Stakes at Royal Ascot (ninth to Soldier's Tale, poorly drawn) next 2 starts: below form after: effective at 5f/6f: acts on fibresand, soft and good to firm ground: patiently ridden. *J. R. Fanshawe*

FIRE ONE (IRE) 3 b.g. Bahri (USA) 125 – Iviza (IRE) 105§ (Sadler's Wells (USA) **67** 132) [2007 p8g⁵ p10g⁵ p10.7g p10.7g Oct 12] fair maiden: left M. Tregoning 18,000 gns after second start: stays 1¼m: raced only on polytrack. *R. McGlinchey, Ireland*

FIRESIDE 2 b.c. (Mar 3) Dr Fong (USA) 128 – Al Hasnaa (Zafonic (USA) 130) [2007 **97 p** 7m⁶ 7m* Oct 5] good-topped, quite attractive colt: third foal: half-brother to winner in Italy by Giant's Causeway: dam unraced sister to smart performer up to 1¼m Alrassaam and half-sister to high-class US performer up to 1¼m Fanmore: useful form: plenty of promise both starts, not clear run when sixth of 19 to Luck Money in valuable sales race at the Curragh, then showed good attitude to win maiden at Newmarket by short head from Slam: will stay 1m: pattern-race performer in the making. *P. W. Chapple-Hyam*

FIRESPIN (USA) 2 ch.f. (Mar 22) Luhuk (USA) 114 – Happy Numbers (USA) (Polish – Numbers (USA)) [2007 p7.1d Dec 28] $6,000Y: first foal: dam US 6f winner: 14/1, tailed off in maiden at Wolverhampton. *M. Botti*

FIRESTORM (IRE) 3 b.g. Celtic Swing 138 – National Ballet (Shareef Dancer (USA) **52** 135) [2007 57: 10.5g 12.1m 12.1m 10d 12s⁴ 16.2s 14.1m 16.1g Oct 3] close-coupled gelding: modest maiden: stays 1½m: acts on firm and soft going: tried blinkered. *C. W. Fairhurst*

FIRESTREAK 2 b.g. (Feb 14) Green Desert (USA) 127 – Flash of Gold 76 (Darshaan **87**
133) [2007 7.1g* 7g⁵ 7m⁶ 6m Sep 15] neat gelding: first foal: dam, maiden (stayed 1½m),
half-sister to smart performer up to 13f Phantom Gold: fairly useful performer: won
maiden at Sandown (beat Donegal by 2½ lengths) in June: only similar form (and signs
of temperament) subsequent starts, gelded after final one: will probably stay 1m: raced
only on good/good to firm going. *R. Hannon*

FIRE UP THE BAND 8 b.g. Prince Sabo 123 – Green Supreme (Primo Dominie 121) **106 d**
[2007 112d: 5.1g* 6m 5m⁴ 5g 5g 6g 5g⁵ 6g 6m Sep 18] lengthy, good-topped gelding:
useful performer nowadays: easily best effort in 2007 when winning minor event at
Nottingham (by ¾ length from Bond City) in April: below form in varied events after:
best at 5f/easy 6f: acts on polytrack, firm and good to soft going, possibly not on soft:
tried visored: has won when sweating: races up with pace. *D. Nicholls*

FIREWALKER 2 b.f. (Apr 20) Bertolini (USA) 125 – Crystal Canyon 59 (Efisio 120) **67**
[2007 6m⁶ 5m³ 5d² 5g⁴ p6g² p5.1d² Dec 17] third foal: dam sprint maiden: fair maiden:
placed at Carlisle, Musselburgh and Wolverhampton (2): will prove best at 5f/6f: acts on
polytrack, good to firm and good to soft ground. *B. Smart*

FIREWORK 9 b.g. Primo Dominie 121 – Prancing 98 (Prince Sabo 123) [2007 53: p7g **53**
p7g* p6g⁶ 7m 7m 8f Aug 9] quite attractive gelding: modest performer: won minor event
at Kempton in February: stays easy 7f: acts on all-weather, firm and soft ground: tried in
headgear: often slowly away. *E. A. Wheeler*

FIRST ABODE 2 br.f. (Jan 18) First Trump 118 – Villa Del Sol 86 (Tagula (IRE) 116) **–**
[2007 5g 5m 6g⁴ Aug 27] 1,200Y: second foal: dam 2-y-o 5f/6f winner: no form.
M. Brittain

FIRST AMONG EQUALS 4 b.f. Primo Valentino (IRE) 116 – Margarets First (Puis- **–**
sance 110) [2007 39: 5.1g May 29] neat filly: poor performer at 3 yrs: well held only start
in 2007, veering right leaving stall: raced only at 5f/6f: acts on good to firm going: tried
blinkered/in cheekpieces. *D. G. Bridgwater*

FIRST AVENUE 2 b.c. (Jan 18) Montjeu (IRE) 137 – Marciala (IRE) (Machiavellian **88 p**
(USA) 123) [2007 8m⁶ 8d* Oct 30] 100,000Y: first foal: dam ran twice
in Ireland: confirmed impressions from Newmarket (sixth to Twice Over) when winning
maiden at Yarmouth in smooth style by 2 lengths from Majeen: will be suited by 1¼m/
1½m: smart prospect. *M. A. Jarvis*

FIRST BLOOM (USA) 3 br.f. Fusaichi Pegasus (USA) 130 – Shy Princess (USA) **–**
117 (Irish River (FR) 131) [2007 71p: 8.3m p12.2g Apr 30] maiden: modest form only
start at 2 yrs: little impact in 2007. *P. F. I. Cole*

FIRST BOY (GER) 8 b.g. Bering 136 – First Smile 104 (Surumu (GER)) [2007 –: f7g **53**
f11g 12s³ Jun 29] modest performer: stayed 1½m: acted on soft ground: winning hurdler:
dead. *D. J. Wintle*

FIRST BUDDY 3 ch.g. Rock of Gibraltar (IRE) 133 – Dance Treat (USA) 115 (Nure- **89**
yev (USA) 131) [2007 76: 8.2g* 8m 8.1m⁴ 8.1m³ 10m Oct 5] rather leggy, close-coupled
gelding: fairly useful performer: on toes/free to post, won maiden at Nottingham in June:
good efforts in frame in handicaps after: should be suited by 1¼m: acts on polytrack and
good to firm ground: front runner: sold 20,000 gns, joined G. A. Swinbank. *W. J. Haggas*

FIRST FRIEND (IRE) 6 b.g. Mark of Esteem (IRE) 137 – Bustira (Busted 134) [2007 **63**
76: p12g⁵ p8g p9.5g⁶ p10g p12g² p10g³ 10.2d 10.2g⁶ 8f⁵ p8.6g 10g Oct 31] leggy **a68**
gelding: fair performer on turf, modest on all-weather: left P. Mitchell 12,000 gns after
fifth start: effective at 1m to 1½m: acts on polytrack and firm ground. *M. Hill*

FIRST FROST 3 ch.f. Atraf 116 – Bless 58 (Beveled (USA)) [2007 –: p6g f6g p8g p7f **–**
p8.6g p10g⁶ 10d 11.5d⁶ 10.1d Oct 30] little form. *M. J. Gingell*

FIRST GENERATION 5 b.g. Primo Dominie 121 – My Cadeaux 93 (Cadeaux Gene- **–**
reux 131) [2007 –: p8.6g Jan 5] strong, angular gelding: of little account. *P. D. Evans*

FIRST IN SHOW 2 b.f. (Apr 24) Zamindar (USA) 116 – Rose Show (Belmez (USA) **–**
131) [2007 6g Nov 2] 5,000Y: seventh foal: half-sister to 3 winners, including smart
1¼m/1½m winner Prize Winner (by Mtoto) and 5-y-o First Show: dam unraced: 33/1,
always behind in maiden at Newmarket. *A. M. Balding*

FIRST LOOK (FR) 7 b.g. Acatenango (GER) 127 – First Class (GER) (Bustino 136) **76 +**
[2007 78: 13.1s³ Oct 4] fair handicapper, very lightly raced on Flat (useful hurdler/fairly
useful chaser): will be suited by 2m: acts on heavy ground. *P. Monteith*

FIRST MATE (IRE) 3 b.g. Desert Style (IRE) 121 – Sail Away (GER) (Platini (GER) **72**
126) [2007 79: 8.1m 8.5d 10d Oct 10] lengthy, useful-looking gelding: fair performer:
may prove best at 6f/7f: acts on soft and good to firm going. *M. Johnston*

FIRST ORDER 6 b.g. Primo Dominie 121 – Unconditional Love (IRE) 104 (Polish **90** Patriot (USA) 128) [2007 97: p6g⁵ p5g p6g⁴ 5m 5m 5m 5d² 6d 6m 5m 5m p6g² 5g³ p5.1g* Dec 8] big, strong gelding: fairly useful handicapper: won at Wolverhampton in December by 2 lengths from Harry Up: effective at 5f/6f: acts on polytrack, firm and good to soft ground: usually visored: has looked tricky ride. *I. Semple*

FIRST PRINCESS (IRE) 3 b.f. King's Best (USA) 132 – Try To Catch Me (USA) **66** (Shareef Dancer (USA) 135) [2007 66: p8g³ p8g³ p10g p9.5g⁶ p7g⁵ p8.6g² 8.1g² f8g⁵ 8.3g 8.1s Jul 13] fair maiden: stays easy 8.6f: acts on polytrack: wears cheekpieces nowadays. *J. S. Moore*

FIRST RHAPSODY (IRE) 5 b.m. Rossini (USA) 118 – Tinos Island (IRE) (Alzao **49** (USA) 117) [2007 63: p8g 8.5m 7.9m⁶ 7.9g⁶ 7d 8v 8s Aug 14] good-bodied mare: poor handicapper nowadays: seems to stay 1m: acts on polytrack and any turf going: sometimes slowly away. *T. J. Etherington*

FIRST SHOW 5 b.g. Cape Cross (IRE) 129 – Rose Show (Belmez (USA) 131) [2007 **66** 85: 8m 7g 8.3m 8.1v p8.6g Jul 30] sturdy gelding: fair handicapper nowadays: may prove best around 1m: acts on polytrack, firm and soft going: tried in cheekpieces, blinkered and tongue tied last 2 starts. *R. A. Harris*

FIRST SLIP 4 b.g. Slip Anchor 136 – Nanouche (Dayjur (USA) 137) [2007 74: 15g **–** 12.1m Sep 7] fair maiden at 3 yrs: well beaten in 2007: barely stays 1½m: acts on polytrack: tried blinkered. *Jonjo O'Neill*

FIRST TO CALL 3 ch.c. First Trump 118 – Scarlett Holly 81 (Red Sunset 120) [2007 **93** –: p7g⁵ 8g* p9.5g⁵ 11d p12g² Oct 12] strong, good-bodied colt: fairly useful performer: won maiden at Bath (by 5 lengths) in June: good second at Lingfield final outing: stays 1½m: acts on polytrack. *P. J. Makin*

FIRST TRIM (IRE) 2 b.g. (Apr 8) Acclamation 118 – Spanker 71§ (Suave Dancer **83** (USA) 136) [2007 6g⁵ 6m³ 6m³ 5.7d p5m Oct 6] 41,000F, 48,000Y: strong gelding: fourth foal: half-brother to 2004 2-y-o 7.5f winner Mastman (by Intikhab) and Irish 1m/1¼m winner Skerries (by Dr Fong), both fairly useful: dam irresolute maiden (stayed 1½m): fairly useful maiden: off almost 4 months after debut, third at Ripon (to Crystany) and Goodwood: should prove best at 5f/6f: acts on good to firm going, below form on good to soft/polytrack last 2 starts (then gelded). *B. J. Meehan*

FIRST VALENTINI 3 b.f. Bertolini (USA) 125 – Oscietra 72 (Robellino (USA) 127) **53** [2007 56: 6v⁵ 5m⁶ 5m⁶ 7.5m⁶ 6m³ 7f⁴ 8m⁵ Oct 8] lengthy filly: modest maiden: stays 7f: acts on firm and good to soft ground: tried blinkered/tongue tied (not in 2007). *N. Bycroft*

FISBERRY 5 gr.g. Efisio 120 – Elderberry (Bin Ajwaad (IRE) 119) [2007 88: 6m 6g 6g **68** 7d p7g 6g Oct 2] lengthy gelding: fair handicapper nowadays: stays 6f: acts on good to firm going (well held both starts on softer than good): waited with. *M. S. Saunders*

FISH CALLED JOHNNY 3 b.g. Kyllachy 129 – Clare Celeste 73 (Coquelin (USA) **71** 121) [2007 85: 8.3m 7d3 6g* 6m p6g⁵ 5m⁶ 5.1s⁵ 5v³ 6v³ 6m⁵ p5.1g p8.6g p6g p7g p6g Dec 19] close-coupled gelding: fair handicapper: claimed from B. Meehan after second outing: won at Ayr in May: needs soft ground at 5f, stays 6f: acts on heavy and good to firm going, probably on polytrack: once tongue tied, sometimes blinkered: none too straightforward. *Peter Grayson*

FISHER BRIDGE (IRE) 4 ch.g. Singspiel (IRE) 133 – Kristal Bridge 75 (Kris 135) **88** [2007 85: 10g² 10d³ 11.8m* p12.2g Oct 2] strong, good sort: fairly useful performer: won handicap at Leicester in August: stays 1½m: acts on good to firm and good to soft ground: sold 30,000 gns, joined N. Meade, Ireland. *W. R. Swinburn*

FISHFORCOMPLIMENTS 3 b.c. Royal Applause 124 – Flyfisher (USA) (River- **99 §** man (USA) 131) [2007 99: p7g 9m³ 8m 8.1d⁴ 10g Jun 21] big, leggy colt: useful performer: best effort at 3 yrs when 2¾ lengths third to Petara Bay in listed race at Newmarket: well held in similar event at Royal Ascot final start: stays 9f: acts on good to firm and good to soft going: temperamental, and has looked hard ride. *R. A. Fahey*

FISTRAL 3 b.g. Piccolo 121 – Fayre Holly (IRE) 57 (Fayruz 116) [2007 –: 8g 9m⁴ **53** 8.3g⁴ 6d² 8.1m 6g³ 8.3g 7g 7d⁵ p7.1g Nov 22] lengthy gelding: modest maiden: left J. Hetherton before final outing: stays 9f: acts on good to firm and good to soft going: tried blinkered. *Ollie Pears*

FITASABUCKSTOAT (IRE) 4 b.g. Fayruz 116 – Bardia 42 (Jalmood (USA) 126) **–** [2007 9m Apr 9] lengthy gelding: little form: tried in cheekpieces/blinkered: dead *K. W. Hogg, Isle of Man*

FITOLINI 2 ch.f. (Mar 15) Bertolini (USA) 125 – Miss Fit (IRE) 87 (Hamas (IRE) **66**
125§) [2007 f5g⁵ p5.1g* 5.1d⁶ p6g⁴ 6m 6s p6g 6s⁶ Oct 4] strong, lengthy filly: third foal: **a72**
half-sister to 3-y-o Crow's Nest Lad: dam 5f/6f winner (including at 2 yrs): fair performer: won maiden at Wolverhampton in May: will be best kept to 5f/6f: acts on polytrack
and soft going: none too consistent. *Mrs G. S. Rees*

FITS OF GIGGLES (IRE) 2 b.f. (Apr 19) Cape Cross (IRE) 129 – Itsibitsi (IRE) **71**
(Brief Truce (USA) 126) [2007 p7.1g* 6g⁶ Aug 27] €30,000F, €22,000Y: third foal: half-
sister to 3-y-o Baltimore Jack and 5f (including at 2 yrs) winner Lyndalee (by Fasliyev):
dam unraced half-sister to smart performer up to 10.5f Siege: fair form: won maiden at
Wolverhampton on debut: stiff task, sixth of 7 to Fat Boy in listed race at Ripon later in
August: stays 7f. *J. G. Given*

FITZROY CROSSING (USA) 2 gr.c. (Mar 3) Cozzene (USA) – Jaded Lady (USA) **89**
(Afleet (CAN)) [2007 5m³ 5s² 6d 6m* 6g 7g²* Sep 24] strong, medium-sized colt: fifth
foal: half-brother to winner in US by El Prado: dam, minor stakes winner in US, half-
sister to US Grade 3 6f winner Commanche Trail: fairly useful form: won maiden at
Haydock in August and minor event at Leicester (arguably fortunate to beat Perfect Stride
by ½ length) in September: will be suited by 1m+: acts on soft and good to firm going.
M. Johnston

FIULIN 2 ch.c. (Mar 19) Galileo (IRE) 134 – Fafinta (IRE) (Indian Ridge 123) [2007 **78 p**
8.2g² Nov 7] big, strong colt: third foal: half-brother to fairly useful 1m winner Furbesta
(by Danehill Dancer): dam, Italian 8.5f and 1¼m winner, half-sister to Falbrav: 5/1,
prominent throughout when second to Laterly in maiden at Nottingham: will stay 1¼m/
1½m: type to progress. *M. Botti*

FIUME 2 ch.c. (Feb 25) Medicean 128 – River Abouali (Bluebird (USA) 125) [2007 8d **66 p**
8d Oct 27] 8,500F: rangy colt: fifth foal: half-brother to several winners, including fairly
useful 2002 2-y-o 5f winner Maugwenna (by Danehill) and 6-y-o Trouble Maker: dam
unraced out of sister to dam of Saffron Walden and Dolphin Street: more promising run
in maidens latter start when eighth to Whistledownwind at Newbury, disputing lead long
way: sort to improve at 3 yrs. *R. Hannon*

FIUMICINO 3 b.f. Danehill Dancer (IRE) 117 – Valhalla Moon (USA) 92 (Sadler's **87**
Wells (USA) 132) [2007 76: p8g² 10m⁵ 10g⁴ 12g⁶ 12m Jul 11] big, lengthy filly: fairly
useful performer: in frame in listed races at Kempton (neck second to Precocious Star)
and Newbury (on toes): flattered in Prix de Malleret at Saint-Cloud penultimate start:
stays easy 1½m: acts on polytrack, soft and good to firm going. *M. R. Channon*

FIVE A SIDE 3 b.g. Lomitas 129 – Fifth Emerald 54 (Formidable (USA) 125) [2007 **90**
84p] 10s 10m 9.8m² 10.5g 12g⁶ Sep 22] sturdy, close-coupled gelding: fairly useful
handicapper: ran as if amiss last 2 starts: stays 9.8f: acts on good to firm and good to soft
going: blinkered final outing: sold 10,000 gns, then gelded. *M. Johnston*

FIVE WISHES 3 b.f. Bahamian Bounty 116 – Due West 56 (Inchinor 119) [2007 62p: **63**
6m⁵ 6g³ 6d² 6.9g² 7.1g² 7.1s 7.2g 6s Oct 4] smallish, strong filly: modest maiden handicapper: stays 7f: acts on good to firm and good to soft going: unseated to post fourth
outing. *M. Dods*

FIXATEUR 5 b.g. Anabaa (USA) 130 – Fabulous Account (USA) (Private Account **–**
(USA)) [2007 f11g 16.1d 10s May 28] ex-French gelding: useful performer when trained
in France by F. Head, winning 4 times, including 2 minor events at Deauville in 2005:
unraced on Flat at 4 yrs, and little form in Britain in 2007: tried blinkered/in cheekpieces:
sold £3,400 in August. *J. G. Given*

FIXATION 3 ch.g. Observatory (USA) 131 – Fetish 85 (Dancing Brave (USA) 140) **62**
[2007 8.3d⁶ p8g⁴ 9.9s⁵ Oct 14] lengthy gelding: modest form in maidens: stays 1¼m:
takes strong hold/hangs left: sold 15,000 gns. *Mrs A. J. Perrett*

FIXBOARD 6 b.g. Bluebird (USA) 125 – Military Tune (IRE) (Nashwan (USA) 135) **104**
[2007 8g* 8s* 10d² 7m 8g 8g 8g⁵ 10g Oct 7] useful performer: progressed very well in
2005, winning 4 handicaps: missed 2006 but improved again on return, winning minor
events at Longchamp (female jockeys) and Chantilly (lady amateurs) in May: respectable
eighth to Giganticus in Bunbury Cup (Handicap) at Newmarket fourth start: below best
afterwards: effective at 7f to 1¼m: acts on soft ground. *F. Poulsen, France*

FIZZLEPHUT (IRE) 5 b.g. Indian Rocket 115 – Cladantom (IRE) 70 (High Estate **83**
127) [2007 86, a82: p5g p5.1g⁵ p5.1g* 5.1f⁴ 5m⁶ p5g p5g⁶ p5g⁶ p5.1d² p5g² p5.1s⁵ Dec
21] lengthy gelding: fairly useful handicapper: won at Wolverhampton in March: best
at 5f: acts on all-weather and firm going: tried in cheekpieces: has flashed tail: races
prominently. *Miss J. R. Tooth*

FIZZY BELLA 3 b.f. Efisio 120 – Tetravella (IRE) (Groom Dancer (USA) 128) [2007 **61** p8.6g f8g³ p7.1g p12g⁶ 11.5d⁵ 10.1m² 10.1g 8.1d² 8m⁴ Aug 27] 11,500F: angular filly: **a66** fourth foal: half-sister to 3 winners, including 4-y-o Island Odyssey: dam French 1½m and 15f winner: fair maiden: stayed 1¼m: acted on all-weather, good to firm and good to soft ground: dead. *M. G. Quinlan*

FIZZY LIZZY 7 b.m. Cool Jazz 116 – Formidable Liz 66 (Formidable (USA) 125) **46 §** [2007 51§: p7g⁴ Jan 3] dipped-backed mare: modest performer at 6 yrs: poor form only start in 2007: stays 7f: acts on polytrack (possibly not fibresand) and firm going: tried in cheekpieces: inconsistent. *H. E. Haynes*

FIZZY LOVER 2 b.f. (Apr 3) Kyllachy 129 – In Love Again (IRE) 86 (Prince Rupert – (FR) 121) [2007 5m Apr 18] 12,000Y: good-bodied filly: half-sister to 4-y-o Silidan, 3-y-o Medici Pearl and 9-y-o Forever My Lord: dam, 2-y-o 5f winner, half-sister to high-class sprinter Hallgate: 40/1, no show (drawn wide) in maiden at Beverley. *T. D. Easterby*

FLAGSTONE (USA) 3 ch.g. Distant View 126 – Navarene (USA) (Known **59** Fact (USA) 135) [2007 10.1m⁶ 12.4m³ 8.2g⁴ 12.1s Jul 3] sturdy gelding: modest maiden: stays 12.4f: acts on good to firm ground. *G. A. Swinbank*

FLAM 2 b.f. (Mar 24) Singspiel (IRE) 133 – Delauncy (Machiavellian (USA) 123) [2007 **74 p** 8m⁵ 8g⁶ Oct 26] rather leggy, lengthy filly: fourth foal: half-sister to smart 1¼m winner who stayed 13.4f Delsarte (by Theatrical), 4-y-o Peppertree and 3-y-o Veenwouden: dam, useful French 2-y-o 1m winner who stayed 1¼m, daughter of Park Hill winner Casey: fair form in maidens at Newmarket and Doncaster (staying-on sixth to Cruel Sea): will benefit from 1¼m/1½m. *J. R. Fanshawe*

FLAME CREEK (IRE) 11 b.g. Shardari 134 – Sheila's Pet (IRE) (Welsh Term 126) **83** [2007 93: f14g⁵ p12g⁶ 16m 14d⁶ 21.7s 16.2s⁶ p13g² p16.5g³ f14d³ f14d Dec 15] fairly useful handicapper on Flat: stays 16.5f: best form on all-weather: tongue tied (ran poorly) final start. *E. J. Creighton*

FLAMESTONE 3 b.g. Piccolo 121 – Renee 55 (Wolfhound (USA) 126) [2007 58: p6g⁴ **46** f7g p6g 7m f8g 6s⁰ 8g³ 8.3d³ 8.2g 8m⁶ 8g 10d Oct 10] close-coupled gelding: just poor maiden in 2007: left J. Bethell after fifth start: stays 1m: acts on polytrack, good to firm and good to soft ground: tried blinkered/in cheekpieces. *A. E. Price*

FLAMING CAT (IRE) 4 b. or br.g. Orpen (USA) 116 – Brave Cat (IRE) (Catrail – (USA) 123) [2007 –: 8.3d⁶ 10.1m⁴ p9.5m 10d 10s Sep 26] tall gelding: little solid form: sometimes wears cheekpieces. *F. Watson*

FLARE STAR 4 ch.f. Nashwan (USA) 135 – Flame Cutter (USA) 79 (Miswaki (USA) **78** 124) [2007 91: 14m⁴ 18.7m 12g 14g Jun 3] just fair performer nowadays: best form up to 1½m: acts on soft and good to firm going. *T. Hogan, Ireland*

FLASH HARRY 3 ch.g. Fantastic Light (USA) 134 – Woodyousmileforme (USA) **59** (Woodman (USA) 126) [2007 –: 6.5d 14g³ 12d 12v⁵ p13.9g⁴ Dec 1] modest maiden: left J. J. Murphy in Ireland, well held when fourth in claimer at Wolverhampton: stays 1¾m: tried blinkered. *M. G. Quinlan*

FLASHIN AMBER 3 ch.g. Kyllachy 129 – Shebasis (USA) (General Holme (USA) – 128) [2007 p5.1g p6g p11g Dec 5] well held in maidens/claimer. *Peter Grayson*

FLASHING FEET (IRE) 3 b.g. Soviet Star (USA) 128 – Delphini (IRE) 69 (Seattle – Dancer (USA) 119) [2007 –: p8.6g 10s p12g Jun 9] little form: left R. Hannon after reappearance: tried in cheekpieces/visor. *Mrs L. C. Jewell*

FLASHING FLOOZIE 4 ch.f. Muhtarram (USA) 125 – High Habit 79 (Slip Anchor **45** 136) [2007 54: p11g p11g p12.2g⁵ 10.2f 12f* 17.2m 11.9s⁶ 12g³ 14g² 8.5g⁴ 14g⁵ 12g² 12g⁴ p12.2g 12.6m 12.1d Sep 25] good-topped filly: poor performer nowadays: won handicap at L'Ancresse (Guernsey) in May when trained by A. Carroll: left Mrs J. Le Brocq in Jersey and rejoined former trainer after fourteenth start: seems to stay 1¾m: acts on polytrack and firm going: tried visored/blinkered. *A. W. Carroll*

FLASH OF COLOUR 2 b.c. (Mar 22) Averti (IRE) 117 – Big Pink (IRE) (Bigstone **67** (IRE) 126) [2007 6g⁶ p8m⁴ p10g² Dec 12] maiden: in frame at Lingfield and Kempton: stays 1¼m: acts on polytrack. *Mrs A. J. Perrett*

FLASH OF FIRE (USA) 2 b.g. (Feb 19) Fantastic Light (USA) 134 – Mistle Thrush – (USA) 90 (Storm Bird (CAN) 134) [2007 6m 6m 6m Jul 13] good-quartered gelding: well held in maidens: bred for middle distances. *J. M. P. Eustace*

FLASHY MAX 2 b.c. (Apr 13) Primo Valentino (IRE) 116 – Be Practical 83 (Tragic **51** Role (USA)) [2007 6d 6f 6m 7.1m⁴ 8g p8.6g⁵ p8.6g² Dec 3] workmanlike colt: modest maiden: best effort when second in nursery at Wolverhampton: stays 8.6f: acts on polytrack. *Jedd O'Keeffe*

FLASHY PHOTON 2 b.g. (May 29) Compton Place 125 – Showboat (USA) (Theatrical 128) [2007 6m 6g* Aug 16] 3,500Y: compact gelding: seventh foal: half-brother to 3 winners in France, including 9f winner Sugar River (by Polish Precedent): dam, French maiden, out of US Grade 1 9f winner Fitzwilliam Place: fair form: better for debut, won maiden at Folkestone: will stay 7f. *H. Candy* **77 +**

FLASHY WINGS 4 ch.f. Zafonic (USA) 130 – Lovealoch (IRE) 108 (Lomond (USA) 128) [2007 115: 8.9g6 8m6 Jun 20] tall, useful-looking filly: had a quick, fluent action: smart performer at 2/3 yrs: below form in pattern company both outings in 2007, leaving impression all wasn't well when sixth to Nannina in Windsor Forest Stakes at Royal Ascot on latter (carried head awkwardly and found little): stayed 1m: acted on good to firm ground, below form on soft: tended to idle: retired in September (reportedly after failing to recover from recurring mucus problem). *M. R. Channon* **102**

FLAVIUS (IRE) 3 b.c. Montjeu (IRE) 137 – Stitching (IRE) 50 (High Estate 127) [2007 10.5g5 10m4 12d* Jun 24] 150,000Y: big, lengthy colt: sixth foal: half-brother to fairly useful 1¼m winner Trueno (by Desert King): dam, Irish maiden, half-sister to very smart 1m/1¼m winner Great Dane: fairly useful form: didn't have to be at best to win maiden at Pontefract in June: well suited by 1½m: looked handful in paddock on debut: sold 34,000 gns in October, sent to Qatar. *Sir Michael Stoute* **85**

FLAWED GENIUS 2 b.c. (Apr 10) Fasliyev (USA) 120 – Talented 112 (Bustino 136) [2007 6d6 7m* 6m4 6g Aug 21] well-made colt: half-brother to 3 winners, including fairly useful 2001 2-y-o 7f winner Zaeema (by Zafonic) and useful French 1m (at 2 yrs) and 1½m winner Friston Forest (by Barathea): dam 1¼m (including Sun Chariot Stakes) winner (stayed 1½m): fairly useful form: won maiden at Salisbury in July: back in trip for nurseries, better effort when fourth at Goodwood (tongue tied final start): should be suited by 1m+. *Sir Michael Stoute* **85 +**

FLAXBY 5 b.g. Mister Baileys 123 – Harryana 79 (Efisio 120) [2007 64: 10g 12g4 8.5g 10g* p7.1g3 Sep 22] strong gelding: modest handicapper: won at Les Landes (Jersey) in August: ran creditably at Wolverhampton final start: stays 1¼m: acts on polytrack, soft and good to firm going: often blinkered: refused to race third outing. *Mrs J. L. Le Brocq, Jersey* **61**

FLAXTON (UAE) 2 b.c. (May 21) Halling (USA) 133 – Yasmeen Valley (USA) 76 – (Danzig Connection (USA)) [2007 7s 7m 6g Aug 24] detached in maidens. *M. Brittain* **–**

FLEETING SPIRIT (IRE) 2 b.f. (Mar 8) Invincible Spirit (IRE) 121 – Millennium Tale (FR) (Distant Relative 128) [2007 5.1m* 5g* 6g2 5m* 6m2 Oct 5] **115**

Fleeting Spirit enjoyed a good two-year-old campaign, winning three of her first four starts and showing herself not far off the best of her age and sex in a close second in the Cheveley Park Stakes at Newmarket on her final appearance. She missed the chance to run at Royal Ascot and in the Prix de l'Abbaye, but she may well be able to add to the two pattern successes she already has in good sprinting company at three.

Fleeting Spirit's campaign got under way in a five-furlong maiden at Nottingham in early-June. She started only third favourite but she won sufficiently

Betfair Molecomb Stakes, Goodwood—Fleeting Spirit and Kingsgate Native pull clear of Captain Gerrard

Polypipe Flying Childers Stakes, Doncaster—Fleeting Spirit is firmly in command as Spirit of Sharjah (stars), Cute Ass and Captain Gerrard (rail) fight out the minor placings

impressively (albeit beating a rival who didn't win until her eighth start) for connections to talk of either the Queen Mary, Windsor Castle or Norfolk as her next engagement. A temperature ruled her out, however, but she showed she would have been well up to the standard when landing the Betfair Molecomb Stakes at Goodwood at the end of July. The Queen Mary runner-up Starlit Sands started favourite, ahead of the Windsor Castle second Kingsgate Native, with the Norfolk Stakes third Spirit of Sharjah also prominent in the betting. Fleeting Spirit was fifth in the betting at 8/1. Quickly recovering from a bump at the stalls, she travelled strongly and battled on gamely to get the better of Kingsgate Native by a neck, with two and a half lengths back to the dual Chester winner Captain Gerrard, with Starlit Sands fourth and Spirit of Sharjah sixth. Clearly a smart performer, there seemed no reason on pedigree why Fleeting Spirit would not stay six furlongs and she was sent next for the Lowther Stakes at York. Kingsgate Native, in the Nunthorpe, and Captain Gerrard went on to success at the York fixture, but Fleeting Spirit managed no better than third behind Nahoodh and Visit (promoted after Visit tested positive for the tranquiliser ACP), racing freely in the lead in a muddling affair and seemingly not seeing out the trip thoroughly. It was no surprise to see Fleeting Spirit back at five furlongs in the Polypipe Flying Childers Stakes at Doncaster in September and she made the most of a straightforward opportunity—Spirit of Sharjah and Captain Gerrard, on the same terms as at Goodwood, were two of her principal rivals—by winning readily, beating Spirit of Sharjah by a length and three quarters.

An altogether more ambitious target was considered next, the Prix de l'Abbaye, in which Fleeting Spirit would have met Kingsgate Native again, but the prospect of soft ground saw her switched to the Cheveley Park instead. Fleeting Spirit clearly had a good chance on form and, despite her Lowther running, she was sent off joint second favourite. Fleeting Spirit showed that it wasn't lack of stamina which beat her at York, running a really game race and just losing out to Natagora, a neck being the winning margin in the Cheveley Park for the fourth year running. In contrast to the three previous years, however, the third was well back, four lengths in fact, and Fleeting Spirit's effort in defeat would have been good enough to win ten of the eleven previous runnings of the Cheveley Park, the exception the one won by Queen's Logic in 2001. The 2002 winner Airwave went on to win the Temple Stakes and reach a place in three Group 1 sprints at three and it wouldn't be overambitious to think about a similar campaign with Fleeting Spirit.

			Green Desert	Danzig
Fleeting Spirit (IRE) (b.f. Mar 8, 2005)	Invincible Spirit (IRE) (b 1997)		(b 1983)	Foreign Courier
		Rafha	Kris
		(b 1987)	Eljazzi
	Millennium Tale (FR) (b 1996)	Distant Relative	Habitat
		(b 1986)	Royal Sister II
		The Bean Sidhe	Corvaro
		(b 1983)	Whiskey Mountain

The compact, attractive Fleeting Spirit is very much a sprinter on looks and provided her sire Invincible Spirit with the two pattern successes so far with his second crop. That didn't quite match the achievements of his first crop, but the Prix du Jockey Club victory of Lawman ensured his star remained in the ascendant. Invincible Spirit's fee for 2008 is €75,000, having been €10,000 in 2003 and

€35,000 in 2007. Fleeting Spirit has twice been through the sale-ring, making €35,000 at the Goffs September Sale as a yearling and 90,000 guineas at the Newmarket April Breeze-Up. She was entered at the latest Newmarket December Sales but was withdrawn as she was 'a little off colour' in the week prior to the sale. Fleeting Spirit is the fifth foal out of her unraced dam Millennium Tale and the second winner after Alone He Stands (by Flying Spur), a fairly useful six- to seven-and-a-half-furlong winner for John Hayden in Ireland in 2007. Hayden also trained Millennium Tale's dam The Bean Sidhe, the most notable member of this family in recent times until Fleeting Spirit came along. The Bean Sidhe was a useful two-year-old and won two notable races at Phoenix Park at three, the One Thousand Guineas Trial and the Hardwicke Cup, both at seven furlongs. The Bean Sidhe produced five winners in France, the most successful the durable middle-distance mare Je Ne Suis Pas La, who won ten and was placed on forty-nine of her more than one hundred starts; the best probably Finir En Beaute, who won at ten furlongs and was fourth in the Prix Penelope before winning over nine furlongs at Santa Anita.

Fleeting Spirit herself is likely to prove best at sprint distances. She has been raced only on good and good to firm going, and is evidently regarded as likely to be less effective on soft. She is owned by a syndicate called The Searchers, whose members include the British Horseracing Authority chairman Paul Roy, well-known jumps owner Andy Stewart and Martin Myers, owner of Mountgrange Stud and Kingsdown Stables. For what exactly the syndicate members are searching is beyond the scope of this book. *J. Noseda*

FLEETWAY (IRE) 2 ch.f. (Apr 19) Fleetwood (IRE) 107 – Eponine 70 (Sharpo 132) – [2007 6m Aug 1] second foal: dam 13f and hurdles winner: tailed off in maiden. *F. Watson*

FLEETWOOD IMAGE 3 b.g. Fleetwood (IRE) 107 – Change of Image 65 (Spectrum (IRE) 126) [2007 55: 12g⁵ Apr 8] modest maiden in 2006: well beaten only start at 3 yrs: sold 1,300 gns in October. *J. R. Weymes* –

FLEMISH ART (IRE) 2 b.c. (Apr 29) Marju (IRE) 127 – Danalia (IRE) 78 (Danehill (USA) 126) [2007 6g Aug 24] 25/1, seemed amiss in maiden at Thirsk: bred for speed. *M. J. Wallace* –

FLEUR DE MONTJEU (IRE) 2 b.f. (Jan 24) Montjeu (IRE) 137 – Dancing Sensation (USA) 72 (Faliraki 125) [2007 7m 7m 8g Oct 26] €90,000Y: small filly: has a scratchy action: sixth foal: half-sister to useful 7f (at 2 yrs)/1m winner Star Sensation (by Sri Pekan) and winner up to 11.5f in Italy by Namaqualand: dam 7f to 1½m and hurdles winner: behind in maidens. *W. R. Swinburn* –

FLEURET 3 b. or br.f. Diktat 126 – Forthwith 104 (Midyan (USA) 124) [2007 8g⁴ 8m 6f² 6g* 7m³ 6m⁶ Oct 4] leggy filly: sixth foal: sister to useful 2004 2-y-o 7f winner Favourita and half-sister to 3 winners, including smart 1½m winner Time Zone (by Shirley Heights): dam 7f (at 2 yrs) and 1¼m winner: fairly useful performer: won maiden at Goodwood in August: 14 lb out of weights when very good sixth to Angus Newz in handicap at Newmarket final start: should prove fully effective at 1m: raced only on good ground or firmer. *Eve Johnson Houghton* **82**

FLEX 2 b.g. (Feb 21) Averti (IRE) 117 – Floppie Disk 82 (Magic Ring (IRE) 115) [2007 p6g 5g 5d⁵ Sep 25] 29,000Y: first foal: dam, 2-y-o 5f winner, half-sister to smart sprinter Ringmoor Down: modest form in maidens and minor event (good speed): will prove best at 5f. *D. J. Murphy* **52**

FLIGHT DREAM (FR) 4 gr.c. Highest Honor (FR) 124 – Flight Night (Night Shift (USA)) [2007 p9.5g p9.5d⁴ Dec 17] poor form in bumpers: fair maiden on Flat: much better effort when fourth to Pelican Waters at Wolverhampton: stays 9.5f: raced on polytrack. *M. G. Quinlan* **65**

FLIGHT PLAN 2 ch.g. (Apr 30) Best of The Bests (IRE) 122 – Cyclone Connie 98 (Dr Devious (IRE) 127) [2007 7m* 7g p7g⁵ 7m p8m Oct 11] close-coupled gelding: second foal: dam, 6f winner, half-sister to smart sprinter Colonel Cotton: fairly useful form: won maiden at Folkestone in August: good fifth in nursery at Lingfield third start, raced too freely last 2 (also swerved badly leaving stall penultimate one): best up to 7f: acts on polytrack and good to firm going: sold 27,000 gns. *C. A. Cyzer* **86**

FLIGHT TO QUALITY 2 ch.c. (Apr 28) Where Or When (IRE) 124 – Southern Psychic (USA) (Alwasmi (USA) 115) [2007 7g 7.1m² 7.5d* Sep 25] 40,000F, €55,000Y: tall colt: half-brother to several winners, including smart 6f (at 2 yrs) to 1m winner Rumpold (by Mister Baileys) and useful 7f (at 2 yrs) to 1¼m winner Wing Commander **84 p**

(by Royal Applause): dam US sprinter: fairly useful form: progressive in maidens, won readily at Beverley despite hanging left across track: will stay at least 1m: should continue on the up. *M. Johnston*

FLIGHTY FELLOW (IRE) 7 ch.g. Flying Spur (AUS) – Al Theraab (USA) 81   **88**
(Roberto (USA) 131) [2007 81: 8.2g⁶ 8m* 8.1m⁵ 8.1s⁵ 8s* 8.5m² 8.3g³ 8g⁴ 8.1g² 10.5s 8.9d Oct 13] big, lengthy gelding: fairly useful handicapper nowadays: won at Pontefract in April and July: good second to Orpen Wide at Haydock ninth outing: best around 1m: acts on firm and soft ground: usually wears headgear (blinkered in 2007): no easy ride (tends to wander): sold 17,000 gns. *T. D. Easterby*

FLINT RIVER 9 b.g. Red Ransom (USA) – She's All Class (USA) (Rahy (USA) 115)   **59**
[2007 79: p7g Jan 24] close-coupled gelding: fairly useful handicapper at best, just modest form only start in 2007: probably best at 7f/1m nowadays: acts on all-weather, firm and soft going: tried blinkered/visored. *H. Morrison*

FLIPANDO (IRE) 6 b.g. Sri Pekan (USA) 117 – Magic Touch (Fairy King (USA))   **108**
[2007 100: 7f⁶ 8f 10.4g⁴ 8.5m* 10m* 8m² 8.9s 8.1m³ 8g 8m 10m 8d Oct 12] tall gelding: useful handicapper: more progress in 2007, winning at Beverley and Redcar (totesport.com Zetland Gold Cup, beat Wind Star by neck) in May: best efforts after when placed, including 4 lengths second of 26 to Royal Oath in Hunt Cup at Royal Ascot on sixth start: stays 10.4f: acts on firm going, not on softer than good. *T. D. Barron*

FLOODLIGHT FANTASY 4 b.g. Fantastic Light (USA) 134 – Glamadour (IRE)   **–**
(Sanglamore (USA) 126) [2007 76: 9.9m f12g⁵ 12d 12.1g p9.5g p9.5g Nov 12] strong gelding: fair performer at 3 yrs: little form in 2007: wears headgear. *Jedd O'Keeffe*

FLOP (IRE) 2 b.f. (Mar 5) Fraam 114 – Confidential 60 (Generous (IRE) 139) [2007   **53**
7d⁵ 7s⁶ 7v³ Jul 26] €4,500Y: leggy filly: fourth foal: half-sister to 3-y-o Confidentiality and 7f winner Confide (by Namid): dam, ran twice, half-sister to smart performers Reprimand (miler) and Wiorno (up to 1½m): modest maiden: third at York: raced only at 7f on going softer than good. *M. Brittain*

FLORAL GUEST 2 b.f. (Jan 31) Barathea (IRE) 127 – Datura 74 (Darshaan 133)   **–**
[2007 7s 7d Oct 16] 22,000F, 35,000U: fourth foal: half-sister to 2 winners abroad: dam 1m winner: well held in maidens: sold 2,500 gns, sent to Kazakhstan. *G. G. Margarson*

FLORENTINE LADY 4 b.f. Medicean 128 – Polytess (IRE) (Polish Patriot (USA)   **§§**
128) [2007 5m 6m p7.1g p6g Oct 5] fifth foal: half-sister to 3 winners, including fairly useful 2000 2-y-o 6f winner Norcroft Lady (by Mujtahid) and 9f/9.7f winner Billy One Punch (by Mark of Esteem): dam second at 1¼m in France: no sign of ability: has refused/virtually refused to race on 3 occasions (slowly away other time), and very much one to avoid. *D. Shaw*

FLORENTINO 3 b.f. Efisio 120 – Sirene Bleu Marine (USA) (Secreto (USA) 128)   **–**
[2007 6.9m 8d 10.1m Aug 24] lengthy filly: sister to useful 1¼m to 13.4f winner Flossy and half-sister to fairly useful 1m/9f winner Down Memory Lane (by Pursuit of Love) and 6f (at 2 yrs) to 1¼m winner Society Girl (by Shavian): dam unraced: well held in maidens. *C. W. Thornton*

FLORES SEA (USA) 3 ch.g. Luhuk (USA) 114 – Perceptive (USA) (Capote (USA))   **83**
[2007 74: p7.1g 6f* 6d⁴ 8.2g 8s⁶ 7g 7g 10g Nov 7] lengthy gelding: fairly useful handicapper: best effort when winning at Thirsk in May: should stay 1m: acts on firm and soft going. *T. D. Barron*

FLORIMUND 4 b.g. Sadler's Wells (USA) 132 – Valentine Girl 109 (Alzao (USA)   **90**
117) [2007 90: 12m⁵ 14g 12m Jun 4] good-bodied gelding: fairly useful handicapper: best effort at 4 yrs when fifth at Newmarket on reappearance: stays 13f: raced on polytrack and good/good to firm going: has raced lazily: joined M. Butler, Ireland, 16,000 gns. *Sir Michael Stoute*

FLORISTA GG (URU) 4 ch.f. Gulpha Gorge (USA) – Flor de Fango (URU) (Villon   **–**
(ARG)) [2007 8m 10m⁶ Aug 11] leggy filly: fifth foal: sister/half-sister to 3 winners in Ururguay: dam Uruguayan Grade 3 winner: ran 3 times at Maronas in 2006, winning maiden and Polla de Potrancas (Uruguayan 1000 Guineas): tailed-off last in handicaps in Britain at 4 yrs: stays 1m: raced only on dirt and good to firm ground: has been early to post. *J. S. Moore*

FLORISTRY 2 b.f. (Mar 6) Fasliyev (USA) 120 – Zaeema 93 (Zafonic (USA) 130)   **106 p**
[2007 6d 7.5g³ 5.7f* 6d* 6g* Oct 27] lengthy filly: has scope: second foal: half-sister to 3-y-o Old Romney: dam, 2-y-o 7f winner on only start, out of Sun Chariot Stakes winner Talented: useful form: improved fast to complete hat-trick in autumn, in maiden at Bath, nursery at York and listed race at Doncaster, in last-named confidently ridden and having

plenty to spare when beating Fateh Field by 1½ lengths: should prove best at 5f/6f: has joined Godolphin: will continue to progress, and should make her mark in pattern races. *Sir Michael Stoute*

FLOR Y NATA (USA) 4 b.f. Fusaichi Pegasus (USA) 130 – Rose of Zollern (IRE) 111 – (Seattle Dancer (USA) 119) [2007 96: 10.1s⁵ 10.1m 9g 10d Aug 25] good-topped filly: useful performer at 3 yrs: well held in 2007: temperament under suspicion. *Sir Mark Prescott*

FLOWER 2 ch.f. (Mar 5) Zamindar (USA) 116 – Time For Tea (IRE) 73 (Imperial Frontier (USA) 112) [2007 p8g p8g 7g⁴ Oct 25] sturdy filly: seventh foal: half-sister to several winners, including 7f to 9f winner Frazzled (by Greensmith), later successful in Spain, and 6-y-o Trifti: dam maiden (stayed 1¼m): fair maiden: will stay 1¼m. *C. A. Cyzer* **66**

FLOWER APPEAL 2 br.f. (Apr 22) Diktat 126 – Flower O'Cannie (IRE) 87 (Mujadil (USA) 119) [2007 6v 7d 7g Aug 17] workmanlike filly: fourth foal: dam 6f (at 2 yrs) to 1½m winner: no form. *M. W. Easterby* –

FLOWER HAVEN 5 b.m. Dr Fong (USA) 128 – Daisy May (In The Wings 128) [2007 p8.6g p12.2g Feb 12] maiden: unraced on Flat in 2006, and little impact both starts on Flat at 5 yrs: stays 1½m: acts on polytrack and good to firm ground. *M. J. Gingell* –

FLOWER OF CORK (IRE) 3 b.f. Noverre (USA) 125 – Scarlet Ribbons 95 (Anabaa (USA) 130) [2007 60: 7.5m 8.1m 5m 5d⁶ 6f 6m⁴ 5.1d 6m 5f Sep 25] small, stocky filly: has a quick action: just poor maiden at 3 yrs: left T. Easterby 1,500 gns after fourth start, Ms J. Doyle after seventh: should stay 7f/1m: acts on all-weather, good to firm and good to soft going: blinkered/in cheekpieces of late. *I. A. Wood* **47**

FLOWER OF KENT (USA) 3 b.f. Diesis 133 – Apple of Kent (USA) 118 (Kris S (USA)) [2007 78p: 10m⁶ p8g Jun 6] leggy filly: fair handicapper, lightly raced: should stay 1¼m: raced only on polytrack and good to firm going: raced freely on reappearance: sold 82,000 gns in December. *J. H. M. Gosden* **69**

FLOWER SONG 2 b.f. (Jan 27) Act One 124 – Sweet Pea 94 (Persian Bold 123) [2007 7d 8g p7m Nov 1] narrow filly: fourth foal: half-sister to 3-y-o Scarlet Runner and Irish 1½m winner Scent (by Groom Dancer): dam 1m winner: modest form in rear in maidens. *A. King* **56**

FLOWING CAPE (IRE) 2 b.c. (Mar 3) Cape Cross (IRE) 129 – Jet Lock (USA) (Crafty Prospector (USA)) [2007 6f⁴ 6m² 6.1m 7g² Oct 27] 40,000 2-y-o: lengthy, good-topped colt: brother to useful 2003 2-y-o 1m winner Malin and half-brother to 2 winners, including 4-y-o Danjet: dam Irish/US maiden: useful form: second to Stimulation in maiden at Newbury and to Kal Barg in nursery at Doncaster: will stay 1m. *R. Hollinshead* **97**

FLUFFY 4 b.f. Efisio 120 – Sirene Bleu Marine (USA) (Secreto (USA) 128) [2007 –: p9.5g⁴ 8.2g² 7g Oct 3] fair maiden: said to have finished lame final outing: will stay at least 1¼m: best effort on polytrack. *K. A. Ryan* **67**

FLUSHED 3 b.g. Foxhound (USA) 103 – Sweet And Lucky (Lucky Wednesday 124) [2007 –: f6g⁵ f8g f8g p6g f7g² f7g⁶ p7.1g f8g 7s 7.5s⁴ 7.5m 6m Sep 1] tall gelding: modest maiden: stays 7f: acts on fibresand: blinkered: has looked wayward. *A. J. McCabe* **50**

FLUTERS HOUSE 3 b.g. Piccolo 121 – Little Tumbler (IRE) 66 (Cyrano de Bergerac 120) [2007 –: 7m p6g 6m 8d⁵ 10.2g Jul 9] workmanlike gelding: no sign of ability: tried blinkered. *S. Woodman* –

FLUTTERING ROSE 3 gr.f. Compton Place 125 – Bethesda 91 (Distant Relative 128) [2007 71: p5g⁴ 5m 6m⁵ p6g 7.1m Sep 15] modest handicapper: sold from R. Charlton 14,000 gns after reappearance: seemed to lose action (blinkered) final start: stays 6f: acts on polytrack, probably on good to firm going: carried head awkwardly third outing. *R. M. Beckett* **61**

FLY BY JOVE (IRE) 4 b.g. Fasliyev (USA) 120 – Flyleaf (FR) (Persian Bold 123) [2007 –: p8g⁶ p8g 8f⁶ 10.2m⁶ 8.1g 8.1d Aug 16] good-topped gelding: poor maiden: stays 1m: acts on polytrack and firm going: blinkered/tongue tied final start. *Jane Southcombe* **46**

FLYING APPLAUSE 2 b.g. (Mar 31) Royal Applause 124 – Mrs Gray 61 (Red Sunset 120) [2007 5g 5.1g⁶ 6m 6g p7g³ 7m³ p7g⁸* Nov 4] 40,000Y: leggy, close-coupled gelding: half-brother to several winners, including useful 2002 2-y-o 6f/7f winner Steelaninch (by Inchinor): dam 2-y-o 7f winner: fair performer: steady progress, won nursery at Lingfield final start: should prove best up to 7f: acts on polytrack and good to firm going. *A. King* **73**

FLYING BANTAM (IRE) 6 b.g. Fayruz 116 – Natural Pearl (Petong 126) [2007 74: p7.1g⁵ f8g³ p7.1g² f7g* p7.1g p7.1g³ p7.1g³ 7f* 7.1m⁶ 7.1m³ 7g² 7.5m* Jun 13] small, **78**

well-made gelding: fair handicapper: won at Southwell in February, Thirsk in April and Beverley in June: best at 7f/1m: acts on all-weather, firm and soft going: tried in cheek-pieces: reliable. *R. A. Fahey*

FLYING CLARETS (IRE) 4 b.f. Titus Livius (FR) 115 – Sheryl Lynn (Miller's Mate **103** 116) [2007 85: 10.9m* 10f² 10.4g² 12g 8.9s² 8d⁴ 9.9g⁶ 8.9f 10m 10.4d* 10d Oct 27] tall, quite good-topped filly: progressed into useful handicapper in 2007, winning at Warwick in April and York in October, best effort when beating The Grey Berry by neck on latter occasion: also ran well when second to Charlie Tokyo in valuable event at latter track on fifth outing: finds 1m too sharp, and stays 1½m: acts on firm and soft going: effective in cheekpieces or not: races prominently: tends to hang, but is tough. *R. A. Fahey*

FLYING DOCTOR 4 b.g. Mark of Esteem (IRE) 137 – Vice Vixen (CAN) (Vice – Regent (CAN)) [2007 –: 13m Aug 2] tall, close-coupled gelding: maiden: well held only start on Flat (winner over hurdles) in 2007. *N. G. Richards*

FLYING ENCORE (IRE) 3 b.f. Royal Applause 124 – Come Fly With Me (Bluebird **71** (USA) 125) [2007 82: 8m⁶ 8.2m⁵ 7s⁶ p6g 7f³ p7g⁵ p7g Sep 5] rather sparely-made filly: fair maiden handicapper: may prove best short of 1m: acts on polytrack and firm going (below form on soft): sometimes wears cheekpieces: sold 3,000 gns, sent to Germany. *W. R. Swinburn*

FLYING GOOSE (IRE) 3 ch.c. Danehill Dancer (IRE) 117 – Top of The Form (IRE) **88** 79 (Masterclass (USA) 116) [2007 74p: 7m³ 7m* 7m³ 7d⁵ 6m³ p7g p7.1g³ Oct 22] sturdy, good-topped colt: fairly useful performer: won maiden at Folkestone in July: third in handicaps after: worth a try at 1m: acts on polytrack and good to firm ground: effective ridden prominently/held up: sold 33,000 gns. *L. M. Cumani*

FLYING GREY (IRE) 3 gr.g. Desert Prince (IRE) 130 – Grey Goddess 117 (Gods- **54** walk (USA) 130) [2007 59: 8.1m 8g* 10.1d⁴ 10.9s⁵ Jul 6] compact gelding: modest performer: won selling handicap at Bath in June: stays 1¼m: acts on polytrack, good to firm and good to soft going: tried blinkered/in cheekpieces: joined C. Down, and gelded. *P. A. Blockley*

FLYING INDIAN 2 ch.f. (Feb 5) Hawk Wing (USA) 136 – Poppadam 87 (Salse (USA) **61** 128) [2007 5.2m 5m⁵ p6g² 5d p5g⁶ p5g p5.1g p6g⁴ Sep 19] 25,000Y: strong filly: fourth foal: half-sister to winner in US by Fantastic Light: dam, 1m winner, half-sister to Irish 1000 Guineas winner Classic Park, herself dam of Derby second Walk In The Park: modest maiden: will be suited by 7f/1m: acts on polytrack and good to firm going. *A. M. Balding*

FLYINGIT (USA) 4 b.f. Lear Fan (USA) 130 – Byre Bird (USA) (Diesis 133) [2007 **78 d** 90: f8g² p8g⁶ p9.5g⁶ 8s 9v 10s 10v Aug 12] sturdy filly: just fair handicapper at best in 2007: left K. Ryan after third start: stays 11f: acts on all-weather and good to firm ground: tried in blinkers/tongue tie earlier in career, sometimes wears cheekpieces: headstrong, and one to be wary of. *Thomas Mullins, Ireland*

FLYING PASS 5 b.g. Alzao (USA) 117 – Complimentary Pass 80 (Danehill (USA) **55** 126) [2007 67: 10g Aug 2] close-coupled gelding: has a quick action: fair maiden handi-capper at best: modest form only start on Flat in 2007: barely stays 1½m: acts on poly-track, firm and good to soft going: tried visored/tongue tied/in cheekpieces. *R. J. Price*

FLYING PRINCESS (IRE) 3 ch.f. Bad As I Wanna Be (IRE) 115 – Baltic Beach – (IRE) (Polish Precedent (USA) 131) [2007 6m 7s 6.9m 6g p5.1g Dec 4] €7,500Y: second foal: half-sister to fairly useful 5f winner Glenviews Youngone (by Namid): dam unraced: no form in maidens: blinkered final start. *A. Berry*

FLYING SOMMELIER (USA) 2 b.g. (Mar 7) Dixieland Band (USA) – Charming **62** Lauren (USA) (Meadowlake (USA)) [2007 6g⁵ Jun 13] $80,000Y: first foal: dam unraced sister/close relation to US 2-y-o Grade 1 8.5f winners Greenwood Lake and Success Express (Breeders' Cup Juvenile): 13/2, immature (very slowly away) when fifth in maiden at Hamilton. *T. D. Barron*

FLYING SPIRIT (IRE) 8 b.g. Flying Spur (AUS) – All Laughter (Vision (USA)) **79** [2007 –: p16g⁵ p13g⁴ p16g 11.9d² 12d² May 27] quite good-topped gelding: fair handi-capper: stays 1½m: acts on polytrack, firm and good to soft going: usually wears head-gear: races up with pace: fairly useful chaser. *G. L. Moore*

FLYING SPUD 6 ch.g. Fraam 114 – Lorcanjo 36 (Hallgate 127) [2007 –: p10g Apr 30] – modest performer at best: little form since 2004. *A. J. Chamberlain*

FLYING TACKLE 9 ch.g. First Trump 118 – Frighten The Life (Kings Lake (USA) **44** 133) [2007 56: p5.1g⁶ p5.1g 5f Jun 7] strong, lengthy gelding: poor performer nowadays:

best at 5f/6f: acts on polytrack and any turf going: wears headgear: tends to get behind: sometimes wanders. *I. W. McInnes*

FLYING TIME 2 b.f. (Feb 26) Mark of Esteem (IRE) 137 – Seagreen (IRE) (Green **70** Desert (USA) 127) [2007 8g 8.5m* 10d⁴ Oct 9] 4,000Y: compact filly: third foal: dam twice-raced daughter of useful 1½m winner Ocean Ballad: fair form: won maiden at Beverley in September: unsuited by steady pace (pulled hard) final start: should stay 1¼m. *M. R. Channon*

FLYING VALENTINO 3 b.f. Primo Valentino (IRE) 116 – Flying Romance (IRE) 68 **78** (Flying Spur (AUS)) [2007 83p: 6g 5g⁴ 8.2g⁶ 6s⁵ 8m³ 6f 7g² 7g 8g⁵ 7g Nov 6] narrow filly: fair handicapper: has form at 1m, but may prove best at shorter: acts on good to firm ground. *G. A. Swinbank*

FLY IN JOHNNY (IRE) 2 b.c. (Jan 22) Fasliyev (USA) 120 – Goodness Gracious **70** (IRE) 93 (Green Desert (USA) 127) [2007 6d⁴ 6.5d⁴ 5.1g Oct 24] 29,000Y: sturdy colt: first foal: dam, 2-y-o 7f winner, half-sister to smart miler Flat Spin: fair maiden: fourth at Windsor and Newbury (behind Fateh Field, went freely in front): may prove best at 5f/6f. *R. Hannon*

FLY KISS 2 b.f. (Mar 25) Arkadian Hero (USA) 123 – Kiss Me Kate 73 (Aragon 118) **83 ?** [2007 5m 5.5d p7g 7m* 7.5g* 7g⁵ Aug 25] 6,000Y: leggy filly: first foal: dam, 1¼m and hurdles winner, half-sister to smart 6f/7f performer Pan Jammer: fairly useful performer: won maiden at Brighton and nursery at Beverley: possibly flattered when 4¾ lengths fifth of 7 to Sense of Joy in falsely-run Prestige Stakes at Goodwood later in August: stays 7.5f: acts on good to firm going. *C. E. Brittain*

FLYLOWFLYLONG (IRE) 4 b.f. Danetime (IRE) 121 – Jellybeen (IRE) 72 (Petar- **73** dia 113) [2007 74: 7.1m⁴ 7.1m 8.3g* 9.1g 8.3g² 6.9d 8.3d Jul 14] good-topped filly: fair handicapper: won at Hamilton in May: reportedly finished lame final start: stays easy 8.6f: acts on polytrack, soft and good to firm going (below form on heavy): visored (ran creditably) final 3-y-o outing: tends to hang right: usually held up. *I. Semple*

FLYOFF (IRE) 10 b.g. Mtoto 134 – Flyleaf (FR) (Persian Bold 123) [2007 –: p16g **–** p16.5g⁶ Feb 2] little form since 2003: used to wear headgear (not in 2007). *Mrs N. Macauley*

FLY SO FREE (IRE) 3 b.f. Fath (USA) 116 – Xania 32 (Mujtahid (USA) 118) [2007 **–** 66: 5d 6d 6v 5m Aug 6] strong, close-coupled filly: maiden: no form at 3 yrs. *D. Nicholls*

FLY TIME 3 b.f. Fraam 114 – Kissing Time 79 (Lugana Beach 116) [2007 65d: 5.7d³ **52 §** 5m 5d⁵ p5.1g⁴ 5.1s² 5.1m 6.1d Aug 16] leggy, workmanlike filly: has a quick action: modest maiden handicapper: stays 5.7f: acts on polytrack, firm and soft going: tried in cheekpieces: unreliable. *Mrs L. Williamson*

FLY WITH THE STARS (USA) 2 ch.g. (Mar 27) Fusaichi Pegasus (USA) 130 – **80** Forest Key (USA) (Green Forest (USA) 134) [2007 8.1s 8.2d⁵ 8.2g³ Nov 7] $100,000Y: tall gelding: has scope: half-brother to several winners, notably very smart US Grade 1 9f winner Gaviola (by Cozzene): dam 1m/8.5f winner in US: fairly useful maiden: progressive form, third to Cuban Missile at Nottingham: will stay 1¼m: gelded, and has joined R. Brookhouse. *M. Johnston*

FOCUS GROUP (USA) 6 b.g. Kris S (USA) – Interim 117 (Sadler's Wells (USA) **88** 132) [2007 98: 8s 12.1g⁵ May 9] strong gelding: lightly raced: has reportedly had shins fired: just fairly useful handicapper in 2007, better effort when close fifth at Beverley: seemingly stays 1½m: acts on firm and good to soft going: often blanketed for stall entry: held up. *J. J. Quinn*

FOLGA 5 b.m. Atraf 116 – Desert Dawn 108 (Belfort (FR) 89) [2007 104: 5.1f² 6.1s 6g **92** 6m 5m 6.1m Sep 15] leggy mare: useful performer at best, just fairly useful nowadays: best effort in 2007 when second in listed event at Bath on reappearance: effective at 5f/6f: acts on polytrack and firm ground, below form on softer than good: sold 33,000 gns in October. *J. G. Given*

FOL HOLLOW (IRE) 2 b.g. (Mar 31) Monashee Mountain (USA) 115 – Constance **92** Do (Risk Me (FR) 127) [2007 5d² 5g² f6g⁴ 5.9g² 6v³ 5g* 6m* 6g⁶ 5m* Aug 28] €3,200F, 2,400Y: strong, compact gelding: third foal: dam French 7f to 9.5f winner: fairly useful performer: thrived in summer, won maiden at Musselburgh, nursery at Goodwood and minor event at Ripon (despite hanging right): gelded after: winner at 6f, probably best at 5f (speedy front runner): acts on good to firm going. *D. Nicholls*

FOLIO (IRE) 7 b.g. Perugino (USA) 84 – Bayleaf 104 (Efisio 120) [2007 95: 10g⁶ 10m **90** 10d 8.9s 10m 9d⁵ 10m⁶ 10.5s² 10d 10.1d⁴ Oct 30] rather leggy, useful-looking gelding: fairly useful handicapper: best effort at 7 yrs when second at Haydock in September:

stays 10.5f: unraced on heavy ground, acts on any other turf and polytrack: usually held up. *W. J. Musson*

FOLK OPERA (IRE) 3 ch.f. Singspiel (IRE) 133 – Skiphall (Halling (USA) 133) **94** [2007 80p: 10m* 11.5g³ May 12] sturdy filly: fairly useful form: won maiden at Newbury in April, then left M. Jarvis: good ¾-length third to Kayah in listed Oaks Trial at Lingfield next time: had ankle chip removed after: stays 11.5f: yet to race on extremes of going on turf. *Saeed bin Suroor*

FOLK (USA) 3 b.f. Quiet American (USA) – Polish Style (USA) (Danzig (USA)) [2007 **114** a8f* a9f* a9f a10f³ a10f a9f⁴ Nov 4] eighth living foal: half-sister to 3 winners, including smart US (at 2 yrs)/UAE 1m/9f winner Danuta (by Sunday Silence): dam, useful French 6f winner (including at 2 yrs), out of US 2-y-o Grade 1 winner Family Style: smart performer: trained by T. Albertrani in USA in 2006, winning maiden at Aqueduct by 10¼ lengths: successful on first 2 starts at Nad Al Sheba in 2007, in UAE 1000 Guineas (by 4¾ lengths from Greetings) in February and UAE Oaks (by 5 lengths from Samba Reggae) in March (left I. Mohammed after): well below form behind Asiatic Boy in UAE Derby there next time (reportedly returned lame on off-fore): off nearly 4 months, creditable 1¼ lengths third to Octave in CCA Oaks at Belmont, then well held in Alabama Stakes at Saratoga and Grade 3 Turnback The Alarm Stakes at Aqueduct: stayed 1¼m: raced only on dirt: usually led: visits A P Indy. *Saeed bin Suroor*

FOLLINGWORTH (IRE) 4 ch.f. Midnish 109 – Pennine Way (IRE) (Waajib 121) **–** [2007 –: p8g f11g Feb 6] compact filly: little form: tried blinkered. *A. D. Brown*

FOLLOWING FLOW (USA) 5 b. or br.g. King of Kings (IRE) 125 – Sign Here **55** (USA) (Private Terms (USA)) [2007 80: p8.6g⁶ p7.1g⁵ p8.6g p8.6g⁴ 9.2g 8m 7m 8.3g 5s 6d⁶ 7.1m 6.9m⁴ 8m⁵ 6g⁴ p7.1g Nov 22] good-topped gelding: one-time fairly useful winner: only modest in 2007, leaving R. Hollinshead after fourth start: stays 8.6f: acts on polytrack, soft and good to firm going: tried visored, often wears cheekpieces. *R. Allan*

FOLLOWMYFOOTSTEPS (USA) 3 bl.c. Giant's Causeway (USA) 132 – Lady **112** Carson (USA) (Carson City (USA)) [2007 72p: 7.5m* 8g⁶ 8m⁵ May 26] third foal: half-brother to winners in USA by Loup Sauvage and Real Quiet: dam US sprinter: won maiden at Tipperary in April: stiff tasks, much better form when 3½ lengths sixth to Astronomer Royal in Poule d'Essai des Poulains at Longchamp and 3 lengths fifth behind Cockney Rebel in Irish 2000 Guineas at the Curragh: stays 1m: raced only on good/good to firm ground. *D. Wachman, Ireland*

FOLLOW ON 5 b.h. Barathea (IRE) 127 – Handora (IRE) 82 (Hernando (FR) 127) **73 d** [2007 84: p16g⁴ p12g³ p13g³ p16g³ 18g 16m p12g p16g p16g⁶ 14.1m³ p16g⁵ 16g⁵ Sep 20] stocky horse: fair maiden handicapper: below form after fourth start in 2007: stays 2m: acts on polytrack and good to firm ground, unraced on going softer than good: tried visored: sometimes slowly away: held up. *A. P. Jarvis*

FOLLOW THE BAND 2 b.c. (Apr 9) Prince Sabo 123 – Pea Green 98 (Try My Best **57** (USA) 130) [2007 6m 6m p6g 8m 6s p8.6g Oct 26] angular colt: modest maiden: seems to stay 1m. *R. Hannon*

FOLLOW THE COLOURS (IRE) 4 b.g. Rainbow Quest (USA) 134 – Gardenia **–** (IRE) (Sadler's Wells (USA) 132) [2007 75: p8.6g p9.5d Dec 7] neat gelding: fair handicapper in 2006: returned to former trainer and tongue tied, well held on Flat in 2007: stays 1¼m: acts on polytrack and soft going. *J. W. Hills*

FOLLOW THE FLAG (IRE) 3 ch.g. Traditionally (USA) 117 – Iktidar 80 (Green **71** Desert (USA) 127) [2007 72: p7g² p7g⁵ p7g⁵ p7g p8.3g 7g⁶ p7g Dec 29] heavy-topped gelding: fair maiden: left. N. Littmoden before final start: stays 7f: acts on polytrack and firm ground: sometimes blinkered. *C. F. Wall*

FOLLOW YOUR SPIRIT 2 b.g. (Jan 21) Compton Place 125 – Ymlaen (IRE) 84 **58 +** (Desert Prince (IRE) 130) [2007 8.1f 7d 7g Oct 16] plain gelding: well held in maidens, but trips possibly too far (showed good speed, and modest form, final start, gelded after): bred to be suited by 5f/6f. *B. Palling*

FOLLY LODGE 3 ch.f. Grand Lodge (USA) 125 – Marika 103 (Marju (IRE) 127) **93** [2007 75: 7g* 7m 8m⁶ 7d² 7m 7d Oct 27] strong, good-bodied filly: has a fluent action: fairly useful handicapper: won at Newbury in May: good second there after: should stay 1m (took strong hold when tried): acts on polytrack, good to firm and good to soft ground. *B. W. Hills*

FONDLED 3 b.f. Selkirk (USA) 129 – Embraced 103 (Pursuit of Love 124) [2007 8.2g⁴ **91** 8d³ 7d² 8g³ 8g* Sep 19] good-topped, quite attractive filly: second foal: half-sister to fairly useful 7.5f/1m winner Caressed (by Medicean): dam, 1m winner (including at

2 yrs), half-sister to very smart 1½m performer Nowhere To Exit: fairly useful form: won handicap at Yarmouth in September: effective at 7f/1m: raced only on good/good to soft going: saddle reportedly slipped third start: slowly away last 2 outings. *J. R. Fanshawe*

FONDNESS 4 ch.f. Dr Fong (USA) 128 – Island Story 88 (Shirley Heights 130) [2007 **65** 70, a–: p12.2g p13.9g² 16m 17.2m 12m⁴ 18d⁴ Aug 16] rather leggy filly: fair maiden: left J. Quinn after second start and J. Broderick in Ireland after fourth: stays 2¼m: acts on polytrack, good to firm and good to soft going: sometimes blinkered/tongue tied: has raced freely. *B. G. Powell*

FONGS GAZELLE 3 b.f. Dr Fong (USA) 128 – Greensand 96 (Green Desert (USA) **91** 127) [2007 74: p11g* 10.2f* 9.9g* 12g⁵ 10m⁵ 10d⁴ 10g 9g* 11m⁴ Aug 4] rangy filly: fairly useful performer: won maiden at Kempton in March and handicaps at Bath in April, Beverley in May and Goodwood in August: seems to stay 1½m: acts on polytrack and any turf going: usually races prominently. *M. Johnston*

FONGSTER 2 b.g. (Feb 18) Dr Fong (USA) 128 – First Lite of Dawn (Green Adventure **–** (USA) 119) [2007 p8g 9d 8.2g Nov 7] lengthy, angular gelding: no form. *A. M. Hales*

FONT 4 b.g. Sadler's Wells (USA) 132 – River Saint (USA) 73§ (Irish River (FR) 131) **100** [2007 94p: 8g³ 10d² 10.9g* 10.4d³ 10d⁴ 12s Oct 13] good-bodied gelding: has a round action: useful performer: won maiden at Warwick in July: better efforts in frame next 2 starts, third to Greek Well in handicap at York and fourth behind King Charles in minor event at Ascot: stays 1¼m: acts on good to soft and good to firm ground: sold 105,000 gns, joined P. Nicholls. *J. R. Fanshawe*

FONTANA AMOROSA 3 ch.f. Cadeaux Genereux 131 – Bella Lambada 87 (Lamm- **104** tarra (USA) 134) [2007 75: p6g* 6g 6g² May 18] angular, good-topped filly: useful performer: won handicap at Kempton in March: very good 3 lengths second to Sakhee's Secret in listed race at Newbury final start: was best at 6f: acted on polytrack and good to soft ground: dead. *K. A. Ryan*

FONTHILL ROAD (IRE) 7 ch.g. Royal Abjar (USA) 121 – Hannah Huxtable (IRE) **113** (Master Willie 129) [2007 113: 6g³ 6g 5g 6v³ 7d² 6d 6v⁶ 7g⁶ 6d⁵ 7d 6d* 6d* Oct 21] strong gelding: smart performer: as good as ever when winning final 2 starts in 2007, namely handicap at York (beat Hoh Hoh Hoh by neck) and quite valuable handicap at the Curragh (by ½ length from Mooretown Lady), both in October: effective at 6f/easy 7f: acts on fibresand, very best turf efforts on good ground or softer: usually held up. *R. A. Fahey*

FOODBROKER FOUNDER 7 ch.g. Groom Dancer (USA) 128 – Nemea (USA) **–** 97 (The Minstrel (CAN) 135) [2007 78: 10m 10m Aug 10] good-bodied gelding: fair handicapper at 6 yrs: well held in 2007: stays 1¼m: acts on firm and good to soft ground: blinkered (took good hold) final start. *D. R. C. Elsworth*

FOOLIN MYSELF 2 b.c. (Jan 21) Montjeu (IRE) 137 – Friendlier (Zafonic (USA) **87 p** 130) [2007 7m⁵ 7g* Nov 2] big, strong colt: first foal: dam unraced half-sister to Oaks and St Leger winner User Friendly: fairly useful form in maidens at Newmarket, fifth to Almajd and winning by 1¼ lengths from Tartan Bearer: will be well suited by 1¼m/1½m: has scope, and bound to go on improving. *B. W. Hills*

paddypower.com Sprint Trophy (Handicap), York—Fonthill Road collars Hoh Hoh Hoh
(whose rider dropped his whip) near the line; Commando Scott takes third

FOOLISH GROOM 6 ch.g. Groom Dancer (USA) 128 – Scared (Royal Academy **70** (USA) 130) [2007 70: 10.9m⁶ 8.1m⁴ 8.2s³ 9g³ 8.1d 8d 8.1m* 8.1d⁵ 8.1f 8.1m Sep 13] quite good-topped gelding: fair handicapper: won ladies event at Chepstow in August: stays 1¼m: acts on polytrack, firm and soft going: tried tongue tied, often visored/in cheekpieces: has raced freely: sold 3,100 gns in October. *R. Hollinshead*

FOOL ME (IRE) 3 b.c. Mull of Kintyre (USA) 114 – Dawn's Folly (IRE) 47 (Bluebird **79** (USA) 125) [2007 82: 6m⁵ 6g 5g May 18] strong, stocky colt: just fair form at 3 yrs, well held last 2 starts: raced only at 5f/6f: yet to race on extremes of going: sold 6,000 gns in October. *E. S. McMahon*

FOOLS GOLD 2 b.c. (Apr 3) Ishiguru (USA) 114 – Sally Green (IRE) 79 (Common **59** Grounds 118) [2007 6d f6d³ Dec 14] deep-girthed colt: modest maiden: better effort when third at Southwell: unlikely to stay much beyond 6f. *T. D. Easterby*

FOOL'S WILDCAT (USA) 2 b. or br.c. (Apr 1) Forest Wildcat (USA) 120 – Nine **94** Flags (USA) (Forty Niner (USA)) [2007 7m⁶ 6m³ p7g⁴ 7m* 7m⁵ Oct 5] 100,000 2-y-o: good-bodied colt: eighth foal: brother to winning US sprinter (including at 2 yrs) and half-brother to several US winners: dam, US 8.5f winner from 2 starts, half-sister to US Grade 2 9f winner Royal Plume: fairly useful form: improved last 2 starts with blinkers and forcing tactics: won maiden at Newbury (beat Confront by 4 lengths) in September, then 5½ lengths fifth of 8 to River Proud in Somerville Tattersall Stakes at Newmarket: stays 7f: acts on good to firm probably polytrack. *B. J. Meehan*

FORBIDDEN (IRE) 4 ch.c. Singspiel (IRE) 133 – Fragrant Oasis (USA) 113 (Rahy **67** (USA) 115) [2007 73: 9.5g 10g 14g 8v p8m² p8g³ p8.6g p8g Nov 21] fair maiden: good efforts in 2007 only when placed at Kempton: stays 1¼m: acts on polytrack and good to firm ground: in cheekpieces third start, tongue tied otherwise. *D. Loughnane, Ireland*

FORCE CELEBRE (IRE) 3 ch.g. Peintre Celebre (USA) 137 – Two Shonas (IRE) **74 d** 94 (Persian Heights 129) [2007 p10g⁵ f11g³ f11g⁵ 14.1s p11g 10.1m Aug 8] €31,000Y: fifth foal: half-brother to Italian 11f/1½m winner Dara Lodge (by Grand Lodge): dam Irish 1m to 11f winner: fair maiden at best: should stay at least 1½m: form only on all-weather: tried blinkered: carried head awkwardly/wandered third start. *M. H. Tompkins*

FORCED UPON US 3 ch.g. Allied Forces (USA) 123 – Zing (Zilzal (USA) 137) **71** [2007 59: 7.1m⁴ 8.2g p10g⁵ p8g³ p8g 8d 8.5m p7m* p6g² 6d p7g p6g Dec 22] compact gelding: fair handicapper: won at Kempton in October: effective at 6f to 1m: acts on polytrack and good to firm ground, possibly not on good to soft: blinkered last 6 starts. *P. J. McBride*

FORCE GROUP (IRE) 3 b.g. Invincible Spirit (IRE) 121 – Spicebird (IRE) 67 (Ela-**70** Mana-Mou 132) [2007 61: 12m² 12g⁶ May 18] close-coupled, good-topped gelding: fair maiden handicapper, lightly raced: stays 1½m: unraced on going softer than good on turf: gelded after final start. *M. H. Tompkins*

FOREIGN AFFAIRS 9 ch.h. Hernando (FR) 127 – Entente Cordiale (USA) (Affirm- **–** ed (USA)) [2007 117: 13.3g⁵ 14g Jun 7] rather leggy, good-topped horse: smart performer at best, winner of 12 races, including 7 listed events: no form in similar contests in 2007: was effective at 1¼m to 1¾m: acted on fibresand, soft and good to firm going: blinkered once: often made running: to stand at Woodlands Stud, Co Galway, Ireland, fee €1,500. *Sir Mark Prescott*

FOREIGN EDITION (IRE) 5 b.g. Anabaa (USA) 130 – Palacegate Episode (IRE) **65** 111 (Drumalis 125) [2007 89: 7g 6g 6s 6m 6m 8.1g 7.5d 8g p7g³ Oct 31] lengthy, useful-looking gelding: just fair performer nowadays: stays 7f: acts on polytrack and good to firm going: sometimes blinkered/in cheekpieces. *Miss J. A. Camacho*

FOREIGN LANGUAGE (USA) 4 ch.f. Distant View (USA) 126 – Binary 109 **80** (Rainbow Quest (USA) 134) [2007 80: p8.6g⁴ p10g Jan 10] fairly useful performer, lightly raced: should stay beyond 8.6f: raced only on polytrack: sold €40,000 in February. *N. A. Callaghan*

FOREIGN RHYTHM (IRE) 2 ch.f. (Mar 20) Distant Music (USA) 126 – Happy **74** Talk (IRE) 74 (Hamas (IRE) 125§) [2007 5s² 5.1d² 5m² 5m³ 5g³ 5.1g⁶ 6.1d Oct 18] 22,000Y: rather leggy, close-coupled filly: second foal: half-sister to 3-y-o Frisky Talk: dam, Irish 1¼m winner, half-sister to US Grade 3 8.5f winner Storm Dream: fair maiden: placed all bar last 2 starts (in nurseries, tongue tied): should be at least as effective at 6f as 5f: acts on soft and good to firm going: sold 2,500 gns. *N. Tinkler*

FOR EILEEN 3 b.f. Dinar (USA) 65 – Dreams of Zena (Dreams End 93) [2007 50: p7g **–** p8g 6g 7.1d 10m Sep 25] maiden: no form at 3 yrs: left M. Quinlan after reappearance: trained by Miss K. Boutflower for fourth start only (rejoined present trainer after): tried tongue tied/in cheekpieces. *G. C. H. Chung*

FORELAND SANDS (IRE) 3 b.g. Desert Sun 120 – Penrose (IRE) 75 (Wolfhound **66**
(USA) 126) [2007 –: p6g³ p6g³ p5g⁶ p8g³ 6f p9.5g⁵ p7m⁴ p6g² Oct 23] fair maiden: stays
7f: best efforts on polytrack: visored last 2 starts. *J. R. Best*

FOREPLAY (IRE) 4 b.f. Lujain (USA) 119 – Watch Me (IRE) 106 (Green Desert **75**
(USA) 127) [2007 86: p7g Jan 3] tall, close-coupled filly: fairly useful handicapper in
2006: just fair form only outing at 4 yrs: stays 7f (raced freely at 1m): acts on polytrack
and good to firm going: wore cheekpieces last 4 starts: sold 52,000 gns in December (in
foal to Red Ransom). *E. A. L. Dunlop*

FORESIGHT 2 ch.c. (Jan 31) Observatory (USA) 131 – Avoidance (USA) 96 (Crypto- **81 p**
clearance (USA)) [2007 8d³ Oct 27] first foal: dam, 2-y-o 7f/1m winner, half-sister to
useful 1¼m performer Averted View: 14/1 and green, promising third to Trianon in
maiden at Newbury, short of room close home: will improve. *Mrs A. J. Perrett*

FOREST DANE 7 b.g. Danetime (IRE) 121 – Forest Maid (Thatching 131) [2007 87: **92**
6m* 6s 6g⁵ 6m³ 6g² 5m⁵ 6g p6g³ p7g² p7m p7g Nov 21] smallish, good-topped gelding:
fairly useful handicapper: won at Folkestone in April: placed 4 times after, including
twice at Lingfield in October: effective at 5f to 7f: acts on polytrack and firm going.
Mrs N. Smith

FOREST EMERALD (IRE) 5 b.m. Desert Sun 120 – Moonbi Range (IRE) 85 (Nor- **–**
dico (USA)) [2007 p11g Oct 17] €12,000 2-y-o: fourth foal: half-sister to 3 winners,
including 1m/1¼m winner Bush Maiden (by Among Men) and 1¼m/1½m winner
Moonbi Ridge (by Definite Article), both useful in Ireland: dam Irish 8.5f to 1¼m winner:
80/1 and fit from hurdling, last in claimer at Kempton on Flat debut. *J. W. Mullins*

FOREST VIKING (IRE) 5 b.g. Orpen (USA) 116 – Berhala (IRE) (Doyoun 124) **–**
[2007 8.5g Aug 15] tall, rather leggy gelding: modest maiden in 2005: unraced in 2006
and well held (in cheekpieces) only start at 5 yrs. *J. S. Wainwright*

FOREVER AUTUMN 4 b.g. Sinndar (IRE) 134 – Photo Call 73 (Chief Singer 131) **59**
[2007 58: 11.7f⁴ p12.2g⁶ Sep 8] quite attractive gelding: modest maiden: stays 1½m: acts
on firm ground. *D. G. Bridgwater*

FOREVER BOLD 3 b.g. Bold Edge 123 – Still In Love 75 (Emarati (USA) 74) [2007 **–**
8.3m 8.3d p7g Sep 5] strong gelding: little form in maidens. *J. G. Portman*

FOREVER CHANGES 2 gr.f. (Apr 20) Bertolini (USA) 125 – Days of Grace 79 **53**
(Wolfhound (USA) 126) [2007 p5g p6g⁴ p5g⁶ Nov 15] second foal: sister to 3-y-o Mogok
Ruby: dam 5f (including at 2 yrs)/6f winner: modest maiden: should prove best at 5f/6f:
raced only on polytrack. *L. Montague Hall*

FOREVER MY LORD 9 b.g. Be My Chief (USA) 122 – In Love Again (IRE) 86 **–**
(Prince Rupert (FR) 121) [2007 14d 16.1m Sep 10] good-bodied gelding: one-time fair
performer: no form in 2007: tried blinkered/in cheekpieces/tongue tied. *W. A. Murphy,
Ireland*

FORFEITER (USA) 5 ch.g. Petionville (USA) – Picabo (USA) (Wild Again (USA)) **61**
[2007 74: p16.5g f12g⁵ p16g p10m² p12g Dec 16] workmanlike gelding: modest performer: stays easy 1½m: acts on all-weather and any turf going: sometimes wears headgear:
tried tongue tied. *C. Gordon*

FORGET IT 2 b.c. (Feb 27) Galileo (IRE) 134 – Queens Way (FR) (Zafonic (USA) **69 p**
130) [2007 8d⁶ Oct 27] €75,000Y, 27,000 2-y-o: fourth foal: half-brother to winner in
Greece by Polish Precedent: dam unraced out of half-sister to Shergar: 25/1, never-
nearer sixth to Trianon in maiden at Newbury: should do better, especially at 1¼m/1½m.
R. Hannon

FORGIVE ME 2 ch.f. (Feb 14) Mark of Esteem (IRE) 137 – Francia 59 (Legend of
France (USA) 124) [2007 8m Sep 21] 17,000Y: seventh foal: half-sister to 8.5f and 1¼m
winner Gracia (by Linamix) and 9f/1¼m winner Suave Performer (by Suave Dancer):
dam 7f (at 2 yrs) and 1½m winner: 66/1, behind in maiden at Newmarket. *C. E. Brittain*

FORGOTTEN VOICE (IRE) 2 b.c. (May 28) Danehill Dancer (IRE) 117 – Asnieres **81 p**
(USA) (Spend A Buck (USA)) [2007 p7g* Oct 24] 230,000Y: closely related to useful
Irish 5f winner Keepers Hill (by Danehill), later successful in US, and half-brother to 2
winners abroad, notably smart French 1m (at 2 yrs) to 10.5f winner Australie (by Sadler's
Wells): dam, French 9f winner, half-sister to Breeders' Cup Classic winner Arcangues
and to dams of Cape Verdi and Aquarelliste: 4/1, good impression when winning maiden
at Lingfield, quickening well after others got first run: will stay 1m: useful prospect.
J. Noseda

FOR LIFE (IRE) 5 b.g. Bachir (IRE) 118 – Zest (USA) (Zilzal (USA) 137) [2007 60§: **84**
f7g p5.1g 7f* 7.6f² 6m* 6m* p6g* Oct 17] strong, lengthy gelding: fairly useful handi-

capper: left Stef Liddiard after second start: much improved after, winning at Yarmouth in July, Folkestone and Brighton in September and Lingfield (beat Bertie Southstreet by ¾ length) in October: will prove as effective at 5f as 6f/7f: acts on all-weather and firm ground: has worn visor/cheekpieces: front runner: has looked temperamental, but did little wrong in 2007. *J. E. Long*

FORMAL DECREE (GER) 4 b.g. Diktat 126 – Formida (FR) (Highest Honor (FR) **119** 124) [2007 117: 9g* 9g* 9g² 8.9g 10g 10g² 10.5m² 8.9f⁶ 9.9d⁵ Sep 26] lengthy, good-topped gelding: smart performer: did well at Nad Al Sheba early in 2007, successful in handicap in January and Dubal Al Rashidiya in February, and also good second to Seihali in Jebel Hatta in March (final start for I. Mohammed): best efforts after when runner-up in Grosser Dallmayr-Preis at Munich (beaten 3 lengths by Soldier Hollow) and Rose of Lancaster Stakes at Haydock (beaten 1¼ lengths by Halicarnassus): stays 1¼m: acts on good to firm and good to soft going: held up: hanging when slipped up on bend at Longchamp fifth start: quirky, but is usually reliable. *Saeed bin Suroor*

FORMATION (USA) 2 ch.g. (Feb 22) Van Nistelrooy (USA) 108 – Miss Valedictor- **80** ian (USA) (With Approval (CAN)) [2007 7d⁶ p8g³ 7.5d³ p7g² p8.6g* Nov 4] $30,000F, 90,000Y: good-bodied gelding: first foal: dam US 6f (at 2 yrs) to 8.5f winner: fairly useful form: placed 3 times prior to winning maiden at Wolverhampton (odds on): gelded after: stays 8.6f: raced only on polytrack and good to soft ground: quirky, flashes tail. *E. A. L. Dunlop*

FORMAX (FR) 5 gr.g. Marathon (USA) 116 – Fortuna (FR) (Kaldoun (FR) 122) [2007 **97** 7.5d* 7.5g⁴ 10.6d² 9.9g 7d 9m² 8m Oct 4] lightly-made gelding: useful performer: won 5 times in France, including handicap at Cagnes-sur-Mer in January: left J-C. Rouget after third start: easily best effort in handicaps in Britain when second to Escape Route at Goodwood in September: stays 9f: acts on soft and good to firm going. *M. P. Tregoning*

FORMIDABLE GUEST 3 b.f. Dilshaan 119 – Fizzy Treat 79 (Efisio 120) [2007 8g **62** 8d p8g p10g* p9.5g² p11g³ p11g p10m⁴ Dec 9] 25,000Y, 5,000 2-y-o: big filly: first foal: dam, 5f/6d winner, sister to useful performer up to 1m Hoh Chi Min: modest handicapper: won at Lingfield in October: stays 11f: acts on polytrack. *J. Pearce*

FORMIDABLE WILL (FR) 5 b.g. Efisio 120 – Shewillifshewants (IRE) (Alzao **–** (USA) 117) [2007 77: f8g⁶ p7.1g⁵ f8g⁴ f6g p5.1g⁶ p6g p6m³ p6g Nov 8] well-made **a63** gelding: modest performer in 2007: said to have finished lame final outing: stayed 8.6f: acted on all-weather, lightly raced on turf in 2006/7: usually wore headgear/tongue strap: was inconsistent: dead. *D. Shaw*

FORREST FLYER (IRE) 3 b.c. Daylami (IRE) 138 – Gerante (USA) (Private **61** Account (USA)) [2007 –: 7m 9.2d⁶ 9.1d 11.1g⁴ 11.1m 16.1g 15.8g³ Oct 30] tall, close-coupled colt: modest maiden: stays easy 2m: unraced on extremes of going. *Miss L. A. Perratt*

FORREST STAR 2 ch.f. (Apr 13) Fraam 114 – Starfleet 66 (Inchinor 119) [2007 6d **–** Sep 20] 4,000F, 15,000Y: third foal: half-sister to 3-y-o Mr Napper Tandy and 4-y-o Wind Star: dam, maiden, half-sister to useful performers Pool Music (stayed 8.5f) and Russian Music (stayed 1¼m): 80/1, soon hampered/stumbled in maiden at Ayr. *Miss L. A. Perratt*

FORROGER (CAN) 4 br.c. Black Minnaloushe (USA) 123 – Count On Romance **99 +** (CAN) (Geiger Counter (USA)) [2007 84: 10.5g* 12g 10.1d 10d² Oct 10] tall, close-coupled colt: useful handicapper: won at Haydock (beat Greek Well by 1¼ lengths) in April: best effort when second to Chantaco at Nottingham final start, travelling strongly but plenty to do: stays 10.5f: raced on good going or softer (acts on soft): took strong hold second/third starts: sold 130,000 gns in October. *M. A. Jarvis*

FORSTERS PLANTIN 3 ch.f. Muhtarram (USA) 125 – Ischia 64 (Lion Cavern **34** (USA) 117) [2007 –: 8m⁵ 8.5s 11.1m Aug 4] neat filly: poor maiden. *J. J. Quinn*

FORSYTE SAGA 2 br.f. (Feb 18) Machiavellian (USA) 123 – First of Many 83 (Dar- **77** shaan 133) [2007 7m² 7.5g² 8.2m⁵ 8g p7g Dec 19] workmanlike filly: second foal: half-sister to useful Irish 7f to 9f winner Many Colours (by Green Desert): dam, ran 3 times (should have stayed 1¼m+), sister to useful performer up to 15f Without A Trace: fair maiden: went wrong way after runner-up first 2 starts (behind Ibn Khaldun at Leicester on debut): should be suited by 1m+. *M. Johnston*

FORT AMHURST (IRE) 3 ch.g. Halling (USA) 133 – Soft Breeze 99 (Zafonic **82** (USA) 130) [2007 81p: 10f* 11g 8m Jul 28] angular, useful-looking gelding: fluent mover: fairly useful performer: won maiden at Windsor in April: stumbled and unseated early on second outing: well below form in handicap final start: stays 1¼m: acts on firm going: sold 15,000 gns in October, and gelded. *E. A. L. Dunlop*

FORT CHURCHILL (IRE) 6 b.g. Barathea (IRE) 127 – Brisighella (IRE) (Al Hareb **98**
(USA) 123) [2007 88, a76: 8s 10g⁵ 10.1g⁶ 12g 9.9g 9m⁴ 10.4d 10m⁴ 9m Oct 6]
big, good-topped gelding: useful handicapper: won at Goodwood (by 5 lengths from
Lisathedaddy) in June: good efforts when fourth at same course and at Pontefract after,
but ran poorly in Cambridgeshire at Newmarket final start: effective at 9f to 1¾m: acts on
polytrack, firm and soft going: blinkered/tongue tied. *B. Ellison*

FORTHEFIRSTIME 2 ch.f. Dr Fong (USA) 128 – Gazebo 68 (Cadeaux Genereux **99 p**
131) [2007 6v⁴ 7d² 6m* Sep 15] tall, good-topped filly: second foal: half-sister to 3-y-o
Oat Cuisine: dam, sprint maiden, half-sister to useful performers up to 7f Injaaz and
Corndavon: useful form: made rapid improvement, winning listed race at the Curragh by
neck from Longing To Dance, leading close home: will prove best up to 7f: should do
better still. *John M. Oxx, Ireland*

FORT HULL (IRE) 2 b.c. (Apr 3) Indian Lodge (IRE) 127 – Pagan Princess 54 **60**
(Mujtahid (USA) 118) [2007 7f 8d⁶ 9s p8m Nov 11] lengthy colt: modest maiden: stays
1m: tried blinkered. *Mrs A. J. Perrett*

FORTRESS 4 b.f. Generous (IRE) 139 – Imperial Bailiwick (IRE) 104 (Imperial Fron- **65**
tier (USA) 112) [2007 66: f6g p6g p8.6g² 8.3g² 9.1d 8.3g⁵ 8d³ 7.6d⁴ Jul 14] fair handicapper: stays 8.6f: acts on polytrack, good to firm and good to soft going: has raced freely:
has worn blinkers. *E. J. Alston*

FORTUITOUS (IRE) 3 ch.g. Tobougg (IRE) 125 – Shallop 55 (Salse (USA) 128) **–**
[2007 10g May 29] 66/1, tailed off in maiden at Redcar. *I. W. McInnes*

FORTUITY (IRE) 2 b.c. (Feb 19) Xaar 132 – Lucky Bet (IRE) 69 (Lucky Guest 109) **81**
[2007 6g p5g³ 6d² 7d p7g* Jul 18] €44,000F, 90,000 2-y-o: useful-looking colt: second
foal: dam Irish 9f to 10.5f winner: fairly useful form: won nursery at Kempton: will
stay 1m: acts on polytrack and good to soft going: sold 6,000 gns, sent to Holland.
J. H. M. Gosden

FORTUNATE ISLE (USA) 5 ch.g. Swain (IRE) 134 – Isla Del Rey (USA) 103 (Nur- **99**
eyev (USA) 131) [2007 93: p10g³ p12.2g 9m 9.8g² 9.9g* 9s* 8.9s 8m 10d Aug 25]
angular gelding: useful handicapper: better than ever when winning at Beverley in May
and Ripon (by ½ length from Full Victory, making all) in June: below form after: stays
1¼m: acts on any going: has worn cheekpieces (including for both wins in 2007): has
sweated. *R. A. Fahey*

FORTUNE DANCER (USA) 12 ch.g. Rahy (USA) 115 – Abeesh (USA) 77 (Nijin- **53**
sky (CAN) 138) [2007 p16g p10g⁵ Jan 29] modest handicapper in Hong Kong for
S. Woods in 2005 (last successful there in 2003): blinkered, better effort in Britain
(modest form) when fifth in seller at Lingfield: stays 11f: acts on dirt, firm and soft
ground: usually wore headgear in Hong Kong. *G. L. Moore*

FORTUNELLA 2 b.f. (Apr 4) Polish Precedent (USA) 131 – Hazy Heights 56 (Shirley **–**
Heights 130) [2007 8.1f Aug 27] third foal: dam, 1m winner, out of sister to smart 1m/
1¼m performer Feminine Wiles: well beaten in maiden at Chepstow. *P. Howling*

FORTUNE POINT (IRE) 9 ch.g. Cadeaux Genereux 131 – Mountains of Mist (IRE) **55 §**
80 (Shirley Heights 130) [2007 66§, a61§: 10s 10.2f 10d p10g⁵ p10g Oct 29] strong,
angular gelding: modest handicapper: stays easy 1½m: acts on all-weather and any turf
going: effective visored or not: tried tongue tied: has found little: unreliable. *A. W. Carroll*

FORTUNES MAID (IRE) 2 b.f. (Feb 25) Raise A Grand (IRE) 114 – Where's The **–**
Money 87 (Lochnager 132) [2007 p7.1g⁶ Nov 23] €9,500Y: sister to fairly useful 5f/6f
winner Lake Chini and half-sister to 3 winners, including fairly useful 5f (at 2 yrs) and
7f winner Promised (by Petardia): dam 2-y-o 5f winner: 25/1, well held in maiden at
Wolverhampton. *M. H. Tompkins*

FORZACURITY 8 ch.g. Forzando 122 – Nice Lady 65 (Connaught 130) [2007 10g **– §**
Jul 10] strong gelding: one-time fair performer: well held only start on Flat (since first since
2003) in 2007: tried in visor/cheekpieces: claimed £6,000 to join Jim Best, won over
hurdles in October. *P. D. Evans*

FORZARZI (IRE) 3 b.c. Forzando 122 – Zarzi (IRE) (Suave Dancer (USA) 136) **51**
[2007 59: 6g 6m Jun 7] modest maiden: likely to stay 1m: unraced on extremes of going.
A. Berry

FOSSGATE 6 ch.g. Halling (USA) 133 – Peryllys 67 (Warning 136) [2007 81: 12g **81**
12m² 11.5d 15.8m 11.8m³ 10m⁵ 11.9g 11.9s Sep 28] angular gelding: fairly useful handicapper: stays 1½m: acts on polytrack, firm and soft going: tried in cheekpieces/visor:
tends to hang right. *J. D. Bethell*

FOUR KINGS 6 b.g. Forzando 122 – High Cut 84 (Dashing Blade 117) [2007 –: 7.1g **52** 7g⁴ 7m 7.1m 5s³ 6m 5m 5m Sep 30] good-topped gelding: modest maiden: stays 1m: acts on soft and good to firm ground: tried tongue tied. *Karen McLintock*

FOUR MIRACLES 3 b.f. Vettori (IRE) 119 – North Kildare (USA) (Northjet 136) **82** [2007 64: 10.1d² 11.1f⁴ 9.2g² 10d* 10d 10g² 10g³ 11.9d² Oct 18] good-bodied filly: fairly useful performer: won maiden at Brighton in July: better efforts when placed in handicaps last 3 starts: stays easy 1½m: acts on fibresand, firm and good to soft going: has looked wayward/flashed tail. *M. H. Tompkins*

FOUR SINS (GER) 3 b.f. Sinndar (IRE) 134 – Four Roses (IRE) (Darshaan 133) **110** [2007 92: 7g² 10g* 12d⁴ 12v 10m* 10f Oct 21] €120,000Y: sturdy, medium-sized filly: has short, unimpressive action: second foal: dam unraced half-sister to smart German 1¼m performer Fabriano and Rockfel Stakes winner Germane: smart performer: won Blue Wind Stakes at Naas (by 2½ lengths from Cherry Hinton) in May and Irish National Stud Blandford Stakes at the Curragh (beat Queen's Best by short head) in September: respectable efforts when 9½ lengths fourth to Light Shift in Oaks at Epsom in between and when 5½ lengths eighth behind Mrs Lindsay in E. P. Taylor Stakes at Woodbine final start: effective at 1¼m/1½m: acts on good to firm and good to soft going, possibly not on heavy: usually races up with pace. *John M. Oxx, Ireland*

FOURSQUARE FLYER (IRE) 5 ch.g. Tagula (IRE) 116 – Isla (IRE) (Turtle Island **71** (IRE) 123) [2007 73: p12.2g* p13.9g Jan 16] angular gelding: fair performer: successful in maidens at Wolverhampton in December 2006 (originally demoted to second, but reinstated as winner on appeal) and January: seems to stay 1¾m: acts on polytrack and firm going. *J. Mackie*

FOURTEENTH 3 b.c. Rainbow Quest (USA) 134 – Valentine Girl 109 (Alzao (USA) **90** 117) [2007 10m² 10g* 11.6m² 11m 12m² Aug 31] compact colt: third foal: brother to useful 1m to 11f winner Public Forum and half-brother to 4-y-o Florimund: dam 7f (at 2 yrs) and 11.4f winner: fairly useful form: won maiden at Windsor in June: good efforts when second in handicaps after: likely to stay 1¾m: raced only on good/good to firm going: sent to Saudi Arabia. *Sir Michael Stoute*

Irish National Stud Blandford Stakes, the Curragh—
a tremendous race between smart fillies Four Sins (left) and Queen's Best

FOUR TEL 3 gr.g. Vettori (IRE) 119 – Etienne Lady (IRE) 67 (Imperial Frontier (USA) **76**
112) [2007 63p: 7m 10.3d p7.1g* 8g p7.1g² p7.1g* Dec 14] fair performer: won at
Wolverhampton in September (maiden) and December (handicap): stays 7f: acts on
polytrack: has made running. *N. J. Vaughan*

FOURTH DIMENSION (IRE) 8 b.g. Entrepreneur 123 – Isle of Spice (USA) 74 **79**
(Diesis 133) [2007 11.6m 14.1m* 16m³ Aug 17] sturdy gelding: fair handicapper nowa-
days: won at Yarmouth in July: barely stays 2m: acts on firm ground, possibly not on soft.
Miss T. Spearing

FOWEY (USA) 3 b. or br.f. Gone West (USA) – Kumari Continent (USA) 114 (Kris S **53**
(USA)) [2007 51: p7.1g⁴ p8g⁶ p10g p8.6g⁶ Nov 5] modest maiden: should stay beyond
1m: raced only on polytrack: has found little: sold 40,000 gns. *Sir Mark Prescott*

FOXHAVEN 5 ch.h. Unfuwain (USA) 131 – Dancing Mirage (IRE) 83 (Machiavellian **112**
(USA) 123) [2007 111: 10g³ 12g³ 12d⁵ 12m⁶ 16g 12.3m² 12m⁵ 11.8d⁴ Oct 29] smallish,
sturdy, lengthy horse: smart performer: several at least creditable efforts in 2007, placed
in listed events at Goodwood (third to Ivy Creek) and Chester (second to Hattan) on
second/sixth outings and fifth behind Galactic Star in similar race at Newmarket on
penultimate start: best at 1¼m/1½m: acts on firm and soft going: visored final 3 outings
in 2007: genuine. *P. R. Chamings*

FOXIES BYCHANCE 2 ch.f. (Mar 2) Zaha (CAN) 106 – Strath Kitten 36 (Scottish **–**
Reel 123) [2007 5m 6g 7d Jun 19] quite good-topped filly: half-sister to winner in Turkey
by Dancing Spree: dam, maiden, stayed 1¼m: no form. *R. D. E. Woodhouse*

FOX'S DEN 2 b.g. (Jan 23) Foxhound (USA) 103 – Milly's Lass 79 (Mind Games 121) **65**
[2007 5g³ 5.1m⁵ 6g 5g⁴ 5.3m⁵ Sep 25] modest maiden: best at 5f: below form in blinkers/
visor. *R. M. Beckett*

FOXXY 3 b.f. Foxhound (USA) 103 – Fisher Island (IRE) 59 (Sri Pekan (USA) 117) **55**
[2007 76d: f7g³ p9.5g 8m 8m 10m 12s⁵ 12s 12m 16m³ 16.1m 16.1g Oct 3] angular filly:
modest handicapper: left K. Ryan after second outing: said to have been in season final
start: stays 2m: acts on soft and good to firm ground: has worn cheekpieces/blinkers.
J. R. Norton

FOXY DIPLOMAT 3 b.g. Foxhound (USA) 103 – Diplomatist 69 (Dominion 123) **57**
[2007 p8g³ p8g p8.6g p7.1g Nov 19] modest maiden: form only when third in claimer
(claimed from I. Wood) on debut: stays 1m: blinkered final start. *Miss J. R. Tooth*

FOXY MUSIC 3 b.g. Foxhound (USA) 103 – Primum Tempus 49 (Primo Dominie 121) **84**
[2007 49: p5.1g 5f² 5.1m³ 5m³ 5.1f 5.1s⁴ 5v* 5g 5g Aug 22] bald, leggy gelding: fairly
useful handicapper: left Peter Grayson after reappearance: made all at Haydock in July:
likely to prove best at 5f/6f: acts on any ground: tried blinkered at 2 yrs: tends to hang.
E. J. Alston

FRAAMINGTON 2 b.g. (Apr 28) Fraam 114 – Patandon Girl (IRE) 66 (Night Shift **41**
(USA)) [2007 5.7g 6f⁶ 7s⁵ p7.1g p5g⁵ 6m 7f 5g³ 6d⁵ 5.1g p6m Dec 10] poor maiden: stays
6f: tried visored. *M. R. Channon*

FRAAMTASTIC TOO 3 gr.f. Fraam 114 – Jilly Woo 60 (Environment Friend 128) **–**
[2007 p7g 8g 8g Jun 1] fifth foal: half-sister to 3 winners, including 1m (at 2 yrs) to
12.2f winner Missie Baileys (by Mister Baileys) and 1½m winner Private Benjamin (by
Ridgewood Ben): dam maiden (stayed 1¼m): well held in maidens first 2 starts: fell
halfway final outing. *Jamie Poulton*

FRACAS (IRE) 5 b.h. In The Wings 128 – Klarifi 91 (Habitat 134) [2007 115: 10m² **115**
10m² 10.5g⁵ 10m* 10s* 12d² 10g² Sep 22] angular, quite good-topped horse: has a round
action: smart performer: won listed event at the Curragh in June and Meld Stakes at
Leopardstown (by ½ length from Red Rock Canyon) in July: also good second in listed
race and Mooresbridge Stakes (to Septimus) at the Curragh, Ballyroan Stakes at Leopardstown (½ length behind Mores Wells) and listed race at Fairyhouse (in cheekpieces,
beaten 1¼ lengths by Arch Rebel): effective at 1¼m/1½m, not 1¾m: acts on heavy and
good to firm going: visored (well held) final 4-y-o outing: often up with pace: consistent:
sent to USA. *D. Wachman, Ireland*

FRACTURED FOXY 3 b.f. Foxhound (USA) 103 – Yanomami (USA) 71 (Slew O' **73**
Gold (USA)) [2007 72: p6g* p7.1g⁶ f7g³ p6g² 6g⁵ p6g³ 7.1g⁵ f6g² 7g⁶ 7d⁵ Aug 1]
smallish filly: fair handicapper: won at Wolverhampton in January: effective at 6f/7f: acts
on all-weather, soft and good to firm going. *J. J. Quinn*

FRAGRANCY (IRE) 3 ch.f. Singspiel (IRE) 133 – Zibet 90 (Kris 135) [2007 83p: **102**
7.5m² 9g⁵ 8.3m* 9g⁵ 8g⁴ 8m² 8.1g² 8g* Oct 6] lengthy filly: useful handicapper: progres-

sive form, winning at Windsor in July and Redcar (beat Observatory Star by 1½ lengths, quickly going clear) in October: probably stays 9f: acts on polytrack and good to firm ground (unraced on softer than good): often makes running. *M. A. Jarvis*

FRAMMENTI 2 br.f. (Mar 10) Fraam 114 – Blushing Victoria 74 (Weldnaas (USA) **50** 112) [2007 p6g 6d p6g⁵ p7.1g6 p8g p7.1g 7g p8.6g f6d Dec 14] 10,000Y: leggy filly: fifth foal: half-sister to 4-y-o Verite: dam 2-y-o 5f winner: modest maiden: seems to stay 7f: acts on polytrack: below form in cheekpieces/blinkers. *A. J. McCabe*

FRANCESCA D'GORGIO (USA) 2 b.f. (Feb 4) Proud Citizen (USA) 122 – Betty's **95** Solutions (USA) (Eltish (USA) 120) [2007 5.1m 5m⁴ 6m⁵ 6m* Jul 28] $250,000Y, $530,000 2-y-o: rangy, well-made filly: has scope: first foal: dam, US 6f and 8.3f winner, out of US Grade 3 8.5f/9f winner Betty Lobelia: useful performer: not seen out after winning maiden at Newmarket in July: fourth of 21 to Elletelle in Queen Mary Stakes at Royal Ascot and fifth of 14 to You'resothrilling in Cherry Hinton Stakes at Newmarket previous 2 outings: may prove best at 5f/6f: raced only on good to firm going: has twice hung left: visored last 2 starts. *J. Noseda*

FRANCESCAS BOY (IRE) 4 b.g. Titus Livius (FR) 115 – Mica Male (ITY) (Law **48** Society (USA) 130) [2007 –: 12m p12.2g6 Sep 14] rather leggy gelding: poor maiden: stays 1½m: unraced on extremes of going on turf. *P. D. Niven*

FRANCESCO 3 ch.g. Vettori (IRE) 119 – Violet (IRE) 77 (Mukaddamah (USA) 125) **53** [2007 57: 11g⁵ 12.1g 10m6 Sep 17] sturdy gelding: modest maiden: ran as if amiss second outing and left M. Bell: stays easy 8.6f: acts on polytrack: tried visored. *Evan Williams*

FRANCHOEK (IRE) 3 ch.g. Trempolino (USA) 135 – Snow House (IRE) (Vacarme **88 +** (USA) 121) [2007 59: 11.7g⁵ 12g³ 16g* 14m³ 16.2f* 16m* Sep 4] good-bodied gelding: fairly useful and progressive handicapper: won at Nottingham and Chepstow in August and Goodwood (beat Strobe 1¾ lengths, travelling well to lead 1f out and going away at finish) in September: stays 2m: acts on firm going: useful juvenile hurdler. *A. King*

FRANKALBERT (IRE) 3 b.c. Fasliyev (USA) 120 – Faribole (IRE) 106 (Esprit du **65 ?** Nord (USA) 126) [2007 6g 8g⁵ 7.5m 7.5m⁵ p7.1g 7.5m⁴ Dec 15] maiden: tongue tied, seemingly fair form when ninth in claimer at Wolverhampton penultimate start. *Emilio Pellegrino, Italy*

FRANK CROW 4 b.g. Josr Algarhoud (IRE) 118 – Belle de Nuit (IRE) 85 (Statoblest **81** 120) [2007 70: 8m² 8m 8m* 9.1d⁵ 10.5m 9.1g⁵ 9.1g 8m 9.8m 7.1s* 7.9g⁴ 8m 10g Oct 6] sturdy, close-coupled gelding: fairly useful handicapper: won at Musselburgh in May and August: stays easy 9f (raced freely over 1¼m): acts on soft and good to firm ground: often held up: none too consistent. *J. S. Goldie*

FRANKSALOT (IRE) 7 ch.g. Desert Story (IRE) 115 – Rosie's Guest (IRE) (Be My **79** Guest (USA) 126) [2007 79: p7.1g p8g⁵ p6g³ p6g⁴ p6g⁴ p7.1g⁴ 7.5m* 6m* 6g 7m⁵ 6m* 7.5m⁵ 7.9d 7.6d⁵ 8m 6.9m 7.5m6 7m 7.5d Sep 25] tall, close-coupled gelding: fair handicapper: won at Beverley in April, Hamilton in May and Pontefract in June: not at best after: effective at 6f to easy 1m: acts on polytrack, firm and good to soft going: tried blinkered/in cheekpieces: tends to edge left: often held up. *I. W. McInnes*

FRANK'S QUEST (IRE) 7 b.g. Mujadil (USA) 119 – Questuary (IRE) 63 (Rainbow **–** Quest (USA) 134) [2007 –, a57: p8g p8g p8g p7g Dec 30] sturdy gelding: modest performer on all-weather in 2006: little form at 7 yrs. *A. B. Haynes*

FRANKY'N'JONNY 4 b.f. Groom Dancer (USA) 128 – Bron Hilda (IRE) 50 (Nam- **–** aqualand (USA)) [2007 58d: 10d6 8d⁴ 10.2s p8g⁵ p8g⁵ 7d p7.1g p8g p10m p12g² p12g **a49** f11d6 p8.6d⁵ Dec 27] poor maiden nowadays: stays 1½m: acts on all-weather, soft and firm going: tried tongue tied: often wears cheekpieces/visor. *M. J. Attwater*

FRATERNAL 3 ch.g. Dr Fong (USA) 128 – Abbey Strand (USA) 78 (Shadeed (USA) **74** 135) [2007 p7g 10g 10d6 14m³ p16g⁵ Aug 29] good-topped gelding: fair maiden: should stay 2m: acts on good to firm and good to soft ground: blinkered final outing: sold 14,000 gns. *R. Charlton*

FRATERNITY 10 b.g. Grand Lodge (USA) 125 – Catawba 98 (Mill Reef (USA) 141) **49** [2007 49: p8g² p8g p8.6g6 p8.6g⁵ f7g Feb 13] poor performer: has form at 1½m, best at 6f to 8.6f: acts on all-weather and good to soft going: tried blinkered/visored (raced freely): front runner. *J. A. Pickering*

FRATT'N PARK (IRE) 4 b.f. Tagula (IRE) 116 – Bouffant (High Top 131) [2007 71: **–** p10g p8g Jan 10] leggy filly: fair handicapper at 3 yrs: below form both starts in 2007: stayed 1¼m: acted on firm and soft going, probably on polytrack: dead. *J. J. Bridger*

FR DOMINIC (USA) 2 b. or br.c. (May 2) Arch (USA) 127 – Collodia (USA) (Leo **90 p**
Castelli (USA)) [2007 7m* Sep 21] $72,000Y, 50,000 2-y-o: big colt: fifth foal: half-
brother to 3 winners abroad, including US winners around 1m by Peaks And Valleys and
Slew City Slew: dam US 2-y-o 1m winner: 10/1, fairly useful form when winning maiden
at Newmarket by ½ length from Virtual, soon prominent: will stay at least 1m: should
progress. *R. M. Beckett*

FREDA'S CHOICE (IRE) 4 b.f. Shinko Forest (IRE) – Marimar (IRE) (Grand Lodge **61**
(USA) 125) [2007 60: p8g* p8.6g p8.6g⁶ 8.5g² 7g* 6.5g⁵ 8m 8g Jun 3] tall filly: modest
handicapper: won at Lingfield in January and Naas in May: stays 9.6f: acts on polytrack
and good to firm going: usually blinkered nowadays: often slowly away. *Patrick Morris,*
Ireland

FREDDY (ARG) 8 ch.h. Roy (USA) – Folgada (USA) (Lyphard's Wish (FR) 124) **62**
[2007 –: p16g 12d 13.3m 14.8d p13.9g p12.2g⁴ 10d Aug 20] lengthy horse: modest handicapper: stays 12.5f: acts on polytrack, sloppy dirt and firm going on turf: usually tongue
tied/blinkered: has hung/shaped as if amiss. *D. K. Ivory*

FRED'S LAD 2 b.g. (Jan 19) Warningford 119 – Lawless Bridget 62 (Alnasr Alwa- **96**
sheek 117) [2007 5.1g* 5g³ 5m* 5m 5g³ 6.1m² p6g Sep 8] 4,000F: lengthy, workmanlike
gelding: fourth foal: half-brother to 4-y-o La Matanza and 5-y-o Melalchrist: dam sprint
maiden: useful performer: won minor events at Nottingham in April and Beverley in
May: held his form well, placed in listed race at York (third to Captain Gerrard) and minor
event at Chester (second to Imperial Mint): will prove best at 5f/easy 6f: acts on polytrack
and good to firm going: races prominently. *M. W. Easterby*

FREEDOM SONG 2 b.f. (Apr 9) Singspiel (IRE) 133 – Girl of My Dreams (IRE) 51 **74**
(Marju (IRE) 127) [2007 p7g² p8g⁴ p8.6g⁴ Nov 17] lengthy, angular filly: sixth foal:
half-sister to smart 2002 2-y-o 6f/7f (Rockfel Stakes) winner Luvah Girl (also won only
US start) and 3-y-o Farley Star, both by Alzao: dam 7f winner: fair maiden: in frame all 3
starts, best efforts first 2: stays 1m: raced only on polytrack. *R. Charlton*

FREE FALLIN 2 b.f. (Mar 24) Desert Prince (IRE) 130 – Dixielake (IRE) 84 (Lake **69**
Coniston (IRE) 131) [2007 7g 7.5m 8m 7.1g Oct 2] leggy filly: fourth foal: half-sister to
3 winners, including useful Irish 5f/6f winner Chief Crazy Horse (by Dansili) and 3-y-o
Provost: dam 1m winner: fair form (but little impact) in maidens and nursery: should
prove best at 6f/7f: sold 1,200 gns. *P. W. Chapple-Hyam*

FREELOADER (IRE) 7 b.g. Revoque (IRE) 122 – Indian Sand (Indian King (USA) **84**
128) [2007 p6g f8g 10.4g May 16] strong, lengthy gelding: fairly useful handicapper:
below best both starts on Flat in 2007: best at 1m/1¼m: acts on all-weather, firm and good
to soft going: useful hurdler successful in June. *R. A. Fahey*

FREE OFFER 3 b.f. Generous (IRE) 139 – Proserpine 95 (Robellino (USA) 127) [2007 **94**
79p: 9.9m⁶ 9m 12d 10f* 9.7m* 10.2f³ 10m² Oct 5] leggy filly: fairly useful handicapper:
won at Newbury in August and Folkestone in September: good placed efforts after: stays
1¼m: acts on firm ground. *J. L. Dunlop*

FREE ROSES (IRE) 4 b.f. Fasliyev (USA) 120 – Ghanaj (Caerleon (USA) 132) [2007 **–**
96: 5g 6.1m 6m Aug 11] lengthy filly: useful performer at 3 yrs: well held in 2007: tried
tongue tied/blinkered: sold 110,000 gns. *J. G. Given*

FREE TO AIR 4 b.g. Generous (IRE) 139 – Petonica (IRE) 77 (Petoski 135) [2007 88: **79**
p12g⁶ 11.9g⁵ Sep 12] big, good-topped gelding: fairly useful performer at 3 yrs, just fair
in 2007: stays 1½m: acts on polytrack, soft and good to firm ground: tried in cheekpieces:
carried head high final outing. *A. M. Balding*

FREGATE ISLAND (IRE) 4 b.g. Daylami (IRE) 138 – Briery (IRE) 66 (Salse (USA) **93**
128) [2007 87: 10.9m³ 11m* 14g 12g² p12g⁵ p12.2g Dec 26] tall, angular gelding: fairly
useful handicapper: won at Goodwood in May: left B. Meehan and off 6 months before
final outing: stays 1½m: acts on polytrack and good to firm going. *J. G. Given*

FREMEN (USA) 7 ch.g. Rahy (USA) 115 – Northern Trick (USA) 131 (Northern **105**
Dancer) [2007 91: p7.1g³ p7g² 7.1m 9s⁶ 8s 8m* 8g* 8g⁵ 7.6m⁴ 8s* 9m Oct 6] big, lengthy
gelding: useful handicapper: better than ever in 2007, winning at Musselburgh and Goodwood in July and Ayr (beat Kinsya in good style by 2½ lengths) in September: stamina
stretched when seventh of 34 to Pipedreamer in Cambridgeshire at Newmarket final start:
effective at 7f to easy 9f: acts on polytrack, firm and soft going: sometimes bandaged in
front: reportedly distressed third start: free-going sort, usually held up. *D. Nicholls*

FRENCH ART 2 ch.c. (Mar 20) Peintre Celebre (USA) 137 – Orange Sunset (IRE) 99 **89 p**
(Roanoke (USA)) [2007 8m⁵ Oct 4] 65,000Y: sturdy, quite attractive colt: third foal: dam,
Irish 1¼m/1½m winner (stayed 1¾m), later successful in US: 22/1, shaped well con-

sidering clear inexperience (including to post) when fifth to Twice Over in maiden at Newmarket: will be suited by 1¼m/1½m: sure to win races. *D. R. C. Elsworth*

FRENCHGATE 6 br.g. Paris House 123 – Let's Hang On (IRE) (Petorius 117) [2007 47: 8f 10.1m Apr 26] maiden: well beaten in 2007: tried in visor/cheekpieces. *I. W. McInnes*

FRENCH OPERA 4 b.g. Bering 136 – On Fair Stage (IRE) 103 (Sadler's Wells (USA) 132) [2007 63: 16.4m³ 16m³ Sep 4] rather leggy gelding: fair maiden, lightly raced: raced freely both starts in 2007: stays 2m, will prove at least as effective at shorter: raced on polytrack and good to firm/firm going: useful novice hurdler. *N. J. Henderson*

77

FRENCH RIVIERA 2 b.c. (Feb 16) Montjeu (IRE) 137 – Arietta's Way (IRE) 71 (Darshaan 133) [2007 8.2g² Nov 7] 150,000Y: close-coupled colt: fifth foal: half-brother to 3 winners, including 7-y-o Midas Way: dam, maiden (should have stayed beyond 1½m), half-sister to Derby Italiano/US Grade 1 1¾m winner Single Empire and smart stayer Court of Honour: 9/2 and green, promising second to Cuban Missile in maiden at Nottingham, finishing well after brief interference: will be well suited by 1½m+: useful prospect. *Sir Michael Stoute*

85 p

FRESH MINT (IRE) 3 b.f. Sadler's Wells (USA) 132 – Valley of Song 74 (Caerleon (USA) 132) [2007 –: 7m 8g 13g⁶ p11m* p12g* p12.2d² Dec 6] well-made filly: second foal: dam, 1¼m winner (her only start), sister to Moyglare Stud Stakes winner Preseli and half-sister to smart 1½m performer Kong (by Sadler's Wells): fairly useful form: off 5 months and left D. Wachman in Ireland, won 2 handicaps at Kempton in November: improved again when second in similar event at Wolverhampton: stays 1½m: acts on polytrack. *M. J. Wallace*

83 +

FRETWORK 3 b.f. Galileo (IRE) 134 – Celtic Cross 100 (Selkirk (USA) 129) [2007 86: 8m³ 9.9d* 10s³ 11.6m⁴ 11.6f⁴ 12m³ 14m⁴ p13.9g* Oct 21] close-coupled filly: useful performer: won maiden at Salisbury in May and handicap at Wolverhampton (by 4 lengths) in October: stays 1¾m: acts on polytrack, firm and soft ground: consistent: sold 60,000 gns. *R. Hannon*

96

FREUDIAN SLIP 2 b.f. (Feb 17) Ishiguru (USA) 114 – Perle d'Azur 91 (Mind Games 121) [2007 6v⁴ 7d² p7g⁴ p7g⁴ 6m³ p6g p7g p6g p8m Nov 24] 1,000Y, resold 1,600Y: rather unfurnished filly: second foal: dam 2-y-o 6f winner: fair maiden: claimed from W. M. Brisbourne £6,000 second start, below form after fifth: stays 7f: acts on polytrack and good to firm going, probably on heavy: tried in blinkers/cheekpieces. *S. Curran*

70

FREYA TRICKS 3 b.f. Noverre (USA) 125 – Trick of Ace (USA) (Clever Trick (USA)) [2007 –: 9.2d² 9g³ 9.2g⁵ 12m⁵ Aug 3] close-coupled filly: fair maiden: stays 1½m: acts on good to firm and good to soft going: has flashed tail. *I. Semple*

72

FRICTION 2 b.f. (Mar 31) Auction House (USA) 120 – Frisson (Slip Anchor 136) [2007 6g 6g 7.5v⁴ 7m⁶ 8.1m p8.6g Oct 5] 3,000Y: workmanlike filly: seventh foal: half-sister to 7f and 9f winner Princes Theatre (by Prince Sabo) and 6-y-o Wanchai Lad: dam unraced out of useful 7f to 9f winner Comic Talent: poor maiden. *J. G. Portman*

39

FRIENDS HOPE 6 ch.m. Docksider (USA) 124 – Stygian (USA) 73 (Irish River (FR) 131) [2007 65: f11d* p9.5g* Dec 26] fairly useful handicapper: improved when winning at Southwell (by 5 lengths) and Wolverhampton (readily) in December: stays 11f: acts on all-weather, firm and soft going: has often been slowly away. *P. A. Blockley*

83

FRIGID 3 b.f. Indian Ridge 123 – Frangy 77 (Sadler's Wells (USA) 132) [2007 7.1m Aug 27] lightly-made filly: third foal: dam, 11.6f/1½m winner, out of half-sister to Fillies' Mile winner and Oaks runner-up Shamshir: 14/1, 7¼ lengths eighth of 12 to Musaalem in maiden at Warwick, racing freely: should do better. *L. M. Cumani*

– p

FRIMLEY'S MATTERRY 7 b.g. Bluegrass Prince (IRE) 110 – Lonely Street 93 (Frimley Park 109) [2007 62: 7m³ 6f 7d 6m³ 5.9g 6m 6g 6m⁵ 8m Sep 18] close-coupled gelding: modest performer: effective at 6f/7f: acts on all-weather, firm and good to soft going: tried visored. *R. E. Barr*

54

FRINGE 4 ch.f. In The Wings 128 – El Jazirah (Kris 135) [2007 93: p12.2g² 12s⁴ 10g² p12g³ 9.9s* Oct 14] useful-looking filly: fairly useful performer on turf, fair on all-weather: won maiden at Goodwood in October: will stay 1¾m: acts on polytrack and heavy ground, unraced on firmer than good. *Jane Chapple-Hyam*

89
a79 +

FRISBEE 3 b.f. Efisio 120 – Flying Carpet 76 (Barathea (IRE) 127) [2007 f7g⁵ Apr 3] third foal: sister to fairly useful 7f/1m winner Casemate and half-sister to useful 6f winner Stanley Goodspeed (by Inchinor): dam, 8.5f winner, out of useful 2-y-o sprinter Flying

57

Squaw: 25/1, 7¾ lengths fifth of 7 to Viami in maiden at Southwell, not knocked about: sold 1,400 gns in December. *T. D. Easterby*

FRISKY TALK (IRE) 3 b.f. Fasliyev (USA) 120 – Happy Talk (IRE) 74 (Hamas (IRE) 125§) [2007 82: p5g⁴ 5g 5d 5s⁴ 5g 6f 5f 5m⁵ Sep 15] leggy filly: fairly useful handicapper: below form after reappearance: best at 5f (has failed to settle over 6f): acts on polytrack and firm going: has made running: can look awkward under pressure: sold 5,000 gns, sent to Saudi Arabia. *B. W. Hills* **81 d**

FRITH (IRE) 5 b.g. Benny The Dip (USA) 127 – Melodist (USA) 118 (The Minstrel (CAN) 135) [2007 p13.9g 12m⁵ 12.4m 11.1d² 12d 10d Sep 20] good-topped gelding: fair maiden nowadays: stays 11f: acts on firm ground, probably good to soft: tried tongue tied/in cheekpieces. *Mrs L. B. Normile* **65 ?**

FRIVOLOUS (IRE) 2 b.f. (Feb 20) Green Desert (USA) 127 – Sweet Folly (IRE) 109 (Singspiel (IRE) 133) [2007 7m 6d⁴ Aug 18] good-bodied, quite attractive filly: first foal: dam, French 10.5f winner, closely related to performer up to 1½m Apprehension and half-sister to smart Coronation Stakes winner Kissing Cousin: much better effort in maidens week apart when fourth to Rinterval at Newbury, making running: should stay 7f/1m. *J. H. M. Gosden* **79**

FRIZZINI 2 b.g. (Apr 18) Bertolini (USA) 125 – Charming Lotte 80 (Nicolotte (118) [2007 5m 5g⁶ 5m p6g p5.1m⁵ p5.1g p5.1g Oct 6] modest maiden: best at 5f: blinkered (tailed off) once. *N. Tinkler* **51**

FROISSEE 3 b.f. Polish Precedent (USA) 131 – Crinkle (IRE) (Distant Relative 128) [2007 72d: 7g⁴ 8s² 8d* 8d* 8s² 8.1d³ 10m p7g⁴ 8.1g⁴ 7d³ Oct 27] lengthy filly: fairly useful handicapper: won at Yarmouth (by 11 lengths) and Pontefract 5 days apart in June: creditable efforts when in frame after: stays 1m: acts on polytrack, soft and good to firm ground: tried in cheekpieces/blinkered: usually held up. *N. A. Callaghan* **85**

FROMSONG (IRE) 9 b.g. Fayruz 116 – Lindas Delight 54 (Batshoof 122) [2007 106: f5g p6g 5f² 5m 6m⁵ 5d⁴ p5g* p6g 5.2f⁶ 5d³ p6g³ p6g⁴ 5m⁵ p5g p6g⁶ p5g⁶ p6g Dec 30] tall, angular gelding: fairly useful handicapper: won at Kempton in July: best at 5f/easy 6f: acts on polytrack, firm and soft going: has worn cheekpieces: tried tongue tied. *D. K. Ivory* **86**

FRONTLINE IN FOCUS (IRE) 3 ch.f. Daggers Drawn (USA) 114 – Christan (IRE) (Al Hareb (USA) 123) [2007 82: p6g Oct 21] rather leggy, workmanlike filly: fairly useful performer at 2 yrs: well held only outing in 2007: effective at 5f/6f: acts on firm and good to soft ground: reportedly bled final 2-y-o start: sold 3,000 gns. *K. R. Burke* **–**

FRONT RANK (IRE) 7 b.g. Sadler's Wells (USA) 132 – Alignment (IRE) 98 (Alzao (USA) 117) [2007 66: 10.5m⁶ 13d⁵ 13m 13g Sep 3] strong, good-bodied gelding: modest maiden handicapper nowadays: stays 13f: acts on fibresand, firm and good to soft going. *Mrs Dianne Sayer* **54**

FROSTY NIGHT (IRE) 3 b.g. Night Shift (USA) – Abla (Robellino (USA) 127) [2007 86: 8g⁶ 10.1g 10m 10m 13.8m⁴ 10.3m 10m 12s³ 10m Oct 22] strong, stocky gelding: type to carry condition: fairly useful handicapper: below form after reappearance: stays 13.8f: acts on soft and good to firm going: blinkered last 2 outings: sold 9,000 gns. *M. Johnston* **85 d**

FROZEN FIRE (GER) 2 b.c. (Feb 19) Montjeu (IRE) 137 – Flamingo Sea (USA) (Woodman (USA) 126) [2007 7d* 8g Oct 27] €250,000Y: lengthy colt: has scope: second foal: dam, German 1m winner, half-sister to several at least useful German winners (all at 1½m+), notably smart Flamingo Road: fairly useful form: good impression when winning maiden at Gowran in August: off 2½ months, well-backed 5/1 but still very green when eighth of 12 behind Ibn Khaldun in Racing Post Trophy at Doncaster, soon off bridle in rear: will be suited by 1½m: type to develop well at 3 yrs. *A. P. O'Brien, Ireland* **90 p**

Ladbrokes Portland (Handicap), Doncaster—jockey P. J. McDonald, successful in the Scottish Grand National earlier in the year, achieves a notable double on Fullandby (spots); they just get up to beat Paradise Isle (rail) with Pearly Wey, Orpsie Boy and Gift Horse (visor) next

FUEL CELL (IRE) 6 b.g. Desert Style (IRE) 121 – Tappen Zee (Sandhurst Prince **58** 128) [2007 49: p12.2g⁴ p10g f8g⁵ p10g⁵ f8g* p8.6g f8g⁵ p9.5g⁵ 9.9m p12g Aug 23] compact gelding: modest performer nowadays: won handicap at Southwell in March: stays 1¼m: acts on all-weather, good to firm and good to soft going: tried tongue tied/in headgear: slowly away seventh outing: has shown signs of temperament. *J. O'Reilly*

FUJIN DANCER (FR) 2 ch.c. (Feb 10) Storming Home 128 – Badaayer (USA) 105 **61 p** (Silver Hawk (USA) 123) [2007 6f 6.1d Oct 18] 18,000Y, 17,500 2-y-o: strong colt: fourth foal: half-brother to 3 winners, including 6-y-o Dancing Lyra and 9f winner Namathej (by Halling), both fairly useful: dam 1m/1¼m winner: inadequate test in maidens (modest form), not knocked about: will do better at 1m+. *R. A. Fahey*

FULFORD 2 ch.g. (Mar 18) Elmaamul (USA) 125 – Last Impression 69 (Imp Society **61** (USA)) [2007 6g 6s² 6m 6m³ 6m 6d Sep 21] workmanlike gelding: modest maiden: placed at York and Ripon: will prove best at 5f/6f: acts on soft and good to firm going. *M. Brittain*

FULLANDBY (IRE) 5 b.g. Monashee Mountain (USA) 115 – Ivory Turner (Efisio **108** 120) [2007 106: 5m⁵ 6m 7s³ 5g⁴ 6v 5d* 6s 6m 5.6m* 6d 6d Oct 20] strong gelding: type to carry plenty of condition: useful handicapper: won at Ayr (by ¾ length from Gallery Girl) in July and Ladbrokes Portland at Doncaster (by head from Paradise Isle, leading late) in September: little impact in Ayr Gold Cup and Bentinck Stakes at Newmarket (poorly drawn) after: effective at stiff 5f to 7f: acts on polytrack, soft and good to firm going: pulled hard fifth outing: has edged right: held up. *T. J. Etherington*

FULL HOUSE (IRE) 8 br.g. King's Theatre (IRE) 128 – Nirvavita (FR) (Highest **99** Honor (FR) 124) [2007 89: 16g* 20m* 21g 18d Oct 20] strong, close-coupled gelding: useful handicapper, lightly raced on Flat in recent years: won at Goodwood in May and Royal Ascot (much improved when beating Juniper Girl by ½ length in Ascot Stakes) in June: below form after, in Cesarewitch at Newmarket on final outing: stays 2½m: acts on polytrack and firm going, probably not on good to soft: tried blinkered: has worn crossed noseband: sometimes races freely: fairly useful hurdler/useful chaser. *P. R. Webber*

FULL MARKS 2 b.f. (Mar 8) Dansili 127 – Flying Wanda 104 (Alzao (USA) 117) **86** [2007 7d² p8g⁴ Oct 29] strong, close-coupled filly: first foal: dam 2-y-o 1m winner (stayed 1¾m): fairly useful maiden: promising second to Laughter at Leicester, making most: possibly found race coming too soon when only fourth at Lingfield (odds on): should stay 1m/1¼m. *J. Noseda*

Ascot Stakes (Handicap), Royal Ascot—
useful chaser Full House shows himself to be just as good on the level;
he's strongly pressed by Juniper Girl (right) and Som Tala, with 2005 winner Leg Spinner (No.7) fourth

FULL OF GOLD (FR) 2 ch.c. (Apr 19) Gold Away (IRE) 125 – Funny Feerie   **109 p**
(FR) (Sillery (USA) 122) [2007 8g⁴ 8g² 8g* 10d* Nov 11]

The winners of Saint-Cloud's pair of back-end Group 1 contests for two-year-olds, the Criterium International and the Criterium de Saint-Cloud, must have provoked very different reactions from the breeding experts. If they were drooling over the blue blood of the winner of the first-named race, Thewayyouare, a King-mambo half-brother to the season's best middle-distance three-year-old filly Peeping Fawn, then they must have been scratching their heads about the Criterium de Saint-Cloud winner Full of Gold. The *Racing Post*'s bloodstock correspondent Tony Morris went so far as to suggest that Full of Gold 'might just qualify as the owner of the year's most remarkable pedigree.' Morris was referring to the fact that his pedigree features a number of duplications or crosses; the one evident from the pedigree table opposite is that of Blushing Groom, who appears twice in the third generation. Go back another generation, and it is Riverman whose name occurs twice. But even leaving the arcana of inbreeding aside, Full of Gold's pedigree is no less remarkable for a couple of other, and perhaps more easily appreciated, reasons.

First though, his racing career, such as it is so far. Full of Gold had three starts in the autumn prior to the Criterium de Saint-Cloud without proving particularly progressive. He was fourth in a newcomers race at Longchamp, second in a maiden at Saint-Cloud to the subsequent listed winner Sceptre Rouge, and then went one better in a similar event at the same track in October by five lengths. That win earned him a supplementary entry into the Criterium de Saint-Cloud, in which he faced five opponents. Of those, only the favourite Hannouma had so much as contested a pattern race before, finishing second in the Prix de Conde on his latest start. The Mick Channon-trained Siberian Tiger, successful in a listed race at Ponte-fract, held similar claims on form but the others all needed to improve considerably. Full of Gold's stable-companion Putney Bridge—the pair started second and third favourite respectively—had won a minor event at Deauville, while Aidan O'Brien relied on a couple of maidens, New Zealand and Tale of Two Cities, the latter the pick of the field on pedigree, being a brother to High Chaparral.

Full of Gold's previous races had all been at a mile on good ground, and he seemed to relish the stiffer test provided by the extra two furlongs, slightly softer conditions and a sound pace. When pacesetter New Zealand was asked to stretch on the home turn, Full of Gold briefly looked in trouble as Putney Bridge was the first of the Head-Maarek runners to lay down a challenge to the leader. But as the runners came down the centre of the track, it was Full of Gold who made the best of his way home, heading his stable-companion over a furlong out and keeping on strongly to the line to win by two lengths. Hannouma collared Putney Bridge to take

Criterium de Saint-Cloud, Saint-Cloud—the final European Group 1 of the year
goes to progressive Full of Gold; he proves suited by the step up in trip and stays on well
ahead of Hannouma (left), Putney Bridge and New Zealand (partially obscured)

second by a short neck, with New Zealand the same distance away fourth ahead of Siberian Tiger and, if proof were needed that pedigrees do not win races, Tale of Two Cities last of all.

As well as being trained by Criquette Head-Maarek, Full of Gold is owned by her father Alec, who bred the colt in partnership with his wife Ghislaine. The Head family's associations with Full of Gold run a lot deeper than that though, because between them they have either owned, bred or trained most of his immediate ancestors—both his sire and dam, all four of his second generation ancestors, and three of his great grandams. Alec Head's connection with Full of Gold's ancestors goes back even further, as the trainer of the aforementioned Riverman, and his contemporary Lyphard (another who appears more than once in Full of Gold's pedigree), and also as the purchaser of Full of Gold's fifth dam Melopee as a yearling. Full of Gold's sire Gold Away, a high-class performer at up to nine furlongs, stands at Alec Head's Haras du Quesnay and is the sire of the high-class mare Alexander Goldrun.

The other no less noteworthy aspect of Full of Gold's pedigree, at least the distaff side of his family, is that most of its success has come over jumps at Auteuil. One race there that recurs in the family's roll of honour is the Prix Finot, a listed contest (run in separate divisions for fillies and colts and geldings) for three-year-old hurdling debutants in September which has been the starting point for a number of good French jumpers. Full of Gold's dam Funny Feerie won the race, as did one of her half-brothers Spanish Wells who was to prove a smart hurdler. Grandam Funny Pearl finished third in it (before going on to four successes over jumps at Auteuil, including over fences), and she was out of a half-sister to two more winners of the Finot, Mediterraneen and Marittimo. The last-named was probably the best of this family's jumpers, who went on to be successful in a number of Auteuil's better hurdle races. Full of Gold's dam Funny Feerie proved a useful hurdler herself (she never ran on the Flat), winning three times at Auteuil and placed there over fences. At stud, she has had three winners from as many foals prior to Full of Gold. The first two, Frejus (by Mansonnien) and First Feerie (by Turgeon), are both winning hurdlers, the latter successful in a mares' novice at Ascot early in 2007. Full of Gold's three-year-old half-sister Funny Line (by Emperor Jones) won her only start on the Flat over thirteen furlongs before showing promise over hurdles at Auteuil in the autumn, starting off naturally enough in the Prix Finot, in which she didn't quite uphold the family tradition, finishing fourth.

		Goldneyev	Nureyev
	Gold Away (IRE)	(b or br 1986)	Gold River
	(ch 1995)	Blushing Away	Blushing Groom
Full of Gold (FR)		(ch 1987)	Sweet Revenge
(ch.c. Apr 19, 2005)		Sillery	Blushing Groom
	Funny Feerie (FR)	(b 1988)	Silvermine
	(b 1995)	Funny Pearl	Irish River
		(ch 1984)	Messenie

Unless he disappoints badly as a three-year-old, it's unlikely that Full of Gold will be sent jumping, though he looks to have the size for it, and wouldn't be the first Criterium de Saint-Cloud winner to go down that route if things didn't go to plan on the Flat—the 1998 winner Spadoun ended up winning over hurdles at Auteuil. Full of Gold has the scope to train on as a three-year-old and will stay a mile and half. He is likely to prove vulnerable to speedier types at a mile and a quarter though, particularly under firmish conditions, and it is worth bearing in mind that two of the first three winners of the Prix du Jockey Club over the race's shortened distance, Shamardal and Lawman, have been milers stepping up in trip. Instead, the Grand Prix de Paris is likely to be Full of Gold's best chance of adding another Group 1 contest to his record. The Criterium de Saint-Cloud form is also some way below that of the Criterium International won by Thewayyouare ten days earlier. In any event, with his very different type of pedigree background, Full of Gold will be a fascinating contender for the good French middle-distance prizes in 2008. *Mme C. Head-Maarek, France*

FULL OF PROMISE (USA) 3 b.f. Street Cry (IRE) 130 – Believe It Beloved (USA) **63** (Clever Trick (USA)) [2007 65p: 10g 7g 8.1m p10g⁴ p12g p12g Nov 19] big, leggy filly: modest maiden: stays 1¼m: form only on polytrack. *Mrs A. J. Perrett*

FULL OF ZEST 5 ch.m. Pivotal 124 – Tangerine 70 (Primo Dominie 121) [2007 71: –
p11g p12g Apr 30] leggy mare: fair maiden at best: well beaten both starts on Flat in
2007: probably stays easy 1½m: acts on polytrack and soft ground: usually wears headgear. *Mrs L. J. Mongan*

FULL SPATE 12 ch.g. Unfuwain (USA) 131 – Double River (USA) (Irish River (FR) **53**
131) [2007 71d: 6.1g 6g⁵ 7.1s 5.7d⁵ 6g 7m Sep 2] tall, good-topped gelding: modest
performer nowadays: stays 7f: acts on any turf going: tried blinkered/cheekpieces (ran
poorly): usually slowly away: usually held up. *J. M. Bradley*

FULL SPEED (GER) 2 b.g. (Mar 16) Sholokhov (IRE) 121 – Flagny (FR) (Kaldoun **73 p**
(FR) 122) [2007 8m 8g² 8g⁵ Oct 19] €67,000Y: good-bodied gelding: type to carry condition: eighth foal: half-brother to several winners in Germany, notably 6.5f (at 2 yrs) to 1m
winner Furstenberg (by Monashee Mountain) and 6f winner Fulminant (by Big Shuffle),
both useful: dam useful French 1m winner: fair form in maidens, second to Redford at
Newcastle: will probably stay 1¼m: sort to progress in 3-y-o handicaps. *G. A. Swinbank*

FULL VICTORY (IRE) 5 b.g. Imperial Ballet (IRE) 110 – Full Traceability (IRE) 53 **91**
(Ron's Victory (USA) 129) [2007 84: 8f p7g 8d³ 8.1g³ 8.1g* 8.1g⁵ 9s² 9.9d⁴ 8s³ 8d⁶ 8g⁶
8.1s⁵ p8.6g² 8.9d 8.3d⁴ p8.6g p9.5g Dec 1] good-topped gelding: fairly useful handicapper: won at Sandown (by 7 lengths) in May: stays 9f: acts on polytrack and heavy
going: tried blinkered, wore cheekpieces last 2 outings: sometimes hangs left (badly so
seventh start). *R. A. Farrant*

FUL OF GRACE (IRE) 3 b.f. Marju (IRE) 127 – Mitawa (IRE) 73 (Alhaarth (IRE) **59**
126) [2007 10.3d⁵ 10m⁶ 8g 11.5m 14.1m 10.5s 11.5d² 10.1d* Oct 30] 12,000Y: small,
leggy filly: first foal: dam, 2-y-o 7f winner, half-sister to useful 1¼m/1½m performer
Balladonia: modest performer: won seller at Yarmouth in October: stays 1¼m: acts on
good to soft going: blinkered last 2 starts: sold 6,000 gns, joined D. Pipe, and won selling
hurdle in December. *M. G. Quinlan*

FULVIO (USA) 7 b.g. Sword Dance – One Tuff Gal (USA) (Lac Ouimet (USA)) [2007 **54 d**
–, a64: p8g³ p9.5g³ p7g p7.1g⁶ p8g³ p7.1g p7.1g⁶ p9.5g p8.6g⁶ p7g⁴ p7g p10g⁴ 8m p8.6g
p12g p10g Sep 11] big gelding: modest performer: stays 1¼m: acts on all-weather, firm
and good to soft going: usually wears headgear. *P. Howling*

FUNFAIR WANE 8 b.g. Unfuwain (USA) 131 – Ivory Bride 86 (Domynsky 110) **76**
[2007 96d: f6g p7.1g f5g 6g 5.9g 6v² 6s 5d* 6s⁴ 6d² 5s² 5d* 5.1m⁶ 5d⁶ 5g³ 5d⁴ 6.1s⁵ Oct
18] strong, lengthy gelding: has a long stride: fair performer nowadays: won seller in July
and handicap in August, both at Hamilton: best at 5f/6f: acts on polytrack, heavy and
good to firm ground: often edgy, tends to sweat and has had 2 handlers/been early to post:
races prominently: formerly unreliable. *D. Nicholls*

FUNGIBLE 2 ch.c. (Apr 1) Compton Place 125 – Highly Liquid 81 (Entrepreneur 123) –
[2007 7s Oct 9] 20/1, tailed off in maiden at Folkestone: sold 1,000 gns. *E. A. L. Dunlop*

FUN IN THE SUN 3 ch.g. Piccolo 121 – Caught In The Rain 66 (Spectrum (IRE) 126) **56 d**
[2007 –: 8f 7d² 7g 7d⁵ 8.1s 7s 7.9m 7f⁵ 7m 8f p8g⁶ 8f³ p10g⁴ 9.1s p9.5g⁵ Oct 27] modest
maiden: left Jane Southcombe after second outing: best form at 7f/1m: acts on firm and
good to soft ground: visored/blinkered nowadays: held up. *P. D. Evans*

FUNNY ME 2 ch.c. (Apr 24) Dr Fong (USA) 128 – Goodie Twosues 91 (Fraam 114) **87**
[2007 6m³ 7.1m 8m² 9d* Sep 26] 65,000Y: rather leggy, attractive colt: second foal:
half-brother to winner in Denmark by Lomitas: dam 2-y-o 6f winner (stayed 8.5f): fairly
useful form: second to Dr Faustus at Thirsk prior to winning maiden at Goodwood by 3½
lengths: will stay 1¼m: sent to USA. *P. W. Chapple-Hyam*

FUNSEEKER (UAE) 2 b. or br.f. (Feb 13) Halling (USA) 133 – Silversword (FR) 102 **76**
(Highest Honor (FR) 124) [2007 8.1s⁵ 7s² p8g³ p8g⁵ p8.6g⁶ p7.1g² Dec 13] good-topped **a65**
filly: seventh foal: closely related to fairly useful 2002 Irish 2-y-o 7f winner Finity
(by Diesis) and half-sister to UAE 8.5f winner Dramatic Edge (by Theatrical): dam,
French 1½m winner, sister to very smart stayer Double Honour: fair maiden: placed at
Folkestone, Kempton and Wolverhampton: will be suited by 1¼m/1½m: raced only on
polytrack and soft going. *M. Johnston*

FUN THAI 3 ch.f. Fraam 114 – Thailand (Lycius (USA) 124) [2007 46: p11g Nov 14] –
neat filly: poor maiden: well held only outing in 2007: stays 7f: acts on firm and soft
going. *A. J. Chamberlain*

FURBESETA 3 b.f. Danehill Dancer (IRE) 117 – Fafinta (IRE) (Indian Ridge 123) **84**
[2007 69+: 7.5g² 10g⁶ p8g* p8g⁵ 7g⁵ 8g p8g Oct 14] compact filly: fairly useful handicapper: won at Lingfield in July: below form last 2 starts: may prove best at 1m: raced
only on polytrack and good ground. *L. M. Cumani*

FURMIGADELAGIUSTA 3 ch.c. Galileo (IRE) 134 – Sispre (FR) (Master Willie **100**
129) [2007 80p: 9.9g⁴ 12s* 14d³ 13.1s 1p12.2g* Oct 22] good-topped colt: useful performer: won maiden at Newbury in July and handicap at Wolverhampton (beat Music
Review a head) in October: stays 1¾m: acts on polytrack and soft ground: sold 115,000
gns, joined K. R. Burke, won over hurdles in December. *L. M. Cumani*

FURNACE (IRE) 3 b.g. Green Desert (USA) 127 – Lyrical Dance (USA) (Lear Fan **94**
(USA) 130) [2007 90: 7m³ 8m 8m⁴ Jul 13] leggy, quite attractive gelding: fairly useful
handicapper: in frame at Newmarket in 2007: suffered infection in a knee joint after, then
gelded: barely stays 1m: unraced on extremes of ground. *M. L. W. Bell*

FURTHER OUTLOOK (USA) 13 gr.g. Zilzal (USA) 137 – Future Bright (USA) **55**
(Lyphard's Wish (FR) 124) [2007 73, a56: f6g⁴ Jan 7] big, strong gelding: carries
condition: fair at 12 yrs: just modest form sole outing in 2007: best at 5f/6f: acts on
all-weather and any turf going: sometimes in cheekpieces (including last 3 starts)/tongue
tied: races up with pace: sometimes hangs right. *Miss Gay Kelleway*

FUSCHIA 3 b.f. Averti (IRE) 117 – Big Pink (IRE) (Bigstone (IRE) 126) [2007 53: **79**
p7.1g* 7g⁴ 6.1m³ 7.1g³ Jul 12] tall, unfurnished filly: fair performer: won maiden at
Wolverhampton in May: creditable efforts in frame in handicaps after: stays 7f: acts on
polytrack and good to firm going. *R. Charlton*

FUSHE JO 3 gr.g. Act One 124 – Aristocratique 71 (Cadeaux Genereux 131) [2007 83p: **86**
10.4g 12g² 14g Aug 23] tall, rather leggy, useful-looking gelding: fairly useful performer:
easily best effort in 2007 when runner-up in handicap at Thirsk: stays 1½m: raced only on
good/good to soft going: placed in juvenile hurdles. *J. Howard Johnson*

FUSILI (IRE) 4 ch.f. Silvano (GER) 126 – Flunder (Nebos (GER) 129) [2007 100: **100**
p12g⁴ p10g* p10g p10f⁵ p10g 9.9g 10.3m⁵ 10.1g³ 10.1d³ p9.5g p12m³ p10g Dec 16]
smallish, close-coupled filly: useful handicapper: won at Lingfield (by ½ length from
Red Spell) in January: best effort after when in frame: stays 1½m: acts on polytrack, soft
and good to firm going: often makes running. *N. P. Littmoden*

FUSTAAN (IRE) 3 b.f. Royal Applause 124 – Alhufoof (USA) 100 (Dayjur (USA) **71**
137) [2007 71p: p6g* p6g p5g Dec 22] well-made filly: won maiden at Lingfield in
January: left M. Tregoning 25,000 gns and off 10 months, well held in handicaps last 2
starts: likely to prove best at 5f/6f. *A. G. Newcombe*

FUTOO (IRE) 6 b.g. Foxhound (USA) 103 – Nicola Wynn 83 (Nicholas Bill 125) **51**
[2007 56: f12g⁵ f12g⁶ f8s⁴ f8g⁴ f11g f12g May 22] tall, useful-looking gelding: modest
performer: stays 1½m: acts on fibresand, good to firm and good to soft going: usually
wears headgear. *D. W. Chapman*

FUTUN 4 b.c. In The Wings 128 – Svanzega (USA) (Sharpen Up 127) [2007 107: p11g **106 §**
12m 10.4g⁵ 12s⁵ 11.9m² 12d 14.1g⁶ 11.8d³ Oct 29] big, strong, close-coupled colt: useful
performer: creditable efforts in 2007 only when placed in Old Newton Cup (Handicap) at
Haydock (½-length second to Dansili Dancer) and minor event at Leicester (third to New
Guinea, again tending to hang) in fifth/final outings: stays 1½m: seems best on good
going or firmer (found little on soft): tried tongue tied: has run well when sweating:
headstrong: one to treat with caution: sold 80,000 gns, sent to Saudi Arabia. *L. M. Cumani*

FUTUNE (IRE) 2 gr.f. (Mar 21) Night Shift (USA) – Splendida Idea (IRE) (Kenmare **55**
(FR) 125) [2007 7m p7g 6m p6g 7g³ Oct 25] good-topped filly: good walker: third foal:
half-sister to Italian 1m/10.5f winner King Celebre (by Peintre Celebre): dam useful
Italian 9f (at 2 yrs) to 10.5f winner: modest maiden: third in nursery at Brighton: should
stay beyond 7f: sold 6,000 gns, sent to Kazakhstan. *B. J. Meehan*

FUTURE DEAL 6 b.m. First Trump 118 – Katyushka (IRE) 73 (Soviet Star (USA) **52**
128) [2007 62: p10g⁶ p10g p10g⁶ p10²g⁶ p8g⁴ p8g⁶ Dec 5] strong, workmanlike mare:
modest performer: stays easy 1¼m: acts on polytrack and good to firm going: has carried
head high: sometimes slowly away. *C. A. Horgan*

FUTURE'S DREAM 4 b.g. Bertolini (USA) 125 – Bahawir Pour (USA) (Green **78 +**
Dancer (USA) 132) [2007 90d: f8g* f8g* 7s 8.5d 9.1v⁴ Oct 26] useful handicapper on **a97**
all-weather, fair on turf: improved to win at Southwell in March and April: shaped as if
needed run final outing: should stay 1¼m: acts on fibresand and soft going: wore cheekpieces final 3-y-o outing: sold 20,000 gns. *K. R. Burke*

FUTURISTIC DRAGON (IRE) 3 b.g. Invincible Spirit (IRE) 121 – Calvia Rose **62 d**
(Sharpo 132) [2007 –p: 6f³ 6.1g⁵ 6d⁶ 6m p6g p5.1m p5.1g Nov 27] close-coupled gelding: fair maiden: well held after second start (gelded after third, left P. Blockley after
sixth): tried blinkered/tongue tied. *D. Shaw*

FU WA (USA) 2 ch.f. (Mar 6) Distant View (USA) 126 – Fire And Shade (USA) 91 **53** (Shadeed (USA) 135) [2007 5v⁶ 6m p6g⁶ p6g Sep 27] 22,000Y: sister to 2003 2-y-o 6f winner Shadowland (later successful in US), closely related to fairly useful 7f winner Miss Shema (by Gulch) and half-sister to 3 winners, including useful 1¼m winner Freedom Flame (by Darshaan): dam, 2-y-o 6f winner, out of Musidora winner Fatah Flare: modest maiden: form only on third start. *M. W. Easterby*

FYODOR (IRE) 6 b.g. Fasliyev (USA) 120 – Royale Figurine (IRE) 107 (Dominion **103** Royale 112) [2007 106, a117: p5g⁵ 5m 5g⁵ p6g Nov 17] tall, good-topped gelding: useful performer nowadays: best efforts in 2007 when fifth in listed race at Lingfield (behind King Orchisios) and handicap at Doncaster (behind Sunrise Safari) first/third outings: stays 6f: acts on all-weather and good to firm going (well beaten on softer than good): held up. *W. J. Haggas*

FYODOROVICH (USA) 2 b.c. (Feb 11) Stravinsky (USA) 133 – Omnia (USA) 85 **74** (Green Dancer (USA) 132) [2007 5f⁶ 5m 7m 6g* 6g Sep 12] $47,000Y: useful-looking colt: half-brother to several winners, including 5-y-o Love Angel and 3-y-o Love Dubai: dam, 7f winner, half-sister to smart performer up to 1m Firm Pledge: fair performer: much improved to win maiden at Thirsk in August: ran badly final outing (reluctant at stall): should stay 7f: raced only on good going or firmer: visored last 2 starts. *J. S. Wainwright*

G

GAABAL (IRE) 2 ch.f. (Feb 15) Frenchmans Bay (FR) 118 – Jazz Up (Cadeaux **62** Genereux 131) [2007 7g⁵ 6m Oct 4] €65,000F, 50,000Y: leggy, lengthy filly: third foal: half-sister to useful Irish 6.5f to 8.5f (including at 2 yrs) winner Jazz Princess (by Bahhare) and 3-y-o Rudry Dragon: dam unraced: better effort in maidens when fifth to Joffe's Run at Salisbury: will stay 1m. *C. E. Brittain*

GABIER 4 b.g. Galileo (IRE) 134 – Contare 108 (Shirley Heights 130) [2007 14d³ 16d² **92** Sep 29] fairly useful form: won minor event at Le Pin-Au-Haras in 2006 when trained by J. Pease in France: good efforts in handicaps in 2007, 2½ lengths second to Samurai Way at Ascot: stays 2m: raced mainly on good ground or softer: fairly useful hurdler, won in December. *G. L. Moore*

GAELIC PRINCESS 7 b.m. Cois Na Tine (IRE) 101 – Berenice (ITY) (Marouble **88** 116) [2007 89: 8d⁵ 8m³ 8d² 8m 7g 9d 7g p8.6g p8.6g² p9.5g* p8g⁴ p8g⁴ p10g* p9.5g⁵ Dec 31] big, good-bodied mare: fairly useful handicapper: won at Wolverhampton in October and Lingfield in December: effective at 7f to easy 1¼m: acts on all-weather, firm and good to soft going: patiently ridden. *A. G. Newcombe*

GAELIC ROULETTE (IRE) 7 b.m. Turtle Island (IRE) 123 – Money Spinner **60** (USA) 61 (Teenoso (USA) 135) [2007 55: p16g² p16g* 16m* p16g³ Jun 20] rather leggy mare: modest performer: won handicaps at Kempton (by 5 lengths) and Lingfield in May: stays 2m: acts on polytrack, best turf form on good going or firmer: often slowly away: hung right on reappearance: reportedly in foal to Val Royal. *J. Jay*

GAIA PRINCE (USA) 2 b. or br.c. (Feb 13) Forestry (USA) 121 – Castlebrook (USA) **69 p** (Montbrook (USA)) [2007 6f⁵ Aug 5] $225,000Y: first foal: dam US 7f (at 2 yrs) to 8.5f (including several minor stakes) winner: 16/1, green and in rear long way when fifth to Cat Junior in maiden at Newbury: will stay 1m: sure to improve. *Mrs A. J. Perrett*

GAINSBOROUGH'S ART (IRE) 2 ch.g. (Apr 7) Desert Prince (IRE) 130 – Cathy **68 p** Garcia (IRE) (Be My Guest (USA) 126) [2007 p7m⁶ Nov 1] €32,000Y: well-made gelding: closely related to useful 5f/5.7f (including at 2 yrs) winner Nights Cross (by Cape Cross) and half-brother to 6f winner (including at 2 yrs) Cantgetyourbreath (by College Chapel): dam Italian 7f winner: 5/1, backward and not knocked about when sixth to Traphalgar in maiden at Lingfield: subsequently gelded: will do better. *D. R. C. Elsworth*

GAINSHARE 2 b.g. (Feb 3) Lend A Hand 124 – Red Shareef (Marju (IRE) 127) [2007 **79** 5m⁴ 5m⁶ 6d⁶ 5.1g³ p6g* Nov 14] quite good-topped gelding: third foal: brother to useful French 1m/9f winner Zylig and half-brother to smart 6f (at 2 yrs) to 7.5f (in UAE) winner Caesar Beware (by Daggers Drawn): dam Italian 1m to 11f winner: fair form: improved in November, and won nursery at Wolverhampton (made all): should prove best at 5f/6f. *T. D. Barron*

Doncaster Audi Stakes (Handicap), Doncaster—Galactic Star, showing further improvement, is driven clear of New Guinea as they draw right away from the remainder

GAITSKELL 2 b.c. (Mar 18) Auction House (USA) 120 – Lady-Love 70 (Pursuit of **68 d** Love 124) [2007 5m⁴ p6g p8.6g³ p7.1g⁶ p8.6g f7d⁵ p7.1g Dec 29] sturdy colt: maiden: fair form on debut (only turf start), modest at best subsequently: should prove best at 5f/ 6f: said to have had breathing problem last 2 starts, tongue tied final one. *R. Hollinshead*

GALA CASINO KING (IRE) 4 ch.g. Elnadim (USA) 128 – Fashion Scout (IRE) **–** (Thatching 131) [2007 60: 15.8m 11.7d May 16] angular gelding: modest maiden at 3 yrs: no form in 2007: best effort at 1¾m: unraced on extremes of going. *Jennie Candlish*

GALA CASINO STAR (IRE) 2 ch.c. (Apr 14) Dr Fong (USA) 128 – Abir 73 (Soviet **66** Star (USA) 128) [2007 6s 6m⁵ 6f² 7g Sep 30] tall colt: fair maiden: runner-up at York: should be suited by 7f/1m: acts on firm going. *R. A. Fahey*

GALACTIC STAR 4 ch.c. Galileo (IRE) 134 – Balisada 115 (Kris 135) [2007 81p: **120** 10d⁵ 10m² 12d* 12m* 12m* 12d⁴ Oct 27] good-bodied, attractive colt: type to carry condition: very smart performer, lightly raced: much improved in 2007, winning handicaps at York (by length from Dunaskin) in August and Doncaster (beat New Guinea by 2½ lengths) in September and listed event at Newmarket (beat Munsef by head) in October: below form in St Simon Stakes at Newbury final outing: stays 1½m: acts on soft and good to firm going: has pulled hard/carried head high: has run well when sweating: held up. *Sir Michael Stoute*

GALA EVENING 5 b.g. Daylami (IRE) 138 – Balleta (USA) 87 (Lyphard (USA) 132) **81** [2007 p16g* 14g May 17] strong, quite attractive gelding: fair hurdler: fairly useful performer on Flat: won handicap at Kempton in May: stays 2m: acts on polytrack, unraced on extremes of going on turf. *J. A. B. Old*

GALA JACKPOT (USA) 4 b. or br.g. Crafty Prospector (USA) – True At Heart **41** (USA) (Storm Cat (USA)) [2007 41: 8f 8.1m 10d⁴ 10.1d 12m p12.2g 9g Aug 30] poor maiden: seemingly stays 1½m: acts on firm ground: tried blinkered. *W. M. Brisbourne*

GALANTOS (GER) 6 b.g. Winged Love (IRE) 121 – Grey Metal (GER) (Secret 'n **58** Classy (CAN)) [2007 65: p16g⁵ p16g² f16s p16g² 17.2m⁵ p16g Sep 7] leggy gelding: **a64** modest performer nowadays: left G. L. Moore after fifth outing: stays 17f: acts on allweather, soft and good to firm ground: tried blinkered. *Jane Southcombe*

GALA SUNDAY (USA) 7 b.g. Lear Fan (USA) 130 – Sunday Bazaar (USA) (Nureyev **70** (USA) 131) [2007 76: 10s 8.3d⁶ 9.8v⁴ 10.1d 9.1s 10g³ 8.3m³ 12.1m⁶ 9.9d⁶ 10g* 10g² Oct 31] smallish, well-made gelding: fair handicapper: won ladies event at Redcar in October: best at 1¼m: acts on polytrack, firm and soft going: blinkered/tongue tied. *M. W. Easterby*

GALAXY OF STARS 3 b.f. Observatory (USA) 131 – Divine Secret (Hernando (FR) **–** 127) [2007 60: p5.1g p5g Oct 24] modest performer at 2 yrs: last both outings in 2007: probably stays 6f: visored last 5 starts: sometimes slowly away. *D. Shaw*

GALAXY STARS 3 b.g. Golden Snake (USA) 127 – Moly 64 (Inchinor 119) [2007 **60 +** 72p: p6g p6g p8g⁵ Jul 17] leggy gelding: fair form sole 2-y-o outing, just modest in handicaps in 2007: should stay 7f+: raced only on polytrack: tongue tied. *P. J. Makin*

GALEOTA (IRE) 5 b.g. Mujadil (USA) 119 – Refined (IRE) 95 (Statoblest 120) [2007 **119** 6f² 5.1d* 7.1m³ 5m* 6m² 6g 6d³ 6m* Nov 10] strong, good-topped gelding: smart performer: unraced in 2006 and went to stud (proved infertile): gelded, won minor event

409

Altium Scarbrough Stakes, Doncaster—the first of Galeota's two listed wins at the course; he leaves it late against Peace Offering

at Nottingham in August and listed races at Doncaster in September (by neck from Peace Offering) and November (beat Borderlescott by short head): also ran well when third to Greek Renaissance in Bentinck Stakes at Newmarket penultimate outing: best at 5f/6f: acts on firm and good to soft going: tried in cheekpieces: usually races prominently. *R. Hannon*

GALIANNA (IRE) 3 b.f. Galileo (IRE) 134 – Ann's Annie (IRE) 78 (Alzao (USA) 117) [2007 10m 10g³ 11.9m* 13m 12d⁶ 14g 12m⁴ 14d⁵ Oct 13] 16,000Y: big, good sort: third foal: closely related to 4-y-o Sgt Schultz and half-sister to 5-y-o Red River Rock: dam, Irish 2-y-o 1m winner, half-sister to smart 6f to 1m winner Pipe Major: fairly useful performer: won maiden at Haydock in June: generally creditable efforts after: stays 1¾m: acts on good to firm and good to soft ground: sold 42,000 gns. *Pat Eddery*   **83**

GALIENT (IRE) 4 b.g. Galileo (IRE) 134 – Endorsement 107 (Warning 136) [2007 107: p16g³ 18.7m 14g 12d⁴ 13.4m Sep 1] tall, good-topped gelding: fluent mover: useful performer: third in handicap at Kempton on reappearance, but regressed: should stay beyond 2m: acts on good to firm and good to soft going: wore cheekpieces third outing: often races prominently: unenthusiastic: joined N. J. Henderson. *M. A. Jarvis*   **96 §**

GALINGALE (IRE) 3 b.f. Galileo (IRE) 134 – Urban Sky (FR) (Groom Dancer (USA) 128) [2007 67: 10m 9.9g⁴ 12.1g⁶ p12g 16g Aug 2] close-coupled filly: maiden: little form at 3 yrs: bred to be suited by 1¼m/1½m. *Mrs P. Sly*   **–**

GALIPETTE 3 b.f. Green Desert (USA) 127 – Arabesque 100 (Zafonic (USA) 130) [2007 79p: 7m⁵ 6m³ 5s⁵ 5f³ 5s Sep 26] strong, compact filly: fair maiden: may prove best at 5f/6f: acts on firm and good to soft ground: has found little/carried head high, and not one to trust: sold 30,000 gns, sent to France. *H. R. A. Cecil*   **70 §**

GALLANTRY 5 b.g. Green Desert (USA) 127 – Gay Gallanta (USA) 112 (Woodman (USA) 126) [2007 94: p8g⁴ p8g⁴ p8f* p7.1g⁴ p7g⁴ p7g 8f 7g 7f² p8g⁴ 7g 7.6m² 7m p8g 6m⁵ 7g p7.1g* p8.6g⁶ Nov 4] strong gelding: useful handicapper: won at Lingfield in February and Wolverhampton (beat Tender The Great by a length) in October: best at 7f/1m: acts on polytrack and firm going: usually held up, and has good turn of foot. *D. Shaw*   **95**

GALLAS (IRE) 6 b.g. Charnwood Forest (IRE) 125 – Nellie's Away (IRE) 72 (Magical Strike (USA) 114) [2007 55: p12.2g⁴ p12.2g³ p12.2g² Jan 21] sturdy gelding: modest maiden: stays easy 1½m: acts on all-weather and good to firm going: usually visored/blinkered: has looked tricky ride. *S. Lycett*   **57**

GALLEGO 5 br.g. Danzero (AUS) – Shafir (IRE) 68 (Shaadi (USA) 126) [2007 70, a61: 10g⁴ 10.5m⁶ 10.2g⁵ 10m⁶ 10.5s⁵ p12g³ 10d² 10d² 8m* 10.5g⁴ 8m⁵ 10m² 12d 10.2m* 12d 10g 10g Nov 7] strong, close-coupled gelding: fair handicapper on turf, modest on all-weather: won at Salisbury (ladies event) in August and Bath in October: effective at   **74 a60**

1m to easy 1½m: acts on polytrack, firm and good to soft going: tried blinkered/visored: often slowly away: held up: tough. *R. J. Price*

GALLERY GIRL (IRE) 4 ch.f. Namid 128 – September Tide (IRE) 58 (Thatching 131) [2007 99: 5m 6g² 6m³ 5m* 5d² 5d 5.6m 5g 5m p5.1g⁴ Oct 2] big, good sort: fairly useful handicapper: dead-heated with Garstang at Ayr in June: good ¾-length second to Fullandby at same course next time: below form after: effective at 5f to 6.5f: acts on polytrack, firm and good to soft going. *T. D. Easterby* **92**

GALLEY LAW 7 ch.g. Most Welcome 131 – Miss Blitz 83 (Formidable (USA) 125) [2007 58: p12.2g f11g p8g Mar 21] sturdy gelding: modest performer at best: little form in 2007. *W. M. Brisbourne* **–**

GALLEY SLAVE (IRE) 2 b.g. (Mar 20) Spartacus (IRE) 107 – Cimeterre (IRE) 49 (Arazi (USA) 135) [2007 5s⁴ 6s 6s 6d⁶ 6s 7m 7m 7g 7.5m 7g 6d 7d p7.1g³ f5d⁶ f7d f5g² Dec 27] workmanlike gelding: modest maiden: claimed from Mrs P. Sly £6,000 fourth start: stays 7f: acts on all-weather and good to firm going: inconsistent. *M. C. Chapman* **63 §**

GALLIC CHARM (IRE) 2 b.f. (Feb 28) Key of Luck (USA) 126 – Kimash (IRE) (Woodman (USA) 126) [2007 p7g⁶ p8m Dec 10] 11,000Y: third foal: dam, ran twice in Ireland, half-sister to useful Irish 7f to 9f winner Definate Spectacle: better effort in maidens (modest form) when sixth of 11 to Dhhamaan, late headway from rear: eased after saddle slipped next time: should stay 1m: remains open to improvement. *D. R. C. Elsworth* **57 p**

GALLILEO FIGARO (USA) 4 b.f. Galileo (IRE) 134 – Temperence Gift (USA) (Kingmambo (USA) 125) [2007 74: 16.1m* 14.8d 16.2v* 18s* 18d⁶ Oct 13] sturdy filly: fairly useful handicapper: won at Newcastle in June and Beverley and York in July: stays 2¼m: unraced on firm going, acts on any other and polytrack: won over hurdles in October. *N. B. King* **81**

GALLOISE (IRE) 3 b.f. Val Royal (FR) 127 – Spring Daffodil 97 (Pharly (FR) 130) [2007 –: 10m 10.2g Jul 9] tall, leggy filly: easily best effort in maidens when eighth of 10 to Wise Little Girl at Lingfield on reappearance. *C. G. Cox* **–**

GALLOWS HILL (USA) 3 b.g. Stravinsky (USA) 133 – Verinha (BRZ) (Baronius (BRZ)) [2007 –: p7.1g 8g 7.9m 7.1s 8m³ 8.5g p9.5g Oct 6] sturdy gelding: modest maiden: stays 1m: acts on good to firm ground: visored/blinkered last 3 outings. *R. A. Fahey* **56**

GALWAY GIRL (IRE) 3 b.f. Namid 128 – Cherry Falls (IRE) 81 (Ali-Royal (IRE) 127) [2007 –: 8g 8m 7g Jul 27] tall filly: modest maiden: probably stays 1m: tried blinkered. *T. D. Easterby* **55**

GALWAY NELLIE (IRE) 9 ch.g. Karaar 74 – Mother Nellie (USA) (Al Nasr (FR) 126) [2007 p6g Feb 17] last of 7 in maiden at Lingfield on debut. *Luke Comer, Ireland* **–**

GAMBLING JACK 2 b.g. (Feb 19) First Trump 118 – Star of Flanders (Puissance 110) [2007 5m May 22] tall, lengthy gelding: 100/1, seventh in maiden at Leicester. *A. W. Carroll* **58**

GAME LAD 5 b.g. Mind Games 121 – Catch Me 75 (Rudimentary (USA) 118) [2007 100: 7m 7g 8f 7g 7v* 7s⁵ 7g Jul 28] big, lengthy gelding: useful handicapper: won at Newcastle (by 3½ lengths from Mezuzah) in June: below form both starts after: stays 1m: acts on any turf going. *T. D. Easterby* **99**

GAME LADY 3 b.f. Mind Games 121 – Highland Gait 63 (Most Welcome 131) [2007 67: 5.1g⁵ p6g* 5.7d 5m⁵ 6s³ 5.1s³ 6d p6g Nov 10] small, sparely-made filly: fair handicapper: won at Wolverhampton in May: possibly amiss final outing: stays 6f: acts on polytrack, soft and good to firm going: often makes running. *I. A. Wood* **70**

GAME PARK (USA) 2 ch.g. (Mar 20) Elusive Quality (USA) – Carefree Cheetah (USA) 66 (Trempolino (USA) 135) [2007 6d⁵ 6d⁵ p7g⁵ Oct 17] 50,000 2-y-o: big, useful-looking gelding: fourth foal: half-brother to US 8.5f (including at 2 yrs) winner Warrior Girl (by War Chant) and US 8.5f winner Screaming Shamal (by Tabasco Cat): dam, maiden (stayed 1¼m), sister to very smart sprinter/miler Arkadian Hero: fair form in maidens, steady progress, and gelded after final start: will stay at least 1m: type to do better in handicaps at 3 yrs. *J. R. Fanshawe* **70 p**

GAMESTERS LADY 4 br.f. Almushtarak (IRE) 122 – Tycoon Tina 61 (Tina's Pet 121) [2007 –: p12.2g² p12g p12.2g* p9.5g p12.2d⁵ p12.2d* Dec 27] sturdy filly: fair handicapper: won at Wolverhampton in November and December: stays 1½m: acts on polytrack, soft and firm going. *W. M. Brisbourne* **74**

GANACHE (IRE) 5 ch.g. Halling (USA) 133 – Granted (FR) 100 (Cadeaux Genereux 131) [2007 p8g⁵ p8.6g⁴ f8g p8g⁶ 10d p10g p11g p7g⁶ p7m⁴ p7g² p7g⁶ p7g³ Nov 14] small **65**

411

gelding: first foal: dam 1m winner who stayed 9f: modest form in bumpers: fair maiden on Flat: stays 8.6f: acts on polytrack: often races prominently. *P. R. Chamings*

GANYMEDE 6 gr.g. Daylami (IRE) 138 – Germane 100 (Distant Relative 128) [2007 **64** 70: p16g³ p16g p16g 12m⁵ p12g p12.2g p12g* 16m² p16g 16.4m Jul 12] close-coupled gelding: modest handicapper: won at Lingfield in May: stays 2m: acts on polytrack, firm and good to soft going: has worn headgear: inconsistent: sold £2,500. *Mrs L. J. Mongan*

GAP PRINCESS (IRE) 3 b.f. Noverre (USA) 125 – Safe Care (IRE) (Caerleon (USA) **71** 132) [2007 69: 5m⁵ 5m⁵ 5v⁶ 6g* 7m³ 7g⁴ p7.1g⁵ 7.2s 7g Oct 3] leggy, unfurnished filly: fair handicapper: dead-heated with Riquewihr at Thirsk in July: likely to prove best at 6f/7f: acts on polytrack and good to firm ground. *R. A. Fahey*

GARAFENA 4 b.f. Golden Snake (USA) 123 – Eclipsing (IRE) 93 (Baillamont (USA) **75 +** 124) [2007 83: p10g⁴ 10d³ p12g* Oct 24] good-bodied filly: fairly useful performer at 3 yrs, just fair in 2007: won maiden at Kempton in October: stays 1½m: acts on polytrack, unraced on extremes of going on turf: sold 18,000 gns. *Pat Eddery*

GARDASEE (GER) 5 gr.g. Dashing Blade 117 – Gladstone Street (IRE) (Waajib 121) **65** [2007 15d⁶ 12s* 10s* 10g Jul 10] big, strong gelding: fair handicapper: won ladies races at Ripon in June and Pontefract in July: stays 1½m: acts on soft ground: fairly useful hurdler. *T. P. Tate*

GARDEN PARTY 3 b.g. Green Desert (USA) 127 – Tempting Prospect 95 (Shirley **70** Heights 130) [2007 p8g 10m 8.3s⁵ p9.5m⁴ p8g⁶ Sep 29] lengthy gelding: fair maiden: gelded after third outing: stays 1¼m: blinkered (showed questionable attitude) final outing: withdrawn after getting very upset in stall prior to intended fourth outing: sold 25,000 gns, joined Jane Chapple-Hyam. *Sir Michael Stoute*

GARDES (IRE) 2 b.c. (Jan 28) Xaar 132 – Golden Honor (IRE) 105 (Hero's Honor **63** (USA)) [2007 7d⁵ p7g⁶ 6d 7d Oct 16] good-topped colt: modest maiden: will be suited by 1m: sold 4,000 gns, sent to Austria. *Jane Chapple-Hyam*

GARIBALDI (GER) 5 ch.g. Acatenango (GER) 127 – Guanhumara (Caerleon (USA) **65** 132) [2007 74: f12g⁵ f8g⁶ 11.5m⁴ 9.9g⁴ 8m 12.1g 10.1m* 9.9d 10m 10g⁴ 10g p10g p12g p11g Nov 28] rangy gelding: fair performer: won handicap at Newcastle in September: seems to stay 16.5f: acts on polytrack (probably on fibresand) and good to firm going: blinkered: tried tongue tied: inconsistent. *J. O'Reilly*

GARLAND 2 ch.f. (Apr 24) Hawk Wing (USA) 136 – Al Persian (IRE) (Persian Bold **64** 123) [2007 7m⁶ 6m Oct 4] 35,000F, 33,000 2-y-o: deep-girthed filly: half-sister to 3 winners, including Irish 1m winner Dicharachera (by Mark of Esteem) and 3-y-o Dowlleh: dam, winner in Spain at 3/4 yrs, half-sister to high-class performer up to 1½m Legal Case: modest form in mid-division in maidens at Newbury and Newmarket: will be suited by 1m. *R. Hannon*

GARLOGS 4 b.g. Hunting Lion (IRE) 115 – Fading (Pharly (FR) 130) [2007 72: f5g⁴ **66** f5g³ f5g³ f5g² f5g⁶ f5g³ p6g⁶ p5.1g⁶ May 14] close-coupled gelding: fair performer: left A. Bailey after sixth start: best at 5f: acts on all-weather, heavy and good to firm ground: tried blinkered: front runner. *R. Hollinshead*

GARNETT (IRE) 6 b.g. Desert Story (IRE) 115 – In Behind (IRE) 52 (Entitled 126) **77** [2007 p16f³ p16g² p16g⁶ 16m³ 16d* 15g⁵ Jul 12] tall gelding: fair handicapper: won at Redcar in June: suited by 2m: acts on polytrack, good to firm and good to soft going: wears headgear. *D. E. Cantillon*

GARNICA (FR) 4 gr.c. Linamix (FR) 127 – Gueridia (IRE) (Night Shift (USA)) [2007 **122** 116: 7v* 6d² 6.5m⁴ 6d* 7d Oct 6] strong, well-made colt: fourth foal: brother to useful French 10.5f/11f winner Gaimix and half-brother to 2 winners in France: dam, ran 3 times (second at up to 1m), out of very smart French performer up to 12.5f Galla Placidia: very smart performer: improved in 2007, winning Prix du Palais-Royal at Longchamp (by length from Ridaar) in May and Prix de Meautry Lucien Barriere at Deauville (best effort, beat Le Cadre Noir 1½ lengths) in August: ran respectably at Deauville in between when length second to Tiza in Prix de Ris-Orangis and 1¾ lengths fourth to Marchand d'Or in Prix Maurice de Gheest: below form in Prix de la Foret at Longchamp final start: best around 6f/7f: acts on heavy and good to firm ground: sold €410,000. *J.-C. Rouget, France*

GARRULOUS (UAE) 4 b.g. Lomitas 129 – Friendly (USA) (Lear Fan (USA) 130) **74** [2007 60: p7g p10g p10g* 11g May 10] fair form, lightly raced: won apprentice handicap at Lingfield (hung left) in April: will stay 1½m: acts on polytrack, unraced on extremes of going on turf: fair hurdler, successful in November. *G. L. Moore*

GARRYA 3 ch.c. Mark of Esteem (USA) – Sherkova (USA) (State Dinner (USA)) **–** [2007 –: 9.5f p12.2g p12.2g Nov 9] good-bodied colt: little form: left R. Verheye in Belgium and returned to Britain after reappearance. *B. P. J. Baugh*

GARSTANG 4 ch.g. Atraf 116 – Approved Quality (IRE) 66 (Persian Heights 129) **82**
[2007 80: p6g p6g f6g p6g² p6f⁵ p6g p6g³ p7g³ p6g p7g 5.1f⁶ 5m* 5d⁶ 5d⁴ 5f* 5g⁴ 5m 5g
Sep 12] rather leggy, workmanlike gelding: fairly useful handicapper: won at Ayr (dead-
heat) in June and Windsor in August: effective at 5f to easy 7f: acts on polytrack, firm and
soft ground: blinkered: signs of temperament. *Peter Grayson*

GARY'S INDIAN (IRE) 4 b.f. Indian Danehill (IRE) 124 – Martino 44 (Marju (IRE) **–**
127) [2007 –: 8.1m 8.1m p8.6g 8.1d p9.5g Sep 21] tall, leggy filly: little form: tried in
cheekpieces. *B. P. J. Baugh*

GASMANFIGHTSBACK 2 b.c. (Mar 2) Primo Valentino (IRE) 116 – Bint Baddi **73**
(FR) (Shareef Dancer (USA) 135) [2007 6g⁵ 5.1d² 5m 6.1m Aug 7] lengthy, workmanlike
colt: fair maiden: second at Bath: dead. *Evan Williams*

GASPAR VAN WITTEL (USA) 2 b.c. (Mar 4) Danehill Dancer (IRE) 117 – Akuna **102**
Bay (USA) 88 (Mr Prospector (USA)) [2007 5.1g* 6.1s* 6m 7.1m³ 6m⁶ Oct 5]
$100,000F, 120,000Y: sturdy colt: fourth foal: half-brother to 3-y-o Sugar Ray and win-
ner in Greece by King of Kings: dam, Irish 2-y-o 7f winner, out of Irish St Leger winner
Dark Lomond: useful form: won maiden in May and minor event in June, both at
Chepstow: ran well when 7 lengths third to Raven's Pass in Solario Stakes at Sandown
and 2¼ lengths sixth of 28 to Exclamation in sales race at Newmarket (did extra well
from low draw): will stay 1m: acts on soft and good to firm going. *N. A. Callaghan*

GATECRASHER 4 gr.g. Silver Patriarch (IRE) 125 – Girl At The Gate 53 (Formid- **56 d**
able (USA) 125) [2007 –: p12.2g⁵ p12g⁴ 16m p16g 15.8m p13.9g p13.9g p13.9g Dec 3]
angular gelding: modest maiden: left P. Eddery after fourth outing: stays 1½m: acts on
polytrack: tried visored/blinkered: hung left second start: unseated rider fifth outing.
G. H. Yardley

GATELAND 4 b. or br.g. Dansili 127 – Encorenous (USA) (Diesis 133) [2007 67: **–**
p12.2g Oct 27] fair maiden at 3 yrs: well beaten only start in 2007: stays easy 1¼m: acts
on polytrack. *B. J. Llewellyn*

GAUDALPIN (IRE) 5 b.m. Danetime (IRE) 121 – Lila Pedigo (IRE) 62 (Classic Sec- **–**
ret (USA) 91) [2007 53: 6g Jul 26] workmanlike mare: modest performer at 4 yrs: well
below form only start in 2007: stays 7f: acts on all-weather and soft going: tried in
cheekpieces/visor: usually tongue tied. *J. McAuley*

GAVANELLO 4 br.g. Diktat 126 – Possessive Artiste 73 (Shareef Dancer (USA) 135) **–**
[2007 –: f11g f12g 12.1d Sep 25] little form: tried tongue tied. *M. C. Chapman*

GAVARNIE BEAU (IRE) 4 b.g. Imperial Ballet (IRE) 110 – Mysticism 79 (Mystiko **73**
(USA) 124) [2007 91, a73: p7g p6g p6g⁵ 6g⁵ 6g⁶ 7g 7s⁵ p7g 5.1s⁵ 6d⁵ p7g p8g p6g Sep
26] well-made gelding: fair handicapper nowadays: stays easy 7f: acts on all-weather,
soft and good to firm going: often blinkered: virtually refused to race eighth outing.
M. Blanshard

GAVROCHE (IRE) 6 b.h. Docksider (USA) 124 – Regal Revolution 105 (Hamas **94**
(IRE) 125§) [2007 106, a97: 12g⁵ 12g 12m⁵ 13.4m Sep 1] close-coupled horse: useful
handicapper at 5 yrs, just fairly useful in 2007: barely stays 13.4f: acts on all-weather and
any turf going: visored once: sometimes slowly away: held up: joined M. Bell. *J. R. Boyle*

GAYANULA (USA) 2 b.f. (Mar 9) Yonaguska (USA) 112 – Betamillion Bock (USA) **56**
(Bet Twice (USA)) [2007 p7.1d p7.1g⁴ Dec 31] 6,500 2-y-o: half-sister to several winners
in USA: dam, US 2-y-o 1m winner, half-sister to US Grade 3 7f winner Noranc: seemingly better effort in maidens at Wolverhampton when fourth. *Miss J. A. Camacho*

GAZBOOLOU 3 b.g. Royal Applause 124 – Warning Star 104 (Warning 136) [2007 **85**
80: 7.1g* 8.3m⁶ 7g 7.5s⁵ 6.9f³ 8g⁶ p8m* p8g p7.1g² Dec 15] sturdy gelding: fairly useful
performer: won maiden at Musselburgh in April and claimer at Kempton (left K. R. Burke
£20,000) in October: effective at 7f/1m: acts on polytrack and firm ground. *David Pinder*

GEE CEFFYL BACH 3 b.f. Josr Algarhoud (IRE) 118 – Miletrian Cares (IRE) 67 **60**
(Hamas (IRE) 125§) [2007 p8g p8g p7g³ f12g⁵ 8.1m⁴ 7d⁴ 8d⁵ 8.3g⁴ 7s p8.6g⁶ p8g Dec 5]
fourth foal: half-sister to fairly useful 1m/1¼m winner Arry Dash (by Fraam): dam sprint
maiden: modest performer: won claimer at Salisbury (claimed from M. Channon) in
May: left John Harris after next outing: stays 1m: acts on polytrack, good to firm and
good to soft ground: has raced freely. *R. C. Guest*

GEE DEE NEN 4 b.g. Mister Baileys 123 – Special Beat 65 (Bustino 136) [2007 90: **94**
p13g³ 16g² 16m* 16g⁴ 16.1v 14.8m⁵ 15.9m* 16d³ 18d 14g* Nov 9] close-coupled, good-
topped gelding: fairly useful handicapper: won at Thirsk (by 5 lengths) in May, Chester
in September and Musselburgh (beat Double Banded by neck) in November: stays 2m:
acts on soft and good to firm going: visored once at 3 yrs: consistent. *M. H. Tompkins*

GEESTRING (IRE) 2 b.f. (Mar 9) Diktat 126 – Change of Heart (IRE) 59 (Revoque **75**
(IRE) 122) [2007 6g⁵ 6s* 6s⁴ 6.5m 7m⁴ Oct 6] 16,000Y: big, lengthy, good-topped filly:
first foal: dam, maiden (stayed 7f), half-sister to useful sprinter Fast Heart: fair performer:
awarded maiden at Newbury (short-head second to Edge of Gold, hampered close home)
in June: fourth in sales race and nursery, both at Newmarket: stays 7f: acts on soft and
good to firm going. *R. Hannon*

GEEZERS COLOURS 2 b.c. (Mar 31) Fraam 114 – Konica 57 (Desert King (IRE) **83**
129) [2007 6d⁵ 7m⁴ 7g⁵ p6g² p7.1g p7g* p7g* p6g² p7.1g* Dec 26] 2,800F, 6,500Y:
compact colt: second foal: dam, maiden (should have stayed 1¼m), half-sister to useful
performers around 7f Abeyr and Boojum: fairly useful performer: progressed to win
nursery and claimer at Lingfield in November and 4-runner minor event at Wolverhampton following month: stays 1m: acts on polytrack: often races prominently. *K. R. Burke*

GEM BIEN (USA) 9 b.g. Bien Bien (USA) 125 – Eastern Gem (USA) (Jade Hunter –
(USA)) [2007 –, a61: f8g p8g f8g⁴ f7g p7.1g² p8.6g p8.6g f8g⁵ p9.5g f7g Jun 5] rather **a54**
leggy gelding: modest performer: effective at 7f to 1¼m: acts on all-weather, soft and
good to firm ground: wears headgear: sometimes slowly away: none too genuine.
D. W. Chapman

GEMOLOGY (USA) 3 b.c. Horse Chestnut (SAF) 119 – Miners Girl (USA) (Miner's **79**
Mark (USA) 120) [2007 90p: 7.5g³ p8.6g² p7.1g Sep 28] fair maiden: stays 8.6f: acts on
polytrack and soft ground: sold 21,000 gns, and sent to USA. *Saeed bin Suroor*

GEMSTONE LASS (FR) 3 b.f. Peintre Celebre (USA) 137 – Mutual Consent (IRE) –
107 (Reference Point 139) [2007 10m Jun 14] €55,000Y: compact filly: sixth foal:
half-sister to 1¼m/1½m winner Prenup (by Diesis): dam French 1m (at 2 yrs) and 1¼m
winner: 50/1 and green, always behind in maiden at Newbury: sold 2,000 gns in
November. *Pat Eddery*

GENARI 4 b.g. Generous (IRE) 139 – Sari 83 (Faustus (USA) 118) [2007 93d: 8.1g⁵ **81**
f8g* 8g⁵ 8.1m p8g 8m Aug 17] big, good-topped gelding: fairly useful handicapper: won **a87**
at Southwell in May: below form last 3 starts: effective at 1m to 11f: acts on fibresand,
firm and good to soft ground: tried blinkered/tongue tied: races prominently: has joined
C. P. Morlock. *P. F. I. Cole*

GENERAL BLUCHER (IRE) 2 br.g. (Mar 12) Marju (IRE) 127 – Restiv Star (FR) **75 p**
108 (Soviet Star (USA) 128) [2007 p7g³ Dec 19] €62,000Y: sixth foal: half-brother to
winner abroad by Linamix: dam, French 1¼m winner, out of smart French 1¼m performer Restiver: 12/1, close third to Parisian Gift in maiden at Lingfield, leading briefly over
1f out: will do better. *P. W. Chapple-Hyam*

GENERAL ELIOTT (IRE) 2 b.c. (Apr 8) Rock of Gibraltar (IRE) 133 – Marlene-D **87 p**
57 (Selkirk (USA) 129) [2007 8d* Oct 19] big, rather leggy, close-coupled colt: fifth foal:
half-brother to 2004 2-y-o 6f/7f winner Shanghai Lily (by King's Best) and 6-y-o Eden
Rock, both useful: dam, Irish 9f winner, half-sister to smart stayer Arden: 6/1 and in fine
shape, won maiden at Newmarket by neck from Sortita, making all: will probably stay
1¼m: open to improvement. *P. F. I. Cole*

GENERAL FEELING (IRE) 6 b.g. General Monash (USA) 107 – Kamadara (IRE) **60**
(Kahyasi 130) [2007 80d: p6g p6g⁶ p7g⁴ p8.6g³ p7.1g⁵ 7d⁶ 8s⁶ 7.1m³ 7m 7m⁴ 6.9g² p7.1g
8g p8.6g³ p8.6g² Nov 2] good-bodied gelding: modest handicapper nowadays: left
M. Mullineaux after fifth start, claimed from K. R. Burke £6,000 after eighth: effective at
6f to 8.6f: acts on polytrack, firm and soft going: tried blinkered/in cheekpieces: often
tongue tied: sometimes slowly away: held up. *S. T. Mason*

GENERAL FLUMPA 6 b.g. Vettori (IRE) 119 – Macca Luna (IRE) 78 (Kahyasi 130) **67**
[2007 65: 10.9m⁴ 10m⁶ 14.1m 11.8m⁴ 11.8s⁵ 10.1d³ 12s 11.5d* 10.1g³ 12.1m 10g⁴ 11.5g
9.9d 10.9g⁶ Oct 2] close-coupled gelding: fair handicapper: won apprentice event at
Yarmouth (by 8 lengths) in July: effective at 1¼m/1½m: acts on all-weather, soft and
good to firm going: sometimes slowly away. *Miss Tor Sturgis*

GENERAL KNOWLEDGE (USA) 4 ch.g. Diesis 133 – Reams of Verse (USA) 121 **87 d**
(Nureyev (USA) 131) [2007 p8g p10g⁶ p12g p12g 8.3f 8.1g² 9.7m* 8g 8.1g 9.7m p10m⁶
p8.6g p8g* p8g Nov 14] rather leggy gelding: useful form at 3 yrs for A. Fabre in France
(sold 32,000 gns), fairly useful at best in 2007: won handicap at Folkestone in May
and claimer at Kempton in November: should prove best at 1m/1¼m: acts on polytrack,
good to firm and good to soft going: tongue tied: races prominently: sold 10,000 gns.
B. G. Powell

GENERAL TING (IRE) 2 b.c. (Apr 28) Daylami (IRE) 138 – Luana 101 (Shaadi **57 p**
(USA) 126) [2007 p7g p7.1g p6g⁵ Oct 6] 86,000Y: brother to 4-y-o King's Ransom and

half-brother to 3 winners, including 5-y-o Hattan: dam, 6f winner, half-sister to Luso, Needle Gun, Warrsan and Cloud Castle: green and showed modest form in maidens (all on polytrack within 3 weeks): likely to prove a different proposition in middle-distance handicaps. *Sir Mark Prescott*

GENERAL TUFTO 2 b.g. (Mar 28) Fantastic Light (USA) 134 – Miss Pinkerton 104 **67 p**
(Danehill (USA) 126) [2007 8m 8m⁶ 8.2d⁵ Oct 10] sturdy gelding: second foal: dam, 6f (at 2 yrs) and 1m winner, out of Coronation Stakes winner Rebecca Sharp: fair form in maidens, fifth to Tajaaweed at Nottingham (gelded after): will stay 1¼m: capable of better. *R. Charlton*

GENERATOR 5 ch.g. Cadeaux Genereux 131 – Billie Blue 63 (Ballad Rock 122) **77**
[2007 71: p7g* Feb 25] fair performer, lightly raced: won handicap at Kempton (hung badly left) in February: stays easy 1m: acts on all-weather. *Dr J. D. Scargill*

GENEROUS BOY 2 b.g. (Mar 26) Fantastic Light (USA) 134 – Supersonic 80 **57**
(Shirley Heights 130) [2007 7.5g 10m 7g Nov 6] 11,000Y: strong gelding: fourth foal: half-brother to 1½m seller winner Whirling (by Groom Dancer): dam, maiden (stayed 10.5f), sister to useful 2m winner Upper Strata: modest maiden: bred to be suited by 1¼m/1½m. *T. D. Easterby*

GENEROUS JEM 4 b.f. Generous (IRE) 139 – Top Jem 85 (Damister (USA) 123) **91**
[2007 62: p12g³ 11.5m² 14.1d 12m³ 12g* 14f* 12m* 12m² 12d⁶ Sep 28] leggy filly: fairly useful handicapper: won at Newbury in August and York and Thirsk within 4 days in September: ran well last 2 starts, sixth to Brisk Breeze in listed race at Ascot on latter: stays 1¾m: acts on polytrack, soft and firm ground: patiently ridden. *G. G. Margarson*

GENEROUS LAD (IRE) 4 b.g. Generous (IRE) 139 – Tudor Loom (Sallust 134) **81**
[2007 74: p12g⁴ p10g³ p10g³ p9.5g³ p10g³ p12g³ 10g² 10.2g³ 10.2g² 11.9d⁶ 12m² 11.9f² p12g* p13g⁴ p12m⁴ p12.2g³ Dec 14] leggy gelding: fairly useful handicapper: won at Lingfield in November: stays 13f: acts on polytrack and firm going: usually wears cheekpieces: effective ridden prominently or held up: consistent. *A. B. Haynes*

GENEROUS THOUGHT 2 b.c. (Apr 26) Cadeaux Genereux 131 – Rosie's Posy **92 p**
(IRE) 86 (Suave Dancer (USA) 136) [2007 6m⁵ 6m³ 6f* 6m* Nov 10] 28,000Y, 95,000 2-y-o: strong, lengthy colt: second foal: dam, 2-y-o 5.7f winner, half-sister to high-class sprinter Tante Rose out of smart performer up to 1m My Branch: fairly useful form: progressed well, won maiden at Pontefract in September and nursery at Doncaster (quickened well from rear) in November: will stay 7f: acts on firm going: tends to drift left: has scope to make an even better 3-y-o. *P. Howling*

GENETHNI 2 b.f. (Feb 21) Primo Valentino (IRE) 116 – Mujadilly 43 (Mujadil (USA) **68**
119) [2007 5m* 6g* p6g⁶ p5.1g³ p6g a6.5g a7.5g³ Dec 28] second foal: half-sister to 4-y-o Guto: dam, maiden best at 7f, half-sister to useful 5f winner Sabre Rattler: fair performer: won seller at Catterick in July and claimer at Hamilton in September: sold from K. Ryan 4,500 gns after fifth start: third in claimer at Deauville final outing: stays 7.5f: acts on all-weather and good to firm going: has hung right. *C. von der Recke, Germany*

GENKI (IRE) 3 ch.g. Shinko Forest (IRE) – Emma's Star (ITY) (Darshaan 133) [2007 **109**
79p: 6g* 6g² 6m* 6d² 6m* 6m² 6d* Sep 28] strong, good-topped gelding: useful performer, progressive: won maiden at Folkestone in April and handicaps at Newmarket in May and Ascot in August (by 2 lengths from Lipocco) and September (beat Sohraab

Coral Sprint (Handicap), Newmarket—the second of Genki's four victories is a very narrow one; Lipocco (striped cap) is still just ahead of him at this point

by short head): should stay 7f: acts on good to firm and good to soft going: tends to get on toes. *R. Charlton*

GENOA STAR 4 b.f. Woodborough (USA) 112 – Naval Dispatch (Slip Anchor 136) [2007 45§: 10m p8.6g f11d⁵ Dec 15] poor maiden at best: well held in 2007: usually wears headgear: temperamental. *D. J. Murphy*   **– §**

GENTLE GURU 3 b.f. Ishiguru (USA) 114 – Soft Touch (IRE) 78 (Petorius 117) [2007 81+: 5g² 6v² 5m* 5g⁶ 7g 7.1m³ Sep 13] good-topped filly: fairly useful handicapper: won at Sandown in July: effective at 5f to 7f: acts on heavy and good to firm going (unraced on firm): versatile regarding tactics. *R. T. Phillips*   **87**

GENTLEMAN'S DEAL (IRE) 6 b.h. Danehill (USA) 126 – Sleepytime (IRE) 121 (Royal Academy (USA) 130) [2007 95, a112: f8g* p8g* p10g* 8s 8d p10m² p10g* Dec 22] big, strong, good-topped horse: has an unimpressive, quick action: smart on all-weather, little form on turf in 2007: winner of 8 of his 9 starts on all-weather, including handicap at Southwell in January, listed race at Kempton in February, Betdirect Winter Derby at Lingfield (beat Grand Passion by neck) in March and, having again been at stud, listed race at Lingfield (beat Grand Passion again, by short head) in December: effective at 1m/1¼m: acts on all-weather, raced only on good ground or softer on turf: has had forelegs heavily bandaged: a credit to connections: standing at Norton Grove Stud, North Yorkshire, fee £1,200, Oct 1st. *M. W. Easterby*   **– a114**

GEOFFDAW 2 b.g. (Feb 5) Vettori (IRE) 119 – Talighta (USA) 62 (Barathea (IRE) 127) [2007 f5g² 5m* p7.1g p7g p6g* 6m 6m Oct 5] rather leggy gelding: fair performer: won maiden at Folkestone in April and nursery at Lingfield in September: best at 5f/6f: acts on all-weather and good to firm going. *M. J. Wallace*   **76**

GEOJIMALI 5 ch.g. Compton Place 125 – Harrken Heights (IRE) (Belmez (USA) 131) [2007 91: 5g* 6m 6s 5g 6d 5s⁶ 6d⁵ 6m⁶ 5.6m² 6d⁶ 6d p7.1g 7m⁴ Nov 10] heavy-topped gelding: fairly useful handicapper: won at Musselburgh in April: good second at Doncaster ninth outing: mainly respectable efforts after: effective at 5f to 7f: acts on polytrack, firm and soft going: hard ride, usually gets behind. *J. S. Goldie*   **89**

GEORDIE DANCER (IRE) 5 b.g. Dansili 127 – Awtaar (USA) 67 (Lyphard (USA) 132) [2007 –§: 6m 6g Sep 3] good-bodied gelding: inconsistent performer. *A. Berry*   **– §**

GEORDIE GIRL 2 b.f. (Apr 1) Tobougg (IRE) 125 – Chiltern Court (USA) (Topsider (USA)) [2007 5f² 6s 6m 6g 7m³ 7d* 7g p7g Nov 4] 8,000Y: small, sturdy filly: half-sister to 1m winner Circlet (by Lion Cavern): dam unraced out of sister to Thatch and Special, latter dam of Nureyev and grandam of Sadler's Wells: fair performer: won nursery at Catterick (dominated) in October, standout effort: stays 7f: acts on firm and good to soft going. *R. C. Guest*   **69**

GEORDIELAND (FR) 6 gr.h. Johann Quatz (FR) 120 – Aerdee (FR) (Highest Honor (FR) 124) [2007 119: p12g² 14.1g⁵ 14g² 20g² 16g⁵ 18m² 18m² Oct 8] strong, close-coupled horse: smart performer: as good as ever in 2007, runner-up in Yorkshire Cup (beaten ¾ length by Sergeant Cecil) at York, Gold Cup at Royal Ascot (best effort, beaten 1½ lengths by Yeats) and Doncaster Cup (5 lengths behind Septimus): 4/1 on, well below form when second to Love Brothers in minor event at Pontefract final outing (reportedly finished distressed): stays 2½m: acts on any turf going: blinkered second 5-y-o outing: reportedly bled when well below form in Melbourne Cup final 5-y-o start: usually held up: travels strongly, but finds little. *J. A. Osborne*   **119 §**

GEORDIE'S POOL 3 b.c. Dilshaan 119 – Last Result (Northern Park (USA) 107) [2007 61: p7g³ p10g p8g p9.5g⁵ p12g³ p12.2g⁵ 12.4d p12g⁶ Oct 24] fair maiden: stays 1½m: raced mainly on polytrack: tried in cheekpieces: sold 8,000 gns, sent to Belgium. *J. W. Hills*   **66**

GEORGE'S FLYER (IRE) 4 b.g. Daggers Drawn (USA) 114 – Winged Victory (IRE) 93 (Dancing Brave (USA) 140) [2007 61, a70: p8.6g 8s p8.6g⁴ p8m p9.5g p8.6g p8.6g Nov 30] sturdy gelding: modest performer nowadays: stays 9.5f: acts on all-weather and good to firm going: blinkered/visored. *R. A. Fahey*   **59**

GEORGES PRIDE 3 b.c. Averti (IRE) 117 – Thaw 74 (Cadeaux Genereux 131) [2007 –: 5.1f 5.1f⁶ 5.1g 6.1s Jun 15] modest form: tried tongue tied/blinkered. *J. M. Bradley*   **50**

GEORGE THE BEST (IRE) 6 b.g. Imperial Ballet (IRE) 110 – En Retard (IRE) 97 (Petardia 113) [2007 71§, a–§: 5g 5.9g 6d 6d⁴ 5.9g 5d⁵ 5.1g² Nov 7] workmanlike gelding: modest handicapper: stays 7f: acts on heavy going, little form on all-weather: tried visored: sometimes slowly away: ungenuine. *Micky Hammond*   **63 §**

Betdirect Winter Derby, Lingfield—one of the highlights of the all-weather season; Gentleman's Deal (right), better than ever at the age of six, wins narrowly from Grand Passion (left) and Illustrious Blue

GEORGE THE SECOND 4 b.c. Josr Algarhoud (IRE) 118 – Pink Champagne **73** (Cosmonaut) [2007 71: p6g* p6g² p6g⁶ p6g⁴ 6s 6g³ 6s p5g* p6g² p5g² 5.1s³ 5g 6d p6g **a82** p6g² p5g⁴ p5g p6g p6m⁶ Dec 7] leggy colt: fairly useful handicapper on all-weather, fair on turf: won at Lingfield in January and July: stays 7f, but seems best at 5f/6f: acts on all-weather, soft and good to firm going: tried tongue tied: usually races prominently. *Mrs H. Sweeting*

GEORGE WASHINGTON (IRE) 4 b.c. Danehill (USA) 126 – Bordighera **124** (USA) 104 (Alysheba (USA)) [2007 133: 8m⁴ 10g³ 8g³ a10s Oct 27]
The dramatic resumption of George Washington's racing career, after he was replaced at Coolmore by the year-younger Holy Roman Emperor in early-spring, must have left Ballydoyle with something of a predicament. Bringing a stallion back to racing presents problems in itself—though it had been done successfully before—but what would be the specific aim if George Washington returned to the form that had made him Horse of the Year in 2006? The Ballydoyle/Coolmore operation is about building the reputations of its racehorses with the aim of standing the successful ones at stud. George Washington had had his chance at stud, albeit an abbreviated one reportedly getting only a handful of mares in foal, and his long-term future as a stallion looked bleak (though there was some talk of giving him another chance). Aidan O'Brien at first intimated that there would be nothing to lose from campaigning George Washington in 'all the top races regardless of the strength of the opposition.' But, if the opposition included other potential top stallion prospects from the Ballydoyle yard, would the presence of a top-form George Washington best serve the wider interests of Coolmore? In the event, George Washington's programme comprised four Group 1 events in which he did not meet any of his leading stablemates, and he missed at least two others which looked tailor-made for him, the Sussex Stakes and the Queen Elizabeth II Stakes, for both of which Ballydoyle's leading three-year-old miler Excellent Art started favourite. The Tattersalls Gold Cup at the Curragh, the International at York and the Irish Champion at Leopardstown were all mentioned as targets for George Washington at one stage or another, but Dylan Thomas ended up being the principal Ballydoyle representative in all three.

417

Given George Washington's wayward tendencies as a racehorse, and the fact that Aidan O'Brien and his team had so expertly managed his temperamental streak, there was never much chance of his going back into training anywhere but Ballydoyle (the States might have been an alternative otherwise). George Washington reportedly didn't, at first, take to being back at Ballydoyle—'he was like a horse with five legs,' according to his trainer—and he needed plenty of coaxing. He couldn't be made ready in time for the Tattersalls Gold Cup and reappeared in the Queen Anne Stakes on the opening day of Royal Ascot. Starting at odds on and handling the preliminaries well (though not fully settled on the way to post), George Washington couldn't quite emulate the 1978 Queen Anne winner Radetzky, who made a successful comeback at 25/1 after a brief, initial spell at stud (brief, in his case, because he failed to attract sufficient interest from breeders). George Washington refused to settle in a muddling Queen Anne and then got going too late, coming fourth in a finish of two short heads and a head behind Ramonti, Jeremy and Turtle Bowl. Although 10 lb or so below the form he had shown at three, when putting up top-class performances in the Two Thousand Guineas and the Queen Elizabeth II Stakes, George Washington shaped as if he was going to be very much the one to beat in the top mile races, allowing for some understandable rustiness. Unfortunately, he didn't fulfil expectations.

George Washington's declaration for the Coral-Eclipse over a mile and a quarter at Sandown in early-July took most punters by surprise after the prospect of softish ground seemed likely to rule him out. Odds in double figures were available ante post on Betfair at one time and other bookmakers reported George Washington as 'friendless'. The fact that he eventually took on the Derby winner Authorized —who started at odds on—was a boost for the sponsors and the racecourse, but the riders of both Authorized and George Washington were outmanoeuvred in the race by Ryan Moore on Notnowcato who made first run on them, switching Notnowcato to race alone on the stand side. Relaxed until going to post, when he proved something of a handful, George Washington looked reluctant in the closing stages, held by Authorized after seemingly travelling the better as the pair moved up to challenge. The distances were a length and a half and a head, George Washington coming out best of a four-strong challenge from Ballydoyle made up of the three-year-olds Yellowstone, Admiralofthefleet and Archipenko, who had all had their limitations exposed in the Derby.

It was thought that George Washington would take part in a rematch with Notnowcato and Authorized in the International at York but, again, Ballydoyle kept its cards close to its chest until it had to show its hand. George Washington was sent instead for the Prix du Moulin at Longchamp in early-September. His rider Kieren Fallon came in for plenty of criticism as George Washington finished strongly into third behind Darjina and Ramonti, after being somewhat trapped in on the home turn and then taking time to get on an even keel as he tended to hang when first asked for his effort. It was widely assumed afterwards that 'Gorgeous George' would, after all, attempt a repeat in Europe's top event at a mile, the Queen Elizabeth II Stakes at Ascot. He was put in as the ante-post favourite for the race but, once more, the first indications that he might not run came when his odds drifted on Betfair, the exchange suspending the market and other bookmakers again following suit. There was no announcement from Ballydoyle for several hours, until a short communication that George Washington was 'unlikely' to run. Ballydoyle reiterated that it had never said George Washington was a definite runner. Ladbrokes, regarded as having its ear to the ground at Ballydoyle, had, perhaps significantly, not priced up the Queen Elizabeth in the week before the race. Gleaning information about stable running plans from the activities of 'in-the-know' bookmakers should be outdated. Ballydoyle tends to deliberate longer than most stables over its plans—and, with most of its horses owned in partnership, it has more owners to consult—but, once plans are finalised, it could perhaps take a leaf out of Godolphin's book. Godolphin's up-to-the-minute website keeps everyone abreast of running plans and its openness brings clear public relations benefits.

The strong, good-topped George Washington, who had an easy action, made his final appearance in a mudbath on the dirt at the Breeders' Cup meeting at Monmouth Park in late-October, tackling the Breeders' Cup Classic (Excellent Art represented Ballydoyle in the Breeders' Cup Mile) for the second time. He was well behind when breaking down in the home straight, suffering severe injuries to his off-fore which necessitated his being put down. George Washington was the second horse from Ballydoyle to lose his life at the Breeders' Cup, following Landseer in the Breeders' Cup Mile in 2002. George Washington made the highest price of his year—1,150,000 guineas—when sent up to the Tattersalls October Yearling Sales and he won four of his five races as a two-year-old, including the National Stakes at the Curragh. His breeders Roy and Gretchen Jackson also bred Barbaro, who won the Kentucky Derby in their colours by six and a half lengths on the same day George Washington won the Two Thousand Guineas. Barbaro is also now dead, a major story which made the front page of the *New York Times* when he had to be put down because of complications in an eight-month battle to save him after he broke a hind leg in the Preakness Stakes, when attempting to follow up his Kentucky Derby victory. Injuries to horses racing on dirt in North America are more common-place than ideally they should be and some tracks are changing to synthetic surfaces, or are in the process of doing so (2008 Breeders' Cup venue Santa Anita is now cushion track). A shortage of horses able to stand racing on the unforgiving dirt surfaces in the 'seventies was at the root of American racing's acceptance of the use of drugs, but the introduction of more resilient artificial surfaces will, hopefully, make that argument redundant. America's permissive policy undoubtedly detracts from the Breeders' Cup's status and makes it very hard for it to live up to its billing as the 'World Championships'.

	Danehill (USA) (b 1986)	Danzig (b 1977)	Northern Dancer
George Washington (IRE) (b.c. 2003)			Pas de Nom
		Razyana (b 1981)	His Majesty
			Spring Adieu
	Bordighera (USA) (ch 1992)	Alysheba (b 1984)	Alydar
			Bel Sheba
		Blue Tip (b 1982)	Tip Moss
			As Blue

A growing mistrust of American horses on the track, at stud and in the sale-ring has created a mood for change, with some leading American breeders vociferous in their condemnation of traditional American thinking on drugs, including furosemide and bute which can effectively be given to any runner nowadays in those states which permit it. Bute is not permitted in New Jersey, which has jurisdiction over Monmouth Park, but all bar three of the one hundred and seventeen runners in the eleven championship Breeders' Cup races ran on furosemide—ostensibly permitted only for 'confirmed bleeders'—with the only exceptions British-trained Passage of Time and Jeremy, and Irish-trained Timarwa, whose connections laudably shunned its use. The chairman of America's Jockey Club, Ogden Mills Phipps, assured its annual Round Table conference that 'there will be no higher priority for the Jockey Club than finding a comprehensive solution to this chronic medication dilemma.' The principal concern at present is with stamping out illegal drugs—leading trainer Patrick Biancone was suspended for a year in October for a variety of offences including possession of snake venom—but, hopefully, this could lead, in time, to America's rules coming into line with those of the other major racing countries where drugs like bute and furosemide are banned. But it will be a very long wait. There are thirty-eight different racing jurisdictions in North America and it will be far from easy for the Jockey Club to persuade—it has no power of enforcement—individual states to take action against illegal drugs, never mind standardise and then reform the use of permitted ones. Trainers with repeated medication-related violations continue to figure prominently in American racing which must cause concern for the sport's integrity. The Jockey Club has suggested making owners more accountable—possibly by imposing suspensions on horses found to have been drugged—in the hope that more will switch from trainers convicted of drug offences. It would be a start.
A. P. O'Brien, Ireland

GEORGIE THE FOURTH (IRE) 2 b.f. (Feb 12) Cadeaux Genereux 131 – Septembers Hawk (IRE) (Machiavellian (USA) 123) [2007 p7g^2 Jul 4] tall, rather unfurnished filly: first foal: dam unraced daughter of Nell Gwyn winner Reunion: 14/1, green but finished strongly when second to Kay Es Jay in maiden at Kempton (reportedly chipped a knee after). *E. J. O'Neill* **79**

GERTIE (IRE) 3 b.f. Redback 116 – Rosalia (USA) 66 (Red Ransom (USA)) [2007 –: **48**
p7.1g p8g⁶ p8g⁶ p8.6g⁵ p10g⁵ p12g⁵ 10.9s³ p12g Aug 28] poor maiden: probably stays
1½m: raced only on polytrack/soft going. *E. J. Creighton*

GETAWAY (GER) 4 b.c. Monsun (GER) 124 – Guernica (Unfuwain (USA) 131) **124**
[2007 112: 15d* 15.5m² 12g⁴ Oct 7]
   Tendon injuries to both Rail Link, winner of the Prix de l'Arc de Triomphe,
and Visindar, a close fifth when a short-priced favourite for the Derby, ultimately
denied a couple of Andre Fabre's best three-year-old colts of 2006 further opportunities for success at four. Visindar was retired after being beaten in a minor event
at Longchamp on his return in May, while Rail Link failed to reappear at all, having
made only slow progress from an earlier setback when needing to have a chip
removed from a joint following his Arc victory. Both colts have been retired to stud,
Rail Link in Britain under his owner's Juddmonte banner and Visindar in Spain.
Their stable-companion Getaway made less of a name for himself as a three-year-
old, but he made excellent progress away from the limelight in a campaign which
culminated in his contesting the top French races for three-year-old stayers.
Narrowly beaten first time out, he went on to win his next four races, stepped up
first to a mile and a quarter and then to fifteen furlongs, making a particularly good
impression at the latter trip in winning a listed race at Deauville and the Prix de
Lutece at Longchamp. Although his three-year-old season ended with a surprise
defeat in the Prix Chaudenay at the Arc meeting, Getaway had done enough to
suggest his prospects at four might be as bright as his then better-known stable-
companions.
   It was, however, well into August before Getaway made his reappearance,
but he could not have returned at a better time so far as his stable's form was
concerned. The yard had hit a purple patch at Deauville and, when Getaway made a
winning return from more than ten months off in the Darley Prix Kergorlay, he was
the last of Andre Fabre's eight pattern winners at the month-long meeting. There
were also four listed wins among a total of twenty-one winners for the stable at
Deauville, with the highlight being Manduro's success in the Prix Jacques le Marois
for Getaway's owner Baron von Ullmann. Only around a length covered the first
five home in the Prix Kergorlay, but Getaway won a shade comfortably after taking
the lead from the odds-on Lord du Sud in the final furlong, having half a length to
spare from the previous year's winner, with Ponte Tresa narrowly holding off Le
Miracle and Varevees for third. Getaway put up an even better performance in the
Prix Gladiateur at Longchamp the following month despite being beaten in a race
he should have won. Although there were only five runners, Getaway found
himself hemmed in on the rail at a crucial time in the straight and was unable to peg
back the filly Varevees once getting clear, though reducing her advantage to a neck

Darley Prix Kergorlay, Deauville—Getaway, back from a near eleven-month absence,
beats the previous year's winner Lord du Sud and the other grey Ponte Tresa

at the line conceding her 10 lb. Assuming he stayed the marathon trip, which his style of racing suggested he would, Getaway's chances of turning the tables on Varevees in the Prix du Cadran on Arc day looked good. However, events earlier in the afternoon on Arc trials day at Longchamp resulted in Getaway missing the Cadran to take his chance in the Arc.

With Manduro sustaining a career-ending injury when winning the Prix Foy, Getaway was supplemented at a cost of €60,000 to replace him in the Arc line-up. With Getaway at 50/1 on the British industry prices and at 27/1 on the pari-mutuel, Andre Fabre can rarely have had a longer-priced runner in the race, but Getaway ran an excellent race on his Group 1 debut over a trip which on available evidence looked unlikely to test his stamina sufficiently. Last of all turning into the straight, in a race which largely favoured the stayers despite conditions being nothing like so testing as those forecast, Getaway stayed on strongly down the outside in the final furlong, failing by just a short head to catch Sagara for third place and beaten little more than a length and a half by the winner Dylan Thomas. The result of the Prix du Cadran later in the afternoon, in which Le Miracle (behind Getaway in the Gladiateur as well as the Kergorlay) narrowly pipped Varevees suggests Getaway might well have missed out on a Group 1 success, but fourth in the Arc probably earned him as much kudos as if he'd won the Cadran. It will also have done his future stallion prospects no harm, and may well mean that, now proven on the fringes of top middle-distance company, his days of contesting staying races are over.

Getaway's career has been one of more or less unremitting improvement so far and, after just nine races, there's no reason to suppose that he won't progress further at five. Getaway shares his sire Monsun with Baron von Ullmann's middle-distance stars of the last couple of seasons, Shirocco and Manduro, who were both better than ever as five-year-olds, and with his old rival Le Miracle who enjoyed his second season in the top flight of stayers as a six-year-old. More about Monsun's excellent year can be found in the essay on Manduro. With the dual Gold Cup winner Royal Rebel being a half-brother to Getaway's unraced dam Guernica, there were good reasons for believing that Getaway would have stayed the trip in the Cadran. His dam has produced three other winners from a total of five foals, including two full sisters to Getaway. The smart Guadalupe won the Oaks d'Italia and finished second to Islington in the Yorkshire Oaks, while three-year-old Guardia showed useful form in listed races in Germany in the autumn. Neither raced beyond a mile and a half, but the dam's other winner Guadalajara (by Acatenango) made her debut for Godolphin as a five-year-old in the Gold Cup, finishing sixth to Yeats after being involved in scrimmaging. She had begun her career in Germany before making into a smart four-year-old in France, when an unlucky second in the Prix de Pomone. Sold out of Jean-Claude Rouget's stable for 800,000 guineas, her best efforts for Godolphin came when winning a minor event at Newmarket and finishing second in the Geoffrey Freer Stakes. The grandam Greenvera was a twice-raced daughter of the speedy French filly Greenway, the great grandam of the high-class mare Alexander Goldrun. A bit further back in this family developed by the Wertheimers is the top-class filly Gold River. Back in the era when it was possible, if rare, to contest both the Cadran (then run in May) and the Arc, she won both races as a four-year-old in 1981.

		Monsun (GER) (br 1990)	Konigsstuhl (br 1976)		Dschingis Khan Konigskronung
Getaway (GER) (b.c. 2003)			Mosella (b 1985)		Surumu Monasia
		Guernica (b 1994)	Unfuwain (b 1985)		Northern Dancer Height of Fashion
			Greenvera (ch 1989)		Riverman Greenway

Getaway is a huge colt, big, angular and heavy-topped, who could easily develop into a high-class five-year-old. His season will presumably be geared around a second attempt at the Arc, while this time he'll have the advantage of being prepared specifically for the race, something at which his trainer excels. It's likely that Getaway will always need a good test at a mile and a half to be seen to best advantage and it may not be until the Arc comes round again that he actually gets one. It will also be interesting to see if he continues to be ridden with plenty of restraint, a tactic which has served him well so far over long distances but may not be to his advantage so much over a mile and a half. Getaway acts on soft and good to firm ground and he has been taken early and/or led to post in the past. *A. Fabre, France*

GET JEALOUS (IRE) 2 ch.f. (Apr 23) Intikhab (USA) 135 – Bauci (IRE) (Desert – King (IRE) 129) [2007 6g May 24] €58,000Y: second foal: dam, unraced, out of sister to Rainbow Quest: 25/1, soon outpaced in maiden at Goodwood. *R. Hannon*

GETRAH 3 ch.g. Barathea (IRE) 127 – Sahara Shade (USA) 79 (Shadeed (USA) 135) 81 [2007 7m⁶ 8g⁵ 8s* 8.9v³ 8g² 7g 9.1v⁶ Nov 3] strong, useful-looking gelding: first foal: dam, 2-y-o 5f/6f winner, sister to smart Scandinavian sprinter Musadif and Queen Mary Stakes winner Nadwah: fairly useful performer: won maiden at Ripon in July: good placed efforts next 2 starts, leaving W. Haggas £19,000 after second occasion: stays 1m: acts on heavy going. *N. Wilson*

GHAFEER (USA) 3 b.g. War Chant (USA) 126 – Hasheema (IRE) 80 (Darshaan 133) 73 [2007 69: 8.2g 7m⁶ 7m² 7g 5s⁶ 7m² 7.1s 8m³ 7g 7g Oct 19] fair maiden: sold from D. Weld in Ireland 15,000 gns after fifth outing: stays 1m: acts on soft and good to firm going: usually in headgear: tried tongue tied: reportedly had breathing problem eighth start. *B. Ellison*

GHAILL FORCE 5 b.g. Piccolo 121 – Coir 'a' Ghaill 38 (Jalmood (USA) 126) [2007 50 p12g p13g p7g 10m⁵ 8.1m p12g⁶ Dec 16] modest maiden: stays 1½m: acts on all-weather and any turf going: tried in headgear/tongue tied: sometimes slowly away. *P. Butler*

GHETTO 2 b.c. (Mar 6) Auction House (USA) 120 – Ellway Queen (USA) 71 (Bahri 97 (USA) 125) [2007 6m⁴ 7s* 8m⁴ 8m p8m³ 8d² 8f⁴ Dec 29] 30,000Y, 66,000 2-y-o: sturdy, deep-girthed colt: second foal: brother to 3-y-o Hythe Bay: dam 1m winner: useful performer: won maiden at Newmarket in June: in frame last 3 starts, in minor events at Kempton and Newmarket (second to Kandahar Run), and, after sold from R. Hannon 145,000 gns, non-graded race at Santa Anita: shapes as if will stay 1¼m: acts on polytrack, soft and good to firm going. *C. Dollase, USA*

GHIZLAAN (USA) 2 b.f. (Mar 18) Seeking The Gold (USA) – Golden Ballet (USA) – p 122 (Moscow Ballet (USA)) [2007 8d Oct 13] $600,000Y: lengthy, angular filly: third foal: dam US 4.5f (minor 2-y-o stakes) to 8.5f (Santa Anita Oaks) winner: 4/1, no show in maiden at York: should benefit from experience. *M. Johnston*

GHOST DANCER 3 ch.c. Danehill Dancer (IRE) 117 – Reservation (IRE) 78 80 (Common Grounds 118) [2007 77: p7.1g 7.1d³ May 12] good-topped colt: fairly useful handicapper: suffered 2 minor injuries after second outing: will stay 1m: acts on polytrack, firm and good to soft going. *L. M. Cumani*

GIANT LOVE (USA) 2 ch.c. (Apr 14) Giant's Causeway (USA) 132 – Morning Dev- 85 otion (USA) 102 (Affirmed (USA)) [2007 6g 7f* 7.1g 7s Oct 14] $250,000Y, 95,000 2-y-o: tall, leggy colt: good mover: closely related to useful 2002 Irish 2-y-o 7f winner Some Kind of Tiger (by Storm Cat) and half-brother to several at least useful winners, notably top-class Oaks/Irish Derby winner Balanchine (2-y-o 7f winner, by Storm Bird): dam 2-y-o 6f winner (stayed 1½m): fairly useful performer: won maiden at York in September: similar form subsequently, seventh in minor event at Sandown and nursery at Goodwood (found little on soft ground): will stay 1¼m/1½m. *M. Johnston*

GIANT SLALOM 3 b.g. Tomba 119 – Fallara (FR) (Tropular) [2007 78p: 8g² f8g² 89 10s⁴ 10d⁴ p8.6g³ 7d³ p7.1g* p7m⁵ 7g* p8g⁵ Nov 30] tall gelding: fairly useful handicapper: won at Wolverhampton in September and Doncaster (apprentices) in October: sold from W. Haggas 26,000 gns prior to final start: best at 7f: acts on all-weather, probably on soft ground: free-going sort, often front runner. *T. G. McCourt, Ireland*

GIANT STAR (USA) 4 b.g. Giant's Causeway (USA) 132 – Vogue Star (ARG) (Ring- 57 aro (USA)) [2007 67: 8m⁵ Sep 1] maiden, lightly raced: fair at 3 yrs for D. Wachman in Ireland: only modest form sole start in 2007. *J. S. Goldie*

GIB (IRE) 3 ch.f. Rock of Gibraltar (IRE) 133 – Saucy Maid (IRE) 69 (Sure Blade 81 (USA) 130) [2007 61p: p10g⁴ 10g³ 9.9s 10m* 10.2s* 10m 11s² 10d⁶ Oct 15] rather leggy filly: fairly useful handicapper: won at Lingfield (by 5 lengths) and Bath in July: stays 11f: acts on soft and good to firm going: front runner: genuine. *B. W. Hills*

GIBSONS 3 ch.g. Tipsy Creek (USA) 115 – Amy Leigh (IRE) 78 (Imperial Frontier – (USA) 112) [2007 50: f8g⁶ f5g⁶ Feb 6] stocky gelding: modest maiden at 2 yrs: little impact in 2007: stays 6f: acts on fibresand. *P. A. Blockley*

GIDDYWELL 3 b.f. Ishiguru (USA) 114 – Understudy 60 (In The Wings 128) [2007 **66** p9.5g⁵ p9.5g⁴ p8.6g⁶ 9.9m⁶ p8.6g 10m⁴ p12.2g 10g 10v* 10.2s³ p12.2g p12.2g³ p12.2g⁶ **a63** p12.2d⁶ Dec 7] fifth foal: half-sister to 6-y-o Bretton and 1¼m winner Castle Ring (by Sri Pekan): dam, placed at 1¼m, half-sister to smart performer up to 1½m Pipsted: fair performer: won seller at Nottingham in July: stays 1½m: acts on polytrack, heavy and good to firm going. *R. Hollinshead*

GIFTED FLAME 8 b.g. Revoque (IRE) 122 – Little Lady Leah (USA) (Shareef **62** Dancer (USA) 135) [2007 78: 8m 7.9m p7g 8m 7.9f⁵ 6.9g 8m 6m 8.5g⁶ p9.5g p9.5g⁵ p8.6g p8.6g f8d 7fd p7.1g⁵ Dec 26] rangy gelding: modest performer nowadays: left T. D. Barron 800 gns after eleventh outing: stays 9f: acts on fibresand, firm and good to soft going: sometimes wears headgear: sometimes slowly away/races freely: waited with. *Miss A. Stokell*

GIFTED GAMBLE 5 b.g. Mind Games 121 – Its Another Gift 64 (Primo Dominie **91 §** 121) [2007 98, a91: p7.1g² p8g f7g² p7.1g⁶ p8g⁵ Mar 17] leggy gelding: fairly useful handicapper: creditable efforts when runner-up in 2007: effective at 6f to 8.6f: acts on all-weather, firm and soft going: tried in cheekpieces, usually blinkered: reportedly struck into final start: best treated with caution. *K. A. Ryan*

GIFTED GLORI 4 ch.g. Vettori (IRE) 119 – Azira 45 (Arazi (USA) 135) [2007 48: **50** f7g² Mar 20] sturdy gelding: modest maiden: should stay 1m: acts on fibresand and good to firm going: has run well when sweating. *T. D. Barron*

GIFTED HEIR (IRE) 3 b.c. Princely Heir (IRE) 111 – Inzar Lady (IRE) (Inzar (USA) **60** 112) [2007 59: p7g p8g² 8m² 10.3m 6g⁵ 8d⁶ p8.6g² Dec 1] small colt: modest performer: left I. Wood after third start: stays 8.6f: acts on polytrack and good to firm going. *A. Bailey*

GIFTED LASS 5 b.m. Bold Edge 123 – Meeson Times 71 (Enchantment 115) [2007 –, **–** a72+: f5g* p5.1g³ p5.1g³ f5g³ p5.1g⁴ p5.1g p5.1g f5g Dec 27] good-bodied mare: fair **a72** handicapper: won at Southwell in January: best at 5f: acts on all-weather, lightly raced and no form on turf: races up with pace. *J. Balding*

GIFTED MUSICIAN 5 b.g. Sadler's Wells (USA) 132 – Photogenic 93 (Midyan **–** (USA) 124) [2007 74: f14g⁶ 12g Jun 1] quite good-topped gelding: fair handicapper at 4 yrs: little form in 2007: stays 1¾m: acts on heavy and good to firm ground. *H. Morrison*

GIFT HORSE 7 ch.g. Cadeaux Genereux 131 – Careful Dancer (Gorytus (USA) 132) **103** [2007 110: 6g 5m³ 6d 6v⁵ 7m 6s 5.6m⁵ 5.6m⁵ 6d 6s⁵ 6g Oct 26] lengthy, angular gelding: poor mover in slower paces: useful performer nowadays: best effort in 2007 when third to Pivotal's Princess in minor event at Beverley second start: often better than bare result after, including when second home on far side in Ayr Silver Cup (won by Utmost Respect) and first home on stand side in handicap at Goodwood (won by Obe Gold) ninth/ tenth outings: stays 6f: unraced on firm going, acts on any other: visored last 5 starts: usually waited with. *D. Nicholls*

GIGANTICUS (USA) 4 ch.g. Giant's Causeway (USA) 132 – Shy Princess (USA) **110** 117 (Irish River (FR) 131) [2007 105: 7m* 7.6m⁴ 7f³ 7m* 7g⁴ 7m* 7.6m 7d Sep 29] rangy gelding: developed into smart handicapper in 2007, winning at Newcastle in April, and at Newmarket in July (Ladbrokes Bunbury Cup, beat King of Argos by neck) and August (best effort, beat Ceremonial Jade by 1¼ lengths): also ran well when fourth to

Ladbrokes Bunbury Cup, Newmarket—Giganticus holds on gamely from King of Argos (second right), Something (diamonds), Dhaular Dhar (right) and Racer Forever (blinkers)

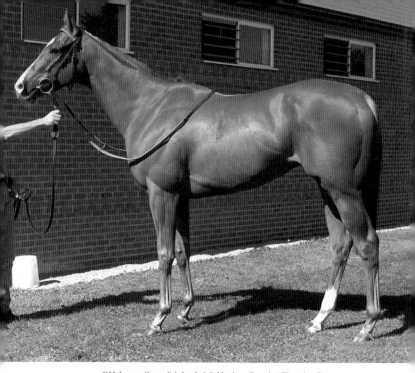

DM James, Cavendish Inv Ltd & Matthew Green's "Giganticus"

Third Set in International Stakes at Ascot fifth start: not at best at Chester and Ascot last 2 outings: stays 7.6f: acts on firm going. *B. W. Hills*

GIGGLING MONKEY 2 b.f. (Apr 7) Fraam 114 – Rewardia (IRE) 66 (Petardia 113) **49** [2007 6.1g² 5m 6d⁴ 7g³ 8.1f 8.2g⁴ p8m p8.6g⁶ p8.6d⁴ p9.5g⁵ p8.6g Dec 31] 5,000Y: leggy filly: sixth foal: sister to 1m winner in Guernsey and half-sister to ungenuine 5f (including seller and at 2 yrs)/6f winner Emaradia (by Emarati): dam maiden, best form at 7f: poor maiden: in frame in sellers/claimer: stays 8.6f: acts on polytrack and firm going: visored/blinkered last 4 starts. *P. D. Evans*

GIGI GLAMOR 5 b.m. Secret Appeal – Gilboa 48 (Shirley Heights 130) [2007 –: **–** 11.9m⁶ 11.7f⁴ 11.5g 15.8g Sep 22] sturdy mare: little solid form. *W. M. Brisbourne*

GIGS MAGIC (USA) 4 ch.g. Gulch (USA) – Magic of Love 99 (Magic Ring (IRE) **74** 115) [2007 60: p8.6g* p10g³ f8g² 8.5m⁴ 10.1d⁶ 12g* 9.8m² 13g* Jun 13] lengthy, good-topped gelding: fair handicapper: won at Wolverhampton in April and Catterick and Hamilton in June: stays 13f: acts on all-weather, firm and good to soft going: usually held up. *M. Johnston*

GILDED COVE 7 b.h. Polar Prince (IRE) 117 – Cloudy Reef 57 (Cragador 110) [2007 **73** 78: f5g p6g² p6g³ 5.7d* 6d⁵ 6g⁵ p6g p7.1m 6.1d p6g⁶ p7.1g³ p6g³ p6g Dec 29] strong horse: reportedly has only one eye: fair handicapper: won at Bath in June: stays 7f: acts on all-weather, soft and good to firm going: held up. *R. Hollinshead*

GILDED YOUTH 3 b.g. Gorse 116 – Nisha (Nishapour (FR) 125) [2007 78p: 6m² 6g³ **78** p7g* p7g Sep 19] lengthy, good-topped gelding: has scope: fair performer: won maiden at Kempton in September: stays 7f: acts on polytrack, soft and good to firm going. *H. Candy*

GILLANS INN 2 b.c. (Apr 10) Rambling Bear 115 – Strat's Quest 65 (Nicholas (USA) **55**
111) [2007 5.1m 5.1g⁶ 5g⁵ Jun 18] tall, lengthy colt: modest maiden: bred mainly for
speed. *J. M. Bradley*

GIMME SOME LOVIN (IRE) 3 b.f. Desert Style (IRE) 121 – Licence To Thrill 83 **69**
(Wolfhound (USA) 126) [2007 6m³ 6g⁶ p6g⁶ 5.1f p6g² p6g* p6g³ p6g⁴ p6m⁴ p7g Dec 29]
second foal: half-sister to 4-y-o Classic Encounter: dam, 5f winner, out of Cherry Hinton
winner Crime of Passion: fair performer: won minor event at Wolverhampton in September: stays 7f: acts on polytrack and good to firm going: tried tongue tied: held up.
D. W. P. Arbuthnot

GIN GENEREUX 2 b.c. (Feb 4) Cadeaux Genereux 131 – Lady Gin (USA) (Saint Bal- **79 §**
lado (CAN)) [2007 5g 5m 6g* 5v⁵ 6m p6g* 5.5m 6s Oct 26] rangy colt: fair performer:
won maiden at Hamilton in June and nursery at Wolverhampton in August: should prove
best at 5f/6f: inconsistent. *M. Johnston*

GINGER FOUNTAIN 2 ch.f. (Apr 14) Generous (IRE) 139 – Gift Fountain 79 **–**
(Greenshift 123) [2007 7.1g p7g Oct 24] second foal: dam maiden (stayed 1¼m): last in
maidens: dead. *H. Candy*

GINGER MINX (IRE) 2 ch.f. (Mar 28) Raise A Grand (IRE) 114 – Glenmalure (IRE) **59 p**
63 (Night Shift (USA)) [2007 p7.1d³ Dec 28] first foal: dam, Irish maiden (stayed 1½m),
half-sister to useful Irish miler Provosky: 9/2, never-nearer third in maiden at Wolverhampton: will be suited by 1m+: open to improvement. *N. J. Vaughan*

GINGER PICKLE 2 ch.g. (Jan 19) Compton Place 125 – Spice Island 68 (Reprimand **77**
122) [2007 7d 5s* 6.1d³ 5m³ 6d⁴ 6g⁵ Sep 23] workmanlike gelding: fair performer: won
maiden at Beverley in July: in frame in 3 nurseries: should stay 7f: acts on soft and good
to firm going: sold 15,500 gns. *J. R. Weymes*

GINGER POP 3 ch.g. Mark of Esteem (IRE) 137 – Norcroft Lady 85 (Mujtahid (USA)
118) [2007 64: p6g² p6g⁵ p5g p6g 6m 6m p7g⁴ p6g Dec 12] rather leggy gelding: modest **a61**
maiden: stays 7f: acts on polytrack: tried visored (ran poorly). *G. G. Margarson*

GINGER PRINCESS (IRE) 5 b.m. Pistolet Bleu (IRE) 133 – Palm Lake (IRE) **59 +**
(Spectrum (IRE) 126) [2007 8.2d 7.5g 7g⁵ 9.5g 5d 7s p8g p7.1g³ Dec 14] well beaten in
bumper/hurdle: modest maiden handicapper on Flat: creditable third at Wolverhampton
final start: stays easy 1m: acts on polytrack and good to soft going: tongue tied last 4
outings. *Oliver McKiernan, Ireland*

GINGHAM 2 b. or gr.f. (Apr 5) Barathea (IRE) 127 – Sianema 62 (Persian Bold 123) **73 p**
[2007 7s 7g³ Oct 6] strong, well-made filly: powerful mover: closely related to 2005
2-y-o 6f winner Sakabula (by King of Kings) and half-sister to 2 winners, including fairly
useful Italian winner up to 1m Sergesto (by Most Welcome): dam, maiden (stayed 1m),
half-sister to very smart middle-distance filly Infamy: green in maidens at Newmarket
and Redcar, shaping well when strong-finishing third to Coachhouse Lady: will be suited
by at least 1m: sure to go on improving. *L. M. Cumani*

GIOVANNI D'ORO (IRE) 3 b.g. Johannesburg (USA) 127 – Maddie G (USA) **59**
(Blush Rambler (USA) 119) [2007 63p: 6m p7.1g⁴ 6m⁶ 8.5s² 10d Jul 12] rather finely-
made, useful-looking gelding: modest maiden: left N. Callaghan after third start: stays
8.5f: acts on polytrack and soft ground: has found little. *Miss M. E. Rowland*

GIPSY PRINCE 2 b.g. (Apr 7) Millkom 124 – Habla Me (IRE) (Fairy King (USA)) **80**
[2007 6.1s 6m 6m⁶ 7m⁴ p6g* p6g⁴ Oct 17] tall, unfurnished gelding: fairly useful performer: improved to win nursery at Kempton in October: should stay 7f: acts on polytrack
and good to firm going: sold 17,500 gns. *M. G. Quinlan*

GIRARDII 4 ch.g. Sinndar (IRE) 134 – Armeria (USA) 79 (Northern Dancer) [2007 68: **–**
p16g Mar 7] well-made gelding: fair maiden at 3 yrs: well held only start in 2007: stays
12.6f: raced on polytrack and good ground or firmer: blinkered last 4 starts. *K. C. Bailey*

GIRL OF PANGAEA (GER) 2 b.f. (Mar 16) Soviet Star (USA) 128 – Genevra (IRE) **70 p**
107 (Danehill (USA) 126) [2007 p8m² Nov 11] €105,000Y: fifth foal: half-sister to 3
winners, including fairly useful 2003 2-y-o 6f winner (stayed 1m) Granato (by Cadeaux
Genereux): dam, German/French 1m winner, out of half-sister to very smart sprinter
Ballad Rock: 9/1 and green (started slowly), shaped well when head second to Burriscarra
in maiden at Kempton: will improve. *E. A. L. Dunlop*

GIVE EVIDENCE 3 b.g. Averti (IRE) 117 – Witness 71 (Efisio 120) [2007 67: 7m 7m **54**
7.1g 8m 7.6s⁵ 9g² p10g 7g⁴ 10s⁶ 10g Oct 8] tall gelding: modest performer nowadays:
reared leaving stall final outing: stays 1¼m: acts on polytrack and soft going: tried
visored: has raced freely/shown signs of temperament. *A. P. Jarvis*

GIVE HER A WHIRL 3 b.f. Pursuit of Love 124 – Peggy Spencer 77 (Formidable –
(USA) 125) [2007 63p: 6m 5m⁶ Jun 8] leggy, useful-looking filly: modest maiden at
2 yrs: little impact in 2007, including in handicap: stays 6f. *G. A. Swinbank*

GIVE ME A BREAK 3 b.c. Danehill Dancer (IRE) 117 – Cream Jug (IRE) (Spectrum 83 +
(IRE) 126) [2007 8m 8d 9.9m* 11s⁴ Oct 4] 62,000Y: good-topped colt: type to carry
condition: third foal: dam unraced half-sister to smart 13.3f winner Dark Shell: fairly
useful form: won maiden at Goodwood in September: good fourth in handicap there final
outing: may prove best at 1¼m: acts on soft and good to firm going: sold 38,000 gns.
P. W. Chapple-Hyam

GIVE ME THE NIGHT (IRE) 4 b.f. Night Shift (USA) – There With Me (USA) 63 85
(Distant View (USA) 126) [2007 83: 7m 6g⁴ 6d 5d⁶ Jun 28] strong filly: fairly useful
handicapper: seems to stay 9f (though all wins at 5f): acts on polytrack/dirt, firm and good
to soft ground. *B. Smart*

GIVEN A CHOICE (IRE) 5 b.g. Trans Island 119 – Miss Audimar (USA) (Mr Lead- 82
er (USA)) [2007 93: 9.1g⁴ 10.1d² 10d p8g³ Nov 14] big, strong gelding: good mover:
fairly useful handicapper: left M. Todhunter after second start: effective at 8.6f to 1½m:
acts on polytrack, good to firm and good to soft ground: tried visored (below form).
J. G. Given

GIZMO 4 b.g. Fasliyev (USA) 120 – Sly Baby (IRE) 59 (Dr Devious (IRE) 127) [2007 57
–: 8.2g 7g⁶ Jul 27] angular gelding: maiden, lightly raced (reported to have suffered stress
fracture in June 2005): seemingly modest form latter outing in 2007: stays 7f. *B. Smart*

GIZMONDO 4 ch.g. Lomitas 129 – India Atlanta (Ahonoora 122) [2007 70: p9.5g⁴ 68
p10g⁵ 10m² 10.1d Jun 19] fair handicapper on turf, modest on all-weather: stays 1¼m: a60
acts on firm ground, below form on polytrack: hung left third 3-y-o start: sold 18,000 gns
in July. *M. L. W. Bell*

GLADIATORUS (USA) 2 b.c. (Mar 28) Silic (FR) 125 – Gmaasha (IRE) (Kris 135) 108
[2007 7m* 6d⁶ 7.5m* 7.5m* 8m* 7.5m² 7.5m* 8g* 8m² Oct 14] $8,000Y: half-brother
to a winner in USA by Mr Prospector: dam unraced half-sister to 2000 Guineas and
Champion Stakes winner Haafhd out of Irish 1000 Guineas winner Al Bahathri: useful
performer: trained by R. Menichetti first 6 starts: successful between June and September
in 2 minor events at Naples and listed races at Naples, Varese, Florence and Rome,
beating Cima On Fly 3½ lengths for last win: ran well final start when ½-length second to
Scintillo in Gran Criterium at Milan, setting good pace and keeping on well when headed:
shapes as though will stay 1¼m: raced mainly on good to firm ground: has had tongue
tied: has joined Godolphin. *Maria R. Salvioni, Italy*

GLAD STAR (GER) 4 br.g. Big Shuffle (USA) 122 – Glady Sum (GER) (Surumu – §
(GER)) [2007 f12g f11g 12m 10m 18m Oct 22] no sign of ability: refused to race fourth
outing: tried blinkered (reluctant to race)/in cheekpieces: temperamental. *D. W. Chapman*

GLAMARAAZI (IRE) 4 b.f. Orpen (USA) 116 – Raazi 46 (My Generation 111) 65
[2007 65: f6g* f7g f6g⁶ p7.1g f7g⁴ 6.1m² 6g May 10] good-topped filly: fair handicapper: won at Southwell in January: stays 7f: acts on all-weather and good to firm going:
tried visored: carried head awkwardly/hung penultimate start: sold 800 gns and joined
P. Beaumont. *R. A. Fahey*

GLAMOROSO (IRE) 2 b.c. (Mar 21) Mull of Kintyre (USA) 114 – Tuneful 89 (Pivo- –
tal 124) [2007 5g 6g Oct 3] sturdy colt: last in maidens 5 months apart. *D. W. Barker*

GLASSHOUGHTON 4 b.g. Dansili 127 – Roseum 102 (Lahib (USA) 129) [2007 83: 92
5g⁵ 5m 6m 5m⁶ 5d 5v* 5s⁴ 5d³ 5g* 5d⁶ 5d Oct 13] smallish, angular gelding: fairly
useful handicapper: won at Beverley in July and Carlisle (beat Sir Noel by 1½ lengths) in
August: best at 5f: acts on heavy and good to firm going: tried in cheekpieces/blinkers:
races prominently. *M. Dods*

GLEAMING SPIRIT (IRE) 3 b.g. Mujadil (USA) 119 – Gleam (Green Desert 75
(USA) 127) [2007 65: f6g⁵ 5m² 5g⁴ 6m³ 6m* 5m⁵ 5d 6d Oct 30] strong gelding: fair
handicapper: won at Yarmouth in August: well held last 2 outings: should prove best at
5f/6f: acts on good to firm ground, probably on polytrack: races prominently. *A. P. Jarvis*

GLENARGO (USA) 4 ch.g. Concerto (USA) 114 – Her Gift (USA) (Saint Ballado 60 d
(CAN)) [2007 66, a59: p5.1g³ p5.1g p5.1g p5.1g 5.7d p8.6g p8.6d Dec 17] modest
performer: left R. Harris after third outing: effective at 5f/6f: acts on polytrack and firm
going: tried tongue tied, often wears cheekpieces: races prominently. *S. T. Lewis*

GLEN AVON GIRL (IRE) 3 b.f. Mull of Kintyre (USA) 114 – Sandystones 60 (Sel- 55
kirk (USA) 129) [2007 55: f5g⁴ p6g⁶ p5.1g⁵ 6g Apr 2] good-topped filly: modest maiden:
barely stays 6f: raced only on all-weather and good/good to soft ground. *T. D. Easterby*

GLENBUCK (IRE) 4 b.g. Mujadil (USA) 119 – Bryna (IRE) (Ezzoud (IRE) 126)   **93**
[2007 89: f7g⁵ f8g 7.1g³ 7m* 6m 7.6m⁶ 7v⁵ 7g⁵ Jul 28] angular, workmanlike gelding:
fairly useful handicapper: won at Yarmouth in April: barely stays 1m: acts on all-weather,
heavy and good to firm going: visored: usually front runner. *A. Bailey*

GLENCAIRN STAR 6 b.g. Selkirk (USA) 129 – Bianca Nera 107 (Salse (USA) 128)   **77**
[2007 84: 5s³ Apr 1] good sort: fair handicapper: slow-starting third at Navan, only outing
of 2007: winner at 6f/7f, best form at 5f: acts on all-weather, soft and good to firm ground:
in cheekpieces last 3 starts. *R. A. Fahey*

GLENCAL 3 ch.f. Compton Place 125 – Raindrop 59 (Primo Dominie 121) [2007 6m⁴   **68**
6g⁵ 5s³ p5g³ 6m² 6.1d* p7g³ p6g³ p7m Oct 11] lengthy filly: third foal: half-sister to 4-y-o
Kasumi: dam maiden (stayed 7f): fair handicapper: won at Chepstow in August: stays 7f:
acts on polytrack, good to firm and good to soft ground: races prominently. *H. Morrison*

GLENCALVIE (IRE) 6 ch.g. Grand Lodge (USA) 125 – Top of The Form (IRE) 79   **82**
(Masterclass (USA) 116) [2007 85: p8f p7g p8g⁵ 8.3f p8g p7g** p8g⁶ 7.6g³ p8g 8.3f* 8m
7f 7v Oct 9] strong, well-made gelding: fairly useful handicapper: won at Lingfield in
May and Windsor in August: stays 8.3f: acts on polytrack and firm going: wears visor/
cheekpieces: often races up with pace: temperament under suspicion. *J. Akehurst*

GLENEAGLES (IRE) 3 ch.g. Pivotal 124 – Embassy 114 (Cadeaux Genereux 131)   **86**
[2007 6m² p7.1g⁵ 7.1d* 7.5s* 8m² 8s⁵ 8s⁶ 8.2g⁵ Nov 7] strong gelding: fairly useful
performer: won maiden at Warwick in June and claimer at Beverley (claimed from
W. Haggas £17,000) in July: good efforts in handicaps next 2 starts: left N. Wilson
£23,000 before final outing: stays 1m: acts on soft and good to firm ground. *T. Wall*

GLENISLAND 3 br.f. Diktat 126 – Glider (IRE) 65 (Silver Kite (USA) 111) [2007 8g⁶   **53**
9.2g⁶ 10.2g Jul 9] 5,500Y: second foal: closely related to 4-y-o Leonardo's Friend: dam,
1m winner, half-sister to Prix Morny winner Bad As I Wanna Be: best effort in maidens
when sixth to First To Call at Bath on debut: stays 1m. *Mrs C. Williamson*

GLENLUJI 2 b.g. (Mar 21) Lujain (USA) 119 – Glenhurich (IRE) 59 (Sri Pekan (USA)   **58**
117) [2007 5g⁶ 6d⁶ 5m* 5m⁶ Aug 2] modest performer: won seller at Musselburgh in
June: should stay 6f: gelded after final start. *J. S. Goldie*

GLENMORE LODGE 4 b.f. Indian Lodge (IRE) 127 – In The Highlands (Petong   **–**
126) [2007 f7g f6g 9.8g Apr 28] fifth foal: half-sister to 3 winners, including fairly useful
2001 2-y-o 5f/6f winner Glenmorangie (by Danzig Connection): dam no form: no sign of
ability. *P. T. Midgley*

GLENMUIR (IRE) 4 b.g. Josr Algarhoud (IRE) 118 – Beryl 77 (Bering 136) [2007   **77**
86: 8.3f 8m 8.3g³ 8.3f 8.1m 8.3g 8.1g 8m Oct 14] angular, well-made gelding: fair handicapper nowadays: stays 8.3f: acts on firm and soft going: tried blinkered: sold 4,500 gns.
B. R. Millman

GLEN NEVIS (USA) 3 b. or br.c. Gulch (USA) – Beating The Buzz (IRE) 96 (Blue-   **99**
bird (USA) 125) [2007 87p: a7f 7.5g³ 10g Jun 21] medium-sized, attractive colt: useful
performer: good third to Mount Hadley in minor event at Nad Al Sheba: left I. Mohammed in UAE, well held in listed Hampton Court Stakes at Royal Ascot final outing: stays
1m: acts on good to soft going, well held only outing on dirt. *Saeed bin Suroor*

GLENRIDDING 3 b.g. Averti (IRE) 117 – Appelone (Emperor Jones (USA) 119)   **70**
[2007 –: 10g 12.1g 11.1g⁶ p9.5g⁴ p9.5g⁵ p8g p8.6g² p10g p8.6d* Dec 27] tall gelding:
fair performer: won maiden at Wolverhampton in December: stays 9.5f: acts on polytrack: tried blinkered. *J. G. Given*

GLENSHEE (IRE) 2 b.g. (Apr 7) Mujadil (USA) 119 – Ancient Secret (Warrshan   **57**
(USA) 117) [2007 5m 6s⁵ 5d³ p7.1g 7g Aug 24] modest maiden: third at Pontefract: best
efforts at 5f/6f. *J. J. Quinn*

GLENTIMON (IRE) 3 ch.g. Mull of Kintyre (USA) 114 – Eliade (IRE) 82 (Flash of   **–**
Steel 120) [2007 p11g 10d p12g⁶ 12.1d Aug 16] workmanlike gelding: little form. *S. Kirk*

GLENVEAGH (IRE) 2 b.c. (Mar 28) Catcher In The Rye (IRE) 115 – Limone (IRE)   **59 p**
(Catrail (USA) 123) [2007 6m 5d³ Aug 19] €4,000F, €7,000Y, 36,000 2-y-o: stocky colt:
third foal: dam unraced sister to useful 7f to 1¼m winner Pretrail: more promise than bare
result in maidens at Haydock and Pontefract, not fully wound up: may prove best at 5f/6f:
capable of better. *K. A. Ryan*

GLENVIEWS YOUNGONE (IRE) 4 b.f. Namid 128 – Baltic Beach (IRE) (Polish   **77**
Precedent (USA) 131) [2007 88: f5g⁵ p5.1g p5g f5g p5.1g f5g⁵ 5m⁶ 5d Jun 25] tall,
close-coupled filly: fairly useful handicapper: below form after reappearance in 2007
(reportedly bled final start): raced at 5f/6f: acts on all-weather and good to soft ground,
probably on firm: tried blinkered, including last 3 starts. *Peter Grayson*

GLITTER BABY (IRE) 4 b.f. Danehill Dancer (IRE) 117 – Gifts Galore (IRE) 88   **101**
(Darshaan 133) [2007 96: 10s⁴ 12.1d 10.9d³ 10.1m⁵ 14g³ 12s⁶ 10.1g 12d Oct 21] quite
good-topped filly: first foal: dam Irish maiden (stayed 1m): useful performer: won
handicap at Limerick at 3 yrs, when trained by D. Weld (sold €100,000): creditable third
to Dash To The Front in listed race at Warwick third start: below form last 4 outings:
effective at 1¼m to 2m: acts on any going: effective with/without blinkers: tongue tied
first 2 appearances at 4 yrs. *M. G. Quinlan*

GLITTERING PRIZE (UAE) 2 b. or br.f. (Jan 22) Cadeaux Genereux 131 – Tanami   **72**
111 (Green Desert (USA) 127) [2007 6g 7m⁴ 6d⁵ 7s² 6.1d² 7d p7.1g* Dec 31] small
filly: seventh foal: sister to useful 2003 2-y-o 6f/7f (Rockfel Stakes) winner Cairns and
half-sister to 2 winners, including useful 5f (including at 2 yrs)/6f winner Machynleth (by
Machiavellian): dam 2-y-o 5f/6f winner: fair performer: won maiden at Wolverhampton
final start: stays 7f: acts on polytrack and soft going: very fractious in stall penultimate
outing. *M. Johnston*

GLOBAL ACHIEVER 6 b.g. Key of Luck (USA) 126 – Inflation 68 (Primo Dominie   **–**
121) [2007 –, a54: p6g p8g⁶ f6g p12m f8d Dec 20] modest at 5 yrs: little form in 2007,
leaving G. Chung after third start: usually blinkered/in cheekpieces: tried tongue tied.
M. J. Gingell

GLOBAL GUEST 3 b.c. Piccolo 121 – By Arrangement (IRE) 60 (Bold Arrangement   **– §**
127) [2007 73§: 7.1g 7d p7.1m p7.1g Sep 21] angular colt: fair but unreliable maiden at
2 yrs: little form in 2007. *A. J. Chamberlain*

GLOBAL STRATEGY 4 b.g. Rainbow Quest (USA) 134 – Pleasuring 68 (Good   **67**
Times (ITY)) [2007 65: f12g* f12g* f14g* 14g⁶ 18g⁶ f14g* 14.1g⁶ 11.9d p13g Nov 4]   **a80**
strong gelding: fairly useful handicapper on all-weather, just fair on turf: won at Southwell in January (2), February and May: well below form final outing: should stay 2m: acts
on fibresand (possibly not on polytrack), raced on good/good to soft going on turf: joined
O. Sherwood. *Rae Guest*

GLOBAL TRAFFIC 3 br.c. Generous (IRE) 139 – Eyes Wide Open 44 (Fraam 114)   **70**
[2007 60: p9.5g* p9.5g* p9.5g* p9.5g⁵ 9.7g 11.6m 11.6m⁵ 10m 10s 12.1s* p12.2g⁶   **a74**
p12.2g⁶ 12.4d⁵ 10g p12.2g⁵ f11d³ Dec 18] strong colt: fair handicapper: won at Wolverhampton (3) in January and Chepstow (amateurs) in July: best around 1½m: acts on
all-weather and soft going: sometimes blinkered/visored: often slowly away. *P. D. Evans*

GLOBE 4 b.f. Agnes World (USA) 123 – Hoist (IRE) 75 (Bluebird (USA) 125) [2007 –:   **40**
p6g p6g p6g p6g 5.1g May 29] poor maiden: stays 6f: acts on polytrack. *Mrs H. Sweeting*

GLORIOUS GIFT (IRE) 2 b.c. (Mar 14) Elnadim (USA) 128 – Queen of Arabia   **86 p**
(USA) (Wild Again (USA)) [2007 6g⁴ 6g² Sep 7] lengthy, heavy-topped colt: first foal:
dam, ran twice, half-sister to very smart German performer up to 1½m Germany: fairly
useful form in maidens at York (eye-catching fourth to Moynahan) and Haydock (met
trouble when runner-up to Errigal Lad): should prove best up to 1m: will improve and
win races. *P. W. Chapple-Hyam*

GLORIOUS VIEW 3 b.g. Observatory (USA) 131 – Prime Property (IRE) 60 (Tirol   **–**
127) [2007 –: 11.5s 12.1s 12.1g Jul 31] good-bodied gelding: little form: tried blinkered.
M. W. Easterby

GLORY BE (ITY) 5 ch.m. Dashing Blade 117 – Hasana (USA) (Private Account   **44**
(USA)) [2007 52: p16g⁵ May 9] tall mare: modest maiden at 4 yrs: just poor form sole
start in 2007: stays 1¾m (probably not 2m): acts on all-weather and firm ground: often
wears headgear. *J. L. Spearing*

GLORY DAYS (GER) 4 b.f. Tiger Hill (IRE) 127 – Glorosia (FR) 109 (Bering 136)   **59**
[2007 p9.5g⁴ p12.2g⁶ Feb 12] third foal: sister to useful German 1¼m/11f winner Gentle
Tiger and half-sister to German 1¼m/11f winner Glorious Storm (by Monsun): dam 7f
(at 2 yrs, also won Fillies' Mile) to 1¼m winner: better effort in maidens at Wolverhampton when over 10 lengths fourth to Metternich, hanging left: may prove best short of
1½m: sold 20,000 gns (in foal to Araafa). *E. A. L. Dunlop*

GLOUCESTER 4 b.g. Montjeu (IRE) 137 – Birdlip (USA) (Sanglamore (USA) 126)   **81**
[2007 12d⁵ 9.9v⁶ 12.1g⁶ 10.1g³ 10.1m⁵ 9.9m* Sep 11] strong ex-French gelding: fairly
useful performer, lightly raced: won minor event at Deauville at 3 yrs (left P. Bary 37,000
gns after): best effort in 2007 when winning handicap at Beverley in September: winner
at 1½m, may prove best at shorter: acts on all-weather and good to firm ground: tried
blinkered/tongue tied: placed both starts over hurdles. *J. J. Quinn*

GLOVED HAND 5 b.m. Royal Applause 124 – Fudge (Polar Falcon (USA) 126)   **105**
[2007 96: 6g⁴ 7g 7d* 6d⁴ 6s² 7g Aug 3] strong mare: useful performer: better than ever in

2007, winning handicap (by neck from Orpen Wide) and minor event in June, both at Newmarket: good 2½ lengths second to Theann in Summer Stakes at York next time: below form in Oak Tree Stakes at Goodwood final outing: best at 6f/7f: acts on polytrack, soft and good to firm going: has been bandaged in front: usually held up: has been blanketed for stall entry: reportedly in foal to Cadeaux Genereux. *R. M. Beckett*

GNILLAH 4 b.f. Halling (USA) 133 – Dimakya (USA) 83 (Dayjur (USA) 137) [2007 59: 7.6g p10g Aug 4] tall, lengthy filly: modest maiden handicapper at 3 yrs: well held in 2007: should be suited by 1¼m+: acts on polytrack and good to firm going: has raced freely. *B. R. Johnson* —

GO AMWELL 4 b.g. Kayf Tara 130 – Daarat Alayaam (IRE) (Reference Point 139) [2007 58: p12.2g p12g p11g³ p12g 16m* p16g* 16s³ 15.8g Oct 30] fair handicapper: won at Goodwood in September and Kempton in October: effective at 1½m to 2m: acts on all-weather, soft and good to firm going: tried visored. *J. R. Jenkins* **65**

GO BUT GO 3 b.g. Tobougg (IRE) 125 – Faraway Lass 94 (Distant Relative 128) [2007 9.8m⁴ 9.2g* 10.3m⁴ 12g³ p13g⁶ 14d Oct 13] 4,500 2-y-o: close-coupled gelding: fourth foal: half-brother to 6-y-o Harry Up: dam 6f winner: fairly useful form, lightly raced: won maiden at Hamilton in June: good third in ladies handicap at Newbury fourth outing: stays 1½m: acts on good to firm going, probably on polytrack: seemed not to handle track (Chester) third start: sold 30,000 gns, joined H. Dunlop. *E. J. O'Neill* **81**

GO DANCING 3 b.f. Golan (IRE) 129 – Torrid Tango (USA) (Green Dancer (USA) 132) [2007 55p: f8g⁴ p10g Apr 14] strong, well-made filly: modest maiden: should stay 1¼m: raced on all-weather and good ground: sold 6,500 gns in July. *P. W. Chapple-Hyam* **59**

GODFREY STREET 4 ch.g. Compton Place 125 – Tahara (IRE) (Caerleon (USA) 132) [2007 94: 6g 5d 5d* 5m p5.1g f5d⁴ f5d⁵ Dec 18] strong, compact gelding: fairly useful handicapper nowadays: won apprentice event at Ascot in October: speedy, and best at 5f/easy 6f: acts on all-weather, soft and good to firm going: blinkered last 5 outings: none too consistent. *K. A. Ryan* **94**

GO DUDE 3 b.g. Mujahid (USA) 125 – Miss Doody 63 (Gorytus (USA) 132) [2007 62: 11.5s 10.1d p11g 10g 11.8g Oct 16] good-topped gelding: fair maiden: possibly flattered third outing: pulled up amiss final start: stays easy 11f: acts on all-weather: usually wears headgear: slowly away first 2 outings. *J. Ryan* **67 ?**

GO FREE 6 b.g. Easycall 115 – Miss Traxdata (Absalom 128) [2007 –, a56: f12g³ 12.1g⁶ Jun 20] modest performer: stays 13f: acts on all-weather, good to firm and good to soft going: tried visored: fairly useful hurdler, successful in September. *J. G. M. O'Shea* — **a60**

GO IMPERIAL (IRE) 3 b.g. Imperial Ballet (IRE) 110 – Miss Divot (IRE) 67 (Petardia 113) [2007 64: 6m 6d⁵ 5g⁵ Jun 22] leggy, workmanlike gelding: modest maiden: should stay 7f: acts on polytrack and good to soft ground: slowly away last 2 outings at 2 yrs: sold 4,500 gns and gelded. *M. G. Quinlan* **52**

GOING SKINT 4 b.g. Elnadim (USA) 128 – Prospering 50 (Prince Sabo 123) [2007 57: p8.6g f6g* f6g³ f7g⁴ f6g 6g 8.1m 8.2s 6m³ 6m 5.7d Jun 16] sturdy gelding: fair performer on all-weather, modest on turf: won maiden at Southwell in January: best form at 6f: acts on fibresand and good to firm going: visored/blinkered last 4 starts: has been slowly away: often races up with pace. *M. Wellings* **59 a71**

GOING TO WORK (IRE) 3 b.f. Night Shift (USA) – Firesteed (IRE) 91 (Common Grounds 118) [2007 58p: 9.7m* 10m³ 8d 9g 10m³ 8m⁴ 10m⁴ 12d⁵ p10g* 10d² Oct 11] tall filly: fairly useful performer: won maiden at Folkestone in April and handicap at Kempton in October: creditable second in handicap at Newbury final outing: likely to prove best up to 1¼m: acts on polytrack, good to firm and good to soft ground: often held up: sold 110,000 gns, joined Venetia Williams. *D. R. C. Elsworth* **89**

GOLAN KNIGHT (IRE) 2 b. or br.c. (Feb 18) Golan (IRE) 129 – Night Rhapsody (IRE) 81 (Mujtahid (USA) 118) [2007 6s* 7g 6s³ 6s³ 6m⁶ 7m* 7d³ Oct 16] €26,000Y: leggy, quite attractive colt: second foal: dam Irish 1m winner: fairly useful performer: won maiden at Leicester in June and nursery at Chester in August: will stay 1m: acts on soft and good to firm going: forces pace: sold 60,000 gns. *K. A. Ryan* **91**

GOLANO 7 gr.g. Linamix (FR) 127 – Dimakya (USA) 83 (Dayjur (USA) 137) [2007 –: p12g⁴ p13.9g³ p13.9g³ p16.5g⁶ p16.5g p16.5g⁵ Dec 3] rather leggy, quite good-topped gelding: fair handicapper: stays 1¾m: acts on polytrack and heavy going: tried visored/in cheekpieces. *P. R. Webber* **78**

GOLAN WAY 3 b.g. Golan (IRE) 129 – Silk Daisy 74 (Barathea (IRE) 127) [2007 78: 10g⁶ 10.3m³ p10g⁴ p10g⁵ p12.2g⁵ Nov 19] fair handicapper: stays 1¼m: acts on polytrack, good to firm and good to soft ground. *I. A. Wood* **78**

GOLBAND 5 b.m. Cadeaux Genereux 131 – Hatheethah (IRE) (Machiavellian (USA) – 123) [2007 –: f5g 5m 5s Oct 9] rather leggy mare: fair performer at 3 yrs: little form since (said to have bled on reappearance, left R. Marvin after): tried blinkered. *J. O'Reilly*

GOLDACRE 2 b. or br.f. (Feb 14) Warningford 119 – Elsie Bamford 57 (Tragic Role – (USA)) [2007 p5g⁶ Jul 10] 1,500Y: third foal: half-sister to fairly useful 7f winner Jane Jubilee (by Mister Baileys): dam, 1¾m winner, out of half-sister to very smart 1m/1¼m performer Radetzky: well held in seller at Lingfield. *Miss D. A. McHale*

GOLDAN JESS 3 b.g. Golan (IRE) 129 – Bendis (GER) (Danehill (USA) 126) **53** [2007 75: f5g³ f7g⁶ 6f Aug 12] just modest form since debut: trained by P. Prendergast in Ireland at 2 yrs: best effort at 5f on heavy going: tried blinkered/visored. *D. Carroll*

GOLD DIGGER MISS (USA) 3 ch.f. Gulch (USA) – Jaramar Miss (USA) (Risen **85** Star (USA)) [2007 p7.1g⁴ p7g⁴ f6g* f7g² 6f* Jun 8] $50,000 2-y-o: sixth foal: closely related to winner in US by Thunder Gulch and half-sister to several winners there: dam, US 2-y-o 6f winner, half-sister to dam of Arlington Million winner Marlin: fairly useful form: won maiden at Southwell in April and handicap at Brighton in June: stays 7f: raced only on all-weather and firm ground: sent to USA. *J. Noseda*

GOLDDIGGING (IRE) 2 b.f. (Mar 25) Acclamation 118 – On The Make (IRE) – (Entrepreneur 123) [2007 p7g 7f Jul 30] €15,000F, 6,000Y: sturdy filly: second foal: half-sister to winner in US by Inchinor: dam unraced out of Oaks d'Italia winner Ivyanna: slowly away and always behind in maidens. *J. G. Portman*

GOLDEN ALCHEMIST 4 ch.g. Woodborough (USA) 112 – Pure Gold 88 (Dilum **65** (USA) 115) [2007 79: p7g³ f8g p10g⁵ p8g 10m⁵ May 25] strong, good-bodied gelding: fair maiden: best form up to 7f: acts on polytrack and good to soft going: tried visored: fair hurdler, successful in July. *M. D. I. Usher*

GOLDEN APPLAUSE (FR) 5 b.m. Royal Applause 124 – Golden Circle (USA) 72 **70** (Theatrical 128) [2007 80: 8d 10.2g³ 10g Jun 13] leggy mare: fair handicapper nowadays: stays 1¼m: acts on firm and good to soft going: tried in cheekpieces: sold 3,000 gns. *Mrs A. L. M. King*

GOLDEN ASHA 5 ch.m. Danehill Dancer (IRE) 117 – Snugfit Annie 49 (Midyan **80** (USA) 124) [2007 96: p6f 6.1s 6g 6g⁵ Jun 2] leggy, lengthy mare: useful performer at 4 yrs: just fairly useful form at best in 2007: stays 6f: acts on firm and good to soft ground: held up. *G. G. Margarson*

GOLDEN BROWN (IRE) 3 b.g. Kyllachy 129 – Sand Grouse (USA) (Arctic Tern **69** (USA) 126) [2007 p7.1g⁵ 7m⁴ 5g³ 5.7g p8g p6g⁶ 7f⁵ p7.1g³ p8g p8g* Oct 24] 20,000F, 10,000Y: sparely-made gelding: half-brother to several winners, notably smart French/ Spanish miler Sand Falcon (by Polar Falcon): dam French 1¼m winner: fair handicapper: won at Kempton in October: stays 1m: acts on polytrack and firm going. *David Pinder*

GOLDEN DAGGER (IRE) 3 ch.f. Daggers Drawn (USA) 114 – Santarene (IRE) 46 **91** (Scenic 128) [2007 85: 11.4m 10g 10.1g³ 12g 10m 10.4d Oct 13] big, strong filly: fairly useful handicapper: best effort when third at Epsom: off 3 months before final appearance: stays 1¼m: acts on good to soft ground: wore cheekpieces fifth outing. *K. A. Ryan*

GOLDEN DANE (IRE) 2 b.g. (Apr 28) Danetime (IRE) 121 – Golden Charm (IRE) **66** 63 (Common Grounds 118) [2007 6g 6f 5.1d⁶ 5.3m² p5.1g* p5.1g⁴ Nov 30] good-topped gelding: fair form: improved gradually, won seller at Wolverhampton (made all) in October: good fourth in claimer there final start: should prove best at 5f/6f: acts on polytrack, good to firm and good to soft going. *I. A. Wood*

GOLDEN DESERT (IRE) 3 b.g. Desert Prince (IRE) 130 – Jules (IRE) 76 (Danehill **96** (USA) 126) [2007 84: p6g² 6g⁶ p6g⁵ 6g⁴ p6m* 5m p6g³ p7g⁴ p7g* Nov 21] strong, lengthy gelding: useful handicapper: won at Lingfield in August and November (beat Danetime Lord by neck): stays easy 7f: acts on polytrack and good to firm going: visored fourth to seventh starts: usually races up with pace. *T. G. Mills*

GOLDEN DIXIE (USA) 8 ch.g. Dixieland Band (USA) – Beyrouth (USA) (Alleged **103** (USA) 138) [2007 100: 5m 6g 5.7f³ 5m* 5d² 5m 5d 6g 6m³ 5.6m* 6g* 5g 5.6m 6d 6g p5.1g⁴ Nov 4] good-bodied gelding: useful handicapper: won at Salisbury in June and Doncaster and Goodwood (beat Mac Gille Eoin by 1½ lengths) in August: creditable fourth to Chief Editor at Wolverhampton final outing: best at 5f/6f: acts on polytrack, firm and good to soft going: tried in cheekpieces: tough. *R. A. Harris*

GOLDEN FEATHER 5 ch.g. Dr Fong (USA) 128 – Idolize 92 (Polish Precedent **85** (USA) 131) [2007 10f⁴ Aug 4] tall, leggy gelding: fairly useful performer, lightly raced on Flat nowadays: modest hurdler/novice chaser: creditable effort only start at 5 yrs: stays 1¼m: acts on soft and firm going: tried visored. *Miss Venetia Williams*

GOLDEN FOLLY 3 ch.g. Polish Precedent (USA) 131 – Height of Folly 81 (Shirley **58**
Heights 130) [2007 57p: 10.1g 9.9g³ p16g 12.4d⁵ p12g Oct 29] modest maiden: should
stay at least 1¾m: raced only on polytrack and good ground or softer: blinkered last 2
starts. *Lady Herries*

GOLDEN GROOM 4 b.g. Groom Dancer (USA) 128 – Reine de Thebes (FR) 67 **66**
(Darshaan 133) [2007 55: 16s⁵ 13d³ 16.1m⁴ 12.1g³ 16m* 16.1m* Sep 10] rather leggy
gelding: fair handicapper: won at Ripon in August and Newcastle in September: stays
2m: acts on firm and soft going: reliable: has joined P. Beaumont. *C. W. Fairhurst*

GOLDEN HOPE (IRE) 3 b.g. Iron Mask (USA) 117 – Ivory Dawn 85 (Batshoof 122) **47**
[2007 –: 5m⁴ 6g 5m 5m 7m Nov 3] poor maiden: below form in handicap at Musselburgh
third start: best effort at 5f on good to firm going: blinkered. *T. G. McCourt, Ireland*

GOLDEN HORUS (USA) 2 ch.g. (Feb 23) Buddha (USA) 122 – Sunburst (Gone **55 p**
West (USA)) [2007 p6g p8m Dec 8] $12,000Y: fifth foal: half-brother to 3 winners
abroad: dam, US 1m winner, out of Oaks d'Italia winner Bright Generation: much better
effort in maidens when eighth at Lingfield (slowly away) second outing: worth a try at 7f:
open to further improvement. *P. J. O'Gorman*

GOLDEN MEASURE 7 b.g. Rainbow Quest (USA) 134 – Dawna 106 (Polish Prece- **–**
dent (USA) 131) [2007 –: p12.2g p16g May 9] good-topped gelding: modest maiden in
2005, lightly raced and little form on Flat since: tried in cheekpieces. *B. P. J. Baugh*

GOLDEN PEACOCK 3 ch.g. Forzando 122 – Flamingo Times 60 (Good Times **–**
(ITY)) [2007 7s p9.5g 10.9g Jul 12] no show in maidens. *M. Appleby*

GOLDEN PENNY 2 b.g. (Feb 22) Xaar 132 – Dog Rose (SAF) (Fort Wood (USA) **78**
117) [2007 6g 6s⁴ 6g⁴ 7g 8m³ 8.3d³ 8m⁵ Oct 22] lengthy, good-topped gelding: has round
action: third foal: half-brother to 3-y-o Colchium: dam, Group 2 winner at 1m in South
Africa, half-sister to Group 1 winner at 1m/9f there: fair maiden: placed in 2 nurseries:
will stay 1¼m: acts on soft and good to firm going: gelded after final start. *H. Morrison*

GOLDEN PLATITUDE (IRE) 4 ch.g. Spinning World (USA) 130 – Rainbow **69**
Dream (Rainbow Quest (USA) 134) [2007 7m² 8g 8.1g p10g⁶ 9.7f Sep 10] fair maiden:
stays 1¼m: acts on polytrack and good to firm ground: tongue tied last 2 starts: refused to
enter stall Sep 25: sold 5,000 gns. *W. R. Swinburn*

GOLDEN PROSPECT 3 b.g. Lujain (USA) 119 – Petonellajill 73 (Petong 126) [2007 **78**
56: 8.1m* 8m* 8m 8d⁴ 7m² 7g 8.3m⁵ Sep 17] fair handicapper: won at Warwick and
Thirsk in May: gelded after final start: stays 1m: acts on good to firm and good to soft
going. *J. W. Hills*

GOLDEN QUEST 6 ch.g. Rainbow Quest (USA) 134 – Souk (IRE) 98 (Ahonoora **102**
122) [2007 –: 14m³ 21.7s³ 16m⁴ 18m 14.6m 18d Oct 20] strong gelding: useful performer
nowadays: creditable efforts when in frame in 2007, including in Queen Alexandra
Stakes at Royal Ascot (third to Enjoy The Moment) and handicap at Ascot (fourth to
Leg Spinner) second/third outings, not disgraced when eleventh of 33 to Leg Spinner in
Cesarewitch at Newmarket final start: stays 2½m: acts on all-weather, soft and good to
firm ground. *M. Johnston*

GOLDEN RIBBONS 3 ch.f. Compton Place 125 – Mim 39 (Midyan (USA) 124) **–**
[2007 –: p5g p8g 5m⁵ 7d May 15] little form: tried blinkered/in cheekpieces. *J. R. Boyle*

GOLDEN SPECTRUM (IRE) 8 ch.g. Spectrum (IRE) 126 – Plessaya (USA) (Nure- **59**
yev (USA) 131) [2007 68: p8.6g⁵ p8.6g³ p9.5g p8.6g* f8g⁵ p8.6g p8.6g³ p8g⁴ p8.6g⁴ **a73**
p8g³ p8.6g³ p9.5g p8.6g³ p8.6g⁴ 8.2s 8m³ p7.1g p9.5g p8.6g³ p8.6g* p8g² p8.6g³ p8.6g²
p8g⁵ p8.6g 8.1f p8.6g⁵ 10m Sep 11] leggy, quite good-topped gelding: fair handicapper
on all-weather, modest on turf: won at Wolverhampton in February and July: stays 9.5f:
acts on all-weather, firm and soft going: blinkered: tried in visor/cheekpieces/tongue
tie: often slowly away: has raced freely: said to have finished distressed final outing.
R. A. Harris

GOLDEN SPRITE 4 b.f. Bertolini (USA) 125 – Shalad'or 97 (Golden Heights 82) **73**
[2007 71: 10m³ 9.9g Aug 15] workmanlike filly: fair handicapper: stays 10.2f: acts on
polytrack and firm going: bolted to post once at 2 yrs, withdrawn after unruly in stalls
Aug 27. *B. R. Millman*

GOLDEN SQUARE 5 ch.g. Tomba 119 – Cherish Me 88 (Polar Falcon (USA) 126) **66 d**
[2007 68: p7g² p8.6g² f8g 8.1m 8.2s 8f p8.6g 8.1f p8g p7g p7m p7.1g Oct 19] workmanlike gelding: fair handicapper: lost form after second start: stays 8.6f: acts on all-weather,
firm and good to soft ground: sometimes wears headgear (including last 5 starts): slowly
away third outing: sometimes races freely: modest hurdler, successful in October.
A. W. Carroll

GOLDEN SURPRICE (IRE) 5 b.h. Indian Lodge (IRE) 127 – Sorpresa (ITY) **79**
(Miswaki (USA) 124) [2007 5s⁴ 6d⁵ 6g* 6g³ 6g² 6g 6g³ 5g* 7.5g² a7g⁵ 8g* p7.1g* p6g
Dec 4] has won 13 races in Italy for various trainers, including minor events at Pisa in
March and Livorno in July and claimer at Milan in November: evens favourite, won seller
on British debut at Wolverhampton in November by 5 lengths: ran as if amiss in claimer
at same track next time: stays 1m: acts on polytrack and soft ground. *Aldo Locatelli, Italy*

GOLDEN TITUS (IRE) 3 ch.c. Titus Livius (FR) 115 – Oraplata (USA) (Silver Hawk **120**
(USA) 123) [2007 107: 8d* 8g* 8s³ 8g 8m² Oct 21] half-brother to 3 winners in Italy:
dam, maiden in USA, half-sister to US Grade 1 9f winner Taylor's Special: very smart
performer: successful in 2006 in newcomers race and listed race race at Rome and Premio
Primi Passi at Milan: also beaten head by Boccassini in Prix Robert Papin at Maisons-
Laffitte: trained on well, winning minor event at Rome in March and Premio Parioli
Gioco del Lotto twice (by ¾ length from Freemusic) in April: placed after in Prix Jean
Prat at Chantilly (4½ lengths third to Lawman) and Premio Vittorio di Capua at Milan
(improved effort, ¾-length second to Linngari): stays 1m: acts on soft ground, best effort
on good to firm. *A. Renzoni, Italy*

GOLDEN TOPAZ (IRE) 3 b.f. Almutawakel 126 – Miss Champagne (FR) (Bering **54**
136) [2007 63: 9.3m 8d⁵ 7m⁶ 6g⁶ Sep 3] modest maiden: best around 7f: acts on firm
going. *J. Howard Johnson*

GOLDEN WAVE (IRE) 3 b.f. Green Desert (USA) 127 – Gold Bust (Nashwan (USA) **73**
135) [2007 p8.6g⁵ 10g⁴ p12.2g² p16g⁴ p13.9g⁴ p12.2g Nov 4] 150,000Y: angular, well-
made filly: third foal: half-sister to fairly useful French 10.5f winner Machinale (by
Kingmambo): dam, useful French 1¼m winner, closely related to smart French miler
Gold Splash: fair maiden: left J. Noseda after fourth outing: barely stays 2m: acts on polytrack. *D. M. Simcock*

GOLD EXPRESS 4 b.g. Observatory (USA) 131 – Vanishing Point (USA) (Caller I D **80**
(USA)) [2007 82p: 5m³ Jun 9] big, strong gelding: fairly useful form: good third in
handicap at Windsor only start in 2007: best form at 5f/6f: acts on good to firm and good
to soft ground. *P. J. O'Gorman*

GOLD FLAME 4 b.g. Gorse 116 – Uae Flame (IRE) (Polish Precedent (USA) 131) **72**
[2007 77: p7g⁴ f6g* 6g 6d 6m Aug 10] tall gelding: fair performer: won maiden at
Southwell in May: well below form after: effective at 6f/7f: acts on all-weather and soft
ground. *H. Candy*

GOLD GUEST 8 ch.g. Vettori (IRE) 119 – Cassilis (IRE) (Persian Bold 123) [2007 60: **–**
p10g⁵ p10g Jan 13] leggy gelding: modest performer at 7 yrs: well below form in 2007:
was effective at 9.5f to 1½m: acted on all-weather, firm and soft going: tried visored/
blinkered: often tongue tied: was sometimes slowly away: dead. *P. D. Evans*

GOLD GUN (USA) 5 b.g. Seeking The Gold (USA) – Possessive Dancer 118 (Shareef **–**
Dancer (USA) 135) [2007 –: p12g Jan 10] big, useful-looking gelding: useful performer
at 3 yrs: lightly raced and little form on Flat since: tried in cheekpieces/blinkers: joined
Mrs A. Thorpe, fair hurdler, successful in July/August. *K. A. Ryan*

GOLDHILL FAIR 2 gr.g. (Mar 3) Bertolini (USA) 125 – May Queen Megan 63 **–**
(Petorius 117) [2007 5d 6g 6d⁶ p6g 7m Sep 11] rather leggy gelding: no form: tried in
cheekpieces. *W. G. M. Turner*

GOLD HUSH (USA) 3 ch.f. Seeking The Gold (USA) – Meniatarra (USA) 68 (Zilzal **96**
(USA) 137) [2007 80p: 8m* 9.9g* 9g⁶ 9.9m⁶ 10.2f² 8d⁵ 10d Oct 19] lengthy filly: useful
performer: won maiden at Thirsk in May and handicap at Salisbury in June: good short-
head second to Six of Diamonds in handicap at Bath fifth outing, bumped close home and
originally awarded race, but placed second again at subsequent inquiry: stays 1¼m: acts
on polytrack and firm ground. *Sir Michael Stoute*

GOLD OPTION 3 ch.c. Observatory (USA) 131 – Minskip (USA) 64 (The Minstrel **91**
(CAN) 135) [2007 93: 10g 9d⁴ Jun 16] well-made colt: fairly useful performer: much
better effort in 2007 when fourth in handicap at Sandown: should stay 1¼m: raced mainly
on good/good to soft going: sold 50,000 gns in October. *J. H. M. Gosden*

GOLD PROSPECT 3 b.g. Rainbow Quest (USA) 134 – Grain of Gold 74 (Mr **87**
Prospector (USA)) [2007 10m⁴ 10m⁵ 10g p10g² p9.5g* 10g 10m⁵ 10.5g⁴ Sep 8] 90,000Y:
close-coupled gelding: first foal: dam, 1¼m winner, out of Irish/Yorkshire Oaks winner
Pure Grain: fairly useful handicapper: won maiden at Wolverhampton in June: gelded
prior to final outing: bred to be suited by 1½m: acts on polytrack and good to firm ground.
M. L. W. Bell

GOLD RESPONSE 3 ch.g. Intikhab (USA) 135 – Razor Sharp (Bering 136) [2007 54: **59** p8.6g³ p9.5g³ p9.5g³ p9.5g⁴ 11g⁶ p12.2g⁶ 8.5g 8.5s Jun 21] workmanlike gelding: modest performer: stayed 11f: acted on polytrack: tried visored: held up: dead. *D. Shaw*

GOLD SOVEREIGN (IRE) 3 b.g. King's Best (USA) 132 – Sassenach (IRE) 68 **97 p** (Night Shift (USA)) [2007 p8g* 10m³ Oct 5] 240,000Y: rather leggy, attractive gelding: has fluent action: fourth foal: half-brother to useful 7.5f and 9.5f winner Fairy of The Night and fairly useful 1¼m winner Night Fairy (both by Danehill): dam, Irish 13f winner, half-sister to smart stayer Far Cry: useful form: won maiden at Lingfield in September: good third to Habalwatan in handicap at Newmarket next time, failing to settle fully, though still going on at finish: gelded after: bred to stay 1½m: open to further improvement. *Saeed bin Suroor*

GO MO (IRE) 5 br.g. Night Shift (USA) – Quiche 83 (Formidable (USA) 125) [2007 **–** 62: p6g f7g Feb 6] quite good-topped gelding: fairly useful handicapper at 3 yrs, on downgrade since: tried tongue tied: sold 800 gns. *R. M. H. Cowell*

GONE FAST (USA) 2 ch.f. (Mar 14) Gone West (USA) – Abita (USA) (Dynaformer **90** (USA)) [2007 6d² 6d* 7m⁶ 6d 6m Oct 5] $230,000Y: good-topped filly: second foal: dam, US 6f to 9f winner, half-sister to smart 1¼m/1½m winner Luhuk: fairly useful form: won maiden at Windsor (by 5 lengths) in July: little impact in pattern events, in Cheveley Park Stakes at Newmarket (twelfth of 14) final start: should stay 7f/1m. *J. R. Fanshawe*

GONE GOLD (USA) 3 ch.c. Seeking The Gold (USA) – Gioconda (USA) (Nijinsky **79 +** (CAN) 138) [2007 10m⁵ p8.6g³ 9.2d* Jun 28] brother to winner in USA and closely related to several winners abroad, notably very smart 1m (Grand Criterium at 2 yrs) to 1½m (US Grade 3) winner Ciro (by Woodman): dam, French 1m winner, half-sister to Bosra Sham and Hector Protector: fairly useful form: visored, won maiden at Hamilton in June: should stay 1¼m: sold 16,000 gns in October. *J. Noseda*

GONE'N'DUNNETT (IRE) 8 b.g. Petardia 113 – Skerries Bell 71 (Taufan (USA) **60 §** 119) [2007 76: f5g 6.1g 8.2s 5.3d² 6s p5g 5.2d 6m* 6f⁵ 5.3d 6g 6m p6g p6g p6g⁵ p6g⁴ f6d⁵ f5d* p6g⁵ Dec 29] strong gelding: modest handicapper: won at Yarmouth in August and Southwell in December: best at 5f/6f: acts on all-weather, firm and good to soft going: wears headgear: has hung left: unreliable. *Mrs C. A. Dunnett*

GONGIDAS 3 b.c. Big Shuffle (USA) 122 – Gonfalon (Slip Anchor 136) [2007 8d² **98** 8.3m* 8.2d* 8g⁶ 8g* 8d Oct 12] well-made colt: brother to several winners, including smart German 8.8f winner Gonlargo and useful 7f to 8.5f winner (including 1m in Germany at 2 yrs) Gonfilia, and half-brother to 3 winners by Lando, including smart German 11f/1½m winner Gonbarda: dam unraced sister to useful stayer Gondolier: useful performer: won maiden at Windsor in June and handicaps at Nottingham in July and Thirsk (again looked wayward when beating Osteopathic Remedy by short head) in August: below form in similar event at York final outing: stays 1m: acts on good to firm and good to soft going: visored last 3 starts: temperament under suspicion. *Saeed bin Suroor*

GOOCHIE (IRE) 3 b.f. Montjeu (IRE) 137 – Royal Ulay (FR) 78 (Selkirk (USA) 129) **62** [2007 –: 10m² 10m⁴ 12s 12v 10m⁴ p10g p12g⁴ Nov 28] 9,500F, €100,000Y: lengthy filly: first foal: dam Irish maiden (stayed 1m): modest maiden handicapper: creditable fourth at Kempton final outing: stays 1½m: acts on polytrack, soft and good to firm going: usually races prominently. *John Joseph Murphy, Ireland*

GOOD ARTICLE (IRE) 6 b.g. Definite Article 121 – Good News (IRE) 61 (Ajraas **70** (USA) 88) [2007 70: 10.2f³ Apr 11] sturdy gelding: blind in near-side eye: fair performer: stays easy 1½m: acts on polytrack and firm going: has worn tongue strap. *D. K. Ivory*

GOODBYE 3 ch.f. Efisio 120 – Blow Me A Kiss 72 (Kris 135) [2007 –: 8g⁴ 7.5g³ 7d⁴ **89** 6.1s³ 7g* 7g* 9.1v³ 7g Nov 3] strong filly: fairly useful performer: won maiden at Thirsk in July and handicap at Newcastle in October: stays 9f, but not short of speed: unraced on going firmer than good (acts on heavy). *G. A. Swinbank*

GOODBYE CASH (IRE) 3 b.f. Danetime (IRE) 121 – Jellybeen (IRE) 72 (Petardia **82** 113) [2007 76: p5g* 6.1m 6s* 7s⁴ 6v⁴ 6s³ p6g⁴ p7m 6v p6g⁴ Dec 30] small, leggy filly: fairly useful handicapper: won at Kempton and Newmarket in May: effective at 5f to 7f: acts on polytrack, heavy and good to firm going: held up. *P. D. Evans*

GOODBYE MR BOND 7 b.g. Elmaamul (USA) 125 – Fifth Emerald 54 (Formidable **97** (USA) 125) [2007 98: 8s 8.1g⁵ 9.1g* 8g² 10m 8m 8.9s⁵ 8m⁴ 8.1m⁵ 9.8m⁵ 8m⁵ 8.9d Oct 13] strong, lengthy gelding: useful handicapper: won at Ayr in May: good efforts when in frame after, especially when fourth to Webbow at Thirsk: needs good test at 1m nowadays, and stays 10.4f: acts on fibresand and any turf going: visored (raced freely) once: waited with: tough. *E. J. Alston*

GOOD CAUSE (IRE) 6 b.g. Simply Great (FR) 122 – Smashing Pet (Mummy's Pet **69 ?**
125) [2007 10m⁵ 10g⁶ f6g Dec 27] workmanlike gelding: little form over hurdles: maiden
on Flat, seemingly fair form first 2 starts: stays 1¼m. *Mrs S. Lamyman*

GOOD EFFECT (USA) 3 ch.g. Woodman (USA) 126 – River Dreams (USA) (River- **80**
man (USA) 131) [2007 66: 9.9s p8g³ p8g* 10g* 9g⁴ Aug 26] strong, useful-looking
gelding: fairly useful handicapper: won at Kempton and Sandown in August: stays 1¼m:
acts on polytrack: sold 32,000 gns in November. *A. P. Jarvis*

GOODENOUGH MOVER 11 ch.g. Beveled (USA) – Rekindled Flame (IRE) **73**
(Kings Lake (USA) 133) [2007 86: 6g 7m 5.7g² 5.1g³ 6d* 6d³ 6m⁴ 7d Oct 9] rangy gelding: fair handicapper nowadays: won at Leicester in August: stays 7f: acts on polytrack,
firm and soft going: blinkered last 6 starts: races prominently. *Andrew Turnell*

GOOD ETIQUETTE 3 b.g. Tipsy Creek (USA) 115 – Aliuska (IRE) 70 (Fijar Tango **–**
(FR) 127) [2007 –: 6m 8.2m Apr 17] leggy gelding: last in maidens. *Mrs S. Lamyman*

GOOD GORSOON (USA) 2 b.c. (May 23) Stravinsky (USA) 133 – Alwaysinbloom **85**
(USA) (Unbridled (USA) 128) [2007 6m⁵ 6g³ 5.7f* 6m 5.1m⁴ p6g³ Oct 29] $35,000Y:
quite good-topped colt: second foal: dam, US 8.3f winner, half-sister to US Grade 1 7f
runner-up Great Notion and useful 2-y-o 7f winner Chester Le Street: fairly useful
performer: won maiden at Bath in August: unlucky fourth in nursery at Bath: likely to
prove best kept to 5f/6f: acts on polytrack and firm going. *B. W. Hills*

GOOD INTENTIONS 5 ch.m. Bien Bien (USA) 125 – Level Headed 68 (Beveled **–**
(USA)) [2007 38: p10g Jan 3] leggy mare: poor maiden at 4 yrs, well held sole start in
2007. *P. W. Hiatt*

GOOD INVESTMENT 5 b.g. Silver Patriarch (IRE) 125 – Bundled Up (USA) **–**
(Sharpen Up 127) [2007 56: f14g 16.1m Jun 2] unfurnished gelding: modest performer at
4 yrs: no show in 2007: tried in cheekpieces, blinkered last 3 starts. *Miss Tracy Waggott*

GOOD LUCK CHIP (IRE) 3 b.f. Princely Heir (IRE) 111 – Surabaya (FR) (Galetto **–**
(FR) 118) [2007 –: 5.7d May 16] well held in maidens/claimer: dead. *I. A. Wood*

GOOD RETURN 2 b.g. (Feb 6) Fasliyev (USA) 120 – Fickle 95 (Danehill (USA) 126) **62**
[2007 8.2d 8.2g Nov 7] rangy gelding: modest form in maidens at Nottingham, forced
strong pace in latter. *Jane Chapple-Hyam*

GOOD WEE GIRL (IRE) 5 b.m. Tagula (IRE) 116 – Auriga 73 (Belmez (USA) 131) **–**
[2007 –: 7m 8m Jun 13] leggy mare: one-time fair performer: little form since 2005:
usually wears cheekpieces/blinkers. *S. Woodman*

GOODWOOD SPIRIT 5 b.g. Fraam 114 – Rechanit (IRE) (Local Suitor (USA) 128) **57**
[2007 –: 7f 8m 7m 6.1g 6m 7.1s 8d⁵ 8.1m² 8f³ 8.1d 8.3m p9.5m 8.1m p9.5g Oct 12] leggy
gelding: modest performer nowadays: stays 1m: acts on firm and good to soft going:
usually wears headgear: takes keen hold. *J. M. Bradley*

GOODWOOD STARLIGHT (IRE) 2 br.c. (Feb 15) Mtoto 134 – Starring (FR) 74 **85 +**
(Ashkalani (IRE) 128) [2007 7d* 8m* Sep 4] 32,000Y: lightly-made colt: second foal:
half-brother to 4-y-o Spinning: dam, second at 1¼m from 2 starts, half-sister to smart
sprinter Watching: fairly useful form: won both starts, maiden at Salisbury in August and
nursery at Goodwood (dead-heated with Townkab having hung markedly left): will stay
1¼m/1½m. *J. L. Dunlop*

GO ON BE A TIGER (USA) 3 br.g. Machiavellian (USA) 123 – Queen's Logic **97**
(IRE) 125 (Grand Lodge (USA) 125) [2007 98p: 10m 11.5g 8g² 8m 7d 6m⁴ 6d Oct 3]
good-topped, attractive gelding: useful performer: in-and-out form in 2007: showed signs of temperament final start: gelded after: best form at 1m: acts on soft ground.
M. R. Channon

GO ON GREEN (IRE) 3 b.c. Kyllachy 129 – Colouring (IRE) 79 (Catrail (USA) **83**
123) [2007 76: p6g* f7g³ p7g⁴ 6g³ 6g⁴ 6s⁵ p6g³ p6g Jul 11] compact colt: fairly useful
handicapper: won maiden at Wolverhampton in February: effective at 6f/7f: acts on all-
weather and good to firm ground: has reportedly had breathing problem, and sometimes
tongue tied: reliable: sold 14,000 gns in October. *E. A. L. Dunlop*

GOOSE CHASE 5 b.g. Inchinor 119 – Bronzewing 103 (Beldale Flutter (USA) 130) **56**
[2007 76: p8.6g⁶ p8g⁶ p7g p9.5g 8.1m 7d May 15] quite good-topped gelding: modest
performer nowadays: left A. Hales 7,000 gns after third outing and P. Blockley after
fourth: stays 1m: acts on all-weather and good to soft going: tried blinkered/in cheekpieces: has raced freely: none too genuine. *B. J. Llewellyn*

GOOSE GREEN (IRE) 3 b.g. Invincible Spirit (IRE) 121 – Narbayda (IRE) 68 (Kah- **72**
yasi 130) [2007 69: p8.6g 8.3m 7.1d² 8.1g 7g 7m⁴ 8.1d p8g⁴ 7g² 7m 7g 6v⁵ p9.5g² p8.6g*

p8.6g³ p7g Dec 1] neat gelding: fair handicapper: won at Wolverhampton in October: stays 9.5f: acts on polytrack and any turf going. *R. J. Hodges*

GORDONSVILLE 4 b.g. Generous (IRE) 139 – Kimba (USA) (Kris S (USA)) [2007 **88** 88: p10g² 13.8m² p12g² p12.2g* Oct 8] tall, good-topped gelding: fairly useful performer: won maiden at Wolverhampton (by 5 lengths) in October: likely to stay 1¾m: acts on polytrack and firm going: sold 32,000 gns. *A. M. Balding*

GO RED 3 b.g. Best of The Bests (IRE) 122 – Boulevard Rouge (USA) 71 (Red Ransom – (USA)) [2007 51: 8m 8g 7m Aug 1] close-coupled, workmanlike gelding: maiden: little form in 2007 (eased as if amiss final outing). *M. W. Easterby*

GORGEOUS GIRL 3 b.f. Generous (IRE) 139 – Zielana Gora (Polish Precedent – (USA) 131) [2007 46: p13.9g Oct 5] poor maiden: bred to stay beyond 7f. *P. W. D'Arcy*

GO SOLO 6 b.g. Primo Dominie 121 – Taza (Persian Bold 123) [2007 96: 14g Jul 31] workmanlike gelding: has a quick action: useful handicapper at 5 yrs: well held sole outing in 2007, looking moody: stays 1½m: acts on firm and good to soft going: fair hurdler. *D. E. Pipe*

GO TECH 7 b.g. Gothenberg (IRE) 117 – Bollin Sophie (Efisio 120) [2007 92: 8m 8m⁵ **89** 9.8m² 12m⁵ 10m³ 10.4d Oct 13] rather leggy, lengthy gelding: shows plenty of knee action: fairly useful handicapper: creditable efforts in 2007 when placed: stays 1½m: acts on polytrack and has form on any turf going, though much better record on good or firmer: sometimes races freely: modest form over hurdles. *T. D. Easterby*

GOT GREEN (FR) 2 ch.f. (Mar 21) Green Tune (USA) 125 – Aphrodisias (FR) **56** (Double Bed (FR) 121) [2007 5.5d 6m 8.1m p10g Oct 24] €32,000Y: sturdy filly: second foal: dam unraced sister to useful French/US performer up to 1m Top Shape: modest maiden: best effort third start: sold 2,500 gns. *R. Hannon*

GO THE DISTANCE (IRE) 5 b.m. Cape Cross (IRE) 129 – Law Student (Preco- – cious 126) [2007 74: p7.1g Mar 2] eighth foal: half-sister to 3 winners, including useful Irish 2002 2-y-o 1m winner (stays 1½m) Askthejudge (by Revoque): dam, maiden, half-sister to Ribblesdale Stakes winner Queen Midas: fair maiden handicapper: runner-up on 4-y-o reappearance, little impact since (left M. O'Brien after final start that year), including at Wolverhampton sole start at 5 yrs: stays 7f: acts on good to soft ground. *Adrian Sexton, Ireland*

GOTHENBURG (UAE) 2 b.c. (Mar 23) Halling (USA) 133 – Poised (USA) (Rahy **111 p** (USA) 115) [2007 7d² 6d* 7f* Aug 5] good-bodied colt: third foal: dam, ran twice in France, sister to Noverre and closely related to Arazi: smart form: won maiden at Ayr in July and nursery at Newbury in August, latter impressively by 7 lengths (value more still, eased): will be suited by 1m/1¼m: has joined Godolphin: pattern-race performer in the making. *M. Johnston*

GOURANGA 4 b.f. Robellino (USA) 127 – Hymne d'Amour (USA) 58 (Dixieland **47** Band (USA)) [2007 72: p13.9g⁴ p12.2g⁶ p12.2d⁴ Dec 28] maiden: fair at 3 yrs, just poor in 2007: barely stays 1½m: acts on good to firm and good to soft ground, probably on polytrack. *A. W. Carroll*

GOVENOR ELIOTT (IRE) 2 ch.g. (Jan 22) Rock of Gibraltar (IRE) 133 – Lac **71 p** Dessert (USA) 91 (Lac Ouimet (USA)) [2007 6f⁵ 7m⁵ 7g⁵ Oct 16] €60,000Y: rather leggy gelding: third reported foal: half-brother to 1m and 1½m winner Exclusive Air (by Affirmed): dam, 2-y-o 7f/7.5f winner, later successful in US: fair form in maidens, not seeing races out thoroughly: gelded after final start: bred to stay 1m: should do better at 3 yrs. *M. Johnston*

GOVERNMENT (IRE) 6 b.g. Great Dane (IRE) 122 – Hidden Agenda (FR) 55 **58** (Machiavellian (USA) 123) [2007 –, a60: f7g f7g* f7g f8g f7g⁴ f7g² f8g* f7g f8g² 10m 10m 8m 8f⁴ p6g 8d 7d7 f8g Dec 27] well-made gelding: modest handicapper: won at Southwell in March and May: stays 1m: acts on fibresand and firm ground: tried blinkered: races prominently: has twice reportedly bled. *M. C. Chapman*

GOWER 3 b.c. Averti (IRE) 117 – Alashaan 73 (Darshaan 133) [2007 78: p6g* p6g⁶ **85** 5.1m⁵ 5g⁴ 5m 5.3d² 5g⁴ 6.3m 5d p5g Oct 19] rather leggy, close-coupled colt: fairly useful performer: won maiden at Wolverhampton in March: left R. Charlton after sixth start: will prove best at 5f/6f: acts on polytrack and good to soft going: tried in headgear. *Ms F. M. Crowley, Ireland*

GOWER BELLE 2 b.f. (Jan 25) Fantastic Light (USA) 134 – Polish Belle (Polish **67** Precedent (USA) 131) [2007 p7g⁶ 6d⁴ 5.7m⁴ p6g² p7.1g⁴ p6g⁵ Oct 15] 16,000Y: small filly: third foal: dam unraced close relation to smart sprinter Danehurst: fair maiden: in frame 4 times, including in nursery: effective at 6f/7f: acts on polytrack, good to firm and good to soft going: tried blinkered. *W. R. Muir*

GOWER SONG 4 b.f. Singspiel (IRE) 133 – Gleaming Water 81 (Kalaglow 132) **108**
[2007 107: 14.1m³ p13m⁶ 10.3m* Nov 10] workmanlike filly: useful performer: close
third to Cape Secret in handicap at Salisbury on reappearance (reportedly suffered
hairline fracture of a cannon bone and off 8 months after): better effort on return when
winning listed race at Doncaster in November by head from Lake Toya: effective at 1¼m
to 1¾m: acts on firm and soft going: reliable. *D. R. C. Elsworth*

GOWNA'S HOPE (IRE) 4 b.g. Distant Music (USA) 126 – Embolden (Warning 136) **–**
[2007 –: 8.1m Aug 7] little form: tried tongue tied. *J. W. Mullins*

GRACE BAY 4 ch.f. Komaite (USA) – Canova's Grace (Ron's Victory (USA) 129) **–**
[2007 p7g p5.1g p5.1g Jan 28] first foal: dam unraced: no sign of ability. *Bob Jones*

GRACECHURCH (IRE) 4 b.g. Marju (IRE) 127 – Saffron Crocus 83 (Shareef **64**
Dancer (USA) 135) [2007 85: 11.7f 8d 8.1g 8d 10.2m⁶ p12g⁴ p13.9g Nov 23] leggy,
useful-looking gelding: fairly useful handicapper in 2006, just modest nowadays: stays
easy 1½m: acts on polytrack, firm and soft going (yet to race on heavy): has sweated.
R. J. Hodges

GRACEFUL DESCENT (FR) 2 b.f. (Apr 15) Hawk Wing (USA) 136 – Itab (USA) **74**
71 (Dayjur (USA) 137) [2007 7v² 7m² 8g³ p8.6g² 8d* 6m Oct 5] 19,000F, 14,000Y:
good-topped filly: fifth foal: half-sister to fairly useful 1½m winner Permanent Way (by
Fantastic Light): dam, 7f winner, half-sister to Poule d'Essai des Pouliches winner Ta
Rib: fair form: placed 4 times prior to winning minor event at Ayr in September:
insufficient test in sales race final start: will be suited by 1¼m/1½m: acts on polytrack,
heavy and good to firm going. *R. A. Fahey*

GRACEFUL FLIGHT 5 gr.m. Cloudings (IRE) 112 – Fantasy Flight (Forzando 122) **–**
[2007 47: 6g May 11] close-coupled mare: poor maiden at 4 yrs: well held sole outing in
2007. *P. T. Midgley*

GRACEFULL MODEL 3 b.f. Erhaab (USA) 127 – Bedtime Model (Double Bed **–**
(FR) 121) [2007 p8g 8d Oct 23] fourth foal: dam unraced: tailed off in maiden and
claimer. *Mrs C. A. Dunnett*

GRACEFUL STEPS (IRE) 3 b.f. Desert Prince (IRE) 130 – Ghassak (IRE) 78 (Per- **79**
sian Bold 123) [2007 61: 8.2g* 10m² 9g* 10m* 11.5g 8m 10m Jul 28] good-topped filly:
fair handicapper: won at Nottingham in April, and Musselburgh and Lingfield in May:
best beyond 1m, and should be suited by 1½m: raced mainly on good/good to firm going:
sold 10,000 gns. *E. J. O'Neill*

GRACIE'S GIFT (IRE) 5 b.g. Imperial Ballet (IRE) 110 – Settle Petal (IRE) (Roi **69**
Danzig (USA)) [2007 69: p8g 7m² 6g⁵ 8d³ 8.1v⁶ 7g⁴ 8g 8d Oct 3] compact gelding: fair
handicapper: stays 1m: acts on all-weather, heavy and good to firm going: tried in
cheekpieces: held up. *A. G. Newcombe*

GRADUATION 3 ch.f. Lomitas 129 – Ceremonial 72 (Lion Cavern (USA) 117) [2007 **102**
7m³ 8.1m* 8g³ 8m 7m² 7d⁵ 6d Oct 19] lengthy filly: second foal: dam, 1m winner,
half-sister to smart middle-distance stayer Sacrament and to dam of very smart 1m/1¼m
performer Chorist: useful performer: won maiden at Warwick in May: much better form
after when placed in listed event at York and handicap at Newmarket (second to Tarteel)
and when fifth to Miss Lucifer in listed race at Ascot: stayed 1m: acted on good to firm
and good to soft going: visits Sakhee. *E. A. L. Dunlop*

GRAFT 8 b.g. Entrepreneur 123 – Mariakova (USA) 84 (The Minstrel (CAN) 135) **–**
[2007 63: p11g Jan 28] quite good-topped gelding: one-time fair handicapper: well held
sole 8-y-o start: tried blinkered, wears cheekpieces nowadays. *Mrs P. Townsley*

GRAFTON (IRE) 4 b.g. Desert Style (IRE) 121 – Gracious Gretclo 54 (Common **58**
Grounds 118) [2007 69d: p7.1g⁴ p6g⁴ f6g⁵ f6g³ f7g f7g Mar 22] strong gelding: modest
performer: stays 7f: acts on all-weather and firm going: blinkered (none too keen) once at
3 yrs: in cheekpieces last 4 outings. *J. O'Reilly*

GRAFTON STREET (IRE) 4 b.c. Danehill (USA) 126 – Bells Are Ringing (USA) **96**
92 (Sadler's Wells (USA) 132) [2007 80: 8.2d² 12m* 20m 12s 12d Oct 21] strong,
good-bodied colt: first foal: dam, Irish 2-y-o 7f winner, half-sister to Breeders' Cup
Juvenile winner Unbridled's Song: useful handicapper: won at the Curragh in April by
length from Grand Revival: well below form after, including at Royal Ascot (whinnying
in paddock, ran as if amiss) next time: stays 1½m well: acts on good to firm and good to
soft going. *A. P. O'Brien, Ireland*

GRAFTY GREEN (IRE) 4 b.g. Green Desert (USA) 127 – Banafsajee (USA) 107 **66**
(Pleasant Colony (USA)) [2007 –: p13.9g 10d⁵ p9.5g 12g⁴ p10g⁴ p11g Nov 28] lengthy **a56**

gelding: fair maiden, lightly raced: stays 1½m: yet to race on extremes of going on turf.
W. M. Brisbourne

GRAHAM ISLAND 6 b.g. Acatenango (GER) 127 – Gryada 93 (Shirley Heights 130) **81**
[2007 90: 12m⁵ 16.2s⁶ Jul 17] strong, lengthy gelding: has a round action: fairly useful
performer: below par in 2007: stays 1¾m: acts on polytrack and good to firm ground (no
form on softer than good): free-going sort: has shown signs of temperament: sold 2,500
gns in October. *G. Wragg*

GRAHAM TWO (IRE) 3 b.g. Agnes World (USA) 123 – Night At Sea 107 (Night **–**
Shift (USA)) [2007 f8g May 1] 100/1, pulled up in maiden at Southwell, soon tailed off.
G. P. Kelly

GRAIL KNIGHT 2 ch.g. (Feb 24) Carnival Dancer 123 – Nashkova (Nashwan (USA) **–**
135) [2007 f8d⁶ Dec 15] 40/1, well held in maiden at Southwell. *Miss Gay Kelleway*

GRANAKEY (IRE) 4 b.f. Key of Luck (USA) 126 – Grand Morning (IRE) 77 (King **66**
of Clubs 124) [2007 63: f8g* f8g f8g* p9.5g⁶ f7g⁵ f8g³ p7m p7g p7.1s⁵ Dec 20] fair
handicapper: won at Southwell in January and February: left M. Quinlan after sixth
outing: stays 1m: raced only on all-weather (best form on fibresand). *M. Wigham*

GRANARY 3 b.f. Singspiel (IRE) 133 – All Grain 102 (Polish Precedent (USA) 131) **67**
[2007 10f 10g⁴ 10.5g⁴ p9.5d² Dec 17] 65,000Y: lengthy filly: second foal: dam, 12.6f
winner, sister to Irish/Yorkshire Oaks winner Pure Grain: fair form in maidens: in frame
3 times: stays 1¼m. *H. Candy*

GRANARY GIRL 5 b.m. Kingsinger (IRE) 94 – Highland Blue 55 (Never So Bold **60**
135) [2007 60: p10g 9.7m² 12g⁴ 10g³ 10g⁶ p10g⁴ p9.5g p9.5d p10g³ Dec 30] leggy
mare: modest handicapper: stays easy 1½m: acts on polytrack and firm going. *J. Pearce*

GRAN CLICQUOT 12 gr.m. Gran Alba (USA) 107 – Tina's Beauty 41 (Tina's Pet **–**
121) [2007 51, a43: p11g Jan 14] modest performer at 11 yrs: well held sole run in 2007:
stays 1½m: acts on polytrack, raced only on good going or firmer on turf: tried in cheekpieces at 7 yrs. *G. P. Enright*

GRANDAD BILL (IRE) 4 ch.g. Intikhab (USA) 135 – Matikanehanafubuki (IRE) **60**
(Caerleon (USA) 132) [2007 –: p9.5g p8.6g 10m 10.1d³ 8m* 8g⁴ 10g Oct 19] rather leggy
gelding: poor mover: modest performer: left W. Musson prior to winning handicap at
Thirsk in September: stays 1¼m: unraced on extremes of going on turf. *J. S. Goldie*

GRAND ART (IRE) 3 b.g. Raise A Grand (IRE) 114 – Mulberry River (IRE) (Blue- **79**
bird (USA) 125) [2007 71: 8.2g³ 8m² 9m⁵ 9g* 10.3m* 10.3m⁶ 11.7g Oct 24] fair performer: won maiden at Yarmouth in July and handicap at Chester in August: stays 1¼m: acts
on good to firm ground: sold 45,000 gns, joined J. Howard Johnson. *M. H. Tompkins*

GRAND ASSAULT 4 b.g. Mujahid (USA) 125 – As Mustard (Keen 116) [2007 59: **62**
p7g² p6g* Dec 13] modest performer, lightly raced: won maiden at Wolverhampton in
December: effective at 6f to 1m: raced only on all-weather: tried in headgear (including
for win): has given trouble at start/refused to enter stall. *G. C. Bravery*

GRAND COURT (IRE) 4 b.f. Grand Lodge (USA) 125 – Nice One Clare (IRE) 117 **45**
(Mukaddamah (USA) 125) [2007 52: p8g 8.1m 10.1d 11.5g Jul 23] poor maiden, lightly
raced: left M. Wallace after third start: seems to stay easy 1¼m: acts on firm going,
probably on good to soft. *Evan Williams*

GRAND CUVEE 2 b.c. (May 4) Efisio 120 – Bel Tempo (Petong 126) [2007 6g 7g 7d⁴ **74**
7s⁴ 7d² Oct 30] 50,000F, 50,000Y, 20,000 2-y-o: useful-looking colt: second foal: dam
twice-raced half-sister to high-class 7f/1m performer Le Vie dei Colori (by Efisio): fair
maiden: ran well in frame in nurseries at Goodwood and Yarmouth last 2 starts: will be
suited by 1m: raced only on good going or softer: sold 33,000 gns. *D. M. Simcock*

GRAND DIAMOND (IRE) 3 b.g. Grand Lodge (USA) 125 – Winona (IRE) 120 **70**
(Alzao (USA) 117) [2007 62: 10.5g 12.1g 8m³ 7.1g³ 8m 6.9g 8m* 7.1m p9.5g⁴ p9.5g⁴
p8.6g Nov 19] good-bodied gelding: fair handicapper: won at Musselburgh in August:
stays 9.5f: raced only on polytrack and good/good to firm going: effective with/without
cheekpieces. *J. S. Goldie*

GRAND DREAM (IRE) 3 ch.g. Grand Lodge (USA) 125 – Tamaya (IRE) (Darshaan **54**
133) [2007 –p: 9.8g⁶ 8m 10g 10s Jul 20] big, good-topped gelding: modest maiden: form
only on reappearance: should be suited by 1¼m+: sold £800 in August. *J. G. Given*

GRANDE CAIMAN (IRE) 3 ch.c. Grand Lodge (USA) 125 – Sweet Retreat (Indian **100 p**
Ridge 123) [2007 85p: p8g 11d⁶ 11d⁶ p13g* p13g* p12m* Dec 9] leggy colt: useful
handicapper, lightly raced: won at Lingfield in November (twice, latter apprentice event)

and December (readily beat Polish Power by length): stays easy 13f: raced only on polytrack and good to soft ground: open to further improvement. *R. Hannon*

GRAND ENTRANCE (IRE) 4 b.g. Grand Lodge (USA) 125 – Alessia (GER) – (Warning 136) [2007 79: 7g Jul 28] fair performer at 3 yrs: well held only outing in 2007: should stay 1m: acts on polytrack, firm and good to soft ground. *C. R. Egerton*

GRAND FLEET 2 b.g. (Mar 3) Green Desert (USA) 127 – Janaat 74 (Kris 135) [2007 **84 p** 5.1m* 6m3 7g2 Sep 22] good-bodied gelding: has scope: eighth foal: half-brother to 3 winners, notably very smart 6f to 1m winner (including at 2 yrs) Lend A Hand (by Great Commotion): dam 1½m winner: fairly useful form: won maiden at Nottingham in April: off 4 months, improvement when second in nursery at Catterick: gelded after: likely to prove best up to 1m. *M. Johnston*

GRAND HEIGHTS (IRE) 3 br.c. Grand Lodge (USA) 125 – Height of Fantasy (IRE) **84** 101 (Shirley Heights 130) [2007 76p: 11.8m2 11.9g4 11.8m* 14m Oct 4] sturdy, good-bodied colt: fairly useful performer: 16/1 on, won 4-runner maiden at Leicester in September: should stay 1¾m+: sold 30,000 gns. *J. L. Dunlop*

GRAND JOUR (IRE) 4 b.g. Grand Lodge (USA) 125 – Reveuse de Jour (IRE) 79 – (Sadler's Wells (USA) 132) [2007 86d: p7.1g 5.7d Aug 19] tall gelding: fairly useful at best: on downgrade: tried blinkered/tongue tied. *B. P. J. Baugh*

GRAND LUCRE 3 b.f. Grand Slam (USA) 120 – Naughty Crown (USA) 84 (Chief's **73** Crown (USA)) [2007 69: p7g* p7.1g p7g 7m4 p8.6g p7g6 p8g2 p7m2 p8.6g Oct 20] unfurnished filly: fair performer: won maiden at Lingfield in March: left J. Hills 17,000 gns after fifth outing: stays 8.6f: acts on polytrack: sometimes slowly away: not straightforward. *G. A. Butler*

GRAND OFFICER (IRE) 3 b.g. Grand Lodge (USA) 125 – Sheer Bliss (IRE) 86 – (Sadler's Wells (USA) 132) [2007 –: p11g 7s May 29] little sign of ability: tried blinkered. *D. J. S. ffrench Davis*

GRAND OPERA (IRE) 4 b.g. City On A Hill (USA) 114 – Victoria's Secret (IRE) 70 **77** (Law Society (USA) 130) [2007 70: 7f4 7d4 7m 8m3 Sep 1] angular, good-topped gelding: has a quick action: fair handicapper: stays 1¼m: acts on firm going, probably on good to soft: blinkered (ran creditably) final outing. *J. Howard Johnson*

GRANDOS (IRE) 5 b.g. Cadeaux Genereux 131 – No Reservations (IRE) 87 – (Commanche Run 133) [2007 54: p8g Mar 17] tall gelding: modest maiden at 4 yrs: well held sole start in 2007: stays 7.5f: acts on firm and soft going: tried in cheekpieces. *Karen George*

GRAND PALACE (IRE) 4 b.g. Grand Lodge (USA) 125 – Pocket Book (IRE) 60 **72** (Reference Point 139) [2007 59: f8g f7g6 p8.6g3 p7.1g* p7.1g2 p7g p6g6 p7.1g p6g p7.1g p7g p6g2 p8.6g p6g2 p6m* p6g3 f6d2 p6g* p6g2 Dec 29] fair handicapper: won at Wolverhampton in January and Lingfield in November and December: effective at 6f to 8.6f: acts on all-weather: visored. *D. Shaw*

GRAND PASSION (IRE) 7 b.g. Grand Lodge (USA) 125 – Lovers' Parlour 83 **106** (Beldale Flutter (USA) 130) [2007 103, a113: p8g2 p10f p10g2 p10g2 10m4 12s5 12m3 **a113** p12g5 9d p10m* p10g2 Dec 22] good-bodied gelding: smart on all-weather, useful on turf: won listed event at Lingfield in November by short head from Gentleman's Deal: ran well otherwise in 2007 when runner-up, including narrow defeats by the same horse in Winter Derby and listed event at Lingfield third/final outings: effective at 1m/1¼m, possibly not 1½m: acts on polytrack, firm and soft going: held up. *G. Wragg*

GRAND PLACE 5 b.g. Compton Place 125 – Comme Ca (Cyrano de Bergerac 120) – [2007 –: 10.2f Jun 10] leggy, lengthy gelding: fair winner at 2 yrs: lightly raced and well held since: tried tongue tied/blinkered. *J. G. Portman*

GRAND REBECCA (IRE) 4 ch.f. Namid 128 – Krayyalei (IRE) 94 (Krayyan 117) – [2007 –: 8d May 30] small filly: little form. *G. A. Huffer*

GRAND SEFTON 4 br.g. Pivotal 124 – Nahlin (Slip Anchor 136) [2007 60: p12g p7g6 **58** p8g 10.2s2 9.7g Aug 16] rangy gelding: modest maiden: stays 1¼m: acts on all-weather and soft ground: tongue tied last 2 starts: sometimes slowly away. *Stef Liddiard*

GRAND SHOW 5 b.g. Efisio 120 – Christine Daae 74 (Sadler's Wells (USA) 132) **89** [2007 94: 5g3 6d3 p6g f5d Dec 11] strong, good-bodied gelding: fairly useful handicapper: effective at 5f/6f: acts on polytrack and good to soft ground: has taken strong hold. *W. R. Swinburn*

GRAND SILENCE (IRE) 4 ch.g. Grand Lodge (USA) 125 – Why So Silent (Mill – Reef (USA) 141) [2007 71: 10d Aug 21] rather leggy gelding: fair maiden at 3 yrs: well held in handicap only start in 2007: tried tongue tied: sold £1,900. *W. R. Swinburn*

GRAND STRATEGY (IRE) 2 b. or br.c. (Mar 25) Singspiel (IRE) 133 – Game Plan **75 p** 118 (Darshaan 133) [2007 8d p7g⁴ Oct 24] close-coupled colt: half-brother to several winners, including Irish 1m (at 2 yrs)/1¼m winner Strategic (by Caerleon) and French 1¼m winner Sobieski (by Polish Precedent), both smart: dam, 1¼m winner and second in Oaks, half-sister to Oaks winner Shahtoush: fair maiden: better than bare result at Newbury (tied up badly on softish ground), and trip possibly too short when fourth at Lingfield: will be suited by 1¼m/1½m: sure to progress. *M. A. Jarvis*

GRAND SYMPHONY 3 ch.f. Zamindar (USA) 116 – Gitane (FR) (Grand Lodge **71** (USA) 125) [2007 –: p6g³ p6g² f6g⁴ 8f² 10.2f³ f8g⁵ 8.3m³ 8d 8g⁵ p8m 8d⁴ Oct 30] sturdy filly: fair maiden: stays 1m: acts on polytrack, firm and good to soft going: tried in cheekpieces: has pulled hard: sold 12,000 gns. *W. Jarvis*

GRAND VALUE (USA) 2 b.f. (Apr 27) Grand Slam (USA) 120 – Privyet Nadya **61** (USA) (Cure The Blues (USA)) [2007 7v⁵ 6m⁶ 7m² Sep 8] $10,000Y: rather leggy, useful-looking filly: third foal: half-sister to winner in US by Mister Baileys: dam unraced out of half-sister to high-class Dante Stakes winner Red Glow: modest form in maidens, runner-up at Thirsk: stays 7f: acts on good to firm going. *T. D. Barron*

GRAND VIEW 11 ch.g. Grand Lodge (USA) 125 – Hemline 77 (Sharpo 132) [2007 **–** 52: p6g⁴ p5.1g⁴ p6g⁶ p6g⁶ p6g⁶ p6g* p6g p6g 6m Aug 24] workmanlike gelding: modest **a54** performer: won minor event at Lingfield in March: best at 6f: acts on all-weather and any turf going: tried blinkered, wears cheekpieces. *J. R. Weymes*

GRAND VIZIER (IRE) 3 b.g. Desert Style (IRE) 121 – Distant Decree (USA) **72 +** (Distant View (USA) 126) [2007 10g p8.6g* 8.1g p8.6g* 8.3g⁶ Sep 24] €33,000Y: sturdy **a83** gelding: second foal: half-brother to 4-y-o Came Back: dam, no form, half-sister to smart performer up to 1½m Triarius: fairly useful on all-weather, fair on turf: won maiden at Wolverhampton in June and dead-heated with Hoh Wotanite in handicap there in July: stays 8.6f: acts on polytrack. *C. F. Wall*

GRAND WELCOME (IRE) 5 b.g. Indian Lodge (IRE) 127 – Chocolate Box 70 **49** (Most Welcome 131) [2007 –: f11g p8g³ p8g p8.6g Apr 28] smallish gelding: just poor nowadays: stays 11f: acts on sand/polytrack, soft and good to firm going: often blinkered/visored: tongue tied: races prominently. *E. J. Creighton*

GRANGEHURST 3 ch.f. Inchinor 119 – My Way (IRE) (Marju (IRE) 127) [2007 58: **–** 10m⁶ a6g a8g a10g Dec 2] modest form in 2-y-o maidens: well held in 2007, sold from Miss J. Gibney 1,700 gns after reappearance (tongue tied in seller). *C. Andersson, Sweden*

GRANGE LILI (IRE) 3 b.f. Daggers Drawn (USA) 114 – Lili Cup (FR) (Fabulous **72** Dancer (USA) 124) [2007 62: p6g⁴ f5g* p5g⁵ p5.1g* p5.1g* f5s³ p5.1g f5g⁶ 5g 5m 5d 5m 5v⁵ p5.1g⁵ 5s⁴ Aug 22] big, workmanlike filly: fair handicapper: won at Southwell and Wolverhampton (2) in January: effective at 5f/6f: acts on all-weather and good to firm ground: usually blinkered: usually slowly away: looks awkward ride. *Peter Grayson*

GRANGE POPPY (IRE) 2 b.f. (Jan 30) Choisir (AUS) 126 – Columbine (IRE) 82 **52** (Pivotal 124) [2007 p5g³ Apr 2] €26,000F, 26,000Y: first foal: dam, 5f (including at 2 yrs)/6f winner, out of half-sister to very smart sprinter Bolshoi: 3/1, third to Thunder Bay in maiden at Lingfield: likely to prove best at 5f/6f. *Peter Grayson*

GRANSTON (IRE) 6 gr.g. Revoque (IRE) 122 – Gracious Gretclo 54 (Common **98** Grounds 118) [2007 98: 8s p8g³ 8g³ 8d³ 8m³ 8m⁵ p8g 8.1s Sep 28] leggy, quite good-topped gelding: useful handicapper: several creditable efforts in 2007, notably when third to Montpellier at Kempton second start: stays 9f: acts on polytrack, firm and soft going: sometimes races freely (has worn crossed noseband), markedly so in visor final 5-y-o start: also tried in cheekpieces: has carried head awkwardly. *J. D. Bethell*

GRANTLEY ADAMS 4 b.g. Dansili 127 – Noble Peregrine (Lomond (USA) 128) **111** [2007 102: 6g⁴ 6.5g* 6.5g⁴ 6m³ 6d⁵ 7m 6m 6m 6m³ 6d 6d 7g⁶ Oct 27] tall gelding: smart handicapper: improved in 2007, winning at Nad Al Sheba in February by 1½ lengths from Sendalam: further progress when third to Beaver Patrol at Newmarket and fifth to Dark Missile in Wokingham Stakes at Royal Ascot (first home in unfavoured group) fourth/fifth outings: well below form last 3 outings: effective at 6f/7f: acts on firm and good to soft going: sold 105,000 gns, joined Godolphin. *M. R. Channon*

GRAPES OF WRATH (UAE) 2 ch.f. (Mar 19) Halling (USA) 133 – Muscadel 103 **53** (Nashwan 135) [2007 p8g p8.6g³ p8g p8.6g f8d² p7.1d Dec 27] sixth foal: sister to French 1½m winner Maelstrom and half-sister to UAE 7.5f winner Festival Queen (by Quiet American), both fairly useful: dam, French 1¼m/1½m winner, out of 1000 Guineas winner Musical Bliss: modest maiden: will be suited by 1¼m/1½m: raced only on all-weather. *M. Johnston*

GRASP 5 b.g. Kayf Tara 130 – Circe 73 (Main Reef 126) [2007 64: f16g^5 p16g^5 Jun 20]   **63**
close-coupled gelding: modest handicapper: stays 17f: acts on all-weather, raced on good
going or softer on turf: tried visored/blinkered: has been tongue tied. *G. L. Moore*

GRAVITAS 4 ch.c. Mark of Esteem (IRE) 137 – Bombazine (IRE) 97 (Generous (IRE)   **118 d**
139) [2007 112: 12g^2 12g^5 10g 10.3m^4 8m Oct 14] leggy, rather lightly-made colt:
half-brother to several winners, including untrustworthy 1¼m winner Dubai Venture (by
Daylami), 1m winner Camelot (by Machiavellian) and French 1½m and 15.5f winner
Affirmative Action (also 8.5f winner in USA, by Rainbow Quest), all useful: dam, 1¼m
winner who stayed 1½m, half-sister to Barathea and Gossamer: smart performer: won
listed races at Saint-Cloud and Toulouse in 2006: left A. Fabre, improved effort when 1¾
lengths second to Quijano in handicap at Nad Al Sheba on reappearance: respectable return
to same rival there next time (raced freely), but below form after: stays 1½m: acts on
heavy and good to firm ground: shaped as if amiss third start. *Saeed bin Suroor*

GRAYLYN RUBY (FR) 2 b.c. (Feb 27) Limnos (JPN) 124 – Nandi (IRE) (Mujadil   **58**
(USA) 119) [2007 p7g 7g 8.1m 8s^5 Sep 26] compact colt: modest maiden: bred to stay
1½m. *J. Jay*

GRAZE ON 5 b.g. Factual (USA) 108 – Queens Check 69 (Komaite (USA)) [2007 96:   **89**
f5g^6 p5f^2 p5g^6 p5.1g Apr 30] lengthy gelding: fairly useful handicapper: was best at 5f/
6f: acted on all-weather, soft and good to firm going: visored/blinkered: raced prominently: dead. *Peter Grayson*

GRAZE ON AND ON 2 ch.f. (May 6) Elmaamul (USA) 125 – Laena 72 (Roman   **–**
Warrior 132) [2007 6m 7g Nov 6] 3,200Y: tall filly: half-sister to 3 winning sprinters by
Clantime, notably useful Cape Merino, herself dam of very smart sprinter Cape of Good
Hope: dam maiden (stayed 7f): no show in maidens. *J. J. Quinn*

GRAZEON GOLD BLEND 4 ch.g. Paris House 123 – Thalya (Crofthall 110) [2007   **78**
92: 5m 5m May 19] big gelding: fairly useful handicapper at 3 yrs: just fair form at best in
2007: effective at 5f/6f: acts on firm and soft going: visored (seemed not to take to it)
once at 3 yrs. *J. J. Quinn*

GRAZIE MILLE 3 b.f. Bertolini (USA) 125 – Daintree (IRE) 66 (Tirol 127) [2007 57:   **–**
7.1m 10g 8g Jun 1] leggy filly: maiden: no form in 2007: tried visored. *R. Berthorton*

GREAT AS GOLD (IRE) 8 b.g. Goldmark (USA) 113 – Great Land (USA) (Friend's   **84**
Choice (USA)) [2007 70: f14g^2 18g^2 21.6m* 18g^2 17.1m^5 18d^2 16.2s^3 21g^6 18m^5 **a58 +**
16.4m 18d Oct 20] good-topped gelding: fairly useful handicapper on turf, modest on
all-weather: won at Pontefract in April and June: stays 21.6f: acts on fibresand, heavy and
good to firm going: has worn cheekpieces/blinkers/tongue tie: usually held up: consistent. *B. Ellison*

GREAT BARRIER REEF (USA) 2 ch.c. (Apr 13) Mr Greeley (USA) 122 – Song   **110**
To Remember (USA) (Storm Cat (USA)) [2007 6g^2 6g^3 7m^5 Sep 16] $550,000Y: good
sort: sixth foal: half-brother to 2 winners abroad, notably smart US Grade 1 9f winner
Magnificent Song (by Unbridled's Song): dam, US maiden, half-sister to US Grade 3
8.5f/9f winner Lech: smart form: taking debut when ¾-length second to Sir Gerry in
Gimcrack Stakes at York: failed to confirm that promise but not discredited continued at
pattern level, close third to Norman Invader in Round Tower Stakes and 8 lengths fifth
to New Approach in National Stakes, both at the Curragh: will stay 1m. *A. P. O'Brien,
Ireland*

GREAT BRITAIN 5 b.h. Green Desert (USA) 127 – Park Appeal 122 (Ahonoora 122)   **118**
[2007 114: 6g^2 6g* Mar 8] close-coupled, good-topped horse: smart performer, lightly
raced: improved again at Nad Al Sheba in 2007, head second to Bad Girl Runs in handicap before winning listed race in March by head from Munaddam, challenging on bridle
over 1f out and needing only hands and heels: has won over 7f, will prove best at 5f/6f:
acts on good to firm and good to soft ground: left Godolphin in May. *Saeed bin Suroor*

GREAT CHARM (IRE) 2 b.g. (May 4) Orpen (USA) 116 – Briery (IRE) 66 (Salse   **72**
(USA) 128) [2007 8m 8d^5 p7.1g^4 Nov 20] big gelding: has scope: fair maiden: fifth to
First Avenue at Yarmouth: stays 1m: gelded after final start. *M. L. W. Bell*

GREAT EXPLORER (IRE) 3 b.c. Indian Danehill (IRE) 124 – Ninth Wonder   **75**
(USA) (Forty Niner (USA)) [2007 58p: p7.1g* Jan 16] better effort in maidens when
winning at Wolverhampton in January by 5 lengths from My Beautaful, still looking
green: looked likely to be suited by 1m: dead. *E. J. O'Neill*

GREAT FUTURE 2 ch.f. (Feb 20) Fantastic Light (USA) 134 – Silvernus (Machia-   **–**
vellian (USA) 123) [2007 8.3g 8g Oct 26] 22,000Y: lengthy, good-topped filly: second

foal: half-sister to 4-y-o Silver Mont: dam, ran 3 times, half-sister to smart miler Dolores: well held in maidens. *H. R. A. Cecil*

GREAT HAWK (USA) 4 b.c. El Prado (IRE) 119 – Laser Hawk (USA) (Silver Hawk **106** (USA) 123) [2007 108p: 12g 10g* 10.4d p12g 9m⁴ Sep 22] strong, good-topped colt: has a fluent, round action: useful performer: won minor event at Ascot (beat Lundy's Lane 2 lengths) in July: creditable efforts after when seventh to Greek Well in handicap at York next time and fourth of 5 to Multidimensional in minor event at Newbury: should stay 1½m: acts on polytrack, unraced on extremes of going on turf: usually visored nowadays. *Sir Michael Stoute*

GREAT MAN (FR) 6 b.g. Bering 136 – Great Connection (USA) (Dayjur (USA) 137) **67** [2007 p12.2g⁴ f12g³ p10g p10g Apr 30] fair performer: won handicap at Le Croise-Laroche in 2004: unraced on Flat at 4/5 yrs: fair form in handicaps in Britain first 2 starts in 2007: stays 1½m: acts on all-weather, raced only on good going or softer on turf: sold 1,600 gns in May. *Noel T. Chance*

GREAT QUEST (IRE) 5 b.m. Montjeu (IRE) 137 – Paparazzi (IRE) 68 (Shernazar **72** 131) [2007 78: 13.8m 12.4m² 14m⁴ 16.1s² 18s 12.1g⁶ 16.1m⁶ Sep 10] half-sister to fairly useful 2002 2-y-o 6f winner Four Jays (by Alzao) and winner in Japan by Seattle Dancer: dam Irish maiden (stayed 1½m): fair handicapper: stays 17f: acts on soft and good to firm going: tried blinkered. *James Moffatt*

GREAT VIEW (IRE) 8 b.g. Great Commotion (USA) 123 – Tara View (IRE) (Wassl **82** 125) [2007 83, a76: 10m 11m 12m⁴ 12d⁵ 10s⁵ 11s* 10.5v² 12s³ 11.8m⁴ 12g 12d Sep 26] **a–** lengthy gelding: fairly useful handicapper on turf, had fair form on all-weather earlier in career: won apprentice event at Newbury in July: stays easy 13f: acts on all-weather and any turf going: usually wears headgear. *Mrs A. L. M. King*

GREATWALLOFCHINA (USA) 2 b.c. (Mar 14) Kingmambo (USA) 125 – Diet- **100** rich (USA) 115 (Storm Cat (USA)) [2007 6g 6g 7m² 7g⁶ 7d Oct 20] strong, close-coupled colt: third foal: half-brother to smart 5f (at 2 yrs)/6f winner Beauty Bright and 7f winner Port of Spain (both in Ireland, by Danehill): dam 5f winner (including King George Stakes and at 2 yrs): useful maiden: stiff tasks, best efforts last 2 starts, 5¼ lengths sixth to Rio de La Plata in Prix Jean-Luc Lagardere at Longchamp and eighth behind New Approach in Dewhurst Stakes at Newmarket: stays 7f. *A. P. O'Brien, Ireland*

GRECIAN SLAVE 2 ch.c. (Mar 1) Spartacus (IRE) 107 – Grecian Halo (USA) 59 **64** (Southern Halo (USA)) [2007 7d 7g⁴ 7s p8.6g⁵ Oct 18] close-coupled colt: modest maiden: stays 8.6f: sold 7,000 gns. *B. Smart*

GREEK EASTER (IRE) 4 b.f. Namid 128 – Easter Heroine (IRE) 72 (Exactly Sharp **85** (USA) 121) [2007 80: 10.5g 12d 9g 8s* 7.8m⁴ 8g* 8.8g⁵ 7g* 8g p12g² p10g* Dec 22] good-topped filly: fairly useful performer: left B. Meehan after third start: won maiden at Hamburg in June, handicap at Bremen in August, minor event at Mannheim in September and, having left C. von der Recke in Germany after ninth start, handicap at Lingfield in December (jinked right late on): stays 1½m: acts on polytrack, firm and soft ground: tended to flash tail final outing at 3 yrs. *D. Myerscough, Ireland*

GREEK ENVOY 3 br.g. Diktat 126 – South Shore 102 (Caerleon (USA) 132) [2007 **113 p** 85: 10s³ 8.9s² 12d 12s* Oct 19] rangy, useful-looking gelding: smart handicapper, lightly raced: won at Leicester (by ½ length from Mad Rush) in June and Newmarket (beat Cutting Crew by neck, leading on bridle final 2f then hanging right and idling): stays 1½m: acts on soft ground: shaped as if amiss penultimate start: remains capable of better still, and should make into a pattern performer. *T. P. Tate*

GREEK GOD 3 b.g. Grand Lodge (USA) 125 – Cephalonia 103 (Slip Anchor 136) **59** [2007 61: p9.5g⁴ f8g² f8g⁵ 12m f11g⁶ May 22] good-topped gelding: good walker: modest maiden: should stay 1½m: acts on all-weather and good to firm going: tried blinkered: sold 12,500 gns in July. *W. Jarvis*

GREEK MYTHOLOGY (USA) 2 b.c. (Mar 29) Mr Greeley (USA) 122 – Tell Me **83** Now (USA) (A P Indy (USA) 131) [2007 6g³ 7m* 6m Jun 19] $800,000Y: rather leggy, quite attractive colt: first foal: dam unraced half-sister to smart 7f performer Wind Cheetah and dam of 4-y-o Confidential Lady out of close relative to Affirmed: fairly useful form: confirmed debut promise (third at Newbury) when winning maiden at Leopardstown in May: unsuited by drop in trip when mid-field behind Henrythenavigator in Coventry Stakes at Royal Ascot, and not seen after: will stay 1m. *A. P. O'Brien, Ireland*

GREEK RENAISSANCE (IRE) 4 b.c. Machiavellian 123 – Athene (IRE) **123** 83 (Rousillon (USA) 133) [2007 108: a6f 6g* 6g³ 6g 6g* 6d* 6m⁵ Nov 10] leggy, quite good-topped colt: very smart performer: further progress in 2007, winning handicap at

Igloos Bentinck Stakes, Newmarket—Greek Renaissance puts up his best performance to date in accounting for Beckermet (third left), Galeota and Borderlescott (fourth left)

Nad Al Sheba (beat Arenti by 2½ lengths) in February (left I. Mohammed, UAE, after fourth start), minor event at Yarmouth in September and Igloos Bentinck Stakes at Newmarket (best effort when beating Beckermet by 2 lengths, running on strongly at finish) in October: respectable fifth to Galeota in listed event at Doncaster final outing: should prove as effective at 5f as 6f: acts on polytrack (well held on dirt on reappearance), soft and good to firm going. *Saeed bin Suroor*

GREEK SECRET 4 b.g. Josr Algarhoud (IRE) 118 – Mazurkanova 63 (Song 132) **63**
[2007 77: f5g 6g 7m 5s 5d⁶ 6m* 6f 5.9g 6m 6m 6f* 5m 6.1m⁵ p6g Oct 14] leggy gelding: modest handicapper: won at Thirsk (ladies) in August and Redcar (apprentices) in September: effective at 5f/6f: acts on polytrack, firm and soft going: tried in cheekpieces, effective blinkered or not: has looked none too genuine. *J. O'Reilly*

GREEK THEATRE (USA) 2 ch.c. (May 4) Smoke Glacken (USA) 120 – Theatre **71**
Flight (USA) 83 (Theatrical 128) [2007 6m⁵ 6m⁵ 7d 7g⁵ p8g² p8g p7g⁵ Nov 30] $37,000Y: tall colt: seventh foal: half-brother to 3 US winners (all at 1m+), including smart 1¼m/1½m Grade 3 winner Sharp Performance (by Kris S): dam, Irish 1¼m/11f winner, half-sister to useful 1½m performer Stereo: fair maiden: best effort when 2½ lengths second to Points of View in nursery at Kempton, almost brought down before halfway: unseated rider leaving stall next time: should be suited by 1m+: acts on polytrack and good to firm ground. *Mrs A. J. Perrett*

GREEK WELL (IRE) 4 b.g. Sadler's Wells (USA) 132 – Hellenic 125 (Darshaan **105**
133) [2007 67p: 10.5g² 12g⁶ 10g* 10g* 8.9s⁴ 9.9g⁵ 10.4d* 10m³ 9m Oct 6] good-bodied gelding: useful handicapper: improved when successful at Sandown (2) in June and York (beat Peruvian Prince by head) in August: excellent third to Monte Alto in John Smith's Stakes at Newbury penultimate start: gone in coat and sweating when running poorly in Cambridgeshire at Newmarket final outing: best around 1¼m: acts on soft and good to firm ground: tongue tied final 3-y-o outing: visored last 3 starts: sold 220,000 gns, then gelded. *Sir Michael Stoute*

GREENBELT 6 b.g. Desert Prince (IRE) 130 – Emerald (USA) (El Gran Senor (USA) **59**
136) [2007 74, a81d: f8g f11g* f11g² f12g f12g f11g 12g⁵ 12.4m Apr 14] fair handicapper **a69**
on all-weather, modest on turf: won at Southwell in February: stays 1½m: acts on all-weather and heavy going: tried in cheekpieces. *G. M. Moore*

GREEN DAY PACKER (IRE) 3 br.g. Daylami (IRE) 138 – Durrah Green 79 (Green **62**
Desert (USA) 127) [2007 64: p9.5g⁶ f12g⁴ 11g 9.9g⁴ 15.8g Sep 22] small, sturdy gelding: modest maiden handicapper: stays 11f, probably not 2m: acts on polytrack and good to firm ground. *P. C. Haslam*

GREEN DIAMOND 2 b.g. (Apr 15) Green Desert (USA) 127 – Balisada 115 (Kris **81**
135) [2007 6g 7g² 7g³ p7m³ Dec 9] 40,000Y: close-coupled gelding: fifth foal: half-brother to 3 winners, including 4-y-o Galactic Star: dam 7f (at 2 yrs) and 1m (Coronation Stakes) winner: fairly useful maiden: placed after debut, best effort when second at Thirsk: likely to stay 1m: gelded after final start. *M. Johnston*

GREEN EARRINGS (IRE) 2 ch.f. (Mar 27) Captain Rio 122 – Kitty Kildare (USA) **54**
68 (Seattle Dancer (USA) 119) [2007 6d⁵ 8.1f⁵ 7.1g Sep 12] 66,000Y: close-coupled filly: fifth foal: half-sister to 3 winners, including fairly useful 6f/7f winner (including at 2 yrs)

Countykat and 9.4f winner Woodboro Kat (both by Woodborough): dam, Irish maiden (stayed 7f), out of sister to smart 7f/1m performer Arjuzah: modest form in maidens: may prove best short of 1m: sold 9,500 gns, sent to Kazakhstan. *R. Charlton*

GREEN IDEAL 9 b.g. Mark of Esteem (IRE) 137 – Emerald (USA) (El Gran Senor (USA) 136) [2007 16s May 12] lightly raced on Flat (useful at 3 yrs), well held only outing in 2007. *Ferdy Murphy* — **–**

GREEN LAGONDA (AUS) 5 gr.g. Crown Jester (AUS) – Fidelis (AUS) (John's Hope (AUS)) [2007 5m 5.2s p6g 5.1s p5g* p6g p5g⁴ p6g p6g* p6g Dec 19] won 3 of his 21 starts in Australia: useful at 2 yrs, but not so good in 2006: fair form in Britain, winning handicap at Kempton in October and claimer at Wolverhampton in December: effective at 5f/6f: acts on polytrack and soft ground. *J. G. Given* — **73**

GREEN MANALISHI 6 b.g. Green Desert (USA) 127 – Silca-Cisa 93 (Hallgate 127) [2007 107: 5.2m* 5g⁵ 5m 5m⁶ 5d 6.1m* 5g 5m⁴ 5.6m⁶ 5m⁵ Oct 4] sturdy gelding: smart performer: better than ever in 2007, winning handicap at Newbury in April and listed event at Chester (beat unlucky Baltic King by short head) in August: creditable fifth to Judd Street in listed event at Newmarket final outing: best at 5f/easy 6f: acts on polytrack and firm going: has hung left. *K. A. Ryan* — **111**

GREENMEADOW 5 b.m. Sure Blade (USA) 130 – Pea Green 98 (Try My Best (USA) 130) [2007 66: 10.2g p8g⁵ 9.7m⁴ p8.6g 9.7m p8g³ p10g p9.5g p10g⁶ p9.5g Dec 3] workmanlike mare: modest handicapper nowadays: stays 1¼m: acts on polytrack and firm going. *S. Kirk* — **54** / **a63**

GREEN OASIS (USA) 2 b.f. (Feb 22) Green Desert (USA) 127 – Class Kris (USA) 117 (Kris S (USA)) [2007 p6g* 6m 6d⁶ Jul 29] \$140,000Y: good-bodied, workmanlike filly: seventh foal: half-sister to 3 winners in US, notably very smart Grade 1 1¼m winner Student Council (by Kingmambo) and Grade 3 8.5f winner Gradepoint (by A P Indy): dam US Grade 2/3 8.5f/9f winner: fairly useful form: won maiden at Wolverhampton in June: upped in class and better form when 3 lengths eighth to You'resothrilling in Cherry Hinton Stakes at Newmarket and 7¼ lengths sixth to Visit in Princess Margaret Stakes at Ascot: will probably stay 7f/1m. *E. J. O'Neill* — **88**

GREEN PARK (IRE) 4 b.g. Shinko Forest (IRE) – Danccini (IRE) 78 (Dancing Dissident (USA) 119) [2007 97: 5m³ 6m 5g⁵ 5m³ 6m 5v* 5v 6s³ 5g 5.6m 6d 5d⁶ Sep 29] useful-looking gelding: useful handicapper: won Gosforth Park Cup at Newcastle (by ½ length from Mecca's Here) in June: good third to Zomerlust in Sky Bet Dash at York eighth start: below form after: raced at 5f/6f: acts on any going. *R. A. Fahey* — **99**

GREEN PIRATE 5 b.g. Bahamian Bounty 116 – Verdura 63 (Green Desert (USA) 127) [2007 67: p8.6g⁶ p8.6g p8g² 8d 9g 8f⁴ p7.1g⁴ p8.6g³ p7.1g² p8.6g p7.1g p6g³ p8.6g⁵ 8m p7.1g² p6g⁴ p7.1g⁴ p7.1s² p7.1g³ Dec 26] leggy, angular gelding: fair on all-weather, modest on turf: stays 8.6f: acts on polytrack and firm going: usually in cheekpieces/visored: has reared in stall: often slowly away, and held up. *W. M. Brisbourne* — **54** / **a70**

GREEN ROOM (FR) 4 b.f. In The Wings 128 – Scarlet Plume 103 (Warning 136) [2007 106: 12m 11.9m³ 12g 12m² Jul 21] leggy filly: useful performer: creditable effort in 2007 only when 1¾ lengths second to Turbo Linn in listed race at Newmarket: stayed 1½m: acted on soft and good to firm ground: tended to hang: stud. *J. L. Dunlop* — **108**

GREEN'S DELIGHT 2 gr.f. (May 18) Hunting Lion (IRE) 115 – Beat Time 78§ (Lion Cavern (USA) 117) [2007 6d 7m Aug 24] well held in maiden/claimer: dead. *M. W. Easterby* — **–**

GREENSLADES 8 ch.h. Perugino (USA) 84 – Woodfield Rose 41 (Scottish Reel 123) [2007 108: 6g 6m⁵ 7d⁵ 6.1s⁴ 6g³ 6m 6g Oct 26] big, strong horse: good walker: useful handicapper: not quite as good in 2007, one of better efforts when third to Golden Dixie at Goodwood fifth outing: effective at 6f/7f: acts on polytrack, soft and good to firm going: races prominently. *P. J. Makin* — **98**

GREEN WADI 2 b.c. (Jan 31) Dansili 127 – Peryllys 67 (Warning 136) [2007 8m² 8.1s³ 8m³ Oct 14] 70,000Y: well-made colt: half-brother to several winners, including useful 6f/7f winner Penelewey (by Groom Dancer) and fairly useful 7f winner Quintrell (by Royal Applause): dam maiden (stayed 1¼m): fairly useful maiden: placed all starts, third to Meer Kat in minor event at Bath final one (finished strongly): will be suited by 1¼m. *M. R. Channon* — **88**

GREENWICH MEANTIME 7 b.g. Royal Academy (USA) 130 – Shirley Valentine 104 (Shirley Heights 130) [2007 102: 18.7m* 16.1v 16g 16m 14g 14.6m⁴ 18d 14g³ Nov 9] sturdy gelding: useful handicapper: won totesport Chester Cup in May by 1½ lengths — **104**

totesport Chester Cup (Handicap), Chester—Greenwich Meantime goes two places better than in 2006; it's close for second between Fair Along (rail) and Enjoy The Moment

from Fair Along: respectable efforts at best after: stays easy 18.7f: acts on polytrack, good to firm and good to soft going (seemingly not on heavy): waited with. *R. A. Fahey*

GREEN WONDER (GER) 2 b.f. (Jan 22) Big Shuffle (USA) 122 – Green Water (Suave Dancer (USA) 136) [2007 p8.6g⁶ Nov 2] €38,000Y, 20,000 2-y-o: fifth foal: sister to 6f winner in Germany: dam, placed up to 1¼m in Germany, half-sister to useful 1m/1¼m winner Prince of Denial: 10/1, well held in maiden at Wolverhampton. *D. M. Simcock* —

GREENWOOD 9 ch.g. Emarati (USA) 74 – Charnwood Queen 61 (Cadeaux Genereux 131) [2007 81, a70: p6g* p7g* 6m p6g 7g⁶ p7g 6g p7g p8g⁵ 7s³ 7.6f 8d p8g⁵ p8g Oct 31] strong, lengthy gelding: fair handicapper: won at Kempton in March and Lingfield in April: stays 7f: acts on all-weather, firm and soft going: formerly blinkered (not since 2003): has worn tongue tie: held up. *P. G. Murphy* **70**

GREMLIN 3 b.g. Mujahid (USA) 125 – Fairy Free (Rousillon (USA) 133) [2007 78: 9.9m* 11g² 10m Jul 12] tall, leggy gelding: has a quick action: fairly useful handicapper: improved form when winning at Salisbury in May, wandering and flashing tail: barely stays 11f: acts on firm and good to soft going. *A. King* **89**

GRENANE (IRE) 4 b.g. Princely Heir (IRE) 111 – Another Rainbow (IRE) 72§ (Rainbows For Life (CAN)) [2007 78: p7.1g Dec 15] fair handicapper at 3 yrs: well held only outing in 2007 (said to have bled): stays easy 7f: acts on polytrack and firm going. *P. D. Evans* —

GRETHEL (IRE) 3 b.f. Fruits of Love (USA) 127 – Stay Sharpe (USA) (Sharpen Up 127) [2007 61: 7m⁶ 8m 7g 6.9g 8.3s 8.5s 7.9f⁵ 9m⁴ 8g³ 9.8g³ 10g 8.5m* 10.3m 8s⁴ 10.5s³ 9.1s³ 8m p8.6g 9.1s* 7.2v Nov 3] leggy, plain filly: fair performer: won minor event at Beverley in September and claimer at Ayr in October: stays 10.5f: acts on soft and good to firm going: often races freely. *A. Berry* **66**

GREY BOY (IRE) 6 gr.g. Medaaly 114 – Grey Perri 103 (Siberian Express (USA) 125) [2007 88: p8g⁴ p7.1g⁴ p8.6g⁴ p8g² 8f 7.1d 7g 6g³ 8.1f 7m⁵ 6.1m Oct 3] tall gelding: fair handicapper: left R. Fahey after fourth start: effective at 6f to 1m: acts on polytrack, firm and good to soft going: races prominently. *A. W. Carroll* **77**

GREYFRIARS ABBEY 3 b.g. Fasliyev (USA) 120 – Mysistra (FR) (Machiavellian (USA) 123) [2007 76p: 7.1d⁴ 8.3d⁵ 7.9m⁵ 9.2m* 9.8g* Aug 27] fairly useful handicapper: won at Hamilton and Ripon in August: gelded after: stays easy 1¼m: yet to race on extremes of going: sometimes slowly away: looks difficult ride: open to further improvement. *M. Johnston* **81 p**

GREY GURKHA 6 gr.h. Kasakov – Royal Rebeka (Grey Desire 115) [2007 8.2m⁶ p7g p9.5g p8g* Dec 16] modest performer, lightly raced: left B. Ellison, won handicap at Kempton in December: stays 1m: acts on polytrack and good to firm going: tried tongue tied: has had breathing problems. *I. W. McInnes* **61**

GREYLAMI (IRE) 2 gr.g. (Mar 4) Daylami (IRE) 138 – Silent Crystal (USA) 94 (Diesis 133) [2007 7.1m⁵ p8g² p7g⁶ Oct 12] 60,000Y: good-topped gelding: first foal: **88**

444

dam, 1m winner (later third in US Grade 2 11f event), half-sister to Canadian 2-y-o Grade 1 8.5f winner Salty You: fairly useful maiden: second to Cordell at Kempton: inadequate test final start: should prove best at 1m/1¼m. *T. G. Mills*

GREY LIGHT (IRE) 3 b.g. Namid 128 – Flying Clouds 40 (Batshoof 122) [2007 f6g **62** p7g 7.1g⁶ 10.5g⁶ 12.1g May 11] workmanlike gelding: modest maiden: left M. Johnston after second outing: should stay 1½m. *L. Lungo*

GREY OUTLOOK 4 ch.f. Observatory (USA) 131 – Grey Galava 64 (Generous (IRE) **70 d** 139) [2007 73: 14g⁴ 14m⁵ 13m⁵ 18g 14m⁶ 13g⁴ 13.1g⁴ 12d⁴ 12.1d⁶ 12.1g 11.1m 17.5s Sep 21] fair handicapper: below form after second outing: stays 2m: acts on heavy and good to firm going: tends to race freely: temperamental. *Miss L. A. Perratt*

GREY REPORT (IRE) 10 gr.g. Roselier (FR) – Busters Lodge (Antwerp City) [2007 **55** 70: p12.2g⁵ Feb 12] lightly-raced maiden on Flat, just modest form only start in 2007: should be suited by 1½m+: raced only on polytrack. *Simon Earle*

GREY SAMURAI 7 gr.g. Gothenberg (IRE) 117 – Royal Rebeka (Grey Desire 115) **70** [2007 12s³ 12.1s* 12.1s⁵ 13m Aug 2] winning hurdler: fair performer, lightly raced on Flat: easily best effort when winning ladies handicap at Beverley in July by 11 lengths: stays 1½m: acts on soft going: tried in cheekpieces. *B. Ellison*

GREYSIDE (USA) 4 gr.g. Tactical Cat (USA) 116 – Amber Gold (USA) (Mr Pros- **–** pector (USA)) [2007 78: p13.9g⁶ f16g⁵ 18g p16.5g Jul 27] good-topped, quite attractive gelding: fair maiden at 3 yrs: little form in 2007: wore cheekpieces last 2 starts: dead. *C. A. Mulhall*

GREYSTOKE PRINCE 2 gr.g. (Apr 12) Diktat 126 – Grey Princess (IRE) 92 **70** (Common Grounds 118) [2007 5s⁶ 6.1s⁴ 6.1d p7g² 7s Oct 14] fair maiden: second in nursery at Lingfield: will prove best up to 7f: acts on polytrack, raced only on ground softer than good on turf: gelded after final start. *W. R. Swinburn*

GREYT BIG STUFF (USA) 3 gr.g. Aljabr (USA) 125 – Dixie Eyes Blazing (USA) **–** 56 (Gone West (USA)) [2007 76: 11.6m 7g 8.3d Aug 1] big gelding: fair performer at 2 yrs: well held in handicaps in 2007: quirky, tried in blinkers. *Miss Gay Kelleway*

GREY VISION 4 gr.f. Grey Desire 115 – Brief Star (IRE) 49 (Brief Truce (USA) 126) **54** [2007 –: 7g 7m⁴ 8f 6.9g 8.5m 10f Sep 17] modest maiden: stays 7f: acts on good to firm going: tried blinkered. *M. Brittain*

GRIMES FAITH 4 b.g. Woodborough (USA) 112 – Emma Grimes (IRE) 54 (Nordico **80** (USA)) [2007 95: p7g* p7g⁶ p6f p7.1g p8g⁶ p8.6g² 7.2s p7.1g⁶ 7m³ p7.1d p6d **a92** Dec 28] good-topped gelding: fairly useful handicapper: won at Lingfield in January: left R. Hannon after sixth start: stays 1m: acts on polytrack, firm and good to soft going: usually blinkered. *K. A. Ryan*

GRIMES HOPE (IRE) 2 ch.c. (Apr 8) Daggers Drawn (USA) 114 – Sharkiyah (IRE) **60** 75 (Polish Precedent (USA) 131) [2007 7m 7m⁴ 5m² 6g 5.8g* 8d a6.8g a6g⁶ a6.8g⁴ Dec 2] sturdy, compact colt: best effort in Britain when second in seller at Windsor (claimed from R. Hannon £6,000): won maiden at Taby in September: stays 5.8f. *C. Bjorling, Sweden*

GRIZEBECK (IRE) 5 b.g. Trans Island 119 – Premier Amour 111 (Salmon Leap **72** (USA) 131) [2007 p12.2g² 10.1m⁴ 11.5d⁶ 14m⁶ 14d⁵ f11d³ Dec 12] big, strong gelding: fair maiden: barely stays 1¾m: acts on good to soft and good to firm going. *R. F. Fisher*

GRIZEDALE (IRE) 8 ch.g. Lake Coniston (IRE) 131 – Zabeta (Diesis 133) [2007 **85 d** 85§: 7g⁶ 7m⁴ 7s⁶ 7g 7.1d 7m⁵ 7v 8s 7g Nov 3] strong gelding: fairly useful handicapper: won at Newmarket in May: well below form after next start: stays 1m: acts on any going: tongue tied: free-going sort: unreliable. *J. Akehurst*

GROOMS AFFECTION 7 b.g. Groom Dancer (USA) 128 – Love And Affection **56** (USA) (Exclusive Era (USA)) [2007 85: p10g⁵ Dec 30] good-bodied gelding: one-time fairly useful handicapper: lightly raced since 2004, modest form in seller only 7-y-o start: stays 1½m: acts on polytrack, soft and good to firm going: tried tongue tied. *K. A. Morgan*

GROSS PROPHET 2 b.g. (Mar 24) Lujain (USA) 119 – Done And Dusted (IRE) 75 **89** (Up And At 'em 109) [2007 p5g 5.1g⁴ 6f³ p6g* p7g³ p6g² 6m* 7g³ 6d⁵ 7d⁵ p6s* Dec 20] workmanlike gelding: third foal: dam 6f/7f winner (latter at 2 yrs): fairly useful performer: won maiden at Wolverhampton in August, nursery at Newbury in September and minor event at Wolverhampton in December: barely stays 7f: acts on polytrack, firm and good to soft going: races prominently: consistent. *Tom Dascombe*

GROUND PATROL 6 b.g. Ashkalani (IRE) 128 – Good Grounds (USA) (Alleged **60** (USA) 138) [2007 68: 10d p10g p12g⁶ p12g Sep 4] good-topped gelding: modest handicapper: stays 1½m: acts on polytrack, firm and good to soft going: tried in headgear/tongue tie: sometimes slowly away. *W. G. M. Turner*

GROUP CAPTAIN 5 b.g. Dr Fong (USA) 128 – Alusha 88 (Soviet Star (USA) 128) **115** [2007 110: 14.1g 12g³ 13.3g³ 12g 12s⁶ 12d* 14d 10s Sep 22] lengthy gelding: smart performer: won handicap at Ascot in July by head from Mull of Dubai: third earlier in Prix d'Hedouville at Longchamp and listed event (to Peppertree Lane) at Newbury: below form last 2 starts: barely stays easy 1¾m: acts on polytrack, firm and soft going: sold 80,000 gns, joined A. King, won on hurdling debut in December. *R. Charlton*

GROUP FORCE (IRE) 3 b.f. Montjeu (IRE) 137 – Allspice (Alzao (USA) 117) **64** [2007 56: 12.1m⁵ p12g³ 16.1g⁵ 13.8g³ 15.8g p13.9g Nov 14] smallish filly: modest handicapper: stays 2m: raced mainly on polytrack and good going or firmer: twice blinkered: has looked a tricky ride. *M. H. Tompkins*

GROUP THERAPY 2 ch.c. (May 5) Choisir (AUS) 126 – Licence To Thrill 83 (Wolf-hound (USA) 126) [2007 5.1f⁶ 5.1g⁵ 5f* 5g² May 21] 30,000Y: good-topped colt: third foal: half-brother to 4-y-o Classic Encounter and 3-y-o Gimme Some Lovin': dam, 5f winner, out of Cherry Hinton winner Crime of Passion: useful form: won maiden at Nottingham in April and minor event at Thirsk (beat New Jersey by 5 lengths) in May: short-head second in minor event at Windsor, then suffered split hind pastern and had 3 screws inserted: will prove best kept to 5f: acts on firm going. *J. A. Osborne*

GROVE CREEK 4 ch.f. Observatory (USA) 131 – Maze Garden (USA) (Riverman **–** (USA) 131) [2007 48: p11g 11.9g 9m May 29] poor maiden: well held at Kempton on reappearance: stays 11f: acts on polytrack and good to soft ground: tried in headgear. *Niall Moran, Ireland*

GROWLER 6 ch.g. Foxhound (USA) 103 – Femme Femme (USA) (Lyphard (USA) **?** 132) [2007 7.5g² a5.5g⁶ 7g³ 7g a6.5g a6g⁴ p7g p6g Dec 12] sturdy gelding: fair performer at best: won twice in Spain in 2006: left P. Haley before tailed off both starts back in Britain in 2007: effective at 5.5f to 1m: acts on firm and soft going: visored earlier in career. *T. D. Walford*

GRUDGE 2 b.c. (Feb 28) Timeless Times (USA) 99 – Envy (IRE) (Paris House 123) **69** [2007 5m 5g⁵ 5m² 5g⁵ 5m⁴ 5g² 5.1g Sep 29] compact colt: fair maiden: second at Carlisle and Catterick: should prove best at 5f: acts on good to firm going: hangs left. *D. W. Barker*

GRYLLS (USA) 2 br.c. (Mar 14) Labeeb 124 – Soupremacist (Lord Carlos **82** (USA)) [2007 6g 5m* 5.1d⁴ 6g 6.5m 6f² Sep 25] 20,000Y: leggy colt: second foal: dam US 5.5f to 8.5f winner: fairly useful performer: won maiden at Sandown in June: second to Dubai Princess in minor event at Folkestone: best at 5f/6f: acts on firm going, probably on good to soft: sold 13,000 gns, sent to USA. *R. Hannon*

GUACAMOLE 3 ch.f. Inchinor 119 – Popocatepetl (FR) 66 (Nashwan (USA) 135) **95** [2007 84: 8.2m p8g⁵ 8m* 8g⁴ 8.1m² p8.6g Oct 21] tall, close-coupled filly: useful handicapper: won at Newmarket in August: good efforts next 2 starts, including 2 lengths second to Ragheed at Warwick: eased as if amiss final outing: should stay beyond 1m: unraced on firm going, acts on any other, and polytrack. *B. W. Hills*

GUADALOUP 5 ch.m. Loup Sauvage (USA) 125 – Rash (Pursuit of Love 124) [2007 **57** 65: f6g⁴ f6g³ 6g⁶ f7g⁶ 7.1d* 8s 7.1g 7m⁶ 6.9f 6.9g Aug 22] big, lengthy mare: modest handicapper: won at Musselburgh in June: effective at 6f/7f: acts on all-weather, good to firm and good to soft ground: has been blinkered/visored. *M. Brittain*

GUADIANA (GER) 5 b.m. Dashing Blade 117 – Gamberaia (IRE) (Konigsstuhl **47** (GER)) [2007 53: 14.1m p9.5g 10g⁴ p12.2g Oct 30] leggy mare: poor performer nowadays: stays 1½m: acts on all-weather, firm and good to soft going: often visored. *A. W. Carroll*

GUARANTIA 3 ch.f. Selkirk (USA) 129 – Maskunah (IRE) (Sadler's Wells (USA) **85** 132) [2007 92: 8.1g 7m 7.1d* p6g Aug 29] lengthy filly: fairly useful performer, lightly raced: didn't need to be anywhere near best to win maiden at Chepstow (edged right) in August: will probably stay 1¼m: acts on good to firm and good to soft ground: tried tongue tied: often makes running. *C. E. Brittain*

GUARDIAN OF TRUTH (IRE) 3 ch.g. Barathea (IRE) 127 – Zarara (USA) **81** (Manila (USA)) [2007 p10g³ 10f² 12m³ 14g 14g² p12.2g⁴ 14g Aug 2] attractive gelding: fairly useful maiden on Flat: stays 1¾m: acts on polytrack and firm ground: often makes running: joined G. L. Moore, won juvenile hurdle in October. *W. J. Knight*

GUERILLA (AUS) 7 b. or br.g. Octagonal (NZ) 126 – Partisan (AUS) (Canny Lad **45 +** (AUS)) [2007 12g⁵ Jul 10] angular gelding: placed on 8 of 10 starts up to 9.5f in Australia: poor form in maiden at Pontefract on Flat debut in Britain: modest hurdler, successful in August. *R. C. Guest*

GUERTINO (IRE) 2 ch.c. (Feb 12) Choisir (AUS) 126 – Isana (JPN) (Sunday Silence **95**
(USA)) [2007 5g⁵ 5m² 5m² 5.9g* 6g⁴ 6g⁶ 6d Oct 12] 57,000F, 14,000Y: tall, good-topped
colt: fluent mover: first foal: dam, third at 6.5f at 2 yrs in France, out of half-sister to
smart miler King of Happiness: useful performer: won maiden at Carlisle in June: best
effort in nurseries when fourth to Cristal Clear at York: should prove best at 5f/6f: acts on
good to firm and good to soft going: joined E. Charpy in UAE. *B. Smart*

GUEST CONNECTIONS 4 b.g. Zafonic (USA) 130 – Llyn Gwynant 115 (Persian **84**
Bold 123) [2007 93: 7f 6m 6g⁴ 6d 6s³ 6g 6m³ 6m² 6m² 5d 7g Oct 20] tall, leggy, attractive
gelding: fairly useful handicapper: effective at 6f/7f: acts on soft and good to firm going:
often visored: often difficult in stall, including when withdrawn before seventh intended
outing: has looked temperamental. *D. Nicholls*

GUILDED WARRIOR 4 b.g. Mujahid (USA) 125 – Pearly River 72 (Elegant Air **94**
119) [2007 73: p6g* 6s³ 7.1s* 7.1s* 7.1s* p8g 7m 7m p7m Nov 1] sturdy gelding: fairly
useful handicapper: much improved in 2007, winning at Kempton in May, Chepstow in
June and Warwick and Chepstow (beat Starlight Gazer by head) in July: below form
after: stays 7f: acts on polytrack, firm and soft going: tried visored: races prominently.
W. S. Kittow

GUILDENSTERN (IRE) 5 b.g. Danetime (IRE) 121 – Lyphard Abu (IRE) 78 **78 d**
(Lyphard's Special (USA) 122) [2007 89: p6f p7g⁵ 7m² 6s 8g⁶ 6g⁶ 6d p7.1g 6g⁴ p6g 6m
p6g⁶ p6g⁵ 5m p6g 6d p6g p6g⁵ Dec 22] well-made gelding: just fair handicapper nowadays: left P. Gilligan after seventh start: effective at 6f/7f, barely at 1m: acts on polytrack,
good to firm and good to soft going: tried visored/in cheekpieces: sometimes tongue tied.
P. Howling

GUILIA 4 ch.f. Galileo (IRE) 134 – Lesgor (USA) 106 (Irish River (FR) 131) [2007 106: **100**
12g 14.6m 10d⁶ p13m³ Nov 1] leggy, light-framed filly: useful performer: should stay 1¾m: acts on
polytrack and good to soft going: held up: sold 87,000 gns. *Rae Guest*

GUISEPPE VERDI (USA) 3 ch.g. Sky Classic (CAN) – Lovington (USA) (Afleet **91**
(CAN)) [2007 85: 8.2m p8.6g* 9.9m* 9.9m⁴ p10g* 11m Aug 4] strong, lengthy gelding:
fairly useful handicapper: successful at Wolverhampton (dead-heated) in April, Beverley
in May and Kempton in June: probably stays 11f: acts on polytrack and good to firm
ground: sold 38,000 gns in October, then gelded. *J. H. M. Gosden*

GULF COAST 2 ch.c. (Feb 24) Dubai Destination (USA) 127 – Lloc 79 (Absalom 128) **65**
[2007 5f⁵ 6g³ 7d⁵ p7g³ 7g p7.1g⁵ p7g⁴ 7.5m⁵ p6g Oct 22] workmanlike colt: fair maiden:
twice in frame in nurseries on polytrack: stays 7f: quirky, ended up in blinkers/visor: sold
6,000 gns. *M. Johnston*

GULF EXPRESS (USA) 3 b.c. Langfuhr (CAN) 124 – Wassifa 95 (Sure Blade (USA) **106 +**
130) [2007 67p: p8.6g* 7.6m² 8.3m⁶ 8m 10s² 10m* 10m* Sep 27] good-topped, attractive colt: useful performer: won maiden at Wolverhampton in April and handicaps at
Newbury and Pontefract (beat Many Volumes by neck) in September: should stay 1½m:
acts on polytrack, soft and good to firm ground. *Sir Michael Stoute*

GULL WING (IRE) 3 ch.f. In The Wings 128 – Maycocks Bay 100 (Muhtarram **101**
(USA) 125) [2007 88: 11.8g² 11.5g⁶ 12m² 10s³ 10.4s* 12g⁴ 10.3m⁵ Nov 10] good-topped
filly: useful performer: won handicap at York (easily by 4 lengths from Sell Out) in July:
good 3¼ lengths fourth to Wannabe Posh in listed race there next time: will stay beyond
1½m: acts on polytrack, soft and good to firm going. *M. L. W. Bell*

GUMLAYLOY 8 ch.g. Indian Ridge 123 – Candide (USA) 74 (Miswaki (USA) 124) **–**
[2007 p12.2g Jul 10] of no account. *G. H. Jones*

GUNFIGHTER (IRE) 4 ch.c. Machiavellian (USA) 123 – Reunion (IRE) 108 (Be My **92 +**
Guest (USA) 126) [2007 f8g³ f8g⁴ 8.1m 6f* 7.9d² 7s⁵ 8s⁴ p7.1g* 7m* p8.6d⁴ Dec 7]
100,000Y, 48,000 3-y-o: big, rangy colt: fourth foal: half-brother to winner in Japan by
Giant's Causeway: dam 6f (at 2 yrs) and 7f (Nell Gwyn) winner: fairly useful and
progressive handicapper: won at Hamilton in June, Wolverhampton in October and
Doncaster (apprentices, readily beat Bahiano by ¾ length) in November: has form at 1m,
probably best at 6f/7f: acts on polytrack, firm and soft going: held up. *J. S. Wainwright*

GUNNADOIT (USA) 2 b. or br.g. (Mar 16) Almutawakel 126 – Gharam (USA) 108 **54**
(Green Dancer (USA) 132) [2007 7d⁶ 7d 8g Oct 24] good-bodied gelding: modest
maiden: bred to stay at least 1m (dam third in Poule d'Essai des Pouliches and Ribblesdale Stakes): tried blinkered. *C. G. Cox*

GUNNER FLY (IRE) 2 b.c. (Mar 1) Noverre (USA) 125 – Anne-Lise 63 (Inchinor **65**
119) [2007 6f p6g² p6g⁴ p6g⁴ p7g⁶ p7g⁶ f8d⁵ Dec 15] fair maiden: in frame all 3 starts at
Wolverhampton, nursery final one: should be suited by 7f/1m. *R. A. Fahey*

GUNNER'S VIEW 3 ch.c. Medicean 128 – Stark Ballet (USA) (Nureyev (USA) 131) **75**
[2007 57: 8f² 8.5m 9.9m² 8d p8g p12g Nov 30] rather leggy, quite attractive colt: has a
quick action: fair maiden: left B. Meehan, said to have had breathing problem final
outing: may prove best up to easy 1¼m: acts on firm going: tried in cheekpieces/tongue
tied: has finished weakly. *A. Ennis*

GUTO 4 b.g. Foxhound (USA) 103 – Mujadilly 43 (Mujadil (USA) 119) [2007 100: **91 d**
5.1m 5g 6g 5g 6g² 6m⁶ 5g⁴ 5g² 5g p6g⁵ Dec 4] quite well-topped gelding: useful
performer at 3 yrs: regressive in 2007, leaving K. Ryan after fifth start: best at 5f/6f: acts
on soft and good to firm going, probably on polytrack: races prominently: tried in
blinkers/cheekpieces. *W. J. H. Ratcliffe*

GWENSEB (FR) 4 ch.f. Green Tune (USA) 125 – La Popesse (USA) (St Jovite (USA) **107**
135) [2007 113: 8s⁵ 8g⁴ 8m 8d² 10d 8g² 8.3d² 8d³ 8s⁵ a7.5g⁶ Nov 22] good-bodied, quite
attractive filly: third foal: sister to French 9f to 11.5f winner Les Annees Pop and
half-sister to French 1¼m/1½m winner Pop Art (by Bering): dam French 1¼m to 12.5f
winner: smart performer at best: won Prix du Bois at Chantilly at 2 yrs and listed race at
Deauville in 2006: just useful form in 2007, best efforts when fourth to Racinger in Prix
du Muguet at Saint-Cloud and ½-length second to Chopastair in listed race at Craon sixth
outing: well held in Windsor Forest Stakes at Royal Ascot third start: stays 1m: acts on
good to firm and good to soft ground: tended to race lazily prior to fitting of
blinkers last 6 starts. *C. Laffon-Parias, France*

GWILYM (GER) 4 b.c. Agnes World (USA) 123 – Glady Rose (GER) (Surumu (GER)) **83**
[2007 76: 6m* 5m² 5m 5m³ 5f⁵ 6f² 5m³ 5m² 6d Sep 26] compact colt: fairly useful
handicapper: won at Windsor (apprentices) in April: best at 5f/easy 6f: acts on polytrack
and firm going: blinkered once at 3 yrs: consistent. *D. Haydn Jones*

GWYLLION (USA) 3 b. or br.f. Red Ransom (USA) – Lady Angharad (IRE) 95 **70**
(Tenby 125) [2007 71p: 6m⁵ p7.1g p7g p8.6d⁵ p8.6d Dec 27] fair maiden, lightly raced:
left J. Gosden after second start, Charles O'Brien in Ireland after third: should stay 1m:
acts on polytrack and good to firm ground: tried blinkered. *B. J. Meehan*

GYPSUM (IRE) 3 gr.g. Desert Style (IRE) 121 – Sassania (IRE) 78 (Persian Bold 123) **–**
[2007 p7g Mar 7] 16/1, well held in maiden at Lingfield. *W. R. Swinburn*

GYPSY BABY (IRE) 2 b.f. (Mar 22) Modigliani (USA) 106 – L-Way First (IRE) 59 **90**
(Vision (USA)) [2007 6m² p7g² 7s* 7.1d 7m² 6g² Aug 23] €8,000F, 30,000Y: leggy filly:
closely related to fairly useful 1997 2-y-o 5f winner First Village (by Danehill) and
half-sister to smart 7f (at 2 yrs) to 1½m (in US) winner Embossed (by Mark of Esteem):
dam Irish maiden (stayed 2m): fairly useful performer: won maiden at Folkestone in
June: improved when second last 2 starts, in nursery at Ascot and St Leger Yearling
Stakes at York (finished fast, beaten length by Dark Angel): will stay at least 1m: acts on
polytrack, soft and good to firm going: sold 135,000 gns, sent to USA. *R. Hannon*

GYRATION (IRE) 3 ch.g. Spinning World (USA) 130 – Tomori (USA) 106 (Royal **58**
Academy (USA) 130) [2007 –: 8m p7.1g 10.1m 8g³ p7g Sep 29] workmanlike gelding:
modest maiden: tried in cheekpieces. *J. G. Given*

GYROSCOPE 3 b.f. Spinning World (USA) 130 – Far Across (Common Grounds 118) **97**
[2007 71p: 8.3m* 7g³ 8.1g² 8m² 9g 8.3m⁴ 10.1g* 10m Oct 5] smallish filly: useful
performer: won maiden at Windsor in April and handicap at Yarmouth (beat Voliere by
1¾ lengths) in September: stayed 1¼m: raced only on polytrack and good/good to firm
going: visits Medicean. *Sir Michael Stoute*

H

HAAJES 3 ch.g. Indian Ridge 123 – Imelda (USA) (Manila (USA)) [2007 61: 6v 5s² 6m **83**
6.7s 5.1d* 6m³ 6m⁵ 5m Sep 14] compact, close-coupled gelding: fifth foal: half-brother
to 2001 2-y-o 6f winner Rapadash (by Boundary), later successful in USA, and 7-y-o
Todlea: dam once-raced half-sister to very smart French miler Shaanxi: fairly useful
handicapper: left D. Weld in Ireland after fourth outing: won at Nottingham in August:
stays 6f: acts on soft and good to firm going: twice below form in blinkers. *D. J. Murphy*

HAARTH SOVEREIGN (IRE) 3 b.g. Alhaarth (IRE) 126 – Summer Queen 80 **79**
(Robellino (USA) 127) [2007 10f³ 10.2f² 10d⁵ 11.6s³ 9.9m Sep 16] 45,000F, 45,000Y:
rangy gelding: fourth foal: half-brother to 3 winners, including fairly useful 5f winner
Chico Guapo (by Sesaro) and 6f winner Party Princess (by Orpen): dam, 7f winner,
half-sister to useful 1m/9f winner Eton Lad: fair maiden: stays 11.6f: acts on firm and soft
going: gelded after final start. *W. R. Swinburn*

*John Guest Diadem Stakes, Ascot—three-year-old Haatef (centre) just comes out on top;
Dark Missile (left) and Assertive fill the minor placings*

HAASEM (USA) 4 b.c. Seeking The Gold (USA) – Thawakib (IRE) 108 (Sadler's **74**
Wells (USA) 132) [2007 8m⁶ 8.1m⁶ 8.1m³ 10m⁶ 9.7s⁴ p8g 8g³ 10g p7g* p7m p10g
Dec 28] sturdy colt: half-brother to several winners, notably top-class 1m (at 2 yrs) to
1½m (Prix de l'Arc de Triomphe) winner Sakhee (by Bahri): dam, 7f (at 2 yrs) and 1½m
(Ribblesdale Stakes) winner, half-sister to top-class middle-distance performer Celestial
Storm: fair handicapper: left E. Dunlop after third start: won at Lingfield in November:
may prove best at 7f/1m: acts on polytrack and good to firm going. *J. R. Jenkins*

HAATEF (USA) 3 b.c. Danzig (USA) – Sayedat Alhadh (USA) (Mr Prospector (USA)) **117**
[2007 113p: 8m 7g* 6v* 8d³ 6g* Sep 30] smallish, sturdy colt: smart performer: won

Mr Hamdan Al Maktoum's "Haatef"

minor event at Naas in June, listed race at Fairyhouse (by 1½ lengths from Moone Cross) in July and John Guest Diadem Stakes at Ascot (best effort, beat Dark Missile a short head, quickening to lead close home) in September: effective at 6f/7f (tenth in 2000 Guineas at Newmarket and below-form third in Desmond Stakes at Leopardstown at 1m): acts on heavy and good to firm ground: tongue tied on second and last 2 starts: missed Irish 2000 Guineas intended second start due to unsatisfactory blood test. *Kevin Prendergast, Ireland*

HAATMEY 5 b.g. Josr Algarhoud (IRE) 118 – Raneen Alwatar 80 (Sadler's Wells (USA) 132) [2007 82d: p16g6 16s p16g4 p16g2 p16g2 p13.9d4 Dec 17] strong, heavy-topped gelding: just modest handicapper nowadays: probably stays 17f: acts on polytrack, firm and good to soft going: usually visored: temperament under suspicion. *P. R. Chamings* **62**

HABALWATAN (IRE) 3 b.c. In The Wings 128 – Mureefa (USA) 73 (Bahri (USA) 125) [2007 87: p8.6g2 p8g5 10.1g4 10.3m3 12m 10g 10m 8g 9.9g3 9.9m3 12m4 10m* Oct 5] compact colt: useful performer: won handicap at Newmarket in October by head from Free Offer: ran well previously when placed, though probably flattered when 3½ lengths third to Admiralofthefleet in Dee Stakes at Chester fourth start: should stay 1½m: acts on polytrack and good to firm ground: used to wear blinkers (not last 4 outings): edgy sort: has looked difficult ride: joined D. Watson in UAE. *C. E. Brittain* **97 +**

HABANERO 6 b.g. Cadeaux Genereux 131 – Queen of Dance (IRE) (Sadler's Wells (USA) 132) [2007 –: p8g Jul 4] good-topped, quite attractive gelding: just fair performer nowadays: best form around 1m: acts on polytrack, firm and good to soft ground: tried tongue tied: front runner: sold 26,000 gns, joined C. A. Mulhall and won over hurdles in August. *A. King* **68**

HABBIE HEIGHTS 2 b.f. (Apr 4) Josr Algarhoud (IRE) 118 – Hello Hobson's (IRE) 67 (Fayruz 116) [2007 5g2 6s Aug 11] 1,500Y: strong, heavy-topped filly: seventh foal: half-sister to 5-y-o Smiddy Hill and 6-y-o Hello Roberto: dam 5f/6f winner, including at 2 yrs: modest maiden: second at Beverley on debut: well held on testing ground 12 days later: should prove best at 5f/6f. *R. Bastiman* **57**

HABSHAN 7 ch.g. Swain (IRE) 134 – Cambara 97 (Dancing Brave (USA) 140) [2007 93: 8m 8m* 8g5 p8.6g4 Oct 8] smallish, good-topped gelding: fairly useful handicapper: won at Newbury in June by 1¼ lengths from Nawaqees: respectable efforts after: stays 8.6f: acts on polytrack, good to firm and good to soft going. *C. F. Wall* **94**

HADAF (IRE) 2 b.c. (May 11) Fasliyev (USA) 120 – Elhida (IRE) 99 (Mujtahid (USA) 118) [2007 5d 5m3 5.1g 5m* p5m* Oct 6] rather unfurnished colt: fourth living foal: half-brother to 6f winner Katheer (by Anabaa): dam 2-y-o 6f winner out of champion Australian older filly (won up to 1m) Nouvelle Star: fairly useful form: progressed to win last 2 starts, maiden at Thirsk in August and nursery at Kempton (with bit in hand): will prove best at 5f/6f: acts on polytrack and good to firm going. *M. P. Tregoning* **93 +**

HADA MEN (USA) 2 b.g. (Feb 27) Dynaformer (USA) – Catchy (USA) (Storm Cat (USA)) [2007 7.1m 8m5 10m3 Oct 8] $300,000Y: stocky gelding: third foal: half-brother to US 2006 2-y-o 6f winner Black Pulpit (by Pulpit): dam, ran once in US, sister to very smart US 2-y-o Hennessy: fair maiden: progressive form, third to Planetarium at Pontefract: gelded after: stays 1¼m. *M. P. Tregoning* **74**

HADRON COLLIDER (FR) 2 ch.c. (Mar 6) Dubai Destination (USA) 127 – Liver de Saron (USA) (Mt Livermore (USA)) [2007 7m6 8.1f 8.3m Oct 8] €90,000Y: useful-looking colt, unfurnished at present: half-brother to French 9.5f/1¼m winner Alluvion (by Highest Honor): dam French 1¼m winner: modest form in maidens, fading: should be suited by 1m: capable of better. *R. Hannon* **64 p**

HAEDI 3 b.f. King's Best 132 – Star Express 80 (Sadler's Wells (USA) 132) [2007 7.5g4 7v 6m* Sep 8] tall, leggy, useful-looking filly: first foal: dam, 11.5f winner in France, sister to smart 7f/1m performer Yalaietanee out of smart 6f performer Vaigly Star, herself half-sister to high-class sprinter Vaigly Great: won maiden at Thirsk in September by ¾ length from Slip Star: tongue tied: sold €9,000. *Saeed bin Suroor* **60**

HAIBAN 5 b.g. Barathea (IRE) 127 – Aquarela (Shirley Heights 130) [2007 48: 13g* 16s 11.9s4 9v2 16g 15s 11.3m5 12g 12.5m Sep 26] quite good-topped gelding: fair handicapper: won at Downpatrick (apprentices) in May: ran respectably at Ayr sixth outing: effective at testing 9f to 13f, not 2m: acts on any turf going: tried tongue tied. *J. J. Lambe, Ireland* **69**

HAIFA (IRE) 4 ch.f. Spectrum (IRE) 126 – Mrs Fisher (IRE) 94 (Salmon Leap (USA) 131) [2007 71: 9.9m4 9.2g 7.9g 9.1s Aug 11] lengthy, good-topped filly: fair handicapper at best: below form after reappearance: stays 1½m: acts on fibresand and heavy going: tried in cheekpieces. *Mrs A. Duffield* **71 d**

HAIL THE CHIEF 10 b.h. Be My Chief (USA) 122 – Jade Pet 90 (Petong 126) [2007 – 96, a107: p8.6g³ p8g⁶ p8.6g p7g p10g 8.3f 8g May 24] rather sparely-made horse: good **a94** mover: just fairly useful in 2007: reportedly finished lame third/sixth outings: effective at stiff 7f to 1¼m: acts on dirt, all-weather, soft and good to firm going: in cheekpieces (well held) final outing: has been bandaged in front: effective held up/making running: sold 13,500 gns. *R. Hannon*

HALF A TSAR (IRE) 3 b.g. Soviet Star (USA) 128 – Villarica (IRE) 76 (Fairy King **46** (USA)) [2007 8g 10d 6f⁵ 6m⁵ p6g 5.7d p6g Oct 4] compact gelding: poor maiden: tried blinkered. *Mark Gillard*

HALFWAY TO HEAVEN (IRE) 2 gr.f. (Apr 25) Pivotal 124 – Cassandra Go (IRE) **94 p** 119 (Indian Ridge 123) [2007 7g² 7m* Nov 4] €450,000Y: lengthy, useful-looking filly: fourth foal: half-sister to 3-y-o Theann and fairly useful 5f winners Neverletme Go and Mannikko (both by Green Desert): dam sprinter: better effort in maidens at Leopardstown (fairly useful form) when winning by head from Charlotte Bronte: not sure to stay 1m: open to further improvement. *A. P. O'Brien, Ireland*

HALFWAYTOPARADISE 4 b.f. Observatory (USA) 131 – Always On My Mind 91 **57** (Distant Relative 128) [2007 66, a56: 7m 7.6g 7d 6s 7m⁵ 7.6s³ 7d² 7d* p7.1g² 7d p7.1g Dec 3] sturdy filly: modest performer: won claimer at Brighton in October: stays 7f: acts on polytrack, firm and soft going: tried visored, wears cheekpieces nowadays: front runner. *W. G. M. Turner*

HALICARNASSUS (IRE) 3 b.c. Cape Cross (IRE) 129 – Launch Time (USA) **117** (Relaunch (USA)) [2007 107: 7m³ 8m 11g* 10.5g 13m⁵ 9.9g 10.5m* 8.9f² 9.9m⁵ 11m* 12f Nov 25] rather leggy colt: smart performer: improved in 2007, winning 3-runner listed race at Goodwood in May, totepool Rose of Lancaster Stakes at Haydock (beat Formal Decree by 1¼ lengths) in August and Dubai Duty Free Arc Trial at Newbury (by neck from Soapy Danger) in September: stays 11f (stiff task in Japan Cup at 1½m): acts on firm ground: sometimes sweats: held up. *M. R. Channon*

HALKERSTON 3 ch.g. Medicean 128 – Summer Daze (USA) (Swain (IRE) 134) **60** [2007 p60: 8.1g³ 8.3m p9.5g p12g Oct 29] strong, good-bodied gelding: regressive maiden: should stay at least 9f: tongue tied second outing: sold 2,200 gns. *C. G. Cox*

HALLAND 9 ch.g. Halling (USA) 133 – Northshiel 85 (Northfields (USA)) [2007 65, – a72: f16g⁶ Mar 19] quite attractive gelding: fair handicapper at 8 yrs: well held only outing in 2007: tried in cheekpieces (well beaten) twice. *T. J. Fitzgerald*

HALLA SAN 5 b.g. Halling (USA) 133 – St Radegund 85 (Green Desert (USA) 127) **102** [2007 86: 13.8m* 16g² 16.1v 12d Jul 29] tall gelding: has a quick action: useful handicapper: won at Catterick in April by 7 lengths from Charlotte Vale: form after only when excellent ¾-length second to Raucous at Ripon next time: stays 2m: acts on soft and good to firm going: changed hands 21,000 gns in December. *R. A. Fahey*

HALLINGDAL (UAE) 2 b.f. (Mar 14) Halling (USA) 133 – Saik (USA) (Riverman **79 p** (USA) 131) [2007 7d* Oct 16] fifth foal: half-sister to 7f winner Wistman (by Woodman): dam, unraced, closely related to dam of Mubtaker out of half-sister to very smart French sprinter Cricket Ball: 7/4, overcame greenness (soon pushed along) to win maiden at Newcastle by 3½ lengths, forging away once getting hang of things: should stay 1m: will improve. *M. Johnston*

Dubai Duty Free Arc Trial, Newbury—
Halicarnassus edges out Soapy Danger (rail) as Papal Bull finishes strongly; Salford Mill (rail) is fourth

HALLINGS OVERTURE (USA) 8 b.g. Halling (USA) 133 – Sonata (Polish Pre- **67** cedent (USA) 131) [2007 66: p12g⁶ p12g² p10g⁴ p12g p12g p12g⁴ p11g⁶ p12g p10g p10g Aug 18] robust gelding: fair handicapper: stays easy 1½m: acts on polytrack, probably on soft going: sometimes slowly away: held up. *C. A. Horgan*

HALL OF FAME 3 b.g. Machiavellian (USA) 123 – Petrushka (IRE) 126 (Unfuwain **73** (USA) 131) [2007 73: f11s³ 10m 10.5s* 13.8g⁵ Nov 6] small, attractive gelding: fair performer: left M. Johnston after reappearance and C. Mann after winning seller at Haydock in October: barely stays 13.8f: acts on soft going. *R. C. Guest*

HALSION CHALLENGE 2 b.c. (Feb 24) King's Best (USA) 132 – Zaynah (IRE) **47** (Kahyasi 130) [2007 7m 7s 6m Sep 17] poor form in maidens (well backed on debut): bred to be suited by 1m+. *J. R. Best*

HALSION CHANCER 3 b.g. Atraf 116 – Lucky Dip 68 (Tirol 127) [2007 p5g* p5g* **92** p5g⁴ 5g p6g⁶ p5g* p5g² p6m* Dec 9] 14,000Y, 18,000 2-y-o: sixth foal: half-brother to 3 winners, including fairly useful 2003 2-y-o 5f winner Fortunately (later won in USA, by Forzando): dam 5f winner: fairly useful performer: won maiden and handicap at Lingfield in February, and handicaps there in November and December: stays 6f: acts on polytrack: races up with pace. *J. R. Best*

HALTON CASTLE 2 ch.g. (Mar 20) Zamindar (USA) 116 – Chilly Start (IRE) (Caerleon (USA) 132) [2007 7.5g 7m 7.1g Sep 12] big, strong gelding: early speed but well beaten in maidens. *E. J. Alston*

HAMAASY 6 b.g. Machiavellian (USA) 123 – Sakha 109 (Wolfhound (USA) 126) **–** [2007 63: f6g⁷ p6g f6g⁵ f6g* f5g⁵ f5g⁴ f6g³ 7.1m 5m Sep 18] quite attractive gelding: **a77** fair on all-weather, no form on turf in 2007: won handicaps at Southwell in January and February: best at 6f/7f: acts on fibresand, firm and good to soft going: tried tongue tied/ visored earlier in career: races prominently. *D. Nicholls*

HAMALKA (IRE) 2 br.f. (Jan 28) Alhaarth (IRE) 126 – Night Owl 73 (Night Shift **69** (USA)) [2007 p7g⁶ 7m² 7m² 7s³ Sep 26] 17,500F, €60,000Y: compact filly: fifth foal: half-sister to useful 7f/1m winner Distant Connection (by Cadeaux Genereux): dam headstrong sprint maiden: fair maiden: placed all turf starts, third at Redcar final one (disputed lead long way with winner Zakhaaref): will prove best up to 1m: acts on soft and good to firm going. *B. W. Hills*

HAMBURG SPRINGER (IRE) 5 b.g. Charnwood Forest (IRE) 125 – Kyra Crown **– §** (IRE) (Astronef 116) [2007 f8g Jan 1] close-coupled gelding: poor performer: tailed off sole 5-y-o outing: usually wears headgear: reluctant to race twice at 3 yrs: one to avoid. *C. J. Teague*

HAMILTON HOUSE 3 b.g. Bahamian Bounty 116 – Grove Dancer 61 (Reprimand **62 d** 122) [2007 –: 7m 8g 7d 7.1g⁵ 8m³ 10.1g 9g⁵ p10g 8d Oct 3] strong gelding: modest maiden: probably stays 1m: acts on good to firm going: tried in blinkers. *M. H. Tompkins*

HAMISH MCGONAGALL 2 b.g. (Mar 4) Namid 128 – Anatase (Danehill (USA) **84** 126) [2007 5d 5g³ 6d⁴ 6g² 6d² 5g* Nov 8] 15,000F, 17,000Y: big, strong, lengthy gelding: fourth foal: half-brother to Swedish winner up to 5f Steelwolf (by Fraam): dam unraced out of Prix Vermeille winner Sharaya: fairly useful performer: in frame 4 times, including second to Calming Influence at York fifth start, prior to winning maiden at Musselburgh: gelded after: should prove best kept to 5f/6f: raced only on good/good to soft going. *T. D. Easterby*

HAMMADI (IRE) 2 b.c. (Feb 16) Red Ransom (USA) – Ruby Affair (IRE) 68 (Night **99** Shift (USA)) [2007 6f⁴ 6g³ 5g² 6m* 5d⁴ 6d Nov 2] 38,000F, 65,000Y: tall, leggy, quite good-topped colt: fifth foal: closely related to 6f (including at 2 yrs)/6.5f winner Khabfair (by Intikhab) and half-brother to 2004 2-y-o 6f winner Francis Cadell (by Cadeaux Genereux), both useful: dam, second at 7f, half-sister to 2000 Guineas winner Island Sands: useful performer: won maiden at Catterick in September by 10 lengths: further improvement when 2¼ lengths fourth to Captain Gerrard in Cornwallis Stakes at Ascot: possibly amiss (weakened quickly and eased) in Criterium de Maisons-Laffitte final start: may prove best at 5f/6f: acts on good to firm and good to soft going. *K. A. Ryan*

HAMMER OF THE GODS (IRE) 7 ch.g. Tagula (IRE) 116 – Bhama (FR) (Habitat **–** 134) [2007 65, a85: p7g p6g⁵ p6g⁴ p6f⁴ f5g⁶ p7g⁶ p6g² p6g⁵ May 9] strong gelding: poor **a77** mover: fair handicapper: best at 5f/easy 6f: acts on polytrack and good to firm going: tried visored, blinkered/tongue tied nowadays: effective held up or ridden prominently. *P. S. McEntee*

HAMOODY (USA) 3 ch.c. Johannesburg (USA) 127 – Northern Gulch (USA) (Gulch **92** (USA)) [2007 106p: 7m 6d p6f² a6.5f Nov 25] strong, lengthy, well-made colt: fluent mover: useful at 2 yrs: below form in listed Free Handicap at Newmarket and Golden

Jubilee Stakes at Royal Ascot first 2 starts in 2007: left P. Chapple-Hyam and off 3½ months, better effort in allowance races after when second at Keeneland in October (only outing for P. Biancone): free-going sort, may prove best at 5f/6f: acts on polytrack and firm going. *Jenine Sahadi, USA*

HAMPSTEAD HEATH (IRE) 2 gr.c. (Jan 30) Daylami (IRE) 138 – Hedera (USA) 90 (Woodman (USA) 126) [2007 7.1g⁶ 7.5g⁴ 8.1m⁵ Sep 13] strong, good-topped colt: closely related to useful French performer up to 11.5f Ivy League (by Doyoun), and half-brother to 1½m winner Heisse (by Darshaan) and 1¼m (including in UAE) winner Hunter's Glen (by Bahri), both useful: dam 2-y-o 7f winner: fairly useful maiden: fourth to Bonjour Allure at Beverley, pulling hard (did so again final start): should stay at least 1m: sold 17,000 gns. *M. Johnston* **81**

HAMPTON COURT 2 ch.g. (Apr 18) King's Best (USA) 132 – Rafting (IRE) 87 (Darshaan 133) [2007 7d 8d Oct 27] 100,000Y: fourth foal: half-brother to 2 winners, including 3-y-o Colorado Rapid: dam, 1½m winner, half-sister to smart stayer Lear White: in need of experience in maidens: gelded after final start. *M. Johnston* **–**

HAMSAT ELQAMAR 2 b.f. (Jan 22) Nayef (USA) 129 – Moon's Whisper (USA) (Storm Cat (USA)) [2007 8m 8.2m⁶ Oct 3] rangy filly: has scope: second foal: half-sister to 3-y-o Yazamaan: dam, unraced, out of very smart French 1m and 10.5f winner East of The Moon, herself half-sister to Kingmambo, out of Miesque: fair form (but clearly green) in maidens at Newmarket and Nottingham: capable of better. *J. H. M. Gosden* **67 p**

HANBRIN BHOY (IRE) 3 b.g. Cape Cross (IRE) 129 – Sea of Stone (USA) 71 (San-glamore (USA) 126) [2007 73+: 8d 11.6d p8g⁴ Dec 1] workmanlike gelding: fair handi-capper, lightly raced: should stay 1¼m: acts on polytrack, firm and soft going. *R. Dickin* **76**

HAND CHIME 10 ch.g. Clantime 101 – Warning Bell 88 (Bustino 136) [2007 –, a69: p8.6g p8.6g p8g p7g⁵ p8.6g p7g² p8.6g p7g p7g Apr 30] angular gelding: modest performer nowadays: left Ernst Oertel after fifth start: stays easy 1m: yet to race on heavy going, acts on any other turf/all-weather: sometimes slowly away: free-going sort: has reportedly bled. *Miss J. Feilden* **–**
a57

HAND OF FATE (IRE) 3 b.f. Jade Robbery (USA) 121 – Destiny Dance (USA) 100 (Nijinsky (CAN) 138) [2007 f8g⁶ Mar 15] half-sister to several winners, notably very smart US performer up to 1¼m Balletto (by Timber Country), US Grade 1 winner at 2 yrs: dam, 11f (US Grade 3 event) to 1½m winner, out of US Grade 1 8.5f/9f winner Althea: 15/8, well-held sixth of 8 in maiden at Southwell: sent to USA. *M. Johnston* **–**

HANDSET (USA) 3 ch.f. Distant View (USA) 126 – Call Account (USA) (Private Account (USA)) [2007 56: 8.3m⁵ 10.9d⁶ 8.2g² 8.3d² p8g³ 8m* Oct 8] good-topped filly: fair performer: won maiden at Pontefract in October: will prove just as effective at 7f as 1m: acts on good to firm going: sold 32,000 gns. *H. R. A. Cecil* **78**

HANDSINTHEMIST (IRE) 2 b.f. (Apr 1) Lend A Hand 124 – Hollow Haze (USA) 90 (Woodman (USA) 126) [2007 6m 6m 5m³ 6g⁶ 5s⁶ 7g 6m 5f* 5g Oct 20] €2,500Y: tall, leggy filly: half-sister to 3-y-o Ella Woodcock and 3 winners abroad, including Italian 10.5f winner Kathy Jet (by Singspiel): dam 8.5f winner: modest performer: won nursery at Redcar in September: should stay 6f/7f: acts on firm going: twice wore cheekpieces (including for win). *P. T. Midgley* **53**

HANDSOME CROSS (IRE) 6 b.g. Cape Cross (IRE) 129 – Snap Crackle Pop (IRE) 87 (Statoblest 120) [2007 95: 5g² 5g⁴ 5d² 5g 5g 5m 5d 5.1m 5d Sep 17] strong gelding: useful handicapper: good efforts first 3 starts, length second to Sunrise Safari at Ayr on third occasion: below form after, failing to impress with attitude: stays easy 6f: acts on firm and good to soft going: races up with pace. *D. Nicholls* **95 d**

HANDSOME FALCON 3 b.g. Kyllachy 129 – Bonne Etoile 94 (Diesis 133) [2007 78p: 7.5m 6g 6m³ 7s⁴ 8.5v⁴ 7.5s* 8m 7m Sep 22] big, angular gelding: fairly useful hand-icapper: best effort when winning at Beverley in July: stays 7.5f: acts on soft and good to firm going. *R. A. Fahey* **84**

HANEEN (USA) 4 b.f. Bahri (USA) 125 – Tamgeed (USA) 66 (Woodman (USA) 126) [2007 67: 7m 8d p8.6g p12g Aug 28] smallish, leggy filly: maiden: no form in 2007. *R. W. Price* **–**

HANELLA (IRE) 4 b.f. Galileo (IRE) 134 – Strutting (IRE) 95 (Ela-Mana-Mou 132) [2007 79: 11.7f* 12.1g² May 28] fairly useful handicapper: won at Bath in May: will be suited by 1¾m: acts on firm going. *R. M. Beckett* **91**

HANGING ON 3 b.f. Spinning World (USA) 130 – Lydia Maria 70 (Dancing Brave (USA) 140) [2007 89: 10g⁴ 11.4m⁵ 12g Jun 21] smallish, workmanlike filly: fairly useful **94**

performer: best effort when 1½ lengths fourth to Silkwood in handicap at Sandown on reappearance: should stay 1½m: acts on polytrack, raced only on good/good to firm ground on turf. *W. R. Swinburn*

HANG LOOSE 4 b.g. Agnes World (USA) 123 – My Cadeaux 93 (Cadeaux Genereux 131) [2007 70: 9.7m p7.1g 5g May 25] maiden: little form in 2007: tried in blinkers/cheekpieces: dead. *S. W. Hall* —

HANNAHBECC 3 ch.f. Singspiel (IRE) 133 – Encorenous (USA) (Diesis 133) [2007 10d⁶ 10.1d⁶ 8.1d p8g p8g 10m p10g p7g³ p7g p7m Nov 26] lengthy, angular filly: modest maiden: left H. Cecil after third start: bred to be suited by 1¼m, but effective at 7f: acts on polytrack and good to soft going: tried tongue tied. *S. C. Williams* **59**

HANNICEAN 3 ch.c. Medicean 128 – Hannah's Music 85 (Music Boy 124) [2007 76p: 10m* 9.9m p8g 8m 10s³ 10d 8g Oct 24] strong, lengthy colt: fair performer: won maiden at Nottingham in April: stays 1¼m: acts on soft and good to firm going. *M. A. Jarvis* **78**

HANSINGER (IRE) 2 b.g. (Mar 23) Namid 128 – Whistfilly 49 (First Trump 118) [2007 5g³ 6m⁵ 6.1s* 7g 6s 7m³ Sep 14] workmanlike gelding: fair performer: won maiden at Nottingham in July: third to Dubai Dynamo in nursery at Doncaster: stays 7f: acts on soft and good to firm going. *B. I. Case* **77**

HANSOMELLE (IRE) 5 b.m. Titus Livius (FR) 115 – Handsome Anna (IRE) 67 (Bigstone (IRE) 126) [2007 63: p11g 8d³ 10m p11g p8g⁶ 8.1m³ 7.6g* p10g³ 7.6f³ 7.6s* 8.1m 8m Sep 4] workmanlike mare: fairly useful handicapper: won at Lingfield in July and August: seems best around 1m: acts on polytrack and any turf going: wears cheekpieces nowadays. *Miss S. West* **81**

HANSOMIS (IRE) 3 b.f. Titus Livius (FR) 115 – Handsome Anna (IRE) 67 (Bigstone (IRE) 126) [2007 69: 6g 6g² 6.9g 7v⁶ 6d Jul 16] leggy, quite attractive filly: modest maiden: stays 7f: acts on heavy and good to firm ground: tried in cheekpieces: races prominently. *B. Mactaggart* **63**

HAOIN AN BOTHAR (IRE) 3 b.g. Bishop of Cashel 122 – Drefflane Ann (IRE) (Petorius 117) [2007 64: p12.2g Mar 2] maiden: stays 9.5f: blinkered on debut, wore cheekpieces (well held at Wolverhampton) only Flat outing in 2007. *Adrian Sexton, Ireland* —

HA'PENNY BEACON 4 ch.f. Erhaab (USA) 127 – Beacon (High Top 131) [2007 68: f12g² f11g³ 14g f14g⁵ 12.1g⁵ p16.5g⁶ p12.2g² p13.9g³ p12.2g⁶ p13.9g 13.8g² 15.8g* Oct 30] sturdy filly: fair handicapper: won at Catterick in October: stays 2m: raced mainly on all-weather and good going (shaped well on heavy on debut): visored last 6 starts: usually held up. *D. Carroll* **74**

HAPPY AS LARRY (USA) 5 b. or br.g. Yes It's True (USA) 116 – Don't Be Blue (USA) (Henbane (USA) 91) [2007 99: p10g⁵ p8g p10g 10.1s 10.9m 8m 8.3g 8d p8.6g⁴ p7g p6g p6m f6d⁵ f8g³ Dec 27] strong gelding: fairly useful handicapper on all-weather, fair on turf: trained by T. Pitt until fifth start: stays 1¼m: acts on all-weather and good to firm going: usually tongue tied, has worn visor/blinkers: held up: said to have had breathing problem final outing. *D. J. Murphy* **77 a91**

HAPPY GO LILY 3 b.f. In The Wings 128 – Lil's Jessy (IRE) 101 (Kris 135) [2007 83p: p10g 10m* 10d⁵ p12g² 11m Aug 4] neat filly: fairly useful handicapper: won at Nottingham in May: stays 1½m: acts on polytrack, good to firm and good to soft going: sold 52,000 gns. *W. R. Swinburn* **89**

HAPPY HACKER (IRE) 2 ch.f. (Feb 20) Captain Rio 122 – Darling Clementine (Lion Cavern (USA) 117) [2007 5.1f⁶ 5.1g 5.7f 6d 5.1m⁴ 6g Aug 27] €16,000Y: close-coupled filly: first foal: dam unraced half-sister to Preis der Diana winner Silvester Lady: poor and temperamental maiden: tried visored. *P. D. Evans* **49 §**

HARALD BLUETOOTH (IRE) 2 b.c. (Feb 4) Danetime (IRE) 121 – Goldthroat (IRE) 79 (Zafonic (USA) 130) [2007 6m⁶ Jul 12] €66,000F, €525,000Y: strong, lengthy colt: second foal: half-brother to 3-y-o New Beginning: dam, Irish 2-y-o 7f winner, out of half-sister to smart miler Killer Instinct: 13/2, shaped well considering greenness and run of race when never-nearer sixth to Spanish Bounty in minor event at Newmarket: suffered minor injury after, likely to stay 7f/1m: will improve. *J. R. Fanshawe* **70 p**

HARARE 6 b.g. Bahhare (USA) 122 – Springs Eternal 69 (Salse (USA) 128) [2007 71: p9.5g⁶ p8.6g³ p8.6g* p8.6g⁶ p7.1g² p8.6g² p8.6g* p8.6g² p7.1g* p8.6g 8.1m³ 8.1m² 7m⁵ 8d⁵ 8.3m Aug 13] workmanlike gelding: fairly useful handicapper: won at Wolverhampton in January, March and April: seems best at 7f to 8.6f: acts on polytrack and firm going: blinkered/visored: usually travels strongly. *R. J. Price* **85**

HARBOUR BLUES 2 ch.c. (Mar 13) Best of The Bests (IRE) 122 – Lady Georgia 94 **82**
(Arazi (USA) 135) [2007 6d² 7g² 7g⁶ 7m 8m⁴ p7.1g³ p6g* p7g Nov 30] 15,000Y:
lengthy, useful-looking colt: fifth foal: half-brother to 5f (including at 2 yrs) winner
Sparkling Eyes (by Lujain) and winner in Greece by Bien Bien: dam 1m winner: fairly
useful performer: easily best effort when winning claimer at Wolverhampton (claimed
from C. Brittain £12,000) in November: best form at 6f: acts on polytrack, yet to race on
extremes of going on turf: tongue tied last 2 starts: races prominently. *A. W. Carroll*

HARCOURT (USA) 7 b.g. Cozzene (USA) – Ballinamallard (USA) 112 (Tom Rolfe) **63 d**
[2007 68: 12m³ p12g 12.1m 12g 16s Oct 14] rangy gelding: modest handicapper at best
in 2007: stays 1½m: acts on polytrack, soft and good to firm going: tried blinkered/in
cheekpieces: fair hurdler. *M. Madgwick*

HARD AS IRON 3 b.g. Iron Mask (USA) 117 – Runs In The Family 69 (Distant Rela- **58 d**
tive 128) [2007 64: p8.6g⁵ p8g p8g p8.6g 7s 10g 10d Oct 9] sturdy, workmanlike gelding:
regressive maiden: stays 8.6f: best efforts on polytrack: tried blinkered. *M. Blanshard*

HARD ROCK CITY (USA) 7 b.g. Danzig (USA) – All The Moves (USA) (A P Indy **114**
(USA) 131) [2007 111: 7m* 8g 7g⁶ 8s² 7v² 8s² 7s* 7.5g⁵ 8.5g² Oct 20] lengthy, quite
attractive gelding: smart performer: won minor event at Gowran in May and valuable
handicap at Galway (by short head from Warriors Key) in August: also ran well when
¾-length second of 4 to Redstone Dancer in Minstrel Stakes at the Curragh fifth start:
effective at 7f/1m: acts on heavy and good to firm going: usually races prominently:
sometimes looks none too keen. *M. J. Grassick, Ireland*

HARD TO CATCH (IRE) 9 b.g. Namaqualand (USA) – Brook's Dilemma 80 (Known **54**
Fact (USA) 135) [2007 65: 5.7m 6m p5g Jul 17] close-coupled gelding: handicapper,
only modest in 2007: effective at 5f to 7f: acts on all-weather, firm and good to soft going:
visored once, often blinkered before 2007: has been slowly away. *Mike Murphy*

HARD TOP (IRE) 5 b.g. Darshaan 133 – Well Head (IRE) (Sadler's Wells (USA) 132) **108 §**
[2007 115: 10g² 9.9g⁶ 12s² 12m⁵ 12g⁴ 14g Aug 25] big, lengthy gelding: just useful and
inconsistent in 2007, placed in minor event at Lingfield (1¼ lengths second to Blue Ksar)
and listed races at Newmarket (2½ lengths second to Classic Punch) and Goodwood
(fourth to Purple Moon): stays 1½m: acts on good to firm and soft ground: pulls hard and
sometimes finishes weakly: temperamental: joined H. Brown in UAE. *Sir Michael Stoute*

HAREEM (IRE) 3 b.g. King's Best (USA) 132 – Knight's Place (IRE) 72 (Hamas **77**
(IRE) 125§) [2007 12.1m⁶ p13.9g* Sep 27] 120,000F, 70,000Y, 85,000 2-y-o: third foal:
dam, Irish maiden (stayed 12.5f), half-sister to smart performers Fife (best around 1½m)
and El Conquistador (stayer): much better effort in maidens when winning at Wolverhampton in September by neck from Vivacita: stays 1¾m: acts on polytrack: sold 20,000
gns, joined M. Keighley then gelded. *J. A. Osborne*

HARLAND 3 b.c. Halling (USA) 133 – White Star (IRE) 108 (Darshaan 133) [2007 **115**
75p: 10.1s* 12d 10d* 10g* Jul 28] tall colt: smart performer, lightly raced: won maiden

Prix Eugene Adam, Maisons-Laffitte—
British challengers Harland (near side) and Regime fight out the finish to Europe's richest Group 2 race

at Newcastle in March, and listed race at Sandown (by head from Tam Lin) and Prix Eugene Adam at Maisons-Laffitte (again showed plenty of resolution when beating Regime a short head) in July: should stay 1½m (still green when tried in King Edward VII Stakes at Royal Ascot): raced only on good going or softer. *M. A. Jarvis*

HARLECH CASTLE 2 b.c. (Mar 22) Royal Applause 124 – Ffestiniog (IRE) 96 **93** (Efisio 120) [2007 5.2m⁴ 5.1f 6f² 6g* p7g³ Sep 5] quite good-topped colt: half-brother to several winners, including 2004 2-y-o 5f to 7f winner Brecon Beacon (stays 1½m, by Spectrum), 6-y-o Eisteddfod, and 7f/1m (including at 2 yrs and in UAE) winner Boston Lodge (by Grand Lodge), all smart: dam 6f (at 2 yrs) to 1m winner: fairly useful performer: won nursery at Newbury in August, hard work but responding: improved again when third to Meeriss in minor event at Lingfield: stays 7f: acts on polytrack and firm going: has looked easier ride when blinkered (twice). *P. F. I. Cole*

HARLEM SHUFFLE (UAE) 2 br.f. (Feb 8) Halling (USA) 133 – Badraan (USA) **80 p** (Danzig (USA)) [2007 p7m* Oct 11] first foal: dam, UAE 6f/7f winner, out of US Grade 3 2-y-o 8.5f winner Gold Sunrise: 8/1, smooth winning debut in maiden at Kempton, in control from 2f out: will be suited by 1m: sure to improve. *M. Johnston*

HARLEQUINN DANSEUR (IRE) 2 b.g. (Mar 10) Noverre (USA) 125 – Nassma **54** (IRE) 95 (Sadler's Wells (USA) 132) [2007 6m 5d⁵ 5m⁶ 6g 8m p8g 8g Oct 3] rather leggy gelding: modest maiden: probably stays 1m: usually tongue tied, tried visored. *N. Tinkler*

HAROLDINI (IRE) 5 b.g. Orpen (USA) 116 – Ciubanga (IRE) (Arazi (USA) 135) **–** [2007 –, a70: p7g f6g² p7.1g⁵ f7g² p7.1g³ p7.1g³ p7.1g⁶ 6.1m p7.1g p7.1g⁶ p7.1g⁵ f7d* **a67** Dec 15] lengthy gelding: fair handicapper on all-weather, lightly raced and little form on turf in recent years: won at Southwell in December: best at 6f/7f: acts on all-weather: wears cheekpieces. *J. Balding*

HARRINGTON BATES 6 ch.g. Wolfhound (USA) 126 – Fiddling 82 (Music Boy **51** 124) [2007 53: p7.1g p5.1g⁵ Oct 20] strong, compact gelding: modest maiden: ran only at Wolverhampton in 2007: best at 5f/6f: acts on polytrack, soft and good to firm going: tried in cheekpieces, often wears visor (not in 2007). *J. J. Lambe, Ireland*

HARRISON GEORGE (IRE) 2 b.c. (Mar 19) Danetime (IRE) 121 – Dry Lightning **79** 63 (Shareef Dancer (USA) 135) [2007 6v² 6m⁴ 7.2g² 6m⁴ 6d³ p6g⁴ Oct 23] €45,000Y: good-topped colt: has plenty of scope: fifth foal: half-brother to several winners, including fairly useful Irish 2006 2-y-o 1m winner Harper Valley (by Val Royal): dam 1¼m winner: fair maiden: in frame all starts, third to Calming Influence at York: raced mainly at 6f, should be well suited by 7f/1m: acts on polytrack, heavy and good to firm going. *R. A. Fahey*

HARRISON'S FLYER (IRE) 6 b.g. Imperial Ballet (IRE) 110 – Smart Pet 77 **81** (Petong 126) [2007 75: 5.3m² 5.1m⁴ 5.5d⁶ 5.7m* 5g³ 5.3f⁶ 5.7d² 5s² 5.3d* 5d⁵ 5m⁶ 5.1s² 5.1g⁵ 5.2f⁴ 5g 5.7d Aug 19] good-topped gelding: fairly useful handicapper: won at Bath in May and Brighton in June: best at 5f/6f: acts on all-weather, firm and soft going: tried blinkered/visored, wears cheekpieces: has shown signs of temperament. *J. M. Bradley*

HARRISON'S STAR 2 gr.g. (Feb 11) Erhaab (USA) 127 – Gentle Gypsy 94 (Junius **–** (USA) 124) [2007 8g 8g⁶ Oct 19] leggy gelding: no show in maidens. *G. M. Moore*

HARRY GEE 2 b.g. (Apr 4) Averti (IRE) 117 – Mentro (IRE) 65 (Entrepreneur 123) **84** [2007 5.1g 6g 6.1m* 6m⁵ 7m⁴ 7s² 7g Oct 27] 7,200F: good-topped gelding: second foal: dam, maiden (stayed 1¼m), out of half-sister to very smart 1¼m/1½m winner Sudden Love: fairly useful performer: won maiden at Chester in August: ran well in frame in nurseries then Goodwood: will stay 1m: acts on soft and good to firm going: blinkered last 3 starts: sold 30,000 gns, then gelded. *W. R. Muir*

HARRY THE HAWK 3 b.g. Pursuit of Love 124 – Elora Gorge (IRE) (High Estate **76 p** 127) [2007 63: 8.5s³ 7m⁶ 8s³ 9.9d² 12.4d* Oct 16] quite good-topped gelding: fair handicapper: won amateur event at Newcastle in October by 1¾ lengths from Right Option, travelling smoothly: stays 1½m: acts on soft and good to firm ground: likely to do better still. *T. D. Walford*

HARRY TRICKER 3 b.g. Hernando (FR) 127 – Katy Nowaitee 112 (Komaite (USA)) **102** [2007 71p: 10g³ p12g³ 9.9m³ 9.9m* 11d* 11.8d² Oct 9] good-topped gelding: developed into a useful handicapper, winning at Goodwood (2) in September, showing good turn of foot when beating Bergonzi by 2 lengths last: future success: very good neck second to Pippa Greene at Leicester after: stays 1½m: acts on polytrack, good to firm and good to soft going on turf: sold 125,000 gns in December. *Mrs A. J. Perrett*

HARRY UP 6 ch.g. Piccolo 121 – Faraway Lass 94 (Distant Relative 128) [2007 94: **93** f5g⁴ p5.1g* p5g 5m⁶ 5g 5m⁶ 5d 5g 5m³ 5m² 5m⁴ 5g² 5g p6g³ p5.1g² p6g⁵ Dec 30] strong gelding: fairly useful handicapper: won at Wolverhampton (by neck from Dig Deep) in January: best at 5f/6f: acts on all-weather, firm and soft ground: tried in blinkers/cheekpieces: front runner. *K. A. Ryan*

HARTING HILL 2 b.g. (May 7) Mujahid (USA) 125 – Mossy Rose 78 (King of Spain **–** 121) [2007 7g Aug 24] short-backed gelding: half-brother to fairly useful 11.6f to 1¾m winner Browning (by Warrshan) and 11.6f winner Bienvenue (by Bien Bien): dam 6f and 1m winner: 20/1, behind in maiden at Newbury. *M. P. Tregoning*

HARTMANN (USA) 3 b.g. El Corredor (USA) 123 – Fearless Wildcat (USA) (Forest **66** Wildcat (USA) 120) [2007 p8g p6g³ p6g⁵ Jun 29] fair maiden: should stay at least 7f: sold 3,500 gns in October. *B. J. Meehan*

HART OF GOLD 3 b.g. Foxhound (USA) 103 – Bullion 85 (Sabrehill (USA) 120) **78** [2007 89: 10m 9g p6g⁵ p6g 7g⁴ 7m* 7m² 7m p6g⁶ p6g Dec 4] good-bodied gelding: just fair performer at 3 yrs: not at best when winning seller at Folkestone (left M. Wallace) in September: stays 7f: acts on polytrack and firm ground: below form all 3 starts in cheekpieces: sometimes edgy, has twice unseated to post: inconsistent. *R. A. Harris*

HARTSHEAD 8 b.g. Machiavellian (USA) 123 – Zalitzine (USA) 98 (Zilzal (USA) **97** 137) [2007 103: 7.5g⁸ 6m 6d 7d 8m² 8m 9.8m 8g Oct 6] tall, leggy gelding: useful handicapper: inconsistent in 2007, good effort when 3 lengths second of 5 to Ragheed at Redcar: stays 1m: acts on firm and good to soft ground: waited with. *G. A. Swinbank*

HARTS IN MO SHUN (IRE) 3 b.g. Spectrum (IRE) 126 – Offshoot (Zafonic (USA) **54** 130) [2007 6g⁶ 6m 7.1g 7s 8m 9.2g 6m Sep 1] big gelding: maiden: well held after reappearance: often blinkered. *A. Berry*

HARVEST JOY (IRE) 3 b.f. Daggers Drawn (USA) 114 – Windomen (IRE) (Forest **80 §** Wind (USA) 111) [2007 89: p8g 11.4m 9.7g 10s 11.6m⁶ 11.6f⁵ 10g Sep 19] lengthy, good-bodied filly: fairly useful performer: left B. R. Millman after sixth outing: seems to stay 11.6f: acts on firm going: wore cheekpieces (clipped heels and unseated) third start: one to treat with caution. *J. Gallagher*

HARVEST QUEEN (IRE) 4 ch.f. Spinning World (USA) 130 – Royal Bounty (IRE) **115** 80 (Generous (IRE) 139) [2007 100: 8m* 8.5d⁵ 8d 8.1g* 8m⁵ Oct 6] tall, good-topped filly: smart performer: progressed again in 2007, winning listed races at Goodwood (by 4 lengths from Expensive) in May and Haydock (further improvement, beat Smart Enough 1¼ lengths) in September: good 2½ lengths fifth to Majestic Roi in Sun Chariot Stakes at Newmarket final outing: raced mostly at 1m: best efforts on good/good to firm going: held up. *P. J. Makin*

Betfredpoker Superior Mile, Haydock—further improvement from Harvest Queen, who quickens from last to first in a steadily-run race to catch Smart Enough (rail)

*Weatherbys Superlative Stakes, Newmarket—Hatta Fort, stepped up in trip,
shows a good turn of foot to beat Declaration of War (star on cap); Ellmau (blaze) is third*

HARVEST WARRIOR 5 br. or gr.g. Mujahid (USA) 125 – Lammastide 93 (Martinmas 128) [2007 93d: 8.1g* 8.5m² 9.8m² 10d⁶ 8.5v* 8.9s⁴ 8.5m⁵ 9.8m⁴ 9.9g⁴ 9.8m 12g Sep 22] tall, leggy gelding: fairly useful handicapper: won at Haydock in May and Beverley in July: stays 1¼m: acts on heavy and good to firm going: has worn blinkers: tricky ride, often slowly away. *T. D. Easterby* **87**

HASANKA (IRE) 3 b.f. Kalanisi (IRE) 132 – Hasainiya (IRE) 109 (Top Ville 129) [2007 88p: 10m 12s² 14d² 12g* Sep 10] lengthy, rather leggy filly: half-sister to several winners, including useful 11f and 13f winner Hasanpour (by Dr Devious): dam Irish 1¼m winner: progressed into a smart performer: runner-up in Give Thanks Stakes at Cork (beaten short head by Downtown) and listed race at the Curragh (to Red Moloney) prior to winning listed race at Galway in September by head from Ezima: stays 1¾m: acts on soft going. *John M. Oxx, Ireland* **112 +**

HASSAAD 4 b.g. Danehill (USA) 126 – Ghazal (USA) 103 (Gone West (USA)) [2007 88: 8m⁴ 10m⁶ 8.1g⁶ 8.9s 10m⁵ 10.3m⁶ 10.4d Oct 13] good-topped gelding: useful handicapper: best effort when winning at Ascot in May by ½ length from Cross The Line: badly hampered when sixth in Zetland Gold Cup at Redcar next time: respectable efforts at best after: stays 1¼m: acts on polytrack and good to firm going, well below form on soft: sometimes wears blinkers/tongue strap: ungenuine (looked reluctant final 3 outings): sold 57,000 gns. *W. J. Haggas* **95 §**

HAS TO BE ABACUS (IRE) 2 br.c. (Feb 15) Indian Lodge (IRE) 127 – No Way (IRE) (Rainbows For Life (CAN)) [2007 7s 8.1m p10g⁵ p10g Dec 12] seemingly modest form in claimer/maiden at Kempton last 2 starts. *A. B. Haynes* **50 ?**

HASTY LADY 2 b.f. (Jan 27) Dubai Destination (USA) 127 – Hasten (USA) (Lear Fan (USA) 130) [2006 6s 6.1g⁵ 6m³ 8.3m 7g⁶ 6g² Oct 19] 70,000F, 31,000 2-y-o: rather leggy filly: second foal: half-sister to winner in Greece by Johannesburg: dam, US maiden, half-sister to smart miler Fantastic View: fair maiden: placed at Ripon and Redcar (5 lengths second to Spinning Lucy): best up to 7f: acts on good to firm going. *K. A. Ryan* **67**

HASTY RETREAT 2 b.g. (Mar 11) King's Best (USA) 132 – Madame Maxine (USA) 89 (Dayjur (USA) 137) [2007 p8m³ p7.1g³ Dec 13] second foal: dam, 5f and (including at 2 yrs) 6f winner, half-sister to smart French miler Panis: fair form in maidens at Lingfield and Wolverhampton, not looking easiest of rides in latter: subsequently gelded. *E. A. L. Dunlop* **68**

HATCH A PLAN (IRE) 6 b.g. Vettori (IRE) 119 – Fast Chick 93 (Henbit (USA) 130) [2007 74: p10g p12g 10.2f 15.4m⁴ 10d³ 11.6m 12g³ 11s⁶ 12m 11.6m⁶ 11.6m p12g⁶ p10g² p10g* p11g Dec 19] leggy, workmanlike gelding: fair handicapper: won at Kempton in November: stays 1½m: acts on polytrack, best efforts on turf on good going or firmer: tried in cheekpieces: held up. *Mouse Hamilton-Fairley* **73**

HATHAAL (IRE) 8 b.g. Alzao (USA) 117 – Ballet Shoes (IRE) 75 (Ela-Mana-Mou 132) [2007 ?: p16g f14g⁵ p16g p12g² p12g² 11s 11.9d 11.8d² 11.6d* Jul 23] good-topped gelding: has a short, unimpressive action: just fair performer nowadays: didn't have to be **61 a68 ?**

at best to win seller at Windsor in July: best at up to 1½m: acts on sand/polytrack, good to firm and good to soft ground: tried blinkered, visored nowadays: usually tongue tied (not final start). *E. J. Creighton*

HATHERDEN 3 b.g. Tobougg (IRE) 125 – Million Heiress (Auction Ring (USA) 123) **69**
[2007 –: p7g* Feb 19] robust gelding: tongue tied, improved form when winning maiden at Lingfield in February: should stay 1m: acts on polytrack: sent to Sweden. *R. A. Kvisla*

HATTA FORT 2 b.c. (Jan 18) Cape Cross (IRE) 129 – Oshiponga 72 (Barathea (IRE) **105**
127) [2007 5m⁵ 5m* 5m³ 7m* 7g⁴ 7d⁶ Oct 20] 135,000F: strong colt: third foal: half-brother to 9f winner Teide Lady (by Nashwan): dam, 9f winner, half-sister to smart performers up to 1½m Tissifer and Sir George Turner: useful performer: won minor event at Windsor in June and Weatherbys Superlative Stakes at Newmarket (beat Declaration of War by neck) in July: off 3 months before running well last 2 starts, 3½ lengths fourth to Rio de La Plata in Prix Jean-Luc Lagardere at Longchamp and 7½ lengths sixth to New Approach in Dewhurst Stakes at Newmarket: will be suited by 1m: acts on good to firm and good to soft going: has joined Godolphin. *M. R. Channon*

HATTAN (IRE) 5 ch.h. Halling (USA) 133 – Luana 101 (Shaadi (USA) 126) [2007 **116**
114: p8.6g* a8f 12g⁴ 12g³ 12g³ p10g 9.8g* 10.3m⁴ 12d⁵ 12d² 10g⁴ 10.4d⁶ 12.3m* 12g⁴
10d Nov 4] leggy horse: smart performer: won minor events at Wolverhampton in January and Ripon in April, and listed event at Chester (by length from Foxhaven) in September: highly tried otherwise in 2007, though generally ran creditably, including when nose second to Sudan in Gran Premio di Milano and 3¾ lengths fourth to Ask in Cumberland Lodge Stakes at Ascot penultimate start: ran poorly in Premio Roma at Rome final outing: effective at 8.6f to 1½m: acts on polytrack (well held on dirt), firm and good to soft going. *C. E. Brittain*

Sheikh Ahmed Al Maktoum's "Hatta Fort"

HATTON FLIGHT 3 b.g. Kahyasi 130 – Platonic 79 (Zafonic (USA) 130) [2007 52: **70** 11g³ 14.1m³ 11.5g⁴ 14m⁵ 13.1f* 14g⁶ p12.2g³ p12g p12g* Oct 29] leggy gelding: fair handicapper: won at Bath in August and Kempton in October: stays 1¾m: acts on polytrack and firm ground: usually in cheekpieces/blinkers: sometimes races freely. *A. M. Balding*

HAVANAVICH 2 b.c. (Apr 3) Xaar 132 – Queen of Havana (USA) (King of Kings **76** (IRE) 125) [2007 p7g p7g⁴ 9d³ p10g Oct 31] lengthy colt: fair maiden: best effort when third to Funny Me at Goodwood, only turf start: stays 9f. *S. Kirk*

HAVING A BALL 3 b.g. Mark of Esteem (IRE) 137 – All Smiles 41 (Halling (USA) **54** 133) [2007 60: 7s⁶ 6s² 6s² p7g⁴ Oct 31] smallish gelding: modest maiden: stays easy 7f: acts on polytrack and soft going. *P. D. Cundell*

HAWAANA (IRE) 2 b.c. (Feb 20) Bahri (USA) 125 – Congress (IRE) 86 (Dancing **87 p** Brave (USA) 140) [2007 6d⁴ 7m* 7m Sep 14] €220,000Y: good-topped colt: half-brother to several winners, including 6-y-o United Nations and Irish 7.5f (at 2 yrs) to 1¼m winner Royal Intrigue (by Royal Applause), both useful: dam, 1m winner, sister to Sprint Cup winner Cherokee Rose: fairly useful form: confirmed debut promise (fourth to Atlantic Sport at Ascot) when winning maiden at Leicester in August by 2 lengths from Doctor Fremantle: stiffish task in sales race at the Curragh final start: will stay 1m: remains likely to do better. *B. W. Hills*

HAWAASS (USA) 2 b.c. (Apr 13) Seeking The Gold (USA) – Sheroog (USA) 77 (Sha- **89 p** reef Dancer (USA) 135) [2007 6g 8.1g* Sep 19] big, leggy, close-coupled colt: brother to 3-y-o Dig Gold and closely related to smart 9f (in UAE) to 1½m winner Sharaf Kabeer and useful 1¼m winner El Mobasherr (both by Machiavellian), and half-brother to 2 winners, notably smart performer up to 1¼m Kabool (by Groom Dancer): dam, 1m winner, sister to dam of Dubai Millennium (by Seeking The Gold): fairly useful form: much improved from debut 4 months earlier when winning maiden at Sandown by short head from Yaddree, battling well: will stay 1¼m: should go on progressing. *M. Johnston*

HAWAII PRINCE 3 b.g. Primo Valentino (IRE) 116 – Bollin Rita 82 (Rambo Dancer **75** (CAN) 107) [2007 72d: 5m* 5v 5s³ 5m⁵ 5g⁴ 5f 5m⁴ 5m Sep 30] fair handicapper: left D. Nicholls and gelded after 2 yrs: won maiden at Catterick in May: probably best at 5f: acts on soft and good to firm ground (below form all starts on firm): often races up with pace: wore cheekpieces final start: has hung left. *S. T. Mason*

HAWA KHANA (IRE) 2 br.f. (Mar 18) Indian Danehill (IRE) 124 – Anearlybird **62** (USA) 53 (Sheikh Albadou 128) [2007 6g 6d⁵ p6g 7d p6g⁶ p8.6g⁴ Dec 3] lengthy, good-topped filly: first foal: dam, maiden (stayed 7f), closely related to useful French sprinter/ miler Always King: modest maiden: stays 8.6f. *N. P. Littmoden*

HAWK AND I (IRE) 2 ch.c. (Mar 27) Hawk Wing (USA) 136 – Dos Talas (USA) (You **?** And I (USA) 118) [2007 6d a6d⁴ Dec 16] trained by R. Kvisla on debut: better effort in maidens when fourth at Taby. *Yvonne Durant, Sweden*

HAWK ARROW 5 ch.g. In The Wings 128 – Barbizou (FR) (Selkirk (USA) **68** 129) [2007 63: p10g⁴ p12g³ p12.2g⁶ p12.2g p12g² p10g² p10g Apr 25] tall, quite good-topped gelding: fair handicapper: stays easy 1½m: acts on polytrack and firm going: tried in cheekpieces: waited with: has shown signs of temperament. *G. L. Moore*

HAWK EYED LADY (IRE) 2 b.f. (Mar 6) Hawk Wing (USA) 136 – Danccini (IRE) **75** 78 (Dancing Dissident (USA) 119) [2007 6f 6d⁵ 6m² 6.5m 7m p6g³ p6g Nov 21] 40,000F, €85,000Y: stocky filly: fifth foal: half-sister to 3 useful winners, including 4-y-o Green Park and 8-y-o Whitbarrow: dam Irish 2-y-o 5f winner: fair maiden: placed at Ripon and Wolverhampton (third to Haybrook): best efforts at 6f: acts on polytrack, good to firm and good to soft going. *J. A. Osborne*

HAWK FLIGHT (IRE) 2 b.c. (Mar 17) Hawk Wing (USA) 136 – Rapid Action **67** (USA) (Quest For Fame 127) [2007 8.2g p8.6g⁶ Nov 17] good-topped colt: fair form in maidens at Nottingham and Wolverhampton: stays 8.6f. *W. R. Muir*

HAWK GOLD (IRE) 3 ch.g. Tendulkar (USA) 114 – Heiress of Meath (IRE) 34 **43** (Imperial Frontier (USA) 112) [2007 –: 8d 9d 12d⁵ 10.5g 12m 10d⁶ 8d Oct 18] good-topped gelding: poor maiden: left M. Sunderland in Ireland after fifth start: probably stays 1½m: tried blinkered. *M. D. I. Usher*

HAWK HOUSE 2 b.g. (Feb 24) Alhaarth (IRE) 126 – Arinaga (Warning 136) [2007 **59** 7m p7g⁶ 7s⁶ Oct 9] 28,000F, €60,000Y: sixth foal: half-brother to useful but untrust- worthy 2001 2-y-o 7f/7.5f winner Lascombes (by Bluebird) and French 6.5f to 1m winner

Jamaicaine (by Emperor Jones): dam, Norwegian 2-y-o 1m winner, out of smart French 1m (at 2 yrs) to 11f winner Brillante, herself half-sister to top-class French miler Bellypha: modest form when mid-field in maidens, off 2½ months prior to final start (gelded after): will stay 1m. *B. W. Hills*

HAWK ISLAND (IRE) 2 b.c. (Jan 14) Hawk Wing (USA) 136 – Crimphill (IRE) 106 **71** (Sadler's Wells (USA) 132) [2007 p7m⁴ Nov 1] 80,000F, 75,000Y: second foal: dam Irish 1¼m/11f winner (stayed 1¾m): 16/1, backward and green (moved poorly to post), fourth to Traphalgar in maiden at Lingfield, wandering: will be suited by 1¼m/1½m. *G. Wragg*

HAWKIT (USA) 6 b.g. Silver Hawk (USA) 123 – Hey Ghaz (USA) (Ghazi (USA)) **82** [2007 80, a73: 9.2g 10.1m² 9.1m⁴ 10.1v 9.2d³ 9.1d 9.2m³ 9.1s* 9.2d* 10g⁶ 9.2s⁶ 9.1v 9.1v² Nov 3] rather leggy gelding: fairly useful handicapper: better than ever when winning at Ayr and Hamilton within 5 days in August: stays 1½m: acts on all-weather, heavy and good to firm going: has been tongue tied: usually waited with. *P. Monteith*

HAWK MOUNTAIN (UAE) 2 b.g. (Mar 16) Halling (USA) 133 – Friendly (USA) **54 p** (Lear Fan (USA) 130) [2007 7g⁴ 6m Oct 22] 9,000Y: strong gelding: third foal: halfbrother to 4-y-o Garrulous: dam unraced out of close relation to 1½m performers Assatis (high class) and Warrshan (smart): inadequate stamina test in maidens, fourth to Reel Buddy Star at Newcastle: will do better at 1m+. *J. J. Quinn*

HAWKSMOOR (IRE) 5 b.g. In The Wings 128 – Moon Cactus 118 (Kris 135) [2007 **–** –: p10g p16g Jan 14] of little account. *L. A. Dace*

HAWKSTAR EXPRESS (IRE) 2 b.g. (Apr 11) Hawk Wing (USA) 136 – Band of **– p** Angels (IRE) (Alzao (USA) 117) [2007 8d 8d Oct 19] 32,000F, 25,000Y: strong gelding: fifth foal: half-brother to Irish 2003 2-y-o 7f winner Dance On The Moon (by Fasliyev) and 11f winner Mont Saint Michel (by Montjeu), both fairly useful: dam unraced halfsister to Derby winner Dr Devious: backward, well held in maidens at Newbury and Newmarket: will probably do better. *J. R. Boyle*

HAWRIDGE KING 5 b.g. Erhaab (USA) 127 – Sadaka (USA) 77 (Kingmambo **88** (USA) 125) [2007 76: 14m* 12.6m² 15.9m⁴ 16.2g² 16d Oct 11] quite good-topped gelding: fairly useful handicapper: won at Haydock in August: improved form when in frame next 3 starts: stays 2m: acts on polytrack, firm and soft ground: visored final 2 starts at 4 yrs: often held up: consistent. *W. S. Kittow*

HAWRIDGE MISS 3 b.f. Piccolo 121 – In The Stocks 59 (Reprimand 122) [2007 7d **70 +** 8f⁴ 7g³ 6g³ 5.7g* Oct 24] sturdy filly: second foal: dam, 1m to 11.5f winner, half-sister to useful sprinter Hill Magic: fair form: improved when readily winning apprentice handicap at Bath in October: best effort at 5.7f: slowly away third outing. *B. R. Millman*

HAWRIDGE PRINCE 7 b.g. Polar Falcon (USA) 126 – Zahwa 72 (Cadeaux Gene-**113 d** reux 131) [2007 120: 14.1g⁴ 16m⁴ 11.6m⁴ 16g 16d⁶ Oct 20] big, lengthy gelding: smart performer: creditable length fourth to Mount Kilimanjaro in listed event at Nottingham on reappearance: below form after (reportedly fell sick and sustained leg problem after second start): stays 2m: acts on good to firm and good to soft going. *B. R. Millman*

HAYBROOK 2 b.c. (Feb 18) Xaar 132 – Miss Brooks 81 (Bishop of Cashel 122) [2007 **88 p** p6g² p6g* p6g* Dec 4] 18,000F, 38,000 2-y-o: first foal: dam, 7f winner, out of half-sister to high-class sprinter Mr Brooks: fairly useful form: confirmed debut promise when winning maiden at Wolverhampton (made all) in November and minor event at Lingfield (showed good attitude to beat Classic Fortune by neck) in December: may prove best at 5f/6f: capable of better still. *E. J. O'Neill*

HAYDENS MARK 2 b.g. (Mar 19) Efisio 120 – Lady In Colour (IRE) 71 (Cadeaux **69 p** Genereux 131) [2007 p7g⁵ Sep 12] fourth foal: half-brother to 7.5f winner Ali Deo (by Ali-Royal): dam, second at 1¼m only start, half-sister to Prix Vermeille winner Pearly Shells: 66/1, green under pressure when fifth to Iguazu Falls in maiden at Kempton: will be suited by 1m+: should do better. *W. J. Haggas*

HAYDOCK EXPRESS (IRE) 3 gr.g. Keltos (FR) 132 – Blusienka (IRE) 102 (Blues **46** Traveller (IRE) 119) [2007 52: f6g p7.1g p6g p5.1g p7.1g⁶ 6m p11g Dec 19] tall gelding: poor maiden: should stay 1m: raced mostly on polytrack: blinkered fourth start. *Peter Grayson*

HAYFIELD FLYER 3 b.f. Wizard King 122 – Diamond Rouge 53 (Puissance 110) **–** [2007 p8.6g 7g 9.8m Sep 1] neat filly: second foal: dam sprint maiden: no show in maidens. *Paul Green*

461

Kleinwort Benson Stakes (Handicap), Newmarket—Hearthstead Maison successfully concedes weight all round, providing the most valuable of 76 wins during the year for champion apprentice Greg Fairley; Man of Vision (left) and Ladies Best (spots on cap) are second and third

HAYLEY'S FLOWER (IRE) 3 b.f. Night Shift (USA) – Plastiqueuse (USA) (Quest **55** For Fame 127) [2007 –: p10g p9.5g p7g⁶ p7.1g* p8g p8g p7.1g³ p7.1g p7g p8g p8.6s Dec 21] sturdy filly: modest performer: won minor event at Wolverhampton in April: should stay 1m: raced only on polytrack since debut at 2 yrs: sometimes blinkered/in cheekpieces: inconsistent. *J. C. Fox*

HAYLEY'S PEARL 8 b.m. Nomadic Way (USA) 104 – Pacific Girl (IRE) 61 (Emm- **–** son 125) [2007 p9.5d Dec 17] no worthwhile form over jumps: well held in maiden at Wolverhampton on Flat debut. *Mrs P. Ford*

HAYWARD'S HEATH 3 ch.f. Allied Forces (USA) 123 – Penny Gold (IRE) (Mill- **57** fontaine 114) [2007 9.9d⁶ 10m 12s⁵ 11.7g⁶ 12g Jul 26] rather leggy filly: third foal: half-sister to 2003 2-y-o 1m winner Katies Tuitor (by Kayf Tara): unraced on Flat, well beaten in bumper: modest maiden: said to have coughed after final start: stays 11.7f. *B. W. Duke*

HAZARAYNA 3 b.f. Polish Precedent (USA) 131 – Hazaradjat (IRE) 82 (Darshaan **70** 133) [2007 10g² 11.8s⁴ 10s² 9g⁴ 10.2f Aug 27] tall filly: half-sister to several winners, including smart Irish 1m/1¼m winner Hazarista (by Barathea) and useful Irish 7f to 9.5f winner Hazariya (by Xaar): dam Irish 7f (at 2 yrs) and 1¼m winner: fair maiden: left H. Cecil after fourth outing: may prove best around 1¼m: acts on firm and soft going: visored final start. *P. D. Evans*

HAZELHURST (IRE) 4 b.f. Night Shift (USA) – Iktidar 80 (Green Desert (USA) **73** 127) [2007 74: 7.1m 8d 6m* 6g⁵ 6m⁵ 7g Oct 30] strong, sturdy filly: has a quick action: fair handicapper: won at Redcar in August: stays 7f: acts on firm and good to soft going. *J. Howard Johnson*

HAZELNUT 4 b.f. Selkirk (USA) 129 – Cashew 80 (Sharrood (USA) 124) [2007 68: **82** 10g* 12d³ 10.3g³ Oct 26] angular, quite attractive filly: fairly useful handicapper, lightly raced: reportedly threw a splint in spring of 2007: won at Newmarket in July: further improvement when third in ladies event at Doncaster final start: stays 1¼m: acts on polytrack and good to soft going: sold 20,000 gns. *J. R. Fanshawe*

HAZELWOOD RIDGE (IRE) 4 b.g. Mozart (IRE) 131 – Aguilas Perla (IRE) **62** (Indian Ridge 123) [2007 60: 5s 5f⁵ 5m 6g 6g 6.5v³ 7d 7g p7.1g Dec 4] good-bodied geld-ing: modest maiden handicapper: below form last 3 starts, including at Wolverhampton: stays 6.5f: acts on any going: none too consistent. *J. G. Fox, Ireland*

HAZY DAYS 3 ch.f. Lomitas 129 – Organza 105 (High Top 131) [2007 p9.5g* 11.5s* **84** 11.6f Aug 4] half-sister to 2 winners, notably very smart 6f (including at 2 yrs)/7f winner Desert Style (by Green Desert): dam, 1¼m winner, half-sister to very smart 7f performer Brocade, dam of Barathea and Gossamer: fairly useful form: won maiden at Wolver-hampton in June and handicap at Lingfield in July: much better effort when beating Jawaaneb by neck at latter track, still looking green (carried head slightly awkwardly): slipped on bend and fatally injured at Windsor next time. *Sir Mark Prescott*

HAZYTOO 3 ch.c. Sakhee (USA) 136 – Shukran 99 (Hamas (IRE) 125§) [2007 8m⁴ **82** p7g³ 8.3m 7.1m² 6f² 6g Oct 8] lengthy colt: fairly useful maiden: best effort when third at Newmarket: stays 1m: acts on polytrack, raced only on good ground or firmer on turf: has looked none too keen. *N. A. Callaghan*

HAZZARD COUNTY (USA) 3 ch.c. Grand Slam (USA) 120 – Sweet Lexy May **97** (USA) (Danzig (USA)) [2007 80: p7g* 7m⁴ 7m² p8g³ 8g p8g³ 8g Nov 3] leggy, quite attractive colt: useful performer: won maiden at Lingfield in March: best effort when third to Troubadour in handicap at Lingfield on penultimate start: free-going type, stays 1m: acts on polytrack, unraced on extremes of going on turf. *D. M. Simcock*

HEADACHE 2 b.c. (Apr 16) Cape Cross (IRE) 129 – Romantic Myth 105 (Mind Games 121) [2007 6m May 26] compact colt: 33/1, always behind in early-season maiden at Newmarket. *B. W. Duke*

HEADLAND (USA) 9 b. or br.g. Distant View (USA) 126 – Fijar Echo (USA) (In Fijar — (USA) 121) [2007 –, a46: f6g p6g f6g Feb 15] well-made gelding: no form in 2007: wears headgear: tongue tied twice. *D. W. Chapman*

HEAD TO HEAD (IRE) 3 gr.g. Mull of Kintyre (USA) 114 – Shoka (FR) 86 (Kal- **58** doun (FR) 122) [2007 44: f5g p5.1g p6g⁶ p5.1g³ f5g⁴ p5g⁵ p5g⁴ p5.1g⁴ p7.1g p8g p6g⁶ p5.1g Jul 6] modest maiden: best at 5f/6f: raced only on all-weather: tried blinkered: sometimes slowly away. *Peter Grayson*

HEAD TO KERRY (IRE) 7 b.g. Eagle Eyed (USA) 111 – The Poachers Lady (IRE) — (Salmon Leap (USA) 131) [2007 p12g p16f Feb 27] lengthy gelding: one-time fair performer: well held in 2007: tried tongue tied/in cheekpieces. *D. J. S. ffrench Davis*

HEART AND HAND (IRE) 3 b.f. Bertolini (USA) 125 – Alchi (USA) 112 (Alleged — (USA) 138) [2007 46: p7.1g f7s Feb 8] maiden: no form in 2007: tried blinkered. *M. G. Quinlan*

HEARTHSTEAD MAISON (IRE) 3 b.c. Peintre Celebre (USA) 137 – Pieds de **115** Plume (FR) (Seattle Slew (USA)) [2007 89p: 9m⁵ 10m* 11.5g² 10m³ 16d 10m* 9.9g 10.5m⁴ 12d 10m* 12g⁶ Sep 23] big, close-coupled colt: smart performer: won handicaps at Newmarket in May and July (by 1¼ lengths from Man of Vision) and Starair Kilternan Stakes at Leopardstown (beat Arch Rebel 1½ lengths in game fashion) in September: never a threat in Preis von Europa at Cologne final start: best form at 1¼m: acts on good to firm going, possibly not on softer than good: usually held up. *M. Johnston*

HEART OF DUBAI (USA) 2 b.c. (Feb 23) Outofthebox (USA) 118 – Diablo's Blend **60** (USA) (Diablo (USA)) [2007 p7g⁵ 7.1g Sep 19] tall colt: modest form (no threat) in minor events at Lingfield and Sandown. *C. E. Brittain*

HEART OF GLASS (IRE) 3 ch.f. Peintre Celebre (USA) 137 – Sallanches (USA) **60** (Gone West (USA)) [2007 –: 8m⁶ 8.2m 12.1m May 22] rangy filly: modest maiden: should be well suited by 1¼m/1½m: unraced on extremes of going: sold 3,500 gns in July, sent to France. *M. L. W. Bell*

HEATHYARDS JOY 6 ch.m. Komaite (USA) – Heathyards Lady (USA) 76 (Mining — (USA)) [2007 36, a51: p12.2g Jan 13] smallish mare: modest maiden at best: well beaten only start in 2007: has worn cheekpieces, including last 5 starts. *R. Hollinshead*

Starair Kilternan Stakes, Leopardstown—Hearthstead Maison, under Ryan Moore this time, gains a first pattern-race victory; he stays on strongly ahead of Arch Rebel (noseband) and Regime (left)

HEATHYARDS PRIDE 7 b.g. Polar Prince (IRE) 117 – Heathyards Lady (USA) 76 **89** (Mining (USA)) [2007 –, a87: f12g³ p12.2g* 12.3g³ 12m³ 11.9f* 12d 11.9g⁵ p12.2g³ **a93** p12.2g⁴ p13.9g² Nov 8] lengthy gelding: fairly useful handicapper: won at Wolverhampton in March and Brighton in August: effective at 11f to easy 2m: acts on all-weather and firm ground (eased off on soft sixth outing): held up (has tended to idle): tough and reliable. *R. Hollinshead*

HEAVEN 2 ch.f. (Feb 28) Reel Buddy (USA) 118 – Wedgewood Star 74 (Bishop of **71** Cashel 122) [2007 5g⁶ 5.7f³ 5.1f* Sep 10] 2,500Y: first foal: dam maiden (stayed 7f): fair form: progressive in maidens, won at Bath final start, rallying: should stay 6f/7f: acts on firm going. *P. J. Makin*

HEAVEN KNOWS 4 ch.g. Halling (USA) 133 – Rambling Rose 111 (Cadeaux **104 +** Genereux 131) [2007 97p: 10.4d 10.3m⁶ 12g⁴ 10d* 12m⁶ Nov 10] strong, close-coupled gelding: useful handicapper, lightly raced: better than ever when winning at Newbury in October by 1¼ lengths from Ajhar, going away at finish having had plenty to do: far from disgraced when sixth to Malt Or Mash in November Handicap at Doncaster final start, travelling best for long way: gelded after: may prove better at 1¼m than 1½m: acts on polytrack, soft and good to firm going: sweating (below form) second outing: held up, and has good turn of foot. *W. J. Haggas*

HEAVENLY SAINT 2 b.f. (Apr 20) Bertolini (USA) 125 – Heavenly Glow (Shavian **59** 125) [2007 5m⁶ 7m³ 7.1m⁴ p8g p8g p8.6g 8.2g* p7.1g³ Nov 5] leggy filly: second foal: dam bumper winner: modest performer: won seller at Nottingham (left M. Channon 6,000 gns) in October: stays 1m: acts on polytrack and good to firm going. *S. Parr*

HEAVEN SENT 4 ch.f. Pivotal 124 – Heavenly Ray (USA) 97 (Rahy (USA) 115) **113** [2007 92: 8m³ 8d* 8m² 10d² 8m³ 10d⁶ 8.1m² 8m³ Oct 6] quite good-topped filly: smart performer: won quite valuable handicap at Ascot (by 2 lengths from Apply Dapply) in May: more improvement after, runner-up to Cheyenne Star in Ridgewood Pearl Stakes at the Curragh and to Championship Point in listed handicap at Royal Ascot: not at best final 3 starts: stays 1¼m: acts on firm and good to soft going: held up: stays in training. *Sir Michael Stoute*

HEAVEN'S GATES 3 ch.g. Most Welcome 131 – Arcady 69 (Slip Anchor 136) [2007 **58** 52: f7g* p7g f7g³ p7.1g⁴ 8.3d 8.3d⁶ 9.8g⁶ 10g 9g Oct 5] modest performer: made all in seller at Southwell in January: stays 8.3f: raced only on all-weather and good/good to soft going: has worn cheekpieces. *K. A. Ryan*

HEAVENS WALK 6 ch.h. Compton Place 125 – Ghost Dancing (Lion Cavern (USA) **72** 117) [2007 82: p5g⁶ 5m p5g⁴ p5g⁴ p5g p5g Aug 29] strong horse: just fair performer nowadays: has form at 6f, races mainly at 5f: acts on polytrack and good to firm going: tried blinkered: tongue tied: has raced freely: usually held up. *P. J. Makin*

HEAVENWARD 3 ch.c. Pivotal 124 – Heavenly Ray (USA) 97 (Rahy (USA) 115) **77 +** [2007 10m 8.3d 10d² 10.3g Oct 26] strong, lengthy, angular colt: fifth foal: brother to smart US 9f/1¼m performer Megahertz and 4-y-o Heaven Sent: dam 7f/1m winner: fair maiden: easily best effort when second at Nottingham: reportedly finished lame final outing: may prove best around 1m: acts on good to soft going: sold 15,000 gns. *Sir Michael Stoute*

HEBENUS 8 b.g. Hamas (IRE) 125§ – Stinging Nettle 90 (Sharpen Up 127) [2007 –: **–** 6g 5.9g 5d Jul 23] lengthy gelding: no form since 2005: tried blinkered/in cheekpieces. *T. A. K. Cuthbert*

HEIDI HI 3 b.f. High Estate 127 – Alwal (Pharly (FR) 130) [2007 49: 6d³ 7s 5g 6m⁵ 7g **51 d** f6d Dec 11] good-topped filly: modest maiden: best efforts at 6f (bred to stay further): acts on good to soft going: tried tongue tied. *J. R. Turner*

HEIGHT OF ESTEEM 4 b.g. Mark of Esteem (IRE) 137 – Biscay 67 (Unfuwain **38** (USA) 131) [2007 54: p9.5g 6g 10.3d 8m 8.5g⁵ Aug 15] poor maiden nowadays: probably stays 1m: acts on polytrack and good to firm ground: tried in cheekpieces: refused to enter stall on intended debut in 2006: said to have had breathing problems (tried tongue tied). *W. M. Brisbourne*

HEIGHT OF FURY (IRE) 4 b.g. Sadler's Wells (USA) 132 – Height of Fantasy **79** (IRE) 101 (Shirley Heights 130) [2007 80: 14.1d⁶ 14.1m⁵ 12m Sep 15] close-coupled gelding: has a short action: fair handicapper: stays 1¾m: acts on heavy and good to firm going: races freely: joined Mrs I. P. Harrington, Ireland. *J. L. Dunlop*

HEIGHT OF SPIRITS 5 b.g. Unfuwain (USA) 131 – Kimono (IRE) (Machiavellian **51** (USA) 123) [2007 56, a69d: p7g p8g⁵ p8g³ p8g² p8g⁵ p8g² 8s³ 9g p8g⁵ p10g Nov 12] modest performer: effective at 1m/1¼m: acts on polytrack and good to firm ground: has worn cheekpieces/blinkers: sometimes carries head awkwardly. *T. D. McCarthy*

HEIGHTS OF GOLAN 3 br.g. Golan (IRE) 129 – Nemesia 111 (Mill Reef (USA) **73** 141) [2007 80: 10d 11m 9.9s p8g p10g p12.2g² p12.2g² p12.2g⁵ p13.9g* p13.9g⁵ p13.9g Oct 30] rather leggy gelding: fair handicapper: won at Wolverhampton in October: shaped as if amiss at same track on final start: stays 1¾m: has usually worn headgear of late: sometimes races freely: sold 21,000 gns. *I. A. Wood*

HELD CAPTIVE (USA) 3 b.f. Red Ransom (USA) – Furajet (USA) 101 (The **89** Minstrel (CAN) 135) [2007 7g⁴ 8d* 8s⁴ 9g Aug 1] strong, close-coupled filly: sister to very smart 6.5f (at 2 yrs, in France) to 9f (in UAE) winner China Visit and useful winner around 1¼m Red Racketeer, and half-sister to 2 useful winners, including 1m winner Dubai Visit (by Quiet American): dam, best at 5f, closely related to 2000 Guineas winner King of Kings: fairly useful form when winning maiden at Newmarket (by 6 lengths from Murbek) in June: below that level in handicaps after: should stay beyond 1m: raced only on good ground or softer. *E. A. L. Dunlop*

HELEN WOOD 4 b.f. Lahib (USA) 129 – Last Ambition (IRE) 29 (Cadeaux Genereux – 131) [2007 52: 11.7f⁵ Jun 10] fair performer at best: well beaten only start on Flat in 2007: stays 1¼m: easily best effort on soft going: fair hurdler/novice chaser. *D. E. Pipe*

HELIOSTATIC (IRE) 4 ch.c. Galileo (IRE) 134 – Affianced (IRE) 109 (Erins Isle **113** 121) [2007 115: 10m³ 8m² 10.5g 8g⁶ Jun 6] lengthy, quite attractive colt: smart performer: placed in listed races first 2 starts in 2007, 4 lengths third to easy winner Dylan Thomas at the Curragh and short-headed by Danak at Leopardstown: well held in Tattersalls Gold Cup at the Curragh and in listed race at Leopardstown after: stayed 1¼m: acted on good to firm ground, probably on soft: blinkered once: tongue tied once: usually raced prominently: to stand at Oak Lodge Stud, Co Kildare, Ireland, fee €6,500. *J. S. Bolger, Ireland*

HELLFIRE BAY 2 b.c. (May 4) Diktat 126 – Composition 82 (Wolfhound (USA) 126) **66** [2007 7g⁶ 6d³ p7.1g² f7d⁵ Dec 14] 16,000Y: good-topped colt: fifth foal: half-brother to fairly useful 7f to 1¼m winner Ephesus (by Efisio), 1½m winner Atriffic Story (by Atraf) and 1m winner Queen Jean (by Pivotal): dam 2-y-o 6f winner: fair maiden: best efforts at Wolverhampton and Southwell last 2 starts: will be well suited by 1m/1¼m. *K. A. Ryan*

HELLO DEAUVILLE (FR) 4 ch.f. Alhaarth (IRE) 126 – Pulpeuse (IRE) (Pursuit of – Love 124) [2007 –: p7g p6g Jan 31] little form. *J. Akehurst*

HELLO IT'S ME 6 ch.g. Deploy 131 – Evening Charm (IRE) (Bering 136) [2007 – 17.1m⁵ 15.9d Jul 14] good-bodied gelding: one-time useful handicapper: well held at 6 yrs: best at up to 13f: acts on polytrack, firm and good to soft going: usually wears cheekpieces/blinkers: fair hurdler, successful in August. *D. McCain Jnr*

HELLO MAN (IRE) 4 b.g. Princely Heir (IRE) 111 – Mignon (Midyan (USA) 124) **75** [2007 84: 5m⁴ 7g⁴ 6.5g 6g a6g⁶ p6g² p6g* Dec 4] fairly useful handicapper on all- **a84** weather, fair on turf: won at Wolverhampton in December: effective at 5f, barely at 7f: acts on polytrack, raced only on good going or firmer on turf: blinkered once at 2 yrs. *E. Tyrrell, Ireland*

HELLO MORNING (FR) 2 gr.c. (Apr 9) Poliglote 121 – Hello Molly (FR) (Sillery **116** (USA) 122) [2007 8g² 7g* 8d* 8s² Nov 1] fourth foal: brother to smart French 1m winner (including at 2 yrs) Hello Sunday and half-brother to useful French winner around 1¼m Hello My Lord (by Anabaa Blue): dam ran once in France: smart performer: won maiden at Chantilly in September and minor event at Saint-Cloud in October: plenty of improve- ment when ½-length second to Thewayyouare (pair clear) in Criterium International at Saint-Cloud final start, looking winner inside final 1f but unable to contain rallying rival: will stay 1¼m: acts on soft ground. *Mme C. Head-Maarek, France*

HELLO NEMO 3 b.c. Hello Mister 106 – Marisa's Pet 46 (Petong 126) [2007 5m⁶ 6m – 6g Jun 23] well held in maidens. *T. E. Powell*

HELLO NOD 3 b.g. Polish Precedent (USA) 131 – Nordan Raider 81 (Domynsky 110) **55** [2007 f7g p7.1g 6m 7s⁵ 7m 8.5g Sep 19] close-coupled gelding: modest maiden: stays 7f: acts on soft and good to firm going: won over hurdles in November. *Miss J. A. Camacho*

HELLO ROBERTO 6 b.m. Up And At 'em 109 – Hello Hobson's (IRE) 67 (Fayruz **61** 116) [2007 78: p6g 5.7d 5m⁶ p6g 5.1g p5g 5.3d³ 5.1m⁴ 5.1f⁵ 6.1m 5.1m⁴ p5.1g 5.7d* p6g 5.7g p5.1g³ p5.1g³ p5m⁴ p5.1s p5.1g⁶ Dec 31] quite good-topped mare: modest handi- capper nowadays: won apprentice event at Bath in October: effective at 5f/6f: acts on all-weather, firm and good to soft going: tried visored/blinkered, wears cheekpieces nowadays: often races prominently. *R. A. Harris*

totepool Beverley Bullet Sprint Stakes, Beverley—
Hellvelyn (near side), the only three-year-old in the field, quickens well to peg back Borderlescott

HELLVELYN 3 gr.c. Ishiguru (USA) 114 – Cumbrian Melody 83 (Petong 126) [2007 **118**
108: 6m 5m* 6g Sep 8] rangy colt: good walker: smart performer: missed first half of
2007, reportedly due to a bruised foot: confirmed reappearance promise (eighth to
Sakhee's Secret in July Cup at Newmarket) when winning listed race at Beverley in
August by short head from Borderlescott, always travelling well: ran poorly in Sprint Cup
at Haydock final start: will prove best at 5f/6f: yet to race on extremes of going. *B. Smart*

HELLZAPOPPIN 2 b.c. (Mar 24) Mtoto 134 – Pure (Slip Anchor 136) [2007 7m 8d **63 p**
Oct 19] useful-looking colt: seventh foal: half-brother to 3 winners, including 5-y-o
Clueless and 7f (at 2 yrs) to 1¼m winner Champions Gallery (by Dansili), both useful:
dam unraced sister to User Friendly: modest form down the field in maidens at Newmarket: will improve at 1¼m/1½m. *B. W. Hills*

HELP (IRE) 2 b.f. (Apr 26) Lend A Hand 124 – Lala Salama (IRE) 62 (College Chapel –
122) [2007 p6g 5d⁶ 7d p7g p8m Nov 24] €2,000Y: good-bodied filly: fourth foal: half-
sister to a winner in Norway by Namid: dam, maiden (stayed 1¼m), half-sister to smart
UAE performer up to 11f Doreg: little form: blinkered: sold £500. *Mrs P. N. Dutfield*

HELVETIO 5 b.g. Theatrical 128 – Personal Love (USA) 103 (Diesis 133) [2007 p16g⁶ –
16g Apr 28] well-made gelding: useful performer for D. Weld in Ireland in 2005 and for
A. de Royer Dupre in France in 2006 (sold 82,000 gns): last both starts in handicaps at 5
yrs: stays 2m: acts on soft and good to firm going: blinkered (ran poorly) final 3-y-o start.
Micky Hammond

HEMISPEAR 3 ch.f. Lear Spear (USA) 124 – Milladella (FR) (Nureyev (USA) 131) –
[2007 68: 11.6m 11.6v⁵ 16g Aug 2] workmanlike filly: fair maiden at 2 yrs: no form
(shaping as though stamina stretched) in 2007: sold 1,700 gns. *Miss J. R. Tooth*

HENNALAINE (IRE) 2 b.f. (Apr 24) Lujain (USA) 119 – Daralaka (IRE) (The **59**
Minstrel (CAN) 135) [2007 p6g Jul 11] 14,000F, 11,000Y: seventh foal: half-sister to 3
winners, including useful 1m to 1½m performer Rehearsal (by Singspiel): dam unraced
half-sister to several useful French 1¼m/1½m performers, including dam of Prix du
Jockey Club winner Darsi: 33/1, outpaced when seventh to Reel Gift in maiden at
Kempton. *P. F. I. Cole*

HENNESSY ISLAND (USA) 2 ch.c. (Mar 22) Hennessy (USA) 122 – Heavenly **47 +**
Dawn (USA) (Holy Bull (USA) 134) [2007 p7g p7g p7m Dec 9] showed a little ability in
maidens at Lingfield. *T. G. Mills*

HENRY BERNSTEIN (USA) 3 b. or br.c. Bernstein (USA) 115 – Hidle (USA) **71**
(Unbridled (USA) 128) [2007 64p: p8.6g 8g⁶ 8m³ 7d Jun 23] well-made colt: fair maiden:
stays 1m: unraced on extremes of going on turf: tried tongue tied: sold 8,000 gns in July.
H. R. A. Cecil

HENRY HALL (IRE) 11 b.h. Common Grounds 118 – Sovereign Grace (IRE) 101 **71 d**
(Standaan (FR) 118) [2007 78: 5f 5g 5m⁴ 5m³ 5m⁶ 5d 5.2m 5d 5m³ 5d 5m⁴ 5m 5m 5m⁶
5g Oct 3] leggy horse: had a round action: useful handicapper in his day, winner of 10 of
his 121 races: just fair at best in 2007: was best at 5f: acted on firm and soft going: visored
(well beaten) once: to stand at Low Moor Stud, Easingwold, North Yorkshire. *N. Tinkler*

HENRY HOLMES 4 b.g. Josr Algarhoud (IRE) 118 – Henrietta Holmes (IRE) 61 **56**
(Persian Bold 123) [2007 64: p12g p10g p12g⁴ p11g⁵ p12g³ p13g⁴ Dec 28] modest
maiden: stays 13f: raced only on polytrack. *Mrs L. Richards*

HENRY JAMES (IRE) 2 b.c. (May 8) Iron Mask (USA) 117 – Izibi (FR) (Saint **63**
Cyrien (FR) 128) [2007 7d⁵ 7g 7v p8g³ Dec 19] lengthy colt: best effort in maidens when
fifth at Gowran: left J. Crowley in Ireland, third at Kempton: stays 1m. *M. Botti*

HENRYTHENAVIGATOR (USA) 2 b. or br.c. (Feb 28) Kingmambo (USA) 125 **115**
– Sequoyah (IRE) 113 (Sadler's Wells (USA) 132) [2007 7m* 6m* 6v² 7d³ Aug 25]
    The ante-post market for the Two Thousand Guineas had an unfamiliar
winter look to it with the Maktoum family owning or having a controlling or
sizeable interest in the first five in the betting, whereas the traditionally strong
Ballydoyle-trained colts are conspicuous by their absence from the head of the
market. Jupiter Pluvius and Henrythenavigator are the leading Ballydoyle candidates quoted and they are available at 16/1 and 20/1 at the time of writing. The
turnaround reflects both increased acquisitiveness on the part of the Maktoums, as
well as the relative lack of success of the Aidan O'Brien-trained juveniles in the
latest season. In 2001, when two-year-old colts from Ballydoyle won nine of the ten
European Group 1s open to them, the O'Brien-trained two-year-olds ran a total of
one hundred and ninety-four times, recording sixty-two wins at an impressive strike
rate of thirty-two per cent. Since then, there has been a downward trend in the
figures, to the extent that in 2007 the Ballydoyle two-year-olds won thirty-four
races from two hundred runs at a rate of seventeen per cent, the colts winning only
three pattern races, none of them at Group 1.
    The first of those three successes at pattern level—the others were by Lizard
Island and Jupiter Pluvius—came when Henrythenavigator justified favouritism in
the Coventry Stakes at Royal Ascot. Despite a field of twenty, including eighteen
individual winners, the latest renewal of the first two-year-old pattern race of the
year in Britain didn't look particularly strong at the time, which was underlined by
the subsequent performances of the principals. As when making a successful debut
in a maiden over seven furlongs at Gowran in May, Henrythenavigator quickly

Coventry Stakes, Royal Ascot—Henrythenavigator gives Aidan O'Brien his fifth win in this contest;
Swiss Franc (light cap), Luck Money (No.14) and Pencil Hill also make the frame

recovered from a tardy start to race handily and he stayed on strongly, always looking likely to hold on, to win by three quarters of a length from Swiss Franc. Following in the footsteps of Harbour Master (1997) and Fasliyev (1999), the first two of O'Brien's five Coventry winners, Henrythenavigator was given a break before running in the Phoenix Stakes at the Curragh, a race Ballydoyle habitually targets with its leading two-year-olds. The latest renewal looked well below the usual standard, but 2/1-on shot Henrythenavigator was never travelling with much fluency in the very testing conditions and went down by a length to Saoirse Abu. Henrythenavigator was returned to the course thirteen days later for the five-runner Futurity Stakes, where again he put in a somewhat laboured performance, possibly not having fully recovered from his hard race in the Phoenix, but he put up his best effort to finish third, three lengths and a neck behind New Approach and Curtain Call. He wasn't seen again.

		Mr Prospector (b 1970)	Raise A Native
Henrythenavigator (USA) (b. or br.c. Feb 28, 2005)	Kingmambo (USA) (b 1990)		Gold Digger
		Miesque (b 1984)	Nureyev
			Pasadoble
	Sequoyah (IRE) (b 1998)	Sadler's Wells (b 1981)	Northern Dancer
			Fairy Bridge
		Brigid (ch 1991)	Irish River
			Luv Luvin'

The smallish, quite good-topped Henrythenavigator is by Kingmambo and hails from an excellent family, being the third foal of a smart filly for O'Brien, Sequoyah, winner of the Moyglare Stud Stakes at the Curragh who went on to finish fourth in both the Irish One Thousand Guineas and Irish Oaks. Sequoyah's sister Listen also found Saoirse Abu too strong when second in the latest Moyglare Stud Stakes but went on to give Ballydoyle its only Group 1 two-year-old win of the year in the Fillies' Mile. Henrythenavigator is a brother to the smart Irish mile winner Queen Cleopatra and a half-brother to the fairly useful Irish seven-and-a-half-furlong winner Abide With Me (by Danehill). Sequoyah's dam, the French mile winner Brigid, is a sister to the useful French winner at up to seven furlongs Or Vision, the dam of the high-class sprinter-miler Dolphin Street and the Aidan O'Brien-trained Irish Two Thousand Guineas winner Saffron Walden, who, like Sequoyah, is by Sadler's Wells. Henrythenavigator, who should stay a mile, won his first two starts on good to firm going and may turn out to be ideally suited by such a surface, though he ran to at least his Coventry form when encountering ground softer than good on his last two outings. *A. P. O'Brien, Ireland*

HENRY THE SEVENTH 3 b.c. Royal Applause 124 – Bombalarina (IRE) (Barathea (IRE) 127) [2007 67: p8g² p8g³ p8g³ 8.3m 8.3m p8g² p8.6g⁶ p11g 10.1d p8g⁴ p8g* p8m⁴ p8g Oct 29] lengthy gelding: fair handicapper: won at Kempton in September: stays 8.6f: acts on polytrack, well held on turf: tried in visor/cheekpieces: sold 10,000 gns. *J. W. Hills* — **a77**

HEPBURN BELL (IRE) 2 ch.f. (Mar 17) Intikhab (USA) 135 – Borsalino (USA) (Trempolino (USA) 135) [2007 7s Oct 4] €42,000F, €70,000Y: first foal: dam, ran once in France, out of winner in France/US up to 11f (including Grade 2 event) Revasser: 25/1, slowly away and no impression (ninth of 11) in maiden at Goodwood: should do better. *J. R. Fanshawe* — **56 p**

HEPHAESTUS 3 b.g. Piccolo 121 – Fragrant Cloud 37 (Zilzal (USA) 137) [2007 75: f7g f6g⁶ 5.1g p5.1g⁶ p5.1g⁶ p5.1g³ p6g p5g Nov 19] close-coupled gelding: modest performer nowadays: left A. Chamberlain after fifth start: stays easy 6f: acts on polytrack, firm and good to soft going: sometimes slowly away. *Peter Grayson* — **50**

HERB PARIS (FR) 3 ch.f. Halling (USA) 133 – Yaya (USA) (Rahy (USA) 115) [2007 72: 10d 7g 8d 6d p6g² p7g p6g p6g p6g Dec 19] leggy filly: fair maiden handicapper: left Maurice Phelan in Ireland after fifth outing: best form at 6f/7f, should be at least as effective at 1m: acts on polytrack and good to firm going: tried in cheekpieces/blinkers. *P. M. Phelan* — **67**

HERE AND HOW 2 b.f. (Mar 30) Where Or When (IRE) 124 – Qilin (IRE) 94 (Second Set (IRE) 127) [2007 7m p8g Sep 19] second foal: dam 6f (including at 2 yrs)/7f winner: well held in maidens. *M. H. Tompkins* — —

HEREDITARY 5 ch.g. Hernando (FR) 127 – Eversince (USA) (Foolish Pleasure (USA)) [2007 –: f12g⁵ p16g Nov 3] poor maiden: should stay beyond 1½m: acts on polytrack: sometimes wears cheekpieces: has been slowly away: fair winning hurdler. *Mrs L. C. Jewell* — **46**

HEREFORD BOY 3 ch.g. Tomba 119 – Grown At Rowan 75 (Gabitat 119) [2007 68: **88** p5g³ f5s⁵ p5g⁴ 5.1g⁴ 5.1f 5.1f² 5.3d* p5g⁴ 5.3m³ 5m 5m 5s* 5d p5g* p5g Oct 31] strong gelding: progressed into fairly useful handicapper: won at Brighton in May, and Goodwood (apprentices) and Lingfield in October: best at 5f: acts on all-weather and soft ground, probably on firm: effective held up or ridden prominently. *D. K. Ivory*

HERE'S BLUE CHIP (IRE) 3 ch.g. Barathea (IRE) 127 – Blasted Heath 105 (That- **62** ching 131) [2007 –: f8g³ f8g⁵ f12g⁶ p8g⁵ 8.2s⁴ p8.6g⁴ 7m Jun 12] modest maiden handicapper: should stay 1¼m: acts on all-weather and soft going: visored last 3 starts: got wedged in stall beforehand and reportedly returned sore third outing: sold 10,500 gns in July. *P. W. D'Arcy*

HERITAGE COAST (USA) 2 b.f. (Apr 28) Dynaformer (USA) – Bristol Channel **79** 113 (Generous (IRE) 139) [2007 7m⁴ p8g² p9.5g² Nov 17] smallish, strong, round-barrelled filly: type to carry condition: fourth foal: dam, 1m (at 2 yrs) to 1½m winner, closely related to Grand Criterium/Dante winner Tenby: fair maiden: runner-up at Lingfield and Wolverhampton (to Dandy Erin, pair well clear): will be suited by 1½m. *Sir Michael Stoute*

HERMANITA 3 b.f. Hernando (FR) 127 – Subjective (USA) (Secretariat (USA)) **64** [2007 9.7m 9.9d 10m⁶ 11.5m 12m 12m* p12g 12m Oct 8] close-coupled filly: half-sister to several winners in USA: dam, 6f (at 2 yrs) to 8.5f (US minor stakes) winner, sister to dam of very smart French sprinter Cherokee Rose and half-sister to smart French stayer Molesnes: modest handicapper: won at Folkestone in September: stays 1½m: acts on good to firm ground. *G. Wragg*

HER NAME IS RIO (IRE) 2 ch.f. (Mar 17) Captain Rio 122 – L'Harmonie (USA) **61** (Bering 136) [2007 6s 6s² 6s 6.3m⁵ 8.3d 6.1d⁴ p6g⁶ f7d² p7.1g⁵ Dec 29] €12,000Y: workmanlike filly: sixth foal: half-sister to Italian 2001 2-y-o 5f winner Dorliska (by Woodborough): dam French maiden: modest maiden on balance: flattered when fourth in nursery at Nottingham sixth start, dictating: stays 7f: acts on fibresand and soft ground, probably on good to firm. *J. S. Moore*

HERNANDO ROYAL 4 b.g. Hernando (FR) 127 – Louis' Queen (IRE) 102 (Tragic **98** Role (USA)) [2007 83: p12g* 12g⁵ 12m⁴ 14g⁴ 12d 12m Oct 6] good-topped gelding: useful handicapper: won at Kempton in May: further improvement next 3 starts, but below par final 2: stays 1¾m: acts on all-weather, heavy and good to firm going: tends to run in snatches: sold 55,000 gns, joined Dr R. Newland. *H. Morrison*

HERNANDO'S BOY 6 b.g. Hernando (FR) 127 – Leave At Dawn (Slip Anchor 136) **82** [2007 67: 14d 13.8g* Nov 6] rather lightly-made, workmanlike gelding: fairly useful handicapper: as good as ever when readily winning at Catterick in November by 3½ lengths from Mighty Moon: best form at 1¾m: acts on soft and good to firm going: fairly useful hurdler. *K. G. Reveley*

HERNINSKI 4 b.f. Hernando (FR) 127 – Empress Dagmar (Selkirk (USA) 129) [2007 **–** –: p8.6g⁴ 10m 10.1m Apr 26] close-coupled filly: maiden: little form since 2 yrs. *M. C. Chapman*

HEROES 3 b.g. Diktat 126 – Wars (IRE) 60 (Green Desert (USA) 127) [2007 88: 7g **99** 7d 8m 10m³ 8.3m² 7.2s² 8m⁵ 7d Oct 19] good-topped gelding: useful handicapper: improved without winning in 2007, best efforts when runner-up at Ayr (beaten ½ length by Commando Scott) and Newmarket (4 lengths behind Blackat Blackitten) sixth/ seventh starts: effective at 7f/1m: shorter: acts on soft and good to firm going: joined Evan Williams. *G. A. Huffer*

HERO HEART 2 ch.c. (Mar 21) Kyllachy 129 – Rainy Day Song 61 (Persian Bold **49 ?** 123) [2007 p5g p5m Nov 24] towards rear in maidens at Lingfield. *Jane Chapple-Hyam*

HEROLDS BAY 2 b.f. (Apr 9) Bertolini (USA) 125 – Prime Property (IRE) 60 (Tirol **–** 127) [2007 5m 5g 5.1g May 11] 5,200Y: compact filly: half-sister to 1¼m/1½m winner Middlethorpe (by Noble Patriarch) and 1½m winner Property Zone (by Cool Jazz): dam 6f winner: last in maidens. *M. W. Easterby*

HERON BAY 3 b.c. Hernando (FR) 127 – Wiener Wald (USA) (Woodman (USA) 126) **107 +** [2007 10m⁶ 10.3m² 11.9m³ 12g* 12g 12d 12m Nov 10] 70,000Y: close-coupled colt: half-brother to several winners, including 6f (in Italy at 2 yrs) winner Riotous Applause (by Royal Applause) and French 9f (at 2 yrs) and 10.6f winner On Reflection (by Rainbow Quest), both useful: dam, US maiden, out of close relative to Storm Cat: useful performer: placed in 2 maidens prior to showing improved form to win King George V Stakes (Handicap) at Royal Ascot (by head from Filios, rallying gamely) in June: not

King George V Stakes (Handicap), Royal Ascot—
Heron Bay (far side) shows improved form to open his account on his handicap debut;
he rallies gamely to get the better of Filios, the pair clear of Walking Talking and Eradicate

discredited when last of 9 in Gordon Stakes at Goodwood next time, but below form last 2 starts: will stay 1¾m: yet to race on extremes of going: held up. *G. Wragg*

HERON (IRE) 2 b.g. (Apr 18) Invincible Spirit (IRE) 121 – Alexander Express (IRE) 102 (Sri Pekan (USA) 117) [2007 p6g⁵ p6m³ 5.1g p5.1g Nov 14] workmanlike gelding: fair maiden: third at Kempton: may prove best at 5f/6f: acts on polytrack. *N. P. Littmoden* **68**

HERRBEE (IRE) 2 b.g. (Feb 15) Mark of Esteem (IRE) 137 – Reematta 75 (Sabrehill (USA) 120) [2007 6g 6g 6g Aug 30] good-bodied gelding: fourth foal: brother to 3-y-o Ebn Reem and half-brother to 2 winners, including fairly useful 2004 2-y-o 6f winner Dahteer (by Bachir): dam, maiden, half-sister to Derby Italiano winner Morshdi: modest form in rear in maidens: sold 6,500 gns, then gelded. *M. P. Tregoning* **57**

HE'S A DECOY (IRE) 3 b.c. In The Wings 128 – Allegheny River (USA) (Lear Fan (USA) 130) [2007 109: 8m⁴ 8m³ 8m Jun 19] rather leggy, good-topped colt: smart performer: fourth to Adagio in Craven Stakes at Newmarket before best effort when 2 lengths third to Cockney Rebel in Irish 2000 Guineas at the Curragh: not discredited when last of 8 behind Excellent Art in St James's Palace Stakes at Royal Ascot final start: not sure to stay beyond 1m: acts on firm going, below form on good to soft: sent to Hong Kong, where renamed Royal Pride. *D. Wachman, Ireland* **114**

HESAGURU (IRE) 3 ch.g. Ishiguru (USA) 114 – Lady Kinvarrah (IRE) 79 (Brief Truce (USA) 126) [2007 –: p8.6g 10g 7g Jun 1] close-coupled gelding: little form: blinkered last 2 starts: dead. *J. O'Reilly* **–**

HE'S A HUMBUG (IRE) 3 b.g. Tagula (IRE) 116 – Acidanthera 81 (Alzao (USA) 117) [2007 86: 6m* 6m 5m 6g 5g 5m p6g Sep 24] rangy, good sort: fairly useful performer: won minor event at Leicester in April: little impact in handicaps after, though showed good speed for long way at Kempton on final start: gelded after: stays 6f: acts on good to firm going: in cheekpieces/blinkered last 3 outings. *K. A. Ryan* **92**

HE'S A ROCKET (IRE) 6 b.g. Indian Rocket 115 – Dellua (IRE) 69 (Suave Dancer (USA) 136) [2007 –, a62d: p5g⁶ p5.1g p5.1g⁴ 5g 5m* 5g p5.1g⁶ p5.1g Sep 20] close-coupled gelding: modest performer: won apprentice handicap at Folkestone in July: left K. R. Burke 3,100 gns after next outing: best at 5f: acts on all-weather, firm and soft ground: usually wears headgear: races prominently. *John R. Upson* **58**

HESIVORTHEDRIVER (GER) 3 b.c. King's Best (USA) 132 – Homing Instinct (Arctic Tern (USA) 126) [2007 p10g⁶ 12s⁴ 12m⁶ p12g³ 14s 11.9d⁴ Oct 18] tall colt: fairly useful maiden: best effort when fourth at Newbury second start: well below form last 2 outings: stays 1½m: acts on soft ground: joined Evan Williams. *Mrs A. J. Perrett* **81**

HE'S MINE TOO 3 b.g. Indian Ridge 123 – Screen Idol (IRE) 86 (Sadler's Wells (USA) 132) [2007 67p: 8g³ 7.5m³ 9.1d p9.5d² Dec 28] leggy, quite good-topped gelding: fair maiden: left J. Bethell before final outing: stays 9.5f: acts on polytrack and good to firm going. *D. G. Bridgwater* **75**

HE'S MY BEST (USA) 3 ch.c. Elusive Quality (USA) – Fair Settlement (USA) (Easy Goer (USA)) [2007 6m³ p6g⁶ p7g Oct 29] angular colt: modest form in maidens: should be suited by 7f+: raced only on polytrack and good to firm going: sold 4,000 gns. *J. Noseda* **63**

HESSIAN (IRE) 3 b.f. Barathea (IRE) 127 – Red Letter 85 (Sri Pekan (USA) 117) [2007 –: p8g³ p8g² f8g³ 7d⁶ 8g 7f p8g* p8g⁴ p7g* p8g⁶ p7.1g* p7.1g Nov 4] sturdy filly: fairly useful performer on all-weather, modest on turf: won claimer (claimed from M. Bell £10,000) in August and handicap in September, both at Lingfield, and handicap at Wolverhampton in November: effective at 7f/1m: acts on polytrack. *P. Howling* **57 a83**

470

HESTER BROOK (IRE) 3 b.f. Soviet Star (USA) 128 – Keen To Please 60 (Keen **49 §**
116) [2007 59: 6m 7d⁴ 10m p8g 10d² 10g Oct 25] quite good-topped filly: poor maiden:
stays 1¼m: acts on firm and good to soft ground: tried in cheekpieces: one to treat with
caution (refused to race third outing). *J. G. M. O'Shea*

HEUREUX (USA) 4 b.c. Stravinsky (USA) 133 – Storm West (USA) (Gone West **73**
(USA)) [2007 82: 7m 8m² 7.9d 5.9m 8m Sep 8] good-topped colt: fair handicapper: stays
1m: acts on firm and good to soft going (well held on soft): often blinkered/visored: has
had breathing problem. *J. Howard Johnson*

HEWAAR (IRE) 4 b.g. Mujadil (USA) 119 – Corynida (USA) (Alleged (USA) 138) **–**
[2007 f8g⁵ 12m f11g May 22] modest form for K. Prendergast in Ireland only 2-y-o
outing: unraced in 2006, and no form at 4 yrs. *J. O'Reilly*

HEY PRESTO 7 b.g. Piccolo 121 – Upping The Tempo (Dunbeath (USA) 127) [2007 **46**
–: 7m p8g⁵ 7.6f 10g p12g p10m p11g Dec 19] strong, good-topped gelding: poor
handicapper nowadays: stays easy 1m: acts on polytrack, raced mostly on good ground or
firmer on turf: tried blinkered/in cheekpieces. *R. Rowe*

HEYWOOD 3 b.g. Tobougg (IRE) 125 – Owdbetts (IRE) 69 (High Estate 127) [2007 **90**
91: p8g 6g³ 6.1m* 7d 6s 7g 6m⁶ 7m⁴ 6d Sep 28] strong, sturdy gelding: fairly useful
handicapper: won at Chester in May: should stay 1m: acts on polytrack and firm going,
possibly unsuited by softer than good: tends to wander, and carry head awkwardly: sold
20,000 gns in October. *M. R. Channon*

H HARRISON (IRE) 7 b.g. Eagle Eyed (USA) 111 – Penrose (IRE) 75 (Wolfhound **90**
(USA) 126) [2007 75: p6g p7.1g* p6g⁴ p7g 7g⁶ 7.1g 7g² 7.1m⁴ 7m* 6m³ 7.1g* 7f* 8m **a71 +**
7.6m 7g 7m* 7.6m⁵ 7m 6m 6g⁵ 7g p7g Oct 14] smallish gelding: fairly useful handicapper on turf, fair on all-weather: won at Wolverhampton, Catterick, Musselburgh
and Chester (2) between March and August: in-and-out form after final success: effective at 6f/7f, barely stays 1m: acts on polytrack, firm and good to soft going: tried
in cheekpieces/blinkers: often hangs left/carries head high: races prominently: tough.
I. W. McInnes

HIATS 5 b.g. Lujain (USA) 119 – Naulakha (Bustino 136) [2007 56: f7g² 8d 5.9g Aug **–**
22] leggy gelding: modest maiden: stays 8.6f: acts on all-weather: has worn cheekpieces. **a54**
R. Craggs

HIAWATHA (IRE) 8 b.g. Danehill (USA) 126 – Hi Bettina 96 (Henbit (USA) 130) **50**
[2007 57: p10g⁵ p12g⁵ Feb 10] modest performer: stays 1½m: acts on all-weather, firm
and soft ground: tried blinkered/in cheekpieces. *A. M. Hales*

HIBIKI (IRE) 3 b.c. Montjeu (IRE) 137 – White Queen (IRE) 86 (Spectrum (IRE) 126) **85**
[2007 8.3m³ 10f² 11.5m* 12m⁵ 11s³ 11.7g* Oct 24] quite attractive colt: first foal: dam,
Irish 1½m winner, half-sister to very smart miler Snow Ridge, out of smart 10.5f to 2m
winner Snow Princess: fairly useful form: won maiden at Lingfield in September and
handicap at Bath (beat Shimoni ¾ length) in October: will stay 1¾m: acts on soft and
good to firm ground: usually held up: sold 120,000 gns, joined P. Hobbs. *J. S. Moore*

HI CALYPSO (IRE) 3 b.f. In The Wings 128 – Threefold (USA) 99 (Gulch (USA)) **114 p**
[2007 80p: 11.6g⁵ 12m* 12d* 14g* 14.6m* Sep 13] big, lengthy filly: progressed into a
smart filly, winning handicaps at Newbury and Salisbury in June, Lillie Langtry Stakes at
Goodwood (beat Wannabe Posh by ½ length) in August and Goffs/DBS Park Hill Stakes

*Goffs/DBS Park Hill Stakes, Doncaster—further improvement from Hi Calypso who completes a four-timer;
All My Loving (rail), Brisk Breeze, Synopsis and Under The Rainbow (grey) fill the next four placings*

at Doncaster (beat All My Loving by neck) in September: will be suited by 2m: unraced on extremes of going: held up: likely to improve further. *Sir Michael Stoute*

HICCUPS 7 b.g. Polar Prince (IRE) 117 – Simmie's Special 75 (Precocious 126) [2007 89: 7g* 7.1d³ 7m⁶ 7f 7.1s³ 7g⁴ 7m 7.2s 7g Oct 30] tall, quite good-topped gelding: fairly useful handicapper: won at Southwell in April: stays 7f: acts on any turf going: has worn visor/cheekpieces: has been difficult at stall: usually waited with: formerly none too reliable. *M. Dods* **89**

HI DANCER 4 b.g. Medicean 128 – Sea Music (Inchinor 119) [2007 61: f11g 14.1d* 12.6s³ 13g³ Sep 3] useful-looking gelding: fair handicapper: much improved over hurdles (fairly useful form) prior to winning at Redcar in June: stays 1¾m: acts on fibresand, firm and good to soft ground: sometimes slowly away: held up. *P. C. Haslam* **66**

HIDDENSEE (USA) 5 b.g. Cozzene (USA) – Zarani Sidi Anna (USA) 113 (Danzig (USA)) [2007 93§: p16g Apr 25] strong, lengthy gelding: one-time useful handicapper: well held only outing on Flat at 5 yrs: tried blinkered/visored: sold £8,000 in June. *M. Wigham* **– §**

HIEROGLYPH 2 b.f. (Apr 11) Green Desert (USA) 127 – Mighty Isis (USA) (Pleasant Colony (USA)) [2007 6g⁶ p7g⁴ 7.1g² p7.1g³ 7.1g* p8g⁵ Dec 4] rather leggy, useful-looking filly: second foal: dam, useful French 10.5f winner who stayed 12.5f, out of very smart 1m to 1½m performer Hatoof: fairly useful form: in frame 3 times prior to winning maiden at Musselburgh (straightforward task) in November: should stay 1m: raced only on polytrack/good going: races prominently. *M. Johnston* **81 a75**

HI FI 9 b.g. Homo Sapien 121 – Baroness Orkzy (Baron Blakeney 83) [2007 p12g⁵ p13g p12.2g Mar 2] modest hurdler/chaser nowadays: ran to similar level in maidens on Flat: likely to prove best at 1½m+: raced only on polytrack: tried in cheekpieces. *Ian Williams* **56**

HIGGY'S BOY (IRE) 2 b.c. (Feb 28) Choisir (AUS) 126 – Pagan Rhythm (USA) (Joanie's Chief (USA)) [2007 5.1f 5f⁶ 6g⁴ p6g⁴ 7m p8m 8m² p10g⁵ Oct 31] strong, close-coupled colt: fair maiden: second in nursery at Pontefract: stays 1m: acts on polytrack and firm going. *R. Hannon* **74**

HIGH AMBITION 4 b.g. High Estate 127 – So Ambitious (Teenoso (USA) 135) [2007 62: f11g⁶ p8.6g² p8.6g 7m* p7g 7g* 7f² 7m Sep 9] fairly useful handicapper: much improved in 2007, winning at Yarmouth in April and May: further progress when 1¼ lengths second to Purus at Brighton (left P. D'Arcy after): best form at 7f: acts on polytrack and firm ground: visored nowadays. *R. A. Fahey* **89**

HIGHBAND 4 b.f. Band On The Run 102 – Barkston Singer 79§ (Runnett 125) [2007 –: 9.9g Aug 15] good-topped filly: of little account. *M. Madgwick* **–**

HIGHBOURNE LADY 3 b.f. Rainbow High 121 – Lady Godiva 69 (Keen 116) [2007 8.2m 12g 11.8s 10.9d Jun 28] unfurnished filly: third foal: dam 2-y-o 1m winner: no sign of ability. *B. N. Pollock* **–**

HIGH BRAY (GER) 6 b.g. Zieten (USA) 118 – Homing Instinct (Arctic Tern (USA) 126) [2007 89: 10f 7m⁵ Sep 2] tall, useful-looking gelding: fairly useful handicapper at best: well held both starts in 2007. *J. D. Frost* **–**

HIGH CLASS PROBLEM (IRE) 4 b.g. Mozart (IRE) 131 – Sarah-Clare 67 (Reach 122) [2007 73: p8g⁶ 8.1g 8.3m 10.9d p8g² 8g p8g⁵ p8g⁶ 7g p8g⁶ p7g⁵ p10g Dec 12] tall, leggy gelding: fair handicapper: left P. Cole after ninth outing: stays easy 8.6f: acts on polytrack and firm ground: tried blinkered/in cheekpieces: sometimes tongue tied. *P. Winkworth* **70**

HIGH COUNTRY (IRE) 7 b.g. Danehill (USA) 126 – Dance Date (IRE) (Sadler's Wells (USA) 132) [2007 57: p9.5g⁶ p13.9g Jan 22] good-topped gelding: just poor maiden handicapper nowadays: stays 2m: acts on good to firm going, probably on polytrack: blinkered last 3 starts in 2005. *Micky Hammond* **40**

HIGH CURRAGH 4 b.g. Pursuit of Love 124 – Pretty Poppy 67 (Song 132) [2007 96: p7g⁴ 7s 6m⁵ 6g 6d⁶ 6s 7.6m³ 6m* 6g³ 6m⁴ 6d 6g Oct 26] strong, lengthy gelding: fluent mover: useful performer: as good as ever when winning handicap at Haydock (by neck from Holbeck Ghyll, travelling strongly into lead) in August: blinkered, below form last 2 starts: best at 6f/7f: acts on polytrack, firm and good to soft going: usually races up with pace: tried in cheekpieces. *K. A. Ryan* **96**

HIGH DAYS (IRE) 2 ch.f. (Mar 16) Hennessy (USA) 122 – Hi Dubai 112 (Rahy (USA) 115) [2007 6g⁵ 6m p6g⁴ p6g* 7.1m⁵ 8d⁵ 8d⁶ a6.5g⁶ Dec 6] lengthy filly: first foal: dam, 1¼m (Pretty Polly Stakes) winner (stayed 1½m), sister to Fantastic Light: fair performer: won nursery at Kempton in August: left Sir Michael Stoute after next outing: stays 1m: acts on all-weather, good to firm and good to soft ground: has had tongue tied. *H.-A. Pantall, France* **77**

HIGH DEE JAY (IRE) 2 b.c. (Feb 18) High Chaparral (IRE) 132 – Brogan's Well – **p**
(IRE) (Caerleon (USA) 132) [2007 9d 8d 8d Oct 11] 16,000F, 35,000Y: useful-looking
colt: sixth foal: half-brother to several winners, including fairly useful 1m (at 2 yrs) to
1½m winner Liquid Form (by Bahhare) and 1¼m winner Joint Destiny (by Desert
Prince): dam unraced half-sister to useful Irish stayer Easy To Please: behind in maidens
(within 16 days): type to do better at 3 yrs at 1¼m/1½m. *R. Hannon*

HIGHEST ESTEEM 3 b.g. Mark of Esteem (IRE) 137 – For More (FR) (Sanglamore **79**
(USA) 126) [2007 7d⁵ 11m p8g p12g⁴ p11g* p12g* Nov 19] good-topped gelding: third
foal: half-brother to useful 1m (including at 2 yrs) winner Humble Opinion and fairly
useful 1½m to 2m winner Junior, both by Singspiel: dam French 9f to 12.5f and hurdles
winner: fair performer: much improved when winning maiden and handicap, both at
Kempton, 5 days apart in November: stays 1½m: acts on polytrack, yet to race on
extremes of going on turf: in cheekpieces last 3 outings. *G. L. Moore*

HIGHEST REGARD 5 b.g. Mark of Esteem (IRE) 137 – Free As A Bird 62 (Robel- –
lino (USA) 127) [2007 72: 12.4m p9.5g May 1] fairly useful handicapper at best: no form
in 2007: tried tongue tied/in cheekpieces: dead. *N. P. McCormack*

HIGH FIVE SOCIETY 3 b.g. Compton Admiral 121 – Sarah Madeline 48 (Pelder **58**
(IRE) 125) [2007 66: 8.2g 8.2g⁶ 8m 10m⁵ 7d² 6d² 6m p9.5g⁴ p7.1g Nov 1] close-coupled **a49**
gelding: modest maiden on turf, poor on all-weather: probably stays 1m: acts on good to
soft going: in cheekpieces/blinkers last 6 starts. *S. R. Bowring*

HIGH FREQUENCY (IRE) 6 ch.g. Grand Lodge (USA) 125 – Freak Out (FR) **43**
(Bering 136) [2007 60: 15.8m 13.8m³ 16s 14d 17.1m Sep 20] tall gelding: poor per-
former nowadays: stays 2m: acts on all-weather and firm going: usually wears headgear.
A. Crook

HIGH HEEL SNEAKERS 4 b.f. Dansili 127 – Sundae Girl (USA) 75 (Green Dancer **107**
(USA) 132) [2007 111: 12s 12m² 12g 14g 12g⁶ 14.6m Sep 13] tall filly: has a quick
action: useful performer: best effort in 2007 when second to Munsef in 4-runner minor
event at Goodwood on second start: form after only when sixth behind Wannabe Posh in
listed event at York penultimate start: stays easy 13f: acts on polytrack, good to firm and
good to soft ground: blinkered last 2 outings: sent to USA. *P. F. I. Cole*

HIGH HOPE (FR) 9 ch.g. Lomitas 129 – Highness Lady (GER) (Cagliostro (GER)) –
[2007 74d: p12g Apr 30] leggy gelding: useful performer at best: well held sole Flat
outing in 2007: tried in cheekpieces, blinkered nowadays. *G. L. Moore*

HIGHLAND DAUGHTER (IRE) 2 b.f. (Apr 15) Kyllachy 129 – Raysiza (IRE) **89**
(Alzao (USA) 117) [2007 6s* 6s³ 6d 6d³ Sep 22] 9,500F, €64,000Y: close-coupled filly:
fourth foal: half-sister to winner up to 1¾m abroad by Generous: dam, useful Italian 7.5f/
9f winner, half-sister to dam of Prix de l'Opera winner Kinnaird: fairly useful performer:
won maiden at Leicester in June: similar form in better company, including when third
in listed race at Newmarket and Firth of Clyde Stakes at Ayr (beaten 2¼ lengths by
Unilateral): likely to stay 7f: raced only on good to soft/soft going. *C. G. Cox*

HIGHLAND HARVEST 3 b.c. Averti (IRE) 117 – Bee One (IRE) 81§ (Catrail (USA) **83**
123) [2007 75: p8g* p8.6g p10g 8.3m² 8m 8.3s⁴ 8.3m² 10m⁴ 10d 7v p8g⁶ Oct 17] close-
coupled colt: fairly useful handicapper: won at Lingfield in January: good efforts when in
frame 4 times (including a minor event) after: barely stays 1¼m: acts on polytrack, soft
and good to firm ground: free-going sort: has hung left. *D. R. C. Elsworth*

HIGHLAND HOMESTEAD 2 b.g. (Mar 25) Makbul 104 – Highland Rossie 67 **69**
(Pablond 93) [2007 6.1g 7g⁶ Jun 23] close-coupled gelding: brother to winner in Greece
and half-brother to 3 winners, including 5f to 7f winner Diet (by Starch Reduced): dam,
7f (at 2 yrs) and 1¼m seller winner, half-sister to dam of useful sprinter Lord Kintyre (by
Makbul): more encouragement than bare result in maidens, looking green: should stay 7f/
1m. *B. R. Millman*

HIGHLAND LADDIE 2 ch.g. (Mar 29) Lomitas 129 – Sirena (GER) (Tejano (USA)) **68 p**
[2007 6f⁴ 7.1m Aug 31] sturdy gelding: fourth foal: closely related to 2 winners by Hernando, including 6-y-o Vinando: dam, German 1m to 9.5f winner, half-sister to high-class
German 1¼m/1½m performer Silvano (by Lomitas): fair form in maidens at Newbury
(fourth to Tajdeef) and Sandown, outpaced after: gelded after: will be well suited by 1¼m/
1½m: should progress. *C. R. Egerton*

HIGHLAND LEGACY 3 ch.c. Selkirk (USA) 129 – Generous Lady 98 (Generous **99 p**
(IRE) 139) [2007 63p: 10.1m 11.6m* 12.1g³ 12s³ 16d* 16s* Oct 18] angular colt: useful
handicapper: won at Windsor in April, and Newbury (by 6 lengths) and Nottingham
(beat Market Forces by 3 lengths, travelling strongly to lead over 3f out), both in October:
stays 2m: acts on soft and good to firm going: held up: remains one to keep on right side.
M. L. W. Bell

HIGHLAND LOVE 2 b.g. (Feb 27) Fruits of Love (USA) 127 – Diabaig 76 (Preco- **62 p** cious 126) [2007 6s p6g³ p6g⁴ Sep 13] 15,000Y: good-bodied gelding: seventh foal: brother to 3-y-o Wester Ross and half-brother to fairly useful 1m winner Ailincala (by Pursuit of Love): dam 1m winner: modest form in maidens, twice in frame at Wolver-hampton, insufficient test: gelded after: will do better at 1m+. *Jedd O'Keeffe*

HIGHLAND SONG (IRE) 4 ch.g. Fayruz 116 – Rose 'n Reason (IRE) (Reasonable **60** (FR) 119) [2007 73: p6g 6g 5g⁵ 5d² 6d 5m³ 5g³ 5g p6g Dec 4] well-made gelding: modest handicapper nowadays: effective at 5f/6f: acts on polytrack, soft and good to firm going: tried in cheekpieces (below form): tends to edge left. *R. F. Fisher*

HIGHLANDS SKYE 3 b.f. Diktat 126 – Manhattan Sunset (USA) 76 (El Gran Senor – (USA) 136) [2007 p11g Nov 14] £1,100Y: half-sister to several winners, including 1¾m/ 2m winner Sun Hill (by Robellino) and 2001 2-y-o 7f winner Tramonto (by Sri Pekan), both fairly useful: dam 2-y-o 7f winner (stayed 1½m): 50/1, well held in maiden at Kemp-ton. *L. Montague Hall*

HIGHLAND WARRIOR 8 b.g. Makbul 104 – Highland Rowena 59 (Royben 125) **89** [2007 93: 5f⁵ 5f 5s* 6v 5s⁴ 5m 5s* 5s 6m 5m 5d⁴ 5.1g 5d Oct 12] big, leggy gelding: fairly useful handicapper: won at Ripon in June and York (beat Blazing Heights by length) in July: best at 5f/6f: acts on any turf going: tried in cheekpieces: often slowly away: usually held up: none too consistent. *P. T. Midgley*

HIGHLINER 5 b.h. Robellino (USA) 127 – Bocas Rose 106 (Jalmood (USA) 126) – [2007 –: 14.1g Apr 21] close-coupled horse: maiden: little form since 2005. *Mrs L. Williamson*

HIGH LITE 3 ch.f. Observatory (USA) 131 – Shall We Run 59 (Hotfoot 126) [2007 – 54p: 10.1g 8s Jun 14] good-topped filly: maiden: well held in handicaps in 2007, not looking straightforward: tried visored. *M. L. W. Bell*

HIGHLY REGAL (IRE) 2 b.c. Halling 133 – High Chaparral (IRE) 132 – Regal Portrait **58** (IRE) 57 (Royal Academy (USA) 130) [2007 p8g⁵ 9s⁵ 8g Oct 25] 24,000 2-y-o: lengthy colt: has scope: closely related to 2001 2-y-o 7f winner (later useful up to 1½m) Atarama and 5-y-o Kingdom of Dreams (both by Sadler's Wells), and half-brother to 2 winners, including 3-y-o Rock Anthem: dam lightly-raced half-sister to King's Theatre and High Estate: modest maiden: will stay 1¼m/1½m. *R. A. Teal*

HIGH 'N DRY (IRE) 3 ch.f. Halling 133 – Sisal (IRE) 84 (Danehill (USA) **76** 126) [2007 72: 7m⁴ 8g⁴ 7m⁴ 8m 7m⁵ 6g* 6d p7g⁶ p8m⁵ p8g p7m⁴ Dec 10] workmanlike filly: fair performer: won maiden at Windsor in October: left C. Cyzer after seventh start: stays 1m: acts on polytrack, unraced on extremes of going on turf: in cheekpieces last 4 starts: signs of temperament. *M. A. Allen*

HIGH PLAINS (FR) 2 ch.c. (Feb 6) Golan (IRE) 129 – Perusha (USA) (Southern **79** Halo (USA)) [2007 6d 6.5d⁶ 7g⁴ p8g⁵ Nov 19] €57,000Y: good sort: type to carry condi-tion: third foal: half-brother to winner abroad by Spinning World: dam US 6f winner (including at 2 yrs): fair maiden: fourth to Naval Review at Doncaster: should stay 1m. *R. Hannon*

HIGH POINT (IRE) 9 b.g. Ela-Mana-Mou 132 – Top Lady (IRE) 83 (Shirley Heights **78** 130) [2007 83: p16g⁴ 16m 16s⁵ 16g 18d⁵ p16g 16m² 16g³ Sep 20] lengthy, leggy gelding: fair handicapper: stays 2¼m: acts on polytrack, soft and good to firm going: tried visored: none too consistent. *G. P. Enright*

HIGH PROFIT (IRE) 3 ch.g. Selkirk (USA) 129 – Spot Prize (USA) 108 (Seattle **77** Dancer (USA) 119) [2007 p7g p8g² Mar 29] seventh foal: brother to useful 7f (at 2 yrs) and 1¼m winner Premier Prize and half-brother to smart 1½m/15f winner Gold Medallist (by Zilzal) and fairly useful 1½m winner Stage Right (by In The Wings): dam, 2-y-o 5f winner, fourth in Oaks: fair form: much better effort (very green on debut) in maidens at Lingfield when second of 4 to Palamoun: gelded after: will stay 1¼m: sold 19,000 gns in October. *D. R. C. Elsworth*

HIGH REACH 7 b.g. Royal Applause 124 – Lady of Limerick (IRE) (Thatching 131) **85 d** [2007 93: 5g⁴ 6g 5g⁴ 5m 5m⁶ 5m⁴ 6d² 6v 6d³ 6d 6m 5m 5m⁶ 6s 6.1s 5g p6g Nov 23] strong, compact gelding: fairly useful handicapper: regressed in second half of year: best at 5f/6f: acts on polytrack, firm and soft going: tried in cheekpieces/blinkers: sold 2,500 gns, joined J. O'Shea. *T. D. Barron*

HIGH REEF (FR) 9 b.m. Shareef Dancer (USA) 135 – Debate (High Line 125) [2007 **95** 92: 10m 12g² 9.9g Aug 26] sturdy mare: useful handicapper: last won in 2005: good short-head second to Forthright at Galway in August: stirred up and sweating, below form in listed event at Goodwood next time: stays 1½m: acts on soft and good to firm going: tried blinkered earlier in career. *C. F. Swan, Ireland*

HIGH RIDGE 8 ch.g. Indian Ridge 123 – Change For A Buck (USA) 83 (Time For A   75
Change (USA)) [2007 84: 6m⁵ 6m 5.7f⁴ p6g 6g 6g⁴ 6g² 6m 5.7f 6.1m p6g Oct 23] big,
lengthy gelding: fair handicapper nowadays: probably best around 6f: acts on polytrack,
firm and soft going: usually wears cheekpieces: blinkered final start: usually waited with:
sometimes races lazily. *J. M. Bradley*

HIGH ROCK (IRE) 2 ch.c. (Mar 5) Rock of Gibraltar (IRE) 133 – Hint of Silver   108 p
(USA) (Alysheba (USA)) [2007 8g³ 8g* 9g* Oct 21] half-brother to several winners in
France, including smart 9.5f to 11f winner Homeland (by Highest Honor) and useful
1¼m/11f winner Hideaway (by Cape Cross): dam, French 2-y-o 7.5f winner, sister to
smart French miler Hill Silver: won maiden at Saint-Cloud in September and Prix de
Conde at Longchamp (kept on well once leading under 2f out, beat Hannouma a length)
in October: will stay 1¼m: should improve again. *J-C. Rouget, France*

HIGH SEASONS 4 b.g. Fantastic Light (USA) 134 – El Hakma 94 (Shareef Dancer   62
(USA) 135) [2007 72: p10g 10.2g Jun 27] close-coupled gelding: modest handicapper
nowadays: left B. R. Millman after reappearance: stays 1¼m: acts on polytrack, good to
firm and good to soft going: tried blinkered/visored. *A. J. Chamberlain*

HIGH STANDING (USA) 2 b. or br.g. (Mar 11) High Yield (USA) 121 – Nena Maka   85 p
(Selkirk (USA) 129) [2007 5m 5.2g p5g 7g⁵ p6g* p6g* Oct 22] $80,000Y, 55,000Y: tall
gelding: has a round action: second foal: dam, 5.5f (in US) to 9f (in France) winner, half-
sister to useful 7f/1m winner Bishr: fairly useful form: much improved to win nurseries at
Kempton and Wolverhampton in October, quickening well and having plenty to spare:
should stay 7f/1m: will go on progressing. *N. A. Callaghan*

HIGH STEPPING (USA) 2 ch.c. (Mar 31) High Yield (USA) 121 – Dance Colony   65 p
(USA) (Pleasant Colony (USA)) [2007 8.2d Oct 10] $100,000Y: well-made colt: closely
related to 2 winners in US by Storm Cat and half-brother to several winners abroad,
including UAE 6f winner Gold Camp (by Mr Prospector): dam US Grade 2 2-y-o 6f/7f
winner: 25/1 and green (unseated behind stall), seventh to Patkai in maiden at Nottingham, going on well at finish: will do better. *E. A. L. Dunlop*

HIGH TREASON (USA) 5 ch.g. Diesis 133 – Fabula Dancer (USA) (Northern   92
Dancer) [2007 86: 10.5g³ 12g² 12g* 12m 12d⁶ 12d 12d Oct 12] tall gelding: fairly useful
handicapper: won at York (by ½ length from Mutawaffer) in May: should stay beyond
1½m: acts on polytrack, firm and soft going: held up: sold 65,000 gns. *W. J. Musson*

HIGH TRIBUTE 3 ch.c. Mark of Esteem (IRE) 137 – Area Girl 76 (Jareer (USA) 115)   76
[2007 68: p6g* p7g² p6g p6g p7g Jul 18] well-made colt: fair performer: won maiden
at Lingfield in January: stays 7f: raced only on polytrack: tongue tied: free-going sort:
usually races prominently: sold 2,000 gns in October. *Sir Mark Prescott*

HIGHWAY TO GLORY (IRE) 4 b.f. Cape Cross (IRE) 129 – Anita Via (IRE)   83
(Anita's Prince 126) [2007 102: p8g⁴ 7g⁵ p8g Nov 28] lengthy filly: useful performer at
3 yrs: only fairly useful in 2007 (tongue tied): best up to 1m: raced on polytrack and good
going or softer: sold 75,000 gns. *M. Botti*

HIGH WINDOW (IRE) 7 b.g. King's Theatre (IRE) 128 – Kayradja (IRE) (Last   –
Tycoon 131) [2007 –: 9.9m 6m 10.3g 7g p8.6g f6g Dec 27] little solid form. *G. P. Kelly*

HI HIGH 2 b.f. (Feb 28) Tumbleweed Ridge 117 – High Finale 85 (Sure Blade (USA)   33
130) [2007 p5.1g p5.1g⁶ Jun 11] first foal: dam 2-y-o 5f winner: poor form in claimer/
seller. *D. K. Ivory*

HILBRE COURT (USA) 2 b. or br.c. (May 24) Doneraile Court (USA) – Glasgow's   85 p
Gold (USA) (Seeking The Gold (USA)) [2007 p8g* p8.6g* p8.6g* Dec 14] $21,000Y,
23,000 2-y-o: rather leggy colt: closely related to useful German 7f winner Croisiere (by
Capote) and half-brother to minor US winners by Mt Livermore and Giant's Causeway:
dam, US sprinter, half-sister to smart French sprinter Abundance out of US Grade 1 8.5f/
9f winner Gorgeous: fairly useful form: successful all 3 starts, in maiden at Lingfield
in October and minor events at Wolverhampton in November and December (beat
Dhhamaan by 1¼ lengths): stays 8.6f: raced only on polytrack: likely to progress further.
B. J. Meehan

HILDEGARDE (IRE) 2 b.f. (May 17) King Charlemagne (USA) 120 – Rose Society   53
(Caerleon (USA) 132) [2007 6s⁵ 5.1d⁵ 7d 6m 7.5g⁵ 6g⁶ 7m Sep 6] €11,000Y: leggy filly:
half-sister to several winners: dam Irish maiden: modest maiden: barely stayed 7.5f: tried
in blinkers/cheekpieces: dead. *T. D. Easterby*

HILLBILLY CAT (USA) 4 ch.g. Running Stag (USA) 124 – Flashy Cat (USA)   –
(Mountain Cat (USA)) [2007 –, a67: f6g⁶ p6g p6g f6g⁶ May 14] modest performer nowa-   a51
days: best at 6f: races mainly on all-weather: tried blinkered: has flashed tail. *R. Ingram*

HILL CLOUD 5 gr.g. Cloudings (IRE) 112 – Hill Farm Dancer 82 (Gunner B 126) **56**
[2007 10.5m 12g⁵ p12g p13.9g p13.9s p12.2d² Dec 28] angular gelding: first foal: dam
1½m winner: modest maiden: seems to stay easy 1¾m: acts on polytrack: tried tongue
tied. *W. M. Brisbourne*

HILL FARM SHANTY 5 b.g. Slip Anchor 136 – Hill Farm Blues 83 (Mon Tresor **–**
113) [2007 f11d Dec 12] no form. *J. T. Stimpson*

HILL OF ALMHUIM (IRE) 4 b.g. City On A Hill (USA) 114 – Kitty Kildare (USA) **51**
68 (Seattle Dancer (USA) 119) [2007 73d: p8g³ p10g p8.6g⁵ p7g⁴ p6g p6g p8.6g
May 1] quite good-topped gelding: modest performer nowadays: barely stays 10.3f:
acts on polytrack, firm and good to soft going: often wears headgear (visored in 2007).
Peter Grayson

HILL OF CLARE (IRE) 5 br. or b.m. Daylami (IRE) 138 – Sarah-Clare 67 (Reach **–**
122) [2007 54: p8.6g 7.1d 10f⁶ 10.2g p9.5g Nov 10] maiden: little form in 2007: tried
tongue tied. *G. H. Jones*

HILL OF LUJAIN 3 b.g. Lujain (USA) 119 – Cinder Hills 72 (Deploy 131) [2007 70: **70**
6.1m 6d p6g p7.1g³ p6d Dec 28] sturdy gelding: fair handicapper: stays 7f: acts on polytrack and good to soft going. *Ian Williams*

HILL QUEEN (IRE) 3 b.f. Montjeu (IRE) 137 – Minodora (IRE) (Marju (IRE) 127) **74**
[2007 p10g 11.6v⁴ p11g³ Aug 1] €160,000Y: useful-looking filly: fourth foal: closely
related to 2 winners in Italy by Barathea, including 9f winner Teofane Il Greco, and half-
sister to Italian winner up to 1¼m Epoca (by Grand Lodge): dam Italian maiden: trained
by B. Grizzetti in Italy at 2 yrs, winning minor event at Varese: fair form in handicaps in
Britain, third at Kempton on final start: stays 11f: acts on sand and polytrack: sent to
USA. *L. M. Cumani*

HILLSIDE SMOKI (IRE) 3 b.f. Soviet Star (USA) 128 – Najeyba 80 (Indian Ridge **–**
123) [2007 –: 7.5m 11.1g 12d⁵ 9.8s 12.1g 10.1m 8m Aug 27] quite good-topped filly: of
little account: tried blinkered. *A. Berry*

HILLS OF ARAN 5 b.g. Sadler's Wells (USA) 132 – Danefair 109 (Danehill (USA) **–**
126) [2007 –: 16m Aug 17] strong, compact gelding: fairly useful performer at best: little
form on Flat since 2005: tried blinkered: fairly useful hurdler, successful in October and
November. *W. K. Goldsworthy*

HILLS PLACE 3 b.g. Primo Valentino (IRE) 116 – Moxby (Efisio 120) [2007 52p: **60**
p6g⁵ p7g³ 10m⁴ p7g³ p8g⁴ p8g⁶ Oct 24] strong gelding: modest maiden handicapper:
stays 1m (pulled hard at 1¼m): acts on polytrack: sold 4,000 gns. *J. R. Best*

HILLTIME (IRE) 7 b.g. Danetime (IRE) 121 – Ceannanas (IRE) 77 (Magical Wonder **58**
(USA) 125) [2007 61: 12g⁵ Jun 11] modest handicapper: stays 1½m: acts on polytrack,
firm and good to soft ground: visored once earlier in career: fairly useful hurdler/chaser.
J. S. Wainwright

HILLTOP FANTASY 6 b.m. Danzig Connection (USA) – Hilltop 45 (Absalom 128) **51**
[2007 52: p6g f8g⁵ f7g p7g⁴ Apr 30] strong mare: modest maiden: stays 1m: acts on
all-weather: tried visored, in cheekpieces last 3 starts. *V. Smith*

HILVERSUM 5 ch.m. Polar Falcon (USA) 126 – Silky Heights (IRE) 67 (Head For **51**
Heights 125) [2007 –: p8.6g* p8.6g Jun 2] modest performer, lightly raced: heavily
backed when winning seller at Wolverhampton in April: stays easy 8.6f: acts on polytrack: in cheekpieces last 3 starts. *Miss J. A. Camacho*

HIMBA 4 b.g. Vettori (IRE) 119 – Be My Wish 80 (Be My Chief (USA) 122) [2007 64: **64 d**
15.4m* 15d 15.4g⁶ 16.4m 16f 16m Aug 17] big, rangy gelding: modest handicapper: won
at Folkestone in April: below form after, looking reluctant last 2 starts: stays 15.4f: acts
on good to firm ground, possibly not good to soft: tried blinkered. *Mrs A. J. Perrett*

HINTERLAND (IRE) 5 b. or br.h. Danzig (USA) – Electric Society (IRE) 107 (Law **104**
Society (USA) 130) [2007 111: 8m 8.2m³ 8v⁵ Jul 26] tall horse: just useful form in 2007,
best effort when third in minor event at Nottingham: should stay 1¼m: acts on good to
firm and good to soft going (well below form on heavy): has given trouble at stall: joined
S. Seemar in UAE. *Saeed bin Suroor*

HINT OF SPRING 3 b.f. Seeking The Gold (USA) – Cherokee Rose (IRE) 122 **70**
(Dancing Brave (USA) 140) [2007 –: 7.5g⁵ 8m³ 9.2s³ 8.2g* Oct 31] unfurnished filly:
fair performer: won maiden at Nottingham in October: stays 8.2f: acts on good to firm
going: has left Godolphin. *Saeed bin Suroor*

HINTON ADMIRAL 3 b.g. Spectrum (IRE) 126 – Shawanni 105 (Shareef Dancer **107**
(USA) 135) [2007 100: p7g* 6d⁵ 7m⁴ 6m² 6m May 20] good-topped gelding: useful
performer: won listed race at Lingfield (by ¾ length from Hurricane Spirit) in March:

good efforts after when fourth to Prime Defender in listed Free Handicap at Newmarket and ½-length second to Hoh Mike in listed race at Ascot: gelded after final start: effective at 6f/7f: acts on polytrack and good to firm going: has been early to post: usually makes running: sold 20,000 gns in October. *M. Johnston*

HIP 2 b.f. (May 3) Pivotal 124 – Hypnotize 103 (Machiavellian (USA) 123) [2007 6f* **78 p** Aug 6] good-topped filly: fourth foal: half-sister to 5-y-o Hypnotic and 4-y-o Macedon: dam, 2-y-o 7f winner, closely related to smart performer up to 1m Dazzle: 7/1, won maiden at Windsor by 1¼ lengths from Street Star, showing inexperience at times: will probably stay 7f/1m: sure to improve. *E. A. L. Dunlop*

HIPPOLYTE (USA) 4 b.f. Monarchos (USA) 129 – Liberty School (USA) (Pine Bluff – (USA)) [2007 49: f8s f8g⁵ f11g Mar 6] lengthy filly: maiden: no form in 2007. *J. G. Given*

HIS MASTER'S VOICE (IRE) 4 ch.c. Distant Music (USA) 126 – Glen of Imaal **83** (IRE) (Common Grounds 118) [2007 80: p7g⁶ p7g² p7g* 7g² p7g² p7g 6m⁶ 7g 7m 6d p7g Oct 15] rather leggy colt: fairly useful maiden: won at Lingfield in March: good efforts when runner-up next 2 starts: stays 7f: acts on polytrack, soft and good to firm going: unruly in stall and withdrawn prior to intended tenth start: sold 20,000 gns, sent to Saudi Arabia. *D. W. P. Arbuthnot*

HISS AND BOO 2 ch.g. (Jan 23) Starborough 126 – Royal Lady (IRE) 65 (Royal **49** Academy (USA) 130) [2007 p8g⁴ Dec 19] 40/1 and blinkered, poor form when fourth in maiden at Kempton, not looking keen. *P. Howling*

HISTORIC PLACE (USA) 7 b.g. Dynaformer (USA) – Captive Island 116 (North- – fields (USA)) [2007 16d 14.6g Oct 26] workmanlike gelding: fairly useful maiden handicapper in 2005: unraced on Flat (fair hurdler) in 2006 and well held both starts at 7 yrs. *J. A. Geake*

HISTORY BOY 3 b.g. Dr Fong (USA) 128 – Goldie 80 (Celtic Swing 138) [2007 84: **88 §** p9.5g p8g p12.2g* p12.2g p12.2g⁵ 12m 9.9d p12.2g Oct 27] leggy, quite attractive gelding: fairly useful handicapper: won at Wolverhampton (never off bridle) in July: little impact after: stays easy 1½m: acts on polytrack: takes strong hold, usually held up: quirky, one to treat with caution: sold 9,000 gns. *D. J. Coakley*

HISTORY PRIZE (IRE) 4 b.g. Celtic Swing 138 – Menominee (Soviet Star (USA) **48** 128) [2007 48: f11g⁴ f11g p16.5g p12.2g³ p12g Dec 19] poor maiden: stays 1½m: raced only on all-weather. *A. G. Newcombe*

HITCHCOCK (USA) 4 ch.c. Giant's Causeway (USA) 132 – Beware of The Cat **109** (USA) (Caveat (USA)) [2007 104+: 9.5m 12s³ 8.9s 14d Aug 22] good-bodied colt: fractured a cannon bone at 2 yrs: useful handicapper: best effort when unlucky third to Pevensey in Duke of Edinburgh Stakes at Royal Ascot, forced to switch and going on strongly: should be suited by further than 1½m (only eleventh in Ebor at York over 1¾m): acts on soft and good to firm going: held up. *A. P. O'Brien, Ireland*

HITCHENS (IRE) 2 b.c. (Mar 22) Acclamation 118 – Royal Fizz (IRE) (Royal **100** Academy (USA) 130) [2007 5d⁴ 6m* 6g³ 7m² 5d⁵ Oct 13] €66,000 2-y-o: good-topped colt: sixth foal: half-brother to useful 7f (at 2 yrs)/1m (in Hong Kong) winner Grand Marque (by Grand Lodge), and winner in Belgium by Brief Truce: dam, French 2-y-o 6.5f winner, half-sister to smart Hong Kong performer up to 1¼m Floral Pegasus: useful performer: won maiden at Folkestone in August: ran well all starts after, unlucky third in nursery at York, second to Luck Money in sales race at the Curragh and 2½ lengths fifth to Captain Gerrard in Cornwallis Stakes at Ascot (barely adequate test): should prove best at 6f/7f: acts on good to firm and good to soft going. *G. L. Moore*

HITS ONLY CASH 5 b.g. Inchinor 119 – Persian Blue 64 (Persian Bold 123) [2007 **76** 74, a80: f6g p7.1g⁵ p8.6g² p7.1g⁶ p8.6g³ p8.6g² 8.5m² 8d⁴ p8.6g⁵ 8d* p8.6g p8.6g* p8.6g⁶ p9.5g Oct 18] close-coupled gelding: fair handicapper: won at Yarmouth in August and Wolverhampton in September: stays 8.6f: acts on polytrack (probably on fibresand), good to firm and heavy ground: tried blinkered: sometimes slowly away: held up. *J. Pearce*

HITS ONLY HEAVEN (IRE) 5 ch.g. Bold Fact (USA) 116 – Algonquin Park (High – Line 125) [2007 91: f8g Jan 1] good-topped gelding: fairly useful handicapper at best: unseated rider when pulling up 4f out only start in 2007: had worn blinkers: dead. *D. Nicholls*

HITS ONLY JUDE (IRE) 4 gr.g. Bold Fact (USA) 116 – Grey Goddess 117 (Gods- **60** walk (USA) 130) [2007 71: p7.1g⁵ p7g p7.1g Dec 1] sturdy, close-coupled gelding: modest maiden handicapper nowadays: stays easy 7f: acts on polytrack, soft and good to firm going: blinkered (pulled hard) on debut. *J. Pearce*

Vodafone 'Dash' Stakes (Handicap), Epsom—Hogmaneigh (quartered cap) finishes well and wins narrowly from Moorhouse Lad (dark cap) and Caribbean Coral (rail)

HITS ONLY LIFE (USA) 4 b.g. Lemon Drop Kid (USA) 131 – Southern Day (USA) (Dixieland Band (USA)) [2007 60: f8g f11g p9.5g 12m² 12.5g³ 11.5g⁵ a14g⁴ a14g² a14g⁶ a11.5g⁶ a11g Oct 20] modest handicapper: left J. Pearce after fourth start: stays 1¾m: acts on sand/fibresand, good to firm and good to soft ground: tends to hang left/has looked none too keen: tried blinkered. *Mme S. Braem, Belgium*   **60**

HIT'S ONLY MONEY (IRE) 7 br.g. Hamas (IRE) 125§ – Toordillon (IRE) 69 (Contract Law (USA) 108) [2007 63: 6g* 6g 6m⁶ 6d 6d⁴ 5.9m 7m⁶ 5.9g⁶ 7.2g 6m 6s Oct 4] workmanlike gelding: usually looks well: modest handicapper: won at Ayr in May: should stay 1m: acts on polytrack, good to firm and good to soft going: tried in cheekpieces/tongue tie. *J. S. Goldie*   **63 d**

HITS ONLY TIME 2 ch.c. (Apr 21) Bertolini (USA) 125 – South Wind 62 (Tina's Pet 121) [2007 6m 8.2d 6d p7g Oct 29] 28,000F, €48,000Y, 40,000 2-y-o: strong colt: fifth foal: half-brother to 2002 2-y-o 6f winner Riverboat Dancer (by Muhtarram) and winner in Greece by Diktat: dam, maiden (stayed 1½m), out of half-sister to Yorkshire Oaks winners Sally Brown and Untold: modest maiden, but has often shaped better than result suggests: should stay 1m: type to progress. *J. Pearce*   **59 p**

HITS ONLY VIC (USA) 3 b. or br.g. Lemon Drop Kid (USA) 131 – Royal Family (USA) (Private Terms (USA)) [2007 –: p6g f8g 9.9m³ Aug 26] workmanlike gelding: left J. Pearce, gelded and off 6 months before seeming to show much improved form when third in maiden at Beverley: stays 1¼m: raced only on polytrack and good/good to firm going. *D. Carroll*   **72 ?**

HIT THE ROAD (IRE) 3 gr.g. Carrowkeel (IRE) 106 – Order of Success (USA) (With Approval (CAN)) [2007 –: p6g 8d 8g Apr 21] modest maiden: ran respectably at Wolverhampton on reappearance: stays 1m. *Michael McElhone, Ireland*   **56**

HIT THE ROOF 2 b.c. (Feb 22) Auction House (USA) 120 – Rave On (ITY) 73 (Barathea (IRE) 127) [2007 6f⁶ 7g p8g⁴ p8g³ 8.3m³ p7g³ Nov 4] small, sturdy colt: fair maiden: third last 3 starts, including in nursery: will prove best up to 1m: acts on polytrack and firm going: has awkward head carriage. *R. Hannon*   **75**

HLA TUN (USA) 2 b.g. (Mar 3) Johannesburg (USA) 127 – Sophie (USA) (Pulpit (USA) 117) [2007 p7g p7m Nov 1] $80,000F, $240,000Y: rather leggy gelding: first foal: dam US 7.5f/1m winner: modest form (but no impact) in maidens at Lingfield, then gelded. *W. R. Swinburn*   **60**

HOBBY 2 b.f. (Mar 24) Robellino (USA) 127 – Wydah (Suave Dancer (USA) 136) [2007 7.1g* 7.1d³ 7.1g² 7d Oct 27] close-coupled filly: fourth foal: sister to winner in Czech Republic: dam unraced out of Pretty Polly Stakes winner Calandra, herself half-sister to Oaks winner Intrepidity: fairly useful form: won maiden at Warwick in July: best efforts when placed at Sandown, third to Muthabara in listed race and second to Billion Dollar Kid in minor event: seemed amiss final start: will be suited by 1m/1¼m: raced only on good/good to soft going. *R. M. Beckett*   **88**

HOBSON 2 b.g. (Apr 9) Choisir (AUS) 126 – Educating Rita 64 (Emarati (USA) 74) [2007 5m² 5.1d⁵ 5m² 5g 5.1d* 6m⁶ 5g⁵ p5m⁴ Oct 6] unfurnished gelding: first foal: dam 5f winner: fair performer: won maiden at Bath in August, having finished ninth in Molecomb Stakes at Goodwood previous outing: held form well in nurseries (blinkered final start, gelded after): probably best at 5f: acts on polytrack, good to firm and good to soft going. *Eve Johnson Houghton*   **78**

HOCINAIL (FR) 3 ch.g. Majorien 118 – Flamme (FR) (Shining Steel 123) [2007 50: – 12.1g 11.5m 12g Aug 16] poor maiden handicapper: should stay 1¼m: raced only on good or firmer going: has raced freely. *P. Winkworth*

HOGAN'S HEROES 4 b.g. Alhaarth (IRE) 126 – Icicle 104 (Polar Falcon (USA) **56** 126) [2007 63: 7.5m 6.7s 10.1g 8f 9.8m Aug 28] angular gelding: modest maiden: ran respectably in Britain third/fourth starts: best form up to 1m: acts on firm going (well held on softer than good): tried in cheekpieces. *Eoin Doyle, Ireland*

HOGMANEIGH (IRE) 4 b.g. Namid 128 – Magical Peace (IRE) 80 (Magical **110** Wonder (USA) 125) [2007 108: 5g³ 5g* 6d 5v⁴ 5d 5m 5g Oct 7] strong, close-coupled gelding: smart handicapper: won Vodafone 'Dash' Stakes at Epsom (by neck from Moorhouse Lad, finishing well to lead late on) in June: fourth in valuable event at the Curragh in July, only good effort after: effective at 5f/6f: acts on soft ground, below form sole start on firmer than good: sometimes bandaged hind joints: held up. *S. C. Williams*

HOH HOH HOH 5 ch.g. Piccolo 121 – Nesting 47 (Thatching 131) [2007 98: 6g⁴ 6m⁶ **114** 6g 5.7g⁵ 5.1f* 5.1d³ 5m² 5d² 5m 5g² 5m⁴ 5g³ 5.6m 5d³ 5m⁶ 6d² 6d Oct 20] good-topped gelding: smart performer: won handicap at Chester in June: improved after, best effort when neck second to Fonthill Road in similar event at York in October, showing good speed before collared close home (jockey dropped whip 1f out): not discredited in Bentinck Stakes at Newmarket final start: effective at 5f/6f: acts on firm and good to soft going: sometimes slowly away: tough and consistent. *R. J. Price*

HOH ME HOH YOU (IRE) 3 ch.g. Redback 116 – Eastern Aura (IRE) 49 (Aho- **46** noora 122) [2007 56: p7.1g p6g⁴ 6.5g* 9.5g* 9s Oct 14] poor performer: sold from S. Kirk 3,000 gns after second start: won minor events at Duindigt in August and Septem- ber: stays 9.5f: acts on good to firm going. *K. Davies, Netherlands*

HOH MIKE (IRE) 3 ch.c. Intikhab (USA) 135 – Magical Peace (IRE) 80 (Magical **118** Wonder (USA) 125) [2007 105: 6m* 6m² 5d* 6v 5g* 5g⁶ 5g Oct 7] strong, lengthy colt: progressed into smart performer: won listed races at Ascot in May and Sandown in June, and Laurent-Perrier Champagne Sprint Stakes at latter track (by ½ length from Wi Dud,

Laurent-Perrier Champagne Sprint Stakes, Sandown—
Hoh Mike storms home after Wi Dud (left) had looked to have it won

getting up late on) in July: finished well again when good 2 lengths sixth to Kingsgate Native in Nunthorpe Stakes at York, but soon behind when down the field in Prix de l' Abbaye at Longchamp final start: will prove best at 5f/6f: acts on good to firm and good to soft ground, possibly not on heavy: held up. *M. L. W. Bell*

HOH WOTANITE 4 ch.c. Stravinsky (USA) 133 – West One 67 (Gone West (USA)) **96 +**
[2007 –, a77: p7.1g⁶ p7.1g⁵ p6g⁵ p6g⁴ 8m⁵ 6.1g p8.6g² p8.6g² p8.6g* 7.6d³ p8.6g* 8.1m³ 8.1m⁶ 8m p8.6g⁵ p8.6g⁵ p8.6g⁴ p9.5g⁴ p8.6g⁵ p8.6g* p8.6g* p9.5g* p9.5g* Dec 31] useful handicapper: progressed through 2007, winning 6 times at Wolverhampton, twice each in July (dead-heated latter occasion), November and December: beat Just Bond by ½ length for final success: stays 9.5f: acts on polytrack, good to soft and good to firm going: wears headgear nowadays (visored last 4 starts): patiently ridden: has hung left. *R. Hollinshead*

HOLBECK GHYLL (IRE) 5 ch.g. Titus Livius (FR) 115 – Crimada (IRE) (Mukad- **86**
damah (USA) 125) [2007 89: 5m⁴ 5m 5g⁴ 5m 5m³ 5m⁴ 5g 6m² 5.7f⁴ 5.1g⁵ p5g⁵ Oct 12] rather leggy, good-topped gelding: fairly useful handicapper: on long losing run, but at least respectable efforts most starts in 2007: best at 5f/6f: acts on polytrack and firm going: sometimes wears cheekpieces, below form only start in blinkers: tricky ride, can be slowly away/headstrong. *A. M. Balding*

HOLBIEN (IRE) 4 b.g. Orpen (USA) 116 – Fading With Music (IRE) (Thatching 131) **87**
[2007 91: p6f 7g⁵ 5m 6.5g² 6.3s 8d² 7d³ 8.5g p7g Sep 27] close-coupled gelding: fairly useful performer: effective at 6.5f to 1m: acts on heavy ground: below form on polytrack, including in listed race at Lingfield on reappearance. *Liam Roche, Ireland*

HOLDEN CAULFIELD (IRE) 2 b.g. (May 7) Catcher In The Rye (IRE) 115 – God **–**
Speed Her (Pas de Seul 133) [2007 7d 6.5d 7g⁶ Oct 25] strong gelding: no form in maidens: should stay at least 1m. *Mouse Hamilton-Fairley*

HOLDEN EAGLE 2 b.c. (Jan 20) Catcher In The Rye (IRE) 115 – Bird of Prey (IRE) **64**
69 (Last Tycoon 131) [2007 7g Oct 26] big, rather leggy colt: 100/1 and very green, modest form when behind in maiden at Doncaster. *A. G. Newcombe*

HOLD THAT CALL (USA) 2 ch.g. (Apr 16) Hold That Tiger (USA) 117 – Rainbow **66**
Master (USA) (Entropy (USA)) [2007 5s 5m 5g³ 5.2g⁶ p6g 6d⁵ p6g Nov 21] strong, good-bodied gelding: fair maiden: should prove best at 5f/6f: acts on good to soft going, probably on polytrack: hard ride. *R. Hannon*

HOLD THE GOLD (IRE) 2 b.c. (Mar 5) Danehill Dancer (IRE) 117 – Ashkirk (Sel- **88**
kirk (USA) 129) [2007 7s⁵ 7m² p6g² p7g² p7m* Dec 9] big, workmanlike colt: sixth foal: half-brother to 3 winners, including Irish 6f winner Antigone (by Cape Cross) and French 1½m winner Apse (by Anabaa): dam, French 1¼m winner, half-sister to useful performer up to 1¼m Heart of Darkness: fairly useful form: runner-up 3 times (beaten neck by Cosmic Art in minor event at Wolverhampton third start) prior to winning maiden at Lingfield: strong-travelling sort, probably better at 6f than 7f: acts on polytrack and good to firm going. *E. J. O'Neill*

HOLIDAY COCKTAIL 5 b.g. Mister Baileys 123 – Bermuda Lily 78 (Dunbeath **72**
(USA) 127) [2007 76: p8.6g p8.6g* p8.6g² 8f 7.9m* 10m² p8.6g 10m Oct 22] quite good-topped gelding: fair performer: won seller at Wolverhampton in March and apprentice handicap at Carlisle in June: stays easy 1¼m: acts on polytrack, firm and soft going: effective visored or not: tongue tied final outing at 4 yrs: fair winning hurdler. *J. J. Quinn*

HOLIDAY ROCK 3 b.g. Rock City 120 – Angie Gold (Mesleh 109) [2007 f8g f11g **–**
11.8s 12d Jun 24] first foal: dam unraced: well held in maidens. *A. J. McCabe*

HOLLOW DREAM (IRE) 2 b.f. (Mar 23) Beat Hollow 126 – Sarah's Dream (IRE) **–**
(Lion Cavern (USA) 117) [2007 p6g p7.1d f8d Dec 21] third foal: dam unraced half-sister to Craven Stakes winner King's Ironbridge: no form in maidens. *R. A. Harris*

HOLLOW JO 7 b.g. Most Welcome 131 – Sir Hollow (USA) (Sir Ivor (USA) 135) **–**
[2007 –, a80: p7g⁵ p5g* p6g p7g p6g p7g p7g p7g⁶ p6g⁶ p6g 6d p6g* p6g 6.1d p6g **a77**
p6g p5g² p6m³ p7g Dec 28] strong, lengthy gelding: fair handicapper: won at Kempton in January and September: effective at 5f to easy 1m: acts on all-weather, little form on turf since 2005: tried tongue tied: tends to wander: usually held up. *J. R. Jenkins*

HOLLOW POINT (IRE) 2 b.c. (Jan 22) Cherokee Run (USA) 122 – Squeak 121 **60 ?**
(Selkirk (USA) 129) [2007 p7.1g f8d p7.1g³ Dec 31] €30,000Y: fourth foal: dam, 7f (at 2 yrs) to 1½m (Lancashire Oaks) winner, later Grade 1 9f/1¼m winner in US: seemingly easily best effort in maidens when third at Wolverhampton, possibly flattered: bred to be suited by 1m+. *M. Johnston*

HOLLOW RIDGE 3 b.f. Beat Hollow 126 – Bolas 118 (Unfuwain (USA) 131) [2007 **94** 91p: 11.4m⁶ 8m 9.9g⁶ 10.4d⁶ Oct 13] lengthy, angular filly: fairly useful performer: best effort when 5¼ lengths sixth to Promising Lead in listed race at Salisbury third start: may prove best short of 1¼m: has sweated: free-going sort: tends to hang right: sold 33,000 gns. *B. W. Hills*

HOLLY GOLIGHTLEY 2 b.f. (Mar 29) Choisir (AUS) 126 – Breakfast Bay (IRE) **56** 80 (Charnwood Forest (IRE) 125) [2007 5m 5m⁶ 5m 6d 6d p5.1g p6d⁴ f5d³ Dec 20] 10,000Y: good-bodied filly: third foal: half-sister to winner in Japan by Montjeu: dam, 2-y-o 7f winner, half-sister to useful French performer up to 1½m Go Boldly: modest maiden: raced only at 5f/6f: tried blinkered. *K. A. Ryan*

HOLLYWOOD GEORGE 3 b.c. Royal Applause 124 – Aunt Tate (Tate Gallery **71** (USA) 117) [2007 75+: p8g³ p7.1g² f7g⁴ p7.1g⁶ p7.1g* Apr 27] fair performer: claimed from W. Haggas £15,000 second start: in cheekpieces, landed odds in seller at Wolver-hampton (sold 13,500 gns) in April: stays easy 7f, but may prove best at shorter: raced only on all-weather. *K. A. Ryan*

HOLY AFFAIRS (IRE) 3 b.g. Bishop of Cashel 122 – Zelda (USA) (Sharpen Up – 127) [2007 –: p12f 11.9g⁶ 13g Jun 8] little form, including in maiden at Lingfield on reappearance: tried blinkered. *Liam Roche, Ireland*

HOLYFIELD WARRIOR (IRE) 3 b.g. Princely Heir (IRE) 111 – Perugino Lady **45** (IRE) 75 (Perugino (USA) 84) [2007 7.1d p8g⁶ 10.1m p10g 8d p8g⁶ Oct 29] poor maiden: stays 1m: form only on polytrack: tried in cheekpieces. *I. A. Wood*

HOLY STORM (IRE) 2 b.g. (Feb 11) Mujahid (USA) 125 – Slupia (IRE) 76 (Indian **49** Ridge 115) [2007 6g 5.7s 6f 8f 6m Sep 17] poor maiden: form at 5f/6f: tried in blinkers. *Eve Johnson Houghton*

HOME 2 b.c. (Jan 27) Domedriver (IRE) 128 – Swahili (IRE) 76 (Kendor (FR) 122) **70 §** [2007 7m 6d³ 6g p7.1g 8m³ 7d³ p8g⁴ p8.6g³ p9.5g² p8.6d² Dec 28] small, close-coupled colt: first foal: dam second at 6f at 2 yrs only start: fair maiden: left E. Dunlop 17,000 gns after sixth outing: stays 9.5f: acts on polytrack, yet to race on extremes of going on turf: in cheekpieces last 3 starts: temperamental. *J. R. Boyle*

HOMEBRED STAR 6 ch.g. Safawan 118 – Celtic Chimes (Celtic Cone 116) [2007 – 54: p11g p8g p8g 10.2f 8f⁶ Jun 8] little form in 2007: often wears cheekpieces/blinkers. *G. P. Enright*

HOMECROFT BOY 3 ch.g. Kyllachy 129 – Quiz Time 90 (Efisio 120) [2007 –: p6g⁶ **48** f7g⁴ p6g⁶ p8g² 8f⁶ p11g⁶ 7s 7.9m 8.3s³ 8.1m⁶ p8.6g p12.2g p8.6d Dec 17] good-bodied gelding: poor maiden: left J. Osborne after third start: stays 8.3f: acts on polytrack and soft going: often wears headgear: held up. *P. D. Evans*

HOMES BY WOODFORD 3 ch.g. Tumbleweed Ridge 117 – Partenza (USA) (Red **64** Ransom (USA)) [2007 71: p7g* p7g⁵ p7.1g⁵ p8g⁵ p8g p8.6g³ p9.5g* 10.9m⁶ p9.5g⁴ 10m **a71** 8.1d 9m⁵ 12s⁵ 10.1g Jul 23] big, good-topped gelding: fair handicapper: won at Lingfield in January and Wolverhampton in April: stays easy 9.5f, not 1½m: acts on all-weather, soft and good firm ground (twice well held on heavy): tried blinkered/in cheekpieces: held up: sold 22,000 gns, sent to Qatar. *R. A. Harris*

HOME SWEET HOME (IRE) 4 b.f. Danehill (USA) 126 – Jungle Moon (IRE) **85** (Sadler's Wells (USA) 132) [2007 95: 8m⁵ 8.3d² 9g 10m Sep 7] workmanlike filly: useful performer at 3 yrs: just fairly useful form in 2007: best at 6f/7f: acts on good to firm and good to soft going, well held on polytrack: has worn cheekpieces. *L. M. Cumani*

HOMETOMAMMY 5 b.g. Diktat 126 – Catania (USA) (Aloma's Ruler (USA)) [2007 **49** –: p12.2g⁵ p9.5g f8g f8g⁴ f7g f8g⁵ f7g⁵ f8g⁵ 10m 10.2f p16g May 2] poor maiden: stays easy 1½m: acts on all-weather: tried in cheekpieces/blinkers. *P. W. Hiatt*

HONDURAS (SWI) 6 gr.g. Daylami (IRE) 138 – High Mare (FR) (Highest Honor – (FR) 124) [2007 97: p12g 12g p16.5g p13g⁶ Nov 15] tall, quite good-topped gelding: useful performer at best: little form in 2007: tried blinkered. *G. L. Moore*

HONEST PROSPECTOR (USA) 3 b.c. Distorted Humor (USA) 117 – Star Nurse **82** (USA) (Eastern Echo (USA)) [2007 8.1m⁴ 8d⁶ p8g² 8m* 8d⁶ Aug 19] $170,000F, $450,000Y: strong, lengthy colt: third foal: brother to winner in USA and half-brother to winner there by Rubiano: dam, US 8.5f winner, half-sister to smart US performer up to 1½m Starry Dreamer: fairly useful form: won maiden at Thirsk in August: will be suited by 1¼m: acts on polytrack and good to firm going: sold 8,000 gns, sent to Bahrain. *Sir Michael Stoute*

HONEST VALUE (IRE) 2 b.g. (Feb 2) Chevalier (IRE) 115 – Sensimelia (IRE) 68 **54 ?**
(Inzar (USA) 112) [2007 p7g 7m 6m 5f⁶ p5g Oct 24] workmanlike gelding: modest
maiden: seemingly best efforts at 5f/6f on going firmer than good. *Mrs L. C. Jewell*

HONEST YANKEE (USA) 2 ch.c. (Feb 13) Yankee Gentleman (USA) – Tresor **–**
(USA) (Pleasant Tap (USA)) [2007 p6g 7g 7.1d p9.5g Nov 17] strong colt: no form: tried
in cheekpieces. *Mrs L. C. Jewell*

HONEYCOTT (IRE) 2 ch.f. (Apr 29) King's Best (USA) 132 – Kingsridge (IRE) 89 **49 ?**
(King's Theatre (IRE) 128) [2007 6s 7m 6f⁵ 7d Oct 9] €35,000Y: good-topped filly: third
foal: half-sister to 3-y-o Lap of Honour: dam, Irish 9f winner, half-sister to smart sprinter
Pharaoh's Delight: maiden: form only when fifth at Redcar, possibly flattered: should
stay 1m. *J. D. Bethell*

HONEY MONSTER (IRE) 2 ch.c. (Mar 23) Choisir (AUS) 126 – Caribbean Escape **71**
(Pivotal 124) [2007 p6g³ 5m 6f³ 6.5m 6g p6g⁶ Oct 27] lengthy colt: fair maiden: twice
third early in campaign: best efforts at 6f: acts on polytrack and firm going. *Miss V. Haigh*

HONEYSTREET (IRE) 7 b.m. Woodborough (USA) 112 – Ring of Kerry (IRE) 67 **–**
(Kenmare (FR) 125) [2007 p8.6g Apr 16] sparely-made mare: one-time modest
performer: well held only start at 7 yrs (first Flat outing since 2004): dead. *D. Burchell*

HONKY TONK SALLY 2 b.f. (Feb 7) Dansili 127 – Flower Girl 108 (Pharly (FR) **86**
130) [2007 6d³ 6m⁵ 6g 5m² 7g* Sep 29] good-topped filly: half-sister to several winners,
including fairly useful 1m winner Roaring Twenties (by Halling) and smart performer
up to 14.6f Eco Friendly (by Sabrehill), 1m winner at 2 yrs: dam 6f winner, including at
2 yrs: fairly useful performer: consistent form, except when highly tried in Lowther
Stakes at York third start, and won maiden at Chester (by 5 lengths, making all): will
probably stay 1m: acts on good to firm and good to soft going. *M. L. W. Bell*

HONOLULU (IRE) 3 b.c. Montjeu (IRE) 137 – Cerulean Sky (IRE) 114 (Dars- **124**
haan 133) [2007 12g³ 12g* 11.3s* 14d² 14.6m³ 12g³ 12f Oct 21]
    Honolulu's performance in finishing second in the Ebor at York on just
his fourth start was the best in any handicap in Britain since 1999 and one good
enough to win many a pattern race, including some recent renewals of the St Leger.
Unfortunately, he wasn't quite able to reproduce it in three subsequent appearances in pattern company and had to settle for third in both the St Leger itself at
Doncaster and the Cumberland Lodge Stakes at Ascot, his performances raising
some concerns about his temperament. Honolulu remains in training as a four-year-
old and, at his best, is certainly good enough to make a successful transition to
pattern company.
    It has long been the case in National Hunt racing that the big handicaps offer
the truest test of the merit of the top performers, particularly steeplechasers. The
likes of Desert Orchid, Carvill's Hill and more recently Azertyuiop, Well Chief
and Denman, winner of the latest renewal of the Hennessy Gold Cup, have produced outstanding performances, sometimes in defeat when conceding plenty of
weight, in the top handicaps. On the Flat, however, handicaps tend to be wrongly
denigrated, which makes it all the more pleasing to report on performances such as
Honolulu's and that of Pipedreamer in the Cambridgeshire, for example. The participation in the Ebor of progressive, potential pattern-race performers is nothing
new but the Ebor is an altogether better race in terms of quality nowadays than that
which Sapience won in 1989 before going on to finish second in the St Leger at Ayr.
Sapience won off a mark of 88 that day and was one of six three-year-olds in the
field, including the favourite Horn Dance, who had the highest mark, one of 99. In
2007, nine of the nineteen Ebor runners had a BHA mark of 100 or higher. In 1999,
the three-year-old Arabian Moon was able to get a run off a mark of 94. Between
2000 and 2004, however, when eleven three-year-olds took part, only the pair that
ran in 2002 got in off a mark below 101. No three-year-old declared was good
enough to get in the field in 2005 or 2006. In going down by three quarters of a
length to Purple Moon off a mark of 111, finishing shortly after being switched,
Honolulu produced not only the best performance by a three-year-old in the Ebor in
recent history, but the best performance in recent years by a horse of any age,
surpassing Geordieland's fourth and Carte Diamond's second in the two preceding
years. Their performances, and indeed some of those by the winners, are as good as
or better than many a pattern-winning effort.

Honolulu earned his place in the Ebor field with a victory in the listed McInerney Homes Martin Molony Stakes at Limerick, in which he responded well to get to the front but then idled in defeating the useful filly Athenian Way a length and a half. Honolulu started favourite there after just a Leopardstown maiden win but Limerick proved to be his final win of the campaign. Honolulu started favourite at Doncaster, and his Ebor performance represented form in advance of Lucarno's in winning the Ebor meeting's recognised Leger trial, the Great Voltigeur. Honolulu's rider was critical of the early gallop in the Leger, though the times confirmed that it was truly run. That said, the race was a relative test of speed under the prevailing underfoot conditions and Honolulu got going too late in finishing third, a length and three quarters behind Lucarno. Honolulu had a pacemaker in the Cumberland Lodge over two furlongs shorter, and at Ascot it appeared that lack of resolution, rather than lack of speed, was his undoing as he was again a beaten favourite in finishing third behind Ask. Ask and Honolulu met again in the Canadian International at Woodbine. Ask finished second but Honolulu, over a mile and a half on firm going, managed only a respectable eighth, never able to get in a blow. Honolulu remains a horse of potential, particularly back at a mile and three quarters or further, though he clearly has a bit to prove.

Honolulu is by Montjeu, which may well explain the quirks, out of Cerulean Sky, a smart performer in France who won the Prix Saint-Alary. He is Cerulean Sky's fourth foal and only winner to date, though this is a notably successful family, mainly at middle distances or further. Cerulean Sky had two superior siblings in L'Ancresse, who was second in the Breeders' Cup Filly & Mare Turf, and Qaatef, a lightly-raced colt who finished third in the two-mile Lonsdale Stakes. Such is the reputation of the family that another half-sister Carisolo, a daughter of Dubai Millennium and a maiden race winner in the States after showing only fair form for

Mr Derrick Smith's "Honolulu"

Sir Michael Stoute, was sold for 1,000,000 guineas at the Newmarket December Sales in 2006. The dam of these four, Solo de Lune, made 775,000 guineas at the same sale, while Solo de Lune's 2005 foal by Dalakhani made 700,000 guineas and, named Moonstone, is in training with Aidan O'Brien. Solo de Lune was an eleven-furlong winner in France and herself related to good winners over middle distances and beyond in Wareed, Truly A Dream and Samurai Way, the last-named winning twice for Luca Cumani in the latest season, including in a two-mile handicap at Ascot. The third dam Truly Special won the Prix du Royaumont and was out of Arctique Royale, winner of the 1981 Irish One Thousand Guineas. Arctique Royale is from the family of the outstanding stayer Ardross.

			Sadler's Wells	Northern Dancer
	Montjeu (IRE)		(b 1981)	Fairy Bridge
	(b 1996)		Floripedes	Top Ville
Honolulu (IRE)			(b 1985)	Toute Cy
(b.c. 2004)			Darshaan	Shirley Heights
	Cerulean Sky (IRE)		(br 1981)	Delsy
	(b 1996)		Solo de Lune	Law Society
			(b 1990)	Truly Special

Honolulu is close coupled in appearance. There is plenty of stamina in his pedigree and he seems sure to stay two miles or more, and could well be a serious Gold Cup candidate should connections choose to go in that direction, though the stable also has Yeats and Septimus for the Cup races. Honolulu won on soft going at Limerick and ran on good to soft in the Ebor, though good to firm seems unlikely to have been the main reason he was a little below that form in the St Leger. *A. P. O'Brien, Ireland*

HONORABLE LOVE 3 ch.f. Highest Honor (FR) 124 – Everlasting Love 100 **80** (Pursuit of Love 124) [2007 9.8g⁵ 10.5g³ 10.1m² 12s² 12s 9.1d⁵ 10.5m* 10.5g Sep 8] €110,000Y: sturdy filly: second foal: half-sister to useful French 7f/1m winner (including at 2 yrs) Samsa (by Zafonic): dam, 2-y-o 7f winner (stayed 1½m), out of half-sister to smart stayer Witness Box: fairly useful handicapper: won at Haydock in August: stays 1½m: acts on soft and good to firm going. *M. Dods*

HONOURED GUEST (IRE) 3 b.c. Danehill (USA) 126 – Wind Silence (USA) (A P **116** Indy (USA) 131) [2007 84: 6.5d* 7m* 8g³ May 13] third foal: half-brother to Japanese 7.5f/8.5f winner Seizan Causeway (by Giant's Causeway): dam French 1m winner: smart performer: won minor event at Limerick in March and listed race at the Curragh (easily, by 1¾ lengths from Alexander Tango) in April: best effort when 2 lengths third to Astronomer Royal in Poule d'Essai des Poulains at Longchamp final start: suffered slight injury after: stays 1m: acts on soft and good to firm going: stays in training. *A. P. O'Brien, Ireland*

HONOUR HIGH 5 gr.g. Cloudings (IRE) 112 – Meant To Be 84 (Morston (FR) 125) **46** [2007 p16g⁶ 17.2f⁵ 16m Sep 16] poor maiden: may prove best at short of 2m: acts on good to firm and good to soft going. *Lady Herries*

HOOBER 6 b.g. Mind Games 121 – Chlo-Jo 65 (Belmez (USA) 131) [2007 8.3d Oct 1] **–** big gelding: no sign of ability over jumps: 100/1, well beaten in maiden at Windsor. *A. W. Carroll*

HOOK MONEY (IRE) 3 b.g. Orpen (USA) 116 – Toi Toi (IRE) 82 (In The Wings **59** 128) [2007 p10g 11.5s 12.1d³ p12.2g² p11g p12.2g⁵ 16.1g 11.8g⁶ 12g p12.2g Nov 14] modest maiden: left D. Arbuthnot after third outing, J. Flint after fourth: should stay 2m: acts on polytrack and good to soft going: tried in cheekpieces/blinkers: difficult ride. *A. J. McCabe*

HO PANG YAU 9 b. or br.g. Pivotal 124 – La Cabrilla 89 (Carwhite 127) [2007 56: **49** 12m 7m 8m 7.9m 8.3g³ 8g⁴ 8.3d 7.1m 12m Aug 30] close-coupled gelding: modest performer: stays 1m: acts on firm and good to soft ground: tried in blinkers/cheekpieces: none too reliable. *J. S. Goldie*

HOPEFUL ISABELLA (IRE) 3 ch.f. Grand Lodge (USA) 125 – Hopeful Sign **41** (Warning 136) [2007 –p: 9.9g 8m⁶ 10.9d Jun 28] big filly: poor maiden. *Sir Mark Prescott*

HOPEFUL PURCHASE (IRE) 4 ch.g. Grand Lodge (USA) 125 – Funoon (IRE) 74 **93** (Kris 135) [2007 102: 10g 8m 8g⁶ p7g 8m Apr 10] sturdy, lengthy gelding: fairly useful performer: likely to prove best at 1m/1¼m: acts on soft and good to firm going: in blinkers/cheekpieces last 3 starts: fair form over hurdles for Evan Williams. *W. J. Haggas*

HOPE ISLAND (IRE) 3 b.f. Titus Livius (FR) 115 – Chapka (IRE) 68 (Green Desert **69** (USA) 127) [2007 8.5m 8s⁶ 9v⁴ 8v 6.3g⁵ p6g⁴ p8g* Nov 6] €270,000Y: useful-looking filly: seventh living foal: half-sister to 3 winners, including smart 5f (including at 2 yrs)/ 6f winner Moon Unit (by Intikhab) and fairly useful 5f and 7f winner Cupids Charm (by Cadeaux Genereux): dam, maiden (stayed 1m), half-sister to Old Vic: fair performer: left D. Wachman in Ireland, won maiden at Lingfield in November: stays 1m: acts on poly-track: sold 67,000 gns. *E. F. Vaughan*

HOPE ROAD 3 ch.g. Sakhee (USA) 136 – Bibliotheque (USA) 79 (Woodman (USA) **80** 126) [2007 70p. 9g⁴ 10m 12d 10.5v³ 8d p12g³ p11m⁵ Oct 11] stocky gelding: fairly useful maiden handicapper: stays 1½m: acts on polytrack and heavy going: didn't handle bend at Windsor second outing (said to have been struck into): sold 20,000 gns. *J. R. Fanshawe*

HOPE'S ETERNAL 4 ro.g. Highest Honor (FR) 124 – Tennessee Moon 73 (Darshaan **–** 133) [2007 –: 17.2m May 21] stocky gelding: no form. *C. L. Popham*

HOPE YOUR SAFE 3 b.f. Tobougg (IRE) 125 – Sunday Night (GER) 51 (Bakharoff **58** (USA) 130) [2007 56: 8.3g 7g⁴ 7m⁴ 7.6s p8g Sep 19] modest maiden: should stay 7f: acts on polytrack, best turf effort on good to firm ground: sold 800 gns. *J. R. Best*

HORA 3 b.f. Hernando (FR) 127 – Applecross 117 (Glint of Gold 128) [2007 –p: p16g³ **67** 16.1g* p16.5g f16d³ Dec 18] fair performer: upped in trip and much improved in handi-caps in 2007, winning at Newcastle in October: stays 2m: acts on all-weather: reportedly lost action third start. *Sir Mark Prescott*

HORATIO CARTER 2 b.c. (Mar 4) Bahamian Bounty 116 – Jitterbug (IRE) (Marju **77** (IRE) 127) [2007 6d 6d⁴ 6m⁶ Nov 10] 40,000F, 61,000 2-y-o: strong, good-topped colt: third foal: half-brother to 4-y-o Pirouetting: dam unraced out of half-sister to smart sprinter Easy Landing: fair maiden: fourth to Calming Influence at York, standout form: will be suited by 7f. *K. A. Ryan*

HORNPIPE 5 b.g. Danehill (USA) 126 – Dance Sequence (USA) 105 (Mr Prospector **–** (USA)) [2007 75d: p5g⁶ p5.1g f5g² f5g⁶ f5g p5.1g 5.1g 5.7d p7.1g⁵ p7.1g⁵ p5g p8.6s⁵ **a69 d** Dec 21] close-coupled gelding: fair performer at best nowadays: left M. Saunders £2,600 after eighth start: barely stays 7f: acts on all-weather and good to firm going: sometimes wears headgear. *M. Hill*

HOROLOGIST 2 ch.g. (Apr 19) Timeless Times (USA) 99 – Georgia (Missed Flight **–** 123) [2007 7d 7d Jul 4] tailed off in maidens. *M. W. Easterby*

HORSEFORD HILL 3 b.g. In The Wings 128 – Love of Silver (USA) 110 (Arctic **89** Tern (USA) 126) [2007 10m⁶ 10d* 14d 12g* 12f⁶ 14m Oct 4] 30,000Y: tall gelding: closely related to 1½m to 2m winner Taxman (by Singspiel) and half-brother to fairly useful 1m winner Silver Bracelet (by Machiavellian): dam 2-y-o 6f/7f winner: fairly useful performer: won maiden in June and handicap in August, both at Newmarket: should stay 1¾m: acts on good to firm and good to soft going. *D. R. C. Elsworth*

HORTICULTURE (USA) 2 ch.f. (Feb 13) Forest Wildcat (USA) 120 – Substance **65** (USA) (Diesis 133) [2007 7m p7g⁶ Oct 24] half-sister to smart 6f/7f winner Demonstrate (by Storm Bird) and fairly useful 9f to 1½m winner Moratorium (by El Gran Senor): dam unraced half-sister to Ribblesdale winner Ballinderry, herself dam of Prix du Jockey Club winner Sanglamore: better run in maidens when sixth at Lingfield: will be suited by 1m+: sold 15,000 gns, sent to USA. *R. Charlton*

HOSTAGE 3 b.f. Dr Fong (USA) 128 – Catatonic (Zafonic (USA) 130) [2007 71p: p8g* **71** 10m 8m 10m⁶ 8s Jul 2] big filly: fair performer: won handicap at Kempton in January: **a75** below form on turf last 3 starts: should stay 1¼m: acts on all-weather: tried visored. *M. L. W. Bell*

HOT AGNES 4 b.f. Agnes World (USA) 123 – Hot Tin Roof (IRE) 112 (Thatching 131) **52** [2007 63: f8g⁵ Jan 25] modest maiden handicapper: best form at 6f/7f: acts on all-weather and good to soft going: tongue tied of late/visored only start at 4 yrs. *H. J. Collingridge*

HOT CHERRY 3 b.f. Bertolini (USA) 125 – Cribella (USA) 71 (Robellino (USA) 127) **–** [2007 –: 6m p7.1g Apr 24] strong filly: little form: tried blinkered. *J. M. P. Eustace*

HOTCHPOTCH (USA) 4 b.g. Dayjur (USA) 137 – Anagram (USA) (Farma Way **60** (USA)) [2007 66: p7g p6g⁴ p6g p7f p6g p7g⁵ p6g⁶ Apr 4] good-bodied gelding: modest performer: stays 7f: acts on polytrack and firm ground: tried visored, in cheekpieces nowadays. *J. R. Best*

HOT DIAMOND 3 b.g. Desert Prince (IRE) 130 – Panna 106 (Polish Precedent (USA) **94** 131) [2007 8g⁶ 10m 8d 10g⁴ p11g⁶ 9.9g* 10.1d⁴ 12m³ 14m³ 14.6g³ Oct 26] 45,000Y: sturdy gelding: second foal: dam, 1¼m winner, half-sister to Pentire: fairly useful handicapper: won at Salisbury in August: ran well last 2 starts: likely to stay 2m: acts on good to firm and good to soft ground: starts slowly and held up/races freely. *D. R. C. Elsworth*

HOTEL DU CAP 4 br.c. Grand Lodge (USA) 125 – Miss Riviera Golf 106 (Hernando (FR) 127) [2007 93: 12g 10m 7m* 8s Nov 1] big, good-topped colt: has scope: useful performer, lightly raced: dropped in trip, best effort when winning listed event at Newbury in September by ½ length from Asset: below form in Prix Perth at Saint-Cloud final start: has won at 1½m, may prove best at 7f/1m: acts on polytrack, good to firm and good to soft ground. *G. Wragg* **109**

HOTEL FELIX 2 ch.c. (Feb 19) Best of The Bests (IRE) 122 – Jaljuli 107 (Jalmood (USA) 126) [2007 8m 8d Oct 19] big, rather leggy, close-coupled colt: last in maidens at Newmarket. *Miss Gay Kelleway* **–**

HOTHAM 4 b.g. Komaite (USA) – Malcesine (IRE) 46 (Auction Ring (USA) 123) [2007 73: 5.1m 5m⁶ 5f 5m* 5g⁶ 5s⁴ 5g⁴ 5d⁴ 5m³ 5m³ 5d² 5m* p6g² p5g⁴ p6g² Nov 10] lengthy, quite attractive gelding: fairly useful handicapper: won at Pontefract in June and September: best at 5f/6f: acts on polytrack, firm and soft going. *N. Wilson* **83**

HOT PROPERTY (IRE) 3 ch.g. Cadeaux Genereux 131 – Tropical Lass (IRE) 67 (Ballad Rock 122) [2007 7d 7g⁴ 9s⁴ 8.3d⁴ p11g 10s 10g Oct 8] lengthy, workmanlike gelding: modest maiden: should stay 9f+: raced only on polytrack and good ground or softer on turf: blinkered (reportedly lame) final start: sold 4,500 gns. *W. R. Muir* **64**

HOUGHTON (IRE) 2 b.c. (May 5) Sadler's Wells (USA) 132 – Love And Affection (USA) (Exclusive Era (USA)) [2007 8.1m Sep 13] 140,000Y: good-topped, attractive colt: half-brother to several winners, notably 3-y-o Yellowstone: dam, US 5f to 1m winner (second in Grade 1 6f event at 2 yrs), closely related to very smart 1¼m performer Zoman: 16/1, needed race when ninth to Silver Regent in maiden at Sandown: will be suited by 1¼m/1½m: sure to improve. *Sir Michael Stoute* **74 p**

HOURI (IRE) 2 b.f. (Mar 29) Alhaarth (IRE) 126 – Witching Hour (IRE) 88 (Alzao (USA) 117) [2007 8m 8g Oct 26] sturdy filly: seventh foal: closely related to 9f winner Unafraid (by Unfuwain) and half-sister to 3 winners, including 5-y-o Night Hour: dam, 2-y-o 6f winner (stayed 1m), half-sister to very smart 1m/1¼m performer Great Dane: green in maidens, better effort when seventh to Cruel Sea at Doncaster: will stay 1¼m. *R. M. Beckett* **72**

HOUSE 2 b.c. (Mar 7) Elusive Quality (USA) – Eurolink Raindance (IRE) 109 (Alzao (USA) 117) [2007 6g 6g² 6m⁴ 7d³ Oct 3] well-made colt: second foal: dam, 6f (at 2 yrs) to 9f (in US, also won Grade 3 1m event) winner, half-sister to smart performers up to 1¼m Mango Mischief and Bonecrusher: fairly useful maiden: in frame 3 times, including second to Young Pretender at Newmarket: should stay 7f/1m. *M. R. Channon* **84**

HOUSE ARREST 3 ch.f. Auction House (USA) 120 – Mentro (IRE) 65 (Entrepreneur 123) [2007 52§: f7g f7s⁶ p7f p6g f7g Mar 13] compact filly: poor maiden: stays 7f: acts on polytrack and firm going: tried in headgear/tongue tie: ungenuine. *A. J. McCabe* **36 §**

HOUSE MAIDEN (IRE) 3 b.f. Rudimentary (USA) 118 – Dahoar 66 (Charnwood Forest (IRE) 125) [2007 68p: 6m p7.1g³ 9g⁴ 10m 8g p9.5g⁴ 10.3g* 10d Oct 11] fair performer: much improved when winning maiden at Chester in September, dictating: stays easy 1¼m: acts on polytrack and good to firm going: tried in cheekpieces: has been early to post: sold 800 gns. *D. M. Simcock* **75**

HOUSE OF TUDOR 2 b.g. (Apr 23) Medicean 128 – Wrong Bride (Reprimand 122) [2007 8m 9d⁵ 10m⁵ Oct 8] 20,000F, 82,000Y: big, lengthy gelding: unfurnished at 2 yrs: sixth foal: half-brother to 3-y-o Opal Noir and 11f/1½m winner Lucky Leo (by Muhtarram), both fairly useful: dam unraced half-sister to one-time smart 8-y-o Funfair Wane: fair maiden: visored, fifth to Planetarium at Pontefract final start: will stay 1½m: sold 24,000 gns. *J. H. M. Gosden* **70**

HOVERING (IRE) 4 ch.f. In The Wings 128 – Orlena (USA) (Gone West (USA)) [2007 100: p12g⁴ 14.1g⁶ 15d⁴ 14m⁵ 10.9d Jun 18] second foal: closely related to temperamental 2004 2-y-o 7f winner Limit (by Barathea): dam, French 2-y-o 7f winner, out of US Grade 3 8.5f/9f winner Cox Orange: useful performer at 3 yrs for J. Bolger in Ireland, winning maiden at Naas: sold 140,000 gns after final start: just fairly useful on balance in 2007, probably flattered in muddling listed race when sixth to Mount Kilimanjaro at Nottingham: probably stays 1¾m: acts on firm ground, has won on good to soft: tongue tied second to fourth 3-y-o starts: tried in cheekpieces/blinkers, looking unenthusiastic in latter: races prominently. *M. G. Quinlan* **91 +**

HOWARDS DREAM (IRE) 9 b.g. King's Theatre (IRE) 128 – Keiko 76 (Generous (IRE) 139) [2007 –: 14g 12.1g Jun 20] little form since 2003. *D. A. Nolan* **–**

HOWARDS HOPE 2 ch.g. (Mar 2) Kyllachy 129 – Howards Heroine (IRE) 70§ **62**
(Danehill Dancer (IRE) 117) [2007 6d⁵ 6s⁵ 7.2g⁶ p6g³ p6g Oct 22] second foal: dam, 7f
to 9.4f winner, one to treat with caution: modest maiden: stays 7f: acts on polytrack and
soft going: ran creditably in blinkers/visor. *I. Semple*

HOWARDS PRINCE 4 gr.g. Bertolini (USA) 125 – Grey Princess (IRE) 92 (Com- **–**
mon Grounds 118) [2007 63: 5m 5m 5f 6g Jun 13] close-coupled gelding: one-time fair
performer: no form in 2007, leaving I. Semple after second start. *D. A. Nolan*

HOWARDS PRINCESS 5 gr.m. Lujain (USA) 119 – Grey Princess (IRE) 92 (Com- **49**
mon Grounds 118) [2007 74d: f6g f6g 7m p5.1g⁶ 5g 5m 6m 5m Sep 11] sparely-made
mare: poor performer nowadays: left J. Hetherton after sixth start (reared and unseated
rider): wears headgear. *J. O'Reilly*

HOWARDS ROCKET 6 ch.g. Opening Verse (USA) 126 – Houston Heiress (USA) **58**
(Houston (USA)) [2007 50: 8.3d³ 8.3d³ 8m 8.3d⁴ 7.9g 8.3m 11.1s Sep 24] modest
maiden: stays 8.3f: acts on polytrack and good to soft ground. *J. S. Goldie*

HOWARDS TIPPLE 3 b.g. Diktat 126 – Grey Princess (IRE) 92 (Common Grounds **76**
118) [2007 75: 7.1g⁴ 6g³ 6m 6f² 5g³ 5s³ 5d² 6m⁵ 5s* 6g³ 6s⁶ 6d⁴ 6v Nov 3] fair handicapper: won at Ayr in August: raced mostly at 5f/6f: acts on firm and soft going: tried
visored, wears cheekpieces nowadays. *I. Semple*

HOWARDS WAY 2 b.g. (Feb 2) Bertolini (USA) 125 – Love Quest (Pursuit of Love **59**
124) [2007 5g⁴ Apr 8] 10/1, fourth in maiden at Musselburgh. *I. Semple*

HOWDIGO 2 b.c. (Apr 28) Tobougg (IRE) 125 – Woodrising 64 (Nomination 125) **83**
[2007 6g 7.1g 6m³ 6m³ p7g³ 7m² 7g p10g² p8g* Nov 14] 29,000F, €55,000Y: good-
topped colt: seventh foal: half-brother to 3 winners, including 4-y-o Rising Cross and
6-y-o Willhego: dam, 1¼m winner, also successful over hurdles: fairly useful performer:
placed 5 times, twice in nurseries, prior to winning maiden at Kempton: stays 1¼m: acts
on polytrack and good to firm going. *J. R. Best*

HOWE'S JACK (IRE) 2 b.g. (Mar 16) Fasliyev (USA) 120 – Berenique (IRE) **–**
(Bering 136) [2007 5m 6m 8m 5d⁶ 5g 7g f6d⁴ f7d Dec 18] stocky gelding: no form.
M. C. Chapman

HOW'S BUSINESS 3 b.f. Josr Algarhoud (IRE) 118 – Love And Kisses 70 (Salse **68**
(USA) 128) [2007 p10g 11.7d⁶ p12g⁶ p16g² 17.2d³ 18m⁴ Oct 8] big filly: second live
foal: half-sister to dam of very smart performer up to 12.5f in France/
USA Dark Moondancer out of high-class sprinter Soba: fair maiden: stays 2¼m: acts on
polytrack, good to firm and good to soft going: sold 30,000 gns. *C. A. Cyzer*

HOW'S SHE CUTTIN' (IRE) 4 ch.f. Shinko Forest (IRE) – Magic Annemarie **95**
(IRE) 75 (Dancing Dissident (USA) 119) [2007 73+: 5m* 5m² 5g* 5s* 5d 5g³ 5g Oct 27]
good-topped filly: useful handicapper: progressed well in 2007, winning at Musselburgh
in April and June and Thirsk in July: good third to King Orchisios at Catterick sixth start:
best at 5f: acts on heavy and good to firm ground: effective blinkered or not: sometimes
carries head high/hangs right. *T. D. Barron*

HOWS THAT 5 ch.m. Vettori (IRE) 119 – Royalty (IRE) (Fairy King (USA)) [2007 50, **–**
a–: 8.1d 8s 7.5v Jul 6] angular mare: modest performer at 4 yrs: little form in 2007:
usually wears cheekpieces. *K. R. Burke*

HOWYA NOW KID (IRE) 3 b.c. Daggers Drawn (USA) 114 – Lear's Crown (USA) **103**
82 (Lear Fan (USA) 130) [2007 97: 7m³ 6g³ 7d* 7m 7m 7g Dec 26] €9,000F: sturdy,
close-coupled colt: fifth foal: half-brother to fairly useful 2002 2-y-o 7f winner Temeritas
(by Tamarisk), later successful in USA, and 7f winner Violent Velocity (by Namid): dam,
1½m winner, out of half-sister to US Grade 1 7f winner Fabulously Fast: useful performer: won listed race at Epsom in June by ¾ length from Solid Rock: left G. Lyons in Ireland
and renamed Fluke, tongue tied when little impression in handicaps in Hong Kong (bled
final start): best form at 7f: acts on firm and soft ground. *A. S. Cruz, Hong Kong*

HUBBLE BUBBLE (USA) 3 ch.c. Giant's Causeway (USA) 132 – Vana Turns **62**
(USA) (Wavering Monarch (USA)) [2007 7.1g³ 7m⁵ 10g⁶ 9.9m 10.3f Jun 12] rangy colt:
modest maiden: stays 1¼m: attitude under suspicion: sold 8,000 gns. *M. Johnston*

HUCKING HARKNESS 2 ch.c. (Feb 24) Dr Fong (USA) 128 – Dalaauna 62 (Cad- **62 p**
eaux Genereux 131) [2007 p5.1g⁵ p5m⁵ Nov 24] 20,000Y: third foal: dam, sprint maiden,
sister to Prix Morny winner Hoh Magic and to dam of Falmouth Stakes winner Rajeem:
similar form in maidens at Wolverhampton and Lingfield, racing wide both times: will
stay 6f: remains open to improvement. *J. R. Best*

HUCKING HARMONY (IRE) 2 b.f. (Feb 23) Spartacus (IRE) 107 – Gute (IRE) **64**
77 (Petardia 113) [2007 p5g³ p5g² 5g 5.2d² 6s⁶ p5g 5.2f⁵ 5m³ p5.1g Oct 2] €16,000Y:
well-grown filly: fourth foal: dam Irish 2-y-o 5f winner: modest maiden: placed 4 times,
in nursery at Goodwood penultimate start: best at 5f: acts on polytrack, soft and good to
firm going: tends to edge right. *J. R. Best*

HUCKING HARRIER (IRE) 2 ch.c. (Feb 17) Hawk Wing (USA) 136 – Dangerous –
Mind (IRE) 104 (Platini (GER) 126) [2007 p7m Oct 3] 12/1, badly needed experience in
maiden at Kempton: bred to stay 1m/1¼m. *J. R. Best*

HUCKING HEAT (IRE) 3 b.g. Desert Sun 120 – Vltava (IRE) 73 (Sri Pekan (USA) **67**
117) [2007 66: p6g⁶ p8g* p8g⁶ 8.3m⁴ 7m 7m 7d⁶ p8g² 7m p7g 8m p8g³ p8g⁶ p8g² p8m⁵ **a74**
p8g³ Dec 28] sturdy gelding: fair handicapper, better on all-weather: won at Lingfield in
March: stays 1m: acts on polytrack, firm and good to soft going: visored last 5 starts:
inconsistent: joined J. Boyle. *J. R. Best*

HUCKING HEIST (IRE) 3 b.g. Desert Style (IRE) 121 – Oriental Queen (GER) (Big Shuf- **80 p**
fle (USA) 122) [2007 7m* Sep 11] 6,000F, 10,000Y: strong, lengthy gelding: first foal:
dam, German 6f winner, half-sister to 7-y-o Orange Touch: 16/1, created good impression
when winning maiden at Lingfield in September by 1¼ lengths from Laura's Best, still
adrift 2f out before running on strongly to lead well inside final 1f: will stay 1m: sure to
improve. *J. R. Best*

HUCKING HERO (IRE) 2 b.c. (Mar 14) Iron Mask (USA) 117 – Selkirk Flyer **79 +**
(Selkirk (USA) 129) [2007 p6g 7f³ p7g* p7g⁶ p8g³ p7g p8g* Dec 1] €8,000F, €10,000Y:
sixth foal: closely related to winner in Italy by Sesaro and half-brother to useful 2004
2-y-o 6f/7f winner Kingsgate Bay (by Desert Sun): dam unraced: fair form: won maiden
in October and nursery in December, both at Lingfield: stays 1m: raced only on polytrack
and firm going. *J. R. Best*

HUCKING HILL (IRE) 3 ch.g. City On A Hill (USA) 114 – Con Dancer (Shareef –
Dancer (USA) 135) [2007 78: 7g p6g⁴ 6f p6g⁴ p6g² p6g² p6m p7g p6g Nov 30] strong, **a79**
useful-looking gelding: type to carry condition: fair handicapper: best at 5f/6f: acts on
polytrack and good to firm going: usually blinkered. *J. R. Best*

HUCKING HOPE (IRE) 3 b.f. Desert Style (IRE) 121 – Amarapura (FR) (Common **69**
Grounds 118) [2007 69: 6d² 6d² 7s⁴ 6g³ 6m 6m⁵ p6g p6g⁴ p6g⁶ p6g⁵ Dec 19] small,
lengthy filly: fair handicapper: stays 7f: acts on polytrack, soft and good to firm ground.
J. R. Best

HUE 6 ch.g. Peintre Celebre (USA) 137 – Quandary (USA) 104 (Blushing Groom (FR) **72**
131) [2007 83: 21.7s 16.1s³ 12v 9m⁶ 12.1g⁵ 12f⁵ 14m³ 13.4g³ 12s⁶ Oct 9] leggy gelding:
fair handicapper: stays 2m: acts on all-weather, soft and firm going: tried in cheekpieces,
often blinkered: hard ride: won over hurdles in October/November/December. *B. Ellison*

HUGHMANBEAN (IRE) 4 ch.g. Elnadim (USA) 128 – Madam Baileys (IRE) –
(Doulab (USA) 115) [2007 p6g⁶ Mar 27] tailed off in maiden at Wolverhampton: dead.
D. Carroll

HUGO QUICK 3 b.g. Zaha (CAN) 106 – Skedaddle 57 (Formidable (USA) 125) [2007 **54**
p8g 8.1d 9.7s⁵ p8g Sep 26] workmanlike gelding: modest maiden: said to have finished
lame final start. *T. M. Jones*

HUGS DESTINY (IRE) 6 b.g. Victory Note (USA) 120 – Embracing 91 (Reference **67**
Point 139) [2007 65: 16m² 12m³ 14.1m p12.2g* 12.4m 14m² 10.5m 13d p13.9g 12m³
12d⁶ 12g* p13.9g⁴ 12.3m³ 14f³ 14m 12m Oct 8] sturdy gelding: fair handicapper: won
amateur events at Wolverhampton in May and Catterick in August: stays 1¾m (seemingly not 2m): acts on polytrack, firm and good to soft going: tried blinkered/in cheekpieces: tongue tied: races prominently. *M. A. Barnes*

HUGS 'N KISSES (IRE) 3 ch.f. Noverre (USA) 125 – La Dolores (GER) (Surumu **75**
(GER)) [2007 82: 8m 11.3g⁵ 12g 10s 7s⁴ 8.5g 8v⁶ 8.5g² 10v 8.5g f12d* Dec 14] medium-
sized filly: fair handicapper: won apprentice event at Southwell in December: stays 1½m:
acts on fibresand, heavy and good to firm going: tried blinkered. *John Joseph Murphy,
Ireland*

HULA BALLEW 7 ch.m. Weldnaas (USA) 112 – Ballon 63 (Persian Bold 123) [2007 **83**
83: 8m⁵ 8.1g 8.5m³ 8m* 8d⁴ 8m 8m 7g 8m 8m 8m⁵ 8.1g Oct 2] smallish mare: fairly
useful handicapper: won at Thirsk in June: stays 9f: acts on any turf going: has worn
cheekpieces. *M. Dods*

HULA HULA 2 ch.f. (May 11) Cadeaux Genereux 131 – Eurolink Sundance 85 (Night –
Shift (USA)) [2007 6d p6g Nov 8] 19,000Y: third foal: half-sister to 4-y-o Mango Music:
dam, 6f winner (including at 2 yrs), half-sister to smart 1¼m performers Bonecrusher and
Mango Mischief: green when behind in maidens: sold 1,000 gns. *E. A. L. Dunlop*

HUMAN TOUCH 2 b.f. (Apr 27) Oasis Dream 129 – Seltitude (IRE) 114 (Fairy King –
(USA)) [2007 6d p6g Dec 1] neat filly: third foal: half-sister to French 1m winner Why
Worry (by Cadeaux Genereux): dam, French 6f/7f winner, out of sister to high-class
middle-distance stayer High Hawk, herself dam of In The Wings: well held in maidens at
Newmarket and Wolverhampton. *E. A. L. Dunlop*

HUMUNGOUS (IRE) 4 ch.g. Giant's Causeway (USA) 132 – Doula (USA) (Gone **113**
West (USA)) [2007 105: p7f p8.6g 8.1g² 8.3m* 8m 8g² 8g 8m⁴ 9m 7g³ Oct 27] tall, rather
leggy gelding: smart handicapper: won at Windsor in June (hung left): excellent 3 lengths
second of 19 to Third Set in totesport Mile at Goodwood sixth start: finds 7f on sharp
side, and stays 1¼m: acts on polytrack, firm and good to soft going: tried blinkered/in
cheekpieces. *C. R. Egerton*

HUNTING HAZE 4 b.g. Foxhound (USA) 103 – Second Affair (IRE) 85 (Pursuit of **59**
Love 124) [2007 65: 12.4m⁴ 13.8m³ 10.1m 12.4d Oct 16] fair maiden: stays 1½m: acts
on firm going. *Miss S. E. Hall*

HUNTING LODGE (IRE) 6 ch.g. Grand Lodge (USA) 125 – Vijaya (USA) (Lear –
Fan (USA) 130) [2007 –: 16.2s⁵ 11.8m⁵ Aug 12] strong gelding: no form since 2005.
H. J. Manners

HUNTING TOWER 3 b.c. Sadler's Wells (USA) 132 – Fictitious 100 (Machiavellian **94**
(USA) 123) [2007 82+: 8.3m² 10.4g 9d 8m* 8.1m⁵ 9g 10m⁵ p10g⁶ Oct 24] leggy colt:
fairly useful handicapper: won at Salisbury in July: stays 1¼m: acts on polytrack, good to
firm and good to soft ground: has shown signs of temperament: sold 15,000 gns, joined
G. T. Lynch in Ireland. *R. Hannon*

HUNT THE BOTTLE (IRE) 2 b.c. (Feb 13) Bertolini (USA) 125 – Zanoubia (USA) **77**
94 (Our Emblem (USA) 114) [2007 6m³ 5d³ 6m⁴ 6d* 6d Oct 11] good-topped, quite
attractive colt: fair performer: won maiden at Haydock in September: will stay 7f: yet to
race on extremes of going. *B. W. Hills*

HURLINGHAM 3 b.g. Halling (USA) 133 – Society (IRE) 73 (Barathea (IRE) 127) **91**
[2007 79: f8g* p8g* p8g⁵ p9.5g² 10.4d 10.5g² 10.3g Oct 26] tall, quite attractive gelding: fairly useful performer: won maiden at Southwell and handicap at Kempton, both in
January: left M. Johnston 19,000 gns after fourth start: stays 10.5f: acts on all-weather,
good to firm and good to soft ground: has looked none too keen: gelded after final outing.
M. W. Easterby

HURRICANE COAST 8 b.g. Hurricane Sky (AUS) – Tread Carefully 51 (Sharpo **54**
132) [2007 81d: p8g p8.6g Sep 8] tall gelding: fairly useful performer at best: below
form both starts in 2007, leaving Ms J. Doyle after reappearance: stays easy 9.5f: acts on
all-weather, firm and soft going: tried tongue tied, wears headgear: quirky. *K. McAuliffe*

HURRICANE DENNIS 3 ch.g. Silver Wizard (USA) 117 – Thatcher's Era (IRE) 57 –
(Never So Bold 135) [2007 –: 10.9s Jul 6] no sign of ability. *Mike Murphy*

HURRICANE HARRIET 2 b.f. (May 1) Bertolini (USA) 125 – Cold Blow 67 (Posse **59 p**
(USA) 130) [2007 6m⁴ Aug 1] seventh foal: half-sister to 3 winners, notably smart 1m to
1¼m winner Katy Nowaitee (by Komaite): dam, second at 7f at 2 yrs, from family of
Yorkshire Oaks winners Sally Brown and Untold: 4/1, fourth in maiden at Redcar,
recovering ground well after slow start: will do better. *R. M. H. Cowell*

HURRICANE HYMNBOOK (USA) 2 b.c. (Feb 13) Pulpit (USA) 117 – April **96 p**
Squall (USA) (Summer Squall (USA)) [2007 6m* 7g² Sep 30] $210,000Y, 60,000 2-y-o:
lengthy colt: third foal: half-brother to winners in US by Dixie Union and Broken Vow:
dam US winner around 1m: useful form: won maiden at Warwick in September: much
improved 2 weeks later when 2 lengths second to Ibn Khaldun in nursery at Ascot, doing
well from wide draw: will stay 1m: should carry on progressing. *B. J. Meehan*

HURRICANE SPIRIT (IRE) 3 b.c. Invincible Spirit (IRE) 121 – Gale Warning **108**
(IRE) (Last Tycoon 131) [2007 103p: p6g³ p7g² 8m May 5] big, good-topped colt: useful
performer: ran well when placed at Lingfield in 2007, 1½ lengths third to Areyoutalkingtome in minor event and ¾-length second to Hinton Admiral in listed race: sweating and
still woolly in coat when last of 24 in 2000 Guineas at Newmarket final outing (said to
have chipped a knee): should stay 1m: acts on polytrack. *J. R. Best*

HURRICANE THOMAS (IRE) 3 b.g. Celtic Swing 138 – Viola Royale (IRE) 90 **80**
(Royal Academy (USA) 130) [2007 78: 9.2d⁴ 10s 12m 14.1m² 14m* 14g 14m³ Sep 30]
big, good-topped gelding: fairly useful handicapper: won at Musselburgh in September:
will stay 2m: acts on polytrack, soft and good to firm going: shaped as if amiss second/
third starts: sold 18,000 gns, joined G. L. Moore. *M. Johnston*

HURSTPIERPOINT (IRE) 2 b.f. (Mar 4) Night Shift (USA) – Double Gamble 76   **62**
(Ela-Mana-Mou 132) [2007 6m⁴ 6g 7d⁵ 7d 7.5g⁶ 7.5m p7.1g² p7g² p8.6g p8.6g²
p8.6g² p8.6g⁶ Nov 24] 10,000Y: smallish filly: second foal: half-sister to sprint winner in
Greece by Gorse: dam, 1½m winner, out of half-sister to very smart performer up to 1¾m
Air Marshall: modest maiden: runner-up 4 times on all-weather (in seller, nursery and
claimers): stays 8.6f: acts on polytrack and good to firm going. *R. A. Fahey*

HUSTLE (IRE) 2 ch.c. (Apr 25) Choisir (AUS) 126 – Granny Kelly (USA) 60 (Irish   **79**
River (FR) 131) [2007 6m 6f³ 7m* 7m⁴ Sep 21] €100,000Y: good sort: sixth foal: half-
brother to fairly useful 6f (at 2 yrs) to 8.5f (in US) winner Six Hitter (by Boundary): dam
Irish maiden: fair form: third to Cat Junior at Newbury prior to winning maiden at
Lingfield in September: fourth in nursery at Newmarket: will be suited by 1m: raced only
on ground firmer than good. *R. Hannon*

HUXLEY (IRE) 8 b.g. Danehill Dancer (IRE) 117 – Biddy Mulligan (Ballad Rock 122)   **48**
[2007 51: p10g p9.5g 10.2f 7d⁶ 8.1m 8m Oct 14] leggy gelding: poor performer nowadays: stays 1¼m: acts on polytrack, firm and soft going: tried blinkered: tongue tied:
sometimes slowly away. *D. J. Wintle*

HUZZAH (IRE) 2 b.c. (Apr 9) Acclamation 118 – Borders Belle (IRE) 96 (Pursuit of   **91**
Love 124) [2007 5m⁴ 6g 7m⁴ 7g² p8g² 7m⁵ 8d* p8m³ 7g⁴ Oct 27] 32,000F, 36,000Y:
strong colt: second foal: dam 1m (at 2 yrs) and 1½m winner: fairly useful performer: won
maiden at Salisbury (by 6 lengths from Meer Kat) in October: in frame after in nurseries
at Kempton and Doncaster: stays 1m: acts on polytrack and good to soft going: usually
forces pace. *B. W. Hills*

HYDE LEA FLYER 2 b.c. (Feb 24) Hernando (FR) 127 – Sea Ridge 65§ (Slip Anchor   **80**
136) [2007 7m⁴ 8.1d 8.2d² Oct 10] 35,000Y: tall, lengthy colt: unfurnished at 2 yrs: first
foal: dam, ran 3 times, closely related to 1m to 1½m performer Safa and Queen's Vase
winner Stelvio, both useful: fairly useful maiden: left A. King, 5 lengths second to
Tajaaweed at Nottingham: will be suited by 1¼m/1½m. *E. S. McMahon*

HYPER VIPER (IRE) 2 b.g. (Mar 2) Atraf 116 – Double Letter (IRE) (M Double M   **63**
(USA)) [2007 5.1m 6g 7s 6d³ p7.1g 8f³ 8g² 8g 8m Oct 22] strong, compact gelding:
modest maiden: second in selling nursery at Yarmouth (left J. S. Moore £5,000): stays
1m: acts on firm and good to soft going: tried in cheekpieces, usually blinkered. *C. Grant*

HYPNOSIS 4 b.f. Mind Games 121 – Salacious (Sallust 134) [2007 79: f5g* 5m² 5m*   **90**
5m 6g³ May 20] leggy filly: fairly useful handicapper: won at Southwell in February and
Catterick in May: effective at 5f/6f: acts on fibresand, firm and soft going: tough and consistent: refused to enter stall prior to final intended outing: sold 6,800 gns. *D. W. Barker*

HYPNOTIC 5 ch.g. Lomitas 129 – Hypnotize 103 (Machiavellian (USA) 123) [2007   **–**
88: p7.1g p8g 7.9d 8s Sep 26] leggy gelding: fairly useful handicapper in 2006: well held
at 5 yrs: tried visored: tongue tied nowadays. *D. Nicholls*

HYPOCRISY 4 b.f. Bertolini (USA) 125 – Glensara (Petoski 135) [2007 85: p7.1g*   **–**
p7g³ p6g⁵ 7g p10.7g 7v p8g² p8g³ p7.1g⁴ Dec 15] good-topped filly: fairly useful handi-   **a83**
capper on all-weather: won at Wolverhampton in February: left D. Carroll after third
start: effective at 6f to 1m: acts on polytrack and good to soft going: tried visored. *Garvan
Donnelly, Ireland*

HYPOTENEUSE (IRE) 3 b.f. Sadler's Wells (USA) 132 – Phantom Gold 119 (Mach-   **86**
iavellian (USA) 123) [2007 72p: 12g² p10g 11.7g* 12s³ 12m³ Sep 8] leggy, lengthy filly:
fairly useful performer: won maiden handicap at Bath in July: ran well final start: stays
1½m: acts on soft and good to firm ground. *Sir Michael Stoute*

HYTHE BAY 3 b.f. Auction House (USA) 120 – Ellway Queen (USA) 71 (Bahri (USA)   **74**
125) [2007 77: p6g⁶ 7g 7m p6g³ 5s³ 5m⁵ 5d⁴ 5s² 5m⁵ 5.3d p5g p6m² p6g Dec 12] tall,
good sort: fair handicapper: effective at 5f/6f: acts on polytrack, firm and soft going: has
been difficult to post: suspect temperament. *J. R. Best*

I

IAMAGREY (IRE) 2 gr.f. (Apr 28) Clodovil (IRE) 116 – Xania 32 (Mujtahid (USA)   **63 d**
118) [2007 p5g³ 5d³ p5g 5g⁵ 6m 5.3m⁶ p7.1g Oct 15] €13,000Y: useful-looking filly:
fourth foal: half-sister to winning sprinters Money Mate (by Mujadil) and Tiffin Deano
(by Titus Livius): dam maiden: modest maiden: regressive form: effective at 5f/6f: tried
in cheekpieces. *J. S. Moore*

IBIS (USA) 2 b. or br.f. (Apr 19) Empire Maker (USA) 129 – Sunlit Silence (USA) **– p**
(Trempolino (USA) 135) [2007 6g Oct 19] $100,000Y, 130,000 2-y-o: leggy filly:
seventh foal: half-sister to 2 winners in US, notably 1m (at 2 yrs) to 9f (Grade 2/3 events)
winner Greek Sun (by Danzig): dam, US 6f to 8.5f winner, half-sister US Grade 3 6.5f
winner Madame Pandit (herself dam of US Grade 1 9f winner Mea Domina): 5/2 and
green (reared/unseated at start), well held behind Spinning Lucy in maiden at Redcar:
open to improvement. *Saeed bin Suroor*

IBN KHALDUN (USA) 2 ch.c. (Feb 14) Dubai Destination (USA) 127 – Gossa- **119 +**
mer 118 (Sadler's Wells (USA) 132) [2007 6d⁴ 7m* 7g* 8s* 8g* Oct 27]
    The near-ecstatic reaction of Authorized's connections to his triumph at
Epsom exemplified the Derby's status as the race that the majority of owners,
trainers and jockeys would still most like to win. One of the more eccentric consequences of this fixation is the way two-year-old colts who win the top late-season
events tend to receive a quote for the classic. There are also those colts from top
stables who have not even run but are rumoured to be exceptional, such as the
Aidan O'Brien-trained William Hogarth who was backed down to 25/1 second
favouritism for the Derby from 40s in August. The best he managed in two starts
was fourth in a Gowran maiden in October. Of rather more interest are colts such as
Ibn Khaldun and Rio de La Plata, respectively second and joint-third favourites for
the Derby at 12/1 and 14/1 by the start of November. Like George Washington two
years before, when he became second favourite for the Derby, both are Group 1
winners, but neither has realistic prospects of staying the Derby distance. That's not
to say the pair have no prospects in the classics. On the contrary, the rate of progress
Ibn Khaldun showed in the space of just over six weeks in the autumn indicates he
should definitely not to be taken lightly in any company.
    Ibn Khaldun's first two races, in maiden events at Yarmouth at the end of
August and Leicester in September, indicated he was a colt with an urge to get on
with the job. He pulled hard both times, running green when fourth to Ancien
Regime on the first occasion and landing the odds unextended from Forsyte Saga
at Leicester. Ibn Khaldun settled much better in his later races, and justified
favouritism under 9-4 in a fifteen-runner nursery at Ascot at the end of the month in
great style, coming through on the bridle in the final furlong and being value for
five lengths, rather than the two by which he beat runner-up Hurricane Hymnbook.
Simon Crisford, racing manager to Godolphin, said 'Ibn Khaldun is likely to have
one more run before we put him away, possibly in the Horris Hill Stakes', which
suggests the colt's rate of progress might have been a surprise—albeit a pleasant
one—to connections. In fact, Ibn Khaldun's first race in pattern company came not

Deloitte Autumn Stakes, Ascot—Ibn Khaldun lands the odds in good style from Redolent and Yahrab

Racing Post Trophy, Doncaster—another step up in class and another convincing win for Ibn Khaldun, who quickens clear of City Leader (grey) and Feared In Flight

in the Horris Hill but in the Deloitte Autumn Stakes back at Ascot a fortnight later. Odds on against such as Meeriss, who had narrowly landed a listed race at Goodwood, and Yahrab, who had finished sixth in the Royal Lodge Stakes, Ibn Khaldun was always going well under a patient ride and beat Redolent by a length after being coaxed ahead in the final furlong. Again, he was value for more than the winning margin.

With a two-year-old in form and progressing, there is nothing to lose and everything to gain from keeping him going, and Godolphin took the bull by the horns by sending Ibn Khaldun to Doncaster for the twelve-runner Racing Post Trophy another fortnight on. He started favourite in a representative renewal, preferred to pattern winners Curtain Call (Beresford Stakes), City Leader (Royal Lodge Stakes) and River Proud (Somerville Tattersall Stakes). Also in the line-up were Declaration of War, who had chased home Rio de La Plata in the Prix Jean-Luc Lagardere, three maiden-race winners, second favourite Frozen Fire and King of Rome from Aidan O'Brien's stable, and Tajaaweed from Sir Michael Stoute's. River Proud ensured a true pace, while Ibn Khaldun was never far away in fifth or sixth. Asked to quicken approaching the two-furlong marker, Ibn Khaldun produced an impressive burst of speed to take up the running and go clear. City Leader tried to respond but Ibn Khaldun looked different class and passed the post with three lengths to spare. Feared In Flight, 66/1 and showing much improved form, was a short head back in third. Ibn Khaldun was promptly cut to 10/1 for the Two Thousand Guineas.

Everything about Ibn Khaldun, not least the pace and acceleration he shows, suggests the Two Thousand Guineas, or the equivalents in Ireland or France, will present him with his best chance of winning a classic. He is something of a rarity in the history of the Racing Post Trophy in being both bred to be a miler and also shaping like one. American Post in 2003 fitted the latter description but was bred to be suited by middle distances. Beauchamp King in 1995 is the closest to Ibn Khaldun in having both elements in his make-up. Beauchamp King raced beyond a mile just three times, with a notable lack of success. Ibn Khaldun is a fairly rare bird in another respect, a Group 1 winner in Europe bred by Darley. His success must have delighted Sheikh Mohammed, whose massive band of broodmares does not produce anything like so many pattern performers as one might expect. Pattern winners in Europe only just reached double figures in the latest season, with West Wind in the Prix de Diane the only other scorer at Group 1 level; there had been just one Group 1 victor in 2005 and one in 2006. By comparison, from a similar total of mares between them the Aga Khan and Princess Zahra, Cheveley Park Stud and the Niarchos Family/Flaxman Holdings bred twenty-two Group 1 winners in the same three-year period. Ibn Khaldun's sire, Dubai Destination, is also in the Darley team. He was a fragile colt but a high-class one whose principal victories in eight starts over three seasons came in the Champagne Stakes as a two-year-old, beating Rock

492

of Gibraltar, and the Queen Anne Stakes, which he won in great style by four lengths two years later. He raced beyond a mile only once, when runner-up and seemingly not staying the trip in the Predominate Stakes. A half-brother to another high-class miler in Librettist out of a half-sister to leading Japanese and European sprinter Agnes World, Dubai Destination has been well patronised at stud. His first crop, from coverings costing £25,000, comprised one hundred and fifteen foals, the top three of which at auction as yearlings were knocked down to John Ferguson acting on behalf of Sheikh Mohammed for a total 1,300,000 guineas. Besides Ibn Khaldun, there is only one other stakes winner so far from the crop, the afore-mentioned Meeriss, though Dubai Time was runner-up in the Prix des Chenes. Dubai Destination's fee is now £15,000, down from £20,000.

		Kingmambo	Mr Prospector
	Dubai Destination (USA)	(b 1990)	Miesque
	(b 1999)	Mysterial	Alleged
Ibn Khaldun (USA)		(b or br 1994)	Mysteries
(ch.c. Feb 14, 2005)		Sadler's Wells	Northern Dancer
	Gossamer	(b 1981)	Fairy Bridge
	(b 1999)	Brocade	Habitat
		(b 1981)	Canton Silk

Given his own attributes on the racecourse, it is unlikely that Dubai Destination will prove a consistent influence for middle-distance stamina, and the same can be said for Ibn Khaldun's dam Gossamer, whose second foal he is. Gossamer's first foal, by Rainbow Quest, was named So Silk, but has not raced for Luca Cumani. Gossamer had a filly by Elusive Quality in 2006 and a colt by Cape Cross in 2007. Gossamer is by Sadler's Wells, most of whose progeny are well suited by middle distances, yet she was precocious as a two-year-old, winning over six furlongs and gaining pattern successes in the Prestige Stakes at Goodwood over seven furlongs and the Fillies' Mile at Ascot. In the latter she beat Maryinsky, who has found fame as dam of Peeping Fawn and Thewayyouare. Conditions were testing at Ascot, and when Gossamer readily landed the Irish One Thousand Guineas. On her only try beyond a mile she finished a creditable fifth in the Breeders' Cup Filly & Mare Turf, beaten two and a half lengths. Gossamer was bred by the late Gerald Leigh, the bulk of whose bloodstock was purchased by Sheikh Mohammed for a reported thirty-five million dollars towards the end of 2003. The fact that the mares pur-chased with Gerald Leigh's bloodstock have also produced Utrecht, winner of the Prix Chloe, and listed winner Criticism hints at the potential when purchasing a stud's broodmares lock, stock and barrel rather than cherry picking individual mares from unrelated families at the sales. The acquisition policy worked for the Aga Khan with the Dupre and Boussac interests, and he followed the same policy when purchasing the bloodstock of Jean-Luc Lagardere. Sheikh Mohammed's purchase of the celebrated White Lodge Stud mares that did so well for the Moller brothers has not so far, however, produced conspicuous results for Darley. Gossamer is well related, and again speed is the main feature of her family. Her dam Brocade was best at up to a mile, gaining her most important victories over seven furlongs in the Prix de la Foret and Challenge Stakes. The best of her seven winners besides Gossamer was the latter's top-class brother Barathea, who was also best at a mile and won the Irish Two Thousand Guineas and Breeders' Cup Mile. Brocade, out of a sprint handicapper who is also grandam of good sprinter Desert Style, foaled two other pattern/graded winners at a lesser level. The family always attracts great interest at the sales—Brocade's daughters Brocatelle and Zibilene fetched 1,700,000 guineas and 1,500,000 guineas respectively at the Newmarket December Sales in 2000 and 2001. Based on his pedigree and the way he races, it will be little short of a miracle if Ibn Khaldun proves effective over a mile and a half; a mile and a quarter looks as far as he is likely to stay, with no certainty of that. Just like his dam, he is on the small side, best described as smallish, strong and sturdy. This lack of stature and scope may be a handicap as his career progresses, though lack of size certainly did not impair Champion Stakes winner Literato for one in the latest season. Given the presence in the Godolphin team of other Guineas prospects Fast Company, Rio de La Plata and McCartney, plus Sheikh Moham-med's purchase of New Approach and a sizeable interest in Raven's Pass, it will surely be difficult keeping the Sheikh's interests separate in the opening months of the season. At the moment, Ibn Khaldun has to be regarded as marginally behind the principal Godolphin colts on form, but not by a great deal. If he improves further, that may well change. His career should be an intriguing one to follow. Frankie Dettori, incidentally, rode Ibn Khaldun to his first three victories, but cried off him at Doncaster to ride at the Breeders' Cup. Godolphin's second jockey Kerrin McEvoy was recalled from Australia to partner him in the Racing Post Trophy. *Saeed bin Suroor*

IBROX (IRE) 2 b.g. (Mar 18) Mujahid (USA) 125 – Ling Lane (Slip Anchor 136) **66 +**
[2007 8d 8g⁴ 8.2g⁴ Nov 7] 5,000Y: good-topped gelding: closely related to 4-y-o Moonstreaker and half-brother to several winners, including 8-y-o Vicious Warrior: dam unraced out of close relation to Irish Oaks winner Bolas: fair maiden: progressive form, fourth at Nottingham final start (briefly threatened to achieve more): may prove best up to 1m. *R. M. Whitaker*

ICANNSHIFT (IRE) 7 b.g. Night Shift (USA) – Cannikin (IRE) 82 (Lahib (USA) **67** 129) [2007 59: p13g⁴ 12m* 11.9m⁶ p16g p12g⁵ p12g 12s* 11.6m 12s* p12g Sep 12] **a55** small, good-bodied gelding: fair handicapper on turf, modest on all-weather: won at Folkestone in April, June and August: effective at 1¼m/1½m: acts on polytrack, firm and soft going: tried visored: front runner. *T. M. Jones*

ICANSINGARAINBOW 3 b.g. Rainbow High 121 – Carole's Choir (Primo Dominie **69** 121) [2007 12.1m p13.9g³ 10d Oct 10] easily best effort in maidens (fair form) when third to Hareem at Wolverhampton: likely to stay 2m. *R. Hollinshead*

ICE AND FIRE 8 b.g. Cadeaux Genereux 131 – Tanz (IRE) 79 (Sadler's Wells (USA) **–** 132) [2007 61: f16g f16s 13.8g p13.9g⁶ p16g* p16.5g Dec 8] quite good-topped gelding: **a56** modest performer: won amateur handicap at Lingfield in December: stays 16.5f: acts on all-weather, good to firm and good to soft ground: wears headgear: tends to edge right: inconsistent. *J. T. Stimpson*

ICE BELLINI 2 ch.f. (Apr 16) Erhaab (USA) 127 – Peach Sorbet (IRE) 77 (Spectrum **57** (IRE) 126) [2007 7g Nov 3] 6,000Y: workmanlike filly: first foal: dam Irish maiden (stayed 7f): 66/1, modest form when thirteenth of 19 in maiden at Newmarket. *J. M. P. Eustace*

ICE BOX (IRE) 3 ch.f. Pivotal 124 – Thaisy (USA) (Tabasco Cat (USA) 126) [2007 **75 +** 63: p8g⁴ p7g 7m³ p8.6g³ 8.3d* Jul 14] sturdy filly: fair handicapper: much improved when winning at Hamilton in July by 7 lengths: should stay 1¼m: acts on polytrack, good to firm and good to soft ground. *M. Johnston*

ICE CHOICE (IRE) 2 b.f. (May 4) Choisir (AUS) 126 – London Pride (USA) 106 **62 ?** (Lear Fan (USA) 130) [2007 8.1f 8m 7m 8.3m 7d² Oct 16] workmanlike filly: half-sister to 3 winners, including 11f winner Bukit Fraser and 1999 2-y-o 7f winner Pekan's Pride (both by Sri Pekan): dam 1m winner: modest maiden: apparent improvement when second to Hallingdal at Newcastle, dictating: stays 7f. *Mark Gillard*

ICED DIAMOND (IRE) 8 b.g. Petardia 113 – Prime Site (IRE) (Burslem 123) [2007 **53** 64, a69: p7.1g p7.1g 7d p8.6g 7m 7.6d 7d p8.6g Nov 11] good-topped gelding: modest handicapper: left W. M. Brisbourne after third start: stays 1m: acts on all-weather and firm going: tried in headgear/tongue tie: held up, and has been flat to handle. *S. Wynne*

ICED TANGO 3 gr.g. Verglas (IRE) 118 – Tangolania (FR) (Ashkalani (IRE) 128) **41** [2007 –: 8.3g 8m³ 8m 6d 8m Aug 9] sturdy gelding: poor maiden: stays 1m: acts on good to firm ground. *F. Jordan*

ICEMAN GEORGE 3 b.g. Beat Hollow 126 – Diebiedale 58 (Dominion 123) [2007 **71** –: 10d 10.1d* 10g 10m 10.3m⁶ p12.2g⁵ 11.6d⁴ p12.2g⁶ Nov 4] compact gelding: fair performer: won maiden at Yarmouth in July: stays easy 1½m: acts on polytrack and good to soft going: visored last 4 starts: inconsistent. *D. Morris*

ICE MOUNTAIN 3 br.g. Kyllachy 129 – Sulitelma (USA) 63 (The Minstrel (CAN) **89** 135) [2007 88: 5f 5g² 5.1s 5m 6m Sep 17] close-coupled gelding: fairly useful handicapper: good second at Redcar, only form in 2007: best at 5f: acts on firm going: reared when stall opened on final outing: sold 1,500 gns. *B. Smart*

ICENI PRINCESS 3 b.f. Victory Note (USA) 120 – Swing Job 58 (Ezzoud (IRE) 126) **–** [2007 –: 8.3g 9g p10g p12.2g p12.2g p13.9g p12g Dec 12] no form. *P. Howling*

ICENI WARRIOR 5 b.g. Lake Coniston (IRE) 131 – Swing Job 58 (Ezzoud (IRE) **–** 126) [2007 47: p10g⁵ p11g⁴ p11g² p13g f11g p16g 10.1m p12.2g Apr 30] modest maiden: **a53** stays 1½m: acts on polytrack: tried blinkered. *P. Howling*

ICE PLANET 6 b.g. Polar Falcon (USA) 126 – Preference (Efisio 120) [2007 99: 6m **102** 6s 6g⁶ 6d* 6v⁴ 6d⁴ 6m 6m⁴ Sep 1] useful-looking gelding: useful handicapper: best effort when winning at Redcar in June by ¾ length from Turnkey: best form around 6f: acts on firm and soft ground: has been bandaged fore joints: tough and consistent. *D. Nicholls*

I CERTAINLY MAY   2 b.g. (Feb 22) Royal Applause 124 – Deep Ravine (USA) 50   **64**
(Gulch (USA)) [2007 6g 7.1g 7m p8g p8g² 8s⁶ p8m⁶ p8g Dec 12] 30,000F, 25,000 2-y-o: quite good-topped gelding: second foal: dam 1½m winner: modest maiden: runner-up in nursery at Kempton: stays 1m: acts on polytrack, probably soft ground. *S. Dow*

IDARAH (USA)   4 gr. or ro.g. Aljabr (USA) 125 – Fatina 98 (Nashwan (USA) 135)   **–**
[2007 97: 13.1s Oct 4] lengthy, useful-looking gelding: useful handicapper at 3 yrs: below form only start on Flat in 2007: barely stays 1½m: acts on soft and good to firm going. *L. Lungo*

IDEALLY (IRE)   3 ch.g. Mark of Esteem (IRE) 137 – Ideal Lady (IRE) (Seattle Slew   **93**
(USA)) [2007 78: 7.1m² 9.8m 10.2g* 10m* 10.3m p12g Sep 24] strong gelding: fairly useful performer: won maiden at Bath in July and handicap at Leicester in August: stays 1¼m: acts on good to firm ground: races up with pace: has hinted at temperament: sold 14,000 gns. *B. W. Hills*

IDESIA (IRE)   3 b.f. Green Desert (USA) 127 – Indaba (IRE) 98 (Indian Ridge 123)   **72**
[2007 8m 8.3g⁵ Jul 9] €280,000Y: first foal: dam, 6f/7f (including in France) winner, half-sister to dam of Shirocco: much better effort in maidens when 5½ lengths fifth to Duchess Royale at Windsor. *W. R. Swinburn*

IDLE NO MORE (USA)   3 ch.c. Mr Greeley (USA) 122 – Idle Rich (USA) 104 (Sky   **93**
Classic (CAN)) [2007 f8g* 9d⁶ 9.9g Aug 16] tall colt: third foal: half-brother to minor 1m winners in USA by Pleasant Tap and Coronado's Quest: dam Irish 7f winner (stayed 1¼m): fairly useful form: won maiden at Southwell in May by 8 lengths: didn't progress, looking temperamental: stays 1m: acts on fibresand: sent to USA. *J. H. M. Gosden*

IDLE POWER (IRE)   9 b. or br.g. Common Grounds 118 – Idle Fancy 79 (Mujtahid   **94**
(USA) 118) [2007 103, a93: 5g 6m 6s 6g 6g⁴ 6s³ p6g² 6g 6d⁵ 6d³ 6s p6g³ Nov 4] close-   **a83**
coupled gelding: fairly useful handicapper: best effort in 2007 when third to Aahayson at Windsor sixth start: effective at 6f/7f: acts on polytrack, firm and soft going: tried blinkered/in cheekpieces prior to 2006: races prominently. *J. R. Boyle*

I DONT DO WALKIN (USA)   2 b. or br.f. (Mar 4) Orientate (USA) 127 – Impeach-   **68**
able Affair (USA) (Colonial Affair (USA) 126) [2007 5m² 6m⁴ 5.1d 6m p7m p6g² p6g⁵ p6g⁵ Oct 31] $11,000F, $37,000Y: compact filly: first foal: dam, US 1m winner, out of useful sprinter Polly Daniels: fair maiden: best at 5f/6f: acts on polytrack and good to firm going: wore blinkers/cheekpieces last 4 starts: sold 4,000 gns. *B. J. Meehan*

IDUN   3 b.f. Robellino (USA) 127 – I Do 81 (Selkirk (USA) 129) [2007 10.3g⁵ p12g⁵   **62**
p8.6g⁵ p8g Dec 29] first foal: dam, 2-y-o 7f winner, half-sister to useful performer up to 1¼m Oblige (by Robellino): modest maiden: easily best effort on debut: stays easy 1¼m. *P. W. Chapple-Hyam*

IFATFIRST (IRE)   4 b.g. Grand Lodge (USA) 125 – Gaily Grecian (IRE) (Ela-Mana-   **65**
Mou 132) [2007 62: p12g* Jan 22] fair handicapper, lightly raced: won at Kempton in January, only start in 2007: stays 1½m: raced on polytrack: tried blinkered: looked tricky ride second outing at 3 yrs: sold 6,500 gns in October. *M. P. Tregoning*

IFTIKHAR (USA)   8 b.g. Storm Cat (USA) – Muhbubh (USA) 108 (Blushing Groom   **–**
(FR) 131) [2007 63: p12g Jun 14] big, strong gelding: modest handicapper: pulled up only start at 8 yrs: effective at 8.6f to 1½m: acts on polytrack and firm ground: blinkered (raced freely) once in 2004. *S. Wynne*

IGNITION   5 ch.m. Rock City 120 – Fire Sprite 83 (Mummy's Game 120) [2007 65:   **65**
7.1m 9.1g 9.2g* 8d 8.3d* 9.2m 7.9f 11.1g 9.2s 8g Oct 5] leggy, close-coupled mare: fair handicapper: won at Hamilton in June and July: stays 9f: acts on polytrack, firm and good to soft going: effective with or without cheekpieces: inconsistent. *W. M. Brisbourne*

IGUACU   3 b.g. Desert Prince (IRE) 130 – Gay Gallanta (USA) 112 (Woodman (USA)   **61**
126) [2007 7d⁶ 7.1m 6g Sep 18] compact, quite attractive gelding: best effort in maidens on debut. *J. L. Spearing*

IGUAZU FALLS (USA)   2 ch.c. (Mar 10) Pivotal 124 – Anna Palariva (IRE) 108   **106 p**
(Caerleon (USA) 132) [2007 6g² p7g* 7m² 7d³ Oct 27] 160,000Y: strong, angular colt: fifth foal: half-brother to 3 winners, including smart French 1m/1¼m winner Advice and fairly useful 7.5f to (in US) 8.5f winner Anglo Saxon (both by Seeking The Gold): dam, French 2-y-o 1m winner (only season to race), out of Park Hill Stakes winner Anna of Saxony: useful form: won maiden at Kempton in September: much improved when placed in Somerville Tattersall Stakes at Newmarket (¾-length second to River Proud)

IHA

and Horris Hill Stakes at Newbury (close third behind Beacon Lodge, patiently ridden): will be suited by 1m: should make a smart 3-y-o. *Saeed bin Suroor*

I HAVE DREAMED (IRE) 5 b.g. Montjeu (IRE) 137 – Diamond Field (USA) 71 (Mr Prospector (USA)) [2007 91: p11g* p12g⁴ 12g p10g⁵ p12g² 12m⁵ p11g² p11g 10d Oct 1] tall gelding: useful handicapper on all-weather, fairly useful on turf: won at Kempton in March: stays 1½m: acts on polytrack and good to firm going: in cheekpieces fourth start, blinkered since: not straightforward: sold 20,000 gns, joined G. L. Moore. *T. G. Mills* **87 a98**

IKE QUEBEC (FR) 2 ch.c. (Mar 1) Dr Fong (USA) 128 – Avezia (FR) (Night Shift (USA)) [2007 6s 6g³ p6g² p7g² p7g* p6s² p6d* Dec 27] €55,000Y: stocky colt: second foal: dam, ran once in France, half-sister to smart 1¼m performer Port Vila: fairly useful performer: won nursery at Lingfield in November and claimer (claimed by J. Boyle £17,000) at Wolverhampton: ran creditably most other starts: stays easy 7f: acts on polytrack: races prominently. *R. Hannon* **80**

IL CASTAGNO (IRE) 4 ch.g. Night Shift (USA) – Cartesian 78 (Shirley Heights 130) [2007 79: 7f³ 7m² 8m³ 8m* 7.1d² 8m 8m 8g 7g Oct 30] sturdy gelding: fairly useful handicapper: won at Redcar in June: stays 1m: acts on firm and good to soft going, probably on soft: usually makes running. *B. Smart* **93**

ILE FACILE (IRE) 6 b.g. Turtle Island (IRE) 123 – Easy Pop (IRE) (Shernazar 131) [2007 p10g³ p10g Jan 27] sturdy gelding: fair performer: stays easy 1½m: acts on all-weather and firm going: effective tongue tied or not: joined P. S. Payne. *B. De Haan* **76**

ILE MICHEL 10 b.g. Machiavellian (USA) 123 – Circe's Isle (Be My Guest (USA) 126) [2007 61: 8m⁶ 9m⁶ p10g* p11g³ 10m p10g Oct 17] good-topped gelding: fair handicapper: won at Lingfield in June: stays easy 11f: acts on polytrack and firm ground: sometimes carries head high/hangs left. *Lady Herries* **70**

ILE ROYALE 2 b.f. (Feb 14) Royal Applause 124 – Island Destiny 79 (Kris 135) [2007 p6g 6m 7m 5g 6m p5g p5g⁴ p5.1g⁶ p6g p8.6g p8g³ p7g³ p7.1d Dec 27] 40,000Y: rather leggy filly: second foal: half-sister to Italian 5f (including at 2 yrs) winner Federica Vegas (by Desert Prince): dam, unreliable sprint maiden, sister to Coronation Stakes winner Balisada: modest maiden: stays 1m: acts on polytrack: blinkered nowadays: often slowly away: irresolute (refused to race tenth outing). *C. N. Allen* **52 §**

I'LL DO IT TODAY 6 b.g. Mtoto 134 – Knayton Lass 94 (Presidium 124) [2007 66: p13.9g⁴ 15.8m* 16g p13.9g p13.9g⁴ Nov 12] modest handicapper: won at Catterick in April: stays 2m: acts on polytrack and good to firm ground: once tongue tied. *J. M. Jefferson* **63 +**

ILLUSIONARY 2 b.c. (Mar 11) Observatory (USA) 131 – Tease (IRE) 81 (Green Desert (USA) 127) [2007 6g 6s 6.1s Jul 27] sturdy colt: poor form in maidens: bred to stay 7f/1m. *J. G. Portman* **44**

ILLUSTRIOUS BLUE 4 b. or br.c. Dansili 127 – Gipsy Moth 99 (Efisio 120) [2007 109: 9g* p10g³ 9m⁴ 8m² 9.9g* 9.9d⁴ 9d p12g³ Nov 3] close-coupled colt: has a rather round action: smart performer: progressed again at 4 yrs, winning handicap at Nad Al Sheba in February and listed race at Goodwood (beat Road To Love) in May: good third to Dansant in listed race at Kempton final start: stays 1½m: acts on polytrack, soft and firm going: held up: genuine. *W. J. Knight* **114**

ILOVETURTLE (IRE) 7 b.g. Turtle Island (IRE) 123 – Gan Ainm (IRE) 92 (Mujadil (USA) 119) [2007 21.6m⁶ Apr 23] workmanlike gelding: unraced on Flat in 2005/6: poor form only start at 7 yrs: probably stays 2m: acts on fibresand, good to firm and good to soft going: tried blinkered/tongue tied: none too reliable. *M. C. Chapman* **–**

ILVIZ (FR) 5 gr.g. Medaaly 114 – Move The Mouse (IRE) (Foxhound (USA) 103) [2007 6.5g 9.5g⁴ 10.8f² 10g³ 9.5g* 9s³ 9g³ 9.5s² 9g⁶ 10.5g 14.5g³ 9s⁶ p12.2d² p12.2g Dec 29] modest performer: winner of 4 races at Duindigt, including amateur minor event in June: left Mrs M. Berrevoets, Holland, after eleventh start: better effort in handicaps at Wolverhampton when runner-up penultimate start: probably stays 14.5f: acts on polytrack, firm and soft ground: tried blinkered. *Ollie Pears* **64**

IL WARRD (IRE) 2 b.c. (Mar 18) Pivotal 124 – Demure (Machiavellian (USA) 123) [2007 6g⁶ 7m⁴ 7g⁶ Aug 1] 240,000Y: tall, useful-looking colt: has scope: sixth foal: half-brother to smart 6f (at 2 yrs)/1m winner Coy and 7-y-o Presumptive (both by Danehill): dam unraced half-sister to very smart 6f/7f performer Diffident: fairly useful form: off 2 months after promising debut, won minor event at Ascot (made most to beat Yahrab by 3 lengths) in July: 11/2, only sixth behind Rio de La Plata in Vintage Stakes at Goodwood 2 weeks later, but helped force strong pace: likely to stay 1m: type to do better at 3 yrs. *M. P. Tregoning* **94 p**

I'M AGENIUS 4 b.f. Killer Instinct 111 – I'm Sophie (IRE) 64 (Shalford (IRE) 124§) **43**
[2007 p8g 8.3d⁶ p8.6g p7m 10.2g p8g Nov 3] workmanlike filly: first foal: dam 6f
winner: poor maiden: stays 1m: suspect temperament. *C. Roberts*

IMAGINEMYSURPRISE 2 b.f. (Apr 30) Mujadil (USA) 119 – Anabaa's Music **56**
(Anabaa (USA) 130) [2007 p6g 5.7m 5.7f⁴ 7.5m p8.6g² p8m⁶ p8.6g p7g p6d Dec 17]
third foal: dam unraced: modest maiden: second in nursery at Wolverhampton: stays 8.6f:
acts on polytrack and firm going. *J. A. Geake*

IMMACULATE RED 4 ch.g. Woodborough (USA) 112 – Primula Bairn 77 (Bairn **–**
(USA) 126) [2007 60: f6g f6g 7g 6v Jul 21] compact gelding: maiden: little form in 2007:
tried blinkered. *R. Bastiman*

IMMINENT VICTORY 4 b.g. Benny The Dip (USA) 127 – Brave Vanessa (USA) **55**
62 (Private Account (USA)) [2007 p11g⁵ p12g* f12d⁶ Dec 12] modest form in bumpers:
modest performer on Flat: best effort when winning maiden at Kempton in November:
stays 1½m: acts on polytrack: wore cheekpieces last 2 starts. *R. M. H. Cowell*

IM OVA ERE DAD (IRE) 4 b.g. Second Empire (IRE) 124 – Eurolink Profile 74 **92**
(Prince Sabo 123) [2007 63: f8g* p8g* p7f⁶ p8g⁴ 8g p8g* 8.1f* p8g⁵ 8.3g⁵ p8g* p7g
p8g⁶ f8d² Dec 14] workmanlike gelding: fairly useful handicapper: won at Southwell in
January, Lingfield in February, Kempton and Chepstow in August, and Lingfield in
October: very good second to Kabeer at Southwell final outing: stays 1m: acts on all-
weather and firm ground: often held up. *D. E. Cantillon*

IMPELLER (IRE) 8 ch.g. Polish Precedent (USA) 131 – Almaaseh (IRE) 63 **106**
(Dancing Brave (USA) 140) [2007 103: a9f⁵ a10f 10g* 10g² p10g³ p8g⁴ p11g 10.1g⁵ 12m
10d 10.4d 10m* 10m 9m Oct 6] tall gelding: useful handicapper: won at Nad Al Sheba in
February and Sandown in September, beat Yarqus by short head in latter: good efforts
otherwise in 2007 when placed, third to Watamu at Lingfield fifth start: effective at 1m/
1¼m: acts on polytrack, firm and good to soft going: blinkered (well below form) once:
held up: carries head high. *J. S. Moore*

IMPENETRABLE (USA) 3 ch.c. Mr Greeley (USA) 122 – Hard Knocker (USA) **–**
(Raja Baba (USA)) [2007 8.3d p8g Sep 18] $440,000F, $950,000Y: closely related to US
2-y-o Grade 3 winner Chimichurri (later Grade 1 runner-up, by Elusive Quality) and half-
brother to several winners, including French 1½m winner Anglona (by Polish Navy):
dam unraced half-sister to very smart middle-distance stayer Mashaallah: little impact
in maidens at Windsor and Lingfield (said to have had breathing problem): has left
Godolphin. *Saeed bin Suroor*

IMPERIAL AMBER 5 ch.m. Emperor Fountain 112 – Bambolona 108 (Bustino 136) **66 ?**
[2007 p9.5g⁴ p8.6g⁶ p7g⁴ p8.6g Nov 22] no promise in bumpers: seemingly best effort in
maidens on second start, well held subsequently. *Karen George*

IMPERIAL BEACH (USA) 3 b.g. Coronado's Quest (USA) 130 – Millie's Trick **53**
(USA) (Phone Trick (USA)) [2007 62: 6m⁶ 7m⁴ 8m 6d 7g Jun 1] leggy, unfurnished
gelding: modest maiden: stays 7f: acts on good to firm going: sold 3,700 gns. *T. D. Barron*

IMPERIAL DECREE 2 b.f. (Jan 26) Diktat 126 – Docklands Princess (IRE) 56 **73**
(Desert Prince (IRE) 130) [2007 6m 7m* 6d 8g⁴ 8d Oct 23] 2,200F, €11,000Y: lengthy
filly: first foal: dam sprint maiden: fair performer: won maiden at Yarmouth in August:
should stay 1m: acts on good to firm going. *John Berry*

IMPERIAL ECHO (USA) 6 b.g. Labeeb 124 – Regal Baby (USA) (Northern Baby **90**
(CAN) 127) [2007 90: 7f² 7.1m 6d⁴ 7v³ 7s² 6d 7.2s⁶ 7g⁴ 7d 7g⁶ 7m Nov 10] leggy,
quite good-topped gelding: fairly useful handicapper: stays 7f: acts on any going: tried
blinkered/visored early in career: sold 17,000 gns. *T. D. Barron*

IMPERIAL GAIN (USA) 4 ch.g. High Yield (USA) 121 – Empress Jackie (USA) **74**
(Mount Hagen (FR) 127) [2007 82: 6s 6g 6g 7g 7d 7.6f 7.1m p6g Oct 5] useful-looking **a–**
gelding: fair handicapper, on downgrade: effective at 6f/7f: acts on polytrack, firm and
good to soft going: often in headgear: none too genuine. *J. M. Bradley*

IMPERIAL HARRY 4 b.g. Alhaarth (IRE) 126 – Serpentara 75 (Kris 135) [2007 70: **77**
11m 11g² 12d 17.1m 12d 11.6m² 11.7d³ Aug 19] tall gelding: fair maiden: stays 1½m:
acts on polytrack, firm and good to soft going: signs of temperament. *V. Smith*

IMPERIAL LUCKY (IRE) 4 b.f. Desert Story (IRE) 115 – Irina (IRE) 91 (Polar **62**
Falcon (USA) 126) [2007 63, a80: f7g⁴ p8g² p8g⁵ 7m p8g⁵ p7g³ p7m 8.3d⁴ 8.3m⁶ Aug 25] **a76**
workmanlike filly: fair handicapper on all-weather, modest on turf: stays 8.3f: acts on
all-weather, firm and good to soft going. *D. K. Ivory*

intercasino.co.uk Magnolia Stakes, Kempton—Imperial Star shows improved form in this listed event on the polytrack; Grand Passion (right), Charlie Cool (rail) and Sri Diamond chase him home

IMPERIAL MARK (IRE) 2 b.c. (Feb 11) Mark of Esteem (IRE) 137 – Farhana 109 – (Fayruz 116) [2007 p6g 6m 9s Oct 14] lengthy colt: well held in maidens: should be suited by 5f/6f. *P. J. O'Gorman*

IMPERIAL MINT (IRE) 2 ch.c. (Apr 12) Tagula (IRE) 116 – Escudo (IRE) 79 **99** (Indian Ridge 123) [2007 6s² 5m* 5g 6g⁴ 6.1m* Sep 1] €50,000Y, 52,000 2-y-o: lengthy, angular colt: moderate mover: sixth foal: half-brother to useful 2006 2-y-o 5f/6f winner Holdin Foldin (by Fayruz) and fairly useful 2005 2-y-o winner Past Tender (by Indian Danehill), later successful in US: dam 2-y-o 5f winner (later stayed 1m in France): useful form: won maiden at Windsor in July and minor event at Chester in September: contested pattern races in between, namely Molecomb Stakes at Goodwood and Gimcrack Stakes at York (4¼ lengths fourth to Sir Gerry): will be best kept to 5f/6f: acts on good to firm going, promise on soft. *K. A. Ryan*

IMPERIAL QUEST 3 ch.f. Rainbow Quest (USA) 134 – Imperial Bailiwick (IRE) **61** 104 (Imperial Frontier (USA) 112) [2007 8.3d² 8.3d Oct 15] useful-looking filly: seventh foal: half-sister to several winners, including 7-y-o Reverence and smart 6f (at 2 yrs) to 1m winner Helm Bank (by Wild Again): dam 2-y-o 5f (including Flying Childers Stakes) winner: much better effort in maidens at Windsor when third to Zero Cool, racing freely: showed signs of temperament next time. *J. R. Fanshawe*

IMPERIAL STAR (IRE) 4 br.c. Fantastic Light (USA) 134 – Out West (USA) 103 **115** (Gone West (USA)) [2007 104: p10g* 9m 9.9g³ 12g² 11.6m³ p12g⁴ Sep 8] good-bodied colt: smart performer: injured back on final 3-y-o start: improved in 2007, winning listed race at Kempton in April comfortably by 1¾ lengths from Grand Passion: reportedly had recurrence of back problem next time: creditable efforts in frame last 4 starts, visored when fourth to Steppe Dancer in September Stakes at Kempton final outing: may prove best short of 1½m: acts on polytrack and firm going: has worn crossed noseband: has joined Godolphin. *J. H. M. Gosden*

IMPERIAL SWORD 4 b.g. Danehill Dancer (IRE) 117 – Hajat 64 (Mujtahid (USA) **64** 118) [2007 92: 6v 6d 7g 6m 6v f7d⁶ Dec 18] close-coupled, useful-looking, dipped-backed gelding: has a quick action: fairly useful handicapper at 3 yrs: just modest at best in 2007: stays 7f: acts on soft ground: tried blinkered: temperament under suspicion (once unseated/bolted to post). *T. D. Barron*

IMPERIUM 6 b.g. Imperial Ballet (IRE) 110 – Partenza (USA) (Red Ransom (USA)) **73** [2007 68: p7.1g² p7g² p7g² p7g⁵ p8g⁶ p6g² p7g⁴ 7.1m* 6g 8f⁶ p6g⁶ 8.1m⁴ 6m p7.1g p7m² p7g⁵ p6g p8g³ Dec 29] leggy gelding: fair handicapper: won at Chepstow in May: stays 1m: acts on all-weather, firm and soft going: sometimes wears headgear, effective without: tried tongue tied: often held up. *Jean-Rene Auvray*

IMPETIOUS 3 b.f. Inchinor 119 – Kauri (USA) 63 (Woodman (USA) 126) [2007 91: **97** 8m 9.9g³ 12g⁵ 12m⁶ 12s 8g* 8d 8g Oct 14] lengthy, workmanlike filly: useful performer: won listed race at Hanover (by short head from Fairyland) in September: best other effort when third to Cosmodrome in similar event at Goodwood: probably stays 1½m: acts on good to firm going: blinkered last 3 starts. *E. Tyrrell, Ireland*

IMPLY 3 b.c. Beat Hollow 126 – Insinuate (USA) 99 (Mr Prospector (USA)) [2007 8m **85** p8.6g* May 3] strong, robust colt: fourth foal: closely related to fairly useful 9.5f winner Indication (by Sadler's Wells) and half-brother to 5-y-o Stronghold: dam, 1m winner, out of Prix du Moulin winner and Oaks runner-up All At Sea: fairly useful form: much better effort (not fully wound up and looked ungainly on debut) when winning maiden at Wolverhampton in May by 5 lengths: sold 7,000 gns. *J. H. M. Gosden*

IMPOSTOR (IRE) 4 b.g. In The Wings 128 – Princess Caraboo (IRE) (Alzao (USA)) **–** 117) [2007 81: f12g Dec 27] sturdy gelding: fairly useful maiden handicapper at 3 yrs: well held only Flat start in 2007: tried visored/blinkered. *R. A. Harris*

IMPRIMIS TAGULA (IRE) 3 b.g. Tagula (IRE) 116 – Strelitzia (IRE) (Bluebird **82** (USA) 125) [2007 65: f6g* f6g* 6m³ Apr 18] big, strong gelding: fairly useful performer: much improved, winning maiden and handicap at Southwell within 3 days in February: chipped a bone in a knee final start: effective at 6f/7f: acts on all-weather and good to firm going. *A. Bailey*

IMPROMPTU 3 b.g. Mujadil (USA) 119 – Pie In The Sky (Bishop of Cashel 122) **81** [2007 80: 6g⁵ 6s* 6d³ 5.7d* p6g⁵ 6d Oct 3] smallish gelding: fairly useful performer: won maiden at Windsor in June and handicap at Bath in August: said to have finished lame final start: stays 6f: acts on firm and soft going, possibly not on all-weather: sold 10,000 gns. *R. M. Beckett*

IMPURE THOUGHTS 2 b.c. (Apr 3) Averti (IRE) 117 – Blooming Lucky (IRE) 40 **–** (Lucky Guest 109) [2007 p7g p5m p6g Dec 29] well held in maidens at Lingfield. *J. R. Best*

IM SPARTACUS 5 b.g. Namaqualand (USA) – Captivating (IRE) 63 (Wolfhound **85** (USA) 126) [2007 81: 9.9g² 10g* May 11] leggy gelding: fairly useful performer: won handicap at Nottingham in May: probably stays 10.5f: acts on all-weather, soft and good to firm going: has worn cheekpieces/blinkers, better without: fairly useful hurdler. *Evan Williams*

INAMINUTE (IRE) 4 ch.f. Spectrum (IRE) 126 – Phantom Ring 62 (Magic Ring **86** (IRE) 115) [2007 80: 8m² 7f 7s 6.9d* 7m⁵ 7d⁵ 7m 7g 7g⁴ 7m Nov 10] workmanlike filly: fairly useful handicapper: won at Carlisle in June: stays easy 1m: acts on all-weather, good to firm and good to soft going: none too consistent. *K. R. Burke*

IN A PICKLE 2 ch.f. (Apr 19) Piccolo 121 – Magic Hanne 55 (Magic Ring (IRE) 115) **60** [2007 7g 7g p6g⁵ p5g⁵ p6g² p5.1g⁵ Oct 22] 8,000Y: compact filly: first foal: dam, sprint maiden, half-sister to sprinter Pool Music and miler Russian Music, both useful: modest maiden: best at 5f/6f: raced only on polytrack/good going: sold 3,000 gns, sent to Sweden. *H. J. L. Dunlop*

INASUS (GER) 3 ch.c. Kornado 120 – Instinctive Dancer (USA) (Spend A Buck **74** (USA)) [2007 58p: 11.1m² 12g² Aug 17] big, strong colt: progressive form in maidens, best effort when second to Yossi at Catterick final start: stays 1½m: sold 10,000 gns. *M. Johnston*

INCARNATION (IRE) 2 b.f. (Mar 15) Samum (GER) 126 – River Patrol 96 (Rou- **55 p** sillon (USA) 133) [2007 7.1g⁵ 7g Sep 29] 35,000F, €65,000Y: tall filly: half-sister to several winners, notably high-class but unreliable 1m to 1½m performer Norse Dancer (by Halling): dam, 1¼m winner, half-sister to smart middle-distance stayer Dry Dock: maiden: some encouragement when fifth at Haydock: seemed amiss only other start: should still do better, especially at 1¼m/1½m. *J. G. Given*

INCA SOLDIER (FR) 4 br.g. Intikhab (USA) 135 – Chrysalu 102 (Distant Relative **72** 128) [2007 –: f6g f6g f8g f8g³ 8f p7.1g* f7g 7m⁴ 7.9m 6g³ 6m* 6d 7m² 6s⁶ 6f* 7g⁵ 6g³ p7.1g⁶ p6g⁴ Dec 29] sturdy gelding: fair handicapper: won at Wolverhampton in April, Ayr in June and Redcar in August: effective at 6f to 1m: acts on all-weather and firm ground, below form all starts on softer than good: very slowly away third outing: free-going sort: held up. *R. C. Guest*

INCH BY INCH 8 b.m. Inchinor 119 – Maid Welcome 81 (Mummy's Pet 125) [2007 **80** 80: p6g² p7g³ p6g Mar 25] smallish mare: fairly useful handicapper: stays easy 7f: acts on all-weather and firm going: blinkered. *P. J. Makin*

INCHCAPE ROCK 5 ch.g. Inchinor 119 – Washm (USA) (Diesis 133) [2007 10.2g **–** Jul 9] lengthy gelding: maiden: well held only Flat start at 5 yrs: stays 1m: acts on soft ground: tried visored/in cheekpieces: free-going sort. *W. K. Goldsworthy*

INCHDHUAIG (IRE) 4 ch.g. Inchinor 119 – Be Thankful (IRE) 98 (Linamix (FR) **56** 127) [2007 56: 10s³ 12m Jun 6] lightly-made gelding: modest maiden: stays 1¼m: acts on fibresand, soft and good to firm going: in cheekpieces at 4 yrs. *P. C. Haslam*

INCHIGEELAGH (IRE) 3 ch.f. Inchinor 119 – Thank One's Stars (Alzao (USA) 117) [2007 54: p7.1g Feb 23] neat filly: modest form in 2-y-o maidens: well held only outing in 2007: should stay 7f. *H. Morrison* –

INCHINATA (IRE) 3 b.f. Inchinor 119 – Caviare (Cadeaux Genereux 131) [2007 –p: 8g p11g² 12d³ 12g⁵ 12m 11.7g³ Oct 24] angular, lengthy filly: fairly useful performer: won maiden at Kempton in July: stays 1½m: acts on polytrack and good to soft ground: sold 13,000 gns, sent to USA. *B. W. Hills* **84**

INCHING WEST 5 ch.m. Inchinor 119 – Key West (FR) (Highest Honor (FR) 124) [2007 14m Aug 10] little form in bumpers/over hurdles: well held in maiden on Flat debut. *C. J. Down* –

INCHLAGGAN (IRE) 3 ch.g. Inchinor 119 – Lakatoi 82 (Saddlers' Hall (IRE) 126) [2007 66p: 10m² 10.5g⁴ 10.3m⁵ 11m³ Sep 16] sturdy, workmanlike gelding: fair maiden: likely to stay 1½m: acts on good to firm ground: joined D. Pipe, won juvenile hurdle in October. *B. W. Hills* **79**

INCHLOCH 5 ch.g. Inchinor 119 – Lake Pleasant (IRE) 90 (Elegant Air 119) [2007 92: p12g⁵ 10d⁵ 12g⁴ 12m Nov 10] leggy gelding: fairly useful handicapper: creditable efforts first 3 starts in 2007: stays 1½m: acts on soft and good to firm ground: looks hard ride. *B. G. Powell* **91**

INCH LODGE 5 ch.h. Grand Lodge (USA) 125 – Legaya 94 (Shirley Heights 130) [2007 86: p10g Mar 9] good-topped horse: fairly useful handicapper at 4 yrs: reportedly struck into when tailed off only start in 2007: stays 1½m: acts on polytrack and firm going: often races prominently. *Miss D. Mountain* –

INCHLOSS (IRE) 6 b.g. Imperial Ballet (IRE) 110 – Earth Charter 60 (Slip Anchor 136) [2007 –: f8g 10m 12s⁶ p13g 12.1m Sep 11] smallish, sturdy gelding: poor performer nowadays: stays 1¼m: acts on soft and good to firm ground. *S. Parr* **45**

INCHMAHOME 4 b.f. Galileo (IRE) 134 – Inchmurrin 114 (Lomond (USA) 128) [2007 61: p9.5g 11.5m* 12m 12m Aug 3] smallish, leggy filly: fair performer: won handicap at Lingfield in May: should stay 1½m: acts on good to firm going: sweated both starts at 3 yrs. *E. F. Vaughan* **72**

INCHMARLOW (IRE) 4 b.g. Cape Cross (IRE) 129 – Glenstal Priory 53 (Glenstal (USA) 118) [2007 54: 7g p8.6d Dec 10] good-topped gelding: maiden: little form in 2007. *T. H. Caldwell* –

INCHNADAMPH 7 b.g. Inchinor 119 – Pelf (USA) 79 (Al Nasr (FR) 126) [2007 93: 14g 20m 15.8m* 18m³ 14g 18d⁵ 16.5m* Nov 10] tall, workmanlike gelding: useful handicapper: won at Catterick in July and Doncaster (best effort, beat Kasthari by 8 lengths) in November: stays 2¼m: acts on firm and soft going: tongue tied. *T. J. Fitzgerald* **100**

INCHPAST 6 ch.g. Inchinor 119 – Victor Ludorum (Rainbow Quest (USA) 134) [2007 14.1g 12m 18m³ 16g⁵ 16p* 16.5g* Dec 3] workmanlike gelding: fairly useful handicapper: won at Wolverhampton in November and December, latter by 4 lengths: stays 16.5f: acts on polytrack and firm ground: blinkered. *M. H. Tompkins* **86**

INCHWALL 3 ch.g. Inchinor 119 – Spoilt Again 91 (Mummy's Pet 125) [2007 p6g p7g p7.1g Mar 30] modest form only on debut. *Peter Grayson* **50**

INCHWOOD (IRE) 2 b.f. (Feb 28) Dubai Destination (USA) 127 – Inchiri 108 (Sadler's Wells (USA) 132) [2007 8.2m⁵ 8d⁵ Oct 23] 200,000Y: strong filly: third foal: half-sister to 3-y-o Celtic Step: dam, 1¼m/1½m winner, out of half-sister to smart performer up to 1m Inchinor: fifth in maidens at Nottingham (shaped well) and Yarmouth (pulled too hard): capable of better. *M. A. Jarvis* **72 p**

INCOMING CALL (USA) 3 b.f. Red Ransom (USA) – Private Line (USA) 105 (Private Account (USA)) [2007 7f³ May 5] fifth foal: half-sister to several winners, including smart French 7f to 10.5f winner Dance Dress (by Nureyev) and useful 1m winner Discuss (by Danzig): dam 7f (at 2 yrs) to 8.5f (in USA) winner: 15/8 and green, third to Ragheed in maiden at Thirsk: sold 56,000 gns in December. *Sir Michael Stoute* **61**

INCOMPARABLE 2 ch.c. (Apr 22) Compton Place 125 – Indian Silk (IRE) 74 (Dolphin Street (FR) 125) [2007 6d⁴ 6.1d⁵ 5.1g² 6m* Nov 10] 20,000Y: big, strong colt: second foal: dam 7f winner: fairly useful form: generally progressive in maidens, second to Chartist at Nottingham prior to winning at Doncaster (left in front close home after Omnicat unseated): should prove best at 5f/6f: type to go on again at 3 yrs. *A. J. McCabe* **81 p**

INDARED 3 ch.c. Daggers Drawn (USA) 114 – Bogus John (CAN) (Blushing John (USA) 120) [2007 p7.1g p12.2g Oct 8] tailed off in maidens. *M. Mullineaux* –

INDECISION 2 b.g. (Apr 3) Muhtarram (USA) 125 – Emma Amour 67 (Emarati **55** (USA) 74) [2007 5m 5g 6g³ 7d* 7.5v² 6v³ 7d⁴ 7m 7g⁶ Aug 24] close-coupled gelding: modest performer: won seller at Redcar in June: will stay 1m: acts on heavy going: tried in cheekpieces. *M. W. Easterby*

IN DECORUM 2 gr.f. (Mar 30) Averti (IRE) 117 – Decorous (IRE) (Runnett 125) **45** [2007 p5g 6g 6g 7m 5f p6g p7g⁴ Dec 19] 4,000Y: fourth foal: half-sister to winner in Macau by King's Signet: dam of little account: poor maiden: probably stays easy 7f: visored last 2 starts. *J. A. Geake*

IN DEEP 6 b.m. Deploy 131 – Bobbie Dee 93 (Blakeney 126) [2007 p16g p16g **–** Aug 1] leggy mare: one-time fair handicapper: little form in 2007: tried blinkered. *Mrs P. N. Dutfield*

INDIAN CHASE 10 b.g. Terimon 124 – Icy Gunner (Gunner B 126) [2007 64d: p16.5g **–** Apr 24] leggy gelding: modest performer in 2006: well held sole Flat outing at 10 yrs: tried visored. *Dr J. R. J. Naylor*

INDIAN DAYS 2 ch.c. (Apr 8) Daylami (IRE) 138 – Cap Coz (IRE) 110 (Indian Ridge **76 §** 123) [2007 6.1g 6s 6.1v⁴ 8s 7.1m* 7g 8g Oct 26] strong, useful-looking colt: fair performer: won nursery at Sandown in September: stays 1m: acts on heavy and good to firm going: ungenuine. *J. G. Given*

INDIAN DIVA (IRE) 2 b.f. (Feb 6) Indian Danehill (IRE) 124 – Katherine Gorge **85** (USA) (Hansel (USA)) [2007 6v⁴ p6g* 6m Nov 10] €40,000Y: workmanlike filly: seventh foal: closely related to 3-y-o Vintage and half-sister to fairly useful 6f (at 2 yrs) to 1m winner Miss Champers (by Grand Lodge) and 5f (including at 2 yrs)/6f winner Straffan (by Shinko Forest): dam unraced out of useful sprinter Katies First, herself out of Irish 1000 Guineas winner Katies: much improved from debut (heavy ground) to win maiden at Lingfield (beat Haybrook by 1½ lengths) in October: well held in nursery at Doncaster: will probably stay 7f: blinkered. *P. A. Blockley*

INDIAN EDGE 6 ch.g. Indian Rocket 115 – Beveled Edge 60 (Beveled (USA)) [2007 **80** 80, a70: p7.1g⁵ p8.6g* 8d⁶ 8.1g⁴ 8.3g² 8g² 8.1s* 7d 8s 8g Oct 24] good-topped gelding: **a70** fairly useful handicapper on turf, fair on all-weather: won at Wolverhampton in April and Chepstow in July: well below form after: effective at 7f to 9.5f: acts on polytrack and soft going: races up with pace nowadays: can be tricky ride. *B. Palling*

INDIAN INK (IRE) 3 ch.f. Indian Ridge 123 – Maid of Killeen (IRE) 97 (Dar- **122** shaan 133) [2007 110: 7m² 8m⁵ 8d* Jun 22]

The timing of the Coronation Stakes at Royal Ascot is ideal for attracting fillies who have made a mark in the European classics over a mile. In the eight runnings this century there has been one classic winner or more every year, and the last two renewals have surpassed all their predecessors. In 2006 Speciosa (One Thousand Guineas), Nightime (Irish One Thousand Guineas), Price Tag (demoted from first place in the Poule d'Essai des Pouliches), Lolita (German Guineas) and Vague (UAE One Thousand Guineas) all tried their luck, only to fail to make the frame behind Nannina. A year later Finsceal Beo (One Thousand Guineas at Newmarket and the Curragh), Darjina, who had beaten Finsceal Beo in the Poule

Coronation Stakes, Royal Ascot—in a race featuring the winners of the English, Irish, French and German 1000 Guineas, Indian Ink routs a quality field; it's close for second between Mi Emma (No.7) and Darjina (noseband), with Arch Swing (stripes) an unlucky fourth

Mr Raymond Tooth's "Indian Ink"

d'Essai des Pouliches, and Mi Emma, a runaway winner of the German Guineas, lined up for the Coronation Stakes but were put firmly in their place by Indian Ink, who triumphed by six lengths. It was consequently regrettable that the winner did not make another public appearance until the December Sales at Newmarket, where she was sold to Sheikh Hamdan's Shadwell Estate Company for 2,000,000 guineas and promptly retired to stud. Not a bad profit on a filly who had fetched only 25,000 guineas at the same venue as a yearling.

Indian Ink had been one of the best, and gamest, of her age as a juvenile, winning three races culminating in a narrow victory over Dhanyata in the Cheveley Park Stakes. Good as this form was, it placed her some way behind the champion Finsceal Beo, and in the first part of her all-too-brief classic campaign Indian Ink still looked far from certain to add to her Group 1 tally. That she had trained on satisfactorily was obvious from her running in the Dubai Duty Free Stakes at Newbury in April. Ridden seemingly to conserve her stamina, she was caught flat-footed when Majestic Roi swept through on the outside and, although she drew clear of the third, Indian Ink could not get to the leader who beat her by a neck. Seven furlongs evidently posed no problem for Indian Ink, and the One Thousand Guineas at Newmarket a fortnight later proved that she was effective at a mile. Indian Ink looked a bit unlucky. She should have finished at least fourth, not fifth, after being stuck behind a rival and switched a furlong and a half out, after which she stayed on well to be beaten just over five lengths by Finsceal Beo.

A planned run in the Irish One Thousand Guineas came to nought after Indian Ink failed to scope cleanly, so the Coronation Stakes was her next appearance. The going at Newmarket was good to firm, as it had been at Newbury. Indian Ink had won on this ground at two but her best form was on soft or good to soft. After rain the day before and a downpour on the day, the Coronation Stakes was run on good to soft. Indian Ink was fourth choice in the betting behind joint favourites Mi Emma, who had won her classic in Germany by nine lengths, and Finsceal Beo, and also behind Darjina. There were other fillies with classic form among the thirteen runners, notably Arch Swing, second at Newmarket, and Rahiyah, third at Longchamp, plus Majestic Roi again and a second French challenger, Missvinski, a close second to Darjina in the Prix de la Grotte. Settled off the pace set by the outsiders Cherry Hinton and Scarlet Runner, Indian Ink was one of the first off the bit when the tempo increased at halfway. However, she was back on it soon after turning for home and, when Mi Emma took it up just over a furlong out, Indian Ink seemed to be going best of all as she made ground on the outside, her jockey oozing confidence. When asked to quicken, Indian Ink responded instantly and sprinted clear of her toiling opponents to win ridden out by six lengths from Mi Emma, who got the better of a battle with Darjina by a head. The winning margin was one of the widest in the history of the race, and the biggest since it was elevated to Group 1 status in 1988; Chimes of Freedom scored by five lengths in 1990. For one reason or another, not all of Indian Ink's opponents ran to their best—Finsceal Beo and Mi Emma were some way below the form they showed in the spring, while the form of Darjina's subsequent win against Ramonti in the Prix du Moulin was superior to any other three-year-old filly. But there is no need to make excuses for everything Indian Ink slammed. It was an imperious performance which encouraged thoughts that she could hold her own against the best of the older fillies and mares at a mile. In the event, after a break—while recovering from pulling some muscles in her back at Ascot—she missed a planned engagement in the Matron Stakes, and the Prix de l'Opera and Sun Chariot Stakes went by without her as well. Her presence would have been most welcome in any of those races.

Indian Ink (IRE) (ch.f. 2004)	Indian Ridge (ch 1985)	Ahonoora (ch 1975)	Lorenzaccio
			Helen Nichols
		Hillbrow (ch 1975)	Swing Easy
			Golden City
	Maid of Killeen (IRE) (b 1996)	Darshaan (br 1981)	Shirley Heights
			Delsy
		Sovereign Touch (b 1989)	Pennine Walk
			Sovereign Dona

The Coronation Stakes was the first of three Group or Grade 1 successes for the offspring of deceased sire Indian Ridge during the year; the others coming from Linngari in the Premio Vittorio di Capua and Daytona in the Hollywood Derby. To update details of Indian Ink's pedigree given in *Racehorses of 2006*, her two-year-old brother Navajo Joe, who cost 180,000 guineas as a yearling, finished eighth of twelve in a maiden race at Newmarket in November on his debut. The dam Maid of Killeen was a stakes-placed winner over nine furlongs. Unavailable (by Alzao), a useful filly who stayed a mile and a quarter, remains her only other winner and her five-year-old daughter Princess Killeen (by Sinndar), last of seventeen on her sole appearance, sold for 140,000 guineas at the December Sales a day after Indian Ink. Maid of Killeen had a filly by Barathea in 2006 and a colt by Azamour in 2007. Indian Ink, a genuine sort, was an imposing presence since she is a big, good-topped filly, just the sort to make an impressive broodmare. Suited by a mile and with a good turn of foot, she had form on good to firm going, but her biggest wins came on good to soft. *R. Hannon*

INDIAN LADY (IRE) 4 b.f. Namid 128 – Lady Eberspacher (IRE) 68 (Royal Abjar (USA) 121) [2007 70: p6g Apr 28] fair performer at 3 yrs: reportedly finished lame only start in 2007: raced only at 5f/6f: acts on firm and good to soft going: often wears headgear: has twice hung left. *Mrs A. L. M. King* –

INDIANNIE MOON 3 b.f. Fraam 114 – Ajig Dancer 86 (Niniski (USA) 125) [2007 8d⁶ Jun 26] fourth foal: sister to fairly useful 2004 2-y-o 5f winner Indiannie Star and half-sister to 4-y-o Ajigolo: dam, 5f (at 2 yrs) to 7f winner, out of sister to smart sprinter Puissance: 12/1, well-held sixth of 7 in maiden at Brighton. *M. R. Channon* –

INDIAN'S FEATHER (IRE) 6 ch.m. Indian Ridge 123 – Mashmoum 85 (Lycius **82** (USA) 124) [2007 79: f7g f8g* f8g³ f8g³ f7g* p8g² 8d⁵ 7d* 8.2v³ 7g 8.3d⁶ p7g³ p7g 7g³ p7g Oct 15] strong, compact mare: fairly useful handicapper: won at Southwell in April and June, and Yarmouth in July: stays 1m: acts on all-weather, heavy and good to firm going: effective blinkered or not. *N. Tinkler*

INDIAN SKIPPER (IRE) 2 b.c. (May 2) Indian Danehill (IRE) 124 – Rosy Lydgate **68 p** 53 (Last Tycoon 131) [2007 8d Oct 19] €9,000F, 26,000Y: close-coupled, workmanlike colt: seventh foal: half-brother to several winners, including 9-y-o Loyal Tycoon and 4-y-o Symbol of Peace: dam maiden half-sister to smart performer up to 11f Supreme Sound and useful stayer Top Cees: 50/1 and backward, seventh to General Eliott in maiden at Newmarket: will improve. *M. H. Tompkins*

INDIAN SPARK 13 ch.g. Indian Ridge 123 – Annes Gift (Ballymoss 136) [2007 73: **64** 6g 6d 5s⁴ 6g⁵ 6m 5s 6v Oct 26] close-coupled gelding: poor mover (reportedly fractured off-fore joint earlier in career): modest handicapper nowadays: stays 7f: acts on any going: often gets behind. *J. S. Goldie*

INDIAN SUNDANCE (IRE) 4 b.g. Namid 128 – Can't Afford It (IRE) 44 (Glow **49** (USA)) [2007 –: p5.1g² f6g p5.1g p8.6g p8g Oct 17] heavy-topped gelding: poor maiden: left R. Fahey after third start: best at 5f: acts on polytrack: tried tongue tied. *K. R. Burke*

INDIAN TRAIL 7 ch.g. Indian Ridge 123 – Take Heart 84 (Electric 126) [2007 112: **115** 7m 6m 6g 6g 7g 6m³ 5s 5g 6g³ 6m³ 5m* 5g* 6d Sep 22] big, strong gelding: smart handicapper: won at Sandown (by 1¾ lengths from Fantasy Believer) and Haydock (beat Judd Street by head) in September: not discredited when eighth to Advanced in Ayr Gold Cup final outing, travelling strongly long way: has won at 7f, best at 5f/6f nowadays: seems best on good ground or firmer: visored nowadays: patiently ridden, and usually travels strongly. *D. Nicholls*

INDIGO DANCER 4 b.g. Groom Dancer (USA) 128 – Violet (IRE) 77 (Mukaddamah **52** (USA) 125) [2007 50: p10g² p10g Jan 31] strong, well-made gelding: modest performer: effective at 8.6f to 11f: acts on polytrack and firm going: blinkered last 4 starts, tongue tied first occasion. *C. F. Wall*

INDIGO MAIL (IRE) 2 b.g. (Apr 22) Modigliani (USA) 106 – Vieux Carre (Pas de **–** Seul 133) [2007 7m Sep 8] 11/1, tailed off in maiden at Thirsk. *M. Brittain*

INDIGO ROSE (IRE) 3 b.f. Cadeaux Genereux 131 – Colourfast (IRE) 88 (Spectrum **66** (IRE) 126) [2007 64p: 8.3m⁶ 10g⁵ 11.7f Sep 10] long-backed, workmanlike filly: fair maiden: should be suited by 1½m+: acts on polytrack and good to firm ground. *J. H. M. Gosden*

INDONESIA 5 ch.g. Lomitas 129 – Idraak (Kris 135) [2007 81: 14m² 17.1m³ 15.8m⁴ **85** 14.8m 16g² 17.1m* 18d Oct 20] strong, useful-looking gelding: fairly useful handicapper: dead-heated with Strobe at Pontefract in September, idling: stays 17f: acts on good to firm and good to soft ground: consistent. *T. D. Walford*

IN DREAM'S (IRE) 5 b.g. Dr Fong (USA) 128 – No Sugar Baby (FR) (Crystal Glit- **–** ters (USA) 127) [2007 15.8m Apr 4] rather unfurnished gelding: modest maiden at 2/3 yrs: well held only start on Flat since: tried in visor/cheekpieces: fairly useful hurdler, successful in May. *G. M. Moore*

INDUSTRIAL STAR (IRE) 6 ch.g. Singspiel (IRE) 133 – Faribole (IRE) 106 (Esprit **78** du Nord (USA) 126) [2007 73: 16m* 16.1s 16m² 16.2g⁵ 16.4m⁴ Sep 9] lengthy gelding: fair handicapper, lightly raced on Flat: won at Ripon in June: stays 2m: acts on good to firm ground: wore cheekpieces in 2007: tends to hang left. *Micky Hammond*

INDY DRIVER 2 ch.c. (Feb 15) Domedriver (IRE) 128 – Condoleezza (USA) 78 **– p** (Cozzene (USA)) [2007 7m Aug 3] 20,000F, €46,000Y: first foal: dam 1¾m winner: 16/1, needed experience when in rear in maiden at Newmarket won by Siberian Tiger: will be suited by 1m+: bound to improve. *J. R. Fanshawe*

INFALLIBLE 2 b.f. (Feb 3) Pivotal 124 – Irresistible 98 (Cadeaux Genereux 131) **81 P** [2007 7g* Nov 3] lengthy filly: has scope: first foal: dam 5f/6f winner (including at 2 yrs) granddaughter of US Grade 1 2-y-o 7f/1m winner Some Romance: 11/2, highly promising win in 20-runner maiden at Newmarket (beat Elmaleeha by 1¾ lengths), green at times but sweeping through under hand ride: likely to stay 1m: will go on to much better things. *J. H. M. Gosden*

INFIDEL (IRE) 7 b.g. Spectrum (IRE) 126 – Implicit View 63 (Persian Bold 123) **–** [2007 p10g 16m May 22] no form on Flat: tried blinkered. *J. R. Best*

INFINITE PATIENCE 2 b. or br.f. (Jan 23) High Chaparral (IRE) 132 – Idma 67 **66**
(Midyan (USA) 124) [2007 p7g 6d⁵ 7g 7m⁶ 8m 7d Oct 30] strong, rangy filly: has scope:
fourth foal: half-sister to winner in US by Peaks And Valleys: dam, US 6f winner, half-
sister to very smart 9f winner Olden Times: fair maiden: staying-on sixth in nursery at
Newmarket: bit better than bare form in similar events both starts after: should be suited
by 1m+. *J. S. Moore*

INFLAGRANTEDELICTO (USA) 3 ch.g. Gentlemen (ARG) 136 – Imprudent **– §**
Love (USA) (Foolish Pleasure) [2007 63: p8.6g⁶ f8g f12g⁶ 9.8s 7m Jul 11] unreliable maiden: no form in 2007: tried blinkered/in cheekpieces. *D. W. Chapman*

INGLEBY ARCH (USA) 4 b.g. Arch (USA) 127 – Inca Dove (USA) (Mr Prospector **99**
(USA)) [2007 101: 6g⁵ 6d³ 6g³ 7g 6d³ 7g 7m 6m 6m⁴ p6g p7.1g⁵ f6d* Dec 12] strong,
well-made gelding: useful handicapper: won by 2½ lengths from Resplendent Alpha at
Southwell in December, making all: best at 6f: acts on fibresand, soft and good to firm
going: tried blinkered (ran poorly)/visored: has high head carriage. *T. D. Barron*

INGLEBY HILL (IRE) 3 b.g. Averti (IRE) 117 – Living Daylights (IRE) 73 (Night **52 d**
Shift (USA)) [2007 –: f7g² 9.9g 14.1m 10m 12s 14.1m 12g Aug 29] good-topped gelding:
modest maiden at best: probably stays 1¾m: acts on fibresand, probably on good to firm
ground. *T. D. Barron*

INGLEBY PRINCESS 3 br.f. Bold Edge 123 – Bob's Princess 69 (Bob's Return **78**
(IRE) 123) [2007 78: 6g⁴ 6s⁶ 6d⁶ 7g⁵ 6m 5g 6g⁵ Oct 30] leggy, angular filly: fair handicapper: effective at 6f, should stay 1m: acts on firm and good to soft going. *T. D. Barron*

INGLEBY STAR (IRE) 2 b.g. (Feb 26) Fath (USA) 116 – Rosy Scintilla (IRE) **77**
(Thatching 131) [2007 5g 5m* 5g p5.1g f5d⁴ Dec 11] chunky, deep-girthed gelding: fair
performer: won maiden at Musselburgh in May: off 6 months after third start, respectable
effort in nursery final one: raced only at 5f: acts on fibresand and good to firm ground.
T. D. Barron

INGRATITUDE (IRE) 4 ch.g. Inchinor 119 – Merci (IRE) (Cadeaux Genereux 131) **83**
[2007 98: 9.9d³ Jun 27] compact gelding: useful handicapper at 3 yrs: fit from hurdling
(fairly useful), shaped as if stamina stretched sole Flat outing in 2007: stays 1m: raced on
good/good to soft going: tried visored: has hung left. *N. J. Henderson*

IN HONOUR (IRE) 2 b.c. (Feb 5) Spartacus (IRE) 107 – Andkit (USA) (Alleged **87**
(USA) 138) [2007 5.1g⁴ 5m³ 6s³ 6f* 6g Aug 21] €16,000F, €42,000Y: stocky colt: third
foal: half-brother to Italian 7f to 8.5f winner by Orpen: dam winner in Italy: fairly useful
form: progressive in maidens, won at Windsor in August: better than bare result (tenth of
17) in well-contested nursery at York, tiring: may prove best at 5f/6f: acts on firm and soft
going. *E. S. McMahon*

INIMICAL 3 b.f. Daggers Drawn (USA) 114 – Mara River 86 (Efisio 120) [2007 54: **43**
p8.6g 8f⁵ 8.1s⁵ 7d a4.8g⁶ Nov 24] sturdy filly: poor maiden nowadays: sold £600 from
W. S. Kittow before final start: may prove best at 5f/6f: tried visored. *Peggy Bastiaens-
Van Cauwenbergh, Belgium*

INKA DANCER (IRE) 5 ch.m. Intikhab (USA) 135 – Grannys Reluctance (IRE) 63 **72**
(Anita's Prince 126) [2007 67, a64: p7g 6g⁵ 6f* 6d² 6s 6d p7.1g⁵ p6g⁶ p6m² p6g⁶ Dec 5] **a65**
small mare: fair handicapper: won at Lingfield in August: stays 7f: acts on polytrack, firm
and good to soft going: has hung right. *B. Palling*

INKJET (IRE) 3 b.f. Beckett (IRE) 116 – Aussie Aisle (IRE) (Godswalk (USA) 130) **54**
[2007 –: p5.1g* p6g p6g p6g p8g Nov 12] smallish filly: modest performer: won seller at
Wolverhampton in January: left Ms Deborah Evans after second start: should be suited
by 6f: acts on polytrack. *P. D. Evans*

INK SPOT 2 b.g. (Jan 27) Diktat 126 – Good Girl (IRE) 100 (College Chapel 122) [2007 **70**
5m 6d² 6s² 6s³ 8s Sep 22] sturdy, close-coupled gelding: fair maiden: placed 3 times,
including third to Sir Gerry at Thirsk, gelded after final start: should prove best at 6f/7f:
acts on soft going. *M. L. W. Bell*

INNER VOICE (USA) 4 gr.g. Cozzene (USA) – Miss Henderson Co (USA) (Silver **57**
Hawk (USA) 123) [2007 –: 8m³ 16m p8g Dec 7] modest maiden: best effort at 1m on
good to firm going: little form over hurdles. *J. J. Lambe, Ireland*

INN FOR THE DANCER 5 b.g. Groom Dancer (USA) 128 – Lady Joyce (FR) **55**
(Galetto (FR) 118) [2007 –: p12g⁴ p11g⁶ May 9] workmanlike gelding: modest maiden
handicapper: stays easy 1½m: acts on polytrack and firm going: tried in cheekpieces.
J. C. Fox

INONTIME (IRE) 2 ch.f. (Mar 16) Golan (IRE) 129 – Phantom Ring 62 (Magic Ring **57**
(IRE) 115) [2007 p6g^6 p7.1d^3 Dec 7] sixth foal: closely related to fairly useful 7f winner
Inaminute and 1m/1¼m winner Double Spectre (both by Spectrum): dam 5f winner:
modest form in maidens at Wolverhampton: likely to stay 1m. *K. R. Burke*

INQUISITRESS 3 b.f. Hernando (FR) 127 – Caribbean Star 81 (Soviet Star (USA) **58**
128) [2007 71: p8g^5 p8g^6 p5g p7g p6g 7m^3 7m p8g^4 p7g^4 p8g^2 p8g^6 p8g 6m^6 7m^3 8d p5g^5 **a69**
p8g* p7m p8g^6 p8g p8g^3 p8g p7m Nov 26] small, workmanlike filly: fair handicapper on
all-weather, modest on turf: won at Kempton in September: stays 1m: acts on polytrack
and good to firm going. *J. J. Bridger*

INSAAF 2 b.f. (Apr 24) Averti (IRE) 117 – Molly Brown 95 (Rudimentary (USA) 118) **96**
[2007 6.5d^4 6d* 6g Nov 2] 130,000Y: good-topped filly: fourth foal: half-sister to 3
winners, notably smart 2006 2-y-o 6f winner Doctor Brown (later successful in Hong
Kong as Helene Brilliant, by Dr Fong): dam 5f (at 2 yrs)/6f winner: useful form: notable
debut in sales race at Ascot (fourth of 22 to Lady Rangali), then won maiden at Newmarket in October: 2/1, disappointing in listed event at Newmarket final start: will stay
7f: raced only on good/good to soft going. *W. J. Haggas*

IN SAFE HANDS (IRE) 3 ch.f. Intikhab (USA) 135 – Safiya (USA) (Riverman **92**
(USA) 131) [2007 87: 8.2g* 10g^2 8m^5 10.1s^2 10m 8.1m 8g Oct 14] €75,000Y: sturdy
filly: half-sister to several winners, including 5f (at 2 yrs)/7f winner Cayman Kai and
sprinter Tajasur (both smart, by Imperial Frontier): dam unraced sister to smart miler
Sulaafah: fairly useful performer: left D. Gillespie in Ireland 90,000 gns after final 2-y-o
start: won maiden at Nottingham in May: good second in listed races at Newbury (1½
lengths behind Measured Tempo) and Newcastle (beaten 7 lengths by Mango Mischief)
second/fourth outings: stays 1¼m: acts on soft and good to firm ground: wore cheekpieces third start. *C. G. Cox*

INSCRIBED (IRE) 4 b.f. Fasliyev (USA) 120 – Fay (IRE) 64 (Polish Precedent (USA) **55**
131) [2007 54: p8.6g^4 p7g f5g^5 p5g^3 p8g 5m^5 7f 6m^2 p7g Sep 12] modest maiden: stays
6f: acts on all-weather and good to firm ground: sometimes blinkered/visored: hung left
final outing. *G. A. Huffer*

INSIDE STORY (IRE) 5 b.g. Rossini (USA) 118 – Sliding (Formidable (USA) 125) **85**
[2007 74: p12.2g^3 p12.2g 9.8m^5 10.3f^3 9.1g^6 p8.6g* 8.1m* 9m^4 10.4m^3 9m^3 p8m^5 p10g^6
p9.5g^4 Dec 15] rather leggy gelding: fairly useful performer: left G. Kelly after second
start: won claimer at Wolverhampton (left M. Easterby) in July and handicap at Haydock
in August: left N. Wilson after ninth start: has won at 1¼m, probably best around 1m:
acts on polytrack, firm and good to soft ground: blinkered: has been slowly away.
M. W. Easterby

INSIGNIA (IRE) 5 b.g. Royal Applause 124 – Amathea (FR) (Exit To Nowhere (USA) **–**
122) [2007 –, a53: f7g^5 p9.5g^3 p9.5g f8g^6 Mar 13] modest maiden: stays 9.5f: acts on **a54**
all-weather, raced only on good/good to firm going on turf: tried in cheekpieces/visor:
joined Mrs A. Thorpe, fair hurdler, successful in July. *W. M. Brisbourne*

INSIYAABI (USA) 3 b.c. Aljabr (USA) 125 – Elle Seule (USA) 122 (Exclusive Native **77**
(USA)) [2007 8d^4 8g Jul 20] angular colt: has a quick, unimpressive action: closely
related to useful 6f (at 2 yrs)/7f winner Khulood (by Storm Cat) and half-brother to
numerous winners, notably July Cup winner Elnadim (by Danzig) and Irish 1000 Guineas
winner Mehthaaf (by Nureyev): dam, French 1m (Prix d'Astarte) to 10.5f winner, half-
sister to dam of Dubai Millennium: better effort in maidens at Newmarket when 5¾
lengths fourth of 9 to Novikov on debut: sold 5,000 gns. *J. L. Dunlop*

INSOMNITAS 2 b.c. (Apr 10) Lomitas 129 – Sleepless 92 (Night Shift (USA)) [2007 **54**
6g 6d^5 6.1s^4 p7g^6 7.5g 9s p10g Oct 24] quite good-topped colt: modest maiden: probably
stays 1¼m: acts on polytrack and soft going. *M. G. Quinlan*

INSPAINAGAIN (USA) 3 ch.g. Miswaki (USA) 124 – Counter Cat (USA) (Hennessy **80**
(USA) 122) [2007 67: 6.1m^4 5d^4 5d* 5m^2 5g 5g Nov 9] attractive gelding: fairly useful
handicapper: won at Musselburgh in June: likely to prove best at 5f: yet to races on
extremes of going. *T. D. Barron*

INSPECTOR CLOUSEAU (IRE) 2 gr.g. (Jan 8) Daylami (IRE) 138 – Claustra **78 +**
(FR) 91 (Green Desert (USA) 127) [2007 7s^4 7m^2 7m* Sep 18] €65,000Y: tall, close-
coupled gelding: third foal: half-brother to 2006 2-y-o 7.5f winner Weld Il Balad (by
Alhaarth) and winner in Hungary by Zafonic: dam, Irish 9f winner, half-sister to smart
French sprinter Wessam Prince: fair form: second to Alexander Castle at Newcastle prior
to winning maiden at Thirsk: will stay 1m: acts on good to firm ground. *T. P. Tate*

INSPIRINA (IRE) 3 b.c. Invincible Spirit (IRE) 121 – La Stellina (IRE) 100 (Marju **75**
(IRE) 127) [2007 73: 7.1g Nov 8] good-topped colt: type to carry condition: fair maiden,
lightly raced: stays 7f: unraced on going softer than good. *R. Ford*

INSTANTLY (IRE) 3 b.f. Dansili 127 – Wigging 96 (Warning 136) [2007 8m p10m **–**
Oct 6] 30,000Y: lengthy filly: half-sister to 7f winner Macaulay (by Zafonic) and 1½m
winner Warbreck (by Selkirk): dam, 7f winner, half-sister to very smart sprinter Bluebook: well held in maidens at Goodwood and Kempton 4 months apart. *W. Jarvis*

INSTINCT 6 b.g. Zafonic (USA) 130 – Gracious Gift 96 (Cadeaux Genereux 131) **–**
[2007 42: 7m May 3] just poor in 2006, and well held sole 6-y-o start. *Micky Hammond*

INSTITUTE 2 ch.c. (Feb 25) Pivotal 124 – Constitute (USA) 85 (Gone West (USA)) **84 p**
[2007 7g⁶ Oct 26] quite attractive colt: second foal: dam, 1m winner, half-sister to smart
performer up to 1¼m Battle Chant: 10/1 and green (including to post), promising sixth to
Speedy Dollar in maiden at Doncaster: will stay 1m: sure to win races. *Sir Michael Stoute*

INSTRUCTOR 6 ch.g. Groom Dancer (USA) 128 – Doctor's Glory (USA) 91 (Elma- **90**
amul (USA) 125) [2007 88: 10m³ 9m⁴ 12d 8.9d Oct 13] good-topped gelding: easy
mover: fairly useful handicapper: best effort in 2007 on reappearance: stays 1½m: acts on
all-weather and good to firm ground, no form on softer than good: often front runner.
R. A. Fahey

INSUBORDINATE 6 ch.g. Subordination (USA) 120 – Manila Selection (USA) **42**
(Manila (USA)) [2007 66: 9.1d 8m 9d 8g Nov 8] leggy gelding: poor performer nowadays: acts on fibresand and any turf going: tried in cheekpieces: usually
slowly away. *J. S. Goldie*

INSURED 2 ch.g. (Apr 22) Intikhab (USA) 135 – Self Assured (IRE) 97 (Ahonoora **–**
122) [2007 5m p6g Jun 13] well held in maidens: bred to stay 1m. *A. J. McCabe*

INTABIH (USA) 2 b. or br.c. (Mar 27) More Than Ready (USA) 120 – Lookaway **67 g**
Dixieland (USA) (Dixieland Band (USA)) [2007 7f Sep 5] $140,000F, $40,000Y:
useful-looking colt: second foal: dam, US 6f (at 2 yrs) to 1m winner, out of half-sister to
US Grade 1 7f winners Hennessy (at 2 yrs) and Pearl City: 16/1, burly and green when
seventh of 8 in maiden at York: will do better. *C. E. Brittain*

INTAVAC BOY 6 ch.g. Emperor Fountain 112 – Altaia (FR) 90 (Sicyos (USA) 126) **65**
[2007 62: p9.5g⁴ 12g³ 12.4m⁶ 12.4m 12.2² 10.1m⁴ 12m⁵ 10.1m 10m 12m⁶ 13.8g 12g²
p12.2g² p12.2g p12.2d⁵ p12.2s⁶ Dec 21] sparely-made gelding: fair handicapper: left
R. Fahey after fourth start: should stay 1¾m: acts on polytrack, firm and good to soft
going: in cheekpieces/visor last 4 outings. *S. P. Griffiths*

INTEGRATION 7 b.g. Piccolo 121 – Discrimination 72 (Efisio 120) [2007 50: f12g **51**
p12.2g⁴ p13g p12.2g p13.9g Nov 12] smallish, quite attractive gelding: modest maiden
on Flat (winning hurdler): stays 1¾m: acts on all-weather, firm and soft going. *Miss
M. E. Rowland*

INTENSIFIER (IRE) 3 b.c. Sinndar (IRE) 134 – Licorne 93 (Sadler's Wells (USA) **62**
132) [2007 –: f8g⁵ f8g⁶ 11g f11g³ 12.1g 11.1m² 11.5m p9.5g⁴ p12.2g⁵ p12g² Oct 29]
modest maiden handicapper: stays 1½m: acts on all-weather and good to firm ground:
usually blinkered: free-going sort. *P. A. Blockley*

INTERACTIVE (IRE) 4 b.g. King's Best (USA) 132 – Forentia 89 (Formidable **78**
(USA) 125) [2007 8f 8.3d p7g⁴ p8.6g⁴ p7g⁴ Dec 29] 75,000F, 150,000Y, 3,500 3-y-o: tall
gelding: fourth foal: half-brother to 7-y-o Tizzy May and 2001 2-y-o 6f winner Access
Denied (by Revoque), both useful: dam, 2-y-o 5f winner, half-sister to Prix Morny and
Middle Park winner Bahamian Bounty: fair maiden: best efforts at 7f on polytrack:
headstrong. *Andrew Turnell*

INTEREST (USA) 3 ch.g. Banker's Gold (USA) 116 – Princess Kris 82 (Kris 135) **–**
[2007 –p: f8g Feb 6] attractive gelding: little form: tried blinkered. *T. D. Barron*

INTERNATIONALDEBUT (IRE) 2 b.c. (Apr 8) High Chaparral (IRE) 132 – **89 p**
Whisper Light (IRE) 74 (Caerleon (USA) 132) [2007 7m² 7.2s 8g Oct 27] €225,000Y:
well-made, attractive colt: good walker: has round action: third foal: dam, Irish 7f winner,
half-sister to useful Irish 2-y-o 6f winner Catch A Glimpse: fairly useful form: shaped
well both starts at Doncaster, second to Newly Elected in minor event and travelled
smoothly long way in Racing Post Trophy (ninth to Ibn Khaldun): ran as if amiss in
maiden (soft ground) in between: stays 1m. *D. J. Murphy*

INTERSKY CHARM (USA) 3 ch.c. Lure (USA) 131 – Catala (USA) (Northern Park **74**
(USA) 107) [2007 10f⁴ 9g⁵ p10g Dec 30] quite good-topped colt: fair form in maidens:
best effort when fifth to Northern Jem at Ripon. *R. M. Whitaker*

INTERSKY MELODY (USA) 2 b.g. (Feb 8) Sky Mesa (USA) 116 – Mayan Maiden **63**
(USA) (Lyphard (USA) 132) [2007 p6g⁵ 7m 7p p7.1g Sep 21] modest maiden: best effort
on debut, only start for K. Ryan: should stay 7f/1m: acts on polytrack. *R. M. Whitaker*

INTERSKY MUSIC (USA) 4 b.g. Victory Gallop (CAN) 130 – Resounding Grace **–**
(USA) (Thunder Gulch (USA) 129) [2007 58p: p11.8m⁶ 10.5m⁶ Aug 9] leggy gelding:
modest form sole 3-y-o start: little form in 2007: modest hurdler. *Jonjo O'Neill*

INTERSKY SPORTS (USA) 3 gr.g. Chester House (USA) 123 – Nightlong (Night **65**
Shift (USA)) [2007 65: f7g* p7.1g⁴ p8g² p8g p8.6d⁶ p8.6d Dec 10] fair performer: won
claimer at Southwell in January: left K. Ryan after fourth start: stays 1m: acts on all-
weather and firm ground: tried blinkered (well beaten), usually in cheekpieces: races up
with pace. *K. J. Burke*

INTER VISION (USA) 7 b.g. Cryptoclearance (USA) – Fateful (USA) 90 (Topsider **100**
(USA)) [2007 100: 5v 5s 5s 7d 6m² 7g 5g 6m⁶ 5m* 6m* 7g p5.1g⁵ Oct 2] tall gelding:
useful handicapper: won at Doncaster (by short head from Yungaburra) and Thirsk (by
2½ lengths from Guest Connections) in space of 5 days in September: effective at 5f to
easy 7f: acts on polytrack, firm and soft ground: wore cheekpieces (ran creditably) once
in 2004. *A. Dickman*

INTIMATE FRIEND (USA) 6 b.m. Expelled (USA) 116 – Intimate (USA) (Topsider **38**
(USA)) [2007 p7g p8g 6m⁶ 7.6s⁴ Aug 18] lengthy, rather sparely-made mare: poor
maiden nowadays: stays 7.6f: acts on good to firm going: usually tongue tied. *Miss Diana
Weeden*

INTIQUILLA (IRE) 3 b.f. Galileo (IRE) 134 – Orinoco (IRE) 53 (Darshaan 133) **91**
[2007 57: 12m* 11.8s* 12d 14g 12s³ 10.3m 12.5s Nov 26] good-topped filly: improved
into a fairly useful performer: won maiden at Salisbury and handicap at Leicester in May:
best effort when seventh in Gower Song in listed race at Doncaster penultimate start:
should stay 1¾m: acts on soft and good to firm going: temperament under suspicion: sold
22,000 gns. *Mrs A. J. Perrett*

INTO ACTION 3 b.c. Sendawar (IRE) 129 – Syrian Dancer (IRE) (Groom Dancer **72 d**
(USA) 128) [2007 75: p12f² 11.8m 11.6m 14g 15g⁴ 16m² p16g 15.4m 18d 16g p16g
Oct 17] close-coupled colt: fair maiden at best: stays 2m: acts on polytrack and good
to firm going, probably on good to soft: tried blinkered (raced freely): usually races
prominently: unreliable: joined W. Storey. *R. Hannon*

INTO THE DARK 6 ch.g. Rainbow Quest (USA) 134 – Land of Dreams 115 (Cadeaux **110**
Genereux 131) [2007 118: 9.9g⁵ 12g⁴ 10s p12g² Nov 3] rather leggy, lengthy gelding:
smart performer: best efforts in 2007 when in frame in listed races at Goodwood (fourth
to Ivy Creek) and Kempton (no tongue tie, neck second to Dansant): best up to 1½m: acts
on polytrack, soft and good to firm going: usually tongue tied: formerly visored: has raced
freely/found little: has left Godolphin. *Saeed bin Suroor*

INTREPID JACK 5 b.h. Compton Place 125 – Maria Theresa (Primo Dominie 121) **114**
[2007 109: 6g² p5g² 6d² 7m 6m Aug 4] lengthy horse: smart performer: good efforts in
2007 when runner-up in handicaps at Newbury (beaten 1¾ lengths by Ripples Maid) and
Royal Ascot (career-best effort, beaten neck by Dark Missile in Wokingham Stakes) first/
third outings: badly hampered when length second to Dazed And Amazed in listed race at
Kempton in between: respectable tenth of 27 to Zidane in Stewards' Cup (Handicap) at
Goodwood final appearance: effective at 5f to 7f: acts on polytrack, soft and good to firm
going: tried visored. *H. Morrison*

INTRICATE DANCE (USA) 3 b.f. Aptitude (USA) 128 – Clog Dance 103 (Pursuit **–**
of Love 124) [2007 7m 7m⁶ May 3] good-topped filly: third foal: half-sister to useful 6f
(at 2 yrs) and 1m winner Short Dance (by Hennessy): dam, maiden (stayed 1¼m),
half-sister to smart Ebor winner Tuning: little form in maidens at Newbury (in need of
race) and Catterick (sweating up badly): sold 30,000 gns in December. *B. W. Hills*

INTRICATE WEB (IRE) 11 b.g. Warning 136 – In Anticipation (IRE) 93 (Sadler's **50**
Wells (USA) 132) [2007 –: p12.2g⁴ p9.5g⁴ Mar 14] sturdy, angular gelding: fairly useful
performer at 9 yrs: lightly raced and modest form at best since: stays 11f: acts on fibresand, firm and soft ground (well beaten on heavy): tried in headgear: tends to race lazily.
E. J. Alston

IN UNIFORM 2 b.c. (Feb 27) Royal Applause 124 – Scarlet Plume 103 (Warning 136) **90**
[2007 5.1f* 5m³ 5g⁶ 6m⁵ 5d* Sep 25] 20,000F, 25,000Y: sturdy, lengthy colt: seventh
foal: half-brother to 4-y-o Green Room, fairly useful 2001 2-y-o 6f winner Scarlet
Ribbons (by Anabaa) and 7f winner Scarlet Invader (by Indian Ridge): dam, 2-y-o 1m
winner, out of Oaks winner Circus Plume: fairly useful form: won maiden at Bath in May

and minor event at Beverley (made all by 3 lengths) in September: ran creditably in between when third to Hatta Fort in minor event at Windsor and sixth to Natagora in Prix du Bois at Maisons-Laffitte (very upset in stall): best at 5f (pulled hard at 6f): acts on firm and good to soft going. *E. S. McMahon*

INVASIAN (IRE) 6 ch.g. Desert Prince (IRE) 130 – Jarrayan 64 (Machiavellian (USA) 123) [2007 93: 9.9d 10d⁶ 12m* 12d p11g³ 10m⁵ 12m 16d p9.5g⁶ p12g³ p12.2g* Dec 14] **96** close-coupled, quite attractive gelding: useful handicapper: trained on reappearance only by A. Lidderdale: won at Newmarket in August and Wolverhampton in December, best effort of 2007 when beating Eumene by 1¾ lengths in latter: stays 1½m: acts on polytrack, good to firm and good to soft ground (below form on soft): usually forces pace: sometimes races freely. *P. W. D'Arcy*

INVASOR (ARG) 5 br.h. Candy Stripes (USA) 115 – Quendom (ARG) (Interprete **132** (ARG)) [2007 133: a9f* a10f* Mar 31]

Winning the world's richest race should, in theory, be the height of any owner's ambition. However, a cursory glance at the roll-call of Dubai World Cup winners might temper that a little. The first two winners, Cigar and Singspiel, fared relatively well after their trips to Dubai. Cigar went on to equal Citation's tally of consecutive victories (since bettered by Silent Witness) and to set a world record for earnings. Singspiel also went on to become a world record holder in an earnings category, his for a British-trained horse. Thereafter, the subsequent record of Dubai World Cup winners becomes patchy. The 1998 winner Silver Charm recorded four subsequent victories but was beaten in each of his later races at the very highest level, including the 1999 Dubai World Cup. The next nine winners managed just three wins (all at Group/Grade 1 level) from twenty-four starts between them. Two of them (Dubai Millennium and Electrocutionist) are now dead, and two never ran again. Included in the latter category is the 2007 winner Invasor.

Invasor was bought for 20,000 dollars as a two-year-old by Pablo Hernandez and brothers Juan Luis and Luis Alberto Vio Bado to race in Uruguay. He raced at that country's premier track, Maronas, winning all five of his starts and becoming Uruguay's first triple crown winner in over a decade, earning only the equivalent of 100,000 dollars. Invasor did, though, catch the eye of Sheikh Hamdan who purchased Invasor for reportedly around 1,400,000 dollars. Transferred to Kieran McLaughlin, Invasor suffered the first and only defeat of his career in the UAE Derby, like the rest of the field on the day no match for an on-song Discreet Cat, though possibly unlucky not to finish second after encountering trouble in running. Invasor went on to prove himself a top-class performer in the States, winning the Pimlico Special (possibly the last running of an historic race, the 2007 edition cancelled due to lack of sponsorship) and the Suburban Handicap (easily by over four lengths from Wild Desert) and Whitney Handicap (by a nose from Sun King). Invasor started third favourite behind the top-class three-year-old Bernardini and

Dubai World Cup Sponsored By Emirates Airline, Nad Al Sheba—the finish of the world's richest race is dominated by the two North American challengers, with Invasor getting the better of Premium Tap; the Hong Kong-trained Bullish Luck is third

Californian-based Lava Man in the Breeders' Cup Classic. In the race itself Lava Man again flopped outside his home domain and Invasor put up his best performance at up to that time to beat Bernardini by a length.

Invasor was prepared for his tilt at the Dubai World Cup in the Donn Handicap, the same race in which Cigar, Captain Steve and Roses In May began their World Cup-winning season. Like Cigar and Captain Steve, Invasor won at Gulfstream and started favourite on the industry prices for the Dubai World Cup, amid speculation about the well-being of market rival Discreet Cat. Those doubts proved well-founded as Discreet Cat trailed in last of the seven runners, the smallest field in the race's history. Instead it was Premium Tap, third behind Invasor at the Breeders' Cup, who ran Invasor closest, the pair drawing clear in a stirring battle which Invasor eventually won by a length and three quarters. Hong Kong's Bullish Luck was another eight lengths back in third with Britain's representative Kandidate sixth. Invasor's winning time was the second fastest in the twelve-year history of the race, bettered only by the outstanding Dubai Millennium.

Invasor (ARG) (br.h. 2002)	Candy Stripes (USA) (ch 1982)	Blushing Groom (ch 1974)	Red God Runaway Bride
		Bubble Company (ch 1977)	Lyphard Prodice
	Quendom (ARG) (bl 1997)	Interprete (b or br 1988)	Farnesio Inaccesible
		Queen of Victory (b or br 1990)	Cipayo Twitch Crown

Invasor's sire Candy Stripes died in February 2007. Relatively undistinguished as a racehorse (second in the Poule d'Essai des Poulains the highlight), Candy Stripes has proved a good advert for South American breeding, siring ten champions worldwide. Invasor's dam Quendom was unraced, her place at stud assured as a sister to a pair of graded winners in Argentina. Invasor is her first foal and her subsequent progeny by Southern Halo and Orpen are as yet unraced. In 2007, Quendom moved to join the Hill 'n' Dale broodmare band in Kentucky and visited Distorted Humor, who will be on a par in 2008 with A P Indy and Storm Cat as the world's most expensive advertised stallion at 300,000 dollars. The rest of Invasor's family on the distaff side includes other Group/Grade 1 winners in a female line that traces back to Pretty Polly. The end of Invasor's career on the track came in his final preparations for a repeat in the Suburban Handicap. He was found to have fractured a hind sesamoid (having suffered a similar injury at the same site on his Uruguayan debut) and was retired to Sheikh Hamdan's Shadwell Farm in Kentucky. The game and genuine Invasor was effective at nine to twelve and a half furlongs and acted in the mud. He will serve a limited book of eighty-five mares (as will all Shadwell stallions) at a fee of 35,000 dollars, live foal, in 2008. *K. P. McLaughlin, USA*

INVENTION (USA) 4 b.g. Lear Fan (USA) 130 – Carya (USA) (Northern Dancer) **90** [2007 91: p12g⁴ p11g 8.1d⁴ 9.9d 9m Aug 4] angular, quite attractive gelding: has a moderate, quick action: fairly useful performer: left W. Knight, creditable fourth in handicap at Sandown third start: below form after: stays 1½m: acts on polytrack, good to firm and good to soft going: visored (well beaten) once at 3 yrs: fair form over hurdles. *Miss E. C. Lavelle*

INVENTOR (IRE) 2 b.c. (Mar 27) Alzao (USA) 117 – Magnificent Bell (IRE) (Octa- **83 p** gonal (NZ) 126) [2007 7.1m 8m³ 10.2d* Oct 1] €27,000F, 72,000Y: short-backed colt: first foal: dam, unraced half-sister to useful 7.5f to 1¼m winner Esyoueffcee (by Alzao), out of half-sister to very smart 1m to 1½m performer All At Sea: fairly useful form: progressive in maidens, won at Bath by 1¼ lengths from Planetarium: will stay 1½m: should do better still. *B. J. Meehan*

INVERTED 3 b.g. Averti (IRE) 117 – Indian Silk (IRE) 74 (Dolphin Street (FR) 125) **–** [2007 49: f6g f5g Mar 20] first foal: dam 7f winner: poor maiden at 2 yrs: well held in 2007: tried visored/in cheekpieces. *Mrs A. Duffield*

INVESTMENT PEARL (IRE) 4 b.f. Desert Sun 120 – Superb Investment (IRE) **59** (Hatim (USA) 121) [2007 66: f11g 10.9d 12.1s 11.7f³ p12.2g Sep 14] modest maiden (trained prior to reappearance by J. Oxx in Ireland): stayed easy 11.6f: acted on firm going: tried blinkered: dead. *D. R. Gandolfo*

William Fry (Handicap), the Curragh—Invincible Force (stars on sleeves), the only British-trained runner, wins this quite valuable prize from Mist And Stone (right) and If Paradise (second right)

INVINCIBLE FORCE (IRE) 3 b.g. Invincible Spirit (IRE) 121 – Highly Respected **105** (IRE) 57 (High Estate 127) [2007 102: 7.1g 6m 7d 6s⁶ 6.1m³ 6m 5g 5g 5m* 5d⁵ 6d 5g p5.1g³ p5.1g Nov 19] close-coupled gelding: useful performer: won quite valuable handicap at the Curragh (by head from Mist And Stone) in September: creditable third in listed race at Chester (to Green Manalishi) and in handicap at Wolverhampton (behind Chief Editor): best at 5f/6f: acts on polytrack, firm and soft ground: tried visored (looked none too keen): saddle slipped seventh outing. *Paul Green*

INVINCIBLE LAD (IRE) 3 b.g. Invincible Spirit (IRE) 121 – Lady Ellen 67 (Horage **61** 124) [2007 6m 5d⁴ 5s² 5.9f 5s Aug 11] modest maiden: raced only at 5f/6f: acts on good to soft ground: tried in cheekpieces: gelded after final start. *E. J. Alston*

INVINCIBLE ROSE (IRE) 2 b.f. (Apr 29) Invincible Spirit (IRE) 121 – Yorkshire **44** Rose (IRE) 82 (Sadler's Wells (USA) 132) [2007 5m 5g⁵ 6s⁵ 7d⁶ 7m⁶ Sep 8] €3,000F, 1,000Y: good-bodied filly: has round action: second foal: dam, maiden, out of half-sister to very smart performer up to 1½m Young Buster: poor maiden: seems to stay 7f. *M. Brittain*

INWAAN (IRE) 4 b.g. King's Best (USA) 132 – Balaabel (USA) 83 (Sadler's Wells **70** (USA) 132) [2007 72: p8g p7f⁶ p6g² p6g 5m³ 5.5d³ p6g 6m⁴ 5.7g p7m Nov 1] lengthy gelding: fair maiden handicapper: effective at 6f, seems to stay 11f: acts on polytrack, heavy and good to firm going: tried blinkered: tongue tied. *P. R. Webber*

INXILE (IRE) 2 b.g. (Feb 8) Fayruz 116 – Grandel (Owington 123) [2007 5g* Sep 7] **94 p** €30,000F, 80,000Y: strong, compact gelding: third foal: half-brother to 5-y-o Tax Free: dam unraced: 33/1, fairly useful form when winning maiden at Haydock by ¾ length from Hammadi, showing good speed and attitude: will prove best at 5f/6f: sure to go on and win more races. *D. Nicholls*

IO (IRE) 2 b.f. (Mar 18) King's Best (USA) 132 – Callisto (IRE) 91 (Darshaan 133) **56** [2007 7m 7s 8d Oct 27] quite attractive filly: second foal: dam, 2m/17.5f winner, half-sister to smart stayer Rain Rider: modest form (no threat, and sometimes looked awkward) in minor event/maidens: will be suited by 1½m+. *J. L. Dunlop*

IOLANTHE 3 ch.f. Vettori (IRE) 119 – Shakalaka Baby (Nashwan (USA) 135) [2007 **75** –: 10m 11.6m p10g² 10.2m 10g² p10g⁵ 9g³ 8d 12f Sep 10] workmanlike filly: fair maiden handicapper: stays 1¼m: acts on polytrack. *B. J. Meehan*

IONIAN 4 b.g. Piccolo 121 – Aegean Flame 86 (Anshan 119) [2007 p7.1g³ 8.2g⁶ 7.1d⁵ **75 d** 8g p7.1g p9.5g Aug 31] good-bodied gelding: fair maiden: easily best effort when third at Wolverhampton on debut: not sure to stay beyond 1m: acts on polytrack and good to soft going: looked hard ride second outing: sold 800 gns. *Pat Eddery*

IONIAN SPRING (IRE) 12 b.g. Ela-Mana-Mou 132 – Well Head (IRE) (Sadler's **64**
Wells (USA) 132) [2007 88: p12.2g⁵ f12g² f12g* Feb 15] sturdy gelding: has reportedly
suffered from broken blood vessels: fairly useful performer at 11 yrs, just modest in 2007:
won claimer at Southwell in February: stays 1½m, at least as effective at 1¼m: acts on
all-weather and any turf going: still a free-going sort, and held up: tends to edge left: has
joined P. D. Evans. *D. Carroll*

IOWEYOU 3 ch.f. Noverre (USA) 125 – Cuore di Aliante (Alhijaz 122) [2007 60: p6g⁶ **57**
p7g p5f² p5g² p5g² 5m⁵ p4g² p5.1g² 5.3d⁵ 5m⁴ p5.1g⁶ Jun 25] rather leggy filly: modest
maiden: runner-up 5 times in 2007: stays 6f: acts on polytrack and good to firm ground:
blinkered nowadays: often races prominently: sold 12,000 gns, sent to Italy. *J. S. Moore*

I PREDICT A RIOT (IRE) 3 b.g. Danehill Dancer (IRE) 117 – Manon's Song (IRE) **77**
(Sadler's Wells (USA) 132) [2007 68: 10f⁵ 12g³ 14g⁵ 15g² 14g⁶ p16g⁶ 12m² 11.6d
Oct 15] big, lengthy gelding: fair maiden: stays 15f: acts on firm and soft ground: in
cheekpieces last 2 starts: sold 60,000 gns. *J. W. Hills*

IRELAND DANCER (IRE) 3 ch.g. Trans Island 119 – Come Dancing 48 (Suave **60**
Dancer (USA) 136) [2007 75: p8.6g p8g⁵ p8g⁶ 7g Jun 12] just modest maiden at 3 yrs:
stays 1m: acts on polytrack and good to firm ground. *P. M. Phelan*

IRISH ARTIST (FR) 2 b.c. (Jan 4) Orpen (USA) 116 – Anchusa (IRE) (Nashwan **71**
(USA) 135) [2007 6g⁶ p7g 7.1m⁶ 8d⁶ Oct 23] €60,000Y: stocky colt: first foal: dam,
lightly-raced French maiden, half-sister to useful French 2-y-o 1m winner Day Or Night:
fair maiden: stays 1m: signs of temperament. *R. Hannon*

IRISH CAPE 4 br.f. Cape Cross (IRE) 129 – Praglia (IRE) 64 (Darshaan 133) [2007
p7g Oct 29] leggy filly: closely related to 1¼m/1½m winner Dash of Magic (by Magic
Ring) and half-sister to winner in Greece by Formidable: dam unreliable sprint maiden:
25/1, well held in maiden at Lingfield, pulling hard. *Mrs N. Smith*

IRISH CONECTION (IRE) 4 b.g. Bold Fact (USA) 116 – Trojan Girl (IRE) 74 (Up **58**
And At 'em 109) [2007 p5.1g⁴ f6g⁵ Dec 27] much better effort in maidens when fourth at
Wolverhampton, not knocked about: bred to prove best at 5f/6f. *T. McLaughlin, Ireland*

IRISH DANCER 3 b.f. Danehill Dancer (IRE) 117 – Gaelic Swan (IRE) 80 (Nashwan **66**
(USA) 135) [2007 6g⁶: 9.7m³ 12.6m⁵ 11.8s⁵ 11m⁴ 9.9s 10.2m⁵ 10d Oct 1] leggy filly: fair
maiden handicapper: stays 12.6f: acts on soft and good to firm going: blinkered last 2
outings: has shown signs of temperament. *J. L. Dunlop*

IRISH JIG (IRE) 2 b.c. (Mar 31) Celtic Swing 138 – Siem Reap (USA) (El Gran Senor **96**
(USA) 136) [2007 5v³ 6m² 6m* 6g 6g⁹* 6s³ Jul 1] €16,000F, 36,000Y: lengthy, useful-
looking colt: has a quick, unimpressive action: third foal: half-brother to 7.5f winner in
Spain by Revoque: dam unraced out of smart Irish sprinter Sunset Reigns: useful
performer: won maiden at Leopardstown in May and listed event at Cork (by head from
May Meeting) in June: below form in listed race at Epsom (upset in stall/ran wide on
turn) in between: good length third of 4 to Lizard Island in Railway Stakes at the Curragh
final start: will stay 7f/1m: acts on soft and good to firm going: sent to Hong Kong.
G. M. Lyons, Ireland

IRISH MAYHEM (USA) 2 b. or br.c. (Mar 7) Woodman (USA) 126 – Adventurous **89**
Di (USA) (Private Account (USA)) [2007 7.1m 8.1g³ 8d² Oct 19] $135,000Y, 80,000
2-y-o: medium-sized, angular colt: brother to useful French 6f (at 2 yrs) to 10.5f winner
Franc and half-brother to 3 winners, including very smart US 6f (at 2 yrs) to 1¼m
(Grade 1) winner Panty Raid (by Include): dam US 9f winner: fairly useful maiden: progressive form, placed at Sandown and Newmarket (neck second to Mukhber): will stay
1¼m. *B. J. Meehan*

IRISH MICKEY 3 b.g. City On A Hill (USA) 114 – Game Leader (IRE) 72 (Mukad- **–**
damah (USA) 125) [2007 6m 5g Jun 22] well held in maiden/seller. *James Moffatt*

IRISH MUSIC (IRE) 2 b.c. (May 14) Namid 128 – Kelly's Tune 63 (Alhaarth (IRE) **61 p**
126) [2007 p6g⁶ Dec 29] first foal: dam maiden (stayed 7f): 25/1, not given hard time
when sixth in maiden at Lingfield, late headway: likely to do better. *A. P. Jarvis*

IRISH PEARL (IRE) 2 b.f. (Jan 17) Statue of Liberty (USA) 115 – Helen Wells (IRE) **86**
72 (Sadler's Wells (USA) 132) [2007 7g⁵ 6d* 6d 6g⁶ Nov 2] lengthy filly: first foal:
dam, Irish maiden, stayed 1½m: fairly useful form: won maiden at Windsor in August:
contributed to overly-strong pace in Firth of Clyde Stakes at Ayr next time, then good
sixth to Spinning Lucy in listed event at Newmarket: should stay 7f/1m: raced only on
good/good to soft going. *K. R. Burke*

IRISH PLANE (IRE) 3 b.g. Barathea (IRE) 127 – Stem The Tide (USA) (Proud Truth (USA)) [2007 11.9g 9.2d May 18] lengthy gelding: well held in maidens at Haydock and Hamilton (jinked left early stages): joined Robert Tyner in Ireland and gelded. *K. R. Burke* —

IRISH QUEST (IRE) 3 b.c. Galileo (IRE) 134 – No Quest (IRE) (Rainbow Quest (USA) 134) [2007 10d 10g 10g 11.7g³ 14g² 16g* 14g* 14.1g² 14m Oct 4] 150,000Y: stocky, compact colt: sixth foal: closely related to 1m (at 2 yrs) to 1¼m winner Rutters Rebel (by Entrepreneur) and half-brother to 2 winners, including smart US performer up to 1½m Macaw (by Bluebird): dam, French maiden, half-sister to very smart French performer up to 1¼m No Pass No Sale: fairly useful handicapper, generally progressive: won at Goodwood in August and Haydock in September: good ½-length second to Aajel at Yarmouth next time: stays 2m: races prominently. *M. A. Jarvis* — 90

IRISH RELATIVE (IRE) 3 b.g. Indian Lodge (IRE) 127 – The Good Life (IRE) (Rainbow Quest (USA) 134) [2007 –p: f7g⁵ f7g⁵ f8g⁶ f8g⁴ 9.8g³ 8g 10g⁴ 8.5s 9.8s³ a8.6g² a8g* a8g Nov 18] modest performer: sold from T. D. Barron 2,800 gns after ninth start: won minor event at Taby in November: stays 1¼m: acts on dirt and soft going. *R. Ohlsson, Sweden* — 55

IRISH SECRET (CZE) 3 ch.g. Secret 'n Classy (CAN) – Irska Sipka (IRE) (Mukaddamah (USA) 125) [2007 p9.5g f11g May 8] well beaten in maidens at Wolverhampton and Southwell. *G. J. Smith* —

IRISH WELLS (FR) 4 b.c. Poliglote 121 – Sign of The Vine (FR) (Kendor (FR) 122) [2007 122: 10s³ 10.5m² 12g⁴ 12g⁴ 12.5d* 12f Oct 21] big, lengthy colt: very smart performer: won Grand Prix de Deauville Lucien Barriere in August for second year running, making most and keeping on gamely to beat Poet Laureate a length: creditable placed efforts at Longchamp first 2 outings in Prix d'Harcourt and Prix Ganay (second to easy winner Dylan Thomas in latter): respectable fourth to Saddex in Grand Prix de Chantilly and to Mountain High in Grand Prix de Saint-Cloud next 2 starts: below form in Canadian International at Woodbine final outing: stayed 12.5f: acted on soft and good to firm ground: had worn ear plugs: made running/raced prominently: to stand at Haras d'Etreham, France, fee €3,500. *Francois Rohaut, France* — 122

IRISH WHISPERS (IRE) 4 b.g. Marju (IRE) 127 – Muneera (USA) 67 (Green Dancer (USA) 132) [2007 67: p16g Mar 25] lengthy gelding: fair maiden handicapper at 3 yrs: below form only start on Flat in 2007: stays 13f: acts on polytrack and firm going. *B. G. Powell* —

IRON CROSS (IRE) 2 b.g. (Mar 14) Cape Cross (IRE) 129 – Alithini (IRE) 75 (Darshaan 133) [2007 7g 8g 8g Oct 25] €58,000Y: big gelding: third foal: dam, French 1½m winner, sister to Park Hill Stakes winner Discreet Brief: no show in back-end maidens: will benefit from 1½m+: sort to flourish in 3-y-o handicaps. *Sir Mark Prescott* — p

IRON DANCER (IRE) 3 b.c. Iron Mask (USA) 117 – Sin Lucha (USA) (Northfields (USA)) [2007 –: 7g 7g 7.1g² p7.1g⁶ p8g 11.5d Oct 23] close-coupled colt: modest maiden: stays 7f: acts on polytrack: tried blinkered. *P. A. Blockley* — 54

IRON PEARL 3 b.f. Iron Mask (USA) 117 – Fast Tempo (IRE) 74 (Statoblest 120) [2007 66: p5.1g p7g⁵ p6g p6g Dec 4] modest performer: left Jane Chapple-Hyam 1,000 gns after third start: probably stays 7f: acts on polytrack: tried tongue tied. *J. Ryan* — 56

IRON RULER (IRE) 3 b.g. Invincible Spirit (IRE) 121 – Blushing Queen (IRE) 75 (Desert King (IRE) 129) [2007 6d May 15] €25,000F, 14,000Y: first foal: dam, maiden who stayed 7f, half-sister to dam of Breeders' Cup Juvenile winner Wilko: 80/1, well held in maiden at Brighton: sold £800 in July. *P. A. Blockley* —

IRONY (IRE) 8 gr.g. Mujadil (USA) 119 – Cidaris (IRE) (Persian Bold 123) [2007 **90** 96: 7g⁴ 7g⁶ 7.1d³ p8g 7m 7m 8.1m⁴ 8.1m⁴ Sep 14] good-topped gelding: fairly useful handicapper: stays 1m: acts on polytrack, firm and good to soft going: tried tongue tied: effective with/without cheekpieces: normally front runner. *A. M. Balding*

IRRIDESCENCE (SAF) 6 b.m. Caesour (USA) 110 – Meretricious (SAF) (Dancing **119** Champ (USA)) [2007 119: 9g³ 8.9g 8m² 9.5d² Aug 11] tall, leggy mare: smart performer: as good as ever when placed in Jebel Hatta at Nad Al Sheba (1¼ lengths third to Seihali), Falmouth Stakes at Newmarket (length second to Simply Perfect) and Beverly D Stakes at Arlington (head second to Royal Highness, just losing out after good battle): below form in Dubai Duty Free at Nad Al Sheba on second outing: stayed 11f: acted on soft and good to firm going: had been mounted on course/got on edge in preliminaries: raced prominently: visits Empire Maker. *M. F. de Kock, South Africa*

IRVING PLACE 2 ch.g. (Jan 29) Compton Place 125 – Prince's Feather (IRE) 77 **80** (Cadeaux Genereux 131) [2007 5.1m² 5f² 5m² 7m 6.1d* 6g 6m⁴ Oct 8] strong, lengthy gelding: fairly useful performer: won nursery at Nottingham in August: best at 5f/6f: acts on firm and good to soft going. *M. L. W. Bell*

ISA'AF (IRE) 8 b.g. Darshaan 133 – Shauna's Honey (IRE) 88 (Danehill (USA) 126) **53** [2007 79: f14g⁶ p13.9g³ p16.5g f12g³ f14g f14g p16g p12g⁶ f12d⁶ Dec 14] neat gelding: modest performer nowadays: effective at 1½m, barely stays 2¼m: acts on all-weather and any turf going. *P. W. Hiatt*

ISABELLA GLYN (IRE) 2 b.f. (Apr 19) Sadler's Wells (USA) 132 – Questina (FR) **75 p** (Rainbow Quest (USA) 134) [2007 7g³ Nov 3] good-bodied, useful-looking filly: closely related to smart French 9f (at 2 yrs) to 10.5f winner Trumbaka (by In The Wings) and half-sister to useful French 1m/1¼m winner Arctic Hunt (by Bering): dam French 1¼m winner: 11/1 and burly, encouraging third to Infallible in maiden at Newmarket, staying on well once in the clear: will be suited by 1¼m/1½m: sure to improve. *J. Noseda*

ISABELLA'S BEST (IRE) 3 ch.f. King's Best (USA) 132 – Spanish Quest (Rainbow **53** Quest (USA) 134) [2007 53: 10g⁵ p12.2g Apr 30] modest maiden: should stay 1½m. *E. J. O'Neill*

ISANDER (USA) 2 b.c. (Mar 12) Grand Slam (USA) 120 – Let Fly (USA) (Flying **61** Paster (USA)) [2007 6g p7g 7m 8g p8m p8g³ p10g⁶ Oct 24] rather leggy colt: modest maiden: barely stays 1¼m: acts on polytrack and good to firm going: blinkered (ran badly) once: sold 10,000 gns, sent to Serbia. *Mrs A. J. Perrett*

ISENT SHE RICH (IRE) 2 ch.f. (Apr 1) Dubai Destination (USA) 127 – Rahika **68** Rose 91 (Unfuwain (USA) 131) [2007 7s² 7g 7d⁴ 10m 8.3d Oct 15] 68,000F, €95,000Y: unfurnished filly: closely related to 3-y-o Lordship and half-sister to 6-y-o Kings Point: dam Irish 7f/1m winner: fair maiden: well held in nurseries: will prove best up to 1m: acts on soft going. *M. G. Quinlan*

ISHETOO 3 b.g. Ishiguru (USA) 114 – Ticcatoo (IRE) 60 (Dolphin Street (FR) 125) **104** [2007 58: 6d⁴ 5g* 5m* 5v⁴ 6m 6v² 5g* 5m* 5.1g³ 5g³ Oct 27] strong gelding: useful handicapper: much improved in 2007, winning at Ayr in May, Catterick (apprentices) and Haydock in June, and Thirsk in August and September (beat Valery Borzov by 1¼ lengths): further good efforts when third after at Chester (behind Topflightcoolracer) and Doncaster (beaten 2 lengths by Sunrise Safari): effective at 5f/6f: acts on heavy and good to firm going: buckle said to have come undone on rein fifth start: troublesome in stall/withdrawn prior to intended eighth outing: races prominently. *A. Dickman*

ISHI ADIVA 3 b.f. Ishiguru (USA) 114 – Nightingale Song 66 (Tina's Pet 121) [2007 **97** 85: 5g³ 5d⁶ 5g 5m* 5m⁵ 6g 5g 5.1m Oct 14] strong filly: useful handicapper: won at Newmarket in July: just respectable efforts at best after: best at 5f: acts on good to firm going: sold 30,000 gns. *Tom Dascombe*

ISHIBEE (IRE) 3 b.f. Ishiguru (USA) 114 – Beauty (IRE) 74 (Alzao (USA) 117) [2007 **64** 63: 6m* 5.9m³ 6m* 6d 6s² 6d⁴ 5.9f 6m* 6g 6d⁴ p6m* p6g 5.3d³ p6g⁵ p7g p6g⁵ Dec 4] sturdy filly: modest performer: won handicap in June and seller in August (sold from Mrs A. Duffield), both at Brighton, and handicap at Kempton in October: barely stays 7f: acts on polytrack, firm and soft going: usually wears cheekpieces: inconsistent. *J. J. Bridger*

ISHIMAGIC 3 ch.f. Ishiguru (USA) 114 – Triple Tricks (IRE) 70 (Royal Academy **41** (USA) 130) [2007 52: 7s 5.3g⁵ 6g Jul 26] modest maiden at 2 yrs, just poor in handicaps in 2007: stays 1m: acts on polytrack and good to soft ground. *J. J. Bridger*

ISHISMART 3 ch.f. Ishiguru (USA) 114 – Smartie Lee 66 (Dominion 123) [2007 –: 8d **–** Jun 16] strong filly: little sign of ability. *R. Hollinshead*

ISIDORE BONHEUR (IRE) 6 b.g. Mtoto 134 – Way O'Gold (USA) (Slew O' Gold **86**
(USA)) [2007 93: 10g 9.8m 8.3g⁵ 8g⁵ 10.5s⁶ p10g Oct 12] big, strong, close-coupled
gelding: fluent mover: fairly useful handicapper: effective at 1m, barely stays 1½m: acts
on firm and good to soft going, probably on polytrack: tried blinkered/tongue tied: races
freely: held up: difficult ride. *G. A. Swinbank*

ISINKSO (IRE) 2 gr.c. (Mar 28) Clodovil (IRE) 116 – Storm Pearl (IRE) 62 (Catrail **–**
(USA) 123) [2007 5g Jun 18] 16/1, no show in maiden at Windsor. *R. M. Beckett*

IS IT ME (USA) 4 ch.g. Sky Classic (CAN) – Thea (GER) (Surumu (GER)) [2007 79: **81**
p16g 11.8m² 12.6m⁶ 12d⁶ Sep 26] sturdy gelding: fairly useful handicapper on turf, just **a56 +**
modest on all-weather: left P. Blockley after reappearance: stays 12.6f: acts on firm and
good to soft going: races prominently: fairly useful hurdler. *A. W. Carroll*

IS IT TIME (IRE) 3 b.f. Danetime (IRE) 121 – Ishaam 76 (Selkirk (USA) 129) [2007 **59**
49: 7.1m⁵ 8.3d 6d p7g⁴ p7g p6g⁴ f5d* Dec 14] workmanlike filly: modest performer: won
handicap at Southwell in December: effective at 5f to 7f: acts on polytrack and good to
firm ground. *Mrs P. N. Dutfield*

ISLAND GREEN (USA) 4 b.g. Cozzene (USA) – Legend of Spring 99 (Night Shift **–**
(USA)) [2007 54: p8.6g f8g* f7g²⁹ 7g p7.1g 7m p7.1g⁴ Nov 19] fair performer: won **a66**
claimer (claimed from B. Curley £5,000) and handicap in March, both at Southwell:
effective at 7f/1m: acts on all-weather, well held all 3 starts on turf: reportedly bled fifth
outing. *D. Carroll*

ISLAND KING (IRE) 4 br.g. Turtle Island (IRE) 123 – Love of Paris (Trojan Fen 118) **49**
[2007 8d⁵ 8d 9m⁵ p12.2g f11d³ Dec 20] sturdy gelding: little encouragement in bumpers/
maiden hurdle for T. Walford: poor maiden on Flat, lightly raced. *R. Bastiman*

ISLAND MUSIC (IRE) 2 b.f. (Mar 5) Mujahid (USA) 125 – Ischia 64 (Lion Cavern **74**
(USA) 117) [2007 6m 6g⁵ 6g³ 7.1g³ Nov 9] close-coupled filly: second foal: dam,
maiden, half-sister to smart performers Attache (best around 7f) and Tadeo (5f/6f): fair
maiden: third at Redcar (to Spinning Lucy) and Musselburgh: stays 7f. *J. J. Quinn*

ISLAND ODYSSEY 4 b.f. Dansili 127 – Tetravella (IRE) (Groom Dancer (USA) 128) **–**
[2007 93: 12d p12g Jun 27] sturdy filly: fairly useful handicapper at 3 yrs: little impact in
2007: stays 1½m: acts on polytrack, firm and good to soft ground: often makes running.
E. A. L. Dunlop

ISLAND VISTA 2 b.f. (Mar 7) Montjeu (IRE) 137 – Colorvista (Shirley Heights 130) **76 p**
[2007 p7g² Sep 7] rather leggy filly: half-sister to several winners, including smart 1997
2-y-o 7f winner Mudeer (by Warning) and fairly useful 13f/14.6f winner Durable (by
Caerleon): dam unraced half-sister to Irish Oaks winner Colorspin, herself dam of
Opera House and Kayf Tara: 4/1, encouraging second to Annie Skates in minor event at
Kempton: will be well suited by 1¼m/1½m: will do better. *M. A. Jarvis*

ISLE DE MAURICE 5 b.g. Sinndar (IRE) 134 – Circe's Isle (Be My Guest (USA) **–**
126) [2007 16d Oct 11] quite good-topped gelding: fair performer at 3 yrs: below form
only start on Flat since: stays 1½m: acts on polytrack: tried blinkered: fair hurdler,
showing signs of temperament. *D. M. Grissell*

ISLE DREAM 5 ch.m. Forzando 122 – La Volta 86 (Komaite (USA)) [2007 p6g Jan 19] **–**
strong mare: of no account. *R. F. Marvin*

ISOBEL ROSE (IRE) 3 b.f. Royal Applause 124 – Total Love 102 (Cadeaux Gene- **57 §**
reux 131) [2007 73§: p7g 5g 8s⁶ p7.1g⁴ 5.1g p7g⁴ p8g f7d Dec 11] quite good-topped
filly: has a quick action: just modest maiden in 2007: left E. Dunlop after fourth outing:
stays 7f: acts on polytrack and firm ground: ran poorly in blinkers/visor: has wandered:
ungenuine. *J. L. Spearing*

ISPHAHAN 4 b.g. Diktat 126 – Waltzing Star (IRE) (Danehill (USA) 126) [2007 80: **69**
p7g 7m 7d⁶ 7.6g 7d 7.1f⁴ 7.1m⁶ 8.1m³ p8g p10g Oct 31] lengthy gelding: fair handicapper
nowadays: barely stays 1¼m: acts on polytrack, firm and good to soft ground: usually
visored/in cheekpieces: races prominently: gelded after final start. *A. M. Balding*

ISTEAD RISE (IRE) 3 b.g. Mull of Kintyre (USA) 114 – Tommys Queen (IRE) **58**
(Ali-Royal 127) [2007 f8g⁴ 7.1s 10.2g Jul 9] best effort in maidens when fourth at
Southwell on debut, slowly away and soon pushed along. *P. A. Blockley*

ISTIBIAN (IRE) 3 b.g. Sakhee (USA) 136 – Cap Coz (IRE) 110 (Indian Ridge 123) **§§**
[2007 9.9m⁵ p10g p10g p9.5g Nov 12] good-topped gelding: left J. Hammond 5,000 gns
after sole start in France at 2 yrs: little impact in Britain: pulled himself up last 2 starts:
thoroughly ungenuine. *Mrs H. Sweeting*

ISTRIA (USA) 2 b.f. (Mar 20) Zavata (USA) 111 – Estri (USA) (Conquistador Cielo **63** (USA)) [2007 p7g⁵ p7.1g⁶ Nov 22] $12,000Y, 19,000 2-y-o: eighth foal: half-sister to several winners in US, including 6f to 8.3f winner Khayelitsha (by Gold Case): dam US 1m winner: better effort in maidens when fifth at Lingfield: will stay 1m. *R. M. Beckett*

ITALIAN ART (IRE) 2 b.c. (Mar 23) Captain Rio 122 – Sallwa (IRE) (Entrepreneur **87 p** 123) [2007 6d³ 6.1d* Oct 18] €66,000F, €40,000Y, resold €24,000Y: well-made colt: second foal: half-brother to 3-y-o Smash N'Grab: dam French 9.5f/11.5f winner: fairly useful form: confirmed debut promise when winning maiden at Nottingham by 1¼ lengths from Lord Sandicliffe, hard driven to assert: will stay 7f/1m: sent to USA: should go on improving. *R. M. Beckett*

ITALIAN GIRL 3 b.f. Danehill Dancer (IRE) 117 – Little Italy (IRE) 103 (Common **97** Grounds 118) [2007 91: 8m* 8m⁴ 8m⁶ 8.1m⁶ 7d⁶ 10d Oct 19] rangy filly: has scope: useful performer: won minor event at Ascot (by 3 lengths from Silver Pivotal) in May: not discredited and often better than bare results suggest in listed races after, including when sixth to Miss Lucifer at Ascot penultimate outing, denied clear run: stays 1m (pulled too hard at 1¼m): acts on good to firm and good to soft going: sent to USA. *A. P. Jarvis*

ITALIAN GODDESS 2 ch.f. (Feb 22) Medicean 128 – Little Italy (IRE) 103 (Com- **68** mon Grounds 118) [2007 8.3m 8.2m⁴ p7g Oct 24] good-topped filly: third foal: half-sister to 3-y-o Italian Girl and French 1¼m winner Cristal Rose (by Montjeu): dam, 6f to 1½m winner, half-sister to smart stayer Romantic Affair: fair maiden: fourth to Classic Legend at Nottingham: inadequate test final start: will be suited by 1¼m/1½m. *M. L. W. Bell*

ITALIAN ROMANCE 4 b.g. Medicean 128 – Polish Romance (USA) 83 (Danzig **80** (USA)) [2007 82: p8.6g* p8.6g* p9.5d⁴ Dec 28] strong, heavy-topped gelding: fairly useful performer: won maiden in January and handicap in April, both at Wolverhampton: stays 9.5f (possibly not 1½m): acts on polytrack: races prominently. *J. W. Unett*

ITALSTAR (IRE) 3 ch.f. Galileo (IRE) 134 – Jorghinia (FR) (Seattle Slew (USA)) **–** [2007 –p: 16.2s Jul 23] little form. *H. Morrison*

ITCANBEDONE AGAIN (IRE) 8 b.g. Sri Pekan (USA) 117 – Maradata (IRE) 68 **58** (Shardari 134) [2007 65: p8.6g f11g p6g³ 10.2f⁶ 8.2s⁶ p8.6g⁴ 10.2d p12.2g⁵ p12.2g³ p12.2g⁵ Jul 16] tall, good-topped gelding: unimpressive mover: modest performer nowadays: stays 1½m: acts on polytrack and any turf going: effective held up or ridden prominently. *Ian Williams*

IT'S A DATE 2 b.c. (Mar 16) Kyllachy 129 – By Arrangement (IRE) 60 (Bold Arrange- **63 p** ment 127) [2007 7m Aug 10] 26,000Y: useful-looking colt: good walker: sixth foal: half-brother to 8-y-o Turbo and 1½m winner Its Your Bid (by Dilum): dam 1m to 2m winner: 50/1, staying-on eighth of 20 to Tanweer in maiden at Newmarket: will be suited by 1m+: capable of better. *A. King*

IT'S A DREAM (FR) 4 b.g. Kaldounevees (FR) 118 – Bahia Mar (USA) (Arctic Tern **86 d** (USA) 126) [2007 83: 8m⁵ 8g⁵ 8.1g 7d 8.5m 7g 8m 8m Sep 20] useful-looking gelding: fairly useful handicapper: better than bare result first 3 outings in 2007: left D. Elsworth, below form after: stays 10.5f (didn't settle at 11.6f): acts on polytrack and good to firm ground: has been slowly away. *M. W. Easterby*

ITSAWINDUP 3 b.g. Elnadim (USA) 128 – Topwinder (USA) (Topsider (USA)) [2007 **–** –: p7g 7m 8m p12g p10m p7g Dec 30] close-coupled gelding: little form: tried visored. *W. J. Knight*

IT'S JOSR 2 b.g. (May 5) Josr Algarhoud (IRE) 118 – It's So Easy 63 (Shaadi (USA) **68** 126) [2007 7g p7m p8g p8.6g² f8d³ Dec 12] fair maiden: runner-up in nursery at Wolver- hampton: stays 8.6f: acts on polytrack. *I. A. Wood*

ITS MOON (IRE) 3 b.f. Tobougg (IRE) 125 – Shallat (IRE) 59 (Pennekamp (USA) **79** 130) [2007 71: 12.1m* 9.9g² 12g 10g² 12d⁶ 12s* 14g 12.1m⁵ 12.1g³ 12s⁴ Oct 9] smallish, workmanlike filly: fair handicapper: won at Beverley in April and Pontefract in July: stays 1½m: acts on soft and good to firm ground: won juvenile hurdles in November/ December. *T. D. Walford*

IT'S MY DAY (IRE) 2 ch.c. (Apr 29) Soviet Star (USA) 128 – Ezana (Ela-Mana-Mou **64** 132) [2007 p6g 7m 7f⁵ p7g* p7g p8.6g⁶ Nov 27] 10,000Y: leggy colt: half-brother to several winners, including smart 7f (at 2 yrs) to 1½m winner Ebaziya (by Darshaan), dam of 3 Group 1 winners, including Gold Cup winner Enzeli and Irish Oaks winner Ebadiyla: dam French 11.5f winner: fair performer: won nursery at Kempton in September: should stay at least 1m: acts on polytrack and firm going: quirky. *Jane Chapple-Hyam*

IT'S NO PROBLEM (IRE) 3 b.f. Averti (IRE) 117 – Polar Rock 66 (Polar Falcon **60 d**
(USA) 126) [2007 60: p10g³ p9.5g p10f* p10g 10.2f³ 14.1g³ 12g 9g 7.1s 8d⁵ 12g 8f p10g
Sep 18] small filly: modest performer: won claimer at Lingfield in February: effective
at 1¼m to 1¾m: acts on polytrack and firm going: tried tongue tied: usually held up.
M. Salaman

IT'S RUMOURED 7 ch.g. Fleetwood (IRE) 107 – Etourdie (USA) (Arctic Tern –
(USA) 126) [2007 –: p16g p16g Jan 29] fair maiden in 2003: lightly raced and little form
since on Flat: blinkered/visored last 3 starts: won over hurdles in February. *Jean-Rene
Auvray*

ITS SENSATIONAL 2 b.f. (Mar 20) Okawango (USA) 115 – Syringa 61 (Lure (USA) –
131) [2007 6m 8.3d Oct 1] rather leggy filly: third foal: half-sister to Danish 7.5f winner
Late Night Love (by Bluebird): dam 2-y-o 5f seller winner: well beaten in sellers.
K. R. Burke

IT'S THE LIMIT (USA) 8 b.g. Boundary (USA) 117 – Beside (USA) (Sportin' Life –
(USA)) [2007 p16g Feb 14] rangy, good sort: useful handicapper at best, lightly raced:
well held only outing in 2007: stayed 2m: acted on firm going: tried in cheekpieces: put
down after breaking down when winning selling hurdle in June. *W. K. Goldsworthy*

IT'S UNBELIEVABLE (USA) 4 b. or br.g. Stravinsky (USA) 133 – Churn Dat **60**
Butter (USA) (Unbridled (USA) 128) [2007 77: p7g 7.1m 6m 8m 8m 5f⁵ 5g⁶ 5m 5m
Sep 18] lengthy gelding: modest performer nowadays: stays 8.5f: acts on firm ground:
tried blinkered/in cheekpieces: can race freely. *P. T. Midgley*

ITSY BITSY 5 b.m. Danzig Connection (USA) – Cos I Do (IRE) (Double Schwartz **50**
128) [2007 p13.9g p12.2g⁶ p10m Nov 11] seventh foal: half-sister to 9-y-o Mind How
You Go: dam unraced: modest form at best in bumpers: similar form on Flat in maiden/
claimers. *W. J. Musson*

IVANA ILLYICH (IRE) 5 ch.m. Tipsy Creek (USA) 115 – Tolstoya (Northfields **46**
(USA)) [2007 –: 7.5m 8d 7v³ 7.1g⁶ 7g 7.9f 8g 10.1g Aug 17] close-coupled mare:
poor maiden: best at 6f/7f: acts on all turf ground: has worn blinkers/cheekpieces.
J. S. Wainwright

IVANASBO 3 gr.g. Cloudings (IRE) 112 – Vonispet (Cotation) [2007 p6g 7.1d 8.2m **48**
p7.1g⁶ Oct 19] leggy gelding: poor maiden: stays 7f. *C. G. Cox*

IVESTAR (IRE) 2 b.g. (Jan 18) Fraam 114 – Hazardous (Night Shift (USA)) [2007 **79**
6m⁶ 6m⁶ 8d² Sep 20] useful-looking gelding, unfurnished at 2 yrs: keen walker: fair
maiden: upped in trip, improved form when short-head second to Graceful Descent in
minor event at Ayr: stays 1m: acts on good to soft going. *D. Nicholls*

IVORY GALA (FR) 4 b.f. Galileo (IRE) 134 – Rubies From Burma (USA) 104 (Forty –
Niner (USA)) [2007 101: 10.4g⁶ 15g Jul 26] quite good-topped filly: useful form at 3 yrs:
below form in Middleton Stakes at York (stiff task) and listed race at Chantilly (failed to
stay) in 2007: stays 1½m: acts on good to firm going. *B. J. Meehan*

IVORY LACE 6 b.m. Atraf 116 – Miriam 59 (Forzando 122) [2007 89: p7g³ p7g p7g⁵ **96**
p8g⁵ 5.1f 6m⁴ 7m³ 7m* 7g* 7s³ 7m³ 7m* 7g 7m* 7.1m 7d p7g⁶ p8m p8m p8g Dec 16]
rather leggy mare: useful performer: much improved in 2007, winning handicaps at
Lingfield and Goodwood in June, Newmarket in August and Goodwood (best effort, beat
Lavenham by length) in September: below form last 5 outings: effective at 6f/7f: acts on
polytrack, firm and soft going: tried in blinkers/cheekpieces: held up. *S. Woodman*

IVORY SILK 2 b.f. (Mar 2) Diktat 126 – Ivory's Joy 109 (Tina's Pet 121) [2007 p8m³ **67**
p7g³ Dec 29] third foal: half-sister to 5f winner Pride of Joy (by Pursuit of Love): dam 5f/
6f winner, including at 2 yrs: fair form when third in maidens at Lingfield, both in
December: bred to be suited by 5f/6f: very slowly away on debut. *D. K. Ivory*

IVORYS SONG 3 b.f. Averti (IRE) 117 – Katy Ivory (IRE) 68 (Night Shift (USA)) –
[2007 45: p5g p6g⁵ Jan 10] poor maiden: best effort at 5f on fibresand. *D. K. Ivory*

IVY BRIDGE (IRE) 4 b.f. Namid 128 – Chinon (IRE) (Entrepreneur 123) [2007 f6g –
p8g Jan 22] heavy-topped filly: little form. *P. A. Blockley*

IVY CREEK (USA) 4 b.c. Gulch (USA) – Ivy Leaf (IRE) 76 (Nureyev (USA) 131) **115**
[2007 110: 9m⁶ 10.3m³ 12g* 12d* 12m⁵ 14g⁴ 10s³ 12d² Oct 27] tall, leggy, attractive
colt: smart performer: suffered back trouble after final 3-y-o outing: won listed races at
Goodwood (by ½ length from Shahin) and Pontefract (beat The Geezer by 1½ lengths,
wandering) in June: creditable efforts in listed race at Ayr (third to Anna Pavlova) and

totesport Pontefract Castle Stakes, Pontefract—
Ivy Creek hangs right but still readily accounts for a smart field

St Simon Stakes at Newbury (1¾ lengths second to Crime Scene) last 2 starts: best at 1¼m/1½m: acts on soft and good to firm going: often takes strong hold: wears crossed noseband/has been early to post: held up. *G. Wragg*

I WILL IF YOU WILL 3 ch.f. Pursuit of Love 124 – Los Alamos 73 (Keen 116) **53** [2007 f8g⁶ p8.6g⁶ 7.5m p8.6g p12.2g Dec 15] sixth foal: sister to useful 7f (at 2 yrs)/1m winner After You and half-sister to 7f winner Rio Branco (by Efisio), later successful in USA: dam 1¾m/15f winner: modest maiden: stays 1m. *K. A. Ryan*

IZABELA HANNAH 3 ch.f. Kyllachy 129 – Papita (IRE) 77 (Law Society (USA) **54** 130) [2007 72+: 5.1g 6.1g⁴ 6d⁵ p7.1g p7g⁵ Oct 17] just modest maiden in 2007: probably stays 7f: acts on good to firm ground: blinkered last 3 starts. *R. M. Beckett*

IZZIBIZZI 2 b.f. (Jan 24) Medicean 128 – Sleave Silk (IRE) 58 (Unfuwain (USA) 131) **86 +** [2007 6m 7g² p7g² 6.5d² Sep 28] €10,000Y: fourth foal: sister to 3-y-o Wickedish: dam, 1½m and 2m winner, half-sister to useful Irish 9f to 1½m winner Lost In The Rain: fairly useful form: progressed well, second in maiden at Folkestone, minor event at Lingfield and 22-runner sales race at Ascot (beaten neck by Lady Rangali): bred to stay 1m+, but has plenty of speed: once withdrawn at stall. *E. A. L. Dunlop*

J

JAADULL 2 b.c. (Feb 4) Dubai Destination (USA) 127 – Saafeya (IRE) 111 (Sadler's **63 p** Wells (USA) 132) [2007 6m⁶ Jul 13] big, strong colt: sixth foal: closely related to 2003 2-y-o 7f winner Manntab (by Kingmambo) and half-brother to 1m winner Janayen (by Zafonic), both useful: dam 1m to 10.5f winner: 11/1, faded into sixth behind Sporting Art in maiden at Ascot: likely to stay 1m: will improve. *M. Johnston*

JAADY (USA) 3 b.g. Coronado's Quest (USA) 130 – Aljawza (USA) 86 (Riverman **79** (USA) 131) [2007 77p: p8g* p10g p10g² p12g⁵ Jun 13] fair performer: won maiden at Lingfield in March: stays 1¼m (didn't settle at 1½m): raced only on polytrack: sold 24,000 gns in July, sent to Czech Republic. *J. H. M. Gosden*

JAASOOS (IRE) 3 ch.c. Noverre (USA) 125 – Nymphs Echo (IRE) (Mujtahid (USA) **86** 118) [2007 87: 7m² 7.1m⁵ 7d⁴ a7f⁵ Dec 21] leggy, useful-looking colt: fairly useful performer: at least respectable efforts in handicaps prior to leaving M. Jarvis before final outing: will stay 1m: acts on good to firm and good to soft going. *D. J. Selvaratnam, UAE*

JAASSEY 4 b.g. Josr Algarhoud (IRE) 118 – Saaryeh 79 (Royal Academy (USA) 130) **–** [2007 66, a–: 7m 8m 10.5m 7d 8m Aug 1] close-coupled gelding: fair performer at 3 yrs: little form in 2007, leaving A. Crook after third outing: tried in cheekpieces. *P. T. Midgley*

JABAL TARIQ 2 ch.c. (Mar 24) Rock of Gibraltar (IRE) 133 – Sueboog (IRE) 109 **80** (Darshaan 133) [2007 7m 7.1g⁵ 7.1m⁶ 7s³ Sep 26] 300,000Y: big, strong colt: closely related to smart 6f (at 2 yrs) to 9f winner Dunhill Star (by Danehill) and half-brother to 3 winners, including very smart 7f (at 2 yrs) to 1¼m winner Best of The Bests (by Machiavellian): dam won Fred Darling Stakes and fourth in Oaks: fairly useful maiden: third to Mazaaya at Redcar: will stay 1m: acts on soft and good to firm going. *B. W. Hills*

JABBARA (IRE) 4 b.f. Kingmambo (USA) 125 – Isle de France (USA) 115 (Nureyev **64** (USA) 131) [2007 65: p6g p7.1g⁶ p6f² f6g⁶ 5d 5.2d 6m* 5g* 6.1m Sep 7] quite good-topped filly: modest handicapper: won at Folkestone and Beverley within 8 days in August: effective at 5f to 7f: acts on all-weather and firm going: often blinkered. *C. E. Brittain*

JABRAAN (USA) 5 b.g. Aljabr (USA) 125 – Miss Zafonic (FR) 98 (Zafonic (USA) **43** 130) [2007 45: f6g 8.5m p8.6g⁵ 7.6d⁶ 8.3d⁴ 8m p5.1g p9.5g Nov 8] good-bodied, angular gelding: poor maiden: stays 8.6f: acts on all-weather, good to firm and good to soft going: sometimes blinkered/in cheekpieces. *D. W. Chapman*

JACARANDA (IRE) 7 ch.g. Bahhare (USA) 122 – Near Miracle (Be My Guest **74** (USA) 126) [2007 10m* 10.9m⁶ Aug 27] fair handicapper: won amateur event at New-market in July: stays easy 1½m, at least as effective at 1¼m: acts on all-weather, firm and soft going: often wears cheekpieces: fair hurdler. *P. J. Hobbs*

JACARANDA RIDGE 3 ch.f. Indian Ridge 123 – Celtic Fling 77 (Lion Cavern **83** (USA) 117) [2007 8.3m⁴ 8.2g³ 8m⁵ 7g* 7m p7m 7d⁴ 8m⁵ Nov 10] sturdy filly: third foal: closely related to 1m/9f winner Toss The Caber (by Dr Devious) and half-sister to smart 7f/1m winner (including at 2 yrs) Celtic Heroine (by Hernando): dam, 1m winner, closely related to Celtic Swing: fairly useful performer: won maiden at Yarmouth in July: creditable efforts in handicaps last 2 starts: stays 1m: unraced on extremes of going: free-going sort, races prominently. *M. A. Jarvis*

JACKADANDY (USA) 5 b.g. Lear Fan (USA) 130 – Chandra (CAN) (Morning Bob **–** (USA)) [2007 12d 15.8m Aug 7] leggy gelding: has a round action: fair maiden in 2005: no form in 2007 (broke down final start). *B. Storey*

JACK DAWKINS (USA) 2 b.c. (Apr 19) Fantastic Light (USA) 134 – Do The **97 p** Mambo (USA) (Kingmambo (USA) 125) [2007 7s⁵ 7m 7m⁴ 8m* 8g* Oct 26] 15,000Y, 40,000 2-y-o: good-topped colt: third foal: half-brother to useful 2005 2-y-o 7f/1m winner Manbala (by Linamix): dam unraced granddaughter of very smart French per-former up to 1¼m Gabina: useful form: much improved to win competitive nurseries at Doncaster in autumn, quickening well both times: will be suited by 1¼m: acts on good to firm going, promise on soft: will continue progressing. *H. R. A. Cecil*

JACK DAWSON (IRE) 10 b.g. Persian Bold 123 – Dream of Jenny 73 (Caerleon **75** (USA) 132) [2007 83: p13.9g⁵ 16m⁵ 15.4m³ Aug 9] neat gelding: fair handicapper nowa-days: stays easy 2m: acts on polytrack, seems best on good going or firmer on turf: held up. *John Berry*

JACKDAY (IRE) 2 b.g. (Apr 12) Daylami (IRE) 138 – Magic Lady (IRE) (Bigstone **65** (IRE) 126) [2007 7.5g 7m⁶ 7s 7g Oct 20] 18,000Y: strong, lengthy gelding: fifth foal: half-brother to French 1¼m/11f winner Etoile Rose (by Montjeu) and 4-y-o Mulligan's Gold: dam unraced half-sister to smart miler Tamburlaine: fair maiden: sweated/slowly away in nursery final start (gelded after): will be well suited by 1m/1¼m. *T. D. Easterby*

JACK GOT EVEN (USA) 2 ch.c. (Mar 20) Stephen Got Even (USA) 125 – Nara **80** (USA) (Green Forest (USA) 134) [2007 p8g 8.1g 8m 8g Oct 26] $175,000Y, $270,000 2-y-o: good-bodied colt: half-brother to several US winners, including minor stakes winners Irish Daisy (9f, by Allen's Alydar) and Irish Silence (up to 1½m, by Seattle Song): dam unraced granddaughter of very smart French 1m/1¼m performer Perlee: maiden: seemingly fairly useful form when seventh to Twice Over at Newmarket third start: too free in front final one (nursery at Doncaster): raced only at 1m: blinkered last 2 starts: sold 14,000 gns. *B. J. Meehan*

JACKIE KIELY 6 ch.g. Vettori (IRE) 119 – Fudge (Polar Falcon (USA) 126) [2007 **75** 79: f14g² f12g⁴ f11g³ f12g⁵ f12g⁵ f11g³ f12g* 10m 10.2g 10g⁵ 9g 10m³ 10m³ 10.2m **a81** 10m² f14d⁴ Dec 11] leggy gelding: fairly useful handicapper on all-weather, fair on turf: won at Southwell in April: stays 2m (all wins at shorter): acts on all-weather, firm and soft going: usually held up: tough and consistent. *R. Brotherton*

JACK JUNIOR (USA) 3 b. or br.c. Songandaprayer (USA) 118 – Ra Hydee (USA) **111** (Rahy (USA) 115) [2007 103: a9f² 8m 10m² 9d Oct 19] leggy, rather lightly-made colt: smart maiden: highly tried most starts, including when 9½ lengths second to Asiatic Boy in UAE Derby at Nad Al Sheba and 5 lengths seventh of 8 to Excellent Art in St James's Palace Stakes at Royal Ascot first 2 starts in 2007: well below form after, including in maiden at Newmarket on first occasion: stays 9f: acts on dirt, unraced on extremes of turf going. *B. J. Meehan*

JACK OF TRUMPS (IRE) 7 b.g. King's Theatre (IRE) 128 – Queen Caroline (USA) **72** 67 (Chief's Crown (USA)) [2007 92: 10d 12.3m 12.1m Aug 26] strong gelding: fairly useful handicapper at 6 yrs, just fair in 2007: free-going sort (wears crossed noseband), but should stay beyond 1½m: acts on polytrack, firm and soft going: tried tongue tied: sometimes finds little. *G. Wragg*

JACK OLIVER 3 ch.g. Compton Place 125 – Glascoed (Adbass (USA) 102) [2007 75: **78 d** p7g p7g⁶ 7m* 7m 7s² 6s⁴ 7g 7s p7g⁶ Oct 24] tall, unfurnished gelding: fair performer: won handicap at Lingfield in May: well below form last 4 starts: stays easy 7f: acts on polytrack, soft and good to firm going: sold 3,500 gns. *B. J. Meehan*

JACK RACKHAM 3 ch.g. Kyllachy 129 – Hill Welcome 52 (Most Welcome 131) **93** [2007 82: 5f* 5g* 5g³ 6d⁵ 5.6m³ 5g p5.1g Oct 2] strong, sturdy gelding: type to carry condition: fairly useful performer: won maiden at Thirsk in April and handicap at Beverley in May: good third (beaten 2 short heads) in handicap at Doncaster fifth start: should stay 6f: acts on firm going. *B. Smart*

JACK ROLFE 5 b.g. Polish Precedent (USA) 131 – Haboobti (Habitat 134) [2007 70: **82** p10g p12g⁶ p13.9g² p13.9g* 12d⁶ 12f² 12m* p12m³ Oct 6] good-topped gelding: fairly useful handicapper: won at Wolverhampton (apprentices) in March and Newbury in September: stays 1¾m: acts on polytrack, firm and good to soft going: fair form over hurdles. *G. L. Moore*

JACK SULLIVAN (USA) 6 ch.g. Belong To Me (USA) – Provisions (USA) (Devil's **116** Bag (USA)) [2007 119: p7.1g² 7g 7.1m* 7g⁵ 8m⁵ a10.5g p8g* Dec 22] strong, good-topped gelding: smart performer: won minor events at Warwick (by ¾ length from Candidato Roy) in August and Lingfield (best effort in 2007, beat Raptor by 3½ lengths) in December: stays 9f, not quite 1¼m: acts on dirt/polytrack, good to firm and good to soft ground: tried in cheekpieces/blinkers: often tongue tied: reportedly suffered from temperature and off 5 months after reappearance. *G. A. Butler*

JACONET (USA) 2 ch.f. (Apr 12) Hussonet (USA) – Radiant Rocket (USA) (Peteski **62** (CAN) 125) [2007 6m³ 6m⁵ p7.1g Sep 28] $50,000Y: good-quartered filly: first foal: dam US maiden: modest form in maidens: best efforts at 6f on good to firm going. *T. D. Barron*

JACQUART (NZ) 5 b.g. Zabeel (NZ) – She Wishes (NZ) (Kenfair (NZ)) [2007 8.1m **82** p7g⁵ p6m⁵ p7.1g Oct 30] useful-looking New Zealand-bred gelding: won maiden at Te Rapa in 2005 and minor event at Tauranga in 2006: fairly useful form in handicaps in Britain in 2007: likely to prove best at 6f: acts on polytrack: wore cheekpieces last 2 starts: sold 800 gns in November. *C. G. Cox*

JADAARA 2 b.f. (Feb 4) Red Ransom (USA) – Beraysim 111 (Lion Cavern (USA) 117) **90 p** [2007 7.5m* Aug 25] third foal: half-sister to useful UAE 6f to 1m winner Almaram (by A P Indy) and fairly useful 9.5f winner Noubian (by Diesis): dam 7f winner: 14/1, won maiden at Beverley by 1½ lengths from Badalona: will stay at least 1m: useful prospect. *M. Johnston*

JADAN (IRE) 6 b.g. Imperial Ballet (IRE) 110 – Sports Post Lady (IRE) 72 (M Double **64** M (USA)) [2007 63: 5m 5.9g 5m 5g² 5d 5g⁵ 5d² 5m³ 5s* 5g 5.1g Oct 31] sturdy gelding: modest handicapper: won at Ayr in October: races mostly at 5f: acts on soft and good to firm ground: tried in cheekpieces, blinkered last 4 starts. *E. J. Alston*

JAFARU 3 b.g. Silver Hawk (USA) 123 – Rafha 123 (Kris 135) [2007 –: 9.9m⁵ 12.1g* **71** 12.1g* 11m² 9.9s³ 12m 16g Nov 8] stocky gelding: fair handicapper: won at Hamilton and Chepstow in May: pulled up at Folkestone on penultimate start: stays 1½m: acts on soft and good to firm going: usually blinkered. *G. A. Butler*

JAFFNA 5 b.m. Makbul 104 – Pondicherry (USA) 64 (Sir Wimborne (USA) 118) [2007 **–** 8.1m f7g p9.5g Jun 30] half-sister to several winners, including useful 1m (at 2 yrs)/

1¼m (in France) winner Teresa Balbi (by Master Willie): dam 7f winner: little form in bumpers/maidens on Flat. *R. T. Phillips*

JAFRA (IRE) 2 ch.g. (Mar 9) Choisir (AUS) 126 – Polish Saga 59 (Polish Patriot (USA) 128) [2007 5m 5s 5d 7.5m 7.1g⁴ Oct 5] good-bodied gelding: modest maiden: stays 7.5f: tried blinkered (has hung). *R. M. Whitaker*   **55**

JAGGER 7 gr.g. Linamix (FR) 127 – Sweetness Herself 106 (Unfuwain (USA) 131) [2007 7d 8.5g 12d p12m⁵ Dec 9] smallish, quite attractive gelding: smart performer in 2005: raced in Australia for D. Hayes in 2006/early-2007, failing to make frame in 10 races: off 6½ months and returned to current trainer, well-held last of 5 in handicap at Lingfield: stays 2¼m: acts on polytrack, firm and good to soft going, possibly unsuited by soft: edgy type: tried tongue tied. *G. A. Butler*   **–**

JAGO (SWI) 4 b.g. Brief Truce (USA) 126 – Jariyah (USA) (It's The One (USA)) [2007 10.8v⁵ 10g³ 8g³ p12g p10m² p10g² Nov 17] tall gelding: winner twice in Switzerland, including minor event at Avenches in 2006, and second in Swiss 2000 Guineas at Diels-dorf earlier that year: left J. Stadelmann after third start, fair form in handicaps in Britain: stays 11f: acts on polytrack, unraced on going firmer than good on turf. *A. M. Hales*   **72**

JAHASH 9 ch.g. Hernando (FR) 127 – Jalsun (Jalmood (USA) 126) [2007 p16g May 2] leggy, quite good-topped gelding: modest handicapper for Sir Mark Prescott in 2002: unseated leaving stall in handicap at Kempton sole Flat start since: effective with or without blinkers. *Simon Earle*   **–**

JAJOLEEN (IRE) 4 ch.f. Titus Livius (FR) 115 – Radeda (IRE) (Great Commotion (USA) 123) [2007 –: 9s 12.1m Sep 7] first foal: dam unraced: poor maiden: left Andrew Oliver in Ireland after reappearance: stays 1½m: acts on firm ground. *P. A. Blockley*   **41**

JAKAM (IRE) 2 b.g. (Apr 2) Diktat 126 – Key Virtue (USA) 78 (Atticus (USA) 121) [2007 f6d⁵ Dec 14] second foal: half-brother to Irish 1¼m winner Alexander Goldmine (by Dansili): dam, maiden (stayed 1m), closely related to very smart miler Among Men: 2/1 favourite, fifth to The Twelve Steps in maiden at Southwell, racing freely and fading: should improve. *E. J. O'Neill*   **54 p**

JAKEINI (IRE) 4 b.g. Rossini (USA) 118 – Talita Kumi (IRE) (High Estate 127) [2007 80: 5f² 5m⁵ 5.1f 5m 5f 5.2d⁴ Aug 26] strong gelding: fairly useful handicapper: good second at Thirsk on reappearance: below form after: should prove as effective at 6f as 5f: acts on polytrack and any turf going: sometimes wears cheekpieces. *E. S. McMahon*   **80**

JALAMID (IRE) 5 b.g. Danehill (USA) 126 – Vignelaure (IRE) 74 (Royal Academy (USA) 130) [2007 98: 6g 8m³ 8d 6g 8m⁵ 10.1g 8m Sep 18] big, strong gelding: useful handicapper at 4 yrs: very much on downgrade in 2007, leaving G. Bravery after sixth start: stays 1m: unraced on extremes of going: usually tongue tied: held up. *M. A. Barnes*   **64 d**

JALANDY (IRE) 4 b.f. Desert Millennium (IRE) – Jaldini (IRE) (Darshaan 133) [2007 12g 14s 9v³ 7s 12.5m⁴ p10m Dec 10] modest maiden: left E. Sheehy in Ireland prior to final start: stays 1½m: acts on polytrack, heavy and good to firm ground. *S. Curran*   **52**

JALEELA (USA) 3 b.f. Kingmambo (USA) 125 – Sultana (USA) (Storm Cat (USA)) [2007 8m³ 8m⁵ 8.2m⁶ p8m Oct 6] unfurnished filly: first foal: dam, US 6f winner, sister to high-class miler Aljabr: fairly useful form: won maiden at Newmarket in May: stayed 1m: acted on good to firm ground: visits Mr Greeley. *W. J. Haggas*   **84**

JALIL (USA) 3 b. or br.c. Storm Cat (USA) – Tranquility Lake (USA) 120 (Rahy (USA) 115) [2007 78p: 10g² 9.8m* p8g² Oct 12] big, good sort: useful form: landed odds in maiden at Ripon in June, idling: much improved when head second to Troubadour in handicap at Lingfield final outing, caught only close home: stays 1¼m: raced only on polytrack and good ground or firmer: open to further improvement. *Saeed bin Suroor*   **102 p**

JALMIRA (IRE) 6 b.m. Danehill Dancer (IRE) 117 – Jaldini (IRE) (Darshaan 133) [2007 93: 10m⁶ 9.5m 9.5m⁵ 11.3s⁵ 10.5d² 9v 8.5g 8g* 10g 9.5g⁴ 8.5g* 8g* p8g³ Nov 16] lengthy mare: smart performer: won 24-runner Irish Cambridgeshire (Handicap) at the Curragh (by ¾ length from Akua'ba) in September and listed events at Cork (by ½ length from Hard Rock City) in October and Newmarket (best effort, beat Tell by neck) in November: seems best at 1m to 10.5f: acts on any going: held up. *C. F. Swan, Ireland*   **112**

JAL MUSIC 2 ch.c. (Apr 19) Ishiguru (USA) 114 – Musica 82 (Primo Dominie 121) [2007 5m 6d⁴ Aug 1] 12,000F, 26,000Y: seventh foal: half-brother to 2002 2-y-o 5f winner Piccatune (by Piccolo) and 1999 2-y-o 5f winner Coco de Mer (by Prince Sabo), both fairly useful: dam 5f winner, including at 2 yrs: better effort in maidens when fourth to Oasis Wind at Leicester: may prove best at 5f/6f: sold 8,500 gns. *L. M. Cumani*   **64**

JALONS BRIDEWELL 2 b.c. (Apr 14) Compton Place 125 – Inflation 68 (Primo   –
Dominie 121) [2007 p7g Oct 23] 50/1, well held in maiden at Lingfield: bred for speed.
M. Quinn

JAMAAHIR (USA) 4 b.g. Bahri (USA) 125 – Elrehaan 96 (Sadler's Wells (USA) 132)   **68 d**
[2007 65: 10d⁶ 9.9g 8.1s 10d⁶ 11.6m 14.1d Aug 16] rather leggy, useful-looking gelding:
has a round action: fair maiden: below form after reappearance: stays 1¼m: acts on soft
going: tried tongue tied: tends to race freely/carry head awkwardly. *S. Lycett*

JAMAALI (USA) 2 ch.f. (Feb 25) Langfuhr (CAN) 124 – Raajiya (USA) 83 (Gulch   **– p**
(USA)) [2007 6m Oct 4] good-bodied filly: has scope: third foal: half-sister to fairly
useful 2005 2-y-o 7f winner Dahaaleez (by Red Ransom): dam, 7f winner, half-sister to
Dewhurst Stakes winner Mujahid: 33/1, upset in/slow from stall when last in maiden at
Newmarket: sent to France: should progress. *M. P. Tregoning*

JAMAAR 5 ch.g. Nashwan (USA) 135 – Kissogram 120 (Caerleon (USA) 132) [2007   –
71: 16g Apr 24] workmanlike gelding: fair maiden handicapper at 4 yrs: well beaten sole
start in 2007: stays 16.5f: acts on polytrack: tried tongue tied: sold 2,000 gns in August,
sent to Sweden. *C. N. Kellett*

JAMAICAN FLIGHT (USA) 14 b.h. Sunshine Forever (USA) – Kalamona (USA)   –
(Hawaii) [2007 50: p16.5g 18g 21.6m 17.1m⁶ p16.5g Nov 12] leggy horse: fairly useful
performer in his prime: firmly on downgrade: tried visored. *Mrs S. Lamyman*

JAMBORETTA (IRE) 3 b.f. Danehill (USA) 126 – Jiving 69 (Generous (IRE) 139)   **94**
[2007 8.2m³ 9g* 8.1g 9g² 10m² Sep 14] 575,000Y: strong, close-coupled filly: fourth
foal: sister to a winner in US and half-sister to 5-y-o Excusez Moi: dam, ran twice, half-
sister to excellent broodmare Hasili: fairly useful form: won maiden at Goodwood in
May: good second in handicaps there and Sandown (beaten ¾ length by Venerable) last 2
starts: stays 1¼m, should prove at least as effective back at 1m. *Sir Michael Stoute*

JAMES CAIRD (IRE) 7 ch.g. Catrail (USA) 123 – Polish Saga 59 (Polish Patriot   **86**
(USA) 128) [2007 96: p11g⁴ 10.1s 8.3f⁵ 10m May 25] leggy gelding: fairly useful
handicapper nowadays: probably stays 11f: acts on polytrack, firm and good to soft
going: tried blinkered: held up: sold 11,500 gns in July and joined J. Clements in Ireland:
poor form over hurdles. *M. H. Tompkins*

JAMES DEAN (IRE) 2 b.c. (Mar 14) Clodovil (IRE) 116 – Karenaragon (Aragon 118)   **83 p**
[2007 p7.1g² Sep 28] €47,000Y: fifth foal: half-brother to 2 winners by Alhaarth, including 3-y-o Zain: dam, of little account, sister to useful sprinter in Britain/US Evening
Promise, out of half-sister to Bandari: 20/1, neck second to Pearl Dealer in maiden at
Wolverhampton, always prominent: will stay 1m: should do better. *P. F. I. Cole*

JAMES'S LASS (IRE) 2 ch.f. (Jan 28) Daggers Drawn (USA) 114 – Kyra Crown   –
(IRE) (Astronef 116) [2007 5g 6m 5m 6s Oct 4] €2,000F: lengthy, angular filly: seventh
foal: sister to fairly useful 5f (including at 2 yrs) winner Sir Ernest and half-sister to 3
winners, including 5-y-o Hamburg Springer: dam French 2-y-o 7.5f winner: no form.
R. A. Fahey

JAMES STREET (IRE) 4 b.g. Fruits of Love (USA) 127 – Humble Mission (Shack   **64**
(USA) 118) [2007 80: p8g p8g 10m 12.6d⁴ p6g p5.1g p8g p8g p8g p7g⁶ f7d⁶ Dec 15]
quite double-topped gelding: modest handicapper nowadays: left J. R. Best after front
start: best at 7f/1m: acts on polytrack, firm and good to soft ground: often wears headgear.
Peter Grayson

JAMIESON GOLD (IRE) 4 b.g. Desert Style (IRE) 121 – Princess of Zurich (IRE)   **93**
(Law Society (USA) 130) [2007 98: 8g 7.1d 7m 7.1d* 7d⁴ 7m 7d Oct 19] useful-looking
gelding: useful handicapper at 3 yrs, fairly useful in 2007: won at Sandown in August:
well below form last 2 starts: stays 7f: acts on soft and good to firm going: sold 10,000
gns. *B. W. Hills*

JA MYFORD 3 b.g. Auction House (USA) 120 – Daleside Ladybird 66 (Tolomeo 127)   **63**
[2007 8g 9.8g 8m 12d² 12s³ 16.2s 12m⁴ p12g 12.4d Oct 16] tall, workmanlike gelding:
modest maiden: stays 1½m (well held at 2m): acts on polytrack, good to firm and good to
soft going: in cheekpieces last 3 starts. *P. T. Midgley*

JANE OF ARC (FR) 3 ch.f. Trempolino 135 – Aerleon Jane 89 (Caerleon   **58**
(USA) 132) [2007 75: 10f 11.6g⁶ 9.1d 7m⁶ 8m⁵ 8g 10g³ 10.1m 9.1s Oct 26] good-bodied
filly: just modest performer in 2007: left M. Tompkins after second outing: stays 1¼m:
acts on good to firm ground. *J. S. Goldie*

JANE'S DELIGHT (IRE) 2 b.f. (Mar 15) Namid 128 – Revolving (USA) 79 (Devil's   **68**
Bag (USA)) [2007 5m p5.1g⁴ 6v* 6m⁶ p6g⁴ Aug 20] 5,500F, 20,000Y: good-bodied filly:

first foal: dam, Irish 2-y-o 5f winner, out of half-sister to dam of Breeders' Cup Sprint winner Elmhurst: fair performer: won seller at Ripon (left P. Haslam 12,800 gns) in July: best form at 6f: acts on polytrack and heavy ground: usually visored. *G. R. Oldroyd*

JANE'S PAYOFF (IRE) 2 b.f. (Jan 26) Danetime (IRE) 121 – Alimony (IRE) 77 – (Groom Dancer (USA) 128) [2007 f7d5 Dec 20] €26,000Y, 8,000 2-y-o: first foal: dam, Irish 7f winner, sister to smart 6f (at 2 yrs)/7f winner Thrilling Day, later successful in Grade 3 8.5f event in USA: 10/1, well held in maiden at Southwell. *Mrs L. C. Jewell*

JANET'S DELIGHT 2 b.f. (Jan 20) Erhaab (USA) 127 – Ishona (Selkirk (USA) 129) **57** [2007 7.1s4 7g 7m6 6m p6g4 p7m5 p7.1g6 p8m Nov 11] fourth foal: half-sister to Irish 1m winner Fields of Green (by Royal Applause): dam unraced: modest maiden: should stay 1m: acts on polytrack and good to firm going. *S. Curran*

JANINA 2 b.f. (Feb 1) Namid 128 – Lady Dominatrix (IRE) 112 (Danehill Dancer (IRE) **96** 117) [2007 5g4 5g6 6g6 Jun 22] 40,000F, 110,000Y: strong, well-made filly: first foal: dam 5f (including at 2 yrs)/6f winner: useful form: won maiden at Haydock in April and listed race at York (by length from Tia Mia) in May: 4/1, stretched by longer trip when sixth to Nijoom Dubai in Albany Stakes at Royal Ascot: not seen after: should prove best at 5f. *B. W. Hills*

JARDINES BAZAAR 3 b.g. Halling (USA) 133 – Alumisiyah (USA) 93 (Danzig **53** (USA)) [2007 50: 10m4 12s Jul 18] tall, leggy gelding: modest maiden: should prove as effective at 1m as 1¼m: acts on good to firm ground. *T. D. Easterby*

JARVO 6 b.g. Revoque (IRE) 124 – Pinkie Rose (FR) (Kenmare (FR) 125) [2007 54: **63** p10g4 p11g4 p12.2g 10.2f2 10.1m* p9.5g* p11g2 10.1m3 9.9m 10m6 p10g Dec 12] sturdy gelding: modest performer: won minor event at Yarmouth in April and apprentice handicap at Wolverhampton in May: stays 11f: acts on polytrack, firm and soft going: tried in tongue tie/headgear. *I. W. McInnes*

JASER 2 ch.c. (May 17) Alhaarth (IRE) 126 – Waafiah 57 (Anabaa (USA) 130) [2007 **71** 7m 8m p8m* Nov 26] good-bodied colt: has moderate, quick action: third foal: brother to 4-y-o Ragad: dam, maiden (stayed 7f), out of Prix Morny winner First Waltz: fair form: much improved to win maiden at Lingfield final start: may prove best up to 1m. *P. W. Chapple-Hyam*

JASMINES HERO (USA) 2 b.c. (May 14) War Chant (USA) 126 – Ryn (USA) (Mr **74** Prospector (USA)) [2007 6m6 6m5 6m4 p7g 7s5 a7f2 Dec 13] rangy colt: has scope: fair maiden: left J. S. Moore before final outing (tongue tied): stays 7f: acts on dirt, soft and good to firm going. *A. Manuel, UAE*

JASOORA 2 b.f. (Mar 5) Mark of Esteem (IRE) 137 – Kotdiji (Mtoto 134) [2007 p7m **64** p8.6g4 p8g Nov 14] 37,000F: second foal: dam unraced half-sister to 1000 Guineas winner Ameerat (by Mark of Esteem): modest form in maidens (all on polytrack): should stay 1m. *M. P. Tregoning*

JASTAANHI 2 b.f. (Apr 6) Superior Premium 122 – Cavern Breeze (Lion Cavern **56** (USA) 117) [2007 5d 6.1s2 5s4 5.2f3 p5.1d6 p7.1d Dec 28] 5,200Y: second foal: half-sister to 4-y-o Cheveley Flyer: dam unraced half-sister to smart sprinter/miler Nigrasine: modest maiden: best efforts when in frame, making running: should prove best at 5f/6f: acts on firm and soft going. *J. A. Pickering*

JAUFRETTE 4 b.f. Kayf Tara 130 – Jucinda 58 (Midyan (USA) 124) [2007 –: p10g – 12.1m p16g p12g Nov 16] little form. *Dr J. R. J. Naylor*

JAWAAB (IRE) 3 ch.g. King's Best (USA) 132 – Canis Star (Wolfhound (USA) 126) **82** [2007 78: 8g5 10d 8.1m6 7d3 7g 7m4 7s4 8.1g* 8.3g3 8d4 10d2 Oct 16] compact gelding: fairly useful handicapper: won at Haydock in September: good efforts in frame after: stays 1¼m: acts on soft and good to firm going: tried in cheekpieces: patiently ridden. *M. A. Buckley*

JAWAANEB (USA) 3 ch.f. Kingmambo (USA) 125 – Khazayin (USA) 74 (Bahri **87** (USA) 125) [2007 8m 7m6 8g6 10.9d* 11.5m2 11.5s2 14g3 15.9m2 15.9m2 16m4 Oct 3] smallish filly: second foal: closely related to useful 2005 2-y-o 6f winner (stays 1¼m) Jaish (by Seeking The Gold): dam, maiden (stayed 1¼m), sister to Sakhee: fairly useful handicapper: won at Warwick in June: good efforts in frame after: stayed 2m: acted on soft and good to firm ground: was effective held up or making running: consistent: visits Medaglia d'Oro. *J. L. Dunlop*

JAYANJAY 8 b.g. Piccolo 121 – Morica 88 (Moorestyle 137) [2007 95, a83: 5g 5m p6g **72** 6s 5.2s 6d* 5d 6f 6d4 p6g3 p6g6 5.3d6 p5m4 5.3d6 p5g Oct 24] close-coupled gelding: **a64** fair handicapper on turf, modest on all-weather: won at Brighton in July: effective at

5f to easy 7f: acts on polytrack, firm and soft going: tried in headgear: held up: none too reliable. *P. Mitchell*

JAYER GILLES 7 br.g. Busy Flight 122 – Jadidh 64 (Touching Wood (USA) 127) **62** [2007 62: 15d 17.2f* 16f 16m⁴ Aug 17] leggy, dipped-backed gelding: fluent mover: modest handicapper: won at Bath (first success) in June: stays 2¼m: acts on polytrack, firm and good to soft going: visored last 3 starts. *Dr J. R. J. Naylor*

JAY GEE WIGMO 2 b.c. (Feb 24) First Trump 118 – Queen of Shannon (IRE) 76 – (Nordico (USA)) [2007 5s 6m 6m 8d Oct 18] stocky colt: no form: should stay 7f/1m. *A. W. Carroll*

JAYZEE (IRE) 3 b.f. Iron Mask (USA) 117 – Golden Concorde (Super Concorde – (USA) 128) [2007 –: f7g Jan 11] little form. *P. D. Deegan, Ireland*

JAZAMATAZ 2 ch.f. (Apr 2) Compton Admiral 121 – Tough Nell (IRE) 61 (Archway – (IRE) 115) [2007 p7g 7m Jul 12] third foal: dam ran 3 times at 5f/6f: well held in maidens: dead. *Tom Dascombe*

JAZENIO 2 b.f. (Mar 19) Auenadler (GER) 114 – Jade Chequer 71 (Green Desert **57** (USA) 127) [2007 p7.1d p6s⁴ Dec 21] 6,000Y: fifth foal: sister to German 2003 2-y-o 7.5f winner Jurako and half-sister to German 2005 2-y-o 7f winner Jade Rheinberg (by Platini): dam, sprint maiden, out of half-sister to Ouija Board: much better effort in maidens at Wolverhampton when fourth to Wise Melody, fading. *K. A. Ryan*

JAZRAWY 5 b.g. Dansili 127 – Dalila di Mare (IRE) (Bob Back (USA) 124) [2007 64: **80** f12g* f12g* f12g* p12g f11g⁴ Mar 28] short-backed, deep-girthed gelding: fairly useful performer: won claimer in January (claimed from P. Hiatt £8,000) and handicaps (2) in February, all at Southwell: stays 1¾m: acts on all-weather, firm and good to soft going: tried tongue tied. *D. Carroll*

JAZZ AT THE SANDS (USA) 4 ch.g. Forest Wildcat (USA) 120 – Dahlia's Krissy – (USA) (Kris S (USA)) [2007 50: p5.1g Jan 15] workmanlike gelding: modest maiden at 3 yrs: well held only start in 2007: tried blinkered, usually visored. *D. Shaw*

JAZZING ABOUT (USA) 2 b. or br.c. (Apr 14) Dixie Union (USA) 121 – Erstwhile **44** (USA) (Arts And Letters (USA)) [2007 5.1g Apr 21] 20/1, hung/weakened when seventh in maiden at Nottingham in spring. *P. A. Blockley*

JAZZ JAM 2 ch.f. (Mar 15) Pivotal 124 – Applaud (USA) 105 (Rahy (USA) 115) [2007 **92** 6d³ 6.1g 7m³ 8f* 8g² Nov 3] stocky filly: seventh foal: half-sister to 3-y-o Reebal and winner in US by Gone West: dam 2-y-o 5f/6f (Cherry Hinton Stakes) winner: fairly useful form: won nursery at Pontefract in September: further improvement when short-head second to Classic Legend in listed race at Newmarket (hung right under pressure): stays 1m: acts on firm going. *P. F. I. Cole*

JAZZ ROMANCE (IRE) 2 ch.f. (Feb 8) Choisir (AUS) 126 – Music In My Life – (IRE) 59 (Law Society (USA) 130) [2007 p6g p6g p6g Sep 13] 21,000Y: half-sister to several winners, including 1m (at 2 yrs) to 2¼m winner Galleon Beach (by Shirley Heights) and Italian 9f to 10.5f winner Musical Score (by Blushing Flame), both useful: dam, maiden (stayed 1m), out of half-sister to very smart 1m/1¼m performer Bach: no form in maidens. *D. Shaw*

JAZZ STICK (IRE) 2 ch.c. (May 11) Choisir (AUS) 126 – Basin Street Blues (IRE) **67 d** 82 (Dolphin Street (FR) 125) [2007 5m⁵ 6m⁵ 5m 6d 7m⁶ 5g³ 6g 7.1d 6s 5g⁵ Nov 8] smallish colt: fair maiden: best effort second start (left T. Stack in Ireland after third, I. Semple after eighth): stays 6f: usually wears headgear: tried tongue tied. *D. A. Nolan*

JEBEL ALI (IRE) 4 b.g. Fruits of Love (USA) 127 – Assertive Lass (USA) (Assert **83** 134) [2007 83: p10g³ p12g² p12g p10g³ Jul 1] tall gelding: fairly useful handicapper: creditable efforts 3 of 4 starts in 2007: stays 1½m: acts on polytrack, good to firm and good to soft ground: tried in headgear. *B. Gubby*

JEBEL TARA 2 b. or ch.c. (Mar 20) Diktat 126 – Chantilly (FR) (Sanglamore (USA) **90** 126) [2007 5m⁵ 6d² 6s* 5m 7m 6.5m 6m⁶ 6m Oct 5] 18,000Y: lengthy, good-topped colt: has scope: fifth foal: dam unraced half-sister to useful 1m/9f winner Penang Pearl: fairly useful performer (ran as Jebel Tarqak on debut): won maiden at Yarmouth in June: always highly tried after, apparent best effort when last of 6 in Mill Reef Stakes at Newbury: probably stays 7f: acts on soft and good to firm going: once tongue tied. *C. E. Brittain*

JEDBURGH 6 b.h. Selkirk (USA) 129 – Conspiracy 98 (Rudimentary (USA) 118) **100** [2007 116: 8.1g 7.1m 7m 7g⁶ 7g 7m³ 7m 7d Oct 19] strong, compact horse: smart performer at 5 yrs, just useful in 2007: pick of efforts at Goodwood fourth to sixth outings, including third to South Cape in handicap: best at 7f: acts on good to firm going, possibly not on good to soft: blinkered: usually held up. *J. L. Dunlop*

JEDEDIAH 2 b.g. (Feb 28) Hernando (FR) 127 – Penelewey 97 (Groom Dancer (USA) 128) [2007 7g⁵ 7.1d² 8.1d* 8.1g⁵ 8s⁵ Oct 13] 10,000F, 35,000Y: smallish, quite attractive gelding: first foal: dam 6f/7f winner: useful performer: won maiden at Sandown (by length from Kandahar Run) in August: good 5 lengths fifth to Ibn Khaldun in Autumn Stakes at Ascot final start (gelded after): will stay 1¼m: raced only on good or softer going (has been heavily bandaged). *A. M. Balding* **95**

JEEPSTAR 7 b.g. Muhtarram (USA) 125 – Jungle Rose 90 (Shirley Heights 130) [2007 82: p16g p13.9g⁵ f16g⁴ 14.1m⁵ 15d² p12g⁵ May 23] leggy, lightly-made gelding: fairly useful handicapper: effective at 1½m to 2m: acts on polytrack, firm and soft ground: wore cheekpieces last 2 outings: front runner: sold 26,000 gns, joined Venetia Williams. *S. C. Williams* **83**

JEER (IRE) 3 ch.g. Selkirk (USA) 129 – Purring (USA) 79 (Mountain Cat (USA)) [2007 78p: 9.8g* 10.4g² 10.1g Jun 2] rather leggy, useful-looking gelding: has a quick, unimpressive action: fairly useful form: won maiden at Ripon in April: much better form when 1¾ lengths second to Spice Route in handicap at York next time: very jarred up after final start, then gelded: stays 10.4f: raced only on polytrack and good/heavy going on turf. *E. A. L. Dunlop* **91**

JELLY MO 2 b.f. (Feb 27) Royal Applause 124 – Flawless 107 (Warning 136) [2007 6g 6d 6d⁵ 7.1g p7g⁵ Oct 31] 16,500F, €38,000Y: leggy filly: fourth foal: half-sister to 3-y-o Duke of Tuscany: dam 2-y-o 7f winner: fair maiden: stays 7f: acts on polytrack and good to soft going. *J. W. Hills* **69**

JELLYTOT (USA) 4 b.f. Minardi (USA) 119 – Dounine (Kaldoun (FR) 122) [2007 68: f7g⁵ f7g 7m f7g⁶ 6.1g² 7m 6s 5d 6m Aug 4] neat filly: fair performer: mostly below form after reappearance: stays 1m, at least as effective at 6f/7f: acts on fibresand, good to firm and good to soft going: tried blinkered. *J. O'Reilly* **66 d**

JEMBER RED 4 b.f. Polish Precedent (USA) 131 – Arabellajill 97 (Aragon (USA) 118) [2007 –: p8.6g f8g f6g⁵ f6g² f6g² 5g 5g p6g f6g⁶ Dec 27] lengthy filly: poor maiden: stays 6f: acts on fibresand: blinkered/visored. *B. Smart* **43**

JEMILIAH 2 b.f. (Mar 19) Dubai Destination (USA) 127 – Cape Cod (IRE) 62 (Unfuwain (USA) 131) [2007 6g p6g 7d p7g Oct 24] 26,000F, 42,000Y: sturdy, close-coupled filly: second foal: dam, maiden, sister to useful 7f/1m winner Abeyr: poor maiden: stays 7f: blinkered final start (flattered): sold 800 gns. *B. J. Meehan* **42**

JEMIMA GODFREY 3 b.f. Ishiguru (USA) 114 – Quantum Lady 79 (Mujadil (USA) 119) [2007 –: p7g p8g⁵ p8g* p8.6g² p10f³ p10g Mar 26] modest performer: won claimer at Lingfield in February: claimed from J. Pearce after fourth outing: stayed easy 1¼m: raced only on polytrack: tongue tied except last 3 starts: dead. *M. J. Gingell* **52**

JEMIMA'S ART 2 b. or br.f. (Mar 13) Fantastic Light (USA) 134 – Subya 107 (Night Shift (USA)) [2007 7s 7g 7f Aug 12] 52,000F, 55,000Y: leggy filly: half-sister to several winners, including smart 1¼m/1½m winner Villa Carlotta (by Rainbow Quest) and fairly useful 7f winner Subyan Dreams (by Spectrum): dam 5f (at 2 yrs) to 1¼m winner: poor maiden: will be suited by middle distances. *M. W. Easterby* **47**

JENDAS JEM 2 b.f. (Feb 14) Josr Algarhoud (IRE) 118 – Miss Hit 82 (Efisio 120) [2007 7g⁵ 7.1d Sep 17] 1,000F, 2,000Y: close-coupled filly: first foal: dam 5f/6f winner: well held in sellers. *Mrs A. Duffield* **–**

JENINSKY (USA) 2 ch.f. (Feb 3) Stravinsky (USA) 133 – Don't Ruffle Me (USA) (Pine Bluff (USA)) [2007 6d³ p6m* Oct 13] $13,000Y, £21,000 2-y-o: big, workmanlike filly: first foal: dam, US stakes-placed winning sprinter (including at 2 yrs), out of half-sister to Kentucky Oaks winner Lite Light: fairly useful form: confirmed debut promise when winning maiden at Kempton by 5 lengths, still green (struggled with bend) but forging clear until eased late on: will prove best at 5f/6f: type to go on improving. *P. J. McBride* **90 p**

JENISE (IRE) 4 b.f. Orpen (USA) 116 – Griqualand (Connaught 130) [2007 51: p8.6g Jan 17] modest maiden at 3 yrs: well below form sole start in 2007: stays 7f: acts on polytrack. *Mark Campion* **–**

JENNIE JEROME (IRE) 2 br.f. (Apr 6) Pivotal 124 – Colourfast (IRE) 88 (Spectrum (IRE) 126) [2007 6m Oct 4] 130,000Y: second foal: dam, Irish 1m winner, half-sister to dam of Shirocco: 7/1, eighth to Shabiba in maiden at Newmarket: will stay 1m: capable of better. *B. J. Meehan* **67 p**

*Betfred Mile, Sandown—Jeremy is confidently ridden stepped up in trip
and has too much finishing speed for Bahia Breeze (second left) and Take A Bow*

JENNIFER'S DREAM (IRE) 2 b.f. (Feb 16) Statue of Liberty (USA) 115 – Elara **80**
(USA) (Spinning World (USA) 130) [2007 6d 5m* 6g⁵ 6g Nov 2] €28,000Y: first foal:
dam, French sprint maiden, half-sister to smart 1¼m winner Flame Valley: fairly useful
performer: won maiden at Ripon in August: stiff task final start (listed race at Newmarket): effective at 5f/6f: acts on good to firm going. *K. A. Ryan*

JENNIFERS JOY (IRE) 2 b.f. (Mar 15) Green Desert (USA) 127 – Perils of Joy **75**
(IRE) 83 (Rainbow Quest (USA) 134) [2007 5g³ 5m* 5g 5m p5g⁵ 6.5m 7g⁴ 7m Oct 6]
€160,000F, €150,000Y: neat filly: half-sister to several winners, including useful Irish/
US 7f/1m winner Hymn of Love (by Barathea): dam Irish 1m winner: fair performer:
won maiden at Warwick in May: stayed 7f: acted on polytrack and good to firm going:
dead. *M. R. Channon*

JENNVERSE 5 b.m. Opening Verse (USA) 126 – Jennelle 97 (Nomination 125) [2007 **42**
57: p7g⁶ Jan 3] modest performer at 4 yrs: just poor form sole start in 2007: effective at
6f, should stay 1m: acts on polytrack and good to soft going. *D. K. Ivory*

JENNY SOBA 4 b.f. Observatory (USA) 131 – Majalis 79 (Mujadil (USA) 119) [2007 **59**
66: 9.9m 9.8g⁵ 9.9g 10s⁴ 10m 8m⁶ 10f* 9.8g 9.8m⁶ 15.8g⁴ 15.8s⁵ p16.5g p12.2g p13.9g
p13.9g³ p12.2s⁵ Dec 21] lengthy filly: modest performer: won seller at Redcar in August:
claimed from R. Whitaker £6,000 after ninth outing: stays 1¾m: acts on polytrack, firm
and soft going: tried visored/in cheekpieces. *Lucinda Featherstone*

JENTRIS GIRL (IRE) 3 b.f. Golan (IRE) 129 – Carranza (IRE) (Lead On Time **59**
(USA) 123) [2007 8g⁴ 9.8g 12m 8.5s 7s³ 7s 7.9m Jul 29] €17,000Y: medium-sized,
strong filly: sixth foal: half-sister to 3 winners, including fairly useful Irish 2000 2-y-o 6f
winner Berlin (by Common Grounds), later successful in USA, and 7-y-o Coustou: dam,
French 1m/9.5f winner, out of half-sister to Derby winner Teenoso: modest maiden:
should stay 1¼m: acts on soft ground: blinkered fourth outing. *T. D. Easterby*

JEREMY (USA) 4 b.c. Danehill Dancer (IRE) 117 – Glint In Her Eye (USA) 76 (Arazi **122**
(USA) 135) [2007 114: 8.1g* 8g⁵ 8m² 8g³ 7d 8s Oct 27] good-bodied colt: impressed in
appearance: had a short, choppy action: very smart performer: won Betfred Mile at
Sandown (readily by 1¼ lengths from Bahia Breeze, confidently ridden) in April: good
efforts when placed behind Ramonti in Queen Anne Stakes at Royal Ascot (short-head
second, leading 1f out before hanging badly right and headed late on) and Sussex Stakes
at Goodwood (¾-length third, challenging on outside): below form last 2 outings, in
Prix de la Foret at Longchamp (seventh to Toylsome, squeezed out on first bend) and
Breeders' Cup Mile at Monmouth (tenth behind Kip Deville): stayed 1m: acted on soft
and good to firm going: had hung right: had good turn of foot: to stand at Irish National
Stud, Co Kildare, Ireland, fee €12,500. *Sir Michael Stoute*

JERMAJESTY (IRE) 2 b.c. (May 11) Touch of The Blues (FR) 125 – Mystic Dispute **–**
(IRE) (Magical Strike (USA) 114) [2007 6p p6g p7g 8.1d 7s p10g Oct 31] compact colt:
little form: tried in cheekpieces/visor. *J. R. Boyle*

JERRY HAMILTON (USA) 2 b. or br.c. (May 9) Cherokee Run (USA) 122 – **74**
Helsinki (Machiavellian (USA) 123) [2007 6m⁵ p7g p7.1g² p7.1g⁴ Nov 24] $120,000Y:
sixth foal: half-brother to 3 winners, notably high-class 6f (at 2 yrs) to 10.5f winner
Shamardal (by Giant's Causeway): dam, useful French 1¼m winner, sister to Dubai

World Cup winner Street Cry out of Irish Oaks winner Helen Street: fair maiden: in frame at Wolverhampton final 2 starts, latter nursery: will stay 1m: has joined R. Brookhouse. *M. Johnston*

JESSICA WIGMO 4 b.f. Bahamian Bounty 116 – Queen of Shannon (IRE) 76 **56** (Nordico (USA)) [2007 49: 5.5s 6m 6d 5.1f p5.1g⁵ p6g p7.1g³ p8m* p7g⁵ p8g Dec 5] good-bodied filly: modest performer: won maiden at Kempton in November: stays 1m: acts on polytrack and good to firm going. *A. W. Carroll*

JETTA JOY (IRE) 2 b.f. (May 22) Hawk Wing (USA) 136 – Woopi Gold (IRE) (Last – Tycoon 131) [2007 7m 7.2s 8f Sep 27] €30,000F, 20,000Y: workmanlike filly: fifth foal: half-sister to 3 winners in Italy at 9f+, including 6-y-o Drizzi: dam useful Italian 1m/1¼m performer: well held in maidens. *Mrs A. Duffield*

JEU DE ROSEAU (IRE) 3 b.g. Montjeu (IRE) 137 – Roseau 75 (Nashwan (USA) – 135) [2007 80: 13g⁶ 13m f12d⁶ Dec 20] fairly useful maiden at 2 yrs: well below form in 2007, leaving K. Condon in Ireland after second outing: should stay 1¼m+: acts on any going: blinkered second start. *A. P. Stringer*

JEU D'ESPRIT (IRE) 4 b.f. Montjeu (IRE) 137 – Cielo Vodkamartini (USA) (Con- **74** quistador Cielo (USA)) [2007 64: f11g* f12g⁵ 10m 8v² 9.8g⁶ p9.5g⁵ Nov 17] fair handicapper, lightly raced: won at Southwell in May: stays 1½m: acts on all-weather and heavy going: sold 16,000 gns, joined Mrs L. J. Mongan. *J. G. Given*

JEVINGTON STAR (IRE) 2 ch.g. (Apr 21) Noverre (USA) 125 – Khalisiyn 96 (Sha- – kapour 125) [2007 6d p7g p7g Sep 18] lengthy gelding: no form. *R. M. Flower*

JEWAAR (USA) 4 ch.f. Diesis 133 – Ringshaan (FR) (Darshaan 133) [2007 84: 8d – May 12] workmanlike filly: fairly useful performer at 3 yrs: well held in handicap at Ascot sole start in 2007: stays 1¼m: acts on good to firm going: wayward first 2 starts at 3 yrs. *M. A. Jarvis*

JEWELLED DAGGER (IRE) 3 b.g. Daggers Drawn (USA) 114 – Cappadoce (IRE) **98** (General Monash (USA) 107) [2007 –: 11g⁶ 8.3m² 8g* 8m* 9m* 9.1m² 8.5v 6.9f² p8.6g **a65** 8.9d* Oct 13] angular gelding: useful handicapper on turf, just fair on all-weather: won at Musselburgh in May (2) and June, and at York (by 3 lengths from Ahlawy) in October: stays 9f: acts on firm and good to soft going: tried visored at 2 yrs, blinkered nowadays: makes running/races prominently. *I. Semple*

JIBAJABA (USA) 3 gr. or ro.g. Aljabr (USA) 125 – Mary's Joy (USA) 74 (Woodman **80** (USA) 126) [2007 7.5m⁴ 7.5m⁵ 8.5s² 8s³ 9.1d² 8.9v⁴ 9m* 9.8m 10d⁵ Sep 22] lengthy, angular gelding: fairly useful performer: good efforts when placed in handicaps fourth/fifth starts prior to landing odds in maiden at Redcar in August: stays 9f (raced freely at 1¼m): acts on soft and good to firm going: sold 10,000 gns. *R. A. Fahey*

JIDAAR (IRE) 4 b.g. Grand Lodge (USA) 125 – Banaadir (USA) 50 (Diesis 133) – [2007 85: p12g p10g Feb 19] fairly useful winner at 3 yrs: no form in 2007: dead. *P. W. Hiatt*

JILL DAWSON (IRE) 4 b.f. Mull of Kintyre (USA) 114 – Dream of Jenny 73 (Caer- **69** leon (USA) 132) [2007 66: 8.1m* 8.3m³ 9g⁴ Aug 2] angular filly: fair handicapper, lightly raced: won apprentice event at Warwick in May: should be suited by 1¼m+: acts on good to firm going: tends to edge left. *John Berry*

JILLY WHY (IRE) 6 b.m. Mujadil (USA) 119 – Ruwy 77 (Soviet Star (USA) 128) **80** [2007 72, a63: f5g⁶ 5m 5m⁴ 5.1f² 6s⁵ 5s³ 6v⁶ p5g⁴ 5g³ 6m⁴ 5g² p6g⁵ 7d* 7g p6g² p6g* **a72** p7.1g p7.1g³ p6g⁴ p8.6g⁴ p6g³ p5.1g⁴ p6g⁴ p6g p6g Dec 29] workmanlike mare: fairly useful handicapper on turf, fair on all-weather: trained by Ms Deborah Evans on reappearance: won at the Curragh in August and Wolverhampton in October: effective at 5f to 7f: acts on all-weather, firm and soft going: tried visored, blinkered nowadays: effective held up or ridden prominently. *Paul Green*

JIMINOR MACK 4 bl.f. Little Jim – Copper Trader 53 (Faustus (USA) 118) [2007 53: **53** p8.6g² p9.5g⁴ p8.6g p12.2g 10.1m 9.9s³ 10v⁶ 8.5s² p8.6g 11.8g Oct 16] modest maiden: stays 1¼m: acts on polytrack and soft going: often blinkered, in cheekpieces last 3 outings. *W. J. H. Ratcliffe*

JIM MARTIN 2 b.g. (Apr 14) Auction House (USA) 120 – Folly Finnesse 80 (Joligen- **82** eration 111) [2007 7d* 8.2d⁴ Aug 14] 18,000Y: seventh foal: half-brother to 3 winners, including 2000 2-y-o 5f/6f winner Quantum Lady (by Mujadil): dam, 6f (at 2 yrs) to 10.8f winner, half-sister to useful sprinter Westcourt Magic: fairly useful form: 33/1, won maiden at Newcastle in July: found little in minor event only other start: gelded after: should stay 1m. *J. R. Weymes*

JIMMY DEAN 2 b.c. (Mar 14) Ishiguru (USA) 114 – Sister Sal 74 (Bairn (USA) 126) [2007 5.7s 6m 7m p7.1g⁶ p7.1g Nov 9] little form: tried blinkered. *M. Wellings* —

JIMMY FALABELLA (IRE) 2 b.g. (Apr 28) Mull of Kintyre (USA) 114 – Super Value (Polar Falcon (USA) 126) [2007 6m p7.1g Oct 27] smallish, sturdy gelding: behind in maidens: sold 1,000 gns, sent to Spain. *N. A. Callaghan* —

JIMMY STYLES 3 ch.g. Inchinor 119 – Inya Lake 101 (Whittingham (IRE) 104) [2007 6m² 6g⁴ 6f* 6m* 6d 6g Oct 26] 32,000Y: strong gelding: fourth foal: half-brother to 4-y-o Lake Hero and 5f winner Special Gold (by Josr Algarhoud): dam 5f (including Molecomb Stakes at 2 yrs) winner: useful performer: reportedly fractured a hind pedal bone and unraced at 2 yrs: won maiden at Windsor and handicap at Newbury (by 3 lengths from Esteem Machine) in August: poorly drawn both starts after, then gelded: raced only at 6f: acts on firm going: remains open to improvement. *C. G. Cox* **102 p**

JIMMY THE GUESSER 4 ch.g. Piccolo 121 – Brush Away (Ahonoora 122) [2007 86, a94: f6g³ f7g³ Jan 23] tall gelding: fairly useful handicapper: creditable efforts in frame both starts in 2007: effective at 5f (given test) to 8.6f: acts on all-weather, firm and soft going: tried blinkered/in cheekpieces. *N. P. Littmoden* **94**

JIM'S BOY (USA) 2 ch.g. (Feb 22) Street Cry (IRE) 130 – Ella Eria (FR) (Bluebird (USA) 125) [2007 8g p9.5g Nov 17] no show in maidens: dead. *M. Johnston* —

JO'BURG (USA) 3 b.g. Johannesburg (USA) 127 – La Martina 100 (Atraf 116) [2007 100: 8m 8.1d³ 8.2m⁴ 8m 8m⁶ 7g 7m⁶ Aug 12] small, strong, good-bodied gelding: useful performer: not discredited in 2000 Guineas at Newmarket on reappearance: creditable efforts next 2 starts, in listed race at Sandown (1½ lengths third of 4 to Massive) and minor event at Nottingham (fourth to Charlie Cool): little impact after: stays 1m, should prove at least as effective back at 7f: acts on polytrack, firm and soft going: has sweated up/given trouble in preliminaries: gelded after final start. *Mrs A. J. Perrett* **100**

JOCHESKI (IRE) 3 b.g. Mull of Kintyre (USA) 114 – Ludovica (Bustino 136) [2007 64: p10g² p9.5g⁵ f11s⁵ 10.1m* 11.7f² p13.9g⁵ 17.2g⁵ Oct 24] fair performer: won claimer at Yarmouth in August: claimed from M. Wallace after fifth outing: stays 11.6f: acts on firm ground, probably on polytrack: visored third outing. *A. G. Newcombe* **72**

JOCKSER (IRE) 6 b.g. Desert Story (IRE) 115 – Pupa Fiorini (ITY) (Indian Ridge 123) [2007 73: 16m⁵ p16g Sep 29] sturdy gelding: fair performer: stays 2m: acts on heavy and good to firm ground: fairly useful hurdler. *J. W. Mullins* **67**

JODRELL BANK (IRE) 4 ch.f. Observatory (USA) 131 – Aravonian 82 (Night Shift (USA)) [2007 63: p7.1g f6g 6m 5.3m 5s Jun 21] rather leggy filly: poor maiden nowadays: best form at 6f: best effort on good ground: blinkered last 2 starts. *J. Ryan* **49**

JOE JO STAR 5 b.g. Piccolo 121 – Zagreb Flyer (Old Vic 136) [2007 61d: p8.6g p9.5g 8f³ Apr 24] compact gelding: modest performer: stays 11.7f: acts on polytrack and firm ground: both wins in cheekpieces. *B. P. J. Baugh* **52**

JOE RICH 3 b.g. Piccolo 121 – Lady Lacey 66 (Kampala 120) [2007 p8g⁵ p10g Dec 30] tailed off in minor event/maiden at Lingfield. *Mrs L. C. Jewell* —

JOFFE'S RUN (USA) 2 ch.f. (Apr 2) Giant's Causeway (USA) 132 – Laguna Seca (USA) (Seattle Slew (USA)) [2007 6d 7g* 7m 8d Oct 26] good-topped filly: seventh foal: sister to winner in Japan and half-sister to 3 winners, including US 6.5f to 8.5f winner Macabe (by Gone West): dam, US 6f to 1m winner, out of US Grade 2 9f winner Topicount: fairly useful form: won maiden at Salisbury in September by 3½ lengths from Shamayel, making all: didn't go on as expected, seventh to Raymi Coya in Oh So Sharp Stakes at Newmarket and last in non-graded event at Monmouth: should stay 1m. *B. J. Meehan* **93**

JOHANNES (IRE) 4 b.g. Mozart (IRE) 131 – Blue Sirocco (Bluebird (USA) 125) [2007 101: 7m 6s Oct 14] good-topped gelding: useful performer at best: just fairly useful in handicaps in 2007, showing away both times: stays 7f: acts on good to firm going: tongue tied (ran as if amiss) final start at 3 yrs. *E. J. O'Neill* **87**

JOHAR JAMAL (IRE) 2 b.f. (Feb 1) Chevalier (IRE) 115 – Miss Barcelona (IRE) 53 (Mac's Imp (USA) 116) [2007 5.1g⁶ 6g* 6m* 6g 6.5m 7.1m⁴ Sep 30] 20,000Y: sturdy, quite attractive filly: third foal: dam, maiden (stayed 1¼m), half-sister to Rockfel Stakes winner Name of Love: fairly useful performer: won maiden at Goodwood in May and nursery at Newmarket in August: also ran well next time when equal-seventh to Dark Angel in sales race at York: looked none too keen final outing: should be suited by 7f/1m: acts on good to firm going: edgy sort, tends to sweat. *M. R. Channon* **83**

JOHN DILLON (IRE) 3 ch.g. Traditionally (USA) 117 – Matikanehanafubuki (IRE) **72**
(Caerleon (USA) 132) [2007 f8g⁴ f8g⁶ 10m⁵ 8.3g³ 8.3s* 10d² 11.9m³ Aug 9] big, strong
gelding: fair handicapper: won at Hamilton (despite very slow start) in July: good efforts
after: stays 1½m: acts on soft and good to firm ground: visored last 3 starts: won over
hurdles in November. *P. C. Haslam*

JOHN KEATS 4 b.g. Bertolini (USA) 125 – Nightingale (Night Shift (USA)) [2007 **80**
83§: 7.1m 6g 6m² 5m⁵ 6m² 6g 5d⁴ 5g 6m² 6g* 6g³ 6m* 5d p6g Oct 19] sturdy, lengthy
gelding: fairly useful handicapper: won at Newcastle in August and Redcar in September:
effective at testing 5f to 7f: acts on good to soft and good to firm going: tried blinkered/in
cheekpieces: has shown signs of temperament. *J. S. Goldie*

JOHNNY FRIENDLY 2 b.g. (Mar 15) Auction House (USA) 120 – Quantum Lady **53**
79 (Mujadil (USA) 119) [2007 5g 5.9d 5v⁶ 7m⁴ p8.6g Oct 12] modest maiden: fourth in
nursery at York: free-going sort, best up to 7f: gelded after final start. *K. R. Burke*

JOHN O'GROATS (IRE) 9 b.g. Distinctly North (USA) 115 – Bannons Dream (IRE) **65**
(Thatching 131) [2007 42: 6m 5g 6d³ 7.1s* 6d Oct 30] tall, close-coupled, good-topped
gelding: fair performer: left W. Harrison after second outing: won handicap at Chepstow
(11 lb out of weights) in July: reportedly went into atrial fibrillation final outing: stays 7f:
acts on firm and soft going: usually wears headgear nowadays. *T. T. Clement*

JOHN POTTS 2 b.g. (Apr 11) Josr Algarhoud (IRE) 118 – Crown City (USA) 56 **55**
(Coronado's Quest (USA) 130) [2007 6g 7.1g p7.1g p6g⁵ p6g⁵ p7.1d⁴ Dec 27] big,
good-topped gelding: modest maiden: stays 7f: acts on polytrack. *B. P. J. Baugh*

JOHNSTON'S DIAMOND (IRE) 9 b.g. Tagula (IRE) 116 – Toshair Flyer 88 **–**
(Ballad Rock 122) [2007 88, a69: 5m 6s 6.1d 6v Nov 3] big, workmanlike gelding: fairly
useful performer at 8 yrs: little form in handicaps in 2007: tried in blinkers/cheekpieces/
tongue tie: dead. *E. J. Alston*

JOHNSTON'S GLORY (IRE) 3 b.f. Desert Sun 120 – Clos de Tart (IRE) (Indian **61**
Ridge 123) [2007 8f⁴ 7.6m 6m p7.1g⁵ 9.1s p8.6g² p8.6g⁴ p8.6g⁵ Dec 14] €2,500Y: second
foal: half-sister to 4-y-o Seesawmilu: dam, Irish maiden, half-sister to useful sprinter
Gorinski: modest maiden: stays 8.6f: acts on polytrack and firm ground. *E. J. Alston*

JOHN TERRY (IRE) 4 b.g. Grand Lodge (USA) 125 – Kardashina (FR) (Darshaan **98 §**
133) [2007 94: 10m³ 10.1d⁵ 11.6s⁶ 12m* 12d 12m² 13.4m 12g⁵ 12m Nov 10] big, good
sort: useful handicapper: won at Newmarket in July: good efforts sixth/penultimate
outings, though found little in latter: should stay beyond 1½m: acts on good to firm and
good to soft going: wore cheekpieces fifth outing: temperamental. *Mrs A. J. Perrett*

JOINEDUPWRITING 2 b.g. (Apr 28) Desert Style (IRE) 121 – Ink Pot (USA) 73 **79**
(Green Dancer (USA) 132) [2007 6d 6m⁵ 6m² 7m* 8s 8m⁴ Oct 14] smallish, strong
gelding: fair form: won nursery at Redcar in September: good fourth to Meer Kat in minor
event at Bath: stays 1m: acts on good to firm going. *R. M. Whitaker*

JOINT AGENCY (IRE) 2 b.f. (Feb 28) Captain Rio 122 – Prima Marta (Primo **41**
Dominie 121) [2007 5v 5g 5g p5.1g⁵ Oct 6] third foal: dam unraced daughter of Nell
Gwyn Stakes winner Martha Stevens: poor maiden: raced only at 5f. *N. Wilson*

JOINT EXPECTATIONS (IRE) 3 b.g. Indian Rocket 115 – Jenny Spinner (IRE) 58 **44**
(Bluebird (USA) 125) [2007 –: p8.6g 8f⁴ 10.1d 8g⁶ p8g p8g 8d Oct 23] workmanlike
gelding: poor performer: won seller at Yarmouth in June: stays 1m: acts on good to soft
going: often visored/blinkered: reportedly struck into final start. *Mrs C. A. Dunnett*

JOJESSE 3 ch.g. Compton Place 125 – Jodeeka 97 (Fraam 114) [2007 52: f5g² f6g³ **60**
p5g* 5m* 5m⁶ 6g⁴ 5m⁴ 5m³ 5g 5g³ 5m³ 5m⁵ p6g f5d Dec 14] workmanlike gelding:
modest handicapper: won at Kempton in March and Musselburgh in April: left
G. A. Swinbank after twelfth start: raced only at 5f/6f: acts on all-weather and good to
firm ground. *Jennie Candlish*

JOLIE FLEUR 2 b.f. (Mar 24) Josr Algarhoud (IRE) 118 – Jenny Rocket (Minster Son **–**
130) [2007 p7g 8.1f Aug 27] medium-sized filly: second foal: dam, hurdles winner, out
of half-sister to smart sprinter Ever Sharp: well held in maidens. *C. Tinkler*

JOLLYHOCKEYSTICKS 2 b.f. (Apr 21) Fantastic Light (USA) 134 – Between The **68**
Sticks 83 (Pharly (FR) 130) [2007 7g 9d⁴ 8g³ 8g Nov 3] sparely-made filly: half-sister to
several winning sprinters, notably 8-y-o Pic Up Sticks: dam 2-y-o 5f winner: fair maiden:
in frame at Goodwood and Bath: out of depth in listed race final start (last of 10): will stay
1¼m/1½m. *M. R. Channon*

JOLLYS JOY 3 b.f. Averti (IRE) 117 – Nest Egg (Prince Sabo 123) [2007 12m⁵ Sep 22]   –
800Y: plain filly: third foal: half-sister to 5-y-o Bee Stinger: dam unraced: 66/1, tailed off
in maiden at Newmarket. *K. F. Clutterbuck*

JOLLY TIPSY 2 ch.f. (Feb 25) Tipsy Creek (USA) 115 – Busy (IRE) (In The Wings   –
128) [2007 5.1g 6m f6g Jun 5] tall filly: first foal: dam unraced close relation to useful
performer up to 1½m Babinda: no form in maidens. *M. W. Easterby*

JOMUS 6 b.g. Soviet Star (USA) 128 – Oatey 68 (Master Willie 129) [2007 –§, a67§:   – §
p10g p8g p8g p8g p8g⁴ Dec 16] close-coupled, quite good-topped gelding: just modest   a53 §
handicapper in 2007: stays 1¼m: acts on all-weather, good to firm and good to soft going:
wears blinkers/cheekpieces: tried tongue tied: sometimes slowly away: patiently ridden:
one to treat with caution. *L. Montague Hall*

JONNY BEHAVE 3 b.g. Erhaab (USA) 127 – Bunty 57 (Presidium 124) [2007 p7g⁴   36
p10f p8.6g p8.6g 8m Jun 17] poor maiden: dead. *I. A. Wood*

JONNY EBENEEZER 8 b.g. Hurricane Sky (AUS) – Leap of Faith (IRE) 65 (North-   –
iam (USA)) [2007 92d: p7.1g Sep 14] tall gelding: smart performer at best: very much on
downgrade: effective at 5f to 7f: acts on all-weather, soft and good to firm going: often
wears headgear. *K. McAuliffe*

JONNY LESTERS HAIR (IRE) 2 b.c. (Feb 14) Danetime (IRE) 121 – Jupiter Inlet   74
(IRE) (Jupiter Island 126) [2007 6.1v⁵ 6s⁴ 7g³ Aug 24] €12,000Y, 14,000 2-y-o: eighth
foal: half-brother to 3 winners in Italy, including fairly useful 7f to 8.5f winner Jupiter
Lighthouse (by Common Grounds): dam useful Italian winner up to 1¾m: fair maiden:
progressive form, third to Rosa Grace at Thirsk: will stay 1m. *T. D. Easterby*

JONTOBEL 2 b.g. (Mar 27) Tobougg (IRE) 125 – Belinda 64 (Mizoram (USA) 105)   –
[2007 8g Oct 19] well beaten in maiden at Redcar: subsequently gelded. *Jedd O'Keeffe*

JOOLS 9 b.g. Cadeaux Genereux 131 – Madame Crecy (USA) (Al Nasr (FR) 126) [2007   69
72d, a64d: p8g⁶ p8.6g⁴ p10g 8.1m p8.6g* 8d⁴ p8g⁶ 8.3m⁵ 8.3g⁵ 8d³ p8.6g 7d 7m⁴ p7g*
p7g³ p8m³ p8g p7g* p7g* p7g⁶ p7g⁵ Dec 16] rather leggy gelding: fair performer: won
minor event at Wolverhampton in May and handicaps at Kempton in September and
November (2, first apprentices): effective at 7f to 1¼m: acts on all-weather, firm and soft
going: visored once at 3 yrs: held up of late. *D. K. Ivory*

JORDANS ELECT 7 ch.g. Fleetwood (IRE) 107 – Cal Norma's Lady (IRE) 87 (Lyp-   68
hard's Special (USA) 122) [2007 77: 8.3m⁴ 10.1m 9.1g³ 13f 9.2s 9.1g⁶ Jul 8] tall, rather
leggy, useful-looking gelding: fair handicapper: effective at 1m/1¼m: acts on firm and
good to soft ground: tried visored: usually races up with pace: none too consistent.
P. Monteith

JORDAN'S LIGHT (USA) 4 gr. or ro.g. Aljabr (USA) 125 – Western Friend (USA)   68
(Gone West (USA)) [2007 81: 8.1m 8m⁴ 10g f11g⁴ May 1] tall gelding: fair handicapper
nowadays: stays 1¼m (seemingly not 11f): acts on all-weather and good to firm going:
often visored. *T. J. Pitt*

JORDANS SPARK 6 ch.g. Opening Verse (USA) 126 – Ribot's Pearl (Indian Ridge   46
123) [2007 62: 7.1m 9.1d 9.1g 8.3g⁵ 9.1g 8g Jul 9] workmanlike gelding: modest performer at 5 yrs, just poor in 2007: stays 1¼m: acts on firm and soft going: tried in headgear.
P. Monteith

JORD (IRE) 3 b.f. Trans Island 119 – Arcevia (IRE) 85 (Archway (IRE) 115) [2007 75:   58 +
f6g f7g⁵ p7g³ p7g f6g³ p6g* f7g 6.1m 6d 6g p6g⁴ p7.1g p6g⁵ p6g p6g⁵ p6g⁴ f8d*   a80
f8d² Dec 21] leggy, plain filly: fairly useful handicapper on all-weather, modest on turf:
won at Wolverhampton in May and Southwell in December: effective at 6f to 1m: acts on
all-weather and firm ground: tried in cheekpieces. *A. J. McCabe*

JOSAMA 3 br.f. Desert Sun 120 – Edge of Darkness 62 (Vaigly Great 127) [2007 5m 6g   –
p8.6g Nov 22] closely related to 4-y-o Fangorn Forest and half-sister to 3 winners,
including fairly useful 1½m/1¾m winner Salford Flyer (by Pharly): dam 1¼m and 2m
winner: well held in maidens. *R. Bastiman*

JOSEPH HENRY 5 b.g. Mujadil (USA) 119 – Iris May 87 (Brief Truce (USA) 126)   99
[2007 95: 7.6m⁵ 6g² 6m Sep 13] well-made gelding: useful handicapper: best effort in
2007 when head second of 27 to Pearly Wey at Goodwood: first home in unfavoured
group when eighth of 20 to Ellens Academy at Doncaster final start: stays 1m, but may
well prove best at shorter: acts on firm and soft going: tried blinkered (ran poorly).
D. Nicholls

JOSEPHINE MALINES 3 b.f. Inchinor 119 – Alrisha (IRE) 90 (Persian Bold 123)   83
[2007 –: 8m² 8d⁶ 10m 10m Sep 14] rather leggy, lightly-made filly: fairly useful maiden:

best effort when second at Salisbury on reappearance: stays 1¼m: acts on good to firm ground: sold 12,000 gns, joined Mrs A. Duffield. *C. G. Cox*

JOSH 5 b.g. Josr Algarhoud (IRE) 118 – Charlie Girl 70 (Puissance 110) [2007 95: p7.1g⁵ p7g⁵ p7g³ p7g⁴ p7g 7.1d⁶ 6m⁵ p6g p9.5g p10g Dec 22] tall, quite good-topped gelding: has a quick, unimpressive action: fairly useful handicapper nowadays: lost form in second half of 2007: stays easy 1m: acts on polytrack, soft and good to firm going: tried in cheekpieces/blinkers. *K. A. Ryan* **85 d**

JOSHUA 2 b.g. (Apr 22) Josr Algarhoud (IRE) 118 – Magic Flute 78 (Magic Ring (IRE) 115) [2007 5.1g p6m⁶ p6g⁶ Dec 26] poor maiden: gelded after debut: left J. Gask after second start. *D. E. Cantillon* **41**

JOSHUA'S GOLD (IRE) 6 b.g. Sesaro (USA) 81 – Lady of The Night (IRE) 54 (Night Shift (USA)) [2007 76: 8f³ f7g⁶ 7m 6m⁶ 7g* 7.2g* 7m 7.5d² p8.6g 7g 8g Oct 24] sturdy, close-coupled gelding: fair handicapper: won at Catterick and Ayr (idled) in August: stays easy 8.6f: acts on all-weather, firm and good to soft going: usually visored. *D. Carroll* **78**

JOSH YOU ARE 4 b.g. Josr Algarhoud (IRE) 118 – Cibenze 74 (Owington 123) [2007 56: p16g* p16g² p13.9g⁴ 8d⁶ p13g* 16f³ p16.5g² 16m Aug 28] tall gelding: fair handicapper: won at Kempton in January and Lingfield in July: stays 16.5f: acts on polytrack, firm and good to soft going. *D. E. Cantillon* **68 a74**

JOSR'S MAGIC (IRE) 3 b.g. Josr Algarhoud (IRE) 118 – Just The Trick (USA) 48 (Phone Trick (USA)) [2007 75: 7m³ p6f⁶ 5m² f6g³ 8d p8g 6f p10g p8g⁵ p10m³ Dec 10] strong, compact gelding: type to carry condition: good mover: modest performer: left Mrs A. Duffield after third start, R. Stronge after fourth and S. Hall after eighth: effective at 5f to 1¼m: acts on polytrack and good to firm going: sometimes blinkered/visored: usually races prominently. *H. J. Collingridge* **61**

JOSS STICK 2 b.g. (May 7) Josr Algarhoud (IRE) 118 – Queen's College (IRE) 57 (College Chapel 122) [2007 5m 5.1d p6g⁶ p6g p5g³ 5.1g p5.1g³ p5m* Dec 8] fair performer: won maiden at Lingfield in December: best efforts at 5f on polytrack: wore cheekpieces last 2 starts. *P. J. Makin* **65**

JOST VAN DYKE 3 b.g. Foxhound (USA) 103 – Interregnum (Interrex (CAN)) [2007 66d: p8.6g⁴ p8.6g⁶ p5.1g⁴ p6g 7.1m Apr 9] close-coupled gelding: just modest performer in 2007: left J. Boyle after third outing: stays 7f: acts on polytrack, firm and good to soft ground: tried in cheekpieces/visored: seems increasingly moody. *J. W. Unett* **52**

JOUSTING 3 b.g. Josr Algarhoud (IRE) 118 – Sweet Wilhelmina 87 (Indian Ridge 123) [2007 –: p7.1g p9.5g f8g² f7g f8g Apr 26] poor maiden: stays 1m: raced only on all-weather: visored last 3 starts: hung left on debut. *V. Smith* **48**

JOY AND PAIN 6 b.g. Pursuit of Love 124 – Ice Chocolate (USA) 77 (Icecapade (USA)) [2007 75: f6g f7g 7g³ 6m 6.1g⁶ 7m 7s² 6g⁵ 6v⁴ 6m 6.1m 8d p7g⁶ p7g* p7g p7m* Nov 26] good-bodied gelding: fair handicapper nowadays: won at Lingfield (2) in November: best at 6f/7f: acts on polytrack, firm and soft ground: usually wears headgear: has looked difficult ride. *M. J. Attwater* **65**

JOYEAUX 5 b.m. Mark of Esteem (IRE) 137 – Divine Secret (Hernando (FR) 127) [2007 75: 6s 5s² 6.1s⁵ 6d³ 5d² 5d³ 6g² 6m² 5g* 5m² 5d p6g⁴ 5.1g⁶ Oct 31] leggy mare: fair handicapper: won at Hamilton in September: effective at 5f to 7f: acts on polytrack, firm and soft ground: effective visored or not: consistent: has joined O. Pears. *J. Hetherton* **78**

JOYFUL TEARS (IRE) 3 ch.f. Barathea (IRE) 127 – Perils of Joy (IRE) 83 (Rainbow Quest (USA) 134) [2007 75p: p7g⁶ 8.3m 7d⁶ 10.2m⁴ 10d 8m⁴ p8.6g⁵ p8.6g Nov 5] good-topped filly: fair maiden handicapper: left E. Dunlop 33,000 gns after second start: likely to prove best at 1¼m+: acts on good to firm and good to soft going. *M. G. Quinlan* **68**

JOY IN THE GUILD (IRE) 4 b.f. Mull of Kintyre (USA) 114 – About Face (Midyan (USA) 124) [2007 60: p10g 10.9m 11.7f² 12s⁵ 12.6m⁵ 10.9g 11.8g⁵ Oct 16] rangy filly: modest performer: stays 1½m: acts on firm ground: tried visored. *W. S. Kittow* **60**

JUBILEE DREAM 5 b.g. Bluebird (USA) 125 – Last Dream (IRE) 80 (Alzao (USA) 117) [2007 54: 14.1m Aug 31] modest maiden at 4 yrs: well held sole start on Flat in 2007: tried blinkered/tongue tied. *Mrs L. J. Mongan* **–**

JUBILEE STREET (IRE) 8 b.g. Dr Devious (IRE) 127 – My Firebird (Rudimentary (USA) 118) [2007 91: 7.1d⁵ 8.5m⁶ 7.6m Aug 5] big gelding: fairly useful handicapper: effective at 7f/1m: acts on firm and good to soft going: tried visored: sometimes slowly away: tends to hang right. *Mrs A. Duffield* **87**

John Smith's Northumberland Plate, Newcastle—Juniper Girl (rail) makes up a lot of ground in the very testing conditions and snatches the prize from Macorville, the pair clear of Tilt and Al Eile

JUCEBABE 4 b.f. Zilzal (USA) 137 – Jucea 77 (Bluebird (USA) 125) [2007 68: 5.7d 5m⁵ 5.7g⁴ 5.1g⁵ 5d⁶ 5.1m³ 6d 5.1d⁴ 5.1f* 5m 5d 5.3d⁴ 5.1s 5.7g⁴ Oct 24] good-bodied filly: fair handicapper: won at Chepstow in August: best at 5f: acts on firm and good to soft going: effective with/without cheekpieces: very slowly away fifth outing. *J. L. Spearing* — **67**

JUCE OF HEARTS 3 b.g. Zilzal (USA) 137 – Jucea 77 (Bluebird (USA) 125) [2007 5.1f 5m⁴ 6m 5.1g 5.7d Jun 16] modest form only on debut: tried in cheekpieces. *J. L. Spearing* — **50 d**

JUDDA 6 b.g. Makbul 104 – Pepeke 78 (Mummy's Pet 125) [2007 p9.5g Jan 19] no form: tried in cheekpieces/tongue tie. *R. F. Marvin* — **–**

JUDD STREET 5 b.g. Compton Place 125 – Pudding Lane (IRE) 64 (College Chapel 122) [2007 104: 5m³ 6.1m 5m* 5g⁶ 5g² 5.6m 5.2m³ 5m* Oct 4] sturdy, close-coupled gelding: smart performer: won handicap at Haydock in August and listed event at New-market (visored, beat Rowe Park by neck) in October: ran well otherwise in 2007 when placed: winner at 6f, best at 5f: acts on polytrack, raced mostly on ground firmer than good on turf (acts on firm): tried tongue tied: tough and reliable. *Eve Johnson Houghton* — **114**

JUDGE NEPTUNE 3 b.g. Ocean of Wisdom (USA) 106 – Princess Louise 86 (Efisio 120) [2007 61: 8m² 9.1d 8m Aug 27] good-bodied gelding: modest maiden: stays 1m: acts on soft and good to firm ground: visored final outing. *J. S. Goldie* — **63**

JUDGETHEMOMENT (USA) 2 br.c. (Feb 17) Judge T C (USA) – Rachael Tennessee (USA) (Matsadoon (USA)) [2007 7.6f⁶ p8g³ 8m³ 10d³ p10g³ Oct 31] smallish, stocky colt: half-brother to several winners, notably smart 7f/1m winner Ecclesiastical (by Bishop of Cashel), later high class up to 1m in Hong Kong as Olympic Express: dam, placed in US, half-sister to top-class miler Lear Fan: fairly useful maiden: third 4 times, possibly flattered in minor event at Newbury third start: will be suited by 1½m. *Jane Chapple-Hyam* — **74 +**

JULATTEN (IRE) 3 b.f. Alhaarth (IRE) 126 – Istibshar (USA) 78 (Mr Prospector (USA)) [2007 –: 6v 8f p7m⁶ p6g 10m³ p13.9g Oct 5] sturdy filly: modest maiden: should stay beyond 1¼m: acts on good to firm going. *D. J. Murphy* — **57**

JULIAN JOACHIM (USA) 3 b.g. Officer (USA) 120 – Seeking The Jewel (USA) (Seeking The Gold (USA)) [2007 6m⁶ 6.2m² 6m Aug 4] modest maiden: should stay 1m: acts on good to firm ground. *G. A. Swinbank* — **63**

JUMBAJUKIBA 4 b.g. Baratea (IRE) 127 – Danseuse du Soir (IRE) 121 (Thatching 131) [2007 92: 9.5m⁴ 8m⁴ 8s* 8.5g 8s* 8m* 8m Oct 6] big gelding: improved into a smart performer: won handicap at the Curragh in July, listed race at Cork in August and Ladbrokes.com Solonaway Stakes at the Curragh (made all, by 1¾ lengths from Cougar Bay) in September: below-form seventh to Creachadoir in Joel Stakes at Newmarket final outing: stays 1m: acts on soft and good to firm going: blinkered last 5 starts. *Mrs J. Harrington, Ireland* — **115**

JUMPIN JOHNNIE 2 ch.g. (Mar 22) Compton Place 125 – Trump Street 77 (First Trump 118) [2007 7g 6m p6g Dec 1] lengthy, good-topped gelding: well held in maidens, then gelded: bred for sprinting. *R. T. Phillips* — **–**

JUNCEA 3 b.f. Elnadim (USA) 128 – Strelitzia (SAF) (Fort Wood (USA) 117) [2007 —
76: 6.1s p6g p5m Oct 13] well-made filly: fair performer at 2 yrs: well held in handicaps
in 2007. *H. Morrison*

JUNEBUG SYMPHONY (IRE) 5 b.m. Indian Lodge (IRE) 127 – Ladies View —
(IRE) 64 (Turtle Island (IRE) 123) [2007 –: p5g Jan 6] maiden: little form since 2005:
tried in cheekpieces. *V. Smith*

JUN FAN (USA) 5 br.g. Artax (USA) 126 – Ringside Lady (NZ) (Clay Hero (AUS)) **52 §**
[2007 63§: p5.1g 6m⁵ 5m⁶ 5m 6s⁵ 5m 5s⁵ 5m 5g Aug 29] big, good-bodied gelding:
modest maiden: best form at 5f: acts on polytrack and firm ground: tried in cheekpieces/
blinkers/tongue tie: has looked quirky: inconsistent. *B. Ellison*

JUNIOR 4 ch.g. Singspiel (IRE) 133 – For More (FR) (Sanglamore (USA) 126) [2007 **96**
85+: 16m* 16s³ p16g* Jul 4] rangy gelding: useful handicapper, lightly raced on Flat:
won at Newbury in April and Kempton in July: stays 2m: acts on polytrack, soft and good
to firm ground: refused to enter stall on intended debut at 3 yrs. *B. J. Meehan*

JUNIPER GIRL (IRE) 4 b.f. Revoque (IRE) 122 – Shajara (FR) (Kendor (FR) 122) **108**
[2007 103+: 14g 20m² 16.1v* 16.4d 20g⁵ Oct 7] lengthy filly: useful performer: further
improvement in 2007, good ½-length second to Full House in Ascot Stakes at Royal
Ascot prior to winning 20-runner John Smith's Northumberland Plate at Newcastle in
June, making up plenty of ground to beat Macorville by short head: better effort in pattern
company after when creditable fifth of 6 to Le Miracle in Prix du Cadran at Longchamp:
needs good test at 2m, and stays 2½m: acts on heavy and good to firm going: raced
freely on reappearance: usually ridden by apprentice Luke Morris (not final outing).
M. L. W. Bell

JUPITER PLUVIUS (USA) 2 b.c. (Mar 30) Johannesburg (USA) 127 – Saratoga **105 p**
Honey (USA) (Boundary (USA) 117) [2007 6d* 7g* Oct 29]
Since Leopardstown's Killavullan Stakes was opened to colts and shortened
to seven furlongs in 1995, it has been won by several promising two-year-olds just
below the top level. The best of the winners have been Grey Swallow (116p),
successful in 2003, before going on to win the Irish Derby, and Footstepsinthesand
(113p in 2004), who won the Two Thousand Guineas on his only subsequent start.
The 2007 victor Jupiter Pluvius is rated only an average winner of the final pattern
race in Ireland, but his rating is a reflection of the unsatisfactory nature of the race
and he looks sure to do better. The early pace was not strong, with most of the field
still in contention on the home turn, and Jupiter Pluvius was unable to show the full
extent of his superiority on the day. He was also one of several to suffer a troubled
passage, though none suffered so much as front-running Amended, who was forced
through the rails, leaving her jockey Shane Gorey with a broken leg. Jupiter Pluvius
was well on top at the finish, beating Famous Name by three quarters of a length
after running on strongly to lead inside the final furlong without having to be hard
ridden.
Like Footstepsinthesand, Jupiter Pluvius made his debut—a winning one—
in a maiden just eight days before the Killavullan Stakes, in his case at the Curragh
rather than Naas. Such a relatively late introduction was, however, not planned,
Jupiter Pluvius the subject of one of the now-familiar gambles on an unraced
two-year-old from the Ballydoyle stable for the Two Thousand Guineas, backed
down from 50/1 into half those odds in July. When Jupiter Pluvius finally made his
debut in October, Aidan O'Brien said that the horse had suffered 'two hold-ups'
and was 'only eighty per cent fit'. Paddock inspection had revealed as much but,
despite being slowly away, Jupiter Pluvius won by a neck from Dahindar. Those
who had taken fancy odds about Jupiter Pluvius were soon able to breathe a relative
sigh of relief with Jupiter Pluvius down to as short as 12/1 for the Guineas after the
Killavullan Stakes.
Jupiter Pluvius' sire, grandsire and great grandsire were precocious and
all ran well in the Breeders' Cup Juvenile, Jupiter Pluvius' sire, Johannesburg,
avenging the narrow defeats of Hennessy (beaten a neck by Unbridled's Song) and
Storm Cat (beaten a nose by Tasso). Johannesburg, Hennessy (who died in 2007)
and Storm Cat were all at their best in their first seasons, Storm Cat's win in a minor
event the only three-year-old victory from a total of just five appearances from all
three. Even Jupiter Pluvius' great-great grandsire, Storm Bird, did not win after his
two-year-old days when he recorded one of the best Dewhurst Stakes wins, beating

Killavullan Stakes, Leopardstown—two wins from as many starts for Jupiter Pluvius (near side), who runs on strongly to lead inside the final furlong

			Hennessy		Storm Cat
		Johannesburg (USA)	(ch 1993)		Island Kitty
		(ch 1999)	Myth		Ogygian
Jupiter Pluvius (USA)			(b 1993)		Yarn
(b.c. Mar 30, 2005)			Boundary		Danzig
		Saratoga Honey (USA)	(b 1990)		Edge
		(b 1996)	High Heeled Honey		Gold Stage
			(b 1986)		Cloud High

subsequent Two Thousand Guineas winner To-Agori-Mou. The distaff side of Jupiter Pluvius' pedigree is noted for speed. His dam Saratoga Honey won once in three starts in minor sprints and produced two colts before Jupiter Pluvius. Rappers Deelite (by Afternoon Deelites) was the first and emulated his dam by winning twice at sprint distances in America. The second, by Favorite Trick, is unraced and Saratoga Honey produced another colt in 2007, this time by Successful Appeal. Saratoga Honey is herself half-sister to two sprint-stakes winners in the States, High Heeled Hope and Koennecker. Jupiter Pluvius is named after a figure in Roman mythology responsible for bringing rain. Connections may, however, be hoping that it keeps dry, jockey Seamus Heffernan having remarked that the colt was better suited by the firmer ground (good) he encountered at Leopardstown than that on his debut (good to soft). The tall, strong, quite attractive Jupiter Pluvius cost 475,000 dollars as a yearling and should stay a mile at three, though it might be as well to keep in mind his speedy pedigree. *A. P. O'Brien, Ireland*

JUST A DANCER (IRE) 2 b.f. (Feb 17) Choisir (AUS) 126 – New Foundation (IRE) **83**
89 (College Chapel 122) [2007 5.1f² 5s* 5.1d³ Jun 16] €22,000F, 32,000Y: first foal:
dam, unreliable 2-y-o 5f winner, half-sister to useful but ungenuine performer up to 7f
Roundtree: fairly useful form: won maiden at Leicester in May: third in minor event at
Bath only subsequent start: should prove best at 5f/6f. *B. W. Hills*

JUST A FLASH (IRE) 3 b.g. Redback 116 – Just Deserts 66 (Alhijaz 122) [2007 –: **–**
p6g p8g p12g Jun 9] no form, including in seller. *B. R. Johnson*

JUST A GIGOLO 7 b.g. Inchinor 119 – Courtisane (Persepolis (FR) 127) [2007 12g –
Apr 2] neat gelding: lightly-raced maiden: no form since 2002: tried in cheekpieces,
usually tongue tied. *P. D. Niven*

JUST AN ANGEL (IRE) 3 b.f. Namid 128 – Changing Partners 58 (Rainbow Quest –
(USA) 134) [2007 p11g⁶ p12g 10g 8m p10g Jul 3] 16,000Y: stocky, workmanlike filly:
type to carry condition: half-sister to several winners, including 1m winner Love Affair
(by Tagula): dam, 1½m winner, half-sister to smart sprinter May Ball: little form.
A. P. Jarvis

JUST BOND (IRE) 5 b.g. Namid 128 – Give Warning (IRE) (Warning 136) [2007 88:   **82**
p8.6g* p9.5g³ p10g 8.1m⁴ 7.9d p8.6g* 10.3d 8m³ p8.6g* p9.5g 8.1g³ p8.6g* p8.6g p8m⁶ **a97**
p9.5g² Dec 31] sturdy gelding: useful handicapper on all-weather, fairly useful on turf:
all wins at Wolverhampton, including in January (apprentices), June, August and October: good second there final start, though hung right: stays easy 9.5f: acts on polytrack,
firm and good to soft ground: tends to start slowly: held up: free-going sort. *G. R. Oldroyd*

JUSTCALLMEHANDSOME 5 ch.g. Handsome Ridge 121 – Pearl Dawn (IRE) 91   **66**
(Jareer (USA) 115) [2007 58: 10s² 10m 10.9d⁴ 10.9d⁶ 9m p9.5g³ p8.6g* p8m* p8.6g⁴
p8g p8.6g³ Nov 27] lengthy, angular gelding: fair performer: won minor event at Wolverhampton in September and handicap at Kempton in October: stays 1¼m, should be
effective at 7f: acts on all-weather, soft and good to firm ground: has worn visor (including for all wins): free-going sort. *D. J. S. ffrench Davis*

JUST CHRISSIE 3 b.f. Classic Cliche (IRE) 128 – Marsh Marigold 65 (Tina's Pet 121) –
[2007 –: 11.8m Apr 12] small filly: no form in maidens nearly a year apart. *G. Fierro*

JUST CRYSTAL 3 b.f. Polar Prince (IRE) 117 – Grandads Dream (Never So Bold 135)   **51**
[2007 p7.1g 8.2m p7.1g p8g⁵ p9.5g⁶ p8.6d Dec 27] close-coupled filly: third foal: dam
unraced: modest maiden: seems to stay 9.5f. *B. P. J. Baugh*

JUST DUST 3 b.g. Makbul 104 – Dusty Bankes 59 (Greensmith 121) [2007 87: 8m 8v   **68**
7d 8s⁶ 7g 8.3m 8m 9.1s Oct 4] workmanlike gelding: just fair performer and inconsistent
in 2007 (said to have finished distressed final outing): seems to stay 1m: acts on firm and
good to soft going: has worn cheekpieces: often races prominently. *M. W. Easterby*

JUSTENJOY YOURSELF 5 b.m. Tipsy Creek (USA) 115 – Habibi 50 (Alhijaz 122) –
[2007 44: 6m Apr 29] poor performer at best: effective at 5f/6f: acts on polytrack, firm
and soft ground: tried in cheekpieces only start in 2007. *R. W. Price*

JUST FLY 7 b.g. Efisio 120 – Chrysalis 66 (Soviet Star (USA) 128) [2007 –, a79: p10g   **51**
p16g⁶ f16s⁶ p7g⁵ p8g⁴ 10.2f p8g⁵ May 31] sturdy gelding: modest handicapper nowa- **a61 d**
days, on long losing run: stays 1¼m: acts on all-weather and good to firm going: usually
visored/blinkered. *Dr J. R. J. Naylor*

JUST INTERSKY (USA) 4 gr.g. Distant View (USA) 126 – Hexane (FR) 108   **68**
(Kendor (USA) 122) [2007 86d: p6g 8m 8g p10m⁶ p10m* Dec 9] just fair handicapper
nowadays: left K. Ryan after reappearance, and R. Whitaker 4,000 gns after third start:
won at Lingfield in December: stays 1¼m: acts on polytrack and soft ground: blinkered
(raced freely) on 4-y-o reappearance. *V. Smith*

JUST JAMES 8 b.g. Spectrum (IRE) 126 – Fairy Flight (IRE) 86 (Fairy King (USA))   **63 §**
[2007 97§: f8g* f8g² f8g 7m f8g⁴ 7m² 7m* 7.1m 8.3g Jun 13] strong, compact gelding: one-
time smart performer, just modest nowadays: won seller in January and claimer in May,
both at Southwell, and apprentice claimer at Newcastle later in May: said to have bled
penultimate outing and again shaped as if amiss final start: effective at 6f to easy 1m: acts
on fibresand, firm and soft going: has worn bandages: temperamental (virtually refused
to race second outing at 7 yrs). *D. Nicholls*

JUST JIMMY (IRE) 2 b.g. (Feb 24) Ashkalani (IRE) 128 – Berkeley Hall 68   **63**
(Saddlers' Hall (IRE) 126) [2007 6m 7d 7m 8f 8g p8.6g Oct 26] angular gelding: modest
maiden: should prove best short of 1m. *P. D. Evans*

JUST JOEY 3 b.f. Averti (IRE) 117 – Fly South (Polar Falcon (USA) 126) [2007 87: 5f   **85**
5g³ 5g 5m 5s⁶ 5g 6g⁶ 6m 6m Sep 8] sturdy filly: fairly useful handicapper: below form
after second start: best at 5f: acts on good to firm and good to soft going: tried blinkered:
none too consistent. *J. R. Weymes*

JUST JULIE (USA) 3 ch.f. Gulch (USA) – Julie Jalouse (USA) 103 (Kris S (USA))   **70 d**
[2007 54: 11.8m³ 12m³ p12g⁴ 12g 11.5s 11.5m Aug 9] neat filly: first foal: dam, Irish
9.5f/1¼m winner, out of smart performer up to 1½m Julie La Rousse: fair maiden: trained
by K. Prendergast in Ireland only 2-y-o start: best efforts when placed first 2 starts in
2007: stays 1½m: acts on good to firm going. *N. A. Callaghan*

JUST LIKE A WOMAN 2 b.f. (Feb 17) Observatory (USA) 131 – Always On My **76**
Mind 91 (Distant Relative 128) [2007 p6g³ 6m⁵ 7g* Oct 20] lengthy, rather unfurnished
filly: fifth foal: sister to 4-y-o Halfwaytoparadise and half-sister to fairly useful 7f/1m
winner Dr Thong (by Dr Fong): dam, 6f winner, half-sister to smart 6f/7f performer Red
Carpet: fair form: won maiden at Catterick final start: will stay 1m. *M. L. W. Bell*

JUST LILLE (IRE) 4 b.f. Mull of Kintyre (USA) 114 – Tamasriya (IRE) (Doyoun **91**
124) [2007 82: 8m 9.9m 8.3m* 10.5m* 9.9m* 8.3d* 9.8v⁵ 12d³ 10g² 12f⁶ Sep 5]
fairly useful performer: won handicaps at Hamilton (jump jockeys event), Haydock and
Beverley, all in May, and minor event at Hamilton in June: effective at 1m to 10.5f: acts
on firm and good to soft ground: in cheekpieces nowadays. *Mrs A. Duffield*

JUST MATTY 4 b.g. Bertolini (USA) 125 – Frisson (Slip Anchor 136) [2007 –: 8f f8g –
Apr 22] little form in maidens. *J. G. M. O'Shea*

JUST MOSSIE 2 ch.g. (Apr 23) Ishiguru (USA) 114 – Marinsky (USA) 63 (Diesis 133) **54**
[2007 6f⁵ 7m 8.3d p6m² p6d³ p8.6g⁴ Dec 31] sturdy gelding: modest maiden: placed in 2
sellers: stays 8.6f: acts on polytrack: tried in cheekpieces. *W. G. M. Turner*

JUST OBSERVING 4 ch.g. Observatory (USA) 131 – Just Speculation (IRE) 86 **83**
(Ahonoora 122) [2007 79: 12m² 12f³ 10f* 12m⁶ 9.9m⁴ 10m⁴ 9.8m⁶ 10m⁴ Aug 10] strong,
close-coupled gelding: fairly useful handicapper: left P. Haslam after reappearance:
won at Pontefract in May: stays 1½m: acts on polytrack, firm and good to soft going:
visored (well held) final 3-y-o outing, in cheekpieces in 2007: has looked tricky ride.
P. T. Midgley

JUST OSCAR (GER) 3 b.g. Surako (GER) 114 – Jade Chequer 71 (Green Desert **72**
(USA) 127) [2007 65: 8.2g 8.3g⁴ 8.3d p7.1g 8f² 8.3g⁵ 7.6s² 7g³ 8.1m² 7.1s 7.6m⁵ 8.1g
p7.1g⁴ p7.1g⁶ p8.6g Oct 30] workmanlike gelding: fair maiden handicapper: will prove
best at 1m: acts on polytrack, firm and soft going: tried visored/in cheekpieces: sometimes slowly away. *W. M. Brisbourne*

JUST PUDDIE 2 b.f. (Apr 13) Piccolo 121 – Miss Laetitia (IRE) (Entitled 126) [2007 **45**
p6g 5d² Jul 19] tall filly: half-sister to 1¼m seller winner Diletia (by Dilum): dam of
little account: poor maiden: second in seller at Leicester: may prove best at 5f/6f
W. G. M. Turner

JUST ROB 2 b.c. (Jan 27) Robellino (USA) 127 – Scapavia (FR) (Alzao (USA) 117) **74**
[2007 8.2d³ 8.2g² Oct 31] workmanlike colt: second foal: dam ran twice: placed behind
Patkai then Turn Left (½-length second) in maidens at Nottingham: will stay 1¼m.
R. Hollinshead

JUST SAM (IRE) 2 b.f. (Apr 15) Mull of Kintyre (USA) 114 – Strawberry Sands 74 **51**
(Lugana Beach 116) [2007 7m 6g⁵ 5m 5g Sep 19] €8,500Y: second foal: dam unreliable
2-y-o 5f winner: modest maiden: should be best at 5f/6f: tried visored. *D. Carroll*

JUST IT 2 b.g. (Mar 29) Averti (IRE) 117 – Lady Kris (IRE) (Kris 135) [2007 **75**
5g* 5g 6m 7d 6m Oct 8] 11,000F, 35,000Y: big, strong gelding: half-brother to 3 winners,
including 7f/1m winner Noon Gun (by Ashkalani) and 1996 2-y-o 6f winner Lima (by
Distant Relative), both useful: dam, Irish 1¼m winner, half-sister to Gimcrack Stakes
winner Bel Bolide: fair performer: won maiden at Leicester in April: off 3 months, well
held in nurseries: should stay 7f. *W. Jarvis*

JUST SPIKE 4 ch.g. Cayman Kai (IRE) 114 – Grandads Dream (Never So Bold 135) **65**
[2007 p6g⁴ f6g p7.1g⁶ p6d p6g Dec 29] fair maiden: stays 7f: raced only on all-weather.
B. P. J. Baugh

JUST SUPERB 8 ch.g. Superlative 118 – Just Greenwich 65 (Chilibang 120) [2007 **45**
p12.2g p16.5g p13.9g⁶ Dec 1] poor maiden on Flat, lightly raced: stays 2m: acts on
polytrack: tried in cheekpieces. *P. A. Pritchard*

JUST TWO NUMBERS 3 b.g. Bahamian Bounty 116 – Khadino (Relkino 131) [2007 **84 p**
–: 10m⁴ 8.3s* 8.1m⁶ 10d⁴ 10.1d⁶ Oct 30] heavy-topped gelding: fairly useful performer:
won maiden at Windsor in June: very much caught the eye fourth outing: needs test at 1m,
and stays 1¼m: acts on soft and good to firm ground: gelded after final start: should still
do better. *W. Jarvis*

JUST WAZ (USA) 5 ch.g. Woodman (USA) 126 – Just Tops (USA) (Topsider (USA)) **67**
[2007 58: 15.8m 12.4m 12m⁵ 14.1m* 14.1d² 16s² 14.1d⁶ 14m 15.8s 14.1g Oct 19] quite
good-topped gelding: fair performer: won claimer at Redcar in June: stays 2m: acts on
soft and good to firm going: tried in cheekpieces/visor. *R. M. Whitaker*

JUXTA POSE 4 b.g. Josr Algarhoud (IRE) 118 – Shi Shi (Alnasr Alwasheek 117) [2007 **39**
p6g p8.6g May 3] modest maiden at 2 yrs: missed 2006, and just poor form at 4 yrs.
P. Winkworth

JUZILLA (IRE) 3 b.f. Marju (IRE) 127 – Mizillablack (IRE) 95 (Eagle Eyed (USA) **72**
111) [2007 57p: 8.3d p7.1g² 8d Oct 3] lengthy, rather sparely-made filly: fair maiden,
lightly raced: stays 7f: acts on polytrack. *W. R. Swinburn*

K

KAATEB (IRE) 4 b.g. Alhaarth (IRE) 126 – Muhaba (USA) 96 (Mr Prospector (USA)) **91**
[2007 7.1d 8d 10m* p12m² p10g* Oct 24] big, good-topped gelding: fairly useful performer, progressing well: won maiden at Sandown in September and handicap at Lingfield
in October: likely to stay 1¾m: acts on polytrack and good to firm ground. *W. J. Haggas*

KABALLERO (GER) 6 ch.g. Lomitas 129 – Keniana (IRE) (Sharpo 132) [2007 8.5m **74**
f8g⁶ Jun 5] ex-German gelding: successful 4 times in native country, including handicap
at Cologne in 2006: easily better effort on Flat in Britain when eighth of 9 in handicap at
Beverley on first outing in 2007: stays 9f: acts on soft going. *S. Gollings*

KABEER 9 ch.g. Unfuwain (USA) 131 – Ta Rib (USA) 116 (Mr Prospector (USA)) **–**
[2007 –, a89: p10g p8g p8g 7m f8d* f8d* f8g⁴ Dec 27] big, lengthy gelding: fairly use- **a94**
ful handicapper: off 8 months, better than ever when winning twice at Southwell in
December: best at 1m: acts on all-weather, lightly raced and little recent form on turf:
tried in cheekpieces: tongue tied: said to have bled fourth start: front runner. *A. J. McCabe*

KABIS AMIGOS 5 ch.g. Nashwan (USA) 135 – River Saint (USA) 73§ (Irish River **80**
(FR) 131) [2007 69: f8g² p9.5g p7.1g* p7.1g* p7.1g* 7m³ 6f 7f² 7f 6.9m⁶ 7.9f* 7.1s⁶ 8m
8m Sep 1] tall, leggy gelding: fairly useful handicapper: won at Wolverhampton (3) in
March and Carlisle in August: stays 1m: acts on all-weather, firm and good to soft going:
tongue tied: front runner: sold 1,200 gns. *D. Nicholls*

KABUKU 2 b.c. (Jan 22) Dr Fong (USA) 128 – Premier Night 102 (Old Vic 136) [2007 **69**
7g 8m⁵ 8f⁵ 8d p8.6g⁵ Oct 30] 10,000Y: neat colt: sixth foal: half-brother to fairly useful
11.5f winner Sir Brastias (by Shaamit) and 1¾m winner Flamenco Bride (by Hernando):
dam 1½m to 2m winner: maiden: fifth at Newmarket (fair form) second start, standout
effort: bred to stay at least 1¼m. *M. H. Tompkins*

KADIA 4 ch.f. Arkadian Hero (USA) 123 – Soba Up 74 (Persian Heights 129) [2007 p8g **54**
f7g f6g* f6g 6g f7g 8s⁵ 8v 8m Sep 1] fourth foal: half-sister to 8-y-o Saint Alebe: dam,
1¼m/1½m winner, half-sister to dam of very smart 1¼m/1½m performer Dark Moondancer out of high-class sprinter Soba: modest performer at best: won 4-runner maiden at
Southwell in April: stays 1m: acts on fibresand and soft going. *P. T. Midgley*

KADOUCHSKI (FR) 3 b.g. Ski Chief (USA) 115 – Douchka (FR) (Fijar Tango (FR) **66**
127) [2007 10g³ 10d⁵ p12g² p6g Dec 19] lengthy gelding: third in maiden at Seiches, only
start for G. Cherel in France: best effort in Britain when fifth in maiden at Windsor (off
over 6 months after): inadequate trip on handicap debut final start. *Miss E. C. Lavelle*

KAFUU (IRE) 3 b.c. Danehill Dancer (IRE) 117 – Nausicaa (USA) (Diesis 133) [2007 **91 p**
84P: 7m 7d Oct 19] tall, quite good-topped colt: has a quick action: impressive maiden
winner sole 2-y-o start: off 12 months/looked very well, eye-catching reappearance when
eighth to Celtic Sultan in handicap at Newmarket, nearest finish after travelling strongly
under patient ride: well held in similar event there 13 days later: will stay 1m: worth
another chance to progress. *J. Noseda*

KAHARA 3 b.f. Sadler's Wells (USA) 132 – Kithanga (IRE) 117 (Darshaan 133) [2007 **100**
70p: 10g* 12m* 14m* 14.6g² Oct 26] rather leggy, useful-looking filly: useful performer,
lightly raced: progressed well, winning maiden at Newbury in August, and handicaps at
Goodwood in September and Newmarket (beat Duty Free by 1½ lengths) in October:
good 1¼ lengths second to Whenever in handicap at Doncaster final outing, again
travelling smoothly: will stay 2m+: acts on good to firm going. *L. M. Cumani*

KAHLUA BEAR 5 b.g. Mister Baileys 123 – Crystal Magic 92 (Mazilier (USA) 107) **58**
[2007 66, a59: p7.1g⁴ p7.1g* p7.1g³ p6g May 3] modest handicapper: won at Wolverhampton in January: effective at 6f to 8.6f: acted on polytrack and firm ground: dead.
Miss K. B. Boutflower

KAHLUA KISS 4 b.f. Mister Baileys 123 – Ring Queen (USA) (Fairy King (USA)) **–**
[2007 103: 10.3m p10m p10g⁶ Dec 22] close-coupled, workmanlike filly: useful
performer at 3 yrs: off a year (reportedly pulled a muscle earlier in season), well below
form in listed races in 2007. *W. R. Muir*

KAICHOU (IRE) 3 b.f. Peintre Celebre (USA) 137 – Lipica (IRE) 99 (Night Shift –
(USA)) [2007 10.1d Jul 5] second foal: closely related to 4-y-o Lipizza: dam 2-y-o 7f
winner: 20/1 and ridden by 7-lb claimer, well-held seventh in maiden at Yarmouth, not
knocked about. *N. A. Callaghan*

KAILASHA (IRE) 3 br.f. Kalanisi (IRE) 132 – Snow Peak (Arazi (USA) 135) [2007   **75**
57p: p9.5g⁵ 10d³ p12g² p11g⁵ Jul 11] tall, close-coupled filly: fair maiden, lightly raced:
stays easy 1½m: raced only on polytrack and good to soft going. *C. F. Wall*

KAIRABA 2 ch.c. (Feb 3) Storming Home 128 – Heaven-Liegh-Grey 90 (Grey Desire   **62**
115) [2007 5m 5m⁶ Apr 23] close-coupled colt: better run in maidens (modest form)
when sixth at Windsor: dead. *J. Pearce*

KALANDA KURL (IRE) 2 ch.f. (Apr 23) Hernando (FR) 127 – Kalanda (Desert   –
King (IRE) 129) [2007 7d 7.5m 6g a9.5g Dec 30] €32,000Y: small, strong filly: second
foal: dam, French maiden, half-sister to very smart sprinter Continent: no form for
J. J. Quinn first 3 starts: mid-division in claimer at Pau final one. *T. Lemer, France*

KALANKARI (IRE) 4 b. or br.c. Kalanisi (IRE) 132 – Stately Princess 70 (Robellino   **102**
(USA) 127) [2007 102: 7.5g* 7.5g⁵ 7.5g³ 8.1m² Apr 17] leggy, quite good-topped colt:
useful performer: won handicap at Nad Al Sheba in January: creditable efforts in similar
event there and in minor event at Warwick (short-head second to Kew Green, reportedly
finishing lame) last 2 starts: effective at 7f/1m: acts on polytrack, firm and soft going:
often front runner. *A. M. Balding*

KALASAM 3 ch.g. Noverre (USA) 125 – Spring Sixpence 60 (Dowsing (USA) 124)   **85**
[2007 79: 8.1m³ 10g 9m⁶ 8m⁴ 8m⁶ 8m⁴ 10d³ 9.8m² 10m* 10g³ 10m³ p9.5g² p12.2g²
Oct 26] strong, smallish gelding: fairly useful handicapper: won apprentice event at Leicester in September: stays 1½m: acts on polytrack, good to firm and good to soft ground:
sold 36,000 gns, then gelded. *W. R. Muir*

KALATIME (IRE) 4 b. or br.f. Kalanisi (IRE) 132 – Dream Time 75 (Rainbow Quest   **60**
(USA) 134) [2007 74: p8g p10g p11g³ f12g⁵ p13.9g Mar 23] rangy filly: modest maiden
nowadays: stays 11.6f: acts on polytrack, good to firm and good to soft going: tried
visored. *M. F. Harris*

KAL BARG 2 b.c. (Mar 10) Medicean 128 – Persian Air (Persian Bold 123) [2007 6g⁴   **98 p**
p7g* 7g³ 7g* Oct 27] 41,000F, 90,000Y: tall, close-coupled, quite attractive colt: half-
brother to several winners, including 5-y-o Turnkey and useful Italian performer up to
1¼m Setmatt (by Rudimentary): dam no form: useful form: developed well, won minor
event at Kempton in September and nursery at Doncaster (by 1¾ lengths from Flowing
Cape) in October: third to Ibn Khaldun in nursery at Ascot in between: likely to stay 1m:
will carry on improving. *M. A. Jarvis*

KALDOUN KINGDOM (IRE) 2 b.c. (Jan 25) King's Best (USA) 132 – Bint   **95**
Kaldoun (IRE) 82 (Kaldoun (FR) 122) [2007 p7g 6m² 6s⁴ 6.1d⁴ 5.5m⁶ 6m* 6.1d³ 6s*
Oct 26] compact colt: fifth foal: half-brother to 7-y-o Shape Up and 4-y-o Zabeel Tower:
dam, maiden (best around 1¼m), half-sister to dam of very smart miler Zafeen: useful
form: much improved in autumn, won nurseries at Brighton and Ayr (by 7 lengths):
should stay 1m: acts on soft and good to firm going: sold 32,000 gns. *E. A. L. Dunlop*

KALHAN SANDS (IRE) 2 b.g. (Apr 2) Okawango (USA) 115 – Night Spirit (IRE)   **85**
78 (Night Shift (USA)) [2007 5.9d 6d* 6m Aug 18] €23,000F, 18,000Y: strong,
workmanlike gelding: sixth foal: half-brother to 2 winners, including 6f winner Victoria
Peek (by Cape Cross): dam 6f winner: fairly useful form: better for debut, won maiden at
Catterick (40/1, beat Feisty Royale by 1¾ lengths) in July: firmer ground, seemed amiss
in minor event final start (gelded after): will probably stay 7f. *G. A. Swinbank*

KALLIGAL 2 br.f. (Apr 30) Kyllachy 129 – Anytime Baby 56 (Bairn (USA) 126)   **75**
[2007 6d⁴ 5m³ 6d² p6m⁵ p5g⁴ Oct 24] 10,000Y: smallish, useful-looking filly: sixth foal:
half-sister to 3 winners, including useful but untrustworthy 2001 2-y-o 5.7f winner
Online Investor (by Puissance): dam 5f winner who became moody: fair maiden: placed
at Sandown and Windsor (second to Seasider): should prove best at 5f/6f: acts on good to
firm and good to soft going, below form on polytrack last 2 starts. *R. Ingram*

KALOKAIRI (IRE) 2 b.f. (Mar 25) Galileo (IRE) 134 – Naziriya (FR) (Darshaan 133)   **54 p**
[2007 7g 8m 8.2d Oct 10] 180,000Y: quite attractive filly: half-sister to several winners,
including smart US Grade 2 1½m winner Nazirali (by Kahyasi) and useful Irish 1¼m
winner Nasafar (by Cape Cross): dam, French 10.5f winner, half-sister to Prix du Jockey
Club winner Natroun: modest form towards rear in maidens: will be well suited by
1½m+: should do better in handicaps. *J. L. Dunlop*

KAMAL 2 ch.g. (Jan 30) Bahamian Bounty 116 – Star Tulip 99 (Night Shift (USA)) **65**
[2007 f5g⁴ 6g p7.1g³ p6d p7g* p6g⁵ Dec 30] 33,000Y: closely related to 9-y-o Texas Gold
and half-brother to several winners: dam 6f winner (including at 2 yrs): fair form: claimed
from K. Ryan £8,000 after third start: improved to win nursery at Kempton in December:
free-going sort, likely to prove best up to 7f: acts on polytrack. *W. R. Muir*

KAMANDA LAUGH 6 ch.g. Most Welcome 131 – Kamada (USA) (Blushing Groom **84**
(FR) 131) [2007 102: 9s⁴ 8.5v⁶ 9.8m 8m 8.1s p8.6g f8g Dec 27] strong gelding: only
fairly useful handicapper in 2007 (reportedly scoped dirty and tended to hang left second/
third starts): stays easy 1¼m: acts on polytrack, good to firm and good to soft going: tried
blinkered: ran as if amiss second/fifth 5-y-o outings. *K. A. Ryan*

KAMES PARK (IRE) 5 b.g. Desert Sun 120 – Persian Sally (IRE) (Persian Bold 123) **100 d**
[2007 96: p13.9g² p13g* p12g* 12g 12.1g² 12.1d⁵ 14m⁵ 13.1m 16.1m 9.2g Sep 23]
lengthy, good-bodied gelding: useful handicapper: won at Lingfield (2) in March, beating Kings Quay by 3 lengths on latter occasion: lost form after second at Beverley in
May, leaving I. Semple after eighth start: stays 1¾m: acts on polytrack, soft and good to
firm going: tried in blinkers/cheekpieces: tends to carry head high: hung sixth outing:
ungenuine. *Mrs H. O. Graham*

KANDAHAR RUN 2 gr.c. (Apr 13) Rock of Gibraltar (IRE) 133 – Kenmist 105 **106 p**
(Kenmare (FR) 125) [2007 8.1d² 8m* 8d* Oct 19] 50,000Y: big, lengthy, good-bodied
colt: has scope: fifth foal: closely related to very smart French 1m (including Prix du
Moulin)/1¼m winner Grey Lilas (by Danehill) and half-brother to 3 winners in France,
notably 6.5f/7f winner Chambord (by Green Desert) and 7f to 1¼m winner Stendhal (by
Polish Precedent), both useful: dam 1m/1¼m winner: useful form: most progressive, won
maiden at Doncaster in September and minor event at Newmarket in October, latter by
3½ lengths from Ghetto (isolated with race sewn up when hung right final 1f): will stay
1¼m, possibly 1½m: pattern-race performer in the making. *H. R. A. Cecil*

KANDIDATE 5 b.h. Kabool 119 – Valleyrose (IRE) (Royal Academy (USA) 130) **114**
[2007 119: a9f* a10f⁶ 10g³ 10d⁵ 10g⁶ 10.5m⁵ 8.9f³ a10.5g Nov 24] strong, good-topped **a119**
horse: impresses in appearance: has a quick action: smart performer: won Maktoum Challenge Round 2 at Nad Al Sheba in February, making all to beat Mullins Bay 5¾ lengths:
best efforts in Britain when third to Red Rocks in Gordon Richards Stakes at Sandown in
April and to Echo of Light in Strensall Stakes at York penultimate start: soundly beaten in
Japan Cup Dirt at Tokyo final outing: stays easy 1½m: acts on polytrack/dirt and firm
going: tried blinkered in 2005: tongue tied. *C. E. Brittain*

KANNON 2 b.f. (Mar 5) Kyllachy 129 – Violet (IRE) 77 (Mukaddamah (USA) 125) **48 p**
[2007 p8m Nov 26] 60,000Y: fourth foal: half-sister to 5-y-o Boo and 4-y-o Indigo
Dancer: dam, 6f and 8.5f winner, half-sister to smart winner up to 1¼m Sobriety: better
than bare result when tenth in maiden at Lingfield (very slowly away): should improve.
W. J. Knight

KANONKOP 3 b.f. Observatory (USA) 131 – Camcorder (Nashwan (USA) 135) [2007 **54**
56: p8g p10g 12.1g⁵ p12g⁵ Jun 30] compact filly: modest maiden: stays 1½m: acts on
polytrack and good to soft going: failed to impress with attitude on reappearance: sold
3,000 gns, joined M. Gingell and won juvenile hurdle in September. *Miss J. R. Gibney*

KANSAS FEATHER (IRE) 4 b.f. Darnay 117 – Kissimmee Bay (IRE) 54 (Brief **–**
Truce (USA) 126) [2007 p8.6g p12.2g Feb 5] second foal: dam sprint maiden: well beaten
only start over hurdles and in maidens at Wolverhampton (slowly away). *B. S. Rothwell*

KANSAS GOLD 4 b.g. Alhaarth (IRE) 126 – Star Tulip 99 (Night Shift (USA)) [2007 **75**
73: f6g 6g 6.1g 8.1g² p9.5g* p9.5g³ p9.5g* p9.5g p9.5g⁵ p9.5d⁶ Dec 17] well-made
gelding: fair handicapper: won at Wolverhampton in September and October: stays 9.5f:
acts on polytrack and firm going. *J. Mackie*

KAPELLMEISTER (IRE) 4 b.g. Mozart (IRE) 131 – March Hare 60 (Groom **–**
Dancer (USA) 128) [2007 88: p10g p7.1g p12.2d Dec 6] sturdy gelding: fairly useful
performer at 3 yrs: little form in 2007: usually in cheekpieces in 2006. *M. S. Saunders*

KAPIL (SAF) 5 b.g. Jallad (USA) 89 – Outstanding Star (AUS) (Bletchingly (AUS)) **117**
[2007 8g³ 8g* 8.9g⁵ 8m 6d 8g⁴ Nov 3] smart performer: successful on 6 of his 8 starts in
South Africa, including Group 2 KZN Guineas at Greyville in 2006: won listed race at
Nad Al Sheba in March by 3¾ lengths from Lord Admiral, readily clear inside final 1f:
off 6 months, better effort at Newmarket in autumn when close fourth to Jalmira in similar
event (blinkered, carried head awkwardly): stays 1m. *M. F. de Kock, South Africa*

KARAOKE QUEEN 3 ch.f. Tumbleweed Ridge 117 – Sodelk (Interrex (CAN)) [2007 **–**
8.2g Oct 31] plain filly: first foal: dam no form on Flat and thoroughly irresolute jumper:
100/1, tailed-off last in maiden at Nottingham. *G. C. Bravery*

KARA TAU 2 b.g. (Apr 1) Efisio 120 – Donna Anna (Be My Chief (USA) 122) [2007 **59 p** 6s⁶ Jul 5] 80,000Y: good-topped gelding: second foal: half-brother to 3-y-o Northern Fling: dam, no form, sister to smart 1m/1¼m performer Donna Viola and half-sister to dam of July Cup winner Frizzante (by Efisio): 12/1 and green, sixth to Legal Eagle in maiden at Newbury: subsequently gelded: will improve. *M. P. Tregoning*

KARATE QUEEN 2 b.f. (Apr 17) King's Best (USA) 132 – Black Belt Shopper (IRE) **58** 82 (Desert Prince (IRE) 130) [2007 7g 8d p7g⁴ Oct 23] 22,000Y: close-coupled filly: second foal: half-sister to 3-y-o Exit Strategy: dam, 6f winner (ran only at 2 yrs, stayed 1m), out of half-sister to smart stayer Arden: modest maiden: should stay 1m. *A. M. Balding*

KARAYEL (IRE) 3 b.c. Fasliyev (USA) 120 – Madamaa (IRE) 88 (Alzao (USA) 117) **–** [2007 94: p6g Mar 31] compact colt: fairly useful performer at 2 yrs: pulled up in minor event at Kempton sole 3-y-o start: stayed 7f: acted on polytrack, firm and good to soft going: dead. *R. Hannon*

KAREEB (FR) 10 b.g. Green Desert (USA) 127 – Braari (USA) 97 (Gulch (USA)) **49** [2007 61: p7.1g⁶ p7.1g Feb 12] smallish, robust gelding: just poor form in 2007: stay- ed 8.6f: acted on polytrack, firm and soft going: tried blinkered (earlier in career)/in cheekpieces: was held up, and reportedly needed tender handling to produce best: dead. *P. A. Blockley*

KARKY SCHULTZ (GER) 2 gr.g. (May 17) Diktat 126 – Kazoo 108 (Shareef **68** Dancer (USA) 135) [2007 6g⁵ 6s³ 6s⁴ 7s 7g p8.6g Nov 9] leggy gelding: fair maiden: in frame at Yarmouth and Newcastle: no impact in nurseries: should stay 1m: acts on soft going. *J. M. P. Eustace*

KARLANI (IRE) 4 br.g. Fantastic Light (USA) 134 – Karliyka (IRE) (Last Tycoon **75 §** 131) [2007 81: 13.1g⁶ 16.2m² 14.1m² 18d⁰ 15.8m⁶ 16m³ 16.1m* 16m⁴ 14m Sep 9] lengthy gelding: fair handicapper: first success at Newcastle in August: stays 2m: acts on heavy and good to firm ground: sometimes visored/blinkered: ungenuine. *G. A. Swinbank*

KARMA LLAMA (IRE) 3 b.f. Intikhab (USA) 135 – Ustka 60 (Lomond (USA) 128) **58** [2007 70: 7.1d 7m 6.9g⁴ p7.1g 7g 7g⁶ Oct 19] good-bodied filly: just modest maiden handicapper in 2007: will stay 1m: acts on firm and good to soft going: tried in cheek- pieces. *B. Smart*

KARMEI 2 b.c. (Apr 28) Royal Applause 124 – Lafite 100 (Robellino (USA) 127) **60** [2007 6f 5m p7.1g⁴ Nov 22] 30,000Y: smallish, robust colt: fourth foal: dam, 1m/1¼m winner, half-sister to very smart 1¼m/1½m performer Imperial Dancer: modest maiden: should stay 7f/1m. *J. W. Hills*

KARMEST 3 ch.f. Best of The Bests (IRE) 122 – Karmafair (IRE) (Always Fair (USA) **60** 121) [2007 54: p9.5g f7g³ 5.9m 6d* 6g p7.1g 7g 6v 7.2v⁴ p11g² p11g³ p10m Dec 10] modest performer: won handicap at Warwick in June: left E. McMahon after next start: stays 11f: acts on all-weather and good to soft ground: tried visored: has carried head awkwardly: inconsistent. *A. D. Brown*

KAROO BLUE (IRE) 3 b.c. Cape Cross (IRE) 129 – Red Conquest 55 (Lycius (USA) **99** 124) [2007 83: p8g³ 11.5g⁶ 7g 7.1d⁴ 8m 8m* p8g² 8g p8g 8g³ Oct 6] strong, useful- looking colt: useful handicapper: won at Redcar (by ½ length from Gleneagles) in August: good third to Fragrancy at Redcar final outing: stays 1m: acts on polytrack, firm and soft ground: tried blinkered: sold 36,000 gns, sent to Bahrain. *C. E. Brittain*

KARRUMBA (IRE) 3 ch.f. Desert Prince (IRE) 130 – Royal Bossi (IRE) (Spectrum **–** (IRE) 126) [2007 9.7m p12.2g Nov 9] first foal: dam, ran once in Ireland, out of half-sister to King's Theatre and High Estate: well held in maidens 7 months apart: said to have returned with sore shins on debut. *B. J. McMath*

KASBAN 3 b.c. Kingmambo (USA) 125 – Ebaraya (IRE) 82 (Sadler's Wells (USA) 132) **78** [2007 –: 10m⁵ 10.2m 11.8s³ 14g⁴ Jun 15] €360,000Y: compact colt: first foal: dam, Irish 1½m winner, sister to Irish Oaks and Prix Royal-Oak winner Ebadiyla, and half-sister to Gold Cup winner Enzeli: fair maiden: trained by D. Weld in Ireland only outing at 2 yrs: will prove best at 1¾m+: sold 85,000 gns in July. *E. A. L. Dunlop*

KASEEMA (USA) 3 b. or br.f. Storm Cat (USA) – Onaga (USA) (Mr Prospector **95** (USA)) [2007 88p: 7m⁴ 8m 8d Jul 27] big, lengthy filly: useful performer, lightly raced: good 1¼ lengths fourth to Scarlet Runner in Nell Gwyn Stakes at Newmarket on reap- pearance: sweating, well held after in 1000 Guineas there and listed race at Ascot: should have stayed 1m: nervy sort: visits Haafhd. *Sir Michael Stoute*

KASHIMIN (IRE) 2 b.c. (May 2) Kyllachy 129 – Oh So Misty (Teenoso (USA) 135) **79 p**
[2007 6m* Oct 22] 8,500F, 11,000Y: fifth foal: dam little form: 12/1, won maiden at
Pontefract easily by 3 lengths from Tito, going strongly before idling once clear: will stay
7f: useful prospect. *G. A. Swinbank*

KASHMINA 2 ch.f. (Mar 7) Dr Fong (USA) 128 – Lady Melbourne (IRE) 76 (Indian **71 §**
Ridge 123) [2007 7g 7g 7s 7m 8f⁵ 7d² 7g 7d Oct 30] 14,000F, 57,000Y: sturdy, lengthy
filly: third foal: half-sister to 3-y-o Dualagi: dam, 6f winner, half-sister to smart performers Crisos Il Monaco (at 1m/1¼m in Italy) and Gay Burslem (stayed 1m in Ireland): fair
maiden: second at Catterick, only sound run in 5 nurseries: should stay 1m: acts on good
to soft going: unreliable. *M. R. Channon*

KASHMIR LADY (FR) 3 ch.f. Rock of Gibraltar (IRE) 133 – Persian Walk (FR) **77**
(Persian Bold 123) [2007 72: p7g⁶ 8.3d⁴ p7g³ 7.1g² 8.3d² 8.1m⁴ 7g 7.5d Sep 25] rangy
filly: fair maiden handicapper: unlikely to stay beyond 8.3f: acts on polytrack, good to
firm and good to soft going. *H. Candy*

KASHOOF 2 b.f. (Feb 9) Green Desert (USA) 127 – Khulood (USA) 103 (Storm Cat **83**
(USA)) [2007 5.1m⁵ 6m² 6g 5g² 5m* Sep 14] smallish, good-topped filly: good walker:
fluent mover: first foal: dam, 6f (at 2 yrs)/7f (Nell Gwyn Stakes) winner, half-sister to
July Cup winner Elnadim and Irish 1000 Guineas winner Mehthaaf out of very smart
French performer up to 1¼m Elle Seule: fairly useful form: runner-up twice at Newmarket, in nursery latterly, prior to winning maiden at Sandown by 4 lengths: will prove
best at 5f/6f: raced only on good/good to firm going. *J. L. Dunlop*

KASSUTA 3 b.f. Kyllachy 129 – Happy Omen (Warning 136) [2007 72: p6g⁴ p6g⁴ p7g⁶ **63**
8.1d 6v² 7.5s 7d³ 7m p7.1g 7d 8d² 9.1s³ 8d* Oct 30] compact filly: modest performer: left
S. Williams after seventh start: won claimer at Yarmouth in October: stays 1m: acts on
polytrack and heavy going: wears headgear: difficult ride. *John A. Harris*

KASTAN 3 ch.g. Auction House (USA) 120 – Cashiki (IRE) 69 (Case Law 113) [2007 **40**
–: 10d 8.1g 8d³ 8.1m p8g p10g 7d Oct 29] lengthy gelding: poor maiden: stays 1m: acts
on good to soft going. *B. Palling*

KASTHARI (IRE) 8 gr.g. Vettori (IRE) 119 – Karliyka (IRE) (Last Tycoon 131) [2007 **104**
112: 14g 16.2m⁶ 20m 18m⁶ 16.1m² 14.6m² 16d⁴ 18d⁶ 16.5m² Nov 10] tall, lengthy gelding: just useful handicapper in 2007: left J. Howard Johnson after reappearance: creditable efforts when in frame, including when by 1¼ lengths second to Dansant in Mallard
Stakes at Doncaster and fourth to Samurai Way at Ascot sixth/seventh starts: stays 2¼m:
has won on soft going, very best efforts on good/good to firm: races prominently.
J. D. Bethell

KASUMI 4 ch.f. Inchinor 119 – Raindrop 59 (Primo Dominie 121) [2007 84: 7g⁴ 7.6g* **91**
8g² 8m* 8m³ p8g⁴ Oct 14] leggy, lengthy filly: fairly useful handicapper: won at Lingfield in June and Brighton (beat Tender The Great by neck) in August: best at 7f/1m: acts
on polytrack, good to firm and good to soft going. *H. Morrison*

KATALAK (IRE) 4 b.c. Desert Prince (IRE) 130 – Katiykha (IRE) 117 (Darshaan 133) **65**
[2007 16m 10m 8m 10s⁵ 10.1g Aug 17] second foal: dam 1½m/1¾m winner: fair maiden:
bred to stay beyond 1¼m: best effort on soft going: twice slowly away. *J. P. Broderick,
Ireland*

KATES GUEST (IRE) 5 b.g. Be My Guest (USA) 126 – Kates Choice (IRE) 86 (Tau- **–**
fan (USA) 119) [2007 –: p12g p9.5g Feb 10] little form: tried in blinkers/cheekpieces.
B. G. Powell

KATESVILLE (IRE) 3 b.f. King's Theatre (IRE) 128 – Great Days (IRE) 52 (Magical **54**
Strike (USA) 114) [2007 65: 10s 7.5m 10m 13.8g² Sep 22] modest maiden: left Frederick
Bowles in Ireland after third outing: stays 1¾m: acts on heavy ground. *R. Ford*

KATHLEEN KENNET 7 b.m. Turtle Island (IRE) 123 – Evaporate 51 (Insan (USA) **52 §**
119) [2007 63: f8g 7.6g⁶ 9.7g⁴ p10g p9.5g⁶ p8g³ p7.1g Nov 22] modest maiden: left Mrs
H. Sweeting after reappearance: effective at 1m, should stay 1½m: acts on polytrack and
good to soft going: has flashed tail/hung: ungenuine. *C. Tinkler*

KATIE BOO (IRE) 5 br.m. Namid 128 – Misty Peak (IRE) 83 (Sri Pekan (USA) 117) **92**
[2007 –: f5g 5m⁶ 6m⁶ 6g⁵ 5d² 6d³ 5f* 5g⁴ 6s² 5s* 5d³ 6v⁴ 6d⁴ 6m* 5d² 5g 6m⁶ 5g⁶
6d 7m Nov 10] lengthy mare: fairly useful handicapper: won at Hamilton in June and
July, and Haydock in August: seemed to run well when sixth in listed race at Hamilton in
September: best at 5f/6f: acts on firm and soft going: tough. *A. Berry*

KATIE CONISTON 3 b.f. Lake Coniston (IRE) 131 – Lycius Touch 50 (Lycius (USA) **43**
124) [2007 p6g p6g 7d 5.7d 7d⁶ p7g Oct 24] 2,000Y: small filly: half-sister to 2000 2-y-o

KAT

6f winner Deceives The Eye (by Dancing Spree) and 5-y-o Ronnies Lad: dam 2-y-o 5f winner: poor maiden. *Dr J. R. J. Naylor*

KATIE KILLANE 5 ch.m. Komaite (USA) – Efficacy 62 (Efisio 120) [2007 52: p5g² **51** p5.1g p5g⁴ f5g p5g May 31] modest performer: best at 5f: acts on all-weather: tried in cheekpieces, often wears visor: tried tongue tied. *M. Wellings*

KATIE KINGFISHER 3 b.f. Fraam 114 – Sonic Sapphire 67 (Royal Academy (USA) **53** 130) [2007 48: 8.1m 7s 8.5g p13.9g⁵ p16g Dec 4] lightly-raced maiden: left R. Beckett after second start: seems to stay 13.9f: acts on polytrack: tried in cheekpieces. *M. Wigham*

KATIE LAWSON (IRE) 4 b.f. Xaar 132 – Idle Chat (USA) 93 (Assert 134) [2007 **52** 70: p7.1g 8m 11.9s⁵ 10.2s p8.6g p7.1g⁶ Dec 3] only modest in 2007: stays 9.5f: acts on all-weather: usually in headgear: withdrawn after unseating rider and bolting prior to second intended outing. *D. Haydn Jones*

KATIES TUITOR 4 b.g. Kayf Tara 130 – Penny Gold (IRE) (Millfontaine 114) [2007 **76** 77: 13.3m⁵ 12d⁶ Sep 28] rangy gelding: fair handicapper: barely stays 13.3f: acts on polytrack and good to firm going. *B. W. Duke*

KATIMONT (IRE) 2 b.f. (Feb 8) Montjeu (IRE) 137 – Katiyfa (Auction Ring (USA) **75** 123) [2007 8.1s² 8d⁴ Oct 19] €260,000Y: strong, good-bodied filly: has quick action: closely related to fairly useful 7f winner Ammenayr (by Entrepreneur) and half-sister to several winners, including smart Irish 1½m/1¾m winner Katiykha (by Darshaan): dam French 1m/1¼m winner: fair form in frame in maidens at Haydock and Newmarket (fourth to Mukhber): will stay 1¼m/1½m: looks highly strung. *B. W. Hills*

KATIYPOUR (IRE) 10 ch.g. Be My Guest (USA) 126 – Katiyfa (Auction Ring **90 d** (USA) 123) [2007 94: p8g² p8g² p7g² p8f⁶ p8g⁴ p6g p8g³ p7g⁴ p8g⁵ p8g⁶ 10m p8g⁴ p7g² p8g p8g⁶ Dec 28] quite attractive gelding: fairly useful handicapper: regressed after third outing in 2007, leaving P. Mitchell after thirteenth start: has won up to easy 1½m, best efforts at 7f/1m: acts on all-weather, firm and good to soft going: tried visored/in cheekpieces: sometimes races freely/carries head high: held up. *B. R. Johnson*

KATRINA BEE (IRE) 2 ch.f. (Mar 17) Captain Rio 122 – Way of Truth (Muhtarram **65 d** (USA) 125) [2007 5.1d³ 5d p5g⁴ Aug 4] 11,000F, £21,000 2-y-o: small filly: second foal: dam twice-raced half-sister to smart performer up to 1m Radwell: maiden: disappointing after debut third at Bath (fair form): raced only at 5f. *R. Hannon*

KATSUMOTO (IRE) 4 ch.g. Muhtarram (USA) 125 – Self Assured (IRE) 97 (Aho- **–** noora 122) [2007 –: p8.6g f8g f12g May 22] big, workmanlike gelding: little form: tried in cheekpieces. *A. J. McCabe*

KATY CARR 3 b.f. Machiavellian (USA) 123 – Khalafiya 104 (Darshaan 133) [2007 **52** 70: p9.5g Jan 26] lightly-raced maiden: easily best effort on debut at 2 yrs. *M. J. Wallace*

KA'U MAUNA KEA 3 ch.f. Observatory (USA) 131 – Musical Twist (USA) 97 **54** (Woodman (USA) 126) [2007 8.3m⁵ 7m p8g p6g Nov 16] 12,000Y: smallish, angular filly: fifth foal: half-sister to winner in Greece by Atticus: dam, maiden (stayed 1m), out of Cherry Hinton/Fred Darling winner Musicale: form only when fifth in maiden at Windsor. *J. A. Geake*

KAVACHI (IRE) 4 b.g. Cadeaux Genereux 131 – Answered Prayer (Green Desert **83** (USA) 127) [2007 74: p7g 8.1g 9.9g³ 10m³ 10d⁶ 8m² 8d³ 10.1d* Oct 30] workmanlike gelding: fairly useful handicapper: won at Folkestone in June and Yarmouth in October: stays 1¼m: acts on firm and soft going (unraced on heavy): has raced freely: held up. *G. L. Moore*

KAVALOTI (IRE) 3 b.g. Kahyasi 130 – Just As Good (FR) (Kaldounevees (FR) 118) **83** [2007 10.5s⁶ 12d 12.5g* 11.5d⁶ 13.5g*⁴ 14g⁴ p16g² Aug 29] good-topped gelding: first foal: dam useful French 1m winner, sister to very smart French 1m/1¼m performer Terre A Terre: fairly useful performer: won maiden at Évreux (by 10 lengths) in May and minor event at Longchamp in June: left Y. de Nicolay in France, creditable efforts in handicaps at Sandown and Kempton both starts in Britain: gelded after: stays 2m: acts on polytrack, raced only on good going or softer on turf: blinkered last 3 starts. *G. L. Moore*

KAVERI (USA) 4 br.f. War Chant (USA) 126 – Valid Bonnet (USA) (Valid Appeal **79** (USA)) [2007 88: p7.1g p7g p7g⁵ 6g 7d² 7m Aug 15] leggy filly: fair handicapper: good test at 6f, and stays 1m: acts on polytrack, firm and good to soft ground. *C. E. Brittain*

KAVI (IRE) 7 ch.g. Perugino (USA) 84 – Premier Leap (IRE) 56 (Salmon Leap (USA) **–** 131) [2007 65: p13g³ p16g² p13g² p16g³ Mar 16] small, strong gelding: fair handicapper **a77** on all-weather: stays easy 2m: acts on polytrack, had form on turf earlier in career: tried blinkered: fair hurdler. *Simon Earle*

KAVINSKY 2 b.c. (Jan 23) Stravinsky (USA) 133 – Khamsin (USA) (Mr Prospector –
(USA)) [2007 7m 7g Oct 26] well-made colt: behind in maidens (favourite on debut).
M. Johnston

KAYAH 3 b.f. Kahyasi 130 – Kristina 92 (Kris 135) [2007 78p: 11.5g* 12d 14.6m⁶ 12s   **103**
Oct 13] sturdy, angular filly: useful performer, lightly raced: won listed Oaks Trial at
Lingfield in May, getting up late to beat Brisk Breeze by ¾ length: best effort when 4½
lengths sixth to Hi Calypso in Park Hill Stakes at Doncaster (on toes) on penultimate
start: will be suited by 2m+: acts on good to firm going (well held in Oaks at Epsom and
Princess Royal Stakes at Ascot on softer than good). *R. M. Beckett*

KAY ES JAY (FR) 2 b.f. (Apr 11) Xaar 132 – Angel Rose (IRE) (Definite Article 121)   **99**
[2007 p7g⁴ p7g⁸ 7.1d⁵ 7m³ 7m 6.5m 8d⁵ 7d⁵ Oct 20] €100,000Y: lengthy, good-topped
filly: third foal: sister to Swedish 6f/1m (including at 2 yrs) winner Xaara: dam Swedish
2-y-o 1m winner: useful performer: won maiden at Kempton in July: generally held form
well in face of stiff tasks, including 1¼ lengths third to Albabilia in Sweet Solera Stakes
and 3 lengths fifth to Kitty Matcham in Rockfel Stakes, both at Newmarket fourth/final
starts: stays 7f (stamina seemed stretched in Fillies' Mile): acts on polytrack and good to
firm going, probably good to soft. *B. W. Hills*

KAYF ARAMIS 5 b.g. Kayf Tara 130 – Ara (Birthright) [2007 81: 17.2f⁵ 16m 18g*   **81**
16g 18d³ 16.2s² 16.2s⁴ 18s⁵ 21g 16.2g⁴ 18d² 16g Nov 2] plain gelding: fairly useful
handicapper: won at York in May: stays 21f well: acts on soft and good to firm ground:
effective with or without cheekpieces: often races prominently: consistent. *J. L. Spearing*

KAYFLAA (IRE) 2 b.f. (Jan 4) Dubai Destination (USA) 127 – Arhaaff (IRE) 101   –
(Danehill (USA) 126) [2007 8.1s 8d Oct 23] second foal: dam, 1m winner, half-sister to
smart performer up to 1½m Subtle Power: dropped away in maidens, on ground softer
than good. *M. R. Channon*

KAY GEE BE (IRE) 3 b.c. Fasliyev (USA) 120 – Pursuit of Truth (USA) 69 (Irish   **103**
River (FR) 131) [2007 80: 8.2m² p8.6g* 8.1m 8.2g⁵ p8m* Oct 6] quite good-topped colt:
useful handicapper: much improved in 2007, winning at Nottingham in April, Wolverhampton in May and Kempton (best effort when beating Amarna) in October: stays 8.6f:
yet to race on firm going, acts on any other turf and polytrack. *M. J. Wallace*

KAYMICH PERFECTO 7 b.g. Sheikh Albadou 128 – Manhattan Diamond 54   –
(Primo Dominie 121) [2007 83: 8m 8m 8s Sep 26] close-coupled gelding: fairly useful
performer at best: no form in 2007: tried in headgear. *R. M. Whitaker*

KAY ONE (IRE) 2 ch.f. (Apr 1) Court Cave (IRE) – Miss Tricks (IRE) (Eagle Eyed   –
(USA) 111) [2007 5.7f p7.1g p7g 6s p8.6g f8d Dec 15] first foal: dam, ran once in Ireland,
closely related to 5-y-o Kay Two: little form. *R. J. Price*

KAYSTAR RIDGE 2 b.c. (Apr 15) Tumbleweed Ridge 117 – Kayartis 57 (Kaytu 112)   **66**
[2007 5g p6g² 6f p5.1m⁶ p6g p6g² p7g Dec 5] workmanlike colt: fair maiden: second at
Wolverhampton and Kempton (nursery): best efforts at 6f: acts on polytrack: inconsistent. *D. W. Ivory*

KAY TWO (IRE) 5 ch.g. Monashee Mountain (USA) 115 – Tricky 66 (Song 132)   **95**
[2007 92: 5g² 5.1m³ 5g 6s 5d 5m 5g* 5.1m² 5g p5.1g p5.1g Nov 19] neat gelding: useful
handicapper: won at Leicester in September and Bath (beat Little Edward by short head)
in October: best at 5f: probably acts on any going: tried blinkered, in cheekpieces last 5
starts: stumbled and unseated rider leaving stall ninth start: races prominently. *R. J. Price*

KAZAKSTAN 3 b.g. Kyllachy 129 – Niseem (USA) (Hennessy (USA) 122) [2007 6.5g   **60**
5f⁵ 6.5d p8g p6g Dec 30] modest maiden: left Edward Lynam in Ireland before final start:
should stay 6f: tried blinkered. *Mrs L. C. Jewell*

KEAGLES (ITY) 4 b.f. Indian Danehill (IRE) 124 – Athens Belle (IRE) 101 (Groom   –
Dancer (USA) 128) [2007 –: p11g 11.5m 14.1d p12m p8g p11g⁶ p10g Dec 19] little form.
J. E. Long

KEELINGS DONABATE 4 b.g. Desert Style (IRE) 121 – Sideloader Special 66   –
(Song 132) [2007 70: 5g May 10] lightly-raced maiden: well beaten in handicap sole
4-y-o start. *K. R. Burke*

KEENES DAY (FR) 2 b. or br.g. (Apr 7) Daylami (IRE) 138 – Key Academy 103   **86**
(Royal Academy (USA) 130) [2007 7.5g⁶ 8m⁵ 8.5m* 8d⁶ p8m⁴ Oct 11] tall, good-
bodied gelding: fourth foal: half-brother to 3-y-o Adaptation and 4-y-o Razed: dam, 1½m
winner, half-sister to Lancashire Oaks/US Grade 1 9f/1¼m winner Squeak: fairly useful
form: won maiden at Beverley in August: well held in listed race at Dusseldorf but

resumed progress when fourth in nursery at Kempton: gelded after: will be suited by 1¼m/1½m: acts on polytrack and good to firm going. *M. Johnston*

KEEPARRYAPPY (IRE) 2 b.g. (Mar 22) Fath (USA) 116 – Coppelia (IRE) (Mac's **72 d**
Imp (USA) 116) [2007 5m 5g³ p6g p6g Sep 7] workmanlike gelding: maiden: third at Musselburgh, only form: should stay 6f/7f: gelded after final start. *K. R. Burke*

KEEP A WELCOME 4 ch.g. Most Welcome 131 – Celtic Chimes (Celtic Cone 116) **–**
[2007 –: f6g 12.1g⁶ 16m May 21] workmanlike gelding: no form: tried in cheekpieces/ blinkers. *S. Parr*

KEEP DISCOVERING (IRE) 2 b.c. (Feb 28) Oasis Dream 129 – Side of Paradise **82**
(IRE) 103 (Sadler's Wells (USA) 132) [2007 6f* 6m Oct 8] 550,000Y: good-bodied colt: second foal: dam, French 1m/9f winner, closely related to Last Tycoon: fairly useful form: won minor event at Folkestone in September: looked to lose action in nursery only other start: not sure to stay much beyond 6f: has left Godolphin. *Saeed bin Suroor*

KEEP SHINING 2 b.f. (Feb 19) Tomba 119 – Turf Moor (IRE) 53 (Mac's Imp (USA) **–**
116) [2007 5m 6g⁵ 5m⁶ Aug 2] fourth foal: half-sister to 6f (at 2 yrs)/7f winner Turf Princess (by Wizard King): dam maiden (stayed 7f): little form (left E. Alston after second start). *J. S. Goldie*

KEEP YOUR DISTANCE 3 b.g. Distant Music (USA) 126 – Queen G (USA) 57 **–**
(Matty G (USA) 119) [2007 67: p8.6g Jan 15] fair maiden at 2 yrs: well held in claimer sole 3-y-o outing: tried tongue tied/in cheekpieces. *K. R. Burke*

KEEP YOUR HEAD (USA) 2 b.f. (Mar 18) Successful Appeal (USA) 118 – Tudor **61**
Guest (USA) (Medieval Man (USA)) [2007 p8.6g⁵ p8g⁶ 7.1g p7.1g Nov 22] $90,000Y: half-sister to several US sprint winners: dam winning US sprinter (including at 2 yrs): modest maiden: bred for speed, but has raced only at 7f/1m. *J. A. Osborne*

KEIDAS (FR) 3 b.f. Lomitas 129 – Kahina (GER) (Warning 136) [2007 74: 8.2m* 8d⁵ **77**
8.3d⁵ 7m p8.6g⁵ Oct 20] sturdy, close-coupled filly: fair handicapper: won at Nottingham in May: stays 8.6f: acts on polytrack, good to firm and good to soft ground. *C. F. Wall*

KEISHA KAYLEIGH (IRE) 4 b.f. Almutawakel (USA) 67 – Awtaar (USA) 67 (Lyphard **72**
(USA) 132) [2007 67: p10g⁵ 9.8g* 8s⁵ 8.3d⁴ 10.1g⁴ 8m² 10s* 10g² 10m⁶ p9.5g² p8.6g³ p12.2d Dec 27] leggy filly: fair performer: won seller at Ripon in April and handicap at Redcar in September: best at 1¼m: acts on polytrack, soft and good to firm ground: wears headgear. *B. Ellison*

KELAMON 3 b.g. Keltos (FR) 132 – Faraway Moon 61 (Distant Relative 128) [2007 **81**
f5g⁵ f6g³ p6g² f6g⁵ 7s³ 6.1s² p6g⁶ 6s* 6v* 6s⁴ p6g 6d p7.1g⁴ p6g p7.1g Oct 30] small, sturdy gelding: third foal: half-brother to fairly useful 2003 2-y-o 6f winner Lunar Wind (by Piccolo), later successful in Austria: dam, maiden who stayed 1m, out of half-sister to Moon Madness and Sheriff's Star: fairly useful handicapper: won at Windsor in June and July: stays easy 7f: acts on polytrack and heavy going (unraced on good or firmer): gelded after final start. *M. D. I. Usher*

KEMPSEY 5 ch.g. Wolfhound (USA) 126 – Mockingbird 64 (Sharpo 132) [2007 81: **70**
p5g p5g* p6g³ p6g⁴ p6g⁴ f5g⁴ p5g³ 5.1f Apr 11] good-bodied gelding: fair handicapper: won at Kempton in January: best at 5f/6f: acts on all-weather, firm and soft ground: wears headgear. *J. J. Bridger*

KENMORE 5 b.g. Compton Place 125 – Watheeqah (USA) 60 (Topsider (USA)) [2007 **89**
96: 6s 5d⁴ 6g 6d 6d 5s* 6s 5s 7g² 8g 7g Oct 20] strong, good sort: has a quick action: fairly useful performer: won claimer at Hamilton (left D. Nicholls) in July: effective at 5f to 1m: acts on soft going: tends to sweat/get on edge, has gone early to post. *J. G. Given*

KENNINGTON 7 ch.g. Compton Place 125 – Mim 39 (Midyan (USA) 124) [2007 78: **61**
p6g p6g 6.1g 5g p7.1g 5.2d 6m² 6f³ p5.1g* p5.1m⁴ 6g⁴ p6g 6d⁴ p6g⁶ p6m³ p5.1g f6d³ p6g² Dec 29] small, sturdy gelding: modest handicapper nowadays: won at Wolverhampton in August: effective at 5f to easy 7f: acts on all-weather and any turf going: often visored/blinkered. *Mrs C. A. Dunnett*

KEN'S GIRL 3 ch.f. Ishiguru (USA) 114 – There's Two (IRE) 85 (Ashkalani (IRE) **78**
128) [2007 70: 5.1f* 6s² 5m 6m p6g p6g Nov 9] tall, leggy filly: fair performer: better on **a68 +**
turf than all-weather: won maiden at Bath in April: stays 6f: acts on firm and soft going. *W. S. Kittow*

KENSINGTON (IRE) 6 b.g. Cape Cross (IRE) 129 – March Star (IRE) 109 (Mac's **68**
Imp (USA) 116) [2007 71: p7.1g⁵ p7g⁴ p7m⁵ f7d* Dec 18] leggy gelding: fair handi- capper: won at Southwell in December: effective at 5f to easy 7f: acts on all-weather, firm and good to soft ground: usually blinkered/in cheekpieces *P. D. Evans*

KENTON STREET 2 ch.c. (May 3) Compton Place 125 – Western Applause 76 **71 p**
(Royal Applause 124) [2007 6g⁴ Nov 2] 38,000Y: half-brother to 3-y-o Encores: dam,
maiden, half-sister to useful performers Western Devil (stays 2m in Germany) and
Just One Look (2-y-o 6f winner): well-backed 12/1, encouraging fourth to Almoutaz in
maiden at Newmarket, travelling strongly but away from main action: will do better.
J. A. R. Toller

KENTUCKY BOY (IRE) 3 b.g. Distant Music (USA) 126 – Delta Town (USA) (San- **68**
glamore (USA) 126) [2007 –: p12.2g³ 12.1s² 16.2s* 17.1d* 16.1g⁶ Oct 3] fair handicapper: won at Beverley in July and Pontefract in August: stays 17f: acts on polytrack and
soft ground. *Jedd O'Keeffe*

KENTUCKY BULLET (USA) 11 b.g. Housebuster (USA) – Exactly So (Caro 133) **–**
[2007 –, a58: f11g f11g³ f12g May 22] leggy, angular gelding: only poor in 2007: barely **a37**
stays 1½m: acts on all-weather, good to firm and good to soft ground: tried blinkered/in
cheekpieces/tongue tied: none too trustworthy. *A. G. Newcombe*

KENWYN 5 b.g. Efisio 120 – Vilany 87 (Never So Bold 135) [2007 8.1g May 29] good- **54**
topped gelding: maiden: unraced on Flat in 2006, and modest form sole 5-y-o start: stays
1m: acts on good to firm going. *K. Bishop*

KEON (IRE) 5 b.g. Rossini (USA) 118 – Lonely Brook (USA) (El Gran Senor (USA) **55**
136) [2007 63: f7g⁴ p8.6g⁵ p8.6g² p8.6g⁶ p8.6g p9.5g p8.6g p8.6d Dec 17] rather leggy
gelding: modest performer: stays 9f: acts on all-weather and soft ground: tried in cheekpieces. *R. Hollinshead*

KERAYASI (FR) 5 b.g. Kahyasi 130 – Good Blend (FR) (Darshaan 133) [2007 11.8s² **75**
10.5s 14.1d⁴ p12g⁶ Sep 3] fair performer: won minor event at Cholet in 2006: left
J. Boisnard in France, better effort in Britain when creditable close fourth in handicap at
Salisbury: stays 1¾m: raced mainly on good ground or softer (acts on heavy): usually
blinkered in France: gelded. *G. L. Moore*

KERRIEMUIR LASS (IRE) 4 b.f. Celtic Swing 138 – Shabby Chic (USA) 114 (Red **96**
Ransom (USA)) [2007 91: 12.3g⁶ 11.6m* 10m 12m p11g⁴ p12g³ p13m Nov 1] strong,
sturdy filly: useful performer: won handicap at Windsor (by 1¾ lengths from Kilimandscharo) in June: should stay 1¾m: acts on polytrack, good to firm and good to soft
ground: in cheekpieces last 2 starts: front runner: sold 58,000 gns. *M. A. Jarvis*

KERRY'S BLADE (IRE) 5 ch.g. Daggers Drawn (USA) 114 – Treasure (IRE) 72 **44 +**
(Treasure Kay 114) [2007 –: 16g⁵ 17.1d 16m⁶ 16.1m 17.1m⁴ Sep 20] tall, leggy gelding:
poor maiden on balance: tried blinkered/in cheekpieces. *Micky Hammond*

KERRY'S DREAM 3 ch.f. Tobougg (IRE) 125 – Jetbeeah (IRE) 95 (Lomond (USA) **75**
128) [2007 84: 6v 5g 6g 5g³ 5d Oct 12] big, lengthy, good-topped filly: only fair handicapper in 2007: best at 5f: acts on firm and soft ground. *T. D. Easterby*

KERSAINT (IRE) 2 b.c. (Mar 5) Catcher In The Rye (IRE) 115 – Quivala (USA) **85**
(Thunder Gulch (USA) 129) [2007 5m* 5m³ 6g⁶ 5.1d² 5.1s³ 6g 7m 6g Oct 6] strong,
sturdy colt: first foal: dam, French 1m winner (only start), out of smart sister to Prix de
Diane winner Caerlina: fairly useful performer: won maiden at Leicester in April: placed
in minor events at Ascot and Chester (2): best at 5f/6f: acts on soft and good to firm going:
blinkered (below form) final start: sent to Macau. *K. A. Ryan*

KERSWELL 3 b.f. Komaite (USA) – Polgwynne 48 (Forzando 122) [2007 64: 7m 7d
Aug 1] good-bodied filly: maiden: no form in 2007. *B. R. Millman*

KERVRIOU (FR) 4 ch.g. Pennekamp (USA) 130 – Good Blend (FR) (Darshaan 133) **71**
[2007 10m 10m 9d p11g Sep 8] tall, workmanlike gelding: fair performer: won minor
events at Marseille Vivaux and Vichy, and handicap on former course in 2006: left
J-M. Capitte in France, form in Britain in 2007 only when eighth in handicap at Sandown
penultimate outing: stays 10.8f: raced mainly on good ground or softer in France: headstrong, often pulls way to front. *A. M. Balding*

KESHYA 6 b.m. Mtoto 134 – Liberatrice (FR) (Assert 134) [2007 74§: p13.9g⁴ p12.2g **49 §**
Jan 19] leggy mare: fair at best, only poor in 2007: stays easy 1¾m: acts on all-weather
and good to soft going: refused to race final 4-y-o outing and virtually refused fifth 5-y-o
start: untrustworthy. *N. P. Littmoden*

KEW GREEN (USA) 9 b. or br.g. Brocco (USA) 124 – Jump With Joy (USA) (Link- **98**
age (USA)) [2007 116: 8.1m* 7s 8g 8.2m⁶ 8m⁵ 10m Sep 1] rangy gelding: smart
performer at best: form in 2007 (useful) only when winning minor event at Warwick in
April by short head from Kalankari, hanging right: stays 10.5f: acts on polytrack, firm
and soft going: tried tongue tied: sometimes races freely. *P. R. Webber*

KEW THE MUSIC 7 b.g. Botanic (USA) – Harmonia (Glint of Gold 128) [2007 65, **68** a70: p8g p8.6g p7g⁴ f7g* f7g⁴ f7g² p7.1g⁴ 7g Apr 3] lengthy gelding: fair handicapper: won at Southwell in March: stayed 1m: acted on all-weather and good to firm ground: sometimes visored: often started slowly/got behind: wasn't one to rely on: dead. *M. R. Channon*

KEYAKI (IRE) 6 b.m. Shinko Forest (IRE) – Woodie Dancer (USA) (Green Dancer **97** (USA) 132) [2007 83: 6f³ 6m³ p6g* 6g² 6g* 6g 7m⁴ 6m 6m 6m Sep 20] leggy mare: useful handicapper: won at Kempton in May and Folkestone (beat Bakhoor by 2 lengths) in June: below form after: stays 7f: acts on polytrack and firm ground, probably on soft. *C. F. Wall*

KEYCAVERN 3 b.f. Key of Luck (USA) 126 – Cavernista 75 (Lion Cavern (USA) **64** 117) [2007 10s² 10s² 9s* 9g² 12g² 9g⁴ 10d² 11d* 14g⁶ 10.1m* Aug 8] ex-Italian trained filly: won handicaps at Pisa in February and Milan in June for A. & G. Botti, and claimer at Yarmouth in August: stayed 1½m: acted on dirt, soft and good to firm going: joined D. Pipe, fell both starts over hurdles, fatally on second occasion. *M. Botti*

KEYNES (JPN) 5 ch.g. Gold Fever (USA) 119 – Eternal Reve (USA) 116 (Diesis 133) **–** [2007 p8g p12g p10g Jul 21] fair maiden at 2 yrs: placed in Spain 3 times in 2005: no form on belated return in 2007. *E. J. Creighton*

KEY PARTNERS (IRE) 6 b.g. Key of Luck (USA) 126 – Teacher Preacher (IRE) 37 **67** (Taufan (USA) 119) [2007 70: p12g p12.2g p12.2g f8g³ f8g p12.2g⁵ 10.9d² 12.6s 9.1s p11g⁵ p12g p12g* p11g⁵ p13.9g Nov 23] quite good-topped gelding: fair performer: left B. Leavy after third start, J. Stimpson after ninth: won handicap at Kempton in October: effective at 1m to 1½m: acts on all-weather, best turf form on ground softer than good: tried tongue tied: shaped as if amiss 4 times in 2007. *P. A. Blockley*

KHANA RAS (IRE) 2 b.c. (Apr 30) Fasliyev (USA) 120 – Siamoise (Caerleon (USA) **65** 132) [2007 5.5d 7.1m⁶ 7.1m p7g⁵ p10g p8.6g* Oct 30] close-coupled colt: fair performer: won claimer at Wolverhampton final start: should stay 1¼m: acts on polytrack and good to firm going: sold 10,000 gns. *E. J. O'Neill*

KHANDALA (IRE) 2 b.f. (Mar 29) Soviet Star (USA) 128 – Khatela (IRE) 91 (Sher- **69** nazar 131) [2007 6f 7.1m³ 6m 7d⁴ p8.6g* Oct 26] good-topped filly: has quick action: fifth foal: half-sister to 3-y-o Massive and French winner around 1¼m Jimbeck (by Night Shift): dam Irish 1m/9f winner: fair form: generally progressive, won nursery at Wolver- hampton final start: stays 8.6f. *M. L. W. Bell*

KHANJAR (USA) 7 ch.g. Kris S (USA) – Alyssum (USA) (Storm Cat (USA)) [2007 **64** 82d: p16.5g p9.5g² p11g² f16g³ p12.2g⁵ May 14] sturdy, attractive gelding: just modest handicapper nowadays: seems to stay easy 2m: acts on all-weather/dirt and firm going: sometimes visored/in cheekpieces: has found little. *J. Pearce*

KHETAAB (IRE) 5 b.g. Alhaarth (IRE) 126 – Liberi Versi (IRE) (Last Tycoon 131) **60** [2007 57: 7f 7.5m⁶ 8.1m 7.9m 8.3g⁴ Jun 13] quite good-topped gelding: modest maiden: stays 1m: acts on polytrack, firm and good to soft going: tried in cheekpieces/blinkers. *E. J. Alston*

KHIBRAAT 2 ch.f. (Apr 20) Alhaarth (IRE) 126 – Nafhaat (USA) 91 (Roberto (USA) **57** 131) [2007 7g 7.5m 8.1s Sep 29] strong filly: closely related to smart 1¼m to 1¾m (Park Hill Stakes) winner Ranin (by Unfuwain) and half-sister to numerous winners, including 1m (at 2 yrs)/1¼m winner Wahchi (by Nashwan) and 7f/1m winner Ghalib (by Soviet Star), both useful: dam 1½m winner: modest form in maidens: will benefit from 1¼m/ 1½m: sold 31,000 gns. *E. A. L. Dunlop*

KHUN JOHN (IRE) 4 b.g. Marju (IRE) 127 – Kathy Caerleon (IRE) (Caerleon (USA) **89** 132) [2007 89+: 10m³ 10.5m³ Jun 7] rangy gelding: fairly useful handicapper: creditable efforts both starts in 2007: stays easy 1¼m: raced on polytrack and good to firm ground. *B. J. Meehan*

KHYBERIE 4 b.f. Kahyasi 130 – Reading Habit (USA) (Half A Year (USA) 130) [2007 **69** 52: p10g p12.2g⁶ p12.2g⁶ p12g² p12g⁴ May 31] leggy filly: fair maiden: will stay 1¾m: raced mainly on polytrack: joined G. Haine. *G. Wragg*

KIAMA 5 b.m. Dansili 127 – Catriona 75 (Bustino 136) [2007 60: p16g p11g p12g p12g⁶ **50** Feb 19] well-made mare: modest maiden handicapper: left M. Johnston after reappear- ance: stays 2m: acts on polytrack, good to firm and heavy ground. *B. G. Powell*

KIBITZER 2 b.c. (May 9) Diesis 133 – Kitza (IRE) 113 (Danehill (USA) 126) [2007 **55 p** p7g Dec 19] 57,000Y: fifth foal: half-brother to 3 winners, including smart 7f (at 2 yrs) and 8.3f winner Fort Dignity (by Seeking The Gold) and fairly useful French 1m/8.3f winner Ascension Island (by Rahy): dam, Irish 6f (at 2 yrs) and 1m winner (later won in USA), half-sister to smart sprinter Marouble: 8/1, tenth in maiden at Lingfield, fading: capable of better. *J. W. Hills*

KICK AND PRANCE 4 ch.g. Groom Dancer (USA) 128 – Unerring (Unfuwain (USA) 131) [2007 61: p13.9g Nov 12] lengthy gelding: modest handicapper: tailed off sole 4-y-o start: stays 1½m: acts on polytrack and good to soft going: tongue tied. *J. A. Geake* —

KID MAMBO (USA) 3 b.c. Lemon Drop Kid (USA) 131 – Spring Pitch (USA) (Storm Cat (USA)) [2007 102+: 10m² 11.5g³ 12g 10g⁴ 7m Dec 1] good-topped colt: smart performer: progressed further in 2007, 1¼ lengths second to Light Shift in minor event at Newbury, 4 lengths third to Aqaleem in Derby Trial at Lingfield, 10¾ lengths seventh to Authorized in Derby at Epsom (given enterprising front-running ride) and close fourth to Zaham in listed Hampton Court Stakes at Royal Ascot: reportedly sold privately from T. Mills, and renamed Viva Hong Kong, last in handicap at Sha Tin final outing: stays 1½m: acts on soft and good to firm going: races prominently. *J. Moore, Hong Kong* **113**

KID'Z'PLAY (IRE) 11 b.g. Rudimentary (USA) 118 – Saka Saka (Camden Town 125) [2007 13m 12.1g 13d 11.1d⁵ 12m Jul 24] workmanlike gelding: fair handicapper in 2005, only poor on return to Flat in 2007: stays 13f: acts on any going: tried in cheek-pieces/visor: sometimes early to post: usually makes running: fairly useful hurdler/chaser at best. *J. S. Goldie* **45**

KIELTY'S FOLLY 3 gr.g. Weet-A-Minute (IRE) 106 – Three Sweeties (Cruise Missile) [2007 8.2g p8.6g⁶ p8.6d⁶ Dec 10] close-coupled gelding: modest form when sixth in maidens at Wolverhampton. *B. P. J. Baugh* **51**

KIHO 2 b.c. (May 4) Dashing Blade 117 – Krim (GER) (Lagunas) [2007 8g⁶ Oct 24] 4,000Y: sixth foal: half-brother to 3 winners by Big Shuffle, including fairly useful 7f (at 2 yrs) and 1½m winner Karlu: dam unraced half-sister to dam of 1000 Guineas and Oaks winner Kazzia: 50/1, needed experience when never-nearer sixth in maiden at Bath: should do better. *Eve Johnson Houghton* **68 p**

KILBURN 3 b.g. Grand Lodge (USA) 125 – Lady Lahar 106 (Fraam 114) [2007 93: 8.1g 8m 8m 8.1g 10m 10.5g⁶ Sep 8] strong, stocky gelding: type to carry condition: fairly useful handicapper: well below form last 3 starts: stays 1m, possibly not 1¼m: acts on good to firm ground: tried in cheekpieces: sold 21,000 gns, then gelded. *C. G. Cox* **83**

KILDARE SUN (IRE) 5 b.g. Desert Sun 120 – Megan's Dream (IRE) 56 (Fayruz 116) [2007 87: p9.5g⁶ 10.5g⁶ 9.8g⁵ 10.1v 9.8m⁵ p9.5g² 8.1m 8g p9.5g Oct 18] well-made gelding: fairly useful handicapper: probably stays 10.5f: acts on polytrack and good to firm ground. *J. Mackie* **84**

KILI LINKS (IRE) 2 b.f. (Jan 24) Bahri (USA) 125 – Hatheethah (IRE) (Machia-vellian (USA) 123) [2007 6f 7s 6m Sep 4] €31,000Y: strong filly: poor mover: fourth foal: half-sister to 5-y-o Golband and a winner in Greece (both by Cadeaux Genereux): dam, maiden, half-sister to useful 7f/1m performer Arzoo: well held in maidens. *R. Hannon* —

KILIMANDSCHARO (USA) 5 b.g. Rahy (USA) 115 – Landaria (FR) (Sadler's Wells (USA) 132) [2007 72: p9.5g* p10g³ p12.2g* 12.1g* 12g³ 11.6m² Jun 9] good bodied ex-German gelding: fairly useful handicapper: further progress in 2007, winning at Wolverhampton in January and February, and Beverley in May: good second to Kerriemuir Lass at Windsor final outing: worth a try at 1¾m: acts on polytrack, good to firm and good to soft going. *P. J. McBride* **91**

KILLALA (IRE) 7 b.g. Among Men (USA) 124 – Hat And Gloves (Wolver Hollow 126) [2007 11.6d Jul 23] workmanlike gelding: poor at best nowadays: well held in seller sole 7-y-o start. *D. J. Wintle* —

KILLCARA BOY 2 b.g. (Mar 21) Tobougg (IRE) 125 – Barakat 93 (Bustino 136) [2007 p8m Nov 26] 34,000Y: half-brother to several winners, including useful 1¼m performer Ta Awun (by Housebuster): dam, 1¾m winner, half-sister to Ibn Bey and Roseate Tern: 25/1 and very green, well held in maiden at Lingfield. *H. Candy* —

KILLENA BOY (IRE) 5 b.g. Imperial Ballet (IRE) 110 – Habaza (IRE) 68 (Shernazar 131) [2007 91: p8g⁴ 8.1d* 8.1g³ 8.1g 8g p8g p8g Oct 12] good-bodied gelding: useful handicapper: won at Sandown in May by 3 lengths from Queen's Best: below form after next outing: has won at 1¼m, best around 1m nowadays: acts on polytrack, soft and good to firm going. *W. Jarvis* **100**

KILLER CLASS 2 ch.f. (Apr 20) Kyllachy 129 – Class Wan 74 (Safawan 118) [2007 – 6d 6d 6f 6s Oct 26] third foal: dam 2-y-o 5f/6f winner: little form. *J. S. Goldie*

KILMEENA DREAM 3 b.f. Foxhound (USA) 103 – Kilmeena Glen (Beveled – (USA)) [2007 p7g Dec 5] sixth foal: half-sister to fairly useful 6f (also at 2 yrs)/7f winner Kilmeena Lad (by Minshaanshu Amad) and 6f winner Kilmeena Star (by So Factual): dam unraced: 50/1 and green, well held in maiden at Kempton. *J. C. Fox*

KILMEENA MAGIC 5 b.m. Fumo di Londra (IRE) 108 – Kilmeena Lady (Inca Chief **50** (USA)) [2007 52: p11g p10g⁶ p8g p10g³ p9.5g⁵ 10.2d p10g⁶ 10.2s⁴ p12g p11g⁶ Nov 21] modest maiden: stays easy 1½m: acts on polytrack and soft ground: tried in cheekpieces. *J. C. Fox*

KILMISTON SATURN 3 ch.g. Trifolio 99 – Sunley Solaire (Aragon 118) [2007 – 10f p12g May 23] well held in maidens at Windsor (started slowly) and Lingfield. *A. M. Hales*

KILVICKEON (IRE) 3 b.g. Daggers Drawn (USA) 114 – Queen of Sweden (IRE) **50** (Solid Illusion (USA) 117) [2007 46: p6g f5g⁶ p5g⁴ 5m² p5g⁵ 5m p6g 5d³ p5.1g 5s⁶ 5g³ 5g 5f 5g⁴ p5m p5.1g p5.1g Dec 31] modest maiden handicapper: stays 7f: acts on all-weather, good to firm and good to soft going: tried blinkered. *Peter Grayson*

KILWORTH (IRE) 4 gr.c. Kalanisi (IRE) 132 – Perugia (IRE) 94 (Perugino (USA) **108** 84) [2007 105: 8f² 7g Oct 6] lengthy, good sort: good walker: useful performer: good efforts both starts in 2007, short-headed by Tell in 4-runner minor event at Bath, though not convincing with attitude: stays easy 1¼m: acts on polytrack, firm and good to soft going: sometimes unimpressive to post: has left Godolphin. *Saeed bin Suroor*

KIMONO MY HOUSE 3 ch.f. Dr Fong (USA) 128 – Roselyn 66 (Efisio 120) [2007 **60** 54: 8s 9m 11.5g⁶ 9.9m² p12.2g Sep 14] modest maiden handicapper: stays easy 1¼m: acts on good to firm ground. *J. G. Given*

KIMPTON CARER 3 b.g. Groom Dancer (USA) 128 – So True 116 (So Blessed 130) **48** [2007 –: 11.5s 15.4g² Aug 16] poor maiden: once refused to enter stall: stays 15.4f: tongue tied. *J. A. Geake*

KIMS ROSE (IRE) 4 b.f. Desert Prince (IRE) 130 – Pinta (IRE) (Ahonoora 122) **60** [2007 46: p6g 7.1s* 8.1m 6d p7.1g p5.1g⁶ p7.1g Dec 4] rather leggy filly: modest handicapper: left D. Burchell prior to winning at Chepstow in July: left R. Price after fourth outing: stays 7f: acts on polytrack and soft going. *R. A. Harris*

KINDALLACHAN 4 b.f. Magic Ring (IRE) 115 – Moore Stylish 65 (Moorestyle 137) **66** [2007 52: 5g 5s 5.2m 6m 5.3d p6m² p6g² p6g* p6g⁶ p6g p6g Nov 9] quite good-topped filly: fair handicapper: won at Wolverhampton in September: stays 6f: acts on polytrack (little form on turf). *G. C. Bravery*

KINDKINTYRE (IRE) 3 b.g. Mull of Kintyre (USA) 114 – Sweet Nature (IRE) 71 **55** (Classic Secret (USA) 91) [2007 p7.1g f6g p9.5g p8g³ f7d² Dec 15] modest maiden: stays 1m: raced only on all-weather. *R. A. Fahey*

KINDLELIGHT BLUE (IRE) 3 gr.g. Golan (IRE) 129 – Kalimar (IRE) (Bigstone **85** (IRE) 126) [2007 70: p8.6g 8m⁵ 8.5g²⁷ 7m p10g⁴ 12m p10g* p10g² 10m⁶ p10g³ p12.2g⁴ p10g* p10g² Dec 4] tall, leggy gelding: fairly useful handicapper: won at Lingfield in August and November: stays 1¼m: acts on polytrack and good to firm ground. *N. P. Littmoden*

KINDLELIGHT DEBUT 7 b.m. Groom Dancer (USA) 128 – Dancing Debut 83 – (Polar Falcon (USA) 126) [2007 92, a105: p10g⁶ p8g⁶ p8.6g⁶ Jan 26] smallish mare: **a100** useful on all-weather, unraced on turf in 2007: creditable efforts in handicaps first 2 starts: stays easy 1¼m: acts on polytrack and firm going: tried in cheekpieces: effective held up or ridden prominently: tough and consistent. *N. P. Littmoden*

KIND OF FIZZY 3 b.f. Efisio 120 – Kind of Light 83 (Primo Dominie 121) [2007 54: **68** 6m⁴ p6g⁵ 6.1s 6d⁴ 7.1g 7m p6g 6s³ 6d⁴ Oct 15] neat filly: fair handicapper: won at Yarmouth in June: stayed 6f: acted on soft and good to firm going: dead. *R. Guest*

KINETA (USA) 4 b.f. Miswaki (USA) 124 – Kibitzing (USA) (Wild Again (USA)) **62 d** [2007 61: p6g⁵ p6g p7.1g 7.5m 7s⁴ 8.2g Jun 13] close-coupled filly: modest maiden: ran poorly after reappearance in 2007: best started at 6f: acts on polytrack, good to soft and good to firm going: tried blinkered. *W. R. Muir*

KINFAYRE BOY 5 b.g. Grey Eagle – Amber Gambler (ITY) (Nijin (USA)) [2007 – 11.1d 12s Jul 18] tall gelding: lightly raced and little form. *K. W. Hogg, Isle of Man*

KING AFTER 5 b.g. Bahamian Bounty 116 – Child Star (FR) 58 (Bellypha 130) [2007 **66**
64: p8g² p6g² p8g⁵ p7g² p8g³ p7f³ p10g* p16g p12g⁵ p10g² p12g⁴ p8g* p8g⁴ p7g 8m⁴
7m p7g⁴ p8g² p7g* p8g p7m p7g⁶ p7m 8m⁴ p8g* Dec 29] leggy gelding: fair performer:
won handicap in March, seller in April, and handicaps in September (dead-heating)
and December, all at Lingfield: effective at 6f to easy 1½m: acts on polytrack, good to
firm and good to soft ground: tried blinkered, usually visored: sometimes races freely.
J. R. Best

KING BATHWICK (IRE) 2 b.g. (Apr 11) Golan (IRE) 129 – Princess Sabaah (IRE) **70**
90 (Desert King (IRE) 129) [2007 5m⁶ 6s⁵ 7s³ 7m⁶ 7f 8m⁴ p8g⁵ 10.2d⁵ Oct 1] 23,000Y:
well-grown gelding: second foal: closely related to 3-y-o Prince Sabaah: dam 6f winner
(ran only at 2 yrs): fair maiden: improved for longer trip when fifth at Bath final start
(gelded after): will stay 1½m: acts on polytrack, firm and soft going. *B. R. Millman*

KING CANUTE (IRE) 3 b.g. Danehill (USA) 126 – Mona Stella (USA) 117 (Nure- **–**
yev (USA) 131) [2007 60: p7g p8g p10g Jun 9] modest maiden at 2 yrs for A. O'Brien in
Ireland: no form in 2007: subsequently gelded. *M. J. Wallace*

KING CHARLES 3 b.g. King's Best (USA) 132 – Charlecote (IRE) (Caerleon (USA) **104**
132) [2007 94p: 9.9m⁴ 10m² 10m 10m² 10d³ 10m³ 10d* Sep 28] strong, close-coupled
gelding: useful performer: often in frame in handicaps prior to winning minor event at
Ascot in September by 2 lengths from Ajhar: should stay 1½m: acts on polytrack, firm
and good to soft going: reliable. *E. A. L. Dunlop*

KING COLUMBO (IRE) 2 ch.c. (Feb 20) King Charlemagne (USA) 120 – Colum- **87**
bian Sand (IRE) (Salmon Leap (USA) 131) [2007 p7g⁵ p8g* 10g⁵ Nov 3] 24,000Y:
strong colt: half-brother to 3 winners, including 7f to 9.4f winner Arc (by Archway): dam
unraced half-sister to useful Italian performer up to 1¼m Arman's Sax: fairly useful form:
won maiden at Kempton in October: better still when fifth to Twice Over in minor event
at Newmarket: will prove best at 1¼m. *Miss J. Feilden*

KINGDOM OF DREAMS (IRE) 5 b.g. Sadler's Wells (USA) 132 – Regal Portrait **78 d**
(IRE) 57 (Royal Academy (USA) 130) [2007 78: 9.8g 10.5m⁵ 10s 11d 10d 10.3g Oct 26]
close-coupled, attractive gelding: fair handicapper: below form after second start: stays
1½m: acts on firm and good to soft going: sometimes tongue tied. *J. Mackie*

KINGDOM OF FIFE 2 b.c. (Mar 19) Kingmambo (USA) 125 – Fairy Godmother 113 **77 p**
(Fairy King (USA)) [2007 7g⁵ Nov 2] fourth foal: dam, 1¼m winner, half-sister to very
smart middle-distance stayer Blueprint: 8/1, promising fifth in maiden at Newmarket,
finishing well while learning: will be suited by 1m/1¼m: sure to win races. *Sir Michael
Stoute*

KINGDOM OF NAPLES (USA) 2 b.c. (Feb 25) Sadler's Wells (USA) 132 – Inkling **95 p**
(USA) 104 (Seeking The Gold (USA)) [2007 8f* Oct 24] fourth foal: brother to 6f winner
in Greece: dam, Irish 2-y-o 6f winner (only start), closely related to Grand Criterium
winner Jade Robbery out of close relative to Nureyev and half-sister to dam of Sadler's
Wells: 5/1, created good impression when winning 14-runner maiden at Navan by 3
lengths from Masiyma, moving through strongly to lead 1f out: not certain to stay 1½m:
smart prospect. *A. P. O'Brien, Ireland*

KING EGBERT (FR) 6 b.g. Fasliyev (USA) 120 – Exocet (USA) (Deposit Ticket **58**
(USA)) [2007 65: 5g 6m⁶ 5d⁴ 5.1s 6d⁶ 5.2d* p5g 5.1m 5m 7g p6g⁴ p6g p5g Oct 29]
lengthy, good-bodied gelding: modest handicapper: left R. Harris after second outing:
won at Yarmouth in August: best at 5f: acts on polytrack, firm and good to soft going:
tried blinkered/tongue tied/in cheekpieces: sometimes slowly away. *R. J. Price*

KING GABRIEL (IRE) 5 b.g. Desert King (IRE) 129 – Broken Spirit (IRE) (Slip **56**
Anchor 136) [2007 61: p11g⁶ 10.9m Apr 9] tall gelding: modest maiden: should stay
1½m: acts on polytrack and soft ground: tried tongue tied. *Andrew Turnell*

KING HAFHAFAH 2 ch.c. (Mar 11) King Charlemagne (USA) 120 – Hafhafah 74 **80 p**
(Shirley Heights 130) [2007 p7g* p7g² Nov 15] 4,000Y, resold 7,000Y: closely related to
winner in Italy by Polar Falcon and half-brother to winner in Greece by Mull of Kintyre:
dam, 1m winner, half-sister to useful 1¼m (including in UAE) winner Islal: fairly useful
form: won maiden at Lingfield in October: improved when head second in nursery there:
will stay 1m: should progress further. *I. A. Wood*

KING HARSON 8 b.g. Greensmith 121 – Safari Park 43 (Absalom 128) [2007 87§: **84 §**
7.1m 7d² 7.1g 7d 7d⁶ 7.6m 7m⁶ 7.1m³ 7g² 7g 7g Nov 6] close-coupled, good-bodied
gelding: fairly useful handicapper: races mainly at 7f nowadays: acts on any going: tried
blinkered, often visored: races prominently: unreliable. *J. D. Bethell*

KING JOCK (USA) 6 b.g. Ghazi (USA) – Glen Kate 118 (Glenstal (USA) 118) [2007 **110**
117: 7.5g² a8f 8g⁵ 8g⁴ 8g³ 8.5g⁴ 7g⁵ 7g² 7m⁴ 7.5g³ 8s* 7m⁵ Nov 4] lengthy, good-topped
gelding: smart performer: won minor event at the Curragh in October comfortably by 1¼
lengths from Belle Artiste: placed earlier in handicap at Nad Al Sheba (¾-length second
to Great Rhythm), took Badener Meile at Baden-Baden (1¼ lengths third to Banknote), Prix
du Pin at Longchamp (1½ lengths second to Sabana Perdida) and Concorde Stakes at
Tipperary (close third behind Eastern Appeal): effective at 7f/1m: acts on any turf going,
well held on dirt: usually held up. *R. J. Osborne, Ireland*

KING JOSHUA (IRE) 3 b.g. King's Best (USA) 132 – Lady Joshua (IRE) 88 (Royal **77**
Academy (USA) 130) [2007 86: 10m⁵ 8.5g³ 11.6g³ 9.8m³ 10m Jul 28] fair maiden:
stayed 11.6f: acted on good to firm and good to soft ground: tried tongue tied: dead.
D. R. C. Elsworth

KING KASYAPA (IRE) 5 b.g. Darshaan 133 – Ezana (Ela-Mana-Mou 132) [2007 68: **69**
11.6f 11.9g Sep 12] good-bodied gelding: fair maiden: stays 1½m: acts on good to soft
going, probably on good to firm: won over hurdles in September. *P. Bowen*

KING KENNY 2 ch.c. (Jan 30) Lomitas 129 – Salanka (IRE) 68 (Persian Heights 129) **86**
[2007 7g⁴ p8.6g² Nov 27] 50,000F, 90,000Y: half-brother to several winners, including
1998 2-y-o 7f winner Penmayne (by Inchinor) and 6f to 1m winner Salamanca (by
Pivotal), both useful: dam 1¼m winner: fairly useful maiden: fourth to Speedy Dollar at
Doncaster: odds on, took bend badly/wandered off bridle when second in minor event at
Wolverhampton (wore eyeshields): should stay at least 1m. *D. J. Murphy*

KINGKOHLER (IRE) 8 b.g. King's Theatre (IRE) 128 – Legit (IRE) (Runnett 125) **65**
[2007 –: 10.5v p13g⁶ p13g³ f14d⁵ Dec 15] lightly raced on Flat, fair form in 2007: seems
to stay easy 13f: acts on all-weather, good to firm and good to soft going: tried in
cheekpieces: has carried head awkwardly. *K. A. Morgan*

KING MARJU (IRE) 5 b.g. Marju (IRE) 127 – Katoushka (IRE) (Hamas (IRE) 125§) **82**
[2007 89, a97: p6g⁵ p7.1g 8d 7m* p7g 7m 6m⁵ 7d Jul 4] lengthy, good-topped gelding:
fairly useful performer nowadays: won seller at Catterick in May: best form at 7f: acts on
polytrack, soft and good to firm going: usually visored: free-going sort: has looked none
to keen: sold 7,000 gns, and sent to Greece, where won at 7f. *K. R. Burke*

KING OF ARGOS 4 b.g. Sadler's Wells (USA) 132 – Wannabe Grand (IRE) 116 **112**
(Danehill (USA) 126) [2007 94: p8g³ 8.3f* 7s 8m* 7m² 7g 8g³ 7g* 8m⁵ Oct 6] close-
coupled, good-topped gelding: smart performer: further improvement in 2007, winning
handicaps at Windsor in April, and Goodwood in June and August, best effort when
beating White Deer by ½ length for final success: nearest finish when respectable fifth to
Creachadoir in Joel Stakes at Newmarket final outing: winner at 1¼m, best form at 7f/
1m: acts on polytrack, firm and good to soft ground: tried visored at 3 yrs: held up: sold
205,000 gns, joined Godolphin. *E. A. L. Dunlop*

KING OF CADEAUX (IRE) 2 br.g. (Feb 26) Cadeaux Genereux 131 – Purple Haze **51**
(IRE) 103 (Spectrum (IRE) 126) [2007 p7g p6g f7d Dec 14] modest form at best in
maidens. *M. A. Magnusson*

KING OF CHARM (IRE) 4 ch.g. King Charlemagne (USA) 120 – Pumpona (USA) **55**
(Sharpen Up 127) [2007 63: p6g p7g⁶ p6g⁵ p6g⁴ p6g* p6g p6g⁶ 7s 5.3m p6g p6g⁶
p7m p6g⁶ Dec 4] modest handicapper: won at Kempton in March: stays easy 7f: raced
mainly on polytrack and ground firmer than good: tried tongue tied, usually blinkered.
G. L. Moore

KING OF CHAV'S (IRE) 4 ch.g. Beckett (IRE) 116 – La Paola (IRE) 68 (Common **32**
Grounds 118) [2007 –: p8.6g 10.1d Jun 19] leggy gelding: poor maiden: tried blinkered.
A. Bailey

KING OF CONNACHT 4 b.c. Polish Precedent (USA) 131 – Lady Melbourne (IRE) **59 d**
76 (Indian Ridge 123) [2007 8.1m⁵ p9.5g f11d⁵ Dec 12] workmanlike colt: easily best
effort in maidens when fifth to Samira Gold at Haydock (only run for B. Baugh): left
J. Unett after next outing: tried in cheekpieces. *M. Wellings*

KING OF DALYAN (IRE) 2 ch.c. (Feb 15) Desert Prince (IRE) 130 – Fawaayid **–**
(USA) 92 (Vaguely Noble 140) [2007 p5g 6v 7d 7m Aug 3] no form: tried visored.
D. Nicholls

KING OF DIXIE (USA) 3 ch.c. Kingmambo (USA) 125 – Dixie Accent (USA) **93 p**
(Dixieland Band (USA)) [2007 7.1m² Aug 7] $200,000Y: brother to US 6f to 8.5f (latter
including minor stakes) winner Mumbo Jumbo and half-brother to several US winners:
dam US 6f (at 2 yrs) to 9f (minor stakes) winner: 20/1, encouraging 1½ lengths second to

Plucky in maiden at Chepstow, pushed along to recover from slowish start and switched before keeping on strongly: will stay 1m: sure to improve. *W. J. Knight*

KING OF KNIGHT (IRE) 6 gr.g. Orpen (USA) 116 – Peace Melody (IRE) 69 **62** (Classic Music (USA)) [2007 67: p10g p9.5g² p10g² p10g p8.6g p8g p10g⁴ 9.7g p9.5m p10g Sep 15] quite good-topped gelding: modest handicapper: best at 1¼m/1½m: acts on polytrack, good to firm and good to soft ground: tried visored/tongue tied: sometimes slowly away. *G. Prodromou*

KING OF LEGEND (IRE) 3 b.c. King Charlemagne (USA) 120 – Last Quarry 52 **64** (Handsome Sailor 125) [2007 7s 8g 8g Jul 20] medium-sized, good-topped colt: has a quick, unimpressive action: modest form in maidens: has been heavily bandaged. *Miss Gay Kelleway*

KING OF MUSIC (USA) 6 ch.g. Jade Hunter (USA) – Hail Roberta (USA) (Roberto **71 d** (USA) 131) [2007 68: p10g* p10g p12g p10g Jul 28] rather leggy, angular gelding: fair performer: won seller at Lingfield in January by 10 lengths for G. Prodromou: well below form after, leaving Gay Kelleway after third start: stays easy 1½m: acts on all-weather and good to firm ground: often visored in 2006. *G. Prodromou*

KING OF PENTACLES 2 b.c. (Feb 8) King's Best (USA) 132 – Maid To Perfection **–** 102 (Sadler's Wells (USA) 132) [2007 8d Oct 27] second foal: half-brother to 3-y-o Perfect Reward: dam 7f (at 2 yrs) and 1¼m winner: 50/1, last in maiden at Newbury. *H. Morrison*

KING OF RHYTHM (IRE) 4 b.g. Imperial Ballet (IRE) 110 – Sharadja (IRE) (Doy- **78** oun 124) [2007 67: p8.6g⁵ 9m³ 10g* 10g⁵ 8.9d Oct 13] sturdy, workmanlike gelding: fair handicapper: won at Ayr in August: stays 1¼m: acts on polytrack, heavy and good to firm going: banned for 40 days under non-triers rule, jockey suspended for 14 days and trainer fined £6,000 after reappearance. *D. Carroll*

KING OF ROME (IRE) 2 b.c. (Apr 8) Montjeu (IRE) 137 – Amizette (USA) (Forty **95 p** Niner (USA)) [2007 8.5d 7.5g* 8g Oct 27] strong, deep-girthed colt: eighth foal: half-brother to UAE 1m winner Rio Hondo (by Storm Cat) and to winners in US by A P Indy and Giant's Causeway: dam, placed in US, sister to US Grade 2 1m/9f winner Twining and half-sister to dam of Green Desert: useful form: won maiden at Tipperary in October by 5½ lengths: 9/1, still looked immature when down the field in Racing Post Trophy at Doncaster: will be suited by 1¼m/1½m: should make a better 3-y-o. *A. P. O'Brien, Ireland*

KING OF THE BEERS (USA) 3 gr. or ro.c. Silver Deputy (CAN) – Pracer (USA) **59** (Lyphard (USA) 132) [2007 58: p9.5g p10g* p9.5g⁶ p10g⁵ p10g⁶ f12g² p10g* p10g⁵ **a70** 12m⁴ f11g² 12.1g p12.2g* 11.9m⁴ 10.9d 12.1s Jul 27] strong colt: fair handicapper on all-weather, modest on turf: won at Lingfield (apprentices) in January, Kempton in March and Wolverhampton in June: left R. Harris before final outing: stays 1½m: acts on all-weather and good to firm going: tried blinkered, usually wears cheekpieces. *C. Roberts*

KING OF THE MOORS (USA) 4 b.g. King of Kings (IRE) 125 – Araza (USA) **84** (Arazi (USA) 135) [2007 91d: 7.1g 8m 8.1g⁴ 9g* 9.8m 8v³ 9.1g² 8s⁵ 8d⁶ 9.1s⁴ p8.6g 10g* 9.1v⁵ 10g 14g⁶ Nov 9] close-coupled gelding: fairly useful handicapper: won at Redcar in May and October: stays 1¼m: acts on soft and good to firm going. *T. D. Barron*

KING OF TRICKS 3 b.g. First Trump 118 – Antithesis (IRE) 75 (Fairy King (USA)) **50** [2007 55: p6g f5g 6.1g 8.5s⁴ 7g⁶ 5m 6m² 6.1d 7d 6g Aug 26] compact gelding: modest maiden: stays 6f: acts on polytrack, good to firm and good to soft going: tried visored. *M. D. I. Usher*

KING OF WESTPHALIA (USA) 2 b.c. (Jan 26) Kingmambo (USA) 125 – Quarter **86** Moon (IRE) 120 (Sadler's Wells (USA) 132) [2007 6g⁵ 7g² 7m⁵ Jul 11] rangy, rather unfurnished colt: has rather round action: second foal: dam, 7f (Moyglare Stud Stakes) winner (later second in Irish 1000 Guineas and English/Irish Oaks), sister to Irish 1000 Guineas winner Yesterday: fairly useful maiden: second at Leopardstown then fifth (to Rio de La Plata) at Newmarket: will stay 1m. *A. P. O'Brien, Ireland*

KING ORCHISIOS (IRE) 4 ch.g. Tagula (IRE) 116 – Wildflower 84 (Namaqualand **109** (USA)) [2007 108: p6f* p5g* 5m 6d 5d 6m 6d 6d⁵ 5g* 5g Oct 27] strong, lengthy gelding: useful performer: won listed races at Lingfield in February/March (best effort to beat Bonus by ½ length in latter) and handicap at Catterick (beat Oldjoesaid by neck) in October: best at 5f/6f: acts on polytrack, good to firm and good to soft going: tried blinkered, wears cheekpieces nowadays: races prominently. *K. A. Ryan*

KING ROY (IRE) 3 b.g. Fruits of Love (USA) 127 – Meranie Girl (IRE) 52 (Mujadil – (USA) 119) [2007 6s⁶ 6f 7.1d Aug 16] workmanlike gelding: well held in maidens. *N. I. M. Rossiter*

KING'S ACCOUNT (USA) 5 ch.g. King of Kings (IRE) 125 – Fighting Countess **61 d** (USA) (Ringside (USA)) [2007 –: p7g 10g 9.9m⁴ 10m⁶ 12s 8.5g 10.9g Oct 2] well-made gelding: just modest at best nowadays: stays 1¼m: acts on soft and good to firm going, well below form on polytrack: tried in cheekpieces/blinkers. *S. Gollings*

KING'S ALCHEMIST 2 b.c. (Apr 20) Slickly (FR) 128 – Pure Gold 88 (Dilum **63 p** (USA) 115) [2007 8d Oct 11] strong colt: fourth foal: half-brother to useful 6f (at 2 yrs) to 9f (including in UAE/US) winner Royal Alchemist (by Kingsinger) and 1m/1¼m winner Swift Alchemist (by Fleetwood): dam, 2-y-o 7f winner (only season to race), out of half-sister to 2000 Guineas winner Don't Forget Me: 66/1 and backward, seventh to Robby Bobby in maiden at Newbury: open to improvement. *M. D. I. Usher*

KING'S APOSTLE (IRE) 3 b.c. King's Best (USA) 132 – Politesse (USA) (Barathea **108 +** (IRE) 127) [2007 80: p7g* p7g² 8m 6m* p6g* 6m³ 6g* 6m* Sep 9] well-made colt: useful performer: won maiden at Lingfield in March and handicaps at Ripon (carried head awkwardly) in June, Kempton in July, Newmarket (drifted left) in August and York (beat Lipocco readily by 1¼ lengths, showing good turn of foot) in September: effective at 6f/easy7f: acts on polytrack and firm ground: usually travels strongly: signs of temperament, but progressive. *W. J. Haggas*

KINGS ART (IRE) 3 b.g. King's Best (USA) 132 – Descant (USA) (Nureyev (USA) **58 §** 131) [2007 64: 8.2m 12.1g 10.3f 9.7g² 10.1d 10m 9g² p10g Oct 10] useful-looking gelding: has a fluent action: modest maiden: stays 9.7f: acts on good to firm ground: tried tongue tied: said to have had breathing problem final start: inconsistent. *W. M. Brisbourne*

KING'S ATTITUDE 3 b.c. King's Theatre (IRE) 128 – Sarah's Dream (IRE) (Lion – Cavern (USA) 117) [2007 –: 7s 7.1d 11.7f Aug 24] well held in maidens/seller. *R. A. Harris*

KING'S BASTION (IRE) 3 b.g. Royal Applause 124 – Aunty Mary 82 (Common **87** Grounds 118) [2007 87: 6m 6g² 5g⁵ 7g⁵ 6s² 6s³ 6d 6m⁵ 6m 6m⁵ p8.6g⁵ 7g* Oct 19] good-topped gelding: fairly useful handicapper: good placed efforts prior to winning off lowest mark at Redcar in October: likely to stay 1m: acts on firm and soft going: tried visored. *M. L. W. Bell*

KINGSCAPE (IRE) 4 br.g. King Charlemagne (USA) 120 – Cape Clear 74 (Slip **87** Anchor 136) [2007 10g⁶ 8m⁵ 10g 10.1d* 10s⁵ 10.1d* 12g³ p11g³ 12d* p12g⁶ Oct 12] rather leggy gelding: fairly useful handicapper: won at Yarmouth in May and July, and Goodwood in September: stays 1½m: acts on polytrack, good to firm and good to soft going: carries head awkwardly: sold 62,000 gns. *J. R. Fanshawe*

KING'S CAPRICE 6 ch.g. Pursuit of Love 124 – Palace Street (USA) 103 (Secreto **103** (USA) 128) [2007 112: p7.1g³ p7g 7.1m 6d 7g 7d 7m 7d 6g⁶ p6g² p6g² p7m p6m⁶ Dec 7] rather leggy gelding: has a round action: useful performer: pick of form in 2007 when third to Border Music in listed event at Wolverhampton on reappearance and second to Ceremonial Jade in handicap at Lingfield eleventh outing: largely well held otherwise: effective at 6f/7f: acts on polytrack, firm and soft going: tried visored: tongue tied: has been mounted on track: races prominently, sometimes freely. *J. A. Geake*

KINGS COLLEGE BOY 7 b.g. College Chapel 122 – The Kings Daughter 79 **73** (Indian King (USA) 128) [2007 84: 5g f5g⁴ f5g 5d 5.2g² 5g 5.1f⁴ 5g 5s⁴ 6d 5s² 5g⁵ 5f⁶ 5g 5m* 5g⁴ 5m 5m 5d 5g² p5.1g Nov 17] strong, well-made gelding: fair handicapper nowadays: won at Beverley in August: best at 5f/6f: acts on fibresand, firm and soft going: usually blinkered/visored: waited with. *R. A. Fahey*

KING'S CONFESSION (IRE) 4 b.g. Danetime (IRE) 121 – Night Rhapsody (IRE) **58 +** 81 (Mujtahid (USA) 118) [2007 67: p8.6g May 3] lightly-raced maiden, going on at finish sole 4-y-o start: stays 8.6f: acts on polytrack. *D. Carroll*

KINGSCROSS 9 ch.g. King's Signet (USA) 110 – Calamanco 71 (Clantime 101) [2007 **78 d** 88, a85: p6g 6m 6s 6m p6g 6v⁵ 6g p6g 7g³ 7d p7g Oct 29] strong, good-bodied gelding: just fair handicapper at best in 2007: stays 7f: acts on polytrack, soft and good to firm going: sometimes slowly away: held up. *M. Blanshard*

KING'S ENVOY (USA) 8 b.g. Royal Academy (USA) 130 – Island of Silver (USA) – 107 (Forty Niner (USA)) [2007 –, a54: 16m³ 14.1g 16g Jun 22] tall gelding: poor at 7 yrs: little form in 2007: tried visored/in cheekpieces. *Mrs J. C. McGregor*

KING'S EVENT (USA) 3 b.c. Dynaformer (USA) – Magic of Love 99 (Magic Ring **98 p**
(IRE) 115) [2007 8m³ 8.3m² 8.3d* 8m³ 10d³ Oct 27] $150,000Y: tall, good sort: second
foal: half-brother 4-y-o Gigs Magic: dam 2-y-o 5f/6f winner: useful performer: won
maiden at Windsor in August by 2½ lengths from Rhyming Slang: creditable third in
handicaps at Newmarket and Newbury after, on both occasions finding stride only late
on: stays 1¼m: acts on good to firm and good to soft ground: very much the type to do
better at 4 yrs. *Sir Michael Stoute*

KING'S GAIT 5 b.g. Mujahid (USA) 125 – Miller's Gait 74§ (Mill Reef (USA) 141) **98**
[2007 103: 6s⁴ 6g 6d³ 6v 6g 6g⁶ Jul 27] leggy, quite good-topped gelding: useful
handicapper: best effort in 2007 when third to Ice Planet at Redcar: stays 6f: best form on
good ground or softer (acts on heavy): usually blinkered: looked ungenuine penultimate
outing. *T. D. Easterby*

KINGSGATE CASTLE 2 b.c. (Apr 19) Kyllachy 129 – Ella Lamees 61 (Statoblest **51**
120) [2007 p6g⁵ p7g⁶ Dec 29] modest form in minor event/maiden (sixth to Whitcombe
Minister) at Lingfield. *J. R. Best*

KINGSGATE NATIVE (IRE) 2 b.c. (Feb 20) Mujadil (USA) 119 – Native Force **122**
(IRE) 82 (Indian Ridge 123) [2007 5m² 5g² 5g* 5g² Oct 7]
    The BHA's weight-for-age scale purports to give an accurate assessment of
'the number of pounds that is deemed the average horse in each group falls short of
maturity at different dates and distances.' The difference between a mature four-
year-old (or older) and an immature two-year-old, for example, at five furlongs in
the second half of March is given on the BHA's scale as 47 lb. The difference is
academic, of course, since there are no opportunities for two-year-olds to race
against older horses at that time of year—in fact there are very few at any stage of
the season—but adding 47 lb back on to a two-year-old's performance at that time
of year would produce some misleadingly inflated ratings, something that can
be noticed when calculating timefigures. Timeform allows 28 lb. The situation is
not quite so extreme by the time the Nunthorpe comes along in August but the
two-year-olds are still remarkably leniently treated receiving 24 lb on the BHA's
scale, compared to 17 lb on Timeform's. It is surprising that such a small number
of two-year-olds race against their elders over five furlongs in races such as the
Nunthorpe—the only pattern race in Britain in which they can do so—and the listed
Scarbrough Stakes at Doncaster's St Leger meeting.
    When Kingsgate Native won the latest edition of the Nunthorpe (sponsored
by Coolmore), he was only the second two-year-old to win the race in half a
century. Since the 1992 success of Lyric Fantasy—the only two-year-old filly to
win the Nunthorpe—only four two-year-olds have contested York's big sprint,
Perugino Bay (100/1) and Speedy James (20/1) in 1998, Enticing in 2006 and
Kingsgate Native in 2007. The first three were no better than useful and all were
well held, though Enticing had won the Molecomb at Goodwood and started 11/1
at York. The twice-raced Kingsgate Native had already shown himself better than
those three, showing smart form, and, with the weight-for-age allowance and the
prospect of improvement, he had a very good chance in the Nunthorpe. Lyric

*Coolmore Nunthorpe Stakes, York—Kingsgate Native becomes only the second two-year-old
to land the race since 1956; Desert Lord (blinkers) and Dandy Man (left) battle it out for second*

Fantasy's Nunthorpe victory followed a game second in the race for another smart two-year-old, Paris House, caught only in the last sixty or seventy yards by Sheikh Albadou, who went on to success in the Breeders' Cup Sprint. That the performances of Paris House and Lyric Fantasy failed to ignite more interest in the Nunthorpe among trainers of leading two-year-old sprinters remains a mystery, but perhaps Kingsgate Native's success will provide impetus.

There was no older sprinter of the calibre of Sheikh Albadou in the latest Nunthorpe, the favourite, Irish-trained Dandy Man, having finished second in the King's Stand and fifth in the July Cup. The Australian challenger Magnus, third in the King's Stand (the Aussie King's Stand winner Miss Andretti had gone back), was second favourite, with the July Cup third Red Clubs and King George Stakes winner Moorhouse Lad, who was supplemented, the only others at odds shorter than 10/1 in a field of sixteen. Kingsgate Native was a 12/1-shot, while the first two in the 2006 Nunthorpe, Reverence and Amadeus Wolf, started at 14/1 and 10/1 respectively, with the previous year's Prix de l'Abbaye winner Desert Lord at 20/1. Kingsgate Native was still a maiden, but he was no ordinary maiden, having been beaten a head (by Drawnfromthepast at 66/1) in the Windsor Castle Stakes at Royal Ascot and a neck (behind Fleeting Spirit, starting 4/1 second favourite) in a strong renewal of the Molecomb Stakes at Goodwood. Kingsgate Native showed further improvement at York. Sweating beforehand, he was driven out firmly after displaying a good turn of foot to win by a length and three quarters and a head from Desert Lord and Dandy Man, with Red Clubs a further three quarters of a length away fourth. Kingsgate Native produced a very smart performance—the best by a two-year-old during the season up to that point—but the BHA's weight-for-age scale favoured him by the equivalent of two lengths and, on that basis, he came out a worse horse at the weights than runner-up Desert Lord. For the record, the three

Mr John Mayne's "Kingsgate Native"

other two-year-olds before Lyric Fantasy to win the Nunthorpe since its inception in 1922 all did so in the 'fifties, High Treason in 1953, My Beau in 1954 and Ennis in 1956. Two-year-olds were barred from the Nunthorpe between 1981 and 1985.

France's top sprint, the Prix de l'Abbaye de Longchamp, was won six times by a two-year-old in the ten-year spell from 1957 to 1966 but has not been won by a juvenile since the filly Sigy succeeded in brilliant style in 1978. More two-year-olds have run in the Abbaye than have run in the Nunthorpe in recent times, though Kingsgate Native was the first to do so since 2002 when July Stakes winner Mister Links, and Molecomb and Flying Childers winner Wunders Dream finished tenth and sixteenth respectively behind Continent. Kingsgate Native started favourite for the latest Prix de l'Abbaye but he was less favourably treated by the weight-for-age scale than in the Nunthorpe, receiving 18 lb from the older horses this time (Timeform allows 14 lb). Significantly, Kingsgate Native couldn't repeat his Nunthorpe form but still came through to take second behind the six-year-old Benbaun, with Desert Lord, also below his York form, edging ahead of the previous year's third Moss Vale to fill the other place. Kingsgate Native was the fourth two-year-old to reach a place in the Abbaye since Sigy's victory, the others being Sicyos (a son of Sigy, third in 1983), Magic Ring (third in 1991) and Superstar Leo (second in 2000). The very speedy Kingsgate Native, who has raced only on good and good to firm going, is a strong, lengthy colt, described by his trainer in an interview before the Nunthorpe as 'a very mature horse, not like a two-year-old', and it remains to be seen whether he has the scope to develop further as a three-year-old. Whatever else he goes on to achieve, Kingsgate Native is assured of a place at stud, having already been purchased to stand at Cheveley Park Stud in Newmarket when his racing days are over.

Kingsgate Native (IRE) (b.c. Feb 20, 2005)	Mujadil (USA) (b 1988)	Storm Bird (b 1978)	Northern Dancer
			South Ocean
		Vallee Secrete (b 1977)	Secretariat
			Midou
	Native Force (IRE) (b 1998)	Indian Ridge (ch 1985)	Ahonoora
			Hillbrow
		La Pellegrina (b 1993)	Be My Guest
			Spanish Habit

It was never the intention that Kingsgate Native's debut would come at Royal Ascot. He was an intended runner in a maiden at York the previous Friday but that two-day meeting (including Timeform Charity Day on the Saturday) was lost through waterlogging. Even before that, Kingsgate Native could have been seen out at Goodwood in May, though he was sent to the racecourse believed to be his stable-companion Kingsgate Castle, the mistake picked up when his markings were found not to match Kingsgate Castle's passport when checked by the racecourse vet, leading to withdrawal. The trainer explained that he had bought both colts—who are in the same ownership—at the St Leger Yearling Sales and had failed to check their respective identities after they came into the yard. He was fined £650 at an inquiry held by the Disciplinary Panel of the Horseracing Regulatory Authority in July. Kingsgate Native cost significantly less than Kingsgate Castle at the sales, fetching 20,000 guineas (having made €28,000 as a foal), and it goes without saying that he has proven a rare bargain. Kingsgate Native's achievements should do wonders for his sire the Cornwallis winner Mujadil, who has been an influence for speed and precocity at stud and enjoyed a remarkable year in 2000 when he had a record thirty-two individual two-year-old winners in Europe. Mujadil's stud record has fluctuated, however, and he covered just five mares in 2006, four of them getting in foal. The median price of Mujadil's yearlings sold in 2007 increased by around half from the previous year to over 30,000 guineas. Kingsgate Native is the second foal of his dam Native Force, who won a Sandown maiden over a mile for Robert Sangster at three, but fetched only 8,000 guineas when sent up to the December Sales later the same year, surplus to Swettenham Stud's requirements. Her first foal, Assumption (by Beckett), gained her only win in a seven-furlong seller at Folkestone and was sold for only 2,500 guineas at the 2006 Newmarket July Sales. Kingsgate Native's grandam La Pellegrina was a disappointing maiden and has produced nothing of note at stud, though she is closely related to Las Meninas (both by a son of Northern Dancer out of Spanish Habit) who carried the Sangster colours to victory in the One Thousand Guineas. The York August meeting was a good one for daughters of King's Stand winner Indian Ridge (sire of Native Force) who were also responsible for the winners of the Gimcrack (Sir Gerry) and the Lowther (Nahoodh). *J. R. Best*

KING'S GENERAL (USA) 2 ch.c. (Jan 11) Langfuhr (CAN) 124 – Jeanie's Gift (USA) (Gulch (USA)) [2007 5d² May 17] $150,000Y: half-brother to 3 winners in USA, including Grade 2 7f winner Elaborate (by Gilded Time): dam unraced: 12/1, strong-finishing second to Sweepstake in maiden at Salisbury: dead. *Mrs A. J. Perrett*   **79**

KING'S HEAD (IRE) 4 b.g. King's Best (USA) 132 – Ustka 60 (Lomond (USA) 128) [2007 103: p16g⁴ Apr 7] useful-looking gelding: useful handicapper: seemed not to stay sole 4-y-o start (fit from hurdling): stays 1½m: acts on good to firm going: effective in cheekpieces. *G. L. Moore*   **–**

KINGS HEIR (IRE) 4 b.g. Princely Heir (IRE) 111 – Unimpeachable (IRE) 65 (Namaqualand (USA)) [2007 76d: p8.6g⁵ Jan 19] leggy, quite attractive gelding: fair performer at best: ended career out of form: dead. *Peter Grayson*   **–**

KINGSHOLM 5 ch.g. Selkirk (USA) 129 – Putuna 98 (Generous (IRE) 139) [2007 93: p8g 8g p8g⁵ 9.2g⁶ 8s p9.5g⁶ p9.5d² p9.5d³ Dec 28] leggy gelding: has a quick action: fairly useful performer: left A. Balding 10,000 gns after fifth outing: stays 1¼m: acts on polytrack, good to firm and good to soft ground: free-going sort: has had bandaged hind joints. *I. W. McInnes*   **84**

KING'S ICON (IRE) 2 b.g. (Mar 25) King's Best (USA) 132 – Pink Sovietstaia (FR) (Soviet Star (USA) 128) [2007 6g² 6g* 6m 6m Aug 4] 28,000F, 62,000Y: good-bodied gelding: fourth living foal: half-brother to 3 fairly useful winners, including 3-y-o Russian Rosie: dam awarded 9f event in France: fair performer: won maiden at Goodwood in June: well beaten after in July Stakes at Newmarket (pulled hard) and nursery, then gelded: will stay 7f. *M. P. Tregoning*   **78**

KING'S KAZEEM 2 b.f. (Mar 9) King's Best (USA) 132 – Kazeem 73 (Darshaan 133) [2007 7m⁴ 8d Oct 27] third foal: half-sister to 3-y-o Azeema: dam, maiden, out of smart performer up to 1½m Kanz: fair maiden: fourth to Rosa Grace in minor event (hung left), better effort at Newbury (possibly unsuited by softer ground second start): should stay 1m. *B. W. Hills*   **73**

KINGSMAITE 6 b.g. Komaite (USA) – Antonias Melody 86 (Rambo Dancer (CAN) 107) [2007 –, a86d: p7.1g f8g⁴ p7.1g f7g⁴ f8g³ p8.6g³ p8.6g³ f7g p7.1g p8.6g f8g³ 7g f7g f7d f7d Dec 15] workmanlike gelding: modest performer on all-weather nowadays, little form on turf since 2005: effective at 6f to 8.6f: acts on all-weather: tried visored, usually blinkered: often tongue tied: none too consistent. *S. R. Bowring*   **– a62**

KING'S MAJESTY (IRE) 5 b.g. King's Best (USA) 132 – Tiavanita (USA) (J O Tobin (USA) 130) [2007 78: p8g 8m 8g 8.2g⁶ 10m⁶ 10m² p10g* Dec 19] close-coupled gelding: fairly useful performer: left L. Dace after third outing: won claimer at Lingfield in December: barely stays 1¼m: acts on polytrack, good to firm and good to soft ground: saddle slipped fifth start. *V. R. A. Dartnall*   **81**

KINGSMEAD (USA) 3 b.g. Kingmambo (USA) 125 – Astor Place (USA) (Deputy Minister (CAN)) [2007 58: p9.5g⁴ 11g 14.1m⁵ 14.1s 11.5g 13.1f⁵ p12.2g p13.9g Oct 5] close-coupled gelding: modest maiden handicapper: stays 1¾m: acts on good to firm ground: in headgear last 5 starts, tongue tied last 3: sold 6,000 gns. *Miss J. Feilden*   **56**

KING'S MINSTREL (IRE) 6 b.g. Cape Cross (IRE) 129 – Muwasim (USA) (Meadowlake (USA)) [2007 p11g⁵ p11g Feb 4] maiden: missed 2006: only poor in 2007: stays 1½m: acts on polytrack: tried tongue tied. *R. Rowe*   **46**

KINGS POINT (IRE) 6 b.h. Fasliyev (USA) 120 – Rahika Rose 91 (Unfuwain (USA) 131) [2007 112: p8.6g⁶ 8m 8g 8g 7.5g 8f⁴ 8g 8s⁴ 8g 8.1m 8g 8.1g⁵ 9d* Sep 17] strong, compact horse: unimpressive mover: smart performer at best: only useful in 2007, easily best effort when fourth to My Paris in handicap at Thirsk sixth outing: won claimer at Musselburgh (joined D. Nicholls) in September: stays 9f: acts on firm and soft ground: usually wears headgear. *R. A. Fahey*   **100**

KINGS QUAY 5 b.h. Montjeu (IRE) 137 – Glen Rosie (IRE) 102 (Mujtahid (USA) 118) [2007 105: p12g² p11g 10.1d 12s 12s⁶ Oct 19] quite attractive horse: has a quick action: useful handicapper: best effort in 2007 when second to Kames Park at Lingfield on return: seems to stay easy 1½m: acts on polytrack, firm and good to soft going: tongue tied: sometimes takes good hold: useful hurdler, successful in July/November. *J. J. Quinn*   **97**

KING'S RANSOM 4 b.g. Daylami (IRE) 138 – Luana 101 (Shaadi (USA) 126) [2007 **78** 73: p10g² p12g* p12g 10g p10g 11.7d⁶ 10s³ 11.6m³ 11.9d³ 16.4m⁶ 11.9m* 12.3m⁶ 14f⁶ 11.9s p8g⁴ p8g p8.6g p8.6g² f11d² Dec 11] rather leggy gelding: fair performer: won maiden at Lingfield in January and selling handicap at Brighton (left W. Muir) in August: stays 1½m: acts on all-weather, soft and good to firm going: tried blinkered/in cheek-pieces: has carried head high (once reported to have breathing problem). *S. Gollings*

KINGS SHILLINGS 3 br.g. Superior Premium 122 – The Kings Daughter 79 (Indian King (USA) 128) [2007 50: f7g³ p7.1g* f7g⁶ p7.1g⁶ p8.6g p8.6g⁴ p7.1g 10f 11g 7m 7d **a57** 7m Aug 12] close-coupled gelding: modest performer: won handicap at Wolverhampton in January: acts 8.6f: acts on all-weather, no form on turf: blinkered/visored: often slowly away. *D. Carroll*

KING'S SPEAR (IRE) 4 b.g. Lear Spear (USA) 124 – First Veil 94 (Primo Dominie **72 d** 121) [2007 68: p9.5g³ f11g p9.5g p12g 10.2m p7.1g Oct 22] well-made gelding: fair maiden: form in 2007 only on reappearance: left P. Chapple-Hyam after third outing: stays 9.5f: acts on polytrack and good to firm going: tried blinkered: sold £900. *Miss J. R. Tooth*

KINGS STORY (IRE) 3 b.c. Royal Applause 124 – Poppy Carew (IRE) 110 (Danehill **69** (USA) 126) [2007 10g 10g 10.2g⁵ 11.9d⁶ Aug 21] workmanlike colt: fair maiden: should stay 1½m: ran in snatches final outing: sold 4,500 gns. *W. R. Swinburn*

KINGS TOPIC (USA) 7 ch.g. Kingmambo (USA) 125 – Topicount (USA) (Private **67** Account (USA)) [2007 65: p9.5g p10g³ p8.6g p10g Nov 19] deep-bodied gelding: fair handicapper: stays 1¼m: acts on polytrack, little form on turf: said to have bled final outing. *A. B. Haynes*

KINGSTYLE (IRE) 2 b.c. (Mar 26) King Charlemagne (USA) 120 – Stylish Clare **55 ?** (IRE) 77 (Desert Style (IRE) 121) [2007 5d⁴ 6m 7d⁶ 7d 6m 7.5g Sep 19] leggy colt: maiden: seemingly modest form second/third starts. *M. Brittain*

KING SUPREME (IRE) 2 b.c. (Mar 23) King's Best (USA) 132 – Oregon Trail **69** (USA) (Gone West (USA)) [2007 6s³ 7m 7s p8g* p8g p8g Nov 7] good-bodied, close-coupled colt: fair performer: won nursery at Kempton in September: stays 1m: acts on polytrack and soft going. *R. Hannon*

KING'S WONDER 2 ch.c. (Mar 24) King's Best (USA) 132 – Signs And Wonders **79** 75§ (Danehill (USA) 126) [2007 6g⁵ 7m³ 7m⁶ Oct 5] 21,000F, 30,000Y: tall, rather leggy colt: half-brother to 2004 2-y-o 5f winner Wonderful Mind (by Mind Games): dam, 1¼m winner, sister to dam of Queen Mary winners Romantic Liason and Romantic Myth: fair maiden: off 4 months before third to Ibn Khaldun at Leicester: should prove best up to 7f. *W. R. Muir*

KING VERTI 3 b.g. Averti (IRE) 117 – Proudfoot (IRE) (Shareef Dancer (USA) 135) **–** [2007 10g 8.3g Jun 13] well held in claimer/seller. *P. C. Haslam*

KING ZEAL (IRE) 3 b.c. King's Best (USA) 132 – Manureva (USA) (Nureyev (USA) **70** 131) [2007 8d 8d 9.8m³ p9.5g⁶ Oct 22] medium-sized, angular colt: fair maiden: left L. Cumani 15,500 gns after debut: stays 1¼m: acts on polytrack and good to firm ground. *M. Wigham*

KINLOCHARD 2 b.f. (Mar 12) Efisio 120 – Rainbow d'Beaute 88 (Rainbow Quest **–** (USA) 134) [2007 5m⁴ 5m Jul 30] 10,000Y: neat filly: second foal: dam 13f winner: well held in minor event/maiden, flashing tail. *Eve Johnson Houghton*

KINNEGO BAY (IRE) 2 ch.c. (Mar 8) Hennessy (USA) 122 – New Music (USA) **76** (Prospector's Music (USA)) [2007 6m⁵ 7m 6d³ Oct 15] €175,000Y: strong colt: type to carry condition: first foal: dam, 5.5f to 7f winner in US, out of half-sister to dam of St Leger winner Mutafaweq: fair form in maidens at Newmarket and Windsor (third to Corrybrough): will prove best up to 7f. *B. W. Hills*

KINOUT (IRE) 2 b.g. (May 10) Invincible Spirit (IRE) 121 – Kinn (FR) (Suave Dancer **74** (USA) 136) [2007 5m⁵ 5g³ 5.1f⁴ p6g 7m³ 6d⁵ 6g Oct 6] quite attractive gelding: has a round action: fair maiden: in frame 3 times, including nursery at Redcar: stays 7f: acts on firm and good to soft going. *K. A. Ryan*

KINSMAN (IRE) 10 b.g. Distant Relative 128 – Besito 79 (Wassl 125) [2007 –, a52: **–** p8g⁵ p8g⁶ p7g³ p8g⁶ p8g³ p8g* p10g p8g* p8g Nov 28] leggy, useful-looking gelding: **a52** modest on all-weather, unraced on turf since 2005: won minor events at Lingfield in April and Kempton in October: stays 1¼m: acts on all-weather, firm and soft going: wears headgear: tried tongue tied: often slowly away: sometimes carries head high/hangs: held up. *T. D. McCarthy*

KINSYA 4 ch.g. Mister Baileys 123 – Kimono (IRE) (Machiavellian (USA) 123) [2007 **103** 96: 8.1m 8s² 8g 8d⁵ 8.3d* 8g² p10m⁵ Nov 24] strong, close-coupled gelding: useful handicapper: won at Leicester in October by 1¾ lengths from Orpen Wide, again carrying head awkwardly: good efforts after, close fifth to Grand Passion in listed event at Lingfield: stays easy 1¼m: acts on soft going, possibly unsuited by firmer than good: held up. *M. H. Tompkins*

KINTBURY CROSS 5 b.g. Kylian (USA) – Cebwob 85 (Rock City 120) [2007 71: **79** p9.5g⁵ 10d² 12g Aug 18] leggy gelding: fair maiden, lightly raced nowadays: stays 11.6f: acts on firm and good to soft going, probably on fibresand. *P. D. Cundell*

KINTYRE LASS (IRE) 2 b.f. (Apr 25) Mull of Kintyre (USA) 114 – Bold Doll (IRE) **53 d** 69 (Dolphin Street (FR) 125) [2007 5.7f 7g³ 6.1s 7m⁴ 6m 7m⁶ p6g Oct 31] €8,500Y: workmanlike filly: second foal: dam, maiden (stayed 7f), half-sister to useful winner up to 1¼m Atlantic Desire: modest maiden: below form after second start, blinkered last 2: stays 7f: sold 1,200 gns. *B. R. Millman*

KIOWA PRINCESS 2 ch.f. (Mar 20) Compton Place 125 – Sunley Stars (Sallust 134) **–** [2007 5g 5g 6d Sep 20] 36,000Y: leggy filly: sister to useful 5f winner (including at 2 yrs) If Paradise, closely related to 1m (in UAE)/9.4f winner Don Sebastian (by Indian Ridge) and half-sister to 1995 2-y-o 5f winner All She Surveys (by Mazilier): dam maiden: well held in maidens. *M. Dods*

KIRIBATI KING (IRE) 2 b.g. (Feb 24) Kalanisi (IRE) 132 – Everlasting (Desert **61** King (IRE) 129) [2007 8d 8d p8g⁶ Nov 14] big gelding: modest maiden: will stay 1¼m: gelded. *M. R. Channon*

KIRKBY'S TREASURE 9 gr.g. Mind Games 121 – Gem of Gold 52 (Jellaby 124) **72** [2007 69: p7.1g⁵ 7d 7.9g⁵ 7.9d⁴ 8g³ 8.3d⁵ 8m* 8f* 7.2g³ 8m² 7.1d* 7.1m⁵ 10g Oct 6] tall, leggy gelding: has a round action: fair performer: won seller at Musselburgh and handicap at Redcar in August and handicap at Musselburgh (sixth course win) in September: stays 1m (raced freely at 1¼m): acts on firm and soft ground: tried in blinkers/cheekpieces: sometimes slowly away/wanders: held up. *G. A. Swinbank*

KIRKHAMMERTON (IRE) 5 ch.g. Grand Lodge (USA) 125 – Nawara 75 (Welsh **56** Pageant 132) [2007 –, a63: f8g⁵ f12g f8g² f11g⁶ f8g p8.6g⁵ p12.2g⁶ 8.1s³ 10v p8.6g⁴ 10m 9.2g⁵ p10g⁶ Sep 18] sturdy gelding: modest performer: effective at 1m, probably stays easy 1¾m: acts on all-weather and soft ground: usually blinkered/visored: races prominently: none too reliable. *A. J. McCabe*

KIRKLEES (IRE) 3 b.c. Jade Robbery (USA) 121 – Moyesii (USA) (Diesis 133) **121 p** [2007 107: 10.3m* 9.9d* Sep 26]
Responsible for three of the four previous winners of the Charles James Homes Foundation Stakes, Godolphin had the odds very much in their favour when they attempted to make it four from five in the latest renewal of the listed event run at Goodwood at the end of September. Godolphin owned three of the five who lined up, including hot favourite, with Dettori on board, Kirklees, the only three-year-old in the field. Stable-companion Windsor Knot, returning from almost a year off, set a fair pace with Kirklees tracking him before taking over after two out, needing to be ridden to do so but soon well on top and three lengths clear at the line, Ordnance Row coming from off the pace to split the pair. It was another improved performance from the lightly-raced Kirklees, who could step up again on the very smart form he showed at Goodwood when he returns to action. A Group 1 winner at two, he is clearly well up to winning more pattern races.

Kirklees raced in Sheikh Mohammed's colours and was trained by Mark Johnston as a two-year-old, when he won a maiden at Catterick and an ordinary renewal of the Gran Criterium at Milan, finishing third in between those wins in both the Vintage Stakes at Goodwood and Royal Lodge Stakes at Ascot and fourth in the Champagne Stakes at York. Eleven months passed after the Gran Criterium before Kirklees was seen again, his lengthy absence explained by his trainer Saeed bin Suroor as being due to a 'tiny problem'. Kirklees returned in a seven-runner minor event at Doncaster's St Leger fixture, one of four in the field who had competed at the highest level at one time or another. Kirklees was much too good for his rivals, taking over from stablemate Gravitas halfway up the straight and going on to win with something to spare by two and a half lengths from Many Volumes.

Charles James Homes Foundation Stakes, Goodwood—a fourth win in five years for Godolphin in this listed event; three-year-old Kirklees proves too good for some smart older rivals, led home by Ordnance Row

		Mr Prospector (b 1970)	Raise A Native
	Jade Robbery (USA) (br 1987)		Gold Digger
		Number (b 1979)	Nijinsky
Kirklees (IRE) (b.c. 2004)			Special
		Diesis (ch 1980)	Sharpen Up
	Moyesii (USA) (b 1997)		Doubly Sure
		Cherokee Rose (b 1991)	Dancing Brave
			Celtic Assembly

Kirklees is by Jade Robbery, one of the leading two-year-olds in France in 1989, and is the second foal of the useful Moyesii who won a nine-furlong maiden for fillies in the French Provinces at three. Her first foal Magic Tree (by Timber Country) was behind in a maiden on her only start; her third, a two-year-old filly by Cape Cross named Artisti, is in training with Mark Johnston but has yet to race. Moyesii is a half-sister to the smart miler Bowman, later a winner over eleven furlongs in the UAE. Their dam Cherokee Rose won the 1995 Haydock Park Sprint Cup for Sheikh Mohammed. Celtic Assembly, the great grandam of Kirklees, was runner-up in the Lupe Stakes and gained her sole success over an extended mile and a quarter. The step up to a mile and a quarter in the latest season looked to suit Kirklees, who settled quite well ridden with more restraint than in his first season. The big, strong Kirklees acts on firm and good to soft ground. *Saeed bin Suroor*

KIRK MICHAEL 3 b.g. Selkirk (USA) 129 – Pervenche (Latest Model 115) [2007 87: 7g⁵ p7.1g* Dec 15] leggy, useful-looking gelding: fairly useful performer, lightly raced: gelded and off 7 months, won maiden at Wolverhampton in December by 12 lengths, setting good pace: may prove best up to 7f: acts on polytrack, yet to race on extremes of going on turf. *H. Candy* **94**

KIRSTYS LAD 5 b.g. Lake Coniston (IRE) 131 – Killick 69 (Slip Anchor 136) [2007 51: 8.1g p9.5g* p9.5g² p9.5g³ p8.6g p8.6g* p9.5g⁴ Dec 14] good-bodied gelding: fair performer: won maiden in October (100/1) and handicap in December, both at Wolverhampton: stays 9.5f: acts on polytrack and good to firm going: tried blinkered. *M. Mullineaux* **68**

KISS CHASE (IRE) 3 b.g. Val Royal (FR) 127 – Zurarah (Siberian Express (USA) 125) [2007 –: 7m 8m 8d* 8g* 9.1s⁶ 10g 8s Sep 20] tall, leggy gelding: fair performer: best efforts when winning sellers at Brighton (left P. Mitchell) and Thirsk (handicap), both in July: stays 1m: acts on good to soft going: tried in cheekpieces, usually in blinkers. *J. S. Goldie* **67**

KISSI KISSI 4 b.f. Paris House 123 – Miss Whittingham (IRE) 68 (Fayruz 116) [2007 43, a57: p7g f6g⁵ f6g p7.1g 6m 7d f5d⁴ f5g⁶ Dec 27] tall, close-coupled filly: just poor in 2007: stays 8.6f: acts on all-weather: often visored: tried tongue tied. *M. J. Attwater* — **a46**

KISSING 3 ch.f. Grand Lodge (USA) 125 – Love Divine 120 (Diesis 133) [2007 p8g⁶ 10d⁵ p9.5g* Nov 10] workmanlike filly: third foal: half-sister to 4-y-o Sixties Icon: dam, 1¼m/1½m (Oaks) winner, out of close relation to Champion Stakes winner Legal Case: easily best effort when winning maiden at Wolverhampton in November by 2½ lengths from Demisemiquaver, not looking keen under pressure: should stay 1½m+. *Sir Mark Prescott* — **84**

KISS THE RING (USA) 2 ch.f. (Feb 28) Touch Gold (USA) 127 – Act Devoted (USA) (A P Indy (USA) 131) [2007 6m Jul 21] $100,000F, $235,000Y, $430,000 2-y-o: well-made filly: fourth foal: half-sister to winner in US by Theatrical: dam unraced half-sister to French 1m/1¼m performer Jeune Homme and sprinter Mutamared, both smart: 11/1, well held in maiden at Newmarket: sent to USA. *B. J. Meehan* — **—**

KITCHEN SINK (IRE) 5 ch.g. Bold Fact (USA) 116 – Voodoo Rocket 56 (Lycius (USA) 124) [2007 66: p5.1g² p5.1g* p6g p6g⁶ p5.1g 6m 10m 5.7m p5g p6g Dec 8] good-bodied gelding: modest performer: won maiden at Wolverhampton in January: left P. Makin after fourth outing, well held after: best at 5f/6f: acts on polytrack, good to firm and good to soft going: tried blinkered: has hung left: none too resolute. *Jean-Rene Auvray* — **59 d**

KITEBROOK 6 b.m. Saddlers' Hall (IRE) 126 – Neptunalia 70 (Slip Anchor 136) [2007 11.5s 11.7d p12g⁶ 10m⁵ p16.5g p13.9g Nov 12] compact mare: fifth foal: half-sister to 3 winners, including fairly useful 1m winner Jarjoor (by Alhaarth) and 7f winner Jabuka (by Shareef Dancer): dam, 1½m winner, half-sister to very smart performer up to 1½m Glory of Dancer: little form. *Mrs Mary Hambro* — **—**

KITTY MATCHAM (IRE) 2 b.f. (May 21) Rock of Gibraltar (IRE) 133 – Imagine (IRE) 119 (Sadler's Wells (USA) 132) [2007 7d⁴ 7m⁴ 7d 6g* 7d* Oct 20] — **102 p**

'The racecourse must not be used as a training ground and all horses including those having their first run, must be ridden to obtain the best possible place . . . [and] the rider of every horse shall take all reasonable and permissible measures to ensure that his/her horse is given a full opportunity to win . . .' These two instructions, both quoted directly from the rules of the Irish Turf Club, are not always applied strictly to the letter. Take a couple of races in the latest season involving finishes between two Ballydoyle runners in the same or similar ownership, on both occasions the noticeably more tenderly-handled horse ridden by Seamus Heffernan. Magna Cum Laude finished a close second to Achill Island in a maiden at Tipperary, subsequent Rockfel Stakes winner Kitty Matcham beat Psalm by a similar margin at Naas. Heffernan didn't draw his whip at all on Magna Cum Laude and used it just once on Psalm. Achill Island (a 7/2-on shot ridden by Kieren Fallon) was strongly ridden, hit five times, while Kitty Matcham was struck eleven times by 7-lb claimer Sean Levey. The post-race actions of Heffernan were as telling as the rides themselves. After Magna Cum Laude's race he went immediately, without

Seriousquitters.co.uk Rockfel Stakes, Newmarket—Kitty Matcham (No.5) shows much improved form and collars Missit near the finish; Royal Confidence (left) is third

being requested, to the stewards' room to explain that the horse had travelled well throughout but had not found as much as expected. Magna Cum Laude is still a maiden after eight races and there is a suspicion that he isn't much of a battler, but, that said, it was still puzzling that he wasn't ridden more vigorously. After the ride on Psalm, Heffernan's post-race comments could have been interpreted as an admission that he had flouted the rules. He was reported as saying 'I suppose if I had really galvanised my filly I might have won, but it was her first run and she was inexperienced and I want her to come forward.' The stewards did not hold an inquiry into the race—probably because it was Psalm's first run—but Psalm should still have won.

	Rock of Gibraltar (IRE) (b 1999)	Danehill (b 1986)	Danzig
Kitty Matcham (IRE) (b.f. May 21, 2005)			Razyana
		Offshore Boom (ch 1985)	Be My Guest
			Push A Button
	Imagine (IRE) (b 1998)	Sadler's Wells (b 1981)	Northern Dancer
			Fairy Bridge
		Doff The Derby (b 1981)	Master Derby
			Margarethen

A late foal, Kitty Matcham herself took four outings to lose her maiden tag, coming fourth in her first two races before looking out of her depth in the C. L. Weld Park Stakes on her third. Kitty Matcham seemed unlikely to be suited by the drop back to six at Naas, having finished fourth at the Curragh and to the impressive Chinese White at Leopardstown on her first two outings. Those fears proved unfounded, though, as mentioned, Kitty Matcham seemed most fortunate to beat her stablemate. Stepped back up to seven furlongs in a substandard Rockfel Stakes at Newmarket, 10/1-shot Kitty Matcham took a long time to weave her way through before catching Missit close home and winning by a neck, with Royal Confidence a further three quarters of a length further back in third.

Like the historical Catherine 'Kitty' Matcham, Kitty Matcham is a sibling of an ill-fated Horatio Nelson. Being by the Danehill stallion Rock of Gibraltar makes Kitty Matcham a close relation of Horatio Nelson (by Danehill), Timeform's champion two-year-old colt of 2005. The other foal out of their dam, Irish One Thousand Guineas and Epsom Oaks winner Imagine, is Red Rock Canyon (a full brother to Kitty Matcham), who ended 2007 as the highest-rated maiden in training. Imagine was without a foal in 2006 and her next representative on the racecourse will, all being well, be a colt by Giant's Causeway foaled in the latest season. Like Horatio Nelson, Kitty Matcham lacks something in stature, being a smallish, good-bodied filly, though she did look in great shape at Newmarket. She has some way to go to match the form of the best of her contemporaries, but it is not beyond the realms of possibility that a mile and beyond may bring out further improvement in Kitty Matcham as a three-year-old. *A. P. O'Brien, Ireland*

KIWI BAY 2 b.g. (Mar 9) Mujahid (USA) 125 – Bay of Plenty (FR) (Octagonal (NZ) 126) [2007 6s² 6m⁵ 7g* 7g⁶ Oct 27] 1,200Y, resold 12,000Y: tall, rather leggy gelding, on weak side at 2 yrs: second foal: closely related to 3-y-o Baylini: dam unraced: fairly useful form: won maiden at Newcastle in October: waited with and too much to do when sixth to Kal Barg in nursery at Doncaster: will stay 1m: acts on soft going, below form on good to firm. *M. Dods* **89 +**

KIWI PRINCESS 2 b.f. (May 2) Vettori (IRE) 119 – The Kings Daughter 79 (Indian King (USA) 128) [2007 6m 7m 7g 7.1m⁵ 7.5m³ p8.6g Nov 9] 3,000Y: half-sister to several winners, including fairly useful 5f/6f winners The Kings Ransom (by Cadeaux Genereux) and Wicked Uncle (by Distant Relative): dam 5f winner: modest maiden: third in nursery at Beverley: should prove best at 6f/7f: acts on good to firm going. *M. Brittain* **59**

KIWI THE CLOWN (IRE) 3 ch.g. Fruits of Love (USA) 127 – Tenby Bay (IRE) (Tenby 125) [2007 p7.1g p9.5g⁶ p6g⁶ p7.1g⁵ Feb 23] modest maiden: slowly away and met trouble in handicap final outing: bred to be suited by 1¼m+: raced only on polytrack. *R. A. Fahey* **58**

KLARITY 2 b.f. (Apr 11) Acclamation 118 – Clarice Orsini (Common Grounds 118) [2007 6g⁴ 5d³ 6d p6g⁶ p5.1g Dec 1] 23,000Y: compact filly: fifth foal: half-sister to 3 winners, including useful 5f to 7.5f winner (at 2 yrs) Johnny Jumpup (by Pivotal): dam French maiden: fair maiden: best efforts in frame first 2 starts: effective at 5f/6f: acts on good to soft going: has raced freely. *J. Pearce* **67**

KLASSEN (USA) 4 br.g. Pine Bluff (USA) – One Great Lady (USA) (Fappiano –
(USA)) [2007 60: 11g 11.9d p8g Jun 27] leggy gelding: modest form in maidens at 3 yrs:
well held in handicaps in 2007: tried blinkered. *A. King*

KNAPTON HILL 3 b.f. Zamindar (USA) 116 – Torgau (IRE) 109 (Zieten (USA) 118) **88**
[2007 60: p7.1g³ f8g p7.1g² 7.1m* 7.5m⁶ p7.1g⁴ 7m⁶ 7.1d⁶ 7.1s⁴ 8d 8d⁶ 7.1m⁵
8.2g⁴ 10.3m Nov 10] quite good-topped filly: fairly useful performer: won handicap at
Warwick in April: often stiff tasks in listed races after: stays 1m: acts on all-weather and
good to firm going, probably on good to soft: sold 17,000 gns. *R. Hollinshead*

KNEAD THE DOUGH 6 b.g. Wolfhound (USA) 126 – Ridgewood Ruby (IRE) 77 **58**
(Indian Ridge 123) [2007 58: p5.1g 6.1s 6m⁴ 6g 5.1f 6f² 6g* 5f⁵ p6g⁵ p7g 5.1g⁶ Nov 7]
smallish, strong gelding: modest performer: won maiden at Yarmouth in September:
effective at 5f/6f: acts on all-weather, firm and good to soft going: tried in cheekpieces/
visor/tongue tie. *A. E. Price*

KNICKYKNACKIENOO 6 b.g. Bin Ajwaad (IRE) 119 – Ring Fence 74 (Polar –
Falcon (USA) 126) [2007 –: 7m p6g p6g p10g p8.6g Nov 27] modest handicapper in
2005, no form since: tried visored. *T. T. Clement*

KNIGHT OF KINTYRE (IRE) 4 b.f. Mull of Kintyre (USA) 114 – Ar Hyd Y Knos **38**
36 (Alzao (USA) 117) [2007 –: 5g⁶ 8.3g⁶ 8.5d 8m Aug 2] fifth foal: dam, maiden,
half-sister to useful performer up to 2m Manama Rose: poor maiden: ran 3 times in
Britain in 2007: likely to prove best short of 1m: tried tongue tied. *Barry Potts, Ireland*

KNIGHT VALLIANT 4 bl.g. Dansili 127 – Aristocratique 71 (Cadeaux Genereux **55**
131) [2007 64: 14.1m 12.4m May 24] close-coupled gelding: modest maiden handicapper: should stay 1½m+: acts on good to firm ground. *J. Howard Johnson*

KNOT IN WOOD (IRE) 5 b.g. Shinko Forest (IRE) – Notley Park 71 (Wolfhound **113**
(USA) 126) [2007 107: 5g⁶ 6d 6d* 6m³ 6d 6g 6d⁶ 6m³ p6m⁵ Nov 24] sturdy gelding:
smart performer: better than ever in 2007, winning handicap at Hamilton (by 3 lengths
from Protector) in July: ran well after when third in Stewards' Cup (Handicap) at Goodwood (to Zindane) and in listed event at Doncaster (to Galeota): likely to prove as
effective at 5f as 6f/7f: acts on firm and soft going, not discredited on polytrack final
outing: tried blinkered, in cheekpieces last 2 starts: effective held up or making running:
tough and reliable. *R. A. Fahey*

KNOW NO FEAR 2 b.g. (Feb 19) Primo Valentino (IRE) 116 – Alustar 71 (Emarati **76**
(USA) 74) [2007 5d⁴ 5v² p5.1g² 5g² 5d* Sep 17] tall gelding: fair form: runner-up in 3
maidens prior to winning nursery at Musselburgh: speedy, raced only at 5f: acts on
polytrack and heavy going. *J. J. Quinn*

KNOW THE LAW 3 b.g. Danehill Dancer (IRE) 117 – Mackenzie's Friend (Selkirk **89**
(USA) 129) [2007 8m 7.5m² 8g³ 8.1d² 8.3m⁴ 8d² 10m³ 11.6g⁶ p12g* p12g⁴ p12g p12m
Dec 7] 64,000F, 105,000Y: sturdy gelding: first foal: dam, unraced half-sister to smart
1¼m winner Arabie, out of smart Princess Royal Stakes winner and Prix Royal-Oak
runner-up Always Friendly: fairly useful performer: won handicap at Lingfield in
October: stays 1½m: acts on polytrack, good to firm and good to soft ground: blinkered 3
of last 4 starts: reliable. *D. R. C. Elsworth*

KOKKOKILA 3 b.f. Robellino (USA) 127 – Meant To Be 84 (Morston (FR) 125) **67**
[2007 9g⁴ 11m⁶ 9.9s³ p12g⁶ Nov 15] fifth foal: dam 1½m and 2m winner (also won over
hurdles): fair form when in frame in maidens at Goodwood: should be suited by 1½m.
Lady Herries

KOLIBRE 4 br.g. Mtoto 134 – Eternal Flame 73 (Primo Dominie 121) [2007 p7g 9m –
May 22] little form in maidens: tried tongue tied. *T. T. Clement*

KOMPETE 3 b.f. Komaite (USA) – Competa (Hernando (FR) 127) [2007 91: 7m 7m **87**
7d 7.1g³ p8m Nov 24] good-topped filly: has a short, unimpressive action: fairly useful **a–**
on turf, fair at best on all-weather: should stay 1m: yet to race on extremes of going on
turf: visored last 2 starts. *V. Smith*

KOMREYEV STAR 5 b.g. Komaite (USA) – L'Ancressaan 67 (Dalsaan 125) [2007 **55**
60, a45: f11g 8.1m 9.1d⁴ 9.1g 8s⁴ 8.1m⁶ p9.5g⁵ p8.6d² f8d⁶ p9.5g⁵ Dec 29] sturdy
gelding: modest handicapper: stays 9.5f: acts on all-weather and any turf going (best
efforts on softer than good): tried in cheekpieces. *R. E. Peacock*

KONDAKOVA (IRE) 3 b.f. Soviet Star (USA) 128 – Solar Star (USA) 93 (Lear Fan **87**
(USA) 130) [2007 77p: p7.1g 7g 6m* 6d⁴ p6g 6m⁶ 5d⁵ p6g 6.1m³ Sep 15] sturdy filly:
fair performer: won handicap at Windsor in June: clearly best effort when third to Blue
Echo in listed race at Chester final outing: best around 6f: acts on polytrack and good to

firm ground: visored last 3 starts: has been bandaged hind joints: probably best treated with some caution (tends to hang left). *M. L. W. Bell*

KONG (IRE) 5 b.g. Sadler's Wells (USA) 132 – Hill of Snow 80 (Reference Point 139) **107 ?**
[2007 12s⁶ 12g 10d⁶ 12m Oct 5] big, lengthy gelding: powerful galloper: smart performer at best: ran twice in USA for N. Drysdale in 2006: just useful form at best at 5 yrs, seemingly best effort when never-dangerous seventh to Galactic Star in listed event at Newmarket final start: barely stays testing 14.6f: acts on soft going: tried blinkered: has hung left: gelded, then sold 65,000 gns. *J. L. Dunlop*

KOOL KATIE 2 b.f. (Mar 24) Millkom 124 – Katie Komaite 54 (Komaite (USA)) **64 p**
[2007 p6s² Dec 21] 1,000Y: second foal: half-sister to 1¼m/1½m winner in Sweden by Forzando: dam 1m to 11f winner: 16/1 and green, 6 lengths second to Wise Melody in maiden at Wolverhampton, finishing well: will stay 7f: likely to improve. *Mrs G. S. Rees*

KORALEVA TECTONA (IRE) 2 b.f. (Apr 10) Fasliyev (USA) 120 – Miss Teak **65**
(USA) 95 (Woodman (USA) 126) [2007 p7g⁶ 8.3g Oct 16] 12,500F, 23,000Y: lengthy filly: first foal: dam, German 11f winner, sister to dam of Cheveley Park Stakes winner Carry On Katie (by Fasliyev): green, mid-field in maidens at Kempton (fair form) and Leicester. *Pat Eddery*

KORCULA 2 ch.g. (Feb 1) Tomba 119 – Misty Goddess (IRE) 63 (Godswalk (USA) **50**
130) [2007 5g 6g 6d p6g⁶ 8.2g⁵ p8.6g Nov 14] good-topped gelding: modest maiden: raced mostly in sellers: stays 8.6f. *M. J. Wallace*

KOROLIEVA (IRE) 4 b.f. Xaar 132 – Dark Hyacinth (IRE) 65 (Darshaan 133) [2007 **–**
–: p8g Jan 10] leggy filly: fair form at 2 yrs: little form in handicaps since: tried blinkered/ in cheekpieces. *K. A. Ryan*

KORTY 3 b.g. Averti (IRE) 117 – Promissory (Caerleon (USA) 132) [2007 –: 8m p7g **–**
p8g 6m p8g² Dec 16] close-coupled gelding: modest maiden: should be as effective at 7f **a52**
as 1m: acts on polytrack, little form on turf: tried tongue tied. *W. J. Musson*

KOSTAR 6 ch.g. Komaite (USA) – Black And Amber 45 (Weldnaas (USA) 112) [2007 **108**
104: p7g 6m* 6g 6m 6m 6m* Aug 18] good-topped gelding: smart handicapper: won at Pontefract (by 5 lengths from Mr Wolf) in April and William Hill Great St Wilfrid at Ripon (beat Obe Brave by short head, making all) in August: best at 6f/7f: acts on polytrack, firm and good to soft ground: withdrawn after unruly in stall once, and sometimes slowly away: has been early to post. *C. G. Cox*

KOTSI (IRE) 2 b.f. (Apr 18) Nayef (USA) 129 – Ingozi 91 (Warning 136) [2007 7s* **103 p**
8m² 8d⁴ Sep 29] big, lengthy filly: has plenty of scope: good mover: closely related to smart performer up to 1½m Sir George Turner (by Nashwan), 7f winner at 2 yrs, and half-sister to several winners, including smart 6f (at 2 yrs) to 1½m winner Tissifer (by Polish Precedent): dam, 7f/1m winner, half-sister to smart 7f/1m performer Inchinor: useful form: won maiden at Newmarket (beat Annie Skates ½ length) in August: much improved when ½-length second to Spacious in May Hill Stakes at Doncaster: possibly not over those exertions 2 weeks later, when 8½ lengths fourth to Listen in Fillies' Mile at Ascot: will stay 1¼m, probably 1½m: acts on soft and good to firm going: sort to progress more at 3 yrs. *E. F. Vaughan*

*William Hill Great St Wilfrid Stakes, Ripon—the far-side runners are in command,
with Kostar (rail) holding on gamely from Obe Brave, Indian Trail, Malcheek and The Tatling (No.2)*

KOVA HALL (IRE) 5 ch.g. Halling (USA) 133 – My Micheline (Lion Cavern (USA) **74**
117) [2007 94: p10g p9.5g p8.6g 12d 9.5g* 10m⁴ Jul 19] compact gelding: fairly useful
performer at best: left M. Harris after third start: won amateur minor event at Mannheim
in June: stays 1¼m: acts on good to firm going: tried blinkered/visored: has been tongue
tied: winning chaser, including in Germany in July: joined Mrs H. R. J. Nelmes 7,000
gns. *C. von der Recke, Germany*

KRAKATAU (FR) 3 b.g. Noverre (USA) 125 – Tomanivi (Caerleon (USA) 132) [2007 **65**
55: p5g⁵ f6g⁴ p9.5g⁴ f8g* 8.2s⁵ f8g³ 6g p8.6g p7g p8g⁵ p8g⁴ Dec 29] lengthy gelding: fair
handicapper: won at Southwell in April: stays easy 9.5f: raced mainly on all-weather
(well held on turf). *D. J. Wintle*

KRASIVAYA (IRE) 3 b.f. Soviet Star (USA) 128 – Damiana (IRE) (Thatching 131)
[2007 8g Jun 1] 14,000Y: third foal: half-sister to fairly useful 7f to 1¼m winner Desert
Cristal (by Desert King): dam, French maiden (stayed 1m), sister to useful French 1m
winner Dirca: 16/1, always behind in maiden at Goodwood, very green. *J. R. Boyle*

KRASIVI'S BOY (USA) 5 b. or br.g. Swain (IRE) 134 – Krasivi (USA) (Nijinsky **63**
(CAN) 138) [2007 56: p12g² p12g* p12g p11g p13g⁵ Dec 28] modest handicapper: won
amateur event at Lingfield in February: stays 2m: acts on polytrack, soft and good to firm
ground: blinkered. *G. L. Moore*

KRIKKET 3 ch.f. Sinndar (IRE) 134 – Star of The Course (USA) 95 (Theatrical 128) **59**
[2007 55p: p7g⁶ 8.1g May 28] smallish filly: modest maiden: bred to be suited by 1¼m/
1½m: has looked handful to post/started very slowly: refused to enter stall intended final
outing in June: sold 4,000 gns. *W. J. Haggas*

KRISNANDO 2 b.f. (Feb 25) Hernando (FR) 127 – Kris Mundi (Kris 135) [2007 p7g **54**
7.1g 8d Oct 23] 25,000 2-y-o: third foal: dam unraced: modest form in rear in maidens:
will stay middle distances. *W. J. Knight*

KRISTALCHEN 5 b.m. Singspiel (IRE) 133 – Crystal Flite (IRE) 76 (Darshaan 133) **46**
[2007 43: 12m⁶ 12m⁶ 12m 15d 13.8m⁵ 12d Jul 4] lightly-made mare: poor performer: stays 1½m: probably acts on any ground: tried in cheekpieces/visor/tongue strap.
D. W. Thompson

KRISTAL GLORY (IRE) 2 ch.c. (Feb 5) Night Shift (USA) – Kristal's Paradise **61**
(IRE) 100 (Bluebird (USA) 125) [2007 6g 6g³ 7m 7g⁴ 8f⁵ Sep 10] good-bodied colt: sixth
foal: brother to 2003 2-y-o 1m winner Kristal's Dream and half-brother to 11f winner
Kristal Dancer (by Charnwood Forest): dam 1¾m/2m winner: modest maiden: in frame
at Goodwood and Salisbury (nursery): will be suited by 1¼m+. *J. L. Dunlop*

KRISTENSEN 8 ch.g. Kris S (USA) – Papaha (FR) 103 (Green Desert (USA) 127) **80 §**
[2007 81§: f14g 14g* 14m* 18g May 17] smallish, sturdy gelding: fairly useful handicapper: won at Musselburgh in April and May: effective at 1¾m to 21f: acts on all-weather,
firm and soft going: usually wears cheekpieces/visor: held up: unreliable overall, but has
a good record at Musselburgh: sold 10,500 gns later in May. *Karen McLintock*

KRISTIANSAND 7 b.g. Halling (USA) 133 – Zonda 100 (Fabulous Dancer (USA) **60**
124) [2007 59: 15d² 16.1m² 16g³ 17.5s² Sep 21] tall gelding: modest handicapper: stays
17.5f: acts on any turf going: won over hurdles in September. *P. Monteith*

KRISTOFFERSEN 7 ch.g. Kris 135 – Towaahi (IRE) (Caerleon (USA) 132) [2007 **–**
66: 10.9m 14.1g 15.8g Jun 1] smallish, well-made gelding: one-time fairly useful performer on Flat: little form in 2007 (said to have finished lame final outing): blinkered
final 4-y-o start. *Ian Williams*

KRUGERRAND (USA) 8 ch.g. Gulch (USA) – Nasers Pride (USA) (Al Nasr (FR) **86**
126) [2007 94: 8m 10m 9.8g⁶ 10d 10g⁴ 8.9s 10f 10.9m p11g⁶ 10d Sep 22] big, lengthy
gelding: fairly useful handicapper: slipped and fell final outing: stays 1¼m: acts on firm
and soft going: tongue tied once at 2 yrs: held up: none too genuine. *W. J. Musson*

KRYPTONITE (IRE) 2 b.c. (Feb 1) Kris Kin (USA) 126 – Brockton Saga (IRE) 61 **67**
(Perugino (USA) 84) [2007 6g 7m p7g⁶ p8.6g* p9.5s Dec 20] fair form: off over 4
months, improved to win nursery at Wolverhampton in December: stays 8.6f. *J. W. Hills*

KUDBEME 5 b.m. Forzando 122 – Umbrian Gold (IRE) 83 (Perugino (USA) 84) [2007 **64**
69: 8.5m⁵ 7m* 7d 6.9d 7m 8d⁴ 8.5s⁶ 8s³ 8m⁶ 7g 9.9m 8s 10g Oct 6] smallish, strong,
sturdy mare: modest handicapper: won at Catterick in June: stays 1m: acts on good to
firm and good to soft ground: blinkered (raced too freely) on 4-y-o reappearance: usually
slowly away: has tended to hang left: reluctant to race last 2 starts. *N. Bycroft*

KUMAKAWA 9 ch.g. Dancing Spree (USA) – Maria Cappuccini 70 (Siberian Express **– §**
(USA) 125) [2007 –§, a54§: f8s² f8g⁴ f7g f11g³ p10g⁶ p11g f8g⁴ f11g⁵ 10.1d Jun 19] tall **a58 §**

gelding: modest on all-weather, little form on turf in recent years: stays easy 11f: acts on fibresand: tried in headgear: difficult ride: unreliable. *N. P. Littmoden*

KUNG HEI 4 b.g. Primo Valentino (IRE) 116 – Cast A Spell (Magic Ring (IRE) 115) **73**
[2007 p5.1g⁶ p5.1g 7g 9.5g⁶ 9g⁵ 9g⁶ 5g 6g⁵ 6d* 6g² 6g* 6d* Oct 21] fair maiden at 2 yrs: missed 2006 and below form first 2 starts on return before sold from Mrs L. Stubbs: trained by H. Grube next 4 outings: won handicaps at Dresden in August and September and Hoppegarten in October: stays 6f: acts on polytrack and good to soft ground: tried blinkered. *G. Lentz, Germany*

KUNTE KINTEH 3 b.g. Indian Lodge (IRE) 127 – Summer Siren (FR) (Saint Cyrien **70**
(FR) 128) [2007 67p: f7g² 7d³ 7s 7s* p8g³ 7.1s⁴ 8s Sep 20] lengthy gelding: fair performer: won maiden at Catterick in July: free-going sort, though stays easy 1m: acts on all-weather, soft and good to firm ground. *D. Nicholls*

KURIYAMA (IRE) 2 ch.c. (May 9) Raise A Grand (IRE) 114 – Gobolino (Don 128) **60**
[2007 8d Oct 19] €10,000F, €14,000Y: strong colt: brother to Irish 9f/1¼m winner Raise Your Heart and half-brother to several winners, including useful Irish 1m to 1½m winner Bolino Star (by Stalker): dam Irish 2-y-o 7f winner: 33/1 and backward, seventh to Mukhber in maiden at Newmarket. *M. H. Tompkins*

KURUMDA 3 b.g. Montjeu (IRE) 137 – Susun Kelapa (USA) 94 (St Jovite (USA) 135) **–**
[2007 –: 11.7d Aug 19] well beaten in 2 maidens 9 months apart: tried in cheekpieces. *C. R. Egerton*

KUSTER 11 b.g. Indian Ridge 123 – Ustka 60 (Lomond (USA) 128) [2007 84: 11.6m **70**
10s⁶ 11.5d² 12.1s⁵ 10g³ Aug 2] good-bodied gelding: unimpressive mover: just fair handicapper nowadays: stays 1½m: acts on firm and soft going: often blinkered: usually held up. *L. M. Cumani*

KWAZULU (USA) 3 br.c. Dynaformer (USA) – De Aar (USA) (Gone West (USA)) **81**
[2007 10g⁶ p12.2g⁶ 12m³ Jul 27] $250,000Y: good-bodied colt: first foal: dam, 1m/8.5f winner in USA, half-sister to very smart US performers up to 1½m Cetewayo and Bowman Mill: fairly useful maiden: barely stays 1½m: never going well on polytrack: blinkered (best effort) final outing: sold 7,000 gns in October. *J. H. M. Gosden*

KYBER 6 ch.g. First Trump 118 – Mahbob Dancer (FR) (Groom Dancer (USA) 128) **66**
[2007 f11g 16m* 14m³ 16m⁶ 14m⁴ 13g⁶ 13.1g* 13.1d³ 13m² 14d* 14m⁵ 14d 14m⁶ Sep 30] fair handicapper: won at Musselburgh in April, Ayr (apprentices) in June and again at Musselburgh (apprentices) in August: stays 2m: acts on polytrack, soft and good to firm ground. *J. S. Goldie*

KYBURG 3 b.f. Silver Patriarch (IRE) 125 – Native Thatch (IRE) 47 (Thatching 131) **34**
[2007 7m p8g f7g⁴ 8f 6s⁵ p10g 8m 8f Sep 10] tall filly: half-sister to useful 8.5f/9.4f winner Celtic Thatcher and 2001 2-y-o 5f winner Celtic Maid (both by Celtic Swing): dam sprint maiden: poor maiden: tried blinkered. *P. F. I. Cole*

KYLAYNE 2 b.f. (Feb 21) Kyllachy 129 – Penmayne 95 (Inchinor 119) [2007 5m* 5m **90**
6m⁶ 6d 6m² 7m⁵ 6.1m³ 6g⁵ 5d p6g* Oct 17] 10,000F, 15,000Y: smallish, workmanlike filly: good walker: fourth foal: half-sister to winner in Sweden by Dr Fong: dam, 2-y-o 7f winner, half-sister to useful performer up to 1¼m Salamanca: fairly useful performer: won maiden at Warwick in April and minor event at Lingfield in October: mostly stiff tasks in between: best at 5f/6f: acts on polytrack and good to firm going: tried blinkered: races prominently. *P. W. D'Arcy*

KYLE (IRE) 3 ch.g. Kyllachy 129 – Staylily (IRE) (Grand Lodge (USA) 125) [2007 **88**
79: p6g³ 6m* 6m* 7.1g⁴ 7d³ p6g³ 7g 6g⁴ 8.1m⁶ 7m 6s⁶ Oct 14] strong, lengthy gelding: has a short, choppy action: fairly useful performer: won maiden at Salisbury and handicap at Haydock in May: best at 6f/7f: acts on polytrack, good to firm and good to soft ground: tried in cheekpieces: tough. *R. Hannon*

KYLE OF LOCHALSH 7 gr.g. Vettori (IRE) 119 – Shaieef (IRE) 66 (Shareef Dancer **–**
(USA) 135) [2007 61: 14m 12.1g 12m 13m 12m 11.1m Aug 31] leggy gelding: handicapper: little form in 2007: tried in cheekpieces/blinkers/tongue tie. *Miss Lucinda V. Russell*

KYLES PRINCE (IRE) 5 b.g. In The Wings 128 – Comprehension (USA) 87§ (Die- **89**
sis 133) [2007 86: p10g² p12g Mar 1] big, strong gelding: fairly useful handicapper: should stay 1¾m: acts on polytrack and soft ground: sold 14,500 gns, joined Evan Williams. *P. J. Makin*

KYLKENNY 12 b.g. Kylian (USA) – Fashion Flow (Balidar 133) [2007 75, a94: p12g **63**
f12g f11g* f12g⁶ f11g f12g f12g⁴ 11s⁴ 10s² 10g⁴ 10g³ f12d* f12g² Dec 27] angular, **a84**

workmanlike gelding: fairly useful handicapper on all-weather, modest on turf: won at Southwell in February and December (sixteenth course win): effective at 1¼m/1½m: acts on fibresand, firm and soft going: tongue tied: free-going sort: sometimes wanders: tough. *H. Morrison*

KYLLACHY STORM 3 b.g. Kyllachy 129 – Social Storm (USA) (Future Storm (USA)) [2007 67: 10.2f⁶ 7m 5.7d 6.1s⁶ 8g² 13.1f Aug 24] compact gelding: modest maiden: stays 1m: acts on good to firm going, probably on polytrack: sometimes wears blinkers. *R. J. Hodges* **55**

KYLLIS 2 b.f. (Apr 1) Kyllachy 129 – Princess Latifa 63 (Wolfhound (USA) 126) [2007 5m³ p6g² p6g⁶ Oct 26] 4,500Y: leggy filly: fourth foal: half-sister to 8.5f winner Book Matched (by Efisio): dam maiden (stayed 7f): fair maiden: placed at Redcar and Wolverhampton: seemed amiss final start: may prove best at 5f/6f. *B. Smart* **66**

KYLOE BELLE (USA) 3 b.f. Elusive Quality (USA) – Besha (USA) (Turkoman (USA)) [2007 60: p10g 10m* 11.5m 10f 10m⁴ 12g 10m⁵ p12m Oct 13] strong filly: fair handicapper: won at Brighton in April: should stay 1½m: acts on firm ground: tried visored/blinkered/tongue tied: sold 5,000 gns after final outing. *Mrs A. J. Perrett* **68**

KYOTO SUMMIT 4 ch.g. Lomitas 129 – Alligram (USA) 61 (Alysheba (USA)) [2007 94: 12g⁴ 12g 8.9s 12v³ 10g⁶ 12d 16.4m 13.4g² 12d⁵ Oct 12] leggy gelding: fairly useful handicapper: best efforts in 2007 when in frame, second to Ainama at Chester in September: should stay 1¾m: acts on polytrack and heavy going. *M. W. Easterby* **90**

KYRENIA GIRL (IRE) 3 b.f. King Charlemagne (USA) 120 – Cherry Hills (IRE) (Anabaa (USA) 130) [2007 52: 6m² f6g 6.9g⁵ 8g Jul 27] modest maiden: should stay 1m: acts on good to firm ground: sold 1,000 gns in October. *T. D. Easterby* **54**

KYRHENA 3 b.f. Desert Prince (IRE) 130 – Kyle Rhea 104 (In The Wings 128) [2007 –: 12s 14.1m 10f 13.8g⁴ Sep 22] poor maiden: has worn blinkers. *C. W. Thornton* **48**

KYRIE ELEISON (IRE) 2 b.c. (Feb 22) Kalanisi (IRE) 132 – Peratus (IRE) 83 (Mujadil (USA) 119) [2007 6m⁴ p7g⁴ 7m p7g³ 7g 8m⁶ Aug 31] sturdy, close-coupled colt: has quick action: fair maiden: in frame 3 times before tried in nurseries: should stay 1m: acts on polytrack and good to firm ground. *R. Hannon* **70**

KYZER CHIEF 2 b.g. (May 13) Rouvres (FR) 117 – Payvashooz 78 (Ballacashtal (CAN)) [2007 6m 6m 6m 5d Oct 9] no form. *R. E. Barr* **–**

L

LAA BAAS (IRE) 2 b.f. (Jan 28) Green Desert (USA) 127 – Baaderah (IRE) 102 (Cadeaux Genereux 131) [2007 6d Oct 23] eighth foal: half-sister to fairly useful 1m winner Badr Rainbow (by Rainbow Quest) and winner in Greece by Singspiel: dam 6f (including at 2 yrs) winner: 20/1, tenth in maiden at Yarmouth, racing alone and weakening: should improve. *M. A. Jarvis* **49 p**

LAA RAYB (USA) 3 b.c. Storm Cat (USA) – Society Lady (USA) 75 (Mr Prospector (USA)) [2007 f8g* 7.1g⁵ 8.1g* 8.1g 8m 7g* 7.6m² 8.1m³ Sep 15] big, lengthy colt: has scope: half-brother to several winners, including 1998 2-y-o 5f/6f winner Bint Allayl (Queen Mary/Lowther Stakes) and 5f/6f (at 2 yrs) and 7f (Jersey Stakes) winner Kheleyf (both by Green Desert): dam, ran 4 times at 2 yrs, half-sister to smart US performer up to 8.5f Time Bandit: useful performer: won maiden at Southwell (hung) in May, handicap at Sandown (by 5 lengths from Gyroscope) in June and minor event at Goodwood (beat Diamond Diva ¾ length) in August: creditable efforts in handicaps at Chester (short-head second to Vanderlin) and Warwick after: stays 1m: acts on fibresand, raced only on good/good to firm ground: has shown signs of temperament. *M. Johnston* **105**

LABELLED WITH LOVE 7 ch.g. Zilzal (USA) 137 – Dream Baby (Master Willie 129) [2007 64: p7g⁴ p6g⁵ p7g³ p8g² p7g² 7g Jun 12] tall gelding: modest performer: left J. Boyle £6,000, reportedly finished lame final outing: effective at 6f to easy 1¼m: acts on all-weather and good to firm going, probably on good to soft: tongue tied nowadays: often slowly away/races freely. *Jean-Rene Auvray* **59**

LA BELLE JOANNIE 2 b.f. (Mar 15) Lujain (USA) 119 – Sea Clover (IRE) 77 (Ela-Mana-Mou 132) [2007 5d 7.5v³ 6v⁵ 7m² p7g 7m⁵ p8m Nov 24] 800Y: leggy filly: eighth foal: half-sister to 5f winner Knockemback Nellie (by Forzando) and 7f/1m winner He Who Dares (by Distinctly North): dam 2-y-o 7f winner: modest maiden: claimed from **50**

P. Midgley £4,000 fourth start: stays 7f: acts on polytrack and good to firm ground. *S. Curran*

LABOR DAY (IRE) 3 b.f. Pivotal 124 – Late Summer (USA) 71 (Gone West (USA)) **73** [2007 8.3m 8.3g⁴ 7d p7g⁶ p8m Nov 24] stocky filly: second foal: dam, maiden (stayed 1¼m), half-sister to Richmond/Champagne Stakes winner Daggers Drawn out of half-sister to Park Hill Stakes winner Madame Dubois: fair maiden: should be suited by 1¼m: acts on polytrack: sold 16,000 gns. *J. H. M. Gosden*

LACALA (IRE) 2 ch.f. (Mar 22) Alhaarth (IRE) 126 – Gazar (Kris 135) [2007 7d **66** p8.6g⁴ p8g Dec 28] 16,000F: fifth foal: half-sister to fairly useful 1m winner Jihaaz (by Elnadim): dam, French 1½m winner, out of sister to Barathea: fair maiden: easily best run when fourth to Conduit at Wolverhampton: should stay 1¼m. *Jane Chapple-Hyam*

LACEWORK 3 ch.f. Pivotal 124 – Entwine 92 (Primo Dominie 121) [2007 79p: 8.3m **91** 8g* 10m* 9.1m³ Jun 23] lengthy filly: fairly useful handicapper: progressed to win at Goodwood and Redcar in May: good third to Samira Gold at Ayr after, taking strong hold: stayed 1¼m: raced only on polytrack and good/good to firm ground: stud. *Sir Michael Stoute*

LA CHICALUNA 2 ch.f. (Mar 13) Cadeaux Genereux 131 – Crescent Moon (Mr **81** Prospector (USA)) [2007 5g 6m² 6m* 6.1s* 7g 7m² 6.5m 7d Oct 9] €28,000F: sturdy filly: fourth foal: dam, French maiden, out of Balanchine: fairly useful performer: won maiden at Pontefract in June and nursery at Chester in July: ran well only once (second at York) in nurseries after: best at 6f/7f: acts on soft and good to firm going: front runner. *J. G. Given*

LA COLLINE (GER) 4 ch.f. Ocean of Wisdom (USA) 106 – La Laja (GER) (Be My **78** Guest (USA) 126) [2007 76p: f7g⁴ p7g Jan 20] compact filly: fair performer: good fourth in handicap at Southwell on reappearance: clipped heels and unseated rider early on only other start in 2007: stays 7f: acts on fibresand, raced only on good to soft going on turf. *W. J. Haggas*

LA COLUMBINA 2 ch.f. (Jan 31) Carnival Dancer 123 – Darshay (FR) 87 (Darshaan **84 +** 133) [2007 6d 8.1d³ 8.1f³ p8g² 10m* Oct 3] 47,000Y: useful-looking filly: half-sister to several winners, including useful 1m (at 2 yrs)/1¼m winner Deal Fair (by Grand Lodge): dam 9f winner in Belgium: fairly useful form: generally progressive, and won nursery at Nottingham final start: stays 1¼m: acts on polytrack, firm and good to soft going. *R. Hannon*

LA COVETA (IRE) 2 b.f. (Mar 1) Marju (IRE) 127 – Colourful Cast (IRE) 93 **74** (Nashwan (USA) 135) [2007 7.1g 7g* Nov 3] 55,000F, 72,000Y: close-coupled filly: third foal: half-sister to 6f (at 2 yrs) to 1m (US minor stakes) winner Golden Balls (by Danehill Dancer) and Irish 1m to 11f winner Morning Glow (by King of Kings): dam Irish 7f winner: fair form: much improved from debut to win maiden at Newmarket (beat Dar Re Mi by neck): will be suited by 1m/1¼m. *B. J. Meehan*

LA CUVEE 3 b.f. Mark of Esteem (IRE) 137 – Premiere Cuvee 109 (Formidable (USA) **48** 125) [2007 –: 7d⁶ 8f⁴ 10g p8.6g⁴ Aug 20] poor maiden: claimed from R. Beckett after reappearance: stays 1¼m: acts on good to soft ground: tried blinkered. *B. G. Powell*

LADIES BEST 3 b.c. King's Best (USA) 132 – Lady of The Lake 104 (Caerleon (USA) **105** 132) [2007 99p: 10d³ 12g 10m³ 9.9g 10.3m³ 12g² 12s Oct 13] good-bodied colt: has a quick action: useful performer: good efforts in handicaps in 2007 when placed, notably when third to Red Gala at Doncaster and neck second to All The Good at Ascot fifth/sixth starts: below form final outing: likely to stay 1¾m: acts on good to firm and good to soft going: sold 210,000 gns. *Sir Michael Stoute*

LADY ALIZE (USA) 3 b.f. Indian Charlie (USA) 126 – Marina Duff (Caerleon (USA) **64** 132) [2007 83: 8.1m³ 9.9d 8.3g 8g a8g* a8g² a8d⁴ Dec 16] leggy, close-coupled filly: just modest performer in 2007: disappointing for R. Kvisla before winning handicap at Taby on debut for new stable in November: stays 1m: acts on dirt and soft going: tongue tied: races freely. *Yvonne Durant, Sweden*

LADY ALTHEA 4 ch.f. Danzig Connection (USA) – Lady Keyser 68 (Le Johnstan **–** 123) [2007 –: 10.1m⁴ Apr 9] no form in 2 maidens. *Mrs C. A. Dunnett*

LADY AMBITIOUS 4 ch.f. Pivotal 124 – Ambitious 98 (Ardkinglass 114) [2007 43: **36** 8f p12.2g⁶ p12g⁵ p12g² p12g p12.2g p10g⁵ p12.2g 10.1d Oct 30] leggy filly: poor **a48** maiden: stays 1½m: acts on polytrack: tried blinkered. *D. K. Ivory*

LADY AMY 2 b.f. (Feb 3) Fleetwood (IRE) 107 – Hartest Rose (Komaite (USA)) [2007 **–** p7g Aug 27] 1,200Y: sturdy filly: first foal: dam unraced: tailed off in maiden at Kempton. *Miss J. Feilden*

LADY AQUITAINE (USA) 2 gr.f. (Apr 16) El Prado (IRE) 119 – Chalamont (IRE)   **97**
88 (Kris 135) [2007 6g⁶ p7g³ 6m* 6d p6g³ 6m Oct 5] tall, leggy, close-coupled filly: has
scope: half-sister to 3 winners, including useful 7f/1m winner Secret Garden (by Danehill): dam, 2-y-o 6f winner, half-sister to Gold Cup winner Gildoran: useful performer:
won maiden at Windsor in July: ran well last 2 starts, length third to Philario in Sirenia
Stakes at Kempton and 6½ lengths seventh to Natagora in Cheveley Park Stakes at
Newmarket: will stay at least 1m: acts on polytrack and good to firm going. *B. J. Meehan*

LADY ASHEENA 2 gr.f. (Jan 29) Daylami (IRE) 138 – Star Profile (IRE) 100 (Sad-   **51**
ler's Wells (USA) 132) [2007 p8g p8.6g⁴ Nov 8] 16,000Y: sister to winner in Greece, and
half-sister to useful 11f/1½m winner Without A Trace and ungenuine 1m winner Just
A Fluke (both by Darshaan): dam, Irish 2-y-o 6f winner, closely related to smart Irish
sprinter Lady Alexander: modest form in maidens. *J. Jay*

LADY ASPEN (IRE) 4 b.f. Elnadim (USA) 128 – Misty Peak (IRE) 83 (Sri Pekan   **66**
(USA) 117) [2007 79: 9g p8.6g² 6s⁴ 6s 5.5s 8d⁴ 8.1g Sep 12] lengthy, angular filly: fair
maiden: left E. Kelly in Ireland after second outing: stays 1m: acts on soft and good to
firm going: blinkered on reappearance. *Ian Williams*

LADY AVENGER (IRE) 2 ch.f. (Feb 14) Namid 128 – Shioda (USA) (Bahri (USA)   **92**
125) [2007 5g* 5g² 5m 6d⁶ 6m Oct 5] €45,000F: angular filly: first foal: dam, ran twice in
France, out of half-sister to high-class 1m/1¼m performer Lahib: fairly useful perform-
er: improvement next 2 starts, in listed race at Sandown (½-length second to Sweepstake) and Queen Mary Stakes at Royal Ascot (seventh to
Elletelle, poorly drawn): off 3 months, below form in Firth of Clyde Stakes at Ayr (softer
conditions) and Cheveley Park Stakes at Newmarket: should prove best kept to 5f/6f: acts
on good to firm going. *J. M. P. Eustace*

LADY AVIATOR 2 b.f. (Apr 23) Averti (IRE) 117 – Flying Carpet 76 (Barathea (IRE)   **–**
127) [2007 f5g May 14] 13,000Y: fourth foal: half-sister to fairly useful 7f/1m winner
Casemate (by Efisio) and useful 6f winner Stanley Goodspeed (by Inchinor): dam, 8.5f
winner, out of useful 2-y-o sprinter Flying Squaw: 50/1, well held in maiden at Southwell.
T. D. Easterby

LADY BAHIA (IRE) 6 b.m. Orpen (USA) 116 – Do The Right Thing 71 (Busted 134)   **70**
[2007 79: p5g² p5g p5.1g⁶ p5.1g⁶ f5g⁴ p5g² f5g* p5g⁵ Mar 26] big, good-topped mare:
has a short, unimpressive action: fair handicapper: won at Southwell and Kempton in
March: best at 5f: acts on all-weather and firm going: blinkered: quirky, often starts
slowly. *Peter Grayson*

LADY BENJAMIN 2 b.f. (Feb 8) Spinning World (USA) 130 – Fresh Look (IRE) 64   **81**
(Alzao (USA) 117) [2007 5m² p5.1g⁴ 6f* 6g² 6d* 6m² 7m 6g² 6s² 6g⁴ 6m Nov 10]
16,000Y: lengthy filly: seventh foal: half-sister to 3 winners, including 3-y-o Estimator
and Irish 2003 2-y-o 6f winner Euro Route (by Desert Style): dam 11.5f winner: fairly
useful performer: won maiden and nursery at Hamilton in June/July: should stay 7f/1m:
acts on firm and soft going, probably polytrack: blinkered (ran creditably) once.
P. C. Haslam

LADY BID 3 ch.f. Auction House (USA) 120 – Lady Ploy 42 (Deploy 131) [2007 p8g   **–**
Jul 21] fourth foal: half-sister to winner up to 1¼m Jakarmi (by Merdon Melody): dam
little form: 50/1, well held in claimer at Lingfield (said to have bled). *B. Palling*

LADY BOWER 2 b.f. (Mar 28) Bertolini (USA) 125 – Noble Water (FR) 46 (Noble-   **59**
quest (FR) 124) [2007 p6g p7g 7g 7m³ p6g 7.1m* p8g⁶ p7.1g³ p7g Dec 19] leggy,
close-coupled filly: third foal: half-sister to winner in Greece by Gothenberg: dam 6f and
(in Belgium) 7f winner: modest performer: won maiden at Musselburgh in August: left
M. Johnston prior to final outing: barely stays 1m: acts on polytrack and good to firm
ground: often races prominently: tends to find little. *J. Ryan*

LADY CALIDO (USA) 2 b. or br.f. (Mar 19) El Prado (IRE) 119 – Hydro Calido   **52 p**
(USA) 117 (Nureyev (USA) 131) [2007 6d p6g⁴ 6d Jul 25] ninth foal: half-sister to
several winners, including smart Japanese performer up to 11f Shinko Calido (by Silver
Hawk) and useful French 7f/1m winner Espereo (by Forty Niner): dam, French miler,
half-sister to Machiavellian and Exit To Nowhere: modest form in sprint maidens:
outpaced: will do better in handicaps at 1m+. *Sir Mark Prescott*

LADY CAROLLINA 2 b.f. (Mar 2) Bertolini (USA) 125 – Carollan (IRE) 68 (Marju   **55 p**
(IRE) 127) [2007 6d⁵ Oct 15] rather unfurnished filly: first foal: dam maiden (stayed
1¼m): 66/1 and green, fifth to Corrybrough in maiden at Windsor: likely to stay 7f/1m:
will improve. *C. F. Wall*

LADY CARTUCCIA 3 b.f. Fasliyev (USA) 120 – Cartuccia (IRE) (Doyoun 124) **47**
[2007 –: p7.1g p6g³ p7.1g Mar 30] poor maiden: should be suited by 7f+: raced only on polytrack. *J. J. Quinn*

LADY CHARLEMAGNE 2 b.f. (Mar 4) King Charlemagne (USA) 120 – Prospering **–**
50 (Prince Sabo 123) [2007 6m p8g p10g Oct 24] 18,000Y, 28,000 2-y-o: half-sister to useful 2004 2-y-o 5f winner Polly Perkins (by Pivotal) and 4-y-o Going Skint: dam, 7f winner, half-sister to useful performers up to 1¼m Skidrow and Skidmark: little form. *N. P. Littmoden*

LADY COBRA 2 ro.f. (May 12) Golden Snake (USA) 127 – Little Emily 48 (Zafonic **–**
(USA) 130) [2007 6g p8g Sep 19] 2,500Y: fifth foal: half-sister to 3 winners, including 3-y-o Benny The Bat: dam, maiden, out of Norfolk Stakes winner Petillante: well held in maidens. *C. E. Brittain*

LADY DEAUVILLE (FR) 2 gr.f. (Feb 10) Fasliyev (USA) 120 – Mercalle (FR) 108 **102**
(Kaldoun (FR) 122) [2007 6d⁵ 7.1d² 7m³ 7m² 6d⁴ 7d* 7d² 6s* Nov 20] €90,000Y: good-topped filly: half-sister to several winners, including fairly useful 1¼m/1¾m winner Jorobaden (by Poliglote) and Japan Cup runner-up Fabulous La Fouine (by Fabulous Dancer): dam French 1m (at 2 yrs) to 2½m (Prix du Cadran) winner: useful performer: won listed races at Newbury (beat Missit ½ length) in October and Fontainebleau (by 1½ lengths from Badaria) in November: 2½ lengths second to Modern Look in Prix Miesque at Maisons-Laffitte in between: likely to stay 1m: acts on soft and good to firm going. *P. A. Blockley*

LADY DEDLOCK 3 b.f. Josr Algarhoud (IRE) 118 – Ideal Candidate 80 (Celestial **63**
Storm (USA) 132) [2007 p8.6g p12.2g 10f⁴ 16g² 14.6m 14s⁶ 12g Oct 24] work-manlike filly: seventh foal: half-sister to 3 winners, including 8-y-o Mission To Mars: dam 1¼m to 2m winner: modest maiden: flattered in Park Hill Stakes at Doncaster fifth outing: stays 17f: acts on good to firm going, probably on soft: reportedly lost a shoe sixth outing: sold 10,000 gns. *C. A. Cyzer*

LADY DIKTAT 5 b.m. Diktat 126 – Scared (Royal Academy (USA) 130) [2007 –: **66**
p12g⁶ 11.7d³ 11.9s³ May 30] lengthy mare: fair maiden, lightly raced: stays 1½m: acts on polytrack, good to firm and good to soft going. *Mouse Hamilton-Fairley*

LADY DOCKER (IRE) 2 ch.f. (May 13) Docksider (USA) 124 – Copper Creek 78 **–**
(Habitat 134) [2007 6m 7.1g p6g p7g Nov 4] leggy filly: half-sister to numerous winners, notably Irish 6f to 1m (including 7f at 2 yrs) winner Abunawwas (by In The Wings), 5f (including at 2 yrs)/6f winner Tipsy Creek (by Dayjur) and 6f/7f (at 2 yrs) to 9f (in UAE) winner Wathik (by Ogygian), all smart: dam 6f winner: well held in maidens. *H. J. L. Dunlop*

LADY DUXYANA 4 b.f. Most Welcome 131 – Duxyana (IRE) (Cyrano de Bergerac **54**
120) [2007 45: 8f² p9.5g⁶ 7m⁴ 8.2s⁴ 7s² p7.1g⁴ 7m 7m³ 8s p8g⁴ 8d 7f 8m⁴ 7.6s⁶ p7g p7m Nov 26] leggy, close-coupled filly: modest maiden handicapper: stays 1m: acts on polytrack, firm and soft ground: visored: often slowly away. *M. D. I. Usher*

LADY EDGE (IRE) 5 ch.m. Bold Edge 123 – Lady Sheriff 90 (Taufan (USA) 119) **63**
[2007 63: p8g p8g f8g⁶ f7g 8.1m 8f⁴ 7m² 7d 8d 7f 7m² 7d⁶ 7m 7.1m⁵ 8m Sep 25] quite good-topped mare: modest handicapper: stays 1m: acts on polytrack, raced mainly on good going or firmer on turf (below form all starts on good to soft): tried visored/blink-ered. *A. W. Carroll*

LADY FAS (IRE) 4 b.f. Fasliyev (USA) 120 – Lady Sheriff 90 (Taufan (USA) 119) **–**
[2007 7.1m p7.1g Nov 1] smallish filly: poor maiden at 2 yrs, little form since. *A. W. Carroll*

LADY FIFER 3 ch.f. Efisio 120 – Amarice 85 (Suave Dancer (USA) 136) [2007 p6g⁵ **57**
p6g p7f⁵ p7g Mar 16] 26,000F, 21,000Y: third foal: half-sister to smart winner in US and France up to 1¾m On The Acorn (by Inchinor): dam, 2-y-o 7f winner (stayed 1¼m), out of half-sister to dam of 1000 Guineas winner Las Meninas: modest form in maidens: stays 7f: raced only on polytrack: sold 15,000 gns in July. *Jane Chapple-Hyam*

LADY FIRECRACKER (IRE) 3 b.f. Almutawakel 126 – Dazzling Fire (IRE) 78 **51**
(Bluebird (USA) 125) [2007 59p: 7m p8g Dec 16] modest maiden: should be suited by 1m+. *J. R. Best*

LADY FLORENCE 2 gr.f. (May 7) Bollin Eric 125 – Silver Fan (Lear Fan (USA) **–**
130) [2007 7m 7g Nov 3] 2,500Y: workmanlike filly: fifth foal: half-sister to 2 Greek sprint winners by Air Express: dam unraced: burly, in rear in maidens at Newmarket. *A. B. Coogan*

LADY FRIEND 5 gr.m. Environment Friend 128 – Lady Prunella (IRE) (Supreme **85**
Leader 123) [2007 p8.6g⁵ 10g² 10.3d⁴ 10d* 10g² p12.2g³ 10.5s⁶ Sep 29] leggy mare:
second foal: dam, unraced on Flat, runner-up only start over hurdles: fairly useful handicapper: won at Windsor in July: good placed efforts next 2 starts: stays 1½m: acts on
polytrack and good to soft ground. *J. W. Hills*

LADY FROM WESTOW 2 b.f. (May 2) Cadeaux Genereux 131 – Dot Com Dot 61 –
(Monsun (GER) 124) [2007 6s 5g Aug 16] 2,000Y: second foal: half-sister to a winner in
Greece by Hernando: dam maiden (best around 1m): tailed off in maidens. *P. T. Midgley*

LADY GEORGETTE (IRE) 4 b.f. Fasliyev (USA) 120 – Georgia Venture 98 (Shir- –
ley Heights 130) [2007 66, a61: p10g Jan 3] lengthy filly: fair maiden handicapper at
3 yrs: well held sole start on Flat in 2007: sold €10,000, joined Miss Mary Quigley in
Ireland. *E. J. O'Neill*

LADY GLORIA 3 b.f. Diktat 126 – Tara Moon (Pivotal 124) [2007 f8g³ f8g* 8.2s² **104**
f8g* 9* 8.2m² 8.2g² 8m 8m 9g³ 8d² 8.3g² 9s* Nov 20] stocky filly: second foal: dam
unraced out of half-sister to smart Scandinavian sprinter Musadif: useful performer: won
maiden at Southwell in February, handicaps there and at Sandown in May, and listed race
at Fontainebleau (by ½ length from In The Light) in November: also ran well when
second to Perfect Star in listed handicap at Ascot eleventh outing: effective at 1m/9f: acts
on fibresand, soft and good to firm going: free-going sort: reportedly struck into eighth
outing. *J. G. Given*

LADY GRACE (IRE) 3 b.f. Orpen (USA) 116 – Lady Taufan (IRE) (Taufan (USA) **104**
119) [2007 91: 7s* 8m 6s³ 7g 6d* Oct 19] lengthy filly: useful performer: won minor
event at Leicester (by 5 lengths from Medley) in June and listed race at Newmarket (beat
Wid by ½ length) in October: creditable third to Theann in Summer Stakes at York third
outing: has won at 1m, may prove best at 6f/7f: acts on polytrack and soft ground:
free-going sort: has been bandaged behind: stays in training (to be covered by Nayef
first). *W. J. Haggas*

LADY GRANTLEY 2 ch.f. (Apr 17) Bertolini (USA) 125 – South Shore 102 (Caer- –
leon (USA) 132) [2007 6g f6g f6g 7s Jul 13] 3,200Y: half-sister to several winners,
including 3-y-o Greek Envoy and useful 7f/1m winner South Rock (by Rock City): dam,
1¼m/1½m winner, half-sister to very smart miler Soviet Line: no form. *M. W. Easterby*

LADY HOPEFUL (IRE) 5 b.m. Lend A Hand 124 – Treble Term 66 (Lion Cavern **54 §**
(USA) 117) [2007 54, a60: p5.1g⁴ p5.1g³ p5.1g² p5.1g p5g⁵ p6g⁵ p5.1g⁵ p5.1g⁵ p5g⁴
5m⁴ 5s⁶ p5.1g⁴ 5s⁵ p5.1g p6g 5f p5g⁵ p5.1g p5.1g⁴ Dec 31] good-topped mare: modest
performer: effective at 5f to easy 7f: acts on all-weather, firm and good to soft ground
(well held on soft/heavy): wears headgear: often slowly away, and not one to trust. *Peter
Grayson*

LADY IN BLUE 3 b.f. Dr Fong (USA) 128 – Dodona 73 (Lahib (USA) 129) [2007 p8g –
8.3d 8.1m Aug 31] first foal: dam 1¼m/11f winner: well held in maidens. *T. D. McCarthy*

LADY IN CHIEF 2 ch.f. (Jan 9) Fantastic Light (USA) 134 – Risque Lady 109 (Ken- –
mare (FR) 125) [2007 7g⁶ 8g Oct 26] 16,000Y: good-topped filly: fourth foal: half-sister
to 2005 2-y-o 7f winner Chris Corsa and 3-y-o Risque Heights (both by Mark of Esteem):
dam, 5f (at 2 yrs)/1m winner, half-sister to smart sprinter To The Roof: well held in
maidens. *Miss J. A. Camacho*

LADY IN THE BATH 3 b.f. Forzando 122 – Dicentra (Rambo Dancer (CAN) 107) –
[2007 10g Oct 6] fifth foal: half-sister to 6f winner Coracle King (by Compton Place),
later winner up to 1½m in France: dam little form: 33/1, well held in seller at Redcar.
P. C. Haslam

LADY JANE DIGBY 2 b.f. (Mar 12) Oasis Dream 129 – Scandalette (Niniski (USA) **96**
125) [2007 7m* 8m⁵ 7d⁶ 8d Oct 23] raw-boned filly: unfurnished at 2 yrs: closely related
to smart 6f (at 2 yrs) to 9f winner Gateman (by Owington) and fairly useful 2005 2-y-o 6f
winner Diablerette (by Green Desert), and half-sister to 2 winners, including smart 7f/1m
winner Surprise Encounter (by Cadeaux Genereux): dam unraced half-sister to high-class
sprinter Polish Patriot: useful performer: won maiden at Doncaster in August: improved
next time when 3 lengths fifth to Spacious in May Hill Stakes there, rallying: possibly
unsuited by softer conditions in C. L. Weld Park Stakes at the Curragh (favourite) and
Prix des Reservoirs at Deauville, weakening: stays 1m: acts on good to firm going.
M. Johnston

LADY JINKS 2 ch.f. (Apr 29) Kirkwall 118 – Art Deco Lady 51 (Master Willie 129) **55 ?**
[2007 6.1s⁵ 6.1d 7g p8.6g⁵ p10g Oct 24] leggy filly: seventh foal: half-sister to 6-y-o

Aperitif and 3-y-o Nassau Style: modest maiden: stays 8.6f: acts on polytrack and soft going. *M. D. I. Usher*

LADY JOHANNA (USA) 3 b. or br.f. Johannesburg (USA) 127 – Bloomin Thunder **44** (USA) (Thunder Gulch (USA) 129) [2007 7d 7g 7.6m Aug 23] €90,000Y: lightly-made filly: fourth foal: dam US maiden half-sister to smart French/US performer up to 1¼m Trishyde: poor maiden: sold 2,000 gns, joined S. Smrczek, Germany. *K. R. Burke*

LADY JOSH 4 b.f. Josr Algarhoud (IRE) 118 – Dee-Lady 93 (Deploy 131) [2007 p8g⁵ 10.2f⁶ May 1] poor maiden. *W. G. M. Turner*

LADY KILLER QUEEN 3 b.f. Killer Instinct 111 – Princess of War (Warrshan **58** (USA) 117) [2007 10m⁶ 10d⁶ Oct 10] first foal: dam bumper winner: better effort in maidens when sixth to Envisage at Nottingham second start: bred to be suited by 1½m+. *D. Carroll*

LADY KINTYRE 3 b.f. Mull of Kintyre (USA) 114 – Lady Sheriff 90 (Taufan (USA) **–** 119) [2007 –: 7d Oct 29] big, strong filly: no form. *M. W. Easterby*

LADY KORRIANDA 6 ch.m. Dr Fong (USA) 128 – Prima Verde 81 (Leading Coun- **47** sel (USA) 122) [2007 47: p11g p12g⁴ 15.4g Aug 16] poor maiden: stays easy 1½m: raced only on polytrack and good/good to soft going. *R. Curtis*

LADY LAFITTE (USA) 3 b.f. Stravinsky (USA) 133 – Ready For Action (USA) **67 §** (Riverman (USA) 131) [2007 73p: p7g 5m² 5g⁵ 5s p5g p6g⁵ p6g⁶ 5.7g p6g Nov 1] good-topped filly: fair maiden: left B. Hills after fifth start: acts on polytrack and good to firm going: tried blinkered/tongue tied/in cheekpieces: has been unruly at start: unreliable. *M. Wellings*

LADY LILY (IRE) 3 ch.f. Desert Sun 120 – Sheila Blige 83 (Zamindar (USA) 116) **94** [2007 90: 6m 5.1f⁵ 6m 5d⁴ 6f* 6m 6m* 6m p6g⁶ Oct 12] sturdy filly: fairly useful handi-capper: won at Redcar (despite hanging left) in August and Pontefract in September: free-going sort, will prove best over 5f/6f: acts on polytrack, firm and good to soft going: sold 45,000 gns. *H. R. A. Cecil*

LADY LIVIUS (IRE) 4 b.f. Titus Livius (FR) 115 – Refined (IRE) 95 (Statoblest 120) **102** [2007 98: p6g* 5.1f 6.1s⁴ 6m 5d 6m⁵ 6g 8.1m 7m⁶ p8m Nov 1] close-coupled, quite good-topped filly: useful performer: won handicap at Lingfield (all-weather debut, by 1¼ lengths from Qadar) in March: below form in listed events/handicaps after: stays 7f: acts on polytrack and good to firm going, not on softer than good: has worn blinkers: inconsistent: sold 105,000 gns. *R. Hannon*

LADY LOCHINVER (IRE) 4 ch.f. Raise A Grand (IRE) 114 – Opening Day (Day Is **–** Done 115) [2007 54: 7.9m 9.9s Jun 21] quite good-topped filly: modest maiden handi-capper at 3 yrs: well beaten in 2007. *Micky Hammond*

LADY LORINS 3 ch.f. Tomba 119 – Charleigh Keary 55 (Sulaafah (USA) 119) [2007 **–** 7.1d p7g p10g p7g Oct 29] leggy filly: third foal: dam 2-y-o 5f winner: little form in maidens. *Andrew Turnell*

LADY LUCAS 4 b.f. Night Shift (USA) – Broadfield Lass (IRE) (Le Bavard **–** (FR) 125) [2007 –: p11g p9.5g 8.1m 10.2d 13.1m p12g May 31] little form: tried tongue tied. *E. J. Creighton*

LADY MAYA 2 br.f. (May 16) Prince Sabo 123 – Monte Mayor Lady (IRE) (Brief **–** Truce (USA) 126) [2007 5.2f 6g 6m p7g 8g Oct 24] 12,500 2-y-o: workmanlike filly: third foal: half-sister to Italian 5.5f (at 2 yrs) to 1m winner La Favola Mia (by Lend A Hand): dam, ran 3 times, out of half-sister to smart stayer Arden: no form. *Dr J. R. J. Naylor*

LADY NIMUE (FR) 3 gr.f. Medaaly 114 – Concert (Polar Falcon (USA) 126) [2007 **45 p** f11d Dec 12] fourth foal: sister to 10.2f to 1½m winner Mae Cigan and half-sister to fairly useful 9.4f (at 2 yrs) to 12.6f winner (stays 2m) Bill Bennett (by Bishop of Cashel): dam unraced close relation to useful 1¼m performer Rudimental: 12/1 and green, well held in maiden at Southwell: should do better. *J. Jay*

LADY NOVA (IRE) 2 b.f. (Feb 2) Noverre (USA) 125 – The Woodstock Lady 90 **79** (Barathea (IRE) 127) [2007 6g 6s⁴ 6s⁵ 6d 7g 6.3m 7v* Oct 28] €6,700F, €33,000Y: strong, good-bodied filly: first foal: dam 2-y-o 7f winner who stayed at least 2m (also winning hurdler): fair performer: left J. S. Moore after sixth start: improved to win minor event at Galway in October: stays 7f: acts on heavy going: tried in cheekpieces. *W. M. Roper, Ireland*

LADY OF KINTYRE (IRE) 2 b.f. (Apr 12) Mull of Kintyre (USA) 114 – Tartan **54**
Lady (IRE) 88 (Taufan (USA) 119) [2007 6g⁴ 5d⁶ 7d Jul 22] €5,500F: well-grown filly:
eighth foal: half-sister to fairly useful 1999 2-y-o 1m winner Scotty Guest (by Distinctly
North) and Irish 1¼m winner Lady For Life (by Rainbows For Life): dam Irish 7f (at
2 yrs) and 9f winner: modest maiden: should stay 1m. *E. J. Alston*

LADY OF PASSION (IRE) 2 b.f. (May 1) Fruits of Love (USA) 127 – Chatsworth **–**
Bay (IRE) (Fairy King (USA)) [2007 5s 7m 5m Sep 2] sister to 4-y-o Trafalgar Bay and
half-sister to 2 winners in Italy: dam unraced: no show in maidens. *M. R. Channon*

LADY OF THE PARK (IRE) 2 ch.f. (Mar 8) Okawango (USA) 115 – Rainstone 57 **57**
(Rainbow Quest (USA) 134) [2007 p7.1g³ 7.1m⁶ 6v⁶ Oct 9] €20,000Y: half-sister to several winners, including useful 1998 2-y-o 5f/6f winner Gipsy Rose Lee (by Marju): dam,
won in Belgium, half-sister to smart 2-y-o sprinter Magic Ring: modest maiden: best
effort on debut (third at Wolverhampton), only all-weather start: stays 7f. *P. A. Blockley*

LADY PETRUS 2 b.f. (Mar 11) Oasis Dream 129 – Odalisque (IRE) (Machiavellian **62 ?**
(USA) 123) [2007 p7g 7g Nov 3] 46,000Y: neat filly: sixth foal: half-sister to French
2004 2-y-o 7.5f winner Fast Enough (by Anabaa) and French 7.5f/8.5f winner Onda Blu
(by Desert King): dam, French 10.5f winner, out of very smart French performer up to
1½m Ode: seemingly modest form in rear in maidens. *H. J. L. Dunlop*

LADY PICKPOCKET 3 b.f. Benny The Dip (USA) 127 – Circe 73 (Main Reef 126) **55**
[2007 –: f11g⁶ 8.3g 10.1g³ 12.1g⁴ 12.1d⁶ 11.6d² 13.8g* 12.4d Oct 16] close-coupled filly:
modest performer: won seller at Catterick (sold from M. Tompkins 7,500 gns) in September: stays 1¾m: acts on fibresand and good to soft going: tried visored. *F. P. Murtagh*

LADY PILOT 5 b.m. Dansili 127 – Mighty Flyer (IRE) (Mujtahid (USA) 118) [2007 –, **–**
a69: p10g p10g³ p16g⁴ p13g⁵ p10g p16g* f14g* f14g* Apr 13] workmanlike mare: fair **a72**
handicapper on all-weather: left Miss J. Doyle £4,500, won at Kempton in March and
Southwell (2) in April: stays 2m: acts on all-weather and good to firm going: sometimes
wears headgear: modest form over hurdles, won in November. *Jim Best*

LADY POMEROL 3 b.f. Josr Algarhoud (IRE) 118 – Queen's College (IRE) 57 **–**
(College Chapel 122) [2007 8.3m p10g 11.5m⁶ Sep 5] stocky filly: first foal: dam sprint
maiden: no form in maidens. *Lady Herries*

LADY RANGALI (IRE) 2 b.f. (Jan 27) Danehill Dancer (IRE) 117 – Promising Lady **87**
91 (Thunder Gulch (USA) 129) [2007 5m⁵ 5m* 5v² 5s* 6m* 6m⁵ 6.5d* Sep 28]
€52,000F, 11,000Y: leggy filly: third foal: dam Irish 1m winner (including at 2 yrs): fairly
useful form: had excellent season, and won maiden at Catterick in May, nurseries at York
in July and Haydock in August and valuable 22-runner Watership Down Stud Sales Race

*Watership Down Stud Sales Race, Ascot—the race unfolds on the far side
and produces a close finish between Lady Rangali, Izzibizzi (No.16), Sophie's Girl and Insaaf*

at Ascot (improved again to beat Izzibizzi by neck) in September: stays 6.5f: yet to race on firm going, acts on any other: tough. *Mrs A. Duffield*

LADY ROCHBONNE 2 b.f. (Apr 12) Superior Premium 122 – French Project (IRE) **72** 84 (Project Manager 111) [2007 p7.1g⁴ 7d² 7m³ p7.1g⁵ p7.1g² 7.1g⁴ 7d⁵ p6g⁴ Oct 19] sixth foal: dam won over hurdles: fair maiden: in frame 6 times, twice in nurseries: better at 7f than shorter: acts on polytrack, good to firm and good to soft going: sold 6,500 gns. *Mrs G. S. Rees*

LADY ROMANOV (IRE) 4 br.f. Xaar 132 – Mixremember (FR) (Linamix (FR) 127) **82** [2007 79: f11g 14g 12d⁴ 10.1d* 12.6s f11d⁶ Dec 18] tall filly: fairly useful handicapper: won at Yarmouth in June: left M. Tompkins prior to final outing: stays 1½m: acts on all-weather and good to soft going (below form both tries on soft). *D. G. Bridgwater*

LADY SANDICLIFFE (IRE) 2 b.f. (Apr 1) Noverre (USA) 125 – Tigava (USA) **63** (Machiavellian (USA) 123) [2007 5.1g⁴ 5.7g³ 6s p7g⁵ p7.1g 7g² p7g⁴ p10g p8g⁶ Dec 12] €9,500Y, resold 17,000Y: angular filly: third foal: half-sister to winner in Italy by Sagamix: dam, French maiden, out of useful 1¼m winner Tiger Flower: modest maiden: claimed from B. Hills £10,000 sixth start: stays 1m: acts on polytrack, best turf form on good going. *Miss Jo Crowley*

LADY SEE (IRE) 2 b.f. (Mar 10) Spartacus (IRE) 107 – Antigonel (IRE) 59 (Fairy – King (USA)) [2007 6s 7s 6m Aug 11] 4,000Y: third foal: half-sister to 4-y-o Lavenham: dam maiden: little form: dead. *T. D. Easterby*

LADY SELKIRK 2 ch.f. (Mar 30) Selkirk (USA) 129 – Hyde Hall 90 (Barathea (IRE) **57 p** 127) [2007 7g 7m Sep 22] 170,000Y: good-topped filly: third foal: dam, 1¼m winner, half-sister to Yorkshire Oaks winner Catchascatchcan, herself dam of very smart but untrustworthy rider Antonius Pius: 14/1, in need of experience in maidens at Salisbury (hampered) and Newbury (modest form): will be suited by 1¼m/1½m: should improve. *R. Charlton*

LADY SHIRLEY HUNT 3 ch.f. Zaha (CAN) 106 – Kathy Fair (IRE) 46 (Nicholas – Bill 125) [2007 –: 8.1m⁶ 7g 7m 7.1s Jul 27] tall, good-topped filly: little form. *A. D. Smith*

LADY'S LAW 4 b.f. Diktat 126 – Snugfit Annie 49 (Midyan (USA) 124) [2007 40: **52** p9.5g p11g f7g⁵ p8.6g⁶ 7g 12d⁵ 10m 12s p13.9g⁶ p12g Nov 21] modest maiden: barely stays 1¾m: acts on polytrack and good to soft ground. *Rae Guest*

LADY SONGBIRD (IRE) 4 b.f. Selkirk (USA) 129 – Firecrest (IRE) 107 (Darshaan **85** 133) [2007 72: 10m 10g³ 12d* 11.5d² 12m⁵ Jul 19] leggy filly: fairly useful handicapper: won at Newbury in May: good second at Carlisle next time: will stay beyond 1½m: acts on good to soft and good to firm going: usually held up: sold 23,000 gns in October. *W. R. Swinburn*

LADY SORCERER 2 b.f. (Feb 10) Diktat 126 – Silk Law (IRE) 80 (Barathea (IRE) **80** 127) [2007 p6g³ 7.2s² p8g* 8d⁴ Oct 19] 10,000Y: leggy, close-coupled filly: second foal: half-sister to 1¼m winner Ms Rainbow Runner (by Josr Algarhoud): dam, 2-y-o 6f/7f winner, out of useful half-sister to smart 7f/1m performer With Reason: fairly useful form: placed twice (second to Boy Blue at Ayr latterly) prior to winning maiden at Kempton in October: again hung right when fourth to Kandahar Run in minor event at Newmarket: stays 1m: acts on polytrack and soft going. *A. P. Jarvis*

LADY SPLODGE 3 b.f. Mark of Esteem (IRE) 137 – La Victoria (GER) (Rousillon **64** (USA) 133) [2007 10.2d³ 10.2g Oct 24] £800Y: half-sister to several winners in Germany, including 1¼m/11f winner Lagoo (by Goofalik): dam, German 1m winner, half-sister to top-class German 1½m performer Lomitas: better effort in maidens at Bath when third to Sharp Dresser. *C. G. Cox*

LADY STARDUST 4 b.f. Spinning World (USA) 130 – Carambola (IRE) 100 (Dane- **95** hill (USA) 126) [2007 90p: p8g 8d⁶ 8s* 8m 8d³ 10s Oct 13] good-topped filly: has scope: useful performer, lightly raced: won handicap at Newmarket in June: creditable third to Whazzis in listed race at Ascot penultimate start: below form final outing: should stay 1¼m: acts on soft going. *J. R. Fanshawe*

LADY SUFFRAGETTE (IRE) 4 b.f. Mull of Kintyre (USA) 114 – Miss Senate **50** (IRE) (Alzao (USA) 117) [2007 51: p11g p12.2g³ p16.5g p13g⁶ f14g⁵ Jun 5] work-manlike filly: modest maiden: stays 1½m: acts on polytrack and good to soft ground: reportedly pulled muscles second 3-y-o outing. *John Berry*

LADY TILLY 10 b.m. Puissance 110 – Lady of Itatiba (BEL) (King of Macedon 126) – [2007 –: 5m 5g May 10] workmanlike mare: no longer of any account. *W. G. Harrison*

LADY TOYAH (IRE) 3 ch.f. Titus Livius (FR) 115 – Secur Pac (FR) (Halling (USA) – 133) [2007 –: p7.1g Aug 20] 800Y: sparely-made filly: second foal: dam unraced: little form. *Mrs L. Williamson*

LADY TRAILL 3 b.f. Barathea (IRE) 127 – Halska (Unfuwain (USA) 131) [2007 63: 56 p12.2g 12.1g⁶ 12.1s³ 16.2s⁴ 16g 16.2f Aug 27] modest maiden handicapper: stays 2m: acts on polytrack and soft ground: tried blinkered. *B. W. Hills*

LADY VALENTINO 3 b.f. Primo Valentino (IRE) 116 – Mystery Night (FR) (Fairy 56 King (USA)) [2007 6f⁴ 7m 7s⁴ 7m⁵ 7.5m² 8.3g² Sep 3] 5,600Y: fourth foal: half-sister to Italian 7f (at 2 yrs) to 1¼m winner Mercuzio (by Vettori): dam unraced half-sister to smart French performer up to 1½m Miss Tahiti: modest maiden: likely to stay 1¼m: yet to race on heavy ground, acts on any other. *M. Dods*

LADY VAN GOGH 2 b.f. (May 18) Dubai Destination (USA) 127 – Sweet Revival – 41 (Claude Monet (USA) 121) [2007 6m 8.1g 8.2m Oct 3] 42,000F: workmanlike filly: half-sister to several winners, notably US Grade 1 9f/1¼m winner Sweet Return (7.5f winner in Britain at 2 yrs, by Elmaamul): dam 1¼m winner: last in maidens. *R. Hannon*

LADY VIBEEKA 2 b.f. (Feb 8) Josr Algarhoud (IRE) 118 – Indian Flag (IRE) 39 64 (Indian Ridge 123) [2007 5s 5.1g 5.1d⁶ 5g² 5.1d 5m p5g² p5g Oct 24] good-quartered filly: third foal: half-sister to 4-y-o Lucayos and 5-y-o Clipper Hoy: dam maiden (stayed 1¼m): modest maiden: second at Lingfield and Kempton: raced only at 5f. *Mrs H. Sweeting*

LADY WARNING 3 b.f. Averti (IRE) 117 – Lady Smith (Greensmith 121) [2007 –: – p5g Jan 3] little form. *W. G. M. Turner*

LADY ZABEEN (IRE) 2 b.f. (Mar 9) Singspiel (IRE) 133 – Britannia House (USA) 70 71 (Diesis 133) [2007 6d⁶ 7g⁶ 7g⁶ Sep 29] 25,000Y, 68,000 2-y-o: good-bodied filly: second foal: dam once-raced half-sister to dam of smart miler Passing Glance: fair maiden: sixth all starts, at Newmarket (behind Don't Forget Faith and Visit) and Goodwood (beaten 5½ lengths by Celtic Slipper) first 2: will stay 1m. *D. M. Simcock*

LADY ZIA (IRE) 3 b.f. Dilshaan 119 – Gift Box (IRE) 63§ (Jareer (USA) 115) [2007 48 7m 6.5g 6g 8d Jul 6] €10,000 2-y-o: leggy filly: sixth foal: half-sister to 7f (at 2 yrs) and 9f (in Saudi Arabia) winner Fadeela (by Desert King): dam, temperamental maiden, half-sister to smart 6f/7f performer Danehill Dancer: poor form in maidens, including at Chester on debut: tried blinkered. *James G. Burns, Ireland*

LA ESPERANZA 3 b.f. Mind Games 121 – Chantilly Myth 81 (Sri Pekan (USA) 117) – [2007 53: p5f 5m 5f Apr 21] smallish, leggy filly: maiden: well held in 2007: tried in cheekpieces. *Miss A. Stokell*

LA ESTRELLA (USA) 4 b.g. Theatrical 128 – Princess Ellen 114 (Tirol 127) [2007 94 90+: 14g⁵ p12.2g⁵ 12g⁴ 12m* 12g⁶ 13.1m⁵ 16.1v 12f 12d 13.1s⁴ 14d p12.2g* 12m p12.2g⁴ Dec 26] lengthy, useful-looking gelding: fairly useful handicapper: won at Pontefract (beat McEldowney by 5 lengths) in May and Wolverhampton in October: left J. Given 32,000 gns, denied clear run last 2 starts: barely stays 13f: acts on polytrack and good to firm going, probably on soft: tried blinkered: races prominently. *D. E. Cantillon*

LA FAMIGLIA 2 ch.f. (Feb 23) Tobougg (IRE) 125 – Sea Isle 73 (Selkirk (USA) 129) 62 p [2007 6m³ Sep 17] 2,000Y: second foal: half-sister to 4-y-o Cativo Cavallino: dam maiden (stayed 1m): 16/1, third in maiden at Leicester, finishing well: will be suited by 7f/1m: should progress. *H. Candy*

LAFONTAINE BLEU 3 b.f. Piccolo 121 – Russell Creek 80 (Sandy Creek 123) [2007 – 66: 5g 6g 6g Sep 23] good-topped filly: modest performer at 2 yrs: well held in 2007: left R. Fahey after second start. *I. Semple*

LA FORTALESA (IRE) 2 b.c. (Mar 29) Rock of Gibraltar (IRE) 133 – Another 74 p Legend (USA) (Lyphard's Wish (FR) 124) [2007 7s⁶ 8d⁴ Oct 13] 27,000F, 100,000Y: tall colt: has high knee action: seventh foal: half-brother to 3 winners, including 2004 2-y-o 5f winner Soviet Legend (by Soviet Star) and French 2001 2-y-o 9.8f winner Celtic Legend (by Celtic Swing): dam US Grade 2 9f winner: fair form in maidens at Redcar and York (fourth to Bright Falcon), travelling well long way before tiring: may prove best up to 1m: type to progress at 3 yrs. *K. A. Ryan*

LAGAN LEGEND 6 gr.m. Midnight Legend 118 – Piecemeal (Baron Blakeney 83) – [2007 14m Aug 10] poor hurdler: blinkered/tongue tied, tailed off on Flat debut. *Dr J. R. J. Naylor*

LA GAZZETTA (IRE) 2 b.f. (Apr 21) Rossini (USA) 118 – Shining Creek (CAN) 59 (Bering 136) [2007 7g p7g Nov 17] €98,000F, 34,000 2-y-o: compact filly: sixth foal:

half-sister to useful 5f/6f winner Cool Creek (by Desert Style): dam Italian winner around 7f, including at 2 yrs: modest form towards rear in maidens. *D. R. C. Elsworth*

LAGO D'ORTA (IRE) 7 ch.g. Bahhare (USA) 122 – Maelalong (IRE) 77 (Maelstrom Lake 118) [2007 79: 8.5m 7.9d 10.4m⁶ 9d⁵ 8g Nov 8] close-coupled, quite good-topped gelding: fair performer at best nowadays: stays 9.3f: acts on firm going: tried tongue tied: often slowly away. *D. Nicholls*   **76 d**

LA GUANCHA 2 b.f. (Feb 28) Timeless Times (USA) 99 – Westcourt Ruby (Petong 126) [2007 5g³ 5m⁵ 5m⁴ 6m³ 6g 5g⁶ 5m 5m 5g 5m³ 5d 7.1g Oct 5] 2,000Y: close-coupled filly: fourth foal: dam, maiden, half-sister to useful sprinter Proud Boast: maiden: left T. D. Barron after fourth start, and little form subsequently: tried in tongue tie/cheek-pieces. *D. A. Nolan*   **60 d**

LAHEEN (IRE) 4 b.f. Bluebird (USA) 125 – Ashirah (USA) (Housebuster (USA)) [2007 60: p10g p10g Mar 5] angular filly: modest maiden: seems to stay 1¼m: acts on polytrack: tried blinkered/visored. *J. R. Best*   **54**

LAISH YA HAJAR (IRE) 3 ch.g. Grand Lodge (USA) 125 – Ya Hajar 106 (Lycius (USA) 124) [2007 75: 7m³ 8g 8.1m² 8.5v 8.1m p7g p8g Dec 1] heavy-topped gelding: fair maiden: good efforts when placed in 2007: left M. Channon 20,000 gns after fourth start: stays 1m: acts on polytrack and good to firm ground. *P. R. Webber*   **76**

LAITH (IRE) 4 b.g. Royal Applause 124 – Dania (GER) (Night Shift (USA)) [2007 71d: f6g f8g p6g³ p7.1g³ p6g⁴ p6g³ 6g p6g 6f 5.2g⁶ 6m 5g p6g Nov 8] big, strong, attractive gelding: has a quick action: modest performer on balance nowadays: stays easy 7f: acts on polytrack and firm going: tried blinkered, often wears cheekpieces: has flashed tail: sold 800 gns. *Miss V. Haigh*   **57**

LAKE CAREZZA (USA) 5 b.g. Stravinsky (USA) 133 – May Wedding (USA) (French Deputy (USA) 118) [2007 p8g p7.1g f8g Feb 15] smallish, strong gelding: maiden, lightly raced: just poor form in 2007: seems to stay 1m. *N. J. Hawke*   **47**

LAKE CHINI (IRE) 5 b.g. Raise A Grand (IRE) 114 – Where's The Money 87 (Lochnager 132) [2007 85: f5g 6m³ 6m⁵ 6g 5s⁵ 5d³ 5d 5s* 5.9g* 5m² 5m² 5g⁶ 6s³ 6.1s 5.1g⁴ Oct 31] strong, good sort: has a round action: fair performer: won claimer at Ayr and amateur handicap at Carlisle in August: stays easy 7f: acts on polytrack, soft and good to firm going: wears cheekpieces/blinkers: races prominently. *M. W. Easterby*   **78**

LAKE HERO 4 b.f. Arkadian Hero (USA) 123 – Inya Lake 101 (Whittingham (IRE) 104) [2007 p6g p6g f5g⁵ p5g⁶ 5m Aug 2] workmanlike filly: fair performer: finished lame behind final start: was best at 5f: acted on all-weather, good to firm and good to soft going: tried blinkered: dead. *M. J. Wallace*   **69**

LAKE NAYASA 2 b.f. (May 2) Nayef (USA) 129 – Lady of The Lake 104 (Caerleon (USA) 132) [2007 8.2g Nov 7] unfurnished filly: sixth foal: half-sister to 3 winners, including 1m (at 2 yrs) and 2m winner Coventina (by Daylami) and 3-y-o Ladies Best, both useful: dam, 2m/17f winner, out of smart performer up to 9f Llyn Gwynant: 66/1 and reluctant at stall, tailed off in maiden at Nottingham. *H. Morrison*   **–**

LAKE POET (IRE) 4 ch.c. Galileo (IRE) 134 – Lyric 58 (Lycius (USA) 124) [2007 98, a83: p10g⁶ p11g⁶ 12g* 10.1d* 10d 9.9g² 14d 12m⁶ 12g Sep 30] leggy, close-coupled   **107 a84 +**

Vodafone Rose Bowl (Handicap), Epsom—
the runners come stand side and Lake Poet, Wovoka, Resonate (No.8) and Tabadul are the first four home

colt: useful handicapper on turf, fairly useful on all-weather: won at Epsom in April and June (beat Wovoka by 1¼ lengths in valuable event): also ran well when second to Championship Point at Goodwood sixth start: below form after: stays 1½m: acts on polytrack (probably on fibresand), firm and soft going. *C. E. Brittain*

LAKE SABINA 2 b.f. (Apr 7) Diktat 126 – Telori 72 (Muhtarram (USA) 125) [2007 **77** 5m³ p5.1g⁶ 6m² 6.1v³ p6g³ Oct 27] neat filly: first foal: dam 7f winner: placed 4 starts, in nursery at Wolverhampton final one: will stay 7f: acts on polytrack, heavy and good to firm going. *E. S. McMahon*

LAKE TOYA (USA) 5 b.m. Darshaan 133 – Shinko Hermes (IRE) (Sadler's Wells **107** (USA) 132) [2007 109: 10.1g⁶ 12d 10.3m² Nov 10] big, strong, good-topped mare: useful performer: best effort in 2007 when head second to Gower Song in listed event at Doncaster final outing, hanging right: stays 13f: acts on polytrack, heavy and good to firm ground: shaped as if amiss penultimate start: has been bandaged: left Godolphin, and sent to USA. *Saeed bin Suroor*

LAKE WAKATIPU 5 b.m. Lake Coniston (IRE) 131 – Lady Broker 54 (Petorius 117) **–** [2007 67: 13g 13.4g 12.4d Oct 16] lengthy mare: fair performer at best: no form in 2007. *M. Mullineaux*

LAKSHMI (IRE) 3 b.f. Efisio 120 – Effie (Royal Academy (USA) 130) [2007 87p: **80** p8g⁶ 10m 8g 8m Sep 8] good-bodied filly: fairly useful performer: below best after reappearance: ran as if amiss final outing: stays easy 1m (found little at 1¼m): acts on polytrack: sold 6,000 gns. *M. R. Channon*

LA LUNETE 3 b.f. Halling (USA) 133 – Miss Pinkerton 104 (Danehill (USA) 126) **74** [2007 p8g 8d⁴ Aug 25] well-made filly: first foal: dam, 6f (at 2 yrs) and 1m winner, out of Coronation Stakes winner Rebecca Sharp: better effort in maidens when fourth to Ezdiyaad at Newmarket: should be suited by 1¼m: sold 26,000 gns. *R. Charlton*

LA MARMOTTE (IRE) 3 b.f. Mujadil (USA) 119 – Zilayah (USA) 79 (Zilzal (USA) **60** 137) [2007 65: p7g⁵ p8g³ 7.5m⁵ 7m 8m 5g⁴ 6d⁶ 7m 5g Aug 17] leggy filly: modest performer: left J. Hills 6,000 gns after second start: stays 1m: acts on all-weather, heavy and good to firm ground: takes keen hold: races up with pace. *R. E. Barr*

LA MATANZA 4 b.f. Hunting Lion (IRE) 115 – Lawless Bridget 62 (Alnasr Alwasheek 117) [2007 79: 7.1g* 7.1g 7.1s² 6m⁶ Sep 20] quite attractive filly: fairly useful **85** handicapper, lightly raced: won at Musselburgh in May: good second there third start: unlikely to stay beyond 7f (raced freely at 1m): acts on soft and good to firm ground: sold 10,000 gns, sent to USA. *T. D. Barron*

LAMBDA (USA) 2 br.f. (Mar 10) Empire Maker (USA) 129 – South of Saturn (USA) **61 p** 91 (Seattle Slew (USA)) [2007 7d Oct 9] good-topped filly: third foal: dam, French 2-y-o 6.5f winner on only start, half-sister to very smart Irish performer up to 1¼m Sportsworld and Queen Mary/Cheveley Park Stakes winner Gay Gallanta: 4/1 and green (got loose in paddock), seventh in maiden at Leicester, not knocked about: will improve. *Sir Michael Stoute*

LAMBENCY (IRE) 4 b.f. Daylami (IRE) 138 – Triomphale (USA) (Nureyev (USA) **61** 131) [2007 61: 6g⁵ 6f 7.1g⁶ 8.3d 6m² 6m⁴ 6g 6m* 7.1m⁵ 6f³ 5d Sep 20] quite good-topped filly: modest handicapper: won at Newcastle (apprentices) in August: stays 7f: acts on polytrack, firm and good to soft going. *J. S. Goldie*

LAMBRINI LACE (IRE) 2 br.f. (Apr 20) Namid 128 – Feather 'n Lace (IRE) 73 **63** (Green Desert (USA) 127) [2007 5.1d⁴ 5d² 5m 6s 6.1d p5.1g³ p5.1g³ p5.1d³ Dec 17] 20,000Y: good-bodied filly: third foal: closely related to Irish 1½m winner Proper Article (by Definite Article): dam 7f winner: modest maiden: placed at Warwick and Wolverhampton (3, including nursery): best form at 5f: acts on polytrack and good to soft going. *Mrs L. Williamson*

LAMISTRELLE (IRE) 2 b.f. (Feb 5) Barathea (IRE) 127 – Samriah (IRE) (Wassl **–** 125) [2007 5d⁶ 7m 6m Sep 10] 57,000Y: smallish filly: sister to useful 2003 2-y-o 6f winner Voile and half-sister to several winners, including fairly useful 1997 2-y-o 5f winner Baby Grand (by Mukaddamah): dam unraced: well held in maidens: tried visored. *Mrs A. Duffield*

LANCASTER LAD (IRE) 2 b.c. (Feb 23) Piccolo 121 – Ruby Julie (Clantime 101) **–** [2007 7m 7.1m 8.1m f8d⁶ Dec 12] good-bodied colt: no form. *A. B. Haynes*

LANCASTER'S QUEST 3 ch.g. Auction House (USA) 120 – Gabibti (IRE) 82 (Dara **57** Monarch 128) [2007 58: p8g p8g⁶ Apr 4] workmanlike gelding: modest maiden: stays 1m: acts on polytrack: gelded after final start. *R. Ingram*

LAND AHOY 3 b.c. Observatory (USA) 131 – Night Haven 99 (Night Shift (USA)) **64** [2007 77: p5g 6m⁵ 5g p6g 5f 6.1d 5.1f p6g p6g⁵ Oct 17] sturdy colt: just modest performer in 2007: raced only at 5f/6f: acts on good to firm going: sold 600 gns. *D. W. P. Arbuthnot*

LANDED GENT (IRE) 2 b.c. (May 2) Kyllachy 129 – Land Ahead (USA) 85 (Distant **47 ?** View (USA) 126) [2007 6g 8g f7d⁴ Dec 20] plain colt: seemingly easily best effort in maidens when fourth at Southwell: bred to prove best up to 7f. *Miss V. Haigh*

LANDIKHAYA (IRE) 2 ch.g. (Feb 2) Kris Kin (USA) 126 – Montana Lady (IRE) 83 **73** (Be My Guest (USA) 126) [2007 6m⁵ 7.1m p7g 7.1g³ 8.3d⁴ 7g p8g Nov 21] stocky gelding: fair maiden: twice in frame in nurseries: left R. Hannon 11,000 gns before final start: gelded after: stays 1m: acts on good to firm and good to soft going. *D. K. Ivory*

LAND 'N STARS 7 b.g. Mtoto 134 – Uncharted Waters 68 (Celestial Storm (USA) **104** 132) [2007 113: 12g 12g 16.4d 16g 13.3d³ 14g³ 14.1g⁴ 18m 16g⁶ 18d Oct 20] leggy, close-coupled gelding: just useful performer nowadays: left Jamie Poulton after second start: several at least respectable efforts in face of stiff tasks after, including in Geoffrey Freer Stakes at Newbury (third to Papal Bull) and Doncaster Cup at Doncaster (seventh to Septimus): tailed off in Cesarewitch at Newmarket final outing: effective at 1½m to 2½m: acts on polytrack, firm and soft going: often races prominently. *R. A. Fahey*

LAND OF LIGHT 4 ch.g. Fantastic Light (USA) 134 – Russian Snows (IRE) 113 **76** (Sadler's Wells (USA) 132) [2007 69: p13g² p16g p12g⁵ Sep 18] good-topped gelding: has a quick action: fair maiden, lightly raced: should stay 2m: acts on polytrack and good to firm ground: sold £1,300 in November. *G. L. Moore*

LAND'S END (IRE) 3 b.g. Danehill Dancer (IRE) 117 – Statistic (USA) (Mr Pros- **58** pector (USA)) [2007 –p: 6m⁵ 6s⁴ 6g⁵ 6g⁵ Oct 19] rangy, good-topped gelding: modest maiden: raced only at 6f: acts on soft and good to firm ground: has raced freely: sold 7,500 gns. *J. Noseda*

LANDUCCI 6 b.g. Averti (IRE) 117 – Divina Luna 96 (Dowsing (USA) 124) [2007 90: **87** 7g p7g 7d³ 8m p7g⁴ p7g² p8g² p7g p8g⁵ Nov 3] big, close-coupled gelding: fairly useful handicapper: won at Kempton in August: good efforts when runner-up next 2 starts: effective at 7f/1m: acts on polytrack, firm and soft going: sometimes wears tongue tie/ cheekpieces: sometimes edges left. *J. W. Hills*

LANFREDO 4 b.g. Fraam 114 – Lana Turrel (USA) (Trempolino (USA) 135) [2007 57: **–** f12g Jan 16] modest maiden at 3 yrs: below form only outing in 2007: tried blinkered, often wears cheekpieces. *Miss M. E. Rowland*

LANGFORD 7 ch.g. Compton Place 125 – Sharpening 72 (Sharpo 132) [2007 105: **95 d** p10g⁴ p10g 10.1g 9m⁶ 8.5m² 8.1g 9m 8.3m p8g² 9m⁴ p10m* Oct 13] well-made gelding: useful performer: creditable efforts in frame in handicaps first/fifth starts in 2007: below form after, not having to be anywhere near best when winning claimer at Kempton in October: best at 1m/1¼m: acts on polytrack and firm going: often finds little: sold 7,000 gns, joined H. Hesse, Germany. *M. H. Tompkins*

LANGHAM HOUSE 2 ch.g. (Feb 28) Best of The Bests (IRE) 122 – Dafne 68§ **70** (Nashwan (USA) 135) [2007 6d 7f⁴ 8.2d⁴ 7d Oct 30] good-topped gelding: second foal: dam 1½m winner: fair maiden: fourth at Folkestone and Nottingham (hurt Patkai): will stay 1¼m: acts on firm and good to soft going: gelded after final start. *J. R. Jenkins*

LANG SHINING (IRE) 3 ch.c. Dr Fong (USA) 128 – Dragnet (IRE) 72 (Rainbow **103 p** Quest (USA) 134) [2007 84p: 8g* 8.1m² 10d⁶ Sep 28] leggy, close-coupled colt: useful form, lightly raced: won maiden at Newmarket in July: good neck second to Cactus Rose in handicap at Sandown next time: below best in minor event at Ascot final outing: should stay 1¼m: acts on good to firm ground, possibly not on good to soft: worth another chance to prove himself capable of better. *Sir Michael Stoute*

LAN KWAI FONG 3 ch.f. Dr Fong (USA) 128 – Lady Pahia (IRE) 81 (Pivotal 124) **46** [2007 7v² 7s⁴ 9.9g⁵ 7g Sep 22] good-topped filly: first foal: dam 7f winner: maiden: poor form only on debut: should stay 1m: tried blinkered. *T. D. Easterby*

LANSDOWN 3 b.f. Lomitas 129 – Reamzafonic 46 (Grand Lodge (USA) 125) [2007 **–** 51: 10f 10s 7g 6d Oct 16] lengthy, unfurnished filly: maiden: no form in 2007: tried in cheekpieces. *R. Johnson*

LANTERNS OF GOLD 2 b.f. (Apr 2) Fantastic Light (USA) 134 – Reason To Dance **74** 96 (Damister (USA) 123) [2007 7.5m⁶ 8m⁴ 9f* 10m Oct 3] 47,000Y: leggy filly: half-sister to several winners, including 5-y-o Diktatorial and fairly useful 9f winner Stands To Reason (by Hernando): dam, 5f (at 2 yrs) and 6.5f (in US) winner, stayed 1¼m: fair performer: fourth to Dr Faustus at Thirsk prior to winning weaker maiden at Redcar in September: favourite, seemed amiss in nursery: should stay 1¼m: acts on firm going. *Mrs A. Duffield*

LA NUAGE 3 gr.f. Tobougg (IRE) 125 – Cole Slaw (Absalom 128) [2007 –: 12m Aug 6] no form in maidens 10 months apart. *T. J. Etherington* —

LAPHONIC (USA) 4 b.g. Labeeb 124 – Speechless (USA) (Hawkin's Special (USA)) 55 [2007 58: p6g 7.1m 6d⁶ 6.9f⁶ p7g² p7g p6m⁵ p8g Oct 17] big, lengthy gelding: modest performer: stays 7f: acts on polytrack, soft and good to firm ground: tried tongue tied: blinkered last 2 outings: reared leaving stall sixth outing: sold 600 gns. *T. J. Etherington*

LAPINA (IRE) 3 ch.f. Fath (USA) 116 – Alpina (USA) 69 (El Prado (IRE) 119) [2007 73 50: 8.2g 10.2f* 10f³ 10g p12g³ 12g² 11.5m³ 14.1d² 12f⁶ p16g⁴ 14.1d³ Oct 3] lengthy filly: fair handicapper: won 4-runner event at Bath in May: improved after, in frame 7 times: stays 2m: acts on polytrack, firm and good to soft ground: blinkered nowadays: held up: has shown signs of temperament. *Pat Eddery*

LAP OF HONOUR (IRE) 3 b.g. Danehill Dancer (IRE) 117 – Kingsridge (IRE) 89 91 (King's Theatre (IRE) 128) [2007 71: 8.2m 8.1m² 8m³ 10.3f 9.7s² 10.1d⁵ 8.1m² 8.5s* 8.2g² 8g* 7d⁸ 8.1m⁴ Sep 15] strong, well-made gelding: has a powerful, rather round action: fairly useful handicapper: won 3 times at Beverley in July and twice at Newmarket in August: effective at 7f, barely stays 1¼m: acts on soft and good to firm going: races up with pace: sold 75,000 gns, joined Jennie Candlish. *N. A. Callaghan*

LAP OF THE GODS 3 b.g. Fleetwood (IRE) 107 – Casarabonela (Magic Ring (IRE) 43 115) [2007 –: 11.5d³ 10.1d p11g⁴ Nov 14] poor maiden: stays 11.5f: raced only on polytrack and good to soft ground: wears cheekpieces: refused to enter stall prior to intended reappearance. *Miss Z. C. Davison*

LA QUINTA (IRE) 3 ch.f. Indian Ridge 123 – Peneia (USA) (Nureyev (USA) 131) 67 [2007 67: p5g* Jan 6] fair performer: won handicap at Lingfield sole start in 2007: effective at 5f, should stay 7f: acts on polytrack and firm ground. *B. J. Meehan*

LARAD (IRE) 6 br.g. Desert Sun 120 – Glenstal Priory 53 (Glenstal (USA) 118) [2007 47 58: 10f⁴ p13.9g⁶ p11g Nov 21] good-bodied gelding: only poor performer in 2007: effective at 9.5f, barely at 2m: acts on all-weather, soft and good to firm ground: tried in cheekpieces, usually blinkered: often held up. *J. S. Moore*

LARKFIELD 2 b.f. (Feb 16) Catcher In The Rye (IRE) 115 – Dominelle 74 (Domynsky — 110) [2007 6m 6f 8g Oct 3] stocky filly: third foal: half-sister to 2004 2-y-o 7f seller Caloosa (by Fraam), later winner up to 9f in Spain: dam sprinter: well held in maidens: tried blinkered. *T. D. Easterby*

LARKY'S LOB 8 b.g. Lugana Beach 116 – Eucharis 41 (Tickled Pink 114) [2007 –, 57 + a73: f6g f7g 5g⁴ 5.9g⁴ 5m 6g p6g p5.1g² Oct 15] leggy, plain gelding: fair handicapper on a73 all-weather, modest on turf: effective at 5f to 7f: acts on all-weather, good to firm and good to soft ground: tried in headgear. *J. O'Reilly*

LA ROCA (IRE) 3 b.f. Rock of Gibraltar (IRE) 133 – Zanella (IRE) 87 (Nordico 83 (USA)) [2007 87: 8.2m³ 8g 8g³ 7.1d⁵ 10s⁶ Jun 26] smallish, sturdy filly: fairly useful handicapper: should be well suited by 1¼m (raced too freely when tried): acts on good to firm ground, probably on good to soft: tried tongue tied. *R. M. Beckett*

LA ROSA NOSTRA 2 ch.f. (Apr 28) Dr Fong (USA) 128 – Rose Quantas (IRE) 76 + (Danehill (USA) 126) [2007 p7g⁶ p7g³ 8.2m* Oct 3] 23,000F, €85,000Y: workmanlike filly: second foal: half-sister to Swedish 1½m winner Evita Quantas (by Zamindar): dam, Swedish 2-y-o 1m winner, sister to useful performer up to 1½m Summerland: fair form: progressive in maidens, won at Nottingham: will stay 1¼m. *W. R. Swinburn*

L'ART DU SILENCE (IRE) 2 b.c. (Apr 1) Xaar 132 – Without Words 71 (Lion 64 Cavern (USA) 117) [2007 5.1d⁴ p6g³ 6s p7g Jul 18] useful-looking colt: modest maiden: in frame first 2 starts, tailed off last 2: should stay 1m: suspect temperament. *J. R. Boyle*

LAS BEATAS 4 b.f. Green Desert (USA) 127 – Dora Carrington (IRE) 106 (Sri Pekan 54 + (USA) 117) [2007 74: 8.3d⁶ Oct 1] small, sturdy filly: easily better effort in maidens only start at 3 yrs: not knocked about only outing in 2007. *W. R. Swinburn*

LASCELLES 3 b.c. Halling (USA) 133 – Poppy's Song 76 (Owington 123) [2007 76p: — p8g Sep 18] fair maiden at 2 yrs: well held but not at all knocked about only outing in 2007. *J. A. Osborne*

LA SPEZIA (IRE) 3 b.f. Danehill Dancer (IRE) 117 – Genoa 96 (Zafonic (USA) 130) 94 [2007 75: p8.6g* 10m³ 10d⁵ 12m⁵ 9.9g Aug 26] leggy, quite good-topped filly: fairly useful performer: won maiden at Wolverhampton in March: best efforts at Newmarket (third to Dalvina in listed event) and Milan (4 lengths fifth to Shot Bless in Premio Mario Incisa) next 2 starts: stays 1¼m: acts on polytrack, good to firm and good to soft ground. *M. L. W. Bell*

LAST ANGEL (IRE) 2 b.f. (Feb 9) King Charlemagne (USA) 120 – Magdalene (FR)   **– p** (College Chapel 122) [2007 p5.1g 6m p6g Oct 2] 14,000Y: small, sturdy filly: fourth foal: half-sister to fairly useful 1½m winner Takhmin (by Almutawakel) and 2005 2-y-o 6f winner Tora Petcha (by Bahhare): dam French maiden: poor form in maidens, off 4 months before final start (considerately handled): will be suited by 7f/1m: likely to do better. *M. Wigham*

LAST DANCE 3 b.f. Sadler's Wells (USA) 132 – Pink Cristal 113 (Dilum (USA) 115)   **–** [2007 12g⁵ May 18] good-topped filly: third foal: closely related to smart 7f (at 2 yrs) to 1½m (US Grade 3 event) winner Always First (by Barathea) and half-sister to fairly useful 1m winner Motaraqeb (by Grand Lodge): dam 7f/1m winner: 10/1, well-held fifth of 9 in maiden at Newmarket, not knocked about. *J. H. M. Gosden*

LAST FLIGHT (IRE) 3 b.f. In The Wings 128 – Fantastic Fantasy (IRE) 85 (Lahib   **81** (USA) 129) [2007 58p: 12.1m 12g⁶ 14.1s² 16.2s* 18s² 17.1m³ 16d⁶ 17.2g² Oct 24] tall filly: fairly useful handicapper: won at Warwick in July: good efforts after: stays 2¼m: acts on soft and good to firm going: visored last 2 starts: consistent. *J. L. Dunlop*

LAST OF THE LINE 2 b.c. (May 13) Efisio 120 – Dance By Night 84 (Northfields   **77** (USA)) [2007 6m 7s p7g p7.1g² p8g* p7g⁶ Nov 30] stocky colt: half-brother to numerous winners, notably very smart French 7f/1m (Poule d'Essai des Pouliches) winner Danseuse du Soir (by Thatching): dam 2-y-o 7f winner: fair form: won maiden at Kempton in November: stays 1m: acts on polytrack. *H. J. L. Dunlop*

LAST PIONEER (IRE) 5 b.g. New Frontier (IRE) 110 – Toordillon (IRE) 69 (Con-   **–** tract Law (USA) 108) [2007 65: 12.3f Jun 12] strong gelding: fair maiden handicapper at 4 yrs: below form sole start on Flat in 2007. *R. Ford*

LAST SOVEREIGN 3 b.c. Pivotal 124 – Zayala (Royal Applause 124) [2007 68p: **79** f6g³ 7m* p8g² p8g⁵ 8m⁶ Aug 9] sturdy colt: has scope: fair handicapper: much improved to win at Catterick (by 5 lengths) in April: at least respectable efforts after: stays 1m: acts on polytrack and good to firm going. *R. Charlton*

LAST THREE MINUTES 2 b.c. (Mar 29) Val Royal (FR) 127 – Circe's Isle   **88 p** (Be My Guest (USA) 126) [2007 8.3g⁴ Oct 16] €16,000F, 47,000Y: useful-looking colt: half-brother to several winners, including smart 7f (at 2 yrs) and 1¼m winner Don Micheletto (by Machiavellian) and useful 1m/1¼m winner Flint Knapper (by Kris): dam unraced close relative of very smart 1¼m performer Sasuru: 16/1, promising fourth to Mountain Pride in maiden at Leicester, getting upsides smoothly before running green: sure to win races. *E. A. L. Dunlop*

LATANAZUL 3 b.f. Sakhee (USA) 136 – Karamah 78 (Unfuwain (USA) 131) [2007   **87** 87: 9.8g² 12g* 12d⁶ 14.8m³ 14.6m⁶ Aug 17] unfurnished filly: fairly useful performer: won maiden at Newmarket in May: ran creditably fourth outing: stays 14.8f: acts on good to firm and good to soft ground: often races freely: sold 4,000 gns. *J. L. Dunlop*

LATERLY (IRE) 2 b.g. (Mar 28) Tiger Hill (IRE) 127 – La Candela (GER) (Alzao   **81** (USA) 117) [2007 7m 7g 8g³ 8g³ 8.2g* Nov 7] €63,000Y: well-made gelding: sixth foal: brother to German 8.7f to 1¼m winner Los Cantos and half-brother to useful German 1m winner La Hermana (by Hernando): dam, German 5f (at 2 yrs) and 7f winner, out of half-sister to high-class German 1½m performer Lomitas: fairly useful form: reared over as stall opened second start: progressed well after and won maiden at Nottingham (made all, found plenty): will stay 1¼m. *T. P. Tate*

LATIF (USA) 6 b.g. Red Ransom (USA) – Awaamir 102 (Green Desert (USA) 127)   **62** [2007 81: 10.5m 9.8m⁶ 10.3f⁶ p8.6g Jul 27] strong, good-topped gelding: fairly useful performer at 5 yrs, just modest handicapper in 2007: effective at 1m to easy 1½m: acts on all-weather, firm and good to soft going (well beaten both starts on soft): tried blinkered/tongue tied: has been slowly away. *Ms Deborah J. Evans*

LATIMER HOUSE (IRE) 2 ch.f. (Mar 3) Observatory (USA) 131 – Tramonto 91   **–** (Sri Pekan (USA) 117) [2007 7f p7.1g p7g Sep 11] 8,000Y: leggy filly: second foal: dam 2-y-o 7f/7.6f winner: well held in maidens. *Dr J. D. Scargill*

LATIN CLASS (USA) 2 b.f. (Feb 2) Carson City (USA) – Latin Lynx (USA) 96   **64** (Forest Wildcat (USA) 120) [2007 5d² 5.1g May 29] first foal: dam 2-y-o 5f winner: better effort in maidens in May when second (of 4, modest form) at Hamilton: should prove best at 5f/6f: sold 1,000 gns in December. *M. Johnston*

LATIN DANCER 2 b.c. (Apr 14) Averti (IRE) 117 – Pieta (IRE) 52 (Perugino (USA) – 84) [2007 5m 6m 6m 6m 6m Sep 18] leggy colt: well held in maidens: tried in cheekpieces. *B. S. Rothwell*

LATIN LAD 2 b.c. (Mar 31) Hernando (FR) 127 – Decision Maid (USA) 105 (Diesis **103** 133) [2007 7m* 7g² 8m² Oct 22] 26,000F, 42,000Y: close-coupled colt: third foal: closely related to 3-y-o Shake On It: dam, 2-y-o 7f winner, closely related to useful 7f/1m winner Miss Ivanhoe: useful form: won maiden at Goodwood in August: improved in listed races, second to Sharp Nephew at Newbury and to Siberian Tiger at Pontefract: will stay 1¼m: raced only on good going or firmer. *R. Hannon*

LATIN SCHOLAR (IRE) 2 ch.g. (Apr 10) Titus Livius (FR) 115 – Crimada (IRE) **70** (Mukaddamah (USA) 125) [2007 6g 5.7g² 6g⁶ 7m p7g Aug 30] big, raw-boned gelding: fair maiden: second at Bath: well held in nurseries (gelded after): should prove best at 5f/ 6f. *A. King*

LA TROUPE (IRE) 2 b.f. (Mar 15) King's Best (USA) 132 – Passe Passe (USA) 78 **73 p** (Lear Fan (USA) 130) [2007 7g⁴ Nov 3] rangy filly: fifth foal: half-sister to 3 winners, including fairly useful 1¼m/1½m winner Magic Instinct (later winner in Australia, by Entrepreneur) and 3-y-o Cabinet: dam, maiden (stayed 1½m), sister to smart 1¼m to 1¾m winner Windermere: 7/1 and not wound up, fourth to Infallible in maiden at Newmarket, racing prominently: will be suited by 1m/1¼m+: sure to improve. *J. H. M. Gosden*

LAUDER 3 ch.f. First Trump 118 – Madam Zando 51 (Forzando 122) [2007 47: 7m 6d⁵ **39** 7g p6g Oct 5] poor maiden: stays 1m: best effort on fibresand. *J. Balding*

LAUGHING GAME 3 b.f. Classic Cliche (IRE) 128 – Ground Game 95 (Gildoran **58** 123) [2007 11.8m p11g p12g² p12.2g 14.1s 12s p12g⁶ Jul 17] fourth foal: half-sister to 6-y-o Magic Sting: dam 1m (at 2 yrs)/1¼m winner: modest maiden: stays 1½m: acts on polytrack: none too reliable. *M. L. W. Bell*

LAUGH 'N CRY 6 b.m. In The Wings 128 – The Kings Daughter 79 (Indian King **55** (USA) 128) [2007 63: p8g p8g⁴ p10g p8g⁴ p10g⁵ p8g⁴ p8.6g⁵ p12.2g⁵ p12g³ p10m⁵ p11g⁴ p11g Nov 7] good-topped mare: modest maiden nowadays: left C. Cyzer 4,000 gns after ninth start: stays easy 1½m: acts on polytrack and good to firm going: tried blinkered: in cheekpieces last 3 starts: reared leaving stall eighth outing: has hung left. *Eoin Doyle, Ireland*

LAUGHTER (IRE) 2 b.f. (Mar 9) Sadler's Wells (USA) 132 – Smashing Review **87 P** (USA) (Pleasant Tap (USA)) [2007 7d* Oct 9] 185,000Y: good-topped filly: fourth foal: half-sister to US winner around 1m by Coronado's Quest: dam 7f and 8.5f (including minor stakes) winner in US: 4/1, made big impression when winning maiden at Leicester (beat Full Marks by ½ length), going smoothly before asserting despite clear greenness: will stay 1¼m, probably 1½m: very much one to follow. *Sir Michael Stoute*

LAUNCH IT LILY 3 b.f. Kyllachy 129 – Bermuda Lily 78 (Dunbeath (USA) 127) **47** [2007 61: p6g p5g⁶ Feb 3] close-coupled filly: maiden: just poor form in 2007: best effort at 6f on good to soft ground. *W. G. M. Turner*

LAURA'S BEST (IRE) 3 b.f. Green Desert (USA) 127 – Lassie's Gold (Seek- **71** ing The Gold (USA)) [2007 75p: 7g 6f³ 6m² 7m² p8g³ 7d³ p8.6g Oct 20] close-coupled filly: fair maiden: placed 5 times in 2007: not sure to stay 1m: acts on polytrack and firm ground: tried blinkered. *W. J. Haggas*

LAUREL DAWN 9 gr.g. Paris House 123 – Madrina 70 (Waajib 121) [2007 –, a54: f5g – f5g p5.1g p5.1g f5g⁶ p5.1g Feb 9] leggy, plain gelding: poor performer at best nowadays: **a38** effective at 5f/6f: acts on all-weather, firm and good to soft going: has worn cheekpieces/ blinkers. *Miss A. Stokell*

LAURELDEAN BREEZE (USA) 2 ch.f. (Mar 1) Good And Tough (USA) 117 – **45** Cozwhy (USA) (Cozzene (USA)) [2007 5m⁵ p6g 6g p8.6g f7d Dec 18] £26,000 2-y-o: half-sister to 2 US winners around 1m, including minor stakes winner Rocker (by Chimes Band): dam, US 1m winner, half-sister to smart French 1¼m performer Seaton Delaval: poor maiden: should stay 1m: tried blinkered. *R. A. Fahey*

LAURELDEAN DREAM (USA) 2 b.f. (Feb 9) Stravinsky (USA) 133 – Classy Women (USA) (Relaunch (USA)) [2007 6d Jun 29] $300,000Y: rather unfurnished filly: half-sister to several winners, notably high-class 6f (at 2 yrs, including Middle Park Stakes) and 1m (Queen Anne Stakes) winner Ad Valorem (by Danzig): dam US Grade 3 8.5f winner: 13/2, pulled up soon after start in maiden at Newmarket (said to have hit stall, giving herself a dead leg). *P. W. Chapple-Hyam*

LAURELDEAN GALE (USA) 2 b. or br.f. (Jan 31) Grand Slam (USA) 120 – **114**
Ravnina (USA) (Nureyev (USA) 131) [2007 6m* 7m² 8g Oct 7] $325,000Y: rather leggy,
quite attractive filly: sixth foal: half-sister to 3 winners, notably useful 7f (at 2 yrs) to
10.4f (Muisidora Stakes) winner Secret History (by Bahri): dam unraced close relative of
smart Irish sprinter Rhine Valley: smart performer: won maiden at Newmarket in July:
plenty of improvement when ½-length second to Proviso in Prix du Calvados at Deauville, clear of remainder: left P. Chapple-Hyam, disappointing favourite (eighth to
Zarkava) in Prix Marcel Boussac at Longchamp final start, reportedly upset by delay
beforehand: should stay 1m. *Saeed bin Suroor*

LAURENTIAN LAD 3 ch.c. Medicean 128 – Cup of Kindness (USA) (Secretariat **54**
(USA)) [2007 10g 10.1d⁵ Jul 5] good-bodied colt: better effort in maidens when fifth to
Miss Marvellous at Yarmouth, not knocked about. *Rae Guest*

LAURENTINA 3 b.f. Cadeaux Genereux 131 – Trois Heures Apres (Soviet Star (USA) **86**
128) [2007 87: p8g⁴ 8.1g 8m³ 8m Jun 20] lengthy filly: fairly useful performer: in frame
in listed races at Kempton and Goodwood: stays 1m: acts on polytrack, good to firm and
good to soft ground. *B. J. Meehan*

LAURO 7 b.m. Mukaddamah (USA) 125 – Lapu-Lapu 62 (Prince Sabo 123) [2007 72, **69**
a66: 8s⁴ 8d* 8.3m 10s⁵ 9.1v Nov 3] strong mare: fair handicapper: won at Redcar in July:
stays 1¼m: acts on all-weather, firm and soft going: tried in cheekpieces (below form):
held up. *Miss J. A. Camacho*

LAUROLLIE 5 b.m. Makbul 104 – Madonna Da Rossi 53 (Mtoto 134) [2007 50: f12g⁶ **49**
p12.2g⁶ p9.5g⁶ f11g⁵ Feb 6] poor performer: stays 1½m: acts on all-weather and firm
going. *B. P. J. Baugh*

LAVANDE 2 b.f. (Mar 4) Tipsy Creek (USA) 115 – Skara Brae 49 (Inchinor 119) [2007 **63**
5m⁴ p6g 5m² p5.1m² p5.1g Oct 22] second foal: dam maiden out of smart performer up
to 1m Tahilla: modest maiden: second at Musselburgh and Wolverhampton: should stay
6f/7f: acts on polytrack and good to firm going. *M. J. Wallace*

LA VARROSA 2 b.f. (Jan 16) Josr Algarhoud (IRE) 118 – Ebony Anne (IRE) (Dane- **46**
time (IRE) 121) [2007 5v⁵ p6g 5.7s p7.1g p7g p7g p7g⁴ p6m⁵ f5g⁶ Dec 27] sturdy
filly: first foal: dam unraced: poor maiden on balance: stays 7f: form only on polytrack.
Mrs P. N. Dutfield

LA VECCHIA SCUOLA (IRE) 3 b.f. Mull of Kintyre (USA) 114 – Force Divine **72**
(FR) (L'Emigrant (USA) 129) [2007 66: p6g 6d 7g⁴ 5g* 5v³ 6m² 5d 5d 5m⁶ 6f³ 8g*
12.4m² 10.3m⁵ 10.3g Sep 29] fair performer: won seller at Musselburgh (sold from
D. Nicholls £6,200) in June and handicap at Newcastle in August: stays easy 1½m: acts
on any ground: usually visored/blinkered (not final outing): races prominently: modest
form over hurdles, successful in December. *R. Johnson*

LAVEMILL (IRE) 2 ch.f. (Apr 28) City On A Hill (USA) 114 – Mackem Beat (Aragon **–**
118) [2007 6m⁵ 6m 6m⁴ p7.1g 7.1d 7g⁶ p8.6g Oct 30] €4,800Y: neat filly: fourth foal:
half-sister to fairly useful Irish 5f (at 2 yrs) to 1½m winner Itsonlywoody (by Woodborough) and 9f/10.5f winner in Italy by Daggers Drawn: dam, no form, half-sister to
useful 2-y-o 5f/6f winner Sumoquinn: little form. *R. F. Fisher*

LAVENDER AND LACE 2 b.f. (Feb 2) Barathea (IRE) 127 – Summertime Legacy **55**
109 (Darshaan 133) [2007 7m p7g Sep 11] tall filly: second foal: dam, French 2-y-o 1m
winner (stayed 1¼m), out of close relative to Derby winner Golden Fleece: modest form
in maidens: will be suited by 1m/1¼m: sold 2,200 gns. *Sir Michael Stoute*

LAVENDER MOON (IRE) 2 b.f. (Apr 9) Anabaa (USA) 130 – Kirana (Niniski **49 §**
(USA) 125) [2007 6m 6d² 6v² Jul 21] 20,000Y: robust filly: half-sister to 2005 2-y-o
6f winner Original Source (by Danehill Dancer) and 9.4f winner Call Me Sunshine (by
Robellino): dam, German 11f/1½m winner, out of half-sister to Danzig: poor maiden:
second in sellers at Thirsk and Ripon (wore cheekpieces, claimed by K. J. Burke £6,000):
will stay 7f: looked reluctant all 3 outings. *K. A. Ryan*

LAVENHAM (IRE) 4 b.f. Kalanisi (IRE) 132 – Antigonel (IRE) 59 (Fairy King **88**
(USA)) [2007 79: p7g⁵ 9g 7m* 8d² 8s³ 7.1s⁴ 7s³ 7m 7m² Sep 4] rather leggy filly: fairly
useful handicapper: improved when winning at Newbury in June: creditable efforts when
placed after: effective at 7f/1m: acts on polytrack, soft and good to firm going: usually
held up: tended to hang right penultimate start: sold 16,000 gns, sent to USA. *R. Hannon*

LAVEROCK (IRE) 5 b.h. Octagonal (NZ) 126 – Sky Song (IRE) (Sadler's Wells **120**
(USA) 132) [2007 123: 12g² 12g⁵ 12g 12m² 12d⁴ 12g⁵ 12m³ 10d Nov 4]
sturdy, attractive horse: very smart performer: runner-up in handicap at Nad Al Sheba
(short head behind Quijano, leaving I. Mohammed in UAE after next outing) and Prin-

Godolphin's "Laverock"

cess of Wales's Stakes at Newmarket (beaten 2½ lengths by Papal Bull): mostly just respectable efforts after: stays 1½m: acts on soft and good to firm going: has worn tongue tie: sometimes finds little: held up: has left Godolphin. *Saeed bin Suroor*

LA VOILE ROUGE 2 ch.g. (Mar 22) Daggers Drawn (USA) 114 – At Amal (IRE) (Astronef 116) [2007 7.1g⁵ p7g* 7m Jul 13] 15,000F, 21,000Y: tall, deep-bodied gelding: seventh foal: half-brother to 7-y-o Bond Becks and winner abroad up to 10.5f by Rainbows For Life: dam unraced: fairly useful form: won maiden at Kempton in June: stiff task in Superlative Stakes at Newmarket, and for long way travelled better than final placing (eighth behind Hatta Fort): will prove at least as effective at 6f as 7f. *B. J. Meehan*   **87 +**

LAWAAHEB (IRE) 6 b.g. Alhaarth (IRE) 126 – Ajayib (USA) 84 (Riverman (USA) 131) [2007 58: 12.1s 10g Jul 20] rangy gelding: modest performer at 5 yrs: just poor on Flat in 2007: stays 1½m: acts on polytrack and good to firm ground: usually wears headgear. *M. J. Gingell*   **45**

LAWDY MISS CLAWDY 3 ch.f. Bold Edge 123 – Long Tall Sally (IRE) 71 (Danehill Dancer (IRE) 117) [2007 5s p6g⁴ 5m 6f⁴ 5f p6g² p6m p6g⁴ p6g³ Dec 29] first foal: dam 6f winner: modest maiden: raced only at 5f/6f: acts on polytrack and firm ground. *D. W. P. Arbuthnot*   **50**

LAW MAKER 7 b.g. Case Law 113 – Bo' Babbity 75 (Strong Gale 116) [2007 71, a86: p5.1g p6g 5m³ 5.5d p6g p6g 5g p6g 5g* p6g Sep 8] good-topped gelding: fair handicapper on all-weather nowadays, modest on turf: effective at 5f/easy 6f: acts on polytrack (seemingly not on fibresand), firm and good to soft going: blinkered/visored often: races up with pace: unseated rider from stall fourth outing: inconsistent. *A. Bailey*   **61 a76**

LAWMAN (FR) 3 b.c. Invincible Spirit (IRE) 121 – Laramie (USA) 63 (Gulch (USA)) [2007 8v² 8g⁴ 9g* 10.5g* 8s* 8g⁶ Aug 12]   **121**
A maximum field of twenty went to post for the Prix du Jockey Club Mitsubishi Motors, making it the largest number of runners for the 'French Derby' since 1978. The large field resulted from the various trials failing to reveal any colt

with outstanding claims beforehand, but, seen from an end-of-season perspective, the field contained plenty of notable performers, even if the form of the actual race was nothing out of the ordinary. Runner-up Literato achieved most subsequently, winning his three remaining starts at a mile and a quarter, notably the Champion Stakes at Newmarket. The pair who finished third and fourth, and had appealed at the time as the two most likely to progress further, were Shamdinan and Zambezi Sun, the former exported to the States where he won the Grade 1 Secretariat Stakes and finished second in the Breeders' Cup Turf, and the latter going on to success in the Grand Prix de Paris. Further down the Jockey Club field were Sagara in seventh, whose season ended with third place in the Prix de l'Arc de Triomphe, and eighth-placed Loup Breton who won the Prix Daphnis on his next start. Even among the tail-enders at Chantilly, Halicarnassus won twice in pattern company later in the year, while Alexander of Hales went on to finish second in the Irish Derby.

Two of the main trials for the Prix du Jockey Club were won by the Aidan O'Brien-trained pair Soldier of Fortune and Anton Chekhov who formed part of Ballydoyle's eight-strong team in the Derby at Epsom twenty-four hours earlier. In their absence, Prix de Guiche winner Lawman started the Prix du Jockey Club, ahead of the Dante Stakes runner-up Raincoat, at 6/1 the shortest-priced of four runners from Britain, and the Prix La Force winner Literato at 13/2. Lawman had won a newcomers race at Saint-Cloud on his only outing at two when the booking of Kieren Fallon was no doubt an indication that he was held in some regard. Lawman was initially prepared for the Poule d'Essai des Poulains, running twice over the course and distance at Longchamp, promoted a place to second behind Chichi Creasy in a minor event on his reappearance and then fourth to the same horse in the main trial for the Poule d'Essai des Poulains, the Prix de Fontainebleau. Defeat caused connections to turn their attentions instead to the Prix du Jockey Club, allowing Lawman a little more time to gain further experience. He was stepped up to nine furlongs in the Prix de Guiche at Chantilly in May and made all for an easy two-and-a-half-length win over six rivals, a performance which represented some of the best form on offer for the Prix du Jockey Club.

Lawman had shaped as though the longer distance would not prove a problem, but it looked unlikely that, in a much larger field and a more competitive race, Lawman would be able to dictate matters quite so easily in the Jockey Club. With Olivier Peslier, who had ridden Lawman on three previous starts, contracted to ride the Wertheimer representative No Dream, Frankie Dettori took the ride. He had a few anxious moments before the race got under way, firstly when Lawman reared and unseated him in the pre-race parade and had to be walked to the start, and then when a false start was declared after Zambezi Sun's stall had failed to open properly. When the field got away at the second attempt, Dettori soon had Lawman at the head of affairs. Dettori gave Lawman a similar ride to Shamardal two years earlier. Interestingly, it was Peslier who kept closest tabs on the leader, probably more aware than anyone of the danger of allowing Lawman his own way in front, but No Dream began to struggle to keep up once the pressure was on after the home

Prix du Jockey Club Mitsubishi Motors, Chantilly—Frankie Dettori's second Derby win of the weekend; he dictates on Lawman, who has enough in reserve to hold off Literato, Shamdinan and Zambezi Sun

*Prix Jean Prat, Chantilly—Lawman completes a hat-trick of all-the-way wins on this course,
the drop back in trip no problem on ground which has become testing;
Stoneside (cheekpieces) and Golden Titus are next*

turn. Dettori was still going well and asked Lawman to quicken around a furlong
and a half out. Although his pursuers were closing at the line, Lawman had a length
and half to spare at the finish over Literato, with short necks back to Shamdinan and
Zambezi Sun who both stayed on well from the rear. Raincoat fared best of the
British-trained runners but managed only eleventh without ever threatening.
Dettori became the latest jockey to complete the Epsom and Chantilly Derby
double in the same year, Pat Eddery having been the last to do so on Quest For
Fame and Sanglamore in 1990. While Dettori's first Epsom Derby had been a long
time in coming, the Prix du Jockey Club had provided one of the biggest successes
of the early part of his career, as he won the race as a twenty-one-year-old on
outsider Polytain in 1992. Dettori returned to Chantilly in the latest season to win
the Prix de Diane on West Wind a week later, becoming the first jockey for fifty-one
years to complete the French Derby-Oaks double.

Lawman did not have to rely on the subsequent exploits of those he beat to
enhance his reputation. He went on to further big-race success himself, returning to
Chantilly five weeks later to land another Group 1, the Prix Jean Prat. Unlike most
of those he beat in the Prix du Jockey Club, Lawman was dropped back in trip
afterwards to race at a mile. In 2005, the first year that the Prix du Jockey Club was
reduced in distance from a mile and a half to a mile and two and a half furlongs,
Shamardal had done the same, returning to a mile to win the St James's Palace
Stakes. Reunited with Peslier, Lawman faced six rivals in the Jean Prat, chief
among them the Poule d'Essai des Poulains winner Astronomer Royal who had
since been beaten in the St James's Palace. The field also included the winner of the
Premio Parioli (Italian Guineas), Golden Titus; the first three from the Prix Paul de
Moussac (won narrowly by British-trained Asperity); and a second British challenger, Tobosa, who had won a valuable handicap under top weight at Haydock last
time. With persistent rain falling through the afternoon, the going was soft by the
time of the big race, but that did not hinder Lawman in the slightest. He completed
a hat-trick of front-running wins with a comfortable three-length defeat of the Paul
de Moussac runner-up Stoneside, leaving his rivals toiling in the last quarter mile.
Third-placed Golden Titus seemed the only other one capable of coping with the
conditions, with the remainder, headed by Astronomer Royal, well held.

The last two Prix du Jockey Club winners had been retired to stud after
managing only one run apiece following their wins at Chantilly. Shamardal suffered a career-ending injury when being prepared for the Eclipse Stakes after his win
at Royal Ascot, while the 2006 winner Darsi was retired after finishing only fifth in
the Irish Derby. Lawman's main target in the second half of the season was the Irish
Champion Stakes, with the possibility of the Prix de l'Arc de Triomphe after that,
but his season too was ended prematurely after a comprehensive defeat in the Prix
Jacques le Marois. Lawman looked Manduro's main rival at Deauville but he
dropped away in the last two furlongs to finish a well-beaten last of the six runners.
A minor liver problem was diagnosed as the cause of Lawman's poor performance
and he wasn't seen again. In September it was announced that Lawman was being
syndicated to stand at Ballylinch Stud in Ireland where his fee will be €25,000,
Oct 1st.

Lawman comes from the first crop of Invincible Spirit, the leading first-
season sire of 2006. Judged purely on his own racing record—he was a very smart

sprinter and never raced beyond seven furlongs—Invincible Spirit might have seemed an unlikely candidate to sire a French Derby winner, even at the race's new distance, though he was out of a Prix de Diane winner, Rafha, and a half-brother to some good horses who have stayed well, including the St Leger fourth Sadian and the Queen's Vase third Aquarius. Sheikh Mohammed purchased a twenty-six per cent share in Invincible Spirit during the summer, and, having stood his first season at €10,000, Invincible Spirit will stand at €75,000 in 2008.

Lawman (FR) (b.c. 2004)	Invincible Spirit (IRE) (b 1997)	Green Desert (b 1983)	Danzig
			Foreign Courier
		Rafha (b 1987)	Kris
			Eljazzi
	Laramie (USA) (b 1994)	Gulch (b 1984)	Mr Prospector
			Jameela
		Light The Lights (b 1985)	Shirley Heights
			Lighted Glory

The same sum had been enough to secure Lawman as a yearling at Deauville, a relatively modest price considering his dam Laramie had already produced a winner of a French classic. That was the 2004 Prix de Diane winner Latice (by Inchinor), who had also been trained by Jean-Marie Beguigne and raced in the colours of one of Lawman's part-owners Enrico Ciampi. Latice was beaten only four lengths when seventh behind Bago in the Prix de l'Arc de Triomphe, though it seems unlikely Lawman would have stayed the trip had he contested the Arc. Latice was bought privately by George Strawbridge towards the end of her three-year-old season and subsequently won twice in the States. The last broodmare to produce winners of both the French Derby and Oaks was Pearl Maiden in the 'thirties. Her Prix de Diane (French Oaks) winner Pearl Cap also won the 1931 Poule d'Essai des Pouliches and the Prix de l'Arc de Triomphe (the first filly to do so), and went on to

C. Marzocco and E. Ciampi's "Lawman"

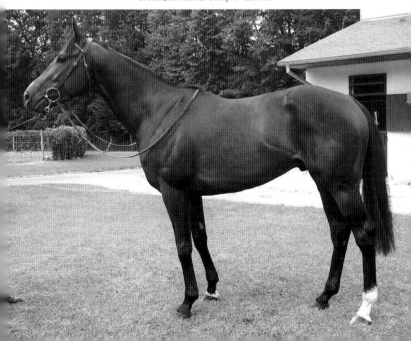

excel at stud as well, producing the Derby winner Pearl Diver. Four years later, Pearl Maiden's son Pearlweed took the Prix du Jockey Club, and, in between, Pearl Maiden also produced a second winner of the Poule d'Essai des Pouliches when Bipearl was successful in 1933. There's time yet for Laramie to come up with a third French classic winner. She had foals by Cape Cross in both 2006 (a colt) and 2007 (a filly), the colt being bought by bloodstock agent Paul Nataf (who had been the buyer of Lawman) for 260,000 guineas at Tattersalls October Yearling Sales. Between Latice and Lawman, Laramie foaled another good winner in stable-companion Satri (by Mujadil), a smart sprinter/miler who won the Prix du Palais-Royal and finished second in the Prix Maurice de Gheest in 2006. He too embarks on a stud career in 2008. In contrast to her stud record, Laramie's racing career was distinctly modest, amounting to two runs in maidens in Ireland, the better of which saw her finish fourth at Tipperary. However, Laramie's dam and grandam, Light The Lights and Lighted Glory, were good fillies in France, both winners of pattern races and placed in Group 1 company. Light The Lights won the Prix de Pomone and finished third in the Prix Vermeille, while Lighted Glory won the Prix de Flore and was runner-up in the Prix Saint-Alary. *J.-M. Beguigne, France*

LAW OF THE LAND (IRE) 3 b.g. Trans Island 119 – Bella's Dream (IRE) (Case Law 113) [2007 65: 8.3m 9m 8m[5] 7.1g[6] 7m 10g[3] p10g 10.1g[6] Sep 19] tall, close-coupled gelding: modest maiden: stays 1¼m: acts on polytrack and firm going: temperament under suspicion. *W. R. Muir* **61**

LAWTON 2 b.c. (Mar 19) Lear Spear (USA) 124 – First Veil 94 (Primo Dominie 121) [2007 7m Sep 22] 66/1, no show in maiden at Newbury. *Miss J. R. Tooth* **–**

LAWYERS CHOICE 3 b.f. Namid 128 – Finger of Light 89 (Green Desert (USA) 127) [2007 69: 6m p7.1g* 8.3d[6] p8g* p8g[2] p10g[4] p8m[2] Nov 24] good-topped filly: fairly useful handicapper: won at Wolverhampton in June and Kempton in September: good efforts in frame after: stays 1¼m: acts on polytrack. *Pat Eddery* **86**

LAWYER TO WORLD 3 gr.c. Marju (IRE) 127 – Legal Steps (IRE) (Law Society (USA) 130) [2007 66: p8g[6] p7g[3] f6g p7g 10g 10m[5] 10.2f 10d* 10m 11.5g 8g[6] 12m[4] p12.2g[5] p9.5g Oct 19] useful-looking colt: modest performer: won claimer at Brighton (claimed by N. Callaghan) in June: stays 1¼m: acts on polytrack, good to firm and good to soft ground: tried in headgear. *Mrs C. A. Dunnett* **59**

LAY DOWN DARLING 2 b.f. (Apr 26) Presidium 124 – Scoffera 63 (Scottish Reel 123) [2007 5m 7d 6v 6m 6g Aug 27] 500 2-y-o: sister to 7-y-o Time To Regret and 2003 2-y-o 5f winner Are You There: dam 1m/1¼m winner: of no account. *N. Tinkler* **–**

LAYED BACK ROCKY 5 ch.g. Lake Coniston (IRE) 131 – Madam Taylor 81 (Free State 125) [2007 58: p7.1g p6g f8g p13.9g f11g[5] p12.2g Mar 27] workmanlike gelding: poor maiden nowadays: stays 8.6f: acts on all-weather and heavy going: tried in cheekpieces/blinkers: reportedly bled third outing. *M. Mullineaux* **49**

LAY THE CASH (USA) 3 ch.g. Include (USA) 121 – Shanade (USA) (Sentimental Slew (USA)) [2007 66: p6g p6g[2] 7m p6g p6g 8f Sep 10] heavy-topped gelding: fair performer on all-weather, little form on turf: best at 6f: acts on polytrack: blinkered: inconsistent. *J. S. Moore* **– a64**

LAZY DARREN 3 b.g. Largesse 112 – Palmstead Belle (IRE) 79 (Wolfhound (USA) 126) [2007 80p: p9.5g[6] p10g[4] p8g[4] 10m 8.1m* 8m 8.1m[3] 8m 8m 8.3f[5] 8g 8m[4] 8.1m[5] 8d[3] 8m[3] Oct 8] close-coupled gelding: fairly useful handicapper: won at Chepstow in May: stays easy 1¼m: acts on polytrack, firm and good to soft going: tried blinkered/visored (tailed off): very upset in stall seventh outing: has hung badly left: held up and difficult ride: sold 17,000 gns, joined C. Grant. *R. Hannon* **89**

LAZY DAYS 2 ch.c. (Apr 8) Bahamian Bounty 116 – Vivianna (Indian Ridge 123) [2007 7m[5] Oct 5] 32,000Y: big, angular, good-bodied colt: has plenty of scope: third foal: half-brother to 3-y-o Diamond Diva and 1¼m winner Kaylianni (by Kalanisi), both useful: dam, French 11f winner, out of champion 3-y-o filly in South Africa Kundalini: 50/1 and green, eye-catching fifth to Fireside in maiden at Newmarket, shaping well under considerate ride: likely to stay 1m, possibly not much further: type to improve considerably, and will win races. *D. R. C. Elsworth* **82 P**

LAZZAZ 9 b.g. Muhtarram (USA) 125 – Astern (USA) 67 (Polish Navy (USA)) [2007 –: p12.2g p12.2g Jul 6] modest handicapper in 2005: lightly raced and little form since: tried blinkered/in cheekpieces. *P. W. Hiatt* **–**

LAZZOOM (IRE) 4 b.g. Zilzal (USA) 137 – Bring On The Choir 87 (Chief Singer – 131) [2007 –: 12g Nov 8] little form since 2 yrs. *Miss Tracy Waggott*

LEADING EDGE (IRE) 2 gr.f. (Mar 24) Clodovil (IRE) 116 – Ja Ganhou (Midyan **70** (USA) 124) [2007 5m⁶ 5.5d⁶ 6d⁵ 6m 5.5m⁴ 6m 7m⁵ p6g⁶ 6s* 6m⁶ 6s 5.1g* p6g³ p6g⁴ Nov 21] €8,000F, 23,000Y: workmanlike filly: first foal: dam, French maiden, half-sister to useful Italian 1½m performer Best Grey: fair performer: won nurseries at Goodwood in October and Nottingham in November: should stay 7f/1m: acts on polytrack, soft and good to firm ground. *M. R. Channon*

LEAH'S PRIDE 6 b.m. Atraf 116 – First Play 59 (Primo Dominie 121) [2007 57: p5.1g – Apr 16] modest performer at 5 yrs: well held only start in 2007: tried tongue tied. *Miss D. A. McHale*

LEAMINGTON (USA) 2 b.f. (Mar 5) Pleasant Tap (USA) – Muneefa (USA) 82 **70** (Storm Cat (USA)) [2007 p8g³ 9s f8d² Dec 21] third foal: dam, 6f winner, half-sister to smart performer up to 1½m Fahal out of US Grade 1 8.5f winner By Land By Sea: fair maiden: placed at Kempton and Southwell, wandering badly in latter: should stay beyond 1m. *M. Johnston*

LEANDER 3 b.c. Kalanisi (IRE) 132 – Guest of Anchor (Slip Anchor 136) [2007 p11g⁴ **74** 12m² 12g 16d Jun 22] 30,000F, 22,000 2-y-o: lengthy colt: has a round action: third foal: half-brother to 1½m and 2m winner Sambaman (by Groom Dancer): dam, useful French 11.5f to 1¾m winner, out of smart performer up to 1¼m Intimate Guest: fair form: in frame in maidens at Kempton and Salisbury first 2 starts: out of depth after in Derby at Epsom (then left B. Johnson) and Queen's Vase at Royal Ascot (tongue tied, said to have finished lame): should stay beyond 1½m: sold £1,000 in November. *K. J. Burke*

LEANDROS (FR) 2 br.c. (Mar 2) Invincible Spirit (IRE) 121 – Logjam (IRE) (Royal **90** Academy (USA) 130) [2007 6g³ 6s* p7g* 6.5m p7g³ Sep 27] €45,000F, 70,000Y: well-made colt: third foal: half-brother to 4-y-o Boris de Deauville: dam French 9.5f winner: fairly useful performer: won maiden at Dundalk in August: good eighth of 22 to Dream Eater in sales race at Doncaster next start: will stay 1m: acts on polytrack and good to firm ground. *G. M. Lyons, Ireland*

LECANVEY 2 b.c. (Mar 26) Where Or When (IRE) 124 – Catch The Flame (USA) **65 p** (Storm Bird (CAN) 134) [2007 6g 5d⁴ 5m⁵ 5m³ 6g Sep 8] 21,000F, €48,000Y: tall, useful-looking colt: seventh foal: half-brother to several winners, including 7-y-o Spark Up: dam unraced half-sister to US 2-y-o Grade 2 6.5f winner Bright Launch: fair form: strong-finishing third in nursery at Sandown: should be well suited by 6f/7f: acts on good to firm going: worth another chance to progress. *R. A. Fahey*

LECHERO (IRE) 2 ch.c. (May 26) Millkom 124 – Lovely Ali (IRE) 69 (Dunbeath – (USA) 127) [2007 6m p8.6g p7.1g⁶ Nov 30] well held in maidens (debut for Ian Williams): bred to stay 1m. *P. A. Blockley*

LE CHIFFRE (IRE) 5 br.g. Celtic Swing 138 – Implicit View 63 (Persian Bold 123) **80** [2007 77: p7.1g³ p6g⁵ f6g p6g⁵ 6m* p5.1g p6g⁵ p7g⁴ p7.1g³ p8.0g* p8g³ p8g* p8g³ p8g² p8.6g⁶ p9.5g Oct 18] tall gelding: fairly useful performer: won sellers at Brighton (sold from K. Burke 5,200 gns) in April and, having left R. Harris £6,000, Wolverhampton in July, and apprentice handicap at Kempton in August: stays 9f: acts on all-weather and firm going: wears cheekpieces/blinkers: reportedly bled second/fourth outings: often races prominently. *S. Curran*

LE CORVEE (IRE) 5 b.g. Rossini (USA) 118 – Elupa (IRE) 98 (Mtoto 134) [2007 88: **82** p12g p10g 10m* 11.6f 10f Aug 8] well-made gelding: fairly useful handicapper nowadays: won amateur event at Newmarket in May: stays 1½m: acts on polytrack and firm ground: fair hurdler, successful twice in September. *A. W. Carroll*

LEDGERWOOD 2 b.g. (Feb 8) Royal Applause 124 – Skies Are Blue 70 (Unfuwain **64** (USA) 131) [2007 5d 6g 6m 7m³ 7g p8g p8g Dec 12] quite attractive gelding: modest maiden: should stay 1m. *J. W. Hills*

LEFT NOSTRIL (IRE) 4 b.f. Beckett (IRE) 116 – Baywood (Emarati (USA) 74) **46** [2007 48: f6g p5.1g* p5.1g f6g* f6g May 14] leggy filly: poor performer: won maiden at Southwell in March: will prove best at 5f/6f: acts on all-weather, good to soft and good to firm going: tried blinkered/tongue tied. *P. S. McEntee*

LEGAL EAGLE (IRE) 2 b.c. (Feb 11) Invincible Spirit (IRE) 121 – Lupulina (CAN) **88 +** (Saratoga Six (USA)) [2007 6m³ 6s* 6g Aug 21] €38,000F, €300,000Y: good-topped colt: half-brother to several winners abroad: dam, German 7f winner, half-sister to smart French stayer Poltarf: fairly useful form: won maiden at Newbury in July by 2 lengths (value extra): well held in nursery at York: likely to stay 7f/1m. *J. H. M. Gosden*

LEGAL LOVER (IRE) 5 b.g. Woodborough (USA) 112 – Victoria's Secret (IRE) 70   **70**
(Law Society (USA) 130) [2007 70: f8g⁵ 8.1m⁶ 8d* 8g 8m² 8.1g Sep 12] sturdy gelding:
fair handicapper: won at Brighton in May: stays 8.6f: acts on all-weather, good to firm
and good to soft going: races prominently. *R. Hollinshead*

LEGAL SET (IRE) 11 gr.g. Second Set (IRE) 127 – Tiffany's Case (IRE) 65 (Thatch-   **57**
ing 131) [2007 54: p6g⁴ p6g⁵ p6g 7m p5.1g⁵ 5g⁴ 5g⁵ 5m⁵ p6g⁵ 5.3m 5g⁴ 5d 6v³ 5d 5.4v³
5g⁶ 6g 6g 5s⁴ 5s p5m p6g Nov 16] rather leggy, close-coupled gelding: modest performer:
seems to stay 1m: races mainly at 5f/6f nowadays: acts on all-weather and any turf going:
tried in cheekpieces, usually blinkered: tried tongue tied. *Miss A. Stokell*

LEGENDARY GUEST 2 b.c. (Feb 16) Bahamian Bounty 116 – Legend of Aragon 67   **75**
(Aragon 118) [2007 5.2m² 5g⁶ 7m⁴ 6m* 7.1m 7m⁶ 6d⁴ 6d⁵ 6.1d⁵ Oct 18] quite
good-topped colt: fair performer: won maiden at Redcar in August: often looked awkward after, but ran creditably in visor last 2 starts (fifth in nurseries): probably best at 6f:
acts on good to firm and good to soft going: sold 9,500 gns. *M. R. Channon*

LEGEND ERRY (IRE) 3 b.g. Act One 124 – Azure Lake (USA) (Lac Ouimet (USA))   **64**
[2007 10d⁵ 10g⁵ 8.3d p9.5g p7g p12g* Dec 12] tall, close-coupled gelding: modest
performer: best effort when winning handicap at Kempton in December: stays 1½m: acts
on polytrack. *Jane Chapple-Hyam*

LEGEND IN HAND (IRE) 5 b.m. Lend A Hand 124 – Living Legend (ITY) (Arch-   **58**
way (IRE) 115) [2007 68d: f12g⁶ Jan 16] fourth foal: half-sister to 2 winners, notably
useful 5f (at 2 yrs) to 1¼m winner Salute Him (by Mull of Kintyre): dam unraced half-
sister to very smart miler Missed Flight: fair maiden at best: just modest form in handicap
at Southwell sole start in 2007: stays 1½m: acts on soft ground: tried in cheekpieces.
Seamus Fahey, Ireland

LEGERETE (USA) 3 b.f. Rahy (USA) 115 – Sea Hill (USA) (Seattle Slew (USA))   **116**
[2007 107p: 8g⁴ 12g* 12g* 10d 12m⁴ 10g³ Oct 7] good-topped filly: smart performer:
successful in June in Prix de Royaumont at Chantilly (by short head from La Hernanda)
and Prix de Malleret - Air Mauritius at Saint-Cloud (by ½ length from Kaloura), leading
inside final 1f both times: in frame at Longchamp after in Prix Vermeille (2½ lengths
fourth to Mrs Lindsay) and Prix de l'Opera (best effort, beaten 2 heads when third to
Satwa Queen): stays 1½m: acts on good to firm ground. *A. Fabre, France*

LEGION D'HONNEUR (UAE) 2 b.c. (Mar 13) Halling (USA) 133 – Renowned   **79**
(IRE) (Darshaan 133) [2007 7.1g 8.2d³ Oct 10] good-bodied colt: fourth foal: half-
brother to fairly useful French 10.5f winner Varsity (by Lomitas): dam unraced sister to
outstanding miler Mark of Esteem: fair maiden: third to Tajaaweed at Nottingham: will
stay 1¼m/1½m: sold 20,000 gns. *M. Johnston*

LEGISLATION 2 b.c. (Apr 6) Oasis Dream 129 – Kite Mark 58 (Mark of Esteem   **85 +**
(IRE) 137) [2007 6m* 7g⁶ 7g⁵ Nov 3] 40,000Y, 140,000 2-y-o: strong, well-made colt:
third foal: half-brother to 3-y-o Daylami Dreams: dam, ran once, half-sister to very smart
Park Hill Stakes winner Madame Dubois: fairly useful form: won maiden at Newmarket
in July: didn't progress as expected, sixth to Fast Company in Acomb Stakes at York and
fifth to Storm Force in minor event at Kempton, but not knocked about once held: should
be suited by 7f/1m. *J. H. M. Gosden*

LEG SPINNER (IRE) 6 b.g. Intikhab (USA) 135 – Road Harbour (USA) (Rodrigo de   **109**
Triano (USA) 130) [2007 20m⁴ 16.1v 16m* 18d* Oct 20] tall gelding: useful handi-
capper: won at Ascot (by 1¼ lengths from Caracciola) in August and 33-runner £2.5
Million totescoop6 Cesarewitch at Newmarket (best effort, beat same rival by ¾ length)

£2.5 Million totescoop6 Cesarewitch (Handicap), Newmarket—
the first four home are all at least as well known as jumpers; Leg Spinner, Caracciola (rail) and Fair
Along fight it out, while Al Eile (No.6) arrives late to take fourth

in October: stays 2½m: acts on firm and good to soft going (ran poorly on heavy second outing): sometimes edges left: fairly useful hurdler. *A. J. Martin, Ireland*

LEG SWEEP 3 ch.g. Compton Place 125 – Radiant Bride (USA) (Blushing Groom (FR) 131) [2007 p6g⁴ p6g² p7g³ p7g⁴ p8g 7m 6s 7m 7g 6g Sep 18] useful-looking gelding: has fluent action: fair maiden on all-weather, modest on turf: well below form last 4 outings: stays 7f: acts on polytrack: tried tongue tied: sold 4,000 gns. *D. R. C. Elsworth* — **62 a71**

LEIGHTON BUZZARD 5 b.g. Cyrano de Bergerac 120 – Winsome Wooster 71 (Primo Dominie 121) [2007 71, a56: p11g³ p13.9g⁵ p16.5g Feb 16] compact gelding: modest handicapper: seems to stay easy 1¾m: acts on polytrack, firm and good to soft going: tried in cheekpieces: usually held up. *N. B. King* — **62**

LEIGHTON (IRE) 7 b.g. Desert Story (IRE) 115 – Lady Fern (Old Vic 136) [2007 p10g p10g p12.2g⁴ p13.9g Nov 23] tall gelding: fairly useful performer in 2004, missed next 3 seasons: just modest form in handicaps at 7 yrs: stayed 1½m: acted on firm going, probably on polytrack: tried tongue tied/in cheekpieces/visored: was none too genuine: dead. *M. S. Saunders* — **61 §**

LEITMOTIF (USA) 2 gr. or ro.c. (Apr 20) Linamix (FR) 127 – First Melody (Vettori (IRE) 119) [2007 7m⁶ 8d 8.2g Oct 31] sparely-made colt: first foal: dam, French 1m winner, out of smart French performer up to 11f Brillante, herself half-sister to Bellypha: fair form when mid-field in maidens: will progress at 1¼m/1½m. *J. L. Dunlop* — **68 p**

LEKIN SEDONA (IRE) 2 ch.g. (May 1) Namid 128 – Abrahamsdotter (IRE) (College Chapel 122) [2007 5v³ 6d⁶ 5d⁴ 5.5m 7d p6g³ Oct 22] workmanlike gelding: modest maiden: effective at 5f/6f: acts on polytrack and heavy going. *J. M. Saville* — **54**

LEKITA 2 b.f. (Apr 11) Kyllachy 129 – Tender Moment (IRE) 78 (Caerleon (USA) 132) [2007 p7g⁵ Oct 24] half-sister to several winners, including 5-y-o Tucker and fairly useful 6f (at 2 yrs)/7f winner Marlo (by Hector Protector): dam 7f winner: 7/2, never-nearer fifth in maiden at Lingfield: will do better. *W. R. Swinburn* — **67 p**

LELLA BEYA 2 b.f. (Feb 1) Diktat 126 – Seamstress (IRE) 72 (Barathea (IRE) 127) [2007 5g 6m p7g⁵ p8g⁶ p8.6g⁴ p6g p7g p7g⁵ Dec 19] quite attractive filly: second foal: half-sister to 3-y-o Elhamri: dam, 7f (at 2 yrs) and 1m (in US) winner, sister to useful performer up to 7f Rag Top: modest maiden: below form in nurseries: stays 8.6f: acts on polytrack. *S. Kirk* — **59**

LE MASQUE 3 b.g. Iron Mask (USA) 117 – Red Millennium (IRE) 102 (Tagula (IRE) 116) [2007 66: f6g² f5g³ p6g⁴ p6g p6g Dec 4] neat, quite attractive gelding: modest maiden: takes strong hold, and will prove best at 5f/6f: acts on all-weather and good to firm ground: sold 1,200 gns. *B. Smart* — **64**

LE MIRACLE (GER) 6 b.g. Monsun (GER) 124 – L'Heure Bleue (IRE) (Kendor (FR) 122) [2007 117: 15.5m² 15.5s⁴ 20g³ 14g 15d⁴ 15.5m³ 20g* 15.5m⁴ Oct 28] — **117**

On the Friday before Arc weekend, a weekend when eleven pattern races are decided at Longchamp, a very different meeting takes place at Saint-Cloud for horses of more modest ability. The entire eight-race card consists of claimers. Perhaps in a bid to remind would-be purchasers of the occasional bargain to be found in such races, each contest is named after a horse who graduated from claiming company to make a name for himself or herself at a much more exalted level. The Prix Polytain, for example, honours the 1992 Prix du Jockey Club winner who made a winning debut in a claimer just months before his classic success at Chantilly. Another race, the Prix Cardmania, takes its name from the 1993 Breeders' Cup Sprint winner, who in his younger days, before his export to the States, had won no fewer than seven claimers in France. In future, perhaps this meeting will also feature a Prix Le Miracle, because, less than eighteen months before his win in the latest Prix du Cadran, the gelding of that name was himself successful in claimers at Longchamp and Saint-Cloud. Entered to be claimed for €16,000 on both occasions, Le Miracle attracted no interest. His connections have picked up more than €350,000 in prize money with him since then.

Anyone not familiar with Le Miracle could be forgiven for thinking he was French rather than German, and not just because of his name. Although German bred, owned and trained, he has been campaigned almost entirely in France for the last three seasons, his now regular partner is a French jockey (Dominique Boeuf), and he last raced in the country of his birth back in the spring of 2005 when making his reappearance as a four-year-old. That run marked a turning-point in his career.

He was still a maiden, had never raced beyond eleven furlongs, and had been campaigned for the most part over a mile, usually in blinkers. Following that reappearance (also over a mile), Le Miracle changed yards, moving to his current trainer. Werner Baltromei decided on a complete change of tack, sending Le Miracle to Chantilly for a minor event over fifteen furlongs which he won by six lengths, showing fairly useful form. Not quite a miracle, but certainly an improvement on previous efforts. A test of stamina was evidently needed to bring out the best in Le Miracle, though a leg injury sustained after his next start and an ensuing absence of almost a year meant that it was not until he was five that Le Miracle's career really took off.

The drop to claiming company came after Le Miracle had been well beaten on his first two starts back from injury but, after those two successes in claimers, he progressed with wins in a minor event at Clairefontaine and a listed race (by six lengths) at Chantilly, and by the autumn of 2006 was showing smart form in the top French staying races. He ran out an impressive five-length winner of the Prix Gladiateur at Longchamp before finishing a close third (pictured in the brown colours on the dust jacket of *Racehorses of 2006*) behind Sergeant Cecil in his first crack at the Prix du Cadran. The Cadran was Le Miracle's main target again in the latest season. In addition, he contested all the other top French staying races, as well as the Gold Cup at Royal Ascot, and made the frame in all of them bar the Prix Maurice de Nieuil at Longchamp in July in which he finished last, reportedly lame. Already proven at the trip and with underfoot conditions in his favour, Le Miracle gave a good account of himself in the Gold Cup and certainly made a nonsense of his odds of 50/1 by finishing five lengths behind Yeats in third, travelling strongly just off the pace and finishing clear of the remainder. Le Miracle had finished behind the two French challengers for the Gold Cup, Lord du Sud and Montare, on his previous start in the Prix Vicomtesse Vigier, but that was on soft ground, and before that he had made an encouraging reappearance in the Prix de Barbeville, also at Longchamp, going down by a neck to Host Nation conceding 8 lb to the winner.

Le Miracle took the same route to the Prix du Cadran as he had the season before, finishing a close fourth behind Getaway in the Prix Kergorlay at Deauville and then beaten around five lengths into third behind the filly Varevees in the Prix Gladiateur, though without advertising his chances for the Cadran in the latter race to anything like the same degree as he had when successful twelve months earlier. The field of six for the Prix du Cadran Casino-Theatre Barriere de Toulouse (let's hope the new sponsors of the Arc meeting in 2008 can agree to less cumbersome race titles) was the smallest since the same number ran in 1995. The presence of Yeats at 5/2-on no doubt scared off a number of would-be challengers, while Getaway was a notable absentee, switched to the Arc to replace injured stable-

Prix du Cadran Casino-Theatre Barriere de Toulouse, Longchamp—German challenger Le Miracle makes much of the running and wins from Varevees, Yeats (No.1), Balkan Knight and Juniper Girl

companion Manduro. Sergeant Cecil was not around to defend his title, having already been retired for the year after some disappointing efforts. The remainder of the field comprised second-favourite Varevees, Goodwood Cup fourth Balkan Knight, the Northumberland Plate winner Juniper Girl and rank outsider Belle Epine. Le Miracle had turned into something of a sitting duck for Sergeant Cecil's strong finish when making the running twelve months earlier but a similarly enterprising ride from Boeuf paid dividends this time. Held up initially, Le Miracle was sent into the lead after passing the post with a circuit to go and made the rest of the running, keeping on strongly and just holding off the late flourish of Varevees to win by a short head. Yeats was three lengths behind in third, a disappointing effort, ahead of Balkan Knight and Juniper Girl. Back at Longchamp three weeks later in the Prix Royal-Oak, Le Miracle, much more patiently ridden this time, ran just about his best race all year when staying on to be beaten little more than a length into fourth behind Allegretto. Varevees was more than two lengths further away in seventh.

Le Miracle (GER) (b.g. 2001)	Monsun (GER) (br 1990)	Konigsstuhl (br 1976)	Dschingis Khan Konigskronung
		Mosella (b 1985)	Surumu Monasia
	L'Heure Bleue (IRE) (b 1993)	Kendor (gr 1986)	Kenmare Belle Mecene
		Loire Princesse (b 1988)	Tate Gallery Admit

A typically late-developing son of his excellent sire Monsun, the tall, leggy Le Miracle is the third foal of his dam L'Heure Bleue, who won five races in Germany at around seven furlongs and a mile. Her offspring have all stayed further than she did herself. Her first two foals were by Platini, Larrimah winning six races in the Czech Republic and Lomicelli showing useful form up to a mile and a quarter in Germany (also pulled up in a beginners chase at Catterick on his only start in Britain). L'Heure Bleue's only other runner to date is Le Miracle's useful stable-companion Loup de Mer (by Law Society), who accompanied his elder half-brother in the Royal-Oak, finishing last after playing a pacemaking role, having put up a career-best effort when sixth in the same race in 2006. The grandam Loire Princesse was a lightly-raced French maiden out of a once-raced daughter of the Oaks runner-up Vals Girl, herself a daughter of the Oaks and Irish One Thousand Guineas winner Valoris.

Le Miracle is effective at around two miles but an even stiffer test of stamina is likely to suit him ideally, making the Gold Cup and the Prix du Cadran his two main objectives again in 2008. He has won on good to soft ground but it looks as though good ground or firmer suits him ideally. Le Miracle hasn't worn blinkers since his three-year-old days but has been fitted with ear plugs more recently than that. Dominique Boeuf had also been associated with another Cadran winner who wore ear plugs, Westerner. Controversy surrounded that horse's run in the Gold Cup when his ear plugs were taken out during the race, something which at the time the French rules permitted but the British regulations did not. However, with effect from September 1st, the French rules have been brought into line with British (and German) ones, allowing ear plugs to be fitted, but not to be removed during a race. Clearly something of a character, Le Miracle has proved mulish at the stalls on more than one occasion and was sweating and on his toes at Ascot, but he has done nothing wrong once racing and is effective either making the running or being held up. *Werner Baltromei, Germany*

LEMONETTE (USA) 4 ch.f. Lemon Drop Kid (USA) 131 – Believability (USA) **98** (Southern Halo (USA)) [2007 p10g⁴ p12.2g*ᵈⁱˢ p10g² p12g² 11m² p12g² 11.6m 12f⁵ 10.9m* 12g³ 10g⁴ Oct 14] good-topped filly: second foal: half-sister to winner in USA by Victory Gallop: dam unraced half-sister to dam of top-class US 9f/1¼m performer Behrens: useful performer: left Mme C. Head-Maarek in France 25,000 gns after final 3-y-o outing: first past post in maiden at Wolverhampton (failed dope test and disqualified) in March and handicap at Warwick (beat Robustian by 1½ lengths) in August: good third past post in listed races at Cologne and Munich (demoted to fourth) after: stays 1½m: acts on polytrack and firm ground: has tended to hang: blinkered final 3-y-o start: reportedly lost a front shoe seventh outing: reliable: sent to USA. *J. W. Hills*

LEM

LEMON N SUGAR (USA) 2 b.f. (Apr 5) Lemon Drop Kid (USA) 131 – Altos de **82 p**
Chavon (USA) (Polish Numbers (USA)) [2007 7g p7g³ Sep 18] $350,000 2-y-o: big,
good-bodied filly: third foal: dam unraced half-sister to high-class US performer up
to 11f Sarafan: fairly useful form: promise in maidens at Goodwood and Lingfield
(third behind Sky Dive and Adversity): will stay at least 1m: type to continue improving.
J. Noseda

LEMON SILK (IRE) 3 ch.g. Barathea (IRE) 127 – Bois de Citron (USA) 88 (Wood- **69 §**
man (USA) 126) [2007 81: 12g 9.1m 8.5v³ 7.5s³ 6m p11g 11.6d Oct 15] sturdy gelding:
fair handicapper: left T. Tate after fifth outing: stays 8.5f: acts on heavy ground: tried
tongue tied/in cheekpieces: headstrong, and was one to treat with caution: improved over
hurdles late in year, winning twice and showing fairly useful form. *K. J. Burke*

LEMPICKA 3 b.f. Bahamian Bounty 116 – Dress Design (IRE) 84 (Brief Truce (USA) **61**
126) [2007 6d⁵ 5v³ 5d³ 6m³ Aug 4] 10,000Y: sturdy filly: fifth foal: half-sister to fairly
useful Italian 5f/6f winner Green Target (by Catrail) and winner in Belgium by Atraf:
dam, Irish 2-y-o 5f winner, granddaughter of 1000 Guineas winner Mrs McArdy: modest
maiden: stays 6f: acts on heavy and good to firm ground: has carried head awkwardly:
tended to hang on debut. *J. J. Quinn*

LENARD FRANK (IRE) 3 b.g. Daggers Drawn (USA) 114 – Princess Sofie 84 **–**
(Efisio 120) [2007 41: f7s p8g⁵ Feb 17] poor maiden: often visored. *M. D. I. Usher*

LENNOXTOWN (IRE) 4 ch.g. Selkirk (USA) 129 – Pump (USA) (Forli (ARG)) **–**
[2007 64: p12g f8g Feb 11] good-topped gelding: modest maiden handicapper at 3 yrs:
well held in 2007: tried blinkered/in cheekpieces: dead. *J. Ryan*

LENOUSKA (IRE) 2 b.f. (Apr 18) Montjeu (IRE) 137 – Crystal City (Kris 135) [2007 **59**
6s 6d 8.1m⁶ p8.6g Oct 12] €19,000F, €19,000Y, resold €20,000Y: rather unfurnished
filly: half-sister to several winners, including useful 1998 2-y-o 5f/6f winner Stoli (by
Night Shift) and fairly useful 1m winner Stoli (by Spectrum): dam, French 1¼m winner,
out of Fillies' Mile and Yorkshire Oaks winner Untold: modest maiden: should stay 1m.
B. De Haan

LEONARD CHARLES 3 b.g. Best of The Bests (IRE) 122 – Iris May 87 (Brief Truce **73 d**
(USA) 126) [2007 77: p7g p8.6g³ p8g 10.2m p7g* 8.5v⁶ 8.1m p7.1g Sep 8] good-
bodied gelding: fair performer: won claimer at Lingfield (claimed from Sir Mark Prescott
£12,000) in June: well below form after: stays easy 8.6f, not 1¼m: acts on polytrack:
blinkered/in cheekpieces last 4 starts: probably not straightforward. *C. R. Dore*

LEONARDO'S FRIEND 4 b.g. Polish Precedent (USA) 131 – Glider (IRE) 65 (Sil- **61**
ver Kite (USA) 111) [2007 p10g p12g 16.4m 16f⁶ 16g Aug 13] lightly raced in Germany
for A. Trybuhl, winning maiden at Munich in 2006: modest form in handicaps in Britain
in 2007: seems to stay 2m: acts on firm going: has been blinkered: tongue tied last 3 starts.
B. G. Powell

LEON KNIGHTS 3 b.g. Inchinor 119 – Valnerina (IRE) (Caerleon (USA) 132) [2007 **75**
70: 7.1g² 8.5g⁴ 8m⁵ 10m p11g p8g Aug 26] strong, lengthy gelding: fair maiden: stays
1¼m: acts on polytrack and good to firm going: blinkered fourth/fifth starts: sold 11,000
gns, sent to Bahrain. *G. A. Butler*

LEOPOLDINE 4 br.f. Desert Prince (IRE) 130 – Beaming 93 (Mtoto 134) [2007 98: **98**
5.1f⁶ 7g² 6m⁵ 7g 7g 6m⁶ 6m⁵ Oct 4] strong, rangy filly: useful performer: good efforts
when second in Chartwell Fillies' Stakes at Lingfield (beaten 3½ lengths by Wake Up
Maggie) and fifth in listed race at Haydock second/third starts: stays easy 7f: acts on
polytrack and good to firm going (unraced on softer than good): races prominently: sold
65,000 gns, sent to USA. *H. Morrison*

LEPIDO (ITY) 3 b.g. Montjeu (IRE) 137 – Luv Is For Sharing (USA) (Miswaki (USA) **89**
124) [2007 10m⁶ May 5] closely related to fairly useful Italian 7f (at 2 yrs) to 11f winner
Sagittifer (by Saddlers' Hall) and half-brother to several winners in Italy: dam, US
maiden, half-sister to US Grade 2 9f winner Lottery Winner: won maiden and minor event
at Milan in 2006 for B. Grizzetti: respectable last of 6 to Salford Mill in listed event at
Newmarket sole start in Britain: suffered stress fracture of tibia after, then gelded: should
stay 1¼m. *L. M. Cumani*

LEPRECHAUN'S GOLD (IRE) 3 ch.g. Spectrum (IRE) 126 – Ashirah (USA) **56**
(Housebuster (USA)) [2007 64: 7m³ 8m⁴ 8.5g 8.3g⁶ 9.2s⁵ 12s 11.7m 12.1d⁴ 9.8m⁴ p12.2g
12.1d² 10d³ 11.8g Oct 16] close-coupled gelding: modest maiden: left M. Johnston 4,000
gns after sixth outing: stays 1½m: acts on fibresand, good to firm and good to soft going:
held up: of suspect attitude. *B. J. Llewellyn*

LEPTIS MAGNA 3 ch.g. Danehill Dancer (IRE) 117 – Dark Eyed Lady (IRE) 82 **81**
(Exhibitioner 111) [2007 69: 8.3d* 8m 8d 8d² 8g³ 8.1m 8g 10d p8g Nov 15] sturdy gelding: fairly useful handicapper: won at Windsor in May: creditable efforts after only when
placed: stays 8.3f, probably not 1¼m: acts on good to soft going: nervy sort: inconsistent.
D. R. C. Elsworth

LE RICHE 3 ch.f. Pivotal 124 – Courtlandt Queen (USA) (Deputy Minister (CAN)) **54**
[2007 6m p6g Jun 29] fourth foal: dam, 8.5f/9f winner in USA, half-sister to US Grade 3
8.5f winner Antoniette: similar form in maidens at Newbury and Wolverhampton (wore
cheekpieces): sold 4,500 gns, then won at 5f in Greece in December. *Miss J. R. Gibney*

LES ALLUES (IRE) 2 b.f. (Mar 10) Chevalier (IRE) 115 – Cwm Deri (IRE) (Alzao –
(USA) 117) [2007 8.1f 8.1m p7g Nov 4] 3,200Y: half-sister to several winners, including
1995 2-y-o 6f winner Kossolian (by Emarati) and 1½m winner Chocstaw (by Mtoto):
dam unraced: well beaten in maidens. *H. S. Howe*

LES ARCS (USA) 7 br.g. Arch (USA) 127 – La Sarto (USA) (Cormorant (USA)) –
[2007 126: 6g May 16] tall, quite good-topped gelding: high-class performer at 6 yrs,
winning Golden Jubilee Stakes at Royal Ascot and July Cup at Newmarket: well below
form in Duke of York Stakes at York only start in 2007: reportedly underwent tendon
surgery after: free-going sort, probably best at 5f to 7f: acts on polytrack, soft and good
to firm going: usually wore headgear earlier in career: has worn tongue tie/crossed
noseband/been bandaged in front. *T. J. Pitt*

LES FAZZANI (IRE) 3 b.f. Intikhab (USA) 135 – Massada 106 (Most Welcome 131) **108**
[2007 83p: 8g⁵ 9.9g p8g* 8.9v* 10g⁶ 10d* Nov 4] workmanlike filly: useful performer:
won handicaps at Kempton and York (beat Smugglers Bay by 4 lengths) in July and listed
event at Rome (by 1½ lengths from Mimetico) in November: also ran well when 3¾
lengths sixth to Turfrose in Premio Lydia Tesio at Rome penultimate outing: stays 1¼m:
acts on polytrack and heavy going. *M. J. Wallace*

LE SINGE NOIR 3 b.g. Averti (IRE) 117 – Prends Ca (IRE) 98 (Reprimand 122) [2007 **75**
75: p7g² 7m p8.6g³ p8.6g³ p9.5g⁶ p8g p7m* Oct 13] close-coupled gelding: fair performer: left D. Simcock 18,000 gns after fourth start: won maiden at Kempton in October: has
form at 8.6f, but best at 6f/7f: acts on polytrack: blinkered last 2 starts: sold 21,000 gns,
joined E. Charpy in UAE. *M. Botti*

LESLINGTAYLOR (IRE) 5 b.g. Orpen (USA) 116 – Rite of Spring 86 (Niniski **84**
(USA) 125) [2007 86: 12g 12d 11.9g² 12s Oct 13] good-topped gelding: fairly useful
handicapper: failed to impress with attitude final outing: stays 1¾m: acts on soft and good
to firm going: useful hurdler, won over fences in 2007. *J. J. Quinn*

LE SOLEIL (GER) 6 b.g. Monsun (GER) 124 – La Blue (GER) 119 (Bluebird (USA) **86**
125) [2007 64: 12.4m* 10g² 12d* 12s⁵ 10.1g⁴ 10d Oct 10] tall, good-topped gelding:
fairly useful handicapper: won at Newcastle in April and Newmarket (hung left) in June:
well below form final outing: has form at 2m, but likely to prove best at 1¼m/1½m: acts
on all-weather, good to soft and good to firm going: withdrawn on veterinary advice prior
to intended return (reportedly lame). *B. J. Curley*

LESSON IN HUMILITY (IRE) 2 b.f. (Apr 4) Mujadil (USA) 119 – Vanity (IRE) 75 **87**
(Thatching 131) [2007 5m* 6m² 6g⁴ 5d² Sep 21] €33,000F, 22,000Y: lengthy, good-
topped filly: third foal: half-sister to fairly useful Irish 2005 2-y-o 6f winner Sensasse (by
Imperial Ballet): dam, sprint maiden, half-sister to dam of smart performers Eisteddfod,
Brecon Beacon and Boston Lodge: fairly useful form: won maiden at Carlisle in July: in
frame in minor event at Ripon (second to Sporting Art) and listed races there and at Ayr:
will prove best kept to 5f/6f: acts on good to firm and good to soft going: quirky, tends to
hang/flash tail. *K. R. Burke*

LETHAL 4 ch.g. Nashwan (USA) 135 – Ipanema Beach 67 (Lion Cavern (USA) 117) **93**
[2007 85: p7g p6g* p6f³ p7g* p7g³ 6m 5g³ 6g 6s 5m f5d Dec 11] good-topped gelding:
fairly useful handicapper: won at Kempton in January and March: left D. Ivory 15,000
gns prior to final start: stays 7f: acts on polytrack, best turf effort on good ground: usually
races up with pace: has been early to post. *R. A. Fahey*

LETHAM ISLAND (IRE) 3 b.f. Trans Island 119 – Common Cause 87 (Polish **79 d**
Patriot (USA) 128) [2007 74: 9.9m² 9.7m³ 12g 7.9d 12d f16d⁶ Dec 18] tall filly: fair
handicapper: good placed efforts first 2 starts in 2007: left M. Johnston 20,000 gns after
fourth outing: should stay 1½m: acts on all-weather, unraced on extremes of going on
turf: races prominently: modest form over hurdles, won in November. *R. M. Stronge*

L'ETINCELLE (IRE) 2 b.f. (Apr 28) Observatory (USA) 131 – Fine Detail (IRE) 93 **65**
(Shirley Heights 130) [2007 7m 7m⁵ p8g Sep 19] compact filly: eighth foal: half-sister

to 3 winners, including useful 1m/1¼m winners Fashionable (by Nashwan) and 7-y-o Artistic Style: dam, 1½m winner only start, half-sister to very smart French performer up to 12.5f De Quest and US Grade 1 9f/1¼m winner Wandesta: fair maiden: should stay 1m/1¼m: sold 4,000 gns. *H. R. A. Cecil*

LET IT BE 6 ch.m. Entrepreneur 123 – Noble Dane (IRE) 79 (Danehill (USA) 126) **73**
[2007 69: 12g² 12.4m⁴ 16.1d⁵ 14.1m³ 14m⁵ 14.1d³ 14.1m⁴ 15.8g⁵ 14.1m* 14.1f² 15.8g*
15.8s² 14.1g Oct 19] lengthy mare: fair handicapper: won at Redcar and Catterick
in September: stays 2m: unraced on heavy going, acts on any other turf: usually races
prominently. *K. G. Reveley*

LE TOREADOR 2 ch.c. (Mar 14) Piccolo 121 – Peggy Spencer 77 (Formidable (USA) **69 p**
125) [2007 5g⁵ 6m⁴ 6g⁴ Aug 24] big, strong colt: has scope: brother to smart 5f (including
Nunthorpe and at 2 yrs)/6f winner La Cucaracha and half-brother to 2002 2-y-o 6f winner
Takes Two To Tango (by Groom Dancer): dam 6f/7f winner: fair form in maidens,
impressing with speed: may prove best at 5f: capable of better. *K. A. Ryan*

LETS GET CRACKING (FR) 3 b. or gr.c. Anabaa Blue 122 – Queenhood (FR) **–**
(Linamix (FR) 127) [2007 76: 12d Jun 29] rather leggy, useful-looking colt: fair performer at 2 yrs: well held in handicap only start in 2007: should stay 1½m: acts on polytrack
and soft going. *A. E. Jones*

LETS GO JO 2 b.g. (Feb 15) Barathea (IRE) 127 – Living Daylights (IRE) 73 (Night **–**
Shift (USA)) [2007 8.2d Oct 10] tailed off in maiden at Nottingham. *Mrs L. Stubbs*

LETS ROLL 6 b.g. Tamure (IRE) 125 – Miss Petronella (Petoski 135) [2007 98: 12g² **95**
12.1d⁶ 14m³ 13.1m⁶ 12v 16m⁶ 14g 13.1s⁴ 13.1s² 14.6g⁴ Oct 26] leggy, close-coupled
gelding: useful handicapper: several creditable efforts in 2007, making frame 5 times:
stays 14.8f: acts on heavy and good to firm going: tough. *C. W. Thornton*

LET US PREY 2 b.c. (Mar 27) Hawk Wing (USA) 136 – Entail (USA) 97 (Riverman **102**
(USA) 131) [2007 5d³ 7m⁴ 6s* 7m⁵ 8d 8m⁶ Oct 22] 42,000Y: big, good-topped colt:
fourth foal: half-brother to 2004 2-y-o 6f winner Entailment (by Kris) and fairly useful
French 1¼m (at 2 yrs) to 1½m winner Grandretour (by Grand Lodge): dam 7f/1m winner:
useful performer: won maiden at Pontefract in July: best efforts in pattern events, 2½
lengths fourth to Hatta Fort in Superlative Stakes at Newmarket, 5½ lengths fifth to
McCartney in Champagne Stakes at Doncaster and 2¼ lengths eighth to City Leader in
Royal Lodge Stakes at Ascot: stays 1m: acts on soft and good to firm going: sold 80,000
gns, sent to USA. *N. A. Callaghan*

LEVERA 4 b.g. Groom Dancer (USA) 128 – Prancing 98 (Prince Sabo 123) [2007 107: **113**
p7g* 7.1g⁵ 8.3d³ 7s² 7s 7g Sep 21] close-coupled gelding: smart performer: further
progress when winning minor event at Lingfield (by ¾ length from Vortex) in April:
creditable efforts after in listed race at Windsor (1½ lengths third to Army of Angels) and
minor event at Leicester (neck second of 3 behind Eisteddfod): poor efforts last 2 outings:
gelded after: barely stays 8.3f: acts on polytrack, soft and firm going: usually makes
running: signs of temperament. *A. King*

LEWIS ISLAND (IRE) 8 b.g. Turtle Island (IRE) 123 – Phyllode (Pharly (FR) 130) **–**
[2007 73: 12g Apr 2] angular, lengthy gelding: fair performer at 7 yrs: well below form in
claimer sole Flat start in 2007: effective at 11.7f to easy 2m: acts on polytrack, soft and
good to firm ground: tried tongue tied: none too reliable. *K. J. Burke*

LEWIS LLOYD (IRE) 4 b.g. Indian Lodge (IRE) 127 – Sandy Fitzgerald (IRE) (Last **56**
Tycoon 131) [2007 59: 8d 7m 7d⁴ 6g 8d 6.9m² 9m⁵ 9.8m Aug 28] strong gelding: modest
performer: effective at 7f to 9.3f: acts on polytrack, good to firm and good to soft ground:
tried blinkered, tongue tied nowadays: sometimes slowly away. *R. E. Barr*

LEXICON 7 ch.m. Weldnaas (USA) 112 – Swift Move (Move Off 112) [2007 6m 8m **–**
Sep 1] no sign of ability. *Mrs J. C. McGregor*

LIAMELISS 5 ch.m. Dr Fong (USA) 128 – Ivory Palm (USA) 93 (Sir Ivor (USA) 135) **–**
[2007 –: 16m 11.5m Aug 10] modest maiden in 2005: little form since: tried visored/
tongue tied. *M. A. Allen*

LIANI (IRE) 2 b.f. (Jan 27) Modigliani (USA) 106 – Well Wisher (USA) (Sanglamore **51**
(USA) 126) [2007 6g² 6d⁵ p7.1g⁵ 7m p7.1g⁴ p6g² 5.3m³ p5.1g⁴ p7.1g⁶ f5d² f5g⁴
Dec 27] 800Y: rather leggy, workmanlike filly: seventh foal: half-sister to winner in
South Africa by Lycius: dam unraced out of half-sister to Known Fact: modest maiden:
left W. M. Brisbourne after sixth start, P. D. Evans after tenth: effective at 5f to 7f: acts on
all-weather and good to firm going. *J. R. Norton*

LIBERMAN (IRE) 9 b.g. Standiford (USA) – Hail To You (USA) (Kirtling 129) [2007 –
–: 21.6m 16m⁶ 16m Aug 17] sturdy gelding: little form since 2004 (reportedly bled on
reappearance). *R. Curtis*

LIBERODE (IRE) 2 b.f. (Apr 18) Statue of Liberty (USA) 115 – Phyllode (Pharly –
(FR) 130) [2007 6m Sep 1] unfurnished filly: half-sister to several winners, including
7f (at 2 yrs) to 1¼m winner Leatherback and 8-y-o Lewis Island (both fairly useful, by
Turtle Island): dam, maiden (stayed 1½m), half-sister to Ribblesdale Stakes winner
Strigida: 100/1, soon outpaced in maiden at Ripon: sold €1,200. *K. A. Ryan*

LIBERTY BELLE (IRE) 2 b. or br.f. (Mar 23) Statue of Liberty (USA) 115 – Enaya **81 d**
99 (Caerleon (USA) 132) [2007 5g⁵ 6g* 6g 6s 5d⁵ p7g p6g Dec 30] €48,000F, €26,000Y:
lengthy, sturdy filly: half-sister to 3 winners, including useful British/UAE 6f to 1m
winner (successful at 7f at 2 yrs) Jila (by Kris) and fairly useful but ungenuine 6f winner
Sulalat (by Hamas): dam, 2-y-o 6f winner (stayed 1¼m), half-sister to very smart miler
Gabr: fairly useful performer: fifth in listed race at York on debut: won maiden at Newmarket later in May, but below form after: should stay 7f: very slowly away last 2 outings:
one to treat with caution. *J. R. Best*

LIBERTY ISLAND (IRE) 2 b.c. (Jan 28) Statue of Liberty (USA) 115 – Birthday **53**
(IRE) (Singspiel (IRE) 133) [2007 6g⁶ 6m Jun 14] big colt: has scope: modest form in
maidens at Newmarket and Newbury. *B. J. Meehan*

LIBERTY RUN (IRE) 5 ch.g. Grand Lodge (USA) 125 – Bathe In Light (USA) 72 **63**
(Sunshine Forever (USA)) [2007 77: p13g⁵ p12g⁵ p12g⁴ 11.9m³ 10d* 10s May 30] neat **a74**
gelding: fair handicapper on all-weather, modest on turf: won at Brighton (apprentices)
in May: pulled up lame final start: stayed 13f: acted on polytrack, good to firm and good
to soft ground: tried tongue tied/visored: dead. *Mouse Hamilton-Fairley*

LIBERTY SHIP 2 b.g. (Apr 2) Statue of Liberty (USA) 115 – Flag (Selkirk (USA) **73**
129) [2007 5m³ 5d² 5f² 5m⁵ Aug 26] good-bodied gelding: fair maiden: placed 3 times:
may prove best kept to 5f: acts on firm and good to firm going: suspect attitude: gelded
after final start. *J. D. Bethell*

LIBERTYTYNE 2 br.f. (Apr 11) Statue of Liberty (USA) 115 – Coffee Time (IRE) 88 **49**
(Efisio 120) [2007 p6g p6m p7.1g⁴ p6g Dec 1] 14,500 2-y-o: second foal: half-sister
to 3-y-o Cuppacocoa: dam, ungenuine sprint maiden, half-sister to useful performers
Middleton Grey (up to 1m) and Fine Silver (up to 1¼m): poor maiden: barely stays 7f:
raced on polytrack. *S. Kirk*

LIBERTY VALANCE (IRE) 2 b.g. (Mar 9) Statue of Liberty (USA) 115 – Tabdea **68 p**
(USA) 106 (Topsider (USA)) [2007 p7.1g⁵ p6g³ Dec 26] 46,000F: half-brother to 3
winners, including smart Irish 1m/9f winner Tolpuddle (by College Chapel) and fairly
useful 7f winner Prevalence (by Cadeaux Genereux), later successful in USA: dam, 6f/
1m winner, half-sister to Poule d'Essai des Pouliches winner Ta Rib: green in maidens at
Wolverhampton, fair form when third (again raced freely): should stay 7f: open to further
improvement. *S. Kirk*

LIBRE 7 b.g. Bahamian Bounty 116 – Premier Blues (FR) 35 (Law Society (USA) 130) **75**
[2007 71, a77: 8s 10d 8.2g⁴ 8.1m² 8d² 10.2m⁴ 8.1m* p9.5g² 8.1g p9.5g Oct 20] leggy
gelding: fair handicapper: won at Chepstow in September: stays easy 1¼m: acts on polytrack and any turf going: tried in blinkers/cheekpieces/tongue tie earlier in career: waited
with. *F. Jordan*

LIEUTENANT PIGEON 2 ch.c. (Mar 3) Captain Rio 122 – Blue Velvet 100 (Form- **76**
idable (USA) 125) [2007 5d* 6g 6s⁶ 5m 6d 5.1g² p5.1g⁵ Nov 30] well-made colt: fair
performer: won maiden at Hamilton in May: left B. Smart after fourth start: second in
nursery at Nottingham: should stay 7f: acts on polytrack and good to soft going: tried
blinkered. *T. D. Easterby*

LIFE'S A WHIRL 5 b.m. Machiavellian (USA) 123 – Spinning Top 105 (Alzao **63**
(USA) 117) [2007 61: 7m p8.6g 8.2s 7.6g² 7d 8g* 7m 7g 7d⁶ p8.6g⁶ p9.5g⁶ Dec 3] close-
coupled mare: modest handicapper nowadays: won at Yarmouth in July: stays 1m: acts
on firm going, below form on all-weather and ground softer than good: wears cheekpieces: races prominently: has looked tricky ride: none too consistent. *Mrs C. A. Dunnett*

LIGHTNING LAD 2 b.c. (Apr 22) Cool Jazz 116 – Cappucino Lady 46 (Prince Sabo –
123) [2007 5m 5s 5.2g 5.2m⁵ Aug 15] rather unfurnished colt: no form. *J. R. Jenkins*

LIGHTNING QUEEN (USA) 3 b.f. Thunder Gulch (USA) 129 – Fairy Dancer **55**
(USA) 94 (Nijinsky (CAN) 138) [2007 56: 11.6m 12g 11.9m³ 12s 14m 18d⁶ p8.6g²
p12.2g Oct 18] rather leggy, quite attractive filly: modest maiden: effective at 1½m to
2¼m: acts on polytrack and good to firm ground. *B. W. Hills*

LIGHTNING STRIKE (GER) 4 ch.g. Danehill Dancer (IRE) 117 – La Capilla – (Machiavellian (USA) 123) [2007 99: 18d Oct 20] big, good-topped gelding: useful performer at 3 yrs: well held in Cesarewitch sole start on Flat in 2007: should stay beyond 2m: acts on polytrack, good to firm and good to soft going: once shied and unseated at flip start: useful form over hurdles, successful in November/December. *Miss Venetia Williams*

LIGHT SEA (IRE) 2 ch.f. (Apr 9) King's Best (USA) 132 – Bint Al Balad (IRE) 63 – p (Ahonoora 122) [2007 8d Oct 23] €82,000Y: half-sister to several winners, including smart 5f (at 2 yrs) to 1m winner Hurricane Alan (by Mukaddamah) and 4-y-o Song of Passion: dam ran twice: 18/1, very green in maiden at Yarmouth: open to improvement. *M. R. Channon*

LIGHT SENTENCE 4 b.g. Fantastic Light (USA) 134 – Almela (IRE) (Akarad (FR) 74 130) [2007 64: 9.9m² 12.4m² p13.9g² 12m* 12m⁴ Aug 6] fair handicapper: won at Musselburgh in July: stays easy 1¾m: acts on polytrack, firm and good to soft going: sold 1,500 gns in October. *G. A. Swinbank*

LIGHT SHIFT (USA) 3 b.f. Kingmambo (USA) 125 – Lingerie (Shirley Heights 121 130) [2007 93: 10m* 11.4m* 12d* 12v² 9.9m³ 10g⁶ Oct 7]

'Absence is to love what wind is to fire; it extinguishes the small, it inflames the great.' The seventeenth century French libertine, Roger de Rabutin, Comte de Bussy, describes more accurately the relationship between absence and love than the sweeping 'Absence makes the heart grow fonder', though both are valid in describing the racing public's affection and admiration for trainer Henry Cecil. In a racing year with more than its usual share of human interest stories, Frankie Dettori's overdue Derby victory attracted the most attention with the general public, bringing incalculable benefit for the sport, but the racing public warmed even more to Henry Cecil's first classic victory for seven years. The Oaks winner Light Shift and ten-times champion trainer Cecil, whose fortunes had declined markedly in recent years, returned to tumultuous scenes in the unsaddling enclosure with calls of 'Three cheers for Henry' not once, but twice. Cecil, who had revealed he was battling stomach cancer, has always been a flamboyant figure but, in contrast to Dettori's ecstatic reaction after the Derby, he seemed overwhelmed and near to tears—if not somewhat embarrassed—by the warmth of the reception afforded to him.

It wasn't the first time Cecil had generated such a reaction after a classic. The Newmarket winner's enclosure rang out to resounding cheers after Bosra Sham's victory in the 1996 One Thousand Guineas, which, as well as acknowledging the filling of the only gap in Pat Eddery's classic riding record, also provided a clear demonstration of public sympathy for Henry Cecil in the wake of Sheikh Mohammed's decision—after a most productive partnership with Cecil over more than a decade—to remove the battalion of his horses from Warren Place. Mark of Esteem had been withdrawn from the Royal Lodge Stakes the previous autumn and sent to Dubai to join the still-small Godolphin team, a move which sparked off problems between owner and trainer, reportedly exacerbated by remarks made by the trainer's then-wife. The Newmarket winner's enclosure produced further memorable scenes after the 1996 Champion Stakes, when another victory for Bosra Sham, after she had come second to Mark of Esteem in the Queen Elizabeth II Stakes, looked as if it might decide the trainers' championship for Cecil in a closely-fought battle with Godolphin's trainer Saeed bin Suroor (who regained the lead and clinched the title with victory in the Racing Post Trophy). In a sporting moment to savour at Newmarket, Sheikh Mohammed, whose family sponsored the Champion Stakes, jokingly shied away from Cecil as he presented him with the trainer's prize, an ornamental Arabian dagger. Cecil joined in by also shrinking back in mock horror, the actions of both men—who have long since reconciled—lightening what looked like being a potentially awkward moment.

The decline of Warren Place from its position of dominance did not stem entirely from the split with Sheikh Mohammed. Cecil hadn't won the trainers' championship since 1993 and was second twice and third once in the years immediately following his second place in 1996, reaching a hundred winners in a season for the fifteenth (and last) time in 1998 and saddling the winners of three of the five British classics in 1999. But between his twenty-third domestic classic success with

Oaks winner Love Divine in the millennium season, and his twenty-fourth, with Light Shift, Cecil's number of winners and prize money fell significantly as the size of his string declined from a full house of over two hundred to around sixty. Part of the decline was due to the demise or reduced operations of some of the British-based owner-breeders who had sustained the Warren Place operation since the days of Cecil's father-in-law Sir Noel Murless, who was champion trainer nine times and won nineteen British classics. Problems in Cecil's personal life also contributed but there were signs of an upturn in the fortunes of Warren Place in 2006 when Multidimensional gave the stable its first pattern victory since 2002 in the Prix Guillaume d'Ornano, and when Passage of Time put herself on the classic short-list when winning the Criterium de Saint-Cloud. Passage of Time's Group 1 victory was an occasion to raise the traditional standard at Warren Place after a Group 1 victory, a flag depicting a family heirloom, the Horn of Leys, said to have been given to one of Cecil's ancestors by Robert The Bruce. It was the first time it had been hoisted since Beat Hollow's victory in the 2000 Grand Prix de Paris.

Passage of Time carries the colours of Khalid Abdulla, whose Juddmonte operation has continued to supply horses for Cecil, and she cemented her position as ante-post favourite for the Oaks when winning the Tattersalls Musidora Stakes, the most prestigious of the recognised Oaks trials, at York in May. Carrying a 3-lb penalty for her Group 1 win, she won by a neck from Sweet Lilly, always doing enough to hold her rival after moving smoothly into the lead over a furlong out. One worry for supporters of Passage of Time, however, was that her trainer reported that she was suffering from a small abscess in her throat which could not be removed so close to the Oaks. Passage of Time was following the path trodden by Cecil-trained Oaks winners Diminuendo, Snow Bride (who got the classic on the disqualification of Aliysa) and Reams of Verse, all of whom won the Musidora. Two other Cecil-trained Oaks winners, Lady Carla and Ramruma, had been warmed up for Epsom with victories in the Lingfield Oaks Trial, while Oh So Sharp, who went on to land

Weatherbys Bank Cheshire Oaks, Chester—
Light Shift quickens past All My Loving (rail) and Fashion Statement

Vodafone Oaks, Epsom—Light Shift, sent for home earlier this time,
finds plenty to hold off Peeping Fawn, the pair clear of All My Loving and Four Sins (blaze)

the fillies' triple crown, was sent straight to the Oaks from the One Thousand Guineas, and Cecil's seventh Oaks winner Love Divine won the Lupe Stakes. Cecil used the Weatherbys Bank Cheshire Oaks to test the Oaks credentials of Light Shift, owned by the Niarchos Family which had also patronised Cecil through the lean years. Light Shift showed fairly useful form at two in fillies maidens at Newmarket, placed twice before winning an above-average one in September, and she showed further improvement when beating Kid Mambo in a minor event at Newbury on her reappearance in April. The Cheshire Oaks has had only listed status in recent times and winning it is seldom a pointer to classic success, though the 1994 winner Bolas won the Irish Oaks after missing Epsom, while the 1995 winner Dance A Dream finished second at Epsom and the 2002 winner Shadow Dancing came third. The last Cecil-trained Cheshire Oaks winner who went on to Epsom, Peplum in 1991, managed eighth of nine. Light Shift and the very well-bred Aidan O'Brien-trained challenger All My Loving dominated the Cheshire Oaks betting—it was 10/1 bar the two—and both earned places at Epsom, Light Shift winning by three quarters of a length from All My Loving with 14/1-shot Fashion Statement (who went on to win the Oaks d'Italia) a neck away third, the first three clear.

Passage of Time started 9/4 favourite for the Vodafone Oaks with Light Shift fourth favourite at 13/2, behind 5/1-shots All My Loving and the Aga Khan's John Oxx-trained Four Sins, who had won the Blue Wind Stakes at Naas. The fourteen runners included other major trial winners Measured Tempo (Swettenham Stud Fillies' Trial at Newbury), Dalvina (Pretty Polly at Newmarket) and Kayah (Lingfield Oaks Trial), as well as the One Thousand Guineas third Simply Perfect. Measured Tempo was the only runner for Godolphin but Ballydoyle sent out three others in addition to All My Loving, namely Peeping Fawn who had finished third in the Irish One Thousand Guineas only five days earlier, the Blue Wind Stakes runner-up Cherry Hinton and the Leopardstown 1000 Guineas Trial runner-up Nell Gwyn, those three sent off at 20/1, 66/1 and 66/1 respectively. When asked about the chances of Passage of Time and Light Shift (who had had a sore joint for a few

598

days the previous week), Cecil said: 'They've never worked together but I think both fillies will run very well . . . in fact I think they should be rather closer to each other in the betting than they are.' The pair were separated more widely in the race itself, Passage of Time dropping away tamely to finish a well-beaten eighth as Light Shift, kept wide and avoiding the trouble that some got into, was sent for home from fully two furlongs out. Ted Durcan, riding his first British classic winner, reported that the Oaks was a rough race and, in the end, he had gone on sooner than he had wanted to. He need not have worried, though, as Light Shift kept on very gamely when challenged throughout the final furlong by Peeping Fawn who had received something of a buffeting and had not got fully opened out until Light Shift had gone clear. That said, it was hard to subscribe to the view that Peeping Fawn was unlucky. She had every chance inside the final furlong. Light Shift held off Peeping Fawn by half a length, with All My Loving adding to her family's fine Oaks record by finishing third, four lengths behind Peeping Fawn. Irish-trained challengers also filled fourth and fifth, Four Sins a further five lengths behind All My Loving with Cherry Hinton beaten another length and a half. There was then an eight-length gap back to the non-staying Simply Perfect in sixth. Kayah came ninth, Dalvina eleventh and Measured Tempo thirteenth.

   Henry Cecil was once an advocate of the first four classics being run later —by up to three weeks for the Derby and Oaks—but if the latest Oaks had been run three weeks later Light Shift would have had her work cut out to beat the most progressive Peeping Fawn. By the time the pair met for a second time, Peeping Fawn had won her first Group 1, taking the Pretty Polly Stakes at the Curragh at the end of June in good style from a back-to-form Speciosa and the Prix de Diane winner West Wind. Peeping Fawn reversed the Epsom form with Light Shift most decisively in the Irish Oaks at the Curragh in July, Light Shift leading only briefly before Peeping Fawn took control to win by three and a half lengths; third-placed All My Loving was two lengths behind Light Shift this time, while Four Sins was back in seventh. The turnaround in Epsom form between Peeping Fawn and Light Shift was even more pronounced on their third meeting, in the Nassau Stakes back at a mile and a quarter at Goodwood in August. The French four-year-old Mand-esha split them, Light Shift snatching third late on and finishing five lengths behind Peeping Fawn. Light Shift did a little better when a staying-on sixth to Satwa Queen, beaten under three lengths, in the Prix de l'Opera at Longchamp in October and there was some talk of her being kept in training at four. Those plans were subsequently changed and she has been retired to stud, with a visit to Dansili getting her new career under way. Light Shift's achievements contributed to the best season for Warren Place stables since 2001 which, at the time, was its worst since Cecil's early training days (eleventh in the table, 48 winners, £736,365 in 1,2,3 earnings). Cecil finished sixteenth in the domestic table in 2007, with 1,2,3 earnings of £694,625; the stable's forty-five winners came at a wins-to-runs ratio of just over one in five. Some way from a return to the glory days, but a welcome improvement nonetheless.

Light Shift (USA) (b.f. 2004)	Kingmambo (USA) (b 1990)	Mr Prospector (b 1970)	Raise A Native
			Gold Digger
		Miesque (b 1984)	Nureyev
			Pasadoble
	Lingerie (b 1988)	Shirley Heights (b 1975)	Mill Reef
			Hardiemma
		Northern Trick (ch 1981)	Northern Dancer
			Trick Chick

   The rather leggy, close-coupled Light Shift, who has a quick action, is no bigger than medium-sized but the fact that she looked in tremendous shape before her races helped to compensate for her rather unprepossessing physique. Light Shift's sire Kingmambo was the product of 'a match made in heaven', between outstanding sire Mr Prospector and Stavros Niarchos's exceptional miler Miesque. After proving himself one of the best of his age, winning the Poule d'Essai des Pou-lains, St James's Palace and Prix du Moulin in the Niarchos colours, Kingmambo has gone on to be a splendid sire. Light Shift's Oaks victory leaves the Derby as the only British classic still to be won by one of Kingmambo's progeny (King's Best won the Two Thousand, Virginia Waters and Russian Rhythm the One Thousand

Niarchos Family's "Light Shift"

and Rule of Law the St Leger). The most notable racemare on the distaff side of Light Shift's pedigree is her grandam the Prix de Diane and Prix Vermeille winner and Prix de l'Arc runner-up Northern Trick who also carried the Niarchos colours with much distinction. Great things must have been expected of Northern Trick at stud but she was lacking in substance as an individual—tall, narrow and sparely made—and bred nothing of note until she was twenty, when she produced the Prix Imprudence winner Onda Nova. Northern Trick was represented successfully in the latest season by her seven-year-old son Fremen, who won three times. Light Shift's dam Lingerie was a maiden, retired after reaching a place five times from twelve starts in France, but she has more than made up for her disappointing racing career. She is now the dam of seven winners, including two others who have made their mark in pattern company for the Niarchos Family. Her first two foals Limnos and Shiva were both bred in Japan, sired by Hector Protector, who was owned and bred by Stavros Niarchos before being sold towards the end of his racing career, after which he was retired to Shadai Farms in Japan. Limnos improved at four, winning the Prix Jean de Chaudenay and the Prix Foy and establishing himself as a very smart middle-distance performer. Shiva did even better for Light Shift's trainer, despite a history of knee problems which restricted her career to ten starts in three seasons. She stayed a mile and a quarter well, revelled in heavy going and was a high-class racemare, her record including victories in the Tattersalls Gold Cup (from Daylami) and the Brigadier Gerard Stakes (very easily), as well as a close third, after encountering plenty of trouble, to Giant's Causeway and Kalanisi in the Eclipse. Probably the pick of Lingerie's other winners is the useful mile- to mile-and-a-quarter filly Burning Sunset (by Caerleon), who won a listed race over a mile at Saint-Cloud after being transferred from Henry Cecil in the autumn of her three-year-old career. Light Shift's brother Erewhon was a winner and placed twice in listed events on turf in North America, and the closely-related Mahasi (by another Mr Prospector stallion Woodman) won a ten-furlong maiden at Pontefract. Light Shift's twice-raced half-sister Leto (by Diesis) was sold for 900,000 guineas at Newmarket in December. Light Shift's year-younger sister Strawberry Fledge finished third in France on her debut for Dominique Sepulchre in the latest season. Lingerie has a 2006 colt by Aldebaran named Hyades. She produced no foal in 2007, but was due to Kingmambo in 2008 and will visit the same stallion again. The genuine Light Shift stayed a mile and a half and acted on heavy going and good to firm. *H. R. A. Cecil*

LIGHTS OF VEGAS 3 b.c. Traditionally (USA) 117 – Catch The Lights 86 (Deploy **74 d** 131) [2007 71: 7m⁴ 8.3m 9.9g 8m 9m Jul 11] strong, sturdy colt: has a quick action: fair maiden: well below form after reappearance: should stay 1m: acts on good to firm ground: jockey lost irons and pulled up second start. *B. J. Meehan*

LIGNE D'EAU 6 ch.g. Cadeaux Genereux 131 – Miss Waterline 77 (Rock City 120) **48** [2007 43: p8g p12.2g⁵ p9.5g⁵ p8.6g Feb 23] sturdy, close-coupled gelding: poor performer: stays easy 1½m: acts on polytrack, good to firm and good to soft going: visored/blinkered. *P. D. Evans*

LII NAJMA 4 b.f. Medicean 128 – Opari (IRE) (Night Shift (USA)) [2007 78, a70: f7g* **75** p7.1g* p7.1g p7g p7.1g⁶ 7d f7g² 8d² p7.1g 8g³ p7m⁴ 7g⁴ 6m⁵ Sep 25] fair handicapper: won at Southwell in January and Wolverhampton in February: stays 1m: acts on all-weather, firm and good to soft ground: front runner. *C. E. Brittain*

LIKE TO GOLF (USA) 3 b. or br.g. Bianconi (USA) 123 – Like To Shimmy (USA) **58** (Shimatoree (USA)) [2007 55: p10g 10m⁶ 12g 10.5s* 12g 10g² Nov 18] strong, good-topped gelding: modest performer: left Mrs A. Perrett, won minor event at Madrid in September: second in handicap there final start: stays 10.5f: acts on soft and good to firm ground: tried in blinkers/cheekpieces. *Ms J. Bidgood, Spain*

LILAC MOON (GER) 3 b.f. Dr Fong (USA) 128 – Luna de Miel (Shareef Dancer **67** (USA) 135) [2007 –: 7.5m⁶ 7m⁶ 7.9m⁴ 7.9f* p9.5g³ p10g³ p10m² p9.5g Dec 14] good-bodied filly: fair performer: won claimer at Carlisle (claimed from A. Duffield £10,000) in August: good placed efforts sixth/seventh outings: stays 1¼m: acts on polytrack and firm going. *N. J. Vaughan*

LILAC STAR 4 ch.f. Observatory (USA) 131 – La Sorrela (IRE) (Cadeaux Genereux **59** 131) [2007 72, a57: p10g⁶ p8.6g⁴ 8g 10m p11g Sep 5] strong, well-made filly: modest maiden handicapper: claimed from Pat Eddery £6,000 after third start: stays easy 1¼m: raced on polytrack and good/good to firm going: tried in cheekpieces. *T. T. Clement*

LILBURN (IRE) 2 b.g. (Feb 8) Statue of Liberty (USA) 115 – Vahine (USA) (Aly- **–** sheba (USA)) [2007 7m Aug 3] €26,000F, €70,000Y: seventh foal: half-brother to several winners, notably French 1¼m to 15f winner Vendangeur (by Galileo): dam unraced half-sister to very smart milers Vacarme and Vin de France: 25/1, needed experience in maiden at Newmarket: gelded after: will be suited by 1m+. *J. R. Fanshawe*

LILLE IDA 2 br.f. (Mar 3) Hawk Wing (USA) 136 – Fur Will Fly 66 (Petong 126) [2007 **73 +** p6g² 6g p6g* Oct 26] rangy filly: half-sister to 2 winners by Inchinor, including smart 6f (including at 2 yrs) winner So Will I: dam sprint maiden: fair form: off 3 months, won maiden at Wolverhampton by 4 lengths: free-going sort, should prove best at 5f/6f. *M. P. Tregoning*

LILLE TUVA 2 ch.f. (May 6) Alhaarth (IRE) 126 – Dipple 80 (Komaite (USA)) [2007 **65** 5.7g⁴ 6d 7m⁴ 8f⁵ Sep 16] first foal: dam 6f (at 2 yrs) to 9f (in Scandinavia) winner: fair maiden: fourth at Bath and Folkestone (to Presbyterian Nun): should stay 1m. *B. R. Millman*

LILY LA BELLE 3 b.f. King Charlemagne (USA) 120 – Corniche Quest (IRE) 74 **55** (Salt Dome (USA)) [2007 7.1m p8.6g p7.1g⁵ p7g Nov 6] lengthy filly: sixth foal: half-sister to 3 winners, including 6-y-o Black Oval: dam 5f to 1m winner: modest maiden: stays 7f. *A. W. Carroll*

LILYMAY 7 b.m. Sovereign Water (FR) – Maysimp (IRE) (Mac's Imp (USA) 116) **–** [2007 11.9m 11.9m 10.5m 10.3m⁶ Aug 31] leggy mare: second foal: dam little form: little form. *B. P. J. Baugh*

LIMBO KING 3 b.g. Barathea (IRE) 127 – Ermine (IRE) 86 (Cadeaux Genereux 131) **80**
[2007 73: 8.3s³ 10d⁴ 10d p12g Sep 5] quite attractive gelding: fairly useful maiden
handicapper: below form last 2 starts: stays 1¼m: raced only on polytrack and going
softer than good: tried visored (looked reluctant). *J. R. Fanshawe*

LIMELIGHT (USA) 2 gr.f. (Mar 28) Dalakhani (IRE) 133 – Last Second (IRE) 121 **45 p**
(Alzao (USA) 117) [2007 6g 6m 7g Jul 27] seventh foal: closely related to 7.5f (at 2 yrs)
and 1¼m winner Approach and 2004 2-y-o 8.5f winner Intrigued (both useful and by
Darshaan), and half-sister to 2 winners, including Poule d'Essai des Poulains winner
Aussie Rules (by Danehill), 6f/7f winner at 2 yrs: dam, won Nassau and Sun Chariot
Stakes, from excellent family: poor form in maidens: will be suited by 1¼m+: sure to
progress at 3 yrs. *Sir Mark Prescott*

LIMESTONE 2 b.g. (Mar 10) Lujain (USA) 119 – Moneymore (IRE) (Bigstone (IRE) **51**
126) [2007 5g 5m⁴ 5m⁶ 6s 6d⁵ 7.1d Sep 17] tall gelding: modest maiden: form only at 5f:
tried blinkered. *J. R. Weymes*

LIMIT DOWN (IRE) 6 b.g. Desert Story (IRE) 115 – Princess Raisa (Indian King **–**
(USA) 128) [2007 48: p7g Jan 22] poor maiden at 5 yrs: well held sole start in 2007
(reportedly bled): tried visored. *John Berry*

LIMONIA (GER) 5 b.m. Perugino (USA) 84 – Limoges (GER) (Konigsstuhl (GER)) **57**
[2007 64: 7.1m 7s⁶ p7.1g 6s* 6s⁶ 6d⁵ 6m⁴ 6d⁴ 5s* 6g 6d 6d p6g 5.1g Nov 7] sturdy mare:
modest handicapper: won at Leicester in June and Folkestone in August: effective at 5f/
6f: acts on all-weather, firm and soft going: tried blinkered: often races prominently: not
straightforward. *Mike Murphy*

LINAS SELECTION 4 ch.c. Selkirk (USA) 129 – Lines of Beauty (USA) (Line In **102 +**
The Sand (USA)) [2007 114: 12.3m⁴ Sep 15] workmanlike colt: smart performer at 3 yrs:
useful form when fourth of 6 to Hattan in listed race at Chester sole start in 2007: stays
1¾m: acts on firm going. *M. Johnston*

LINCOLNEUROCRUISER 5 b.g. Spectrum (IRE) 126 – Rush Hour (IRE) (Night **77 d**
Shift (USA)) [2007 82: f8g 8g 7m⁵ 7.6g 7m 7d 7m 8m 7m⁴ 7m 7g³ 10m p8.6g p7.1g
p7.1g Dec 14] good-topped gelding: fair handicapper at best nowadays: stays 8.6f: acts
on all-weather, firm and soft going: has worn cheekpieces/visor (in latter last 7 starts).
Mrs N. Macauley

LINDA GREEN 6 b.m. Victory Note (USA) 120 – Edge of Darkness 62 (Vaigly Great **82**
127) [2007 78: 6f 6m³ 5.7d⁴ 6g⁶ 7m⁶ p6g 7s⁴ 6d² 6m⁵ 6f⁴ 6d 6d 6d⁶ 6d 6d⁵ 6d p6g Nov 27]
rather leggy mare: fairly useful handicapper: won at Bath in May: best at 6f: acts on
all-weather and any turf going: held up: tough. *M. R. Channon*

LINDA'S COLIN (IRE) 5 b.g. Xaar 132 – Capable Kate (IRE) (Alzao (USA) 117) **75**
[2007 79: p8.6g⁵ p10g⁵ p10g² p8g* p8g² p7g⁵ p8.6g 9m 7.6m p8.6g 8.1m p8.6g p7m*
Oct 11] lengthy gelding: fair performer: claimed from R. Harris £6,000 after third start:
won seller at Lingfield in February and, having left K. R. Burke after seventh start, handicap at Kempton in October: has form at 1¼m, but best at 7f/1m: acts on polytrack, firm
and good to soft going: tried in cheekpieces: has hung: said to have bled several times.
R. A. Harris

LINDA'S LAD 4 b.c. Sadler's Wells (USA) 132 – Colza (USA) 89 (Alleged (USA) **110**
138) [2007 116: 12m⁵ 9f 11f⁴ 12f 8.5d⁴ Nov 23] rangy colt: smart performer: somewhat
disappointing since winning Derby Trial at Lingfield in 2006 (reportedly suffered fractured pelvis after final start that year): just fair efforts in 2007, including in Jockey Club
Stakes at Newmarket on reappearance (last of 5 to Sixties Icon, final start for A. Fabre)
and when behind Cloudy's Knight at Woodbine in Grade 2 Sky Classic Stakes (fourth)
and Canadian International (eleventh) on third/fourth outings: should stay 1½m: acts on
soft and good to firm ground: thoroughly mulish before going to post for Derby at Epsom
in 2006: looks hard ride, tends to hang left. *E. Kenneally, USA*

LINDBERGH 4 b.g. Bold Edge 123 – Halland Park Girl (IRE) 106 (Primo Dominie **74**
121) [2007 92: p6g 5g 5d 5m 5g⁵ 5s p5g⁶ p6g Oct 29] lengthy, good-topped gelding:
fairly useful performer at 4 yrs: just fair at best in 2007: best form at 5f: acts on polytrack, good to firm and good to soft going: tried blinkered, in cheekpieces last 4 starts.
A. J. Lidderdale

LINDELAAN (USA) 2 ch.f. (Mar 7) Rahy (USA) 115 – Crystal Symphony (USA) **80 p**
(Red Ransom (USA)) [2007 5.1g⁴ p6g² Nov 12] $480,000 2-y-o: sturdy filly: third foal:
sister to US 1m winner Classic Campaign and half-sister to 9f winner in US by Theatrical:
dam US Grade 3 1m winner: shaped well, finishing strongly, in maidens at Nottingham

and Wolverhampton (second to Haybrook): will be suited by 1m: useful prospect, sure to win races. *Sir Michael Stoute*

LINDEN LIME 5 ch.m. Double Trigger (IRE) 123 – Linden Grace (USA) 88 (Mister **76** Baileys 123) [2007 76: p16g* p16g 14.6g Oct 26] quite good-topped mare: fair handicapper: won at Kempton in January: stays easy 2m: acts on polytrack, firm and good to soft going. *Jamie Poulton*

LINDEN'S LADY 7 b.m. Compton Place 125 – Jubilee Place (IRE) 76 (Prince Sabo **56** 123) [2007 64d: 8d² 8g⁵ 8m² 8m 6.9g 8m* p8.6g 8ɪɪɪ 7g Sep 22] leggy mare: modest performer: won apprentice handicap at Musselburgh in August: stays 1m: acts on firm and good to soft going (no form on all-weather): wears headgear: reportedly lost a shoe and finished lame fourth start. *J. R. Weymes*

LINDHOVEN (USA) 3 gr.c. Monarchos (USA) 129 – Bevel (USA) (Mr Prospector **62** (USA)) [2007 57p: p10g f8g⁵ p8.6g⁵ 11.5s 7m⁵ Aug 9] neat colt: modest maiden: best efforts at 1m: acts on all-weather: tried blinkered: sold 4,500 gns. *C. E. Brittain*

LINDORO 2 b.g. (Feb 10) Marju (IRE) 127 – Floppie (FR) (Law Society (USA) 130) **91** [2007 6g* 6m 6m⁵ 7.1m 6.5m⁵ 6g 5d Oct 13] 60,000F, 72,000Y: lengthy, quite attractive gelding: half-brother to several winners, notably smart sprinter Ringmoor Down (by Pivotal): dam French 1m winner: fairly useful performer: won maiden at Goodwood in May: mostly stiff tasks after, only sound effort when fifth of 22 to Dream Eater in sales race at Doncaster on fifth outing: stays 6.5f: acts on good to firm going: tongue tied last 3 starts, also visored final one, when saddle slipped: subsequently gelded: pulls hard: inconsistent. *W. R. Swinburn*

LINDY LOU 3 b.f. Hernando (FR) 127 – Daylight Dreams 77 (Indian Ridge 123) [2007 **70** –: 12m² 12d⁶ 10g⁶ 12f Sep 10] close-coupled filly: fair maiden: stays 1½m: acts on good to firm and good to soft going: tried tongue tied: sold 4,000 gns. *C. A. Cyzer*

LINKSLADE LAD 3 b.g. Mujahid (USA) 125 – Goodwood Lass (IRE) 71 (Alzao **– §** (USA) 117) [2007 64§: p6g Jul 11] compact gelding: modest and irresolute maiden at 2 yrs: should stay 7f: usually in blinkers/cheekpieces: often reluctant (including sole outing in 2007), once refused to race. *W. R. Muir*

LINLITHGOW (IRE) 3 gr. or br.g. Linamix (FR) 127 – Diarshana (GER) (Darshaan **58** 133) [2007 56: 9.7g⁶ 11g² 12g⁴ 14g Jun 15] angular gelding: modest maiden: should stay 1¾m: sold 13,000 gns in July, then gelded. *J. L. Dunlop*

LINNET PARK 2 b.f. (Jan 27) Compton Place 125 – Shifty Mouse 44 (Night Shift **63 d** (USA)) [2007 p5.1g 5.1m⁶ 5d³ 5m 5f⁴ p5.1g 5.1g Nov 7] strong filly: fifth foal: half-sister to 5-y-o Mimi Mouse and winner in Hungary by Eagle Eyed: dam ran twice: modest maiden: below form after third start: should prove best kept to 5f: acts on firm and good to soft going. *J. G. Given*

LINNGARI (IRE) 5 ch.h. Indian Ridge 123 – Lidakiya (IRE) 105 (Kahyasi 130) [2007 **124** 120: 8g* 8.9g² 8m⁶ 8g⁴ 7d 8m* Oct 21] rather leggy, quite attractive horse: very smart performer: won Al Fahidi Fort at Nad Al Sheba for second successive year (by 3¼ lengths from Seihali) in February and Premio Vittorio di Capua at Milan (by ¾ length from Golden Titus) in October: best efforts in between when ½-length second to Admire Moon in Dubai Duty Free at Nad Al Sheba (left H. Brown after next start) and 4 lengths fourth to Darjina in Prix du Moulin at Longchamp: effective at 6f to 9f: acts on polytrack, firm and good to soft going: has rejoined H. Brown. *A. de Royer Dupre, France*

LINTON DANCER (IRE) 4 b.f. Mujadil (USA) 119 – Daisy Grey 46 (Nordance **50** (USA)) [2007 60: p9.5g⁶ 7.1g Apr 8] modest maiden: stays easy 1¼m: acts on polytrack and firm going: tried blinkered/tongue tied. *J. R. Weymes*

LION RIDGE (IRE) 3 b.c. Montjeu (IRE) 137 – Guardiagrele (IRE) (Persian Heights **67** 129) [2007 11.9m⁵ 10d⁵ Jun 22] easily better effort in maidens when fifth to Set The Scene at Brighton on debut, taking strong hold: sent to USA. *L. M. Cumani*

LION SANDS 3 b.c. Montjeu (IRE) 137 – Puce 112 (Darshaan 133) [2007 80p: 11.9m* **116** 12d⁴ 12g⁵ p12g³ 14m* Oct 4] neat, attractive colt: smart and progressive form: won maiden at Haydock in May and listed race at Newmarket (beat Spanish Hidalgo by 2½ lengths) in October: also ran well when fifth in Gordon Stakes at Goodwood (behind Yellowstone) and 1½ lengths third to Steppe Dancer in September Stakes at Kempton: likely to stay 2m: acts on polytrack, good to firm and good to soft ground. *L. M. Cumani*

LIPIZZA (IRE) 4 b.f. Spinning World (USA) 130 – Lipica (IRE) 99 (Night Shift **76** (USA)) [2007 81: 6g⁵ 6m⁶ 6m 7d Oct 29] strong filly: fair performer nowadays: best

efforts at 5f/6f: acts on polytrack, heavy and good to firm going: sold 4,500 gns.
N. A. Callaghan

LIPOCCO 3 br.g. Piccolo 121 – Magical Dancer (IRE) 53 (Magical Wonder (USA) **111**
125) [2007 87: 6m* 6m² 6m 6m² 6m² 5.6m Sep 15] lengthy, good-topped gelding: smart
handicapper: much improved in 2007, winning at Salisbury (by length from Oldjoesaid,
making all) in May: good efforts after when second at Newmarket, Ascot (to Genki)
and York (beaten 1¼ lengths by King's Apostle): ran poorly in Portland at Doncaster
final start: best form at 6f, should be effective back at 5f: acts on firm and soft going.
R. M. Beckett

LIQUID LOVER (IRE) 5 b.g. Night Shift (USA) – New Tycoon (IRE) (Last Tycoon –
131) [2007 59: p12.2g Feb 12] sturdy gelding: modest maiden at best: well held only start
on Flat in 2007: tried in cheekpieces/blinkers. *W. M. Brisbourne*

LISATHEDADDY 5 br.m. Darnay 117 – Erith's Chill Wind 61 (Be My Chief (USA) **94**
122) [2007 86: p10g* p10g* 10f³ 12d⁵ 9.9g² 9.9g³ 9g⁴ 9d 10.3m³ 10m² 12s⁶ Oct 4]
workmanlike mare: fairly useful handicapper: won at Lingfield in February and March:
mainly respectable efforts on turf after: stays easy 1½m, probably better at shorter: acts
on polytrack and firm ground: held up. *B. G. Powell*

LI SHIH CHEN 4 ch.g. Dr Fong (USA) 128 – Mad Annie (USA) (Anabaa (USA) 130) **67 d**
[2007 75: p7g p7g 7g 7g p7g p12.2g Jul 30] neat gelding: fair performer: regressed in
2007: barely stays 1m: acts on polytrack, best efforts on turf on good going: tried visored:
sold 2,200 gns in August. *A. P. Jarvis*

LISKAVEEN BEAUTY 4 gr.f. Danehill Dancer (IRE) 117 – Smooth Princess (IRE) **37**
63 (Roi Danzig (USA)) [2007 48: p8g p7g Jun 14] strong, lengthy filly: poor maiden:
effective at 6f to 1m: acts on fibresand, good to firm and good to soft ground: blinkered
last 2 starts: has shown signs of temperament. *T. J. Fitzgerald*

LISS ARD (IRE) 6 b.h. In The Wings 128 – Beguine (USA) 77 (Green Dancer (USA) –
132) [2007 87: 14m 20m Jun 19] big, good-topped horse: one-time useful performer:
little impact in minor event at Tipperary and Ascot Stakes (Handicap) at Royal Ascot
(blinkered) in 2007: stays 1¾m: acts on heavy and good to firm going. *John Joseph
Murphy, Ireland*

LISSELAN DANCER (USA) 3 b.f. Outflanker (USA) 83 – Sambacarioca (USA) –
(Irish Tower (USA)) [2007 –: 12.1g⁵ f11g May 22] well-made filly: little form.
J. R. Weymes

LISSELAN PROSPECT (USA) 2 b.c. (Mar 19) Suave Prospect (USA) 118 – Right **61**
Again Rose (USA) (Royal And Regal (USA)) [2007 6g 6g 6g⁵ 7g 7.5g⁵ 7s* Nov 25]
rather leggy colt: modest form for Mrs A. Perrett first 4 starts: won maiden at Madrid in
November: stays 7f. *Ms J. Bidgood, Spain*

LISTED ART 2 ch.g. (Feb 19) Night Shift (USA) – Saturnalia (Cadeaux Genereux 131) **58**
[2007 p6g 6d p6g Oct 12] modest maiden: bred to stay 7f/1m. *B. J. Meehan*

LISTEN (IRE) 2 b.f. (Feb 3) Sadler's Wells (USA) 132 – Brigid (USA) (Irish **117 p**
River (FR) 131) [2007 6s* 7v² 7g² 8d* Sep 29]
    By its own exceptional standards Ballydoyle experienced a substandard
season with its two-year-old colts. For the first time since Aidan O'Brien took over
at Ballydoyle in 1996 the colts won no Group 1 races—the tally over the eleven
previous years was thirty-eight, plus Johannesburg in the Breeders' Cup Juvenile—
and the relative lack of success wasn't for want of trying. Fourteen attempts in the
best races yielded just one place, a second for Henrythenavigator in the Phoenix
Stakes (Achill Island finished second in the Breeders' Cup Juvenile Turf but that
race is not yet graded.) The fact that O'Brien's sole runner in the Dewhurst Stakes,
Greatwallofchina, started at 100/1, and his two shortest-priced contenders for
the National Stakes, Lizard Island and Great Barrier Reef, were both 25/1-shots
sums up a highly unusual year. Jupiter Pluvius, winner of the Killavullan Stakes, is
undoubtedly promising but the saving grace for Ballydoyle was the performance of
the fillies. You'resothrilling won the Cherry Hinton Stakes, Kitty Matcham landed
the Rockfel Stakes, Savethisdanceforme finished a creditable fourth in the Prix
Marcel Boussac before notching a listed event at the Curragh by nine lengths and,
best of all, Listen developed into one of the best of her age with the highlight a
victory in the Meon Valley Stud Fillies' Mile. Whatever happens in the colts'

classics—and Coolmore's aim on the track is to produce stallions—O'Brien undoubtedly has plenty to look forward to with his fillies.

Just like her sister Sequoyah, who was started off in the Railway Stakes, Listen was thrown in at the deep end, in the listed Saoire Stakes at the Curragh in June. Unlike Sequoyah, she won, moving through to lead over a furlong out and not being fully extended to defeat Tuscan Evening by a length and a quarter despite edging left. Odds on Saoirse Abu was only fifth. Stepped up in distance to seven furlongs, two reverses followed for Listen. Odds on both times, she failed to justify favouritism in the Debutante Stakes and the Moyglare Stud Stakes, both at the Curragh. In both races she finished strongly after being held up, giving the strong impression that, as with the vast majority of her sire Sadler's Wells's progeny at two, a mile would suit her better. In the Debutante Stakes Listen went down by a neck to Campfire Glow and in the Moyglare she had to be switched left as Saoirse Abu, already successful in the Phoenix Stakes, took it up over a furlong out. Listen ran on but never looked likely to get to the leader, who beat her by a length and a half.

The Meon Valley Stud Fillies' Mile has, by some margin, turned out in recent times to be the most important guide to the future among European pattern races for juvenile fillies, leaving the Prix Marcel Boussac and the traditional leader in this category, the Cheveley Park Stakes, some way behind. Since 1995 there have been three classic winners and three other Group 1 scorers among those who won at Ascot, while fillies in the frame in the same period have notched six classics and four other Group 1s. None of the races involved was so strongly contested as the latest edition, which had very promising Prix du Calvados winner Proviso, a rare French challenger for the Fillies' Mile, as a short-priced favourite, with Listen, Saoirse Abu, May Hill Stakes runner-up Kotsi and the fourth in that race, Sugar Mint, also in the line-up. Completing the field were the useful Kay Es Jay and the unraced Wadlia, who started at 100/1 for Clive Brittain. Listen, who has raced only on good going or softer, got involved in some scrimmaging with the favourite early on, which resulted in Proviso's dropping back. Listen was ridden close to what was only a steady pace, lying fourth as they turned for home, and once moved out and asked to quicken she responded in great style. Going past Saoirse Abu under two furlongs out, she stayed on with tremendous gusto as Proviso attempted to launch a challenge after being forced to come wide, but the latter made no significant ground through the final furlong. Listen passed the post a length to the good with Saoirse Abu a one-paced third, two and a half lengths away. A cracking performance and, all other things being equal, an outstanding trial for the classics, with the winner and second likely to prove tough nuts to crack. For some reason, Listen's victory did not initially lead to her being made favourite for the One Thousand Guineas —Proviso still held the call with one major firm—but Listen was at the head of affairs before long at a best-priced 8/1, not unattractive odds given her looks, form, breeding and connections. She was also 7/1 favourite for the Oaks. The best

Meon Valley Stud Fillies' Mile, Ascot—the first three are well clear of the rest;
Listen gallops on strongly ahead of Proviso and Saoirse Abu in an above-average renewal

French-trained filly, Zarkava, has not been mentioned as a likely contender for the Guineas but another clash between Listen and Proviso, with Natagora thrown in for good measure, would make for a classic confrontation in every sense of the term. On the face of it, Listen, a tall, leggy filly who did not look the finished article at Ascot and has the scope to develop, is the one to beat. She is a most exciting prospect.

			Northern Dancer	Nearctic
Listen (IRE) (b.f. Feb 3, 2005)	Sadler's Wells (USA) (b 1981)		(b 1961)	Natalma
		Fairy Bridge	Bold Reason
		(b 1975)	Special
	Brigid (USA) (ch 1991)	Irish River	Riverman
		(ch 1976)	Irish Star
		Luv Luvin' (ch 1977)	Raise A Native
			Ringing Bells

The Oaks trip should be within Listen's compass. Sadler's Wells is essentially an influence for stamina and even though Sequoyah, who won the Moyglare Stud Stakes, seemed to have more speed than Listen possesses, she put up her best effort as a three-year-old when beaten under two lengths into fourth place behind Lailani in the Irish Oaks. There is speed on the dam's side of the pedigree. Brigid herself won a race over a mile at Compiègne and is well bred. Her sister Or Vision stayed a mile and won two listed events, notably the Prix Imprudence. Or Vision has produced three Group or Grade 1 winners—high-class sprinter-miler Dolphin Street (by Bluebird), successful in the Prix de la Forêt, Saffron Walden (by Sadler's Wells), who won the Irish Two Thousand Guineas, and Insight (also by Sadler's Wells), who struck gold in the E. P. Taylor Stakes over a mile and a quarter. Two half-sisters of Brigid's were stakes winners and Sequoyah has made a good start at

Mr D. Smith, Mrs J. Magnier & Mr M. Tabor's "Listen"

stud with Queen Cleopatra, third in the Irish One Thousand Guineas and Prix de Diane, and Coventry Stakes winner Henrythenavigator. Brigid, who was sold for 140,000 guineas as a four-year-old, has foaled two other winners including useful sprinter Oyster Catcher (by Bluebird), and her yearling by Sadler's Wells (named Liffey Dancer) set a record for a filly sold in Europe of 2,500,000 guineas when bought on behalf of Purple Moon's owner Craig Bennett at the Newmarket October Sales. In passing, claims that this shattered the world record price for a yearling filly held by the unraced Storm Cat filly Moon's Whisper, who fetched 4,400,000 dollars at Keeneland in 2000, are inaccurate because they ignore the exchange rates prevailing at the time. In January 2000 the rate was $1.64 to the pound, whereas in September the rate was $1.42. If the contemporaneous figure is used, Moon's Whisper cost the equivalent of 2,951,040 guineas. Brigid also has a colt foal by Sadler's Wells—what price that one? If Listen does as well as anticipated, the sky should be the limit. *A. P. O'Brien, Ireland*

LISVALE (IRE) 2 b.c. (May 2) Danehill Dancer (IRE) 117 – Farthingale (IRE) 67 **100** (Nashwan (USA) 135) [2007 7g⁴ 7s* 7.5s* 7m⁴ 8d⁵ Sep 30] €270,000Y: lengthy, good-topped, quite attractive colt: first foal: dam, Irish maiden (stayed 1½m), out of half-sister to very smart Irish 6f/7f performer Desert Style: useful performer: won maiden at the Curragh in June and listed race at Tipperary (beat Achill Island by 1¼ lengths) in August: good fifth to Curtain Call in Beresford Stakes at the Curragh final start: stays 1m: acts on soft going. *D. Wachman, Ireland*

LITALIA (IRE) 4 b.f. Monsun (GER) 124 – Libertad (GER) (Lagunas) [2007 103: – 13.4m⁶ May 11] half-sister to several winners in Germany, including 6f (at 2 yrs) to 9f winner Linara (by Windwurf): dam German 6f (at 2 yrs) and 1¼m winner: useful performer: won maiden at Baden-Baden in 2006: also good third in Prix de Malleret at Saint-Cloud and in Fahrhofer Stutenpreis at Hamburg: left P. Schiergen in Germany 220,000 gns, tailed off in Ormonde Stakes at Chester only start in Britain: stays 1½m: acts on good to soft ground. *P. W. Chapple-Hyam*

LITERATO (FR) 3 gr.c. Kendor (FR) 122 – La Cibeles (FR) 103 (Cardoun (FR) **127** 122) [2007 103p: 8s² 10g* 10.5g² 10m* 10g* 10d* Oct 20]

Not all the traffic between Britain and France was one way over the weekend in mid-October which saw England taking on South Africa in the Rugby World Cup final in Paris. The French had been knocked out of that tournament a week earlier, but their three runners at Newmarket on the day of the final had a much more successful time of it. Royal And Regal won the Jockey Club Cup and Literato, part-owned by French defence minister Herve Morin, proved himself beyond reasonable doubt the best three-year-old colt trained in France by winning the Emirates Airline Champion Stakes in a stirring finish with Eagle Mountain. The other cross-Channel raider, Doctor Dino, came third. Given his range of attributes, notably a fine turn of foot, the ability to act on soft and good to firm ground and tremendous consistency—he has won nine of his eleven races, finishing second in the other two—Literato should have another good season as a four-year-old, which is likely to begin in Dubai following his sale to Godolphin in December.

For a colt unbeaten in five starts as a two-year-old Literato was still something of an unknown quantity when he embarked on his classic campaign. That, though, is not unusual for trainer Jean-Claude Rouget, who trains at Pau, only thirty miles from the border with Spain, and habitually heads the French trainers' table in number of races won. He has been training since 1978 and in April passed Martin Pipe's European record of 4,183 winners. In the last fifteen years Rouget has saddled more than 2,700 winners, with a high of two hundred and forty-two in 1994 when Millkom provided him with his first Group 1 wins in the Prix Jean Prat and Grand Prix de Paris. Rouget's latest tally was two hundred and seventeen, which put him sixty-seven ahead of Andre Fabre numerically—he still couldn't catch the perennial champion trainer in earnings though. There have been plenty of pattern successes for Rouget since Millkom, notably with Shaka in the Criterium de Saint-Cloud and Ask For The Moon, Germance and Coquerelle in the Prix Saint-Alary, but many of his two-year-olds begin their careers in the Provinces rather than on the Parisian tracks. US Ranger won all his three races as a juvenile at odds on, at Bordeaux and Toulouse (two), and Literato raced from May to Novem-

Emirates Airline Champion Stakes, Newmarket—
the grey Literato crowns another fine season while Eagle Mountain makes it a 1,2 for the three-year-olds;
Doctor Dino (noseband) and Creachadoir also make the frame

ber, dead-heating in a maiden race at Tarbes, adding minor events at Vichy and Deauville, and concluding his campaign by picking up the listed Criterium de Lyon and the Criterium du Languedoc at Toulouse. Like US Ranger and various other classic hopefuls Rouget has had, including Prix Hocquart winner Maille Pistol and Prix Noailles winner Ruwi, Literato reappeared on a metropolitan track. The race was the Prix Omnium II at Saint-Cloud towards the end of March and Literato was ridden for the first time by Christophe Lemaire, engaged by Rouget early in the year to ride all his horses on the Parisian tracks. This was bad luck on the colt's former rider Ioritz Mendizabal, the champion French jockey of 2004 with a record two hundred and twenty wins (thanks largely to Rouget) who had done nothing wrong on him. Mendizabal, who finished a clear runner-up to Stephane Pasquier in the latest table, might have been excused a smile after the Prix Omnium, since Literato lost his unbeaten record by two lengths to a more-enterprisingly ridden but, as things turned out, significantly inferior rival, Hurricane Fly. Literato got back on the winning trail in the Prix La Force at Longchamp, the waiting tactics that suit him so well being used much more effectively this time as he quickened to join issue in the final furlong and beat Chinese Whisper by three quarters of a length. There were better trials than this for the Prix du Jockey Club and Literato started only third favourite at Chantilly. He was caught a bit flat-footed when Lawman quickened clear with two furlongs to go and, despite running on well, he was unable to pose a threat to the leader, going down by a length and a half.

If the Prix du Jockey Club had represented the high point of Literato's campaign his connections would have had nothing to complain about, but it wasn't the high point by a long chalk. Immediately after the classic Rouget identified the Champion Stakes as a long-term target. Given a break through July and most of August, like so many leading French-trained three-year-olds down the years, Literato came back better than ever. Not that he needed to show any improvement to win either the Prix Guillaume d'Ornano-Haras d'Etreham at Deauville or the Prix du Prince d'Orange-Lucien Barriere Hotels et Casinos at Longchamp. He started a short-priced favourite for each, odds on in the latter, and showed his customary turn of foot to catch and beat Spirit One by half a length at Deauville and Indian Choice, giving weight all round, by three quarters of length despite idling in front at Longchamp. For one reason or another the Champion Stakes a month after Longchamp lacked the three best winners over the trip during the year—Manduro, Dylan Thomas and Authorized—and Lawman had already been retired, but it still represented Literato's toughest assignment. His eleven rivals included triple Group 1 winner Notnowcato, two other classic runners-up, Eagle Mountain (Derby) and Creachadoir (Poule d'Essai des Poulains and Irish Two Thousand Guineas); and Man o'War Stakes victor Doctor Dino. Multidimensional, winner of the Prix Guillaume d'Ornano in 2006 but having only his second race of the year following an injury, was at 7/1. Not all Literato's opponents ran to form, notably Notnowcato and Creachadoir, and Doctor Dino should have finished closer, but the best horse on the day undoubtedly won. Waited with again, Literato came with his trademark run after Eagle Mountain was sent on over two furlongs out and he got upsides the leader a hundred and fifty yards out. After going a neck up, Literato had only a short head to spare over the rallying runner-up at the finish. Doctor Dino, who was given plenty to do and received a buffeting on his way through, was three lengths away third over Creachadoir, for whom neither the trip nor the soft ground was ideal, the same distance back in fourth. Notnowcato was not a factor in the closing stages, finishing sixth.

		Kenmare	Kalamoun
	Kendor (FR)	(gr 1975)	Belle of Ireland
	(gr 1986)	Belle Mecene	Gay Mecene
Literato (FR)		(b 1982)	Djaka Belle
(gr.c. 2004)		Cardoun	Kaldoun
	La Cibeles (FR)	(b 1989)	Cable Car
	(b 1997)	Douberta	Don Roberto
		(ch 1989)	Dourenne

Literato, a small, sturdy colt who cost only €40,000 at Deauville as a yearling, is not quite the best of his sire's progeny. That honour goes to Keltos, a fine miler whose moment of glory came when landing the Lockinge Stakes decisively in 2002. The sire Kendor, who died from a haemorrhage four days after the Prix du Jockey Club, won the Grand Criterium and Poule d'Essai des Poulains and has tended to get horses who aren't true middle-distance performers. However, Literato, who stays ten and a half furlongs, may be worth trying over a bit further given that he is amenable to restraint. Kendor's only other Group 1 scorer is Charge d'Affaires, successful in the Prix Morny from Xaar. Literato is the first foal of La Cibeles, a tough racemare who ran thirty-one times over four seasons, mostly in south-west France and Spain, winning five races from six furlongs to eleven furlongs and being placed in eighteen. She finished third in the Prix Fille de l'Air as a four-year-old. Her subsequent foals are the two-year-old colt Aldaketa (by Victory Note), who showed only a modicum of ability in races at Chantilly and Saint-Cloud in the autumn, and a yearling sister to Literato named Candidata who fetched €220,000 at Deauville in August. La Cibeles' dam Douberta was the best three-year-old filly in Spain in 1992, when she won that country's versions of the One Thousand Guineas and Oaks. This hardly made her a household name other than in Spain, and the fact that there is little else of note close up in the pedigree makes Literato's achievements all the more creditable. *J-C. Rouget, France*

LIT ET MIXE (FR) 4 gr.g. Linamix (FR) 127 – Lit (IRE) (Danehill (USA) 126) [2007 68: p10g 8d Oct 1] ex-French gelding: no form in handicaps in Britain: raced on polytrack and good going or softer on turf. *Noel T. Chance*   –

LITHAAM (IRE) 3 ch.g. Elnadim (USA) 128 – Elhida (IRE) 99 (Mujtahid (USA) 118) [2007 6m p6g⁶ 7.1m p7.1m p6g Oct 10] big, strong gelding: modest form: best effort on second start. *J. M. Bradley*   **64**

LITIGIOUS 10 b.m. Mtoto 134 – Kiomi 65 (Niniski (USA) 125) [2007 p12.2g Dec 15] temperamental maiden: tailed off in handicap only outing since 2003: tried visored. *B. P. J. Baugh*   **– §**

LITTLE ANGEL (IRE) 2 b. or br.f. (Mar 22) Auction House (USA) 120 – Green Sea (Groom Dancer (USA) 128) [2007 p6g 5.2g³ 5m Jun 16] 2,000 2-y-o: first foal: dam unraced: poor maiden: third in seller: blinkered. *Miss V. Haigh*   **36**

LITTLE BIG BOY (IRE) 2 b.g. (Mar 25) Danetime (IRE) 121 – Beverley Macca 73 (Piccolo 121) [2007 5m* 5.1s² 5g* 6g Sep 8] 15,000Y: smallish, close-coupled gelding: second foal: dam, 5f (including at 2 yrs) winner, half-sister to very smart sprinter Airwave: fair form: won maiden at Haydock in May and nursery at Newmarket in August: should prove best at 5f/6f: acts on soft and good to firm going: sold 10,000 gns, sent to Spain. *R. Hannon*   **78**

LITTLE BOB 6 ch.g. Zilzal (USA) 137 – Hunters of Brora (IRE) 102 (Sharpo 132) [2007 66: 9.1d⁶ 10.1d 9.1v* Nov 3] good-topped gelding: fair handicapper: won at Ayr in November: stays 1¼m: acts on any going: blinkered. *J. D. Bethell*   **67**

LITTLE BONES 2 ch.f. (Feb 25) Tobougg (IRE) 125 – City Gambler 74 (Rock City 120) [2007 6m 6d 6f³ 7m 6g² 7g⁵ p7.1g⁴ Nov 12] smallish filly: fourth foal: half-sister to 1¼m/11.5f seller winner River of Diamonds (by Muhtarram): dam 7.6f to 1¼m winner: modest maiden: second in seller at Ripon (left Rae Guest £6,000), only start in tongue tie: stays 7f: acts on polytrack. *J. F. Coupland*   **55**

LIT

LITTLE BY LUCK (IRE) 2 b.f. (Mar 22) Key of Luck (USA) 126 – Concept **37** (Zafonic (USA) 130) [2007 5.1d p7.1g⁴ 5.1g 7d³ Jul 17] €7,000Y: first foal: dam unraced sister to useful 1m (including in US)/1¼m winner Zante: poor maiden: in frame in sellers: will stay 1m: tried in cheekpieces. *W. G. M. Turner*

LITTLE CARMELA 3 gr.f. Beat Hollow 126 – Carmela Owen (Owington 123) [2007 **71** –: 6m 8.1d 10m² 11.9d² p11g* p12m⁶ 11.6d Oct 15] strong filly: fair handicapper: won at Kempton in September: stays 1½m: acts on polytrack, good to firm and good to soft ground. *S. C. Williams*

LITTLE CASCADE 2 b.f. (Mar 11) Forzando 122 – Dash Cascade (Absalom 128) **53** [2007 p5.1g⁴ p6g Sep 21] 2,000Y: eighth foal: half-sister to several winners, notably useful 6f (including at 2 yrs) winner Ingleton (by Komaite): dam unraced: modest form in seller and maiden at Wolverhampton. *E. S. McMahon*

LITTLE DARLIN 3 b.f. Mujahid (USA) 125 – Distant Cheers (USA) 77 (Distant **–** View (USA) 126) [2007 p12.2g 10d³ 12m⁴ 8m⁴ 8.3g 11.8d 8.2g⁶ p8.6g Nov 24] work-manlike filly: second foal: dam 8.5f winner: of no account. *G. J. Smith*

LITTLEDODAYNO (IRE) 4 b.f. Mujadil (USA) 119 – Perfect Welcome (Taufan **67** (USA) 119) [2007 79: p7.1g p6g p6g⁶ 5.5d 5.7m 5m 6f 6f⁴ 7d⁵ 6m p6g² p6g⁴ p6g² p6m* Nov 11] smallish, leggy, close-coupled filly: fair handicapper: won at Kempton in November: stays 7f: acts on polytrack and firm going: tried in cheekpieces: sometimes slowly away: held up. *M. Wigham*

LITTLE EDWARD 9 gr.g. King's Signet (USA) 110 – Cedar Lady (Telsmoss 91) **99** [2007 95: 5d⁶ 5m 5g 5g⁴ p6g* p6g² 5.7f* 5g 5.1m² 5g p6g³ p6g⁶ p6m p6m Dec 7] angular gelding: useful handicapper: won at Lingfield in August and Bath (beat Even Bolder by 2 lengths) in September: flattered when seventh to Maltese Falcon in listed race at Lingfield penultimate outing: best at stiff 5f/6f: acts on polytrack, firm and good to soft going: tried in cheekpieces: held up. *R. J. Hodges*

LITTLE EVIE 2 b.f. (May 12) First Trump 118 – Cedar Lady (Telsmoss 91) [2007 5.1f **50** 7m 5.7f⁴ p5.1g Oct 2] half-sister to 2 winners, notably 9-y-o Little Edward: dam, of little account, sister to smart sprinter Hard To Figure: modest maiden: will prove best at 5f/6f. *R. J. Hodges*

LITTLE FINCH (IRE) 2 b.f. (Mar 31) Acclamation 118 – Hard To Lay (IRE) 60 **44 §** (Dolphin Street (FR) 125) [2007 5m 5g⁶ 5m 6m* 5m 6m⁴ 6m⁵ 6g 6m⁵ 7g 5g p8.6g⁶ p6g² p6m p7g f5g Dec 27] strong filly: first foal: dam, maiden (stayed 1m), winning hurdler: poor performer: won seller at Catterick in May: stays 6f: acts on polytrack and good to firm going: tried visored, usually blinkered: untrustworthy (once veered and unseated rider). *R. C. Guest*

LITTLE FIRECRACKER 2 b.f. (Apr 18) Cadeaux Genereux 131 – El Hakma 94 **60** (Shareef Dancer (USA) 135) [2007 6d* p6g 6g⁶ 8m p6g⁵ p6d⁶ p7.1g³ p8.6d³ Dec 28] close-coupled filly: third foal: half-sister to fairly useful Irish 2006 2-y-o 7f/8.5f winner Porto Calero (by Tobougg) and 4-y-o High Seasons: dam, 1½m winner, sister to smart Italian performer up to 1¼m Snake Snap: modest performer: won seller at Thirsk (left G. M. Moore 10,000 gns) in June: left L. Cumani after fourth start: should be suited by 1m+: acts on polytrack and good to soft going. *Miss M. E. Rowland*

LITTLE HOTPOTCH 3 b.f. Erhaab (USA) 127 – Berzoud 69 (Ezzoud (IRE) 126) **–** [2007 –: 6d p10g Nov 12] smallish, good-bodied filly: little form: left J. Jenkins after reappearance. *M. J. Gingell*

LITTLE IRIS 3 ch.f. Inchinor 119 – Galanthus (USA) 59 (Rahy (USA) 115) [2007 **54** 50p: p7.1g 10s 8.5s⁶ Nov 3] quite good-topped filly: modest maiden: sold 800 gns from L. Cumani before final start: should be suited by 1¼m+. *J. Pubben, Holland*

LITTLE JIMBOB 6 b.g. Desert Story (IRE) 115 – Artistic Licence (High Top 131) **88** [2007 85, a77: p8.6g p10g⁶ 8m² 8m 9.3g* 9g² 9.8m 9.8m⁶ 9.9m² 9m² Sep 30] close- **a69 +** coupled gelding: fairly useful performer on turf, fair on all-weather: won claimer at Carlisle in June: stays 1¼m: acts on polytrack, firm and good to soft going: front runner: won over hurdles in October. *R. A. Fahey*

LITTLE KNICKERS 2 b.f. (Feb 19) Prince Sabo 123 – Pants 78 (Pivotal 124) [2007 **77** p5g⁶ 5.1g* 6d p6g p5m p6g⁵ Oct 17] compact filly: first foal: dam 7f winner: fair per-former: won maiden at Bath in July: left D. Ivory after fourth start: should prove best at 5f/easy 6f. *Andrew Reid*

LITTLE LILY MORGAN 4 gr.f. Kayf Tara 130 – Cool Grey 49 (Absalom 128) **–** [2007 –: f14g Jan 7] compact filly: poor maiden at 3 yrs: well held only start in 2007. *R. Bastiman*

LITTLE LOVELY (IRE) 2 ch.f. (Apr 18) Mizzen Mast (USA) 121 – Copper Play 59 (USA) (Fast Play (USA)) [2007 5.1g p5g³ Nov 15] €40,000Y: seventh foal: half-sister to several winners, including 5-y-o Play The Ball and 4-y-o Spell Casting: dam, US sprinter, half-sister to smart sprinter Tipsy Creek: modest form in maidens at Bath and Lingfield: likely to stay 7f/1m. *A. G. Newcombe*

LITTLEMADGEBOB 3 b.f. Primo Valentino (IRE) 116 – Midnight Orchid (IRE) 74 – (Petardia 113) [2007 –: f7g 5m 5m 6m Sep 1] little form: reportedly bled second start: tried blinkered. *J. R. Norton*

LITTLEMISSDYNAMITE 4 b.f. Observatory (USA) 131 – Once In My Life (IRE) 44 114 (Lomond (USA) 128) [2007 8d⁶ p10g 9g 7.6m⁵ p10g Oct 14] 10,000F, 2,500Y: half-sister to 1m winner Genius (by Lycius) and French 12.5f winner The Good Life (by Rainbow Quest): dam French 6.5f (at 2 yrs) and 1m (Prix de Sandringham) winner: poor maiden: left J. McAuley after fourth start: stays 7.5f. *S. W. Hall*

LITTLE MISS LILI 6 b.m. Danzig Connection (USA) – Little Miss Rocker 65 (Rock – Hopper 124) [2007 10.2f May 1] no form. *Miss Z. C. Davison*

LITTLEMISSSUNSHINE (IRE) 2 b.f. (Apr 24) Oasis Dream 129 – Sharp Catch 93 (IRE) 98 (Common Grounds 118) [2007 5m⁴ 5m² 5g² 5m⁶ 5m* 5g⁵ 5.2m 5d 5s⁵ Oct 22] €78,000F, 54,000Y: neat filly: fluent mover: fourth foal: half-sister to 6f winner Bohola Flyer (by Barathea), Irish 2004 2-y-o 7f winner Cappa Blanca (by Giant's Causeway) and 3-y-o Slate: dam, Irish 5f (at 2 yrs) and 1m winner, half-sister to smart sprinter Catch The Blues: fairly useful performer: won maiden at Folkestone in July: best form on starts either side, 1½ lengths sixth to Elletelle in Queen Mary Stakes at Royal Ascot and 5¼ lengths fifth to Fleeting Spirit in Molecomb Stakes at Goodwood: speedy, raced only at 5f: acts on good to firm and good to soft going: in cheekpieces last 5 starts. *J. S. Moore*

LITTLE MISS TARA (IRE) 3 b.f. Namid 128 – Circled (USA) 83 (Cozzene (USA)) 74 [2007 75: p8g⁵ 8.3m 10s 8g 10m³ 10d⁶ 9.9m⁶ 10.2m p8.6d p8.6g⁶ p10g* Dec 30] leggy filly: fair performer: won seller at Lingfield in December: stays 1¼m: acts on polytrack, firm and good to soft going: tried visored/blinkered. *A. B. Haynes*

LITTLE NIPPER 3 b.g. Conclude (USA) 107 – Emma May (Nicholas Bill 125) [2007 53 7m f8g⁶ 10.1m 7.5v² 9.8s⁶ 8.5s Jul 23] sturdy gelding: modest maiden: stays 7.5f: acts on fibresand and heavy ground: tried in cheekpieces/blinkered. *W. J. H. Ratcliffe*

LITTLE PASO (FR) 7 b.g. Jeune Homme (USA) 120 – Seguedille (FR) (Lou Piguet 51 (FR) 126) [2007 a6.5g⁵ a7.5g⁶ a6.5g³ a7g p7.1g p8.6g Jul 10] ex-French gelding: modest performer: won handicap at Pau in 2006 for D. Soubagne: left C. Gourdain before poor form in Britain last 2 starts: stays 1m: acts on all-weather: usually blinkered/visored. *B. N. Pollock*

LITTLE PETE (IRE) 2 ch.g. (May 2) City On A Hill (USA) 114 – Full Traceability 75 (IRE) 53 (Ron's Victory (USA) 129) [2007 5m p5g* 5.1m² 5m 5.1d⁵ Jun 30] lengthy gelding: fair performer: won maiden at Kempton in May: likely to prove best at 5f: acts on polytrack and good to firm going. *R. A. Farrant*

LITTLE RED ROASTER (USA) 3 b.f. Red Ransom (USA) – Pine Rob (USA) 41 (Pine Bluff (USA)) [2007 59: 7.6m⁶ 10m p12.2g Oct 12] $20,000Y: leggy filly: first foal: dam ran twice in USA: maiden: left C. Collins in Ireland after 2 yrs: just poor form in 2007. *P. D. Evans*

LITTLE RICHARD (IRE) 8 b.g. Alhaarth (IRE) 126 – Intricacy 65 (Formidable 68 (USA) 125) [2007 71: p13.9g² p13.9g f12g p12.2g p13.9g⁴ p12g⁶ p13.9g³ p12.2g⁵ p13.9d* p13.9g⁵ Dec 31] small, workmanlike gelding: fair handicapper: won at Wolverhampton in December: effective at 1½m to 16.5f: acts on all-weather and good to firm going: wears headgear: consistent. *M. Wellings*

LITTLE RUTLAND 3 ch.g. Mark of Esteem (IRE) 137 – Prickly Poppy 72 (Lear Fan – (USA) 130) [2007 55: 10.1g 9.9g Aug 15] maiden: no form in 2007. *E. J. O'Neill*

LITTLE TASK 9 b.g. Environment Friend 128 – Lucky Thing (Green Desert (USA) – 127) [2007 –: 12.1g Jun 20] smallish, close-coupled gelding: poor performer: lightly raced and no form on Flat since 2005: tried blinkered (not since 2001). *J. S. Wainwright*

LITTLE TINY TOM 3 b.g. Tobougg (IRE) 125 – Villa Del Sol 86 (Tagula (IRE) 116) – [2007 44: f7g p7.1g 8g 10.9s Jul 6] sturdy gelding: maiden: no form in 2007: usually in blinkers/cheekpieces. *C. N. Kellett*

LITTLETON ALDOR (IRE) 7 b.g. Pennekamp (USA) 130 – Belle Etoile (FR) 52 (Lead On Time (USA) 123) [2007 46: 10m 11.6d² 11.9m p12.2g⁶ Aug 13] modest maiden: should stay 1½m: acts on polytrack and good to soft ground. *Mark Gillard*

LITTLETON TELCHAR (USA) 7 ch.g. Atticus (USA) 121 – Miss Waikiki (USA) **74**
(Miswaki (USA) 124) [2007 89, a82: p7.1g p8g³ p7.1g⁵ 6g⁵ 8g Oct 29] quite good-topped
gelding: just fair handicapper in 2007: effective at 6f to 1¼m: acts on polytrack and firm
going: tried in cheekpieces. *S. W. Hall*

LITTLE TOTO 2 b.c. (Mar 19) Mtoto 134 – Moonlight Seas 36 (Sabrehill (USA) 120) **63**
[2007 5.7s 7g³ 7f 9s⁴ p8g Nov 7] neat colt: first foal: dam winning hurdler: modest
maiden: will be suited by 1¼m/1½m: acts on polytrack and soft going. *C. G. Cox*

LITTLE WHITE LIE (IRE) 3 b.g. Orpen (USA) 116 – Miss Informed (IRE) (Dane- **103**
hill (USA) 126) [2007 90: 7v* 7d² 7s⁵ 7s³ Aug 5] lengthy gelding: improved into a useful
handicapper, winning at the Curragh in March by 3 lengths from Out of The Red: good
placed efforts after at Epsom (length second to Vitznau) and Galway (¾-length third to
Hard Rock City): stays 7f: goes well on ground softer than good (acts on heavy): usually
races up with pace. *G. M. Lyons, Ireland*

LITTLE WING (IRE) 2 b.c. (Mar 7) Hawk Wing (USA) 136 – Hartstown House **66**
(IRE) 83 (Primo Dominie 121) [2007 6g 6m 5d⁶ Jul 26] €120,000F, €215,000Y: rather
leggy, useful-looking colt: third foal: half-brother to fairly useful Irish 2003 2-y-o 6f
winner Sheltingham (by Intikhab): dam, Irish 2-y-o 5f winner, half-sister to smart 7f/1m
winners Corinium and Fa-Eq: fair form in mid-field in maidens, not knocked about: will
be suited by 7f/1m. *J. A. Osborne*

LITTLE WISHES 4 b.f. Most Welcome 131 – Zac's Desire (Swing Easy (USA) 126) **–**
[2007 –: p13.9g Jan 27] neat filly: no form in maidens. *S. Parr*

LITTONFOUNTAIN (IRE) 2 b.g. (Mar 10) Desert Style (IRE) 121 – Idle Chat **–**
(USA) 93 (Assert 134) [2007 6d Oct 12] sturdy gelding: burly, detached in maiden at
York (gelded after). *K. R. Burke*

LITZINSKY 9 b.g. Muhtarram (USA) 125 – Boulevard Girl 80 (Nicholas Bill 125) **–**
[2007 f14g p16g May 2] rather leggy, lengthy gelding: fair in 2002, lightly raced and little
form since. *Mrs L. J. Young*

LIVALEX 3 b.f. Zamindar (USA) 116 – Evie Hone (IRE) 69 (Royal Academy (USA) **52**
130) [2007 50: 10.1m⁴ 7.5m 5.9m Jun 4] modest maiden, lightly raced: seems to stay
1¼m: acts on firm going. *M. Dods*

LIVIA (IRE) 6 b.m. Titus Livius (FR) 115 – Passing Beauty 83 (Green Desert (USA) **– §**
127) [2007 11.9m Aug 8] modest and unreliable maiden in 2004: no show on only Flat
start since: tried in headgear. *B. J. Llewellyn*

LIVING ON A PRAYER 4 b.f. Josr Algarhoud (IRE) 118 – Denton Lady 49 **60**
(Inchinor 119) [2007 –, a56: 14d² p16g⁵ 12g* p13.9g Dec 3] modest handicapper: left
M. McElhone, won amateur event at Musselburgh in November: stays 2m: acts on poly-
track and good to soft going. *T. McLaughlin, Ireland*

LIVVY INN (USA) 2 ch.c. (Feb 2) Woodman (USA) 126 – London Be Good (USA) **63**
76 (Storm Bird (CAN) 134) [2007 6g 8.3d⁶ 7.2g⁵ Aug 29] modest maiden: should stay
1m. *Miss Lucinda V. Russell*

LIZARAZU (GER) 8 b.g. Second Set (IRE) 127 – Lilly (GER) (Motley (USA) 123) **68 d**
[2007 82, a–: 6m 7.1m⁶ 7d 8m 8.1g 7.1s 8g⁴ 8g 6g⁵ 8.1m 7m p8g Sep 4] close-coupled **a–**
gelding: useful at best, very much on downgrade: effective at 6f, had form at 1¼m earlier
in career: acts on polytrack, firm and soft going: tried blinkered, usually wears
cheekpieces: sold £2,000. *R. A. Harris*

LIZARD ISLAND (USA) 2 b.c. (Apr 15) Danehill Dancer (IRE) 117 – Add (USA) **114**
(Spectacular Bid (USA)) [2007 6s² 6s* 7g² 7m⁴ 8d⁶ Sep 30] lengthy colt: unfurnished at
2 yrs: half-brother to several winners, notably smart 2005 Irish 2-y-o 7f winner (stays
1¼m) Arabian Prince (by Fusaichi Pegasus): dam, 6.5f to 1m winner in US, half-sister to
Grand Criterium winner Jade Robbery from excellent family of Nureyev and Sadler's
Wells: smart performer: won 4-runner Anheuser-Busch Adventure Parks Railway Stakes
at the Curragh (beat South Dakota by ¾ length) in July: ran well in Vintage Stakes at
Goodwood (2 lengths second to Rio de La Plata) and National Stakes at the Curragh (5
lengths fourth to New Approach): evens favourite, only sixth in Beresford Stakes at the
Curragh final start: should stay 1m: acts on soft and good to firm going: reportedly sold
privately, initially joined J. S. Moore and taken to UAE, then joined A. Manuel there.
A. P. O'Brien, Ireland

LIZ LONG 2 b.f. (Mar 28) Reel Buddy (USA) 118 – Surrealist (ITY) (Night Shift **45**
(USA)) [2007 6d 6f p6g⁶ p7.1g p6g⁶ Nov 6] 3,700Y: smallish filly: seventh foal: half-
sister to 3 winners, including fairly useful but unreliable 5f/6f (including at 2 yrs) winner

Mitsuki (by Puissance) and 4-y-o Crafty Fox: dam unraced half-sister to smart Italian sprinter Arranvanna: maiden: form (poor) only at 6f. *P. Howling*

LIZZIE ROCKET 7 gr.m. Paris House 123 – Jane's Affair (Alleging (USA) 120) [2007 –: p6g f6g f8g Mar 13] modest winner at 5 yrs: little form since: blinkered/visored. *J. O'Reilly* —

LLAB NALA 2 gr.g. (Feb 18) Tobougg (IRE) 125 – Zilkha 50 (Petong 126) [2007 7g 6d 5.7s 7m 5.1m* 6m³ 6m⁵ 5g p7g³ p7.1g⁵ 7g p7g⁴ p8m⁴ p8m³ Nov 24] strong gelding: modest performer: won seller at Bath in August: stays 1m: acts on polytrack and good to firm going: tried visored: ungenuine. *M. R. Channon* 57 §

LLAMADAS 5 b.g. Josr Algarhoud (IRE) 118 – Primulette 82 (Mummy's Pet 125) [2007 87: p12g p16g⁶ Jan 20] rather leggy, close-coupled gelding: fairly useful handicapper at 4 yrs: well held in 2007: has worn headgear. *C. Roberts* —

LLIZAAM 3 b.f. Foxhound (USA) 103 – Mazilla 59 (Mazilier (USA) 107) [2007 p9.5g p9.5g 10.5g Sep 12] smallish filly: second known foal: dam 7f to 11f winner: well held in maidens. *J. T. Stimpson* —

LOBBY 2 ch.c. (Feb 3) Dr Fong (USA) 128 – Real Trust (USA) (Danzig (USA)) [2007 7m⁵ 7d Jul 27] lengthy colt: first foal: dam, useful French maiden (best around 7f), half-sister to smart French performers Art Master (7f/1m) and Latent Heat (7f), out of US Grade 2 9f winner True Flare: fair form (but no threat) in maidens at Salisbury and Ascot. *Mrs A. J. Perrett* 68

LOBENGULA (IRE) 5 b.g. Spectrum (IRE) 126 – Playwaki (USA) (Miswaki (USA) 124) [2007 70, a67: p9.5g p9.5g* p10g⁵ p10g 8d 8s⁵ 8m⁵ 9.9d* 10m p9.5g³ p9.5g* p9.5g* p9.5g* p9.5g⁶ Dec 31] good-topped gelding: fairly useful handicapper: progressed well in 2007, winning at Wolverhampton in January, Beverley (amateurs) in September and Wolverhampton in October, November (2) and December: ran as if amiss final start: stays 10.5f: acts on polytrack, soft and firm ground: tried in cheekpieces: enthusiastic front runner. *I. W. McInnes* 94

*Anheuser-Busch Adventure Parks Railway Stakes, the Curragh—
a race run in driving rain but Lizard Island makes light of the conditions;
his stable-companion South Dakota (left) edges out Irish Jig for second*

LOCAL POET 6 b.g. Robellino (USA) 127 – Laugharne (Known Fact (USA) 135) **66**
[2007 82d: p7.1g p7.1g p7.1g[2] 7.1m 6g[5] 6f 6g[4] 6g[2] 6s[2] 8.3d[2] 6.9m 6s p7.1g p7.1g[6] p7.1g[6] **a74**
p8.6g[5] Nov 20] sturdy gelding: fair performer: stays 1m: acts on all-weather, soft and
good to firm going: has worn cheekpieces/tongue tie, usually blinkered: has joined Ollie
Pears. *I. Semple*

LOCH AWE 4 b.f. Inchinor 119 – Lochbelle 70 (Robellino (USA) 127) [2007 50: 10.1m **50**
14.1m[5] 12m Jun 6] big, close-coupled filly: modest maiden: seems to stay 1¼m: acts on
good to firm and good to soft going: tried in cheekpieces. *R. E. Barr*

LOCHIEL 3 b.g. Mind Games 121 – Summerhill Special (IRE) 80 (Roi Danzig (USA)) **74**
[2007 9.2d[4] 9.2d 11.1d[2] 12.4d[3] 12g[3] Nov 9] fair maiden: stays 1½m: raced only on good/
good to soft ground. *Mrs S. C. Bradburne*

LOCH JIPP (USA) 2 b.f. (Mar 13) Belong To Me (USA) – Miss Keyonna (USA) **95**
(Septieme Ciel (USA) 123) [2007 5m[5] 5g[6] 5g* 6g 6m[4] 6d[4] 6d 6d Oct 13] $27,000Y:
strong, workmanlike filly: has scope: fourth foal: half-sister to winners in US by Will's
Way and Sahm: dam unraced half-sister to US Grade 3 6f winner Willa On The Move:
useful performer: won maiden at Pontefract in April and listed event at Beverley (by
2½ lengths from only other rival to race stand side) in May: creditable fourth in
Cherry Hinton Stakes at Newmarket (1½ lengths behind You'resothrilling) and Princess
Margaret Stakes at Ascot (beaten 4¼ lengths by Visit): should prove best at 5f/6f: acts on
good to firm and good to soft going: races prominently: often hangs. *J. S. Wainwright*

LOCHSTAR 3 b.c. Anabaa (USA) 130 – Lochsong 129 (Song 132) [2007 5.1f[5] p6g* **91**
May 31] sixth foal: closely related to 4-y-o Loch Verdi and half-brother to useful 6f/7f
winner Lochridge (by Indian Ridge): dam, high-class sprinter, best at 5f: won maiden at
Lingfield in May by 1½ lengths fom Obstructive, travelling best and well on top at finish:
not seen out again: likely to prove best at 5f/6f. *A. M. Balding*

LOCH TAY 3 b.g. Cape Cross (IRE) 129 – Taysala (IRE) (Akarad (FR) 130) [2007 78: **66**
8.3m[6] 8.5g 8d Jun 22] leggy gelding: fair handicapper: stays 8.3f: sold 6,500 gns, won at
7f in Greece in November. *M. L. W. Bell*

LOCH VERDI 4 b.f. Green Desert (USA) 127 – Lochsong 129 (Song 132) [2007 95: **103**
5g[2] 5g 5m 5d 6m[4] 5.6m[4] 5f* 5g* 5m Oct 4] strong, smallish, lengthy filly: useful performer: won handicap at Folkestone and listed race at Hamilton (best effort when beating
Pivotal's Princess by length, racing alone towards stand-side rail), both in September:
all wins at 5f, has form at 6f: acts on firm and good to soft going: makes running.
A. M. Balding

LOCKERLEY MAN 4 b.g. Man Among Men (IRE) – Branston Lucy 65 (Prince Sabo **57**
123) [2007 p7g 8f[5] 10.2m 8f Jun 10] well held in bumpers: modest form in maidens first
2 starts on Flat: looks awkward. *W. S. Kittow*

LOCKSTOCK (IRE) 9 b.g. Inchinor 119 – Risalah (Marju (IRE) 127) [2007 69, a57: **53**
p9.5g f12g p9.5g 8.1m 8.1g 8f Jun 10] quite good-topped gelding: handicapper, modest
at best in 2007: stays easy 9.5f: acts on all-weather, heavy and good to firm going: usually
wears blinkers/cheekpieces: races prominently: none too reliable. *M. S. Saunders*

LOCUM 2 ch.g. (Mar 8) Dr Fong (USA) 128 – Exhibitor (USA) 68 (Royal Academy **66**
(USA) 130) [2007 5.2d 7.5g[5] p7m[2] Oct 3] 8,000F, 5,000Y: second foal: half-brother to
3-y-o Axiom: dam 1¼m winner: fair maiden: progressive form, runner-up at Kempton:
gelded after: will be suited by 1m/1¼m. *M. H. Tompkins*

LODI (IRE) 2 ch.g. (Mar 24) Bertolini (USA) 125 – Lady of Leisure (USA) 76 (Diesis **88 +**
133) [2007 7m[4] 7g[3] p6g* 6m 7g[5] Oct 27] strong, compact gelding: fifth foal: half-brother
to smart German sprinter Omasheriff (by Shinko Forest) and 1½m winner Dances With
Angels (by Mukaddamah): dam 1¼m winner: fairly useful form: won maiden at Kempton in September: did well from unfavourable draw when fifth to Kal Barg in nursery at
Doncaster final start: free-going sort, best up to 7f. *B. J. Meehan*

LOGSDAIL 7 b.g. Polish Precedent (USA) 131 – Logic 94 (Slip Anchor 136) [2007 78: **85**
7g 9g* 9m* 7.9d 9m p8g* p8g Sep 24] good-topped gelding: fairly useful performer: won
handicaps at Goodwood in May and June and claimer at Kempton in September: effective
at 1m/easy 1¼m: acts on polytrack, good to firm and good to soft going, probably on soft:
usually wears cheekpieces: patiently ridden. *G. L. Moore*

L'OISEAU DE FEU (USA) 3 b.g. Stravinsky (USA) 133 – Off You Go (USA) **78 d**
(Seattle Slew (USA)) [2007 78: p8g[2] p9.5g[3] p7g[6] 10.9m 8.1g p8.6g 10.9g Oct 2] good-
topped gelding: fair maiden at best: below form after reappearance, leaving E. Dunlop
following third start: stays 1m: acts on polytrack, raced only on good going or firmer on
turf: tried visored/in cheekpieces: one to treat with caution. *Mrs K. Waldron*

LONE WOLFE 3 b.c. Foxhound (USA) 103 – Fleet Hill (IRE) 99 (Warrshan (USA) **100** 117) [2007 p7g* 8.1g³ 7.1g³ 8m⁴ 7g² 8m³ 7m 7d Oct 19] 22,000F, €55,000Y: heavy-topped colt: fifth foal: half-brother to several winners, including smart 1m to 10.3f winner African Dream (by Mark of Esteem) and 4-y-o Cresta Gold: dam, 6f (at 2 yrs) to 9f (in US) winner: useful performer: won maiden at Kempton in January: better form after, including when second in handicap at Newmarket and when third to Vertigineux in listed race at Deauville sixth start: well below form last 2 starts: stays 1m: acts on polytrack and good to firm going. *Jane Chapple-Hyam*

LONG DISTANCE (FR) 2 b. or br.g. (Apr 13) Storming Home 128 – Lovers Luck **78** (IRE) (Anabaa (USA) 130) [2007 7g 7.5d² 8g² Oct 19] €50,000F, 50,000 2-y-o: leggy, useful-looking gelding: second foal: dam French 1¼m winner: fair form in maidens, second at Beverley and Redcar (gelded after): will stay 1¼m. *J. R. Fanshawe*

LONGEVITY 2 b.c. (Feb 16) Olden Times 121 – Gevity 76 (Kris 135) [2007 8d 7g Oct **68** 26] big, good-topped colt: third foal: dam, 8.5f winner, half-sister to useful performers Shaindy (sprinter), Fast Manouvre (at 1¼m) and Cephalonia (stayer): fair form towards rear in maidens at Newbury and Doncaster. *W. Jarvis*

LONG GONE 4 b.f. Mtoto 134 – Absentee 66 (Slip Anchor 136) [2007 10g 10s 11.8d⁴ – 14.1d 11.8g f11d Dec 20] close-coupled filly: second foal: dam unreliable 1¾m winner: little sign of ability: in cheekpieces last 4 starts. *John A. Harris*

LONGHILL TIGER 4 b.c. Tiger Hill (IRE) 127 – Lauren (GER) (Lightning (FR) **64** 129) [2007 83: 10.1m³ p16g 11.8m p12g³ 12d 11.5d Jul 5] strong colt: just modest maiden nowadays: stays easy 1½m: acts on polytrack and firm going: joined E. Kurdu, Germany. *G. G. Margarson*

LONGORIA (IRE) 2 b. or br.f. (Jan 20) Fasliyev (USA) 120 – Shangri La (IRE) 97 **70** (Sadler's Wells (USA) 132) [2007 5m 5m 5.2g* 5m³ 5.3f⁴ 6g⁶ 6g p5.1g⁶ f6d* p7.1g² Dec 29] leggy filly: first foal: dam, Irish maiden (best at 7f), half-sister to smart Scandinavian sprinter Hanzano out of sister to Irish 1000 Guineas winner Trusted Partner: fair performer: won seller at Yarmouth in May and claimer at Southwell in December: stays 7f: acts on all-weather and firm going. *M. G. Quinlan*

LONGQUAN (IRE) 3 b.g. Invincible Spirit (IRE) 121 – Pipers Pool (IRE) 94 (Mtoto **102** 134) [2007 92: 6g* 6m 6g Aug 3] strong, close-coupled gelding: useful handicapper: gelded, improved when winning at Newmarket (beat by 3 lengths from Luscivious) in May: just respectable efforts after, racing too freely second start: will prove best at 5f/6f: raced only on good/good to firm going: sent to Hong Kong, where renamed Win-A-Lot. *P. J. Makin*

LONGSPUR 3 br.g. Singspiel (IRE) 133 – Bunting 102 (Shaadi (USA) 126) [2007 10d³ **87** 12m² p12g* Aug 29] tall, good sort: has plenty of scope: half-brother to several winners, including 1m (at 2 yrs) and 1¼m winner Mot Juste (by Mtoto) and 6f (at 2 yrs) and 1¼m (including in UAE) winner Parasol (by Halling), both smart: dam 1m (at 2 yrs)/1¼m winner: fairly useful performer: won maiden at Kempton in August all out by neck from Tropical Strait: stays 1½m: sold 72,000 gns, and gelded. *Saeed bin Suroor*

LONGY THE LASH 4 b.g. Contract Law (USA) 108 – Hello Hobson's (IRE) 67 – (Fayruz 116) [2007 –: 8g Nov 8] sturdy gelding: no sign of ability. *Paul Murphy*

LOOK BUSY (IRE) 2 b.f. (Mar 9) Danetime (IRE) 121 – Unfortunate 55§ (Komaite **95** (USA)) [2007 5g 5m⁴ 5.1f² 5s³ 5.1d³ 5m* 5m* 5m² 6.1m⁴ 5d² 6d³ 6g⁵ Oct 27] €7,500Y: sturdy filly: third foal: sister to 4-y-o The City Kid and half-sister to winner in Greece by Raise A Grand: dam untrustworthy 6f winner, including at 2 yrs: useful performer: won maiden at Musselburgh in July and nursery at Thirsk in August: held form well after, placed 4 times including in listed races at Ayr (second to Captain Gerrard) and York (third to Max One Two Three) eleventh/twelfth starts: effective at 6f, but may prove best at 5f: acts on good to firm and good to soft going: usually races up with pace: has been slowly away: tough. *A. Berry*

LOOKER 4 b.f. Barathea (IRE) 127 – Last Look (Rainbow Quest (USA) 134) [2007 – 71: p9.5g 10d Oct 11] leggy filly: fair performer at 2/3 yrs: well below form in 2007. *J. Gallagher*

LOOK FAR 3 ch.f. Observatory (USA) 131 – Marani 106 (Ashkalani (IRE) 128) [2007 **71** p9.5g³ Aug 12] 5,000 2-y-o: first foal: dam 9f/1½m winner: 50/1 and green, 1¼ lengths third to Salsa Verdi in maiden at Wolverhampton: dead. *N. J. Vaughan*

LOOK HERE 2 b.f. (Feb 28) Hernando (FR) 127 – Last Look (Rainbow Quest (USA) **84 p** 134) [2007 8d* Oct 3] lengthy, angular filly: half-sister to several winners, including 5-y-o Daniel Thomas and 3-y-o Look So: dam unraced out of half-sister to Pursuit of

Love: 16/1, won maiden at Salisbury in good style by 2½ lengths from Doctor Fremantle: will stay 1¼m: should make a useful 3-y-o. *R. M. Beckett*

LOOK OF EAGLES 5 b.m. Fraam 114 – Dreamtime Quest (Blakeney 126) [2007 –, **65** a71: p8g p10g² Jul 28] fair handicapper: left P. Cole after reappearance: stays 1¼m: acts on all-weather and firm going: blinkered (well held) once. *C. J. Mann*

LOOKS COULD KILL (USA) 5 b. or br.g. Red Ransom (USA) – Mingling Glances **74 §** (USA) 106 (Woodman (USA) 126) [2007 85§: 7d 7m 7d² 6s* 6s p7g⁶ p7.1g 6v² p7g⁶ p7g Nov 19] good-topped gelding: just fair nowadays: won claimer at Ripon (left E. Alston) in June: effective at 5f to 1m: acts on polytrack, heavy and good to firm going: tried blinkered/in cheekpieces/tongue tied: sometimes sweats: often slowly away: usually held up: tends to find little. *A. B. Haynes*

LOOK SO 3 b.f. Efisio 120 – Last Look (Rainbow Quest (USA) 134) [2007 p8g 7g* 7s* **81** 7.1d 7m 8.9v⁵ Jul 26] lengthy filly: sixth foal: half-sister to several winners, including useful 1¼m winner Look Again (stays 1½m, by Zilzal): dam unraced out of half-sister to Pursuit of Love: fairly useful performer: won maiden at Newbury (100/1) in May and handicap at Leicester in June: below form after: bred to stay 1m: acts on soft going. *R. M. Beckett*

LOOKS THE BUSINESS (IRE) 6 b.g. Marju (IRE) 127 – Business Centre (IRE) 58 **70** (Digamist (USA) 110) [2007 69: 11.5d⁶ p12.2g⁶ p12g² Aug 28] workmanlike gelding: fair performer: stays 1½m: acts on polytrack and firm going: has worn cheekpieces: tongue tied in 2003/4. *W. G. M. Turner*

LOOKTHEOTHERWAY (IRE) 3 br.f. Val Royal (FR) 127 – Gold Stamp (Golden **63** Act (USA) [2007 10m⁵ 12.1s 10d⁵ 14m⁶ Sep 1] angular filly: half-sister to several winners, including fairly useful 11f/1½m winner Brad's House (by Rossini): dam unraced half-sister to Nell Gwyn Stakes winner Reunion: modest maiden: stays 1¼m: acts on good to firm and good to soft ground. *J. G. M. O'Shea*

LOOSE CABOOSE (IRE) 2 b.f. (Apr 27) Tagula (IRE) 116 – Tama (IRE) 58 (Indian **68** Ridge 123) [2007 6d p7.1g 7g p6m* p7g⁵ p6g² 6d² p6g⁴ p5.1g⁵ 5.1g⁵ Nov 7] 900 2-y-o: first foal: dam, maiden (stayed 7.5f), out of half-sister to Yorkshire Oaks winner Catchas-catchcan: fair performer: won seller at Lingfield in August and nursery at Wolverhampton in November: best at 5f/6f: acts on polytrack and good to soft going: often wears cheekpieces, as good without. *A. J. McCabe*

LOOTER (FR) 2 b.g. (Feb 26) Red Ransom (USA) – Water Echo (USA) 79 (Mr **60** Prospector (USA)) [2007 7d 7m⁵ 8.3m⁶ Oct 8] €50,000Y: close-coupled, quite attractive gelding: second foal: half-brother to winning US sprinter by War Chant: dam, 2-y-o 6f winner, closely related to useful 2-y-o 6f winner Enthused, out of Coronation Stakes winner Magic of Life: modest form in maidens (subsequently gelded): should prove best up to 1m. *J. L. Dunlop*

LOPINOT (IRE) 4 br.g. Pursuit of Love 124 – La Suquet 72 (Puissance 110) [2007 80: **77** p7g² p7g* p8g* p8g* p8g 8g 8m 7m 8.3m p8g p8g Dec 30] robust gelding: fairly useful **a87** performer on all-weather, fair on turf: won maiden at Kempton (despite hanging markedly left) in January and handicaps at Lingfield (2) in March: left P. Makin after ninth start: stays 1m: acts on polytrack and good to firm going: usually races prominently. *M. R. Bosley*

L'ORAGE 2 b.f. (Jan 25) Storming Home 128 – Rosa Canina 91 (Bustino 136) [2007 **–** 5m 6s 7s Aug 24] 3,000Y: tall, leggy filly: fifth foal: half-sister to 5-y-o Thorny Mandate: dam, 1¾m to 2¼m winner, half-sister to useful 1m (at 2 yrs) to 1¼m winner Golden Sparrow: no form (made debut in Queen Mary Stakes). *J. Ryan*

LORD ADMIRAL (USA) 6 b.h. El Prado (IRE) 119 – Lady Ilsley (USA) (Trempo- **113** lino (USA) 135) [2007 115: 8g⁶ 9g⁶ 8g² 8m² 7m⁵ 7g* 10s³ 8d⁴ 8m³ 10g² 7m* Nov 4] rather leggy, close-coupled, quite attractive horse: smart performer: won Ballycorus Stakes (by head from Modeeroch) in June and listed race (by length from Excelerate) in November, both at Leopardstown: also creditable efforts when placed on same course in Amethyst Stakes (to Danak) and Meld Stakes (behind Fracas) and at the Curragh in Solonaway Stakes (to Jumbajukiba) fourth/seventh/ninth starts: effective at 7f to 1¼m: acts on firm and soft going: effective blinkered or not. *Charles O'Brien, Ireland*

LORD ADONIS (IRE) 4 b.g. Galileo (IRE) 134 – Flaming June (USA) 69 (Storm **–** Bird (CAN) 134) [2007 –: p12.2s Dec 21] good-bodied gelding: little form on Flat: tried tongue tied. *S. A. Brookshaw*

LORD BLUE BOY 3 gr.g. Atraf 116 – Flair Lady 55 (Chilibang 120) [2007 51: 7d –
p5.1g Aug 30] tall, lengthy gelding: maiden: well held in sellers in 2007: tried blinkered/
visored. *W. G. M. Turner*

LORD CHAMBERLAIN 14 b.g. Be My Chief (USA) 122 – Metaphysique (FR) **49**
(Law Society (USA) 130) [2007 68, a74: p7.1g p8.6g p9.5g p7.1g p7.1g p8g 8f Apr 24]
big gelding: just poor nowadays: effective at 7f to easy 9.5f: acts on all-weather and any
turf going: blinkered: sometimes slowly away: usually held up. *J. M. Bradley*

LORD CONYERS (IRE) 8 b.m. Inzar (USA) 112 – Primelta 55 (Primo Dominie 121) –
[2007 –: 6s 9m 7m Sep 6] leggy mare: little form since 2005: tried in headgear.
G. Woodward

LORD DEEVERT 2 br.g. (Feb 28) Averti (IRE) 117 – Dee-Lady 93 (Deploy 131) **64**
[2007 p5g 5.2m 5.3m⁴ 6s³ p5g* p5m³ p5g p6g* p6g p7g⁴ p6g 8.2g² p7.1g f7d³
p7.1g³ Dec 29] strong gelding: modest performer: won seller at Lingfield in June and
claimer at Wolverhampton in August: barely stays 1m: acts on polytrack, soft and good
to firm going: tried in cheekpieces/visor: takes strong hold (saddle slipped twice).
W. G. M. Turner

LORD DU SUD (FR) 6 gr.h. Linamix (FR) 127 – Marseillaise (FR) (Esprit du Nord **119**
(USA) 126) [2007 116: 12.5d⁴ 15.5s* 20g⁶ 15d² 15.5m Oct 28] leggy, angular horse:
smart performer: won Prix Vicomtesse Vigier at Longchamp in May by 2½ lengths from
Ponte Tresa: easily best effort afterwards when ½-length second to Getaway in Prix
Kergorlay at Deauville: below-form sixth to Yeats in Gold Cup at Royal Ascot in between
and well held in Prix Royal-Oak at Longchamp final outing: stayed 15.5f: went well on
soft/heavy going: sometimes wore cheekpieces: usually made running: to stand at Haras
d'Etreham, France, fee €3,000. *J-C. Rouget, France*

LORD LAING (USA) 4 br.g. Chester House (USA) 123 – Johanna Keene (USA) **61**
(Raise A Cup (USA)) [2007 64: p12g⁴ p12g p12.2g 14.1m 10g p12g⁵ p12g⁶ p12.2g*
p11g Nov 28] workmanlike gelding: modest handicapper: won at Wolverhampton in
November: stays 1½m: acts on polytrack: tried visored: said to have coughed after final
outing. *H. J. Collingridge*

LORD MAYOR 6 b.g. Machiavellian (USA) 123 – Misleading Lady (Warning 136) –
[2007 96d: p12.2g Jan 29] quite good-topped gelding: useful performer in 2005: was on
downgrade: wore cheekpieces once in 2006: dead. *B. N. Pollock*

LORD NELLSSON 11 b.g. Arctic Lord 114 – Miss Petronella (Petoski 135) [2007 **57**
p16.5g p16.5g⁶ 17.2f⁴ 17.2m 17.2f³ p16.5g⁶ Jul 27] modest handicapper: stays 2¼m: acts
on firm and good to soft going: tried blinkered: inconsistent. *Andrew Turnell*

LORD OF DREAMS (IRE) 5 ch.g. Barathea (IRE) 127 – The Multiyorker (IRE) 72 –
(Digamist (USA) 110) [2007 73: p9.5g³ p9.5g⁴ p9.5g⁴ 8d p8.6g² p8.6g p8.6g⁴ p8.6g⁴ **a73**
p10g⁴ p10g* p11m³ p9.5g⁵ Nov 16] tall, strong gelding: fair performer: left D. Arbuthnot
prior to winning seller at Lingfield in September: barely stays easy 11f: acts on polytrack
and soft going, seemingly not on firmer than good: tried in cheekpieces/blinkers: held up.
G. L. Moore

LORD OF ESTEEM 2 ch.c. (Jan 30) Mark of Esteem (IRE) 137 – Lady Rockstar 90 **50**
(Rock Hopper 124) [2007 7m p8g⁴ 8m 7d Oct 29] close-coupled, good-bodied colt:
modest maiden: stays 1m: best effort on polytrack. *J. Ryan*

LORD OF THE EAST 8 b.g. Emarati (USA) 74 – Fairy Free (Rousillon (USA) 133) – §
[2007 89§, a81§: p7.1g 6m Aug 27] lengthy gelding: inconsistent and temperamental
handicapper: no form at 8 yrs: tried tongue tied/blinkered/in cheekpieces (not after 2003):
dead. *I. W. McInnes*

LORD OF THE LAKE 3 b.g. Lake Coniston (IRE) 131 – Loriner's Lass 80 (Sad- –
dlers' Hall (IRE) 126) [2007 10m p12.2g Nov 9] workmanlike gelding: well held in
maidens. *P. J. McBride*

LORD OF THE REINS (IRE) 3 b.g. Imperial Ballet (IRE) 110 – Waroonga (IRE) **76**
(Brief Truce (USA) 126) [2007 f6g 5.1m p6g³ 5d 5s* 5d⁵ p6g* p6g* p6g³ p6g² p5.1g³
p6g p6g Dec 29] good-topped gelding: fair performer: won maiden at Leicester in July,
and handicaps at Lingfield in August and September: stays 6f: acts on polytrack and soft
going: held up: consistent. *D. Shaw*

LORD OF THE WING 2 b.c. (Apr 9) Daggers Drawn (USA) 114 – Brangane (IRE) **57 d**
(Anita's Prince 126) [2007 5.1f 5m⁴ 5.1g⁵ p6g 5.3f 6.1d 6s 5g p6g p8.6g p8.6d Dec 10]
neat colt: maiden: little form after third outing, leaving R. Beckett after sixth: best efforts
at 5f: tried blinkered/in cheekpieces. *P. T. Midgley*

LORD OROKO 3 ch.g. Lord of Men 116 – Wannaplantatree 72 (Niniski (USA) 125) **81** [2007 72: p9.5g 10s⁴ 12m 13.1f* 16m² 17.2g² 16g³ Nov 2] rather leggy, quite attractive gelding: fairly useful handicapper: left K. Ryan after reappearance: won amateur maiden event at Bath in September: stays 2m: acts on all-weather, firm and soft going: sometimes races freely: held up. *J. G. M. O'Shea*

LORD ORPEN (IRE) 3 b.g. Orpen (USA) 116 – Kenyane (IRE) 82 (Kahyasi 130) **51** [2007 –: f8g 10s 8m 8d 12.5m 12m Sep 4] modest form: well held at Southwell on reappearance: sometimes blinkered. *Patrick Morris, Ireland*

LORD ORPHEUS 3 b.g. Auction House (USA) 120 – Lady of The Realm (Prince **–** Daniel (USA)) [2007 –: p6g 8.8g 8s Nov 4] tall, close-coupled gelding: little sign of ability: sold 800 gns from B. Hills after reappearance. *Patrick Morris, Ireland*

LORD PETER FLINT (IRE) 2 b.c. (Apr 7) Cadeaux Genereux 131 – Bibi Karam **81** (IRE) 104 (Persian Bold 123) [2007 7s⁵ 7m² 7.1g* Oct 2] €90,000Y: strong, well-made colt: second foal: half-brother to fairly useful Irish 1¼m/11f winner Bold Bibi (by Hernando): dam Irish 1m winner: fairly useful form: shaped well at Newmarket and Newbury prior to winning maiden at Warwick (made all to beat Detonator by 1½ lengths): will stay 1m: acts on soft and good to firm going: joined A. Schutz in Hong Kong, where renamed Noble de Best. *B. J. Meehan*

LORD SANDICLIFFE (IRE) 2 ch.c. (Mar 16) Spartacus (IRE) 107 – Devious Miss **86** (IRE) (Dr Devious (IRE) 127) [2007 6m⁶ 6.1m⁶ 6.1d² 6d* Oct 29] 26,000Y: compact colt: second foal: dam, of no account in Ireland, half-sister to useful Irish 7f performer Little White Lie: fairly useful form: progressive in maidens, won at Leicester by neck from Alwaabel (pair clear): likely to stay 7f/1m. *B. W. Hills*

LORD'S BIDDING 2 b.c. (Apr 25) Auction House (USA) 120 – Lady Ploy 42 **58** (Deploy 131) [2007 5m 7g p7m p10g p8m² p9.5g Nov 17] lengthy colt: modest maiden: runner-up in nursery at Kempton: stays 1m: acts on polytrack: blinkered last 2 starts. *R. Ingram*

LORDSHIP (IRE) 3 b.g. King's Best (USA) 132 – Rahika Rose 91 (Unfuwain (USA) **74** 131) [2007 59: 7.1d 8f 8.1d² 7d³ 7.1g* 8.1v³ 8m 8.3d 7g³ 7s* 7.1m 8.5d 7d⁶ 7g⁶ 8g Nov 2] sturdy, close-coupled gelding: fair handicapper: won at Warwick in July and Folkestone in August: best at 7f: acts on heavy going, below form on firmer than good: headstrong. *A. W. Carroll*

LORD SNOOTY (IRE) 2 b.c. (Mar 30) Traditionally (USA) 117 – Actualite (Polish **68 p** Precedent (USA) 131) [2007 6m Sep 21] 15,000F, 42,000Y: strong colt: eighth foal: half-brother to several winners, including smart 1m (at 2 yrs)/1¼m winner Shamrock City (by Rock City) and 7-y-o Ali Bruce: dam French 10.5f winner: 11/4, seventh in maiden at Newmarket (broke blood vessel): will stay 1m: sent to USA: capable of better. *P. W. Chapple-Hyam*

LORDSWOOD (IRE) 3 b.g. Mark of Esteem (IRE) 137 – Dinwood (Charnwood **55** Forest (IRE) 125) [2007 67: p7g³ p7g p10g p7g 7g 8m 6s⁶ 6m⁶ 7f 8f p7g p10g⁶ p10g⁶ p10g⁵ p11g Nov 21] rangy gelding: modest performer: left A. Balding after reappearance: seems to stay easy 1¼m: acts on polytrack. *J. J. Bridger*

LORD THEO 3 b.g. Averti (IRE) 117 – Love You Too 88 (Be My Chief (USA) 122) **82** [2007 84: 6m 7.1m* p7g⁶ 6m⁴ 6g 6m⁶ 7d⁶ 10.5g³ 8.3m² 8.5d p8.6g³ Oct 8] tall, close-coupled gelding: fairly useful handicapper: won at Warwick in May: stays 8.6f: acts on polytrack and good to firm going, probably on good to soft. *N. P. Littmoden*

LORIKEET 8 b.g. Rainbow Quest (USA) 134 – Destiny Dance (USA) 100 (Nijinsky **77** (CAN) 138) [2007 –: p13g* p12g³ p16g* p16g³ p16f² p16g* 17.2f³ p10m⁵ Dec 8] ex-Irish gelding: fair handicapper: won at Lingfield in January (2) and March: stays easy 17f: acts on polytrack and firm ground: tried in cheekpieces/blinkers. *Noel T. Chance*

LOS NADIS (GER) 3 b.g. Hernando (FR) 127 – La Estrella (GER) (Desert King (IRE) **84** 129) [2007 9.5v² 9.8m 12m* 11s 13s 13.1s⁶ 16g³ Nov 8] first foal: dam, German 1m winner, half-sister to Deutsches Derby winner Lavirco: won maiden at Vannes in May: left E. Libaud in France after next start: fairly useful form in handicaps in Britain: may prove best at short of 2m: acts on heavy and good to firm ground: blinkered third/fourth starts: fairly useful juvenile hurdler. *P. Monteith*

LOST ALL ALONE 3 b.c. Bertolini (USA) 125 – Wandering Stranger 69 (Petong **58** 126) [2007 –: p7.1g p6g² 6m³ 7d 6g⁵ p7g⁶ p6m* Nov 24] modest handicapper: won at Lingfield in November: best form at 6f: acts on polytrack and good to firm going. *D. M. Simcock*

LOST IN WONDER (USA) 3 b.f. Galileo (IRE) 134 – Arutua (USA) (Riverman **88**
(USA) 131) [2007 82p: 11.4m 9.9g⁴ 12g Jun 21] strong, good-bodied filly: fairly useful
performer: best effort when fourth to Cosmodrome in listed race at Goodwood: visored,
well held in Ribblesdale Stakes at Royal Ascot next time: stays 1¼m: temperament under
suspicion. *Sir Michael Stoute*

LOST SOLDIER THREE (IRE) 6 b.g. Barathea (IRE) 127 – Donya 74 (Mill Reef **111**
(USA) 141) [2007 114: 9g⁵ 12g 10g 12g⁶ 12g³ Mar 1] close-coupled gelding: smart
performer: easily best effort at Nad Al Sheba in 2007 when 3¾ lengths third to Quijano in
Dubai City of Gold Stakes, dictating: stays 2m: acts on firm and soft going: tried visored:
usually waited with. *D. Nicholls*

LOUGH NEAGH (USA) 4 b.g. Giant's Causeway (USA) 132 – Saytarra (USA) 111 **62**
(Seeking The Gold (USA)) [2007 p8g⁵ p8g⁵ p7f p8g 8d May 30] sold (unraced) from
Saeed bin Suroor 1,500 gns in 2006: modest maiden: tried blinkered: sent to Bahrain.
Miss D. Mountain

LOUISIADE (IRE) 6 b.g. Tagula (IRE) 116 – Titchwell Lass 57 (Lead On Time (USA) **68**
123) [2007 57, a71: f8g⁴ p7.1g p7.1g² p7.1g* f7g* p8g⁵ f7g* 7g⁵ p8.6g* f8d Dec 20]
strong, lengthy gelding: fair performer: won sellers at Wolverhampton and Southwell in
February, handicap at Southwell in March and claimer (amateurs) at Wolverhampton (left
K. Ryan after) in April: effective at 6f to 8.6f: acts on all-weather and firm ground: tried
blinkered/tongue tied, usually wears cheekpieces. *John A. Harris*

LOUIS SEFFENS (USA) 2 b.c. (Apr 23) Elusive Quality (USA) – Miss Seffens **80 p**
(USA) (Dehere (USA) 121) [2007 7g² Oct 26] $50,000Y, resold 30,000Y, 40,000 2-y-o:
close-coupled colt: second foal: dam US sprint winner (including minor stakes and at
2 yrs): 10/1, encouraging neck second to Naval Review in maiden at Doncaster, finishing
strongly: will stay 1m: should do better. *G. A. Swinbank*

LOULWA (IRE) 3 b.f. Montjeu (IRE) 137 – Refined (IRE) 95 (Statoblest 120) [2007 **103**
82p: 10m⁴ 12s² 11.1d* 12s p13m* Nov 1] good-bodied filly: useful performer: won
maiden at Hamilton in July and listed race at Lingfield (beat Market Forces by ¾ length)
in November: respectable seventh to Trick Or Treat in Princess Royal Stakes at Ascot in
between: likely to be suited by 1¾m+: acts on polytrack and soft ground: tongue tied.
J. Noseda

LOUPHOLE 5 ch.g. Loup Sauvage (USA) 125 – Goodwood Lass (IRE) 71 (Alzao **82**
(USA) 117) [2007 77: p6g* p6g* p6g⁶ 6m⁶ 6m⁴ p6g² 6d⁴ p6g 6m⁵ p6g⁵ Nov 10] close-
coupled gelding: fairly useful handicapper: won at Kempton in January and Lingfield
in February: has form at easy 1m, better at shorter: acts on polytrack and firm going.
P. J. Makin

LOUVIERE 3 b.f. Alhaarth (IRE) 126 – Binche (USA) 51 (Woodman (USA) 126) **80**
[2007 10m³ 12s² 10.9g³ 11.7d⁴ 14g⁵ p13.9g p10m Oct 6] lengthy, good-topped filly: first
foal: dam twice-raced half-sister to smart performers up to 1¼m Binary File and Hawksbill, out of useful French/US 9f/1¼m winner Binary: fairly useful maiden: probably
stayed 1¾m: acted on soft and good to firm going: visored (well below form) last 2 starts:
stud. *Pat Eddery*

LOVE ALWAYS 5 b.m. Piccolo 121 – Lady Isabell 62 (Rambo Dancer (CAN) 107) **79**
[2007 81: 12g* 11.7f² 12d 11.6m 12m² 14m³ 12m 12d⁴ 10.9m 12m² 11.5g 14.1d Oct 3]
tall, good-bodied mare: fair handicapper: won at Folkestone in April: barely stays 1¾m:
acts on firm and good to soft going. *S. Dow*

LOVE AND AFFECTION 4 b.g. Groom Dancer (USA) 128 – Fox Star (IRE) 61 **–**
(Foxhound (USA) 103) [2007 –: 12d 8d 10.1f Jul 30] little form: left P. McEntee after
second start: tongue tied since second.3-y-o outing. *Miss K. B. Boutflower*

LOVE AND GLORY (FR) 2 b.c. (May 11) Intikhab (USA) 135 – La Splendide (FR) **56 p**
(Slip Anchor 136) [2007 5.1g p6g⁶ p5g Nov 15] €50,000Y: half-brother to several
winners, including 1m winner Le Fantasme (by Fairy King) and useful French performer
up to 15f Le Nomade (by Nashwan): dam, French 15f winner, half-sister to Japan Cup
winner Le Glorieux: faced seemingly inadequate tests in maidens, modest form when
seventh at Lingfield final start: will do better at 1m+. *G. L. Moore*

LOVE ANGEL (USA) 5 b. or br.g. Woodman (USA) 126 – Omnia (USA) 85 (Green **56**
Dancer (USA) 132) [2007 68: p16g p16g 17.2m May 21] good-topped gelding: just
modest handicapper nowadays: seems to stay easy 2m: acts on polytrack and any turf
going: tried blinkered/visored: fair hurdler. *J. J. Bridger*

LOVE BROTHERS 3 b.g. Lomitas 129 – Morning Queen (GER) (Konigsstuhl **80**
(GER)) [2007 76: p10g 10.9m² 12m³ 12g p10g 11.7m* 12g 12m⁶ p16g³ 12.1g⁶ 16m⁵

18m* 18m Oct 22] tall, angular gelding: fairly useful performer: won apprentice handicap at Bath in August and minor event at Pontefract in October: stays 2¼m: acts on polytrack, heavy and good to firm going: sold 50,000 gns. *M. R. Channon*

LOVE CAT (USA) 2 b. or br.g. (Feb 1) Stormin Fever (USA) 116 – Remuda (USA) (Gilded Time (USA)) [2007 7m 7.1g 7g Oct 26] unfurnished gelding: looked weak at 2 yrs, well held in maidens (seemingly modest form final start): subsequently gelded. *K. A. Ryan* **56 ?**

LOVE DANCER (IRE) 2 b.g. (Mar 8) Fasliyev (USA) 120 – L'Amour (USA) 81 (Gone West (USA)) [2007 6m 7m 6d 8.2d Oct 10] well-made gelding: little form in maidens. *M. L. W. Bell* **–**

LOVE DUBAI (USA) 3 b. or br.c. E Dubai (USA) 124 – Omnia (USA) 85 (Green Dancer (USA) 132) [2007 94: p10g* a9f p9f 9.5f⁵ 10f 10d⁵ 9f 9f³ 14f Dec 9] close-coupled, useful-looking colt: useful performer: won handicap at Lingfield in January (left M. Johnston since): at least respectable efforts in varied company in US, including when fifth in Secretariat Stakes at Arlington (9 lengths behind Shamdinan) on sixth start: stays 1¼m: acts on polytrack, firm and good to soft going: blinkered nowadays. *M. J. Maker, USA* **96**

LOVE EMPIRE (USA) 2 b.c. (Apr 6) Empire Maker (USA) 129 – Gioconda (USA) (Nijinsky (CAN) 138) [2007 p8m f8d Dec 15] $120,000Y: half-brother to several winners, notably very smart 1m (Grand Criterium at 2 yrs) to 1½m (US Grade 1) winner Ciro (by Woodman): dam, French 1m winner, half-sister to Bosra Sham and Hector Protector: well held in maidens at Lingfield and Southwell. *M. Johnston* **–**

LOVE GALORE (IRE) 2 b.c. (Apr 10) Galileo (IRE) 134 – Lobmille (Mill Reef (USA) 141) [2007 8m⁴ 8.3g* Sep 23] good-topped colt: closely related to 2 winners by Barathea, including useful French 11f/1½m winner Lyndaar, and half-brother to several winners, notably smart French miler Lone Bid (by Priolo): dam unraced: fairly useful form: confirmed promise from Newbury (fourth to Alfathaa) when winning maiden at Hamilton by 6 lengths: will be suited by 1¼m/1½m: will go on improving. *M. Johnston* **92 p**

LOVEINANELEVATOR 2 ch.f. (Apr 16) Dr Fong (USA) 128 – Londonnetdotcom (IRE) 101 (Night Shift (USA)) [2007 6g May 18] 80,000Y: strong filly: first foal: dam, 7f (at 2 yrs)/1m winner, out of close relative to very smart 7f/1m winner Greensmith: 8/1, very green in maiden at Newmarket (seventh of 8): not seen out again. *M. L. W. Bell* **53**

LOVE IN MAY (IRE) 3 ch.f. City On A Hill (USA) 114 – May Hinton 82 (Main Reef 126) [2007 78: p6g² p6g³ Feb 7] strong, useful-looking filly: fairly useful performer: stays 6f: best efforts on polytrack: consistent. *J. S. Moore* **80**

LOVELACE 3 b.c. Royal Applause 124 – Loveleaves 93 (Polar Falcon (USA) 126) [2007 80: 8.3m⁵ 6g³ 7.1m* 7m* 7d* 7m* 7d 7d Oct 20] tall colt: has scope: smart performer: progressed well when winning handicaps at Haydock (tended to idle) in May, and Leicester and Newbury in August and Charlton Hunt Supreme Stakes at Goodwood (beat Dunelight by neck) in September: creditable seventh to Candidato Roy in valuable handicap at Ascot next time: below form in Challenge Stakes at Newmarket final outing: stays 7f: yet to race on extremes of ground. *M. Johnston* **115**

Charlton Hunt Supreme Stakes, Goodwood—Lovelace, stepping up in class, completes a four-timer; Dunelight (visor), Bygone Days (right) and Mac Love (checked cap) are among those breathing down his neck

LOVE OF DUBAI (USA) 2 b.f. (Apr 16) More Than Ready (USA) 120 – Diamond **91**
Kris (USA) (Prospect Bay (CAN) 117) [2007 5m² 5.4m⁴ 7.1g* 7d⁶ Oct 20] rather leggy
filly: fourth foal: dam unraced half-sister to US Grade 2 winner Square Cut: fairly useful
form: won maiden at Warwick in October: stiff task, progressed again when 3¾ lengths
sixth to Kitty Matcham in Rockfel Stakes at Newmarket, dictating: stays 7f. *C. E. Brittain*

LOVEOFMYLIFE 2 gr.f. (Mar 20) Dr Fong (USA) 128 – True Love (Robellino –
(USA) 127) [2007 p7.1g⁵ Nov 9] 5,000F, 31,000Y: fifth foal: half-sister to fairly useful
2006 2-y-o 7.5f winner Hucking Hot (now useful around 1m in US, by Desert Prince):
dam unraced half-sister to smart sprinter Hellvelyn: 8/1, dropped away tamely in maiden
at Wolverhampton. *R. M. Beckett*

LOVE ON SIGHT 3 b.f. Beat Hollow 126 – Greek Dream (USA) 79 (Distant View **85 §**
(USA) 126) [2007 93: p7g² 7m 7.1m³ 7m 7g 9.7m 8s Sep 21] deep-girthed filly: fairly
useful maiden handicapper: should stay 1m: acts on good to firm ground: temperamental
(took little interest final outing). *A. P. Jarvis*

LOVERS KISS 3 b.f. Night Shift (USA) – Evening Promise 108 (Aragon 118) [2007 **50**
52: 6g 7.1g 5v⁶ 6d Jul 23] good-topped filly: modest performer: stays 7f: acts on fibresand
and soft going: blinkered: none too consistent. *N. Wilson*

LOVES BIDDING 3 b.g. Auction House (USA) 120 – Charlottevalentina (IRE) 80 **72 d**
(Perugino (USA) 84) [2007 73: 5g 7m 7m 6v³ 5d⁵ 5.1f p7.1g 6g p6g 6d Oct 23] small,
close-coupled gelding: fair handicapper: creditable effort in 2007 only on fifth outing:
best at 5f/6f: acts on any going: tried visored: temperamental. *R. Ingram*

LOVE VALENTINE (IRE) 2 b.f. (Jan 15) Fruits of Love (USA) 127 – Ridotto (Salse **69**
(USA) 128) [2007 7.1g p8g* 6d 8m p8g⁶ Nov 7] lengthy, good-bodied filly: fourth foal:
half-sister to useful 2004 2-y-o 5f winner Salsa Brava (by Almutawakel) and 3-y-o
Stagehand: dam French maiden: fair performer: won maiden at Kempton in September:
little impact in nurseries: stays 1m: acts on polytrack and good to soft going. *M. Johnston*

LOVE YOU ALWAYS (USA) 7 ch.g. Woodman (USA) 126 – Encorenous (USA) **50**
(Diesis 133) [2007 63: p9.5g³ p11g p12g 12g⁶ 10d⁵ 12d 9g 8.1d 8s 10.1f Jul 30] lengthy
gelding: modest handicapper: stays 12.6f: acts on polytrack and good to firm going:
tongue tied: sometimes slowly away/races freely: has shown signs of temperament.
Miss J. Feilden

LOW CLOUD 7 b.g. Danehill (USA) 126 – Raincloud (Rainbow Quest (USA) 134) –
[2007 70: p9.5g Jan 21] useful-looking gelding: fair handicapper at 6 yrs: well held only
Flat outing in 2007: stays 1¼m: acts on polytrack, firm and good to soft going: often
visored/in cheekpieces: has raced freely: fair hurdler. *J. J. Quinn*

LOW FLYER (USA) 2 gr. or ro.g. (Jan 17) Runaway Groom (USA) – To The Right **66**
(USA) (Saint Ballado (CAN)) [2007 6s³ 7d⁵ 6m Aug 18] good-topped gelding: fair
maiden: encouraging third at Newcastle: raced too freely subsequent starts (gelded after):
likely to prove best at 5f/6f. *T. D. Barron*

LOWRY'S ART 2 b.f. (Feb 2) Night Shift (USA) – Creme Caramel (USA) 88 (Sep- **60**
tieme Ciel (USA) 123) [2007 5d⁴ 6m⁶ 6d p7g⁴ Sep 29] 32,000Y: quite attractive filly:
half-sister to 2003 2-y-o 7f winner Monte Bianco (by King of Kings), later successful in
US, and 7f winner Soft Focus (by Spectrum): dam, 2-y-o 7f winner, half-sister to smart
performer up to 1m Robellation: modest maiden: best efforts (first 2 starts) at 5f/6f.
R. M. Beckett

LOYAL KNIGHT (IRE) 2 ch.g. (Apr 13) Choisir (AUS) 126 – Always True (USA) **81**
67 (Geiger Counter (USA)) [2007 6g 7.1g³ 8.1m³ 6m p7.1g* Oct 18] €8,000F: leggy
gelding: fifth foal: half-brother to 4-y-o Blues In The Night and French 11f winner Touch
And Dream (by Bering): dam Irish 2-y-o 1m winner: fairly useful form: mid-field in
28-runner sales race at Newmarket prior to winning maiden at Wolverhampton: best up
to 7f: acts on polytrack and good to firm going. *S. Kirk*

LOYAL ROYAL (IRE) 4 b.g. King Charlemagne (USA) 120 – Supportive (IRE) **82**
(Nashamaa 113) [2007 98: 6s 7m 6d p6g Oct 21] leggy gelding: useful performer in 2006:
fairly useful at best in handicaps in 2007, leaving A. Balding after second start: best at 5f/
6f: acts on firm and good to soft going: has flashed tail/carried head awkwardly under
pressure. *J. M. Bradley*

LOYAL TYCOON (IRE) 9 br.g. Royal Abjar (USA) 121 – Rosy Lydgate 53 (Last **71**
Tycoon 131) [2007 77: f6g p6g⁵ p7g Jan 24] robust, close-coupled gelding: fair handicapper: effective at 6f/7f: acts on all-weather, firm and soft going: tried visored/blinkered:
effective held up or making running. *D. K. Ivory*

intercasino.co.uk Rosebery Stakes (Handicap), Kempton—Luberon bounces back to form;
Woolfall Blue is his nearest pursuer

LUBERON 4 b.g. Fantastic Light (USA) 134 – Luxurious (USA) (Lyphard (USA) 132) **110 d**
[2007 109: 12g 12g a10f p11g* 10.1g 12.1d 8.9s 11.9m 10.4d 10m Sep 1] angular
gelding: smart handicapper at best: won at Kempton in April by 2½ lengths from Woolfall
Blue: well held all other starts: gelded after final outing: stays 13.4f: acts on polytrack
and firm going: usually makes running: unreliable. *M. Johnston*

LUCARNO (USA) 3 b.c. Dynaformer (USA) – Vignette (USA) 93 (Diesis 133) **121**
[2007 8m² p8g* 10m* 12g⁴ 12d² 12m⁴ 12d* 14.6m* Sep 15]
    The St Leger's return to Doncaster after the course's multi-million-pound
redevelopment drew a large and typically enthusiastic crowd, confirming the race's
continued popularity with the public. The attendance on St Leger day itself was
31,000, a record for recent years when the crowd has been between 25,000 and
27,000. There would have been no more fitting sight for the return to Town Moor
than that of the Derby winner attempting to confirm himself as the best of his
generation, or, indeed, of a three-year-old attempting the traditional triple crown
last achieved by Nijinsky or the fillies' triple crown last landed by Oh So Sharp. It
was, of course, futile to entertain such hopes. Thirty-seven years had elapsed since
Nijinsky won the St Leger, twenty-two since Oh So Sharp became the last horse to
win three English classics, and twenty years since a Derby winner (Reference
Point) ran in the St Leger (only three Oaks winners, Diminuendo, Ramruma and
User Friendly have gone on to the St Leger since Oh So Sharp, User Friendly
completing the double and the two others finishing second).
    In truth, the latest Ladbrokes St Leger was a below-par edition, even by
modern-day standards, run without any of the placed horses from the Derby, Irish
Derby or Prix du Jockey Club (there hasn't been a French challenger of any sort
since the supplemented Vertical Speed in 1997). Ladbrokes also sponsor the Great
Voltigeur Stakes at York which again proved the best St Leger trial, Lucarno
becoming the fourth to complete the Voltigeur/St Leger double since Reference

Ladbrokes Great Voltigeur Stakes, York—Lucarno is chased by the stable-companions
Yellowstone (third left), Macarthur (light cap), Acapulco (right) and Mahler (rail)

Ladbrokes St Leger Stakes, Doncaster—the Voltigeur proves the key trial as Lucarno comes out on top again; the O'Brien-trained pair Mahler (second right) and Honolulu (No.3) are placed, ahead of Regal Flush (second left), Veracity (star on cap) and Macarthur (rail)

Point (Bob's Return in 1993, Milan in 2001 and Rule of Law in 2004 were the others). Seven of the last eleven St Leger winners have run in the Great Voltigeur, the others, apart from Milan, Rule of Law and Lucarno, being Silver Patriarch (second in 1997), Mutafaweq (fourth in 1999), Bollin Eric (third in 2002) and Brian Boru (second in 2003). Aidan O'Brien, who had won three of the six previous St Legers, with Milan, Brian Boru and Scorpion, saddled the second, third, fourth and fifth behind Lucarno in the Great Voltigeur and three of them, third-placed Macarthur, fourth-placed Acapulco and fifth-placed Mahler, were in the St Leger line-up, a fourth Ballydoyle representative Honolulu starting 13/8 favourite after a splendid second under a big weight for a three-year-old in the Ebor Handicap. Second favourite Lucarno and Mahler, who had won the Queen's Vase, were the only St Leger runners with a pattern victory to their name, the ten-strong line-up also including the supplemented Regal Flush, a progressive sort who had won valuable handicaps at Goodwood and Haydock on his last two starts, the Gordon Stakes third Raincoat and the Queen's Vase and Goodwood Cup runner-up Veracity. Raincoat had started second favourite for the Prix du Jockey Club but was held on form by his stablemate Lucarno, who had won the Voltigeur from the Gordon Stakes winner Yellowstone (sent to America for the Man o'War Stakes instead of running in the St Leger). Lucarno and Raincoat were the first runners their trainer had had in the St Leger since 1996 when he won with Shantou, an unwilling racehorse at times who has the singular claim to fame of being the only winner of a British classic to carry the infamous Timeform squiggle alongside his rating going into the race (it was removed after the St Leger in which a superb Frankie Dettori made up Shantou's mind for him).

Shantou did not race at two and the St Leger was his eighth outing as a three-year-old. Lucarno didn't see a racecourse at two either, but had also had plenty of experience by St Leger time. He progressed rapidly after finishing second at 50/1 to Diamond Tycoon in a good Newbury maiden in April on his debut (the race in which stable-companion Pipedreamer, much the shorter-priced of the pair, also made his first appearance). After wide-margin wins in a maiden on the polytrack at Kempton and the onerailway.com Fairway Stakes at Newmarket, the first at a mile, the second at a mile and a quarter, Lucarno fully vindicated the late decision of his connections to run him in the Derby (a race in which Shantou finished third at 25/1). Starting at 16/1, Lucarno finished fourth of seventeen, just over seven and a half lengths behind the winner Authorized, despite hanging markedly left after three furlongs out. Lucarno's busy campaign continued with the King Edward VII Stakes at Royal Ascot (second to Boscobel when favourite) and the Princess of Wales's Stakes at Newmarket (fourth to Papal Bull). The six-week break between the Princess of Wales's Stakes and the Great Voltigeur was the longest between any of his races and Lucarno returned a performance at York at least as good as any he had produced at up to that time, travelling well throughout and winning by a length from Yellowstone, the Voltigeur result also boosting the St Leger claims of Derby third Aqaleem who had run Yellowstone to a neck, con-

Mr George Strawbridge's "Lucarno"

ceding 3 lb, in the Gordon Stakes. Yellowstone wasn't bred to stay the St Leger trip, which was why he was eventually sent for the Man o'War. Ballydoyle's Irish Derby winner Soldier of Fortune remained ante-post favourite for the St Leger after the Voltigeur.

The decision to train Soldier of Fortune for the Prix de l'Arc de Triomphe, coupled with an injury which ruled Aqaleem out of the St Leger, were blows to the Doncaster executive and to the St Leger's sponsors. Even Lucarno's participation was in doubt for some time because of concerns, justified on pedigree, that he might have stamina limitations, although he had shaped as if he would stay beyond a mile and a half, particularly in the Derby and the Princess of Wales's Stakes. Lucarno's American owner-breeder George Strawbridge insisted, while others wavered, that the colt took his place in the line-up. The proven Mahler set a sound gallop—Honolulu's jockey claimed afterwards that the field went 'far too slow for the first six furlongs'—and the timefigures recorded in the race by the principals, Lucarno's equivalent to a timerating of 117, confirmed that the race was truly run. That said, stamina had not been at a premium on Doncaster's new surface during the earlier part of the week, the course looking in tremendous shape but the going decidedly on the firm side of good. The entire Flat track had been levelled and re-seeded, and some of the drains realigned, during the course's closure. Under a well-judged ride by Jimmy Fortune, winning his first British classic, Lucarno, having his eighth race in five months, was produced smoothly to lead over a furlong out and kept on to win by a length from Mahler, who stumbled and lost his action briefly a furlong out, with the steadily-closing Honolulu a further three quarters of a length away third. Regal Flush, Veracity and Macarthur were only a neck, a short head and a neck further behind in a bunched finish. Lucarno's stablemate Raincoat weakened as though all was not well, trailing in last. 'His class saw him through,' was trainer John Gosden's view of Lucarno's performance and he announced that Lucarno would have a programme of races at a mile and a half in 2008, the Coronation Cup and the King George VI and Queen Elizabeth Stakes likely targets.

			Roberto	Hail To Reason
	Dynaformer (USA)		(b 1969)	Bramalea
	(b or br 1985)		Andover Way	His Majesty
Lucarno (USA)			(b or br 1978)	On The Trail
(b.c. 2004)			Diesis	Sharpen Up
	Vignette (USA)		(ch 1980)	Doubly Sure
	(b 1995)		Be Exclusive	Be My Guest
			(b 1986)	Exclusive Fable

The big, strong, close-coupled Lucarno—'too damned big to make a two-year-old'—is by the Roberto stallion Dynaformer, a Grade 2 winner at nine and ten furlongs on dirt, but also a winner on turf at a mile and a half. He is best known as the sire of ill-fated Kentucky Derby winner Barbaro, but has also been represented by good performers on turf including the Grade 1-winning fillies Riskaverse, Film Maker and Sand Springs, as well as an Epsom Derby third in Beat All, his best representative in Europe until Lucarno. The concerns about Lucarno's stamina arose largely from the distaff side of his pedigree. His dam Vignette was a sprinter, a promising juvenile who held some lofty entries when with John Gosden and, after being transferred to Neil Drysdale following a short-lived three-year-old campaign, won at five and a half and six and a half furlongs on turf in the States at four and five, one of her successes coming at listed level. Lucarno is Vignette's third live foal and her second winner, following Minute of Fame (by Olympio) who won on dirt (at a mile and a quarter) and turf (a five-furlong maiden at three) in the States. Lucarno's grandam Be Exclusive also began her racing career in Europe, winning the Prix Chloe over nine furlongs, before being switched to the States where she won in listed company at eight and a half furlongs on turf. Be Exclusive bred numerous winners, the pick of them Be Elusive and On A Cloud, listed winners at a mile in the States and France respectively, and Totally Cosmic who was placed in the Prix Cleopatre (ten and a half furlongs) and the Prix Chloe. One of Be Exclusive's half-sisters produced Lexicon, a leading sprinter in California. Lucarno travels strongly (has worn a crossed noseband) and, like several recent St Leger winners, is not short of speed for racing at a mile and a half. He has a round, unimpressive action and acts on polytrack, good to firm and good to soft going. He often races prominently. *J. H. M. Gosden*

LUCAYAN DANCER 7 b.g. Zieten (USA) 118 – Tittle Tattle (IRE) 80 (Soviet Lad **91** (USA)) [2007 91: p8g 10.1s³ 10g³ 10.1g 8f 10.3m 9.8g 10d⁵ 10.3d* 9m 12d 10m⁵ 10.3m 8.9d Oct 13] close-coupled gelding: has a markedly round action: fairly useful handicapper: won at Chester in July: effective at 1m to 1½m: acts on any going: tried in cheekpieces/blinkers at 3 yrs: has flashed tail: has run well when sweating: usually held up, but also effective ridden prominently. *D. Nicholls*

LUCAYOS 4 ch.g. Bahamian Bounty 116 – Indian Flag (IRE) 39 (Indian Ridge 123) **90** [2007 81§: p6g³ p6g* p6g² p6f* p6g* p6g⁶ 6m² 6m 6g⁶ 6s* 6g 6g 6s⁶ 6m 6m 6g p6g **a100** p6g* p6m² p6g Dec 28] sturdy gelding: useful handicapper: won at Lingfield in January, February and March, Brighton in May and Lingfield (beat Hello Man by short head) in November: best at 5f/6f: acts on all-weather, soft and good to firm going: has been blinkered: races prominently nowadays. *Mrs H. Sweeting*

LUCEFER (IRE) 9 b.g. Lycius (USA) 124 – Maharani (USA) (Red Ransom (USA)) **51** [2007 –: 10d 10.1d² Jun 19] leggy gelding: modest performer: stays 1½m: acts on polytrack, firm and soft going: tried blinkered in cheekpieces, often tongue tied at 5 yrs: sometimes carries head high. *G. C. H. Chung*

LUCIFER SAM (USA) 2 b.c. (Mar 5) Storm Cat (USA) – Rafina (USA) (Mr Pros- **99** pector (USA)) [2007 7s⁵ 7v² 7s* 7g² 7m 8d Sep 30] strong, angular colt: fifth foal: half-brother to 3 winners, including 3-y-o Admiralofthefleet and useful Irish 2001 2-y-o 8.5f winner Canberra (by Sadler's Wells): dam, French maiden, sister to Machiavellian, and half-sister to Exit To Nowhere: useful performer: won maiden at Galway in July: kept pattern company after, best effort when 3½ lengths second to Fast Company in Acomb Stakes at York: should stay 1m/1¼m: acts on heavy going. *A. P. O'Brien, Ireland*

LUCIUS VERRUS (USA) 7 b.g. Danzig (USA) – Magic of Life (USA) 118 (Seattle
Slew (USA)) [2007 –, a67: f7g² f6g² f6g* p6g* f6g² p7f³ p6g p6g p7g⁶ p7.1g² f7g p7g
p7.1g² 7m p7.1g p7.1g p8m f7d⁴ Dec 11] fair handicapper on all-weather: won minor
event at Southwell in January and handicap at Wolverhampton in February: effective at
6f to 8.6f: acts on all-weather, little form on turf: visored: held up (sometimes slowly
away). *D. Shaw* **– a69**

LUCK BE A LADY (IRE) 3 b.f. Alhaarth (IRE) 126 – Khamseh 85 (Thatching 131)
[2007 7m 7m⁴ Jul 21] 400,000Y: good-topped filly: fifth foal: half-sister to 4-y-o Third
Set, 7-y-o Bonus and fairly useful 7f/1m winner Corky (by Intikhab): dam, 7f winner,
half-sister to high-class performer up to 1½m Predappio: fair form in maidens at
Newmarket, off 3 months prior to 3¼ lengths fourth to Medicea Sidera, again taking
fierce hold (wore crossed noseband)/carrying head awkwardly: sent to USA. *J. Noseda* **74**

LUCK MONEY (IRE) 2 b.c. (Feb 15) Indian Ridge 123 – Dundel (IRE) 82 (Machiavellian (USA) 123) [2007 6m* 6m³ 7m* 7d⁵ Oct 20] €160,000Y: strong, rangy colt: has
plenty of scope: sixth foal: half-brother to several winners, including useful French 2006
2-y-o 6f/7f winner Charlotte O Fraise (by Beat Hollow) and 17f winner Lodgician (by
Grand Lodge): dam, 7f winner, out of sister to high-class middle-distance stayer High
Hawk, herself dam of In The Wings: useful form: won maiden at Newmarket in May and
valuable sales race at the Curragh (beat Hitchens by 2½ lengths) in September: ran well
other starts, ¾-length third to Henrythenavigator in Coventry Stakes at Royal Ascot and
7¼ lengths fifth to New Approach in Dewhurst Stakes at Newmarket: will probably stay
1m: acts on good to firm and good to soft going: front runner. *P. F. I. Cole* **108**

LUCK WILL COME (IRE) 3 b.f. Desert Style (IRE) 121 – Petite Maxine 70
(Sharpo 132) [2007 70: p6g⁵ 6m* 6m⁴ p6g³ p7.1g² Sep 21] fair performer: won maiden at
Hamilton in August: stays 7f: acts on polytrack and good to firm ground: hung right/
flashed tail final outing. *M. J. Wallace* **68**

LUCKY BEE (IRE) 3 b.f. Indian Danehill (IRE) 124 – All Laughter (Vision (USA))
[2007 78: f6g 6m 6f⁴ Jun 7] close-coupled filly: fair performer at 2 yrs, little form in 2007.
G. A. Swinbank **–**

LUCKY CLIO (IRE) 3 gr.f. Key of Luck (USA) 126 – Special Lady (FR) (Kaldoun
(FR) 122) [2007 8s 7d⁵ 8s 7v⁴ 7d⁴ p7.1g³ Dec 1] €130,000Y: lengthy filly: fourth foal:
half-sister to very smart French 7f (at 2 yrs) to 1¼m winner Special Kaldoun (by Alzao):
dam ran once in France: modest maiden handicapper: should stay at least 1m: acts on
polytrack and heavy ground: sold 17,000 gns. *M. J. Grassick, Ireland* **59**

LUCKY DANCEUSE (IRE) 2 b. or br.f. (Jan 29) Mujadil (USA) 119 – Kristal Dancer (IRE) 84 (Charnwood Forest (IRE) 125) [2007 7m Sep 2] first foal: dam 11f winner
out of useful stayer Kristal's Paradise: 100/1, tailed off in maiden at Folkestone: sold
1,500 gns, sent to Spain. *H. J. L. Dunlop* **–**

LUCKY FIND (IRE) 4 b.f. Key of Luck (USA) 126 – Recherchee (Rainbow Quest
(USA) 134) [2007 50: 12.1g⁴ 12.4m 16s 12.1g Jul 31] lengthy filly: poor maiden.
M. Mullineaux **38**

Parknasilla Hotel Goffs (C&G) Million, the Curragh—
Luck Money leads throughout, with Hitchens and Major Willy making it a 1,2,3 for British-trained runners

LUCKYLOVER 4 b.c. Key of Luck (USA) 126 – Hang Fire (Marju (IRE) 127) [2007 **82**
74: p10g⁵ f8g* p8.6g² p8.6g f8g² f8g* f8g* f8g² 8g⁴ 7.1d³ 8d⁴ Jun 28] quite good-topped **a94**
colt: fairly useful handicapper: progressive in first half of 2007, winning at Southwell
in January, April and May (beat Orpen Wide by 1¾ lengths): stays easy 1¼m: acts on
all-weather, soft and good to firm going: often tongue tied: usually races prominently:
consistent: sold 30,000 gns in July. *M. G. Quinlan*

LUCKY STREAM 2 b.f. (Apr 15) Tamayaz (CAN) 121 – Call Me Lucky 65 (Magic **50 ?**
Ring (IRE) 115) [2007 5m 6g 5.9g 5g Sep 19] 500Y: fifth foal: half-sister to 6-y-o Steel
Grey: dam 2-y-o 6f winner: behind in maidens, seemingly modest form final outing.
M. Brittain

LUCKY TERN 4 b.g. Sooty Tern 79 – Miss Money Spider (IRE) 65 (Statoblest 120) **–**
[2007 –: 7g 6m Apr 29] small gelding: no form. *J. M. Bradley*

LUCY BABE 4 ch.f. Groom Dancer (USA) 128 – La Puce Volante (Grand Lodge **39**
(USA) 125) [2007 40: 10.1d⁶ Oct 30] poor maiden: stays 11f. *G. Prodromou*

LUCY REBECCA 3 b.f. Diktat 126 – Crown Water (USA) (Chief's Crown (USA)) **–**
[2007 61p: 10m 10g 14.1g May 11] big, strong filly: has quick action: maiden: little form
at 3 yrs: twice slowly away. *M. R. Channon*

LUDOVICO 4 b.g. Zilzal (USA) 137 – Devastating 70 (Bluebird (USA) 125) [2007 93: **–**
8.1m 5.7f Jun 10] tall gelding: no form in 2007: dead. *J. M. Bradley*

LUJANO 2 b.g. (Mar 13) Lujain (USA) 119 – Latch Key Lady (USA) 48 (Tejano **64**
(USA)) [2007 p7.1g p6g* f6d³ Dec 21] modest performer: won seller at Wolverhampton
in December: will prove best at 5f/6f: raced only on all-weather. *Ollie Pears*

LUJIANA 2 b.f. (Apr 6) Lujain (USA) 119 – Compact Disc (IRE) 48 (Royal Academy **–**
(USA) 130) [2007 5m⁵ 5.4m Sep 9] 1,800Y, resold 2,000Y: neat filly: half-sister to
several winners, including Irish 2005 2-y-o 5f winner Mother's Day and 2006 2-y-o 1m
seller winner Emergency Services (both by Foxhound): dam 2-y-o 7f winner: well held in
maidens 5 months apart. *M. Brittain*

LULA (IRE) 3 ch.f. Tagula (IRE) 116 – Sodfahh 65 (Lion Cavern (USA) 117) [2007 **45**
p5.1g² 5s⁵ Jul 25] 8,000Y: second foal: sister to a winner in Spain: dam, Irish maiden, out
of useful winner up to 7f Balwa: form only when second of 2 finishers to stable-
companion Savanagh Forest in seller at Wolverhampton: sold £450. *M. Quinn*

LULLABY LADY 2 b.f. (Feb 3) Piccolo 121 – Musetta (IRE) 107 (Cadeaux Genereux **75 p**
131) [2007 5.1d⁵ p7g³ Oct 24] 34,000Y, 60,000Y: strong, lengthy filly: half-sister to
several winners, including 2001 2-y-o 6f winner Mameyuki (by Zafonic) and 1¼m
winner Mineko (by Nashwan), both fairly useful: dam, 7f (at 2 yrs) and 1¼m winner,
fourth in Oaks: fair maiden: improved from debut (green) when third at Lingfield 2 weeks
later: likely to stay 1m: should continue to progress. *B. W. Hills*

LULOAH 4 b.f. Mujahid (USA) 125 – Bangles 83 (Chilibang 120) [2007 63d: f5g⁴ f6g **52**
5.1g³ 5g² 5.1g 5.1s p5.1g³ p6g f5d Dec 14] modest performer: left P. McEntee after
second start: best at 5f/easy 6f: acts on all-weather and good to firm going: tried
blinkered/in cheekpieces: sometimes front runner. *J. G. M. O'Shea*

LUMINOUS GOLD 2 b.f. (Apr 22) Fantastic Light (USA) 134 – Nasaieb (IRE) 89 **62**
(Fairy King (USA)) [2007 7g 7d⁶ 6v² Oct 9] 115,000Y: rather leggy filly: fourth foal:
half-sister to useful 2004 2-y-o 5f winner Kissing Lights (by Machiavellian): dam, 2-y-o
5f winner, half-sister to smart 7f/1m performer Raise A Grand: modest maiden: dropped
in trip, runner-up at Folkestone: will prove best at 5f/6f: acts on heavy going. *C. F. Wall*

LUNA DANZA 3 gr.f. Danehill Dancer (IRE) 117 – Sita (IRE) 112 (Indian Ridge 123) **55**
[2007 7m 8g 9g p10g 10.8g³ 8.8g² 9.3g² 10.3d³ Oct 13] 52,000Y: close-coupled filly:
first foal: dam, Irish 1m/1¼m winner, out of half-sister to St Leger winner Moon Madness
and Coronation Cup winner Sheriff's Star: modest maiden: sold from B. Meehan 4,500
gns after fourth start: placed subsequent outings, including in handicap: should stay 1½m.
C. von der Recke, Germany

LUNA LANDING 4 ch.g. Allied Forces (USA) 123 – Macca Luna (IRE) 78 (Kahyasi **88**
130) [2007 84: p9.5g⁵ 12g 12m* 13.1m 12.3m² 12f⁵ 12.3m 12m⁵ p12.2g⁶ Oct 21] **a73 +**
close-coupled gelding: fairly useful handicapper on turf, fair on all-weather: won at
Thirsk in June: stays 1½m: acts on good to firm and good to soft going: usually makes
running. *Jedd O'Keeffe*

LUNAR LASS 2 b.f. (Feb 23) Fraam 114 – Easter Moon (FR) (Easter Sun 122) [2007 **–**
6d 5m⁶ 6s⁶ 5.1g Nov 7] 2,500F, €3,000Y: unfurnished filly: half-sister to several winners

in USA/Scandinavia, including 6-y-o Emilio: dam French 2-y-o 7f winner: little form (debut for D. J. Murphy). *G. Woodward*

LUNAR LIMELIGHT 2 b.c. (Feb 5) Royal Applause 124 – Moon Magic 62 (Polish Precedent (USA) 131) [2007 5m 5s⁵ 7s p7g Sep 26] smallish, strong colt: good walker: modest maiden: should stay 7f/1m. *P. J. Makin*   **55 +**

LUNAR PROMISE (IRE) 5 b.g. Mujadil (USA) 119 – Lunadine (FR) (Bering 136) [2007 73: p10g⁸ Jan 13] big gelding: fairly useful performer: lightly raced: well backed, best effort when winning handicap at Lingfield in January: stays 1¼m: acts on polytrack and good to firm going. *Ian Williams*   **83**

LUNAR RIVER (FR) 4 b.f. Muhtathir 126 – Moon Gorge 78 (Pursuit of Love 124) [2007 73: 10m p10g p10g⁴ p10g* 10g p8g p10g³ 9g 10m⁵ p8.6g³ p9.5m p9.5g³ p9.5g Oct 5] big filly: fair handicapper on all-weather, modest on turf: won at Lingfield in May: acts on polytrack and good to firm going: tongue tied: tried visored: said to have had breathing problem fifth start: none too consistent. *David Pinder*   **61**   **a73**

LUNATICO (GER) 2 b.g. (Mar 16) Bertolini (USA) 125 – La Playa (Shavian 125) [2007 6d 6g 7s Jul 25] behind in maidens (then gelded). *S. C. Williams*   **–**

LUNCES LAD (IRE) 3 gr.g. Xaar 132 – Bridelina (FR) (Linamix (FR) 127) [2007 85: 7m 7m⁶ 7d⁴ 7d 7m² 7m⁴ 7d 7m³ 7f.1m Sep 13] lengthy, good-topped gelding: fairly useful handicapper: raced only at 7f, will be suited by 1m: acts on good to firm and good to soft going: usually held up. *M. R. Channon*   **87**

LUNDY'S LANE (IRE) 7 b.g. Darshaan 133 – Lunda (IRE) 60 (Soviet Star (USA) 128) [2007 108, a104: a8f a8f 8g⁴ 8g 10g⁶ 8m 8.1g⁶ 10g² 11.9m⁴ 13.4m² 12.3m³ 12g 12m Nov 10] lengthy, good-topped gelding: useful performer: left S. Seemar in UAE after fifth outing: mainly creditable efforts after, including 3 lengths third to Hattan in listed event at Chester eleventh start: effective at 1m to 13.4f: acts on all-weather and dirt, raced only on good going or firmer on turf: tried blinkered/visored/tongue tied. *A. M. Balding*   **103**

LUSCIOUS LIPS 2 b.f. (Mar 15) Mujahid (USA) 125 – Zing (Zilzal (USA) 137) [2007 5m 6g³ 5g² 5v* 6m 6m⁵ 6s⁴ 5.1m Oct 14] neat filly: second foal: half-sister to 3-y-o Forced Upon Us: dam unraced half-sister to useful sprinter Cool Question: fair performer: won maiden at Windsor in July: will prove best at 5f (given test)/6f: acts on heavy and good to firm going. *R. Hannon*   **75**

LUSCIVIOUS 3 ch.g. Kyllachy 129 – Lloc 79 (Absalom 128) [2007 99: 5.1m⁴ 6g² 6m⁵ 5d 6m 5g 5g p6g⁶ 5g Oct 27] small gelding: useful handicapper: creditable efforts in 2007 only in handicaps at Newmarket second/third starts: effective at 5f/6f: acts on soft and good to firm going: usually blinkered, in cheekpieces penultimate start: has hung right. *A. J. McCabe*   **96**

LUSH (IRE) 2 b.f. (Mar 20) Fasliyev (USA) 120 – Our Hope (Dancing Brave (USA) 140) [2007 6g³ 7s⁵ Jun 26] €30,000F, €60,000Y: tall, angular filly: has scope: half-sister to useful Irish 7f (at 2 yrs) to 9f winner Derivative (by Erins Isle) and Irish 1½m winner Dochas Mor (by Project Manager): dam, unraced, out of smart Irish winner up to 1¼m Calandra, herself half-sister to Oaks winner Intrepidity: fair maiden: promising third to Johar Jamal at Goodwood: unsuited by stiffer test at Newbury: likely to prove best at 5f/6f. *R. Hannon*   **68**

LUSH LASHES 2 b.f. (Feb 20) Galileo (IRE) 134 – Dance For Fun 74 (Anabaa (USA) 130) [2007 7m* Sep 14]   **103 P**

First outing, first win, £670,068 in the kitty—has there ever been a more lucrative start to a racing career? Lush Lashes was the only newcomer in a field of twenty-two for the Parknasilla Hotel Goffs Fillies Million, one of two very valuable sales races (the other for colts and geldings worth the same) run at the Curragh on a Friday afternoon in September. The Goffs Million races shared third place in the table of Europe's richest races—only the Prix de l'Arc and the Derby were worth more—and were the most valuable for two-year-olds anywhere in the world, apart from the Golden Slipper Stakes in Australia. The Fillies Million line-up was typical of a valuable sales race, the large field attracting runners of wide-ranging ability (more than half of them started at odds ranging from 25/1 to 66/1). There were two pattern winners, the Debutante Stakes winner Campfire Glow and the Sweet Solera winner Albabilia (the latter one of ten British-trained challengers). They headed the market at 3/1 and 5/1 respectively, with Newbury maiden winner Rinterval, who had form with Albabilia, the only other runner sent off at shorter than 10/1. There was support for Lush Lashes at those odds, encouragement provided with stable-

Parknasilla Hotel Goffs Fillies Million, the Curragh—Lush Lashes, the only newcomer in the field, stamps herself as a highly promising prospect; Rinterval, Carribean Sunset and Žeu Tin Tin follow in that order

jockey Kevin Manning riding her instead of stablemate Allicansayis Wow who had finished a place behind Albabilia when that pair filled fourth and fifth in the Moyglare Stud Stakes. Lush Lashes stamped herself a highly promising prospect, always prominent and leading two furlongs out to win readily by a length and a half from Rinterval, with 25/1-shot Carribean Sunset, a stablemate of Campfire Glow, a further length away third. Campfire Glow herself came fifth and Albabilia last (found to be 'clinically abnormal'). The form was no better than useful but Lush Lashes—whose debut had been delayed because 'she got a shin'—was introduced into the One Thousand Guineas betting straight afterwards, the odds offered against her emulating stable-companion Finsceal Beo (only sixth in the Curragh race the year before) ranging from between 16/1 and 25/1. At the time of writing, Lush Lashes stands as low as 12/1 with some bookmakers for Newmarket and at a general 16/1 for the Oaks.

		Sadler's Wells (b 1981)	Northern Dancer
	Galileo (IRE)		Fairy Bridge
	(b 1998)	Urban Sea (ch 1989)	Miswaki
Lush Lashes			Allegretta
(b.f. Feb 20, 2005)		Anabaa (b 1992)	Danzig
	Dance For Fun		Balbonella
	(b 1999)	Hilaris (ch 1994)	Arazi
			Carnival Spirit

The lengthy, good-topped Lush Lashes made €80,000 as a yearling, less than half the average for Galileo's yearling fillies in 2006. She is the first foal out of Dance For Fun who won a maiden over a mile at Lingfield on the first of only two starts. The grandam of Lush Lashes, the unraced Hilaris, died after producing only two foals, the first of them Dance For Fun. The breeder of Lush Lashes, Ann Jenkins, acquired Hilaris from Sheikh Mohammed after the death of Fiesta Fun, the fourth dam of Lush Lashes and the dam of Prix de l'Arc winner Saumarez (bred by Lush Lashes' breeder when she had Heatherwold Stud). 'I didn't have a daughter but Sheikh Mohammed had bought Fiesta Fun's daughter Carnival Spirit [great grandam of Lush Lashes] and I asked if I could buy one of her daughters.' The winning miler Carnival Spirit has bred several winners for Sheikh Mohammed, including the smart Exaltation, who never won at further than a mile and a quarter but was a good fifth to Galileo in the Irish Derby. Exaltation's sister the useful Carniola won at a mile and a half, as did another useful half-sister Bustling. Fiesta Fun was a half-sister to the smart six- and seven-furlong performer Derrylin but she won three races at a mile and a quarter before putting up her best effort when a close

Mrs J. S. Bolger's "Lush Lashes"

third in the Yorkshire Oaks. There is stamina on both sides of Lush Lashes' pedigree and she will stay middle distances as a three-year-old. The going was good to firm at the Curragh. *J. S. Bolger, Ireland*

LU'S WOMAN 2 b.f. (May 1) Lujain (USA) 119 – Business Woman (Primo Dominie 121) [2007 5g⁴ 7g 7d⁵ Oct 16] 4,800Y: leggy filly: third foal: half-sister to 3-y-o Best Woman: dam little sign of ability: modest form in maidens: may prove best at 5f/6f. *M. W. Easterby* **59**

LUXURIX (FR) 6 gr.g. Linamix (FR) 127 – Luxurious (USA) (Lyphard (USA) 132) [2007 p10g⁵ p12.2g* Mar 5] ran 6 times in France in 2004 when trained by J-C. Rouget: unraced in 2005/2006: fairly useful form in Britain at 6 yrs, winning handicap at Wolverhampton (reared leaving stall) in March: should stay 1¾m: acts on polytrack and soft going. *P. R. Webber* **80 +**

LYNFORD LADY 4 b.f. Zaha (CAN) 106 – Little Miss Rocker 65 (Rock Hopper 124) [2007 60: 9.7m 12g p13.9g p11g Sep 5] workmanlike filly: poor maiden: stays 1½m: acts on polytrack and good to soft going: tried in headgear. *P. W. D'Arcy* **45**

LYON'S HILL 3 ch.g. Generous (IRE) 139 – New Abbey 104 (Sadler's Wells (USA) 132) [2007 12.4d 12g² Nov 6] modest form in maidens, 4 lengths second to Ashwell Rose at Catterick: stays 1½m. *M. Mullineaux* **57**

LYRICAL SYMPHONY 2 b.f. (Feb 11) Captain Rio 122 – Musical Key 71 (Key of Luck (USA) 126) [2007 7g⁶ 7g p6g⁶ p5g p6g Nov 30] 50,000Y: first foal: dam, sprint maiden, half-sister to smart Hong Kong performers Firebolt (sprinter) and Industrialist (best at 1¼m): modest maiden: left W. Knight 3,000 gns before final start (tongue tied): stays 7f. *W. Power, Ireland* **59**

LYSANDER'S QUEST (IRE) 9 br.g. King's Theatre (IRE) 128 – Haramayda (FR) (Doyoun 124) [2007 57: p16g² p16g⁶ p12g⁴ p16.5g⁶ p16g⁵ 15.4m 16m p16g p16g **55**

MAC

Nov 14] tall gelding: modest handicapper: stays 17f: acts on polytrack, firm and good to soft going: has worn headgear: waited with. *R. Ingram*

LYTHAM (IRE) 6 b.g. Spectrum (IRE) 126 – Nousaiyra (IRE) (Be My Guest (USA) **58** 126) [2007 f7g f7g p12.2g⁴ p10g* p8.6g Oct 26] tall gelding: modest performer: won minor event at Lingfield in July: stays 1¼m: acts on polytrack, firm and soft going. *D. J. Wintle*

LYTTON 2 b.c. (May 14) Royal Applause 124 – Dora Carrington (IRE) 106 (Sri Pekan **92 p** (USA) 117) [2007 6m* p6g 6d⁵ Oct 13] well-made colt: third foal: dam, 2-y-o 6f winner (including Cherry Hinton Stakes), half-sister to Middle Park winner Primo Valentino: fairly useful form: won maiden at Windsor in August: shaped better than bare result in Sirenia Stakes at Kempton (poorly drawn, seventh to Philario) and listed race at York (softer ground, faded into fifth behind Max One Two Three): likely to prove best at 5f/6f: will do better still. *W. R. Swinburn*

M

MAAHE (IRE) 2 b.f. (Apr 30) Namid 128 – Almond Flower (IRE) (Alzao (USA) 117) **42** [2007 5d 5s 5m 7m Sep 18] 30,000Y: sister to 5f winner Sweet Namibia and half-sister to several winners, including useful 7f winner Macaroon (by Tagula): dam Irish 2-y-o 5f winner: poor maiden. *R. A. Fahey*

MA AL SALAMAH (IRE) 2 ch.f. (Mar 21) Noverre (USA) 125 – Tres Sage (Repri- **62 p** mand 122) [2007 5m⁶ 6g Sep 19] 38,000Y: well-made filly: half-sister to 3 winners, including 3-y-o Makshoof: dam, French 1m winner, closely related to smart performer up to 1m Aragon: shaped better than bare result in mid-field in maidens at Sandown and Yarmouth within a week: likely to stay 1m: will do better. *C. E. Brittain*

MABAAHEJ (USA) 3 b.f. Belong To Me (USA) – Tabheej (IRE) 100 (Mujtahid **69** (USA) 118) [2007 7m p8g³ 7s p8g⁶ Aug 1] good-topped filly: third foal: half-sister to 7f winner Tawajud (by Dixieland Band): dam, 2-y-o 5f/6f winner, sister to useful 2-y-o 5f winner Mubhij: fair maiden: should have been as effective at 7f as 1m: form only on polytrack: visits Forestry. *B. W. Hills*

MABEL (IRE) 4 b.f. In The Wings 128 – Ma N'Ieme Biche (USA) (Key To The King- **71** dom (USA)) [2007 78: 14m⁵ 14d 14.1m² 16g 12m⁴ 13.8g Oct 20] tall, useful-looking filly: fair handicapper: stays 1¾m: acts on firm and good to soft ground: has shown signs of temperament: sold 11,000 gns. *S. C. Williams*

MACADEMY ROYAL (USA) 4 b.g. Royal Academy (USA) 130 – Garden Folly **–** (USA) (Pine Bluff (USA)) [2007 68: p5g* f6g⁶ 5m p5g 5.1s p5.1g² p6g² p7g Dec 1] quite **a76** good-topped gelding: fair performer: won maiden at Lingfield in March: stays 6f: acts on all-weather, well held all 3 starts on turf: tongue tied: mulish final 3-y-o outing (report-edly had sore shins): said to have bled final outing. *H. Morrison*

MACARONI GIN (IRE) 3 b.g. Grand Slam (USA) 120 – Polyandry (IRE) 99 (Penne- **59** kamp (USA) 130) [2007 69: 10.5g 12.1d 9m⁴ Sep 6] lengthy, workmanlike gelding: maiden: just modest form in 2007: stays 1m. *J. Howard Johnson*

MACARTHUR 3 b.c. Montjeu (IRE) 137 – Out West (USA) 103 (Gone West (USA)) **117** [2007 95P: 10m³ 10m³ 12d³ 14.6m⁶ Sep 15] good-bodied, useful-looking colt: smart performer: progressed well in 2007, best efforts when 1½ lengths third to Lucarno in Great Voltigeur Stakes at York and 2¼ lengths fifth behind same rival in St Leger at Doncaster (short of room for much of final 2f) last 2 starts: will stay 2m+: acts on heavy and good to firm ground. *A. P. O'Brien, Ireland*

MACCABEUS 2 b.c. (Mar 29) Bold Edge 123 – Birthday Venture 65 (Soviet Star **56** (USA) 128) [2007 5.2g 6m 6g⁶ p5.1g⁴ 5.4m Sep 9] modest maiden: free-going sort, should prove best at 5f/6f. *P. J. O'Gorman*

MAC DALIA 2 b.f. (Feb 6) Namid 128 – Maugwenna 85 (Danehill (USA) 126) [2007 **71** 5.2d⁵ p6g 5g* 5m⁶ 6s f5d³ f5g* Dec 27] 9,000Y: first foal: dam, 2-y-o 5f winner, should have stayed 6f: fair performer: won maiden at Lingfield in July and seller at Southwell in December: creditable third in nursery at Southwell: free-going sort, best at 5f: acts on fibresand and good to firm going. *M. G. Quinlan*

MACEDON 4 b.g. Dansili 127 – Hypnotize 103 (Machiavellian (USA) 123) [2007 89: **88** 8m⁴ 8.1m 8m 7g⁴ 8m⁶ 7m Nov 10] big, strong gelding: fairly useful handicapper: stays 1m: acts on firm and soft going: held up. *J. S. Moore*

631

John Roarty Memorial Scurry Handicap, the Curragh—a valuable win for the David Nicholls-trained Machinist, who has four lengths to spare over Nastrelli (spots); the winner's stable-companion Bahamian Pirate (far left) is fourth

MAC FEDERAL (IRE) 5 b.g. In The Wings 128 – Tocade (IRE) (Kenmare (FR) 125) **66** [2007 p13g⁵ Feb 14] fair maiden: in frame 3 of 4 starts in Italy at 2/3 yrs: fifth at Lingfield on British Flat debut: should stay 1¾m: fairly useful hurdler. *Miss S. West*

MAC GILLE EOIN 3 b.c. Bertolini (USA) 125 – Peruvian Jade 76 (Petong 126) [2007 **101** 79+: 6m² 6.1m⁵ p5g³ 6m² 6g* p6g* 5m 5g 6g² p6g⁵ 6m* 7d Sep 29] improved into a useful handicapper: won at Goodwood and Kempton within 6 days in June and Goodwood again (beat Esteem Machine by short head) in September: well below form final outing: may prove best at 6f: acts on polytrack and good to firm going: versatile regarding tactics. *J. Gallagher*

MACHINATE (USA) 5 b. or br.g. Machiavellian (USA) 123 – Dancing Sea (USA) 80 **69** (Storm Cat (USA)) [2007 –: p9.5g p9.5g p8.6g² p8.6g⁴ f7g p8.6g² 8.1m p7.1g² p8.6g 7s³ 7.5m⁶ p8.6g⁵ 8s 6.9f⁵ 7.1m p8.6g² p7g⁶ p8.6g² p8.6g⁶ p8.6g* p8.6g² p8.6g² p9.5s p8.6d* Dec 27] leggy gelding: fair performer: won handicaps at Wolverhampton in November and December: stays 8.6f: acts on polytrack, firm and soft going: tried visored/tongue tied: held up. *W. M. Brisbourne*

MACHINIST (IRE) 7 br.g. Machiavellian (USA) 123 – Athene (IRE) 83 (Rousillon **110** (USA) 133) [2007 98: a6f a5f⁴ p6g⁵ 6m³ 7s 5g 6g* 6.3s* 6m 7g Aug 23] good-topped gelding: smart handicapper: won at Hamilton (by 1½ lengths from Trojan Flight) in June and the Curragh (beat Nastrelli by 4 lengths in valuable event) in July: below form in Stewards' Cup at Goodwood and listed event at York after: effective at stiff 5f to 6.3f: acts on polytrack/dirt, firm and soft going: sometimes slowly away. *D. Nicholls*

MACLEYA (GER) 5 b.m. Winged Love (IRE) 121 – Minaccia (GER) (Platini (GER) **115** 126) [2007 105: 15.5g⁴ 10g* 10.5s² 14g³ 12.5m* 12m⁵ 15.5m² 12g Dec 9] second foal: half-sister to German 9f to 11f winner Midas (by Selkirk): dam, useful German 6f (at 2 yrs) to 1m winner, half-sister to useful German performer up to 1¾m Mendosino: smart performer: won 3 times for A. Schutz in Germany in 2005 before sold €46,000: won minor event at Clairefontaine and listed race at Chantilly in 2006: further progress in 2007, winning Prix Allez France at Chantilly (by length from Satwa Queen) in May and Prix de Pomone at Deauville (led on line to beat Pearl Sky short head) in August: good short-neck second to Allegretto in Prix Royal-Oak at Longchamp before well held in Hong Kong Vase at Sha Tin last 2 starts: effective at 1¼m to 15.5f: acts on soft and good to firm ground: blinkered final 3-y-o start: usually races in touch. *A. Fabre, France*

MAC LOUGH (USA) 5 br.g. Exploit (USA) 117 – Bundle of Gold (USA) (Seeking –
The Gold (USA)) [2007 –: p16g May 9] fair form at best in maidens: little form since
3-y-o reappearance: stays 1½m: tried in cheekpieces. *E. Tyrrell, Ireland*

MAC LOVE 6 b.g. Cape Cross (IRE) 129 – My Lass 91 (Elmaamul (USA) 125) [2007 **114**
109: 6.5g² 6.5g⁵ 6g⁴ 7.1g³ 7s 7g⁶ 7m⁶ 7m⁴ 7m⁵ 7d Oct 20] strong, compact gelding: smart
performer: best efforts in 2007 when second to Munaddam in handicap at Nad Al Sheba
and close fourth to Lovelace in Supreme Stakes at Goodwood eighth outing: below form
in Park Stakes at Doncaster (pulled too hard) and Challenge Stakes at Newmarket final 2
starts: effective at 6f to 1m: acts on polytrack and firm going, not on softer than good:
edgy, free-going sort (has been early to post/worn crossed noseband): held up. *J. Noseda*

MACORVILLE (USA) 4 b.g. Diesis 133 – Desert Jewel (USA) (Caerleon (USA) **113 ?**
132) [2007 99: 9.8g⁶ 16g⁶ 12g⁶ 16.1v² 14s² 14m⁴ 18d Oct 20] leggy, workmanlike gelding: has a markedly round action: useful performer: second in handicaps at Newcastle
(short-headed by Juniper Girl in Northumberland Plate) and York (¾ length behind Wing
Collar in listed contest) in July: seemed to run very well when fourth to Yeats in Irish
St Leger at the Curragh next time, though prominent long way in steadily-run race: tailed
off in Cesarewitch at Newmarket final start: stays 2m: acts on heavy and good to firm
going: usually up with pace. *G. M. Moore*

MADAAREK (USA) 3 b.c. Kingmambo (USA) 125 – Hachiyah (IRE) 91 (Generous **86**
(IRE) 139) [2007 76: p8g³ 9.9m* 11g⁴ 14g* 15.9d⁵ 13.3m⁶ p12g Sep 24] good-topped,
quite attractive colt: fairly useful handicapper: won at Beverley in April and Sandown in
May: tongue tied, well beaten at Kempton final start (reportedly had breathing problem):
stays easy 1¾m: acts on good to firm going: said to have finished distressed fifth outing:
sold 22,000 gns, sent to Bahrain. *E. A. L. Dunlop*

MAD ABOUT YOU (IRE) 2 b.f. (Jan 28) Indian Ridge 123 – Irresistible Jewel (IRE) **103**
115 (Danehill (USA) 126) [2007 7g* 7s² 7g³ 8g³ Oct 7] lengthy filly: first foal: dam,

Moyglare Stud Farms Ltd's "Mad About You"

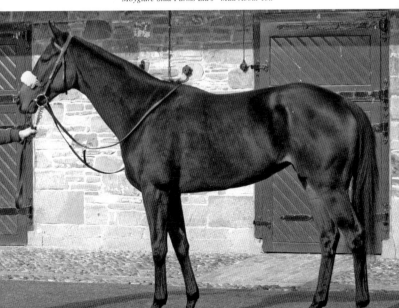

1¼m/1½m (Ribblesdale Stakes) winner, half-sister to useful Irish winners Diamond Trim (1¼m/1½m) and Legal Jousting (1m): useful form: won maiden at Leopardstown in June: progressed well, third in Moyglare Stud Stakes at the Curragh (2 lengths behind Saoirse Abu) and Prix Marcel Boussac at Longchamp (beaten 4 lengths by Zarkava): will stay 1¼m/1½m. *D. K. Weld, Ireland*

MADAM CARWELL 2 b.f. (Feb 28) King's Best (USA) 132 – Delirious Moment (IRE) 90 (Kris 135) [2007 7m 6f⁴ 6.5d Sep 28] 9,000Y: fifth foal: half-sister to 6-y-o Mith Hill and 1¼m winner Nuwara Eliya (by Grand Lodge), both fairly useful: dam, 1m winner, out of half-sister to very smart Irish performer up to 1¼m Executive Perk: modest maiden: possibly flattered when fourth to Maramba at Redcar: stiff task (sales race) final start: will stay 1m+. *J. G. Given* **55 ?**

MADAME BOUNTIFUL 2 ch.f. (Mar 13) Bahamian Bounty 116 – Madame Crecy (USA) (Al Nasr (FR) 126) [2007 7d p6g 6d Oct 29] close-coupled filly: closely related to 9-y-o Jools and 1¼m winner French Lieutenant (both useful by Cadeaux Genereux) and half-sister to 2 winners: dam, French maiden, half-sister to high-class sprinter/miler Polar Falcon: poor form in maidens. *A. King* **49**

MADAME HOI (IRE) 2 ch.f. (Apr 30) Hawk Wing (USA) 136 – Lindesberg 71 (Doyoun 124) [2007 7m⁵ 8.2m² 8s² Oct 26] 46,000Y: lengthy, angular filly: fourth foal: half-sister to 3 winners, including Phoenix Stakes second (later winner in Singapore) Amadeus Mozart (by Mozart) and Irish 7f winner Dolce Voche (by Intikhab): dam, sprint maiden, half-sister to smart 7f/1m performer Gothenberg: fairly useful maiden: second to Classic Legend at Nottingham and to Silk Affair at Ayr (beaten short head, having made most): will prove best up to 1m: acts on soft and good to firm going. *M. R. Channon* **86 +**

MADAME MONTOM (USA) 2 b.f. (Apr 12) French Envoy (USA) – Sticky Fingers (USA) (Crafty Prospector (USA)) [2007 p5g p6g p8.6g Nov 14] $37,000Y: stocky filly: second foal: sister to US 2-y-o sprint winner: dam US winner around 1m: no form. *S. W. Hall* **–**

MADAME RIO (IRE) 2 b.f. (Jan 27) Captain Rio 122 – Glenviews Purchase (IRE) 77 (Desert Story (IRE) 115) [2007 5s 6m⁶ 7g⁴ p6g p6g Oct 22] €12,000F, €33,000Y: lengthy filly: first foal: dam, 2-y-o 5.7f winner (stayed 1¼m), half-sister to useful 1¼m performer Resplendent Star: modest maiden: fourth at Chester: well beaten in nurseries (on polytrack): should prove best up to 7f. *K. R. Burke* **59**

MADAM PATTI 4 b.f. Monashee Mountain (USA) 115 – Thabeh 57 (Shareef Dancer (USA) 135) [2007 46: 6d⁶ 5s⁶ 6s⁵ Jul 28] leggy filly: poor maiden: effective at 6f to 8.6f: acts on all-weather, firm and soft ground. *R. Ingram* **43**

MADAM SUPERIOR 2 b.f. (Mar 20) Superior Premium 122 – Amy Leigh (IRE) 78 (Imperial Frontier (USA) 112) [2007 5m 5.5d 5m 7m Aug 8] 2,200Y: small filly: fourth foal: half-sister to 2001 2-y-o 5f/6f winner Katy O'Hara and 5-y-o Benny The Bus (both by Komaite): dam 5f (including at 2 yrs)/6f winner: little form in maidens. *D. J. S. ffrench Davis* **–**

MADAM VOUVRAY 3 ch.f. Vettori (IRE) 119 – April Stock 97 (Beveled (USA)) [2007 8m p10g⁴ p11g 10g 16.2f Aug 27] lengthy filly: first foal: dam 1½m winner: fair maiden at best: should be suited by 11f+: acts on polytrack: joined B. Powell. *B. J. Meehan* **68 d**

MADAM ZORRO 2 gr.f. (Mar 9) Weet-A-Minute (IRE) 106 – Capponicus (IRE) 73 (Woodborough (USA) 112) [2007 p5.1g 7d⁴ p7.1g⁶ Jun 29] second foal: dam 2-y-o 5f winner: little form in sellers. *S. Parr* **–**

MADDIE'S PEARL (IRE) 2 b. or gr.f. (May 14) Clodovil (IRE) 116 – Perle d'Irlande (FR) (Top Ville 129) [2007 5.2g 6m Jun 9] leggy filly: half-sister to several winners, including smart French 1¼m winner Paraiyor (by Lomitas) and useful Irish 7f winner Excelerate (by Mujadil): dam, French 1m (at 2 yrs) and 1¼m winner, half-sister to Prix Marcel Boussac/Vermeille winner Sierra Madre, herself dam of high-class miler Aljabr: well held (pulled hard) in minor event and maiden. *M. R. Channon* **–**

MADDY 2 b.f. (Mar 7) Daggers Drawn (USA) 114 – Summer Lightning (IRE) 81 (Tamure (IRE) 125) [2007 5m⁵ p6g* p6g⁴ 6m 6m⁵ p7g Oct 31] lengthy, angular filly: first foal: dam 5f (including at 2 yrs)/6f winner: fair performer: won maiden at Lingfield in July: often better than bare result in nurseries: should stay 7f/1m: acts on polytrack and good to firm going: sold 7,000 gns. *R. M. Beckett* **66**

MADEMOISELLE 5 b.m. Efisio 120 – Shall We Dance 83 (Rambo Dancer (CAN) 107) [2007 60: p10g² p9.5g² p8g³ f8g³ f8g p8.6g² p8.6g⁵ f8g² f8g* f8g p8g⁵ p8.6g⁴ **66**

Jul 10] lengthy mare: fair performer: claimed from R. Curtis £5,000 after reappearance: won handicap at Southwell in March: stays 1¼m: acts on all-weather and heavy going: effective in cheekpieces or not: sold £4,200. *R. A. Harris*

MADE TO RANSOM 2 b.c. (Apr 6) Red Ransom (USA) – Maid For The Hills 101 **93 p** (Indian Ridge 123) [2007 8m³ Oct 4] well-made colt: seventh foal: half-brother to several winners, including 7f (at 2 yrs) to 1¼m winner Maid To Perfection (by Sadler's Wells), 2002 2-y-o 7f winner Artistic Lad (stayed 1½m, by Peintre Celebre) and 3-y-o Maid To Believe, all useful: dam 2-y-o 6f winner: 10/3 and fluently to post, plenty of promise when third to Twice Over in maiden at Newmarket, going strongly close up: will stay 1¼m: sure to improve and win races. *J. H. M. Gosden*

MADIBA 8 b.g. Emperor Jones (USA) 119 – Priluki 65 (Lycius (USA) 124) [2007 58, **58** a70: p16g f16s⁴ 15.4m² 16.1d³ 15.4g² 16.4m p16.5g² 15.4m⁶ p16.5g⁵ p16g⁶ Sep 15] **a62** leggy, useful-looking gelding: modest handicapper: stays 2¼m: acts on all-weather, firm and soft going: formerly visored/blinkered. *P. Howling*

MADISON HEIGHTS (IRE) 2 ch.g. (Mar 20) Monashee Mountain (USA) 115 – **70** Stormchaser (IRE) (Titus Livius (FR) 115) [2007 6m⁵ 7d⁴ 7d² 7m² 8m Aug 27] €13,000F: strong, lengthy gelding: fair maiden: second at Catterick and Newcastle (nursery): gelded after final start: stays 7f: acts on good to firm and good to soft going. *J. Howard Johnson*

MAD MAN WILL (IRE) 2 b.g. (Feb 24) Namid 128 – Native Queen (FR) (Desert **57** King (IRE) 129) [2007 p6g⁵ Dec 13] 15,500Y: first foal: dam, French 1¼m winner, out of half-sister to very smart 1¼m performer/Champion Hurdle winner Alderbrook: better effort in maidens at Wolverhampton (gelded in between) when last of 5. *S. C. Williams*

MADRIGALE 3 b.f. Averti (IRE) 117 – Shy Minstrel (USA) (The Minstrel (CAN) **74** 135) [2007 61: p6g³ p6g² p7g⁵ p7g² p7g* p7g⁴ Apr 30] fair performer: won maiden at Lingfield in March: will stay 1m: acts on polytrack and firm ground: carried head awkwardly on debut: races prominently. *G. L. Moore*

MAD RUSH (USA) 3 b.c. Lemon Drop Kid (USA) 131 – Revonda (IRE) (Sadler's **103 p** Wells (USA) 132) [2007 10g³ 10.5g* 10s² 12d² Jun 27] $80,000Y: big, rangy colt: half-brother to several winners, including useful Italian 1¼m winner Nashatara (by Nashwan) and 1½m winner Dinofelis (by Rainbow Quest): dam unraced sister to smart 7f/1m winner Yalaietanee: useful and progressive performer: won maiden at Haydock (by 3½ lengths from Coastal Command) in May: runner-up after in handicaps at Leicester (beaten ½ length by Greek Envoy) and Salisbury (short headed by Hi Calypso having looked sure to win): suffered setback after (said to have recovered): stays 1½m: raced only on good going or softer: looks type to do well at 4 yrs. *L. M. Cumani*

MAE CIGAN (FR) 4 gr.g. Medaaly 114 – Concert (Polar Falcon (USA) 126) [2007 76: **75** p12g 10g² 10.2d⁴ 10.2g⁵ 10s⁶ 10.5v⁴ 9.9g⁴ p11g² p12g⁶ 11.9s* p12g⁵ 11.7g⁶ Oct 24] angular gelding: fair handicapper: won at Haydock in September: stays 1½m: acts on polytrack, heavy and good to firm going: tried visored at 2 yrs: often held up. *M. Blanshard*

MAEVE (IRE) 3 b.f. Tomba 119 – Boozy 111 (Absalom 128) [2007 53: 6g 5.7d⁶ f6g⁵ **47** p6g⁶ f7d Dec 15] poor maiden. *E. J. Creighton*

MAFAHEEM 5 b.g. Mujahid (USA) 125 – Legend of Aragon 67 (Aragon 118) [2007 **85** p7f p8g 5m⁶ 6m 5.7d⁸ 6v* 6d⁵ 5.1s⁵ 7s⁴ p6g p6g⁴ Dec 8] strong, well-made gelding: fairly useful performer: won sellers at Bath (sold from S. Dow 5,000 gns) in June and Windsor in July, and claimer at Wolverhampton in October (final start for P. D. Evans): stays 7f: unraced on firm going, acts on any other turf and polytrack: said to have finished lame ninth start: none too reliable. *A. B. Haynes*

MAFASINA (USA) 2 b.f. (Apr 7) Orientate (USA) 127 – Money Madam (USA) (A P **72** Indy (USA) 131) [2007 p7g* p8g⁴ Dec 4] $60,000Y, 45,000 2-y-o: seventh foal: half-sister to minor Japanese stakes winner around 9f Feminine Girl (by Kingmambo) and 2 winners in US: dam, US 9f winner, half-sister to US Grade 2 6f winner Funistrada: fair form: won maiden at Lingfield in November: respectable effort in nursery there only other outing. *Christian Wroe*

MAFEKING (UAE) 3 b.g. Jade Robbery (USA) 121 – Melisendra (FR) (Highest **93** Honor (FR) 124) [2007 80: p10g² 11g⁵ 9.9g p8g⁴ p8g³ p8.6g² p10g³ p10g² p10g³ p10m* Dec 8] useful-looking gelding: fairly useful handicapper: won at Lingfield in December: stays 1¼m: raced only on polytrack and good ground: reliable. *M. R. Hoad*

MAFIOSO 2 b.c. (Mar 8) Red Ransom (USA) – Lamarque (IRE) (Nureyev (USA) 131) **88 p** [2007 6g 6.1m³ p7g² p7.1g* Nov 9] stocky colt: fifth foal: half-brother to fairly useful winner around 1¼m (including at 2 yrs) La Mouline (by Nashwan): dam unraced close relation to Arc winner Carnegie out of Arc winner Detroit: fairly useful form: placed at Nottingham and Kempton (second to Adversity) prior to winning maiden at Wolverhampton by 3 lengths from Jerry Hamilton: should progress at 1m/1¼m. *M. Johnston*

MAGDALENE 3 ch.f. Act One 124 – Three Terns (USA) (Arctic Tern (USA) 126) **76** [2007 63: 10d⁴ 8.5s² 8.5s⁴ 10.1d* p12.2g⁴ p9.5g Oct 15] tall, good-topped filly: fair handicapper: won at Yarmouth in August: stays 1½m: acts on polytrack and soft going. *Rae Guest*

MAGGIE KATE 2 b.f. (Feb 6) Auction House (USA) 120 – Perecapa (IRE) 44 (Arch- **61** way (IRE) 115) [2007 p6g⁶ p7.1d² Dec 28] 1,500Y: third foal: dam 11f winner: modest form in maidens at Kempton and Wolverhampton: should stay beyond 7f. *R. Ingram*

MAGICAL FANTASY (USA) 2 ch.f. (Mar 24) Diesis 133 – Kissing Gate (USA) 62 **78** (Easy Goer (USA)) [2007 7m p7g⁴ p8g² p8.6g² p8m* Nov 26] strong filly: type to carry condition: sixth foal: half-sister to several winners, including smart 1m (including at 2 yrs) winner Forward Move (by Dr Fong) and fairly useful 13f/1¾m winner Turnstile (by Linamix): dam, 2-y-o 8.5f winner, half-sister to very smart sprinter Keen Hunter and smart performers up to 1¼m Altibr and Marnor, all by Diesis: fair performer: runner-up at Kempton and Wolverhampton (clear with Mystery Star) before winning maiden at Lingfield: should stay 1¼m. *J. Nicol*

MAGICAL MUSIC 4 b.f. Fraam 114 – Magical Flute 75 (Piccolo 121) [2007 62, a96: **70** p8.6g⁴ p10g p10g³ 8m p8g 8d 8s* 8g 8.2g³ 8d³ p8g* 8g p8g⁵ p8.6g⁵ p9.5g Dec 1] strong **a94** filly: fairly useful handicapper on all-weather, fair on turf: won at Pontefract in July and Kempton (valuable event, beat Evident Pride by neck) in September: stays 1¼m: acts on all-weather, soft and good to firm ground: held up. *J. Pearce*

MAGICALMYSTERYTOUR (IRE) 4 b.g. Sadler's Wells (USA) 132 – Jude 53 **100** (Darshaan 133) [2007 93: 12m 11.6m³ 10d² 12m 13.3m* Aug 17] strong, good-bodied gelding: useful handicapper: best effort when winning at Newbury in August by 1¾ lengths from Silver Suitor, travelling strongly: stays 13.3f: acts on heavy and good to firm going. *W. J. Musson*

MAGICAL SONG 2 ch.c. (Apr 19) Forzando 122 – Classical Song (IRE) 69 (Fayruz **45** 116) [2007 p6g⁶ 6m p6g p8g Nov 21] poor maiden: left E. O'Neill after third start: probably stays 1m. *P. A. Blockley*

MAGICAL SPEEDFIT (IRE) 2 ch.g. (Mar 31) Bold Fact (USA) 116 – Magical **71** Peace (IRE) 80 (Magical Wonder (USA) 125) [2007 5m² 5d² 5m 5s² 5.2g² 6f⁴ 5m² 5.1g 6m Oct 5] sturdy gelding: fair maiden: runner-up 4 times: gelded after final start: effective at 5f/6f: acts on firm and soft going. *G. G. Margarson*

MAGICAL WORLD 4 b.f. Agnes World (USA) 123 – Otaru (IRE) (Indian Ridge **–** 123) [2007 –: p5.1g 7g Apr 3] smallish, lengthy filly: of no account. *J. M. Bradley*

MAGIC AMIGO 6 ch.g. Zilzal (USA) 137 – Emaline (FR) 105 (Empery (USA) 128) **65** [2007 79, a67: p12g² p12g f11g 11.5m 10.1d⁵ p11g 10.1d⁴ 10.1d⁴ 10.1m⁵ p10g⁵ p10g⁴ p10g⁴ p11g p12g³ Dec 12] tall, leggy gelding: fair handicapper: stays easy 1½m: acts on all-weather, heavy and good to firm ground: often wears cheekpieces/visor nowadays: sometimes races freely. *J. R. Jenkins*

MAGIC AMOUR 9 ch.g. Sanglamore (USA) 126 – Rakli 84 (Warning 136) [2007 71: **67** f6g³ f5g* p7.1g⁴ p6g² p6g* p6g* p5.1g³ p5.1g³ Apr 21] strong, lengthy gelding: fair performer: won seller at Southwell in January and seller and claimer (within 24 hours) at Wolverhampton in March: effective at 5f to 1m: acts on all-weather and firm going, well held on softer than good: blinkered/visored nowadays: usually races up with pace. *P. A. Blockley*

MAGIC BOX 9 b.g. Magic Ring (IRE) 115 – Princess Poquito (Hard Fought 125) [2007 – 8.3d Jul 14] strong, good-bodied gelding: one-time fair performer: well held in 2 runs on Flat since 2001: tried in visor/cheekpieces/tongue tie. *A. M. Crow*

MAGIC CLOVER (ARG) 6 ch.h. Candy Stripes (USA) 115 – Magnanimity (ARG) **82 +** (Babas Fables (USA)) [2007 12m Sep 21] ex-Argentinian horse: won 4 of 15 starts in native country, including handicap at San Isidro in 2006: off 18 months (seemingly in need of run) and 20/1, fairly useful form when eighth in handicap at Newbury on British debut: stays 11f: acts on dirt and any turf ground. *P. R. Webber*

MAGIC ECHO 3 b.f. Wizard King 122 – Sunday News'n'echo (USA) 78 (Trempolino **84** (USA) 135) [2007 76: 8.2s³ 9.9m³ 10g* 9.9s* 10.3s⁵ 8m 10d² 10d⁶ Oct 11] close-coupled, compact filly: fairly useful handicapper: won at Nottingham and Beverley (3 ran) in June: stays 1¼m: acts on soft and good to firm going: usually makes running. *M. Dods*

MAGIC GLADE 8 b.g. Magic Ring (IRE) 115 – Ash Glade (Nashwan (USA) 135) **95** [2007 91: f5g* p5.1g³ p6g⁵ f6s* p5f* p6g 5g 5m³ 5g⁴ 5g 5.1d 5m 5g³ p6g² p6g* p6g* p5.1g³ f5d Dec 11] compact gelding: useful performer: won 6 times in 2007, namely handicap and claimer at Southwell, handicaps at Lingfield and Thirsk, and claimers at Kempton and Wolverhampton (left Tom Dascombe): effective at 5f/6f: acts on allweather, firm and soft going: tried in cheekpieces/blinkers: has bled: usually held up. *Peter Grayson*

MAGIC MOTH 4 b.c. Mtoto 134 – Majoune (FR) 105 (Take Risks (FR) 116) [2007 **77** 73: 11.7f⁴ p12.2g³ 13.1g 13f Jun 7] fairly useful on all-weather, fair on turf: lightly raced: **a82** creditable efforts in handicaps first 2 starts in 2007: should be suited by 1¾m: acts on polytrack and firm ground: tried blinkered: has shown signs of temperament: sold 7,000 gns, joined John Joseph Hanlon, Ireland. *M. Johnston*

MAGIC MOUNTAIN (IRE) 3 b.c. Dr Fong (USA) 128 – Hard Task 82 (Formidable **86 d** (USA) 125) [2007 82: 8.1g⁵ 7.6m⁵ 10d⁴ 8.1g 7s² 8.3f 8.1d³ 10g⁴ p11g p11g⁶ p11g² Oct 17] stocky colt: fairly useful performer: below form after third outing: stays 11f: acts on polytrack, soft and good to firm ground: tried blinkered: won only start in a tongue tie: sold 10,000 gns. *R. Hannon*

MAGIC RUSH 5 b.g. Almaty (IRE) 113§ – Magic Legs 54 (Reprimand 122) [2007 88: **87** f6g⁶ p8g p8g² p6g Apr 20] fairly useful handicapper: good second at Lingfield third start: stays 1m: acts on polytrack and soft going: often races prominently: successful over hurdles in October. *Mrs Norma Pook*

MAGIC SHOW 3 b.c. Marju (IRE) 127 – White Rabbit 99 (Zilzal (USA) 137) [2007 **89 +** 10g 8.3m⁶ p8g 10.1d² p12g* 11.5g* Sep 18] 115,000Y: strong, lengthy colt: first foal: dam 2-y-o 6f winner who stayed 1m: fairly useful and progressive form: left J. Gosden 15,000 gns after debut: won handicaps at Lingfield and Yarmouth (readily by 3 lengths) in September: stays 1½m: acts on polytrack and good to soft ground. *Jane Chapple-Hyam*

MAGIC STING 6 ch.g. Magic Ring (IRE) 115 – Ground Game 95 (Gildoran 123) – [2007 90: 9.9g 8m 11.5d 10.1v 9.8v⁶ 10.1d 8m 10s Sep 26] smallish, workmanlike gelding: fairly useful handicapper at best: little form in 2007 (said to have bled once): tried visored. *B. S. Rothwell*

MAGIC WARRIOR 7 b.g. Magic Ring (IRE) 115 – Clarista (USA) 67 (Riva Ridge **49 +** (USA)) [2007 68, a76: p10g p8g p8.6g⁵ p10g³ p8g² p8g² p8g³ 9g⁶ p8g⁵ p10g⁵ p8g⁶ **a76** p8g p8g p8.6g p8g⁵ p8g³ p10m⁶ p9.5s* p10g⁴ Dec 28] strong, compact gelding: fair performer, better on all-weather than turf: won at Wolverhampton in December: stays easy 1¼m: acts on polytrack and firm ground: tried blinkered: held up: twice said to have bled. *J. C. Fox*

MAGNIFICO (FR) 6 b.g. Solid Illusion (USA) 117 – Born For Run (FR) (Pharly (FR) – 130) [2007 p13.9g⁶ Jan 27] fourth in 15f maiden at Fontainebleau for G. Cherel on debut at 4 yrs: well held in similar event at Wolverhampton only Flat start since: fairly useful but unreliable hurdler. *Mrs K. Waldron*

MAGNOL 2 gr.f. (Apr 30) Tobougg (IRE) 125 – Magnolia 52 (Petong 126) [2007 5s **49** f6g⁶ 7d² p7g p10g 8.2g⁶ Oct 31] sixth foal: half-sister to 1m winner One Upmanship (by

Bahamian Bounty) and Italian 9f/1¼m (at 2 yrs) winner Lujarun (by Lujain): dam, ran twice, half-sister to smart 7f winner Naahy: poor maiden: second in seller at Redcar (left M. Jarvis £6,000): should stay 1¼m: acts on polytrack and good to soft going: none too keen. *J. G. M. O'Shea*

MAGNUM OPUS (IRE) 5 b.g. Sadler's Wells (USA) 132 – Summer Breeze 101 **62** (Rainbow Quest (USA) 134) [2007 –: 12.1s 17.1d⁶ 14.1d⁵ 13.1f³ p16g 10m 9.9d 10g Oct 19] sturdy gelding: modest handicapper nowadays: left J. S. Moore after reappearance: stays 15f (seemingly not 17f): acts on good to soft going: tried in headgear/tongue strap. *D. J. Murphy*

MAGNUS (AUS) 5 b.h. Flying Spur (AUS) – Scandinavia (AUS) 116 (Snippets **122** (AUS)) [2007 5g² 5.5g³ 6g⁴ 5.5d* 5m³ 6d 5g Aug 23] strong horse: third foal: dam Australian Group 2 6f winner: very smart performer: has won 4 of his 14 starts in Australia, including Group 2 The Age Classic at Flemington in 2006 and Group 1 Bisley Workwear Galaxy Handicap at Warwick Farm (by short neck from Fast 'n' Famous) in March: in frame earlier in 2007 in Lightning Stakes (1½ lengths second to Miss Andretti) at Moonee Valley, and Oakleigh Plate (½-length third to Undue) and Newmarket Handicap (½-length fourth behind Miss Andretti), both at Caulfield: very good 2 lengths third to Miss Andretti in King's Stand Stakes at Royal Ascot in June, headed 1f out: below that form after, in Golden Jubilee Stakes, also at Royal Ascot, and Nunthorpe Stakes at York (ninth behind Kingsgate Native): effective at 5f/6f: acts on soft and good to firm going: blinkered all 3 starts in Britain. *Peter G. Moody, Australia*

MAGNUSHOMESTWO (IRE) 2 b.g. (May 4) Val Royal (FR) 127 – Classy Act **–** 76 (Lycius (USA) 124) [2007 5d 6d 5f 6d 5d p5.1g Oct 22] little form: tried blinkered. *A. Berry*

MAGROOM 3 b.g. Compton Place 125 – Fudge (Polar Falcon (USA) 126) [2007 p8g **75** p7g 10f 6m 7d* 7m* 7d² 7d⁴ 7g³ 8m⁵ 8m p7g* p8g⁴ 8d² 8m* p8.6g² p8g Dec 1] fair performer: won sellers at Brighton in May and June (sold from B. Johnson 8,200 gns), and handicaps at Lingfield in September (dead-heated) and Bath in October: stays 8.6f: acts on polytrack, good to firm and good to soft going: usually in cheekpieces/visor in first half of season. *R. J. Hodges*

MAHADEE (IRE) 2 b. or br.g. (Feb 3) Cape Cross (IRE) 129 – Rafiya 89 (Halling **67** (USA) 133) [2007 7m 7.5g 7m² 7.1g 8d Oct 23] 50,000Y: tall, quite attractive gelding: second foal: half-brother to 1¾m winner Riff Raff (by Daylami): dam, 1½m winner, out of smart 1¼m and 13.5f winner Nemesia: ran creditably in nursery at Warwick next start: should stay 1¼m/1½m. *C. E. Brittain*

MAHLER 3 b.c. Galileo (IRE) 134 – Rainbow Goddess (Rainbow Quest (USA) 134) **119** [2007 10g 10m* 12m* 12g 16d* 12d⁵ 14.6m² 16g³ Nov 6] 140,000Y: good-bodied colt: third foal: dam, German 1¼m winner, sister to dam of 2000 Guineas winner Footstepsinthesand: smart performer: won maiden at Leopardstown in April, minor event at Gowran in May and Queen's Vase at Royal Ascot (beat Veracity by 3½ lengths) in June: better form after, including when placed in St Leger at Doncaster (length second to Lucarno) and Melbourne Cup (Handicap) at Flemington (3 lengths third to Efficient): stays 2m: acts on good to firm and good to soft going: tends to sweat: races up with pace. *A. P. O'Brien, Ireland*

MAHMJRA 5 b.g. Josr Algarhoud (IRE) 118 – Jamrat Samya (IRE) 79 (Sadler's Wells **65** (USA) 132) [2007 –: f12g² p13.9g f12g³ f11g* f12g⁴ f11g* f11g³ f11g³ 10g 14m f11g* **a76** 12.6s⁵ 12.3s⁶ 12m 16f 11.6m p11g p12m 11.9g Oct 25] big, strong gelding: fair handicapper: won at Southwell in February, March and June: stays 1¾m: acts on fibresand and good to firm going: effective with/without visor: tried tongue tied: usually makes running: sold 7,000 gns. *C. N. Allen*

Queen's Vase, Royal Ascot—Mahler bounces back after the Derby, and is in control from Veracity (right) and Secret Tune

MAHUSAY (IRE) 2 b.c. (Feb 6) Noverre (USA) 125 – Saada One (IRE) 66 (Polish **80** Precedent (USA) 131) [2007 5s* 6s5 6g4 7m 8g Oct 26] smallish, compact colt: first foal: dam, maiden (stayed 1m), half-sister to 6-y-o Lost Soldier Three: fairly useful form: won maiden at Leicester in May: fourth at Pontefract, best effort in nurseries (off 3 months before final start): should stay at least 1m: acts on soft going: sold 12,000 gns. *L. M. Cumani*

MAIA 3 ch.f. Observatory (USA) 131 – Preference (Efisio 120) [2007 5f3 7m 6m* 6d **69** 6m* Jul 11] angular filly: third foal: half-sister to 6-y-o Ice Planet: dam unraced sister to smart 6f/7f performer Casteddu: fair performer: won maiden in May and handicap in July, both at Catterick: should stay 7f: acts on good to firm ground. *D. Nicholls*

MAIDANNI (USA) 5 b. or br.g. Private Terms (USA) – Carley's Birthday (USA) **67 +** (Marfa (USA)) [2007 p8m Dec 10] rangy gelding: fair performer for Saeed bin Suroor at 2 yrs: ran as if in need of race on belated return: stays 1m. *J. R. Gask*

MAIDEN INVESTOR 4 b.f. Orpen (USA) 116 – Actress 73 (Known Fact (USA) 135) **54** [2007 54: p9.5g f7g 6g 6d6 p8.6d5 p8.6g* p8.6g5 Dec 29] lengthy filly: modest performer: left M. Saunders after fourth start: won maiden at Wolverhampton in December: stays easy 8.6f: acts on polytrack. *Stef Liddiard*

MAIDEN MISS (IRE) 2 b.f. (Apr 19) Xaar 132 – Cheeky Weeky (Cadeaux Genereux **51** 131) [2007 6d6 7m5 6g5 p7g6 Sep 29] €21,000Y: leggy filly: half-sister to several winners, including 3-y-o Pretty Majestic and 1¼m winner Cellarmaster (by Alhaarth): dam, French maiden (stayed 1½m), out of close relative of Mujadil/half-sister to Fruits of Love: modest maiden: should stay 1m: looks awkward: sold 800 gns. *M. R. Channon*

MAID IN BLOOM 2 b.f. (Mar 3) Averti (IRE) 117 – Fille de Fleurie 63 (Whittingham **60** (IRE) 104) [2007 5m4 5f3 5m6 f5d5 Dec 20] 2,000Y: first foal: dam sprint maiden: modest form in maidens, staying on: will be suited by 6f. *B. Smart*

MAID OF ALE (IRE) 3 b.f. Barathea (IRE) 127 – Borders Belle (IRE) 96 (Pursuit of **57** Love 124) [2007 61: 8.3d 8.1m 10g Aug 30] rather leggy filly: modest maiden: probably stays 8.3f: acts on good to firm going: tried blinkered. *A. King*

MAID OF LAMANCHA 2 ch.f. (Jan 27) Bahamian Bounty 116 – Golden Fortune **–** 102 (Forzando 122) [2007 7g Oct 3] 5,000Y: fifth foal: half-sister to several winners, including 5-y-o Along The Nile and 1¼m winner Fortune's Princess, both by Desert Prince and fairly useful: dam 6f (at 2 yrs) to 7.5f winner: 20/1, finished lame in maiden at Newcastle. *J. R. Weymes*

MAID TO BELIEVE 3 b.f. Galileo (IRE) 134 – Maid For The Hills 101 (Indian Ridge **106** 123) [2007 73: 10.5g 10d* 10s4 11.6m3 11.6f* 12m* 12d4 Sep 28] leggy, close-coupled filly: improved into a useful performer: won handicaps at Windsor in May, and Windsor and Salisbury (by 3 lengths from Fourteenth) in August: ran very well when 3½ lengths fourth to Brisk Breeze in listed race at Ascot final outing: will stay 1¾m: acts on firm and soft going: edgy sort (often sweats). *J. L. Dunlop*

MAIMOONA (IRE) 2 ch.f. (Apr 8) Pivotal 124 – Shuruk 73 (Cadeaux Genereux 131) **82** [2007 6d2 6d2 Sep 28] rather leggy, close-coupled filly: has a moderate quick action: third foal: dam, 2-y-o 6f winner, half-sister to very smart French/US performer up to 1½m Volochine: fairly useful form when second in maidens at Newmarket (to Upton Grey) and Haydock: likely to stay 7f/1m. *W. J. Haggas*

MAIREAD'S BOY (IRE) 2 ch.c. (Jan 10) Noverre (USA) 125 – Welltold (IRE) 64 **60** (Danehill (USA) 126) [2007 5.1d 5.7g 6m 7m 5m p6g3 p6g p6g2 p7g2 p6g4 p6g4 p8g2 Dec 12] sturdy colt: modest maiden: left J. S. Moore, good second in nursery at Kempton final outing, making most: stays 1m: acts on polytrack: usually wears headgear. *P. Butler*

MAISON DIEU 4 br. or b.g. King Charlemagne (USA) 120 – Shining Desert (IRE) 82 **67** (Green Desert (USA) 127) [2007 68: 6g* p6g3 7m6 6m5 6d p7.1g 6m 7m2 6f 7.6m4 7.1m 8g p6g p6g3 Nov 1] useful-looking gelding: fair handicapper: won at Southwell in April: stays 7f: acts on polytrack and firm going: tried in cheekpieces/blinkers: has been slowly away: none too consistent. *E. J. Alston*

MAJEEN 2 ch.c. (Apr 23) Rock of Gibraltar (IRE) 133 – Guilty Secret (IRE) 109 (Kris **83 p** 135) [2007 8m 7g2 8d2 Oct 30] big, useful-looking colt: half-brother to several winners, including useful 1m/9.3f winner Mawsoof (by Alzao) and fairly useful 1½m winner Abyssinian Wolf (by Dr Devious): dam 1½m winner and second in Park Hill Stakes: fairly useful form in maidens, shaping well when second at Leicester and Yarmouth (beaten 2 lengths by First Avenue): bred to stay 1¼m, not short of speed: type to progress at 3 yrs. *W. J. Haggas*

MAJEHAR 5 b.g. Marju (IRE) 127 – Joonayh 81 (Warning 136) [2007 50, a61: f8g² **56 +** f8g* p8g⁵ f8g³ 10m p8g⁴ p8.6g⁴ p10g* p12g* 10m⁴ p10g* p11m³ Nov 11] fair handi- **a69** capper on all-weather, modest on turf: won at Southwell in February, Lingfield in July and August, and Kempton in October: stays 1½m: acts on all-weather, good to firm and good to soft going: often held up. *A. G. Newcombe*

MAJESTAS (IRE) 3 b.g. Val Royal (FR) 127 – Pantera Piceno (IRE) (College Chapel **–** 122) [2007 71: 8.2s 11.6d Jul 23] smallish, rather leggy gelding: fair maiden at 2 yrs: well held in 2007, in seller latter outing: tried tongue tied. *Evan Williams*

MAJESTICAL (IRE) 5 b.g. Fayruz 116 – Haraabah (USA) 99 (Topsider (USA)) **62** [2007 59, a73: p6g p6g p6g⁵ p5.1g⁴ p6g⁵ p6g⁴ p6g p5g p6g p5.1g* 5m 5.3d⁵ 6s* p5g⁴ 5.2d* 7m⁴ 6m⁵ p6g p6g⁴ 6d p7g² p6m² p7g³ p7g³ Nov 21] tall gelding: modest handi-capper: left J. M. Bradley, won at Wolverhampton in May, Folkestone (claimer) in June and Yarmouth in July: effective at 5f to easy 7f: acts on polytrack, firm and soft going: tried blinkered/in cheekpieces: often slowly away: has wandered/carried head high: held up. *V. Smith*

MAJESTIC CHEER 3 b.g. Royal Applause 124 – Muwasim (USA) (Meadowlake **73** (USA)) [2007 75: p6g³ 6g⁶ 5g 6f⁴ 5m p8g p6m p10.7g Dec 5] quite good-topped geld-ing: fair handicapper: left M. Channon after fifth start and E. Dunlop (1,000 gns) after seventh: will prove best up to 7f: acts on polytrack and firm going, probably on soft: tongue tied final outing: often slowly away/finds little. *W. Power, Ireland*

MAJESTIC CHIEF 3 b.g. Xaar 132 – Grand Splendour 79 (Shirley Heights 130) **72** [2007 –: 8.2m⁴ 12f f8g⁶ p12.2g⁵ 10m² Jul 27] heavy-topped gelding, type to carry plenty of condition: fair maiden: left K. Ryan after third outing: stays 1¼m: acts on good to firm going: wore cheekpieces last 2 starts: won juvenile hurdle in August, then sold 20,000 gns. *P. D. Niven*

MAJESTIC MARAUDER (USA) 2 b. or br.c. (Feb 4) War Chant (USA) 126 – Rose **80 p** Bourbon (USA) (Woodman (USA) 126) [2007 7d Jul 27] $200,000Y: strong, well-made colt: closely related to Irish 8.5f winner Georgina (by Polish Precedent) and half-brother to 2 winners, including useful 2002 2-y-o 7f winner Bourbonnais (by Singspiel), later successful in US: dam, useful French maiden (should have stayed 1m), half-sister to Poule d'Essai des Pouliches winner Baiser Vole: 7/4, more promise from bare result (seventh to City Leader) in maiden at Ascot, green and poorly positioned: will be suited by 1m/1¼m: has joined Godolphin: bound to improve. *Sir Michael Stoute*

MAJESTIC ROI (USA) 3 ch.f. Street Cry (IRE) 130 – L'Extra Honor (USA) **122** (Hero's Honor (USA)) [2007 86p: 7m* 8g² 8d 7g⁵ 7m⁴ 8m* Oct 6]
Approaching the first weekend in October, the owner/trainer combination of Jaber Abdullah and Mick Channon would probably have considered 2007 to have been a successful campaign. The trainer had bettered his count of recent seasons with seven pattern winners in Britain and Ireland, no fewer than four of them in the now-familiar royal blue and white colours of Abdullah, including those of emerging One Thousand Guineas hopes Nijoom Dubai and Nahoodh. However, things were about to get even better. Not only did the Abdullah/Channon flag-bearer Youmzain belie long odds when going down narrowly in the Prix de l'Arc de Triomphe, but twenty-four hours earlier Majestic Roi provided the partnership with its first home Group 1 success since Zafeen won the St James's Palace Stakes in 2003 as she sprung a surprise herself in the Kingdom of Bahrain Sun Chariot Stakes.
Some recent renewals of the Sun Chariot haven't proved so competitive as they might with many fillies over the top by that late stage of the season. The first four in the market all ran well below form the previous year as the outsider of the five-strong field Spinning Queen came home a wide margin winner. Paddock inspection suggested that would not be repeated in the latest season, with the entire field impressing in appearance. There was plenty of depth too. In betting order: the late-maturing Echelon had thrived since mid-summer, making the breakthrough to Group 2 and then Group 1 success in the Celebration Mile and Matron Stakes respectively; the Fillies' Mile winner Simply Perfect had returned to finish third in the Guineas and since added another top-level success in the Falmouth Stakes; whilst 2006 Coronation Stakes winner Nannina and that year's One Thousand Guineas winner Speciosa also went off at single figure odds, the former having shown she retained all of her old sparkle with an authoritative success in the

*Kingdom of Bahrain Sun Chariot Stakes, Newmarket—in a strong renewal,
Majestic Roi shows plenty of improvement to beat Nannina (far side), Echelon and Simply Perfect (rail)*

Windsor Forest Stakes at Royal Ascot, and the latter defending a good record on the Rowley Mile, with her only defeat from four starts there coming at the hands of Manduro in the spring. Majestic Roi was joint-sixth favourite at 16/1 in a field of nine but it became apparent at around halfway that her backers were going to have a good run for their money. In what appeared a soundly-run race, the front-running Speciosa had lost her chance soon after halfway and, with three furlongs to run, matters must have looked to some to be between the Cheveley Park Stud-owned pair of Nannina and Echelon as they swept past Simply Perfect. Majestic Roi was finding her stride against the rail in fifth, though, and, as Nannina edged to her right in front, tightening up Echelon, Majestic Roi was switched wide and came with a sustained run to cut her down in the final hundred yards, going away at the line to win by three quarters of a length, with Echelon a further length back in third.

Majestic Roi's Sun Chariot success might well have come as something of a surprise, but it wasn't the first she had inflicted. Reported by her trainer to be backward at two, put away as early as June after winning a maiden at Hamilton on her second start, Majestic Roi upset Indian Ink when coming from last to first to win the Dubai Duty Free Stakes (Fred Darling) at Newbury by a neck at odds of 25/1. Majestic Roi held an entry in the Oaks and not the One Thousand Guineas at the time, with her connections also having Sweet Lilly in the latter, but the speed she showed marked her down as one likely to do best at around the shorter trip. Plans to supplement her for the Poule d'Essai des Pouliches came to nothing but she did go to France (where her bizarrely masculine name must have caused some confusion) for her next outing, in the Group 2 Prix de Sandringham at Chantilly in June, only to find a steady gallop counting against her as she stayed on to go down by two and a half lengths to all-the-way winner All Is Vanity. Majestic Roi's bare form left her with something to find in the Coronation Stakes, in which Indian Ink scored an impressive success, and she had no luck in running on her next two starts, doing well to finish as close as fifth behind Wake Up Maggie in the Oak Tree Stakes at Goodwood, quickening once belatedly in the clear, and fourth to Medley in a listed race at Doncaster, going on strongly after another moderate run through.

Majestic Roi is from the second crop of Dubai World Cup winner Street Cry, who is fast making a name for himself at stud. With three other individual Group or Grade 1 winners in the latest season, including Kentucky Derby winner Street Sense, his fee has doubled for 2008 to 100,000 dollars. Majestic Roi is the ninth foal of her dam, and the fifth to win a race. Of the four others, none won more than once, though a half-brother Heza Gone West (by Gone West), was placed in a Grade 3 over a mile at two in the States, and a half-sister Hiddnah (by Affirmed), showed useful form to be placed three times in listed company for Mark Johnston, and finished sixth in the Park Hill Stakes. Their dam, L'Extra Honor, won twice at a

Mr Jaber Abdullah's "Majestic Roi"

	Street Cry (IRE) (br 1998)	Machiavellian (b 1987)	Mr Prospector / Coup de Folie
Majestic Roi (USA) (ch.f. 2004)		Helen Street (b 1982)	Troy / Waterway
	L'Extra Honor (USA) (ch 1987)	Hero's Honor (b 1980)	Northern Dancer / Glowing Tribute
		L'Extravagante (b 1973)	Le Fabuleux / Fanfreluche

mile and a half as a four-year-old in France, including a listed event, and was very well connected herself being a half-sister to very smart mile-and-a-quarter winner Montelimar, who went on to sire two Grand National winners. The second dam L'Extravagante was third in the Canadian Oaks and comes from one of the best Canadian families, being a half-sister to no fewer than five stakes winners in North America, including L'Enjoleur (dual Horse of the Year in Canada) and D'Accord, who also proved themselves in the States as juvenile Grade 1 and 2 winners respectively. Another of L'Extravagante's half-sisters is dam of Holy Roman Emperor. The family traces back one more generation to Fanfreluche, who earned the titles of Canadian Horse of the Year and United States Co-Champion Three-Year-Old Filly in 1970, and later made the headlines when sold as a broodmare prospect for a then-world-record price of 1,300,000 dollars. That wasn't the last time Fanfreluche made the news, famously being abducted from Claiborne Farm in Kentucky seven years later and only retrieved after more than five months. A lengthy, good-topped filly, who did well physically throughout the campaign, Majestic Roi looks the type to come back at least as good as ever at four. At the time of writing she is reported to have the Dubai Carnival as her first target, a path connections took unsuccessfully in the latest season with Flashy Wings. There will be plenty of options for Majestic Roi at around a mile in Europe—her form is better, for example, than that achieved at the end of her three-year-old season by subsequent Lockinge winner Red Evie. Majestic Roi won a maiden on firm going, but has done the majority of her racing on good and good to firm. Judged on pedigree, there is a chance she will stay a mile and a quarter if connections decide to step her up in trip. *M. R. Channon*

MAJESTIC TIMES (IRE) 7 b.g. Bluebird (USA) 125 – Simply Times (USA) 64 **104** (Dodge (USA)) [2007 116: 6m 6.3s 7v⁴ 6v³ 7s⁴ p6g⁴ 6d 6d 5g p6g p7g p6g Dec 7] tall, lengthy gelding: useful performer: several creditable efforts in 2007, including in listed race at Fairyhouse (third to Haatef) and Ayr Gold Cup (seventh to Advanced) fourth/ seventh outings: well below form after: probably best at 5f/6f: acts on polytrack and any turf going: occasionally blinkered. *Liam McAteer, Ireland*

MAJIGAL 2 b.f. (Apr 26) High Estate 127 – Face The Judge (USA) 59 (Benny The Dip **51** (USA) 127) [2007 5m⁵ 5.1g 6m 7d Jul 4] close-coupled filly: second foal: dam, maiden (stayed 1¼m), out of sister to Mujadil and half-sister to Fruits of Love: modest maiden: will stay 1m. *M. W. Easterby*

MAJIK 8 ch.g. Pivotal 124 – Revoke (USA) 70 (Riverman (USA) 131) [2007 –, a72: **63** f6g² f5g² f6g 5.5s a4.8g* 5.5m 5f 4g³ 5.5d⁵ a6.5g a6.5g Dec 12] close-coupled gelding: modest performer: sold from P. Midgley 3,400 gns after third start: won minor event at Mons in April: best up to 6.5f: acts on all-weather, heavy and good to firm going: tried tongue tied, wears headgear. *Stal Lannoo, Belgium*

MAJOLICA 3 br.f. Lujain (USA) 119 – Marjorie's Memory (IRE) 76 (Fairy King **36** (USA)) [2007 –: p5g Feb 3] close-coupled filly: poor form in maidens 7 months apart. *N. P. Littmoden*

MAJOR CADEAUX 3 ch.c. Cadeaux Genereux 131 – Maine Lobster (USA) 71 **116** (Woodman (USA) 126) [2007 104: 7m* 8m⁶ 7s² 6.5m⁵ Aug 5] big, strong, lengthy colt: won Lane's End Greenham Stakes at Newbury (impressively by 3½ lengths from Dutch Art, dictating and sprinting clear once shaken up over 1f out) in April: creditable efforts

N. A. Woodcock, A. C. Pickford & David Mort's "Major Cadeaux"

in 2000 Guineas (3 lengths sixth to Cockney Rebel, reportedly spread a plate on morning of race and came back sore on same foot) and Criterion Stakes (head second to Silver Touch), both at Newmarket, before respectable fifth to Marchand d'Or in Prix Maurice de Gheest at Deauville: takes strong hold, but stays 1m: acts on soft and good to firm going: has been bandaged in front. *R. Hannon*

MAJOR EAZY (IRE) 2 b.c. (Apr 24) Fasliyev (USA) 120 – Castilian Queen (USA) **98** 82 (Diesis 133) [2007 5m³ 5m⁴ 5g⁵ 5m 5s* 5.5m 5g 6d* 6d Oct 13] €70,000Y: well-made colt: eighth foal: half-brother to 3 winners, notably very smart 5f winner (including at 2 yrs) Carmine Lake (by Royal Academy): dam, 2-y-o 6f winner, out of Breeders' Cup Mile winner Royal Heroine: useful performer: won maiden at Lingfield in June and minor event at Salisbury (beat Berbice by length) in October: mostly ran in listed/pattern company otherwise: should prove best at 5f/6f: acts on soft and good to firm going. *B. J. Meehan*

MAJOR LEAGUE (USA) 5 b.g. Magic Cat (USA) – Quick Grey (USA) (El Prado **62** (IRE) 119) [2007 –: 8m 10g 8d³ 8g 8d p8.6g 8f⁵ 7.6m 7m Sep 11] big, strong gelding: modest handicapper: stays 1m: acts on dirt/polytrack, firm and good to soft going: none too consistent. *D. Morris*

MAJOR MAGPIE (IRE) 5 b.g. Rossini (USA) 118 – Picnic Basket (Pharly (FR) 130) **90** [2007 83: 7m² 8.1g* Apr 28] close-coupled gelding: fairly useful handicapper: won at Haydock in April: underwent colic surgery after: stays 1¼m: acts on firm and good to soft going: held up. *M. Dods*

MAJOR MELODY (IRE) 5 b.g. Fayruz 116 – Chiming Melody 71 (Cure The Blues **–** (USA)) [2007 11.3m 7d⁵ 9d p8.6s Dec 21] little form, including in handicap at Wolverhampton final start: virtually refused to race on debut. *J. J. Lennon, Ireland*

MAJOR WILLY 2 b.c. (Feb 2) Xaar 132 – Dame Blanche (IRE) 67 (Be My Guest **96** (USA) 126) [2007 5m⁴ 6m² 6d³ 7m³ 7d⁶ Oct 13] lengthy, useful-looking colt: first foal: dam, maiden (stayed 1m), half-sister to smart Irish 1m/9f performer Luas Line: useful maiden: placed 3 times, much improved when third to Luck Money in valuable sales race at the Curragh fourth start: will stay 1m: acts on good to firm going, didn't find much on good to soft: sold 55,000 gns, sent to Qatar. *W. Jarvis*

MAJOUNES SONG 3 gr.f. Singspiel (IRE) 133 – Majoune (FR) 105 (Take Risks (FR) **104** 116) [2007 86: 7.5m⁵ 9g³ 10m³ 12g⁶ 12m 11g⁴ 10g Oct 7] strong, good-bodied filly: useful performer: improved to win Walther J. Jacobs-Stutenpreis at Bremen (by head from Ioannina) in August: not discredited when sixth to Silkwood in Ribblesdale Stakes at Royal Ascot fourth start, making running: out of depth in Prix de l'Opera at Longchamp final outing: best form at up to 11f: raced only on good ground or firmer: has raced freely: carries head awkwardly. *M. Johnston*

MAJURO (IRE) 3 b.c. Danetime (IRE) 121 – First Fling (IRE) 63 (Last Tycoon 131) **103** [2007 97: p7g⁸ p8g⁶ 8g⁶ 8.1m⁶ 8m 7g⁵ 7d⁵ p6g² 7m³ 6d⁵ p6m p7g⁵ Oct 24] good-topped colt: useful performer: won 3-runner minor event at Lingfield (by short head from Cesc) in April: good efforts eighth to tenth starts, in handicaps at Kempton (½-length second to Edge Closer), Doncaster (third to Danehill Sundance) and Ascot (fifth to Genki): has won at 8.6f, finds 6f a minimum: acts on polytrack, firm and good to soft going: sold 75,000 gns. *M. R. Channon*

MAKAASEB (USA) 2 b.f. (Apr 2) Pulpit (USA) 117 – Turn And Sparkle (USA) **96 p** (Danzatore (CAN) 120) [2007 8m²* 7d Oct 20] $370,000F: big filly: sixth foal: half-sister to minor US winners by Gilded Time and Silver Ghost: dam, US 1m (at 2 yrs) winner, half-sister to Turn And Dance (third in Grade 1 8.5f event): useful form: impressive debut when winning maiden at Newmarket in September by ¾ length from Queen of Naples, pair clear: 11/8 but gone in coat/edgy, 4 lengths seventh of 10 to Kitty Matcham in Rockfel Stakes on same course, not punished once held: will probably stay 1¼m: remains a smart prospect. *M. A. Jarvis*

MAKABUL 4 b.g. Makbul 104 – Victoria Sioux 54 (Ron's Victory (USA) 129) [2007 **82** 84: p7g⁵ 5f 6m⁴ 6m* 6m 5m² 6s* 6g* 5d 6m 6m 6d² p6g Oct 17] rather leggy, lengthy gelding: fairly useful performer: won claimer in May and handicaps in June and July, all at Windsor: stays 6f: acts on soft and good to firm ground: tried tongue tied/blinkered. *B. R. Millman*

MAKAI 4 ch.g. Cayman Kai (IRE) 114 – Young Sue 76 (Local Suitor (USA) 128) [2007 **72 d** 66, a73: p10g p10g⁴ f12g p12g p10g⁴ p10g 11g 11.9d³ 10s 10m² p11g 11s 8g 10d Jul 25] rather leggy gelding: fair handicapper: below form after second outing: stays easy 13f: acts on all-weather, firm and soft going: usually blinkered: none too consistent. *J. J. Bridger*

MAKE A BID 2 b.f. (Mar 18) Superior Premium 122 – Make Ready 76 (Beveled – (USA)) [2007 6g p7.1g Nov 20] fourth foal: half-sister to 2003 2-y-o 1m winner Xpressions (by Turtle Island): dam 5f (at 2 yrs)/6f winner: well held in maiden and claimer (visored). *J. R. Norton*

MAKE ACQUAINTANCE 2 ch.f. (Apr 11) Reel Buddy (USA) 118 – Spindara (IRE) – 64 (Spinning World (USA) 130) [2007 6d p8.6g⁵ Nov 4] 6,000Y: close-coupled filly: second foal: half-sister to 3-y-o Spinning Game: dam, maiden, half-sister to useful 7f/1m performer Sporting Lad: no form in maidens. *M. Mullineaux*

MAKE HASTE (IRE) 3 b.g. Sadler's Wells (USA) 132 – Mosaique Bleue (Shirley **91** Heights 130) [2007 66p: 11m⁵ 10g 12d* 12.1m* 16m³ Oct 3] big, strong gelding: has scope: fairly useful handicapper: won at Pontefract in July and Beverley in August: further progression when third at Nottingham final outing: stays 2m: acts on good to firm and good to soft ground: races lazily: sold 165,000 gns, then gelded. *R. Charlton*

MAKE MY DREAM 4 b.g. My Best Valentine 122 – Sandkatoon (IRE) (Archway **72** (IRE) 115) [2007 62: p7g 6.1g 6g² 6d² 6f³ 6f² 6g⁴ p6g⁵ 5.3d² 5.3d⁴ 5.1g* p5g⁶ p5g p6m p6g⁴ Dec 12] close-coupled gelding: fair handicapper: won (first success) at Nottingham in October: effective at 5f/6f: acts on polytrack, firm and good to soft going: tried blinkered/visored: effective held up or ridden prominently. *J. Gallagher*

MAKE MY HAY 8 b.g. Bluegrass Prince (IRE) 110 – Shashi (IRE) 79 (Shaadi (USA) – 126) [2007 –: p16g Jan 14] leggy, sparely-made gelding: modest performer at best: lightly raced and no form on Flat since 2005: tried blinkered. *J. Gallagher*

MAKER'S MARK (IRE) 3 b.g. Invincible Spirit (IRE) 121 – Certain Impression **92** (USA) (Forli (ARG)) [2007 85: 5.2f* 5g 6m 5g⁵ 5.1m 5m⁶ Oct 22] sturdy gelding: fairly useful handicapper, lightly raced: won at Newbury in August: creditable efforts last 3 starts: should prove best at 5f/6f: unraced on going softer than good (acts on firm): visored final outing: sold 7,000 gns, sent to Belgium. *H. Candy*

MAKFLY 4 b.g. Makbul 104 – Flying Flip 67 (Rolfe (USA) 77) [2007 90d: 8.1g 8.5m – 12.3f 10.9d Jun 28] workmanlike gelding: fairly useful performer at 3 yrs: little impact in handicaps in 2007: best form at 6f: acts on heavy ground: tried in cheekpieces/blinkered. *R. Hollinshead*

MAKING MUSIC 4 b.f. Makbul 104 – Crofters Ceilidh 101 (Scottish Reel 123) [2007 **72** 72: 7.5m 7.1m 5.9g 5s 5d⁴ 5m* 5m* 5m* 5m⁴ Sep 27] lengthy, good-topped filly: fair handicapper: won at Newcastle and Hamilton in August and Beverley in September: best at 5f/6f: acts on firm going: tried blinkered (including for wins)/in cheekpieces: sometimes wanders: races up with pace nowadays. *T. D. Easterby*

MAKSHOOF (IRE) 3 b.g. Kyllachy 129 – Tres Sage (Reprimand 122) [2007 84: 6g* **87** 5d 5g⁶ 6d 7m⁶ Nov 10] good-topped gelding: has a fluent action: fairly useful handicapper: won at Haydock in May: left M. Jarvis 42,000 gns after next start: ran creditably final outing: may prove best short of 7f: acts on firm and soft ground. *K. A. Ryan*

MAKTAVISH 8 b.g. Makbul 104 – La Belle Vie 73 (Indian King (USA) 128) [2007 –, – a87: f5g² f5g f5g⁶ f5g f5g f5g p5.1g 5.1m 5.1g f5d Dec 14] close-coupled gelding: fair **a71 d** handicapper at best in 2007: best at 5f: acts on all-weather and probably any turf going (all 6 turf wins on good or softer): wears headgear: has run well when sweating: tends to hang right: speedy front runner. *R. Brotherton*

MALAATH (IRE) 3 b.f. Green Desert (USA) 127 – Mouwadh (USA) 64 (Nureyev **69** (USA) 131) [2007 78p: 7.1d⁶ 7f⁵ 7d Aug 26] fair performer: disappointing in handicaps in 2007, leaving Saeed bin Suroor after reappearance: raced only around 7f: acts on polytrack: slowly away final outing: sent to France. *E. A. L. Dunlop*

MALAKIYA (IRE) 4 b.g. Sadler's Wells (USA) 132 – State Crystal (IRE) 114 (High **77** Estate 127) [2007 80: 18g³ Apr 10] fair handicapper: stays 2¼m: acts on good to firm going: has wandered: not straightforward: fairly useful hurdler. *Jonjo O'Neill*

MALAPROPISM 7 ch.g. Compton Place 125 – Mrs Malaprop 83 (Night Shift (USA)) **93** [2007 93: 5.1f⁶ 5m⁶ 5m 5m 5.3f 5g³ 5.2s³ 5v⁴ 5m² 5m* 5m² 5.2f³ 5f⁵ 5g⁵ 5m³ 5g⁵ 5f⁴ 5g* 5m* 5d* 5.1g 5d 5m⁴ 5g⁶ Nov 9] well-made gelding: fairly useful handicapper: won at Windsor in July and Beverley, Newmarket and Goodwood within 8 days in September: best at 5f/easy 6f: acts on dirt, firm and soft going: visored nowadays: sometimes rears in stall: has hung/carried head awkwardly: often races prominently. *M. R. Channon*

MALCHEEK (IRE) 5 br.g. Lend A Hand 124 – Russland (GER) (Surumu (GER)) **98** [2007 94: 7f³ 7f* 7s 7m⁵ 7f 7g 7g 6m* 6m⁴ 6m 6g 6g Oct 26] tall, lengthy gelding: useful handicapper: won at Thirsk in May and Ripon in August: good equal-second to Damika

645

at latter course tenth outing: well held after: effective at 6f/7f: acts on polytrack and firm ground: sometimes edges right/races freely: often races prominently: has reportedly bled, including final outing. *T. D. Easterby*

MALECH (IRE) 4 b.g. Bahhare (USA) 122 – Choral Sundown 81 (Night Shift (USA)) – [2007 74: 10.1m 10m 10f Sep 17] lengthy gelding: fair performer at 3 yrs, below form in 2007 (reportedly had breathing problem on reappearance). *K. G. Reveley*

MALGURU 3 b.g. Ishiguru (USA) 114 – Vento Del Oreno (FR) 67 (Lando (GER) 128) **58** [2007 9m 8g 10f⁶ 14.1m 12s Jul 2] deep-girthed gelding: modest maiden: probably stays 1¼m: has joined A. Foster. *G. A. Swinbank*

MALIBU GIRL (USA) 2 b.f. (Feb 16) Malibu Moon (USA) – Gale The Queen (USA) **81 p** (Dr Blum (USA)) [2007 p7g* Oct 24] $170,000Y: eighth foal: half-sister to several winners in US, including 1m/9f winner Phone The King (by Phone Trick) and 1m winner Jazzy Ginger (by Mecke): dam, US 6f winner, half-sister to US Grade 1 7f winner King's Swan: 8/1, won maiden at Lingfield by 1¾ lengths with something to spare, quickening well: likely to stay 1m: will improve. *E. A. L. Dunlop*

MALIBU (IRE) 6 b.g. Second Empire (IRE) 124 – Tootle (Main Reef 126) [2007 68d: **51** p16.5g⁶ p13.9g⁵ p16.5g Jul 27] tall, good-topped gelding: modest handicapper nowadays: left M. Appleby after reappearance: stays 16.5f: acts on polytrack and good to firm ground: tried in headgear. *S. Lycett*

MALINSA BLUE (IRE) 5 b.m. Desert Style (IRE) 121 – Talina's Law (IRE) 83 (Law **75** Society (USA) 130) [2007 69: 7m 10m⁴ 8f* 9.9g* 10m⁵ 8v⁶ 9.2d 8.5g 7m³ 8m* 8.1g Oct 2] workmanlike mare: fair handicapper: won at Pontefract and Beverley in May and Pontefract again in September: stays 1¼m: acts on firm going, possibly not good to soft: tried blinkered: in cheekpieces last 3 starts. *B. Ellison*

MALT EMPRESS (IRE) 2 b.f. (Mar 11) Second Empire (IRE) 124 – Sunset Malt – (IRE) (Red Sunset 120) [2007 p7m Dec 9] fourth foal: dam, Irish maiden, half-sister to useful Irish sprinter Miss Provider: 66/1, last in maiden at Lingfield. *B. W. Duke*

MALTESE FALCON 7 b.g. Mark of Esteem (IRE) 137 – Crime Ofthecentury 80 – (Pharly (FR) 130) [2007 109: f5g p6g² p5g² p5g² p5g⁴ p6g* p6g⁴ 5.2m 6g 6s p6g⁴ p6m* p6g⁴ **a116** Dec 28] strong, good-topped gelding: smart performer on all-weather, little form on turf in 2007: won handicap in April (by ½ length from Ajigolo) and listed race in November (by ½ length from Borderlescott), both at Lingfield: effective at 5f/6f: acts on polytrack, good to firm and good to soft going: tongue tied: tried blinkered: races prominently nowadays. *P. F. I. Cole*

Play Casino At ladbrokes.com Stakes (Golden Rose), Lingfield—
the inaugural running of this listed race on the all-weather is won by Maltese Falcon,
who accounts for some smart performers led home by Borderlescott

totesport.com November Stakes (Handicap), Doncaster—the progressive Malt Or Mash gains his fourth success of the year; Sanbuch is about to take second off Night Crescendo (dark colours); Tropical Strait (partially hidden near rail) is fourth, while further down the field is Akarem, the final ride of Kevin Darley's career

MALT OR MASH (USA) 3 gr.c. Black Minnaloushe (USA) 123 – Southern Tradition (USA) (Family Doctor (USA)) [2007 80: p8g² 9.9g* 10m* 12g⁴ 14g 12m* 12m* Nov 10] big, lengthy colt: progressed into a smart handicapper: won at Goodwood in June, Sandown (dead-heated with Six of Diamonds) in July, Newmarket (by ½ length from Sanbuch) in October and Doncaster (totesport.com November Stakes, beat same rival by 1½ lengths) in November: stays 1½m: acts on good to firm going: open to further improvement. *R. Hannon*   **114 p**

MALYANA 3 b.f. Mtoto 134 – Pass The Peace 116 (Alzao (USA) 117) [2007 79: 8.5g* 8g⁶ 8.2m 9.8g* 10m 8.9d Oct 13] strong, good-bodied filly: type to carry condition: fairly useful handicapper: won at Epsom in April and Ripon in August: well below form final outing: will stay 1½m: acts on polytrack. *M. A. Jarvis*   **89**

MAMA LEO 2 ch.f. (Apr 26) Forzando 122 – Milady Lillie (IRE) 65 (Distinctly North (USA) 115) [2007 p5g⁴ 5m⁴ 5g 6d⁴ 5.1g² 5.2m² p5.1g p6g f6d⁶ Dec 14] 10,500Y: leggy filly: fourth foal: half-sister to 2005 2-y-o 6f seller winner Savannah Pride (by Namid): dam, 7f winner, out of Irish 1000 Guineas runner-up Millingdale Lillie: modest maiden: runner-up in sellers at Bath (left P. D. Evans) and Yarmouth (nursery, left K. J. Burke): best form at 5f: acts on good to firm going: sometimes visored. *J. G. M. O'Shea*   **51**

MAMBAZO 5 b.g. Dansili 127 – Kalindi 102 (Efisio 120) [2007 –, a85: p6g⁵ p6g⁶ p5.1g p6g p5.1g⁶ p6g p6g³ p5g p5.1g³ p6g* p6g* p6g³ p6g* p6g 5m 6f p6g p5g p5g p5g⁶ Dec 22] stocky gelding: fairly useful handicapper on all-weather, modest on turf: won at Lingfield and Wolverhampton in June and Kempton (apprentices, by 5 lengths) in July: effective at 5f/6f: acts on all-weather: tried blinkered: has started slowly: can race freely. *S. C. Williams*   **51 a85**

MAMBOMOON 3 b.c. Zaha (CAN) 106 – Moontime (FR) (Habitat 134) [2007 –: 6f⁵ 6m 6g 5.9m* 6d 6m⁴ Aug 9] tall colt: modest performer: won handicap at Carlisle in June: raced only around 6f: acts on good to firm going: blinkered last 5 starts: tried tongue tied: reportedly lost a shoe at start final outing. *T. D. Easterby*   **60**

MAMBO SPIRIT (IRE) 3 b.g. Invincible Spirit (IRE) 121 – Mambodorga (USA) (Kingmambo (USA) 125) [2007 84: 5.2m* 6m 5s⁴ p6g² 5s² 5g p6g⁴ 6m⁶ 6d⁶ p5g Oct 12] tall, good-topped gelding: fairly useful handicapper: won at Yarmouth (dead-heated) in April: creditable efforts last 4 outings: should prove best at 5f/6f: acts on polytrack, firm and soft going. *J. G. Given*   **93**

MAMBO SUN 4 b.g. Superior Premium 122 – The Manx Touch (IRE) 70 (Petardia 113) [2007 71: p9.5g p7.1g f8g⁵ f8g⁴ Mar 22] leggy gelding: fair handicapper: stays easy 11f: acts on all-weather and firm going: effective with or without blinkers/cheekpieces. *P. A. Blockley*   **66**

MAMICHOR 4 br.g. Mamalik (USA) 115 – Ichor 52 (Primo Dominie 121) [2007 50: p12g 10d³ 7s 8f* p8g 10d⁶ 8m⁶ 8m p10g⁵ Sep 11] good-topped gelding: modest performer: won claimer at Brighton in June: stays 1¼m: acts on polytrack, firm and good to soft ground: has worn blinkers/cheekpieces: tended to hang left final 3-y-o start. *B. R. Johnson*   **50**

MAMONTA 4 b.f. Fantastic Light (USA) 134 – Mamoura (IRE) 97 (Lomond (USA) **65** 128) [2007 63: p16g² p16g⁵ Jan 29] fair maiden: stays 2m: acts on polytrack and good to firm ground. *M. J. Wallace*

MANAAL (USA) 3 b.f. Bahri (USA) 125 – Muwakleh 115 (Machiavellian (USA) 123) **93 +** [2007 88p: 8g* 10f⁴ 8d 7g⁵ p8g* Oct 24] good-topped filly: fairly useful performer: won handicaps at Ripon in April and Lingfield in October: stayed 1¼m: acted on polytrack, firm and good to soft going: visits Elusive Quality. *Sir Michael Stoute*

MANALITO 2 b.c. (Mar 27) High Chaparral (IRE) 132 – Brush Strokes (Cadeaux **73 p** Genereux 131) [2007 8d⁵ 8.2g⁶ Oct 31] rangy colt: fifth foal: closely related to useful 1½m winner Kassiopeia (by Galileo) and half-brother to winner around 1¼m in France and Bahrain Craft Fair (by Danehill): dam, unraced, out of half-sister to Irish Oaks winner Colorspin, herself dam of Opera House and Kayf Tara: fair form in mid-field in maidens at Newmarket and Nottingham, needing experience: will be suited by 1¼m/1½m: will do better. *M. R. Channon*

MAN APPEAL 2 ch.f. (Mar 11) Mark of Esteem (IRE) 137 – Emma Peel 113 (Emarati **–** (USA) 74) [2007 6m Sep 11] good-topped filly: fourth foal: half-sister to useful Norwegian 7f (at 2 yrs)/1m (Norsk 1000 Guineas) winner Females Fun (by Diktat): dam 5f/ 6f (latter including at 2 yrs) winner: 66/1, well held in maiden at Lingfield won by Missit. *B. J. Meehan*

MANASSAS (IRE) 2 b.c. (Feb 5) Cape Cross (IRE) 129 – Monnavanna (IRE) 109 **92** (Machiavellian (USA) 123) [2007 6g³ 6g* 7g Oct 7] second foal: closely related to Norwegian 5.5f (at 2 yrs) to 1m winner Massenzio (by Green Desert): dam, 6f to 1m winner, half-sister to smart 1m/1¼m performer Monturani: fairly useful form: third to Young Pretender at Newmarket, then won maiden at Yarmouth in September: stiff task, improved again when seventh to Rio de La Plata in Prix Jean-Luc Lagardere at Longchamp, though no threat: will stay 1m. *B. J. Meehan*

MANATHON (FR) 4 b.g. Marathon (USA) 116 – Fleurissante (FR) (Legend of France **69** (USA) 124) [2007 p9.5m p9.5d⁴ Dec 17] won handicap at La Teste in 2006: in frame 6 of 7 other starts that year, leaving M. Roussel in France after second in claimer at Saint-Cloud on final outing: fair form in 2 handicaps on Flat in 2007 (no show over hurdles): stays 10.5f. *A. E. Jones*

MANBAR (USA) 3 b.c. Dynaformer (USA) – Devil's Nell (USA) (Devil's Bag (USA)) **82** [2007 10g³ 12g* 10d Jul 26] $100,000Y: closely related to US Grade 3 8.5f winner Kiss The Devil (by Kris S) and half-brother to 2 winners abroad, including fairly useful French 5.5f/6f winner Tailspin (by Tale of The Cat): dam US 4.5f (at 2 yrs)/6f winner: fairly useful form: confirmed debut promise when winning maiden at Goodwood in May: reportedly suffered breathing problem when tailed off at Sandown on handicap debut final outing: stays 1½m: sold only 6,000 gns in October. *Sir Michael Stoute*

MANCEBO (GER) 4 b.g. Acambaro (GER) 118 – Marsixa (FR) (Linamix (FR) 127) **–** [2007 12.1s Jul 27] placed 3 times up to 1½m from 5 starts for A. Wohler in Germany in 2006: well held sole Flat start in 2007. *R. Curtis*

MANCHURIAN 3 b.g. Singspiel (IRE) 133 – Royal Passion 78 (Ahonoora 122) [2007 **96** 92: 7.1m⁶ 8m⁴ 10m⁵ 9.9m 7m p8g Oct 12] smallish gelding: useful handicapper: best efforts at 3 yrs on second/final outings: probably stays 1¼m: acts on polytrack and good to firm going. *M. J. Wallace*

MANDALAY KING (IRE) 2 b.c. (Apr 18) King's Best (USA) 132 – Mahamuni **49** (IRE) (Sadler's Wells (USA) 132) [2007 p7g p7.1g Oct 15] poor form in maiden and seller. *Jane Chapple-Hyam*

MANDALAY PRINCE 3 b.g. Tobougg (IRE) 125 – Autumn Affair 100 (Lugana **66** Beach 116) [2007 p7g⁴ 7.1m p8.6g p8g 8.5s⁵ 9.9s* 10g⁵ p11g p12.2g p9.5g p12.2d⁴ Dec 7] well-made gelding: fair handicapper: won at Goodwood in July: stays 1¼m: acts on polytrack and soft going: sometimes slowly away: held up. *W. J. Musson*

MANDARINKA 2 ch.g. (Feb 17) Kyllachy 129 – Lihou Island 89 (Beveled (USA)) **61** [2007 5.1g 5m 6d⁶ 6m p6g⁵ p6g p5g p5g Oct 24] smallish gelding: modest maiden: raced only at 5f/6f: looked hard ride, including when blinkered. *P. Winkworth*

MANDARIN ROCKET (IRE) 4 ch.g. Titus Livius (FR) 115 – Two Thousand (IRE) **64** (Polish Patriot (USA) 128) [2007 59: 5g 9.1g² 8.3f⁶ 9.1g 9.1m⁶ 9.2s² 8.3d² 8.3d 9.2m⁵ 9.1s 9.9m⁵ 9.2m² 10.1m 9.2s 8g* Oct 5] modest handicapper: won apprentice event at Musselburgh in October: stays 1¼m: acts on firm and soft going: ran well in cheekpieces sixth start. *Miss L. A. Perratt*

MANDARIN SPIRIT (IRE) 7 b.g. Primo Dominie 121 – Lithe Spirit (IRE) 74 **81** (Dancing Dissident (USA) 119) [2007 86: p6g³ p7.1g³ p7g⁵ f7g* p7.1g⁵ p7g 6m⁵ 7g p6g⁴ **a88** 6m⁴ 5m⁶ p7m p7.1g⁶ p6g⁴ p7g p8m Nov 26] compact gelding: fairly useful handicapper: won at Southwell in February: effective at 5.7f to 7f: acts on all-weather, firm and good to soft going: usually wears headgear: sometimes slowly away: held up. *G. C. H. Chung*

MANDELIEU (IRE) 2 b.g. (Apr 11) Acclamation 118 – Notley Park 71 (Wolfhound **69** (USA) 126) [2007 5.1g 5.2g² 6g⁶ 5d⁴ p5.1g⁴ p5.1g⁵ Dec 1] good-topped gelding: fair maiden: in frame 3 times: free-going type, should prove best at 5f/6f: blinkered first 2 starts (gelded last 2). *W. J. Haggas*

MANDESHA (FR) 4 b.f. Desert Style (IRE) 121 – Mandalara (IRE) (Lahib (USA) **122** 129) [2007 124: 10.5s* 12g² 9.9m² 12m² 12g Oct 7] strong, stocky filly: very smart performer: best 3-y-o filly in 2006: not in same heart in 2007, though won Prix Corrida at Saint-Cloud in May by ¾ length from Macleya (who rec. 4lb): runner-up afterwards to Mountain High in Grand Prix de Saint-Cloud (beaten 1½ lengths), Peeping Fawn in Nassau Stakes at Goodwood (left with ground to make up on winner, went down by 1½ lengths) and Manduro in Prix Foy at Longchamp (beaten 2½ lengths): in cheekpieces, below-form seventh to Dylan Thomas in Prix de l'Arc de Triomphe at Longchamp final outing: effective at 1m to 1½m: acted on soft and good to firm ground: slowly away first 2 outings: held up, and had good turn of foot: visits Kingmambo. *A. de Royer Dupre, France*

MANDRAGOLA 3 b.g. Machiavellian (USA) 123 – Viz (USA) (Kris S (USA)) [2007 **85** –: p10g* 10g 12.3m⁴ 12d 11.6g³ p12.2g² Oct 21] good-topped gelding: fairly useful performer: won maiden at Lingfield in April: good efforts in handicaps last 3 outings: stays easy 12.3f: acts on polytrack, good to firm and good to soft going: got upset in stall fourth outing: sold 50,000 gns, sent to Saudi Arabia. *B. W. Hills*

MANDRIANO (ITY) 3 b.g. Averti (IRE) 117 – My Penny (USA) (Gulch (USA)) **35** [2007 52: f5g 6f⁵ 7m 8.3m⁵ 5m 5s⁵ 6g Aug 22] workmanlike gelding: poor maiden at 3 yrs: best at 5f: tried in cheekpieces/visor. *D. W. Barker*

MANDURAH (IRE) 3 b.g. Tagula (IRE) 116 – Fearfully Grand (Grand Lodge (USA) **79** 125) [2007 53: p6g³ 6g* 5m² 5m 5g* 5g³ 6m³ 5m⁴ 5m⁵ 5m² 6g Sep 23] strong, sturdy gelding: fair handicapper: won at Southwell and Haydock in April, and Carlisle in July: has won at 6f, best at 5f: acts on polytrack and good to firm going: races prominently. *D. Nicholls*

MANDURO (GER) 5 b.h. Monsun (GER) 124 – Mandellicht (IRE) (Be My Guest **135** (USA) 126) [2007 123: 9m* 9.3s* 10m* 8g* 12m* Sep 16]

When a trainer describes a horse as the best he has trained, the identity of the trainer is every bit as important as that of the horse, maybe even more so. When the trainer is Andre Fabre, in his twenty-first consecutive season as France's champion trainer, and with nearly two hundred horses in his care each year, owned by a selection of the world's top owners, he has more candidates to choose from than most. Unlike some trainers whose assessments of their horses can sound suspiciously like a sales pitch or advertising material for a future stallion career, Fabre is not given to handing out such accolades lightly. It was only in 2006, as the opening lines of the essay on Shirocco highlighted, that the trainer expressed his reluctance to compare that horse with the stable's other top older middle-distance performer Hurricane Run. That the trainer's opinions on his horses, or any subject for that matter, are available to the British media, be it in newspapers or on tele-vision, is perhaps taken too much for granted, because, on the other side of the Channel, much to the frustration of French racing journalists, Fabre has a long-standing policy of not communicating with the media. This results in the bizarre situation of the French media having to report second-hand information gleaned from their British colleagues, rather than from the trainer himself. For example, readers of *Paris Turf* found out two days after readers of the *Racing Post* that Fabre considered Manduro the best horse he had trained.

A trainer's idea of the best horse he has trained is not necessarily based on, or backed up by, evidence from the racecourse and the form-book. Henry Cecil, for example, another trainer who has had more top-class candidates than most to choose from during his career, nominated his One Thousand Guineas and Cham-pion Stakes winner Bosra Sham as the best he has trained, even though a number of the trainer's other horses, headed by his Derby, King George and St Leger winner

Prix d'Ispahan, Longchamp—Manduro is a five-length winner from Turtle Bowl and Stormy River

Reference Point, have achieved higher ratings. Similarly, Andre Fabre has trained a couple of Prix de l'Arc de Triomphe winners who have achieved ratings on a par with, or even superior to Manduro, in Trempolino (also 135) and Peintre Celebre (137). Ironically, the question of which of the trainer's pair was better, Shirocco or Hurricane Run, became less of an issue after the 2006 Arc in which both were beaten by their three-year-old stablemate Rail Link. Maybe not even Fabre himself could have known then that within twelve months Manduro would have improved sufficiently to trump all of them in his estimation.

Manduro was described as a late-developer in some quarters, and in the sense that he did not reach the height of his powers until his five-year-old season, that description fits him well. But, at the same time, it's hardly an accurate portrayal of a horse who was, after all, champion two-year-old in Germany. Two-year-old racing in Germany may not be so competitive as in Britain, Ireland and France, but Manduro won both his starts that season and showed smart form, taking a maiden at Munich by six lengths and the country's top two-year-old contest, the Preis des Winterfavoriten, by five. As well as standing out among his contemporaries (he was rated 7 lb clear of the next-best German trained two-year-old, the filly Paita who won the Criterium de Saint-Cloud), his Timeform rating of 115p remains the highest given to a German two-year-old since lists of ratings for the top horses abroad were first published in *Racehorses of 1993*. Manduro was described in *Racehorses*, at the end of his two-year-old campaign, as 'a first-rate Deutsches Derby prospect', but, in truth, his three-year-old season was something of a disappointment, even though he ended it rated 118. He was slow to come to hand and the Derby was long gone by the time he made his reappearance in September. Manduro kept his unbeaten record for a couple more starts, winning a listed race at Munich and a Group 3 event at Hoppegarten, but disappointed on his final outing when only fourth to stable-companion Soldier Hollow (whom he'd beaten the time before) in the Premio Roma. That was to be the only time that Manduro finished out of the first three in his career.

During 2005, Manduro's owner Baron Georg von Ullmann switched his previous year's Deutsches Derby winner Shirocco from Andreas Schutz in Germany to Andre Fabre, a move which paid dividends when Shirocco won the Breeders' Cup Turf at Belmont that autumn. Manduro, who had been trained in Germany by Peter Schiergen, was among several more of the owner's horses to make the move to Fabre before the 2006 season. Manduro's four-year-old campaign began with a win in the Prix d'Harcourt at Longchamp but the rest was a frustrating episode in which he had to settle for place money in the Prix Ganay, the Prix d'Ispahan, the Prince of Wales's Stakes, the Prix Messidor, the Prix Jacques le Marois, the Prix du Moulin and the Prix Dollar. In the last-named at Longchamp, Manduro looked something of an unlucky loser when beaten a neck, ironically by his former stable-companion Soldier Hollow, after that rival had got first run. Manduro's four-year-old season must have been shaped to some extent by his connections having Shirocco to contest the top mile and a half races. Manduro was not raced over a mile and a half himself, though he shaped as if he might stay the trip. Manduro was, nonetheless, at home doing duty instead over a mile and a quarter, though in his three starts over a mile, in the Messidor, Jacques le Marois and Moulin (all won by Librettist), Manduro looked in need of a longer trip.

Manduro came closest to beating Librettist, running one of his best races all that season, when going down by a neck at Deauville, the combination of soft ground and a sound pace both in Manduro's favour, in contrast to a more tactical affair on good ground in the Moulin at Longchamp the following month.

Manduro began the latest season with a rating of 123, indicative of his having made further improvement at four, but still leaving him some way short of top class and giving little indication of the progress he was to make as a five-year-old. With Hurricane Run and Shirocco already retired to stud and a setback keeping Rail Link out of action until he too was retired later in the year, Manduro had the stage to himself among the Fabre stable's top older horses for much of the season. He renewed a successful partnership with Stephane Pasquier which was maintained throughout the year. The only occasion that Manduro had been ridden by Pasquier as a four-year-old was when he won the Prix d'Harcourt; Christophe Soumillon and Olivier Peslier had taken the ride on subsequent starts. Manduro returned with an emphatic win in the Weatherbys Earl of Sefton Stakes at Newmarket in April when he coasted home by four lengths from the previous season's One Thousand Guineas winner Speciosa and there was soon further confirmation that he was an improved horse when he ran out a five-length winner of the Prix d'Ispahan at Longchamp the following month, showing top-class form. Beaten a short neck by Laverock in a more keenly contested renewal of the same race twelve months earlier, Manduro had only two credible opponents among those that took him on this time, and one of them was Turtle Bowl, a reliable yardstick who was readily left behind in the last two furlongs as Manduro beat him easily by five lengths to land the first Group 1 of his career.

Andre Fabre nominated Manduro's performance in his next race, the Prince of Wales's Stakes, as the horse's best effort in 2007 and it is not easy to disagree. Manduro had run a good race when third at 12/1 in the same race the year before, beaten half a length and three quarters of a length by Ouija Board (who visits Manduro's sire in 2008 after producing a colt by Kingmambo) and Electrocutionist in what was the race of the Royal meeting. The line-up for the latest renewal was every bit as select, if not even stronger. Only the ex-Italian 25/1 outsider Pressing had not won in Group 1 company, though he was successful at that level by the end of the year. It says something for the strength of the field that the previous season's Derby winner Sir Percy was only fifth choice in the market, though the betting was also indicative of his disappointing effort in the Coronation Cup. Manduro's three other rivals were all in top form. Notnowcato had narrowly got the better of the Prix Ganay winner Dylan Thomas in the Tattersalls Gold Cup at the Curragh last time out, but it was the latter who challenged Manduro for favouritism, Manduro eventually sent off at 15/8 and Dylan Thomas at 2/1. The line-up was completed by the 2006 Breeders' Cup Turf winner Red Rocks, third favourite on 4/1, who had made a successful reappearance in the Gordon Richards Stakes. Sir Percy set the pace, chased by Notnowcato, with Manduro poised behind them in third. With the leader folding tamely two furlongs out and Notnowcato lacking the pace to take

Prince of Wales's Stakes, Royal Ascot—Manduro puts up the best performance of the year to account for Dylan Thomas, Notnowcato and Red Rocks

Prix du Haras de Fresnay-le-Buffard-Jacques le Marois, Deauville—
Manduro doesn't need to reproduce his best dropped back to a mile; Holocene (rail) stays on well
to take second off Turtle Bowl; Toylsome and Stormy River are next

advantage, Manduro and Dylan Thomas, on his outer, swept to the front, Manduro showing a fine turn of foot and winning by a length and a quarter. Dylan Thomas tended to hang right, in behind Manduro, but he still pulled four lengths clear of Notnowcato, with Red Rocks never able to land a blow in fourth, ahead of Pressing and Sir Percy, the last-named making what proved to be his final racecourse appearance.

The placed horses in the Prince of Wales's Stakes advertised the form in no uncertain terms before Manduro was seen out again, Dylan Thomas returning to Ascot to win the King George VI and Queen Elizabeth Stakes by four lengths and Notnowcato getting the better of Authorized and George Washington in a tactical Eclipse Stakes at Sandown. Before Manduro's sights were set on the Arc in the autumn, he was given another crack at a top mile race in the Prix Jacques le Marois again at Deauville in August. The Jacques le Marois is usually France's top all-aged mile contest, if not Europe's, but the latest renewal was substandard, with the likes of Darjina, Ramonti and George Washington all clashing instead in the Prix du Moulin at Longchamp the following month. Of those who did take on Manduro, neither of his rivals from the d'Ispahan, Turtle Bowl and Stormy River, was at his best this time, while Manduro's main threat beforehand, three-year-old Lawman who had won the Prix du Jockey Club and Prix Jean Prat, was a long way below form and finished last. With the German-trained eight-year-old Toylsome, in the same ownership as Manduro, employed as his pacemaker and yet to show the form he produced in the autumn, that left Manduro to beat the useful three-year-old colt Holocene (carrying the Niarchos colours of race sponsors the Haras de Fresnay-le-Buffard). Manduro did so with little fuss, leading over a furlong out and keeping on strongly despite wandering markedly in front. He had three lengths to spare over Holocene at the line, not having to run to anything like his best form. Turtle Bowl was another half length back in third, well clear of Toylsome and Stormy River.

With a month to go before the Arc, Manduro was second favourite in most bookmakers' lists, though he had not been entered for the race in May and was due to be put in at the supplementary stage. Manduro was also in the unusual position for a leading Arc contender, certainly for an older horse, of not yet having run at a mile and a half. Manduro's Arc trial, the Prix Foy at Longchamp in September, was therefore potentially a trial in the truest sense of the word and likely to be a much more informative race than usual. There was a serious rival in Mandesha, even though she had yet to find her best three-year-old form, while the previous year's Derby runner-up Dragon Dancer was another on trial for the Arc after a listed win at Windsor. The five-runner field was completed by Italian challenger Distant Way and, once again, a German-trained pacemaker for Manduro, this time Sommertag. Manduro came through with flying colours, typically racing with plenty of zest before joining issue three-wide rounding the home turn and quickening away smartly from two furlongs out to beat Mandesha by two and a half lengths, with Dragon Dancer another three lengths behind in third. Nothing untoward was immediately apparent with him and, as a trial for the Arc, it seemed that things could hardly have gone more smoothly, the only quibble perhaps being that despite the presence of the pacemaker, the field had not gone much of a pace, resulting in the Foy, run in a slower time than either the Prix Niel or the Prix Vermeille, turning into essentially a sprint up the straight and being far from a true test of stamina, still leaving something of a question mark, in the eyes of some, over Manduro's absolute effectiveness at a mile and a half.

Within hours, though, Manduro's victory proved sadly pyrrhic; a fracture to his off-hind cannon bone was detected, putting paid to the Arc and what was scheduled to have been his final appearance at the Breeders' Cup, probably in the Classic. In hindsight, missing the mudbath at Monmouth might have been no bad thing, but being ruled out of the Arc, a race his owner is particularly keen to win, was much more regrettable. The fact that Manduro changed his legs approaching the winning post in the Foy was perhaps an indication that he was feeling his injury, while earlier in the straight there had been an incident in which Distant Way was tight for room between Manduro and his pacemaker. The contact was enough to cause Pasquier to look down and to his right for a moment or two, while Distant Way's rider was quick to accept the situation after being hampered. Whether or not the incident played any part in Manduro's injury is impossible to say, especially as the ground at Longchamp on Arc trials day also came in for criticism. The going was good to firm (Soldier of Fortune set a race record time in the Prix Niel) and in the opinion of Mandesha's trainer Alain de Royer-Dupre, who reported that his filly had had some stiffness after the Foy, the ground had not been watered sufficiently in the preceding week.

Surgery on Manduro's leg, a two-hour operation which required the insertion of four screws, was reported to have gone well and Manduro will begin his stud career at Darley's Kildangan Stud in Ireland at a fee of €40,000. Manduro ran his final race still carrying Baron von Ullmann's colours but he had been purchased for breeding after the Jacques le Marois by Sheikh Mohammed in a deal rumoured to be worth €23,000,000. Manduro's sire Monsun, who also raced for Baron von Ullmann, has been at stud at Gestut Schlenderhan since 1996, but it is only in the last couple of seasons that he has emerged as a major force, so much so that his fee doubled to €120,000 in 2007, making him the most expensive sire standing in continental Europe, and his fee has been raised again to €150,000 for 2008. Baron

Prix Foy Gray d'Albion Barriere, Longchamp—Manduro keeps his unbeaten record for the season stepped up to a mile and a half, but is found to have suffered a career-ending injury; Mandesha is second, clear of Dragon Dancer and Sommertag (rail)

MAN

von Ullmann broke the Baden-Baden sales record when paying €710,000 for a yearling son of Monsun, named North Star, in September. Manduro is part of a major investment by Sheikh Mohammed in sons of Monsun; a year earlier, Shirocco made the same move as Manduro, from racing in Baron von Ullmann's colours to standing under the Darley banner at stud, while the purchase of the 2006 Deutsches Derby winner Schiaparelli to race for Godolphin in 2008 makes him a third potential Monsun stallion for Sheikh Mohammed in due course. As well as Manduro and Schiaparelli (winner of two Group 1 events in Germany and one in Italy in the latest season), Monsun's high profile in 2007 was maintained by Getaway (Manduro's understudy in the Arc), the Prix du Cadran winner Le Miracle and the Beverly D Stakes winner Royal Highness, as well as several other lesser pattern winners.

		Konigsstuhl (br 1976)	Dschingis Khan
	Monsun (GER) (br 1990)		Konigskronung
		Mosella (b 1985)	Surumu
Manduro (GER) (b.h. 2002)			Monasia
		Be My Guest (ch 1974)	Northern Dancer
	Mandellicht (IRE) (b 1994)		What A Treat
		Mandelauge (b 1989)	Elektrant
			Mandriale

The lengthy, useful-looking Manduro was bought for €130,000 as a yearling at Baden-Baden. His family has produced numerous winners in Germany, though nothing anywhere near so good as Manduro. Being by Monsun made him an attractive proposition to Baron von Ullmann, though so too, apparently, was the fact that his foaling date of March 9th also happened to be the Baron's mother's birthday! Manduro's dam Mandellicht gained her only win in a seven-and-a-half-furlong maiden at Mulheim but showed form verging on useful and was placed in listed races at up to nine furlongs and finished fifth in the German One Thousand Guineas. She produced two winners before Manduro. Maraschino (by Dashing Blade) was a two-year-old seven-furlong winner who later won over hurdles in Italy, while the filly Mandela (by Acatenango) was a useful middle-distance performer who won in listed company and finished third in the Preis der Diana (German Oaks) and the Prix de Pomone. Since Manduro, Mandellicht has produced the fairly useful mile winner Madura (by Dashing Blade), the three-year-old gelding Manduras (by Tiger Hill), third on his only start so far in Germany, an unraced two-year-old colt named Manaba (by Anabaa), owned by Manduro's breeder and also in training with Fabre, and a filly foal by Danehill Dancer. Mandellicht was one of seven winners out of Mandelauge, a winner over a mile (at two) and eleven furlongs. The best of Mandelauge's five winning siblings was Mandelbaum who won the first six races of his career, notably the Mehl-Mulhens-Rennen (German 2000 Guineas) and one of the main German Derby trials, the eleven-furlong Union-Rennen at Cologne.

Manduro's rise to fame resulted in a frenzy of interest in other members of this hitherto unremarkable family at various end-of-year sales, resulting in a total of more than five million guineas changing hands in a matter of weeks for a collection of his relatives. First up was Manduro's older half-sister Mandela who briefly set a record for a German-bred broodmare when sold to Japanese interests for 1,400,000 dollars at Keeneland in November. At the same sale, Mandela's filly foal by Dynaformer was sold for 700,000 dollars to Sheikh Mohammed's bloodstock advisor John Ferguson. Ferguson had also tried to acquire a Monsun colt out of Mandamou, a half-sister to Manduro's dam, at Tattersalls Foal Sales but, when the bidding stopped at 450,000 guineas, somewhat surprisingly it was Demi O'Byrne who came out on top, registering Coolmore's first interest in Monsun. At Tattersalls December Sales, Manduro's younger half-sister Madura (in foal to Monsun) was sold for 710,000 guineas (after making 170,000 guineas at the same venue twelve months earlier), and his dam's half-sister Mandelhush (in foal to Shirocco), another Japanese purchase at 200,000 guineas, were joined by a late addition to the catalogue, Manduro's own dam Mandellicht, also in foal to Monsun again. Not surprisingly, Mandellicht smashed her daughter Mandela's record for a German mare when sold for 3,000,000 guineas.

Manduro's win in the Prix Foy may have gone some way at least to answering unequivocally the question about his effectiveness at a mile and a half but the

Baron G. von Ullmann's "Manduro"

fact that he never ran again posed others. How would he have fared in the Arc itself? There's little doubt that the Arc would have been a sterner test of stamina than the Foy, given that in general it was the staying types who came to the fore. The Foy second and third finished only seventh and ninth in the Arc, beaten considerably further by the winner Dylan Thomas than they had been by Manduro. On the other hand, the fact that Manduro had given a sound beating to Dylan Thomas, albeit at a shorter trip, at Royal Ascot in the summer must have left Manduro's connections thinking what might have been. Andre Fabre has proved a master at preparing horses for the Arc using the established trials; all six of his three-year-old winners of the race contested the Prix Niel beforehand (Peintre Celebre the only one not to win the Niel, though an unlucky loser), while Fabre's other Arc winner, four-year-old Subotica, finished second in the Foy beforehand. It seems more than likely that whatever Manduro showed in the Foy, he could have been expected to be more fully tuned up for the Arc itself, in which maybe he would have given a public performance to back up his trainer's assessment of him as the best he has trained. But that's speculation, and Manduro achieved enough in reality without having to dwell too much on what else he might have done. He was a top-class racehorse, in our experience the best to come out of Germany, ahead of the 1975 Arc winner Star Appeal (rated 133), whose career began in Ireland. Manduro's record of finishing out of the first three only once, when fourth, speaks for itself, and, while better at a mile and a quarter than a mile, and probably capable of proving as good at a mile and a half, he was given the opportunity to show rare versatility in a top racehorse these days, winning important races at eight, nine, ten and twelve furlongs on ground ranging from soft to good to firm. *A. Fabre, France*

MANDY'S MAESTRO (USA) 3 br.g. Brahms (USA) 118 – Belle Masque (USA) **57 d**
(Devil's Bag (USA)) [2007 62: 5g 5g 7m 6d⁵ 5v 6v 5m⁵ 5s 7.5m Aug 26] compact
gelding: modest maiden: below form after reappearance: should stay 7f: acts on soft
ground: tried blinkered: sold £1,500. *R. M. Whitaker*

MANEKI NEKO (IRE) 5 b.g. Rudimentary (USA) 118 – Ardbess (Balla Cove 119) **73 §**
[2007 82: 12f⁵ 13m 14g⁵ 12m² 12m 14.1f⁶ 13.4g Sep 29] close-coupled gelding: fair
handicapper: barely stays 1¾m: acts on firm and good to soft going: blinkered (below
form) once: often let down by attitude. *E. W. Tuer*

MANGANO 3 b.g. Mujadil (USA) 119 – Secret Dance (Sadler's Wells (USA) 132) **60**
[2007 –: p6g f5g² f6g⁴ 5m 5m 5g² 6d 5m⁴ 5g³ 5m⁶ 5d 6d² 6g² 6d 6v³ 6.9m⁵ 5.9f² 6m⁵
7.1s* 6g⁵ 8m⁴ 8.5m 9.1s⁶ Oct 4] sturdy gelding: modest handicapper: won at Musselburgh in August: stays 1m: acts on fibresand and any turf ground: held up. *A. Berry*

MANGHAM (IRE) 2 b.c. (Feb 7) Montjeu (IRE) 137 – Lovisa (USA) 55 (Gone West **67**
(USA)) [2007 7d² 7s⁵ 7.1g³ Oct 5] 75,000F, 70,000Y: big, strong colt: second foal: dam,
ran once in Ireland, out of useful performer up to 1m Musicale: fair form in maidens,
placed at Redcar and Musselburgh: free-going sort, but bred to be suited by 1m+.
B. Smart

MANGO MASHER (IRE) 3 ch.g. Danehill Dancer (IRE) 117 – Shariyfa (FR) (Zay- **66 §**
yani 119) [2007 p6g p7.1g⁴ p7g⁴ f8g⁴ 10g 11.6s 11.5g⁵ 15.8m² 7.1f 10.2m 10.2m p13.9g⁴
p12.2g⁶ p16g⁴ Dec 4] good-topped gelding: fair maiden: left C. Egerton after eighth
outing, J. M. Bradley after eleventh: stays easy 2m: acts on polytrack and good to firm
ground: usually blinkered/in cheekpieces: one to treat with caution. *J. L. Flint*

MANGO MISCHIEF (IRE) 6 ch.m. Desert King (IRE) 129 – Eurolink Mischief 84 **108**
(Be My Chief (USA) 122) [2007 107: 12s⁵ 11.9m⁵ 10.9d⁴ 10.1s* 10.1m 10.4s⁵ 10d 10m
9.5g Oct 5] tall, leggy mare: useful performer: won listed event at Newcastle (by 7 lengths
from In Safe Hands) in June: seemingly good fifth to Stage Gift in York Stakes at York
sixth outing: below form after: best around 1¼m: acts on soft and good to firm going:
usually races up with pace: sometimes hangs right. *M. R. Channon*

MANGO MUSIC 4 ch.f. Distant Music (USA) 126 – Eurolink Sundance 85 (Night **90**
Shift (USA)) [2007 90: 5.1f 6g⁵ 6.1s 6m 6m² 6d³ 6m⁴ 6s p6g³ p6g Nov 16] angular filly: **a75 +**
fairly useful performer on all-weather, fair on turf: effective at 5f/6f: acts on firm and soft
going: races prominently: sold 7,000 gns. *M. R. Channon*

MANGO PICCLE 3 ch.g. Piccolo 121 – Starliner (IRE) 57 (Statoblest 120) [2007 p6g **–**
Oct 23] 50/1, well held in seller at Lingfield. *L. Wells*

MANGROVE CAY (IRE) 5 b.g. Danetime (IRE) 121 – Art Duo 86 (Artaius (USA) **54**
129) [2007 f11g² f8g f8g 16g⁵ 15.8m f12g² 12m⁵ 12.1g Aug 16] modest maiden: reportedly finished lame final outing: probably stays easy 2m: acts on all-weather, unraced on
extremes of going on turf: tried visored: tends to wander/find little. *A. J. Lockwood*

MANHATTAN BOY (GER) 5 ch.g. Monsun (GER) 124 – Manhattan Girl (USA) **64 +**
(Vice Regent (CAN)) [2007 11d Oct 11] won minor event at Krefeld and handicaps at
Cologne and Krefeld in 2006: left A. Trybuhl in Germany, just modest form in handicap
at Newbury on British Flat debut: stays 11f: acts on soft ground: fairly useful form over
hurdles. *P. J. Hobbs*

MANHATTAN DREAM (USA) 2 b.f. (Apr 18) Statue of Liberty (USA) 115 – **72 p**
Vallee Des Reves (USA) (Kingmambo (USA) 125) [2007 6d 7s 6m³ Sep 21] rangy filly:
sixth foal: closely related to smart 7f (at 2 yrs)/1m winner Maids Causeway (by Giant's
Causeway), and half-sister to 2 winners, including 4-y-o Corum: dam unraced half-sister
to very smart French performers Vetheuil (miler) and Verveine (up to 1½m), latter dam of
very smart winner up to 13.5f Vallee Enchantee: fair form in maidens, third to Red
Rumour at Newmarket: will stay 1m: has scope to make a better 3-y-o. *B. W. Hills*

MANIPULATE 4 b.c. Machiavellian (USA) 123 – Balalaika 108 (Sadler's Wells **72**
(USA) 132) [2007 85p: 10.5g p8.6g May 21] good-topped colt: fairly useful maiden at
3 yrs: just fair form in handicaps in 2007: should stay 1¼m: raced on good/good to firm
going on turf: sold 16,000 gns, sent to Greece. *L. M. Cumani*

MANNELLO 4 b.f. Mamalik (USA) 115 – Isle of Sodor 63 (Cyrano de Bergerac 120) **59**
[2007 62: 6g 6.1m 6.1g 7g² 7.1s² 7d⁶ p7g p7g 6m 5f p7g⁵ p6g² p5.1g⁴ p6g⁵ p6g⁵ p6g
Dec 19] leggy filly: modest maiden: left B. Palling after fifth outing, Mrs C. Dunnett after
ninth: stays 7f: acts on polytrack, soft and good to firm going: tried in headgear. *Jim Best*

MAN OF GWENT (UAE) 3 b.g. In The Wings 128 – Welsh Valley (USA) 64 (Irish —
River (FR) 131) [2007 10m May 25] 50/1 and burly (bandaged hind joints), tailed-off last
in maiden at Newmarket: subsequently gelded. *G. A. Huffer*

MAN OF VISION (USA) 3 b.c. Kingmambo (USA) 125 – Nalani (IRE) 104 (Sadler's   **101**
Wells (USA) 132) [2007 74p: p8g² p9.5g² p10g* 11.8g* 12g 10m² 12g³ Aug 1] neat colt:
improved into a useful handicapper: won at Lingfield in March and Leicester (beat Gull
Wing by 1¾ lengths) in April: good efforts when placed after at Newmarket (1¼ lengths
second to Hearthstead Maison, not clear run) and Goodwood (BGC Stakes, 2 lengths
third to Regal Flush): may prove best at 1¼m: raced only on polytrack and good/good to
firm going: fractious in stall first 3-y-o outing: has joined Godolphin. *M. R. Channon*

MANOR PARK (IRE) 2 b.c. (Mar 10) Hernando (FR) 127 – Campiglia (IRE) (Fairy   **73 p**
King (USA)) [2007 7.1m 8.1s Sep 29] €105,000Y: rangy, attractive colt: has scope:
fourth foal: half-brother to French 2005 2-y-o 9.5f winner Arborea (by Fantastic Light):
dam, French maiden (stayed 1½m), half-sister to high-class performer up to 1½m Tobougg, out of Prix de Diane winner Lacovia: more promise than bare result in mid-field in
maidens at Sandown and Haydock, insufficient test: will be well suited by 1¼m/1½m:
sold 47,000 gns: type to thrive at 3 yrs. *C. G. Cox*

MANSII 2 b.c. (Feb 10) Dr Fong (USA) 128 – Enclave (USA) (Woodman (USA) 126)   **81**
[2007 5.2m⁵ 5m³ p6g 6f⁴ 6m² 6f⁴ p6g⁶ 6.1m² Oct 3] 42,000F, 25,000Y: tall colt: fourth
foal: half-brother to 3-y-o Paradise Walk: dam, ran twice in France, half-sister to smart
performer up to 1¼m Comfy: fairly useful maiden: in frame 5 times, second to Prohibit at
Nottingham final start: will stay 7f/1m: acts on firm going: has hung. *C. E. Brittain*

MANUKA BEE 2 b.g. (Mar 5) Xaar 132 – Legend 74 (Belmez (USA) 131) [2007 7s³   **62**
7.2s 7d⁴ Oct 16] 10,000F, €40,000Y: good-topped gelding: fourth foal: half-brother to 7f
winner in Greece by Royal Applause: dam, maiden (stayed 1½m), half-sister to smart
stayer Arabian Story: modest maiden: will stay at least 1m: raced only on going softer
than good. *J. Howard Johnson*

MANYRIVERSTOCROSS (IRE) 2 b.c. (Feb 22) Cape Cross (IRE) 129 – Alex-   **58 P**
andra S (USA) (Sadler's Wells (USA) 132) [2007 8d⁵ Oct 3] good sort: third foal: half-
brother to fairly useful 1m winner Fantastisch (by Fantastic Light): dam, ran twice, sister
to Irish Derby second Glyndebourne out of half-sister to Breeders' Cup Turf winner
Northern Spur: 66/1, eye-catching fifth to Huzzah in maiden at Salisbury, green and
considerably handled but keeping on: will do much better. *A. King*

MANY VOLUMES (USA) 3 b.c. Chester House (USA) 123 – Reams of Verse (USA)   **113**
121 (Nureyev (USA) 131) [2007 93: 10g* 11.5g⁴ 10m⁵ 10m 9.9g⁵ 10m* 10.3m² 10m²
Sep 27] big, strong, close-coupled colt: fluent mover: developed into a smart performer:
won maiden at Leicester in April and minor event at Newmarket (by 2½ lengths from
Snoqualmie Boy) in August: ran well when second after, in minor event at Doncaster (2½
lengths behind Kirklees) and handicap at Pontefract (neck behind Gulf Express): well
worth a try at 1½m: acts on good to firm ground. *H. R. A. Cecil*

MANZILA (FR) 4 ch.f. Cadeaux Genereux 131 – Mannsara (IRE) (Royal Academy   **102**
(USA) 130) [2007 6s⁵ 6s 6m* 5m⁶ 5g⁶ 5m 6d 5.5d Oct 8] €10,000 2-y-o: raw-boned filly:
third foal: half-sister to French 2004 2-y-o 1m winner Mannsar (by Sendawar): dam,
French maiden, half-sister to smart French miler Massigann: useful performer: trained by
G. Henrot in 2006, winning maiden at Royan and handicap at Chantilly: improved when
winning listed race at Chantilly in April by length from Val Jaro: well held last 3 starts, in
King's Stand Stakes at Royal Ascot first of them: left F. Head before final outing: has won
at 1m, best at 5f/6f: acts on soft and good to firm ground. *A. de Royer Dupre, France*

MARAAGEL (USA) 4 b.c. Danzig (USA) – Hasnaael Reef (USA) (Seattle Slew   **51**
(USA)) [2007 –: p8g p5m f7d⁵ f6g³ Dec 27] lightly-raced maiden: modest in 2007
(trained by C. Drew second start only): tried tongue tied. *S. C. Williams*

MARAAHEL (IRE) 6 b.h. Alzao (USA) 117 – Nasanice (IRE) 97 (Nashwan (USA)   **121**
135) [2007 126: 12m* 10.3m* 12d³ 12d8* 12g³ 10m⁵ 10d Oct 20] quite good-topped
horse: has a fluent, round action: very smart performer: won 3 of first 4 starts in 2007,
namely Dubai Tennis Championships Stakes (John Porter, by neck form Mighty) at
Newbury in April, Akkroball Huxley Stakes at Chester (for third successive year, beat
Blue Bajan a head) in May, and Hardwicke Stakes at Royal Ascot (for second successive
year, beat Scorpion by ½ length) in June: at least respectable third in Coronation Cup at
Epsom (1¾ lengths behind Scorpion) and King George VI and Queen Elizabeth Stakes at
Ascot (beaten 7½ lengths by Dylan Thomas), but poor efforts in Irish Champion Stakes

Hardwicke Stakes, Royal Ascot—Maraahel (left) reverses Coronation Cup form with Scorpion, on terms 5 lb better, to gain his second successive win in the race; Mighty (right) is third with Admiral's Cruise (centre) fourth and Blue Bajan (noseband) fifth

at Leopardstown and Champion Stakes at Newmarket final 2 outings: effective at 1¼m/1½m, probably at 14.6f with emphasis on speed: acts on firm and good to soft going (well held on dirt in Dubai World Cup in 2006): blinkered/visored nowadays: has looked none too keen: stays in training. *Sir Michael Stoute*

MARACA (IRE) 3 b.c. Danehill Dancer (IRE) 117 – Marasem 86 (Cadeaux Genereux 131) [2007 82p: p9.5g⁶ Apr 24] sturdy colt: fair winner at 2 yrs: well below form sole start in 2007: stays 8.6f: acts on polytrack: sold 4,500 gns in October. *J. H. M. Gosden*   **–**

MARACANA BOY (IRE) 2 ch.g. (Apr 24) Captain Rio 122 – Mary's Way (GR) 78 (Night Shift (USA)) [2007 5g⁶ 5.1m⁴ 5d³ 6d⁶ 5m p5.1g Sep 13] good-topped gelding: fair maiden: third at Musselburgh in June: lost form after: tried in blinkers/tongue tie: best efforts at 5f: sold 2,000 gns, sent to Sweden. *M. Dods*   **71 d**

MARAJAA (IRE) 5 b.g. Green Desert (USA) 127 – Ghyraan (IRE) 106 (Cadeaux Genereux 131) [2007 101: p8g⁴ p7f⁶ p8.6g⁴ p7g⁵ 8m⁵ p8g 8.1g 8m³ 8g 7.1d⁵ p7g⁵ p8g Sep 8] good-topped gelding: fairly useful handicapper: mainly respectable efforts in 2007: stays 1m: acts on polytrack, heavy and good to firm ground. *W. J. Musson*   **93**

MARAKAI (IRE) 2 b.g. (Jun 7) Cayman Kai (IRE) 114 – Emmajoun 69 (Emarati (USA) 74) [2007 6f Aug 8] strong, close-coupled gelding: 100/1, well beaten in maiden at Pontefract. *C. Grant*   **–**

MARAMBA (USA) 2 ch.f. (Apr 17) Hussonet (USA) – Coco (USA) 105 (Storm Bird (CAN) 134) [2007 p6g⁴ 6f* 7d³ Oct 27] fourth foal: closely related to 11f winner Missouri (by Gulch) and half-sister to 2004 2-y-o 7f winner Minnesota (by Silver Hawk): dam, 1m winner, later successful in US: progressive form: won maiden at Redcar in September by 3 lengths from Tobar Suil Lady: third behind Lady Deauville and Missit in listed race at Newbury, still green and nearest finish: will be suited to 1m: acts on firm and good to soft going: already useful, and will go on improving. *Sir Michael Stoute*   **97 p**

MARBAA (IRE) 4 b.g. Peintre Celebre (USA) 137 – Bahareeya (USA) (Riverman (USA) 131) [2007 75: p10g⁵ p10g³ p10g f11g 8m 9g p10g 10m p10g⁵ 10.2s⁶ 11.9m³ 7.6s Aug 18] smallish gelding: regressive maiden: stays easy 1¼m: acts on polytrack and good to firm going: has worn crossed noseband: visored/in cheekpieces last 3 starts: has been slowly away/looked reluctant. *S. Dow*   **75 d**

MARCHAND D'OR (FR) 4 gr.g. Marchand de Sable (USA) 117 – Fedora (FR) (Kendor (FR) 122) [2007 121: a6f 8g 7g* 6m⁴ 6.5m* 6g² 7d³ 6g⁶ Dec 9]   **123**

It was a case of same again for the leading French-trained six- and seven-furlong performer Marchand d'Or in 2007. He repeated wins from the previous year in the Group 3 Prix de la Porte Maillot at Longchamp in June and the Group 1 Prix Maurice de Gheest at Deauville in August, in the latter putting up as good a performance as any in his career. Marchand d'Or also made the frame in three other Group 1 events, the July Cup, the Haydock Sprint Cup and the Prix de la Foret. His efforts in Britain were on a par with his performance at Deauville.

The Porte Maillot provided an ideal opportunity for Marchand d'Or to regain the winning thread. He had appeared twice earlier in the year, shaping well in the Golden Shaheen at Nad Al Sheba over six furlongs on his first start on dirt in March, then finding a mile beyond him in the Prix du Muguet at Saint-Cloud in

Prix Maurice de Gheest, Deauville—Marchand d'Or (left) gains a second successive win in the race, reversing July Cup form with Dutch Art; next home are Silver Touch (striped sleeves), Garnica (between second and third) and Major Cadeaux (star on cap)

May. Significantly, in the Porte Maillot, he was unpenalised for his Group 1 win the previous summer and faced mainly useful older rivals, his chief rival on form Satri not having been out since finishing second to him in the Maurice de Gheest. Marchand d'Or didn't have to be at his best to win in good style by two and a half lengths. He was held up to utilise his good turn of foot, as he had been since the Maurice de Gheest and as became the pattern.

The field for Marchand d'Or's second Maurice de Gheest provided an altogether more rigorous test, with a strong cross-Channel representation, headed by Dutch Art, with the very smart Australian sprinter Bentley Biscuit also among the opposition. The trio had met the previous month in the July Cup at Newmarket, where Marchand d'Or finished fourth behind Sakhee's Secret, two places and a length and a half behind the three-year-old Dutch Art, with Bentley Biscuit tenth. Marchand d'Or was a 25/1-chance at Newmarket, though that hardly reflected his chance and the pari-mutuel odds at Deauville were a much closer guide to the chances of the trio, Dutch Art favourite ahead of Marchand d'Or, with the pair dominating the market. They dominated the finish as well, Dutch Art produced to lead entering the final furlong before Marchand d'Or, produced widest of all, swept past to win by a length. The proximity of Silver Touch and Garnica in third and fourth suggested that the runner-up was below his Newmarket form but it was still a very smart effort by the winner. Marchand d'Or and Dutch Art should have met again at Haydock but concerns about the ground at the course, discussed in the essays on Dutch Art and Sakhee's Secret, meant Dutch Art was an absentee. Marchand d'Or was there, however, and ran a fine second, collared late on by Red Clubs and beaten three quarters of a length. Marchand d'Or ran twice subsequently, not at his best when third behind the unconsidered pacesetters Toylsome and Welsh Emperor in the Prix de la Foret or when sixth, albeit the first foreign runner past the post, in the Hong Kong Sprint. The locals at Sha Tin sent him off a 100/1 chance, assuredly not a true reflection of his ability.

Marchand d'Or (FR) (gr.g. 2003)	Marchand de Sable (USA) (b 1990)	Theatrical (b 1982)	Nureyev
			Tree of Knowledge
		Mercantile (b 1983)	Kenmare
			Mercuriale
	Fedora (FR) (gr 1998)	Kendor (gr 1986)	Kenmare
			Belle Mecene
		Far But Near (b 1989)	Far North
			Kesar Queen

The quite good-topped Marchand d'Or is the best offspring by his sire Marchand de Sable, whose only winner in Britain has been the smart two-mile chaser Andreas. Marchand de Sable has had one other Grade 1 winner in the 2004 E. P. Taylor Stakes winner Commercante and he himself won the Criterium de Saint-Cloud at two before compiling a consistent record of placed efforts over middle distances at three and four. Marchand d'Or's dam Fedora failed to earn any prize money in six starts at three but has already more than rewarded her owner with her efforts at stud. Marchand d'Or is her first foal, the third Saga d'Or (by Sagacity) winning over a mile at Saint-Cloud on her second start in October, also trained by Freddie Head. Both the grandam Far But Near and third dam Kesar Queen won on the Flat in Britain, Far But Near winning a six-furlong maiden at Yarmouth on her only outing, Kesar Queen landing her biggest success in the Coronation Stakes. Far But Near bred five winners in Britain and in France, the best of them probably the fairly useful Corniche. Marchand d'Or clearly doesn't stay so well as might have been expected from his breeding and he can be expected to have a similar campaign in 2008, looking likely to continue to play a significant role in the top races at around six and seven furlongs. He has yet to race on firm going but acts on any other. *F. Head, France*

MARCH MATE 3 b.g. Warningford 119 – Daira 72 (Daring March 116) [2007 9m⁵ 7s⁶ 8m³ 9.8m⁵ Sep 1] lengthy, unfurnished gelding: third foal: half-brother to 5-y-o Spring Time Girl: dam 1½m winner: modest form in maidens: stays 1m: likely to do better, particularly in handicaps. *B. Ellison* **57 p**

MARCHPANE 2 b.f. (Mar 2) Olden Times 121 – Ecstasy 81 (Pursuit of Love 124) [2007 5.7s 7g* 7m⁶ 7m Oct 6] workmanlike filly: third foal: half-sister to 3-y-o Abounding: dam, 7f (at 2 yrs) to 10.2f winner, out of half-sister to smart performers Gaelic Storm (sprinter) and Waterfield (1½m to 2m): fair form: 40/1, won maiden at Newbury in August: well held in minor event and nursery (took little interest): will stay 1¼m+. *R. M. Beckett* **70**

MARCUS ANDRONICUS (USA) 4 b.c. Danehill (USA) 126 – Fiji 125 (Rainbow Quest (USA) 134) [2007 117: 7m³ 8g May 19] small, strong, attractive colt: just useful form in 2007 when ¾-length third to Mustameet in Gladness Stakes at the Curragh: ran as if amiss in Lockinge Stakes at Newbury next time: stays 1m: acts on soft and good to firm going. *A. P. O'Brien, Ireland* **107**

MARDI 3 b.g. Montjeu 137 – Portorosa (USA) (Irish River (FR) 131) [2007 73p: 10g 11.6s⁵ p11g 10g³ 12m 11.8g Oct 16] leggy, quite attractive gelding: fair performer: probably stays 11.6f: acts on fibresand, probably on soft ground: sold 9,000 gns. *W. J. Haggas* **74**

MARDOOD 2 b.g. (Jan 24) Oasis Dream 129 – Gaelic Swan (IRE) 80 (Nashwan (USA) 135) [2007 8.3g 7d³ Oct 30] 60,000F: good-topped gelding: second foal: dam, maiden (stayed 1½m), sister to smart 1¼m/1½m winner Mary Stuart and half-sister to dam of Golan: fair form in maidens at Leicester (green) and Yarmouth (close third to Tasheba): gelded after: stays 1m: should do better still. *W. J. Haggas* **74 p**

MARFENG 2 ch.f. (Mar 24) Mark of Esteem (IRE) 137 – Chilly Waters (Polar Falcon (USA) 126) [2007 6.5d p7.1g 7g Nov 3] 8,000Y: small, close-coupled filly: third foal: half-sister to fairly useful 2003 2-y-o 5f/6f winner Milly Waters (by Danzero) and winner in Holland by Sabrehill: dam, Italian 1¼m/11f winner, out of half-sister to dam of Oh So Sharp: well held in sales race/maidens: sold 800 gns. *W. M. Brisbourne* **–**

MARIA ANTONIA (IRE) 4 ch.f. King's Best (USA) 132 – Annieirwin (IRE) 94 (Perugino (USA) 84) [2007 64: f12g* f12g² p13.9g 12g⁴ 12m f13g 14.1m p11g⁶ p13.9g 11.8g² 11.9g³ p12g⁶ p12m⁵ f12d Dec 14] fair handicapper: won at Southwell in January: stays 1½m: acts on all-weather and soft ground: takes good hold: usually held up. *P. A. Blockley* **67**

MARIAS BUDDY 2 b.f. (Mar 29) Reel Buddy (USA) 118 – Mitsuki 91§ (Puissance 110) [2007 5m³ p5g² 5m² 5f⁵ 5s⁵ 5f⁶ Sep 13] 5,500Y: compact filly: first foal: dam 5f/6f winner (including at 2 yrs): modest maiden: placed first 3 starts, including at Kempton: will prove best kept to 5f. *E. Tyrrell, Ireland* **61**

MARIAVERDI 3 b.f. Diktat 126 – Belinda 64 (Mizoram (USA) 105) [2007 51: 6m⁵ p8g⁵ p10m p11g³ p12g⁵ Dec 16] modest maiden: barely stays easy 1½m: raced only on polytrack and good to firm going. *P. G. Murphy* **57**

MA RIDGE 3 ch.c. Tumbleweed Ridge 117 – Ma Barnicle (IRE) 76 (Al Hareb (USA) 123) [2007 –: 9m p7g⁴ 7f p8g Dec 16] modest maiden: probably stays easy 7f: crashed into rail/unseated rider third outing, seemingly amiss final one. *T. D. McCarthy* **55**

MARIE CAMARGO 2 b.f. (May 4) Kyllachy 129 – Wheeler's Wonder (IRE) 43 (Sure Blade (USA) 130) [2007 5.1m 7d⁵ Oct 30] close-coupled filly: eighth foal: half-sister to 4-y-o Anna Pavlova and 1m/9f winner Cyclonic Storm (by Catrail): dam 1½m/2m and hurdles winner: modest maiden: will stay at least 1m. *R. A. Fahey* **58**

MARIE CLAUDE 2 b.f. (Apr 25) Where Or When (IRE) 124 – Lalique (IRE) (Lahib — (USA) 129) [2007 p6s Dec 21] 30,000Y: fifth foal: half-sister to 2003 2-y-o 5f winner Mister Marmaduke (by Marju) and 7f seller winner Maid In England (by Mujadil): dam unraced half-sister to smart French 7f to 1¼m performer Goofalik: 5/1 and green, well held in maiden at Wolverhampton. *J. Noseda*

MARIESCHI (USA) 3 b.g. Maria's Mon (USA) 121 – Pennygown 91 (Rainbow Quest **68** (USA) 134) [2007 10g⁴ 10d 8.3m⁴ Jul 30] tall gelding: third foal: dam, 1½m winner, half-sister to very smart pair Craigsteel (best at 1½m/1¾m) and Invermark (stayed 2½m): best effort in maidens when fourth at Lingfield on debut: will be suited by 1½m+: sold 13,000 gns, joined R. Fisher and gelded. *H. R. A. Cecil*

MARIE TEMPEST 2 b.f. (Feb 24) Rock Of Gibraltar (IRE) 133 – Hakkaniyah 84 (Machiavellian **– p** (USA) 123) [2007 7g Nov 3] useful-looking filly: has scope: sixth foal: half-sister to winner abroad by Grand Lodge: dam 2-y-o 6f winner: 12/1, towards rear in maiden at Newmarket: will improve with experience. *B. W. Hills*

MARINO PRINCE (FR) 2 b.c. (Mar 3) Dr Fong (USA) 128 – Hula Queen (USA) **70** (Irish River (FR) 131) [2007 p7.1g⁶ p7m p7.1g p7.1g* p8.6g* p8.6g* p9.5s³ Dec 20] fair performer: progressed to win seller and 2 claimers at Wolverhampton in November, left W. Turner £9,000 after second success and A. Haynes £13,000 after third: creditable third in nursery there final outing: stays 9.5f: raced only on polytrack. *T. Wall*

MARIOTTO (USA) 3 b.c. Swain (USA) 134 – Shamaat Hayaaty (IRE) (Sadler's Wells **109** (USA) 132) [2007 96p: 10d* 12g 12s Oct 13] good-topped colt: useful performer: left M. Johnston, won handicap at Sandown in July by head from Ballinteni, disputing running: ran in valuable handicaps after, at Goodwood (seemed amiss) and Ascot (every chance when breaking down 2f out, subsequently put down): stayed 1¼m: acted on good to soft going: tongue tied in 2007. *Saeed bin Suroor*

MARIST MADAME 3 ch.f. Tomba 119 – Linda's Schoolgirl (IRE) (Grand Lodge **47** (USA) 125) [2007 44: p7.1g³ p7.1g² 7d⁴ 6m⁴ p7g p8.6g p7.1d Dec 27] strong filly: poor maiden: left D. Ivory after sixth start: stays 7f: acts on polytrack, good to firm and good to soft going: looks tricky ride. *T. J. Pitt*

MARJU'S GOLD 3 b.c. Marju (IRE) 127 – Dubious (Darshaan 133) [2007 52: p8g f8g **61** 11g³ 12.6m³ 12g 9m³ 11.7d Jun 16] modest maiden: stays 12.6f: acts on good to firm going (seemed not to handle fibresand): pulls hard, and not an easy ride: sold 10,000 gns, joined D. McCain Jnr. *E. J. O'Neill*

MARKAB 4 b.c. Green Desert (USA) 127 – Hawafiz (Nashwan (USA) 135) [2007 7.6m **86** p7g Dec 28] fairly useful performer: won maiden at Maisons-Laffitte in 2006: placed all 4 starts in minor events later that year: left F. Head 33,000 gns, better effort in handicaps in Britain at 4 yrs when seventh at Lingfield final start: stays 1m: acts on heavy going, probably on good to firm. *K. A. Morgan*

MARKER 7 ch.g. Pivotal 124 – Palace Street (USA) 103 (Secreto (USA) 128) [2007 **51** 80d: 6g 8.1s 7g p6g Sep 15] sturdy, close-coupled gelding: modest handicapper nowadays: stays 7f: acts on firm and soft going: tried in headgear. *J. D. Frost*

MARKESTINO 4 b.g. Mark of Esteem (IRE) 137 – Mademoiselle Chloe 106 (Night **58** Shift (USA)) [2007 56: 6.1g³ 6m 6d Jul 25] strong, well-made gelding: modest performer: effective at 6f, seems to stay 8.5f: acts on fibresand and firm ground: tried tongue tied. *T. D. Easterby*

MARKET FORCES 3 b.f. Lomitas 129 – Quota 102 (Rainbow Quest (USA) 134) **107** [2007 75p: 12.1g* 11.8s⁴ 12d² 14.8m* 14d* 16s² p13m² Nov 1] rather leggy, lengthy filly: useful performer: won maiden at Beverley (by 11 lengths) in May and handicaps at Newmarket in July and York (by 4 lengths from Casual Affair) in October: at least creditable efforts after, beaten 3 lengths by Highland Legacy in handicap at Nottingham and ¾ length by Loulwa in listed race at Lingfield final outing: stayed 2m: acted on polytrack, soft and good to firm going: genuine: stud. *H. R. A. Cecil*

MARKET WATCHER (USA) 6 b.g. Boundary (USA) 117 – Trading (USA) (A P **81 d** Indy (USA) 131) [2007 73: p13.9g³ 16g 16s 11.9s³ 12d 17.8m p10.7g p16.5g p12.2g Nov 20] strong gelding: fairly useful handicapper: good third at Wolverhampton on reappearance, but well below form after: stays 16.5f: acts on polytrack, soft and good to firm going: tried blinkered: tongue tied: none too consistent. *Seamus Fahey, Ireland*

MARK OF LOVE (IRE) 3 ch.g. Mark of Esteem (IRE) 137 – Dazilyn Lady (USA) **78** 105 (Zilzal (USA) 137) [2007 p7g p8g p8.6g p8g p8g² 8.2g² p8g* 8m³ 8.2s 8.1g 8.1d⁴ 8s* 8.3g 8.1v² 10m 8g⁶ 8m³ 8m⁴ Sep 6] sturdy, quite attractive gelding: fair handicapper: won at Kempton in May and Newbury in July: stays 1m: acts on polytrack, heavy and good to firm ground: free-going sort, effective ridden prominently or held up: joined R. Phillips. *M. R. Channon*

MARK OF THE FEN 3 b.g. Mark of Esteem (IRE) 137 – Krisalya 98 (Kris 135) **60**
[2007 p8.6g p8g⁶ p12.2g⁵ p9.5g 10.1d² Oct 30] modest maiden: stays 1¼m: raced only on polytrack/good to soft going: sold 6,000 gns. *Rae Guest*

MARKO JADEO (IRE) 9 b.g. Eagle Eyed (USA) 111 – Fleeting Quest (Rainbow **83**
Quest (USA) 134) [2007 82, a90: p7.1g⁶ p6g* f7g⁶ p7g⁵ p6g⁴ p7g p7.1g³ 6f 6m² 6m³ 6g 6s⁶ 7.1s³ p6g⁶ p6g 6f⁴ 6m³ 6m Sep 2] workmanlike gelding: fairly useful performer: won claimer at Wolverhampton in January: effective at 6f to easy 1m: acts on sand, polytrack, firm and good to soft ground: tried in cheekpieces: usually slowly away and held up. *R. A. Harris*

MARLENA (IRE) 2 b. or br.f. (Feb 3) Marju (IRE) 127 – Red Rosie (USA) 83 (Red **60**
Ransom (USA)) [2007 6s⁶ 6m 7f⁵ 7m Sep 9] €30,000Y: second foal: half-sister to 2006 2-y-o 5f winner Major Third (by Daggers Drawn): dam, 1¼m winner, half-sister to US Grade 3 8.5f winner Gentleman Beau: modest maiden: will stay 1m. *T. D. Easterby*

MARLYN RIDGE 3 b.g. Tumbleweed Ridge 117 – Kayartis 57 (Kaytu 112) [2007 –: **67**
p8g⁴ 10g⁴ p12g Jul 17] lengthy, unfurnished gelding: fair maiden: stays 1¼m: acts on polytrack: hung right second start, played up in stall and ran as if amiss final outing. *D. K. Ivory*

MARMITE (IRE) 2 b. or br.f. (Feb 2) Vettori (IRE) 119 – Marliana (IRE) (Mtoto 134) **60**
[2007 5m f6g⁵ 7s 7d* p7.1g* p8g p8.6g⁴ p10g⁵ Oct 24] third foal: half-sister to 2005 2-y-o 6f winner Zambach (by Namid): dam, French 2-y-o 6f winner, out of useful French sprinter Mahalia: modest form: won sellers at Brighton and Wolverhampton in July: stays 1¼m: acts on polytrack and good to soft going: usually blinkered/visored: has her share of temperament. *E. F. Vaughan*

MARMOOQ 4 ch.g. Cadeaux Genereux 131 – Portelet 91 (Night Shift (USA)) [2007 **65**
82, a69: p7.1g p7.1g⁶ p8.6g f7g p7g* 7m p7g⁵ p7g² 7d³ 7m⁶ 7m⁶ 7.6f p7.1g⁴ p8.6g³ p8m⁴ 6d p7m p7g p7.1g Nov 19] tall gelding: just fair at best nowadays: won claimer at Lingfield in March: left J. Gallagher after ninth outing: stays 7f: acts on polytrack, firm and good to soft going: tried visored/in cheekpieces: often races prominently: said to have bled twelfth outing. *M. J. Attwater*

MARNING STAR 2 b.c. (Mar 18) Diktat 126 – Mustique Dream 87 (Don't Forget Me **72**
127) [2007 6m 7d² 7.1s 7g 8m³ 8m⁵ Sep 4] leggy, lengthy colt: fair maiden: placed at Thirsk and Newcastle (nursery): stays 1m: acts on good to firm and good to soft going. *M. R. Channon*

MAROMITO (IRE) 10 b.g. Up And At 'em 109 – Amtico (Bairn (USA) 126) [2007 **59**
50: 5g* p5g² 5g 5d 5m³ 5m 5m⁵ 5s 5.1g p5g³ Nov 19] well-made gelding: modest performer: won seller at Musselburgh in May: best at 5f: acts on all-weather, firm and good to soft going: tried blinkered at 6 yrs: has hung left: often front runner. *R. Bastiman*

MAROUSSIES ROCK 3 b.f. Rock of Gibraltar (IRE) 133 – Maroussie (FR) 115 **–**
(Saumarez 132) [2007 8m Apr 14] 50,000Y: fifth foal: half-sister to 4-y-o Maroussies Wings, useful 7f to 9f winner Mamounia and fairly useful 1m to 1¼m winner Clipperdown (both by Green Desert): dam French 1¼m winner: 16/1, behind in maiden at Newcastle: sold 11,000 gns in December. *P. C. Haslam*

MAROUSSIES WINGS (IRE) 4 b.f. In The Wings 128 – Maroussie (FR) 115 **98**
(Saumarez 132) [2007 111: 10.4g⁴ 11.9m⁴ May 26] good-topped filly: smart performer at 3 yrs: below form in Middleton Stakes at York and listed race at Haydock in 2007, still not right in coat and again looked ungainly under pressure in latter: stayed 1¾m: acted on heavy and good to firm going: stud. *P. C. Haslam*

MAROZI 3 ch.c. Forest Wildcat (USA) 120 – Chitka (USA) (Jade Hunter **91**
(USA)) [2007 81p: p6g* 6d⁴ 5g* 5m Sep 1] well-made colt: useful performer: won maiden at Lingfield in July and handicap at Goodwood (beat Morinqua by ¾ length, travelling strongly but drifting right) in August: may prove best at 5f: acts on polytrack, probably on good to firm and good to soft going: sent to USA. *M. A. Jarvis*

MARQUEE (IRE) 3 b.c. Mark of Esteem (IRE) 137 – Queen's Ransom (IRE) 70 (Last **69**
Tycoon 131) [2007 54: 10m 8m³ 10.9d³ 12.1s³ p8.6g⁴ Aug 12] tall colt: fair maiden: barely stays testing 1½m: acts on polytrack, soft and good to firm ground: hung left third start. *P. A. Blockley*

MARRAASI (USA) 2 ch.f. (Mar 25) Rahy (USA) 115 – Bashayer (USA) 103 (Mr **69**
Prospector (USA)) [2007 7d p7g⁶ p7g² Nov 17] sturdy filly: seventh foal: closely related to 2 winners by Arazi, including fairly useful 1¾m winner Awtaan, and half-sister to 3

winners, including useful 1m winner Mosayter (by Storm Cat): dam, 1m winner (including at 2 yrs) who stayed 11.4f, closely related to Nayef and half-sister to Unfuwain and Nashwan: fair form in maidens at Lingfield last 2 starts: will be suited by 1m+. *M. P. Tregoning*

MARRAMED 2 ch.f. (Mar 24) Medicean 128 – Marrakech (IRE) 103 (Barathea (IRE) – 127) [2007 7f Aug 12] 27,000Y: first foal: dam 1m/1½m and hurdles winner: 20/1, always behind in maiden at Redcar: sold 2,000 gns. *E. J. O'Neill*

MARRIAJ (USA) 3 b. or br.c. Giant's Causeway (USA) 132 – Be My Sweetheart **84** (USA) (No Robbery) [2007 80+: 8.2m⁶ 9.1m p8g³ a10f* a8g⁵ a10f³ Dec 20] leggy colt: fair performer: left B. Smart, won handicap at Nad Al Sheba in November: stays 1¼m: acts on dirt and soft going. *A. Al Raihe, UAE*

MARRON FLORE 4 ch.f. Compton Place 125 – Flore Fair (Polar Falcon (USA) 126) **44** [2007 46: p8g⁶ p8g f7g Feb 1] poor maiden: stays 1m: raced on all-weather: wears cheekpieces/tongue tie. *A. J. Lidderdale*

MARRYL 3 b.g. Warningford 119 – Nordico Princess 71 (Nordico (USA)) [2007 –: 10v – 8.5g Aug 15] quite good-topped gelding: no form: tried blinkered. *M. W. Easterby*

MARSAM (IRE) 4 gr.g. Daylami (IRE) 138 – Dancing Prize (IRE) 99 (Sadler's Wells **79** (USA) 132) [2007 96: 9.7f⁵ 14d p10g f12d² Dec 12] raced in 2006 for D. Weld in Ireland (sold 70,000 gns): only fair form in handicaps on Flat in 2007: stays 1½m: acts on fibresand, firm and soft ground: winning hurdler. *M. G. Quinlan*

MARSHMAN (IRE) 8 ch.g. College Chapel 122 – Gold Fly (IRE) (Be My Guest **76 d** (USA) 126) [2007 98d: 7d 7g 7d 7.5d Sep 25] good-topped gelding: useful handicapper at best, on downgrade: stays 7f: acts on polytrack, firm and soft going: blinkered (below form) once in 2004: usually held up. *M. H. Tompkins*

MARTINET (IRE) 3 b.g. Jade Robbery (USA) 121 – Insistent (USA) (Diesis 133) – [2007 10.3m 12.1g⁵ 10g 8d⁶ Jul 3] angular, workmanlike gelding: little form in maidens/seller: tongue tied first 2 starts: has hung/pulled hard. *P. D. Evans*

MARTINGRANGE BOY (IRE) 2 b.g. (Jan 24) Danetime (IRE) 121 – Coloma **73** (JPN) (Forty Niner (USA)) [2007 p5m f6d² p6g* f5g² Dec 27] fair form: made all in seller at Lingfield in December: likely to prove best at 5f/6f: tongue tied last 3 starts. *D. J. Murphy*

MARTYR 2 b.c. (Mar 12) Cape Cross (IRE) 129 – Sudeley 65 (Dancing Brave (USA) **79 p** 140) [2007 8d 7g p8.6g² p9.5s* Dec 20] 47,000F, 62,000Y: sturdy colt: closely related to Irish 2000 2-y-o 7f winner Katherine Seymour (by Green Desert) and half-brother to 7f to 1¼m winner Etmaam (by Intikhab), both useful: dam, 11.5f winner, half-sister to Coronation Cup winner Quiet Fling: fair form: won nursery at Wolverhampton in December by 2½ lengths: likely to stay beyond 9.5f: acts on polytrack: will do better again. *R. Hannon*

MARVIN GARDENS 4 b.g. Largesse 112 – En Grisaille 53 (Mystiko (USA) 124) **49** [2007 48: 8m³ 12m Aug 30] poor maiden: stays 1m: acts on good to firm ground. *John Berry*

MARWAH 2 b.f. (Feb 18) King's Best (USA) 132 – Mubkera (IRE) 100 (Nashwan **76** (USA) 135) [2007 7g³ 7m⁴ Aug 17] lengthy, useful-looking filly: fluent mover: second foal: half-sister to French 1½m winner Manjam (by Almutawakel): dam 2-y-o 1m winner (stayed 1½m): fair form in frame in maidens at Newmarket and Doncaster (fourth to Lady Jane Digby): will stay at least 1m: sold 14,000 gns, sent to USA. *E. A. L. Dunlop*

MARY FROM MARYHILL (IRE) 3 b.f. Fath (USA) 116 – Kentucky Wildcat 64 **35** (Be My Guest (USA) 126) [2007 6g 6m 7v Jun 29] sturdy filly: half-sister to several winners: dam staying maiden: poor form in maidens. *Miss L. A. Perratt*

MARY MONTAGU (IRE) 2 b.f. (Feb 6) Danehill Dancer (IRE) 117 – Epistoliere **70 p** (IRE) (Alzao (USA) 117) [2007 6.5d p7g⁵ Oct 24] rather unfurnished filly: second foal: closely related to 11f winner in Italy by Indian Danehill: dam, French maiden (stayed 1¼m), sister to smart French performer up to 13f Epistolaire and half-sister to smart French stayer Epitre: encouragement in sales race at Ascot (tenth of 22 to Lady Rangali) and maiden at Lingfield (not clear run): will be suited by 1m+: sent to USA: capable of better. *J. W. Hills*

MARYOLINI 2 b.f. (Apr 9) Bertolini (USA) 125 – Mary Jane 77 (Tina's Pet 121) [2007 **78** 5.1f⁶ p6g* 6.1m² p6g⁵ p6g³ p6d* Dec 28] 13,000Y: second foal: dam 5f (including at 2 yrs)/6f winner: fair performer: won maiden in July and nursery in December, both at Wolverhampton: placed in nurseries at Chepstow and Kempton: stays 6f: acts on polytrack and good to firm going. *N. J. Vaughan*

MARYQUEENOFSCOTS (IRE) 2 b.f. (Mar 4) Fantastic Light (USA) 134 – Marie **80 +**
de Blois (IRE) (Barathea (IRE) 127) [2007 7.1g* Sep 12] €40,000Y, 65,000 2-y-o:
sparely-made filly: second foal: half-sister to smart French 7f (at 2 yrs) to 11f winner
Shujoon (by Sakhee): dam, German 1m/8.5f winner, half-sister to useful French 1m/1¼m
performer Kilometre Neuf: 13/2, won maiden at Haydock by ¾ length from dead-heaters
Ballochroy and Blue Boy (both successful next time), picking up well from rear: will be
suited by 1m/1¼m. *M. L. W. Bell*

MARZELLINE (IRE) 3 ch.f. Barathea (IRE) 127 – Juno Marlowe (IRE) 100 (Dane- **102**
hill (USA) 126) [2007 8.3m⁶ 10m* 12g⁵ 10.1m⁶ 12f⁴ p11g² 10.1g 8.3g³ Oct 16] useful-
looking filly: has scope: third foal: half-sister to 5-y-o Fairmile and 4-y-o Constant
Cheers: dam, 7f winner, sister to smart performer up to 10.5f Leporello: useful performer:
won maiden at Lingfield in June: best effort when fifth to Silkwood in Ribblesdale Stakes
at Royal Ascot next time: stays 1½m: acts on firm going: visored (ran creditably) final
outing: sent to USA. *W. R. Swinburn*

MASAALEK 2 b.c. (May 12) Green Desert (USA) 127 – Hammiya (IRE) 103 (Dars- **90**
haan 133) [2007 6g² May 19] smallish colt: first foal: dam 8.5f/11.4f winner: 16/1,
promising second to Coasting in maiden at Newbury, weaving through from rear: will
stay 1m. *M. P. Tregoning*

MASADA (IRE) 2 br.f. (Mar 16) Key of Luck (USA) 126 – Desert Bloom (IRE) **85 p**
(Pilsudski (IRE) 134) [2007 5.1g* 6g Nov 2] second foal: dam unraced out of useful
daughter of outstanding broodmare Hellenic: fairly useful form: won maiden at Bath in
October: improvement when 4 lengths seventh to Spinning Lucy in listed race at Newmarket: will be suited by 1m+: should do better still. *B. J. Meehan*

MASAI MOON 3 b.g. Lujain (USA) 119 – Easy To Imagine (USA) (Cozzene (USA)) **96**
[2007 79: 8.1m⁴ 6g³ 7m* 7.1g² 7d 7m 6d* 7d⁴ 6g Oct 26] tall, rather leggy gelding: improved into a useful handicapper: won at Leicester in May and Salisbury (beat Rainbow
Mirage by ½ length) in October: good fourth to Damika at Newmarket next time:
effective at 6f/7f: acts on firm and soft going: usually races prominently. *B. R. Millman*

MASHAAHED 4 b.c. In The Wings 128 – Patacake Patacake (USA) 67 (Bahri (USA) **117**
125) [2007 112: 10g² 10g³ 12m 10.4s 9d² 10g* Nov 3] lengthy, quite attractive colt: has a
quick, unimpressive action: smart performer: won 6-runner listed event at Newmarket in
November by neck from Fairmile, making all: ran well earlier when placed in Brigadier
Gerard Stakes at Sandown (beaten 2 short heads behind Take A Bow) and Darley Stakes
at Newmarket (beaten ¾ length by Windsor Knot) second/fifth starts: barely stays 1½m:
acts on firm and good to soft going: joined E. Charpy in UAE. *B. W. Hills*

MASHRAI (IRE) 2 b.c. (Feb 16) Dubai Destination (USA) 127 – Largo (IRE) 94 **68**
(Selkirk (USA) 129) [2007 8m⁶ 10m Oct 8] strong colt: better effort in maidens when
sixth to Alfathaa at Newbury: should stay 1¼m: sold 8,000 gns, sent to Czech Republic.
M. R. Channon

MASKED (IRE) 6 b.g. Soviet Star (USA) 128 – Moon Masquerade (IRE) 69 (Dar- **87**
shaan 133) [2007 p12g³ Dec 19] good-bodied, quite attractive gelding: fairly useful
handicapper: first start for well over 2 years when good ½-length third at Lingfield, not
looking straightforward: stays 2m: acts on polytrack, soft and firm going. *R. M. Beckett*

MASLAK (IRE) 3 b.g. In The Wings 128 – Jeed (IRE) 86 (Mujtahid (USA) 118) [2007 **77**
86: p12g² 10m³ 9.2d³ p8g 9.7s² p12.2g³ p12g⁶ p12.2g² p11m² 10.3g⁴ p13.9g³ p16.5g **a86**
f12d* f12g³ Dec 27] good-bodied gelding: fairly useful performer: left E. Dunlop after
fourth start: won maiden at Southwell in December: stays 1¾m: acts on all-weather, good
to firm and good to soft going. *P. W. Hiatt*

MASON ETTE 3 br.f. Grand Lodge (USA) 125 – Karlaska (Lashkari 128) [2007 78: **82**
p7.1g 6d* 6m 6g³ 6d 6d Oct 3] leggy filly: fairly useful handicapper: won at Salisbury in
May: should stay 7f: acts on good to firm and good to soft going, below form on polytrack. *C. G. Cox*

MASRA 4 b.g. Silver Patriarch (IRE) 125 – Go Sally Go (IRE) 46 (Elbio 125) [2007 **55**
12.4d⁶ Oct 16] 8/1, modest form when sixth to Snake's Head in maiden at Newcastle on
Flat debut (fairly useful form when runner-up all 4 starts in bumpers). *G. A. Swinbank*

MASSAMS LANE 3 b.g. Lahib (USA) 129 – Night Trader (USA) (Melyno 130) [2007 **63**
p7g 6m⁴ 6m⁶ p8.6g⁴ p8g⁵ Nov 6] tall, unfurnished gelding: modest maiden: left
P. McEntee after third start: stays 1m. *G. C. Bravery*

MASSEY 11 br.g. Machiavellian (USA) 123 – Massaraat (USA) (Nureyev (USA) 131) **–**
[2007 –, a57: f6g f7g Feb 1] big gelding: one-time useful performer: little form in 2007.
C. R. Dore

MASSIF CENTRALE 6 ch.g. Selkirk (USA) 129 – Madame Dubois 121 (Legend of – France (USA) 124) [2007 101: p16g Jan 17] big, lengthy gelding: useful performer at best: tailed off in claimer only start in 2007: tongue tied. *D. R. C. Elsworth*

MASSIVE (IRE) 3 b.c. Marju (IRE) 127 – Khatela (IRE) 91 (Shernazar 131) [2007 **103** 103: 9m⁶ 8.1s 8g Jul 28] well-made colt: has a short action: useful performer: form in 2007 only when winning listed race at Sandown in May by neck from Charlie Farnsbarns, dictating and battling on well: clearly amiss last 2 starts, including in visor: stays 1¼m: raced mainly on good going or softer, well held both starts on good to firm: joined D. Selvaratnam in UAE. *M. R. Channon*

MASTA PLASTA (IRE) 4 b.g. Mujadil (USA) 119 – Silver Arrow (USA) 67 **104** (Shadeed (USA) 135) [2007 103: 5g 5g 5m⁴ 5g³ 5g⁴ 5.1d³ 6g² 6d 5.5d 6d Oct 21] good-topped gelding: useful performer: creditable efforts in 2007 when in frame, including close fourth to Only Answer in listed race at Deauville and ¾-length second to Greek Renaissance in minor event at Yarmouth fifth/seventh outings: best at 5f/easy 6f: acts on good to firm and good to soft going. *D. Nicholls*

MASTER AT ARMS 4 ch.g. Grand Lodge (USA) 125 – L'Ideale (USA) (Alysheba **73** (USA)) [2007 9g 13g 12m 8m 10m⁶ 10.5g⁴ 9v 12v p12g³ p12g³ p12.2g* Nov 20] fair handicapper: won at Wolverhampton in November: stays 1½m: acts on polytrack and good to firm ground, possibly not on heavy. *D. Loughnane, Ireland*

MASTER BEN (IRE) 4 b.g. Carrowkeel (IRE) 106 – Java Jive 63 (Hotfoot 126) [2007 **56 ?** –: f8g f7g p6g² f7g⁶ p12.2g Oct 30] useful-looking gelding: modest maiden at best: stays 8.6f: acts on polytrack: usually blinkered, tried tongue tied. *S. R. Bowring*

MASTER CHEF (IRE) 2 b.c. (Feb 9) Oasis Dream 129 – Miss Honorine (IRE) 109 **98** (Highest Honor (FR) 124) [2007 5m⁵ 6g³ p6g³ 6m* 6g⁶ 7d⁵ p6g 7m⁶ 5g³ 6g⁶ Oct 27] 240,000F: strong colt: first foal: dam, Irish 1m/1¼m winner, out of sister to US Grade 1 8.5f winner Louis Cyphre: useful performer: won maiden at Ascot in July: highly tried at times, but best efforts in nurseries, third to Mesmerize Me at Windsor: effective at 5f to 7f: acts on good to firm and good to soft going, probably on polytrack: blinkered last 7 starts: sold 60,000 gns. *J. H. M. Gosden*

MASTER HALLING 3 ch.g. Halling (USA) 133 – Red Empress 88 (Nashwan (USA) **82 d** 135) [2007 10m³ 11.9m 10m 11.6g Oct 8] 65,000Y: big, strong gelding: third foal: dam, 1½m winner, closely related to smart 1¼m/1½m performer Happy Valentine out of smart sister to Salsabil: green, easily best effort when third to Dansant in maiden at Windsor: gelded, failed to handle track there final outing: should be suited by 1½m+: sold 18,000 gns. *R. Charlton*

MASTER JOBS 3 b.g. Singspiel (IRE) 133 – Pure Misk 55 (Rainbow Quest (USA) **55** 134) [2007 p12g⁵ p8g p12g May 23] modest form in maidens only on debut: gave trouble at stall and looked none too keen second outing: sold 2,800 gns later in May. *S. C. Williams*

MASTER MALARKEY 4 b.g. Tipsy Creek (USA) 115 – Girl Next Door 58 (Local **56** Suitor (USA) 128) [2007 64: 6m⁶ 6v 5.2d⁶ 6f 5.3d² 5.2d² p6g³ p6m p5g Oct 29] workmanlike gelding: modest maiden handicapper: best at 5f/6f: acts on polytrack and good to soft going: usually blinkered: often races prominently. *Mrs C. A. Dunnett*

MASTER'N COMMANDER 5 ch.g. Zafonic (USA) 130 – Magical Retreat (USA) **68** 115 (Sir Ivor (USA) 135) [2007 71: p12g⁶ p13g² p12.2g³ p10g p12g³ 9m Nov 3] tall gelding: fair maiden handicapper: left C. Cyzer after fifth outing: stays 13f: acts on polytrack and good to firm ground: tends to race freely. *John Joseph Hanlon, Ireland*

MASTER NIMBUS 7 b.g. Cloudings (IRE) 112 – Miss Charlie 59 (Pharly (FR) 130) **54** [2007 56: 12.1g⁴ 12m³ p12.2g² Sep 14] strong, angular gelding: modest handicapper: stays easy 1¾m: acts on polytrack, firm and good to soft going: fairly useful hurdler, successful twice in October. *J. J. Quinn*

MASTER OF ARTS (USA) 2 b. or br.g. (Jan 29) Swain (IRE) 134 – Grazia 111 **54 p** (Sharpo 132) [2007 6.1m p6g p6g Sep 5] 110,000Y: fifth foal: half-brother to Irish 7f (including at 2 yrs) winner Caprarola (by Rahy): dam, 6f (including at 2 yrs) winner, closely related to Halling: no show in maidens within 2 weeks (gelded after): will be suited by at least 1m: likely to prove a different proposition at 3 yrs. *Sir Mark Prescott*

MASTEROFTHECOURT (USA) 4 ch.g. Horse Chestnut (SAF) 119 – Great **78** Verdict (AUS) (Christmas Tree (AUS)) [2007 84: p11g² 12d 10.2d⁶ p8g 7d³ 7g⁶ p10g⁶ **a88** f8d f8g² Dec 27] sturdy gelding: type to carry condition: fairly useful handicapper on all-weather, fair on turf: should stay 1½m: acts on all-weather and good to firm ground, probably on good to soft: unseated leaving stall penultimate start. *H. Morrison*

MASTER OF THE RACE 5 ch.g. Selkirk (USA) 129 – Dust Dancer 116 (Suave **77** Dancer (USA) 136) [2007 89: 8g 10g Jun 7] strong, close-coupled gelding: fair maiden handicapper: stays 1¼m: acts on good to firm and good to soft going, probably on poly-track: in cheekpieces in 2007: appeared reluctant to go by on final outing at 3 yrs: sold 11,500 gns, sent to Greece. *Tom Dascombe*

MASTER PEGASUS 4 b.g. Lujain (USA) 119 – Seeking Utopia 76 (Wolfhound **92** (USA) 126) [2007 91: 7m⁴ 8g⁶ 8.1g² p7g⁵ 8d 8.3m p9.5g³ 10d⁶ p8.6g* p8.6d³ p8g⁵ Dec 30] big, lengthy gelding: fairly useful handicapper: won at Wolverhampton in November: stays easy 9.5f: acts on polytrack, soft and good to firm ground. *C. F. Wall*

MASTERSHIP (IRE) 3 ch.g. Best of The Bests (IRE) 122 – Shady Point (IRE) 76 **99** (Unfuwain (USA) 131) [2007 86: p8g² p6g* p7g⁴ 7m⁴ 8g 7d⁴ 6m 6m 6g p6m p7g Oct 24] good-topped gelding: useful performer: won handicap at Lingfield (beat Si Foo by 3 lengths) in February: several creditable efforts after, including when 1½ lengths fourth to Hinton Admiral in listed race on same course next time: effective at 6f to 8.6f: acts on polytrack, firm and soft ground: blinkered: tends to idle, and probably best produced late: sold 67,000 gns, then gelded. *C. E. Brittain*

MASTER SPY 2 br.c. (Apr 3) Cape Cross (IRE) 129 – Secret Seeker (USA) (Mr **61 p** Prospector (USA)) [2007 p7g⁶ Nov 17] closely related to useful 7f (including at 2 yrs)/1m winner Hidden Oasis (by Green Desert) and half-brother to 2 winners, including useful 7f (at 2 yrs)/1m winner Sekari (by Polish Precedent): dam, 6f winner in USA, sister to Gone West and Lion Cavern: 13/2, 3½ lengths sixth to Wasan in maiden at Lingfield: should improve. *J. H. M. Gosden*

MASTER WELLS (IRE) 6 b.g. Sadler's Wells (USA) 132 – Eljazzi 92 (Artaius **72** (USA) 129) [2007 12.1s* Jul 13] smallish, close-coupled gelding: fair handicapper nowa-days: won apprentice event at Chepstow only Flat start in 2007: stays 17.5f: acts on soft ground. *J. D. Frost*

MATARAM (USA) 4 b.g. Matty G (USA) 119 – Kalinka (USA) (Mr Prospector **71 +** (USA)) [2007 –, a84: p10g* p11g³ p10g p10g² p8g³ 7.5m p8g p8m⁶ p8g⁴ Dec 16] tall, **a90** leggy, long-backed gelding: fairly useful handicapper on all-weather, lightly raced and just fair on turf: won at Lingfield in January: good third at Kempton fifth start: effective at 1m to 11f: acts on polytrack, probably on good to firm ground. *W. Jarvis*

MATARAZZO (IRE) 5 gr.g. Linamix (FR) 127 – Altamira (FR) (Highest Honor (FR) **57 ?** 124) [2007 a12g⁵ a12g² a12g* a12g⁴ a12g* 13.5g 12.5d⁶ 13.5d⁴ 12g* 11d p10g⁶ p12g 11.9d Oct 18] won handicaps at Cagnes-sur-Mer in January, Toulouse in April and Salon de Provence in May: left J. M. Capitte in France, modest form at best in 3 runs in Britain: stays 1½m: acts on all-weather, and good to soft going: tried blinkered. *G. L. Moore*

MATERIAL WITNESS (IRE) 10 b.g. Barathea (IRE) 127 – Dial Dream (Gay **81** Mecene (USA) 128) [2007 93, a81: 7g 7m⁶ 7g³ p8g 7.1s² 7d 7m 7g⁶ 7m⁵ Sep 11] angular gelding: fairly useful handicapper, on long losing run: effective at 6f/7f: acts on polytrack, firm and soft going: tried in headgear: carries head high: front runner. *W. R. Muir*

MATHOOL (IRE) 2 b.f. (Apr 19) Alhaarth (IRE) 126 – Mathaayl (USA) 79 (Shadeed **–** (USA) 135) [2007 6g 8s Oct 26] closely related to useful 1m (at 2 yrs)/1½m winner Sahool (by Unfuwain) and half-sister to 3 winners, including useful Irish 9f winner Nasanice (by Nashwan), now dam of 6-y-o Maraahel: dam 6f/1¼m winner: well held in maidens. *C. W. Thornton*

MATINEE IDOL 4 ch.f. In The Wings 128 – Bibliotheque (USA) 79 (Woodman **48** (USA) 126) [2007 62d: 12m 16s 12g³ 17.1m⁵ 18m 12g 12g⁴ Nov 6] sturdy filly: maiden, only poor in 2007: should stay 1¾m: tried in cheekpieces. *Mrs S. Lamyman*

MATSUNOSUKE 5 b.g. Magic Ring (IRE) 115 – Lon Isa 80 (Grey Desire 115) [2007 **107** 88: 5m⁵ 5m 5m 5m 5g⁶ 5.1g 5f 5g* 6g 5m² 5f³ 5m* 5m² 5g³ p5.1g* p5g* 5g6m Oct 27] workmanlike gelding: useful handicapper: better than ever in 2007, winning at Sandown in August and September, and Wolverhampton (by 3 lengths from Tamagin) and Lingfield (beat Osiris Way by length, showing good turn of foot) in October: has won at 6f, best form at 5f: acts on polytrack, firm and good to soft going: patiently ridden, and travels strongly. *A. B. Coogan*

MATTEROFACT (IRE) 4 b.f. Bold Fact (USA) 116 – Willow Dale (IRE) 89 (Dane- **67** hill (USA) 126) [2007 70: p6g 5.7d² 5g* 5m³ 5m* 5.7d⁶ 5s⁵ p7.1g 5d 5s p5.1g⁶ p5.1g⁴ p5.1g Dec 3] strong filly: fair handicapper: won at Goodwood (apprentices) in May and Lingfield in June: best at 5f/6f: acts on firm and good to soft going, probably on polytrack. *M. S. Saunders*

MATTY TUN 8 b.g. Lugana Beach 116 – B Grade 59 (Lucky Wednesday 124) [2007 **77** 79: 5m 5d³ 5d 5s⁵ 5s Jul 13] strong gelding: fair handicapper: best at 5f: acts on fibresand and any turf going: tongue tied once at 3 yrs: in cheekpieces third outing (ran poorly): sometimes slowly away: tends to carry head awkwardly/idle. *J. Balding*

MATUZA (IRE) 4 ch.c. Cadeaux Genereux 131 – Aoife (IRE) 83 (Thatching 131) **83** [2007 88: 7m⁵ f7g³ 6s 5.7g* 6m p6g² p6g 6m⁴ 8.3m Aug 25] big, strong colt: useful **a95** handicapper on all-weather, fairly useful on turf: won at Bath in June: good second at Wolverhampton sixth start: stays 7f: acts on all-weather and firm going: blinkered (hung and well beaten) once at 3 yrs: sometimes carries head high: sold 4,000 gns. *W. R. Muir*

MAUD'S CAT (IRE) 4 b.f. Black Minnaloushe (USA) 123 – Tree House (USA) **–** (Woodman (USA) 126) [2007 62: 9m Jun 8] tall, sparely-made filly: maiden handicapper: well held sole 4-y-o outing: best up to 1¼m: acts on good to firm and good to soft going: edgy type. *A. P. Jarvis*

MAUNBY ROLLER (IRE) 8 b.g. Flying Spur (AUS) – Brown Foam (Horage 124) **–** [2007 f12g May 1] strong gelding: modest performer in 2003: well beaten in seller only Flat outing since: wears headgear. *K. A. Morgan*

MAWAARED 3 b.f. Machiavellian (USA) 123 – Inaaq 109 (Lammtarra (USA) 134) **61** [2007 p7g⁶ p8g⁴ 10d³ Jun 16] sparely-made filly: third foal: half-sister to 5-y-o Maya-deen: dam, 1¼m winner, half-sister to Dubai World Cup winner Almutawakel and 1000 Guineas runner-up Muwakleh (both by Machiavellian): encouragement in maidens at Lingfield first 2 starts, fourth to Zar Solitario in latter: off 4 months, remote third of 4 at Sandown only subsequent outing: should stay 1¼m/1½m. *M. P. Tregoning*

MAXIMIX 4 gr.g. Linamix (FR) 127 – Time Will Show (FR) (Exit To Nowhere (USA) **65** 122) [2007 72: p12g p12g Sep 18] useful-looking gelding: fair handicapper at 3 yrs for B. Hills: below form both Flat starts (8 months apart) in 2007: stays 1½m: acts on poly-track and good to soft going. *G. L. Moore*

MAXIM'S (ARG) 6 b.h. Lode (USA) – Mari's Ballerina (USA) (Mari's Book (USA)) **99** [2007 90: p5g a5g² a6g² a6f* 5.8m⁵ 6g⁶ a6g² a6g* 5.8g* a6g* Oct 11] useful performer: left R. Kvisla after well held on reappearance: won listed races at Jagersro in May and August (dead-heated) and minor event at Taby (dead-heated) in August and handicap at Jagersro in October: effective at 5f/6f: acts on dirt and good to firm ground: often blinkered: has worn tongue tie. *L. Reuterskiold, jnr, Sweden*

MAXIMUS AURELIUS (IRE) 2 b.c. (Mar 27) Night Shift (USA) – Dame's Violet **76** (IRE) (Groom Dancer (USA) 128) [2007 6g⁶ 6m 7.1m³ 7g* 6m 8.3d Oct 15] small, close-coupled colt: fair performer: won nursery at Catterick in September: should stay 1m: acts on good to firm going. *J. Jay*

MAXOLINI 4 ch.g. Bertolini (USA) 125 – Evening Falls 82 (Beveled (USA)) [2007 –: **–** 6g May 29] quite good-topped gelding: no form. *J. J. Quinn*

MAX ONE TWO THREE (IRE) 2 b.f. (Apr 9) Princely Heir (IRE) 111 – Dakota **102 p** Sioux (IRE) 90 (College Chapel 122) [2007 6m* 7m³ 6d* Oct 13] €23,000Y: useful-looking filly, unfurnished at 2 yrs: second foal: dam, 7f/1m winner, half-sister to useful 7f/1m (latter in Hong Kong when named Stay Young) performer Romancero (by Princely Heir): useful form: developed well, won maiden at Salisbury in August and listed race at York (beat Maze by 2 lengths, Eastern Romance fourth) in October: probably better at 6f than further: quirky (tail flasher), but should continue to progress. *Tom Dascombe*

MAXWIL 2 b.c. (Feb 23) Storming Home 128 – Lady Donatella 57 (Last Tycoon 131) **85 p** [2007 7m 8.1d⁶ 7.1g⁴ 7g* Oct 25] 45,000Y, 55,000 2-y-o: workmanlike colt: fourth foal: half-brother to 4-y-o Dark Moon: dam, maiden (stayed 1½m), half-sister to very smart 1m/9f performer Right Wing: fairly useful form: fourth to Billion Dollar Kid in minor event at Sandown prior to winning maiden at Brighton (seemed uncomfortable on track, hanging badly left) by head from Connor's Choice, pair clear: should stay 1m: will improve further. *G. L. Moore*

MAYAAR (USA) 2 ch.f. (Feb 7) Grand Slam (USA) 120 – Kovna (USA) (Seattle Slew **64** (USA)) [2007 6d⁶ 5v³ 5m⁴ 5.1d Oct 10] $130,000Y: tall filly: sister to winner in US and half-sister to several winners abroad, including German 5f to 7f winner Kalaheo (by Crafty Prospector): dam unraced sister to Coronation Stakes winner Magic of Life: modest maiden: in frame at Ripon and Sandown: sweating, reportedly banged head on stall final start: should stay 6f/7f: acts on heavy and good to firm going: sent to USA. *P. W. Chapple-Hyam*

MAYADEEN (IRE) 5 b.g. King's Best (USA) 132 – Inaaq 109 (Lammtarra (USA) **62** 134) [2007 77d: p12.2g 12m 9.2g⁶ 8m³ 8.3f⁴ 8.3g 9.2s* 8.3d⁶ 8m 9.1s⁶ 10.1g⁵ 11.1m⁴

11.1s p12.2d* Dec 10] good-topped gelding: just modest performer nowadays: won handicap at Hamilton in July and seller at Wolverhampton in December: stays 1½m: acts on polytrack, soft and firm going: tried in cheekpieces/visor, usually blinkered: held up. *I. Semple*

MAYBE I WILL (IRE) 2 b.f. (Jan 12) Hawk Wing (USA) 136 – Canterbury Lace **69** (USA) (Danehill (USA) 126) [2007 5g⁶ p6g⁴ p7g* 7.1m 8m⁶ 7m 7g Oct 25] 62,000F: small filly: first foal: dam unraced sister to Irish 2-y-o 1m winner Chevalier and 3-y-o Alexander of Hales, both smart, and half-sister to 1000 Guineas winner Virginia Waters: fair performer: won maiden at Kempton in July: little impact in nurseries: should stay 1m: acts on polytrack: signs of temperament. *R. Hannon*

MAYBE I WONT 2 b.c. (Mar 26) Kyllachy 129 – Surprise Surprise 91 (Robellino **71** (USA) 127) [2007 5g 6m³ 6g² 6d² p5g⁴ 6m p6g⁶ 6g p5g⁶ 5g p5.1g p5g⁴ p6g* p7g⁶ p6g⁵ p8m² p6g² p6m* p7.1g² Dec 14] good-topped colt: fair performer: successful in claimers at Lingfield in October and, having been claimed from S. Dow £6,000 after fifteenth start, December: effective at 6f to 1m: acts on polytrack, good to firm and good to soft going. *R. M. Stronge*

MAY DAY QUEEN (IRE) 2 b.f. (Feb 18) Danetime (IRE) 121 – Birthday Present **79** (Cadeaux Genereux 131) [2007 5g³ 6d³ 6g 6s⁴ p6g* p6g Oct 17] €6,000F, 28,000Y: strong, good-bodied filly: type to carry condition: second foal: dam unraced half-sister to smart sprinter Border Subject: fair performer: third behind You'resothrilling and Saoirse Abu in Swordlesown Stud Sprint Stakes at Naas second start: easily best effort after when winning maiden at Lingfield in July: should prove best at 5f/6f: acts on polytrack and good to soft going. *R. Hannon*

MAYIRENEYRBEL 3 ch.f. Auction House (USA) 120 – Travel Secret (Blakeney **60** 126) [2007 58: p7g 10f 10.2f* 10m⁶ 12m⁵ 12f⁴ 10d 10g 10g 10g Oct 25] rather leggy filly: modest performer: won seller at Bath in May: barely stays 1½m: acts on firm ground: has been slowly away: said to have bled final outing. *J. Akehurst*

MAYONGA (IRE) 4 ch.f. Dr Fong (USA) 128 – Mayara (IRE) 85 (Ashkalani (IRE) **96** 128) [2007 104: a7.5g Jan 3] useful performer: tenth in listed race at Deauville sole 4-y-o outing: should stay 1¼m: acts on all-weather, raced only on good going or firmer on turf. *Sir Mark Prescott*

MAYSARAH (IRE) 3 b.f. Green Desert (USA) 127 – Royale (IRE) 102 (Royal **77** Academy (USA) 130) [2007 72: 6g* 5.7g p6g² p7.1g⁴ p6g³ p7g² p6g³ Dec 5] £175,000Y: rather leggy, lengthy filly: fair performer: won maiden at Hamilton in May: in frame in handicaps last 5 starts: will prove best up to 7f: acts on polytrack. *G. A. Butler*

MAYS LOUISE 3 ch.f. Sir Harry Lewis (USA) 127 – Maysimp (IRE) (Mac's Imp – (USA) 116) [2007 p7.1g p8.6g p7.1g p9.5g Nov 10] third foal: dam little form: well held in maidens/claimer at Wolverhampton. *B. P. J. Baugh*

MAYSRIDGE OFKUWAIT 3 b.f. Tumbleweed Ridge 117 – Kuwait Dawn (IRE) 98 – (Pips Pride 117) [2007 6m 6f 5g 8.3d 7m a14g a4.8g⁵ a7.5g Dec 1] 2,100 2-y-o: first foal: dam 1m winner: little form: left A. Berry after fifth start. *R. Simoens, Belgium*

MAYVIEW 2 b.f. (May 17) Royal Applause 124 – Just Ice 90 (Polar Falcon (USA) 126) **50** [2007 5.1d⁶ p5g Oct 24] 10,000Y: neat filly: half-sister to 3 winners, including useful sprinter Jezebel (by Owington): dam 2-y-o 5f/6f winner: modest maiden, better run on debut: likely to prove best at 5f/6f. *Rae Guest*

MAYYAS 7 b.g. Robellino (USA) 127 – Amidst 86 (Midyan (USA) 124) [2007 55: **55** p12.2g⁵ f14g Jan 25] modest maiden: should be suited by 1¾m+: raced on all-weather: tongue tied. *C. C. Bealby*

MAZAAYA (USA) 2 b.f. (Mar 28) Cozzene (USA) – Mariamme (USA) 66 (Verbatim **81** (USA)) [2007 7s* 6d⁶ 8g⁴ Oct 26] $120,000Y: tall filly: eighth foal: sister to useful winner Cozy Maria and half-sister to several minor winners in US: dam, US winner up to 1¼m, half-sister to Breeders' Cup Turf winner Miss Alleged: fairly useful form: won maiden at Redcar (by short head from Tiger Dream) in September: ran creditably in competitive nurseries at York and Doncaster (equal-fourth to Jack Dawkins): will stay 1¼m: raced only on good going or softer. *M. Johnston*

MAZARA (IRE) 2 ch.g. (May 4) Alhaarth (IRE) 126 – Azdihaar (USA) 81 (Mr Prospector (USA)) [2007 7m 8d Oct 3] good-topped gelding: half-brother to several winners, including useful 7f/1m winner (including at 2 yrs, and in UAE) Alshawameq (by Green Desert): dam, 7f winner, half-sister to 1000 Guineas winner Shadayid: behind in maidens at Newbury and Salisbury. *J. L. Dunlop*

MAZE (IRE) 2 ch.c. (Mar 29) Dr Fong (USA) 128 – Aryadne (Rainbow Quest (USA) **104 §**
134) [2007 6m* 7g* 7.1m⁶ 7m 6d² 6g Oct 27] 28,000Y: leggy, workmanlike colt: third
foal: brother to 5-y-o Count Kristo: dam unraced sister to Derby winner Quest For Fame:
useful performer: won maiden at Newcastle and listed event at Royal Ascot (by neck
from Pegasus Again, wandered) in June: only good run subsequently when second to
Max One Two Three in listed race at York, swerving left in front: stays 7f: acts on good
to firm and good to soft going: headstrong, gets worked up and usually early to post:
untrustworthy. *B. Smart*

MAZORAN (FR) 3 ch.g. Majorien 118   Isgala (FR) (Galetto (FR) 118) [2007 –: 10g   **–**
12.1g May 28] workmanlike gelding: well held in 4 maidens: tried in cheekpieces.
D. G. Bridgwater

MAZZANTI 2 b.c. (Mar 9) Piccolo 121 – Feather Boa (IRE) 81 (Sri Pekan (USA) 117) **86**
[2007 5m⁴ 5m² 5d* 6m⁶ 6g 6m⁶ 6d Oct 13] 26,000Y: smallish, sturdy colt: first foal: dam,
2-y-o 6f winner, half-sister to useful miler Wagtail: fairly useful performer: won maiden
at Musselburgh in June: seemed to run well in sales race at York (3½ lengths ninth to Dark
Angel) and minor event at Doncaster (sixth to Spitfire): will be suited by 7f: acts on good
to firm and good to soft going: sold 18,500 gns, sent to Serbia. *K. A. Ryan*

MCCARTNEY (GER) 2 b.c. (Feb 2) In The Wings 128 – Messina (GER) (Dash- **116**
ing Blade 117) [2007 7.1d³ 8.3d* 8m* 7m* 7d Oct 20]
     Mark Johnston sent out one hundred and sixty-one winners in Britain, a
personal best, but he dropped to seventh in the domestic trainers' championship,
the lowest he has finished in any season since 1999. Three domestic pattern wins—
none at the highest level—is some way below the total usually achieved by the yard
which, for the second year running, had over a hundred individual winners, just
over half of them two-year-olds. Whilst the two-year-olds picked up plenty of
races in the latest campaign—playing their part in making it the fourteenth year in
succession that the stable has completed a century of domestic winners—they
failed, on the whole, to make much of an impact once stepped up in grade. The
notable exception, however, was McCartney, who provided one of those three
pattern wins when scoring in good style in the Urban-i Champagne Stakes at
Doncaster in September.
    McCartney shaped well on his debut in a maiden at Sandown, looking in
need of the experience, and looked all the better for that run when stamping himself
an exciting prospect in a novice event at Hamilton in August, quickening impressively to beat Doon Haymer by seven lengths. He then again justified favouritism in the listed Weatherbys Bank Stonehenge Stakes over a mile at Salisbury later in
the month, running around a bit after getting to the front over a furlong out, still
looking green, and just holding on by a head from Scintillo. In terms of quality, the
latest Champagne Stakes was rather overshadowed by the National Stakes at the
Curragh the following day, but McCartney still put himself on the fringe of the
leading juveniles with a clear-cut win. Dropped back to seven furlongs and sensibly
kept in touch, he showed good speed to settle matters, eventually having two and a
half lengths in hand of Alexander Castle at the line. McCartney's performance was,
if anything, above average for a Champagne winner and he started fourth favourite
at 15/2 for the Dewhurst at Newmarket, where he met most of the leading juveniles
in an excellent renewal. However, he managed only seventh of ten behind New

*Urban-i Champagne Stakes, Doncaster—McCartney turns in an above-average winning performance
for the race to beat Alexander Castle, One Great Cat (fifth right) and Tajdeef (striped cap)*

Sheikh Mohammed's "McCartney"

Approach and failed to give his running, the return to softer conditions possibly a factor, although he might also have been past his best for the year.

McCartney (GER) (b.c. Feb 2, 2005)	In The Wings (b 1986)	Sadler's Wells (b 1981)	Northern Dancer / Fairy Bridge
		High Hawk (b 1980)	Shirley Heights / Sunbittern
	Messina (GER) (ch 1998)	Dashing Blade (b 1987)	Elegant Air / Sharp Castan
		Monamira (br 1981)	Kashmir / Monacchia

Mark Johnston won't be training McCartney as a three-year-old. Sheikh Mohammed has transferred him to Godolphin, for whom he looks just the type to do well over middle distances. The workmanlike McCartney will probably turn out to be the best performer from the eight foals that made up the now-deceased In The Wings' final crop. McCartney was bred in Germany and cost €90,000 as a yearling at Baden-Baden, the second foal of Messina, a German seven-furlong winner, and a half-brother to the German mile winner Milana (by Highest Honor). Messina is a half-sister to the useful German six- and seven-furlong performer My King. McCartney is unraced on extremes of going. *M. Johnston*

MCCONNELL (USA) 2 ch.c. (Apr 14) Petionville (USA) – Warsaw Girl (IRE) **75** (Polish Precedent (USA) 131) [2007 7m⁴ 6m⁵ 7s⁴ p8g² Dec 28] $52,000Y: good-topped colt: second foal: dam, US 6f winner, half-sister to Derby winner Motivator: fair form in maidens: stays 1m. *J. R. Best*

MCCORMACK (IRE) 5 b.g. Desert Story (IRE) 115 – La Loba (IRE) 73 (Treasure Kay 114) [2007 55: 9.9s 6.9m 10f Aug 12] close-coupled gelding: maiden: no form in 2007: tried visored. *Micky Hammond* —

MCELDOWNEY 5 b.g. Zafonic (USA) 130 – Ayodhya (IRE) (Astronef 116) [2007 97: 12m² 15g³ 20m 16.1v 13d³ Jul 13] useful-looking gelding: fairly useful handicapper: stays 21f: acts on fibresand and any turf going: blinkered (below form) once at 2 yrs: lazy sort. *M. Johnston* — **91**

MCHEPPLE 2 b.f. (Mar 26) Fleetwood (IRE) 107 – Roleover Mania (Tragic Role (USA)) [2007 7f 7g 7s 7d 5g³ Nov 8] fourth foal: half-sister to winner in Sweden by Up and At 'em: dam unraced: maiden: probably flattered when third at Musselburgh. *W. Storey* — **50 ?**

MCNAIROBI 4 b.f. Josr Algarhoud (IRE) 118 – Bonita Bee 50 (King of Spain 121) [2007 87: p7g* 8d⁴ 7g³ 7.1d⁵ Jun 16] tall filly: fairly useful handicapper: won at Lingfield in March: stays 1m: acts on polytrack and good to soft ground, probably on firm. *P. D. Cundell* — **89**

MCQUEEN (IRE) 7 ch.g. Barathea (IRE) 127 – Bibliotheque (USA) 79 (Woodman (USA) 126) [2007 –: 15s² 16.2m⁵ 14m⁴ p16g 15.8s⁶ 13.8g* 12g Oct 30] lengthy gelding: fair handicapper: won at Catterick in October: stays 2m: acts on all-weather, heavy and good to firm ground: tried visored. *J. T. Stimpson* — **68**

MEADFOOT 3 b.f. Averti (IRE) 117 – Rivermead (USA) (Irish River (FR) 131) [2007 p7.1g⁶ p7.1g p7f p10g f6g 7d 5.1g 7.1g³ p8g⁸ 8f p8g 10d⁵ Oct 10] compact filly: second foal: dam unraced out of half-sister to US Grade 1 winners Tis Juliet and Stella Madrid: poor maiden: stays 1m: acts on polytrack: tried tongue tied/in cheekpieces: sometimes slowly away. *B. R. Millman* — **47**

MEADOW SOPRANO (IRE) 5 b.m. Imperial Ballet (IRE) 110 – Good Aim (IRE) (Priolo (USA) 127) [2007 53: 8g 9m Sep 30] modest maiden: creditable seventh in claimer at Musselburgh final outing: stays 1¼m: probably acts on soft going: tried in cheekpieces/blinkers/tongue tie. *M. P. Sunderland, Ireland* — **53**

MEANTIME (USA) 4 b.g. Point Given (USA) 134 – Interim 117 (Sadler's Wells (USA) 132) [2007 64: p12g 11.9g p12.2g Nov 1] close-coupled, deep-girthed gelding: modest maiden at 3 yrs: little form in 2007: sometimes in headgear. *G. Prodromou* —

MEASURED RESPONSE 5 ch.g. Inchinor 119 – Seal Indigo (IRE) 93 (Glenstal (USA) 118) [2007 74d: 8.1s³ 10g² 10.2m p9.5g 10g Oct 31] lengthy gelding: modest maiden: stays 1¼m: acts on polytrack and soft ground: has reared in stall: tried in cheekpieces. *J. G. M. O'Shea* — **61**

MEASURED TEMPO 3 b.f. Sadler's Wells (USA) 132 – Allez Les Trois (USA) 114 (Riverman (USA) 131) [2007 100P: 10g* 12d 9.9g Aug 26] big, good-topped filly: useful performer, lightly raced: won listed race at Newbury in May by 1½ lengths from In Safe Hands, idling (flicked tail under whip): disappointing after in Oaks at Epsom (said to have had abscess on a foot in week before, still green in paddock, increasingly edgy to post and didn't settle in race) and listed handicap at Goodwood (reluctant to go through with effort, hanging right): should stay 1½m: left Godolphin, and sent to USA. *Saeed bin Suroor* — **95**

MEATHOP (IRE) 3 b.g. Imperial Ballet (IRE) 110 – Jacobina 71 (Magic Ring (IRE) 115) [2007 –: p7.1g⁵ p6g p7.1g p8.6g 7g⁵ 6s Jul 18] modest maiden: stays 7f. *R. F. Fisher* — **57**

MECCA'S MATE 6 gr.m. Paris House 123 – Clancassie (Clantime 101) [2007 110: 6d 5.2m 6m 5v² 6v⁶ 5g* 6s⁵ 5d 5g 6d 5d Sep 29] leggy, lengthy mare: useful performer: ran well in 2007 only when second in Gosforth Park Cup (Handicap) at Newcastle (beaten ½ length by Green Park) and winning listed race at Ayr (by head from Final Dynasty) in July: best at 5f/6f: acts on polytrack, good to firm and heavy ground: tried in cheekpieces: unseated rider and ran loose before ninth outing: held up: sold 75,000 gns. *D. W. Barker* — **107**

MEDIA STARS 2 gr.c. (Apr 16) Green Desert (USA) 127 – Starine (FR) 123 (Mendocino (USA) 108) [2007 p7g⁶ Oct 29] 35,000Y: second foal: dam 1m (at 2 yrs in France) to 1¼m (Breeders' Cup Filly & Mare Turf) winner: 20/1, sixth to Adversity in maiden at Kempton, slowly away and not knocked about: will stay 1m: capable of better. *J. A. Osborne* — **65 p**

MEDICEA SIDERA 3 b.f. Medicean 128 – Broughtons Motto 75 (Mtoto 134) [2007 p7g 7m² 8m² 7m⁶ 7m* 7m* 7m⁵ 6m p7.1g⁵ Oct 22] 14,500Y: good-bodied filly: first foal: dam 5f (at 2 yrs) to 1¼m winner: reportedly chipped a knee in 2006: fairly useful performer: successful at Newmarket in maiden in July (sweating and edgy) and handicap in August: stays 1m: races up with pace. *E. F. Vaughan* — **92**

MEDICI CODE 3 ch.g. Medicean 128 – Fiveofive (IRE) 61 (Fairy King (USA)) [2007 **116**
59: f8g* p8.6g* f8g* a9f⁶ 8f²ᵈ 8.5f*ᵈⁱˢ 9f* a8.5f⁵ 10f² 9f³ Dec 30] vastly improved, and
developed into a smart performer, first past post in handicaps at Southwell (by 14 lengths)
and Wolverhampton in January, and Southwell in February (10/1 on, by 5 lengths, left
H. Morrison for reported private sale of £300,000 after), and La Jolla Handicap in August
(failed dope test and disqualified) then Del Mar Derby (beat Augment ¾ length) in
September, both Grade 2 events at Del Mar: good efforts behind Daytona last 2 starts, in
Hollywood Derby (½-length second) and Grade 2 San Gabriel Handicap at Santa Anita
(2½ lengths third): stays 1¼m: acts on all-weather and firm going. *D. Vienna, USA*

MEDICI GOLD 2 ch.f. (Mar 15) Medicean 128 – Silence Is Golden 120 (Danehill **49 p**
Dancer (IRE) 117) [2007 p7g 6f 7d⁶ Aug 21] smallish, rather leggy filly: first foal: dam
7f to 1¼m winner: poor form in maidens: will be suited by 1m/1¼m: should do better.
B. J. Meehan

MEDICINE PATH 3 b.c. Danehill Dancer (IRE) 117 – Indian Mystery (IRE) 69 **106**
(Indian Ridge 123) [2007 110: 10m⁶ 10.5g 9g⁶ 8.2g* Nov 7] good-topped, attractive colt:
smart performer at 2 yrs: useful form at best in 2007, winning minor event at Nottingham
in November by 1¼ lengths from Fajr: best at 1m (last in Prix du Jockey Club at Chantilly
at 10.5f): winner on firm ground, best efforts on good or softer: looked tricky ride at 2 yrs:
free-going sort. *E. J. O'Neill*

MEDICI PEARL 3 b.f. Medicean 128 – In Love Again (IRE) 86 (Prince Rupert (FR) **81**
121) [2007 f6g³ 7m⁴ 7.5m² 7.5g* 8.1s⁴ 7d⁴ 7m⁴ 7.5s* 6.9f 8d 8.1s 10.3g 7m Nov 10]
11,000Y: good-topped filly: sixth living foal: half-sister to fairly useful 2005 2-y-o 6f/7f
winner Silidan (by Dansili) and 9-y-o Forever My Lord: dam, 2-y-o 5f winner, half-sister
to high-class sprinter Hallgate: fairly useful performer: won maiden in May and handicap
in July, both at Beverley: lost form after: barely stays 1m: acts on soft and good to firm
going. *T. D. Easterby*

MEDICI TIME 2 ch. or gr.c. (Apr 9) Medicean 128 – Pendulum 82 (Pursuit of Love **58**
124) [2007 7d 7d 7m⁵ 8m Aug 27] big, good-topped colt: has round action: modest
maiden: should stay 1m: looks awkward. *T. D. Easterby*

MEDIEVAL MAIDEN 4 gr.f. Zaha (CAN) 106 – Brillante (FR) 118 (Green Dancer **59**
(USA) 132) [2007 78: p9.5g⁶ p9.5g⁵ p9.5g⁵ p12.2g* 11.8s p11g³ 11.6g 11.5g⁶ **a74**
p12g p11m⁶ p11m p12.2g⁵ Dec 29] lengthy, quite good-topped filly: fair handicapper on
all-weather, modest on turf: won at Wolverhampton in May: stays easy 1½m: acts on
polytrack, best effort on turf on good going. *W. J. Musson*

MEDITATION 5 ch.m. Inchinor 119 – Trojan Desert 97 (Troy 137) [2007 88: p7g p7g⁴ **77**
p7g p7g f7g p7g p7m* 7d 7m p7.1g p8.6g³ p7g p8g p8g p8g² p7g p8g* p8g⁵
p8m² p10g² p10g⁶ Dec 22] workmanlike mare: fair handicapper: won at Lingfield in
August and November: stays 1¼m: acts on polytrack, firm and good to soft going: tried
in cheekpieces/blinkers: often races up with pace. *I. A. Wood*

MEDLEY 3 ch.f. Danehill Dancer (IRE) 117 – Marl 94 (Lycius (USA) 124) [2007 95: **102**
6m³ 7s² 6d² 7m³ 7m* 7g⁶ 7m* 8f⁵ Oct 8] strong, angular filly: has a round action: useful
performer: won handicap at Newmarket in July and listed race at Doncaster (by head
from Our Faye) in September: left R. Hannon before final outing: effective at 6f/7f: acts
on soft and good to firm ground: reliable. *C. Clement, USA*

MEERISS (IRE) 2 b.c. (Apr 7) Dubai Destination (USA) 127 – Bless The Bride (IRE) **96**
82 (Darshaan 133) [2007 5g* 6g 7g³ 8s p7g* 8m* 8s⁶ Oct 13] 90,000Y: rather leggy,
close-coupled colt: fourth foal: dam, 1¼m winner, closely related to smart performer up
to 1¼m Millennium Dragon: useful performer: generally progressive, won maiden at
Hamilton in May and minor event at Lingfield and listed race at Goodwood (beat Eastern
Gift by neck, dictated) in September: creditable 6 lengths sixth to Ibn Khaldun in Autumn
Stakes at Ascot final start: likely to stay 1¼m: acts on polytrack and good to firm going,
probably on soft. *M. R. Channon*

MEER KAT (IRE) 2 b.c. (Mar 2) Red Ransom (USA) – Bush Cat (USA) 93 (King- **90**
mambo (USA) 125) [2007 7m 8.1f² 8m³ 8d² 8m* 8f³ Nov 23] 90,000Y: close-coupled
colt: first foal: dam, 2-y-o 7f winner (stayed 11.4f), out of sister to smart 6f/7f performer
Nicholas: fairly useful form: placed in 3 maidens prior to winning minor event at Bath in
October: sold from R. Charlton 90,000 gns, creditable 5 lengths third to The Leopard in
Grade 3 Generous Stakes at Hollywood final start: will stay 1¼m: acts on firm going.
B. D. A. Cecil, USA

MEETING OF MINDS 3 b.f. Mind Games 121 – Turn Back 73 (Pivotal 124) [2007 **53**
50: p7.1g⁵ 8s 8g 8m⁴ 8d⁴ p10g p8g f8d* Dec 20] modest performer: won seller at Southwell in December: stays 1m: acts on all-weather and good to soft ground: sometimes
slowly away (markedly so sixth outing). *W. Jarvis*

ME FEIN 3 gr.g. Desert Prince (IRE) 130 – Attachment (USA) (Trempolino (USA) 135) **61**
[2007 –: p12g* 12m p11g⁵ p12.2g³ Dec 15] lengthy, good-bodied gelding: modest
performer, lightly raced: upped in trip and well backed, won minor event at Lingfield
(heavily eased) in August: ran as if amiss next 2 starts (when trained by B. Curley): stays
1½m: acts on polytrack. *A. P. Stringer*

MEGA DAME (IRE) 3 b.f. Iron Mask (USA) 117 – Easter Girl (Efisio 120) [2007 **65**
p8.6g p9.5g⁶ p8.6g² 10f p9.5g p9.5g Aug 31] fourth foal: half-sister to 7f (at 2 yrs) to
12.6f winner Eastborough (by Woodborough) and 6-y-o Spring Goddess: dam unraced
half-sister to smart 6f/7f performer Bollin Knight: fair maiden: stays 8.6f: acts on polytrack: blinkered/tongue tied final outing. *D. Haydn Jones*

MEGALALA (IRE) 6 b.g. Petardia 113 – Avionne 59 (Derrylin 115) [2007 60: p6g 9g **56**
7s p8g 7d⁴ p10g 10g² p8g Dec 16] lengthy gelding: modest performer: effective at 7f to
1¼m: acts on polytrack, good to firm and good to soft going: tried in cheekpieces: often
held up. *J. J. Bridger*

MEGALO MANIAC 4 b.g. Efisio 120 – Sharanella (Shareef Dancer (USA) 135) **64**
[2007 51: f6g* f7g* f7g³ 7.1g 6s⁴ 7.1v 6.9g⁴ p7.1g* 7.2s⁵ p6g Nov 9] fair performer on **a72**
all-weather, modest on turf: won handicaps at Southwell in April and May and claimer at
Wolverhampton in September: stays 7f: acts on all-weather, soft and good to firm going.
R. A. Fahey

MEGATON 6 ch.g. Nashwan (USA) 135 – Pan Galactic (USA) 105 (Lear Fan (USA) **75**
130) [2007 75: 14.1m* p16g Jul 4] deep-girthed ex-French trained gelding: fair performer: won handicap at Nottingham in June: said to have been struck into subsequent
Flat outing: stays 1¾m: acts on soft and firm ground: winning hurdler/chaser.
P. Bowen

MEGA WATT (IRE) 2 b.c. (Apr 5) Acclamation 118 – Kilshanny 70 (Groom Dancer **67 p**
(USA) 128) [2007 6d 7m³ Aug 13] 19,500Y: tall, good-topped colt: seventh foal: half-
brother to 3 winners, including fairly useful but ungenuine 2002 2-y-o 5f winner (stayed
1¼m) Leitrim Rock (by Barathea) and 6-y-o Shinko Femme: dam 1½m winner: promise
in maidens at Ascot (mid-field behind Atlantic Sport) and Thirsk (third having travelled
best): may prove best up to 7f: capable of better still. *W. Jarvis*

MEIKLE BARFIL 5 b.g. Compton Place 125 – Oare Sparrow 75 (Night Shift (USA)) **55**
[2007 69: 5.1m 5.1m 5g p5g 5.7m 5g⁵ 5.1f p5.1g² p5.1g p6m Oct 3] strong, good-bodied
gelding: modest performer: best at 5f: acts on polytrack, good to firm and good to soft
ground: tried blinkered, usually wears cheekpieces: tongue tied last 5 starts. *J. M. Bradley*

MEJHAR (IRE) 7 b.g. Desert Prince (IRE) 130 – Factice (USA) 78 (Known Fact **61**
(USA) 135) [2007 12m⁶ p12g p11g p12.2g Nov 19] fairly useful performer in 2003:
lightly raced since, and just modest in 2007: stays 1½m: acts on sand, firm and soft
ground: tried blinkered. *E. J. Creighton*

MELALCHRIST 5 b.g. Almaty (IRE) 113§ – Lawless Bridget 62 (Alnasr Alwasheek **91**
117) [2007 78d: p5.1g p6g⁴ f5g² 6g² 5.1m³ 5g³ f5g⁶ f6g⁴ 6v⁶ 5d⁵ 5s⁴ 5s* 5g² 5g* 5.1m⁵ **a74**
5g 5m Oct 22] compact gelding: fairly useful handicapper on turf, fair on all-weather:
won at Hamilton and Beverley in July, and Beverley in August: effective at 5f/6f: acts on
all-weather, heavy and good to firm going: wears headgear: often makes running: has
been slowly away. *K. A. Ryan*

MELANDRE 5 b.m. Lujain (USA) 119 – Talighta (USA) 62 (Barathea (IRE) 127) **53**
[2007 –: f5g p5.1g 5m 6m 5m 5m Aug 7] close-coupled mare: fair handicapper in 2005,
little impact since. *M. Brittain*

MELLIFLUOUS (IRE) 2 b.f. (Feb 2) Noverre (USA) 125 – Danestar 64 (Danehill **–**
(USA) 126) [2007 p7g 7g Nov 3] 22,000Y: sturdy filly: second foal: dam maiden (stayed
1¼m): last in maidens (tongue tied in latter). *J. W. Hills*

MELODRAMATIC (IRE) 2 b.f. (Jan 23) Sadler's Wells (USA) 132 – My Branch **92 p**
111 (Distant Relative 128) [2007 7g⁴ Aug 18] good-bodied filly: sixth foal: closely related to high-class 6f (including Sprint Cup and at 2 yrs)/7f winner Tante Rose (by Barathea)
and half-sister to 3 winners, including useful 2003 2-y-o 6f/7f winner Bay Tree (by
Daylami): dam, 5f (at 2 yrs) to 7f winner, also third in Irish 1000 Guineas: 7/1 and green,
shaped very well when length fourth to Sharp Nephew (Latin Lad and Scintillo others in
frame) in listed event at Newbury, briefly looking bigger threat: had slight setback after:
will stay 1m: good prospect, sure to win races. *R. Charlton*

MELPOMENE 4 ch.f. Peintre Celebre (USA) 137 – Lady Joyce (FR) (Galetto (FR) **95**
118) [2007 90: p13.9g* p16g p12g⁶ 16.2m³ 20m Jun 19] useful handicapper, lightly
raced: won at Wolverhampton in January: creditable effort after only when third at Haydock: stays 2m: acts on all-weather, soft and good to firm ground. *M. Johnston*

MELT (IRE) 2 b.f. (Apr 8) Intikhab (USA) 135 – Kindle (Selkirk (USA) 129) [2007 6d⁵ **70** 6.1d⁶ p5g² p8g Oct 31] rather unfurnished filly: fourth foal: half-sister to useful 1¾m/2m winner Numero Due (by Sinndar) and winner in Spain by Dansili: dam, French maiden, half-sister to smart stayer Arden: fair maiden: best run on debut: should be suited by 1¼m+. *R. Hannon*

MELVINO 5 b.g. Josr Algarhoud (IRE) 118 – Safe Secret 50 (Seclude (USA)) [2007 69: **77** p12.2g² p12.2g* p12.2g⁵ p12.2g⁴ Feb 26] rather leggy gelding: fair handicapper: won at Wolverhampton in January: stays 1½m: acts on all-weather, firm and soft going: tried visored/in cheekpieces: sometimes slowly away: has his quirks, though is largely consistent: sold 16,000 gns, joined J. K. Price. *T. D. Barron*

MELWOOD DREAMS 2 ch.g. (Feb 13) Domedriver (IRE) 128 – Hertha (Hernando – (FR) 127) [2007 6.1m 6m 6g 8s p7.1g p7.1g³ p7.1g⁶ p8.6g p7.1g p8.6g Dec 31] quite **a56 ?** good-topped gelding: modest maiden: third in seller: bred to stay at least 1m: form only on polytrack: tried visored. *Paul Green*

ME ME ME 2 b.g. (Mar 3) Red Ransom (USA) – Jalousie (IRE) 108 (Barathea (IRE) – 127) [2007 5.2g 6d p8g⁶ Aug 29] no form in maidens: bred to be suited by 1m+. *M. J. Wallace*

MEMORATA 3 b.f. Montjeu (IRE) 137 – Polish Lake (Polish Precedent (USA) 131) – [2007 p9.5g 10.9d May 12] second foal: dam unraced half-sister to high-class 1¼m/1½m performer Powerscourt: well held in maidens: sold 3,000 gns. *R. Charlton*

MEMPHIS CITY (USA) 2 ch.g. (Mar 5) Langfuhr (CAN) 124 – Fleet Wahine (CAN) **79** (Afleet (CAN)) [2007 7m 6g⁵ 6d³ p8g* Nov 9] $27,000F, €85,000Y: heavy-topped gelding: half-brother to several winners in North America: dam US sprinter: fair form: progressed in maidens, at Newmarket first 3 starts (for J. Noseda), then won at Dundalk by neck from Croi Mo Ri: stays 1m: acts on polytrack. *Andrew Oliver, Ireland*

MEMPHIS KATE 2 ch.f. (Mar 6) Bahamian Bounty 116 – Halloa 88 (Wolfhound – (USA) 126) [2007 5m 5m 5m Sep 20] 16,000F, 32,000Y, 50,000 2-y-o: third foal: half-sister to winner in Greece by Diktat: dam, 2-y-o 6f winner, half-sister to smart performer up to 1½m Counsel's Opinion: little form: dead. *M. L. W. Bell*

MEMPHIS MAN 4 b.g. Bertolini (USA) 125 – Something Blue (Petong 126) [2007 **84** 79: 5.1m 5m³ 6g³ 6.1g 6g p7.1g⁶ p5.1g⁶ 6d 5.9g 6d* 7g⁴ 6d* 6v* 6d³ 6v p6g* p6g p5.1s² p6d⁴ Dec 28] leggy, close-coupled gelding: fairly useful handicapper: left W. M. Brisbourne after eighth start (reluctant to race): won at Brighton, Yarmouth and Ayr, all in October, and at Wolverhampton in November: effective at 5f to 7f: acts on all-weather, heavy and good to firm going: tried in cheekpieces: held up: not straightforward. *P. D. Evans*

MEMPHIS MARIE 3 b.f. Desert Sun 120 – Spirito Libro (USA) 89 (Lear Fan (USA) **57** 130) [2007 –: p8.6g⁶ 9m⁴ 10.1m 11.5m p7.1g** p7.1g⁶ p6g Nov 10] workmanlike filly: modest performer: won maiden at Wolverhampton in August: stays 9f: acts on polytrack. *C. N. Allen*

MENADHA (USA) 2 ch.c. (Feb 9) Carson City (USA) – Wiedniu (USA) 106 (Danzig **90** Connection (USA)) [2007 5g⁵ 5m⁴ p6g³ 7m* 7g 7m⁶ p8.6g* Oct 18] $55,000F, $150,000Y: rangy, good-topped colt: has scope: closely related to 2 winners, including fairly useful Irish 7f (at 2 yrs)/1m winner Queen's Love (by Kingmambo), and half-brother to 3 winners in USA: dam fairly useful former: won maiden at Newmarket (dead-heated with Autocue) in July and nursery at Wolverhampton in October: stays 8.6f: acts on polytrack and good to firm going: joined D. Selvaratnam in UAE. *M. R. Channon*

MENELAUS 6 b.g. Machiavellian (USA) 123 – Mezzogiorno 108 (Unfuwain (USA) **59** 131) [2007 –: 18d p16g Oct 4] modest maiden on Flat, lightly raced: stays 2¼m: acts on good to firm and good to soft ground: wears cheekpieces: fair hurdler. *K. A. Morgan*

MENKAURA 4 b.g. Pivotal 124 – Nekhbet 74 (Artaius (USA) 129) [2007 79: p9.5g – p12.2g Nov 24] maiden: no form in 2007: stays 7f: acts on good to firm ground: tried blinkered/visored. *John R. Upson*

ME NO PUPPET 3 b.f. Mtoto 134 – Puppet Play (IRE) 82 (Broken Hearted 124) [2007 – –: 10m p9.5d⁵ Dec 17] little form in maidens. *E. J. Alston*

MENORCA (IRE) 2 b.f. (Feb 6) Hawk Wing (USA) 136 – Saskya's Dream (IRE) – (Ashkalani (IRE) 128) [2007 p9.5g Nov 17] €70,000Y: third foal: half-sister to winner in France by Barathea: dam, useful French 1m winner, half-sister to dam of very smart miler Zafeen: 66/1 and green, well held in maiden at Wolverhampton. *Jane Chapple-Hyam*

MEON MIX 3 b.f. Kayf Tara 130 – Millennium Dash 94 (Nashwan (USA) 135) [2007 **61**
10d⁴ p10g 12.1m⁵ 9.9s⁴ Oct 14] third foal: closely related to smart but temperamental 1m
(at 2 yrs)/1¼m winner Dash To The Top (by Montjeu) and half-sister to 4-y-o Dash To
The Front: dam, 1¼m winner, out of top-class miler Milligram: modest maiden: should
stay 1½m+: tends to edge left. *J. R. Fanshawe*

MERCHANT BANKES 4 b.c. Observatory (USA) 131 – Lady Bankes (IRE) 69 **58**
(Alzao (USA) 117) [2007 71: 8m 10.2g 14.1d 14.1s⁶ 14.1m 13.1f p16g Sep 29] workmanlike colt: just modest maiden handicapper nowadays: stays 1¾m: acts on polytrack, soft
and good to firm ground: has looked no easy ride. *W. G. M. Turner*

MERCHANT NAVY 2 b.g. (Jan 21) Green Desert (USA) 127 – Khalkissa (USA) 98 **79**
(Diesis 133) [2007 6g 6g⁶ 6.1g⁴ p6g p7g⁶ 6m* 7g³ Oct 20] small, good-bodied gelding:
fair form: won nursery at Pontefract in October: free-going type, likely to prove best up
to 7f: acts on polytrack and good to firm going: sold 20,000 gns. *E. A. L. Dunlop*

MERCHANT OF DUBAI 2 b.c. (Mar 11) Dubai Destination (USA) 127 – Chame- **77**
leon 79 (Green Desert (USA) 127) [2007 6.1g⁶ 6m² 7m⁴ Aug 8] 135,000F, 21,000
2-y-o: good-bodied colt: third living foal: dam, 7f winner (stayed 1¼m), sister to very
smart sprinter Owington: fair form: won maiden at Ayr in July: favourite, not much room
when fourth in nursery at Newcastle: will stay 1m. *G. A. Swinbank*

MERCURY BLUE 3 b.f. Montjeu (IRE) 137 – Rowan Flower (IRE) 67 (Ashkalani **68 d**
(IRE) 128) [2007 9.9d² 11.9m 11.7g 12d Aug 16] 74,000Y: first foal: dam, 7f winner,
half-sister to 1¼m winner Muakaad and 1¼m to 1½m winner Suhaad, both smart: fair
form on debut: little impact after: should stay 1½m: acts on good to soft ground. *S. Kirk*

MERDIFF 8 b.g. Machiavellian (USA) 123 – Balwa (USA) 101 (Danzig (USA)) [2007 **46**
46, a64: p7.1g p8g p7.1g⁵ f7g f7g p8.6g⁵ Mar 24] big gelding: poor performer nowadays:
stays 8.6f: acts on all-weather and firm ground: tongue tied (won) once. *W. M. Brisbourne*

MERIDIAN GREY (USA) 3 gr.c. More Than Ready (USA) 120 – Love Rhythm **54**
(CAN) (Seeking The Gold (USA)) [2007 62: 6m⁴ 7.5m 8m 6s 6d 7m Aug 1] strong colt:
modest maiden: stays 7f: acts on good to firm going: blinkered last 3 starts: carried head
high on 3-y-o reappearance. *K. A. Ryan*

MERIDIAN LINE (IRE) 2 b.f. (Apr 1) Trans Island 119 – Meranie Girl (IRE) 52 **79**
(Mujadil (USA) 119) [2007 6m 5v² 6m 5.7s² 5.7m* 5m 6g³ 6.5d Sep 28] €6,000Y, resold
17,000Y: lengthy, workmanlike filly: sister to fairly useful 6f (including in Germany)
winner Transaction and half-sister to 2003 2-y-o 6f (including seller) winner Cheverak
Forest (by Shinko Forest): dam, sprint maiden, out of sister to very smart sprinter Hever
Golf Rose: fair performer: won maiden at Bath in August: good third in nursery at
Leicester: effective at 5f/6f: acts on heavy and good to firm going. *J. G. Portman*

MERLIN'S DANCER 7 b.g. Magic Ring (IRE) 115 – La Piaf (FR) (Fabulous Dancer **100 §**
(USA) 124) [2007 106: p5g* 5.2m⁶ 5m⁵ 5g 6d 5m 6g⁵ 5m⁶ 5g 5.1m³ p5.1g p6g Oct 15]
good-bodied gelding: unimpressive mover: useful handicapper: won at Lingfield (beat
Talbot Avenue by ¾ length) in March: left D. Nicholls after third start: mostly below form
after: effective at easy 6f, better at 5f: acts on polytrack, firm and good to soft ground:
blinkered (below form) once: front runner: inconsistent. *S. Dow*

MERLINS DREAMS 4 b.g. Dansili 127 – Red Leggings 84 (Shareef Dancer (USA) **–**
135) [2007 –: p8.6g p9.5g 8.3g Jun 13] stocky gelding: no form. *P. C. Haslam*

MERLINS QUEST 3 b.c. Wizard King 122 – Wonderland (IRE) 55 (Dolphin Street **48**
(FR) 125) [2007 60: f5g 6g 7.1m 6.1m 8g p6g p6g Nov 28] strong, lengthy colt: just poor
maiden at 3 yrs: effective at 5f/6f: acts on firm and good to soft going: blinkered last 2
starts. *J. M. Bradley*

MERRYMADCAP (IRE) 5 b.g. Lujain (USA) 119 – Carina Clare (Slip Anchor 136) **78**
[2007 83: 8f⁴ p9.5g³ 8d⁴ 8.1g² 8.1g 8g⁵ 8.1s 8.1d⁶ p8.6g p8.6g⁴ p8g p9.5m* p8.6g⁴
Sep 20] leggy gelding: fair handicapper: won at Wolverhampton in September: effective
at 1m to 9.5f: acts on polytrack, firm and soft ground: tried blinkered: patiently ridden,
and has tended to idle. *M. Blanshard*

MERRYMAKER 7 b.g. Machiavellian (USA) 123 – Wild Pavane (Dancing Brave **70 +**
(USA) 140) [2007 81: 15.9m⁴ 15.9m⁶ 13.4g 12s² p16.5g 15.8g⁴ p13.9g* p13.9g* **a80**
p16.5g Dec 8] angular gelding: fairly useful handicapper: won at Wolverhampton (2) in
November: stays easy 2m: acts on polytrack, firm and soft going: tried visored/blinkered:
held up: has run in snatches. *W. M. Brisbourne*

MERSEY SOUND (IRE) 9 b.g. Ela-Mana-Mou 132 – Coral Sound (IRE) 67 (Glow **88**
(USA)) [2007 88: 14.1m Apr 26] good-topped gelding: fairly useful handicapper at best:

well below form only start in 2007: should stay 2¼m: acts on polytrack, firm and good to soft going: tried visored: held up. *D. R. C. Elsworth*

MERU CAMP (IRE) 3 ch.g. Loup Sauvage (USA) 125 – Morgan Le Fay 70 (Magic Ring (IRE) 115) [2007 61: 7m 7m Jun 3] sturdy gelding: maiden: well held in sellers in 2007: tried blinkered. *P. Winkworth*

MESBAAH (IRE) 3 b.g. Noverre (USA) 125 – Deyaajeer (USA) 64 (Dayjur (USA) **104** 137) [2007 93: 8m³ 8g 8m³ 9m⁵ 8m⁶ Oct 14] strong, lengthy gelding: type to carry condition: useful performer: good efforts in handicaps at Doncaster (third to Webbow) and Goodwood (fifth to Escape Route) third/fourth outings: respectable sixth to Smart Enough in minor event at Bath final outing: stays 9f: raced only on good going or firmer: in cheekpieces last 2 starts at 2 yrs: sold 35,000 gns. *M. A. Jarvis*

MESMERIZE ME 2 b.g. (Mar 19) Mind Games 121 – Exotic Forest 66 (Dominion **94** 123) [2007 5m 5.7s* 6f² 5d⁵ 5g* Oct 8] good-topped, attractive gelding: half-brother to several winners, notably useful 5f (at 2 yrs) to 1m winner Threezedzz (by Emarati): dam 1m winner: fairly useful form: won maiden at Bath in July and nursery at Windsor (beat Ancien Regime by ½ length) in October: will prove best at 5f/6f: acts on firm and soft going: sold 27,000 gns. *E. S. McMahon*

MESSIAH GARVEY 3 b.c. Lear Fan (USA) 130 – Maid of Camelot 102 (Caerleon **70** (USA) 132) [2007 77: 7g 7.1m⁶ 8d 7d p7g⁴ Dec 16] sturdy colt: just fair form at best in handicaps in 2007: free-going type, but should stay 1m: acts on polytrack. *M. R. Channon*

MESSIAS DA SILVA (USA) 2 b. or br.f. (Mar 8) Tale of The Cat (USA) 113 – Indy **89 p** Power (USA) (A P Indy (USA) 131) [2007 p6g² p6g* Oct 29] $250,000Y, $700,000 2-y-o: good-quartered filly: fourth foal: half-sister to winners in US by Royal Academy and El Corredor: dam, US maiden, out of US Grade 3 2-y-o 6f winner Clever Power: fairly useful form: shaped promisingly both starts, at Lingfield, second in maiden and winning minor event by 1½ lengths from Ramatni, showing sharp turn of foot: may prove best at 5/6f: will continue to progress. *J. Noseda*

METAL GURU 3 ch.f. Ishiguru (USA) 114 – Gemtastic 70 (Tagula (IRE) 116) [2007 **75** 65: 5.1f² 5.1g⁵ p6g* 5g 5.1f 6d³ 6.1s p6g⁴ p6g⁶ p5.1s Dec 20] fair handicapper: won at Wolverhampton in July: in-and-out form after: best at 5f/easy 6f: acts on polytrack, firm and good to soft ground: has tended to hang. *R. Hollinshead*

METAL MADNESS (IRE) 2 b.c. (May 12) Acclamation 118 – Dosha 47 (Touching **54** Wood (USA) 127) [2007 6s⁵ 6d⁵ 6m Aug 9] modest form in maidens: should be suited by 5f/6f. *M. G. Quinlan*

METAPHORICAL 2 b.c. (Mar 11) Bahri (USA) 125 – Shinko Hermes (IRE) (Sadler's **72** Wells (USA) 132) [2007 7d⁶ 7.1m 8m Sep 21] lengthy, unfurnished colt: best effort in maidens when seventh at Sandown: broke leg next time: dead. *M. Johnston*

METAPHORIC (IRE) 3 b.g. Montjeu (IRE) 137 – Virgin Hawk (USA) (Silver Hawk **109** (USA) 123) [2007 85P: 10m* 12.3m⁴ 16d⁶ 14d⁴ 14g³ 14.1g³ 14m⁶ Oct 4] big, good-topped, attractive gelding: useful performer: won handicap at Newmarket by neck from Regal Flush) in April: good efforts after when third in similar events at York (3¼ lengths behind Speed Gifted in Melrose Stakes) and Yarmouth (¾ length behind Aajel): visored, below form in listed race at Newmarket final start: will be suited by return to 2m: acts on soft and good to firm going: tongue tied last 3 outings: gelded, then runner-up on hurdling debut in November. *M. L. W. Bell*

METHAALY (IRE) 4 b.g. Red Ransom (USA) – Santorini (USA) (Spinning World **79** (USA) 130) [2007 76: p7g p7.1g⁵ p7g³ p6g* 5.1m⁴ 6m⁵ p6g 6d² p6g⁶ p6g* 5.1m² 5m* 5g p6g³ p6g 5g⁵ 5d p6g³ p7.1g⁵ p6g³ p6g³ p6g² Dec 15] compact gelding: fair performer: won handicap at Kempton in March, claimer at Wolverhampton (left Jane Chapple-Hyam £10,000) in July and handicap at Musselburgh in August: effective at 5f to 7f: acts on polytrack, good to firm and good to soft going: effective ridden prominently or held up. *M. Mullineaux*

METHODICAL 5 b.m. Lujain (USA) 119 – Simple Logic 73 (Aragon 118) [2007 –: **–** 18d Aug 16] close-coupled mare: modest maiden in 2005: lightly raced and little form on Flat since. *B. G. Powell*

METHUSALEH (IRE) 4 b.g. Mutamam 123 – Madamaa (IRE) 88 (Alzao (USA) **61** 117) [2007 80: p7.1g p7g p8.6g⁶ p9.5g f8g⁴ f7g p7g 7m³ 8f p7.1g² 8.2s⁵ 8d f7g 7d⁶ 8s Jul 3] sturdy, quite attractive gelding: fairly useful at best, only modest nowadays: effective at 7f to 1¼m: acts on polytrack, firm and good to soft going: tried visored (looked far from keen): usually waited with. *D. Shaw*

METROPOLITAN CHIEF 3 b.g. Compton Place 125 – Miss Up N Go (Gorytus **68** (USA) 132) [2007 –: p7g⁵ 7m⁵ p8g 7g⁵ 8d³ 8m⁴ 7g⁵ 7f³ p7.1g* p7m⁶ p7.1g³ p7g Dec 29] tall gelding: fair handicapper: won at Wolverhampton in September: left D. Simcock 15,000 gns before final outing: stays 1m: acts on polytrack, firm and good to soft ground: sometimes blinkered, including for win. *P. Burgoyne*

METROPOLITAN MAN 4 ch.c. Dr Fong (USA) 128 – Preceder (Polish Precedent **115** (USA) 131) [2007 109: 9g³ 8g 7s 8m² 8.1g⁴ 8m² 8m⁶ Oct 6] close-coupled colt: smart performer: good efforts in listed race at Haydock (fourth to Harvest Queen) and handicap at Doncaster (head second to The Illies) fifth/sixth outings: below-form sixth to Creachadoir in Joel Stakes at Newmarket final start: stays 9f: acts on soft and good to firm going: reliable. *D. M. Simcock*

METTERNICH 3 b.c. Machiavellian (USA) 123 – Jomana (IRE) 113 (Darshaan 133) **78** [2007 p9.5g* 9.8g⁶ a8g⁵ Aug 28] very green (hung to stand rail) when winning maiden at Wolverhampton in February by 5 lengths: sold from M. Johnston 30,000 gns following month, in rear in 2 minor events at Taby. *A. McLaren, Sweden*

MEXICAN BOB 4 b.g. Atraf 116 – Eskimo Nel (IRE) 75 (Shy Groom (USA)) [2007 **75** 71: p10g⁶ 10.5m² 13.1f⁴ Sep 10] strong, good-bodied gelding: type to carry condition: fair maiden handicapper, lightly raced: stays 10.6f (stamina stretched over 13f): acts on polytrack, firm and good to soft going: fairly useful form over hurdles, successful in October (2) and December. *A. King*

MEXICAN PETE 7 b.g. Atraf 116 – Eskimo Nel (IRE) 75 (Shy Groom (USA)) [2007 **79** 82: p12.2g³ Jul 10] close-coupled gelding: fair handicapper: creditable third sole start on Flat in 2007: stays 12.6f: acts on polytrack, firm and good to soft going: fairly useful hurdler. *A. King*

MEXICAN VENTURE 2 b.c. (Feb 10) Tobougg (IRE) 125 – Nacho Venture (FR) 88 **–** (Rainbow Quest (USA) 134) [2007 6m Sep 21] compact colt: good mover: first foal: dam maiden (should have stayed 1½m): 50/1, very green in maiden at Newmarket. *W. Jarvis*

MEXILHOEIRA 3 ch.f. Observatory (USA) 131 – With Music In Mind (Mind Games 121) [2007 6g⁶ Aug 25] leggy filly: first foal: dam unraced half-sister to useful 7f/1m winner Russian Rhapsody: 16/1 and green (including in paddock), 10 lengths sixth of 7 to Fleuret in maiden at Goodwood. *C. G. Cox*

MEY BLOSSOM 2 ch.f. (Jan 28) Captain Rio 122 – Petra Nova 51 (First Trump 118) **84** [2007 5d⁶ 5g² 5g* 5m⁴ 6.5m 6d⁶ 6g Nov 2] 15,000Y: sturdy, deep-girthed filly: third foal: half-sister to 5-y-o Paris Heights and 1m seller winner Tafilah (by Foxhound): dam sprint maiden: fairly useful performer: won maiden at Beverley in August: good sixth to Max One Two Three in listed event at York (raced wide): will prove best at 5f/6f: unraced on extremes of going. *R. M. Whitaker*

MEYDAN DUBAI (IRE) 2 b.c. (Apr 17) Alzao (USA) 117 – Rorkes Drift (IRE) 55 **92 ?** (Royal Abjar (USA) 121) [2007 6m³ 7g⁶ 5m³ 6m² Aug 25] €11,000F, €40,000Y: strong colt: second foal: dam, Irish maiden, half-sister to smart performer up to 1½m Sobriety: easily best effort when sixth to Maze in listed race at Royal Ascot: placed in lesser company all other starts, probably inadequate test: will be suited by 1m. *J. R. Best*

MEYDAN PRINCESS (IRE) 2 b.f. (Apr 25) Choisir (AUS) 126 – Miss Assertive 88 **80 p** (Zafonic (USA) 130) [2007 6g⁵ 6m⁶ p6g* Oct 15] €50,000Y: good-bodied filly: has quick action: first foal: dam, 2-y-o 6f winner, half-sister to useful performer up to 1¼m Ascertain: progressive form in maidens, won at Lingfield by 1½ lengths (value extra), quickening well: likely to prove best at 5f/6f: will do better still. *J. Noseda*

MEYNELL 3 br.f. Sakhee (USA) 136 – In Full Cry (USA) (Seattle Slew (USA)) [2007 **78** p10g⁵ p11g 8d² 8.1m² p8g³ Sep 18] 65,000Y: lengthy filly: half-sister to several winners, including useful 6f (at 2 yrs)/7f winner Saville Road (by Mozart) and dam of Oaks d'Italia winner Menhoubah: dam, US 6f (at 2 yrs) and 8.5f winner, half-sister to Sussex Stakes winner Posse: fair maiden: easily best effort on fourth outing: probably stays 1¼m: acts on good to firm ground. *M. A. Jarvis*

MEZUZAH 7 b.g. Barathea (IRE) 127 – Mezzogiorno 108 (Unfuwain (USA) 131) **93 §** [2007 91§: 8s⁵ 7m³ f7g 6g 8g 8d⁴ 7v² 7s⁶ 8.2v² 7g 8g 7.6m 8s² 7g 8.3d⁶ Oct 29] lengthy gelding: useful handicapper: creditable efforts in 2007 when placed: barely stays 1¼m: acts on any going: tried tongue tied/blinkered: often races prominently: unreliable. *M. W. Easterby*

MEZZANISI (IRE) 2 b.g. (Feb 28) Kalanisi (IRE) 132 – Mezzanine (Sadler's Wells **74 p** (USA) 132) [2007 8m 8.2d³ Oct 18] €45,000Y: medium-sized, well-made gelding: fifth foal: half-brother to several winners, including 7-y-o The Kiddykid and 13f/2m winner

Annus Iucundus (by Desert King): dam unraced: fair maiden: third at Nottingham (gelded after): shapes as if 1¼m/1½m will suit: will do better still. *M. L. W. Bell*

MGANGA 2 b.g. (Jan 13) Dr Fong (USA) 128 – Hannalou (FR) 70 (Shareef Dancer **72 +** (USA) 135) [2007 7.1g 7d 7.1m 7.5m 8s* 10m⁵ Oct 3] lengthy gelding: fair form: won nursery at Redcar in September: better still when fifth in similar event at Nottingham: stays 1¼m: acts on soft and good to firm going. *M. R. Channon*

MIACARLA 4 b.f. Forzando 122 – Zarzi (IRE) (Suave Dancer (USA) 136) [2007 44: **66** p5.1g 5m 5g⁴ 5d* 5d³ 5d³ 6v 5s 5d 5g² 5g⁵ 5m⁴ 5m* p5.1g 5s 5.1s Oct 18] workmanlike filly: fair handicapper: won at Redcar in June and Thirsk in September: free-going sort, will prove best at 5f: acts on heavy and good to firm going (ran poorly all starts on all-weather). *A. Berry*

MIA HARIA 2 b.f. (Mar 28) Dr Fong (USA) 128 – Pantita 74 (Polish Precedent (USA) **–** 131) [2007 6f 8.1f p7g Sep 11] compact filly: first foal: dam maiden: well held in maidens. *B. R. Millman*

MIAMI TALLYCE (IRE) 3 b.f. Montjeu (IRE) 137 – Altishaan (Darshaan 133) **53** [2007 55: 12.1m p10g May 11] lightly-made filly: modest maiden handicapper: probably stays 1½m: sold 5,500 gns, joined Frau M. Rotering, Germany. *E. J. O'Neill*

MIA'S BOY 3 b.c. Pivotal 124 – Bint Zamayem (IRE) 95 (Rainbow Quest (USA) 134) **80** [2007 73p: p7g³ 10m⁶ 7d* 8g⁶ Aug 18] big, deep-girthed colt: fairly useful form: landed odds in maiden at Thirsk in June: good sixth in handicap at Newmarket final outing: stays 1m (not 1¼m): acts on polytrack, good to firm and good to soft ground. *P. W. Chapple-Hyam*

MICHABO (IRE) 6 b.g. Robellino (USA) 127 – Mole Creek 91 (Unfuwain (USA) **–** 131) [2007 97: 14d 16.1m⁵ Aug 11] strong, good sort: useful handicapper at 5 yrs: below form in 2007: stays 1¾m: acts on firm and soft going: free-going sort, usually makes running: fair form over fences. *P. Bowen*

MICHAELS DREAM (IRE) 8 b.g. Spectrum (IRE) 126 – Stormswept (USA) 74 **– §** (Storm Bird (CAN) 134) [2007 –§: 16.2v Jul 7] smallish gelding: unreliable performer: little form on Flat since 2005 (fair winning hurdler): usually in headgear. *N. Wilson*

MICHITA (USA) 2 b. or br.f. (Mar 15) Dynaformer (USA) – Thunder Kitten (USA) **84 p** (Storm Cat (USA)) [2007 8d* Oct 23] fourth foal: half-sister to 3 winners in US, including 6f to 1m winner Thunder Mission (by Pulpit): dam, US 6.5f to 8.5f (including Grade 3) winner, half-sister to Japanese Grade 1 1m winner Nobo True out of US Grade 1 winner up to 1¼m Nastique: 11/1, overcame greenness to win maiden at Yarmouth by ½ length, wearing down long-time leader Dove: will stay 1¼m: sure to improve. *J. H. M. Gosden*

MICKEY PEARCE (IRE) 5 b.g. Rossini (USA) 118 – Lucky Coin 73 (Hadeer 118) **–** [2007 f12g Feb 15] close-coupled gelding: lightly-raced maiden, well held only Flat start in 2007: modest hurdler, successful in October. *J. G. M. O'Shea*

MICK IS BACK 3 b.g. Diktat 126 – Classy Cleo (IRE) 102 (Mujadil (USA) 119) [2007 **68** 53: p6g² p8g⁴ p8g⁵ p7.1g³ p7.1g⁶ p8.6g³ p10f⁴ p7.1g* 7g² 8.3g² p7.1g⁶ 7s* 7.1s* 8d* 7.1g⁵ 7.1g* 10.1d 7d⁴ 8g⁴ p8g⁶ p8g Dec 5] workmanlike gelding: fair performer: won seller at Wolverhampton in March (claimed from P. D. Evans after next start) and claimers at Leicester in May, Chepstow (awarded race) and Newmarket, both in June, and Sandown (claimed from J. Boyle) in August: stays 8.6f: acts on polytrack and soft going: wears headgear: has hung right. *G. G. Margarson*

MICKLEBERRY (IRE) 3 b.f. Desert Style (IRE) 121 – Miss Indigo 62 (Indian Ridge **58** 123) [2007 66: p7.1g⁴ f5g³ 5m 5m⁶ 5m² p5.1g* 5.1g⁴ p5.1g⁴ p5.1g² Dec 31] leggy, lengthy filly: modest performer: won maiden at Wolverhampton in September: effective at 5f/6f: acts on all-weather and good to firm going. *J. D. Bethell*

MICKMACMAGOOLE (IRE) 5 b.g. Sadler's Wells (USA) 132 – Musk Lime **79** (USA) 97 (Private Account (USA)) [2007 12m⁶ 14m* 16s 14.1m⁵ 16.4d 11.7g Oct 24] strong gelding: fairly useful handicapper: won at Haydock in June and Yarmouth in August: stays 1¾m: acts on all-weather and good to firm going: joined Evan Williams, fair form over hurdles, won twice in November. *Seamus G. O'Donnell, Ireland*

MICK'S DANCER 2 b.c. (Apr 26) Pivotal 124 – La Piaf (FR) (Fabulous Dancer **70** (USA) 124) [2007 p7g p8m⁴ Dec 7] 65,000Y: half-brother to several winners, including 7f/1m winner Gilded Dancer (by Bishop of Cashel) and 8-y-o Merlin's Dancer, both useful: dam, French 2-y-o 7.5f winner (later winner in USA), half-sister to very smart US 9f/1¼m performer Golden Apples (by Pivotal): much better effort in maidens at Lingfield when fourth to Crosstar. *W. R. Muir*

MICKY MAC (IRE) 3 b.g. Lend A Hand 124 – Gazette It Tonight 63 (Merdon **54**
Melody 98) [2007 –: p6g⁵ p8.6d⁴ Dec 27] smallish, lengthy gelding: modest maiden:
likely to stay 1¼m: tried blinkered. *T. D. Walford*

MIDAS WAY 7 ch.g. Halling (USA) 133 – Arietta's Way (IRE) 71 (Darshaan 133) **–**
[2007 105: p12g⁵ 16d Sep 29] leggy, close-coupled gelding: smart at best, well held in
handicaps in 2007: stays 2m: acts on firm and soft going: visored (well beaten) once: fair
hurdler. *P. R. Chamings*

MIDDLE EASTERN 5 b.g. Mujahid (USA) 125 – Swissmatic 54 (Petong 126) [2007 **65**
65: f7g⁴ 6g f7g* f8g⁵ p7g p7.1m Sep 6] big, leggy gelding: fair handicapper: won apprentice event at Southwell in May: stays 1m, may prove best at shorter: acts on all-weather,
good to firm and good to soft going: tried in cheekpieces/blinkers. *P. A. Blockley*

MIDDLEMARCH (IRE) 7 ch.g. Grand Lodge (USA) 125 – Blanche Dubois (Nash- **85**
wan (USA) 135) [2007 81: 8m 8m 7d⁵ 8.3g⁶ 8d⁵ 8d⁶ 7g* 7g* 8g Oct 6] tall, angular
gelding: fairly useful handicapper: won at Ascot (ladies event) in July and Newcastle in
August: effective at 7f to 1¼m: acts on polytrack, firm and good to soft going: usually
wears headgear (has won without): ran as if amiss second outing. *J. S. Goldie*

MIDDLETON GREY 9 gr.g. Ashkalani (IRE) 128 – Petula 103 (Petong 126) [2007 **63**
77, a89: 7.1v⁶ 6g 7m⁶ p7.1g p8.6g Nov 20] leggy gelding: fairly useful handicapper
at 8 yrs, just modest form in 2007: effective at 6f to 8.6f: acts on all-weather, good to
firm and good to soft going: wears headgear: sometimes slowly away: often held up.
A. G. Newcombe

MIDMAAR (IRE) 6 b.g. Cape Cross (IRE) 129 – Khazinat El Dar (USA) 78 (Slew O' **60**
Gold (USA)) [2007 62: p7g⁵ p6g p7.1g² p6g p7.1g f6g p7.1g p6g² p6g² p7g³ p6g³ p6g³
p7m⁶ p6g⁴ p7g Dec 30] modest performer: stays 7f: acts on all-weather: wears headgear:
has reportedly bled. *M. Wigham*

MIDNIGHT FLING 2 b.f. (Feb 7) Groom Dancer (USA) 128 – Perfect Night 79 **66**
(Danzig Connection (USA)) [2007 5.1m³ 5.7f³ Jun 10] first foal: dam 6f/7f winner: third
in minor event (to Waveline) and maiden at Bath (suffered a fracture): will probably stay
1m: stays in training. *R. Charlton*

MIDNIGHT MUSE (USA) 2 b.c. (Feb 11) Swain (IRE) 134 – Witching Hour (FR) **84 p**
(Fairy King (USA)) [2007 7d³ 7d* Jul 22] $17,000Y: quite good-topped colt: fifth foal:
half-brother to smart French miler Holocene (by Lemon Drop Kid) and winner in US
by Kris S: dam, French 1¼m winner, half-sister to smart French performer up to 1½m
Kathmandu: fairly useful form: third behind Sourire and Gothenburg in maiden at
Catterick, then won similar event at Redcar (by neck from The Oil Magnate): will stay at
least 1m: capable of better still. *T. D. Barron*

MIDNIGHT MYSTIQUE (IRE) 2 b.f. (Feb 2) Noverre (USA) 125 – Dark Hyacinth **–**
(IRE) 65 (Darshaan 133) [2007 7f 6g Aug 24] half-sister to 3 winners, including useful
Italian 1m/9f winner Dark Indian (by Indian Ridge) and 4-y-o Korolieva: dam Irish
maiden (stayed 13f): well held in maidens. *T. D. Barron*

MIDNIGHT OASIS 2 b.f. (Feb 22) Oasis Dream 129 – Midnight Shift (IRE) 73 **49 p**
(Night Shift (USA)) [2007 5g⁵ 5.1f 5.1g Oct 31] sturdy filly: closely related to 3-y-o
Midnight Sky, and half-sister to several winners, including 6-y-o Out After Dark: dam, 6f
winner, half-sister to very smart sprinter Owington: poor form in maidens, not fully
wound up: will prove best at 5f/6f: should do better. *Rae Guest*

MIDNIGHT SKY 3 b.f. Desert Prince (IRE) 130 – Midnight Shift (IRE) 73 (Night **51**
Shift (USA)) [2007 52p: 5s³ 5m 5m* 5g 5m Sep 11] modest performer: won maiden at
Beverley in August: likely to prove best at 5f/6f: acts on good to firm ground. *Rae Guest*

MIDNITE BLEWS (IRE) 2 gr.g. (Feb 10) Trans Island 119 – Felicita (IRE) 97 **63**
(Catrail (USA) 123) [2007 5m⁴ 5.7g⁴ 7s² 7.1s⁵ 7f⁵ 8f p7g Sep 18] modest maiden: in
frame first 3 starts, seemed amiss on final 2: stays 7f: acts on firm and soft going: below
form in cheekpieces. *A. B. Haynes*

MID OCEAN 3 ch.f. Sakhee (USA) 136 – Wavy Up (IRE) (Brustolon 117) [2007 61: **57**
p8.6g⁶ 6m 5.1g Apr 21] well-made filly: modest maiden: stays 8.6f: acts on polytrack:
tongue tied last 2 starts. *P. W. D'Arcy*

MIDSHIPS (USA) 2 gr.c. (Feb 11) Mizzen Mast (USA) 121 – Interim 117 (Sadler's **87**
Wells (USA) 132) [2007 6m* 7g 7f³ Aug 5] well-made colt: seventh foal: half-brother to
several winners, including 1¼m/1½m winner Staging Post (by Pleasant Colony), later
smart up to 1¾m in US, and 6-y-o Focus Group: dam 1m to 1½m (US Grade 2) winner:
fairly useful performer: won maiden at Newbury in June: didn't progress as expected,

seventh (behind Raven's Pass) in listed race at Ascot and third in minor event at New-bury: will stay at least 1m. *Mrs A. J. Perrett*

MIDSUMMER FUN (USA) 3 b.f. Gone West (USA) – Windsharp (USA) 123 (Lear **58** Fan (USA) 130) [2007 10f³ 11.7d 9.8f⁵ 15g² Oct 21] good-topped filly: fourth foal: sister to top-class US performer up to 1½m (dead-heated in Breeders' Cup Turf) Johar and half-sister to US Grade 1 9f winner Dessert (by Storm Cat): dam US Grade 1 1¼m/1½m winner: modest maiden: placed at Windsor on debut (left Saeed bin Suroor after next outing) and Segre final start: stays 15f. *H.-A. Pantall, France*

MID VALLEY 4 ch.g. Zilzal (USA) 137 – Isabella d'Este (IRE) 65 (Irish River (FR) **58** 131) [2007 56: p7g p8g² p8g⁶ p8g f8g* f7g⁴ p8g⁵ f8g² 10.2f f8g⁶ p8g p8.6g p12g p10g p12g⁴ p12g p12g² p12g⁴ Dec 19] modest performer: won minor event at Southwell in February: stays 1½m: acts on all-weather and firm going: tried in cheekpieces/visor: often held up. *J. R. Jenkins*

MI EMMA (GER) 3 b.f. Silvano (GER) 126 – Mi Anna (GER) (Lake Coniston (IRE) **118** 131) [2007 7d³ 8g* 8g* 8d² 8d 8g* Aug 28] leggy, rather sparely-made filly: fourth foal: half-sister to 3 winners in Germany, including 6.5f to 7.5f winner Mi Juanito (by Lavirco) and 8.5f to 1¼m winner Mi Violetta (by Grand Lodge): dam, German 7f/7.5f (listed race) winner, ran only at 2 yrs: smart performer: won maiden at Mulheim in March and 9-length winner of listed race and AKDOV Stutenpreis German 1000 Guineas (took strong hold, readily quickened clear from Mystic Lips) both at Dusseldorf in April: below best next 2 starts in Coronation Stakes at Royal Ascot (6 lengths second to Indian Ink) and Prix d'Astarte at Deauville: back to form when making all (beat Soldier Hollow 2 lengths) in Darley Oettingen-Rennen at Baden-Baden in August: stays 1m: raced only on good/good to soft ground. *A. Wohler, Germany*

MIESKO (USA) 2 b.c. (Apr 30) Quiet American (USA) – Polish Style (USA) (Danzig **88** (USA)) [2007 7m² 6m⁶ 6m p6g² 6m⁵ 5d* 5.1m* Oct 14] useful-looking colt: brother to 3-y-o Folk, and half-brother to 3 winners, including useful 1m (including at 2 yrs in USA)/9f (UAE Oaks) winner Danuta (by Sunday Silence): dam, French 6f winner (including at 2 yrs), out of US Grade 1 2-y-o 6f to 8.5f winner Family Style: fairly useful form: dropped in trip, much improved to win maiden at Catterick and nursery at Bath (always in control) in October: best at 5f: acts on polytrack, good to firm and good to soft going. *M. Johnston*

MIGHT BE MAGIC 2 b.g. (Jan 23) Fraam 114 – Modelliste (Machiavellian (USA) **–** 123) [2007 7m Oct 5] 50/1 and burly, well held in maiden at Newmarket: subsequently gelded. *P. W. Chapple-Hyam*

MIGHTY 4 ch.c. Pivotal 124 – Miswaki Belle (USA) 73 (Miswaki (USA) 124) [2007 **117** 68: p10g* p10g* p10g* p10f³ p10g⁴ 12m² 12m³ 10g² 12d³ 14m⁵ Sep 15] strong, good-bodied colt: smart performer: progressed in 2007, winning maiden in January and 2 handicaps in February, all at Lingfield: better efforts in frame in listed/pattern races after, including when neck second to Maraahel in John Porter Stakes at Newbury, short-head second to Take A Bow in Brigadier Gerard Stakes at Sandown and 3 lengths third to Maraahel in Hardwicke Stakes at Royal Ascot: only respectable fifth to Yeats in Irish St Leger at the Curragh final appearance: stays 1½m: acts on polytrack, good to firm and good to soft ground: sometimes wears bandages. *Jane Chapple-Hyam*

MIGHTY ALFRED (IRE) 2 gr.c. (Mar 20) Kendor (FR) 122 – Night Shifter (IRE) **–** 74 (Night Shift (USA)) [2007 6g Jun 8] quite attractive colt: unfurnished at 2 yrs: 14/1, last in maiden at Goodwood. *M. R. Channon*

MIGHTY KITCHENER (USA) 4 br.g. Mighty (USA) 118 – Libeccio (NZ) (Danza- **58** tore (CAN) 120) [2007 68: f11g² p11g³ p9.5g p13.9g* p12.2g² p12g³ p12.2g² p12g 10g **a74** p10g 12g⁴ p13.9g* p12.2g* 16.1m p13.9g⁵ p13.9g p13.9g p13.9g p12.2g⁶ p12.2g Dec 29] tall gelding: fair performer on all-weather, modest on turf: won maiden in January and 2 handicaps in August, all at Wolverhampton: stays 1¾m: acts on all-weather: has hung/carried head awkwardly. *P. Howling*

MIGHTY MISSOURI (IRE) 3 b.g. Danehill (USA) 126 – Pietra Dura 96 (Cadeaux **68** Genereux 131) [2007 66: 8.2g 8.2m² May 2] sturdy, angular gelding: fair maiden: stays 8.2f: raced only on good/good to firm ground: wore cheekpieces final outing: sold 1,000 gns in October. *W. R. Swinburn*

MIGHTY MOON 4 gr.g. Daylami (IRE) 138 – Moon Magic 62 (Polish Precedent **88** (USA) 131) [2007 90: 13.8m⁴ 12.3g⁵ 14g⁶ 12m 14.1d 16.2s⁵ 10g⁴ 13.8m³ 14f² 12g⁴ 14s 14d⁴ 14.6g 13.8g² Nov 6] small, leggy gelding: fairly useful handicapper: stays 1¾m, possibly not 2m: acts on fibresand, and any turf going: sometimes blinkered/in cheek-pieces, usually tongue tied: sold 35,000 gns. *J. O'Reilly*

MIGHTY MOVER (IRE) 5 ch.g. Bahhare (USA) 122 – Ericeira (IRE) (Anita's **67** Prince 126) [2007 11.7g p12.2g 11.9m p9.5g⁴ p9.5g² p9.5g* p9.5g² p12.2d Dec 6] fair performer: won handicap at Wolverhampton in November: stays 9.5f: acts on polytrack: races prominently. *B. Palling*

MIGRATION 11 b.g. Rainbow Quest (USA) 134 – Armeria (USA) 79 (Northern **55** Dancer) [2007 p13.9g 12g 12g6] tall gelding: modest performer nowadays: stays 1½m: acts on soft and good to firm going: tried in cheekpieces. *Mrs S. Lamyman*

MIKAO (IRE) 6 b.g. Tagula (IRE) 116 Oumaladia (IRE) 84 (Waajib 121) [2007 99: **98** 14g² 12s 13.4m⁴ 12g 12m 12s Oct 19] rather leggy, useful-looking gelding: useful handicapper: creditable efforts when in frame in 2007: effective at 1½m to 2m, possibly not 18.7f: acts on polytrack, soft and good to firm going. *M. H. Tompkins*

MIKHAIL FOKINE (IRE) 2 b.c. (Mar 27) Sadler's Wells (USA) 132 – Rain Flower **82** (IRE) (Indian Ridge 123) [2007 7d³ 8m 8m² p8g⁵ Oct 19] close-coupled, quite attractive colt: unfurnished at 2 yrs: fourth foal: half-brother to 2004 2-y-o 5f winner Sumora and Irish 2006 2-y-o 7f winner Fleeting Shadow, both useful and by Danehill: dam unraced close relative to Derby winner Dr Devious and half-sister to smart performer up to 1½m Hill Country: fairly useful maiden: placed at Leopardstown and Navan, easily best efforts: tended to hang at Doncaster in between: stays 1m. *A. P. O'Brien, Ireland*

MILANOLLO 2 b.f. (Mar 31) Soviet Star (USA) 128 – Military Tune (IRE) (Nashwan **49** (USA) 135) [2007 7m p8g Sep 19] 105,000Y: eighth foal: closely related to useful 7f winner Play That Tune (by Zilzal) and half-sister to several winners, including 7f to 1¼m winner Nice Tune (by Diktat) and 6-y-o Fixboard, both useful: dam unraced half-sister to Prix Royal-Oak winner Mersey and Prix Saint-Alary winner Muncie: poor form in maidens. *M. L. W. Bell*

MILEAMINUTEMURPHY 2 b.g. (Feb 12) Fasliyev (USA) 120 – Shining Hour **–** (USA) 104 (Red Ransom (USA)) [2007 6g 7f Aug 9] last in maidens: bred for speed. *R. Hannon*

MILITARY CROSS 4 b.g. Cape Cross (IRE) 129 – Tipsy 95 (Kris 135) [2007 102: 8m **106 +** p8g* Nov 17] close-coupled, quite attractive gelding: useful handicapper: shaped as if in need of run in Hunt Cup at Royal Ascot on reappearance: improved form when winning at Lingfield (by ½ length from Troubadour) in November: stays 1¼m: acts on polytrack and good to firm going (below form on softer than good). *L. M. Cumani*

MILITARY POWER 2 b.c. (Apr 17) Dubai Destination (USA) 127 – Susun Kelapa **77 p** (USA) 94 (St Jovite (USA) 135) [2007 7.1g³ 7f⁵ Sep 5] rather leggy, quite attractive colt: half-brother to 3 winners, including fairly useful Irish 7f winner Monsusu (by Montjeu): dam, Irish 1m (at 2 yrs)/9f winner, out of half-sister to dam of high-class French miler Green Tune and smart French sprinter Pas de Reponse: fair form in maidens at Sandown (encouraging third to Campanologist) and York: will stay 1m: should progress. *J. W. Hills*

MILK AND SULTANA 7 b.m. Millkom 124 – Premier Princess 45 (Hard Fought 125) **62** [2007 62: p10g⁴ p9.5g p11g⁴ p12g² Feb 19] modest performer: stays easy 1½m: acts on all-weather, firm and good to soft going. *G. A. Ham*

MILLACHY 3 b.f. Kyllachy 129 – Millazure (USA) 71 (Dayjur (USA) 137) [2007 65p: **65** 5.1f³ 6m 6d Jun 18] leggy filly: fair maiden: best form at 5f: acts on firm ground: sold 3,500 gns in July. *B. W. Hills*

MILLAGROS (IRE) 7 b.m. Pennekamp (USA) 130 – Grey Galava 64 (Generous **65** (IRE) 139) [2007 76: p12.2g⁵ Jan 12] lengthy, good-bodied mare: fair handicapper nowadays: stays 2m: acts on polytrack, firm and soft going: tried in visor/cheekpieces: has hung left: signs of temperament: fairly useful hurdler. *I. Semple*

MILLA'S ROCKET (IRE) 3 b.f. Galileo (IRE) 134 – Tenable (Polish Precedent **86** (USA) 131) [2007 53: f8g² p9.5g² f11s² p9.5g* 8s* 10.3s² 8m⁶ 8d⁵ 9g Oct 21] sturdy filly: fairly useful performer: won maiden at Wolverhampton in February and handicap at Thirsk in July: left K. Ryan, stiff task in listed race at Longchamp final start: has form at 11f, but better at shorter (winner at 1m): acts on all-weather and soft ground: effective blinkered or not: has rejoined K. Ryan. *N. Clement, France*

MILLBROOK STAR (IRE) 4 b.g. Orpen (USA) 116 – Lady Bodmin (IRE) (Law **–** Society (USA) 130) [2007 46: f6g Feb 20] lengthy gelding: poor maiden at 3 yrs: well held only start in 2007: has been blinkered/visored. *M. C. Chapman*

MILL BY THE STREAM 5 b.g. Lujain (USA) 119 – Lonesome 60 (Night Shift **69** (USA)) [2007 57: p6g f7g² f6g* f6g* f6g f7g⁵ p6g f6g⁶ 7d p7g May 23] close-coupled gelding: fair performer on all-weather (well below form only start on turf at 5 yrs): won 2 handicaps at Southwell in January: left Tom Dascombe after eighth outing: effective at 5.9f to 1m: acts on all-weather and firm going: tried in headgear: hung right second outing: sold £2,000 in July. *A. M. Hales*

MILL CREEK 2 ch.f. (Mar 26) Ishiguru (USA) 114 – Hollia 72 (Touch Boy 109) [2007 **31** 6g 5g 5g 6m⁴ 6g³ 5g⁴ Sep 19] quite good-topped filly: half-sister to several winners, including fairly useful 1996 2-y-o 5f winner Fredrik The Fierce (by Puissance): dam 2-y-o 5f winner: poor maiden: in frame in selling events, including in visor/blinkers final 2 starts: raced only at 5f/6f. *B. Smart*

MILLE FEUILLE (IRE) 2 b.f. (Jan 19) Choisir (AUS) 126 – Watch The Clock 93 **65 p** (Mtoto 134) [2007 6m³ Sep 4] €52,000F, €110,000Y: rather leggy filly: fifth foal: half-sister to 3 fairly useful winners, including 7f winner (including at 2 yrs) Go Padero (by Night Shift) and 1½m/2m winner E Minor (by Blushing Flame): dam 2-y-o 6f/7.5f winner who stayed 1¼m: 5/1, third in maiden at Goodwood, knowing job and showing speed: open to improvement. *R. M. Beckett*

MILLENIUM SUN (IRE) 3 b.g. Tendulkar (USA) 114 – Millenium Love (IRE) 75 **61 d** (Great Commotion (USA) 123) [2007 81d: 5g 6g p5g 6d p8g 5g 5.1d Aug 19] small gelding: fairly useful form at 2 yrs, clearly best effort when winning maiden at Cork: just modest form in handicaps in 2007, leaving P. Prendergast in Ireland/gelded after second start: raced mainly at 5f/6f: acts on good to soft going. *E. J. Creighton*

MILLENNIUM STORM (GER) 2 b.c. (Apr 25) Samum (GER) 126 – Millennium **–** Dawn (IRE) (Cadeaux Genereux 131) [2007 7.1g 6.1d p10g p8m Nov 11] sturdy colt: little form. *M. F. Harris*

MILLERS JEWEL 4 b.f. Sly – Old Castle Liziann (The Dissident 85) [2007 p7.1g **–** May 21] first foal: dam unraced: well held both starts in bumpers for C. Price: 200/1 and tongue tied, tailed off in maiden at Wolverhampton on Flat debut. *K. G. Wingrove*

MILLESTAN (IRE) 3 b.f. Invincible Spirit (IRE) 121 – Atnab (USA) 64 (Riverman **91** (USA) 131) [2007 87: 8.2g 7m 8m⁵ 7.1g³ 7g³ 8m³ 8m Oct 8] compact filly: fairly useful handicapper: creditable efforts when third in 2007: stays 8.3f: acts on firm and good to soft going: sold 35,000 gns. *H. R. A. Cecil*

MILLFIELD (IRE) 4 br.g. Elnadim (USA) 128 – Eschasse (USA) (Zilzal (USA) 137) **78** [2007 79d: p7.1g⁴ p7g p7g⁶ 7m⁶ 7m* p7.1g² 7.1m 7.1m p7m p7g³ p7g* p8.6g³ p7g* p7m² p9.5g³ Dec 15] tall, close-coupled gelding: fair performer: won handicaps at Brighton in August, Lingfield in November and Kempton in December: stays 8.6f: acts on polytrack and good to firm going: blinkered (very slowly away) once. *P. R. Chamings*

MILLFIELDS DREAMS 8 b.g. Dreams End 93 – Millfields Lady 75 (Sayf El Arab **73** (USA) 127) [2007 70: p6g⁵ p6g p6g³ p6g⁵ 5f⁴ 6f p5g 5g⁴ p6g³ p6g Oct 18] tall gelding: fair performer: won handicap at Wolverhampton in January: best at 5f/6f: acts on all-weather, firm and good to soft going: tried in cheekpieces. *M. G. Quinlan*

MILLIEGAIT 3 b.f. Tobougg (IRE) 125 – Miller's Gait 74§ (Mill Reef (USA) 141) **81** [2007 81: 8m 8.2m 10g³ 10.4s³ 8g⁶ 10.3m 10.3g 8g Nov 9] tall, unfurnished filly: fairly useful handicapper: creditable efforts in 2007 only when third: should stay 1½m+: acts on soft going. *T. D. Easterby*

MILLIE'S ROCK (IRE) 2 b.f. (Feb 20) Rock of Gibraltar (IRE) 133 – Miletrian **56** (IRE) 113 (Marju (IRE) 127) [2007 8.2g Nov 7] workmanlike filly: third foal: dam, 9f (at 2 yrs) to 14.6f (Park Hill Stakes) winner, half-sister to very smart 1½m/13f winner Mr Combustible: 14/1, seventh in maiden at Nottingham: will be suited by 1¼m/1½m. *M. R. Channon*

MILLINSKY (USA) 6 ch.m. Stravinsky (USA) 133 – Millyant 114 (Primo Dominie **65** 121) [2007 85: f5g Jan 9] sturdy mare: fairly useful handicapper at 5 yrs: well below form only start in 2007: best at 5f: acts on polytrack and firm going: tried blinkered (looked none too genuine): slowly away second/fourth 5-y-o starts. *Rae Guest*

MILLION PERCENT 8 b.g. Ashkalani (IRE) 128 – Royal Jade 82 (Last Tycoon 131) **81** [2007 72, a76: p8g p8g* p7g⁶ 7m² 7m 7m* p7g³ p7g³ p7g² 7m² 8.1m³ p7.1g⁴ Sep 8] small, strong gelding: fairly useful performer: won handicaps at Lingfield in February and Catterick in May: reportedly finished lame final outing: effective at 6f to 1m: acts on polytrack, firm and soft going: tried in headgear: has been slowly away: consistent. *C. R. Dore*

MILLISECOND 3 b.f. Royal Applause 124 – Milligram 130 (Mill Reef (USA) 141) **85 +** [2007 77: 7g⁵ p6g³ 6f* 5m* 5m⁴ 5m Oct 22] lengthy filly: fairly useful performer: won maiden at Lingfield in August and handicap at Folkestone in September: creditable seventh in handicap at Pontefract final outing: will prove best at 5f/6f: acts on polytrack and firm going: races up with pace. *M. A. Jarvis*

MILLOAKS (IRE) 2 b.f. (Apr 30) Tamayaz (CAN) 121 – Jaldini (IRE) (Darshaan – 133) [2007 6m Sep 11] €4,000F: unfurnished filly: half-sister to 6-y-o Jalmira: dam unraced: last in maiden at Lingfield. *E. J. Creighton*

MILLSINI 3 b.f. Rossini (USA) 118 – Millyant 114 (Primo Dominie 121) [2007 –p: **55** 5.1m⁵ 5g⁶ p5.1g p5.1g⁵ 5g p6g p5.1g⁶ Oct 30] modest maiden: will prove best at 5f/6f: blinkered final outing. *Rae Guest*

MILLVILLE 7 ch.g. Millkom 124 – Miss Top Ville (FR) (Top Ville 129) [2007 115: – p12g² a10g⁵ 12g 12s 11.8d⁵ p10m³ p10g⁴ Dec 22] tall, leggy gelding: smart performer on **a113** all-weather, little form on turf in 2007: good ½-length second to Sri Diamond in handicap at Lingfield on reappearance: below form after: stays 1¾m: acts on polytrack, firm and soft going: has been bandaged hind joints: held up. *M. A. Jarvis*

MILLYJEAN 3 ch.f. Whittingham (IRE) 104 – Taken Aback (IRE) (Robellino (USA) **52** 127) [2007 52: p6g p7f 8s p8g 8m 7s Aug 24] sturdy filly: modest maiden: best efforts at 6f on polytrack: tried blinkered. *John Berry*

MILNE BAY (IRE) 2 b.g. (Feb 17) Tagula (IRE) 116 – Fiction 59 (Dominion 123) – [2007 6s Jun 14] 33/1, very green (hung badly left) in maiden at Yarmouth: subsequently gelded. *D. M. Simcock*

MILNE GRADEN 3 b.g. Montjeu (IRE) 137 – Glen Rosie (IRE) 102 (Mujtahid (USA) **97 p** 118) [2007 9.9g* 10.3g* Oct 26] 230,000Y: third foal: brother to 5-y-o Kings Quay: dam 2-y-o 5f winner (stayed 1m): useful form: unbeaten in maiden at Beverley (overcame greenness) in August and handicap at Doncaster (by neck from Ella Woodcock, picking up smartly to lead close home after being hemmed in) in October: gelded after: stays 10.3f: open to further improvement. *J. Noseda*

MILSON'S POINT (IRE) 3 b.g. Fasliyev (USA) 120 – Hilbys Brite Flite (USA) **66** (Cormorant (USA)) [2007 76: 5g⁶ 6g 8.1m 6d⁵ 6g² 8.3d² 7.9m 6s 7.2g 8.3g* Sep 3] good-topped gelding: fair handicapper: won at Hamilton in September: was effective at 6f to 8.3f: acted on polytrack and good to soft ground: tried blinkered: had suspect attitude: dead. *I. Semple*

MILTONS CHOICE 4 b.g. Diktat 126 – Starosta (Soviet Star (USA) 128) [2007 65: – p6g Mar 24] workmanlike gelding: fair handicapper at 3 yrs: well held only start in 2007: best at 5f/6f: acts on soft and good to firm going. *J. M. Bradley*

MILTON'S KEEN 4 gr.g. Largesse 112 – Not A Word (Batshoof 122) [2007 61: 7m **65** 6s² 8.1s² 7.1s² 8.1m⁶ 6g 7.1f³ p8g 8.1m Sep 13] leggy, quite attractive gelding: fair maiden: left John Berry after second start: effective at 6f to 1m: acts on any turf going, lightly raced on all-weather. *M. Salaman*

MIMI MOUSE 5 br.m. Diktat 126 – Shifty Mouse 44 (Night Shift (USA)) [2007 91: **91** 5f² 5m³ 5m⁵ 5m* 5s³ 5s⁵ 5.6m 5g² 5g Sep 23] smallish, close-coupled mare: fairly useful performer: won handicap at Thirsk in June: good second in similar event at Haydock penultimate start: best form at 5f: acts on firm and soft ground: sometimes on toes/early to post: races up with pace: tends to hang right. *T. D. Easterby*

MIMISEL 3 ch.f. Selkirk (USA) 129 – Milly-M (Cadeaux Genereux 131) [2007 84: **92** 7m⁵ 7.1d³ 8.1g 6.5v 7v p7g Dec 19] leggy filly: fairly useful performer: ran only in listed races in 2007, improved efforts first 3 starts, third to Ponty Rossa at Warwick: well held after: barely stays 1m: acts on soft and good to firm going. *Rae Guest*

MIMTON (IRE) 2 b.f. (Apr 8) Shinko Forest (IRE) – Playa Del Sol (IRE) (Alzao – (USA) 117) [2007 f5g 6s 5s 7m 6m p5.1g⁶ Aug 31] €9,000Y: good-bodied filly: fourth foal: half-sister to 5-y-o Comeintothespace: dam Italian 1¼m winner: little form. *N. Wilson*

MINA 5 ch.m. Selkirk (USA) 129 – Midnight Shift (IRE) 73 (Night Shift (USA)) [2007 **68** 73: p6g³ Jan 14] tall mare: fair handicapper: stays 7f, but raced mainly at 6f: acts on all-weather, good to firm and good to soft: none too consistent. *Rae Guest*

MINA A SALEM 5 b.g. Singspiel (IRE) 133 – Amber Fizz (USA) (Effervescing **60 +** (USA)) [2007 83, a101: p7g 7m⁴ p8g Jul 18] leggy, workmanlike gelding: reportedly **a89** partially sighted in left eye: just fairly useful nowadays, better on all-weather than turf: effective at 7f to 1¼m: acts on polytrack, firm and good to soft going: often makes running: sold 6,500 gns in October. *C. E. Brittain*

MINAASH (USA) 3 b.c. Dixie Union (USA) 121 – Metanoia (USA) (Seeking The **87** Gold (USA)) [2007 84: p7g⁶ p7.1g⁴ p6m p6g* p6g³ p7g² p7g Nov 21] workmanlike colt: fairly useful handicapper: left J. Noseda after second start: won at Kempton in August: good efforts next 2 outings: stays 7f: acts on polytrack and good to firm going: often races prominently. *D. M. Simcock*

MIND ALERT 6 b.g. Mind Games 121 – Bombay Sapphire (Be My Chief (USA) 122) [2007 –, a65: f6g² f6g² f6g³ p6g³ f6g⁴ f6g p6g p6g² p6g³ p7g³ f6g 6m p7g p6g p6m p6g⁴ p7g⁵ Dec 30] good-topped gelding: modest handicapper: stays 7f: acts on all-weather, good to firm and good to soft ground: wears headgear (visored nowadays): none too genuine. *D. Shaw* —
a58

MIND HOW YOU GO (FR) 9 b.g. Hernando (FR) 127 – Cos I Do (IRE) (Double Schwartz 128) [2007 p16g* 16m⁵ 16s⁶ 18g 16.4m⁶ 16d⁴ Oct 11] fairly useful handicapper, lightly raced on Flat: won apprentice event at Lingfield in March: stays 2m, seemingly not 2¼m: acts on polytrack, soft and good to firm going: has hung: winning hurdler. *J. R. Best* 80

MIND THAT FOX 5 b.g. Mind Games 121 – Foxie Lady 77 (Wolfhound (USA) 126) [2007 –: p6g p5.1g⁴ p5.1g⁵ p5.1g p5.1g f5g p5.1g p5.1g⁵ p5.1g⁴ p5.1g p5g p8.6g Nov 27] modest maiden: may prove best at 5f/6f: form only on polytrack: tried blinkered. *T. Wall* —
a54

MIND THE STYLE 3 b.g. Mind Games 121 – Sioux Lady (Petong 126) [2007 78: p6g⁵ 5.1f 5m* p5g⁶ 5.7d⁴ 5.1g⁵ p5.1g⁶ 5m Aug 6] good-bodied gelding: fair performer: won claimer at Folkestone in April: well below form after: barely stays easy 6f: acts on polytrack, good to firm and good to soft going: tried in cheekpieces/blinkers/tongue strap. *W. G. M. Turner* 74 d

MINE BEHIND 7 b.g. Sheikh Albadou 128 – Arapi (IRE) 89 (Arazi (USA) 135) [2007 93: 5.1m 7.6m 5.7f 6g³ f6d 6g 6g p6g² p6g⁶ p6m⁶ p7m⁴ Dec 8] lengthy gelding: fairly useful handicapper: creditable efforts when placed in 2007: effective at 5f (given a test) to 7f: acts on polytrack, firm and soft going: tried in cheekpieces: usually held up. *J. R. Best* 87
a80

MINE (IRE) 9 b.h. Primo Dominie 121 – Ellebanna 69 (Tina's Pet 121) [2007 117: 8g 7.1m* 7s⁶ 7m 8g 7g⁴ 8m⁶ 7d Sep 29] tall, useful-looking horse: smart performer: won listed race at Haydock (by ½ length from Beckermet) in June: creditable efforts in Criterion Stakes at Newmarket (sixth to Silver Touch) and listed event at York (fourth to Duff) third/sixth outings: well below form in valuable handicap at Ascot final start: effective at 7f/1m: acts on firm and soft going, possibly not on heavy: visored: held up/travels strongly. *J. D. Bethell* 112

MINERAL RIGHTS (USA) 3 ch.g. Gulch (USA) – Long Vacation (IRE) (Thatching 131) [2007 69p: 8m 7.1g⁴ 7.2g 7.1d p6g² Oct 5] big, rangy gelding: modest maiden: barely stays 8.6f: acts on polytrack, unraced on extremes of going on turf. *I. Semple* 61

MINERAL STAR (IRE) 5 b.g. Monashee Mountain (USA) 115 – Summit Talk (Head For Heights 125) [2007 82: 8d* 8.2g 8m 8s⁴ p7.1g⁵ p7g⁴ 8d p7g Dec 5] tall, leggy, angular gelding: fairly useful performer: won handicap at Yarmouth in June: well below form last 2 starts, leaving M. Tompkins 13,000 gns before final one: stays 1m: acts on polytrack, soft and good to firm ground: tried visored/blinkered: free-going sort: held up: sometimes finds little. *R. Donohoe, Ireland* 83 d

Bank of Scotland Corporate Stakes (John of Gaunt), Haydock—
Mine shows he still retains plenty of ability at the age of nine; Beckermet is second

MINE THE BALANCE (IRE) 4 b.g. Desert Style (IRE) 121 – Dia (IRE) (Astronef **67 d** 116) [2007 62: p7g p6g² p6g⁶ p6g p8g² p7.1g f8g p8.6g⁶ p7g⁵ p8.6g p7g⁶ 7m 6m⁵ p8.6g 7.1s p6g³ p7g⁵ 5.1s 7m Aug 12] leggy gelding: fair performer: claimed from J. R. Best £6,000 fifth start: not at best after: got loose beforehand and withdrawn prior to intended final run: stays easy 1m: acts on polytrack and heavy going: often blinkered: tried tongue tied. *H. J. Manners*

MING VASE 5 b.g. Vettori (IRE) 119 – Minstrel's Dance (CAN) (Pleasant Colony **59** (USA)) [2007 54: p10g⁶ 12m f8g⁴ f8g⁴ 10s⁵ 10d⁵ 8s³ 8s 8.5s³ 8.1m⁴ 9.2g 8.1g 8m 10g³ Oct 6] strong gelding: modest performer: stays 11f: acts on all-weather, firm and soft going: tried in headgear: sometimes hangs: races prominently. *P. T. Midgley*

MINI MOSA 3 b.f. Indian Ridge 123 – Baldemosa (FR) (Lead On Time (USA) 123) **73** [2007 8.1d 7m² 8.1m p7g³ 8g p10g⁴ Nov 21] good-bodied filly: sixth foal: half-sister to 9-y-o Caustic Wit and 6-y-o Seldemosa: dam, French 1m winner, half-sister to very smart French sprinter Balbonella (dam of Anabaa and Key of Luck): fair maiden: left C. Laffon-Parias in France after sole outing at 2 yrs: barely stays 1m: acts on polytrack and good to firm going. *J. H. M. Gosden*

MINIMUM FUSS (IRE) 3 b.f. Second Empire (IRE) 124 – Jamis (IRE) (Be My **56** Guest (USA) 126) [2007 60: f6g⁵ f5g 5m³ f5g 5m 5g 5m⁶ 5m 5d 5g 5d p5.1g f5g Dec 27] tall filly: modest performer: free-going sort, best at 5f/6f: acts on fibresand, firm and good to soft going: effective with/without blinkers: hangs left: inconsistent and of suspect temperament. *M. C. Chapman*

MINISTEROFINTERIOR 2 b.g. (Mar 2) Nayef (USA) 129 – Maureen's Hope **–** (USA) (Northern Baby (CAN) 127) [2007 8.1s Sep 29] good-bodied, compact gelding: 40/1, backward in maiden at Haydock (gelded after). *C. F. Wall*

MINJIM 2 b.c. (Apr 19) Kyllachy 129 – Sarabah (IRE) 83 (Ela-Mana-Mou 132) [2007 **–** p7g⁵ 7g Sep 19] 50,000Y: half-brother to several winners, including useful 7f (at 2 yrs) and 1¼m winner Saratov (by Rudimentary): dam 1¼m winner: well held in minor event/ maiden. *C. E. Brittain*

MINKOWSKI 4 b.g. Galileo (IRE) 134 – Abitara (IRE) 114 (Rainbow Quest (USA) **100** 134) [2007 10.5g² 10.5d² 12s* 10g⁴ 14d⁴ 12d Oct 4] angular gelding: first foal: dam 1¼m to 13.5f (Prix de Pomone) winner: useful performer: won newcomers race at Longchamp and minor event at Maisons-Laffitte in 2006, and minor event (amateurs) at Dieppe in June: ran well when fourth to Purple Moon in Ebor Handicap at York (stayed on steadily) penultimate start: stays 1¾m: acts on soft ground: has had tongue tied: joined Jonjo O'Neill, and gelded, pulled up in hurdling debut. *J. E. Hammond, France*

MINNEAPOLIS 2 b.c. (Mar 4) Sadler's Wells (USA) 132 – Teggiano (IRE) 108 (Muj- **100** tahid (USA) 118) [2007 7d⁵ 7s³ 7s⁴ 7m p7g* 7g p7g⁴ Oct 12] 400,000Y: good-topped, quite attractive colt: third foal: dam 2-y-o 6f to 1m (including Fillies' Mile) winner, later second in Ribblesdale Stakes: useful performer: won maiden at Gowran in June and minor event at Dundalk (beat Rock Moss by 3 lengths) in September: subsequently last in Prix Jean-Luc Lagardere at Longchamp and respectable fourth to Great War Eagle in listed race at Dundalk (slowly away): will be suited by at least 1m: acts on polytrack and soft ground. *A. P. O'Brien, Ireland*

MINNIE MILL 3 b.f. Mind Games 121 – Sometime Never (IRE) (College Chapel 122) **56** [2007 60: p7.1g⁵ p6g 6g p6g 6.1d⁴ 6.1m p6g⁵ p7g p7.1g Oct 19] modest maiden: should stay 7f: acts on polytrack and good to soft ground: tried in cheekpieces. *B. P. J. Baugh*

MINNIS BAY (CAN) 3 b.g. Royal Academy (USA) 130 – Aly's Daylite (USA) (Day- **87** jur (USA) 137) [2007 83: 10g 12d p7g⁶ 8m* p8g² 8m⁵ p8g Sep 24] leggy gelding: fairly useful handicapper: won at Bath in August: good second at Kempton next time: stays 1m: acts on polytrack and good to firm going: often races prominently. *E. F. Vaughan*

MINNOW 3 b.f. Averti (IRE) 117 – Tharwa (IRE) 63 (Last Tycoon 131) [2007 76p: 6m **56** 5.4v 5.1m⁶ 5g p6g⁶ p5g⁴ p5m⁵ p5g² p5g p6m⁶ p7.1g p5m³ p6g Dec 29] big, lengthy **a64** filly: has scope: modest handicapper, better on all-weather than turf: best at 5f/6f: acts on polytrack and firm ground: sometimes wears headgear: sometimes slowly away. *S. C. Williams*

MINORITY REPORT 7 b.g. Rainbow Quest (USA) 134 – Queen Sceptre (IRE) 97 **104** (Fairy King (USA)) [2007 104: 8f³ 8m 7g³ 7g 7m 7d 8m³ 7g Oct 27] stocky gelding, type to carry condition: useful performer: creditable third in minor events at Goodwood (beaten by Laa Rayb) and Bath (behind Smart Enough) third/seventh outings: below form in similar event at Doncaster final start: effective at 7f/1m: acts on firm and good to soft going: usually held up. *L. M. Cumani*

MINOS (IRE) 3 ch.c. Grand Lodge (USA) 125 – Miniver (IRE) (Mujtahid (USA) 118) –
[2007 90: 10m 10m 8d 8.3g p8g Oct 17] deep-girthed colt: fluent mover: fairly useful
performer at 2 yrs: little impact in handicaps in 2007: sold 11,000 gns. *R. Hannon*

MINSHAR 2 ch.f. (Mar 31) Noverre (USA) 125 – Reine de Neige 96 (Kris 135) [2007 **84**
6s³ 7v⁴ 6d* Oct 29] 12,500F, 26,000Y: sturdy, compact filly: half-sister to 7-y-o Oeuf A
La Neige and 1999 2-y-o 5f winner Stylish Beauty (by Night Shift): dam, 1m winner, out
of half-sister to dam of Fantastic Light: fairly useful performer: off 3 months, much improved
to win maiden at Leicester by neck from Provence, getting up close home: should be
suited by 7f/1m: raced only on going softer than good. *L. M. Cumani*

MINSTREL FLYER (IRE) 5 b.m. Brave Act 119 – Miss Sabre (Sabrehill (USA) –
120) [2007 8.2s p7.1g 10d 11.9m 12m Sep 30] 1m winner in Spain in 2005: no form in
Britain: tried blinkered. *E. J. Creighton*

MINT 4 b.f. Bahamian Bounty 116 – Tick Tack (Primo Dominie 121) [2007 77: 5m 6m **57**
6.1m 6m 5m 5s² Oct 4] smallish filly: modest handicapper nowadays: stays 6f: acts on
soft and good to firm going: tried in cheekpieces: none too consistent. *D. W. Barker*

MINUS FIFTEEN (IRE) 2 ch.c. (Apr 25) Trans Island 119 – Bumble (Rainbow **70**
Quest (USA) 134) [2007 6d 6m² Nov 10] 60,000F: tall, good-topped colt: fourth foal:
half-brother to 4-y-o Northern Empire and 5-y-o Scutch Mill: dam unraced half-sister to
Racing Post Trophy winner Be My Chief: fair form in maidens at Newmarket and
Doncaster (neck second to Premier Danseur): may prove best at 5f/6f. *K. A. Ryan*

MINWIR (IRE) 2 b.c. (Mar 22) Green Desert (USA) 127 – Elshamms 107 (Zafonic **68**
(USA) 130) [2007 6m 6d⁶ 6m 6s³ Oct 4] fair maiden: third in nursery at Goodwood: will
be at least as effective at 5f as 6f: sold 16,000 gns. *M. A. Jarvis*

MI ODDS 11 b.g. Sure Blade (USA) 130 – Vado Via 56 (Ardross 134) [2007 –, a75d: f8g –
f12g f12g⁴ f12g f12g f12g 10v Jul 20] tall gelding: little form in 2007. *Mrs N. Macauley*

MIO FIORE 2 b.f. (Jan 9) Bertolini (USA) 125 – Queenie 82 (Indian Ridge 123) [2007 –
7d p6g 7d p8.6g Oct 30] 13,000Y: lengthy filly: second foal: dam, 1m winner, out of
useful 1¼m performer Bint Zamayem: little form. *M. Blanshard*

MIRACLE BABY 5 b.m. Atraf 116 – Musica 82 (Primo Dominie 121) [2007 –: p7.1g –
p6g Jan 19] strong mare: maiden: little form since 2005. *A. J. Chamberlain*

MIRACLE RIDGE (IRE) 12 ch.g. Indian Ridge 123 – Highly Delighted (USA) **67**
(Verbatim (USA)) [2007 78: p6g* p6g⁴ p6g 5g 6.5g 5.8d 6g 5g 5v 6.7s 6.5d a6g* Sep 6] **a80**
workmanlike gelding: fair performer on all-weather, fair on turf: won seller at Wolverhampton in January and handicap at Laytown in September: effective at 5f to 7f: acts
on all-weather/sand and any turf going: tried tongue tied: usually blinkered. *Adrian
McGuinness, Ireland*

MIRACLE SEEKER 2 br.f. (Mar 11) Rainbow Quest (USA) 134 – Miracle (Ezzoud **82**
(IRE) 126) [2007 8.1s² 8g³ Oct 26] leggy, useful-looking filly: third foal: half-sister to
1¼m winner/very smart hurdler Katchit (by Kalanisi) and Irish 1¼m winner Prince Erik
(by Indian Ridge): dam, French/US 1m winner, out of half-sister to smart Irish 7f/1m
winner Manntari: fairly useful form in maidens at Haydock (second, beaten a neck, after
drifted left) and Doncaster (third to Cruel Sea): will stay 1¼m/1½m. *C. G. Cox*

MIRAMARE (GER) 3 b.f. Rainbow Quest (USA) 134 – Minaccia (GER) (Platini **103**
(GER) 126) [2007 11g* p12g⁴ Nov 3] fourth foal: half-sister to 3 winners in Europe,
including 5-y-o Macleya: dam, useful German 6f (at 2 yrs) to 1m winner, half-sister to
useful German performer up to 1¾m Mendosino: useful performer: won maiden at
Krefeld on debut (by 6 lengths from subsequent Group 3 winner Avanti Polonia) in May:
left J. Hirschberger in Germany, creditable 3 lengths fourth to Dansant in listed race at
Kempton on British debut, racing freely in clear lead and rallying when challenged: stays
1½m: refused to enter stall when favourite for Preis der Diana at Dusseldorf in June.
B. J. Curley

MIRIN 3 b.f. Generous (IRE) 139 – Musetta (IRE) 107 (Cadeaux Genereux 131) [2007 **84**
70p: 9.7m 12s* 12f⁶ 12m³ Sep 21] unfurnished filly: fairly useful performer: won maiden
at Newbury in June: seemingly good last of 6 to Queen's Best in listed race at Newbury
next time: will stay 1¾m: acts on firm and soft going. *G. Wragg*

MIRJAN (IRE) 11 b.g. Tenby 125 – Mirana (IRE) (Ela-Mana-Mou 132) [2007 102: **99**
16d³ 16m 16.1m* 18d⁵ Oct 13] strong, sturdy gelding: useful handicapper: won at Newcastle (for second successive year, beat Kasthari by short head) in August: below form
final outing: stays 2¼m: acts on firm and soft going: effective blinkered or not. *L. Lungo*

MIRKO 3 b.c. Dansili 127 – Marithea (IRE) (Barathea (IRE) 127) [2007 –: p6g⁶ 6s **54** 7.1d⁴ p10g Sep 3] modest maiden: stays 7f: acts on polytrack: tongue tied last 2 starts. *B. R. Millman*

MIRTHFUL (USA) 3 b.f. Miswaki (USA) 124 – Musicanti (USA) (Nijinsky (CAN) **85** 138) [2007 75p: 10m⁶ 11.8s³ 11.7g* 11.9m* 14.8s³ 11.9g⁵ Sep 7] lengthy filly: fairly useful performer: won maiden at Bath in June and handicap at Haydock in August: stayed 14.8f: acted on soft and good to firm ground: stud. *B. W. Hills*

MISAINE (IRE) 3 b.g. Fasliyev (USA) 120 – Rose Paille (FR) (General Holme (USA) **53** 128) [2007 59: p5g³ 5.9g Jun 18] strong, lengthy gelding: modest maiden: was best at 5f: acted on good to firm ground: dead. *T. J. Etherington*

MISARO (GER) 6 b.g. Acambaro (GER) 118 – Misniniski (Niniski (USA) 125) [2007 **95** 84, a75: f5g² p5.1g² f6g⁵ p5.1g⁵ 6m³ 5.3m* 5.5d* 5d* 6s³ 5.7d p6g* 6g⁴ 5d 5g 5.6m 5.1m⁴ 5f 5.7f⁵ 6d p5g Oct 12] leggy gelding: useful handicapper: won at Brighton in April, Warwick and Hamilton in May and Kempton (had run of things) in July: effective at 5f/6f: acts on all-weather, firm and soft going: tried visored, blinkered nowadays: usually races prominently. *R. A. Harris*

MIS CHICAF (IRE) 6 b.m. Prince Sabo 123 – Champagne Season (USA) 54 (Vaguely **51** Noble 140) [2007 –: 5g 6m 5g 8m 8m 7.5d 6s³ p7.1g³ p7.1g Nov 1] strong, workmanlike mare: modest performer nowadays: stays easy 7f: acts on polytrack, soft and good to firm ground: tongue tied at 5 yrs. *D. Carroll*

MISCHIEF MAKING (USA) 2 b. or br.f. (Apr 27) Lemon Drop Kid (USA) 131 – **49** Fraulein 117 (Acatenango (GER) 127) [2007 p8m Nov 26] second foal: closely related to 3-y-o Sister Maria: dam 7f (at 2 yrs) to 1¼m (E. P. Taylor Stakes) winner: 12/1 and green, poor form when ninth in maiden at Lingfield. *E. A. L. Dunlop*

MISK HILLS 2 b.g. (Feb 15) Warningford 119 – Classical Jazz (FR) (Celtic Swing **–** 138) [2007 6g 7d⁶ p7.1g Jun 29] no form. *P. T. Midgley*

MISPHIRE 4 b.f. Mister Baileys 123 – Bombay Sapphire (Be My Chief (USA) 122) **86** [2007 87: 5g 6d⁵ 7s³ 6d 6s* 6s³ 6d⁵ 6m³ 6s Oct 14] big, good-topped filly: fairly useful handicapper: won at Haydock in June: good third at Newmarket penultimate start: stays 7f: acts on soft and good to firm going: in cheekpieces/blinkered nowadays: has looked none too keen. *M. Dods*

MISPLACED FORTUNE 2 b.f. (Apr 8) Compton Place 125 – Tide of Fortune **62** (Soviet Star (USA) 128) [2007 6d⁶ 6m⁵ 6m⁴ 6f³ 6f 7d³ Oct 16] 9,000Y: half-sister to 3 winners, including fairly useful 2000 2-y-o 6f winner Starbeck (by Spectrum): dam unraced granddaughter of top-class 1m to 1¼m performer Rose Bowl: modest maiden: in frame 3 times: should prove best at 5f/6f. *N. Tinkler*

MISSABEAT (IRE) 2 b.f. (Mar 20) Distant Music (USA) 126 – Dear Catch (IRE) 69 **–** (Bluebird (USA) 125) [2007 5.1m 6d 6m Aug 1] 26,000Y: tall, good-topped filly: second foal: dam, Irish 9f winner, sister to smart Irish sprinter Catch The Blues: behind in maidens. *T. D. Easterby*

MISS ADMIRAL 3 ch.f. Compton Admiral 121 – Frisky Miss (IRE) 70 (Fayruz 116) **–** [2007 f7g Apr 26] seventh foal: dam, 5f/6f (latter including at 2 yrs) winner, half-sister to useful 2-y-o 6f/7f winner Smittenby: 33/1 and green, well beaten in maiden at Southwell, slowly away. *S. R. Bowring*

MISS ANDRETTI (AUS) 6 b.m. Ihtiram (IRE) 114 – Peggie's Bid (AUS) **127** (Marooned 89) [2007 118: 5g* 6g* 6g* 5m* 6d 6g* 6g* 6g Dec 9]
      For the top sprinters in particular, the world has shrunk considerably in just the last five years. For the third time since 2003, a sprinter trained in Australia was successful at Royal Ascot. Choisir caused an upset when winning the King's Stand Stakes at 25/1 before following up in the Golden Jubilee Stakes four days later, but the lesson was quickly learned by bookmakers and punters alike not to underestimate Australian-trained sprinters at the Royal meeting, particularly after Takeover Target's win in the 2006 King's Stand showed that Choisir's achievements were not a flash in the pan. Bookmakers were taking no chances with the latest raiding party of Australian sprinters, one firm going a shade of odds on that one of their number would win either of the meeting's big sprints. It was just 5/2 that both the King's Stand and the Golden Jubilee would go to the visitors. The bookmakers' caution was understandable given that numerically the four-strong Australian team was the most impressive yet. Takeover Target was back again, fresh from a Group 1

win at Doomben, and joined by Bentley Biscuit, who had beaten him a short neck in a similar event at the same track earlier in May, and by Magnus, also successful in a Group 1 last time out at Warwick Farm. Magnus had also twice finished in the frame behind Miss Andretti, whose hat-trick of Group 1 wins early in the year led to her being widely considered the best of the Australian sprinters. Miss Andretti's trainer Lee Freedman had gained some idea of the standard required for Royal Ascot when his stable's Falkirk dead-heated for a close fourth behind Takeover Target in the King's Stand the year before. Freedman was previously best known outside Australia as the trainer of Makybe Diva for the last two of her three consecutive Melbourne Cup victories.

In Miss Andretti, though, Freedman had a mare at the opposite end of the distance spectrum, one who had broken track records over five and six furlongs in completing her Group 1 hat-trick. The first of those came in the Coolmore Lightning Stakes at Moonee Valley (where she won by a length and half from Magnus) and the second in the Seppelt Wines Newmarket Handicap at Caulfield after another win at Moonee Valley in the Timbercorp Australia Stakes. At Caulfield, where she won by a head, Miss Andretti was giving the runner-up Gold Edition 7 lb, with Magnus a close fourth. As a measure of how much Miss Andretti had improved in twelve months, she had finished only eleventh to Takeover Target in the same race (run at Flemington) the year before in receipt of more than a stone from the winner. Both Choisir and Takeover Target had also won the Lightning Stakes in the season they were successful at Royal Ascot. By following up in the Australia Stakes, Miss Andretti made a flying start in the Global Sprint Challenge, with wins in the first two legs of the series.

Unlike Choisir and Takeover Target, Miss Andretti was not asked to shoulder a Group 1 penalty in the King's Stand due to a change in the race conditions for the latest renewal, interpreted as a step towards restoring the race's Group 1 status which it last had in 1987. The King's Stand will, indeed, be back as a Group 1—deservedly so—in 2008 after a successful application to the European Pattern Committee. The Australian sprinters took three of the first five places in the betting in the twenty-runner field, with Miss Andretti the 3/1 favourite, Takeover Target on 11/2 and Bentley Biscuit at 9/1. The only European runners at single-figure odds were the well-backed Dandy Man, who had dead-heated for fourth the year before, on 15/2, and the impressive Bath listed winner Enticing on 8/1. Miss Andretti justified favouritism with little fuss, positioned just off the pace from her high draw and picking off the leaders approaching the final furlong to win going away by a length and three quarters. Dandy Man raced on his own up the stand side for most of the way before running on for second, with Magnus and Takeover Target completing the frame for Australia, a neck and half a length further behind respectively. Bentley Biscuit reportedly returned jarred up when trailing in last of all. Conditions

King's Stand Stakes, Royal Ascot—Miss Andretti gives Australia a third win in the race in five years; Dandy Man (right) is the only European in the first four as Magnus (blinkers) finishes third ahead of 2006 winner Takeover Target (noseband)

The Age Classic, Flemington—
sixth win of the year for Miss Andretti (left), who gets the better of Gold Edition

were on the firm side on the opening day of the Royal meeting, so much so that Miss Andretti took 2.35 seconds off Takeover Target's winning time (also on good to firm ground) in the first running on the redeveloped course the year before. But, by the Saturday of the meeting, conditions were softening, with a heavy burst of rain falling prior to the Golden Jubilee Stakes. There was no shortage of confidence in Miss Andretti handling the good to soft ground as she was made the 2/1 favourite to account for twenty rivals, including Magnus and Takeover Target again, but she was struggling to stay in touch with the leaders over two furlongs out and finished well down the field, just behind Magnus. However, Takeover Target almost pulled off another success for Australia, leading inside the final furlong but collared on the line and beaten a head by Soldier's Tale.

For Miss Andretti and Takeover Target, their European campaigns were over, but their compatriots contested Europe's other top summer sprints, albeit without making any impact. Magnus started second favourite for the Nunthorpe Stakes at York but finished only ninth, while Bentley Biscuit proved disappointing twice more, finishing in mid-division in the July Cup and Prix Maurice de Gheest. The July Cup also saw the debut in Europe of a fifth Australian sprinter, Mutawaajid, who joined Mick Channon from Gai Waterhouse for four races in Britain. His best efforts came when finishing fourth in the Sprint Cup at Haydock and the World Trophy at Newbury. As for Miss Andretti, she was given a four-month break after Royal Ascot before her next two starts back in Australia. She kept her unbeaten home record for the year with wins in the Group 2 Schweppes Stakes at Moonee Valley in October and then the Group 1 The Age Classic at Flemington in November. On both occasions she was chased home by her old rival from earlier in the year, Gold Edition. The pair of them dominated throughout in both races, Gold Edition making the running with Miss Andretti shadowing her before being produced to lead inside the final furlong. Over the straight six at Flemington, Gold Edition's rider tried to give Miss Andretti the slip by suddenly taking his mount to race on the far rail, but Miss Andretti was switched to cover the move before running out the winner by three quarters of a length, the pair five lengths clear of the rest. There were just five runners in the Schweppes and six in The Age Classic, the small fields just one result of the outbreak of equine influenza which had a severe impact on the racing and breeding industries in Australia after it was first detected at the end of August. Travel restrictions to prevent spread of the disease meant, for example, that Takeover Target, based in one of the worst-hit states, New South Wales, was unable to travel to Melbourne for either of these races. A fuller account of the repercussions of the EI outbreak is given in the Australia and New Zealand section of 'Top Horses Abroad' at the back of the annual.

Miss Andretti made her final appearance of the year in the Hong Kong Sprint at Sha Tin, starting second favourite to the eventual winner, locally-trained Sacred Kingdom, who put up a top-class performance. Miss Andretti's connections blamed the right-handed track for a disappointing effort which saw her finish only tenth of the thirteen runners. Her jockey reported that she was never comfortable and on her 'Melbourne leg' (where all the tracks are left-handed) all the way. In fact, things seemed to go wrong for Miss Andretti well before the first turn, as she broke quickly but fought strongly for her head when her rider tried to restrain her in the early stages. Her trainer also felt that the time Miss Andretti was required to spend in quarantine in Australia and then a two-week stay at Sha Tin had been detrimental. Nonetheless, Miss Andretti had already done enough to clinch the Global Sprint Challenge title, succeeding Hong Kong's Cape of Good Hope (whose wins in the series came in the Australia Stakes and the Golden Jubilee) in 2005 and Takeover Target in 2006. The July Cup has been added as a third British leg of the series in 2008, while The Age Classic replaces the Australia Stakes as the second of the two Australian races in the competition. Miss Andretti's owners had to find room for more trophies on their mantlepiece at the end of the year. As well as being

P. S. Buckley, D. B. Meuller & Ms G. Guenzi's "Miss Andretti"

named Champion Sprinter and Most Popular Racehorse for 2006/7, Miss Andretti became the first sprinter for twenty years to be named Australian Racehorse of the Year.

We have become used to Australian sprinters in the Choisir mould, strong types like Takeover Target, Bentley Biscuit and Magnus. Miss Andretti fills the eye a lot less, being just smallish and leggy in appearance. She certainly doesn't have a sprinter's pedigree either, with three of her four great grandsires all successful in the King George VI and Queen Elizabeth Stakes! The only horse close in her pedigree to excel over short distances is her grandsire, the July Cup and Breeders' Cup Mile winner Royal Academy, though even he was an unusually speedy son of Nijinsky. Miss Andretti's sire Ihtiram (a half-brother to the Grand Criterium winner Second Empire from the family of Salsabil and Marju) was a smart performer in Britain for John Dunlop for whom he won four races at up to a mile and a quarter (the best of them a listed race at Newbury) and probably stayed a mile and a half. After an unsuccessful spell in the UAE, he was moved on to Australia where he won five more races at up to around eleven furlongs, the last of them as a seven-year-old. Miss Andretti was reportedly one of fewer than thirty foals in his 2000 crop. There is little to say about Miss Andretti's distaff family; of the three mares on the bottom line of her pedigree, only grandam Time To Bid raced, and she saw the racecourse only twice, finishing unplaced on both her starts. Miss Andretti's dam Peggie's Bid was by the British-bred sire Marooned, a winner of the old Bess-borough (now the Duke of Edinburgh) Stakes at Royal Ascot for Michael Stoute before being bought by Robert Sangster for an Australian career, improving there and winning the Group 1 Sydney Cup over two miles. Marooned is also a half-brother to the very smart stayer Arctic Owl, whose wins included the Irish St Leger. Peggie's Bid has bred two more winners in Australia since her first foal Miss Andretti. The better of them is Miss Andretti's gelded brother Charlie Beau, who gained his first placing in a pattern race when second in the Group 2 Winterbottom Stakes over six furlongs at Ascot (the one in Perth) in December, a race Miss Andretti herself won two years earlier.

Miss Andretti (AUS) (b.m. 2001)			
Ihtiram (IRE) (b 1992)	Royal Academy (b 1987)	Nijinsky	
		Crimson Saint	
	Welsh Love (b 1986)	Ela-Mana-Mou	
		Welsh Flame	
Peggie's Bid (AUS) (b or br 1996)	Marooned (b 1981)	Mill Reef	
		Short Rations	
	Time To Bid (b or br 1990)	Alytime	
		Without Reserve	

Miss Andretti's pedigree therefore sheds little light on why Australian-bred sprinters should have proved more than a match for their British counterparts. She is far from unique among them, however, in having a middle-distance performer for a sire; Takeover Target is by the Prix du Jockey Club winner Celtic Swing, while Bentley Biscuit (better than he was able to show in Europe) is by another winner of that race Peintre Celebre. The last-named pair, like Choisir (by Danehill Dancer), were by European sires on shuttle duty in Australia, so in terms of pedigree, at least in the top half, they are no different from plenty of European-bred horses. It is not just in Britain either that Australian-bred sprinters have made their mark abroad. Miss Andretti may have disappointed at Sha Tin, but the first five home in the Hong Kong Sprint were all Hong Kong-trained, but Australian-bred. All nine runnings of the Hong Kong Sprint have now gone to Australian-bred horses and three of the most recent winners, Silent Witness, Absolute Champion and Sacred Kingdom, all had strong claims to be considered the world's best sprinter in the years they were successful.

Miss Andretti's connections reportedly regretted not prolonging her stay in Britain for the July Cup, and it looks as though she may be campaigned in Britain again in 2008; at any rate, connections seem in no hurry to retire her to the paddocks. Miss Andretti began her career in Western Australia where she won eight of her first ten starts (runner-up in the two others) but it was not until she joined Lee Freedman after her second start in 2006 that her career took off, her first Group 1 success coming in September of that year in the Manikato Stakes at Moonee Valley, another win gained in course-record time. One of Miss Andretti's early wins came at seven furlongs but she is best at five or six. She acts on firm going, and, although the ground was blamed for her defeat in the Golden Jubilee, she has won on soft going at up to Group 3 level in Australia. She is a tough mare with an admirable record of nineteen wins from twenty-nine starts, and her King's Stand victory was one of the highlights of the Royal meeting. *Lee Freedman, Australia*

MISS ANTROPIST (IRE) 2 b.f. (Apr 25) Fath (USA) 116 – Perfect Welcome 43 (Taufan (USA) 119) [2007 p5g⁶ 5m⁵ p5.1g⁵ 6.1g³ 6m³ p5.1g p7.1g Jun 29] €15,000Y: angular filly: half-sister to several winners, including Irish 6f winner (including at 2 yrs) Immovable Option (by Fairy King) and 1m/1¼m winner Leave Me Alone (by Nashwan), both useful: dam, Irish 7f winner, half-sister to high-class miler Chalon: poor maiden: placed in sellers: best at 5f/6f: acts on polytrack and good to firm ground: tried blinkered. *R. A. Harris*

MISS BEATRIX (IRE) 3 b.f. Danehill Dancer (IRE) 117 – Miss Beabea (IRE) 105 – (Catrail (USA) 123) [2007 106: 8m May 6] neat filly: useful performer at 2 yrs, winning 3 times, including Moyglare Stud Stakes and very valuable sales race, both at the Curragh: behind in 1000 Guineas at Newmarket (reportedly very sick after) sole start in 2007: stays 7f: probably acts on any going: usually held up. *Kevin Prendergast, Ireland*

MISS BOOTYLISHES 2 b.f. (Jan 24) Mujahid (USA) 125 – Moxby (Efisio 120) 87 § [2007 6d* 6m⁴ 6v³ 7m⁵ 6.5m 7m 7d⁵ Oct 27] neat filly: third foal: half-sister to 2004 2-y-o 6f winner Bow Wave (by Danzero): dam unraced sister to useful 7f performer Abbey's Gal: fairly useful performer: won maiden at Brighton in June: seemed to run well when seventh in nursery at Doncaster and fifth in listed race at Newbury fifth/final starts: stays 7f: acts on heavy and good to firm going: temperamental. *A. B. Haynes*

MISS BOUGGY WOUGGY 2 b.f. (Feb 23) Tobougg (IRE) 125 – Polly Golightly 84 58 (Weldnaas (USA) 112) [2007 6m 7m 8.1s p7.1g⁵ p8.6g² p8.6g⁵ p8.6g⁶ Dec 4] lengthy, good-topped filly: third foal: half-sister to 2004 2-y-o 5f winner Piper Lily (by Piccolo): dam 5f winner, including at 2 yrs: modest maiden: runner-up at Wolverhampton (hung): stays 8.6f: form only on polytrack. *M. Blanshard*

MISS BRONTE 2 b.f. (Apr 9) Ishiguru (USA) 114 – Gemtastic 70 (Tagula (IRE) 116) 58 [2007 p5.1g⁴ 5g Aug 16] second foal: sister to 3-y-o Metal Guru: dam 5f (at 2 yrs)/6f winner: modest maiden: much better run when fourth at Wolverhampton: likely to prove best at 5f/6f. *R. Hollinshead*

MISS BRUSH 4 b.f. Foxhound (USA) 103 – Tattinger 85 (Prince Sabo 123) [2007 60: p6g Dec 30] useful-looking filly: fair winner at 2 yrs: lightly raced since, well held in claimer sole 4-y-o outing: should stay 6f: acts on polytrack and good to soft going. *J. R. Fanshawe*

MISS CAPRICORN 3 b.f. Forzando 122 – Miss Flirtatious 75 (Piccolo 121) [2007 –: 41 6.1m 5g⁶ 5d Jun 23] good-bodied filly: poor maiden: tried tongue tied. *K. A. Ryan*

MISS CRUISECONTROL 2 b.f. (Jan 28) Hernando (FR) 127 – Wenda (IRE) 93 – (Priolo (USA) 121) [2007 p7g 7g 8.1d Aug 16] 7,500F: rather unfurnished filly: fourth foal: half-sister to a winner in Greece by Zilzal: dam, 2-y-o 6f winner (stayed 11.5f), sister to useful Irish 1½m performer Carnelly: no show in maidens: should be suited by middle distances. *J. R. Best*

MISS DAAWE 3 b.f. Daawe (USA) 103 – Feiticeira (USA) 79 (Deposit Ticket (USA)) 62 [2007 –: 6m⁶ 6f⁶ 8.2g 5v⁵ 6g⁵ 5d³ 5.9f⁴ 5g³ 5m³ 5m³ 6g² 5g⁴ Oct 3] close-coupled, workmanlike filly: modest maiden handicapper: left S. Parr after third start: may prove best at 5f/6f: acts on any going. *B. Ellison*

MISS DEEDS (IRE) 2 b.f. (Mar 28) Invincible Spirit (IRE) 121 – Aseelah 72 (Nash- – wan (USA) 135) [2007 p7g 5d 6d 5.4m Sep 9] 25,000Y, 44,000 2-y-o: good-topped filly: first foal: dam, maiden (best effort at 7f), half-sister to smart French performer up to 1¼m Chaibia out of close relative of Erhaab: no form. *N. P. Littmoden*

MISS DELILA (USA) 2 b. or br.f. (Feb 21) Malibu Moon (USA) – Staraway (USA) – (Star de Naskra (USA)) [2007 7g 7m Aug 4] fourth live foal: half-sister to 3-y-o Sander Camillo and winner in US by King of Kings: dam Canadian 6f to 9f winner: well held in maidens at Newmarket. *K. A. Ryan*

MISS EMMA MAY (IRE) 2 b.f. (Mar 30) Hawk Wing (USA) 136 – For Example 84 (USA) 66 (Northern Baby (CAN) 127) [2007 6g⁴ 5.1m² 6g 7m⁴ 7s⁴ 8m 7.1g² 8d* Oct 23] 180,000Y, 220,000Y: big, close-coupled filly: half-sister to several winners, including smart 1m (at 2 yrs) to 1½m winner Forbearing (by Bering) and useful 1½m winner Viz (by Darshaan): dam, Irish maiden (stayed 1¼m), closely related to dams of Zilzal and

Polish Precedent: fairly useful form: improvement in visor final 2 starts, second to Love of Dubai in maiden at Warwick prior to winning similar event at Yarmouth by 3 lengths despite pulling hard early: will stay 1¼m: acts on soft and good to firm going: edgy sort. *D. R. C. Elsworth*

MISS FIREFLY 2 b.f. (Mar 13) Compton Place 125 – Popocatepetl (FR) 66 (Nashwan (USA) 135) [2007 5m³ 6m² 5s⁶ 7g⁴ 7m 5.7f⁵ 5.5m³ 6.5m Sep 25] 27,000Y: leggy filly: fluent mover: second foal: half-sister to 3-y-o Guacamole: dam maiden (stayed 1¾m): fair maiden: stays 7f: acts on firm going: ungenuine. *M. R. Channon* — 73 §

MISS GIBRALTAR 3 b.f. Rock of Gibraltar (IRE) 133 – Photogenic 93 (Midyan (USA) 124) [2007 7g Jun 12] fifth foal: half-sister to 5-y-o Gifted Musician: dam, Irish 2-y-o 6f/7f winner, out of half-sister to Bella Colora (dam of Stagecraft) and Colorspin (dam of Kayf Tara and Opera House): 12/1, well beaten in maiden at Salisbury, soon ridden along but not knocked about: sold 3,000 gns in December. *L. M. Cumani* —

MISS GLORY BE 9 b.m. Glory of Dancer 121 – Miss Blondie (USA) (Stop The Music (USA)) [2007 –, a62: p9.5g p8.6g⁶ 12.1m 10.9g Oct 2] just poor form at best in 2007, leaving Ernst Oertel after second start: effective at 1m to 11f: acts on all-weather, firm and good to soft going: tried visored (tailed off), wears cheekpieces nowadays: has bled. *C. J. Down* — a42

MISS GORICA (IRE) 3 b.f. Mull of Kintyre (USA) 114 – Allegorica (IRE) (Alzao (USA) 117) [2007 40: 7.5m 7.5m³ 7m* 8g² 7m* 8m 7g³ 8g³ 7m³ p7g² p7g⁴ p7g Nov 9] sturdy, compact filly: useful handicapper: vastly improved, and won at Gowran and Leopardstown in May: well below form at Royal Ascot sixth start: good efforts in frame at Dundalk tenth/eleventh outings, ½-length second to Dynamo Dancer on first occasion: effective at 7f, barely at 1m: acts on polytrack and good to firm going: travels strongly close up. *Ms Joanna Morgan, Ireland* — 100

MISS HABERSHON 3 b.f. Baryshnikov (AUS) – Mighty Squaw 58 (Indian Ridge 123) [2007 8.1d⁴ 9.9m⁶ 10m 10.2d 10g⁶ Oct 8] lengthy filly: fifth foal: dam, maiden who stayed 1½m, half-sister to smart US miler Mighty Forum: fair form on debut: failed to progress after, in seller final start. *A. King* — 67 d

MISS HAVISHAM (IRE) 3 b.f. Josr Algarhoud (IRE) 118 – Agony Aunt 81 (Formidable (USA) 125) [2007 –: 11g 12.4m 9.3g⁴ 10.1d* 9.1d 11.1m* 10.1g p12.2g 11.1s Sep 24] big, strong filly: modest handicapper: won at Yarmouth (seller) in June and Hamilton in August: stays 11f: acts on good to firm and good to soft going. *J. R. Weymes* — 58

MISS HIGHJINKS (USA) 4 ch.f. Stravinsky (USA) 133 – Ready For Action (USA) (Riverman (USA) 131) [2007 92: a7.5g Jan 3] strong filly: fairly useful performer: well held sole 4-y-o start: stays 1m, seemingly not 1¼m: acts on polytrack, raced only on going softer than good on turf. *E. J. O'Neill* —

MISS HOLDERNESS 2 ch.f. (Apr 4) Millkom 124 – Miles (Selkirk (USA) 129) [2007 7.5g 9f 7.5d Sep 25] 1,000Y: good-topped filly: third foal: dam ran twice: tailed off in maidens. *J. O'Reilly* —

MISS HOLLY 8 b.m. Makbul 104 – Seraphim (FR) 48 (Lashkari 128) [2007 63: f12g² f16g* f16g⁴ f16s³ f14g Feb 28] fair handicapper: won at Southwell in January: stays 2m: acts on fibresand, good to firm and good to soft ground. *D. Carroll* — 71

MISS HOOLIE 3 b.f. Danehill Dancer (IRE) 117 – Silky Dawn (IRE) 100 (Night Shift (USA)) [2007 –p: p7.1g⁶ f6g Dec 27] poor form in 3 maidens. *W. G. M. Turner* — 32

MISSIE BAILEYS 5 ch.m. Mister Baileys 123 – Jilly Woo 60 (Environment Friend 128) [2007 66: p12g³ p12.2g 11.5m² p12g⁵ p13.9g⁶ p10g⁶ 10s³ 11.6m* p12g⁴ p13g⁶ 11.9m² 12.1m p10g⁵ p12g 10g p12g⁵ p12m³ Dec 8] close-coupled mare: modest performer: won claimer at Windsor in June: best at 1¼m/1½m: acts on polytrack, firm and soft going: wears headgear. *Mrs L. J. Mongan* — 63

MISS IMPERIOUS 4 b.f. Imperial Ballet (IRE) 110 – Birthday Belle 70 (Lycius (USA) 124) [2007 50: p7.1g a6g⁶ 5.8g² a8g⁴ 6.5g* 8g* a8g² 11d a8.6g⁴ Oct 20] quite good-topped filly: modest performer: left B. Smart after reappearance: won handicaps at Copenhagen and Ovrevoll in August: stays 1m: acts on fibresand/dirt, soft and good to firm going. *L. Herlin, Sweden* — ?

MISS INVINCIBLE 3 b.f. Invincible Spirit (IRE) 121 – Zagaleta 81 (Sri Pekan (USA) 117) [2007 p7g p8g⁶ 10m p8g⁴ 10.1m³ p13.9g Sep 27] 90,000Y: second foal: half-sister to Irish 9f winner Sweet Petite (by Mark of Esteem): dam, 1¼m winner, out of sister to high-class performer up to 1¼m Bold Arrangement: modest maiden: claimed from — 51

A. Jarvis £12,000 after fifth start: stays 1¼m: raced only on polytrack and good to firm going: tried visored. *Mrs A. L. M. King*

MISSION CONTROL (IRE) 2 ch.c. (Jan 23) Dubai Destination (USA) 127 – Stage Manner 104 (In The Wings 128) [2007 p7.1g p8.6g* Dec 31] fair form: left M. Johnston 8,000 gns, won seller at Wolverhampton in December (still looked green): will be suited by 1¼m. *J. R. Boyle*   **66 +**

MISSIONER (USA) 2 b.c. (Jan 29) Rahy (USA) 115 – Magic Mission 117 (Machiavellian (USA) 123) [2007 7d³ 7m³ Aug 4] lengthy colt: has a quick action: first foal: dam 1m (US Grade 3 event) to 9f (in France) winner: fairly useful form when third in maidens at Ascot (1¼ lengths behind City Leader) and Goodwood (beaten length by Latin Lad): will be suited by 1m/1¼m: sure to improve and win races. *M. Johnston*   **85 p**

MISSION IMPOSSIBLE 2 b. or gr.g. (Apr 17) Kyllachy 129 – Eastern Lyric 93 (Petong 126) [2007 5m² 6g⁴ 6m³ 7d⁵ 6m 7g p5.1g² p6g* f6d⁴ Dec 21] tall gelding: fair performer: won maiden at Wolverhampton in December: respectable fourth in nursery at Southwell final start: best at 5f/6f: acts on all-weather and good to firm going: often races prominently. *P. C. Haslam*   **74**

MISSION MAN 6 b.g. Revoque (IRE) 122 – Opopmil (IRE) 68 (Pips Pride 117) [2007 p9.5g p7.1g⁶ f7g Feb 15] big, strong gelding: fairly useful at best: missed 2005/6: just modest form at 6 yrs: stayed 1m: acted on soft and good to firm ground (probably on polytrack): dead. *M. G. Rimell*   **59**

MISSION TO MARS 8 b.g. Muhtarram (USA) 125 – Ideal Candidate 80 (Celestial Storm (USA) 132) [2007 p12g⁶ p12g p12g p13.9g Mar 10] quite good-topped gelding: useful performer in 2004: unraced on Flat in 2005/06: left P. Hedger, little impact in handicaps at 8 yrs: stayed 1½m: acted on all-weather and good to firm ground: dead. *P. G. Murphy*   **–**

MISS IPPOLITA 3 b.f. Diktat 126 – Isabella d'Este (IRE) 65 (Irish River (FR) 131) [2007 73: 8g 6s⁴ p6g⁶ 6d² 6s² 5m 6m 6g⁶ Nov 2] tall, lengthy filly: fairly useful performer: good second in handicaps at Yarmouth and Warwick: raced mainly at 6f: acts on soft going (well held on good to firm). *J. R. Jenkins*   **84**

MISSIT (IRE) 2 b.f. (Jan 21) Orpen (USA) 116 – High Spot 73 (Shirley Heights 130) [2007 5m² 6m* 6m⁵ 7d² 7d² Oct 27] 35,000Y: tall, good-topped filly: third foal: half-sister to Irish 2005 2-y-o 7f winner Night Sphere (by Night Shift): dam, maiden (should have stayed 1½m), half-sister to useful performer up to 1¾m Allergy: useful form: won maiden at Lingfield in September: continued progress, 5¼ lengths fifth to Natagora in Cheveley Park Stakes at Newmarket and second in Rockfel Stakes there (beaten a neck by Kitty Matcham) and listed race at Newbury (½ length behind Lady Deauville): will stay 1m: has joined B. Cecil in USA: has plenty of scope, and should do better still at 3 yrs. *M. R. Channon*   **101 p**

MISS JENNY (IRE) 3 b.f. Desert Prince (IRE) 130 – Please Believe Me 93 (Try My Best (USA) 130) [2007 83: 8.2m 7m p7.1g Aug 13] compact filly: type to carry condition: handicapper: well held at 3 yrs: blinkered final outing: sold 1,500 gns. *B. J. Meehan*   **–**

MISS JOLYON (USA) 2 b.f. (Feb 1) Johannesburg (USA) 127 – Konvincha (USA) (Cormorant (USA)) [2007 6m 7m⁴ p7g² 8.3d Oct 15] $31,000Y, resold €85,000Y: sturdy filly: eighth foal: half-sister to smart 1m/1¼m (including in US) winner Askham (by El Gran Senor) and fairly useful 1½m winner Schapiro (by Nureyev): dam, US winner up to 9f, half-sister to US Grade 2 7f winner Lottsa Talc: fair maiden: runner-up at Kempton: should stay 1m. *M. A. Jarvis*   **69**

MISS KIN (IRE) 2 b.f. (Apr 15) Kris Kin (USA) 126 – Pipewell (IRE) 84 (Lake Coniston (IRE) 131) [2007 5m 5g Apr 28] €9,000Y: leggy filly: third foal: half-sister to 5-y-o Piper General: dam Irish 6f winner: well held in sprint maidens. *T. J. Pitt*   **–**

MISS LADYBIRD (USA) 6 b. or br.m. Labeeb 124 – Bird Dance (USA) (Storm Bird (CAN) 134) [2007 p8.6g p10g Mar 5] quite good-topped mare: lightly raced and no recent form. *T. J. Etherington*   **–**

MISS LIGHTNING 4 b.f. Mujahid (USA) 125 – Salu 65 (Ardross 134) [2007 8m f8g 9.8m⁵ 16d Jun 22] fifth foal: half-sister to fairly useful 8.5f to 2m winner Clarinch Claymore (by Sabrehill) and 1¼m to 1½m winner Merryvale Man (by Rudimentary): dam 1½m to 2m winner: little form. *R. Bastiman*   **–**

MISS LOVAT 4 b.f. Wizard King 122 – Cantina 103 (Tina's Pet 121) [2007 p7.1g 6g p7.1g 9.2g 12m⁶ 10f⁶ 9.8m⁵ 10f Sep 17] rather leggy filly: poor performer nowadays: seemingly stays 1¼m: acts on polytrack and good to firm going: tried in headgear/tongue tie. *W. M. Brisbourne*   **49**

VC Bet Challenge Stakes, Newmarket—the progressive Miss Lucifer justifies the decision to supplement;
Al Qasi takes second off Toylsome (rail)

MISS LUCIFER (FR) 3 b.f. Noverre (USA) 125 – Devil's Imp (IRE) 84 (Cadeaux **119**
Genereux 131) [2007 86p: 7m² 7.1m² 7g⁴ 7m² 7g² 7m² 7d* 7d* Oct 20] good-topped
filly: smart performer: progressive form, runner-up 5 times in handicaps, including at
Salisbury (to Perfect Star) and Doncaster (short head behind Danehillsundance) on last
2 occasions prior to winning listed race at Ascot (by ¾ length from Diamond Diva) in
September and VC Bet Challenge Stakes at Newmarket (beat Al Qasi by 1¼ lengths,
quickening to lead over 1f out, despite drifting left) in October: stays 7f: acts on good to
firm and good to soft going: has joined Godolphin. *B. W. Hills*

MISS MARVELLOUS (USA) 3 ch.f. Diesis 133 – Sue Warner (USA) (Forli (ARG)) **78 +**
[2007 –p: 8.2m 10.1d* 10.2s⁶ 9.7m⁴ Sep 2] angular filly: fair form: won maiden at Yarmouth in July: stays 1¼m: acts on good to firm and good to soft going. *J. R. Fanshawe*

MISS MONICA (IRE) 6 ch.m. Grand Lodge (USA) 125 – Bea's Ruby (IRE) 86 (Fairy **56**
King (USA)) [2007 54: p9.5g p10g² p11g³ p10g⁵ Mar 9] rather sparely-made mare:
modest performer: stays 11f: acts on polytrack, firm and good to soft going. *P. W. Hiatt*

MISS MOZART 2 b.f. (Mar 2) Bahamian Bounty 116 – Papillon de Bronze (IRE) **50**
(Marju (IRE) 127) [2007 6d 6m Sep 4] good-topped filly: first foal: dam unraced sister to
useful Hong Kong 6f to 1m winner Northern Gold Ball: looked awkward in maidens at
Windsor and Goodwood (modest form). *H. Morrison*

MISS MUJAHID TIMES 4 b.f. Mujahid (USA) 125 – Stealthy Times 80 (Timeless **59 d**
Times (USA) 99) [2007 59: p5.1g² 6g p5.1g 5m 5s 7.1m p6g² p6g⁴ p6g p7.1g Nov 1]
modest performer: stays easy 6f: acts on all-weather, best turf efforts on good going:
wears headgear. *A. D. Brown*

MISS MUJANNA 2 b.f. (Mar 23) Mujahid (USA) 125 – Robanna 60 (Robellino **71**
(USA) 127) [2007 p6g³ p7g² p7g² p7g² Dec 29] third foal: half-sister to fairly useful 6f (at
2 yrs)/7f winner Aastral Magic (by Magic Ring): dam, maiden (stayed 1¾m), half-sister
to Jersey Stakes winner Lots of Magic: fair maiden: placed all 3 starts: will stay 1m: raced
only on polytrack. *J. Akehurst*

MISS ODD SOX 4 ch.f. Primo Valentino (IRE) 116 – Dam Certain (IRE) 61 (Damister **56**
(USA) 123) [2007 62: p9.5g⁶ Mar 27] modest maiden: stays 9.5f: raced only on polytrack. *W. M. Brisbourne*

MISS OKALOOSA 2 b.f. (Mar 29) Hawk Wing (USA) 136 – Shalimar (IRE) 95 **59**
(Indian Ridge 123) [2007 p8g 8.1s p7m Nov 1] 23,000Y: big, useful-looking filly: fourth
foal: dam, out of useful half-sister to very smart 1½m/1¾m performer
Gamut: behind in maidens, refusing to settle, though showed ability at Lingfield final
start. *D. M. Simcock*

MISS OLIVIA 2 ch.f. (May 19) Dr Fong (USA) 128 – Beleaguer 88 (Rainbow Quest **51**
(USA) 134) [2007 7m 5m 5.4m⁶ Sep 9] €5,000Y: close-coupled filly: third foal:
half-sister to fairly useful French 7f winner Vulnerable (by Hector Protector): dam, 1m
winner, sister to Racing Post Trophy winner/St Leger runner-up Armiger: modest form in
maidens, inadequate test after debut: should be suited by 1m. *P. W. Chapple-Hyam*

MISSOULA (IRE) 4 b.f. Kalanisi (IRE) 132 – Medway (IRE) 60 (Shernazar 131) **90**
[2007 79: 10.5g 12g 11.5d 12f⁶ 16.4m² 15.9m* 17.2d⁴ 18d* Oct 13] leggy, useful-looking
filly: fairly useful handicapper: won at Chester in September and York in October: stays

2¼m: acts on good to firm and good to soft going: sold 110,000 gns, joined Miss Suzy Smith. *M. H. Tompkins*

MISSOURI (USA) 4 b.g. Gulch (USA) – Coco (USA) 105 (Storm Bird (CAN) 134) [2007 60: p11g 10.2m 12m 10.1m 13g Sep 3] rather leggy gelding: no longer of any account. *M. A. Barnes* —

MISS PERCY 3 b.f. Mark of Esteem (IRE) 137 – Anabaa's Music (Anabaa (USA) 130) [2007 64p: 8.5g 12s 8d⁵ 10.5m⁶ 10.3m⁴ 8.3g Sep 3] sturdy filly: modest maiden handicapper: stays 1m: acts on soft going: tried in cheekpieces: sold 2,200 gns. *R. A. Fahey* — **63**

MISS PHOEBE (IRE) 2 b.f. (Mar 10) Catcher In The Rye (IRE) 115 – Stroke of Six (IRE) 84 (Woodborough (USA) 112) [2007 6d p7m⁵ p7.1g p7g³ p10g⁶ p7.1d* Dec 28] second foal: dam, 6f (at 2 yrs) and 1m winner, half-sister to smart 1¼m performer Revelation: dam won maiden at Wolverhampton final start: will stay 1m: raced only on polytrack after debut. *S. Kirk* — **73**

MISS POLAND 3 b.f. Polish Precedent (USA) 131 – Robellino Miss (USA) (Robellino (USA) 127) [2007 9g May 20] closely related to useful 1998 2-y-o 6f winner Chief Rebel (by Chief's Crown) and half-sister to several winners, including useful 7f/1m winner Miss Ivanhoe (by Selkirk) and 1999 2-y-o 7f winner Decision Maid (by Diesis): dam won up to 9f in USA: 50/1, last in maiden at Ripon: sold 7,500 gns in July. *J. G. Given* —

MISS POPPY 2 b.f. (Apr 24) Averti (IRE) 117 – Pretty Poppy 67 (Song 132) [2007 6m 5.7d³ p6g⁶ p5.1g Oct 22] 65,000Y: smallish filly: sister to 3-y-o Pretty Miss and half-sister to numerous winners, notably high-class 5f performer Kyllachy (by Pivotal): dam 2-y-o 5f winner: fair maiden: should prove best at 5f/6f: acts on polytrack and good to soft going. *P. R. Chamings* — **68**

MISS PORCIA 6 ch.m. Inchinor 119 – Krista 73 (Kris 135) [2007 61: 10.2s³ 7s⁶ p9.5g⁴ 11.6d⁴ 8m² 8.3m p10g p10g Oct 10] tall, lengthy mare: modest performer: stays 11.6f, effective at shorter: acts on polytrack and any turf going: tried tongue tied/visored/in cheekpieces. *P. A. Blockley* — **57**

MISS REDACTIVE 4 b.f. Whittingham (IRE) 104 – Gold And Blue (IRE) (Bluebird (USA) 125) [2007 46: p8g p5.1g f7g p7g⁴ p6g p7f p8.6g Feb 26] close-coupled filly: poor maiden: stays 7f: acts on polytrack and good to firm ground: tried visored. *M. D. I. Usher* — **46**

MISS ROCHESTER (IRE) 2 b.f. (Mar 5) Montjeu (IRE) 137 – Pilgrim's Way (USA) 84 (Gone West (USA)) [2007 7s Aug 24] €320,000Y: good-topped, quite attractive filly: fourth foal: half-sister to UAE 1¼m winner Liwa (by Mozart): dam, 7f/1m winner, sister to smart 6f and 1m winner Mugharreb out of very smart miler Marling: 7/1, mid-division in maiden at Newmarket won by Kotsi, not knocked about: will be suited by 1m+: sure to improve. *Sir Michael Stoute* — **58 p**

MISS SAAFEND PLAZA (IRE) 3 b.f. Danetime (IRE) 121 – Coup de Coeur (IRE) (Kahyasi 130) [2007 83: p10g² p8g⁵ p10g² p10g³ 11.6m 10m⁵ 10s Jun 25] lengthy, good-topped filly: fair maiden: stays easy 1¼m: acts on polytrack and good to firm going: tried blinkered: joined G. L. Moore, and poor form in juvenile hurdles, then sold 1,500 gns in November. *R. Hannon* — **74**

MISS SILVER SPURS 3 gr.f. Mujahid (USA) 125 – Wakeful Night (FR) (Linamix (FR) 127) [2007 –: p8g 10.9s 8.1s Jul 13] close-coupled filly: little form: visored last 2 starts. *M. D. I. Usher* —

MISS SKYCAT (USA) 2 gr. or ro.f. (May 7) Tale of The Cat (USA) 113 – Gigi's Skyflyer (USA) (Skywalker (USA)) [2007 5.9d 7f 6f Sep 17] $62,000Y: first foal: dam US 6f to 7.5f winner: well held in maidens: sold 1,600 gns, sent to Denmark. *T. D. Barron* —

MISS SOLO 2 b. or br.f. (Jan 25) Intikhab (USA) 135 – American Rouge (IRE) (Grand Lodge (USA) 125) [2007 6v⁴ 6s p7g⁵ p10g Nov 19] 29,000Y: second foal: dam unraced half-sister to useful 2-y-o 7f winner Chez Cherie: modest maiden: best efforts at 6f on turf (raced on soft/heavy going). *P. C. Haslam* — **58**

MISS SPIRIT (IRE) 4 b.f. King Charlemagne (USA) 120 – Joyfullness (USA) (Dixieland Band (USA)) [2007 –: 5s 6g 5.8f⁴ 5m⁶ 5d 5g³ 5d⁴ p6g Oct 18] modest maiden: ran poorly in claimer at Wolverhampton final start: stays 6f: acts on firm and soft going. *Michael Mulvany, Ireland* — **59**

MISS ST ALBANS 6 b.m. Robellino (USA) 127 – Alieria (IRE) (Lomond (USA) 128) [2007 p8.6g Nov 17] no sign of ability. *G. C. H. Chung* —

MISS SUDBROOK (IRE) 5 ch.m. Daggers Drawn (USA) – Missed Opportunity (IRE) (Exhibitioner 111) [2007 –: p10g³ p11g p10g p8g⁶ p8g 10.2f p8.6g Apr 16] poor maiden: stays 1¼m: acts on polytrack: tried visored/tongue tied. *A. W. Carroll* — **49**

MISS SUNSHINE 2 b.f. (Mar 9) Piccolo 121 – Rhinefield Beauty (IRE) 52 (Shalford **39** (IRE) 124§) [2007 6g 6d 6d 5f 6g Oct 19] fifth foal: half-sister to 2 winners, including 4-y-o Rothesay Dancer: dam sprint maiden: poor maiden. *J. S. Goldie*

MISS SURE BOND (IRE) 4 ch.f. Danehill Dancer (IRE) 117 – Desert Rose (Green **60** Desert (USA) 127) [2007 67: 7m 6v⁶ 9.9m⁴ 11.1g⁶ p9.5g³ p8.6g 12g p9.5g Nov 22] tall, lengthy filly: modest maiden: stays 1¼m: acts on polytrack and good to firm going: sometimes wears headgear: inconsistent. *G. R. Oldroyd*

MISS TABOO (IRE) 3 b.f. Tobougg (IRE) 125 – Miss Croisette 69 (Hernando (FR) **56** 127) [2007 –: 6f³ 6m² 6m⁴ 6d² 6g 7s² 7m² 6m 7g⁴ p7g Oct 4] smallish filly: modest maiden: stays 7f: acts on soft and good to firm ground: tried in cheekpieces. *P. T. Midgley*

MISS TILEN 2 ch.f. (Apr 1) Tipsy Creek (USA) 115 – Ashleen (Chilibang 120) [2007 **44** 5d 5m⁶ 5m² 6g⁶ 6m⁵ Jun 3] close-coupled filly: fourth foal: dam maiden: poor maiden: fell on debut: runner-up in seller: effective at 5f/6f. *V. Smith*

MISSUS MOLLY BROWN 3 b.f. Mind Games 121 – Prim N Proper (Tragic Role **53** (USA)) [2007 p7.1g⁵ f6g⁶ p6g f7g³ 7m⁶ 6d³ 5.9m² 5d 6v⁴ 5.9f* 5.9g 7g⁶ 6s Oct 4] 2,000Y: third foal: sister to 5-y-o Primarily: dam ran 3 times: modest handicapper: won at Carlisle in August: stays 7f: acts on fibresand and any turf going: tried blinkered/in cheekpieces. *R. A. Fahey*

MISS VERSATILE (IRE) 2 b.f. (Apr 20) Alhaarth (IRE) 126 – Liberi Versi (IRE) **94** (Last Tycoon 131) [2007 5m² 6m³ 6g 5d³ p5.5f 6.5f³ 8f⁵ Nov 24] €10,000Y: lengthy filly: fourth foal: half-sister to winner in Spain by Soviet Star: dam, Italian 7.5f winner, half-sister to very smart performer up to 1m Missed Flight: fairly useful maiden: 1½ lengths third to Western Art in listed race at Sandown on fourth start, then left J. S. Moore: ran well when fifth to Sea Chanter in Grade 3 Miesque Stakes at Hollywood final outing: stays 1m: acts on firm and good to soft going: blinkered sixth appearance. *B. D. A. Cecil, USA*

MISSVINSKI (USA) 3 b.f. Stravinsky (USA) 133 – Miss U Fran (USA) (Brocco **116** (USA) 124) [2007 a6.5g* 8g² 8d⁵ 8d² 9f 8f Oct 14] $8,000F, 36,000Y: close-coupled filly: second foal: half-sister to French 2005 2-y-o 6f winner Le Retour (by Tale of The Cat): dam, ran twice in US, out of sister to top-class 1½m performer Cacoethes: smart performer: improved in 2007, winning listed race at Deauville in March: runner-up after to Darjina in Prix de la Grotte at Longchamp (beaten short neck) and Prix d'Astarte at Deauville (best effort when going down by ½ length): below form when fifth to Indian Ink in Coronation Stakes at Royal Ascot in between and in Garden City Stakes at Belmont (left J-C. Rouget, France subsequently) and non-graded handicap at Santa Anita last 2 starts: stays 1m: acts on all-weather and soft ground. *J. C. Canani, USA*

MISS WEDGE 4 b.f. Fraam 114 – Tough Nell (IRE) 61 (Archway (IRE) 115) [2007 64: **51** 7.1m⁶ p7g May 23] tall, angular filly: modest maiden: stays 8.5f: acts on polytrack and firm ground: visored final 3-y-o start: races prominently: edged left on reappearance: signs of temperament. *Tom Dascombe*

MISS WILLOUGHBY 2 b.f. (Mar 28) First Trump 118 – Jeanette Romee 61 (Victory **49 d** Note (USA) 120) [2007 5m³ 5f⁵ 5m⁶ f5g⁶ 5.2g⁴ p5.1g³ 7s* 7d³ p7.1g³ 6d³ 5.2m⁴ p7.1g 6f p6m⁵ p6g 6g 8g 8.2g Oct 31] leggy, close-coupled filly: first foal: dam sprint maiden: poor performer: raced 18 times, mainly in sellers, winning at Yarmouth in June: below form after tenth start: stays 7f: acts on polytrack and soft going. *J. Ryan*

MISS WOLF 7 b.m. Wolfhound (USA) 126 – Jussoli (Don 128) [2007 p12.2g p9.5g – p12.2g 6m 9g p6g Oct 5] little sign of ability. *G. H. Jones*

MISTA ROSSA 2 br.c. (Mar 10) Red Ransom (USA) – Cloud Hill (Danehill (USA) **65 p** 126) [2007 8d 8d 8g Oct 24] 32,000Y: good-bodied colt: second foal: half-brother to winner in Greece by Inchinor: dam unraced half-sister to St Leger runner-up High And Low and dam of smart French miler American Post: backward, steady progress in maidens in October, fair form at Bath (seventh to Colony) final start: raced only at 1m, not sure to stay much further: sort to do better in 3-y-o handicaps. *H. Morrison*

MISTBLACK 7 b.m. Wizard King 122 – Dear Heart (Blakeney 126) [2007 10.3m – Aug 31] no form. *B. P. J. Baugh*

MISTER ALWAYS 3 b.g. Titus Livius (FR) 115 – Pieta (IRE) 52 (Perugino (USA) **59** 84) [2007 48: p7g p6g³ p10g 7.5m p5.1g⁴ p6g³ p7m f6d⁴ p7.1d* Dec 27] modest handicapper: left Ms J. Doyle after second start, B. Baugh after fifth and K. McAuliffe after sixth: won at Wolverhampton in December: stays 7f: acts on all-weather and firm ground: tried in cheekpieces/blinkers/tongue tie: looks hard ride: said to have had breathing problem first outing at 3 yrs. *I. W. McInnes*

MISTER ARJAY (USA) 7 b.g. Mister Baileys 123 – Crystal Stepper (USA) (Fred **81** Astaire (USA)) [2007 73: 12m* 14m⁴ 14g⁴ 16.2m⁴ 14.1m* 14g² p13.9g 15.8m 16.2g³ **a64 +** 16.1m⁶ 16.4m* 14m 14.6g Oct 26] smallish, good-bodied gelding: fairly useful handicapper on turf, modest on all-weather: won at Catterick in April, Redcar in May and York in September: effective at 1½m to 2¼m: acts on polytrack, firm and soft going: tried blinkered: has hung right: races up with pace. *B. Ellison*

MISTER BEANO (IRE) 2 b.c. (Feb 14) Mull of Kintyre (USA) 114 – Subtle Move **60** (USA) 60 (Known Fact (USA) 135) [2007 6m 6d 6d² p5.1g⁵ p6g p5g⁵ p7.1g² p7.1g² f8d⁵ p7.1d⁶ Dec 27] smallish colt: modest maiden: second 3 times in sellers: left V. Smith after eighth outing: stays 1m: acts on all-weather and good to soft going: tried in cheekpieces, best form in visor: signs of temperament. *R. J. Price*

MISTER BECKS (IRE) 4 b.g. Beckett (IRE) 116 – Cappuchino (IRE) 59 (Roi Dan- **35** zig (USA)) [2007 49: f7g f6g⁵ f6g f6g Feb 20] strong gelding: poor performer: stays 6f: acts on fibresand: races prominently: tried blinkered. *M. C. Chapman*

MISTER BENEDICTINE 4 b.g. Mister Baileys 123 – Cultural Role 95 (Night Shift **82** (USA)) [2007 82: p7g p8g⁶ 9m² 8m Aug 31] sturdy, quite attractive gelding: fairly useful handicapper: stays 9f: acts on polytrack and firm going: sometimes races freely: fairly useful hurdler, successful in September/October. *B. W. Duke*

MISTER BENJI 8 b.g. Catrail (USA) 123 – Katy-Q (IRE) 58 (Taufan (USA) 119) **–** [2007 –, a71: f8g⁵ f8g³ p7.1g⁸* p8.6g f7g p7.1g⁵ p7.1g p7.1g⁴ 7.6d p8.6g p8.6d⁵ p7.1d⁵ **a64** Dec 27] quite good-topped gelding: modest performer: won handicap at Wolverhampton in February: stays 8.6f: acts on all-weather, little recent form on turf: sometimes wears headgear. *B. P. J. Baugh*

MISTER CAFNEX (IRE) 2 b.c. (Feb 3) Royal Applause 124 – Makelovelast (IRE) **–** 74 (Darshaan 133) [2007 5.1f p5g 5d 7d 8f 10m p8m p8.6d Dec 10] little form: tried in cheekpieces. *B. W. Duke*

MISTER CASTLEFIELD (IRE) 3 gr.g. Mujahid (USA) 125 – Woodland Garden **57 d** (Godswalk (USA) 130) [2007 62: 6.5d⁶ 10m 9g 10m⁵ 10m 11d⁴ 7g⁵ 7v 8v⁶ 12m 8m Oct 8] modest maiden at best: well held in claimer at Pontefract final start: stays 1¼m: acts on good to firm ground: tried blinkered. *Mrs A. M. O'Shea, Ireland*

MISTER CHRISTIE 2 b.g. (Feb 5) Auction House (USA) 120 – Dazzling Quintet 73 **65** (Superlative 118) [2007 6s 6g⁴ 5s* 6.1m p6g Nov 19] sturdy gelding: fair performer: won claimer at Beverley (left N. Tinkler £12,000) in July: best at 5f: acts on soft ground. *J. G. Given*

MISTER COMPLETELY (IRE) 6 b.g. Princely Heir (IRE) 111 – Blue Goose **73** (Belmez (USA) 131) [2007 65: p16g* p16g³ p16g 14.1g³ p13.9g* p16g² p16g 16.2s⁵ p13.9g 16m* p16g⁵ 15.4m² p16.5g* 16m⁶ 16.2m³ 16m² 15.9m⁵ 16.2g 16d² p13.9g³ 14.6g 16g f16d⁵ Dec 18] sturdy gelding: fair performer: won handicap at Kempton in January, seller at Wolverhampton in June and handicaps at Lingfield in July and Wolverhampton in August: stays easy 16.5f: acts on all-weather, firm and good to soft going: blinkered (raced freely) once, usually visored. *Ms J. S. Doyle*

MISTER ELEGANT 5 b.g. Fraam 114 – Risky Valentine 68 (Risk Me (FR) 127) **62** [2007 66: p7g⁴ p7.1g p7g f7g p6g p6g³ 6g⁵ 6m p6m² p6g³ p6g⁶ p6m p6g⁵ p6g⁴ f6d* f6d³ Dec 21] modest performer: won seller at Southwell in December: best at 6f/7f: acts on all-weather, good to firm and good to soft going: tried blinkered: clipped heels and unseated fifth start. *J. L. Spearing*

MISTER FIPS (IRE) 2 b.c. (Apr 13) Chevalier (IRE) 115 – Blue Holly (IRE) 83 **86** (Blues Traveller (IRE) 119) [2007 5s 5d⁶ 5m² 5m 6d 5d* 6m p5m³ Oct 6] 40,000 2-y-o: sturdy colt: second foal: half-brother to 3-y-o Suzieblue: dam sprinter: fairly useful performer: won maiden at Pontefract in August: good third in nursery at Kempton final start: should prove best kept to 5f/6f: acts on polytrack, good to firm and good to soft going. *Jane Chapple-Hyam*

MISTER FIZZBOMB (IRE) 4 b.g. Lend A Hand 124 – Crocus (IRE) 70 (Mister **72** Baileys 123) [2007 63: 14.1m 12d 10f² 12.1d* 12m 12g³ p9.5d⁴ Dec 7] smallish, sturdy gelding: fair performer: won seller at Beverley in September and apprentice claimer at Catterick in October: stays 1½m: acts on good to firm and good to soft going: blinkered/visored nowadays: often races prominently. *J. S. Wainwright*

MISTER HARDY 2 b.c. (Mar 16) Kyllachy 129 – Balladonia 103 (Primo Dominie **90** 121) [2007 5d⁵ 5m* 6g 7g³ 6g⁵ 6.5m 6g⁵ 6d Oct 13] 30,000Y: smallish, close-coupled colt: third foal: half-brother to 6f (at 2 yrs) to 1m (in Hong Kong) winner Zaal (by Alhaarth): dam 9f winner: fairly useful performer: won minor events at Newcastle in

March and April: held form well in listed/sales races, including fifth of 23 to Dubai Dynamo in Two-Year-Old Trophy at Redcar penultimate start: barely stays 7f: untried on extremes of going: tough. *R. A. Fahey*

MISTER INCREDIBLE 4 b.g. Wizard King 122 – Judiam 74 (Primo Dominie 121) **58** [2007 –, a68: p7g p7.1g f6g³ f7g* f6g* p6g f6g⁵ f6g² f6g³ 6.1g 6m⁵ 5s* 6v⁴ 5.1g 5d Jul 13] lengthy gelding: modest performer: won seller and claimer (claimed from V. Smith £5,000) at Southwell in February and minor event at Beverley in June: effective at 5f to 7f: acts on all-weather, heavy and good to firm ground: usually wears headgear: sometimes finds little. *J. M. Bradley*

MISTERISLAND (IRE) 2 b.c. (May 30) Spectrum (IRE) 126 – Carranita (IRE) 111 **55** (Anita's Prince 126) [2007 6.1m Aug 23] 11/1, eighth in maiden at Chester, outpaced. *J. A. Osborne*

MISTER JINGLES 4 ch.g. Desert Story (IRE) 115 – Fairy Free (Rousillon (USA) **68** 133) [2007 50: 5g f6g³ f7g³ p8.6g⁶ 8s 7.1m* 6.9f* 7.1s³ 7.5m* 8m 7.1g 7.2s Oct 26] lengthy, workmanlike gelding: fair performer: won claimer at Musselburgh (hung markedly left) in July and handicaps at Carlisle and Beverley in August: stays 7.5f: acts on all-weather, firm and soft ground: often wears headgear. *R. M. Whitaker*

MISTER MAQ 4 b.g. Namaqualand (USA) – Nordico Princess 71 (Nordico (USA)) **50 §** [2007 65, a53: f8g p8.6g³ p9.5g⁵ 12g 7m⁶ 9.3g 7.5v⁴ 8.5s 8m 12.1d Sep 25] leggy gelding: modest performer: stays 1¼m: acts on polytrack and any turf going: wears cheekpieces/blinkers: unreliable. *A. Crook*

MISTER MARMADUKE 6 b.g. Marju (IRE) 127 – Lalique (IRE) (Lahib (USA) **46 §** 129) [2007 41§: 6m 5m 5g 5s 5g 5d 7.1m 5g Oct 5] poor handicapper nowadays: tried tongue tied, often wears cheekpieces: temperamental. *D. A. Nolan*

MISTER MINTY (IRE) 5 b.g. Fasliyev (USA) 120 – Sorb Apple (IRE) 79 (Kris 135) **40** [2007 –: 7m 8.5m⁴ 9.9g 8.5m 7.5v Jul 6] very big, plain gelding: poor maiden: best effort at 8.5f on good to firm going, though flattered. *Mrs S. Lamyman*

MISTER NEW YORK (USA) 2 b.c. (Apr 10) Forest Wildcat (USA) 120 – Shebane **60** (USA) 108 (Alysheba (USA)) [2007 p6g p6g⁴ p7g⁴ Dec 29] £20,000 2-y-o: third foal: dam French 1½m winner (stayed 15f and later successful in US): modest form in maidens/minor event at Lingfield: will stay beyond 7f. *Noel T. Chance*

MISTER PETE (IRE) 4 b.g. Piccolo 121 – Whistfilly 49 (First Trump 118) [2007 –: **57** 9.8g⁴ 8s 10g⁴ 8g Nov 8] compact gelding: modest maiden: will be suited by 1½m+: raced only on good going or softer: won over hurdles in November. *W. Storey*

MISTER RIGHT (IRE) 6 ch.g. Barathea (IRE) 127 – Broken Spirit (IRE) (Slip **84** Anchor 136) [2007 84: p12g² 16m 16g 10d 12m* 12m⁴ Sep 15] lengthy, plain gelding: fairly useful handicapper: won apprentice event at Newbury in September: stays 1¾m: acts on polytrack and firm going: tried tongue tied: won over hurdles in September/October. *D. J. S. ffrench Davis*

MISTER TROUBRIDGE 5 ch.g. Mister Baileys 123 – So True 116 (So Blessed 130) **47** [2007 p13.9g⁵ Oct 8] strong gelding: poor maiden handicapper: stays 1¾m: acts on polytrack, good to firm and good to soft going: has shown signs of temperament. *J. A. Geake*

MISTRAL SKY 8 b.g. Hurricane Sky (AUS) – Dusk In Daytona 64 (Beveled (USA)) **73** [2007 73: p6g⁵ p6g² p7g p6g³ p6g p6g⁴ p6g³ p7.1g⁴ p6g p7.1g p6g² p6g³ p7.1g 6m⁴ p6g* 6m 6.1g⁴ p6g³ p7.1g⁵ p6g 6v³ p6g² 6d³ p6g p6g³ p6g* p6g p6g³ p7g⁵ Nov 19] angular gelding: fair performer: won claimer at Wolverhampton in June and handicap at Kempton in October: best at 6f/7f: acts on polytrack and any turf ground: wears headgear: tends to wander: usually races prominently. *Stef Liddiard*

MISTRESS BAILEY (IRE) 4 b.f. Mister Baileys 123 – Carson Dancer (USA) 52 **92** (Carson City (USA)) [2007 93: 8d f8g 7s² 9v 10s⁶ 10v Aug 12] sturdy filly: fairly useful performer: in-and-out form at 4 yrs, leaving D. Shaw after second start: stays 9f: acts on heavy ground: twice blinkered at 2 yrs: often held up. *Nicholas Cox, Ireland*

MISTRESS COOPER 2 b. or br.f. (Feb 1) Kyllachy 129 – Litewska (IRE) 86 (Muja- **71** dil (USA) 119) [2007 5g 5m⁵ 5m⁶ 6.1d⁶ 5.5m² 5.5m² 5g* Sep 19] 15,000Y: good-topped filly: first foal: dam 5f (including at 2 yrs)/6f winner: fair form: progress in nurseries, twice runner-up at Warwick before winning at Sandown: will prove best at 5f/6f: acts on good to firm going. *W. J. Musson*

MISTRESS EVA 2 b.f. (Feb 23) Diktat 126 – Foreign Mistress (Darshaan 133) [2007 **72** 7s* 7.1g⁶ Oct 2] 20,000Y: half-sister to several winners, including 1m winner Mistress Twister (by Pivotal) and 2001 2-y-o 6f winner Lihou Island (by Beveled): dam Italian maiden: fair form: won maiden at Folkestone in August: sixth in nursery at Warwick only other start: will be suited by 1m. *P. Winkworth*

MISTRESS GREELEY (USA) 2 ch.f. (Mar 26) Mr Greeley (USA) 122 – My Reem (USA) (Chief's Crown (USA)) [2007 6.1g* 7g⁶ Aug 25] $250,000: rangy filly: has scope: sixth foal: half-sister to US 1m/9f winner (also second in Grade 3 1m event) Willard Straight (by Lion Cavern): dam unraced half-sister to smart performer up to 1½m Knoosh: fairly useful form: won maiden at Nottingham (by ¾ length, with something to spare) in August: 11/2, still green and unsuited by steady pace (didn't settle) when 5 lengths sixth to Sense of Joy in Prestige Stakes at Goodwood: will be suited by 1m: very much type to progress at 3 yrs. *Sir Michael Stoute* **83 p**

MISTRESS RIO (IRE) 2 ch.f. (Mar 26) Captain Rio 122 – Bu Hagab (IRE) (Royal Academy (USA) 130) [2007 6.1g 6m Aug 18] €6,000Y: smallish filly: half-sister to several winners, including 5-y-o Take A Mile and 4-y-o Earl Kraul: dam unraced: no form in maidens. *J. G. Given* **–**

MISTY DANCER 8 gr.g. Vettori (IRE) 119 – Light Fantastic 66 (Deploy 131) [2007 11.6m⁴ 12g² 13.1m* 12d⁴ 11.9m³ 14g Sep 8] good-topped gelding: has reportedly had sinus problems: useful handicapper: won at Ayr in June: good third to Dansili Dancer in Old Newton Cup at Haydock after: should stay 1¾m: acts on good to firm and good to soft ground: sometimes races freely. *Miss Venetia Williams* **99**

MISU BOND (IRE) 4 b.c. Danehill Dancer (IRE) 117 – Hawala (IRE) 97 (Warning 136) [2007 114: 6v⁶ 7d⁴ 7g Jul 31] strong, good-topped colt: smart performer at best: below form at 4 yrs: stayed 1m: acted on soft and good to firm going: to stand at Hedgeholme Stud, Co Durham, fee £2,500. *B. Smart* **101**

MISWADAH (IRE) 4 b.f. Machiavellian (USA) 123 – Khulan (USA) 103 (Bahri (USA) 125) [2007 62: p7g* 6m p6g⁵ 5d Jun 4] medium-sized filly: fair performer: won handicap at Lingfield in March: left D. Simcock and rejoined former trainer prior to final outing: best at 7f: acts on polytrack: tried visored. *Kevin F. O'Donnell, Ireland* **68**

MITANNI (USA) 4 b.g. Lear Fan (USA) 130 – Maria Dolores (USA) (Prized (USA)) [2007 71: 8.3m⁴ 10.1d⁴ 8g³ 7s Jul 28] workmanlike gelding: fair maiden handicapper: stays 1¼m: acts on polytrack, firm and good to soft ground: blinkered last 2 outings: sold 8,500 gns. *Mrs A. J. Perrett* **74**

MITH HILL 6 b.g. Daylami (IRE) 138 – Delirious Moment (IRE) 90 (Kris 135) [2007 16s⁴ 21.7s Jun 23] smallish gelding: fairly useful handicapper: stays 2m: acts on polytrack, probably on soft ground. *Ian Williams* **84**

MIXING 5 gr.g. Linamix (FR) 127 – Tuning 114 (Rainbow Quest (USA) 134) [2007 67d: 9g 9g 10d 11.9g* p11g⁴ p12g² p11g² p13g Dec 28] close-coupled gelding: modest performer: left W. Jarvis, won apprentice handicap at Brighton in October: stays 1½m: acts on polytrack and soft ground: tried blinkered: reluctant to race once at 4 yrs. *J. Akehurst* **62**

MIX N MATCH 3 b.c. Royal Applause 124 – South Wind 62 (Tina's Pet 121) [2007 6.1m 7.5m p6g 8.5s⁴ 8m⁶ 8.1d Aug 16] stocky colt: modest maiden: left W. Haggas 12,000 gns after fourth start: stays 8.5f: acts on soft ground. *R. M. Stronge* **58**

MIYASAKI (CHI) 5 br.h. Memo (CHI) 118 – Cantame Al Oido (CHI) (Yendaka (USA)) [2007 a8g* a8.7f 8s* 8g⁵ 8g 9m⁵ 10g 7m³ 5.5d 7d Oct 21] useful performer: successful 4 times in Chile in 2005, including in Group 1 event: won minor events at Ovrevoll in April and May: creditable 3½ lengths third to Hotel du Cap in listed race at Newbury eighth start, hanging left whilst rallying: well held last 2 starts: effective at 7f, has won up to 9.5f: acts on dirt, soft and good to firm going: often blinkered: has had tongue tied. *Rune Haugen, Norway* **101**

MIZOOKA 2 b.f. (Mar 26) Tobougg (IRE) 125 – Tetravella (IRE) (Groom Dancer (USA) 128) [2007 5d⁵ 6s⁵ 5.7s³ 7g* 8m² 8s Sep 22] 35,000Y: sturdy filly: fifth foal: half-sister to 3 winners, including 4-y-o Island Odyssey and 1½m winner Ellerslie Tom (by Octagonal): dam, French 1½m and 15f winner, half-sister to useful performer up to 1½m Torcello: fair form: won nursery at Salisbury in August: second to Siberian Tiger in similar event there next time: likely to stay 1½m: acts on good to firm going, probably on soft. *R. M. Beckett* **77**

MIZZLE (USA) 3 ch.f. Rahy (USA) 115 – Loving Claim (USA) 110 (Hansel (USA)) [2007 69: p9.5g⁴ p8.6g² p9.5g p8.6g Apr 16] modest maiden: should stay 1¼m: sold 26,000 gns. *M. Johnston* **60**

MOAYED 8 b.g. Selkirk (USA) 129 – Song of Years (IRE) 89 (Shareef Dancer (USA) 135) [2007 86, a105: p6g p7f p8.6g p7g⁵ p6g⁴ 7g p7g 7m 7m p7g p7g Sep 11] workman- **70 a95 d**

like gelding: useful handicapper at best, better on all-weather than turf: regressive form at 8 yrs: winner at 9f, best form at shorter nowadays (effective at 6f): acts on all-weather and any turf going: usually wears blinkers: effective with/without tongue tie: best held up, and tends to miss break. *N. P. Littmoden*

MOCHA JAVA 4 b.g. Bertolini (USA) 125 – Coffee Cream 87 (Common Grounds 118) – [2007 76, a–: p8g 8m 7f p7g Nov 14] good-topped gelding: fair performer at best: well held at 4 yrs, leaving Mrs L. Mongan after reappearance: stays 8.3f: acts on polytrack, firm and soft going: tried in cheekpieces. *B. G. Powell*

MO CHROI 4 ch.f. Observatory (USA) 131 – Away To Me (Exit To Nowhere (USA) – 122) [2007 –: p11g p8g p10g p12g Apr 1] compact, close-coupled filly: no solid form: tried in cheekpieces. *J. J. Bridger*

MODARAB 5 b.g. Barathea (IRE) 127 – Jathaabeh 99 (Nashwan (USA) 135) [2007 **64 d** 10.1m³ 11.9m 10.1m 13.1g⁶ 10d Sep 20] tall gelding: well held in bumpers/maiden hurdle: best effort on Flat when third in maiden at Haydock on debut. *Mrs L. B. Normile*

MODERN LOOK 2 b.f. (Mar 7) Zamindar (USA) 116 – Prophecy (IRE) 109 (Warning **109 p** 136) [2007 8g⁴ 7g* 7d* 7d* Nov 2] closely related to 6f winner Arabesque and 5f/6f winner (latter at 2 yrs) Threat (both useful, by Zafonic) and half-sister to 2 winners, including 3-y-o Rule of Life: dam, 2-y-o 5f/6f (latter including Cheveley Park Stakes) winner (stayed 1m), out of Lancashire Oaks winner Andaleeb: useful form: won maiden at Chantilly in September, minor event there in October and Prix Miesque at Maisons-Laffitte (always prominent, beat Lady Deauville 2½ lengths) in November: should prove as effective at 1m as 7f: open to further improvement. *D. Smaga, France*

MODERN PRACTICE (IRE) 2 br.c. (Feb 5) Modigliani (USA) 106 – Practice **58 ?** (USA) 97 (Diesis 133) [2007 p6d⁴ Dec 27] 40/1, slowly away when last of 4 in claimer at Wolverhampton. *Miss V. Haigh*

MODERN VERSE 4 b.g. Pleasant Tap (USA) – Sandalwood (USA) (El Gran **64** Senor (USA) 136) [2007 f6g⁴ p8g⁶ 6m³ 11.1m⁴ f7g⁵ 7.9g Jun 18] sturdy gelding: modest maiden: stays 11f: acts on all-weather and good to firm going: played up at start on second outing: sold 5,500 gns. *G. A. Swinbank*

MODHANA (IRE) 2 b. or br.f. (Mar 27) Modigliani (USA) 106 – Stridhana 70 (Indian – Ridge 123) [2007 7g Jul 26] third foal: dam, 6f winner, out of useful sprinter French Gift, herself out of high-class sprinter Soba: last in maiden at Folkestone. *M. G. Quinlan*

MOFARIJ 3 ch.c. Bering 136 – Pastorale 91 (Nureyev (USA) 131) [2007 92p: 8g* **95** 8.3m⁴ 7d⁶ p7m Nov 1] well-made colt: useful performer: won maiden at Nad Al Sheba in March: best subsequent effort when respectable seventh on handicap debut at Lingfield final start (tongue tied): stays 1m: yet to race on extremes of going on turf. *Saeed bin Suroor*

MOGOK RUBY 3 gr.g. Bertolini (USA) 125 – Days of Grace 79 (Wolfhound (USA) **79** 126) [2007 72: p5g⁵ p5g⁴ p5g³ p5g⁴ Dec 22] fair performer: barely stays 6f: acts on polytrack and good to firm ground: effective ridden prominently or held up: has looked awkward. *L. Montague Hall*

MOHEEBB (IRE) 3 b.g. Machiavellian (USA) 123 – Rockerlong 112 (Deploy 131) **80** [2007 –: 5v² 8s 6d⁵ 7m 7.1s² 7.9g* 8m p7.1m⁵ p8.6g 8.5d* 9.1s* 9.1v p9.5g f8d⁴ Dec 20] **a69** heavy-bodied gelding: fairly useful handicapper on turf, fair on all-weather: won at Carlisle in August, Beverley in September and Ayr in October: likely to stay 1¼m: acts on polytrack and heavy going. *D. W. Chapman*

MOKSI 2 b.c. (Apr 1) Olden Times 121 – Yasalam (IRE) (Fairy King (USA)) [2007 6d⁶ **77 p** Oct 1] rangy colt: has scope: third foal: half-brother to 2005 2-y-o 6f winner Tawaaf (by Medicean): dam once-raced half-sister to smart performer up to 1½m Sri Diamond: well-backed 5/2, much more promise than bare result (sixth to Seasider) in maiden at Windsor, doing well to recover from very slow start: will be suited by 1m: bound to improve. *P. W. Chapple-Hyam*

MOLLY ANN (IRE) 2 b.f. (Mar 13) Medicean 128 – Molly Mello (GER) 106 (Big **68** Shuffle (USA) 122) [2007 8g 8.2g p7.1g² f7d² p7.1g² Dec 31] 40,000Y: good-bodied filly: first foal: dam German 7f winner, including at 2 yrs: fair maiden: stays 7f: acts on all-weather. *T. D. Easterby*

MOLLYATTI 2 b.f. (Mar 22) Medicean 128 – Tolyatti (Green Desert (USA) 127) [2007 **72** 7m 7g p7g⁴ p6g³ 6g Sep 24] 9,000Y: strong, angular filly: third foal: dam, ran twice in France, out of half-sister to dam of 1000 Guineas winner Wince: fair maiden: in frame at Kempton and Lingfield (nursery): should prove best up to 7f: acts on polytrack and good to firm going. *Miss V. Haigh*

MOLUCCELLA 2 b.f. (Mar 30) Marju (IRE) 127 – Pine Needle 89 (Kris 135) [2007 **49** p7m p9.5g Nov 17] 9,000F, 38,000Y: good-topped filly: half-sister to 3 winners, including 9-y-o Dumaran and 1¼m winner Pine Cone (by Dr Fong), both useful: dam, 1m (at 2 yrs) to 1¾m winner, half-sister to dam of very smart middle-distance performer Border Arrow: poor form in maidens. *H. Morrison*

MOMAHA 3 b.g. Dinar (USA) 65 – Virginia Stock (Swing Easy (USA) 126) [2007 – p8.6g Dec 1] 66/1, no sign of ability in seller at Wolverhampton. *J. M. Bradley*

MOMENT OF CLARITY 5 b.g. Lujain (USA) 119 – Kicka (Shirley Heights 130) **73** [2007 12.3f 10s 10g³ 10s⁵ 10f⁴ 9.9m² 12.1m 10m⁴ 10m⁵ p12.2g* p9.5d* p9.5g² Dec 14] lengthy gelding: fair handicapper: won at Wolverhampton in November and December: stays 1½m: acts on polytrack and firm going, well held on soft: in cheekpieces last 6 starts. *R. C. Guest*

MOMENT'S NOTICE 2 ch.g. (Jan 26) Beat Hollow 126 – Figlette (Darshaan 133) **79** [2007 7s⁴ p8g³ 7m⁴ 7g p8g³ p8.6g* Nov 9] 18,000Y: sturdy gelding: first foal: dam unraced half-sister to smart performers up to 1¼m Marbush and Sublimity (also Champion Hurdle winner): fair form: won nursery at Wolverhampton final start: will stay 1¼m: acts on polytrack, soft and good to firm going: reported breathing problem fourth start. *S. Kirk*

MONAAZALAH (IRE) 2 b.f. (Apr 19) Green Desert (USA) 127 – Karamah 78 (Un- **81** fuwain (USA) 131) [2007 6m* 5m 7m 6m p6g⁵ Oct 31] big, strong, close-coupled filly: has round action: second foal: half-sister to 3-y-o Latanazul: dam, sprint maiden, out of half-sister to 1000 Guineas winner Shadayid: fairly useful form: won maiden at Haydock in May: struck into in Queen Mary Stakes at Royal Ascot: ran creditably (without threatening) 2 of 3 starts in nurseries, racing freely: should prove best up to 7f: acts on polytrack and good to firm going. *B. W. Hills*

MONACHELLO (USA) 3 b.g. Lemon Drop Kid (USA) 131 – Antoniette (USA) **75** (Nicholas (USA) 111) [2007 80: 9.9m⁵ 11g 9.9m 10.1m⁴ Jul 17] leggy, quite attractive gelding: fair performer: probably stays 1¼m: acts on good to firm ground: sold 16,000 gns, sent to Qatar. *Mrs A. J. Perrett*

MONADREEN FLYER (IRE) 2 b.g. (Apr 8) Atraf 116 – First Kiss (GER) 65 (Night **77** Shift (USA)) [2007 5f³ 6g* 6s³ 6m⁴ 6m³ 5f⁴ p6g p6g³ Dec 7] compact gelding: fair performer: won maiden at Cork in June: in frame most other starts, including in minor event at Newcastle on fourth: effective at 5f/6f: acts on polytrack, firm and soft going: below form in cheekpieces. *D. Loughnane, Ireland*

MONASHEE BRAVE (IRE) 4 b.g. Monashee Mountain (USA) 115 – Miss Butter- **79** field (Cure The Blues (USA)) [2007 80: f5g p5.1g 5g² 5g 6d 5v⁵ 5d⁵ 5f 5m 7.1d 5g⁶ 5.1s² 5g* p5.1g⁶ p7m⁵ f6d* Dec 21] tall, attractive gelding: fair performer: won sellers at Musselburgh (left J. Quinn 7,000 gns) in November and Southwell in December: best at 5f/6f: acts on all-weather, firm and soft going: has carried head high: tried in visor/cheek-pieces/tongue strap. *R. A. Harris*

MONASHEEMINI (IRE) 4 gr.f. Monashee Mountain (USA) 115 – Ivory's Promise – 74 (Pursuit of Love 124) [2007 5m Aug 25] third foal: dam 2-y-o 5f winner: 16/1, well held in maiden at Beverley. *Mrs N. Macauley*

MONASHEE PRINCE (IRE) 5 ch.g. Monashee Mountain (USA) 115 – Lodema **73** (IRE) (Lycius (USA) 124) [2007 72: p8g p6g⁵ 5m⁴ 6m 6g p6m⁴ p6g* 6d⁵ p7g p6g p6g⁶ p6g Dec 19] tall, leggy gelding: fair handicapper: won at Lingfield in October and Wolverhampton in November: seemingly stays easy 1¼m, but races mostly at shorter (winner at 5f): acts on polytrack, good to firm and good to soft going: sometimes visored. *J. R. Best*

MONASHEE RIVER (IRE) 4 b.f. Monashee Mountain (USA) 115 – Dixie Jazz 51 **58** (Mtoto 134) [2007 58: f11g f8g 9g* 10.5m 10m 8.1d⁶ p7g Jul 18] tall filly: modest performer: won amateur handicap at Goodwood in June: stays 9f: acts on polytrack, best effort on turf on good going. *Miss V. Haigh*

MONASHEE ROCK (IRE) 2 b.f. (Mar 12) Monashee Mountain (USA) 115 – Polar **75** Rock 66 (Polar Falcon (USA) 126) [2007 8g³ 7m³ 8d⁵ 6d³ p7g² Nov 4] useful-looking filly: second foal: half-sister to 3-y-o It's No Problem: dam, maiden (stayed 7f), sister to 7-y-o Cold Turkey: fair maiden: placed 4 times: free-going sort, should prove best up to 1m: acts on polytrack, good to firm and good to soft going. *M. Salaman*

MONASH LAD (IRE) 5 ch.g. General Monash (USA) 107 – Story Time (IRE) (Man- – sooj 118) [2007 71: 15.8m Aug 7] rather leggy gelding: fair performer at best: tailed off only Flat start at 5 yrs: stays 1½m: yet to race on heavy ground, acts on any other turf: tried blinkered. *Mrs K. Waldron*

MONDA 5 b.m. Danzig Connection (USA) – Fairey Firefly 64 (Hallgate 127) [2007 48: **61** f6g f6g² p6g² f6g 6g⁴ 6g² 6s² p6g⁶ 6v p6g Nov 20] workmanlike mare: modest handicapper: stays 7f: acts on all-weather and soft ground: refused to enter stall once: sold 1,500 gns. *Miss J. A. Camacho*

MONDAY MORNING (IRE) 2 b.f. (Mar 15) Touch of The Blues (FR) 125 – Thats **60** Your Opinion 48 (Last Tycoon 131) [2007 5.1g⁵ p5.1g⁶ Jul 30] €56,000Y, resold €55,000Y: good-topped filly: fifth foal: half-sister to 4-y-o Balthazaar's Gift: dam Irish maiden (stayed 1¾m): modest maiden: much better run when fifth at Nottingham (reportedly returned jarred up). *M. J. Wallace*

MONET'S LADY (IRE) 3 gr.f. Daylami (IRE) 138 – Wide Range (IRE) (Spectrum **51** (IRE) 126) [2007 –: 10.1m p12.2g⁵ 14.1m² May 28] angular filly: modest maiden: stays 1¾m: raced only on polytrack and good to firm going. *R. A. Fahey*

MONETS MASTERPIECE (USA) 4 b.g. Quiet American (USA) – Math (USA) **67 §** (Devil's Bag (USA)) [2007 78§: p10g³ p10g p13g⁴ p12g⁶ Mar 7] lengthy, good-topped gelding: fair maiden: stays 13f: raced only on polytrack and good/good to firm going: tried blinkered/tongue tied: upset at stall on final 2-y-o outing: ungenuine: joined P. Kelsall, £6,000. *G. L. Moore*

MONKEY GLAS (IRE) 3 b.c. Mull of Kintyre (USA) 114 – Maura's Pet (IRE) 58 **88** (Prince of Birds (USA) 121) [2007 78: 8.2m 8m 8m⁵ 8.1m 8m* 8.1m³ 8g 8m⁶ p8m⁵ p8g⁶ p7.1g³ Dec 31] strong, lengthy colt: fairly useful handicapper: won at Pontefract in August: free-going sort, but stays 1m: acts on polytrack and firm ground. *K. R. Burke*

MONKSTOWN ROAD 5 b.g. Makbul 104 – Carolside 108 (Music Maestro 119) **– §** [2007 64d: p12.2g p12.2g Jan 21] good-topped gelding: unreliable performer: no form in 2007: wears headgear. *C. N. Kellett*

MONMOUTHSHIRE 4 b.g. Singspiel (IRE) 133 – Croeso Cariad 107 (Most Wel- **55** come 131) [2007 63?: p9.5g f12g f11g f14g⁶ f14g 10.2f* p11g⁵ 10.2d⁶ 10.2f 10.2d Jun 16] good-topped gelding: modest handicapper: won at Bath in April: stays 1¼m: acts on all-weather and firm going: often visored. *R. J. Price*

MONOLITH 9 b.g. Bigstone (IRE) 126 – Ancara 109 (Dancing Brave (USA) 140) **89** [2007 89: 13m* 15g² 18d⁴ 16.1v 16d⁶ 13.1s 18d Oct 13] smallish gelding: fairly useful handicapper: won at Hamilton in May: stays 2½m: acts on good to firm and heavy ground: useful hurdler. *L. Lungo*

MON PETITE AMOUR 4 b.f. Efisio 120 – Food of Love 109 (Music Boy 124) [2007 **67** 58: p8g² p8g² p10g* p10g p9.5g* 12g³ 9.7m p10g p10g⁵ p10g⁴ p10g p10m p10m³ p10g² Dec 28] deep-girthed filly: fair handicapper: won at Lingfield in February and Wolverhampton in March: stays easy 1½m: acts on all-weather, good to firm and good to soft going: tried visored/in cheekpieces: has had breathing problem. *D. W. P. Arbuthnot*

MON PLAISIR (USA) 2 b. or br.c. (Apr 16) Pleasant Tap (USA) – Coquine (USA) **73** (Gone West (USA)) [2007 7g³ 7f³ 8.2d Oct 10] strong colt: fifth foal: half-brother to minor US winners by Favourite Trick and Honour And Glory: dam unraced granddaughter of Prix Saint-Alary winner Smuggly: fair maiden: third at Newmarket and Folkestone (behind Billion Dollar Kid): should stay 1m: acts on firm going, seemed unsuited by good to soft final start. *J. L. Dunlop*

MONROE GOLD 7 ch.g. Pivotal 124 – Golden Daring (IRE) (Night Shift (USA)) **–** [2007 8m Aug 27] close-coupled gelding: poor maiden: usually wears headgear/tongue tie. *Jennie Candlish*

MONSHERAMIE (IRE) 5 b.g. Desert Style (IRE) 121 – Sheramie (IRE) 33 (Sherna- **–** zar 131) [2007 51: p13.9g Dec 1] modest maiden at 4 yrs: little impact in claimer at Wolverhampton sole start in 2007: stays 1¾m: acts on firm ground. *T. G. McCourt, Ireland*

MONSIEUR DUMAS (IRE) 3 b.g. Iron Mask (USA) 117 – Serenity 98 (Selkirk **61** (USA) 129) [2007 68: 12f⁴ 10m 12s 8.5g 8.5m² p9.5g Oct 6] strong, workmanlike gelding: modest maiden: left T. Tate after third start: probably stays 1¼m: acts on polytrack and good to firm going. *R. Bastiman*

MONSIEUR REYNARD 2 ch.g. (Apr 17) Compton Place 125 – Tell Tale Fox (Tel **71** Quel (FR) 125) [2007 6s³ 6m 6s Aug 24] attractive gelding: fair maiden: third at Salisbury on debut: may prove best at 5f/6f: acts on soft going: suspect temperament. *B. J. Meehan*

MONSIGNOR FRED 5 b.g. Fraam 114 – Monsoon 66 (Royal Palace 131) [2007 70: **–** 11.8m 10g Jun 13] tall, leggy gelding: maiden: little form in 2007: stays 9f: acts on good to firm ground. *H. Candy*

John Smith's Stakes (Handicap), Newbury—the improving three-year-old Monte Alto is too good for older rivals Speedy Sam (left), Greek Well (behind winner), Bolodenka (disc on body) and Invasian (No.17)

MONSOON WEDDING 3 b.f. Monsun (GER) 124 – Hyabella 111 (Shirley Heights 130) [2007 75: 12f³ 10s³ 10d 9.2s* 10.1d 8g Nov 9] fair performer: won maiden at Hamilton in September: may prove best short of 1½m: acts on soft ground: often front runner. *M. Johnston* **75**

MONTAGNE D'OR (IRE) 2 b.c. (Feb 8) Montjeu (IRE) 137 – Muschana 100 (Deploy 131) [2007 7s* 7g Jul 28] €35,000Y: good-bodied colt: third living foal: half-brother to fairly useful 1½m/13f winner Mpenzi (by Groom Dancer) and 2005 2-y-o 5f winner Peace And Love (by Fantastic Light): dam, 1¼m winner, half-sister to Melbourne Cup winner Jeune and King Edward VII Stakes winner Beneficial: fairly useful form: won minor event at Catterick (beat Shannersburg by 1½ lengths) in July: coltish and still green (pulled hard) when well held in listed race won by Raven's Pass at Ascot 10 days later: underwent successful colic surgery after, but later broke his hip: should have been suited by 1¼m/1½m: dead. *M. Johnston* **90**

MONTALEMBERT (USA) 3 b. or br.g. Kalanisi (IRE) 132 – Garendare 105 (Vacarme (USA) 121) [2007 86: 10g 8g May 6] lengthy, good-topped gelding: fairly useful performer: stiff tasks and far from discredited in German pattern races at 3 yrs: stays 1¼m: acts on polytrack and good to firm going: gelded after final start. *J. S. Moore* **90 ?**

MONTANA SKY (IRE) 4 b.g. Peintre Celebre (USA) 137 – Catch The Lights 86 (Deploy 131) [2007 –: p10g² p10g p11g Nov 28] modest maiden: stays 1¼m: acts on polytrack and good to firm going. *R. A. Harris* **55**

MONTAQUILA 2 b.g. (Apr 10) Hawk Wing (USA) 136 – Intellectuelle (Caerleon (USA) 132) [2007 6g³ 6g³ 6s* 7m 8s⁶ Sep 22] 75,000Y: tall, good-topped gelding: good walker and mover: sixth foal: half-brother to useful French 6f winner Fastidia (by Fasliyev) and Irish 1¼m winner Strike One (by Danehill Dancer): dam, French 2-y-o 1m winner, half-sister to smart French performer up to 10.5f Audacieuse and useful stayer Lord Jim: fairly useful performer: won minor event at Newcastle (dictated) in June, standout effort: may prove best short of 1m: acts on soft going: gelded after final start. *J. Howard Johnson* **93**

MONTARE (IRE) 5 b.m. Montjeu (IRE) 137 – Contare 108 (Shirley Heights 130) [2007 116: 10s 15.5s³ 20g⁵ 12.5m³ 12m⁶ 12g* Oct 21] tall, leggy mare: smart performer: gained all 7 career wins in autumn and won Prix du Conseil de Paris (for second time) at Longchamp in October by nose from Arch Rebel: creditable efforts previously when third in Prix Vicomtesse Vigier at Longchamp (beaten 2½ lengths by Lord du Sud) and Prix de Pomone at Deauville (idled and caught close home, beaten short head and nose behind Macleya): staying-on fifth to Yeats in Gold Cup at Royal Ascot on third start, forced to wait for run on bend and meeting trouble in straight: needed minimum of 1½m and stayed at least 15.5f: acted on soft and good to firm ground: tended to carry head awkwardly, had hung and flashed tail: wore cheekpieces: held up: stud. *J. E. Pease, France* **115**

MONTBRETIA 2 b.f. (Feb 22) Montjeu (IRE) 137 – Bayswater 76 (Caerleon (USA) 132) [2007 8d⁴ Oct 23] fourth foal: half-sister to fairly useful 1m winner Art Work and 7f winner Portland (both by Zafonic): dam, 1½m winner, sister to Tenby: 7/2, fourth to Michita in maiden at Yarmouth: will be suited by 1¼m/1½m: sure to improve. *H. R. A. Cecil* **69 p**

MONTCHARA (IRE) 4 b.g. Montjeu (IRE) 137 – Mochara (Last Fandango 125) **75 d** [2007 60: p9.5g³ p12.2g* 12d 10.2s 10g 12s⁶ 9.7f Sep 10] lengthy, angular gelding: fair handicapper: won at Wolverhampton in April: stays 1½m: acts on polytrack and good to soft ground: sold 19,000 gns, joined M. Todhunter. *G. Wragg*

MONTE ALTO (IRE) 3 b.c. Danehill Dancer (IRE) 117 – Peruvian Witch (IRE) **110** (Perugino (USA) 84) [2007 83p: 7m* 7m³ 8.1g³ 10g³ 9.7g* 10f² 9.9m² 10m* 9m⁶ Oct 6] good-bodied colt: smart performer: progressed well, winning maiden at Lingfield in May, and handicaps at Folkestone in July and Newbury (John Smith's Stakes, beat Speedy Sam 1¼ lengths) in September: creditable sixth to Pipedreamer in Cambridgeshire at Newmarket final start, best of those towards far rail: best at 1¼m: acts on firm and good to soft ground: held up: reliable. *L. M. Cumani*

MONTE CASSINO (IRE) 2 ch.c. (Mar 21) Choisir (AUS) 126 – Saucy Maid (IRE) **–** 69 (Sure Blade (USA) 130) [2007 7g 5.1g Nov 7] big, workmanlike colt: well held in maidens. *J. O'Reilly*

MONTECRISTO 14 br.g. Warning 136 – Sutosky 78 (Great Nephew 126) [2007 48: **48** p16g p11g⁴ p11g p13g³ f11g⁶ p12.2g⁵ f14g Jun 5] leggy, close-coupled gelding: poor performer: effective at 11f to 2m: acts on all-weather and any turf going: held up. *Rae Guest*

MONTEFIORE (IRE) 2 b.c. (May 16) Orpen (USA) 116 – Tokurama (IRE) (Mtoto **57** 134) [2007 7g⁴ p8g Oct 31] lengthy colt: tongue tied but reported breathing problem in maidens, fourth at Newcastle on debut (modest form): should stay 1m. *M. Botti*

MONTE MAJOR (IRE) 6 b.g. Dockside (USA) 124 – Danalia (IRE) 78 (Danehill **71** (USA) 126) [2007 59: p5g p5.1g* p5.1g³ p5.1g⁴ p6g⁵ p5.1g² 6g p5.1g* 5.1d³ 5g p5g⁶ **a75** p5.1g* 5g³ 5.2s² 5s⁵ 5.1g p5.1g³ p6g p5.1g² p6m³ p5.1s² Dec 20] strong, sturdy gelding: fair performer: won amateur handicap in January, claimer in April and handicap in June, all at Wolverhampton: effective at 5f to 7f: acts on all-weather, soft and good to firm going: effective with/without visor. *D. Shaw*

MONTE MAYOR BIRDIE (IRE) 2 b.f. (Feb 23) Captain Rio 122 – Ascoli (Sky- **58** liner 117) [2007 p6g 7v² 6d⁴ Aug 1] €18,000Y: half-sister to several winners, including useful 6f (including at 2 yrs)/7f winner Spencers Wood (by Pips Pride) and 1m to 15f winner Precious Mystery (by Titus Livius): dam Irish winner up to 1¼m and over hurdles: modest maiden: in frame at Lingfield (second to Safari Sunup) and Leicester: stays 7f: acts on heavy going. *D. Haydn Jones*

MONTEMAYORPRINCESS (IRE) 3 b.f. Fath (USA) 116 – Blonde Goddess **53** (IRE) (Godswalk (USA) 130) [2007 59: 6.1g⁵ p5.1g 5.1s⁶ 5.7m⁶ 5.1f 7g* 7g p9.5g⁴ Dec 3] modest performer: won seller at Leicester in September: barely stays 9.5f: acts on all-weather, firm and good to soft going: in cheekpieces last 5 starts. *D. Haydn Jones*

MONTERRICO 2 b.c. (Apr 28) Dubai Destination (USA) 127 – Mezzogiorno 108 **72 p** (Unfuwain (USA) 131) [2007 6m 7d³ Oct 16] well-made colt: seventh foal: half-brother to 3 winners, including smart 1m/1¼m winner Monturani (by Indian Ridge) and useful 6f/7f winner Monnavanna (by Machiavellian): dam, 7f (at 2 yrs) and 1¼m winner, third in Oaks: fair form: off 2 months then promising third to Prime Exhibit in maiden at Leicester: will stay 1m: should go on progressing. *G. Wragg*

MONT ETOILE (IRE) 4 b.f. Montjeu (IRE) 137 – Troyes 81 (Troy 137) [2007 112: **105** 8m² 12m⁵ 12f³ 10.1g⁵ 12d Sep 28] sturdy filly: smart performer at 3 yrs: best effort in 2007 when fifth to Turbo Linn in Lancashire Oaks at Newmarket on second start: should be suited by 1¾m: acts on good to firm going: has been bandaged: tried visored: sold 575,000 gns. *W. J. Haggas*

MONTGOMERY 6 b.g. In Command (IRE) 114 – Lightening Reef (Bon Sang (FR) **49** 126) [2007 17.2f⁴ 15.4g* Aug 16] poor performer: off 2½ years before return: won minor event at Folkestone in August: stays 15.4f: tried in cheekpieces. *A. G. Newcombe*

MONTIBOLI (IRE) 2 ch.f. (Feb 2) Bahamian Bounty 116 – Aunt Sadie 71 (Pursuit of **60** Love 124) [2007 6g² 6g³ p6g³ 6m 6s Aug 24] €39,000Y, 28,000Y: leggy, close-coupled filly: fourth foal: half-sister to 4-y-o Shaydreambeliever: dam sprint maiden: modest maiden: placed first 3 starts, seemed amiss final 2 (last one in cheekpieces): likely to prove best at 5f/6f. *K. A. Ryan*

MONTICELLI (GER) 7 b.g. Pelder (IRE) 125 – Marcelia (GER) (Priamos (GER) **–** 123) [2007 8d Oct 3] good-topped gelding: won 3 times in Germany in 2004: well held on Flat return in handicap at Salisbury: stays 11f: acts on heavy going: fairly useful hurdler for P. Hobbs/S. Earle. *J. R. Gask*

MONTILLIA (IRE) 5 b.m. Monashee Mountain (USA) 115 – Steel Tap (IRE) (Flash –
of Steel 120) [2007 58: p5g May 31] modest performer: well held only start at 5 yrs:
front runner, best at 5f: acts on polytrack and firm going: sold 2,000 gns, sent to Greece.
J. W. Unett

MONTIONA 3 b.g. Montjoy (USA) 122 – Lady Iona 50 (Weldnaas (USA) 112) [2007 –
f8g p9.5g f7s Feb 8] no sign of ability. *John A. Harris*

MONTJEU'S MELODY (IRE) 3 b.f. Montjeu (IRE) 137 – Pride of Place (IRE) 71 **74**
(Caerleon (USA) 132) [2007 –p: 9g³ p10g⁵ 10g⁴ 11.6m 14.1m⁵ Aug 31] rather leggy filly:
fair maiden: barely stays 1¾m: acts on polytrack and good to firm ground. *J. W. Hills*

MONTOSARI 8 ch.g. Persian Bold 123 – Sartigila 67 (Efisio 120) [2007 63, a75: p12g **68**
p12g⁴ p16g⁴ p13g Jul 10] fair handicapper: effective at 1½m to 2m: acts on all-weather
and firm going: reportedly finished lame final outing. *P. Mitchell*

MONTPELLIER (IRE) 4 b.g. Montjeu (IRE) 137 – Ring of Esteem (Mark of Esteem **99**
(IRE) 137) [2007 89: 8s 10m p8g* 8.5d² 8m 8.1g p8g² 8g⁵ 8g⁵ p8g Sep 8] big, rangy
gelding: useful handicapper: won at Kempton in May by 1¼ lengths from Unshakable:
mainly creditable efforts subsequently, including when head second to Samarinda in
minor event at Lingfield on seventh start: stays 8.5f: acts on polytrack, good to firm and
good to soft ground: travels strongly, but hasn't always impressed with finishing effort:
sent to UAE. *E. A. L. Dunlop*

MONTRACHET 3 ch.f. Singspiel (IRE) 133 – Riberac 110 (Efisio 120) [2007 10m **85**
8.2g⁴ 8.1s² 8.1s* 8.3d* 9.2d² 8.9d⁴ 7d⁵ 8v⁶ Nov 3] sturdy filly: second foal: half-sister to
4-y-o Emilion: dam 5f (at 2 yrs) to 1¼m winner: fairly useful handicapper: won at
Chepstow and Windsor in July: should stay 1¼m: acts on soft ground: has carried head
awkwardly/hung right. *M. L. W. Bell*

MONTREAL (GER) 2 b.f. (May 11) Boreal (GER) 126 – Margie's Darling (USA) –
(Alydar (USA)) [2007 8g Oct 26] tall filly: closely related to German 7f winners
Masvingo (at 2 yrs in 2002) and Margie's Gold (both by Java Gold) and half-sister to
several winners in Germany, including useful 9f/11f winner Margosto (by Acatenango):
dam unraced: 28/1, towards rear in maiden at Doncaster. *H. R. A. Cecil*

MONTROSE MAN 3 ch.g. Foxhound (USA) 103 – Don't Jump (IRE) 71 (Entitled **77**
126) [2007 56p: 8.2g p10g³ Nov 21] rangy gelding: best effort in maidens when third to
Alpes Maritimes at Lingfield: stays easy 1¼m: acts on polytrack. *B. J. Meehan*

MONTZANDO 4 b.g. Forzando 122 – Clashfern (Smackover 107) [2007 60: p5.1g⁶ **54**
6m⁵ 6m 6g 5.7d 5.2s⁵ Jun 26] good-topped gelding: modest performer: best efforts at 5f:
acts on firm going: often wears headgear. *B. R. Millman*

MONZANTE (USA) 3 gr. or ro.g. Maria's Mon (USA) 121 – Danzante (USA) 107 **101**
(Danzig (USA)) [2007 110p: 10m³ 10.3m⁴ 10m⁶ a8.5f* Nov 25] unfurnished gelding:
useful performer: creditable efforts when in frame in minor event at Newbury (2¼ lengths
third to Light Shift) and Dee Stakes at Chester (5¼ lengths fourth to Admiralofthefleet):
well below form in listed race at Newmarket, then left R. Charlton 100,000 gns: won
allowance race at Hollywood in November: stays 1¼m: acts on polytrack/cushion track
and good to firm going. *M. R. Mitchell, USA*

MOODY TUNES 4 b.g. Merdon Melody 98 – Lady-Love 70 (Pursuit of Love 124) **96**
[2007 87: 8m 8.1g² 8.1m⁴ 8g* 8m 8.1s* 8s² 8.1g 8.5g⁴ 8s 9m 8d Oct 12] lengthy, good-
topped gelding: useful handicapper: won at Yarmouth in May and Haydock (beat Vacation by length) in June: stays 8.5f: winner on good to firm ground, best efforts on good or
softer (acts on heavy): blinkered once in 2005: usually travels strongly. *K. R. Burke*

MOOKHLESA 2 b. or br.f. (Mar 28) Marju (IRE) 127 – Ikhlas (IRE) (Lahib (USA) **94 p**
129) [2007 5m* Apr 19] smallish, lengthy filly: has a quick action: first foal: dam unraced
sister to useful 7f/1m performer La-Faah and half-sister to useful sprinter Afaan: 8/1, won
maiden at Newmarket by ½ length (Missit second, Spinning Lucy third), going strongly:
looks a useful prospect. *B. W. Hills*

MOON BIRD 5 b.m. Primo Dominie 121 – Time For Tea (IRE) 73 (Imperial Frontier –
(USA) 112) [2007 –, a68: p6g p7g⁶ p7g p8g³ p8g p8g p8g⁴ Jul 3] modest performer: stays **a63**
1m: acts on polytrack, lightly raced on turf: free-going sort: sold 4,500 gns. *C. A. Cyzer*

MOON BOUND (IRE) 2 b.c. (Feb 18) Observatory (USA) 131 – Inspiring (IRE) **71**
(Anabaa (USA) 130) [2007 p6d⁴ p6g² Dec 29] 29,000Y: second foal: half-brother to
smart 5f/6f (latter at 2 yrs) winner Dixie Belle (by Diktat): dam unraced out of useful 7f/
1m winner Mareha: fair maiden: better effort when second to at Lingfield, making most.
W. R. Muir

MOONE CROSS (IRE) 4 b.f. Cape Cross (IRE) 129 – Cannikin (IRE) 82 (Lahib **102**
(USA) 129) [2007 102: 6v² 6s⁵ 6d 5g⁶ 6m 5d⁶ 5g Oct 7] lengthy filly: useful performer:
good efforts when second in listed race at Fairyhouse in July and sixth to Benbaun in
Flying Five Stakes at the Curragh: seems best at 5f/6f: acts on heavy and good to firm
going: blinkered last 2 starts: inconsistent (ran as if amiss at Pontefract on third appearance): sold 65,000 gns. *Mrs J. Harrington, Ireland*

MOON EMPEROR 10 b.g. Emperor Jones (USA) 119 – Sir Hollow (USA) (Sir Ivor **73 d**
(USA) 135) [2007 82d: p16.5g* p16.5g³ p16g⁵ 16m p16g p16g⁴ p16g f16d⁴ Dec 18] tall,
close-coupled gelding: fair handicapper: won at Wolverhampton in February: below form
after next start: stays 16.5f: acts on all-weather, lightly raced on turf nowadays: usually
wears headgear: sometimes looks none too keen: held up. *J. R. Jenkins*

MOON EMPRESS (FR) 4 gr.f. Rainbow Quest (USA) 134 – Diamoona (FR) (Last **84**
Tycoon 131) [2007 72p: p12g² p12.2g² p12.2g² p12g* 12d* May 17] fairly useful
performer: improved to win maiden at Lingfield in April and handicap at Salisbury in
May: stays 1½m: acts on polytrack and good to soft going: reportedly in foal to Tiger Hill.
W. R. Muir

MOONFINDER (IRE) 3 b.f. Galileo (IRE) 134 – Callisto (IRE) 91 (Darshaan 133) **–**
[2007 9.9d 10m 12s⁶ 12m Aug 4] 21,000F: first foal: dam, 2m/17.5f winner, half-sister to
smart stayer Rain Rider: signs of ability on debut, but well held subsequently: sold 3,000
gns. *J. L. Dunlop*

MOON FOREST (IRE) 5 br.g. Woodborough (USA) 112 – Ma Bella Luna 76 (Jal- **58**
mood (USA) 126) [2007 64: f8g p6g⁴ 7.1m⁴ 6.1g² 7g⁴ 7.1s⁶ p7.1g 7s 7g p6g⁴ 7g⁵ 7.1m
Sep 7] good-topped gelding: modest handicapper: effective at 6f/7f: acts on polytrack,
soft and good to firm going: wears cheekpieces. *J. M. Bradley*

MOONHAWK 4 b.g. Montjeu (IRE) 137 – Enclave (USA) (Woodman (USA) 126) **78**
[2007 75: 9.2d⁶ 7s⁴ 8d² 10d⁶ Sep 22] strong gelding: fair maiden handicapper: best efforts
at 7f/1m: acts on good going. *J. Howard Johnson*

MOONLIGHT ANGEL 2 b.f. (Feb 21) Kyllachy 129 – Far Post (USA) (Defensive **65**
Play (USA) 118) [2007 6m p7g³ Jul 12] 17,000F, 36,000Y: first foal: dam French maiden:
fair form in maidens at Lingfield, third to Dusty Moon: stays 7f. *W. R. Swinburn*

MOONLIGHT APPLAUSE 3 b.f. Royal Applause 124 – Antonia's Choice 73 **58**
(Music Boy 124) [2007 46: f6g⁶ f5g³ 5m⁵ f5g² 5g⁵ 6d 5m² 5d² p5.1g³ 5d⁶ 5s³ 5m*
Aug 18] modest performer: won maiden at Ripon in August: should prove best at 5f/6f:
acts on all-weather, soft and good to firm ground. *T. D. Easterby*

MOONLIGHT FANTASY (IRE) 4 b.g. Night Shift (USA) – County Girl (IRE) **67**
(Prince Rupert (FR) 121) [2007 58: 10m p8.6g 10.1m 10.1d 10f² 10.1g³ 9.8m* 9.5m⁶
9.9d p8m p9.5g* p9.5g⁵ p9.5g⁵ Dec 29] sturdy gelding: fair performer: left
N. Tinkler after third start: won seller at Ripon (sold from T. D. Barron 8,800 gns) in
August and handicaps at Wolverhampton in November and December: stays 1¼m: acts
on polytrack and firm ground: tried in cheekpieces: held up and travels strongly: has hung
left. *Lucinda Featherstone*

MOONLIGHT GAMBLER (IRE) 2 ch.c. (Mar 28) Captain Rio 122 – Bound To **45**
Glitter (USA) (Boundary (USA) 117) [2007 5m 6m 5s⁵ 7.5g 6m⁶ 7.8g* Nov 9] poor performer: sold from T. Easterby 1,200 gns before winning maiden at Arhus in November:
stays 7.8f: tried blinkered. *T. Christensen, Denmark*

MOONLIGHT MAN 6 ch.g. Night Shift (USA) – Fleeting Rainbow 65 (Rainbow **99**
Quest (USA) 134) [2007 –: p7g 8.1d⁵ 8.3m⁴ 7.1d⁴ 7m² 8s⁴ p6g⁶ p6g p7.1g Oct 22] good- **a86**
topped gelding: useful handicapper on turf, fairly useful on all-weather: best effort at
6 yrs when second to Bomber Command at Ascot: claimed from R. Hannon £18,000 after
sixth start: stays 1m: acts on polytrack, firm and good to soft ground: tried blinkered.
C. R. Dore

MOON MELODY (GER) 4 b.g. Montjeu (IRE) 137 – Midnight Fever (IRE) (Sure **–**
Blade (USA) 130) [2007 57: 15.8m 12.1g Aug 16] modest maiden in 2006: well held in
sellers at 4 yrs. *M. E. Sowersby*

MOON QUEST (IRE) 3 ch.g. Rainbow Quest (USA) 134 – Midnight Line (USA) 114 **90**
(Kris S (USA)) [2007 10m* 12d⁴ Jun 27] strong gelding: third foal: dam, 7f (at 2 yrs) to
1½m (in USA) winner and third in Oaks, out of May Hill winner Midnight Air: won
maiden at Windsor in June by 1¾ lengths from Fourteenth: some improvement when 3¾
lengths fourth to Hi Calypso in handicap at Salisbury next time: underwent surgery for
ankle chip after, then gelded: will probably stay beyond 1½m. *Saeed bin Suroor*

MOONSHINE BEACH 9 b.g. Lugana Beach 116 – Monongelia 98 (Welsh Pageant **67**
132) [2007 –: p13.9g 16.2g 16s⁴ 18m⁴ p16g p16.5g⁵ p16g⁵ Dec 4] leggy, lengthy gelding:
fair handicapper: stays 2¼m: acts on polytrack, firm and good to soft going: tried visored/
in cheekpieces: often races prominently. *P. W. Hiatt*

MOONSHINE BILL 8 ch.g. Master Willie 129 – Monongelia 98 (Welsh Pageant 132) **52 d**
[2007 52: p16.5g p13.9g p12g p13.9g Mar 5] lengthy, workmanlike gelding: modest
performer: below form after reappearance: stays 1½m: acts on polytrack, soft and good to
firm ground: often races prominently. *P. W. Hiatt*

MOONSHINE CREEK 5 b.g. Pyramus (USA) 78 – Monongelia 98 (Welsh Pageant **59**
132) [2007 58: 10s² 11.8s 10m³ 11.9d⁴ 10.1f 9.9m p10g Aug 29] leggy gelding: modest
maiden handicapper: stays 1¼m, seemingly not 1½m: acts on soft and good to firm going:
races prominently. *P. W. Hiatt*

MOONSHINE VIXEN 6 ch.m. Deploy 131 – Monongelia 98 (Welsh Pageant 132) **–**
[2007 12s p12g 12.1m Sep 7] lengthy mare: half-sister to several winners, including
9-y-o Moonshine Beach: dam 1m to 1¼m winner: poor form in bumpers: no form on Flat.
P. W. Hiatt

MOON SISTER (IRE) 2 b.f. (Feb 12) Cadeaux Genereux 131 – Tanz (IRE) 79 (Sad- **52**
ler's Wells (USA) 132) [2007 6g Nov 2] sister to fairly useful 1½m winner Ball Boy
and half-sister to several winners, including useful 7f winner (stayed 11.4f) Tanzilla (by
Warning) and fairly useful 11.9f to 1¾m winner Tarxien (by Kendor): dam, 1½m winner,
sister to smart middle-distance stayer Spring and closely related to Pentire: 20/1, green
and insufficient test in maiden at Newmarket (eighth): will benefit from 1m+. *W. Jarvis*

MOON SPRAY (USA) 2 ch.c. (Apr 21) Malibu Moon (USA) – Sun Spray (USA) **48**
(Woodman (USA) 126) [2007 6g⁶ 7m 6m Aug 25] poor form in maidens (best effort at
7f). *K. A. Ryan*

MOON STAR (GER) 6 b.g. Goofalik (USA) 118 – Maria Magdalena (GER) (Alkalde **–**
(GER)) [2007 11g May 10] fairly useful performer at best: successful 5 times up to
1¼m in Italy/Switzerland for K. Schafflutzel: no show on British Flat debut: fair hurdler.
A. M. Hales

MOONSTREAKER 4 b.g. Foxhound (USA) 103 – Ling Lane (Slip Anchor 136) **60**
[2007 71: 9.8m 8s⁴ 8m 8.3m 8s 7g² 9.1v p8.6g² f8d⁴ Dec 12] tall, leggy gelding: just
modest nowadays: stays 8.6f: acts on all-weather and good to firm going, probably on
soft: takes keen hold. *R. M. Whitaker*

MOON VALLEY 4 ch.f. Halling (USA) 133 – Crescent Moon (Mr Prospector (USA)) **79**
[2007 79: 10s³ 8.1d 10m³ 10d² p12.2g Aug 31] angular filly: fair maiden: should stay
1½m: acts on good and good to soft ground: blinkered last 2 outings, very slowly
away final one. *W. J. Haggas*

MOONWALKING 3 b.g. Danehill Dancer (IRE) 117 – Macca Luna (IRE) 78 (Kah- **78**
yasi 130) [2007 78: 10m⁴ 12f³ 12g³ 12g 12m 12d Oct 12] angular, quite good-topped
gelding: fair handicapper: will probably stay beyond 1½m: acts on firm and good to soft
going. *Jedd O'Keeffe*

MOORHOUSE LAD 4 b.g. Bertolini (USA) 125 – Record Time 69 (Clantime 101) **121**
[2007 92: f5g* p5g³ 5g³ 5m² 5g² 5m 5m* 5g* 5g Aug 23] neat gelding: progressed into
very smart performer in 2007, winning handicaps at Southwell in January and New-

*Audi Stakes (King George), Goodwood—a very smart performance from Moorhouse Lad,
who is a clear-cut winner from Enticing (third right), Tax Free (second right) and Wi Dud (noseband)*

market in July and Audi Stakes (King George) at Goodwood (much improved when beating Enticing by 2 lengths) in August: only eleventh behind Kingsgate Native in Nunthorpe Stakes at York final outing: best at 5f: acts on all-weather, raced only on good going or firmer (acts on firm) on turf: often races prominently: has been bandaged behind. *B. Smart*

MOORLANDER (USA) 3 ch.g. Cozzene (USA) – Forest Key (USA) (Green Forest **64** (USA) 134) [2007 74: 8g 8g 10s⁶ p10g Oct 4] lengthy, good-bodied gelding: maiden handicapper: just modest at best in 2007: probably stays 1m: acts on good to firm ground: tongue tied last 3 starts. *Mrs A. J. Perrett*

MOORS MYTH 6 b.g. Anabaa (USA) 130 – West Devon (USA) (Gone West (USA)) – [2007 56: p6g Jan 19] big, good-topped gelding: one-time fair performer: well beaten in claimer (tongue tied) sole 6-y-o start. *B. G. Powell*

MOOSLEY (IRE) 2 b.c. (Feb 1) Marju (IRE) 127 – Shauna's Honey (IRE) 88 **77 p** (Danehill (USA) 126) [2007 p7.1s² Dec 21] 100,000F, 100,000Y: half-brother to 11f to 2m winner Isa'af (by Darshaan) and winner around 1m in Hong Kong by Indian Ridge: dam, Irish 7f winner, half-sister to smart French performer up to 10.5f Ahohoney: evens favourite, green when promising length second to Fadhb Ar Bith in maiden at Wolverhampton, finishing well: will be suited by 1m+: sure to improve. *P. W. Chapple-Hyam*

MOOTAMARESS (IRE) 3 b.g. Fath (USA) 116 – Perle d'Irlande (FR) (Top Ville – 129) [2007 74: 6.1g 6m 6.1v 7.1m Sep 15] deep-girthed, close-coupled gelding: fair maiden at 2 yrs for K. Prendergast in Ireland: no form in 2007: tried blinkered/visored. *Mrs A. L. M. King*

MOOTHIR (USA) 2 gr.c. (Apr 25) Elusive Quality (USA) – Alattrah (USA) (Shadeed **70 p** (USA) 135) [2007 p7g³ Nov 17] fifth foal: dam unraced sister to 1000 Guineas winner Shadayid: 5/1, close third to Wasan in maiden at Lingfield, keeping on: will probably stay 1m: should improve. *M. Johnston*

MORAINE 3 br.f. Rainbow Quest (USA) 134 – Cantilever 107 (Sanglamore (USA) **71** 126) [2007 12m* 12m Jun 14] sparely-made filly: second foal: half-sister to 1¾m winner Levitator (by Sadler's Wells): dam, French 1¼m/1½m (Prix de Royaumont) winner, out of sister to Irish Oaks winner Princess Pati and high-class middle-distance performer Seymour Hicks: fair form: overcame greenness to win maiden at Folkestone in April by ½ length from Lindy Lou, under pressure long way out: well held in handicap at Newbury next time: would have stayed 1¾m: stud. *R. Charlton*

MORAL CODE (IRE) 3 ch.c. Danehill Dancer (IRE) 117 – Scruple (IRE) (Catrail **75 d** (USA) 123) [2007 63p: p9.5g³ 8d 10d p8.6g³ p12.2g⁵ Nov 27] heavy-topped colt: fair maiden: stays 9.5f: acts on polytrack: refused to race second outing, reluctant to do so next time: one to treat with caution. *E. J. O'Neill*

MORAL DUTY (USA) 2 ch.c. (Jan 22) Silver Deputy (CAN) – Shoogle (USA) 86 (A **73** P Indy (USA) 131) [2007 6d⁵ 6m⁶ 6m⁵ 6d* Oct 15] close-coupled colt: fair form: won maiden at Windsor final start: will stay 1m: acts on good to soft going: sould 22,000 gns, sent to Czech Republic. *Pat Eddery*

MORBICK 3 ch.g. Kyllachy 129 – Direcvil (Top Ville 129) [2007 f6g⁴ 7m⁵ 7.5m **58** 8.3s 9.1d p9.5g² p8.6g³ Dec 29] lengthy, heavy-topped gelding: modest maiden: left M. Johnston and gelded after fifth start: stays 9.5f: acts on polytrack and good to firm ground. *W. M. Brisbourne*

MORESTEAD (IRE) 2 ch.c. (Apr 5) Traditionally (USA) 117 – Itsy Bitsy Betsy **75 §** (USA) (Beau Genius (CAN)) [2007 7d 7g 7m⁶ 7.1g Oct 2] rangy colt: maiden: fair form on debut, but went wrong way after (including temperamentally): raced at 7f. *B. G. Powell*

MORES WELLS 3 b.c. Sadler's Wells (USA) 132 – Endorsement 107 (Warning 136) **116** [2007 90p: 10g* 10m* 10m⁴ 12s⁵ 12g 12d* 14m³ 15d⁶ Oct 6] 220,000Y: close-coupled, quite attractive colt: third foal: closely related to 4-y-o Galient and 2004 2-y-o 7f winner Road Rage (by Giant's Causeway): dam 1½m/1¾m winner: smart performer: won maiden and P. W. McGrath Memorial Ballysax Stakes (beat Ferneley by ½ length) in April, and Ballyroan Stakes (by ½ length from Fracas, drifting left) in August, all at Leopardstown: also ran well when 3 lengths seventh to Yellowstone in Gordon Stakes at Goodwood and 5 lengths third to Yeats in Irish St Leger at the Curragh fifth/seventh starts: stays 1¾m: acts on good to firm and good to soft going (below-form fifth in Irish Derby on soft): usually tongue tied. *Kevin Prendergast, Ireland*

MORE VOTES (IRE) 6 b.g. Victory Note (USA) 120 – Mardi Gras Belle (USA) 65§ **64** (Masked Dancer (USA)) [2007 66: p9.5g 12m 9.5m² 13m³ 12m Jun 11] modest handicapper: well below form at Wolverhampton on reappearance: stays 13f: has form on good to soft going, best efforts on firmer than good: ran poorly in cheekpieces final start. *Eoin Doyle, Ireland*

MORFORWYN 2 br.f. (Mar 31) Averti (IRE) 117 – Rash Gift 78 (Cadeaux Genereux 131) [2007 6g p6g p6g p7.1g p9.5s Dec 20] 14,000Y: seventh foal: sister to Italian 7f (at 2 yrs)/1m winner Accussi Grande and half-sister to useful performer up to 1¾m Allergy (by Alzao), 1m winner at 2 yrs, and 6-y-o Nightspot: dam maiden (stayed 1¼m): little form: left J. Osborne prior to final start: tried blinkered. *A. Bailey* –

MORINQUA (IRE) 3 b.f. Cadeaux Genereux 131 – Victoria Regia (IRE) 90 (Lomond (USA) 128) [2007 82: 5.1g* 5g² 5.1m² 5g* 5g* 5d³ 5g³ 5.1s² 5g² 5g⁴ 5m 5g Sep 23] small, good-quartered filly: useful performer: much improved in 2007, winning handicaps at Nottingham in April and York in May, and minor event at Beverley (beat Siren's Gift by length) later in May: creditable efforts next 4 starts: ran as if amiss final outing: best at 5f: acts on soft and good to firm going: front runner: consistent. *J. G. Given* **98**

MORMEATMIC 4 b.g. Orpen (USA) 116 – Minining 83 (Tower Walk 130) [2007 80: 5f 5g f5g 5.1d⁶ May 12] good-topped gelding: handicapper, only modest in 2007: best form at 5f: acts on good to soft going, below form on firmer than good. *M. W. Easterby* **63**

MORNING FAREWELL 3 br.g. Daylami (IRE) 138 – Got To Go 99 (Shareef Dancer (USA) 135) [2007 74: p9.5g² p10g⁵ 11.6m* 12.3m⁵ p10g Nov 4] smallish, unfurnished gelding: fair performer: won handicap at Windsor in April: reported in July to be suffering from sore shins and below form after 6-month break final outing: stays 11.6f: acts on polytrack and good to firm going: found little second start. *P. W. Chapple-Hyam* **79**

MORNIN RESERVES 8 b.g. Atraf 116 – Pusey Street Girl 87 (Gildoran 123) [2007 5m May 5] tall, angular gelding: one-time useful performer: lightly raced and little form since 2004: tried in cheekpieces/tongue tie. *W. G. Harrison* –

MOROCCHIUS (USA) 2 b.c. (May 18) Black Minnaloushe (USA) 123 – Shakespearean (USA) (Theatrical 128) [2007 7d⁵ p7m⁴ p7g Oct 24] compact colt: fair maiden: should prove best up to 7f: sold 17,000 gns. *R. M. Beckett* **72**

MORRISTOWN MUSIC (IRE) 3 b.f. Distant Music (USA) 126 – Tongabezi (IRE) 75 (Shernazar 131) [2007 71: 6f⁴ 5m⁴ 5m 5v* 5m 5g 5g 5m 5.1s⁵ 5v* Oct 26] close-coupled filly: fair handicapper: won at Newcastle in June (one of 2 to race far side) and Ayr in October: should prove best at 5f/6f: acts on good to firm going, but both wins on heavy. *J. S. Wainwright* **70**

MORSE (IRE) 6 b.g. Shinko Forest (IRE) – Auriga 73 (Belmez (USA) 131) [2007 86: p6g² p6g³ p6g⁶ p6g 6d 6.1s Oct 18] close-coupled gelding: fairly useful handicapper, better on all-weather than turf nowadays: effective at 6f to 1m: acts on polytrack, soft and good to firm going. *J. A. Osborne* **a81** –

MOSCOW OZNICK 2 b. or br.c. (Feb 1) Auction House (USA) 120 – Cozette (IRE) 49 (Danehill Dancer (IRE) 117) [2007 8g 8d Oct 30] compact colt: better effort in maidens when seventh to First Avenue at Yarmouth latterly: may prove best up to 1m. *N. J. Vaughan* **65**

MOSSMANN GORGE 5 b.g. Lujain (USA) 119 – North Pine (Import 127) [2007 72, a68: f14g f12g³ p12.2g f12g Jan 25] quite good-topped gelding: modest performer nowadays: left M. Wellings after reappearance: stays 1½m: acts on all-weather, soft and good to firm going: wears headgear: usually held up: tricky ride, often finds little. *R. A. Harris* **56**

MOSS VALE (IRE) 6 b.h. Shinko Forest (IRE) – Wolf Cleugh (IRE) 65 (Last Tycoon 131) [2007 126: 6g 6m² 5g² 5g³ 5m 6.5m 5g³ 6m² 5g⁴ Oct 7] big, strong, lengthy horse: had a quick action: high-class performer at his best: just smart in 2007: creditable second in Greenlands Stakes at the Curragh, Temple Stakes at Sandown and Renaissance Stakes at the Curragh (beaten ¾ length by Benbaun): also ran creditably when in frame behind Benbaun in Flying Five Stakes at the Curragh and Prix de l'Abbaye at Longchamp seventh/final starts: was effective at 5f/6f: acted on heavy and good to firm going: usually raced prominently: retired, and to stand at Rathbarry Stud, Co Cork, Ireland, fee €5,000. *D. Nicholls* **117**

MOSS WAY 2 b.g. (Feb 15) Zaha (CAN) 106 – Ruwaya (USA) 80 (Red Ransom (USA)) [2007 f6g p6g 6d Aug 26] no show in maidens, then gelded: bred to be suited by middle distances (dam stayed 1¾m). *W. J. Musson* –

MOSTANAD 5 b.g. Alhaarth (IRE) 126 – Jeed (IRE) 86 (Mujtahid (USA) 118) [2007 64, a48: p6g p8g f6g 6f 7.1m p8.6g 5.7d Oct 1] lengthy gelding: modest maiden: left **53**

J. M. Bradley after third start: stays 6f: acts on firm and soft going, only poor form on polytrack: tried blinkered/in cheekpieces. *R. A. Harris*

MOSTARSIL (USA) 9 ch.g. Kingmambo (USA) 125 – Naazeq 80 (Nashwan (USA) 135) [2007 79: 10g 12m 14d 14m⁵ 11.9f 16m⁴ 16m Sep 16] workmanlike gelding: fair handicapper: inconsistent in 2007, said to have finished lame last 2 starts: stays 17f, effective at 1½m: acts on polytrack, firm and soft going: tried blinkered/visored, usually wears cheekpieces: usually races prominently. *G. L. Moore* **68**

MOST BECOMING 4 b.f. Most Welcome 131 – Bertie's Girl (Another Realm 118) [2007 p8.6g p9.5g Feb 2] fifth foal: half-sister to 9f to 11.5f winner Berzoud (by Ezzoud): dam ran once: well held in maidens at Wolverhampton. *S. Parr* **–**

MOST DEFINITELY (IRE) 7 b.g. Definite Article 121 – Unbidden Melody (USA) (Chieftain) [2007 90: p12g p16g³ 16m⁵ 16g⁵ 13.3m⁶ 14.8d 14.1d⁵ Aug 16] good-bodied gelding: fair handicapper: effective at 1½m to 17f: acts on fibresand, firm and good to soft going: tried blinkered/in cheekpieces: held up: tends to finish weakly, and is best treated with caution. *R. M. Stronge* **78 §**

MOTAFARRED (IRE) 5 ch.g. Machiavellian (USA) 123 – Thurayya (Nashwan (USA) 135) [2007 81d: 10.1m 9.8m 7.5m² 9.1g⁵ p7g* p8g² 6.9m⁴ 8.3m* 8m² 9.9m⁶ 8g Oct 6] leggy, workmanlike gelding: fair handicapper: won at Kempton (apprentices) in July and Leicester in August: stays 1½m, effective at much shorter: acts on polytrack and firm ground: tried tongue tied. *Micky Hammond* **78**

MOTARJM (USA) 3 br.g. Elusive Quality (USA) – Agama (USA) 44 (Nureyev (USA) 131) [2007 10m f8g 9g 8g⁶ 7f⁵ 8.1m⁴ 10.1d⁵ p11g² Sep 12] tall gelding: fair maiden handicapper: left M. Jarvis after third outing: stays easy 11f: acts on polytrack, firm and good to soft ground: tongue tied last 5 starts. *H. J. Collingridge* **72**

MOTHER'S DAY 4 b.f. Foxhound (USA) 103 – Compact Disc (IRE) 48 (Royal Academy (USA) 130) [2007 –: 5s 5m 8.3m p6g Sep 5] small filly: half-sister to 3 winners, including 8-y-o Turibius: dam 2-y-o 7f winner: fair performer at 2 yrs, winning maiden at Tipperary (for M. Browne): little solid form since, leaving Frederick Bowles in Ireland after second start in 2007: tried blinkered/in cheekpieces. *L. A. Dace* **–**

MOTHERWELL 2 b.f. (Feb 21) Tamayaz (CAN) 121 – Mother Corrigan (IRE) 64 (Paris House 123) [2007 6g 7d 7d Jul 22] 500Y: first foal: dam 7f winner: no form. *M. Brittain* **–**

MOTIVE (FR) 6 ch.g. Machiavellian (USA) 123 – Mistle Song 112 (Nashwan (USA) 135) [2007 99: 12g⁵ 10m May 28] lengthy, good-topped gelding: useful at best: lightly raced and only fairly useful in 2007: stays 1½m: acts on good to firm going. *J. Howard Johnson* **93**

MOTU (IRE) 6 b.g. Desert Style (IRE) 121 – Pink Cashmere (IRE) (Polar Falcon (USA) 126) [2007 69: p7g p7.1g p7.1g* 7.1m² 7f⁶ 7.1m² 8.3m² May 6] good-topped gelding: fair handicapper: won at Wolverhampton in March: stays 1m: acts on polytrack, firm and good to soft going: tried blinkered, visored nowadays: sometimes hangs left. *I. W. McInnes* **75**

MOUNAFES 3 ch.c. Barathea (IRE) 127 – Guilty Secret (IRE) 109 (Kris 135) [2007 10.3m p12g⁵ 11.5m³ 12d p12.2g 17.2g Oct 24] sturdy colt: modest maiden: stays 1½m: acts on polytrack and good to firm ground: tried blinkered: sold 6,000 gns, sent to Germany. *G. A. Butler* **64**

MOUNTAIN CAT (IRE) 3 b.g. Red Ransom (USA) – Timewee (USA) (Romanov (IRE) 119) [2007 53: p8.6g⁵ p8.6g* 8d p8g* p8.6g* p8.6g* p8m 8g Nov 2] stocky gelding: fairly useful handicapper: much improved in 2007, winning at Wolverhampton in June, Kempton in July, and Wolverhampton in August and September: not discredited back on turf final outing: stays 8.6f: acts on polytrack: races prominently. *W. J. Musson* **85**

MOUNTAIN CLIMB (IRE) 5 ch.g. Monashee Mountain (USA) 115 – Fancied 62 (Dominion 123) [2007 48: p8g⁵ 8f* p10g⁶ p8.6g⁶ p9.5g³ p8.6g Dec 1] poor performer: won minor event at Bath in April: stays easy 1¼m: acts on polytrack and firm ground: tried blinkered: has hung markedly: said to have finished lame final outing. *J. D. Frost* **47**

MOUNTAIN FAIRY 4 ch.f. Daylami (IRE) 138 – Mountain Spirit (IRE) (Royal Academy (USA) 130) [2007 p12.2g f16g Mar 19] third foal: half-sister to fairly useful French 1m winner (including at 2 yrs) Mountain Stream (by Vettori): dam, French 12.5f winner, half-sister to Prix Saint-Alary winner Muncie and Prix Royal-Oak winner Mersey: fair maiden: left E. Lellouche after fourth start in 2006 and D. Sepulchre after **–**

final one: little form in Britain, visored and looked none too keen before pulled up final outing: stays 1½m: tried blinkered. *B. S. Rothwell*

MOUNTAIN HIGH (IRE) 5 b.h. Danehill (USA) 126 – Hellenic 125 (Darshaan **123** 133) [2007 124: 10g⁵ 12s* 12g³ 12g* 12g Sep 2]

For the second time in four years a late-maturing five-year-old bay horse trained by Sir Michael Stoute and ridden by Kieren Fallon won the Grand Prix de Saint-Cloud. And they are not the only similarities between Mountain High and the 2004 winner Gamut, as both are products of the Ballymacoll Stud and neither had won a Group 1 event previously. Gamut at least had a pattern-race victory to his name, successful in the Jockey Club Stakes on his previous start. Mountain High's most important victory prior to the Grand Prix in June had come in a listed event at Ascot six weeks earlier.

Mountain High had shown very smart form at Group 2 level, though, when runner-up in the Hardwicke Stakes and Princess of Wales's Stakes in 2006. In the light of his relative lack of experience—he was making only his eighth appearance in the Princess of Wales's, which proved to be his final race that season—the chances were that he would prove at least as good in 2007. When Mountain High returned in the Gordon Richards Stakes at Sandown in April, not surprisingly he shaped as if in need of his first race for over nine months, and he showed the benefit of that run at Ascot the following month. Mountain High had comfortably the best form of the seven who contested the Bovis Homes Buckhounds Stakes, and he started odds on for it despite concerns about the soft ground, having failed to come up to expectations on the only occasion he had encountered such a surface previously. The ground was not a problem as it turned out, and neither was the opposition, Mountain High setting a steady pace and drawing away in the closing stages, despite edging left, to win by four lengths. Akarem, successful in the same race twelve months earlier, finished second. Mountain High followed with a respectable third to Saddex in the Grand Prix de Chantilly, again edging left under pressure, and then came the Grand Prix de Saint-Cloud. Mountain High and Ponte Tresa were the outsiders in a six-runner field, the favourite being the 2006 Prix Vermeille winner Mandesha bidding to become the first odds-on shot to win it since Montjeu in 2000. There had been no fewer than five odds-on failures in the interim, Egyptband, Aquarelliste and Bago all finishing third, Sulamani fifth and Hurricane Run, ridden by Fallon, beaten a head by Pride in 2006. Mountain High returned to his best to ensure that Mandesha became the sixth to bite the dust. Still tracking the leader Irish Wells when the pace was stepped up on the home turn, Mountain High was sent on over two furlongs out and ran on well, keeping a straight course this time and never really being threatened in winning by a length and a half from Mandesha. Mountain High's five-year-old campaign ended with a below-par performance in the Grosser Preis von Baden, in which he was already looking held when hampered over a furlong out. It turned out to be Mountain High's last race. He has been retired to stand as a jumps stallion in Ireland, following in the footsteps of Gamut (who won the Princess of Wales's Stakes at six after being placed in it at four).

Mountain High's dam Hellenic won three races including the Ribblesdale Stakes and Yorkshire Oaks, and also finished runner-up to Snurge in the St Leger. She has proved high class as a broodmare, too, and Mountain High is her third Group 1 winner, following on from Islington and Greek Dance, both of whom are

Grand Prix de Saint-Cloud, Saint-Cloud—Mountain High upsets the odds on Mandesha, the sixth such favourite beaten in the race in the last seven runnings; Prince Flori, Irish Wells and Youmzain are next

Mrs John Magnier & Mr M. Tabor's "Mountain High"

Mountain High (IRE) (b.h. 2002)	Danehill (USA) (b 1986)	Danzig (b 1977)	Northern Dancer
			Pas de Nom
		Razyana (b 1981)	His Majesty
			Spring Adieu
	Hellenic (b 1987)	Darshaan (br 1981)	Shirley Heights
			Delsy
		Grecian Sea (ch 1978)	Homeric
			Sea Venture

by Sadler's Wells. Islington surpassed Hellenic by winning the Yorkshire Oaks twice, and was also successful at the top level in the Breeders' Cup Filly & Mare Turf; Greek Dance won the Grosser Dallmayr-Preis as a five-year-old. Of Hellenic's five other winners, four are also by Sadler's Wells. They include the stayer Election Day and middle-distance performer New Morning, both smart, and two who were successful in the latest season, Greek Well and Praxiteles. Three-year-old Praxiteles was having only his second start when running out an impressive winner of a maiden at Lingfield in November, and he looks one who could further enhance Hellenic's already impressive stud record in the next season. Hellenic's dam and grandam were both useful and finished in the frame in Group 3 races. Mountain High stayed a mile and a half and acted on soft and good to firm going. A good-topped, attractive individual, he will be standing at Coolmore's Beeches Stud at a fee of €4,000. *Sir Michael Stoute*

MOUNTAIN PASS (USA) 5 b.g. Stravinsky (USA) 133 – Ribbony (USA) (Dayjur (USA) 137) [2007 65, a74d: p7g* p7.1g⁴ p7g⁶ 7.1m⁵ p7g p8g p7m⁵ p7.1g* p8g⁵ Dec 28] fair performer: won handicap at Lingfield in January and seller at Wolverhampton in

713

December: effective at 5f to 1m: acts on polytrack, firm and soft going: wears headgear: tried tongue tied: sometimes slowly away. *B. J. Llewellyn*

MOUNTAIN PRIDE (IRE) 2 b.c. (Jan 24) High Chaparral (IRE) 132 – Lioness 74 **93 p** (Lion Cavern (USA) 117) [2007 7s³ 7m⁵ 8.3g* Oct 16] €80,000Y: light-bodied colt: has moderate, quick action: third foal: half-brother to 5-y-o Wilford Maverick: dam, maiden (stayed 9f), half-sister to smart French 7f/1m performer Puppeteer: fairly useful form: confirmed earlier promise (third to Yankadi at Newmarket) when winning maiden at Leicester by 2½ lengths from Cuban Missile, forging away once switched clear: will be suited by 1¼m/1½m: acts on soft going: useful prospect. *J. L. Dunlop*

MOUNT HADLEY (USA) 3 b.c. Elusive Quality (USA) – Fly To The Moon (USA) **102** 90 (Blushing Groom (FR) 131) [2007 92: a7f³ 7.5g* 8m³ Sep 14] tall, good-topped colt: useful performer, lightly raced: best effort when winning minor event at Nad Al Sheba in March by neck from Truly Royal (then left I. Mohammed in UAE): off 6 months, visored and tongue tied, ran as though amiss in minor event at Doncaster final outing: stays 7.5f: acts on dirt and good to soft going: sold 70,000 gns. *Saeed bin Suroor*

MOUNT HERMON (IRE) 3 b.g. Golan (IRE) 129 – Machudi (Bluebird (USA) 125) **82** [2007 79p: f7g* p7.1g⁶ p8g* 8d Sep 28] big, strong, heavy-bodied gelding: fairly useful performer: won maiden at Southwell (simple task) in March and handicap at Lingfield in September: stays 1m: acts on all-weather and firm ground. *H. Morrison*

MOUNT KILIMANJARO (IRE) 4 b.c. Sadler's Wells (USA) 132 – Hill of Snow **110** 80 (Reference Point 139) [2007 96p: 14.1g* 16.4d⁴ May 29] strong, lengthy colt: smart performer, lightly raced: won listed race at Nottingham in April by neck from The Last Drop: sweating slightly, hung left over 2f out when respectable fourth to Allegretto in Henry II Stakes at Sandown subsequent outing: probably stayed 2m: acted on soft and good to firm going: retired. *J. L. Dunlop*

MOUNT LAVINIA (IRE) 2 b.f. (Feb 8) Montjeu (IRE) 137 – Havinia (Habitat 134) **–** [2007 7g 8.2d Oct 10] 24,000F, 55,000Y: unfurnished filly: closely related to smart Swedish 8.5f/1½m winner Highway (by King's Theatre) and fairly useful 1¼m winner Cill Droichead (by Entrepreneur) and half-sister to 2 winners, including smart French/US 1m to 1¼m winner Lord Cromby (by Risen Star): dam French 1m winner: well held (and none too keen) in maidens. *R. M. Beckett*

MOUNT NELSON 3 b.c. Rock of Gibraltar (IRE) 133 – Independence 116 (Selkirk **–** (USA) 129) [2007 114p: 10d Oct 20] big, strong, close-coupled colt: smart performer, lightly raced: won Criterium International at Saint-Cloud at 2 yrs: reported in May to be on 'easy list', and looked in need of run when well held in Champion Stakes at Newmarket only 3-y-o start: shapes as if will stay at least 1¼m. *A. P. O'Brien, Ireland*

MOUNT PLEASURE (USA) 2 ch.c. (Mar 18) Mt Livermore (USA) – Private Beach **98** (USA) (Unaccounted for (USA) 124) [2007 5m* 5m* 6g³ 6m⁵ Jun 19] $42,000F, €39,000Y: leggy, short-backed colt: third foal: dam unraced half-sister to useful 2-y-o 5f/ 6f winner Snowy Owl: useful form: won maiden at Windsor in April and minor event at Ascot in May: further improvement in listed race at Epsom (third to Declaration of War) and Coventry Stakes at Royal Ascot (3 lengths fifth to Henrythenavigator, best of those drawn low): shapes as if 7f will suit: raced only on good/good to firm going: joined D. Watson in UAE. *J. A. Osborne*

MOUNT USHER 5 br.g. Polar Falcon (USA) 126 – Division Bell (Warning 136) [2007 **80 §** 80: 8m 8m² 8.1m³ 9.9g⁴ May 30] lengthy gelding: fairly useful handicapper: best at 1m/ 1¼m: acts on polytrack, firm and good to soft ground: ungenuine. *G. A. Swinbank*

MO (USA) 3 br.c. Cherokee Run (USA) 122 – Mambo Mate (USA) (Kingmambo (USA) **75** 125) [2007 75: 8.1g 8f a6g⁶ a6g³ a6g a6g* a8g* a8g² Oct 4] rather leggy, close-coupled colt: fair performer: left R. Kvisla after seventh to Champollion in Swedish 2000 Guineas at Taby second start: won minor events at Taby in August and September: stays 1m: acts on polytrack/dirt, firm and good to soft going: tongue tied in Britain: has looked awkward. *Yvonne Durant, Sweden*

MOUSEEN (IRE) 4 ch.g. Alhaarth (IRE) 126 – Marah 93 (Machiavellian (USA) 123) **56** [2007 65: f6g⁵ f7g³ f6g⁶ f6g 8.1m 10.2g Jun 1] only modest at best in 2007, leaving R. Harris after fourth start: stays 7.5f: acts on fibresand, soft and good to firm going: tried in cheekpieces/blinkers/tongue tie: very slowly away penultimate start. *R. J. Price*

MOUSE WHITE 2 bl. or gr.g. (Mar 31) Auction House (USA) 120 – Petinata (Petong **–** 126) [2007 5.7g 7s Jul 25] well beaten in maidens (blinkered in latter). *H. Candy*

MOVE OVER DARLING (IRE) 4 b.f. Singspiel (IRE) 133 – Darling Harbour **65** (USA) (Candy Stripes (USA) 115) [2007 f11g² 13.1m⁶ May 21] tall, close-coupled filly:

fair maiden: stays 11f: acts on fibresand and good to soft going: sold 8,000 gns in July. *P. F. I. Cole*

MOVES GOODENOUGH 4 ch.g. Woodborough (USA) 112 – Rekindled Flame **76** (IRE) (Kings Lake (USA) 133) [2007 73: p7.1g³ p8g 8m 8g* 8g² 10d⁴ p9.5g 8g p7.1g Nov 4] compact gelding: fair handicapper: won at Bath in June: stays 1¼m: acts on polytrack, good to firm and good to soft ground: can race freely: often blinkered. *Andrew Turnell*

MOVIE MOGUL 3 b. or br.f. Sakhee (USA) 136 – Norfolk Lavender (CAN) 80 (Ascot **62** Knight (CAN) 130) [2007 p8.6g 8.2g p8.6g Jun 2] €100,000Y, 28,000 2-y-o: tall filly: sixth foal: half-sister to 3 winners, including useful 1m (at 2 yrs) to 1½m winner Celtic Mission (by Cozzene) and fairly useful 7f/1m winner In The Pink (by Indian Ridge): dam, 1m/8.5f (latter minor US Stakes) winner, out of 1000 Guineas winner Nocturnal Spree: modest form in maidens, not knocked about last 2 starts: should be suited by 9f+. *M. L. W. Bell*

MOVILLE (IRE) 2 b.g. (Apr 21) Alhaarth (IRE) 126 – No Sugar Baby (FR) (Crystal **84 p** Glitters (USA) 127) [2007 7d 8m² 8m⁵ Sep 12] 32,000F: rather leggy, quite attractive gelding: brother to French 9.5f winner Nampala, closely related to 3 winners by Unfu-wain, notably useful 1½m to 2m winner Sweetness Herself, and half-brother to 3 winners abroad: dam French maiden: fairly useful maiden: second to Centennial at New-market (race worked out well): gelded after final start: will stay 1¼m: capable of better. *B. W. Hills*

MOVING STORY 4 b.g. Desert Story (IRE) 115 – Arianna Aldini (Habitat 134) [2007 **51** –: 10g⁵ 9.9s⁶ 8s 7.9g 10.4m 10f⁶ 10g Oct 25] strong gelding: modest maiden: stays 1¼m: acts on firm and soft ground. *P. T. Midgley*

MOVING TARGET (IRE) 8 ch.g. Karaar 74 – Lucky Noire 73 (Aragon 118) [2007 **63** –: p12g⁶ p13g⁶ p10g⁴ f11g 10m Jun 3] modest maiden: very lightly raced: best effort when fourth in handicap at Lingfield: probably stayed 13f: said to have had a breathing problem only start at 7 yrs: dead. *Luke Comer, Ireland*

MOWADEH (IRE) 3 ch.g. In The Wings 128 – Jazmeer 88 (Sabrehill (USA) 120) **73** [2007 11m 12m⁴ 12m² 12g² 11.7g 11.5s⁵ 12m⁴ 16g 15.9m⁶ p9.5g Nov 1] stocky gelding: fair maiden: left M. Channon before final outing: should stay 1¾m: acts on soft and good to firm going: in cheekpieces final start: lazy. *J. R. Gask*

MOYENNE CORNICHE 2 ch.c. (Feb 12) Selkirk (USA) 129 – Miss Corniche 104 **72 p** (Hernando (FR) 127) [2007 8.2g⁴ Oct 31] big, lengthy colt: first foal: dam, 7f (at 2 yrs) and 1¼m winner, sister to useful 1m winner Miss Riviera Golf: 11/1 and green, encourag-ing fourth in maiden at Nottingham, coming wide from last: will be suited by 1¼m: sure to improve. *G. Wragg*

MOYNAHAN (USA) 2 ch.c. (Jan 25) Johannesburg (USA) 127 – Lakab (USA) 74 **104 p** (Manila (USA)) [2007 6g⁴ 6g* Aug 22] $200,000Y, 150,000 2-y-o: big, good-bodied colt: half-brother to several winners, including US 8.5f (including at 2 yrs and a minor stakes) winner European Rose (by Nureyev): dam, 7.6f winner, half-sister to very smart 1m/9f performer Wixm and smart 1m/1¼m winner Run Softly: useful form: shaped well when fourth to Shallal at Goodwood, then impressively won maiden at York by 2½ lengths from Iguazu Falls: will stay 7f/1m: pattern performer in the making. *P. F. I. Cole*

MOYNE PLEASURE (IRE) 9 b.g. Exit To Nowhere (USA) 122 – Ilanga (IRE) 92 **53** (Common Grounds 118) [2007 –: f12g³ f14g³ f14g f11g⁴ f12g⁴ 12d⁴ 12d² 15.8s Oct 9] small, sparely-made gelding: modest performer: stays 2m: acts on fibresand, firm and soft ground (well held on heavy): tried in cheekpieces: sometimes looks none too keen, refused to race final 6-y-o outing. *R. Johnson*

MOYOKO (IRE) 4 b.f. Mozart (IRE) 131 – Kayoko (IRE) 74 (Shalford (IRE) 124§) **64** [2007 64: p8g⁴ p8g p8g⁶ p8g 7.1s⁵ 8f⁴ 8.1d⁴ 9.7f⁵ p9.5g* p10g p10g p9.5g Nov 12] close-coupled filly: modest handicapper: won at Wolverhampton in September: stays 9.5f: acts on polytrack, firm and good to soft ground. *M. Blanshard*

MOZAKHRAF (USA) 5 b.g. Miswaki (USA) 124 – Anakid (USA) (Danzig (USA)) **72** [2007 73: p7.1g p6g* p6g p6g 6g⁴ 7.1g 7s 6d⁴ p6g* 6s 7.2s p6g⁵ p6g⁶ p7g⁶ p7m p6g⁶ f6d² Dec 21] good-topped gelding: fair handicapper: won at Lingfield (amateurs) in January and Hamilton and Wolverhampton in July: best at 6f/7f: acts on all-weather, firm and good to soft going: tried in cheekpieces: often races freely: sometimes finds little. *K. A. Ryan*

MR AITCH (IRE) 5 b.g. Soviet Star (USA) 128 – Welsh Mist 102 (Damister (USA) **79** 123) [2007 83: 12.3m⁵ 12.3m Aug 23] big, good-topped gelding: fairly useful handicapper: stays 1½m: acts on polytrack and firm going (seemingly not good to soft): tongue tied nowadays. *R. T. Phillips*

MR AVIATOR (USA) 3 b. or br.c. Lear Fan (USA) 130 – In Bloom (USA) (Clever **98** Trick (USA)) [2007 80p: 8.1g 9g* 9.9m² 8m 8g⁴ 9.9g² 10m 10s³ 10d Oct 27] tall colt: has a short action: useful handicapper: won at Goodwood in May: good efforts after when in frame, including when second to Pipedreamer in Alphameric Vase at same course sixth start: worth a try at 1½m: acts on polytrack, soft and good to firm ground. *R. Hannon*

MR BELVEDERE 6 b.g. Royal Applause 124 – Alarming Motown (Warning 136) **50 §** [2007 –§, a56§: p8.6g⁶ p12g p8.6g p10m Oct 13] sturdy gelding: modest performer: stays easy 1½m: acts on polytrack, firm and good to soft ground: wears headgear: has hung left: unreliable. *A. J. Lidderdale*

MR BOUNTIFUL (IRE) 9 b.g. Mukaddamah (USA) 125 – Nawadder 73 (Kris 135) **–** [2007 f6g f8g f7g³ f7g⁶ f8g f8g f7g Mar 20] angular gelding: poor performer on balance: **a44** best at 6f/7f: acts on all-weather, firm and soft going: often wears headgear/tongue tie. *C. J. Teague*

MR CELLOPHANE 4 ch.g. Pursuit of Love 124 – Fresh Fruit Daily 92 (Reprimand **85** 122) [2007 85: 6f² p6g² 6m 6d³ 6d⁴ p6g 7m⁴ 7d⁶ 6m 6.1s² 6d p6g⁴ Dec 5] tall, lengthy gelding: fairly useful handicapper: best at 5f/6f: acts on polytrack, firm and good to soft going: tried visored. *J. R. Jenkins*

MR CHOCOLATE DROP (IRE) 3 b.g. Danetime (IRE) 121 – Forest Blade (IRE) **–** (Charnwood Forest (IRE) 125) [2007 –: f8g² f8g f8g⁴ f7s* f8g f7g⁴ p7.1g⁴ f8g 8.5s 7.6g **a55** 7g 10.1d f7d⁵ f8d Dec 20] modest performer on all-weather, no form on turf: won seller at Southwell in February: left M. Attwater after eighth outing: stays 1m: acts on all-weather: sometimes wears headgear: tried tongue tied. *Miss M. E. Rowland*

MR CRYSTAL (FR) 3 ch.g. Trempolino (USA) 135 – Iyrbila (FR) (Lashkari 128) **66** [2007 –: f7g⁶ 9.8g 12.1m⁶ 12.1m* 12s⁶ 14.1m³ 14.1m³ Aug 25] fair handicapper: won at Beverley in June: stays 1¾m: acts on good to firm going: gelded, fairly useful winner over hurdles. *Micky Hammond*

MR ED (IRE) 9 ch.g. In The Wings 128 – Center Moriches (IRE) 74 (Magical Wonder **–** (USA) 125) [2007 –: 16.2m 16.1m⁶ Aug 11] tall, angular gelding: one-time fairly useful handicapper: little impact since 2005: wears cheekpieces. *P. Bowen*

MR EXCEL (IRE) 4 b.g. Orpen (USA) 116 – Collected (IRE) (Taufan (USA) 119) **–** [2007 86: p13.9g⁶ p12.2d⁶ p12.2g Dec 22] good-topped gelding: fairly useful at best, lightly raced: well below form in 2007. *G. A. Ham*

MR FANTOZZI (IRE) 2 br.c. (Apr 20) Statue of Liberty (USA) 115 – Indian Sand **65 ?** (Indian King (USA) 128) [2007 6d⁴ 6d 7m Aug 3] tall colt: maiden: probably flattered when fourth in minor event at Yarmouth on debut: bred to stay 1m. *Miss J. Feilden*

MR FORTHRIGHT 3 b.c. Fraam 114 – Form At Last (Formidable (USA) 125) [2007 **57** 55: 6g 7.1m 6.1m 5.1m* 6.1m⁶ 5.7g⁴ 5.1s* 5f⁵ 5g⁶ 5.1f⁶ 5.7g p6m p7.1g Dec 1] big, lengthy colt: modest performer: won maiden in May and handicap in July, both at Bath: best at 5f/6f: acts on firm and soft going, probably on polytrack. *J. M. Bradley*

MR FUNSHINE 2 b.g. (Jan 28) Namid 128 – Sunrise Girl 62 (King's Signet (USA) **63** 110) [2007 5.7g 5.1g 5m p6g 5d⁴ p5.1g Oct 22] good-topped gelding: modest maiden: best efforts at 5f: gelded after final start. *Mrs P. N. Dutfield*

MR GARSTON 4 b.g. Mull of Kintyre (USA) 114 – Ninfa of Cisterna (Polish Patriot **92** (USA) 128) [2007 92: 7.1d² 8g May 24] fairly useful performer, very lightly raced: stays 7f: acts on polytrack, good to firm and good to soft going. *M. P. Tregoning*

MR GRAND LODGE (FR) 3 ch.c. Grand Lodge (USA) 125 – Legende d'Or (FR) **78** (Diesis 133) [2007 p7g 9g p8.6g⁴ 9.9d p8.6g* p8.6g² Aug 12] useful-looking colt: fair performer: improved to win handicap at Wolverhampton in July: stays 8.6f: acts on polytrack (well held starts on turf): tends to wander: sold 17,000 gns, joined D. Watson in UAE. *L. M. Cumani*

MR JOE PLATINUM (IRE) 5 b.g. Pierre – Hurgill Lady 62 (Emarati (USA) 74) **–** [2007 p12.2d⁶ Dec 28] fair form first 2 starts in bumpers, but well held (including over hurdles) since, and showed nothing in maiden at Wolverhampton on belated Flat debut (tongue tied). *E. J. Creighton*

MR KEPPEL (IRE) 2 b.c. (Feb 12) Royal Applause 124 – Oh Hebe (IRE) 74 (Night **90** Shift (USA)) [2007 6m 6m⁵ 6m³ 7d* 6g* 6m* 6g Oct 6] 58,000F, 85,000Y: sturdy, compact colt: type to carry condition: fifth foal: half-brother to smart 5f (at 2 yrs) to 9f (in US) winner Devious Boy (by Dr Devious) and useful 6f/7f winner Special Lad (by Spectrum): dam, 7f winner, half-sister to smart performers Leporello (at 1¼m) and Poppy Carew (at 1¼m/1½m): fairly useful form: won maiden at Brighton in August and nurseries at Haydock (from Art Sale and Eastern Romance) and Newbury in September: wide throughout from low draw when seventh of 23 to Dubai Dynamo in listed Two-Year-Old Trophy at Redcar final start: winner at 7f, probably best at 6f: acts on good to firm and good to soft going: sold 155,000 gns. *J. A. Osborne*

MR KLICK (IRE) 3 b.g. Tendulkar (USA) 114 – Lake Poopo (IRE) 79 (Persian –
Heights 129) [2007 79: 6m 6g 8v⁵ 5v Jul 15] tall gelding: fair performer at 2 yrs: no form in 2007: wore cheekpieces (mulish stall, hung left) final outing. *N. Wilson*

MR LAMBROS 6 ch.g. Pivotal 124 – Magical Veil 73 (Majestic Light (USA)) [2007 –, –
a105: a7f 5.2g p6g p7.1g 5g p5.1g⁵ p6d* Dec 28] good-topped gelding: fairly useful **a86 +**
handicapper nowadays: reportedly bled and also locked a stifle at Nad Al Sheba on reappearance (left A. Balding and off 7 months after): won handicap at Wolverhampton final start: best at 6f/7f: acts on polytrack and firm ground: visored last 4 starts, tongue tied last 6: often races prominently. *Miss Gay Kelleway*

MR LOIRE 3 b.g. Bertolini (USA) 125 – Miss Sancerre 95 (Last Tycoon 131) [2007 75: **76 d**
p6g³ p6g⁵ p6g* p7g p6g 5.3s⁴ 5.3m² p6g⁵ 5.3d⁶ 5d⁶ 5.7m* 5.7d p6g⁶ p6g p7.1g 5.7g 5.1g p6m p6g⁵ Dec 19] rather leggy gelding: fair performer: left R. Charlton after second start: won handicap at Wolverhampton in March and claimer at Bath (left H. Dunlop after next start) in August: below form in handicaps after: should stay 7f: acts on polytrack and firm ground, probably on soft: tried visored, usually blinkered. *A. J. Chamberlain*

MR LU 2 b.g. (Mar 21) Lujain (USA) 119 – Libretta (Highest Honor (FR) 124) [2007 **51**
5m⁶ 6.1s 6m³ Sep 22] modest maiden: beaten 13 lengths when third at Catterick: likely to stay 7f. *G. A. Swinbank*

MR MINI SCULE 3 b.g. Piccolo 121 – Courtisane (Persepolis (FR) 127) [2007 56: **44**
p6g 7g 7.1m⁶ 6m 5.7d 8.3s⁵ 7.9f Aug 6] small gelding: poor maiden: left A. Haynes after fifth start: stays 7f: acts on polytrack and firm ground: tried blinkered. *S. Wynne*

MR MISCHIEF 7 b.g. Millkom 124 – Snow Huntress 80 (Shirley Heights 130) [2007 **67**
f14g² f12g* 18g 9g 10.1d⁶ 11.6g 10g⁵ 11.6m³ 11.6f⁵ 17.1d³ 16m² 14.1m³ 12.1m⁴ 15.8s⁴ **a77**
p13.9g* p16.5g³ Nov 12] leggy gelding: fair performer: won seller at Southwell (left P. Haslam) in May and handicap at Wolverhampton in October: effective at 1¼m to 17f: acts on all-weather, firm and good to soft ground: has hung left. *M. C. Chapman*

MR NAPOLEON (IRE) 5 gr.g. Daylami (IRE) 138 – Dathuil (IRE) 97 (Royal Aca- **74**
demy (USA) 130) [2007 62: 10s 9.5g⁵ 11.9g 13g 10g 10.1m³ 10.1m p10g³ p10g 10g p10m p10g* p10g* Dec 28] rather leggy gelding: fair handicapper: left D. Weld in Ireland after fourth start, G. Prodromou after tenth: improved to win at Kempton and Lingfield in December: should stay 1½m: acts on polytrack, heavy and good to firm ground: tried in blinkers/cheekpieces: has carried head awkwardly. *G. L. Moore*

MR NAPPER TANDY 3 ch.c. Bahamian Bounty 116 – Starfleet 66 (Inchinor 119) **107**
[2007 84p: p8g² 8g² 7m² 7m² 6.5f⁵ 8f* 8f² Dec 26] sturdy colt: useful performer: further progress when runner-up first 4 starts in 2007, in handicaps first 2 outings, then 3 lengths behind Creachadoir in Tetrarch Stakes at the Curragh and 1½ lengths behind Tariq in listed race at Newmarket (off bridle before halfway): left M. Channon after: won optional claimer at Santa Anita in November: creditable length second to Monterey Jazz in Grade 3 Sir Beaufort Stakes on same course final outing: stays 1m: acts on polytrack, firm and soft going: consistent. *J. Carava, USA*

MR PLOD 2 ch.g. (Mar 9) Silver Patriarch (IRE) 125 – Emily-Mou (IRE) 80 (Cadeaux –
Genereux 131) [2007 p7g Nov 17] 50/1, well held in maiden at Lingfield, slowly away. *Andrew Reid*

MR ROONEY (IRE) 4 b.g. Mujadil (USA) 119 – Desert Bride (USA) (Key To The **71**
Kingdom (USA)) [2007 78: 5f 5g² 5.3m⁶ 5s 5d 6m 6g⁶ 5m⁴ 5s² 5g² 5.1s Oct 18] strong gelding: fair handicapper: best at 5f/6f: acts on firm and soft going: tried tongue tied: races prominently. *D. Nicholls*

MRS LINDSAY (USA) 3 ch.f. Theatrical 128 – Vole Vole Monamour (USA) **117**
(Woodman (USA) 126) [2007 11s* 10.5g* 10.5m² 12.5g⁶ 12m* 10f* Oct 21]
In 1980, the Ian Balding-trained Mrs Penny enjoyed a tremendous season, the twin highlights of which were successes in France's two top middle-distance races for three-year-old fillies, the Prix de Diane at Chantilly and the Prix Vermeille at Longchamp. Mrs Penny had already established herself as the top two-year-old

Prix Vermeille Lucien Barriere, Longchamp—Mrs Lindsay is given a fine enterprising ride by Johnny Murtagh, one of ten Group/Grade 1 successes for the jockey in 2007; West Wind looks unlucky in second, with Passage of Time (rail) and Legerete next

filly the previous season, winning the Cherry Hinton Stakes, the Lowther and the Cheveley Park, while in the spring she had finished third in the One Thousand Guineas and its Irish equivalent. In addition, between her two wins in France, she ran with great credit in defeat in top open company, beaten three quarters of a length by Ela-Mana-Mou in the King George VI and Queen Elizabeth Stakes and not getting the best of runs when fourth behind Master Willie in the Benson and Hedges Gold Cup at York. Mrs Penny was tough, game and consistent, as well as high class, and the field she beat in the Vermeille was outstanding, containing as it did the next two winners of the Prix de l'Arc de Triomphe, Detroit (an unlucky third) and Gold River (fourth), as well as that autumn's Champion Stakes winner Cairn Rouge in fifth.

Twenty-seven years and four generations later, a much more modest renewal of the Prix Vermeille was won by Mrs Penny's great-great-granddaughter Mrs Lindsay. Like Mrs Penny, Mrs Lindsay had also contested the Prix de Diane, and, while victory had eluded her at Chantilly, she had made a bold bid and beaten a dozen others, making the running until over a furlong out when headed by West Wind and keeping on for second to finish a length and a half behind the winner after looking like being swallowed up. There had been few other similarities between Mrs Lindsay and Mrs Penny up to that point however. Mrs Lindsay was a much later developer who had finished third in a newcomers race at Longchamp over a mile on her only outing at two. She earned her place in the Diane field by winning both her starts in the spring, a maiden at Fontainebleau and then the Prix Penelope at Saint-Cloud in which she pulled hard for a long way behind the steady pace before wearing down the leader Sismix near the line for a short-neck success. Although Mrs Lindsay's progressive profile was maintained in the Diane, she was sent off the complete outsider in the ten-runner field in the Vermeille after her improvement had seemingly come to an end at Deauville in August where she finished only sixth in the Prix Minerve, having been several lengths clear before the home turn.

In contrast, the Deauville meeting witnessed the disappointing Andre Fabre-trained Prix de Diane favourite Vadapolina restoring her reputation with an impressive win in the Prix de Psyche and she started favourite again (coupled with her pacemaker) for the Vermeille, while progressive stable-companion Tashelka, also successful at Deauville, in the Prix de la Nonette, was coupled in second spot in the betting with the Diane winner West Wind. In theory, the Prix Vermeille should be a more competitive race these days than it was in Mrs Penny's day, now that the race is open to older fillies and mares as well, though the two five-year-olds in the line-up, Macleya (also trained by Fabre, responsible for half the field in all) and Montare (runner-up the year before), although smart, promised to be suited by a bit more of a test, conditions on the day putting the emphasis on speed. The previous year's winner Mandesha, who was warmed up for the Arc in the Prix Foy later on the card instead, was the chief absentee among the older generations, while leading three-year-old middle-distance filly Peeping Fawn and her Oaks conqueror

Light Shift were others whose absence gave the race a substandard look. However, Light Shift's stable-companion, Passage of Time, who had been suffering from a throat abscess when a disappointing favourite for the Oaks, ensured the field was not all French.

Mrs Lindsay's win owed plenty to a fine ride by Johnny Murtagh who had also partnered her on her last two starts. Murtagh soon had the strong-galloping Mrs Lindsay tracking the steady pace set by Vadapolina's pacemaker Takaniya before committing to get her name turning into the straight. That proved a decisive move, as at the same time, West Wind, who proved to be Mrs Lindsay's biggest danger, was well down the field and struggling to extricate herself from a position on the rail. Mrs Lindsay kept on well up the straight to hold off the challenge of Passage of Time, until West Wind, finally in the clear and finishing strongly, stayed on to finish three quarters of a length behind the winner, passing third-placed Passage of Time inside the final furlong. With Vadapolina and Tashelka both disappointing, another Fabre filly Legerete took fourth ahead of Macleya and Montare.

It turned out that Mrs Penny's career had reached its peak in the Vermeille. She finished down the field in the Prix de l'Arc de Triomphe next time and enjoyed a much less successful season kept in training at four, disappointing in the Coronation Cup and Hardwicke Stakes, though winning in Grade 3 company after continuing her career in the States. Mrs Lindsay wasn't even entered in the Arc and nor were connections tempted to supplement her. Instead, she was sent to contest the E. P. Taylor Stakes at Woodbine where once again she wasn't the first from her family to get her name on the roll of honour. The relative she emulated this time was Hatoof, a daughter of Mrs Penny's half-sister Cadeaux d'Amie, and winner of the E. P. Taylor in 1992. For Hatoof, winner of the One Thousand Guineas and the Prix d'Opera (then run over an extended nine furlongs), the mile and a quarter of the Canadian race was the furthest distance she had tackled at that stage of her career. For Mrs Lindsay, it was a step down in trip, which didn't seem likely to be in her favour. However, the strong pace, resulting in the track record being broken, made it a good test and helped the free-going Mrs Lindsay to be settled better than she had in more sedate affairs at home. Initially looking held when the top local filly Sealy Hill went over a length up approaching the final furlong, Mrs Lindsay responded well for Murtagh to get on top well inside the last furlong, going on to win by half a length. The other European challenger, Blandford Stakes winner Four Sins, weakened to finish eighth of the ten runners. Mrs Lindsay's win was part of a remarkable international treble for her stable, as Ricine, in a Group 3 at Baden-Baden, and Young Tiger, in an important race at Madrid, were successful for the yard on the same day. With Mrs Lindsay following on from the likes of Pearly Shells, Turtle Bow, Whortleberry, Torrestrella and Tie Black, trainer Francois Rohaut hasn't been without a good filly in his stable over the last five seasons or so. Pearly Shells won the yard's first Prix Vermeille in 2002, while Torrestrella in 2004 and Tie Black (awarded the race in 2006) were both winners of the Poule d'Essai des Pouliches.

			Nureyev	Northern Dancer
Mrs Lindsay (USA) (ch.f. 2004)	Theatrical (b 1982)		(b 1977)	Special
		Tree of Knowledge (b 1977)	Sassafras
			Sensibility
	Vole Vole Monamour (USA) (ch 1998)	Woodman (ch 1983)	Mr Prospector
			Playmate
		A Votre Sante (ch 1993)	Irish River
			Mrs Jenney

The female line connecting Mrs Lindsay to her fourth dam Mrs Penny hangs by something of a thread because Mrs Penny's daughter Mrs Jenney produced just two foals, the only filly being Mrs Lindsay's grandam A Votre Sante. In turn, A Votre Sante was scarcely more productive, managing just three foals, her only filly being Mrs Lindsay's dam Vole Vole Monamour. Mrs Jenney won twice for Henry Cecil over six furlongs at two before two more wins in minor stakes company over an extended mile in the States. She took her name from Bettina Jenney, Mrs Lindsay's owner-breeder, whose late husband Marshall Jenney founded Derry Meeting Farm in Pennsylvania where Mrs Penny was bred. Derry Meeting was also the birthplace of Danzig and Storm Cat, as well as Lucarno, whose St Leger win came just a day before Mrs Lindsay's success in the Prix Vermeille. Returning to the equine Mrs Jenney, her colt foal was the very smart American dirt performer Unaccounted For, who won the Whitney Handicap and was placed behind Cigar in the Jockey Club Gold Cup and Breeders' Cup Classic. Mrs Jenney's daughter A Votre Sante showed useful form for Criquette Head, winning a listed race over a mile at Saint-Cloud and finishing fourth in the Poule d'Essai des Pouliches before failing to stay in the Prix de Diane. Her daughter Vole Vole Monamour dead-heated in a mile-and-a-quarter minor event at Chantilly on her only start and, so far at least, Vole Vole Monamour has proved no more productive than her dam and grandam so far as female offspring are concerned, Mrs Lindsay, her second foal, being her only filly to date. First foal General Sherman (by War Chant) has won in the States and she has a yearling colt by Tale of The Cat.

Mrs Lindsay stays in training, with the Prix de l'Arc de Triomphe reported to be her main target in 2008. Of the two relatives whom she emulated to some degree in the latest season, connections will be hoping Mrs Lindsay takes more after Hatoof than Mrs Penny as a four-year-old. Hatoof improved again at that age, winning three more races, notably the Champion Stakes at Newmarket, while the decision to keep her in training again at five paid off with wins in the Prix d'Astarte at Deauville and the Beverly D Stakes at Arlington and a second in the Breeders' Cup Turf, her two fine performances in the States earning her an Eclipse award as champion turf mare. A big, strong filly (if anything, more like a jumper on looks), who has had only seven races, Mrs Lindsay should win another good prize or two, particularly if progressing a bit more. The Arc looks to be aiming a bit high at this stage, but there are more options for older fillies in Europe now than there were in Mrs Penny's and Hatoof's day, and it would be no surprise to see Mrs Lindsay campaigned across the Atlantic again later in the year. Mrs Lindsay acts on firm and soft ground and is effective at a mile and a quarter to a mile and a half. She was very much on her toes at Longchamp, when her rider was given permission to take her to the start early, and she is keen to get on with things once racing too, which means a good pace is always likely to suit her best. *Francois Rohaut, France*

MRS SNOW 4 ch.f. Singspiel (IRE) 133 – Shining Vale (USA) (Twilight Agenda (USA) 126) [2007 100: 9m⁵ 8g³ 6.5d⁶ 8g 8g 8m Oct 14] lengthy filly: second foal: dam unraced half-sister to smart German 1m/1¼m performer Walzerkoenigin: useful performer: only success in maiden at Cologne at 2 yrs: respectable fifth to Dahlia Stakes at Newmarket on reappearance: ¾-length third to Desabina in listed race at Frankfurt next time but lost form afterwards: probably stays 9f: acts on soft going, probably on good to firm: blinkered (ran poorly) third/fourth outings: none too consistent. *M. Hofer, Germany*   **98**

MRS SOLESE (IRE) 4 b.f. Imperial Ballet (IRE) 110 – Sugar (Hernando (FR) 127) [2007 63: p10g Dec 28] leggy, close-coupled filly: modest maiden: well held sole run in 2007: stays 1¼m: acts on polytrack and good to soft ground: sometimes slowly away, including only 4-y-o outing. *J. R. Boyle*   –

MRS SUMMERSBY (IRE) 2 ch.f. (Mar 1) King's Best (USA) 132 – Kournikova (SAF) (Sportsworld (USA) 121) [2007 p8m² p8g⁵ Dec 28] €45,000Y: first foal: dam won South African 1000 Guineas: better effort in Lingfield maidens when second to Jaser in November, finishing strongly: bit reluctant to enter stall next time: remains open to improvement. *H. Morrison*   **64 p**

MR VELOCITY (IRE) 7 b.g. Tagula (IRE) 116 – Miss Rusty (IRE) (Mukaddamah (USA) 125) [2007 –: p8g Mar 30] compact, quite attractive gelding: fairly useful handicapper in 2005: well held both outings since. *E. F. Vaughan*   –

MR WALL STREET 3 b.g. Efisio 120 – La Suquet 72 (Puissance 110) [2007 58d: 10m 8.3d 7.5s⁶ Jul 17] good-topped gelding: regressive maiden: no form in 2007 (said to have had breathing problem second outing): tried in cheekpieces/blinkers: hard ride. *M. W. Easterby*   –

MR WHOPPIT 3 b.g. Lake Coniston (IRE) 131 – Miss Runaway 73 (Runnett 125) [2007 f6g⁵ f6g 6m⁵ Apr 4] modest form in maidens: dead. *T. D. Easterby*   **56**

MR WOLF 6 b.g. Wolfhound (USA) 126 – Madam Millie 99 (Milford 119) [2007 102: 6m² 5.1m 6d 6v 6g⁵ 5s³ 5g 5m⁵ 5m 6d Sep 21] tall, leggy gelding: useful handicapper: best at 5f/6f: acts on firm and soft going: effective with or without cheekpieces: tends to hang left: often front runner: sold 10,000 gns. *D. W. Barker*   **91**

MTOTO GIRL 3 b.f. Mtoto 134 – Shalati (FR) (High Line 125) [2007 p8g p10m p7g — Oct 24] £3,200 3-y-o: medium-sized filly: half-sister to several winners, including 1¼m winner Kewarra (by Distant Relative) and 7f (at 2 yrs)/1m winner Shalad'or (by Golden Heights), both useful: dam French 1m winner: well held in maidens/claimer. *Ms J. S. Doyle*

MUARA 5 ch.m. Wolfhound (USA) 126 – Darussalam 78 (Tina's Pet 121) [2007 64: **73 d** f5g³ p6g* f6g⁴ p5.1g⁵ 6.1m⁴ 5d 5m 5m⁶ 6m 6f p6g Aug 31] smallish, strong mare: fair handicapper: won at Wolverhampton in January: below form after: effective at 5f/6f: acts on all-weather and any turf going: tried in cheekpieces. *D. W. Barker*

MUBAASHIR (IRE) 3 ch.c. Noverre (USA) 125 – Birdsong (IRE) 73 (Dolphin Street **86** (FR) 125) [2007 97: 7m 7m p7g⁵ 7d 8g p8g Sep 24] rather leggy, quite good-topped colt: impresses in appearance: fluent mover with a round action: just fairly useful form in handicaps in 2007: stays 7f: acts on polytrack and good to firm going: sold 8,000 gns, sent to Italy. *E. A. L. Dunlop*

MUBHER 2 b.c. (Jan 30) Bahri (USA) 125 – Hawriyah (USA) 103 (Dayjur (USA) 137) **57** [2007 7m 7m p8g 8s Sep 26] tall, rather leggy colt: modest maiden: eighth at Newmarket second start, only form. *J. L. Dunlop*

MUCHO LOCO (IRE) 4 ch.g. Tagula (IRE) 116 – Mousseux (IRE) (Jareer (USA) **53** 115) [2007 65: p8.6g⁶ p9.5g 10m 12s p10m⁶ Dec 10] lengthy gelding: modest maiden handicapper: stays easy 1¼m: acts on all-weather, firm and soft going: often wears cheekpieces/blinkers. *R. Curtis*

MUDAWIN (IRE) 6 b.g. Intikhab (USA) 135 – Fida (IRE) (Persian Heights 129) [2007 **101** 102: 10g 12m⁶ 14g³ 16d⁵ 14d 15.5m⁵ 18d Oct 20] big, lengthy, good-topped gelding: has a round action: useful handicapper: creditable efforts when third to Sentry Duty at Newmarket and fifth to Odiham at Ascot third/fourth starts: below form otherwise in 2007: stays easy 2m: acts on polytrack, good to firm and good to soft going. *Jane Chapple-Hyam*

MUDHISH (IRE) 2 b.c. (Apr 21) Lujain (USA) 119 – Silver Satire (Dr Fong (USA) **77** 128) [2007 6g⁶ p6g² 6m⁴ 7f* p7g 6m 6m³ p6m³ Dec 7] good-topped colt: fair performer: won maiden at Brighton in August: blinkered, third in nurseries at Doncaster and Lingfield: stays 7f: acts on polytrack and firm going. *C. E. Brittain*

MUD MONKEY 3 ch.g. Muhtarram (USA) 125 – Tenderfoot 61 (Be My Chief (USA) **51** 122) [2007 71: 9.7m⁴ 11.6d 10m p12.2g 11.9g⁵ Oct 25] tall gelding: maiden: only modest form in handicaps in 2007: should stay 1½m: fair winner over hurdles. *B. G. Powell*

MUFASA 2 ch.c. (May 4) Cayman Kai (IRE) 114 – Petticoat Rule (Stanford 121§) [2007 **58** 7.2v 8g Nov 9] little impact in maidens (modest form on debut) within a week. *Miss L. A. Perratt*

MUFFETT'S DREAM 3 b.f. Fraam 114 – Loveless Carla (Pursuit of Love 124) [2007 — 60: 11.6m 9.9d 12.1g 14g Jun 15] maiden: well held in 2007. *J. A. Geake*

MUGA (SPA) 2 ch.f. (Jan 24) Ski Wells – Hot Doris (IRE) (Fayruz 116) [2007 p8g — p7.1g p6g Oct 12] second foal: half-sister to 3-y-o Zaafira: dam 4.5f to 1m winner in Spain: of no account. *E. J. Creighton*

MUGEBA 6 b.m. Primo Dominie 121 – Ella Lamees 61 (Statoblest 120) [2007 68: 7m³ **67** f6g⁴ 7g⁶ 7m 6s² 6s³ 7s* 7d⁴ 6.1s⁴ 7.6g² 6d 8d 7g² 6d² 6d 7.2v* Nov 3] workmanlike mare: fair handicapper: won at Newmarket (apprentices) in June and Ayr in November: barely stays 1m: acts on all-weather and any turf going: tongue tied: tried in headgear. *Miss Gay Kelleway*

MUHAJAAR (IRE) 2 b.c. (Apr 10) Cape Cross (IRE) 129 – Ya Hajar 106 (Lycius **75 p** (USA) 124) [2007 6m³ Jun 8] good-bodied colt: second foal: dam, 6f and 7f (Prix du Calvados) winner at 2 yrs, half-sister to very smart miler Zafeen: 5/2, promising third in maiden at Haydock in June, travelling strongly (slightly jarred up after): should improve. *L. M. Cumani*

MUHANNAK (IRE) 3 b.g. Chester House (USA) 123 – Opera 84 (Forzando 122) **89** [2007 –: p8g² p8.6g* p8.6g³ 10f* 10g⁴ 9.9m 12d p12m* p12g³ Oct 12] sturdy gelding: fairly useful performer: won maiden at Wolverhampton in July and handicaps at Windsor in August and Kempton (apprentices) in October: stays 1½m: acts on polytrack and firm ground: blinkered last 2 starts: waited with: sold 75,000 gns, and gelded. *G. A. Butler*

MUHARJAM 2 b.c. (Apr 22) Diktat 126 – Elsie Plunkett 92 (Mind Games 121) [2007 **68** 7g 7s⁶ 8g Oct 25] fair maiden: lost action final start (blinkered): stays 7f. *C. E. Brittain*

MUJAADEL (USA) 2 ch.c. (Apr 6) Street Cry (IRE) 130 – Quiet Rumour (USA) **88** (Alleged (USA) 138) [2007 7d² 7m⁴ 7m* 8m⁶ Sep 21] 160,000 2-y-o: tall colt, unfurnished at 2 yrs: seventh foal: half-brother to 3 winners in US, including 8.5f winner Beebe Lake (by Grand Slam): dam unraced sister to very smart French performer up to 1½m Contested Bid and half-sister to US 2-y-o Grade 1 9f winner Only Queen: fairly useful form: in frame in maidens at Newmarket (including fourth to Rio de La Plata) prior to winning similar race at Lingfield in September: longer trip, found little in minor event at Newbury: should stay 1m. *E. A. L. Dunlop*

MUJADA 2 b.f. (Apr 20) Mujahid (USA) 125 – Catriona 75 (Bustino 136) [2007 f5g² **46** 5g f5g⁶ 5.9g⁶ Jun 18] 800Y: fifth foal: half-sister to 5f winner Cheney Hill (by Compton Place): dam 7f winner: poor maiden: best efforts at 5f on fibresand. *M. Brittain*

MUJAHAZ (IRE) 3 b.g. Act One 124 – Sayedati Eljamilah (USA) 64 (Mr Prospector **72** (USA)) [2007 68p: 11g* 12m Jun 14] strong, useful-looking gelding: fair performer: won handicap at Newbury in May: well held in similar event there subsequent Flat start: should stay 1½m: sold 24,000 gns, joined P. Bowen and gelded. *J. L. Dunlop*

MUJAHOPE 2 b.g. (Apr 8) Mujahid (USA) 125 – Speak 63 (Barathea (IRE) 127) [2007 **68** p7g p8g p8.6g³ p8.6g² f8d⁴ Dec 12] good-topped gelding: fair maiden: in frame last 3 starts (wore cheekpieces), twice in claimers: stays 8.6f: raced only on all-weather. *M. Botti*

MUJAMEAD 3 b.g. Mujahid (USA) 125 – Island Mead 86 (Pharly (FR) 130) [2007 51: **–** f8g 11g Apr 24] lightly-raced maiden: well held in handicaps in 2007: not bred to stay 1m: tried visored: won over hurdles in November (sold 6,500 gns after) and December. *P. C. Haslam*

MUJART 3 b.f. Mujahid (USA) 125 – Artifact 73 (So Factual (USA) 120) [2007 58: **58** 5.1g 7m⁶ 8.1m 5.1m⁴ 6s* 6d 5s 5d 7m f5d Dec 14] close-coupled filly: modest handicapper: won at Leicester in June: effective at 5f/6f: acts on polytrack, soft and good to firm going. *J. A. Pickering*

MUJINDA 2 b.f. (Apr 27) Mujahid (USA) 125 – Arminda (Blakeney 126) [2007 5f⁶ 7d **–** 7d 7.5g Sep 19] 2,200Y: half-sister to several winners, including 7f (at 2 yrs) to 1½m winner Carburton (by Rock City) and 1997 2-y-o 7f winner Optimistic (by Reprimand), both fairly useful: dam unraced half-sister to high-class 1¼m/1½m performer Madam Gay: no form. *M. Brittain*

MUJMA 3 b. or gr.c. Indian Ridge 123 – Farfala (FR) 106 (Linamix (FR) 127) [2007 66: **71 §** 8.1m⁵ 11g 10.3f³ 10.9d Jun 24] lengthy, good-topped colt: fair maiden handicapper: stays 10.3f: acts on firm going: visored last 2 starts: looked thoroughly ungenuine final outing, and one to leave well alone: sold 26,000 gns, joined D. J. Murphy. *Sir Michael Stoute*

MUJOBLIGED (IRE) 4 b.g. Mujadil (USA) 119 – Festival of Light (High Top 131) **48** [2007 –: p7g p7g p11g⁵ Dec 19] tall gelding: poor maiden: left Seamus O'Donnell in Ireland and gelded after second start: stays easy 11f: acts on polytrack: tried tongue tied/ in cheekpieces. *J. R. Best*

MUJOOD 4 b.g. Mujahid (USA) 125 – Waqood (USA) 75 (Riverman (USA) 131) [2007 **97** 91: p7g 6m³ f7g⁶ 6m⁴ 6s⁶ 6d 6m⁴ p7g⁴ p6g 6s⁶ 7g 6g⁶ 6m 6g 6m⁶ 7f² 6d 6g Oct 25] quite **a87** good-topped gelding: useful handicapper: won at Goodwood (beat Saviours Spirit by 1¾ lengths) in May: in-and-out form after: has form at 1¼m, but races mostly at 6f/7f nowadays: acts on all-weather, firm and good to soft ground: usually wears headgear. *Eve Johnson Houghton*

MUKHBER 2 br.g. (Mar 19) Anabaa (USA) 130 – Tarbiyah 89 (Singspiel (IRE) 133) **92 p** [2007 8d* Oct 19] strong, well-made gelding: first foal: dam, 1m winner on only start, half-sister to 1000 Guineas winner Lahan: 7/2, won maiden at Newmarket by neck from Irish Mayhem, looking green and held before storming home on meeting rising ground: not sure to stay much beyond 1m: sure to improve. *J. H. M. Gosden*

MUKTASB (USA) 6 b.g. Bahri (USA) 125 – Maghaarb 104 (Machiavellian (USA) **–** 123) [2007 52, a63: p5g⁴ p5g³ p6g⁴ p5.1g⁵ p5.1g³ p5g⁴ f5g⁶ p6g³ p6g⁴ p6g⁵ p5.1g⁶ p5.1g **a63** 5.2d p6g p6g² p5.1g² p7.1g⁶ p5g* p5.1g³ p6g p6g³ p6g* Dec 29] good-topped gelding: has a quick action: modest performer: won minor event at Kempton in November and handicap at Lingfield in December: effective at 5f, should stay 7f: acts on all-weather and good to firm going: wears headgear (visored nowadays): often slowly away: held up: signs of temperament. *D. Shaw*

MULAAZEM 4 b.g. King's Best (USA) 132 – Harayir (USA) 119 (Gulch (USA)) **73** [2007 82+: p12.2g 12m 10.5m 10d 12m⁵ 10.5g² 10m Oct 3] medium-sized, quite attractive gelding: just fair handicapper in 2007: should stay 1½m: acts on polytrack and good to firm going: has taken keen hold. *J. Mackie*

MULBERRY LAD (IRE) 5 b.g. Entrepreneur 123 – Taisho (IRE) 96 (Namaqualand **63** (USA)) [2007 54, a64: p6g⁵ p6g⁶ p7.1g p6g* p7g² f6g p7.1g⁴ p7f⁵ f6g p6g⁶ p6g* p7g p7.1g p7m p6g p6g⁴ p6m p7m⁵ p6g p7m⁶ p6g² p7g Dec 30] stocky gelding: fair performer: won claimer in January and handicap in March, both at Lingfield: effective at 6f to 1m: acts on all-weather and firm going: tried in tongue tie/blinkers/cheekpieces. *P. W. Hiatt*

MULLEIN 2 b.f. (May 10) Oasis Dream 129 – Gipsy Moth 99 (Efisio 120) [2007 6d **74** Jul 27] 45,000Y: strong filly: fifth foal: half-sister to several winners, including 4-y-o Illustrious Blue, 7-y-o Romany Nights and Irish 7f winner Fly Free (by Halling): dam, 5f performer, half-sister to useful 1m winner Heavenly Whisper: 11/1, needed experience (last and driven at halfway) when seventh to Albabilia in maiden at Ascot. *R. M. Beckett*

MULLIGAN'S GOLD (IRE) 4 b.g. Fasliyev (USA) 120 – Magic Lady (IRE) (Big- **72** stone (IRE) 126) [2007 72: 5m⁵ 6g² 6m² 5g 5d 6m⁴ 5d⁴ 5m 6m⁴ 5g p6g⁵ Nov 1] lengthy gelding: fair handicapper: raced at 5f/6f: acts on polytrack, good to firm and good to soft ground: wore cheekpieces last 5 starts. *T. D. Easterby*

MULLIGAN'S PRIDE (IRE) 6 b.g. Kahyasi 130 – Babs Mulligan (IRE) (Le Bavard **58** (FR) 125) [2007 63: 15.8m³ 16g 15.8m 16g⁵ Jun 22] strong, good-bodied gelding: modest handicapper: stays 2m: acts on firm going: disappointing nowadays. *James Moffatt*

MULLIGANS PURSUIT (IRE) 3 b.g. Musical Pursuit 113 – Anna Mong Men **66** (Man Among Men (IRE)) [2007 60: 8m 7m⁵ p6g p8g p8.6g p6g Nov 4] fair maiden on **a58** turf, modest on all-weather: left M. Sunderland in Ireland after second outing: stays 7f: acts on good to firm going, probably on heavy: tried blinkered/visored: has raced freely. *M. D. I. Usher*

MULLINS BAY 6 b.h. Machiavellian (USA) 123 – Bella Colora 119 (Bellypha 130) **114** [2007 107: a9f² a8f³ 8.9f⁵ 9.9m³ 10d Oct 20] big, close-coupled horse: smart performer: left A. O'Brien after final start in 2005: 5 lengths second to Ramonti in Premio Ribot at Rome only outing in 2006 (for J. Hammond): best efforts in 2007 when third in Godolphin Mile at Nad Al Sheba (4 lengths behind Spring At Last) and Select Stakes at Goodwood (beaten ½ length by Stotsfold, hanging right and carrying head awkwardly): below form in Champion Stakes at Newmarket final start: effective at 1m to 10.4f: acts on dirt, soft and good to firm going: has been tongue tied (including last 2 starts)/bandaged in front. *M. F. de Kock, South Africa*

MULL OF DUBAI 4 b.g. Mull of Kintyre (USA) 114 – Enlisted (IRE) 83 (Sadler's **100** Wells (USA) 132) [2007 78: 11.7f³ 12.1g⁴ 12g³ 10v* 10.9s* 12d² 12d⁴ 14.1g Sep 20] sturdy gelding: useful handicapper: improved in 2007, winning at Windsor and Warwick within 4 days in July: good efforts next 2 starts (including head second to Group Captain at Ascot) but ran as if amiss final outing: stays 1½m: acts on any going: blinkered final 2-y-o start: held up: reliable. *J. S. Moore*

MULLZIMA (IRE) 4 b.f. Mull of Kintyre (USA) 114 – Habaza (IRE) 68 (Shernazar **–** 131) [2007 –: p16.5g Jan 28] tall, lightly-made filly: maiden: well held both starts since 2005. *M. A. Doyle*

MULTAHAB 8 b. or br.g. Zafonic (USA) 130 – Alumisiyah (USA) 93 (Danzig (USA)) **75** [2007 72: 5.3m⁵ 5g 5.3m⁴ 5.2m² 5f 5.3d p5.1m* 5m p5m³ p5.1g Oct 21] smallish gelding: fair handicapper: left Miss D. McHale after fifth start: won at Wolverhampton in September: effective at 5f/6f: acts on all-weather and firm ground: tried blinkered/in cheekpieces: tongue tied. *M. Wigham*

MULTAKKA (IRE) 4 b.g. Alhaarth (IRE) 126 – Elfaslah (IRE) 107 (Green Desert **85** (USA) 127) [2007 90: p8g² p7g* Nov 4] strong, rangy, attractive gelding: keen walker: fairly useful performer: won maiden at Lingfield in November easily by 6 lengths from Takaamul: should stay 1¼m: yet to race on heavy going, acts on any other turf and polytrack: carried head awkwardly on reappearance: possibly not straightforward (blinkered final 3-y-o start). *M. P. Tregoning*

MULTICULTURAL 4 bl.g. Singspiel (IRE) 133 – Three Piece (Jaazeiro (USA) 127) **83** [2007 p8g² p9.5g* 10m 10g³ p11g⁶ 14s p12m p9.5g⁶ Nov 1] leggy, lengthy gelding: fairly useful performer: won maiden at Wolverhampton in March: ran well in handicaps after only when close third at Newmarket: stays 1¼m: acts on polytrack, best turf effort on good ground (travelled with no fluency only start on soft). *D. M. Simcock*

MULTIDIMENSIONAL (IRE) 4 b.c. Danehill (USA) 126 – Sacred Song (USA) **118 p** 116 (Diesis 133) [2007 115p: 9m* 10d⁵ Oct 20] smallish, well-made colt: smart performer, lightly raced: reported in April to have sustained hairline fracture of his pelvis: has won 4 of his 6 starts, including minor event at Newbury (beat Oracle West by a neck) in September: met trouble after again patiently ridden when 6½ lengths fifth behind Literato in Champion Stakes at Newmarket next time: will stay 1½m: acts on soft and good to firm ground: hangs right under pressure: remains open to improvement. *H. R. A. Cecil*

MULTITUDE (IRE) 3 b.g. Mull of Kintyre (USA) 114 – Sea Modena (IRE) (Mac's Imp (USA) 116) [2007 65: 6g⁶ 6m* 6g⁶ 6d³ 7.6s⁵ 6m 6g p7.1g 7g Oct 19] sturdy gelding: fair handicapper: won at Newcastle in May: should stay 7f: acts on good to firm and good to soft going: tried blinkered. *T. D. Easterby* — **68**

MUMAATHEL (IRE) 4 b.g. Alhaarth (IRE) 126 – Alhufoof (USA) 100 (Dayjur (USA) 137) [2007 84: 6g p7g p6m Nov 26] rather leggy gelding: fairly useful maiden at 3 yrs: little form in 2007, racing too freely. *M. A. Buckley* — **60**

MUMBLESWERVE (IRE) 3 b.c. City On A Hill (USA) 114 – Dolcezza (FR) (Lichine (USA) 117) [2007 67: p8g⁵ Jan 13] lengthy colt: fair maiden, lightly raced: probably stays 1m (took strong hold at the trip). *W. Jarvis.* — **62**

MUMBLING (IRE) 9 ch.g. Dr Devious (IRE) 127 – Valley Lights (IRE) (Dance of Life (USA)) [2007 p13g⁶ p16g p16g³ p13g⁴ p16f p13.9g p16.5g Mar 14] strong, lengthy gelding: fair performer: stayed 17f: acted on polytrack, firm and soft ground: tried blinkered: dead. *B. G. Powell* — **68**

MUM'S MEMORIES 3 ch.g. Zaha (CAN) 106 – Trevorsninepoints 71 (Jester 119) [2007 50: f8g p10g f7g p8.6g May 1] good-topped gelding: poor maiden: probably stays easy 7f. *W. J. Musson* — **43**

MUMS THE BEST 2 ch.f. (May 16) Best of The Bests (IRE) 122 – Super Sally 108 (Superlative 118) [2007 5m 6g May 18] rather leggy filly: sixth foal: half-sister to useful 1996 2-y-o 7f winner (stayed 1¼m) Shii-Take and fairly useful 1¼m winner Shii-Take's Girl, both by Deploy: dam, 1m/1¼m winner, half-sister to smart performer up to 1¼m (including in US) Unanimous Vote: behind in maidens. *A. B. Coogan* — **–**

MUNADDAM (USA) 5 ch.g. Aljabr (USA) 125 – Etizaaz (USA) 117 (Diesis 133) [2007 109: 6.5g* 6.5g* 6g² 7.1g* 7s 8g Aug 1] sturdy gelding: smart performer: much improved in 2007, successful in handicaps at Nad Al Sheba in January and February (beat Ashdown Express by 4 lengths) and listed race at Haydock (in great shape, beat Excusez Moi by 1¼ lengths) in May: well below form in pattern company after: effective at 6f/7f: acts on good to firm going (well below form all starts on softer than good): returned to UAE, joining E. Charpy. *E. A. L. Dunlop* — **117**

MUNCASTER CASTLE (IRE) 3 b.g. Johannesburg (USA) 127 – Eubee (FR) (Common Grounds 118) [2007 54: p6g⁵ p7.1g⁶ p8.6g* p10g 8.2m⁶ 8.3d³ 8.3g³ p8.6g Dec 4] lengthy gelding: modest handicapper: won at Wolverhampton in March: stays 8.6f: acts on polytrack, soft and good to firm going: races prominently. *R. F. Fisher* — **61**

MUNCHING MIKE (IRE) 4 br.g. Orpen (USA) 116 – Stargard (Polish Precedent (USA) 131) [2007 64: 10d 9s² 10m Oct 22] modest maiden handicapper: left C. Swan in Ireland after second start: stays 1¼m: acts on soft and good to firm going: tried in cheekpieces. *K. M. Prendergast* — **63**

MUNDO'S MAGIC 3 b.g. Foxhound (USA) 103 – Amber's Bluff 80 (Mind Games 121) [2007 76: 5g² 6d³ 6g² 6m⁵ 6m⁴ 6d 6f⁶ 6f 7g³ 6m⁶ 5g Sep 19] big, close-coupled gelding: fair handicapper: stays 7f: acts on firm and good to soft going: tried in cheekpieces: races prominently. *G. M. Moore* — **74**

MUNGO JERRY (GER) 6 b.g. Tannenkonig (IRE) 111 – Mostly Sure (IRE) (Sure Blade (USA) 130) [2007 –: p16g Mar 26] tall gelding: lightly raced and little form on Flat since 2005. *B. N. Pollock* — **–**

MUNSEF 5 b.g. Zafonic (USA) 130 – Mazaya (IRE) 105 (Sadler's Wells (USA) 132) [2007 119: 12m³ 14g⁶ 12m* 12s³ 12g 14.1g² 12m² Oct 5] strong, close-coupled gelding: smart performer: landed odds in 4-runner minor event at Goodwood (beat High Heel Sneakers by 3½ lengths) in June: best efforts in 2007 when 1½ lengths third to Maraahel in John Porter Stakes at Newbury and head second to Galactic Star in listed event at Newmarket first/final starts, unlucky in latter, finishing well after winner had got first run: should stay 1¾m: acts on soft and good to firm going: tried blinkered, including at Goodwood: often held up: ungenuine. *J. L. Dunlop* — **119 §**

MUNSTER MOUNTAIN (IRE) 3 ch.g. Monashee Mountain (USA) 115 – The Voice (ITY) (Catrail (USA) 123) [2007 58: p7.1g Sep 3] strong gelding: modest maiden at 2 yrs: well held only Flat outing in 2007: will stay 1m: tried in cheekpieces. *James Moffatt* — **–**

MUNTAMI (IRE) 6 gr.g. Daylami (IRE) 138 – Bashashah (IRE) 83 (Kris 135) [2007 **76** –: f11g* f12g* f11g f12g⁶ 14.1d³ 14.8d² 14.8m⁴ 16.2g⁴ Aug 15] sturdy, close-coupled gelding: fair handicapper: won at Southwell in February and March: stays 1¾m: acts on fibresand and heavy going: tried blinkered/visored: fair winning hurdler. *John A. Harris*

MUQADAM (IRE) 3 b.c. Rock of Gibraltar (IRE) 133 – Onereuse (Sanglamore **73** (USA) 126) [2007 9.8g 10.2g³ 9.9g² 9.9m² 9.2s² Sep 24] 300,000F: fourth foal: half-brother to smart French 1¼m (Prix Saint-Alary) winner Fidelite (by In The Wings) and French 1¼m/11f winner Amour Multiple (by Poliglote): dam, French maiden, half-sister to Irish Derby winner Winged Love: fair maiden: outbattled last 2 starts, in visor final one: likely to stay 1½m: acts on soft and good to firm going: sold 20,000 gns. *Sir Michael Stoute*

MUQARRAR (IRE) 8 ch.g. Alhaarth (IRE) 126 – Narjis (USA) 87 (Blushing Groom **–** (FR) 131) [2007 –: f12g p12g p12g Jun 14] workmanlike gelding: no form since 2005. *T. J. Fitzgerald*

MURACO 3 b.g. Bertolini (USA) 125 – Miss Honeypenny (IRE) (Old Vic 136) [2007 **76** 10g 10d 10g³ 11.7g 11.5m* 12.6m⁵ p12g Sep 18] close-coupled gelding: fair handi-capper: won at Lingfield in August: stays 1½m: acts on good to firm going, probably on good to soft: sold 11,000 gns. *R. M. Beckett*

MURAQEB 7 ch.g. Grand Lodge (USA) 125 – Oh So Well (IRE) (Sadler's Wells (USA) **40** 132) [2007 f14g⁶ Mar 15] sturdy gelding: poor maiden: stays 1¾m: acts on fibresand, soft and good to firm ground: tried in headgear: has looked none too keen. *Mrs Barbara Waring*

MURBEK (IRE) 3 b.c. Dansili 127 – Flagship 84 (Rainbow Quest (USA) 134) [2007 **86** 88: 10m 8g² 10g² 8d² 7g² a7.5f⁴ Dec 13] useful-looking colt: fairly useful maiden: left M. Jarvis before final outing: stays 1m: acts on good to firm and good to soft ground, unraced on extremes: often finds little. *M. Al Muhairi, UAE*

MURDOCH 3 b.g. Mutamarkiz (IRE) 77 – Miss Pharly (Pharly (FR) 130) [2007 77: **58** 10.1s 10m⁴ p8.6g 8g Jun 1] useful-looking gelding: maiden: just modest form at 2 yrs: stays 1m: raced freely on reappearance. *E. S. McMahon*

MURDOL (IRE) 3 ch.g. Traditionally (USA) 117 – Rock Abbey (IRE) (College **39** Chapel 124) [2007 48: p8.6g⁴ f8g p12g Jun 9] poor maiden. *C. R. Dore*

MUREE QUEEN 3 b.f. Diktat 126 – Bright Future (FR) (Akarad (FR) 130) [2007 49: **53** p9.5g f8g f7g⁵ p8.6g* f8g³ 11g f8g Apr 26] leggy filly: modest performer: won seller at Wolverhampton in March: left R. Hollinshead after next start: barely stays 11f: acts on all-weather and good to firm going: tried in cheekpieces. *Miss J. S. Davis*

MURFREESBORO 4 b.c. Bahamian Bounty 116 – Merry Rous 66 (Rousillon (USA) **100** 133) [2007 99: p6g 6m⁴ 5d p6m 8m p6m⁶ p7g⁴ Dec 1] useful-looking colt: good walker: useful performer: creditable fourth to Abraham Lincoln in minor event at the Curragh second start: left M. Halford in Ireland after third outing: flattered when sixth to Maltese Falcon in listed race at Lingfield penultimate start: best at 5f/6f: acts on polytrack and good to firm going: tried visored/blinkered. *K. J. Burke*

MURRIN (IRE) 3 b. or br.g. Trans Island 119 – Flimmering (Dancing Brave (USA) **82** 140) [2007 74: p7g⁴ 8.5g⁶ 8m* 8.1m 8m 10d Oct 15] close-coupled gelding: fairly useful handicapper: won at Goodwood in June: free-going type, stays 1m: acts on polytrack and good to firm going. *T. G. Mills*

MURRISK 3 ch.g. Groom Dancer (USA) 128 – Food of Love 109 (Music Boy 124) **64** [2007 74: 7.5m 8.2g 8g 6d 6.1d⁶ p6g⁵ p7.1g⁴ p8m⁴ Nov 11] maiden handicapper, just modest in 2007, including at Wolverhampton/Kempton: acts on polytrack and good to soft ground: tried blinkered/tongue tied: usually makes running. *E. Tyrrell, Ireland*

MURRUMBIDGEE (IRE) 4 gr.g. Bluebird (USA) 125 – Blanche Neige (USA) (Lit **68** de Justice (USA) 125) [2007 70: p8g⁴ 8.1m² 9g² 9g⁵ 10m⁴ p8g⁵ 8d 8f 9g 8.5m⁴ Sep 11] good-topped gelding: fair handicapper: effective at stiff 1m to 1¼m: acts on polytrack and firm going: tried visored/tongue tied/in cheekpieces: has looked ungenuine: joined Miss C. Caroe. *J. W. Hills*

MURTAAD 3 b.c. Soviet Star (USA) 128 – Zulfaa (USA) 97 (Bahri (USA) 125) [2007 **71** p8g⁶ Apr 30] 9/2, looked green throughout when sixth to Premio Loco in maiden at Lingfield, slowly away and not knocked about: sold 11,000 gns, joined Miss Susan A. Finn in Ireland. *W. J. Haggas*

MUSAALEM (USA) 3 gr.g. Aljabr (USA) 125 – Atyab (USA) (Mr Prospector (USA)) **80 P** [2007 7.1m* Aug 27] rangy gelding: has scope: fourth foal: brother to 5-y-o Dysonic: dam once-raced sister to US Grade 2 7f winner Kayrawan and half-sister to dam of 3-y-o

Haatef: 11/10 favourite, most encouraging debut when winning maiden at Warwick in August by 1¾ lengths from Batchworth Blaise, pulling hard and galloping on strongly after leading over 1f out: open to considerable improvement. *W. J. Haggas*

MUSADIF (USA) 9 ch.g. Shadeed (USA) 135 – Tadwin 109 (Never So Bold 135) – [2007 105: 6g 8m Aug 17] lengthy gelding: one-time smart performer: well held in handicaps in 2007: best up to 7f: acts on good to firm ground: tongue tied nowadays: edgy sort, has gone early to post: reportedly withdrawn after bolting to post intended second outing. *R. A. Kvisla*

MUSANGO 4 b.g. Night Shift (USA) – Imbabala (Zafonic (USA) 130) [2007 66: p7f⁵ **76** p10g² p12g* p12g⁵ p12g³ 11.6m p10g³ p16g p12g* p11g p13g⁵ p12g* p12m³ f11d³ p12.2g⁴ Dec 22] leggy gelding: fair performer: won handicap in March, claimer in August and seller in November (left B. Johnson after), all at Lingfield: stays easy 1½m: acts on all-weather (ran as if amiss only turf outing): usually tongue tied: twice said to have had breathing problem. *Miss Gay Kelleway*

MUSASHI (IRE) 2 ch.c. (Apr 26) Hawk Wing (USA) 136 – Soubrette (USA) (Opening **75** Verse (USA) 126) [2007 6f 6g⁶ 7m⁴ 8.3d a7f⁴ Dec 13] sturdy colt: fair maiden: best effort third start: left J. S. Moore before final outing: should stay 1m. *A. Manuel, UAE*

MUSCA (IRE) 3 b.g. Tendulkar (USA) 114 – Canary Bird (USA) 59 (Catrail (USA) **85** 123) [2007 88p: 7g³ 6m⁶ 8v⁴ 7.5s⁴ 7g⁶ 6m Sep 18] angular gelding: fairly useful performer at best: ran creditably in 2007 only on reappearance (left J. Howard Johnson and gelded after second start): bred to be suited by further than 7f: acts on soft ground. *J. Wade*

MUSCARI 5 ch.m. Indian Ridge 123 – Desert Serenade (USA) (Green Desert (USA) **60** 127) [2007 68: p6g Jan 14] fair performer in 2006: little impact only outing at 5 yrs: effective at 6f to 1m: acts on polytrack and firm going. *S. Woodman*

MUSCOVADO (USA) 3 b.f. Mr Greeley (USA) 122 – Only Royale (IRE) 121 (Caer- **71 p** leon (USA) 132) [2007 10.2g p10g⁵ Nov 30] seventh foal: half-sister to winners in USA and Japan by Kingmambo: dam 1m to 1½m (including Yorkshire Oaks twice) winner: much better effort in maidens when fifth at Lingfield, shaping as though will be suited by 1½m: likely to improve further. *L. M. Cumani*

MUSETTE (IRE) 4 b.f. Mujadil (USA) 119 – Repique (USA) 88 (Sharpen Up 127) **54** [2007 43: 6m 6m 7g³ 8m⁵ 7g 6.9m⁶ 10f 9.8m Aug 28] small filly: modest maiden: stays 1m: acts on good to firm going: tried in cheekpieces. *R. E. Barr*

MUSHTAAQ (USA) 2 b.c. (Apr 19) Dynaformer (USA) – Siyadah (USA) 106 (Mr **92** Prospector (USA)) [2007 8m³ 8g⁴ 10m² Oct 8] compact colt: sixth foal: half-brother to smart 9f winner Musanid (by Swain) and fairly useful 1m winner Tasjeel (by Aljabr): dam, 1¼m winner, out of Yorkshire Oaks winner Roseate Tern, herself half-sister to Ibn Bey: fairly useful form in frame in maidens, clear of rest when second to Planetarium at Pontefract: will stay 1½m. *M. A. Jarvis*

MUSICAL AFFAIR 3 b.f. Alflora (IRE) 120 – Song For Jess (IRE) (Accordion) [2007 – 52: 7m May 3] lengthy filly: maiden in 2006: well held only start at 3 yrs. *F. Jordan*

MUSICAL BEAT 3 ch.f. Beat Hollow 126 – Warbler 110 (Warning 136) [2007 75+: **85** p8g 8m³ 8f* 8.5g⁵ 8g⁴ 8d f8g² 8m⁴ 8.2g⁴ 9.7g³ 7m* p8g⁴ 10.4s 8m 7g* 8m Sep 8] angular filly: fairly useful handicapper: won at Thirsk (drifted left) in April, and Catterick in July and August: best form at 7f: acts on polytrack and firm going. *Miss V. Haigh*

MUSICAL BOX 3 b.f. Ballet Master (USA) 92 – Houston Heiress (USA) (Houston **42** (USA)) [2007 6m⁶ p7g⁵ f7g 8d⁵ Jun 19] fifth foal: half-sister to 11f winner Simplified (by Lend A Hand) and winner in Spain by Opening Verse: dam Italian maiden: form only when fifth at Kempton second start: stays 7f: acts on polytrack. *G. Prodromou*

MUSICAL CHARM (IRE) 2 b.f. (Apr 30) Distant Music (USA) 126 – Fairybird **69** (FR) 70 (Pampabird 124) [2007 5m⁴ 5m⁴ p6g Aug 13] 4,500F: close-coupled filly: half-sister to several winners, including 5-y-o Piddies Pride: dam 2-y-o 5f winner: fair maiden: fourth at Pontefract and Thirsk (behind Starlit Sands): should stay 6f/7f. *T. D. Easterby*

MUSICAL CHIMES 4 b.f. Josr Algarhoud (IRE) 118 – Sally Slade 80 (Dowsing **48** (USA) 124) [2007 45: 8.1m⁵ 7.5g 7.1d³ 5.5s⁶ 6.9m⁶ 6m 7.6m Aug 23] good-bodied filly: poor maiden on balance: stays 7f: acts on firm and good to soft going: inconsistent. *W. M. Brisbourne*

MUSICAL FEUD (IRE) 2 b.g. (Mar 24) Distant Music (USA) 126 – Family At War – (USA) 71 (Explodent (USA)) [2007 p7g Dec 19] 33/1 and blinkered, always behind (started slowly) in maiden at Lingfield. *Jane Chapple-Hyam*

MUSICAL GIANT (USA) 4 ch.g. Giant's Causeway (USA) 132 – Music House **55**
(USA) (Sadler's Wells (USA) 132) [2007 –: 8m⁴ 10.1m f11g⁶ 8.3d 9.2s Sep 24] strong,
lengthy gelding: modest maiden at best: left J. Howard Johnson after third start: tried
blinkered/tongue tied. *J. Wade*

MUSICAL GIFT 7 ch.g. Cadeaux Genereux 131 – Kazoo 108 (Shareef Dancer (USA) **46**
135) [2007 –, a57: f6g⁵ p8g⁴ 10.2g⁶ p9.5g Sep 21] sturdy gelding: poor performer nowadays: left P. Blockley £2,100 after second start: stays easy 1¼m: acts on all-weather:
usually visored/in cheekpieces. *M. Hill*

MUSICAL LAND (IRE) 3 ch.g. Distant Music (USA) 126 – Esquiline (USA) (Gone **63**
West (USA)) [2007 76: 10.1m⁵ 9g 9m² 9.9m⁴ 9.2m⁴ 12d p12.2g 10g p9.5g Oct 19]
close-coupled gelding: modest maiden: stays 9f: acts on firm and soft ground: blinkered
last 2 starts: no easy ride: sold 7,500 gns. *J. R. Weymes*

MUSICAL LOCKET (IRE) 3 b.f. Distant Music (USA) 126 – My Lucy Locket **56**
(IRE) 96§ (Mujadil (USA) 119) [2007 p7g³ p8.6g⁴ p8g³ 7d p9.5g p7m p8g Oct 29]
€1,000Y: first foal: dam 5f (at 2 yrs) to 1m winner: modest maiden: left R. Hannon after
fourth start: no form after: stays 8.6f: raced mostly on polytrack. *J. C. Fox*

MUSICAL MIRAGE (USA) 3 b.f. Royal Anthem (USA) 135 – Fantasy 80 (Cadeaux **83**
Genereux 131) [2007 83: 8g⁵ 10f⁶ 8m f8g 8.5d 6g Oct 20] unfurnished filly: fairly useful
performer: lost form after reappearance, leaving G. A. Swinbank following fourth outing:
races freely, but stays 1m: acts on good to soft ground: often held up. *N. Meade, Ireland*

MUSICAL PARKES 3 b.f. Piccolo 121 – Top of The Parkes 60 (Mistertopogigo (IRE) **59 d**
118) [2007 6m⁶ 6m 5.1m³ p6g 5d 5g 5d 7g 5g Nov 6] 1,200Y: sturdy filly: second foal:
half-sister to winner in Jersey by Pursuit of Love: dam sprint maiden: modest maiden:
well held last 4 starts: likely to prove best at 5f/6f: acts on good to firm ground: tried
blinkered. *W. J. H. Ratcliffe*

MUSICAL ROMANCE (IRE) 4 b.f. Mozart (IRE) 131 – Dear Girl (IRE) 105 (Fairy **–**
King (USA)) [2007 76: 5.1f 6g Jun 2] sturdy filly: fair handicapper in 2006: well held
both starts at 4 yrs: blinkered nowadays: sold 62,000 gns in July (reportedly in foal to
Dr Fong). *B. J. Meehan*

MUSICAL SCRIPT (USA) 4 b.g. Stravinsky (USA) 133 – Cyrillic (USA) 106 (Irish **65**
River (FR) 131) [2007 72: 6m 5.5d⁵ 5g⁵ p5g³ 6g p6g 6d 6f⁶ 6g³ 5m⁵ 6.1m p6g² 6d² p5m²
p5g⁴ p6g⁶ p6g² p6g⁵ Dec 12] sturdy gelding: fair handicapper: free-going sort, best at 5f/
6f: acts on polytrack, firm and soft going: blinkered/in cheekpieces nowadays: difficult
ride. *Mouse Hamilton-Fairley*

MUSICAL WAY (FR) 5 ch.m. Gold Away (IRE) 125 – Mulika (FR) (Procida (USA) **112**
129) [2007 112: 10.5s³ 10g 10s 10d⁴ 10g* 10g* 9.8d* 10g³ 10g³ Dec 9] €16,500 2-y-o:
fifth foal: half-sister to useful French 1¼m winner Murray River (by Esprit du Nord):
dam French maiden: smart performer: in good form in autumn, winning listed race at
Chantilly (made all, beat Touch of Land a length), La Coupe de Maisons-Laffitte (for
second year running, beat Kocab ½ length) and Prix Dollar Casino Barriere de Montreux
at Longchamp (beat demoted Rhenus a length): good keeping-on third last 2 starts, in
Premio Lydia Tesio at Rome (length behind Turfrose) and Hong Kong Cup at Sha Tin
(beaten 3 lengths by Ramonti): has won at 1½m, races mainly around 1¼m nowadays:
acts on all-weather, soft and good to firm ground: wears cheekpieces: ridden prominently
when successful in 2007. *P. Van de Poele, France*

MUSIC BOX EXPRESS 3 b.g. Tale of The Cat (USA) 113 – Aly McBe (USA) **66**
(Alydeed (CAN) 120) [2007 6g p6g³ p5.1g* p5.1s³ Dec 20] fair form: confirmed earlier
promise when winning maiden at Wolverhampton in December: poorly drawn on handicap debut there next time: will stay 7f: acts on polytrack. *D. J. Murphy*

MUSIC CELEBRE (IRE) 7 b.g. Peintre Celebre (USA) 137 – Marwell 133 (Habitat **66**
134) [2007 81: p12g p10g p10g 8.1m³ 8.1d⁴ p8.6g⁵ 8f p8g 8d Oct 23] just fair performer
nowadays: stays 1m: acts on firm and soft ground: usually blinkered, has worn cheekpieces. *S. Curran*

MUSIC IN EXILE (USA) 2 ch.f. (Mar 23) Diesis 133 – Royal Occasion (USA) 56 **58 p**
(El Gran Senor (USA) 136) [2007 7g Nov 3] tall filly: second foal: dam twice-raced
sister to Rodrigo de Triano: looked weak only 2-y-o start, 33/1 and mid-field in maiden at
Newmarket: will progress. *B. W. Hills*

MUSICMAESTROPLEASE (IRE) 4 b.g. Rossini (USA) 118 – Who Told Vicky **70 d**
(IRE) 50 (Anita's Prince 126) [2007 70: 7g² p8.6g⁶ 7.1m 7.5m p7.1g 8f 6.9g p7.1g⁵
p8.6g⁵ p8.6g p12.2g Nov 1] sturdy, close-coupled gelding: fair performer: below form

after reappearance: stays easy 8.6f: acts on all-weather and firm going: sometimes slowly away: often held up: gelded after final start. *S. Parr*

MUSIC NOTE (IRE) 4 b.c. Indian Ridge 123 – Samara Middle East (FR) 87 (Marju **88** (IRE) 127) [2007 90: p8g 8.3f³ 8m⁴ 8g p8g 7d 8m⁶ 7.1d 8m⁶ Sep 4] leggy, attractive colt: fairly useful handicapper: creditable efforts in 2007 when in frame at Windsor and Ascot second/third outings: stays 8.3f: acts on firm and soft going, probably on polytrack: has been bandaged: tongue tied last 5 starts: reportedly bled fourth outing (below form after): front runner. *Miss Gay Kelleway*

MUSIC REVIEW 3 b.f. Singspiel (IRE) 133 – Vivid Concert (IRE) 73 (Chief Singer **87** 131) [2007 8m⁵ 10g³ 10d⁴ 12s² 12s⁴ 12.1g* 12.1g⁴ p12g³ 12.1g* 11.8d⁶ p12.2g² p10g² Nov 15] 17,000 2-y-o: smallish, close-coupled filly: half-sister to several winners, notably smart US performer up to 8.5f Extended Applause (by Exbourne): dam 2-y-o 5f winner: fairly useful handicapper: won at Beverley in August and September: further improvement when runner-up last 2 starts: likely to stay beyond 1½m: acts on polytrack and soft ground: effective held up or forcing pace: sold 55,000 gns. *R. A. Fahey*

MUSSOORIE (FR) 4 gr.f. Linamix (FR) 127 – Fascinating Hill (FR) (Danehill (USA) **103** 126) [2007 108: 10g 12g³ 14.6m 10d⁵ p13m 10.3m Nov 10] tall, angular filly: useful performer: left R. Gibson in France after reappearance: best efforts in Britain in listed races at York (third to Wannabe Posh) and Newmarket (fifth to Short Skirt): stays 1½m: acts on good to firm and good to soft going, yet to race on extremes. *J. H. M. Gosden*

MUSTAJED 6 b.g. Alhaarth (IRE) 126 – Jasarah (IRE) 70 (Green Desert (USA) 127) **94** [2007 91: p11g p12g 10.1s² 10m³ 11.6m⁶ 12m⁴ 12m* 16.1v 14g 12m⁴ p11g* p11g⁴ 12g **a88** Sep 30] sturdy gelding: fairly useful handicapper: reportedly suffered a second fractured pastern after only outing in 2006: won at Salisbury in June and Kempton in August: stays 1½m, not 1¾m: acts on polytrack, soft and good to firm ground: visored once: often races prominently: consistent. *B. R. Millman*

MUSTAKHLAS (USA) 6 ch.g. Diesis 133 – Katiba (USA) 99 (Gulch (USA)) [2007 **53** 59: p16.5g³ p16.5g p16g 14m p13.9d Dec 17] rangy gelding: modest performer: stays 16.5f: acts on polytrack: tried in cheekpieces. *B. P. J. Baugh*

MUSTAMAD 4 b.g. Anabaa (USA) 130 – Nasanice (IRE) 97 (Nashwan (USA) 135) **–** [2007 74: 10m Apr 30] big, strong, lengthy gelding: fair form in maidens at 3 yrs: well held in handicap only Flat outing in 2007 (no form over hurdles): will stay 1½m: unraced on extremes of going. *Miss A. M. Newton-Smith*

MUSTAMEET (USA) 6 b.h. Sahm (USA) 112 – Hamasah (USA) 83 (Irish River (FR) **116** 131) [2007 123: 7m* 10m⁶ 10.5g⁶ May 27] lengthy horse: smart performer in 2007, winning Castlemartin & Louviere Studs Gladness Stakes at the Curragh (bandaged hind legs) in April by ¾ length from An Tadh: below form after in Mooresbridge Stakes and Tattersalls Gold Cup on same course: stayed 1¼m: acted on heavy and good to firm going: reportedly lost 2 teeth when banging head in stall on 4-y-o reappearance: sometimes edged right: held up: retired. *Kevin Prendergast, Ireland*

MUSTAMMER 4 b.g. Fasliyev (USA) 120 – Alazima (USA) 64 (Riverman (USA) **57** 131) [2007 51: f6g⁵ p6g p5.1g* p5.1g⁵ 6m p6g p5.1g Jul 2] sturdy, close-coupled gelding: modest performer: won seller at Wolverhampton in February: best at 5f/6f: acts on polytrack: has worn visor. *D. Shaw*

MUSTANG DU GUESLAN (FR) 7 b.g. Passing Sale (FR) 125 – Arzel du Marais **–** (FR) (Djarvis (FR)) [2007 11.8d⁵ p12.2g Aug 13] good-topped gelding: placed twice in non-thoroughbred events in French Provinces in 2005 for F. Belmont: well held in claimer/seller on Flat in Britain (no form over hurdles). *D. W. Thompson*

MUSTARD BENN 4 b.g. Golden Snake (USA) 127 – Mysterious Maid (USA) 76 **–** (L'Emigrant (USA) 129) [2007 p10g⁶ p13g p8g p6g 10s 8d 10.2s Jul 26] fourth foal: dam 1¼m to 1¾m winner: little solid form. *Mouse Hamilton-Fairley*

MUST BE KEEN 8 b.g. Emperor Jones (USA) 119 – As Mustard (Keen 116) [2007 57: **56** p5g⁵ p6g* p5.1g⁶ p6g f7g 5.2s⁴ p6g 5.1s 6m 6m p6g Sep 20] modest performer: won minor event at Kempton in January when trained by E. Oertel: in-and-out form for several trainers after: effective at 6f, probably stays 1¼m: acts on polytrack and good to soft going: tried tongue tied: wears headgear: often slowly away. *Miss Diana Weeden*

MUTABAYEN (USA) 2 b. or br.c. (Mar 29) Doneraile Court (USA) – La Frou Frou **93** (IRE) (Night Shift (USA)) [2007 6m² 7m⁵ 7f⁴ Aug 5] 30,000 2-y-o: stocky, useful-looking colt: third foal: half-brother to winner in US by El Corredor: dam, French/US 1m to 9.5f winner, half-sister to smart 7f/1m winner Madid: fairly useful form: won maiden at Redcar in June: much improved when 3 lengths fifth to Hatta Fort in Superlative Stakes at Newmarket, rallying: firmer ground, soon off bridle when disappointing favourite in minor event at Newbury: will be suited by 1m: joined A. Al Raihe in UAE. *B. Smart*

MUT'AB (USA) 2 b.c. (Jan 15) Alhaarth (IRE) 126 – Mistle Song 112 (Nashwan **84** (USA) 135) [2007 7.1d³ 7.1g² 7g Aug 21] 37,000Y: rangy, good-topped colt: fifth foal: half-brother to 3 winners, including 6-y-o Motive and 4-y-o Wassfa: dam 1½m/14.6f (Park Hill Stakes) winner: fairly useful form: placed in maidens at Sandown: stiff task, last of 7 (beaten 8¾ lengths) behind Fast Company in Acomb Stakes at York: will be suited by 1¼m+. *C. E. Brittain*

MUTADARREJ (IRE) 3 ch.c. Fantastic Light (USA) 134 – Najayeb (USA) (Silver **91** Hawk (USA) 123) [2007 91p: 10m⁵ 10.4g 10d² 12g 12d 12g 12f² Sep 25] leggy, sparely-made colt: fairly useful handicapper: good efforts when runner-up in 2007, beaten 3½ lengths by Sahrati at Sandown and 1½ lengths behind Samsons Son at Folkestone: stays 1½m: acts on firm and good to soft going: tried blinkered: has been bandaged in front: sold 42,000 gns in October. *J. L. Dunlop*

MUTAJARRED 3 ch.g. Alhaarth (IRE) 126 – Bedara 93 (Barathea (IRE) 127) [2007 **112** 73P: 8.1s* 8s* 8.2v* 8s⁴ 10s² Oct 13] big, strong gelding: smart and generally progressive form: won maiden at Haydock in June, and handicaps at York (beat Novikov by 9 lengths) and Nottingham (9/4 on, didn't have to be at best to beat Mezuzah by 6 lengths in 4-runner event) in July: very good length second to Night Crescendo in handicap at Ascot final start: stays 1¼m: raced only on ground softer than good (acts on heavy). *W. J. Haggas*

MUTAKARRIM 10 ch.g. Mujtahid (USA) 118 – Alyakkh (IRE) 78 (Sadler's Wells **112** (USA) 132) [2007 112: 12m* 14m² 14s⁵ 14v 12g 16m Nov 4] good-topped gelding: smart performer: as good as ever when winning handicap at Leopardstown in May: second to Yeats in listed race at Leopardstown later in month, but little impact after: stays 1¾m: acts on any going: usually blinkered. *D. K. Weld, Ireland*

MUTAMAASEK (USA) 5 b. or br.g. Swain (IRE) 134 – Tamgeed (USA) 66 (Wood- **75** man (USA) 126) [2007 71: p12g 12.4d p10g³ p10m* p12g* Dec 19] smallish, strong gelding: fair handicapper: won twice at Lingfield in December: stays easy 1½m: acts on polytrack, firm and good to soft going: tried visored/in cheekpieces/tongue tied. *Lady Herries*

MUTAMARED (USA) 7 ch.g. Nureyev (USA) 131 – Alydariel (USA) (Alydar **106** (USA)) [2007 115: 6.5g 6g p6g³ 6m⁵ 6m² 6d 6m p6g 6m⁶ 6g p6g Nov 16] lengthy gelding: just useful performer in 2007, best efforts third to fifth starts, ¾-length second to Beaver Patrol in handicap at Newmarket: not at best after, though badly hampered at the Curragh and Doncaster before leaving K. Ryan prior to final start: best form at 6f: acts on dirt, polytrack, good to firm and good to soft going: tried tongue tied at 3 yrs. *Mrs Sandra McCarthy, Ireland*

MUTANASEB (USA) 3 b.g. Mr Greeley (USA) 122 – Rose Rhapsody (USA) **99** (Pleasant Colony (USA)) [2007 87p: p7g* 7.1d* 8.1g⁵ 7m⁴ 7d 7d Oct 19] tall gelding: useful performer: successful in maiden at Kempton in May and handicap at Sandown (beat Endiamo by 1¼ lengths) in June: blinkered/in cheekpieces, little impact in handicaps last 2 starts: gelded after: barely stays 1m: acts on polytrack and good to soft going: joined A. Al Raihe in UAE. *M. A. Jarvis*

MUTAWAAJID (AUS) 4 b.c. Redoute's Choice (AUS) – Elated Lady (AUS) (Vain **121** (AUS)) [2007 5.5g* 6g* 7g* 8g⁴ 6m 7g 6g⁴ 5.2m⁴ Sep 22] very big, strong colt: half-brother to several winners in Australia, including Group 2 6f winners Adeewin and Fatoon (both by Snaadee): dam unraced: very smart performer: won his first 5 races, namely maiden at Wyong, handicaps at Canterbury and Randwick (latter in January), and Group 2 events Royal Sovereign Stakes at Randwick (by length from Sniper's Bullet) and Hobartville Stakes at Rosehill (beat Gold Edition by a neck), both in February: left Gai Waterhouse in Australia after next start: best efforts in Britain when fourth on last 2 starts, in Sprint Cup at Haydock (beaten 2½ lengths by Red Clubs, tending to hang left) and World Trophy at Newbury (sweating, 1¾ lengths behind Rowe Park): may prove ideally suited by 6f/7f: raced only on good/good to firm going: has returned to Gai Waterhouse. *M. R. Channon*

MUTAWAFFER 6 b.g. Marju (IRE) 127 – Absaar (USA) 76 (Alleged (USA) 138) **97** [2007 97: 8s³ 12g² 14d Aug 22] strong, well-made gelding: useful handicapper, on long losing run: creditable efforts this year when 5 lengths third to Very Wise in Lincoln at Newcastle in March and ½-length second to High Treason at York in May: seemed not to stay when well held in Ebor at York final outing: stays 1½m: acts on soft and good to firm going: tongue tied once. *R. A. Fahey*

MUTAWASSEL (USA) 6 b.h. Kingmambo (USA) 125 – Danzig Darling (CAN) **95**
(Danzig (USA)) [2007 a6g* a9g² a16g a11g⁴ a12g³ a11g² a9g* a12g* 9.9d⁵ 10m⁴ p11g⁶
8g² 10g 7g⁶ Dec 27] tall, good-topped, quite attractive horse: has a round action: useful
performer: winner of 15 races in Qatar from 4 yrs to 6 yrs, successful in January, April
and May in 2007: returned to original trainer (B. Hills), best effort in 3 handicaps in
Britain when creditable fourth to Pathos at Newmarket: returned to Qatar for last 3 starts:
stays 1½m: unraced on extremes of going on turf: has hung right/flashed tail: blinkered
(ran poorly) final start in 2004. *M. Al Attiya, Qatar*

MUTAYAM 7 b.g. Compton Place 125 – Final Shot 91 (Dalsaan 125) [2007 –: 5g 5g 5d **59**
5d⁶ 6g 5m 5g⁵ 5d 5g Sep 23] modest handicapper: races mainly at 5f: tongue tied nowadays: has worn cheekpieces. *D. A. Nolan*

MUTHABARA (IRE) 3 b.f. (Mar 4) Red Ransom (USA) – Hureya (USA) 82 (Wood- **104 p**
man (USA) 126) [2007 7s* 7.1d* Jul 26] good-topped filly: third foal: half-sister to 3-y-o
Aqmaar and fairly useful 9f winner Estiqraar (by Alhaarth): dam, 1m winner, half-sister
to very smart performer up to 1¼m Muqbil out of half-sister to high-class miler Bahri:
useful form: made good impression winning both starts, namely maiden at Newbury
(by 5 lengths) in June and listed race at Sandown (beat Lady Deauville by ¾ length),
quickening well: suffered an injury in late-August: will stay 1m: should make her mark in
pattern company. *J. L. Dunlop*

MUTOON (IRE) 3 b.f. Erhaab (USA) 127 – Nafhaat (USA) 91 (Roberto (USA) 131) **64**
[2007 52: p8g² p8g p8g f8g³ p7g 8.1m⁵ 10.1g² 11.5m Aug 9] modest maiden handicapper: stays 1¼m: acts on polytrack, best effort on turf on good going. *S. C. Williams*

MUTUAL FRIEND (USA) 3 gr.g. Aljabr (USA) 125 – Dubai Visit (USA) 101 (Quiet **84**
American (USA)) [2007 71p: p7g⁵ p8g⁵ p10g* 10f² p10g⁴ 10v³ Jul 2] tall gelding: fairly
useful handicapper: won at Lingfield in May: better efforts after, third to Mull of Dubai at
Windsor, carrying head rather awkwardly and wandering under pressure: stays 1¼m: acts
on polytrack and any turf going: often races freely: sold 72,000 gns, joined D. Pipe and
gelded. *E. A. L. Dunlop*

MUZMIN (USA) 2 b. or br.c. (Feb 2) Seeking The Gold (USA) – In On The Secret **75 p**
(CAN) (Secretariat (USA)) [2007 8m⁵ Sep 8] $285,000Y: tall, leggy colt: closely related
to smart 1m (in UAE) to 10.4f winner Royal Tryst (by Kingmambo) and half-brother to
several winners, including US Grade 3 8.5f winner Ask Me No Secrets (by Seattle Slew):
dam, stakes-placed winner up to 9f in North America, out of Canadian Oaks second In
My Cap: 12/1, encouraging fifth to Dr Faustus in maiden at Thirsk: will stay 1¼m: sure
to improve. *M. Johnston*

MWINDAJI 2 b.g. (Jun 7) Hunting Lion (IRE) 115 – Gayane 125 (Nureyev (USA) 131) **69**
[2007 6m 7m* 8d⁵ Oct 23] close-coupled gelding: fair form: won seller at Leicester (left
M. Channon 10,500 gns) in September: fifth in nursery at Yarmouth: stays 1m. *Mrs P. Sly*

MY ARCH 5 b.g. Silver Patriarch (IRE) 125 – My Desire 88 (Grey Desire 115) [2007 **94**
88: 7m 12.3g 9.8g* 12g 12s⁴ 12m 11.9m Aug 11] big, good-bodied gelding: fairly useful
handicapper: improved to win at Ripon (beat Fortunate Isle by head, hung right) in
May: best effort after when fourth to Arc Bleu at the Curragh fifth start: stays 1½m: acts
on soft going: blinkered at Ripon, in cheekpieces last 2 starts: has joined M. Todhunter.
K. A. Ryan

MY AUNT FANNY 2 b.f. (Mar 16) Nayef (USA) 129 – Putuna 98 (Generous (IRE) **75 p**
139) [2007 p7g³ Sep 7] tall, quite attractive filly: fifth foal: half-sister to 5-y-o Kingsholm: dam, 8.5f/1¼m winner, half-sister to useful 2-y-o sprinter Lochonica: 20/1, never-
nearer third to Annie Skates in minor event at Kempton: will stay 1m/1¼m: should do
better. *A. M. Balding*

MY BEAUTAFUL 3 ch.f. Classic Cliche (IRE) 128 – Ginger Rogers 71 (Gildoran 123) **56**
[2007 49p: p7.1g² p8.6g³ p9.5g p12.2g Oct 12] modest form when placed in maidens at
Wolverhampton first 2 starts in 2007: tailed off last 2 outings: should be suited by 1¼m+:
raced only on polytrack on Flat. *Miss J. S. Davis*

MYBOYCHARLIE (IRE) 2 b.c. (Apr 20) Danetime (IRE) 121 – Dulceata (IRE) **118**
(Rousillon (USA) 133) [2007 6s* 6.3v* 6d* 7m³ Sep 16]
With the obvious exception of the now-deceased Danehill, Coolmore has
not enjoyed the best of results with the leading sprinters it has stood over the last
decade. Lake Coniston failed to cut the mustard and is now in South Africa;
Stravinsky, sire of Benbaun and Soldier's Tale, is shuttling between Japan and New
Zealand; and Mozart died after just one season, leaving behind enough above-

average runners, headed by Dandy Man and Amadeus Wolf, to suggest his loss was significant. Among the others, champion juvenile Fasliyev has been represented by just one Group 1 winner in five crops and has been exported to Japan, and Choisir was near the top of the numerical table for first-season sires without getting much in the way of potential pattern horses. Danehill Dancer, who was best at distances short of a mile, is certainly doing well, but the average winning distance of his progeny is more than a mile and he is not exactly a 'speed' sire. Perhaps the aim of obtaining another top sprinter for its ever-expanding team was one of the reasons behind Coolmore's purchase of Myboycharlie for an undisclosed sum after his second start. Successful in the Prix Morny on his first appearance for his new owners, Myboycharlie has little in common with Excellent Art, a rare Coolmore two-year-old purchase a year before, in that he gives the strong impression sprinting will be his metier.

Coolmore's enthusiasm for Myboycharlie was understandable based on the style in which he won the Dubai Duty Free Anglesey Stakes. He arrived for the race at the Curragh in mid-July the winner of his only start, a maiden at the same course at the end of the previous month—a relatively late start for a colt with as much speed, with Royal Ascot a memory. Myboycharlie showed great promise in the maiden, overcoming greenness to win unextended by three lengths after travelling strongly from the outset. The Anglesey Stakes, for which Myboycharlie was second choice in the betting, had only four other runners, none of whom boasted top form. The favourite was Railway Stakes runner-up South Dakota from Aidan O'Brien's stable and the others were the filly Tuscan Evening, second to Listen in a listed race, newcomer Chun Tosaigh and Abolition trained by Mark Johnston. Myboycharlie outclassed them, held up and taking a keen hold before leading a furlong from home and running right away to score driven out by seven lengths from Tuscan Evening. Given his apparent aptitude over six furlongs, two obvious options existed—the Phoenix Stakes, for which Myboycharlie would have to be supplemented, and the Darley Prix Morny. The latter, which consistently takes as much winning as any race for two-year-olds in France, was chosen. With Winker Watson withdrawn because of the soft ground, Myboycharlie's five opponents consisted of three no-hopers, two of them from Spain, and two of the best French-trained juveniles seen out to that point. They were Prix du Bois and Prix Robert Papin winner Natagora and Alexandros, successful in the Prix de Cabourg. Myboycharlie started favourite and justified the confidence in style. Settled behind the trail-blazing Natagora, he was pulled out to challenge over a furlong out and made Natagora look almost one paced as he stretched out impressively for a ready two-length success. Alexandros finished half a length away third. One thing Natagora does not lack is speed and, although her subsequent form in the Cheveley Park

Darley Prix Morny, Deauville—Myboycharlie keeps his unbeaten record on his first outing for his new owners; pattern-race winners Natagora (right) and Alexandros (centre) are next

Stakes was superior, Myboycharlie's performance to beat her in the Prix Morny was a fine display.

Tommy Stack had sent out two Group 1 winners previously, Las Meninas (One Thousand Guineas) and Tarascon (1998 Irish One Thousand Guineas). Unlike the arrangement with Excellent Art, who joined Aidan O'Brien's team after being with Neville Callaghan as a juvenile, Tommy Stack, whose son Fozzy is a godson of Ballydoyle/Coolmore boss John Magnier, will continue training Myboycharlie. In the wake of the Prix Morny, Myboycharlie was promoted by William Hill to ante-post joint-favouritism for the Two Thousand Guineas at 7/1, a position he held for a month. Until, in fact, he contested the National Stakes at the Curragh again, and had his limitations exposed, at least over seven furlongs. The race was run on good to firm going, the firmest Myboycharlie had encountered. Up against New Approach and Rio de La Plata, he started joint-second favourite of the nine runners and was held up as usual. This time, however, he could not get to the front when asked to quicken two furlongs from home, always being held and coming three and a half lengths adrift of New Approach with Rio de La Plata ahead of him in second. Myboycharlie was a bit below his best form, and he was almost certainly not helped by being stepped up in distance. Given the lopsided arrangement of the pattern system for sprinters, mentioned in the essay on Dark Angel, connections will have the opportunity to try Myboycharlie over seven furlongs again to test whether it is worth making a challenge for the Two Thousand Guineas, for which Myboycharlie was quoted at a best-priced 20/1 at the end of the season. In truth, his chances of staying a mile look slim and, if he trains on and makes normal improvement, he should do well as a sprinter as a three-year-old.

		Danehill	Danzig
	Danetime (IRE)	(b 1986)	Razyana
	(b 1994)	Allegheny River	Lear Fan
Myboycharlie (IRE)		(b 1987)	Allesheny
(b.c. Apr 20, 2005)		Rousillon	Riverman
	Dulceata (IRE)	(b 1981)	Belle Dorine
	(b 1988)	Snowtop	Thatching
		(b 1983)	Icing

Myboycharlie, a quite good-topped, useful-looking colt, is by the now-deceased Danetime, a smart colt who showed form over seven furlongs but put up his best runs at six, notably when landing the Stewards' Cup and finishing second (demoted to third) in the Haydock Sprint Cup as a three-year-old and third in the July Cup as a four-year-old. Danetime has been a strong influence for speed at stud. Around three quarters of his offspring's wins have been at five or six furlongs, with only a handful beyond a mile; Two Thousand Guineas runner-up Vital Equine is his best performer at a mile. Myboycharlie's dam Dulceata was last of ten in a maiden at Newmarket on her only start as a three-year-old but she comes from a successful family, one in which speed has been to the fore. Myboycharlie, who cost €13,000 as a foal at Goffs and 54,000 guineas as a yearling at Doncaster, is her sixth winner. None of the others has been any great shakes but all of them have shown a relative lack of stamina, even Byzantium (by influence for stamina Shirley Heights), who won at a mile and a quarter but did most of his later racing at around a mile. Dulceata's yearling filly by Imperial Ballet was entered in three auctions during the year, being knocked down for €1,800 at Goffs February Sales, withdrawn at the same venue in October, then bought by Stack for what seemed a bargain price of 38,000 guineas at the Newmarket December Sales. Myboycharlie's grandam Snowtop won at six furlongs at two and three, the latter in a listed handicap, and is also grandam of the very smart sprinter Asset and Snowland, whose tally includes a Group 1 event over five and a half furlongs in Australia. The next dam, Icing, foaled ten winners, most notably Al Hareb, successful in the William Hill Futurity, and Dr Somerville who won La Coupe de Maisons-Laffitte. There was give in the ground for all three of Myboycharlie's wins and he won the Anglesey on heavy. *T. Stack, Ireland*

MY CAUSEWAY DREAM (IRE) 4 ch.f. Giant's Causeway (USA) 132 – Meritorious (USA) (St Jovite (USA) 135) [2007 –: 10.1m 10.1m 12d⁶ 11.1m 14.1m Aug 11] maiden: left C. Roche in Ireland, little form in 2007: often blinkered/visored. *J. S. Wainwright*

MYCENEAN PRINCE (USA) 4 b.g. Swain (IRE) 134 – Nijinsky's Beauty (USA) **49**
(Nijinsky (CAN) 138) [2007 49: p9.5g f7g 8.5g p8g⁴ p10g⁴ p8.6g Nov 27] strong,
compact gelding: poor maiden: stays 1¼m: acts on all-weather, unraced on extremes of
going on turf: visored/blinkered nowadays. *R. C. Guest*

MY DROP (IRE) 3 b.c. Danetime (IRE) 121 – Notluckytochange (IRE) 91 (King of **70**
Clubs 124) [2007 52p: f5g* f6g⁶ 5g⁶ 5.3d⁴ 5.3s³ 5g⁴ Jun 20] fair performer: won maiden
at Southwell in January: raced only at 5f/6f: acts on fibresand and soft going: sold 10,000
gns, sent to Bahrain. *E. J. O'Neill*

MY FLAME 2 b.c. (Apr 28) Cool Jazz 116 – Suselja (IRE) 53 (Mon Tresor 113) [2007 **52**
6d 7s 6d p6g p6d Dec 6] workmanlike colt: modest maiden: visored, well beaten in
nurseries: should prove best up to 7f. *J. R. Jenkins*

MYFRENCHCONNECTION (IRE) 3 b.g. Tendulkar (USA) 114 – Papinette **71**
(IRE) (Maelstrom Lake 118) [2007 63: 7m 7m⁴ 8m 8g³ 7.9f³ 9.9g⁵ 7.5m* 8.5g* 8m² 8g²
Oct 25] strong gelding: fair handicapper: won in August (claimer) and September, both at
Beverley: stays 8.5f: acts on firm ground: tried in cheekpieces. *P. T. Midgley*

MY FRIEND FRITZ 7 ch.g. Safawan 118 – Little Scarlett 54 (Mazilier (USA) 107) **58**
[2007 p16g⁶ f12g³ Jan 30] limited encouragement from 2 starts in bumpers: better effort
on Flat (modest form) when third in claimer at Southwell: stays 1½m: raced only on
all-weather. *P. W. Hiatt*

MY GACHO (IRE) 5 b.g. Shinko Forest (IRE) – Floralia 81 (Auction Ring (USA) **86**
123) [2007 93: 6m* 6m 6g 6m 6m 6m Sep 22] good-topped gelding: fairly useful handicapper: won at Thirsk in May: little impact after: best at 6f: acts on all-weather and firm
ground: visored/blinkered: races prominently. *T. D. Barron*

MY JEANIE (IRE) 3 ch.f. King Charlemagne (USA) 120 – Home Comforts (Most **62**
Welcome 131) [2007 46+: p8g⁵ p8g* Dec 16] modest performer: won handicap at Kempton in December: stays 1m: raced only on polytrack since debut. *J. C. Fox*

MY KAISER CHIEF 2 bl.c. (Mar 29) Paris House 123 – So Tempted (So Factual **68**
(USA) 120) [2007 5m⁴ 5m⁴ 5.1g f5d⁵ f5g⁶ Dec 27] lengthy colt: fair maiden: likely
to prove best kept to 5f: raced only on fibresand and good/good to firm ground.
W. J. H. Ratcliffe

MY LEARNED FRIEND (IRE) 3 b.g. Marju (IRE) 127 – Stately Princess 70 **72**
(Robellino (USA) 127) [2007 86: p8g⁶ 8.3m 7.1m 6d p7.1g⁵ Nov 1] close-coupled,
useful-looking gelding: just fair form in handicaps in 2007: stays 7f, seemingly not 1m:
unraced on extremes of going on turf: gelded after final start. *A. M. Balding*

MY LEGAL EAGLE (IRE) 13 b.g. Law Society (USA) 130 – Majestic Nurse 80 **56**
(On Your Mark 125) [2007 62, a–: 14.1g⁴ 14.1m³ 11.8s² p12g 14.1d⁶ 12.1s² 12.1s 14m⁵
16.2m 12.1m³ 12.6m² 17.2d⁵ 16s⁶ Oct 14] smallish gelding: modest performer nowadays
(no wins since 2004): effective at 1½m to 17f: acts on fibresand, heavy and good to firm
going: tried blinkered: patiently ridden. *E. G. Bevan*

MY LOVE THOMAS (IRE) 3 b.f. Cadeaux Genereux 131 – Flanders (IRE) 110 **84**
(Common Grounds 118) [2007 77p: 6d⁴ 6.1m² p6m 5m Sep 1] rather leggy filly: fairly
useful performer: best effort when second in handicap at Nottingham: probably best at 6f:
acts on polytrack and good to firm ground: slowly away final outing. *E. A. L. Dunlop*

MY MAITE MICKEY 3 b.g. Komaite (USA) – Mrs Plum 72 (Emarati (USA) 74) **–**
[2007 –: 5d 6d 6m 6g Aug 29] rather leggy gelding: little form: visored last 2 starts: sent
to Spain. *R. C. Guest*

MY MATE MAX 2 b.g. (Apr 8) Fraam 114 – Victory Flip (IRE) 67 (Victory Note **75 p**
(USA) 120) [2007 p7.1g* Dec 13] first foal: dam maiden: 25/1, won
maiden at Wolverhampton by 1¾ lengths from Funseeker: will stay 1m: should improve.
R. Hollinshead

MY MATE PETE (IRE) 2 b.g. (Apr 23) Captain Rio 122 – Lady Peculiar (CAN) **76 p**
(Sunshine Forever (USA)) [2007 5.1d p5.1g³ p6g* Dec 29] €20,000Y, 30,000 2-y-o:
well-made gelding: half-brother to several winners, including smart Irish 2006 2-y-o 7f
winner Summit Surge (by Noverre): dam Canadian 6f winner: fair form: upped in trip,
won maiden at Lingfield: will stay 7f: acts on polytrack: should continue to progress.
R. M. Beckett

MY MENTOR (IRE) 3 b.g. Golan (IRE) 129 – Vanille (IRE) 72 (Selkirk (USA) 129) **71 +**
[2007 p7g f7g p7.1g p10g² p8g* p8g Jul 17] fair performer: best effort when winning
handicap at Lingfield in June: stays 1¼m: raced only on polytrack. *Sir Mark Prescott*

MY MICHELLE 6 b.m. Ali-Royal (IRE) 127 – April Magic (Magic Ring (IRE) 115) **67** [2007 60: p8.6g* p9.5g³ p9.5g⁴ p8.6g* p9.5g² p9.5g p8.6g⁴ 8d p7.1g⁶ p9.5g p9.5g² **a74** 8.1d² p8.6g p8.6g⁶ p9.5g² p8.6g² p8.6g* p8.6d⁶ Dec 6] leggy, quite good-topped mare: fair handicapper: won at Wolverhampton in January, February and November: stays easy 9.5f: acts on polytrack, good to firm and good to soft going: often makes running. *B. Palling*

MY MIRASOL 3 ch.f. Primo Valentino (IRE) 116 – Distinctly Blu (IRE) 70 (Distinctly **68** North (USA) 115) [2007 72: f7g⁴ p8.6g² p8.6g² p8.6g² p8.6g* p10f⁶ p10g p10g 10m⁵ 10.2f p8.6g³ p10m Dec 9] lengthy filly: fair performer: landed odds in seller at Wolverhampton in February: left K. Ryan after sixth outing: stays 8.6f: acts on all-weather, heavy and good to firm ground: usually wears cheekpieces (well held without in 2007): reportedly bled seventh outing. *D. E. Cantillon*

MY MONNA 3 b.f. Josr Algarhoud (IRE) 118 – Albarsha 75 (Mtoto 134) [2007 –: p8g **59** 11.9m p10g² p10g p10g⁴ p12g⁴ p10g p16g Dec 4] modest maiden handicapper: stays 1½m: acts on polytrack (raced only twice on turf). *Miss S. West*

MYMUMSAYSIMTHEBEST 2 b.c. (Mar 21) Reel Buddy (USA) 118 – Night **89** Gypsy 74 (Mind Games 121) [2007 6g 7m² 7.1g⁴ 6g⁶ Aug 23] 24,000Y, 32,000 2-y-o: lengthy colt: third foal: half-brother to 4-y-o Safari Mischief: dam 2-y-o 5f winner (only season to race): improved form when 2½ lengths sixth of 20 to Dark Angel in sales race at York: should prove best up to 7f: raced only on good/good to firm going. *R. Hannon*

MYND 7 b.g. Atraf 116 – Prim Lass 65 (Reprimand 122) [2007 73, a55: p5.1g 5.1g **48** May 29] workmanlike gelding: fair performer at best: well below form both starts at 7 yrs: effective at 5f/6f: acts on all-weather and heavy going: tried in cheekpieces/visor: sometimes slowly away. *B. Palling*

MY PARIS 6 b.g. Paris House 123 – My Desire 88 (Grey Desire 115) [2007 110: p8.6g **106** 8s⁵ 8m 8f* 8g² 8m⁶ 8s⁵ 7m 8g 8g 8s 9m Oct 6] leggy, lengthy gelding: useful handicapper: won at Thirsk in May by neck from Bustan: good efforts next 2 starts, second to European Dream at Ripon when sixth of 26 to Royal Oath in Hunt Cup at Royal Ascot: mostly below form after: effective at 7f, and stays 1¼m: acts on firm and soft going, lightly raced on all-weather: tried blinkered/in cheekpieces: races prominently. *K. A. Ryan*

MY PIN UP 2 b.f. (Feb 1) Forzando 122 – Victoria Sioux 54 (Ron's Victory (USA) 129) **67** [2007 p5g⁵ p6g² p6s⁵ Dec 21] sixth foal: half-sister to fairly useful 5f (at 2 yrs)/6f winner Makabul and 7f winner Bint Makbul (both by Makbul) and to 6f/7f winner Brave Chief (by Komaite): dam sprint maiden: fair maiden: best effort when second at Kempton: stays 6f: very slowly away on debut. *Christian Wroe*

MY PORTFOLIO (IRE) 5 b.g. Montjeu (IRE) 137 – Elaine's Honor (USA) (Chief's **55 ?** Crown (USA)) [2007 –: 14g 13d p16.5g Oct 20] maiden: just modest form on Flat since 2004: best efforts at 1m: acts on good to soft going. *J. J. Lambe, Ireland*

MY RASCAL (IRE) 5 b.g. Imperial Ballet (IRE) 110 – Derena (FR) (Crystal Palace **–** (FR) 132) [2007 51: f7g May 22] big, strong gelding: modest handicapper at 3 yrs: little impact since: best effort at 6f on good ground: usually wore headgear: dead. *J. Balding*

MYRIOLA 2 ch.f. (Feb 5) Captain Rio 122 – Spaniola (IRE) (Desert King (IRE) 129) **61** [2007 5m⁵ 5m f6g⁶ 5g³ 6.1d⁶ p5.1g³ p6g p6g Oct 22] 10,000Y: attractive filly: first foal: dam ran once: modest maiden: left J. Given after fourth start: best form at 5f: acts on polytrack and good to firm going. *B. Palling*

MYRTLE BAY (IRE) 4 bl.g. Pennekamp (USA) 130 – Moneypenny (GER) (Neshad **58 d** (USA) 108) [2007 62: p10g⁴ p10g⁵ p10g p12g⁶ 10.2d p10g p10g Nov 19] useful-looking gelding: modest maiden: stays 2m: acts on polytrack and good to firm going: tried in visor/cheekpieces: no easy ride. *J. C. Tuck*

MY SARA 3 b.f. Mujahid (USA) 125 – Ancestry (Persepolis (FR) 127) [2007 55: p6g **58** f8g⁴ p9.5g⁴ f8g* f8g⁵ 11g 12.1m 12m³ p12.2g f11d⁵ f11d⁶ Dec 21] sturdy filly: modest handicapper: won at Southwell in February: effective at 1m, barely stays 1½m: acts on all-weather: often visored, blinkered final outing: difficult ride. *R. A. Fahey*

MY SECRETS 3 b.c. Fantastic Light (USA) 134 – St Radegund 85 (Green Desert **81** (USA) 127) [2007 85: 10.9m⁴ 10.5g² 12f² 11.6g 12m⁵ 12m p12.2g³ p12.2g² Jul 10] sturdy colt: fairly useful handicapper: in frame 5 times in 2007, blinkered final outing (sold 16,000 gns after): stays 1½m: acts on polytrack and firm ground (well held on heavy): races up with pace. *M. Johnston*

MY SHADOW 2 b.c. (Jan 24) Zamindar (USA) 116 – Reflections (Sadler's Wells **70** (USA) 132) [2007 7.5d⁴ p7.1g p8m p8g⁴ Dec 28] 25,000Y: first foal: dam once-raced half-sister to smart performers Erudite (up to 2m) and Vortex (7f/1m): fair maiden: left E. McMahon 15,000 gns after second start: stays 1m. *S. Dow*

MY SHEILAS DREAM (IRE) 2 b.f. (Mar 9) Acclamation 118 – Triphibious 69 **50** (Zafonic (USA) 130) [2007 5m* 5m 5m⁵ 6d³ 5s⁵ 5.1m 5m⁵ Aug 25] €15,000Y: lengthy filly: dam, maiden, out of sister to smart 1¼m/1½m performer Talented: modest performer: won seller at Catterick (off J. Spearing 7,000 gns) in April: probably best at 5f: acts on good to firm going: tried in cheekpieces. *W. G. M. Turner*

MY SILVER MONARCH (IRE) 3 b.f. Bertolini (USA) 125 – April View (USA) **–** (Distant View (USA) 126) [2007 –: 6m 8g Jun 1] smallish filly: little impact in maidens: sold 800 gns, sent to Spain. *H. S. Howe*

MY SPRING ROSE 3 b.f. Lake Coniston (IRE) 131 – Diamond Jayne (IRE) (Royal **52** Abjar (USA) 121) [2007 8.3m 8d 8.3g p10g p8g 8.3d 11.9g p8g Dec 16] angular filly: second foal: dam no form: modest maiden: form only at 1m. *J. R. Jenkins*

MYSTERIOUS WORLD (IRE) 3 ch.c. Desert Prince (IRE) 130 – Salligram (Salse **62** (USA) 128) [2007 8d 10.5g⁵ 10m⁵ 12.4d p12.2g p13.9g Dec 1] rangy colt: modest maiden: stays 1¼m: yet to race on extremes of going on turf: unseated rider early on on fourth start: sold 8,500 gns. *Mrs K. Walton*

MYSTERY OCEAN 3 b.f. Dr Fong (USA) 128 – Tiriana (Common Grounds 118) **87** [2007 86: p8g³ 7g 7d 8s⁵ 7s³ Jul 25] leggy, lengthy filly: fairly useful performer: best effort when third to Precocious Star in listed race at Kempton: below form in handicaps after, looking reluctant to race final outing (well held in 4-runner race): stays easy 1m: acts on polytrack and good to firm going: one to treat with some caution. *R. M. Beckett*

MYSTERY PIPS 7 b.m. Bin Ajwaad (IRE) 119 – Le Shuttle 49 (Presidium 124) [2007 **56** 71: p5.1g f5g f5g f5g f5g 5g* p5.1g 5m⁴ p5.1g⁶ 5g 5g 5g⁴ p5.1g 5m p5.1g Sep 20] modest performer: won minor event at Ayr in May: best at bare 5f: acts on all-weather, firm and good to soft going: has worn blinkers, visored nowadays: often forces pace. *N. Tinkler*

MYSTERY RIVER (USA) 3 ch.f. Dr Fong (USA) 128 – Bacinella (USA) (El Gran **83** Senor (USA) 136) [2007 78: p8.6g³ p8.6g⁴ 8g 10.3f⁵ 9.7m⁵ 10g 10.2d⁵ Aug 19] good-bodied filly: fairly useful handicapper: improved when winning at Folkestone (by 5 lengths) in July: stays 1¼m: acts on polytrack, firm and soft going: often makes running: sold 16,000 gns, sent to Saudi Arabia. *B. J. Meehan*

MYSTERY SAIL (USA) 2 b.f. (May 1) Mizzen Mast (USA) 121 – Questonia 107 **80 p** (Rainbow Quest (USA) 134) [2007 7m* Sep 22] rangy filly: seventh foal: half-sister to several winners, including 5-y-o Sharp Reply and French 1¼m winner Common Request (by Lear Fan): dam, 1m winner, out of half-sister to Xaar: 7/1, won maiden at Newbury by head from Lord Peter Flint, digging deep to lead close home: will be suited by 1m+: open to improvement. *Mrs A. J. Perrett*

MYSTERY STAR (IRE) 2 ch.c. (Apr 18) Kris Kin (USA) 126 – Mystery Hill (USA) **85** 72 (Danehill (USA) 126) [2007 8m² 8d³ p8.6g* Nov 10] €23,000Y: close-coupled colt: fourth foal: half-brother to Irish 5f/6f winner Lilly Be (by Titus Livius) and 2006 2-y-o 6f winner Shebang (by Trans Island): dam UAE 7f winner: fairly useful form in maidens, placed at Newmarket (second to Tomintoul Flyer) and York prior to winning at Wolverhampton (wandered): will stay 1¼m. *M. H. Tompkins*

MYSTIC 3 ch.f. Bahamian Bounty 116 – Sweet Myrtle (USA) (Mutakddim (USA) 112) **43** [2007 –: 7m⁵ 5.9m 6g Aug 29] workmanlike filly: poor maiden: stays 7f. *D. W. Barker*

MYSTICAL AYR (IRE) 5 br.m. Namid 128 – Scanno's Choice (IRE) 54 (Pennine **76** Walk 120) [2007 65: 8.3m⁶ 9.2g² 9.1d 9.1g³ 8.3g⁴ 9.2g² 9.1g² 10.1v⁵ 9.1g 9.1d⁴ 9.2m 9.1s* 8s² 8.3g² 7.2s³ 9.2s² 8g² 9.1v 7.2v⁶ Nov 3] sturdy mare: fair handicapper: won at Ayr in August: stays 1¼m: acts on heavy going: tried in cheekpieces final 4-y-o start: none too resolute, but consistent. *Miss L. A. Perratt*

MYSTICAL MOON 3 b.g. Medicean 128 – Moon Carnival 94 (Be My Guest (USA) **64** 126) [2007 69p: 10.2m⁶ 10.2f 11.5m p12g p16g p12m Oct 3] quite good-topped gelding: modest maiden handicapper: stays 1½m: acts on polytrack, good to firm and good to soft going: blinkered last 3 starts. *Lady Herries*

MYSTIC ART (IRE) 2 b.g. (May 8) Peintre Celebre (USA) 137 – Mystic Lure 70 **83** (Green Desert (USA) 127) [2007 6m 6m p7g⁵ Sep 18] 45,000Y: rather unfurnished gelding: eighth foal: half-brother to 3 winners, including useful 6f winner (including at 2 yrs) Entrap (by Phone Trick) and 4-y-o Reeling N' Rocking: dam, maiden (stayed 7f), half-sister to top-class French 1m/9f winner Thrill Show: fairly useful maiden: much improved when fifth to Sky Dive at Lingfield: gelded after: will stay 1m. *C. R. Egerton*

MYSTIC DANCER 3 ch.c. Machiavellian (USA) 123 – Mystic Goddess (USA) 94 **79** (Storm Bird (CAN) 134) [2007 79p: 10m⁴ 8m May 19] tall, attractive colt: has a fluent, round action: fair form in maidens: not given hard time when fourth at Windsor on reappearance, but well held on handicap debut next time: stays 1¼m: acts on polytrack, unraced on extremes of going on turf: sold 11,500 gns in October. *Sir Michael Stoute*

MYSTICKHILL (IRE) 2 ch.f. (Feb 7) Raise A Grand (IRE) 114 – Lady Eberspacher **70** (IRE) 68 (Royal Abjar (USA) 121) [2007 f5g⁴ 5m³ 5f³ 5g p6g⁴ p6g³ p6g² Oct 22] 5,000Y: close-coupled filly: third foal: half-sister to 4-y-o Indian Lady: dam sprint maiden: fair maiden: in frame 6 of 7 starts (first 4 for T. Pitt, tongue tied after): will prove best at 5f/6f: acts on all-weather and firm going. *D. J. Murphy*

MYSTIC LIPS (GER) 3 b.f. Generous (IRE) 139 – Majorata (GER) (Acatenango **113** (GER) 127) [2007 8g³ 8g² 11g* 10d⁴ 10g⁴ 10g⁵ Oct 28] fifth foal: half-sister to German 1¼m/1½m winner Major Roi (by Roi Danzig): dam once-raced half-sister to smart German 1½m performers Malinas and Masterplayer out of Preis der Diana winner Majoritat: smart performer: 9 lengths second to Mi Emma in German 1000 Guineas at Dusseldorf before making all in Henkel Preis der Diana on same course (beat Dominante 5 lengths) in June: best effort afterwards when creditable 1¾ lengths fourth to Satwa Queen in Prix de l'Opera at Longchamp penultimate start: will stay 1½m: raced only on good/good to soft ground. *Andreas Lowe, Germany*

MYSTIC MAN (FR) 9 b.g. Cadeaux Genereux 131 – Shawanni 105 (Shareef Dancer **68** (USA) 135) [2007 89d: p7.1g⁴ p7g⁶ p7g² p8g⁴ p7g³ p8g⁵ p7g* p7.1g p7g Mar 26] strong, angular gelding: just fair handicapper nowadays: won at Kempton in February: stays 1m: acts on all-weather, soft and good to firm going: wears headgear: tried tongue tied early in career: held up, tends to race freely: none too reliable. *I. W. McInnes*

MYSTIC SPIN (IRE) 3 b.c. Tendulkar (USA) 114 – Mystical Jumbo (Mystiko (USA) **–** 124) [2007 p8g Nov 6] very slowly away when tailed off in maiden at Lingfield. *K. J. Burke*

MYSTIC STORM 4 b.g. Medicean 128 – Mrs Nash 66 (Night Shift (USA)) [2007 77: **77** p10g 10m 11.6f² 12g⁴ 14.1m 12d Sep 28] big, good-bodied gelding: fair handicapper: good second to Wait For The Will in amateur event at Windsor in August: stays 1½m (failed to settle only try at 1¾m): acts on polytrack, firm and good to soft going: sometimes tongue tied: sold 18,000 gns in November. *Lady Herries*

MYSTIFIED (IRE) 4 b.g. Raise A Grand (IRE) 114 – Sunrise (IRE) 58 (Sri Pekan **59** (USA) 117) [2007 62: 16g⁴ 16m² 14.1m⁵ 14.1g⁵ 16s 15.8m* 15.8s 13.8g Nov 6] useful-looking gelding: modest performer: won seller at Catterick in August: races mainly around 2m nowadays: acts on polytrack, good to firm and good to soft ground: tried in cheekpieces, usually blinkered: inconsistent. *R. F. Fisher*

MYSTIK MEGAN 6 gr.m. Wizard King 122 – Sian's Girl (Mystiko (USA) 124) [2007 **–** 10.5m Aug 9] workmanlike mare: second foal: sister to 7.2f winner Wizard of Us: dam unraced: modest form in bumpers: tailed off in maiden at Haydock on Flat debut. *M. Mullineaux*

MYTHICAL CHARM 8 b.m. Charnwood Forest (IRE) 125 – Triple Tricks (IRE) 70 **66** (Royal Academy (USA) 130) [2007 68: p8g p8g 9g⁶ 9m 7m 8s* p7g 7s* 9m 9g 8g 8d⁴ 7d p8g⁴ p7g p8g³ p8g p10g⁶ p7g³ Dec 30] good-topped mare: fair handicapper: won amateur events at Goodwood and Salisbury in July: effective at 7f to easy 1¼m: acts on all-weather, firm and soft ground: tongue tied: patiently ridden. *J. J. Bridger*

MYTHICAL FOSROC (USA) 2 b.f. (Mar 6) Najran (USA) – Green Boulevard **–** (USA) 57 (Green Forest (USA) 134) [2007 5m 6m Oct 22] $45,000Y: lengthy filly: half-sister to winners in US by Royal Academy and Favorite Trick: dam, 5f winner, half-sister to Prix Royal-Oak winner Assez Cuite and to dam of St Leger winner Michelozzo: well held in maidens. *J. S. Moore*

MYTHICAL KID (USA) 3 b. or br.c. Lemon Drop Kid (USA) 131 – Myth To Reality **102** (FR) (Sadler's Wells (USA) 132) [2007 111p: 11.5g⁵ 10m⁴ May 26] good-topped colt: trained by Sir Michael Stoute at 2 yrs: failed to progress as expected in 2007, shaping as if stamina stretched both starts, better effort when fifth of 7 to Aqaleem in Derby Trial at Lingfield: likely to prove best around 1m: acts on soft ground. *Saeed bin Suroor*

MYTHICAL STORY (IRE) 3 br.f. Alhaarth (IRE) 126 – Dreams 88 (Rainbow Quest **75** (USA) 134) [2007 10m⁶ 10d³ 12g⁴ Nov 9] leggy filly: seventh foal: half-sister to 3 winners, including winner around 1¼m First Fantasy (by Be My Chief) and 1m/1¼m winner Front Stage (by Grand Lodge), both useful: dam, untrustworthy 1¼m winner, half-sister to Melbourne Cup winner Jeune: best effort in maidens (fair form) when 3¼ lengths third to Abydos at Nottingham second start, clear of remainder: shaped like non-stayer final start: stays 1¼m: sold 18,000 gns. *J. R. Fanshawe*

MYTHS AND VERSES 4 b.f. Primo Valentino (IRE) 116 – Romantic Myth 105 **62** (Mind Games 121) [2007 65: p8g Jan 10] good-bodied filly: has a short, unimpressive action: modest maiden handicapper: said to have bled only start in 2007: stays 8.6f, effective at shorter: acts on polytrack and any turf going: sometimes wears cheekpieces. *K. A. Ryan*

MY TIGER LILLY 3 ch.f. Tobougg (IRE) 125 – Ashantiana 64 (Ashkalani (IRE) 128) **56** [2007 56: 6m² 5.1g⁶ 6m p8g 7f 6f Sep 10] modest maiden: left W. Knight after fifth start: best form at 6f: acts on polytrack and firm going (unraced on softer than good). *R. A. Teal*

MYTTON'S DREAM 5 br.m. Diktat 126 – Courtisane (Persepolis (FR) 127) [2007 **–** 46: p9.5g p8.6g f7g Feb 13] leggy mare: little form in 2007: sometimes blinkered. *Miss Joanne Priest*

MYTTON'S PRIDE 4 b.g. Tagula (IRE) 116 – Pictina (Petong 126) [2007 66d: p7.1g **–** 5g May 10] leggy gelding: has a quick action: fair handicapper at best: no form in 2007: tried in cheekpieces/blinkers. *A. Bailey*

MY TWO GIRLS (IRE) 3 b.f. Danetime (IRE) 121 – Sanctuary Line (IRE) (Lake **49** Coniston (IRE) 131) [2007 61: 5m 5f⁵ 5m⁵ 6m May 3] close-coupled filly: poor maiden: should stay 6f: acts on firm ground: tried in cheekpieces. *P. T. Midgley*

N

NAAYLA (IRE) 3 br.f. Invincible Spirit (IRE) 121 – Pink Cashmere (IRE) (Polar **76** Falcon (USA) 126) [2007 85: p6g⁴ Jan 20] medium-sized, robust filly: just fair form only start in 2007: strong-travelling type, will prove best at 5f/6f: acts on polytrack and good to firm ground (well held on soft): blinkered last 3 outings. *B. J. Meehan*

NABIR (FR) 7 gr.g. Linamix (FR) 127 – Nabagha (FR) (Fabulous Dancer (USA) 124) **55** [2007 65: f12g⁵ Apr 22] modest handicapper nowadays: stays 11f: acts on all-weather and soft going: tried in cheekpieces: tongue tied last 3 starts. *P. D. Niven*

NABRA 3 b.f. Kyllachy 129 – Muja Farewell 94 (Mujtahid (USA) 118) [2007 65: p6g⁶ **52** 6d 5m 5m 7g Sep 22] just modest maiden at 3 yrs: left J. Gosden 2,000 gns after second start: likely to prove best at 5f/6f: yet to race on extremes of going on turf: tried blinkered. *M. Brittain*

NACHO LIBRE 2 b.c. (Apr 4) Kyllachy 129 – Expectation (IRE) 59 (Night Shift **95** (USA)) [2007 5.2m⁶ 6m* 6s² 6g⁵ 6.1m³ 6.5m 6g³ Oct 27] 49,000F, £150,000Y: strong, good-bodied colt: has scope: sixth foal: closely related to fairly useful 2003 2-y-o 6f winner Enford Princess (by Pivotal) and half-brother to 3 winners, notably smart 2005 2-y-o 5f/6f winner Always Hopeful and useful Irish 6f winner Extraterrestrial (both by Mind Games): dam sprint maiden: useful performer: won maiden at Windsor in June: ran well when 5½ lengths fifth to Sir Gerry in Gimcrack Stakes at York and third to Floristry in listed race at Doncaster fourth/final starts: will prove best at 5f/6f: acts on soft and good to firm ground. *B. W. Hills*

NADAWAT (USA) 3 b.f. Kingmambo (USA) 125 – Tashawak (IRE) 118 (Night Shift **94** (USA)) [2007 80: 8m* 8g 7d 7f* 7m⁴ 7m² 6m⁴ 7g⁴ Nov 3] leggy, close-coupled filly: fairly useful performer: won maiden at Newcastle in April and handicap at Lingfield (beat Ficoma by 5 lengths) in August: won over 1m, but best form at 7f: acted on firm going: visits Swain. *J. L. Dunlop*

NAHLASS 4 ch.f. Bluegrass Prince (IRE) 110 – Nahla (Wassl 125) [2007 58: 12m⁶ p16g **–** p16g May 9] lengthy, plain filly: maiden: little form in 2007. *Ms J. S. Doyle*

NAHOODH (IRE) 2 gr.f. (Jan 24) Clodovil (IRE) 116 – Mise (IRE) (Indian Ridge **116 p** 123) [2007 6m 6d³ 6g* Aug 23]
Given his continued success with juvenile fillies, the One Thousand Guineas looks the race most likely to provide Mick Channon with his best chance of finally winning a British classic, though it must be a race which Channon approaches with some lack of optimism. He had the ante-post favourites in both 1999 and 2002, with Bint Allayl and Queen's Logic respectively, each of them the

Jaguar Cars Lowther Stakes, York—a muddling race goes to Nahoodh (fourth right) from the subsequently disqualified Visit (second left), Fleeting Spirit (far left), Unilateral (third right) and Festoso (third left)

best two-year-old fillies of their year. Neither made it to Newmarket, the former fracturing a shoulder on the gallops before the season got under way and the latter, after maintaining her unbeaten record in the Fred Darling, found to be lame the day before the Guineas. In between, Channon's Cheveley Park winner Seazun finished fourth at Newmarket, and that is as well as any of his nine One Thousand Guineas runners have fared since, including Treat in the latest edition. Channon's best hopes of winning the One Thousand Guineas in 2008 would appear to rest with the Lowther Stakes winner Nahoodh and Albany Stakes winner Nijoom Dubai. Neither has raced since those victories, Nahoodh retired for the season after returning a bit stiff from York and Nijoom Dubai kept out of the Cheveley Park by a bout of coughing, though both are set to be back in action in the spring.

Four of the last ten runnings of the Lowther have gone to Channon-trained fillies, Nahoodh following Bint Allayl, Queen's Logic and Flashy Wings, the last-two owned by Jaber Abdullah, as are Nahoodh and Nijoom Dubai. Unlike her trainer's previous Lowther winners, Nahoodh was still a maiden going into the race, though she probably shouldn't have been. Thrown in at the deep end and too green to do herself justice in the Cherry Hinton Stakes at Newmarket on her debut, Nahoodh started favourite for a maiden at Ascot later in July but was given an overly-confident ride, especially in view of her inexperience, and was beaten into third behind Albabilia and newcomer Naomh Geileis. Held up well away from the first two, Nahoodh didn't quicken as instantly as might have been expected but almost got up nonetheless, the distances a head and a short head. Where others might have been inclined to look to another maiden for consolation, Nahoodh's connections adopted a fighting policy and returned her to Group 2 company for the Jaguar Cars Lowther Stakes at York—'Jaber is not worried about winning maidens,' said Channon. Six of her nine opponents were winners, three of them in pattern company, namely Visit (Princess Margaret), Fleeting Spirit (Molecomb) and You'resothrilling (Cherry Hinton). They headed the betting in that order, Visit the 6/4 favourite, and after those three came Nahoodh at 15/2, the form of her Ascot maiden having been boosted in the meantime by Albabilia's victory in the Sweet Solera Stakes. The Lowther was a somewhat unsatisfactory contest in that You'resothrilling lost all chance when badly hampered two furlongs out, with Visit short of room at this point as Nahoodh, after proving difficult to settle held up in rear, avoided trouble by being switched wide by Jamie Spencer. Making good headway to take the lead off Fleeting Spirit entering the final furlong, Nahoodh sustained her effort despite hanging left and held on by half a length from Visit who ran on strongly once in the clear. Fleeting Spirit was a further three quarters of a length back in third followed closely by 100/1-shot Unilateral and Festoso. With less than four lengths covering the first eight home, the bare form cannot be rated very high, but there isn't much doubt that the first three at least are smart fillies. Fleeting Spirit, promoted to second after Visit tested positive for a tranquiliser, went on to win the Flying Childers Stakes and finished a close second in the Cheveley Park, a place ahead of Festoso in the latter. Others from the race to win afterwards also included Unilateral and sixth-placed Fashion Rocks, successful in Group 3 and listed events respectively. However, seventh-placed 150/1-chance Romantic Destiny finished last in two listed races subsequently (once behind

Fashion Rocks), having been beaten off BHA marks in the seventies earlier, while eighth-placed Thought Is Free was a beaten favourite in a maiden at Lingfield on her next start, both underlining the dubious nature of the bare form of the Lowther.

Nahoodh (IRE) (gr.f. Jan 24, 2005)	Clodovil (IRE) (gr 2000)	Danehill (b 1986)	Danzig / Razyana
		Clodora (gr 1994)	Linamix / Cloche d'Or
	Mise (IRE) (b 2000)	Indian Ridge (ch 1985)	Ahonoora / Hillbrow
		Misbegotten (b 1991)	Baillamont / Mistreat

After the Lowther, Spencer, who had also partnered 50/1-shot Nijoom Dubai when that filly beat You'resothrilling by a length and a quarter in the Albany, was reported as saying that 'Nahoodh feels smart, but I would still prefer Nijoom Dubai—she has got an attitude you would die for. If Nahoodh was as relaxed as her, she would be a star.' Nahoodh has been raced only at six furlongs so far, and she does need to learn to settle if she is to stay a mile, a trip which should be within her compass judged on pedigree. By the Poule d'Essai des Poulains winner Clodovil, Nahoodh is the first foal of Mise, an unraced half-sister to the useful French performers at up to a mile and a half Not Just Swing and Minuit Noir out of the Prix de l'Opera runner-up Misbegotten. A €30,000 foal who was resold for 19,000 guineas as a yearling, Nahoodh has already proved herself a bargain and, as a rangy filly with scope, there is every chance that she will train on into an even better three-year-old. *M. R. Channon*

NAKED SPARK (IRE) 2 b.f. (Mar 7) Spartacus (IRE) 107 – Naked Poser (IRE) 83 (Night Shift (USA)) [2007 5g 7m Aug 5] €8,200Y: leggy filly: half-sister to several winners, including useful Irish 7f/1m winner Artist's Muse (by Cape Cross): dam, 2-y-o 6f winner, half-sister to useful sprinter Damalis: well beaten in maidens. *W. G. M. Turner* —

NAKHEEL 4 b.c. Sadler's Wells (USA) 132 – Matiya (IRE) 116 (Alzao (USA) 117) [2007 107: p10g 9.8g³ 12m² 12g⁴ 12g 12s 10d³ 10g⁴ Jul 28] strong, sturdy colt: useful performer: suffered from a pelvic problem early in 2006: almost as good as ever in 2007 when in frame in minor event at Ripon and handicaps at Newmarket (second to Wannabe Posh) and York: well below form after (often missing break): stays 1½m: acts on good to firm and good to soft going: tried blinkered: tends to sweat, and has looked ungenuine: sold only 3,000 gns in December. *M. Johnston* **106 d**

NALEDI 3 b.g. Indian Ridge 123 – Red Carnation (IRE) 103 (Polar Falcon (USA) 126) [2007 7d⁴ 8.2g p8.6d⁵ f8g⁴ Dec 27] modest maiden: stays 1m: blinkered first 3 starts: signs of temperament. *J. R. Norton* **59**

NAMARIAN (IRE) 3 b.f. Namid 128 – Zalamera 45 (Rambo Dancer (CAN) 107) [2007 58: p8.6g 8.5s⁵ 12.1g² 14m 12.1d⁵ Sep 25] big, leggy filly: poor maiden handicapper: stays 1½m: best efforts on good ground: blinkered last 3 starts: has looked difficult ride: sold 2,000 gns. *T. D. Easterby* **49**

NAMED AT DINNER 6 ch.g. Halling (USA) 133 – Salanka (IRE) 68 (Persian Heights 129) [2007 13f⁶ 15s⁴ 13g Sep 3] close-coupled gelding: modest maiden handicapper: lightly raced on Flat in recent seasons (missed 2006): stays 15f: acts on firm and soft ground: tried in headgear. *Miss Lucinda V. Russell* **50**

NAMIBIAN PINK (IRE) 3 b.f. Cape Cross (IRE) 129 – Sky Pink (Warning 136) [2007 55: 7d³ 8m⁶ p8.6g Nov 20] close-coupled filly: modest maiden: should stay 1m: tried blinkered: sold £1,300. *R. M. Beckett* **60**

NAMID REPROBATE (IRE) 4 br.g. Namid 128 – Morning Surprise 58 (Tragic Role (USA)) [2007 89: p7g 7d⁴ p7g 8.1m³* p8g 8s 8.2g⁶ Oct 31] compact gelding: fairly useful handicapper: back to best when winning at Sandown (by ½ length from Optimus) in September: below form after: stays 1m: acts on polytrack, soft and good to firm going: tried blinkered (below form). *P. F. I. Cole* **89**

NAMIGUEST (IRE) 3 b.f. Namid 128 – Gentle Guest (IRE) (Be My Guest (USA) 126) [2007 –: 5m p8.6g p12.2g p8.6d Dec 27] little sign of ability, leaving D. Hassett in Ireland after reappearance. *Paul Green* —

NAMING PROBLEMS 2 ch.f. (Feb 28) Forzando 122 – Basheera 46 (Bahhare (USA) 122) [2007 5d p7.1g p7.1g⁴ p6m³ p7.1d⁶ p7.1g Dec 14] 1,600Y: first foal: dam, **44**

sprint maiden, granddaughter of US Grade 1 9f winner Lucky Lucky Lucky: poor maiden: in frame in sellers: stays 7f: acts on polytrack: tried visored/blinkered. *K. J. Burke*

NAMIR (IRE) 5 b.g. Namid 128 – Danalia (IRE) 78 (Danehill (USA) 126) [2007 74: p6g⁵ 5.1d* 5m⁶ 5m* 5m⁶ 5d² 5d⁵ 5v 5s² 6g 5g⁶ p6g 5m Sep 27] strong, good-topped gelding: fairly useful handicapper: won at Nottingham and Beverley in May: good efforts when runner-up after: stays 6f: acts on polytrack, firm and soft going: tried in cheek-pieces, visored/tongue tied nowadays: held up. *D. Shaw*   **84**

NAMROUD (USA) 8 b.g. Irish River (FR) 131 – Top Line (FR) (Top Ville 129) [2007 92: f8g³ f8g⁴ f8g p8.6g³ p8.6g³ Apr 16] tall gelding: just fair performer nowadays: claimed by D. Carroll (£8,000) after final start: best efforts at 7f/easy 1m: acts on all-weather, heavy and good to firm going: tried in cheekpieces/blinkers. *R. A. Fahey*   **77**

NANCYMAY 2 b.f. (Apr 3) Millkom 124 – Just Eliza (Hector Protector (USA) 124) [2007 5.7f⁶ 5.3m Sep 25] first foal: dam unraced: well held in maiden/seller. *J. Ryan*   **–**

NANDO'S DREAM 4 ch.f. Hernando (FR) 127 – Dream Quest 102 (Rainbow Quest (USA) 134) [2007 82: p12g⁶ Jan 10] fairly useful performer in 2006: ran poorly only outing at 4 yrs: stays 13f: raced only on polytrack: has raced freely. *J. Noseda*   **–**

NAN JAN 5 b.m. Komaite (USA) – Dam Certain (IRE) 61 (Damister (USA) 123) [2007 –, a63: f7g² p8g* p9.5g⁵ p8g* p7.1g² p8g* p8g* p8g p8.6g Aug 20] compact mare: fairly useful handicapper on all-weather, lightly raced on turf: won at Lingfield in May, June and July and at Kempton (best effort, beat Motafarred by head) later in July: stays easy 1m: acts on all-weather and good to firm going: tongue tied: tried blinkered: held up. *R. Ingram*   **–** **a80**

NANNINA 4 b.f. Medicean 128 – Hill Hopper (IRE) 106 (Danehill (USA) 126) [2007 119: 8.5d³ 8m* 8m⁴ 9.9m 8m² Oct 6] sturdy, attractive filly: powerful galloper: had a round action: very smart performer: won Coronation Stakes at Royal Ascot in 2006: better than ever when winning Windsor Forest Stakes there (beat Satwa Queen by 3 lengths) in June: also ran well when ¾-length second to Majestic Roi in Sun Chariot Stakes at Newmarket final start, collared late after again hanging right in front: below form otherwise, including in Falmouth Stakes at Newmarket and Nassau Stakes at Goodwood in between: was effective at 1m/1¼m: acted on good to firm going, not at best on softer than good: visits Pivotal. *J. H. M. Gosden*   **121**

NANOSECOND (USA) 4 ch.g. Kingmambo (USA) 125 – Easy 'n Gold (USA) (Slew O' Gold (USA)) [2007 61: p7.1g p10g Dec 28] well-made gelding: modest maiden, very lightly raced: best effort at 1¼m on good to firm ground. *N. A. Callaghan*   **51**

NANS BEST (IRE) 3 b.g. Rock of Gibraltar (IRE) 133 – Hawas 93 (Mujtahid (USA) 118) [2007 60: 7.5m 10m³ 11d⁴ 8.5d³ p8g⁶ 8m² 10m⁶ 8s* 8f⁵ 8g Oct 29] quite good-topped gelding: fair handicapper: won at Ayr in September: stays 11f: acts on polytrack, firm and soft going: tried in cheekpieces/blinkered: often front runner. *Liam McAteer, Ireland*   **79**

NANS JOY (IRE) 3 b.f. In The Wings 128 – True Joy (IRE) (Zilzal (USA) 137) [2007 74: p7g² p7g³ p7.1g⁴ 10m* 9.2d* 8.5d⁴ 7.1d² Jun 24] smallish, lengthy filly: sixth foal: half-sister to 3 winners abroad, including fairly useful French 6.5f to 1¼m winner Torbato (by Machiavellian): dam once-raced half-sister to Green Desert: useful performer: trained by L. McAteer in Ireland at 2 yrs: won maiden at Hamilton in May: much improved efforts last 2 starts, fourth to Echelon in Princess Elizabeth Stakes at Epsom and neck second to Ponty Rossa in listed race at Warwick, on both occasions racing prominently in tactical affairs: stays 9.2f: acts on polytrack, good to firm and good to soft ground. *E. J. O'Neill*   **95**

Windsor Forest Stakes, Royal Ascot—Nannina wins at the Royal meeting for the second year in a row; Satwa Queen (noseband) and Sabana Perdida (right) are in vain pursuit

NANS LADY (IRE) 4 b.f. Mozart (IRE) 131 – Embers of Fame (IRE) (Sadler's Well **69**
(USA) 132) [2007 78: p10g 7d 6m⁴ 6d³ 6g³ p6g Sep 8] tall filly: fair maiden handicapper:
left Liam McAteer in Ireland after 3 yrs: should be at least as effective at 7f as shorter:
acts on soft and good to firm ground. *E. J. O'Neill*

NANTON (USA) 5 gr. or ro.g. Spinning World (USA) 130 – Grab The Green (USA) **95**
(Cozzene (USA)) [2007 92: 7m 8m 9.8g³ 8m⁴ 8m⁵ 10.4d⁵ 10s 8g⁶ p8.6g⁶ Oct 21] leggy,
quite good-topped gelding: useful handicapper: several creditable efforts in 2007, fifth
to Greek Well at York sixth start: stays 1¼m: acts on polytrack, firm and good to soft
going (well held both starts on soft): held up. *N. Wilson*

NAOMH GEILEIS (USA) 2 ch.f. (Feb 20) Grand Slam (USA) 120 – St Aye (USA) **95**
90 (Nureyev (USA) 131) [2007 6d² 6f* 7m⁴ p6g⁵ 8s⁴ Oct 13] $90,000Y: big, lengthy,
angular filly: first foal: dam, US 8.5f winner, half-sister to smart Irish 1½m performer
Andros Bay and dam of high-class 1¼m performer Oratorio: useful performer: split
Albabilia and Nahoodh in maiden at Ascot prior to winning similar event at Pontefract in
August: kept pattern company after and twice finished fourth, in Prix du Calvados at
Deauville (9 lengths behind Proviso) and Autumn Stakes at Ascot (beaten 4 lengths by
Ibn Khaldun): will stay 1¼m: acts on polytrack, firm and soft going. *M. Johnston*

NAPOLEON DYNAMITE (IRE) 3 b.c. Danetime (IRE) 121 – Anita's Contessa **82**
(IRE) 68 (Anita's Prince 126) [2007 70: 6m⁵ p6g² p6g² p7g* p7g⁶ p7.1m* p7.1g⁴ p6g²
p6m⁶ p7.1g⁴ Oct 30] fairly useful performer: won maiden at Lingfield in June and
handicap at Wolverhampton in September: unlucky 2 outings later: stays easy 7f: acts on
polytrack, lightly raced on turf: tends to have left: sold 16,500 gns. *J. W. Hills*

NAPOLETANO (GER) 6 b.g. Soviet Star (USA) 128 – Noble House (GER) (Siberian **64**
Express (USA) 125) [2007 62: p8g p7f f7g 6m 7m 9g⁵ 8d 7m⁵ 7m³ 7m³ 7m⁴ 7m* 7.6g
p8g 8d p8g² Dec 29] strong gelding: modest handicapper: won at Lingfield in June:
gelded before final start: stays 8.8f: acts on polytrack, firm and soft ground: tried blinkered, in cheekpieces nowadays: often races freely. *S. Dow*

NARMEEN 2 b.f. (Mar 29) Royal Applause 124 – Protectorate 91 (Hector Protector **67**
(USA) 124) [2007 5.1m⁴ p7g³ p7g⁶ 6m 7m³ 6g 6m⁴ Sep 22] 34,000Y: tall, useful-looking
filly: second foal: half-sister to French 1m and 9.5f winner Castellina (by Medicean):
dam, 5f (at 2 yrs)/6f winner who stayed 1m, out of half-sister to Irish Oaks winner
Possessive Dancer: fair maiden: stays 7f: acts on polytrack and good to firm going: sold
5,000 gns. *M. R. Channon*

NASAQ (USA) 2 b.c. (Jan 21) Gulch (USA) – Irtahal (USA) 94 (Swain (IRE) 134) **79 p**
[2007 p7g³ Oct 24] first foal: dam, 1m winner (stayed 1¼m), out of sister to Dayjur: 15/2,
¾-length third to Forgotten Voice in maiden at Lingfield: will stay 1m: sure to improve.
M. P. Tregoning

NASHHARRY (IRE) 3 b.f. Ishiguru (USA) 114 – Abbey Park (USA) 71 (Known Fact **66**
(USA) 135) [2007 61: p7g 8.3d p7.1g* p7g² p6g 7f p6g p7g Sep 5] narrow filly: fair
handicapper: won at Wolverhampton in June: well beaten last 3 starts, eased as if amiss
final one: stays easy 7f: acts on polytrack. *S. Kirk*

NASRAWY 5 b.g. Grand Lodge (USA) 125 – By Charter 104 (Shirley Heights 130) **–**
[2007 11.1d Jul 19] has shown more temperament than ability in bumpers (refused to race
once): well held in maiden at Hamilton on Flat debut. *J. J. Lambe, Ireland*

NASSAR (IRE) 4 b.c. Danehill (USA) 126 – Regent Gold (USA) (Seeking The Gold **60**
(USA)) [2007 65: p10g² Mar 5] compact colt: modest maiden: close second in handicap
at Lingfield only start in 2007 (said to have finished lame): stays 1¼m: acts on polytrack
and firm going: tried visored/in cheekpieces: has looked wayward. *G. Prodromou*

NASSAU STYLE 3 ch.g. Bahamian Bounty 116 – Art Deco Lady 51 (Master Willie **80**
129) [2007 7.1d⁴ 7.1s* 8m⁵ p8g Aug 27] 26,000F, 30,000Y: angular gelding: sixth foal:
half-brother to 6-y-o Aperitif: dam maiden (stayed 1¾m): fairly useful form: won maiden
at Warwick in July by ½ length from Trees of Green: below that form in handicaps after:
should stay 1m: acts on soft ground. *J. R. Fanshawe*

NASSMAAN (IRE) 3 b.c. Alhaarth (IRE) 126 – Just In Love (FR) (Highest Honor **80**
(FR) 124) [2007 79: p8g* p10g⁴ 9.9m⁴ 9.9g Jun 15] medium-sized colt: fairly useful
handicapper: won at Lingfield in February: creditable efforts next 2 starts: stays 1¼m:
acts on polytrack: sold 22,000 gns in July. *P. W. Chapple-Hyam*

NATAGORA (FR) 2 gr.f. (Feb 18) Divine Light (JPN) – Reinamixa (FR) **116**
(Linamix (FR) 127) [2007 4.5g² 5.5d* 5g* 5g* 5.5m* 6d² 6m* Oct 5]
Pascal Bary has been at the top of his profession in France for fifteen years,
sending out five winners of the Prix du Jockey Club and saddling three successful
horses—Miss Alleged, Domedriver and Six Perfections—at the Breeders' Cup, a

skybet.com Cheveley Park Stakes, Newmarket—Natagora (right) provides trainer Pascal Bary with his first winner in Britain; Fleeting Spirit is clear of Festoso (centre, epaulets), Perfect Polly (diamonds on cap), Missit (dark cap towards left), Elletelle (second right) and Lady Aquitaine (right)

score that puts him level with Sir Michael Stoute and Aidan O'Brien and behind only Andre Fabre in the European list at the meeting. Like so many French trainers, though, and unlike their British and Irish-based counterparts going the other way, he has not paid a lot of attention to British races. Overall, between 1990 and the end of 2007, horses trained in Britain have won well over one hundred French Group 1 events, compared with fewer than half that number of French successes in Britain, of which Fabre has trained twenty. Bary, on the other hand, had only four runners— none successful—in any kind of pattern event between 1990 and 2000. Since then the number had increased, as he had saddled another seven without success, two defeats for top-notch filly Six Perfections, in the One Thousand Guineas and Queen Anne Stakes, and one for Domedriver in the Lockinge Stakes, no doubt particularly disappointing. The tide finally turned at Newmarket in October, when Natagora showed her customary speed to win the Cheveley Park Stakes, giving a performance that also hinted of enough stamina to give her trainer food for thought about a challenge for the One Thousand Guineas.

The skybet.com Cheveley Park Stakes is not the guide it used to be to the following year's classics. Indian Ink's victory in the Coronation Stakes was the first in a three-year-old Group 1 event for a filly on the race's roll of honour since 1992 winner Sayyedati, who landed the One Thousand Guineas and the Prix Jacques le Marois the following year. For the record, Sayyedati died in August. The latest Cheveley Park Stakes attracted a field of fourteen, and was up to the usual standard, although nine of the runners started at 20/1 or longer. The market was headed by Visit, winner of the Princess Margaret Stakes and second past the post in the Lowther, from Natagora and Fleeting Spirit (Molecomb Stakes and Flying Childers Stakes), with Elletelle (Queen Mary Stakes) and maiden race winner Missit next in the betting. Soon in front, travelling strongly, Natagora had the measure of all her rivals except Fleeting Spirit entering the Dip. The pair drew clear in the final furlong and, although Fleeting Spirit tried her utmost, Natagora never looked like surrendering her advantage and had a neck to spare at the line. The third horse, 33/1-shot Festoso, was a long-looking four lengths back. The form looked smart and the winner returned a timefigure of 0.61 fast, equivalent to a timerating of 115, which provided confirmation that Natagora's performance was the best seen in the race for over a decade, apart from that of 2001 when Queen's Logic. Natagora was still available at 14/1 for the One Thousand Guineas afterwards, attractive odds providing she comes to Newmarket and that she stays the trip. Natagora's jockey Christophe Lemaire apparently is not optimistic about the latter, being quoted as saying 'She has a lot of natural speed so it will be difficult for her to stay the mile. Her trainer will see what he can do to make her stay, but he will have a hard job I think.' Natagora shows plenty of speed but she is not by any means headstrong or a tearaway. Providing her natural exuberance continues to be contained, as it was at Newmarket, she has prospects of proving effective at a mile.

Natagora's form in the Cheveley Park was her best by some margin, but she had shown plenty on home soil. She was out early and by the end of May had finished second in a newcomers race at Saint-Cloud and won a minor event at Chantilly. Stepped up in class after that, she landed the first listed prize of the year for juveniles in France, the Prix La Fleche at Longchamp in June, by four lengths and then went on to win the first pattern event, the Prix du Bois at Maisons-Laffitte in July, by three quarters of a length from Wilki. This was Bary's sixth success in the Prix du Bois, putting him level with two of French racing's greatest trainers, Etienne Pollet and Francois Mathet. Divine Proportions won the Prix du Bois for Bary in 2004 before going on to much better things, starting with the Prix Robert Papin at Maisons-Laffitte later in July, and Natagora followed suit. She started odds on against six opponents, including four from Britain led by Norfolk Stakes runner-up Art Advisor and fifth Strike The Deal, plus unbeaten Italian filly Magritte, successful in the Premio Primi Passi. Leading from the off, Natagora had all the others off the bridle with two furlongs to go and came home three quarters of a length ahead of Magritte, the pair clear. Natagora started second favourite for the Prix Morny in August behind runaway Anglesey Stakes winner Myboycharlie. She couldn't cope with him but ran creditably, leading as usual and keeping on once Myboycharlie went past her a furlong out, going down by two lengths.

Natagora (FR) (gr.f. Feb 18, 2005)	Divine Light (JPN) (b 1995)	Sunday Silence (b or br 1986)	Halo
			Wishing Well
		Meld Sport (ch 1979)	Northern Taste
			Shadai Prima
	Reinamixa (FR) (gr 1994)	Linamix (gr 1987)	Mendez
			Lunadix
		Reine Margie (ch 1981)	Margouillat
			Reine Des Sables

Mr Stefan Friborg's "Natagora"

The influence of Japanese-bred and Japanese-raced horses on the sport has been significant in the last decade, though there have been no Group 1 victories in Europe since 2000. Natagora's sire Divine Light is by Sunday Silence, easily the most influential sire to have stood in Japan in the history of the sport, champion there every year from 1995 to the present. However, Divine Light was not one of that stallion's most important winners. Divine Light won four races, including a listed event in Tokyo over a mile, and finished second, just ahead of July Cup and Prix de l'Abbaye winner Agnes World, in the Group 1 Takamatsunomiya Kinen over six furlongs. With this background, the Haras de Lonray was taking a bit of a chance standing Divine Light even at €2,500. Divine Light's first crop comprised only eight foals but matters have improved, with twenty-three in 2006 then thirty-eight. Even so, he will be standing in Turkey in 2008. The rangy, angular Natagora, who has the scope to develop, is one of three winners from that first crop. They include Nera Divine, also tough, winner of five races from seventeen starts. Predictably, Natagora attracted fairly modest interest at the sales, fetching €30,000 at Deauville as a yearling. Her half-sister Baila Morena, by Agnes Kamikaze, another Haras de Lonray-based son of Sunday Silence, set a sale record when going for €330,000 at Deauville in October. The dam Reinamixa was no great shakes on the track, landing a claimer over ten and a half furlongs in the mud at Saint-Cloud. A half-sister to listed-winning miler Reinstate, out of Reine Margie who won over a mile as a juvenile, Reinamixa is also dam of Smile Dream (by Lyphard's Wish), a minor multiple winner at up to an extended thirteen furlongs, and Sel Et Poivre, a winning jumper by the same sire. Reine Margie was a half-sister to the dam of Resless Kara, successful in the Prix de Diane. The stamina on the distaff side of the pedigree supports the view that the tough and reliable Natagora, who acts on good to firm and good to soft going, may stay a mile. A meeting between her, Listen and Proviso in the One Thousand Guineas could be worth going a long way to see. At the time of writing, Natagora looks likely to take her place in the line-up at Newmarket, provided she comes satisfactorily through a planned preparatory outing in the Prix Imprudence at Maisons-Laffitte in April. That race was used as a warm-up for Six Perfections, who went on to finish an unlucky second, encountering all sorts of trouble in running, in the 2003 running of the One Thousand Guineas. Victory for Natagora would be sweet compensation. *P. Bary, France*

NATAL LAD (IRE) 2 b.c. (Apr 27) Acclamation 118 – Gentle Guest (IRE) (Be My Guest (USA) 126) [2007 5s 5g* 6g* 5g² 5g* 7.5m⁴ 7.5m³ 5g⁵ 6g⁴ 7d Oct 27] 1,200Y, €22,000 2-y-o: half-brother to 1m winner Freedom Chance (by Lahib) and 2m winner Engstrum (by Grand Lodge): dam unraced: fairly useful form: won maiden at Naples and minor events at Rome and Naples in June/July: creditable efforts in listed races next 3 starts: left G. Bietolini in Italy, well beaten in Horris Hill Stakes at Newbury (tongue tied) final outing: stays 7.5f. *M. G. Quinlan* **81**

NATCO 3 b.f. Cois Na Tine (IRE) 101 – Young Sue 76 (Local Suitor (USA) 128) [2007 7m 8d⁶ 8g⁴ p8g Oct 29] strong filly: third foal: half-sister to 1m/1¼m winner Makai (by Cayman Kai): dam 9f winner: modest form only on second start: sold 600 gns. *M. Johnston* **52**

NATHAN DEE 2 ch.c. (Jan 17) Guys And Dolls 113 – Blu Air Flow (ITY) (Entrepreneur 123) [2007 5m 6s⁶ p5.1g⁴ p7g p7.1g⁶ 9d⁶ Sep 26] workmanlike colt: modest maiden: left R. Hannon £2,600 after second start, claimed from P. McEntee £6,000 after next: seems to stay 9f: best efforts on ground softer than good: tried blinkered/tongue tied. *Mrs H. Sweeting* **58**

NATHAN JONES 8 b.g. Emperor Jones (USA) 119 – Brightside (IRE) 99 (Last Tycoon 131) [2007 –: 8.5d 6s 6.5d 5m⁴ 6.3d⁶ p5g Nov 19] poor handicapper: left P. Fahy in Ireland prior to final start: effective at 5f/6f: acts on soft and good to firm ground. *M. G. Quinlan* **49**

NATIONAL DAY (IRE) 3 b.f. Barathea (IRE) 127 – Rise And Fall (Mill Reef (USA) 141) [2007 p10g Dec 30] 320,000Y: half-sister to several winners, including very smart miler Fly To The Stars (by Bluebird) and smart 7f (at 2 yrs)/1m winner Fallen Star (by Brief Truce): dam, maiden, out of smart sister to outstanding broodmare Highclere: 16/1, poor form when eighth of 12 in maiden at Lingfield. *D. R. C. Elsworth* **48**

NATIVE AMERICAN 5 b.g. Indian Lodge (IRE) 127 – Summer Siren (FR) (Saint Cyrien (FR) 128) [2007 61: p10g p10g Jan 31] quite attractive gelding: modest handicapper in 2006: well held both starts on Flat at 5 yrs: won over hurdles in July (modest form). *T. D. McCarthy*

NATIVE TALENT 2 b.c. (Mar 25) Beat Hollow 126 – Native Justice (USA) 115 – (Alleged (USA) 138) [2007 7.1g Jun 15] useful-looking colt: well held in maiden at Sandown (hung badly): dead. *B. W. Hills*

NATIVE TITLE 9 b.g. Pivotal 124 – Bermuda Lily 78 (Dunbeath (USA) 127) [2007 **74** 87: p5.1g⁵ f6s⁵ p6g⁶ p6g Mar 24] big, close-coupled gelding: has had breathing operation: fairly useful performer at 8 yrs: just fair form at best in 2007: best at 5f/6f: acts on all-weather, firm and soft going: blinkered once at 4 yrs: held up. *D. Nicholls*

NATMANA 2 b.c. (Mar 23) Alhaarth (IRE) 126 – Gracious Gift 96 (Cadeaux Genereux **80** 131) [2007 6m⁶ 6d² 6m⁵ 5.3f² 5m² p6g⁴ 6d 6m³ p6g² Oct 27] fairly useful maiden: placed 5 times, 4 in nurseries: may prove best kept to 5f/6f: acts on polytrack and firm going: sold 26,000 gns. *M. R. Channon*

NATURAL ACTION 3 b.c. Diktat 126 – Naskhi 102 (Nashwan (USA) 135) [2007 8m **78** p8.6g⁴ 9m³ 10g⁶ 11.5d² 14m* p16g 14m Oct 4] 32,000Y: big, angular colt: fourth foal: half-brother to fairly useful 11f winner Nassiria (by Singspiel) and 1m winner in Italy by Machiavellian: dam 1m (at 2 yrs)/1¼m winner: fair form: won maiden at Lingfield in August: shaped as if amiss after: stays 1¾m: carried head high fourth start. *W. Jarvis*

NATURAL RHYTHM (IRE) 2 ch.c. (Apr 28) Distant Music (USA) 126 – National- **66** artgallery (IRE) (Tate Gallery (USA) 117) [2007 5f⁵ 5g³ 6m 5d⁶ 6m⁵ 5m 7g* 7g³ 8m⁶ 7m 7.5m² 8s² 10m 8m⁶ p7.1g³ p8.6g⁵ f8d⁶ f7d² p8.6g⁴ Dec 26] good-topped colt: fair performer: won seller at Catterick (left Mrs A. Duffield 6,000 gns) in August: placed 4 times in nurseries: stays 1m: acts on all-weather, soft and firm going: tried in headgear: signs of temperament. *D. W. Chapman*

NAUGHTY FRIDA (IRE) 2 b.f. (Mar 12) Royal Applause 124 – Nausicaa (USA) **78** (Diesis 133) [2007 6g 6m⁴ 6g² p6g* 5m⁶ Oct 28] 42,000Y: second foal: half-sister to 3-y-o Kafuu: dam 7f (in France at 2 yrs)/1m (in US) winner: fair performer: won maiden at Lingfield in October: stiff task in listed race at Longchamp (sixth to Eastern Romance) final start: should prove best at 5f/6f: acts on polytrack and good to firm going. *E. A. L. Dunlop*

NAUGHTY NOD (IRE) 4 b.g. Intikhab (USA) 135 – Quelle Celtique (FR) (Tel Quel **60** (FR) 125) [2007 f12g 9.8g⁶ 15d⁴ 14.1m⁴ p16.5g Nov 19] leggy gelding: modest maiden handicapper: stays 15f: acts on good to firm and good to soft going: tried visored/blinkered: has looked awkward ride (including only try over hurdles). *K. R. Burke*

NAUGHTY THOUGHTS (IRE) 3 b.f. Grand Lodge (USA) 125 – Gentle Thoughts **71** 73 (Darshaan 133) [2007 69: 8.2m⁵ 8.5g 7m p8g³ p9.5g p7m p10g Dec 28] sparely-made filly: fair maiden handicapper: left K. Ryan after third start: should be suited by 1¼m: acts on polytrack, heavy and good to firm ground. *Andrew Turnell*

NAUTICAL 9 gr.g. Lion Cavern (USA) 117 – Russian Royal (USA) 108 (Nureyev **78 d** (USA) 131) [2007 88, a81: 8s 6f 6m 8g 7f⁵ 5.7g³ 6g⁶ 6d⁴ 6m 6g⁶ p6g² p6g⁴ p6g p6g³ p8.6g Oct 20] good-topped gelding: fair handicapper nowadays: raced up to 1¼m, best around 6f: acts on dirt, polytrack, firm and good to soft going: tried in headgear/tongue strap: has carried head awkwardly: usually held up (disputed running when running poorly final start at 9 yrs). *A. W. Carroll*

NAVAJO JOE (IRE) 2 ch.c. (Mar 31) Indian Ridge 123 – Maid of Killeen (IRE) 97 **69 p** (Darshaan 133) [2007 7g Nov 2] 180,000Y: fifth foal: brother to 3-y-o Indian Ink and half-brother to fairly useful 2003 2-y-o 6f and 1m winner who stays 1¼m Unavailable (by Alzao): dam Irish 2-y-o 9f winner (stayed 1½m): 11/2, eighth to demoted Classic Descent in maiden at Newmarket: will stay at least 1m: should do better. *B. J. Meehan*

NAVAL REVIEW (USA) 2 b. or br.c. (Jan 28) Storm Cat (USA) – Arutua (USA) **87 p** (Riverman (USA) 131) [2007 7g* Oct 26] quite good-topped colt: half-brother to several winners, including 7f (at 2 yrs) and 1½m winner Juliette (by Sadler's Wells) and 6f (at 2 yrs) and 1m winner Plato (by Lure), both useful in Ireland: dam unraced out of top-class middle-distance mare All Along: 11/4 and tongue tied, won maiden at Doncaster by neck from Louis Seffens, quickening through from last before idling in front: will stay 1m/1¼m: useful prospect. *Sir Michael Stoute*

NAVENE (IRE) 3 b.f. Desert Style (IRE) 121 – Majudel (IRE) (Revoque (IRE) 122) **57** [2007 8g 6m⁶ 6d² p7g 6g² Oct 19] €26,000Y, 52,000 2-y-o: good-topped filly: first foal: dam unraced: modest maiden: best form at 6f: unraced on extremes of going on turf: raced freely/carried head high second outing. *C. F. Wall*

NAVIGATION (IRE) 5 ch.g. Bahamian Bounty 116 – Bridge Pool 74 (First Trump **54**
118) [2007 63d: p6g² p5.1g⁴ p5.1g 6g 5m 5s 5g 5g³ p6g Oct 17] lengthy gelding: modest
performer: effective at 5f/6f: acts on polytrack, firm and soft going: blinkered/visored in
2007: tried tongue tied (looked ungenuine): sold 700 gns, sent to Sweden. *T. J. Ether-*
ington

NAWAAFF 2 ch.c. (Feb 3) Compton Place 125 – Amazed 58 (Clantime 101) [2007 6g² **80**
6g³ 5.9d² 6d² 5m* 6m p5m 6g Nov 6] 120,000Y: leggy, quite good-topped colt: third foal:
half-brother to 3-y-o Dazed And Amazed: dam, sprint maiden, sister/half-sister to smart
sprinters Bishops Court and Astonished: fairly useful performer: won maiden at Thirsk in
August: mid-field in nurseries: should prove best at 5f/6f: acts on good to firm and good
to soft going: sold 17,000 gns. *M. R. Channon*

NAWAMEES (IRE) 9 b.g. Darshaan 133 – Truly Generous (IRE) 104 (Generous (IRE) **91**
139) [2007 97: p16g³ p13.9g³ 12g 12m³ 12d⁵ 12m p12.2g* p12m* p12.2g* Dec 22]
close-coupled gelding: fairly useful performer: won claimers at Wolverhampton (apprentices) in October and Lingfield and Wolverhampton in December: effective at 1½m to
easy 2m: acts on polytrack, soft and good to firm going: tried blinkered, wears cheekpieces nowadays: effective held up/ridden prominently: fairly useful hurdler. *G. L. Moore*

NAWAQEES 4 b.c. Danehill (USA) 126 – Elrafa Ah (USA) 105 (Storm Cat (USA)) **89**
[2007 65: 8.1g 8g* 8m² 9.9d⁶ 8m 8g Jul 31] quite good-topped colt: fairly useful handicapper: much improved in 2007, winning at Goodwood (by ¾ length from Ebert, despite
edging left) in May, then unlucky second to Habshan at Newbury: below form after (said
to have finished lame final start): stays 1m: acts on soft and good to firm going: held up:
sold 3,000 gns in December. *J. L. Dunlop*

NAWAYEA 4 b.f. Lujain (USA) 119 – Shallat (IRE) 59 (Pennekamp (USA) 130) [2007 **51**
47: p5.1g⁶ p5g⁶ f6g 5.1m³ p5g³ 5s² p5.1g² 5.2d 6m⁵ 6m p5.1g⁶ 6f⁶ p6g⁶ p8.6g p7.1g² p8m
f7d³ p8.6g f6d p7g Dec 30] modest maiden: effective at 5f to 7f: acts on all-weather, firm
and soft going: tried blinkered: tongue tied nowadays. *C. N. Allen*

NAWOW 7 b.g. Blushing Flame (USA) 109 – Fair Test 95 (Fair Season 120) [2007 73, **83**
a77: p13g* p12g³ p12g³ 16m⁶ 14.1d* May 12] tall, good-topped gelding: fairly useful
handicapper: won at Lingfield in January and Nottingham in May: effective at 1½m to
easy 2m: acts on all-weather, soft and good to firm going: has hung. *P. D. Cundell*

NAYARNA 2 b.f. (Apr 7) Nayef (USA) 129 – Dimakya (USA) 83 (Dayjur (USA) 137) **49 p**
[2007 7m⁶ Aug 7] 100,000 2-y-o: half-sister to several winners, including useful French
2006 2-y-o 5.5f winner Mpumalanga (by Observatory) and 7-y-o Golano: dam French
7.5f winner: 7/1, needed experience in maiden at Catterick: will do better. *Mrs A. Duffield*

NAYEF STAR 2 b.c. (Mar 23) Nayef (USA) 129 – Satin Bell 99 (Midyan (USA) 124) **73 p**
[2007 7g⁶ Nov 2] 80,000Y: seventh foal: closely related to fairly useful 1m/9f winner
Strawberry Leaf (by Unfuwain) and half-brother to 3 winners, including useful 6f (at
2 yrs) to 11f (in Hong Kong) winner Zabaglione (by Zilzal): dam 7f winner: 11/1 and
green (reared leaving stall), encouraging sixth to Foolin Myself in maiden at Newmarket:
will stay 1m: sure to improve. *J. Noseda*

NAYODABAYO (IRE) 7 b.g. Definite Article 121 – Babushka (IRE) (Dance of Life **62**
(USA)) [2007 f14g² f16g Jan 16] maiden on Flat, only modest nowadays: should stay 2m:
acts on fibresand and heavy going: tried blinkered: joined Miss H. Lewis after winning
selling hurdle in July. *Evan Williams*

NAYYIR 9 ch.g. Indian Ridge 123 – Pearl Kite (USA) 106§ (Silver Hawk (USA) 123) **–**
[2007 116: 8g 8m⁵ 9.9g Jul 31] strong, lengthy, angular gelding: had a round action:
high-class performer at his best: well below form in 2007, in listed races at Nad Al Sheba
and Goodwood and handicap on latter course: was effective at 7f to easy 1¼m: acted on
polytrack, firm and soft going: blinkered/in cheekpieces/tongue tied last 4 starts: had
worn creased noseband/had 2 handlers: held up: reportedly retired. *G. A. Butler*

NDOLA 8 b.g. Emperor Jones (USA) 119 – Lykoa (Shirley Heights 130) [2007 56: **56**
p12.2g* p12g⁶ Oct 31] rather leggy, quite good-topped gelding: modest performer: won
minor event at Wolverhampton in October: stays 1½m: acts on all-weather, best turf effort
on good going: sometimes blinkered/visored. *B. J. Curley*

NEARDOWN BEAUTY (IRE) 4 br.f. Bahhare (USA) 122 – Habla Me (IRE) (Fairy **91**
King (USA)) [2007 93: p8g⁶ 8s 8f⁶ 8m³ 7.1g² 8g⁴ 8m⁶ 8s⁶ p8g⁵ 8m 8g p7.1g Nov 30]
leggy filly: fairly useful handicapper: best efforts at 4 yrs when placed fourth/fifth starts:
left I. Wood after tenth outing: stays 1m: acts on polytrack, firm and soft going (best form
on good or firmer): tongue tied at 2 yrs: tried in cheekpieces: held up: tends to carry head
high: joined A. J. McCabe. *R. E. Barr*

NEAR GERMANY (IRE) 7 b.g. Germany (USA) 124 – Night Year (IRE) (Jareer **68** (USA) 115) [2007 9.7m² 10g⁵ 11.8s³ 10s Jun 16] winner of 3 races in Germany, including handicaps at Dortmund and Hamburg in 2005: well held in 2006, then left T. Gibson: fair form in handicaps in Britain at 7 yrs: stays 11.8f: acts on soft and good to firm going. *R. Curtis*

NEBDI (IRE) 6 b.g. Fayruz 116 – Miss Nutwood (IRE) 77 (Prince Rupert (FR) 121) – [2007 62: p6g Jan 4] modest performer at 5 yrs: well held only start in 2007: tried in blinkers/cheekpieces. *E. J. Alston*

NEBOISHA 3 ch.f. Ishiguru (USA) 114 – Mariette 35 (Blushing Scribe (USA) 107) **56** [2007 p7g² p10g p7.1g p8g p7g Oct 31] half-sister to 7-y-o Azreme: dam ran 3 times: modest form on debut: little impact after: stays 7f: raced only on polytrack. *P. Howling*

NECKAR VALLEY (IRE) 8 b.g. Desert King (IRE) 129 – Solar Attraction (IRE) 60 **56** (Salt Dome (USA)) [2007 p12.2g⁶ 12g⁵ 16m⁶ Sep 16] lengthy, quite good-topped gelding: fair performer in 2005: unraced at 7 yrs: just modest form in 2007: stays 1½m: acts on soft and good to firm going, probably on polytrack. *J. G. Portman*

NED LUDD (IRE) 4 b.g. Montjeu (IRE) 137 – Zanella (IRE) 87 (Nordico (USA)) **89** [2007 83: 16m² 16s² 21.7s⁴ 14s⁴ 18d 16.5m Nov 10] leggy, close-coupled gelding: fairly useful performer: best effort when fourth in Queen Alexandra Stakes at Royal Ascot third start: below form after: stays 2¾m: acts on soft and good to firm ground. *J. G. Portman*

NEIDEEN (IRE) 5 ch.m. Elnadim (USA) 128 – Mynador (USA) 90 (Forty Niner – (USA)) [2007 –: p7g Jan 24] lengthy mare: fair maiden at 3 yrs: lightly raced and little form since: dead. *J. Akehurst*

NEIL'S LEGACY (IRE) 5 br.m. Second Empire (IRE) 124 – Eliade (IRE) 82 (Flash **76** of Steel 120) [2007 58: 8.3m 9.2g 9.1d 9.1g⁴ 10.1m⁶ 8.3g² 9.2g 9.1g* 8.3d² 9.1d* 9.1s⁵ 10.1m³ 10g⁴ 9.9m 9.2s* 10.1d 9.1v⁶ 7.2v³ 8g⁶ Nov 9] leggy mare: fair handicapper: won at Ayr in July and Hamilton in September: stays 1¼m: acts on all-weather, heavy and good to firm going: usually carries head high. *Miss L. A. Perratt*

NELL GWYN (IRE) 3 b.f. Danehill (USA) 126 – Offshore Boom 96 (Be My Guest **97** (USA) 126) [2007 85: 7g 8m² 12d 8g 10g⁴ p10.7g Nov 9] strong, well-made filly: useful performer: good efforts in frame in Derrinstown Stud 1000 Guineas Trial (3 lengths second to Alexander Tango) and listed race (fourth to Ezima), both at Leopardstown: was effective at 1m/1¼m (never a threat in Oaks at Epsom at 1½m): acted on good to firm ground: usually held up: inconsistent: visits Galileo. *A. P. O'Brien, Ireland*

NELLIE 3 b.f. Lake Coniston (IRE) 131 – Boomerang Blade 100 (Sure Blade (USA) – 130) [2007 –: 7f p6g Jul 27] rangy filly: no sign of ability. *R. M. Whitaker*

NELL TUPP 4 b.g. Killer Instinct 111 – Eternal Triangle (USA) 76 (Barachois (CAN)) – [2007 –: 8f 10s Sep 26] medium-sized, well-made gelding: little form: tried in cheekpieces/blinkers/tongue tie. *G. Woodward*

NELLY'S GLEN 3 b.f. Efisio 120 – Ravine 81 (Indian Ridge 123) [2007 p8g 8.3m³ **71** 8m⁶ 7d* 7.1s³ 7d Oct 27] 150,000Y: quite attractive filly: third foal: half-sister to 5-y-o Captain Hurricane: dam, 6f/7f winner, half-sister to 1000 Guineas second Niche: fair performer: won handicap at Brighton in July: barely stays 1m: acts on good to firm and good to soft going. *R. Hannon*

NELSONS COLUMN (IRE) 4 b.g. Benny The Dip (USA) 127 – Sahara Rose (Green **86** Desert (USA) 127) [2007 93: 10g 12.1g⁶ 12m 12v⁴ 12m 12.1m⁴ 14d 12g⁴ Oct 5] strong gelding: fairly useful handicapper: stays 1½m: acts on any going: has carried head awkwardly (has no left eye): often makes running: none too consistent. *G. M. Moore*

NEMO SPIRIT (IRE) 2 gr.c. (Jan 28) Daylami (IRE) 138 – La Bayadere 83 (Sadler's **82 p** Wells (USA) 132) [2007 8d³ 8d² Oct 27] 20,000Y: workmanlike colt: first foal: dam, Irish 12.5f winner, sister to smart 1½m winner Xtra: fairly useful form placed in maidens at Salisbury and Newbury (head second to Trianon): should do better still at 1¼m/1½m. *W. R. Muir*

NEON 3 b.f. Fantastic Light (USA) 134 – River Saint (USA) 73§ (Irish River (FR) 131) **61** [2007 69: 6.1m p10g Jun 9] leggy, quite attractive filly: modest maiden: bred to be suited by 1m+: sold 9,000 gns, sent to Qatar. *J. W. Hills*

NEON BLUE 6 b. or br.g. Atraf 116 – Desert Lynx (IRE) 79 (Green Desert (USA) 127) **80** [2007 80: 7d³ 7g² 7g⁴ 8m 7s³ 7d 7m⁵ 7m⁴ 7m* 7.2s⁶ 7g Nov 3] smallish, compact gelding: fairly useful handicapper: won at York in September: stays 7f: acts on firm and soft going: tried in headgear: saddle reportedly slipped penultimate outing. *R. M. Whitaker*

NEPOS 3 b.g. Piccolo 121 – Blushing Victoria 74 (Weldnaas (USA) 112) [2007 64: f6g⁶ 5g Jun 22] sturdy gelding: modest maiden at 2 yrs: well held in claimer/seller in 2007. *A. J. McCabe* —

NEPRO (IRE) 5 b.g. Orpen (USA) 116 – My Gray (FR) (Danehill (USA) 126) [2007 75: f5g p6g² p7.1g⁶ p6g⁴ 5.1g 6f 5m Apr 24] sturdy gelding: fair performer: stayed 1m: acted on all-weather/dirt, firm and good to soft going: tried in visor/cheekpieces: tongue tied: dead. *E. J. Creighton* — **75**

NERO'S RETURN (IRE) 6 b.g. Mujadil (USA) 119 – Snappy Dresser (Nishapour (FR) 125) [2007 89: 12g² 11m⁶ p12g⁶ 12g⁶ 11.6m Jun 11] rather leggy gelding: fair performer nowadays: left M. Johnston £10,000 after reappearance: stays 1½m: acts on any turf going, probably on polytrack: below form both starts in blinkers: often sweats: sometimes slowly away. *G. L. Moore* — **77**

NERO WEST (FR) 6 ch.g. Pelder (IRE) 125 – West River (USA) (Gone West (USA)) [2007 13f⁴ 13g² 16.1s* 15.9d* 21g 14m⁴ 17.5s⁴ 13.1s⁵ 16g Nov 8] good-topped gelding: fair handicapper: won at Newcastle in June and Chester in July: stays 2m: acts on soft and good to firm ground: in cheekpieces/blinkers nowadays: races prominently: ungenuine. *I. Semple* — **75 §**

NESHLA 4 ch.f. Singspiel (IRE) 133 – Nordica 99 (Northfields (USA)) [2007 –p: f11g³ p9.5g p8.6g Feb 21] poor maiden: may prove best around 1¼m: raced on all-weather: in cheekpieces last 3 starts: has shown signs of temperament. *C. E. Brittain* — **49**

NESNAAS (USA) 6 ch.g. Gulch (USA) – Sedrah (USA) 82 (Dixieland Band (USA)) [2007 p8g p16g Jul 28] big, workmanlike gelding: fair maiden at 2 yrs: lightly raced and little form in handicaps on Flat since: fair hurdler, modest form over fences. *M. G. Rimell* —

NESNO (USA) 4 ch.g. Royal Academy (USA) 130 – Cognac Lady (Olympio (USA)) [2007 81: 10.1s 10g 8.1m⁶ 14m 12d 10.1d Jul 28] big, lengthy gelding: fairly useful handicapper at best, only fair in 2007: stays 11f: acts on polytrack and firm going: tried blinkered/visored: has shaped as if amiss on more than one occasion. *J. D. Bethell* — **67**

NESTOR PROTECTOR (IRE) 2 b.c. (May 9) Bold Fact (USA) 116 – Irma La Douce (IRE) 62 (Elbio 125) [2007 5m* 5.1m 6.1s³ 6v⁴ p7.1g Aug 13] compact colt: modest performer: won seller at Warwick in April: best at 5f/6f: acts on soft and good to firm going: somewhat wayward. *A. B. Haynes* — **54**

NETWORKER 4 ch.g. Danzig Connection (USA) – Trevorsninepoints 71 (Jester 119) [2007 74: p8g p8g 7m⁴ 8.5m* 8d* 8.3f* 7.9d³ p8g² 8m⁴ p8g⁴ 8m Aug 8] workmanlike gelding: fairly useful handicapper: won at Beverley and Yarmouth (by 7 lengths) in May and Hamilton in June: stays 8.6f: acts on polytrack, firm and good to soft going: held up: consistent. *P. J. McBride* — **83**

NEUTRINO 5 b.g. Mtoto 134 – Fair Seas 72 (General Assembly (USA)) [2007 81: 10.5m⁴ 10g Aug 9] rather leggy, good-topped gelding: fairly useful handicapper at best: just modest form only Flat start in 2007: stays 1½m: acts on firm and soft ground: tried visored/blinkered: has carried head awkwardly: fair form over fences for G. A. Swinbank, successful in November. *P. C. Haslam* — **64**

NEVADA DESERT (IRE) 7 b.g. Desert King (IRE) 129 – Kayanga (Green Desert (USA) 127) [2007 81, a91: 8.1g 8f 8.5m⁴ f8g³ 8m 8s* 8.5m* 8m² 8.1m⁴ 8g 8g⁵ 8s⁵ 8.1s³ 8d 8.3d Oct 29] useful-looking gelding: useful handicapper: won at York (claimer) and Beverley within 4 days in July, making all both times: creditable efforts when placed after: stays 11f, races mainly around 1m nowadays: acts on all-weather and any turf going: tried in cheekpieces: tends to carry head high. *R. M. Whitaker* — **96**

NEVE LIEVE (IRE) 2 b.f. (Apr 9) Dubai Destination (USA) 127 – Love of Silver (USA) 110 (Arctic Tern (USA) 126) [2007 p7g 7g³ 7.5m 8f⁴ Sep 16] €62,000Y: good-topped filly: half-sister to 1½m to 2m winner Taxman (by Singspiel), 1m winner Silver Bracelet (by Machiavellian) and 3-y-o Horseford Hill, all fairly useful: dam 2-y-o 6f/7f (Prestige Stakes) winner: modest maiden: in frame at Thirsk and Bath (nursery, wore cheekpieces): will stay 1¼m+. *M. Botti* — **64**

NEVER CATCHER (IRE) 2 b.f. (Feb 2) Catcher In The Rye (IRE) 115 – Never End 74 (Alzao (USA) 117) [2007 6d⁶ Oct 29] €10,000Y: close-coupled filly: second foal: half-sister to 4-y-o Aboyne: dam, 2-y-o 7f winner, out of half-sister to Derby winner Quest For Fame: 50/1 and green, sixth in maiden at Leicester: open to improvement. *P. A. Blockley* — **61 p**

NEVER SAY DEYA 4 b.f. Dansili 127 – Dream On Deya (IRE) (Dolphin Street (FR) 125) [2007 55: 6g p12.2g Jun 11] tall, leggy filly: modest maiden at 3 yrs: below form in handicaps in 2007: stays 1m: acts on polytrack, firm and soft going: reportedly in foal to Bahamian Bounty. *M. J. Wallace* —

NEVER SO EASY 4 b.g. Easycall 115 – Polistatic 53 (Free State 125) [2007 p8g Feb 25] 14/1, visored and reluctant to enter stall, never dangerous in maiden at Kempton: should stay 1¼m. *E. S. McMahon* **54**

NEVER SOLD OUT (IRE) 2 ch.c. (Apr 22) Captain Rio 122 – Vicious Rosie (Dancing Spree (USA)) [2007 5f 5.5d p5g² p7.1g* p7g p8.6g p7g Oct 31] modest performer: claimed from Pat Eddery £6,000 third start: won seller at Wolverhampton in June: stays 7f: acts on polytrack. *J. G. M. O'Shea* **54 d**

NEVER WITHOUT ME 7 ch.g. Mark of Esteem (IRE) 137 – Festival Sister (Belmez (USA) 131) [2007 74: f5g⁴ 5g 5m³ f6g 5s 6f² 5d* 5m⁴ 5m 5m 5.1g Oct 31] tall gelding: fair handicapper: won at Pontefract in August: effective at 5f/6f: acts on fibresand, firm and good to soft going: tried visored/blinkered: has bled, including on penultimate outing. *J. F. Coupland* **75**

NEVINSTOWN (IRE) 7 b.g. Lahib (USA) 129 – Moon Tango (IRE) 81 (Last Tycoon 131) [2007 55: f6g f6g² f6g f7g 7m⁶ 8d⁵ 8m² 7.9m³ 8s⁴ 8s 6.9f 6s p7.1g Oct 19] modest performer: stays 1m: acts on fibresand and good to firm going: tried in headgear/tongue tied: inconsistent. *C. Grant* **54**

NEW APPROACH (IRE) 2 ch.c. (Feb 18) Galileo (IRE) 134 – Park Express 123 (Ahonoora 122) [2007 7v* 7s* 7d* 7m* 7d* Oct 20] **127**

Please stop us if you have heard this before. A two-year-old colt sired by Galileo and trained by Jim Bolger makes a successful debut in a maiden at the Curragh in mid-July. In an unbeaten campaign he adds four races to his tally, the Tyros Stakes at Leopardstown, the Futurity Stakes and the National Stakes at the Curragh and the Dewhurst Stakes at Newmarket, proving himself the best of his generation with a hard-fought victory in the last-named. He is installed as a pretty warm favourite for the Two Thousand Guineas and Derby. Familiar? It ought to be, because that is not only the profile of the 2006 champion juvenile Teofilo but also of his successor, New Approach—a slightly ironic name in the circumstances. Imitation is supposed to be the sincerest form of flattery but there's no flattery intended in stating that New Approach seems to hold as good a chance in the classics as Teofilo did at the same stage of his career. Let's hope things turn out better for New Approach than they did for Teofilo, who never even made it to the track as a three-year-old.

As with Teofilo, New Approach's first three races take little describing. He started joint-second favourite to Lucifer Sam from the Aidan O'Brien stable on his debut on Irish Oaks day and, after travelling strongly throughout, found plenty under pressure to beat the favourite going away by two lengths. In its first running as a Group 3 race, having been upgraded from listed, the Tyros Stakes nearly a fortnight later attracted only four runners. The soft going might have been a factor in this particular shortfall, but as a rule none of the pattern events open to two-year-old colts in Ireland attracts many runners. The latest Railway Stakes had four, the Anglesey Stakes five, the Phoenix Stakes six and the Futurity Stakes five. In the last decade three of those races have not once managed a field in double figures, the exception being the Phoenix Stakes, which did so three times. A warm favourite

Galileo EBF Futurity Stakes, the Curragh—
odds-on New Approach stays on strongly to beat Curtain Call (rail) and Henrythenavigator

for the Tyros Stakes, New Approach made all to beat Tipperary maiden winner Brazilian Star by two lengths. New Approach appeared an uncomplicated ride, and nothing that happened subsequently altered that impression. Some temperamental quirks, however, soon became evident, starting in the Galileo EBF Futurity Stakes at the end of August. With only five runners, three of whom started at 25/1 and upwards, the race was not strongly contested on the face of it, the betting dominated by New Approach at 11/8-on and the Coventry Stakes winner and Phoenix Stakes runner-up Henrythenavigator at 11/10. New Approach was accompanied by two handlers in the preliminaries and did a 'George Washington' by digging in his heels on the way to the parade ring and having to be cajoled in backwards. He was mounted early and went down freely but, as before, there was nothing to criticise in the race itself. In front from the outset, initially harried by Henrythenavigator's stable-companion Warsaw, New Approach was in command two furlongs out and stayed on strongly to beat the maiden Curtain Call by three lengths with Henry-thenavigator running his best race a further neck away in third.

In the wake of the Futurity Stakes, Jim Bolger might have been excused for reflecting wistfully on the recent past as well as anticipating the future. Just over three weeks earlier the trainer had been forced to concede defeat over Teofilo and retire him. It is appropriate here to relate the story of what had happened to the colt spoken of over the winter as a possible triple crown winner. The first public doubts emerged nearly three weeks before the Two Thousand Guineas and only hours after Bolger had told the press '(Teofilo) is well on target for Newmarket next month and we'll see how things go there first regarding Epsom.' From mid-afternoon on the same day, Teofilo's odds for the first classic on the Betfair betting exchange drifted from 2.58 to 11 before ending up at 6. The leading High Street bookmakers temp-orarily suspended betting on the Guineas and Derby, though by the end of the day Ladbrokes were quoting Teofilo at 5/4 and 5/2 for the two races. The next day Bolger announced that Teofilo had had 'a minor setback' with soreness behind his off-fore knee and would be restricted to walking and swimming for a week. He concluded 'I'm confident Teofilo will be fit and ready to run at Newmarket' before adding 'My only concern at this stage is that with a niggling injury it might recur, or could be the start of something more serious'. Nothing untoward arose from then until two days before the Guineas when, with Teofilo at 2/1, Bolger did not declare him for the race. He explained 'Teofilo had a blow-out this morning at 6.30am over five furlongs and moved with his usual fluency. He gave every indication that he was fit and ready to run. Unfortunately at 9am there was excessive heat, and some soreness at the back of his off-fore knee.' Disappointment was matched by a furore about the ante-post losses incurred by punters which were variously estimated to be between £1,000,000 and £2,500,000. Irish bookmakers Paddy Power announced that they were going to return all losing single ante-post bets on Teofilo, an action hardly likely to become common practice. While strongly denying accusations that he had been less than frank about Teofilo's prospects of lining up at Newmarket, Bolger admitted that staff at his stable were probably laying Teofilo on Betfair when the problems first came to light. He added 'It was the first time that it has happened, and I would expect it to be the last.'

In some circumstances, private policing of misuse of inside information is probably at least as effective as official action in preventing the misuse. The use of information for pecuniary advantage when it is not in the public domain has exercised the racing world almost as much as it has occupied the wider financial world, especially with the advent of betting exchanges which, even with close monitoring, potentially allow a much wider section of the racing community the opportunity to profit from inside information. While leading economists, including Milton Friedman, believe insider dealing in financial markets should not be a criminal offence, it is penalised heavily, with the rules in Ireland, for instance, allowing maximum penalties of a fine of €10,000,000 and/or imprisonment for a term not exceeding ten years. Prosecutions are uncommon although, in 2005, the Financial Services Authority found evidence that almost twenty-five per cent of announcements about company takeovers in Britain were preceded by some insider dealing. The figure in the States in the same year was around forty per cent. There are inevitable difficulties in obtaining proof and enforcing the rules on every misuse of inside information, small and medium in scale as well as large. In July, the

Bank of Scotland (Ireland) National Stakes, the Curragh—
a good renewal with New Approach again making all; Rio de La Plata (right), Myboycharlie (dark colours), Lizard Island (left) and Great Barrier Reef (striped sleeves) chase him home

Horseracing Regulatory Authority (now part of the BHA) announced the findings of its wide-ranging consultation into misuse of inside information. A raft of proposals to try to stamp out the practice included better education, harsher penalties, looking at the circumstances in which it is acceptable for those within the industry to lay a horse to lose, and cutting delays in informing the public about non-runners. Paul Scotney, HRA Director of Security and chairman of the working group, also said there was an intention to discuss with Bolger what had happened regarding Teofilo 'We are looking at who, if anybody, did lay that horse on inside information. We will contact the trainer and ask him at what time he found the horse to be wrong and then we will look at who laid it after that time and we will know if they were acting on inside information.' Bolger, with a shade more flippancy than was perhaps justified in the circumstances, commented 'If they want to come and talk to me I'll give them tea and buns.'

Whatever the outcome of any meeting with the Horseracing Regulatory Authority, there was no tea and buns to celebrate a return to the track for Teofilo. Soon after the Two Thousand Guineas it was revealed he would be on the easy list for six weeks, missing the Derby, then at the start of August an unsatisfactory scan on the off-fore knee led to his retirement. Soon afterwards, Sheikh Mohammed's Darley Stud arranged to stand Teofilo as a stallion, though he was still in his trainer's ownership. Just over a week after the Futurity Stakes, news came that Darley had purchased a half-share in New Approach, though that colt continued to race in

751

Darley Dewhurst Stakes, Newmarket—most of the leading two-year-olds in the line-up and New Approach (right) keeps his unbeaten record; Fast Company is an excellent second and the imposing Raven's Pass (rail) third; Rio de La Plata (hidden against rail) and Luck Money are next

the colours of Bolger's wife Jackie. Sheikh Mohammed's bloodstock advisor John Ferguson provided an interesting insight into Darley's methods when he said '(New Approach) was a very good-looking yearling, and he has a great pedigree, so we made note of him quite a while ago.' Bolger reportedly mulled over the possibility of running New Approach in the Goffs Million but really there was only one likely target for New Approach—the Bank of Scotland (Ireland) National Stakes, the race which almost sets the Irish juvenile season in stone each year. The latest renewal was a good one, with three of the top five juvenile colts in Europe lining up. New Approach was favourite ahead of Godolphin's Vintage Stakes winner Rio de La Plata and Myboycharlie, successful in the Prix Morny. Four of the six other runners were trained by Aidan O'Brien, including Lizard Island, runner-up to Rio de La Plata at Goodwood. As confirmation of New Approach's highly-strung nature, he had an equine companion, ridden by Bolger's assistant, throughout the preliminaries, including when being saddled and going down to the start. Accompanying a runner with an outrider is common practice 'going down' in America, but not in the parade ring. The theory is that company helps ensure that the principal horse remains calm and under control. Following approval by the Horseracing Regulatory Authority, the practice became permissible in Britain in May 2006; Haydock had run a trial almost a year previously. 'Ponying' had been used occasionally in Ireland before this, and Bolger had tried it before New Approach with the smart Heliostatic. Whether the practice catches on widely in Europe remains to be seen—with a handful of exceptions the configuration of European tracks is nothing like so compact as in the States. The thought of having thirty or so ponies around at the start of the Stewards' Cup, for instance, would surely not be popular with jockeys, stalls handlers or starters. Even with the presence of the pony, New Approach refused to walk through the arch leaving the pre-parade ring at the Curragh, despite being hooded, and racegoers at the paddock missed seeing him altogether as he was taken back to the stable yard and thence on to the course. By the time the other runners were being mounted, New Approach had already arrived at the stalls. New Approach was once again admirably straightforward in the race, bounced out and settling well in the lead, his jockey gradually winding up the pace after a quarter of a mile before New Approach forged clear in the last two furlongs to beat Rio de La Plata readily by a length and three quarters, staying on strongly. Myboycharlie was the same distance away third. The runner-up might have finished closer had he raced closer to the pace, but it was, nonetheless, a cracking run by the winner which stamped him as the best of his age.

After the National Stakes, the odds about New Approach for the Two Thousand Guineas were shortened to as low as 7/2 with Coral; he had been available at 8/1 beforehand. Bolger told the racing media 'Last year, the Dewhurst had the edge in prestige over today's race, and after winning the National Stakes Teofilo went there to make sure he would be European champion. It's a different story this year. This is the place and the race this year, and there won't be the same urgency or need to send New Approach to Newmarket.' However, a week or so before the Darley Dewhurst Stakes the race was on the agenda. One thing not known to punters at the time, but reported by the trainer after the Dewhurst, was that he had 'had Derbys in mind over the last couple of weeks training (New Approach) and all his work was just lobbing and loitering. I thought we had better get him to settle and we hadn't really settled on the Dewhurst until around ten days ago. I decided not to rev him before the race and we didn't do any fast work with him, except a half-speed the other day.' This piece of information would have been useful beforehand. Anyone expecting New Approach to adopt his usual front-running style was in for a surprise as he raced in a different style and had to work much harder for victory. Bolger had not bargained for the Dewhurst being more strongly contested than the National Stakes. There was, however, no room for argument on that score, the field at Newmarket having greater strength in depth and representing a higher overall level of form. New Approach started 6/4 favourite in a field of ten containing six other pattern winners led by Rio de La Plata, who had easily landed the Prix Jean-Luc Lagardere after his second in the National Stakes. Dark Angel, far from certain to stay the distance, had won the Middle Park, while McCartney, Fast Company, Hatta Fort and second favourite Raven's Pass had been successful respectively in the Champagne Stakes, Acomb Stakes, Superlative Stakes and Solario Stakes. Luck Money's claim to fame was victory in the Goffs Million while the 100/1 shots included Aidan O'Brien's contender Greatwallofchina. Again accompanied by a pony throughout the preliminaries, New Approach was down at the start well ahead of the others.

If the intention in training, as Bolger had suggested, was to get New Approach to race more tractably it worked almost too well. Awkwardly away as Dark Angel set off in front, New Approach was restrained in mid-division and took time to get going when asked to make headway from halfway. He came under the whip over two furlongs out before challenging Raven's Pass, who had looked the likely winner when taking it up, with Rio de La Plata also threatening. Once New Approach had managed to see off that pair less than a furlong from home, a more dangerous challenge appeared on the outside in the form of Fast Company. Kevin Manning needed to show all his strength, and New Approach all his resolution, to get the partnership home by half a length. Raven's Pass was third, two and a half lengths back, with Rio de La Plata the same distance away in fourth. Manning was banned for five days by the stewards for excessive use of the whip. New Approach never really looked like losing, and deserves full credit for a game and high-class run, one in which he posted the best timefigure of the year by a two-year-old of 1.00 fast, equivalent to a timerating of 125, the same as Teofilo twelve months earlier.

Those he beat at Newmarket are likely to prove even tougher rivals at three. The good to soft ground did not cause New Approach any problems—it was good to firm for the National Stakes but he had won on heavy on his debut—but it appeared to be against Raven's Pass and Rio de La Plata while Raven's Pass, as well as Fast Company, were less experienced and can be expected to improve. Moreover, all three of those look likely to be trained specifically for the Two Thousand Guineas. New Approach will still be a formidable opponent in the Guineas and may well prove capable of winning, but the 5/2 available at the time of writing are hardly odds to snap up. He will be racing in the colours of Princess Haya as a three-year-old, as Sheikh Mohammed bought the other half of him in November. New Approach stays with Bolger.

Mention of the triple crown was much more circumspect with New Approach than it had been with Teofilo—Bolger made no quoted reference on the subject to the press—but, after the Dewhurst, VC Bet quoted New Approach at 12/1, the same odds as his predecessor had been at the same stage of his career. There is no need to pursue the matter here, though the question of how far New Approach is likely to stay is of some moment regarding the Derby if nothing else. His sire Galileo headed the combined juvenile earnings table for Britain and Ireland thanks mainly to the victory of the Bolger-trained Lush Lashes in the Goffs Fillies Million, which had first prize money of just over £670,000. Galileo does not get much in the way of precocious stock and he is still without a single winner over shorter than seven furlongs. His best three-year-olds and upwards, led by Allegretto, Galactic Star, Mahler, Purple Moon, Red Rocks, Sixties Icon, Soldier of Fortune and The Last Drop, have all shown form at a mile and a half or more. Based on such a record, it will be remarkable if New Approach fails in the Derby through want of stamina, especially as his dam Park Express, who had been blind since 1999 and died in 2006, was effective at the trip. By the sprinter Ahonoora, responsible for a Derby winner in Dr Devious, Park Express was a very smart filly—also trained by Bolger—whose tally of five wins included the Irish Champion Stakes, Nassau Stakes and Lancashire Oaks; she also finished runner-up in the Yorkshire Oaks. Park Express's seven other winners at stud are led by Shinko Forest, sired by noted influence for speed Green Desert and successful in the Group 1 Takamatsunomiya Kinen over six furlongs. Dazzling Park (by Warning) was also well above average, winning the Matron Stakes and reaching a place in the Irish One Thousand Guineas and Irish Champion Stakes. However, there have been some costly failures, such as Park Express's Desert Prince colt Dubai Sun, who cost 2,300,000 guineas and showed just a modicum of ability in six starts in Dubai after being unraced for Godolphin, and Thunder Rock (by King's Best), a 775,000-guinea purchase who won an eleven-furlong maiden at Yarmouth before eventually having his attention turned to jumps. He won over fences at Ludlow just over a month after the Dewhurst.

			Sadler's Wells	Northern Dancer
	Galileo (IRE)		(b 1981)	Fairy Bridge
	(b 1998)		Urban Sea	Miswaki
New Approach (IRE)			(ch 1989)	Allegretta
(ch.c. Feb 18, 2005)			Ahonoora	Lorenzaccio
	Park Express		(ch 1975)	Helen Nichols
	(br 1983)		Matcher	Match
			(br 1966)	Lachine

Perhaps because of the mixed record of Park Express as a broodmare, and her advanced age, the tall, quite attractive New Approach, fetched only €430,000

Mrs J. S. Bolger's "New Approach"

as a yearling at Goffs. His breeder Seamus Burns, evidently believing the colt should have sold for more, promptly bought back half of him, an inspired move as things turned out. It was Burns's half of the colt which was first sold to Sheikh Mohammed. For the record, the only twenty-two-year-old mare to have produced a Derby winner was Ferina back in 1869. The oldest dam of a Derby winner was Horatia, who was twenty-five when foaling Paris, successful in 1806. New Approach's grandam Matcher ran only twice and foaled another stakes winner, the useful two-year-old Myra's Best, who became grandam of Waky Nao (Premio Vittorio di Capua). This is also the family of the tough middle-distance performer Bandari. The main questions about New Approach's stamina revolve more around his racing character than around his breeding. His high-mettled behaviour may prove a drawback in the drawn-out preliminaries that invariably accompany the classics, particularly at Epsom. Similarly, the tendency he had to get on with things once a race was under way—a trait also seen in Teofilo—might count against him if manifested over middle distances. Bolger had evidently made some progress in curbing this before the Dewhurst. In New Approach's favour, as discussed above, he has shown no hint of quirkiness in his races, and he is by no means a tearaway. On balance, he can be expected to stay a mile and a half and must be viewed as the one to beat in the Derby. Not that the 4/1 available about New Approach for the Derby at the time of writing looks any better value than the odds for the Guineas. *J. S. Bolger, Ireland*

NEW BALLS PLEASE (IRE) 2 ch.g. (Apr 18) Titus Livius (FR) 115 – Kilkee Bay (IRE) 61 (Case Law 113) [2007 p5g⁵ p5g⁴ 5d 6m 6m 5f² p5g⁶ p5g 5.1g⁴ Nov 7] small gelding: modest maiden: best efforts at 5f: acts on polytrack and firm going: usually wears cheekpieces or blinkers. *P. M. Phelan* — 55

NEW BEGINNING (IRE) 3 b.c. Keltos (FR) 132 – Goldthroat (IRE) 79 (Zafonic (USA) 130) [2007 82: p9.5g² p8.6g⁴ f7g⁵ 10m* 11.8g³ 10.4g 9.8m³ 10m⁴ 10d⁵ 12m² Jul 27] good-topped colt: useful performer: won handicap at Leicester (dead-heated with Zar Solitario) in April: seemed to improve when ½-length second to Classic Punch in minor event at Newmarket final outing: stays 1½m: acts on polytrack, soft and good to firm going: somewhat edgy in preliminaries eighth start (ran well): often held up. *Mrs S. Lamyman* — 101 ?

NEWCASTLE SAM 2 b.g. (Jun 11) Atraf 116 – Ballyewry (Prince Tenderfoot (USA) 126) [2007 p5g 6g p8g 6m Sep 11] temperamental maiden, no form. *J. J. Bridger* — – §

NEWCASTLES OWEN (IRE) 4 b.g. Elnadim (USA) 128 – Brittas Blues (IRE) 52 (Blues Traveller (IRE) 119) [2007 34: f7g⁴ f6g 5m 6v 5s² 5d Jul 13] fair maiden: possibly flattered in claimer at Hamilton penultimate start: stays 7f: acts on fibresand and soft ground. *R. Johnson* — 67 ?

NEW COLOSSUS 2 b.g. (Mar 13) Statue of Liberty (USA) 115 – Daisy Do (IRE) 77 (Danehill (USA) 126) [2007 5g 6s May 30] poor form in maidens (favourite for debut): bred to stay 1m: sold 800 gns, sent to Spain. *E. J. O'Neill* — 49

NEWCORP LAD 7 b.g. Komaite (USA) – Gleam of Gold (Crested Lark 78) [2007 62: p9.5g f12g 8m 8.3d 8s⁶ 10.5m⁶ 12.1g 11.1m⁵ 10m p12.2g⁶ Nov 4] strong gelding: poor handicapper nowadays: probably stays 1½m: acts on polytrack and any turf going: has worn visor/cheekpieces. *Mrs G. S. Rees* — 48

NEW DIAMOND 8 ch.g. Bijou d'Inde 127 – Nannie Annie 60 (Persian Bold 123) [2007 –: 8.1f p9.5m 10m p13.9g Oct 25] lightly raced on Flat, retains little ability: tried blinkered. *Mrs P. Ford* — –

NEWGATE PARISIEN 4 b. or gr.g. Paris House 123 – Gemgem 54 (Lochnager 132) [2007 6m 8.3d p7.1g p5.1g Oct 30] little sign of ability: said to have finished lame final outing. *Mark Campion* — –

NEW GUINEA 4 b.g. Fantastic Light (USA) 134 – Isle of Spice (USA) 74 (Diesis 133) [2007 110p: 12m² 16g⁴ 11.8d* 12m⁵ Nov 10] sturdy, compact gelding: smart performer: improved again in 2007, winning minor event at Leicester (by ¾ length from Young Mick, made all) in October: better than bare result when fifth to Malt Or Mash in November Handicap at Doncaster final outing, not best of runs: likely to stay 1¾m (stamina stretched at 2m second start): acts on fibresand, good to firm and good to soft going: races prominently. *Saeed bin Suroor* — 110 +

NEW JERSEY (IRE) 2 br.c. (Feb 14) Statue of Liberty (USA) 115 – Shinkoh Rose **93**
(FR) 67 (Warning 136) [2007 5g⁴ 5f² 5g* 5g⁴ 5d² 5.5m⁶ 6g 5d⁶ 6g Oct 6] strong, good-
topped colt: half-brother to several winners, including 2002 2-y-o 6f/7f (in Ireland)
winner Oh So Rosie (by Danehill Dancer) and 5f (at 2 yrs) to 7f winner Vienna's Boy (by
Victory Note): dam third at 9f in Ireland: fairly useful performer: won
minor event at York in May: ran well next 3 starts, in listed races at Sandown (second to
Western Art latterly) and Prix Robert Papin at Maisons-Laffitte (sixth to Natagora):
probably best at 5f: acts on good to firm and good to soft going: edgy type, and has flashed
tail under pressure: sold 50,000 gns, joined D. Watson in UAE. *K. A. Ryan*

NEWKEYLETS 4 b.f. Diktat 126 – Jay Gee Ell 78 (Vaigly Great 127) [2007 63: p6g⁵ **58 §**
f6g³ f5g 5g³ 6d⁶ 6d 6m⁴ 6d³ 5m⁵ 5s Oct 4] modest maiden: best at 5f/6f: acts on all-
weather, soft and good to firm ground (below form on heavy): tried blinkered, often wears
cheekpieces: once withdrawn (unruly at start): ungenuine. *I. Semple*

NEW LIGHT 3 ch.f. Generous (IRE) 139 – May Light 62 (Midyan (USA) 124) [2007 **55**
56: 6g 9s³ 10.1g 8.3d 8.1d 10m³ p12g⁶ 9.9s 8.2g Oct 31] neat filly: modest maiden: stays
1¼m: acts on soft and good to firm going: none too consistent. *Eve Johnson Houghton*

NEWLY ELECTED (IRE) 2 b.c. (Mar 13) Acclamation 118 – Assafiyah (IRE) 62 **102 p**
(Kris 135) [2007 6m* 7m* Sep 12] strong, sturdy colt: fifth foal: half-brother to 1m
winner in Italy by Salse: dam, maiden (stayed 1½m) out of half-sister to Prix de Diane
winner Rafha, herself dam of Invincible Spirit: useful form: won maiden at Newbury
(trained by E. McMahon) in August and minor event at Doncaster, in latter picking up
well (after hampered early) to beat Internationaldebut by 1¼ lengths: will stay 1m: joined
J. Moore in Hong Kong, where renamed Able Too: should progress further. *C. G. Cox*

NEW MINERTON (IRE) 2 b.f. (Feb 28) Trans Island 119 – Irish Lover (USA) (Irish **–**
River (FR) 131) [2007 5m 7s 6d Aug 18] 10,000F, 24,000Y: third foal: half-sister to
winner abroad by Mujadil: dam, Italian 1¼m winner, half-sister to 4-y-o Flashy Wings:
well held in maidens. *B. R. Millman*

NEWNHAM (IRE) 6 ch.g. Theatrical 128 – Brief Escapade (IRE) 95 (Brief Truce **88**
(USA) 126) [2007 81: p12.2g p12.2g p16g⁴ p16f* p13.9g p16g* p16g² 16g p16g⁵ p16g*
14.8s² Aug 24] lengthy gelding: fairly useful handicapper: won at Lingfield in February
and Kempton in March and August: good second at Newmarket final outing: stays easy
2m: acts on all-weather, soft and good to firm going: tried visored/in cheekpieces: slipped
on bend eighth start: held up. *J. R. Boyle*

NEW OPTIONS 10 b.g. Formidable (USA) 125 – No Comebacks 70 (Last Tycoon **–**
131) [2007 –, a66: p5g p5.1g p5.1g p5g² p5.1g p5.1g³ p5g p5g p5.1g p5.1g p5.1g May 21] **a59**
strong gelding: modest performer: stays easy 7f, races mainly at 5f nowadays: acts on
all-weather/dirt, firm and soft going: tried in cheekpieces, blinkered nowadays: tends to
carry head high/finish weakly. *Peter Grayson*

NEWPARK SPIRIT (IRE) 4 b.g. Desert Style (IRE) 121 – Newpark Lady (IRE) 105 **41**
(Foxhound (USA) 103) [2007 –: p5g p6g 5g Oct 20] poor maiden: little impact in Britain
first 2 starts in 2007, leaving P. Morris after: form only at 5f/6f: tried in cheekpieces.
Emmanuel Hughes, Ireland

NEWPORT BOY (IRE) 4 b.g. Montjeu (IRE) 137 – Dream Chaser 92 (Record Token **–**
128) [2007 67, a62: f12g⁶ p9.5g Jan 19] rather leggy, attractive gelding: fair maiden at
3 yrs: well below form in handicaps in 2007: tried in cheekpieces/blinkers. *R. A. Harris*

NEWPORT LASS (IRE) 3 b.f. Mull of Kintyre (USA) 114 – Mari-Ela (IRE) 60 **37**
(River Falls 113) [2007 52: f7g 7g Jun 1] lightly-raced maiden: poor form in 2007: should
be as effective at 5f as 6f: acts on good to firm ground. *K. R. Burke*

NEW PROPOSAL (IRE) 5 b.g. Orpen (USA) 116 – Woodenitbenice (USA) (Nasty **57**
And Bold (USA)) [2007 –: p7g⁴ f6g p7g p6g² 7m⁵ p6g Jul 30] lengthy gelding: modest
maiden: stays 7f: acts on polytrack and good to firm going. *A. P. Jarvis*

NEW REALM (USA) 5 b.g. Red Ransom (USA) – Mystery Rays (USA) 122 (Nijin- **–**
sky (CAN) 138) [2007 p9.5g Apr 21] tall gelding: fair maiden in 2005: tailed off only Flat
start since: tried blinkered. *R. A. Farrant*

NEW SEEKER 7 b.g. Green Desert (USA) 127 – Ahbab (IRE) 81 (Ajdal (USA) 130) **117 d**
[2007 115: 7g* 8.3d⁵ 7.1m 7g 9m⁵ Sep 22] tall, good sort: impresses in appearance: smart
performer: as good as ever when winning listed race at Leicester (beat Excusez Moi 1¾
lengths) in April: last all starts after: stays 1m: acts on good to firm and good to soft
ground: effective with or without blinkers: tried visored: front runner: formerly tough and
genuine, but one to treat with caution nowadays. *P. F. I. Cole*

NEWS OF THE DAY (IRE) 3 ch.f. Diesis 133 – Etoile Ascendante (USA) (Arctic **71** Tern (USA) 126) [2007 61: p8.6g* f8g p8g* p9.5g³ 10f² 9.9m² 11.1f² 8.3d³ 13d⁶ 12.1d⁵ 10g 10.1d Oct 16] tall filly: fair performer: sold at Wolverhampton in January and Lingfield in February: left M. Johnston after sixth start: stays 11f: acts on polytrack, firm and soft going: often races prominently: winning juvenile hurdler. *P. Monteith*

NEW SPIRIT (IRE) 3 b.f. Invincible Spirit (IRE) 121 – Rainbow Java (IRE) (Fairy **67** King (USA)) [2007 84: 5s 12g 10v 8.5g p7g p5g⁵ Dec 16] €3,000F, €18,000Y: fourth foal: half-sister to a winner in Italy by Glen Jordan: dam, won in Italy, half-sister to Gold Cup winner Mr Dinos: fairly useful maiden at 2 yrs: just fair form at best in 2007 (refused to enter stall once): may prove best up to 8.5f: acts on heavy going. *John Joseph Murphy, Ireland*

NEWSROUND 5 ch.g. Cadeaux Genereux 131 – Ring The Relatives 75 (Bering 136) **42** [2007 56: 6g 7.1g 8v 6d 8f Aug 12] well-made gelding: poor performer nowadays: stays 7f: acts on fibresand and good to soft going: usually wears blinkers/cheekpieces: often slowly away. *D. W. Chapman*

NEW STAR (UAE) 3 b.g. Green Desert (USA) 127 – Princess Haifa (USA) 69 (Mr **83** Prospector (USA)) [2007 10.3m p8.6g 10.3d³ 10.3m* 10.9m 10d⁵ 10.3g Oct 26] workmanlike gelding: fairly useful handicapper: won at Chester in August: stays 1¼m: acts on good to firm and good to soft ground. *W. M. Brisbourne*

NEWTONIAN (USA) 8 ch.g. Distant View (USA) 126 – Polly Adler (USA) (House- **69** buster (USA)) [2007 12g f12g⁴ f11g⁴ f12g* f11g Jun 5] well-made gelding: fair performer: won handicap at Southwell (drifted right) in May: reportedly finished lame final outing: will stay 1¾m: acts on fibresand, little form on turf: in cheekpieces last 2 starts: very slowly away on reappearance. *M. Brittain*

NEW WAVE 5 b.g. Woodman (USA) 126 – Vanishing Point (USA) (Caller I D (USA)) **–** [2007 10m p8.6g Oct 20] useful-looking gelding: fair maiden in 2005: unraced on Flat at 4 yrs: little impact in handicaps in 2007: tried in cheekpieces. *R. Lee*

NEW WORLD ORDER (IRE) 3 b.c. Night Shift (USA) – Kama Tashoof 72 (Mtoto **88** 134) [2007 88: p7.1g³ p7.1g² p8.6g³ 8m 9.1m 10.3s⁴ 12g p9.5m² p8.6g* 9.2g² p8.6g p8m² f12g³ Dec 19] fairly useful performer: ran in Ireland at 2 yrs then left D. Gillespie: won maiden at Wolverhampton in September: claimed £10,000 final start: stays 10.3f: acts on polytrack and soft going: tongue tied last 6 starts. *K. R. Burke*

NEW YEAR (IRE) 3 ch.g. Traditionally (USA) 117 – Zelah (IRE) 91 (Alzao (USA) **56** 117) [2007 6m⁶ 6m 8.1s⁴ 8s 7m Aug 3] 8,000F, 14,500Y: workmanlike gelding: fifth foal: half-brother to 3 winners, including fairly useful 6f (at 2 yrs) to 8.5f (including in Sweden) winner Pollinwilline (by Mull of Kintyre): dam, lightly-raced 7f winner, out of smart French/US performer up to 1¼m Marie Noelle: modest form only on third outing. *T. P. Tate*

NEW YORK OSCAR (IRE) 3 b.g. Tobougg (IRE) 125 – Special Dissident (Dancing **93** Dissident (USA) 119) [2007 68: p5g² p6g* f6g 5g⁵ 6m p5.1g⁴ p5g* 5g p6g⁶ 5d³ 5v p5.1g⁴ p6g* p5g* p6g⁵ p5.1g⁶ p6g⁶ f5d⁵ f6d⁵ Dec 21] compact gelding: fairly useful handicapper: won claimer (rejoined former trainer from A. Hales) in January and handicaps in May and October (2), all at Lingfield: raced only at 5f/6f: acts on all-weather and good to soft ground: usually wears headgear: hung fourth outing: quirky. *A. J. McCabe*

NEW ZEALAND (IRE) 2 ch.c. (Feb 9) Galileo (IRE) 134 – Worlds Apart (Darshaan **104** 133) [2007 8s⁴ 7s² 8v² p8g⁴ 10d⁴ Nov 11] 75,000F, 200,000Y: tall, good-topped colt: fifth foal: half-brother to Italian 7f/1m (including at 2 yrs) winner Matibru (by Turtle Island): dam unraced granddaughter of Oaks/Irish Oaks winner Unite: useful maiden: second at Naas and Tralee in August: much improved when 2½ lengths fourth of 6 to Full of Gold in Criterium de Saint-Cloud final outing, making most: will stay 1½m: below form on polytrack, raced only on ground softer than good on turf. *A. P. O'Brien, Ireland*

NEXT BEST 2 b.f. (May 1) Best of The Bests (IRE) 122 – Lone Pine (Sesaro (USA) 81) **41** [2007 5m⁶ 6m⁵ p5.1g² 6d³ 5m³ 5s 5d³ 5m⁵ Aug 30] 3,000Y: leggy filly: first foal: dam maiden: poor maiden: effective at 5f/6f: acts on polytrack, good to firm and good to soft going: sometimes wears cheekpieces. *A. Berry*

NEXT FLIGHT (IRE) 8 b.g. Woodborough (USA) 112 – Sans Ceriph (IRE) 75 (That- **52** ching 131) [2007 –: 15.8m⁴ 16g 16m Aug 28] good-bodied gelding: modest handicapper: stays 2m: acts on fibresand, heavy and good to firm ground: visored once (well beaten). *R. E. Barr*

NEXT OF KIN (IRE) 2 b.g. (May 4) Kris Kin (USA) 126 – Lady of Shalott 61 (Kings **55 p** Lake (USA) 133) [2007 6m⁶ 6m 8.3g⁵ Sep 23] €6,200F, €10,000Y: sturdy gelding: half-brother to several winners, including smart German sprinter Meliksah (by Thatching): dam maiden (stayed 1m): modest form in maidens: caught the eye on debut, and gelded after final start: should do better at 1m+. *G. A. Swinbank*

NEYRAAN 2 b.f. (Jan 29) Lujain (USA) 119 – Zaynaat 71 (Unfuwain (USA) 131) **53** [2007 p8g p8m⁶ Dec 10] first foal: dam, maiden (stayed 1m), sister to Musidora/Nassau Stakes winner Zahrat Dubai: still in need of run, much better effort in maidens when sixth of 10 to Bauhaus Bourbon at Lingfield, finding little: raced at 1m, may prove effective over shorter. *M. Johnston*

NEZAMI (IRE) 2 b.g. (Mar 20) Elnadim (USA) 128 – Stands To Reason (USA) 80 **96** (Gulch (USA)) [2007 5.7s 7.6f² 7g⁴ 7f² 6g* Sep 23] €37,000F, 30,000Y: second foal: dam, sprint maiden, out of smart French 2-y-o 6f winner Sheer Reason: fairly useful form: runner-up in maidens at Lingfield and Folkestone (beaten ¾ length by Billion Dollar Kid), and won nursery at Hamilton final start: stays 7.6f: acts on firm going. *B. J. Meehan*

NIBBLES (IRE) 5 b.g. Soviet Star (USA) 128 – Tumbleweed Pearl 96 (Aragon 118) **–** [2007 p13.9g⁵ Jun 1] well held in claimer/seller nearly 3 years apart. *D. W. Chapman*

NICADA (IRE) 3 ch.g. Titus Livius (FR) 115 – Rhapsani (IRE) 24 (Persian Bold 123) **74** [2007 73: 8.3m⁴ 8.3s² 8s⁴ 8.1v⁵ 8m² p8g⁴ 8d⁵ p10g⁶ p8g² p7.1d⁴ p7g Dec 16] work- **a79** manlike gelding: fair handicapper: left J. S. Moore after eighth outing: stays 8.3f: acts on all-weather, firm and soft ground: usually wears cheekpieces: signs of temperament. *Stef Liddiard*

NICE DREAM 2 b.f. (Mar 26) Oasis Dream 129 – Have Fun (Indian Ridge 123) [2007 **–** f6g Jun 5] 35,000Y: second foal: dam, French 7.5f and 11f winner, half-sister to useful French performer up to 1½m Day Or Night: 12/1, green and well held in maiden at Southwell. *C. E. Brittain*

NICE TO KNOW (FR) 3 ch.f. Machiavellian (USA) 123 – Entice (FR) 111 (Selkirk **83** (USA) 129) [2007 66p: 7g⁴ 7g⁴ 8s⁶ 7m* 7g* 8.1g⁶ p8m⁴ Nov 24] big, leggy filly, weak at 3 yrs: fairly useful handicapper: left E. Dunlop, improved to win at Folkestone and Goodwood in August: good fourth at Lingfield final start: stays 1m: acts on polytrack and good to firm ground: held up. *G. L. Moore*

NICE WEE GIRL (IRE) 2 b.f. (Apr 24) Clodovil (IRE) 116 – Neat Dish (CAN) 90 **67** (Stalwart (USA)) [2007 p6g⁴ p7g⁶ p6g³ p7g³ p7.1g⁴ p8m² p7.1g² Dec 26] 20,000Y: half-sister to several winners, including 1m (at 2 yrs) to 1¾m winner Riddlesdown (by Common Grounds) and 3-y-o Vitznau, both smart: dam, 1¼m 2-y-o 6f/7f winner, half-sister to US Grade 1 1m runner-up Western Winter: fair maiden: in frame 6 times: stays 1m: raced only on polytrack. *S. Kirk*

NICKEL SILVER 2 ro.c. (Feb 10) Choisir (AUS) 126 – Negligee 94 (Night Shift **80** (USA)) [2007 6g² 6m² 6f⁵ 6s⁴ Oct 4] quite good-topped colt: fairly useful maiden: second to Bespoke Boy at Ripon on debut: below form after: will prove at least as effective at 5f as 6f. *B. Smart*

NICK'S NIKITA (IRE) 4 ch.f. Pivotal 124 – Elaine's Honor (USA) (Chief's Crown **109** (USA)) [2007 101: 10m⁴ 9.5m⁵ 10g³ 12g* 14s² 12s³ 12d⁴ Aug 19] good-topped filly: useful performer: won Kerry Group Noblesse Stakes at Cork in June by comfortable length from Athenian Way: in frame most other starts, including when 3 lengths second to Peppertree Lane in Curragh Cup: stays 1¾m: acts on soft and good to firm ground: usually held up: consistent. *M. Halford, Ireland*

NICOMEDIA (IRE) 3 br.f. Key of Luck (USA) 126 – Ladylishandra (IRE) 82 (Muja- **78** dil (USA) 119) [2007 76: p8g³ p7g³ p7g³ 9.7m² p8.6g* p10g* 10.2m⁴ 10g 9.7s⁵ p10g⁶ 10f⁶ Aug 5] strong, compact filly: fair handicapper: won at Wolverhampton in April and Lingfield in May: stays 10.2f: acts on polytrack and firm ground (well held both starts on ground softer than good): blinkered last 2 starts: sold 4,000 gns. *R. Hannon*

NIGELLA 4 b.f. Band On The Run 102 – Yabint El Sham 83 (Sizzling Melody 117) **72** [2007 90: 5m 5m Jul 21] strong, good-bodied filly: fairly useful performer at best: lightly raced nowadays and only fair in handicaps in 2007: raced mainly at 5f: acts on polytrack and firm going. *E. S. McMahon*

NIGHT CRESCENDO (USA) 4 br. or b.g. Diesis 133 – Night Fax (USA) (Known **105** Fact (USA) 135) [2007 102: 8m 9m³ 9.9g 9m 10s* 10d⁶ 12m³ Nov 10] tall, useful-looking gelding: useful handicapper: won at Ascot (by length from Mutajarred, finding plenty) in October: creditable third to Malt Or Mash in November Handicap at Doncaster final outing: stays 1½m: acts on polytrack, soft and good to firm ground. *Mrs A. J. Perrett*

NIGHT CRU 4 b.g. Night Shift (USA) – Jouet 71 (Reprimand 122) [2007 78: 8m 8m² **103** 10m* p10g2 10d* 10d⁴ 10d* 9m Oct 6] strong, compact gelding: useful handicapper: successful at Windsor and Newmarket in June and Newmarket again (beating Apply Dapply by short head, pair clear) in August: ran poorly in Cambridgeshire there final outing: stays 1¼m: acts on polytrack, firm and good to soft going (below form on soft): said to have suffered irregular heartbeat on reappearance: joined Jonjo O'Neill. *C. F. Wall*

NIGHT CRUISE (IRE) 4 b.g. Docksider (USA) 124 – Addaya (IRE) (Persian Bold **89** 123) [2007 80p: p16g³ p16g* p16g⁵ Mar 31] fairly useful handicapper, lightly raced: won at Lingfield in February: below form at Kempton next time: sustained an injury after: stays easy 2m: raced on polytrack. *J. A. Osborne*

NIGHT FALCON 3 b.f. Act One 124 – Original Spin (IRE) 91 (Machiavellian (USA) **50** 123) [2007 –: p8g p10g f11g⁵ 6g⁶ 8f Jun 10] angular, useful-looking filly: modest maiden: stays 1¼m: acts on polytrack: tried visored. *H. Morrison*

NIGHT GROOVE (IRE) 4 b.g. Night Shift (USA) – Taysala (IRE) (Akarad (FR) **62** 130) [2007 63: p12g p10g 11.5m⁵ p12g p12g p13g Dec 28] sturdy gelding: modest performer: left N. Littmoden after fourth start: stays 11.5f: acts on polytrack (probably fibresand), yet to race on extremes of going on turf: usually in cheekpieces/blinkered. *P. Butler*

NIGHT HOUR (IRE) 5 b.g. Entrepreneur 123 – Witching Hour (IRE) 88 (Alzao **101** (USA) 117) [2007 12g⁵ 12g³ 14g⁵ 12d² p12g⁴ 12g* Oct 27] strong, rangy gelding: useful handicapper: unraced at 4 yrs: improved form when winning at Doncaster (by 3 lengths from Bandama) in October: stays easy 1¾m: acts on good to firm and good to soft ground: tried in cheekpieces: has shown signs of temperament: sold 62,000 gns, joined Godolphin. *J. H. M. Gosden*

NIGHTIME (IRE) 4 ch.f. Galileo (IRE) 134 – Caumshinaun (IRE) 114 (Indian Ridge **103** 123) [2007 113: 10.5g May 27] leggy, lightly-made, plain filly: smart performer, lightly raced: successful twice in 2006, notably in Irish 1000 Guineas at the Curragh by 6 lengths: reportedly pulled a muscle final start that year: below-form eighth of 9 to Not-nowcato in Tattersalls Gold Cup at the Curragh only outing in 2007: best effort at 1m on heavy going: in foal to Holy Roman Emperor. *D. K. Weld, Ireland*

NIGHT IN (IRE) 4 b.g. Night Shift (USA) – Sherannda (USA) (Trempolino (USA) **69** 135) [2007 75: 6g⁵ 7m 6d* 6g 6m 7g p7.1g⁵ 6s p6g⁵ Oct 12] tall, good-topped gelding: fair handicapper: won at Hamilton in June: best at 5f/6f: acts on firm and good to soft ground: tried visored: usually tongue tied: inconsistent: sent to Spain. *N. Tinkler*

NIGHT MYSTERY 2 ch.c. (Mar 23) Observatory (USA) 131 – Highland Gait 63 **–** (Most Welcome 131) [2007 6.1v 6m Aug 1] no form in maidens. *T. D. Easterby*

NIGHT PREMIERE (IRE) 2 b.f. (Apr 1) Night Shift (USA) – Star Studded (Cad- **57 +** eaux Genereux 131) [2007 6m⁶ 5m Sep 13] 45,000F, 46,000Y, 80,000 2-y-o: sturdy filly: first foal: dam unraced sister to smart 5f performer Land of Dreams: modest form when mid-division in maidens at Goodwood and Sandown (good speed from wide draw): should prove best at 5f/6f. *R. Hannon*

NIGHT PROSPECTOR 7 b.g. Night Shift (USA) – Pride of My Heart 74 (Lion **71** Cavern (USA) 117) [2007 92: p6g f6g⁴ f7g p5g* p6g p6g³ p6f 5f 6m 5.3f 5.7d p6g **a87** 5.7m 5.3d⁴ 6g Aug 26] close-coupled, good-topped gelding: fairly useful on all-weather, fair on turf: won claimer at Lingfield in January: trained by B. Palling fourth to sixth starts only: best at 5f/6f: acts on all-weather, firm and good to soft going: tried blinkered, usually wears cheekpieces: tends to wander: has looked difficult ride: none too consistent. *R. A. Harris*

NIGHT RAINBOW (IRE) 4 ch.f. Night Shift (USA) – Teresita (Rainbow Quest **–** (USA) 134) [2007 60: 7m Aug 12] close-coupled filly: modest maiden at best: well held in seller only start in 2007: stays easy 7f: acts on polytrack and firm going. *P. G. Murphy*

NIGHT REVELLER (IRE) 4 b.f. Night Shift (USA) – Tir-An-Oir (IRE) (Law **–** Society (USA) 130) [2007 –: f11g f7g f7g 11.6m 10f 9.8m Aug 28] compact filly: of little account. *M. C. Chapman*

NIGHT RIDER 3 b.g. Night Shift (USA) – Lady Emmaline (IRE) (Charnwood Forest **–** (IRE) 125) [2007 p6g p8m Nov 11] well held in maidens at Wolverhampton and Kemp-ton. *Miss J. Feilden*

NIGHT ROBE 2 b.f. (May 28) Robellino (USA) 127 – Camp Fire (IRE) 81 (Lahib **47** (USA) 124) [2007 5v⁶ 5.1s³ 6.1s 6.1m p6g⁵ 7d p7.1g f6d* f6d⁶ Dec 21] narrow filly: second foal: dam, 2-y-o 6f winner, out of half-sister to Irish 2000 Guineas winner Flash of Steel: poor performer: won nursery at Southwell in December: stays 6f: acts on fibre-sand and soft ground. *P. D. Evans*

Albany Stakes, Royal Ascot—50/1-shot Nijoom Dubai upsets the favourite You'resothrilling;
Baffled (right), Aide Memoir (No.2) and Cute (striped cap) come next

NIGHT SKIER (IRE) 2 ch.f. (Feb 9) Night Shift (USA) – Ski For Me (IRE) 88   **85**
(Barathea (IRE) 127) [2007 6g 6m⁵ 7g* 7m p8m Oct 11] close-coupled filly: has a quick
action: second foal: dam, 2-y-o 1m winner (stayed 1½m), out of half-sister to US Grade 1
1¼m winner Bequest: fairly useful form: won maiden at Folkestone in July by 5 lengths:
well beaten in nurseries 2 months apart: should stay 1m. *J. L. Dunlop*

NIGHTSPOT 6 ch.g. Night Shift (USA) – Rash Gift 78 (Cadeaux Genereux 131) [2007   **84**
80: 10d* 10.2g² 10.5m² 10g³ 10m⁴ p11g* 9.9g⁵ 9.9m⁵ 10d² 12d Oct 27] tall, quite attractive gelding: fairly useful handicapper: won at Newbury in May and Kempton in August:
stays 1½m: acts on polytrack, firm and soft ground: tried visored/in cheekpieces: front
runner: consistent. *Eve Johnson Houghton*

NIGHTSTRIKE (IRE) 4 b.f. Night Shift (USA) – Come Together 68 (Mtoto 134)   **63**
[2007 68: p8g p7g p7g p7g² 7.6g Jul 28] fair winner at 3 yrs, only modest in handicaps in
2007: stays 7f: acts on polytrack and good to firm ground: tried blinkered. *Luke Comer,
Ireland*

NIGHT WOLF (IRE) 7 gr.g. Indian Ridge 123 – Nicer (IRE) 113 (Pennine Walk 120)   **67 §**
[2007 55§: p8g⁴ p7f* p7g 8m* 7f p7g⁴ p7g³ p8g Dec 29] fair handicapper: won at Lingfield in February and Brighton in April: stays 1m: acts on polytrack and firm going:
tongue tied of late: often makes running/races prominently: inconsistent. *Jamie Poulton*

NIJOOM DUBAI 2 b.f. (Mar 8) Noverre (USA) 125 – Aileen's Gift (IRE) (Rainbow   **104 p**
Quest (USA) 134) [2007 5.2g² 6g³ 6g* Jun 22] 19,000Y: close-coupled, useful-looking
filly: third foal: half-sister to winner in Greece by Xaar: dam unraced out of half-sister
to high-class performer up to 1m Golden Opinion: useful form: placed in minor event at
Newbury and maiden at Folkestone: 50/1 and worked up in preliminaries, much
improved when winning 20-runner Albany Stakes at Royal Ascot by 1¼ lengths from
You'resothrilling, slowly away but coming strongly through: reportedly suffered from
cough after: will stay 7f/1m: should continue to progress. *M. R. Channon*

NIKINDI (IRE) 2 b.g. (Mar 5) Mull of Kintyre (USA) 114 – Alma Latina (IRE) 73   **85**
(Persian Bold 123) [2007 5g* 5m⁴ 6d⁴ 6.5m 6g Oct 27] strong, good-bodied gelding:
fairly useful form: won maiden at Folkestone in April: fourth in minor event at Newmarket 2 weeks later: off 4 months, stiff tasks on return: best at 5f/6f: acts on good to firm
going: sold 17,000 gns. *J. S. Moore*

NIKINOO 4 b.f. Averti (IRE) 117 – Tzarinassilouhette 42 (Puissance 110) [2007 f7g   **–**
p8.6g 7d 7m May 22] close-coupled filly: second foal: dam sprint maiden: little form:
tried blinkered. *B. Palling*

NIKKI BEA (IRE) 4 ch.f. Titus Livius (FR) 115 – Strong Feeling (USA) (Devil's Bag   **70**
(USA)) [2007 63: p8g⁴ p8g p8g p8g³ p8g³ p7g⁶ p8g² p7g* p8g⁵ p7g* p7g p8g p7g 6f
p7m³ p7g⁵ p6g p7g p7g⁵ Dec 29] leggy filly: fair performer: won seller in April and
handicap in May, both at Lingfield: effective at 7f to 1¼m: acts on polytrack and firm
going. *Jamie Poulton*

NIKOLAIEVICH (IRE) 2 b.c. (May 3) Xaar 132 – Seren Quest 90 (Rainbow Quest **67**
(USA) 134) [2007 7m 8.1f⁶ p8g 10.2d Oct 1] strong colt: half-brother to several winners,
notably smart 1¼m to 11.6f winner Saddler's Quest (by Saddlers' Hall): dam 1¼m
winner: fair maiden: should be suited by 1¼m/1½m: acts on polytrack and firm going.
P. F. I. Cole

NIMBELLE (IRE) 2 b. or br.f. (Feb 19) Namid 128 – Bellissi (IRE) 77 (Bluebird **51**
(USA) 125) [2007 5.1g Nov 7] half-sister to several winners, including useful Irish 5f
winner Belleinga (by Orpen): dam, Irish 7f winner, half-sister to Moyglare Stud Stakes
winner Priory Belle: 25/1 and burly, eighth in maiden at Nottingham. *T. F. Lacy, Ireland*

NIMELLO (USA) 11 b.g. Kingmambo (USA) 125 – Zakota (IRE) (Polish Precedent – §
(USA) 131) [2007 –§, a70§: f12g³ f11g² f12g* f11g⁵ f12g⁶ Apr 22] smallish, well-made **a64 §**
gelding: one-time useful performer: modest nowadays: won apprentice handicap at
Southwell in March: stays 1½m: acts on all-weather, has won on firm ground but best turf
efforts on softer than good: tried blinkered: held up: temperamental. *A. G. Newcombe*

NIMRANA FORT 4 b.g. Indian Ridge 123 – Ninotchka (USA) 110 (Nijinsky (CAN) –
138) [2007 60: p9.5g 9m 9.8g Apr 28] leggy, dipped-backed gelding: just modest maiden
at 3 yrs: little form in 2007: stays 1¼m: best effort on good going: in cheekpieces/visor
last 3 starts. *J. S. Wainwright*

NIMRA (USA) 4 gr. or ro.f. Cozzene (USA) – Purity (USA) (Fappiano (USA)) [2007 **83**
85: 18g 12.1s⁵ 14g² 15g* 14.8m⁶ 14d⁶ Sep 17] good-topped filly: fairly useful handicapper: won at Warwick in July: below form after: stays 15f: acts on polytrack, firm and
good to soft going: blinkered last 4 outings: sent to Bahrain. *G. A. Butler*

NINA BLINI 3 b.f. Bertolini (USA) 125 – Film Buff 60 (Midyan (USA) 124) [2007 90: –
6m 7m Apr 18] strong filly: fairly useful performer at 2 yrs: changed hands 70,000 gns in
January: last in minor event at Leicester and Nell Gwyn Stakes at Newmarket (blinkered)
in 2007: effective at 5f/6f, bred to stay further: acts on good to firm going, probably on
polytrack. *B. J. Meehan*

Mr Jaber Abdullah's "Nijoom Dubai"

NINEFINEIRISHMEN (IRE) 2 b. or br.c. (Feb 18) Statue of Liberty (USA) 115 – 72
Tallassee 60 (Indian Ridge 123) [2007 6d 7.2v² Nov 3] €35,000Y: compact colt: first
foal: dam, maiden (stayed 11f), sister to very smart 1m/1¼m performer Handsome Ridge:
fair form in maidens at York and Ayr (second to Doon Haymer): will stay 1m. *K. R. Burke*

NINE STORIES (IRE) 2 b.g. (Mar 27) Catcher In The Rye (IRE) 115 – Irinatinvidio 85
(Rudimentary (USA) 118) [2007 6d⁴ 6d* 7d² 8.3d³ 6g 6d⁶ Sep 21] €13,500F, 40,000Y:
big gelding: has scope: first foal: dam Italian 2-y-o 1¼m winner: fairly useful performer:
won maiden at Ayr in May: held form well, placed in nursery at Catterick and minor event
at Hamilton (third to McCartney): stays 1m: raced only on good/good to soft going:
gelded after final start. *J. Howard Johnson*

NINETYNINETREBLE (IRE) 4 b.g. Grand Lodge (USA) 125 – Licorne 93 70
(Sadler's Wells (USA) 132) [2007 p9.5g² f11g⁴ f8g 10g⁵ 12d⁶ 14.1m 15.8g Sep 22] tall
gelding: fair maiden: left D. Nicholls after fourth outing: stays 1¼m: acts on polytrack.
Grant Tuer

NINO COCHISE (IRE) 2 b.g. (Feb 20) High Chaparral (IRE) 132 – Lady Scarlett 72 ?
(Woodman (USA) 126) [2007 p8m p7m f7d³ Dec 14] 75,000Y: third foal: half-brother to
smart 5f/6f winner Sunrise Safari (by Mozart): dam unraced half-sister to Poolesta (useful
sprinter in Britain/Grade 3 8.5f winner in USA) and Desert Fox (smart Irish/Hong Kong
performer up to 1½m: seemingly easily best effort in maidens when third at Southwell,
nearest finish: gelded after: should stay at least 1m. *C. R. Egerton*

NINTH HOUSE (USA) 5 b.h. Chester House (USA) 123 – Ninette (USA) 101 (Alle- 88
ged (USA) 138) [2007 93: p8.6g² p8g 8m 8m p8g p8g p7.1g⁴ p7.1g² p8g⁵ p8.6d* p8g*
Dec 28] good-topped horse: fairly useful performer: won claimers at Wolverhampton
and Lingfield in December: stays 9.5f: acts on polytrack and firm going: often blinkered
(including for last 2 wins): usually tongue tied: has reportedly had breathing problems.
N. P. Littmoden

NIQAAB 3 ch.f. Alhaarth (IRE) 126 – Shanty 94 (Selkirk (USA) 129) [2007 70p: 10d⁴ 72
10s³ 11.6m p9.5g p12g⁵ Nov 28] useful-looking filly, unfurnished at 3 yrs: fair maiden:
left B. Hills 13,000 gns after second outing: stays 1½m: acts on polytrack and good to soft
going: has made running. *W. J. Musson*

NISBAH 2 ch.f. (Apr 16) Kyllachy 129 – Amazing Bay 100 (Mazilier (USA) 107) [2007 –
6m p6g Jul 18] 16,000Y: smallish, strong filly: seventh foal: half-sister to several
winners, including useful Italian miler Scartozz (by Barathea): dam 2-y-o 5f/6f winner:
green and behind in maidens. *C. E. Brittain*

NISTAKI (USA) 6 ch.g. Miswaki (USA) 124 – Brandywine Belle (USA) (Trempolino 52
(USA) 135) [2007 72: p6g p5g Oct 24] strong, compact gelding: fairly useful performer
at best: just modest in 2007: best form at 6f/7f: acts on polytrack, soft and good to firm
going: reportedly bled on 4-y-o reappearance. *D. Shaw*

NITEOWL LAD (IRE) 5 ch.g. Tagula (IRE) 116 – Mareha (IRE) 95 (Cadeaux Gene- 67
reux 131) [2007 77: 5.1d 5m 5m⁶ 5s⁶ 5m⁴ 5.1s³ 5.1g⁵ Oct 31] lengthy gelding: fair
handicapper: best at 5f: acts on firm and soft going: tongue tied last 3 starts at 4 yrs.
J. Balding

NIZA D'ALM (FR) 6 b. or br.m. Passing Sale (FR) 125 – Bekaa II (FR) (Djarvis (FR)) –
[2007 –: p12.2g 12m 15.8g Oct 30] no form. *A. Crook*

NOAH JAMEEL 5 ch.g. Mark of Esteem (IRE) 137 – Subtle One (IRE) (Polish Patriot 59
(USA) 128) [2007 –: f11g⁶ p8g 9.7g⁵ p10g³ p11g* Dec 19] modest performer, lightly
raced: dead-heated in handicap at Kempton in December: stays 11f: acts on polytrack and
good to soft ground. *A. G. Newcombe*

NOBELIX (IRE) 5 gr.g. Linamix (FR) 127 – Nataliana 103 (Surumu (GER)) [2007 90: 94
20m 14.8m* 16m 12m* p12g⁵ p12g³ Oct 29] compact gelding: fairly useful performer:
won handicap in July and claimer (claimed from J. Fanshawe £30,000) in September,
both at Newmarket: stays 14.8f: acts on polytrack, firm and good to soft going. *J. R. Gask*

NOBILISSIMA (IRE) 3 b.f. Orpen (USA) 116 – Shadow Smile (IRE) 74 (Slip 88
Anchor 136) [2007 71: 6g² 6.1m³ 6.1g* 6g 6s* 6d⁵ 6g 6d² p7m Oct 6] lengthy filly: fairly
useful handicapper: won at Chepstow in May and Warwick in July: should stay 7f: acts
on soft and good to firm ground: genuine. *J. L. Spearing*

NOBLE CALLING (FR) 10 b.g. Caller I D (USA) – Specificity (USA) 103 (Alleged 38
(USA) 138) [2007 –: 10.2f 10f² 17.2f Jun 10] angular gelding: one-time fair performer:
lightly raced and only poor form on Flat since 2004: stays 17.2f: acts on firm and good to
soft going: sometimes blinkered/visored. *R. J. Hodges*

NOBLE CITIZEN (USA) 2 b.c. (Feb 24) Proud Citizen (USA) 122 – Serene Nobility **85** (USA) (His Majesty (USA)) [2007 7s 7m⁶ p7g² 7m* p8m⁵ Oct 11] $190,000Y: good-topped, angular colt: half-brother to several winners, notably smart 6f to 1m (at 2 yrs) winner Mutaahab (by Dixieland Band): dam US 6f to 9f winner, including several minor stakes: fairly useful performer: won nursery at Newmarket in September: should prove best up to 1m: acts on polytrack and good to firm going, probably soft. *D. M. Simcock*

NOBLE EDGE 4 ch.g. Bold Edge 123 – Noble Soul 67 (Sayf El Arab (USA) 127) **56** [2007 68d: 8d 7.9m⁴ 10.1d 8m 11.1m Aug 31] sturdy gelding: modest performer nowadays: stays 1½m: acts on all-weather, good to firm and good to soft going: tried blinkered, often wears cheekpieces. *Karen McLintock*

NOBLE MINSTREL 4 ch.g. Fantastic Light (USA) 134 – Sweetness Herself 106 **82** (Unfuwain (USA) 131) [2007 68: p12g⁵ p16g* p16g* 16g² 14.8d 14.8m² 21g 18m 16.4m p16.5g² p12.2g⁵ Dec 26] lengthy gelding: fairly useful handicapper: won at Kempton in January and February: further improvement when runner-up after: stays 2¼m: acts on polytrack and good to firm going: tongue tied. *S. C. Williams*

NOBLE MOUNT 6 b.g. Muhtarram (USA) 125 – Our Poppet (IRE) 58 (Warning 136) **–** [2007 52: 6m 6d p7g Dec 30] modest performer at best: no form in 2007: usually wears cheekpieces. *A. B. Haynes*

NOBLE NOVA 4 br.f. Fraam 114 – Noble Destiny 89 (Dancing Brave (USA) 140) **48** [2007 69: f8g Feb 15] useful-looking filly: fair handicapper at 3 yrs: below form sole start in 2007: stays 8.3f: acts on any turf going. *G. A. Swinbank*

NOBLE PLUM (IRE) 3 b.f. King's Best (USA) 132 – Perfect Plum (IRE) 113 (Dar- **84 +** shaan 133) [2007 p9.5g p11g² p12.2g* p12.2s³ Dec 20] good-topped filly: second foal: dam, 2-y-o 1m winner, out of half-sister to top-class sprinter Marwell: fairly useful form: won maiden at Wolverhampton in December: good third in handicap there next time: stays 1½m: raced only on polytrack: very slowly away on debut. *Sir Mark Prescott*

NOCHE DE REYES 2 b.c. (Mar 12) Foxhound (USA) 103 – Ashleigh Baker (IRE) 68 **–** (Don't Forget Me 127) [2007 5.1g Oct 31] 20/1, backward in maiden at Nottingham. *E. J. Alston*

NO COMMISSION (IRE) 5 b.g. General Monash (USA) 107 – Price of Passion 83 **– §** (Dolphin Street (FR) 125) [2007 –§: 12m Aug 7] sturdy gelding: lightly raced and little form on Flat since 2005: reluctant, and one to leave alone. *R. F. Fisher*

NODDIES WAY 4 b.g. Nomadic Way (USA) 104 – Sharway Lady 50 (Shareef Dancer **76** (USA) 135) [2007 67: p16g³ p16g⁴ 21.6m² 16g³ 16.2m 16m³ 21g³ 16m⁵ 16m² 18m Oct 22] leggy gelding: fair maiden handicapper: stays 21.6f: acts on polytrack and good to firm going: tried blinkered (below form): unruly in stall and withdrawn once at 3 yrs. *J. F. Panvert*

NODDLEDODDLE (IRE) 3 b.f. Daggers Drawn (USA) 114 – En Retard (IRE) 97 **39** (Petardia 113) [2007 53: 6v⁶ 5m 5g 10.1g 7.1g⁴ 8m 5d⁶ p7m 5g p6g f5d Dec 14] big, useful-looking filly: poor maiden: stays 1m: acts on polytrack and good to soft going: in blinkers/cheekpieces last 5 starts: usually tongue tied. *J. Ryan*

NODSERVATORY 2 ch.f. (Apr 5) Observatory (USA) 131 – Nordan Raider 81 **–** (Domynsky 110) [2007 p7.1d Dec 7] sixth foal: half-sister to 7.5f to 1¼m winner Nod's Nephew (by Efisio) and fairly useful 5f to 7f (latter at 2 yrs) winner Sir Nod (by Tagula): dam, 6f winner, half-sister to useful 7f/1m performer Hi Nod: 66/1, well held in maiden at Wolverhampton. *Miss J. A. Camacho*

NOD'S STAR 6 ch.m. Starborough 126 – Barsham 94 (Be My Guest (USA) 126) [2007 **–** 47: p16g* f14g² p16.5g² p16.5g p16.5g² p16g² f14g⁵ 15.4m 16m Sep 5] close-coupled **a57** mare: modest on all-weather, poor on turf: won minor event at Kempton in January: stays 16.5f: acts on all-weather and good to soft going: tongue tied. *Mrs L. C. Jewell*

NO GREATER LOVE (FR) 5 b.g. Take Risks (FR) 116 – Desperate Virgin (BEL) **57** (Chief Singer 131) [2007 f11g* Jan 11] ran 4 times for A. Fabre in 2005, in frame on all starts (fair form): won maiden at Southwell on British Flat debut in January: stays 14.5f: acts on fibresand, has run only on good/good to soft going on turf: winning hurdler/chaser. *Ian Williams*

NO GROUSE 7 b.g. Pursuit of Love 124 – Lady Joyce (FR) (Galetto (FR) 118) [2007 **65** 70, a63: 7m 6g³ 6d³ 6d⁵ 6m 6m 7g² 7.1m* 7m 7.1g p7.1g p7.1g Nov 1] strong, round-barrelled gelding: fair handicapper: won at Musselburgh in September: effective at 6f to 7.5f: acts on all-weather, good to firm and good to soft going: tried in cheekpieces: held up. *E. J. Alston*

NO GUILT (IRE) 2 b.f. (May 5) Viking Ruler (AUS) – Icefern 88 (Moorestyle 137) –
[2007 6s 6d Jul 5] €16,000Y: half-sister to numerous winners, including useful 1m
winner Iamus (by Most Welcome) and fairly useful 2003 2-y-o 5f winner Mac The Knife
(by Daggers Drawn): dam sprinter: well held in maiden and seller. *J. L. Spearing*

NO INKLING (IRE) 4 b.f. Xaar 132 – No Tippling (IRE) 72 (Unblest 117) [2007 –, –
a37: f7g⁶ f7g f6g 9.9s p9.5g Nov 12] plain filly: poor maiden at best: tried visored/in
cheekpieces. *Miss M. E. Rowland*

NOISY SILENCE (IRE) 3 b.c. Giant's Causeway (USA) 132 – Golightly (USA) 88
(Take Me Out (USA)) [2007 79: 8.3m* 10.3m⁴ 8.9d Oct 13] leggy, close-coupled colt:
fairly useful performer: won maiden at Windsor in August: good fourth in handicap at
Chester next time: stays 10.3f: acts on good to firm and good to soft going: sold 13,000
gns, joined A. Manuel in UAE. *E. F. Vaughan*

NOK TWICE (IRE) 6 b.g. Second Empire (IRE) 124 – Bent Al Fala (IRE) 59 (Green 67
Desert (USA) 127) [2007 6d 6s⁶ p8.6g² p7.1g Nov 9] fair handicapper: won at Limerick
and Cork in 2005: only creditable effort in 2007 when runner-up: P. Casey in Ireland and unraced at 5 yrs:
2007 when runner-up: stays 8.6f: acts on polytrack/sand, firm and good to soft ground:
has worn tongue tie/cheekpieces. *D. Carroll*

NOMOREBLONDES 3 ch.f. Ishiguru (USA) 114 – Statuette 57 (Statoblest 120) 75
[2007 54: p6g⁵ 5g³ 5m⁴ 5m⁴ 5g² 5m* Aug 27] fair performer: won handicaps at
Musselburgh (apprentices) in July and Newcastle in August: may prove best at 5f/6f: acts
on polytrack and good to firm ground: wore cheekpieces last 4 outings: races up with
pace: reliable. *P. T. Midgley*

NONA 4 ch.f. Halling (USA) 133 – Zarma (FR) (Machiavellian (USA) 123) [2007 –: –
p12g p12g Feb 10] quite good-topped filly: modest maiden at 2 yrs: lightly raced and
little form since. *S. Dow*

NON COMPLIANT 3 b.c. Lujain (USA) 119 – Flourish (Selkirk (USA) 129) [2007 92
88: p6g³ 6g 7g⁶ Jun 17] leggy colt: fairly useful performer: good third in handicap at
Lingfield on reappearance: below form after: was best at 5f/6f: acted on polytrack and
good to firm going: dead. *J. W. Hills*

NO NINES 2 b.g. (Apr 29) Noverre (USA) 125 – Amber Mill 96 (Doulab (USA) 115) 66
[2007 5.2m p5g⁶ f5g³ p6g 8s³ p8m 8g Dec 9] sturdy gelding: fair maiden: third at Southwell and Redcar (nursery): sold from B. Hills 12,000 gns before final start: stays 1m: acts
on fibresand and soft going. *J. Calderon, Spain*

NO NO NINETTE 2 b.f. (Feb 5) Oasis Dream 129 – Madam Ninette (Mark of Esteem –
(IRE) 137) [2007 6f 6m p7g Oct 10] 42,000Y: compact filly: first foal: dam unraced
half-sister to very smart sprinter Bolshoi: little form: tried in blinkers/cheekpieces.
C. R. Egerton

NON SUCRE (USA) 2 b. or br.c. (Apr 25) Minardi (USA) 119 – Vieille Rose (IRE) 77
(Dancing Spree (USA)) [2007 5g 5m² p7.1g² 7f³ 6.1d* 6g Oct 6] lengthy colt: fair form:
placed 3 times, including in nursery at Newbury, prior to winning maiden at Chepstow in
August (first of 2 starts in blinkers, stiff task other): stays 7f: acts on polytrack, firm and
good to soft going. *P. A. Blockley*

NO NUKES 2 b.g. (Mar 21) Where Or When (IRE) 124 – Intellibet One 74 (Compton –
Place 125) [2007 p8.6g⁶ 8.2g p8.6g Nov 8] leggy gelding: little form. *P. D. Evans*

NOOJOOM (IRE) 3 ch.f. Machiavellian (USA) 123 – Abeyr 106 (Unfuwain (USA) 88
131) [2007 75p: p8g* 9.9g 10s² 12d* 13.3m Aug 17] big, lengthy filly: fairly useful
performer: won maiden at Lingfield in January and handicap at Ascot in July: stayed
1½m: acted on polytrack and soft ground: dead. *M. P. Tregoning*

NOORA (IRE) 6 ch.m. Bahhare (USA) 122 – Esteraad (IRE) 90 (Cadeaux Genereux 86
131) [2007 86: 9.9g⁴ p12g⁶ p10g 9g p12g³ 12.1m* p16g⁶ p13.9g* Oct 15] good-topped
mare: fairly useful performer: won claimer at Chepstow in September and handicap at
Wolverhampton in October: stays 1¾m: acts on polytrack, firm and good to soft going:
tried blinkered/visored nowadays: sometimes starts slowly/looks none too keen: sold 800
gns in November. *C. G. Cox*

NO PAGE (IRE) 2 b.f. (Apr 16) Statue of Liberty (USA) 115 – Esligier (IRE) 87 81
(Sabrehill (USA) 120) [2007 6f⁴ 5g⁴ 6d* 6m Oct 8] useful-looking filly: has a quick
action: first foal: dam, 2-y-o 5f winner, half-sister to useful performer up to 1m Achilles
Star: fairly useful form: won maiden at Haydock (beat Maimoona by neck) in September:
seemed amiss in nursery: likely to stay 7f: acts on good to soft going. *B. W. Hills*

NOPLACE FOR A LADY 2 ch.f. (Apr 26) Compton Place 125 – Pusey Street Girl **45 +**
87 (Gildoran 123) [2007 6g 6m 7f⁶ Aug 12] 22,000Y: rather leggy, lengthy filly: half-
sister to several winners, including 8-y-o Mornin Reserves: dam 7f winner: poor form in
maidens: will prove best up to 7f. *N. Tinkler*

NO POINT (IRE) 2 ch.f. (Apr 29) Point Given (USA) 134 – Youngus (USA) (Atticus **51**
(USA) 121) [2007 5.1f* 5m⁵ 6g⁴ 5m⁴ p5.1g² 5g p6g Nov 20] €5,000Y: quite good-topped
filly: first foal: dam, French maiden, closely related to smart French performer up to 7f
Diableneyev: modest performer: won seller at Bath in April: should stay 6f/7f: acts on
polytrack and firm going. *P. A. Blockley*

NORA CHRISSIE (IRE) 5 br.m. Bahhare (USA) 122 – Vino Veritas (USA) 72 **74**
(Chief's Crown (USA)) [2007 –: 12m⁶ 13m⁶ 12d⁴ 12.9g* 13g⁵ 12v³ 12v³ 12v⁶ 12m⁴
12m p12.2g⁵ p12g² Dec 7] fair performer: won handicap at Down Royal in June: below
form in similar event at Wolverhampton penultimate start: stays 13f: acts on polytrack
and heavy going, probably on good to firm: tried in cheekpieces/visor, usually blinkered:
sometimes slowly away. *Niall Moran, Ireland*

NORAVANA (IRE) 3 b.f. Namid 128 – Kirvana (IRE) (Lycius (USA) 124) [2007 f8g **49**
p7g p8.6g⁴ f12g 9.3m⁶ 8f 6s 7g 7.1g 7.6s Aug 18] tall, leggy filly: poor maiden: temperament under suspicion. *Miss V. Haigh*

NORCROFT 5 b.g. Fasliyev (USA) 120 – Norcroft Joy 82§ (Rock Hopper 124) [2007 **65**
81: p6g⁵ p6g⁴ p7.1g³ 6m⁴ p7.1g⁶ p6g⁵ p6g² 6m³ 6d⁵ p6g³ p6g² 6g 6d p6g* p6g p6d⁶ **a76**
Dec 28] leggy, good-topped gelding: fair handicapper nowadays: won at Wolverhampton in November: stays 1m, races mainly at 6f nowadays: acts on all-weather, firm
and good to soft ground: tried blinkered, wears cheekpieces: often races prominently.
Mrs C. A. Dunnett

NORDIC AFFAIR 3 b.g. Halling (USA) 133 – Affair of State (IRE) 99 (Tate Gallery **85 d**
(USA) 117) [2007 85: p7g⁴ 10m 9.9m 10v 8m Oct 14] tall gelding: fairly useful performer: well below form after reappearance: stays 1m: acts on polytrack: tried blinkered:
sold 3,000 gns. *D. R. C. Elsworth*

NORDIC COMMANDER (IRE) 2 b.c. (Mar 8) Viking Ruler (AUS) – Rising Lady **68**
(Alzao (USA) 117) [2007 7d p7.1g⁴ p7g⁵ Nov 16] 6,000F, 12,000Y: half-brother to 3
winners, including 1m/1¼m winner Okay and 1¼m winner Church House Lady (both
in Ireland, by Treasure Kay): dam Irish maiden: fair form in maidens: will stay 1m.
E. A. L. Dunlop

NORDIC LIGHT (USA) 3 b. or br.g. Belong To Me (USA) – Midriff (USA) (Naevus **81**
(USA)) [2007 65: p7g p6g* 6m* 6g⁵ 6s⁴ May 29] small, strong gelding: fairly useful
performer: much improved to win handicaps at Wolverhampton in March and Folkestone
in April: below form in similar events after: should prove best at 5f/6f: acts on polytrack
and good to firm going: sold 6,000 gns in October. *P. W. Chapple-Hyam*

NORDWIND (IRE) 6 b.g. Acatenango (GER) 127 – Narola (GER) (Nebos (GER) **90**
129) [2007 91: 12g⁶ 18.7m 14g 12m⁶ 16.2g Oct 2] tall, quite attractive gelding: fairly
useful performer: reportedly jarred a knee final 5-y-o outing: in-and-out form in
2007: stays 2m: acts on polytrack and firm going: sold 26,000 gns, joined Evan Williams,
modest form on hurdling debut in December. *W. R. Swinburn*

NORISAN 3 ch.g. Inchinor 119 – Dream On Deya (IRE) (Dolphin Street (FR) 125) **96**
[2007 97: p8g⁴ p8g³ 10g 8m 8m 7s* 7.1g⁵ 7s* p8g² Sep 5] lengthy colt: useful performer:
good third to Fares in listed race at Lingfield second outing: won claimers at Salisbury in
July and Newmarket in August: stays 1m: acts on polytrack, soft and good to firm going:
blinkered last 4 starts: tried tongue tied: often races prominently. *R. Hannon*

NORMAN NORMAN 5 b.g. Double Trigger (IRE) 123 – Nour El Sahar (USA) (Sag- **–**
ace (FR) 135) [2007 –: p12.2g 12s Jun 29] modest maiden at 3 yrs: well held since.
W. S. Kittow

NORMAN THE GREAT 3 b.g. Night Shift (USA) – Encore du Cristal (USA) 82 **85**
(Quiet American (USA)) [2007 51: p8g² p10g² 8.2m³ 8d p10g⁴ 12d⁵ 10m² p11g* 10.2d⁴
10.9m 10d p10g Oct 24] close-coupled gelding: fairly useful handicapper: won at Kempton in August: at least respectable efforts after: stays 1½m: acts on polytrack, good to firm
and good to soft going: sold 45,000 gns. *Jane Chapple-Hyam*

NORMAN TRADITION 3 ch.f. Traditionally (USA) 117 – Normandy (CHI) (Great **48**
Regent (CAN)) [2007 –: p7.1g⁴ p8g Sep 26] poor form in maidens. *A. M. Balding*

NORTELCO (IRE) 4 ch.g. Titus Livius (FR) 115 – Irish Moss (USA) (Irish River **–**
(FR) 131) [2007 9.8g 10.1g 9.8m 8m Sep 18] big, workmanlike gelding: little form: tried
tongue tied. *Micky Hammond*

NORTHERN BOLT 2 b.c. (Mar 27) Cadeaux Genereux 131 – Shafir (IRE) 68 (Shaadi (USA) 126) [2007 6m 6d* Sep 20] 30,000 2-y-o: sturdy colt: eighth foal: half-brother to several winners, including 5-y-o Gallego and 7-y-o Toledo Sun: dam 2-y-o 5f winner: fairly useful form: much improved from debut to win maiden at Ayr by 2 lengths from Elizabeth Swann, making all: should prove best at 5f/6f: will do better again. *D. Nicholls* **92 p**

NORTHERN BOY (USA) 4 ch.g. Lure (USA) 131 – Catala (USA) (Northern Park (USA) 107) [2007 88: 8m⁶ 8m³ 8f⁵ 8.5m 8.3f 12d⁵ 10s 8.1v p7.1g² p7.1g² p7.1g* p7g⁴ p8.6d⁵ Dec 6] quite good-topped gelding: fair handicapper nowadays: left T. D. Barron after eighth start: won at Wolverhampton in November: effective at 7f/1m: acts on polytrack, soft and good to firm going: often held up. *M. W. Easterby* **74**

NORTHERN CANDY 3 ch.g. Sugarfoot 118 – Thalya (Crofthall 110) [2007 –: 6f 5g⁴ 5d 5m Aug 6] poor maiden: tried in cheekpieces. *A. Dickman* **47**

NORTHERN CHORUS (IRE) 4 ch.g. Distant Music (USA) 126 – Nationalartgallery (IRE) (Tate Gallery (USA) 117) [2007 77: f5g 5m 5.1d 5d 6m⁶ 5g³ 6m 5g⁴ 5m Sep 18] angular gelding: fair handicapper: stays 6f: acts on firm and good to soft ground: tried blinkered, usually visored: has looked none too straightforward. *J. O'Reilly* **66**

NORTHERN DARE (IRE) 3 b.g. Fath (USA) 116 – Farmers Swing (IRE) (River Falls 113) [2007 –: f6g 6f* 5m³ 7m 5d* 6d³ 6v* 6m² 6g³ 6d² Sep 21] useful performer, progressive: won maiden at Thirsk in April and handicaps at Ayr and York (by 2½ lengths from Ishetoo) in July: excellent 1½ lengths second of 26 to Utmost Respect in Ayr Silver Cup (Handicap) final outing: sometimes races freely (pulled too hard fourth start), and best at 5f/6f: acts on any turf going: races prominently. *D. Nicholls* **101 +**

NORTHERN DESERT (IRE) 8 b.g. Desert Style (IRE) 121 – Rosie's Guest (IRE) (Be My Guest (USA) 126) [2007 –, a95: p8.6g³ p8g³ 8.1m* p8g p8g 8.3d⁵ p8g p7.1g⁴ p8g² Dec 28] lengthy, quite good-topped gelding: fairly useful handicapper on all-weather and turf: won at Warwick in April: left P. Hiatt after seventh start: stays 8.6f: acts on polytrack, firm and soft going: usually patiently ridden. *S. Curran* **68 a80**

NORTHERN DUNE (IRE) 3 b.g. Dilshaan 119 – Zoudie 79 (Ezzoud (IRE) 126) [2007 –: p10g p9.5g f8g Feb 15] well held in maidens/handicap: modest form over hurdles. *B. J. Curley* **–**

NORTHERN EMPIRE (IRE) 4 ch.g. Namid 128 – Bumble (Rainbow Quest (USA) 134) [2007 84: 5.2m 5g 5g⁴ 5g 6d 5d p5.1g⁵ f5d* Dec 11] strong, good-topped gelding: useful performer, lightly raced: left B. Meehan after second start: won handicap at Southwell in December: best at 5f/6f: acts on fibresand and firm going: tried blinkered: has been early to post. *K. A. Ryan* **97**

NORTHERNER (IRE) 4 b.c. Mark of Esteem (IRE) 137 – Ensorceleuse (FR) (Fabulous Dancer (USA) 124) [2007 63: f12g Mar 6] tall colt: modest maiden at best: tailed off only start in 2007. *J. O'Reilly* **–**

NORTHERN FLING 3 b.g. Mujadil (USA) 119 – Donna Anna (Be My Chief (USA) 122) [2007 87: 6m³ 6m 6g* 6g² 6m⁶ 5g 5g* 6d Sep 21] tall, quite good-topped gelding: useful handicapper: won at Ripon in April and York (beat Special Day by neck) in August: eased as if amiss in Ayr Silver Cup final outing: best at 5f/6f: acts on polytrack and good to firm going: sometimes looked tricky ride at 2 yrs. *D. Nicholls* **100**

NORTHERN JEM 3 b.g. Mark of Esteem (IRE) 137 – Top Jem 85 (Damister (USA) 123) [2007 86: 8m³ 10m³ 9g* 10m 9.7g² 9.8m 10.3g Sep 29] leggy, close-coupled gelding: fairly useful performer: won maiden at Ripon in May: good second in handicap at Folkestone fifth start: gelded after final outing: stays 1¼m: acts on good to firm and good to soft ground: hung left fourth outing. *G. G. Margarson* **93**

NORTHERN SPY (USA) 3 b.c. War Chant (USA) 126 – Sunray Superstar 101 (Nashwan (USA) 135) [2007 8.2m* 9.1v p10g² Dec 16] well-made colt: has scope: first foal: dam, 1½m winner, sister to Prix Saint-Alary winner Nadia: useful form: won maiden at Nottingham in October: left Saeed bin Suroor, best effort when 1¼ lengths second to Evident Pride in handicap at Kempton final start, plenty to do: stays 1¼m: acts on polytrack and good to firm going. *S. Dow* **98 +**

NORTH FLEET 4 b.g. Bertolini (USA) 125 – Rhiann (Anshan 119) [2007 64: p6g⁴ 5g p6g² 6.1g 6s p6g p5.1g 7m 7d Oct 1] good-topped gelding: modest performer: no form after third start: stayed 6f: acted on polytrack and good to soft ground: tried blinkered/in cheekpieces: dead. *J. M. Bradley* **54 d**

NORTHGATE LODGE (USA) 2 ch.c. (Mar 6) Hold That Tiger (USA) 117 – Sabaah Elfull 75 (Kris 135) [2007 5d 5m⁶ 5f⁴ 7m 7m 7m Sep 9] big, strong colt: modest maiden: form only at 5f on going firmer than good: tried blinkered. *M. Brittain* **55**

NORTHGATE MAISIE 2 b.f. (May 8) Sugarfoot 118 – Chasetown Cailin 59 (Suave —
Dancer (USA) 136) [2007 8.2d 8g Oct 19] smallish filly: fourth foal: dam maiden who
stayed 1¼m: well held in maidens. *Jedd O'Keeffe*

NORTH PARADE 2 b.c. (Feb 28) Nayef (USA) 129 – Queen Sceptre (IRE) 97 (Fairy **94 p**
King (USA)) [2007 8.1g⁶ 8m² Sep 21] €70,000Y: strong, lengthy colt: sixth reported
foal: half-brother to 7-y-o Minority Report: dam, 2-y-o 5f/6f winner, out of half-sister to
smart Irish middle-distance colt Topanoora: fairly useful form in minor events at Haydock and Newbury, in latter beaten length by Centennial after moving upsides smoothly:
not sure to stay much beyond 1m: tongue tied: should go on improving, and sure to win
races. *B. J. Meehan*

NORTH SOUTH DIVIDE (IRE) 3 b.g. Namid 128 – Bush Rose (Rainbow Quest **72 p**
(USA) 134) [2007 p8g p7g p7g³ Dec 5] 16,000F, 10,500Y, £4,200 3-y-o: good-topped
gelding: sixth foal: dam unraced half-sister to smart 1¼m/1½m winner Young Buster:
best effort in maidens when seventh to Swop at Lingfield second start (trained by
P. Mitchell): denied clear run at Kempton final outing: stays 7f: raced only on polytrack:
stumbled and unseated on debut: capable of better. *R. A. Teal*

NORTH STARS (IRE) 3 b.g. Soviet Star (USA) 128 – Rania (Aragon 118) [2007 9m⁶ **42**
7f p6g⁶ Oct 15] form in maidens only when in cheekpieces at Wolverhampton final start.
J. O'Reilly

NORTH WALK (IRE) 4 b.g. Monashee Mountain (USA) 115 – Celtic Link (IRE) 66 **58**
(Toca Madera 111) [2007 86: p12g³ p12.2g⁶ p8.6g p8.6g Jul 27] good-topped gelding:
fairly useful in 2006 for K. Ryan, only modest in 2007: seems to stay 1½m: acts on
polytrack, firm and soft going: tried in cheekpieces. *Jennie Candlish*

NORTHWEST 2 b.g. (Mar 21) Reel Buddy (USA) 118 – Adorable Cherub (USA) 58 —
(Halo (USA)) [2007 5.9g 5s 6s⁵ 7g⁶ 7g Nov 6] little form. *A. Berry*

NORTUNE (USA) 2 b.c. (Apr 25) Street Cry (IRE) 130 – Gilded Leaf (USA) (Lyphard —
(USA) 132) [2007 7g Oct 26] small colt: 66/1 and heavily bandaged behind, in rear in
maiden at Doncaster (reportedly finished lame). *B. Smart*

NO RULES 2 b.c. (Mar 14) Fraam 114 – Golden Daring (IRE) (Night Shift (USA)) **70**
[2007 8d 7d⁵ Oct 30] 5,000F, €6,500Y: workmanlike colt: half-brother to 3 winners,
including Irish 1m winner Monroe Gold (by Pivotal): dam Italian 2-y-o 6f winner: mid-
field in maidens at Newmarket and Yarmouth (fair form, fifth to Tasheba): should be
suited by 1m+. *M. H. Tompkins*

NORWEGIAN 6 b.g. Halling (USA) 133 – Chicarica (USA) 112 (The Minstrel (CAN) **61**
135) [2007 –, a54: p8.6g⁴ p8.6g* p8.6g³ p9.5g* p8.6g³ f8g² p9.5g² p9.5g* 9.7m* p9.5g² **a68**
10g⁶ 8.1m 10m⁶ 9m⁵ p9.5g 8m p9.5g p8.6g p9.5g⁴ p9.5g p9.5g⁴ Dec 29] good-topped
gelding: fair performer on all-weather, modest on turf: won 2 handicaps and a seller
at Wolverhampton between January/March and handicap at Folkestone in April: stays
1¼m: acts on all-weather, raced mainly on good/good to firm going on turf: usually wears
headgear. *Ian Williams*

NOSFERATU (IRE) 4 b.g. In The Wings 128 – Gothic Dream (IRE) 113 (Nashwan **99**
(USA) 135) [2007 84p: 11.6m* 12g* 16.1v 14g 14d 12s Oct 13] strong gelding: good
mover: useful handicapper, lightly raced: won at Windsor in May and Epsom (beat Misty
Dancer by 1¼ lengths) in June: should stay 1¾m: acts on good to firm and good to soft
going: sold 80,000 gns, joined J. Howard Johnson. *Mrs A. J. Perrett*

NOTA BENE 5 b.g. Zafonic (USA) 130 – Dodo (IRE) 90 (Alzao (USA) 117) [2007 —
102: 5g 6d Jun 23] strong gelding: smart performer at 3 yrs, lightly raced since: gelded,
well held in handicaps in 2007: should prove just as effective at 5f as 6f: acts on soft and
good to firm going: tongue tied once: reportedly bled final 3-y-o start. *D. R. C. Elsworth*

NOTABILITY (IRE) 5 b.h. King's Best (USA) 132 – Noble Rose (IRE) 113 (Caerleon **102**
(USA) 132) [2007 116: a8f 9g⁶ 8m 8m⁶ Jul 22] leggy, quite good-topped horse: improved
into smart performer in 2006 for M. Jarvis: just useful in 2007, best effort when sixth to
Illustrious Blue in handicap at Nad Al Sheba second start: bred to stay beyond 1m: acts
on polytrack, heavy and good to firm going: has left Godolphin. *Saeed bin Suroor*

NOTA LIBERATA 3 b.g. Spinning World (USA) 130 – Kyda (USA) 78 (Gulch **72**
(USA)) [2007 72: 8.2g 7.5m 7m² f8g³ 9.8m⁵ 7.1g⁵ 8.3s⁵ 9.1d* 10.3m⁵ 10m Sep 20] leggy
gelding: fair handicapper: won at Ayr in July: stays 9f, not 1¼m: acts on fibresand, heavy
and good to firm going: tongue tied last 3 outings: tends to race freely: sold 6,500 gns,
joined Ollie Pears. *G. M. Moore*

NOT ANOTHER CAT (USA) 3 ch.g. Hennessy (USA) 122 – Isle Be Loving You **68** (USA) (Stuka (USA) 116) [2007 75: 8g Jul 20] medium-sized, angular gelding: fair maiden, very lightly raced: stays 7f: best run on polytrack. *K. R. Burke*

NOTEPAD 2 b.f. (Mar 13) King's Best (USA) 132 – Petite Epaulette 80 (Night Shift **63** (USA)) [2007 5d⁵ 6m Jun 9] 72,000Y: leggy filly: half-sister to several winners, including useful 2002 2-y-o 5f to 7f winner Rag Top (by Barathea): dam, 5f winner, ran only at 2 yrs: modest maiden: better run when fifth at Newmarket: should stay 6f/7f. *W. Jarvis*

NOTE PERFECT 2 b.f. (Apr 19) Diktat 126 – Better Still (IRE) (Glenstal (USA) 118) **46** [2007 5g 5m 6v Jun 30] sturdy filly: sister to 5-y-o Word Perfect and half-sister to 2 winners, including useful 5f (at 2 yrs) to 10.5f winner Strong Hand (by First Trump): dam maiden: poor form in maidens. *M. W. Easterby*

NOTHING IS FOREVER (IRE) 3 b.g. Daylami (IRE) 138 – Bequeath (USA) **64** (Lyphard (USA) 132) [2007 70: 10.2m p11g 14m p12g Sep 4] sturdy gelding: maiden: modest at best in handicaps in 2007: should stay 1¼m: sold 8,000 gns. *Mrs A. J. Perrett*

NOTHING LIKEA DAME 2 ch.f. (Apr 13) Bahamian Bounty 116 – Dame Jude 76 **65 d** (Dilum (USA) 115) [2007 5.7f² p6g⁴ 6m p6g 7m p6g p7.1g⁶ p8.6g⁶ Dec 31] leggy filly: fifth foal: half-sister to 2003 2-y-o 7f winner Bertocelli (by Vettori): dam 2-y-o 5f winner: maiden: second at Bath on debut, but lost her way after: best form at 6f: acts on polytrack and firm ground. *D. J. Coakley*

NOTHING TO ADD 2 b.g. (Apr 12) Noverre (USA) 125 – Gaijin 97 (Caerleon (USA) **53** 132) [2007 6s p5.1g 7m⁶ f7d⁴ Dec 18] strong, good-bodied gelding: modest maiden: gelded after third start: blinkered, only form when fourth in seller at Southwell (looked very hard work). *K. A. Ryan*

NOTHINGTODECLAIRE 3 b.c. Tobougg (IRE) 125 – Double Fault (IRE) 54 **78 d** (Zieten (USA) 118) [2007 8m 8d p10g⁴ 9m 9g⁶ 6g⁶ p10g Sep 29] stocky colt: maiden: form only when fourth at Lingfield: stays 1¼m: acts on polytrack: tried blinkered. *G. A. Huffer*

NOTICEABLE (IRE) 3 b.c. Night Shift (USA) – Nawaji (USA) 45 (Trempolino **89 §** (USA) 135) [2007 8m 9.7m* 11g² 12g 10m 9.7g 11m 10.3m² 10m 10.2f⁶ 9.7f² 10m p12.2g⁶ Oct 22] well-made colt: fairly useful performer: won maiden at Folkestone in May: best efforts when runner-up in handicaps: stays 11f: acts on firm going: suspect temperament and one to treat with caution: sold 35,000 gns. *M. R. Channon*

NO TIME (IRE) 7 b.h. Danetime (IRE) 121 – Muckross Park 41 (Nomination 125) **73** [2007 67, a82: p6g p5g p6g p5g⁴ 5.1m² 5m* 5g⁶ 5m² 5.1d² 5m³ 5m² 6g⁶ 5g 5m p5g⁵ p6g 5m² 5m² 5g* 5s⁶ p5.1g 5g⁴ p5g p6m³ p5.1g p6m* p6g⁶ p7g³ Dec 28] smallish, good-topped horse: fair handicapper: won at Folkestone in April, Newcastle in October and Lingfield in December: effective at 5f, and stays easy 7f: acts on dirt/polytrack, firm and good to soft going: tried in cheekpieces: usually held up: sometimes flashes tail. *A. J. McCabe*

NOT MY CHOICE (IRE) 2 ch.c. (Feb 20) Choisir (AUS) 126 – Northgate Raver **84** (Absalom 128) [2007 5d⁴ 5.1m⁵ 5g 5.1g* 6s⁶ p5m 5g⁶ Oct 20] €40,000Y: good-topped, quite attractive colt: sixth foal: half-brother to several winners abroad: dam, of little account, half-sister to dam of smart sprinter Carol's Treasure: fairly useful performer: trained by T. Pitt first 2 starts: won nursery at Chester (made all) in September: best at 5f: acts on soft and good to firm going: once tongue tied. *D. J. Murphy*

NOTNOWCATO 5 ch.h. Inchinor 119 – Rambling Rose 111 (Cadeaux Genereux **128** 131) [2007 126: 10g⁴ 10.5g* 10m³ 10g* 10.4d³ 10d⁶ Oct 20]
    In the brief period in the last century when Britpop ruled the musical world, the question was often asked as to whether Blur or Oasis was the best band. Some thought the smart answer was Pulp. Similarly, in any debate as to whether Seb Sanders or Jamie Spencer was the better jockey, following their closely run contest for the Jockeys' Association's 2007 Flat jockeys' title, some might suggest that Ryan Moore was better than either. Moore, the 2006 champion, lost his title before his defence had begun, missing the first part of the turf season after suffering a broken right elbow in a fall at Lingfield in March. When he returned in the summer, Moore showed a capacity time and again to win races through tactical awareness and strength in the saddle that others might not have done. His record made him popular with punters, as he returned a level-stake profit at starting price on his rides for both his main stables, those of Sir Michael Stoute and Richard Hannon, figures that were even more impressive when two-year-olds were excluded. At Goodwood,

where trouble in running is a regular hazard and a jockey's skills are tested more than at most tracks, Moore won on more than one in four of his mounts. It could be argued that in the context of the season as a whole he made the difference several times in pattern events. On Echelon in the Matron Stakes at Leopardstown, making first run on the Spencer-ridden Red Evie was a vital contribution to victory; under different circumstances, Moore timed things perfectly when sweeping by late to win the Prix Royal-Oak at Longchamp by a short neck on Allegretto; and Moore got the co-operation of the often unwilling Papal Bull to land the Princess of Wales's Stakes at Newmarket. All three of those wins came for Stoute and it came as no great surprise when Moore was named as Stoute's retained jockey for 2008. Moore is a hot favourite at the time of writing to regain his jockeys' crown.

Another Stoute-Moore victory that owed plenty to the rider's initiative was Notnowcato's success in the Coral-Eclipse Stakes at Sandown in July. The main focus beforehand was the return to the fray of the impressive Derby winner Authorized, along with the top three-year-old of 2006 George Washington, having his second start after his unexpected comeback. Eight in all went to post. George Washington was joined by three stable companions, Admiralofthefleet, Archipenko and Yellowstone, who had all finished well behind Authorized at Epsom. Authorized himself had a pacemaker in the supplemented Champery. The line-up was completed by two five-year-olds, Notnowcato and Kandidate, third over course and distance in the Gordon Richards Stakes in the spring (Notnowcato, in need of the run, had come fourth). On his best form, Notnowcato, with a proven record at Group 1 level, appeared the only danger to the two principals. Such had been the impression of Authorized's success at Epsom that he started odds on, with George Washington a 4/1 chance, and Notnowcato at 7/1.

The Eclipse turned on tactics. Yellowstone and Archipenko harried Champery for the lead early on before they were steadied back and effectively left Champery marooned in front and largely ineffective after a couple of furlongs. Champery served no useful purpose in Authorized's cause as the main body of the field was left playing cat and mouse with the gallop just fair. Turning for home, Moore on Notnowcato made the decisive move, his actions in sending his mount on and in bringing him to the stand side in the straight making the difference between victory and defeat. The rest remained on the far side, Authorized holding off George Washington by a head, but it was only for second. Notnowcato responded really well to his rider's urgings once sent on and was still a length and a half up at the line. Even though he had ridden on the track the previous day, Moore had

Tattersalls Gold Cup, the Curragh—Notnowcato (left) gamely holds off Dylan Thomas

Coral-Eclipse Stakes, Sandown—Ryan Moore outmanoeuvres the opposition (and the photographers!) as Notnowcato, brought to race alone on the stand side, makes first run, while on the other side of the course (inset) Authorized (left) just gets the better of George Washington for second

walked the course before racing. Authorized's rider, Frankie Dettori, reportedly had not. That said, the fact that Moore outmanoeuvred his rivals, when making first run and gaining a couple of lengths, was arguably more crucial than the fact that he brought Notnowcato to race wide of the others on the stand side. The riders in the races after the Eclipse followed Moore's example but, in truth, there seemed to be little or no ground bias, emphasised when Soft Morning (ridden by Seb Sanders) won the final race when the only runner to stay far side.

Notnowcato gave Sir Michael Stoute his fifth Eclipse win, all of them gained with examples highlighting the trainer's skill in maximising the potential of older horses. Like Notnowcato, the trainer's 1993 winner Opera House won the Eclipse as a five-year-old having been runner-up the previous year. Opera House was a top-class performer at that age, as was the 1997 winner Pilsudski, another five-year-old, both of them multiple Group 1 winners. Yet another five-year-old Ezzoud, successful in the 1994 Eclipse, was also a dual winner of the International Stakes. The four-year-old winner in this quintet was Medicean, successful in 2001, when he won the Lockinge and the then-Group 2 Queen Anne Stakes before his Sandown success. Who knows what Medicean might have achieved kept in training a further year? Coincidentally, both Ezzoud and Pilsudski also had a Derby winner in their wake, Erhaab finishing third to the former and Benny The Dip runner-up (ahead of odds-on Bosra Sham) to the latter.

The Eclipse was Notnowcato's third Group 1 success. He had landed a substandard renewal of the International at York the previous summer, giving Moore his first Group 1 success, and in May, before Moore returned from injury, he won the Tattersalls Gold Cup at the Curragh, Ireland's first Group 1 of the season for older horses. Notnowcato started at 7/1 that day as well, with Dylan Thomas, already successful twice earlier in the spring, notably in the Group 1 Prix Ganay, a 2/1-on chance. Notnowcato showed gameness under pressure to prevail by a head from Dylan Thomas, with Youmzain four lengths back in third. Notnowcato's performances at the Curragh and Sandown were the best of his career.

Notnowcato's defeats of Dylan Thomas and Authorized were, in different ways, thrilling and highly commendable but, on balance, high class as it is, his best form is inferior to the pick of theirs and both subsequently gained revenge of sorts.

Defeats in the Prince of Wales's Stakes at Royal Ascot and in the International at York illustrated Notnowcato's limitations. At Ascot, in the strongest mile-and-a-quarter event of the year, Notnowcato finished third, a length and a quarter and four lengths behind Manduro and Dylan Thomas, swamped for speed two furlongs out after being ridden less enterprisingly than would have been ideal in top company. At York, bidding to repeat the previous year's victory, he had no such excuse, sent on into the straight but simply not good enough against Authorized and Dylan Thomas, beaten a length and three. Notnowcato's season ended on a low note. Two months on from York, he started favourite for the Champion Stakes at Newmarket, but, as he had the previous year, he ran well below his best, again sweating and going in his coat beforehand. Notnowcato could be edgy in the preliminaries and was sometimes sent out first in the parade for Group 1 events as a result, though he matured with age, not untypically for a runner from his stable.

Notnowcato (ch.h. 2002)	Inchinor (ch 1990)	Ahonoora (ch 1975)	Lorenzaccio
			Helen Nicholls
		Inchmurrin (b 1985)	Lomond
			On Show
	Rambling Rose (ch 1995)	Cadeaux Genereux (ch 1985)	Young Generation
			Smarten Up
		Blush Rambler (ch 1988)	Blushing Groom
			Nikitina

The strong, lengthy Notnowcato has been retired to stand at Stanley House Stud in Newmarket at a fee of £8,000, a larger version of his sire, the now-deceased Inchinor, the last stallion to stand there. Notnowcato is a stouter stayer than his sire, who raced exclusively at seven furlongs to a mile after his debut, and, given the stamina on the dam's side of his pedigree, it is slightly surprising that Notnowcato was never tried beyond ten and a half furlongs—his last eleven races were all at around a mile and a quarter. Notnowcato's year-younger half-brother Heaven Knows (by Halling) showed useful form in 2007, winning at a mile and a quarter and running creditably in the November Handicap. Their dam Rambling Rose's fourth foal (the first Rosacara, by Green Desert, failed to win) is Maigold Lass (by Mark of Esteem), who was in training with Stoute but failed to make it to the track. Rambling Rose, also trained by Stoute, was a smart performer herself, being placed in the Ribblesdale Stakes and Lancashire Oaks before winning the Galtres Stakes. She was one of seven winners out of the Irish mile-and-a-half winner Blush Rambler, many of them also trained by Stoute (quite a few were later sent hurdling with Renee Robeson). Three showed useful form on the Flat, Kiftsgate, Magnifico and Ponderon, the last named successful at two miles (and trained by Fulke Johnson Houghton). Blush Rambler was a half-sister to some even stouter stayers, notably the Queen Alexandra Stakes runner-up Excellenza. The third dam Nikitina was a useful mile-and-a-quarter winner in Ireland.

Notnowcato was raced mainly on going ranging from good to firm to good to soft. He gained his first win, in a handicap, on his only start on firm going, and was untried on soft or heavy. Despite his edgy nature, he was a thoroughly genuine racehorse. For the second year running, he was the highest earner for the Stoute stable, his Tattersalls Gold Cup win and his 1,2,3 earnings in Britain together worth £483,316. The strength of its older horses continues to serve the yard well and the latest campaign was no exception with six-year-old Maraahel, five-year-olds Mountain High and Echelon, and four-year-olds Allegretto, Ask and Papal Bull also among the leading earners in a year when four-year-olds and upwards accounted for the lion's share of the stable's prize money. With Maraahel, Allegretto, Papal Bull and Ask, as well as Galactic Star, Hi Calypso and Promising Lead among the older horses remaining in training with Stoute in 2008, there should be plenty for his new stable jockey Ryan Moore to look forward to. *Sir Michael Stoute*

NOT NOW LEWIS (IRE) 3 b.g. Shinko Forest (IRE) – Pearl Egg (IRE) 55 (Mukad- **66** damah (USA) 125) [2007 p6g³ f6g⁵ p6g³ p7g³ p10g⁴ p8g² p9.5g⁵ p8.6d Dec 7] €22,000Y: first foal: dam, Irish maiden (stayed 7f): fair maiden: stays 7f: raced only on all-weather. *J. A. Osborne*

NO TO TRIDENT 2 b.g. (Apr 3) Zilzal (USA) 137 – Charmante Femme 53 (Bin **78** Ajwaad (IRE) 119) [2007 5.7f 8.1m² p8.6g⁵ p8.6g² 8d² Oct 13] leggy, close-coupled gelding: fair maiden: runner-up 3 starts, including final 2 at Wolverhampton (in control until veered right) and York (3 lengths behind Bright Falcon): stays 8.6f: acts on polytrack, good to firm and good to soft going. *P. D. Evans*

NOT TO KNOW 3 b.g. Mujahid (USA) 125 – Little Tramp (Trempolino (USA) 135) **77** [2007 68: p7.1g4 10s* 8g 9v p10.7g* p12g3 14g Oct 29] fair performer: below form at Wolverhampton on reappearance: won handicap at Navan in April and claimer at Dundalk in September: stays 1½m: acts on polytrack and soft ground: held up. *John A. Quinn, Ireland*

NOT TOO TAXING 3 b.g. Forzando 122 – Areish (IRE) 66 (Keen 116) [2007 67: **66 d** p7.1g2 p8g2 p7g p7g p8g 8.2m p8g p8g Aug 8] sturdy gelding: maiden: regressed in 2007, leaving R. Hannon after sixth start and became one to avoid: stays 1m: raced only on polytrack and good to firm ground: tried blinkered/tongue tied. *G. A. Ham*

NOU CAMP 3 ch.g. Compton Place 125 – Real Popcorn (IRE) 52 (Jareer (USA) 115) **59 §** [2007 59: p7g p5g3 f5g 5m3 5g5 5m6 6d4 p7.1g5 6m 7d p8g4 8d5 8g 5g5 Dec 30] well-made gelding: modest maiden: sold from N. Callaghan 5,000 gns after twelfth start: stays 7f: acts on polytrack and good to firm ground: tried blinkered: often races freely: temperamental. *J. Salguero, Spain*

NOUVEAU (GER) 3 b.g. Desert Style (IRE) 121 – Night Care (GER) (Caerwent 123) **84** [2007 p7g 8.3s 6s5 5.7g2 p8g4 6g* 6m* 6m6 p6g3 p6g4 6d* p7g4 Oct 15] sturdy gelding: fairly useful handicapper: much improved when winning at Folkestone (apprentices) in July, Haydock in August and Windsor in October: stays 7f: acts on polytrack, good to firm and good to soft ground: sold 16,000 gns, joined J. Carr in Ireland. *R. Hannon*

NOUVELLE NOVA (IRE) 2 b.f. (Apr 24) Noverre (USA) 125 – Uhud (IRE) (Mujtahid (USA) 118) [2007 p7g Sep 11] lengthy filly: sixth foal: half-sister to useful 5f (at 2 yrs)/6f (in Sweden) winner Pitch Up (by Cape Cross) and winner in Italy by Distinctly North: dam unraced out of half-sister to smart Irish 6f/7f winner Prince Echo: 10/1, last in maiden at Lingfield. *G. G. Margarson*

NOVAS (IRE) 2 b.c. (Feb 6) Noverre (USA) 125 – Coolrain Lady (IRE) 74 (Common – Grounds 118) [2007 7m Sep 21] leggy colt: tailed off in maidens. *M. R. Channon*

NOVA TOR (IRE) 5 b.m. Trans Island 119 – Nordic Living (IRE) 53 (Nordico (USA)) – [2007 61: p5.1g f5g Feb 1] small, strong, close-coupled mare: modest performer at 4 yrs: no form in 2007: often in cheekpieces/blinkers. *Peter Grayson*

NOVELLEN LAD (IRE) 2 b.c. (May 21) Noverre (USA) 125 – Lady Ellen 67 (Hor- **59 p** age 124) [2007 6m6 Nov 10] £50,000 2-y-o: tall colt: half-brother to several winners, including smart sprinters Ellens Academy (12-y-o) and Ellens Lad (by Polish Patriot): dam, sprint maiden, half-sister to Indian Ridge: 10/1, sixth in maiden at Doncaster, racing freely: should progress. *E. J. Alston*

NOVESTAR (IRE) 2 ch.c. (Feb 21) Noverre (USA) 125 – Star of Cayman (IRE) (Un- **47** fuwain (USA) 131) [2007 6d4 5s 6m 7m3 8g4 p8.6g f7d Dec 14] neat colt: maiden: seemingly easily best effort when third in seller at Leicester (claimed from Mrs A. Duffield £6,000): claimed from G. L. Moore £5,000 next time: should stay 1m: acts on good to firm going: tried in cheekpieces. *G. J. Smith*

NOVIKOV 3 ch.g. Danehill Dancer (IRE) 117 – Ardisia (USA) 87 (Affirmed (USA)) **91** [2007 8g 8g5 8m3 8d* 8s2 10s5 Aug 18] 65,000Y: strong, good-bodied gelding: half-brother to several winners, including smart 1¾m winner Ashgar (by Bien Bien) and fairly useful 11.5f winner Halcyon Daze (by Halling): dam, 1¼m winner, half-sister to Oaks winner Ramruma: fairly useful performer: improved to win maiden at Newmarket in June: stays testing 1m: acts on soft going: gelded after final start. *J. H. M. Gosden*

NOVISTA (IRE) 3 b.g. Anabaa Blue 122 – Bistranova (USA) (Torrential (USA) 117) – [2007 73: 10.1d Oct 30] lightly-raced maiden: refused to settle when well held in handicap sole 3-y-o outing: should stay 1m: signs of temperament: sold 800 gns, sent to Spain. *M. H. Tompkins*

NOWAIRA (IRE) 2 b.f. (Feb 3) Daylami (IRE) 138 – Shallat (IRE) 59 (Pennekamp **77** (USA) 130) [2007 7.1m 8.3m* 7g Sep 30] rather unfurnished filly: third foal: half-sister to 3-y-o Its Moon: dam, maiden (stayed 1½m), half-sister to 1000 Guineas third Hathrah and smart performers abroad up to 1½m Ivan Luis and Zero Problemo: fair form: won maiden at Leicester in September: ran poorly in nursery at Ascot: will stay 1¼m/1½m. *M. Johnston*

NOW LOOK OUT 3 gr.g. Bahamian Bounty 116 – Where's Carol 67 (Anfield 117) **65** [2007 77p: 5g 5g6 5f 5g p5.1g Oct 15] close-coupled gelding: good walker: fair winner at 2 yrs: little impact in handicaps in 2007: likely to prove best at 5f/6f: tried visored/tongue tied: sold 2,000 gns. *E. S. McMahon*

NO WORRIES YET (IRE) 3 b.f. Orpen (USA) 116 – Charming Victoria (IRE) **64** (Mujadil (USA) 119) [2007 69: 5.7d* 5m* 5.1g 5.7g 5.1s* Jul 26] angular filly: modest performer: won claimer at Bath and seller at Beverley in May, and claimer at Bath in July: raced mainly at 5f: acts on firm and soft going: shaped as if amiss third start. *J. L. Spearing*

NOW YOU SEE ME 3 b.f. Anabaa (USA) 130 – Bright Vision (Indian Ridge 123) **60** [2007 p7g⁵ 7g Jun 12] first foal: dam unraced daughter of useful French sprinter Bright Finish: better effort in maidens when 4¾ lengths fifth to Madrigale at Lingfield, refusing to settle: will be suited by 5f/6f. *K. McAuliffe*

NOWZDETIME (IRE) 2 b.c. (May 17) Statue of Liberty (USA) 115 – Sensitive **43** (IRE) 86 (Posen (USA)) [2007 p7g Dec 29] €48,000Y, 38,000 2-y-o: fifth foal: half-brother to Irish 1¼m winner Senseansensibility (by Capote) and to winner in Japan by Stravinsky: dam, Irish 1½m winner, half-sister to dam of Breeders' Cup Turf winner Theatrical: 25/1 and green, seventh in maiden at Lingfield: bred to be suited by 1m+. *M. G. Quinlan*

NUFOUDH (IRE) 3 b.g. Key of Luck (USA) 126 – Limpopo 49 (Green Desert (USA) **68** 127) [2007 66d: 6m 6m⁵ 5m⁴ 6d 6v 5.9f 6f⁵ 7.1s³ 7g³ 6m⁴ 7g⁶ 6m⁵ 7m 7.1g⁴ Oct 5] workmanlike gelding: fair maiden handicapper: stays 7f: acts on firm and soft going. *Miss Tracy Waggott*

NUIT SOMBRE (IRE) 7 b.g. Night Shift (USA) – Belair Princess (USA) (Mr Pros- **88** pector (USA)) [2007 80, a68: 10.2m* 11.6m⁶ 8.5v⁵ 8.2d⁵ 8m 7.5d* 7g* 7g³ 7g* p7.1d Dec 6] good-topped gelding: fairly useful on turf, fair on all-weather: won claimer at Chepstow (left J. O'Shea after next start) in May and handicaps at Beverley in September and Catterick in October and November: stays 10.5f, though best recent form around 7f: acts on polytrack and any turf going: usually wears headgear: often races up with pace. *G. A. Harker*

NUMERICAL (IRE) 3 ch.g. Numerous (USA) – Conspiracy 98 (Rudimentary (USA) **–** 118) [2007 56: 7.1s Jul 6] robust gelding: modest maiden at 2 yrs: well held only outing in 2007: blinkered final 2-y-o start. *J. L. Dunlop*

NUR TAU (IRE) 3 b.g. Peintre Celebre (USA) 137 – Litchfield Hills (USA) (Relaunch **97** (USA)) [2007 80: 11m⁶ 10m* 10m⁶ Sep 22] quite attractive gelding: useful handicapper, lightly raced: easily best effort when winning at Sandown in August by 1¼ lengths from Sugar Ray, making all: likely to stay 1½m: unraced on going softer than good: sold 82,000 gns. *M. P. Tregoning*

NUSOOR (IRE) 4 b.g. Fasliyev (USA) 120 – Zulfaa (USA) 97 (Bahri (USA) 125) **78 §** [2007 79: p6g p5.1g² p5.1g² p6g f5g³ f5g p5.1g² 5f⁴ 5f³ 5m⁵ 5d⁵ 5m⁴ 5d 5d⁴ 5s⁶ 5d⁶ 5.1m³ 5g⁴ p6g* p6g p6g p6g p6g p5g Dec 22] sturdy gelding: fair handicapper: won at Wolverhampton in September: best at 5f/6f: acts on all-weather, firm and good to soft ground: usually blinkered: often slowly away: sometimes races freely: ungenuine. *Peter Grayson*

NUTKIN 3 gr.f. Act One 124 – Cashew 80 (Sharrood (USA) 124) [2007 8g p8g⁴ 9.7s* **77** 10s⁴ Sep 26] big, leggy filly: half-sister to several winners, most at least useful, including 1m (including at 2 yrs)/1¼m winner Macadamia (by Classic Cliche) and 6f (at 2 yrs) to 1m (in UAE) winner Azarole (by Alzao), both smart: dam 1m winner: fair performer: won maiden at Folkestone in August, still green: good fourth in handicap at Redcar next time: stays 1¼m: acts on soft going. *J. R. Fanshawe*

NYLLA 2 b.f. (Feb 16) Bertolini (USA) 125 – Eljariha 71 (Unfuwain (USA) 131) [2007 **73** 6d⁵ p6g³ 5v* 6g 6g⁴ Sep 24] 10,000Y: compact filly: third foal: dam, ran once, out of useful performer up to 1m Hiwaya: fair performer: won maiden at Ripon in July: will stay 7f: acts on polytrack and heavy going: sold 6,000 gns. *M. R. Channon*

O

OAKBRIDGE (IRE) 5 b.g. Indian Ridge 123 – Chauncy Lane (IRE) 90 (Sadler's **63** Wells (USA) 132) [2007 57: p7.1g p9.5g* f8d Dec 21] tall, lengthy gelding: modest performer: won handicap at Wolverhampton in February (final run for D. Wintle): stays easy 9.5f: acts on polytrack and good to firm ground: tried blinkered (raced freely): somewhat temperamental. *R. Brotherton*

OAKLEY ABSOLUTE 5 ch.g. Bluegrass Prince (IRE) 110 – Susie Oakley VII –
(Damsire Unregistered) [2007 66, a73: p10g p10g p9.5g Nov 12] strong, lengthy gelding:
fair handicapper at best: well held in 2007, leaving R. Hannon after second start: tried
visored/in cheekpieces. *J. C. Fox*

OAKLEY HEFFERT (IRE) 3 b.g. Titus Livius (FR) 115 – Daftiyna (IRE) 74 (Dars- **85**
haan 133) [2007 81: 9.9m² 11.6g² 12d 11.6g⁴ 10g³ 10d 11.7g p10g p10g⁴ p10g³ Dec 19]
stocky gelding: has a short, scratchy action: fairly useful handicapper: should stay 1½m:
acts on polytrack and firm going, below form on good to soft: often blinkered. *R. Hannon*

OARSMAN 2 ch.c. (Feb 13) Selkirk (USA) 129 – Felucca 94 (Green Desert (USA) 127) **80 p**
[2007 p7g² Sep 12] half-brother to smart 1m (at 2 yrs) to 10.4f winner Lateen Sails (by
Elmaamul) and winning sprinter in Scandinavia by Zafonic: dam, 2-y-o 6f winner, half-
sister to very smart French performer up to 1½m Radevore: 9/1, promising second to
Iguazu Falls in maiden at Kempton, slowly away and wide: will stay 1m: sure to go on
and win races. *R. Charlton*

OASIS DAVIS 2 b.c. (Feb 21) Oasis Dream 129 – Panarea (FR) (Highest Honor (FR) **70**
124) [2007 6s⁶ 5m⁶ 6f p6g⁵ Oct 26] rather leggy, quite attractive colt: fair maiden: should
prove best at 5f. *K. A. Ryan*

OASIS SUN (IRE) 4 ch.f. Desert Sun 120 – Albaiyda (IRE) (Brief Truce (USA) 126) –
[2007 53: p10g p8g³ p10g* p10g⁶ p10g⁶ p10g 9.7g p12g p10g p10g⁶ p12g³ p11g* p12g³ **a61**
Dec 19] modest performer: won minor event in January and handicap in November, both
at Kempton: stays 1½m: acts on polytrack: usually visored/blinkered. *J. R. Best*

OASIS WIND 2 b.c. (Jan 31) Oasis Dream 129 – Haibah (Rainbow Quest (USA) 134) **96**
[2007 6g³ 6d* 6g² 6.5m⁶ 6d³ Oct 3] 95,000Y: rather leggy, close-coupled colt: first foal:
dam unraced out of sister to 5f (Queen Mary Stakes) to 1m (US Grade 2 event) winner
Dance Parade: useful form: won maiden at Leicester in August: improved after, placed in
nursery at York (neck second to Cristal Clear) and minor event at Salisbury, and in
between second home far side (sixth overall behind Dream Eater) in sales race at Doncaster: should prove best at 5/6f: acts on good to soft and good to firm going. *P. F. I. Cole*

OAT CUISINE 3 b.f. Mujahid (USA) 125 – Gazebo 68 (Cadeaux Genereux 131) [2007 **63**
p8.6g p8g² p8g* Oct 15] 20,000Y: first foal: dam sprint maiden: modest performer: won
maiden at Lingfield in October: stays 1m: raced only on polytrack. *M. L. W. Bell*

OBE BOLD (IRE) 6 b.m. Orpen (USA) 116 – Capable Kate (IRE) (Alzao (USA) 117) –
[2007 65d: p5.1g f6g Feb 1] small, lengthy mare: fair performer at best: no form in 2007:
tried tongue tied/in headgear: sold 5,000 gns in foal to Needwood Blade, sent to Qatar.
A. Berry

OBE BRAVE 4 b.g. Agnes World (USA) 123 – Pass The Rose (IRE) (Thatching 131) **110**
[2007 107: 7.5g* 7.5g 6.5g 6m² 6d 6d 6d 6d Oct 20] strong gelding: has a quick action: smart
handicapper: won at Nad Al Sheba (beat Sendalam a length) in January: off 6 months,
form after only when good short-head second to Kostar in Great St Wilfrid at Ripon: stays
7.5f: acts on soft and good to firm going: races up with pace: sometimes hangs right: sold
42,000 gns. *M. R. Channon*

OBE GOLD 5 b.g. Namaqualand (USA) – Gagajulu 75 (Al Hareb (USA) 123) [2007 **98**
110: 6g⁵ 6.5g⁴ 7m 6m 6s 6m 6g⁶ 6g⁴ 6m² 6m⁶ 6m⁵ 7.2s 7g 6s* 6g⁶ 6g⁵ Oct 24] tall,
useful-looking gelding: useful handicapper: won at Goodwood in October by 1¼ lengths
from Chjimes: effective at 6f/7f: acts on soft and good to firm going: tried blinkered,
effective visored or not: sold 35,000 gns. *M. R. Channon*

OBE ONE 7 b.g. Puissance 110 – Plum Bold 83 (Be My Guest (USA) 126) [2007 61: **50**
6m 7.1m 6f 6g 7.1d 6.9m⁵ 6s 6g 6m³ p6g³ 6s⁴ 6v f6d Dec 11] leggy gelding: modest
performer: stays 7f: acts on polytrack and any turf going: tried in cheekpieces/blinkers:
usually held up. *A. Berry*

OBERLIN (USA) 2 ch.c. (Feb 16) Gone West (USA) – Balanchine (USA) 131 (Storm **79**
Bird (CAN) 134) [2007 p8.6g² 8g⁵ 8g⁶ Oct 25] rather leggy, attractive colt: sixth foal:
closely related to smart French 1¼m/10.5f winner Gulf News (by Woodman) and UAE
9f/1¼m winner Ibtecar (by Seeking The Gold): dam, Oaks and Irish Derby winner, also
7f winner at 2 yrs: fair maiden: encouraging second to Conduit at Wolverhampton, but
disappointing on turf subsequently: will stay 1¼m. *M. Johnston*

OBE ROYAL 3 b.g. Wizard King 122 – Gagajulu 75 (Al Hareb (USA) 123) [2007 75d: **72**
p5.1g⁴ 6g 6d² 7d³ 7.2s² p7.1g⁴ p7.1g⁴ p8.6g⁵ p7.1g p7.1g² Dec 26] close-coupled gelding:
fair maiden: stays 1m: acts on polytrack and any turf going: wears cheekpieces/blinkers
nowadays: sometimes slowly away. *P. D. Evans*

OBEZYANA (USA) 5 ch.g. Rahy (USA) 115 – Polish Treaty (USA) (Danzig (USA))   **87**
[2007 88: 8f 9.1g 7f Jun 12] quite good-topped gelding: fairly useful handicapper: stays
easy 1¼m: acts on polytrack, best efforts on turf on good going: often tongue tied/blink-
ered: reportedly finished lame on reappearance in 2006. *A. Bailey*

OBRIGADO (USA) 7 b.g. Bahri (USA) 125 – Glorious Diamond (USA) (His Majesty   **82 §**
(USA)) [2007 102§: p10g p10m³ p10g Dec 19] big, leggy gelding: useful performer at
best, only fairly useful in handicaps in 2007: stays 1¼m: acts on polytrack, firm and good
to soft going: visored once: tends to sweat: free-going sort, held up: ungenuine. *Karen
George*

OBSCENE 4 b.g. Key of Luck (USA) 126 – Scene (IRE) 87 (Scenic 128) [2007 53:   **–**
p10g p9.5g Jan 8] leggy, good-topped gelding: maiden: well held in 2007, including in
blinkers. *A. J. McCabe*

OBSERVATORY RIDGE 2 ch.f. (Feb 1) Observatory (USA) 131 – Chiasso (USA)   **58**
58 (Woodman (USA) 126) [2007 5m 6.1s⁴ 6d³ 7g p7g p7.1g⁶ p8g⁶ p10g⁴ Oct 24]
15,000Y: good-topped filly: first foal: dam, maiden (stayed 1m), closely related to 10-y-o
Quito: modest maiden: stays 1¼m: acts on polytrack and soft going: sold 8,000 gns, sent
to UAE. *M. D. I. Usher*

OBSERVATORY STAR (IRE) 4 br.g. Observatory (USA) 131 – Pink Sovietstaia   **89**
(FR) (Soviet Star (USA) 128) [2007 74: 6m² 6g³ 5.9m⁶ 7m² 8m* 8.1s² 8g² 8.3d⁵ Oct 29]
fairly useful handicapper: won at Redcar in August: stays 1m: acts on firm and soft going:
blinkered/in cheekpieces nowadays: held up: sometimes races lazily. *T. D. Easterby*

OBSTRUCTIVE 3 ch.g. Zilzal (USA) 137 – Emily-Mou (IRE) 80 (Cadeaux Genereux   **101**
131) [2007 80: p7g³ p6g² 5m* 5d² 5.1s* 5g 5d Sep 29] workmanlike gelding: useful
handicapper: won at Windsor in June and Chester (made all to beat Morinqua by 1¾
lengths) in July: good short-head second to Sundae at Newmarket in between: left
D. Ivory after sixth outing: likely to prove best at 5f/6f: acts on soft and good to firm
going: refused to enter stall prior to intended reappearance. *Andrew Reid*

O'CASEY (IRE) 2 b.g. (Apr 19) Bold Fact (USA) 116 – Miss Scott (IRE) (Be My   **48**
Guest (USA) 126) [2007 5.1f 5m³ 6g⁶ 6.1g⁶ 5.1g⁶ Jul 9] big, workmanlike gelding: poor
maiden: best effort at 5f: wore cheekpieces final start: gelded after. *J. G. M. O'Shea*

OCEANA BLUE 2 b.f. (Feb 26) Reel Buddy (USA) 118 – Silken Dalliance 91 (Rambo   **63**
Dancer (CAN) 107) [2007 p6g⁶ p8.6g³ p8g⁵ p7g⁶ p8m⁵ p7.1d⁵ Dec 27] fifth foal:
half-sister to 3-y-o Oceana Gold and 4-y-o Snake Skin: dam 6f and 1m winner: modest
maiden: stays 8.6f: raced only on polytrack: visored final start. *A. M. Balding*

OCEANA GOLD 3 ch.g. Primo Valentino (IRE) 116 – Silken Dalliance 91 (Rambo   **97**
Dancer (CAN) 107) [2007 73: 8g* 8m³ 8m⁶ 8.1g* 8m⁴ 8d² Sep 28] strong, close-coupled
gelding: useful handicapper: won at Newmarket in May and Sandown (beat Ballroom
Dancer by neck) in August: very good second to Bankable at Ascot final outing: stays
1m: acts on good to firm and good to soft going, unraced on extremes: once refused to
enter stall: races prominently. *A. M. Balding*

OCEAN AVENUE (IRE) 8 b.g. Dolphin Street (FR) 125 – Trinity Hall 67 (Hallgate   **84**
127) [2007 84: p12g³ 11.6m 11.6m* 12m⁶ 11.6f⁶ p11g p11m⁴ p12g⁵ Nov 6] strong
gelding: fairly useful handicapper: won at Windsor in June: just respectable efforts after:
effective at 11f to 14.4f: acts on polytrack and firm going: front runner. *C. A. Horgan*

OCEAN BLAZE 3 b.f. Polar Prince (IRE) 117 – La Belle Vie 73 (Indian King (USA)   **83**
128) [2007 71: 5.1g 5.1f⁵³ 5.1g* 5m² 5.5s² 5.1s⁴ 5g 5m* 5m⁵ 5g* Oct 6] strong, lengthy
filly: fairly useful handicapper: won at Bath in June, Goodwood in September and Redcar
in October: speedy, and will prove best at 5f: acts on firm and soft ground: usually front
runner. *B. R. Millman*

OCEAN GIFT 5 b.g. Cadeaux Genereux 131 – Sea Drift (FR) 72 (Warning 136) [2007   **73 d**
87: 7f 5f⁴ 6m⁶ 6m⁵ 6g 6g⁴ 6m p7.1g⁶ p6g⁵ p7.1g p6g p6g⁶ Nov 20] quite good-topped
gelding: just fair performer nowadays: left N. Tinkler after third outing, P. D. Evans after
sixth: best at 6f/7f: acts on firm going: tried in cheekpieces: tends to race lazily. *N. Tinkler*

OCEAN GLORY (IRE) 2 b.g. (Jan 24) Redback 116 – Finty (IRE) (Entrepreneur   **65 ?**
123) [2007 5m* 5.1g p5m p6g p8g p8g f5d⁶ Dec 20] sturdy gelding: form only on debut,
when winning maiden at Warwick in September. *Peter Grayson*

OCEANICO DOT COM (IRE) 5 br.m. Hernando (FR) 127 – Karen Blixen (Kris   **–**
135) [2007 –: p5.1g Jan 15] small, sturdy mare: fair handicapper in 2005, well held since:
tried tongue tied/in cheekpieces. *A. Berry*

OCEAN LEGEND (IRE) 2 b.c. (Feb 25) Night Shift (USA) – Rose of Mooncoin **66**
(IRE) 99 (Brief Truce (USA) 126) [2007 6m p7g³ Aug 27] workmanlike colt: has scope:
fair maiden: better for debut, third to Copywriter at Kempton: stays 7f. *Miss J. Feilden*

OCEAN OF CHAMPAGNE 3 ch.f. Arkadian Hero (USA) 123 – Champagne **45**
Grandy 84 (Vaigly Great 127) [2007 59: f6g 5.9m⁶ 6.9g 6g 6s 10f 13.8g⁵ Sep 22] good-
topped filly: poor maiden: left A. Dickman after fifth outing: stays 6f: acts on heavy
ground: wears headgear. *Micky Hammond*

OCEAN OF DREAMS (FR) 4 b.g. Ocean of Wisdom (USA) 106 – Tifosa (USA) **77**
(Hickman Creek (USA)) [2007 78: p7.1g⁵ f7g⁶ p7.1g³ p8.6g f6g f7g 13m² 6g* 8g* 7d⁴
8g³ 5.5d* Oct 26] strong, stocky gelding: fair performer: sold from J. Bethell 4,000 gns
after sixth outing: won amateur minor event at Bad Harzburg in July, handicap at Baden-
Baden in August and claimer at Le Croise-Laroche (joined P. Monfort, France €10,555)
in October: best up to 1m: acts on all-weather and good to soft ground: visored final start
in Britain. *C. von der Recke, Germany*

OCEAN PRIDE (IRE) 4 b.g. Lend A Hand 124 – Irish Understudy (ITY) (In The **69**
Wings 128) [2007 86: p13g⁵ p12g⁶ Jun 30] strong, neat gelding: just fair form at best in
2007: barely stays 13f: acts on polytrack, heavy and good to firm going: has been blinkered, in cheekpieces final outing: often let down by temperament over hurdles. *D. E. Pipe*

OCEAN TRANSIT (IRE) 2 b.f. (Feb 12) Trans Island 119 – Wings Awarded 67 **82**
(Shareef Dancer (USA) 135) [2007 f5g 5.1f 5m 6.1g* 6m² 6m 6m* 6g⁶ 6g² 7d⁴ Oct 16]
5,500F, 2,000Y: strong, compact filly: fourth foal: half-sister to winner around 1m
(including at 2 yrs) Leonor de Soto (by Fraam): dam 1m to 1½m winner: fairly useful
performer: won seller at Chepstow in May and nursery at Windsor in August: ran well in
frame in nursery and minor event at Leicester final 2 starts: stays 7f: acts on good to firm
and good to soft ground. *W. G. M. Turner*

OCEAN VALENTINE 4 gr.g. King Charlemagne (USA) 120 – Dolly Bevan 53 **49**
(Another Realm 118) [2007 43: 10.9g p9.5g p8.6g p11g p8.6g p12.2d⁴ p13.9s⁶ Dec 20]
poor maiden: stays easy 1½m: acts on polytrack and good to firm going: often held up.
J. T. Stimpson

OCEAN WAVES (IRE) 4 ch.f. Barathea (IRE) 127 – We've Just Begun (USA) (Hug- **50**
uenot (USA) 121) [2007 –: 9.5m 6.5g⁴ 7m² 8d⁶ 7s 6.3d p7g p12g p8.6d³ Dec 10] modest
maiden handicapper: left Michael Cunningham in Ireland after sixth outing: stays 1¼m:
acts on firm going: tried blinkered (raced freely). *Miss Tor Sturgis*

OCHENVAY 2 gr.f. (Feb 12) Tobougg (IRE) 125 – Bogus Mix (IRE) 52 (Linamix (FR) **50**
127) [2007 6d p7.1g³ p7.1g 8g⁶ p7g p10g⁶ 8.2g Oct 31] 8,000Y: close-coupled,
workmanlike filly: fourth foal: half-sister to 2005 2-y-o 7f seller winner Dispol Shabama
(by Bahamian Bounty) and winner in Macau by Petong: dam maiden: modest maiden:
seems to stay 1¼m. *M. Quinn*

OCHOA (IRE) 2 b.f. (Feb 17) Okawango (USA) 115 – Karakorum (IRE) 94 (Fairy **66**
King (USA)) [2007 6.1d 6m² 7m Sep 14] €24,000F, €50,000Y: lengthy filly: fourth foal:
half-sister to minor US winner by Smart Strike: dam Irish 2-y-o 6f/7f winner: fair maiden:
runner-up at Goodwood: stiff task at the Curragh (Goffs Fillies Million) final start: should
stay 7f: sold 5,000 gns, sent to USA. *C. G. Cox*

OCHRE BAY 4 b.c. Polar Prince (IRE) 117 – Cloudy Reef 57 (Cragador 110) [2007 82: **80**
f7g 7.1d⁶ p7.1g² p7.1g p7.1g⁴ p7.1g³ p6g⁵ Nov 8] good-bodied colt: fairly useful
performer: stays 7f: acts on polytrack, best turf form on good ground: effective with/
without cheekpieces. *R. Hollinshead*

OCHRE (IRE) 3 b.f. Diktat 126 – Cox Orange (USA) 108 (Trempolino (USA) 135) **82**
[2007 p8g⁵ p8g³ p8.6g³ p8g³ p7.1g⁵ p9.5g p9.5g³ p8.6g* p8.6d³ f8g* p8g Dec 30] sister
to useful 7f/1m winner Vista Bella and half-sister to 2 winners, including French 1999
2-y-o 7f winner Orlena (by Gone West): dam, 7f (at 2 yrs in France) to 9f (US Grade 3
events) winner, half-sister to Prix Marcel Boussac winner Amonita: fairly useful performer: left M. Jarvis 75,000 gns after fifth outing: won handicaps at Wolverhampton
(amateurs) in November and Southwell in December: raced only on all-weather: should
stay 1¼m: tried blinkered/in cheekpieces/tongue tie. *R. A. Fahey*

OCTOBER BEN 4 b.f. Killer Instinct 111 – Birmania (IRE) (Rainbow Quest (USA) **68**
134) [2007 72: p8g⁶ p8g p7g⁶ p8g p8g⁵ 9m³ p8.6g² Sep 8] tall, leggy, close-coupled filly:
fair handicapper: should stay 1¼m: acts on polytrack and good to firm going: often
slowly away: held up: joined Conor O'Dwyer, Ireland. *M. D. I. Usher*

ODDSMAKER (IRE) 6 b.g. Barathea (IRE) 127 – Archipova (IRE) (Ela-Mana-Mou **90**
132) [2007 78: 13.8m⁶ 14g³ 9.9m⁶ 14g* 11.5d* Jun 27] angular gelding: fairly useful

handicapper: won at Musselburgh and Carlisle in June: effective at 1½m to 2m: acts on firm and soft going: tried in headgear: tongue tied: front runner, can be headstrong: sometimes hangs. *M. A. Barnes*

ODESSA STAR (USA) 4 gr.f. Stravinsky (USA) 133 – Cryptocari (USA) (Crypto- **71** clearance (USA)) [2007 78: p9.5g p8g⁶ f8g⁵ 10.2f⁵ p9.5g 10.2m Oct 14] fair handicapper: stays 1¼m: acts on polytrack and firm ground: none too consistent: sold 1,300 gns. *J. G. Portman*

ODIHAM 6 b.g. Deploy 131 – Hug Me 96 (Shareef Dancer (USA) 135) [2007 102: **98** p16g* 16m⁵ 18.7m 20m⁵ 16.1v 16d* 16m⁵ 16d 18d Oct 20] tall, deep-girthed gelding: **a104** useful handicapper: won at Kempton (by neck from Salute) in April and Ascot (by ½ length from Thewhirlingdervish, dictating) in July: stays 2½m: acts on polytrack, firm and soft going: blinkered twice, effective visored or not: has been bandaged hind joints: sold 55,000 gns, joined Dr R. Newland. *H. Morrison*

O'DWYER (IRE) 3 ch.g. Namid 128 – Leopardess (IRE) 79 (Ela-Mana-Mou 132) **53 d** [2007 68d: p6g³ p6g⁶ p5g 7.1m⁶ 7g p7g 7.5v 6.9m Jul 29] close-coupled, workmanlike gelding: just modest maiden at best at 3 yrs: stays 6f: acts on polytrack and good to soft going: often wears cheekpieces/blinkers. *A. D. Brown*

OEDIPUSS (IRE) 3 b.c. Mujadil (USA) 119 – Evrobi (IRE) 84 (Grand Lodge (USA) **–** 125) [2007 –: p9.5g p10g p12.2g Jul 16] sturdy colt: maiden: little form in 2007 (tongue tied). *K. J. Burke*

OEUF A LA NEIGE 7 b.g. Danehill (USA) 126 – Reine de Neige 96 (Kris 135) [2007 **67** 59: 7.1m 5m⁴ 6g² 7.1m³ 5d³ 6f⁶ 6g⁶ 5.9g⁴ 6m 7.1d⁵ 6g⁶ 5d⁶ 6d⁴ 6d⁵ 6d 6d 6g⁶ 6g² 8.3m* 7.1m 6m³ 7.1d⁴ 5d 9m* 8g³ 7.2s³ 9.1v⁶ 8g² Nov 8] leggy gelding: fair performer: won handicap at Hamilton in August and claimer at Musselburgh in September: stays 9f: acts on polytrack, soft and good to firm going: tried blinkered/in cheekpieces: has been slowly away. *Miss L. A. Perratt*

OFARABY 7 b.g. Sheikh Albadou 128 – Maristax 74 (Reprimand 122) [2007 107: **–** p10g⁶ 10.4d 10s Oct 13] leggy gelding: useful performer at best: lost way in handicaps in 2007. *M. A. Jarvis*

OFFICER 3 b.c. Medicean 128 – Appointed One (USA) (Danzig (USA)) [2007 10m **89** 10f² 10g 10m⁵ 8.3m* p8g* 8g³ p8.6g⁶ a7f² Dec 21] big, strong colt: fifth foal: half-brother to several winners, notably smart 2002 2-y-o 7f/1m winner Battle Chant (by Coronado's Quest), later successful in USA: dam, US 1m minor stakes winner, sister to smart miler Emperor Jones: fairly useful performer: won maiden at Windsor in July and apprentice handicap at Kempton in September: left Sir Michael Stoute 110,000 gns before good second at Jebel Ali (tongue tied) final outing: effective at 7f/1m: acts on dirt/polytrack and firm ground: visored last 5 starts in Britain: front runner. *H. Brown, South Africa*

OFFICER MATERIAL (IRE) 3 b.g. Barathea (IRE) 127 – Alserna (IRE) 98 (Alha- **55** arth (IRE) 126) [2007 6.1g 7g⁶ 8.1g 8.3d p9.5g⁴ p9.5g Oct 22] small, sturdy gelding: modest maiden: stays 9.5f: acts on polytrack: blinkered last 2 outings. *C. G. Cox*

OFFSHORE STAR (IRE) 2 b.c. (Mar 16) Spartacus (IRE) 107 – Alvilda (IRE) **–** (Caerleon (USA) 132) [2007 p6g Oct 19] 20/1, well beaten in maiden at Wolverhampton: bred to stay 1m. *P. A. Blockley*

OFF STAGE (IRE) 4 ch.f. Danehill Dancer (IRE) 117 – Safe Exit (FR) (Exit To **–** Nowhere (USA) 122) [2007 58: f12g Apr 22] second foal: half-sister to useful 1¼m winner One To Win (by Cape Cross): dam, French 11.5f winner, half-sister to dam of Prix Vermeille winner Volvoreta: lightly-raced maiden: left D. Wachman in Ireland after modest form at 3 yrs: well beaten in handicap only Flat start in 2007: stays 7.5f: acts on firm and soft ground. *Carl Llewellyn*

OFF THE RECORD 3 b.c. Desert Style (IRE) 121 – Record Time 69 (Clantime 101) **103** [2007 70p: f6g* f5g* f5g* 6m² 5s 6g² 5.6m 6d Sep 28] compact colt: useful performer: much improved in handicaps in 2007, winning at Southwell in April (2) and May: good efforts when runner-up at Newmarket after, beaten a neck by Shmoockh then ½ length by King's Apostle: made running in unfavoured group in Portland Handicap at Doncaster penultimate outing: will prove best at 5f/6f: acts on fibresand and good to firm ground (below form on softer than good): front runner. *J. G. Given*

O FOURLUNDA 3 b.f. Halling (USA) 133 – Lunda (IRE) 60 (Soviet Star (USA) 128) **71** [2007 6m³ 5.7f² 6g³ 8.2m 6d Oct 23] leggy, lengthy filly: half-sister to several winners, notably very smart 1m (at 2 yrs) to 11f winner Blue Monday and 6-y-o Lundy's Lane, both by Darshaan: dam, maiden, half-sister to several at least smart 1½m performers, notably high-class Warrsan and Luso: fair maiden: below form after second start: should be suited by further than 6f. *C. E. Brittain*

OGEE 4 ch.g. Generous (IRE) 139 – Aethra (USA) 89 (Trempolino (USA) 135) [2007 **101** 100: 12m p10g⁴ 12s⁴ 14s* 16d⁴ 14d 13.4m⁶ 14.6m⁵ Sep 14] well-made gelding: useful handicapper: won 4-runner event at Goodwood in July by head from Swan Queen: best effort otherwise in 2007 when fourth to Odiham at Ascot next time: effective at 1¼m to easy 2m: acts on polytrack, soft and good to firm going: tried visored: looks hard work: temperament under suspicion: joined Mrs P. Robeson. *Sir Michael Stoute*

OGMORE JUNCTION (IRE) 2 b.c. (Apr 9) Catcher In The Rye (IRE) 115 – Fairy **62 p** Berry (IRE) (Fairy King (USA)) [2007 6m p8g Oct 31] €22,000Y, 48,000 2-y-o: third foal: half-brother to 3-y-o Dolly Coughdrop: dam, Italian maiden, half-sister to smart 1½m performer Pencader: better effort 3 months apart when seventh in maiden at Kempton, making running: should progress further. *P. D. Cundell*

OGRE (USA) 2 b. or br.f. (Apr 1) Tale of The Cat (USA) 113 – Soverign Lady (USA) **71** (Aloha Prospector (USA)) [2007 6m 6m 7.1g p7.1g⁴ p8.6g² p8g* Dec 12] $60,000F, $95,000Y: sturdy filly: third foal: half-sister to winning US sprinter by Belong To Me: dam minor US sprint stakes winner: fair form: steady progress, won nursery at Kempton (idled in front) final start: stays 8.6f: acts on polytrack. *J. A. Osborne*

OHANA 4 b.g. Mark of Esteem (IRE) 137 – Subya 107 (Night Shift (USA)) [2007 75d: **59 §** f8g⁴ f7g Jan 16] strong, close-coupled gelding: modest handicapper: stays easy 1¼m: acts on all-weather: has worn cheekpieces/blinkers: reportedly bled sixth start at 3 yrs: one to be wary of: joined N. Gifford, successful over hurdles in November. *Miss Gay Kelleway*

OH DANNY BOY 6 b.g. Cadeaux Genereux 131 – Final Shot 91 (Dalsaan 125) [2007 – 66: 10m f11g 8d 9.9d p9.5g⁶ Nov 12] sturdy gelding: fair performer at best: little form in 2007: stays 1¼m: acts on polytrack and good to firm ground. *M. C. Chapman*

OH GLORY BE (USA) 4 b.f. Dixieland Band (USA) – Long View (USA) (Damascus **97** (USA)) [2007 90: 12g 9.9d² 14g⁶ p12g⁶ 12s⁴ 12s⁴ 12g* Nov 2] angular filly: useful handicapper: visored, won at Newmarket in November by ½ length from Vale de Lobo: stays 1½m: acts on good to soft ground: none too consistent: sold 145,000 gns, sent to USA. *R. Hannon*

OH GRACIOUS ME (IRE) 3 b.c. Traditionally (USA) 117 – Classic Jenny (IRE) 69 – (Green Desert (USA) 127) [2007 –: 7g May 19] sturdy colt: little impact in 3 maidens: bred to stay at least 1m. *P. A. Blockley*

OH MARY (IRE) 3 b.f. Anabaa (USA) 130 – Contradictive (USA) (Kingmambo **58** (USA) 125) [2007 p8g⁴ 8m 6s Jun 14] tall, sparely-made filly: first foal: dam unraced half-sister to smart French performer up to 10.5f Gracioso: modest form in maidens: sold 3,000 gns. *W. J. Haggas*

OH SO SAUCY 3 b.f. Imperial Ballet (IRE) 110 – Almasi (IRE) 96 (Petorius 117) **60** [2007 58: p6g³ p7.1g⁵ p7g³ 6d³ 7m 7g⁴ Sep 19] sturdy filly: modest maiden handicapper: stays easy 7f: acts on polytrack and good to firm ground, probably on good to soft. *C. F. Wall*

OI VAY JOE (IRE) 3 b.g. Namid 128 – Nuit Des Temps (Sadler's Wells (USA) 132) **81** [2007 84: 7g 6g 5m p6g Sep 24] strong, heavy-topped gelding: fairly useful handicapper: should stay 7f: acts on good to firm and good to soft ground: looked very wayward final start. *W. Jarvis*

OKAFRANCA (IRE) 2 b.g. (Apr 19) Okawango (USA) 115 – Villafranca (IRE) (In **55** The Wings 128) [2007 7.6f 7g 8d Oct 18] 40,000F: fifth foal: half-brother to 3 winners, including 1m winner Sweet Potato (by Monashee Mountain): dam, French 1¼m winner, out of half-sister to Arlington Million winner Mill Native and high-class 1m/9f performer French Stress: modest form in maidens, then gelded: should be suited by 1m/1¼m. *W. R. Muir*

OKIKOKI 3 b.g. Ishiguru (USA) 114 – Crofters Ceilidh 101 (Scottish Reel 123) [2007 **85** 77: 7.1m³ 8m⁵ 7d 7.6s³ 8g 8g⁴ 7s 7.1m² 8d⁶ p8g 7g² p7.1d⁶ Dec 6] quite good-topped **a74 +** gelding: fairly useful handicapper on turf, fair on all-weather: stays 1m: acts on polytrack, firm and good to soft going, probably on soft: sometimes blinkered. *W. R. Muir*

OLD ETONIAN (UAE) 3 ch.g. Jade Robbery (USA) 121 – Favoured 78 (Chief's **86 d** Crown (USA)) [2007 p10g² 12g⁴ p10g Dec 30] rangy gelding: fourth foal: brother to winner and half-brother to winner by Timber Country, both in Japan: dam, maiden, half-sister to smart French 1¼m performer Barbola: easily best effort in maidens when neck second to Pippa Greene at Lingfield, making most but idling: gelded, sold from M. Johnston 16,000 gns after second start: one to treat with caution. *Peter Grayson*

OLDJOESAID 3 b.g. Royal Applause 124 – Border Minstral (IRE) 69 (Sri Pekan (USA) 117) [2007 97: 6m² 5m 5d* 5g² Oct 20] rather leggy gelding: smart handicapper: improved further in 2007, winning at Haydock (by 2 lengths from Efistorm) in September: best effort when neck second to King Orchisios at Catterick final outing: will prove best at 5f/6f: acts on soft and good to firm going. *H. Candy* **113**

OLDRIK (GER) 4 b.g. Tannenkonig (IRE) 111 – Onestep (GER) (Konigsstuhl (GER)) [2007 10.2g 10.2s³ 10.2g² Jun 27] won maiden at Bremen at 2 yrs: last of 4 in minor event at Dortmund only Flat outing in 2006, left Frau E. Schnakenberg in Germany after: fair form in handicaps in Britain: stays 1¼m: acts on soft ground: hung left final outing: fair novice hurdler. *P. J. Hobbs* **73**

OLD ROMNEY 3 br.c. Halling (USA) 133 – Zaeema 93 (Zafonic (USA) 130) [2007 92: 10d 11.9m⁵ p13g³ 10g 8m 10.3m² 10.3m⁵ 10.5s 10d 10g Nov 7] tall, lengthy colt: fairly useful performer: left M. Johnston after third start, G. Huffer after seventh and N. Callaghan after eighth: stays 1½m: acts on good to firm going, probably on good to soft. *M. W. Easterby* **84**

OLGARENA (IRE) 3 b.f. Xaar 132 – Copine (Selkirk (USA) 129) [2007 –: 12.1m 8.3m May 6] smallish filly: little form: tried blinkered. *T. D. Easterby* **–**

OLI JAMES (USA) 2 ch.c. (Mar 11) Officer (USA) 120 – Post It (USA) 112 (Notebook (USA)) [2007 7m p7g 8.3m p7.1g p8m⁴ p8m⁵ Nov 24] leggy colt: maiden: seemingly best effort on debut: probably stays 1m: tried blinkered: sold 6,500 gns, sent to Holland. *P. F. I. Cole* **67 d**

OLIMPO (FR) 6 ch.g. Starborough 126 – Emily Allan (IRE) (Shirley Heights 130) [2007 83: 12d 11.6m² 10.2s* 12.6s* 14m* 14.1d² 11.9g 18d Oct 20] rather leggy gelding: fairly useful handicapper: won at Chepstow in June and Warwick and Sandown in July: stays 1¾m: acts on firm and soft ground. *B. R. Millman* **90**

OLLIE GEORGE (IRE) 4 ch.g. Fruits of Love (USA) 127 – The Iron Lady (IRE) (Polish Patriot (USA) 128) [2007 85: 11.7f* 14.1m² 14g⁵ May 19] good-topped gelding: fairly useful handicapper: won at Bath in April: creditable efforts after: stays 1¾m: acts on polytrack, firm and good to soft going: often visored in 2006: looked none too keen first 2 appearances in 2006, but has looked genuine since. *A. M. Balding* **94**

OLYMPIAN ODYSSEY 4 b.c. Sadler's Wells (USA) 132 – Field of Hope (IRE) 119 (Selkirk (USA) 129) [2007 120: 9g⁴ 9g⁵ 8d³ 8.1g⁶ 9m³ 8m Oct 6] tall colt: smart performer: trained by I. Mohammed in UAE first 2 starts, best effort of year when 1½ lengths fifth to Seihali in Jebel Hatta Stakes at Nad Al Sheba: off 5 months, respectable third to Pride of Nation in Sovereign Stakes at Salisbury next time: disappointing after, failing to impress with attitude: free-going sort, barely stays 1¼m: acts on soft and good to firm going: visored last 2 starts: one to treat with caution. *Saeed bin Suroor* **117 §**

OMMADAWN (IRE) 3 b.f. Montjeu (IRE) 137 – Bonheur (IRE) 93 (Royal Academy (USA) 130) [2007 72p: 9.9d⁵ 10g 10.1d⁶ p12m* Oct 3] fair performer, lightly raced: tongue tied, best effort when winning handicap at Kempton in October: stays 1½m: acts on polytrack. *J. R. Fanshawe* **73**

OMNICAT (USA) 2 br.c. (Mar 31) Storm Cat (USA) – Onaga (USA) (Mr Prospector (USA)) [2007 6m Nov 10] big, rangy, angular colt: brother to 3-y-o Kaseema, closely related to 7f winner Aragorn (by Giant's Causeway), subsequently high-class winner up to 9f in US, and half-brother to 2 winners abroad: dam, US maiden, sister to dam of very smart performer up to 7f One Cool Cat (by Storm Cat): 9/2 and tongue tied, would have won maiden at Doncaster but for swerving right and unseating near finish (had hung badly left before that): will stay 1m. *Saeed bin Suroor* **88**

ON AIR (USA) 4 gr. or ro.f. Cozzene (USA) – Cumulate (USA) 69 (Gone West (USA)) [2007 71d: p8.6g Feb 26] rather leggy, lengthy filly: maiden handicapper, fair at best: well held sole 4-y-o outing. *J. W. Hills* **–**

ONATOPP (IRE) 3 b.f. Soviet Star (USA) 128 – Blueprint (USA) (Shadeed (USA) 135) [2007 67: 6m² 7m² 7m 6d* 6g 6f⁴ 6.9g³ 8m⁴ 8s 10g Oct 6] strong, good-bodied filly: fluent mover: fair performer: won maiden at Catterick in July: stays 1m: acts on firm and soft going: has shown temperament, including when unruly in stall prior to being withdrawn on intended reappearance. *T. D. Easterby* **75**

ONE AND GONE (IRE) 3 b.g. Machiavellian (USA) 123 – Bright Smile (IRE) 83 (Caerleon (USA) 132) [2007 63p: 8.2g 8m 8.3s 11.1m 10f f7d Dec 15] sturdy gelding: **–**

779

maiden: little form at 3 yrs: left R. Fahey prior to final start: should be suited by 1¼m: tried in cheekpieces. *Miss M. E. Rowland*

ONE CALLED ALICE   2 ch. or gr.f. (Apr 26) Zilzal (USA) 137 – Boadicea The Red   **58** (IRE) 72 (Inchinor 119) [2007 p6g⁴ p6g³ p6g⁵ p7.1g³ 7d Oct 29] 1,500Y: compact filly: third foal: sister to winner in Greece: dam 6f/7f winner: modest maiden: third in nursery at Wolverhampton fourth start: will prove best up to 7f: acts on polytrack. *J. R. Holt*

ONE FOR GRETTA (IRE)   5 ch.m. Timeless Times (USA) 99 – Bay of Bengal (IRE)   **–** 55 (Persian Bold 123) [2007 f11g Mar 6] of no account. *J. Hetherton*

ONEFOURSEVEN   14 b.g. Jumbo Hirt (USA) 90§ – Dominance (Dominion 123)   **–** [2007 p13.9g Nov 12] angular gelding: poor handicapper in 2003: tailed off on belated return: tried blinkered/tongue tied. *Lucinda Featherstone*

ONE GIANT LEAP (IRE)   3 ch.f. Pivotal 124 – Petite Epaulette 80 (Night Shift   **73** (USA)) [2007 7m³ 6.9m* 8.1f 7d³ 7g⁴ Oct 19] rangy filly: half-sister to several winners, including useful 2002 2-y-o 5f to 7f winner Rag Top (by Barathea) and fairly useful 7.5f and (in USA) 1m winner Red Top (by Fasliyev): dam 2-y-o 5f winner: fair performer: won maiden at Carlisle in July: stays 7f: acts on good to firm and good to soft going. *H. Morrison*

ONE GREAT CAT (USA)   2 br.c. (Feb 26) Storm Cat (USA) – Blissful (USA) (Mr   **108 p** Prospector (USA)) [2007 6s³ 6v* 6g³ 7m³ Sep 15] lengthy colt: has scope: fifth foal: brother to fairly useful Irish 2005 2-y-o 5f winner (later useful up to 9f in UAE) Where's That Tiger: dam, ran 3 times in USA, sister to Kentucky Derby winner Fusaichi Pegasus out of sister to Preakness Stakes winner Pine Bluff: useful form: won maiden at Fairyhouse in July: continued improvement, 2¾ lengths equal-third to Strike The Deal in Richmond Stakes at Goodwood and 3¾ lengths third to McCartney in Champagne Stakes at Doncaster (had to switch around entire field): will be suited by 1m: acts on heavy and good to firm going: smart prospect. *A. P. O'Brien, Ireland*

ONE HOUR   3 b.c. Halling (USA) 133 – Mingora (USA) 89 (Mtoto 134) [2007 p8g*   **100** 8g³ 9d* 10d⁵ 10g³ Jul 28] strong, lengthy colt: has plenty of scope: first foal: dam, twice-raced half-sister to smart 7f winner Beraysim, out of half-sister to Belmont/Preakness winner Risen Star: useful performer: won maiden at Lingfield in January and handicap at Sandown (made most to beat Royal Rationale by ¾ length) in June: good 2¼ lengths third of 5 to Great Hawk in minor event at Ascot final outing, dictating: stays 1¼m: acts on polytrack, raced only on good/good to soft ground on turf: joined D. Selvaratnam in UAE. *M. P. Tregoning*

ONE MORE ROUND (USA)   9 b.g. Ghazi (USA) – Life of The Party (USA) (Pleas-   **100 §** ant Colony (USA)) [2007 111§: p5g⁵ p5g p6g³ p7g³ 6m 7s 6d 6m 6m 6g* 5.6m p6m p6g p6g* p7m² p6g² Dec 30] rather leggy gelding: useful performer: won minor event at Haydock (by ½ length from Come Out Fighting) in September and claimer at Lingfield (left N. Littmoden) in November: has form at 8.5f, races mainly over shorter: acts on all-weather, firm and good to soft going: tried in cheekpieces, blinkered nowadays: held up: sometimes slowly away/looks none too keen, and best treated with caution. *Ollie Pears*

ONENIGHTINLISBON (IRE)   3 br.f. Bold Fact (USA) 116 – Mickey Towbar (IRE)   **79** 41 (Mujadil (USA) 119) [2007 86: p6m p7g p7.1g⁴ p7g³ p7m* p7m² p7g⁶ Dec 29] leggy, short-backed filly: fair performer: won claimer at Lingfield (left K. R. Burke) in November: stays 7f: acts on polytrack, good to firm and good to soft going. *J. R. Boyle*

ONE NIGHT IN PARIS (IRE)   4 b. or br.f. Danetime (IRE) 121 – Forget Paris (IRE)   **82** (Broken Hearted) [2007 75: p8g* p8g* p7g p7g p7g p8.6g* p8.6g² Nov 5] sturdy filly: fairly useful handicapper: won at Kempton in January, Lingfield in February and Wolverhampton in October: stays 9.5f: acts on polytrack and good to soft going. *M. J. Wallace*

ONE PUTRA (IRE)   5 b.h. Indian Ridge 123 – Triomphale (USA) (Nureyev (USA)   **–** 131) [2007 112: 6d 5m Jul 14] strong horse: smart performer in 2006: below form in handicaps at Ascot at 5 yrs: effective at 5f/6f: acts on soft and good to firm ground: effective tongue tied or not: edgy type, tends to sweat: races prominently. *M. A. Jarvis*

ONE TO FOLLOW   3 b.g. Mtoto 134 – Becalmed (Dilum (USA) 115) [2007 87+:   **75** 9.9m 11d 14d 17.2g Oct 24] lengthy gelding: fair performer, little impact in handicaps in 2007: best effort at 7f. *C. G. Cox*

ONE TOU MANY   2 b.f. (Apr 25) Tobougg (IRE) 125 – Reine de Thebes (FR) 67   **–** (Darshaan 133) [2007 5m Apr 14] half-sister to several winners, including 7f (at 2 yrs) and 1½m winner King's Welcome (by Most Welcome) and 5f (at 2 yrs) to 7f winner

Boldly Goes (by Bold Arrangement), both useful: dam, 1m to 11f winner, half-sister to smart French middle-distance performer Sand Reef: last in minor event at Newcastle. *C. W. Fairhurst*

ON EVERY STREET 6 b.g. Singspiel (IRE) 133 – Nekhbet 74 (Artaius (USA) 129) **53**
[2007 53: f12g 16g 14g 14.1m⁵ 12m² p13.9g Nov 12] close-coupled gelding: modest performer nowadays: probably stays 1¾m: acts on fibresand and firm going: tried blinkered/tongue tied, often visored. *R. Bastiman*

ONE WAY TICKET 7 ch.h. Pursuit of Love 124 – Prima Cominna 86 (Unfuwain **77**
(USA) 131) [2007 88, a64: 5.3m³ 5m p5.1g² 5.3f³ 5f² 6f³ 5m 5g 5.7f 5.1m⁵ p6g³ p6g **a60**
p5m³ p5g Nov 21] lengthy, workmanlike horse: fair handicapper on turf, modest on all-weather: stays 6f: acts on polytrack, firm and soft going: wears cheekpieces/blinkers: carries head high: usually makes running. *J. M. Bradley*

ONE WHITE SOCK 3 b.f. Compton Admiral 121 – Night Gypsy 74 (Mind Games **42**
121) [2007 49: p5.1g⁶ p5.1g⁵ 5.7f 7g Sep 24] neat filly: poor maiden: stays 6f: acts on polytrack and good to firm going: often visored/blinkered: none too genuine. *J. L. Spearing*

ON INSTINCT (IRE) 2 b.f. (Apr 20) Clodovil (IRE) 116 – Julius (IRE) 96 (Persian **67**
Bold 123) [2007 5m⁶ 5g³ 6m⁴ 7d⁶ 6v Nov 3] €32,000Y: third foal: half-sister to fairly useful 1m (at 2 yrs in Ireland) and 13f winner Heart of Svetlana (by Linamix): dam 1¼m/1½m winner: fair maiden: caught the eye when fourth at Newcastle: softer ground, well held in nurseries: will be suited by 1m+: acts on good to firm going. *B. Smart*

ONIZ TIPTOES (IRE) 6 ch.g. Russian Revival (USA) 125 – Edionda (USA) (Magical **70 d**
Strike (USA) 114) [2007 12g⁴ 14.1m⁶ 13m⁶ 12.1m Sep 11] close-coupled gelding: fair maiden: seemingly best effort on reappearance: stays 1½m: raced only on good going or firmer on turf: in headgear nowadays: winning hurdler/chaser. *J. S. Wainwright*

ONLY A GAME (IRE) 2 b.c. (Feb 14) Foxhound (USA) 103 – Compendium (Puis- **74**
sance 110) [2007 p5g* 6g* 6m² 5.5m p7g² p6d² Dec 28] strong colt: fair form: won sellers at Lingfield and Yarmouth in July: left E. O'Neill 7,000 gns, good second in nurseries at Lingfield and Wolverhampton: stays 7f: acts on polytrack and good to firm going. *Miss M. E. Rowland*

ONLY A GRAND 3 b.f. Cloudings (IRE) 112 – Magic Orb 81 (Primo Dominie 121) **63**
[2007 63: 7m 5d 5m 6g 6d 5.9f⁶ 6s 7d² p7.1g³ f8d* f8g² Dec 27] strong filly: modest performer: won handicap at Southwell in December: stays 1m: acts on fibresand, good to firm and good to soft going: usually blinkered. *R. Bastiman*

ONLY A SPLASH 3 b.g. Primo Valentino (IRE) 116 – Water Well 96 (Sadler's Wells **– §**
(USA) 132) [2007 53§: 5g 8d 6d Jul 23] sparely-made gelding: ungenuine maiden: no form in 2007. *D. W. Chapman*

ONLY HOPE 3 b.f. Marju (IRE) 127 – Sellette (IRE) 88 (Selkirk (USA) 129) [2007 65, **57**
a53: 7m 10m 8d p12g⁴ Dec 16] big, workmanlike filly: modest maiden: left P. McEntee after reappearance: stays 1½m: acts on polytrack, probably on good to soft ground: usually wears headgear: said to have been in season second start. *Miss Diana Weeden*

ONLY IF I LAUGH 6 ch.g. Piccolo 121 – Agony Aunt 81 (Formidable (USA) 125) **52**
[2007 64: p7g⁴ p7.1g p7.1g p7g 6f 6f p8.6g⁶ p7m⁶ f7d⁴ p8g p7g Dec 30] big, strong gelding: modest performer: stays 7.6f: acts on all-weather, firm and good to soft going: has worn headgear. *M. J. Attwater*

ONLY IN JEST 2 b.f. (Apr 8) Averti (IRE) 117 – Silver Purse 67 (Interrex (CAN)) **73**
[2007 p5g² p5.1g 5m* 5.1d⁴ 5.1s⁴ 5g 5.3f p5.1g 5.1m Oct 14] 3,000Y: smallish filly: sixth foal: closely related to winner in Turkey by Piccolo and half-sister to 2 other winners abroad: dam 2-y-o 5.7f winner: fair performer: won maiden at Leicester in May: best at 5f: acts on polytrack, soft and good to firm going: sometimes tongue tied: inconsistent. *W. G. M. Turner*

ON THE MAP 3 b.f. Agnes World (USA) 123 – Noor El Houdah (IRE) 61 (Fayruz 116) **63**
[2007 64: 8m p8g p7g* p7g⁵ 5.9f 6m³ 6g p7.1g Oct 22] modest performer: won handicap at Kempton in June, dictating: stays 7f: acts on polytrack and good to firm ground: often visored: sold 3,500 gns, joined J. Saville. *A. P. Jarvis*

ON THE TRAIL 10 ch.g. Catrail (USA) 123 – From The Rooftops (IRE) (Thatching **–**
131) [2007 39, a50: p6g f6g Apr 26] strong gelding: no form in 2007: has been blinkered/tongue tied, often wears cheekpieces. *D. W. Chapman*

ON WATCH 3 b.f. Josr Algarhoud (IRE) 118 – Sole Control (Jupiter Island 126) [2007 **55 d**
–: 9.9d 11.7g 12g 16.2f Aug 27] close-coupled filly: form only when seventh in maiden
at Salisbury on reappearance: visored (raced too freely) final start. *H. Candy*

ONYERGO (IRE) 5 b.g. Polish Precedent (USA) 131 – Trick (IRE) 76 (Shirley **64**
Heights 130) [2007 68: 16.1d³ᵈ May 15] sturdy gelding: fair handicapper: disqualified
after rider failed to weigh in on sole 5-y-o outing: effective at 1½m to 2m: acts on firm
and soft going: tried in cheekpieces/blinkers. *J. R. Weymes*

OPAL HAZE (USA) 3 gr. or ro.f. With Approval (CAN) – Summer Mist (USA) 75 **94**
(Miswaki (USA) 124) [2007 10.1d³ p12g* p12.2g* 13.1s⁴ 12s⁵ Oct 4] third foal: half-
sister to useful 9f/1¼m winner Climate Change (by Langfuhr): dam, US 8.5f winner,
closely related/half-sister to several at least useful winners, including dam of Poule
d'Essai des Pouliches winner Matiara: fairly useful performer: won maiden at Kempton
in July and handicap at Wolverhampton (beat Vallemeldee by ½ length) in September:
stays 13f: acts on polytrack and soft ground: folded tamely final outing: often makes
running: sold 80,000 gns, sent to USA. *J. H. M. Gosden*

OPAL NOIR 3 b.g. Lujain (USA) 119 – Wrong Bride (Reprimand 122) [2007 86: 6g⁴ **67**
6d 6m 7.2s 5v⁶ Oct 26] close-coupled gelding: just fair handicapper in 2007, leaving
J. Howard Johnson after second start: should stay 7f: acts on firm going, probably on soft:
tried in cheekpieces. *I. Semple*

OPAL WARRIOR 4 b.f. Orpen (USA) 116 – Indian Wardance (ITY) (Indian Ridge **–**
123) [2007 59: p8g p10g p8g Feb 4] modest performer at best: no form in 2007: visored
last 2 starts. *Jane Southcombe*

OPENIDE 6 b.g. Key of Luck (USA) 126 – Eyelet (IRE) (Satco (FR) 114) [2007 70: **59**
p16g⁵ p16g 18d⁵ Aug 16] sturdy, close-coupled gelding: maiden handicapper on Flat,
only modest in 2007: probably stays 17f: acts on good to firm going: fairly useful hurdler/
chaser. *B. W. Duke*

OPENING ACT 2 br. or gr.c. (Mar 3) Daylami (IRE) 138 – Bluebelle 80 (Generous **– p**
(IRE) 139) [2007 p8.6g⁶ Nov 24] fifth foal: dam, 1½m winner, half-sister to useful
German winner up to 11f (Preis der Diana) Centaine: 12/1 and very green, well held in
maiden at Wolverhampton: bred to need further than 1m: should improve. *P. F. I. Cole*

OPERA CAPE 4 b.g. Barathea (IRE) 127 – Optaria 83 (Song 132) [2007 –: 7d⁵ 8v⁴ 6d* **106**
6d Oct 20] close-coupled gelding: smart performer at 2 yrs when trained by S. Kirk:
lightly raced since: best effort in 2007 (useful form) when winning minor event at Hamilton in September by 2 lengths from Come Out Fighting: well held in Bentinck Stakes at
Newmarket final outing: should stay 1m: acts on good to firm and good to soft going:
tongue tied nowadays: often races freely: left Godolphin, then gelded. *Saeed bin Suroor*

OPERACHY 2 b.g. (Mar 14) Kyllachy 129 – Sea Music (Inchinor 119) [2007 6m 6m⁶ **65 p**
5.1d⁵ Oct 10] 32,000Y: rather leggy gelding: third foal: half-brother to 4-y-o Hi Dancer
and 3-y-o Power Ballad: dam unraced out of half-sister to smart performers up to 1½m
White Heart and Kind Regards: fair maiden: never-nearer fifth at Nottingham (gelded
after): should be suited by 7f/1m: open to further improvement. *B. R. Millman*

OPERA CROWN (IRE) 3 b.g. Grand Lodge (USA) 125 – Silly Goose (IRE) 77 **76 d**
(Sadler's Wells (USA) 132) [2007 84: 9.9m⁶ 10.2m 11.9m⁶ p13g 10s 10g p12.2g p12m
Oct 13] good-bodied gelding: fair handicapper: well below form after reappearance: stays
1¼m: acts on good to firm going: tried blinkered/tongue tied: sold 4,500 gns. *P. F. I. Cole*

OPERA MUSIC 3 b.g. Kirkwall 118 – Optaria 83 (Song 132) [2007 94: 8.1g⁴ 7d 8m **92**
7m 10m⁴ 10m⁴ 10m³ Oct 5] sturdy gelding: fairly useful handicapper: creditable efforts
last 3 starts: stays 1¼m: acts on soft and good to firm ground: sold 30,000 gns. *S. Kirk*

OPERA PRINCE 2 b.c. (May 11) Kyllachy 129 – Optaria 83 (Song 132) [2007 8m 6g **58**
Nov 2] smallish colt: modest maiden: better effort (2 months after debut) when seventh at
Newmarket, good speed: will prove best at 5f/6f. *S. Kirk*

OPERA WRITER (IRE) 4 b.g. Rossini (USA) 118 – Miss Flite (IRE) (Law Society **67**
(USA) 130) [2007 74: f12g3 f14g⁴ p12.2g f12g⁶ f12g p12.2g³ p12.2g³ p12.2d⁶ p13.9g²
Dec 31] strong, compact gelding: fair handicapper: stays 1¾m: acts on all-weather and
good to firm going: tried visored/in cheekpieces. *R. Hollinshead*

OPTICAL ILLUSION (USA) 3 b.g. Theatrical 128 – Paradise River (USA) (Irish **71 §**
River (FR) 131) [2007 69p: 8.5g⁶ p7g⁵ 7m 7.1s³ 9m⁵ 8m 6g 9.2s Sep 24] smallish
gelding: fair maiden: left E. Dunlop after fourth outing: subsequently lost way: gelded
after final start: stays 8.5f: acts on polytrack and soft going: suspect temperament (finds
little). *I. Semple*

OPTICAL SECLUSION (IRE) 4 b.g. Second Empire (IRE) 124 – Theda 61 **58**
(Mummy's Pet 125) [2007 61: p5.1g³ p5.1g⁵ p5g⁴ f5g 5m Sep 10] useful-looking gelding:
modest maiden: may prove best at 5f/6f: acts on polytrack, good to firm and good to soft
going: blinkered: tried tongue tied: none too genuine. *T. J. Etherington*

OPTIMISTIC ALFIE 7 b.g. Afzal 83 – Threads (Bedford (USA) 109) [2007 11.8m² **55**
p13.9g 14s p16g Oct 17] modest maiden, lightly raced: tried blinkered: signs of temperament. *B. G. Powell*

OPTIMUM (IRE) 5 b.g. King's Best (USA) 132 – Colour Dance (Rainbow Quest **–**
(USA) 134) [2007 69: f14g Feb 28] close-coupled gelding: fair handicapper at best: well
held sole 5-y-o start: stays 1¾m: acts on all-weather: visored final start at 4 yrs: races up
with pace. *J. T. Stimpson*

OPTIMUS (USA) 5 ch.g. Elnadim (USA) 128 – Ajfan (USA) 112 (Woodman (USA) **89**
126) [2007 86: 8.1g 11.6m⁵ 10m⁵ 10g 10.2s⁵ 10.3d⁴ 8.1m* 8.3m² 9g² 8.1m² 8.1g³ p10m*
p12g⁵ Nov 17] sturdy gelding: fairly useful performer: won claimer at Sandown in July
and handicap at Lingfield in November: effective at 1m to 1½m: acts on polytrack and
firm going: tried blinkered/tongue tied: usually held up: consistent. *B. G. Powell*

OPUS MAGNUS (IRE) 4 b.g. Mozart (IRE) 131 – Bold As Love (Lomond (USA) **–**
128) [2007 62: p8.6g p7g p9.5g Dec 3] modest in maidens at 3 yrs: little form in 2007.
P. J. Makin

ORACLE WEST (SAF) 6 b.g. Western Winter (USA) 116 – Noble Prophet (SAF) **122**
(Noble Ambition (USA)) [2007 116: 9g³ 12g² 12g² 10m⁶ 10d⁶ 9m² 12f⁵ Oct 21] good-
topped gelding: very smart performer: successful first 3 outings in 2006 at Nad Al Sheba,
notably in Dubai City of Gold: ran twice for J. Hammond in France later in year: rejoined
former trainer, in good form again at Nad Al Sheba early in 2007, excellent 1¼ lengths
second to Vengeance of Rain in Dubai Sheema Classic third start: below form next 3
outings in Queen Elizabeth II Cup at Sha Tin, Singapore Airlines International Cup at
Kranji and 5-runner minor event at Newbury (trip on short side when neck second to
Multidimensional): back to near best when 1¾ lengths fifth to Cloudy's Knight in Canadian International at Woodbine final start: suited by 1½m: acts on firm and good to soft
going. *M. F. de Kock, South Africa*

ORAMA'S GHOST 3 b.f. Golan (IRE) 129 – Orange Sunset (IRE) 99 (Roanoke **77 d**
(USA)) [2007 8.3m³ 10.9d³ 10m³ 11.7g p10g⁵ Aug 11] €40,000Y: second foal: dam, Irish
1¼m/1½m winner, later won in USA: fair maiden: should stay at least 1½m: tends to edge
left: found little final start. *Sir Michael Stoute*

ORANGE 3 ch.f. Giant's Causeway (USA) 132 – Shopping For Love (USA) (Not For **–**
Love (USA)) [2007 54p: 7m Aug 17] angular filly: behind in maidens 12 months apart.
W. J. Haggas

ORANGE PIP 2 ch.f. (Apr 27) Bold Edge 123 – Opopmil (IRE) 68 (Pips Pride 117) **70 p**
[2007 6m² Nov 10] tall, lengthy filly: fifth foal: sister to 4-y-o Don't Tell Sue and 6-y-o
Mission Man: dam, maiden, sister to very smart sprinter Pipalong: 8/1 and green (soon
off bridle), second to Incomparable in maiden at Doncaster: likely to prove best at 5f/6f:
will do better. *R. Hannon*

ORANGES AND LEMONS (FR) 4 b.f. Zafonic (USA) 130 – Tarte Aux Pommes **–**
(USA) (Local Talent (USA) 122) [2007 –: p6g Jan 8] angular, workmanlike filly: no form
since 2-y-o debut. *C. E. Brittain*

ORANGE SQUARE (IRE) 2 br.c. (May 26) King Charlemagne (USA) 120 – Unaria **68**
(Prince Tenderfoot (USA) 126) [2007 p7g p8m³ p5m² Dec 8] 15,000Y: half-brother to
several winners, including useful 5f/6f (including at 2 yrs and in US) winner Mujado
(by Mujadil): dam French maiden: fair maiden: raced only at Lingfield, best effort when
equal-third to Jaser: may prove best at 6f/7f. *R. Hannon*

ORANGE TOUCH (GER) 7 b.g. Lando (GER) 128 – Orange Bowl (General Assem- **–**
bly (USA)) [2007 104: p12g⁴ Feb 3] well-made gelding: one-time smart listed winner:
well held in handicap at Lingfied sole 7-y-o start: stays 1¾m: acts on soft and good to
firm going: sold 9,000 gns in July, joined Eric McNamara in Ireland. *Mrs A. J. Perrett*

ORANMORE CASTLE (IRE) 5 b.g. Giant's Causeway (USA) 132 – Twice The **85**
Ease 46 (Green Desert (USA) 127) [2007 87: 5g 5f* 5m 5g 5g 6g 5m 6m² 5m⁶ 6d Sep 26]
good-topped gelding: has a quick action: fairly useful handicapper: won at Thirsk in May:
left D. Nicholls after sixth start: effective at 5f/6f: acts on firm and soft going: sometimes
tongue tied: sometimes makes running: inconsistent. *R. A. Fahey*

ORBITAL ORCHID 2 b.f. (Feb 11) Mujahid (USA) 125 – Carati 86 (Selkirk (USA) – 129) [2007 p5.1g 5.7f p6g 8.1m Sep 13] fifth foal: half-sister to 4-y-o Sea Salt: dam 2-y-o 6f winner: little form. *W. S. Kittow*

ORCADIAN 6 b.g. Kirkwall 118 – Rosy Outlook (USA) 79 (Trempolino (USA) 135) – § [2007 115§: 14g May 18] well-made gelding: fluent mover: smart performer: fit from hurdling (had been showing useful form), well beaten in Yorkshire Cup at York sole Flat outing in 2007: stays 1¾m: acts on heavy and good to firm going (went in snatches and weakened tamely only outing on polytrack): usually makes running: temperamental and untrustworthy. *J. M. P. Eustace*

ORCHARD HOUSE (FR) 4 b.g. Medaaly 114 – Louisa May (IRE) (Royal Abjar – (USA) 121) [2007 45: f12g³ f14g* 14.1d 11.6d Jul 23] leggy, sparely-made gelding: **a59** modest performer: won handicap at Southwell in June, despite hanging left: stays 1¾m: acts on fibresand: usually blinkered: looked most unwilling final outing. *J. Jay*

ORCHARD SUPREME 4 ch.g. Titus Livius (FR) 115 – Bogus Penny (IRE) 80 (Pen- **95** nekamp (USA) 130) [2007 88, a109: p10g⁴ p8g⁴ p7f⁴ p8.6g* p10g p8g³ 8.1g p10g⁵ 8g* **a111** 8s⁵ p8g⁴ p8g⁴ p7g² p8m⁵ p8g² Dec 29] good-topped gelding: smart on all-weather, useful on turf: won handicaps at Wolverhampton (beat Bomber Command ½ length) in March and Ascot (by neck from River Tiber) in September: good second to Baharah in minor event at Kempton and Atlantic Story in handicap at Lingfield, both in December: stays easy 1¼m: acts on polytrack, soft and good to firm going: ran creditably only try in visor, blinkered thirteenth/fourteenth starts: effective held up or making running: has good turn of foot. *R. Hannon*

ORCHESTRATION (IRE) 6 ch.g. Stravinsky (USA) 133 – Mora (IRE) 100 (Second – Set (IRE) 127) [2007 46, a63: f6g⁴ f5g f6g p5.1g* p6g f5g⁶ p6g f5g p6g f6g² p5g⁶ **a56** p5.1g⁶ Dec 31] compact gelding: modest on all-weather, unraced on turf in 2007: left M. Attwater after reappearance: second run in 24 hrs, won at Wolverhampton in Feb- ruary: left K. J. Burke after eighth outing: best at 5f/6f: acts on all-weather and firm going: usually wears headgear. *S. Parr*

ORCHESTRATOR (IRE) 3 b.g. Docksider (USA) 124 – Summerhill (Habitat 134) **72** [2007 –p: 8g⁵ 7s² p7g p7.1g² p6m Sep 6] lengthy gelding: fair maiden: free-going sort, but stays easy 1m: best effort on good ground. *T. G. Mills*

ORCHESTRION 2 ch.f. (Mar 12) Piccolo 121 – Mindomica 63 (Dominion 123) [2007 **67 p** 6m³ Sep 10] eighth foal: closely related to fairly useful 2006 2-y-o 5f winner Dimboola (by Averti) and half-sister to 3 winners: dam, 7f winner (including at 2 yrs), half-sister to Fred Darling winner/Oaks fourth Sueboog, herself dam of very smart 1m/1¼m performer Best of The Bests: 12/1, third to Atabaas Pride in maiden at Newcastle: should progress. *G. A. Swinbank*

ORDINANCE (USA) 2 b.c. (Apr 10) Orientate (USA) 127 – Moody's Cat (IRE) 97 **88** (Alzao (USA) 117) [2007 6g⁴ p7g² 7m³ 7d⁶ 7m⁴ p8g* Sep 7] well-made colt: fairly useful form: in frame 4 times, including fourth to Relative Order in nursery at Ascot, prior to winning maiden at Kempton: stays 1m: acts on polytrack, good to firm and good to soft going: sent to Hong Kong, where renamed Master Gunner. *T. G. Mills*

ORDNANCE ROW 4 b.g. Mark of Esteem (IRE) 137 – Language of Love 63 (Rock **115** City 120) [2007 100: 7s 7g³ 8.5d³ 8.5g⁵ 8m³ 8d* 8.1g* 8d² 10m⁵ 9.9d² 9d⁵ Oct 19] close-coupled gelding: smart performer: progressed again in 2007, winning handicaps at Salisbury in June and Sandown (totescoop6 Stakes, by ½ length from Colorado Rapid) in

totescoop6 Stakes (Handicap), Sandown—a smart performance from Ordnance Row;
Colorado Rapid (cross-belts) finishes strongly for second in front of Unshakable (No.8),
Pride of Nation (No.3, right) and Mutanasab (striped cap)

July: good efforts when runner-up after, in Sovereign Stakes at Salisbury (beaten 1¼ lengths by Pride of Nation) and listed race at Goodwood (went down by 3 lengths to Kirklees): stays easy 1¼m: unraced on firm going, acts on any other turf: tough: sold 110,000 gns. *R. Hannon*

ORIENTAL GIFT (FR) 3 ch.g. Orientate (USA) 127 – Golden Queen (USA) (Gold Fever (USA) 119) [2007 8s 10.5m 8g⁶ 7f⁶ Sep 17] workmanlike gelding: no form in maidens. *J. R. Norton* —

ORIENTAL GIRL 2 b.f. (Jan 17) Dr Fong (USA) 128 – Zacchera 82 (Zamindar (USA) 116) [2007 p8g p7m p7g Nov 17] €17,000Y: tall filly: first foal: dam, 6f winner, half-sister to 3-y-o Sakhee's Secret: modest form in maidens. *J. A. Geake* **58**

ORIENTALIST ART 2 b.c. (Feb 23) Green Desert (USA) 127 – Pink Cristal 113 (Dilum (USA) 115) [2007 6m² May 26] 50,000Y: rangy colt: has plenty of scope: fourth foal: half-brother to smart 7f (at 2 yrs) to 1½m (US Grade 3) winner Always First (by Barathea) and fairly useful 1m winner Motaraqeb (by Grand Lodge): dam 7f/1m winner: 5/1, promising second to Luck Money in maiden at Newmarket, going on well at finish: suffered sore shins after: will stay 7f/1m: useful prospect, all being well. *P. W. Chapple-Hyam* **85 p**

ORIENTOR 9 b.h. Inchinor 119 – Orient 106 (Bay Express 132) [2007 114: 5m⁵ 5g 5v⁵ 5d³ 5d 5m⁴ 5.6m 6d 5d Sep 29] close-coupled horse: smart performer at best, winning 5 times during career: reportedly fractured a bone final 8-y-o outing: just useful handicapper in 2007, best effort when 1¼ lengths third to Fullandby at Ayr: winner at 7f, best at 5f/6f: probably acted on any going: usually got behind: to stand at Portbury Stud, near Bristol, fee £3,000, Oct 1st. *J. S. Goldie* **101**

ORKNEY (IRE) 2 b.g. (Apr 30) Trans Island 119 – Bitty Mary 49 (Be My Chief (USA) 122) [2007 8g p9.5g⁴ Nov 17] 20,000 2-y-o: good-bodied gelding: third foal: dam maiden (stayed 1¼m): fair maiden: fourth at Wolverhampton, going smoothly: stays 9.5f: should do better still. *Miss J. A. Camacho* **67 p**

ORONSAY 2 ch.f. (Mar 12) Elmaamul (USA) 125 – Glenfinlass (Lomond (USA) 128) [2007 6.1s 7d⁶ 5.1f p7g Sep 29] rather leggy filly: sister to useful 6f to 9f winner (including in Scandinavia) Blue Mountain: dam unraced close relation of high-class hurdler Pridwell and half-sister to smart 1½m performer Prize Giving: maiden: form (modest) only when sixth at Salisbury: will stay 1m. *B. R. Millman* **60 ?**

OROTUND 3 b.g. Orpen (USA) 116 – Soyalang (FR) (Alydeed (CAN) 120) [2007 –: f7g 5s⁵ 5d² 5v⁵ 5d³ 6v* 6m⁴ 6g 6g² 6m* 6f 6d⁶ Oct 16] lengthy gelding: modest performer: successful in maiden handicap at Ripon in July and seller in September: should stay beyond 6f: acts on heavy and good to firm going. *T. D. Easterby* **63**

ORPEN BID (IRE) 2 b.f. (Apr 30) Orpen (USA) 116 – Glorious Bid (IRE) (Horage 124) [2007 8s⁵ 7.2v⁶ Nov 3] half-sister to winner up to 11.5f in Italy by Turtle Island: dam ran once: modest maiden: probably stays 1m. *A. M. Crow* **55**

ORPEN FIRE (IRE) 2 b.f. (Apr 10) Orpen (USA) 116 – Feet of Flame (USA) 59 (Theatrical 128) [2007 p7.1g* p8.6g⁴ Nov 27] €11,000Y: third foal: dam maiden (stayed 1¼m): fair form: 33/1, won maiden at Wolverhampton in October: fourth to Hilbre Court in minor event there: stays 8.6f. *E. S. McMahon* **71**

ORPENINDEED (IRE) 4 b. or br.c. Orpen (USA) 116 – Indian Goddess (IRE) (Indian Ridge 123) [2007 6m² 8m* 8d⁵ 8m p7m⁴ p7m⁶ p6m³ p6g⁶ Dec 28] 4,500Y: tall colt: second foal: dam unraced half-sister to Deutsches Derby winner All My Dreams: useful performer: won minor event at Merano in July: left A. & G. Botti in Italy after fourth start: raced only in handicaps at Lingfield after, best efforts last 2 starts: stays 1m: acts on polytrack and good to firm ground: tongue tied last 3 outings. *M. Botti* **98**

ORPENLINA (IRE) 4 b.f. Orpen (USA) 116 – Westlife (IRE) 32 (Mind Games 121) [2007 57: 5g p5.1g p5.1g 5s Aug 11] lengthy filly: just poor form in 2007: best effort at 5f on soft ground. *Peter Grayson* **33**

ORPEN QUEST (IRE) 5 b.g. Orpen (USA) 116 – Pursuit of Truth (USA) 69 (Irish River (FR) 131) [2007 69: p10g 10.9m⁵ p9.5g p8.6g f8g 10m 10.2g⁴ 10.9d⁴ 12.6s p12.2g⁶ 10.2s* p10g p16.5g Aug 13] strong gelding: modest performer nowadays: won seller at Bath in July: stays 1½m: acts on all-weather, soft and good to firm going: often visored/in cheekpieces, effective without: said to have bled sixth start. *M. J. Attwater* **61**

ORPEN'S ART (IRE) 2 b.c. (Apr 22) Invincible Spirit (IRE) 121 – Bells of Ireland (UAE) (Machiavellian (USA) 123) [2007 5m⁶ 5m 6.1g 5m⁵ 5.3f 5g 6m⁴ p5.1g² 5g p6g f5d Dec 11] quite good-topped colt: modest maiden: best at 5f: acts on polytrack and firm going: tried blinkered. *N. A. Callaghan* **55 a60**

ORPEN'S ASTAIRE (IRE) 4 b.g. Orpen (USA) 116 – Rhythm And Style (USA) 53 – (Keen 116) [2007 61: 10g 9.1g 7.9g 8s Jun 21] strong gelding: maiden handicapper: well held in 2007. *Jedd O'Keeffe*

ORPEN WIDE (IRE) 5 b.g. Orpen (USA) 116 – Melba (IRE) 62 (Namaqualand 96 (USA)) [2007 89: p8.6g f8g⁴ f7g 7m² 7f f8g² 8g³ f8g⁴ 7d² 10g 7m² 6m⁵ 6g⁴ 9.8m 8.1g* 8m 8d⁴ 8.3d² Oct 29] strong, lengthy gelding: fairly useful hurdler: useful handicapper on Flat: better than ever when winning at Haydock (by 2 lengths from Flighty Fellow) in September: ran well last 2 starts: best efforts at 7f/1m: acts on all-weather and any turf going: tried tongue tied, usually blinkered/visored nowadays: tough. *M. C. Chapman*

ORPHAN BOY 2 b.g. (Mar 26) Tipsy Creek (USA) 115 – Miss Jingles 73 (Muhtarram – (USA) 125) [2007 f5g Dec 27] 18/1, always behind in seller at Southwell. *M. G. Quinlan*

ORPHAN (IRE) 5 b.g. Orpen (USA) 116 – Ballinlee (IRE) (Skyliner 117) [2007 79: – 5.9m 6f 8s Jul 9] big, good-topped gelding: fairly useful handicapper at best: well held in 2007, falling final outing (blinkered). *E. J. Alston*

ORPHINA (IRE) 4 b.f. Orpen (USA) 116 – Keralba (USA) (Sheikh Albadou 128) 57 [2007 61: p12g⁶ p9.5g 10.2f 10.2f⁴ 8.1m 12.1m⁵ 12g* 12g 11.9m Sep 25] neat filly: modest handicapper: won at Folkestone in August: stays easy 1½m: acts on polytrack, firm and soft going: tried in headgear: usually tongue tied (not final start): has looked no easy ride. *B. G. Powell*

ORPHIR (IRE) 4 b.g. Orpen (USA) 116 – Silver Moon (Environment Friend 128) – [2007 –: f11g p16g p16g f12g⁵ 14.1m 10d 11.8d⁶ Jul 19] close-coupled gelding: little solid form: tried in headgear. *Mrs N. Macauley*

ORPSIE BOY (IRE) 4 b.g. Orpen (USA) 116 – Nordicolini (IRE) 64 (Nordico (USA)) 103 [2007 94: p6g* 6g* 6m* 6m 7m 5.6m⁴ p6m⁵ p6g³ Dec 28] big, useful-looking gelding: useful handicapper: won at Lingfield in April, Salisbury in May and Ascot (beat Roman Maze 1¼ lengths) in July: creditable efforts last 3 starts, including when fourth to Fullandby in Portland at Doncaster and third to Ebraam at Lingfield: should stay 7f: acts on polytrack and firm ground: has been tongue tied/blinkered (not in 2007): said to have irregular heartbeat after poor effort fifth outing. *N. P. Littmoden*

ORTON PARK 2 ch.c. (Feb 19) Bahamian Bounty 116 – Whittle Woods Girl 80 69 (Emarati (USA) 74) [2007 5g⁴ Jun 18] lengthy colt: fourth in maiden at Windsor: dead. *Mrs P. Sly*

OSCAR IRELAND (IRE) 6 b. or br.g. Oscar (IRE) 122 – Distinctly Scarlet (IRE) 53 (Import 127) [2007 p12g³ p12.2g⁵ Jul 6] well beaten over jumps: better effort on Flat when third to Treetops Hotel in seller at Lingfield: stays 1½m. *R. M. Beckett*

OSCARSHALL (IRE) 3 ch.g. Halling (USA) 133 – Mafaatin (IRE) (Royal Academy 77 (USA) 130) [2007 63: 7m³ 7s* 7s⁴ 8.1g p7g 8m p12.2g⁴ Oct 27] sparely-made gelding: fair handicapper: won at Newmarket in May: below form after: should stay 1m: acts on soft going: sold 6,000 gns. *M. H. Tompkins*

OSCAR SNOWMAN 4 b.g. Selkirk (USA) 129 – Chilly Start (IRE) (Caerleon (USA) 90 132) [2007 62+: p8g⁴ p10g* p12g⁶ 10m² 8d Jun 28] angular gelding: fairly useful performer, lightly raced: won handicap at Lingfield in February: very good second to Night Cru in similar event at Windsor, despite hanging badly right: in cheekpieces, well below form final outing: worth another chance at 1½m: acts on polytrack and good to firm ground. *M. P. Tregoning*

OSCILLATOR 4 b.g. Pivotal 124 – Craigmill 85 (Slip Anchor 136) [2007 79: p9.5g² 79 May 1] strong gelding: fair performer, lightly raced: creditable effort in handicap only outing in 2007: should stay 1½m: acts on polytrack and soft going. *G. A. Butler*

OSIRIS WAY 5 ch.g. Indian Ridge 123 – Heady (Rousillon (USA) 133) [2007 45: p8.6g 91 p6g* 6g* 6d* 6.1s³ p5g² p5g³ p6g Nov 30] fairly useful handicapper, lightly raced: much improved to win at Lingfield in May and Goodwood and Newmarket (beat Barney McGrew by neck) in June: effective at 5f/6f: acts on polytrack and good to soft going: said to have finished lame final outing. *P. R. Chamings*

OSOLOMIO (IRE) 4 b.g. Singspiel (IRE) 133 – Inanna 105 (Persian Bold 123) [2007 92 70: 12.4m⁴ 12f* 13m³ 13.8m² 12m* 14.8m³ 13.8m* p13g⁵ 12g³ Sep 22] good-bodied a86 gelding: fairly useful handicapper: progressed in 2007, winning at Thirsk in April, Ripon (sweating) in June and Catterick in August: just respectable efforts last 2 starts: stays 14.8f: acts on polytrack and firm going: front runner: sold 45,000 gns, joined Jennie Candlish. *G. A. Swinbank*

OSTEOPATHIC REMEDY (IRE) 3 ch.g. Inchinor 119 – Dolce Vita (IRE) 85 (Ela- 90 Mana-Mou 132) [2007 86p: 6g 7g⁶ 7.1m 6d 8s² 6v⁵ 6.9f⁶ 8g² 8s³ 8.1s⁴ 7g 8v⁴ Nov 3] sparely-made gelding: fairly useful handicapper: mostly good efforts when in frame in 2007: needs further than 6f, and stays 1m: acts on soft going (below form on firmer than good). *M. Dods*

OSTFANNI (IRE) 7 b.m. Spectrum (IRE) 126 – Ostwahl (IRE) 97 (Waajib 121) [2007 **70** 72: 15.8m 16g* 16m Aug 4] compact mare: fairly useful handicapper on Flat: won at Musselburgh (amateurs, third course success) in June: stays 2m: acts on firm going. *M. Todhunter*

OSTINATA (IRE) 2 ch.f. (Feb 18) Spartacus (IRE) 107 – Poly Dancer (Suave Dancer **49** (USA) 136) [2007 6g 6g 5.7g⁵ p8g 8f p8.6g* Dec 3] €16,000Y: smallish filly: half-sister to several winners, including useful Italian 5f (at 2 yrs) to 8.5f winner Golden Sensation (by Turtle Island): dam no form: poor performer: won nursery at Wolverhampton: stays 8.6f: raced only on polytrack and good ground or firmer. *B. W. Duke*

OTAARED 2 b. or br.c. (Feb 6) Storm Cat (USA) – Society Lady (USA) 75 (Mr Pros- **79 p** pector (USA)) [2007 6g⁶ Aug 22] strong, angular colt: powerful galloper: brother to 3-y-o Laa Rayb and half-brother to several winners, including 1998 2-y-o 5f/6f winner Bint Allayl and 5f (at 2 yrs) and 7f (Jersey Stakes) winner Kheleyf (both smart, by Green Desert): dam, maiden: half-sister to smart US performer up to 8.5f Time Bandit out of champion Canadian filly La Voyageuse: 8/1, sixth to Moynahan in maiden at York, green and nearest finish: will improve and win races. *M. A. Jarvis*

OTAKI (IRE) 3 gr.f. King's Best (USA) 132 – On Call 103 (Alleged (USA) 138) [2007 **41 +** –p: p7.1g f8g p11g⁶ Dec 19] poor maiden: off 11 months before final start (shaped as if amiss). *Sir Mark Prescott*

OTRIAD (RUS) 4 b.g. Dotsero (USA) – Oshma (RUS) (Observation Post 121) [2007 **–** f8g Mar 28] Russian-bred gelding: maiden: runner-up 3 times at Moscow at 2/3 yrs: joined W. Hickst in Germany for last 3 starts in 2006, best placing when fourth at Hoppe- garten: well held in handicap at Southwell on only outing in 2007: probably stays 9f: sold 1,000 gns in July. *B. J. Curley*

OUR ACQUAINTANCE 2 ch.g. (Feb 17) Bahamian Bounty 116 – Lady of Limerick **70** (IRE) (Thatching 131) [2007 5s³ 5m⁴ 5g³ 6g² 6s p5.1m* 6d 5g Oct 8] lengthy gelding: fair performer: won maiden at Wolverhampton in September: stiff tasks in nurseries after (then gelded): should prove best at 5f/6f: acts on polytrack, soft and good to firm going. *W. R. Muir*

OUR ARCHIE 3 b.g. Kyllachy 129 – Oriel Girl 65 (Beveled (USA)) [2007 –: 7g p5.1g **49** 5.7f 5g 5.3d p5.1g f5d Dec 14] poor maiden: best form at 5f: usually visored/in cheekpieces. *M. J. Attwater*

OUR BLESSING (IRE) 3 b.g. Lujain (USA) 119 – Berenice (ITY) (Marouble 116) **84** [2007 78: p5g* p6g⁴ 6m p6g 5m⁴ 6.9f 6g³ 6m Sep 13] tall, close-coupled gelding: fairly useful handicapper: won at Kempton in January: ran well penultimate start: will prove best at 5f/6f: acts on polytrack, soft and good to firm ground: inconsistent. *A. P. Jarvis*

OUR CHAIRMAN (IRE) 2 b.c. (Feb 6) Okawango (USA) 115 – Lucky For Me **77** (USA) (King of Kings (IRE) 125) [2007 6g 6.1d² 7d p7g² 7g⁵ 5m* Dec 16] neat colt: fair performer: sold from R. Hannon 22,000 gns prior to winning minor event at Dos Hermanas in December: stays 7f: acts on polytrack, good to firm and good to soft going. *J. Calderon, Spain*

OUR CHOICE (IRE) 5 b.g. Indian Danehill (IRE) 124 – Spring Daffodil 97 (Pharly **–** (FR) 130) [2007 75: p16g Sep 7] tall, good-topped gelding: fair handicapper in 2006: well held only outing on Flat in 2007: stays 2m: acts on polytrack, firm and good to soft going. *C. J. Mann*

OUR DOLLY 2 b.f. (May 5) Lomitas 129 – Amidst 86 (Midyan (USA) 124) [2007 **42** p7.1g⁶ Nov 5] 2,500Y: eighth foal: half-sister to 3 winners, including fairly useful 7f winner Aploy (by Deploy) and 7f winner Atwirl (by Pivotal): dam 6f (at 2 yrs) and 1m winner: 66/1, sixth in maiden at Wolverhampton: will stay at least 1m. *S. Parr*

OUR FAYE 4 b.f. College Chapel 122 – Tamara 83 (Marju (IRE) 127) [2007 74: 7m* **103** 7s* 7s* 6m* 8d⁵ 7g⁵ 7m² 7d Sep 29] angular filly: useful performer: vastly improved in 2007, winning handicaps at Salisbury in June, Goodwood and Salisbury in July and Ascot (badly hampered start, beat Dark Missile by ¾ length) in August: further progress when head second to Medley in listed race at Doncaster penultimate outing: best at 7f: acts on polytrack, soft and good to firm going. *S. Kirk*

OUR FLOSSIE (IRE) 4 b.f. Midhish 109 – Buckalgo (IRE) (Buckskin (FR) 133) **–** [2007 8.5m f12g May 1] showed little in bumpers and sellers on Flat: blinkered final outing. *A. D. Brown*

OUR FUGITIVE (IRE) 5 gr.g. Titus Livius (FR) 115 – Mystical Jumbo (Mystiko **75** (USA) 124) [2007 85: 5f⁵ 5.1d 5m 5m2 5.1s* 5.1d 5s p5.1g⁵ 5s p5.1g³ p5.1g* Dec 3] leggy gelding: just fair handicapper in 2007, winning at Chepstow in July and Wolverhampton in December: effective at 5f/6f: acts on polytrack, soft and good to firm going: tried blinkered: races prominently: often carries head awkwardly: has joined C. Gordon. *A. W. Carroll*

OUR GEORGIA 4 b.f. Mind Games 121 – Our Krissie 65 (Kris 135) [2007 –: p5.1g⁴ **–** Feb 21] little form in maidens: said to have bled last 2 starts. *T. D. Barron*

OUR GLENARD 8 b.g. Royal Applause 124 – Loucoum (FR) 93 (Iron Duke (FR) 122) **– §** [2007 50§: p11g p12.2g Jan 21] smallish, sturdy gelding: untrustworthy performer: well held in 2007: tried tongue tied. *J. E. Long*

OUR HERBIE 3 b.g. Tobougg (IRE) 125 – Trevillari (USA) (Riverman (USA) 131) **68** [2007 83: 8.2m 8g 8.1g⁵ 8.3g⁶ p8g² 7.1g² 7g³ p8g p8g 10g⁴ p11g⁶ Oct 17] well-made gelding: just fair performer in 2007: stays 1m: acts on polytrack and good to soft ground: often visored, tried tongue tied: held up: has looked difficult ride: sold 4,500 gns. *J. W. Hills*

OUR JOAN 2 ch.f. (May 10) Starborough 126 – Aonach Mor (Anabaa (USA) 130) **–** [2007 6m⁵ p8g 6f Sep 27] 1,500Y: fourth foal: half-sister to 8.5f selling winner Mercari (by Bahamian Bounty): dam unraced: no form. *P. T. Midgley*

OUR KALLY 2 b.f. (Jan 19) Kyllachy 129 – Rendition 95 (Polish Precedent (USA) **56** 131) [2007 5d 5g⁶ 5.1d⁴ p6g p5.1g 5m Sep 13] 20,000F, 4,000Y: smallish filly: third foal: dam, 7f winner, half-sister to US Grade 1 9f winner Jovial: modest maiden: probably best at 5f. *M. D. I. Usher*

OUR KENNY 5 b.g. Overbury (IRE) 116 – Auntie Alice (Uncle Pokey 116) [2007 **–** 10.1m Apr 14] modest form over hurdles: well held in maiden at Newcastle on Flat debut. *C. W. Thornton*

OUR KES (IRE) 5 gr.m. Revoque (IRE) 122 – Gracious Gretclo 54 (Common Grounds **73** 118) [2007 –, a75: p10g p7g p7.1g⁵ p8.6g* p10g* f11g⁴ f8g⁴ p8g³ p8.6g⁵ 10.2g* 10.2f⁶ 7m 8g⁶ p8g² p7g 8d⁵ 10.2m³ p9.5g* p9.5g⁵ p7.1g⁴ p8.6g⁴ p9.5g² p9.5g⁵ Dec 26] strong, lengthy mare: fair handicapper: won at Wolverhampton in February, Lingfield in March, Bath in June and Wolverhampton in October: stays 1¼m: acts on all-weather/dirt and good to firm going: tried blinkered: tough and consistent. *P. Howling*

OUR LAMENT 2 ch.g. (Mar 27) Compton Place 125 – Glider (IRE) 65 (Silver Kite **53** (USA) 111) [2007 p6g 6m Sep 17] modest form (but no impact) in maidens: subsequently gelded. *G. C. Bravery*

OUR LITTLE SECRET (IRE) 5 ch.m. Rossini (USA) 118 – Sports Post Lady (IRE) **104** 72 (M Double M (USA)) [2007 76: 5m 5m⁶ 5m⁴ 5m* 5s⁴ 5.1d* 5g⁵ 5.1d* Jul 14] leggy mare: useful performer: vastly improved in 2007, winning handicaps at Catterick and Chester in June, and listed race at Chester (beat Fathom Five by ½ length) in July: front runner, best at 5f: acts on polytrack, firm and soft going: tried in cheekpieces: sold 30,000 gns, reportedly in foal to Mind Games. *A. Berry*

OUR MONOGRAM 11 b.g. Deploy 131 – Darling Splodge (Elegant Air 119) [2007 **–** 82: p16g 16m⁶ p16g 16f Jul 30] big, strong gelding: fairly useful handicapper in 2006: little impact at 11 yrs. *R. M. Beckett*

OURNINA 2 b.f. (Apr 28) Hunting Lion (IRE) 115 – Ella's Charm (Charmer 123) [2007 **–** 7s 7g Oct 19] smallish filly: first foal: dam unraced half-sister to useful winner up to 8.5f Stoppes Brow: last in maiden/claimer. *C. R. Wilson*

OUR PICCADILLY (IRE) 2 b.f. (Mar 9) Piccolo 121 – Dilys 84 (Efisio 120) [2007 **78 +** 6d² 6d² p6g* Sep 21] leggy filly: first foal: dam 2-y-o 6f winner: fair form: second in maidens at Leicester and Windsor prior to winning similar event at Wolverhampton: will be at least as effective at 5f as 6f. *W. S. Kittow*

OUR PUTRA 4 b.g. King's Best (USA) 132 – Prima Volta 80 (Primo Dominie 121) **–** [2007 89: 7g 7g Jun 2] fairly useful performer in 2006: well held at 4 yrs: often tongue tied at 3 yrs, when reportedly had irregular heartbeat once. *M. A. Jarvis*

OUR RUBY 3 b.f. Diktat 126 – Almost Amber (USA) 88 (Mt Livermore (USA)) [2007 **73** 77: 8.3m⁵ 8g 8d 8.3d³ 7.6f⁶ 6v³ 7d Oct 23] sturdy filly: fair handicapper: probably stays 8.3f: acts on good to soft ground: blinkered last 4 starts. *P. W. Chapple-Hyam*

OUR SION 7 b.g. Dreams End 93 – Millfields Lady 75 (Sayf El Arab (USA) 127) [2007 **–** 5.1s Jul 27] of no account. *G. C. H. Chung*

OURS (IRE) 4 b.g. Mark of Esteem (IRE) 137 – Ellebanna 69 (Tina's Pet 121) [2007 **65** 68: p7.1g p7.1g⁶ p7.1g 7m⁵ 6.9m 6.9f 8.5g² p8g* 10g⁶ p8.6g² p8.6g³ f8d² p8.6s³ Dec 21] strong, close-coupled gelding: fair performer: left J. Bethell after sixth start: won minor event at Kempton in October: stays 8.6f: acts on all-weather and firm going: effective in blinkers/cheekpieces or not. *John A. Harris*

OUR SUNNIE 2 b.g. (Mar 17) Averti (IRE) 117 – Barawin (FR) (Fijar Tango (FR) 127) **65 §** [2007 5m⁶ 6s² 6s 6d³ 5m² p6g Aug 1] 11,000Y: leggy gelding: fair maiden: placed 3 times: effective at 5f/6f: acts on soft and good to firm going: irresolute. *D. Nicholls*

OUR TALLULAH (IRE) 2 b.f. (May 25) Piccolo 121 – Savannah Belle 84 (Green **–** Desert (USA) 127) [2007 5.7f 6m 6.5d Sep 28] 15,000Y: good-topped filly: fourth foal: half-sister to 3 winners, including 3-y-o Salient and 4-y-o Dixieland Boy: dam, 2-y-o 5f winner, out of Ribblesdale winner Third Watch: well held in maidens/sales race. *C. G. Cox*

OUR TEDDY (IRE) 7 ch.g. Grand Lodge (USA) 125 – Lady Windley (Baillamont **82** (USA) 124) [2007 91: p11g 11.7f 13.8m³ May 26] sturdy, lengthy gelding: fairly useful handicapper: stays 1½m: acts on polytrack, best turf form on good ground or firmer: tried in headgear. *P. A. Blockley*

OUR TOY SOLDIER 3 b.g. Forzando 122 – The Wild Widow 84 (Saddlers' Hall **– §** (IRE) 126) [2007 62§: 7s 6.1m Jun 6] strong, compact gelding: temperamental maiden: well held in 2007: blinkered final start. *B. Smart*

OUT AFTER DARK 6 b.g. Cadeaux Genereux 131 – Midnight Shift (IRE) 73 (Night **106 §** Shift (USA)) [2007 110: 6m 6g³ 6d 5d⁵ 5m 6m 5m 6d 6g Oct 26] strong, useful-looking gelding: has a quick action: just useful handicapper at best in 2007, third to Ripples Maid at Newbury in May: well below form last 5 starts: needs good test at 5f nowadays, and stays 6.5f: acts on firm and soft going: tried in blinkers, wears cheekpieces: ungenuine. *C. G. Cox*

OUTER HEBRIDES 6 b.g. Efisio 120 – Reuval 102 (Sharpen Up 127) [2007 76, a90: **79** 7g⁵ 6s⁵ 6m 5.7d³ 6g⁵ 5.7g 6g 6m 7d⁶ 8.1m³ 7g* 7.6m 8g 7g 8m Oct 14] sturdy gelding: has a round action: fair handicapper: made all at Salisbury (apprentices) in August: effective at 5.7f to 1m: acts on all-weather, firm and soft going: often wears headgear: effective tongue tied or not. *J. M. Bradley*

OUT FOR A STROLL 8 b.g. Zamindar (USA) 116 – The Jotter 99 (Night Shift **67** (USA)) [2007 71: p7.1g⁶ p7g p8.6g⁴ 7g 8.3m p8g* 7s⁵ 8g⁵ p8g 8f⁶ 7m⁵ 7m* 8.1f Aug 27] sturdy, deep-girthed gelding: fair handicapper: won at Kempton in June and Yarmouth in August: best at 7f/1m: acts on polytrack, firm and good to soft going: sometimes slowly away. *S. C. Williams*

OUTLOOK 4 ch.g. Observatory (USA) 131 – Area Girl 76 (Jareer (USA) 115) [2007 **–** 82: a8.8g a11g 8g a11g p7.1g Dec 15] close-coupled gelding: fairly useful performer in 2006: well held in Spain for J. L. Eyre (sold 1,500 gns in October) and on British return final start: often blinkered in Britain. *P. T. Midgley*

OUT OF COURT 3 b.g. Hernando (FR) 127 – Shot At Love (IRE) 79 (Last Tycoon **77** 131) [2007 8.3m p12g³ 9.9m Sep 4] rather leggy gelding: fair form in maidens: best effort when 1½ lengths third to Longspur at Kempton: every chance when breaking down badly 1f out at Goodwood next time: may prove best at 1¼m. *C. A. Cyzer*

OUT OF TOWN 3 ch.g. Namid 128 – Superstore (USA) (Blushing Groom (FR) 131) **–** [2007 –: 10f 7g Sep 24] last on all 3 outings, including in sellers in 2007: withdrawn after playing up at start on intended reappearance. *R. C. Guest*

OUTSIDE EDGE (IRE) 2 b.g. (Feb 10) Danetime (IRE) 121 – Naraina (IRE) (Desert **78** Story (IRE) 115) [2007 5.1g⁶ 5m⁵ 6g* May 25] 30,000Y: first foal: dam unraced half-sister to very smart performer up to 1½m Narwala: fair form: much improved to win maiden at Goodwood (quickened well) in May: not seen out again (gelded): not certain to stay much beyond 6f. *W. R. Swinburn*

OVERBAY 3 b.f. Overbury (IRE) 116 – On The Bay (Carlton (GER) 116) [2007 10d **–** Oct 18] small filly: second foal: dam second in bumper: 125/1, well-held last in maiden at Nottingham (unruly at start). *E. J. Alston*

OVERFIELDS 7 b.g. Overbury (IRE) 116 – Honey Day (Lucky Wednesday 124) **–** [2007 p12.2g f14g⁶ Mar 6] well held both outings on Flat. *G. J. Smith*

OVER ICE 4 b.f. Mister Baileys 123 – Oublier L'Ennui (FR) 79 (Bellman (FR) 123) **67 d** [2007 70: 10.2d⁵ 10.2g 11.5m⁶ p9.5g Sep 13] close-coupled filly: fair maiden: below form after reappearance: stays 1¼m: acts on good to firm and good to soft going: wore cheekpieces final outing. *Karen George*

OVERRULE (USA) 3 b.g. Diesis 133 – Her Own Way (USA) 87 (Danzig (USA)) **93**
[2007 –p: 10m* 10m⁵ 10m⁶ 10.3g Sep 29] strong, lengthy gelding: fairly useful performer: won maiden at Windsor in April: creditable efforts in handicaps last 2 starts: stays 1¼m, likely to prove at least as effective back at shorter: raced only on good/good to firm going: sold 48,000 gns, then gelded. *J. Noseda*

OVERSIGHTED (GER) 6 b.g. Selkirk (USA) 129 – Obvious Appeal (IRE) 82 (Danehill (USA) 126) [2007 82: p6g Nov 22] fairly useful winner at best: raced freely when well held in handicap at Wolverhampton only outing at 6 yrs: probably stays 9.5f: acts on any ground: often blinkered. *Mrs Y. Dunleavy, Ireland*

OVERSTAYED (IRE) 4 ch.g. Titus Livius (FR) 115 – Look Nonchalant (IRE) 61 **86 d** (Fayruz 116) [2007 91: 5.1m 5g 5v 5g 5m 5m p5.1g p5.1s Dec 20] strong, close-coupled gelding: fairly useful handicapper at best: well below form after reappearance, leaving I. Semple after sixth start: best form at 5f: acts on heavy and good to firm going: tried in cheekpieces/blinkers: has looked unwilling. *M. Mullineaux*

OVER TO YOU BERT 8 b.g. Overbury (IRE) 116 – Silvers Era 72 (Balidar 133) **58** [2007 –: p8g* p8.6g² p8g² p9.5g² p8g⁴ p6g² p7.1g* p8g⁶ 8f² 6g 7m² p7g 8g p8.6g² p7g⁶ Jul 18] modest performer: won minor event at Kempton (awarded race) in January and handicap at Wolverhampton in March: effective at 6f to easy 9.5f: acts on all-weather, soft and good to firm going: tried in cheekpieces/visor at 4 yrs. *R. J. Hodges*

OVERWING (IRE) 4 b.f. Fasliyev (USA) 120 – Sierva (GER) (Darshaan 133) [2007 **78** 84: p5.1g² p6g⁶ 5.2g⁶ 5m 5d⁵ 5.2m 6m³ 6m³ 5s³ 5g p6g 5m⁴ 6d² 5.1s p6g p6g Nov 27] leggy filly: just fair handicapper at 4 yrs: effective at 5f/6f: acts on polytrack, firm and good to soft going: often makes running: has been slowly away. *R. M. H. Cowell*

OVTHENIGHT (IRE) 2 b.c. (Feb 19) Noverre (USA) 125 – Night Beauty 80 (King **65** of Kings (IRE) 125) [2007 7.1g 7s⁶ 8.1d p8g 10m⁴ p10g Oct 24] good-topped colt: fair maiden: stays 1¼m: acts on good to firm and good to soft going. *Mrs P. Sly*

OWED 5 b.g. Lujain (USA) 119 – Nightingale (Night Shift (USA)) [2007 –, a81d: f6g* **–** f7g² f7g³ 6g f7g² f6g* f6g⁴ f6g May 24] good-topped gelding: fairly useful performer on **a82** all-weather: successful at Southwell in seller in January and handicap in May: effective at 6f/7f (seemingly not 1m): acts on all-weather, lightly raced and no form on turf: usually tongue tied: visored/in cheekpieces last 4 starts: races up with pace: sometimes hangs left/flashes tail. *R. Bastiman*

OWN BOSS (USA) 3 b.c. Seeking The Gold (USA) – Ameerat 116 (Mark of Esteem **89** (IRE) 137) [2007 8.3s 8g² 7m³ 7.1m³ 7.1m* Aug 27] sturdy, attractive colt: has a quick action: first foal: dam 7f (at 2 yrs) and 1m (1000 Guineas) winner: fairly useful performer: best effort when winning maiden at Warwick in August by 5 lengths from Hazytoo: stays 1m: acts on good to firm going: joined D. Selvaratnam in UAE. *M. A. Jarvis*

OWN GIFT 3 b.f. Rahy (USA) 115 – Zahrat Dubai 114 (Unfuwain (USA) 131) [2007 **–** 8.2g 7m 7g Sep 22] 4,000 2-y-o: small filly: fourth foal: half-sister to 2005 2-y-o 1m winner Shariki (by Spectrum): dam 1¼m (Musidora/Nassau Stakes) winner: well held in maidens. *S. Parr*

OXBRIDGE 2 ch.c. (Mar 10) Tomba 119 – Royal Passion 78 (Ahonoora 122) [2007 7g **62** 7.1g⁶ 8.3m⁴ 8d Oct 23] sturdy, lengthy colt: modest maiden: free-going sort, should prove best up to 1m: acts on good to firm going: sold 7,200 gns. *B. J. Meehan*

OYSTERMOUTH 3 b.f. Averti (IRE) 117 – Alessia 91 (Caerleon (USA) 132) [2007 **74** 5.1m² p6g⁵ 5.7f* Sep 10] tall filly: sixth foal: sister to Avonbridge and half-sister to 9-y-o Patavellian, both very smart sprinters (Prix de l' Abbaye winners): dam, 2-y-o 7f winner (stayed 1¼m), sister to Park Hill winner Casey: easily best effort in maidens when winning at Bath in September by ¾ length from O Fourlunda, travelling smoothly and leading over 1f out: would have proved best at 5f/6f: acted on firm going: withdrawn after unseating and injuring jockey prior to intended third outing: stud. *R. Charlton*

P

PAB SPECIAL (IRE) 4 b.g. City On A Hill (USA) 114 – Tinos Island (IRE) (Alzao **80** (USA) 117) [2007 78: p8.6g² p10g⁵ p8.6g⁵ 8f² 8.1g³ 10.5m⁴ 8m p8.6g⁵ p8.6g² p8g f8g⁶ p7g⁶ Dec 28] good-topped gelding: fairly useful handicapper: creditable efforts when placed in 2007: stays 8.6f, possibly not 1¼m: acts on polytrack, firm and soft going: tried visored/in cheekpieces. *K. R. Burke*

PACEMAN (USA) 3 b.c. Diesis 133 – Innes (USA) (A P Indy (USA) 131) [2007 82: **92**
10g⁵ 9m³ 8.3s* 8m⁵ 8.1s Sep 28] lengthy colt: fairly useful performer: won handicap at
Windsor in June: stayed 9f: acted on soft and good to firm going: dead. *R. Hannon*

PACHELLO (IRE) 5 b.g. Priolo (USA) 127 – Most Charming (FR) (Darshaan 133) **–**
[2007 79: 6m 7.1m 6.1g 8.3d 8.1f Aug 27] good-topped gelding: fair at best in Britain: no
form in 2007: tried tongue tied/in cheekpieces/visored. *J. M. Bradley*

PACIFIC PRIDE 4 b.g. Compton Place 125 – Only Yours 113 (Aragon 118) [2007 **96 d**
105: 5g 6g 6s 5g 6g 6g 6d Sep 21] big, strong gelding: useful handicapper: below form
after reappearance: best at 6f: acts on good to firm and good to soft going: tried blinkered/
visored. *J. J. Quinn*

PACIFISM (UAE) 2 ch.g. (Mar 31) Halling (USA) 133 – African Peace (USA) (Rob- **63 p**
erto (USA) 131) [2007 8.3g 7g Nov 2] rangy gelding: has scope: brother to smart 1¼m/
1½m winner Mkuzi and useful 9f/1¼m winner Swiss Cottage, and half-brother to several
winners, including smart French 6f (at 2 yrs) to 10.5f winner Alliteration: dam, French
1½m winner, out of very smart French performer up to 13.5f Galla Placidia: mid-field in
maidens at Leicester (shaped well) and Newmarket: will be suited by 1¼m/1½m: type to
thrive at 3 yrs. *M. A. Jarvis*

PACKERS HILL (IRE) 3 b.g. Mull of Kintyre (USA) 114 – Head For The Stars (IRE) **77**
(Head For Heights 125) [2007 70: 8m* 10m 7.5s Jul 17] good-topped gelding: fair
performer: won handicap at Newcastle (carried head awkwardly) in May: stays 8.5f: acts
on good to firm ground: reportedly finished lame second outing: gelded after final start.
G. A. Swinbank

PACO BOY (IRE) 2 b.c. (Mar 24) Desert Style (IRE) 121 – Tappen Zee (Sandhurst **98 p**
Prince 128) [2007 p6g³ 6m* 6g* Nov 2] €18,000F, €21,000Y, resold €16,000Y, 30,000
2-y-o: compact colt: brother to fairly useful Irish 7f winner Zacholiv and 6-y-o Fuel Cell,
and half-brother to 2 winners, including useful 7f/1m winner Mawingo (by Taufan): dam,
Irish 7f winner, half-sister to smart 7f (at 2 yrs) to 1¼m winner Cape Town (by Desert
Style): useful form: progressed well, won maiden at Newbury in September and minor
event at Newmarket (beat 3-y-o Wid by ¾ length) in November: will stay 1m: should go
on improving. *R. Hannon*

PACTOLOS WAY 4 b.g. Docksider (USA) 124 – Arietta's Way (IRE) 71 (Darshaan **73**
133) [2007 75: p9.5g 10d 11.6m⁵ p10g⁴ 10m⁵ p11g² 9.9g⁵ p8g² p8.6g Oct 20] close-
coupled gelding: fair handicapper: stays 11.6f: acts on polytrack, soft and good to firm
going. *P. R. Chamings*

PADDY JACK 2 ch.g. (Mar 19) Rambling Bear 115 – Bayrami 39 (Emarati (USA) 74) **71**
[2007 6g³ 6m6 6f³ 5g³ p5.1g 5m² 5d² Oct 9] close-coupled, workmanlike gelding: fair
maiden: placed 5 times: should prove best at 5f: acts on firm and good to soft going: front
runner. *J. R. Weymes*

PADDYMCTUME 5 b.m. Overbury (IRE) 116 – Esterelle (USA) § (Trempolino **–**
(USA) 135) [2007 p10g p12.2g Mar 2] first foal: dam temperamental maiden: well held
both starts on Flat. *H. J. Manners*

PADDY MOON 4 b.g. Lujain (USA) 119 – Tara Moon (Pivotal 124) [2007 44: f8s f8g **–**
Feb 15] tall gelding: maiden: no form in 2007. *J. G. Given*

PADDY RIELLY (IRE) 2 b.g. (Mar 11) Catcher In The Rye (IRE) 115 – The Veil **55**
(IRE) (Barathea (IRE) 127) [2007 f5g 7s⁵ 8.1f Aug 27] modest maiden: should stay 1m.
P. D. Evans

PADDY'S ISLE (IRE) 4 b.g. Trans Island 119 – Remember Mulvilla (Ballad Rock **–**
122) [2007 7g 7d 6s p9.5g Nov 12] sturdy gelding: little sign of ability, leaving Patrick
Allen in third at third start. *A. J. McCabe*

PADDYWACK (IRE) 10 b.g. Bigstone (IRE) 126 – Millie's Return (IRE) 71 (Ballad **69**
Rock 122) [2007 71: p6g 6g 5.1m 5g* 7.5m 5m 5m² 5g 5v 5s⁶ 5s⁵ 5g 5f⁴ 5d² 5m⁶ p6g **a62**
p5.1m⁶ 5m 6s⁵ 5.1s p7.1g p6d⁴ f7d Dec 18] small gelding: fair handicapper on turf,
modest on all-weather: won at Ripon (apprentices) in April and Redcar in September:
effective at 5f/6f: acts on all-weather and any turf going: tried in cheekpieces/visor,
usually blinkered: often slowly away and held up. *D. W. Chapman*

PADLOCKED (IRE) 3 b.c. Key of Luck (USA) 126 – Accelerating (USA) 76 (Lear **98**
Fan (USA) 130) [2007 p8g² 9m* 9.9m⁵ 8g* 8.1m² 10d Sep 28] 62,000F, €75,000Y:
deep-girthed, useful-looking colt: second foal: dam 1¼y-o 7f winner, half-sister to
useful French performer up to 1m Primrose Place, out of very smart French/US 1m/9f
performer Fitzwilliam Place: useful performer: won maiden at Kempton and handicap at

Lingfield, both in May, and having left J. Noseda, handicap at Salisbury (hung left) in August: good length second to Amarna in handicap at Sandown penultimate start: best form at 1m: acts on polytrack and good to firm ground. *D. M. Simcock*

PADRAO LIMA (BRZ) 4 ch.g. Exile King (USA) – Karakatu (BRZ) (Minstrel Glory (USA)) [2007 a6f 6.5g 7m 6m a5f⁵ a6f Dec 13] won 3 of his 4 starts in Uruguay in 2006, including Grade 3 event: best effort in 2007 (fairly useful form) when fifth in 5f minor event at Jebel Ali penultimate outing: little impact in handicaps in Britain for J. S. Moore third/fourth starts: probably stays 1m: tongue tied in UAE. *A. Manuel, UAE*   **87**

PADRE NOSTRO (IRE) 8 ch.g. Grand Lodge (USA) 125 – Meglio Che Posso (IRE) 93 (Try My Best (USA) 130) [2007 65: f12g⁵ f12g⁴ f11g⁴ f11g f11g 12.1s³ 12.1s 12.6m Sep 15] sturdy gelding: modest performer: left J. Holt 6,000 gns after fifth start: stays 13f: acts on fibresand, firm and soft going: tried tongue tied. *M. Sheppard*   **53**

PAGAN BELIEF 3 b.g. Fraam 114 – Au Contraire § (Groom Dancer (USA) 128) [2007 8g 7g* 7g 7.1m p7g⁶ Oct 15] rangy gelding: fair performer: won maiden at Salisbury in June: should stay 1m: acts on polytrack. *J. A. R. Toller*   **75**

PAGAN CREST 4 ch.g. Indian Ridge 123 – Maria Theresa (Primo Dominie 121) [2007 79: 11m 10m 10d 10d p10m Nov 1] quite good-topped gelding: good walker: has a moderate, quick action: fair handicapper at 3 yrs: little form in 2007: tried blinkered/in cheekpieces. *Mrs A. J. Perrett*   **–**

PAGANO (IRE) 4 b.g. Night Shift (USA) – Frippet (IRE) 87 (Ela-Mana-Mou 132) [2007 79: 10.9m⁴ 11.4d² May 12] sturdy gelding: fairly useful handicapper: creditable efforts in frame both starts in 2007: stays easy 1¾m: acts on polytrack, soft and good to firm going: progressive form over hurdles, winner in December. *A. King*   **83**

PAGAN ROSE (IRE) 3 ch.f. Medicean 128 – Countess Sybil (IRE) 73 (Dr Devious (IRE) 127) [2007 8g 8.1m 11.8m³ p9.5g Oct 6] 26,000Y: leggy filly: third foal: half-sister to Italian winner by Mister Baileys: dam Irish 1¾m winner: well held in maidens/handicap. *J. A. R. Toller*   **–**

PAGAN RULES (IRE) 3 b.g. Desert Prince (IRE) 130 – Fernanda 95 (Be My Chief (USA) 122) [2007 64: 12g 11.9m² 11.6s⁴ 9.9s Jul 2] good-topped gelding: fair maiden handicapper: stays 1½m: acts on soft and good to firm going: blinkered at 3 yrs: sold 13,000 gns and joined J. Mackie, successful over hurdles in December. *Mrs A. J. Perrett*   **65**

PAGAN STARPRINCESS 3 b.f. Robertico 111 – Pagan Star (Carlitin 50) [2007 61p: 8g 9.8g 8.5g 12.1s⁶ 12s³ 16g 15.8s* Oct 9] tall filly: fair handicapper: won at Catterick in October: stays 15.8f: acts on soft and good to firm ground: in cheekpieces last 2 starts: won over hurdles in November. *G. M. Moore*   **66**

PAGAN SWORD 5 ch.g. Selkirk (USA) 129 – Vanessa Bell (IRE) (Lahib (USA) 129) [2007 95: p10g³ p10g⁴ 10.1g 10m² 10.5m 9.7m⁶ 9m² 10m² p11g⁵ 10m⁵ 10m 10m p10g³ Oct 24] tall, well-made gelding: fairly useful handicapper nowadays: should stay 1½m: acts on polytrack, firm and good to soft going: often visored/in cheekpieces: sometimes slowly away, markedly so fifth start: tricky ride: sold 40,000 gns, joined D. Bridgwater, modest form over hurdles. *Mrs A. J. Perrett*   **94**

PAIN IN THE NECK (IRE) 4 br.g. Orpen (USA) 116 – Ravishing (IRE) 88 (Bigstone (IRE) 126) [2007 61: p7g Jan 10] modest maiden at 3 yrs: visored, well held in handicap sole start in 2007. *M. J. Wallace*   **–**

PAINTED SKY 4 ch.g. Rainbow Quest (USA) 134 – Emplane (USA) 101 (Irish River **84** (FR) 131) [2007 12d p7.1d* Dec 6] fourth foal: half-brother to 5-y-o Early March and French 11f winner Coach Lane (by Barathea): dam, 1m winner, sister to smart 1¼m performer Boatman out of half-sister to Irish 1000 Guineas winner Al Bahathri, herself dam of Haafhd: fairly useful performer: sold from Mme C. Head-Maarek 18,000 gns after final start at 3 yrs: better effort in Britain when winning handicap at Wolverhampton in December: seemingly effective at 7f, stays 1½m: acts on polytrack and soft ground. *R. A. Fahey*

PAINT STRIPPER 2 b.g. (Mar 3) Prince Sabo 123 – Passing Fancy (Grand Lodge **62** (USA) 125) [2007 6s 6s 5m 7d⁶ 6s² 6v* Nov 3] modest performer: gradual progress, won nursery at Ayr final start: best efforts at 6f: acts on heavy going. *W. Storey*

PAINT THE TOWN RED 2 b.c. (Apr 25) Mujahid (USA) 125 – Onefortheditch **61** (USA) 79 (With Approval (CAN)) [2007 8.2d Oct 10] 50/1 and backward, eighth behind Tajaaweed in maiden at Nottingham. *H. J. Collingridge*

PAIRUMANI PRINCESS (IRE) 3 b.f. Pairumani Star (IRE) 110 – Persian Fantasy **72** 94 (Persian Bold 123) [2007 75p: p10g⁶ 11.6v³ 11.5m³ 12g⁴ 14.1d³ p13.9g⁶ Sep 13] close-coupled filly: fair handicapper: will be suited by 2m: acts on polytrack, heavy and good to firm ground: hung markedly right fourth start: possibly not straightforward. *E. A. L. Dunlop*

PAJADA 3 b.f. Bertolini (USA) 125 – Last Ambition (IRE) 29 (Cadeaux Genereux 131) **48** [2007 –: p7g p10g p7f p8g⁴ p8.6g⁴ 8f 8m 8.1d 6g p10g 8d⁴ 7d p8m p7g⁶ p7m p10m Dec 9] leggy filly: poor maiden: stays 8.6f: acts on polytrack: visored nowadays. *M. D. I. Usher*

PAKTOLOS (FR) 4 b.g. Dansili 127 – Pithara (GR) (Never So Bold 135) [2007 p9.5g² **95** p12g* p13g³ 12m 11.6s Jun 30] lengthy gelding: useful handicapper: trained in France by C. Laffon-Parias in 2006, successful at Longchamp: won at Lingfield (by 2 lengths from Jebel Ali) in March: ran as if amiss last 2 starts: stays 1½m: acts on polytrack, soft and good to firm going. *A. King*

PALAIS POLAIRE 5 ch.m. Polar Falcon (USA) 126 – Palace Street (USA) 103 **61 §** (Secreto (USA) 128) [2007 61: 8.1m p7g p7g² p8g⁵ p7g p7g² p7g⁶ p7m⁴ p7g⁵ Dec 30] rather leggy mare: modest maiden handicapper: stays 7f: acts on all-weather, good to firm and good to soft ground: tried in cheekpieces: temperamental. *J. A. Geake*

PALAMOUN 3 b.c. Mtoto 134 – Princess Minnie (Mistertopogigo (IRE) 118) [2007 **86** 86: p8g* 8f Sep 30] strong, close-coupled colt: fairly useful performer: won 4-runner maiden at Lingfield (by 3 lengths, eased) in March: sold 25,000 gns in July, well held in allowance race at Bay Meadows only subsequent start: travels strongly, will prove best up to 1m: raced only on polytrack and good or firm going: refused to enter stall on intended debut. *B. D. A. Cecil, USA*

PALANOVERRE (IRE) 3 ch.f. Noverre (USA) 125 – Palavera (FR) (Bikala 134) **72 d** [2007 64: 5s 8m³ 7.5m⁵ 10m⁵ 10d 10d p11g 10.2s⁴ 8.1m 12g⁶ 10.2m p8g⁵ Oct 4] €60,000Y: leggy filly: half-sister to several winners abroad, including useful French 6f (at 2 yrs) and 1m winner Palafairia (by Always Fair): dam, French 1m winner (including at 2 yrs), sister to Prix du Jockey Club winner Polytain: fair maiden handicapper: left Francis Ennis in Ireland after sixth outing: stays 1¼m: acts on heavy and good to firm ground: tried blinkered/in cheekpieces/tongue tied. *D. J. S. ffrench Davis*

PALM COURT 2 b.c. (May 6) Green Desert (USA) 127 – Amenixa (FR) 73 (Linamix **86** (FR) 127) [2007 6g 6m⁴ 6m³ p7.1g* 7m⁴ 7d 8f* 8g⁶ p8m² p8.6g⁶ Oct 18] good-topped, **a92** quite attractive colt: fairly useful performer: won nurseries at Wolverhampton in July and Bath in September: head second to Bronze Cannon in similar event at Kempton: stays 1m: acts on polytrack and firm going: not straightforward (tried blinkered): sold 40,000 gns, joined A. Al Raihe in UAE. *R. Charlton*

PALMERIN 2 b.c. (Apr 7) Oasis Dream 129 – Armorique (IRE) (Top Ville 129) [2007 **85** 7m 7d⁴ p8g* p7g⁴ 10d² Oct 9] 85,000F, £45,000 2-y-o: neat colt: has a quick action: half-brother to several winners, including fairly useful 7f winner Camaret (by Danehill): dam, French 1½m winner, half-sister to very smart French 1½m winner Modhish, out of Irish 1000 Guineas winner Arctique Royale: fairly useful form: won maiden at Kempton in August: subsequently in frame in minor events there and Leicester (second to Tomintoul Flyer): stays 1¼m: acts on polytrack and good to soft going. *R. Hannon*

PALMER'S GREEN 2 b.g. (Apr 16) Mujahid (USA) 125 – Moss (Alzao (USA) 117) **–** [2007 8g⁶ 7d p8g Nov 14] sturdy gelding: no form. *Mrs C. A. Dunnett*

PALMETTO POINT 3 ch.g. Bahamian Bounty 116 – Forum 86 (Lion Cavern (USA) **79** 117) [2007 –: f8g 7g³ 8.1d* 9m⁴ 7.9m³ 8f* p8g* 8m⁴ 8m³ Oct 14] strong gelding: fair handicapper: won at Warwick in June, and Bath and Lingfield (odds on) in August: further improvement when in frame after: stays 9f: acts on polytrack, firm and good to soft going: wears cheekpieces nowadays: has been slowly away: not straightforward. *H. Morrison*

PAMIR (IRE) 5 b.g. Namid 128 – Mijouter (IRE) (Coquelin (USA) 121) [2007 81: f5g **65** p5g⁶ p5m 5.3d p5g Oct 24] good-topped gelding: just fair handicapper nowadays: best at 5f/6f: acts on polytrack and heavy going: tried in cheekpieces, usually blinkered: sold 2,000 gns. *P. R. Chamings*

PAMPAS (USA) 2 ch.f. (May 7) Distant View (USA) 126 – Alvernia (USA) (Alydar **69** (USA)) [2007 p7g⁵ 7m⁶ p8m³ Nov 11] sister to 9f/1¼m winner Exterior and half-sister to 3 winners, including 1m to 11f winner Acrobatic (by Storm Boot) and 1m winner Verbose (by Storm Bird), all useful: dam, US 8.5f/9f winner, half-sister to dam of Poule d'Essai des Pouliches winner Matiara: fair form in maidens, off 4 months before third at Kempton, rallying: will stay 1¼m: sold 33,000 gns. *R. Charlton*

PANADIN (IRE) 5 b.g. Desert King (IRE) 129 – Strident Note 89 (The Minstrel (CAN) **–** 135) [2007 10m p12g Aug 28] little form: in cheekpieces last 3 outings. *Mrs L. C. Jewell*

PANAMAR BESAR (IRE) 2 b.g. (Feb 20) Bahri (USA) 125 – Paradise Blue (IRE) **–** 63 (Bluebird (USA) 125) [2007 7d Jun 23] 12/1, detached in maiden at Redcar (gelded after). *J. Howard Johnson*

PANDA POWER 3 b.f. Pursuit of Love 124 – Golden Panda 77 (Music Boy 124) [2007 **49** 8.3m 10d 8.3g 10.1m 10.1m⁶ Aug 15] sturdy filly: half-sister to 3 winners, including 1996 2-y-o 6f winner Pandiculation (by Statoblest): dam 8.2f winner: poor maiden: tried visored. *S. C. Williams*

PANGO'S LEGACY 3 ch.g. Bertolini (USA) 125 – Sans Egale (FR) (Lashkari 128) **71** [2007 71: 6d³ 7m 6d 6f Aug 6] stocky gelding: fair maiden: stayed 6f: acted on firm and good to soft going: reportedly struck into on second outing: dead. *H. Morrison*

PANSHIR (FR) 6 ch.g. Unfuwain (USA) 131 – Jalcamin (IRE) (Jalmood (USA) 126) **49** [2007 62: 7m p7.1g p11g 10.1d⁶ 8.1d⁵ 7s p8g 7d 8m Aug 8] tall, leggy gelding: modest handicapper at 5 yrs, only poor in 2007: stays 1m: acts on good to firm and good to soft going: tried tongue tied: often races freely: usually waited with: reportedly had breathing problem penultimate start. *Mrs C. A. Dunnett*

PANTHERII (USA) 2 ch.f. (Apr 6) Forest Wildcat (USA) 120 – Saraa Ree (USA) 102 **60** (Caro 133) [2007 5.2g⁴ 5.1m⁵ 7m 8f Sep 27] 80,000Y: strong filly: half-sister to several winners, notably high-class 6f (at 2 yrs in US) winner Sarafan (by Lear Fan): dam, 7f winner, out of sister to Irish River: modest maiden: should stay 1m. *P. F. I. Cole*

PANTOMIME PRINCE 4 b.g. Royal Applause 124 – Floppie (FR) (Law Society **49** (USA) 130) [2007 52: p8g⁵ p8g p8g Feb 4] poor maiden: stays 1m: acts on polytrack and good to firm going: tried in cheekpieces. *John Berry*

PAPAL BULL 4 b.c. Montjeu (IRE) 137 – Mialuna (Zafonic (USA) 130) [2007 **121 §** 120: 12m⁴ 10g⁵ 12m* 13.3d* 11m³ 2f Nov 25]
  Papal Bull is a particularly difficult ride, and, of the five jockeys who have ridden him, only Kieren Fallon and Ryan Moore have won on him. Fallon's four victories on Papal Bull came in 2005 and 2006 (when he won the Chester Vase and

Princess of Wales's wbx.com Stakes, Newmarket—although a law unto himself at times, Papal Bull (left) shows he's capable of very smart form at his best; Laverock (second left) and Shahin dead-heat for second, ahead of Lucarno

CGA Geoffrey Freer Stakes, Newbury—Papal Bull continues his resurgence under Ryan Moore, defeating Shahin (right) by further than at Newmarket

King Edward VII Stakes), and in his enforced absence Moore and Papal Bull struck up a successful partnership in the latest season. Moore will be following in Fallon's footsteps as the retained jockey at Freemason Lodge in 2008 and his prowess on Papal Bull probably played a part in his appointment. With Moore on the sidelines in the spring, Papal Bull made an inauspicious start to the season when running below form in the Jockey Club Stakes at Newmarket and Brigadier Gerard Stakes at Sandown in May, tending to run in snatches and looking disinclined to battle. Reunited with Moore in a strong renewal of the Princess of Wales's wbx.com Stakes at Newmarket in July, Papal Bull again highlighted his temperamental streak, labouring in rear six furlongs out and then appearing in two minds as Moore finally coaxed him into making headway, before then veering right across to the stand rail after he got to the front inside the final furlong. This idiosyncratic performance from Papal Bull still produced a career-best effort as he beat dead-heaters Laverock and Shahin by two and a half lengths. Papal Bull put up another very smart performance over a longer trip in the CGA Geoffrey Freer Stakes at Newbury next time, winning by four lengths from Shahin, seemingly suited by having longer to get going and keeping straighter as he again came from well back. Dropped back to a mile and three furlongs in the Arc Trial at the same course next time, Papal Bull's quirks were once again in evidence as he came home strongly to finish a close third to Halicarnassus. Although Papal Bull might have found a mile and a half on firm going an insufficient test in the Japan Cup on his final outing, he managed only seventh to Admire Moon. Papal Bull had run only once before in Group 1 company, when meeting trouble in running when tenth in Sir Percy's Derby, but he had no such excuses at Tokyo, never a threat after a slow start.

		Sadler's Wells	Northern Dancer
	Montjeu (IRE)	(b 1981)	Fairy Bridge
	(b 1996)	Floripedes	Top Ville
Papal Bull		(b 1985)	Toute City
(b.c. 2003)		Zafonic	Gone West
	Mialuna	(b 1990)	Zaizafon
	(b 1997)	Mamaluna	Roberto
		(ch 1986)	Kadesh

Papal Bull's dam Mialuna was sold for 255,000 guineas at the latest December Sales after changing hands for just 12,500 guineas three years earlier. Mialuna has a yearling by Allied Forces but failed to get in foal to Montjeu in 2007. That aside, there is nothing to add to the detailed description of the good-bodied Papal Bull's pedigree that can be found in *Racehorses of 2006*. Papal Bull tends to take time to warm to his task, and he also hangs and often looks moody during his races. While Papal Bull is something of a law unto himself and needs treating with caution, it may be that campaigning him at trips around a mile and three quarters, and possibly even two miles, could prove the making of him if he is given the chance. He acts on good to firm and good to soft going. *Sir Michael Stoute*

PAPARAAZI (IRE) 5 b.g. Victory Note (USA) 120 – Raazi 46 (My Generation 111) **68** [2007 79, a70: p9.5g² p8.6g³ f12g⁴ p10g³ 8.5m⁴ 10.1d 10.1f 12m* 12m p12g 12m⁴ 12m 12g Oct 20] lengthy gelding: fair performer: claimed from R. Fahey £8,000 after third outing: won claimer at Catterick in August: stays 1½m: acts on all-weather, firm and soft going: tried in headgear. *I. W. McInnes*

PAPA'S PRINCESS 3 b.f. Mujadil (USA) 119 – Desert Flower (Green Desert (USA) **61** 127) [2007 7.1g⁴ 6.9m 9.2g⁴ 8.5m⁵ 9g Oct 5] 18,000Y: third foal: half-sister to 1½m winner Fleetfoot Mac (by Fleetwood): dam unraced sister to smart 2-y-o sprinter Magic Ring: modest maiden: stays 9.2f: slowly away second outing. *J. S. Goldie*

PAPEETE (GER) 6 b.m. Alzao (USA) 117 – Prairie Vela (Persian Bold 123) [2007 72: – p16g p12g Sep 4] leggy, close-coupled mare: fair handicapper at best: little form in 2007: below form in blinkers. *Mrs N. Smith*

PAPER TALK (USA) 5 gr.h. Unbridled's Song (USA) 125 – Journalist (IRE) 102 **106** (Night Shift (USA)) [2007 104: 7.5g³ 7m Oct 6] tall, useful-looking horse: has a quick action: useful handicapper: good close third to Vortex at Nad Al Sheba on reappearance (only outing for I. Mohammed in UAE): off 6 months, ran poorly at Newmarket final outing, troublesome at stall and slowly away: stays 1m: acts on firm and good to soft going: joined A. Al Raihe in UAE. *Saeed bin Suroor*

PAPILLIO (IRE) 2 b.c. (Mar 6) Marju (IRE) 127 – Danish Gem (Danehill (USA) 126) **82** [2007 6g² 6m³ 6d Aug 25] €100,000Y: quite good-topped colt: second foal: half-brother to 3-y-o Ponty Rossa: dam, French 9f winner, out of unraced half-sister to smart 1¼m winner Dartney: fairly useful maiden: placed at Hamilton and Newmarket (third to Captain Brilliance): down the field in sales race at the Curragh: will stay 7f. *K. R. Burke*

PAPPAS IMAGE 3 b.g. Arkadian Hero (USA) 123 – Fair Attempt (IRE) (Try My Best **55** (USA) 130) [2007 54: p5g⁶ f6g³ f5g³ f5g⁵ f6g f5g f8g f6d⁴ Dec 21] modest maiden: stays 6f: raced only on all-weather: usually wears headgear. *A. J. McCabe*

PAPPAS RUBY (USA) 4 b.f. Red Ransom (USA) – Pappa Reale 104 (Indian Ridge **63** 123) [2007 52: f6g³ f7g f7g* p7.1g⁵ 6.1g⁵ 6s⁵ Jun 16] leggy, quite attractive filly: modest performer: won handicap at Southwell in May: best form at 6f/7f: acts on all-weather and heavy ground: tried in headgear. *R. M. Beckett*

PAPRADON 3 b.g. Tobougg (IRE) 125 – Salvezza (IRE) 97 (Superpower 113) [2007 –: **67** p10g³ p12g p10g⁴ p10m* p12m⁶ p13.9g² p13.9g³ p12g⁵ Nov 19] fair performer: won minor event at Kempton in October: stays 1¾m: raced only on polytrack since debut: visored last 5 starts. *J. R. Best*

PAPUAN PRINCE (IRE) 2 b.c. (Feb 25) Tagula (IRE) 116 – Pussie Willow (IRE) 77 – (Catrail (USA) 123) [2007 6m Aug 17] good-topped colt: 100/1, in rear in maiden at Newbury. *S. Kirk*

PARADISE DANCER (IRE) 3 b.f. Danehill Dancer (IRE) 117 – Pintada de Fresco **76** (FR) (Marignan (USA) 117) [2007 7.1d³ 7.1s⁵ 7m³ p8.6g² 8m³ p7g p10g² p10g³ p10g⁶ Dec 30] 58,000Y, resold 40,000Y: big, strong filly: second foal: dam useful French 1m (at 2 yrs) to 1¼m winner: fair maiden: left Pat Eddery after sixth outing: stays 1¼m: acts on polytrack and good to firm going, probably on good to soft. *J. A. R. Toller*

PARADISE EXPECTED 4 ch.f. North Briton 67 – Phenomenon (Unfuwain (USA) – 131) [2007 69: 9.9m Apr 26] tall, unfurnished filly: fair performer at 3 yrs: well held in handicap only start in 2007: should stay 1¼m: acts on polytrack. *C. Grant*

PARADISE ISLAND (IRE) 2 b.f. (Jan 21) Green Desert (USA) 127 – Meadow Pipit **76 p** (CAN) 113 (Meadowlake (USA)) [2007 7d⁴ Oct 9] tall, deep-girthed filly: sister to 5-y-o Desert Commander, closely related to fairly useful 2000 2-y-o 7f winner Paiyda (by Danehill) and half-sister to 2 winners by Key of Luck, including useful 7f (including at 2 yrs) winner Lucky Pipit: dam 7f to 1¼m winner: 12/1, encouraging fourth in maiden at Leicester, possibly needing run: will do better. *E. A. L. Dunlop*

PARADISE ISLE 6 b.m. Bahamian Bounty 116 – Merry Rous 66 (Rousillon (USA) **112** 133) [2007 112: 6g² 6g⁵ 6m³ 5m 6m⁶ 5.6m² 6d Oct 19] lengthy mare: smart performer: good efforts when placed in 2007, including in handicaps at Nad Al Sheba (beaten nose by Conceal) and Doncaster (Portland, head second to Fullandby, leading for much of final 1f) on first/sixth outings: below form in listed event at Newmarket final start: stays 6f:

acts on firm and good to soft going: tends to carry head high/swish tail: ridden up with pace nowadays: none too consistent: sold 130,000 gns. *C. F. Wall*

PARADISE WALK 3 b.f. Sakhee (USA) 136 – Enclave (USA) (Woodman (USA) 126) [2007 68: p7g³ 8.3d 10m 12m 9.9g* 9.9m* 12.1g⁴ Sep 19] good-bodied filly: fair performer: left R. Charlton 10,000 gns after third outing: won 2 handicaps at Beverley in August: stays 1½m: acts on good to firm ground. *E. W. Tuer* **76**

PARAGUAY (USA) 4 b.g. Pivotal 124 – Grisonnante (FR) (Kaldoun (FR) 122) [2007 86: p8g⁵ p8g⁶ 8m³ 7f⁵ 10m 8m 9.9g⁴ 9m 10f⁵ 9m 9g 7m 7.1d Sep 17] small, leggy gelding: fairly useful handicapper: below form after third start: stays 9f: acts on polytrack, firm and soft going: visored last 2 starts (well below form): held up: has pulled hard. *Miss V. Haigh* **80 d**

PARA SIEMPRE 3 b.f. Mujahid (USA) 125 – Miriam 59 (Forzando 122) [2007 81+: f6g* f6g* 6d⁵ 7m 8g⁵ 7d Oct 19] strong filly: useful performer: won 2 handicaps at Southwell in January: well held in similar event final outing: stays 1m: acts on fibresand, best turf effort on good going: blinkered. *B. Smart* **95**

PARBYBLOS (FR) 4 b.f. Milford Track (IRE) 110 – Biblos (FR) (Vorias (USA) 114) [2007 12g⁴ 12g² 12g* 11.6m 11.6d Jul 23] rather leggy filly: fifth foal: half-sister to French 1¼m winner Made In Love (by Video Rock): dam unraced: won non-thoroughbred event at Paray-Le-Monial in May: left J-P. Gallorini in France, well held in sellers in Britain: stays 1½m. *John Allen* **?**

PARCHMENT (IRE) 5 ch.g. Singspiel (IRE) 133 – Hannalou (FR) 70 (Shareef Dancer (USA) 135) [2007 66: 9.9m⁶ 12.1s⁵ 12.1g⁶ 15.8g³ 14.1m⁴ 12.1m* 14.1f 9.9d 13.8g 12g Oct 30] smallish gelding: fair handicapper: won ladies event at Beverley in September: effective at stiff 1½m to 2m: acts on firm going, probably on soft: often blinkered. *A. J. Lockwood* **65**

PAR EXCELLENCE 4 gr.f. Wizard King 122 – Great Intent (Aragon 118) [2007 55: p7g p6g p6g Mar 16] leggy filly: poor performer nowadays: effective at 5f/6f: acts on polytrack, good to firm and good to soft going: tried tongue tied: in cheekpieces last 2 starts. *W. G. M. Turner* **42**

PARIS BELL 5 gr.g. Paris House 123 – Warning Bell 88 (Bustino 136) [2007 86: 6g 6m 6m 6d* 6v 6g⁶ 6s² 6d⁶ 6d⁶ 6g 6m 5d⁶ 6v* Nov 3] leggy gelding: fairly useful handicapper: won at Warwick in June and Ayr in November: effective at 6f/7f: acts on any going: tends to race freely: often slowly away: none too consistent. *T. D. Easterby* **85**

PARIS HEIGHTS 5 gr.g. Paris House 123 – Petra Nova 51 (First Trump 118) [2007 60: p9.5g Jan 12] quite good-topped gelding: modest performer at 4 yrs: well held in claimer sole Flat start in 2007: tried visored/in cheekpieces. *Mrs A. M. Thorpe* **–**

PARISIAN DREAM 3 b.c. Sakhee (USA) 136 – Boojum 101 (Mujtahid (USA) 118) [2007 56p: 7g³ 7g* 8m² 8d* 10.3m 10.3g Sep 29] strong, deep-girthed colt: fairly useful performer: won maiden at Salisbury in June and handicap at Pontefract in August: tailed off in handicap at Chester final outing: best up to 1m: acts on good to firm and good to soft ground: possibly not straightforward: sold 35,000 gns. *B. W. Hills* **92**

PARISIAN GIFT (IRE) 2 b.g. (May 2) Statue of Liberty (USA) 115 – My Micheline (Lion Cavern (USA) 117) [2007 6d p7g* Dec 19] €60,000Y: fourth foal: half-brother to 3-y-o Sues Surprise and 5-y-o Kova Hall: dam unraced out of sister to dam of Zafonic: fair form: well backed, won maiden at Lingfield by neck, leading final 1f having taken time to settle: bred to stay 1m: open to further improvement. *Tom Dascombe* **76 p**

PARISIENNE GEM 2 b.f. (May 1) Rock City 120 – Miss Pigalle 55 (Good Times (ITY)) [2007 8s Oct 26] second foal: sister to 4-y-o City Miss: dam 7f winner: tailed off in maiden at Ayr. *Miss L. A. Perratt* **–**

PARK ROYAL (UAE) 2 b. or br.f. (Mar 19) Cape Cross (IRE) 129 – Shbakni (USA) (Mr Prospector (USA)) [2007 7g³ 6g 6m⁴ 7g p7g Nov 4] leggy, workmanlike filly: seventh foal: closely related to winner in Saudi Arabia by Green Desert: dam, French/UAE maiden (stayed 9f), out of Kentucky Derby winner Winning Colors: fair maiden: third at Goodwood on debut, but disappointing after: will stay 1m: seems temperamental. *M. Johnston* **74**

PARKSIDE PURSUIT 9 b.g. Pursuit of Love 124 – Ivory Bride 86 (Domynsky 110) [2007 77: 5g 5f⁶ p5g⁶ 5m 6g p6g p6m Nov 24] lengthy, dipped-backed gelding: modest performer at best nowadays: best at 5f/6f: acts on firm and good to soft going, probably on polytrack: held up: rider lost irons on reappearance. *J. M. Bradley* **53**

PARK'S PRODIGY 3 b.g. Desert Prince (IRE) 130 – Up And About 77 (Barathea **55**
(IRE) 127) [2007 f8g f8g 10m⁶ 11g⁴ 14.1m⁴ 12.1m³ p16.5g⁶ Dec 8] big, workmanlike
gelding: modest maiden: stays 16.5f: acts on polytrack and good to firm going: tongue
tied last 4 outings: won over hurdles in November. *P. C. Haslam*

PARK VALLEY PRINCE 3 ch.c. Noverre (USA) 125 – Santorini (USA) (Spinning **63**
World (USA) 130) [2007 7d 9.9m⁶ p8g p7g p7g³ p7m* p8m³ p7.1s⁴ Dec 20] close-
coupled colt: modest performer: won handicap at Lingfield in November: stays easy 1m:
acts on polytrack: said to have bled third start. *W. R. Muir*

PARKVIEW LOVE (USA) 6 b. or br.g. Mister Baileys 123 – Jerre Jo Glanville **71 §**
(USA) (Skywalker (USA)) [2007 70, a78: f8g² p8.6g⁵ p8.6g⁵ f6g³ f8g³ p7.1g² p8g* f7g⁵ **a80 §**
p8g* p8g³ 7g³ p8g² p8.6g⁵ p7.1g² 7g 6g 7m² p7.1g p7.1g* p7.1d f8d⁵ p6d³ Dec 28] leggy,
good-topped gelding: fairly useful handicapper on all-weather, firm and good to soft going:
won at Lingfield (2) in March and Wolverhampton in November: effective at 7f to 11f: acts on
all-weather, firm and good to soft going: usually wears headgear: finds little. *D. Shaw*

PARLIAMENTARY (JPN) 2 b.c. (Feb 21) Diktat 126 – Rebuff 107 (Kris 135) [2007 **71**
7d⁶ 7d³ 7m⁴ 8s 7g³ Oct 20] strong, compact colt: fair maiden: in frame 3 times: stays 7f:
acts on good to firm and good to soft going: sold 9,500 gns. *M. Johnston*

PARMA (IRE) 3 ch.f. Grand Lodge (USA) 125 – Braari (USA) 97 (Gulch (USA)) **–**
[2007 p9.5g p8g Apr 1] €140,000Y: half-sister to several winners, notably smart 2000
2-y-o 6f winner Shaard (by Anabaa): dam 2-y-o 6f winner: well held in maidens. *M. Botti*

PARNASSIAN 7 ch.g. Sabrehill (USA) 120 – Delphic Way 63 (Warning 136) [2007 80: **77**
10d⁴ 10g³ 10g 10.1d⁶ 10d⁴ 8d Oct 3] angular, sparely-made gelding: fair handicapper:
stays 1¼m: acts on any turf going, but goes particularly well on good or softer: visored
last 5 starts: has carried head awkwardly: usually waited with. *J. A. Geake*

PARSONAGEHOTELYORK (IRE) 3 b.f. Danehill (USA) 126 – Makarova (IRE) **62**
(Sadler's Wells (USA) 132) [2007 8d³ Jul 29] €60,000Y: third foal: dam unraced sister to
useful Irish performer up to 1¾m French Ballerina and half-sister to Fillies' Mile winner/
Irish Oaks runner-up Sunspangled: 5/1, 5 lengths third of 5 to Twilight Star in maiden at
Pontefract, racing freely and fading: suffered injury after: stud. *R. A. Fahey*

PARSON'S PUNCH 2 b.g. (Apr 25) Beat Hollow 126 – Ordained 66 (Mtoto 134) **69 p**
[2007 p8g³ Nov 19] 6,500Y, 20,000 2-y-o: fourth foal: dam 1¼m/1½m winner: 11/2, 3¼
lengths third to Last of The Line in maiden at Kempton, travelling well out wide long
way: bred to stay at least 1¼m: should improve. *P. D. Cundell*

PARTHENOPE 4 gr.f. Namid 128 – Twosixtythreewest (FR) 69 (Kris 135) [2007 43: **53**
p6g 7m p7g⁴ 8s 8m* p7g³ Sep 12] tall, leggy filly: modest handicapper: won apprentice
event at Brighton in August: stays 1m: acts on polytrack and good to firm ground: has
hung/started slowly. *J. A. Geake*

PARTNERS IN JAZZ (USA) 6 ro.g. Jambalaya Jazz (USA) 111 – Just About **106**
Enough (USA) (Danzig (USA)) [2007 109: f7g⁴ 7s⁴ 7.1g 7m³ 7d³ 6m⁶ 6d 7d 8d p7m
Nov 24] tall gelding: useful handicapper: reportedly suffered a splint after final 5-y-o
outing: creditable efforts in 2007 when in frame, including at Southwell (fourth to Wise
Dennis) and Newmarket (third to Giganticus) on first/fifth outings: below form last 5
starts: best at 6f (given test)/7f: acts on fibresand, soft and good to firm going: starts
slowly on occasions: held up: genuine. *T. D. Barron*

PARTY BOSS 5 gr.h. Silver Patriarch (IRE) 125 – Third Party 63 (Terimon 124) [2007 **113**
100: p6g⁶ p8g² p8g³ f7s* p8g* p10f⁴ p7.1g p7g p8g p7m Nov 24] tall, close-coupled
horse: smart performer: won handicap at Southwell (by short head from Waterside) and
minor event at Lingfield (back to best when beating Ceremonial Jade by length), both in
February: below form in listed races/handicaps after: effective at 7f/1m: acts on all-
weather, probably on firm ground: tried tongue tied: races up with pace. *C. E. Brittain*

PARTY IN THE PARK 2 b.g. (Jan 25) Royal Applause 124 – Halland Park Girl (IRE) **78**
106 (Primo Dominie 121) [2007 5.2m³ 5m² 5d³ 5m 6g 5m Sep 16] strong, good-topped
gelding: fair maiden: placed 3 times in spring: lost his way, blinkered final start (gelded
after): should prove best at 5f/6f. *R. Hannon*

PARTY (IRE) 3 ch.f. Cadeaux Genereux 131 – Forty Belles (USA) (Forty Niner **97**
(USA)) [2007 92: 10d² 12g 10d 12s Oct 13] strong, lengthy filly: useful performer: good
length second to Kaloura in listed race at Fontainebleau on reappearance: stiff tasks but
well below form after: stays 1¼m: acts on firm and soft going, probably on polytrack:
sold 160,000 gns. *R. Hannon*

Tattersalls Musidora Stakes, York—Passage of Time (centre) cements her place at the head of the Oaks market with a smooth success; Sweet Lilly (left) is second ahead of Sues Surprise

PARTY PALACE 3 b.f. Auction House (USA) 120 – Lady-Love 70 (Pursuit of Love **57** 124) [2007 54: p9.5g⁵ p8.6g⁴ p8g⁴ p10g³ 10f 10.2f⁵ p11g⁴ 10g p11g p12g⁶ p13.9g² p13.9g² Nov 14] small, sparely-made filly: modest performer: left J. Osborne after third start: stays 1¾m: acts on polytrack and firm going: tried in cheekpieces: has made running/raced freely. *H. S. Howe*

PARTY PLOY 9 b.g. Deploy 131 – Party Treat (IRE) 69 (Millfontaine 114) [2007 p12g **–** Jan 10] small gelding: poor mover: fair handicapper at best: little impact only start since 2005: tried in visor/cheekpieces. *K. R. Burke*

PASO DOBLE 9 b.g. Dancing Spree (USA) – Delta Tempo (IRE) (Bluebird (USA) **–** 125) [2007 46, a66: f8g² f8g* f8g f8g⁴ f8g* f8g p8g p8.6g f8g 8.5m Apr 18] smallish, **a67** strong gelding: fair on all-weather, little recent form on turf: won handicap in January and seller in February (sold from D. Ivory 4,500 gns), both at Southwell: effective at 1m to 11f: acts on all-weather and firm going: usually wears headgear: has looked none too keen. *R. Bastiman*

PASSAGE OF TIME 3 b.f. Dansili 127 – Clepsydra 78 (Sadler's Wells (USA) 132) **115** [2007 113p: 10.4g* 12d 12m³ 11s³ Oct 27] tall, useful-looking filly: smart performer: successful in Criterium de Saint-Cloud at 2 yrs: won Tattersalls Musidora Stakes at York (beat Sweet Lilly by neck, idling) in May: disappointing favourite when eighth behind stable-companion Light Shift in Oaks at Epsom next time (subsequently treated for throat abscess): back to best last 2 starts, third in Prix Vermeille at Longchamp (1½ lengths behind Mrs Lindsay) and Breeders' Cup Filly & Mare Turf at Monmouth (beaten a length by Lahudood, chasing winner from home turn): stays 1½m: acts on soft and good to firm ground. *H. R. A. Cecil*

PASSAGER (FR) 4 b.g. Anabaa (USA) 130 – Passionnee (USA) 90 (Woodman (USA) **117** 126) [2007 117: 8s³ 8g³ 8g³ 8m³ Jun 10] strong, good-topped gelding: smart performer: at least creditable efforts when third all starts in 2007, in Prix Edmond Blanc at Saint-Cloud (beaten length by Racinger), Prix du Muguet at same course (beaten 1¾ lengths by same rival), Lockinge Stakes at Newbury (beaten 2 heads by Red Evie and Ramonti) and Prix du Chemin de Fer du Nord at Chantilly (3 lengths behind Spirito del Vento): best at 1m: acts on soft and good to firm ground: consistent. *Mme C. Head-Maarek, France*

PASSING HOUR (USA) 3 b.f. Red Ransom (USA) – Timely 104 (Kings Lake (USA) **80** 133) [2007 76: 7m³ 8g* 9.9d² p11g 10f p9.5g Oct 18] tall, lengthy filly: fairly useful performer, lightly raced: won maiden at Goodwood in June: good second in handicap at Salisbury next time: stays 1¼m: acts on good to soft ground: tried blinkered: sold 40,000 gns. *G. A. Butler*

PASSING TRUE (IRE) 3 b.f. Barathea (IRE) 127 – Nambucca 69 (Shirley Heights **67** 130) [2007 p11g 10.5m⁵ 9m³ 8g p9.5g⁵ Nov 10] angular filly: fourth foal: half-sister to Irish 7f winner San Giustino (by Night Shift): dam, maiden (stayed 1¼m), closely related to useful stayer Cephalonia: fair maiden: form only when third at Redcar third start, dictating: stays 9f: acts on good to firm ground. *M. Johnston*

PASSIONATELY ROYAL 5 b.g. Royal Applause 124 – Passionelle 56 (Nashwan **49** (USA) 135) [2007 –: 8f 7m 8d 8m⁴ 8g² 8m 8m⁶ Sep 18] strong, close-coupled gelding: poor performer: stays 1m: acts on good to firm and good to soft going: tried blinkered: reportedly finished distressed sixth start. *M. Brittain*

PASSION FRUIT 6 b.m. Pursuit of Love 124 – Reine de Thebes (FR) 67 (Darshaan **91** 133) [2007 89: 7f 8.3g³ 7g⁶ 7s 8m³ 8d³ 6.9d² 7s 7d⁴ 7m* 7g 7m³ 8d 7g Oct 6] close-coupled, good-topped mare: fairly useful handicapper: won at Redcar in August: flattered when ¾-length third to Medley in listed race at Doncaster twelfth start: stays 8.3f: acts on soft and good to firm going: has worn blinkers: held up. *C. W. Fairhurst*

PASS THE PORT 6 ch.g. Docksider (USA) 124 – One of The Family 73 (Alzao (USA) **90** 117) [2007 86: f12g⁵ p12.2g* p13.9g² p12.2g⁴ p12m² p12.2g² Dec 26] leggy gelding: fairly useful handicapper: won at Wolverhampton in February: good efforts in frame after: stays 1¾m: acts on all-weather and soft going: tried visored/in cheekpieces. *D. Haydn Jones*

PASTA PRAYER 2 b.c. (Mar 15) Bertolini (USA) 125 – Benedicite (Lomond (USA) **–** 128) [2007 6m Jul 16] strong, stocky colt: 20/1 and burly, last in maiden at Windsor. *N. A. Callaghan*

PATAVELLIAN (IRE) 9 b.g. Machiavellian (USA) 123 – Alessia 91 (Caerleon **115** (USA) 132) [2007 115: 5.1g³ 6g⁵ 5g 6m 6d³ 5g⁵ 6d 6d Nov 2] tall, useful-looking gelding: smart performer: creditable efforts in 2007 when fifth in minor event at Haydock (behind Sierra Vista) and Prix de l'Abbaye at Longchamp (behind Benbaun): never on terms in Prix de Seine-et-Oise at Maisons-Laffitte final start: best at 5f/6f: acts on firm and soft going: blinkered nowadays: has worn crossed noseband/been bandaged in front: has run well when sweating. *R. Charlton*

PATAVIAN (IRE) 3 b.g. Titus Livius (FR) 115 – Five of Wands 71 (Caerleon (USA) **64** 132) [2007 72: 9m⁶ 11.1m* 12m 11.1g⁴ 12.1s 11.1d³ 12.1g Jul 31] rather leggy gelding: fair performer: won maiden at Hamilton in May: stays 1½m: acts on good to firm going: tried in cheekpieces/blinkers: joined J. Wade. *I. Semple*

PATAVIUM (IRE) 4 b.g. Titus Livius (FR) 115 – Arcevia (IRE) 85 (Archway (IRE) **63** 115) [2007 58: 9.9g³ 12.4m³ 13f³ 12s⁵ 16.2v 12d³ 12.1g Aug 15] good-topped gelding: modest maiden handicapper: stays 13f: acts on polytrack and firm going: races prominently: has looked temperamental: fairly useful hurdler, won in December *E. W. Tuer*

PATAVIUM PRINCE (IRE) 4 ch.g. Titus Livius (FR) 115 – Hoyland Common (IRE) **46** (Common Grounds 118) [2007 75, a70: 7s 6.1s p5g p7m p6g Dec 19] compact gelding: just poor handicapper in 2007: left J. R. Best after third start: effective at 5f to 7f: acts on polytrack, firm and good to soft going: tried visored: often held up. *Miss Jo Crowley*

PATHOS (GER) 3 b.g. Danehill Dancer (IRE) 117 – Panthere (GER) 94 (Acatenango **101 p** (GER) 127) [2007 10m⁵ 9g* 12d⁴ 10g² 10m* Aug 4] €36,000Y: big, angular gelding: has scope: fifth foal: half-brother to German 5f to 1m winner Passionate Dancer (by Peintre Celebre) and German 1¼m winner Petrovski (by Night Shift): dam German 2-y-o 6f/7f winner: useful form: won maiden at Musselburgh in June and handicap at Newmarket (by ¾ length from Galactic Star) in August: will probably prove best at 1¼m: unraced on extremes of going: unruly in stall and withdrawn on intended debut: races prominently: should do well at 4 yrs. *D. R. C. Elsworth*

PATH TO GLORY 3 b.c. Makbul 104 – Just Glory (Glory of Dancer 121) [2007 51: **62** 6f⁶ 6g 10d² 8.3d p11g p8g⁵ p8g p12m Oct 13] sturdy, workmanlike colt: modest maiden: left Mrs L. Mongan after second start: stays 1¼m (well held both starts over further): acts on polytrack and good to soft going: tried in cheekpieces. *Miss Z. C. Davison*

PATHWAY TO GLORY 3 b. or br.c. Auction House (USA) 120 – Nopalea 75 (Warr- **44** shan (USA) 117) [2007 p6g p6g 5.7f p5.1g p6g Oct 15] poor maiden: best effort on fourth start: visored last 2 outings. *M. Quinn*

PATIO 2 b.f. (Apr 5) Beat Hollow 126 – Maze Garden (USA) (Riverman (USA) 131) **81** [2007 6s⁴ 6d 7m³ 7.5g* Sep 19] compact filly: seventh foal: half-sister to 3 winners, including 7-y-o Roman Maze and 10.5f (in France)/15f winner Crossed Wire (both by Lycius): dam useful French 1m winner: fairly useful form: won maiden at Beverley final start: will stay 1m: sold 41,000 gns. *Mrs A. J. Perrett*

PATITIRI (USA) 4 ch.f. Rahy (USA) 115 – Dharma (USA) (Zilzal (USA) 137) [2007 –
–: p8g 8d 6v Jul 2] leggy filly: no form: tried in cheekpieces/tongue tie. *Mrs C. A. Dunnett*

PATKAI (IRE) 2 ch.c. (Mar 15) Indian Ridge 123 – Olympienne (IRE) (Sadler's Wells **79 p**
(USA) 132) [2007 8.1g⁶ 8.2d* Oct 10] good-bodied colt: first foal: dam unraced sister/
half-sister to very smart middle-distance performers Islington, Greek Dance and Mountain High, out of Yorkshire Oaks winner Hellenic: confirmed debut promise when winning maiden at Nottingham by 1¼ lengths from Etruscan, sweeping through off steady
pace and going away at finish: will be suited by 1¼m/1½m: one to follow. *Sir Michael
Stoute*

PATSYMARTIN 2 ch.g. (Apr 27) Bertolini (USA) 125 – Souadah (USA) (General –
Holme (USA) 128) [2007 5m 5m Jun 5] close-coupled gelding: well beaten in maidens.
J. Ryan

PATTERNMAKER (USA) 5 b.g. Elnadim (USA) 128 – Attasliyah (IRE) (Marju **47**
(IRE) 127) [2007 66: p6g Jan 4] fair performer at 4 yrs: below form at Wolverhampton
only Flat start in 2007 (reportedly lost a shoe): tried blinkered/visored. *A. M. Hales*

PATTHEPAINTER (GER) 2 ch.c. (Feb 9) Alhaarth (IRE) 126 – Picturesque (Polish –
Precedent (USA) 131) [2007 6g 6d 7d Oct 16] smallish, sturdy colt: well held in maidens:
bred for middle distances. *K. R. Burke*

PAT WILL (IRE) 3 b.f. Danetime (IRE) 121 – Northern Tara (IRE) 84 (Fayruz 116) **51**
[2007 60: p5.1g⁸ p6g p6g 6m² 6m² 5.7d⁵ 6m 5.1g⁶ 6s 5.7d 5g 7g Sep 24] leggy filly:
modest performer: effective at 5f/6f: acts on polytrack and firm going: often blinkered/
visored. *P. D. Evans*

PATWISH 3 b.f. Best of The Bests (IRE) 122 – Sagina (Shernazar 131) [2007 –: 8d 8s **57**
p12.2g⁶ 13g⁴ 13d² 13d² 12v 10m⁵ Sep 5] quite good-topped filly: modest maiden: below
form in handicap at Wolverhampton third start: stays 13f: acts on good to firm and good
to soft going: often races prominently. *E. M. D. Kelly, Ireland*

PAULA LANE 7 b.m. Factual (USA) 108 – Colfax Classic 48 (Jareer (USA) 115) [2007 –
p12g 5g Jun 4] no longer of any account. *R. Curtis*

PAULINE'S PRINCE 5 b.h. Polar Prince (IRE) 117 – Etma Rose (IRE) (Fairy King **68**
(USA)) [2007 66, a76: f7d⁴ p8.6d² Dec 27] leggy horse: fair handicapper: stays 8.6f:
acts on all-weather, firm and soft going: tried blinkered/in cheekpieces/tongue tied.
R. Hollinshead

PAULS PLAIN 6 b.g. Young Buster (IRE) 120 – On The Wagon (Then Again 126) –
[2007 12s Jul 5] good-topped gelding: well held in maidens over 2 years apart: modest
hurdler, won in October. *S. Curran*

PAUL THE CARPET (UAE) 2 ch.c. (Apr 16) Halling (USA) 133 – Favoured 78 –
(Chief's Crown (USA)) [2007 7.1g p8g 8.1m Sep 7] lengthy colt: behind in maidens.
P. F. I. Cole

PAUVIC (IRE) 4 b.g. Fayruz 116 – Turntable (IRE) 59 (Dolphin Street (FR) 125) [2007 **57**
76: f5g p5.1g p6g 5g f6g p6g f6d Dec 11] workmanlike gelding: fair handicapper at 3 yrs:
modest at best in 2007: effective at 5f/6f: acts on all-weather: sometimes wears visor/
cheekpieces. *Mrs A. Duffield*

PAVEROC 2 b.c. (Apr 7) Royal Applause 124 – Take Liberties 110 (Warning 136) **90**
[2007 5s⁵ 5m⁴ 5m⁵ 6g⁶ 6g* 6g⁶ 6.5m 7m⁶ 8s Oct 13] 50,000Y: rangy, attractive colt: has
scope: fifth foal: half-brother to winners abroad by Hennessy, Galileo and Gone West:
dam French 2-y-o 6f winner (stayed 1¼m): fairly useful performer: won maiden at Salisbury in August: highly tried and little impact after: should stay 1m: acts on good to firm
going: tried in cheekpieces: lazy sort: joined A. Manuel in UAE. *J. S. Moore*

PAVERSHOOZ 2 b.g. (Apr 23) Bahamian Bounty 116 – Stormswept (USA) 74 (Storm **75**
Bird (CAN) 134) [2007 6d⁵ 7.2v⁴ Nov 3] workmanlike gelding: fair maiden: 100/1, better
effort when fifth to Calming Influence at York: should stay 7f. *N. Wilson*

PAVLOVIA 3 b.f. Diktat 126 – Waseyla (IRE) 71 (Sri Pekan (USA) 117) [2007 69: 6m –
9.3m Jun 4] lengthy filly: fair form in maidens at 2 yrs: well held in handicaps in 2007:
should stay 7f/1m: sold 700 gns in August. *M. Dods*

PAWAN (IRE) 7 ch.g. Cadeaux Genereux 131 – Born To Glamour (Ajdal (USA) 130) **90**
[2007 84, a90: f5g³ f5g⁵ f7g p6g³ p6f⁶ f5g⁵ 6f 5g f5g f6g⁵ 6s² f7g³ 6g 6s² p6g f5d² f5d³
Dec 18] lengthy, angular gelding: fairly useful performer: has won at 9f, but races mainly
at 5f/6f nowadays: acts on all-weather and any turf going: tried in cheekpieces, blinkered
nowadays: sometimes slowly away: usually trainer ridden: tough but none too consistent.
Miss A. Stokell

Prix de Saint-Georges, Longchamp—
Peace Offering (right) confirms himself better than ever while beating Beauty Is Truth

PAWN IN LIFE (IRE) 9 b.g. Midhish 109 – Lady-Mumtaz (Martin John) [2007 –, a67d: f8g⁶ f7g⁶ f7g* f8g³ f7g f8g f7g³ 8.2d⁶ 7.5m Aug 25] lengthy gelding: poor performer nowadays: won minor event at Southwell in February: left S. Parr after seventh start, G. Woodward after eighth: effective at 7f/1m: acts on all-weather: wears headgear: sometimes slowly away. *D. W. Chapman* — a49

PAYMASTER GENERAL (IRE) 3 b.g. Desert Style (IRE) 121 – Khawafi 86 (Kris 135) [2007 65: f7g² p10g* 10d 10g f8g⁴ 10g 9.9s⁵ 10d⁵ 10m 12m⁴ p12g² p12.2g⁶ p12g Oct 12] big, lengthy gelding: fairly useful handicapper on all-weather, modest on turf: won at Lingfield in April: stays 1½m: acts on polytrack, soft and good to firm ground: held up: no easy ride (headstrong, tends to hang): sold 22,000 gns in November. *M. D. I. Usher* — 64 / a82

PAYNE RELIEF (IRE) 2 b. or br.f. (Feb 21) Desert Prince (IRE) 130 – Saffron Crocus 83 (Shareef Dancer (USA) 135) [2007 6d 6g p7g Oct 24] €56,000F, 65,000Y: workmanlike filly: half-sister to several winners, including smart 7f (at 2 yrs) to 1¼m winner Boule d'Or (by Croco Rouge) and useful 1½m to 2m winner Knockholt (by Be My Chief): dam Irish 1½m/13f winner: modest form in maidens: will be suited by 1m+. *M. L. W. Bell* — 53

PAY ON (IRE) 4 ch.g. Danehill Dancer (IRE) 117 – Richly Deserved (IRE) (Kings Lake (USA) 133) [2007 61: p8.6g Jan 13] workmanlike gelding: modest maiden at 3 yrs: below form only Flat start in 2007: seems to stay 1¼m: acts on firm ground: visored last 3 starts. *A. C. Whillans* — –

PAY OR PAY 5 b.g. Atraf 116 – Petinata (Petong 126) [2007 9.2g Jun 20] well beaten in bumpers, and in maiden at Hamilton on Flat debut. *P. S. McEntee* — –

PAY PARADE 2 b.f. (May 11) Mujahid (USA) 125 – Bollin Sophie (Efisio 120) [2007 5f³ May 5] compact filly: half-sister to several winners, including 7-y-o Go Tech and 5f/6f (including at 2 yrs) winner Travelling Times (by Timeless Times): dam, maiden, half-sister to St Leger winner Bollin Eric and smart sprinter Bollin Joanne: 14/1, third to Group Therapy in minor event at Thirsk, only start (refused to enter stall Jul 7). *T. D. Easterby* — 57

PAY PAY PAY 2 ch.f. (Feb 14) Reel Buddy (USA) 118 – Marabela (IRE) 79 (Shernazar 131) [2007 6s 7.1s⁴ 6s⁶ 6.5d 8d 8.2g Oct 31] 9,000Y: rangy filly: fifth foal: half-sister to fairly useful 2003 2-y-o 7f winner Betty Stogs (by Perugino): dam 1m winner: little form: tried visored. *P. D. Evans* — –

PAYS D'AMOUR (IRE) 10 b.g. Pursuit of Love 124 – Lady of The Land 75 (Wollow 132) [2007 –§: 6g 6f 5d 6g Aug 29] strong gelding: no longer of any account. *D. A. Nolan* — – §

PAY THE GREY 2 g.f. (Mar 2) Daylami (IRE) 138 – Dance Clear (IRE) 99 (Marju (IRE) 127) [2007 8g 10.2d Oct 1] 22,000Y: lengthy filly: fourth foal: half-sister to 5-y-o Rosecliff and 4-y-o Dyanita: dam 6f (in Ireland at 2 yrs) to 9f (in US) winner: well held in maidens. *R. Hannon* — –

PAY TIME 8 ch.m. Timeless Times (USA) 99 – Payvashooz 78 (Ballacashtal (CAN)) [2007 72: 7m 7m³ 8d⁴ 7.1g 6.9m* 7m 7g⁴ 6.9g* 7m 7.1d Sep 17] dipped-backed mare: fair handicapper: won at Carlisle in July and August: stays 7f: acts on fibresand and firm going: tried tongue tied. *R. E. Barr* — 71

PEACE OFFERING (IRE) 7 b.g. Victory Note (USA) 120 – Amnesty Bay 63 (That- **117** ching 131) [2007 113: 5m2 5m* 5g2 5s4 5.1d4 5m3 5m2 5g Oct 7] good-topped gelding: smart performer: won Prix de Saint-Georges at Longchamp (by ½ length from Beauty Is Truth) in May: also good efforts in 2007 when runner-up in Palace House Stakes at Newmarket (beaten short head by stable-companion Tax Free), Prix du Gros-Chene at Chantilly (2½ lengths behind Beauty Is Truth) and listed race at Doncaster (beaten neck by Galeota): below-form ninth to Benbaun in Prix de l'Abbaye at Longchamp final outing: best at 5f: acts on polytrack and any turf going: tried in blinkers/cheekpieces early in career: has been early to post: races up with pace. *D. Nicholls*

PEAK DISTRICT (IRE) 3 b.c. Danehill (USA) 126 – Coralita (IRE) 98 (Night Shift **104** (USA)) [2007 6v 5s 7.5m 5m* 5.8d2 5g3 5g Oct 7] good-quartered colt: fourth foal: brother to fairly useful Irish 2005 2-y-o 5f winner Always A Star: dam, Irish 2-y-o 5f winner, out of half-sister to high-class filly up to 1½m Little Bonny: useful performer: won handicap at Tipperary in May: good placed efforts in similar events at Navan and York (third of 20 to Northern Fling) next 2 starts: stiff task, below form in Flying Five Stakes at the Curragh final outing: travels strongly and will prove best at 5f: acts on good to firm and good to soft ground. *D. Wachman, Ireland*

PEAK SEASONS (IRE) 4 ch.g. Raise A Grand (IRE) 114 – Teresian Girl (IRE) 52 **42** (Glenstal (USA) 118) [2007 61: f8g f11g f8g May 15] leggy gelding: just poor form at best in 2007: stays 1¼m: acts on firm and soft going: blinkered/visored nowadays: races prominently. *M. C. Chapman*

PEARL DEALER (IRE) 2 b.c. (Jan 18) Marju (IRE) 127 – Anyaas (IRE) 99 (Green **84** Desert (USA) 127) [2007 p7.1g* 7s Oct 14] first foal: dam 7.5f winner in UAE: fairly useful form: won maiden at Wolverhampton in September: worked up, pulled hard in nursery at Goodwood: likely to prove best up to 7f: sold 20,000 gns. *Saeed bin Suroor*

PEARL FARM 5 b.m. Foxhound (USA) 103 – Trinity Hall 67 (Hallgate 127) [2007 57: **64** p6g2 p6g p8g* p7g3 p7g 7.6f p7g Oct 10] modest handicapper: won at Lingfield in April: stays 1m: acts on polytrack, good to firm and good to soft going: tried tongue tied. *C. A. Horgan*

PEARL (IRE) 3 b.f. Daylami (IRE) 138 – Briery 66 (Salse (USA) 128) [2007 **79** 67p: 8d4 10.5g2 10.3g2 10.2g* p12.2g3 p9.5g4 p11g* Dec 5] rather leggy filly: fair per- former: won maiden at Bath in October and claimer at Kempton in December: stays 1½m: acts on polytrack: races prominently. *W. J. Haggas*

PEARL OF ESTEEM 4 ch.f. Mark of Esteem (IRE) 137 – Ribot's Pearl (Indian Ridge **–** 123) [2007 56: p8.6g 7g p12m p12g Oct 14] maiden: no form in 2007. *Mrs C. A. Dunnett*

PEARL'S GIRL 4 gr.f. King's Best (USA) 132 – Karsiyaka (IRE) (Kahyasi 130) [2007 **86** 80: 8d3 7.8s 8.3s Jun 30] lengthy filly: fairly useful performer, lightly raced: best effort when third to Tarteel in handicap at Newmarket: stays 1m: acts on firm and soft going. *W. J. Haggas*

PEARL TRADER (IRE) 2 ch.f. (Feb 6) Dubai Destination (USA) 127 – Vintage **67** Tipple (IRE) 117 (Entrepreneur 123) [2007 7.2g3 9f5 8d3 9.5d3 Nov 24] 200,000Y: first foal: dam, Irish 7f (at 2 yrs) to 1½m (Irish Oaks) winner, out of half-sister to smart 1½m performer Overbury: fair form: left M. Johnston before third in minor events at Lyon-Parilly and Bordeaux last 2 starts: should stay 1¼m. *H-A. Pantall, France*

PEARL VALLEY 3 b.f. Indian Rocket 115 – Indigo 86 (Primo Dominie 121) [2007 **37** 6m 6f f7g5 8.3g Jun 20] half-sister to several winners, mostly sprinters, notably smart pair Astonished (by Weldnaas) and Bishops Court (by Clantime) and 7-y-o Cape Royal: dam 5f winner: poor maiden: tried visored. *R. A. Fahey*

PEARLY WEY 4 b.g. Lujain (USA) 119 – Dunkellin (USA) (Irish River (FR) 131) **104** [2007 99: 6d5 6m 6g* 6m 6g3 6g* 5.6m3 6d Sep 22] close-coupled gelding: useful handi- capper: won at Folkestone in June and 27-runner Turf Club Stewards' Sprint Stakes at Goodwood (beat Joseph Henry by head) in August: good 1¼ lengths third to Fullandby in Portland Handicap at Doncaster next time: should be as effective at 5f as 6f: acts on firm and good to soft going: early to post: has been slowly away (reared leaving stall final outing): held up. *C. G. Cox*

PEARO (IRE) 2 b.f. (Mar 27) Captain Rio 122 – Westlife (IRE) 32 (Mind Games 121) **52** [2007 6m3 6d* p5g2 8.3d p6g Oct 24] lengthy filly: second foal: half-sister to 4-y-o Orpenlina: dam, maiden, half-sister to useful sprinter Pepperoni: modest performer: won seller at Yarmouth in May: effective at 5f/6f: acts on good to soft going, probably on poly- track. *J. S. Moore*

PEARSON GLEN (IRE) 8 ch.g. Dolphin Street (FR) 125 – Glendora (Glenstal – (USA) 118) [2007 –: 10m Apr 23] good-topped gelding: modest in 2005: well held both Flat outings since: tried visored/in cheekpieces/tongue tied: won over hurdles in May. *James Moffatt*

PEAS IN A POD 2 ch.g. (Apr 20) Kyllachy 129 – Entwine 92 (Primo Dominie 121) – p [2007 6m 6d 6m Sep 21] 55,000Y: sturdy gelding: fourth foal: closely related to 3 at least fairly useful winners by Pivotal, including 2004 2-y-o 5f/6f winner Cyclical and 6f (at 2 yrs) to 8.3f winner Envision, both useful: dam, 2-y-o 5f winner, half-sister to smart sprinter Feet So Fast out of smart sprinter Splice: behind in maidens, probably needing experience: type to do better. *J. R. Fanshawe*

PEAS 'N BEANS (IRE) 4 ch.g. Medicean 128 – No Sugar Baby (FR) (Crystal Glitters – (USA) 127) [2007 62: p9.5g 12.4m 11.5d 16m Jun 8] leggy gelding: modest maiden at best: well held in 2007. *T. Keddy*

PECULIAR PRINCE (IRE) 5 b.g. Desert Prince (IRE) 130 – Lady Peculiar (CAN) 95 (Sunshine Forever (USA)) [2007 85: 10m* 8d⁵ 8.5g⁶ 8g² 8g 10s⁶ p10.7g⁵ 10f³ p10.7g p8g² Nov 30] useful handicapper: won at the Curragh in May: ran creditably at Ayr sixth start, and also ran well when placed: effective at 1m/1¼m: acts on polytrack and any turf going: often races prominently: game. *Liam McAteer, Ireland*

PEDIMENT 2 b.f. (Mar 25) Desert Prince (IRE) 130 – White Palace 80 (Shirley 75 p Heights 130) [2007 p7g 7f⁶ p8g² Sep 26] compact filly: half-sister to 1m/1¼m winner Ice Palace (by Polar Falcon), 7f winner (including at 2 yrs) Palatial (by Green Desert) and 4-y-o Portal, all useful: dam 1m winner: fair form in maidens, second to Ballora at Kempton: stays 1m: open to further improvement. *J. R. Fanshawe*

PEE JAY'S DREAM 5 ch.g. Vettori (IRE) 119 – Langtry Lady 91 (Pas de Seul 133) 66 [2007 66: f12g² Apr 22] sturdy gelding: fair handicapper: effective at 1½m to 2m: acts on all-weather, heavy and good to firm going: tried blinkered. *M. W. Easterby*

PEEPHOLE 4 ch.g. Pursuit of Love 124 – Goodwood Lass (IRE) 71 (Alzao (USA) – 117) [2007 68, a54: p13.9g p12.2g Nov 24] good-bodied gelding: fair performer at best: well held both Flat starts in 2007, leaving Mrs A. Thorpe in between: usually in headgear. *M. A. Allen*

PEEPING FAWN (USA) 3 b.f. Danehill (USA) 126 – Maryinsky (IRE) 107 126 (Sadler's Wells (USA) 132) [2007 8s³ 8m³ 8g² 8g* 8g³ 12d² 10s* 12v* 9.9m* 12d* Aug 22]

The enhanced programme of pattern races for fillies and mares introduced in Europe in 2004 can be judged a success of sorts against its primary aim of encouraging owners and breeders to keep their fillies and mares in training after the age of three, instead of retiring them. However, creating more Group 1 opportunities for good fillies and mares to race against their own sex has the potential to damage the competitiveness of open championship races to which top three- and four-year-old fillies have made a valuable contribution. The tradition in Europe of running leading fillies in open Group 1s is likely to continue at least with some top owners who find it more satisfying to take on the opposite sex and beat them than to campaign a top filly solely in restricted races. In the long term, however, European racing must be in danger of mimicking its North American cousin. American racegoers aren't used to seeing a top filly like Rags To Riches, for example—owned by Ballydoyle/Coolmore partners Derrick Smith and Michael Tabor—taking on the leading colts. The Santa Anita Oaks and Kentucky Oaks winner got the better of the Preakness winner Curlin in a thrilling duel in the Belmont Stakes, becoming the first filly to win the race since 1905. The last filly to be named Horse of The Year in the States, Azeri in 2002, recorded seventeen wins from twenty-four starts but made only two appearances against colts. One of the part owners of Rags To Riches, Michael Tabor, is also part owner of the top middle-distance filly to race in Europe, the three-year-old Peeping Fawn who, by coincidence, comes from the same family as Rags To Riches. Peeping Fawn did not take on the colts as a three-year-old but, after winning four Group 1s, she has nothing more to prove against her own sex. She stays in training and, in the form she showed as a three-year-old, would be a leading contender for the top open races in receipt of the weight-for-sex allowance. Her participation in races such as the King George VI and Queen Elizabeth Stakes and the Prix de l'Arc de Triomphe might, however, be just as dependent

Audi Pretty Polly Stakes, the Curragh—Peeping Fawn starts her Group 1 winning spree; Speciosa (left) is second, ahead of West Wind and Timarwa

on plans for the Ballydoyle colts at the time as on whether she herself trains on from three to four. She could still enjoy a lucrative campaign without meeting the colts.

Peeping Fawn was given time to grow into her huge frame and was not seen out as a two-year-old. It took her four races to get off the mark as a three-year-old, placed in fillies maidens at Navan, the Curragh and Gowran in April before finally winning one at Naas in May. Peeping Fawn's racing career was eight weeks old when she had her first outing outside maiden company in the Irish One Thousand Guineas at the Curragh. Starting at 12/1, she was always prominent and stuck to her guns to finish third to Finsceal Beo, stepping up by a stone on her best previous form. There was another stone's improvement when Peeping Fawn turned up somewhat surprisingly later the same week at Epsom as part of a four-strong Ballydoyle challenge for the Oaks. At 20/1, she was the second shortest in the betting of the O'Brien runners, behind the Cheshire Oaks runner-up All My Loving, the joint second favourite, and ahead of 66/1-shots Cherry Hinton and Nell Gwyn. Peeping Fawn and All My Loving filled second and third behind Cheshire Oaks winner Light Shift, Peeping Fawn going down by half a length, four lengths in front of her stable companion, after being buffeted at least twice in a rough race and not getting going until Light Shift was clear. Peeping Fawn made good headway to have every chance inside the final furlong but Light Shift was always holding her and there didn't seem a strong argument for Peeping Fawn's being regarded as an unlucky loser.

Having seemingly benefited from the step up to a mile and a half at Epsom, Peeping Fawn was aimed at the Darley Irish Oaks for a second meeting with Light Shift. She displayed her toughness by winning the Audi Pretty Polly Stakes at the Curragh in the interim. In its fourth year as a Group 1, the Pretty Polly is run over a mile and a quarter but Peeping Fawn wasn't at all inconvenienced by the step back in trip and won by two lengths and the same from the previous year's One Thousand Guineas winner Speciosa and the Prix de Diane winner West Wind. The Irish Oaks, run at the Curragh two weeks after the Pretty Polly, was Peeping Fawn's eighth outing of the season but she reversed Epsom form with Light Shift in no uncertain manner, improving again and clearly thriving on the exacting programme laid out for her. The going was heavy at the Curragh where the twelve-runner Irish Oaks featured the first four from Epsom, the Oaks fourth Four Sins joined in a three-pronged challenge from the John Oxx stable by another Aga Khan-owned stablemate Timarwa, who had finished a creditable fourth in the Pretty Polly on only her third start. The most notable absentee was the sidelined Silkwood who had thrashed All My Loving in the Ribblesdale. The Oaks principals filled the first three places again at the Curragh, Peeping Fawn produced to lead a furlong out, after the favourite Light Shift had led briefly, before keeping on—edging over to the rail once in front—to win by three and a half lengths, with All My Loving a further two lengths away third, Timarwa fourth and Four Sins seventh. Peeping Fawn showed signs of coming into season on the morning of the Irish Oaks, information relayed to Curragh racegoers over the loudspeakers after the stewards sought her trainer's views when she was a morning drifter on the betting exchanges. O'Brien had also had to find a replacement for stable-jockey Kieren Fallon who was due to partner Peeping Fawn for the first time but was injured the previous evening in a fall from Eagle Mountain in the Grand Prix de Paris. Johnny Murtagh replaced Fallon and went on to remain unbeaten on Peeping Fawn as she completed her campaign in the Blue Square Nassau Stakes and the Darley Yorkshire Oaks in Britain, where Fallon was unable to ride. The three victories on Peeping Fawn were among ten Group/Grade 1s won by Murtagh in 2007 after he had drawn a blank in 2006 when, after two years spent mostly riding in Britain, he did nearly all his riding in Ireland (only twenty-two rides, no winners, in Britain). Murtagh rode six Group 1 winners in Britain in the latest season, which also included Dylan Thomas in the King George and Listen in the Fillies' Mile, both for O'Brien, and Soldier's Tale in the Golden Jubilee and Simply Perfect in the Falmouth. His haul worldwide was completed by Notnowcato in the Tattersalls Gold Cup and Mrs Lindsay in the Prix Vermeille and the E. P. Taylor. Murtagh was also placed in three British classics (on Simply Perfect, Eagle Mountain and Honolulu) and finished second to Frankie Dettori in the jockeys' prize-money table despite having only one hundred and thirty-one rides (twenty-one winners) in Britain.

Peeping Fawn met Light Shift for a third time in the Nassau at Goodwood, which also attracted three other Group 1 winners, the four-year-olds Speciosa, Nannina and French-trained Mandesha, who had been the top three-year-old filly of 2006. Peeping Fawn brushed aside the new challenge from Mandesha and also confirmed her superiority over Light Shift, winning from that pair by a length and a half and three and a half lengths, idling after taking the lead and probably value for more. The Nassau is a strong counter-attraction to the King George VI and Queen Elizabeth Stakes nowadays for the leading middle-distance fillies and the top-form

Darley Irish Oaks, the Curragh—Peeping Fawn reverses Epsom form with Light Shift as All My Loving again takes third; Timarwa (right) is fourth

Blue Square Nassau Stakes, Goodwood—Peeping Fawn defeats four Group 1 winners, including Mandesha and Light Shift (second right); Sweet Lilly (rail) is fourth

Peeping Fawn would have given her stablemate (in similar ownership) Dylan Thomas a better race than those who chased him home at Ascot.

It was on to York after Goodwood, and the Yorkshire Oaks looked like producing a clash between Peeping Fawn and her stable-companion the previous year's Oaks, Irish Oaks and Yorkshire Oaks winner Alexandrova, who was due to make a belated reappearance, but the latter was an overnight withdrawal after suffering a slight setback. Starting at 9/4-on, Peeping Fawn won virtually unchallenged, cruising to the front two furlongs out and coasting home by four lengths from the four-year-old Allegretto, who had won the Henry II Stakes and the Goodwood Cup and went on to win the Prix Royal-Oak afterwards. Silkwood was second favourite at York but ran no sort of race on her first start since the Ribblesdale, finishing last of seven. One issue raised at the York Ebor meeting was the state of the going—'like jumping ground in mid-winter' in the view of trainer Mark Johnston—and it was certainly true that the ground had more give in it on the round course on the first two days (the Yorkshire Oaks was run on the second) than the official description of 'good (good to soft in places)'. The holes that were being filled in by a large team at the end of the day were more pronounced than those normally found after racing on good ground. It is always frustrating for owners, trainers, racegoers and punters alike when official going descriptions turn out to be manifestly inaccurate. York wasn't the only course to come in for criticism in one of the wettest summers on record for issuing misleading going descriptions. The controversy over the official description of the going at Haydock in the run up to and on Sprint Cup day, the ground a little softer than the official probably as a result of watering earlier in the week, is discussed in the essay on Sakhee's Secret. Clerks of the course have a wide-ranging job, particularly at the Grade 1 tracks, and, because of the element of subjectivity, there are bound to be differences between Timeform's own going assessments and the 'official' descriptions on occasions. However, the need for accurate going descriptions should be afforded greater importance than it sometimes is by clerks of the course for whom the interests of punters are not always a priority. York is set to close for nine months for

Darley Yorkshire Oaks, York—a fourth Group 1 proves easy pickings; Allegretto (visor) is second, with Trick Or Treat (checked cap) and Under The Rainbow (white cap) next; Silkwood (right) is a disappointing last of seven

large-scale drainage work on the track after the 2008 Ebor meeting. That fixture has been extended to a fourth day, with the Yorkshire Oaks moving from Ebor day to Thursday and the Nunthorpe being run on the fourth day, Friday.

Peeping Fawn (USA) (b.f. 2004)	Danehill (USA) (b 1986)	Danzig (b 1977)	Northern Dancer Pas de Nom
		Razyana (b 1981)	His Majesty Spring Adieu
	Maryinsky (IRE) (b 1999)	Sadler's Wells (b 1981)	Northern Dancer Fairy Bridge
		Blush With Pride (ch 1979)	Blushing Groom Best In Show

The big, strong, attractive Peeping Fawn, who has a powerful, round action, still looked in fine shape before the Yorkshire Oaks but she was not seen out again, the Breeders' Cup Filly & Mare Turf having been announced as her main end-of-season target. Rags To Riches also missed the Breeders' Cup—where she would probably have run in the Distaff (on dirt)—after suffering a hairline fracture of her off-fore pastern when second in the Gazelle Stakes at Belmont in mid-September. Peeping Fawn, from the final crop of Danehill, and Rags To Riches, by the outstanding North American sire A P Indy, are out of the half-sisters Maryinsky and Better Than Honour, the latter successful in the Grade 2 Demoiselle Stakes at two and placed in two Grade 1s at three, and also the dam of the 2006 Belmont Stakes winner Jazil. Maryinsky has some way to go to match her half-sister's historic achievement but she is going the right way, her second foal being Peeping Fawn's year-younger half-brother Thewayyouare (by Kingmambo), whose four wins in the latest season included two big races at Saint-Cloud, the Prix Thomas Bryon and the

Mr M. Tabor & Mrs John Magnier's "Peeping Fawn"

PEG

Group 1 Criterium International. Thewayyouare has taken more after his dam than Peeping Fawn in that Maryinsky also did well as a two-year-old, winning at seven furlongs and finishing second in the Fillies' Mile at Ascot. She failed to make the expected progress as a three-year-old, though she ran in the One Thousand Guineas in both Britain and Ireland, and in the Oaks, finishing ninth of seventeen at Newmarket, seventh of fifteen at the Curragh and twelfth of fourteen at Epsom. Maryinsky recorded her best effort at three when fourth in the Matron Stakes, at the time a Group 3 event, but since promoted, firstly to Group 2 and then to Group 1 in 2004 as part of the widening of the restricted big-race programme for fillies and mares.

Peeping Fawn and Rags To Riches are following in the footsteps of their grandam Blush With Pride, who won the Kentucky Oaks after winning the Santa Susana Stakes (now run as the Santa Anita Oaks). Blush With Pride had a top-class pedigree to go with her racing performance, being by Blushing Groom out of the renowned mare Best In Show, who also bred numerous performers who made their mark for Ballydoyle in the era of Vincent O'Brien, including Gielgud, Malinowski, Monroe (the dam of Xaar) and Try My Best and El Gran Senor, the two last-named out of the unraced Sex Appeal, a daughter of Best In Show. The family is packed with winners and is well and truly back in the limelight as it now includes the top Australian stallion Redoute's Choice, who is by Peeping Fawn's sire and has Best In Show as his fourth dam. Blush With Pride and Better Than Honour were both recruited to the Coolmore broodmare band, Blush With Pride at a cost of 635,000 dollars at the age of eighteen, two years before she produced Maryinsky, and Better Than Honour at a cost of 2,000,000 dollars in 2004. Rags To Riches was a Coolmore purchase as a yearling a year later for 1,900,000 dollars. Blush With Pride's career at stud took some time to get off the ground, three of her first six foals being unraced and the three others minor winners in the States. Her seventh foal, however, was the smart miler Smolensk, who came second in the Coronation Stakes before winning the Prix d'Astarte (another race that has been a Group 1 since 2004). The foal by Deputy Minister that Blush With Pride was carrying at the time of her purchase by Coolmore interests turned out to be Turnberry Isle, who won the Beresford Stakes and finished second in the Royal Lodge for Aidan O'Brien in 2000. Maryinsky had a filly by Fusaichi Pegasus in 2006 and a colt by Kingmambo in 2007. Peeping Fawn, who has worn a crossed noseband, is effective at a mile and a quarter and a mile and a half, and she acts on heavy and good to firm going. *A. P. O'Brien, Ireland*

PEERESS 6 ch.m. Pivotal 124 – Noble One 107 (Primo Dominie 121) [2007 124: 8g⁶ May 19] strong, rangy mare: had a quick action: very smart performer at best: won Sun Chariot Stakes at Newmarket in 2005 and Lockinge Stakes at Newbury in 2006: finished distressed when sixth to Red Evie in latter race on only outing at 6 yrs: was best at 1m: had won on firm ground, went well on soft: bandaged hind joints: tended to idle: visits Oasis Dream. *Sir Michael Stoute* **102**

PEER PRESSURE 2 gr.c. (Apr 23) Verglas (IRE) 118 – Mystery Quest (IRE) (Rainbow Quest (USA) 134) [2007 7.1d p6g 7f p7g 6d⁴ 7d Oct 29] lengthy colt: modest maiden: best form at 6f: acts on good to soft going, probably on polytrack. *P. Mitchell* **61**

PEGASUS AGAIN (USA) 2 b.c. (Apr 11) Fusaichi Pegasus (USA) 130 – Chit Chatter (USA) (Lost Soldier (USA) 103) [2007 7g² p8g* 7.1m⁵ Sep 1] $50,000Y, £75,000 2-y-o: leggy, useful-looking colt: first foal: dam US 7f to 8.5f winner: useful form: won maiden at Lingfield in August: ran very well either side, neck second of 12 to Maze in listed race at Royal Ascot and 8¾ lengths fifth to Raven's Pass in Solario Stakes at Sandown (tended to swish tail): should be suited by 1m/1¼m: sweating and edgy first/third starts. *T. G. Mills* **96**

PEGASUS DANCER (FR) 3 b.g. Danehill Dancer (IRE) 117 – Maruru (IRE) (Fairy King (USA)) [2007 76: 5f⁴ 6d⁵ 7m⁶ 6g³ 6m⁴d 5g 5m³ 5g 5m³ 5g p6g³ p6g² p5g* Dec 22] quite good-topped gelding: fairly useful performer: won handicap at Lingfield in December: effective at 5f/6f: acts on polytrack, firm and good to soft going: wears cheekpieces/blinkers nowadays: often races prominently: edgy sort. *K. A. Ryan* **82**

PEGASUS PRINCE (USA) 3 b.g. Fusaichi Pegasus (USA) 130 – Avian Eden (USA) (Storm Bird (CAN) 134) [2007 –: p6g 8g³ 10m 8.3g⁵ p9.5g³ Oct 6] modest maiden handicapper: should stay 1¼m: acts on polytrack. *Miss J. A. Camacho* **55**

PEGGLE 2 b.f. (Feb 18) Tobougg (IRE) 125 – Grove Dancer 61 (Reprimand 122) [2007 – p7g Nov 17] third foal: dam, 2-y-o 6f winner, half-sister to smart performer up to 1m Winisk River: 33/1, well held in maiden at Lingfield. *M. H. Tompkins*

PEGGYS FIRST 5 b.g. Wolfhound (USA) 126 – Peggys Rose (IRE) 65 (Shalford – (IRE) 124§) [2007 –, a55: p5g³ p6g⁴ p7g⁵ f6g⁴ a6g² a6g² a6g* a6s² a6.8g² 5.8g* 8d 5.8g² **a48** a6s⁶ a5g⁴ 5.8g Sep 27] poor performer: sold from D. Cantillon 2,000 gns after fourth start: won minor event and handicap at Jagersro in April and minor event at Taby in June: effective at 5f to 1m: acts on dirt/all-weather: tried in cheekpieces/blinkered. *Annelie Larsson, Sweden*

PEGGYS FLOWER 3 b.f. Arkadian Hero (USA) 123 – Peggys Rose (IRE) 65 (Shal- **47 §** ford (IRE) 124§) [2007 65§: 6g p7.1g⁶ p7.1g³ Apr 27] just poor performer in 2007: stays easy 7f: acts on polytrack and firm going: tried in cheekpieces: irresolute. *M. Wigham*

PEINTRE'S WONDER (IRE) 3 b.f. Peintre Celebre (USA) 137 – Ring The Rela- **70** tives 75 (Bering 136) [2007 70: 8.2g 9.2g⁴ 13d 10g⁴ Aug 29] workmanlike filly: fair maiden handicapper, lightly raced: should stay beyond 1¼m: raced mainly on good ground or softer (acts on heavy). *E. J. O'Neill*

PELHAM CRESCENT (IRE) 4 ch.g. Giant's Causeway (USA) 132 – Sweet Times **72** 60 (Riverman (USA) 131) [2007 70: p10g⁴ p10g p9.5g⁶ p8.6g⁵ 8.1m² 7g 8.1d³ p9.5g* p10g⁴ 8m³ 7d⁵ p8.6g* p8.6g³ p8.6g⁵ Nov 14] close-coupled gelding: fair handicapper: won at Wolverhampton in August (apprentices) and October: stays 9.5f: acts on poly-track, good to firm and good to soft ground: tried in cheekpieces/blinkers: has been withdrawn after unruly at stall. *B. Palling*

PELICAN KEY (IRE) 3 b.f. Mujadil (USA) 119 – Guana Bay (Cadeaux Genereux **80** 131) [2007 80: 5f p6g 7s² 7m⁶ 6m Jul 30] rather leggy, useful-looking filly: fairly useful handicapper: seems to stay 7f: acts on firm and soft going: reportedly distressed when tailed off once at 2 yrs: said to have bled final outing. *D. M. Simcock*

PELICAN PRINCE 2 b.c. (Feb 12) Fraam 114 – Nightingale Song 66 (Tina's Pet 121) **85** [2007 5m² 6m* 6s³ 6m* 6g 6g 6g³ Oct 6] 41,000Y: lengthy colt: has scope: fourth foal: brother to fairly useful 2005 2-y-o 6f winner Lindus Atenor and half-brother to 3-y-o Ishi Adiva: dam 5f/6f (at 2 yrs) winner: fairly useful performer: won maiden at Newcastle in May and nursery at Ascot in July: good third of 23 to Dubai Dynamo in listed Two-Year-Old Trophy at Redcar final start, always prominent: should prove best at 5f/6f: acts on good to firm going. *K. R. Burke*

PELICAN WATERS (IRE) 3 b.f. Key of Luck (USA) 126 – Orlena (USA) (Gone **94** West (USA)) [2007 82: 8g 5d³ 5s 6s 6m 7g 8m³ p7g⁶ p8g p9.5d* Dec 17] close-coupled, quite good-topped filly: fairly useful performer: placed in handicaps at Navan and Leo-pardstown: left Mrs J. Harrington in Ireland 34,000 gns, straightforward task to win maiden at Wolverhampton (by 9 lengths) in December: stays 9.5f: acts on polytrack, good to firm and good to soft going: tried in blinkers/cheekpieces. *E. F. Vaughan*

PELLEAS 3 b.g. Mark of Esteem (IRE) 137 – Questabelle (Rainbow Quest (USA) 134) **71** [2007 –: 10m 11.9m⁶ Jun 8] close-coupled gelding: lightly-raced maiden, fair form at best: sold 16,000 gns in July. *R. Charlton*

PELTRE 2 b.f. (Mar 7) Bertolini (USA) 125 – Pewter Lass 56 (Dowsing (USA) 124) – [2007 f5g 6s 6m Aug 9] 2,200Y: quite good-topped filly: seventh foal: sister to 4-y-o Signor Peltro and half-sister to 2 winners, including 1999 2-y-o 5f/6f seller winner Tinsel Winner (by Piccolo): dam sprint maiden: no form. *M. Brittain*

PEMBO 2 b.g. (Jan 19) Choisir (AUS) 126 – Focosa (ITY) (In The Wings 128) [2007 – p7.1g 8.2g Oct 31] good-bodied gelding: well held in maiden/seller. *B. Palling*

PENANG CINTA 4 b.g. Halling (USA) 133 – Penang Pearl (FR) 106 (Bering 136) **79** [2007 64: p12.2g³ p9.5g* p9.5g⁵ p9.5g² p9.5g* 11.8m* 10.2g⁴ p13.9g⁶ 12g 12 3m² 12m Sep 15] smallish gelding: fair handicapper: left A. Chamberlain after reappearance: won at Wolverhampton in February and April, and Leicester in May: stays 1½m: acts on poly-track and good to firm going: tried blinkered/in cheekpieces: sometimes carries head awkwardly: quirky, but consistent. *P. D. Evans*

PENANG (IRE) 3 b.f. Xaar 132 – Badawi (USA) 103 (Diesis 133) [2007 p10g 10.3m **57** 10.3m⁴ 10m Sep 25] big, long-backed filly: half-sister to several winners, mostly useful, including 2004 2-y-o 7f winner Fox (by Diktat) and 1m winner Badagara (by Warning): dam 1m/9f winner: modest maiden: will be suited by 1½m: sent to France. *C. E. Brittain*

PENCHESCO (IRE) 2 b.c. (Mar 22) Orpen (USA) 116 – Francesca (IRE) (Perugino **77** (USA) 84) [2007 6s 7m⁵ p7g⁵ p7.1g² Nov 20] lengthy colt: fair maiden: runner-up at Wolverhampton: will stay 1m: acts on polytrack and good to firm going. *Pat Eddery*

PENCIL HILL (IRE) 2 b.c. (May 3) Acclamation 118 – Como (USA) 95 (Cozzene **103** (USA)) [2007 6g* 5m* 6m⁴ 7g Oct 29] 8,000Y, resold 8,000Y: lengthy colt: third foal: half-brother to 6f winner Arzaag (by Bertolini): dam 6f winner: useful performer: won minor event at Naas and listed race at the Curragh (by 1¾ lengths from You'resothrilling) in May: good 1½ lengths fourth to Henrythenavigator in Coventry Stakes at Royal Ascot: off 4 months, well held in Killavullan Stakes at Leopardstown: best at 5f/6f: acts on good firm going. *Miss T. A. M. Collins, Ireland*

PENDULUM STAR 3 gr.f. Observatory (USA) 131 – Pendulum 82 (Pursuit of Love **89 p** 124) [2007 8.1m² 8.3g⁶ 8m⁶ p8g* p8g² Nov 3] 21,000Y: leggy filly: second foal: dam 7f winner: fairly useful performer: off 4 months, improved when winning handicap at Lingfield in October: good neck second to Waterline Twenty in similar event at Kempton next time, racing freely: stays 1m: acts on polytrack: should do better still. *W. R. Swinburn*

PENEL (IRE) 6 b.g. Orpen (USA) 116 – Jayess Elle 55 (Sabrehill (USA) 120) [2007 **58** 58: f6g³ f6g³ f7g f6g³ f7g² f7g f7g⁶ 7m⁵ 6f³ 7g 7.5m³ 8d² f7g 7.5m 6s⁴ 7.1d⁶ 7.5v³ 8.5s 6m⁵ 6.9f 8m* 9.9d³ Sep 25] smallish gelding: modest performer: won claimer at Newcastle in August: effective at 6f to 1¼m: acts on all-weather and good to firm going, probably on heavy: wears headgear (in cheekpieces nowadays). *P. T. Midgley*

PENICUIK 3 b.f. Hernando (FR) 127 – Barari (USA) (Blushing Groom (FR) 131) – [2007 p12.2g⁶ Apr 5] half-sister to several winners, including 6f to 1¼m (US Grade 1 event) winner White Heart (by Green Desert) and 7.5f (at 2 yrs) to 1½m winner Kind Regards (by Unfuwain), both smart: dam unraced half-sister to very smart French/US performer up to 10.5f Colour Chart: 9/2 and green, well held in maiden at Wolverhampton: sold 80,000 gns in July. *M. Johnston*

PENMARA 4 b.f. Mtoto 134 – Pendulum 82 (Pursuit of Love 124) [2007 59: 10.5m 9g – Jul 23] good-bodied filly: modest maiden at best: showed nothing in 2007 (blinkered second outing): dead. *Miss J. E. Foster*

PENMON POINT (IRE) 4 b.g. Foxhound (USA) 103 – Brandon Princess (Waajib – 121) [2007 8.3d 10s 15.8g Oct 30] little sign of ability: tried in tongue strap/cheekpieces. *R. Johnson*

PENNY ARCADE 2 ch.f. (Feb 26) Arkadian Hero (USA) 123 – Concentration (IRE) – (Mind Games 121) [2007 5v⁶ 5g 7g⁶ 5m 5f Sep 11] 1,000Y: quite good-topped filly: first foal: dam unraced out of half-sister to top-class sprinter Lochnager: no form. *M. E. Sowersby*

PENNY FROM HEAVEN (IRE) 3 b.f. Machiavellian (USA) 123 – Flying Kiss **72** (IRE) (Sadler's Wells (USA) 132) [2007 75: 8.3m 8.1g⁶ 10g³ p11g Aug 1] fair maiden: stayed 1¼m: acted on polytrack: looked reluctant penultimate start: dead. *E. A. L. Dunlop*

PENNYGEE 3 b.f. Bertolini (USA) 125 – Samadilla (IRE) 83 (Mujadil (USA) 119) – [2007 p6g f6g Dec 27] 2,000Y, resold 6,000Y: second foal: dam 2-y-o 5f/6f winner: last in maidens. *S. R. Bowring*

PENNY GLITTERS 4 br.f. Benny The Dip 127 – Lucy Glitters (USA) 60 **44** (Cryptoclearance (USA)) [2007 63, a56: p7.1g 7f 8m p8.6g 7d⁵ p7g Nov 19] smallish filly: just poor on balance in 2007: stays 7f: acts on polytrack: blinkered/visored last 4 starts. *S. Parr*

PENNY POST (IRE) 3 b.f. Green Desert (USA) 127 – Blue Note (FR) 122 (Habitat **78** 134) [2007 93p: p6g⁴ p6g² p6g 6.1m³ 7.1g⁴ 6s⁵ May 27] lengthy filly: fairly useful handi- **a88** capper: should stay 7f: best form on polytrack: races prominently. *M. Johnston*

PENNYROCK (IRE) 3 b.c. Rock of Gibraltar (IRE) 133 – Inforapenny 111 (Deploy **64** 131) [2007 62: p9.5g 7.5m⁴ 7m² 7m* 7m p6g 5.9f 8m³ 7.5m³ Aug 26] close-coupled colt: modest performer: left K. Ryan after reappearance: won maiden at Catterick in May: worth a try over 1¼m: acts on firm going: sometimes races freely: claimed £10,000, joined A. E. Jones. *J. J. Quinn*

PENNYSPIDER (IRE) 2 b.f. (Mar 30) Redback 116 – Malacca (USA) (Danzig **51** (USA)) [2007 5g 5s 5.1g 5.1s³ Jul 26] 27,000Y: eighth foal: half-sister to 3 winners, including fairly useful Irish 2000 2-y-o 5f winner Patinham (by Mujtahid) and 1998 2-y-o 5f winner Hit The Beach (by Turtle Island): dam unraced: modest maiden: will prove best at 5f. *M. S. Saunders*

PENRICE CASTLE 2 br.f. (Mar 7) Averti (IRE) 117 – Stormont Castle (USA) (Irish **70** River (FR) 131) [2007 5.7g p6g⁴ p5g* p6g 6m² 5.5m 5g 6.1d Oct 18] rather leggy filly: first foal: dam unraced out of half-sister to US Grade 1 winners Tis Juliet and Stella Madrid: fair performer: won maiden at Lingfield in June: second at Windsor, only sound effort in nurseries: should prove best at 5f/6f: acts on polytrack and good to firm going. *R. Hannon*

PENTANDRA (IRE) 2 b.f. (Mar 16) Bahri (USA) 125 – Miss Willow Bend (USA) **63**
(Willow Hour (USA)) [2007 7.1g 7g Nov 3] rather leggy filly: half-sister to several
winners, including fairly useful 5f/6f (including at 2 yrs) winner Willow Dale (by Danehill): dam US sprint winner: well held in maidens at Haydock and Newmarket, modest
form in latter. *J. G. Given*

PENTASILEA 4 b.f. Nashwan (USA) 135 – Isabella Gonzaga 75 (Rock Hopper 124) **75**
[2007 70: p12.2g* 10d 14m² p16g p13.9g³ 12g Aug 24] lengthy, angular filly: third foal:
half-sister to 5-y-o Annibale Caro: dam 1¼m/1½m winner: fair performer: left J. Oxx in
Ireland after 3 yrs: won maiden at Wolverhampton in April: inconsistent in handicaps
after: stays 1¾m (seemingly not 2m): acts on polytrack and good to firm going: visored
(too free) final outing. *H. J. L. Dunlop*

PENTATHLON (IRE) 2 b.g. (Jan 22) Storming Home 128 – Nawaiet (USA) (Zilzal **62 p**
(USA) 137) [2007 p7g Dec 19] closely related to several winners by Machiavellian,
notably very smart miler No Excuse Needed (7f winner at 2 yrs) and useful 5f (at 2 yrs) to
1m (in UAE) winner Skywards: dam, French 6f winner, half-sister to high-class French
middle-distance filly Fitnah, out of very smart sprinter Greenland Park: 5/1, seventh to
Parisian Gift in maiden at Lingfield: should be better for experience. *M. Johnston*

PENTATONIC 4 b.f. Giant's Causeway (USA) 132 – Fascinating Rhythm 85 (Slip **100**
Anchor 136) [2007 86p: 10m 9.9g² 12m* 14g⁵ Aug 2] tall, useful-looking filly: useful
performer: progressed well in 2007, winning handicap at Folkestone in July by 2 lengths
from Crossbow Creek: good 5¼ lengths fifth to Hi Calypso in Lillie Langtry Stakes at
Goodwood final outing: stays 1¾m: acts on good to firm ground. *L. M. Cumani*

PENTECOST 8 ch.g. Tagula (IRE) 116 – Boughtbyphone 62 (Warning 136) [2007 109: **102**
7.5g⁴ 8g 7s⁶ 8m 8d 8m³ 8m³ 8f⁴ 8g Sep 30] sturdy gelding: useful handicapper: shaped
better than result on several occasions in 2007, including when third to Benandonner at
Ascot seventh start: well below form last 2 outings (looked unwilling final one): stays 9f:
yet to race on heavy going, acts on any other turf: tried visored (not since 2003), in
cheekpieces last 4 starts: free-going sort (has worn dropped noseband), and usually held
up. *A. M. Balding*

PENWELL HILL (USA) 8 b.g. Distant View (USA) 126 – Avie's Jill (USA) (Lord –
Avie (USA)) [2007 –, a70d: f8g⁶ f8g f8g f8g p10g p12.2g⁴ p13.9g Jul 16] quite good- **a55**
topped gelding: fairly useful at best: only modest form in 2007: best form at 7f to 8.5f: acts
on all-weather and firm ground: usually blinkered/visored: inconsistent front runner.
Miss M. E. Rowland

PENZO (IRE) 4 gr.g. Shinko Forest (IRE) – Thatchabella (IRE) (Thatching 131) [2007 –
73: 7m 9.2d 9.1d Jul 23] maiden: little form in 2007, leaving J. Howard Johnson after
reappearance. *J. Wade*

PEOPLETON BROOK 5 b.h. Compton Place 125 – Merch Rhyd-Y-Grug (Sabrehill **89**
(USA) 120) [2007 89: 5m 5m 5m⁶ 5m* 5.2g³ 5m⁵ 5g 5.2f 5m 5g p5.1g p5g p5g Nov 12]
leggy horse: fairly useful handicapper: won at Haydock (apprentices) in May: below form
after: best at 5f: acts on firm and soft ground: tried in blinkers/cheekpieces. *J. M. Bradley*

PEP IN HER STEP (IRE) 4 b.f. Cape Cross (IRE) 129 – Monzitta (GER) (Monsun **53**
(GER) 124) [2007 67: p6g 9.5m 5d 5d³ 6s 5g⁴ Aug 31] modest maiden: well held in
handicap at Wolverhampton on reappearance, then left E. Tyrrell: effective at 5f to easy
1m: acts on polytrack, good to firm and good to soft ground: tried blinkered/in cheekpieces: sometimes slowly away/wanders. *Andrew Oliver, Ireland*

At The Races Curragh Cup, the Curragh—
Peppertree Lane lands a substandard renewal from Nick's Nikita and Alfie Flits

Mr P. D. Savill's "Peppertree Lane"

PEPPERMINT GREEN 3 b.f. Green Desert (USA) 127 – One So Wonderful 121 **65** (Nashwan (USA) 135) [2007 73p: 8m 8g 11.9d Aug 21] strong filly: lightly-raced maiden: ran poorly in handicaps last 2 starts. *L. M. Cumani*

PEPPER ROAD 8 ch.g. Elmaamul (USA) 125 – Floral Spark 69 (Forzando 122) [2007 **48** 47: f8g f7g 8.5m⁵ 8d³ 8m Aug 2] poor performer: effective at 7f to 8.5f: acts on polytrack, firm and good to soft going: tried in cheekpieces/tongue tied: often early to post. *R. Bastiman*

PEPPER'S GHOST 2 gr.c. (Apr 12) Act One 124 – Mill On The Floss 117 (Mill Reef **57** (USA) 141) [2007 7f p8g 8m Sep 21] unfurnished colt: modest maiden: bred to be suited by 1½m+. *Miss J. Feilden*

PEPPERTREE 4 b.f. Fantastic Light (USA) 134 – Delauncy (Machiavellian (USA) **96** 123) [2007 95: 14.1m⁴ 14m⁶ 10m* p13m Nov 1] rather leggy, lengthy filly: useful performer, lightly raced: left J. Fanshawe, won handicap at Newbury (by length from Lisathedaddy) in September: little impact in listed race at Lingfield (all-weather debut) subsequent outing: stays 1½m: acts on firm going (well held on soft). *E. F. Vaughan*

PEPPERTREE LANE (IRE) 4 ch.c. Peintre Celebre (USA) 137 – Salonrolle (IRE) **116** 103 (Tirol 127) [2007 111: 15.5g 12g* 13.4m⁴ 13.3g* 12d³ 14s* 14d⁶ 14v⁵ Sep 30] rather leggy, quite attractive colt: good walker: smart performer: won minor event at Ripon in April, listed race at Newbury (by ¾ length from Day Flight) in May and At The Races Curragh Cup (allowed to dictate, beat Nick's Nikita by 3 lengths) in June: long way below form in listed race at the Curragh (said to have been sore behind) and Deutsches St Leger at Dortmund last 2 starts: stays 1¾m: has form on good to firm going, but all wins on good or softer (acts on heavy): tends to wander/carry head awkwardly: usually races up with pace. *M. Johnston*

PEPPIN'S GOLD (IRE) 3 b.f. King Charlemagne (USA) 120 – Miss Senate (IRE) **51** (Alzao (USA) 117) [2007 63d: f7g f7s³ f8g⁵ p10g* Mar 27] lightly-made filly: modest performer: won seller at Lingfield in March: stays 1¼m: acts on all-weather and good to soft ground: often tongue tied: slowly into stride. *B. R. Millman*

PEQUENO DINERO (IRE) 2 b.f. (Apr 11) Iron Mask (USA) 117 – Mrs Kanning 61 **59** (Distant View (USA) 126) [2007 f5g 5g 7.5v* 7d³ 7.5g 8s⁴ Sep 26] 2,500Y: sparely-made filly: second foal: half-sister to 3-y-o Sad Times: dam maiden: modest performer: won claimer at Beverley in July: twice in frame in nurseries: stays 1m: acts on heavy going. *C. W. Fairhurst*

PERCUSSIONIST (IRE) 6 b.g. Sadler's Wells (USA) 132 – Magnificient Style **110** (USA) 107 (Silver Hawk (USA) 123) [2007 121: 14g⁴ 16.4d⁶ Aug 21] tall, close-coupled gelding: has a powerful, round action: just smart form on Flat in 2007: better effort when fourth to Sergeant Cecil in Yorkshire Cup at York on reappearance (had won race in 2006): stays 2m: acts on soft going, well below form last 3 starts on firmer than good: tried blinkered: wears crossed noseband: has worn earplugs/American halter: has reportedly had breathing problem over hurdles: edgy sort, tends to sweat and has had 2 handlers: hard ride: fairly useful chaser. *J. Howard Johnson*

PERCY DOUGLAS 7 b.g. Elmaamul (USA) 125 – Qualitair Dream 80 (Dreams To **46 §** Reality (USA) 113) [2007 62§: f5g f5g f6g p5.1g f8g² p5.1g f5g f5d f5g p5.1g Dec 31] good-topped gelding: poor nowadays: effective at 5f/6f: acts on all-weather, firm and soft ground: usually wears headgear: often tongue tied: sometimes bleeds (including in 2007): unreliable. *Miss A. Stokell*

PEREGRINE FALCON 3 b.c. In The Wings 128 – Island Race 93 (Common **76** Grounds 118) [2007 77: p9.5g³ f12g³ Feb 28] fair handicapper, lightly raced: stays 1½m: raced only on all-weather: sold 17,000 gns in March, sent to Germany. *M. Johnston*

PEREZ PRADO (USA) 2 b.c. (Feb 17) Kingmambo (USA) 125 – Marisa (USA) **54** (Swain (IRE) 134) [2007 7g Nov 2] $260,000Y: first foal: dam unraced half-sister to very smart 1m/1¼m performer Russian Rhythm (by Kingmambo): 33/1, eighth in maiden at Newmarket. *W. Jarvis*

PERFECT ACT 2 b.f. (Mar 8) Act One 124 – Markova's Dance 64 (Mark of Esteem **89** (IRE) 137) [2007 7g* 7m² 6m⁵ 7d⁴ Oct 27] 26,000Y: smallish, sturdy filly: third foal: dam, sprint maiden, half-sister to smart middle-distance stayers Azzilfi and Khamaseen: fairly useful form: won maiden at Newbury in August: ran well in sales race at Newmarket (fifth of 28 to Exclamation) and listed event at Newbury (fourth to Lady Deauville): free-going type, but should stay 1m: acts on good to firm and good to soft going. *C. G. Cox*

PERFECT CAUSE (USA) 3 b. or br.f. Giant's Causeway (USA) 132 – Possibly **53** Perfect (USA) 122 (Northern Baby (CAN) 127) [2007 8.1m 12m⁴ Sep 22] tall filly: fifth living foal: half-sister to several winners, including US 8.5f (at 2 yrs) and 9f (Grade 3 event) winner Promontory Gold (by Gone West) and 4-y-o Right To Play: dam, champion turf mare in USA, multiple Grade 1 winner at 9f/1¼m: better effort in maidens when eighth to Angel Kate at Sandown on debut, green: sent to USA. *J. H. M. Gosden*

PERFECT COURTESY (IRE) 3 ch.g. Danehill Dancer (IRE) 117 – Kate Maher **74** (IRE) (Rainbow Quest (USA) 134) [2007 74: 8.2g² 8.3d 8.1m⁵ 7s 10d² 10g* 10g³ 8d Oct 7] lengthy, workmanlike gelding: fair performer: sold from G. A. Swinbank 15,000 gns after fourth start: won maiden at Baden-Baden in August: stays 1¼m: acts on good to firm and good to soft going: tried blinkered: seemed to lose action second outing. *W. Kujath, Germany*

PERFECT FLIGHT 2 b.f. (Mar 28) Hawk Wing (USA) 136 – Pretty Girl (IRE) 103 **84** (Polish Precedent (USA) 131) [2007 5m⁵ 6g⁴ 5.1d⁵ 5m* 5m² 6g³ 6m 6d² Oct 11] neat filly: second foal: dam, Scandinavian 4.5f (at 2 yrs) to 8.5f winner, half-sister to very smart 1½m performer Mutamam: fairly useful performer: won nursery at Haydock in August: placed in 3 similar events after: effective at 5f/6f, bred to stay further: acts on good to firm and good to soft going. *M. Blanshard*

PERFECT PAULA (USA) 2 b. or br.f. (Feb 12) Songandaprayer (USA) 118 – Ra **93** Hydee (USA) (Rahy (USA) 115) [2007 5g⁴ 5m 5.1g² 5g 5.2m³ p5g* 5m Sep 12] strong, workmanlike filly: fourth foal: sister to 3-y-o Jack Junior and half-sister to winner in US by Devil's Bag: dam US 8.5f winner: fairly useful performer: won nursery at Lingfield in August: mostly stiff tasks otherwise, seemingly best effort when third to Cake in listed event at Newbury: speedy, raced only at 5f: acts on polytrack and good to firm going: sold 56,000 gns, sent to USA. *B. J. Meehan*

PERFECTPERFORMANCE (USA) 5 ch.h. Rahy (USA) 115 – Balistroika (USA) **107** (Nijinsky (CAN) 138) [2007 107+: 10d* 12g²¹ 10s⁴ Oct 13] strong, good-bodied horse: type to carry condition: has fluent, quick action: smart performer at 2 yrs: has run only 5 times since, and just useful nowadays: won 4-runner minor event at Nottingham in July by ½ length from Tucker: stays 1½m: acts on firm and good to soft going, probably on soft: sometimes blanketed for stall entry: tends to edge right: has left Godolphin. *Saeed bin Suroor*

PERFECT PICTURE 8 b.g. Octagonal (NZ) 126 – Greenvera (USA) (Riverman (USA) 131) [2007 12m⁶ 10.5m Jun 8] leggy, lengthy gelding: fair maiden at best in 2002: lightly raced and little form on Flat since: tried tongue tied/in cheekpieces. *P. T. Midgley* –

PERFECT POLLY 2 b.f. (Mar 26) Efisio 120 – Nashira 78 (Prince Sabo 123) [2007 5s⁶ 6d* 6g² 6m⁴ 6d Nov 2] 6,500Y: strong filly: second foal: dam 2-y-o 5f winner: useful performer: won maiden at the Curragh in August: improved in Round Tower Stakes at the Curragh (head second to Norman Invader) and Cheveley Park Stakes at Newmarket (5¼ lengths fourth to Natagora): below form back under more testing conditions in Criterium de Maisons-Laffitte final outing: should prove best at 5f/6f: winner on good to soft going, best efforts on good/good to firm. *Andrew Oliver, Ireland* **99**

PERFECT PRACTICE 3 ch.f. Medicean 128 – Giusina Mia (USA) (Diesis 133) [2007 54: p7g⁶ p7f⁶ p8g 10m p7g² p8g⁶ Dec 16] modest maiden handicapper: left J. Toller/off 6 months before penultimate start: best form at 7f: acts on polytrack. *C. G. Cox* **62**

PERFECT PUNCH 8 b.g. Reprimand 122 – Aliuska (IRE) 70 (Fijar Tango (FR) 127) [2007 60: 12.1g⁶ Aug 16] handicapper: well held in selling event only Flat start at 8 yrs. *K. G. Reveley* –

PERFECT REFLECTION 3 b.f. Josr Algarhoud (IRE) 118 – Surrealist (ITY) (Night Shift (USA)) [2007 –: 5g⁵ 7g Jun 1] no sign of ability. *A. Berry* –

PERFECT REWARD 3 b.c. Cadeaux Genereux 131 – Maid To Perfection 102 (Sadler's Wells (USA) 132) [2007 62: 10d² p11g⁴ p12m² 11.6d* Oct 15] close-coupled colt: fairly useful handicapper: much improved in 2007, winning at Windsor in October, despite jinking right final 1f: stays 1½m: acts on polytrack and good to soft going: sold 40,000 gns. *Mrs A. J. Perrett* **80 +**

PERFECT SILENCE 2 b.f. (Apr 10) Dansili 127 – Perfect Echo 81 (Lycius (USA) 124) [2007 7g Nov 3] tall, close-coupled filly: first foal: dam, 1m winner, out of useful sprinter Perfect Timing: 9/1, modest form when mid-field in maiden at Newmarket won by Infallible: type to do better at 3 yrs. *C. G. Cox* **58 p**

PERFECT STAR 3 b.f. Act One 124 – Granted (FR) 100 (Cadeaux Genereux 131) [2007 84p: 10s⁵ 8m* 7.1d² 7.1g² 7g* 8d* Sep 29] rather leggy filly: improved into a useful handicapper: won at Salisbury in July and September, and Ascot (beat Lady Gloria by 2½ lengths in listed event) later in September: has form at 1¼m, better at 7f/1m: acts on good to firm and good to soft ground: races up with pace. *C. G. Cox* **105**

PERFECT STORM 8 b.g. Vettori (IRE) 119 – Gorgeous Dancer (IRE) (Nordico (USA)) [2007 12.1m⁶ 12.6m⁶ 12m³ Sep 30] lengthy gelding: unraced on Flat in 2005/6: modest performer nowadays: stays 1½m: acts on firm and soft going: blinkered (well beaten) once. *W. G. M. Turner* **61**

PERFECT STORY (IRE) 5 b.m. Desert Story (IRE) 115 – Shore Lark (USA) (Storm Bird (CAN) 134) [2007 93: p6g² 6g² 6.1s² 6m 7d 6s 6m Aug 11] good-topped mare: useful performer: second to Firenze in listed event at Nottingham third start, below form after: effective at 6f to 1m: acts on polytrack, firm and soft ground: waited with: visored penultimate outing. *J. A. R. Toller* **95**

Space Property Rosemary Stakes (Handicap), Ascot—
Perfect Star (left) improves again to beat Lady Gloria and Contentious (USA) (right)

PERFECT STRIDE 2 b.c. (Apr 8) Oasis Dream 129 – First (Highest Honor (FR) 124) **97 p** [2007 7.1m* 7g² Sep 24] 135,000F, 440,000Y: good sort: third foal: half-brother to useful French 1¼m winner Next (by In The Wings) and useful French 2006 2-y-o 6f winner Law Lord (by Diktat): dam, French 1m winner, half-sister to smart performers up to 7f Bluebook and Myself: useful form: good impression when winning maiden at Sandown (beat Bold Choice by short head) in August: unlucky second in minor event at Leicester, going strongly but caught out by late charge of Fitzroy Crossing: will stay 1m: sure to improve and win more races. *Sir Michael Stoute*

PERFECT TREASURE (IRE) 4 ch.f. Night Shift (USA) – Pitrizza (IRE) (Machia- **85** vellian (USA) 123) [2007 77, a66: 5.3f⁴ 6d³ 7f* 7d* 8.1m 6m³ 7v⁵ 6g p7g⁵ Nov 12] sturdy filly: fairly useful handicapper: won twice at Brighton in August: stays 1m: acts on polytrack, firm and good to soft going: tried tongue tied. *J. A. R. Toller*

PER INCANTO (USA) 3 b.c. Street Cry (IRE) 130 – Pappa Reale 104 (Indian Ridge **111** 123) [2007 7m* 6m* 6m* 7d⁶ 6g Sep 8] medium-sized, quite attractive colt: fourth foal: half-brother to 2 winners in Italy, notably smart sprinter Patapan (by Stravinsky): dam Italian 5f to 1m winner: smart performer: winner of 5 of his 8 starts in Italy, including minor events at Rome in March, Milan in April and Premio Tudini at Rome (beat Sakhee's Song by 2 lengths) in May: left R. Brogi in Italy, below form in Hungerford Stakes at Newbury and Sprint Cup at Haydock last 2 starts: stays 7f: acts on soft and good to firm going. *J. L. Dunlop*

PERKS (IRE) 2 b.g. (Apr 19) Selkirk (USA) 129 – Green Charter 77 (Green Desert **72 p** (USA) 127) [2007 7d 7s 7m⁴ Sep 21] big, close-coupled gelding: has a round action: sixth foal: half-brother to 3 winners, including 9f winner Manouche (by Highest Honor) and 2001 2-y-o 7f winner Safe Trip (by Hector Protector): dam, 2-y-o 7f winner, closely related to 1¼m to 2m winner First Charter and half-sister to middle-distance performer Private Charter, both smart: fair form in maidens, again not knocked about when fourth to Fr Dominic at Newmarket (gelded after): will be suited by 1¼m+: type to do better in handicaps. *J. L. Dunlop*

PERLACHY 3 b.g. Kyllachy 129 – Perfect Dream 72 (Emperor Jones (USA) 119) **68** [2007 76: p5g³ p6g p5.1g⁵ f5s⁴ f5g⁵ 5.1g f5g⁴ 6g⁴ 7g 5m³ 5m⁶ p6g³ p5.1g² p6g⁴ p6g² p5.1g³ p6d² p6g* Dec 22] quite good-topped, close-coupled gelding: fair handicapper: belated first win at Wolverhampton in December: best at 5f/easy 6f: acts on all-weather and firm going: usually visored. *Mrs N. Macauley*

PERRY'S PRIDE 3 b.f. Perryston View 114 – Caspian Morn 63 (Lugana Beach 116) **38** [2007 p8.6g p8.6g p6g p6g 8.2m 6v Oct 26] 500Y: fourth foal: half-sister to 1m/11f winner Caspian Dusk (by Up And At 'em) and 11f/1½m winner Precaster (by Factual): dam 6f winner: poor maiden. *Mrs G. S. Rees*

PERSIAN EXPRESS (USA) 4 b.f. Bahri (USA) 125 – Istikbal (USA) (Kingmambo **97** (USA) 125) [2007 76, a97: p8g⁶ 9m 8d 8g 8.3m* 8m* 8m p7g p8m Nov 1] compact filly: useful handicapper: won at Windsor in August and Newmarket (beat South Cape by 1½ lengths) in September: best efforts around 1m: acts on polytrack and firm going: sold 35,000 gns, sent to USA. *B. W. Hills*

PERSIAN FOX (IRE) 3 b.g. King Charlemagne (USA) 120 – Persian Mistress (IRE) **62 §** (Persian Bold 123) [2007 73: 10.1g⁵ 8m 7g³ 10g⁵ 7g Oct 16] leggy gelding: modest performer nowadays: left G. Huffer after fourth start: stays 1m: acts on firm going: tried in cheekpieces: has carried head high/found little: one to treat with caution. *A. G. Juckes*

PERSIAN PERIL 3 br.g. Erhaab (USA) 127 – Brush Away (Ahonoora 122) [2007 77: **78** 12g⁴ 10m 11.9m⁵ 12g Aug 18] strong, close-coupled gelding: fair handicapper: should stay 1¾m: acts on fibresand, unraced on extremes of going on turf. *G. A. Swinbank*

PERSISTENT (IRE) 2 b.c. (Mar 13) Cape Cross (IRE) 129 – Insistent (USA) (Diesis **56** 133) [2007 p7g⁶ 6m f7d⁶ Dec 14] sturdy colt: modest maiden: left M. Johnston 5,200 gns after debut: will stay 1m. *P. T. Midgley*

PERSONA (IRE) 5 b.m. Night Shift (USA) – Alonsa (IRE) 69 (Trempolino (USA) **68** 135) [2007 68: f12g³ p10g Oct 31] unfurnished mare: fair maiden handicapper on Flat: stays 1½m: acts on fibresand and good to soft going: reportedly had breathing problem on 4-y-o reappearance. *B. J. McMath*

PERSONAL CHOICE 2 ch.f. (Mar 5) Choisir (AUS) 126 – Bonkers 63 (Efisio 120) **49** [2007 5g⁴ 6s 6s 6m Aug 9] 5,500Y: attractive filly: first foal: dam, 2-y-o 5f winner (later successful up to 7f abroad), half-sister to useful performers up to 1¼m Skidmark and Skidrow: poor maiden. *M. Brittain*

PERSONAL COLUMN 3 ch.g. Pursuit of Love 124 – Tromond 94 (Lomond (USA) **75** 128) [2007 76p: f12g⁴ p10g 11.6m⁴ 11.6d⁴ 14.1s p10g* p11g Aug 1] lengthy gelding:

fair handicapper: won at Lingfield in July: stays 1½m: acts on all-weather and good to soft ground: won over hurdles in September, then joined Mrs J. Harrington in Ireland. *T. G. Mills*

PERSONIFY 5 ch.g. Zafonic (USA) 130 – Dignify (IRE) 105 (Rainbow Quest (USA) **77** 134) [2007 81: 8f⁵ 8d 8.3f 8.1f³ 8m Sep 20] rather leggy gelding: fair handicapper: stays 9f: acts on firm going: tried visored/tongue tied, wears cheekpieces nowadays: said to have bled final outing: sold 4,000 gns. *C. G. Cox*

PERTEMPS GREEN 4 b.g. Green Desert (USA) 127 – Pure Misk 55 (Rainbow Quest **–** (USA) 134) [2007 69: p8g 7s 7.6f 10g 7d Oct 1] leggy, close-coupled gelding: lightly-raced maiden: well held in 2007, leaving M. Saunders after third start. *Stef Liddiard*

PERTEMPS NETWORKS 3 b.g. Golden Snake (USA) 127 – Society Girl 73 **60 +** (Shavian 125) [2007 57: 12.1v⁵ 9.9d f11d² Dec 21] tall, workmanlike gelding: modest maiden handicapper on Flat (winning hurdler): stays 11f: acts on fibresand and good to firm ground. *M. W. Easterby*

PERTEMPS POWER 3 b.g. Zaha (CAN) 106 – Peristyle 59 (Tolomeo 127) [2007 **59** 11.7g⁶ p12g⁴ 14m⁵ 16.2f p13.9g⁴ p12.2g⁴ Sep 27] modest maiden handicapper: stays 1¾m: acts on polytrack. *A. D. Smith*

PERUVIAN PRINCE (USA) 5 b.g. Silver Hawk (USA) 123 – Inca Dove (USA) (Mr **102** Prospector (USA)) [2007 89: p9.5g p10g 12g 10.5m* 10.9s³ 9.9g³ 9m³ 10.4d² 10m 12s Oct 13] strong, well-made gelding: useful handicapper: improved again in 2007, winning at Haydock (by 3½ lengths from Nightspot) in June: excellent head second to Greek Well at York eighth start: stays 10.5f, probably not 1½m: acts on polytrack, good to firm and good to soft going: tried visored. *R. A. Fahey*

PERUVIAN STYLE (IRE) 6 b.g. Desert Style (IRE) 121 – Lady's Vision (IRE) 93 **63** (Vision (USA)) [2007 66, a58: 5.3m⁵ 5.1g 5.1s³ 5.7m³ 6g 5.1f 6.1m 6d p6g Oct 4] strong gelding: modest performer: best at 5f to easy 7f: acts on polytrack, firm and soft ground: tried blinkered earlier in career. *J. M. Bradley*

PETARA BAY (IRE) 3 b.c. Peintre Celebre (USA) 137 – Magnificient Style (USA) **106** 107 (Silver Hawk (USA) 123) [2007 89p: 9m* 10g 12g Jun 2] big, good sort: useful performer: easily best effort when winning listed race at Newmarket (beat Salford Mill by head) in April: disappointing after in Classic Trial at Sandown (mulish at stall) and Derby at Epsom (reportedly returned slightly sore): should be suited by 1¼m/1½m: acts on good to firm going: suspect temperament. *T. G. Mills*

PETER ISLAND (FR) 4 b.g. Dansili 127 – Catania (USA) (Aloma's Ruler (USA)) **85** [2007 85: p6g⁴ p6g⁶ 6g p6g 5m 5.2f² 6f* 5.6m 5.1m⁴ 5.1m⁴ p5g p5g p5g Nov 12] smallish, strong gelding: fairly useful handicapper: won at Brighton in August: best at 5f/6f: acts on polytrack and firm going: usually visored/blinkered: races prominently. *J. Gallagher*

PETER'S JOY (USA) 2 b.g. (Mar 1) Stravinsky (USA) 133 – Jadarah (USA) 62 (Red **–** Ransom (USA)) [2007 5m p7g Dec 29] close-coupled, workmanlike gelding: well held in maidens 6½ months apart, reportedly finishing lame on debut. *Jean-Rene Auvray*

PETER'S STORM (USA) 2 ch.c. (Apr 28) Van Nistelrooy (USA) 108 – Fairy Land **81** Flyer (USA) (Lyphard's Wish (FR) 124) [2007 6d⁵ p5.1g* 6m Nov 10] strong, workman-like colt: type to carry condition: fairly useful form: won maiden at Wolverhampton in October: early speed but well held in nursery at Doncaster: may prove best kept to 5f/6f. *K. A. Ryan*

PETIDIUM 2 b.f. (May 6) Presidium 124 – Efipetite 54 (Efisio 120) [2007 6m 6g **–** Oct 19] 1,000Y: small filly: sixth foal: sister to 3 winners, including 6-y-o Dium Mac and 9-y-o Efidium: dam 1m winner: well held in maidens. *N. Bycroft*

PETITE ARVINE (USA) 3 b.f. Gulch (USA) – Grapevine (IRE) 88 (Sadler's Wells **–** (USA) 132) [2007 8.2m 9g f11g May 22] $80,000Y: good-bodied filly: fourth foal: dam, US 9.5f and 11f winner, half-sister to smart performer up to 1½m Theatre Script out of half-sister to high-class sprinter Committed: well held in maidens: sold 9,000 gns in July. *M. L. W. Bell*

PETITE MAC 7 b.m. Timeless Times (USA) 99 – Petite Elite 47 (Anfield 117) [2007 **66** 74: 7g 5d⁶ 5.9m⁶ 5m 5.9g 7d* 7s 6d 6g⁵ 6m 6m 6m² 7m⁶ 6f² 6s⁶ 5g p6g Oct 30] small **a–** mare: fair performer: won claimer at Redcar in June: probably best at 6f/7f nowadays: acts on fibresand, firm and good to soft going: tried blinkered/in cheekpieces: often claimer ridden. *N. Bycroft*

Duke of Edinburgh Stakes (Handicap), Royal Ascot—the first three pull clear in the soft ground with Pevensey (centre) gaining a narrow verdict over Solent (left) and Hitchcock

PETITE MUSIC (IRE) 2 b.f. (Mar 26) Distant Music (USA) 126 – Petite Maxine 70 (Sharpo 132) [2007 6d 6g Oct 19] €22,000Y: sparely-made filly: half-sister to several winners, including fairly useful 5f (including at 2 yrs)/6f winner Pipadash (by Pip's Pride): dam, maiden (stayed 7f), out of smart 2-y-o 5f winner Penny Blessing: 100/1 and no show in maidens. *T. D. Easterby* —

PETITO (IRE) 4 b.g. Imperial Ballet (IRE) 110 – Fallacy (Selkirk (USA) 129) [2007 65: 10v⁶ 10s 8.2g 7m³ 7.1f 7g Sep 19] strong gelding: fair maiden handicapper: stays 1¼m: acts on good to firm ground: unseated rider leaving stall third outing: sold 4,500 gns. *J. L. Spearing* **67**

PETIT PARC 2 b.f. (Mar 10) Bahamian Bounty 116 – Alkarida (FR) (Akarad (FR) 130) [2007 p6g⁴ 6m⁴ p6g Oct 23] 25,000Y, £20,000 2-y-o: fifth foal: half-sister to 3 winners, including fairly useful 7f winner Kali (by Linamix) and 3-y-o Emefdream: dam French 1m winner: fair maiden: twice fourth at Lingfield: off 4 months, weakened final start: likely to prove best at 5f/6f. *R. A. Teal* **67 +**

PETOMIC (IRE) 2 ch.c. (Mar 31) Dubai Destination (USA) 127 – Petomi 75 (Presidium 124) [2007 p7g Dec 19] 33/1, modest form when ninth in maiden at Lingfield (slowly away). *Christian Wroe* **60**

PETROSIAN 3 b.g. Sakhee (USA) 136 – Arabis 88 (Arazi (USA) 135) [2007 63§: f8g³ f12g* 11.6m 12.1g⁵ May 11] fair handicapper: won at Southwell in March: stays 1½m: acts on fibresand and good to firm ground: blinkered (ran poorly) third start: carries head high, and best treated with caution. *M. Johnston* **68 §**

PETROVICH (USA) 4 ch.c. Giant's Causeway (USA) 132 – Pharma (USA) 118 (Theatrical 128) [2007 111p: p10m 8.2g⁴ p12m Dec 7] good-topped colt: very lightly raced: smart at 3 yrs for J. Noseda: off 15 months (reportedly suffered from disease), showed —

little in 2007, claimed from B. Curley £15,000 after reappearance: tried blinkered. *Jane Chapple-Hyam*

PEVENSEY (IRE) 5 b.g. Danehill (USA) 126 – Champaka (IRE) (Caerleon (USA) 132) [2007 98: 10.4g 12s* 8.9s 14d 10s⁵ 12s Oct 13] compact gelding: useful handicapper: won Duke of Edinburgh Stakes at Royal Ascot in June by head from Solent: ran well after only when fifth at Ayr: should stay 1¾m: acts on firm and soft going, probably on polytrack: tried blinkered early in career: often slowly away: useful hurdler, pulled up in November/December. *J. J. Quinn* **105**

PHA MAI BLUE 2 b.c. (May 14) Acclamation 118 – Queen of Silk (IRE) 93 (Brief Truce (USA) 126) [2007 7m³ 7m 7d⁵ 6m² 5.7d p6g Oct 17] quite attractive colt: fair maiden: will prove best up to 7f: acts on good to firm going. *W. J. Knight* **74**

PHANTOM WHISPER 4 b.g. Makbul 104 – La Belle Vie 73 (Indian King (USA) 128) [2007 94: p6g p5.1g³ 6s 6g 5m² 6s² 5d³ 6g 6m* 5m 5g 6s Oct 14] workmanlike gelding: useful handicapper: best effort when winning at Windsor in August by 1¼ lengths from Beaver Patrol, making all: raced at 5f/6f: acts on polytrack, soft and good to firm ground: tried blinkered at 2 yrs: none too consistent. *B. R. Millman* **102**

PHARAOH PRINCE 6 b.g. Desert Prince (IRE) 130 – Kinlochewe 102 (Old Vic 136) [2007 58: p11g³ p12.2g p12g p11g p8g⁶ Mar 21] modest performer: stays 1½m: acts on polytrack, firm and good to soft ground: tried tongue tied, sometimes blinkered/visored. *G. Prodromou* **51**

PHARAOHS JUSTICE (USA) 2 br.c. (Mar 17) Kafwain (USA) 118 – Mary Linoa (USA) 113 (L'Emigrant (USA) 129) [2007 p8.6g p8m⁵ f8d⁷ Dec 21] $77,000F, $150,000Y: half-brother to 3 winners, including smart French 1m/1¼m performer Marrast (by Groom Dancer): dam won Prix Marcel Boussac: fairly useful form: progressive in maidens, won at Southwell final start: will be suited by 1¼m: raced only on all-weather. *Jane Chapple-Hyam* **81**

PHARAOHS QUEEN (IRE) 2 b.f. (Apr 3) Bahri (USA) 125 – Medway (IRE) 60 (Shernazar 131) [2007 p7g³ p8g² Nov 19] 14,500Y: eighth foal: half-sister to several winners, including 4-y-o Missoula and fairly useful 1½m winner Settlement Craic (by Ela-Mana-Mou): dam, 1½m winner, half-sister to top-class Hong Kong performer up to 1½m Indigenous: fair form: placed in maidens at Lingfield and Kempton (better effort): will stay 1¼m/1½m. *E. A. L. Dunlop* **70 +**

PHEIDIAS (IRE) 3 ch.g. Spectrum (IRE) 126 – Danse Grecque (IRE) (Sadler's Wells (USA) 132) [2007 p10g p10g 10d Oct 10] good-topped gelding: modest form in maidens: left M. Tregoning and gelded prior to final outing. *Mrs P. Sly* **55**

PHILANTHROPY 3 ch.g. Generous (IRE) 139 – Clerio 108 (Soviet Star (USA) 128) [2007 96: 12g 11.6s³ 14g 12f* 12m³ 10.3g⁴ 12m Nov 10] lengthy gelding: useful handicapper: left M. Johnston 45,000 gns after second start: won at York (by 2½ lengths from Sanbuch, making all) in September: should stay 1¾m: acts on firm and good to soft ground: ran as if amiss final outing at 2 yrs/reappearance: races prominently. *K. A. Ryan* **98**

PHILARIO (IRE) 2 ch.c. (Mar 9) Captain Rio 122 – Salva 73 (Grand Lodge (USA) 125) [2007 5m* 6m² 6g p6g* 6m⁴ Sep 22] 27,000Y: tends not to impress in appearance: fourth foal: half-brother to 7f winner Saxon Lil (by Second Empire): dam maiden (stayed 8.5f): useful form: won maiden at Carlisle in June and totescoop6 Sirenia Stakes at Kempton (made all to beat Red Alert Day by length) in September: creditable length fourth to Dark Angel in Dubai Duty Free Mill Reef Stakes at Newbury: should prove best at 5f/6f: acts on polytrack and good to firm going. *K. R. Burke* **104**

totescoop6 Sirenia Stakes, Kempton—Philario (second left) puts up his best performance to beat the unlucky Red Alert Day (fourth left), the grey Lady Aquitaine (left) and Sporting Art (right)

PHILATELIST (USA) 3 b.c. Rahy (USA) 115 – Polent (Polish Precedent (USA) 131) **96**
[2007 11m⁶ 10.3m³ p12g* 11.9m² 12g 12g⁶ 9.9m⁵ Aug 25] tall, lengthy colt: sixth foal:
closely related to fairly useful Irish 1¾m winner Tentpole (by Rainbow Quest) and
half-brother to 2 winners, including fairly useful stayer Querido (by Spectrum), 7f winner
at 2 yrs: dam, French 13f/15.5f winner, half-sister to Oaks winner Snow Bride, herself
dam of Lammtarra: useful performer: won maiden at Lingfield in May: much better form
in handicaps all starts after, second at Haydock: should stay 1¾m: acts on polytrack,
raced only on good/good to firm ground on turf: blinkered final outing: sold 95,000 gns.
M. A. Jarvis

PHILHARMONIC 6 b.g. Victory Note (USA) 120 – Lambast 70 (Relkino 131) [2007 **109**
115: 6s⁴ 6m 5d* 6d p7m p6g³ Dec 30] strong, lengthy gelding: useful performer nowadays: easily best effort in 2007 when winning minor event at Beverley in September
by ¾ length from Bond City: effective at 5f to 7f: acts on any turf going: waited with.
R. A. Fahey

PHINERINE 4 ch.g. Bahamian Bounty 116 – Golden Panda 77 (Music Boy 124) [2007 **–**
71: f5g³ p5.1g⁴ p5.1g⁵ p6g* p6g⁴ p6g⁴ 6f⁵ 6.1g 6d p6g⁶ p6g p5.1g⁵ p6g f6d² f5d⁴ Dec 14] **a61**
modest performer: won seller at Wolverhampton in February: left R. Harris after next
start: best at 5f/6f: acts on all-weather and good to firm going: usually blinkered: has
hung. *Miss J. E. Foster*

PHLUKE 6 b.g. Most Welcome 131 – Phlirty (Pharly (FR) 130) [2007 97: 7m³ 7.1d* **101**
7m* 7g 7f⁶ p8g⁶ 7g 7.6m 7d 7m 7g⁶ p7m Oct 6] good-bodied gelding: useful handicapper: won at Warwick and Catterick (beat Zomerlust by head) in May: below form after:
best at 7f/1m: acts on all-weather, firm and good to soft going. *Eve Johnson Houghton*

PHOENIX BAY 2 b.f. (Mar 15) Reel Buddy (USA) 118 – Bollin Victoria 51 (Jalmood **–**
(USA) 126) [2007 5g p5.1g Oct 6] 1,200Y: half-sister to several sprint winners, including
useful 2003 2-y-o 5f winner Axis (by Pivotal): dam maiden (stayed 7f): last in maiden/
seller. *J. J. Quinn*

PHOENIX EYE 6 b.g. Tragic Role (USA) – Eye Sight 67 (Roscoe Blake 120) [2007 **–**
56: p16.5g Jan 5] close-coupled gelding: modest performer: well held only Flat outing in
2007: modest winning hurdler. *M. Mullineaux*

PHOENIX FACTOR (IRE) 4 b.f. Indian Ridge 123 – Alassio (USA) 90 (Gulch **–**
(USA)) [2007 74: p10g f8g Feb 22] €95,000Y: first foal: dam, Irish 9f winner, out of
Oaks/Irish Oaks runner-up Royal Ballerina: maiden handicapper: left M. Grassick in
Ireland, well held in 2007: tried blinkered. *J. S. Moore*

PHOENIX FLIGHT (IRE) 2 b.g. (May 5) Hawk Wing (USA) 136 – Firecrest (IRE) **74 p**
107 (Darshaan 133) [2007 7d³ p7.1g* Jul 2] €110,000Y: fourth foal: half-brother to 12.4f
winner Grey Plover (by Alzao) and 4-y-o Lady Songbird, both fairly useful: dam, 1½m
winner, half-sister to smart stayer Anak Pekan: promise both starts in maidens, won at
Wolverhampton (made all but still green), and subsequently gelded: will be suited by
1¼m/1½m: sure to improve further. *Sir Mark Prescott*

PHOENIX HILL (IRE) 5 b.g. Montjeu (IRE) 137 – Cielo Vodkamartini (USA) (Con- **62**
quistador Cielo (USA)) [2007 65: p16g⁶ 16m p16g⁵ p13.9g p12g⁵ p13.9g Dec 31] quite
good-topped gelding: modest maiden handicapper: stays easy 2m: acts on polytrack and
good to soft going: tried tongue tied. *D. R. Gandolfo*

PHOENIX NIGHTS (IRE) 7 b.g. General Monash (USA) 107 – Beauty Appeal **–**
(USA) (Shadeed (USA) 135) [2007 –: 13.8m⁶ 9.3g⁶ 10d 9m⁶ Aug 11] smallish, workmanlike gelding: little form since 2003. *A. Berry*

PHOENIX TOWER (USA) 3 b.c. Chester House (USA) 123 – Bionic 105 (Zafonic **106 +**
(USA) 130) [2007 85p: 7m* 8.3m* May 7] quite good-topped colt: unbeaten in 3 starts,
including handicap at Newbury (impressive, beating Jaasoos 4 lengths) in April and
minor event at Windsor (easily landed odds in 4-runner race) in May: effective at 7f/1m:
swerved left once in front sole 2-y-o start: looked likely to go on to better things, but
reported in June to have suffered a setback: stays in training. *H. R. A. Cecil*

PHONE CALL 4 b.f. Anabaa (USA) 130 – Phone West (USA) (Gone West (USA)) **–**
[2007 p12g 11d Oct 11] third foal: sister to French 5.5f winner Payphone and French
2-y-o 6.5f/1m winner Conference Call (both useful): dam placed all 3 starts in France
(1m to 10.5f), out of smart close relative to Danehill: fairly useful maiden: twice in frame
at Saint-Cloud at 3 yrs: left P. Bary in France 19,500 gns, well held in handicaps in 2007:
stays 1½m: raced on good/good to soft ground on turf. *Mouse Hamilton-Fairley*

PHONE IN 4 b.g. Sinndar (IRE) 134 – Patria (USA) 76 (Mr Prospector (USA)) [2007 **50**
74: 14.1m 10s⁶ 11.8s 11.9d f12d⁵ Dec 15] big, good-bodied gelding: maiden handicapper
on Flat: only modest in 2007: stays 13f: acts on polytrack and firm going: tried blinkered/
in cheekpieces: successful over hurdles in September. *R. Brotherton*

PHOTOGRAPHER (USA) 9 b. or br.g. Mountain Cat (USA) – Clickety Click (USA) **–**
(Sovereign Dancer (USA)) [2007 p13.9g⁶ p16g Jan 29] close-coupled gelding: fairly
useful performer at 3 yrs: first runs on Flat since 2002 when well held in handicaps in
2007. *S. Lycett*

PHREEZE 3 gr.c. Sadler's Wells (USA) 132 – Showdown 65 (Darshaan 133) [2007 **89 +**
7.1g f8g² 10.3m f11g³ 12d* 14d 14.6m* Aug 17] 55,000Y: good-topped colt: first foal:
dam once-raced sister to useful performers up to 1½m Approach and Intrigued and
half-sister to Poule d'Essai des Poulains winner Aussie Rules out of very smart 1¼m
performer Last Second: fairly useful performer: successful in handicaps at Newmarket in
June and Doncaster in August: stays 14.6f: acts on fibresand, good to firm and good to
soft going: carried head awkwardly second outing: sold 60,000 gns. *G. A. Swinbank*

PIANOFORTE (USA) 5 b.g. Grand Slam (USA) 120 – Far Too Loud (CAN) (No **74**
Louder (USA)) [2007 74: 9g 8m 8s⁶ 8s 8m² 8f⁶ 8m 10g³ 8.3m⁶ 8.1g⁶ 10g⁶ 9.2g³ 8g 8g
10g 8g p8g² p8g p7.1g⁶ Dec 14] strong, close-coupled gelding: fair performer: probably
best up to 9f: acts on all-weather and firm ground: has been visored/blinkered: often
slowly away: held up: not straightforward. *E. J. Alston*

PIANO KEY 3 ch.f. Distant Music (USA) 126 – Ivorine (USA) (Blushing Groom (FR) **51**
131) [2007 –: 8.3m 6m p12.2g 8m⁶ 8.1d³ 8.5s⁶ 10.2s⁵ 16g⁶ 7.6s³ p12g⁶ f11d⁴ p13.9s³
Dec 20] modest maiden: seems to stay 1¾m: acts on all-weather and soft going: tried
visored. *M. D. I. Usher*

PIANO MAN 5 b.g. Atraf 116 – Pinup 44 (Risk Me (FR) 127) [2007 57: 10.2d² 10s⁴ **66**
10m⁴ p10g⁶ 10d⁴ 10.2s Jul 26] smallish, sturdy gelding: fair maiden: stays 1¼m: acts on
polytrack, soft and good to firm going: tried blinkered. *B. G. Powell*

PIANO SONATA 2 b.f. (May 4) Observatory (USA) 131 – Matinee (Sadler's Wells **59 p**
(USA) 132) [2007 7g Nov 3] good-topped filly: third foal: dam, unraced, out of useful
1¾m winner Totality, herself sister to Derby winner Commander In Chief and half-sister
to Warning, Dushyantor and Deploy: 8/1, eleventh of 20 to Infallible in maiden at Newmarket: will do better, especially at 1¼m/1½m. *B. W. Hills*

PICACHO (IRE) 4 b.f. Sinndar (IRE) 134 – Gentle Thoughts 73 (Darshaan 133) [2007 **75**
74: 16.2d³ 14d⁴ Jul 6] quite good-topped filly: fair handicapper: stays 2m: acts on soft
ground (successful on firm over hurdles): joined M. Rolland in France. *P. J. Hobbs*

PICADOR 4 b.g. Pivotal 124 – Candescent (Machiavellian (USA) 123) [2007 64: **84**
p8.6g* f8g² p9.5g p8.6g Feb 2] fairly useful handicapper: won at Wolverhampton and
Southwell in January: said to have bled when pulled up final outing: stayed 1¼m: acted
on all-weather: dead. *Sir Mark Prescott*

PICCLEYES 6 b.g. Piccolo 121 – Dark Eyed Lady (IRE) 82 (Exhibitioner 111) [2007 **52**
64: f7g⁵ f6g f6g f6g⁴ f6g³ f6g⁶ f5g f5g f7g⁴ f6g⁴ f8g f7g Jun 5] modest performer: best at
5f/6f: acts on all-weather, good to firm and good to soft going: usually blinkered: has
hung right. *A. J. McCabe*

PICCOLO DIAMANTE (USA) 3 b. or br.g. Three Wonders (USA) – Bafooz (USA) **61**
48 (Clever Trick (USA)) [2007 59: 5m 5m⁶ 5f⁴ p6g⁴ p6g p6g* p7g⁵ p7m³ f7d⁶ p7.1s³ Dec
20] modest handicapper: won at Kempton in November: stays 7f: acts on polytrack:
usually tongue tied. *D. J. Murphy*

PICCOLOMINI 5 b.g. Diktat 126 – La Dama Bonita (USA) 87 (El Gran Senor (USA) **52**
136) [2007 –: f14g 16g⁶ 15.8m⁶ 16m⁴ f14g⁴ 14.1d 14.1m Aug 11] good-bodied gelding:
modest maiden handicapper: barely stays 2m: acts on soft and good to firm going: often
blinkered, tried in cheekpieces. *E. W. Tuer*

PICCOLO PETE 2 b.c. (Apr 4) Piccolo 121 – Goes A Treat (IRE) 82 (Common **54**
Grounds 118) [2007 5f 7m 5m⁴ 5f 6g⁴ Oct 3] close-coupled colt: modest maiden: likely
to prove best at 5f/6f: tried in visor. *J. J. Quinn*

PICCOLO PRIDE 2 ch.g. (May 3) Piccolo 121 – Jaycat (IRE) 56 (Catrail (USA) 123) **–**
[2007 p6g Dec 29] 25/1, always behind in maiden at Lingfield. *B. G. Powell*

PICCOLO PRINCE 6 ch.g. Piccolo 121 – Aegean Flame 86 (Anshan 119) [2007 64: **47**
f6g f6g³ f8g p7.1g f6g 5s Jun 21] strong, stocky gelding: only poor nowadays, left
P. Blockley after fourth start: effective at 5f/6f: acts on all-weather and any turf going:
tried in cheekpieces. *Mrs Marjorie Fife*

PICCOSTAR 4 b.f. Piccolo 121 – Anneliina 80 (Cadeaux Genereux 131) [2007 75: **59**
p6g⁵ 6m 7.1m³ p7g⁶ 7m 7f⁴ 7m⁴ p5g* 6f 5.1f 6.1m 5.3d⁶ p6g⁶ p5m Dec 9] quite good-
topped filly: modest handicapper: won at Kempton in July: effective at 5f to 7f: acts on
polytrack and firm ground: usually blinkered/visored. *A. B. Haynes*

PICK A NICE NAME 5 ch.m. Polar Falcon (USA) 126 – Opuntia (Rousillon (USA) **85**
133) [2007 75: f5g 6g 5m³ 7s 6s* 6.1s² 6s⁵ Jul 14] strong, lengthy mare: fairly useful
handicapper: won at Pontefract in July: should stay 7f: acts on soft and good to firm going
(seemed to resent kickback on fibresand): awkward ride: reportedly in foal to Monsieur
Bond. *R. M. Whitaker*

PICKERING 3 br.g. Prince Sabo 123 – On The Wagon (Then Again 126) [2007 67: **80**
5.1g* 6g⁴ 5g 7.1g⁴ 6v 6f² 6g 6m⁶ Sep 8] big, strong, lengthy gelding: fairly useful handicapper: won at Nottingham in April: effective at 5f to 7f: acts on firm ground. *E. J. Alston*

PICKLEDALLNUTS 3 ch.f. Piccolo 121 – Salinas 65 (Bay Express 132) [2007 f7g –
8m p7.1g Apr 27] sister to Swedish 6f/7f winner Wonky Donkey: dam sprint maiden:
well held in maidens/seller. *Miss J. A. Camacho*

PICK OF THE CROP 6 ch.g. Fraam 114 – Fresh Fruit Daily 92 (Reprimand 122) –
[2007 –: p8g Jan 3] tall gelding: poor performer in 2005: well beaten both starts since:
tried visored/tongue tied *I R. Jenkins*

PICKY 3 b.g. Piccolo 121 – Passerella (FR) (Brustolon 117) [2007 p7.1g³ p9.5g⁵ **68**
p10g⁶ p10g³ 11.5m 10m 10.1m³ p10g⁵ p10g* p12g p10g* Oct 14] fair performer: left
J. Osborne after fourth start: won minor event in September and apprentice handicap
(landed gamble) in October, both at Lingfield: stays 1¼m: acts on polytrack and good to
firm ground: visored last 5 starts: sold 12,000 gns. *C. Tinkler*

PICOT DE SAY 5 b.g. Largesse 112 – Facsimile 67 (Superlative 118) [2007 52: p13.9g **53**
10.9g Oct 2] unfurnished gelding: modest performer: stays 11.5f: acts on soft ground.
C. Roberts

PICTURE FRAME 3 ch.g. Fraam 114 – Floral Spark 69 (Forzando 122) [2007 69: **69**
5.1g⁶ 5g⁴ 6m Jun 11] lengthy gelding: fair performer: bred to be suited by 7f/1m: acts on
firm and good to soft going. *J. T. Stimpson*

PIC UP STICKS 8 gr.g. Piccolo 121 – Between The Sticks 83 (Pharly (FR) 130) [2007 **89**
96: 5g 5m³ 6g 5.7g⁶ 6g 5.7f⁶ 5m⁶ 5g 6g 5m⁴ 5g* 5.7f³ 5m⁴ p5g Oct 23] tall gelding: fairly
useful handicapper: won at Salisbury in September: effective at 5f to 6.5f: acts on firm
and good to soft going, probably on polytrack: tried in cheekpieces: none too consistent.
B. G. Powell

PIDDIES PRIDE (IRE) 5 b.m. Indian Lodge (IRE) 127 – Fairybird (FR) 70 (Pampa- **62**
bird 124) [2007 65, a–: p6g* 6m⁶ p6g⁵ 6m⁵ 6s³ 6d 6m⁶ Aug 9] smallish, lengthy mare: **a56 +**
modest handicapper: won at Kempton in March: stays 7f: acts on polytrack, firm and soft
going: wears headgear. *Miss Gay Kelleway*

PIECE OF MY HEART 2 b.f. (Apr 11) Fasliyev (USA) 120 – Cultured Pearl (IRE) **69**
72 (Lammtarra (USA) 134) [2007 5m* 5d³ 5m a6.5g p6s⁴ Dec 20] lengthy filly: fourth
foal: half-sister to 1½m/1¾m winner Pearl's A Singer (by Spectrum) and 2005 2-y-o 6f
winner Culture Queen (by King's Best): dam, maiden, out of Prix Marcel Boussac and
Poule d'Essai des Pouliches winner Culture Vulture: fair form: won maiden at Warwick
in April: off 6 months after well beaten (hampered) in Queen Mary Stakes at Royal Ascot:
much better effort on return when creditable seventh in minor event at Deauville: stays
6.5f. *P. F. I. Cole*

PIE O MY (IRE) 2 gr.c. (Apr 14) Nayef (USA) 129 – Sea Drift (FR) 72 (Warning 136) –
[2007 p8.6g Nov 10] last in maiden at Wolverhampton. *J. Jay*

PIERMARINI 2 b.c. (Feb 15) Singspiel (IRE) 133 – Allespagne (USA) (Trempolino **77 ?**
(USA) 135) [2007 8.2d⁵ 8m⁴ 8.2g Nov 7] 52,000Y: small, sturdy colt: fifth foal: brother
to smart 1¼m to 2¾m winner Cruzspiel and half-brother to 1½m winner Larousse (by
Unfuwain): dam, useful French performer up to 1¾m, out of smart Spanish mare up to
1½m: Teresa: fair maiden: seemingly easily best effort when fourth to Kandahar Run at
Doncaster, dictating: will be suited by 1½m+. *M. Johnston*

PIETER BRUEGHEL (USA) 8 b.g. Citidancer (USA) – Smart Tally (USA) (Smar- **89**
ten (USA) 99, a89: f5g² f6g p5f⁶ f5g³ 6g⁵ f5g 6m 5d 5g³ 6v² 5g² 5g⁵ 5g³
Dec 30] big, good-topped gelding: fairly useful performer nowadays: left D. Nicholls
after eleventh start: effective at 5f to easy 7f: acts on all-weather and any turf going: has
been tongue tied: usually races prominently: has bled, including final outing in Britain.
P. Haley, Spain

PIETERSEN (IRE) 3 ch.g. Redback 116 – Faye 79 (Monsanto (FR) 121) [2007 59: **73** p7.1g² p6g* p6g³ p7.1g* 7.5m* 8.2m⁴ 7m⁴ 8.5g⁶ p7.1g⁴ 7g p7.1d p7g² Dec 16] compact, good-quartered gelding: has a quick action: fair handicapper: won at Wolverhampton in January and February, and Beverley in April: effective at 6f, probably at 8.5f: acts on polytrack, heavy and good to firm going: usually blinkered. *T. D. Barron*

PIGEON FLIGHT 3 ch.g. Compton Admiral 121 – Fervent Fan (IRE) 65 (Soviet Lad **69** (USA)) [2007 68: 10.1m* 12m⁶ 9.9m⁴ 10.3f 8s Jul 9] strong, workmanlike gelding: fair performer: won 4-runner maiden at Yarmouth in April: stays 1¼m: acts on soft and good to firm going: takes strong hold: sold 21,000 gns, joined Eugene M. O'Sullivan in Ireland. *M. L. W. Bell*

PIKABOO 4 ch.f. Pivotal 124 – Gleam of Light (IRE) 81 (Danehill (USA) 126) [2007 **–** 62: p7.1g f6g⁵ Feb 6] regressive maiden: sold 30,000 gns in December, reportedly in foal to Ishiguru. *S. C. Williams*

PILLAR OF HERCULES (IRE) 3 b.c. Rock of Gibraltar (IRE) 133 – Sabreon 85 **90** (Caerleon (USA) 132) [2007 8d² 7g² 8f* 8.1m Sep 14] 78,000F, 165,000Y, 400,000 2-y-o: well-made colt: second foal: dam, 1¼m winner, half-sister to high-class miler Landseer and very smart 1m/1¼m performer Ikhtyar: reportedly suffered problem with a suspensory in 2006: fairly useful performer, lightly raced: won maiden at Pontefract (by 3½ lengths from Zifaaf) in August: stays 1m: acts on firm ground. *H. R. A. Cecil*

PINCHBECK 8 b.g. Petong 126 – Veuve Hoornaert (IRE) 88 (Standaan (FR) 118) **84** [2007 83, a89: f6g⁵ p6g p6g Feb 10] strong, good sort: fairly useful handicapper: best at 6f: acts on all-weather, good to firm and good to soft ground: usually in cheekpieces/blinkers. *M. A. Jarvis*

PINCH OF SALT (IRE) 4 b.g. Hussonet (USA) – Granita (CHI) (Roy (USA)) [2007 **69 +** 81: 11.6m 10d⁵ p12g* p11m* p12g p11g² p12.2g⁴ Dec 14] big, lengthy gelding: has **a100** reportedly had wind operation: useful handicapper on all-weather, fair on turf: won at Kempton in September and October: unlucky second three penultimate start: stays 1½m: acts on polytrack, soft and good to firm ground: tried tongue tied. *A. M. Balding*

PINDAR (GER) 3 b.g. Tertullian (USA) 115 – Pierette (GER) (Local Suitor (USA) **59 p** 128) [2007 –: f6g p7.1g p9.5g* Oct 12] well-backed favourite, much improved, though still green, when winning minor event at Wolverhampton in October by 1¾ lengths from Fantastic Delight: will stay 1¼m: raced only on all-weather: should progress further. *B. J. Curley*

PINEAPPLE POLL 3 b.f. Josr Algarhoud (IRE) 118 – Petrovna (IRE) 78 (Petardia **–** 113) [2007 –: f8g p9.5g Jan 15] good-topped filly: no sign of ability: tried blinkered. *P. L. Gilligan*

PINEWOOD LULU 2 bl. or br.f. (Apr 20) Lujain (USA) 119 – Lucy Glitters (USA) **70 ?** 60 (Cryptoclearance (USA)) [2007 7d⁵ 6m⁴ f6d⁶ Dec 14] 4,200F, €11,000Y: smallish, workmanlike filly: fifth foal: half-sister to 4-y-o Penny Glitters and winner in Italy by Unfuwain: dam, sprint maiden, out of half-sister to smart performer up to 9f Hoy: fair maiden: seemingly easily best effort on debut. *R. C. Guest*

PINKABOUT (IRE) 3 br.f. Desert Style (IRE) 121 – Dinka Raja (USA) (Woodman **86** (USA) 126) [2007 85: 6s³ 7.1d⁵ 6.5v 6d Oct 19] leggy, lengthy filly: fairly useful performer, lightly raced: left J. Gosden 105,000 gns after second start: stays 6f: acts on polytrack and good ground. *J. S. Moore*

PINK BAY 5 b.m. Forzando 122 – Singer On The Roof 62 (Chief Singer 131) [2007 57: **–** p7g 8d 8m 10d Aug 21] leggy mare: fair at best, little form in 2007: sometimes visored/blinkered. *K. F. Clutterbuck*

PINKINDIE (USA) 2 ch.c. (Feb 3) Smart Strike (CAN) 121 – Only Princesses (USA) **87 p** (Chief's Crown (USA)) [2007 7m³ 7.1m³ 8g* Sep 20] $85,000Y, 120,000 2-y-o: sturdy colt: fifth foal: closely related to minor US sprint winner (including at 2 yrs) by Crafty Prospector and half-brother to winner in Japan by Meadowlake: dam, US 8.5f and 11f winner, half-sister to US Grade 1 9f/1¼m winner Tactile: fairly useful form in maidens, third at Newmarket and Sandown (to Perfect Stride), and winning at Yarmouth by neck from Robby Bobby: will stay 1¼m: good prospect. *E. A. L. Dunlop*

PINK NOTES 3 ch.g. Bandmaster (USA) 97 – Pink Petal (Northern Game) [2007 –: **–** 10d 11.7d Aug 19] workmanlike gelding: well held in maidens, then gelded. *R. J. Hodges*

PINK SALMON 3 ch.f. Dr Fong (USA) 128 – West Humble 93 (Pharly (FR) 130) **59 d** [2007 –: p6g 8.1m⁶ 9.7f p7g p10g Dec 19] leggy filly: modest maiden: best effort on second start. *Mrs L. J. Mongan*

Bloor Homes Spring Cup (Handicap), Newbury—Pinpoint lands a gamble from Royal Oath, Heaven Sent (No.18) and Macedon (third from near rail)

PINNACLE POINT 2 ch.g. (Mar 27) Best of The Bests (IRE) 122 – Alessandra 101   **62 p**
(Generous (IRE) 139) [2007 7.1m 8.1m 7s Oct 4] lengthy, workmanlike gelding: sixth
foal: closely related to 3-y-o Whenever, and half-brother to 5-y-o Alessano and fairly
useful 5f to 1m winner Kryssa (by Kris): dam, 1½m winner, half-sister to dam of very
smart sprinters Avonbridge and Patavellian: behind in maidens, showing ability on debut:
should do better. *G. L. Moore*

PINOT NOIR (GER) 4 b.c. Dictator's Song (USA) 106 – Princesse Aga (IRE) (Acate-   **–**
nango (GER) 127) [2007 95: 10d Oct 20] useful maiden: better effort in listed races in
2006 when third to Storm Mountain at Milan: left E. Kurdu and off 17½ months, out of
depth in Champion Stakes at Newmarket only start in 2007: stays 1¼m: acts on soft and
good to firm ground. *L. Ottofulling, Germany*

PINPOINT (IRE) 5 b.g. Pivotal 124 – Alessia (GER) (Warning 136) [2007 106: 8m*   **117**
9m² 10g⁴ 8g 9m 10g³ Nov 3] tall, close-coupled gelding: has a round action: smart handicapper: further improvement in 2007, won Spring Cup at Newbury (by 1¼ lengths from
Royal Oath) in April: very good short-head second to Supaseus in quite valuable event at
Newmarket next time, tending to wander: easily best effort after when third to Mashaahed
in listed race at Newmarket final outing: best at 1m/1¼m: acts on good to firm and good
to soft going: waited with: said to have bled fourth start. *W. R. Swinburn*

PINTANO 2 ch.g. (Mar 6) Dr Fong (USA) 128 – Heckle 47 (In The Wings 128) [2007   **72**
6m³ 6m⁵ 6f Sep 27] strong gelding: fair maiden: went wrong way after debut third at
Haydock: will stay 7f. *J. Howard Johnson*

PINTLE 7 b.m. Pivotal 124 – Boozy 111 (Absalom 128) [2007 96: 8.1g* 8g 8d* 8.1m 8d   **103**
Sep 29] workmanlike mare: useful performer: won handicap at Sandown (made all,
by 2½ lengths from Master Pegasus) in June and listed race at Bath (by ¾ length from
Sesmen) in August: well held otherwise in 2007: should prove as effective at 7f as 1m:
acts on firm and good to soft going: has reportedly bled: usually races up with pace.
J. L. Spearing

PIPEDREAMER 3 b.c. Selkirk (USA) 129 – Follow A Dream (USA) 90 (Gone   **120 p**
West (USA)) [2007 8m⁶ 8g* 10m* 10m⁴ 9.9g* 9m* Oct 6]
    In a season which featured some fine handicap performances, there were
few that promised so much as Pipedreamer's victory in the totesport.com Cambridgeshire at Newmarket in October, a very smart effort that would have been
more than good enough to win quite a few pattern races. With potential for further
improvement at four, Pipedreamer has excellent prospects of following three of the
last four three-year-olds to win the race in scoring a subsequent pattern victory.
    In the build-up to the Cambridgeshire, Pipedreamer's participation was in
some doubt. He had been withdrawn from a very valuable handicap at Newbury the

previous month because of concerns about the firmness of the ground and his trainer John Gosden stressed that he needed to be satisfied with the state of the going before allowing Pipedreamer to take his chance at Newmarket. This all seemed rather curious, given that Pipedreamer had already shown himself effective on good to firm going. After walking the course on the morning of the race, Gosden declared Pipedreamer would be allowed to take his chance. The punters duly took their cue, Pipedreamer sent off a strong 5/1 favourite in a field of thirty-four. Rarely, in a supposedly competitive handicap, can layers of the favourite have been resigned to their fate at such an early stage. Pipedreamer was in complete command soon after two furlongs out and, though the winning margin over the strong-finishing Docofthebay was only a length, the outcome was never in doubt. Pipedreamer was one of five three-year-olds in the first six, with the four-year-old Yarqus in fourth denying a clean sweep for the younger brigade. Teslin was third and, to bring further gloom to the bookmakers, particularly those paying each way on the fifth, The Illies, the quintet consisted of five of the first six in the market. Pipedreamer's success evoked comparisons with Gosden's previous Cambridgeshire winner Halling, who landed the prize as a three-year-old in 1994. Halling's useful performance in winning the race doesn't compare with Pipedreamer's, but he improved nearly two stone as a four-year-old and ended up a dual winner of both the Eclipse and the International. It is asking a lot of Pipedreamer to match that level of achievement, but all three three-year-olds to have won the race since Halling have managed at least a win at listed level. Cap Juluca, plagued by problems after his Cambridgeshire victory in 1995, won a three-runner listed race, but the other pair did rather better. Lear Spear, successful in 1998, gained three pattern-race wins at four, including the Prince of Wales's Stakes, while the 2006 victor Formal Decree, who also showed very smart form and won as easily as Pipedreamer, won in Group 3 company at Nad Al Sheba before finishing second in a Group 1 in Germany after joining Godolphin.

The Cambridgeshire was Pipedreamer's sixth and final start of the year and his fourth win—a possible run in a listed event subsequently coming to nothing. He won a mile maiden at Goodwood on his second start and a mile-and-a-quarter handicap at Pontefract on his third, both times seemingly green, though a tendency to idle towards the finish in the Cambridgeshire suggests he may benefit from being covered up for longer than he has been in his races so far. On his fifth start Pipedreamer showed an excellent turn of foot to land a valuable three-year-old heritage handicap at Glorious Goodwood. This particular event has more heritage than some with that tag, having for many years been run as the Extel Handicap (last under that banner in 1989). Until the advent of betting shop pictures, Extel provided commentaries and betting shows for the off-course industry, so, in a way, the race has come full circle as the 2007 sponsors were Alphameric, partners in TurfTV, which is in competition with SIS, Extel's successor, as the sole provider of betting shop pictures and shows.

Pipedreamer's two defeats are both worthy of comment. The first came when sixth behind Diamond Tycoon in a mile maiden at Newbury in April on his debut. It proved a very strong race of its type, with his stable companion and subsequent St Leger winner Lucarno the runner-up at 50/1. The second defeat was in a

Alphameric Vase (Handicap), Goodwood—
Pipedreamer (blaze) quickens well to beat Mr Aviator (stars) and Six of Diamonds (left)

totesport.com Cambridgeshire (Handicap), Newmarket—reminiscent of Halling, as the John Gosden-trained Pipedreamer beats fast-finishing Docofthebay (No.20), Teslin (far right) and Yarqus (striped cap)

very competitive three-year-old heritage handicap at the Newmarket July meeting. That too proved very strong form, with nine of the first eleven showing themselves useful or better subsequently, but, perhaps the pertinent point with regard to Pipedreamer's future, is that he seemed to spoil his chance by failing to settle after getting little cover. Pattern races, with their usually smaller fields and a different tempo, are likely to present a challenge which Pipedreamer will need to adapt to if he's to realise his potential fully.

Pipedreamer (b.c. 2004)	Selkirk (USA) (ch 1988)	Sharpen Up (ch 1969)	Atan Rocchetta
		Annie Edge (ch 1980)	Nebbiolo Friendly Court
	Follow A Dream (USA) (b 1998)	Gone West (b 1984)	Mr Prospector Secrettame
		Dance A Dream (b 1992)	Sadler's Wells Exclusive Order

Pipedreamer is an imposing sort physically, just the type to improve from three to four, a big, strong, useful-looking colt. He could turn out to be the best offspring of his sire Selkirk, who has been at stud since 1993. Selkirk was a high-class seven-furlong and one-mile performer himself, though, with the exception of the one-time very smart sprinter The Trader and the Champagne Stakes winner Etlaala, his very best performers have been effective over a fair bit further. They include an Irish St Leger winner in Kastoria and a St Leger runner-up in Highest, as well as two Italian Group 1 winners Altieri, twice winner of the Premio Presidente della Repubblica, and Leadership, who won the Gran Premio di Milano, and the Prix d'Ispahan winner Prince Kirk. Pipedreamer's dam Follow A Dream was also a seven-furlong and one-mile performer, finishing second four times from six starts at those distances, showing fair form but suspect resolution. Pipedreamer is her first foal, and the second, a Pivotal filly named Explore, was unraced at two. Follow A Dream's third foal, a colt by Pivotal, was bought back for 120,000 guineas at the yearling sales in the autumn and has since been named Dreamcoat. Follow A Dream's dam, Dance A Dream, was rather more able on the track, finishing second in the Oaks, and she is a sister to the Two Thousand Guineas winner Entrepreneur and half-sister to the Coronation Stakes winner Exclusive, the dam of Echelon, in whose essay further details on this family are to be found. Pipedreamer may well be campaigned at a mile to a mile and a quarter, and the Earl of Sefton Stakes over the Cambridgeshire course and distance seems an obvious starting point. Pipedreamer has so far raced only on good or good to firm going. A round action and his trainer's comments with regard to the ground may suggest improvement on a softer surface, though that is far from certain. Pipedreamer showed a tendency to sweat in his later races. *J. H. M. Gosden*

PIPER GENERAL (IRE) 5 br.g. General Monash (USA) 107 – Pipewell (IRE) 84 – (Lake Coniston (IRE) 131) [2007 71: f12g f11g⁵ f8g p9.5g p12.2g Jul 30] fairly useful at best: lightly raced and little impact in handicaps since 2005: once tongue tied. *J. Balding*

PIPERMAN 3 b.g. Zamindar (USA) 116 – Heather Mix 84 (Linamix (FR) 127) [2007 58 9.8g 6m 8m Jun 12] quite good-topped gelding: form only when seventh to Zonta Zitkala in maiden at Pontefract on second start: sold 1,000 gns in October. *M. Dods*

PIPER'S SONG (IRE) 4 gr.g. Distant Music (USA) 126 – Dane's Lane (IRE) (Dane-86 hill (USA) 126) [2007 73: 10m² 10g 10.2g⁶ 10g⁶ 8.3f³ 8m 8g² 7g* p7g Oct 14] big

826

gelding: fairly useful handicapper: won at Leicester (apprentices) in September: seems to stay 1¼m, both wins at 7f: acts on polytrack and firm going: sometimes slowly away: visored last 3 starts: sold 40,000 gns. *H. Candy*

PIPPA GREENE 3 b.c. Galileo (IRE) 134 – Funny Girl (IRE) 78 (Darshaan 133) [2007 **106 +** p10g* 10s* 11.8d* 12m Nov 10] 48,000Y: tall colt: second foal: dam maiden (stayed 1¼m): useful form: unbeaten first 3 starts, in maiden at Lingfield in March and handicaps at Newbury (beat Gulf Express by 2 lengths) in August and Leicester (further improvement when beating Harry Tricker by neck, again edging right) in October: respectable eighth of 21 to Malt Or Mash in November Handicap at Doncaster final outing: stays 1½m: acts on polytrack and soft ground. *P. F. I. Cole*

PIPPBROOK GOLD 2 ch.g. (Feb 27) Golden Snake (USA) 127 – Chiaro (Safawan **60** 118) [2007 p7g⁵ Dec 29] 100/1, modest form when fifth in maiden at Lingfield: likely to stay 1m+. *J. R. Boyle*

PIPPINS CORNER 5 b.m. Piccolo 121 – Newlands Corner 65 (Forzando 122) [2007 **–** p8m Oct 11] tailed off in maiden at Lingfield and claimer at Kempton over 2 years apart: tongue tied. *M. A. Allen*

PIPS ASSERTIVE WAY 6 ch.m. Nomadic Way (USA) 104 – Return To Brighton 51 **–** (Then Again 126) [2007 –: p9.5g⁶ Sep 21] little form on Flat: modest hurdler, successful in October. *A. W. Carroll*

PIQUET 9 br.m. Mind Games 121 – Petonellajill 73 (Petong 126) [2007 43, a52: p8g³ **49** p8g⁴ p8g p10g p11g p7m p8g Dec 16] poor performer: effective at 1m to 1½m: acts on polytrack and firm going: tried in cheekpieces. *J. J. Bridger*

PIRNER'S BRIG 3 b.g. Warningford 119 – Loch Maree 65 (Primo Dominie 121) **67** [2007 64: f6g⁴ p6g³ f6g³ f6g³ p5.1g⁴ f5g* 5.1g f5g⁴ f5g 5g⁶ p6g⁵ 5d Jul 4] workmanlike gelding: fair performer: won handicap at Southwell in March: stays 6f: acts on all-weather: effective blinkered or not: races up with pace: sold 4,000 gns. *M. W. Easterby*

PIROUETTING 4 b.f. Pivotal 124 – Jitterbug (IRE) (Marju (IRE) 127) [2007 81: **74** 10.3f⁵ 8g 8.3m⁴ p8g 8.3g⁴ 8g⁴ Oct 24] big filly: fair performer nowadays: stays 1¼m: acts on polytrack, soft and good to firm going: sold 24,000 gns. *B. W. Hills*

PISCEAN (USA) 2 b. or br.c. (Mar 23) Stravinsky (USA) 133 – Navasha (USA) **82** (Woodman (USA) 126) [2007 6d 5m⁴ 5m³ 7d 5m* p5m² 6d 6m Nov 10] $75,000F, £40,000 2-y-o: sturdy, close-coupled colt: second foal: half-brother to US 1m winner Silver Navasha (by Silver Hawk): dam unraced from good family of Cape Cross: fairly useful performer: won nursery at Goodwood in September: best at 5f/6f: acts on polytrack, good to firm and good to soft going: blinkered fifth to seventh starts: usually gets behind. *T. Keddy*

PITBULL 4 b.g. Makbul 104 – Piccolo Cativo 67 (Komaite (USA)) [2007 65: p6g 7g⁶ **69** 6s⁶ 7m³ p8.6g⁵ 7g 6.9g* p8.6g⁶ p8.6g⁶ 10m* p12.2g⁶ Nov 19] smallish, good-bodied gelding: fair handicapper: won at Carlisle in August and Pontefract (veered left when hitting front) in October: stays 1¼m: acts on polytrack and firm going: often slowly away: wears cheekpieces nowadays. *Mrs G. S. Rees*

PIVERINA (IRE) 2 b.f. (Mar 23) Pivotal 124 – Alassio (USA) 90 (Gulch (USA)) **57** [2007 6d⁵ 6g Oct 19] 44,000Y: third foal: dam, Irish 9f winner, out of Oaks/Irish Oaks runner-up Royal Ballerina: modest form in maidens: will probably stay 1m. *T. D. Barron*

PIVOTAL ANSWER (IRE) 3 ch.f. Pivotal 124 – Begueule (FR) (Bering 136) [2007 **101** 8.2g³ p9.5g² 10.2g* p10g² p11g* p12g² 12s² p13m⁴ p12g² Dec 1] €90,000Y: lightly-made filly: first foal: dam useful French 7f/1m winner: useful performer: won maiden at Bath (dead-heat) in July and handicap at Kempton in September: better efforts after, including in listed races at Lingfield (fourth to Loulwa) and Kempton (5 lengths second to Dansant) last 2 starts: stays 13f: acts on polytrack, raced only on good going or softer on turf: sold 62,000 gns. *J. Noseda*

PIVOTAL ERA 4 ch.g. Pivotal 124 – Femme Savante 89 (Glenstal (USA) 118) [2007 **65** 8.1m p6g⁴ 7.6g p7.1g p7g p6g p6g⁵ p7m Nov 26] strong, well-made gelding: fair maiden: left C. Wall after third start: suffered fatal fall: stayed 1m: acted on polytrack and good to firm ground: tried in cheekpieces/blinkers. *Jim Best*

PIVOTAL FLAME 5 b.h. Pivotal 124 – Reddening 82 (Blushing Flame (USA) 109) **–** [2007 118: 6d Mar 31] strong, good-topped horse: usually looks well: smart performer in 2006: well below form in listed race at Newcastle only start at 5 yrs: suffered niggling problems after: has form at 6f/7f, probably best at 5f: acts on soft and good to firm going: tried in blinkers/visor, usually in cheekpieces nowadays: races prominently: often wanders under pressure. *E. S. McMahon*

PIVOTALIA (IRE) 3 b.f. Pivotal 124 – Viscaria (IRE) 97 (Barathea (IRE) 127) [2007 **74**
63p: p8.6g² p7.1g² p8g³ 8.3d p8g⁵ p8.6g³ p9.5g* Sep 28] sturdy filly: fair performer:
visored, won handicap at Wolverhampton (hung right) in September: should stay 1¼m:
raced mainly on polytrack: sold 14,000 gns. *W. R. Swinburn*

PIVOTAL POINT 7 b.g. Pivotal 124 – True Precision 84 (Presidium 124) [2007 119: **109**
6m⁴ 5m 6m⁵ Sep 15] big, strong, close-coupled gelding: has a quick, fluent action: one-
time very smart performer, only useful in 2007: best effort when fourth to Sakhee's Secret
in listed race at Salisbury on reappearance: effective at 5f/6f: acts on firm going, below
form only outing on softer than good: usually races up with pace. *P. J. Makin*

PIVOTAL QUEEN (IRE) 2 ch.f. (Feb 15) Pivotal 124 – Queen of Norway (USA) **75 p**
(Woodman (USA) 126) [2007 6d³ 6.1g³ Aug 2] second foal: dam, useful French/US 1m
(including at 2 yrs) to 9f winner, out of half-sister to very smart French/US performer up
to 1½m Contested Bid: third in maidens at Yarmouth and Nottingham (length behind
Mistress Greeley): will be suited by 7f/1m: should do better. *L. M. Cumani*

PIVOTAL'S PRINCESS (IRE) 5 ch.m. Pivotal 124 – Art Princess (IRE) (Fairy King **107**
(USA)) [2007 106: 5m* 5m* 5g⁶ 5m 5m⁶ 5g² 5m Oct 4] small, sturdy mare: useful performer: won handicap in April (by ¾ length from Cape Royal) and minor event in May
(readily beat Baron's Pit by 1¼ lengths), both at Beverley: not at best after, though not
discredited in listed races last 2 starts, length second to Loch Verdi at Hamilton on first
occasion: stays easy 6f: yet to race on heavy ground, acts on any other: sold 65,000 gns.
E. S. McMahon

PIVOTAL TRUTH 3 ch.f. Pivotal 124 – Home Truth 98 (Known Fact (USA) 135) **75**
[2007 p7g⁴ 7g 7m p7.1g* p8g Sep 29] sparely-made filly: half-sister to several winners,
including very smart 6f/7f performer Susu (by Machiavellian) and useful 6f winner Cadeaux Cher (by Cadeaux Genereux): dam 7f/1m winner: fair performer: won maiden at
Wolverhampton in September: below form on handicap debut final start: raced only at 7f/
1m: acts on polytrack. *B. W. Hills*

PIX 4 b.f. Bertolini (USA) 125 – Fair Kai (IRE) (Fayruz 116) [2007 39: p6g Sep 15] –
sparely-made maiden at 2 yrs: lightly raced and little form since: tried
blinkered. *Michael McElhone, Ireland*

PIXIE PRINCESS (IRE) 3 b.f. Imperial Ballet (IRE) 110 – Tereed Elhawa 75 –
(Cadeaux Genereux 131) [2007 7m 7s p6g 8m 8.5g 11.1g 7g⁶ Sep 6] plain
filly: third foal: half-sister to 4-y-o European Dream: dam, 2-y-o 6f winner, half-sister to
useful French 2006 2-y-o 5.5f winner Mpumalanga (by Observatory): little form.
Miss V. Haigh

PIXIE'S BLUE (IRE) 2 br.f. (Feb 3) Hawk Wing (USA) 136 – Isle of Flame (Shirley **75**
Heights 130) [2007 p5g 6g² 6g² p7g⁶ 7m⁵ 6m⁵ Aug 13] 30,000Y: rather leggy filly: half-
sister to several winners, including smart French 9f/1¼m winner Thattinger (by Salse),
stayer Dorothy's Friend (by Grand Lodge) and 2004 2-y-o 9f winner Kindling (by Dr
Fong), latter 2 useful: dam unraced: fair maiden: twice runner-up at Newmarket: should
stay 1m: acts on good to firm going, probably polytrack. *J. H. M. Gosden*

PLAKA (FR) 2 gr.f. (Apr 18) Verglas (IRE) 118 – Top Speed (IRE) (Wolfhound (USA) **55**
126) [2007 5.1m p6g⁴ 6m p7g p6g p6g p7.1d Dec 27] 62,000Y: lengthy filly: sixth foal:
half-sister to several winners, including useful French sprinter/milers Toamasina (by
Marju) and Lady Weasley (by Zieten): dam, German 7f winner, half-sister to Deutsches
Derby winner All My Dreams: modest maiden: left J. Osborne 3,000 gns before final
start: should stay 1m. *W. M. Brisbourne*

PLANE PAINTER (IRE) 3 b.g. Orpen (USA) 116 – Flight Sequence 88 (Polar **86**
Falcon (USA) 126) [2007 83: p8.6g⁴ 10m³ 9.8m⁶ 9.1m⁵ p8g 9.7g⁵ 11.7m³ 14.6m² 12.3m²
p16g⁵ 14d⁴ 17.2d* Oct 1] tall gelding: fairly useful handicapper: won at Bath in October:
effective at 1¼m to 17f: acts on good to firm and good to soft going, probably on polytrack: consistent. *M. Johnston*

PLANETARIUM 2 gr.c. (Feb 25) Fantastic Light (USA) 134 – Karsiyaka (IRE) (Kah- **99 p**
yasi 130) [2007 10.2d² 10m* 10g² Nov 3] 120,000F: leggy, lengthy colt, unfurnished at
2 yrs: fifth foal: half-brother to useful 7f winner (including at 2 yrs) Contractor (by Spectrum), 3-y-o Altos Reales and 4-y-o Pearl's Girl: dam unraced half-sister to French
winner up to 11f Karliyka: useful form: won maiden at Pontefract in October by 1½
lengths from Mushtaaq, pair well clear: second to Twice Over in minor event at Newmarket, rallying: will be suited by 1½m: type to make a better 3-y-o. *M. Johnston*

PLANET PARADISE (IRE) 2 b.f. (Apr 24) Spinning World (USA) 130 – Just Heav- **37**
ens Gate 106 (Slip Anchor 136) [2007 p5.1g p5g 5.1g³ 5s⁴ Jul 23] €14,000F, 3,500Y: first
foal: dam 6f/7f winner abroad: poor maiden: will stay 6f/7f. *D. Shaw*

PLANET QUEEN 2 ch.f. (Jan 29) Bahamian Bounty 116 – Ash Moon (IRE) 92 **50** (General Monash (USA) 107) [2007 6g⁵ 6g⁶ 5.1s Jul 13] 10,000F, 19,000Y: lengthy filly: second foal: dam 2-y-o 5f/6f winner (stayed 1½m): modest maiden: may prove best at 5f/6f. *K. R. Burke*

PLANTERS PUNCH (IRE) 6 br.g. Cape Cross (IRE) 129 – Jamaican Punch (IRE) **54** (Shareef Dancer (USA) 135) [2007 66: f12g 13d Jun 28] strong, useful-looking gelding: modest at best in 2007, leaving G. M. Moore after reappearance: barely stays 15.8f: acts on firm and good to soft ground: tried visored: sometimes slowly away. *N. G. Richards*

PLAN (USA) 2 ch.c. (Apr 13) Storm Cat (USA) – Spain (USA) 123 (Thunder Gulch **97 p** (USA) 129) [2007 7g⁵ 7g* Oct 29] medium-sized, quite attractive colt: third foal: dam US Grade 1 7f to 9f (Breeders' Cup Distaff) winner: useful form: confirmed debut promise when winning 17-runner maiden at Leopardstown later in October impressively by 5½ lengths from Tarkari, leading 1f out and forging clear: will stay 1m: open to further improvement. *A. P. O'Brien, Ireland*

PLATEAU 8 b.g. Zamindar (USA) 116 – Painted Desert 89 (Green Desert (USA) 127) **74** [2007 91d: f8g p7.1g⁵ p7.1g³ p7g⁴ p7g 7g 7g³ 7g⁵ 7m p7.1g³ p8g 6f⁵ 6m* 6m⁶ 6.1m³ 6v p6g³ p6g p6m p6g Dec 29] good-bodied gelding: fair handicapper nowadays: won at Redcar in August: best at 6f/7f: acts on polytrack, firm and good to soft going: often held up. *C. R. Dore*

PLATINUM CHARMER (IRE) 7 b.g. Kahyasi 130 – Mystic Charm (Nashwan **65** (USA) 135) [2007 71d: 12m⁶ 12m⁵ 14.1m⁴ p12g Oct 12] compact gelding: modest performer nowadays: left K. R. Burke after third start: stays 1¾m: acts on all-weather, firm and soft going: usually wears cheekpieces: sometimes wanders. *Ms Joanna Morgan, Ireland*

PLAUSABELLE 6 b.m. Royal Applause 124 – Sipsi Fach 100 (Prince Sabo 123) **–** [2007 –, a65: p7g Jan 10] lengthy mare: fair performer at 5 yrs: just modest form sole **a52** start in 2007: stays 10.2f: acts on polytrack, firm and soft ground: tried blinkered. *G. G. Margarson*

PLAVIUS (USA) 2 b. or br.c. (Mar 7) Danzig (USA) – Sharp Minister (CAN) (Deputy **– p** Minister (CAN)) [2007 7d Oct 16] $9,200,000Y (fifth highest-priced yearling ever sold at public auction): compact colt: fifth foal: brother to 3-y-o Dijeerr and half-brother to winner in US by Capote: dam, ran twice in US, sister to very smart French/US performer up to 1½m Flag Down: 9/4, seemed unable to cope with softish ground in maiden at Leicester, eased: should do better. *Saeed bin Suroor*

PLAYERS PLEASE (USA) 3 ch.g. Theatrical 128 – Miss Tobacco (USA) 106 (Forty **104** Niner (USA)) [2007 p9.5g* p11g* 10m⁴ 10g 8m p8g⁵ 9.9g⁴ 10.4d 10m⁶ 12m* 10m 12s³ Oct 13] €37,000Y: well-made gelding: second foal: dam, German 1m winner, half-sister to dam of Irish 2000 Guineas winner Bachelor Duke: useful performer: won maiden at Wolverhampton in January, and handicaps at Kempton in February and Thirsk (beat Generous Jem by 3 lengths) in September: creditable close third to Buccellati in valuable handicap at Ascot final start: gelded after: best form at 1½m: acts on polytrack, soft and good to firm ground: has hung right/folded: often races prominently. *M. Johnston*

PLAYFUL 4 b.f. Piccolo 121 – Autumn Affair 100 (Lugana Beach 116) [2007 p5g 5.1m **90** p5.1g Nov 19] tall, close-coupled filly: good walker: fairly useful performer: seems best at 5f: acts on good to firm and good to soft going. *R. M. Beckett*

PLAYFUL DANE (IRE) 10 b.g. Dolphin Street (FR) 125 – Omicida (IRE) (Danehill **83** (USA) 126) [2007 5m 5g⁶ 5m 6m⁶ Jun 8] good-topped gelding: fairly useful handicapper: best at bare 5f: acts on fibresand, firm and good to soft ground: has been slowly away: often races up with pace. *K. A. Ryan*

PLAY MASTER (IRE) 6 b.g. Second Empire (IRE) 124 – Madam Waajib (IRE) **66** (Waajib 121) [2007 72: 10.2f p13.9g⁴ 10.8g⁴ Oct 2] tall, rather leggy, useful-looking gelding: fair handicapper: should stay 1½m: acts on all-weather and soft going: tried visored: has raced freely/idled. *C. Roberts*

PLAY STRAIGHT 3 ch.f. Piccolo 121 – Align 69 (Petong 126) [2007 69: p7.1g p9.5g **–** 7.5m 8m 10g 10m⁴ 9.8s 10.1m Aug 8] sturdy filly: fair winner at 2 yrs: little form in 2007: tried in cheekpieces. *I. W. McInnes*

PLAY THE BALL (USA) 5 ch.g. Boundary (USA) 117 – Copper Play (USA) (Fast **62** Play (USA)) [2007 78: p9.5g 9.5g 11.9g 9g Jun 6] just modest handicapper at 5 yrs: stays 1m: acts on polytrack: tried blinkered/in cheekpieces: none too consistent. *J. J. Lambe, Ireland*

PLAYTOTHEAUDIENCE 4 b.g. Royal Applause 124 – Flyfisher (USA) (Riverman **60 §** (USA) 131) [2007 –: 8m 5.9m p6g⁵ p7g 11.1m 9.1s 7.1m⁴ 10f 10s 10g² p12g 10g Oct 19] tall, useful-looking gelding: modest performer nowadays: seems to stay 11f: acts on polytrack and firm going: tried blinkered: has been slowly away: none too keen. *R. A. Fahey*

PLAY UP POMPEY 5 b.g. Dansili 127 – Search For Love (FR) (Groom Dancer (USA) 128) [2007 62: p10g³ p10g* p10g p10g⁶ p10g 10.2g p11g 10g p8m⁵ p10g p10g p11g p10g p10m⁴ p10m* p10g⁶ Dec 28] angular gelding: modest handicapper: won at Lingfield in January and December: stays 1¼m: acts on polytrack, firm and good to soft going: sometimes slowly away. *J. J. Bridger* — a64

PLEASING 4 b.f. Dr Fong (USA) 128 – Trounce (Barathea (IRE) 127) [2007 80+: 7g May 12] smallish, useful-looking filly: fairly useful performer at 3 yrs: well held in Chartwell Fillies' Stakes at Lingfield only start in 2007: seems to stay 1¼m: acts on polytrack and soft going. *C. E. Brittain* —

PLEASING GIFT 4 b.f. Largesse 112 – Pleasure Dome 77 (Most Welcome 131) [2007 58: 10.1m Aug 15] leggy filly: modest maiden at 3 yrs: well below form only start in 2007: stays 8.6f: acts on polytrack and good to firm ground: tried blinkered. *J. M. P. Eustace* —

PLEASURE PURSUIT 3 b.g. Pursuit of Love 124 – Glen Falls (Commanche Run 133) [2007 –: 11.8m Apr 12] big gelding: no signs of ability: tried blinkered. *K. A. Ryan* —

PLENTY CRIED WOLF 5 b.g. Wolfhound (USA) 126 – Plentitude (FR) (Ela-Mana-Mou 132) [2007 69: f11g³ p12.2g³ f14g³ f14g⁵ Apr 3] workmanlike gelding: fair performer at best, only modest in 2007: stayed 1¾m: acted on all-weather, soft and good to firm going: often raced prominently: dead. *R. A. Fahey* — 61

PLENTY OF ACTION (USA) 2 b. or br.f. (Feb 12) Hennessy (USA) 122 – Mary Had A Lot (USA) (Double Zeus (USA)) [2007 p5m⁴ p6g⁴ Dec 26] $50,000Y: half-sister to several winners in US, including Grade 3 6.5f winner Native Heir (by Makin) and minor sprint stakes winner A Lot of Mary (by Clever Champ): dam stakes-placed US sprinter: modest form in maidens: should prove suited to 5f/6f. *M. J. Wallace* — 56

PLUCKY 3 b.f. Kyllachy 129 – Pizzicato 64 (Statoblest 120) [2007 7d³ 7m² 7.1m* 7g² 6m² 6d⁶ 7d⁶ Oct 27] 300,000Y: medium-sized, lengthy filly: had a quick action: fourth foal: half-sister to 2002 2-y-o 5f (Molecomb/Flying Childers) winner Wunders Dream (by Averti), 4-y-o Grecian Dancer, both useful, and fairly useful 6f (at 2 yrs)/7f winner Go Between (by Daggers Drawn): dam, 5f winner, half-sister to smart performers in Britain/Hong Kong Volata (sprinter) and Mensa (up to 1¼m): fairly useful form: won maiden at Chepstow in August: better form after in handicaps/listed race: stayed 7f: unraced on extremes of going: visits Dutch Art. *J. H. M. Gosden* — 93

PLUMAGE 2 b.f. (Feb 12) Royal Applause 124 – Cask 99 (Be My Chief (USA) 122) [2007 p8m Dec 7] 36,000Y: fifth living foal: half-sister to useful French 7f/1m winner Jardin Bleu (by Diesis): dam 7f to 8.5f (including in US) winner: 50/1, modest form when ninth in maiden at Lingfield. *M. Blanshard* — 59

PLUM PUDDING (IRE) 4 b.g. Elnadim (USA) 128 – Karayb (IRE) 93 (Last Tycoon 131) [2007 104: p10g⁵ 8m 8g* 8.5d 8m 8.1g 10.4d 8g 8m 10d Oct 27] strong, good-topped gelding: impresses in appearance: useful handicapper: won at Newmarket (by neck from Goodbye Mr Bond) in May: below form after: probably stays 1¼m: acts on polytrack and good to firm going, not on softer than good: usually races prominently. *R. Hannon* — 102

PLUSH 4 ch.g. Medicean 128 – Glorious (Nashwan (USA) 135) [2007 64: 6m Aug 10] modest maiden at 3 yrs: blinkered, ran poorly in claimer only Flat start in 2007. *B. P. J. Baugh* —

POCHARD 4 br.f. Inchinor 119 – Pomorie (IRE) 67§ (Be My Guest (USA) 126) [2007 69: 12g⁶ 11.5d May 30] modest maiden, lightly raced: should stay 1¾m: acts on polytrack and firm going, ran poorly on good to soft final start. *J. M. P. Eustace* — 63

POCKET TOO 4 b.g. Fleetwood (IRE) 107 – Pocket Venus (IRE) (King's Theatre (IRE) 128) [2007 66: p16g* p16g³ p16.5g 12.1s² 21g 12d² p16g⁵ f12d⁵ Dec 12] close-coupled gelding: fair performer: won claimer at Lingfield in January: effective at 1½m, seemingly stays 21f: acts on polytrack and soft going: sometimes wears blinkers/cheekpieces. *M. Salaman* — 70

POCKETWOOD 5 b.g. Fleetwood (IRE) 107 – Pocket Venus (IRE) (King's Theatre (IRE) 128) [2007 –: p16g 16m 12d² 12g* 11.5d 11.6g p12g 12d⁶ p13.9g⁴ Dec 3] well-made gelding: fairly useful handicapper on turf, fair on all-weather: won at Folkestone in June: stays 1¾m: acts on polytrack and soft going. *Jean-Rene Auvray* — 81 a73

POET LAUREATE 3 gr.c. Highest Honor (FR) 124 – Desired (Rainbow Quest (USA) 134) [2007 10s* 12.5g* 12.5d² Aug 26] fifth foal: half-brother to smart French 1¼m/ — 120 p

1½m winner Desideratum (by Darshaan) and French 10.5f winner Covet (by Polish Precedent): dam unraced half-sister to high-class 7f/1m winner Charnwood Forest and Racing Post Trophy winner Medaaly (by Highest Honor): progressive form: won maiden at Compiegne on reappearance in July and listed race at Deauville (shade comfortably by 2½ lengths from Shujoon) in August: plenty more improvement when keeping-on length second to Irish Wells in Grand Prix de Deauville: stays 12.5f: has joined Godolphin: looks sure to win good races as 4-y-o. *A. Fabre, France*

POINT OF ORIGIN (IRE) 10 b.g. Caerleon (USA) 132 – Aptostar (USA) (Fappiano (USA)) [2007 p13.9g⁶ f14g Jan 25] maiden hurdler/winning chaser: no form on Flat. *John A. Harris* —

POINTS OF VIEW 2 b.g. (Jan 21) Galileo (IRE) 134 – On Point 72 (Kris 135) [2007 7s 7.1g p7g p7g* p8g* p8.6g² Nov 9] 115,000Y: tall, lengthy gelding: first foal: dam, 5f winner, half-sister to useful sprinters Violette and Silca's Gift: fairly useful form: won nurseries at Lingfield in October and Kempton in November: will stay 1¼m/1½m: gelded after final start: has scope, should continue progressing. *Sir Mark Prescott* **89 p**

POISIEDON (IRE) 3 b.g. King's Best (USA) 132 – Lizanne (USA) (Theatrical 128) [2007 61: 6v 7m⁴ 6d³ 6g³ 6g⁶ 5d² 6v⁵ p5g⁶ 5d p6g⁵ Oct 12] good-topped gelding: fair maiden: has form at 7f, better at 5f/6f: acts on polytrack, good to firm and good to soft ground: sometimes races freely. *Liam McAteer, Ireland* **76**

POLAR ANNIE 2 b.f. (Mar 2) Fraam 114 – Willisa 67 (Polar Falcon (USA) 126) [2007 6m⁵ 5.7s⁴ 5.1d p7g² Oct 31] 10,000F, 10,000Y: sixth foal: half-sister to 5f (at 2 yrs) to 1m winner Waterpark (by Namaqualand): dam 7f winner: fair form: won nursery at Kempton in September: second to Points of View in similar event at Lingfield: should prove best up to 7f: acts on polytrack and soft going. *M. S. Saunders* **74**

POLAR CIRCLE (USA) 2 b.f. (Feb 4) Royal Academy (USA) 130 – Polar Bird 111 (Thatching 131) [2007 5.2g⁸ 5m 6s* 6d 6m Oct 5] strong, angular filly: sister to smart 6f/7f winner Fokine and useful (at 2 yrs) 6f winner Arctic Burst, and half-sister to 2 winners, including smart 1996 2-y-o 5.5f (Prix Robert Papin)/6f winner Ocean Ridge (by Storm Bird): dam sprinter: fairly useful form: won minor event at Newbury (by 1½ lengths from Nijoom Dubai) in May and listed race at Newmarket in June: little impact in Princess Margaret Stakes at Ascot and Cheveley Park Stakes at Newmarket (pulled hard) 2½ months apart: will prove best at 5f/6f: acts on soft and good to firm going: sent to USA. *P. W. Chapple-Hyam* **92**

POLAR FORCE 7 ch.g. Polar Falcon (USA) 126 – Irish Light (USA) 91 (Irish River (FR) 131) [2007 74: p6g⁸ p5.1g⁵ p6g p6g 6s² 6g² 6v* 6m 5.1s⁶ 6d p5.1g⁵ p6g Dec 22] neat gelding: fair handicapper: won at Lingfield in July: best at 5f/6f: acts on polytrack, heavy and good to firm going: races prominently. *Mrs C. A. Dunnett* **67**

POLAR FOX 4 ch.g. Pivotal 124 – Niseem (USA) (Hennessy (USA) 122) [2007 67: f5g f5g p5.1g p7.1g Apr 27] maiden: fair form at times for A. Oliver in Ireland at 2/3 yrs: no form in 2007: tried visored/blinkered/tongue tied. *D. Shaw* —

POLE DANCER 4 b.g. Polish Precedent (USA) 131 – Pounelta 91 (Tachypous 128) [2007 10.2g 12.1m p12g Aug 28] maiden: missed 2006: little form at 4 yrs. *W. S. Kittow* —

POLICE OFFICER 2 b.c. (Mar 19) Mark of Esteem (IRE) 137 – No Rehearsal (FR) (Baillamont (USA) 124) [2007 6d p7.1g p7g⁵ Nov 12] poor form in maidens, probably green: bred to be suited by 1m+. *W. J. Musson* **47 ?**

POLISH EMPEROR (USA) 7 ch.g. Polish Precedent (USA) 131 – Empress Jackie (USA) (Mount Hagen (FR) 127) [2007 89d: f6g p7.1g p5.1g p6g 7m 5m 5g 6d⁶ 6m 6.9f 6g 6g Sep 3] lengthy gelding: handicapper: on downgrade: best at 5f/6f: acts on all-weather, firm and soft going: often wears headgear, also tongue tied seventh start: often starts slowly: one to treat with caution. *D. W. Barker* **70 d**

POLISH INDEX 5 b.g. Polish Precedent (USA) 131 – Glossary (Reference Point 139) [2007 76: p6g May 23] leggy, angular gelding: handicapper: just modest form sole start at 5 yrs: effective at 6f to 1m: acts on good to firm going: wears cheekpieces: has hung right. *J. R. Jenkins* **56**

POLISH MYTH 3 b.c. Polish Precedent (USA) 131 – Myth 89 (Troy 137) [2007 13.8m⁴ Jul 11] 10/1, well-held fourth of 7 to Blue Jet in maiden at Catterick. *J. G. Given* —

POLISH POWER (GER) 7 br.h. Halling (USA) 133 – Polish Queen (Polish Precedent (USA) 131) [2007 87: p12g³ f12g² p12g* p13g⁶ p12g³ 12g 11.6m 12m⁴ 11.6s⁴ 12v⁵ 10d⁵ 12g p11g p12g* 12d³ p12g² p12m² Dec 9] tall horse: useful handicapper on all-weather, fairly useful on turf: won at Lingfield in March and October: stays easy 1¾m: **83 a96**

acts on all-weather, heavy and good to firm going: tried in cheekpieces, often blinkered in Germany earlier in career: held up (sometimes slowly away). *J. S. Moore*

POLISH PRIORY (IRE) 2 b.f. (May 5) Polish Precedent (USA) 131 – Glenstal Priory 53 (Glenstal (USA) 118) [2007 5m 5m 6d 6d 5.7f³ 6g p7.1g⁴ p6g 6s p7.1g p6g Dec 4] €12,000Y: unfurnished filly: half-sister to several winners, including fairly useful 1999 2-y-o 5f winner Duke of Aston (by Shalford) and 6-y-o Larad: dam 2m/2¼m winner: fair maiden: below form after third start: will stay at least 1m: acts on firm and good to soft going: wore visor/blinkers end of year. *P. D. Evans* **67 d**

POLISH PRIZE 3 b.g. Polish Precedent (USA) 131 – Forest Prize 77 (Charnwood Forest (IRE) 125) [2007 8.3s p8g 7g p6g p5g⁶ p6g f5d Dec 14] sturdy gelding: modest maiden. *W. R. Swinburn* **56**

POLISH PROSPECT (IRE) 3 ch.f. Elnadim (USA) 128 – Always True (USA) 67 (Geiger Counter (USA)) [2007 –: 10.2m 7d 10.2g p7g p7g 8f⁵ 10g⁶ p8g³ p9.5g Nov 16] poor maiden: stays 1m: acts on polytrack and firm ground. *H. S. Howe* **42**

POLISH RED 3 b.g. Polish Precedent (USA) 131 – Norcroft Joy 82§ (Rock Hopper 124) [2007 75: 11.6m⁶ 12m 11.6s* 11.6g* 12d Jul 29] good-topped gelding: fairly useful handicapper: improved to win at Windsor in June and July: stays 11.6f: acts on soft going: usually waited with. *G. G. Margarson* **85**

POLISH STAR 3 b.g. Polish Precedent (USA) 131 – Apennina (USA) (Gulch (USA)) [2007 –: p6g p6g⁶ 7.1g 8m⁵ 8m 8.3g Jun 20] big, strong gelding: poor maiden on balance: stays 1m: acts on good to firm going: has looked tricky ride: refused to race final outing: one to avoid. *J. S. Wainwright* **46 §**

POLISH WELCOME 4 ch.f. Polish Precedent (USA) 131 – Three White Sox 73 (Most Welcome 131) [2007 56: 10.1g Jul 23] lightly-made filly: maiden handicapper: poor form sole 4-y-o start: stays 1½m: acts on polytrack and firm going. *S. C. Williams* **–**

POLISH WORLD (USA) 3 b.g. Danzig (USA) – Welcometotheworld (USA) (Woodman (USA) 126) [2007 52p: p6g⁶ p6g* 7m² 6m p6g p8g Sep 12] medium-sized, stocky gelding: fair handicapper: won at Lingfield in April: left E. Dunlop after fourth start: effective at 6f/7f: acts on polytrack and good to firm ground. *T. J. Etherington* **74**

POLITEIA (USA) 2 b. or br.f. (Mar 30) Mr Greeley (USA) 122 – Ujane (USA) (Theatrical 128) [2007 6m 7g 7g Sep 6] $38,000F, €65,000Y: leggy, close-coupled filly: second foal: dam unraced out of half-sister to dam of top-class US 9f/1¼m performer Cigar: fair form in maidens, never dangerous: will stay 1m: should do better. *R. Hannon* **67 p**

POLITE SOCIETY (IRE) 2 b.f. (Mar 11) Seeking The Gold (USA) – Born Something (IRE) 105 (Caerleon (USA) 132) [2007 5d⁶ 6.1g³ p7g Jul 12] compact filly: first foal: dam, French 2-y-o 1m winner, half-sister to smart French 1¼m performer Gold Sound: fair maiden: third to Easy Target at Nottingham: should be suited by 1m/1¼m. *M. Johnston* **73**

POLLY JONES (USA) 3 b.f. Lear Fan (USA) 130 – Polly's Link (USA) (Phone Trick (USA)) [2007 48: p7g p7g⁶ Jan 17] workmanlike filly: poor performer: stays 6f: acts on polytrack: sometimes slowly away. *G. L. Moore* **–**

POLLY ROCKET 3 ch.f. Tendulkar (USA) 114 – Celts Dawn (Celtic Swing 138) [2007 –: p6g⁵ f7s 6m 5m⁴ May 22] second foal: dam, little form, half-sister to smart 5f performer Repertory: poor maiden: best efforts at 5f/6f: acts on polytrack: tried in cheekpieces. *P. D. Niven* **38**

POLMAILY 2 b.c. (Mar 22) Hawk Wing (USA) 136 – Hampton Lucy (IRE) 65 (Anabaa (USA) 130) [2007 6m² 8d³ Oct 19] 55,000Y: medium-sized, good-topped colt: first foal: dam, 6f winner, half-sister to useful French performers Okabango (1½m) and Shigeru Summit (5f to 7f): fairly useful form placed in maidens at Newmarket 2½ months apart, second to Captain Brilliance on debut: stays 1m. *B. J. Meehan* **86**

POLONIUS 6 b.g. Great Dane (IRE) 122 – Bridge Pool 74 (First Trump 118) [2007 87: p12.2g f8g p8.6g 7g Apr 2] fairly useful performer at best: no form in 2007: tried blinkered. *G. J. Smith* **–**

POLYCHROME 2 b.f. (Mar 29) Polish Precedent (USA) 131 – Pantone 92 (Spectrum (IRE) 126) [2007 p6g⁶ Dec 1] first foal: dam, 7f to 1½m winner, out of useful 1½m winner Tinashaan: 80/1, sixth in maiden at Wolverhampton, very slowly away: will be suited by 1m+: should do better. *John Berry* **48 p**

POLYGONAL (FR) 7 b.g. Octagonal (NZ) 126 – Sectarine (FR) (Maelstrom Lake 118) [2007 100: p13.9g Dec 1] quite good-topped gelding: useful handicapper at 6 yrs: off 17 months, well beaten in claimer only 2007 start: effective at 1¼m/1½m: acts on polytrack, firm and good to soft going: tried blinkered. *Miss Gay Kelleway* **–**

POLYGRAPH (IRE) 2 ch.g. (Feb 23) Pivotal 124 – Dear Girl (IRE) 105 (Fairy King **72** (USA)) [2007 6g 5.7g⁵ 6m² 7m⁵ 7g Sep 30] close-coupled gelding: fair maiden: second at Ascot: well beaten in nurseries: should stay 7f/1m: sold 12,000 gns, sent to USA. *A. M. Balding*

POLYQUEST (IRE) 3 b.f. Poliglote 121 – Seren Quest 90 (Rainbow Quest (USA) **73** 134) [2007 6g: p9.5g 10m* 12m 10.9d⁶ 9.2d p10g⁴ p12m* p12g* p11g² p12g⁵ Dec 19] fair handicapper: left P. Cole after reappearance: won at Pontefract in May and twice at Kempton (within 5 days) in October: stays 1½m: acts on polytrack and good to firm going. *G. A. Butler*

POMELLATO (GER) 2 br.c. Big Shuffle (USA) 122 – Passata (FR) (Polar Falcon **110** (USA) 126) [2007 6.5d* 7g* 8m⁴ 6d* Nov 2] second foal: half-brother to German 1m winner Passato (by Lando): dam, German 1m winner, out of smart French performer up to 1½m Premier Amour: smart form: won maiden at Frankfurt and Maurice Lacroix-Trophy at Baden-Baden (made all, beat Peace Royale ¾ length) in August, and Criterium de Maisons-Laffitte (best effort, led after halfway, drifted right when going clear to beat Norman Invader 3 lengths) in November: best effort at 6f, not discredited when fourth to Scintillo in Gran Criterium at Milan over 1m third start: acts on good to soft ground. *P. Schiergen, Germany*

POMFRET LAD 9 b.g. Cyrano de Bergerac 120 – Lucky Flinders 77 (Free State 125) **57** [2007 81: f8g⁵ f6g Feb 1] good-topped gelding: fair performer nowadays: stays 7f: acts on firm and soft going: tried blinkered/visored: none too reliable. *J. J. Quinn*

POMPOM 3 ch.f. Polish Precedent (USA) 131 – Slipper 94 (Suave Dancer (USA) 136) **53** [2007 10g⁶ Jul 10] smallish, lengthy filly: fifth foal: half-sister to several winners, including useful French 1m (at 2 yrs)/10.5f winner Cartier Opera (by Zilzal) and fairly useful 1¼m/1½m winner Cordier (by Desert Style): dam 1½m winner: 33/1, 15½ lengths sixth of 10 to Dar Es Salaam in maiden at Pontefract, green when ridden. *J. G. Given*

PONDAPIE (IRE) 2 b.g. (Mar 9) Highest Honor (FR) 124 – Fruhling Feuer (FR) 80 **68** (Green Tune (USA) 125) [2007 8d⁵ 8d Oct 13] compact gelding: fair maiden, looked green both starts: gelded after: will stay 1¼m. *R. M. Whitaker*

PONDER ANEW (IRE) 2 b.f. (Jan 5) Namid 128 – Luisa Demon (IRE) (Barathea **61** (IRE) 127) [2007 5m 5s⁴ 5d⁴ Jun 27] €32,000Y: fourth foal: half-sister to 3-y-o Everymanforhimself: dam, Italian 2-y-o 5f/6f winner, half-sister to useful sprinters Fred Bongusto and Atlantic Viking: modest maiden: will prove best at 5f/6f: sold only 800 gns. *K. R. Burke*

PONIARD (IRE) 3 b.g. Daggers Drawn (USA) 114 – It's Academic 73 (Royal Aca- **60 §** demy (USA) 130) [2007 64§: f7g⁶ f7g* f7g³ p9.5g f8g 8g⁵ 8m May 21] small, good-bodied gelding: modest handicapper: won at Southwell in February: stays 7f: acts on fibresand and soft going: in cheekpieces nowadays: unreliable, sometimes runs as if amiss. *D. W. Barker*

PONT DES SOUPIRS (USA) 2 b.c. (Mar 6) Harlan's Holiday (USA) 124 – Flirted **65 p** (USA) (Relaunch (USA)) [2007 6d Oct 1] $100,000Y, 320,000 2-y-o: rangy colt: has scope: first foal: dam unraced half-sister to high-class sprinter Committed: 15/2, eighth to Unbreak My Heart in maiden at Windsor: likely to stay 1m: will improve. *Saeed bin Suroor*

PONTEFRACT GLORY 4 b.g. Lujain (USA) 119 – Final Glory (Midyan (USA) **50** 124) [2007 45: p7.1g⁵ f7g⁴ f8g⁵ p7g 7g Apr 24] close-coupled gelding: modest maiden: stays 7f: acts on polytrack and firm ground: wears cheekpieces/blinkers. *M. Dods*

PONTE VECCHIO (IRE) 3 b.g. Trans Island 119 – Gino Lady (IRE) 79 (Perugino **54** (USA) 84) [2007 –: p8g⁶ p8g⁶ p8g p9.5g² Dec 13] tall, close-coupled gelding: modest maiden: stays 9.5f: acts on polytrack. *J. R. Boyle*

PONT WOOD 3 b.g. Iron Mask (USA) 117 – Bajan Rose 89 (Dashing Blade 117) [2007 **51** 63: p6g⁴ 6s 7f p6m p8.6g p7g p8g p8g p8.6g Nov 17] smallish gelding: modest maiden: left M. Blanshard after sixth start: stays 1m: acts on polytrack. *Mrs N. S. Evans*

PONTY ROSSA (IRE) 3 ch.f. Distant Music (USA) 126 – Danish Gem (Danehill **96** (USA) 126) [2007 89: 6g⁶ 7g² 8.1m 7.1d* Jun 24] sturdy, lengthy filly: useful performer: improved, winning listed race at Warwick in June by neck then Nans Joy: also ran well earlier when ½-length second to Shmookh in handicap at York: bred to stay 1m: acts on polytrack, good to firm and good to soft going: effective held up or ridden handily. *T. D. Easterby*

POP MUSIC (IRE) 4 b.g. Tagula (IRE) 116 – Easy Pop (IRE) (Shernazar 131) [2007 **77** 70: p9.5g* p8.6g* p9.5g² p8.6g⁶ p8.6g p9.5g⁴ 9.7m⁴ p8.6g⁶ p10m p8.6g p8.6g⁵ p9.5d*

Dec 28] rather leggy gelding: fair handicapper: won at Wolverhampton in January, February and December: stays 9.5f: acts on polytrack and good to firm ground: tried blinkered/tongue tied, normally wears cheekpieces. *Miss J. Feilden*

POPOLO (IRE) 3 b.f. Fasliyev (USA) 120 – Delisha (Salse (USA) 128) [2007 66: f6g² **64** p7g⁵ f6g² f6g² Feb 28] rather leggy, lengthy filly: modest maiden: left M. Bell after second start: needs to settle to stay 7f: acts on fibresand and good to firm ground: wandered final start. *P. W. Chapple-Hyam*

POPPETS SWEETLOVE 3 b.f. Foxhound (USA) 103 – Our Poppet (IRE) 58 (Warn- **73** ing 136) [2007 7.1m 7.5m 8m 7.1d* 7.6f 7.1m⁴ 8d* 8m⁴ Oct 14] lightly-made filly: third foal: half-sister to fairly useful French 7f winner Poppet's Bounty (by Bahamian Bounty) and 5f/6f winner Noble Mount (by Muhtarram): dam, ran once, out of very smart 1¼m/1½m winner Upend: fair form: won maiden at Warwick in June and handicap at Bath in October: stays 1m: acts on good to firm and good to soft going. *A. B. Haynes*

POPPY DEAN (IRE) 2 ch.f. (Apr 4) Night Shift (USA) – Miss Devious (IRE) 51 (Dr **58** Devious (IRE) 127) [2007 5g 6g⁴ p7m⁴ p8.6g² Oct 26] 11,000Y: compact filly: first foal: dam, Irish 1½m to 2m winner, out of sister to smart 1¼m/1½m performer Monsajem: modest maiden: will stay 1½m: tongue tied first 2 starts. *J. G. Portman*

POPPY PERFECT 2 b.f. (Jan 18) Lujain (USA) 119 – Sea Jade (IRE) 56 (Mujadil – (USA) 119) [2007 6f 6g 7d⁴ p7.1g p5.1g Aug 31] unfurnished filly: first foal: dam, maiden, sister to useful performer up to 8.5f Sir Ferbet: little form: tried blinkered. *J. M. P. Eustace*

POPPY RED 2 ch.f. (Apr 10) Lear Spear (USA) 124 – Pooka's Daughter (IRE) 63 – (Eagle Eyed (USA) 111) [2007 p7.1g Oct 18] first foal: dam, 7f (at 2 yrs) to 8.5f seller winner, out of half-sister to smart 1m/1¼m performers Bachir, Elliot's World and Albu-hera: no show in maiden. *Miss J. R. Tooth*

POPPY'S ROSE 3 b.f. Diktat 126 – Perfect Peach 100 (Lycius (USA) 124) [2007 p6g⁶ **71** 6m* 7m 6m⁶ 6d* 6f⁵ 5d 7.2s⁵ 6g² 6d⁶ Oct 9] lengthy, workmanlike filly: second foal: half-sister to fairly useful 1¼m winner Thumpers Dream (by Cape Cross): dam, 5f (at 2 yrs) and 7f winner, out of useful sprinter Perfect Timing: fair performer: won maiden at Pontefract in April and handicap at Redcar in June: stays 7f: acts on soft and good to firm ground: quirky, has twice hung badly left. *I. W. McInnes*

PORJENSKI 3 ch.f. Piccolo 121 – Stygian (USA) 73 (Irish River (FR) 131) [2007 46: – 8f 8d⁵ Jul 3] poor maiden: stays 6f: acts on polytrack. *A. B. Haynes*

PORTAL 4 b.f. Hernando (FR) 127 – White Palace 80 (Shirley Heights 130) [2007 105: **108** 10.4g³ 10.9d 12m³ 12m⁴ p11g⁴ Aug 27] rather leggy filly: useful performer: good efforts when third in Middleton Stakes at York (beaten narrowly by Topatoo) and Lancashire Oaks at Newmarket (4¼ lengths behind Turbo Linn): below form last 2 starts: would have stayed 1¾m: acted on good to firm ground: held up: reportedly finished lame second outing: visits Azamour. *J. R. Fanshawe*

PORTHOLE (USA) 2 gr. or ro.c. (Apr 18) Mizzen Mast (USA) 121 – Privity (USA) **84 p** 114 (Private Account (USA)) [2007 7m³ Oct 5] leggy, short-backed colt: has a quick action: seventh foal: brother to US 7.5f and 8.5f winner Trimaran, closely related to useful 2005 2-y-o 6f and 7.5f winner Private Business (by Cozzene) and half-brother to useful French 5.5f and 1m winner Private War (by Danzig): dam, 7f winner (in France at 2 yrs) to 1½m (Prix de Malleret) winner, out of Princess Royal Stakes winner Sylph: 9/2, promising third in Almajd in maiden at Newmarket, finishing well from rear: will be suited by 1m+: bound to improve and win races. *B. W. Hills*

PORT LUANDA (IRE) 3 ch.g. Docksider (USA) 124 – Lady Angola (USA) 83 (Lord – At War (ARG)) [2007 –: 9m 8d⁴ 7s⁶ Jun 29] no form in maidens. *R. M. Flower*

PORT MACQUAIRIE (IRE) 3 b.g. Val Royal (FR) 127 – Hishmah 79 (Nashwan – (USA) 135) [2007 52: p8g p9.5g p12.2g Sep 22] maiden: little form in 2007: left R. Beckett after second start: tried in blinkers/cheekpieces. *J. W. Mullins*

PORTMEIRION 6 b.m. Polish Precedent (USA) 131 – India Atlanta (Ahonoora 122) **86** [2007 96: 5m³ 6m Jun 9] leggy, good-topped mare: useful performer at 5 yrs: easily better effort in 2007 (fairly useful form) when third of 6 to Sierra Vista in handicap at Haydock (9 lb out of weights) on reappearance: effective at 5f/6f: acts on polytrack, good to firm and good to soft going. *S. C. Williams*

PORT 'N STARBOARD 6 ch.g. Polar Falcon (USA) 126 – Sally Slade 80 (Dowsing **69** (USA) 124) [2007 75: p10g⁴ p10g³ p9.5g⁶ p12.2g p10g p12g Aug 28] fair performer: stays 1¼m: acts on polytrack: tried visored: hung markedly right second/fifth starts at 4 yrs: very slowly away final start in 2007: sold 1,000 gns in October, sent to Spain. *C. A. Cyzer*

PORTODORA (USA) 2 b.f. (Feb 1) Kingmambo (USA) 125 – High Walden (USA) **78 p**
111 (El Gran Senor (USA) 136) [2007 7d³ Oct 9] strong, sturdy filly: type to carry condition: third foal: half-sister to fairly useful 1m winner Heather Moor (by Diesis): dam,
1m (at 2 yrs)/9f (in US) winner, closely related to Oaks winner Reams of Verse and
half-sister to Eclipse Stakes winner Elmaamul: 6/1, encouraging close third in maiden at
Leicester, ending up isolated once going on over 1f out: will be suited by at least 1m:
useful performer in making. *H. R. A. Cecil*

PORT QUIN 2 ch.c. (Feb 3) Dr Fong (USA) 128 – Saphila (IRE) 72 (Sadler's Wells **84**
(USA) 132) [2007 7m 7g* p7g⁶ Nov 30] 82,000Y: strong, sturdy colt: first foal: dam,
maiden (stayed 1¾m), sister to useful performers up to 1½m Kisses For Me and Poseidon
Adventure: fairly useful form: better for debut, won maiden at Leicester in October by ½
length from Majeen: unsuited by test of speed in minor event at Lingfield: will benefit
from 1¼m/1½m. *G. Wragg*

PORTRUSH STORM 2 ch.f. (Mar 25) Observatory (USA) 131 – Overcast (IRE) 72 **68**
(Caerleon (USA) 132) [2007 5d³ Mar 31] 4,500Y: lengthy, workmanlike filly: half-sister
to several winners, including useful 7f and 8.5f winner Thunder Sky (by Zafonic) and
1¼m winner Tata Naka (by Nashwan): dam, Irish 1m winner, closely related to smart
Irish middle-distance performer Phantom Breeze: 20/1, third to Mister Hardy in minor
event at Newcastle, refusing to settle. *D. Carroll*

PORTWAY LANE 2 ch.f. (Apr 9) Tobougg (IRE) 125 – Interregnum (Interrex (CAN)) **43**
[2007 5g 5.1f² 5f⁴ p5.1g 5.2g⁶ May 31] leggy, plain filly: fourth foal: half-sister to 3-y-o
Jost Van Dyke: dam, maiden, half-sister to useful miler Lilli Claire: poor maiden: raced
only at 5f. *W. G. M. Turner*

POSEIDON'S SECRET (IRE) 4 b.g. Night Shift (USA) – Chita Rivera 61 (Chief **81 d**
Singer 131) [2007 68: p12.2g* p12g⁵ p12g⁴ 11.7f⁶ p12.2g 11.6f p12m 12d Oct 27] big,
strong, useful-looking gelding: has a round action: fairly useful performer: won maiden
at Wolverhampton in February: lost form after third start: will stay 1¾m: acts on polytrack, below form on turf: tried in cheekpieces/blinkers: looked difficult ride latter 3-y-o
start: sold 16,000 gns in November, joined C. Mann. *Pat Eddery*

POSITANO (IRE) 7 b.h. Polish Precedent (USA) 131 – Shamaya (IRE) (Doyoun 124) **–**
[2007 10f Aug 5] winner of 5 races in Norway for W. Neuroth, latest in 2005: well held
only Flat outing in 2007: has won at 1½m, raced mainly around 1m: acts on dirt and good
to soft ground: tried in cheekpieces: modest winning hurdler. *M. Scudamore*

POSITIVE PROFILE (IRE) 9 b.g. Definite Article 121 – Leyete Gulf (IRE) (Slip **78**
Anchor 136) [2007 f16g5 p13.9g* p16g⁵ 14g Apr 8] angular gelding: fair performer
nowadays: won handicap at Wolverhampton in January: effective at 1¾m to 2½f: acts on
all-weather, firm and soft going: has shown signs of temperament, hung and flashed tail
for latest win. *J. J. Quinn*

POSTAGE STAMPE 4 b.f. Singspiel (IRE) 133 – Jaljuli 107 (Jalmood (USA) 126) **87**
[2007 95: 10m 9.9g⁵ 9.7m³ 12g³ Nov 2] rather leggy filly: fairly useful handicapper: stays
1½m: acts on polytrack and good to firm going. *D. M. Simcock*

POSTAGE (USA) 4 b. or br.g. Chester House (USA) 123 – Nimble Mind (USA) 103 **–**
(Lyphard (USA) 132) [2007 62: p8g⁶ Apr 2] maiden: well held in seller sole 4-y-o start:
in cheekpieces last 3 starts at 3 yrs. *K. A. Morgan*

POSTGRADUATE (IRE) 5 b.g. Almutawakel 126 – Institutrice (IRE) 87 (College **80**
Chapel 122) [2007 96: 8.3f 8g May 24] tall, good-topped gelding: useful handicapper at
best: little impact in 2007 (said to have finished lame final outing): stays 1m: acts on
polytrack, soft and good to firm going: tried visored: banned for 40 days, trainer fined
£3,000 and jockey suspended for 14 days after HRA inquiry into running at Windsor on
reappearance: sold 5,500 gns, sent to Greece, where won at 6f and 7f. *W. J. Knight*

POSTMASTER 5 b.g. Dansili 127 – Post Modern (USA) (Nureyev (USA) 131) [2007 **64**
60: p7g⁵ p7.1g⁵ p8.6g* p8g* p9.5g p8g² 9.7m⁴ 9g⁴ 8d⁶ p8g p8.6g⁶ 7s p8g² 7.6f⁴ p8g 7g
p8m² p8g p8.6g⁵ p8.6g⁴ p8m Dec 9] good-bodied gelding: modest handicapper: won at
Wolverhampton in February and Lingfield in March: stays 1½m, races mainly around 1m
nowadays: acts on polytrack and firm going: tried in cheekpieces/visor: formerly tongue
tied: held up. *R. Ingram*

POSTSPROFIT (IRE) 3 b.g. Marju (IRE) 127 – Housekeeper (IRE) 97 (Common **71 §**
Grounds 118) [2007 69: 9.7m² p8.6g³ 8g p10g 7d⁵ 10g³ 8m 10.1d 9.7f⁴ 8g⁴ p8.6g⁵ 7d
Oct 23] good-topped gelding: has a round action: fair maiden: stays 1¼m: acts on polytrack, probably on firm ground: tried in cheekpieces: has raced freely/hung: one to treat
with caution: sold 10,000 gns, sent to Belgium. *N. A. Callaghan*

POTEMKIN (USA) 2 b. or br.g. (Mar 9) Van Nistelrooy (USA) 108 – Bolshoia (USA) **56** (Moscow Ballet (USA)) [2007 7m 7.1m 7.1g 7d Oct 29] close-coupled gelding: modest maiden: bred to prove best up to 7f. *A. King*

POTENTIALE (IRE) 3 ch.g. Singspiel (IRE) 133 – No Frills (IRE) 62 (Darshaan **81** 133) [2007 55: 9.9g* 12.1m² 11.7d² 11.5g² 10.1m² 10.2f p11g* p12.2g² Oct 6] sturdy gelding: fairly useful performer: improved in 2007, winning minor event at Beverley in May and handicap at Kempton in September: stays 1½m: acts on polytrack, good to firm and good to soft ground: wore cheekpieces last 2 starts. *J. W. Hills*

POTHOS WAY (GR) 4 ch.g. Wadood (USA) 97 – Evropi's Way (Sanglamore (USA) **73** 126) [2007 65: p10g² p10g⁵ p11g* 11.6m p12g p12g p9.5g* p11m Nov 11] fair handicapper: won at Kempton in June and Wolverhampton in October: stays easy 11f: acts on polytrack (below form both turf starts). *P. R. Chamings*

POTWASH 7 b.m. Piccolo 121 – Silankka 70 (Slip Anchor 136) [2007 a7.5g p5g⁴ 7s **55** 8d* 8d³ 9.3m 9s May 29] modest performer: fourth in claimer at Lingfield second start: left A. Hermans before winning similar event at Compiegne in April: effective at 5f to 1m: acts on polytrack/sand, heavy and good to firm going: tried blinkered: has carried head awkwardly/flashed tail. *Stal Lannoo, Belgium*

POUND SIGN 4 ch.g. Singspiel (IRE) 133 – Profit Alert (IRE) 97 (Alzao (USA) 117) **–** [2007 84: 10.9s⁶ Jul 5] fairly useful form at 2/3 yrs: off 14 months (reportedly suffered knee problems), tailed off sole Flat start in 2007. *Evan Williams*

POWER AGAIN (GER) 6 b.m. Dashing Blade 117 – Pik Konigin (GER) (Konigs- **65** stuhl (GER)) [2007 11.7d² 16.4m² p16.5g Aug 18] ex-German mare: first foal: dam, German winner around 9f, half-sister to smart German miler Power Flame (by Dashing Blade): won handicaps at Hanover and Baden-Baden for G. Sybrecht in 2005: unraced in 2006: modest form when runner-up in handicaps in Britain in 2007: stays 16.5f: acts on soft and good to firm ground: has worn blinkers, including for last win. *P. R. Chamings*

POWER ALERT 3 b.g. Averti (IRE) 117 – Crystal Power (USA) (Pleasant Colony **53** (USA)) [2007 47: f7s² p6g³ f7g⁴ 7g 5.5s a4.8g³ a7.5g* a7.5g Dec 13] close-coupled gelding: modest performer: sold from B. R. Millman 3,000 gns after third start: won maiden at Mons in December: stays 7.5f: acts on dirt/fibresand: has worn cheekpieces/blinkers. *L. Braem, Belgium*

POWER BALLAD 3 ch.f. Titus Livius (FR) 115 – Sea Music (Inchinor 119) [2007 67: **79 p** p8g* Sep 26] fair form: better effort in maidens 14 months apart when winning at Kempton in September, making all and going readily clear despite edging left: should progress further. *W. J. Knight*

POWER BROKER 4 b.g. Mark of Esteem (IRE) 137 – Galatrix 72 (Be My Guest **–** (USA) 126) [2007 –: p8g May 4] tall, rather leggy gelding: has a quick, unimpressive action: fair maiden at 2 yrs: well held since: tongue tied/blinkered last 2 starts: sold 1,500 gns in July. *P. F. I. Cole*

POWER DESERT (IRE) 2 b.g. (Feb 11) Anabaa (USA) 130 – Legende d'Or (FR) **–** (Diesis 133) [2007 6g Oct 3] strong gelding: sixth foal: half-brother to 3-y-o Mr Grand Lodge and 6f/7f winner in Hungary (both by Grand Lodge): dam, French 2-y-o 7f winner, half-sister to Prix Marcel Boussac winner Amonita (by Anabaa): 16/1, green (hung left) when well held in maiden at Newcastle: held up well 800 gns. *M. Johnston*

POWER OF FUTURE (GER) 4 ch.f. Definite Article 121 – Pik Konigin (GER) **88** (Konigsstuhl (GER)) [2007 89: 14.1m* 14g 14m 16s 12g⁵ 16m⁵ Nov 4] tall, leggy filly: fairly useful performer: won handicap at Yarmouth in April: left H. Cecil after third outing: stays 1¾m, not quite 2m: acts on polytrack, good to firm and good to soft going. *Andrew Oliver, Ireland*

POWER PLAYER 3 b.g. Diktat 126 – Royal Patron 78 (Royal Academy (USA) 130) **77** [2007 9m⁵ p9.5g² p12g⁴ p9.5g² p10g³ Nov 30] fair maiden: stays 1¼m: acts on polytrack. *D. J. Coakley*

POWER SHARED (IRE) 3 gr.g. Kendor (FR) 122 – Striking Pose (IRE) 77 (Dar- **71** shaan 133) [2007 10d 10s⁶ p12g⁴ 11.6d Oct 15] quite good-topped gelding: fair maiden: left D. Weld in Ireland after second start: stays 1½m: acts on polytrack, raced only on going softer than good on turf: gave trouble at start third outing. *P. G. Murphy*

POWER TRIP (IRE) 3 b.g. Namid 128 – Graten (IRE) 84 (Zieten (USA) 118) [2007 **–** 7g Sep 22] 25/1, tailed-off last in maiden at Catterick (said to have finished lame): sold 800 gns. *Miss V. Haigh*

POWYS LAD 2 b.c. (Mar 19) Diktat 126 – Cheyenne Squaw (IRE) (Night Shift (USA)) **54 ?**
[2007 6m 6m[4] 6s 7.5m 6s p7g 7g Oct 19] rangy colt: maiden: seemingly modest form at
best: tried visored. *K. R. Burke*

POYLE KIERA 3 b.f. Diktat 126 – Poyle Amber 55 (Sharrood (USA) 124) [2007 56: **54**
p12g[5] 10.2d[6] 11.8g Oct 16] modest maiden: stays 1¼m: acts on polytrack, firm and good
to soft ground: difficult ride. *M. Blanshard*

POYLE RUBY 3 b.f. Josr Algarhoud (IRE) 118 – Poyle Jezebelle 58 (Sharpo 132) **52**
[2007 –: p8g p8g p8g p8g 10.1m 8d Aug 21] modest maiden: raced mostly at 1m: form
only on polytrack. *M. Blanshard*

PRACTICAL JOKE (IRE) 3 b.g. Alhaarth (IRE) 126 – Trick (IRE) 76 (Shirley **64**
Heights 130) [2007 p7g 8g 8d[3] 8g[4] 8g[4] 8d[3] 6.5g[5] a7.5g Dec 13] modest maiden: sold from
W. Knight after second start: stays 1m. *W. Kujath, Germany*

PRACTICALLYPERFECT (IRE) 3 b.f. King Charlemagne (USA) 120 – Morn- **82**
ingsurprice (USA) (Future Storm (USA)) [2007 78: 8m[5] 8.2g[3] 8.1g[3] 9g[6] p8g Oct 17]
compact filly: fairly useful performer: left H. Cecil after third start: worth a try back at 7f:
raced only on polytrack and good/good to firm going: visored final start. *P. D. Evans*

PRAGMATISM 2 b.c. (Mar 12) Kingmambo (USA) 125 – Sheer Reason (USA) 110 **69**
(Danzig (USA)) [2007 7d[3] 8d[5] Oct 27] fifth foal: half-brother to 4-y-o Faith And Reason
and 2006 2-y-o 7f winner I'm Right (by Rahy), both fairly useful: dam, French 2-y-o 6f
winner, out of half-sister to dam of Fantastic Light: fair form in maidens at Brighton (third
to Mr Keppel) and Newbury 2 months apart: should be suited by 1m/1¼m. *M. Johnston*

PRAGMATIST 3 b.f. Piccolo 121 – Shi Shi (Alnasr Alwasheek 117) [2007 8m 6g* 6v[5] **68**
6d* p6g[5] 6d Oct 9] smallish filly: third foal: dam French 1½m winner: fair performer:
won maiden at Lingfield in June and handicap at Salisbury in August: stays 6f: acts on
good to soft going (probably on polytrack). *P. Winkworth*

PRAIRIE LAW (GER) 7 b.g. Law Society (USA) 130 – Prairie Charm (IRE) (Thatch- **–**
ing 131) [2007 p12.2g f14g Mar 6] modest performer at best: no form in 2007: has worn
blinkers/cheekpieces. *B. N. Pollock*

PRAIRIE MOON 3 ch.f. Halling (USA) 133 – Warning Shadows (IRE) 113 (Cadeaux **47**
Genereux 131) [2007 p8g Mar 24] lengthy filly: seventh foal: half-sister to 1m winner
Shady Point (by Unfuwain) and 1¼m winner Dark Planet (by Singspiel): dam 7f and
1¼m (Sun Chariot Stakes) winner and second in Irish 1000 Guineas: 16/1 and fit, very
much in need of experience when 8¾ lengths ninth of 10 to Warm Embraces in maiden at
Lingfield: sold 8,500 gns in December. *C. E. Brittain*

PRAIRIE STORM 2 b.g. (Apr 4) Storming Home 128 – Last Dream (IRE) 80 (Alzao **70**
(USA) 117) [2007 8g[5] 8.2g[5] Nov 7] neat gelding: seventh foal: half-brother to several
winners, including useful French 8.5f winner Last Cry (by Peintre Celebre): dam, Irish
1½m winner, half-sister to Grand Criterium winners Lost World and Fijar Tango, latter
also high class up to 1½m: fair form in maidens, then gelded: will stay 1¼m/1½m.
A. M. Balding

PRAIRIE SUN (GER) 6 b.m. Law Society (USA) 130 – Prairie Flame (IRE) 85 **70**
(Marju (IRE) 127) [2007 81, a–: 16.1s[6] 15.8m Jul 11] quite good-topped mare: just fair
handicapper in 2007: stays 17f: acts on good to firm and good to soft ground: tried
visored/in cheekpieces. *Mrs A. Duffield*

PRAIRIE TIGER (GER) 3 b.c. Tiger Hill (IRE) 127 – Prairie Lilli (GER) (Acaten- **88 p**
ango (GER) 127) [2007 10m[4] p10m* 10.3g[6] Oct 26] €180,000Y: attractive, heavy-
topped colt: third foal: half-brother to 2 winners abroad by Dashing Blade: dam, German
1¼m/11f winner, half-sister to smart German stayer Pinot: fairly useful form: still green
when winning maiden at Kempton in October by ½ length from Abydos: had 2 handlers
and on toes, race not run to suit when creditable sixth to Milne Graden on handicap debut
at Doncaster final start: will stay 1½m+: acts on polytrack: remains open to improvement.
N. J. Vaughan

PRAVDA STREET 2 ch.c. (Apr 21) Soviet Star (USA) 128 – Sari 83 (Faustus (USA) **76 p**
118) [2007 p7g[2] Nov 16] 18,000Y: fourth foal: closely related to fairly useful 5f (at
2 yrs)/6f winner Saristar (by Starborough) and half-brother to 4-y-o Genari: dam 7f
winner (including at 2 yrs): 3/1, green throughout when second to Dhhamaan in maiden
at Lingfield: will improve. *P. F. I. Cole*

PRAXITELES (IRE) 3 b.c. Sadler's Wells (USA) 132 – Hellenic 125 (Darshaan 133) **90 P**
[2007 10g[6] p12g* Nov 15] lengthy colt: has scope: brother to several at least smart
performers, including 1¼m winner Greek Dance and 1¼m/1½m winner Islington, both

very smart, and half-brother to useful 7f/1m winner Desert Beauty (by Green Desert) and 5-y-o Mountain High: dam won Yorkshire Oaks and second in St Leger: plenty of promise in maidens 6 months apart, impressive winner at Lingfield by 3½ lengths from Wraith, overcoming trouble: stays 1½m: potentially smart, and sure to win more races. *Sir Michael Stoute*

PRECEPT 3 b.f. Polish Precedent (USA) 131 – Anna of Brunswick 78 (Rainbow Quest **70** (USA) 134) [2007 10g 11.5s² 12m⁵ p12g⁵ p12m Oct 6] rather leggy filly: seventh foal: half-sister to several winners, including fairly useful 1½m winner Goslar (by In The Wings): dam, 1¼m winner (stayed 1¾m), half-sister to dams of very smart performers up to 1½m Annaba and Annus Mirabilis: fair maiden: should stay 1½m+: acts on soft ground: sold 7,000 gns in October. *H. Candy*

PRECIOUS BOY (GER) 2 br.c. Big Shuffle (USA) 122 – Pretty Su (IRE) (Surumu **111 p** (GER)) [2007 6.5g⁴ 7s* 8g* Oct 14] fourth foal: half-brother to 3 winners, including Irish 7f/1m winner Poppyfield (by Waky Nao) and German 1¼m winner Pretty Smart (by Law Society): dam German 9f/9.5f winner: unbeaten in maiden at Krefeld in July, listed race there in September and Christlacke-Preis des Winterfavoriten at Cologne (came from rear to lead in final 1f, beat Liang Kay ½ length, pair clear) in October: stays 1m: should progress further. *W. Hickst, Germany*

PRECIOUS METTLE 3 gr.f. Golden Snake (USA) 127 – Silver Fan (Lear Fan (USA) **–** 130) [2007 11.8s Jun 4] fourth foal: half-sister to 2 winners in Greece: dam unraced: 40/1, well held in maiden at Leicester: sold 2,000 gns in July, and joined J. Turner: dead. *H. R. A. Cecil*

PRECOCIOUS STAR (IRE) 3 ch.f. Bold Fact (USA) 116 – Flames (Blushing Flame **88** (USA) 109) [2007 91: a7f a8f p8g* 7m 8m 7s⁵ 7m p8m p8g p8g Dec 16] strong, work-manlike filly: fairly useful performer: won listed race at Kempton by neck from Fiumicino) in March: mostly at least respectable efforts in varied company after: stays easy 1m: acts on polytrack, good to firm and good to soft going (well below form on dirt first 2 starts in 2007). *K. R. Burke*

PRE EMINANCE (IRE) 6 b.g. Peintre Celebre (USA) 137 – Sorb Apple (IRE) 79 **42** (Kris 135) [2007 12m 10d⁶ 8s 12m 14.1g p16.5g Dec 8] useful-looking gelding: maiden: poor at best in 2007, leaving J. Wainwright after third start: stays 1½m: acts on firm ground: usually tongue tied, tried in blinkers/cheekpieces. *L. R. James*

PRELUDE 6 b.m. Danzero (AUS) – Dancing Debut 83 (Polar Falcon (USA) 126) [2007 **77** 9.9m⁶ 11.5m⁵ 11.8s 12.3f* 12s 12.3s* 12s² 12.3m³ 12.3m* 15.9m⁵ 13.4g⁴ Sep 29] good-topped mare: fair handicapper: better than ever in 2007, winning at Chester in June, July and August: stays 1½m (not 2m): acts on firm and soft going: often races prominently. *W. M. Brisbourne*

PREMIER CLASS (IRE) 2 b.g. (Mar 14) Indian Danehill (IRE) 124 – Shams Wa **44** Matar (Polish Precedent (USA) 131) [2007 5m 6m 7d 7d 8g 7g Oct 19] poor maiden. *J. S. Wainwright*

PREMIER CRU 4 b.g. King's Best (USA) 132 – No Rehearsal (FR) (Baillamont **37** (USA) 124) [2007 –: p10g 7d Oct 29] close-coupled gelding: poor maiden. *Andrew Turnell*

PREMIER DANSEUR (IRE) 2 b.c. (Apr 24) Noverre (USA) 125 – Destiny Dance **71 p** (USA) 100 (Nijinsky (CAN) 138) [2007 6g² 6m* Nov 10] good-bodied colt: closely related to useful Irish 7f (at 2 yrs) to 1¼m winner Dearly (by Rahy) and half-brother to 3 winners, including very smart US Grade 1 2004 2-y-o 8.5f winner Balletto (by Timber Country): dam, 11f (US Grade 3 event) to 1½m winner, out of US Grade 1 8.5f/9f winner Althea: fair form: won maiden at Doncaster by a neck, getting up close home: will be well suited by 1m: should go on progressing. *M. Johnston*

PREMIER YANK (USA) 2 b.c. (Feb 24) Johannesburg (USA) 127 – Sallybrooke **– p** (USA) (Dehere (USA) 121) [2007 5.7d Oct 1] $220,000Y: second foal: half-brother to winner in US by Honour And Glory: dam, US 1m (at 2 yrs)/8.5f winner, out of half-sister to Breeders' Cup Sprint winner Safely Kept: 25/1, very slowly away and met trouble in maiden at Bath: will do better. *J. A. Osborne*

PREMIO LOCO (USA) 3 ch.g. Prized (USA) – Crazee Mental 107 (Magic Ring **105** (IRE) 115) [2007 58p: 8m⁵ p8g* 8m 7m* Sep 22] lengthy gelding: useful form, lightly raced: won maiden at Lingfield (by 5 lengths) in April and handicap at Newbury (beat Big Noise by 1¾ lengths, asserting readily) in September: stays 1m: raced only on poly-track and good to firm ground: has been early to post. *C. F. Wall*

PREMIUM PORT 2 b.g. (Apr 30) Superior Premium 122 – The Barnsley Belle (IRE) **56 ?**
63 (Distinctly North (USA) 115) [2007 6f⁵ 5d 6g 5d⁵ Jul 19] modest maiden: dead.
A. Berry

PRESBYTERIAN NUN (IRE) 2 b.f. (Mar 14) Daylami (IRE) 138 – Conspiracy 98 **86 p**
(Rudimentary (USA) 118) [2007 7g 7m² 7m* 7m Oct 6] lengthy, unfurnished filly:
half-sister to 3 winners, notably 6-y-o Jedburgh and useful 1¼m/11.6f winner In Disguise
(by Nashwan): dam, 2-y-o 5f winner, closely related to high-class sprinter Gayane: fairly
useful form: second to Sense of Joy at Newmarket prior to winning maiden at Folkestone
in September by neck from Lady Deauville: seemingly over the top (not take eye) in
nursery at Newmarket: will be suited by 1m+: type to improve more at 3 yrs. *J. L. Dunlop*

PRESENT 3 ch.f. Generous (IRE) 139 – Miss Picol (Exit To Nowhere (USA) 122) **57**
[2007 49: 10m 12.1m 14.1g⁶ 10.1g p12.2g⁶ p11g 12m p12.2g 10.1g* p12m Oct 3] good-
topped filly: modest performer: won seller at Yarmouth (left D. Morris) in September:
probably stays 1½m: acts on polytrack, probably on good to firm ground: tried in
cheekpieces/visor: often forces pace. *M. J. Gingell*

PRESENT ORIENTED (USA) 6 ch.g. Southern Halo (USA) – Shy Beauty (CAN) **–**
(Great Gladiator (USA)) [2007 11.6m Aug 13] strong, close-coupled gelding: has a
fluent, round action: lightly-raced maiden on Flat: no form since 2004: fair form over
fences. *M. C. Chapman*

PRESIDENT DAN 3 b.c. Polish Precedent (USA) 131 – Mill Line 71 (Mill Reef **61**
(USA) 141) [2007 p10g p12f⁶ p12g⁴ 12m 11.5s⁶ p12g 12g* 15.4m⁵ 14m⁴ 11.9d⁴ 12.4m⁶
12g 16.1g p16g Oct 17] well-made colt: modest handicapper: won at Folkestone in July:
stays 1¾m: acts on polytrack and good to firm ground: tried visored (ran poorly): held up.
M. R. Channon

PRESIDENT ELECT (IRE) 2 b.c. (Mar 19) Imperial Ballet (IRE) 110 – Broadway **78 p**
Rosie 101 (Absalom 128) [2007 5m⁶ 5d² 5g³ Oct 20] €21,000F, 36,000Y: good-topped
colt: half-brother to several winners, notably smart 6f (including at 2 yrs) winner Eastern
Purple (by Petorius): dam Irish 5f to 7f winner: fair form in maidens: twice placed at
Catterick, including short-head second to Miesko: will prove best at 5f/6f: should do well
at 3 yrs. *T. D. Barron*

PRESIDIUM STAR 2 b.f. (Apr 5) Presidium 124 – Pagan Star (Carlitin 50) [2007 5m **–**
5d 5g⁵ Aug 29] compact filly: third reported foal: half-sister to 3-y-o Pagan Starprincess:
dam unraced: well held in maidens. *G. M. Moore*

PRESKANI 5 b.g. Sri Pekan (USA) 117 – Lamarita 92§ (Emarati (USA) 74) [2007 –, **–**
a65: f8g f7g f7g⁴ f7d p7.1g Dec 26] fair at 5 yrs: poor at best in 2007: stays 1m: acts on **a39**
fibresand, rarely tried on turf: usually wears cheekpieces/visor. *Mrs N. Macauley*

PRESQUE PERDRE 3 ch.g. Desert Prince (IRE) 130 – Kindle (Selkirk (USA) 129) **41**
[2007 –: 8.2g 8.5s 10.1m⁵ Aug 8] good-topped gelding: poor maiden: bred to be suited by
1½m+. *K. G. Reveley*

PRESS EXPRESS (IRE) 5 ch.g. Entrepreneur 123 – Nawaji (USA) 45 (Trempolino **72**
(USA) 135) [2007 82d: 7m⁶ 8f⁶ 10s* 12d² 12d⁵ Jul 4] strong gelding: fair performer
nowadays: won at Leicester in May: effective at 9.7f to 1½m: acts on soft and good
to firm going: visored seventh 4-y-o outing: edgy, free-going sort: sold 17,000 gns, joined
C. von der Recke in Germany. *R. A. Fahey*

PRESSING (IRE) 4 b.c. Soviet Star (USA) 128 – Rafif (USA) 68 (Riverman **120**
(USA) 131) [2007 102: 10m* 10m* 10m* 10m² 10m⁵ 10d 12d² 11d* 10d* Nov 4]
He's no Rakti, but the latest colt purchased from Italy by Gary Tanaka and
sent to Michael Jarvis has given his new connections plenty to celebrate in the short
time they have had him. Pressing developed into a very smart performer in the latest
season, capping it with a victory in a Group 1 event, the Premio Roma At The Races
at Rome. Rakti won six Group 1 events in all, including the Champion Stakes, Prince
of Wales's Stakes, Queen Elizabeth II Stakes and Lockinge Stakes, but races
of that quality look beyond the reach of Pressing, and he will probably continue to
be campaigned extensively abroad in search of further big-race successes.

Pressing was trained by Roberto Feligioni when based in Italy and managed
only one win in his first two seasons before quickly taking his total to four on his
return in 2007, picking up a couple of minor events at Milan and completing his
hat-trick on the same course in April in the Premio Ambrosiano, upgraded for the
first time to Group 3. Pressing had been sold to Tanaka by the time of the Premio
Presidente della Repubblica at Rome the following month, a race Rakti had won on

*Premio Roma At The Races, Rome—Pressing gains his fifth success of the year,
and his second for Michael Jarvis; outsider Monachesi (second right) is followed by
Boris de Deauville (centre), Cherry Mix (right) and Vol de Nuit (rail)*

his debut for the Jarvis stable. Pressing himself joined Jarvis after the race, in which
he showed further improvement to finish a half-length second to Distant Way. Not
up to troubling the likes of Manduro and Dylan Thomas in the Prince of Wales's
Stakes at Royal Ascot on his first appearance for Jarvis, and last of seven in the
Arlington Million on his second, Pressing made a far greater impact in his three
subsequent races, the first of which took place in Turkey. The Bosphorus Cup at
Veliefendi attracted a smart field of international performers following a huge
increase in prize money, over £80,000 of which went to Pressing's connections
after he'd finished second to German challenger Bussoni, beaten two lengths.
Pressing's stamina seemed stretched on what was only his second race over as far
as a mile and a half—he'd been well held in the Derby Italiano on his first—and he
showed better form over shorter on his last two outings, both of which were in Italy.
In the Premio Federico Tesio, a Group 3 contest run over eleven furlongs at Milan
in September, Pressing won easily by three and a half lengths from Gimmy, making
all. Five weeks later Pressing, partnered by Neil Callan who had won the Oaks
d'Italia on Pressing's stable-companion Fashion Statement, was ridden a bit more
patiently in winning the Premio Roma over a mile and a quarter. Taking it up around
two furlongs out, Pressing ran on well to win by a length and a half from rank
outsider Monachesi.

			Nureyev (b 1977)	Northern Dancer
	Soviet Star (USA) (b 1984)			Special
			Veruschka (b 1967)	Venture VII
Pressing (IRE) (b.c. 2003)				Marie d'Anjou
	Rafif (USA) (b or br 1990)		Riverman (b 1969)	Never Bend
				River Lady
			Reves Celestes (b 1979)	Lyphard
				Tobira Celeste

Pressing, who cost only €35,000 as a yearling, is closely related to the
three-year-old Make Me An Offer (by Fasliyev), a winner at six to eight furlongs in
Spain in the latest season; and he is a half-brother to two useful winners in Rajam
(by Sadler's Wells) and Kadir (by Unfuwain), the former at a mile and a half and
the latter at a mile and three quarters. Pressing's dam Rafif raced only at three,
putting up easily her best performance when winning a maiden over a mile and a
quarter at Sandown. Rafif is a daughter of the fairly useful one-mile winner Reves
Celestes and granddaughter of Tobira Celeste, successful at up to nine furlongs in
France. Tobira Celeste is also the dam of the King George VI and Queen Elizabeth
Stakes runner-up Celestial Storm and the Ribblesdale Stakes winner Thawakib, the
latter the dam of Sakhee. Pressing, a leggy, useful-looking individual, acts on good
to firm and good to soft going. *M. A. Jarvis*

PRESS THE BUTTON (GER) 4 b.g. Dansili 127 – Play Around (IRE) 105 (Niniski **96**
(USA) 125) [2007 92: 8m 10.1d 8d³ 9.7m³ 8g 10.2d* 10d⁴ 10m² 9.7f* 10s⁵ 10d Oct 27]
workmanlike gelding: useful handicapper: won at Bath in August and Folkestone in
September: stays 10.2f: acts on polytrack, firm and soft ground: ran poorly in cheekpieces
(on edge): free-going sort, often makes running. *J. R. Boyle*

PRESTO LEVANTER 2 b.f. (Jan 24) Rock of Gibraltar (IRE) 133 – Presto Vento 103 **69**
(Air Express (IRE) 125) [2007 5m² 5g 5d* 5d 6m 5m Aug 31] smallish, stocky filly: first
foal: dam 5f (at 2 yrs) and 7f winner: fair performer: won maiden at Sandown in May:
well held in nurseries (said to have been struck into final outing): best at 5f: acts on good
to firm and good to soft going. *R. Hannon*

PRESTO SHINKO (IRE) 6 b. or br.g. Shinko Forest (IRE) – Swift Chorus (Music **114**
Boy 124) [2007 119: 5m⁴ 5g 6m³ 6d 6d 5g 6f* 6d⁴ 7m Sep 4] tall gelding: smart performer: won minor event at Windsor (by ½ length from Galeota) in August: creditable
efforts otherwise only when fourth in Palace House Stakes at Newmarket (behind Tax
Free) and third in listed race at Salisbury (behind Sakhee's Secret) first/third outings:
effective at 5f/6f: acts on polytrack and any turf going: often wears cheekpieces/visor:
sold 27,000 gns. *R. Hannon*

PRESUMPTIVE (IRE) 7 b.g. Danehill (USA) 126 – Demure (Machiavellian (USA) **103**
123) [2007 97: p7g⁶ p7g* 8.1d³ 7f 7v 7g³ 7m² 7d⁴ Sep 29] leggy, useful-looking gelding:
useful handicapper: won at Lingfield (by ½ length from Ceremonial Jade) in May: good
efforts in frame last 3 starts, including second at Goodwood (short head behind South
Cape) and fourth to Candidato Roy in valuable event at Ascot, finishing well: stays 1m:
acts on polytrack, good to firm and good to soft going: blinkered (seemed to take little
interest) once at 4 yrs: held up. *R. Charlton*

PRET A PORTER (UAE) 3 b. or br.f. Jade Robbery (USA) 121 – Velour 94 (Mtoto **72**
134) [2007 73: p10g* p10g³ 10.9m⁵ 10.2f⁴ 12.6m* 12m 16d Jun 22] close-coupled filly:
fair performer: won handicaps at Lingfield in January and Warwick in May: very stiff
task, well held in Queen's Vase at Royal Ascot final outing: stays easy 12.6f: acts on
polytrack and firm ground: effective blinkered or not. *P. D. Evans*

PRET A TOUT 2 ch.f. (Mar 22) Ishiguru (USA) 114 – Pretiosa (IRE) 47 (Royal Abjar **–**
(USA) 121) [2007 6m 6m 8.5m Sep 11] 3,000F, 3,000Y: strong filly: third foal: closely
related to 4-y-o Prettilini: dam maiden (stayed 10.4f): no show in maidens. *P. J. McBride*

PRETTILINI 4 ch.f. Bertolini (USA) 125 – Pretiosa (IRE) 47 (Royal Abjar (USA) 121) **56**
[2007 70: f7g⁶ f8g f6g⁶ f6g⁴ f7g⁵ f6g² p7.1g p5.1g⁶ 6.1g f7g⁶ 6s⁶ 5m 6m Aug 9] smallish,
workmanlike filly: modest performer: left R. Brotherton after seventh outing: stays 7f:
acts on all-weather and good to firm going. *A. W. Carroll*

PRETTY BALLERINA (USA) 2 b.f. (Mar 4) Swain (IRE) 134 – Hawzah (Green **76**
Desert (USA) 127) [2007 6g² 6d⁴ 6g⁶ 7d⁵ p6g⁶ Dec 4] $65,000F: smallish filly: sixth foal:
half-sister to fairly useful miler Sharplaw Autumn (by Red Ransom): dam unraced sister
to smart 1m/1¼m winner Fahim: fair maiden: fourth to Yu'resothrilling in Swordlestown Stud Sprint Stakes at Naas: lost form after (final start in minor event at Lingfield):
should stay 1m: acts on good to firm going. *John Joseph Murphy, Ireland*

PRETTY BONNIE 2 b.f. (Apr 4) Kyllachy 129 – Joonayh 81 (Warning 136) [2007 5d **54**
5m³ 5.2d⁴ p6g p7.1g 6m⁶ 5.3m p6g⁶ p7.1g⁵ Nov 5] 8,000F: close-coupled filly: fourth
foal: half-sister to 5-y-o Majehar and 3-y-o Xalted: dam, 2-y-o 6f winner, half-sister to
smart 7f performer Millennium Force: modest maiden: probably best at 6f: acts on
polytrack, good to firm and good to soft going. *J. G. Portman*

PRETTY DEMANDING (IRE) 3 b.f. Night Shift (USA) – Absolute Glee (USA) **84**
100 (Kenmare (FR) 125) [2007 9.7m⁶ p7.1g 8.1m 10.1g⁵ 11.5m* 11.5s* 12s 12g⁵ 10s³
12.1m² 12m⁴ 11.9s⁵ 12d⁴ 14g Oct 29] €17,500 3-y-o: sturdy filly: fifth foal: half-sister to
useful Irish 7f winner Absolute Image (by Indian Ridge): dam Irish 1m (at 2 yrs) and
1¼m winner: fairly useful handicapper: won at Lingfield and Yarmouth in June: at least
respectable efforts when in frame after: stays 1½m: acts on soft and good to firm ground:
tongue tied third appearance: usually held up. *M. G. Quinlan*

PRETTY GAME 3 b.g. Mind Games 121 – Catwalk Girl 53 (Skyliner 117) [2007 –: **40**
p9.5g f7g⁴ f8d⁶ Dec 20] poor maiden. *K. A. Ryan*

PRETTY MAJESTIC (IRE) 3 b.f. Invincible Spirit (IRE) 121 – Cheeky Weeky **92**
(Cadeaux Genereux 131) [2007 92: 7m⁶ 6m 6m 7g 6m 6m⁴ 6m Oct 4] angular, useful-
looking filly: fairly useful performer: below form after reappearance: best up to 7f: acts
on good to firm going: tried visored. *M. R. Channon*

PRETTY MISS 3 b.f. Averti (IRE) 117 – Pretty Poppy 67 (Song 132) [2007 76: 5m* 5g **80**
5m³ 5m² 5f⁶ 5m³ 5m² 5m⁶ Sep 22] small filly: fairly useful performer: won maiden at
Folkestone in May: improved form in handicaps after, notably last 2 starts: may prove
best kept to 5f: raced only on good going or firmer: tried visored: often races up with
pace: reliable. *H. Candy*

PRETTY OFFICER (USA) 2 b.f. (Mar 23) Deputy Commander (USA) 124 – La **–**
Samanna (USA) (Trempolino (USA) 135) [2007 p6g p7g 6d Oct 29] €50,000Y, 15,000
2-y-o: lengthy, unfurnished filly: fourth foal: half-sister to US winner by Forest Wildcat:
dam, US 8.5f winner, half-sister to useful Irish 2-y-o 5f winner Irrawaddy: well held in
maidens. *Rae Guest*

PRETTY ORCHID 2 b.f. (Feb 6) Forzando 122 – Dunloe (IRE) 54 (Shaadi (USA) **55**
126) [2007 7d Oct 9] sturdy filly: seventh foal: half-sister to 3 winners, including 6-y-o Bridgewater Boys and 4-y-o Tilly's Dream: dam, 1m winner from 3 starts,
out of useful miler Kates Cabin: 100/1, seventh to Laughter in maiden at Leicester.
G. C. H. Chung

PRETTY POSEY 3 b.f. Dolpour 128 – Aegean Glory 53 (Shareef Dancer (USA) 135) **–**
[2007 8.1s 10.2g 10d Jul 23] compact filly: second foal: dam maiden best at 1¼m: well
held in maidens. *J. G. M. O'Shea*

PRETTY SELMA 3 b.f. Diktat 126 – Brave Vanessa (USA) 62 (Private Account **49 §**
(USA)) [2007 –: f5g⁴ f5g³ f5g² p5.1g⁶ f5g* 5m Apr 4] poor performer: won handicap
at Southwell in March: best form at 5f: acts on fibresand: wears headgear: ungenuine.
R. M. H. Cowell

PREVAILING WIND 2 b.c. (Mar 12) Gone West (USA) – Royal Alchemist (USA) **81 P**
(Royal Academy (USA) 130) [2007 6m⁴ Aug 3] 320,000Y: first foal: dam, US maiden,
half-sister to Sprint Cup winner Dowsing and Beverly D Stakes winner Fire The Groom,
herself dam of Stravinsky: 9/1, very promising fourth to Captain Brilliance in maiden
at Newmarket, running green before finishing strongly under hand riding: likely to
prove best up to 1m: open to considerable improvement, and is sure to win races.
J. R. Fanshawe

PRICELESS MELODY (USA) 3 b. or br.c. Orientate (USA) 127 – Regatta Queen **50**
(USA) (Danzig Connection (USA)) [2007 44: p6g² p6g p5f³ p5g 6g 5m⁵ May 3] strong,
good-bodied colt: modest maiden: effective at 5f/6f: acts on polytrack: blinkered:
probably temperamental: sent to USA. *Mrs A. J. Perrett*

PRICELESS SPEEDFIT 2 b.f. (Jan 29) Barathea Guest 117 – Princess Speedfit (FR) **56**
77 (Desert Prince (IRE) 130) [2007 7s 7.1m² 7m³ 8d 7d Oct 29] tall filly: first foal: dam,
1m winner, half-sister to smart French/UAE performer up to 12.5f Sibling Rival: modest
maiden: placed at Musselburgh and Thirsk: should stay 1m: acts on good to firm going:
tried in cheekpieces: sold 7,000 gns, sent to Serbia & Montenegro. *G. G. Margarson*

PRICEOFLOVE (IRE) 4 ch.f. Inchinor 119 – Piaf 62 (Pursuit of Love) [2007 72: **71**
p8g² p8g⁴ p6f⁵ 8s 6v 7s Jul 25] good-topped filly: fair maiden handicapper: left P. Makin
after third outing: effective at 6f to 1m: acts on polytrack and firm ground, well held on
soft/heavy: often tongue tied. *Liam McAteer, Ireland*

PRIDE OF INDIA (USA) 2 b.c. (Mar 27) Johannesburg (USA) 127 – How Could **62 p**
You (USA) (Boundary (USA) 117) [2007 6m May 26] $210,000Y: lengthy, useful-
looking colt: has scope: fourth foal: brother to a winner in USA and half-brother to US 6.5f
winner I Want You (by Phone Trick) and winner in Japan by Giant's Causeway: dam US
6f to 8.3f winner: 5/1 and tongue tied, ninth to Luck Money in maiden at Newmarket,
very green off bridle: looked sure to improve. *J. Noseda*

PRIDE OF JOY 4 ch.f. Pursuit of Love 124 – Ivory's Joy 109 (Tina's Pet 121) [2007 **66**
73: p5.1g⁸ p5.1g⁵ p5.1g f5g p5g* p5g² p5.1g p5.1g⁵ 5g p5g p5g⁵ p5g p5.1m Sep 6]
smallish filly: fair performer: won maiden at Wolverhampton in January and claimer at
Lingfield in March: left D. Ivory 4,800 gns after eleventh outing: best at 5f: acts on polytrack: tried in cheekpieces (below form): usually races up with pace. *M. A. Buckley*

PRIDE OF NATION (IRE) 5 b.h. Danehill Dancer (IRE) 117 – Anita Via (IRE) **116**
(Anita's Prince 126) [2007 106: 8g³ 7g⁶ 8.1g⁴ 8v* 8d* 8d 7d Oct 20] tall, quite attractive
horse: smart performer: improved to win minor event at York (by 2½ lengths from
Shumookh) in July and totesport.com Sovereign Stakes at Salisbury (beat Ordnance
Row by 1¼ lengths, in control when hanging into runner-into) in August: run best ignored
when seventh to Spirito del Vento in Prix Daniel Wildenstein at Longchamp next
time, persistently hemmed in early in straight: below form in Challenge Stakes at Newmarket final outing: effective at 7f/1m: has form on good to firm ground, all wins on good

or softer (acts on heavy): sometimes wears ear plugs in preliminaries: joined J. Hills. *L. M. Cumani*

PRIDE OF NORTHCARE (IRE) 3 b. or gr.g. Namid 128 – Pride of Pendle 80 **63** (Grey Desire 115) [2007 p6g^6 f8g^4 p7g^4 7g^5 7d Oct 9] close-coupled gelding: modest maiden: stays 7f: acts on polytrack: races freely: reportedly returned lame second/final outings. *G. A. Huffer*

PRIGSNOV DANCER (IRE) 2 ch.g. (Mar 24) Namid 128 – Brave Dance (IRE) **72** (Kris 135) [2007 5m^5 5m^2 5m^2 5s^2 6g 7m^5 5g* 6d^6 5g^2 6m Nov 10] small, strong, close-coupled gelding: fair performer: won selling nursery at Beverley in September, then left P. Haslam: good second in minor event at Catterick penultimate start: best at 5f/6f: acts on soft and good to firm going: often wears cheekpieces. *J. O'Reilly*

PRIMA BALLERINA 3 b.f. Pivotal 124 – Kirov 87 (Darshaan 133) [2007 8.3m 8.2g **73** May 11] lengthy filly: first foal: dam, 1m winner, half-sister to smart French 1¼m performer Cheshire: much better effort in maidens when seventh to Gyroscope at Windsor on debut, keeping on well not knocked about: run best ignored next time, losing all chance when hampered: sold 6,500 gns in December. *J. H. M. Gosden*

PRIMA LUCE (IRE) 2 b.f. (Feb 22) Galileo (IRE) 134 – Ramona (Desert King (IRE) **91** 129) [2007 8s^5 7v^5 7d* 8m Sep 13] 270,000Y: angular, good-bodied filly: third foal: half-sister to 1¼m winner Home You Stroll (by Selkirk) and 6f winner Sheer Silk (by Fasliyev), both in Ireland: dam unraced half-sister to smart performers Cassandra Go (best at 5f) and Verglas (won Coventry Stakes): fairly useful performer: won minor event at the Curragh in August: firmer ground, firmly held in May Hill Stakes at Doncaster final start: should stay 1m: acts on good to soft going. *J. S. Bolger, Ireland*

PRIMARILY 5 b.g. Mind Games 121 – Prim N Proper (Tragic Role (USA)) [2007 67: **55** p5g* p5.1g p5.1g^2 p6g^6 f5g* p6g^5 f5g^5 p6g^3 p6g^4 p5.1g^3 p7g Jun 21] leggy, quite good-topped gelding: modest performer: won minor event at Kempton in January and handicap at Southwell in March: effective at 5f to 7f: acts on all-weather and any turf going: effective in cheekpieces/visored or not: reportedly finished lame final outing. *Peter Grayson*

PRIME ASPIRATION (USA) 2 b. or br.c. (Apr 27) Tale of The Cat (USA) 113 – **79** Bank On Her (USA) 76 (Rahy (USA) 115) [2007 6g p7g 5.7d^2 6d^4 p6g^4 Oct 29] close-coupled colt: fair maiden: in frame last 3 starts, in minor event at Lingfield (fourth to Messias da Silva) final one: should stay 7f: acts on polytrack and good to soft going. *Christian Wroe*

PRIME CONTENDER 5 b.g. Efisio 120 – Gecko Rouge (Rousillon (USA) 133) **83 d** [2007 81: p11g^5 p12g^6 p11g 9.7m^6 10m p10g 11.7g p12g Dec 19] tall, quite good-topped gelding: fairly useful handicapper: well below form after first 2 starts in 2007: stays 1½m: acts on polytrack and soft going, probably on firm: tried blinkered. *G. L. Moore*

PRIMED AND POISED (USA) 2 b. or br.f. (Mar 8) More Than Ready (USA) 120 – **72** Sierra Madre (USA) (Mr Prospector (USA)) [2007 5m^5 p6g^3 6m^2 p6g^2 6.5f Oct 20]

$30,000F, €23,000Y: sparely-made filly: half-sister to several minor US sprint winners: dam unraced: fair maiden: runner-up at Goodwood and Kempton: left J. Hills before final outing: should prove best at 5f/6f. *P. Gallagher, USA*

PRIME DEFENDER 3 ch.c. Bertolini (USA) 125 – Arian Da 81 (Superlative 118) **115** [2007 108: p8g² 7m* 8m 6m* 6m² 6m 5g⁵ 6m³ 6g Sep 30] strong, good-bodied colt: impresses in appearance: good walker: powerful mover, with a round action: smart performer: won listed races at Newmarket (Sporting Index European Free Handicap by short head from Tobosa) in April and Haydock (beat Hoh Mike 1½ lengths) in May: good 4 lengths second to Sakhee's Secret in similar event at Salisbury next time: respectable efforts in pattern races next 3 outings, but below form in Diadem Stakes at Ascot final start: probably best at 6f/7f: acts on polytrack, soft and good to firm going. *B. W. Hills*

PRIME EXHIBIT 2 b.c. (Mar 7) Selkirk (USA) 129 – First Exhibit (Machiavellian **94 P** (USA) 123) [2007 8.1s⁴ 7d⁴ Oct 16] 92,000Y, resold 135,000Y: rangy colt: has scope: second foal: dam unraced out of Yorkshire Oaks/Prix Vermeille winner My Emma, herself half-sister to St Leger/Gold Cup winner Classic Cliche: plenty of promise both starts in maidens, winning easily by 1½ lengths from Endless Luck at Leicester despite again pulling hard: will stay at least 1¼m, provided he settles better with experience: pattern-race performer in the making. *R. Charlton*

PRIME NUMBER (IRE) 5 gr.g. King's Best (USA) 132 – Majinskaya (FR) 110 **81** (Marignan (USA) 117) [2007 85: 7.1d 8d⁶ 8m 10g⁴ 12m³ 10m² 10m* 10g p12g⁶ Dec 19] sturdy gelding: fairly useful handicapper: won at Nottingham (amateurs) in October: stays 1½m: acts on polytrack, firm and good to soft going: tried tongue tied. *J. Akehurst*

PRIME PERFORMER (IRE) 2 b.f. (Feb 21) Acclamation 118 – Storming Kate **79 p** (IRE) (Lion Cavern (USA) 117) [2007 5m³ 5d³ Sep 25] 18,000F, 25,000Y: first foal: dam unraced close relative to high-class 1¼m/1½m performer Storming Home: fair form: won maiden at Beverley in May: off 4 months, faded finish when third to In Uniform in minor event there: likely to prove best at 5f/6f: should still do better. *B. Smart*

S. Falle, M. Franklin & J. Sumsion's "Prime Defender"

PRIME POWERED (IRE) 6 b.g. Barathea (IRE) 127 – Caribbean Quest 90 (Rainbow Quest (USA) 134) [2007 83: p12g⁶ p12g p12g⁶ 11m⁴ 12d 9.9g 11.6g⁵ 10d³ 10d* 10d Sep 22] close-coupled gelding: had a round action: fairly useful handicapper: won at Windsor in August: fell next time: stayed 1½m: acted on polytrack, good to firm and good to soft ground: sometimes wore cheekpieces/blinkers: tried tongue tied: was sometimes reluctant to race/hung left: dead. *R. M. Beckett*   **81**

PRIME RECREATION 10 b.g. Primo Dominie 121 – Night Transaction 59 (Tina's Pet 121) [2007 –§, a61§: p5g f5g⁵ f5g 5.2d⁶ f5d⁶ Dec 14] strong, rangy gelding: poor performer: best at 5f: acts on all-weather, heavy and good to firm going: tried in cheekpieces: front runner: unreliable. *P. S. Felgate*   **– §**
a40 §

PRIMER LUGAR 2 b.f. (Mar 22) Primo Valentino (IRE) 116 – Up Front (IRE) 61 (Up And At 'em 109) [2007 6m 7s p6g Dec 4] small filly: first foal: dam 2-y-o 6f seller winner: little form. *W. J. H. Ratcliffe*   **–**

PRIMESHADE PROMISE 6 ch.m. Opening Verse (USA) 126 – Bonnie Lassie 74 (Efisio 120) [2007 65: 7.1s⁴ 8.1m p9.5g p8g² p8.6g Nov 27] lengthy, angular mare: fair at 5 yrs, only poor in 2007: stays 8.6f: acts on polytrack, soft and good to firm going: tried in cheekpieces. *J. L. Flint*   **48**

PRIMITIVE ACADEMY 5 b.h. Primitive Rising (USA) 113 – Royal Fontaine (IRE) 84 (Royal Academy (USA) 130) [2007 70: 10g Apr 28] tall horse: fair maiden at 4 yrs: ran poorly only start on Flat in 2007: may prove best short of 1½m: acts on polytrack and good to firm going: modest hurdler, successful in December. *J. R. Holt*

PRIMO HEIGHTS 2 b.f. (Feb 11) Primo Valentino (IRE) 116 – Harrken Heights (IRE) (Belmez (USA) 131) [2007 5g* 5.1m⁴ 5g² May 30] small, sturdy filly: sixth foal: half-sister to 3 winners, including 4-y-o Blazing Heights and 5-y-o Geojimali: dam maiden: fairly useful form: won maiden at Musselburgh in April: in frame in listed events at Chester and Beverley, in latter apparent improvement when beaten, but one of only 2 to race stand side (along with winner Loch Jipp): should prove best at 5f/6f. *J. S. Goldie*   **87 ?**

PRIMONDO (IRE) 5 b.g. Montjeu (IRE) 137 – Tagiki (IRE) (Doyoun 124) [2007 71: p16g p13.9g Mar 5] smallish gelding: fair handicapper at 4 yrs: modest form at best in 2007: stayed 2m: acted on polytrack, good to firm and good to soft going: often held up: tried visored: probably wasn't straightforward: dead. *A. W. Carroll*   **60**

PRIMOS DREAM 2 b.g. (Apr 8) Primo Valentino (IRE) 116 – Compton Amber 78 (Puissance 110) [2007 p5.1g f6d⁶ Dec 12] no form in maiden/claimer. *Ollie Pears*   **–**

PRIMO WAY 6 b.g. Primo Dominie 121 – Waypoint 95 (Cadeaux Genereux 131) [2007 87, a78: p9.5g⁴ 10m⁶ 8d⁴ 9.1d* 9.1g⁶ 8.3g 9g⁴ 9.1g 8m 8.3d* Aug 15] tall gelding: fair performer: won handicap at Ayr in May and claimer at Hamilton in August: effective at 7f to easy 9.5f: acts on polytrack, soft and good to firm going: sometimes wears headgear, effective without: sometimes slowly away. *I. Semple*   **78**

PRIMUS INTER PARES (IRE) 6 b.g. Sadler's Wells (USA) 132 – Life At The Top 107 (Habitat 134) [2007 –: f8g Feb 13] smallish, close-coupled gelding: one-time useful performer, just fair form sole outing on Flat in 2007: stays 1m: acts on polytrack and good to firm going: tried visored: suspect temperament: fair hurdler/chaser. *N. Wilson*   **79**

PRINCE AFRAM 2 b.c. (Mar 13) Fraam 114 – Miletrian Cares (IRE) 67 (Hamas (IRE) 125§) [2007 6m Aug 31] 20/1, seventh to Max One Two Three in maiden at Salisbury: will stay 1m. *R. M. Beckett*   **57**

PRINCE AMONG MEN 10 b.g. Robellino (USA) 127 – Forelino (USA) 62§ (Trempolino (USA) 135) [2007 17.2m⁴ 13g Sep 3] sparely-made gelding: modest maiden handicapper nowadays (unraced on Flat 2002-2006): stays 17f: acts on soft and good to firm going: tried blinkered: fair winning hurdler. *N. G. Richards*   **58**

PRINCE CHARLEMAGNE (IRE) 4 br.g. King Charlemagne (USA) 120 – Ciubanga (IRE) (Arazi (USA) 135) [2007 89: p12g⁵ p10g⁵ p9.5g⁴ p10g⁴ p10g⁶ p11g⁵ 10m⁵ p12g 10m 11.5d Jun 27] quite good-topped gelding: fairly useful handicapper on all-weather, fair on turf: stays 1½m: acts on polytrack, good to firm and good to soft ground: held up: has joined K. R. Burke. *N. P. Littmoden*   **79**
a89

PRINCE DAYJUR (USA) 8 b. or br.g. Dayjur (USA) 137 – Distinct Beauty (USA) (Phone Trick (USA)) [2007 82: p7.1g p8g p7g⁶ p8g³ p8.6g⁵ p7.1g² p8.6g⁵ p8.6g 7.6s Aug 18] close-coupled, quite attractive gelding: fair performer nowadays: stays 7f: acts on all-weather and good to firm ground: tried visored: hasn't always impressed with attitude. *J. Pearce*   **78**

PRINCE DESIRE (IRE) 2 b.c. (Feb 21) Fasliyev (USA) 120 – No Quest (IRE) (Rainbow Quest (USA) 134) [2007 6g 7s 7m⁶ 8s⁶ 7m 8f* 6m Oct 5] 58,000Y: good-topped   **87**

colt: seventh foal: half-brother to several winners, notably smart US performer up to 1½m Macaw (by Bluebird), earlier useful 1m/1¼m winner in Britain, and 3-y-o Irish Quest: dam, French maiden, half-sister to very smart French performer up to 1¼m No Pass No Sale: fairly useful performer: first-time blinkers, improved to win maiden at Pontefract (made all to beat Downhiller by 4 lengths) in September: inadequate test in sales race final start: stays 1m: acts on firm and soft going. *B. W. Hills*

PRINCE DES NEIGES (FR) 4 b.g. Milford Track (IRE) 110 – Miss Smith (FR) (Grand Lodge (USA) 125) [2007 p9.5g 10.2f² 10s² 10s² 11.6m⁴ 14.1g² 12s p16g 11.9m² 10.9g p12g Dec 12] angular gelding: fair performer: left Ian Williams after fourth start: stays 1¾m: acts on firm and soft going: tried in cheekpieces: ungenuine (has refused to race). *M. R. Hoad* — **68 §**
— **a– §**

PRINCE EVELITH (GER) 4 b.g. Dashing Blade 117 – Peace Time (GER) (Surumu (GER)) [2007 82p: 8.1m⁵ 9.1g³ 7.9d² 9.1g 8.5m⁴ Jul 31] workmanlike gelding: fairly useful handicapper: will stay 1¼m: acts on soft and good to firm going. *G. A. Swinbank* — **85**

PRINCE FLORI (GER) 4 b.c. Lando (GER) 128 – Princess Liberte (GER) (Nebos (GER) 129) [2007 119: 12g³ 11g* 12g³ 12g 12g 11g⁴ Oct 20] tall colt: very smart performer: close third to Saddex in Gerling-Preis at Cologne (gave weight to first 2) before winning Grosser Mercedes-Benz-Preis at Baden-Baden in May by ½ length from Egerton: ran well when keeping-on 2 lengths third to Mountain High in Grand Prix de Saint-Cloud next time: below form last 3 starts, in King George VI and Queen Elizabeth Stakes at Ascot (stirred up beforehand/reluctant at stall, last of 7), Grosser Preis von Baden at Baden-Baden (won race year before) and when fourth to Egerton in Baden-Wurttemberg-Trophy at Baden-Baden: stays 1½m: acts on soft going. *S. Smrczek, Germany* — **120**

PRINCE FOREVER (IRE) 3 b.c. Giant's Causeway (USA) 132 – Routilante (IRE) 96 (Rousillon (USA) 133) [2007 96p: 7m³ May 26] strong, good sort: useful form in just 3 starts: reportedly returned with sore shins after final 2-y-o outing: best effort when 1¾ lengths third to Tariq in listed race at Newmarket only appearance in 2007, again racing too freely: subsequently suffered an injury: raced at 7f: stays in training. *M. A. Jarvis* — **107**

PRINCE GOLAN (IRE) 3 b.c. Golan (IRE) 129 – Mohican Princess (Shirley Heights 130) [2007 95: 10.4g⁶ 9.1m⁶ 10.3s 12g⁶ p13.9g Dec 1] good-topped colt: just fairly useful performer at best in 2007: probably stays 9f: acts on heavy and good to firm going: tried in cheekpieces. *K. A. Ryan* — **81 d**

PRINCE HAMLET (IRE) 2 b.c. (Feb 1) Fantastic Light (USA) 134 – Hamsaat Hi Haat (USA) (Hennessy (USA) 122) [2007 p7.1g³ f8d* Dec 15] first foal: dam, US/UAE maiden, out of half-sister to high-class performer up to 10.5f Ekraar: fair former: sharper for debut, won maiden at Southwell: will stay 1¼m: should continue on the up. *B. Smart* — **76 p**

PRINCE KALAMOUN (IRE) 2 ch.g. (Apr 2) Desert Prince (IRE) 130 – Grenouillere (USA) (Alysheba (USA)) [2007 7d³ 7g² 7.2g⁴ 8.5m⁴ Sep 11] fair maiden: in frame all starts, gelded after final one: will stay 1¼m. *G. A. Swinbank* — **70**

PRINCELET (IRE) 5 b.g. Desert Prince (IRE) 130 – Soeur Ti (FR) 109 (Kaldoun (FR) 122) [2007 16s* 20m Jun 19] leggy gelding: has no near eye: fairly useful performer, very lightly raced (unraced on Flat in 2006): improved to win handicap at Ascot in May: creditable seventh in Ascot Stakes (Handicap) at Royal Ascot only other Flat start in 2007: barely stays 2½m: acts on soft and good to firm ground: fairly useful hurdler. *N. J. Henderson* — **90**

PRINCELY GREEN (IRE) 2 b.c. (Apr 21) Princely Heir (IRE) 111 – Greenmount Lady (IRE) (Mac's Imp (USA) 116) [2007 5d⁴ p5g³ Jul 10] poor form in frame in maiden/seller. *I. A. Wood* — **40**

PRINCELY ROYAL 3 b.g. Prince Sabo 123 – Premium Princess 78 (Distant Relative 128) [2007 62: p5g p6g 7d 5.3m⁶ Jun 3] maiden: no form in 2007: blinkered last 2 starts. *J. J. Bridger* — **–**

PRINCELY TED (IRE) 6 b.g. Princely Heir (IRE) 111 – Just Out (IRE) (Bluebird (USA) 125) [2007 55: 10m² 10d²ᵈ 11.9m³ 12m** 11.1m⁶ p8g⁶ p9.5g⁶ p12.2g³ 10.2m p13.9g* p13.9g⁵ Nov 27] fair handicapper: left R. Farrant after third start: won at Musselburgh in August, and having left P. Blockley after next start, Wolverhampton in November: stays 1¾m: acts on sand/polytrack and good to firm going: tried visored/tongue tied: races prominently. *D. Burchell* — **67**

PRINCELY VALE (IRE) 5 b.g. Princely Heir (IRE) 111 – Lomalou (IRE) (Lightning Dealer 103) [2007 62: 6m² 5.1g 6s⁵ 6s 6m 6m Sep 3] leggy gelding: modest performer at best nowadays: effective at 6f/easy 7f: acts on polytrack, firm and soft ground: usually wears headgear: hung markedly left fifth start. *W. G. M. Turner* — **58 d**

PRINCE NAMID 5 b.g. Namid 128 – Fen Princess (IRE) 72 (Trojan Fen 118) [2007 **92** 101: p5.1g 5g⁴ 6g² 6g 5v⁶ 5v 6s⁴ 6d³ 7d 6m⁴ 5m 7g 7g⁵ Nov 6] quite good-topped gelding: fairly useful handicapper nowadays: best at 5f/6f: acts on any turf going: tried in visor/ cheekpieces: sometimes slowly away. *Mrs A. Duffield*

PRINCE NOEL 3 b.g. Dr Fong (USA) 128 – Baileys On Line 60 (Shareef Dancer **75** (USA) 135) [2007 56: 7.1m f8g⁴ 8g² 7g⁵ 9m⁶ 8.5s 8.1m⁶ 9.8m² 10d⁵ 10s⁵ 9g* p9.5g* p9.5g³ p8.6g* p9.5g* p8.6g² Nov 20] short-backed gelding: fair performer: won seller at Musselburgh and minor event at Wolverhampton in October, and handicaps (2) at Wolverhampton in November: stays 1¼m: acts on all-weather, soft and good to firm going: tried in cheekpieces/blinkers. *N. Wilson*

PRINCE NUREYEV (IRE) 7 b.g. Desert King (IRE) 129 – Annaletta 89 (Belmez **88** (USA) 131) [2007 p10g p11g⁴ 10m 10m² 10g⁴ 10g⁴ 11.6g² 13.3m p11g Sep 8] quite good-topped gelding: has a short, choppy action: fairly useful handicapper: unraced in 2006 (reportedly underwent stem-cell surgery on tendons): creditable efforts when in frame at 7 yrs: effective at 1¼m, barely at 1¾m: acts on polytrack, firm and soft ground: races freely: held up. *B. R. Millman*

PRINCE OF CHARM (USA) 3 ch.g. Mizzen Mast (USA) 121 – Pretty Clear (USA) **71** 89 (Mr Prospector (USA)) [2007 74: p7g³ p7g³ 8.5g 7m 7g* 8.3v⁶ p7g p8m Dec 10] neat gelding: fair handicapper: trained by P. Mitchell first 3 starts: won at Salisbury in June: slowly away all outings after: stays 1m: acts on polytrack and good to soft going: tried blinkered, usually wears cheekpieces. *R. A. Teal*

PRINCE OF DELPHI 4 b.c. Royal Applause 124 – Princess Athena 119 (Ahonoora **79** 122) [2007 67: 6m² 6s 6g² p6m² Oct 11] strong, good-bodied colt: fair maiden: left H. Candy after second start: will prove best at 5f/6f: acts on polytrack and good to firm going. *R. M. Beckett*

PRINCE OF ELEGANCE 3 b.c. Cape Cross (IRE) 129 – Elegant Lady 89 (Selkirk **–** (USA) 129) [2007 92: 7.1g 8g 9.9g 9g 7.1m Sep 13] good-topped colt: fairly useful performer at 2 yrs: little impact in handicaps in 2007: tried in cheekpieces/blinkers: sold 2,000 gns, sent to Sweden. *Mrs A. J. Perrett*

PRINCE OF GOLD 7 b.g. Polar Prince (IRE) 117 – Gold Belt (IRE) 61 (Bellypha **61** 130) [2007 51, a60: p7.1g* p7.1g p7.1g² p7.1g⁴ p7.1g² 8.5m Apr 18] good-topped geld- ing: modest performer: won seller at Wolverhampton in January: effective at 6f to 1m: acts on all-weather, firm and good to soft ground: usually wears headgear: usually waited with. *R. Hollinshead*

PRINCE OF LIGHT (IRE) 4 ch.g. Fantastic Light (USA) 134 – Miss Queen (USA) **108** (Miswaki (USA) 124) [2007 112: 8m 9m 10m 8m 10d Jun 22] good-topped gelding: has a quick action: smart performer at best, just useful form in handicaps in 2007: best efforts at Newmarket (seventh to Supaseus) and Redcar (2¼ lengths eighth to Flipando in Zetland Gold Cup, weakening) second/third starts: well below form at Royal Ascot last 2 starts (gelded after final one): barely stays 1¼m: winner on good to soft going, best form on good/good to firm: blinkered last 3 starts: often races prominently. *M. Johnston*

PRINCE OF MEDINA 4 ch.g. Fraam 114 – Medina de Rioseco 70 (Puissance 110) **60** [2007 63, a69: 10m 15.4g³ 16f 12g⁶ 14.1m² p11g p12g p13.9g⁴ p12g⁶ p13.9s* Dec 20] rangy gelding: modest performer: won maiden at Wolverhampton (hung left) in Decem- ber: will stay beyond 2m: acts on polytrack and good to firm going. *J. R. Best*

PRINCE OF THEBES (IRE) 6 b.g. Desert Prince (IRE) 130 – Persian Walk (FR) **97** (Persian Bold 123) [2007 104: 8m 8.1g³ 7s 8.5d 8d⁵ 8.1g 8g 8m 7g 7m⁴ 8g 8d² 7d 8g⁴ Nov 3] good-topped gelding: useful handicapper: creditable efforts in 2007 when placed: effective at 7f/1m: acts on firm and good to soft going: sometimes fractious in paddock: races prominently. *J. Akehurst*

PRINCE ROSSI (IRE) 3 b.g. Royal Applause 124 – Miss Rossi (Artaius (USA) 129) **67** [2007 79: 6g 7m 6m 6d⁵ 7m² 6.1v² 5.9f 6s⁵ p7.1g p7.1g³ Dec 4] neat gelding: has a quick action: fair handicapper: stays 7f: acts on polytrack, heavy and good to firm going: wears cheekpieces nowadays: races prominently: sold 10,000 gns. *J. D. Bethell*

PRINCE SABAAH (IRE) 3 b.c. Spectrum (IRE) 126 – Princess Sabaah (IRE) 90 **97** (Desert King (IRE) 129) [2007 82: p9.5g* 10g 10m² 12d² 14.1d⁴ 12m² 12g⁶ 11.8d⁵ 14.6g⁶ Oct 26] big, lengthy colt: useful handicapper: won at Wolverhampton in April: good sixth at Doncaster final outing: barely stays 14.6f: acts on polytrack, unraced on extremes of going on turf: tried tongue tied at 2 yrs: has looked difficult ride. *R. Hannon*

PRINCE SAMOS (IRE) 5 b.g. Mujadil (USA) 119 – Sabaniya (FR) (Lashkari 128) **90** [2007 96: 8s⁴ 8f 10.3m 8g⁴ 10.1d 8g 9m⁵ 8.3d⁶ 9.2g² 8s 10.3g² Oct 26] neat gelding:

fairly useful handicapper: stays 10.6f: acts on polytrack, soft and good to firm going: tried blinkered (ran well)/visored. *D. Nicholls*

PRINCE'S DECREE 2 br.c. (Feb 19) Diktat 126 – Rock Face 77 (Ballad Rock 122) **60** [2007 6g⁵ 7.1s 6d Jul 25] 7,500Y: half-brother to 2 winners, including fairly useful 7f (at 2 yrs) to 1¼m winner Sheer Face (by Midyan): dam 1¼m to 1¾m winner: modest maiden: will stay at least 1m. *G. M. Moore*

PRINCESS AIMEE 7 b.m. Wizard King 122 – Off The Air (IRE) 54 (Taufan (USA) **56** 119) [2007 10.2m 10.2g p9.5g⁶ p12.2g 12.1m Sep 7] fourth foal: half-sister to winner up to 11f in Italy by Contract Law: dam 5f to 9.4f winner: modest maiden: tried in cheek-pieces/visor. *D. Burchell*

PRINCESS ARWEN 5 b.m. Magic Ring (IRE) 115 – Absolutelystunning 63 (Aragon **49** 118) [2007 43: p6g p7.1g² p7g p8g f7g p7.1g 7m 6s 10m Sep 17] close-coupled mare: poor performer: stays 7f: acts on all-weather: tried in cheekpieces, often blinkered. *Mrs Barbara Waring*

PRINCESS AUGUSTA (USA) 2 b.f. (May 29) Silic (FR) 125 – Tri Anytime (USA) **–** (Tri Jet (USA)) [2007 6d p8m p7g Dec 29] lengthy filly: half-sister to 3 winners in US, including sprinter Torch Relay (by Gold Fever): dam, US sprint winner, half-sister to Breeders' Cup Juvenile winner Brocco: well held in maidens: will prove best up to 7f. *A. M. Balding*

PRINCESS CHARLMANE (IRE) 4 b.f. King Charlemagne (USA) 120 – Bint **33** Alreeys (Polish Precedent (USA) 131) [2007 7.5m 5v 5m⁵ Aug 25] quite good-topped filly: poor maiden. *C. J. Teague*

PRINCESS CLEO 4 ch.f. Mark of Esteem (IRE) 137 – Classy Cleo (IRE) 102 (Muja- **66** dil (USA) 119) [2007 75: f5g⁵ f6g 6d⁴ 5m² 5s 5d⁶ 5m⁶ 5g 5g³ 6m Sep 10] sturdy filly: fair handicapper: raced at 5f/6f: acts on fibresand, good to firm and good to soft going: in cheekpieces last 3 starts: tends to wander: sold 8,000 gns. *T. D. Easterby*

PRINCESS COCOA (IRE) 4 b.f. Desert Sun 120 – Daily Double (FR) (Unfuwain **83** (USA) 131) [2007 81: 9.9s³ 9.9v⁵ 10m³ 9.8g² 10.5s³ p8.6g* 10.3g⁵ p9.5g² Dec 1] sturdy filly: fairly useful handicapper: reportedly underwent sinus operation after 3 yrs: won at Wolverhampton in October: effective at 8.6f to 1½m: acts on polytrack and any turf going: consistent. *R. A. Fahey*

PRINCESS DANEHILL (IRE) 3 b.f. Indian Danehill (IRE) 124 – A La Longue **54** (GER) (Mtoto 134) [2007 8.3g p8.6g³ p12m p8g⁶ p6g Nov 28] €43,000F, 45,000Y: fourth foal: half-sister to useful Italian 7f (at 2 yrs) to 1¼m winner Le Giare (by Mona-shee Mountain): dam German maiden: modest maiden: stays 8.6f: tried blinkered/tongue tied. *P. F. I. Cole*

PRINCESS ELLIS 3 ch.f. Compton Place 125 – Star Cast (IRE) 82 (In The Wings **84** 128) [2007 64: 6g⁵ 6m² 6g⁴ 5g* 6d⁴ 5m 5m⁵ 6d⁶ 5d³ 5m⁴ 5g² 5m³ 5m* 5g* 5d* 5g Oct 27] lengthy filly: improved into a fairly useful handicapper: won at Ayr in May, Musselburgh in September and October, and York later in October: best at 5f: acts on firm and soft going: free-going sort, usually races prominently: sometimes carries head high: reliable. *E. J. Alston*

PRINCESS FLAVIA (IRE) 3 ch.f. Redback 116 – Malacca (USA) (Danzig (USA)) **–** [2007 6m May 7] 11,000 2-y-o: seventh foal: half-sister to 3 winners, including fairly useful Irish 2000 2-y-o 5f winner Patinham (by Mujtahid): dam unraced: 33/1, well held in maiden at Windsor: sold £700 in November. *M. Quinn*

PRINCESS GEE 2 b.f. (Mar 25) Reel Buddy (USA) 118 – Queen G (USA) 57 (Matty **–** G (USA) 119) [2007 8d p8.6g Nov 10] 5,500Y: second foal: dam, 11f winner, out of half-sister to dam of top-class miler Observatory: in rear in maidens. *B. J. McMath*

PRINCESS ILEANA (IRE) 3 b.f. Danetime (IRE) 121 – Uhud (IRE) (Mujtahid **62** (USA) 118) [2007 68: 5d⁵ 5g³ 6m 5d⁶ 5.7g⁶ Jul 9] quite good-topped filly: modest maiden handicapper: best at bare 5f: acts on polytrack and firm going: visored penultimate start: sold 4,000 gns in July, joined C. von der Recke in Germany. *K. R. Burke*

PRINCESS INDIA (IRE) 2 ch.f. (Apr 5) Hawk Wing (USA) 136 – Litchfield Hills **78** (USA) (Relaunch (USA)) [2007 6s p6g 6d⁶ p7g* 6.3m³ Sep 18] €38,000Y, 50,000 2-y-o: stocky filly: fourth living foal: half-sister to 3-y-o Nur Tau and 6-y-o Clearing Sky: dam US 1m/8.5f winner: fair performer: won nursery at Lingfield in September: will be suited by 1m: acts on polytrack and good to firm going. *P. Winkworth*

PRINCESS KAI (IRE) 6 b.m. Cayman Kai (IRE) 114 – City Princess 62§ (Rock City **49 §** 120) [2007 50: f5g⁴ f6g p6g 6m⁵ 5.1g 6s⁵ Jun 29] poor performer nowadays: best at 5f/6f: acts on all-weather, firm and good to soft ground: has worn blinkers/cheekpieces: sometimes slowly away (virtually refused to race second start): ungenuine. *R. Ingram*

PRINCESS KIOTTO 6 b.m. Desert King (IRE) 129 – Ferghana Ma 62 (Mtoto 134) **72**
[2007 13.1g³ 16.2v⁴ 13.1d⁴ 16.1m⁵ 16m 16.2m* Aug 27] rather leggy mare: fair handicapper: won at Warwick in August: stays 2¼m: acts on fibresand, good to firm and good
to soft going. *W. M. Brisbourne*

PRINCESS LAVINIA 4 ch.f. Fraam 114 – Affaire de Coeur 55 (Imperial Fling (USA) **75 §**
116) [2007 72: p8g³ p10g* 10m 12g⁴ 9.7m³ 10.1m* 11.1g⁵ 8m Sep 20] useful-looking
filly: fair handicapper: won at Kempton in May and Yarmouth in August: barely stays
1½m: acts on polytrack, good to firm and good to soft going: one to treat with caution.
G. Wragg

PRINCESS LOMI (IRE) 2 b.f. (Apr 9) Lomitas 129 – Athlumney Lady 98 (Lycius **70 p**
(USA) 124) [2007 7.6f³ Aug 4] third foal: half-sister to useful 2006 2-y-o 5f/6f winner
Princess Iris (by Desert Prince) and 1½m winner Lady Gregory (by In The Wings): dam
Irish 2-y-o 7f/1m winner: 12/1, third to Al Muheer in maiden at Lingfield, plenty to do:
will be suited by 1m+: capable of better. *E. J. O'Neill*

PRINCESS MARIA (USA) 2 b.f. (Jan 26) Giant's Causeway (USA) 132 – Passive **–**
Action (USA) (Double Negative (USA)) [2007 7.2s 6g 6g Oct 19] sixth foal: half-sister
to 3 winning US sprinters, including minor stakes winners Sherpa Guide (by Ends Well)
and Fait Accompli (by Louis Quatorze): dam unraced: well held in maidens. *R. A. Fahey*

PRINCESS NAMID (IRE) 2 br.f. (Feb 3) Namid 128 – Banutan (IRE) 73 (Charn- **–**
wood Forest (IRE) 125) [2007 5.7f Jun 10] €12,000Y: first foal: dam Irish maiden (stayed
7f): always behind in maiden at Bath. *R. A. Harris*

PRINCESS OF AENEAS (IRE) 4 b.f. Beckett (IRE) 116 – Romangoddess (IRE) **–**
(Rhoman Rule (USA)) [2007 61: p8g p13.9g Nov 16] close-coupled filly: modest winner
in 2006: last in handicaps both 4-y-o starts: tried in cheekpieces. *Peter Grayson*

PRINCESS PALATINE (IRE) 3 b.f. Iron Mask (USA) 117 – Kitty Kildare (USA) **67**
68 (Seattle Dancer (USA) 119) [2007 74: f7g⁴ 7m 8d 7.5s Jul 17] tall filly: fair maiden:
no show after reappearance, in claimer final outing: barely stays 1m: acts on fibresand
and soft going: tried visored/tongue tied: sold 1,000 gns. *K. R. Burke*

PRINCESS RHIANNA (IRE) 2 ch.f. (Apr 21) Fath (USA) 116 – Persian Sally (IRE) **66**
(Persian Bold 123) [2007 5g² 5m 5d* p6g⁶ 5.1g Nov 7] €21,000 2-y-o: compact filly:
sixth foal: half-sister to several winners, including 5-y-o Kames Park and Italian 6f
to 1m winner Mr Picchio (by Cois Na Tine), both useful: dam unraced: fair performer:
left K. R. Burke, won maiden at Catterick in October: will prove best at 5f/6f: acts on
polytrack and good to soft ground. *Mrs G. S. Rees*

PRINCESS TAYLOR 3 ch.f. Singspiel (IRE) 133 – Tapas En Bal (FR) (Mille Balles **82**
(FR) 124) [2007 70: 7s³ 8m² 8g² 8.3m* p8m³ p8g Dec 4] leggy filly: fairly useful handicapper: won at Leicester in September: will be suited by 1¼m: acts on polytrack, soft and
good to firm going: tried in cheekpieces: tongue tied. *M. Botti*

PRINCESS VALERINA 3 ch.f. Beat Hollow 126 – Heart So Blue (Dilum (USA) 115) **88**
[2007 94p: p8g⁵ 7m 8m 7s³ 7m³ 7.1g⁴ 7g p7g 7d p7g Nov 21] tall filly: fairly useful
handicapper: barely stays 1m: acts on polytrack, good to firm and good to soft ground.
B. W. Hills

PRINCESS ZADA 3 ch.f. Best of The Bests (IRE) 122 – Barnacla (IRE) 83 (Bluebird **75**
(USA) 125) [2007 64: 8.2g 8.1g* 8.3m 7s⁵ 8.1s² 7.1s² 8g⁵ 7.1m⁵ 8d Oct 1] leggy filly:
fair handicapper: won at Chepstow in May: stays 1m: acts on soft going: races freely: has
hung left: twice lost action at 2 yrs. *B. R. Millman*

PRINCESS ZAHA 5 b.m. Zaha (CAN) 106 – Otaru (IRE) (Indian Ridge 123) [2007 **50**
10s p7g p9.5g⁴ Dec 13] modest maiden, lightly raced: stays 9.5f: acts on polytrack.
A. G. Newcombe

PRINCESS ZHUKOVA (IRE) 2 b.f. (May 6) Terroir (IRE) 110 – Miss Bussell 65 **–**
(Sabrehill (USA) 120) [2007 p7.1s⁶ Dec 21] half-sister to 6-y-o Red Lancer and 6f winner
Mannora (by Prince Sabo): dam 1m winner: 100/1, well held in maiden at Wolverhamp-
ton. *R. J. Price*

PRINCE TAMINO 4 b.g. Mozart (IRE) 131 – Premiere Dance (IRE) (Loup Solitaire **101**
(USA) 117) [2007 115: a6f 6.5g⁴ 6g 6f⁴ p6g Aug 27] good-topped gelding: smart performer at 3 yrs, just useful in 2007: best efforts when fourth in handicap at Nad Al Sheba
(4 lengths behind Grantley Adams) and, having left I. Mohammed in UAE after third
start, minor event at Windsor (2¼ lengths behind Presto Shinko): best at 5f/6f: acts on
polytrack and firm going: visored final outing: returned to UAE, joined A. Al Raihe.
Saeed bin Suroor

PRINCE TUM TUM (USA) 7 b.g. Capote (USA) – La Grande Epoque (USA) 120 **92**
(Lyphard (USA) 132) [2007 92: p6g² f7g⁴ f6g³ f6g⁶ Feb 13] lengthy gelding: fairly useful
handicapper: creditable efforts in frame first 3 starts in 2007: has won at 9f, but best
efforts at 6f to 1m: acts on all-weather, firm and good to soft ground: effective blinkered/
visored or not: has been tongue tied: sometimes reluctant to post: formerly none too
reliable. *D. Shaw*

PRINCE VALENTINE 6 b.g. My Best Valentine 122 – Affaire de Coeur 55 (Imperial **60**
Fling (USA) 116) [2007 63: p7g 8m⁶ 8d 10s⁶ 8s⁴ 8g 8d⁴ 8f² 8m³ p8g³ 8m* p7m⁶ Nov 1] **a47**
lengthy gelding: modest handicapper, better on turf than all-weather: won at Brighton in
September: best at 1m: acts on polytrack and any turf going: tried tongue tied/blinkered,
wears cheekpieces nowadays: held up. *G. L. Moore*

PRINCE VECTOR 5 b.g. Vettori (IRE) 119 – The In-Laws (IRE) 90 (Be My Guest –
(USA) 126) [2007 91: p10g p12.2g⁶ Feb 21] tall gelding: fairly useful performer at best:
well below form on Flat in 2007: tried in visor/blinkers: sold 10,000 gns and joined Mrs
A. Thorpe. *A. King*

PRINCE VETTORI 5 b.g. Vettori (IRE) 119 – Bombalarina (IRE) (Barathea (IRE) –
127) [2007 –, a69: p8.6g Jan 13] angular gelding: fair performer at 4 yrs: well below form
only start in 2007: stays 1¼m: acts on all-weather, little form on turf. *Mrs Norma Pook*

PRINCE WOODMAN (USA) 4 br.g. Woodman (USA) 126 – Queen Mama (USA) **107**
(Seattle Slew (USA)) [2007 6g⁶ 6m a8.3f⁴ 8f* 8.5f* Nov 3] close-coupled, useful-
looking gelding: useful form: off 18 months, excellent 2¼ lengths sixth to Sierra Vista in
minor event at Haydock on reappearance, slowly away: failed to settle when last in listed
race at Windsor next time, then left B. Meehan: successful at Laurel in allowance race in
October and optional claimer in November: stays 8.5f: acts on firm and good to soft
going. *H. G. Motion, USA*

PRINCE ZAFONIC 4 ch.g. Zafonic (USA) 130 – Kite Mark 58 (Mark of Esteem **87**
(IRE) 137) [2007 69: 10m 12.3f 12s² 12s⁴ 14d² 13.1f² 16g² 16d⁵ 18d³ Oct 13] big, strong
gelding: fairly useful maiden handicapper: improved form in 2007, runner-up 4 times:
stays 2m (seemed stretched by 2¼m): acts on soft and firm going: tongue tied at 4 yrs.
Miss Gay Kelleway

PRIVATE CODE 2 br.f. (Jan 30) Fasliyev (USA) 120 – Aunt Pearl (USA) (Seattle **64**
Slew (USA)) [2007 p5g⁶ 5.2m p7g³ p7g Oct 31] small filly: closely related to 3 winners,
including smart 2003 2-y-o 6f to 1m winner Pearl of Love (by Peintre Celebre) and
half-sister to a winner in US by Sadler's Wells: dam US sprint winner: modest maiden:
trained by T. Pitt first 2 starts: stays 7f: acts on polytrack: sold 55,000 gns. *B. J. Meehan*

PRIVATE PEACHEY (IRE) 3 b.g. Shinko Forest (IRE) – Adamas (IRE) 75 (Fairy **70**
King (USA)) [2007 56: 11g 10g 7m* 8.1m² 8.1g³ 8f* p8g⁴ 8m Aug 9] leggy gelding: fair
handicapper: won at Folkestone in May and Bath in June: pulled up final outing: stayed
1m: acted on polytrack and firm going: usually raced prominently: dead. *B. R. Millman*

PRIVATE REASON (USA) 3 b.c. Red Ransom (USA) – Sultry Lass (USA) (Private **70**
Account (USA)) [2007 75: 9g⁵ p12.2g⁵ 12s Jul 18] strong, sturdy colt: fair maiden: may
prove best short of 1½m: acts on polytrack and good to soft ground: tried in cheekpieces.
K. A. Ryan

PRIVATE SOLDIER 4 gr.g. Dansili 127 – Etienne Lady (IRE) 67 (Imperial Frontier **58**
(USA) 112) [2007 6.9m 7.1m 9.9g⁴ p9.5g* p9.5g³ p8.6g³ Sep 28] modest performer: won
minor event at Wolverhampton in May: stays 9.5f: acts on polytrack. *N. J. Vaughan*

PRIZE FIGHTER (IRE) 5 b.g. Desert Sun 120 – Papal (Selkirk (USA) 129) [2007 **92**
p9.5g 10m 9.8g 10s* 10.9s⁴ 10f³ 10d⁵ 10m² a8g⁶ Nov 24] tall gelding: fairly useful
handicapper nowadays: left D. Carroll after reappearance: won at Leicester in June: sent
to Belgium before final start: will prove best up to 1¼m: acts on fibresand, firm and soft
going: blinkered last 5 starts: sometimes looks reluctant. *H. R. A. Cecil*

PROCRASTINATE (IRE) 5 ch.g. Rossini (USA) 118 – May Hinton 82 (Main Reef **50**
126) [2007 –: p8.6g 8d³ 9.3g 7.1d 7m 9d⁶ p8.6g⁴ Sep 28] quite good-topped gelding:
modest maiden: stays 1m: acts on polytrack, heavy and good to firm going: tried in
blinkers/cheekpieces: has been slowly away. *R. F. Fisher*

PROFESSOR TWINKLE (IRE) 3 ch.c. Dr Fong (USA) 128 – Shining High 90 (Shirley **76**
Heights 130) [2007 72: p10g⁴ p10g* p8g² p10g⁵ 8.5g 10d⁶ 8d² 10g⁶ 9.7g⁴ 9.9m p10g p8g
Oct 29] compact colt: fair handicapper: won at Lingfield in February: stays 1¼m: acts on
polytrack and soft ground: visored last 6 starts: often races prominently: sold 10,000 gns.
W. J. Knight

PROHIBIT 2 b.c. (Feb 14) Oasis Dream 129 – Well Warned 104 (Warning 136) [2007 **85 +** p7g² p7g⁶ 6.1m* Oct 3] strong, sturdy colt: half-brother to useful French 6f/7f (including at 2 yrs) winner Prior Warning (by Barathea): dam, 2-y-o 6f winner, sister to useful 7f/1m performer Out of Reach: fairly useful form: confirmed earlier promise (neck second to Kal Barg in minor event at Kempton) when winning maiden at Nottingham: should prove best kept to 6f/7f. *J. H. M. Gosden*

PROJECT SUNSHINE (GER) 4 b. or br.g. Xaar 132 – Prada (GER) (Lagunas) **–** [2007 –: p12g Jul 4] lengthy gelding: little form. *C. P. Morlock*

PROMISED GOLD 2 ch.g. (Feb 12) Bahamian Bounty 116 – Delphic Way 63 (Warn- **62** ing 136) [2007 8d 8g 8.2g Oct 31] workmanlike gelding: modest form in maidens, stamina stretched: subsequently gelded: may prove best at 6f/7f. *J. A. Geake*

PROMISING LEAD 3 b.f. Danehill 126 – Arrive 109 (Kahyasi 130) [2007 **117** 7m* 8g² 10.1s⁴ 9.9g* 10g² Oct 7] good-bodied filly: second foal: dam, 1¼m to 15f win- ner, sister to outstanding broodmare Hasili and half-sister to dam of high-class US miler Leroidesanimaux: smart performer: won maiden at Newbury (seemed to idle) in April and listed race at Salisbury (beat Sell Out by 2½ lengths) in August: improved when head second to Satwa Queen in Prix de l'Opera at Longchamp final outing, caught on line: stays 1¼m: acts on good to firm going: stays in training. *Sir Michael Stoute*

PROPAGANDA (IRE) 3 b.f. Sadler's Wells (USA) 132 – Pearly Shells 121 (Efisio **76** 120) [2007 12s³ 11.5s⁵ 10.2d 11.9d³ 12g² p12.2g² f11d² Dec 20] 450,000Y: first foal: dam won Prix Vermeille: fair maiden: runner-up last 3 starts: will stay beyond 1½m: acts on polytrack and soft ground: none too keen. *L. M. Cumani*

PROPER ARTICLE (IRE) 5 b.g. Definite Article 121 – Feather 'n Lace (IRE) 73 **61** (Green Desert (USA) 127) [2007 73: f12g⁴ f12g⁴ p13.9g Dec 3] modest handicapper: stays 1½m: acts on fibresand, soft and good to firm ground: blinkered/tongue tied. *Miss J. E. Foster*

PROPER (IRE) 3 b.g. Rossini (USA) 118 – Pardoned (IRE) 74 (Mujadil (USA) 119) **79** [2007 70: p6g⁶ p7g⁴ p7g⁵ p7.1g² 7m* 7m* 7.6m f7g⁶ 7g 7g p7g* p7g⁴ p8g p7g⁶ p8g⁶ p8g 8g p8g 8m⁴ p7.1g⁵ p7.1g² Oct 25] lightly-made gelding: fair performer: won at Brighton in April, Catterick in May and Kempton in July: stays 1m: acts on polytrack and good to firm going: often takes good hold: sold 14,000 gns. *M. R. Channon*

PROPONENT (IRE) 3 b.g. Peintre Celebre (USA) 137 – Pont Audemer (USA) 108 **99** (Chief's Crown (USA)) [2007 100P: 10.4g⁵ 9.9g 12f⁴ 8s⁶ Sep 22] tall, close-coupled gelding: useful performer: best effort in 2007 (ran poorly in Dante Stakes on reappear- ance) when seventh to Pipedreamer in Alphameric Vase (Handicap) at Goodwood second start: should be suited by 1½m: gelded after final outing. *R. Charlton*

PROPOSAL 3 b.f. Tobougg (IRE) 125 – Patiala (IRE) (Nashwan (USA) 135) [2007 52: **59** 11.6m 12g³ 11.5m⁴ 11.9d⁴ 10m³ Jul 18] sturdy filly: modest maiden handicapper: stays 1½m: acts on good to firm and good to soft going. *A. W. Carroll*

PROSPECT COURT 5 ch.g. Pivotal 124 – Scierpan (USA) 86 (Sharpen Up 127) **88** [2007 64: f7g 6g 7m⁵ 5.9g² 6v* 5v* 6s* 5.4v* 5.1g 6d 6v⁴ Nov 3] close-coupled gelding: fairly useful handicapper: won at Newcastle in June and Beverley and York (2) in July: seems best at stiff 5f/6f: acts on good to firm going, has very good record on soft/heavy: tried blinkered (well below form). *A. C. Whillans*

PROSPECT PLACE 3 b.g. Compton Place 125 – Encore My Love 68 (Royal Appl- **78** ause 124) [2007 86: 6g 5g 6m⁴ 6g³ 6g⁶ 5d⁵ 6s⁵ 6v 6g 6g Sep 23] small, strong gelding: just fair handicapper in 2007: effective at 5f/6f: acts on soft and good to firm ground: held up: sold 3,000 gns. *M. Dods*

PROTECTOR (SAF) 6 b.g. Kilconnel (USA) 99 – Mufski (SAF) (Al Mufti (USA) **111** 112) [2007 6.5f* 6g 7.5g a5f³ 6d 6v* 6d² 6m 8.3d Sep 24] big gelding: smart performer: winner in South Africa in 2004 and successful in minor event at Vichy for D. Lowther in 2006: won handicaps at Nad Al Sheba in January and, having left H. Brown after fourth start, Newcastle (by 5 lengths) in June: creditable second to Knot In Wood at Hamilton before respectable ninth to Zidane in Stewards' Cup at Goodwood, final start for Gay Kelleway: trip too far final start: stays 6.5f: acts on dirt and any turf going: blinkered/ visored fourth/fifth starts: edgy type, and sometimes early to post. *A. de Royer Dupre, France*

PROUD KILLER 4 b.g. Killer Instinct 111 – Thewaari (USA) 68 (Eskimo (USA)) **78** [2007 73: 7.1d 6g 6d² 6g 6v* 6d f5d⁴ Dec 18] big, rather leggy, useful-looking gelding: fair handicapper: won at Folkestone in October: should stay 7f: acts on fibresand and heavy going: visored final start (seemingly good effort). *J. R. Jenkins*

PROUD LINUS (USA) 2 b.c. (Feb 13) Proud Citizen (USA) 122 – Radcliffe Yard **91**
(USA) (Boston Harbor (USA) 122) [2007 5g⁴ 6m Oct 5] $20,000Y, £40,000 2-y-o: rather
leggy, useful-looking colt: first foal: dam, US sprinter (6f winner at 2 yrs), out of US
Grade 3 6f/7f winner Forest Fealty: fairly useful form: stiff tasks both starts, in listed race
at York (fourth to Captain Gerrard) and Middle Park Stakes at Newmarket (walked to
post, pulled hard in race): withdrawn from Flying Childers Stakes in between after bolting to post and crashing through rail: eager sort, likely to prove best at 5f/6f. *D. Carroll*

PROUD SCHOLAR (USA) 5 br. or b.m. Royal Academy (USA) 130 – Proud Fact **58**
(USA) 108 (Known Fact (USA) 135) [2007 58: p13.9g p12g p9.5m⁴ p12.2g Sep 14]
leggy mare: modest maiden handicapper: left R. Kvisla after second start: seems to stay
easy 1¾m: acts on polytrack and good to firm ground: tried tongue tied/in cheekpieces/
blinkered. *M. A. Magnusson*

PROVENCE 2 b.f. (Mar 14) Averti (IRE) 117 – Prowse (USA) 55 (King of Kings (IRE) **83**
125) [2007 6m⁴ 6d³ 6d² Oct 29] 11,000Y, 38,000 2-y-o: close-coupled filly: has a quick
action: first foal: dam, maiden, half-sister to US Grade 1 1¼m winner Chelsey Flower:
fairly useful form in frame in maidens at Newmarket (2) and Leicester (neck second to
Minshar): likely to stay 7f. *B. W. Hills*

PROVISION 2 ch.f. (Feb 7) Cadeaux Genereux 131 – Brand (Shareef Dancer (USA) **63 p**
135) [2007 7m Sep 22] rather unfurnished filly: half-sister to several winners, including
useful 6f (at 2 yrs) and 1m winner Royal Warrant (by Royal Applause) and 5-y-o Banknote: dam, unraced half-sister to useful winner up to 1½m Clever Cliche, out of sister to
Height of Fashion, herself dam of Nashwan, Unfuwain and Nayef: 8/1 and looking weak,
ran green when seventh to Mystery Sail in maiden at Newbury: will stay 1m: sure to
progress. *A. M. Balding*

PROVISO 2 b.f. (Feb 8) Dansili 127 – Binche (USA) 51 (Woodman (USA) 126) **116 p**
[2007 7d* 7m* 8d² Sep 29]
    Decorum would appear to be high on trainer Andre Fabre's list of qualities
for a jockey. He was reportedly angered by Christophe Soumillon's much-publicised antics—gesturing to his posterior and sticking his tongue out at the stands—after
winning the 2006 King George VI and Queen Elizabeth Stakes on Hurricane Run.
Another of Fabre's jockeys hit the headlines in similar circumstances in the
latest season. Stephane Pasquier was reported to have labelled Johnny Murtagh a
'connard' after an incident just after the start of the Fillies' Mile, also at Ascot.
Pinpointing a precise definition of the term is beyond the scope of this book; it is,

Prix du Calvados - Haras de Capucines, Deauville—
Proviso and Laureldean Gale are well clear of the opposition

not to put too fine a point on it, more derogatory than the 'chauffard' (reckless driver) that Pasquier later claimed actually to have uttered. Pasquier seemingly reacted quickly enough to escape the wrath of Fabre, issuing hurried retractions and offering an in-depth interview to the *Racing Post*, expressing shock at the allegations of using coarse language.

The incident that caused the furore occurred when Murtagh angled his mount (eventual winner Listen) across from a wide draw at Ascot, the chief sufferer from this action being Pasquier's mount Proviso. While the incident left Proviso further back than proved ideal, and also led her being forced wide to make ground, Listen won the Meon Valley Stud Fillies' Mile on merit. Proviso was sent off 11/10 favourite, her form setting a high standard in an above-average renewal of a race that is regularly a strong pointer to the classics. Proviso slammed a field of newcomers at Deauville in July and then landed the odds in the Group 3 Prix du Calvados in which only Laureldean Gale offered any resistance, the two fillies pulling six lengths clear of Lady Deauville, as Proviso ran out a half-length winner. After the early scrimmaging at Ascot, Proviso recovered well and was as close to Listen two furlongs out as she was at the line, seeming just to lack the required acceleration. Proviso went down by a length, with dual Group 1 winner Saoirse Abu two and a half lengths back in third, clear of the rest in a race run in faster time than the Royal Lodge on the same day.

			Danehill (b 1986)	Danzig
	Dansili (b 1996)			Razyana
			Hasili (b 1991)	Kahyasi
Proviso				Kerali
(b.f. Feb 8, 2005)			Woodman (ch 1983)	Mr Prospector
	Binche (USA) (ch 1999)			Playmate
			Binary (ch 1993)	Rainbow Quest
				Balabina

The rangy Proviso, who has the scope to train on, is a Juddmonte homebred, by Dansili out of Binche, who showed a glimmer of ability in two outings at three. Binche herself is a half-sister to several winners, chiefly among them smart miler (in Scandinavia nowadays) Binary File and Hawksbill, who showed smart form at up to a mile and a quarter. Proviso's grandam Binary was a useful performer in France at around a mile and a quarter, and also won a minor event in the States. Binary is a sister to the smart mile-and-a-half performer Bequeath, from a very good family, Coronation Cup winner Quiet Fling and Sandown Classic Trial winner Peacetime both being brothers of Binary's dam Balabina. Proviso's presence in what looks like being a highly competitive One Thousand Guineas would be welcome, though the Prix de Diane is reportedly being considered as an alternative target. Proviso should stay the Prix de Diane trip and, wherever she turns up at three, looks an outstanding prospect to win good races. *A. Fabre, France*

PROVOST 3 ch.g. Danehill Dancer (IRE) 117 – Dixielake (IRE) 84 (Lake Coniston (IRE) 131) [2007 66p: 8m* Apr 9] much better effort in maidens when winning 15-runner event at Yarmouth (impressively by 1½ lengths from Apple Blossom) only start in 2007: stays 1m: sold 15,000 gns in October, since gelded. *M. Johnston* **88**

PRUNES 2 ch.f. (Mar 31) Cadeaux Genereux 131 – Sahara Shade (USA) 79 (Shadeed (USA) 135) [2007 6g³ 6s⁵ 7.1d⁴ p7.1g³ 7.1m⁶ 6s⁴ 7d 7g³ p8.6g 6v⁴ p6g p6g p7.1d⁵ Dec 6] second foal: half-sister to 3-y-o Getrah: dam, 2-y-o 5f/6f winner, sister to smart Scandinavian sprinter Musadif and Queen Mary Stakes winner Nadwah: fair maiden: best effort on debut: claimed from Sir Mark Prescott £6,000 fourth start: stays 7f: acts on polytrack and soft going: tried in cheekpieces/blinkers. *A. Berry* **65 d**

PSALM (IRE) 2 b.f. (Feb 22) Sadler's Wells (USA) 132 – Litani River (USA) (Irish River (FR) 131) [2007 6g² Oct 14] sister to useful Irish 1m winner Queen Titi and half-sister to smart 1m and 8.5f (in US) winner The Editor (by Alzao): dam, French maiden, sister to useful dam of Irish 2000 Guineas winner Saffron Walden (by Sadler's Wells) and high-class sprinter/miler Dolphin Street: 6/1, neck second of 18 to stable-companion Kitty Matcham in maiden at Naas, smooth headway to challenge 1f out but ridden out only with hands and heels (should have won): will stay at least 1m: open to considerable improvement, and sure to win races. *A. P. O'Brien, Ireland* **83 P**

PSYCHIC STAR 4 b.f. Diktat 126 – Southern Psychic (USA) (Alwasmi (USA) 115) [2007 87: 8m⁵ 8.3g⁶ 12m May 21] leggy filly: just fair handicapper in 2007: barely **70**

stays 9.7f: acts on good to firm going: none too resolute: sold 6,500 gns. *Miss Lucinda V. Russell*

PSYCHO CAT 4 b.g. Hunting Lion (IRE) 115 – Canadian Capers 70 (Ballacashtal – §
(CAN)) [2007 65§: p12.2g p7.1g 10.2d Jun 16] fair but ungenuine performer at best: little
form in 2007: tried in cheekpieces/blinkers: sold £2,000 in November. *S. T. Lewis*

PTARMIGAN RIDGE 11 b.h. Sea Raven (IRE) 75 – Panayr (Faraway Times (USA) 78
123) [2007 86§: 5g⁵ 5g⁵ 5d 5m⁵ 5g⁶ 5m 5d³ 5g² 5d⁴ 5d⁵ 5g Aug 22] quite good-topped
horse: fairly useful handicapper at best, just fair in 2007: was probably best at 5f: acted on
any going: sometimes hung: put down after reportedly fracturing off-fore in September.
Miss L. A. Perratt

PUBLIC EYE 6 b.g. Zafonic (USA) 130 – Stardom (Known Fact (USA) 135) [2007 –
p11g p10g Jan 20] sturdy gelding: modest maiden at 4 yrs: unraced on Flat in 2006: little
impact at 6 yrs. *L. A. Dace*

PUGGY (IRE) 3 b.f. Mark of Esteem (IRE) 137 – Jakarta (IRE) 79 (Machiavellian 99
(USA) 123) [2007 95: 7m 8m 8.5d 8d 7g 6d⁵ Aug 19] smallish, workmanlike filly: useful
performer: little impact in 2007 (often highly tried), best effort when eighth to Finsceal
Beo in 1000 Guineas at Newmarket second start: stays 1m: acts on good to firm and good
to soft ground: tongue tied. *R. A. Kvisla*

PUGNACIOUS LADY 3 b.f. Hernando (FR) 127 – Simacota (GER) (Acatenango 70
(GER) 127) [2007 9.9d² 11.9m⁵ 11.7g³ 16g⁶ p12.2g 14s p12g³ Oct 24] 50,000Y: leggy
filly: second foal: half-sister to 1½m winner Germanicus (by Desert King): dam, German
10.5f winner, sister to very smart German/US performer Sabiango and half-sister to
high-class German 1¼m/1½m performer Silvano: fair maiden: will prove best at short of
2m: acts on polytrack, good to firm and good to soft going. *J. W. Hills*

PUGNACITY 3 b.f. Zilzal (USA) 137 – Attention Seeker (USA) 75 (Exbourne (USA) 52
125) [2007 p7g 8g p8.6g 8d⁶ 10.9s² Jul 6] unfurnished filly: second foal: half-sister
to 1m winner in US by Diktat: dam, French 10.5f winner, out of half-sister to US Grade 1
1¼m/1½m winner Vanlandingham: modest maiden: stays 10.9f: acts on soft ground.
S. C. Williams

PUISSANT PRINCESS (IRE) 3 b. or br.f. Rock of Gibraltar (IRE) 133 – Toroca 71
(USA) 112 (Nureyev (USA) 131) [2007 52p: p7g 7g 7m p8g² p8g 8d 8.1m⁵ Sep 13]
useful-looking filly: fair maiden: stays 1m: acts on polytrack and good to firm ground:
often races freely: held up. *J. W. Hills*

PUKKA TIQUE 4 b.g. Groom Dancer (USA) 128 – Surf Bird (Shareef Dancer (USA) 60
135) [2007 71: p9.5g p12.2g⁴ p16.5g Aug 13] good-topped gelding: modest maiden
nowadays: left R. Hollinshead after second start: seems to stay easy 1½m: acts on polytrack and good to soft ground: tried blinkered. *Miss J. S. Davis*

PULSATE 3 ch.f. Inchinor 119 – Salanka (IRE) 68 (Persian Heights 129) [2007 8m 8.3s 52
7m Jul 12] 28,000F: lengthy, angular filly: sister to 1998 2-y-o 7f winner Penmayne and
winner around 1m Salinor, both fairly useful, and half-sister to 3 winners, including
useful 6f (at 2 yrs)/1m winner Salamanca (by Pivotal): dam 1¼m winner: modest form in
maidens: stays 8.3f. *Mrs A. J. Perrett*

PULSE 9 b.g. Salse (USA) 128 – French Gift 99 (Cadeaux Genereux 131) [2007 p5g⁴ 57
p5.1g⁴ 5m 5.1m 5.7m 5.3d⁴ Jun 26] modest performer nowadays: best at 5f/6f: acts
on all-weather and any turf going: tried blinkered, usually wears cheekpieces. *Miss
J. R. Tooth*

PUNCHING 3 b.g. Kyllachy 129 – Candescent (Machiavellian (USA) 123) [2007 8m 69
6m⁴ 6m 5g p6g 5.7f⁴ 6f³ p7m p5.1g⁵ p6g* p6g⁵ p6m⁶ p5m⁵ Dec 9] good-topped gelding:
fair handicapper: won at Wolverhampton in November: best at 5f/6f: acts on polytrack
and firm going: tried blinkered/tongue tied: front runner. *Eve Johnson Houghton*

PUNTA GALERA (IRE) 4 b.g. Zafonic (USA) 130 – Kobalt Sea (FR) (Akarad (FR) 79
130) [2007 93: 10m p8g 9.9g 10m 10.3d³ 8.1s⁴ 10.3d⁵ 8s 8.1m p12.2g² p12.2d³
p12.2g³ p12.2d⁶ Dec 27] big, strong, close-coupled gelding: fair handicapper nowadays:
left R. Hannon after sixth start: stays 1½m: acts on polytrack, good to firm and good to
soft going: well held in headgear. *Paul Green*

PURE IMAGINATION (IRE) 6 ch.g. Royal Academy (USA) 130 – Ivory Bride 86 81
(Dominsky 110) [2007 79: 8.3f² Apr 16] workmanlike gelding: fairly useful handicapper: good second at Windsor only start at 6 yrs: effective at 6f to 8.6f: acts on polytrack,
firm and soft going: often blinkered nowadays. *J. M. Bradley*

PURE SCANDAL 2 b.g. (Feb 24) Barathea (IRE) 127 – Sharena (IRE) 78 (Kahyasi 130) [2007 6g p7g p8g Sep 24] well-made gelding: behind in maidens: bred for middle distances. *M. W. Easterby* —

PURE VELVET (IRE) 3 b.f. Mull of Kintyre (USA) 114 – Velvet Slipper 50 (Muhtafal (USA)) [2007 –p: 8g 12.1s p8.6g⁵ p8g p8g⁶ p7.1g⁵ p9.5g Oct 27] modest maiden: sold 800 gns. *S. Kirk* 52

PURPLE EMPEROR (USA) 3 b.c. Red Ransom (USA) – Checkerspot (USA) (Affirmed (USA)) [2007 10m² 10g² 9s* 11m⁵ Aug 4] $500,000Y: good-topped, useful-looking colt: third foal: half-brother to 3 winners in USA, including minor 2-y-o stakes winner Salty Romance (by Salt Lake): dam unraced: useful form: landed odds in maiden at Goodwood in July by 7 lengths: ran well when fifth to Sanbuch on handicap debut there final start: should stay 1½m: acts on soft and good to firm ground: tongue tied last 2 starts. *Saeed bin Suroor* 96

PURPLE MOON (IRE) 4 ch.g. Galileo (IRE) 134 – Vanishing Prairie (USA) 93 (Alysheba (USA)) [2007 103: 10d⁴ 12g* 14d* 12g⁶ 16g² Nov 6] 118

When Purple Moon was bought at the Autumn Sales in 2006 to go hurdling for a record-breaking 440,000 guineas, his new connections can scarcely have imagined that just over a year later they would be watching him come as close as any British-trained horse before him to winning the Melbourne Cup. It was easy to see why Purple Moon attracted so much attention at the sales as he had developed into a useful performer for Sir Michael Stoute at three, and is a good type physically. However, time was called on Purple Moon's hurdling career after just two starts for Nicky Richards, both over two miles at Musselburgh, his form fairly useful but his jumping lacking fluency. It was back on the Flat and in the hands of Luca Cumani that he fulfilled his potential, progressing really well in the latest season, putting up a career-best effort when second to Efficient in the Emirates Melbourne Cup at Flemington. The only British-trained horse to match Purple Moon's feat in coming so close was Central Park in 1999. Trained by Saeed bin Suroor, Central Park was rerouted to that year's Melbourne Cup after Kayf Tara suffered a setback and he also finished a half-length second, at 50/1, to Rogan Josh.

Purple Moon made a promising reappearance over a trip short of his best in the Wolferton Handicap at Royal Ascot when a running-on and not-knocked-about fourth to Championship Point, form he left behind at Goodwood six weeks later. Having won the 2004 renewal with another who began his career with Sir Michael Stoute, Alkaased, Cumani won the mile-and-a-half Coutts Glorious Stakes for the second time in four years since it was changed back to a non-handicap listed event. Purple Moon looked a much improved performer in beating Imperial Star by two and a half lengths despite idling once he hit the front. With just a 4-lb penalty to shoulder, Purple Moon held outstanding claims in the totesport Ebor, over two furlongs further, later in the month and he was very well supported ante-post as well as on the day. He didn't need to improve much on the form of his Goodwood effort to win a strong renewal of Europe's richest handicap by three quarters of a length from Honolulu. The longer trip at York posed no problems and Purple Moon won in the style of a horse capable of making his mark at a higher level, his rider needing to get serious only in the closing stages as he idled once again after going clear.

totesport Ebor (Handicap), York—Purple Moon (blaze) provides his trainer with a third victory in the race; Honolulu (left) runs an excellent race for a three-year-old to be second, ahead of Scriptwriter (centre) and Minkowski (right)

Purple Moon's preparation for the Melbourne Cup included a staying-on sixth, not getting a clear run, to Master O'Reilly, already favourite for the Melbourne Cup itself, in the Caulfield Cup in October. At Flemington seventeen days later Purple Moon was 9/2 second favourite, with dual Melbourne Cup-winning jockey Damien Oliver in the saddle. Purple Moon was a third of the way down the field in a race run at a steady pace before taking closer order on the home turn and leading over a furlong out, being caught by the fast-finishing Efficient in the last seventy-five yards. The race wasn't the test of stamina it might have been, the pace only steady, the time the second slowest recorded in the last twelve years.

Purple Moon (IRE) (ch.g. 2003)	Galileo (IRE) (b 1998)	Sadler's Wells (b 1981)	Northern Dancer / Fairy Bridge
		Urban Sea (ch 1989)	Miswaki / Allegretta
	Vanishing Prairie (USA) (ch 1990)	Alysheba (b 1984)	Alydar / Bel Sheba
		Venise (ch 1985)	Nureyev / Virunga

The tall, quite good-topped Purple Moon, who is a good walker and a fluent mover, is Vanishing Prairie's eighth foal. She showed fairly useful form when winning at a mile and a quarter and a mile and a half in Ireland and is a half-sister to the very smart French performers Vetheuil, who was best at a mile, and Verveine, who stayed a mile and a half and to the dam of Coronation Stakes winner Maids Causeway. Purple Moon is closely related to the smart French winner at around a mile and a quarter La Sylphide (by Barathea) and a half-brother to several winners, notably the high-class mile- to mile-and-a-quarter winner Vespone (by Llandaff). Purple Moon stays two miles and acts on firm and soft going. He has worn ear plugs in the preliminaries. *L. M. Cumani*

PURPLE RANSOM (IRE) 2 b.g. (Apr 28) Intikhab (USA) 135 – Brittas Blues (IRE) 52 (Blues Traveller (IRE) 119) [2007 p5g⁶ 6s 6d⁴ 6f Aug 5] modest maiden: bred to stay 1m. *I. A. Wood* **58**

PURPLE SANDS (IRE) 3 b.g. Desert Prince (USA) 130 – Violet Spring (IRE) 32 (Exactly Sharp (USA) 121) [2007 55: p7.1g f5g Mar 20] maiden: no form at 3 yrs. *J. Hetherton* **–**

PURUS (IRE) 5 b.g. Night Shift (USA) – Pariana (USA) (Bering 136) [2007 90: f7g p7g 6m⁵ 7g p7g³ 7f* 7d* 7m³ 8g 7f³ 7m⁵ 7d⁵ 7g* Nov 3] close-coupled gelding: fairly useful handicapper: left P. Mitchell 8,500 gns after second start: won at Brighton (2) in June and Newmarket in November: will prove best short of 1m: acts on polytrack, firm and soft going: tried tongue tied: often races prominently. *R. A. Teal* **94**

PUSEY STREET LADY 3 b.f. Averti (IRE) 117 – Pusey Street Girl 87 (Gildoran 123) [2007 56: p5g⁵ 6m* 6.1m* 6d³ 6m⁶ p6m 6d⁴ 6.1m 6d Sep 21] unfurnished filly: fairly useful performer: won maiden at Windsor in May and handicap at Nottingham in June: raced mainly at 6f: acts on polytrack, good to firm and good to soft going. *J. Gallagher* **90**

PUSKAS (IRE) 4 b.g. King's Best (USA) 132 – Chiquita Linda (IRE) (Mujadil (USA) 119) [2007 94: 5m⁶ f5g 5g³ 5d⁶ 5.3d⁴ 5m 5.1g 5f 5m 5d 6.1m 5.1s p6g p5.1g Dec 3] strong gelding: fairly useful handicapper, in decline in 2007: effective at 5f/6f: acts on firm and good to soft going: often wears cheekpieces/visor. *J. M. Bradley* **84 d**

PUSSYCAT BOW 2 ch.f. (Feb 5) Bertolini (USA) 125 – Bow Peep (IRE) 74 (Shalford (IRE) 124§) [2007 5m 6d 5v⁵ Jul 7] workmanlike filly: second foal: sister to useful 2005 2-y-o 5f winner Bow Bridge: dam 5f/6f winner: no form in maidens: tried blinkered. *M. W. Easterby* **–**

PUT IT ON THE CARD 3 ch.r. Bertolini (USA) 125 – Madame Jones (IRE) 79 (Lycius (USA) 124) [2007 59: p5.1g² p6g* p7.1g* p7.1g³ 7m 5m 6d p7.1g f6d Dec 21] close-coupled rig: fair performer: won claimers at Wolverhampton in January and February (left P. D. Evans £6,000): stays 7f: acts on polytrack and good to firm going: wears headgear. *J. S. Wainwright* **– a66**

PUTRA LAJU (IRE) 3 b.c. Trans Island 119 – El Corazon (IRE) (Mujadil (USA) 119) [2007 72: 8.5g 8.5g 8.1g 10g p8g 8d p8g² p8.6g² p8.6g³ p8.6d* Dec 6] compact colt: fair handicapper: won at Wolverhampton in December: stays 8.6f: acts on polytrack: in cheekpieces nowadays. *J. W. Hills* **77**

PUTRA SQUARE 3 b.g. Cadeaux Genereux 131 – Razzle (IRE) 68 (Green Desert **91** (USA) 127) [2007 87: p8g⁶ 10m² 11.8g 10.3m⁴ 10.1g p10g³ p12g² Oct 14] big, good- **a81** topped gelding: fairly useful maiden: should stay 1½m: acts on polytrack, good to firm and good to soft going: breathing problem third outing, tongue tied next time: has looked none too keen, including when blinkered final start: subsequently gelded. *P. F. I. Cole*

PUY D'ARNAC (FR) 4 b.g. Acteur Francais (USA) 118 – Chaumeil (FR) (Mad **64** Captain 117) [2007 10g⁶ 11g* 10s* 10g⁴ 10d 12d⁶ 10s Sep 26] ex-French gelding: won minor events at Angouleme in April and Libourne in May: left J-F. Bernard, better effort in handicaps in Britain when sixth at Musselburgh penultimate start: stays 11f: acts on soft ground. *G. A. Swinbank*

Q

QAASI (USA) 5 ch.g. Rahy (USA) 115 – Recording (USA) (Danzig (USA)) [2007 71, **65** a65: f12g⁴ p9.5g p13.9g² p16.5g⁴ 12.1g² 14.1d⁴ 13d⁴ 12v⁶ 16m⁶ p13.9g⁶ 14.1f 15.8g⁵ p13.9g Oct 8] lengthy gelding: fair handicapper: effective at 1½m and easy 2m: acts on polytrack, good to soft and good to firm ground: tried blinkered/visored/tongue tied: weak finisher. *M. Brittain*

QADAR (IRE) 5 b.g. Xaar 132 – Iktidar 80 (Green Desert (USA) 127) [2007 109: p6g* **100** p6g⁴ p6g* f6g² p5g³ p5g⁵ p6f³ p6g² p5g p6g² a6f⁶ 6m 5.6m⁶ 7m 5.6m p6m³ 5.1m³ p6g⁵ **a109** Dec 28] strong, good sort: useful handicapper, better on all-weather: won at Wolverhampton and Lingfield (by short head from Maltese Falcon) in January: effective at 5f to 7f: acts on polytrack (probably on fibresand) and firm going: usually wears headgear: tried tongue tied: held up. *N. P. Littmoden*

QASAYED (USA) 2 b.f. (Jan 29) Diesis 133 – Bright And Cheery (USA) (Event of The **55 p** Year (USA) 125) [2007 p7g⁵ Sep 11] $15,000F, 32,000Y: good-topped filly: has a round action: first foal: dam unraced out of half-sister to very smart 1¼m performers Grise Mine (in France) and Kostroma (in US): 25/1, needed experience when fifth in maiden at Lingfield: will stay at least 1m: should do better. *C. E. Brittain*

QATAR WAY (GR) 3 ch.f. Harmonic Way 121 – Sea Shell (IRE) (Unfuwain (USA) **–** 131) [2007 p7g 7g p6g Nov 16] first foal: dam unraced half-sister to high-class 1½m/ 1¾m performer Hellenic (later dam of Islington, Greek Dance and Mountain High): well held in maidens. *P. R. Chamings*

QUAGLINO WAY (GR) 3 b.g. Mark of Esteem (IRE) 137 – Pringipessa's Way 72 **75** (Machiavellian (USA) 123) [2007 8g 8.3m 8.3d⁵ 8.3g p8g³ p8.6g* Oct 25] good-bodied gelding: fair performer: won maiden at Wolverhampton in October: likely to stay 1¼m: acts on polytrack, unraced on extremes of going on turf. *P. R. Chamings*

QUAI DU ROI (IRE) 5 ch.g. Desert King (IRE) 129 – Emly Express (IRE) (High **76 §** Estate 127) [2007 93: p7.1g p8g³ 8m⁴ 8m 8m a7g* 8s Sep 21] fairly useful handicapper: **a91 §** left K. Ryan after fourth start: won at Laytown in September (no stalls): very slowly away/refused to race other starts: effective at 7f to 11.5f: acts on polytrack/sand and any going on turf: tried blinkered: one to treat with plenty of caution. *D. Nicholls*

QUAKER BOY 4 b.g. Agnes World (USA) 123 – La Brise (IRE) (Llandaff (USA)) **–** [2007 60: 7.9m 6d 5g Jul 8] good-topped gelding: modest maiden: no form at 4 yrs: tried in cheekpieces: sold 900 gns. *A. C. Whillans*

QUALIFY 4 b.g. Mark of Esteem (IRE) 137 – Raneen Alwatar 80 (Sadler's Wells **78** (USA) 132) [2007 –: 12s³ 10g² Sep 19] strong, close-coupled gelding: fair handicapper, lightly raced: placed both starts at 4 yrs: should stay 1½m: acts on soft and good to firm going, probably on polytrack. *Miss S. West*

QUALITAIR WINGS 8 b.g. Colonel Collins (USA) 122 – Semperflorens (Don 128) **63** [2007 74: 9.2g⁵ 10g⁵ 10m⁴ May 25] lengthy, quite good-topped gelding: modest handi- capper: stays 1¼m: acts on polytrack, firm and soft going: tried in cheekpieces/blinkers: sometimes starts slowly/wanders: held up. *J. Hetherton*

QUALITY STREET 5 ch.m. Fraam 114 – Pusey Street Girl 87 (Gildoran 123) [2007 **80** 86, a77: p6g² p6g² p6g 5g⁶ 6g p5g³ p6g* p6g* p6g⁴ p6g⁶ p6g 5m Sep 14] lengthy, rather leggy mare: fairly useful handicapper: won at Lingfield (twice) in July: stays easy 6f: acts on polytrack, raced mainly on good going or firmer on turf: usually in cheekpieces, tried visored: edgy type, tends to sweat. *P. Butler*

totesport.com Winter Hill Stakes, Windsor—Queen's Best (blaze) makes a successful step up to pattern company; Winged Cupid (rail) is second with Cougar Bay third

QUAM CELERRIME 2 b.c. (Apr 14) Xaar 132 – Divine Secret (Hernando (FR) 127) [2007 p8g⁵ p8g² 7s* 6d Nov 2] €65,000Y: useful-looking colt: fourth foal: half-brother to 3 winners, including useful Italian 6f to 1m winner Adorabile Fong (by Dr Fong): dam unraced out of sister to smart sprinter Monde Bleu: fairly useful form: won maiden at Folkestone in October: stiff task, seventh to Pomellato in Criterium de Maisons-Laffitte: stays 1m: acts on polytrack and soft going. *P. A. Blockley* **89 ?**

QUANTUM LEAP 10 b.g. Efisio 120 – Prejudice 83 (Young Generation 129) [2007 79: p7g p7g p7g 7g² 7d* p7g⁶ 7m² 7f³ 6g⁵ 7s 7g p7g 7d³ p7g 7g p7m p7g* p7g* p8m² p7g Dec 29] quite good-topped gelding: fair handicapper: won at Salisbury (apprentices) in May and Lingfield in October/November: has won at 1¼m, probably best at 7f/1m: acts on polytrack, good to firm and good to soft going: wears visor/cheekpieces: waited with. *S. Dow* **76**

QUAROMA 2 ch.f. (May 5) Pivotal 124 – Quiz Time 90 (Efisio 120) [2007 5.1g³ 5.1g* Nov 7] 14,000 2-y-o: neat filly: sister to 5-y-o Countdown, closely related to useful 2002 2-y-o 5f/6f winner Cool Question (by Polar Falcon) and half-sister to winner in Spain by Pursuit of Love: dam 2-y-o 5f winner: fair form: confirmed debut promise (third to Chartist at Nottingham) when winning maiden there week later, good speed both times: will prove best at 5f. *Jane Chapple-Hyam* **74**

QUARRYMASTER (IRE) 2 b.g. (May 8) Captain Rio 122 – Partenza (USA) (Red Ransom (USA)) [2007 5m⁵ 5m 6m Aug 10] close-coupled gelding: little form: sold 2,500 gns, sent to Denmark. *J. Howard Johnson* **–**

QUE BEAUTY (IRE) 2 b.f. (Feb 9) Val Royal (FR) 127 – Ardbess (Balla Cove 119) [2007 6f 7d 6m Oct 22] €8,000F, €20,000Y: smallish, workmanlike filly: third foal: half-sister to 5-y-o Maneki Neko: dam unraced out of useful Irish 1m/1¼m winner Bonnie Bess: well held in maidens. *R. C. Guest* **–**

QUEEN BE 2 ch.f. (Mar 18) First Trump 118 – Madam Zando 51 (Forzando 122) [2007 6d 5d 5.2f Jul 30] 2,100 2-y-o: tall filly: sixth foal: half-sister to 6-y-o Uig and 5f/6f winner Largs (by Sheikh Albadou): dam sprint maiden: no form. *I. W. McInnes* **–**

QUEEN EXCALIBUR 8 ch.m. Sabrehill (USA) 120 – Blue Room 70 (Gorytus (USA) 132) [2007 p12.2g Jun 25] rather leggy mare: poor performer: unraced on Flat in 2005/6: effective at 7f to 11f: acts on soft and good to firm going: tried in cheekpieces/blinkers. *C. Roberts* **–**

QUEEN NOVERRE (IRE) 3 b.f. Noverre (USA) 125 – Tafrah (IRE) 71 (Sadler's Wells (USA) 132) [2007 83: 7m p7g 7m* p8.6g⁵ p9.5m³ 10g* p10g Oct 12] leggy, quite attractive filly: fairly useful performer: won maiden at Redcar in August and handicap at Sandown in September: stays 1¼m: acts on polytrack and good to firm going: in cheekpieces last 3 starts: reportedly lost a shoe fifth outing. *J. W. Hills* **86**

858

QUEEN OF DIAMONDS (IRE) 4 b.f. Fruits of Love (USA) 127 – Royal Jubilee **41**
(IRE) 81 (King's Theatre (IRE) 128) [2007 53: f11g⁵ f14g Apr 13] tall, sturdy filly: poor
maiden: stays 1½m: acts on heavy going. *Mrs K. Walton*

QUEEN OF NAPLES 2 b.f. (Mar 6) Singspiel (IRE) 133 – Napoleon's Sister (IRE) **94 p**
101 (Alzao (USA) 117) [2007 8m² 8g 8g³ Nov 3] 190,000Y: strong, attractive filly: fifth
foal: half-sister to 3 fairly useful winners, including 2-y-o 1m winners Louis Napoleon
(in 2002, by Indian Ridge) and Elise (in 2005, by Fantastic Light): dam, 1¼m winner,
half-sister to Derby winner Oath and high-class performer up to 10.5f Pelder: fairly useful
form: placed in maiden and listed race (½-length third to Classic Legend) at Newmarket,
and ran well when 7¾ lengths seventh to Zarkava in Prix Marcel Boussac at Longchamp
in between: will be suited by 1¼m/1½m: should improve further, and sure to win races.
J. H. M. Gosden

QUEEN'S BEST 4 b.f. King's Best (USA) 132 – Cloud Castle 119 (In The Wings 128) **110**
[2007 95: p10g³ 8.1d² 10.9d² 12f* 10m* 10m² 12s² Oct 13] smallish, close-coupled filly:
smart performer: progressed well at 4 yrs, winning listed race at Newbury and Winter Hill
Stakes at Windsor (by ½ length from Winged Cupid), both in August: good efforts when
runner-up in Blandford Stakes at the Curragh (beaten short head by Four Sins) and
Princess Royal Stakes at Ascot (beaten ½ length by Trick Or Treat) last 2 starts: effective
at 1¼m/1½m: unraced on heavy going, acts on any other turf and polytrack: sometimes
carries head awkwardly: stays in training. *Sir Michael Stoute*

QUEEN SCARLET (IRE) 2 b.f. (Mar 23) Redback 116 – Hill Hopper (IRE) 106 **92**
(Danehill (USA) 126) [2007 7g* 7m⁴ Aug 11] 270,000Y: close-coupled filly: half-sister
to several winners, notably 4-y-o Nannina: dam 6f/7f winner: fairly useful form: won
maiden at Newmarket in July: improved when 3¼ lengths fourth to Albabilia in Sweet
Solera Stakes there: should have stayed 1m: dead. *B. J. Meehan*

Cheveley Park Stud's "Queen's Best"

QUEEN'S COMPOSER (IRE) 4 b.g. Mozart (IRE) 131 – Queen Leonor (IRE) 72 **68**
(Caerleon (USA) 132) [2007 82: 7d 8d 7m 7d 7.2s⁶ Oct 26] rangy gelding: just fair handicapper in 2007, gelded after second start: effective at 7f/1m: acts on any going. *B. Smart*

QUEEN'S ECHO 6 b.m. Wizard King 122 – Sunday News'n'echo (USA) 78 (Trempo- **60**
lino (USA) 135) [2007 62: 7m² 7.1m² 9.1d³ 9.1g 8.3f 7.2v Nov 3] modest performer:
claimed from M. Dods £7,000 after reappearance: stays easy 9f: acts on heavy and good
to firm going: tried tongue tied: none too reliable. *P. Monteith*

QUEENSGATE 3 b.f. Compton Place 125 – Ring Queen (USA) (Fairy King (USA)) **43**
[2007 60: 6m p6g 5.7d 5m Jul 19] good-bodied filly: poor maiden: effective at 5f/6f: acts
on polytrack and firm going. *M. Blanshard*

QUEEN'S LODGE (IRE) 7 ch.m. Grand Lodge (USA) 125 – Manilia (FR) (Kris **69**
135) [2007 –: 6s 6d 7f Jul 30] deep-girthed mare: fair performer, lightly raced nowadays:
both wins at 6f: acts on good to firm going: tried in cheekpieces. *I. W. McInnes*

QUEENS MANTLE 2 b.f. (Jan 16) Bold Edge 123 – Queen Shirley (IRE) (Fairy King **53**
(USA)) [2007 6d p6g p5g⁶ p5.1g⁴ p5m³ Dec 8] 10,000Y: lengthy filly: fifth foal: half-
sister to 2002 2-y-o 5f winner Blues Princess (by Bluebird): dam unraced out of half-
sister to Cherry Hinton Stakes winner Crime of Passion: modest maiden: best at 5f: acts
on polytrack. *P. J. Makin*

QUEENS QUAY 3 b.f. Grand Lodge (USA) 125 – Nirvana 82 (Marju (IRE) 127) [2007 **53**
–: 10.2m 9.9d 12.1g May 29] close-coupled filly: modest maiden: sold 18,000 gns in July.
R. Hannon

QUEEN'S SPEECH (IRE) 2 b.f. (Mar 1) Medicean 128 – Jazan (IRE) 94 (Danehill **61 p**
(USA) 126) [2007 p8.6g⁵ Nov 1] 38,000Y: second foal: closely related to winner in
Greece by Best of The Bests: dam maiden (stayed 8.5f): 16/1, fifth to Fandangerina in
maiden at Wolverhampton, not knocked about: will do better. *J. H. M. Gosden*

QUEEN'S TREASURE (IRE) 2 b.f. (Apr 4) Bahamian Bounty 116 – Daltak (Night **50**
Shift (USA)) [2007 5m 6m 6g Aug 15] 30,000Y, 70,000 2-y-o: rather unfurnished filly:
sixth foal: half-sister to 2003 2-y-o 6f winner Scarlet Empress (by Second Empire):
dam, unraced, closely related to smart sprinter Ya Malak out of half-sister to Cadeaux
Genereux: modest maiden: likely to prove best at 5f/6f: sold 7,000 gns, joined S. Dow.
M. P. Tregoning

QUEL FONTENAILLES (FR) 9 b.g. Tel Quel (FR) 125 – Sissi Fontenailles (FR) **–**
(Pampabird 124) [2007 p12g p13.9g p16.5g Mar 14] compact gelding: modest handicapper: missed 2006 and well held at 9 yrs. *L. A. Dace*

QUEST FOR SUCCESS (IRE) 2 b.c. (May 8) Noverre (USA) 125 – Divine Pursuit **97**
69 (Kris 135) [2007 5d³ 6d³ 6s² 6g 6.5m 6s* Oct 4] €17,000F, 25,000Y: rather leggy,
close-coupled colt: half-brother to 1¼m winner Blazing The Trail (by Indian Ridge) and
winner in US by Marju: dam, maiden (stayed 8.5f), sister to smart French sprinter Divine
Danse and half-sister to Pursuit of Love: useful performer: placed in 3 maidens and
mid-division in 2 sales races before winning maiden at Ayr by 5 lengths: bred to stay 1m,
but has plenty of speed: acts on soft going, probably on good to firm. *R. A. Fahey*

QUICKLIME 3 b.f. Gorse 116 – Linden Grace (USA) 88 (Mister Baileys 123) [2007 **–**
7g⁶ p8g Sep 18] second foal: half-sister to 5-y-o Linden Lime: dam 7f (at 2 yrs)/1m
winner: well held in maidens at Lingfield. *Jamie Poulton*

QUICK OFF THE MARK 2 b.f. (Feb 3) Dr Fong (USA) 128 – Equity Princess 106 **66 +**
(Warning 136) [2007 p7.1g³ 6m Aug 3] €24,000Y: fifth foal: half-sister to fairly useful
7f (at 2 yrs) and 9f winner Market Trend (by Selkirk): dam, 1m (at 2 yrs) and 9f winner,
out of useful stayer Hawait Al Barr: fair maiden: much better effort when third at Wolverhampton: will need to settle to stay 1m (bred to). *J. G. Given*

QUICK RELEASE (IRE) 2 b.c. (May 2) Red Ransom (USA) – Set The Mood (USA) **89**
(Dixie Brass (USA)) [2007 6.1g² 7m* 8m 7g⁴ p7g³ Nov 3] €53,000Y: close-coupled colt:
third foal: dam unraced half-sister to Oaks winner Casual Look and smart French 1¼m
winner Shabby Chic (both by Red Ransom): fairly useful performer: won maiden at
Chester in August: seemed to have problem next 2 starts, but improved final one in minor
event at Kempton (third to Storm Force): should stay 1m: acts on polytrack and good to
firm going. *D. M. Simcock*

QUICK SANDS (IRE) 2 b.f. (Jan 19) Redback 116 – Winning Note (IRE) 66 (Victory **70**
Note (USA) 120) [2007 5m 5m⁵ 7s⁴ 7m² 7f² 7g 8f³ 8.3d 8.3d Oct 15] 40,000Y: close-
coupled filly: first foal: dam, maiden (should have stayed 1m), out of half-sister to 2000

Guineas winner Island Sands: fair maiden: placed 3 times, twice in nurseries: stays 1m: acts on firm and soft going: sold 4,200 gns. *R. Hannon*

QUICKS THE WORD 7 b.g. Sri Pekan (USA) 117 – Fast Tempo (IRE) 74 (Statoblest 120) [2007 54: 6g³ 8.3g 5.9g³ 6g* 6d 5.9g⁵ 6m* 6s Oct 4] rather leggy gelding: modest handicapper: won at Ayr in July and Newcastle in September: best form at 6f: acts on heavy and good to firm going: tried blinkered: none too consistent. *T. A. K. Cuthbert* **62**

QUICUYO (GER) 4 ch.g. Acatenango (GER) 127 – Quila (IRE) (Unfuwain (USA) 131) [2007 9.5g² 9.2d 11.1d⁴ 11.1m 15s 17.5s⁵ Sep 21] second foal: brother to 5-y-o Quijano: dam German 2-y-o 6f winner: second in maiden at Hanover on debut for T. Reineke: little impact on Flat in Britain, though successful over hurdles in October: stays 15f. *P. Monteith* **52**

QUIDOR WAY (GR) 3 br.g. Harmonic Way 121 – Jollity Way (GR) (Wadood (USA) 97) [2007 9m Jul 18] Greek-bred gelding: 11/1, well held in maiden at Lingfield, slowly into stride: returned to Greece. *P. R. Chamings* **–**

QUIET ELEGANCE 2 b.f. (Apr 11) Fantastic Light (USA) 134 – Imperial Bailiwick (IRE) 104 (Imperial Frontier (USA) 112) [2007 5.1d* Oct 10] strong filly: half-sister to several winners, including 6-y-o Reverence and smart 6f (at 2 yrs) to 1m winner Helm Bank (by Wild Again): dam 2-y-o 5f (including Flying Childers Stakes) winner: 11/1 and looking backward, won maiden at Nottingham in smooth style: should prove best at 5f/6f: useful prospect. *E. J. Alston* **79 p**

QUIET READING (USA) 10 b.g. Northern Flagship (USA) 96 – Forlis Key (USA) (Forli (ARG)) [2007 64: f8g Jan 9] big, lengthy gelding: poor handicapper: has form at 15f, best at 7f to 8.5f: acts on fibresand and any turf going: wears headgear: held up: often a weak finisher. *M. R. Bosley* **45**

QUIET TIMES (IRE) 8 ch.g. Dolphin Street (FR) 125 – Super Times (Sayf El Arab (USA) 127) [2007 –, a95: f6g p6g p6g⁵ f6g⁵ p6g* f6g³ p6g p5.1g p6g² p6g² f6d³ Dec 11] strong gelding: fairly useful performer: won claimer at Wolverhampton in February: best at 5f/6f: acts on all-weather, heavy and good to firm going: wears headgear: often slowly away, has refused to race 3 times (including once in 2007) and needs treating with caution. *K. A. Ryan* **– §** **a89 §**

QUIJANO (GER) 5 ch.g. Acatenango (GER) 127 – Quila (IRE) (Unfuwain (USA) 131) [2007 112p: 12g* 12g* 12g* 12g 10d 11g* 12g* 12f³ 12g² Dec 9] **122**

For a time, it seemed as though Quijano might emulate his own sire Acatenango as he started to compile a lengthy sequence of wins. Acatenango was much the best horse of his time in what was then West Germany, to the extent that he managed to run up a sequence of twelve wins over the best part of two seasons as a three- and four-year-old in 1985 and 1986. At a time when there were far fewer international options for a horse such as Acatenango, and when German trainers were less in the habit of taking advantage of opportunities abroad, Acatenango proved a big fish in the relatively small pond of German racing. His twelve wins in a row included six Group 1 victories, among them the Deutsches Derby and one of two editions of the Grosser Preis von Baden that he won, though his success wasn't confined to his own country as the Grand Prix de Saint-Cloud was part of that run. Acatenango finally met his match when sent to France again for a very hotly-contested Prix de l'Arc de Triomphe at the end of his four-year-old season in which he finished a creditable seventh behind Dancing Brave. Acatenango also ran abroad twice more as a five-year-old, both times in Britain, finishing third in the Coronation Cup and sixth in the King George VI and Queen Elizabeth Stakes.

As well as being a son of Acatenango, Quijano carries the same colours as his sire, the yellow, black sleeves of the Gestut Fahrhof. While Acatenango owed his run of success to being the best around in his part of the world and proving tough and consistent, Quijano's winning streak was the result of constant improvement which took him from a maiden at Hanover to the riches of the Dubai Carnival. Although seen as a potential German Derby horse at the time, he made an inauspicious debut when tailed-off last of five in what turned out to be his only race as a three-year-old. By the time he was seen out again, more than twelve months later, he had been gelded. From then on, though, Quijano made remarkable progress, staying unbeaten in seven races as a four-year-old: a maiden, five handicaps and a listed race. In his final race that season, a handicap at Baden-Baden, he showed smart form (earning a rating of 112p), and the signs were that he was still improv-

*Grosser Preis von Baden, Baden-Baden—Quijano (black sleeves) finds extra
to hold off the German Derby winner Adlerflug (left) to gain his twelfth win from fifteen starts;
Egerton (second right) is third ahead of Youmzain (white cap, hidden by Quijano)*

ing. The German handicappers had struggled to keep up with Quijano's progress, and their colleagues in Dubai soon had the same problem. Quijano was still largely unknown outside Germany, but three wins at the Dubai International Carnival earned him a much higher profile. He made a really good impression when winning a handicap on his reappearance and defied a 10-lb higher mark in a similar event a fortnight later, though this time having only a short head to spare over the previous season's dual European Group 1 winner Laverock. Quijano made it ten wins in a row when showing further improvement to win the Intikhab Dubai City of Gold, the trial for the Dubai Sheema Classic, by a length and a quarter from the previous season's winner Oracle West, taking the lead two furlongs out and just needing riding with hands and heels to maintain his advantage. Like Acatenango, Quijano was anything but discredited when his sequence of wins was finally brought to an end when he finished seventh in the Dubai Sheema Classic, the world's joint-richest race on turf, behind the Hong Kong-trained Vengeance of Rain in a field which also included Derby winner Sir Percy, Breeders' Cup Turf winner Red Rocks and the Japanese-trained Melbourne Cup runner-up Pop Rock.

Quijano's efforts in Dubai showed that he was well up to competing in pattern company, though his first start back in Europe yielded a disappointing effort in the Grand Prix de Vichy. The trip was on the short side for him and it was his first start for nearly four months, and Quijano soon put that run behind him with a win in the listed race at Cologne in August that he had won the year before. The following month, Quijano made his European Group 1 debut in the Grosser Preis von Baden. Despite its status as Germany's most prestigious race, the lack of a sponsor meant that prize money was only a third of what it had been twelve months earlier, leaving it well behind the Deutsches Derby in value. Mercedes-Benz, who sponsored the Grosser Preis von Baden between 1996 and 2000, are set to renew their patronage in 2008. The winner of the Deutsches Derby, Adlerflug, was made favourite, ahead of the British-trained runners Mountain High, winner of the Grand Prix de Saint-Cloud, and Youmzain, who had finished third in the Sheema Classic. Quijano was next in the betting in a field of nine which also included the previous year's winner Prince Flori and the Grand Prix de Paris runner-up Axxos. The favourite's pace-maker Sommertag did his job until the home turn, where the field fanned wide. One of several with chances in the straight, Quijano hung right briefly under the whip into his stable-companion Axxos (who in turn hampered Mountain High), but found plenty inside the final furlong to hold off Adlerflug by a neck, the pair pulling three and a half lengths clear of Egerton, who made the frame in the race for the third time, just ahead of the staying-on Youmzain. Quijano was reportedly the first gelding to win the Grosser Preis von Baden, and, as a gelding, he was barred from running in the Arc as his sire had done. Instead, Quijano was sent outside Europe again for his last two starts and ran well in defeat on both occasions. In the Canadian International at Woodbine he was beaten only a length into third behind Cloudy's Knight and Ask, and in the Hong Kong Vase at Sha Tin he fared best of the three German runners when a length and a half second to Doctor Dino. Quijano stayed on well in both races, the short straight at Sha Tin not making it easy to come from well off the pace.

Quijano (GER) (ch.g. 2002)	Acatenango (GER) (ch 1982)	Surumu (ch 1974)	Literat
			Surama
		Aggravate (b 1966)	Aggressor
			Raven Locks
	Quila (IRE) (ch 1997)	Unfuwain (b 1985)	Northern Dancer
			Height of Fashion
		Quest of Fire (b 1991)	Rainbow Quest
			Vallee Dansante

Quijano's pedigree is fairly academic now that he has been gelded, but he comes from a fine family and one that had an excellent season in 2007 thanks to Authorized's exploits; Quijano's grandam, the French nine-furlong winner Quest of Fire, is a half-sister to the dam of the Derby winner. Quest of Fire has produced six winners to date. As well as Quijano's dam the German two-year-old six-furlong winner Quila, the others include a couple of three-parts brothers to Quijano by Acatenango. One of them, Querido, won over a mile in Germany in the latest season. The other is Quorum, a €400,000 yearling (then a record for a German yearling) who was unraced for Godolphin but has since won at a mile and nine furlongs on the dirt at Nad Al Sheba, showing fairly useful form. Quijano is his dam's first foal, her only other runner so far being the year-younger full brother to Quijano, Quicuyo, who is just a modest maiden on the Flat but has won his first two starts over hurdles for Peter Monteith. Quijano stays a mile and a half well and acts on firm and soft ground. He is held up, and reportedly has the Dubai Sheema Classic as his main target again early in the year. *P. Schiergen, Germany*

QUINCE (IRE) 4 b.g. Fruits of Love (USA) 127 – Where's Charlotte 53 (Sure Blade (USA) 130) [2007 92: p12g² p12g² p12.2g⁴ p13g² p11g 12m 10m⁴ 10.5m⁶ p13.9g⁴ 12m 12g Oct 27] strong, close-coupled gelding: fairly useful handicapper: stays 1¾m, at least when emphasis on speed: acts on polytrack, good to firm and good to soft going: effective in cheekpieces/visor or not: usually held up: quirky. *J. Pearce* **93**

QUINMASTER (USA) 5 gr.g. Linamix (FR) 127 – Sherkiya (IRE) (Goldneyev (USA) 114) [2007 113: 8m⁴ 8m⁴ 8g* 8.5g 8s Aug 6] smart performer: made all in listed race at Leopardstown in June, beating Cheyenne Star by a head: long way below form after in handicap at Galway and listed race at Cork: seems best around 1m: acts on good to firm and good to soft ground, not on soft/heavy: occasionally tongue tied/in cheekpices (both last 2 starts). *M. Halford, Ireland* **112**

QUIRINA 2 b.f. (Mar 6) Red Ransom (USA) – Qirmazi (USA) 113 (Riverman (USA) 131) [2007 7g⁴ Nov 3] good-topped, quite attractive filly: closely related to fairly useful 2-y-o 1m winner (stays 2m) Quartino (by Dynaformer), and half-sister to several winners, including 10-y-o Quito: dam French 6f (at 2 yrs) and 9f winner: 22/1 and better for race, fourth to La Coveta in maiden at Newmarket, nearest finish: will stay at least 1m: sure to improve. *J. H. M. Gosden* **67 p**

QUITE A SPLASH (USA) 3 b.g. Smart Strike (CAN) 121 – Easy Sunshine (IRE) 96 (Sadler's Wells (USA) 132) [2007 10m 10m 10.2m 12.1g 8.5s p8g p10g Oct 10] neat gelding: little form: tried blinkered. *S. Curran* **–**

QUITO (IRE) 10 b.r. Machiavellian (USA) 123 – Qirmazi (USA) 113 (Riverman (USA) 131) [2007 121: 6m 7.1g⁶ 6g 7.1m⁴ 6d 6m Jul 13] tall, leggy rig: just smart performer in 2007, best effort when fourth to Mine in listed event at Haydock in June: well held last 2 starts, in Golden Jubilee Stakes at Royal Ascot and July Cup at Newmarket (reportedly returned home very sore and underwent stem-cell treatment after): needs testing conditions at 6f, and stays 1m: acts on dirt/all-weather, soft and good to firm going: wears blinkers: tried tongue tied earlier in career: has been bandaged fore joints/worn crossed noseband/been on toes: sometimes slowly away: held up, and best in well-run race: very tough and genuine. *D. W. Chapman* **111**

QUORN MASTER 5 b.g. Bal Harbour 113 – Queen of The Quorn 53 (Governor General 116) [2007 8.2m p7.1g Oct 22] big, workmanlike gelding: well held in bumper (for M. Easterby): seemingly modest form on Flat. *Mrs P. Ford* **51 ?**

QUOTATION 2 b.f. (Apr 13) Medicean 128 – Eloquent 94 (Polar Falcon (USA) 126) **83 p**
[2007 7m² 8d⁴ Oct 23] big, rather leggy filly: has a fluent, round action: third foal: sister
to fairly useful 2005 2-y-o 7f winner Commentary: dam 2-y-o 6f winner from 3 starts:
shaped well in maidens at Doncaster (second to Lady Jane Digby) and Yarmouth (fourth
after hampered): stays 1m: will make a useful 3-y-o. *Sir Michael Stoute*

QWERTYUIOP (IRE) 2 ch.c. (Apr 14) Noverre (USA) 125 – French River (Bering   **–**
136) [2007 5d⁶ p7.1g Jul 2] last in maidens, blinkered latterly. *K. J. Burke*

R

RAAQIA 2 b.f. (Apr 6) Sakhee (USA) 136 – Crown Water (USA) (Chief's Crown   **–**
(USA)) [2007 8d Oct 23] 40,000Y: half-sister to several winners abroad: dam US 2-y-o
1m winner: 33/1, detached in maiden at Yarmouth. *B. J. Meehan*

RABBIT 6 b.m. Muhtarram (USA) 125 – Ninia (USA) 102 (Affirmed (USA)) [2007   **– §**
14.1d Aug 16] rather leggy mare: poor maiden: has twice refused to enter stall, and has
served a temporary ban: one to treat with caution. *M. Sheppard*

RABBIT FIGHTER (IRE) 3 ch.c. Observatory (USA) 131 – Furnish 87 (Green   **83**
Desert (USA) 127) [2007 91: p8.6g* 10m 8.5v⁵ 8s p7g p8.6g p8.6g p7.1g p7.1g² p7g³
p7g² p7.1g⁶ p6g* p6g* Dec 19] strong, close-coupled colt: fairly useful performer: won
maiden at Wolverhampton in March and, having left P. Blockley after fourth start, 2
handicaps at Kempton in December: effective at 6f to 8.6f: acts on polytrack and good to
firm going: visored last 4 starts. *D. Shaw*

RABEERA 2 b.f. (Apr 9) Beat Hollow 126 – Gai Bulga 110 (Kris 135) [2007 8m Sep   **62 p**
21] 60,000Y: strong filly: half-sister to 3 winners, including useful 1m to 1¼m winner
Chivalry (by Mark of Esteem) and 3-y-o Darfour: dam, 1¼m winner, half-sister to dam of
2000 Guineas winner Footstepsinthesand: 66/1, seventh to Makaaseb in maiden at Newmarket, getting hang of things late: will be suited by 1¼m: should progress. *A. M. Balding*

RACCOON (IRE) 7 b.g. Raphane (USA) 102 – Kunucu (IRE) 94 (Bluebird (USA)   **87**
125) [2007 76§: 5.1m* 5m* 6.1g 5d⁵ 5m* 5g⁴ 5m 5m⁵ 5g⁵ 5s² 5g* 5.1m 5m 5s³ 5g Oct 6]
strong, good-quartered gelding: has been tubed: fairly useful performer: rejuvenated at 7
yrs, winning handicaps at Nottingham and Catterick in May and Musselburgh in June and
claimer at Catterick in August: best at bare 5f: acts on firm and soft going: sometimes
visored: tried tongue tied: tends to edge right: races up with pace: formerly ungenuine.
D. W. Chapman

RACER FOREVER (USA) 4 b.g. Rahy (USA) 115 – Ras Shaikh (USA) 105 (Sheikh   **118**
Albadou 128) [2007 106: p7g³ 7g 7m⁵ 7g² 7g³ 7m 7.1m⁴ 7g⁶ Oct 6] attractive, well-made
gelding: smart performer: best efforts when 1¼ lengths second of 27 to Third Set in
International Stakes at Ascot in July and when close third to Duff in listed event at
York next time, hanging left: not at best after: stays 7f: acts on polytrack, yet to race on
extremes of going on turf: sweating and on edge second outing (below form): has hung
right: blinkered of late: held up: suspect attitude. *J. H. M. Gosden*

RACE THE MOON 2 b.c. (Apr 25) Danetime (IRE) 121 – Arbitration (IRE)   **72**
(Bigstone (IRE) 126) [2007 5d 6d 7.1d 7m⁶ 7g p8m³ p8.6g* Oct 12] strong colt: fair
performer: improved to win nursery at Wolverhampton final start, race run to suit: stays
8.6f: acts on polytrack: tried in cheekpieces: hard ride: sent to USA. *V. Smith*

RACEY RACHEL (IRE) 2 b.f. (Feb 15) Marju (IRE) 127 – Paris Song (IRE) 69   **49**
(Peintre Celebre (USA) 137) [2007 6g p6g 8.3d⁵ 8.2g p10g p7.1g Nov 27] €16,000Y:
lengthy filly: first foal: dam, Irish maiden (stayed 9f), half-sister to smart French performer up to 1½m Papago: poor maiden: stays 1m: in blinkers (pulled hard/saddle slipped)
final start: sold 600 gns. *E. F. Vaughan*

RACIE GRACIE 2 gr.f. (Mar 20) Dr Fong (USA) 128 – Maxizone (FR) (Linamix (FR)   **54**
127) [2007 6m 6d Oct 19] unfurnished filly: fourth foal: half-sister to Scandinavian 7f (at
2 yrs, also in Britain)/1m winner Big Player (by Noverre): dam unraced out of half-sister
to Prix Jacques le Marois winner Miss Satamixa: backward in maidens at Newmarket
(modest form debut). *John Berry*

RACINGER (FR) 4 b.c. Spectrum (IRE) 126 – Dibenoise (FR) (Kendor (FR) 122)   **119**
[2007 112: 8s* 8g* 8m⁶ 8m 8d² Oct 6] €40,000Y: good-topped colt: fifth foal: half-
brother to very smart French winner around 1¼m (including Prix Ganay) Corre Caminos
(by Montjeu): dam unraced out of Poule d'Essai des Pouliches runner-up Boreale: smart

performer: improved on return at Saint-Cloud, winning Prix Edmond Blanc in April and Prix du Muguet in May, both by neck from Turtle Bowl: below form at Ascot next 2 starts, in Queen Anne Stakes (Turtle Bowl third) and Summer Mile Stakes (looked none too keen): back to form when 2 lengths second to Spirito del Vento in Prix Daniel Wildenstein at Longchamp final start: best at 1m/9f: acts on heavy ground, probably on good to firm: races prominently: sold €665,000, joined D. Watson in UAE. *F. Head, France*

RACING STRIPES (IRE) 3 ch.g. Night Shift (USA) – Swan Lake (IRE) 65 (Waajib **61** 121) [2007 75: 5.2m⁴ p6g p8g p7g Dec 16] big, lengthy gelding: fair winner at 2 yrs: left J. S. Moore after reappearance (said to have bled), and well held after: best at 5f: acts on firm going: tried blinkered. *K. O. Cunningham-Brown*

RACING TIMES 3 b.g. Danetime (IRE) 121 – Cartesian 78 (Shirley Heights 130) **72** [2007 78: p8g⁴ f7g² p6g³ p7g⁶ 7f Aug 4] rangy maiden: fair maiden: left B. Meehan after second start: will prove at least as effective at 6f as 7f/1m: acts on all-weather and good to firm going: edgy sort: has found little: sold 6,500 gns. *W. J. Knight*

RADIATOR ROONEY (IRE) 4 br.g. Elnadim (USA) 128 – Queen of The May **59** (IRE) 80 (Nicolotte 118) [2007 73: p5g p6g³ f6g 6g 5m⁶ 5g³ 5.8f 5s² 6d 5m⁵ 5g 5f p8.6g **a67** p7.1g⁵ p5.1s⁴ Dec 20] good-topped gelding: fair handicapper on all-weather, modest on turf: best at 5f/6f: acts on all-weather and firm ground: usually wears cheekpieces/blinkers. *Patrick Morris, Ireland*

RADICAL VIEWS 3 ch.g. Machiavellian (USA) 123 – Nawaiet (USA) (Zilzal (USA) **81** 137) [2007 72: 10f f7g* 8.2g⁴ 10.3s⁶ 10s p8g Oct 24] strong, compact gelding: fairly **a86** useful handicapper: won at Southwell in May: likely to prove best around 7f/1m: acts on fibresand, best turf form on good going (ran poorly on soft): sold 19,000 gns. *B. W. Hills*

RAFFAAS 3 b.g. Green Desert (USA) 127 – Felawnah (USA) 111 (Mr Prospector **94** (USA)) [2007 71: 11m⁴ p13g* 12g 14.6m⁴ Jul 13] tall, good-topped gelding: fairly useful handicapper: gelded and off 9 months, successful at Goodwood in June and Lingfield (by 6 lengths) in July: likely to prove best short of 14.6f: acts on polytrack and good to firm going: blinkered final 2-y-o start: joined D. Selvaratnam in UAE. *M. P. Tregoning*

RAFFERTY (IRE) 8 ch.g. Lion Cavern (USA) 117 – Badawi (USA) 103 (Diesis 133) **–** [2007 –, a94d: p7.1g² p7g p8g² p8g f7g⁶ p8g f7g⁴ p8g³ p7g⁵ p7g³ p7g³ p8g 8.1s⁶ **a56** 10m p10g p7g p7g⁵ p7g⁴ p7.1g⁶ p7m⁶ p6g⁶ Dec 19] angular gelding: modest performer nowadays: claimed from T. D. Barron £6,000 after reappearance: best up to 8.5f: acts on all-weather, firm and soft going: tried in headgear. *S. Dow*

RAFFISH 5 ch.g. Atraf 116 – Valadon 72 (High Line 125) [2007 –: 11.8m⁵ 12.6s* **78** 14.1d² 12v* 14m⁵ 14.1d² Aug 16] close-coupled gelding: fair handicapper: won at Warwick and York, both in July: stays 1¾m: acts on polytrack, good to firm and heavy going: in cheekpieces last 4 starts. *M. Scudamore*

RAGAD 4 b.c. Alhaarth (IRE) 126 – Waafiah 57 (Anabaa (USA) 130) [2007 74+: f6g³ **70** a7f* a5.5f³ a6.5f² Dec 20] sturdy colt: fair performer: left W. Jarvis after reappearance: off 9 months, won handicap at Nad Al Sheba in November: stays 7f: acts on dirt/fibresand. *D. Watson, UAE*

RAGAMUFFIN MAN (IRE) 2 gr.c. (Feb 15) Dalakhani (IRE) 133 – Chamela Bay **80 p** (IRE) 106 (Sadler's Wells (USA) 132) [2007 8.1g 8d³ 8g* Oct 24] lengthy colt: second foal: dam, Irish 1½m winner, sister to smart middle-distance stayer Chiang Mai and half-sister to Prix de Diane winner Rafha: fairly useful form: encouragement at Sandown and Salisbury (third behind Look Here and Doctor Fremantle), then won maiden at Bath: will be suited by 1¼m/1½m: has the scope for further progress. *W. J. Knight*

RAGHEED (USA) 3 ch.c. Rahy (USA) 115 – Highbury (USA) (Seattle Slew (USA)) **109 +** [2007 p6g 7f* 7.1g⁶ 8m* 8m* 8g² 8.1m* Sep 15] $190,000Y: lengthy, rather leggy colt: third foal: half-brother to winner in South Africa by Giant's Causeway: dam, French 1¼m/10.5f winner, half-sister to US Grade 1 9f winner Gal In A Ruckus: useful and progressive form: won maiden at Thirsk in May, and handicaps at Newmarket in July, Redcar in August and Warwick (beat Guacamole by 2 lengths) in September: stays 1m: raced only on polytrack and good or firmer going on turf: tongue tied on debut: makes running/races prominently: joined E. Charpy in UAE. *W. J. Haggas*

RAGLAN COPENHAGEN 3 b.g. Lahib (USA) 129 – Peperonata (IRE) 91 (Cyrano **72** de Bergerac 120) [2007 –: 6g³ 6s* 6m Aug 17] strong, deep-girthed gelding: fair performer, lightly raced: won maiden at Salisbury in July: raced too freely next time: should prove at least as effective at 5f as 6f: acts on soft going. *B. R. Millman*

RAG TAG (IRE) 4 b.g. Tagula (IRE) 116 – Lovat Spring (USA) (Storm Bird (CAN) **50** 134) [2007 82: p5.1g⁴ 5g Sep 19] strong gelding: fairly useful performer at best: just modest form in 2007: raced mainly at 5f: acts on firm going: tongue tied: sold 1,400 gns in October. *A. M. Balding*

RAGUANY (IRE) 5 ch.m. Pennekamp (USA) 130 – Roots Sister (USA) (Green Dancer (USA) 132) [2007 9g⁵ 11.1d⁴ 10f Aug 12] poor form in maiden hurdles in Ireland: no form on Flat in Britain. *B. Mactaggart* —

RAHAAN (USA) 2 b.f. (Mar 30) Forestry (USA) 121 – Jordanesque (USA) (Mr Prospector (USA)) [2007 8.2m Oct 3] $150,000Y: close-coupled filly: fifth foal: half-sister to 2 US sprint winners by Cherokee Run: dam unraced half-sister to smart US/UAE performer up to 1¼m Essence of Dubai, out of Breeders' Cup Juvenile Fillies' winner Epitome: 50/1 and burly, seventh to Classic Legend in maiden at Nottingham. *C. E. Brittain* **65**

RAHERE (IRE) 2 ch.c. (Mar 6) King's Best (USA) 132 – Ascot Cyclone (USA) 93 (Rahy (USA) 115) [2007 6f³ Jun 7] €27,000Y: fifth foal: half-brother to 3 winners, including useful 2002 2-y-o 6f winner Fancy Lady (by Cadeaux Genereux) and fairly useful 1¼m winner Daylami Star (by Daylami): dam, 5.7f (at 2 yrs) and 7f winner, half-sister to smart performer up to 1¼m Magellan: 9/2, length third to Lady Benjamin in maiden at Hamilton, soon disputing lead: will stay 1m: suffered minor injury after: should improve. *M. Johnston* **71 p**

RAHIYAH (USA) 3 ch.f. Rahy (USA) 115 – Meiosis (USA) 98 (Danzig (USA)) [2007 105p: 8g³ 8d 8m⁵ 7m⁵ 7g² Oct 6] strong, lengthy, attractive filly: smart performer: good 1¾ lengths third to Darjina in Poule d'Essai des Pouliches at Longchamp on reappearance: creditable effort after only when neck second to Appalachian Trail in listed race at Redcar, taking while to pick up after racing freely: stayed 1m: had won on good to firm ground, very best efforts on good/good to soft: had worn crossed noseband: had swished tail/got stirred up in paddock: stud in USA. *J. Noseda* **113**

RAIDING PARTY (IRE) 2 b.f. (May 11) Orpen (USA) 116 – Lady Angola (USA) 83 (Lord At War (ARG)) [2007 p6g⁴ p6g* p6g* 8f Dec 30] €20,000Y: second foal: dam, 1½m winner, half-sister to dam of US Grade 1 9f winner Honor In War: fairly useful form: progressed to win maiden and nursery at Wolverhampton in September/October, both with something to spare: left J. Hills, well held in non-graded stakes at Santa Anita final start: should stay 1m: acts on polytrack. *J. M. Cassidy, USA* **82**

RAIHANAH 3 b.f. Dr Fong (USA) 128 – Al Shadeedah (USA) 86 (Nureyev (USA) 131) [2007 p8.6g p6g Nov 19] fifth foal: half-sister to fairly useful 9f/1¼m winner Shirazi (by Mtoto) and French 9f winner Safeer (by Lion Cavern): dam, 1m winner, out of Australian Group 1 1m winner Copperama: tailed off in maidens. *D. Shaw* —

RAILWAY EXPRESS (IRE) 3 br.g. Lend A Hand 124 – Deerussa (IRE) (Jareer (USA) 115) [2007 60: 10s 7v³ 8s p8g⁶ p7g Nov 16] poor maiden handicapper: stays 1m: acts on polytrack and probably any turf going: tried in cheekpieces. *Bernard Lawlor, Ireland* **49**

RAIN AND SHADE 3 ch.g. Rainbow Quest (USA) 134 – Coretta (IRE) 118 (Caerleon (USA) 132) [2007 52: p9.5g² p10g² p12f 9.9m 12f May 2] tall, good-topped gelding: fair maiden: left M. Johnston after third start: no form subsequently: gelded after final start: should stay 1½m: acts on polytrack: tried tongue tied. *E. W. Tuer* **77 d**

RAINBOW BAY 4 b.g. Komaite (USA) – Bollin Victoria 51 (Jalmood (USA) 126) [2007 77: 6g⁴ 6g 6m* p6g 6.1g⁴ 6g* 6m* 5.7f⁵ 6m 5d² 5g 6m⁶ 5g 5m⁵ p6g⁴ p6g⁶ 5.1g p6g p6g² p6g Dec 29] smallish, close-coupled gelding: fairly useful performer: won apprentice claimer (left E. O'Neill £7,000) in May and handicaps (2) in June, all at Catterick: effective at 5f/6f: acts on polytrack, firm and good to soft going: usually wears headgear. *P. D. Evans* **81**

RAINBOW FLAME 3 b.g. Alhaarth (IRE) 126 – Rainbow d'Beaute 88 (Rainbow Quest (USA) 134) [2007 10g p12g⁶ 11.8s⁵ 11.9d 10.1g² 13.1f p12g p9.5g⁵ Oct 25] rangy gelding: modest maiden: left W. Swinburn after fifth start: stays 1½m: acts on polytrack and soft ground: usually blinkered/visored: sold 5,000 gns in November. *Tom Dascombe* **61**

RAINBOW FOX 3 b.g. Foxhound (USA) 103 – Bollin Victoria 51 (Jalmood (USA) 126) [2007 79: f6g 7.1m 6d³ 7m⁶ 6d⁴ 6m⁶ 6d⁴ 6m² 6s³ 6m² 6m* 6m⁴ 6g⁵ 6d³ 6g p6g⁵ Nov 14] smallish, good-topped gelding: fair handicapper: won at Ayr in July and Hamilton in August: seems best at 6f: acts on polytrack, soft and good to firm going: tried in headgear. *R. A. Fahey* **78**

RAINBOW MIRAGE (IRE) 3 b.c. Spectrum (IRE) 126 – Embers of Fame (IRE) 92 (Sadler's Wells (USA) 132) [2007 98: 6m 6m 7g 6m³ 7m 6d² p6g³ p6g⁶ p7.1g² Nov 30] strong colt: fairly useful handicapper: placed 4 times: stays 7f: acts on polytrack, soft and good to firm going: tried blinkered. *E. S. McMahon* **92**

RAINBOW PRINCE 4 b.g. Desert Prince (IRE) 130 – Eve 81 (Rainbow Quest (USA) –
134) [2007 50: p10g 10.1d Oct 30] strong, workmanlike gelding: poor maiden: no form
in 2007. *M. J. Gingell*

RAINBOW PROMISES (USA) 3 b. or br.f. Came Home (USA) 122 – To Be A **99**
Lover (USA) (The Minstrel (CAN) 135) [2007 99P: 7g 8d Aug 19] well-made filly:
excellent impression when winning maiden at Lingfield only outing at 2 yrs: changed
hands privately after and reportedly suffered 2 minor setbacks: better than result in Oak
Tree Stakes at Goodwood on belated return, dropped out and not clear run: last in listed
race at Bath only subsequent start: should stay at least 1m. *B. J. Meehan*

RAINBOW'S CLASSIC 4 b.g. Muhtarram (USA) 125 – Legend of Aragon 67 (Ara- –
gon 118) [2007 70: p8.6g f6g f8g Mar 13] strong gelding: fair maiden at best: no form in
2007: tried in blinkers/cheekpieces/tongue tie. *P. Beaumont*

RAINBOWS GUEST (IRE) 4 ch.f. Indian Lodge (IRE) 127 – Maura's Guest (IRE) **73**
(Be My Guest (USA) 126) [2007 75: f7g² Jan 16] strong filly: fair performer: stays 1m:
acts on fibresand: visored last 5 starts. *A. M. Balding*

RAINCOAT 3 b.c. Barathea (IRE) 127 – Love The Rain (Rainbow Quest (USA) 134) **115**
[2007 91p: 10.1g* 10.4g² 10.5g 12g³ 14.6m Sep 15] rangy colt: smart performer: won
4-runner minor event at Epsom in April by 4 lengths from Dubai Twilight: kept pattern
company after, best form when 4 lengths second to Authorized in Dante Stakes at
York and length third to Yellowstone in Gordon Stakes at Goodwood: below form in
Prix du Jockey Club at Chantilly and St Leger at Doncaster otherwise, folding as though
all wasn't well in latter: should stay 1¾m: raced only on good/good to firm ground.
J. H. M. Gosden

RAINES BOY 2 ch.c. (May 3) Dr Fong (USA) 128 – Come To The Point (Pursuit of –
Love 124) [2007 7d p8.6g Oct 30] sturdy colt: no form. *N. P. Littmoden*

RAIN STOPS PLAY (IRE) 5 b.g. Desert Prince (IRE) 130 – Pinta (IRE) (Ahonoora **86 §**
122) [2007 97§: p10g 8s 8.1m⁵ 8.1g⁶ 8g 8.5d 8d 8g² 8.2g 8m⁶ 8m⁵ 8.3d 8g p8.6g⁴ Nov 14] **a73 §**
leggy gelding: fairly useful handicapper on turf, fair on all-weather: stays 9f: acts on firm
and soft going: visored (below form) once: front runner: sometimes hangs/carries head
awkwardly: unreliable. *M. Quinn*

RAISE AGAIN (IRE) 4 b.g. Raise A Grand (IRE) 114 – Paryiana (IRE) (Shernazar **57**
131) [2007 72: 8.7g 8.5m p8g 10d p7g⁴ p10m f8g⁵ Dec 27] modest handicapper: left
P. Prendergast in Ireland after second start: stays 1m: acts on polytrack and probably any
turf going: tried blinkered. *Mrs P. N. Dutfield*

RAISE THE GOBLET (IRE) 3 b.g. Almutawakel 126 – Saninka (IRE) 82 (Doyoun **82**
124) [2007 60: 10.1g* 11.5s² 12s p11g* 11.5m² p12g² Sep 5] workmanlike gelding: fairly
useful handicapper: won at Yarmouth in May and Kempton in August: stays 1½m: acts
on polytrack, soft and good to firm ground: usually races up with pace, below form when
held up in visor third start (raced freely): sold 110,000 gns in October. *W. J. Haggas*

RAISE THE HEIGHTS (IRE) 4 b.g. Orpen (USA) 116 – Blue Heights (IRE) **73**
(Persian Heights 129) [2007 67: p11g² f12g² f14g p12.2g p12g² 11.8g Oct 16] fair handicapper: left J. Portman after third outing, C. Tinkler after fifth: stays 1½m: raced only
on all-weather and good/good to soft ground: tried tongue tied: has been slowly away.
B. J. Llewellyn

RAJAM 9 b.g. Sadler's Wells (USA) 132 – Rafif (USA) 68 (Riverman (USA) 131) –
[2007 63d: 14.1m⁶ 11.1m Aug 31] sturdy gelding: modest handicapper at 8 yrs: lightly
raced and no form on Flat in 2007: has worn headgear: tried tongue tied: fair hurdler/
chaser for W. Goldsworthy. *P. C. Haslam*

RAJAYOGA 6 ch.g. Kris 135 – Optimistic 90 (Reprimand 122) [2007 53: p16g⁴ 15.8m⁶ **56**
p16.5g⁴ 16f⁵ 18d* 16g Sep 20] modest handicapper: won maiden event at Chepstow in
August: stays 2¼m: acts on polytrack, firm and good to soft going. *M. H. Tompkins*

RAJEH (IRE) 4 b.g. Key of Luck (USA) 126 – Saramacca (IRE) 54 (Kahyasi 130) **93**
[2007 89: 12d³ Aug 21] sturdy gelding: fairly useful performer: good 4 lengths third to
Galactic Star in handicap at York sole run on Flat in 2007 (fairly useful hurdler): should
stay 1¾m: acts on good to firm and good to soft ground. *J. L. Spearing*

RAKATA (USA) 5 b.m. Quiet American (USA) – Haleakala (IRE) 99 (Kris 135) [2007 **83**
83: p8g³ 9m 8d 8.3m⁴ 8m⁶ p8g Oct 14] good-topped mare: fairly useful performer: stays
1m: acts on polytrack, soft and good to firm going: tried tongue tied: free-going sort.
P. F. I. Cole

RAKEEKAH 2 b.f. (Apr 17) Bahri (USA) 125 – Amanah (USA) 100 (Mr Prospector **66 p**
(USA)) [2007 7s⁶ 8d⁶ p7g Nov 17] half-sister to 3 winners, notably 7f (Rockfel Stakes)/
1m (1000 Guineas winner) Lahan (by Unfuwain): dam, 1m winner, out of US Grade 1 1m
and 8.5f winner Cheval Volant: fair form in maidens: should be suited by 1m: capable of
better. *J. H. M. Gosden*

RALLYING CRY (USA) 3 b. or br.c. War Chant (USA) 126 – Turning Wheel (USA) **105**
108 (Seeking The Gold (USA)) [2007 110: a8f³ a9f³ a9f⁴ 10d² 8m Aug 4] rangy, quite
good-topped colt: just useful performer in 2007, best efforts in UAE Derby at Nad Al
Sheba (5 lengths third to Asiatic Boy on reappearance, left I. Mohammed after next start)
and minor event at Leicester (off 3½ months, length second of 3 to Big Robert): reportedly lost action when well held in listed race at Goodwood final start: stays 1¼m: acts on
polytrack, firm and good to soft going: tongue tied last 2 outings. *Saeed bin Suroor*

RAMAAD 2 ch.g. (Feb 23) Dr Fong (USA) 128 – Artifice 80 (Green Desert (USA) 127) **77 p**
[2007 6m² Sep 21] 70,000Y: attractive gelding: third foal: dam, 6f winner, sister to smart
7f/1m performer Ardkinglass: 9/1, promising second to Red Rumour in maiden at
Newmarket, closing in wide and late: will stay 7f/1m: sure to improve. *W. J. Haggas*

RAMATNI 2 b.f. (Mar 10) Green Desert (USA) 127 – Wardat Allayl (IRE) 87 (Mtoto **88**
134) [2007 5m² 5m² 5m⁵ 6d² 6g³ 6m* 6m 6m² p6g² 6g* Nov 6] well-made filly: third
foal: sister to 3-y-o Shot Gun: dam, 2-y-o 7f winner, half-sister to smart performers Bint
Allayl (leading 2-y-o filly in 1998) and Kheleyf (6f/7f performer), both by Green Desert:
fairly useful performer: generally progressive, won nurseries at Hamilton in August and
Catterick in November: should prove best kept to 5f/6f: acts on polytrack and good to
firm going: front runner. *M. Johnston*

RAMBLIN BOB 2 b.c. (Apr 3) Piccolo 121 – Bijan (IRE) 75 (Mukaddamah (USA) **69**
125) [2007 5m 5g⁴ 6g* 7m 6.1m⁵ 5.5m p7g³ p6g³ p8.6g p7g Dec 19] quite attractive colt:
fair performer: won maiden at Salisbury in June: left R. Beckett 7,500 gns after eighth
start: best up to 7f: acts on polytrack and good to firm going: ran creditably in blinkers.
W. J. Musson

RAMBLING LIGHT 3 b.g. Fantastic Light (USA) 134 – Rambler 74 (Selkirk (USA) **87**
129) [2007 69p: p8g³ p8.6g* p8g⁴ Jul 11] smallish, well-made, attractive gelding: progressive form: won maiden at Wolverhampton in March: still green when good fourth to
Electric Warrior on handicap debut at Kempton final start (gelded after): may prove best
up to 8.6f: raced only on polytrack and good ground. *A. M. Balding*

RAMBLING SOCKS 4 ch.f. Rambling Bear 115 – Cledeschamps 46 (Doc Marten **44**
104) [2007 42: p7.1g p8.6g p9.5g 7g⁵ 8m Jun 12] leggy filly: poor maiden: best at 5f/6f:
acts on all-weather: often blinkered/in cheekpieces/tongue tied. *S. R. Bowring*

RAMONA CHASE 2 b.c. (Mar 31) High Chaparral (IRE) 132 – Audacieuse 113 **99**
(Rainbow Quest (USA) 134) [2007 5g² 7g⁴ 7g⁶ 8g* 8m 8s 7d Oct 27] 90,000Y: leggy
colt: second foal: dam, French 1m to 10.5f winner, half-sister to useful stayer Lord Jim:
useful performer: ran well in listed races at Royal Ascot (fourth to Maze) and Newbury
(sixth to Sharp Nephew) prior to winning minor event at Salisbury in September: unseated rider early next time, well below form last 2 starts: free-going sort, best up to 1m.
S. Kirk

RAMONTI (FR) 5 b.h. Martino Alonso (IRE) 113§ – Fosca (USA) (El Gran Senor **126**
(USA) 136) [2007 122: 8g² 8m* 8g* 8g² 8d* 10g* Dec 9]
　　Asked after the success of Ramonti in the Sussex Stakes for a response to
media criticism that Godolphin was 'underperforming', racing manager Simon
Crisford said that he and the training team 'can only play with the cards we've been
dealt.' As a defence of those handling the horses it was fair enough, but the analogy
seemed somewhat incongruous given that Godolphin comes to the table with a
bigger bank than any other player and has a reputation for discarding a weak hand,
if it has one, and dealing itself another. While many of the expensive private
purchases made by Godolphin in recent seasons have not come up to the mark, its
latest hand turned out to contain an ace from one of the least likely sources, the
domestic Italian racing scene. Italy relies fairly heavily on imports, particularly
from Britain and Ireland, for its racing stock, the standing of its breeding industry
nowhere near so high as it once was. Those top-class ex-Italians Falbrav and Rakti
were fine recent adverts for the country where they started their racing careers but
both were by stallions based outside Italy. Ramonti, on the other hand, is by an
Italian-raced and -based stallion out of an Italian mare. Ramonti's sire Martino

Alonso was bred by Godolphin but it was Ramonti's racing record, rather than his pedigree, that must have made him look an attractive purchase. Eight wins from thirteen starts for Alduino and Giuseppe Botti included the Premio Parioli (Italian Two Thousand Guineas) and three domestic pattern races at a mile as a four-year-old, the Premio Emilio Turati, the Premio Vittorio di Capua (Group 1) and the Premio Ribot. Ramonti ran twice for the Bottis outside his native country, finishing seventh behind Godolphin's Librettist in the Prix Jacques le Marois at Deauville and a creditable third in the Hong Kong Mile at Sha Tin on his final start.

Front-running Ramonti was beaten only a head in the Derby Italiano on his only start beyond nine furlongs, but Godolphin planned his campaign as a five-year-old around the top mile races for his type in Britain and France. He contested all four Group 1s at the distance in Britain open to horses above the age of three, winning three of them, and then crowned his campaign when landing the mile-and-a-quarter Hong Kong Cup, the most valuable of the four Group 1 events at Hong Kong's international meeting in December, becoming the second to win that race in Godolphin's colours, following Fantastic Light in 2000. Ramonti kept his form very well in a campaign which stretched from May to December and his record is hard to fault. He finished second on his two other appearances, in the Lockinge and the Prix du Moulin, and was most genuine and consistent. That said, Ramonti's four victories included particularly close calls in the Queen Anne and the Sussex Stakes, and Frankie Dettori's tactical awareness and strength played a big part in his overall success. Dettori's quote after the Hong Kong Cup—'he's the toughest battler I've ever ridden, and I'm very good on him'—may have sounded immodest but it was a valid assessment. The only race in which Dettori's tactical handling of Ramonti could have been criticised—but only in hindsight—was in the Lockinge at Newbury on his reappearance. He probably rode Ramonti with a little too much restraint and also kept him a little isolated from the other runners. The race developed into a muddling affair in which Red Evie held Ramonti's strong finish by a head in a three-way photo also involving 20/1-shot Passager. That Passager finished so close underlined the latest Lockinge's shortcomings as a Group 1. Ramonti's form in the Lockinge wasn't far behind the pick of his Italian form and he looked fit beforehand. It was far from obvious that he was even going to become one of the leading lights in his stable, let alone make a wider impact. *Timeform Perspective* concluded after the Lockinge: 'It will be a surprise if any of these are challenging for top miling honours come the end of the season.'

Queen Anne Stakes, Royal Ascot—two short heads and a head separate Ramonti, Jeremy (far side), Turtle Bowl (nearest camera) and George Washington (No.2)

BGC Sussex Stakes, Goodwood—Ramonti (left) gets first run on Excellent Art;
Jeremy (second right) and the South African-trained Asiatic Boy are next

Dettori admitted that he 'didn't really know Ramonti when I rode him in the Lockinge . . . my friend Endo Botti who rode him last year told me afterwards to be brave because the horse stays well.' Dettori was peerless on Ramonti next time, in the Queen Anne Stakes at Royal Ascot, a race won six times before by Godolphin's trainer Saeed bin Suroor and five times before by Dettori (including in the first year out of his apprenticeship in 1990). The Queen Anne, which did not become a Group 1 until 2003 (the Lockinge was made a Group 1 in 1995), attracted Red Evie and the fifth in the Lockinge, Jeremy, who had won the previous year's Jersey Stakes, as well as Racinger and Turtle Bowl, the first two in the Group 2 Prix du Muguet (in which Passager had come third) and the previous year's Royal Hunt Cup winner Cesare, supplemented after winning a listed event impressively over the course and distance on his reappearance. All eyes, though, were on the 2006 Horse of The Year George Washington, odds on for his first appearance since being put back into training after suffering fertility problems at stud. Ramonti was third favourite at 5/1 (behind Cesare in the betting but at shorter odds than Red Evie) in what looked a below-par renewal beforehand, with the probable exception of George Washington. With front-running tactics readopted, Dettori was able to dictate things on Ramonti who responded very gamely under the whip once the race began in earnest in the home straight, especially after being headed by Jeremy. Ramonti's cause was helped when Jeremy spoiled his finishing effort by hanging right and, with Dettori at his most forceful, Ramonti battled back to win in a blanket finish from Jeremy, Turtle Bowl and George Washington, the last-named getting going too late, the distances in a pulsating finish a short head, a short head and a head. Cesare finished on the heels of the first four, with Racinger and Red Evie next.

Ramonti's victory was Godolphin's first in a Group 1 in Britain since Punctilious won the Yorkshire Oaks in 2005, and Dettori's first British Group 1 in Godolphin's colours since Sulamani in the Juddmonte International in 2004. There was a sting in the tail for Dettori, though, as he was referred by the Royal Ascot stewards to the Horseracing Regulatory Authority for using his whip with excessive frequency and without giving his mount time to respond. The Royal Ascot stewards considered that Dettori's offence—he struck Ramonti around twenty-five times in the last two furlongs—warranted more than the seven days they could have imposed. When the Shaftesbury Avenue hearing was finally heard in early-July, Dettori was punished with a fourteen-day ban, despite offering a defence that Ramonti was an experienced older horse and had continued to respond to the whip. Veterinary evidence was also submitted by Godolphin that Ramonti 'returned to the stable in good condition' and ate up and walked and jogged the next day. Jeremy's rider also received a two-day ban and George Washington's rider a one-day ban for whip offences in the finish to the Queen Anne, illustrating, if nothing else, the unworkability of the idea that the mounts of jockeys found guilty of whip offences should be disqualified; third-placed Turtle Bowl would have been declared the winner from fifth-placed Cesare and sixth-placed Racinger if such a rule had been in force. The whip was under the spotlight for a good part of the season as more riders than usual came into conflict with the racing authorities over the issue. A new style of shock-absorbing whip became compulsory from April 1st but some jockeys considered it was not so effective as its predecessors and needed using more often and with greater force. Most, however, supported the new whip, which was less hard on horses and reduced the risk of them being marked. 'We are all using the same whip so nobody is being disadvantaged,' seemed to be the majority view among jockeys. In another high profile case, Eddie Ahern was banned for three months for bringing racing into disrepute when deliberately flouting the whip guidelines at Southwell in December in order to bring forward a suspension impending under the 'totting-up' rules.

Ramonti showed absolutely no ill-effects from his race in the Queen Anne Stakes when making his next appearance six weeks later in the BGC Sussex Stakes at Goodwood, where Ballydoyle saddled the St James's Palace Stakes winner Excellent Art. The Sussex Stakes used to be regarded as virtually the British miling championship until it began to be challenged after the mid-'eighties by the Queen Elizabeth II Stakes at Ascot. The Queen Elizabeth was raised to Group 1 in 1987, with the runners meeting at strict weight-for-age, and soon provided strong competition to the Sussex for the right to be regarded as the most important of Britain's open-aged mile races. Since 1987, the three-year-olds have had the upper hand over the older horses in both races, four-year-olds and upwards winning nine of the twenty-one renewals of the Sussex and eight renewals of the Queen Elizabeth. The three-year-olds Warning (1988), Zilzal (1989) and Bigstone (1993) were the only horses before Ramonti to complete the Sussex/Queen Elizabeth double during the period that both have been Group 1s. The last horse above the age of three to win both races in the same year was the four-year-old Jimmy Reppin in 1969 when, incidentally, he was beaten in the Lockinge and the Queen Anne (in both of which, because of penalties and allowances, he came out the best horse at the weights, in the Lockinge dividing Habitat and that year's Two Thousand Guineas runner-up Tower Walk). Jimmy Reppin, who won six of his ten races in 1969, contested the Queen Elizabeth only because the going was too firm for his stablemate the Two Thousand Guineas winner Right Tack. The latest Sussex Stakes wasn't seen at the time as a duel between Royal Ascot's two Group 1-winning milers. Excellent Art started favourite, with Jeremy and the South African-trained challenger Asiatic Boy (winner of the UAE 2000 Guineas and Derby) also at shorter odds than Ramonti in the field of eight. However, it was the two Royal Ascot winners who came to the fore, Dettori outmanoeuvring Spencer on Excellent Art by making first run two furlongs out after two stablemates of Excellent Art had dictated the pace. Excellent Art was gaining on Ramonti with every stride at the finish but Ramonti held on by a head, with Jeremy, who kept much straighter than at Royal Ascot, pipping Asiatic Boy for third, a further length and three quarters back, the first four clear.

Queen Elizabeth II Stakes, Ascot—Ramonti is given another excellent ride by Frankie Dettori to again get the better of Excellent Art (dark colours, right of centre); Duke of Marmalade (rail), Cesare (centre left), the grey Stormy River, Blue Ksar and Darjina (right) are next

Cathay Pacific Hong Kong Cup, Sha Tin—Ramonti (left) holds off odds-on Viva Pataca (dark colours) to gain his fourth Group 1 success of the year

Ramonti faced Excellent Art and Ballydoyle's St James's Palace runner-up Duke of Marmalade in the Queen Elizabeth II Stakes at Ascot in September, when he also met the top French three-year-old filly Darjina three weeks after she had beaten him into second (with George Washington third) in the Prix du Moulin de Longchamp. There were only seven runners in the Queen Elizabeth for which Excellent Art, who had not run since the Sussex, started favourite, with Darjina second favourite and Ramonti third best, just ahead of Cesare, a good second in the Celebration Mile at Goodwood on his latest appearance, and Duke of Marmalade. Another copybook ride by Dettori, who took the initiative early in the home straight before Excellent Art had hit top pace, saw Ramonti home by half a length. Ramonti found plenty as Excellent Art stormed home, after being hemmed in briefly two furlongs out by Darjina, having too much to do and looking unlucky. The front-running Duke of Marmalade virtually reproduced his St James's Palace form with Excellent Art, finishing another half a length back in third, a head in front of Cesare with Darjina, clearly well below her best on the day, last.

Ramonti's victory in the Queen Elizabeth took his prize money earnings for the season on home soil to £489,333, which accounted for just under a third of the total won by the Godolphin stable in Britain in 2007. Godolphin finished top of the owners' table and Saeed bin Suroor, who saddled seventy-three winners at an impressive ratio of winners to runners of over one in four, ended the season in sixth place in the trainers' table, the same as in the two other seasons since he won his third title in 2004. Plans for Ramonti after Ascot remained uncertain at first—'it's been a tough six months for him with no let-up'—but he reportedly came out of the race in fine form and was aimed at the Hong Kong international meeting in preference to the Breeders' Cup. While new acquisition Creachadoir represented Godolphin in the Hong Kong Mile (finishing second, with Darjina third and Excellent Art eighth), Ramonti was pitted against local champion Viva Pataca in an unusually small field for the Cathay Pacific Hong Kong Cup. Viva Pataca, who raced as Comic Strip as a two-year-old in Britain, had improved since his fourth in the race the previous year, having beaten Dubai Sheema Classic winner Vengeance of Rain and the Japanese-trained Dubai Duty Free winner Admire Moon in the Queen Elizabeth II Cup in the spring and won the main trial for the Hong Kong Cup in November. Vengeance of Rain, who won the Hong Kong Cup in 2005 and finished third in 2006, was also in the line-up but was only third favourite. Viva Pataca started at 100/30-on and Ramonti at 38/10. Ramonti didn't quite have to match his best form at a mile to get the better of Viva Pataca, Dettori settling him in third and keeping Viva Pataca in a pocket behind the two front runners before sending on Ramonti a furlong out. Ramonti held off Viva Pataca, who had to be switched to get a run, by half a length, with French challenger Musical Way a further two and a half lengths back in third and Vengeance of Rain sixth. The stewards looked into the incident involving Ramonti and Viva Pataca in the straight, connections enduring a lengthy wait before Ramonti was confirmed the winner.

Ramonti (FR) (b.h. 2002)	Martino Alonso (IRE) (b 1994)	Marju (br 1988)	Last Tycoon, Flame of Tara
		Cheerful Note (b 1987)	Cure The Blues, Strident Note
	Fosca (USA) (b 1995)	El Gran Senor (b 1981)	Northern Dancer, Sex Appeal
		La Locandiera (b 1986)	Alleged, Moon Ingraver

Ramonti is not a particularly striking individual, being rather leggy and useful-looking, but he usually impresses in appearance and looked in tremendous shape before both the Sussex Stakes and the Queen Elizabeth II Stakes. His sire Martino Alonso, who stands at the Azienda Agricola Antezzate at Brescia at a fee of €10,000, was bought by BBA Italia for just IR 6,400 guineas as a yearling at the Tattersalls Ireland September Sales. He was kept in training until he was six, winning nine of his thirty-three races, successful in listed company at a mile and a

Godolphin's "Ramonti"

mile and a quarter and placed in two Group 1s, the Premio Vittorio di Capua and the
mile-and-a-quarter Premio Roma, and was seemingly effective from a mile to a
mile and three quarters. Martino Alonso was a smart racehorse but he invariably
found little and was ungenuine. Ramonti is from Martino Alonso's small first crop
and is the third foal out of the El Gran Senor mare Fosca, who ran only twice but is
doing considerably better at stud, having produced the Italian winners Fosglen
(by Glen Jordan) and Foscallo (by Tibullo) before Ramonti. Fosca is a half-sister to
Black Wood, the dam of Premio Parioli-placed Ceprin. Ramonti's grandam La Loc-
andiera was a listed winner at nine furlongs in Italy and his great grandam Moon
Ingraver won the Prix d'Astarte over a mile when that event was a Group 3. Moon
Ingraver's dam Engraving was out of a half-sister to the Derby winner Charlottown.
The usually tongue-tied Ramonti, who is effective at a mile and a mile and a quarter,
acts on good to firm and good to soft ground. He stays in training. *Saeed bin Suroor*

RAMPALLION 4 b.g. Daylami (IRE) 138 – Minute Waltz (Sadler's Wells (USA) 132) **102**
[2007 106p: 12m⁵ 12g⁵ 12m Nov 10] big, good-topped gelding: useful handicapper, very
lightly raced: easily best effort in 2007 when 2½ lengths fifth to All The Good at Ascot
second start: stays 1½m: acts on good to soft going (below form both starts on good to
firm): joined E. Charpy in UAE. *Saeed bin Suroor*

RAMPANT RONNIE (USA) 2 b.r. (Apr 9) Honor Glide (USA) 119 – Jalfrezi 103 **59**
(Jalmood (USA) 126) [2007 7f p8g⁵ 6m p8m p8.6g³ Oct 26] modest maiden on balance:
third in nursery at Wolverhampton: stays 8.6f: acts on polytrack. *P. W. D'Arcy*

RAMVASWANI (IRE) 4 b.g. Spectrum (IRE) 126 – Caesarea (GER) (Generous (IRE) **63**
139) [2007 –: p12m⁴ Oct 3] left R. Watson in Ireland and fit from hurdling, best effort in
maidens when 9 lengths fourth to Top Tiger at Kempton sole Flat start in 2007: stays
1½m: acts on polytrack. *N. B. King*

RANAVALONA 3 br.f. Diktat 126 – Syrian Queen 82 (Slip Anchor 136) [2007 54: p7g² **56**
p8g p7f² p7g² f7g⁴ p7.1g⁴ 10m³ 11g 10f 11.6m³ 10m 10.3m 9.8m³ 12.1m 10f⁴ 12.1d⁶
Sep 25] good-topped filly: modest maiden: claimed from A. Balding sixth start: stays
11.6f: acts on polytrack and good to firm going: visored early in 2007, tongue tied later:
sometimes races freely: has twice had breathing problem. *C. Smith*

RANDAMA BAY (IRE) 2 b. or br.c. (Apr 24) Frenchmans Bay (FR) 118 – Randama **74**
77 (Akarad (FR) 130) [2007 7g 6f p7g² p7g⁵ Nov 7] fourth foal: dam, staying maiden/
winning hurdler, half-sister to very smart French/US middle-distance performer Rainbow Dancer: fair maiden: runner-up at Lingfield (66/1, dictated): will stay at least 1m.
I. A. Wood

RANGALI BELLE 3 b.f. Diktat 126 – Dalaauna 62 (Cadeaux Genereux 131) [2007 **–**
68p: 8m 9m 7m p8g p8g p6g Nov 28] workmanlike filly: maiden: little form since only
outing at 2 yrs: carries head high. *C. A. Horgan*

RANKAYO HITAM (USA) 2 b.c. (Apr 2) Yonaguska (USA) 112 – Catala (USA) **71 p**
(Northern Park (USA) 107) [2007 p7m⁵ p8g³ Dec 28] $130,000F, $100,000Y: third foal:
half-brother to 4-y-o Northern Boy: dam US winner around 1m: fair form in maidens
at Lingfield, not run of race when third to Age of Reason: stays 1m: capable of better.
J. S. Moore

RANN NA CILLE (IRE) 3 b.f. Agnes World (USA) 123 – Omanah (USA) (Kayra- **72**
wan (USA) 91) [2007 67: f6g² f6g³ p6g⁴ p6g 7.1g p6g³ 7m³ 7.5s⁵ p6g 5m* 5g 6g⁶ 5g⁶
5m⁴ 5m² 6s p5.1g³ p6g Nov 14] fair handicapper: won selling event at Ripon in August:
left K. Ryan 3,500 gns before final start: stays 1m, mostly races at shorter (effective at
5f): acts on all-weather, good to firm and good to soft going: wears cheekpieces/blinkers.
P. T. Midgley

RANNOCH 2 ch.c. (Feb 9) Best of The Bests (IRE) 122 – Concubine (IRE) 76 (Dane- **40 ?**
hill (USA) 126) [2007 p5g 7g p5g⁴ 6g 6f⁴ Jul 30] poor maiden: fourth in sellers: bred to
stay 7f. *Miss D. A. McHale*

RANSOM CAPTIVE (USA) 3 b.f. Red Ransom (USA) – Cap Rouge (USA) (Sum- **91**
mer Squall (USA)) [2007 85p: p8g 10g³ 10m⁶ 10.1s³ 8.1m 9m Sep 15] strong, close-
coupled filly: fairly useful performer: mostly creditable efforts in 2007, third in listed
races at Newbury and Newcastle: stays 1¼m: acts on soft and good to firm going: sold
115,000 gns, sent to USA. *M. A. Magnusson*

RANSOM STRIP (USA) 4 b.g. Red Ransom (USA) – L'Extra Honor (USA) (Hero's –
Honor (USA)) [2007 71: 14m May 4] fair performer: well beaten sole start in 2007:
should stay 1½m: acts on polytrack and firm ground. *R. A. Fahey*

RAPID CITY 4 b.g. Dansili 127 – West Dakota (USA) (Gone West (USA)) [2007 87p: **97**
p10g² p10g* p10g² p8g⁴ 8m Apr 21] lengthy gelding: useful handicapper: successful 3 of
first 4 outings in Britain, including at Lingfield in January: good 1¾ lengths second to
Mighty at same course next time: ran as though needing further than 1m final 2 starts:
stays 1¼m: acts on polytrack. *Miss J. Feilden*

RAPID FLOW 5 b.g. Fasliyev (USA) 120 – Fleet River (USA) 93 (Riverman (USA) **53**
131) [2007 47: p6g³ p5.1g p8.6d⁴ Dec 10] lengthy, workmanlike gelding: modest maiden:
probably stays 8.6f: acts on polytrack: inconsistent. *J. W. Unett*

RAPIDITY 2 b.c. (Feb 27) Mind Games 121 – Lunasa (IRE) 82 (Don't Forget Me 127) **60**
[2007 6s⁶ 7d⁶ 7g⁶ Aug 17] fifth foal: half-brother to 3 winners, including fairly useful
6f (at 2 yrs) and 7.5f winner Voodoo Moon (by Efisio) and 9.7f winner Moonfleet (by
Entrepreneur): dam, Irish 1¾m winner, out of half-sister to St Leger winner Moon Madness: modest form in maidens: stays 7f. *E. J. O'Neill*

RAPTOR (GER) 4 b.c. Auenadler (GER) 114 – Royal Cat (Royal Academy (USA) **106**
130) [2007 8s⁴ 9m 7d³ p8g³ p8g² Dec 22] big, good-topped colt: brother to smart German
sprinter Raffelberger and half-brother to 6f winner (including at 2 yrs) Trustthunder (by
Selkirk) and German 1m winner Rebecca Rheinberg (by Surako): dam unraced: useful
performer: won 3 times in Germany at 3 yrs for M. Hofer: generally ran well in 2007,
particularly when third to Ventura in listed race at Kempton penultimate start: should stay
1¼m: acts on polytrack and heavy going, probably good to firm. *K. R. Burke*

RAQUEL WHITE 3 b.f. Robellino (USA) 127 – Spinella (Teenoso (USA) 135) [2007 **71**
57: p8.6g³ p7.1g⁴ p8.6g⁴ p10g p9.5g³ p8.6g⁶ 12.1g³ 11.5m⁵ 12.1s* 12.1s³ 11.6f p12.2g²
p12g³ p13.9g⁶ p12.2d³ Dec 27] workmanlike filly: fair performer: claimed from
P. D. Evans after reappearance: won handicap at Beverley in June: stays 1½m: acts on
polytrack and soft going: tried blinkered: free-going sort. *J. L. Flint*

RARE BREED 4 b.g. Foxhound (USA) 103 – Rare Indigo 80 (Timeless Times (USA) **66**
99) [2007 85: 5g p5.1g 5m 5.2d 5.1d³ 5m⁶ 5m Aug 31] good-topped gelding: fair
performer nowadays: speedy, raced only at 5f: acts on good to soft going, probably on
firm. *Mrs L. Stubbs*

RARE COINCIDENCE 6 ch.g. Atraf 116 – Green Seed (IRE) 78 (Lead On Time **76**
(USA) 123) [2007 66: f14g³ 12g* 14.1m* 13.1d² 11.1d² 12d³ p16.5g 13g* 12.1m³ 12d
12s p13.9g² p16.5g³ Dec 3] quite good-topped gelding: fair handicapper: won at Southwell (apprentices) in April, Nottingham in May and Hamilton (amateurs) in September:
stays 2m: acts on all-weather, firm and soft ground: wears cheekpieces: tongue tied once:
front runner. *R. F. Fisher*

RARE CROSS (IRE) 5 b.m. Cape Cross (IRE) 129 – Hebrides (Gone West (USA)) **73**
[2007 87: 5.3f 5g⁵ 5s² 5d 5g Jul 27] sturdy mare: fair handicapper: left R. Teal after third
start: headstrong, best at 5f: probably acts on any going: reportedly in foal to Iceman.
D. Shaw

RASAMAN (IRE) 3 b.g. Namid 128 – Rasana 74 (Royal Academy (USA) 130) [2007 **90**
73: p6g* p6g* p6g³ p6g⁴ 5g⁴ 5g 5m³ 5.1g Sep 29] sturdy gelding: type to carry condition:
fairly useful performer: won maiden in April and handicap in May, both at Lingfield:
best effort when third in similar event at Sandown seventh start: effective at 5f/6f: acts on
polytrack, raced only on good/good to firm ground on turf: sold 25,000 gns in October.
M. A. Jarvis

RASCASSE 2 b.c. (Apr 13) Where Or When (IRE) 124 – Sure Flyer (IRE) (Sure Blade –
(USA) 130) [2007 6m⁶ Sep 22] 100/1, well held in maiden at Catterick. *Garry Moss*

RASHIDA 5 b.m. King's Best (USA) 132 – Nimble Lady (AUS) (Fairy King (USA)) **55**
[2007 73d: 12.1s⁶ 11.5m⁵ Aug 10] rangy mare: modest handicapper: stays 8.6f: acts on
polytrack and good to firm going: tried in cheekpieces/visor/tongue tie. *S. Lycett*

RASH JUDGEMENT 2 b.c. (Apr 26) Mark of Esteem (IRE) 137 – Let Alone 78 **88 p**
(Warning 136) [2007 5m³ 6f² 6m* 6m 6m² Nov 10] 38,000Y: deep-girthed colt: fourth
foal: half-brother to 2 winners, including 4-y-o Tabulate: dam, 1m winner, out of half-
sister to very smart 1½m performer Urgent Request: fairly useful form: won minor event
at Windsor in August: good second to Generous Thought in nursery at Doncaster final
start, travelling strongly long way: likely to stay 7f/1m: acts on firm going: will go on
improving. *W. S. Kittow*

RAS LAFFAN 2 b.c. (Apr 10) Vettori (IRE) 119 – Supreme Angel 85 (Beveled (USA)) **58**
[2007 7d 7f⁵ 7g⁶ p8g p8.6g⁵ Oct 12] modest maiden: stays 8.6f: acts on polytrack and
firm going. *E. S. McMahon*

RASLAN 4 b.g. Lomitas 129 – Rosia (IRE) (Mr Prospector (USA)) [2007 89: 20m 18d **90**
Oct 20] lengthy gelding: has a round action: fairly useful handicapper: much better effort
on Flat (useful hurdler) when good eighth of 20 to Full House in Ascot Stakes at Royal
Ascot: stays 2½m: acts on polytrack and good to firm ground: visored (below form) final
start. *D. E. Pipe*

RASMANI 3 ch.f. Medicean 128 – Rasmalai 71 (Sadler's Wells (USA) 132) [2007 p8m **–**
p12g f11d p8.6d Dec 27] third foal: dam, maiden (stayed 8.5f), half-sister to smart Irish
performers up to 1¼m Raiyoun and Rayouni: little form: tried visored: tongue tied: said
to have had breathing problem second start. *Miss Gay Kelleway*

RATHMOLYON 2 ch.f. (Mar 18) Bahamian Bounty 116 – Feather Circle (IRE) 64 **73 ?**
(Indian Ridge 123) [2007 p6g⁶ 6d⁶ 5.7m² 5.1f² p5.1m³ 5g Oct 8] 3,500F: workmanlike
filly: first foal: dam Irish maiden (stayed 1½m): fair maiden: second twice at Bath, seemingly easily best effort on latter occasion: should prove best at 5f/6f: acts on firm going.
D. Haydn Jones

RATIONALE (IRE) 4 b.g. Singspiel (IRE) 133 – Logic 94 (Slip Anchor 136) [2007 **88**
93: 11.6m⁶ 13.1m 14.8m⁶ 10m⁴ 12d Oct 12] tall, lengthy gelding: fairly useful handicapper: stays 1¾m: acts on good to firm and good to soft ground: tried tongue tied.
S. C. Williams

RATTAN (USA) 2 ch.c. (Feb 19) Royal Anthem (USA) 135 – Rouwaki (USA) (Mis- **85 p**
waki (USA) 124) [2007 7.1g² 8.1m² 9s² Oct 14] good-topped colt: second foal: dam, US
maiden, half-sister to US Grade 1 9f/1¼m winner Flute: fairly useful form in maidens:
runner-up all starts, beaten short head by Cool Judgement at Goodwood final one: stays
9f: acts on soft and good to firm going: should do better still. *H. R. A. Cecil*

RAUCOUS (GER) 4 b.g. Zinaad 114 – Roseola (GER) (Acatenango (GER) 127) **90**
[2007 89p: 16g* 14g⁶ 20m Jun 19] tall, leggy gelding: fairly useful handicapper, lightly
raced: won at Ripon (beat Halla San by ¾ length, making all) in April: better effort after
when creditable sixth to Sentry Duty at Newmarket: stays 2m: raced mostly on good
going or firmer: usually races prominently. *T. P. Tate*

RAUL SAHARA 5 br.g. Makbul 104 – Sheraton Heights 52 (Deploy 131) [2007 –: **55**
p8.6g² 8.1m May 7] modest maiden: stays easy 9.5f: acts on polytrack and good to firm
ground. *J. W. Unett*

RAVARINO (USA) 3 ch.f. Unbridled's Song (USA) 125 – Sous Entendu (USA) **96**
(Shadeed (USA) 135) [2007 57P: p9.5g³ 9g² 10m² p9.5g³ p10g* 9.9g* 10.3m Sep 12]
good-topped filly: useful performer: won handicaps at Lingfield in July and Beverley
(beat Zonergem by length) in August: eased as if amiss final start: likely to stay 1½m:
raced only on polytrack and good to firm ground. *Sir Michael Stoute*

RAVENHILL RALPH (IRE) 3 b.g. Raphane (USA) 102 – Winter Dolphin (IRE) 58 **55**
(Dolphin Street (FR) 125) [2007 7g 8.1s⁵ 10.2g 10.2m³ p8g Oct 4] modest maiden: stays
1¼m: acts on good to firm going. *J. G. M. O'Shea*

RAVENNA 3 ch.f. Compton Place 125 – Cultural Role 95 (Night Shift (USA)) [2007 **85**
50p: p7g³ p7g⁵ 8.1g 7g p12g* p11g* 11.5g* 12m* 12g⁵ 12m² 12.1g⁵ p12.2g Oct 2] good-
bodied filly: fairly useful performer: much improved once upped in trip, winning seller at
Lingfield in June and handicaps at Kempton and Yarmouth in July, and Thirsk in August:
good second at Thirsk after: stays 1½m: acts on polytrack, raced only on good/good to
firm ground on turf: well below form in blinkers/cheekpieces third/fourth starts, looking
none too keen in former. *M. P. Tregoning*

RAVEN RASCAL 3 b.f. Zaha (CAN) 106 – Eccentric Dancer 47 (Rambo Dancer **45**
(CAN) 107) [2007 –: f7g f8g* 9.8g 8.3m⁶ 10m 10g May 29] poor performer: won selling
handicap at Southwell in March: stays 1m: acts on fibresand. *J. F. Coupland*

RAVEN'S PASS (USA) 2 ch.c. (Feb 17) Elusive Quality (USA) – Ascutney **125 p**
(USA) (Lord At War (ARG)) [2007 7m* 7g* 7.1m* 7d³ Oct 20]
    No two-year-old performance in 2007 quite took the breath away like the
seven-length success of Raven's Pass in the Group 3 Iveco Solario Stakes at
Sandown in September, a very smart effort backed up by an excellent timefigure.
While Raven's Pass wasn't quite able to match that form when third to New
Approach in the Dewhurst Stakes at Newmarket the following month, he still looks

like making up into a top-class miler at three and makes plenty of appeal at odds of around 7/1 at the time of writing for the Two Thousand Guineas.

Raven's Pass first appeared at Newbury in June but was withdrawn at the start after breaking through his stall on his intended debut and he was ridden by David Kinsella, who had done a lot of work with the horse to help him overcome an aversion to the stalls, when winning a maiden at Yarmouth in July at 20/1. Jimmy Fortune took over when Raven's Pass appeared later the same month in a listed race at Ascot. He was 9/2 third favourite in a fairly useful field for the Kleenex Winkfield Stakes in which eight of the nine other runners had won previously but Raven's Pass made short work of them, really imposing himself on the race after halfway and beating Unnefer by five lengths. That effort, with the promise of substantial further improvement to come, saw Raven's Pass start a short-priced favourite for the Solario. In truth, the field was not particularly strong for the long-established event, with the pick of the opposition the Chesham Stakes first and second Maze and Pegasus Again and the Ascot maiden winner City Leader. Raven's Pass won in more imperious style than at Ascot, again travelling strongly close to the pace before drawing right away after two furlongs out, winning most impressively from City Leader, still looking to have plenty of running in him at the line. It was the best performance in the Solario since it became a pattern event in 1986 and Raven's Pass returned an exceptional timefigure for a juvenile below Group 1 level of 0.89 fast, equivalent to a timerating of 122. While the opposition was weakened by the poor showing of Maze, City Leader did his bit to boost the form, winning the Royal Lodge back at Ascot later in the month.

'Not particularly strong' were not words that could remotely be applied to the Dewhurst field, containing as it did many of the best two-year-old colts seen out. Raven's Pass, firmly in the public eye now, was a well-backed second favourite and for a long way looked the most likely winner, still travelling strongly, and the last on the bridle, when sent to the front two furlongs out. However, he was unable to sustain his effort and was beaten half a length and two and a half lengths by the favourite New Approach and Fast Company. The obvious explanation for Raven's Pass's floundering late on was the softer ground than any he had previously encountered, a view also put forward by jockey and trainer. Raven's Pass may handle softish ground better with maturity, but he has a real chance of reversing placings with the first two in the Guineas if there is a dry spring.

				Gone West		Mr Prospector
	Elusive Quality (USA)			(b 1984)		Secrettame
	(b 1993)			Touch of Greatness		Hero's Honor
Raven's Pass (USA)				(b 1986)		Ivory Wand
(ch.c. Feb 17, 2005)				Lord At War		General
	Ascutney (USA)			(ch 1980)		Luna Da Miel
	(b or br 1994)			Right Word		Verbatim
				(b 1982)		Oratorio

Raven's Pass has an imposing physique and was the pick of the Dewhurst field on looks. A big, strong colt, he impressed in appearance each time he ran and has the scope to train on well. His pedigree, like that of his Kentucky-based owners-breeders, is all-American. He is the sixth foal of the Grade 3 two-year-old mile winner Ascutney. She has produced two winners in the States, including the

Grade 3 mile winner Gigawatt (by Wild Again). Raven's Pass's year-older half-sister by Storm Cat, named Gentle Gale, was in training with Gosden, as now is a younger one. Ascutney is a sister to the minor stakes-winning filly Words of War, who has produced a couple of above-average performers in the very smart performer at up to a mile and a quarter E Dubai and the useful French miler No Matter What, who later won the Grade 1 Del Mar Oaks. Raven's Pass is the best European-raced runner so far by his sire Elusive Quality, the best previously being the Prix Morny winner Elusive City, though Raven's Pass has some way to go to match his best runner overall, the Kentucky Derby and Preakness Stakes winner Smarty Jones. Raven's Pass will stay a mile but wouldn't be certain to get a mile and a quarter. He may prove best on good going or firmer. A share in Raven's Pass was sold to Sheikh Mohammed for an undisclosed sum prior to the Dewhurst. *J. H. M. Gosden*

RAVINIA (USA) 3 ch.f. Rahy (USA) 115 – Reverie (USA) (Nijinsky (CAN) 138) **59**
[2007 72p: 7g 7s p8g⁶ 6.5f Dec 30] strong filly: just modest form in 2007: left B. Meehan before final start: bred to stay 1m: acts on polytrack, probably on good to firm going, well below form on soft (though said to have been in season). *B. D. A. Cecil, USA*

RAVI RIVER (IRE) 3 ch.c. Barathea (IRE) 127 – Echo River (USA) 101 (Irish River **85** (FR) 131) [2007 91+: p7g² 8g 7.1g 7.1d⁶ Jul 25] strong, good-bodied colt: fairly useful performer: left B. Hills after third start: stays 7f (stamina stretched over 1m): acts on polytrack and good to firm going. *J. R. Boyle*

RAWAABET (USA) 5 b.g. Bahhare (USA) 122 – Haddeyah (USA) 68 (Dayjur (USA) **62** 137) [2007 65: f8g p11g 11.6m⁴ 10m⁶ 11s 10.9d Jun 28] good-topped gelding: modest handicapper: stays 11.6f: acts on fibresand, good to firm and good to soft going: very slowly away final start: has run well when sweating. *P. W. Hiatt*

RAWDON (IRE) 6 b.g. Singspiel (IRE) 133 – Rebecca Sharp 122 (Machiavellian **79** (USA) 123) [2007 85: 10.5g 10g⁵ 12g⁴ 10.1d⁶ 10d⁶ 10.5m³ 10.1m³ 10.5g* 10m³ 10d³ 10g⁴ Nov 7] tall, good-topped gelding: fair handicapper nowadays: won amateur event at Haydock in September: stays 1½m: acts on polytrack, soft and good to firm going: usually visored: tends to find little. *M. L. W. Bell*

RAYDAN (IRE) 5 b.g. Danehill (USA) 126 – Rayseka (IRE) 112 (Dancing Brave **62** (USA) 140) [2007 64: p11g* p11g p12g Nov 19] modest handicapper, lightly raced: left J. Oxx after 4 yrs: won at Kempton in May: stays 13f: acts on polytrack and any turf going: blinkered twice (including for win). *D. R. Gandolfo*

RAY DIAMOND 2 ch.g. (Apr 4) Medicean 128 – Musical Twist (USA) 97 (Woodman **–** (USA) 126) [2007 7.1g 7.1m 8d Oct 30] well held in maidens: sold £2,000, then gelded. *N. P. Littmoden*

RAYHANI (USA) 4 b.g. Theatrical 128 – Bahr Alsalaam (USA) (Riverman (USA) **105** 131) [2007 99: 12m* 16g 14g⁵ 12m⁴ Sep 15] big, strong, attractive gelding: useful handicapper, lightly raced: gelded, improved form when winning at Newmarket in May by 4 lengths (value extra) from Castle Howard: best effort after when respectable fourth to Galactic Star at Doncaster: stays 1½m, (below form over further): acts on good to firm going: blinkered (raced freely) final start at 3 yrs. *M. P. Tregoning*

RAYMI COYA (CAN) 2 b.f. (Mar 14) Van Nistelrooy (USA) 108 – Something Mon **100** (USA) (Maria's Mon (USA) 121) [2007 5m* 6m³ 6g³ 7m* Oct 6] 16,000 2-y-o: leggy filly: third foal: half-sister to US sprint winners by Alydeed and Cape Town: dam unraced half-sister to smart miler Somethingdifferent: useful performer: won maiden at Lingfield in June and Finnforest Oh So Sharp Stakes at Newmarket (improved and not all out to beat Step Softly by ½ length) in October: third in minor event at Haydock and listed race at Salisbury (length behind Fashion Rocks) in between: stays 7f: raced only on good/good to firm going. *M. Botti*

RAZAANA (USA) 3 ch.f. Dixieland Band (USA) – Jinaan (USA) 72 (Mr Prospector **50** (USA)) [2007 7m Apr 20] smallish filly: second foal: dam once-raced granddaughter of Salsabil: 25/1, eighth of 16 to Promising Lead in maiden at Newbury: sold 6,000 gns in July, re-sold 3,500 gns in December. *J. L. Dunlop*

RAZA CAB (IRE) 5 b.g. Intikhab (USA) 135 – Laraissa (Machiavellian (USA) 123) **68** [2007 –, a85: p8g p7g* p7.1g⁶ p7g² 7g p7g 7.6g 8.1m Aug 7] heavy-topped gelding: **a82** fairly useful handicapper on all-weather, fair at best on turf: won at Lingfield in March: stays 1m: acts on polytrack, good to firm and good to soft going: blinkered once (raced freely) at 3 yrs: held up. *Karen George*

RAZED 4 b.g. King's Best (USA) 132 – Key Academy 103 (Royal Academy (USA) – 130) [2007 59: f8g p11g⁶ p9.5g Feb 9] big, leggy gelding: little form in 2007. *P. L. Gilligan*

RAZZANO (IRE) 3 b.f. Fasliyev (USA) 120 – Shewillifshewants (IRE) (Alzao (USA) **61** 117) [2007 63?: p7g² p6g² p7g⁶ p8g⁵ p7.1g³ 8.5g² 9m⁵ 11.5m 8d² 8.1m 7f* 6g³ 7g³ p6g⁶ p6g⁵ Oct 29] stocky filly: modest performer: left P. D. Evans after reappearance: won maiden handicap at Brighton in August: stays 8.5f: acts on polytrack and firm going. *A. M. Hales*

REACHING OUT (IRE) 5 b.g. Desert Prince (IRE) 130 – Alwiyda (USA) (Trempo- **73** lino (USA) 135) [2007 71: p10g⁴ p10g² p12.2g³ p10g⁶ p10g⁴ 10g 9g p12.2g⁶ 9.5g Oct 5] smallish, close-coupled gelding: fair handicapper: first past post at Lingfield in January (demoted after causing interference): left N. Littmoden after eighth start: effective at 1¼m/1½m: acts on polytrack, firm and soft going: blinkered of late: often slowly away: sometimes races freely. *G. Keane, Ireland*

READY TO CROWN (USA) 3 b.f. More Than Ready (USA) 120 – Dili (USA) 73 **57** (Chief's Crown (USA)) [2007 p8.6d² p10g Dec 30] $28,000Y, resold $50,000Y, 7,000 2-y-o: sixth foal: half-sister to winners in US by Honour And Glory and Crafty Friend: dam French 1½m winner: won bumper in November: better effort in maidens when second to Red Blossom at Wolverhampton: will be suited by 1½m+. *Andrew Turnell*

REAL CHIEF (IRE) 9 b.g. Caerleon (USA) 132 – Greek Air (IRE) 107 (Ela-Mana- – Mou 132) [2007 –, a59: p13g Mar 5] poor hurdler: no form on Flat since early-2006: blinkered once. *Miss M. E. Rowland*

REALISM (FR) 7 b.g. Machiavellian (USA) 123 – Kissing Cousin (IRE) 116 (Danehill **98** (USA) 126) [2007 104: 10.3m 10.3d* 10g⁵ 11.9m 12d 10.4m* 12g² 12m 12m Nov 10] strong, good-bodied gelding: useful performer: easy winner of claimers at Chester in June and York (claimed from R. Fahey £30,000) in September: good second to Dzesmin in handicap at Catterick next time: stays easy 1½m: acts on fibresand, good to firm and good to soft going: has run well when sweating: tried tongue tied/in cheekpieces. *M. W. Easterby*

REALLY REALLY WISH 2 b.c. (Apr 7) Bertolini (USA) 125 – Shanghai Lil 57 **76** (Petong 126) [2007 5g⁶ 5m⁵ p5g* Sep 29] €19,000F, €20,000Y: sturdy colt: fifth foal: dam 6f to 1½m winner: fair form: off 3½ months, won maiden at Kempton final start: should be suited by 6f/7f. *J. R. Best*

REAL PEARL 2 ch.g. (Apr 9) Reel Buddy (USA) 118 – Pearls (Mon Tresor 113) [2007 – 8m Sep 12] good-topped gelding: 100/1 and burly, last in maiden at Doncaster. *T. D. Easterby*

REALT NA MARA (IRE) 4 b. or br.g. Tagula (IRE) 116 – Dwingeloo (IRE) 83 (Dan- **77 +** cing Dissident (USA) 119) [2007 8v 5m a7g⁵ p6g* p6m³ p6g* Dec 15] strong gelding: fair form: left P. Verling in Ireland after third start: much improved to win maiden at Kempton in October and handicap at Wolverhampton in December: should stay 7f: acts on polytrack. *H. Morrison*

REALLY NAUGHTY (IRE) 3 b.c. Night Shift (USA) – Naughty Reputation (IRE) 31 **68** (Shalford (IRE) 124§) [2007 67?: p6g p7g p8g⁴ p8g³ 6m⁴ 7m 7s 7g² 6m² 7d 7g⁴ p7g 7f 7f⁴ a4.5g Nov 23] compact colt: fair maiden handicapper: left B. Powell before final start: stays 1m: acts on polytrack and firm going: tends to hang. *L. Braem, Belgium*

REASON (IRE) 9 b.g. Sadler's Wells (USA) 132 – Marseillaise (Artaius (USA) 129) **55** [2007 p12g f14g 9.9s² 13d⁴ 16s⁴ Jul 3] close-coupled, quite attractive gelding: just modest handicapper nowadays: stays 2m: acts on soft going: tried visored/blinkered. *D. W. Chapman*

REBALLO (IRE) 4 b.g. King's Best (USA) 132 – Lyrical Dance (USA) (Lear Fan **78 +** (USA) 130) [2007 69: 7g⁶ p8g⁶ p7g² p8g p8g⁵ Oct 17] stocky gelding: fair maiden handicapper: stays 1m: raced only on polytrack and good ground: sold 8,500 gns. *J. R. Fanshawe*

REBEL ACLAIM (IRE) 2 b.f. (Feb 25) Acclamation 118 – Tribal Rite 95 (Be My **64** Native (USA) 122) [2007 5.1g² 5.1g³ 5g² 6s 5.1m³ 5.5m 5f Sep 17] good-topped filly: half-sister to several winners, including 2005 2-y-o 7f winner Arminius by Shinko Forest) and 1997 2-y-o 6f and 1m winner Silent Tribute (by Lion Cavern), both useful: dam Irish 6f (at 2 yrs) to 1¼m winner: modest maiden: placed 4 times: effective at 5f/6f: acts on soft and good to firm going. *M. G. Quinlan*

REBEL DUKE (IRE) 3 ch.g. Namid 128 – Edwina (IRE) 63 (Caerleon (USA) 132) **84**
[2007 76: p6g⁵ f5s* 5f² 5g 6s⁶ 5d⁵ p5.1g³ 5g³ p5.1g⁵ Nov 22] angular gelding: fairly useful handicapper: won at Southwell in February: left M. Quinlan 9,000 gns after seventh
start: best at 5f: acts on all-weather, firm and good to soft going: tried blinkered/tongue
tied. *D. W. Barker*

REBELLIOUS SPIRIT 4 b.g. Mark of Esteem (IRE) 137 – Robellino Miss (USA) **69**
(Robellino (USA) 127) [2007 74: f8g* f8g² p8g* p8g² f7g⁴ p8f² p7.1g p8g⁵ 10m 8.2d **a94 d**
p8g 8.3m p8g⁶ p8g* p8g f8d³ f8g Dec 27] tall, quite good-topped gelding: fairly useful
performer: won handicaps at Southwell and Kempton in January and claimer at Kempton
in November: stays 1m: acts on all-weather, good to firm and good to soft going: often
races prominently. *P. W. Hiatt*

REBEL PEARL (IRE) 3 b.f. Barathea (IRE) 127 – Rebel Clan (IRE) (Tagula (IRE) **71**
116) [2007 69+: p7g⁵ 8.2g 7s² 8s³ 7.1g* 8.3s³ 8.1s 7g 7.2s f8d p7.1g Dec 26] fair
handicapper: won at Musselburgh in June: stays 8.3f: acts on polytrack and soft going:
blinkered (well held) final start: front runner. *M. G. Quinlan*

REBEL RAIDER (IRE) 8 b.g. Mujadil (USA) 119 – Emily's Pride (Shirley Heights **58**
130) [2007 p12g³ Feb 19] modest performer: effective at 8.6f to easy 1½m: acts on polytrack and soft going: fairly useful hurdler, successful in April. *B. N. Pollock*

RECALCITRANT 4 b.g. Josr Algarhoud (IRE) 118 – Lady Isabell 62 (Rambo Dancer **64**
(CAN) 107) [2007 61: p12g³ p13g p10g⁴ 12m² 11.9m² 11.7d³* 11.8s 13.3m 11.9d³ 11.9d⁵
11.6m⁴ 10m* 10d⁵ 10g³ 9.7f 10m⁴ p12g³ p10g p11g² p12g⁶ p10m Dec 9] workmanlike
gelding: modest handicapper: won at Bath in May and Brighton in August: best at 1¼m/
1½m: acts on polytrack, good to firm and good to soft going: free-going front runner.
S. Dow

RECAST (IRE) 2 ch.f. (Feb 21) Traditionally (USA) 117 – Rag Top (IRE) 101 (Bara- **–**
thea (IRE) 127) [2007 p8g p8g Oct 12] rather unfurnished filly: first foal: dam 2-y-o 5f to
7f winner: well held in maidens. *R. Hannon*

RECENT TIMES 2 b.f. (Mar 8) Dansili 127 – Forever Times 98 (So Factual (USA) **75**
120) [2007 6g³ 5.1d² 5.1g⁶ Nov 7] workmanlike filly: first foal: dam, 5f (at 2 yrs) to 7f
winner, half-sister to 8-y-o Welsh Emperor and smart sprinter Majestic Times: fair maid-
en: placed at Thirsk and Nottingham (second to Quiet Elegance): will prove best at 5f/6f.
T. D. Easterby

RECIPROCATION (IRE) 3 ch.c. Singspiel (IRE) 133 – Tekindia (FR) (Indian Ridge **80**
123) [2007 p9.5g³ p9.5g³ p12.2g* p12g² p12.2g⁴ p12g³ 14g Jun 15] fair performer:
awarded maiden at Wolverhampton in March: left M. Johnston 36,000 gns after fourth
start: below par subsequently: stays 1½m, not 1¾m: acts on polytrack: tried tongue tied/
visored: has sweated: free-going sort: sold 12,500 gns in October. *K. McAuliffe*

RECLAMATION (IRE) 2 b.f. (Mar 5) Red Ransom (USA) – Overruled (IRE) 91 **69 p**
(Last Tycoon 131) [2007 6d⁶ p8g⁶ 8d Oct 23] good-topped filly: seventh foal: half-sister
to smart Irish 7f (at 2 yrs) to 1½m (Irish Oaks) winner Vintage Tipple (by Entrepreneur),
2000 2-y-o 7f/1m winner Spettro (by Spectrum, later successful up to 1½m in Italy), and
3-y-o Record Breaker: dam, 1m (at 2 yrs)/1¼m winner (stayed 1¾m), half-sister to smart
performer up to 1½m Overbury: fair form in maidens: will be suited by 1¼m/1½m: sort
to thrive in 3-y-o handicaps. *Sir Mark Prescott*

RECOIL (IRE) 2 b.c. (Mar 28) Red Ransom (USA) – Dazilyn Lady (USA) 105 (Zilzal **58**
(USA) 137) [2007 7m 7.1m 7.1m 8s p8m Oct 3] big, strong colt: modest maiden: should
stay at least 1m: blinkered final start: sold £1,500, joined R. Johnson. *Christian Wroe*

RECORD BREAKER (IRE) 3 b.g. In The Wings 128 – Overruled (IRE) 91 (Last **98**
Tycoon 131) [2007 81p: 9m* 11g* 12g⁶ 12d⁵ 12d⁴ 9.9m 14g Sep 8] tall gelding: has
scope: improved into a useful performer: won maiden at Musselburgh in April and
handicaps at Goodwood in May and Pontefract (beat Night Hour by 3 lengths) in August:
should stay 1¾m: acts on good to firm and good to soft going: races prominently: ran in
snatches final outing (gelded after). *M. Johnston*

RECOVERY MISSION 3 b.g. Foxhound (USA) 103 – Have Fun (Indian Ridge 123) **–**
[2007 6m 7m 6d 7.5s Jul 17] workmanlike gelding: no form in maidens/claimer.
G. M. Moore

RED 3 ch.f. Fraam 114 – Great Tern 59 (Simply Great (FR) 122) [2007 68: 12.1m⁴ 14.1g **68**
11.6v² 16.2f p13.9s⁴ Dec 20] leggy filly: fair maiden handicapper: left R. Beckett before
final start: stays 1½m: acts on polytrack, heavy and good to firm going. *R. M. Stronge*

RED ALERT DAY 2 b.c. (Mar 8) Diktat 126 – Strike Hard (IRE) 108 (Green Desert **106**
(USA) 127) [2007 6m³ 6m² 5g³ 7m* 7d³ p6g² 6m⁴ Oct 5] 40,000Y: strong colt: type to
carry condition: fourth living foal: half-brother to winner in Japan by Singspiel: dam Irish
6f winner, including at 2 yrs: useful performer: won nursery at Newmarket in August:
continued improvement, length second to Philario in Sirenia Stakes at Kempton (badly
hampered start) and 2¼ lengths fourth to Dark Angel in Middle Park Stakes at Newmarket: stays 7f: acts on polytrack, good to firm and good to soft ground. *N. A. Callaghan*

RED AMARYLLIS 2 ch.f. (Mar 4) Piccolo 121 – Passiflora 75 (Night Shift (USA)) **69**
[2007 p6g 6m⁵ 6m³ 7m 6d⁴ p6g² p6g Nov 28] sturdy filly: fifth foal: sister to fairly useful **a55**
2002 2-y-o 6f winner Bond Royale, and half-sister to 5-y-o Zomerlust and 6f (at 2 yrs)
to 1m (US Grade 2 event) winner Passified (by Compton Place): dam, 2-y-o 6f winner,
half-sister to very smart 6f/7f performer Harmonic Way: fair maiden, better form on turf
than all-weather: should prove best at 5f/6f. *H. J. L. Dunlop*

RED AND WHITE (IRE) 2 b.f. (Apr 26) Red Ransom (USA) – Candice (IRE) 101 **91 p**
(Caerleon (USA) 132) [2007 6s² 6d* Jun 28] 40,000Y: third foal: half-sister to fairly
useful French 1½m winner Sweet Shop (by Grand Lodge): dam, 2-y-o 1m winner (stayed
1¼m), out of useful half-sister to top-class miler Markofdistinction: fairly useful form:
shaped well in maidens in June, second to Highland Daughter at Leicester before winning
at Hamilton by 6 lengths: suffered fracture after, but said to have made full recovery: will
be suited by 1m+. *M. Johnston*

RED ARMY COMMANDER (IRE) 2 b.g. (Mar 15) Soviet Star (USA) 128 – **–**
Penny Fan 58 (Nomination 125) [2007 7d Aug 16] good-topped gelding: 50/1, last in
maiden at Salisbury (gelded after). *Christian Wroe*

REDARSENE 2 ch.c. (Mar 18) Sakhee (USA) 136 – Triple Zee (USA) (Zilzal (USA) **67**
137) [2007 p8g⁶ 7s 7g Nov 2] 40,000F, €68,000Y: tall colt: sixth foal: half-brother
to useful 2000 2-y-o 7f winner Cauvery (by Exit To Nowhere) and 7.5f winner Three
Pennies (by Pennekamp): dam unraced: fair maiden: encouraging debut (sixth at Kempton), but too free subsequent starts: stays 1m. *M. G. Quinlan*

REDBACKCAPPUCHINO (IRE) 2 b.f. (Mar 3) Redback 116 – Cappuchino (IRE) **46**
59 (Roi Danzig (USA)) [2007 p5g 5m 6d³ 7s³ Jun 14] €7,000: half-sister to 3 winners,
including useful 1999 2-y-o 7f winner Blue Bolivar (by Blues Traveller) and 5f winner
Cayman Expresso (by Fayruz): dam, 7f winner, half-sister to 9-y-o Chookie Heiton: poor
maiden: third in sellers at Yarmouth: stays 7f: acts on soft going. *J. L. Spearing*

RED BARNET 3 ch.g. Tipsy Creek (USA) 115 – Heather Valley 47 (Clantime 101) **56**
[2007 6s⁶ 6d⁶ 7g⁵ 7m p7.1g 8.5m p9.5g Nov 2] modest maiden: probably stays 7f.
M. W. Easterby

RED BIRR (IRE) 6 b.g. Bahhare (USA) 122 – Cappella (IRE) 75 (College Chapel 122) **81**
[2007 83: p8g p8g⁵ p8g p8.6g* p10g p8.6g⁴ p12g³ p8.6g* p8.6g⁵ Oct 2] leggy, quite
good-topped gelding: fairly useful handicapper: won at Wolverhampton in February
and September: barely stays easy 1½m: acts on polytrack, good to firm and good to soft
going: front runner. *P. R. Webber*

RED BLOODED WOMAN (USA) 3 b.f. Red Ransom (USA) – Maskaya (IRE) 92 **65**
(Machiavellian (USA) 123) [2007 71p: 7.6m* 7m⁴ p10g Oct 4] smallish, sturdy filly: fair
performer: won maiden at Chester in August: stays 7.6f (raced freely at 1¼m): acts on
good to firm going: sold 60,000 gns. *J. Noseda*

RED BLOSSOM 3 b.f. Green Desert (USA) 127 – Red Camellia 116 (Polar Falcon **70 §**
(USA) 126) [2007 7.5m³ 7v p8g⁵ 6.9m² 7m⁴ 8m² 7m³ 8.3d² 8.2g³ p8.6g² p8.6d* p7g
Dec 19] lengthy filly: has scope: fifth foal: half-sister to smart 7f to 1¼m (including
Fillies' Mile) winner Red Bloom (by Selkirk) and 4-y-o Red Gala: dam, 2-y-o 6f/7f
(Prestige Stakes) winner, out of half-sister to Ibn Bey and Roseate Tern: fair performer:
won maiden at Wolverhampton in December: flattered in listed race at Kempton final
start: stays 8.6f: acts on polytrack, good to firm and good to soft ground: tried visored,
blinkered last 5 starts: temperamental, tends to find little. *Sir Mark Prescott*

REDBRICK GIRL 2 b.f. (Apr 19) Bahamian Bounty 116 – Once Removed 65 **60 d**
(Distant Relative 128) [2007 f5g⁵ 5f² 5m⁶ p7.1g p6g² p5.1g Nov 30] 8,000Y: sparely-
made filly: fourth foal: half-sister to 3 winners, including 4-y-o The Jailer: dam maiden
(stayed 7f): modest maiden: below form after second outing: best efforts at 5f: acts on
fibresand and firm going: tried blinkered. *K. A. Ryan*

RED BRICK ROAD (IRE) 3 ch.g. Medicean 128 – Dacian (USA) (Diesis 133) [2007 **47**
p7g 7g 8.1g 8.1d 10m Jul 18] angular gelding: poor maiden: tried cheekpieces.
A. J. Lidderdale

RED CAPE (FR) 4 b.g. Cape Cross (IRE) 129 – Muirfield (FR) (Crystal Glitters (USA) **104**
127) [2007 99: p6g² f6g⁴ p6f⁴ p6g p7g* p7g⁴ Apr 14] big, rangy gelding: useful performer: won handicap at Lingfield in March by 1½ lengths from Yarqus: creditable
fourth in minor event there subsequent outing: effective at 6f to 1m: acts on polytrack (not
discredited sole try on fibresand), and good to firm going: has edged left. *Jane Chapple-
Hyam*

RED CAULDRON 2 ch.c. (Jan 27) Choisir (AUS) 126 – First Musical 107 (First **65**
Trump 118) [2007 7d³ 7d³ 7m⁴ Aug 13] 40,000F, 29,000Y: big, strong colt: fourth foal:
half-brother to 5.7f winner Casterossa (by Rossini) and 3-y-o Avertuoso: dam 5f/6f
winner at 2 yrs: fair maiden, in frame all starts: should prove best up to 7f. *E. J. O'Neill*

RED CHAIRMAN 5 br.g. Red Ransom (USA) – Chine 100 (Inchinor 119) [2007 66d: **73 §**
7.9g 6v 10.1v⁶ 9.2d* 8s² 11.1m³ 12m 10.1m² 11.1g³ 16.1m⁵ 13.4g Sep 29] good-topped,
close-coupled gelding: fair handicapper: won at Hamilton in July: seems to stay 2m: acts
on polytrack, soft and good to firm going: usually wears headgear: tried tongue tied: has
been slowly away, but usually front runner: ungenuine: won over hurdles in October: sold
11,000 gns, joined Eugene M. O'Sullivan in Ireland. *R. Johnson*

REDCHETE 2 b.f. (Feb 2) Red Ransom (USA) – Zacheta (Polish Precedent (USA) **–**
131) [2007 6v Oct 9] €12,000Y: second foal: half-sister to 3-y-o Dawn Sky: dam unraced
half-sister to Prix de l'Arc de Triomphe winner Marienbard: 15/2, soon outpaced in
maiden at Folkestone: will be suited by 1m+. *C. E. Brittain*

REDCLIFF (GER) 3 ch.g. Lomitas 129 – Rhode Island (GER) (Waajib 121) [2007 75: **–**
8.2s 10g 14m Jul 19] workmanlike gelding: fair performer at 2 yrs: no form in 2007,
looking none too keen (including when blinkered): left M. W. Easterby before final start.
C. von der Recke, Germany

RED CLUBS (IRE) 4 br.c. Red Ransom (USA) – Two Clubs 111 (First Trump **125**
118) [2007 119: 6g² 5g 6d⁴ 6m³ 5g⁴ 6g* 7d Oct 6]
    If at first you don't succeed . . . Red Clubs finally landed a Group 1 at the
twelfth attempt when he won the Betfred Sprint Cup at Haydock in September. His
success was fine reward for a tough colt with a solid record. It was a pity that the
success of Red Clubs was overshadowed by the brouhaha over the ground, discussed in the essay on Sakhee's Secret, officially good to firm but well watered
(*Timeform* returned the ground as good) which allegedly spoilt the chances of some
of the runners including the favourite Sakhee's Secret. The prospect of firmish
ground had earlier led to the withdrawal at the forty-eight-hour stage of Dutch Art,
who had finished second to Sakhee's Secret in the July Cup at Newmarket. Red
Clubs finished third then, a length and three quarters behind the winner. Sakhee's

*Betfred Sprint Cup, Haydock—a deserved first Group 1 win for Red Clubs,
who is well on top close home from Marchand d'Or (right), Balthazaar's Gift (left),
Mutawaajid (dark colours) and favourite Sakhee's Secret (blaze)*

Mr R. J. Arculli's "Red Clubs"

Secret was 11/8 favourite at Haydock, with Red Clubs, a creditable fourth behind Kingsgate Native in the Nunthorpe at York in the interim, a 9/1-chance. Separating them in the market were three who had finished behind Red Clubs in the July Cup, the fourth Marchand d'Or, who had since beaten Dutch Art in the Prix Maurice de Gheest, the sixth Asset, who was being tried in blinkers for the first time, and the eighth Hellvelyn, who was making a belated reappearance at Newmarket and had subsequently won a listed event at Beverley. There were reasons why that trio might reverse placings with Red Clubs, but none of them proved able to as Red Clubs took advantage of the favourite's below-par showing, travelling well under a patient ride before quickening to lead in the final furlong and pass the post well on top. Red Clubs beat Marchand d'Or by three quarters of a length with a couple of July Cup also rans Balthazaar's Gift and Mutawaajid third and fourth. Sakhee's Secret was only fifth, with Asset sixth and Hellvelyn last, running as if amiss.

Red Clubs's campaign had begun in the Duke of York Stakes at York in May, when he was beaten a length and a quarter by Amadeus Wolf, to whom he was conceding 4 lb. Red Clubs's connections, if not Red Clubs himself, must have been sick of the sight of Amadeus Wolf by now. Red Clubs had beaten him into third in the 2005 Coventry Stakes at York, and the Duke of York was the eighth time since then that they had met, Amadeus Wolf finishing ahead of him on all eight occasions. They had been first and second in both the Gimcrack and Middle Park at two and Red Clubs had finished behind Amadeus Wolf in most of the top sprints in 2006. They were to meet four more times but the Duke of York was the last time Red Clubs finished behind. After coming last of eight, reportedly lame, in the Temple Stakes at Sandown, Red Clubs had Amadeus Wolf well behind when fourth to Soldier's Tale in the Golden Jubilee Stakes at Royal Ascot, as well as at Newmarket and in the Nunthorpe. Red Clubs made just one more appearance after Haydock. Having finished ninth over five furlongs in the 2006 Prix de l'Abbaye, he was stepped up to seven at the 2007 Arc meeting but made no greater impact in the Prix de la Foret, behind throughout and coming last of thirteen. Red Clubs has been retired to stand at the Tally-Ho Stud in Ireland at a fee of €12,500. He is small but well made and, given his precocity and his record of pattern-race success at two, three and four, he seems likely to be a popular choice for commercial breeders.

	Red Ransom (USA) (b 1987)	Roberto (b 1969)	Hail To Reason
			Bramalea
Red Clubs (IRE) (br.c. 2003)		Arabia (b 1977)	Damascus
			Christmas Wind
	Two Clubs (br 1996)	First Trump (ch 1991)	Primo Dominie
			Valika
		Miss Cindy (br 1975)	Mansingh
			Iridium

Red Clubs's pedigree should stand him in good stead too. His sire Red Ransom has a fairly good overall record and his dam Two Clubs was a smart six-furlong performer for William Jarvis, out of Miss Cindy, a fairly useful five- to seven-furlong performer, who was a sister to the high-class sprinter Petong. Petong worked his way up through the ranks at three and four, progressing through handicaps to win both the Wokingham and the Stewards' Cup before landing the then Group 2 Vernons Sprint Cup at Haydock. Another notable sprinter in the family is Two Clubs's half-brother Gipsy Fiddler who was useful at up to seven furlongs and gained his biggest success in the Windsor Castle Stakes. Two Clubs is also half-sister to some lesser winners who stay a fair bit further than the aforementioned relatives, including Miss Camellia, who stayed a mile and three quarters. Among Two Clubs's half-sisters are the dams of the useful mile- to mile-and-a-quarter filly Joint Aspiration and the one-time smart hurdler at up to two and a half miles Genghis, who won the Scottish Champion Hurdle. Red Clubs is Two Clubs's second foal. The first, by Bahri, has yet to race, while the third, Elusive Hawk (by Noverre), made his belated debut in December after being unraced for Godolphin. Two Clubs's 2005 filly by Hawk Wing, Flying Hawk, a 90,000-guinea yearling, didn't run at two. Another filly, by Fasliyev, was sold for 75,000 guineas at the Newmarket October Sales. Red Clubs himself went through the sale-ring at Newmarket twice, making 40,000 guineas both as a foal and a yearling.

In addition to his wins in the Coventry and Sprint Cup, Red Clubs won two pattern events at three, the Greenham Stakes at Newbury and the Diadem Stakes at Ascot. Although he had form at five and seven furlongs, his optimum trip was probably six. He acted on good to firm going and, although a little below form in two outings on soft (one when he had plenty of use made of him under the conditions in the 2006 Sprint Cup), he shaped as if effective on it. *B. W. Hills*

RED CONTACT (USA) 6 b.g. Sahm (USA) 112 – Basma (USA) 104 (Grey Dawn II 132) [2007 –, a91: f8g 7.1g 8s p7.1g p8.6g³ p7.1m⁴ p7.1g p9.5g f8d³ f8d Dec 21] leggy gelding: fair handicapper: effective at 7f to easy 1¼m: acts on all-weather, lightly raced (and little form) on turf nowadays: tried blinkered/tongue tied, wears cheekpieces: inconsistent. *A. Dickman* — **a79**

RED CURRENT 3 b.f. Soviet Star (USA) 128 – Fleet Amour (USA) (Afleet (CAN)) [2007 72: 8m⁴ 8.3g³ 7s 7s 8d² p8g* p10g p8g 10.2m² 10.2m* 10m* 10d³ p9.5g p9.5g² p11g⁴ p9.5d p9.5g⁶ Dec 26] leggy, close-coupled filly: fair performer: won claimer at Lingfield (left J. Fanshawe £9,000) in July and handicaps at Chepstow and Pontefract (apprentices) in September: stays 1¼m: acts on polytrack, good to firm and good to soft going. *R. A. Harris* — **75 a68**

RED DELIGHT (IRE) 2 b.f. (Apr 29) Redback 116 – Lindas Delight 54 (Batshoof 122) [2007 6s⁵ 5d⁴ 6m Aug 8] €7,200Y, resold 13,000Y: half-sister to several winners, including 9-y-o Fromsong: dam 2-y-o 6f seller winner: modest form in maidens: likely to prove best at 6f/7f: acts on soft going. *R. A. Fahey* — **54**

RED DUNE (IRE) 2 b.f. (May 3) Red Ransom (USA) – Desert Beauty (IRE) 103 (Green Desert (USA) 127) [2007 8g⁴ Oct 26] €1,050,000Y: good-topped filly: fifth foal: half-sister to 3-y-o Rose of Petra and 2 winners abroad by Machiavellian: dam, 7f/1m winner, half-sister to very smart middle-distance performers Greek Dance, Islington and **77 p**

Mountain High: 12/1 and not fully wound up, promising fourth to Cruel Sea in maiden at Doncaster, going strongly in lead before tiring: not certain to stay much beyond 1m: will improve and win races. *M. A. Jarvis*

REDDY RONNIE (IRE) 3 b.g. Redback 116 – Daffodil Dale (IRE) 78 (Cyrano de **52** Bergerac 120) [2007 8m⁶ 8d p7.1g Sep 20] workmanlike gelding: modest form in maidens: slowly away final outing. *D. Carroll*

REDEEMED 2 b.f. (Mar 21) Red Ransom (USA) – Pastel 95 (Lion Cavern (USA) 117) **73** [2007 6d 7m³ p7g Sep 24] close-coupled filly: second foal: dam 2-y-o 5f winner: fair maiden: third to Cape Amber at Newmarket: stays 7f. *B. J. Meehan*

REDESDALE 2 b.g. (Apr 8) Pursuit of Love 124 – No Candles Tonight 74 (Star Appeal **58** 133) [2007 6d 7s⁶ p8.6g 10m p10g⁴ Oct 24] close-coupled gelding: modest maiden: stays 1¼m: acts on polytrack and soft going: quirky, tends to hang. *P. W. D'Arcy*

REDESIGNATION (IRE) 2 b.c. (Mar 5) Key of Luck (USA) 126 – Disregard That **89 p** (IRE) (Don't Forget Me 127) [2007 6g 7g* 8d Sep 20] €75,000Y: tall, good-topped colt: eighth foal: brother to 3 winners, notably smart Irish/French 6f winner (including at 2 yrs) Miss Emma, and half-brother to 2 winners: dam unraced: fairly useful form: won maiden at Newmarket (beat Timetable by neck, pair clear) in August: odds on, fell early (clipped heels) in minor event at Ayr: should stay 1m: sold 75,000 gns: capable of better. *R. Hannon*

RED EVIE (IRE) 4 b.f. Intikhab (USA) 135 – Malafemmena (IRE) 96 (Nordico **117** (USA)) [2007 117: 8g* 8m 8m 7d* 8m² 7d Oct 6]

When she won the Juddmonte Lockinge Stakes at Newbury in May, it seemed that Red Evie, one of the most progressive horses in training in 2006, might continue in the same vein as a four-year-old. However, her performance in a

Juddmonte Lockinge Stakes, Newbury—Red Evie makes a successful reappearance, having a head and the same to spare over Ramonti (nearest camera) and Passager (far side)

below-par renewal of the Lockinge, which provided her with her eighth win in nine starts had required no improvement on the pick of her three-year-old efforts. Red Evie's form was below that of recent Lockinge winners of her sex, Russian Rhythm and Peeress, and even further behind the top-class performances of Hawk Wing and Rakti. As it transpired, Red Evie did not manage to show form at any stage in the latest season in advance of that she had produced in 2006. What the Lockinge lacked in quality, however, it made up for a cracking finish as Red Evie, travelling with typical fluency from the start, quickened well and kept on to beat Ramonti by a head, with the same distance to Passager in third. On her next two starts, Red Evie was unplaced, beaten just over three lengths by Ramonti in the Queen Anne Stakes at Royal Ascot, and about six lengths by Simply Perfect in the Falmouth Stakes at Newmarket, on both occasions disadvantaged by being held up in muddling races. It was back at Newbury that Red Evie recorded the final victory of her career. Dropped back to seven furlongs in the CGA Hungerford Stakes, she overcame trouble in running and won by a short head from the front-running Welsh Emperor who had been successful in the race twelve months previously. Red Evie was narrowly denied a repeat success herself when beaten a length and a half by Echelon in the Matron Stakes at Leopardstown, coming from further back than the winner in a steadily-run race. As in the Sun Chariot at Newmarket on her final outing at three, Red Evie performed poorly on her final start in the latest season, this time in the Prix de la Foret at Longchamp.

Red Evie (IRE) (b.f. 2003)	Intikhab (USA) (b 1994)	Red Ransom (b 1987)	Roberto Bramalea
		Crafty Example (b 1987)	Crafty Prospector Real Crafty Lady
	Malafemmena (IRE) (b 1992)	Nordico (b 1981)	Northern Dancer Kennelot
		Martinova (b 1978)	Martinmas Pavlova

Red Evie had been entered in the December Mares' Sales at the end of 2006, before being withdrawn to stay in training. She was also entered in the same sale after her four-year-old campaign but, after being led out unsold for 1,000,000 guineas, she was purchased by Coolmore in a private deal. There is little to add to the in-depth appraisal of Red Evie's pedigree in *Racehorses of 2006*, although it is perhaps worth mentioning that her sire Intikhab enjoyed a slightly better time of things in 2007, with stablemates Red Evie and Hoh Mike leading the way. Whilst the latter is a sprinter purely and simply, Intikhab also sired the Cesarewitch winner Leg Spinner. The big, lengthy Red Evie, who was held up, was campaigned exclusively at seven furlongs and a mile, and acted on firm and soft going. Her hind joints were usually bandaged. *M. L. W. Bell*

RED EXPRESSO (IRE) 2 ch.g. (Feb 12) Intikhab (USA) 135 – Cafe Creme (IRE) (Catrail (USA) 123) [2007 5f³ 5m May 7] strong, compact gelding: fair maiden: encouraging third at Windsor on debut, disappointing on same course only subsequent start (gelded after): should stay 6f. *M. L. W. Bell* — **70**

RED FLARE (IRE) 3 b.g. Redback 116 – Cwm Deri (IRE) (Alzao (USA) 117) [2007 54: 7m⁴ 8g⁴ 8m 8m² 9.9s² 12m³ 10m⁵ 16g Aug 2] well-made gelding: modest maiden handicapper: stays 1½m, probably not 2m: acts on soft and good to firm going: joined A. King, won over hurdles in December. *M. R. Channon* — **60**

REDFLO 3 b.f. Redback 116 – Button Hole Flower (IRE) (Fairy King (USA)) [2007 –: p5g p5.1g⁴ p5g p5f⁵ p5g p5g p5g f5g 5.1g p5g 5.1g 5.5s Jul 6] poor maiden handicapper: generally regressed in 2007: raced only at 5f, mostly on polytrack. *Ms J. S. Doyle* — **46 d**

RED FLYER (IRE) 8 br.g. Catrail (USA) 123 – Marostica (ITY) (Stone 124) [2007 f8g Apr 30] close-coupled gelding: modest at best on Flat, lightly raced nowadays: well held only Flat outing in 2007: sometimes starts slowly/carries head high. *B. P. J. Baugh* — **–**

REDFORD (IRE) 2 b.c. (Apr 2) Bahri (USA) 125 – Ida Lupino (IRE) (Statoblest 120) [2007 7m 7d⁴ 8g* Oct 3] 32,000F, €57,000Y, 82,000 2-y-o: good-topped colt: fourth foal: half-brother to Italian 5f (including at 2 yrs) to 1m winner Imperial Valley (by Marju): dam, no form, half-sister to Chester Vase winner High Baroque: fairly useful form: fourth to Spacious at Leicester, then won maiden at Newcastle easily by 2 lengths (value plenty extra): stays 1m: will make his mark in better company. *M. L. W. Bell* — **88 p**

RED GALA 4 b.c. Sinndar (IRE) 134 – Red Camellia 116 (Polar Falcon (USA) 126) **108**
[2007 90: 10m* 10.3m* 12s⁵ 12d⁵ Oct 27] good-bodied colt: useful performer: further
progress in 2007, winning handicaps at Newbury (by 1¼ lengths from Samurai Way,
flashing tail) in April and Doncaster (beat Fairmile by length, taking while to find stride)
in September: plenty to do when creditable fifth to Buccellati in similar event at Ascot
next time: below form in St Simon Stakes at Newbury 2 weeks later: effective at 1¼m/
1½m: acts on polytrack, soft and good to firm going: has worn crossed noseband. *Sir
Michael Stoute*

RED ICON 2 b.f. (Mar 30) Red Ransom (USA) – Blue Icon (Peintre Celebre (USA) **76**
137) [2007 p7g² 8.1s⁴ Sep 29] medium-sized, good-bodied filly: first foal: dam, French
11f winner, closely related to very smart French 1m to 10.5f winner Bright Sky out of
very smart French 1½m/13.5f winner Bright Moon: fair form in frame in maidens at
Lingfield and Haydock: will stay 1¼m. *R. M. Beckett*

RED LANCER 6 ch.g. Deploy 131 – Miss Bussell 65 (Sabrehill (USA) 120) [2007 **90**
102d: 10.1g 8f 10m⁵ 10.1d⁶ 10.3f² 12s⁶ 12.3m 10.4d⁵ Oct 13] small, stocky gelding: just
fairly useful handicapper nowadays: stays 13f: acts on all-weather, soft and firm going:
has got on edge and been early to post: tends to edge left: patiently ridden. *D. Nicholls*

RED LANTERN 6 ch.g. Young Ern 120 – Croft Sally (Crofthall 110) [2007 47: f8g **47**
p7.1g 7g⁵ 7m⁴ 7.9m 7.5g 9.9m Aug 25] sturdy gelding: poor maiden: stays 9.5f: acts on
polytrack and good to firm going: tried in cheekpieces/visor/tongue tie. *M. W. Easterby*

RED LEAVES 2 b.g. (Feb 28) Rock of Gibraltar (IRE) 133 – Brigadiers Bird (IRE) **64**
(Mujadil (USA) 119) [2007 8g⁴ 7d⁵ Oct 16] strong, useful-looking gelding: modest
maiden: prominent long way when fifth to Prime Exhibit at Leicester: should prove best
up to 1m. *P. F. I. Cole*

RED LILY (IRE) 2 b.f. (Apr 3) Red Ransom (USA) – Panna 106 (Polish Precedent **61 p**
(USA) 131) [2007 7m 8f 8.2d⁶ Oct 10] small, sturdy filly: third foal: half-sister to 3-y-o
Hot Diamond: dam, 1¼m winner (stayed 1½m), half-sister to top-class 1¼m/1½m performer Pentire: modest form in maidens, looking to be learning: will be suited by 1¼m/
1½m: should do better. *J. R. Fanshawe*

RED MERLIN (IRE) 2 ch.g. (Mar 21) Soviet Star (USA) 128 – Truly Bewitched **75**
(USA) 81 (Affirmed (USA)) [2007 7d 7.1g⁵ 7m Oct 5] rather leggy, attractive gelding:
fair form in maidens: fifth to Redolent at Sandown, racing freely: off 2 months, faded
final start (gelded after): will prove best up to 1m. *C. G. Cox*

RED MOLONEY (USA) 3 b.g. Sahm (USA) 112 – Roja (USA) (L'Enjoleur (CAN)) **117**
[2007 8m⁵ 10m* 10s* 14d* 12g³ p10.7g* Nov 9] rather leggy, useful-looking gelding:
half-brother to several winning US sprinters: dam, US sprint maiden, out of half-sister to
US Grade 1 1½m winner Lieutenant's Lark: smart performer: won maiden at Roscommon in June, handicap at Naas in July and listed races at the Curragh (by 3 lengths from
Hasanka) in August and Dundalk (by 1¼ lengths from Ezima) in November: below-form
third behind Hasanka in similar event at Galway on penultimate start: effective at 1¼m to
1¾m: acts on polytrack, best turf efforts on soft/good to soft going. *Kevin Prendergast,
Ireland*

REDOLENT (IRE) 2 ch.c. (Mar 4) Redback 116 – Esterlina (IRE) 95 (Highest Honor **105**
(FR) 124) [2007 7m² 7.1g* 7m 8s² 8s³ Nov 1] 22,000F, €120,000Y: useful-looking colt:
second foal: dam, Irish 1m winner, out of close relation to Fillies' Mile winner/Oaks third
Leap Lively: useful performer: won maiden at Sandown in August: much improved final
2 starts, length second to Ibn Khaldun in Autumn Stakes at Ascot and 6½ lengths third
to Thewayyouare in Criterium International at Saint-Cloud: stays 1m: acts on soft going,
promise on good to firm: front runner. *R. Hannon*

RED OPERA 5 ch.g. Nashwan (USA) 135 – La Papagena (Habitat 134) [2007 13g⁴ **65**
17.2d Oct 1] big, lengthy, good-topped gelding: fair handicapper, lightly raced: stays
13.8f: acts on good to firm ground. *D. E. Pipe*

RED PETAL 3 ch.f. Medicean 128 – Red Garland (Selkirk (USA) 129) [2007 67: p9.5g **80**
f11s* f12g² 11.6d 16m Jul 18] well-made filly: fairly useful handicapper: won at Southwell in February: stays easy 1½m: acts on fibresand: tongue tied final outing: not straightforward, has hung/flashed tail. *Sir Mark Prescott*

RED RAPTOR 6 ch.g. Polar Falcon (USA) 126 – Star Precision 103 (Shavian 125) **57**
[2007 57: p8g³ p8g⁶ f8s⁵ f7g 9.7g p10g Nov 12] little form in bumpers/hurdles: modest
maiden handicapper: stays 1m: acts on polytrack and good to firm ground: tongue tied.
J. A. Geake

Betfred Gordon Richards Stakes, Sandown—Red Rocks gives weight and a beating to Mashaahed (rail) and Kandidate; Notnowcato (right) and Mountain High (dark colours) come next

RED RIVER BOY 2 ch.g. (Feb 23) Bahamian Bounty 116 – Riviere Rouge (Forzando 122) [2007 5m 5m Jul 24] sturdy gelding: well held in maidens, modest form latterly (gelded after): bred for sprinting. *C. W. Fairhurst* **50**

RED RIVER REBEL 9 b.g. Inchinor 119 – Bidweaya (USA) 45 (Lear Fan (USA) 130) [2007 58, a61: f14g f14g 16g 11.8s* 12.1v* 12.1s² 12.1g Jul 31] tall, leggy gelding: modest handicapper: won at Leicester (apprentices) in May and Beverley in July: effective at 11.8f to 2m: acts on all-weather, heavy and firm going: tried visored earlier in career: races up with pace. *J. R. Norton* **62**

RED RIVER ROCK (IRE) 5 b.g. Spectrum (IRE) 126 – Ann's Annie (IRE) 78 (Alzao (USA) 117) [2007 56: f14g* f16s⁵ f14g f14g⁴ f14g⁶ p16g⁶ f14g 14g² 12g³ Aug 12] modest performer: won minor event at Southwell in January: below form in handicaps after, leaving T. Fitzgerald before placed in Jersey last 2 starts: stays 1¾m (possibly not 2m): acts on all-weather, best effort on turf on good going: usually blinkered. *R. A. Maletroit, Jersey* **56**

RED ROCK CANYON (IRE) 3 b.c. Rock of Gibraltar (IRE) 133 – Imagine (IRE) 119 (Sadler's Wells (USA) 132) [2007 105: 10m² 10d² 12g 10s² 10s² 10m³ Sep 8] well-made colt: smart maiden: best efforts on last 2 starts, ½-length second to Fracas in Meld Stakes and 3½ lengths third to Dylan Thomas in Irish Champion Stakes, both at Leopardstown: favourite when runner-up in maidens/minor event earlier: stays 1¼m: acts on soft and good to firm going: tried in cheekpieces/blinkers: often makes running. *A. P. O'Brien, Ireland* **113**

RED ROCKS (IRE) 4 b. or br.c. Galileo (IRE) 134 – Pharmacist (IRE) 108 (Machiavellian (USA) 123) [2007 124: 12g 10g* 10m⁴ 10m⁴ 12s³ 12g Dec 9] rather leggy, attractive colt: has a quick, fluent action: won Breeders' Cup Turf at Churchill Downs in 2006: successful in 2007 in Betfred Gordon Richards Stakes at Sandown in April by 2 lengths from Mashaahed: not at best subsequently, just respectable efforts when fourth to Manduro in Prince of Wales's Stakes at Royal Ascot next time and when 7¾ lengths third to English Channel in Breeders' Cup Turf at Monmouth: only ninth in Hong Kong Vase at Sha Tin final outing: effective at 1¼m/1½m: acts on firm and soft going: has worn crossed noseband: sometimes sweats/edgy: versatile tactically. *B. J. Meehan* **124**

RED ROMEO 6 ch.g. Case Law 113 – Enchanting Eve 67 (Risk Me (FR) 127) [2007 90: 7v⁴ 7s 7m⁴ 6g p8.6g³ p7.1g² 7g⁶ p7.1g p7.1g* Dec 31] tall gelding: fairly useful handicapper: won at Wolverhampton in December: best at 7f/1m: acts on polytrack, heavy and good to firm going: tried in blinkers/cheekpieces: often races prominently. *N. Wilson* **92**

RED RUDY 5 ch.g. Pivotal 124 – Piroshka (Soviet Star (USA) 128) [2007 77: 8.1g 7.1s⁵ 8s 8.3m³ 7d⁵ 7.1f* 8.1m² p8.6g Sep 20] tall, close-coupled gelding: fair handicapper: won at Chepstow in August: effective at 7f, barely stays 9.7f: acts on polytrack, firm and good to soft going: very slowly away third start. *A. W. Carroll* **76**

RED RUMOUR (IRE) 2 b.c. (Mar 14) Redback 116 – Church Mice (IRE) 82 (Petardia 113) [2007 6g 6m* 6g⁵ Nov 2] 30,000Y: good-topped colt: second foal: dam sprinter: fairly useful form: sharper for debut, won maiden at Newmarket (beat Ramaad by 2½ lengths) in September: outpaced in finish in minor event there (fifth to Paco Boy): will be suited by 7f. *R. M. Beckett* **85**

RED SAIL 6 ch.m. Dr Fong (USA) 128 – Manhattan Sunset (USA) 76 (El Gran Senor **60**
(USA) 136) [2007 62: p8g⁵ p10g⁵ 12m* Aug 3] angular mare: modest handicapper: won
at Newmarket in August: stays 1½m: acts on polytrack and firm going: blinkered:
reportedly in foal to Domedriver. *Dr J. D. Scargill*

REDSENSOR 2 b.c. (Mar 31) Redback 116 – Xtrasensory 96 (Royal Applause 124) **73**
[2007 6f² 6g² 6g 6m⁵ 7g⁴ p6g⁴ p7g* p8g⁵ Nov 21] good-bodied, attractive colt: fair
performer: won claimer at Lingfield in November: best at 6f/7f: acts on polytrack and
firm going: blinkered (below form) once: sold 12,000 gns. *R. Hannon*

RED SKIPPER (IRE) 2 ch.g. (May 7) Captain Rio 122 – Speed To Lead (IRE) 90 **62**
(Darshaan 133) [2007 5g 6m⁴ 6m 6d p7.1g 8m 6v² Nov 3] strong, compact gelding:
modest maiden: second in nursery at Ayr: form only at 6f: acts on heavy ground.
N. Wilson

RED SOMERSET (USA) 4 b.g. Red Ransom (USA) – Bielska (USA) (Deposit **91**
Ticket (USA)) [2007 94: 8.1g³ 7.6m 8g 10v 8m⁴ 10f 8.1m 8.3g* 7v² 8g² 8.2g* Oct 31]
strong, good-bodied gelding: fairly useful handicapper: won at Leicester in September
and Nottingham (beat Apex by 5 lengths) in October: should stay 1¼m: acts on polytrack
and good to firm going. *R. J. Hodges*

RED SPELL (IRE) 6 ch.g. Soviet Star (USA) 128 – A-To-Z (IRE) 101 (Ahonoora **–**
122) [2007 102, a111: p8.6g² p10g² p8g* p8g⁴ p8g³ Feb 17] good-topped gelding: smart **a112**
on all-weather, useful on turf: won handicap at Lingfield in January by length from Party
Boss: below form last 2 starts: effective at 7f to easy 1¼m: acts on polytrack, soft and
good to firm going: tried blinkered/in cheekpieces. *R. Hannon*

REDSTONE DANCER (IRE) 5 ch.m. Namid 128 – Red Affair (IRE) 95 (Generous **115**
(IRE) 139) [2007 102: 7d³ 7s* 7s* 7v* 7g³ Aug 3] sturdy, lengthy mare: smart performer:
improved again in 2007, winning quite valuable handicap at the Curragh in June, and

*Irish Stallion Farms EBF Brownstown Stakes, Leopardstown—the second of three wins during the season
for the in-foal Redstone Dancer, who beats She's Our Mark (right) and Modeeroch*

Irish Stallion Farms EBF Brownstown Stakes at Leopardstown (by 2½ lengths from She's Our Mark) and 4-runner Emirates Airline Minstrel Stakes at the Curragh (by length from Hard Rock City) in July: creditable 2 lengths third to Wake Up Maggie in Oak Tree Stakes at Goodwood final outing: best form at 7f: acts on any going: successful in cheekpieces in 2006: reportedly in foal to Refuse To Bend. *Miss S. Collins, Ireland*

RED SUN 10 b.g. Foxhound (USA) 103 – Superetta 65 (Superlative 118) [2007 66: 13d⁶ **59** 14g⁵ 12d⁴ 12.1g⁴ 15.8g 17.1m⁶ p13.9g p16.5g Oct 20] smallish gelding: just modest handicapper in 2007: stays 17f: acts on all-weather, good to firm and good to soft going: tried in cheekpieces: usually tongue tied: often makes running: modest hurdler, successful in November. *R. C. Guest*

RED TARN 2 gr.g. (Apr 28) Fraam 114 – Cumbrian Melody 83 (Petong 126) [2007 7s⁴ **66** 7d⁵ 7.2v Nov 3] 23,000F, 37,000Y: big gelding: has plenty of scope: half-brother to several winners, notably 3-y-o Hellvelyn: dam 2-y-o 5f/6f winner: fair maiden: best effort on debut (fourth to Zakhaaref at Redcar), and gelded after final start: should prove best up to 7f: raced on ground softer than good. *B. Smart*

RED TWIST 2 b.c. (Mar 18) Red Ransom (USA) – Spinning The Yarn 70 (Barathea **73 p** (IRE) 127) [2007 8d⁶ 8d p8.6g⁵ Nov 17] 52,000Y: big, good-topped colt: fifth foal: half-brother to smart 2003 2-y-o 7f (including Moyglare Stud Stakes) winner Necklace (by Darshaan): dam, ran once, closely related to Kayf Tara and Opera House: fair form in maidens, taking strong hold: will be suited by 1¼m+ (provided he settles down): type to make a better 3-y-o. *H. Morrison*

RED VIXEN (IRE) 4 b.f. Agnes World (USA) 123 – West Escape 95 (Gone West **–** (USA)) [2007 57: p8g Jan 14] smallish filly: modest performer: well below form only outing in 2007: stays 7f: acts on polytrack and firm ground, well beaten on soft: blinkered last 2 starts. *C. N. Allen*

RED WINE 8 b.g. Hamas (IRE) 125§ – Red Bouquet (Reference Point 139) [2007 f12g⁶ **71** f14g⁶ p16g⁶ 14.1d 12d p11g 12v²ᵈ 14m³ 12.1g² p12g⁴ p13.9g Sep 28] smallish, leggy gelding: one-time useful handicapper, fair nowadays: reportedly sustained hairline fracture of pelvis in 2004 and off nearly 3 years: effective at 1½m to 2m: acts on all-weather and any turf going: tried blinkered. *A. J. McCabe*

RED WINGS (IRE) 2 ch.f. (Feb 7) Titus Livius (FR) 115 – Canosa (IRE) 53 (Catrail **68** (USA) 123) [2007 5m⁵ 5m² 5g⁴ 5g⁴ Aug 29] €20,000Y: smallish, sturdy filly: first foal: dam sprint maiden: fair maiden: second to Hadaf at Thirsk: will prove best kept to 5f: sold 7,500 gns. *G. A. Swinbank*

REDWOOD ROCKS (IRE) 6 b.g. Blush Rambler (USA) 119 – Crisp And Cool **67** (USA) (Ogygian (USA)) [2007 75: p7.1g 7.1m⁶ 8s⁶ 7.2g Aug 29] rather leggy gelding: fluent mover: fair handicapper: stays 1m: acts on polytrack, firm and good to soft going: tried blinkered: headstrong front runner. *B. Smart*

REEBAL 3 b.c. Danehill (USA) 126 – Applaud (USA) 105 (Rahy (USA) 115) [2007 86: **82** p6g⁴ p5g 5g May 21] smallish, good-topped colt: fairly useful handicapper: will prove best kept to 5f/6f: acts on polytrack and soft going: often blinkered: sent to Saudi Arabia. *B. J. Meehan*

REEL BUDDY BLAZE 2 ch.g. (Feb 16) Reel Buddy (USA) 118 – Hope Chest 70 **73** (Kris 135) [2007 6m 7d⁴ 8.5m³ 7.5d⁶ Sep 25] sturdy gelding: fair maiden: in frame at Newcastle and Beverley: stays 8.5f: sold 15,000 gns. *T. P. Tate*

REEL BUDDY STAR 2 ch.g. (Mar 9) Reel Buddy (USA) 118 – So Discreet (Tragic **74 p** Role (USA)) [2007 7m² 7g* 7g² Oct 20] 6,000Y: big, good-bodied gelding: second foal: dam unraced half-sister to smart 7f/1m performer Gothenberg: fair form: claimed from T. Tate £6,000 after debut: won maiden at Newcastle in October: shaped better still when second in nursery at Catterick, insufficient test: will be suited by 1m/1¼m: sort to do well in handicaps at 3 yrs. *G. M. Moore*

REEL CLASSY 2 ch.f. (Mar 18) Reel Buddy (USA) 118 – Classy Lassie (IRE) 70 **–** (Goldmark (USA) 113) [2007 7.5g 6d Sep 28] 7,000Y: first foal: dam 6f winner: tailed off in maidens. *M. A. Peill*

REEL COOL 2 b.f. (May 2) Reel Buddy (USA) 118 – Waterfowl Creek (IRE) 88 (Be **–** My Guest (USA) 126) [2007 7g 7d 7.1g Nov 9] sixth living foal: half-sister to several winners, including useful 1¼m winner Maid of Camelot (by Caerleon) and 3-y-o Dark Energy: dam, 1m winner, closely related to smart miler Inchmurrin, herself dam of Inchinor: well held in maidens. *B. Smart*

REEL GIFT 2 b.f. (Apr 2) Reel Buddy (USA) 118 – Its Another Gift 64 (Primo Domi- 101 ?
nie 121) [2007 p6g* 6d² p6g 6.5m⁴ 6.5d 5d Oct 13] 37,000Y: strong, sturdy filly: has a
fast, fluent action: fourth foal: half-sister to 5-y-o Gifted Gamble and fairly useful 2006
2-y-o 5f winner Scented Present (by Foxhound): dam sprint maiden: useful performer:
won maiden at Kempton in July: much improved when 1½ lengths second to Visit in
Princess Margaret Stakes at Ascot, soon dominating: failed to confirm that form, but
often better than bare result, including when fourth of 22 to Dream Eater in St Leger 2-y-o
Stakes at Doncaster (stamina stretched after forcing ride): will prove best at 5f/6f: acts on
polytrack, good to firm and good to soft going. *R. Hannon*

REELING N' ROCKING (IRE) 4 b.f. Mr Greeley (USA) 122 – Mystic Lure 70 82
(Green Desert (USA) 127) [2007 77+: p8g p7.1g 8m⁴ 7m⁴ p7g² p7g* p7g p8g² p8g² p8g
p7g* Dec 28] big, lengthy filly: fairly useful handicapper: won at Lingfield in July and
December: stays 1m: acts on polytrack and good to firm going. *B. W. Hills*

REEL MADAM 2 b.f. (Apr 17) Reel Buddy (USA) 118 – Prim N Proper (Tragic Role –
(USA)) [2007 7m 7.1d⁶ Sep 17] 800Y: lengthy filly: fourth foal: half-sister to 5-y-o
Primarily and 3-y-o Missus Molly Brown: dam maiden: no form in sellers. *K. A. Ryan*

REEL MAN 2 ch.g. (Feb 21) Reel Buddy (USA) 118 – Yanomami (USA) 71 (Slew O' 56
Gold (USA)) [2007 6m 6m p7m Oct 3] big, strong gelding: modest form in maidens, not
knocked about: likely to prove best at 6f/7f: sold 9,000 gns, then gelded. *R. Hannon*

REEL STAR 2 ch.c. (Mar 14) Reel Buddy (USA) 118 – Waltzing Star (IRE) (Danehill 63
(USA) 126) [2007 7g p8.6g⁶ 8d⁶ Oct 18] good-topped colt: modest maiden: probably
stays 8.6f: sold 5,000 gns, sent to Germany. *S. Kirk*

REFINEMENT (IRE) 8 b.m. Oscar (IRE) 122 – Maneree (Mandalus 110) [2007 –
10.5g 10.2g Oct 24] good-bodied mare: second living foal: dam winning hurdler/chaser
up to 3m: smart staying hurdler, winning Grade 1 at Punchestown in April: trip too short
when behind in maidens at Haydock and Bath: will be suited by 1½m+. *Jonjo O'Neill*

REFLECTING (IRE) 4 gr.f. Daylami (IRE) 138 – Church Light 88 (Caerleon (USA) –
132) [2007 69: 7.1m 8m 7m Jun 9] rather leggy, close-coupled filly: fair maiden at best:
no form in handicaps in 2007, visored and eased as if amiss final outing: stays easy 1¼m:
acts on polytrack and good to firm going: sold 8,500 gns in August. *A. W. Carroll*

REFLECTIVE GLORY (IRE) 3 ch.f. City On A Hill (USA) 114 – Sheznice (IRE) 49
58 (Try My Best (USA) 130) [2007 60: 9.3m⁴ 12.1m 8d⁶ 7.9f 8g f11d⁶ Dec 20] good-
topped filly: just poor maiden nowadays: should stay 7f/1m: acts on firm and good to soft
going: in cheekpieces last 4 starts. *J. S. Wainwright*

REFLEX BLUE 10 b.g. Ezzoud (IRE) 126 – Briggsmaid 70 (Elegant Air 119) [2007 –
17.2f Jun 10] lengthy, angular gelding: modest handicapper in 2005: unraced on Flat in
2006: soundly beaten only Flat outing in 2007: stays 2m: acts on all-weather, firm and
good to soft going: often visored: poor and temperamental winning jumper. *R. J. Price*

REGAL BEST (IRE) 2 b.c. (Mar 20) King's Best (USA) 132 – Carranza (IRE) (Lead 68 p
On Time (USA) 123) [2007 7d⁴ Oct 16] 45,000Y: good-topped colt: seventh foal: half-
brother to 3 winners, including 5.5f (in US)/6f (in Ireland at 2 yrs) winner Berlin (by
Common Grounds) and 7-y-o Coustou: dam, French 1m/9.5f winner, out of half-sister to
Derby winner Teenoso: 50/1, encouraging fourth to Prime Exhibit in maiden at Leicester,
left rather isolated wide: will stay 1m: capable of better. *Mrs A. J. Perrett*

REGAL BIRD (USA) 2 b. or br.f. (Apr 18) Grand Slam (USA) 120 – Storm Ring 75
(USA) 100 (Storm Bird (CAN) 134) [2007 6g² p7g² p7m² Dec 9] $190,000Y: fifth foal:
sister to a winner in US and half-sister to 2 winners there: dam, 2-y-o 6f winner, out of
half-sister to Champion Stakes winner Northern Baby: fair maiden: runner-up at Goodwood (to Johar Jamal, then absent 6 months) and Lingfield (2): stays 7f. *M. A. Magnusson*

REGAL CHEER 3 b.f. Royal Applause 124 – Local Abbey (IRE) (Primo Dominie 47
121) [2007 6m⁶ p6g p6g 5s Oct 4] 24,000Y, 21,000 2-y-o: compact filly: second foal:
half-sister to fairly useful 2005 2-y-o 5f winner Local Fancy (by Bahamian Bounty): dam
unraced half-sister to smart 7f to 9f winner Lonesome Dude: poor maiden. *C. F. Wall*

REGAL CURTSY 3 b.f. Royal Applause 124 – Giant Nipper (Nashwan (USA) 135) 67
[2007 67: p7g 8.1d⁵ 7d Oct 18] smallish filly: lightly-raced maiden, fair at best: seems to
stay 1m: best efforts on soft/good to soft going. *P. R. Chamings*

REGAL DREAM (IRE) 5 b.g. Namid 128 – Lovely Me (IRE) 70 (Vision (USA)) 67
[2007 75: p7.1g p7.1g p8.6g⁶ 8.1m 7.6m² p7.1g 7.1m 7d⁴ Oct 9] fair handicapper on turf, a53 +
modest on all-weather: should stay 1m: acts on polytrack and firm going, probably on
good to soft: tried tongue tied/visored. *J. W. Unett*

BGC Stakes (Handicap), Goodwood—Regal Flush proves suited by the step up in trip, beating Camps Bay (right), Man of Vision (left) and the grey Malt Or Mash

REGAL ESTATE 3 b.f. Pivotal 124 – Lady High Havens (IRE) 102 (Bluebird (USA) 125) [2007 8.3g May 21] 220,000Y: lengthy filly: first foal: dam, 2-y-o 7f winner (stayed 1¼m), half-sister to smart Irish 1m winner Middlemarch out of half-sister to Irish 2000 Guineas winner Indian Haven: 12/1, well held in maiden at Windsor: sold 32,000 gns in December. *M. A. Jarvis* **–**

REGAL FLUSH 3 b.c. Sakhee (USA) 136 – Ruthless Rose (USA) (Conquistador Cielo (USA)) [2007 83p: 10m² 10g⁶ 10.1g 12g* 14g* 14.6m⁴ Sep 15] strong, close-coupled colt: has a quick action: smart performer: much improved to win valuable handicaps at Goodwood (BGC Stakes, by ¾ length from Camps Bay) in August and Haydock (beat Samurai Way by 2 lengths in betfredcasino.com Old Borough Cup) in September: good 2 lengths fourth to Lucarno in St Leger at Doncaster final outing, nearest finish: should stay 2m: acts on good to firm and good to soft going: patiently ridden nowadays: sold privately, and has joined Godolphin. *Sir Michael Stoute* **117**

REGAL OVATION 3 b.g. Royal Applause 124 – Briggsmaid 70 (Elegant Air 119) [2007 60: 10g 12g p10g 16.2f⁶ p13.9g⁵ 13.8g³ p13.9g p16g Oct 17] sturdy gelding: modest maiden: stays 1¾m: raced only on polytrack and good going or firmer: tried blinkered: sold 12,000 gns. *W. R. Muir* **56**

REGAL PARADE 3 ch.g. Pivotal 124 – Model Queen (USA) 76 (Kingmambo (USA) 125) [2007 p7.1g* f7g* 7m* 8.1m 8m 7.1g⁴ 7g 7g 8g⁶ 9m⁴ Dec 28] 430,000Y: strong, lengthy gelding: has scope: second foal: half-brother to French 9.7f winner Sister Sylvia (by Fantastic Light): dam, 7.5f winner, out of half-sister to dam of Zafonic: useful performer: won first 3 starts, namely maiden at Wolverhampton in January, and handicaps at Southwell in February and Newmarket (beat Miss Lucifer by 2 lengths despite carrying head awkwardly) in May: ran creditably in handicaps after when fourth at Sandown and Goodwood: stays 9f: acts on all-weather and good to firm going: took no interest final outing: not one to trust: sold 16,000 gns. *M. Johnston* **98 §**

REGAL QUEST (IRE) 3 b.f. Marju (IRE) 127 – Princess Sceptre (Cadeaux Genereux 131) [2007 83: 7.1g⁶ 7s² 8g 7g 7g³ 7m 7g² p8m⁶ p7g⁴ Dec 28] good-bodied filly: fairly useful performer: left S. Kirk 13,000 gns after seventh outing: free-going sort, probably best up to 7f: acts on polytrack and soft ground: tongue tied (ran well) last 2 starts. *S. C. Williams* **91**

REGAL RAIDER (IRE) 4 b.g. King's Best (USA) 132 – Alegranza (IRE) 106 (Lake Coniston (IRE) 131) [2007 84: 8.1g 7d 6f 6g 6d² 7.1m 6g⁴ 6g p7.1g⁵ p6g p6g³ p6g⁵ p6g⁴ p6m* p7m* Dec 8] leggy gelding: fair handicapper: claimed from I. Semple £4,000 eleventh start: won at Lingfield in November and December: best at 6f/7f: acts on polytrack, firm and good to soft going: wears cheekpieces nowadays. *A. M. Hales* **80**

REGAL RHYTHM (IRE) 2 b.g. (Jan 20) Namid 128 – King of All (IRE) (King of Clubs 124) [2007 5f⁵ 5g⁵ 5.1d* p6g 6g³ 6d³ 6d Oct 11] 23,000F, 19,500Y: strong gelding: third foal: half-brother to fairly useful 2004 2-y-o 6f winner Haunting Memories (by **82**

Barathea): dam, Italian 6f/7f winner, out of sister to high-class miler Noalcoholic: fairly useful performer: won maiden at Bath in May: third in nurseries at Newbury and Haydock: best at 5f/6f: acts on good to soft going, promise on firm and polytrack: sold 10,000 gns. *B. J. Meehan*

REGAL ROYALE 4 b.g. Medicean 128 – Regal Rose 110 (Danehill (USA) 126) [2007 **83 d** 98: p8g p6g⁶ p8f p7g p7g⁶ p6g p6g 6m⁶ 6g³ 6m⁵ p6g⁴ 6d p6g p7.1g p6m p6g³ p6g³ p6g p7g Dec 30] well-made gelding: useful at best, just fairly useful in 2007: below form after third start: stays 1m: acts on polytrack and good to firm going: tried visored/blinkered: none too genuine. *Peter Grayson*

REGAL STEP 2 b.f. (Jan 21) Royal Applause 124 – Two Step 60 (Mujtahid (USA) **85** 118) [2007 5.1m* 5m 5d⁵ Jul 6] strong, good-bodied filly: has scope: fourth foal: half-sister to 3 winners, including fairly useful but irresolute 2005 2-y-o 5f winner Smooch (by Inchinor) and 3-y-o Corlough Mountain: dam 5f/7f winner: fairly useful form: won maiden at Nottingham (beat Unilateral by 2 lengths) in June: had excuses for failure to progress, found to be in season after Queen Mary Stakes at Royal Ascot and went off too fast in listed race at Sandown: will prove best at 5f/6f. *R. M. H. Cowell*

REGAL SUNSET (IRE) 4 b.g. Desert Prince (IRE) 130 – Sunsetter (USA) 94 (Diesis **64** 133) [2007 73: 12d p8.6g 10.1f* 10.1m⁶ Aug 15] close-coupled, good-topped gelding: just modest handicapper in 2007: won at Yarmouth (ladies event) in July: stays 1¼m: acts on polytrack, firm and good to soft going: tried in headgear: sold 5,000 gns. *D. E. Cantillon*

REGAL TRADITION (IRE) 2 b.c. (Apr 30) Traditionally (USA) 117 – Dathuil **68** (IRE) 97 (Royal Academy (USA) 130) [2007 p6g p7.1g³ p7.1g³ Oct 27] fair maiden: twice third at Wolverhampton: will stay 1m: raced only on polytrack. *P. A. Blockley*

REGAL VEIL 2 b.f. (Feb 8) Royal Applause 124 – Shararah 87 (Machiavellian (USA) **–** 123) [2007 6d p6g p7.1g Oct 27] stocky filly: first foal: dam 6f winner: no show in maidens. *S. C. Williams*

betfredcasino.com Old Borough Cup Stakes (Handicap), Haydock—Regal Flush follows up off a mark 9 lb higher; Samurai Way (No.3) is second with Dansili Dancer (rail) third

*Betfredpoker Classic Trial, Sandown—Regime shows a good turn of foot
to start his season off in good style; Striving Storm and Asperity (hidden) are placed*

REGENCY RED (IRE) 9 ch.g. Dolphin Street (FR) 125 – Future Romance (Distant **64**
Relative 128) [2007 64: p12.2g⁶ p12.2g² p12.2g⁶ 12g³ p12.2g⁴ p12.2g⁵ 11.9d⁶
p12.2g 12.1g³ p12.2g* 11.6f⁴ p9.5g 12.1g* 12m⁶ 12d³ p12.2g⁴ p12.2g³ p12.2d p12.2s³
p12.2g³ Dec 29] lengthy gelding: modest performer: won sellers at Wolverhampton
(amateurs) in June and Beverley (handicap) in August: stays 2m, races mainly at 1½m:
acts on all-weather, firm and good to soft going: sometimes finds little, but is consistent.
W. M. Brisbourne

REGENT'S SECRET (USA) 7 br.g. Cryptoclearance (USA) – Misty Regent (CAN) **83**
(Vice Regent (CAN)) [2007 89: 7.1g 10.1g 9.1g 8.3f 8.3g³ 7.9g* 7.9d 8m 9.2m² 8.3g 10g
9.9m⁵ 9.2s⁵ Sep 24] leggy, useful-looking gelding: fairly useful handicapper: won
at Carlisle in June: stays 1¼m: acts on polytrack, firm and soft going (well beaten on
heavy): tried visored at 3 yrs, usually in cheekpieces nowadays: often slowly away:
waited with. *J. S. Goldie*

REGIME (IRE) 3 b.c. Golan (IRE) 129 – Juno Madonna (IRE) (Sadler's Wells (USA) **115**
132) [2007 106: 10g* 12g 10g² 10m⁵ 10m³ 12d³ Oct 27] well-made colt: has a quick
action: smart performer: won Betfredpoker Classic Trial at Sandown in April by 2 lengths
from Striving Storm: good efforts when placed after, in Prix Eugene Adam at Maisons-
Laffitte (beaten short head by Harland), Kilternan Stakes at Leopardstown (1¾ lengths
third behind Hearthstead Maison) and St Simon Stakes at Newbury (2 lengths third to
Crime Scene, still on bridle when winner kicked clear): stays 1½m: acts on good to firm
and good to soft ground: held up: said to have suffered minor injury when thirteenth in
Derby at Epsom second start. *M. L. W. Bell*

REGISTRAR 5 ch.g. Machiavellian (USA) 123 – Confidante (USA) 95 (Dayjur (USA) **64**
137) [2007 8.2g 8g 7m 6g⁴ 5.2d³ 6f p6g⁴ p6g 6d 5.1g³ 5.1g* p6g Nov 23] lengthy,
good-topped gelding: fair handicapper: won at Nottingham in November: effective at 5f
to 9f: acts on polytrack, good to firm and good to soft ground: held up. *Mrs C. A. Dunnett*

REGULUS WAY (GR) 2 ch.c. (Jan 27) Harmonic Way 121 – Exotic Way (GR) (Flash **–**
N Thunder (USA) 115) [2007 p8g Oct 29] workmanlike Greek-bred colt: last in maiden
at Lingfield (pulled hard). *P. R. Chamings*

REHEARSED (IRE) 4 ch.f. In The Wings 128 – Emilia Romagna (GER) (Acatenango **81**
(GER) 127) [2007 79: p16g 12m* 14.1s² 14.1d⁵ 14.1d* 12d* 14g⁴ Nov 9] strong filly:
fairly useful handicapper: won at Salisbury in July and October and Newbury (ladies)
later in October: effective at 1½m to 2m: acts on polytrack, soft and good to firm ground:
consistent. *H. Morrison*

REIGNING MONARCH (USA) 4 b.g. Fusaichi Pegasus (USA) 130 – Torros Straits **61**
(USA) 82 (Boundary (USA) 117) [2007 –: 8d 6g 7s⁴ 7.1s⁴ 6f* 6f 7f Sep 10] leggy gelding:
fair handicapper: left A. O'Brien in Ireland 5,000 gns after debut at 3 yrs: won at Lingfield in August: stays 7f: acts on firm and soft going. *Miss Z. C. Davison*

RELATIVE ORDER 2 b.c. (Feb 26) Diktat 126 – Aunt Ruby (USA) 67 (Rubiano **83**
(USA)) [2007 6m 6s⁶ 6m⁴ 7m* 7m⁶ Sep 14] 29,000Y: big, strong colt: third foal:
half-brother to 4-y-o South Cape: dam 7f seller winner: fairly useful performer: much
improved to win nursery at Ascot (worked out well) in August: best excused final start:
will stay 1m: acts on good to firm going. *J. R. Best*

RELATIVE STRENGTH (IRE) 2 ch.c. (Feb 25) Kris Kin (USA) 126 – Monalee **70**
Lass (IRE) 72 (Mujtahid (USA) 118) [2007 p10g* Dec 12] 5,800F, 11,500Y: first foal:
dam Irish 5f to 1m winner: 12/1, won maiden at Kempton, dictating: not sure to stay much
beyond 1¼m. *A. M. Balding*

RELINQUISHED 2 b.f. (Feb 28) Royal Applause 124 – Marl 94 (Lycius (USA) 124) **80**
[2007 6g⁴ 6m 7d² 7m³ 7.5g* p7.1g³ 8m⁴ 9m⁴ 7g* 8g Nov 3] 22,000F: big, strong filly:
eighth foal: sister to 2004 2-y-o 6f winner Marching Song and half-sister to several
winners, including smart 7f to 8.5f (in US) winner Green Line (by Green Desert) and
3-y-o Medley: dam 2-y-o 5f winner: fairly useful performer: won maiden at Beverley in
July and nursery at Brighton in October: stiff task in listed race final start: probably best
at 7f/1m: acts on polytrack, good to soft and good to firm going. *J. Noseda*

RELIX (FR) 7 gr.g. Linamix (FR) 127 – Resleona (Caerleon (USA) 132) [2007 15.8s **–**
Oct 9] modest staying hurdler: no form on Flat. *A. M. Crow*

RELOCATION (IRE) 6 b.g. Grand Lodge (USA) 125 – Olean (Sadler's Wells (USA) **52**
132) [2007 –: 14g 12s⁴ 11.1d³ 12m Sep 4] modest maiden: third in handicap at Hamilton:
pulled up final outing: probably stayed 1¾m: acted on firm and good to soft going: dead.
J. J. Lambe, Ireland

REMARK (IRE) 3 b.g. Machiavellian (USA) 123 – Remuria (USA) 93 (Theatrical **–**
128) [2007 50: p8.6g 12s 9.9g 9.8m Aug 28] unfurnished gelding: maiden: little form in
2007: tried tongue tied: said to have had breathing problem second start. *M. W. Easterby*

REMINISCENT (IRE) 8 b.g. Kahyasi 130 – Eliza Orzeszkowa (IRE) 69 (Polish **–**
Patriot (USA) 128) [2007 –, a65: p16.5g² p13.9g* p13.9g³ p16.5g 14.1g p13.9g p13.9g⁴ **a66**
p13.9d p13.9g Dec 31] rather leggy gelding: fair handicapper: won at Wolverhampton in
January: stays 16.5f: acts on all-weather, little recent form on turf: usually wears headgear. *B. P. J. Baugh*

REMIS VELISQUE 4 ch.f. Fraam 114 – Charming Tina (IRE) (Indian Ridge 123) **–**
[2007 p12g p12g Jan 27] first foal: dam unraced on Flat (no sign of ability over jumps):
well held in bumpers/maidens at Lingfield. *B. G. Powell*

RENEGADE (IRE) 6 b.g. Fasliyev (USA) 120 – Arcade (Rousillon (USA) 133) [2007 **–**
64, a–: p8g⁵ 6m Apr 9] modest performer in 2006: no form in 2007: often in cheekpieces/
blinkers. *Mrs L. J. Mongan*

REN'S MAGIC 9 gr.g. Petong 126 – Bath 76 (Runnett 125) [2007 11.6d 10f 11.9m **–**
p12g Aug 28] angular gelding: no form in Britain since 2003 (won handicap at Dos
Hermanas in 2006): tried in visor/cheekpieces/tongue tie. *E. J. Creighton*

REPLICATOR 2 b.c. (Mar 26) Mujahid (USA) 125 – Valldemosa 81 (Music Boy 124) **71**
[2007 p5g p5g⁴ 5.1m⁶ p6g⁵ 6v⁵ p6g² p6g⁴ 6d* Oct 1] compact colt: fair performer: in
frame in nurseries at Kempton and Lingfield prior to winning maiden at Brighton: should
prove best at 5f/6f: acts on polytrack, good to firm and good to soft going. *Pat Eddery*

REQUISITE 2 ch.f. (Apr 18) Pivotal 124 – Chicarica (USA) 112 (The Minstrel (CAN) **72 +**
135) [2007 5.1g⁵ p6g² Dec 1] 15,000 2-y-o: attractive filly: half-sister to several winners,
including fairly useful 2001 2-y-o 5f winner Morouj (by Gone West) and fairly useful
6f (at 2 yrs) to 1m (in France) winner Court Lane (by Machiavellian): dam won Cherry
Hinton Stakes: fair form in maidens at Nottingham and Wolverhampton (runner-up,
forced wide). *Jane Chapple-Hyam*

RESAASS (USA) 4 b. or br.g. Seeking The Gold (USA) – Sheroog (USA) 77 (Shareef –
Dancer (USA) 135) [2007 12g⁶ p13.9g 10d Oct 10] stocky gelding: well held in maidens.
J. O'Reilly

RESCUE ME 2 b.f. (Feb 28) Red Ransom (USA) – Duchcov 101 (Caerleon (USA) **64**
132) [2007 p5g* 7.1d 8s Aug 24] 38,000Y: angular filly: second foal: half-sister to winner
in Denmark by Diesis: dam 1¼m winner (including in US): modest performer: won
maiden at Kempton in May: stiff tasks in listed race and nursery after: should stay 1m.
R. Hannon

RESOLUTE DEFENDER (IRE) 2 b.g. (Apr 29) Namid 128 – Snowspin 75 (Car- **58**
white 127) [2007 6s 6m 6s Aug 24] modest maiden: raced only at 6f, bred for further
(dam stayed 2m). *J. Howard Johnson*

RESONATE (IRE) 9 b.h. Erins Isle 121 – Petronelli (USA) (Sir Ivor (USA) 135) **92**
[2007 89, a79: 10.1d³ 8.9s⁶ 10m³ p11g³ 10.3m⁴ 10d⁴ p10g⁵ Dec 4] useful-looking horse: **a81**
fairly useful handicapper, better on turf than all-weather: best at 1¼m/1½m: acts on
polytrack, firm and soft going: held up: consistent. *A. G. Newcombe*

RESOUNDING GLORY (IRE) 2 b.c. (Feb 2) Honour And Glory (USA) 122 – **92**
Resounding Grace (USA) (Thunder Gulch (USA) 129) [2007 6m 5m³ 6g* 7g Oct 27]
$50,000F, €58,000Y: rangy colt, unfurnished at 2 yrs: second foal: dam, French/US
maiden, half-sister to smart performer up to 1¼m Flat Spin: fairly useful form: left Mrs
A. Duffield after debut: much improved to win maiden at Newcastle in October by 1¼
lengths from Hamish McGonagall (pair clear): much better than bare result in nursery at
Doncaster, poorly drawn: should stay 7f/1m. *R. A. Fahey*

RESPLENDENT ACE (IRE) 3 b.c. Trans Island 119 – Persian Polly 99 (Persian **70**
Bold 123) [2007 88p: p7g⁵ p8.6g² p8g* p10g³ 9g 10g p8g p8g p7g⁶ p8g p10g² p10m p10g **a79**
p10g p10g⁵ Dec 28] sturdy colt: fair performer: won maiden at Kempton in March: stays
easy 1¼m: raced mostly on polytrack. *P. Howling*

RESPLENDENT ALPHA 3 ch.g. Best of The Bests (IRE) 122 – Sunley Scent 85 **92**
(Wolfhound (USA) 126) [2007 97: a6.5g⁶ p7g³ 6m 6f⁶ 6m p6g 6m 6g⁴ p6g⁶ p6g p6g f6d²
f6d² p7.1g⁶ Dec 31] lengthy gelding: fairly useful performer: should be suited by 7f: acts
on all-weather: tried tongue tied: sometimes slowly away. *P. Howling*

RESPLENDENT LIGHT 2 b.c. (Jan 27) Fantastic Light (USA) 134 – Bright Halo **80 +**
(IRE) (Bigstone (IRE) 126) [2007 7g p7g⁴ 7.1g⁶ 8m* Oct 22] 85,000Y: good-topped colt:
fourth foal: half-brother to useful 6f (at 2 yrs) and 1m winner Nantyglo (by Mark of
Esteem): dam, French 1¼m winner, half-sister to very smart Irish performer up to 1½m
L'Ancresse, Prix Saint-Alary winner Cerulean Sky (dam of 3-y-o Honolulu) and smart
stayer Qaatef: fairly useful form: developed well, won nursery at Pontefract final start:
will be suited by 1¼m/1½m. *W. R. Muir*

RESPLENDENT NOVA 5 b.g. Pivotal 124 – Santiburi Girl 77 (Casteddu 111) [2007 **85**
90: p7.1g² p7g² 8s 8.1g 7g p7g² p7g³ 8d 7g² 7d* 8m p7g* 8g Sep 19] sturdy gelding: **a95**
useful handicapper on all-weather, fairly useful on turf: won at Yarmouth in July and
Kempton (beat Blackat Blackkitten by short head, making all) in August: best at 7f: acts
on polytrack, soft and good to firm going: tried visored (ran poorly): versatile tactically.
P. Howling

RESTLESS GENIUS (IRE) 2 b.c. (Apr 18) Captain Rio 122 – Mainmise (USA) –
(Septieme Ciel (USA) 123) [2007 6m Jul 16] good-topped colt: 40/1, shaped as if needing
run in maiden at Windsor. *A. M. Balding*

RESTLESS SOUL 3 b.f. Singspiel (IRE) 133 – Seasonal Splendour (IRE) 95 (Prince **77 +**
Rupert (FR) 121) [2007 –: p10g⁵ p12.2g 10m⁴ 12g 12g 9.9m⁴ 10.2d⁴ 10d 10.2g⁶ 10.3m⁶
p12.2g* p12g Dec 1] rather leggy filly: fair performer: won maiden at Wolverhampton in
November: sometimes highly tried (and flattered) earlier: bred to stay beyond 1½m: acts
on polytrack, good to firm and good to soft going: troublesome in stall/pulled up fourth
outing: sold 20,000 gns, sent to USA. *C. A. Cyzer*

RESTLESS SWALLOW 2 gr.g. (May 5) Bandmaster (USA) 97 – Pink Petal (North- –
ern Game) [2007 7.1m Sep 13] tailed off in maiden at Chepstow. *C. J. Down*

RESURGE (IRE) 2 b.c. (May 7) Danehill Dancer (IRE) 117 – Resurgence (Polar **77 p**
Falcon (USA) 126) [2007 7m Oct 5] 100,000F: tall, close-coupled colt: fourth foal: half-
brother to 3 winners, notably high-class miler Araafa (by Mull of Kintyre) and 3-y-o Blue
Monkey: dam unraced sister to Pivotal: 14/1 and backward, in touch until running green
when seventh to Almajd in maiden at Newmarket: may prove best up to 7f: will improve.
J. Noseda

RETALIATE 3 br.f. Wizard King 122 – Retaliator 80 (Rudimentary (USA) 118) [2007 **52**
75: p8g p7.1g 5g f6g⁴ 6d 7s⁴ 6m Aug 15] strong, workmanlike filly: just modest performer in 2007: bred to stay 7f, though speedy front runner: acts on firm and good to soft
going: sold 800 gns. *M. Quinn*

RETIREMENT 8 b.g. Zilzal (USA) 137 – Adeptation (USA) (Exceller (USA) 129) **51**
[2007 –: p10g² p8g p10g p11g⁶ p9.5g 12g⁵ 8.5g 8.5g 8.5g* 8.5g Aug 27] leggy, good-
topped gelding: unimpressive mover: just modest nowadays: left R. Stronge after fifth
start: subsequently ran at Les Landes (Jersey), winning handicap in August: effective at
1m, seems to stay 1½m: acts on all-weather, soft and good to firm going: tried in cheekpieces. *Mrs B. Powell, Jersey*

RETTORICAL LAD 2 gr. or ro.c. (Jan 22) Vettori (IRE) 119 – Reciprocal (IRE) 88 **–**
(Night Shift (USA)) [2007 8d Oct 11] tall, angular colt: 50/1, reported breathing problem
in maiden at Newbury. *Jamie Poulton*

REUNITE (IRE) 4 ch.f. Kingmambo (USA) 125 – Allez Les Trois (USA) 114 (River- **99**
man (USA) 131) [2007 111: 10.1g³ Sep 19] useful-looking filly: smart performer at 3 yrs:
suffered minor setback and off 13 months, not discredited when 1½ lengths third to
Samira Gold in listed event at Yarmouth sole 4-y-o outing, travelling well before faltering
at finish: stays 1½m: acts on any going: has left Godolphin. *Saeed bin Suroor*

REVELINO (IRE) 8 b.g. Revoque (IRE) 122 – Forelino (USA) 62§ (Trempolino **–**
(USA) 135) [2007 p12.2g p16g p16g Oct 4] useful-looking gelding: fairly useful in 2002
for E. Dunlop: well held in 4 Flat outings since. *Mrs N. S. Evans*

REVERENCE 6 ch.g. Mark of Esteem (IRE) 137 – Imperial Bailiwick (IRE) 104 **116 +**
(Imperial Frontier (USA) 112) [2007 127: 5g⁵ 6d⁶ 5g Aug 23] strong, heavy-bodied gelding: takes eye in appearance: has reportedly fractured pelvis twice: high-class performer
at best: further significant improvement in 2006, last 2 wins in Nunthorpe Stakes at York
and Sprint Cup at Haydock: reportedly underwent treatment on knee during winter (off 9
months) and only smart at best in 2007, fifth to Hoh Mike in Sprint Stakes at Sandown
and sixth to Balthazaar's Gift in Hackwood Stakes at Ascot: effective at 5f/6f: has form
on good to firm going, all wins on good or softer (yet to race on heavy): reportedly bled in
Nunthorpe Stakes at York final outing: game and genuine. *E. J. Alston*

REVEUR 4 b.f. Rossini (USA) 118 – Without Warning (IRE) (Warning 136) [2007 69: **58**
p7.1g⁴ p8g⁶ p8.6g⁶ 8.1m⁶ 9.2g p8.6g 9.7g⁶ p7g⁵ p9.5g⁴ p9.5g* p8.6g³ p9.5g⁶ p8.6g
Nov 30] angular filly: modest performer: trained fifth to seventh starts by K. R. Burke:
won minor event at Wolverhampton in October: stays 10.5f: acts on polytrack, raced
mainly on going firmer than good on turf: held up. *M. Mullineaux*

REVE VERT (FR) 2 b.c. (Apr 18) Oasis Dream 129 – Comme d'Habitude (USA) 72 **49**
(Caro 133) [2007 6m 6.1m 7g Oct 16] strong colt: behind in maidens, poor form on debut.
A. W. Carroll

REVISIONIST (IRE) 3 b.g. Indian Danehill (IRE) 124 – Lady of Dreams (IRE) 84 **65**
(Prince Rupert (FR) 121) [2007 67: 11.6m 11.6d 11.5m p10g* p11g 12v 12d Sep 11] big,
strong gelding: fair handicapper: form on Flat in 2007 only when winning at Lingfield in
June: left R. Hannon after next start: stays 1¼m: acts on polytrack, soft and good to firm
going: tried visored. *Seamus Lynch, Ireland*

REVIVALISM 2 b.c. (Feb 26) Where Or When (IRE) 124 – Revival 86 (Sadler's Wells **67**
(USA) 132) [2007 6g May 19] sturdy, useful-looking colt: fourth foal: half-brother to
fairly useful Irish 8.7f winner Uva Fragola (by Nashwan) and 3-y-o Danalova: dam, 1¼m
winner, half-sister to very smart sprinter Pivotal: 11/1 and better for race,fair form when
mid-field behind Coasting in maiden at Newbury, only start. *J. H. M. Gosden*

REVOLVE 7 b.g. Pivotal 124 – Alpine Time (IRE) 85 (Tirol 127) [2007 63: p10g³ p10g⁵ **66**
9.7m⁵ p10g p10g² 9g³ p11g p10g 8g Oct 25] fair performer: best form at 1¼m: acts on
polytrack, good to firm and good to soft ground: usually blinkered/in cheekpieces: has
bled, including seventh/final outings. *Mrs L. J. Mongan*

REVOLVING WORLD (IRE) 4 b.g. Spinning World (USA) 130 – Mannakea **60**
(USA) (Fairy King (USA)) [2007 55: 12m* 12.1g⁵ 14m Sep 30] modest handicapper:
won at Ripon (selling event) in June: stays 1½m: acts on good to firm going: tried in
blinkers/cheekpieces: tongue tied. *L. R. James*

REVUE PRINCESS (IRE) 2 b.f. (Apr 20) Mull of Kintyre (USA) 114 – Blues Queen **64**
85 (Lahib (USA) 129) [2007 5m⁵ 5s³ 5v² 5g* Jul 31] €13,000Y: strong, sturdy filly: sixth
foal: half-sister to 3 winners, including fairly useful 2003 2-y-o 6f winner Waterline Blue
(by Mujadil) and 2002 2-y-o 6f winner Speed Queen (by Goldmark): dam 2-y-o 6f

winner: modest form: won maiden at Beverley (flashed tail): should prove best kept to 5f: signs of temperament. *T. D. Easterby*

REWSKI (IRE) 2 b.g. (Apr 6) Beckett (IRE) 116 – Miraculous (IRE) (Marju (IRE) **42** 127) [2007 p6g 5m Jul 29] poor form in maidens: dead. *Ms Deborah J. Evans*

RHAAM 3 b.c. Fantastic Light (USA) 134 – Elhilmeya (IRE) 94 (Unfuwain (USA) 131) **87** [2007 80p: 10m[6] 11.9g[3] 11.9m[4] 12g* 12.3m* 14g 11.9g Sep 12] lengthy colt: fairly useful performer: won maiden at Pontefract in July and handicap at Chester in August: should stay 1¾m: unraced on extremes of going: wandered final outing: sold 32,000 gns, sent to Qatar. *B. W. Hills*

RHADEGUNDA 2 b.f. (Mar 21) Pivotal 124 – St Radegund 85 (Green Desert (USA) **65 p** 127) [2007 p7g Nov 17] fifth foal: half-sister to 3 winners, including 3-y-o My Secrets and 5-y-o Halla San: dam, 7f winner, out of 1000 Guineas and Sussex Stakes winner On The House: 4/1 and green, seventh to Fantasy Princess in maiden at Lingfield: will do better. *J. H. M. Gosden*

RHAPSILIAN 3 b.f. Dansili 127 – Rivers Rhapsody 104 (Dominion 123) [2007 p6g **66** 6g[4] 6m 5f[6] 6d 6d[5] 7d p6g* p7g[4] p6m[6] p6g[2] Dec 19] tall filly: sister to 4-y-o Ripples Maid and half-sister to several winners, including 2003 2-y-o 6f/7f winner Peak To Creek (by Mujadil) and 5f (at 2 yrs) to 1m winner For Your Eyes Only (by Pursuit of Love), both smart: dam 5f winner, including at 2 yrs: fair handicapper: won at Lingfield (apprentices) in October: barely stays 7f: acts on polytrack and good to soft going. *J. A. Geake*

RHODE ISLAND RED (USA) 2 ch.f. (Jan 23) Tale of The Cat (USA) 113 – Miss **52** Sobriety (CAN) (Temperence Hill (USA)) [2007 p7g 7m 5.1f Aug 24] $160,000Y: stocky filly: eighth foal: closely related to US 2-y-o Grade 1 7f/8.5f winner Habibti (by Tabasco Cat) and half-sister to US 6.5f to 8.5f winner Skeete's Bay (by Bold Ruckus): dam unraced half-sister to Kentucky/Canadian Oaks winner Gal In A Ruckus: modest maiden, form only on debut: likely to stay 1m: once tongue tied. *B. J. Meehan*

RHONDDA VALLEY 3 ch.f. Inchinor 119 – Morgannwg (IRE) 86 (Simply Great **61** (FR) 122) [2007 10m p11g Jul 4] 15,000Y: lengthy filly: sister to fairly useful 1¼m and 2m winner Incursion and half-sister to several winners, including 5f/6f winner Black Army (by Aragon): dam, 7f winner, sister to useful Irish performer up to 1¾m General Cloney: better effort in maidens when seventh at Lingfield on debut. *Mrs A. J. Perrett*

RHUBY RIVER (IRE) 5 b.m. Bahhare (USA) 122 – Westside Flyer 59 (Risk Me (FR) **49** 127) [2007 p8g[5] Dec 16] poor maiden: should stay 1¼m+: acts on polytrack. *R. Dickin*

RHUEPUNZEL 3 b.f. Elnadim (USA) 128 – Fairy Story (IRE) 80 (Persian Bold 123) **86** [2007 62p: 8.5s* 7.1g* 9g 8.3d* 8m p7.1g 7d Oct 27] leggy, lengthy filly: fairly useful performer: much improved in 2007, winning maiden at Beverley in June, and handicaps at Warwick in July and Windsor in August: free-going sort, but stays 8.5f: acts on soft ground: slowly away penultimate outing. *G. A. Butler*

RHYMING SLANG (USA) 3 b. or br.c. Street Cry (IRE) 130 – Purr Pleasure (USA) **90** (El Gran Senor (USA) 136) [2007 63p: p8g 8.3d[2] p8g* p10g[6] Oct 12] sturdy colt: fairly useful performer, lightly raced: won maiden at Lingfield in September: stays 1¼m: raced only on polytrack and good to soft going: sold 24,000 gns. *J. Noseda*

RICCI DE MARE 2 b.f. (Feb 8) Cadeaux Genereux 131 – Procession 72 (Zafonic **55** (USA) 130) [2007 6d[5] p6g p6g Nov 21] lengthy filly: second foal: half-sister to winner in Sweden by Rock of Gibraltar: dam, maiden stayed 1¼m, out of Cherry Hinton winner Applaud: modest form in sprint maidens, all within a month. *Sir Mark Prescott*

RICHARDS CLAIRE (IRE) 6 b.m. Darazari (IRE) 123 – Loquacious (IRE) 79 (Dis- **–** tinctly North (USA) 115) [2007 –: p10g Jan 20] lightly-raced maiden on Flat: no form since 2005: tried tongue tied. *D. P. Keane*

RICHARDTHESECOND (IRE) 2 b.g. (Mar 6) Acclamation 118 – Tahlil 46 **68** (Cadeaux Genereux 131) [2007 5m 6g[3] 5.1d[6] 6g[5] 6m[2] p5.1g[6] p6g[4] p5g[2] Oct 24] robust **a61** gelding: fair maiden on turf, modest on all-weather: left W. M. Brisbourne after third start: second in nurseries at Lingfield and Kempton (blinkered): effective at 5f/6f: acts on polytrack and good to firm going: quirky: sold 2,000 gns, rejoined former trainer. *R. M. Beckett*

RICHCAR (IRE) 2 b.c. (Mar 29) Almutawakel 126 – Gerobies Girl (USA) 86 (Deposit **63** Ticket (USA)) [2007 6d 7g Aug 24] €45,000F, 33,000 2-y-o: strong colt: second foal: dam, Irish 8.5f winner, half-sister to smart performer up to 1½m Santillana: modest form in mid-field in maidens at Ascot and Newbury (tired/eased): will stay at least 1m. *R. M. Beckett*

RICHELIEU 5 b.g. Machiavellian (USA) 123 – Darling Flame (USA) 101 (Capote **81**
(USA)) [2007 69: p5.1g p9.5g p7.1g 5.8f* 7f⁴ 6g² 6d² 7v 5g p7.1g³ p8.6g⁶ Oct 20] fairly **a62**
useful handicapper on turf, modest on all-weather: won at Navan in April: best effort in 5
runs at Wolverhampton in 2007 when third: seems best around 6f: acts on polytrack, firm
and good to soft ground, possibly not on heavy: usually held up. *J. J. Lambe, Ireland*

RICH HARVEST (USA) 2 b. or br.c. (Apr 6) High Yield (USA) 121 – Mangano **–**
(USA) (Quiet American (USA)) [2007 p7g Dec 29] 33/1, well held in maiden at Lingfield, failing to settle. *A. P. Jarvis*

RICH JAMES (IRE) 2 b.g. (Feb 23) Ishiguru (USA) 114 – Mourir d'Aimer (USA) **60 d**
(Trempolino (USA) 135) [2007 6g⁶ 6m 5v⁴ 6m⁶ 7.1d p6g⁶ f6d² Dec 14] quite good-
topped gelding: modest maiden: best effort second start: best at 5f/6f: acts on fibresand,
heavy and good to firm going. *J. D. Bethell*

RICH KID (IRE) 2 b.c. (Mar 16) Spartacus (IRE) 107 – Sea Glen (IRE) (Glenstal **71**
(USA) 118) [2007 5.1g 6m 6f⁶ 7m* p7.1g² Nov 20] round-barrelled colt: fair form: won
nursery at Leicester in September, then left R. Hannon: stays 7f: acts on good to firm
going. *R. A. Harris*

RICH LORD 3 b.g. Zamindar (USA) 116 – Al Corniche (IRE) 62 (Bluebird (USA) **71**
125) [2007 f8g* p8.6g 8.2s f8g⁵ May 22] fair performer: best effort when winning maiden
at Southwell in February: raced only around 1m: acts on fibresand: blinkered final outing:
sold 6,500 gns, joined Ferdy Murphy. *J. D. Bethell*

RICHTEE (IRE) 6 ch.m. Desert Sun 120 – Santarene (IRE) 46 (Scenic 128) [2007 **54 §**
76d: 12f⁴ p12.2g 12g⁶ 12.3f 13d 10s³ 12.1s 10.1d 10.1f p9.5g p12.2g Oct 18] strong,
good-topped mare: modest handicapper nowadays: left R. Fahey after sixth outing:
stays easy 13f: acts on firm and soft going: sometimes in cheekpieces/blinkers: sometimes slowly away: unreliable. *I. W. McInnes*

RICKETY BRIDGE (IRE) 4 ch.g. Elnadim (USA) 128 – Kriva 69 (Reference Point **77**
139) [2007 p12.2g* p12g³ p12g⁴ 12m 11.9d⁶ p13.9g* p13.9g² Nov 27] modest form only
outing in bumper: fair performer on Flat: won maiden at Wolverhampton (wandered)
in April and amateur handicap there in November: stays 1¾m: best form on polytrack.
P. R. Chamings

RIDE A WHITE SWAN 2 gr.c. (May 16) Baryshnikov (AUS) – The Manx Touch **66 ?**
(IRE) 70 (Petardia 113) [2007 7m 7.1g 7g Aug 24] down the field in maidens, seemingly
fair form at Sandown second start. *P. A. Blockley*

RIDGE DANCE 2 b.c. (Jan 31) Selkirk (USA) 129 – Pearl Dance (USA) 102 (Nureyev **105**
(USA) 131) [2007 6m⁶ 6m 7.1m* 7g* 8d⁴ 8g Oct 27] close-coupled, attractive colt: first
foal: dam, 2-y-o 6f winner (stayed 1m), half-sister to useful German stayer Ocean Sea:
useful performer: won maiden at Sandown in August and nursery at Yarmouth (by 5
lengths) in September: further progress when close fourth to City Leader in Royal Lodge
Stakes at Ascot, finishing strongly: seemed amiss (eased right off) in Racing Post Trophy
at Doncaster: stays 1m: acts on good to firm and good to soft going. *J. H. M. Gosden*

RIDGE ROSE 3 b.f. Sadler's Wells (USA) 132 – Fig Tree Drive (USA) 94 (Miswaki **75**
(USA) 124) [2007 10s⁴ 10d⁵ 12m⁵ Aug 6] 270,000Y: big, strong filly: closely related to
5-y-o Estate and half-sister to smart 1m/1¼m winners Marbush (including in UAE, by
Linamix) and Sublimity (by Selkirk), latter also Champion Hurdle winner: dam 2-y-o 6f
winner only start: best effort in maidens when fifth to Alaghiraar at Leicester: plenty to
do final start: sent to USA. *L. M. Cumani*

RIDGEWAY JAZZ 2 b.f. (Apr 8) Kalanisi (IRE) 132 – Billie Holiday (Fairy King **49**
(USA)) [2007 f5g⁴ p6g p7.1g p10g p8.6g³ f8d* Dec 15] third foal: dam, maiden,
half-sister to smart Irish performers up to 1m/1¼m Rayouni and Raiyoun: poor performer:
won nursery at Southwell final start: should stay 1¼m: raced only on all-weather.
M. D. I. Usher

RIDGEWAY PLACE 3 br.f. Compton Place 125 – Rockstine (IRE) 61 (Ballad Rock **–**
122) [2007 p7g 7m p10g Jun 9] 8,000F, 4,500Y: leggy filly: fifth foal: half-sister to 2
winners, including fairly useful French 1¼m (at 2 yrs) to 15.5f winner Kimosabe (by
Mtoto): dam 8.5f and 1¼m winner: no form in maidens at Lingfield: poorly to post
second outing: sold £500. *A. B. Haynes*

RIDGEWAY STAR 3 b.g. Tumbleweed Ridge 117 – Princess Starla (Stetsen) [2007 **–**
p7g p9.5g p8g p10g p16g Oct 17] little sign of ability: tried blinkered. *R. Ingram*

RIDGEWELL (USA) 3 b.f. Rahy (USA) 115 – Voladora (USA) (Hickory Ridge **69**
(USA)) [2007 p7.1g³ p8g⁵ p8.6g* 8m⁶ p7.1g Jun 30] $70,000F, $225,000Y: second foal:

half-sister to winner in US by Saint Ballado: dam US 5.5f to 8.5f minor stakes winner: fair performer: won maiden at Wolverhampton (despite flashing tail) in March: likely to stay 1¼m: acts on polytrack and good to firm ground: tongue tied third and final outings: hung left on debut: sent to USA. *B. J. Meehan*

RIDGE WOOD DANI (IRE) 2 b.g. (Mar 14) Invincible Spirit (IRE) 121 – Dani **69** Ridge (IRE) 92 (Indian Ridge 123) [2007 5.1g 5m⁵ 5.7g 6s⁴ 6m⁵ 5.5m* 6g⁴ 5g² 5.1g⁵ 6m Nov 10] lengthy, workmanlike gelding: first foal: dam, 6f winner, sister to useful 7f/1m winner Blomberg: fair performer: won nursery at Warwick in August: will prove best kept to 5f/6f: acts on good to firm going. *E. J. Alston*

RIDLEY DIDLEY (IRE) 2 b.g. (Feb 16) Tagula (IRE) 116 – Dioscorea (IRE) (Pharly **–** (FR) 130) [2007 6d Sep 20] tailed off in maiden at Ayr. *N. Wilson*

RIEVAULX VALENTINO 2 b.c. (Feb 13) Primo Valentino (IRE) 116 – Distinctly **75** Blu (IRE) 70 (Distinctly North (USA) 115) [2007 5f⁶ 5m³ 5g² 5g² 5f* p6g 6g p6g⁶ f6d² **a69** p6g⁶ Dec 22] lengthy colt: fair performer: won maiden at Carlisle in August: should prove best at 5f/6f: acts on fibresand and firm going: in cheekpieces last 3 starts. *K. A. Ryan*

RIFLEMAN (IRE) 7 ch.g. Starborough 126 – En Garde (IRE) 82 (Irish River (FR) **63** 131) [2007 –: 12d³ 12s Jul 18] compact gelding: lightly raced on Flat nowadays and just modest handicapper: stays 1½m: tried visored/in cheekpieces/tongue tied: acts on polytrack and good to firm going: joined R. Lee. *D. W. Thompson*

RIGAT 4 b.g. Dansili 127 – Fudge (Polar Falcon (USA) 126) [2007 72: 7m³ 8d 7s 6.9m **70** 6g 6m 7.1m 8g⁵ 10.1d⁵ 12g³ 12g² p9.5g² p9.5g* p9.5d Dec 17] tall, good-topped gelding: fair handicapper: won at Wolverhampton in December: stays easy 1½m: acts on polytrack, firm and good to soft going: sometimes slowly away/held up. *T. D. Barron*

RIGGINS (IRE) 3 b.c. Cape Cross (IRE) 129 – Rentless (Zafonic (USA) 130) [2007 **97** p7.1g* Apr 27] €130,000Y: first foal: dam, Italian 7f (at 2 yrs) to 1m winner, sister to useful 1¼m/1½m winner Yawmi: 4/1, created good impression when winning maiden at Wolverhampton in April by 7 lengths from Diksie Dancer, forging clear under hands and heels: not seen out again: should stay 1m. *L. M. Cumani*

RIGHTCAR ELLIE (IRE) 2 b.f. (Jan 11) Namid 128 – Maid To Order (IRE) 83 **65** (Zafonic (USA) 130) [2007 p5g⁶ 5.1d³ p5.1g p5.1g 5f* p5.1g⁴ 6d p5g³ p5.1g Nov 2] 16,000Y: first foal: dam, Irish 1m winner, half-sister to useful Irish 2-y-o 6f winner Catch A Glimpse: fair performer: won nursery at Folkestone in September: should stay 6f: acts on polytrack, firm and good to soft going: blinkered last 5 starts. *Peter Grayson*

RIGHTCAR LEWIS 2 ch.f. (May 7) Noverre (USA) 125 – Abeyr 106 (Unfuwain **–** (USA) 131) [2007 p6g p6m Oct 13] €25,000Y: half-sister to several winners, including 7f winners Raheibb (by Lion Cavern) and Makfool (including at 2 yrs, by Spectrum), both useful, and 3-y-o Noojoom: dam 7f/1m winner: last in maidens. *Peter Grayson*

RIGHTFUL RULER 5 b.g. Montjoy (USA) 122 – Lady of The Realm (Prince Daniel **61** (USA)) [2007 16g⁶ 13d⁶ p16.5g⁵ p16.5g Nov 12] modest maiden: unraced on Flat in 2006: best form up to 1¼m: acts on polytrack and firm going: tried in cheekpieces: won over hurdles in August. *N. Wilson*

RIGHT OPTION (IRE) 3 b.g. Daylami (IRE) 138 – Option (IRE) 52 (Red Ransom **78** (USA)) [2007 64: p10g² p10g⁶ p11g³ p12g* p12g 11.6m⁶ 11.6d³ 8.1m 12.1d² 16.2f² 16m* p16g⁵ p13.9g² 12.4d² p12.2g* p13.9g⁵ p16.5g⁵ p16.5g⁴ f12g⁶ Dec 27] smallish, close-coupled gelding: fair performer: won seller in June and (having left S. Dow £6,000 after seventh start) handicap in September, both at Lingfield, and handicap at Wolverhampton in October: stays 16.5f: acts on polytrack, firm and good to soft ground: tried in cheekpieces/blinkers. *J. L. Flint*

RIGHT TED (IRE) 4 b.f. Mujadil (USA) 119 – Islandagore (IRE) 97 (Indian Ridge **–** 123) [2007 78d: p9.5g p8.6g p8.6g 10m Jun 6] smallish, compact filly: modest performer: on downgrade: probably stays 9.5f: acts on polytrack and good to firm going. *T. Wall*

RIGHT TO PLAY (USA) 4 b. or br.c. Kingmambo (USA) 125 – Possibly Perfect **100** (USA) 122 (Northern Baby (CAN) 127) [2007 71: 11.8m* p12.2g² 14m* May 26] big, good-topped colt: useful form: much improved to win maiden at Leicester in April and handicap at Newmarket in May: stays 1¾m: acts on polytrack and good to firm going: sold 32,000 gns, sent to Germany. *J. H. M. Gosden*

RIGUEZ DANCER 3 b.g. Dansili 127 – Tricoteuse (Kris 135) [2007 56p: f8g⁴ 10.1s⁴ **79** 10.3f 10s⁶ 12m* 11.9g³ Sep 7] workmanlike gelding: fair performer: won handicap at Ripon in August: suited by 1½m: acts on good to firm ground. *P. C. Haslam*

RIKI WIKI WHEELS 2 b.c. (Apr 28) Elmaamul (USA) 125 – Madam Wurlitzer – (Noble Patriarch 115) [2007 p7.1g⁵ 6g p7.1g⁶ Nov 20] little form. *P. T. Midgley*

RIKOCHET 3 ch.g. Generous (IRE) 139 – Narva (Nashwan (USA) 135) [2007 70: p11g Aug 1] big, good-topped gelding: has a fluent action: fair maiden in 2006: tailed off only start at 3 yrs: should stay 1¼m. *Mrs A. L. M. King*

RILEY BOYS (IRE) 6 ch.g. Most Welcome 131 – Scarlett Holly 81 (Red Sunset 120) **88 d** [2007 93: 8m 8.5v² 8.5m⁶ 9.9g 8g 9.9m p8.6g 10g Nov 7] close-coupled gelding: fairly useful handicapper: below form after second start: stays 1¼m: acts on fibresand and any turf going: tried in cheekpieces/visor: reportedly severed a hind tendon final outing at 5 yrs: very slowly away on reappearance (stumbled after jockey late removing blindfold). *J. G. Given*

RIMROCK (IRE) 2 gr.g. (Jan 14) Royal Applause 124 – Hotelgenie Dot Com 107 **62** (Selkirk (USA) 129) [2007 6g 6m 6m Jun 9] sturdy gelding: modest maiden: gelded after final start: will stay 7f/1m: sold 1,000 gns. *J. Noseda*

RING OF CHARM 5 b.m. Magic Ring (IRE) 115 – Pink Petal (Northern Game) [2007 **38** 7.1m 5.7f p5.1g p7g Nov 4] strong mare: poor form in maidens. *C. J. Down*

RINGO (IRE) 7 b.g. Norwich 118 – Fairly Lively (IRE) (Remainder Man 126§) [2007 – 10.1m Jun 2] failed to complete in 2 points in 2006: soundly beaten over hurdles, and in maiden at Newcastle on Flat debut. *R. Johnson*

RINGSIDER (IRE) 6 ch.g. Docksider (USA) 124 – Red Comes Up (USA) (Blushing **73** Groom (FR) 131) [2007 –: p10g⁶ p12g 12s 12s Aug 24] close-coupled gelding: fair handicapper: respectable efforts in handicaps at Kempton first 2 starts: stays easy 13f: acts on polytrack and firm going: tried in cheekpieces/tongue tie: sometimes slowly away. *Declan Gillespie, Ireland*

RINTERVAL (IRE) 2 ch.f. (Mar 3) Desert Prince (IRE) 130 – Interpose (Indian Ridge **95** 123) [2007 6d⁴ 6d* 7m² Sep 14] €36,000Y: strong, lengthy filly: fourth foal: sister to fairly useful 7f and 1¼m winner Go Figure and half-sister to French 11.5f winner Betwixt (by Sinndar): dam unraced half-sister to smart French winner up to 12.5f Short Pause out of very smart winner up to 1m Interval: useful form: won maiden at Newbury in August: progressed again when 1½ lengths second of 22 to Lush Lashes in Goffs Fillies Million at the Curragh, always prominent: will stay 1m. *R. Hannon*

RIODAN (IRE) 5 ch.m. Desert King (IRE) 129 – Spirit of The Nile (FR) 72 (Generous **66** (IRE) 139) [2007 82: 18g 15.8g⁵ 14d Oct 13] just fair performer in 2007: stays 17f: acts on soft and good to firm going. *J. J. Quinn*

RIO DE JANEIRO (IRE) 6 b.g. Sadler's Wells (USA) 132 – Alleged Devotion **74** (USA) (Alleged (USA) 138) [2007 78: 14.1d⁵ Oct 3] sturdy gelding: fair handicapper: suited to polytrack, firm and good to soft going: has wandered: fairly useful hurdler. *Miss E. C. Lavelle*

RIO DE LA PLATA (USA) 2 ch.c. (Mar 26) Rahy (USA) 115 – Express Way **120 +** (ARG) (Ahmad (ARG)) [2007 6d³ 7m* 7g* 7m² 7g* 7d⁴ Oct 20]

Godolphin's three-year-olds did little to boost the stable's cause, with mid-season purchase Creachadoir providing the only pattern victory, in the Joel Stakes at Newmarket in October. With an eye to the future, the juveniles did much better, with Group 1 victories for Ibn Khaldun in the Racing Post Trophy and Rio de La

Veuve Clicquot Vintage Stakes, Goodwood—
Rio de La Plata impresses in beating Lizard Island, Donegal (right) and Scintillo (hooped sleeves)

Prix Jean-Luc Lagardere (Grand Criterium), Longchamp—
Rio de La Plata again displays a good turn of foot; Declaration of War, Shediak (rail), Hatta Fort,
Young Pretender (No.4) and Greatwallofchina (No.7) are next

Plata in the Prix Jean-Luc Lagardere supplementing earlier pattern successes. This improved significantly what can only be called an ordinary record in the best races for two-year-olds over the thirteen years Godolphin has been functioning. There had been just four Group 1 or Grade 1 wins between 1994 and 2006, from Dubawi (2004 National Stakes), Tempera (2001 Breeders' Cup Juvenile Fillies), Aljabr (1998 Prix de la Salamandre) and Medaaly (1996 Racing Post Trophy), plus nine in Group/Grade 2 company. Initially, Godolphin did not have many two-year-olds (none at all in some years), but there was a noticeable increase in 2004, with ninety-one individual runners, and in 2005, with seventy-three. The figures have been cut back in the last two seasons, with twenty and twenty-eight respectively. Apart from Ibn Khaldun and Rio de La Plata, among the twenty-six others are the promising Calming Influence, Iguazu Falls and Storm Force, so with them and all the purchased additions, notably Fast Company, there is plenty for the Dubai-based operation to look forward to.

Rio de La Plata was just about the best of the two-year-olds that have raced for Godolphin from the start. He was the second Godolphin two-year-old to run, clearly needing the experience and handled sympathetically in a maiden race at Newmarket in June in which he finished third to Shifting Star. The benefit of that run showed in a similar event with nineteen runners at the July meeting on the same course, Rio de La Plata leaving his rivals for dead out of the Dip and winning by a long-looking five lengths from Fifteen Love. The turn of foot Rio de La Plata displayed at Newmarket, and the fluent way he moved to post, were eye-catching, and he gave a repeat performance when moved up in grade in the Veuve Clicquot Vintage Stakes at Goodwood three weeks later. There were only seven runners but all had won at least once, including Lizard Island in the Railway Stakes, while Ellmau had finished third in the Superlative Stakes and both Donegal and Il Warrd were promising. Rio de La Plata started at 13/8-on and justified the confidence in style, responding instantly when asked to quicken less than a quarter of a mile from home and always holding Lizard Island despite running a bit green and drifting right, beating him driven out by two lengths, the pair clear. Winners of the Vintage Stakes, which was elevated in status to Group 2 in 2003, have as good a record as those in any race for two-year-olds in Europe. In the last twenty years, eleven of the winners have gone on to win at least one Group 1 race and four have run second in top company. Rio de La Plata's first attempt to join the Group 1 winners in that list, including Dr Devious, Mister Baileys, Alhaarth, Aljabr, Shamardal and Sir Percy, met with failure, but the National Stakes at the Curragh in mid-September still produced his best run of the campaign. Running in the National Stakes in preference to the Champagne Stakes at Doncaster, even though he had to be supplemented at a cost of €30,000, Rio de La Plata was waited with again but this time, after quickening to chase the leader New Approach over a furlong out, he could find no extra and went down by a length and three quarters.

Rio de La Plata soon gained his first Group 1 win, in the Prix Jean-Luc Lagardere (Grand Criterium) at Longchamp, which was not so strongly contested as the National Stakes. Rio de La Plata's presence was in some doubt in the run-up to the race because of the softish going, his connections expressing the view that such conditions do not suit him. On the day, however, the ground was good and he duly lined up. There was only one French-trained contender, Prix La Rochette runner-up Shediak from the Andre Fabre stable, and the challenge from Aidan O'Brien, who had landed five of the six previous runnings, was much weaker than usual as he relied on maiden Greatwallofchina and maiden/minor winner Minneapolis. There were two other pattern winners in the field of eight, Young Pretender, successful in the Prix La Rochette, and Hatta Fort, who had won the Superlative Stakes at Newmarket, notably New Approach. Heavy for another Longchamp hopeful, Declaration of War. Rio de La Plata started at 5/4-on and once he managed to get a run halfway up the straight the result was in no doubt. He quickened for a single smack of the whip and passed the post two and a half lengths clear of Declaration of War with Shediak a close third. The temptation must have been not to run Rio de La Plata again, especially as the Maktoums had complete or partial ownership of other colts likely to play a leading part in the Darley Dewhurst Stakes at Newmarket, notably New Approach. Heavy rain during the week before the Dewhurst left the final decision about Rio de La Plata's participation until the day of the race and, judging that the ground had dried sufficiently, connections let him take his chance. Rio de La Plata started third favourite and, over a furlong out, looked set to take a hand in proceedings when trying to come through between New Approach and Raven's Pass. However, the gap closed as Rio de La Plata began to run out of steam and he was not knocked about, coming home under six lengths behind New Approach in fourth. There is a good chance that the going did not suit Rio de La Plata, and that he is better than he showed in the Dewhurst.

	Rahy (USA)	Blushing Groom	Red God
	(ch 1985)	(ch 1974)	Runaway Bride
Rio de La Plata (USA)		Glorious Song	Halo
(ch.c. Mar 26, 2005)		(b 1976)	Ballade
	Express Way (ARG)	Ahmad	Good Manners
	(b 1993)	(br 1975)	Azyade
		Escaline	Hawk
		(b 1987)	Escolastica

Godolphin's "Rio de La Plata"

Rio de La Plata, a rangy, good-topped colt, was one of the cheaper purchases among the latest Godolphin two-year-olds, costing 170,000 guineas at the
Breeze Up Sale at Newmarket in April, where another colt, Pont des Soupirs, who
showed a bit of promise on his only appearance was bought for 320,000 guineas.
Another bought as a two-year-old, the maiden Wolgan Valley, who did not race
after July, cost 1,450,000 dollars and another pair, Silver Trigger and Seventh
Street, who cost 1,000,000 dollars apiece, did not race. Sheikh Mohammed's
spending had also been prolific at the yearling sales in 2006. John Ferguson
purchased on his behalf thirty-nine yearlings at Keeneland and Saratoga for a total
of 63,220,000 dollars and twenty-three at the Newmarket October Sales for
6,745,000 guineas. There isn't much to show from the highest priced of those so
far—Meydan City, Emirates Flyer, Nawakhida, Perfect Chance and an unnamed
Storm Cat filly, who cost more than 31,000,000 dollars between them, have yet to
reach the racecourse. Plavius, a 9,200,000 dollar buy, finished ninth of ten in a
maiden at Leicester in October on his only start for Godolphin. Rio de La Plata had
been through the ring twice before Newmarket, making 65,000 dollars as a foal and
75,000 dollars as a yearling, both at Keeneland. He might have been sold elsewhere
as a two-year-old, since he was entered as lot 81 in the Baden-Baden Spring Sales
in May. Part of the appeal of Rio de La Plata came from his sire Rahy, who had been
responsible for five notable members of the Godolphin team in the eight previous
years. Fantastic Light won six Group/Grade 1 events, Noverre and Perfectperformance each picked up a Group 2 at two before Noverre went on to land the Sussex
Stakes, City On A Hill won the July Stakes and Hi Dubai finished second in the
Prix Saint-Alary. They are probably the pick of Rahy's progeny in Europe. The
family of Rio de La Plata's dam Express Way is Argentinian and, given the
achievements in recent years of horses foaled in that country, in the United States in
particular, there is every reason to pay attention to it. Like dual Eclipse Award
winner Paseana, Express Way is a daughter of Ahmad, who did most of his winning
at a mile to a mile and a quarter and was twice champion sire in Argentina. Express
Way was placed in Argentina and has foaled four other winners, notably El
Expresivo, a Grade 1 winner over seven furlongs as a two-year-old. Rio de La Plata
is closely related to El Expresivo since the latter is by Invasor's sire Candy Stripes,
like Rahy a son of Blushing Groom. Rio de La Plata's grandam Escaline was unraced and foaled two minor winners, but she was well related. Her dam Escolastica
was a stakes-winning half-sister to dual Group 1 winner Espadana from a family
that has produced a host of major winners in Argentina and South Africa. On the
whole, Rahy is not an influence for stamina—Fantastic Light stayed a mile and a
half but he was out of a mare by Nijinsky—and two thirds of the sire's winners aged
three and above in Europe have done their winning at distances short of a mile and
a quarter. Despite the claim by his connections after the Vintage Stakes that Rio de
La Plata is 'quite stoutly bred', there is precious little about him to indicate that he
is a colt who will shine over middle distances early on as a three-year-old, or
necessarily at any stage. Be that as it may, however, at around a mile under suitable
conditions, his sharp turn of foot should continue to make him a potent force at the
highest level. *Saeed bin Suroor*

RIO (IRE) 5 ch.g. Namid 128 – Renashaan (FR) (Darshaan 133) [2007 74: p9.5g³   **66**
p9.5g⁶ 10.1m p9.5g Jun 11] ex-Irish gelding: fair maiden: left K. Prendergast 16,000 gns
and gelded prior to reappearance: may prove best around 1m: acts on heavy and good to
firm going, probably on polytrack: blinkered final 4-y-o start: sold 1,800 gns. *J. Balding*

RIOLO (IRE) 5 ch.g. Priolo (USA) 127 – Ostrusa (AUT) (Rustan (HUN)) [2007 65: 8d   **48**
6m 7d⁵ 6m p8.6g p8.6d⁵ Dec 27] tall, workmanlike gelding: poor performer at 5 yrs: stays
7f: acts on firm going, probably on polytrack: blinkered/in cheekpieces nowadays: not an
easy ride. *K. F. Clutterbuck*

RIO L'OREN (IRE) 2 ch.f. (Mar 17) Captain Rio 122 – Princess Sofie 84 (Efisio 120)   **–**
[2007 5.1m Aug 7] €2,500Y, resold 14,000Y: second foal: dam 2-y-o 5f winner: tailed off
in maiden at Chepstow. *N. J. Vaughan*

RIO NOVO 2 b.g. (Mar 18) Nayef (USA) 129 – Dead Certain 123§ (Absalom 128)   **–**
[2007 Aug 15] 28/1, last in minor event at Hamilton. *J. Howard Johnson*

RIO PRINCESS (IRE) 2 ch.f. (Jan 23) Captain Rio 122 – Prince's Passion 80 (Brief   **70**
Truce (USA) 126) [2007 5.2g³ p5g² p6g³ p6g 5g⁴ 5m p7.1g Sep 21] €52,000Y, £41,000

2-y-o: sturdy, compact filly: has a fluent action: first foal: dam 2-y-o 5.7f winner (stayed 1¼m): fair maiden: placed first 3 starts: effective at 5f/6f: acts on polytrack and good to firm going: sold 3,000 gns, sent to Austria. *T. G. Mills*

RIO RIVA 5 b.g. Pivotal 124 – Dixie Favor (USA) 82 (Dixieland Band (USA)) [2007 **111** 103: 8s² 8g⁵ 8.5d 8s* 8.1g 8v³ 8m 9m Oct 6] tall gelding: smart handicapper: further progress in 2007, second to Very Wise in Lincoln at Newcastle and won there in June emphatically, beating Moody Tunes by 5 lengths: below form after: should stay 1¼m: has form on polytrack and good to firm ground, best efforts on good or softer: edgy sort: held up. *Miss J. A. Camacho*

RIO ROCKET (IRE) 2 b. or br.f. (Apr 28) Captain Rio 122 – Special One 66 (Aragon **56** 118) [2007 5m⁶ 6d⁶ 5m⁴ 5g⁶ p5.1g⁶ p5g p7.1g⁵ p6g⁵ Dec 4] €10,500F: seventh foal: half-sister to several winners, including useful 5f winners Inya Lake (including Molecomb Stakes at 2 yrs) and Old Blue Eyes (at 2 yrs in 2001), both by Whittingham: dam 2-y-o 5f winner: modest maiden: left G. A. Swinbank after sixth start: may prove best at 5f: acts on polytrack, good to firm and good to soft going: tried blinkered. *Tom Dascombe*

RIORUN (IRE) 2 b.g. (Apr 16) Captain Rio 122 – Sulaka (Owington 123) [2007 5.7g **59 ?** 6m 6f p7g p7g Oct 10] workmanlike gelding: modest maiden: seemingly best effort second start. *J. G. Portman*

RIO SABOTINI 2 ch.c. (Feb 11) Captain Rio 122 – Sabotini 62 (Prince Sabo 123) **60** [2007 5m 5g 6d 6s⁴ Oct 26] sturdy colt: modest maiden: raced only at 5f/6f. *G. A. Swinbank*

RIO SANDS 2 b.g. (Mar 19) Captain Rio 122 – Sally Traffic 57 (River Falls 113) [2007 **70** 5d⁵ 6m 6f⁵ 6d 5g Oct 20] quite good-topped gelding: fair maiden: should prove best at 5f/6f: acts on firm going: gelded after final start. *R. M. Whitaker*

RIO TAFFETA 2 b.g. (Mar 19) Diktat 126 – Taffeta (IRE) 69 (Barathea (IRE) 127) **62** [2007 p5g⁵ 5m³ 5.1g³ 5.3m⁵ p5.1g² 6g² 6s² 5m 6g* 6.1s³ 7d* 7m p6g p7.1d⁶ Dec 6] stocky gelding: modest performer: claimed from M. Channon £6,000 sixth start: won sellers at Windsor in June and Catterick in July: stays 7f: acts on polytrack, soft and good to firm ground: blinkered once. *Peter Grayson*

RIOTOUS APPLAUSE 4 b.f. Royal Applause 124 – Wiener Wald (USA) (Woodman **104** (USA) 126) [2007 100p: 6.1s 6m³ 5m³ 5g⁴ 6m Oct 4] leggy, attractive filly: useful performer, lightly raced: best effort when third to Siren's Gift in minor event at Leicester third start: effective at 5f/6f: acts on good to firm going (below form only start on soft): often held up: usually attended by stablehand at start. *J. R. Fanshawe*

RIOTOUS (IRE) 3 b.g. Royal Applause 124 – Takarna (IRE) 70 (Mark of Esteem **–** (IRE) 137) [2007 69: 6g May 29] smallish, sturdy gelding: fair maiden in 2006: well held in handicap only start at 3 yrs: may prove best at 5f: acts on firm going: sold 1,200 gns. *A. Dickman*

RIPPLES MAID 4 b.f. Dansili 127 – Rivers Rhapsody 104 (Dominion 123) [2007 106: **109** p6g p6g³ 6m 6g* 6d⁶ 6m² 6d 6m 6d* 6.1m⁵ 6g 6d Oct 19] sturdy filly: useful performer: further progress at 4 yrs, winning handicap at Newbury in May and listed race at Ponte-fract (beat Diamond Diva by 1¼ lengths) in August: below form after: races mainly at 6f, should be as effective at 5f: acts on polytrack, good to firm and good to soft ground. *J. A. Geake*

RIQAAB (IRE) 2 b.c. (May 17) Peintre Celebre (USA) 137 – Jeed (IRE) 86 (Mujtahid **68 p** (USA) 118) [2007 7g Oct 26] sturdy colt: fourth foal: half-brother to useful 2005 2-y-o 6f winner Nidhaal (by Observatory) and Maslak: dam, 2-y-o 6f winner, out of half-sister to Irish St Leger winner Eurobird and Prix du Jockey Club winners Bikala and Assert: 15/2, more promise than bare result (seventh to Naval Review) in maiden at Doncaster, wide throughout but good speed: will do better. *E. A. L. Dunlop*

RIQUEWIHR 7 ch.m. Compton Place 125 – Juvenilia (IRE) 55 (Masterclass (USA) **79** 116) [2007 82: p7g⁶ 6g⁵ 6m 6s² 6s⁴ 5v⁵ 7s* 6s 6g* 7m³ 7m 6d 7g Aug 23] quite good-topped mare: fair handicapper, better on turf than all-weather: won at York and Thirsk (dead-heat) in July: flattered final start: effective at 6f/7f: acts on polytrack and any turf going: often wears cheekpieces: reportedly in foal to Monsieur Bond. *J. S. Wainwright*

RISING CROSS 4 bl.f. Cape Cross (IRE) 129 – Woodrising 64 (Nomination 125) **113 d** [2007 115: 14g 12d⁴ 20g 12m 12.5m 14v⁶ 12s 12g⁵ Nov 11] small, sparely-made filly: smart performer: did very well at 3 yrs, proving tough and genuine, and winning twice, including Park Hill Stakes at York: not in same heart at 4 yrs, showing similar form only when fourth to Scorpion in Coronation Cup at Epsom: well below form last 6 starts,

Mr Gary A. Tanaka's "Rising Cross"

including at Aqueduct final outing: stays 15.5f: acts on polytrack, good to firm and good to soft going: to remain in USA. *J. R. Best*

RISING FORCE (IRE) 4 b.g. Selkirk (USA) 129 – Singing Diva (IRE) (Royal Academy (USA) 130) [2007 72: 8d⁴ 8.5d² p8g 8s p9.5g⁶ Dec 8] fair handicapper: second at Galway in August, only creditable effort in 2007: left D. Weld in Ireland 8,000 gns prior to final start (well held at Wolverhampton): effective at 1m/1¼m: acts on firm and good to soft ground: tried blinkered. *J. L. Spearing*   **74**

RISING SHADOW (IRE) 6 b.g. Efisio 120 – Jouet 71 (Reprimand 122) [2007 113: 6d* 6g⁴ 6d 6v⁴ 6m 6d⁶ 6d 7g 6d 6m⁶ Nov 10] close-coupled gelding: smart performer: won listed race at Newcastle (beat Sierra Vista by ¾ length) in March: creditable efforts after at York (fourth to Amadeus Wolf in Duke of York Stakes), Newcastle (fourth to Confuchias in Chipchase Stakes) and, having left T. D. Barron, Doncaster (sixth to Galeota in listed race, nearest finish): best at 6f: acts on heavy and good to firm going: held up. *N. Wilson*   **113**

RISK CHALLENGE (USA) 5 ch.g. Mt Livermore (USA) – Substance (USA) (Diesis 133) [2007 –: 8.1m May 25] stocky gelding: fairly useful bumper winner/poor hurdler: well held in maidens. *C. J. Price*   **–**

RISKIE BLUE (IRE) 2 b.f. (Apr 1) Iron Mask (USA) 117 – Riskie Things 62 (Risk Me (FR) 127) [2007 5m⁶ 5.1f³ 6.1g May 28] 2,800Y: unfurnished filly: fourth foal: half-sister to 2 winners, including fairly useful 2002 2-y-o 5f/6f winner Notty Bitz (by Darnay): dam sprinter: poor form in sellers: tried in cheekpieces. *J. S. Moore*   **39**

RISQUE HEIGHTS 3 b.g. Mark of Esteem (IRE) 137 – Risque Lady 109 (Kenmare (FR) 125) [2007 72: 8.3m⁶ 7m⁵ 7.1d² 7.1g p11g² p10g* 10s⁴ 10m³ p10g* p12.2g³ p12g⁴ p11g p8g p8g Dec 30] medium-sized gelding: useful performer: much improved in second half of 2007, winning maiden in August and handicap in October, both at Lingfield: stays 1½m: acts on polytrack, soft and good to firm going: tried blinkered/tongue tied: held up: sometimes looks none too genuine. *G. A. Butler*   **95**

RITA PETITE 3 gr.f. Primo Valentino (IRE) 116 – Most Uppitty 69 (Absalom 128) – [2007 8.3d 6g p6m Sep 6] 500Y: sparely-made filly: half-sister to German 5.5f/7.5f winner Lady Fly (by Revoque): dam 5f (at 2 yrs)/6f winner: last in maidens: withdrawn after unseating rider to post prior to intended debut. *D. W. Chapman*

RIVER ALHAARTH (IRE) 5 b.h. Alhaarth (IRE) 126 – Sudden Interest (FR) (Highest Honor (FR) 124) [2007 103: 14g 16.2m² 16.1v⁵ Jun 30] smallish, close-coupled horse: useful handicapper: cracked cannon bone only start in 2005: stays 2m: acts on good to firm and good to soft going: tried visored/blinkered: sold 40,000 gns in December. *P. W. Chapple-Hyam* **99**

RIVER ARDECHE 2 b.g. (Apr 20) Elnadim (USA) 128 – Overcome (Belmez (USA) 131) [2007 6s* Jul 28] fourth foal: brother to 3-y-o Bridget's Team and half-brother to 5-y-o Brace of Doves: dam, German 1¼m winner, out of unraced half-sister to Deutsches Derby winners Orofino and Ordos: 15/2, won substandard maiden at York by 6 lengths only 2-y-o start (slipped and fell through rail after line): likely to stay 7f/1m: will progress all being well. *P. C. Haslam* **82 p**

RIVER BOUNTY 2 b.f. (Feb 3) Bahamian Bounty 116 – Artistic Merit (Alhaarth (IRE) 126) [2007 p7g⁵ p7g⁵ 6m* 6g⁴ 6m⁴ 7g 6m p6g⁵ p5.1g² Dec 5] 5,000Y: lengthy filly: third foal: dam unraced half-sister to useful 1m/9f winner Gryffindor: fair performer: won maiden at Haydock in August and claimer at Kempton in December: best at 5f/6f: acts on polytrack and good to firm going: visored last 2 starts. *A. P. Jarvis* **71**

RIVER BRAVO (IRE) 4 b.c. Indian Ridge 123 – Sheer Spirit (IRE) 86 (Caerleon (USA) 132) [2007 100: 7m 6s⁵ Jul 5] good-bodied colt: useful handicapper at best, very lightly raced: just fairly useful form at 4 yrs: bred to stay at least 1m: acts on soft going: sold 3,000 gns. *P. W. Chapple-Hyam* **83**

RIVER CITY (IRE) 10 b.g. Norwich 118 – Shuil Na Lee (IRE) (Phardante (FR) 123) [2007 71: 16d p12g⁶ Nov 6] rangy gelding: fairly useful hurdler/smart chaser: fair maiden on Flat: little impact at 10 yrs. *Noel T. Chance* –

RIVER CLUB 3 ch.g. Kyllachy 129 – Amused 78 (Prince Sabo 123) [2007 –: 6m 7.5m 5d² 6g 5.9g 6g⁶ Aug 29] sturdy gelding: modest maiden: would have proved best at 5f/6f: acted on good to soft ground: dead. *G. A. Swinbank* **61**

RIVER DEUCE 3 b.g. Zaha (CAN) 106 – Light Hand 80 (Star Appeal 133) [2007 71: 10.5g p12g³ p12g² 10m p12g³ p12g³ Nov 6] close-coupled, workmanlike gelding: fairly useful performer on all-weather, modest on turf: won maiden at Lingfield in October: stays 1½m: acts on all-weather: gelded after final start. *M. H. Tompkins* **60 a84**

RIVER FALCON 7 b.g. Pivotal 124 – Pearly River 72 (Elegant Air 119) [2007 101: 5.2m² 5m² 5m² 5g 5v⁴ 5d⁶ 6s 5m 5g* 5.6m 6d⁶ 6d⁶ 6d⁴ 6g Oct 26] useful-looking gelding: useful handicapper: runner-up 3 times prior to winning at York (by length from Hoh Hoh Hoh) in August: effective at 5f/6f: acts on polytrack, probably on any turf ground: looked none too keen in cheekpieces eighth outing: held up. *J. S. Goldie* **105**

RIVER GLEAM (IRE) 2 b.f. (Mar 25) Trans Island 119 – Gleam (Green Desert (USA) 127) [2007 p6g⁵ 7m³ 6m² 6d p6m⁶ Oct 13] 7,000Y: stocky filly: fourth foal: half-sister to 3-y-o Gleaming Spirit: dam unraced out of half-sister to smart sprinter Zarani Sidi Anna: fair maiden: placed at Yarmouth and Ripon: stays 7f: acts on polytrack and good to firm going. *A. P. Jarvis* **67**

RIVER GYPSY 6 b.g. In The Wings 128 – River Erne (USA) (Irish River (FR) 131) [2007 58, a68: p16g 12.1s Jul 27] modest maiden: well held at 6 yrs. *J. D. Frost* –

RIVERHILL (IRE) 4 b.g. Mull of Kintyre (USA) 114 – Thrill Seeker (IRE) (Treasure Kay 114) [2007 56: 7.1m⁴ 7.9g⁴ Jun 18] well-made gelding: modest maiden: effective at 7f to 11f: acts on heavy and good to firm ground. *J. Howard Johnson* **56**

RIVER HUNTER (IRE) 3 b.f. Desert Prince (IRE) 130 – Carmenta (IRE) (Unfuwain (USA) 131) [2007 9m p8.6g 10d Jul 3] €58,000Y: second foal: dam, ran twice in US, half-sister to useful 6f (at 2 yrs) to 7.5f (in Italy) winner Darwin: well held in maidens. *S. Kirk* –

RIVER KENT 2 b.g. (May 17) Fantastic Light (USA) 134 – Ciboure 74 (Norwick (USA) 125) [2007 8.2d Oct 10] good-topped gelding: 50/1 and backward, well held in maiden at Nottingham. *Mrs A. Duffield* –

RIVER KIROV (IRE) 4 b.g. Soviet Star (USA) 128 – Night Shifter (IRE) 74 (Night Shift (USA)) [2007 87: 6m⁴ 6m² 6g 6d 6d 6g 6d p6g⁶ p6g⁶ Nov 24] strong gelding: fairly useful handicapper at best: good efforts in frame first 2 starts at 4 yrs: lost his form, leaving P. Chapple-Hyam after sixth start: effective at 6f/7f: acts on good to firm going: virtually refused to race fifth/sixth outings, and one to treat with plenty of caution. *M. Wigham* **94 d**

RIVER LOGIC (IRE) 4 b.g. Fasliyev (USA) 120 – Grey Again 63 (Unfuwain (USA) **51** 131) [2007 65: f11g 12.4m May 24] quite good-topped gelding: fair performer at 3 yrs, only modest in handicaps in 2007: stays 11f: raced only on good ground or firmer on turf: tried in cheekpieces: fairly useful hurdler. *A. D. Brown*

RIVER N' BLUES (IRE) 2 ch.f. (Mar 31) Touch of The Blues (FR) 125 – Feather **58** River (USA) (Strike The Gold (USA) 123) [2007 7g 8g 7g⁵ p6g⁵ Nov 21] sparely-made filly: fifth foal: half-sister to 2 winners in Italy, notably useful 7f/1m winner Kill Cat (by Catrail): dam unraced: modest maiden: probably flattered when fifth at Newmarket third start: should stay 1m. *Dr J. R. J. Naylor*

RIVER PRINCE 3 br.g. Riverwise (USA) – Princess Penny 46§ (King's Signet (USA) **71** 110) [2007 55: p6g* p6g* Feb 21] fair performer: won seller at Lingfield (left W. Turner) in January and claimer at Wolverhampton (joined J. Boyle) in February: stays 6f: acts on polytrack: fractious in stall and withdrawn intended debut: ran loose prior to actual debut: slowly away and unbalanced final 2-y-o outing. *A. B. Haynes*

RIVER PROUD (USA) 2 b.c. (Mar 15) Proud Citizen (USA) 122 – Da River Hoss **111** (USA) (River Special (USA)) [2007 6m* 6m² 7m 7m* 8g Oct 27] $75,000Y: strong, good-bodied colt: has scope: sixth foal: half-brother to winner in US by Forest Camp: dam unraced half-sister to dual Breeders' Cup Mile winner Da Hoss: smart performer: won maiden at Newbury in June and Somerville Tattersall Stakes at Newmarket (beat Iguazu Falls by ¾ length) in October: best effort when short-head second to Winker Watson in July Stakes at Newmarket: seemingly over the top for year (wintry in coat) in Racing Post Trophy at Doncaster, weakening into seventh behind Ibn Khaldun: should stay 1m: raced only on good/good to firm going: prominently ridden: banged head in stall when well held in Champagne Stakes third start. *P. F. I. Cole*

RIVERSCAPE (IRE) 2 ch.f. (Apr 21) Peintre Celebre (USA) 137 – Orinoco (IRE) 53 **75** (Darshaan 133) [2007 p7g³ 8.2m² 8d⁵ Oct 23] tall filly: third foal: half-sister to 4-y-o Bandama and 3-y-o Intiquilla: dam once-raced half-sister to Irish Oaks winner Winona: fair form in maidens: neck second to La Rosa Nostra at Nottingham: will be well suited by 1¼m/1½m. *Mrs A. J. Perrett*

RIVERSIDE 2 b.f. (Jan 24) Kyllachy 129 – My Cadeaux 93 (Cadeaux Genereux 131) **–** [2007 6d Sep 20] €22,000Y: fifth foal: half-sister to 6f winner Milly Fleur (by Primo Dominie): dam, 6f winner, closely related to very smart sprinter Prince Sabo: soon detached in maiden at Ayr. *M. Brittain*

RIVERSIDE DANCER (USA) 3 ch.f. Stravinsky (USA) 133 – Odori (USA) (The **78** Minstrel (CAN) 135) [2007 85: 6g 7m⁵ 7g² 6f* 7f² 7m⁶ p6g Aug 5] tall, rather leggy filly: has a powerful, round action: fair performer: won claimer at Hamilton (claimed from K. Ryan) in June: effective at 5f to 7f: acts on polytrack and firm going: tried in cheekpieces/blinkers: often slowly away. *G. A. Huffer*

RIVER THAMES 4 b.g. Efisio 120 – Dashing Water 87 (Dashing Blade 117) [2007 **90** 85: 5f⁴ 6m 5m 6d⁶ 5s⁶ 6d* 6d⁴ 6m 5.1g² p5.1g f6d⁶ Dec 12] sturdy, useful-looking geld- **a77** ing: fairly useful handicapper on all-weather, just fair on turf in 2007: won at Ayr in July: best at 5f/6f: acts on polytrack, firm and soft going: tried in cheekpieces (ran poorly): none too consistent. *K. A. Ryan*

Somerville Tattersall Stakes, Newmarket—River Proud shrugs off Iguazu Falls (rail) only in the closing stages as Yankadi and Bazergan stay on well for third and fourth respectively

RIVER TIBER 4 b.g. Danehill (USA) 126 – Heavenly Whisper (IRE) 105 (Halling **108** (USA) 133) [2007 90: 10g 8v 8m* 8g⁴ 10.4d 8g² 9m Oct 6] good-topped gelding: useful handicapper: left D. Gillespie in Ireland after second start: won at Ascot (by short head from Waterside) in July: good efforts in frame 2 of next 3 starts, gelded prior to neck second to Orchard Supreme at same course: respectable ninth of 34 to Pipedreamer in Cambridgeshire at Newmarket final outing: stays 9f: acts on soft and good to firm going: waited with: sold 120,000 gns, joined Godolphin. *L. M. Cumani*

RIVIERA RED (IRE) 7 b.g. Rainbow Quest (USA) 134 – Banquise (IRE) (Last **52** Tycoon 131) [2007 44: p8g⁶ p8g⁴ p8g p7g⁴ Dec 30] modest performer: should stay beyond 1m: acts on polytrack: often visored. *L. Montague Hall*

RIVINGTON PIKE (IRE) 2 b.g. (Feb 22) Catcher In The Rye (IRE) 115 – Bean **67** Island (USA) (Afleet (CAN)) [2007 6f⁴ 7g 8.1s Sep 29] big, strong gelding: fair maiden: failed to build on debut promise (fourth to Naomh Geileis at Pontefract): should be suited by 7f/1m. *J. J. Quinn*

ROAD TO LOVE (IRE) 4 ch.g. Fruits of Love (USA) 127 – Alpine Flair (IRE) (Tirol **112** 127) [2007 118: 9g 9g 8.1g⁴ 8m⁵ 9.9g² 10d Jun 22] strong, close-coupled gelding: smart performer: clearly best effort in 2007 when ¾-length second to Illustrious Blue in listed race at Goodwood: well held in listed handicap at Royal Ascot final outing: strained a fetlock joint after: best around 1¼m: acts on firm going, winner on good to soft: usually front runner. *M. Johnston*

ROAD TO RECOVERY 3 b.g. Mujahid (USA) 125 – Legend of Aragon 67 (Aragon **–** 118) [2007 66: p6g 6m⁵ 7s⁶ May 29] leggy gelding: maiden: little form on Flat in 2007: visored last 4 starts. *A. M. Balding*

ROARING FORTE (IRE) 2 b.c. (Jan 29) Cape Cross (IRE) 129 – Descant (USA) **89 P** (Nureyev (USA) 131) [2007 7m⁴ p7g* Nov 12] 25,000Y: strong, rangy colt: seventh foal: half-brother to 6f winner Climate Control (by Mt Livermore) and 9-y-o Far Note, both fairly useful: dam unraced half-sister to Zafonic: fairly useful form: caught the eye when fourth to Almajd in maiden at Newmarket, then simple task in weaker event at Lingfield: likely to stay 1m: will improve considerably and make his mark in higher grade. *W. J. Haggas*

ROBBIE SCOTT 3 b.g. Robellino (USA) 127 – Milly of The Vally 93 (Caerleon **–** (USA) 132) [2007 68p: 10f 11.1s Sep 24] fair form in maidens at 2 yrs: tailed off in handicaps in 2007: sold 2,700 gns in November. *M. Johnston*

ROBBMAA (FR) 2 br. or bl.c. (Feb 28) Cape Cross (IRE) 129 – Native Twine 114 (Be **53** My Native (USA) 122) [2007 p8g 7.1g⁶ Oct 2] compact colt: modest form in maidens, looking reluctant: should stay 1m: sold 10,000 gns. *M. A. Jarvis*

ROBBY BOBBY 2 ch.c. (Apr 16) Selkirk (USA) 129 – Dancing Mirage (IRE) 83 **92 p** (Machiavellian (USA) 123) [2007 8g² 8d* Oct 11] 80,000Y: tall colt: fourth foal: half-brother to 3 winners, including 5-y-o Foxhaven and 3-y-o Swiss Act: dam, 2-y-o 7f winner, out of half-sister to very smart French miler Shaanxi: fairly useful form: plenty of promise in maidens, neck second to Pinkindie at Yarmouth before winning by 3 lengths, with plenty to spare, at Newbury (hung right): will stay 1¼m/1½m: sure to go on improving. *M. Johnston*

ROBEMA 4 b.f. Cadeaux Genereux 131 – Germane 100 (Distant Relative 128) [2007 **89** 88: 6s² 7m³ 7.6m* 7.6m 8s 8m Oct 4] big, strong filly: fairly useful handicapper, lightly raced: won at Chester (by short head from Gallantry) in August: effective from testing 6f to 1m: acts on firm and soft going. *J. J. Quinn*

ROBERT BURNS (IRE) 2 b.c. (Apr 27) Invincible Spirit (IRE) 121 – Double Red **68 p** (IRE) 70 (Thatching 131) [2007 7d⁶ Oct 30] 120,000Y: second foal: dam, 1¼m and hurdles winner, half-sister to useful performers Duty Paid (sprinter) and Lady Miletrian (1m winner): 7/2, encouraging sixth in maiden at Yarmouth, looking big threat before tiring: will do better. *J. H. M. Gosden*

ROBERT THE BRAVE 3 b.g. Primo Valentino (IRE) 116 – Sandicliffe (USA) 66 **85** (Imp Society (USA)) [2007 69: p9.5g⁵ 10.5g p8.6g* p9.5g* p12.2g* p12.2g⁶ Dec 26] rangy gelding: fairly useful performer: left A. McCabe, improved when winning handicaps at Wolverhampton in October (2) and November: effective at 8.6f to 1½m: acts on polytrack, well held both turf starts (reluctant at stall on second occasion). *P. R. Webber*

ROBINZAL 5 b.g. Zilzal (USA) 137 – Sulitelma (USA) 63 (The Minstrel (CAN) 135) **72** [2007 73: 8.5g 12g⁵ 7g⁶ p7.1g⁴ p8.6g² p7.1g⁶ p7.1d Dec 6] tall, close-coupled gelding: fair handicapper: left Mrs J. Le Brocq in Jersey after fourth start: should stay 1¼m: acts on polytrack, soft and good to firm ground: tried tongue tied. *A. W. Carroll*

ROB

ROBSCARVIC (IRE) 2 b.g. (Mar 6) Statue of Liberty (USA) 115 – Calypso Run **89**
(Lycius (USA) 124) [2007 6v* 7s³ 8f⁵ 8f⁵ Nov 23] €21,000Y: leggy gelding: seventh
foal: half-brother to fairly useful 1½m to 2m winner Bendarshaan and French 1½m
winner Newtown (both by Darshaan): dam ran once: fairly useful form: won maiden at
Newcastle in June: left G. A. Swinbank after next start: ran well in US, fifth to The Leopard in Grade 3 Generous Stakes at Hollywood final start: stays 1m: acts on any going.
P. Gallagher, USA

ROBSLASTCALL 2 br.f. (Apr 21) Timeless Times (USA) 99 – Lavernock Lady **–**
(Don't Forget Me 127) [2007 6f⁶ 5g 7.1m Aug 30] 2,500Y: sixth foal: sister to several 5f
winners: dam no form: of no account. *A. Berry*

ROBUSTIAN 4 b.g. Robellino (USA) 127 – Pontressina (USA) (St Jovite (USA) 135) **95**
[2007 88: 8m* 10m⁵ 10m⁶ 10m⁶ 8m⁴ 9.7m p8g 8m 10.9m² 10m* 10.9m 10m³ Sep 27] **a79 +**
workmanlike gelding: useful handicapper on turf, just fair form so far on all-weather
(both runs on polytrack): won at Pontefract in April and Sandown (amateurs) in September: stays 11.6f: raced only on good ground or firmer on turf (acts on firm): blinkered last
5 starts: reliable: sold 48,000 gns, joined George Baker. *Eve Johnson Houghton*

ROCAMADOUR 5 b.h. Celtic Swing 138 – Watch Me (IRE) 106 (Green Desert (USA) **–**
127) [2007 110: 8m 9m 8g May 20] good-topped horse: had a quick action: smart
performer at best: little impact in handicaps in 2007: was effective at 1m to 10.5f: acted
on firm and soft going: tried visored: often raced prominently: retired. *M. R. Channon*

ROCA REDONDA (IRE) 3 b.f. Fasliyev (USA) 120 – Devil's Crown (USA) (Chief's **44**
Crown (USA)) [2007 62: p8g p8g 11g 12.1m 9.9g 10g⁵ 8d Jun 19] lengthy, good-topped
filly: poor maiden on balance in 2007, leaving M. Wallace after second start: seems to
stay 11f: tried visored/in cheekpieces: joined W. Storey. *V. Smith*

ROCHEFORT (IRE) 2 b.c. (Apr 5) Red Ransom (USA) – Sombreffe 71 (Polish **87**
Precedent (USA) 131) [2007 7s² 8m³ p8g³ 8.3m* Oct 8] 105,000F: smallish, strong colt:
has moderate, quick action: seventh foal: brother to 2002 2-y-o 6f winner Ransom O'War,
later smart performer up to 1½m in Germany, and half-brother to 1m winner Madame
Cerito (by Diesis) and 1¼m winner Uliana (by Darshaan), both useful: dam 7f winner:
fairly useful form: won maiden at Windsor (made all) final start: placed in 3 similar
events, notably third to Kandahar Run at Doncaster second outing: will stay 1¼m: acts on
polytrack, soft and good to firm going. *J. H. M. Gosden*

ROCHEPORT 2 ch.g. (Jan 26) Reel Buddy (USA) 118 – Just A Gem (Superlative 118) **65**
[2007 5d³ 6m⁴ 5g³ 6d 5g⁶ 5f Sep 17] sturdy gelding: fair maiden: effective at 5f/6f: acts on
good to firm going: blinkered (nearly fell leaving stall) final outing. *J. Howard Johnson*

ROCK ANTHEM (IRE) 3 ch.g. Rock of Gibraltar (IRE) 133 – Regal Portrait (IRE) **83**
57 (Royal Academy (USA) 130) [2007 78: 8.5g 8.3d² 9.9m* 10m⁶ 11.9f⁴ 10m⁶ 11s Oct 4]
leggy, close-coupled gelding: fairly useful handicapper: won at Goodwood in June:
seems to stay 1½m: acts on good to firm and good to soft going: sold 16,000 gns and
gelded. *J. L. Dunlop*

ROCK DIVA (IRE) 3 ch.f. Rock of Gibraltar (IRE) 133 – Merlannah (IRE) (Shy **61**
Groom (USA)) [2007 –: 6m 7g² 6.9g⁴ p7.1g Sep 3] sturdy filly: modest maiden: stays 7f.
P. C. Haslam

ROCKELLIO (IRE) 2 b.f. (Mar 15) Rock of Gibraltar (IRE) 133 – Lillibits (USA) **58**
(Kingmambo (USA) 125) [2007 6m Jul 13] quite attractive filly: first foal: dam unraced
out of Mill Reef and Coronation Stakes winner Magic of Life: 20/1, mid-division in
maiden at Newmarket won by Laureldean Gale: will be suited by 1m. *B. W. Hills*

ROCKER 3 b.g. Rock of Gibraltar (IRE) 133 – Jessica's Dream (IRE) 114 (Desert Style **78**
(IRE) 121) [2007 70: p5g² p5g* p6g⁵ 5m⁵ 6g⁵ 5d³ 5.3d³ 5g 5f 5d³ 5m² p7g 5m p5g
Nov 12] smallish gelding: fair handicapper: won at Lingfield in March: acts at 5f: acts on
polytrack, good to firm and good to soft going: usually visored: has looked none too keen.
B. R. Johnson

ROCKET FORCE (USA) 7 ch.g. Spinning World (USA) 130 – Pat Us (USA) **61**
(Caucasus (USA) 127) [2007 80: 12s⁶ 12.1g Aug 15] well-made gelding: fairly useful
performer at 6 yrs, only modest in 2007: stays 1¾m: acts on good to firm and good to soft
ground: tried visored: sold 1,600 gns in October. *N. Wilson*

ROCKETRY 2 ch.c. (Feb 15) Desert Prince (IRE) 130 – Moon Search 110 (Rainbow **–**
Quest (USA) 134) [2007 6.5d 5.1g Oct 31] strong colt: well held in maidens, probably
inadequate test (dam, won Prix de Royallieu, half-sister to Brian Boru). *T. Keddy*

910

ROCKFIELD LODGE (IRE) 2 b.g. (Apr 16) Stravinsky (USA) 133 – La Belle   **77**
Simone (IRE) (Grand Lodge (USA) 125) [2007 p7.1g⁴ p7g² 6m² p6g* 7g⁶ Sep 18] leggy
gelding: fair performer: won maiden at Lingfield in August: ran as though something
wrong in nursery final start (gelded after): stays 7f: acts on polytrack and good to firm
going: not straightforward. *J. A. Osborne*

ROCKFIELD TIGER (IRE) 2 b.c. (Mar 21) Dubai Destination (USA) 127 – Alja-   **69**
zeera (USA) 91 (Swain (IRE) 134) [2007 6g⁴ 6m⁵ 6m p8g⁶ Aug 29] close-coupled colt:
fair maiden: stays 1m: tongue tied once. *J. A. Osborne*

ROCK HAVEN (IRE) 5 b.g. Danehill Dancer (IRE) 117 – Mahabba (USA) 74 (Elocu-   **66**
tionist (USA)) [2007 56: p9.5g² p12.2g 10.2d⁴ p8.6g 8s² 10m 12.1m⁶ 8.5g⁶ p12.2g 10g⁵
Oct 25] workmanlike gelding: fair performer: left G. Bridgwater after sixth outing,
J. Unett after ninth: stays 11f: acts on polytrack, soft and good to firm going: tried in
cheekpieces: said to have bled seventh outing: sold £4,700 in November. *G. H. Yardley*

ROCKING 2 b.f. (May 8) Oasis Dream 129 – Council Rock 74 (General Assembly   **79**
(USA)) [2007 5m⁴ 5g* 5m³ 5.2m 6m Sep 7] neat filly: half-sister to several winners,
including smart 2005 2-y-o 5f winner Superstar Leo (by College Chapel) and useful 6f to
8.5f winner (7f winner at 2 yrs) Royal Artist (by Royal Academy): dam, maiden (stayed
7f), half-sister to dam of 2000 Guineas winner Footstepsinthesand: fair performer: won
maiden at Windsor in June: went wrong way after (tried blinkered): should prove best at
5f/6f: acts on good to firm going: sold 38,000 gns. *W. J. Haggas*

ROCKJUMPER 2 br.c. (May 28) Cape Cross (IRE) 129 – Bronzewing 103 (Beldale   **–**
Flutter (USA) 130) [2007 8.3g 8.2g Oct 31] close-coupled colt: half-brother to numerous
winners, including 6f (at 2 yrs) to 1m winner Snow Goose (by Polar Falcon) and stayer
(7f winner at 2 yrs) Dusky Warbler (by Ezzoud), both smart, and 3-y-o Double Banded:
dam 6f/1m winner: backward, well held in maidens. *H. Morrison*

ROCK ME (IRE) 2 ch.c. (Feb 11) Rock of Gibraltar (IRE) 133 – Final Farewell (USA)   **43**
(Proud Truth (USA)) [2007 p8g 8m 8.2d 7d⁶ p8m f7d⁵ Dec 18] strong colt: poor maiden:
should stay 1m: often blinkered. *N. A. Callaghan*

ROCKNEST ISLAND (IRE) 4 b.f. Bahhare (USA) 122 – Margin Call (IRE) 75   **70**
(Tirol 127) [2007 56: f14g p16.5g* 15.8m⁵ 16.1d⁴ 16m³ 17.1m⁴ 16d² 16.2v² 18s⁶ 17.1d⁵
Aug 19] small, close-coupled filly: fair handicapper: left G. Lyons in Ireland after 3 yrs:
won at Wolverhampton in April and Newcastle in May: stays 2¼m: acts on polytrack and
any turf going: wears cheekpieces nowadays. *P. D. Niven*

ROCK 'N' ROLLER (FR) 3 b. or br.g. Sagacity (FR) 125 – Diamond Dance (FR)   **83**
112 (Dancehall (USA) 127) [2007 75: 11m⁴ 12.4m* 14s 16d Oct 11] tall, lengthy gelding:
fairly useful performer: won maiden at Newcastle (by 5 lengths) in May: gelded, little
impact in handicaps after: stays 12.4f: best efforts on good to firm going. *W. R. Muir*

ROCK OF ROCHELLE (USA) 2 br.c. (May 13) Rock of Gibraltar (IRE) 133 –   **102**
Recoleta (USA) (Wild Again (USA)) [2007 6d² 6g* 6m* 6m Oct 5] tall, close-coupled
colt: sixth foal: closely related to useful 2005 2-y-o 7f winner Silent Times (by Danehill
Dancer) and half-brother to Irish 1½m winner Mr Smooth (by Diesis): dam, US 1m
winner, sister to very smart US performer up to 1¼m Offlee Wild, out of half-sister to
Dynaformer: useful performer: won maiden and listed event (beat Domingues by short
head) at the Curragh in September: below-form seventh behind Dark Angel in Middle
Park Stakes at Newmarket final start: will be suited by 7f/1m: tongue tied after debut.
Andrew Kinsella, Ireland

ROCK OF TARIK (IRE) 3 ch.g. Rock of Gibraltar (IRE) 133 – Molasses (FR)   **68**
(Machiavellian (USA) 123) [2007 8d⁵ 7g 8.5g p8.6g⁶ Nov 16] fair maiden: best effort on
debut: tongue tied, last of 6 in handicap at Wolverhampton final start: gelded after: stays
1m: acts on good to soft going: tried blinkered. *M. J. Grassick, Ireland*

ROCK OF VEIO (IRE) 3 b.c. Rock of Gibraltar (IRE) 133 – Al Saqiya (USA) 68   **88**
(Woodman (USA) 126) [2007 6d* 8g 8m² 10g⁶ Nov 3] strong, sturdy colt: third foal:
half-brother to French 1¼m and 15f winner Cashel Blue (by Aljabr): dam, maiden
(should have stayed 1¼m), half-sister to smart US performer up to 8.5f Buffythecentre-
fold: won maiden at Rome in March: eighth in listed race there next time: left R. Brogi in
Italy, seemingly fairly useful form when 7 lengths second of 4 to Tobosa in minor event at
Doncaster: stiff task, well held in listed race at Newmarket final outing: stays 1m.
P. W. Chapple-Hyam

ROCK PEAK (IRE) 2 b.c. (Mar 2) Dalakhani (IRE) 133 – Convenience (IRE) (Ela-   **79 P**
Mana-Mou 132) [2007 8.1m⁴ Sep 13] €42,000Y, resold 110,000Y: rather leggy colt: fifth
foal: half-brother to useful 2002 2-y-o 6f winner (stayed 1¼m) Dust Cover (by Desert

Story): dam unraced half-sister to smart sprinter Fire Dome: 33/1, shaped very well when fourth to Silver Regent in maiden at Sandown, considerably handled while finishing strongly from rear: will stay 1¼m: open to plenty of improvement and is one to follow. *H. Morrison*

ROCKY REPPIN 7 b.g. Rock City 120 – Tino Reppin 46 (Neltino 97) [2007 52§: f7g⁴ f7g f7g² f7g⁶ f7g Feb 22] leggy, close-coupled gelding: poor performer: effective at 7f/1m: acts on fibresand and good to firm ground: wears headgear: unreliable. *J. Balding* **49 §**

RODEO 4 ch.g. Pivotal 124 – Flossy 107 (Efisio 120) [2007 83: 9.1g 8.5v³ 8s 8d³ 7.5s² 8.5m Jul 31] tall, useful-looking gelding: has a moderate, round action: fairly useful maiden handicapper: will stay 1¼m: acts on heavy and good to firm going: blinkered of late: temperamental. *C. W. Thornton* **83 §**

ROGERS LODGER 3 b.g. Cyrano de Bergerac 120 – Bertrade 75 (Homeboy 114) [2007 –: p6g⁶ p6g p7g p7g⁵ 6g⁶ p6g p7g 7.6s Aug 18] modest maiden: stays 7f: acts on polytrack: tried blinkered. *J. Akehurst* **55**

ROGER'S REVENGE 2 ch.g. (May 7) City On A Hill (USA) 114 – Resemblance (State Diplomacy (USA)) [2007 7d 7g⁵ Nov 6] good-topped gelding: modest maiden: hung badly both starts (over 3 months apart), better effort when close-up fifth at Catterick: will stay 1m. *B. Smart* **58**

ROGUE 5 b.m. Royal Applause 124 – Mystique (Mystiko (USA) 124) [2007 74: p6g 6g² 6m⁴ 7m² Jun 17] strong mare: fair maiden: stays 7f: raced only on good ground or firmer on turf. *Jane Southcombe* **68**

ROI DE L'ODET (FR) 7 b.g. Grape Tree Road 122 – Fanfare du Roi (Rusticaro (FR) 124) [2007 12d Jun 22] ex-French gelding: won 5 times from 1m to 11f on Flat in native country at 3 yrs: tailed off in handicap at Newmarket only Flat start at 7 yrs: fair hurdler. *N. J. Henderson* **–**

ROJABAA 8 b.g. Anabaa (USA) 130 – Slava (USA) (Diesis 133) [2007 12.1s Jul 17] lengthy gelding: poor performer: unraced on Flat in 2005/6: stays easy 1½m: acts on firm going: tried in cheekpieces. *M. Mullineaux* **–**

ROKER PARK (IRE) 2 b.g. (May 3) Choisir (AUS) 126 – Joyful (IRE) 71 (Green Desert (USA) 127) [2007 5m* 5m 6g 5g Aug 22] strong, good-bodied gelding: half-brother to 1m winner Cooden Beach (by Peintre Celebre) and French 7f and 9f winner Dorset (by Sadler's Wells): dam 7f winner: fairly useful form: won maiden at Ripon in June: little impact facing stiff tasks (in pattern/listed events) subsequently, then gelded: likely to prove best at 5f/6f: raced only on good/good to firm going. *K. R. Burke* **89**

ROLEXA 3 br.f. Pursuit of Love 124 – Dunkellin (USA) (Irish River (FR) 131) [2007 8m³ 8.3g 7m⁶ p8g² 10.2g⁵ Oct 24] sturdy, good-topped filly: has scratchy action: half-sister to several winners, including smart 1m/1¼m winner Green Card (by Green Dancer) and 4-y-o Pearly Wey: dam US sprinter: fairly useful maiden at best: left C. Cox after third start: stays 1m: acts on polytrack and good to firm going. *C. F. Wall* **80 d**

ROLL EM OVER 4 b.f. Tamure (IRE) 125 – Miss Petronella (Petoski 135) [2007 9.2d 11.9m p12.2g 11.1d⁵ 12s Jul 18] seventh foal: sister to 2 winners, including 6-y-o Let's Roll and half-sister to 2 winners, including 2¼m winner Lord Nellson (by Arctic Lord): dam unraced: well held only start in bumpers, and on Flat: blinkered last 2 starts. *C. W. Thornton* **–**

ROLLIN 'N TUMBLIN 3 ch.c. Zaha (CAN) 106 – Steppin Out 63 (First Trump 118) [2007 p7g p8g p7g⁵ p11g p11g³ p10g³ Dec 30] fair maiden: stays 11f: raced only on polytrack. *W. Jarvis* **73**

ROMAN ARMY (IRE) 5 b.g. Trans Island 119 – Contravene (IRE) 64 (Contract Law (USA) 108) [2007 61: 11.1m³ 16.1m Jun 2] leggy gelding: modest maiden: left D. Marnane in Ireland prior to reappearance: stays 13.3f: acts on heavy and good to firm ground: tried blinkered/in cheekpieces. *James Moffatt* **61**

ROMAN BOY (ARG) 8 ch.g. Roy (USA) – Roman Red (USA) (Blushing Groom (FR) 131) [2007 60: p9.5g p8g² p8.6g f8g² p8g³ p8g⁴ p8g f8g⁶ p7g p8g⁴ 9.7f 8m⁶ p10g³ p8g⁶ Oct 17] fair handicapper: stays easy 1¼m: acts on all-weather, good to firm and good to soft ground: tried visored/blinkered: sometimes races freely. *Stef Liddiard* **65**

ROMAN EMPIRE 7 b.g. Efisio 120 – Gena Ivor (USA) (Sir Ivor (USA) 135) [2007 65: f8g f6g Jan 30] lengthy, good-bodied gelding: fair performer at best: tailed off in handicaps at 7 yrs: wears visor/blinkers: has looked hard ride. *P. A. Blockley* **–**

ROMAN FUN (IRE) 3 b.f. Peintre Celebre (USA) 137 – Tuscaloosa (Robellino **50**
(USA) 127) [2007 8s 8g⁵ 8.3m 11.1g 12m Sep 30] fourth foal: dam unraced out of useful
Irish sprinter Title Roll: form only when fifth to Dawla in maiden at Listowel second
start, final start for T. Stack in Ireland: tried in cheekpieces/blinkered. *I. Semple*

ROMAN HISTORY (IRE) 4 b.g. Titus Livius (FR) 115 – Tetradonna (IRE) 102 **60**
(Teenoso (USA) 135) [2007 60: 10.1m 9.1d 8m 9m² 10.1g 12m⁴ 10.1m⁴ 9d 10g Oct 6]
sturdy gelding: modest performer: stays 1½m: acts on good to firm going: often wears
cheekpieces: tried visored: has shown temperament. *Miss Tracy Waggott*

ROMAN LEGION (IRE) 2 gr.c. (Feb 4) Spartacus (IRE) 107 – Singhana (IRE) **74**
(Mouktar 129) [2007 7d³ 8g² 7.2v³ Nov 3] fair maiden: placed all starts, second to Colony
at Bath: stays 1m: raced only on good ground or softer. *P. A. Blockley*

ROMAN MAZE 7 ch.g. Lycius (USA) 124 – Maze Garden (USA) (Riverman (USA) **98**
131) [2007 94: 6m* 7.1d⁴ 6g 5.7f* 7f⁵ 6m² 6g² 6g 6m 7.6m 6m⁵ 5.1m⁴ p7g p7m⁵ p6g **a91**
p7.1g Nov 30] good-bodied gelding: useful handicapper on turf, fairly useful on all-
weather: won at Windsor in April and Bath in June: needs good test at 6f, and stays 7.6f:
acts on all-weather, firm and good to soft going: usually held up. *W. M. Brisbourne*

ROMAN QUEST 4 b.g. Lujain (USA) 119 – Roma 61 (Second Set (IRE) 127) [2007 **79**
79: 6f 5m⁵ 6d 6m 7s² 7m⁶ 7g p7g 6d⁵ 6d² 6.1s⁶ Oct 18] tall, good-topped gelding: fair
handicapper: stays 7f: acts on soft and good to firm ground: free-going sort: held up: sold
14,000 gns. *H. Morrison*

ROMAN QUINTET (IRE) 7 ch.g. Titus Livius (FR) 115 – Quintellina 83 (Robellino **76**
(USA) 127) [2007 82: 7m 6g³ 6m* 6m² 6m⁵ 5g⁶ 5m⁵ 6g p7.1g Oct 12] big, lengthy
gelding: fair handicapper: won at Haydock in June: stays easy 1m: acts on all-weather,
firm and good to soft going: tried tongue tied/in headgear: free-going sort, usually races
prominently: quirky. *R. J. Price*

ROMANTIC DESTINY 2 b.f. (Jan 24) Dubai Destination (USA) 127 – My First **90 ?**
Romance 61 (Danehill (USA) 126) [2007 5s³ 6m² 6d² 6d² 7d⁴ 6m⁵ 6g 6g 5d Sep 21]
lengthy, good-bodied filly: half-sister to several winning sprinters, including Queen Mary
winners Romantic Myth (in 2000, by Mind Games) and Romantic Liason (in 2002, by
Primo Dominie): dam ran twice: fair maiden: runner-up 3 times, including in nursery:
flattered (set pace) in Lowther Stakes at York seventh start: best at 5f/6f: acts on good to
firm and good to soft going: blinkered end of season. *K. A. Ryan*

ROMANTIC GIFT 5 b.m. Cadeaux Genereux 131 – Last Romance (IRE) (Last **–**
Tycoon 131) [2007 8m p6g 6g Jun 23] rather leggy mare: modest maiden: unraced in
2005/6: well beaten completed starts in 2007: dead. *Mrs C. A. Dunnett*

ROMANTIC VERSE 2 b.f. (Feb 1) Kyllachy 129 – Romancing 79 (Dr Devious (IRE) **61**
127) [2007 6d⁶ p7.1g* Nov 5] second foal: dam, maiden (stayed 1¼m), granddaughter of
US Grade 1 2-y-o 7f/1m winner Some Romance: modest form: won maiden at Wolverhampton latter stage: may prove best up to 7f. *W. J. Haggas*

ROMANY NIGHTS (IRE) 7 b.g. Night Shift (USA) – Gipsy Moth 99 (Efisio 120) **85**
[2007 94, a–: p6g p6g* p6g 6m p7g⁵ 6d 7f p6g* p6g² p6g 6m 6f⁴ p6g 6m⁵ 6d 6.1d p6g **a77**
Dec 5] strong gelding: fairly useful handicapper on turf, fair on all-weather nowadays:
won at Kempton in January (changed hands 20,000 gns following month) and June:
effective at 6f/7f: acts on all-weather, firm and good to soft going: tried visored, blinkered
nowadays: usually tongue tied. *Miss Gay Kelleway*

ROMANY PRINCESS (IRE) 2 b.f. (Apr 7) Viking Ruler (AUS) – Fag End (IRE) **76**
88 (Treasure Kay 114) [2007 5m 5g³ 6s² 6m³ 6m p7g* 7g Sep 30] 13,000F, 65,000Y:
good-topped filly: has scope: half-sister to several winners, including 2005 2-y-o 7f
winner Bellsbank (by Beckett): dam 2-y-o 6f/7f winner: fair performer: placed 3 times,
including third in listed race at Goodwood and nursery at Ascot, prior to winning maiden
at Lingfield in September: stays 7f: acts on polytrack, soft and good to firm going.
R. Hannon

ROMFORD CAR TWO 2 b.c. (Feb 20) Josr Algarhoud (IRE) 118 – Film Buff 60 **54 ?**
(Midyan (USA) 124) [2007 p7g 7s 7d Oct 30] tall colt: seemingly modest maiden: raced
only at 7f, should be suited by further (dam stayed 1¾m). *Miss J. Feilden*

ROMIL STAR (GER) 10 b.g. Chief's Crown (USA) – Romelia (USA) (Woodman **45**
(USA) 126) [2007 57, a73d: f12g⁵ f12g⁴ f16g⁶ f14g⁶ Jan 25] strong, workmanlike gelding: just poor form at 10 yrs: stays 1¾m: acts on all-weather and heavy going: usually
wears headgear: joined Mrs C. Ikin. *M. Wellings*

RONALDSAY 3 gr.f. Kirkwall 118 – Crackling 57 (Electric 126) [2007 80: p8g 10m² **108** 9.9g 8m³ 9g² 9.9g⁴ 10m² 10.5s* 10d² Oct 19] leggy filly: useful performer: progressed well at 3 yrs, in frame 4 starts prior to winning handicap at Haydock in September by 2 lengths from Sunisa: very good ½-length second to Short Skirt in listed race at Newmarket final start: will stay 11f: acts on polytrack, firm and soft going: reportedly had an irregular heartbeat third outing: held up. *R. Hannon*

RONDEAU (GR) 2 ch.g. (Jan 31) Harmonic Way 121 – Areti (GR) (Wadood (USA) **70** 97) [2007 p8g⁵ p8g p7g Nov 16] Greek-bred gelding: fair maiden: fifth at Kempton on debut, standout effort: stays 1m: starts slowly. *P. R. Chamings*

RONDO 4 b.g. Piccolo 121 – Flourish (Selkirk (USA) 129) [2007 75d: f6g 7.1d 7.1g⁴ **58 §** 6d* 6d³ 6d⁴ 6g 6g Aug 22] tall, good-topped gelding: modest handicapper: won apprentice event at Hamilton in July: stays 7f: acts on firm and good to soft going: has worn blinkers: refused to race penultimate outing and again reluctant on final appearance: one to avoid: sold 1,400 gns, sent to Denmark. *T. D. Barron*

RON IN ERNEST 3 ch.g. Medicean 128 – Viewfinder (USA) (Boundary (USA) 117) **48** [2007 61: 7.1g 7.6g 13.1f p10g Sep 11] lengthy gelding: maiden: just poor form in 2007. *J. A. Geake*

RONNIE FROM DONNY (IRE) 7 b.g. Eagle Eyed (USA) 111 – New Rochelle **–** (IRE) 65 (Lafontaine (USA) 117) [2007 –: f6g f6g Jan 30] sturdy, useful-looking gelding: no longer of any account. *C. J. Teague*

RONNIE HOWE 3 b.g. Hunting Lion (IRE) 115 – Arasong (Aragon 118) [2007 72: **70** f5g² f5g* f5g⁴ 5g⁵ 5g⁶ 5g² 5v 5s Jul 18] sturdy gelding: fair performer: won maiden at Southwell in February: best at 5f: acts on fibresand, firm and good to soft going. *M. Dods*

RONNIES GIRL 3 b.f. Tobougg (IRE) 125 – Tryptonic (FR) (Baryshnikov (AUS)) **–** [2007 7d 7g Jul 27] 7,000Y: first foal: dam, French 1m winner, out of useful French 2-y-o sprinter Shining Molly: tailed off in maidens. *C. J. Teague*

RONNIES LAD 5 b.g. Lake Coniston (IRE) 131 – Lycius Touch 50 (Lycius (USA) **50** 124) [2007 40: p8.6g p9.5g⁶ f11g⁵ f12g p12.2g Mar 27] modest performer: seems to stay 1½m: acts on all-weather and firm going: tried in cheekpieces/visor. *J. R. Norton*

RONSAI (USA) 2 b. or br.f. (Mar 25) Black Minnaloushe (USA) 123 – Roundtree **61** (IRE) 98 (Night Shift (USA))) [2007 6m 5m² 5m⁴ 5.7m 5.1f⁴ p5g Sep 29] close-coupled filly: first foal: dam 5f (at 2 yrs)/6f winner (US 5.5f winner): modest maiden: best form (in frame 3 times) at 5f: acts on firm going: said to have finished lame fourth outing. *R. Hannon*

RONSARD (IRE) 5 b.g. Spectrum (IRE) 126 – Touche-A-Tout (IRE) (Royal Academy **73** (USA) 130) [2007 71d: p12g 10.2f³ p9.5g 14.1m² 11.7d 17.2m²* 16m² 15.8g⁴ 14m⁶ 13d³ **a64** 16.2s³ 14.1d³ 16.2s* 18s⁴ 16m 16m 14.1m p16g p16g p16.5g⁴ p16g³ p16.5g* p16g³ p13.9g* p16.5g f12d³ p13.9d⁵ p13.9g Dec 31] leggy gelding: fair performer on turf, modest on all-weather nowadays: left J. Tuck after reappearance: won amateur handicap at Bath in May and claimer at Chepstow in July: stays 2¼m: acts on all-weather, firm and soft going: tried in headgear: held up: tough. *P. D. Evans*

ROOD BOY (IRE) 6 b.g. Great Commotion (USA) 123 – Cnocma (IRE) 58 (Tender **–** King 123) [2007 f12g f12g f11g May 8] modest performer: unraced in 2006: well held at 6 yrs: stays 11f: acts on fibresand. *Simon Earle*

ROODOLPH 3 ch.g. Primo Valentino (IRE) 116 – Roo 97 (Rudimentary (USA) 118) **82 §** [2007 84p: p7g⁴ 7.1m⁴ 7g 6m 7m⁵ 8.3g² Oct 8] big, lengthy gelding: fairly useful handicapper: stays 1m: raced only on polytrack and good going or firmer (acts on firm): tried tongue tied: blinkered final start: ungenuine. *Eve Johnson Houghton*

ROOKWITH (IRE) 7 b.g. Revoque (IRE) 122 – Resume (IRE) 69 (Lahib (USA) 129) **65** [2007 82: p9.5g 8d 9v 8.5d 10d a7g⁴ 7g 9m³ p9.5g p7g⁶ Dec 5] tall gelding: modest performer: well held at Wolverhampton on reappearance and penultimate outing: effective at 7f to 1¼m: acts on any turf going, all-weather and sand: occasionally wears headgear: sometimes finds little. *T. G. McCourt, Ireland*

ROONAH (FR) 4 b.f. Xaar 132 – Caer Mecene (FR) (Caerwent 123) [2007 –: 12m 16g **49** 12m⁴ 16g] poor maiden: stays 1½m: acts on good to firm ground: tried blinkered/visored: sold 2,500 gns, sent to Kazakhstan. *Karen McLintock*

ROPE BRIDGE (IRE) 2 b.c. (Mar 13) Orpen (USA) 116 – Carhue Journey (IRE) 77 **56** (Barathea (IRE) 127) [2007 f5g 5s 5s³ 6g 5g⁴ 5m* p5.1g 6d³ Oct 9] unfurnished colt: modest performer: won seller at Musselburgh (dead heat) in August: best at 5f/6f: acts on soft and good to firm going: usually blinkered. *T. D. Easterby*

RORY BOY (USA) 2 b.g. (Mar 9) Aldebaran (USA) 126 – Purr Pleasure (USA) (El **64** Gran Senor (USA) 136) [2007 7m 8m Oct 4] big, quite good-topped gelding: well held in maidens at Yarmouth and Newmarket (seemingly modest form) 3 months apart: should be suited by 1m. *E. A. L. Dunlop*

ROSA DE MI CORAZON (USA) 3 ch.f. Cozzene (USA) – Rose of Zollern (IRE) **86** 111 (Seattle Dancer (USA) 119) [2007 f6g* f7g* f7g* Feb 20] second foal: half-sister to useful 2005 2-y-o 7f winner Flor Y Nata (by Fusaichi Pegasus): dam, German 7f (at 2 yrs)/1m (stayed 11f and later won in US): fairly useful form: unbeaten in 3 starts, namely maiden in January and 2 handicaps in February, all at Southwell: still green, landed odds by short head from Captain Jacksparra for final success: would have stayed 1m: stud. *Sir Mark Prescott*

ROSA GRACE 2 gr.f. (Feb 18) Lomitas 129 – Night Haven 99 (Night Shift (USA)) **96** [2007 7g* 7m* 7m⁵ 7d⁴ Oct 20] 30,000Y: rather leggy, quite attractive filly: third foal: half-sister to 4-y-o Secret Night: dam 5f (at 2 yrs)/6f winner: useful form: won maiden at Thirsk in August and minor event at Newbury in September: better still when length fifth to Raymi Coya in Oh So Sharp Stakes (unsuited by steady pace) and 2¾ lengths fourth to Kitty Matcham in Rockfel Stakes (had to weave through), both at Newmarket: will stay 1m: unraced on extremes of going. *Rae Guest*

ROSALEEN (IRE) 2 b.f. (Feb 4) Cadeaux Genereux 131 – Dark Rosaleen (IRE) **88** (Darshaan 133) [2007 7g⁴ 7g* 7g⁴ 7m Oct 6] 70,000Y: medium-sized filly: second foal: half-sister to 3-y-o Rosbay: dam unraced: fairly useful form: won maiden at Thirsk in July: stiff tasks after in Prestige Stakes at Goodwood (muddling race, 3 lengths fourth to Sense of Joy) and nursery at Newmarket (mid-field): likely to stay 1m: acts on polytrack and good to firm going. *B. J. Meehan*

ROSANDWIL (IRE) 3 b.f. Muhtarram (USA) 125 – Anne-Sophie 65 (First Trump – 118) [2007 f11d Dec 12] second foal: dam 9f/1¼m winner: tailed off in bumper/maiden. *A. D. Brown*

ROSBAY (IRE) 3 b.g. Desert Prince (IRE) 130 – Dark Rosaleen (IRE) (Darshaan 133) **94** [2007 87: 8g⁴ 10.4g³ 10.3s* 12g 12g² 12f⁵ 10s 10.3g Sep 29] strong gelding: fairly useful handicapper: won at Chester in July: stays 1½m: acts on any going: gelded after final outing. *T. D. Easterby*

ROS CUIRE (IRE) 2 br.c. (May 29) Expelled (USA) 116 – Haven Island (IRE) **55** (Revoque (IRE) 122) [2007 6d p7.1g⁵ p7.1g⁶ Dec 13] quite good-topped colt: modest maiden: seemingly best effort at Wolverhampton final start. *W. A. Murphy, Ireland*

ROSE BIEN 5 b. or br.m. Bien Bien (USA) 125 – Madame Bovary 82 (Ile de Bourbon **70** (USA) 133) [2007 70: p16g⁵ 14.1g 18g⁴ 16m⁵ 14.8d⁴ Jun 23] sparely-made mare: fair performer: stays 2¼m: acts on polytrack, firm and good to soft going: usually wears cheekpieces, blinkered final outing at 4 yrs. *P. J. McBride*

ROSECLIFF 5 b.g. Montjeu (IRE) 137 – Dance Clear (IRE) 99 (Marju (IRE) 127) **72** [2007 –: p12.2g 18s 12.1g Aug 15] good-topped gelding: fair performer, lightly raced nowadays: stays 1½m: acts on polytrack, good to firm and good to soft going: often wears headgear: tried tongue tied: joined N. Wilson. *Heather Dalton*

ROSE DE RITA 2 br.f. (Apr 29) Superior Premium 122 – Rita's Rock Ape 87 (Mon – Tresor 113) [2007 6d 5.1d 5.1g Nov 7] sturdy filly: second foal: dam 5f winner: no form. *L. P. Grassick*

ROSEIN 5 b.m. Komaite (USA) – Red Rosein 97 (Red Sunset 120) [2007 69, a86: f5g – f6g² f7g² p6g 6g p6g Aug 30] big, heavy-topped mare: fairly useful handicapper on **a86** all-weather, fair at best on turf: stays 7f: acts on all-weather, soft and good to firm going: sometimes slowly away. *Mrs G. S. Rees*

ROSEMARY AND THYME 3 ch.f. Medicean 128 – Marie La Rose (FR) (Night – Shift (USA)) [2007 p7g 8.3m 10m 8.2g Oct 31] 27,000Y: well-made, stocky filly: half-sister to 3 winners, including French 1m (at 2 yrs)/1¼m winner Contemporary Art (by Blushing Flame): dam, French 1¼m winner, out of half-sister to Prix Ganay winner Vert Amande and Prix Vermeille winner Indian Rose: well held in maidens, leaving J. Hills 5,500 gns after second start. *Mrs S. Lamyman*

ROSE MUWASIM 4 ch.f. In The Wings 128 – Muwasim (USA) (Meadowlake (USA)) **57 d** [2007 71: p10g p9.5g² p9.5g⁵ p10g⁴ 11.7f⁵ p9.5g³ 10s 10g 9.9s 10v p10g 9.9m p10g Sep 11] small filly: modest maiden: left K. J. Burke after fourth outing: stays 1¼m: acts on polytrack: usually in headgear: sometimes fails to impress with attitude: sold 800 gns. *S. Parr*

ROSENTRAUB 2 b.c. (Jan 30) Dansili 127 – Ambrosine 81 (Nashwan (USA) 135) **60 p**
[2007 7m p7g Oct 24] first foal: dam, 1¼m/1½m winner, half-sister to 6-y-o Camrose
out of half-sister to Most Welcome: better than bare result in mid-division in maidens at
Lingfield: will be suited by 1m+: open to improvement. *H. J. L. Dunlop*

ROSE OF INCHINOR 4 b.f. Inchinor 119 – Rosa Canina 91 (Bustino 136) [2007 70: **41**
6m 6m⁶ 6g 6m 6m Sep 8] leggy filly: fair maiden at best: well below form in 2007: bred
to be suited by at least 1m: best form on good ground: visored final start. *R. E. Barr*

ROSE OF PETRA (IRE) 3 b.f. Golan (IRE) 129 – Desert Beauty (IRE) 103 (Green **91**
Desert (USA) 127) [2007 88: 8.1g 9m⁴ 9.7g* 9.7m⁴ 11.6f³ Aug 4] angular, useful-looking
filly: fairly useful handicapper: won at Folkestone in June: good efforts after: stays 11.6f:
acts on polytrack and firm going. *Sir Michael Stoute*

ROSE ROW 3 gr.f. Act One 124 – D'Azy 91 (Persian Bold 123) [2007 p7g 10m p10g⁵ **64 +**
Dec 30] sparely-made filly: half-sister to several winners, notably very smart 1m (at
2 yrs) to 13.3f winner Presenting (by Mtoto): dam 2-y-o 7f winner: modest form in
maidens, fifth at Lingfield: refused to race on debut: will stay 1½m. *Mrs Mary Hambro*

ROSE SIOG 2 ch.f. (Apr 23) Bahamian Bounty 116 – Madame Sisu 47 (Emarati (USA) **85**
74) [2007 5m* 5g⁵ 5s² 5m* 6s³ Aug 24] 7,500Y: lengthy filly: fifth foal: sister to 5f
winners Bahamian Duke and Treasure Cay, latter useful: dam, ran twice, out of half-sister
to high-class 1m/1¼m performer Bijou d'Inde: fairly useful performer: won maiden in
May and nursery in August, both at Musselburgh: again travelled strongly long way when
third to Edge of Gold in sales race at Newmarket: effective at 6f, probably ideally suited
by 5f: acts on soft and good to firm going. *R. A. Fahey*

ROSE STREET (IRE) 3 b.f. Noverre (USA) 125 – Archipova (IRE) (Ela-Mana-Mou **94 p**
132) [2007 p10g* 10.1d² Oct 30] 60,000F, 55,000 2-y-o: fourth foal: half-sister to very
smart 1m/1¼m performer Autumn Glory (by Charnwood Forest) and fairly useful 1m
(including at 2 yrs) to 1¾m winner Oddsmaker (by Barathea): dam, fairly useful winner
up to 15f in Italy, sister to useful 1½m performer Abyaan and half-sister to smart Irish
performer up to 1¾m Sadlers Wings: fairly useful form: won maiden at Kempton in June:
better effort when length second to Kavachi in handicap at Yarmouth next time: bred to
be suited by 1½m: useful prospect. *M. A. Jarvis*

ROSHANAK (IRE) 3 b.f. Spinning World (USA) 130 – Desert Bloom (IRE) (Pilsud- **81**
ski (IRE) 134) [2007 91p: p6g⁴ 7g p6g Jun 13] strong, compact filly: fair performer:
below form after reappearance at 3 yrs: should be suited by 7f/1m: acts on polytrack and
good to soft going. *B. J. Meehan*

ROSIE CROSS (IRE) 3 b.f. Cape Cross (IRE) 129 – Professional Mom (USA) **73**
(Spinning World (USA) 130) [2007 64: p8g³ p7g 6f³ 5.3d⁶ p5.1g* p6g 5g² 5.1f³ p5.1m³
p5g* p6g p5m⁶ p6g p5g⁵ p6g Nov 27] fair handicapper: won at Wolverhampton in July
and Kempton in September: best at 5f: acts on polytrack and firm going. *Eve Johnson
Houghton*

ROSIE SAYS NO 2 b.f. (Apr 10) Catcher In The Rye (IRE) 115 – Curlew Calling (IRE) **50 p**
51 (Pennine Walk 120) [2007 6d p6g⁴ p6g Nov 28] 1,500F: stocky filly: seventh foal:
half-sister to 6f winner Bold Cheverak (by Bold Edge): dam once-raced half-sister to
smart performers Dusky Warbler (stayer), Merry Merlin (up to 1¼m) and Snow Goose
(miler): modest maiden: type to do better at 1m+. *R. M. H. Cowell*

ROSIE'S GLORY (USA) 3 b. or br.f. More Than Ready (USA) 120 – Cukee (USA) **78 d**
(Langfuhr (CAN) 124) [2007 79: 7m p11g 10f 12.1m 12.1m⁵ 10m³ Sep 17] well-made
filly: fair maiden at best: stays 1¼m: acts on firm ground: joined M. Harris. *B. J. Meehan*

ROSIE'S RESULT 7 ch.g. Case Law 113 – Precious Girl 76 (Precious Metal 106) **43 §**
[2007 52§: 5f 5m 5g 5g 5d 5g 6m 5m 5m Aug 31] sparely-made gelding: poor handicapper: best at 5f: acts on firm and good to soft going: tried visored/in cheekpieces:
unreliable. *M. Todhunter*

ROSSALL POINT 6 b.g. Fleetwood (IRE) 107 – Loch Clair (IRE) 53 (Lomond (USA) **–**
128) [2007 12m Jul 24] fair maiden at 3 yrs: lightly raced and no form since. *Karen
McLintock*

ROSSIN GOLD (IRE) 5 b.g. Rossini (USA) 118 – Sacred Heart (IRE) 45 (Catrail **–**
(USA) 123) [2007 55: 12.1g 14g⁶ Jul 9] modest handicapper at best: no form in 2007:
blinkered at 2 yrs: has shown signs of waywardness. *P. Monteith*

ROSSINI BYLINE (IRE) 2 b.f. (May 5) Rossini (USA) 118 – Byliny (IRE) (Arch- **58 p**
way (IRE) 115) [2007 6g Sep 19] leggy filly: half-sister to winner in Italy by Monashee
Mountain: dam unraced granddaughter of Irish 1000 Guineas winner Miralla: 100/1,

promising early speed (before faded into ninth) in maiden at Yarmouth: will prove best at 5f/6f: should progress. *J. L. Spearing*

ROSSINI'S DANCER 2 b.c. (Apr 22) Rossini (USA) 118 – Bint Alhabib (Nashwan (USA) 135) [2007 6f p5.1g⁶ Oct 22] 1,000F, €7,500 2-y-o: half-brother to French 1½m winner Chocolate Cake (by Daggers Drawn): dam once-raced half-sister to smart 1½m/1¾m performer Gallery God: modest form in maidens, insufficient test: will benefit from 7f/1m: capable of better. *R. A. Fahey* — **64 p**

ROSS IS BOSS 5 gr.g. Paris House 123 – Billie Grey 72 (Chilibang 120) [2007 –: f7g 12g⁶ 8m 7.9m Jun 4] tall gelding: no form. *C. J. Teague* — **–**

ROSS MOOR 5 b.g. Dansili 127 – Snipe Hall 93 (Crofthall 110) [2007 74+: p13.9g⁴ p12.2g p13.9g² p12.2g² p13.9g⁶ p12g² p12g⁴ 11.6m 10g 12g² p12g³ 12m p13.9g⁶ Oct 15] big, strong, close-coupled gelding: fair handicapper: left N. Littmoden after fourth start: likely to stay 2m: acts on polytrack, raced only on good/good to firm ground on turf: tried blinkered. *Mike Murphy* — **77**

ROSY ALEXANDER 2 ch.f. (Feb 3) Spartacus (IRE) 107 – Sweet Angeline 74 (Deploy 131) [2007 p7g 7g⁶ 7f* Jul 30] sturdy filly: first foal: dam 1½m winner: fair performer: raced only in July, winning maiden at Yarmouth: will be suited by 1m/1¼m. *N. A. Callaghan* — **72 +**

ROSY ANNE 5 b.m. Paris House 123 – Common Rock (IRE) 44 (Common Grounds 118) [2007 f11g Mar 6] second foal: dam 2-y-o 7f seller winner: well held in bumpers/seller. *J. R. Turner* — **–**

ROSY DAWN 2 ch.f. (Mar 1) Bertolini (USA) 125 – Blushing Sunrise (USA) (Cox's Ridge (USA)) [2007 6g 7m⁴ 7.6f p7g p8g p7g⁶ p10g* p8m p10g² Nov 19] 14,000F, 12,000Y: sixth foal: half-sister to 1m/9f winner Sharp Needle (by Mark of Esteem), later successful in US: dam US 6.5f winner: modest performer: won claimer at Lingfield (left H. Dunlop £5,000) in October: stays 1¼m: acts on polytrack and good to firm ground: usually visored/blinkered. *Ms J. S. Doyle* — **51**

ROTATION (IRE) 3 b.g. Galileo (IRE) 134 – Termania (IRE) (Shirley Heights 130) [2007 –: 10.1g 10.1d⁶ 10.5d* 11g 12d* 14.5g²* 13d⁵ 15s⁵ Nov 25] sturdy gelding: little form in Britain: sold from J. Hills 4,500 gns after second start: won maiden at Dresden in August and claimer at Nancy and minor event at Duindigt (Dutch St Leger) in September: claimed from C. von der Recke €20,500 after next start: stays 14.5f. *T. Callejo, Spain* — **67**

ROTHESAY DANCER 4 b.f. Lujain (USA) 119 – Rhinefield Beauty (IRE) 52 (Shalford (IRE) 124§) [2007 73: 5m⁴ 5m 5d³ 5m³ 5m⁶ 5g 5g⁶ 5g³ 5d² 5d² 5g 5g* 5d² 6d³ 6g 5m⁴ 5g⁵ 5m⁶ 5d 5d 5d 6s² 5d 6v 6v Nov 3] leggy filly: has a quick action: fair handicapper: won at Musselburgh (second outing in 24 hrs) in July and Hamilton in August: effective at 5f/6f: acts on polytrack, firm and soft going (well held on heavy): tried blinkered, wore cheekpieces in 2006: held up: tough. *J. S. Goldie* — **73**

ROTUMA (IRE) 8 b.g. Tagula (IRE) 116 – Cross Question (USA) 84 (Alleged (USA) 138) [2007 63, a–: 10.1m⁶ 10.1m 10d* 9.1g 10.1d⁴ 10.1g 12m Aug 30] smallish, useful-looking gelding: modest performer nowadays: won claimer at Redcar in June: best around 1¼m: acts on polytrack and any turf going: blinkered: has worn tongue tie: tends to carry head awkwardly. *M. Dods* — **61 a–**

ROUGH ROCK (IRE) 2 ch.g. (Mar 28) Rock of Gibraltar (IRE) 133 – Amitie Fatale (IRE) (Night Shift) [2007 5.2m 5m⁴ 5d⁵ 7m p7g 6f* 6s⁶ 6f 6.1d Oct 18] close-coupled gelding: fair performer: won seller at Yarmouth (left B. Meehan 28,600 gns) in July: best up to 7f: acts on firm and soft going: blinkered last 5 starts, tongue tied last 3: front runner. *Miss Gay Kelleway* — **74**

ROUGH SKETCH (USA) 2 b.g. (Jan 31) Peintre Celebre (USA) 137 – Drama Club (IRE) (Sadler's Wells (USA) 132) [2007 p7g 6d p7g Oct 12] 105,000Y: useful-looking gelding: first foal: dam, French maiden, half-sister to smart 2003 2-y-o 6f to 1m winner Pearl of Love (by Peintre Celebre): green and not knocked about in maidens in autumn (gelded after final start): likely to prove a different proposition in middle-distance handicaps. *Sir Mark Prescott* — **– p**

ROUNDTHETWIST (IRE) 2 b.g. (Mar 18) Okawango (USA) 115 – Delta Town (USA) (Sanglamore (USA) 126) [2007 p6g² Dec 26] €30,000Y: seventh foal: half-brother to 3 winners, including 7f (at 2 yrs) to 10.5f winner Kentucky Blue (by Revoque) and 1m/8.5f (latter including at 2 yrs and in US) winner Missatacama (by Desert Style): dam, ran twice in France, out of smart French filly up to 1¼m Daeltown: 8/1, encouraging neck second to Annes Rocket in maiden at Wolverhampton, briefly short of room: should improve. *K. R. Burke* — **69 p**

ROURKE STAR 5 b.g. Presidium 124 – Mirror Four Sport 59 (Risk Me (FR) 127) – [2007 11.1d⁶ 12m⁶ 8.3d Aug 15] fair form in bumpers at 3 yrs, tailed off in similar event on return: little form in maidens on Flat. *B. Storey*

ROWAAD 2 ch.c. (Jan 15) Compton Place 125 – Level Pegging (IRE) 48 (Common 74 Grounds 118) [2007 p7m p7g⁴ Oct 29] 45,000Y: fourth foal: half-brother to 4-y-o Even Bolder: dam twice-raced sister to smart sprinter Flanders: fair form in maidens at Kempton, fourth to Adversity: may prove best at 5f/6f. *M. P. Tregoning*

ROWANBERRY 5 b.m. Bishop of Cashel 122 – Raintree Venture (Good Times (ITY)) 49 [2007 50, a59: p5.1g³ Jan 15] modest performer at best: not discredited only outing at 5 yrs: effective at 5f/6f, should stay 7f: acts on polytrack, firm and good to soft going: has hung left. *R. M. H. Cowell*

ROWAN DANCER 2 b.f. (Mar 27) Medicean 128 – Golden Seattle (IRE) (Seattle – Dancer (USA) 119) [2007 p7g⁶ 6v⁵ p7m Nov 1] rather leggy filly: fourth foal: half-sister to 5-y-o Rowan Warning and 6-y-o Rowan Pursuit: dam Italian 2-y-o 5f/6f winner: no form in maidens. *J. R. Boyle*

ROWAN LODGE (IRE) 5 ch.g. Indian Lodge (IRE) 127 – Tirol Hope (IRE) 100 71 (Tirol 127) [2007 79: f8g³ f8g⁵ 10s⁴ 8d³ 8d⁴ 8.1s² 10.1d⁴ 10.2m* 8d² p8g 8d⁶ p8g Nov 6] sturdy gelding: fair performer: left M. Tompkins after sixth start: won seller at Chepstow in September: stays 1¼m: acts on fibresand, heavy and good to firm going, probably on polytrack: sometimes blinkered/visored: free-going sort: joined Ollie Pears. *J. R. Boyle*

ROWAN PURSUIT 6 b.m. Pursuit of Love 124 – Golden Seattle (IRE) (Seattle Danc- – er (USA) 119) [2007 –, a56: p8g p8g p11g⁵ 12m p7g⁵ 8f⁵ 8m⁶ 7d Aug 21] small mare: **a46** poor performer nowadays: left C. Horgan after third start: stays 1¼m: acts on polytrack and firm ground: usually blinkered, tried in cheekpieces: has carried head awkwardly. *E. A. Wheeler*

ROWAN RIVER 3 b.f. Invincible Spirit (IRE) 121 – Lemon Tree (USA) (Zilzal (USA) 79 137) [2007 62: p8.6m⁴ 10m⁴ 10g³ 10f³ 10g* 10m 12d Sep 26] workmanlike gelding: fair handicapper: won at Newmarket (flashed tail before hanging violently right) in August: stays 1¼m, probably not 1½m: acts on polytrack and firm going: quirky. *M. H. Tompkins*

ROWAN WARNING 5 b.g. Diktat 126 – Golden Seattle (IRE) (Seattle Dancer (USA) 64 119) [2007 67: p8g³ p10g⁴ p10g p10g p12g³ p10g p10g⁴ p11g⁵ Jun 13] close-coupled, quite good-topped gelding: modest handicapper nowadays: stays 1½m, at least with emphasis on speed: acts on polytrack and firm ground: tried in headgear: usually held up. *J. R. Boyle*

ROWE PARK 4 b.g. Dancing Spree (USA) – Magic Legs 54 (Reprimand 122) [2007 119 77+: p5.1g² f5g* p6g² 6m⁶ 5m* 5g* p5g³ 5m³ 5.2m* 5m² Oct 4] lengthy gelding: developed into smart performer in 2007, winning handicaps at Southwell in February and Lingfield and Goodwood in May, and Dubai International Airport World Trophy at Newbury (beat Enticing by ½ length) in September: very good neck second to Judd Street in listed event at Newmarket final start: best at 5f: acts on all-weather and good to firm going: sometimes sweats: races prominently. *Mrs L. C. Jewell*

Dubai International Airport World Trophy, Newbury—the improving Rowe Park causes a 25/1 upset; Enticing (right), Judd Street (second left), Mutawaajid and Desert Lord (hidden by winner) are next

ROXIE PRINCESS (IRE) 3 b.f. Inchinor 119 – Pagan Princess 54 (Mujtahid (USA) **68** 118) [2007 8g 8g³ 8g 10d p8g p10g p10g Nov 19] compact filly: second foal: dam, maiden, half-sister to useful performer up to 1¾m Hambleden: fair maiden: stays 1m. *J. A. R. Toller*

ROXY SINGER 3 b.f. Erhaab (USA) 127 – Rainy Day Song 61 (Persian Bold 123) **49** [2007 –: 11m p12g 10.1d² 12.1g⁵ 15.4g⁵ p12g 10d⁶ Oct 10] leggy, close-coupled filly: poor maiden: stays 1¼m: acts on good to soft going: often visored: refused to enter parade ring and geed up on reappearance, refused to enter stall intended seventh outing. *W. J. Musson*

ROYA 4 b.c. Daylami (IRE) 138 – Aegean Dream (IRE) 97 (Royal Academy (USA) 130) **–** [2007 72: 10g 10g p9.5g Aug 13] lightly-made colt: fair maiden handicapper at 3 yrs: little impact in 2007. *Miss Gay Kelleway*

ROYAL ACCLAMATION (IRE) 2 b.c. (Jan 30) Acclamation 118 – Lady Abigail **63 p** (IRE) (Royal Academy (USA) 130) [2007 5g 6g⁵ 6m⁴ Nov 10] €41,000F, 44,000 2-y-o, resold 28,000 2-y-o: good-topped colt: third foal: half-brother to 2005 2-y-o 7f winner Waiting For Mary (by Tagula) and winner in Norway by Inchinor: dam unraced half-sister to smart sprinter Lionhearted: modest form in maidens (not knocked about), never-nearer fourth to Premier Danseur at Doncaster: will stay 7f: should continue to progress. *G. A. Harker*

ROYAL AMNESTY 4 b.c. Desert Prince (IRE) 130 – Regal Peace 94 (Known Fact **–** (USA) 135) [2007 –, a87: p10g p9.5g⁵ p8g⁶ 7m p8g p7g p7g⁵ 10.1m p8.6g p11g p8g⁴ **a77 d** p8g⁵ p10m⁵ Nov 26] close-coupled colt: fair handicapper on all-weather nowadays (below form after third start), little form on turf: stays easy 1½m: acts on polytrack: tried blinkered: patiently ridden, and has found little. *G. C. H. Chung*

ROYAL AND REGAL (IRE) 3 b.c. Sadler's Wells (USA) 132 – Smart 'n Noble **116** (USA) (Smarten (USA)) [2007 97P: 11g² 12v* 12s 15g³ 15d³ 16d* Oct 20] tall, good-topped, attractive colt: smart performer: won listed race at Longchamp in May and Jockey Club Cup at Newmarket (improved effort when beating Balkan Knight by 1¼ lengths) in October: also placed in 3 pattern races at Longchamp, including when beaten a head in Prix Hocquart: well-held eighth in Irish Derby at the Curragh third start: stays 2m: raced only on good ground or softer (acts on heavy). *A. Fabre, France*

ROYAL APPLORD 2 b.c. (Mar 27) Royal Applause 124 – Known Class (USA) **74** (Known Fact (USA) 135) [2007 7m³ 7m⁵ 6f² 7d 8g⁴ Nov 9] strong colt: has a quick action: fair maiden: second to Generous Thought at Pontefract: should stay beyond 6f: acts on firm going. *K. A. Ryan*

ROYAL AUDITON 6 ch.m. First Trump 118 – Loriner's Lass 80 (Saddlers' Hall (IRE) **61** 126) [2007 –: f14g p16f 11.5m³ 11.5m⁶ p12g Jun 14] modest maiden handicapper: said to have pulled muscles final outing in 2007: stays 1¾m: acts on polytrack, good to firm and good to soft going: has worn cheekpieces. *T. T. Clement*

ROYAL AXMINSTER 12 b.g. Alzao (USA) 117 – Number One Spot 71 (Reference **48** Point 139) [2007 52, a60: p16g p12g p10g³ p12g p12g Oct 31] useful-looking gelding: poor performer nowadays: stays 1½m: acts on all-weather, firm and good to soft going: tried blinkered/in cheekpieces. *Mrs P. N. Dutfield*

ROYAL BECKY (IRE) 3 gr.f. Beckett (IRE) 116 – Annahala (IRE) (Ridgewood Ben **59** 113) [2007 –: p6g⁴ p6g⁵ p6g⁴ 6.5d 6g 5m 5d* 5g 6g 5m p5.1g Oct 20] €1,500F, €3,500Y: second foal: half-sister to useful Irish 5f/6f winner Lady Orpen (by Orpen): dam ran twice in Ireland: modest handicapper: won at Navan (apprentices) in June: best at 5f/6f: acts on polytrack and good to soft ground: tried in cheekpieces. *Patrick Morris, Ireland*

Jockey Club Cup, Newmarket—the French-trained Royal And Regal gains his first pattern-race success; he is followed by Balkan Knight, Veenwouden and Distinction

ROYAL CHALLENGE 6 b.g. Royal Applause 124 – Anotheranniversary 95 **86**
(Emarati (USA) 74) [2007 92: 5m 5g 6g 5m 6m 5g⁶ 5g⁶ 5.1m 6m 5m p6m⁴ p6g⁵ p6g³
p6g⁶ p6g² p6d* p6g⁵ p6d Dec 28] well-made gelding: fairly useful handicapper: left
M. Tompkins after thirteenth start: won at Wolverhampton in December: effective at 5f to
easy 7f: acts on polytrack, firm and good to soft going, possibly not on soft/heavy: tried
blinkered. *I. W. McInnes*

ROYAL CHOIR 3 ch.f. King's Best (USA) 132 – Harmonic Sound (IRE) (Grand **–**
Lodge (USA) 125) [2007 76: p8g⁶ 6f 7d Oct 23] maiden: little form in 2007. *C. E. Brittain*

ROYAL CITADEL (IRE) 4 b.f. City On A Hill (USA) 114 – Royal Baldini (USA) **60 §**
(Green Dancer (USA) 132) [2007 75d: 8.3m 10.1m⁵ 10.5m 9.1g² 9.1g⁴ 8m⁶ 9.1s³ 9.9m
10.1m 9.2s⁶ Sep 24] rather leggy, close-coupled filly: modest maiden handicapper: stays
1¼m: acts on soft and good to firm going: usually wore headgear at 3 yrs: unreliable.
Mrs L. B. Normile

ROYAL COMPOSER (IRE) 4 b.g. Mozart (IRE) 131 – Susun Kelapa (USA) 94 (St **67**
Jovite (USA) 135) [2007 72: 7m 6g² 6f 5m* 5g² 5g³ Oct 30] lengthy, good-topped
gelding: has a quick action: fair performer: won maiden at Beverley in August: placed in
handicaps both starts after: stays 8.5f, effective at 5f: acts on firm going: tried visored (on
edge): blinkered last 3 starts: signs of temperament. *T. D. Easterby*

ROYAL CONFIDENCE 2 b.f. (Feb 22) Royal Applause 124 – Never A Doubt 107 **99**
(Night Shift (USA)) [2007 5d² 5.1g⁵ 6g² 5g* 6.5m* 7m⁴ 7d³ Oct 20] rangy, good sort:
second foal: dam, 2-y-o 5f (including Prix Robert Papin) winner, out of half-sister to
smart 5f/6f winner Acclamation (by Royal Applause): useful form: won maiden at
Sandown in August and nursery at Doncaster (beat Crystany by head) in September:
ongoing progress, length fourth to Raymi Coya in Oh So Sharp Stakes (left with plenty to
do) and length third to Kitty Matcham in Rockfel Stakes, both at Newmarket: will prove
best up to 7f: acts on good to firm and good to soft going. *B. W. Hills*

ROYAL DAGGER (IRE) 3 gr.g. Daggers Drawn (USA) 114 – September Tide (IRE) **48**
58 (Thatching 131) [2007 f5g³ p5f⁴ p5g f5g 5.1g⁶ 5g⁶ p5.1g Jul 2] poor maiden: raced
only at 5f on polytrack and good going on turf. *Rae Guest*

ROYAL DEGREE 2 b.c. (Mar 9) Royal Applause 124 – First Degree 50 (Sabrehill **79 p**
(USA) 120) [2007 5m² Aug 4] 40,000F, 60,000Y: strong colt: third foal: closely related
to fairly useful 7f and 1¼m winner Keel (by Carrowkeel) and half-brother to 3-y-o Zelos:
dam, maiden, half-sister to smart performers up to 1m Auditorium and Mister Cosmi
(both by Royal Applause): 9/4, promising neck second to Nawaaff (pair clear) in maiden
at Thirsk: will probably stay 6f/7f: joined E. Charpy in UAE: sure to improve. *B. Smart*

ROYAL DIGNITARY (USA) 7 br.g. Saint Ballado (CAN) – Star Actress (USA) **102**
(Star de Naskra (USA)) [2007 95: f8g⁵ p7g² 7.1g⁶ 7.1m³ 7s 8m* 7.1g³ 8s 8g 8g⁴ 8s
Sep 22] useful-looking gelding: useful handicapper: won at Ripon in June: good fourth to
The Illies at York in August: best at 7f/1m: acts on dirt/polytrack and firm going, unsuited
by softer than good: tried blinkered/visored: often forces pace. *D. Nicholls*

ROYAL EMBRACE 4 b.g. Bertolini (USA) 125 – Tight Spin (High Top 131) [2007 **65**
61: p8.6g³ p8g p8g* p8.6g³ p8g² p7.1g Dec 14] strong, compact gelding: fair handicapper: won at Kempton in October: good efforts when placed next 2 starts: stays 9.5f:
raced only on all-weather since 2005: visored nowadays: held up. *D. Shaw*

ROYAL ENCORE 3 b.f. Royal Applause 124 – Footlight Fantasy (USA) 68 (Nureyev **59 p**
(USA) 131) [2007 6m⁴ Sep 8] 40,000Y: quite attractive filly: half-sister to several win-
ners, including 7f/1m winner Unscrupulous (by Machiavellian) and 1998 2-y-o 6f winner
Dominant Dancer (by Primo Dominie), both useful: dam, 7f winner, out of top-class miler
Milligram: slowly away but getting hang of things throughout (not knocked about)
when fourth in maiden at Thirsk: will be suited by 7f: should be capable of better.
J. R. Fanshawe

ROYAL ENGINEER 4 b.g. Royal Applause 124 – Iris May 87 (Brief Truce (USA) **71**
126) [2007 p6g p7g 6g⁶ Jun 20] sturdy gelding: fair handicapper, lightly raced: missed
2006: should prove best at 5f/6f: acts on firm going. *M. Johnston*

ROYAL ENVOY (IRE) 4 b.g. Royal Applause 124 – Seven Notes (Zafonic (USA) **69**
130) [2007 82: p7.1g p7.1g p6g⁴ p6g³ 6g p5.1g p7.1g³ p7.1g p8g p6g p7g² p8g² p7g*
p8.6g⁶ Dec 4] strong, lengthy gelding: fair performer nowadays: won minor event at
Kempton in October: will prove best at short of 1m: acts on polytrack, firm and good to
soft going: often slowly away: inconsistent. *D. Shaw*

ROYAL FANTASY (IRE) 4 b. or br.f. King's Best (USA) 132 – Dreams 88 (Rainbow **83**
Quest (USA) 134) [2007 75: 8m* 8m 8m⁵ 10m⁶ 10m² p10m³ p9.5g⁵ Nov 8] leggy filly:
fairly useful handicapper, lightly raced: won at Yarmouth in April: best efforts when plac-

ed, fast-finishing third at Lingfield in November: stays 1¼m: acts on polytrack and good to firm ground (unraced on going softer than good): patiently ridden. *J. R. Fanshawe*

ROYAL FLYNN 5 b.g. Royal Applause 124 – Shamriyna (IRE) (Darshaan 133) [2007 **85** 70: 10g³ 10.1m* 10.1m 10m⁵ 10.5s* 10.1v³ 9.9v* 10.5v* 10.1d 10d⁵ Aug 1] rather leggy, close-coupled gelding: fairly useful handicapper: improved in 2007, winning at Newcastle in May, Haydock in June, and Beverley and Haydock (best effort, beat Great View by 2½ lengths) in July: stays 1½m: has form on good to firm ground, possibly ideally suited by much more testing conditions (acts on heavy): tried in cheekpieces: usually patiently ridden: sold 28,000 gns in October. *M. Dods*

ROYAL GAME 5 b.g. Vettori (IRE) 119 – Ground Game 95 (Gildoran 123) [2007 12m **–** Aug 30] maiden: unraced on Flat in 2006, well held only outing at 5 yrs. *M. Todhunter*

ROYAL GUEST 3 b.g. Royal Applause 124 – Bajan Blue 59 (Lycius (USA) 124) **64 §** [2007 55: p7f⁴ p8g 8.5g p7.1g⁵ p8g 7g 7.6g 8m³ 6.1d² 5.1f 7m 7f p5g 7g 5.7d² 5s⁴ 5.3d 5v⁵ p8g² p7g Dec 30] quite attractive gelding: modest maiden handicapper: left M. Channon prior to penultimate start: stays easy 1m: acts on polytrack, soft and good to firm ground: tried visored: often slowly away: temperamental. *J. R. Jenkins*

ROYAL INDULGENCE 7 b.g. Royal Applause 124 – Silent Indulgence (USA) **69** (Woodman (USA) 126) [2007 63: 9g⁶ 10g⁴ 9.1g⁶ 10.3d 9m⁶ 10d⁵ 10.2f* 10g* 10.2m 10m 10m⁵ 10m⁴ Sep 27] sturdy gelding: fair handicapper: won at Chepstow and Lingfield (apprentices) within 4 days in August: stays 10.3f: acts on polytrack and firm going: tried in cheekpieces/blinkers: often starts slowly. *W. M. Brisbourne*

ROYAL INTRUDER 2 b.c. (Feb 13) Royal Applause 124 – Surprise Visitor (IRE) (Be **86** My Guest (USA) 126) [2007 6m 5d* 5m⁴ Aug 31] 62,000Y: sturdy colt: sixth foal: brother to 2003 2-y-o 7f winner Tashkil and half-brother to several winners, including French 4.5f (at 2 yrs)/5f winner Ziria (by Danehill Dancer), both useful: dam, French maiden, half-sister to dam of very smart miler Swallow Flight: fairly useful form: won maiden at Sandown in July: improved again when close fourth in nursery there: should prove best at 5f/6f. *R. Hannon*

ROYALIST (IRE) 2 b.c. (Feb 22) King's Best (USA) 132 – Nebraas (Green Desert **85 p** (USA) 127) [2007 6g⁵ Jul 31] €425,000Y: good-bodied colt: first foal: dam unraced half-sister to high-class sprinter Malhub: 4/1, shaped well when fifth to Shallal in maiden at Goodwood which worked out well, looking threat before running green: certain to improve and win races. *M. A. Jarvis*

ROYAL JASRA 3 b.c. Royal Applause 124 – Lake Pleasant (IRE) 90 (Elegant Air **87 p** 119) [2007 10.1m² 10.5g* Sep 12] 57,000F, 62,000Y: strong colt: half-brother to several winners, including useful 7f (at 2 yrs) to 1½m winner Serpentine (by Grand Lodge) and 5-y-o Inchloch: dam, 2-y-o 6f winner, half-sister to useful sprinter Power Lake: fairly useful form: confirmed debut promise when winning maiden at Haydock (by 1¼ lengths from Pearl, asserting over 1f out) in September: stays 10.5f: useful prospect. *E. A. L. Dunlop*

ROYAL JET 5 b.g. Royal Applause 124 – Red Bouquet (Reference Point 139) [2007 **102** 96: p12g* p12g³ p11g Apr 7] leggy gelding: useful handicapper: better than ever in 2007, winning at Lingfield (beat Eva Soneva So Fast 2½ lengths) in February: met trouble both starts after: will stay 1¾m: acts on polytrack, firm and good to soft going: tried visored. *M. R. Channon*

ROYAL MANOR 2 b.f. (Feb 2) King's Best (USA) 132 – She's Classy (USA) **–** (Boundary (USA) 117) [2007 7m Sep 11] 30,000Y, 50,000 2-y-o: compact filly: third foal: half-sister to winner in US by Saint Ballado: dam, useful 2-y-o winner in US (placed in Grade 1s at 7f/8.5f), out of half-sister to Coronation Cup winner Be My Native: 25/1, needed experience in maiden at Leicester won by Ibn Khaldun. *N. J. Vaughan*

ROYAL MASTER 5 b.g. Royal Applause 124 – High Sevens 90 (Master Willie 129) **56** [2007 64: 9.9g 9.9m⁶ Aug 25] strong gelding: modest maiden handicapper: stays 1¼m: acts on polytrack and firm ground: tried visored/in cheekpieces. *P. C. Haslam*

ROYAL MELBOURNE (IRE) 7 ch.g. Among Men (USA) 124 – Calachuchi 74 **65** (Martinmas 128) [2007 65, a46: p12.2g* p12.2g p12.2g⁶ 13.8g⁵ p13.9g³ Nov 5] lengthy, workmanlike gelding: fair handicapper: won at Wolverhampton (by 8 lengths) in September: stays 1¾m: acts on polytrack and soft ground: often races freely: none too straightforward. *A. D. Brown*

ROYAL MUSKETEER (IRE) 2 b.g. (Jan 15) Chevalier (IRE) 115 – Cayman **–** Expresso (IRE) 79 (Fayruz 116) [2007 7d 8d 7g Oct 20] close-coupled gelding: well beaten in maidens: subsequently gelded. *T. D. Easterby*

Royal Hunt Cup (Handicap), Royal Ascot—Royal Oath is improved in blinkers and runs away with the prize; Flipando (fifth right), Vortex (second right) and Supaseus (far left) chase him home

ROYAL OATH (USA) 4 b.c. Kingmambo (USA) 125 – Sherkiya (IRE) (Goldneyev (USA) 114) [2007 100: 8m² 9m 8m* 8m² 7g 8.9f⁴ Sep 5] strong, good-bodied colt: has a quick action: smart performer: improved form once blinkered in 2007, winning 26-runner Royal Hunt Cup at Royal Ascot in June by 4 lengths from Flipando: good 1¼ lengths second to Cesare in Summer Mile on same course next time, but below best in similar company final 2 starts: likely to stay 1¼m: acts on polytrack and good to firm going: often tongue tied at 3 yrs: patiently ridden. *J. H. M. Gosden* **117**

ROYAL ORISSA 5 b.g. Royal Applause 124 – Ling Lane (Slip Anchor 136) [2007 72d: p7.1g³ f5g³ p6g f6g⁶ 5.7m p7.1g* p7.1g p6g³ 6g 6v⁶ p7g p6g p8.6g p8g p7g p6g f7d⁴ Dec 15] leggy gelding: modest handicapper: won at Wolverhampton in June: below form after eighth outing: stays 7f: acts on all-weather, firm and soft ground: has worn tongue strap/blinkers/cheekpieces: has been slowly away. *D. Haydn Jones* **64 d**

ROYAL PARDON 5 b.m. Royal Applause 124 – Miss Mercy (IRE) 62 (Law Society (USA) 130) [2007 61: 7.1d³ 6s 7m 8.3d Jul 19] sturdy mare: modest maiden handicapper: stays 9f: acts on good to firm and good to soft going: wears headgear nowadays. *M. Dods* **55**

ROYAL POWER (IRE) 4 b.c. Xaar 132 – Magic Touch (Fairy King (USA)) [2007 108: 7.5g 8g 7.5g³ 8.1g 7g 7.1m 7d 7d Oct 19] tall colt: good sort: useful performer: creditable efforts in 2007 when third to National Captain in handicap at Nad Al Sheba on third start and when down the field in listed races fifth/sixth starts: stays 1m: acts on polytrack, good to firm and good to soft going: none too consistent: sold 45,000 gns later in October. *M. R. Channon* **103**

ROYAL PREMIER (IRE) 4 b.g. King's Theatre (IRE) 128 – Mystic Shadow (IRE) 80 (Mtoto 134) [2007 65: p13.9g⁶ 11.5m* 11g* 11.6m 10m p12.2g⁵ 11.5g⁴ p12g p13.9g p13.9g p12g* Dec 19] quite good-topped gelding: fair handicapper: improved (by 7 lengths) in April, Goodwood in May and Kempton in December: stays 1½m: acts on polytrack, soft and good to firm going: tried in cheekpieces. *H. J. Collingridge* **74 a66**

ROYAL RAINBOW 3 ch.g. Rainbow Quest (USA) 134 – Royal Future (IRE) (Royal Academy (USA) 130) [2007 9.7s 10d Oct 10] tall gelding: well held in maidens, leaving T. Mills after debut. *P. W. Hiatt* **–**

ROYAL RATIONALE (IRE) 3 b.g. Desert Prince (IRE) 130 – Logic 94 (Slip Anchor 136) [2007 79: p8.6g² 9m* 9d² Jun 16] strong, good-bodied gelding: fairly useful performer: won maiden at Lingfield in May: better form when ¾-length second to One Hour in handicap at Sandown final start: likely to stay 1¼m: acts on polytrack, good to firm and good to soft going: sold 78,000 gns in July, joined D. Pipe. *W. J. Haggas* **84**

ROYAL ROCK 3 b.g. Sakhee (USA) 136 – Vanishing Point (USA) (Caller I D (USA)) [2007 8m p7.1g³ 7m* 7m² p6g* 6d* 6g⁶ Aug 18] strong, well-made gelding: third foal: half-brother to 4-y-o Gold Express: dam US 6f (including at 2 yrs)/6.5f winner: useful form: easily won maiden at Lingfield in May, and handicaps at Kempton in June and Windsor (further progress when beating Crystal Gazer by 3½ lengths, again travelling strongly and quickening impressively) in July: respectable sixth to King's Apostle at Newmarket final start: will prove best at 6f/7f: acts on polytrack, good to firm and good to soft ground. *C. F. Wall* **105**

ROYAL SAILOR (IRE) 5 b.g. Bahhare (USA) 122 – Old Tradition (IRE) 76 (Royal Academy (USA) 130) [2007 –, a53: p16g⁵ f11g⁴ p12.2g 17.2m 10m 10m 8.1d⁵ 12.6d⁵ 8s 10f 12.3m 13g 12g p13.9g⁵ p12g p13.9g Dec 3] tall gelding: poor maiden handicapper on turf, modest on all-weather: stays easy 2m: acts on all-weather, firm and good to soft ground: sometimes wears blinkers/cheekpieces. *J. Ryan* **40 a57**

ROYAL SECRETS (IRE) 3 b.f. Highest Honor (FR) 124 – Marble Maiden 117 (Lead On Time (USA) 123) [2007 10.9d⁵ 8g² 8g* 8.3m Jul 16] €180,000Y: rangy, attractive filly: seventh foal: half-sister to useful French 6f (at 2 yrs) and 1m winner Vernoy (by Forty Niner): dam French/US 9f/1¼m winner: fair form, lightly raced: confirmed promise of first 2 starts when winning maiden at Goodwood in June by 1¼ lengths from Castara Bay: shaped as if amiss in handicap at Windsor only subsequent start: should stay 1¼m: unraced on extremes of ground. *E. A. L. Dunlop*

ROYAL SENGA 4 b.f. Agnes World (USA) 123 – Katyushka (IRE) 73 (Soviet Star (USA) 128) [2007 67: p7g 6m 6m Sep 3] fair maiden at 3 yrs, no form in 2007. *C. A. Horgan* —

ROYAL SHAKESPEARE (FR) 8 b.g. King's Theatre (IRE) 128 – Persian Walk (FR) (Persian Bold 123) [2007 p12g Oct 10] little impact both starts on Flat in Britain: tried visored: useful hurdler/chaser. *S. Gollings* —

ROYAL SOVEREIGN (IRE) 2 b.g. (Apr 20) Invincible Spirit (IRE) 121 – Ombry Girl (IRE) (Distinctly North (USA) 115) [2007 5g⁶ 5g⁶ 5m 6g Sep 3] modest maiden: will probably stay 7f/1m. *J. Howard Johnson* 55

ROYAL STORM (IRE) 8 b.h. Royal Applause 124 – Wakayi 87 (Persian Bold 123) [2007 107: 06m 7g 6d p6g⁵ 7g 7g 7d 6g 7m Sep 4] tall, lengthy horse: useful performer at best, very much on downgrade: effective at 6f/7f: acts on polytrack, firm and soft going: usually races up with pace/makes running: sold 4,000 gns, joined B. R. Millman, *Mrs A. J. Perrett* 90 d / a73

ROYAL STRAIGHT 2 ch.g. (Feb 19) Halling (USA) 133 – High Straits 74 (Bering 136) [2007 8d 8g⁵ Oct 24] 37,000F: rangy gelding: first foal: dam, 1m and (in France) 1¼m winner, out of sister to dam of Poule d'Essai des Pouliches winner Matiara: fair form in maidens at Newbury and Bath (fifth to Colony): will stay at least 1¼m. *A. M. Balding* 69

ROYAL TARTAN (USA) 2 b.f. (Mar 28) Lemon Drop Kid (USA) 131 – Castellina (USA) (Danzig Connection (USA)) [2007 7.1g Sep 19] workmanlike filly: half-sister to useful 8.3f (at 2 yrs) to 1¼m winner Blaise Hollow (by Woodman), useful 2002 2-y-o 1m winner Blaise Castle and fairly useful 1¼m winner Castle River (both by Irish River): dam, US 8.5f winner, half-sister to US Grade 1 1¼m winner Chelsey Flower: 66/1 and very green in minor event at Sandown. *G. L. Moore* —

ROYAL TAVIRA GIRL (IRE) 4 b.f. Orpen (USA) 116 – Just Like Annie (IRE) 65 (Mujadil (USA) 119) [2007 62: 8g⁵ 8f 8m 8.1m⁶ 7g 7d⁵ Oct 1] lengthy filly: modest maiden: stays 8.5f: acts on polytrack and firm ground, probably good to soft: tried blinkered: sometimes slowly away: held up. *M. G. Quinlan* 55

ROYAL TENDER (IRE) 3 gr.f. Woods of Windsor (USA) – Tender Guest (IRE) (Be My Guest (USA) 126) [2007 –: p8g⁵ p9.5g² 12.6m p12.2g p10g p12g p12g 12g p12g Aug 23] modest maiden at best: stays 1¼m: acts on polytrack: tried blinkered. *B. G. Powell* 62 d

ROYALTIES 5 b.m. Mujahid (USA) 125 – Rock Face 77 (Ballad Rock 122) [2007 –: p13.9g⁶ p10g p12g Nov 30] no sign of ability. *M. A. Allen* —

ROYLE DANCER 4 b.g. Makbul 104 – Foxtrot Pie 77 (Shernazar 131) [2007 67: p9.5g Jan 8] strong, close-coupled gelding: modest maiden: said to have bled sole outing in 2007: stays 1m: acts on polytrack, firm and good to soft going. *R. Hollinshead* —

ROYMAR 3 b.f. Muthahb (IRE) – Tapper (IRE) (Elbio 125) [2007 8m 10d 10.9g⁵ 11.9m⁴ 11.7f Aug 24] leggy filly: second foal: dam unraced: little form. *M. Appleby* —

RSMIYA 2 b.f. (Feb 5) Diktat 126 – Scenic Venture (IRE) (Desert King (IRE) 129) [2007 p8.6g 7g⁵ Oct 25] 4,000Y: second foal: dam unraced half-sister to smart Irish sprinter Lidanna: no show in maidens, not knocked about. *C. E. Brittain* —

RUBBER DUCK (IRE) 3 b.f. Daggers Drawn (USA) 114 – Dhuhook (USA) 96 (Dixieland Band (USA)) [2007 –: p6g p7.1g f5g⁶ Feb 11] little form. *Peter Grayson* —

RUBENSTAR (IRE) 4 b.g. Soviet Star (USA) 128 – Ansariya (USA) 83 (Shahrastani (USA) 135) [2007 85: 8m 7g⁵ 7m³ 7.9d 8m p8g⁶ 7m⁶ 8.3g² p8m⁶ p8g Oct 24] strong gelding: fairly useful handicapper: stays 1m: acts on polytrack, soft and good to firm going: has raced freely: usually held up: sold 12,000 gns later in October. *M. H. Tompkins* 83

RUBILINI 3 ch.f. Bertolini (USA) 125 – Aunt Ruby (USA) 67 (Rubiano (USA)) [2007 58: p7f p7g⁴ p8g 6d 8.1s⁴ 7.6g⁴ 8m⁶ 7.6s² 8d p7g 10d⁴ 8d³ p7m Nov 1] leggy, lengthy filly: modest maiden: will prove best at 7f/1m: acts on polytrack, soft and good to firm going: races freely. *M. R. Channon* 59

RUBIROSA (IRE) 2 b.c. (Mar 19) Acclamation 118 – Bendis (GER) (Danehill (USA) **91**
126) [2007 6g* 6d³ 6g⁵ 6m² 6g 6d² 6d Oct 12] 33,000F, 19,500Y: useful-looking colt:
second foal: dam, German 7f winner, half-sister to useful German performer up to 11f
Basilea Gold: fairly useful performer: won maiden at Ripon in May: second in nurseries
at Newmarket and Ayr (beaten neck by Cape Vale after troubled passage): likely to prove
best at 5f/6f: acts on good to firm and good to soft going. *M. Dods*

RUB OF THE RELIC (IRE) 2 b.c. (Apr 1) Chevalier (IRE) 115 – Bayletta (IRE) 41 **70**
(Woodborough (USA) 112) [2007 5.1g f5g² f6g³ 6s² 7.1s³ 6g² 6.1v² 6s⁴ 8s p6g³ p6g³ 7g³ **a78**
Oct 25] lengthy colt: fair maiden: placed 9 of 12 starts, in blinkers final one: should stay
1m. *P. A. Blockley*

RUBY BROWN 5 b.m. Polar Falcon (USA) 126 – Raspberry Sauce 65 (Niniski (USA) **67**
125) [2007 p10g Jan 27] fair maiden: little impact sole outing in 2007: sold £1,000 in
June. *C. A. Cyzer*

RUBY DELTA 2 b.g. (Feb 27) Delta Dancer – Picolette 56 (Piccolo 121) [2007 6g 5m⁴ **68**
7g² p6g⁴ 7s² 7f⁴ 7s⁶ 7m Sep 11] tall, short-backed gelding: fair maiden: in frame second
to sixth (nursery) starts: gelded after final one: stays 7f: acts on polytrack, firm and soft
going. *P. D. Cundell*

RUBY LEGEND 9 b.g. Perpendicular 119 – Singing High 87 (Julio Mariner 127) **60**
[2007 67: 10m 10f 10.1m 10.1m³ 10g³ 10d 10v² 10.1g* 10m 10.1d Oct 16] leggy gelding:
modest performer nowadays: won seller at Newcastle in August: stays 10.5f: acts on any
turf ground: usually wears blinkers/cheekpieces: unseated rider leaving stall final outing.
K. G. Reveley

RUBY LIGHT 2 b.f. (Feb 1) Fantastic Light (USA) 134 – Rumpipumpy 80 (Shirley **59**
Heights 130) [2007 7m⁶ p8.6g Sep 3] 125,000Y: fourth foal: half-sister to fairly useful 6f/
7f winner Banjo Patterson (by Green Desert) and 2002 2-y-o 7f winner Persian Jasmine
(by Dynaformer): dam, US Grade 2 9f winner, half-sister to Irish 1000 Guineas winner
Classic Park, herself dam of very smart 1½m performer Walk In The Park: modest form
in maidens at Newmarket (sixth to Sense of Joy) and Wolverhampton: should be suited
by 1m+: sent to Germany. *Sir Michael Stoute*

RUBY'S DREAM 5 b.m. Tipsy Creek (USA) 115 – Sure Flyer (IRE) (Sure Blade **55**
(USA) 130) [2007 62, a53: p5.1g⁴ 5g p5.1g p5.1g³ 5.1g 5.7d⁶ 5s p5.1g³ 5m² 5g p5.1g
Aug 30] workmanlike mare: modest performer: stays 6f: acts on polytrack and any turf
going: wears blinkers/cheekpieces: races prominently. *J. M. Bradley*

RUBY'S RAINBOW (IRE) 2 b.f. (Feb 22) Fayruz 116 – Sweet Finesse (IRE) 53 **–**
(Revoque (IRE) 122) [2007 5m 6m p5.1g Oct 6] €4,200Y, resold €4,800Y: first foal:
dam, maiden, half-sister to useful 2-y-o 6f/7f winner Smittenby: no form. *J. Balding*

RUBY'S SMILE 2 b.f. (Mar 12) Bold Edge 123 – Funny Wave 65 (Lugana Beach 116) **–**
[2007 5g 5m 5.1m Aug 9] fifth foal: half-sister to fairly useful 5f (at 2 yrs)/6f winner
Nivernais (by Forzando) and 2005 2-y-o 5f winner Nivelle (by Imperial Ballet): dam ran
once: of no account. *R. Brotherton*

RUBY SUNRISE (IRE) 5 ch.m. Polish Precedent (USA) 131 – Kinlochewe 102 (Old **48**
Vic 136) [2007 50: f11g³ f11g Jan 11] leggy mare: poor mover: poor maiden: stayed 11f:
acted on all-weather: tried blinkered: had been slowly away: reportedly finished lame
final start: in foal to Storming Home. *B. P. J. Baugh*

RUBYTWOSOX (IRE) 2 b.f. (Feb 6) Redback 116 – Policy (Nashwan (USA) 135) **60**
[2007 p5g 5s⁵ 6f⁴ p7g 7m p7g⁶ 8.3d p7.1g⁶ Oct 15] €9,000F: good-bodied filly: second
foal: dam unraced half-sister to useful 2-y-o 7f winner Queen of Poland: modest maiden:
may prove best at 5f/6f: acts on polytrack, firm and soft going. *W. R. Muir*

RUDI'S PET (IRE) 13 ch.g. Don't Forget Me 127 – Pink Fondant (Northfields (USA)) **44**
[2007 79: 5m 5g⁶ 5m⁶ 5m Aug 7] strong gelding: one-time smart winner: just poor form
in 2007: best at 5f: acts on firm and soft going: effective blinkered/visored or not: usually
races prominently. *D. Nicholls*

RUDRY DRAGON (IRE) 3 b.c. Princely Heir (IRE) 111 – Jazz Up (Cadeaux Gene- **86**
reux 131) [2007 75: 8.3m* 8m 7m⁶ 8.1m⁴ 9.7g³ 8.1g⁴ 10.5m⁶ 9.8m⁵ p8m⁶ 10d² 9.1v²
9.1v³ Nov 3] leggy colt: has a quick action: fairly useful handicapper: won at Windsor in
April, despite looking wayward in front: stays 1¼m: acts on heavy and good to firm
ground: sometimes races freely. *P. A. Blockley*

RUDRY WORLD (IRE) 4 ch.g. Spinning World (USA) 130 – Fancy Boots (IRE) 62 **79**
(Salt Dome (USA)) [2007 51: p10g³ f6g⁴ 7g³ p12.2g* f12g⁵ p12.2g² 12.1v² p12g* 12.1s
13m⁴ 14m³ 12.1d* 12.1g* 11.9s² 12d⁴ p12.2g⁴ Oct 26] workmanlike gelding: fair performer: won apprentice seller at Wolverhampton in April and, having been claimed

from P. Blockley £5,000 after sixth start, handicaps at Lingfield in July and Hamilton (2) in August: stays easy 1¾m: acts on all-weather, heavy and good to firm going. *M. Mullineaux*

RUE SOLEIL 3 ch.f. Zaha (CAN) 106 – Maria Cappuccini 70 (Siberian Express (USA) 125) [2007 63: 6m 5m² 6m 5g³ 6m 5d³ 6d⁴ 5d* 6d⁶ 5m⁵ 5v² 5g Oct 30] tall filly: modest performer: won maiden at Hamilton in July: best at 5f/6f: acts on heavy and good to firm ground: none too consistent. *J. R. Weymes*   **63**

RUFF DIAMOND (USA) 2 b. or br.c. (Mar 11) Stormin Fever (USA) 116 – Whalah (USA) 76 (Dixieland Band (USA)) [2007 5s⁴ 6g* 6m 7m⁴ Jul 14] $70,000Y: big, close-coupled, good-topped colt: third foal: half-brother to winner in US by Grand Slam: dam, 1¼m winner, out of US Grade 1 9f winner Firm Stance: fairly useful performer: won maiden at Folkestone (Nijoom Dubai third) in June: firmer ground, below form in Coventry Stakes at Royal Ascot (lost action) and minor event at same course (stamina stretched): possibly best at 5f/6f. *J. R. Best*   **89**

RUFFIE (IRE) 4 b.f. Medicean 128 – Darling Lover (USA) 56 (Dare And Go (USA) 125) [2007 –, a72: p9.5g⁴ p8g⁶ f8g* p9.5g f8g³ f11g⁵ 8d 7s⁴ 7d p7.1g³ f7d² f8d⁴ Dec 20] fair performer on all-weather, modest on turf: won handicap at Southwell in March: stays 9.5f: acts on all-weather and good to firm going: tried visored. *Miss Gay Kelleway*   **57 a72**

RUGGTAH 6 gr.m. Daylami (IRE) 138 – Raneen Alwatar 80 (Sadler's Wells (USA) 132) [2007 16m Jul 18] quite good-topped filly: fair at best on Flat: fit from chasing (no form for various trainers), no show sole run in 2007. *M. G. Rimell*   **–**

RULE FOR EVER 5 br.g. Diktat 126 – Tous Les Jours (USA) 70 (Dayjur (USA) 137) [2007 71§: p16g p16.5g* p16g⁴ f16g* 18g⁵ 21.6m⁴ 15.8m² 16.2m⁶ 16g⁴ Jun 22] big, lengthy gelding: fair handicapper: won at Wolverhampton (wandered) and Southwell (by 13 lengths, left M. Johnston after) in March: stays 2¼m: acts on all-weather, soft and good to firm going: tried blinkered/visored/tongue tied: moody, and one to treat with caution. *I. W. McInnes*   **73 §**

RULE OF LIFE 3 br.c. Dansili 127 – Prophecy (IRE) 109 (Warning 136) [2007 80: p7.1g* 7m 8m² 8s³ 8.1g 9d* 9g³ Aug 26] strong, sturdy colt: has a round action: fairly useful performer: won maiden at Wolverhampton in April and handicap at Sandown in August, making all when beating Uig by 2½ lengths in latter: will stay 1¼m: acts on poly-track, soft and good to firm ground: tried blinkered: joined D. Watson in UAE. *B. W. Hills*   **94**

RUMAN (IRE) 5 b.g. Fayruz 116 – Starway To Heaven (ITY) (Nordance (USA)) [2007 67: 6.1g 6m³ p6g* p6g³ p6g* Nov 19] lengthy gelding: fair handicapper: won at Kempton in October and November: should stay 7f: acts on all-weather and good to soft ground. *M. J. Attwater*   **73**

RUMBLED 3 b.f. Halling (USA) 133 – Tatanka (IRE) (Lear Fan (USA) 130) [2007 62: p7g³ 7s 7m 7g 11.7m⁴ 12s⁵ Aug 22] lengthy filly: fair maiden handicapper: seems to stay 11.6f: acts on polytrack and good to firm ground: visored/in cheekpieces last 3 starts. *J. A. Geake*   **70 d**

RUM JUNGLE 3 b.g. Robellino (USA) 127 – Anna Karietta 82 (Precocious 126) [2007 8.3d⁴ Oct 15] big, strong gelding: half-brother to several winners, including 2004 2-y-o 5f winner Moscow Music (by Piccolo) and German 6f/7f performer Just Heaven's Gate (by Slip Anchor), both useful: dam 6f/7f winner: 12/1 and green, 6 lengths fourth of 13 to Shadowy Figure in maiden at Windsor: should do better. *H. Candy*   **68 p**

RUMPUS (GER) 3 ch.g. Medaaly 114 – Roseola (GER) (Acatenango (GER) 127) [2007 11g* 14.1g 12m Jun 2] heavy-topped gelding: fair form when winning maiden at Southwell in April: below that level in handicaps after: stays 11f. *T. P. Tate*   **68**

RUN FOR EDE'S 3 b.f. Peintre Celebre (USA) 137 – Raincloud (Rainbow Quest (USA) 134) [2007 66p: 8g³ 9g 9.7g⁶ p8g⁵ 7g⁶ p8g² p11g p8g² p8.6d Dec 10] leggy, close-coupled filly: fair maiden: may prove best up to 1¼m: raced only on polytrack and good/good to soft ground on turf: in cheekpieces last 5 starts: races freely: carries head high: ungenuine. *P. M. Phelan*   **74 §**

RUN FREE 3 b.g. Agnes World (USA) 123 – Ellie Ardensky 100 (Slip Anchor 136) [2007 77: 8g⁶ 8m² 8.1m 9.1d⁶ 8m 8s 12g p9.5g³ p8.6g⁴ p9.5d⁶ f7d³ Dec 18] good-bodied gelding: fair maiden: probably stays 9.5f: acts on all-weather, soft and good to firm going: usually races prominently. *N. Wilson*   **72**

RUN FROM NUN 2 b.f. (Apr 4) Oasis Dream 129 – Nunatak (USA) (Bering 136) [2007 p7.1g p6g p7.1g⁶ p7.1g⁵ Nov 8] 28,000Y: half-sister to several winners, including 7f (in France at 2 yrs) to 8.5f (US Grade 3 event) winner Nunatall (by Night Shift): dam French 9f winner: poor maiden: probably stays 7f: raced only on polytrack: sold 6,000 gns. *J. A. Osborne*   **49**

RUNNING BUCK (USA) 2 b.c. (Feb 12) Running Stag (USA) 124 – Dinghy (USA) **50** (Fortunate Prospect (USA)) [2007 p6g 5d 6f 5.5m 5g⁶ Sep 19] sturdy colt: modest maiden, sporadic form: raced only at 5f/6f: tried in blinkers. *N. P. Littmoden*

RUNNING ON EMPTY 4 b.g. College Chapel 122 – Abstone Queen 66 (Presidium **–** 124) [2007 8m p12g Jun 21] of little account. *P. D. Evans*

RUNNING RINGS 3 br.f. Synefos (USA) 114 – Madame Gehenne (IRE) (Lord **–** Americo) [2007 p12g 12m 14m Aug 10] angular, close-coupled filly: second known foal: dam ran over hurdles in Ireland: well held in maidens. *P. W. D'Arcy*

RUNS RIOT (IRE) 3 b.g. Spinning World (USA) 130 – Chasing Rainbows (Rainbow **55** Quest (USA) 134) [2007 –: 8g 12d² 12.5m⁶ 13.8g Oct 20] close-coupled gelding: modest maiden: ran creditably at Catterick final start: stays 1¾m: acts on good to soft ground. *Andrew Oliver, Ireland*

RUNSWICK BAY 2 b.c. (Mar 12) Intikhab (USA) 135 – Upend 120 (Main Reef 126) **85** [2007 5d⁵ 5m³ 6d³ 6m³ 7d* 6g* 7m⁴ 7d Aug 25] big, useful-looking colt: half-brother to several winners, including smart 1m winner Musicanna (by Cape Cross) and useful 1m (at 2 yrs) to 1½m winner Al Azhar (by Alzao): dam, 1¼m/1½m (St Simon Stakes) winner, half-sister to dam of high-class stayer/Champion Hurdle winner Royal Gait: fairly useful performer: won maiden at Redcar in June and nursery at Pontefract in July: will stay 1m: acts on good to firm and good to soft going. *G. M. Moore*

RUSE 4 b.f. Diktat 126 – Reuval 102 (Sharpen Up 127) [2007 66: f11g⁴ p12g Oct 10] **58** modest maiden: stays easy 1½m: acts on polytrack (probably on fibresand), raced on good/good to firm ground on turf: tried in cheekpieces. *J. R. Fanshawe*

RUSSIAN CONSORT (IRE) 5 ch.g. Groom Dancer (USA) 128 – Ukraine Venture **–** 96 (Slip Anchor 136) [2007 88: 10m Apr 21] lengthy gelding: useful performer at 2 yrs, lightly raced since: well beaten sole Flat outing in 2007. *A. King*

RUSSIAN DREAM (IRE) 4 b.g. Xaar 132 – Summer Dreams (IRE) 79 (Sadler's **67** Wells (USA) 132) [2007 75: p12g f12g⁶ 10.2f⁴ Apr 11] fair maiden: stays 1¾m: acts on all-weather and firm ground: wore cheekpieces final start. *W. R. Swinburn*

RUSSIAN EPIC 3 b.g. Diktat 126 – Russian Rhapsody 100 (Cosmonaut) [2007 10m **83** 8g² 7s* 9d³ 10v⁴ 8.1g⁵ Aug 2] good-topped gelding: first foal: dam 7f/1m winner: fairly useful performer: won maiden at Leicester in May: gelded after final start: probably stays 1¼m: acts on heavy ground: usually races prominently. *M. A. Jarvis*

RUSSIAN GIFT (IRE) 3 b.f. Soviet Star (USA) 128 – Birthday Present (Cadeaux **75** Genereux 131) [2007 68: 5.1g² 6m 5.7g 5d⁴ 5m Aug 31] rangy filly: fair maiden handicapper: should prove best at 5f/6f: acts on good to firm ground: sold 1,000 gns in November. *C. G. Cox*

RUSSIAN INVADER (IRE) 3 ch.g. Acatenango (GER) 127 – Ukraine Venture 96 **84** (Slip Anchor 136) [2007 10.5m² p12g 10.5g³ 11.6g* Oct 8] 50,000Y: good-bodied gelding: fifth foal: half-brother to several winners, including 5-y-o Russian Consort, 6f (at 2 yrs)/7f winner Indian Steppes (by Indian Ridge) and 4-y-o Urban Tiger, latter 2 fairly useful: dam 1¼m winner: fairly useful form: best effort when winning handicap at Windsor in October by neck from Watchful: will stay 1½m: raced only on polytrack and good/good to firm ground: successful over hurdles in November. *A. King*

RUSSIAN MIST (IRE) 4 gr.g. Xaar 132 – Cape Mist (USA) (Lure (USA) 131) [2007 **51** 69: p8g p8g p8g Mar 7] tall gelding: fair maiden at 3 yrs, only modest in 2007: stays 9.5f: acts on polytrack: joined A. Martin in Ireland. *M. J. Wallace*

RUSSIAN REEL 2 b.c. (Apr 23) Reel Buddy (USA) 118 – Charlie Girl 70 (Puissance **90 §** 110) [2007 6d³ 6m* 5m 6.1s² 6.1m⁵ 6g 6g² 5d⁴ 6g p6s³ Dec 20] 45,000Y: strong, good-topped colt: fifth foal: half-brother to 3 winners, including 5-y-o Josh: dam, 2-y-o 5f winner, out of half-sister to high-class French 1¼m performer Creator: fairly useful performer: won maiden at Ripon in June: runner-up in nurseries at Chester and Haydock (to Craggy Cat): best at 6f: acts on soft and good to firm going: tends to hang right, markedly so when well below form on polytrack: one to treat with caution. *K. A. Ryan*

RUSSIAN ROCKET (IRE) 5 b.g. Indian Rocket 115 – Soviet Girl (IRE) (Soviet Star **76** (USA) 128) [2007 85: p5g⁴ p6g 5.1m⁵ p6g⁶ 5.2m p6g 6.1d p5.1g 6d⁵ p5.1g² p6g Dec 22] small, leggy gelding: fair handicapper: stays 6f: acts on all-weather, firm and soft going. *Mrs C. A. Dunnett*

RUSSIAN ROSIE (IRE) 3 b.f. Traditionally (USA) 117 – Pink Sovietstaia (FR) **105** (Soviet Star (USA) 128) [2007 90: 7m 8g⁴ 10m² 8.1g 9.9g³ 9.9g³ 10.1g p10f⁵ Nov 10] sparely-made filly: useful performer: good efforts when in frame in listed races at York,

Newbury (¾-length second to Darrfonah), Salisbury (third to Promising Lead) and Goodwood (handicap, best effort, 1½ lengths third to Samira Gold, despite hanging left): not discredited last 2 starts, including in valuable non-graded event at Woodbine final one: stays 1¼m: acts on good to firm and good to soft going (below form on soft): consistent. *J. G. Portman*

RUSSIAN SILK 3 b.f. Fasliyev (USA) 120 – Queen of Silk (IRE) 93 (Brief Truce (USA) 126) [2007 76: 5g 5m 6m 5m Aug 24] good-topped filly: fair performer at 2 yrs: well held in handicaps in 2007: tried blinkered. *Jedd O'Keeffe* —

RUSSIAN SYMPHONY (USA) 6 ch.g. Stravinsky (USA) 133 – Backwoods Teacher (USA) (Woodman (USA) 126) [2007 83: 6m 6g 7g⁴ 7g 7g p7g² p7m p6g⁵ p6m⁴ Dec 9] lengthy gelding: fairly useful handicapper nowadays: raced only at 6f/7f: acts on polytrack and firm going: tried in cheekpieces/blinkers: tends to race freely: inconsistent. *C. R. Egerton* **88**

RUSSKI (IRE) 3 b.c. Fasliyev (USA) 120 – Rose of Mooncoin (IRE) 99 (Brief Truce (USA) 126) [2007 88p: 7.1g 8.1g⁶ 8m p8g³ 8g p8g* 8.1g* 8m³ p8.6g* Oct 21] big, strong colt: useful performer: won claimer at Kempton (left Mrs A. Perrett) in September, and handicaps at Warwick and Wolverhampton in October: stays 8.6f: acts on polytrack and good to firm ground: blinkered nowadays: has looked difficult ride, and hung left penultimate start. *D. M. Simcock* **96**

RUSTENBERG 3 b.f. Dr Fong (USA) 128 – River City Moon (USA) (Riverman (USA) 131) [2007 8g Jun 1] sixth foal: half-sister to 1m (at 2 yrs) to 1½m winner McBain (by Lear Fan) and a winner in USA by Theatrical: dam, US 2-y-o 1m winner, out of half-sister to very smart sprinter Dowsing and US Grade 1 9.5f winner Fire The Groom (dam of Stravinsky): 33/1 and green, well held in maiden at Goodwood: sold 3,000 gns, sent to Greece. *E. F. Vaughan* —

RUST EN VREDE 8 b.g. Royal Applause 124 – Souveniers (Relko 136) [2007 –: f11g⁵ May 1] tall gelding: fair performer at best, lightly raced and little form on Flat since 2004: tried visored: modest hurdler. *J. J. Quinn* —

RUSTIC FLAME (IRE) 3 b.f. Danehill Dancer (IRE) 117 – Soviet Artic (FR) 84§ (Bering 136) [2007 7g⁶ 8m⁴ 7d* 7m Jul 11] tall filly: has scope: fourth foal: closely related to smart Irish 2-y-o 5f winner Russian Blue (by Danehill): dam, French 1¼m winner, out of half-sister to very smart middle-distance performer Antheus: fairly useful form: easily best effort when winning maiden at Salisbury in June: folded tamely on handicap debut final outing: stays 7f: acts on good to soft ground: races freely: sent to USA. *C. R. Egerton* **92**

RUSTIC GOLD 3 ch.g. Tobougg (IRE) 125 – Suave Shot (Suave Dancer (USA) 136) [2007 –: p10g⁴ 10m 8m 10g² 9.9d* 9.7s³ 12m⁵ 10m* 11s⁵ 11d Oct 11] rather leggy gelding: fair handicapper: won at Salisbury in June and Windsor in July: stays 1¼m: acts on polytrack, soft and good to firm ground: held up: sold 38,000 gns. *J. R. Best* **76**

RUSTLER 5 b.g. Green Desert (USA) 127 – Borgia 91 (Machiavellian (USA) 123) [2007 12m³ Jul 19] good-topped gelding: has a fluent, round action: fairly useful performer: unraced at 4 yrs: creditable third only Flat start in 2007: stays 1½m: acts on firm and good to soft ground: tried visored: looked none too keen sixth 3-y-o start. *N. J. Henderson* **83**

RUSTY ROOF 4 ch.f. Zaha (CAN) 106 – Parisian Lady (IRE) 91 (Paris House 123) [2007 p7g⁴ p7g⁶ p9.5g p13.9g Nov 12] first foal: dam 6f (at 2 yrs) and 1m winner: little form. *Rae Guest* —

RUTBA 2 b.f. (Mar 25) Act One 124 – Elhilmeya (IRE) 94 (Unfuwain (USA) 131) [2007 p10g p8g Nov 14] fifth foal: half-sister to 5-y-o Alfie Flits and 3-y-o Rhaam: dam 10.5f winner: well held in maidens on polytrack: will be suited by 1½m+: should do better. *M. P. Tregoning* **– p**

RUTHLES PHILLY 3 b.f. Primo Valentino (IRE) 116 – Compton Amber 78 (Puissance 110) [2007 58: 7m² 7m³ 8m 7m⁴ 6f 7.1s⁶ 5g p6g⁵ p7g Nov 14] leggy filly: modest maiden: left D. Barker after seventh outing: should stay 1m: acts on good to firm going: has carried head high. *G. L. Moore* **58**

RUWAIN 3 b.g. Lujain (USA) 119 – Ruwaya (USA) 80 (Red Ransom (USA)) [2007 8.2g p8m p8.6g⁵ p11g Dec 19] close-coupled gelding: modest maiden: stays 8.6f. *W. J. Musson* **53**

RYAN'S FUTURE (IRE) 7 b.h. Danetime (IRE) 121 – Era 70 (Dalsaan 125) [2007 95: 10d 12g p10g⁴ p10g⁴ Dec 30] leggy, useful-looking horse: useful handicapper at best: just fair on balance of form in 2007: stays 1¼m: acts on polytrack, heavy and good to firm going: often slowly away. *J. S. Moore* **70 +**

RYAN'S ROCK 2 b.g. (Apr 1) Lujain (USA) 119 – Diamond Jayne (IRE) (Royal Abjar – (USA) 121) [2007 7.1g p8g⁵ 7s p7m Dec 9] tall gelding: no form: gelded after final start. *T. D. McCarthy*

RYDAL MOUNT (IRE) 4 b.f. Cape Cross (IRE) 129 – Pooka 65 (Dominion 123) **82** [2007 80: p7g² 7s⁶ 6g² 6g⁶ p7g 7d* 7m Nov 10] smallish, sturdy, angular filly: has a quick action: fairly useful handicapper: won at Leicester (apprentices) in October: stays 7f: acts on polytrack, soft and good to firm ground: tried visored: races up with pace: inconsistent. *W. S. Kittow*

RYDAL (USA) 6 ch.g. Gilded Time (USA) – Tennis Partner (USA) (Northern Dancer) **78** [2007 ?: 6m² 5g² 5d⁴ 6d p6g² p6g p6g² Oct 29] good-topped gelding: fair performer nowadays: runner-up in 4 claimers in 2007: effective at stiff 5f to 8.5f: acts on all-weather, firm and good to soft going: tried in headgear/tongue tie: sold 12,000 gns and joined Miss J. Crowley. *J. A. Osborne*

RYE BEAU (IRE) 2 b.g. (Feb 21) Catcher In The Rye (IRE) 115 – Belle of Honour – (USA) (Honour And Glory (USA) 122) [2007 5.1m p5.1g 5d 6v Jul 21] close-coupled gelding: of no account. *Mrs A. Duffield*

RYEDALE OVATION (IRE) 4 b.g. Royal Applause 124 – Passe Passe (USA) 78 **72** (Lear Fan (USA) 130) [2007 062: 7m⁴ 7g⁵ 7.5m 5d 5s⁶ 5g p11g* Nov 7] big, useful-looking gelding: fair handicapper: left T. Easterby after sixth start: won at Kempton in November: stays easy 11f: acts on polytrack, good to firm and good to soft ground: tried blinkered/in cheekpieces. *M. Hill*

RYEDANE (IRE) 5 b.g. Danetime (IRE) 121 – Miss Valediction (IRE) (Petardia 113) **77** [2007 77: 5.1m 5g⁴ 5m⁵ p5.1g⁴ p6g³ 6d² 6m³ 5f³ 6m² 6g* p6g* p6g³ p6g Oct 19] tall, leggy gelding: fair handicapper: won at Catterick in August and Wolverhampton in September: effective at 5f/6f: acts on polytrack, firm and good to soft going: usually blinkered nowadays: often races prominently: reliable. *T. D. Easterby*

RYHOPE CHIEF (IRE) 4 b.g. Indian Danehill (IRE) 124 – Rachel Pringle (IRE) – (Doulab (USA) 115) [2007 –: p13.9g⁵ p16.5g Jan 28] little form: tried blinkered/tongue tied. *M. Sheppard*

RYTHM N RHYME (IRE) 8 ch.g. Danehill Dancer (IRE) 117 – Valley Heigh (IRE) – (Head For Heights 125) [2007 –: 11.8d 9.9g⁶ Aug 15] workmanlike gelding: little form: tried in cheekpieces. *John A. Harris*

S

SAAFEND GEEZER 2 ch.g. (Mar 24) Kyllachy 129 – Kindred Spirit (IRE) (Cadeaux **54 p** Genereux 131) [2007 7.1m 7d 6d Oct 19] 21,000Y: good-topped gelding: fourth foal: half-brother to Irish 11f winner Magic Princess (by Bahhare): dam unraced half-sister to useful miler Holly Blue: modest form in maidens, not knocked about: not sure to stay much beyond 7f: sort to progress in handicaps. *B. J. Meehan*

SAAMEQ (IRE) 6 b.g. Bahhare (USA) 122 – Tajawuz 82 (Kris 135) [2007 61: p13.9g **53** p12.2g⁵ p12.2g³ Sep 14] strong gelding: modest performer: stays 1½m: acts on polytrack and good to firm going: wore cheekpieces sixth/seventh 4-y-o starts. *D. W. Thompson*

SAARATT 3 ch.f. Mark of Esteem (IRE) 137 – Cambara 97 (Dancing Brave (USA) **70** 140) [2007 60p: 8m⁴ p9.5g⁶ 8.2g⁵ 8m³ p8g p10g³ p9.5g⁶ Oct 25] close-coupled, quite attractive filly: fair maiden: left M. Tregoning after second start: stays 1¼m: acts on polytrack and good to firm ground. *J. W. Hills*

SABAH 4 ch.f. Nashwan (USA) 135 – Massorah (FR) 108 (Habitat 134) [2007 91: 8.5d – Jun 1] big, strong, angular filly: fairly useful performer at 3 yrs: very stiff task, last of 10 behind Echelon in Princess Elizabeth Stakes at Epsom only start in 2007: best form around 1m: acts on firm ground. *A. M. Balding*

SABANA PERDIDA (IRE) 4 b.f. Cape Cross (IRE) 129 – Capriola (USA) (Mr Pros- **112** pector (USA)) [2007 106: 8.5m 7g* 7v 8m³ 7g* Sep 9] €38,000Y: workmanlike filly: closely related to fairly useful Italian 7f/1m winner Salumee (by Desert Prince) and half-sister to several winners abroad: dam unraced half-sister to very smart hurdler Absalom's Lady: smart performer: winner of 6 races in Italy (left R. Feligioni after fourth outing at 3 yrs): improved again in 2007, winning minor event at Longchamp in May and Qatar Airways Prix du Pin on same course (led near finish to beat King Jock 1½ lengths) in September: creditable 3¾ lengths third to Nannina in Windsor Forest Stakes at Royal Ascot fourth outing: effective at 7f/1m: acts on good to firm and good to soft ground, also successful on sand. *A. de Royer Dupre, France*

SABANCAYA 2 b.f. (Feb 23) Nayef (USA) 129 – Serra Negra 83 (Kris 135) [2007 7g Nov 3] neat filly: second foal: dam, 1m winner, half-sister to useful Irish 1¼m performer Royal Intrigue, out of sister to Sprint Cup winner Cherokee Rose: 10/1, mid-field in maiden at Newmarket: should stay at least 1m: will improve. *W. J. Haggas* — **58 p**

SABO PRINCE 5 ch.g. Atraf 116 – Moving Princess 71 (Prince Sabo 123) [2007 50: f6g f6g Apr 13] good-bodied gelding: modest performer at best: no form in 2007: tried blinkered, usually wears cheekpieces. *J. M. Bradley* — **–**

SABRE LIGHT 2 b.g. (Mar 29) Fantastic Light (USA) 134 – Good Grounds (USA) (Alleged (USA) 138) [2007 7.1g p7g 7m⁵ 8.3d 7g Oct 25] compact gelding: fifth foal: half-brother to 3 winners, including 6-y-o Ground Patrol: dam unraced: fair maiden: should be suited by 1¼m/1½m: gelded after final start. *G. L. Moore* — **66**

SABRE'S EDGE (IRE) 6 b.g. Sadler's Wells (USA) 132 – Brave Kris (IRE) 104 (Kris 135) [2007 p6g Jun 21] quite good-topped gelding: fairly useful form in 2-y-o maidens: very lightly raced and well held on Flat since. *R. J. Hodges* —

SACRE COEUR 3 b.f. Compton Place 125 – Take Heart 84 (Electric 126) [2007 90p: 6.1s 6s 6g 6m² 6m 6m² 6g Oct 25] useful-looking filly: fairly useful handicapper: good efforts when runner-up in 2007: likely to prove best at 5f/6f: acts on good to firm going: slowly away fifth outing: none too reliable: sold 16,000 gns. *J. L. Dunlop* — **84**

SACRED KINGDOM (AUS) 4 b.g. Encosta de Lago (AUS) – Courtroom Sweetie (AUS) (Zeditave (AUS)) [2007 5g* 5m* 6m* 6m⁴ 5m* 6m* 6g* Dec 9] vastly improved and developed into a top-class sprinter, winning 8 of his 9 starts at Sha Tin from December 2006, including handicaps in January, March and May, Group 3 Sha Tin Sprint Trophy (Handicap) in October, Group 2 Cathay Pacific International Sprint Trial (by 2¾ lengths from Absolute Champion, quickening clear impressively and breaking track record) in November and Cathay Pacific Hong Kong Sprint (beat Absolute Champion shade comfortably by 2¼ lengths, quickening from well off pace to lead ½f out) in December: effective at 5f/6f: raced only on good or good to firm ground: tongue tied. *P. F. Yiu, Hong Kong* — **131**

SACRILEGE 2 ch.g. (Feb 25) Sakhee (USA) 136 – Idolize 92 (Polish Precedent (USA) 131) [2007 p7g⁶ Dec 9] fourth foal: half-brother to useful 1m winner Golden Feather (by Dr Fong): dam, 1m (at 2 yrs) and 1¼m winner, sister to very smart performer up to 1½m Riyadian out of Irish Oaks winner Knight's Baroness: 22/1 and green, sixth to Parisian Gift in maiden at Lingfield: will be suited by 1m+: should improve. *D. R. C. Elsworth* — **68 p**

SADDEX 4 b.c. Sadler's Wells (USA) 132 – Remote Romance (USA) (Irish River (FR) 131) [2007 113: 12g* 12g* 12d* 12g⁶ 12f Nov 25] €115,000Y: second foal: dam, French 7f/1m winner, closely related to dam of top-class miler Spinning World, half-sister to very smart miler Chimes of Freedom and very smart French/US performer up to 1½m Denon: very smart performer: won 3 races in 2006, including listed events at Dortmund and Bremen, and in frame in Deutsches Derby at Hamburg and Grosser Preis von Baden at Baden-Baden: won first 3 starts in 2007, namely Gerling-Preis at Cologne (by head from Bussoni) in April, Grand Prix de Chantilly Mitsubishi Motors (best effort, by 1½ — **124**

Rheinland-Pokal der Sparkasse KolnBonn, Cologne—third win in a row for Saddex, who holds off First Stream (armlets), Bussoni (right), Laverock (second right) and Egerton (partially hidden)

lengths from Vison Celebre) in June and Rheinland-Pokal der Sparkasse KolnBonn at Cologne (by 1¼ lengths from First Stream, leading after halfway) in August: respectable sixth to Dylan Thomas in Prix de l'Arc de Triomphe at Longchamp, then below form in Japan Cup at Tokyo last 2 starts: stays 1½m: acts on soft ground: consistent. *P. Rau, Germany*

SADEEK 3 ch.c. Kyllachy 129 – Miss Mercy (IRE) 62 (Law Society (USA) 130) [2007 – 98: 7m 6d 6g Oct 26] strong, lengthy colt: easy walker: has a quick action: useful performer at 2 yrs: well below form in handicaps in 2007. *B. Smart*

SADLER'S HILL (IRE) 3 b.g. Sadler's Wells (USA) 132 – Dedicated Lady (IRE) – 101 (Pennine Walk 120) [2007 –: p10g p12.2g 15.4m 11.9m⁶ p11g⁶ p12g Dec 19] little form: tried blinkered. *M. J. McGrath*

SADLER'S KINGDOM (IRE) 3 b.c. Sadler's Wells (USA) 132 – Artful Pleasure **97** (USA) (Nasty And Bold (USA)) [2007 p9.5g⁵ p9.5g p9.5g 9.9g⁶ 12.1m* 12m⁴ 12s² 10d* 12s* 11.9m⁴ 11.9g² 13s* 16d Oct 21] 130,000Y: good-topped colt: fifth foal: half-brother to 2 winners in US, notably Grade 1 7f winner Peeping Tom (by Eagle Eyed): dam, US 1m/1¼m minor stakes winner, half-sister to US Grade 1 1m winner Traitor: useful handicapper: won at Beverley in May, Nottingham and Galway in July, and Hamilton (best effort to beat Dustoori by ½ length) in September: below form in Irish Cesarewitch at the Curragh final outing: stays 13f: acts on soft and good to firm going. *R. A. Fahey*

SADLER'S LEAP (IRE) 4 b.f. Sadler's Wells (USA) 132 – Leaping Flame (USA) **67** (Trempolino (USA) 135) [2007 10d 12.1s² 12s⁵ p12g² p13.9g⁵ p16g Nov 3] lightly-made filly: third foal: half-sister to fairly useful 9f winner Firesong (by Dansili) and 6-y-o Zaffeu: dam, French 7f winner, half-sister to smart performers up to/around 1m Apple of Kent and War Zone: fair maiden: stays 1½m: raced on polytrack and good to soft/soft going: sold 8,000 gns. *Pat Eddery*

SADLER'S STAR (GER) 4 b.g. Alwuhush (USA) 121 – Sadlerella (IRE) (King's Theatre (USA) 128) [2007 p12g Feb 17] fairly useful performer in Germany in 2006 (trained by H. Groschel), winning maiden at Dresden: well held in handicap at Lingfield on British Flat debut: stays 11f: raced only on good/good to soft going on turf. *B. G. Powell*

SAD TIMES (IRE) 3 b.f. Tendulkar (USA) 114 – Mrs Kanning 61 (Distant View **55 §** (USA) 126) [2007 7f§: 7m³ 7g 8d³ 8g⁵ Jun 27] workmanlike filly: modest performer: stays 1m: acts on polytrack, firm and soft going: often in cheekpieces, visored final start: refused to race once at 2 yrs: ungenuine: won juvenile hurdle in August. *W. G. M. Turner*

SAFARI 4 b.f. Namaqualand (USA) – Breakfast Creek 63 (Hallgate 127) [2007 44: p6g – 7g 10.9d 8.1s Jul 5] poor maiden: tried blinkered. *A. J. Chamberlain*

SAFARI DANCER (IRE) 2 b.g. (Mar 30) Indian Danehill (IRE) 124 – Umlani (IRE) **59 p** (Great Commotion (USA) 123) [2007 7g 7m⁵ 6d⁶ Sep 20] €14,000F, 16,000Y: second foal: half-brother to fairly useful 2004 2-y-o 5f winner Safari Sunset (by Fayruz): dam unraced: more encouragement than bare result in maidens: should be suited by 7f/1m: capable of better. *I. Semple*

SAFARI MISCHIEF 4 b.g. Primo Valentino (IRE) 116 – Night Gypsy 74 (Mind **88** Games 121) [2007 77: 5.7m³ 5.3f* 5g⁶ p5g* 5g⁶ 5f⁵ 5m³ p5g⁴ Oct 12] fairly useful handicapper: won at Brighton in June and Lingfield in July: good efforts in frame last 2 outings: best at 5f: acts on polytrack and any turf going. *P. Winkworth*

SAFARI SUNDOWNER (IRE) 3 b.g. Daggers Drawn (USA) 114 – Acadelli (IRE) **65** 71 (Royal Academy (USA) 130) [2007 65: 8.1g p12g p12g Oct 23] strong, useful-looking gelding: fair maiden: stays 1½m: acts on polytrack and good to firm ground. *P. Winkworth*

SAFARI SUNUP (IRE) 2 b.c. (Apr 26) Catcher In The Rye (IRE) 115 – Nuit Des **97** Temps (Sadler's Wells (USA) 132) [2007 p7g⁵ 7v* 7g² 8.3d* 8g Oct 26] €16,000F, 36,000Y: compact colt: ninth foal: half-brother to several winners, including useful Irish 7f/7.5f winner (including at 2 yrs) Mrs Evans (by College Chapel) and 3-y-o Oi Vay Joe: dam, ran once in Ireland, half-sister to useful French performer up to 1¼m Night Watch: useful performer: won maiden at Lingfield in July and nursery at Windsor in October: stays 1m: acts on polytrack and heavy going. *P. Winkworth*

SAFARI TIME (IRE) 2 b.f. (Apr 18) Danetime (IRE) 121 – Laurel Delight 104 (Presi- **58** dium 124) [2007 p5m² 5.1f⁴ Aug 24] €35,000Y: seventh foal: half-sister to 3 winners, notably smart US performer up to 11f Mr O'Brien (by Mukaddamah): dam, 5f winner (including at 2 yrs), half-sister to very smart sprinter Paris House: modest form in frame in minor event at Lingfield (second to Toolittleyourlate) and maiden at Bath: likely to prove best at 5f/6f. *P. Winkworth*

SAFEBREAKER 2 b.g. (Apr 26) Key of Luck (USA) 126 – Insijaam (USA) 112 **78**
(Secretariat (USA)) [2007 6s³ 6s² p7.1g² p7.1g³ f7d* Dec 14] half-brother to several
winners, notably smart 7f (at 2 yrs) to 11f winner (including in US) Pictavia (by Sinndar)
and useful 7f to 9f winner Master Marvel (by Selkirk): dam, French 9f (at 2 yrs) and 1¼m
winner, half-sister to very smart 1m to 1½m performer Hatoof: fair form: consistent in
maidens, placed all starts (left M. Johnston 13,000 gns after third) before winning at
Southwell: will be suited by 1m: acts on all-weather and soft going. *N. Tinkler*

SAFE INVESTMENT (USA) 3 b.g. Gone West (USA) – Fully Invested (USA) 99 **85 d**
(Irish River (FR) 131) [2007 94p: p8g⁵ 10m 9m 8m p7g Oct 15] small gelding: fairly
useful performer: below form after reappearance in 2007, leaving J. Gosden after third
start: should stay 1¼m: raced only on polytrack and good to firm going: has been early to
post. *B. N. Pollock*

SAFIN (GER) 7 b.g. Pennekamp (USA) 130 – Sankt Johanna (GER) (High Game) **56**
[2007 f11g p9.5g p12g p12.2g Nov 12] ex-Swiss gelding: one-time useful performer
when trained by C. von der Recke, successful 5 times: below that form in 2006 (left Frau
C. Bocskai after final outing), and just modest form in handicaps in Britain at 7 yrs: stays
11f: acts on sand and heavy ground. *F. Jordan*

SAFIYEH 2 b.f. (Feb 25) Golden Snake (USA) 127 – Safinaz 50 (Environment Friend **–**
128) [2007 p7g 7v 7m Aug 9] third foal: closely related to winner in Spain by Bertolini:
dam maiden: tailed off in maidens. *M. J. Attwater*

SAFRANINE (IRE) 10 b.m. Dolphin Street (FR) 125 – Webbiana (African Sky 124) **52**
[2007 63: 7.1m⁵ 7.1g⁶ 7s⁵ f7g 5.5s⁴ 7.1g⁴ 6d⁶ 7.1m⁶ 7g 5s p6g p6g Dec 29] rather leggy
mare: modest performer: effective at 5f to 7f: acts on all-weather, firm and soft ground:
tried tongue tied/in headgear: saddle reportedly slipped eighth start. *Miss A. Stokell*

SAFWA (IRE) 3 b.f. Green Desert (USA) 127 – Nasanice (IRE) 97 (Nashwan (USA) **85**
135) [2007 8g⁵ 7d⁴ 8d² 8.1d* 8.1m⁴ 7d Oct 27] stocky filly: fifth foal: half-sister to 3
winners, including 6-y-o Maraahel and smart 7f/1m winner Mostashaar (by Intikhab):
dam Irish 9f winner: fairly useful performer: won maiden at Sandown in August: better
effort in handicaps after when fourth at Sandown: stayed 1m: acted on good to firm and
good to soft going: visits Medicean. *Sir Michael Stoute*

SAGARA (USA) 3 b.c. Sadler's Wells (USA) 132 – Rangoon Ruby (USA) 105 **124**
(Kingmambo (USA) 125) [2007 10.5d* 10d² 10.5g 12g³ 12.5d⁵ 12m² 12g³ Oct 7]
    When Sagara returns in the next season the colours worn by his rider will be
a different shade of blue, the colt having been bought privately by Godolphin from
the Niarchos family in November. Sagara won't have come cheap, his stock having
risen considerably following his performance on the final outing of his three-year-
old campaign, when third in the Prix de l'Arc de Triomphe. His new connections
were evidently impressed by what they saw at Longchamp and, judged on the very
smart form he showed in the Arc, Sagara is well up to winning good races over a
mile and a half as a four-year-old. There remains a suspicion that Sagara, whose
only success to date was gained in a maiden, might have been flattered to some
degree, though for now he has been given full credit for his effort. What wasn't in
doubt in the Arc was that Sagara is a hard ride, racing lazily as has become the norm
with him.
    Once-raced at two (beaten a neck in a newcomers race at Compiegne),
Sagara was stepped up markedly in class after making a successful return at
Maisons-Laffitte in April, his next race the Prix Greffulhe in which he went down
by a short neck to Quest For Honor at Saint-Cloud. Even at this early stage,
Sagara's attitude was giving cause for concern, and it was not a complete surprise
to see him fitted with cheekpieces in the Prix du Jockey Club at Chantilly. They
didn't bring about any improvement in form, though, and Sagara raced without
headgear on his four subsequent starts. He finished seventh to Lawman at Chantilly,
and ran to similarly useful form on his next appearance when third to the impressive Zambezi Sun in the Grand Prix de Paris at Longchamp, finishing well and
giving the impression he might well have come second with a clear passage.
Following a disappointing run in the Grand Prix de Deauville, Sagara was returned
to Longchamp for the Prix Niel, a race which has proved a significant pointer to the
Arc in recent years, which this time around centred on Soldier of Fortune and
Zambezi Sun. Sagara, the outsider of the six who took part, left his previous form
well behind and split the pair, getting to within a length and a half of Soldier of

Fortune as he snatched second place near the finish. The performance was enough to earn Sagara his place in the Arc, though, in a field which also included Authorized, it looked long odds about his proving the best of the three-year-olds, never mind winning the race outright. Yet Sagara wasn't far off doing both. Only the four-year-olds Dylan Thomas and Youmzain were ahead of him at the line, the distances a head and a length and a half. For much of the way it seemed unlikely that Sagara would finish so close as he did but, as in the Niel, the strong gallop helped bring out the best in him. Sagara was detached in last place and off the bridle over half a mile from home, but he made very good headway in the straight, managing to obtain a clear run towards the rail until slightly short of room approaching the finish, still running on strongly at the time. His performance had similarities to that of another three-year-old, Acropolis, who excelled himself in finishing fourth in the 2004 Arc. At least Sagara should go on to prove a good deal more successful than Acropolis. The latter has failed to win any of his sixteen starts since the Arc, three of them over hurdles!

			Northern Dancer (b 1961)	Nearctic
Sagara (USA) (b.c. 2004)	Sadler's Wells (USA) (b 1981)			Natalma
		Fairy Bridge (b 1975)	Bold Reason
				Special
	Rangoon Ruby (USA) (b 1996)	Kingmambo (b 1990)	Mr Prospector
				Miesque
		Imperfect Circle (b or br 1988)	Riverman
				Aviance

Sagara, who is by Sadler's Wells, is likely to stay beyond a mile and a half if required to do so. A mile was as far as his dam Rangoon Ruby was bred to stay and even that trip seemed beyond her. Rangoon Ruby gained her only win over seven furlongs, in a minor event at Longchamp at three, and went on to show herself at least as effective over six when in the frame in the Prix de Ris-Orangis and Prix de Seine-et-Oise. A half-sister to the top-class miler Spinning World, Rangoon Ruby is a daughter of the Firth of Clyde Stakes winner and Cheveley Park Stakes runner-up Imperfect Circle, who in turn is a half-sister to the very smart miler Chimes of Freedom. The next dam in what is an excellent family is the Phoenix Stakes winner Aviance, a daughter of a half-sister to Sex Appeal, the dam of Try My Best and El Gran Senor. This is the Best In Show family which is discussed in more detail in the essays on Peeping Fawn and Thewayyouare. Sagara is the second foal of Rangoon Ruby. Her first, a filly by Dream Well named Spectralia, never raced and was sold at Newmarket in December 2005 for 70,000 guineas. Sagara, a medium-sized, good-bodied colt, acts on good to firm and good to soft going. *J. E. Pease, France*

SAGASSA 3 b.f. Largesse 112 – Sally's Trust (IRE) 51 (Classic Secret (USA) 91) [2007 **47** –: p12g 10d 10m 8.3m Aug 25] leggy filly: poor maiden. *W. de Best-Turner*

SAGREDO (USA) 3 b.g. Diesis 133 – Eternity 77 (Suave Dancer (USA) 136) [2007 **106** 95p: p12g⁶ 10.3s³ 10d* 10g* 13.4m³ 14g 14m 12.5d⁶ Oct 22] tall, useful-looking gelding: useful handicapper: won at Pontefract in July and Nottingham (by 1¼ lengths from Top Mark) in August: good 2¼ lengths third to Bauer in listed handicap at Chester next time: below form in listed races at Newmarket and Deauville last 2 starts: probably stays 1¾m: acts on polytrack, soft and good to firm going: patiently ridden nowadays: sold 310,000 gns. *Sir Mark Prescott*

SAGUNT (GER) 4 ch.g. Tertullian (USA) 115 – Suva (GER) (Arazi (USA) 135) [2007 **72** 7g 6f p7g 7.1m⁶ 8g* p11m p11g Dec 19] workmanlike gelding: fair performer: lightly **a–** raced for W. Hickst in Germany prior to 2007, winning maiden at Bremen at 2 yrs: well backed, easily best effort in Britain when winning handicap at Brighton in October: should stay 1¼m. *S. Curran*

SAHAADI 2 b.f. (May 6) Dansili 127 – Shardette (IRE) (Darshaan 133) [2007 6s⁵ 7s⁵ **73** 7g⁴ 7m* Sep 25] workmanlike filly: first foal: dam French 10.5f winner: fair form: won maiden at Brighton: will stay 1m: acts on soft and good to firm going. *R. Hannon*

SAHARA DAWN (IRE) 3 b.f. Desert Sun 120 – Sharadja (IRE) (Doyoun 124) [2007 **46** 53: p8g 7.9f⁴ 7.5m 8m 8m 10d Oct 10] leggy filly: poor maiden: tried blinkered/visored. *D. Carroll*

SAHARA PRINCE (IRE) 7 b.g. Desert King (IRE) 129 – Chehana 78 (Posse (USA) **52** 130) [2007 –, a57: p7g² p8g p10g² p10g 7.6f 8.1d³ p10g⁵ Sep 18] tall gelding: fairly useful performer at best, just modest nowadays: stays 1¼m: acts on polytrack, firm and soft going: usually wears headgear. *K. A. Morgan*

SAHARA SILK (IRE) 6 b.m. Desert Style (IRE) 121 – Buddy And Soda (IRE) 75 **71**
(Imperial Frontier (USA) 112) [2007 62, a83: p6g 5m* 6s 5s Jul 3] well-made mare: fair
handicapper: won at Beverley in June: effective at 5f/6f: acts on all-weather and firm
ground (below form on soft last 2 starts): visored: tends to edge left: usually races prominently: reportedly in foal to Bahamian Bounty. *D. Shaw*

SAHF LONDON 4 b.g. Vettori (IRE) 119 – Lumiere d'Espoir (FR) 81 (Saumarez 132) **55**
[2007 51: p11g* p10g Jan 20] modest performer: won minor event at Kempton in January: stays 1½m: acts on polytrack: tried blinkered. *G. L. Moore*

SAHRATI 3 ch.c. In The Wings 128 – Shimna 62 (Mr Prospector (USA)) [2007 81: **98**
p8g⁶ p8g⁴ 10m³ 11.8g⁴ 10d* 12g 10g² 10m* 9.9g 14g 10.3g³ Sep 29] leggy colt: useful
handicapper: won at Sandown in May and Newmarket in July: good third to Buccellati
at Chester final outing, hanging left: stays 11.8f: yet to race on heavy going, acts on any
other turf and polytrack. *C. E. Brittain*

SAILING BY 2 b.g. (Jan 28) Mull of Kintyre (USA) 114 – Rainbow Spectrum (FR) 57 **45**
(Spectrum (IRE) 126) [2007 5m 6.1g⁵ 6g³ 5.1g⁴ 5.1m⁵ Aug 9] sturdy gelding: poor
maiden: blinkered, in frame in sellers: bred to stay 1m. *B. R. Millman*

SAILOR AT SEA (USA) 2 b.c. (Jan 27) Mizzen Mast (USA) 121 – Merida (Warning **87**
136) [2007 5s⁶ 5m* 5.1s* 5g⁶ 6.1m⁶ 6m Sep 15] well-made, attractive colt: closely
related to useful 6f winner Como (by Cozzene) and half-brother to fairly useful 2004
2-y-o 5f winner Piper's Ash (by Royal Academy): dam, French/US 1m winner, half-sister
to smart performer up to 1m Tychonic: fairly useful performer: won maiden at Sandown
and minor event at Bath in July: sixth to Captain Gerrard in listed race at York next time,
but seemed to have problem after: should prove best at 5f/6f: acts on soft and good to firm
going: sold 8,000 gns. *R. Charlton*

SAILOR KING (IRE) 5 b.g. King's Best (USA) 132 – Manureva (USA) (Nureyev **86**
(USA) 131) [2007 87: p6g⁶ p6g⁶ p6g p7g⁵ p7g³ 6f p7.1g* p8g² 7g p7g* p7g p8g⁴
7d² 7.1d⁶ 7d p7g⁵ p7m³ p7.1g Oct 22] leggy gelding: fairly useful handicapper: won at
Wolverhampton in May and Kempton in June: stays 1m: acts on polytrack, heavy and
good to firm ground: hung left eighth 5-y-o start. *D. K. Ivory*

SAINGLEND 2 b.c. (Feb 28) Galileo (IRE) 134 – Verbal Intrigue (USA) (Dahar (USA) **83**
125) [2007 7.1d⁴ 8.1f³ 8.1m⁶ 8.3d⁴ Oct 1] 40,000 2-y-o: tall colt: seventh foal: half-
brother to several winners in US, notably Grade 2 11f winner Monkey Puzzle (by Country
Pine): dam US 8.5f winner: fairly useful maiden: in frame 3 starts, in nursery at Windsor
(staying-on fourth to Safari Sunup) final one: will be suited by 1¼m/1½m: acts on firm
and good to soft going. *H. Candy*

SAINT ALEBE 8 b.g. Bishop of Cashel 122 – Soba Up 74 (Persian Heights 129) [2007 **–**
94+: 14g May 19] heavy-topped gelding: poor mover: one-time useful performer: well
beaten in handicap at Newmarket sole start in 2007, tending to hang: should stay beyond
2m: acts on firm and soft going: has run well when sweating. *D. R. C. Elsworth*

SAINTLY PLACE 6 ch.g. Compton Place 125 – Always On A Sunday 101 (Star **58 §**
Appeal 133) [2007 45§: p5.1g p5.1g⁴ p7.1g f6g p5.1g 6f* 5.1g⁵ 5.3m 5.7d⁴ 6v⁵ 8.1m
6f Aug 11] lengthy gelding: modest performer: won 4-runner handicap at L'Ancresse
(Guernsey) in May: was effective at 5f to 7f: acted on all-weather and firm ground: tried
blinkered/visored/tongue tied: was unreliable: dead. *A. W. Carroll*

SAINTLY THOUGHTS (USA) 12 b. or br.g. St Jovite (USA) 135 – Free Thinker **45**
(USA) 100 (Shadeed (USA) 135) [2007 p16.5g p16g Mar 26] good-bodied gelding:
modest performer in 2005: unraced at 11 yrs: only poor form on return: stays 17.4f: acts
on all-weather, good to firm and good to soft going: wears headgear. *R. J. Hodges*

SAINT REMUS (IRE) 3 b.g. Diktat 126 – Fur Will Fly 66 (Petong 126) [2007 –: **45**
p5.1g p6m⁶ p8.6g p6g p5.1g p6g⁶ Dec 13] poor maiden: best form at 6f: raced only on
polytrack: blinkered last 3 starts. *Peter Grayson*

SAITAMA 5 b.m. Pursuit of Love 124 – Sea Ballad (USA) (Bering 136) [2007 –: p16g **–**
f14g 12g Apr 22] fair performer for Mme M. Bollack-Badel in France in 2005: well held
all starts since, including in Jersey final one: stays 1½m: often blinkered. *A. M. Hales*

SAKE (IRE) 5 b.g. Shinko Forest (IRE) – Drosera (IRE) (Thatching 131) [2007 80: 7g **76**
8m 8d³ 7s 7s² 7.5s⁴ 7m⁴ 8m 7m Sep 9] sturdy, deep-girthed gelding: fair handicapper:
effective at 7f/1m: acts on firm and soft ground: tried tongue tied/visored: tends to race
freely: usually races up with pace. *N. Tinkler*

SAKHACITY 2 b.f. (Apr 30) Sakhee (USA) 136 – Subtle One (IRE) (Polish Patriot **65**
(USA) 128) [2007 6g⁶ 6s³ 6m⁶ 6d² Oct 15] 10,000Y: sturdy, close-coupled filly: has an

unimpressive action: sixth foal: half-sister to 5-y-o Noah Jameel and 1½m winner Chara
(by Deploy): dam, no form, closely related to smart performer up to 11f Air Smap and
half-sister to very smart performer up to 2m Manhattan Cafe, both in Japan: fair maiden:
runner-up at Windsor (made most): bred to stay at least 1m, but has plenty of speed: acts
on soft going. *J. R. Jenkins*

SAKHEE'S SECRET 3 ch.c. Sakhee (USA) 136 – Palace Street (USA) 103 **128**
(Secreto (USA) 128) [2007 104p: 6m* 6g* 6m* 6m* 6g⁵ Sep 8]
Fast-improving three-year-olds are a nightmare for the British Horseracing
Authority's handicappers, and there must have been relief in that department when
Sakhee's Secret, allotted a mark of 93 after his two-year-old campaign, was moved
up to conditions races after contesting just one handicap. The race concerned, at
Newmarket in April, indicated that the promise Sakhee's Secret had shown in his
first season, chiefly when trouncing fourteen opponents in a Windsor maiden by
six lengths, was well on the way to being realised. Sakhee's Secret's official mark
underestimated his ability by a long way. Nonetheless, the way in which he made
light of 8-12, starting favourite in a field of eighteen, was breathtaking as he
quickened clear to beat Aahayson by five lengths. If this was good, Sakhee's
Secret's subsequent form was in a different league as he added three more races,
culminating in the Darley July Cup, proving himself the best sprinter in Europe
who will continue to take all the beating in the top races as a four-year-old.
Sakhee's Secret's next race, a month after Newmarket, was the listed Ultimate Travel Stakes at Newbury, in which he started at long odds on against only
four opponents and had no difficulty accounting for Fontana Amorosa by three
lengths. The Ultimate Travel Stakes (registered as the Carnarvon Stakes) was
upgraded to listed status in 2002, the year in which Sakhee's Secret's next target,
the Axminster Carpets Cathedral Stakes at Salisbury, was inaugurated with the
same status. The lack of opportunities for good three-year-old sprinters in the first
part of the year and for above-average fillies and mares suited by a test of stamina
is something which is bemoaned in other essays, but, generally speaking, the seemingly relentless proliferation of pattern and listed races in Britain is a cause for
concern in that it devalues the standing of such races and of the pattern system as a
whole. Those owners who demand more prestigious and rewarding opportunities
for their horses are probably delighted with the 292 pattern and listed races in
Britain which earned 'black type' in 2007, over 100 more than in 1990. To those
who regard the level of form shown by a runner in a race as the only true guide to his
or her ability, the status of an event, listed or otherwise, is largely inconsequential.
Sakhee's Secret's performance in the Cathedral Stakes proved the point, since the
form value of his win was more in keeping with that of a Group 1 race. In fact, it
was the best in a listed contest for a long while, ahead of that shown by such as
Imperial Stride, Grandera, Ikhtyar, Mamool and Trade Fair in listed races over the
last decade. Although Sakhee's Secret's opponents Ashdown Express, Patavellian,
Pivotal Point and The Trader were not the forces of old, that quartet were still
capable of at least useful form. Another opponent Presto Shinko had run creditably
when fourth in the Palace House Stakes and the only other three-year-old in the
race, Prime Defender, had shown smart form when landing the Free Handicap and
Sandy Lane Stakes. Prime Defender started a short-priced favourite but he hardly
saw the way Sakhee's Secret went as the latter settled the issue in a matter of strides
after being switched outside over a furlong out, passing the post an easy four-length
winner.
This was a first-rate victory, judged on form as well as style, one backed
up by Sakhee's Secret's timefigure of 0.61 fast, equivalent to a timerating of 115.
The decision to go for the July Cup next was a welcome boost to that race which
was missing the Royal Ascot winners Soldier's Tale and Miss Andretti, as well as
Miss Andretti's Australian compatriot Takeover Target. Not that the July Cup was
weakly contested, with runners representing six countries among the field of
eighteen. Sakhee's Secret was second favourite behind Asset, successful in the
Abernant Stakes and third in the Golden Jubilee Stakes. After them came Middle
Park winner Dutch Art, coming back in distance after running well in Group 1 races
at a mile, King's Stand Stakes runner-up and regular participant in top sprints
Dandy Man, and Amadeus Wolf, winner of the Duke of York Stakes. Besides

Dandy Man, the foreign challenge consisted of: Bentley Biscuit, successful in three Group 1 races in Australia in the spring but last of twenty in the King's Stand Stakes; 2006 Prix Maurice de Gheest winner Marchand d'Or; and smart German sprinter Electric Beat. Though trained by Mike de Kock, Drayton had never raced in South Africa, while there was an ex-Australian in the shape of Mutawaajid, now with Mick Channon after landing two Group 2 events in February. Others in the line-up included Prime Defender, Red Clubs, second to Amadeus Wolf at York, and a couple of well-above-average juveniles from 2006, Hellvelyn and Sander Camillo. In a race that saw the field bunched together in the centre of the track, there was some scrimmaging at halfway that did not help Dutch Art for one. Sakhee's Secret was waited with as Drayton took them along and, sweeping through to take over from Red Clubs a furlong out, Sakhee's Secret drifted left—as he had on his reappearance—but still did not need to be subjected to anything like maximum pressure to beat the strong-finishing Dutch Art by half a length. Red Clubs was a length and a quarter further away third followed by Marchand d'Or. The form was on a par with Sakhee's Secret's at Salisbury and up to the level of recent years for the July Cup, though not so good as when Stravinsky and Mozart won the race. It was the second time Hughie Morrison had landed the race, having trained Pastoral Pursuits in 2005.

Pastoral Pursuits did not race again after winning the July Cup as a four-year-old but there was no question of retirement for Sakhee's Secret, with Morrison mentioning the Nunthorpe Stakes and the Betfred Sprint Cup as possible targets. Sakhee's Secret had not raced over five before—seven had almost certainly been too far for him on his final start at two—and it was decided to stick to six and go to Haydock to attempt a double last achieved by Ajdal twenty years before. In the interim, Marchand d'Or beat Dutch Art in the Prix Maurice de Gheest, but Sakhee's Secret was sent off a hot favourite against thirteen rivals, including Marchand d'Or, in the Sprint Cup, seven of whom he had defeated at Newmarket. Dutch Art and Soldier's Tale had been taken out earlier in the week because the going was forecast to be good to firm and Al Qasi was withdrawn on the day for the same reason. Sakhee's Secret finished just under three lengths fifth behind Red Clubs and Marchand d'Or after being unable to quicken in customary fashion when asked to challenge just over a furlong out. A furore followed. Officially the going was good to firm, good in places, but good all round would have been a more accurate assessment. The difference from the forecast going—the connections of the supplemented (at a cost of £17,500) Per Incanto had reportedly been assured before entering that the going would be 'on the fast side'—was not because of rain but because of watering, clerk of the course Kirkland Tellwright accused, among other things, of misleading owners and trainers. Some trainers including Morrison, Barry Hills and Mick Channon claimed that the ground was loose and soft, while Luca Cumani for one thought it was perfect. Inaccurate assessments of the state of the going are not hard to find—based on Timeform's analysis there were around thirty in August alone—though with the vast majority the difference was marginal rather than dramatic. Haydock, by the way, could point to the fact that only five horses were withdrawn on the Sprint Cup day programme from ninety declared (and they

Darley July Cup, Newmarket—Sakhee's Secret (blaze) confirms himself a high-class sprinter; Dutch Art (on winner's left), Red Clubs (second right), Marchand d'Or (right), Dandy Man (dark colours, centre), Asset (armlets) and Borderlescott (left) are next

included Dutch Art on the grounds that the going was considered too firm!). In certain respects, clerks are on a hiding to nothing with the ground, since they are under instructions to ensure that the conditions on their courses are 'safe'. Thinking on such matters seems to be led by trainers who often perceive firm going to be unsafe almost by definition. For example, after his remark quoted above, Cumani added: 'I would much rather have safe ground than firm ground', implying that the one precludes the other.

Granted an even surface and a good covering of grass a sound thoroughbred can race safely on firm going, though that's not the same as saying all would be equally effective on it. If there is indeed a problem with firm going being unsafe in the twenty-first century it can hardly be blamed on the vagaries of the British climate, which has always been unpredictable. A more likely explanation is that the grass on some tracks is not copious enough or consistent enough for the job. The blame for this could lie with any, or all, of the following: indifferent turf husbandry, excessive wear and tear due to more and more racing, or excessive watering. Frequent watering can lead to the grass roots being closer to the surface and a decline in quality and consistency. There are inevitable differences in soil structure and drainage which can affect watering as it did at Warwick just before the Haydock meeting, when a card had to be abandoned because of a false patch of going. Mark Johnston queried current practices in his stable magazine during the summer: 'Is watering ruining our tracks? I think it may well be! Here in Middleham we have more grass on the gallops than we have ever had and the wonderful cushion allows us to work when the ground is firm but also holds the turf together when the rain comes. I cannot understand why we should find it the best ever summer for growing grass on the gallops but (the) courses are struggling to meet their usual standards.' Why indeed? To get back to Sakhee's Secret, Morrison's claim that the colt needs good to firm ground is unconvincing—Sakhee's Secret had won on good at Windsor (as a two-year-old) and Newbury. Perhaps the explanation is that Sakhee's Secret simply had an off-day, which can happen with any horse. Fortunately, he stays in training and can, and with luck will, prove the point.

		Bahri	Riverman
	Sakhee (USA)	(b 1992)	Wasnah
	(b 1997)	Thawakib	Sadler's Wells
Sakhee's Secret		(b 1990)	Tobira Celeste
(ch.c. 2004)		Secreto	Northern Dancer
	Palace Street (USA)	(b 1981)	Betty's Secret
	(ch 1987)	Majestic Street	Majestic Prince
		(ch 1972)	Beaver Street

In terms of his distance requirements, Sakhee's Secret takes more after his dam Palace Street than his sire Sakhee whose first crop also contained the useful sprinters Royal Rock and Sakhee's Song, the latter in Italy, and three stakes performers who are suited by a mile and a half or more, Darsha, Regal Flush and Shujoon. Sakhee spent his time aged three and upwards racing over middle distances, with his principal victories—brilliant ones—coming in the Juddmonte International at a mile and a quarter and the Prix de l'Arc de Triomphe at a mile and a half. Three of the best sprinters in the last sixty years were also by horses who were effective over at least a mile and a half—Abernant (by Derby and Gold Cup winner Owen Tudor), Pappa Fourway (by November Handicap winner Pappageno) and Flirting Around (by Round Table, who stayed thirteen furlongs). Sakhee's Secret's dam Palace Street was bought by Sakhee's Secret's owner-breeder for 145,000 guineas at the end of her two-year-old campaign. Even though sired by Derby winner Secreto, she was not tried beyond a mile and did most of her racing at shorter distances, showing useful form in winning the John of Gaunt Stakes and Cammidge Trophy and finishing second in the Supreme Stakes. She was tough and most of her seven successful progeny have displayed the same trait, with Ca d'Oro (by Cadeaux Genereux), Marker (by Pivotal), Duke of Modena (by Salse) and King's Caprice (by Pursuit of Love) winning twenty-two of their one hundred and ninety starts collectively. Better than any of those was Palace Street's second foal by Pursuit of Love, the smart filly Palace Affair, whose nineteen starts were highlighted by wins in five listed events from five to seven furlongs, including the 2002 Cathedral Stakes. Palace Street comes from a good family since her dam Majestic Street won twice as a two-year-old and was second in a minor stakes race over seven and a half furlongs the following year. Majestic Street foaled seven other winners including Stramusc, successful in the Criterium di Roma, and useful handicapper Indian Trail, who won the Extel Handicap and ran second in the Cambridgeshire. The next dam Beaver Street also produced Kentucky Oaks winner Native Street, dam of Florida Derby winner Royal And Regal. Native Street's daughter Prospector's Fire appears in the bottom line of the pedigrees of Stravinsky and Dowsing, both very good sprinters. Sakhee's Secret, a tall, strong colt who looked in outstanding shape at Newmarket, should be effective at five furlongs, although with such as Benbaun and Kingsgate Native around, he will need to be at his best if tackling that distance. Whatever Sakhee's Secret's fate over the minimum trip, at six furlongs it will take a very good sprinter among the up-and-coming three-year-old crop, or an exceptional raider from Australia, to prevent Sakhee's Secret's dominating the scene over six furlongs in races such as the Golden Jubilee Stakes and the July Cup again. *H. Morrison*

SALAASA (USA) 3 ch.c. Swain (IRE) 134 – Jawla 97 (Wolfhound (USA) 126) [2007 **90** 79p: 10m* 10g 10m⁵ May 28] useful-looking colt: fairly useful form: landed odds in maiden at Pontefract in April: disappointing in handicaps after, typically carrying head awkwardly: stays 1¼m: acts on good to firm and good to soft ground: sold 38,000 gns and joined E. McNamara in Ireland. *M. Johnston*

SALAWAT 4 b.f. Tomba 119 – Galadriel (Fairy King (USA)) [2007 –: p12.2g⁶ p16.5g **–** Nov 19] no form. *T. T. Clement*

SALEIMA (IRE) 2 b.f. (Apr 10) Rock of Gibraltar (IRE) 133 – Lumber Jill (USA) 75 **82** (Woodman (USA) 126) [2007 8m³ 8d² 8g Nov 3] 80,000Y: neat filly: third foal: dam, French 11f/1½m winner, out of Yorkshire Oaks runner-up Bineyah: fairly useful form: placed in maidens at Newmarket and Newbury (second to Strategic Mission): well-backed 6/1 but not take eye and no impression in listed race at Newmarket: will stay 1¼m. *J. Noseda*

SALEROSA (IRE) 2 b.f. (Apr 5) Monashee Mountain (USA) 115 – Sainte Gig (FR) **65** (Saint Cyrien (FR) 128) [2007 7.1g⁴ Nov 9] fifth foal: dam unraced half-sister to smart French/US 1m/1¼m performer Val des Bois: 10/1, one-paced fourth in maiden at Musselburgh: will stay 1m. *Mrs A. Duffield*

SALFORD MILL (IRE) 3 b.c. Peintre Celebre (USA) 137 – Razana (IRE) 71 (Kah **116** yasi 130) [2007 80p: p10g* 9m² 10m* 12g⁶ 12d 10.3m³ 11m⁴ Sep 21] big, strong, angular colt: smart performer: won maiden at Lingfield in January and listed race at Newmarket (beat Acapulco 1¼ lengths) in May: creditable efforts after in Derby at Epsom (9 lengths sixth to Authorized, never nearer), minor event at Doncaster (3¾ lengths third to Kirklees) and Arc Trial at Newbury (fourth to Halicarnassus): worth trying beyond 1½m: acts on polytrack and good to firm going: reportedly suffered from foot infection after fifth start: reportedly sold privately, and joined A. Cruz in Hong Kong, where renamed Helene Mascot. *D. R. C. Elsworth*

SALIENT 3 b.c. Fasliyev (USA) 120 – Savannah Belle 84 (Green Desert (USA) 127) **98** [2007 85: p8g 8.3m³ 7d³ 7d⁵ 8m² 8g 8m³ 8m² 7.1m* 7m 7d p7m² p7m⁵ p8m² p7g³ Dec 28] sturdy, compact colt: useful handicapper: won at Sandown in September: creditable efforts otherwise when placed: stays 1m: acts on polytrack, good to firm and good to soft going: often races prominently: consistent. *J. Akehurst*

SALINGERS STAR (IRE) 2 b.f. (Apr 24) Catcher In The Rye (IRE) 115 – Head For **78** The Stars (IRE) (Head For Heights 125) [2007 6d* 7m⁴ Aug 25] €7,000Y: half-sister to several winners, including Irish 8.5f/9f winner In Other Words (by Lake Coniston) and 3-y-o Packers Hill: dam maiden: fair form: won maiden at Pontefract in June: off 2 months, fourth to Screen Star in minor event at Redcar: will stay 1m. *G. A. Swinbank*

SALINGER (USA) 5 b.g. Lear Fan (USA) 130 – Sharp Flick (USA) (Sharpen Up 127) **50** [2007 58: p12g p11g Feb 25] leggy gelding: modest performer: stays easy 1¼m: acts on polytrack, good to firm and good to soft going: tried in cheekpieces/blinkers. *Mrs L. J. Mongan*

SALISBURY PLAIN 6 b.h. Mark of Esteem (IRE) 137 – Wild Pavane (Dancing Brave **53** (USA) 140) [2007 59: 9g 7d 7m 8d 8.3v⁴ 8.1s p10g Aug 29] smallish horse: modest performer nowadays: stays easy 1½m: acts on polytrack and good to firm ground: tried in cheekpieces. *N. I. M. Rossiter*

SALISBURY WORLD (IRE) 4 ch.g. Spinning World (USA) 130 – Dinka Raja **– §** (USA) (Woodman (USA) 126) [2007 47§: 9.9s 9m Aug 11] rather leggy gelding: temperamental maiden: well held in 2007. *J. F. Coupland*

SALONGA (IRE) 4 b.f. Shinko Forest (IRE) – Alongside 58 (Slip Anchor 136) [2007 **77**
65: 8m p9.5g³ 10.1d² Jul 5] tall, quite good-topped filly: fair handicapper: improved form
when placed last 2 outings: stays 1¼m: acts on polytrack, good to firm and good to soft
ground. *C. F. Wall*

SALOON (USA) 3 b.c. Sadler's Wells (USA) 132 – Fire The Groom (USA) 115 **72**
(Blushing Groom (FR) 131) [2007 –p: 11.9d² Oct 18] better effort in maidens when 1¾
lengths second to Crimson Monarch at Brighton sole start at 3 yrs: sold 16,000 gns. *Sir
Michael Stoute*

SALSADAR 3 ch.f. Zamindar (USA) 116 – Flaming Salsa (FR) 93 (Salse (USA) 128) **68**
[2007 f12g² p12g p10.7g 10v Oct 3] first foal: dam, 1½m winner, half-sister to smart
winner up to 1½m Bahamian Dancer (including in Hong Kong as Industrial Success): fair
form when runner-up on debut: little form after, leaving J. Gosden after second start: stays
1½m: acts on fibresand. *J. C. McConnell, Ireland*

SALSA STEPS (USA) 3 ch.f. Giant's Causeway (USA) 132 – Dance Design (IRE) **84**
119 (Sadler's Wells (USA) 132) [2007 80p: 8.3g⁴ 8d⁵ 6f* 6d Oct 19] big, useful-looking
filly: fairly useful performer: won maiden at Folkestone (by 5 lengths) in September:
stays 6f: acts on firm and good ground: tongue tied last 2 starts. *H. Morrison*

SALSA TIME 2 b.f. (Mar 5) Hernando (FR) 127 – Kabayil 75 (Dancing Brave (USA) **70 p**
140) [2007 7s² Sep 26] rather leggy filly: sister to 9.5f winner Spanish Lace and half-
sister to 3 winners, notably 10-y-o Dancing Bay: dam 1¼m and hurdles winner: 18/1, 7
lengths second to Zakhaaref in maiden at Redcar: will be suited by 1¼m+: should do
better. *Miss J. A. Camacho*

SALSA VERDI (USA) 3 b.f. Giant's Causeway (USA) 132 – Cape Verdi (IRE) 126 **80**
(Caerleon (USA) 132) [2007 p10g² p11g³ p9.5g* Aug 12] smallish filly: fourth foal:
sister to 4-y-o Benandonner: dam, 6f (at 2 yrs) to 1m (1000 Guineas) winner, out of sister
to Breeders' Cup Classic winner Arcangues: fairly useful form: won maiden at Wolverhampton in August: stayed 11f: raced only on polytrack: hung under pressure first 2
outings: dead. *Saeed bin Suroor*

SALTO CHICO 3 b.g. Fraam 114 – Miss Tango 61 (Batshoof 122) [2007 53: 11g **49**
p12.2g⁵ 11.5m⁶ 16.2f 14m⁴ Sep 1] just poor maiden handicapper in 2007: barely stays
1¾m: seems to act on soft and good to firm going. *W. M. Brisbourne*

SALT OF THE EARTH (IRE) 2 b.c. (Mar 31) Invincible Spirit (IRE) 121 – Get The **74 p**
Accountant (Vettori (IRE) 119) [2007 p6g³ Nov 21] €45,000Y, £50,000 2-y-o: first foal:
dam, ran 3 times, half-sister to useful 2-y-o sprinter Magic of Love: 10/1, 1¾ lengths third
to Classic Fortune in maiden at Lingfield: should improve. *T. G. Mills*

SALUSCRAGGIE 5 b.m. Most Welcome 131 – Upper Caen (High Top 131) [2007 **62**
60: 10m* 10g⁴ 10.5s⁴ 13.1d⁵ 12s Jul 20] workmanlike mare: modest handicapper: won
apprentice event at Nottingham in June: effective at 1¼m to 1¾m: acts on soft and good
to firm going: tried in cheekpieces: has flashed tail, and doesn't look easiest of rides.
K. G. Reveley

SALUTE (IRE) 8 b.g. Muhtarram (USA) 125 – Alasib 93 (Siberian Express (USA) **88**
125) [2007 89, a82: p13.9g* p16g² 16m 14.1m⁵ p16g⁴ 14.8m⁴ 14.1d³ 12.6m* 12d
p13.9g² p13.9g⁴ p13.9g* Dec 1] lengthy, quite attractive gelding: fairly useful performer:
won handicap at Wolverhampton in March and claimers at Warwick in September and
Wolverhampton in December: stays 16.5f: acts on all-weather, firm and soft going: tried
in headgear: edgy sort, has carried head awkwardly. *P. G. Murphy*

SALUTE THE GENERAL 4 ch.g. Mark of Esteem (IRE) 137 – Oiselina (FR) (Lina- **–**
mix (FR) 127) [2007 91: 10.3g Oct 26] tall, leggy gelding: fairly useful handicapper at
3 yrs: well below form sole outing in 2007: stays 1½m: acts on all-weather, soft and good
to firm going: often waited with. *Micky Hammond*

SALUT SAINT CLOUD 6 b.g. Primo Dominie 121 – Tiriana (Common Grounds **66**
118) [2007 75: f16g⁴ p16g p16g⁴ p16g⁵ p16g* p16g² p16g⁶ 18g p12g p10g p12g Dec 19] **a77**
close-coupled gelding: fair handicapper: won at Kempton in March: stays 16.5f: acts on
all-weather, firm and soft going: often wears headgear: fairly useful hurdler. *G. L. Moore*

SALVESTRO 4 b.g. Medicean 128 – Katy Nowaitee 112 (Komaite (USA)) [2007 67: **56**
10.9m p8.6g 8.1m 10s⁵ 8g 11.9d 7f 8.1d⁶ 8f 10.2m⁵ 10g⁶ Oct 25] smallish, useful-looking
gelding: modest maiden: stays 10.2f: acts on polytrack, firm and soft going: tried blinkered: often slowly away. *A. W. Carroll*

SALYM (FR) 6 ch.g. Limnos (JPN) 124 – Tina's Crest (FR) (Ocean Falls 113) [2007 **52**
56: f11g³ f12g f12g⁴ p16g Sep 29] big, workmanlike gelding: one-time fairly useful
winner in France: modest form in Britain: stays 12.5f: acts on fibresand and soft going:
usually blinkered. *D. J. S. ffrench Davis*

SAMAHIR (USA) 3 b.f. Forest Wildcat (USA) 120 – Saabga (USA) 83 (Woodman **62**
(USA) 126) [2007 71: 7d⁵ 8.2g⁵ p7g⁶ p10g⁶ Nov 30] sturdy filly: underwent surgery for
hairline fracture of leg after only start at 2 yrs: should stay 7f: raced only on polytrack and good ground or softer. *T. T. Clement*

SAMARINDA (USA) 4 ch.g. Rahy (USA) 115 – Munnaya (USA) 101 (Nijinsky **96**
(CAN) 138) [2007 76: p10g² p10g⁴ p8.6g* 8m p8g* p8g* p8g* p8g³ 8g³ p8g Oct 12] **a102**
good-topped gelding: useful performer: much improved in 2007, winning handicaps at
Wolverhampton in March, Kempton in June and July and minor event at Lingfield (by
head from Montpellier) later in July: good close third to Magical Music in valuable
handicap at Kempton next start: effective at 1m/1¼m: acts on polytrack, easily best effort
on turf on good going. *Mrs P. Sly*

SAMDANIYA 3 b.f. Machiavellian (USA) 123 – Cloud Castle 119 (In The Wings 128) **73**
[2007 79: 8.2m 6s 7m⁵ 9.7m* 9.7m⁵ 11.5g Sep 18] good-bodied filly: fair performer: won
handicap at Folkestone in August: stays 9.7f (well held over 11.5f): acts on good to firm
ground: sometimes races freely. *C. E. Brittain*

SAMIRA GOLD (FR) 3 ch.f. Gold Away (IRE) 125 – Capework (USA) (El Gran **107**
Senor (USA) 136) [2007 8.1m* 9.1m* 10.1m² 12g 9.9g* 10.1g* 12s³ Oct 13] €65,000Y:
useful-looking filly: second foal: dam unraced out of half-sister to high-class French
1¼m and 13.5f winner Marie de Litz and dam of Polar Falcon: useful performer: won
maiden at Haydock and handicap at Ayr in June, listed handicap at Goodwood (by ½
length from Cliche) in August and listed race at Yarmouth (beat Shorthand by 1½ lengths)
in September: creditable 1¾ lengths third to Trick Or Treat in Princess Royal Stakes at
Ascot final outing, staying on well: stays 1½m: acts on soft and good to firm ground:
edgy sort: held up. *L. M. Cumani*

SAMIZDAT (FR) 4 b.g. Soviet Star (USA) 128 – Secret Account (FR) (Bering 136) **–**
[2007 14.1g 15.8m Jul 11] fair performer: won newcomers race at Saumur when trained
in France at 3 yrs by E. Libaud: last in handicaps in Britain in 2007, leaving H. Morrison
in between: stays 15f: raced only on good/good to soft going: blinkered/visored. *James Moffatt*

SAM LORD 3 ch.g. Observatory (USA) 131 – My Mariam 79 (Salse (USA) 128) [2007 **81**
86: 8.3m 9.9g 9.8m⁴ Jun 5] stocky, close-coupled gelding: fairly useful performer: respectable efforts in handicaps in 2007: may prove best at short of 1¼m: acts on good to firm
ground: sold 27,000 gns and joined A. King. *J. H. M. Gosden*

SAMMY THE SNAKE (IRE) 2 b.c. (Feb 2) Diktat 126 – Love Emerald (USA) **83 p**
(Mister Baileys 123) [2007 5v* Mar 25] €35,000F: second foal: dam unraced half-sister
to useful Irish performer up to 9f Lil's Boy, from family of Mr Prospector: 12/1 and ran
loose at start, won maiden at the Curragh in March by ½ length from Scupio, rallying:
suffered strained suspensory on gallops after, but was back in light work by end of year:
will stay 6f/7f: should improve. *B. W. Duke*

SAMORRA (IRE) 3 b.f. In The Wings 128 – Walesiana (GER) (Star Appeal 133) **80**
[2007 74p: 9g 9.9g a8f⁶ Dec 20] well-made filly: fairly useful form: better than result in
handicaps first 2 starts in 2007 (not knocked about), then left M. Tregoning: should stay
1¼m. *D. J. Selvaratnam, UAE*

SAM'S CROSS (IRE) 2 b.c. (Mar 6) Cape Cross (IRE) 129 – Fancy Lady 99 (Cad- **89**
eaux Genereux 131) [2007 6f² 6m* 7d³ 6g Oct 27] €95,000Y: rather leggy colt: first foal:
dam, 2-y-o 6f winner, out of half-sister to smart 1m/1¼m performer Magellan: fairly
useful form: won maiden at Goodwood in September: stiff tasks in minor event at Ascot
(good if remote third behind Confront and Stimulation) and listed race at Doncaster: will
prove best up to 7f: acts on firm and good to soft going. *W. R. Swinburn*

SAMSONS SON 3 b.g. Primo Valentino (IRE) 116 – Santiburi Girl 77 (Casteddu 111) **91**
[2007 p7g p8g 7m³ 7.1g 7d* 7g* 8m³ 7.6g 9g⁵ 12f* Sep 25] close-coupled gelding: third
foal: half-brother to 5-y-o Resplendent Nova and winner in Greece by Foxhound: dam 7f
(at 2 yrs) to 11f winner: fairly useful performer: won maiden at Yarmouth in June, and
handicaps at Newmarket in July and Folkestone in September: effective at 7f to 1½m:
acts on firm and good to soft ground. *J. R. Best*

SAM'S SECRET 5 b.m. Josr Algarhoud (IRE) 118 – Twilight Time (Aragon 118) **84**
[2007 73: 8m* 7m* 7.5m⁴ 8m* 8m* 7.1m* 7m⁶ 8m² 8g⁶ Sep 19] quite good-topped mare:
fairly useful performer: successful 5 times in 2007, namely sellers at Musselburgh and
Redcar in May, and handicaps at Musselburgh in July and Redcar and Musselburgh in
August: free-going sort, stays 1m: acts on polytrack and firm ground: tried in visor/cheek-
pieces: tough. *G. A. Swinbank*

SAM

SAMUEL 3 ch.c. Sakhee (USA) 136 – Dolores 111 (Danehill (USA) 126) [2007 54: **111**
11m³ 11.9m² 13m³ 14g² 14.6m Sep 15] lengthy colt: on weak side at 3 yrs: smart maiden:
best effort when length third to Tranquil Tiger in listed race at Newmarket third start,
switching left before finishing well: respectable 6 lengths second to Tungsten Strike in
similar event at Goodwood next time, plenty to do: will be suited in St Leger at Doncaster
final outing: will stay 2m: acts on good to firm ground. *J. L. Dunlop*

SAMUEL CHARLES 9 b.g. Green Desert (USA) 127 – Hejraan (USA) 73 (Alydar **80**
(USA)) [2007 89: p8.6g p8.6g p8g* p8g⁶ p9.5g⁵ p8g* p8.6g⁴ p8.6g² 10g p8.6g³ p7.1g*
p7g² p8.6g² p8.6g* p8g³ p7.1g* p7g* p8g⁴ p8g⁵ p7g Dec 29] tall gelding: fairly useful
performer: won claimers (4) and handicaps (2) at Lingfield and Wolverhampton between
February/October: effective at 7f to 8.6f: acts on all-weather, firm and good to soft going:
wears headgear: sometimes slowly away: carries head awkwardly. *C. R. Dore*

SAMURAI WARRIOR 2 br.g. (Jan 30) Beat All (USA) 120 – Ma Vie 69 (Salse **70**
(USA) 128) [2007 7g p8.6g² p7g Oct 23] compact gelding: fair maiden: second at Wolverhampton: stays 8.6f. *P. J. Makin*

SAMURAI WAY 5 b.g. Darshaan 133 – Truly Special 116 (Caerleon (USA) 132) [2007 **111**
79: 10m² 12m* 12m² 14g² 14g² 16d* 18d Oct 20] angular gelding: smart performer,
lightly raced: much improved in 2007, winning maiden at Thirsk (very easily) in May and
handicap at Ascot (beat Gabier by 2½ lengths) in September: also ran well when runner-
up in between, notably behind Regal Flush in Old Borough Cup at Haydock: poorly
drawn when well held in Cesarewitch at Newmarket final start: should stay 2¼m: acts on
good to firm and good to soft going: sold 100,000 gns, and gelded. *L. M. Cumani*

SAMYA 3 b.f. Invincible Spirit (IRE) 121 – Special Society (IRE) (Imp Society (USA)) **98**
[2007 6m* 6m* 8g* 8m⁵ 7g 7d Oct 18] lengthy ex-Italian filly: third foal: half-sister to
Italian 2003 2-y-o 7.5f/9f winner Valperto (by Inchinor): dam Italian 6f/7f winner: useful
performer: won maiden at Milan at 2 yrs, minor events at Pisa and Milan in March and
listed race at Rome in April: respectable fifth to Lokaloka in Premio Regina Elena at
Rome next time: behind last 2 starts in Oak Tree Stakes at Goodwood (though not
discredited on final start for E. Borromeo) and listed race at Chantilly: stays 1m: acts on
good to firm ground: has had tongue tied. *P. Bary, France*

SAN ANTONIO 7 b.g. Efisio 120 – Winnebago 63 (Kris 135) [2007 84, a98: p10g **80**
p8g 8m³ 8m 8.3g⁶ Jun 18] strong, well-made gelding: has a round action: fairly useful **a86**
handicapper nowadays: in-and-out form in 2007: stays 1m: acts on polytrack, soft and
firm going: usually blinkered: tried in cheekpieces: often races prominently. *Mrs P. Sly*

SA NAU 4 b.g. Generous (IRE) 139 – Trellis Bay 100 (Sadler's Wells (USA) 132) [2007 **66**
67: p13.9g⁵ 14.1m⁶ 14.1m³ 16f⁴ 14.1m⁴ 17.1d² 16.2m⁴ 16.1m⁴ 16d Oct 11] rather leggy,
quite good-topped gelding: fair handicapper: stays 17f: acts on firm and good to soft
going. *T. Keddy*

SANBUCH 3 b.c. Tobougg (IRE) 125 – Monte Calvo 85 (Shirley Heights 130) [2007 **111 +**
83p: p9.5g³ 11g⁴ 11.9m⁴ 11m* 12f² 12m² 12m² Nov 10] strong, lengthy colt: type to carry
condition: progressive form in handicaps in 2007, winning at Goodwood (visored, by ½
length from Coeur de Lionne): good efforts when runner-up after at York (2½ lengths
behind Philanthropy), Newmarket (beaten ½ length by Malt Or Mash) and Doncaster
(November Handicap, beaten 1½ lengths by last-named rival): will stay 1¾m/2m: raced
only on polytrack and good or firmer ground: not entirely straightforward. *L. M. Cumani*

SANDALPHON (USA) 4 b.g. King Cugat (USA) 122 – Noumea (USA) (Plugged —
Nickle (USA)) [2007 p8g⁴ Mar 23] well held in 2 bumpers: 20/1, tailed off in maiden at
Lingfield on Flat debut, missing break: sold £450 in August. *J. A. Geake*

SANDARKAN (USA) 3 b.g. Rahy (USA) 115 – True Fantasy (USA) (Seeking The —
Gold (USA)) [2007 8f⁶ Aug 8] good-topped gelding: 20/1, tailed-off last in maiden at
Pontefract. *G. A. Swinbank*

SAND CAT 4 b.g. Cadeaux Genereux 131 – Desert Lynx (IRE) 79 (Green Desert (USA) **94**
127) [2007 7.5g 6g⁴ 6.5g³ a7f 5g 7g 6g p6g p5g⁵ p7g p6g³ p6m Dec 9] smallish, strong
gelding: fairly useful handicapper: left C. Wroe in UAE after fifth start: creditable third at
Lingfield penultimate start: effective at 6f to 8.5f: acts on dirt/polytrack and good to firm
going: visored once. *G. L. Moore*

SAN DENG 5 gr.g. Averti (IRE) 117 – Miss Mirror 77 (Magic Mirror 105) [2007 72: **59**
12m⁴ Apr 25] tall gelding: fair handicapper at 4 yrs: below form only start on Flat in
2007: stays 1½m: acts on polytrack, good to firm and good to soft going: possibly none
too resolute. *Micky Hammond*

SANDER CAMILLO (USA) 3 b.f. Dixie Union (USA) 121 – Staraway (USA) (Star **101 d**
de Naskra (USA)) [2007 116p: 7m² 8g 6m 7g Aug 3] medium-sized, well-made filly:

carried condition: fluent mover with a quick action: smart performer at 2 yrs, winning twice, including Cherry Hinton Stakes at Newmarket (by 5 lengths): just useful form when neck second to Scarlet Runner in Nell Gwyn Stakes at Newmarket on reappearance: second favourite, missed 1000 Guineas at Newmarket reportedly after being found in season on the day: very disappointing subsequently, in Poule d'Essai des Pouliches at Longchamp, July Cup at Newmarket (visored) and Oak Tree Stakes at Goodwood: should have stayed 1m: acted on good to firm going: sold 3,200,000 gns in December: reportedly visits Street Cry. *J. Noseda*

SANDERS BOY 4 gr.g. Arkadian Hero (USA) 123 – Rising of The Moon (IRE) 82 **49** (Warning 136) [2007 41: p8.6g Jan 5] leggy gelding: poor maiden: seems to stay 8.6f: acts on all-weather, probably on good to firm going. *J. R. Norton*

SANDIES CHOICE 2 ch.f. (Feb 28) Tobougg (IRE) 125 – Nijmah 71 (Halling (USA) – 133) [2007 5m⁵ 6g 6s 6m Sep 18] 5,000Y: first foal: dam, maiden, half-sister to smart 7f/1m winner On The Ridge: little form. *M. Brittain*

SAND MAIDEN (IRE) 2 ch.f. (Apr 13) Desert Prince (IRE) 130 – Maka (USA) (Die- **58** sis 133) [2007 6s 7m 7g⁵ 7.5m⁶ Sep 11] €7,000Y: lengthy filly: third foal: dam unraced sister to very smart 1¼m performer Knifebox: modest maiden: will stay 1m: acts on good to firm going. *T. D. Easterby*

SAND REPEAL (IRE) 5 b.g. Revoque (IRE) 122 – Columbian Sand (IRE) (Salmon **73** Leap (USA) 131) [2007 77: f14g³ f12g³ p16g³ 18g⁶ 16g² 15.4g* 16.2s⁴ 14.1m⁴ 12s 12d⁴ 16s⁵ f12d⁴ Dec 14] leggy gelding: fair handicapper: won apprentice event at Folkestone in June: stays easy 2m: acts on all-weather, heavy and good to firm ground: in cheekpieces final 4-y-o outing, visored nowadays: usually races prominently. *Miss J. Feilden*

SANDREY (IRE) 3 b.g. Noverre (USA) 125 – Boudica (IRE) (Alhaarth (USA) 126) **91** [2007 80: 6g* 6m 6m p7g Oct 24] useful-looking gelding: fairly useful performer: won handicap at Lingfield in May: little impact in similar events next 3 starts, though raced in unfavoured group and not clear run on second occasion: will prove best up to 7f: raced only on polytrack and good/good to firm going: said to have finished lame second outing: gelded after final start. *P. W. Chapple-Hyam*

SANDS CROONER (IRE) 4 b.g. Imperial Ballet (IRE) 110 – Kurfuffle (Bluebird **67** (USA) 125) [2007 –, a80: p5g⁵ p6g⁴ p7.1g p6g f5g p5g 5.1d⁴ p6g⁶ p5.1g⁵ 5g 5.1g* 5.2m⁶ **a76** 5.1g 5.1d p5m* p5.1s⁵ Dec 20] workmanlike gelding: fair handicapper: won at Bath in July and Lingfield in December: best at 5f/6f: acts on all-weather, soft and good to firm going: visored: formerly tongue tied: has hung: moody. *D. Shaw*

SANDS OF BARRA (IRE) 4 gr.g. Marju (IRE) 127 – Purple Risks (FR) 80 (Take **81** Risks (FR) 116) [2007 82, a73: 8.1m 7m 7m⁵ 7.1g² 7.1g 7m 7.5g 7m 7g 7.6m* 7.1d² 7.2s* 7.1m⁶ p7.1g⁵ 7.2s Oct 26] quite good-topped gelding: fairly useful handicapper: won at Chester in August and Ayr in September: effective at 7f/easy 1m: acts on polytrack, firm and soft going: tried blinkered/in cheekpieces. *I. W. McInnes*

SANDWITH 4 ch.g. Perryston View 114 – Bodfari Times 72 (Clantime 101) [2007 75: **73** p5.1g⁴ p5g 5f 5d 5f⁵ 5g⁶ 5d 5m* p5.1g* 5g⁵ p5.1g⁵ Dec 3] fair handicapper: won at Musselburgh in September and Wolverhampton in October: best at 5f: acts on polytrack, firm and good to soft ground: wears cheekpieces nowadays: tended to wander fourth start. *J. S. Wainwright*

SANDY PAR 2 ch.g. (Apr 27) No Excuse Needed 123 – Nesting 47 (Thatching 131) **60** [2007 5.1g² 6g³ 5m 5.5m p6g Oct 10] tall gelding: modest maiden: should prove best at 5f/6f: acts on polytrack and good to firm going. *P. Winkworth*

SANGFROID 3 gr.g. With Approval (CAN) – Affaire d'Amour 100 (Hernando (FR) **57 §** 127) [2007 –p: 12.1s⁴ 16.2s 14.1m⁵ 12g* 14.1m p12m Oct 3] angular gelding: modest handicapper: won at Catterick in August: should stay beyond 1½m: acts on good and good to firm ground: blinkered final outing: ungenuine: sold 14,000 gns. *Sir Mark Prescott*

SANGREAL 3 ch.f. Medicean 128 – La Belle Dominique 76 (Dominion 123) [2007 **65 d** 66: 8m⁴ 8.1m 7.1g 8.5s 8g⁴ 8.5g 9g Oct 5] neat filly: fair maiden: well below best after reappearance: seems to stay easy 1m: acts on all-weather, soft and good to firm going: sold 1,200 gns, sent to Denmark. *K. R. Burke*

SAN SILVESTRO (IRE) 2 b.c. (Apr 24) Fayruz 116 – Skehana (IRE) 69 (Mukad- **68** damah (USA) 125) [2007 7g* Nov 6] 40,000Y, 14,500 2-y-o: compact colt: first foal: dam 2-y-o 7f winner, half-sister to 8-y-o Fayr Jag: 6/1, won maiden at Catterick by a head, knowing his job: may prove best up to 7f. *Mrs A. Duffield*

SANTA CLARA 2 b.f. (Apr 25) Night Shift (USA) – Mena 58 (Blakeney 126) [2007 **59** 6m 6v³ p7g f6d⁴ Dec 14] seventh foal: half-sister to 3 winners, including 1m/1¼m winner

My Maite (by Komaite): dam maiden (probably stayed 11.5f): modest maiden: best efforts at 6f: acts on fibresand and heavy going. *Jane Chapple-Hyam*

SANTAVERTI 4 br.g. Averti (IRE) 117 – Santa Vida (USA) 64 (St Jovite (USA) 135) **a63**
[2007 p10g⁵ p10g² p12g⁵ 11g 10s p6g Jun 6] modest form in maidens first 3 outings, no form after: stays 1½m: acts on polytrack: blinkered last 2 starts. *G. L. Moore*

SANTERA (IRE) 3 br.f. Gold Away (IRE) 125 – Sainte Gig (FR) (Saint Cyrien (FR) **49**
128) [2007 –: 12m⁴ 10d p8.6g⁶ p9.5g Dec 13] poor maiden. *Mrs A. Duffield*

SAOIRSE ABU (USA) 2 ch.f. (Mar 20) Mr Greeley (USA) 122 – Out Too Late **108**
(USA) (Future Storm (USA)) [2007 6g³ 6g* 6d² 6s⁵ 7s³ 6v* 7g* 8d³ Sep 29]
Jim Bolger's repetition of a winning formula with New Approach, who followed the similarly-bred Teofilo, wasn't the only one in his team of two-year-olds. A year after his Mr Greeley filly Finsceal Beo had proved herself conclusively the best of her age in Europe, with successes in the Prix Marcel Boussac and Rockfel Stakes, Bolger produced another filly by the same sire out of the hat. In terms of the prestige of the races she won in her first season, Saoirse Abu outpointed her predecessor as her tally included two Group 1s, the Phoenix Stakes and Moyglare Stud Stakes. However, the form she showed was some way behind that of Finsceal Beo and her prospects of emulating the latter with a classic victory, let alone two, are not very high. Still, credit where it is due—in a tough campaign the genuine Saoirse Abu did herself and her trainer proud, earning nearly £300,000 and more than recouping her 260,000-dollar purchase price as a yearling.

With just one win from five starts and defeats in lesser races on her last three runs, Saoirse Abu started the 25/1 rank outsider of six runners in the Independent Waterford Wedgwood Phoenix Stakes at the Curragh in August. Her only victory, an easy one by four lengths, had come in a twelve-runner maiden at the Curragh at

Independent Waterford Wedgwood Phoenix Stakes, the Curragh—in very testing conditions Saoirse Abu (blinkers) floors the odds laid on Henrythenavigator; Elletelle is third and The Loan Express fourth

Moyglare Stud Stakes, the Curragh—Saoirse Abu captures another Group 1 from a Ballydoyle odds-on shot, this time Listen; Mad About You (No.5) takes third off Albabilia (rail)

the end of May on her second appearance. She was then beaten in the Swordlestown Stud Sprint Stakes at Naas, in which You'resothrilling beat her by a length and in listed races at the Curragh (fifth to Listen) and Leopardstown. In the last-named she started at longer odds than her stable-companion Kayd Kodaun and kept on to be third behind Triskel. Saoirse Abu's form was the best part of a stone below that usually required to win the Phoenix Stakes, but one difference was that Saoirse Abu wore headgear for the first time in the Phoenix, and perhaps this was the key to her improvement. Her five rivals included two fillies who had played a prominent role in the Queen Mary at Royal Ascot, winner Elletelle and third-placed The Loan Express. The colts were Coventry Stakes winner Henrythenavigator, 2/1-on to give Aidan O'Brien his ninth Phoenix Stakes victory, listed winner Warsaw from the same stable and the sole challenger from Britain, five-length Ripon maiden winner Captain Royale. Saoirse Abu was close up on the rail throughout and, after Henrythenavigator took it up a furlong from home, she rallied under strong driving and got on top near the finish to score by a length. Elletelle was third, nearly two lengths away. Only one other winner of the Phoenix Stakes, Pianissimo in 1969, had started at such long odds in the long history of the race. Bolger, who had trained another filly, Eva Luna, to win the race in 1994, memorably summed up the outcome. He said: 'It took Henry The Navigator fifteen attempts to get round the Cape of Good Hope, so I decided it was worth having a shot at his namesake. We were hoping it might happen, but I can't say I was expecting it.' The headgear probably was a factor, but the heavy ground might well have assisted Saoirse Abu as well as inconveniencing some of the other runners. Henrythenavigator for one was never travelling with any real fluency.

Judged by the betting for the Moyglare Stud Stakes at the Curragh three weeks later, the Phoenix Stakes form had been taken with a pinch of salt. Blinkered once more, Saoirse Abu was only third favourite of nine behind odds-on Listen and Albabilia, successful in the Sweet Solera Stakes, just ahead of Silver Flash Stakes runner-up Mad About You. Two of the other contenders, Allicansayis Wow and

Solas Na Greine, were also trained by Bolger. Never far away, Saoirse Abu took it up just over a furlong out and stayed on strongly to beat Listen by a length and a half with Mad About You third. The Moyglare was inaugurated in 1973 and this was only the second time a filly had completed the Phoenix-Moyglare double, Minstrella in 1976 being the first. There were no excuses for any of the beaten horses this time, unless a lack of speed over a distance too short can be used as a possible excuse for Listen. Seven furlongs proved no problem for Saoirse Abu and her run in the Fillies' Mile later in September showed that she stays a mile. The trip at Ascot suited Listen much better than the seven furlongs of the Moyglare, though, and she and the favourite Proviso had little difficulty seeing off Saoirse Abu. Equipped with a visor, Saoirse Abu was always prominent and led just over two furlongs out, though the writing was on the wall even then. Listen and Proviso swept by and, although Saoirse Abu kept on, finishing five lengths clear of the fourth, she was no match for the principals and was beaten three and half lengths. To all intents and purposes the Fillies' Mile exposed the limitations of Saoirse Abu, a sturdy filly who acts on heavy going and has yet to race on ground firmer than good. She will need to improve significantly to beat the leaders of her generation as a three-year-old.

Saoirse Abu (USA) (ch.f. Mar 20, 2005)	Mr Greeley (USA) (ch 1992)	Gone West (b 1984)	Mr Prospector
			Secrettame
		Long Legend (ch 1978)	Reviewer
			Lianga
	Out Too Late (USA) (ch 1997)	Future Storm (ch 1990)	Storm Cat
			Sea Sands
		Morning Has Broken (ch 1974)	Prince John
			A Wind Is Rising

Ennistown Stud's "Saoirse Abu"

A yearling by Mr Greeley sold for 2,200,000 dollars in Kentucky during the summer, more than eight times the sum Saoirse Abu had made at Keeneland in 2006. Finsceal Beo had cost only €340,000, so clearly Bolger has managed to obtain excellent value. Another Mr Greeley filly, a foal, was sold for 200,000 guineas at the Newmarket December Sales and will eventually go into training with Bolger. Saoirse Abu is the third foal of Out Too Late, whose only other runner, So Busted (by Tiznow), has won twice from twenty starts in the States. Considering that Saoirse Abu had already won the Phoenix Stakes and the Moyglare Stud Stakes, it was slightly surprising that her yearling half-brother by Indian Charlie should fetch only 50,000 dollars at Keeneland in September. Out Too Late never ran, while the next dam, Morning Has Broken, was twice unplaced. Another daughter of Morning Has Broken, Morning Devotion, became the dam of Sun Chariot winner Red Slippers (herself dam of Prix de Diane winner West Wind) and of Oaks and Irish Derby winner Balanchine. A good pedigree coupled with her racing record gives Saoirse Abu plenty in her favour for when she is retired to stud, whatever she achieves as a three-year-old. *J. S. Bolger, Ireland*

SAOODAH (IRE) 2 b.f. (Mar 18) Green Desert (USA) 127 – Saeedah 75 (Bustino 136) [2007 5g p6g⁵ 6m⁶ Aug 9] small, sturdy filly: fifth foal: sister to fairly useful 2003 2-y-o 6f winner Dallaah: dam twice-raced sister to smart performer up to 1¼m Bulaxie and half-sister to very smart performer up to 1½m Zimzalabim: modest maiden: best effort at 6f on polytrack. *M. A. Jarvis*   **59**

SAPPHIRE DREAM 5 b.m. Mind Games 121 – Bombay Sapphire (Be My Chief (USA) 122) [2007 –, a46: 6s Jun 16] close-coupled, quite good-topped mare: poor in 2006: well held sole start at 5 yrs: tried in visor/cheekpieces. *A. Bailey*   **–**

SARAH PARK (IRE) 2 ch.f. (Apr 23) Redback 116 – Brillano (FR) 75 (Desert King (IRE) 129) [2007 p6g⁵ 7g 6m p8g Sep 15] 15,000Y: first foal: dam 2-y-o 7f winner: modest maiden: stays 1m: seems a lazy sort. *B. J. Meehan*   **57**

SARAH'S ART (IRE) 4 gr.g. City On A Hill (USA) 114 – Treasure Bleue (IRE) (Treasure Kay 114) [2007 79: p6g p5.1g 5.3m p7g⁴ p7g Nov 21] lengthy gelding: left Miss D. McHale and off 5 months, form in 2007 only when winning at Kempton in September: effective at 5f to 7f: acts on polytrack and firm going: usually blinkered (not last 2 starts): sometimes slowly away: said to have finished lame final outing: has looked wayward. *Stef Liddiard*   **61**

SARAH'S BOY 2 ch.g. (Mar 14) Nayef (USA) 129 – Bella Bianca (IRE) 78 (Barathea (IRE) 127) [2007 8d 8d Oct 19] very big, strong gelding: well held in maidens. *S. Dow*   **–**

SARAH'S FIRST 2 ch.f. (Apr 27) Cadeaux Genereux 131 – Band (USA) (Northern Dancer) [2007 8.2m 8d⁵ p7m⁶ Nov 1] 125,000Y: strong, lengthy filly: half-sister to several winners, including 1995 2-y-o 5f/6f (Cherry Hinton Stakes) winner Applaud (by Rahy) and 1¼m winner Glam Rock (by Nashwan), both useful: dam, US maiden, out of high-class sprinter Swingtime: fair maiden: fifth to Mukhber at Newmarket: stays 1m. *E. A. L. Dunlop*   **68**

SARA MANA MOU 4 b.f. Medicean 128 – Sarabah (IRE) 83 (Ela-Mana-Mou 132) [2007 41: f14g Mar 28] big, strong filly: poor maiden: well held sole 4-y-o outing: retired, reportedly in foal to Dubawi. *J. G. Portman*   **–**

SARANOME (IRE) 2 b.c. (Apr 10) Statue of Liberty (USA) 115 – My Gray (FR) (Danehill (USA) 126) [2007 6.5d 5.1g⁴ 5.1g Nov 7] €31,000F, 40,000Y: big colt: fifth foal: half-brother to 5-y-o Nepro and 5f (at 2 yrs) to 1m winner Mrs Moh (both fairly useful, by Orpen): dam French maiden: fair maiden: not knocked about all starts (within a month), fourth to Masada at Bath: will be suited by 7f/1m: type to progress in handicaps. *R. Charlton*   **71 p**

SARATEE 2 b.f. (Apr 11) Mark of Esteem (IRE) 137 – Salalah 62 (Lion Cavern (USA) 117) [2007 7.5g⁶ 7.1g⁶ Oct 2] 22,000Y: fourth foal: half-sister to useful 6f (including at 2 yrs) winner Intoxicating (by Mujahid) and 1½m winner Faraway Echo (by Second Empire): dam 7f winner: modest form in maidens: will stay at least 1m. *C. E. Brittain*   **55 +**

SARRAAF (IRE) 11 ch.g. Perugino (USA) 84 – Blue Vista (IRE) (Pennine Walk 120) [2007 64: 8.3d⁴ 9.2m⁴ 8s 7.1m² 9d⁴ 9m 7.1g p8.6g 8g⁴ p7.1g² p8.6g³ p8.6s Dec 21] smallish, strong gelding: modest performer: effective at 7f to 1¼m: acts on all-weather and any turf going: tried in blinkers/visor. *I. Semple*   **63**

SARWIN (USA) 4 gr. or ro.g. Holy Bull (USA) 134 – Olive The Twist (USA) 94 (Theatrical 128) [2007 60, a70: p9.5g² p9.5g* Feb 23] strong gelding: fairly useful handicapper   **–**   **a76**

on all-weather, modest at best on turf: won at Wolverhampton in February: stays 1¼m: acts on polytrack and good to firm ground: has looked no easy ride. *W. J. Musson*

SASSY GAL (IRE) 2 ch.f. (Feb 15) King's Best (USA) 132 – Dancing Prize (IRE) 99   **82**
(Sadler's Wells (USA) 132) [2007 6m³ 8s³ 7g² 7d 7d² p8g* Oct 31] good-topped filly: half-sister to several winners, notably 1¼m/1½m winner Dancing Phantom (by Darshaan), 4-y-o Marsam and UAE 7.5f to 1¼m winner Seeking The Prize (by Zafonic), all useful: dam, maiden (stayed 11.5f), half-sister to smart performer up to 9f Polar Bear: fairly useful performer: best effort when seventh to Eva's Request in C. L. Weld Park Stakes at the Curragh: placed in maidens other starts, then won at Kempton in December: will stay 1¼m: acts on polytrack, soft and good to firm going. *John Joseph Murphy, Ireland*

SATAN'S SISTER 6 ch.m. Tout Ensemble – Winter Greeting (Hello Gorgeous (USA)   **–**
128) [2007 11.5s 10.5m Aug 9] leggy mare: second reported foal: dam unraced: well held in maidens. *Ian Williams*

SATIN BRAID 3 b.f. Diktat 126 – Beading 82 (Polish Precedent (USA) 131) [2007 73:   **78**
8.2m⁴ 7m⁴ 8.1m⁴ 8.3m p8g p8g* p8.6d² p7g Dec 16] well-made filly: fair handicapper: left A. Carroll after fourth start: won apprentice event at Lingfield in November: stays 1m: acts on polytrack and good to firm ground. *D. R. C. Elsworth*

SATINDRA (IRE) 3 b.g. Lil's Boy (USA) 109 – Voronova (IRE) 71 (Sadler's Wells   **71**
(USA) 132) [2007 63: 7m 10s p9.5g⁶ 10.1d³ p9.5g³ p11g³ f11d* f12g⁵ Dec 27] fair performer: left J. Bolger in Ireland 800 gns after second start: won maiden at Southwell in December: stays 11f: acts on all-weather and good to soft going: often in cheekpieces/tongue tied. *John A. Harris*

SATULAGI (USA) 3 b.f. Officer (USA) 120 – Shawgatny (USA) 83 (Danzig Con-   **97**
nection (USA)) [2007 98: a7f² a8f 8m 8g⁵ 8m 8g 8.1m 12s Oct 13] good-topped filly: useful performer: several creditable efforts in 2007, including when second to Greetings in minor event at Nad Al Sheba and ninth in 1000 Guineas at Newmarket on third start: likely to stay 1¼m: acts on dirt, firm and good to soft going: tends to race lazily. *J. S. Moore*

SATURDAY BOY 2 b.c. (Apr 11) Josr Algarhoud (IRE) 118 – Prideway (IRE) 78§   **58**
(Pips Pride 117) [2007 6m 6s 6m 7.5g p8.6g p8.6g p8.6g⁴ Dec 4] sturdy colt: modest maiden: stays 8.6f: acts on polytrack. *Paul Green*

SATWA BARON 3 b.c. Singspiel (IRE) 133 – Crown of Spring (USA) (Chief's Crown   **–**
(USA)) [2007 p6g p6g 10d Jul 3] no form in maidens, leaving D. Elsworth after second outing. *D. J. Daly*

SATWA QUEEN (FR) 5 ch.m. Muhtathir 126 – Tolga (USA) 75 (Irish River (FR)   **115**
131) [2007 120: 10g² 8m² 10d* 10g* Oct 7]

The Prix de l'Abbaye has long been almost an 'offshore' British pattern race. But if the latest Arc meeting was anything to go by, the five other Group 1s on the card are also becoming dominated numerically by horses from outside France. French-trained horses accounted for just six of the seventeen runners in the Abbaye (four of them from one stable, that of Robert Collet), only four of the ten in the Prix Marcel Boussac were French-trained, just one of the eight in the Prix Jean-Luc Lagardere, five of the eleven in the Prix de l'Opera, four of the twelve in the Arc itself and two of the six in the Prix du Cadran. That made just twenty-two French-trained horses among the sixty-four horses who contested the six races. The remainder were split between Britain (twenty-six), Ireland (eleven) and Germany (five) and there were winners trained in all four of the countries represented. There were also just four French-trained horses in the thirteen-strong field for the highlight of the weekend's Saturday card, the Prix de la Foret in which runners from Germany, Britain, France and Ireland took the first four places. In a year when the idea of holding the Breeders' Cup in Europe was seemingly finally ruled out, and there was a debate about Britain staging its own version of the Breeders' Cup or some sort of end-of-season equivalent, it could be said that a European Breeders' Cup in all but name is already well established (although the Prix du Cadran is to be run on Saturday from now on, making way for a race for Arab horses on the Arc day programme).

The Prix de l'Opera Casino Barriere d'Enghien Les Bains, the Group 1 on Arc day with the greatest percentage of French-trained runners, had a French-trained, and French-bred, winner. Satwa Queen was contesting the Opera for the third year running. As a three-year-old she had finished fifth behind the shock British-trained winner Kinnaird after winning the Prix Vanteaux at Longchamp and Prix de Psyche at Deauville and coming seventh in the Prix de Diane. Satwa Queen improved as a four-year-old and, in a much stronger renewal of the Opera, was beaten three quarters of a length by Mandesha, with Oaks winner Alexandrova third. Satwa Queen also won the Prix Jean Romanet at Deauville as a four-year-old, when her four other appearances were outside Europe. She finished second twice at the Dubai International Carnival early in the year and, after the Opera, wasn't entirely discredited when fifth to Ouija Board in the Breeders' Cup Filly & Mare Turf and sixth to Pride in the Hong Kong Cup.

Satwa Queen was given a less ambitious campaign in the latest season, a light one aimed specifically at making it third time lucky in the Prix de l'Opera. She made an eyecatching reappearance in the Prix Allez France at Chantilly in May, giving 9 lb to most of her rivals and threading her way through the field from the rear to be beaten a length by the more handily-ridden Macleya. The following month Satwa Queen started one of the co-favourites for the Windsor Forest Stakes at Royal Ascot but she failed to settle in the falsely-run mile contest and was beaten three lengths into second by Nannina. Back at a mile and a quarter, Satwa Queen was successful for the third year running at Deauville's August meeting when winning the Prix Jean Romanet for the second time. It was a closely-run thing, however, as Satwa Queen justified favouritism by a short head, in a race in which a stronger pace would probably have suited her better. Even if the photo-finish verdict had gone against her, though, there was a good chance that Satwa Queen would have got the race in the stewards' room as the British-trained runner-up Bahia Breeze hung into her in the final furlong.

Satwa Queen came out best in another tight finish in the Prix de l'Opera in which all ten of her rivals were three-year-old fillies. With One Thousand Guineas winner Finsceal Beo and Oaks winner Light Shift in the line-up, the latter starting favourite at 17/10 ahead of Satwa Queen on 3/1, her task wasn't straightforward, though the well-being of both classic winners was in some doubt and the leading three-year-old middle-distance filly Peeping Fawn and the previous year's winner

Prix de l'Opera Casino Barriere d'Enghien Les Bains, Longchamp—on her third attempt at the race Satwa Queen (between horses), the only one above the age of three in the field, gains her first Group 1 success; she has a head and the same to spare over Promising Lead and Legerete (nearest camera); German Oaks winner Mystic Lips is fourth

Mandesha (running in the Arc instead) were absentees. French classic form was represented by the Prix de Diane third Diyakalanie and the disappointing favourite at Chantilly, Vadapolina, though both had been out of the money in the Prix Vermeille last time, while the first two from Germany's Oaks, Mystic Lips and Dominante, were also in the field. None of those with form in classics figured in the photo-finish to the Opera, Satwa Queen's victory over Salisbury listed winner Promising Lead and the Vermeille fourth Legerete, by a head and the same, requiring no improvement on the form she had shown in defeat in the race the year before. Promising Lead looked the most likely winner when sent on over a furlong out but Satwa Queen responded well to collar her on the line as Legerete finished best of all from a long way back on their outside. Less than four lengths covered the first seven home, with the front-running Mystic Lips holding on for fourth ahead of Finsceal Beo and Light Shift.

	Muhtathir (ch 1995)	Elmaamul (ch 1987)	Diesis
			Modena
		Majmu (b 1988)	Al Nasr
Satwa Queen (FR) (ch.m. 2002)			Affirmative Fable
	Tolga (USA) (ch 1982)	Irish River (ch 1976)	Riverman
			Irish Star
		Light of Realm (b 1977)	Realm
			Some Thing

Satwa Queen's racing career ended on a high note in the Opera. The option of sending her to race in Hong Kong again was rejected in favour of a date at Tattersalls December Sales, one that proved far more lucrative for her owner as she was sold for 3,400,000 guineas to Sheikh Mohammed. That broke the European record for a filly or mare in training which had been held briefly by 2006 Albany Stakes and Cherry Hinton Stakes winner Sander Camillo, sold earlier in the day, also to Sheikh Mohammed, for 3,200,000 guineas. The previous record of 3,000,000 guineas had been set by the Sun Chariot Stakes winner Spinning Queen at the same sale twelve months earlier. The European record for a broodmare is held by Magical Romance, who was sold for 4,600,000 gns, also in 2006. Satwa Queen's sire Muhtathir gained his biggest win as a five-year-old, successfully taking the place of his Godolphin stablemate Dubai Millennium in the Prix Jacques le Marois after that horse had suffered his career-ending injury eight days earlier. Muhtathir had not sired a winner at the top level until the latest season when Satwa Queen's win in the Prix de l'Opera came soon after the first of two Grade/Group 1 wins for another French-trained five-year-old, Doctor Dino, in the Man o'War Stakes at Belmont. Satwa Queen's dam Tolga was just a fair maiden for Ian Balding at seven furlongs and a mile who was sold for 42,000 guineas at the same sales twenty-two years earlier. She has produced eight winners at stud so far and they have proved a mixed bunch to say the least. Satwa Queen became Tolga's second Group 1 winner after the 1998 Criterium de Saint-Cloud winner Spadoun. He failed to progress at three, winning only in listed company and, unusually for a Group 1 winner on the Flat, ended up winning over hurdles before embarking on a career as a sire of jumpers. Another of Tolga's winners, Fier Danseur (by Fabulous Dancer), was useful over jumps in France (and at up to eleven furlongs on the Flat), while her other Flat winners (two of them in Morocco!) include Anbella (by Common Grounds), who won a seven-furlong listed race at Deauville as a two-year-old. Incidentally, Satwa Queen's full brother and stable-companion Satwa King is still seeking his first win at the age of four and ended the season in claimers. Tolga is a half-sister to the dam of the smart French miler Signe Divin and a daughter of another smart performer, the Prix des Reservoirs winner Light of Realm. Great grandam Some Thing was a sister to the Prix d'Ispahan winner La Troublerie. The leggy, close-coupled Satwa Queen was best at a mile and a quarter, though shaped as though she would have stayed further. She acted on soft ground (won on each of her three starts under those conditions) and good to firm and was held up. *J. de Roualle, France*

SATYRICON 3 b.c. Dr Fong (USA) 128 – Belladera (IRE) 82 (Alzao (USA) 117) **87** [2007 72: p7g* p8g³ p8g² p7g⁵ 8g 7m³ 7m* 7m 7m⁶ p8g⁵ p7g⁴ p7m Dec 10] sturdy colt: fairly useful handicapper: won at Kempton (apprentices) in February and Redcar (hung right) in June: stays easy 1m: raced only on polytrack and good/good to firm going: blinkered/visored. *M. Botti*

SAUCY 6 b.m. Muhtarram (USA) 125 – So Saucy 59 (Teenoso (USA) 135) [2007 56: **60**
p8g* p10g² p10g p8g³ 9.5m 10g⁵ 10m 8s 10m⁶ p10g 9m³ p9.5g Nov 22] sturdy mare:
modest handicapper: won at Kempton in January: left A. Carroll after fourth start: effective at 1m to 1½m: acts on polytrack and good to firm ground: tried blinkered early in
career: often held up. *D. Loughnane, Ireland*

SAUNDERS ENCORE 2 b.f. (Apr 20) Piccolo 121 – Magical Dancer (IRE) 53 **–**
(Magical Wonder (USA) 125) [2007 p6d⁶ Dec 6] sixth foal: sister to 3-y-o Lipocco and
fairly useful 2003 2-y-o 7f winner Scotch N' Dry: dam, 1m winner, half-sister to smart
sprinter Don't Worry Me: 25/1, well held in maiden at Wolverhampton. *M. S. Saunders*

SAUZE D'OULX 2 b.g. (Apr 7) Makbul 104 – Bewails (IRE) 53 (Caerleon (USA) **91**
132) [2007 5g⁴ 5f* 5m⁶ 5.1m⁴ 6d* 6m² 7.1m⁶ 8.1g Sep 8] 4,000Y: good-topped gelding:
tenth foal: dam twice-raced granddaughter of Yorkshire Oaks winner Attica Meli: fairly
useful performer: won maiden at Windsor in April and nursery at Leicester in July: stays
7f: acts on firm and good to soft going: sold 26,000 gns. and gelded. *B. R. Millman*

SAVANAGH FOREST (IRE) 3 b.f. Shinko Forest (IRE) – Adieu Cherie (IRE) (Bus- **47**
tino 136) [2007 –: p5g p5.1g* 5m 6m⁶ 5f² p6g Oct 23] poor performer: won 3-runner
seller at Wolverhampton in April: bred to stay 7f: acts on polytrack and firm ground.
M. Quinn

SAVANNAH 4 b.c. Sadler's Wells (USA) 132 – La Papagena (Habitat 134) [2007 104d: **–**
p12g⁵ 10m 11.9g⁴ May 12] smallish, attractive colt: useful at best: little form in 2007,
including at Lingfield: stays 1½m: acts on good to firm ground: tried blinkered. *Luke
Comer, Ireland*

SAVANNAH BAY 8 ch.g. In The Wings 128 – High Savannah 77 (Rousillon (USA) **–**
133) [2007 93: 14g 13s 18d Oct 20] good-topped gelding: one-time smart performer:
little form in 2007: tried blinkered/tongue tied. *B. Ellison*

SAVARAIN 2 b.c. (Apr 4) Rainbow Quest (USA) 134 – Frangy 77 (Sadler's Wells **87 p**
(USA) 132) [2007 8m⁴ 8d⁴ Oct 27] 100,000Y: close-coupled, quite attractive colt: fourth
foal: dam, 11.6f/1½m winner, out of half-sister to Fillies' Mile winner and Oaks runner-
up Shamshir: fairly useful form: fourth in maidens at Newmarket (promising, 5¼ lengths
behind Twice Over) and Newbury (still green): will be suited by 1¼m/1½m: sure to go on
and win races. *L. M. Cumani*

SAVETHISDANCEFORME (IRE) 2 b.f. (Mar 26) Danehill Dancer (IRE) 117 – **108 p**
Bex (USA) 116 (Explodent (USA)) [2007 7g³ 7d⁴ 6m p6g* 8g⁴ 8d* Oct 21] 330,000Y:
well-made, quite attractive filly: half-sister to several at least useful winners, including
smart French 1¼m/1½m winners Hijaz (by Sadler's Wells) and Crimson Quest (by
Rainbow Quest): dam 1m to 10.5f winner: useful form: most progressive last 3 starts,
winning maiden at Dundalk in September and listed race at the Curragh (beat Maryellen's
Spirit by 9 lengths, smooth headway to lead well over 1f out) in October: ran well when
6½ lengths fourth of 10 to Zarkava in Prix Marcel Boussac at Longchamp in between:
stays 1m: acts on polytrack and good to soft going: has had 2 handlers: capable of better
still. *A. P. O'Brien, Ireland*

SAVILE'S DELIGHT (IRE) 8 b.g. Cadeaux Genereux 131 – Across The Ice (USA) **52**
(General Holme (USA) 128) [2007 70: p6g p5.1g f6g f7g f7g⁴ f7g 5.1g⁴ 7.1s f6d⁶ Dec 11]
modest performer: left Miss Joanne Priest prior to final start: effective at 5f to 7f: acts
on all-weather, heavy and good to firm going: often wears headgear/tongue tie. *Tom
Dascombe*

*Lanwades & Staffordstown Studs Stakes, the Curragh—Savethisdanceforme shows improved form to win
by a wide margin from Maryellen's Spirit (noseband, on right) and Queen Jock (noseband, on left)*

SAVIOUR SAND (IRE) 3 b.g. Desert Sun 120 – Teacher Preacher (IRE) 37 (Taufan **82** (USA) 119) [2007 76: p6g⁶ 8m² 8d⁵ p8g p10g⁴ p9.5d³ Dec 17] good-topped gelding: fairly useful maiden: seems to stay easy 1¼m: acts on polytrack and good to firm going. *D. R. C. Elsworth*

SAVIOURS SPIRIT 6 ch.g. Komaite (USA) – Greenway Lady (Prince Daniel (USA)) **84** [2007 81, a98: p6g⁶ f6g² f2f⁵ 6f* 6m² 5.7f Jun 10] good-topped gelding: useful handi- **a95** capper on all-weather, fairly useful on turf: won at Windsor in April, doing well to overcome very slow start: effective at 5f to 7f: acts on all-weather, yet to race on heavy going but acts on any other turf: often races prominently. *T. G. Mills*

SAVOY CHAPEL 5 br.g. Xaar 132 – Royal Gift (Cadeaux Genereux 131) [2007 –, **51** a54: p8g p8g p8g² p8g p7.1g p8g⁴ p7g³ p8g⁴ p10g p8g² 8f 8f⁴ p7g 10m² 10d³ 10m⁵ 10.2s Jul 26] lengthy gelding: modest performer: stays 1m: acts on all-weather, probably on good to soft going: tried blinkered/tongue tied, often visored. *A. W. Carroll*

SAWPIT SOLITAIRE 2 gr.f. (Apr 8) Daylami (IRE) 138 – Balleta (USA) 87 (Lyp- **–** hard (USA) 132) [2007 8.2g Nov 7] €40,000Y: small filly: sister to 5-y-o Gala Evening and half-sister to several winners, including smart French/US performer up to 1m Barricade (by Riverman) and useful 1¾m winner War Cabinet (by Rainbow Quest): dam, 1m/1¼m winner (including in US), sister to Dancing Brave: tailed off in maiden at Nottingham. *J. L. Spearing*

SAWPIT SUNSHINE (IRE) 2 b.f. (Mar 10) Mujadil (USA) 119 – Curie Express **71** (IRE) 65 (Fayruz 116) [2007 5m⁴ 5.7g 6.1s³ 6s* 6s Oct 4] €30,000Y: half-sister to several winners, including 1998 2-y-o 5f winner Acuria (by Contract Law): dam 2-y-o 5f winner: fair performer: won nursery at Leicester in July: off 2½ months, seemed amiss final start: likely to stay 7f: acts on soft going. *J. L. Spearing*

SAWWAAH (IRE) 10 ch.g. Marju (IRE) 127 – Just A Mirage 76 (Green Desert (USA) **86** 127) [2007 75§: p8.6g⁴ f8g⁴ p8.6g* p10g* 7m* 8.5m⁴ 10.2m² 10s³ 10m* 10m* 8m* p8.6d² p10g² Dec 19] big, useful-looking gelding: fairly useful performer: won sellers at Wolverhampton and Lingfield in March and Catterick in April, and, having left D. Nicholls after sixth start, handicaps at Brighton and Newbury (ladies) and apprentice claimer at Brighton in June: stays easy 1¼m: acts on all-weather, firm and soft going: usually wears headgear: often slowly away, and no easy ride. *Tom Dascombe*

SAXON SAINT 4 b.g. Josr Algarhoud (IRE) 118 – Antithesis (IRE) 75 (Fairy King **–** (USA)) [2007 –: 5m 6g Jun 18] close-coupled gelding: has a quick action: fair performer at 2 yrs, lightly raced and well held since. *M. D. I. Usher*

SAYEDATI ELHASNA (IRE) 2 b.f. (Apr 22) Alhaarth (IRE) 126 – Sayedati Elja- **66** milah (USA) 64 (Mr Prospector (USA)) [2007 7s³ 7d⁶ 7g⁶ Nov 3] close-coupled filly: fourth foal: half-sister to fairly useful 2-y-o 6f winners by Green Desert, Motarassed (in 2004), later successful in Spain, and Nudrah (in 2005), and 3-y-o Mujahaz: dam, ran twice, half-sister to Derby winner Erhaab: fair form in maidens: will stay at least 1m: raced only on good going or softer. *J. L. Dunlop*

SAYYEDATI SYMPHONY (USA) 2 b.f. (May 15) Gone West (USA) – Sayyedati **87 ?** 122 (Shadeed (USA) 135) [2007 7g² 8d³ 8g⁶ Nov 3] compact filly: half-sister to several winners, including smart 2002 2-y-o 7f winner Almushahar (by Silver Hawk) and useful 2005 2-y-o winner Lonely Ahead (by Rahy): dam, 6f (Cheveley Park Stakes) to 1m (1000 Guineas) winner, half-sister to high-class 1¼m/1½m performer Golden Snake: fairly useful maiden: placed at Chester and Newbury: apparent improvement when 1¾ lengths sixth to Classic Legend in listed race at Newmarket: may stay 1m. *C. E. Brittain*

SCAMPERDALE 5 br.g. Compton Place 125 – Miss Up N Go (Gorytus (USA) 132) **83** [2007 67: p8.6g⁴ p9.5g⁶ p9.5g* p9.5g² p8.6g* 8.1g⁵ p9.5g² p8.6g³ p10g⁴ p8.6g⁵ 8.3m⁵ p9.5m⁵ p9.5d* Dec 17] good-topped gelding: fairly useful handicapper: successful in March, April and December, all at Wolverhampton: stays 1¼m: acts on polytrack and good to firm ground: often wears cheekpieces: waited with: sometimes looks awkward under pressure, but is reliable. *B. P. J. Baugh*

SCANNO (IRE) 2 b.c. (Feb 24) Captain Rio 122 – In Denial (IRE) (Maelstrom Lake **66 p** 118) [2007 5s⁵ Jul 17] €55,000F, 35,000Y: third foal: half-brother to fairly useful 2003 2-y-o 6f/7f winner Overdrawn (by Daggers Drawn): dam ran once in Ireland: 11/2, prom- inent most of way when fifth in maiden at Beverley: may prove best at 5f/6f: open to improvement. *K. R. Burke*

SCARAMOUSHCA 4 gr.g. Most Welcome 131 – Kinraddie (Wuzo (USA) 99) [2007 **60** –: f11g⁵ p13.9g³ p12.2g⁴ f14g⁵ p11g⁴ p12g Dec 12] modest maiden: left P. McEntee after fourth start: seems to stay 1¾m: raced on all-weather: tried blinkered. *G. C. Bravery*

SCARLET FLYER (USA) 4 b.g. Gilded Time (USA) – Tennis Partner (USA) (Northern Dancer) [2007 83: 6m 8.1g 7g 7g* 7g⁴ 7g³ 8m 8.1m⁶ 7f p8g³ Oct 17] good-topped gelding: fairly useful handicapper: won at Goodwood in May: stays easy 1m: acts on polytrack and firm going: usually wears headgear: held up. *G. L. Moore* **81**

SCARLET KNIGHT 4 b.g. Lujain (USA) 119 – Gem 58 (Most Welcome 131) [2007 87§: 6g 6m 6g6 7g 7f⁴ 7g 7f⁴ p8g³ 8d Oct 3] good-topped gelding: fair handicapper: stays 1m: acts on polytrack and any turf going: tried blinkered/in cheekpieces: has raced freely: quirky and inconsistent. *P. Mitchell* **72 §**

SCARLET OAK 3 b.f. Zamindar (USA) 116 – Flamenco Red 93 (Warning 136) [2007 p8g⁶ p7g p5f* p6g² 6m p6g⁵ 5.7g³ p7m p7g 6d* 6.1s 8g Oct 24] 11,000 2-y-o: angular filly: third foal: half-sister to useful French 2005 2-y-o 1m/9f winner Customary (by Anabaa): dam, 6f (at 2 yrs) and 1m winner, half-sister to smart 1m/1¼m performer Spanish Don: fair performer: won maiden at Lingfield in February and handicap at Leicester in October: best at 5f/6f: acts on polytrack and good to soft going. *D. J. S. ffrench Davis* **75**

SCARLET ROYAL 2 b.f. (Apr 21) Red Ransom (USA) – Royal Future (IRE) (Royal Academy (USA) 130) [2007 7d 5m 5g Aug 16] leggy filly: half-sister to several winners, including 4-y-o They All Laughed: dam unraced half-sister to very smart miler Where Or When and smart performer up to 1¾m All The Way: poor maiden: form only at 5f, but bred to stay 1m+. *Mrs Marjorie Fife* **43**

SCARLET RUNNER 3 b.f. Night Shift (USA) – Sweet Pea 94 (Persian Bold 123) [2007 103: 7m* 8m 8d⁶ 7g⁶ 6g 6g Sep 30] strong, good-topped filly: wasn't a good walker: useful performer: won Shadwell Nell Gwyn Stakes at Newmarket in April by neck from Sander Camillo, racing on far rail and making most: mostly creditable efforts in face of stiff tasks after, seventh in 1000 Guineas at Newmarket, sixth in Coronation Stakes at Royal Ascot, sixth to Wake Up Maggie in Oak Tree Stakes at Goodwood and eighth to Red Clubs in Sprint Cup at Haydock, before folding tamely in Diadem Stakes at Ascot: would have proved best short of 1m: acted on firm and good to soft going: edgy sort, often had 2 handlers: stud. *J. L. Dunlop* **102**

SCARLETT HEART (IRE) 3 b.f. Lujain (USA) 119 – Scarlett Ribbon 104 (Most Welcome 131) [2007 55: p5g³ p5g² p5g⁵ p5g* p5g⁶ 5.1g* 6m⁵ p6g⁵ 5f² 5.1m⁴ 5.1f⁵ p5g p5m p5.1g p6g* p6g⁴ Dec 15] leggy filly: fair performer: won handicap at Kempton in April, claimer at Bath (left P. Makin) in May and seller at Lingfield in October: left J. Gallagher prior to final start (carried head awkwardly): effective at 5f/6f: acts on polytrack and firm ground: often held up. *James G. Burns, Ireland* **72 a66**

SCARRABUS (IRE) 6 b.g. Charnwood Forest (IRE) 125 – Errazuriz (IRE) 94 (Classic Music (USA)) [2007 54: 15.8m 12f⁵ 16.1d May 15] angular, good-topped gelding: maiden: little form in 2007: tried in cheekpieces. *A. Crook* **–**

SCAR TISSUE 3 ch.f. Medicean 128 – Possessive Lady 62 (Dara Monarch 128) [2007 55p: 8.3g⁵ p10g² 10f p10g Aug 23] close-coupled filly: modest maiden: left Tom Dascombe after second start: probably stays 1¼m. *E. J. Creighton* **63**

SCARY 3 ch.g. Peintre Celebre (USA) 137 – Danlu (USA) (Danzig (USA)) [2007 p11g³ f11d⁵ Dec 20] half-brother to several winners, notably very smart 1¼m to 1¾m winner Strategic Choice (by Alleged): dam Irish 1m (at 2 yrs)/8.5f winner: much better effort in maidens when 4¼ lengths third to Highest Esteem at Kempton, soon prominent: will stay 1½m. *P. F. I. Cole* **67**

SCATINA (IRE) 3 b.f. Samum (GER) 126 – Silvassa (IRE) (Darshaan 133) [2007 8g² 11g* 11d³ 12m 11g⁴ 14v² 10s² Nov 11] fifth foal: dam, German 7f winner, out of Preis der Diana winner Slenderella: smart performer: won maiden at Bremen at 2 yrs and Schwarzgold-Rennen at Cologne (set slow pace, beat Scoubidou ½ length) in May: placed afterwards in Oaks d'Italia at Milan (2 lengths third to Fashion Statement), Deutsches St Leger at Dortmund (beaten ½ length by El Tango) and Hessen Pokal at Frankfurt (best effort, beaten 2 lengths by Fair Breeze): below form in Lancashire Oaks at Newmarket (edgy beforehand) fourth start: has form up to 1¾m: acts on heavy ground: often races prominently: sold 330,000 gns. *M. Hofer, Germany* **109**

SCENE THREE 3 gr.f. Act One 124 – Ferber's Follies (USA) (Saratoga Six (USA)) [2007 –: 6m p9.5g 10.1d Oct 30] little sign of ability. *J. J. Quinn* **–**

SCHERMULY (IRE) 3 b.g. Fruits of Love (USA) 127 – Express Account 78 (Carr de Naskra (USA)) [2007 p8g Jan 13] 11/1, eighth in maiden at Lingfield, seeming green: sold 1,400 gns in May. *M. Johnston* **–**

SCHIAPARELLI (GER) 4 ch.c. Monsun (GER) 124 – Sacarina (Old Vic 136) **120**
[2007 116: 12g 11g³ 11v* 12g* 12g* 12m* Oct 14]

Among the plethora of big middle-distance races that take place in the
autumn, Milan's Gran Premio del Jockey Club is one that struggles most for
international recognition but, one way or another, it is a contest which Godolphin
keeps a close eye on. Kutub in 2001 and Cherry Mix in 2005 have won the race for
Saeed bin Suroor, and it has also been a source of recruits for the stable. Electrocutionist first came to prominence in the 2004 renewal, when beaten a short head,
before ultimately joining Godolphin in 2006 for what proved a highly successful
campaign in which he won the Dubai World Cup and finished second in the Prince
of Wales's Stakes and the King George VI and Queen Elizabeth Stakes, before his
death from a heart attack in September of that year. The following month, Laverock
won the Gran Premio del Jockey Club for Carlos Laffon-Parias in the colours of
Gainsborough Stud before he too was recruited by Godolphin for the latest
campaign, one which proved somewhat disappointing in Europe after a promising
start in Dubai.

Godolphin now have the 2007 Gran Premio del Jockey Club winner
Schiaparelli, and it will be a surprise if he doesn't prove a lot more successful than
Laverock for his new connections. Schiaparelli's purchase no doubt involved the
longer-term aim of standing him at stud, Sheikh Mohammed having already
invested heavily in sons of Monsun, purchasing Shirocco (the horse who beat
Electrocutionist at Milan) and Manduro for Darley towards the end of their racing
careers. In Schiaparelli he has a son of Monsun who should have more to offer as a
racehorse first. That will certainly be true if Schiaparelli takes after Shirocco and
Manduro and enjoys his most successful season as a five-year-old. Schiaparelli
ended his four-year-old campaign in top form, completing a hat-trick of Group 1
wins when successful at Milan, his fourth win in a row in all and his ninth from
thirteen starts in the last two seasons.

With his Italian name (his astronomical namesake discovered the so-called
'canals' on the surface of Mars), Schiaparelli might have been mistaken for one of
the locals at Milan, but he is German-bred and had done all his racing for trainer
Peter Schiergen in Germany before then. Schiaparelli won five races as a three-
year-old, notably the Deutsches Derby at Hamburg, and ended that year by taking
the Deutsches St Leger as well. Germany's St Leger is only a Group 3 race nowadays, and Schiaparelli had been the first German Derby winner to contest the race
for fifteen years and the first to win it since 1983. On his first two starts on his return
in the spring, Schiaparelli was beaten in races won by horses who had finished
behind him in the Derby the year before. After a disappointing reappearance, for
which he was sent off favourite but finished last of eight behind the Derby fourth
Saddex in the Gerling-Preis at Cologne, Schiaparelli ran a much better race when
two lengths third to Prince Flori in the Grosser Mercedes-Benz-Preis at Baden-
Baden a month later. Prince Flori had finished only ninth in the Deutsches Derby,
but had subsequently beaten Schiaparelli in the Grosser Preis von Baden and had
also finished in front of him at Cologne.

*Deutschlandpreis, Dusseldorf—a race that featured the first three from the 2006 Deutsches Derby,
but the three-year-old Conillon gives Schiaparelli (left) most to do on this occasion*

IVG - Preis von Europa, Cologne—another Group 1 for Schiaparelli; the blinkered Poseidon Adventure finishes strongly to take second with Ioannina (rail), First Stream (armlets) and Egerton (centre) next

Schiaparelli's winning sequence began in the mud at Hamburg in June when conditions were so bad that starting stalls could not be used for the Idee Hansa-Preis. Schiaparelli had won a maiden on heavy ground, so the going was no problem, and nor was the opposition, as Schiaparelli successfully gave weight all round in the Group 2 contest and stayed on strongly to beat the former Aidan O'Brien-trained colt Poseidon Adventure by two and a half lengths. Schiaparelli's next appearance, in the Deutschlandpreis at Dusseldorf in July, featured a rematch with the pair who had chased him home in the Derby the year before, Dickens and Oriental Tiger. However, one of the current three-year-old generation gave Schiaparelli most to do but he gamely held off the persistent challenge of Conillon to win by a head, leading early in the back straight and gradually increasing the pace. Most of Schiaparelli's races had taken place on good ground but conditions were considered too firm for him to take his chance in Germany's most important race, the Grosser Preis von Baden in early-September. Schiaparelli had finished only sixth when a short-priced favourite behind Prince Flori at Baden-Baden the year before and, in his absence, the latest edition went to his stable-companion Quijano. Schiaparelli was kept instead for the IVG - Preis von Europa at Cologne later in the month. With another front runner in the field, Schiaparelli tracked the leader Ioannina before wearing her down over a furlong out and then stayed on to hold off Poseidon Adventure, having three quarters of a length to spare over his old rival this time, with Ioannina a neck back in third.

Schiaparelli's three wins in Germany revealed little new about him but the Gran Premio del Jockey Club was illuminating in two respects. Firstly, although officially 'good', race times suggest that the ground at Milan was on the firm side, conditions which Schiaparelli had so far not encountered. Also, with Laverock in the field, seeking to repeat his 2006 win, as well as the smart French colt Champs Elysees and Italy's dual Premio Presidente della Repubblica winner Distant Way, Schiaparelli faced his biggest test so far. The three three-year-olds in the line-up looked out of their depth but Germany also fielded Bussoni, who had narrowly beaten Champs Elysees in the Prix Maurice de Nieuil at Longchamp in the summer and had since held Laverock behind him when winning the valuable Bosphorus Cup in Turkey. Bussoni often leads as well but Schiaparelli was sent straight into the lead and made all the running, really stepping up the pace from two furlongs out and keeping on strongly to beat Champs Elysees by a length and three quarters, with Laverock beaten a total of three lengths in third, Bussoni fourth and Distant Way last of the eight runners. It was Schiaparelli's best effort to date and further proof of his genuineness.

		Konigsstuhl (br 1976)	Dschingis Khan
	Monsun (GER) (br 1990)		Konigskronung
		Mosella (b 1985)	Surumu
Schiaparelli (GER) (ch.c. 2003)			Monasia
		Old Vic (b 1986)	Sadler's Wells
	Sacarina (ch 1992)		Cockade
		Brave Lass (ch 1974)	Ridan
			Bravour II

When winning the Deutsches Derby, Schiaparelli followed in the footsteps of his older brother Samum who won at Hamburg six years earlier and took his unbeaten record to six races when following up in the Grosser Preis von Baden, showing high-class form. Their unraced dam Sacarina has produced a third German classic winner by Monsun, the smart filly Salve Regina, successful in the 2002 Preis der Diana (German Oaks) and runner-up in both the Deutsches Derby and the Grosser Preis von Baden. The same mating also resulted in the filly who, at €750,000, was the most expensive yearling sold at Deauville's August sale in 2006. Named Sortita and purchased on behalf of Hamdan Al Maktoum, she is further evidence of the Maktoum family's investment in Monsun's offspring. Sortita made a promising debut for Michael Jarvis when second in a maiden at Newmarket less than a week after her elder brother's win at Milan. Their dam has also produced minor winners in Germany by Platini and Dashing Blade. Sacarina was out of the smart two-year-old sprinter Brave Lass, herself a daughter of another German classic winner, Bravour II, successful in the Schwarzgold-Rennen, as the German One Thousand Guineas was then known. Schiaparelli will get an early chance to prove his worth for new connections as he is reportedly to be aimed at the Dubai Sheema Classic at Nad Al Sheba in March, though presumably the top mile-and-a-half prizes in Europe will be on his agenda after that. He would need to show a bit more improvement to win in Dubai, but, as we have said, that is by no means out of the question and he is now proven on good to firm ground as well as heavy. The thoroughly game and genuine Schiaparelli seems best making the running or being ridden close to the pace and has proved a tough horse to pass. *P. Schiergen, Germany*

SCHOENBERG (USA) 3 ch.c. Johannesburg (USA) 127 – Bahia Gold (USA) **64** (Woodman (USA) 126) [2007 7.1m⁶ 7.1m⁴ 8.3d p8g Nov 14] rangy colt: modest maiden: should stay 1m: acts on good to firm ground: in cheekpieces (ran poorly) last 2 starts. *C. R. Egerton*

SCIENTIFIC 2 b.g. (Feb 26) Fraam 114 – Lady Butler (IRE) (Puissance 110) [2007 **57** 5m 7g 6g⁵ 7.1d 7g⁵ p7.1g⁴ p8.6d² p8.6g² Dec 31] rather leggy gelding: modest maiden: blinkered, improvement in frame in claimers/seller at Wolverhampton last 3 starts: stays 8.6f: acts on polytrack. *R. A. Fahey*

SCINTILLO 2 ch.c. (Feb 6) Fantastic Light (USA) 134 – Danseuse du Soir (IRE) 121 **109** (Thatching 131) [2007 6g⁵ 7g 7.1d* 7g⁴ 7g³ 8m² 8d³ 8m* Oct 14] 30,000Y: strong,

Gran Criterium, Milan—the prize goes abroad for the twelfth year running as Scintillo beats Gladiatorus (right), the latter subsequently joining Godolphin

good-topped colt: good walker: half-brother to 3 winners, including smart 6f (at 2 yrs) and 1m winner Jumbajukiba (by Barathea): dam French 5f (at 2 yrs) to 1m (Poule d'Essai des Pouliches) winner: useful performer: won maiden at Sandown in July and Gran Criterium at Milan (beat Gladiatorus ½ length) in October: in frame in listed/pattern company in between, including close third to City Leader in Royal Lodge Stakes at Ascot penultimate start: stays 1m: acts on good to firm and good to soft going: genuine. *R. Hannon*

SCORPION (IRE) 5 b.h. Montjeu (IRE) 137 – Ardmelody (Law Society (USA) 130) [2007 111: 13.4m² 12d* 12d² 12g⁵ 14m² Sep 15]   **125**

Scorpion's career echoes an earlier time. His Group 1 victories have come in the Grand Prix de Paris and St Leger as a three-year-old and, in the latest season, the Coronation Cup. None of these three historic races enjoys quite the lustre it once did, the sturdy defenders of the St Leger having to fight against calls for change and the Grand Prix de Paris having gone through two alterations in distance since its days as one of the world's greatest races when it was run over one mile seven furlongs. Scorpion is essentially a stayer, susceptible to rivals with a better turn of foot over a mile and a half, and he has usually been ridden enterprisingly, including when winning the Coronation Cup at Epsom in June (tried to stalk the winner when beaten by Ask in the Ormonde at Chester on his reappearance). Although positioned behind his front-running, better-fancied stablemate Septimus, who set something of a stop-start gallop to the home turn, Scorpion was kicked clear early in the straight and held on gamely. Despite the disappointing performances of the 2006 St Leger winner Sixties Icon and the 2006 Derby winner Sir Percy, the Coronation Cup did belatedly show that Scorpion retained all of his ability after his four-year-old campaign had been delayed by a fractured hind pastern.

Scorpion started at 5/4-on, conceding 5 lb all round, in the Hardwicke Stakes at Royal Ascot next time, and ran well in defeat, at least matching the form of his win at Epsom when beaten half a length by Maraahel. In the King George VI and Queen Elizabeth Stakes at the same course the following month, Scorpion started 3/1 second favourite behind his stablemate Dylan Thomas at 5/4. Scorpion was ridden from the front to make full use of his stamina, setting a strong pace. Whilst he had made all in the St Leger, such forcing tactics were different to how he'd been ridden in the meantime and, niggled along from a fair way out to maintain the tempo, he failed to give his running, finishing eleven lengths fifth of seven to Dylan Thomas. With stable-companions Yeats and Septimus proving themselves

Vodafone Coronation Cup, Epsom—in a meeting of three British classic winners, Scorpion comes out best and wins from his stable-companion Septimus; Maraahel (left) is third while Sir Percy (rail) and Sixties Icon (last) disappoint

high-class stayers, Scorpion did not get the chance to race at a mile and three quarters and beyond until taking on Yeats in the Irish St Leger at the Curragh. Scorpion was again ridden positively, though not so forcefully as at Ascot. He had Yeats in trouble when forging a few lengths clear around three furlongs out but was caught close home, carrying his head to one side and jinking left—something he did in the St Leger at Doncaster as well—inside the final furlong, possibly feeling the firmish ground.

		Sadler's Wells	Northern Dancer
	Montjeu (IRE)	(b 1981)	Fairy Bridge
	(b 1996)	Floripedes	Top Ville
Scorpion (IRE)		(b 1985)	Toute Cy
(b.h. 2002)		Law Society	Alleged
	Ardmelody	(br 1982)	Bold Bikini
	(b 1987)	Thistlewood	Kalamoun
		(gr 1979)	Le Melody

Scorpion was set to take in the Melbourne Cup at Flemington in November after his Irish St Leger second but suffered an injury to his off-hind a couple of weeks before, prompting his retirement. He is set to stand at Castle Hyde Stud in County Cork for €6,000, taking his place on Coolmore's roster of National Hunt stallions. Scorpion's dam Ardmelody died while foaling in 2004 and there is nothing to add to the detailed description of Scorpion's pedigree that can be found in *Racehorses of 2005*. The tall, rangy Scorpion was effective at a mile and a half to an extended mile and three quarters, and acted on soft and good to firm going (won a maiden on heavy on his debut). An edgy sort, he had run well when sweating and on his toes. *A. P. O'Brien, Ireland*

SCOTCH PANCAKE 4 ch.f. Selkirk (USA) 129 – Galette 94 (Caerleon (USA) 132) – [2007 74: f8g Apr 30] tall, useful-looking filly: fair maiden at best: tailed off in cheekpieces sole 4-y-o outing: stays easy 1¼m: acts on polytrack, raced on good/good to firm going on turf: sold 14,000 gns in July. *E. A. L. Dunlop*

SCOTLAND THE BRAVE 7 ch.m. Zilzal (USA) 137 – Hunters of Brora (IRE) 102 **82** (Sharpo 132) [2007 76: 7m 7.1d⁵ 7s⁶ 7.1v* 7.5s⁵ Jul 23] leggy, lengthy mare: fair handicapper: won at Haydock (made all) in July: stays 1m: has form on any going, goes well on soft/heavy: wears cheekpieces/visor. *J. D. Bethell*

SCOTLAND YARD (UAE) 4 b.g. Jade Robbery (USA) 121 – Aqraba 69 (Polish – Precedent (USA) 131) [2007 93: 20m Jun 19] quite good-topped gelding: fluent mover: fairly useful handicapper at 3 yrs: visored, well held in Ascot Stakes at Royal Ascot on only Flat start in 2007: should be suited by 1¾m+: acts on polytrack and firm going: fair winning hurdler. *D. E. Pipe*

SCOTS W'HAE 2 b.c. (Apr 18) Piccolo 121 – Ionian Secret 56 (Mystiko (USA) 124) – [2007 p6g Nov 21] 66/1, well held in maiden at Lingfield, not knocked about. *S. C. Williams*

SCOTT 6 gr.g. Polar Falcon (USA) 126 – Circled (USA) 83 (Cozzene (USA)) [2007 –: – f11g⁶ f14g p12.2g Sep 14] fair handicapper at best: lightly raced and well held since 2005. *J. Jay*

SCOTTISH RIVER (USA) 8 b.g. Thunder Gulch (USA) 129 – Overbrook 95 (Storm **75** Cat (USA)) [2007 69§, a73§: p9.5g* p8.6g⁵ p11g⁵ f8g⁴ p9.5g* p8.6g* p8.6g² 10d⁵ 10m 10m³ 12.6d² 11s⁵ p8.6g⁶ 10m Jul 27] strong gelding: fair handicapper: won in January (amateurs) and twice in April, all at Wolverhampton: effective at 1m to 1½m: acts on all-weather, firm and soft going: tried visored earlier in career: better attitude nowadays, but often slowly away: held up. *M. D. I. Usher*

SCOTTISH SPIRIT (IRE) 3 b.g. Invincible Spirit (IRE) 121 – Triphibious 69 – (Zafonic (USA) 130) [2007 –: 6g 5g Nov 8] of no account. *J. S. Haldane*

SCOTT SUMMERLAND (HOL) 4 b.g. Bretigny (FR) – Licence Summerland **61** (Lion Cavern (USA) 117) [2007 11.9g⁶ 7d 10g⁵ 11.9s 7g p9.5g⁶ Dec 14] sturdy, lengthy gelding: won minor event and listed race at Duindigt in 2006: left J. Pubben in Holland, fair form at best in Ireland/Britain, little impact in handicaps last 3 starts, at Wolverhampton final one: probably stays 1¼m. *Mervyn Torrens, Ireland*

SCOTTY'S FUTURE (IRE) 9 b.g. Namaqualand (USA) – Persian Empress (IRE) **59 §** 51 (Persian Bold 123) [2007 68§: p13.9g 12g 7.5v* 10g⁵ 8.1v 8.5s³ 7.5g 7.9f 8.5g 7.9g⁵ 9.9d 10g 10m 8v⁵ Nov 3] close-coupled, quite good-topped gelding: modest performer:

won seller at Beverley in July: stays 1½m: acts on polytrack and any turf going: visored once: edgy sort: held up: temperamental. *A. Berry*

SCRAP N'DUST 2 b.f. (Jan 23) Averti (IRE) 117 – Happy Lady (FR) 72 (Cadeaux **35** Genereux 131) [2007 5.1f⁴ 6.1g p5.1g⁵ 6g Jun 18] workmanlike filly: third living foal: half-sister to 6f (at 2 yrs)/7f winner Chorus Beauty and 1m seller winner Homme Dangereux (both by Royal Applause): dam, maiden, half-sister to smart performer up to 2m Rainbow Ways: poor maiden, raced only in sellers: best effort at 5f on polytrack. *W. G. M. Turner*

SCREAMING REEL 4 b.g. Dr Fong (USA) 128 – Heart of India (IRE) (Try My Best **–** (USA) 130) [2007 8.1m 8.1m⁶ 8.3m 8d p12.2g Sep 8] workmanlike gelding: little form. *M. Wellings*

SCREENPLAY 6 ch.g. In The Wings 128 – Erudite 114 (Generous (IRE) 139) [2007 **69** 69: 16m 14.8d⁵ 14m⁴ 21g 16m⁶ Sep 5] smallish, sturdy gelding: has a rather round action: fair handicapper: stays 2½m: acts on polytrack, soft and good to firm going: has worn cheekpieces: said to have finished lame final outing. *G. L. Moore*

SCREEN STAR (IRE) 2 gr.f. (Mar 25) Tobougg (IRE) 125 – Actoris (USA) (Diesis **110 p** 133) [2007 7m* Aug 25] sixth foal: half-sister to 8-y-o Activity and a winner in Greece by Green Desert: dam, useful French 1m winner, out of half-sister to smart miler Sensation, herself out of Breeders' Cup Juvenile Fillies' winner Outstandingly: 7/2, remarkable debut (smart form) when winning minor event at Redcar most impressively by 11 lengths from Thompsons Walls, making running and merely pushed clear: will stay 1m: has joined Godolphin: will prove a force at pattern level. *M. Johnston*

SCRIPTED (USA) 3 br.c. Theatrical 128 – Val Gardena (CHI) (Roy (USA)) [2007 8m **69** 10d⁶ Jul 19] sturdy, useful-looking colt: has scope: fourth foal: brother to US 2004 2-y-o 7.5f winner Our Leading Lady: dam won several Grade 1s in Chile, including Oaks and Derby: better effort in maidens when seventh to Jaleela at Newmarket on debut: folded tamely next time: bred to stay at least 1¼m. *L. M. Cumani*

SCRIPTWRITER (IRE) 5 b.g. Sadler's Wells (USA) 132 – Dayanata (Shirley **113** Heights 130) [2007 111: 12.1d⁸ 12s⁶ 14g* 14d³ Aug 22] tall gelding: smart handicapper, lightly raced: further progress in 2007, winning at Hamilton (beat Camrose a short head in listed event) in May and Goodwood (by 2½ lengths from Samurai Way) in July: travelled strongly long way when creditable 3¼ lengths third to Purple Moon in Ebor at York final outing: stays 1¾m: acts on firm and soft going: wore cheekpieces final start in 2006: quirky (has carried head high): sold 35,000 gns, joined J. Howard Johnson, fair form on hurdling debut. *Saeed bin Suroor*

SCROLL 4 b.g. Mark of Esteem (IRE) 137 – Bella Bellisimo (IRE) 84 (Alzao (USA) **55** 117) [2007 61, a77: p7g p7g p10g p9.5g⁵ 9.7m 8m 8m 7m p7g² 7m p7g⁵ p8.6g Jul 10] **a62** angular, useful-looking gelding: modest performer: should stay 9.5f: raced only on polytrack and good ground or firmer: usually visored, tried blinkered: has looked none too keen. *P. Howling*

SCRUFFY (IRE) 3 b.g. Second Empire (IRE) 124 – Karakapa (FR) (Subotica (FR) **–** 131) [2007 7d 7s 6.9m 9m⁶ p9.5g f7d Dec 15] strong gelding: no form: tried visored. *C. J. Teague*

SCRUFFY SKIP (IRE) 2 b.g. (Apr 27) Diktat 126 – Capoeira (USA) (Nureyev (USA) **65** 131) [2007 5.9g 6m⁴ 6m⁵ 6s 7g Oct 20] workmanlike gelding: fair maiden: should stay 7f: acts on good to firm going: tried in cheekpieces. *M. Dods*

SCUBA (IRE) 5 b.g. Indian Danehill (IRE) 124 – March Star (IRE) 109 (Mac's Imp **67** (USA) 116) [2007 75: p7.1g⁴ p6g 6.1g f7g³ p8g² p8g⁶ p7g⁵ p7.1g³ p7.1g⁶ Sep 22] well-made gelding: fair handicapper: stays easy 1m: acts on all-weather, best effort on turf on good going (ran poorly on heavy): blinkered. *H. Morrison*

SCUFFLE 2 gr.f. (Feb 1) Daylami (USA) 138 – Tantina (USA) 115 (Distant View (USA) **77 P** 126) [2007 8d⁵ Oct 27] first foal: dam, 7f winner, out of smart 7f to 8.5f (in US) performer Didina, herself out of half-sister to Xaar: 7/1, highly promising third to Whistledownwind in maiden at Newbury, needing experience (took time to settle) but going on strongly at finish: will stay 1¼m: useful prospect, and sure to win races. *R. Charlton*

SCURRA 8 b.g. Spectrum (IRE) 126 – Tamnia 106 (Green Desert (USA) 127) [2007 **–** 56d: p12.2g 13d 14d 12m Sep 30] leggy gelding: fair at best: little form in 2007: tried in cheekpieces. *A. C. Whillans*

SCUTCH MILL (IRE) 5 ch.g. Alhaarth (IRE) 126 – Bumble (Rainbow Quest (USA) **69** 134) [2007 73: 10.9m³ 12g p13.9g⁶ p12.2g Nov 20] leggy gelding: fair handicapper: stays easy 1¾m: acts on polytrack and firm going: tongue tied nowadays: often slowly away (markedly so third start): fair winning hurdler. *P. C. Haslam*

SCUZME (IRE) 4 br.g. Xaar 132 – Decatur (Deploy 131) [2007 58: p10g⁴ p16g⁴ p10g⁶ **58 d**
p12.2g p16g⁴ p16g p12g 12d Jul 25] leggy gelding: modest performer: left Miss S. West
after seventh outing: stays easy 2m: acts on polytrack, good to firm and good to soft
going: often in cheekpieces: has been slowly away. *M. A. Barnes*

SEA ADMIRAL 2 b.g. (Mar 1) Sinndar (IRE) 134 – Overboard (IRE) 73 (Rainbow **70 p**
Quest (USA) 134) [2007 7.1g 8g Oct 24] 60,000Y: second foal: dam, maiden (placed
at 1½m), half-sister to smart performer up to 1½m Red Sea out of smart winner up to
1½m Up Anchor: fair maiden: probably insufficient tests at 2 yrs, but shaped well on
debut (third to Hustle at Lingfield): will be suited by 1¼m/1½m: should do better.
R. Charlton

SEABOW (USA) 4 b.c. Rainbow Quest (USA) 134 – Dream Bay (USA) (Mr Prospec- **104**
tor (USA)) [2007 91p: 10d³ 10m⁶ 10m* 9m 10d Oct 27] close-coupled colt: useful
handicapper, lightly raced: improved in 2007, best effort when winning at Sandown in
September by ½ length from Press The Button: likely to stay 1½m: unraced on extremes
of going: tongue tied: has left Godolphin. *Saeed bin Suroor*

SEA COOKIE 3 b.f. Largesse 112 – Maylan (IRE) 47 (Lashkari 128) [2007 –: 10f **49**
8.3m⁵ 10.5s⁶ 10g Oct 8] lengthy filly: poor maiden: should stay 1¼m. *W. de Best-Turner*

SEA COVE 7 b.m. Terimon 124 – Regal Pursuit (IRE) 61 (Roi Danzig (USA)) [2007 **37**
f14g⁵ Jan 25] workmanlike mare: modest maiden in 2004: poor form only Flat outing
since: stays easy 1½m: acts on fibresand and good to firm ground. *G. A. Swinbank*

SEAFIELD TOWERS 7 ch.g. Compton Place 125 – Midnight Spell 79 (Night Shift **61**
(USA)) [2007 5m 7.1m 5g 6d 5d 5s 5m 6g⁶ 5m 5m 5m⁵ 5m 5d 5d 5m Sep 30]
good-bodied gelding: just modest performer nowadays: effective at 5f/6f: acts on firm
and good to soft ground: tried blinkered, usually wears cheekpieces: difficult ride.
Miss L. A. Perratt

SEAFLOWER REEF (IRE) 3 b.f. Robellino (USA) 127 – Sankaty Light (USA) 55 **64**
(Summer Squall (USA)) [2007 68: 8.3d⁴ 7g Aug 15] rather leggy filly: fair maiden,
lightly raced: should be suited by 1m: acts on polytrack, firm and good to soft going.
A. M. Balding

SEA FROLIC (IRE) 6 b.m. Shinko Forest (IRE) – Centre Travel (Godswalk (USA) **48**
130) [2007 48: f7g 7.9m 8.1d p9.5g⁵ 7m 10m p12.2g⁶ p13.9g⁵ p13.9g Nov 16] rather
leggy mare: poor performer: seems to stay easy 1¾m, all wins at 1m: acts on all-weather,
firm and good to soft going: tried in headgear. *Jennie Candlish*

SEA LAND (FR) 3 ch.g. King's Best (USA) 132 – Green Bonnet (IRE) (Green Desert **77**
(USA) 127) [2007 79p: p7g* p8g 8.3s 6g 6m⁵ Aug 3] well-made gelding: fair performer:
won maiden at Lingfield in February (edged left): left M. Tregoning after fourth outing:
stays 7f: visored (below form) third/fourth starts. *B. Ellison*

SEAL POINT (USA) 3 ch.c. Point Given (USA) 134 – Maudie May (USA) (Gilded **91**
Time (USA)) [2007 79: 7.5g* a9f 7d 10m 8g⁶ 10d p8g p10g Nov 4] big, good-topped
colt: fairly useful performer: won maiden at Nad Al Sheba in February: stays 1¼m: acts
on polytrack, probably on good to firm ground: tried in blinkers/cheekpieces. *Christian
Wroe*

SEA MAP 5 ch.g. Fraam 114 – Shehana (USA) 86 (The Minstrel (CAN) 135) [2007 **67**
p16.5g⁴ p16g⁵ p16g⁶ p16g⁵ p16.5g Feb 16] tall, leggy gelding: fair performer: left
D. Cantillon after second start: stays 2m: acts on polytrack, heavy and good to firm
ground: blinkered (ran poorly) once: none too consistent. *Miss S. West*

SEA MARK 11 gr.g. Warning 136 – Mettlesome (Lomond (USA) 128) [2007 f8g p12g³ **56**
Apr 25] big, rangy gelding: has a round action: handicapper: off nearly 3 years, only
modest in 2007: finds 7f a minimum, and stays easy 1½m: acts on firm and good to soft
going: blinkered once in 2002: usually held up. *A. D. Brown*

SEAMUS SHINDIG 5 b.g. Aragon 118 – Sheesha (USA) (Shadeed (USA) 135) [2007 **82**
88: p7g⁴ 6s⁴ 6g² p6g⁵ 6g⁴ 6g⁵ Jul 27] small, sturdy gelding: fairly useful handicapper:
stays 7f: acts on polytrack, firm and good to soft going: in cheekpieces (said to have
finished distressed) final 4-y-o outing. *H. Candy*

SEAN OG (IRE) 5 gr.g. Definite Article 121 – Miss Goodbody (Castle Keep 121) – **–**
[2007 64d: p10g Jan 3] maiden: well behind sole 5-y-o outing: tried in cheekpieces/blinkers.
E. J. Creighton

SEA ROVER (IRE) 3 b.c. Jade Robbery (USA) 121 – Talah 87 (Danehill (USA) 126) **78**
[2007 6f* 6m² 5g⁵ 7m⁵ Jun 12] tall, useful-looking colt: fair performer: won maiden at
Thirsk in April: bred to stay 1m, but not short of speed. *M. Brittain*

SEA SAGA (IRE) 4 ch.f. Generous (IRE) 139 – Winter Pageant 65 (Polish Precedent **?**
(USA) 131) [2007 9.5v⁵ a8g* 9d* 8m⁵ 8m⁴ 10.1d Oct 30] won maiden at Dax in 2006
(when trained in France by D. de Watrigant) and amateur minor events at Albenga in February and Florence in May: left M. Gasparini in Italy, well held in handicap at Yarmouth
on British debut: stays 10.5f: acts on sand and good to soft ground. *L. M. Cumani*

SEA SALT 4 b.g. Titus Livius (FR) 115 – Carati 86 (Selkirk (USA) 129) [2007 82: 6d⁴ **81**
5g⁵ 5d 5d 6v p6g⁶ p7.1g Dec 15] good-topped gelding: fairly useful handicapper: effective at 5f/6f: acts on firm and good to soft ground, probably on soft. *R. A. Fahey*

SEASIDER 2 b.c. (Jan 8) Zamindar (USA) 116 – Esplanade 77 (Danehill (USA) 126) **95 p**
[2007 6d* p7g² Nov 3] well-made colt: first foal: dam, 1¼m winner, sister to useful performer up to 1m Kithira and half-sister to smart French performer up to 1½m Tenuous:
useful form: good impression when winning maiden at Windsor in October: still green,
further promise when second to Storm Force in minor event at Kempton: will be suited
by 1m/1¼m: sure to go on improving. *Sir Michael Stoute*

SEA STORM (IRE) 9 b.g. Dolphin Street (FR) 125 – Prime Interest (IRE) (Kings **78**
Lake (USA) 133) [2007 –: 7.1m⁵ 8.1g 7.2s Sep 20] big, strong gelding: fair handicapper
nowadays: stays 1m: acts on firm going, soft and polytrack: sometimes wears cheekpieces, blinkered once. *James Moffatt*

SEATON SNOOKS 3 b.g. Diktat 126 – Buck's Fizz (Kris 135) [2007 65: 5m 7.5m 7m **45**
6m⁴ 6m⁵ May 28] angular gelding: poor maiden nowadays: should stay 7f/1m: acts on
soft and good to firm going: tried blinkered. *T. D. Easterby*

SEATTLE STORM (IRE) 2 b.c. (Jan 27) Robellino (USA) 127 – Seattle Ribbon **76 p**
(USA) 70 (Seattle Dancer (USA) 119) [2007 p8m² p8g² Dec 19] brother to 2003 2-y-o 6f
winner Robocop and 9f/1¼m winner Seattle Robber and half-brother to 2 winners, including 5-y-o Snoqualmie Boy: dam, maiden (stayed 1¼m), sister to Racing Post Trophy
winner Seattle Rhyme: fair form when runner-up in maidens at Lingfield and Kempton:
will do better. *D. R. C. Elsworth*

SEA WALL 5 b.g. Giant's Causeway (USA) 132 – Spout 115 (Salse (USA) 128) [2007 **–**
14g May 19] big, strong gelding: useful performer in 2005: unraced on Flat in 2006: well
beaten in handicap at Newmarket sole Flat start at 5 yrs: stays 1½m, probably not 1¾m:
acts on firm and good to soft going: fairly useful hurdler, successful in September. *Jonjo
O'Neill*

SEA WILLOW (IRE) 3 b.g. Tamarisk (IRE) 127 – Willow Dale (IRE) 89 (Danehill **59**
(USA) 126) [2007 6s 7.1s⁶ 7m p8g 8d⁴ 7g p10g Oct 17] big, lengthy gelding: fifth foal:
half-brother to 2 winners, including 4-y-o Matterofact: dam 5f/6f winner, including at
2 yrs: modest maiden: seems to stay 1m. *D. R. C. Elsworth*

SECAM (POL) 8 gr.g. Alywar (USA) – Scytia (POL) (Euro Star) [2007 60: p8g f11g **48**
p10g⁴ 9g Jun 1] poor handicapper nowadays: stays 1¼m: acts on all-weather, lightly
raced on turf: usually wears cheekpieces/blinkers. *Mrs P. Townsley*

SECOND OPINION (IRE) 2 ch.f. (Jan 25) Dr Fong (USA) 128 – Second To Go **69**
(USA) 81 (El Prado (IRE) 119) [2007 6.1g⁴ 5.1f Aug 24] 70,000Y: first foal: dam 7f
winner: better effort in maidens (dictated and likely flattered) when fourth to Mistress
Greeley at Nottingham: may prove best at 5f/6f. *J. M. P. Eustace*

SECOND REEF 5 b.g. Second Empire (IRE) 124 – Vax Lady 98 (Millfontaine 114) **65 d**
[2007 62: p8.6g⁵ p9.5g³ p9.5g p9.5g p8.6g 12m 12g⁴ 12m 9g⁶ 8g Nov 8] good-topped
gelding: fair performer: regressive form at 5 yrs, leaving E. Alston after third outing,
J. Weymes after ninth: stays 1¼m: acts on all-weather and firm going: sometimes wears
headgear: tried tongue tied. *T. A. K. Cuthbert*

SECONDS OUT (IRE) 2 b.g. (Feb 27) Marju (IRE) 127 – Next Round (IRE) 83 **65**
(Common Grounds 118) [2007 f5g⁵ p7g 7.1m p8g² 7g⁶ Oct 19] tall, workmanlike gelding: fair maiden: runner-up in claimer at Lingfield: stays 1m: acts on polytrack: blinkered
last 2 starts: sold 10,000 gns. *Sir Mark Prescott*

SECRET ASSET (IRE) 2 gr.g. (Apr 27) Clodovil (IRE) 116 – Skerray 71 (Soviet **98**
Star (USA) 128) [2007 5m 5m³ 5m* 5m* 5d³ Sep 17] 5,000Y: sturdy gelding: fifth foal:
half-brother to useful 5f (at 2 yrs) to 9f (in Hong Kong) winner Chinsola (by Inchinor)
and smart French sprinter Desert Ocean (by Desert Sun): dam, maiden (stayed 1m),
half-sister to smart performer up to 1m Ardkinglass: useful performer: won maiden at
Haydock in June and nursery at Beverley in August: good third in nursery at Musselburgh
final start: will prove best kept to 5f: acts on good to firm and good to soft going: once
refused to enter stall intended fourth outing. *W. M. Brisbourne*

Invesco Perpetual Goodwood Stakes (Handicap), Goodwood—the versatile Secret Ploy makes all; another successful jumper, Afrad (noseband), is second

SECRET GEM (IRE) 2 b.f. (Apr 28) Cape Cross (IRE) 129 – Orlena (USA) (Gone **66** West (USA)) [2007 7g⁶ 8.2m⁶ 7g Nov 3] 72,0000 2-y-o: close-coupled filly: fourth foal: half-sister to 3 winners, including 3-y-o Pelican Waters and 4-y-o Hovering: dam, French 2-y-o 7f winner, out of US Grade 3 8.5f/9f winner Cox Orange: fair form in maidens: shapes as if 1¼m+ will suit. *C. G. Cox*

SECRET LIAISON 4 gr.g. Medicean 128 – Courting 108 (Pursuit of Love 124) [2007 **91** 89: f8g⁵ p7g* 7d⁶ 9.9d* p9.5g⁵ Nov 10] leggy gelding: fairly useful performer: won handicap at Kempton in June and claimer at Salisbury (left Sir Mark Prescott £24,000) in October: effective at 7f to 1¼m: acts on polytrack and any turf going: usually races up with pace, ridden more patiently last 2 starts: carries head high. *S. Parr*

SECRET MEANING 2 b.f. (Apr 6) Mujahid (USA) 125 – Hidden Meaning 66 **59** (Cadeaux Genereux 131) [2007 5m⁴ 5.2g² 6m² 7s⁴ 6d* 6d² 6.1m⁴ 6g Aug 24] leggy, close-coupled filly: third foal: half-sister to useful French 9.5f/1¼m winner Becher (by Vettori), also successful in Qatar: dam, maiden (stayed 7f), half-sister to 1000 Guineas runner-up Niche: modest performer: won seller at Yarmouth in July: in frame in nurseries next 2 starts: best at 6f: acts on good to firm and good to soft going: in cheekpieces 4 of last 5 starts (not for win): edgy sort. *W. G. M. Turner*

SECRET NIGHT 4 gr.f. Dansili 127 – Night Haven 99 (Night Shift (USA)) [2007 88, **–** a99: p6g p7g³ p7g² p7g 6m 7d p6g⁵ p7g Dec 19] tall, useful-looking filly: fairly useful **a92** handicapper, better on all-weather than turf: stays easy 1m: acts on polytrack and good to firm going. *J. A. R. Toller*

SECRET PLOY 7 b.g. Deploy 131 – By Line 64 (High Line 125) [2007 12f* 21.7s⁶ **82** 14.1d⁴ 21g* 17.2f³ 18d Oct 20] leggy, attractive gelding: smart in bumpers, fairly useful hurdler: lightly raced and fairly useful on Flat: won maiden at Thirsk in May and quite valuable handicap at Goodwood in August: below form in Cesarewitch at Newmarket final outing: stays 21f: acts on firm and soft going: difficult ride. *H. Morrison*

SECRET TUNE 3 b.c. Generous (IRE) 139 – Sing For Fame (USA) 90 (Quest For **102** Fame 127) [2007 10m² 10.1d* 12m* 16d³ 12g 14g Aug 25] well-made colt: first foal: dam, 9f winner, out of half-sister to Prince of Wales's Stakes winner Two Timing: useful performer: successful in maiden at Newcastle in May and handicap at Musselburgh (beat Gull Wing by ½ length) in June: good 3¾ lengths third to Mahler in Queen's Vase at Royal Ascot next time: below form last 2 starts: stays 2m: acts on good to firm and good to soft going. *Pat Eddery*

SECRET VISION (USA) 6 ch.m. Distant View (USA) 126 – Secret Angel (Halo **–** (USA)) [2007 –: p6g Jan 20] well held sole start in 2007: effective with/without cheekpieces. *R. M. H. Cowell*

SECRET WORLD (IRE) 4 ch.g. Spinning World (USA) 130 – Classic Park 115 **111** (Robellino (USA) 127) [2007 106: 9m 8g⁴ 8v⁶ 8d Aug 16] big, strong, lengthy gelding: smart performer, lightly raced: reportedly suffered stress fracture after final 3-y-o start: easily best effort in 2007 when 2½ lengths fourth to Red Evie in Lockinge Stakes at Newbury: should stay beyond 1m: raced mainly on good/good to firm going (well below form on ground softer than good last 2 starts): gelded. *J. Noseda*

SEDGE (USA) 7 b.g. Lure (USA) 131 – First Flyer (USA) (Riverman (USA) 131)   **80**
[2007 71: p7.1g p7.1g² 7m* 7m⁵ 7.5m p7.1g* 7s 7m⁵ 7m 7.5m 7m² 7.5d p7.1g* p7.1g³
Nov 1] good-topped gelding: fairly useful handicapper: won at Thirsk in May and Wolverhampton in July and October: effective at 7f, probably at 9f: acts on all-weather, firm
and good to soft ground: usually wears cheekpieces/blinkers: inconsistent. *P. T. Midgley*

SEDGWICK 5 b.g. Nashwan (USA) 135 – Imperial Bailiwick (IRE) 104 (Imperial   **77**
Frontier (USA) 112) [2007 59: p7.1g² f6g³ p8.6g p8g 10s* 11.8m⁶ 9.1g² 9m² 9.1g 9.1d⁶
10.1g 10.1d² Oct 16] tall, strong gelding: fair handicapper: won at Nottingham (maiden
event) in May: best up to 1¼m: acts on polytrack and soft ground: joined Ian Williams.
J. G. Given

SEDUCTIVE WITCH 2 ch.f. (Feb 26) Zamindar (USA) 116 – Thicket 87 (Wolf-   **51**
hound (USA) 126) [2007 5v 6d p5g⁵ p5.1d⁵ Dec 17] lengthy filly: fifth foal: half-sister to
winners around 5f Diminuto (fairly useful and including at 2 yrs, by Iron Mask) and
Baileys Applause (by Royal Applause): dam 2-y-o 5f winner: modest maiden: off 3
months after debut (reportedly bled): should be suited by 6f. *M. D. I. Usher*

SEEIN'RED (IRE) 2 b.g. (Apr 20) Redback 116 – Red Keane (IRE) 46 (Red Sunset   **55 ?**
120) [2007 5m³ 5m 5m Aug 4] close-coupled gelding: maiden: form only when third in
claimer: bred to stay 7f/1m: tried in cheekpieces. *P. T. Midgley*

SEEKING STAR (IRE) 2 b.c. (Mar 26) King's Best (USA) 132 – Firedrake (USA)   **98**
(Kris S (USA)) [2007 6m⁴ 6m* 7g⁵ 7d* 7d Oct 27] 65,000Y: rangy colt: second foal:
dam, French maiden (raced only around 1¼m), out of useful half-sister to Breeders' Cup
Classic winner Skywalker: useful form: won maiden at Windsor in June and minor event
at Leicester (comfortably) in October: pulled too hard in Horris Hill Stakes at Newbury
(eighth behind Beacon Lodge) final start: will be suited by 1m: acts on good to firm and
good to soft going. *M. R. Channon*

SEEKING THE BUCK (USA) 3 b.c. Seeking The Gold (USA) – Cuanto Es (USA)   **95**
(Exbourne (USA) 125) [2007 –: 8g⁶ 7.5m⁵ 10f* 10g² 10m² 11m³ 12g² 10.5g* 10.1g Sep
19] close-coupled colt: useful handicapper: won at Brighton in June and Haydock (by 4
lengths from Hurlingham) in September: stays 1½m: raced only on good ground or firmer
(acts on firm): blinkered last 3 starts: tongue tied nowadays: reliable: sold 90,000 gns.
M. A. Magnusson

SEEKING THE STAR (CAN) 2 b.g. (Mar 18) Seeking The Gold (USA) – Water   **70 ?**
Music (CAN) (Danzig (USA)) [2007 6m p6g⁵ p7g p6g⁶ Aug 1] lengthy gelding: fair
maiden: seemingly easily best effort when fifth in minor event at Kempton: should stay
7f/1m: tried blinkered: gelded after final start. *D. M. Simcock*

SEESAWMILU (IRE) 4 b.g. Almutawakel 126 – Clos de Tart (IRE) (Indian Ridge   **52**
123) [2007 54: p7.1g⁴ 8m p7.1g⁵ 5s 6d⁵ 6d⁵ 6m p6g 7g⁵ p6g⁴ Oct 22] sturdy gelding:
modest performer: stays 7f: acts on polytrack, good to firm and good to soft ground: tried
blinkered. *E. J. Alston*

SEGAL (IRE) 2 b.c. (Apr 9) Cadeaux Genereux 131 – Camcorder (Nashwan (USA)   **72 +**
135) [2007 6.5d p7m³ p7g² Nov 17] sturdy colt: fair maiden: twice placed at Lingfield,
finishing well both times: will be suited by 1m: acts on polytrack. *J. Noseda*

SEHOYA (IRE) 5 b. or br.m. Second Empire (IRE) 124 – Blue Jazz (IRE) 70 (Bluebird   **–**
(USA) 125) [2007 51: f8g Feb 15] modest handicapper: left Eoin Doyle in Ireland, well
held only start in 2007 (said to have bled): stays 1¼m: acts on good to firm going: tried
tongue tied. *R. C. Guest*

SEKULA PATA (NZ) 8 b.g. Pompeii Court (USA) – Torquay (NZ) (Wharf (USA))   **66**
[2007 76: 8s 10.2m⁵ p10g² p9.5g 9m p9.5g⁴ p10g* p10g Nov 7] good-topped gelding:
fair handicapper: left Christian Wroe after reappearance: won at Kempton in October:
stays 1½m: acts on polytrack, soft and good to firm going: often wears headgear: tried
tongue tied. *E. J. Creighton*

SELDEMOSA 6 br.m. Selkirk (USA) 129 – Baldemosa (FR) (Lead On Time (USA)   **55**
123) [2007 55: p7.1g² f7g⁴ p7.1g⁵ p7.1g³ f7g² f7g p6g⁵ p7.1g⁶ f8g p8g 7.6g Jun 23] big,
workmanlike mare: modest handicapper: stays 9.5f: acts on all-weather, best effort on
turf on good going: tried visored/blinkered: sometimes finds little. *M. S. Saunders*

SELECT COMMITTEE 2 b.g. (Apr 15) Fayruz 116 – Demolition Jo 89 (Petong 126)   **72**
[2007 5m³ 5m² 5v³ 5s 6g Aug 17] sturdy gelding: fair maiden: placed first 3 starts: will
probably prove best at 5f/6f: acts on heavy and good to firm going. *J. J. Quinn*

SELECTIVE 8 b.g. Selkirk (USA) 129 – Portelet 91 (Night Shift (USA)) [2007 79: 8m   **–**
Apr 23] good-bodied gelding: fair handicapper in 2006: well held sole 8-y-o start: effec-

tive at 7f/1m: acts on polytrack, firm and soft going: tried in cheekpieces/visor, sometimes tongue tied: has run well when sweating: carries head awkwardly: waited with: sold 2,400 gns in May. *A. W. Carroll*

SELEET (IRE) 3 b.c. Sakhee (USA) 136 – Summerhill Parkes 105 (Zafonic (USA) **74** 130) [2007 8.5m* 7m p10g 11s Oct 4] lengthy, useful-looking colt: fair performer: won maiden at Beverley in April (reportedly returned a bit sore): disappointing in handicaps after: stays 8.5f: sold 6,500 gns, sent to Italy. *M. A. Jarvis*

SELINKA 3 b.f. Selkirk (USA) 129 – Lady Links 100 (Bahamian Bounty 116) [2007 **110** 95: 8m 8m² 8.1g* 7g⁴ 8g⁴ 10g⁶ Sep 22] leggy filly: smart performer: improved when winning listed race at Sandown in July by 1¾ lengths from Barshiba: respectable efforts after only when fourth at Goodwood in Oak Tree Stakes (to Wake Up Maggie) and Celebration Mile (behind Echelon): stays 1m (behind throughout in Prix du Prince d'Orange at Longchamp over 1¼m): acts on good to firm and good to soft going: looks hard ride, and needs treating with some caution. *R. Hannon*

SELIQUE 3 b.f. Selkirk (USA) 129 – Elle Questro 61 (Rainbow Quest (USA) 134) **55** [2007 p9.5g Apr 28] fourth foal: half-sister to 3 winners abroad: dam, 1½m winner, half-sister to Be My Chief: 20/1, ninth in maiden at Wolverhampton, not settling early on: sold 2,500 gns in July. *E. A. L. Dunlop*

SELKIRK GRACE 7 b.g. Selkirk (USA) 129 – Polina 69 (Polish Precedent (USA) **72** 131) [2007 f12g p12g² p12g⁵ 12s² p13g² 9.9m* 12g 11d³ 12d⁴ Oct 27] tall, angular gelding: fair handicapper: won at Beverley (apprentices) in August: stays easy 13f: acts on polytrack, good to firm and good to soft going: in cheekpieces last 4 starts: has pulled hard: looked quirky last 2 outings. *K. A. Morgan*

SELKIRK SKY 3 b.f. Selkirk (USA) 129 – Arctic Air 79 (Polar Falcon (USA) 126) **65** [2007 7g* 8m⁴ 6.9g Aug 22] good-topped filly: fourth foal: half-sister to 5-y-o Andronikos: dam, 2-y-o 7f winner, half-sister to smart performers Barrow Creek (effective at 6f to 1m) and Last Resort (7f) out of smart 6f/7f winner Breadcrumb: won maiden at Thirsk in July: just respectable efforts in handicaps after: stays 7f. *R. A. Fahey*

SELL OUT 3 gr.f. Act One 124 – Nordica 99 (Northfields (USA)) [2007 76p: 10m⁵ f8g **104** p8g 10s* 10.4s² 9.9g² 10.1g⁴ 10d⁴ Oct 19] big, useful-looking filly: has a round action: useful performer: won handicap at Newbury in June by ½ length from Noojoom, looking none too keen: in frame in listed races last 3 starts, best efforts when 2½ lengths second to Promising Lead at Salisbury and ¾-length fourth to Short Skirt at Newmarket final one: will stay 1½m: acts on polytrack and soft going: held up: has looked hard ride. *G. Wragg*

SELSEY 2 b.f. (Mar 2) Selkirk (USA) 129 – Louella (USA) (El Gran Senor (USA) 136) **61 p** [2007 7g Nov 3] close-coupled filly: fifth foal: sister to very smart 7f (at 2 yrs) to 1½m winner Leadership and half-sister to 2 winners, including 1½m/1¾m winner in Germany by Hector Protector: dam, French maiden, sister to useful 1¼m performer Himself: 16/1 and better for race, mid-field in maiden at Newmarket: will be suited by 1¼m/1½m: bound to improve. *Sir Michael Stoute*

SEMAH HAROLD 2 b.g. (Apr 9) Beat All (USA) 120 – Semah's Dream 39 (Gunner **76** B 126) [2007 p7.1g* 8.2d³ p8.6g³ p8m p7.1g⁶ Nov 24] fair performer: won maiden at Wolverhampton in July: below form in nurseries last 2 starts: should prove best up to 1m: acts on polytrack and good to soft going. *E. S. McMahon*

SEMI DETACHED (IRE) 4 b.g. Distant Music (USA) 126 – Relankina (IRE) (Brok- **65** en Hearted 124) [2007 72: p8g⁶ p8.6g p10g⁴ p9.5g⁵ p8.6g⁵ p8.6g Nov 22] tall, quite good-topped gelding: fair maiden: left J. Boyle after third outing: stays easy 1¼m: acts on polytrack and soft ground: tried tongue tied. *J. W. Unett*

SEMPRE LIBERA (IRE) 2 b.f. (Feb 23) Statue of Liberty (USA) 115 – Lucky **64** Oakwood (USA) 75 (Elmaamul (USA) 125) [2007 p6g² p6g³ p6g³ Dec 29] €10,000F, 15,000Y: fifth foal: half-sister to 1¼m winner in Japan by Grand Lodge: dam, 2-y-o 7f winner, closely related to useful 1¼m winner Gisarne: modest maiden: placed all 3 starts: raced only at 6f on polytrack. *P. W. Chapple-Hyam*

SENDALAM (FR) 5 ch.g. Sendawar (IRE) 129 – Alamea (IRE) (Ela-Mana-Mou 132) **103** [2007 108: 7.5g² 7.5g 6.5g² a6f 7g 8.1m 7g Dec 23] good-bodied gelding: useful performer: left F. Fouin in France after 2006: runner-up to Obe Brave and Grantley Adams in handicaps at Nad Al Sheba early in year (for H. Brown): well held both starts in Britain in summer, leaving J. S. Moore before final outing: stays 1¼m, races mainly at shorter: acts on all-weather and soft ground. *A. Manuel, UAE*

SENDALI (FR) 3 b.g. Daliapour (IRE) 122 – Lady Senk (FR) (Pink (FR) 123) [2007 **52** 75: 12f⁶ 12.4m⁵ 12s⁵ 16.2s 14m⁶ 14.1m Aug 25] rather leggy gelding: modest maiden: worth another try at 2m: acts on good to firm going. *J. D. Bethell*

SENDEFAA (IRE) 2 b. or br.f. (Mar 2) Halling (USA) 133 – Patruel 93 (Rainbow **63** Quest (USA) 134) [2007 8.3m p8g p10g⁴ Oct 31] €52,000Y: attractive filly: fourth foal: dam, 9f winner, out of Coronation Stakes winner Kissing Cousin: modest form in maidens: stays 1¼m. *M. Botti*

SENDINPOST 4 b.f. Dansili 127 – Colleville 97 (Pharly (FR) 130) [2007 71: p12.2g⁴ **77** 15.4g⁵ p16g* p16g³ Jul 4] sturdy filly: fair handicapper: won at Kempton in June: stays 2m well: acts on polytrack and firm ground: sold 38,000 gns, joined Venetia Williams. *S. C. Williams*

SENESCHAL 6 b.g. Polar Falcon (USA) 126 – Broughton Singer (IRE) 61 (Common **75** Grounds 118) [2007 76: p6g p6g p7g* p6g p6g³ p7g p7g³ p7g p8g² 8.1m* 8m 8.1g⁶ 9m 7.1f p8g p8g⁵ p8g* 7d* 8g⁶ p8g p7g Dec 16] big, leggy gelding: fair performer: won claimer at Lingfield in February, and handicaps at Chepstow in May and Lingfield (apprentices) and Yarmouth in October: stays 1m: acts on polytrack, soft and good to firm going: tried in cheekpieces earlier in career: often makes running. *A. B. Haynes*

SENORA LENORAH 3 ch.f. Tumbleweed Ridge 117 – Blue Diamond (First Trump **–** 118) [2007 –: 6d 5g 5d 5m 5s 6g 8m 5g Oct 5] little sign of ability. *D. A. Nolan*

SENORA'S BEST 2 ch.f. (Mar 6) Best of The Bests (IRE) 122 – Hispaniola (IRE) **–** (Barathea (IRE) 127) [2007 5g 6g Oct 3] smallish filly: second foal: dam French maiden (stayed 11f): well held in maidens. *M. W. Easterby*

SENOR BENNY (USA) 8 br.h. Benny The Dip (USA) 127 – Senora Tippy (USA) (El **111** Gran Senor (USA) 136) [2007 112: 6v 7m⁶ 5m 5v³ 6v⁵ 5s* p6g³ 5g⁴ 6m⁵ 6d² 5g* 6d 6m p6g p6g Dec 7] lengthy, angular horse: smart performer: won handicap at Tipperary in August and listed race there (by 2½ lengths from City of Tribes) in October: in frame in handicap at Dundalk, Flying Five Stakes at the Curragh (fourth to Benbaun) and listed contest at the Curragh (3½ lengths second to US Ranger) in between: below form last 4 starts, in listed race at Doncaster on second occasion: best at 5f/6f: acts on sand, polytrack and heavy going: blinkered once early in career. *M. McDonagh, Ireland*

SENOR BOND (USA) 6 ch.g. Hennessy (USA) 122 – Troppa Freska (USA) (Silver **–** Hawk (USA) 123) [2007 10d⁵ Jun 26] smallish, good-bodied gelding: fair in 2005: unraced in 2006, and below form in claimer sole 6-y-o start. *A. M. Hales*

SENOR EDUARDO 10 gr.g. Terimon 124 – Jasmin Path (Warpath 113) [2007 –: 8m **–** Aug 30] good-topped gelding: modest in 2005: well held both starts since: often wears cheekpieces. *Mrs H. O. Graham*

SENORITA PARKES 2 ch.f. (Feb 12) Medicean 128 – Lucky Parkes 108 (Full Extent **– p** (USA) 113) [2007 6d Jul 16] sixth foal: half-sister to 3 winners, including useful 5f winner Charlie Parkes (by Pursuit of Love) and fairly useful 2002 2-y-o 5f/6f winner Robinia Parkes (by Robellino): dam, prolific 5f winner (including at 2 yrs), half-sister to useful performers Summerhill Parkes (stayed 6f) and My Melody Parkes (stayed 7f): 9/1, much better than bare result (ninth to Merchant of Dubai) in maiden at Ayr, showing good speed from poor draw: twice subsequently withdrawn following trouble at start: will prove best at 5f/6f: capable of better. *K. A. Ryan*

SENSASSE (IRE) 4 b.f. Imperial Ballet (IRE) 110 – Vanity (IRE) 75 (Thatching 131) **83** [2007 p7g⁶ p7g⁴ May 9] €8,000Y: first foal: dam, sprint maiden, half-sister to dam of smart performer up to 7f Eisteddfod: fairly useful winner at 2 yrs for D. Watchman in Ireland: unraced in 2006: better effort at 4 yrs when creditable fourth in handicap at Kempton: stays 7f: acts on polytrack and soft ground. *Mrs A. J. Perrett*

SENSE OF JOY 2 b.f. (Feb 12) Dansili 127 – Bonash 110 (Rainbow Quest (USA) **108 P** 134) [2007 7m* 7g* Aug 25]
     John Gosden has a very good record at Ascot's September meeting, in the two-year-old events particularly. He has saddled the winner of the Fillies' Mile on three occasions since 2000, winning with Crystal Music, Playful Act and Nannina, and he would have had prospects of supplementing those successes in the latest season with Sense of Joy. Sense of Joy is still unbeaten and looks a cracking prospect for 2008, having missed the Fillies' Mile, her reported objective after winning the Prestige Stakes at Goodwood in August, when the Fabre-trained Proviso was rerouted from the Prix Marcel Boussac at Longchamp. With Proviso and Sense of

Joy both in the ownership of Khalid Abdulla, their intended targets were reversed, with Sense of Joy becoming an intended runner in the Prix Marcel Boussac. In the intervening week, however, Sense of Joy suffered a setback which ended her season.

Sense of Joy made her debut in a fillies' maiden at Newmarket in August, along with some other well-bred newcomers from top stables. She could hardly have been more impressive, soon tracking the leaders on the bridle after jinking right on leaving the stalls and needing merely to be nudged along to pull five lengths clear of Presbyterian Nun, edging right but still recording a useful time-figure in the process. Sense of Joy started at 7/4-on three weeks later in the totescoop6 Prestige Stakes at Goodwood, facing six rivals who had all won a race, five of them having done so on their latest outing. Sense of Joy set for speed in a slowly-run race and won with more in hand than the half-length margin over the staying-bred runner-up Celtic Slipper, who pressed on two furlongs out but was always covered by Sense of Joy.

		Danehill	Danzig
	Dansili	(b 1986)	Razyana
	(b 1996)	Hasili	Kahyasi
Sense of Joy		(b 1991)	Kerali
(b.f. Feb 12, 2005)		Rainbow Quest	Blushing Groom
	Bonash	(b 1981)	I Will Follow
	(b 1991)	Sky Love	Nijinsky
		(b or br 1985)	Gangster of Love

Sense of Joy is the sixth living foal out of the smart French mile- to mile-and-a-half (Prix de Malleret) winner Bonash who, like Proviso, was owned by Khalid Abdulla and trained by Andre Fabre. Sense of Joy isn't the only filly out of Bonash to end her two-year-old season unbeaten and with a Timeform large 'P'. Bionic (by Zafonic) looked a most exciting prospect when winning a maiden at Goodwood in 1998, like Sense of Joy recording a particularly good timefigure, only to be ruled out of both the Fillies' Mile and Prix Marcel Boussac with a thrown splint. Bionic was prominent in the betting for both the One Thousand Guineas and the Oaks over the winter but was never seen on a racecourse again, suffering a hairline fracture of the pelvis the following spring and promptly retired to stud. The best of Bionic's winners as a broodmare is the unbeaten three-year-old colt Phoenix Tower. Sense of Joy is also a half-sister to the very smart mile-and-a-quarter to mile-and-five-furlong winner Day Flight (by Sadler's Wells), who often didn't look particularly straightforward but was successful in four pattern events and finished out of the frame just once in his fifteen-race career. Bonash is a sister to the dam of Raincoat, placed in the Dante and Gordon Stakes in the latest season, and to the smart mile-and-a-half listed winner Quenched (by Dansili), as well as a half-sister to the dam of the Prix de Diane and Prix du Moulin winner Nebraska Tornado and the Prix Eugene Adam winner Burning Sun.

Sense of Joy has all the attributes to go right to the top, a well-made filly who looks very much the type to train on. She will be suited by at least a mile and must have good prospects of staying a mile and a half. At the time of writing she is available at 16/1 for the One Thousand Guineas and 14/1 for the Oaks. *J. H. M. Gosden*

SENSIBLE 2 ch.f. (Mar 17) Almutawakel 126 – Opera 84 (Forzando 122) [2007 p8m[4] **57 p** Nov 11] €35,000Y: sixth foal: half-sister to fairly useful 8.6f to 1½m winner Muhannak (by Chester House) and 2 winners in US by Gold Case: dam, 2-y-o 7f/1m winner, later 6f winner in USA: 16/1, fourth to Burriscarra in maiden at Kempton: should improve. *M. J. Wallace*

SENTIERO ROSSO (USA) 5 b.g. Intidab (USA) 115 – Kheyrah (USA) 100 (Dayjur **65** (USA) 137) [2007 76: p8.6g 7g f8g[6] 8.1g f8g[6] 7.1m[4] May 21] small, strong gelding: fair handicapper: stays 1m: acts on all-weather, heavy and good to firm going: tried in blinkers/cheekpieces, often tongue tied: has looked reluctant: sold 11,000 gns. *B. Ellison*

SENTRY DUTY (FR) 5 b.g. Kahyasi 130 – Standing Around (FR) (Garde Royale **106** 120) [2007 14g* 16.1v Jun 30] useful performer: won minor events at Chantilly and Clairefontaine in 2006 for E. Libaud in France: fit from hurdling, best effort when winning handicap at Newmarket in May by 2½ lengths from Mikao: well held in Northumberland Plate subsequent outing: stays 15f: acts on soft ground: gelded. *N. J. Henderson*

SEPIA 2 b.f. (Jan 15) Dansili 127 – Spanish Sun (USA) 119 (El Prado (IRE) 119) [2007 **–** 7m Sep 21] smallish filly: first foal: dam, 7f (at 2 yrs) and 1½m (Ribblesdale Stakes) winner from 3 starts, out of useful half-sister to smart French middle-distance performers Apogee and Daring Miss: 5/1, weakened as if amiss in minor event at Newbury. *B. W. Hills*

SEPTIMUS (IRE) 4 b.c. Sadler's Wells (USA) 132 – Caladira (IRE) 81 (Darshaan **128** 133) [2007 121: 10m* 12d[2] 16.4d* 18m* Sep 14]

With established top performers rarely seen in British handicaps on the Flat nowadays, and rarely asked to shoulder sizeable penalties in Group 2 or Group 3 races either, it is uncommon for the highest-rated performance in any category in a season to come outside Group 1 company. It is, however, more common among the sprinters and stayers, no doubt partly because there are fewer Group 1s for these specialists compared to those available for the milers and middle-distance horses. Dayjur's victory in the Group 2 King's Stand Stakes in 1990 was his top-rated performance in Britain that year, as was Elnadim's in the 1996 Group 2 Diadem Stakes. Miss Andretti's run in the latest King's Stand Stakes was within a whisker of champion Sahkee's Secret's joint best, one of which, exceptionally, came in the listed Cathedral Stakes at Salisbury. Among the stayers, Double Trigger showed better form in winning the Group 2 Goodwood Cup and the then-Group 3 Doncaster Cup in 1995 than he needed in the Gold Cup, as did Yeats in landing the Goodwood Cup in 2006. A year on, the top staying performance of the season was not Yeats's at the Royal meeting but that of Septimus in the Doncaster Cup (Group 2 since 2003), in which, on only his second start at a trip of two miles or more, he put up a stunning display to trounce a representative field by five lengths.

Weatherbys Insurance Lonsdale Cup, York—Septimus marks his arrival on the staying scene by beating Balkan Knight (blaze), Anna Pavlova and Distinction

GNER Doncaster Cup, Doncaster—Septimus puts up a high-class performance with a runaway success from Geordieland, Allegretto (left) and Distinction (hidden behind runner-up)

With Septimus, Yeats and Melbourne Cup third Mahler all in his stable, Aidan O'Brien has an exceptionally strong hand for the best long-distance events. Not that Septimus needs two miles plus to make a mark—he is undoubtedly effective over shorter, as he showed on his first two starts. As reported in *Racehorses of 2006*, he injured a shoulder when twelfth in the Derby, a race in which he looked to hold a good chance based on an eight-length victory in the Dante Stakes. Septimus did not race again that year and remained on the sidelines until May when starting second favourite to Gladness Stakes winner Mustameet in the seven-runner High Chaparral EBF Mooresbridge Stakes over a mile and a quarter at the Curragh. Septimus won in fine style, racing close up behind Championship Point and idling markedly once taking over with more than a furlong to go, eventually defeating Fracas by a length and a half. A year earlier Septimus had looked ill at ease on the Epsom course but, in hindsight, that was probably because of the injury rather than any problems with Epsom's lay-out and camber. His run in the Coronation Cup suggested as much because he beat everything except his stable-companion Scorpion. Septimus made much of the running and, after being tapped for speed when Scorpion went past over two furlongs out, he rallied well, going down by a length and a quarter.

Septimus was staying on at Epsom and it was no surprise to see him moved up in trip on his next appearance, in the Weatherbys Insurance Lonsdale Cup at York over two and a half months later. The race has had some good winners since being made a pattern event in 1998, notably Persian Punch, Celeric, Royal Rebel, Bollin Eric, Millenary and Sergeant Cecil. The latest edition was over a slightly longer trip than previously but the distance caused Septimus no problems—indeed, he seemed well suited by it. Starting a hot favourite and opposed by proven Cup horses Distinction, Percussionist and Sergeant Cecil, Septimus could be named the winner as he took closer order, going easily, three furlongs out. Driven on approaching the final furlong, he was soon in command and had no difficulty defeating Balkan Knight by a length with Anna Pavlova third. The fact that several of his better-known rivals, including the proven trio mentioned above, were not at their best detracted a little from Septimus's victory, but he still started at 11/10 for the GNER Doncaster Cup three weeks later, carrying a penalty and giving weight all round. His seven opponents on this occasion included Goodwood Cup winner Allegretto, Gold Cup runner-up Geordieland, Finalmente, who had been in the frame in both those races, and Balkan Knight and Distinction again. Thanks to Finalmente, the race was a true test of stamina and Septimus proved well suited by it, travelling with great ease four or five lengths off the pace and accelerating in a style reminiscent of Yeats at his best—not a common sight in top-flight staying events—as he took the lead over a furlong from home. Ridden out, Septimus left his rivals for dead, passing the post five lengths clear of Geordieland, with Allegretto plugging on for third. This was the best performance in the Doncaster Cup since the days of Ardross and Le Moss getting on for thirty years earlier. The timefigure of 0.82 fast, equivalent to a timerating of 121, was the best by a horse over two miles or more since Persian Punch won the Jockey Club Cup in 2000, confirming impressions that Septimus's success heralded the arrival of potentially an exceptional Cup performer.

Septimus (IRE) (b.c. 2003)	Sadler's Wells (USA) (b 1981)	Northern Dancer (b 1961)	Nearctic
			Fairy Bridge
		Fairy Bridge (b 1975)	Bold Reason
			Special
	Caladira (IRE) (br 1991)	Darshaan (br 1981)	Shirley Heights
			Delsy
		Cape Race (b 1974)	Northern Dancer
			Sticky Case

Given that there is no shortage of stamina in the pedigree, Septimus's effectiveness over long distances can scarcely have come as a surprise. Sadler's Wells is essentially an influence for stamina and he has sired two Gold Cup winners (dual winners Kayf Tara and Yeats), two winners of the St Leger (Brian Boru and Milan) and two of the Prix Royal-Oak (Braashee and Ebadiyla). His three-year-old son Royal And Regal showed himself one of the best French-trained stayers when landing the Jockey Club Cup. The dam Caladira, by Darshaan, readily won a maiden race over a mile and a quarter on soft going at the Curragh on her debut but ran only once afterwards, when reasonably close up in seventh in a listed event. Septimus apart, her record at stud is mediocre, with two minor winners from eight foals. One of these is two-year-old Hollow Hill (by Orpen), who did not progress after winning a minor event at Sligo in August, finishing well beaten in the Goffs Fillies Million and running as if something was amiss when last in a nursery at Dundalk. A yearling brother to Septimus—there is also a foal—sold for 140,000 guineas at the Newmarket December Sales. The next dam, Cape Race, was a daughter of Falmouth Stakes runner-up Sticky Case and won a modest maiden over a mile. She foaled nine winners including one in listed company in Sweden. Cape Race was a half-sister to high-class mile- to mile-and-a-quarter performer Lord Gayle, and to the dam of One Thousand Guineas third Seraphima, ancestress of Deutsches Derby winner Nicaron. Septimus is a sturdy colt who acts on soft and, as he showed once and for all at Doncaster, also on good to firm going. Septimus can be expected to stay two and a half miles and he holds excellent prospects of giving his sire a fifth Gold Cup win if given the chance. Equally, he should not be ignored over shorter trips and, with or without Soldier of Fortune, another crack at the Coronation Cup, providing there is a strong gallop, may be a good option in the first part of the year. *A. P. O'Brien, Ireland*

SERENA'S STORM (IRE) 2 b.f. (Apr 28) Statue of Liberty (USA) 115 – Princess **87** Serena (USA) 48 (Unbridled's Song (USA) 125) [2007 6m⁵ 7d* 6d 6.5m⁵ 7.1m² 7d Oct 27] €30,000Y: leggy, lightly-made filly: has a quick action: first foal: dam, US 1m winner, out of twice-raced sister to high-class US performer up to 1¼m Serena's Song (dam of Coronation Stakes winner Sophisticat): fairly useful form: won maiden at Catterick in July: ran well in nurseries at Doncaster (fifth to Royal Confidence, first home far side) and Musselburgh (second to Sourire): should prove best at 6f/7f: acts on good to firm and good to soft going. *J. J. Quinn*

SERENE DANCER 4 b.f. Danehill Dancer (IRE) 117 – Bliss (IRE) 75 (Statoblest 120) **58** [2007 59: 7.1d 8m³ 6d p8g Sep 18] big, angular filly: modest maiden: stays 1m: acts on good to firm ground: said to have finished lame final outing. *Mrs P. N. Dutfield*

SERENE HIGHNESS (IRE) 3 b.f. Highest Honor (FR) 124 – Dollysister (FR) **–** (Alydar (USA)) [2007 66: 8m 9m Jul 11] lightly-raced maiden: fair at 2 yrs, no form in 2007: should stay at least 1m: slowly away on reappearance. *J. L. Dunlop*

SERENGETI 3 b.c. Singspiel (IRE) 133 – Tanzania (USA) (Darshaan 133) [2007 80p: **105** p10g² p10g* 9.9m* 16d⁴ Jun 22] rangy colt: has scope: useful performer, lightly raced: much improved in handicaps in 2007, winning at Lingfield in April and Goodwood (very stiff to post, beat Oakley Heffert 7 lengths) in May: not at best when fourth in Queen's Vase at Royal Ascot subsequent outing: will stay at least 1½m: acts on polytrack and good to firm going. *M. Johnston*

SERGEANT CECIL 8 ch.g. King's Signet (USA) 110 – Jadidh 64 (Touching Wood **120** (USA) 127) [2007 120: 12m⁴ 14g* 20g 12g⁶ 16.4d⁵ Aug 21] workmanlike gelding: very smart performer: won Emirates Airline Yorkshire Cup at York in May by ¾ length from

Emirates Airline Yorkshire Cup, York—Sergeant Cecil shows himself to be as good as ever and reverses 2006 running with Percussionist (hooped cap), who is only fourth this time; the enigmatic Geordieland (right) is second with Bulwark (left) third

Geordieland: well below form after, only 10 lengths fifth to Septimus in Lonsdale Cup at same course final outing: reportedly suffered lung infection after: stays 2½m: acts on firm and soft going: ran poorly in cheekpieces once in 2003: sometimes races freely/carries head awkwardly: has good turn of foot, and usually held up. *B. R. Millman*

SERGEANT SHARPE 2 ch.g. (Feb 6) Cadeaux Genereux 131 – Halcyon Daze 82 **66** (Halling (USA) 133) [2007 7m 7m⁴ 7s⁶ Sep 26] 14,000Y: well-made gelding: third foal: dam, 11.5f winner, half-sister to smart 1¾m winner Ashgar out of half-sister to Oaks winner Ramruma: fair maiden: gelded after final start: will be suited by 1m+. *M. H. Tompkins*

SERHAAPHIM 3 gr.f. Erhaab (USA) 127 – Salinova (FR) (Linamix (FR) 127) [2007 **67** 11g² 10.1d⁴ 9m⁶ 12.1s 16.2s³ 16g³ p16g³ Nov 14] sixth foal: half-sister to 8-y-o Shabernak and fairly useful 1¾m winners Silver Sash (by Mark of Esteem) and Souffleur (by In The Wings): dam unraced sister to useful French 1½m winner Six Zero: fair maiden: left M. Bell after sixth start: stays 2m: acts on polytrack and soft ground: won over hurdles in November. *N. B. King*

SERIAL HABIT (IRE) 4 b.f. Lahib (USA) 129 – Satire 53 (Terimon 124) [2007 9.8m – Sep 1] sturdy filly: first foal: dam, maiden who stayed 1¼m, half-sister to Cheshire Oaks winner Shadow Dancing: 100/1, well held in maiden at Ripon. *M. Brittain*

SERIEUX 8 b.g. Cadeaux Genereux 131 – Seranda (IRE) (Petoski 135) [2007 81§: f6g – § f6g⁶ Jan 30] strong, lengthy, useful-looking gelding: ungenuine performer: fairly useful at best in 2006: no form at 8 yrs: tried in cheekpieces/visor. *D. Nicholls*

SERIOUS CHOICE (IRE) 2 b.g. (Mar 15) Choisir (AUS) 126 – Printaniere (USA) **60** (Sovereign Dancer (USA)) [2007 7s 8d p8g Oct 31] modest form in maidens, then gelded: may prove best up to 1m. *J. R. Boyle*

SERIOUSLY LUCKY (IRE) 3 b.g. Key of Luck (USA) 126 – Serious Delight **41** (Lomond (USA) 128) [2007 –: 6m 5m May 22] angular, quite good-topped gelding: poor maiden, lightly raced: should stay 7f+. *D. Nicholls*

SERPENTARIA 3 b.f. Golden Snake (USA) 127 – French Spice 85 (Cadeaux **89** Genereux 131) [2007 p8g* p10g⁴ 14.1g² 12g 12m⁴ 16.2s² 16.2g² 14g 17.2f⁴ Sep 16] lengthy, leggy filly: fourth foal: half-sister to 1½m seller winner Gentian (by Generous) and winner in Greece by Hector Protector: dam, 8.5f to 1½m winner, half-sister to Gold Cup winner Celeric: fairly useful performer: won maiden at Lingfield in January: generally progressive in handicaps after, second at Nottingham and Beverley (2): stays 2m: acts on polytrack, soft and good to firm going: sold 57,000 gns. *Sir Mark Prescott*

SERRAMANNA 6 ch.m. Grand Lodge (USA) 125 – Spry 84 (Suave Dancer (USA) **55**
136) [2007 67: p16g⁶ p12g p16g Jan 24] leggy mare: handicapper, only modest in 2007:
stays 2m: acts on polytrack, firm and soft ground: tried blinkered. *Ms J. S. Doyle*

SESARO EXPRESS (IRE) 6 b.g. Sesaro (USA) 81 – Curie Express (IRE) 65 (Fayruz **–**
116) [2007 p13.9g Nov 14] maiden, lightly raced on Flat: well held in handicap at Wolverhampton sole start in 2007: stays 1¾m: best efforts on good ground: tried blinkered.
John A. Quinn, Ireland

SESMEN 3 gr.f. Inchinor 119 – Poetry In Motion (IRE) 76 (Ballad Rock 122) [2007 106: **102**
7m⁶ 8g⁶ 6s 7g 8d² 7m p8m* Nov 1] neat filly: useful performer: in-and-out form in 2007,
winning listed race at Lingfield in November by head from Fidelia: creditable sixth to
Darjina in Poule d'Essai des Pouliches at Longchamp on second start: stays 1m: acts on
polytrack, good to firm and good to soft going: often tongue tied: has been early to post:
front runner. *M. Botti*

SET ALIGHT 6 b.m. Forzando 122 – Me Spede (Valiyar 129) [2007 59, a74: f8g Jan 7] **–**
big mare: fair performer at best: no show sole run in 2007: stays 1m: acts on all-weather
and good to firm going: wears visor/cheekpieces: looks hard ride. *Mrs C. A. Dunnett*

SETA PURA 2 b.f. (Apr 16) Domedriver (IRE) 128 – Sulitelma (USA) 63 (The Minstrel **58**
(CAN) 135) [2007 7.1g⁶ 6g⁵ 6g* Oct 30] smallish, sturdy filly: half-sister to several
winners, including Irish 5f winner Neeze (by Cadeaux Genereux), 6-y-o Tromp and 3-y-o
Ice Mountain, all fairly useful: dam, 2-y-o 5f winner, out of half-sister to Petoski: modest
form: won maiden at Catterick final start: should be suited by 7f/1m. *Mrs A. Duffield*

SETEEM (USA) 3 ch.g. Diesis 133 – Inscrutable Dancer (USA) (Green Dancer (USA) **– §**
132) [2007 74: 10.1s⁶ 9.9m 10.3m 8m 9.1s Oct 4] sturdy gelding: maiden: well held in
2007, looking increasingly wayward. *N. Tinkler*

SET THE SCENE (IRE) 3 b.f. Sadler's Wells (USA) 132 – Margarula (IRE) 120 **79**
(Doyoun 124) [2007 74p: p9.5g⁶ 10.9d² 11.9m* 10m Jun 14] lengthy filly: fair performer:
won maiden at Brighton in June: stays 1½m: acts on good to firm and good to soft ground:
signs of temperament. *J. H. M. Gosden*

SEVEN NO TRUMPS 10 ch.g. Pips Pride 117 – Classic Ring (IRE) 50 (Auction Ring **59**
(USA) 123) [2007 66: 5g⁶ p5.1g p5.1g 5.1g* 5f³ 5.1g 5d⁴ 6d⁶ 5.1s² 5.7m⁵ 5g 5.1f 5m
Aug 31] rangy, good-topped gelding: modest performer: won claimer at Chepstow in
May: effective at 5f/6f: acts on polytrack and any turf going: blinkered once at 3 yrs, tried
in cheekpieces: edgy sort: tends to carry head high. *J. M. Bradley*

SEVENTH CLOUD (IRE) 2 br.f. (Feb 28) Septieme Ciel (USA) 123 – Wana Doo **61 d**
(USA) (Grand Slam (USA) 120) [2007 5f 5m p5g³ 6s p7g p6g 6m 5m³ p6g p7.1g Nov 5]
16,000Y: neat filly: first foal: dam, French 6.5f and 1m winner (latter at 2 yrs), out of
useful French performer up to 10.5f Wedding Gift: modest maiden: below form after third
start: best efforts at 5f: acts on polytrack and good to firm going: tried visored. *A. P. Jarvis*

SEVENTH HILL 2 ch.c. (Feb 5) Compton Place 125 – Dream Baby (Master Willie **75**
129) [2007 7m 7m⁶ 8d Oct 3] workmanlike colt: fair maiden: sixth at Newbury, standout
effort: best short of 1m: acts on good to firm going. *M. Blanshard*

SEW IN CHARACTER 3 ch.g. Woodborough (USA) 112 – Elegant Rose 72 (Noalto **44**
120) [2007 –: p8.6g p12.2g⁵ p8g p8.6g Jul 27] poor form: tried blinkered. *M. Blanshard*

SEW'N'SO CHARACTER (IRE) 6 b.g. Imperial Ballet (IRE) 110 – Hope And **80**
Glory (USA) 87 (Well Decorated (USA)) [2007 95: p8.6g⁵ 8m 8.1g Apr 28] good-topped
gelding: fairly useful handicapper: effective at 7.5f to 10.5f: acts on polytrack, soft and
good to firm going: blinkered once: waited with. *M. Blanshard*

SEXY LADY (GER) 4 ch.f. Danehill Dancer (IRE) 117 – Sky Dancing (IRE) (Exit To **101**
Nowhere (USA) 122) [2007 107: 10d 10.1m⁴ 8g⁵ 10m 8g Sep 9] first foal: dam useful
German 7f (at 2 yrs) to 1¼m winner: useful performer: won maiden at Hanover, handicap
at Frankfurt, listed race at Baden-Baden and Prix Chloe at Maisons-Laffitte (awarded
race after being beaten 1½ lengths by Mandesha) in 2006: mostly disappointing in 2007,
best effort when 2¼ lengths fourth to Yaqeen in listed race at Yarmouth: stays 1¼m: acts
on soft and good to firm ground. *P. Rau, Germany*

SFORZANDO 6 b.m. Robellino 127 – Mory Kante (USA) (Icecapade (USA)) **76**
[2007 81: 10.1s 12.4m 12f² 11.7f⁴ 10.5m⁵ 9.1m⁵ 11.5g 10.5m* 10.1m⁶ 11.9g⁴ 10g 10.1d³ **a70**
10g* p12.2g Nov 12] well-made mare: fair handicapper: won at Haydock in August and
Nottingham in November: stays 1½m: acts on polytrack, firm and good to soft going:
sometimes slowly away: tried blinkered: not entirely straightforward. *Mrs L. Stubbs*

SGT SCHULTZ (IRE) 4 b.g. In The Wings 128 – Ann's Annie (IRE) 78 (Alzao **90**
(USA) 117) [2007 75, a78: p12g* p12g* p12g⁶ p12g⁴ p10g⁴ p12g* p12g³ 10g⁴ 10g⁴ p12g
10m⁶ 12m³ 12g p12m* Dec 7] big, good-topped gelding: fairly useful performer: won
maiden in January, and handicaps in February, March and December, all at Lingfield:
effective at 1¼m to easy 1¾m: acts on polytrack and firm going: consistent. *J. S. Moore*

SHAABAN (IRE) 6 b.g. Woodman (USA) 126 – Ashbilya (USA) (Nureyev (USA) **–**
131) [2007 –: 10.2m Sep 13] good-bodied gelding: little form since 2005: has worn
cheekpieces/blinkers. *R. J. Price*

SHAAMA ROSE (FR) 2 gr.f. (Jan 15) Verglas (IRE) 118 – River Ballade (USA) (Irish **–**
River (FR) 131) [2007 8.1f⁶ 8.3m Sep 11] €75,000Y: neat filly: half-sister to 3 winners,
including useful French 5.5f to 7.5f winner (including at 2 yrs) Kenkaye (by Kendor):
dam unraced: no show (very green) in maidens. *M. R. Channon*

SHABAHAR (IRE) 3 b.g. Hernando (FR) 127 – Shara (IRE) 75 (Kahyasi 130) [2007 **84**
78: 8d* 10g⁵ 10s 8d 8s 10g⁶ Nov 7] strong gelding: fairly useful performer: won maiden
at Thurles in March: left J. Oxx 85,000 gns after third start (gelded after final one): stays
1¼m: acts on good to soft ground. *M. J. McGrath*

SHABERNAK (IRE) 8 gr.g. Akarad (FR) 130 – Salinova (FR) (Linamix (FR) 127) **–**
[2007 109: p16g⁵ 14g May 19] smallish, lengthy gelding: smart performer at best: well
held in handicaps in 2007: stayed 2m: acted on firm and soft going: raced prominently:
retired due to recurring leg problems and now at Moorcroft Racehorse Welfare Centre,
West Sussex. *M. L. W. Bell*

SHABIBA (USA) 2 b.f. (Mar 6) Seeking The Gold (USA) – Misterah 105 (Alhaarth **89 p**
(IRE) 126) [2007 6m² 6m* Oct 4] strong, well-made filly: easy mover: second foal: dam
6f (at 2 yrs)/7f (Nell Gwyn Stakes) winner: confirmed debut promise
when winning maiden at Newmarket by ½ length from Elizabeth Swann (Spinning Lucy
head back in third): will stay 7f/1m: will continue to improve. *M. P. Tregoning*

SHABNAAM 2 b.f. (Feb 27) Diktat 126 – Noble View (USA) 68 (Distant View (USA) **50**
126) [2007 5g⁴ 5.9g p6g p6d⁵ Dec 6] tall, rather unfurnished filly: second foal: half-sister
to 3-y-o Silver Hotspur: dam, maiden, half-sister to Poule d'Essai des Pouliches winner
Houseproud: modest maiden: should be suited by 6f/7f. *K. A. Ryan*

SHADED EDGE 3 b.g. Bold Edge 123 – Twilight Mistress 84 (Bin Ajwaad (IRE) 119) **68**
[2007 49: p7g⁴ p6g* p6g² p7g* p6g⁴ Oct 14] fair performer: successful at Lingfield
in maiden in July and handicap in September: stays 7f: raced only on polytrack.
D. W. P. Arbuthnot

SHADES OF BLUE 4 b.f. Bandmaster (USA) 97 – Just Sidium 46 (Nicholas (USA) **–**
111) [2007 7.1m 7.1m Aug 27] fourth foal: dam sprint maiden: well beaten in maidens.
C. J. Down

SHADOW ASPECT 4 b.c. Nashwan (USA) 135 – Hedonic (Gone West (USA)) [2007 **50**
59: p7.1g⁶ p8.6g³ p10g p10g 13m 12g 12.5m Aug 27] quite good-topped colt: modest
maiden: stayed 1¼m: acted on polytrack: blinkered final outing: dead. *Eoin Doyle,
Ireland*

SHADOW CABINET (IRE) 2 b.c. (Feb 10) Noverre (USA) 125 – Shadow Roll **78**
(IRE) 79 (Mark of Esteem (IRE) 137) [2007 6m 7g⁵ p7g⁵ 7m² 7.1g² 8.3d³ Oct 15] tall,
unfurnished colt: second foal: brother to fairly useful 2006 2-y-o 6f winner Undertone:
dam, maiden best at 6f/7f at 2 yrs, out of smart performer up to 1¼m Warning Shadows:
fair maiden: placed in nurseries last 3 starts: stays 1m: acts on good to firm and good to
soft going: sold 46,000 gns. *M. L. W. Bell*

SHADOW JUMPER (IRE) 6 b.g. Dayjur (USA) 137 – Specifically (USA) (Sky **58**
Classic (CAN)) [2007 71: f6g f6g f6g f6g p8.6g⁵ f8g² f7g f8g⁴ p8.6g f7g² 6d 7.1g⁵ 8.3d
8.5s p10g p8.6g⁴ p9.5g p9.5g⁶ p8.6d f7d² p7.1d Dec 27] modest performer nowadays:
stays 1m: acts on all-weather and good to soft ground: tried tongue tied: usually wears
headgear: often races prominently: none too consistent. *J. T. Stimpson*

SHADOWS FALL (USA) 2 b.c. (Apr 23) Dynaformer (USA) – Not Bashful (USA) **66**
(Seattle Slew (USA)) [2007 p8g⁵ 8g p8g 10.2d⁶ p10g p8g⁴ p8.6g⁴ p8.6g Dec 3] strong
colt: fair maiden: stays 8.6f: acts on polytrack, probably on good to soft going: sold
20,000 gns. *P. F. I. Cole*

SHADOW THE WIND (IRE) 3 b.g. Val Royal (FR) 127 – Kesh Kumay (IRE) 76 **82**
(Danehill (USA) 126) [2007 7d³ 6m* 7m⁴ 9.9m² 10d⁵ Oct 15] lengthy gelding: fairly
useful handicapper: won maiden at Newbury in June: off 2 months and upped in trip, best
effort when second to Harry Tricker at Goodwood after: stays 1¼m: unraced on extremes
of going: failed to handle bend at Windsor final outing. *E. F. Vaughan*

SHADOWY FIGURE 3 b.c. Machiavellian (USA) 123 – Renashaan (FR) (Darshaan **82 p** 133) [2007 8.3d* Oct 15] 400,000Y: good-topped, attractive colt: brother to smart miler Medecis and half-brother to several winners, notably very smart 5f (at 2 yrs) to 1¼m (including Prix de l'Opera and Hong Kong Cup) winner Alexander Goldrun (by Gold Away): dam, French 1m and (at 2 yrs) 9f winner, out of half-sister to dam of Gold Cup winner Royal Rebel: 7/4 favourite, overcame greenness when winning maiden at Windsor in October by ½ length from Red Blossom, coaxed along to lead final 1f after taking good hold in rear: should go on to better things. *Saeed bin Suroor*

SHADY BAY 3 b.f. Sure Blade (USA) 130 – French Project (IRE) 84 (Project Manager – 111) [2007 7f 10d 9.1s p13.9g Nov 14] 800Y: lengthy, workmanlike filly: fifth foal: dam, maiden (stayed 1½m), hurdle winner: no form: has been withdrawn twice after being unruly at start (refused to enter stall first occasion). *D. W. Chapman*

SHADY GLOOM (IRE) 2 b.c. (Feb 6) Traditionally (USA) 117 – Last Drama (IRE) **50 p** (Last Tycoon 131) [2007 8.2g Nov 7] big, lengthy colt: half-brother/closely related to several winners, including US performer up to 1¼m Self Feeder (by Lycius), French 1m and 1½m winner King's Drama (by King's Theatre) and 2005 2-y-o 6f winner Rosinka (by Soviet Star), later successful up to 11f (Grade 3) in US, all smart: dam useful French 1¼m winner: 14/1, eleventh in maiden at Nottingham having forced good pace: will do better. *K. A. Ryan*

SHADY GREEN (IRE) 3 b.g. Kalanisi (IRE) 132 – Albacora (IRE) 98 (Fairy King – (USA)) [2007 69: f8g⁵ 7m p12.2g Jun 1] close-coupled, good-topped gelding: maiden: well held at 3 yrs: dead. *M. W. Easterby*

SHAFRONS CANYON (IRE) 4 b.f. Lend A Hand 124 – Carroll's Canyon (IRE) – (Hatim (USA) 121) [2007 –: p7.1g Dec 14] modest maiden at best: left G. Lyons prior to handicap at Wolverhampton, only outing in 2007. *P. M. Rogers, Ireland*

SHAFTESBURY AVENUE (USA) 4 ch.c. Fusaichi Pegasus (USA) 130 – Little **60** Firefly (IRE) 97 (Danehill (USA) 126) [2007 p12.2g f6g² f7g* f7g 8f Aug 12] modest performer: won maiden at Southwell in March: may prove best at 7f/1m: blinkered since debut, also tongue tied last 3 starts. *J. O'Reilly*

SHAFTESBURY (IRE) 2 b.g. (May 1) Lomitas 129 – Vivid Concert (IRE) 73 (Chief **65** Singer 131) [2007 9d 8g p8m Nov 26] lengthy, rather unfurnished gelding: mid-field in maidens, fair form at Bath second start (raced alone): will stay 1¼m. *M. Johnston*

SHAHADAH (IRE) 5 b.m. Daylami (IRE) 138 – Mafaatin (IRE) (Royal Academy **46** (USA) 130) [2007 8.1m 6s p8.6g 8.1d p12g Aug 28] lengthy ex-Irish mare: second foal: dam unraced granddaughter of Arc winner All Along: lightly-raced maiden: missed 2006: poor form at 5 yrs: stays 8.6f: acts on polytrack and firm going. *R. J. Price*

SHAHEER (IRE) 5 b.g. Shahrastani (USA) 135 – Atmospheric Blues (IRE) 91 **62** (Double Schwartz 128) [2007 57, a62: p10g p9.5g p10g* p10g² p10g² p10g⁶ 11.5m 11.9m⁴ 10s³ 10.2f² 10d² p8g p10g⁶ p10m p10m² p10g Dec 12] sturdy gelding: fluent mover: modest performer: won handicap at Lingfield in February: stays 1½m: acts on all-weather, firm and soft ground: tried tongue tied/in headgear (often visored of late). *J. Gallagher*

SHAHIN (USA) 4 b.c. Kingmambo (USA) 125 – String Quartet (IRE) 109 (Sadler's **115** Wells (USA) 132) [2007 102: 12g² 12d⁴ 12m² 13.3d² p12g⁶ Sep 8] tall, quite attractive colt: smart performer, lightly raced: injured off-hind fetlock joint after sole 3-y-o outing: improved on return in 2007, best efforts when ½-length second to Ivy Creek in listed race at Goodwood, 2½ lengths equal-second to Papal Bull in Princess of Wales's Stakes at Newmarket and 4 lengths second to same rival in Geoffrey Freer Stakes at Newbury: below form in September Stakes at Kempton final start, seeming to lose interest (report- edly returned lame): stays 13f: unraced on extremes of going on turf: visored third/fourth starts. *M. P. Tregoning*

SHAIKA 4 b.f. Almushtarak (IRE) 122 – Subtle Girl (Selkirk (USA) 129) [2007 60, a44: **§§** 10s⁵ 11.5d⁵ 10.1d 11.5d 11.9m Aug 14] modest performer at best: tried in cheekpieces/ blinkers: virtually refused to race last 3 outings: one to leave alone. *G. Prodromou*

SHAKE ON IT 3 b.g. Lomitas 129 – Decision Maid (USA) 105 (Diesis 133) [2007 80: **84** 8f* 8.3m 7m⁵ 8m⁴ 7f⁵ 8m³ 10g* 10m 10.2f⁵ Sep 16] sparely-made gelding: fairly useful performer: won maiden at Bath in April and handicap at Lingfield in August: gelded after final start: stays 1¼m: raced only on good ground or firmer: tongue tied: travels strongly, and sometimes finds little. *Eve Johnson Houghton*

SHAKER (IRE) 2 b.f. (Apr 25) Key of Luck (USA) 126 – Gravieres (FR) (Saint **89 +** Estephe (FR) 123) [2007 6d* 7.1d 7m 7d² 8g Nov 3] €155,000Y: leggy, quite attractive filly: half-sister to several winners by Sadler's Wells, including 9f winner Coliseum and 1999 2-y-o 1m winner Homer, both useful in Ireland: dam 5.5f (at 2 yrs in France) to 9f (US Grade 2 event) winner: fairly useful form: won maiden at Yarmouth in July: best efforts last 2 starts, second to Seeking Star in minor event at Leicester and seventh to Classic Legend in listed race at Newmarket (not clear run): stays 1m: acts on good to soft going. *M. L. W. Bell*

SHAKESPEARE'S SON 2 b.g. (Mar 29) Mind Games 121 – Eastern Blue (IRE) 68 **59** (Be My Guest (USA) 126) [2007 6.1d p6g⁴ p5g⁴ p6g p6d⁵ f5d⁴ Dec 20] angular gelding: modest maiden: should prove best at 5f/6f: acts on all-weather. *H. J. Evans*

SHALLAL 2 b.c. (Apr 24) Cape Cross (IRE) 129 – First Waltz (FR) 117 (Green Dancer **101 p** (USA) 132) [2007 6m³ 6g* Jul 31] strong, sturdy colt: half-brother to several winners, including 1m winners Atlantic Rhapsody (10-y-o) and Gaitero (in France, by Groom Dancer), and 5f/6f winner Gimasha (by Cadeaux Genereux), all useful: dam won Prix Morny: useful form: promising debut at Newmarket, then won maiden at Goodwood by ½ length from Eastern Gift (Dream Eater third, Moynahan fourth), showing good attitude: likely to stay 7f: will go on to better things. *P. W. Chapple-Hyam*

SHALOO DIAMOND 2 b.g. (Apr 21) Captain Rio 122 – Alacrity 62 (Alzao (USA) **68** 117) [2007 6m⁶ 7m³ 7.2s⁴ Sep 21] well-made gelding: fair maiden: in frame at Redcar (minor event) and Ayr: gelded after: will stay 1m: acts on heavy and good to firm going. *R. M. Whitaker*

SHAMAYEL 2 b.f. (Feb 28) Pivotal 124 – Mauri Moon 104 (Green Desert (USA) 127) **85** [2007 7g² p7g* 7d⁶ Oct 27] 380,000Y: good-bodied filly: second foal: half-sister to 2006 2-y-o 7f winner Capannina (by Grand Lodge): dam, 6f (at 2 yrs) to 1m winner, half-sister to useful French 1¼m performer All Glory: fairly useful form: confirmed encouragement from Salisbury (second to Joffe's Run) when winning maiden at Kempton in September: still rather green when sixth to Lady Deauville in listed event at Newbury, not knocked about once held: will stay 1m. *B. W. Hills*

SHAMDINAN (FR) 3 ch.c. Dr Fong (USA) 128 – Shamdara (IRE) 111 (Dr Devious **118** (IRE) 127) [2007 10g* 10.5m² 10.5g³ 12s 10d³ 11f⁵ 9f⁵ 12s² Oct 27] good-topped colt: first foal: dam, French 1¼m/10.5f winner, half-sister to smart French 1½m to 2½m performer Shamdala: smart performer: won maiden at Saint-Cloud in April and, having left A. de Royer Dupre after fourth outing, Secretariat Stakes at Arlington in August, latter by ½ length from Red Giant (who gave 4 lb), edging left before quickening to lead near finish: good efforts when placed in Prix du Jockey Club at Chantilly (1¾ lengths third to Lawman, staying on well) and Breeders' Cup Turf at Monmouth (7 lengths second behind English Channel) on third and final outings: below form otherwise, including in Irish Derby at the Curragh (well-held ninth) fourth start and in Man o'War Stakes at Belmont (fifth behind Doctor Dino, left D. O'Neill afterwards) sixth outing: needs further than 9f, and stays 1½m: very best efforts on good going or softer: usually held up, but ridden more prominently final start. *A. Penna jnr, USA*

SHAMROCK BAY 5 b.m. Celtic Swing 138 – Kabayil 75 (Dancing Brave (USA) 140) **53** [2007 73d: p12g⁶ p16g³ p13.9g Nov 16] close-coupled mare: modest performer nowadays: barely stays 2m: acts on soft and good to firm ground, probably on polytrack: tried tongue tied: formerly headstrong: held up. *C. R. Dore*

SHAMROCK LADY (IRE) 2 b.f. (Mar 17) Orpen (USA) 116 – Shashi (IRE) 79 **71** (Shaadi (USA) 126) [2007 5m³ 5g² 5m⁵ 6s* 7.1d 6g 6s 6g Nov 2] compact filly: half-sister to 8-y-o Make My Hay: dam 5f (at 2 yrs) to 7f winner: fair performer: won maiden at Goodwood in July: stiff tasks afterwards: should stay 7f/1m: acts on soft going. *Pat Eddery*

SHAM RUBY 5 ch.m. Tagula (IRE) 116 – Bistro (USA) (Strawberry Road (AUS) 128) **44** [2007 34: p6g⁵ p6g p6g p6g³ p6g 6m³ 7m 6g 6m⁶ 7d Aug 21] poor maiden: stays 6f: acts on polytrack and good to firm going: usually tongue tied. *M. R. Bosley*

SHAMWARI FIRE (IRE) 7 ch.g. Idris (IRE) 118 – Bobby's Dream 53 (Reference **– §** Point 139) [2007 42§: 10m Jun 3] poor performer: stays 1¼m: acts on firm and good to soft ground, little recent form on all-weather: tried visored, blinkered last 5 starts in 2006: unreliable. *I. W. McInnes*

SHANAFARAHAN (IRE) 2 b.g. (Mar 22) Marju (IRE) 127 – Sedna (FR) (Bering **74** 136) [2007 7s⁵ 7d 7g⁵ Oct 26] €48,000Y: compact gelding: fourth foal: half-brother to 4-y-o Braddock: dam, French 10.5f winner, out of smart French filly up to 10.5f Sheba Dancer: fair maiden: pulled hard when fifth to Naval Review at Doncaster final start (gelded after): will be suited by 1m/1¼m: raced only on good going or softer. *T. P. Tate*

SHANDELIGHT (IRE) 3 b.f. Dilshaan 119 – By Candlelight (IRE) 84 (Roi Danzig **60**
(USA)) [2007 –: 8f⁴ f8g* 8f 8.3g² 8.3s 9.1d⁴ 12m² Aug 3] deep-girthed filly: modest
performer: won minor event at Southwell in May, hanging right: stays 1½m: acts on
fibresand, soft and good to firm going: usually wears cheekpieces (not final start).
Mrs A. Duffield

SHANEHILL (IRE) 5 b.g. Danehill (USA) 126 – Shunaire (USA) 81 (Woodman **–**
(USA) 126) [2007 8.1m Aug 7] little form over jumps: 33/1, well held in seller at Chepstow on Flat debut. *Evan Williams*

SHANNERSBURG (IRE) 2 b. or br.c. (Mar 17) Johannesburg (USA) 127 – Shah- **79**
oune (USA) (Blushing Groom (FR) 131) [2007 5s 6.1g⁵ 7s² 7.5g² 8.2d* 8.3d⁴ Aug 15]
28,000Y: leggy colt: half-brother to several winners, including smart French 1m winner
Bouccaneer (by Hero's Honor): dam French maiden: fair form: won minor event at
Nottingham in August: fourth to McCartney in similar race at Hamilton following day:
stays 1m: raced only on good ground or softer. *E. J. O'Neill*

SHANNON ARMS (USA) 6 b.g. Wolf Power (SAF) – Cresta's Best (USA) (Cresta **51**
Rider (USA) 124) [2007 74d: p8.6g f8g⁶ p8.6g⁶ 8f p8.6g² p9.5g⁶ p8.6g p12g⁶ p8.6g
Nov 20] modest performer nowadays: stays 8.6f: acts on polytrack and soft going: tried
blinkered/in cheekpieces: usually makes running: not straightforward. *R. Brotherton*

SHANTINA'S DREAM (USA) 3 b.f. Smoke Glacken (USA) 120 – J'Aime Jeblis **54**
(USA) (Jeblar (USA)) [2007 60: 5.3d⁶ 5g p5.1g p7.1g p6g p7g p8g p9.5g* Dec 13]
lengthy filly: modest performer: left H. Morrison after third start: won minor event at
Wolverhampton in December: stays 9.5f: acts on polytrack: tried tongue tied: has given
trouble at stall (once withdrawn) and sometimes slowly away (reared leaving stall second
outing). *J. R. Boyle*

SHANZU 2 b.f. (Apr 14) Kyllachy 129 – Limuru (Salse (USA) 128) [2007 6m⁶ 7d² 7s⁵ **69**
Oct 9] close-coupled filly: third foal: half-sister to 3-y-o Shimoni: dam unraced sister to
very smart Italian/US performer up to 1½m Timboroa out of half-sister to Efisio: fair
maiden: runner-up at Goodwood: stays 7f: acts on good to soft going. *H. Candy*

SHAPE UP (IRE) 7 b.g. Octagonal (NZ) 126 – Bint Kaldoun (IRE) 82 (Kaldoun (FR) **83**
122) [2007 86d: f12g f11g* f11g² 10g* 12.4m 10.5m³ 12m⁵ 12d⁴ Jun 19] close-coupled,
quite good-topped gelding: fairly useful handicapper: won at Southwell in March and
Nottingham in April: stays 1½m: acts on all-weather and any turf going: blinkered/visor-
ed: races prominently. *R. Craggs*

SHARAAB (USA) 6 b. or br.g. Erhaab (USA) 127 – Ghashtah (USA) (Nijinsky (CAN) **64**
138) [2007 52: 17.2f² 16.4m⁴ 16f* 16g² 16.1m³ Sep 10] tall, rather leggy gelding: has a
quick action: modest handicapper: won at Yarmouth in July: stays 17f: acts on polytrack,
firm and good to soft going: usually tongue tied. *D. E. Cantillon*

SHARBASIA (IRE) 4 b.f. King's Best (USA) 132 – Sharbata (IRE) (Kahyasi 130) **–**
[2007 14.1d Jul 12] winning hurdler: lightly-raced maiden on Flat: left J-P. Gallorini in
France, well beaten sole start in 2007. *H. J. Evans*

SHARE THE FEELING (IRE) 5 b.m. Desert King (IRE) 129 – Antapoura (IRE) 82 **80**
(Bustino 136) [2007 68: p13.9g* p13.9g² f14g³ p13.9g³ p13.9g⁶ Mar 10] fairly useful
handicapper: won at Wolverhampton in January: stays 2m: acts on all-weather and firm
going, probably on soft. *J. W. Unett*

SHARMY (IRE) 11 b.g. Caerleon (USA) 132 – Petticoat Lane (Ela-Mana-Mou 132) **65**
[2007 –: 11.6m 10s³ 10.9d² 10.9d⁵ 10f² 12m⁵ Sep 7] close-coupled, quite attractive gelding: fair handicapper nowadays: stays 1½m: acts on any going. *Ian Williams*

SHARPATTACK 3 ch.g. Auction House (USA) 120 – Sharp Decision 67 (Greensmith **58**
121) [2007 f7g p7g 6m² 5d p6g 8m p8g Sep 4] leggy gelding: maiden: modest maiden:
clear best effort at 6f on good to firm ground: tried tongue tied. *M. Botti*

SHARPAZMAX (IRE) 3 b.c. Daggers Drawn (USA) 114 – Amour Toujours (IRE) **84**
(Law Society (USA) 130) [2007 86p: 8m⁶ 7.1g Jun 7] tall colt: fairly useful performer:
lightly raced in 2007: should stay 1¼m: acts on polytrack and good to firm ground.
P. J. Makin

SHARP DRESSER (USA) 3 ch.f. Diesis 133 – A La Mode (USA) 77 (Known Fact **80 p**
(USA) 135) [2007 80p: 10m² 10.2d* Oct 1] fairly useful form in maidens, winning at
Bath in October easily by 6 lengths from Anthea: stays 1¼m: acts on polytrack, good to
firm and good to soft ground: sold 28,000 gns, joined Venetia Williams: open to further
improvement. *Mrs A. J. Perrett*

SHARPE IMAGE (IRE) 4 b.f. Bluebird (USA) 125 – Silvretta (IRE) 73 (Tirol 127) **–**
[2007 –: 11.8m⁴ Sep 17] leggy filly: little form. *G. Woodward*

SHARP HAT 13 ch.g. Shavian 125 – Madam Trilby (Grundy 137) [2007 61, a55: p5g **56** p5.1g⁴ 5g³ 5.1m 5m 5m² 5m⁴ 5g⁴ 5d 5d 5s⁴ 5m 5g p6g 5s 5g Nov 6] leggy, angular **a49** gelding: has raced 217 times (considered to be a record in Britain), winning 24 races: modest performer nowadays: best at 5f/6f: acts on all-weather and any turf going: tried in cheekpieces/blinkers: sometimes goes freely, including to post: sometimes slowly away. *D. W. Chapman*

SHARP LIQUOR (IRE) 4 br.g. Fruits of Love (USA) 127 – Pazza Idea (IRE) (Caer- **50** leon (USA) 132) [2007 40: p8.6g⁶ p7.1g Dec 14] modest maiden handicapper: stays 8.6f: acts on polytrack and firm ground: blinkered nowadays. *G. T. Lynch, Ireland*

SHARP NEPHEW 2 ch.c. (Jan 29) Dr Fong (USA) 128 – Snap Crackle Pop (IRE) 87 **105** (Statoblest 120) [2007 6g* 7g* 8d Sep 29] €65,000F, 155,000Y: leggy, useful-looking colt: sixth foal: half-brother to 6-y-o Handsome Cross and 2001 2-y-o 6f winner Snip Snap (by Revoque): dam, 2-y-o 5f winner, granddaughter of Cheveley Park Stakes winner Jacinth: useful form: won maiden at Windsor in July and listed event at Newbury (by head, beat Latin Lad and Scintillo) in August: 9/2, appeared unsuited by softer ground (eased once held) in Royal Lodge Stakes at Ascot: should stay 1m. *B. J. Meehan*

SHARP REPLY (USA) 5 b.g. Diesis 133 – Questonia 107 (Rainbow Quest (USA) **82** 134) [2007 80: 14d² 16g⁵ Nov 8] lengthy gelding: fairly useful handicapper: should stay 2m: acts on firm and soft going: has been visored: fairly useful hurdler. *Mrs S. C. Bradburne*

SHARPS GOLD 2 ch.f. (Mar 3) Twice As Sharp 99 – Toking N' Joken (IRE) (Mukad- **54** damah (USA) 125) [2007 5.2g⁵ 6g⁵ 6d⁶ p6g* p6g⁶ 7d p6g p5.1g p8.6g³ Dec 31] big, workmanlike filly: second foal: half-sister to Belgian 1m winner Deep Swing (by Pursuit of Love): dam ran twice: modest performer: won seller at Lingfield in September: effective at 6f to 8.6f: acts on polytrack: tongue tied after debut. *P. J. McBride*

SHARP TUNE (USA) 5 ch.g. Diesis 133 – Moonflute (USA) 82 (The Minstrel (CAN) **–** 135) [2007 –: p8g Mar 21] little form. *J. D. Frost*

SHATTER RESISTANT (IRE) 2 b.g. (Mar 20) Fath (USA) 116 – Beech Bramble **69 §** (IRE) (Cyrano de Bergerac 120) [2007 5.1f³ 5m³ 5.1d² 6s³ 6f³ 5d² 5g⁴ p5.1g³ 5.1d 5m⁴ Aug 30] fair maiden: in frame 9 of 10 starts: effective at 5f/6f: acts on polytrack, firm and soft going: tried visored: ungenuine. *M. R. Channon*

SHAVA 7 b.g. Atraf 116 – Anita Marie (IRE) (Anita's Prince 126) [2007 57: p7.1g* p6g⁵ **57** p7.1g⁴ f6g² p6g⁶ p8.6g⁵ f6g p7g⁵ p7g p7g f7d³ Dec 15] modest handicapper: won at Wolverhampton in January: effective at 6f to 8.6f: acts on all-weather and good to firm going: tried in cheekpieces/blinkers/tongue tie: often carries head awkwardly. *H. J. Evans*

SHAVANSKY 3 ch.g. Rock of Gibraltar (IRE) 133 – Limelighting (USA) 107 (Alleged **83** (USA) 138) [2007 10m 10.2m² 10g⁶ Jun 7] tall, attractive gelding: third foal: closely related to 2005 2-y-o 1m winner Los Cabos (stayed 1¾m, by Mozart): dam 1¼m winner: fairly useful form in maidens: best effort when length second to Venerable at Chepstow, going on at finish under hands and heels: again not knocked about final start: sold 13,000 gns in October, and gelded. *J. H. M. Gosden*

SHAVOULIN (USA) 3 b. or br.g. Johannesburg (USA) 127 – Hello Josephine (USA) **77** (Take Me Out (USA)) [2007 79: a7f³ a7f⁶ a8f 8g³ 7d 7m p6g p6g Dec 5] close-coupled, leggy gelding: first foal: dam US 6f winner (including minor stakes at 2 yrs): fair maiden: stays 7f: acts on dirt and soft going: tried blinkered/visored: edgy. *Christian Wroe*

SHAWHILL 3 b.f. Dr Fong (USA) 128 – Speremm (IRE) (Sadler's Wells (USA) 132) **93** [2007 p10g⁴ p12f³ p11g² 10f* 11.6m² 11.6d² 11.5g² 12g 14s³ 14m Oct 4] 5,000Y, £1,250 2-y-o: tall, rather unfurnished filly: fifth foal: half-sister to fairly useful 1m (at 2 yrs) to 14.4f winner Constantine (by Linamix) and useful Italian 7f/1m winner Indian Filly (by Indian Ridge): dam Italian 11f and 1¾m winner: fairly useful performer: won claimer at Windsor (claimed from A. Hales £17,000) in April: very good length second to Orion Girl in listed race at Le Lion d'Angers on seventh outing: respectable efforts at best after: best form up to 1½m: acts on polytrack, firm and good to soft ground: races prominently. *Tom Dascombe*

SHAYDREAMBELIEVER 4 ch.g. Daggers Drawn (USA) 114 – Aunt Sadie 71 **68** (Pursuit of Love 124) [2007 74: p9.5g⁶ f11d* Dec 15] big, strong, workmanlike gelding: fair performer: won claimer at Southwell in December: stays 11f: acts on fibresand, firm and good to soft going, probably on soft: said to have bled final start at 3 yrs. *R. A. Fahey*

SHEA'S ROUND 3 b.c. Josr Algarhoud (IRE) 118 – Elms Schoolgirl 79 (Emarati **–** (USA) 74) [2007 –: p10g⁵ p10g Jan 17] little sign of ability. *G. L. Moore*

SHEEKEY (IRE) 2 b.c. (Mar 16) Okawango (USA) 115 – My Darling Dodo (IRE) **83 +** (Anita's Prince 126) [2007 6m² 7.1m* 8s³ Sep 22] €31,000Y: lengthy colt: unfurnished at present: second foal: dam little form: fairly useful form: won maiden at Musselburgh in September: more progress when third to Cobo Bay in nursery at Ayr: stays 1m: acts on soft and good to firm going. *G. A. Swinbank*

SHEER BLUFF (IRE) 2 b.g. (Feb 1) Indian Ridge 123 – Sheer Bliss (IRE) 86 (Sadler's Wells (USA) 132) [2007 7m 6f⁶ 8m⁶ Aug 17] smallish, strong, stocky gelding: second foal: dam, 2-y-o 1m winner, closely related to Derby winner Oath and high-class 1m/1¼m performer Pelder: fair form in maidens at Newmarket (2) and Newbury, all worked out well: free-going sort, likely to prove best up to 1m: raced only on ground firmer than good: gelded after final start: should do better. *D. R. C. Elsworth* — **70 p**

SHEER FANTASTIC 2 b.g. (Apr 27) Fantastic Light (USA) 134 – Sheer Bliss (USA) (Relaunch (USA)) [2007 7d p8.6g⁴ p10g* Nov 19] good-topped gelding: modest form: won claimer at Kempton in November: will stay 1½m: acts on polytrack: visored/blinkered after debut. *P. C. Haslam* — **63**

SHEIK'N'KNOTSTERD 2 ch.g. (Feb 23) Zaha (CAN) 106 – Royal Ivy 71 (Mujtahid (USA) 118) [2007 5m³ 6g⁶ 6m³ 7g⁶ 6v⁶ p7g Sep 4] lengthy gelding: modest maiden: best at 5f/6f: acts on good to firm going: tried blinkered: sold 4,500 gns, joined J. Coupland, and gelded. *J. Akehurst* — **63**

SHEKAN STAR 5 b.m. Sri Pekan (USA) 117 – Celestial Welcome 96 (Most Welcome 131) [2007 62: 9.9m 12.4m 13f Jun 7] smallish, close-coupled mare: modest handicapper: stays 13f: acts on polytrack, firm and soft going: often slowly away: tough. *K. G. Reveley* — **54**

SHE KNOWS TOO MUCH 3 ch.f. Tobougg (IRE) 125 – How Do I Know 91 (Petong 126) [2007 –: p8g p7g Oct 29] leggy filly: no form in maidens. *A. M. Hales* — **–**

SHELA HOUSE 3 ch.g. Selkirk (USA) 129 – Villa Carlotta 110 (Rainbow Quest (USA) 134) [2007 8d⁶ 7m² 8.1d³ 8.3d³ 10d* 10d³ Oct 10] lengthy gelding: has a round action: second foal: half-brother to fairly useful 1¼m winner Villa Sonata (by Mozart): dam 1¼m/1½m winner: useful performer: won handicap at Windsor in October: good third in similar event at Nottingham final outing: will stay 1½m: acts on good to firm and good to soft ground. *J. R. Fanshawe* — **97 +**

SHEPHERDESS (USA) 3 ch.f. Stravinsky (USA) 133 – Hushi (USA) (Riverman (USA) 131) [2007 55: p5.1g³ p5g⁴ f5g⁴ Feb 6] modest maiden: raced only at 5f/6f on all-weather: sold 11,000 gns. *D. M. Simcock* — **53**

SHEPHERDS WARNING (IRE) 2 ch.f. (May 7) Vettori (IRE) 119 – Sky Red 75 (Night Shift (USA)) [2007 5g⁶ 5m² 5m² 5m* p5.1g 8d⁴ 8f 7d⁵ p7.1g* p7.1g* Dec 29] 5,500Y: plain filly: sixth foal: half-sister to Irish 2006 2-y-o 5f winner Rose of Battle (by Averti) and 1½m winner Chronomatic (by Mister Baileys), both fairly useful: dam, 5f winner, sister to useful sprinter Night Haven: fair performer: claimed from P. D. Evans £6,000 second start: won claimers at Thirsk (left R. Stronge £8,000) in May and Wolverhampton (2) in December: stays 1m: acts on polytrack, good to firm and good to soft going: often races prominently. *N. J. Vaughan* — **69**

SHERIFF'S DEPUTY 7 b.g. Atraf 116 – Forest Fantasy 61 (Rambo Dancer (CAN) 107) [2007 53: p8.6g 8.5m f11g 10s 10.1d Aug 26] strong gelding: poor performer nowadays: stays 10.5f: acts on all-weather, firm and good to soft ground: tried tongue tied/in cheekpieces. *C. N. Kellett* — **41**

SHERIFF'S SILK 3 b.g. Forzando 122 – Sylhall (Sharpo 132) [2007 63: f7g* f7g³ f6g² f6g² f7g⁵ 7d Jun 23] tall gelding: fair performer: won seller at Southwell in January: good efforts when runner-up in handicaps after: best at 6f/7f: acts on fibresand, well held both starts on turf: blinkered at 3 yrs: hung right fourth outing. *B. Smart* — **a77**

SHERIFF STAR 4 b.f. Killer Instinct 111 – Westcourt Ruby (Petong 126) [2007 –: 8.1m 7d 5g Jul 31] tall filly: no sign of ability. *G. P. Kelly* — **–**

SHERJAWY (IRE) 3 b.g. Diktat 126 – Arruhan (IRE) 87 (Mujtahid (USA) 118) [2007 63: p8g⁴ 7g 6m⁶ 5.7d 5.3m⁴ 6s⁵ 5d 6.1d 5d⁴ p6g⁴ Oct 23] stocky gelding: modest maiden: stays 7f: acts on polytrack, good to firm and good to soft going: blinkered: refused to race seventh outing: one to treat with caution. *Miss Z. C. Davison* — **57 §**

SHE'S A SOFTIE (IRE) 3 b.f. Invincible Spirit (IRE) 121 – New Tycoon (IRE) (Last Tycoon 131) [2007 –: 6m 6g⁶ 8s Jun 14] close-coupled filly: well held in maidens/handicap. *C. F. Wall* — **–**

SHE'S DUNNETT 4 b.f. Diktat 126 – College Night (IRE) 54 (Night Shift (USA)) [2007 60: p6g p8g 7m 10.1m 8d 6f 6m 6f⁶ 8d Oct 23] tall, leggy filly: maiden: poor at best in 2007: stays 7f: acts on good to firm and good to soft ground: tongue tied last 6 starts. *Mrs C. A. Dunnett* — **48**

SHESHA BEAR 2 b.f. (Jan 29) Tobougg (IRE) 125 – Sunny Davis (USA) 71 (Alydar **67** (USA)) [2007 p7g⁴ p7g Nov 16] 16,000Y: half-sister to several winners, including useful 6f (at 2 yrs) to 1m (in Sweden) winner Warming Trends (by Warning) and fairly useful 1¼m winner Dance In The Sun (by Halling): dam 2-y-o 7f winner: fair maiden: encouraging fourth at Lingfield, better effort (hampered next time): will stay 1m. *W. R. Muir*

SHES MILLIE 3 b.f. Auction House (USA) 120 – Wintzig 72 (Piccolo 121) [2007 51: **47** p7.1g⁵ p8g f8g Feb 15] unfurnished filly: poor performer: probably stays 1m: acts on firm ground: tried visored. *J. G. M. O'Shea*

SHES MINNIE 4 b.f. Bertolini (USA) 125 – Wintzig 72 (Piccolo 121) [2007 82: 5.1f **90** p6g² 6g⁴ 6d² 6g³ 6s⁴ 6.1s* 6m 6m² 5g² 5d* 6m⁵ 5g 6d⁴ 6m Oct 4] strong filly: fairly useful performer: won at Nottingham in July and Windsor in August: trained by P. Blockley ninth to eleventh starts before rejoined former trainer: stays 6f: acts on polytrack and any turf going: below form in visor/cheekpieces: often held up: consistent. *J. G. M. O'Shea*

SHE'S MY OUTSIDER 5 b.m. Docksider (USA) 124 – Solar Flare (IRE) (Danehill **–** (USA) 126) [2007 82: 6m p8g Dec 30] lengthy, useful-looking mare: fairly useful performer at 4 yrs: well held both starts in 2007, leaving I. Wood in between: effective at 6f to 1m: acts on polytrack, good to firm and good to soft going: free-going sort. *A. W. Carroll*

SHE'S OUR BEAUTY (IRE) 4 b.f. Imperial Ballet (IRE) 110 – Eleonora d'Arborea **58** 78 (Prince Sabo 123) [2007 58: f5g⁵ p5.1g f5g⁴ p5.1g 5g² 5m⁵ 5s³ 5v³ 5d* 5s 5g⁵ f5d **a47** Dec 14] modest performer on turf, poor on all-weather: won claimer at Catterick in July: best at 5f: acts on fibresand and heavy ground: has been visored, wears cheekpieces nowadays: usually front runner: none too consistent. *S. T. Mason*

SHE'S OUR DREAM 2 b.f. (Mar 17) Statue of Liberty (USA) 115 – Mainly Sunset **54** (Red Sunset 120) [2007 5.1g⁵ 5m 5g³ 6m 5f⁶ 6g 6d p7.1g Nov 8] 15,000Y: sturdy filly: half-sister to several winners, including 5f winner Antonia's Double (by Primo Dominie) and Irish 5f/6f winner Musical Sunset (by Music Boy), both fairly useful: dam once-raced half-sister to very smart sprinter Bolshoi: modest maiden: best efforts at 5f: acts on firm going: sometimes tongue tied. *R. C. Guest*

SHE'S OUR LASS (IRE) 6 b.m. Orpen (USA) 116 – Sharadja (IRE) (Doyoun 124) **81** [2007 80: p7.1g⁵ 8m f8g p8.6g 8.1f⁶ 8m⁴ 8m⁵ 10d* 8.9d 11.7g 10g Nov 7] sturdy mare: fairly useful handicapper: won at Ayr in September: stays 1¼m: acts on fibresand (probably on polytrack) and any turf going: tried visored: held up. *D. Carroll*

SHE'S OUR MARK 3 ch.f. Ishiguru (USA) 114 – Markskeepingfaith (IRE) 86 **106** (Ajraas (USA) 88) [2007 74: 6.7g* 8g* 7d² 7s² 9v² 8s² 8d* 7.5m⁴ 8m 9.5g⁵ Oct 5] quite good-topped filly: useful performer: won maiden at Limerick and handicap at the Curragh (by 4 lengths from Miss Gorica) in May and Desmond Stakes at Leopardstown (by ½ length from Eastern Appeal) in August: not discredited last 2 starts, in Matron Stakes at Leopardstown (seventh to Echelon) on penultimate outing: effective at 7f to 9.5f: acts on heavy and good to firm going: usually held up. *Paul Flynn, Ireland*

SHE'S SO PRETTY (IRE) 3 ch.f. Grand Lodge (USA) 125 – Plymsole (USA) 84 **68** (Diesis 133) [2007 65: 10m 10.2f³ 10g⁵ 8g 9.7m⁴ 12m p11g p12m³ p12m³ 13.8g Oct 20] angular, useful-looking filly: fair maiden handicapper: stays 1½m: acts on polytrack and firm going: tried in cheekpieces/visored: sold 7,500 gns. *W. R. Swinburn*

SHEVALINA (IRE) 5 b.m. Blue Ocean (USA) 87 – First Time Round (IRE) 64 (Elbio **36** 125) [2007 38: 6.9m⁴ p9.5g p9.5g 5f Sep 25] poor maiden nowadays: stays 7f: acts on good to firm going: tried blinkered/in cheekpieces. *Adrian Sexton, Ireland*

SHEVCHENKO (IRE) 3 b. or br.g. Rock of Gibraltar (IRE) 133 – Hula Angel (USA) **109** 111 (Woodman (USA) 126) [2007 85p: 7m³ p7g² 7m* 7.1d* 7.1g* 7d² Sep 29] well-made, attractive gelding: has a quick, unimpressive action: useful performer: progressed well in 2007, winning maiden at Thirsk in June, and handicaps at Sandown in July and August (beat Perfect Star 1½ lengths): further improvement when ¾-length second of 23 to Candidato Roy in valuable handicap at Ascot final outing, faring best of main group: bred to be suited by 1m: acts on polytrack, good to firm and good to soft going: has worn crossed noseband: sold 205,000 gns, joined P. F. Yiu in Hong Kong and renamed Hurricane Dash. *J. Noseda*

SHE WHISPERS (IRE) 4 b.f. Royal Applause 124 – Zariyba (IRE) (In The Wings **40** 128) [2007 54: f6g f7g 7.1s⁶ 5.5s 5d 6m⁵ Aug 14] strong, sturdy filly: poor performer nowadays: effective at 6f to 8.6f: acts on polytrack, firm and soft going. *R. Hollinshead*

SHE WONT WAIT 3 b.f. Piccolo 121 – Who Goes There 63 (Wolfhound (USA) 126) **47** [2007 61d: p8g 5.7d 6m⁶ 5g 6f Sep 10] unfurnished filly: maiden: only poor form in 2007: tried blinkered. *T. M. Jones*

SHIFTING STAR (IRE) 2 ch.g. (Mar 8) Night Shift (USA) – Ahshado 70 (Bin **82** Ajwaad (IRE) 119) [2007 6m³ 6d* 6m² 7g⁶ 6g Aug 21] €41,000F, €82,000Y: strong, sturdy gelding: first foal: dam, Irish maiden (stayed 1½m), half-sister to multiple US Grade 1 winner up to 1¼m In Excess: fairly useful form: won maiden at Newmarket in June: ran well in nurseries at Ascot (unlucky second) and Goodwood (drawn wide, sixth to Coasting): should prove best up to 7f: acts on good to firm and good to soft going: gelded after final start. *W. R. Swinburn*

SHIFTY 8 b.g. Night Shift (USA) – Crodelle (IRE) (Formidable (USA) 125) [2007 67, **74 d** a78: f8g f7g f7g⁶ f8g² f8g⁶ f8g⁶ p8.6g p8.6g f7d f8d² Dec 20] well-made gelding: has a round action: fair handicapper: below form after fourth start: best at 7f/1m: acts on all-weather and any turf going: tried blinkered/visored (not since 2004). *D. Carroll*

SHIITAKE 4 b.f. Cayman Kai (IRE) 114 – Petticoat Rule (Stanford 121§) [2007 65: **72** 10.1m² 9.1m² 9.1g Jul 8] lengthy, angular filly: fair maiden: stays 1¼m: acts on good to firm ground: said to have had breathing problem final 3-y-o/4-y-o starts. *Miss L. A. Perratt*

SHIMONI 3 b.f. Mark of Esteem (IRE) 137 – Limuru (Salse (USA) 128) [2007 75p: **88** 11.5g⁴ 9.9g⁶ 16d 13m 14d p12g⁵ p12g 11.7g² 12g p12m⁶ Dec 7] big, good-topped filly: fairly useful performer: good efforts when in frame in listed Oaks Trial at Lingfield and handicap at Bath: stays 1½m: acts on polytrack, good to firm and good to soft going: visored last 4 outings: has been slowly away. *W. J. Knight*

SHINDY (FR) 2 b.f. (Apr 6) Intikhab (USA) 135 – Sheriya (USA) (Green Dancer **74** (USA) 132) [2007 7g p7g³ Nov 17] sturdy filly: seventh foal: half-sister to 2 winners, including useful 6f to 1m winner Shersha (by Priolo): dam unraced: fair form in maidens, third at Lingfield: will stay 1m. *J. A. R. Toller*

SHINE AND RISE (IRE) 3 b.c. Marju (IRE) 127 – Ela Cassini (IRE) (Ela-Mana- **97** Mou 132) [2007 62p: 8f 8m 10m⁶ 12m⁵ 12m² 14m² p16g* p16g² 16m* Oct 3] close-coupled colt: useful and progressive handicapper: much improved once upped in trip, winning at Kempton in August and Nottingham (beat Lord Oroko easily by 2½ lengths) in October: free-going sort, but stays 2m: acts on polytrack and good to firm going: joined J. Moore in Hong Kong, where renamed Rise And Shine. *C. G. Cox*

SHINE LIKE A STAR 3 b.f. Fantastic Light (USA) 134 – Fallen Star 112 (Brief Truce **60** (USA) 126) [2007 10m 10g 10m⁶ 11.6s Jun 25] 60,000Y: sparely-made filly: first foal: dam, 7f (at 2 yrs)/1m winner, half-sister to very smart miler Fly To The Stars: modest maiden: best effort on third start. *J. L. Dunlop*

SHINING ARMOUR (IRE) 2 b.c. (Mar 9) Green Desert (USA) 127 – Perfect Touch **95** (USA) 107 (Miswaki (USA) 124) [2007 6g⁵ 7m 6g* 6d Oct 13] sturdy colt: type to carry condition: first foal: dam, 7f winner, half-sister to smart 7f/1m performer King Jock, out of smart US 6f/7f winner Glen Kate: useful form: won maiden at Fairyhouse in September: well held under softer conditions in listed race at York next time: likely to prove best at 5f/6f: blinkered last 2 starts. *D. K. Weld, Ireland*

SHINKO FEMME (IRE) 6 b.m. Shinko Forest (IRE) – Kilshanny 70 (Groom Dancer **–** (USA) 128) [2007 38: f8g p8.6g Feb 26] tall mare: little form in 2007. *J. O'Reilly*

SHINKO (IRE) 4 b.f. Shinko Forest (IRE) – Sharp Circle (IRE) 83 (Sure Blade (USA) **–** 130) [2007 60: p7g⁵ p8g 8d p8g May 31] quite good-topped filly: modest performer at 3 yrs: no form in 2007: has worn cheekpieces/blinkers. *Miss J. Feilden*

SHIPBOARD ROMANCE (IRE) 2 b.f. (Mar 27) Captain Rio 122 – In Other Words **42** (IRE) 76 (Lake Coniston (IRE) 131) [2007 5.1m⁵ 5.1f 6m² 6g⁶ 5d³ 6g³ 7g² 7m p7.1g Nov 5] €2,500F, €12,500Y: close-coupled filly: first foal: dam Irish 8.5f/9f winner: poor maiden: placed in sellers: stays 7f: acts on good to firm and good to soft going: tried visored. *P. D. Evans*

SHIPS WATCH (IRE) 3 b.f. Night Shift (USA) – Bel 83 (Darshaan 133) [2007 p7g **–** May 4] quite attractive filly: first foal: dam, 1½m winner, half-sister to useful French winner up to 11.5f Leros: 25/1 and very green, well held in maiden at Lingfield, not knocked about: sold 2,000 gns in December. *R. Charlton*

SHIRE (IRE) 5 br.g. Trans Island 119 – Trebles (IRE) (Kenmare (FR) 125) [2007 12m **–** 10m Jul 27] big, heavy-topped gelding: fair maiden in 2005: missed 2006, and well held both starts at 5 yrs. *D. R. C. Elsworth*

SHIRLEY A STAR (USA) 3 b.f. Cozzene (USA) – Fashion Star (USA) (Chief's **85** Crown (USA)) [2007 8g p10g 10m* Jun 14] tall filly: fifth foal: half-sister to 3 winners, including very smart US performer up to 1¼m Eddington (by Unbridled) and fairly useful

1m winner Star Crowned (by Kingmambo): dam, US 1m to 9f winner (Grade 3 placed up to 1½m), half-sister to Criterium de Saint-Cloud winner Miserden: fairly useful form: blinkered, much improved when winning maiden at Newbury in June by 1½ lengths from Circle of Love: stays 1¼m: acts on good to firm going: sent to USA. *B. J. Meehan*

SHIRLEY OAKS (IRE) 9 b.m. Sri Pekan (USA) 117 – Duly Elected (Persian Bold **32** 123) [2007 56: p7g p8g Feb 3] small, sparely-made mare: poor performer nowadays: effective at 5f to easy 1m: acts on all-weather, good to firm and good to soft going: has been blinkered/visored/tongue tied. *Miss Z. C. Davison*

SHISHIO 2 b.c. (Apr 2) Largesse 112 – Sachiko 54 (Celtic Swing 138) [2007 7g p8g 8m **–** Sep 21] good-topped colt: little form. *W. de Best-Turner*

SHIVERING 2 b.f. (Feb 27) Royal Applause 124 – Snowing 88 (Tate Gallery (USA) **80** 117) [2007 5g⁴ 5g* 5g 6g⁵ 5v² 5m² Aug 30] 20,000Y: lengthy, useful-looking filly: seventh foal: half-sister to 9-y-o The Trader and fairly useful 2003 2-y-o 5f winner Molly Moon (by Primo Dominie): dam Irish 5f winner: fairly useful performer: won maiden at Tipperary in April: contested listed/minor events after (including at York third start), twice runner-up at Tipperary: probably best at 5f: acts on heavy and good to firm going. *T. Stack, Ireland*

SHMOOKH (USA) 3 b.c. Green Desert (USA) 127 – Elrafa Ah (USA) 105 (Storm Cat **106** (USA)) [2007 85: 7.1m* 7g* 8m 6m* 7g³ 6m⁶ Sep 15] sturdy, good-bodied colt: useful form: won maiden at Warwick in April, and handicaps at York in May and Newmarket (beat Off The Record by neck) in July: good 1¾ lengths third to Docofthebay in similar event at Goodwood next time: well below form in listed race there final outing: stays 7f: acts on good to firm and good to soft going: joined D. Watson in UAE. *J. L. Dunlop*

SHOGUN PRINCE (IRE) 4 b.g. Shinko Forest (IRE) – Lady of Dreams (IRE) 84 **86** (Prince Rupert (FR) 121) [2007 88: 10d⁴ 11.7g⁴ Oct 24] sturdy, compact gelding: useful handicapper: creditable efforts both starts at 4 yrs: effective from 1m to 1½m: acts on polytrack and good to soft ground: tried visored: sold 20,000 gns. *A. King*

SHOOT OUT 4 b.g. Killer Instinct 111 – Icy 44 (Mind Games 121) [2007 9.2d 7m 9g **–** Jun 22] no form. *C. W. Thornton*

SHOOT PONTOON (IRE) 2 b.g. (Apr 15) Danehill Dancer (IRE) 117 – Burmese **56** Princess (USA) 64 (King of Kings (IRE) 125) [2007 p8m f7d Dec 14] modest form in maidens at Lingfield and Southwell, slowly away both times: subsequently gelded. *N. A. Callaghan*

SHOPFITTER 4 b.g. Sugarfoot 118 – Madam Wurlitzer (Noble Patriarch 115) [2007 **–** 49: p8.6g f8d Dec 20] good-bodied gelding: poor maiden at best: well held in 2007: usually wears headgear. *P. T. Midgley*

SHORE THING (IRE) 4 b.g. Docksider (USA) 124 – Spicebird (IRE) 67 (Ela-Mana- **78** Mou 132) [2007 82: 12m² 13.3m Aug 17] big, strong gelding: fair handicapper: said to have had irregular heartbeat final start: stays 1¾m: acts on firm going: sometimes finds little. *C. R. Egerton*

SHORTCAKE 3 b.f. Sure Blade (USA) 130 – Confection (Formidable (USA) 125) **–** [2007 p5g p5f p6g 6m 6m 8m Sep 25] sister to useful 6f (at 2 yrs) to 8.3f winner Aggrava- tion and half-sister to several winners, including 1995 2-y-o 5f/6f winner Anthelia and 1m to 1¼m winner Athenian, both useful and by Distant Relative: dam ran twice: little form, leaving D. Ivory after second start. *M. R. Hoad*

SHORTHAND 3 b.f. Diktat 126 – Much Too Risky 87 (Bustino 136) [2007 95p: 10.4g⁴ **100** 12g 9.9g⁴ 10.1g² 10d Oct 19] leggy, useful-looking filly: useful performer: best effort when 1½ lengths second to Samira Gold in listed race at Yarmouth: stays 1¼m (stamina stretched at 1½m in Ribblesdale Stakes at Royal Ascot): raced only on good/good to soft going: sold 260,000 gns. *Sir Michael Stoute*

SHORT SKIRT 4 br.f. Diktat 126 – Much Too Risky 87 (Bustino 136) [2007 117: 10d* **109** 10g Oct 28] tall, quite good-topped filly: smart performer at 3 yrs for Sir Michael Stoute (sold 1,400,000 gns): off 12 months, didn't have to be at best to win listed event at Newmarket in October by ½ length from Ronaldsay: below form in Premio Lydia Tesio at Rome 9 days later: stays 1½m: acts on soft going: tends to look awkward under pres- sure: left Godolphin, and sent to USA. *Saeed bin Suroor*

SHOTFIRE RIDGE 4 ch.g. Grand Lodge (USA) 125 – Darya (USA) (Gulch (USA)) **–** [2007 80p: 10d p8g Jul 21] lengthy, angular gelding: fairly useful performer: suffered fatal injuries in claimer at Lingfield: stayed 8.5f. *M. Wigham*

totesport.com Stakes (Handicap), Newmarket—the stand-side group come out on top as Shmookh (striped cap) resumes his progression; Off The Record is second ahead of Utmost Respect (hidden against rail), Celtic Sultan (stars on sleeves) and Siren's Gift (noseband)

SHOT GUN 3 b.g. Green Desert (USA) 127 – Wardat Allayl (IRE) 87 (Mtoto 134) **90**
[2007 p8g² 7.1g⁵ 8.5g* 9g⁶ p8g⁴ p8g² 8m 8m Aug 4] unfurnished gelding: second foal: dam, 2-y-o 7f winner, half-sister to smart performers Bint Allayl (leading 2-y-o filly in 1998) and Kheleyf (6f/7f performer), both by Green Desert: fairly useful performer: won maiden at Epsom in April: stays 9f: acts on polytrack and good to firm going: joined D. Selvaratnam in UAE. *M. R. Channon*

SHOTLEY MAC 3 ch.g. Abou Zouz (USA) 109 – Julie's Gift (Presidium 124) [2007 **71** 63: 8m 5m 10d 9.8s 7.5s² 7.5g² 9m³ 9.9g² 10m 8m² 10.4m⁵ 8.5d⁴ 8m² 7g² Oct 19] workmanlike gelding: fair maiden: runner-up 6 times in 2007: may prove best at 7f/1m: acts on soft and good to firm ground: blinkered of late: front runner. *N. Bycroft*

SHOT THROUGH (USA) 2 b.g. (Mar 6) Golden Missile (USA) 123 – Halo's Gleam **47** (USA) (Halo (USA)) [2007 7g 6m 7m⁴ p8m⁶ Nov 11] tall, unfurnished gelding: poor maiden: stays 1m: tried visored. *P. C. Haslam*

SHOT TO FAME (USA) 8 b.g. Quest For Fame 127 – Exocet (USA) (Deposit Ticket **88** (USA)) [2007 98d: p7g 8s³ 8m⁵ 7g³ 7m⁴ 9.1d⁴ 8.1g³ 7f⁴ 7.9d 8v² 7s 7.2s³ 8.3d Oct 29] angular, rangy gelding: fairly useful handicapper: several creditable efforts in 2007: effective at 7f to 9f: acts on any turf going, probably on polytrack: tried visored (well beaten), tongue tied nowadays: makes running. *D. Nicholls*

SHOULDNTBETHERE (IRE) 3 ch.g. Soviet Star (USA) 128 – Octomone (USA) **56** 74 (Hennessy (USA) 122) [2007 69: p10g 8.3m p10g⁶ 10g 9m p8g² 8g p8g p10g⁵ p9.5g **a71** p8g² f8g Dec 27] good-topped gelding: fair handicapper on all-weather, modest on turf: best at 1m: acts on all-weather: held up. *Mrs P. N. Dutfield*

SHOUT (IRE) 4 ch.f. Halling (USA) 133 – Spout 115 (Salse (USA) 128) [2007 83: 8.1g **86** 10m² 9.9g⁶ Jun 1] strong, lengthy filly: fairly useful performer, lightly raced: stays 1½m: acts on polytrack and good to firm going: sent to USA. *J. W. Hills*

SHOW BUSINESS (IRE) 3 ch.g. Distant Music (USA) 126 – Gertie Laurie (Lomond **53 §** (USA) 128) [2007 –: f7g⁶ p6g⁴ 7g 7d 10s 8m Jun 17] modest maiden: left Sir Mark Prescott 1,200 gns after second start: will prove best at 7f+: acts on polytrack: tried tongue tied/in headgear: temperamental: sold 500 gns. *P. Butler*

SHOW ME THE LOLLY (FR) 7 b.m. Sri Pekan (USA) 117 – Sugar Lolly (USA) **53 d** (Irish River (FR) 131) [2007 51: p10g² p8g⁵ p8g p8.6g³ 8d p9.5m p9.5g Oct 12] leggy mare: modest performer: left P. McBride after fourth start, J. McAuley after fifth: stays 1¼m: acts on polytrack and good to firm going: tried visored/tongue tied. *S. W. Hall*

SHOWTIME ANNIE 6 b.m. Wizard King 122 – Rebel County (IRE) 97 (Maelstrom **50** Lake 118) [2007 –: f8g 9.1g 10.1m p12.2g² 11.6d⁵ 9.2g⁶ 9.9m⁶ p9.5g Sep 27] goodbodied mare: modest performer: stays 1½m: acts on all-weather, soft and good to firm going: wears headgear. *A. Bailey*

SHOWTIME ICE 2 b.f. (Feb 23) Lujain (USA) 119 – Rebel County (IRE) 97 (Mael- **72** strom Lake 118) [2007 5.1f⁵ p6g² p6g⁶ p7m⁵ Dec 10] fifth foal: half-sister to 6-y-o Showtime Annie: dam 6f to 1¼m winner: fair maiden: second at Wolverhampton, standout effort: may prove best at 5f/6f: acts on polytrack: suspect temperament. *M. J. Wallace*

SHOW TRIAL (IRE) 3 b.f. Jade Robbery (USA) 121 – Court Lane (USA) 81 (Mach- **61** iavellian (USA) 123) [2007 61: p6g² p7g Feb 4] close-coupled filly: modest performer: stays 7f: acts on all-weather and good to soft ground. *D. J. S. ffrench Davis*

SHRAAYEF 2 b.f. (Feb 14) Nayef (USA) 129 – Gorgeous Dancer (IRE) (Nordico – (USA)) [2007 8m Sep 21] 30,000Y: lengthy filly: eighth foal: half-sister to several at least useful winners (all at 1¼m/1½m), notably very smart Imperial Dancer (5f winner at 2 yrs, by Primo Dominie): dam, Irish 1m winner (stayed 1¾m), out of half-sister to Irish Oaks winner Give Thanks: 50/1, behind in maiden at Newmarket. *M. Botti*

SHREDDY SHRIMPSTER 3 ch.f. Zilzal (USA) 137 – Empress Dagmar (Selkirk **51** (USA) 129) [2007 57: p7g p6g⁵ 5m² 5.1g Jun 1] unfurnished filly: modest maiden: best efforts at 5f: acts on polytrack and good to firm going: sold £600. *A. B. Haynes*

SHREWD DUDE 3 b. or br.c. Val Royal (FR) 127 – Lily Dale (IRE) 78 (Distinctly **55** North (USA) 115) [2007 54: p9.5g² p9.5g⁵ Jan 27] workmanlike colt: modest maiden: will stay 1½m: acts on polytrack and good to soft ground: blinkered final start. *Carl Llewellyn*

SHRINE MOUNTAIN (USA) 5 b.g. Distorted Humor (USA) 117 – Fancy Ruler **70 d** (USA) (Half A Year (USA) 130) [2007 60, a72: p8g* p10g³ p7.1g p7.1g p8g⁵ 8d p7g p7.1g Jul 2] good-topped gelding: fair performer: won seller at Lingfield in January: below form since, leaving R. Harris £6,000 after fifth start: stays 10.8f, better at shorter: acts on all-weather, good to firm and good to soft ground: usually visored/blinkered: tried tongue tied: free-going sort. *Miss J. S. Davis*

SHUMOOKH (IRE) 4 b.g. Mujahid (USA) 125 – Midway Lady (USA) 126 (Alleged **110** (USA) 138) [2007 108: 8.2m² 8v² Jul 26] close-coupled, rather lightly-made gelding: smart form: good second in minor events at Nottingham (beaten 2 lengths by Charlie Cool) and York (went down by 2½ lengths to Pride of Nation) in 2007: should stay 1¼m: acts on heavy and good to firm going (hung left on firm on debut): front runner: sold 9,000 gns, sent to Spain. *M. A. Jarvis*

SHUNKAWAKHAN (IRE) 4 b.g. Indian Danehill (IRE) 124 – Special Park (USA) **59** (Trempolino (USA) 135) [2007 61: p6g⁶ f7g³ f8g² f8g p8g² p8g⁴ 8m⁴ p7g⁴ p7g³ p8g³ p7g³ p8g p10g⁵ f8g Dec 27] quite good-topped gelding: modest maiden handicapper: stays 1m (raced freely at 1¼m): acts on all-weather, firm and good to soft going: blinkered/in cheekpieces nowadays. *G. C. H. Chung*

SHUSTRAYA 3 b.f. Dansili 127 – Nimble Fan (USA) (Lear Fan (USA) 130) [2007 84: **96** p6g* 6g⁴ p6g⁶ p6m⁵ 7g⁶ 7m p7m* p7.1g Oct 22] sturdy, close-coupled filly: fairly useful handicapper: won at Lingfield in January and Kempton in October: stays easy 7f: acts on polytrack. *P. J. Makin*

SHY 2 ch.f. (Feb 1) Erhaab (USA) 127 – Shi Shi (Alnasr Alwasheek 117) [2007 p8g³ Sep **74** 26] fourth foal: half-sister to 3-y-o Pragmatist: dam French 1¼m winner: 50/1, third to Ballora in maiden at Kempton, always prominent: likely to stay 1¼m/1½m. *P. Winkworth*

SHYBUTWILLING (IRE) 2 ch.f. (Mar 2) Best of The Bests (IRE) 122 – Reticent – Bride (IRE) 71 (Shy Groom (USA)) [2007 p6g Jun 13] €7,000F, €8,000Y: half-sister to several winners, including fairly useful 6f winner Barnacla (by Bluebird) and fairly useful but ungenuine 1½m winner Palua (by Sri Pekan): dam, Irish 6f winner, sister to Lowther winner Miss Demure: tailed off (looked reluctant) in maiden. *Mrs P. N. Dutfield*

SHY GLANCE (IRE) 5 b.g. Red Ransom (USA) – Royal Shyness 104 (Royal Acad- **84** emy (USA) 130) [2007 72+: 8f* p7.1g⁵ 8m⁵ 9.1g² 9.1g⁶ 10.1d 7.9f² 8.3g⁴ 8g⁶ 9.2g⁴ 8g Oct 3] good-topped gelding: fairly useful handicapper: won at Thirsk in April: left G. A. Swinbank after next start: effective at 7f, barely stays 10.5f: acts on polytrack and good to soft going: reportedly had breathing problem third start at 4 yrs, tongue tied next 3 outings. *P. Monteith*

SIAMESE CAT (IRE) 3 ch.f. Rock of Gibraltar (IRE) 133 – Real Cat (USA) (Storm **82** Cat (USA)) [2007 99: 8.3g² 7.1d 8.3g² p7f* a8.5f³ Nov 24] smallish, good-bodied filly: just fairly useful performer at 3 yrs: left B. Meehan, won maiden at Keeneland in October: stays 8.5f: acts on polytrack, soft and good to firm going. *H. G. Motion, USA*

SI BELLE (IRE) 2 gr.f. (Apr 10) Dalakhani (IRE) 133 – Stunning (USA) 103 (Nureyev **61 p** (USA) 131) [2007 f8d⁴ Dec 15] third foal: dam, French 6f (at 2 yrs)/7f winner, out of US Grade 1 8.5f/9f winner Gorgeous: 11/1 from 33/1, fourth to Prince Hamlet in maiden at Southwell, some late headway not knocked about: should do better. *Rae Guest*

SIBERIAN TIGER (IRE) 2 b.c. (Mar 24) Xaar 132 – Flying Millie (IRE) 99 (Flying **103**
Spur (AUS)) [2007 6m⁴ p6g⁵ 7m³ 7m* 8m* 8m 8m* 10d⁵ Nov 11] €60,000Y: tall, angular colt: second foal: half-brother to 3-y-o Fabuleux Millie: dam 5f (at 2 yrs)/6f winner:
useful performer: won maiden at Newmarket and nursery at Salisbury in August and
listed event at Pontefract (beat Latin Lad by ¾ length) in October: good 3 lengths fifth to
Full of Gold in Criterium de Saint-Cloud final start, never nearer: will probably stay
1½m: acts on good to firm and good to soft going. *M. R. Channon*

SIBO BAGGINS (IRE) 3 ch.g. Docksider (USA) 124 – Isadora Duncan (IRE) (Sad- **62**
ler's Wells (USA) 132) [2007 8g 8d³ 8d⁵ p7g Nov 21] modest maiden: stays 1m: acts on
good to soft going. *J. S. Moore*

SIEGFRIEDS NIGHT (IRE) 6 ch.g. Night Shift (USA) – Shelbiana (USA) (Chief- **50**
tain) [2007 56: f11g⁶ 11.5d 12.1s Jul 17] quite good-topped gelding: modest handicapper:
probably stays 15.8f: acts on fibresand and firm ground, probably on good to soft: wore
tongue strap last 2 starts at 5 yrs. *M. C. Chapman*

SIENA 2 b.f. (Feb 24) Lomitas 129 – Sea Lane (Zafonic (USA) 130) [2007 8d Oct 30] **–**
first foal: dam unraced out of Rockfel Stakes winner Yawl: tailed off in maiden at Yarmouth. *Mrs C. A. Dunnett*

SIENA STAR (IRE) 9 b.g. Brief Truce (USA) 126 – Gooseberry Pie 63 (Green Desert **74**
(USA) 127) [2007 70: p10g⁶ p10g p10g* p10g 10.2f* 9.7m 10m⁵ 9.9m 10m⁶ p9.5g
10.2m² p9.5g⁶ p9.5g⁴ 10g p11m⁴ p10m⁴ p9.5d⁵ p9.5g p10g Dec 28] close-coupled gelding: has a quick action: fair handicapper: won at Lingfield in February and Bath in June:
stays easy 1½m: acts on polytrack, firm and soft going: tried blinkered: waited with. *Stef
Liddiard*

SIENNA STORM (IRE) 4 b.g. Peintre Celebre (USA) 137 – Saint Ann (USA) 66 **86 d**
(Geiger Counter (USA)) [2007 101: 14.1g 12g 14g 11.6s⁵ 12m⁶ 12g 10m⁶ 10.4m² 9d³
10.5s⁴ 10g⁵ Oct 6] well-made gelding: just fairly useful at best in 2007: below form in
claimers/sellers last 4 starts: stays 1½m: acts on soft and good to firm going: tried blink-
ered/visored: sold 25,000 gns. *M. H. Tompkins*

SIERRA ROSE 3 b.f. Auction House (USA) 120 – Young Whip (Bold Owl 101) [2007 **54**
10d p9.5g 8d p12.2g Sep 22] plain filly: half-sister to useful 7f to 1¼m winner Elmhurst
Boy and 7f/1m winner Mountgate (both by Merdon Melody): dam unraced: modest
maiden: best effort on debut. *P. J. McBride*

SIERRAS FUTURE 3 b.g. Fusaichi Pegasus (USA) 130 – Sierra Virgen (USA) (Stack **65**
(USA)) [2007 11.1d 8.3d 9.2g³ Aug 22] fair form: best effort when third to El Coto in
claimer at Hamilton: stays 9.2f: blinkered. *I. Semple*

SIERRA VISTA 7 ch.m. Atraf 116 – Park Vista (Taufan (USA) 119) [2007 108: 6d² 6m **114**
6g* 5m* 5g* 6v⁵ 5g 5g 6g Sep 8] leggy mare: smart performer: better than ever at 7 yrs,
winning minor event and handicap at Haydock (beat River Falcon by 2½ lengths) and
Betfair Temple Stakes at Sandown (beat Moss Vale by 1¼ lengths), all in May: also ran
well when eighth to Kingsgate Native in Nunthorpe Stakes at York penultimate start: well

*Betfair Temple Stakes, Sandown—Sierra Vista continues her improvement at the age of seven
and gains her third win in a row; Moss Vale and Firenze chase her home*

below form in Sprint Cup at Haydock final outing: best at 5f/6f: acts on polytrack, firm and soft going: tried in cheekpieces: usually makes running: genuine: sold 115,000 gns. *D. W. Barker*

SIESTA (IRE) 3 ch.f. King Charlemagne (USA) 120 – Quiescent 88 (Primo Dominie **58** 121) [2007 –p: 6.1g 6g³ p6g² p6g 6m p7g² Oct 4] lengthy filly: modest maiden: stays 7f: acts on polytrack: looks quirky: joined W. Kujath in Germany. *J. R. Fanshawe*

SI FOO (USA) 3 ch.g. Fusaichi Pegasus (USA) 130 – Ascension (IRE) 110 (Night Shift **90** (USA)) [2007 79p: p7.1g* p7g* p6g² p7g 6m⁴ Apr 18] sturdy gelding: fairly useful performer: off 6 months (reportedly had knee problem), won handicaps at Wolverhampton and Lingfield in January: fourth to Sakhee's Secret in handicap at Newmarket final start: gelded after: effective at 6f/7f: acts on polytrack and firm ground: races prominently: sent to Macau. *A. M. Balding*

SIGN OF THE CROSS 3 b.g. Mark of Esteem (IRE) 137 – Thea (USA) 95 (Marju **91** (IRE) 127) [2007 77p: 8d⁴ 8.2g*⁸ 8s⁴ 8m p8g p10g² 10.3g⁴ Oct 26] good-topped gelding: fairly useful performer: won maiden at Nottingham in June: best effort in handicaps after on penultimate start: stays 1¼m: acts on polytrack and good to soft ground: free-going sort. *J. R. Fanshawe*

SIGNORA (IRE) 2 ch.f. (Feb 5) Indian Ridge 123 – Lady Catherine 107 (Bering 136) **51 p** [2007 6m⁵ Nov 10] medium-sized, workmanlike filly: first foal: dam French/Italian 1m winner (second in Oaks d'Italia): 14/1 and green, fifth in maiden at Doncaster: will be suited by 1m+: should do better. *M. Johnston*

SIGNOR PANETTIERE 6 b.g. Night Shift (USA) – Christmas Kiss 82 (Taufan **– §** (USA) 119) [2007 ?: p5.1g p6g f5g p5.1g 5g 5g Oct 3] well-made gelding: has reportedly had wind operation: untrustworthy handicapper, firmly on downgrade: tried tongue tied: has worn cheekpieces. *A. D. Brown*

SIGNOR PELTRO 4 b.g. Bertolini (USA) 125 – Pewter Lass 56 (Dowsing (USA) **96** 124) [2007 100: 7g⁶ 7g 6g* Jul 27] strong, rangy gelding: useful handicapper: blinkered, back to form when winning at Newmarket in July by ¾ length from Roman Maze: effective at 6f/easy 7f: acts on polytrack, soft and good to firm ground. *H. Candy*

SIGNOR WHIPPEE 4 ch.g. Observatory (USA) 131 – Revoltosa (IRE) (Catrail **44 §** (USA) 123) [2007 64§: 5m 6f⁶ 5s 5g 5s⁶ 6m Sep 1] smallish gelding: poor performer: best at 5f: acts on polytrack, soft and good to firm ground: blinkered: unreliable. *A. Berry*

SIGNS OF LOVE (FR) 4 b.g. Poliglote 121 – Severina (Darshaan 133) [2007 p9.5g⁴ **–** Nov 10] second once from 3 starts in France in 2005/6: fairly useful form in juvenile hurdles in early-2007: well-held fourth to Kissing in maiden at Wolverhampton only Flat start at 4 yrs: will be suited by 1½m+. *Noel T. Chance*

SILCA CHIAVE 3 ch.f. Pivotal 124 – Silca-Cisa 93 (Hallgate 127) [2007 106: 7m⁵ 7m **90** Jun 20] good-topped filly: just fairly useful form when fifth in Fred Darling Stakes at Newbury, then shaped as if amiss when last in Jersey Stakes at Royal Ascot (subsequently found to have a chip in a hock): stayed 7f: acted on good to firm and good to soft ground: reportedly retired. *M. R. Channon*

SILCA DESTINATION 2 b.f. (Mar 4) Dubai Destination (USA) 127 – Golden Silca **59** 115 (Inchinor 119) [2007 6m⁵ 6f⁶ 5.1f⁶ 6s p6g 7d⁴ p8m² p8g Dec 12] sturdy filly: second foal: dam, 5f (at 2 yrs) to 9f winner, sister to Prix Morny winner Silca's Sister and half-sister to 6-y-o Green Manalishi: modest maiden: second in nursery at Kempton: stays 1m: acts on polytrack and firm going: tried visored. *M. R. Channon*

SILCA ELEGANCE 3 b.c. Selkirk (USA) 129 – Parisian Elegance 90 (Zilzal (USA) **77** 137) [2007 8.1g⁶ 7g⁵ 6m² 6s³ 6d* 6s⁵ 6m² 5d² 6m⁴ 5d⁶ Aug 16] lengthy, useful-looking colt: impresses in appearance: fair performer: won maiden at Redcar in June: mainly creditable efforts in handicaps after: will prove best at 5f/6f: acts on soft and good to firm ground: consistent: sold 9,000 gns. *M. R. Channon*

SILCA KEY 3 ch.f. Inchinor 119 – Baalbek 76 (Barathea (IRE) 127) [2007 77: p10g⁶ **94** p11g⁵ p8g p9.5g⁶ 8g⁶ p10g p8g⁵ p12g 9m² 10s* 9.1d* 9g⁶ 9.8g p8g⁴ p10g³ 10d* 10d **a75** 10g⁵ 10.3m p10g⁵ Nov 15] lightly-made filly: fairly useful performer on turf, fair on all-weather: won handicaps at Pontefract and Ayr within 4 days in July, and Newbury in October: stiff tasks in listed races next 3 starts, far from discredited third last occasion: stays 1¼m: acts on polytrack, soft and good to firm going: often held up. *M. R. Channon*

SILENCIO (IRE) 6 b.g. Sillery (USA) 122 – Flabbergasted (IRE) (Sadler's Wells **64** (USA) 132) [2007 17.2m³ May 21] poor maiden: stays 17f: acts on good to firm going: fairly useful hurdler. *A. King*

SILENT APPLAUSE 4 b.g. Royal Applause 124 – Billie Blue 63 (Ballad Rock 122) **77**
[2007 77: 8d² 8m⁶ 8m³ 8g⁴ 8m Sep 20] lengthy gelding: fair maiden handicapper: stays
1m: acts on firm and good to soft going: tried visored: has wandered/looked difficult ride.
Dr J. D. Scargill

SILENT BEAUTY (IRE) 3 b.f. Intikhab (USA) 135 – Precedence (IRE) 88 (Polish **59 d**
Precedent (USA) 131) [2007 –: 6.1g 12.1d p8.6g⁵ p9.5g³ p9.5g⁶ p12.2g p8g 11.9g p9.5g
Oct 27] sturdy filly: modest maiden at best: stays 9.5f: acts on polytrack. *S. C. Williams*

SILENT LUCIDITY (IRE) 3 ch.g. Ashkalani (IRE) 128 – Mimansa (USA) (El Gran **68**
Senor (USA) 136) [2007 –: 8.3m* 11.1f³ Jun 7] fair performer: trained by G. Lyons in
Ireland at 2 yrs: won seller at Hamilton in May: stays 11f: acts on firm going. *P. D. Niven*

SILENT MASTER (USA) 2 b.c. (Mar 20) Cherokee Run (USA) 122 – Polent (Polish **79**
Precedent (USA) 131) [2007 6g⁶ 7.2s p7m² p8g² p7m³ Dec 10] 34,000Y: rather leggy
colt: half-brother to several winners, including 3-y-o Philatelist and fairly useful 2004
2-y-o 7f winner (stays 2m) Querido (by Spectrum): dam, French 13f/15.5f winner, half-
sister to Oaks winner Snow Bride, herself dam of Lammtarra: fair maiden: placed 3 times
at Lingfield, twice in nurseries: will stay 1¼m: acts on polytrack. *M. Johnston*

SILENT STORM 7 ch.g. Zafonic (USA) 130 – Nanda 83 (Nashwan (USA) 135) [2007 **85 d**
79, a82: p8g p8g² p7g* p7g³ p6g⁴ 8.3g p6g p6g p8.6g p8g p7.1g⁶ p8g p7g f6d Dec 11]
sturdy gelding: fairly useful handicapper: won at Lingfield in February: left C. Cyzer
10,000 gns after fifth start: below form after: free-going sort, but stays easy 1m: acts on
all-weather and firm going: tried visored (well below form). *Peter Grayson*

SILENT STREET 4 b.g. Celtic Swing 138 – Smart Spirit (IRE) 71 (Persian Bold 123) **47**
[2007 12g 9.9g 12.4m⁶ 16.1m 14.1d 15.8m Aug 7] big gelding: poor maiden: stays 1½m:
acts on good to firm ground. *K. G. Reveley*

SILIDAN 4 b.g. Dansili 127 – In Love Again (IRE) 86 (Prince Rupert (FR) 121) [2007 **–**
–: 6m 6m 8.1m 6f Sep 17] compact gelding: fairly useful performer at best: firmly on
downgrade. *M. Brittain*

SILK AFFAIR (IRE) 2 b.f. (Mar 15) Barathea (IRE) 127 – Uncertain Affair (IRE) 79 **87**
(Darshaan 133) [2007 8.1s⁶ 8s* 8v⁵ Nov 24] 80,000Y: tall, good-topped filly: sister to
fairly useful winner around 11f Subtle Affair and half-sister to several winners, including
smart 1½m/1¾m winner Lochbuie (by Definite Article) and useful Irish stayer Direct
Bearing (by Polish Precedent): dam Irish 1¾m winner: fairly useful form: won maiden at
Ayr in October: creditable 2½ lengths fifth to Vadsalina in listed event at Saint-Cloud:
will be suited by 1¼m/1½m: raced only on soft/heavy going. *M. G. Quinlan*

SILK BLOSSOM (IRE) 3 ch.f. Barathea (IRE) 127 – Lovely Blossom (FR) (Spin- **–**
ning World (USA) 130) [2007 107: 7m 8d 7m Sep 13] rather leggy, close-coupled filly:
useful performer at 2 yrs when successful in Lowther Stakes at York and Goffs Fillies
Five Hundred at the Curragh (awarded race): well held in 2007 in Fred Darling Stakes at
Newbury, Coronation Stakes at Royal Ascot and listed race at Doncaster: should stay 1m:
acts on soft and good to firm going: on toes at York, slipped over in parade ring at the
Curragh: bandaged hind joints: sold 450,000 gns. *B. W. Hills*

SILK DRESS (IRE) 3 b.f. Gulch (USA) – Zvezda (USA) (Nureyev (USA) 131) [2007 **74 d**
91: 10m 8g 10d⁴ 10d⁶ 10v 12v⁵ 8d 6g⁶ p6g Oct 5] €110,000Y: angular filly: first foal:
dam, French maiden, sister to Dewhurst Stakes third Zentsov Street: maiden: fairly useful
form at 2 yrs: disappointing in 2007, well held in listed race at Newmarket on reappearance: seems to stay 1¼m: tried blinkered. *John Joseph Murphy, Ireland*

SILK DRUM (IRE) 2 gr.g. (Mar 22) Intikhab (USA) 135 – Aneydia (IRE) (Kenmare **68**
(FR) 125) [2007 6s³ 7d⁴ 8f Sep 27] workmanlike gelding: fair maiden: in frame at Ripon
and Catterick (fourth to Sourire): should stay 1m: acts on soft going. *J. Howard Johnson*

SILKEN SPELL 2 b.f. (Mar 9) Tobougg (IRE) 125 – Walsham Witch 61 (Music Maes- **–**
tro 119) [2007 7f 5g Sep 7] 4,500Y: close-coupled filly: half-sister to several winners
up to 7f, including fairly useful 6f winner Mishka (by Mistertopogigo): dam 6f winner
(stayed 2m): well held in maidens. *Mrs A. Duffield*

SILK GALLERY (USA) 2 b.f. (Mar 1) Kingmambo (USA) 125 – Moon Flower (IRE) **57 p**
95 (Sadler's Wells (USA) 132) [2007 6g Sep 7] strong, good-topped filly: fifth foal:
half-sister to 2 winners, including smart 11f to 12.5f winner Fantastic Love (by Peintre
Celebre): dam, Irish 1m/1¼m winner, half-sister to top-class sprinter/miler Last Tycoon:
80/1 and backward, eighth in maiden at Haydock: will be suited by 1m/1¼m: sure to
progress. *M. L. W. Bell*

SILK HALL (UAE) 2 b.c. (Mar 9) Halling (USA) 133 – Velour 94 (Mtoto 134) [2007 **77**
p8g⁵ p8g⁴ p7m Oct 11] 22,000Y: rather leggy colt: sixth foal: half-brother to French
2002 2-y-o 1m winner Verneau (by Lion Cavern) and 3-y-o Pret A Porter: dam, 2-y-o 7f
winner, out of useful half-sister to Preakness and Belmont Stakes winner Risen Star: fair
form: staying-on fourth at Kempton: will be suited by 1¼m/1½m: raced only on polytrack. *D. W. P. Arbuthnot*

SILKIE SMOOTH (IRE) 3 b.f. Barathea (IRE) 127 – Whassup (FR) (Midyan (USA) **61 §**
124) [2007 83: p6g⁴ 7m 5s Jul 5] rangy filly: has a quick, unimpressive action: just
modest form at 3 yrs, leaving B. Hills 10,000 gns after reappearance: stays 7f: acts on
polytrack and good to firm going: virtually refused to race final outing, and is one to treat
with caution. *G. M. Lyons, Ireland*

SILKWOOD 3 b.f. Singspiel (IRE) 133 – Wood Vine (USA) (Woodman (USA) 126) **116**
[2007 p9.5g* p10g² 10g* 12g* 12d Aug 22] tall, sparely-made filly: fourth live foal: half-
sister to useful 2001 2-y-o 6f (including Cherry Hinton Stakes) winner Silent Honor and
1¼m seller winner Contemplation (both by Sunday Silence): dam unraced half-sister to
useful French 1½m winner Maeander out of sister to Miesque: smart form: won maiden
at Wolverhampton in February, handicap at Sandown in April and Ribblesdale Stakes at
Royal Ascot (much improved when beating All My Loving by 5 lengths, readily asserting
despite again carrying head high and edging left): reported in early-July to have scoped
badly: looked well but ran poorly when last of 7 behind Peeping Fawn in Yorkshire Oaks
at York final outing, hanging left and finding nothing (said to have been unwell for few
days after): stays 1½m: acts on polytrack: has joined Godolphin. *M. A. Jarvis*

SILKY STEPS (IRE) 2 gr.f. (Feb 12) Nayef (USA) 129 – Legal Steps (IRE) (Law **72**
Society (USA) 130) [2007 6d p6g p7m⁴ Nov 1] lengthy filly: half-sister to several
winners, including smart 6f winner (including at 2 yrs) Stormont (by Marju) and fairly
useful 1m winner Stilett (by Tirol): dam Irish 12.5f winner: fair maiden: improved for
longer trip when fourth at Lingfield: will be suited by 1m+. *P. J. Makin*

SILLY GILLY (IRE) 3 b.f. Mull of Kintyre (USA) 114 – Richly Deserved (IRE) **65**
(Kings Lake (USA) 133) [2007 51: f7g⁵ p7.1g 6m 5m 6s 5g² 5v² 5d* 5m³ 5m² p5.1g³ 6g⁴
5.1m⁵ 5g⁵ Oct 5] unfurnished filly: fair handicapper: won at Redcar in July: effective at
5f to easy 7f: acts on fibresand, heavy and good to firm going: tried in cheekpieces: races
prominently: sold 3,100 gns. *K. R. Burke*

SILMI 3 gr.c. Daylami (IRE) 138 – Intimaa (IRE) 104 (Caerleon (USA) 132) [2007 81p: **71**
11.9g 12m Jun 14] neat colt: fair maiden: stays 1½m: acts on polytrack: sold 9,000 gns,
won over hurdles for M. Harris. *E. A. L. Dunlop*

SILVABELLA (IRE) 4 gr.f. Monashee Mountain (USA) 115 – Siva (FR) (Bellypha **–**
130) [2007 –: p8.6g⁶ p9.5g p8.6g Nov 24] tall, close-coupled filly: no form: often wears
headgear. *D. Haydn Jones*

SILVANUS (IRE) 2 b.c. (Mar 22) Danehill Dancer (IRE) 117 – Mala Mala (IRE) 104 **79 p**
(Brief Truce (USA) 126) [2007 6g⁵ 5g Sep 7] 140,000F, 140,000Y: angular, useful-
looking colt: unfurnished at 2 yrs: third foal: brother to useful Irish 5f/6f winner Contest:
dam, Irish 5f winner, half-sister to very smart 1¼m performer Mister Monet and Irish
1000 Guineas winner Tarascon: fair form in maidens at York (promising fifth to Moynahan) and Haydock (odds on, inadequate test): should prove best at 6f/7f: capable of better.
W. J. Haggas

*Ribblesdale Stakes, Royal Ascot—Silkwood is an emphatic winner
from the Oaks third All My Loving (white cap); Dalvina (No.4) is third*

SILVER APPRAISAL 3 gr.f. Royal Applause 124 – Arinaga (Warning 136) [2007 61:   **48**
6m⁶ 6g p6g Sep 15] smallish filly: just poor maiden in 2007: stays 6f: acts on firm ground,
probably on fibresand. *Pat Eddery*

SILVER BLUE (IRE) 4 ch.g. Indian Lodge (IRE) 127 – Silver Echo (Caerleon (USA)   **72 §**
132) [2007 99d: 8.3f 8m 8m⁴ 8.1m⁵ 9m⁵ p8g⁴ p12g Sep 12] good-topped gelding: fair
performer nowadays: claimed from R. Hannon £5,000 prior to final outing: stays 1¼m:
acts on polytrack, soft and good to firm going: tried blinkered: unreliable. *C. R. Dore*

SILVER DEAL 2 b.f. (Apr 2) Lujain (USA) 119 – Deal In Facts 61 (So Factual (USA)   **40**
120) [2007 5d⁴ 6d p5.1m p6d f5g⁵ Dec 27] second foal: dam sprint maiden: poor maiden:
raced at 5f/6f. *J. A. Pickering*

SILVER DIAMOND 2 b.f. (Mar 15) Josr Algarhoud (IRE) 118 – Silvermour (Aydi-   **–**
mour) [2007 7.1g Oct 2] third foal: dam unraced: 66/1, behind in maiden at Warwick.
W. Jarvis

SILVER DREAMER (IRE) 5 b.m. Brave Act 119 – Heads We Called (IRE) (Blue-   **47**
bird (USA) 125) [2007 p12g p13.9g p13g 18d 16m⁵ p12g p13g Dec 28] leggy mare: poor
maiden: effective at 1½m to 2m: acts on polytrack: tried visored. *H. S. Howe*

SILVER FLAME 3 ch.f. Dr Fong (USA) 128 – Pastel 95 (Lion Cavern (USA) 117)   **–**
[2007 55: 5.1g 6.1g 6.1d 8d 5.7f Sep 10] leggy, close-coupled filly: has a quick action:
modest form at 2 yrs: well held in 2007: blinkered final start. *A. W. Carroll*

SILVER GUEST 2 br.g. (Jan 26) Lujain (USA) 119 – Ajig Dancer 86 (Niniski (USA)   **94 §**
125) [2007 5g² 5m² 5m³ 6g² 5m⁴ 5.1s⁴ Jul 13] 42,000Y: tall, good-topped gelding: has a
quick action: fifth foal: half-brother to fairly useful 2004 2-y-o 5f winner Indiannie
Star (by Fraam) and 4-y-o Ajigolo: dam, 5f (at 2 yrs) to 7f winner, out of sister to smart
sprinter Puissance: fairly useful maiden: in frame all starts, including Norfolk Stakes at
Royal Ascot (2¼ lengths fourth to Winker Watson) on penultimate: gelded after final
outing: effective at 5f/6f: acts on good to firm going: no battler, and needs treating with
caution. *M. R. Channon*

SILVERHAY 6 b.g. Inchinor 119 – Moon Spin 83 (Night Shift (USA)) [2007 82:   **77**
p12.2g⁵ f11g Feb 6] well-made gelding: fair handicapper: effective at 1¼m/1½m: acts on
polytrack and any turf going: in cheekpieces of late: usually races prominently: consistent: successful over hurdles for M. Harris prior to rejoining former trainer. *L. Corcoran*

SILVER HOTSPUR 3 b.g. Royal Applause 124 – Noble View (USA) 68 (Distant   **61**
View (USA) 126) [2007 70: f6g f8g³ 5m 5d⁵ p6g⁴ p7g 5g 6v⁶ p7.1g* p7.1d⁶ Dec 27] neat
gelding: modest performer: won minor event at Wolverhampton in November: stays 7f:
acts on polytrack, good to firm and good to soft ground: tried blinkered: trainer fined
£7,500, jockey suspended for 33 days and horse banned for 40 days under non-triers rule
fourth start: has shown temperament. *M. Wigham*

SILVER MITZVA (IRE) 3 b.f. Almutawakel 126 – Ribblesdale 80 (Northern Park   **95**
(USA) 107) [2007 55: 9.7m⁵ 10g⁵ 11.5m² 11.5s³ p11g² 12m⁴ 11.5m* p12g* 12.1g² 12d²
12.5s³ Nov 26] big filly: useful performer: won handicaps at Yarmouth in August and
Kempton in September: plenty of improvement when placed in listed events at Milan and
Fontainebleau last 2 starts: stays 1½m: acts on polytrack, soft and good to firm ground: in
headgear nowadays, tongue tied on debut: usually races up with pace (not final start):
sometimes looks none too keen: sold 90,000 gns. *M. Botti*

SILVER MONT (IRE) 4 b.g. Montjeu (IRE) 137 – Silvernus (Machiavellian (USA)   **62**
123) [2007 59: f12g f14g⁶ f14g⁵ p12.2g³ 14.1g⁶ f12g* 15.8g* f14g² p16.5g 16g⁴ 15.8s
Oct 9] heavy-topped gelding: modest performer: won minor event at Southwell in May
and handicap at Catterick in June: effective at 1½m to 2m: acts on all-weather, firm and
good to soft going: tried in visor/tongue tie, blinkered nowadays. *S. R. Bowring*

SILVER PIVOTAL (IRE) 3 br.f. Pivotal 124 – Silver Colours (USA) 94 (Silver   **108**
Hawk (USA) 123) [2007 73p: p8.6g* 8m² 8g* May 18] tall, close-coupled filly: useful
form: won maiden at Wolverhampton in April and listed race at York (by neck from
Promising Lead) in May: suffered setback after: will be suited by 1¼m: acts on polytrack
and good to firm going. *G. A. Butler*

SILVER PRELUDE 6 b.g. Prince Sabo 123 – Silver Blessings (Statoblest 120) [2007   **88**
73: 5f 5.1d 5g p5.1g² 5.3m p6g² 5.2m* 6f 5.1d⁵ p5g p6g² p5.1m² p5.1g* 5m p5.1g²
5.1g p5g⁵ p5g* p5.1d* Dec 7] good-bodied gelding: fairly useful handicapper: won at
Yarmouth in July, Wolverhampton in September, Lingfield in November and Wolverhampton in December: stays easy 6f, all wins at 5f: acts on polytrack and firm going:
probably on good to soft: forces pace. *D. K. Ivory*

SILVER REGENT (USA) 2 b.c. (Jan 29) Silver Deputy (CAN) – Alexine (ARG) **86** (Runaway Groom (CAN)) [2007 6m 7.1m⁴ 8.1m* 8g⁶ Oct 26] lengthy colt: has scope: first foal: dam Argentinian/US 1m to 11f winner: fairly useful form: won maiden at Sandown in September: creditable sixth to Jack Dawkins in nursery at Doncaster (not much room): will stay 1¼m/1½m. *Mrs A. J. Perrett*

SILVER RIME (FR) 2 gr.c. (Feb 28) Verglas (IRE) 118 – Severina (Darshaan 133) **85** [2007 7m 7s⁴ 7d* Sep 26] €100,000: rather leggy colt: third foal: dam, French maiden, out of close relation to very smart French performer up to 10.5f Secret Form: fairly useful form: fourth to Yankadi in maiden at Newmarket prior to winning weaker event at Goodwood readily by 2 lengths: will stay 1m: acts on soft going. *R. Hannon*

SILVER SAIL 4 gr.f. Daylami (IRE) 138 – Fiveofive (IRE) 61 (Fairy King (USA)) **49** [2007 44: 10.1m 10m 9.9s 10g 8.5s Jul 23] small, compact filly: poor maiden handicapper: probably stays 1¼m: acts on firm and good to soft going: usually wears cheekpieces, visored final start. *J. S. Wainwright*

SILVER SNIPE 3 b.g. Piccolo 121 – Baileys Silver (USA) (Marlin (USA) 124) [2007 **63** –: 6g 6.7g² 7.5m 6d 6g⁵ 6v 5g⁶ p7g² Nov 3] good-topped gelding: modest maiden handicapper: second at Kempton final start: stays 7f: acts on polytrack, best turf effort on good going. *John Joseph Murphy, Ireland*

SILVER SPRITE 2 gr.g. (Jan 26) Best of The Bests (IRE) 122 – Nightingale (Night **55** Shift (USA)) [2007 p8.6g p7.1g⁴ p6g p7g f8d³ Dec 15] modest maiden: third in nursery at Southwell: stays 1m: raced only on all-weather. *D. Shaw*

SILVER SUITOR (IRE) 3 b.g. Swain (IRE) 134 – Taatof (IRE) (Lahib (USA) 129) **97 p** [2007 8g 10g⁵ 10m⁵ 12m* 13.3m² Aug 17] big, unfurnished gelding: second foal: dam unraced out of Princess Royal Stakes winner Labibeh: useful form: won maiden at Newmarket in July: further improvement when 1¾ lengths second to Magicalmysterytour in handicap at Newbury final start: stays 13.3f: acts on good to firm going, yet to race on softer than good: remains capable of better still. *D. R. C. Elsworth*

SILVER SURPRISE 3 gr.f. Orpen (USA) 116 – Dim Ofan 80 (Petong 126) [2007 **53** 8.3m 8g 7g 8g 8m 9.9s 10f 12d 14.1m 11m⁵ p12g p11m p12g p13g Dec 28] lengthy filly: third foal: half-sister to Scandinavian winners Rue d'Alsace (won Norsk Oaks, by Danehill Dancer) and winner up to 10.5f by Second Empire: dam 6f (at 2 yrs) and 1m winner: modest maiden: stays 1½m: acts on polytrack. *J. J. Bridger*

SILVER TIDE (USA) 3 ch.f. Silver Hawk (USA) 123 – Soaring Bay (USA) (Boone's **76** Mill (USA) 115) [2007 12s 10s 9v² 12s³ 8s⁴ 10v² 10d² p8.6g* Nov 17] sturdy, lengthy filly: third foal: dam ran once: fair performer: won maiden at Wolverhampton in November: stays 1¼m, seemingly not 1½m: raced only on polytrack and ground softer than good. *M. J. Grassick, Ireland*

SILVER TOUCH (IRE) 4 b.f. Dansili 127 – Sanpala (Sanglamore (USA) 126) [2007 **115** 111: 6m 7s* 6.5m³ 7d⁵ 6g Sep 30] strong, good-bodied filly: smart performer: won Criterion Stakes at Newmarket in June by head from Major Cadeaux despite hanging left: very good third to Marchand D'Or in Prix Maurice de Gheest at Deauville next time: not at best after in Hungerford Stakes at Newbury and Diadem Stakes at Ascot: has form at 1m, raced mainly at shorter: acts on soft and good to firm going: held up. *M. R. Channon*

SILVERTOWN 12 b.g. Danehill (USA) 126 – Docklands (USA) (Theatrical 128) **–** [2007 89: p16g Jan 20] lengthy gelding: fairly useful handicapper at 11 yrs: pulled up only start in 2007: stays 2m: acts on all-weather, firm and good to soft going: makes running: has tended to flash tail. *L. Lungo*

SILVER WATERS 2 ro.c. (Jan 29) Fantastic Light (USA) 134 – Silent Waters (Polish **59 p** Precedent (USA) 131) [2007 p6g³ Nov 6] 10,000Y: first foal: dam, maiden, half-sister to useful middle-distance performers Faraway Waters, Gower Song and Prince of Denial: 9/1 and green, third in maiden at Lingfield, outpaced: will improve for stiffer stamina test (likely to stay 1¼m/1½m). *D. R. C. Elsworth*

SILVER WIND 2 b.g. (Mar 21) Ishiguru (USA) 114 – My Bonus 79 (Cyrano de Ber- **87** gerac 120) [2007 5d 5m 6s² 6g³ 6m* 7g 6g 6m² 6m² 6d⁵ Sep 28] small, strong, compact gelding: fairly useful performer: won minor event at Folkestone in July: twice runner-up in nurseries at Newbury in September: gelded after final start: best at 6f: acts on soft and good to firm going: usually visored/blinkered. *P. D. Evans*

SIMBA'S PRIDE 3 b.g. Dansili 127 – Welcome Aboard 68 (Be My Guest (USA) 126) **–** [2007 11.1d 8m 9.2g 8.5m 9g Oct 5] stocky gelding: little form. *Miss L. A. Perratt*

SIMBA SUN (IRE) 3 b.g. Intikhab (USA) 135 – Lions Den (IRE) 76 (Desert Style **88**
(IRE) 121) [2007 90: p8g 8.3m⁶ 10m 10d⁴ Oct 1] lengthy, sparely-made gelding: fairly
useful handicapper: stays 1¼m: acts on polytrack, firm and good to soft going: joined
A. King. *R. M. Beckett*

SIMONDIUN 4 b.g. Hernando (FR) 127 – Jetbeeah (IRE) 95 (Lomond (USA) 128) **86**
[2007 97: 12g p16g⁶ Jul 4] good-topped gelding: useful performer at 3 yrs: just fairly
useful at best in 2007: stays 1¾m: acts on good to soft going: visored final outing: joined
P. Nicholls, modest form on hurdling debut. *W. J. Haggas*

SIMONE MARTINI (IRE) 2 b.g. (Jan 20) Montjeu (IRE) 137 – Bona Dea (IRE) **73 p**
(Danehill (USA) 126) [2007 8d⁵ 8d⁴ 8.2g⁵ Nov 7] 85,000Y: compact gelding: first foal:
dam, ran twice in Ireland, sister to useful Irish performer up to 1¼m Darina: fair form in
maidens, catching the eye when fourth to Trianon at Newbury: will be suited by 1¼m/
1½m: gelded after final start: type to progress in handicaps. *R. Charlton*

SIMPLE JIM (FR) 3 b.g. Jimble (FR) – Stop The Wedding (USA) (Stop The Music **62**
(USA)) [2007 11.5s³ 11.3g 10.5s* 11.5g⁵ 12s* 11s⁴ 11.5g a12g² p13.9g⁶ Nov 23] won
maiden at Erbray in July and claimer at Rochefort-sur-Loire in August: left J. Thibault in
France, fair form when sixth in handicap at Wolverhampton on British debut: stays 1½m:
acts on all-weather and soft ground. *A. D. Brown*

SIMPLETON 4 b.g. Easycall 115 – Ok Babe 68 (Bold Arrangement 127) [2007 7g⁶ 9m **–**
p6g p6g⁶ 7m⁶ p10g Sep 18] signs of a little ability. *J. R. Best*

SIMPLIFIED 4 b.f. Lend A Hand 124 – Houston Heiress (USA) (Houston (USA)) **52**
[2007 55: p11g⁶ p10g⁴ p11g* p12g p11g p10g Mar 26] sparely-made filly: modest performer: won minor event at Kempton in February: stays 11f: acts on polytrack and good to
firm going: consistent. *N. B. King*

Mr Jaber Abdullah's "Silver Touch"

SIMPLIFY 5 b.g. Fasliyev (USA) 120 – Simplicity 93 (Polish Precedent (USA) 131) – §
[2007 61d: 9.7m 7m 6m 7g p7m p12m Dec 8] sturdy, quite attractive gelding: modest and
unreliable handicapper at 4 yrs: no impact in 2007: usually wears headgear. *T. M. Jones*

SIMPLY PERFECT 3 gr.f. Danehill (USA) 126 – Hotelgenie Dot Com 107 **116**
(Selkirk (USA) 129) [2007 110: 8m³ 12d⁶ 8m* 8d³ 8m⁴ 11s Oct 27]
        Simply Perfect was given a ride to match her name by Johnny Murtagh
when gaining a third pattern-race victory, and second at Group 1, in the UAE Hydra
Properties Falmouth Stakes at Newmarket in July. The late withdrawal of the 2006
One Thousand Guineas winner Speciosa not only reduced the field to seven but
also left doubts as to how the race would be run, with the South African mare
Irridescence, having her first start in Britain, seeming the one most likely to set the
pace in the absence of confirmed front runner Speciosa. Simply Perfect's jockey
Johnny Murtagh had other ideas, though. He had adopted patient tactics when
winning the Falmouth on Soviet Song in 2004 and 2005, but on this occasion he
had Simply Perfect in front from the start and proceeded to dictate matters.
Steadying the pace after a couple of furlongs or so, Murtagh wound it up again from
around halfway and then found Simply Perfect more than ready to play her part
when her pursuers, led by the favourite Nannina, threatened approaching the final
furlong. Put under stronger pressure, Simply Perfect responded most gamely and
ran on strongly to hold off Irridescence and Arch Swing, as Nannina weakened into
fourth, Simply Perfect's winning margin a length. Murtagh's salute as he passed the
post showed his delight at a job well done. It was the highlight of Simply Perfect's
second and final season, one which had begun at Newmarket in May in the One
Thousand Guineas.
        Despite having won the May Hill Stakes and the Fillies' Mile on her last
two starts in 2006, Simply Perfect was rather overshadowed by her stablemate
Sander Camillo in the run-up to the Guineas. In the end, Sander Camillo, who
proved most disappointing at three, didn't even take her place in the field while
Simply Perfect acquitted herself well in taking third behind Finsceal Beo and Arch
Swing, beaten three and three quarter lengths by the winner. A mile and a half
proved too far for Simply Perfect in the Oaks, but she confirmed herself a smart
miler on her next three starts. The Falmouth was the first of those, and that was followed by good efforts in two more Group 1 contests, the Prix d'Astarte at Deauville
in July and the Sun Chariot Stakes at Newmarket in October. At Deauville, Simply
Perfect finished third behind Darjina and Missvinski, beaten half a length and the
same; and in the Sun Chariot she finished fourth behind Majestic Roi, Nannina and

*UAE Hydra Properties Falmouth Stakes, Newmarket—Simply Perfect returns to a mile and is given
an excellent front-running ride by Johnny Murtagh; the well-travelled Irridescence (noseband)
is second with Arch Swing (left) and Nannina (white sash) next*

Echelon, unable to make the running with Speciosa in opposition this time and getting to the front only briefly under three furlongs out. Simply Perfect was given another chance at a trip beyond a mile in the Breeders' Cup Filly & Mare Turf over eleven furlongs at Monmouth Park. However, she turned in a most headstrong display, pulling her way into the lead before running very wide on the turn into the back straight, carrying two others out with her, Murtagh pulling her up soon after. One of those two fillies, Precious Kitten, won the Grade 1 Matriarch Stakes next time. A few days after the Breeders' Cup it was announced that Simply Perfect had been retired and would be joining the broodmare band at Coolmore. She visits Galileo.

Simply Perfect (gr.f. 2004)	Danehill (USA) (b 1986)	Danzig (b 1977)	Northern Dancer
			Pas de Nom
		Razyana (b 1981)	His Majesty
			Spring Adieu
	Hotelgenie Dot Com (gr 1998)	Selkirk (ch 1988)	Sharpen Up
			Annie Edge
		Birch Creek (gr 1982)	Carwhite
			Deed

Judged on pedigree, Simply Perfect was far from certain to get a mile and a half. She is the second foal of Hotelgenie Dot Com who was at her best at two, winning a minor event at Sandown and being placed in the Moyglare Stud Stakes and Fillies' Mile. Simply Perfect's grandam, the highly-tried maiden Birch Creek, showed useful form in France and Italy, including when third in a Group 3 over a mile, while the next dam, Deed, gained her sole win over five furlongs as a juvenile. Hotelgenie Dot Com's first foal never ran. Her third, Rimrock (by Royal Applause), was gelded after failing to reach a place in three starts in maidens and was sold for just 1,000 guineas at Newmarket, one month before Hotelgenie Dot Com's filly foal by Green Desert fetched 240,000 guineas at the December Sales there. Simply Perfect, a smallish, lengthy filly, acted on good to firm and good to soft going. She was often on edge in the preliminaries, and was free under strong restraint to post prior to the Oaks, though she was calm before the Falmouth Stakes. *J. Noseda*

SIMPLY ST LUCIA 5 b.m. Charnwood Forest (IRE) 125 – Mubadara (IRE) 80 (Lahib (USA) 129) [2007 –, a63: f8g 11.1d* 12d⁵ Jul 29] modest performer nowadays: won claimer at Hamilton in July: stays 11f: acts on all-weather and good to soft ground: tried blinkered/in cheekpieces: races prominently. *J. R. Weymes* — **61**

SIMPSONS GAMBLE (IRE) 4 b.g. Tagula (IRE) 116 – Kiva (Indian Ridge 123) [2007 60: p7g p7g⁵ p8g p10g⁴ p8g³ p8g³ p6g 9g p7g⁵ p8g⁵ p8m² p8g² Dec 16] strong gelding: modest maiden: left M. Flower after eighth start: stays easy 1¼m: acts on poly-track, no form on turf: tried blinkered/in cheekpieces. *R. A. Teal* — **a60**

SIMPSONS ROSS (IRE) 4 b.g. Imperial Ballet (IRE) 110 – Brunswick (Warning 136) [2007 64: p8g⁴ Jan 10] leggy gelding: modest maiden: stayed 1m: acted on polytrack and firm going: tried blinkered: dead. *R. M. Flower* — **51**

SINAAF 2 b.f. (Feb 7) Nayef (USA) 129 – Elutrah (Darshaan 133) [2007 p7g p7g⁶ Nov 17] second foal: dam, unraced sister to Rockfel Stakes winner Sayedah (stayed 1½m), out of half-sister to US Grade 2 7f winner Kayrawan: fair form latter start in maidens at Lingfield: will be suited by 1m/1¼m. *M. P. Tregoning* — **65**

SINATAS (GER) 4 b.g. Lomitas 129 – Sylvette (USA) (Silver Hawk (USA) 123) [2007 11g⁴ 9.2d⁵ 13.1d⁶ 15s⁵ Aug 11] better effort in maidens at 3 yrs for P. Schiergen when second at Dresden: left S. Stokes in Germany after reappearance: modest form in Britain: stays 15f: acts on soft ground: tried blinkered. *P. Monteith* — **59**

SINBAD THE SAILOR 2 b.c. (Apr 10) Cape Cross (IRE) 129 – Sinead (USA) (Irish River (FR) 131) [2007 7m 7.1m⁵ 8.1g Sep 19] 40,000F, €50,000Y: compact colt: sixth foal: half-brother to 5-y-o Art Modern: dam, US 2-y-o 8.5f winner, half-sister to dam of Preakness Stakes winner Red Bullet: fair form in maidens, fifth to Ridge Dance at Sandown: should be suited by 1m+. *J. W. Hills* — **72**

SIN CITY 4 b.g. Sinndar (IRE) 134 – Turn of A Century 85 (Halling (USA) 133) [2007 78: 10f² 14m² Jun 2] rather leggy, close-coupled gelding: has a quick action: fairly useful handicapper, lightly raced: further improvement when runner-up both starts in 2007: stays 1¾m: raced only on good ground or firmer. *R. A. Fahey* — **85**

SINEAD OF AGLISH (IRE) 2 ch.f. (Apr 7) Captain Rio 122 – Final Favour (IRE) **75** (Unblest 117) [2007 5m² 5g² 5m³ 5.1m³ 6g² 6f² 5d* 6g 6f⁴ 6g p5.1g³ p6m⁵ Dec 7] €14,000Y: compact filly: good walker: second foal: half-sister to 3-y-o Sister Etienne: dam unraced: fair performer: won maiden at Warwick in June: left A. Haynes after tenth start (wore blinkers subsequently): effective at 5f/6f: acts on polytrack, firm and good to soft going. *Peter Grayson*

SINGER OF SONGS (IRE) 2 ch.c. (Feb 8) Spartacus (IRE) 107 – Waratah (IRE) **61 ?** (Entrepreneur 123) [2007 6g 7s 6.1s⁶ p8g Sep 5] strong colt: maiden: form (modest) only when sixth at Chepstow: bred to be suited by 1m/1¼m. *P. A. Blockley*

SINGHALONGTASVEER 5 b.g. Namaqualand (USA) – Felinwen (White Mill 76) **55** [2007 50: 16m* 16.1m 16s³ Jul 3] compact gelding: modest handicapper: won at Musselburgh in May: left W. Storey prior to final start: stays 2m: acts on soft and good to firm going: usually tongue tied/visored/in cheekpieces: fair hurdler, won in December. *G. A. Charlton*

SINGLEB (IRE) 3 b.g. Intikhab (USA) 135 – Bubble N Squeak (IRE) 91 (Catrail **67** (USA) 123) [2007 f7g³ p7.1g⁶ f6g 7g* 7g⁵ 10g Oct 31] fair performer: won maiden at Catterick in September: stays 7f: acts on fibresand, raced only on good going on turf. *T. D. Barron*

SINTENIS MAC (GER) 4 ch.g. Pivotal 124 – Sintenis (GER) (Polish Precedent **65** (USA) 131) [2007 6g² p6g⁴ f6g⁴ Dec 27] big, good-topped gelding: fair maiden: similar form first 2 starts, fourth to Tubby Isaacs at Wolverhampton: will stay 7f. *P. J. O'Gorman*

SION HILL (IRE) 6 b.g. Desert Prince (IRE) 130 – Mobilia 67 (Last Tycoon 131) **55** [2007 51: f6g⁶ f8g 7g 8.5g³ 8.5g p8g² p8.6g* p7.1g⁴ p8g p7.1g² p7.1g² p8g² f8d Dec 20] well-made gelding: modest performer: left Mrs N. Macauley after second start: won (first success) minor event at Wolverhampton in September: stays 9.5f: acts on all-weather and good to firm going: usually wears headgear: races prominently: hung markedly right and virtually pulled up at Kempton ninth outing. *John A. Harris*

SIRAJ 8 b.g. Piccolo 121 – Masuri Kabisa (USA) 48 (Ascot Knight (CAN) 130) [2007 **61** 70: f6g⁶ 6d⁴ 7m p5g⁶ p6g p6g p6g⁴ p6g⁴ Nov 1] good-bodied gelding: modest performer nowadays: best at 6f: acts on all-weather and any turf going: usually wears headgear: tried tongue tied. *J. Ryan*

SIR ARTHUR (IRE) 4 ch.g. Desert Prince (IRE) 130 – Park Express 123 (Ahonoora **82** 122) [2007 83: 10.1s 12m³ 9.9g² 10g⁵ 9.9m² 11.5d 9.9v³ 10d Aug 1] big, lengthy gelding: fairly useful handicapper: left M. Johnston 20,000 gns prior to final start: stays 1½m: acts on any going: tried blinkered: has awkward head carriage: usually forces pace: modest form in hurdling debut. *B. Ellison*

SIR BOND (IRE) 6 ch.g. Desert Sun 120 – In Tranquility (IRE) (Shalford (IRE) 124§) **67** [2007 72: p9.5g⁵ p8.6g 8f² 7.5m 7m² 8.5m 8m 8d 7.6d p8.6g p8.6g p8.6s* Dec 21] lengthy, heavy-bodied gelding: fair handicapper: won at Wolverhampton in December: stays 9.5f: acts on all-weather, firm and soft ground: tried in cheekpieces/tongue tie: often held up: sometimes slowly away: flashes tail: none too consistent. *G. R. Oldroyd*

SIR DON (IRE) 8 b.g. Lake Coniston (IRE) 131 – New Sensitive (Wattlefield 117) **64** [2007 63: p5.1g p6g* Dec 19] sparely-made gelding: modest handicapper: won at Lingfield in December: effective at 5f/6f: acts on polytrack, firm and good to soft going: usually wears headgear: has found little. *E. S. McMahon*

SIR DOUGLAS 4 ch.c. Desert Sun 120 – Daintree (IRE) 66 (Tirol 127) [2007 80: **79** p7.1g² p7g⁵ f6g⁵ p7.1g² p7.1g² p7g² p7.1g p6g* p6g³ 5.1f p6g p6g p6g⁵ p7m⁶ Dec 8] strong colt: fair handicapper: claimed from J. Osborne £8,000 after reappearance: won at Wolverhampton (hung left) in March: effective at 6f/7f: acts on all-weather: tried in cheekpieces: sometimes takes strong hold (has worn crossed noseband). *R. A. Harris*

SIR DUKE (IRE) 3 b.g. Danehill (USA) 126 – Dimanche (IRE) (Sadler's Wells (USA) **67** 132) [2007 –: p9.5g 10m 10m* 10g⁵ 12d p12g⁵ 14.1m⁵ 11.5m⁶ 16m³ 16g⁴ p12.2g* Oct 12] angular gelding: fair performer: won handicap at Redcar in June and minor event at Wolverhampton in October: effective from 1½m to 2m: acts on polytrack, unraced on extremes of going on turf: tried visored: has wandered under pressure. *P. W. D'Arcy*

SIREN CALL 2 b.f. (May 19) Fantastic Light (USA) 134 – Fleet Amour (USA) (Afleet **50** (CAN)) [2007 7m 8m 8.2m Oct 3] lightly-made filly: eighth foal: half-sister to several winners, including useful 7f winner Affaire Royale (by Royal Academy) and fairly useful 7.5f to 1¼m winner Fleet of Light (by Spectrum): dam, US maiden, closely related to US Grade 1 1m winner Quiet American: modest form in maidens: sold 2,200 gns. *W. J. Haggas*

*Ireland Gimcrack Stakes, York—Sir Gerry quickens sharply from last place
to beat the newcomer Great Barrier Reef with Swiss Franc (right) third*

SIREN'S GIFT 3 ch.f. Cadeaux Genereux 131 – Blue Siren 113 (Bluebird (USA) 125) **103**
[2007 98: 5g² 5d⁴ 6m⁵ 6m⁴ 5m* 5.2m⁶ p6m⁴ Oct 6] lengthy filly: useful performer: won
minor event at Leicester (by neck from The Jobber) in September: creditable fourth to
Bonus in handicap at Kempton final outing, racing wide: effective at 5f/easy 6f: acts on
polytrack, firm and soft going: withdrawn after giving trouble at start (ran loose) intended
fifth outing. *A. M. Balding*

SIR GEORGE (IRE) 2 b.c. (Apr 19) Mujadil (USA) 119 – Torrmana (IRE) (Ela- **71**
Mana-Mou 132) [2007 6s² 6d Aug 25] quite good-topped colt: fair maiden: runner-up at
Yarmouth: 5/1, well held in sales race at the Curragh 2 months later: will stay 7f/1m.
P. W. Chapple-Hyam

SIR GERRY (USA) 2 ch.c. (Apr 20) Carson City (USA) – Incredulous (FR) 95 (Indian **112 +**
Ridge 123) [2007 6s* 6m⁴ 6g* 6m Oct 5] $75,000Y, 100,000 2-y-o: good-topped colt:
has scope: third foal: half-brother to French 2006 2-y-o 7f winner Unbeliever (by Bahri):
dam, 1m winner, half-sister to useful performers up to 1¼m Be Mindful and Mythic:
smart form: won maiden at Thirsk in July and Ireland Gimcrack Stakes at York in August,
in latter quickening sharply switched round the field to beat Great Barrier Reef by ¾
length: 2/1 favourite, seemingly had problem (laboured display) when only eighth in
Middle Park Stakes at Newmarket: will stay 7f, possibly 1m: successes on good and soft
going, but probably acts on good to firm also. *J. R. Fanshawe*

SIR HAYDN 7 ch.g. Definite Article 121 – Snowscape (Niniski (USA) 125) [2007 –, **70**
a83: p10g 10.1d 10.1d 10.1g p10g⁴ p10g⁵ p11g⁴ p12g² p12g p12.2g³ p10g⁶ p10m⁵ p11g*
Dec 19] big, leggy gelding: fair handicapper nowadays: won (dead-heated) at Kempton
in December: stays 1½m: acts on all-weather, firm and soft ground: usually wears headgear: held up: sometimes finds little: fair winning hurdler. *J. R. Jenkins*

SIR IKE (IRE) 2 b.c. (Apr 5) Xaar 132 – Iktidar 80 (Green Desert (USA) 127) [2007 **60 +**
6m⁴ 6d Oct 15] well-made colt: modest form in maidens at Ascot (tongue tied, fourth to
Master Chef) and Windsor 3 months apart: will stay 7f. *W. S. Kittow*

SIR JAKE 3 b.c. Killer Instinct 111 – Waikiki Dancer (IRE) 48 (General Monash (USA) **–**
107) [2007 10.9g 10f Aug 6] angular colt: no form in maidens at Warwick and Windsor.
T. T. Clement

SIR JOEY 2 ch.g. (Mar 2) Forzando 122 – Estabella (IRE) 67 (Mujtahid (USA) 118) **52 §**
[2007 p5g⁵ p6g 6d 5.1g p6g p7.1g⁴ p9.5g⁶ p8.6g Dec 31] strong, workmanlike gelding:
modest maiden: stays 7f: acts on polytrack: tried blinkered (looked difficult ride).
J. T. Stimpson

SIRJOSHUA REYNOLDS 2 b.c. (Jan 31) Kyllachy 129 – Alzianah 102 (Alzao **88 +**
(USA) 117) [2007 5g p5g 6g⁵ 6s* 6d⁴ 5d⁶ 6.8g⁶ 8g* 8d* a6.8g* Nov 6] 60,000Y: well-
grown colt: half-brother to several winners, including fairly useful sprinters Desperate
Dan (by Danzero) and Leozian (by Lion Cavern): dam 5f/6f winner, including at 2 yrs:
fairly useful performer: won maiden at Brighton in May and, having been sold from
N. Callaghan 72,000 gns after sixth start, 3 minor events at Taby in autumn (all by wide
margins): stays 1m: acts on dirt and soft going: blinkered last 3 starts. *Yvonne Durant,
Sweden*

SIR LIAM (USA) 3 b.g. Monarchos (USA) 129 – Tears (USA) (Red Ransom (USA)) **77**
[2007 77: p10g* p10g⁵ 11g 8m p10g⁵ p11g⁶ 10g 10m Aug 31] well-made gelding: has
scope: fair handicapper: won maiden at Kempton in March: in-and-out form in handicaps
after: should stay beyond 1¼m: acts on polytrack and firm going: in cheekpieces last 2
starts: gelded after final outing. *P. Mitchell*

SIR LOIN 6 ch.g. Compton Place 125 – Charnwood Queen 61 (Cadeaux Genereux 131) **63**
[2007 64: p5g⁴ p5.1g⁶ f5g p5.1g 5.1m 6.1g p5.1g* p5.1g p5.1g 5g³ 5s 5g⁴ 5d⁴ 6m⁶ p7g
p6g p5g³ p5m² p5.1g p5m p6g⁴ p6g⁴ Dec 29] leggy gelding: modest handicapper: won at
Wolverhampton in June: left N. Tinkler after fourteenth start: best at 5f: acts on polytrack,
good to firm and good to soft going (well beaten on soft/heavy): usually wears headgear:
races prominently. *P. Burgoyne*

SIR MIKEALE 4 b.c. Easycall 115 – Sleep Standing (IRE) (Standaan (FR) 118) [2007 **–**
50: p7g p6g f7d Dec 12] good-topped colt: little form in 2007. *G. Prodromou*

SIR MONTY (USA) 5 ch.g. Cat's Career (USA) – Lady of Meadowlane (USA) (Pan- **70 +**
cho Jay (USA)) [2007 89: p12g p16g⁶ Mar 7] leggy, workmanlike gelding: fairly useful
handicapper at 4 yrs: just fair form in 2007: effective at 1½m: acts on
polytrack, firm and soft going: has run well when sweating: has worn crossed noseband:
sold 8,000 gns and joined P. Bowen, fairly useful form over hurdles, won in November.
Mrs A. J. Perrett

SIR NOD 5 b.g. Tagula (IRE) 116 – Nordan Raider 81 (Domynsky 110) [2007 87: 6d **89**
6m² 5g² 5m 5d⁴ p6g² p6g Nov 16] lengthy gelding: fairly useful handicapper: creditable
efforts in 2007 when in frame: effective at 5f/6f: acts on polytrack, firm and good to soft
ground: often races prominently. *Miss J. A. Camacho*

SIR ORPEN (IRE) 4 gr.g. Orpen (USA) 116 – Yalciyna 92 (Nishapour (FR) 125) **77**
[2007 81: 7m* 7m⁵ 7d 6m⁶ 7d 6g 6m 7m p7.1g Oct 12] lengthy, good-topped gelding:
fair handicapper: won at Catterick in April: effective at stiff 6f to 1m: acts on firm and
soft going: tried blinkered/in cheekpieces: sold 6,000 gns. *T. D. Barron*

SIR PERCY 4 b.c. Mark of Esteem (IRE) 137 – Percy's Lass 120§ (Blakeney 126) **122**
[2007 129: 12g⁴ 12d⁶ 10m⁶ Jun 20]
    According to Timeform's weight-for-age scale, a four-year-old at the
beginning of June should be 13 lb better at a mile and a half than at the same time
as a three-year-old. That is a measure of the improvement made by the average
thoroughbred in the intervening twelve months, but the fact that the first four
classics are run relatively early favours the more mature three-year-olds, hence the
reason that very few classic winners prove capable of making more than the normal
improvement from three to four. The 2006 Derby winner Sir Percy was more
precocious than most modern-day Derby winners, going unbeaten through a
two-year-old campaign which culminated in a neck win over the unlucky Horatio
Nelson in the Dewhurst which, as usual, attracted the strongest field for any juvenile event in Britain. Sir Percy showed he had trained on well when second of
fourteen to George Washington in the Two Thousand Guineas. Sir Percy's victory
at Epsom in probably the closest finish in Derby history—the first four separated
by a short head, a head and a short head—made him the first Derby winner since
Generous in 1991 even to have run in the Two Thousand Guineas. He was also the
first Derby winner since Dr Devious in 1992 to have won the Dewhurst, a race also
won by Generous. Unfortunately, Sir Percy returned 'stiff' and 'jarred up' from
Epsom and ran only once more at three, when a long way below form in the
Champion Stakes. His four-year-old campaign was an anti-climax too after a
creditable fourth of fourteen, beaten a length and three quarters, despite a rough
passage (sustaining several cuts), behind Vengeance of Rain in the Dubai Sheema
Classic at Nad Al Sheba in March. Sir Percy didn't even make the frame in his two
subsequent races, making no impression in the Coronation Cup at Epsom and

folding tamely when forcing tactics were tried in the Prince of Wales's Stakes at Royal Ascot. An announcement that he had been retired was made in August and he will be standing at Lanwades Stud, Newmarket, in 2008 at a fee of £8,000 (October 1st special live foal).

		Darshaan	Shirley Heights
	Mark of Esteem (IRE)	(br 1981)	Delsy
	(b 1993)	Homage	Ajdal
Sir Percy		(b 1989)	Home Love
(b.c. 2003)		Blakeney	Hethersett
	Percy's Lass	(b 1966)	Windmill Girl
	(b or br 1984)	Laughing Girl	Sassafras
		(b 1973)	Violetta III

The close-coupled Sir Percy, a good mover with a fluent action, cost his connections only 16,000 guineas as a yearling, his dam the very smart racemare Percy's Lass having a stud record that was ordinary at best before Sir Percy came along. Percy's Lass, weeded out of Darley Stud in 1998, was descended from Horama, the legendary foundation mare of the Moller brothers' White Lodge Stud, and had come into Darley when Sheikh Mohammed bought the Moller bloodstock on the death of Eric Moller in 1989. Sir Percy's grandam the Oaks fourth Laughing Girl was a half-sister to Irish One Thousand Guineas winner Favoletta, Oaks runner-up Furioso, the dam of 1983 Derby winner Teenoso, and to the dams of other Group 1 winners in Give Thanks, Ashayer and Nicolotte. Sir Percy's great grandam Violetta III (a granddaughter of Horama) dead-heated in the Cambridge-shire and bred nine winners in all. Sir Percy (whose sire the top miler Mark of Esteem seems to have been forced into early retirement) was the fifth male-line descendant of his great-great grandsire Mill Reef to win the Derby, and the only one to match Mill Reef's victories in the Dewhurst and the Derby. Mill Reef sired two Derby winners himself, Shirley Heights and Reference Point, and Shirley Heights in turn sired the 1985 winner Slip Anchor and is the sire of High Estate whose son High-Rise won the 1998 Derby. British-bred Derby winners like Sir Percy are rare nowadays but the fact that his pedigree is largely free of the influence of Northern Dancer and Mr Prospector—in fact largely free of any American influence close up—makes it straightforward to find suitable mares for him. Let's hope that Lanwades, which has a splendid record with its stallions, can provide a launching pad for Sir Percy to make his mark at stud. If he imparts a measure of precocity, Sir Percy may well make the early impression which will be needed to retain the faith of breeders. *M. P. Tregoning*

SIR ROYAL (USA) 2 b.c. (Mar 4) Diesis 133 – Only Royale (IRE) 121 (Caerleon (USA) 132) [2007 7.2s⁵ Sep 21] 24,000Y: medium-sized, good-bodied colt: eighth foal: half-brother to 6f winner in Japan and 1m winner in US (both by Kingmambo): dam, 1m to 1½m (including dual Yorkshire Oaks) winner, out of smart Irish 6f/7f winner Etoile de Paris, herself half-sister to high-class 1m to 1½m performer Northern Treasure: 25/1 and green, never-nearer fifth to Boy Blue in maiden at Ayr: will be suited by 1m/1¼m: sure to improve. *G. A. Swinbank* **65 p**

SIR SANDICLIFFE (IRE) 3 b.g. Distant Music (USA) 126 – Desert Rose (Green Desert (USA) 127) [2007 74: p8g p9.5g² p9.5g 10.3s 9m⁶ 12g³ p12.2g⁴ p12.2g⁶ p13.9g p12g p12g p12g² p12.2d p12.2s* p12.2g² Dec 29] workmanlike gelding: fair performer: left B. Hills 11,000 gns after second start: won handicap at Wolverhampton in December: stays 1½m: acts on polytrack and good to firm ground: usually held up. *W. M. Brisbourne* **68**

SIR XAAR (IRE) 4 b. or br.g. Xaar 132 – Cradle Brief (IRE) (Brief Truce (USA) 126) [2007 103: 7m 6m 7d² 8.1m 8g 7g 7m² p7m Nov 1] good-topped filly: has a quick action: useful handicapper: creditable efforts in 2007 only when runner-up, beaten length by Celtic Sultan at Newmarket seventh start: gelded after final outing: effective at 6f/7f: acts on good to firm and good to soft going: tongue tied nowadays: blinkered last 2 outings: ungenuine. *B. Smart* **101 §**

SIRYENA 2 b.f. (Feb 3) Oasis Dream 129 – Ard Na Sighe (IRE) (Kenmare (FR) 125) [2007 6m 7m⁶ p7g⁶ p7g Sep 20] 20,000F: good-topped filly: sixth foal: half-sister to 3 winners, including useful Irish 6f winner Dr Dignity (by Dr Devious) and fairly useful 2006 2-y-o 6f winner Pixie Ring (by Pivotal): dam unraced half-sister to top-class sprinter Marwell, herself dam of very smart miler Marling: modest maiden: stays 7f. *E. A. L. Dunlop* **54**

SISTER ACT 3 b.f. Marju (IRE) 127 – Kalinka (IRE) 88 (Soviet Star (USA) 128) [2007 **85**
7m² 8.2g 8d³ 7d 8.1g⁵ p8g* Oct 10] strong, rangy filly: fifth foal: sister to high-class miler
Soviet Song and half-sister to 2 winners, including fairly useful 1m (at 2 yrs)/1¼m and
Triumph Hurdle winner Penzance (by Pennekamp): dam 2-y-o 7f winner (stayed 1¼m):
fairly useful performer: made all in maiden at Kempton in October: will probably stay
beyond 1m: acts on polytrack and good to firm ground, probably on good to soft:
reportedly lost action second/fourth starts. *J. R. Fanshawe*

SISTER AGNES (IRE) 3 ch.f. Dr Fong (USA) 128 – Nibbs Point (IRE) 107 (Sure **65**
Blade (USA) 130) [2007 10d 11.8s 12g³ 11.7g 14s⁵ Oct 4] lengthy filly: half-sister to
several winners, including very smart but untrustworthy 1¼m/1½m performer Border
Arrow (by Selkirk), 9.4f to 1½m winner Shingles (by Desert Prince) and French 9f
winner Hatem (by Zafonic), latter 2 fairly useful: dam 1¼m/1½m winner: fair maiden:
left J. Fanshawe 22,000 gns after fourth outing: stays 1¾m: raced only on good ground or
softer (acts on soft): blinkered final start. *Jane Chapple-Hyam*

SISTER ETIENNE (IRE) 3 b.f. Lend A Hand 124 – Final Favour (IRE) (Unblest **54**
117) [2007 68: f5g* f5g⁵ 5.1g Apr 4] compact filly: just modest performer in 2007: won
seller at Southwell (sold from T. D. Barron) in February: raced mainly at 5f: acts on fibresand and good to firm going: tends to wander. *J. T. Stimpson*

SISTER GEE (IRE) 5 b.m. Desert Story (IRE) 115 – My Gloria (IRE) (Saint Estephe **–**
(FR) 123) [2007 46: f5g⁷ Feb 13] sturdy mare: poor maiden: effective at 5f/6f: acts on
fibresand and good to soft going. *R. Hollinshead*

SISTER MARIA (USA) 3 b. or br.f. Kingmambo (USA) 125 – Fraulein 117 (Acate- **89**
nango (GER) 127) [2007 75: 8g⁴ 9g⁶ 10g³ 10s* 10.4s⁵ 9.8g³ p12.2g² 10m* 12g⁵ Nov 2]
leggy filly: fairly useful handicapper: won at Windsor in June and Newmarket in October:
stays easy 1½m: acts on polytrack, soft and good to firm ground: often races prominently.
E. A. L. Dunlop

SISTER MOONSHINE 2 b.f. (Mar 30) Averti (IRE) 117 – Cal Norma's Lady (IRE) **65**
87 (Lyphard's Special (USA) 122) [2007 5.7d⁵ p6g Oct 15] 80,000Y: half-sister to several
winners, notably double 5f/6f winner (including Cheveley Park Stakes) Donna Blini (by
Bertolini) and 6-y-o Bijou Dan: dam 2-y-o 6f/7f winner (stayed 1¼m): mid-field in
maidens at Bath (fair form) and Lingfield: will stay 7f/1m. *W. R. Muir*

SISTOS FASCINATION 2 b.g. (Feb 27) Fasliyev (USA) 120 – Sierra Virgen (USA) **60**
(Stack (USA)) [2007 6s 6m 5m⁵ 5d⁶ p6g p6g Nov 14] compact gelding: modest maiden:
will stay beyond 6f: acts on polytrack and good to firm going: tried tongue tied/in cheek-
pieces/blinkered: gelded. *M. Botti*

SITULA (IRE) 3 ch.f. Pairumani Star (IRE) 110 – Suspiria (IRE) 87 (Glenstal (USA) **64**
118) [2007 73: 8.5g 10.2m 7g 7g⁶ p10.7g Dec 5] smallish filly: fair performer at 2 yrs:
only modest in handicaps in 2007, leaving H. Dunlop after third outing: should stay 1m:
acts on polytrack. *P. Henley, Ireland*

SIVOTA (IRE) 3 b.g. Sakhee (USA) 136 – Mamara Reef 71 (Salse (USA) 128) [2007 **75**
77p: 12g 12s⁶ 16.2g* 15.9m³ Sep 15] neat gelding: fair performer: won handicap at
Beverley in August: stays 2m: acts on soft and good to firm ground: sold 40,000 gns in
October. *T. P. Tate*

SIX DAY WAR (IRE) 3 b.g. Barathea (IRE) 127 – Risarshana (FR) (Darshaan 133) **85**
[2007 p10g³ p9.5g⁵ f8g* f12g* 12.3m⁶ 12g May 19] tall, close-coupled gelding: fourth
foal: half-brother to useful 1½m winner Selebela (by Grand Lodge): dam, ran once in
France, granddaughter of smart French performer up to 10.5f Restiver: fairly useful performer: won maiden in January and handicap in February, both at Southwell: below form
in handicaps after (reportedly returned with severe muscle problems final outing): stays
1½m: acts on fibresand: sold 42,000 gns in October, joined O. Sherwood. *J. A. Osborne*

SIXFIELDS FLYER (IRE) 3 gr.f. Desert Style (IRE) 121 – Gratclo 65 (Belfort (FR) **66**
89) [2007 p7g 7.1m 8.1m⁶ 8.1m³ p8.6g 10g 10m Aug 10] 75,000Y: lengthy filly: half-
sister to several winners, including 1996 2-y-o 6f (July Stakes) winner Rich Ground (by
Common Grounds) and 5f/6f winner (including at 2 yrs) Bandanna (by Bandmaster),
both useful: dam 6f (including at 2 yrs)/7f winner: fair maiden: stays 1m: acts on good to
firm going: wore cheekpieces final outing: sold 1,000 gns. *Pat Eddery*

SIX OF DIAMONDS (IRE) 3 b.c. Redback 116 – Villa Nova (IRE) 55 (Petardia 113) **99**
[2007 7.1m³ p8g⁴ 7m⁴ 10.2m* 9.9g⁴ 10m* 9.9g³ 9.9m 10.2f* 9.7f³ Sep 25] €48,000Y:
sturdy colt: fourth foal: half-brother to useful 5f (at 2 yrs) to 8.5f (in UAE) winner Prince
of Denmark (by Danetime) and fairly useful 11f winner Star of Canterbury (by Beckett):
dam Irish maiden (stayed 9f): useful handicapper: won at Bath in May, Sandown (dead-

heat) in July and Bath (beat Gold Hush by short head, edging left, bumping runner-up close home and originally demoted, but reinstated as winner on appeal) in September: stays 1¼m: acts on firm ground: usually makes running: joined A. Cruz in Hong Kong, where renamed Really Happy. *J. A. Osborne*

SIX OF HEARTS 3 b.g. Pivotal 124 – Additive (USA) 81 (Devil's Bag (USA)) [2007 **66** p7.1g² f8g⁵ 7g³ p7.1g 7.1g p8g⁵ p8g³ p8g³ p9.5g Sep 28] good-topped colt: fair maiden: stays 1m: acts on polytrack: wore cheekpieces last 2 outings: sold 11,000 gns. *J. A. Osborne*

SIX OF TRUMPS (IRE) 3 b.g. Fasliyev (USA) 120 – Run To Jane (IRE) (Doyoun **61** 124) [2007 –: f6g² p6g⁴ 7f⁶ p7.1g² Aug 30] useful-looking gelding: modest maiden: raced only at 6f/7f: acts on polytrack and firm ground: wandered on reappearance: sold 3,000 gns in November. *J. A. Osborne*

SIX SHOTS 3 b.c. Josr Algarhoud (IRE) 118 – Captive Heart (Conquistador Cielo **84** (USA)) [2007 67: p9.5g² p9.5g* p10g² p8g⁴ p11g³ p10g³ 9g 8.5f³ 8.5f² 8.5f 12f p9.5f Oct 13] good-bodied colt: fairly useful performer: won maiden at Wolverhampton in January: left J. Osborne after sixth start: stays 11f: acts on polytrack and firm going. *D. Douglas, USA*

SIXTIES ICON 4 b.c. Galileo (IRE) 134 – Love Divine 120 (Diesis 133) [2007 **125** 125: 12m⁵ 12m* 12d 12m Jul 12]

And it was all looking so rosy in May! The 2006 St Leger winner Sixties Icon seemed set for another very successful season when making an impressive return in the Jockey Club Stakes at Newmarket, but two dismal performances followed and he wasn't seen out after July. Sixties Icon's three-year-old season had

StanJamesUK.com Jockey Club Stakes, Newmarket—
the 2006 St Leger winner Sixties Icon makes a successful reappearance;
Admiral's Cruise (right), Mighty, Papal Bull (left) and Linda's Lad make up the field

ended on a low note, the colt finishing seventh of eight in the Prix de l'Arc de Triomphe for which he had been supplemented at a cost of €60,000. His Arc run was all forgotten after Newmarket. Shouldering a Group 1 penalty and giving weight to his four rivals, Sixties Icon confirmed himself a high-class performer in the StanJamesUK.com Jockey Club Stakes, a Group 2 event run over a mile and a half. Papal Bull, also making his seasonal reappearance, shaded favouritism ahead of Sixties Icon, but was already well held when Sixties Icon moved smoothly to the front two furlongs out. Given one backhander as Admiral's Cruise threatened briefly, Sixties Icon quickened away and was three lengths clear at the line, still running on strongly. The Coronation Cup had already been mentioned as Sixties Icon's first big-race target, and he turned up at Epsom in superb shape and looking to have a first-rate chance. Sent off the 11/8 favourite, he performed in markedly contrasting fashion to Newmarket, his effort early in the straight short-lived before he trailed home last of seven behind Scorpion. Excuses were readily available. It was the first time he had been raced on ground softer than good, while the undulating Epsom track was also put forward as a reason for his lacklustre display, though Sixties Icon hadn't fared too badly on it when seventh in the Derby twelve months earlier. Whatever the reason, most were prepared to forgive Sixties Icon this most disappointing run and he started favourite again in the Princess of Wales's Stakes at Newmarket in July. His supporters knew their fate even earlier this time, with Sixties Icon performing even more dismally than at Epsom. Sweating freely, as he'd done before the Arc, Sixties Icon dropped away tamely over three furlongs out in a race won by Papal Bull. The veterinary officer on duty reported that Sixties Icon had finished in a distressed state. The colt has since undergone a breathing operation, and he stays in training.

Sixties Icon (b.c. 2003)	Galileo (IRE) (b 1998)	Sadler's Wells (b 1981)	Northern Dancer Fairy Bridge
		Urban Sea (ch 1989)	Miswaki Allegretta
	Love Divine (b 1997)	Diesis (ch 1980)	Sharpen Up Doubly Sure
		La Sky (b 1988)	Law Society Maryinsky

Sixties Icon, a 230,000-guinea yearling, is the second foal of Oaks winner Love Divine. Her third foal, the three-year-old filly Kissing (by Grand Lodge), won a maiden over nine and a half furlongs at Wolverhampton in November. Her 2005 colt by Red Ransom, Divine Song, was unplaced in two races in Japan in the latest season. She produced a colt by Cape Cross in 2006 and a filly by Montjeu in 2007. The next dam La Sky won over a mile and a quarter on her first two starts and was second in the Lancashire Oaks and third in the March Stakes on her only subsequent outings. La Sky is closely related to Champion Stakes winner Legal Case out of Maryinsky who won twice at up to nine furlongs in the States. The strong, well-made, attractive Sixties Icon, who has a quick action, stays a mile and three quarters and acts on good to firm going. He usually wears a crossed noseband. *J. Noseda*

SIYABONA (USA) 2 b.f. (Mar 8) Kingmambo (USA) 125 – Relish (IRE) 101 (Sadler's **77 p** Wells (USA) 132) [2007 7d² 8d² Oct 23] tall, useful-looking filly: first foal: dam, Irish 1¼m winner, closely related to useful 2-y-o sprinter Loyalize out of US Grade 1 9f/1¼m winner Reloy: fair form: second in maidens at Leicester and Yarmouth: will be suited by 1¼m/1½m: should do better still. *Saeed bin Suroor*

SIYASA (USA) 2 ch.f. (Feb 21) Rahy (USA) 115 – Jood (USA) 87 (Nijinsky (CAN) **– p** 138) [2007 7m Aug 4] sister to top-class 7f (at 2 yrs) to 1½m winner Fantastic Light and smart 1¼m winner Hi Dubai, and half-sister to 3 winners: dam, third at 7f (at 2 yrs) and 1¼m on only starts, out of Canadian Oaks winner Kamar, herself half-sister to dam of Swain: 11/10 on, bumped leaving stall and took strong hold when seventh to Sense of Joy in maiden at Newmarket, not knocked about: will be suited by 1¼m/1½m: bound to progress. *Saeed bin Suroor*

SKADRAK (USA) 2 ch.c. (Feb 24) Forest Camp (USA) 114 – Occhi Verdi (IRE) 77 **96 p** (Mujtahid (USA) 118) [2007 6d² Jul 29] $50,000Y, 48,000 2-y-o: big, strong colt: fourth foal: half-brother to US 7.5f/1m (latter at 2 yrs) winner Palistar (by Royal Academy): dam 5f (at 2 yrs) to 1m (in US) winner: 2/1 favourite, useful form when short-head second to Atlantic Sport in newcomers event at Ascot, responding well while looking green: will stay 1m: has joined B. Meehan: exciting prospect, and sure to win good races. *P. W. Chapple-Hyam*

SKHILLING PRIDE 2 ch.f. (Apr 10) Kyllachy 129 – Twilight Time (Aragon 118) – [2007 5m Jun 9] 13,000F, 26,000Y: seventh foal: closely related to winner abroad by Pivotal and half-sister to several winners, including 6-y-o Dispol Katie and 5f winner Paradise Eve (by Bahamian Bounty): dam unraced half-sister to smart middle-distance performer Punishment: 28/1, well held in maiden at Haydock. *T. D. Barron*

SKHILLING SPIRIT 4 b.g. Most Welcome 131 – Calcavella 75 (Pursuit of Love **103 §** 124) [2007 101: 6d³ 6m 7s² 8m 7s³ 6s 6m 6d 8d⁶ Oct 12] strong, close-coupled gelding: has a short, unimpressive action: useful performer: good efforts when third in listed race at Newcastle (2½ lengths behind Rising Shadow) and second in fairly valuable handicap at Ascot (4 lengths behind Wise Dennis) first/third outings: creditable sixth to Amarna in handicap at York final start: best at 6f/7f: has won on good to firm going, seems best on good to soft/soft nowadays: tried blinkered/visored: temperamental (refused/virtually refused to race sixth/seventh outings), and one to treat with caution. *T. D. Barron*

SKIDDAW FOX 3 ch.c. Foxhound (USA) 103 – Stealthy Times 80 (Timeless Times – (USA) 99) [2007 –: 6m 6.1m 5.1g f5d Dec 14] neat colt: little form: tried in cheekpieces. *Mrs L. Williamson*

SKIDDAW JONES 7 b.g. Emperor Jones (USA) 119 – Woodrising 64 (Nomination **49 §** 125) [2007 10m³ 12.1m Sep 11] good-topped gelding: poor handicapper: stays 10.5f: acts on firm ground: tongue tied last 4 starts: unreliable. *M. A. Barnes*

SKI FOR LUCK (IRE) 3 br.g. Key of Luck (USA) 126 – Ski For Me (IRE) 88 **54** (Barathea (IRE) 127) [2007 –: 10g 11.5m⁶ p12g Jun 21] modest maiden: stays 11.5f. *J. L. Dunlop*

SKIP OF COLOUR 7 b.g. Rainbow Quest (USA) 134 – Minskip (USA) 64 (The Min- **66** strel (CAN) 135) [2007 65: f5g f7g² p7.1g p7.1g Feb 5] fair performer: stays 7f: acts on all-weather and good to soft ground: tried tongue tied: races up with pace. *P. A. Blockley*

SKI SCHOOL (IRE) 2 b.g. (Apr 12) Montjeu (IRE) 137 – Teller (ARG) (Southern **73** Halo (USA)) [2007 7m 6m 6m⁴ 8g 6m 7g⁴ Oct 25] lengthy, useful-looking gelding: fair maiden: better than ease result in nurseries, visored (raced freely) final start: should prove best at 7f/1m: acts on good to firm going: sold 6,000 gns. *W. J. Haggas*

SKI SUNDAY 2 b.c. (Feb 23) King's Best (USA) 132 – Lille Hammer 110 (Sadler's – Wells (USA) 132) [2007 7.1g p7g Oct 17] 60,000Y: half-brother to several winners in France, including 1¼m to 11.5f winner Olimpic Girl (by Darshaan) and 1m to 1½m winner L'Olympique (by Machiavellian), both useful: dam 1m (at 2 yrs) to 1¾m winner: well held in maidens: bred to be well suited by middle distances. *M. A. Jarvis*

SKODGER (IRE) 4 b.c. Nashwan (USA) 135 – Ghay (USA) 61 (Bahri (USA) 125) – [2007 –: 8m 8s Jul 9] no form. *G. Woodward*

SKY BEAM (USA) 3 b.f. Kingmambo (USA) 125 – Weekend In Seattle (USA) (Seat- **56** tle Slew (USA)) [2007 –: p12.2g⁵ 10.1g 12.1m⁴ 16.2s⁵ Jul 23] tall, leggy, quite good-topped filly: modest maiden: stays 2m: acts on polytrack, soft and good to firm ground. *J. L. Dunlop*

SKY CHART (IRE) 3 ch.g. Fantastic Light (USA) 134 – Marion Haste (IRE) 69 (Ali- **60** Royal (IRE) 127) [2007 8m 8.2g⁶ 8.1s 10.9g⁴ 12g p8.6g Dec 29] sturdy gelding: modest maiden: gelded prior to final start: barely stays 1½m: tried in cheekpieces: swerved left and unseated on debut. *N. J. Vaughan*

SKYCRUISER (IRE) 2 ch.g. (Jan 25) Dubai Destination (USA) 127 – Maskunah **74** (IRE) (Sadler's Wells (USA) 132) [2007 7g 7s³ p7g⁶ Oct 24] 625,000Y: sturdy colt: fourth foal: half-brother to 3-y-o Guarantia: dam unraced close relative of Nell Gwyn Stakes winner Cloud Castle (stayed 1½m) and half-sister to Luso, Warrsan and Needle Gun: fair maiden: third at Folkestone: will stay 1m: acts on soft going. *Saeed bin Suroor*

SKY DIVE 2 ch.c. (Feb 13) Dr Fong (USA) 128 – Free Flying 52 (Groom Dancer (USA) **92 p** 128) [2007 7s⁶ p7g* Sep 18] big, strong, good sort: has a quick action: first foal: dam, ran twice, closely related to smart 1m to 1½m winner Freequent and half-sister to Fillies' Mile winner/Oaks second Shamshir: fairly useful form: confirmed Newmarket promise (sixth to Yankadi) when winning maiden at Lingfield by length from Adversity, going away at finish: will be suited by 1¼m/1½m: type to improve for some time. *L. M. Cumani*

SKYE BUT N BEN 3 b.g. Auction House (USA) 120 – Island Colony (USA) (Pleasant **63** Colony (USA)) [2007 47: p9.5g³ f8g³ f8g⁴ p8.6g² 11g² 10g* 9g⁵ 10g* 10.3f 9.1d 8.3m⁵ 10g⁵ p9.5g³ 9g⁵ 10g Oct 6] lengthy, quite attractive gelding: good walker: modest performer: won handicap at Nottingham in April and claimer at Redcar in May: stays 11f: acts on polytrack, best turf efforts on good going: blinkered: often races prominently: sold 6,000 gns. *T. D. Barron*

SKYELADY 4 b.f. Dansili 127 – Song of Skye 84 (Warning 136) [2007 83: p8.6g⁵ 8m⁴ **86**
8m⁶ 9.9g³ 8.5m 7.1g* 7s* 7m⁶ 7s⁵ Jul 28] close-coupled, rather lightly-made filly: has a quick action: fairly useful handicapper: left Miss J. Camacho after fifth outing: won at Musselburgh in June and Thirsk in July: best form at 7f/1m: acts on polytrack, heavy and good to firm going: tried in cheekpieces/blinkers: reportedly in foal. *T. D. Barron*

SKYLARKER (USA) 9 b.g. Sky Classic (CAN) – O My Darling (USA) 76 (Mr
Prospector (USA)) [2007 11.5d Jun 27] tall, rather leggy gelding: fairly useful handicapper in 2005: reportedly finished lame only outing since: tried in cheekpieces/visor.
T. A. K. Cuthbert

SKY MASTERSON 3 ch.g. Traditionally (USA) 117 – Katina (USA) 68 (Danzig **73**
(USA)) [2007 8m⁶ f8g² f8g² 7s 7d p7.1g⁶ Aug 30] sturdy gelding: fair maiden: stays 1m: acts on fibresand and good to firm ground: tried in cheekpieces: sold 4,000 gns, joined F. Breuss in Germany. *J. H. M. Gosden*

SKY MORE 3 b.c. Xaar 132 – Jathaabeh 99 (Nashwan (USA) 135) [2007 f8g* 8.2s* **89**
8m May 25] useful-looking colt: third foal: dam, 1m winner, half-sister to smart 2-y-o 7f winner Kareymah out of half-sister to Cape Cross: fairly useful form: created very good impression when winning maiden at Southwell in April and handicap at Nottingham (beat Lady Gloria by 6 lengths, eased) in May: broke leg in last 50 yards at Pontefract next time: raced only at 1m: won on fibresand and soft going: dead. *M. A. Jarvis*

SKYNDA 2 b.f. (Feb 8) Domedriver (IRE) 128 – Skimra 91 (Hernando (FR) 127) [2007 **–**
7m 8.3m Sep 11] smallish filly: fourth foal: dam, 1½m winner, out of half-sister to Petoski: well held in maidens: sold 800 gns, sent to Serbia. *Rae Guest*

SKY QUEST (IRE) 9 b.g. Spectrum (IRE) 126 – Rose Vibert (Caerleon (USA) 132) **80**
[2007 83: p10g³ p10g⁴ p10g⁵ p8g 10g² 10g* 10m⁵ 10m³ 8.1m 8m p10m⁶ Nov 1] smallish, quite good-topped gelding: fairly useful handicapper: won apprentice event at Sandown in August: effective at 1¼m/1½m: acts on polytrack, firm and good to soft going: used to wear cheekpieces/tongue tie: has carried head awkwardly/found little. *J. R. Boyle*

SKY WALK 4 b.g. Josr Algarhoud (IRE) 118 – Jamrat Samya (IRE) 79 (Sadler's Wells **57**
(USA) 132) [2007 –: p12g⁴ p13g p16g Mar 16] smallish, compact gelding: modest maiden: probably stays easy 13f: raced on polytrack. *Jamie Poulton*

SLAM 2 b.c. (Apr 7) Beat Hollow 126 – House Hunting (Zafonic (USA) 130) [2007 7g⁵ **96**
8m² 7m² 7g³ Oct 26] big, strong, well-made colt: fifth foal: half-brother to winner up to 7f in Greece by Kahyasi: dam unraced daughter of Poule d'Essai des Pouliches winner Houseproud: useful form: fifth to Sharp Nephew in listed event at Newbury on debut, then placed in 3 maidens, including short-head second to Fireside at Newmarket penultimate start: should be suited by 1m/1¼m. *B. W. Hills*

SLATE (IRE) 3 b.c. Rock of Gibraltar (IRE) 133 – Sharp Catch (IRE) 98 (Common **98**
Grounds 118) [2007 78p: 7m² 7.1d* 7g* 8m 8m Aug 17] rather leggy colt: useful handicapper: won at Warwick in May and Folkestone in June: ran poorly at Royal Ascot and Doncaster after, leaving J. Osborne 40,000 gns in between: travels strongly, though stays 7f: acts on good to firm and good to soft ground: sent to Qatar. *Miss V. Haigh*

SLAVONIC LAKE 3 b.g. Lake Coniston (IRE) 131 – Slavonic Dance (Muhtarram **53**
(USA) 125) [2007 56: 10.1g p12g p10g² 10.1m⁴ p8g⁴ p9.5g² p9.5g⁶ p10m Dec 9] modest performer: stays easy 1¼m: acts on polytrack and firm going: tried blinkered: tongue tied in 2007: has raced prominently. *I. A. Wood*

SLAVONIC (USA) 6 ch.g. Royal Academy (USA) 130 – Cyrillic (USA) 106 (Irish **51**
River (FR) 131) [2007 –: 7.9m² 8.3m 14g 12s 8m Aug 2] strong, close-coupled gelding: fair performer at 4 yrs: lightly raced and modest at best since: stays 1¼m: acts on polytrack, soft and good to firm going: usually wears headgear: has looked difficult ride.
B. Storey

SLEEPY HOLLOW 2 b.g. (Apr 13) Beat Hollow 126 – Crackling 57 (Electric 126) **78 p**
[2007 8.1m 8d 8.2d* Oct 18] 20,000Y, 32,000 2-y-o: good-topped, attractive gelding: sixth foal: half-brother to several winners, including fairly useful 6f (at 2 yrs) to 1¼m winner Crackle (by Anshan) and 3-y-o Ronaldsay: dam, 9f and 1½m winner (stayed 2m), half-sister to useful 2-y-o performers Bianca Nera (Moyglare Stud Stakes winner) and Hotelgenie Dot Com (third in Fillies' Mile, dam of 3-y-o Simply Perfect): fair form: improved to win maiden at Nottingham final start, but looked awkward most of way: gelded after: will be suited by 1¼m/1½m: should do better still provided temperament holds. *H. Morrison*

SLEW CHARM (FR) 5 b.g. Marathon (USA) 116 – Slew Bay (FR) (Beaudelaire **62** (USA) 125) [2007 p8g⁴ p12g Sep 19] fair maiden when trained by C. Gourdain in France in 2005: unraced on Flat in 2006 (fairly useful hurdler): only modest in handicaps on Flat in 2007: should stay 1½m: acts on polytrack and heavy going (yet to race on firmer than good): tried tongue tied. *Noel T. Chance*

SLING BACK (IRE) 6 b.m. Desert Style (IRE) 121 – Arabian Princess (Taufan (USA) **85** 119) [2007 87: 7g⁶ 6m³ 5g 7m³ 8m 7d 7d 8m⁴ 8g a7g⁴ p8g p5g Oct 19] strong mare: fairly useful handicapper: none too consistent in 2007: effective at 6f to easy 1m: acts on all-weather/sand and firm going: tried in visor/blinkers. *E. Tyrrell, Ireland*

SLIP 2 b.c. (May 2) Fraam 114 – Niggle 65 (Night Shift (USA)) [2007 p8g p7g 8d⁴ Oct 3] **64 +** compact colt: modest form in maidens, best of stand-side group when fourth to Look Here as if 1¼m will suit. *M. P. Tregoning*

SLIPASEARCHER (IRE) 3 b.f. Danetime (IRE) 121 – Imperialist (IRE) 93 (Imper- **65 §** ial Frontier (USA) 112) [2007 76d: p6g⁵ p6g⁴ 6m⁴ 5.1f⁴ 6.1m* 6.1m⁵ 5.7d⁵ 7s 5.9m⁴ 6m⁶ 6m 7.1f 6.1m⁴ Sep 7] unfurnished filly: fair handicapper: second run in 2 days, won at Nottingham in May: best around 6f: acts on polytrack and firm ground, probably on good to soft: wears headgear: ungenuine: sold 6,000 gns. *P. D. Evans*

SLIP SILVER 3 gr.f. Slip Anchor 136 – New Wind (GER) (Windwurf (GER)) [2007 **50** 8.3m p10g 10g p12.2g⁶ p13.9g p12g p12.2g⁶ p13.9g Dec 1] big filly: sixth foal: sister to useful 1½m to 2¼m winner Swift Sailor and half-sister to useful 8.5f (at 2 yrs) to 1½m winner Stunning Force (by Ezzoud) and fairly useful 1½m winner Winds of Change (by King's Best): dam, German 6f (at 2 yrs) and 1m winner, half-sister to useful German 1¼m performer No Dancer: modest maiden: stays 1½m: acts on polytrack: in cheekpieces last 5 starts: often races prominently. *P. J. Makin*

SLIP STAR 4 b.f. Slip Anchor 136 – Shiny Kay 65 (Star Appeal 133) [2007 –: p12.2g⁶ **58** p13.9g 7.5g 7g³ 7m³ 7m 7.6m⁴ 6m² 7g Sep 22] quite good-topped filly: modest maiden: stays 7f: acts on good to firm ground. *T. J. Etherington*

SLO MO SHUN 3 b.f. Polish Precedent (USA) 131 – Malvadilla (IRE) 77 (Doyoun **52** 124) [2007 45: 8d³ p9.5m⁵ 7g⁶ Sep 24] tall filly, unfurnished at 2 yrs: modest maiden: barely stays easy 9.5f: acts on polytrack and good to soft ground. *H. J. L. Dunlop*

SLUGGER O'TOOLE 2 br.g. (Feb 26) Intikhab (USA) 135 – Haddeyah (USA) 68 **64 +** (Dayjur (USA) 137) [2007 6.1m Oct 3] tall gelding: has a short, scratchy action: 20/1 and gone in coat, green and faded into ninth in maiden at Nottingham: subsequently gelded. *G. A. Huffer*

SMALL FORTUNE 3 b.f. Anabaa (USA) 130 – New Assembly (IRE) 99 (Machia- **81** vellian (USA) 123) [2007 74p: 8.2m* 9.9g³ 11.9m Jun 9] good-topped filly: fairly useful form: won maiden at Nottingham in May: much better effort in handicaps after when third at Salisbury: stays 1¼m (possibly not 1½m): raced only on good/good to firm going. *R. Charlton*

SMALL STAKES (IRE) 5 b.g. Pennekamp (USA) 130 – Poker Chip 106 (Bluebird **76** (USA) 125) [2007 78: p7g³ p7g⁶ 6g p7g 7m⁵ 7.1f 8.3g Oct 8] strong gelding: fair handi- capper: stays 7f: acts on polytrack and good to soft going: usually tongue tied/visored: sold 6,500 gns. *P. J. Makin*

SMART ANGUS 3 gr.g. Agnes World (USA) 123 – She's Smart 88 (Absalom 128) **–** [2007 –: 7m May 3] good-topped gelding: well held in maidens/seller. *R. A. Fahey*

SMART ASS (IRE) 4 b.f. Shinko Forest (IRE) – Jayess Elle 55 (Sabrehill (USA) 120) **89** [2007 91: p8.6g 8d⁶ 8m* 8m² 8d⁶ Aug 19] quite good-topped filly: fairly useful perfor- mer: won handicap at Newmarket in August: possibly flattered in listed event at Bath final outing: stays 8.6f: acts on all-weather, firm and good to soft going: held up, and has good turn of foot. *J. S. Moore*

SMART CASSIE 4 ch.f. Allied Forces (USA) 123 – Katy-Q (IRE) 58 (Taufan (USA) **45** 119) [2007 69d: p8.6g 6.1g 5m 5.1d 5f³ p6g p5.1g³ p5g Nov 19] just poor in 2007: best at 5f: acts on firm going: tried in cheekpieces/blinkers. *H. J. Evans*

SMART CAT (IRE) 4 ch.f. Barathea (IRE) 127 – Lioness 74 (Lion Cavern (USA) 117) **63** [2007 55p: p12g⁵ p12.2g⁵ 10g⁴ p10g⁵ 11.6m 7m⁵ 8.1m² 9g p10g 8s 7g p7g⁴ 8d Oct 30] tall filly: modest maiden: stays 1¼m: acts on good to firm ground: sometimes visored. *A. P. Jarvis*

SMART ENOUGH 4 gr.c. Cadeaux Genereux 131 – Good Enough (FR) 109 (Muk- **114** addamah (USA) 125) [2007 113: 8g 8.1g² 8d 8m* 8g⁶ Nov 3] tall, lengthy colt: has scope: smart performer: won minor event at Bath (by 1½ lengths from Dijeerr, readily) in October: only other creditable effort in 2007 when 1¼ lengths second to Harvest

Queen in listed race at Haydock: stays 1m: acts on soft and good to firm going: exuberant type, tends to sweat and usually makes running: has been blanketed for stall entry. *M. A. Magnusson*

SMARTERTHANUTHINK (USA) 2 b.c. (May 5) Smart Strike (CAN) 121 – Dance Gaily (USA) (Nureyev (USA) 131) [2007 6g⁶ 5g 5d Oct 9] modest form in sprint maidens: will be suited by 7f/1m. *R. A. Fahey* **59**

SMART INSTINCT (USA) 3 ch.g. Smart Strike (CAN) 121 – Smile N Molly (USA) (Dixieland Band (USA)) [2007 100: 7g⁴ 8.1m⁵ 8.9s⁵ 9.9g 9.9m 10.3g⁶ Sep 29] strong, lengthy gelding: has scope: useful handicapper: several creditable efforts in 2007, including when eighth to Pipedreamer in Alphameric Vase at Goodwood fourth outing: stays 1¼m: acts on soft and good to firm going: wore cheekpieces (took strong hold) final outing. *R. A. Fahey* **101**

SMART JOHN 7 b.g. Bin Ajwaad (IRE) 119 – Katy-Q (IRE) 58 (Taufan (USA) 119) [2007 –: 12.1s 11.6f 12.6m Aug 27] good-topped gelding: modest handicapper nowadays: stays 12.6f: acts on good to firm going: has shown signs of temperament. *H. J. Evans* **63**

SMART PICK 4 ch.f. Piccolo 121 – Nevita (Never So Bold 135) [2007 p7g⁶ p8.6g p6g⁶ p7.1g 8.5m 11.1m 6m⁵ 7m⁵ 8d 7.6d² 6d⁴ 6.9f⁴ 7.2g⁵ 8m⁵ 10.3g p9.5g³ p8m p8.6g⁶ p8.6d Dec 17] close-coupled filly: modest maiden: left J. Holt after fourth start: stays easy 1¼m: acts on polytrack, firm and good to soft going: tried blinkered: sometimes slowly away. *Mrs L. Williamson* **57**

SMASH HIT (IRE) 4 ch.g. Grand Lodge (USA) 125 – Rainbow Lyrics (IRE) (Rainbow Quest (USA) 134) [2007 8.3d 7m p7.1g⁴ 10.2m p8g p8g p8m Dec 9] well-made gelding: modest maiden: best form around 7f: dead. *David Pinder* **68**

SMASH N'GRAB (IRE) 3 ch.f. Jade Robbery (USA) 121 – Sallwa (IRE) (Entrepreneur 123) [2007 63: p6g⁶ 8m p6g 6.9g³ 6d 8g² 7d⁴* 7.5m 7g⁴ 7g p8g⁴ 8d p7g f7d p7g⁶ Dec 30] good-topped, quite attractive filly: modest performer: won claimer at Leicester in August and, having left K. Ryan, handicap at Kempton in October: stays 1m: acts on polytrack, good to firm and good to soft going: tried in cheekpieces: has found little. *J. R. Jenkins* **64**

SMETANA 2 b.c. (Apr 18) Kylian (USA) – Shimmer 55 (Bustino 136) [2007 8.2g p8g f8d Dec 12] 22,000Y: half-brother to fairly useful 2001 2-y-o 5f/6f winner Young Lion (by Lion Cavern): dam, maiden (should have stayed 1½m), out of smart sister to Highclere: modest form in maidens: will probably stay 1¼m/1½m. *H. Morrison* **59**

SMIDDY HILL 5 b.m. Factual (USA) 108 – Hello Hobson's (IRE) 67 (Fayruz 116) [2007 79: 5f 5m 5m 5d 5m 5g 5m Sep 18] lengthy mare: fair handicapper at 4 yrs: modest at best in 2007: best at bare 5f: acts on polytrack and firm going: has given trouble in preliminaries. *R. Bastiman* **52**

SMILEFORAWHILE (IRE) 2 b.g. (Apr 14) Green Desert (USA) 127 – Woodyousmileforme (USA) (Woodman (USA) 126) [2007 5f 5g² 6.1g p5.1g 6m⁵ Aug 31] smallish, sturdy gelding: has a moderate, quick action: fair maiden: second at Hamilton: regressed after, showing temperament, and tried in cheekpieces/blinkers: best form at 5f. *K. A. Ryan* **68 §**

SMILE FOR US 4 b.g. Whittingham (IRE) 104 – Don't Smile 76 (Sizzling Melody 117) [2007 73: p7g p7.1g p6g⁵ 6m² 6.1g 6f Aug 11] fair handicapper: best at 5f/6f: acts on all-weather and good to firm going: tried in cheekpieces, blinkered nowadays: has shown signs of temperament. *C. Drew* **69**

SMILING TIGER 3 b.g. Contract Law (USA) 108 – Nouvelle Cuisine 64 (Yawa 122) [2007 p7g p10g 8m f11g Apr 30] no form. *M. J. Gingell* **–**

SMILODON 2 ch.f. (Mar 26) Reel Buddy (USA) 118 – Timoko (Dancing Spree (USA)) [2007 5m 5d 5v 5g 6g a7.5g³ Sep 23] 500Y, resold 1,200Y: workmanlike filly: third foal: dam maiden: little form for A. Berry: third in minor event at Mons final start: stays 7.5f. *L. Braem, Belgium* **?**

SMIRFYS GOLD (IRE) 3 ch.g. Bad As I Wanna Be (IRE) 115 – Golden Jorden (IRE) (Cadeaux Genereux 131) [2007 58: 5m² 15g⁶ 5m³ 5f⁴ 5d p5g² Sep 15] good-topped gelding: modest maiden handicapper: best at 5f: acts on polytrack, firm and good to soft ground: visored: tried tongue tied. *E. S. McMahon* **61**

SMIRFY'S SILVER 3 b.g. Desert Prince (IRE) 130 – Goodwood Blizzard 97 (Inchinor 119) [2007 62d: 7m 10.1g* 11.5m² 10.1d³ Aug 26] short-backed gelding: fair performer: left W. M. Brisbourne after reappearance: won handicap at Yarmouth in July: stays 11.5f: acts on good to firm and good to soft going: made running last 3 outings. *E. S. McMahon* **68**

SMIRFYS SYSTEMS 8 b.g. Safawan 118 – Saint Systems 68 (Uncle Pokey 116) **58**
[2007 58: p7.1g⁵ p7.1s Dec 20] close-coupled, workmanlike gelding: modest handicapper: stays 7f: acts on polytrack, firm and good to soft going: blinkered once at 5 yrs:
free-going sort. *E. S. McMahon*

SMITH ESQUIRE (USA) 2 b.g. (Mar 23) Giant's Causeway (USA) 132 – Makam **60**
(IRE) 68 (Green Desert (USA) 127) [2007 f6g 7.1g⁶ p8g⁴ 10m Oct 3] leggy geld-
ing: modest maiden: stays 1m: acts on polytrack: sold 4,500 gns, sent to Belgium.
W. R. Swinburn

SMOKEY OAKEY (IRE) 3 b.c. Tendulkar (USA) 114 – Veronica (Persian Bold 123) **107**
[2007 89: 7g 10d⁴ 9.9g 10.4d⁶ 10.3m³ 10s⁴ 10.3g⁵ 8v* Nov 3] smallish, leggy colt: useful
handicapper: won at Newmarket (by short head from Eradicate) in May and at Ayr (best
effort, beat Emerald Bay by 6 lengths) in November: effective at 1m to 1¼m: acts on
polytrack, heavy and good to firm going. *M. H. Tompkins*

SMOKEYOURPIPE (IRE) 2 ch.g. (Apr 12) Bold Fact (USA) 116 – Gi La High 68 **51**
(Rich Charlie 117) [2007 5m 5.2m* p6g⁵ 6m p6g p7.1g p8m Nov 24] angular gelding:
modest performer: won seller at Yarmouth (left J. Spearing 4,600 gns) in August: left
C. Tinkler after sixth start: effective at 5f/6f: acts on polytrack and good to firm going:
difficult ride (has been tried in visor/cheekpieces). *R. M. Stronge*

SMOKEY RYE 2 b.f. (Apr 10) Bertolini (USA) 125 – Another Secret 87 (Efisio 120) **78**
[2007 6g 6g 7m² 6s 7g p7g³ p6g* p7m² p6g² Dec 30] good-topped filly: first foal: dam,
1m winner, out of half-sister to high-class sprinter Mr Brooks: fair performer: progress in
blinkers last 4 starts, won maiden at Kempton in November: second in nurseries at Lingfield after: stays 7f: acts on polytrack and good to firm going: tail flasher. *G. L. Moore*

SMOKEY THE BEAR 5 ch.g. Fumo di Londra (IRE) 108 – Noble Soul 67 (Sayf El **63**
Arab (USA) 127) [2007 p10g² p8g³ p10m⁵ p12g* p13g³ Dec 28] modest performer,
lightly raced on Flat: won handicap at Kempton in December: stays 13f: acts on polytrack
and firm ground: tried in cheekpieces/blinkers. *Miss S. West*

SMOKIN BEAU 10 b.g. Cigar 68 – Beau Dada (IRE) 66 (Pine Circle (USA)) [2007 93: **79**
p5.1g f6g p5f 5f³ 6m 5.7g 5g 5.1d p5g⁴ 7d p5g* p5g* Dec 12] smallish, robust gelding:
fairly useful handicapper nowadays: best at Kempton in November and December: best
at 5f/6f: acts on all-weather and any turf going: tried in headgear: usually races prominently: has reportedly bled. *N. P. Littmoden*

SMOKIN JOE 6 b.g. Cigar 68 – Beau Dada (IRE) 66 (Pine Circle (USA)) [2007 –, a80: **–**
p8g p10g p8g p7.1g p10g² p8g⁶ p8g* p8g⁶ p8g⁵ p8g³ p8m³ p7g* p10g² p7g² Dec 29] **a85**
small, quite attractive gelding: fairly useful handicapper: won at Kempton in November
and December: effective at 7f to easy 1¼m: acts on all-weather, little form on turf: tried
visored, usually blinkered: sometimes slowly away: usually held up. *J. R. Best*

SMOOTH AS SILK (IRE) 2 b.f. (Apr 22) Danehill Dancer (USA) 117 – Doula (USA) **64**
(Gone West (USA)) [2007 6f 7m⁵ Sep 2] €240,000Y: tall, useful-looking filly: fourth
foal: half-sister to 3 winners, including 4-y-o Humungous: dam, US 1m winner, half-
sister to US Grade 1 2-y-o 8.5f winner Dixie Chatter out of Breeders' Cup Juvenile
Fillies' winner Phone Chatter: better effort in maidens when fifth to Presbyterian Nun at
Folkestone: will stay 1m. *C. R. Egerton*

SMOOTHIE (IRE) 9 gr.g. Definite Article 121 – Limpopo 49 (Green Desert (USA) **54**
127) [2007 59: p12g p11g* f11g 12m p12g Dec 16] close-coupled gelding: modest performer: won minor event at Kempton in February: stays 16.5f: acts on all-weather, firm
and soft going: tried blinkered/in cheekpieces: held up: none too consistent. *E. G. Bevan*

SMUGGLERS BAY (IRE) 3 b.g. Celtic Swing 138 – Princess Mood (GER) **81**
(Muhtarram (USA) 125) [2007 67: 8f 12g 8.5g⁵ 8.5s* 8.5v² 9.8v² 8.9v² 12g⁴ 9.8m⁴ 9.9m³
Sep 11] useful-looking gelding: shows plenty of knee action: fairly useful handicapper:
won at Beverley in June: good efforts when placed after: stays 1¼m: acts on heavy and
good to firm going: tried blinkered: won juvenile hurdle in October. *T. D. Easterby*

SNAAFY (USA) 3 b.c. Kingmambo (USA) 125 – Nafisah (IRE) 109 (Lahib (USA) **94**
129) [2007 p6p: 7m* 8m 8.1m² 8.1m³ 10m³ 10m⁵ Oct 5] good-topped colt: has a quick
action: fairly useful form: won maiden at Newmarket in April: good efforts when placed
in handicaps after: stays 1¼m: raced mainly on good to firm going: joined M. Al Muhairi
in UAE. *B. W. Hills*

SNAKE HIPS 3 b.g. Golden Snake (USA) 127 – Royal Loft 105 (Homing 130) [2007 **59**
p9.5g⁴ p9.5g⁶ p8.6g⁵ 10g p12.2g 10s³ 10.9d p12.2g 11.7f 10.2m 10d⁵ p11g Dec 5] neat
gelding: modest maiden: stays 1¼m: acts on polytrack and soft going: tried blinkered/in
cheekpieces. *B. Palling*

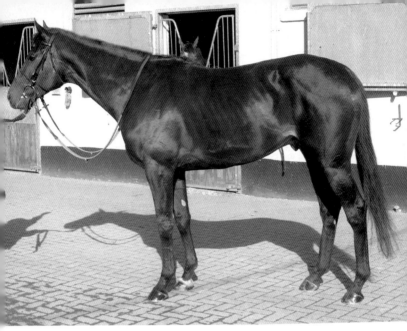

Mrs R. J. Jacobs' "Soapy Danger"

SNAKE'S HEAD 3 b.f. Golden Snake (USA) 127 – Satin Bell 99 (Midyan (USA) 124) **77**
[2007 81: 9.7m² 9m² p12g³ 11.7g⁴ 14m⁴ 11.7f² 12.4d* Oct 16] rather leggy, attractive
filly: fair performer: won maiden at Newcastle in October: stays 12.4f: acts on firm and
good to soft going: usually races prominently: sold 20,000 gns. *J. L. Dunlop*

SNAKE SKIN 4 ch.f. Golden Snake (USA) 127 – Silken Dalliance 91 (Rambo Dancer **68**
(CAN) 107) [2007 59: p12g p11g³ 11.9s* 10m² p11g⁴ 11.5g 12.1m³ 12g⁵ p11g Sep 5]
leggy, workmanlike filly: fair handicapper: won at Brighton in May: effective at 1¼m/
1½m: acts on all-weather and any turf going: has run poorly in blinkers/cheekpieces.
J. Gallagher

SNARK (IRE) 4 b.g. Cape Cross (IRE) 129 – Agoer 61 (Hadeer 118) [2007 82: p10g⁴ **83**
p12.2g⁶ 10d 8m 8.3m⁶ 7.6g 10m⁴ 10f* 9g* 10.5g³ 12d³ 10m⁴ Oct 3] lengthy gelding:
fairly useful handicapper: won amateur events at Pontefract and Goodwood in August:
stays 1½m: acts on polytrack, firm and good to soft going: tried in visor/cheekpieces/
tongue tie: sold 18,000 gns. *P. J. Makin*

SNICKERS FIRST 2 ch.f. (Apr 9) Presidium 124 – Mirror Four Sport 59 (Risk Me **–**
(FR) 127) [2007 7g 7m⁶ 7d Oct 16] workmanlike filly: fifth foal: dam, 1m to 11f winner,
closely related to useful 6f/7f performer Madly Sharp: little form in maidens.
M. W. Easterby

SNOQUALMIE BOY 4 b.g. Montjeu (IRE) 137 – Seattle Ribbon (USA) 70 (Seattle **105**
Dancer (USA) 119) [2007 111: 9m⁵ 8m⁴ 9.9g⁴ 10m² 9g 9m Oct 6] rangy, good-bodied,
attractive gelding: useful performer nowadays: best efforts in 2007 when 7½ lengths fifth
to Manduro in Earl of Sefton Stakes at Newmarket and 3½ lengths fourth to Championship Point in quite valuable handicap at Goodwood first/third starts: below form after, in
Cambridgeshire at Newmarket on final outing: best form at 9f/1¼m: acts on firm going,
probably on good to soft: tends to get on toes: sold 75,000 gns, joined J. S. Moore and
gelded. *D. R. C. Elsworth*

SNOW BALLERINA 3 b.f. Sadler's Wells (USA) 132 – Snow Bride (USA) 121 **57**
(Blushing Groom (FR) 131) [2007 61p: p12.2g⁴ 12g⁵ 12.1s Jun 21] modest maiden: stays
1½m. *E. A. L. Dunlop*

SNOWBERRY HILL (USA) 4 b.g. Woodman (USA) 126 – Class Skipper (USA) **62**
(Skip Trial (USA)) [2007 59: p16.5g⁶ p13.9g* f14d⁴ Dec 15] workmanlike gelding:
modest performer: won handicap at Wolverhampton in November: stays 13⁄4m: acts on
all-weather and firm going: tried blinkered/in cheekpieces. *Lucinda Featherstone*

SNOW BUNTING 9 ch.g. Polar Falcon (USA) 126 – Marl 94 (Lycius (USA) 124) **59**
[2007 69: p7.1g 7.1m⁴ 7.1m⁵ 6m 7.1g 7m 6.9g⁶ 7.1m p6g⁵ p6g* p7.1g⁴ p6g p7.1g⁵ Dec 3]
leggy gelding: modest performer: won minor event at Wolverhampton in October: stays
7f: acts on polytrack and firm going: held up: none too consistent. *Jedd O'Keeffe*

SNOW DANCER (IRE) 3 b.f. Desert Style (IRE) 121 – Bella Vie (IRE) (Sadler's **74**
Wells (USA) 132) [2007 69: p9.5g⁴ p8.6g³ p8.6g⁴ 9g 8.5g* 8.1m³ 10.3f⁴ 8.1s 8.1v 10.3m²
8.5d 8m* Oct 8] leggy filly: fair performer: won handicap at Beverley in May and claimer
at Pontefract in October: stays 1¼m: acts on polytrack and any turf going: held up.
A. Berry

SNOWED UNDER 6 gr.g. Most Welcome 131 – Snowy Mantle 54 (Siberian Express **83**
(USA) 125) [2007 88: 10m⁶ 10f 10m³ 10d* 10m 9.8m⁴ 10.9m⁴ 10d Oct 16] good-topped
gelding: fairly useful handicapper: won at Leicester (fifth course success) in August:
stays 1½m: acts on polytrack, firm and good to soft going: often races prominently.
J. D. Bethell

SNOWFLIGHT 3 b.c. Danehill Dancer (IRE) 117 – Sadler's Song 54 (Saddlers' Hall **66**
(IRE) 126) [2007 71: 9.2d 8s⁵ 8.1v⁶ 10f³ 11.1g⁵ p11g 12d⁵ p12.2g Sep 27] unfurnished
colt: fair maiden: stays 1¼m: acts on firm and soft going: sold 5,000 gns. *R. A. Fahey*

SNOW GRETEL (IRE) 4 b.f. Green Desert (USA) 127 – Snow Princess (IRE) 111 **101**
(Ela-Mana-Mou 132) [2007 81: p7g⁴ 8m³ 8g* 10d Jun 3] 120,000Y: fifth foal: half-sister
to 3 winners, notably 7f/1m winner (including Royal Lodge Stakes, also second in 2000
Guineas) Snow Ridge (by Indian Ridge) and fairly useful Irish 1½m winner White Queen
(by Spectrum): dam 10.5f to 16.5f winner: useful performer: won maiden at Roscommon
in 2006 when trained by J. Oxx in Ireland: best effort when winning listed race at Hanover
(by neck from Jalta) in May: respectable seventh to Wickwing in Premio Paolo Mezza-
notte at Milan final outing: stays 1¼m: acts on polytrack, good to firm and good to soft
ground: tried blinkered/tongue tied. *M. Botti*

SNOWY DAY (FR) 4 b.g. Pennekamp (USA) 130 – Snow White (Polar Falcon (USA) **78**
126) [2007 73p: p10g³ p9.5g² p12.2g Feb 26] fair handicapper, lightly raced: left
W. Haggas after second outing: stays 1¼m: raced on all-weather. *Grant Tuer*

SNOWY INDIAN 2 b.f. (Feb 8) Indian Ridge 123 – Snow Princess (IRE) 111 (Ela- **76**
Mana-Mou 132) [2007 7g³ 8.1s⁶ p8.6g³ Nov 1] unfurnished filly: sister to 7f/1m winner
(including Royal Lodge Stakes, also second in 2000 Guineas) Snow Ridge and half-sister
to 3 winners, including fairly useful Irish 1½m winner White Queen (by Spectrum) and
4-y-o Snow Gretel: dam 10.5f to 16.5f winner: fair maiden: best effort at Salisbury (third
to Joffe's Run) on debut: should be suited by 1m+. *Sir Michael Stoute*

SOAPY DANGER 4 b.c. Danzig (USA) – On A Soapbox (USA) 119 (Mi Cielo (USA)) **117**
[2007 120: 11m² 12m³ 15.5m Oct 28] strong, good-bodied colt: fluent mover: very smart
performer at 3 yrs, winning 5 times: fractured near-fore pastern final start that season and
underwent surgery, having 4 screws inserted: at least respectable efforts first 2 starts in
2007, neck second to Halicarnassus in Arc Trial at Newbury and length third to Galactic
Star in listed race at Newmarket: only eighth to Allegretto in Prix Royal-Oak at Longchamp final outing: effective at 1½m to 2m: acts on firm and good to soft going: makes
running/races prominently. *M. Johnston*

SOBA JONES 10 b.g. Emperor Jones (USA) 119 – Soba 127 (Most Secret 119) [2007 **62**
71: f6g⁴ f6g² f6g⁴ f6s² f6g⁴ f6g* f6g* 6g f6g⁵ f6g⁴ f6g May 15] tall gelding: modest
performer: won handicap in February and claimer in March, both at Southwell: best at 5f/
6f: acts on fibresand and any turf going: tried in blinkers/cheekpieces: slowly away ninth
outing at 10 yrs. *J. Balding*

SOCCERJACKPOT (USA) 3 b.g. Mizzen Mast (USA) 121 – Rahbaby (USA) (Rahy **93**
(USA) 115) [2007 6f² 7f² 7.5m* 8m³ 8m⁵ 8g⁴ Oct 6] $10,000F: quite good-topped geld-
ing: fourth foal: half-brother to US 4.5f to 6.5f winner Rahy Cat (by Tabasco Cat): dam
US 5.5f to 7f (including at 2 yrs) winner: fairly useful performer: landed odds in maiden
at Beverley in May: good efforts in frame in handicaps after: stays 1m: unraced on going
softer than good (acts on firm): sometimes carries head awkwardly. *G. A. Swinbank*

SOCCEROO 2 b.f. (Jan 21) Choisir (AUS) 126 – Silca Boo 99 (Efisio 120) [2007 5g⁴ **65** p6g⁴ Oct 6] 46,000Y: compact filly: first foal: dam, 2-y-o 5f/6f winner, half-sister to useful sprinter Zilch: fair maiden: fourth at Haydock (to Janina, for T. Pitt) and Wolverhampton (too free) over 5 months apart: should prove best at 5f/6f. *D. J. Murphy*

SOCIAL HEIGHT (IRE) 2 ch.g. (Apr 19) Monashee Mountain (USA) 115 – Yiayia's **–** Girl (Smackover 107) [2007 6g 6v 6m 7g 7m Aug 24] good-topped gelding: of no account: dead. *A. Berry*

SOCIAL RHYTHM 3 b.f. Beat All (USA) 120 – Highly Sociable 56 (Puissance 110) **81** [2007 75+: p7g⁶ 6g* 7.1m 6d⁵ p6g 6g³ 7g Nov 6] sturdy filly: fairly useful handicapper: won at Southwell (turf debut) in April: effective at 6f/7f: acts on polytrack and good to soft going. *H. J. Collingridge*

SOCIAL SPIRIT 2 br.f. (Apr 2) Auction House (USA) 120 – Sibilant (Selkirk **49** (USA) 129) [2007 7g 8.3g⁴ 8g Oct 3] 12,000Y: fifth foal: half-sister to 3 winners, including 2004 2-y-o 6f winner Sweet Coincidence (by Mujahid) and 4-y-o Solicitude: dam, French maiden, out of half-sister to very smart 7f to 1¼m performer Tinners Way: poor maiden: stays 1m. *J. R. Weymes*

SOCIETY MUSIC (IRE) 5 b.m. Almutawakel 126 – Society Fair (FR) (Always Fair **80** (USA) 121) [2007 77: 8m⁵ 8m* 8.3f 8d⁴ 8s² 8s 8.1m² 8.1m² 8g² 8m* 9.2s⁴ Sep 24] leggy mare: fairly useful handicapper: won at Pontefract in May and Thirsk in September: stays 1m: acts on any going: tried blinkered, usually wears cheekpieces nowadays: tends to wander/race lazily. *M. Dods*

SOCIETY VENUE 2 b.g. (Feb 6) Where Or When (IRE) 124 – Society Rose 88 (Sad- **70** dlers' Hall (IRE) 126) [2007 7g³ 6g 6f⁶ 7.1g⁵ Oct 2] tall, angular gelding: fair maiden: will stay 1m: acts on firm going: gelded after final start. *Jedd O'Keeffe*

SOFIA ROYALE 3 b.f. Royal Applause 124 – Once In My Life (IRE) 114 (Lomond **61** (USA) 128) [2007 51: 8.2g 8.3g 10g 8.5s p8g p8.6g Dec 8] lengthy, angular filly: modest maiden: not sure to stay beyond 1m. *B. Palling*

SOFIA'S STAR 2 b.c. (Apr 3) Lend A Hand 124 – Charolles 82 (Ajdal (USA) 130) **85** [2007 6g⁴ 6m* 6m⁵ 7g 7.1m 6d⁴ Oct 11] 20,000Y: short-backed colt: half-brother to several winners, including fairly useful 6f (at 2 yrs)/7f winner Chantilly Myth (by Sri Pekan): dam, maiden (stayed 1m), half-sister to high-class French performer around 1¼m Creator: fairly useful performer: won maiden at Goodwood in June: best effort in nurseries when fourth at Newbury: should prove best up to 7f: acts on good to firm and good to soft going: blinkered (ran creditably) once. *P. Winkworth*

SOFIE TUCKER 3 b.f. Erhaab (USA) 127 – Bollin Sophie (Efisio 120) [2007 8.1m³ **64** 8m² 8m² 8.5s³ 10s⁶ Jul 20] strong filly: half-sister to several winners, including 7-y-o Go Tech and 5f/6f (including at 2 yrs) winner Travelling Times (by Timeless Times): dam, maiden, half-sister to St Leger winner Bollin Eric and smart sprinter Bollin Joanne: modest maiden: should stay 1¼m: acts on soft and good to firm going. *T. D. Easterby*

SOFINELLA (IRE) 4 gr.f. Titus Livius (FR) 115 – Mystical Jumbo (Mystiko (USA) **69** 124) [2007 66: p5g p5.1g p5.1g p5.1g⁶ f5g⁶ 5.3d p5.1g² p5.1g* 5.3d* p5.1g p5.1g⁵ Nov 9] leggy filly: fair handicapper: won at Wolverhampton in September and Brighton in October: best at 5f: acts on polytrack, good to firm and good to soft going: tried tongue tied/in cheekpieces: often races prominently: has given trouble at stall, once withdrawn. *A. W. Carroll*

SOFTLY KILLING ME 2 b.f. (Apr 6) Umistim 119 – Slims Lady 59 (Theatrical **61** Charmer 114) [2007 6m 7.1s³ 7s⁴ 8.1d p7g 8.2d⁶ Oct 10] workmanlike filly: second foal: half-sister to 2003 2-y-o 8.5f seller winner Killing Me Softly (by Kingsinger): dam maiden (stayed 1½m): modest maiden: stays 1m: acts on polytrack and soft going. *J. Gallagher*

SOFT MORNING 3 b.f. Pivotal 124 – Summer Night 94 (Nashwan (USA) 135) [2007 **104** 75p: p7.1g* p8g² 10g 10g* 11m 10.3m² 10g⁵ 9s³ a9.5g* a9.5g⁴ Dec 12] lengthy filly: much improved in 2007, and developed into a useful performer: won maiden at Wolverhampton in January, handicap at Sandown (only runner to stay far side) in July and listed race at Deauville (by 2 lengths from Daralara) in December: good fourth to Willywell in similar event on same course final outing: stays 1¼m: acts on all-weather, soft and good to firm ground: usually makes running. *Sir Mark Prescott*

SOGGY DOLLAR 2 ch.g. (Feb 2) Bahamian Bounty 116 – Ninia (USA) 102 (Affirm- **76** ed (USA)) [2007 7m 7m² 7s² 8s⁵ 8d³ Oct 18] strong, angular gelding: fair maiden: twice second at Folkestone: stays 1m: acts on soft and good to firm going: gelded after final start. *M. H. Tompkins*

SO GLAMOROUS 2 b.f. (Apr 4) Diktat 126 – Gena Ivor (USA) (Sir Ivor (USA) 135) – [2007 6d Oct 1] 4,500F, 5,000Y: sister to winner in Italy and half-sister to several winners, including fairly useful 1m winner Joint Statement (by Barathea): dam US 6f to 8.5f winner: 33/1, well held in maiden at Windsor. *C. F. Wall*

SOHO SQUARE 4 ch.g. Generous (IRE) 139 – Stardance (USA) (Rahy (USA) 115) **56** [2007 80: 14g 8.3m 10.1m 9.1g p12g 10f⁶ 14v Oct 29] rather leggy gelding: formerly fairly useful, only modest in 2007: left L. Lungo after fourth start: stays 1½m: acts on polytrack and soft ground: tried blinkered: temperament under suspicion. *John Joseph Hanlon, Ireland*

SOHRAAB 3 b.g. Erhaab (USA) 127 – Riverine (Risk Me (FR) 127) [2007 69p: p6g⁶ **100** p5g* f6g² p5g² p6g² 5g² 6s² 5d² 5m² 5g 6d² 7d Oct 19] compact gelding: improved into a useful maiden: won maiden at Lingfield in February and handicap at Southwell in March: runner-up 7 of next 9 starts, best effort when beaten short head by Genki at Ascot penultimate outing: upped in trip, not discredited at Newmarket final start: bred to stay 7f+, but not short of speed and effective at 5f: acts on all-weather, good to firm and good to soft going: tough and reliable. *H. Morrison*

SOINLOVEWITHYOU (USA) 2 b.f. (Mar 27) Sadler's Wells (USA) 132 – Love **79** Me True (USA) 99 (Kingmambo (USA) 125) [2007 7g⁶ 7s 7d⁴ 8m 7g* 8d Oct 21] deep-girthed filly: third foal: half-sister to 3-y-o Duke of Marmalade: dam, Irish 1m winner, half-sister to very smart performer up to 1¾m Shuailaan, out of half-sister to Wolfhound: fair performer: won maiden at Gowran in October: often highly tried, including when eighth in May Hill Stakes at Doncaster fourth start: will stay 1¼m/1½m: acts on soft and good to firm going. *A. P. O'Brien, Ireland*

SOIZIC (NZ) 5 ch.m. Istidaad (USA) 114 – Nellie May (NZ) (Babarooom (USA)) **65** [2007 76: p10g p7g 10m 9m p11g Sep 5] neat mare: fair form at best in Britain: left C. Cox 2,100 gns after reappearance in 2007: stays 9.5f: acts on polytrack: sold £1,200 in October. *L. A. Dace*

SOKOKE 6 ch.g. Compton Place 125 – Sally Green (IRE) 79 (Common Grounds 118) – [2007 50: 5m 5g 5d 5m 5m 5m Aug 31] workmanlike gelding: little form in 2007. *D. A. Nolan*

SOLARIAS QUEST 5 b.g. Pursuit of Love 124 – Persuasion 79 (Batshoof 122) [2007 – –: p13.9g Jan 16] sturdy gelding: fairly useful performer in 2005: lightly raced and little form on Flat since. *A. King*

SOLAR SPIRIT (IRE) 2 b.c. (May 2) Invincible Spirit (IRE) 121 – Misaayef (USA) **75 p** 82 (Swain (IRE) 134) [2007 7d² Oct 16] €11,000F, €22,000Y, 15,500 2-y-o: first foal: dam 10.5f winner: 22/1, encouraging second to Collection in maiden at Newcastle, travelling smoothly long way: not sure to stay much beyond 7f: will do better. *G. A. Swinbank*

SOLDIER FIELD 3 b.g. Fantastic Light (USA) 134 – Khambani (IRE) 80 (Royal **61** Academy (USA) 130) [2007 –: p8g p8.6g⁵ p10g p8g⁴ 8.1m p8.6g p12.2g³ p11g p11g² f11d⁴ Dec 20] leggy gelding: fair maiden: left A. Balding after penultimate start: stays easy 11f: acts on polytrack: tried in cheekpieces: hung left sixth start. *J. S. Wainwright*

SOLDIER HOLLOW 7 br.h. In The Wings 128 – Island Race 93 (Common **121** Grounds 118) [2007 119: 10s⁴ 10m³ 8.8g* 10g* 8g² Aug 28]

One of the longest and most consistently successful careers of recent seasons in European pattern races came to an end at Baden-Baden in August when Soldier Hollow was retired from racing at the age of seven. Although campaigned internationally—he won good races in France and Italy and also competed in Hong Kong and the States—his travels never took him to Britain, which largely accounts for why his exploits are in danger of being overlooked in the country where he was bred. Soldier Hollow enjoyed recognition at home in Germany though, where he was voted Horse of The Year in 2004. Though Soldier Hollow could never be credited with showing better than very smart form, he remained as good as ever in the latest season, and by the end of his career could boast ten wins in pattern races (four of them at Group 1 level), winning at least one pattern event every season since his three-year-old days; he was also a national listed winner at two. Not the least of Soldier Hollow's claims to fame was that he was the last horse to lower Manduro's colours, inflicting a neck defeat on his former stable-companion in the Prix Dollar at Longchamp on his penultimate start in 2006.

Grosser Dallmayr-Preis – Bayerisches Zuchtrennen, Munich—Soldier Hollow (right) repeats his 2005 success; Formal Decree is second with Dominante (centre) and Hattan (striped cap) next

Soldier Hollow began the latest season back at Longchamp with a good fourth to Boris de Deauville in the Prix d'Harcourt and followed that with a third successive appearance in the Premio Presidente della Repubblica at Rome. He finished a length and a half behind Distant Way in third, after finishing a length second to the same rival the year before. Soldier Hollow had an even better record in Rome's other Group 1 mile-and-a-quarter contest, the Premio Roma, a race he won in 2004 and 2005. The Premio Roma is run in November, and, in general, Soldier Hollow tended to run his best races from the summer onwards. The other highlight of Soldier Hollow's career outside Germany was his third behind The Tin Man in the Arlington Million in 2006. Less successful was his venture to Sha Tin for the Hong Kong Cup at the end of his four-year-old season, but that was one of only four occasions in his whole career that he failed to make the frame.

Soldier Hollow's last three races all took place on home turf. At Dortmund in June he made the most of an easier task than usual when beating British-trained Banknote (racing in the Royal colours) a length in the Group 3 Grosser Preis der Wirtschaft. Soldier Hollow followed that with a return to Group 1 company the following month in the Grosser Dallmayr-Preis – Bayerisches Zuchtrennen at Munich, a race he had already won two years earlier. He was a short-priced favourite to account for eight younger rivals and did so in clear-cut fashion after leading over a furlong out, coming home three lengths ahead of Godolphin's Formal Decree, with the German Oaks runner-up Dominante and the other British challenger Hattan completing the frame. For most of his career, Soldier Hollow was campaigned at a mile and a quarter. He was never tried at a mile and a half, despite the many more opportunities that would have provided for him at Group 1 level in Germany (he was demoted for causing interference when first past the post in the Hansa-Preis at Hamburg in 2005 on a rare try at eleven furlongs). Soldier Hollow bowed out at Baden-Baden over a mile, running right up to his best and giving a performance in defeat which would have won him virtually any other mile race in Germany during the years in which he has been running. Unfortunately for Soldier Hollow, one of his four rivals was the smart three-year-old filly Mi Emma, a nine-length winner of the German 1000 Guineas. Soldier Hollow chased Mi Emma throughout but the concession of 15 lb (Germany's weight-for-age scale does no favours to older horses) to his younger rival proved too much and he went down by two lengths.

				Northern Dancer
			Sadler's Wells	Fairy Bridge
	In The Wings		(b 1981)	Shirley Heights
	(b 1986)		High Hawk	Sunbittern
Soldier Hollow			(b 1980)	Kris
(br.h. 2000)			Common Grounds	Sweetly
	Island Race		(b 1985)	Caerleon
	(b 1995)		Lake Isle	Inisfree
			(br 1989)	

Soldier Hollow was sold at Newmarket as a yearling for 75,000 guineas. He is his dam's first foal, and the closest any of his younger siblings have come to him in ability is half-brother Day Walker (by Dr Devious). Now trained in Norway, Day

Walker was also bought to race in Germany initially and showed smart form when winning the Group 3 Furstenberg-Rennen at Baden-Baden over a mile and a quarter. Soldier Hollow's three-year-old full brother Peregrine Falcon won a Wolverhampton maiden for Mark Johnston at two before being sold to Russia where he won over a mile and a quarter in the latest season, while the dam's four-year-old Pivotal colt, Hurst Point, is a seven-furlong winner in Italy. A two-year-old close relative to Soldier Hollow, Sea Chorus (by Singspiel) was in training with Michael Bell but she has yet to race. Soldier Hollow's dam Island Race won twice at six furlongs for James Fanshawe, while Vincent O'Brien trained the twice-raced grandam Lake Isle who was a seven-furlong winner. O'Brien was synonymous with the better-known names in this family a bit further back. Soldier Hollow's great grandam Inisfree was an unraced half-sister to the National Stakes winner Fatherland out of the Coronation Stakes winner Lisadell, herself a sister to July Cup winner Thatch. Soldier Hollow's grandsire Sadler's Wells is a member of the same family, being a grandson of another of Lisadell's sisters, Special. More recent descendants of Lisadell include the top-class Japanese horse El Condor Pasa and the Irish Two Thousand Guineas winner Bachelor Duke, so Soldier Hollow has the pedigree to go with his racing record in his new career at stud. He is to stand at Gestut Rottgen at a fee of €6,500. A reliable racehorse who acted on firm and soft ground, Soldier Hollow was a credit to his connections. *P. Schiergen, Germany*

SOLDIER OF FORTUNE (IRE) 3 b.c. Galileo (IRE) 134 – Affianced (IRE) 109 **131** (Erins Isle 121) [2007 114p: 10.5m* 12.3m* 12g⁵ 12s* 12m* 12g⁵ Oct 7]

For the second year running, one of the Ballydoyle classic three-year-olds improved out of all recognition between Epsom and the Curragh to run away with the Irish Derby. The improvement shown by Soldier of Fortune, one of eight Derby runners saddled at Epsom by Ballydoyle, was even more pronounced than that shown the previous year by Dylan Thomas who, after finishing third to Sir Percy in a blanket finish at Epsom, went on to win the Irish Derby by three and a half lengths, much more patiently ridden at the Curragh. Soldier of Fortune started at over twice the odds at Epsom of his stablemates Eagle Mountain and Archipenko who were second and third favourite behind Authorized. Soldier of Fortune's odds of 14/1 at Epsom, the same as another of his stable companions Admiralofthefleet, seemed a fair reflection of his chance. A progressive two-year-old, runner-up to Passage of Time in the Criterium de Saint-Cloud on the last of three starts, Soldier of Fortune had earned his place in the Derby field with wins in small fields in the Prix Noailles at Longchamp (from the Criterium de Saint-Cloud fourth Spirit One) and the MBNA Chester Vase (narrowly landing the odds, conceding 4 lb all round penalised for his Noailles win). Michael Kinane, who rode Soldier of Fortune at Chester, where he also partnered Dee Stakes winner Admiralofthefleet, was on the Derrinstown Stud Derby Trial winner Archipenko at Epsom. Soldier of Fortune had still not fully come to himself at Chester, where he was not quite right in his coat, but he looked in good shape at Epsom where, soon well positioned under Wayne Lordan, he had every chance and simply seemed not quite good enough. He finished second best among the Ballydoyle octet, coming fifth of seventeen, three places behind Eagle Mountain, but beaten over eight lengths by the winner Authorized.

Eagle Mountain and Soldier of Fortune both lined up four weeks after Epsom for the Budweiser Irish Derby—the twenty-second and last to be sponsored by the US corporation Anheuser-Busch—and, with Authorized being kept for the Eclipse and with Prix du Jockey Club winner Lawman also missing, Eagle Mountain started 6/4 favourite, ridden by Kieren Fallon, just back from serving a world-wide six-month suspension (Soldier of Fortune in the Criterium de Saint-Cloud had turned out to be his final mount before the revelation that he had failed a drug test). Fallon's prediction after the Criterium de Saint-Cloud that Soldier of Fortune would 'surely turn into a top-class three-year-old' was fulfilled in no uncertain manner at the Curragh. He started second favourite at 5/1, ahead of the two French-trained challengers, Royal And Regal and the Prix du Jockey Club third Shamdinan, and the supplemented (at a cost of €150,000) King Edward VII Stakes winner Boscobel, the six remaining runners starting at odds of 12/1 or longer. Boscobel carried the colours of Sheikh Mohammed but Frankie Dettori missed the opportunity to attempt an historic Derby treble (he had won on Authorized and

Lawman) when failing to apply in time to the Horseracing Regulatory Authority for the deferral of a riding ban picked up at Royal Ascot. Michael Kinane did apply in time and his Royal Ascot ban, incurred like Dettori's in the Prince of Wales's Stakes, was successfully deferred, allowing him to take the mount, among others, on the Ballydoyle third string in the Irish Derby, Alexander of Hales, who had finished down the field in the Prix du Jockey Club after winning the Gallinule Stakes. A fourth Ballydoyle runner, 50/1-shot Spanish Harlem, was employed essentially as a pacemaker to ensure a truly-run race. Soldier of Fortune was waited with, travelling well, before moving through from the middle of the field to hit the front two furlongs out, by which time Eagle Mountain was already under pressure after being forced wide on the home turn. Soldier of Fortune stretched clear in magnificent style, pushed along in the final furlong, to win by nine lengths from the staying-on Alexander of Hales who pipped Eagle Mountain by a short head for second. Boscobel finished three and a half lengths behind Eagle Mountain in fourth, with Royal And Regal and Shamdinan well beaten in eighth and ninth.

The going on Irish Derby day was soft and Soldier of Fortune's superiority might have been exaggerated a little by the conditions. However, the attempts afterwards to write off or denigrate Soldier of Fortune's performance were both unfair and unwarranted. The ground was far from bottomless at the Curragh and his performance was, by Timeform's reckoning, the best in the race since Sinndar scored by the same margin in 2000, also on going on the soft side. Only St Jovite, a twelve-length winner on good to firm in 1992, has won the Irish Derby by further than Sinndar and Soldier of Fortune since the race became fully recognised as one of international importance (its value was boosted significantly for the first time by major sponsorship in 1962). Soldier of Fortune showed himself a top-class mile-and-a-half horse at the Curragh and, at the time, there looked to be very little between him and Authorized on their respective Derby performances.

The Irish Derby was a personal triumph for Soldier of Fortune's trainer Aidan O'Brien who saddled the first three, the fourth time he has done so in an Irish classic, following the Irish Two Thousand Guineas in 2001 (Black Minnaloushe, Mozart and Minardi) and in 2002 (Rock of Gibraltar, Century City and Della Francesca) and the Irish Derby in 2002 (High Chaparral, Sholokhov and Ballingarry). O'Brien also had a one, two, three in two other Group 1s in the latest season, the St James's Palace Stakes and the Irish Champion Stakes, and also achieved the feat in the Dewhurst and the Criterium de Saint-Cloud in 2001. Apart from O'Brien, only Saeed bin Suroor (who saddled the first three in the Eclipse in 1998) has had a one, two, three in a Group 1 Flat race in Britain since the pattern was introduced in 1971. The last time a trainer had the first three in a British classic was in 1918 when Alec Taylor saddled Gainsborough, My Dear and Prince Chimay in a St Leger run at Newmarket. Frank Butters trained the first, second, fourth and fifth (all for the Aga Khan) in the 1932 St Leger. Aidan O'Brien's victory in the latest Irish St Leger with Yeats (who won from stablemate Scorpion) enabled him to join his Ballydoyle predecessor Vincent O'Brien and British trainer Dick Hern in completing a full set of the ten British and Irish classics. Aidan O'Brien achieved his first classic victory in 1997, with Classic Park in the Irish One Thousand Guineas, twenty-four hours

Budweiser Irish Derby, the Curragh—a 1,2,3 for Aidan O'Brien as Soldier of Fortune runs away from Alexander of Hales (light colours, centre) and Eagle Mountain (striped sleeves); Boscobel (star on cap) is fourth

Prix Niel Casino Barriere d'Enghien Les Bains, Longchamp—Soldier of Fortune comes through his Arc trial in satisfactory style; Sagara rail takes second off Zambezi River

before Desert King—who went on to win the Irish Derby—completed a Guineas double for the trainer. The current master of Ballydoyle has taken less time than his illustrious predecessor (who had a much smaller string) to win all the British and Irish classics and he now needs twelve more to match Vincent O'Brien's twenty-seven Irish classic victories and three more to match his British total of sixteen.

Vincent O'Brien enjoyed the most successful training career of modern times but Aidan O'Brien now needs only three more Irish trainers' championships on the Flat to match Vincent O'Brien and Michael Dawson, who, according to *The Sweeney Guide To The Irish Turf* by Tony and Annie Sweeney, hold the record jointly with thirteen titles. As well as being champion trainer in Ireland again in 2007 (the ninth year in a row), Aidan O'Brien was also champion for the third time in Britain, following successes in 2001 and 2002, and remains the only overseas-based trainer to win the British title since Vincent O'Brien did so for the second time in 1977 (when he too was also champion in Ireland). Another Irish-based trainer Paddy Prendergast was champion for three successive years in Britain, in 1963, 1964 and 1965 (also champion in Ireland in 1963 and 1965), but Aidan O'Brien is the only trainer to be champion at least three times in both Britain and Ireland. Ballydoyle had another splendid year, winning fifteen Group 1 races, the restricted availability of the stable's number-one jockey Kieren Fallon resulting in O'Brien adopting a policy of 'using the best available on the day'. Seven different jockeys rode Group 1 winners for the stable including long-standing regular Seamus Heffernan, who recorded his second Irish classic win on Soldier of Fortune in the Irish Derby, six years after 16/1-shot Imagine to victory in the Irish One Thousand Guineas. The most successful jockey for Ballydoyle in Group 1 races in 2007, incidentally, was Johnny Murtagh with five wins, followed by Kieren Fallon with four and Michael Kinane with two. Christophe Soumillon, Colm O'Donoghue and Jamie Spencer also rode one. It was announced at the end of January that Murtagh had been appointed stable jockey following Fallon's eighteen-month worldwide ban for failing another drug test in France.

Soldier of Fortune was Aidan O'Brien's fifth Irish Derby winner—one short of Vincent O'Brien's total—but, unlike his four previous winners, there were no plans to bring Soldier of Fortune back to race at a mile and a quarter afterwards. Desert King went on to finish second in the International at York and in the Irish Champion; Galileo won the King George VI and Queen Elizabeth Stakes before reverting to a mile and a quarter for the Irish Champion (beaten narrowly by Fantastic Light) and the Breeders' Cup Classic on dirt (sixth of thirteen); High Chaparral's training after the Irish Derby was interrupted by coughing but he was an intended runner in the Irish Champion before being withdrawn on the day of the race because his trainer was unhappy with the results of a blood test (after finishing third in the Prix de l'Arc, he won the Breeders' Cup Turf); Dylan Thomas won the

Mrs John Magnier, Mr M. Tabor & Mr D. Smith's "Soldier of Fortune"

Irish Champion after finishing fourth in the International (on his final start he flopped on dirt in the Jockey Club Gold Cup). Soldier of Fortune looked tailor-made for the St Leger, a race won in three of the six previous years by Aidan O'Brien, but, after being announced 'a definite possible' and being installed for a time as ante-post favourite, he missed Doncaster in favour of an orthodox preparation for the Prix de l'Arc. He won the Prix Niel Casino Barriere d'Enghien Les Bains, a race which has been a significant pointer to the Arc in recent times. After Song of Hiawatha had done a grand job as pacemaker, Soldier of Fortune took over coming round the home turn and ran on strongly to win in a record time for the race by a length and a half and three quarters of a length from Sagara and the Grand Prix de Paris winner Zambezi Sun, the first three clear. Connections wouldn't confirm Soldier of Fortune a definite runner for the Arc at first, his jockey Johnny Murtagh expressing the view that he might need more give in the ground (it was good to firm for the Niel). The Arc was run on good going and Ballydoyle provided two pacemakers, Yellowstone and the supplemented Song of Hiawatha, to ensure a thorough test of stamina at the trip. Soldier of Fortune wasn't discredited, tracking the pacemakers until going on over two furlongs out but beginning to weaken when forced to check by his stable-companion Dylan Thomas close home. Dylan Thomas won the race for Ballydoyle, surviving a stewards' inquiry after also hampering Zambezi Sun, with Soldier of Fortune beaten just over two lengths into fifth. Soldier of Fortune was some way below his Irish Derby form, which remains a fair bit in advance of anything else he has achieved, but he will have opportunities as a four-year-old to allay continuing suggestions that his Curragh performance flatters him. He is game and genuine but lacks the turn of foot of High Chaparral and Dylan

Thomas, the two other Aidan O'Brien-trained Irish Derby winners who remained in training, and is clearly very well suited by testing conditions and a strongly-run race at a mile and a half.

		Sadler's Wells	Northern Dancer
	Galileo (IRE)	(b 1981)	Fairy Bridge
	(b 1998)	Urban Sea	Miswaki
Soldier of Fortune (IRE)		(ch 1989)	Allegretta
(b.c. 2004)		Erins Isle	Busted
	Affianced (IRE)	(b 1978)	Chemise
	(b 1998)	La Meilleure	Lord Gayle
		(ch 1985)	Gradille

The strong, attractive Soldier of Fortune is from the second crop of Galileo and the third classic winner sired by him, following St Leger winner Sixties Icon and Irish One Thousand Guineas winner Nightime. Galileo looks like turning out to be essentially an influence for stamina at stud and Soldier of Fortune's dam the very useful Affianced stayed a mile and three quarters, though she did not win beyond a mile and a quarter. Affianced is by the Busted stallion Erins Isle who was second in the Irish St Leger before winning five Grade 1s in the States, including the San Juan Capistrano Handicap over a mile and three quarters. Soldier of Fortune is the second foal out of Affianced, the first being his brother Heliostatic, a smart performer who pulled hard when a creditable seventh in Dylan Thomas's Irish Derby and was kept to shorter distances for the rest of his career. Affianced was also represented on the racecourse in the latest season by the Jim Bolger-trained Ard Fheis (by Lil's Boy) who was placed once in four starts and showed signs of temperament. Affianced is a sister to the useful Irish mile-and-a-quarter winner Irish Summit and a half-sister to the Irish Derby and Eclipse runner-up Sholokhov, who is by Soldier of Fortune's grandsire Sadler's Wells, and to several other winners, including the useful Napper Tandy, a listed winner at a mile and a quarter in Ireland who finished seventh of nine in Alamshar's Irish Derby. Soldier of Fortune's grandam La Meilleure won at seven furlongs and a mile in Ireland and stayed a mile and a quarter, while his great grandam Gradille was out of a half-sister to the top-class sprinter Double Form and the Lupe Stakes winner Scimitarra who would have been placed in the Oaks but for fracturing her off-fore cannon bone a furlong out. Scimitarra, incidentally, was saved for stud and has bred four minor winners. *A. P. O'Brien, Ireland*

SOLDIERS QUEST 3 b.c. Rainbow Quest (USA) 134 – Janaat 74 (Kris 135) [2007 **86 d** p10g^2 p12.2g* 11.8g^5 9.2g p12.2g Sep 8] fairly useful performer: confirmed debut promise when winning maiden at Wolverhampton (by 11 lengths) in March: not discredited when fifth on handicap debut at Leicester next time: left M. Johnston, well beaten in claimer/seller last 2 starts (said to have finished lame both occasions): should stay 1¾m: acts on polytrack. *Peter Grayson*

SOLDIERS ROMANCE 4 b.g. Allied Forces (USA) 123 – Still In Love 75 (Emarati **53** (USA) 74) [2007 54: p9.5g^6 f8g f7g 5m^5 p5.1g May 21] tall, good-topped gelding: modest maiden: stays 9.5f: acts on polytrack. *T. D. Easterby*

SOLDIER'S TALE (USA) 6 ch.h. Stravinsky (USA) 133 – Myrtle 96 (Batshoof **126** 122) [2007 6g^3 7.1m^3 6d* Jun 23]

Soldier's Tale has managed just eight starts in four years, missing entirely as a five-year-old and not seen out in any season later than early-July. Minor setbacks, more serious problems and concerns about his effectiveness on firmish ground have all severely limited his opportunities. He has, however, rewarded the skill and patience of his connections by showing himself a high-class sprinter when able to make it to the track and he crowned his career in the latest season with victory in the Group 1 Golden Jubilee Stakes at Royal Ascot.

The stop-start pattern of abundant promise and frustrating absences was established early. Soldier's Tale ran just twice as a three-year-old, finishing second in a Newmarket maiden on his debut in April before going one better in a similar event at York the following month. A setback led to his missing the Jersey Stakes at Royal Ascot and further, more serious problems meant he failed to return in the autumn either. He suffered a fracture to his leg so serious that he was nearly put down. That was followed by two bouts of colic, the first of which led to part of his stomach being removed. At four, Soldier's Tale again won at York's May meeting, in a handicap this time, and, missing the Wokingham back at York because of firm ground, he followed up in the Group 3 Chipchase Stakes at Newcastle. Again he looked a potential star, overcoming a difficult passage to win readily after showing an impressive turn of foot, and he started joint favourite for the July Cup at Newmarket just a week later. Despite a poor draw, he did well to finish fourth to Pastoral Pursuits, isolated from the main action. Soldier's Tale appeared among the five-day entries for the Challenge Stakes at Newmarket that autumn but failed to meet the engagement. He wasn't seen out again until the latest season, his 2006 campaign delayed at first by minor setbacks and then by unsuitable ground, while an abscess on a foot meant he missed his main target the Sprint Cup at Haydock too.

When Soldier's Tale finally returned to action, it was in familiar surroundings, at York for the May meeting, at which he contested the Duke of York Stakes. Soldier's Tale showed he had lost none of his ability, running a race full of promise in finishing third to Amadeus Wolf and Red Clubs, running on without being given a hard time. That was followed by, so far, the only disappointing run of his career. Starting odds on for the listed John of Gaunt Stakes at Haydock three weeks later, he could finish only third behind Mine, running in snatches and wandering under pressure.

Soldier's Tale was racing on good to firm going at Haydock for the first time, which offered an obvious explanation for his below-par effort, though when he lined up at Royal Ascot he was equipped with a visor. Amadeus Wolf and Red Clubs were again in the field, Amadeus Wolf the shortest-priced British-trained runner at 13/2 in a market dominated by Australian challengers. The impressive King's Stand Stakes winner Miss Andretti started a warm favourite at 2/1, with fellow antipodeans Magnus and Takeover Target, third and fourth in her wake earlier in the week, 15/2 and 8/1 respectively. Smart handicapper Al Qasi, sixth in the Duke of York on his reappearance, was also at 8/1, with Soldier's Tale, despite his Haydock flop, the only other at single-figure odds at 9/1. On ground somewhat softer than at the start of the meeting, neither Miss Andretti nor Magnus ran close to their earlier form, while Al Qasi and Amadeus Wolf were well below the form they showed on their reappearances at York. Magnus made the running, the majority of

Golden Jubilee Stakes, Royal Ascot—Soldier's Tale (visor) repays his stable's patience; Takeover Target (noseband) is placed for the second year running as Asset and Red Clubs (left) also make the frame

the field of twenty-one well grouped in the centre of the track. Those involved in the finish were, as in so many races on the straight course at Ascot since its reopening, well placed throughout. Takeover Target was the first to press for home, headed narrowly by Red Clubs before getting back in front in the final furlong. Soldier's Tale looked an unlikely winner a furlong out, though still handy, but responded well to his rider's urgings and caught Takeover Target near the line, winning by a head, with Asset running on in third, half a length down, and Red Clubs the same margin back in fourth. The field for the Golden Jubilee was thoroughly representative, containing nearly all the leading established sprinters, and Soldier's Tale's performance was as good as any produced by a runner in the latest Golden Jubilee, excepting Miss Andretti's in the King's Stand. Only Sakhee's Secret, the winner of the July Cup, produced a better performance at six furlongs in 2007. Although Asset eventually proved disappointing, others upheld the Golden Jubilee form: Takeover Target returned to action in December, winning twice at Randwick and Red Clubs ran well when third in the July Cup before winning the Sprint Cup at Haydock. Soldier's Tale, though, went missing again. Connections bypassed the July Cup due to the ground, the Prix Maurice de Gheest after a slight setback, the Sprint Cup again due to the ground that was forecast, and finally the Prix de la Foret after another minor setback. That might have been that, but it was reported early in 2008 that Soldier's Tale was back in light training, with a view to yet another appearance at the York May meeting.

	Stravinsky (USA) (b 1996)	Nureyev (b 1977)	Northern Dancer Special
Soldier's Tale (USA) (ch.h. 2001)		Fire The Groom (b 1987)	Blushing Groom Prospector's Fire
	Myrtle (b 1993)	Batshoof (b 1986)	Sadler's Wells Steel Habit
		Greek Goddess (b 1986)	Young Generation Cassandra

The strong, good-bodied Soldier's Tale, despite his frailties and a pretty humdrum immediate family on the distaff side, ought to have a future at stud when his racing career is finally over. His sire, the July Cup and Nunthorpe Stakes winner Stravinsky, one of the best sprinters of the last decade but now based in Japan, had his most successful season in 2007, with Benbaun also landing a Group 1 sprint. In addition Stravinsky sired runners-up in Group 1 events at a mile in France (Missvinski) and Japan (Kongo Rikishio). His other Group 1 winner in Britain, Balmont, who was awarded the 2003 Middle Park Stakes, was also trained by Soldier's Tale's trainer Jeremy Noseda. Soldier's Tale is the second foal out of the useful two-year-old seven-and-a-half furlong winner Myrtle, who later won in the States. Her 2003 foal Bayberry King (by Lear Fan) is a maiden on the Flat, yet to be placed, though he finished second over hurdles in November. Devil's Ruse, a brother to Soldier's Tale, was in training with Noseda as a three-year-old in 2007 but failed to make the track. Myrtle's dam, the fair maiden sprinter Greek Goddess, produced two other winning two-year-olds, including Myrtle's brother Dalmeny Dancer who later won at up to a mile in the then-Yugoslavia. It is necessary to go back to the third dam Cassandra to find other useful performers in this family. Cassandra was a daughter of the smart sprinter Matinee, who won the Portland Handicap, and her useful siblings included Melodrama, who won at up to a mile, and the two-year-old seven-furlong winner Candide. Cassandra herself showed useful form at up to a mile and three quarters, making her something of an aberration in this family, though she was by Troy. That said, Cassandra isn't the stoutest stayer in the family by any means. Matinee's Lowther Stakes-winning half-sister Kittyhawk is the dam of the Cesarewitch winner and Queen Alexandra Stakes runner-up Nomadic Way, who was a dual Champion Hurdle runner-up and also won the Stayers' Hurdle at Cheltenham. *J. Noseda*

SOLEMN 2 b.c. (Jan 31) Pivotal 124 – Pious 74 (Bishop of Cashel 122) [2007 p7g p6g³ **61** Oct 26] modest maiden: third at Wolverhampton: may prove best up to 7f: sold 14,000 gns. *Sir Mark Prescott*

SOLENT (IRE) 5 b.g. Montjeu (IRE) 137 – Stylish (Anshan) 119) [2007 105: 12g² **110** 14.1m⁶ 12s² 12d⁵ 14d 13.4m 16g* Sep 30] big, good-topped gelding: impresses in appearance: smart performer: dead-heated with Distinction in listed event at Ascot (rallied gamely) in September: some good efforts in handicaps otherwise in 2007, head second to Pevensey in Duke of Edinburgh Stakes at Royal Ascot third outing: stays 2m: acts on heavy and good to firm going: often early to post: has run well when sweating: usually makes running: sold 155,000 gns. *R. Hannon*

SOLENT RIDGE (IRE) 2 b.c. (Apr 5) Namid 128 – Carrozzina 70 (Vettori (IRE) **90** 119) [2007 6g⁶ 7s p6g² p7g³ 6.1m* p7g* 7.1g⁵ p8m⁶ p7g⁶ Oct 12] 9,500F, £11,000 2-y-o: good-topped colt: second foal: dam, 2-y-o 7f winner, half-sister to useful performers Hockney (French stayer) and Right Again (2-y-o 7f winner) out of half-sister to smart sprinter Titus Livius: fairly useful performer: won nursery at Chepstow and minor event at Lingfield in August: sixth to Great War Eagle in listed race at Dundalk final start: probably stays 1m: acts on polytrack and good to firm going. *J. S. Moore*

SOLICITUDE 4 ch.f. Bertolini (USA) 125 – Sibilant (Selkirk (USA) 129) [2007 –, **–** a62: p7.1g⁵ p8.6g³ p8.6g f7g³ p8g p7g* p8m p7m² p7.1g⁶ Dec 1] workmanlike filly: **a61** modest handicapper: won at Kempton in September: stays 8.6f: acts on all-weather, little form on turf: often wears cheekpieces/blinkers. *D. Haydn Jones*

SOLIDGOLDESYACTION 3 b.f. Intikhab (USA) 135 – Keltech Star (IRE) 62 **50** (Bigstone (IRE) 126) [2007 f6g p6g p7.1g* p7.1g⁵ Apr 27] 800Y: fourth foal: dam, maiden (stayed 1½m), half-sister to smart miler Waajib: modest performer: won seller at Wolverhampton in April: will stay 1m: acts on polytrack. *P. A. Blockley*

SOLID ROCK (IRE) 3 b.g. Rock of Gibraltar (IRE) 133 – Sheer Spirit (IRE) 86 **101** (Caerleon (USA) 132) [2007 100: p8g⁵ 6m⁴ 7d² 7m 6m Jul 11] close-coupled gelding: useful performer: good ¾-length second to Howya Now Kid in listed race at Epsom in June: below form at Royal Ascot (stiff task in Jersey Stakes) and Newmarket (poorly drawn in valuable handicap) after: effective at 6f to 1m: acts on polytrack, good to firm and good to soft going: has raced freely: gelded, then sold 16,000 gns. *T. G. Mills*

SOLID SILVER 6 ch.g. Pharly (FR) 130 – Shadows of Silver 89 (Carwhite 127) [2007 **–** 10.1m Jun 2] fair form when successful in bumper: 33/1, well held in maiden at Newcastle on Flat debut: will be suited by 1½m. *K. G. Reveley*

SOLO CITY 3 b.g. Averti (IRE) 117 – Surakarta 67 (Bin Ajwaad (IRE) 119) [2007 –: **–** f8g⁵ p8.6g⁶ Jan 8] little form. *P. A. Blockley*

SOLO FLIGHT 10 gr.g. Mtoto 134 – Silver Singer 65 (Pharly (FR) 130) [2007 95: **90** p10g⁴ p10g⁶ 12m 12g p12g⁵ p10g⁵ Oct 24] angular gelding: fairly useful handicapper nowadays: effective at 1¼m/1½m: acts on polytrack, firm and good to soft going: sometimes finds little, and best produced late. *H. Morrison*

SOLO RIVER 2 b.f. (Feb 20) Averti (IRE) 117 – Surakarta 67 (Bin Ajwaad (IRE) 119) **60** [2007 5.1f³ 6m⁴ p6m⁴ p5g Oct 24] 2,000Y: second foal: dam, maiden (stayed 1m), out of half-sister to dam of Prix du Jockey Club winners Sulamani and Dream Well: modest maiden: will stay 7f: acts on polytrack and firm going. *P. J. Makin*

SOL ROJO 5 b.g. Efisio 120 – Shining Cloud 73 (Indian Ridge 123) [2007 66, a80: **72** 10m³ 10m 10m 10f⁵ 8.5g² 10.5g⁶ 10m Oct 3] lengthy gelding: fair handicapper: effective at 1m to easy 1¾m: acts on all-weather, soft and firm going: usually wears headgear: often slowly away: usually ridden by Mr S. Pearce. *J. Pearce*

SOMARINI 2 b.f. (Mar 14) Bertolini (USA) 125 – Lake Pleasant (IRE) 90 (Elegant Air **–** 119) [2007 6m 6.1g 7m 7m p6g p6g Dec 1] 9,000Y: leggy filly: half-sister to several winners, including useful 7f (at 2 yrs) to 1½m winner Serpentine (by Grand Lodge): dam, 2-y-o 6f winner, half-sister to useful sprinter Power Lake: little form: left J. Given after fourth start: tried blinkered. *T. T. Clement*

SOMERSET FALLS (UAE) 2 b.f. (Mar 27) Red Ransom (USA) – Dunnes River **76 p** (USA) 84 (Danzig (USA)) [2007 7.1g² Nov 9] third foal: half-sister to 3-y-o Boscobel and fairly useful 2005 2-y-o 1m winner Crested (now smart up to 1¼m in US, by Fantastic Light): dam, 1m winner only outing, out of smart French 1m/9f performer Elizabeth Bay: 12/1, second to stable-companion Hieroglyph in maiden at Musselburgh, making running: will be suited by 1m/1¼m: sure to improve. *M. Johnston*

SOMETHING (IRE) 5 b.g. Trans Island 119 – Persian Polly 99 (Persian Bold 123) **115** [2007 114: 6m³ 6d⁴ 7m³ 6m 6g³ Sep 18] big, lengthy gelding: smart performer: good efforts in frame in listed race at Windsor (third to Assertive) and valuable handicaps at Royal Ascot (Wokingham, fourth to Dark Missile) and Newmarket (Bunbury Cup, close third to Giganticus): below form after: effective at 6f/7f: acts on polytrack, good to firm and good to soft going: races prominently. *T. G. Mills*

SOMETHING SIMPLE (IRE) 4 ch.g. Raise A Grand (IRE) 114 – Baccara (IRE) –
(Sri Pekan (USA) 117) [2007 67: p12.2g 10m Jun 3] fair maiden at best: little impact in
handicaps in Britain: tried blinkered. *R. Ford*

SOMNUS 7 b.g. Pivotal 124 – Midnight's Reward 84 (Night Shift (USA)) [2007 115:   **104**
7d⁶ 7g 6g 6d 7g⁵ Oct 27] good-topped gelding: high-class performer at best, winner of 3
Group 1s: just useful form in 2007, best effort when 1¾ lengths fifth to Appalachian Trail
in minor event at Doncaster final outing: best at 6f/7f: acts on soft and good to firm going:
tongue tied last 2 starts. *T. D. Easterby*

SOM TALA 4 ch.c. Fantastic Light (USA) 134 – One of The Family 73 (Alzao (USA)   **99**
117) [2007 97: 18.7m⁵ 20m³ 21g⁵ 18m 16.1m³ 18d Oct 20] workmanlike colt: useful
handicapper: good efforts when third at Royal Ascot (to Full House in Ascot Stakes) and
Newcastle (to Mirjan) in 2007: never a threat in Cesarewitch at Newmarket (unseated and
ran loose at start) final outing: stays 21f: acts on firm and good to soft going: formerly not
an easy ride. *M. R. Channon*

SONARA (IRE) 3 b.g. Peintre Celebre (USA) 137 – Fay (IRE) 64 (Polish Precedent   **79**
(USA) 131) [2007 60p: 10g³ 12f* 12.1g⁴ 12.1g² 10g 11.5g 12m 14.1m* 14m³ 14g⁴ 14m²
17.2g Oct 24] strong, good-bodied gelding: fair handicapper: won at Pontefract in May
and Redcar in August: stays 1¾m: acts on firm ground: sold 75,000 gns, joined J. Howard
Johnson. *M. H. Tompkins*

SONAR SOUND (GER) 3 b.g. Slickly (FR) 128 – Samothrace (IRE) (Arazi (USA)   –
135) [2007 79: 9g 8.1s 7.5s 7.5g Jul 31] big gelding: maiden: well held at 3 yrs. *T. P. Tate*

SONDERBORG 6 b.m. Great Dane (IRE) 122 – Nordico Princess 71 (Nordico (USA))   –
[2007 52: f8g Jan 25] workmanlike mare: modest performer at 5 yrs: well below form
only start in 2007: wears headgear. *J. Mackie*

SONG OF HIAWATHA 3 b.c. Sadler's Wells (USA) 132 – Sabria (USA) (Miswaki   **110**
(USA) 124) [2007 70p: 10d* 12.9g² 10.4d 12m⁶ 12g Oct 7] smallish colt: closely related
to very smart 1m/1¼m winner Ikhtyar (by Unfuwain) and half-brother to several winners,
notably high-class miler Landseer (by Danehill): dam unraced half-sister to smart
middle-distance performer King Sound: smart performer: won minor event at Navan in
June: improved when ½-length second to Temlett in quite valuable handicap at Down
Royal next time: acted as pacemaker after when last in Juddmonte International Stakes at
York (far from discredited), and Prix Niel and Prix de l'Arc de Triomphe at Longchamp:
stays 13f: acts on good to soft ground. *A. P. O'Brien, Ireland*

SONG OF PASSION (IRE) 4 b.f. Orpen (USA) 116 – Bint Al Balad (IRE) 63 (Aho-   **104**
noora 122) [2007 100: p7g⁵ 7.6m³ 6g* 7g 7d⁵ 6d 6.1m Sep 15] sturdy, lengthy filly:
useful performer: won handicap at Epsom (by 2 lengths from Prince Namid) in June and
minor event at Chester (beat Fonthill Road by ¾ length, dictated) in July: ran poorly last
2 starts, including in blinkers (said to have come loose) final outing: effective at 6f to 7.6f:
acts on polytrack, good to firm and good to soft going: sold 95,000 gns. *R. Hannon*

SONIC ANTHEM (USA) 5 b.g. Royal Anthem (USA) 135 – Whisperifyoudare   –
(USA) (Red Ransom (USA)) [2007 –, a72: f8g* f8g p9.5g Dec 14] tall, good-topped   **a67**
gelding: fair performer on all-weather, modest at best on turf: won claimer at Southwell
in March: left P. Haslam after second start: free-going sort, but stays 11f: acts on fibresand
and firm ground. *J. T. Stimpson*

SONNING STAR (IRE) 3 b.g. Desert Prince (IRE) 130 – Fantazia 100 (Zafonic   **79**
(USA) 130) [2007 –: 8d⁴ 7s³ 8g⁵ 8.3m² 10.3m 8.5d³ 8m² Oct 8] tall, useful-looking
gelding: fair maiden: should stay 1¼m: acts on soft and good to firm ground: sold 35,000
gns, joined N. Gifford. *D. R. C. Elsworth*

SONNY MAC 4 b.c. Pivotal 124 – Sea Drift (FR) 72 (Warning 136) [2007 74: p12g   –
10.2d p13g Jul 10] rather leggy, close-coupled colt: fair maiden at best: well held in
handicaps in 2007: tongue tied: tried in headgear. *M. J. McGrath*

SONNY PARKIN 5 b.g. Spinning World (USA) 130 – No Miss Kris (USA) (Capote   **82**
(USA) [2007 87, a75: p10g⁵ p8g³ p8g⁴ 7m 8g 12d 8d³ 8g⁴ 8m³ 10m³ 8m* 8g p10g   **a79**
Oct 24] tall, leggy gelding: fairly useful handicapper: all 3 wins at Newmarket, including
in August: stays 1¼m: acts on polytrack, soft and good to firm ground: wears headgear,
visored nowadays: held up. *G. A. Huffer*

SONNY RED (IRE) 3 b.c. Redback 116 – Magic Melody 62 (Petong 126) [2007 100:   **114**
8m² 8m 7m⁶ 6d³ 6m⁴ 6g 5g Oct 7] well-made colt: good walker: smart performer: best
efforts in 2007 when 1½ lengths second to Adagio in Craven Stakes at Newmarket and 2
lengths third to Balthazaar's Gift in Hackwood Stakes at Ascot: below form last 3 starts,
in Goldene Peitsche at Baden-Baden, Diadem Stakes at Ascot and Prix de l'Abbaye at
Longchamp: effective at 6f to 1m: acts on soft and good to firm going. *R. Hannon*

SONNY SAM (IRE) 2 b.g. (Mar 3) Black Sam Bellamy (IRE) 121 – Purple Risks **52**
(FR) 80 (Take Risks (FR) 116) [2007 7m 8m Sep 21] smallish, strong gelding: backward,
modest form in maidens: bred to stay at least 1m: gelded after final start. *M. H. Tompkins*

SON OF GREEK MYTH (USA) 6 b.g. Silver Hawk (USA) 123 – Greek Myth (IRE) –
58 (Sadler's Wells (USA) 132) [2007 –: p16g Mar 16] sturdy, quite attractive gelding:
maiden on Flat: well beaten both outings since 2005 (ungenuine hurdler): tried blinkered.
G. L. Moore

SON OF SPARTACUS (IRE) 2 ch.c. (Apr 15) Spartacus (IRE) 107 – Classic Silili –
(ITY) (Be My Guest (USA) 126) [2007 5m 7g 5m⁵ 5g⁵ p7.1g 7g Oct 19] compact colt:
little form: tried in blinkers/cheekpieces: sold 800 gns, sent to Serbia. *Mrs L. Stubbs*

SONOMA (IRE) 7 ch.m. Dr Devious (IRE) 127 – Mazarine Blue (USA) (Chief's **46**
Crown (USA)) [2007 15.4g⁴ Aug 16] sturdy mare: poor on Flat nowadays: stays 2m: acts
on good to firm and good to soft ground, seemingly not on soft: tried visored in 2005.
B. G. Powell

SONSUE 2 ch.f. (Mar 8) Auction House (USA) 120 – Sontime 65 (Son Pardo 107) [2007 –
5.1g 6.1g May 28] second foal: sister to 2006 2-y-o 5f winner Auction Time: dam 2-y-o
5f/6f winner: well beaten in maiden and seller (veered left). *B. Palling*

SOOPACAL (IRE) 2 b.g. (Jan 21) Captain Rio 122 – Fiddes (IRE) 52 (Alzao (USA) **79**
117) [2007 5v* p6g³ 6g⁵ 7g 7d⁵ 6m Nov 10] sturdy, deep-girthed gelding: fair on turf, **a88**
won maiden at Beverley in July: best effort (fairly useful form) when third in minor event
at Wolverhampton next time, only all-weather start: probably stays 7f: acts on polytrack
and heavy going: gelded after final start. *B. Smart*

SOPHIA GARDENS 3 ch.f. Barathea (IRE) 127 – Lovely Lyca 76 (Night Shift **70**
(USA)) [2007 72: p7g 7g⁴ p7m² p7.1g p7g p8m⁵ p8g Dec 29] fair maiden: stays 1m: acts
on polytrack, good to firm and good to soft ground. *D. W. P. Arbuthnot*

SOPHIE'S DREAM 3 b.g. Averti (IRE) 117 – Sophielu 80 (Rudimentary (USA) 118) **63**
[2007 57: f7g² p8g* f8g⁵ p8.6g 8.3g p8g Sep 12] sturdy gelding: modest performer: left
J. Given after reappearance: won claimer at Kempton in January: below form after:
free-going sort, stays easy 1m: acts on all-weather and good to soft going: has refused to
enter stall. *A. M. Hales*

SOPHIE'S GIRL 2 b.f. (Apr 1) Bahamian Bounty 116 – Merry Rous 66 (Rousillon **94**
(USA) 133) [2007 5.1m⁴ 5m² 6g 5m* 6m* 6.5m⁶ 6.5d³ 6g⁴ Nov 2] 50,000Y: unfurnished
filly: sister to 3 winners (all at least useful), including 6-y-o Paradise Isle and 4-y-o
Murfreesboro, and half-sister to several winners, including fairly useful 1994 2-y-o 5f
winner Bruton Stream (by Taufan): dam, 2-y-o 6f winner, half-sister to very smart sprinter Tina's Pet: fairly useful form: won maiden at Thirsk and nursery at Ripon in August:
ran well last 2 starts, third of 22 to Lady Rangali in sales race at Ascot and fourth to
Spinning Lucy in listed event at Newmarket: stays 6.5f: acts on soft and good to firm
going: races prominently. *P. W. Chapple-Hyam*

SOPHIES SECRET 2 b.f. (Mar 17) Superior Premium 122 – Funky 69 (Classic Music –
(USA)) [2007 7g 6f 8.1f Aug 27] stocky filly: second foal: dam, maiden (stayed 1m),
winning hurdler: no form. *J. R. Holt*

SOPRAN GATH (ITY) 4 b.f. Galileo (IRE) 134 – Theano (IRE) 114 (Thatching 131) **77**
[2007 74: p8.6g⁴ f8g⁴ 10d 10.2g⁴ p8g 8g 7f p12g⁵ p12g⁴ 11.9m³ p12.2g⁴ p12g³ p10g³
Oct 31] €35,000Y, €20,000 2-y-o: half-sister to 8-y-o Dexileos: dam Irish 6f to 9f winner:
fair maiden handicapper: trained by C. Collins in Ireland in 2006: stays 1½m: acts on all-
weather, good to firm and good to soft going: tried tongue tied: travels strongly: possibly
not straightforward. *J. W. Hills*

SORBIESHARRY (IRE) 8 gr.g. Sorbie Tower (IRE) 120 – Silver Moon (Environ- –
ment Friend 128) [2007 –, a62d: f12d⁵ p13.9d f8g³ Dec 27] leggy gelding: poor mover: **a47**
poor performer nowadays: effective at 1m to 1½m: acts on all-weather, raced only on
good ground or firmer on turf: often wears visor/cheekpieces. *Mrs N. Macauley*

SORREL POINT 4 b.c. Bertolini (USA) 125 – Lightning Princess (Puissance 110) **61**
[2007 62: p7m 7d Oct 23] modest maiden: stays 1m: acts on polytrack and good to soft
going. *H. J. Collingridge*

SORTITA (GER) 2 b.f. (May 4) Monsun (GER) 124 – Sacarina (Old Vic 136) [2007 **81 p**
8d² Oct 19] €750,000Y: smallish, angular filly: sister to Deutsches Derby winners
Samum (high class, also 7f/1m winner at 2 yrs) and Schiaparelli (very smart, also winner
up to 1¾m) and smart German 8.5f/11f (Preis der Diana) winner Salve Regina, and
half-sister to 2 winners in Germany: dam unraced: 15/2, neck second to General Eliott in
maiden at Newmarket, finishing strongly once getting hang of things: will be well suited
by 1¼m/1½m: sure to improve and win races. *M. A. Jarvis*

SOSUEME NOW 3 ch.f. Foxhound (USA) 103 – So Discreet (Tragic Role (USA)) **47**
[2007 –: 11.9m⁴ 12.1d⁵ 11.7f⁵ Aug 24] poor maiden: probably stays 11.7f: acts on firm
and good to soft ground. *A. B. Haynes*

SO SWEET (IRE) 3 b.f. Cape Cross (IRE) 129 – Announcing Peace (Danehill (USA)) **91**
126) [2007 97: 11.4m⁴ 9.9g 8m Jun 20] smallish, quite attractive filly: just fairly useful at
3 yrs: 7 lengths fourth to Light Shift in listed Cheshire Oaks at Chester on reappearance:
raced too freely after: stays easy 11.4f: acts on good to firm going: sold €125,000 in November. *M. R. Channon*

SOTIK STAR (IRE) 4 b.g. Elnadim (USA) 128 – Crystal Springs (IRE) 79 (Kahyasi **66**
130) [2007 92: f8g⁵ 8.1g 7g Nov 3] strong gelding: fairly useful at 3 yrs: fair form at best
in 2007: stays 1m: acts on polytrack, unraced on extremes of going on turf: tried tongue
tied: tends to hang. *P. J. Makin*

SOTO 4 b.g. Averti (IRE) 117 – Belle of The Blues (IRE) (Blues Traveller (IRE) 119) **72**
[2007 83: 5g 5f⁵ 6m 5m 6s⁶ 6d 6d⁵ 6m 6s 5.9g² 6m 5g⁴ 5g⁵ 6v⁵ Oct 26] small, leggy gelding: fair handicapper: won at Yarmouth in June: best form at 6f: acts on fibresand, firm
and soft going: sometimes starts awkwardly: usually races prominently. *M. W. Easterby*

SOUBRIQUET (IRE) 4 b.g. Daylami (IRE) 138 – Green Lucia 116 (Green Dancer **62**
(USA) 132) [2007 76d: 12g³ 10.1m 16.1m Sep 10] angular gelding: regressive maiden:
tongue tied last 3 starts, tried blinkered. *M. A. Barnes*

SOUL ANGEL 3 ch.g. Tipsy Creek (USA) 115 – Over Keen 58 (Keen 116) [2007 7m **54**
9.2s⁵ 9g⁴ 12.4d 9.1s⁶ Oct 26] modest maiden: left R. Hannon after debut: should stay
1¼m: tried in cheekpieces. *Miss S. E. Forster*

SOULARD (USA) 4 b.c. Arch (USA) 127 – Bourbon Blues (USA) (Seeking The Gold **–**
(USA)) [2007 76: p13.9g Feb 21] fair performer: blinkered, well held sole Flat start
in 2007: stays easy 13.8f: acts on firm ground: successful in visor: races freely.
J. L. Spearing

SOUL BLAZER (USA) 4 b.g. Honour And Glory (USA) 122 – See You (USA) **69 d**
(Gulch (USA)) [2007 74: p12g⁵ p12.2g⁴ 8m p8g 10.1d Aug 26] tall, good-bodied gelding:
regressive maiden: left A. Balding after second outing: may prove best short of 1½m: acts
on polytrack: tried in cheekpieces/visor. *Miss Gay Kelleway*

SOUL MOUNTAIN (IRE) 3 b.f. Rock of Gibraltar (IRE) 133 – Qhazeenah 101 **88**
(Marju 127) [2007 7m 10m³ 10.3d² 10g⁴ 10.5m* 9.8g⁴ 9.8m* 10.2f⁴ 12m p12.2g⁴
Oct 22] €220,000F: rather leggy, lengthy filly: fourth foal: half-sister to US Grade 2 8.5f
winner Girl Warrior (by Elusive Quality): dam, 6.5f (at 2 yrs)/7f winner, half-sister to Park
Hill Stakes winner Ranin: fairly useful performer: won maiden at Haydock in
August and handicap at Ripon (by length from Kalasam) in September: should be well
suited by 1½m+: acts on good to firm going, probably on polytrack. *B. W. Hills*

SOUNDASAPOUND 3 b.f. Pursuit of Love 124 – Blue Nile (IRE) 70 (Bluebird **–**
(USA) 125) [2007 60d: 9.8s 16.2s Jul 23] good-topped filly: little form since second start
at 2 yrs: tried in blinkers/cheekpieces. *I. W. McInnes*

SOUNDBYTE 2 b.g. (Apr 17) Beat All (USA) 120 – Gloaming 74 (Celtic Swing 138) **–**
[2007 8.2g Nov 7] angular gelding: tailed off in maiden at Nottingham. *J. Gallagher*

SOUND OF NATURE (USA) 4 b.c. Chester House (USA) 123 – Yashmak (USA) **101**
118 (Danzig (USA)) [2007 78p: 7m* 7m³ 10m* May 22] good-topped, attractive colt:
useful handicapper: won at Leicester in April (idled) and May (by 1¼ lengths from Shout,
always travelling easily): stays 1¼m: raced only on good/good to firm ground: has looked
highly strung at times: looked sort to make his mark in much stronger company, but
reportedly suffered injuries in horsebox on way to Royal Ascot in June. *H. R. A. Cecil*

SOURIRE 2 b.f. (Apr 26) Domedriver (IRE) 128 – Summer Night 94 (Nashwan (USA) **94 +**
135) [2007 p6g 7d* p7g² 7.1d p7g² p7g² 7m³ 7.1m* Sep 30] smallish filly: half-sister to
several winners, including smart performer up to 14.6f Songerie (7f/1m winner at 2 yrs),
4-y-o Souvenance (both by Hernando) and 3-y-o Soft Morning: dam, 6f winner from 2
starts, out of half-sister to Petoski: fairly useful form: won maiden at Catterick in July and
nursery at Musselburgh in September: will be suited by 1m: acts on polytrack, good to
firm and good to soft going: quirky, sometimes flashes tail. *Sir Mark Prescott*

SOUTHANDWEST (IRE) 3 ch.g. Titus Livius (FR) 115 – Cheviot Indian (IRE) 71 **94**
(Indian Ridge 123) [2007 93: 6m² 6g 6.1d² 7.1d⁶ 7m 5g⁵ 6m⁴ Aug 11] strong, lengthy
gelding: fairly useful performer: best effort in handicap at Ascot final start: free-going
sort, best at 5f/6f: acts on firm and good to soft going. *J. S. Moore*

SOUTH CAPE 4 b.g. Cape Cross (IRE) 129 – Aunt Ruby (USA) 67 (Rubiano (USA)) **103**
[2007 102: 8s 7s 7g* 7g⁵ 8m 7g 8m⁴ 8.1m⁵ 7m* 8m² 7g* 7m 7d 8g Nov 3] small, leggy
gelding: useful handicapper: won at Folkestone in June and Goodwood and Chester (beat
Thabaat by ½ length) in September: below form after: stays 1m: acts on any going:
sometimes races freely. *M. R. Channon*

SOUTH DAKOTA (IRE) 2 b.c. (Apr 19) Danehill Dancer (IRE) 117 – Moon Drop **97**
103 (Dominion 123) [2007 5m* 6g² 6m 6s² 6.3v⁴ 6m⁵ Sep 16] strong, lengthy colt:
closely related to 3 winners by Danehill, including useful Irish 2003 2-y-o 5f winner
Devil Moon and 3-y-o Abraham Lincoln, and half-brother to several winners, including
1996 2-y-o 6f winner Dancing Drop (by Green Desert) and 5f (at 2 yrs) to 7f winner
Moon King (by Cadeaux Genereux), both useful: dam sprinter: useful performer: won
maiden at Tipperary in May: mid-division in Coventry Stakes at Royal Ascot third start:
better efforts after when ¾-length second of 4 to Lizard Island in Railway Stakes and 1½
lengths fifth to Rock of Rochelle in listed race, both at the Curragh: will be suited by 7f:
acts on soft and good to firm going, below form on heavy: joined A. Cruz in Hong Kong.
A. P. O'Brien, Ireland

SOUTHERN BAZAAR (USA) 6 ch.g. Southern Halo (USA) – Sunday Bazaar **–**
(USA) (Nureyev (USA) 131) [2007 –: 12.1s 14.1m Sep 6] good-bodied gelding: modest
at 4 yrs, little form since: tried tongue tied/blinkered. *M. C. Chapman*

SOUTHERN MISTRAL 2 b.g. (Feb 17) Desert Prince (IRE) 130 – Hyperspectra 91 **71**
(Rainbow Quest (USA) 134) [2007 6f p6g⁴ p7g³ 8.3d⁵ Oct 1] good-bodied gelding: fair
maiden: twice in frame at Kempton: should be suited by 1m: acts on polytrack and good
to soft going: wore cheekpieces (didn't settle) final start: sold 22,000 gns. *W. J. Haggas*

SOUTHERN REGENT (IND) 6 b.g. Razeen (USA) – Allinda (IND) (Treasure Leaf **95**
(USA)) [2007 10g 9.8m 13.1s p12.2g² Oct 2] deep-girthed gelding: winner of 9 of his 32
starts in India for S. Ganapathy, notably Indian Derby at Mumbai in 2005: successful at
same course on reappearance in 2006 before placed several times in graded events: well
held in handicap at Nad Al Sheba on reappearance in 2007, only outing for S. Seemar in
UAE: off nearly 7 months, best effort in handicaps in Britain when 3 lengths second to
Tropical Strait at Wolverhampton: effective at 1m, has won up to 1¾m: acts on polytrack,
firm and soft going. *G. A. Swinbank*

SOUTH HILL 4 b.f. Marju (IRE) 127 – Briggsmaid 70 (Elegant Air 119) [2007 –: f8g **–**
Mar 15] neat filly: little form: reared and unseated rider leaving stall sole 4-y-o start.
R. J. Price

SOUTH O'THE BORDER 5 b.g. Wolfhound (USA) 126 – Abbey's Gal 100 (Efisio **75**
120) [2007 84: 12.3g May 11] good-topped gelding: fairly useful performer: seemed to
find stamina stretched sole 5-y-o outing: best form at 9f/1¼m: acts on polytrack, firm and
soft ground: has run well when sweating: tends to hang: races up with pace: consistent.
Miss Venetia Williams

SOUTHPAW LAD 2 b.c. (Feb 8) Diktat 126 – Ashantiana 64 (Ashkalani (IRE) 128) **74 +**
[2007 p7g⁴ p7g³ p7g* Nov 7] second foal: dam, maiden (stayed 1¼m), half-sister to smart
performer up to 9f Missile: fair form: won maiden at Kempton (did well after dropped
out) final start: will stay 1m: raced only on polytrack. *J. R. Best*

SOUTHSIDE STAR 3 ch.f. Singspiel (IRE) 133 – Samara (IRE) 108 (Polish Patriot **–**
(USA) 128) [2007 10m 10d 8.1d⁶ Aug 16] sparely-made filly: little sign of ability: dead.
H. J. L. Dunlop

SOUTHWARK NEWSBOY (IRE) 2 b.g. (Feb 5) Chevalier (IRE) 115 – Canoe **–**
Cove (IRE) 55 (Grand Lodge (USA) 125) [2007 7v 7f Jul 30] well held in maidens.
Mrs C. A. Dunnett

SOUTHWARKNEWSFLASH 3 b.f. Danetime (IRE) 121 – Enchanting Wood (IRE) **59**
(Woodborough (USA) 112) [2007 6m⁶ p7.1g³ p6m* p7.1g Sep 21] 1,500 2-y-o: first foal:
dam unraced out of half-sister to Rock of Gibraltar: modest performer: won maiden at
Wolverhampton in September: stays 6f: acts on polytrack: usually tongue tied (ran poorly
without final outing). *Mrs C. A. Dunnett*

SOUTHWEST STAR (IRE) 2 b.g. (Mar 10) No Excuse Needed 123 – Christening- **70**
present (IRE) (Cadeaux Genereux 131) [2007 p5g⁵ 5.1f⁵ p6g⁶ 6d 6g p7g² p6g² p6g²
p7.1g⁵ p7.1d⁴ p6g⁴ Dec 30] good-topped gelding: fair maiden: runner-up in 3 nurseries at
Kempton: effective at 6f/7f: acts on polytrack and firm going. *J. S. Moore*

SOUVENANCE 4 b.f. Hernando (FR) 127 – Summer Night 94 (Nashwan (USA) 135) **101**
[2007 110: 14g² 13m* 16v 16.4d 14g⁶ 12g² Sep 23] lengthy filly: useful performer: won
minor events at Killarney and Wexford (simple tasks) in May and listed race at Cologne

(by ¾ length from Rinconada, making most) in September: stays 2¼m: acts on good to firm and good to soft going: usually races prominently. *Sir Mark Prescott*

SOVEREIGN'S HONOUR (USA) 2 ch.f. (Mar 28) Kingmambo (USA) 125 – **65 p**
Chiming (IRE) 110 (Danehill (USA) 126) [2007 7m⁶ Aug 11] $550,000Y: big, strong
filly: first foal: dam Irish 7f to 1¼m winner: 11/2 and backward, sixth to Cape Amber in
maiden at Newmarket, best work late: will be suited to 1m/1¼m: sure to improve. *Sir Michael Stoute*

SOVEREIGN SPIRIT (IRE) 5 b.g. Desert Prince (IRE) 130 – Sheer Spirit (IRE) 86 **70**
(Caerleon (USA) 132) [2007 61, a77: p13g p13.9g 12.1m² p12.2g⁶ p12g⁴ p16g² p16g³
Oct 17] leggy gelding: fair handicapper: stays 2m: acts on all-weather, good to firm and
good to soft going: usually tongue tied nowadays, ran poorly only start in cheekpieces:
sold 16,000 gns, joined C. Gordon. *W. R. Swinburn*

SOVEREIGNTY (JPN) 5 b.g. King's Best (USA) 132 – Calando (USA) 110 (Storm **56**
Cat (USA)) [2007 77: p7.1g p7g p6g p7.1g p6g p7m⁵ p6g⁶ p6g⁴ p7g Dec 30] lengthy
gelding: just modest in 2007: stays 1m: acts on all-weather and good to firm going:
visored (found little) once at 4 yrs: tends to wander. *D. K. Ivory*

SOVIET PALACE (IRE) 3 b.g. Jade Robbery (USA) 121 – Daisy Hill (Indian Ridge **85**
123) [2007 88: 7m⁵ 7.1m⁴ 7g⁵ 7g 6g 7m 7g p8.6d* Dec 10] big, good-topped gelding:
fairly useful handicapper: won at Wolverhampton in December, wandering: stays 8.6f:
acts on polytrack and good to firm going: often races prominently. *K. A. Ryan*

SOVIET SCEPTRE (IRE) 6 ch.g. Soviet Star (USA) 128 – Princess Sceptre (Cad- **62**
eaux Genereux 131) [2007 60: 10.2d² 12.1m⁴ 10.2m Sep 7] lengthy gelding: modest
handicapper: effective at 1¼m to 1¾m: acts on polytrack, soft and good to firm going:
tongue tied. *Evan Williams*

SOVIET SOUND (IRE) 3 ch.g. Soviet Star (USA) 128 – Orange Grouse (IRE) 105 **55**
(Taufan (USA) 119) [2007 51: 6m 6d⁵ 5.9m⁵ 6s³ p7.1g 6d 6v 7m 8g Aug 13] good-bodied
gelding: modest maiden handicapper: stays 6f: acts on soft ground: tried blinkered. *Jedd O'Keeffe*

SOVIETTA (IRE) 6 b.m. Soviet Star (USA) 128 – La Riveraine (USA) 90 (River- **60**
man (USA) 131) [2007 61, a–: 12g 10.9d³ 11s⁵ 12.6s² 12.1s⁴ 14m p16g⁶ Nov 3]
modest handicapper: should stay 2m: acts on heavy and good to firm going: tongue tied.
A. G. Newcombe

SOVIET THREAT (IRE) 6 ch.g. Soviet Star (USA) 128 – Veiled Threat (IRE) 105 **52**
(Be My Guest (USA) 126) [2007 58: p8.6g p9.5g p8.6g⁴ f8g May 14] modest performer:
stays 8.6f: acts on polytrack: tried in cheekpieces/blinkers. *A. G. Juckes*

SOWDREY 3 b.g. In The Wings 128 – Baaderah (IRE) 102 (Cadeaux Genereux 131) **74**
[2007 77p: p12.2g² p12g³ 12g² 11.9g⁵ 12g² 11.9m³ 14g⁶ 14g⁴ 13.1f² 14.1m³ Aug 31]
leggy, attractive gelding: fair maiden: well worth a try at 2m: acts on firm ground, probably on polytrack: consistent: gelded, joined Evan Williams. *M. R. Channon*

SOWERBY 5 b.g. Grey Desire 115 – Brief Star (IRE) 49 (Brief Truce (USA) 126) [2007 **45**
46: f7g f7g⁶ f7g May 1] quite good-topped gelding: poor maiden: stays easy 7f: best
efforts on good going: tried blinkered. *M. Brittain*

SOXY DOXY (IRE) 2 ch.f. (Apr 14) Hawk Wing (USA) 136 – Feather Bride (IRE) **– p**
(Groom Dancer (USA) 128) [2007 8.2m Oct 3] €70,000Y: half-sister to several winners,
notably smart 7f (at 2 yrs)/1m (US Grade 3) winner Millennium Dragon (by Mark of
Esteem): dam French 10.5f winner: 16/1, needed run in maiden at Nottingham: should be
suited to 1m/1¼m: capable of better. *M. Johnston*

SOYLENT GREEN 3 b.f. Primo Valentino (IRE) 116 – Slipperose 72 (Persepolis (FR) **–**
127) [2007 –: 8.2g 8.3s 10f p9.5g 13.8g⁶ Sep 22] close-coupled filly: no form. *S. Parr*

SPACE PIRATE 2 b.c. (Apr 5) Bahamian Bounty 116 – Science Fiction (Starborough **58**
126) [2007 6m 7m 7g⁶ 8m⁵ 7g² 8d³ p8.6g Dec 3] leggy, close-coupled colt: has a round
action: modest maiden: placed in nurseries at Yarmouth: left M. Bell 16,000 gns before
final start: stays 1m: acts on good to firm and good to soft going. *J. Pearce*

SPACIOUS 2 b.f. (Apr 18) Nayef (USA) 129 – Palatial 101 (Green Desert (USA) **106 p**
127) [2007 7d* 8m* Sep 13]
    Given the fine record of his dam Height of Fashion, there was always a
certain degree of expectation attached to Nayef, firstly as a racehorse and now as a
stallion. Nayef proved a fine racehorse, nearly as good as his illustrious
half-brothers Unfuwain and Nashwan, but by the time Nayef put up his career-best
performance when second to Golan in the King George, both of those half-brothers

Frenchgate First For Fashion May Hill Stakes, Doncaster—Spacious and Kotsi (noseband), both daughters of Nayef, are first and second; Celtic Slipper (left) is third

were dead. Nashwan was put down after suffering complications during a routine operation on a hind-leg just six months after Unfuwain had died from a neurological condition. Both did well at stud, Nashwan's progeny headed by the top-class pair Bago and Swain, Unfuwain responsible for classic winners Lahan and Petrushka and a champion two-year-old in Alhaarth. It is now up to Nayef to maintain Height of Fashion's legacy and he has made a promising start, with seven individual two-year-old winners in his first crop. Though not the best of her sire's progeny (that honour going to the smart Confront), Spacious led home an impressive one, two for Nayef in the May Hill Stakes at Doncaster, beating Kotsi by half a length.

Spacious got her career off to a successful start in a maiden against colts at Leicester where she won by four lengths from Dr Faustus, with Alfathaa (also by Nayef) and Redford close behind in third and fourth, eight lengths clear of the remainder. The first four were all successful on their next start. Spacious then started favourite for the Frenchgate First For Fashion May Hill Stakes at Doncaster, Dr Faustus and Alfathaa having already franked her form. In the paddock beforehand she took the eye as a big, rangy, good sort, though still rather unfurnished. Confidently handled throughout by Jamie Spencer, she looked like running out a comfortable winner entering the final furlong, only to run green and edge left before getting the better of the runner-up. Celtic Slipper, Sugar Mint and Lady Jane Digby filled third, fourth and fifth, the first five pulling clear in a truly-run race, the form of which looks well up to standard. Celtic Slipper went on to win the Group 3 Premio Dormello at Milan by over five lengths next time.

Spacious (b.f. Apr 18, 2005)	Nayef (USA) (b 1998)	Gulch (b 1984)	Mr Prospector
			Jameela
		Height of Fashion (b 1979)	Bustino
			Highclere
	Palatial (b 1998)	Green Desert (b 1983)	Danzig
			Foreign Courier
		White Palace (b 1992)	Shirley Heights
			Blonde Prospect

Spacious' trainer James Fanshawe also trained most of her family, including the dam Palatial and year-older half-brother Artimino, both useful at seven furlongs and a mile. Palatial has two half-sisters of similar merit to herself in Ice Palace (a listed winner at a mile and a quarter) and Portal (listed-placed at up to a mile and a half in the latest season). It is early days to be predicting Nayef's propensity to transmit stamina, though it is probably fair to assume he will prove a stronger influence than Artimino's sire, Medicean. Given how well Spacious travelled on both her two-year-old starts, the One Thousand Guineas may prove her best chance of winning a domestic classic, though she should stay a mile and a quarter in due course. Spacious has plenty of physical scope and looks sure to train on, though she'll need to progress significantly to make a mark at Newmarket. The going was good to soft when she made her debut and good to firm at Doncaster. *J. R. Fanshawe*

SPANISH ACE 6 b.g. First Trump 118 – Spanish Heart 86 (King of Spain 121) [2007 **94** 90d: 5.1f* 5m* 5f⁶ f5g 5m⁴ 5m² 5.7g⁴ 5g 5g 5.6m 5.1m 6m 5g 6d 5.1m Oct 14] rather leggy, close-coupled gelding: fairly useful handicapper: won at Bath and Warwick in April: effective at 5f/6f: acts on firm and good to soft going: often wore headgear in 2004/5. *J. M. Bradley*

SPANISH AFFAIR 3 b.g. Pursuit of Love 124 – Catalonia (IRE) 76 (Catrail (USA) **–** 123) [2007 –: p8.6g f8g Mar 19] no form: dead. *Jedd O'Keeffe*

SPANISH AIR 3 b.f. Muhtarram (USA) 125 – Spanish Heart 86 (King of Spain 121) **–** [2007 57: p8.6g p6g⁵ 7m May 3] close-coupled filly: modest maiden at 2 yrs: well held in 2007: tried tongue tied. *J. W. Hills*

SPANISH BOUNTY 2 b.g. (Mar 10) Bahamian Bounty 116 – Spanish Gold 82 **90 ?** (Vettori (IRE) 119) [2007 5d 5.7g* 5.1d² 6m* 7g⁶ 6g p6g Sep 8] sturdy gelding: first foal: dam 8.5f winner: fairly useful performer: won maiden at Bath in June and minor event at Newmarket in July: below form after in listed/pattern races: best at 5f/6f: acts on good to firm and good to soft going: gelded after final start. *J. G. Portman*

SPANISH CONQUEST 3 b.g. Hernando (FR) 127 – Sirena (GER) (Tejano (USA)) **68** [2007 –p: p12m² p12g* p16g² p13.9g⁶ Nov 5] tall, leggy, useful-looking gelding: fair handicapper: won at Lingfield in October: stays 2m, will prove at least as effective at shorter: acts on polytrack. *Sir Mark Prescott*

SPANISH DIVA 3 b.f. Singspiel (IRE) 133 – Allespagne (USA) (Trempolino (USA) **86** 135) [2007 10m p11g 7m 11.5m³ 14g² 14m⁵ Sep 30] compact filly: fourth foal: sister to smart 1¼m to 2¾m winner Cruzspiel and half-sister to 1½m winner Larousse (by Unfuwain): dam, useful French 1½m/1¾m winner, out of smart Spanish mare up to 1½m Teresa: fairly useful maiden: stays 1¾m: raced only on polytrack and good/good to firm ground on turf: hung left penultimate start. *S. C. Williams*

SPANISH DON 9 b.g. Zafonic (USA) 130 – Spanish Wells (IRE) (Sadler's Wells **83** (USA) 132) [2007 –: 8g⁶ 8.5d 10d 9.7m⁵ 8.3f⁴ Aug 6] big, lengthy gelding: smart performer at best, fairly useful handicapper nowadays: stays 1¼m: acts on firm and soft ground: blinkered once: usually waited with: reportedly struck into on second outing. *D. R. C. Elsworth*

SPANISH HEROINE 2 br.f. (May 5) Kyllachy 129 – Spanish Heart 86 (King of Spain **–** 121) [2007 6m p6g 8.3m Sep 11] 25,000Y: close-coupled filly: half-sister to several winners, including 6-y-o Spanish Ace and 7f/1m winner Bold King (by Anshan), both useful: dam, 7f/1m winner, half-sister to smart sprinter Northern Goddess: last in maidens: tried in cheekpieces: sold 3,500 gns, sent to Spain. *P. Winkworth*

SPANISH HIDALGO (IRE) 3 b.c. Night Shift (USA) – Spanish Lady (IRE) 61 **111** (Bering 136) [2007 94: 10d³ 12v* 12g⁵ 14g⁶ 14m² 14d* 14d Nov 18] sturdy colt: improved this year as a smart performer, winning handicap in July and listed St Leger Italiano at Milan (made all, beat Ryan 1¾ lengths) in October: best efforts when sixth to Speed Gifted in Melrose Stakes (Handicap) at York and 2½ lengths second to Lion Sands in listed race at Newmarket in between: stays 1¾m: acts on any turf going. *J. L. Dunlop*

SPANISH MOON (USA) 3 b.c. El Prado (IRE) 119 – Shining Bright 98 (Rainbow **104 p** Quest (USA) 134) [2007 97p: 10.4d⁶ Oct 12] tall, attractive colt: won maiden at Newmarket only outing at 2 yrs: off 12 months (reported in mid-March to have suffered a setback), good 6 lengths sixth to Fairmile in minor event at York sole 3-y-o start, off bridle turning in: will be suited by 1½m: remains a smart prospect. *Sir Michael Stoute*

SPANISH NEEDLE 3 b.f. Green Desert (USA) 127 – Hasta (USA) (Theatrical 128) **68** [2007 p6g³ p6g 6m p7.1g³ p7.1g Nov 9] 57,000Y: small, quite attractive filly: fifth foal: half-sister to 1½m winner Exclusive Danielle (by Thunder Gulch) and 6f (at 2 yrs)/7f winner Stormy Monday (by Cadeaux Genereux): dam US 7f/8.5f winner: fair maiden: should stay at least 1m: acts on polytrack: very slowly away second and final outings: sold 8,000 gns. *P. R. Webber*

SPANISH SPRINGS (IRE) 2 b.f. (Apr 30) Xaar 132 – Crystal Gazing (USA) 114 (El Gran Senor (USA) 136) [2007 p7g³ Nov 4] half-sister to several winners, including smart UAE sprinter Conroy (by Gone West) and fairly useful Irish 1¼m winner Dark Veil (by Gulch): dam 6f/7f winner (including Rockfel and Nell Gwyn Stakes) and third in 1000 Guineas: 10/3, third in maiden at Lingfield: will stay 1m: open to improvement. *J. H. M. Gosden* **69 p**

SPARES AND REPAIRS 4 b.g. Robellino (USA) 127 – Lady Blackfoot 108 (Prince Tenderfoot (USA) 126) [2007 12g³ p12.2g³ f12d⁴ f12g⁴ Dec 27] good-bodied gelding: modest in bumpers: fair maiden on Flat: likely to be suited by 1¾m+: acts on all-weather. *Mrs S. Lamyman* **72**

SPARKBRIDGE (IRE) 4 b.g. Mull of Kintyre (USA) 114 – Persian Velvet (IRE) (Distinctly North (USA) 115) [2007 56: 8m 8.1s 10.2s 12.1m Sep 7] good-topped gelding: inconsistent maiden on Flat/over hurdles: left R. Fisher after reappearance: tried blinkered/tongue tied. *S. C. Burrough* **–**

SPARKLER 2 b.f. (Mar 15) Best of The Bests (IRE) 122 – Gem 58 (Most Welcome 131) [2007 5.7f Aug 24] 12,500Y: sixth foal: sister to 3-y-o Sun of The Sea and half-sister to 4-y-o Scarlet Knight: dam, maiden (stayed 9f), sister to useful stayer Wilcuma: 14/1, seventh to Good Gorsoon in maiden at Bath, plenty to do and not knocked about: will stay 7f/1m: capable of better. *P. Winkworth* **59 p**

SPARKLING EYES 3 b.f. Lujain (USA) 119 – Lady Georgia 94 (Arazi (USA) 135) [2007 77: p6g⁴ 6g² 5.2m* 6.1m² 6g⁵ 6m 6m⁵ 6g 5g 5m³ 5m⁶ p6g⁴ 7.1g⁴ Nov 8] leggy filly: fairly useful handicapper on turf, fair on all-weather: dead-heated at Yarmouth in April: stays easy 7f: acts on polytrack, good to firm and good to soft going. *C. E. Brittain* **80 a74**

SPARKLING MONTJEU (IRE) 2 b.f. (Feb 5) Montjeu (IRE) 137 – Dart Board (IRE) (Darshaan 133) [2007 7m p8.6g⁶ 8.1s⁴ Sep 29] 40,000Y: big, good-bodied filly: fourth foal: dam, French 1m/11f winner, half-sister to smart French miler Trojan Sea: modest form in maidens, staying-on fourth at Haydock: will be well suited by 1¼m/1½m: likely to make better 3-y-o. *J. W. Hills* **63 p**

SPARKLING SILVER 2 gr.f. (Mar 18) Silver Patriarch (IRE) 125 – Full English (Perugino (USA) 84) [2007 p6g p8m Dec 10] first foal: dam ran twice: well held in maidens at Kempton and Lingfield: should stay 1m. *D. K. Ivory* **–**

SPARK UP 7 b.m. Lahib (USA) 129 – Catch The Flame (USA) (Storm Bird (CAN) 134) [2007 64: p8.6g⁴ p8.6g⁶ p7.1g⁴ p6f⁴ Feb 24] smallish, quite attractive mare: modest handicapper: stays 8.6f: acts on all-weather, good to firm and good to soft going: wears headgear: sometimes slowly away. *J. W. Unett* **61**

SPARKWELL 5 b.g. Dansili 127 – West Devon (USA) (Gone West (USA)) [2007 76: p6g⁵ p5.1g p5g 5d 6f Aug 11] good-topped gelding: fair handicapper: effective at 5f to 7f: acts on polytrack and good to firm ground: said to have bled on first and final starts. *D. Shaw* **66**

SPARKY VIXEN 3 b.f. Mujahid (USA) 125 – Lucy Glitters (USA) 60 (Cryptoclearance (USA)) [2007 –: 7m³ 8m⁴ 7.1g⁵ 6m 7g 7d³ Oct 29] quite good-topped filly: modest maiden: stays 1m: acts on good to firm ground. *G. A. Swinbank* **57**

SPARTAN DANCE 3 ch.g. Groom Dancer (USA) 128 – Delphic Way 63 (Warning 136) [2007 65: 11.6d 11.7g 11.5s Jul 25] usual-looking gelding: maiden: soundly beaten in handicaps in 2007, refusing to settle: visored last 2 starts. *J. A. Geake* **–**

SPARTON DUKE (IRE) 2 b.c. (Apr 20) Xaar 132 – Blueberry Walk (Green Desert (USA) 127) [2007 6g 6m Jun 12] 42,000Y: half-brother to several fairly useful winners, including 1m winner Basserah (by Unfuwain) and French 1m (at 2 yrs)/1¼m winner Jungle Rambler (by Charnwood Forest): dam unraced sister to useful stayer Hawait Al Barr: modest form towards rear in maidens at Goodwood and Redcar (favourite): will be suited by 7f+. *E. J. O'Neill* **58**

SPATE RIVER 2 b.g. (Apr 13) Zaha (CAN) 106 – Rion River (IRE) (Taufan (USA) 119) [2007 6d Oct 15] sturdy gelding: 16/1, well held in maiden at Windsor: bred to stay 1m. *C. F. Wall* **–**

SPA WELLS (IRE) 6 ch.g. Pasternak 111 – La Tache 58§ (Namaqualand (USA)) [2007 48: 14m 7f 7g⁵ 17.8m 10.1m Sep 10] modest hurdler: lightly raced on Flat, easily best effort when fifth in maiden at Down Royal: tried blinkered, visored (well held in handicap at Newcastle) final outing. *Barry Potts, Ireland* **60**

SPEAGLE (IRE) 5 ch.g. Desert Sun 120 – Pohutakawa (FR) (Affirmed (USA)) [2007 **77** 89: p11g 8s 10.9m⁵ p16g 10g 10d 8.3m⁴ 10.2f⁵ 11.1m² 10.4m p10m⁶ p12.2g² p12.2d p9.5d⁵ p12.2d⁵ Dec 27] strong gelding: fair performer: left D. Carroll after twelfth start: stays 1½m: acts on all-weather/sand and firm going: usually forces pace. *A. J. Chamberlain*

SPECIAL BRANCH AMI (IRE) 2 ch.c. (Feb 28) Galileo (IRE) 134 – Helena's **57** Paris (IRE) (Peintre Celebre (USA) 137) [2007 p7g Sep 12] 190,000Y: first foal: dam, French 11f winner, half-sister to smart French 9f/1¼m winner Hidalguia: 12/1, middivision in maiden at Kempton won by Iguazu Falls: will be suited by 1¼m/1½m. *C. R. Egerton*

SPECIAL DAY 3 b.f. Fasliyev (USA) 120 – Mustique Dream 87 (Don't Forget Me **95** 127) [2007 79: 6g³ 6m² 6g² 6g⁵ 5g² 5g 6m Oct 4] leggy, lengthy filly: useful handicapper: placed 4 times in 2007: stays 6f: raced only on good/good to firm going: held up. *B. W. Hills*

SPECIAL FEATURE (IRE) 2 b.g. (Apr 5) Montjeu (IRE) 137 – Starring Role (IRE) **–** (Glenstal (USA) 118) [2007 8.3m 8g p7.1g⁴ Nov 9] sturdy gelding: little form in maidens: gelded after final start. *C. R. Egerton*

SPECIAL PLACE 4 b.g. Compton Place 125 – Petarga 87 (Petong 126) [2007 72: p7g **72** p8g p7g³ p8g² p7g* p7g³ p8g⁶ 7g 7m p8g³ p7g p7m⁴ p7g Nov 17] sturdy gelding: fair handicapper: won at Lingfield in April: stays 1m: acts on polytrack, lightly raced on turf: held up: not straightforward. *J. A. R. Toller*

SPECIAL RESERVE (IRE) 2 b.c. (Feb 4) Sadler's Wells (USA) 132 – Ionian Sea **– p** (Slip Anchor 136) [2007 8d Oct 19] 130,000Y: big, good-bodied colt: brother to Derby runner-up The Great Gatsby, also 8.5f winner at 2 yrs, and smart Irish 2003 2-y-o 7.5f winner Magritte, and half-brother to several winners, including useful French 11f/12.5f winner Ithaca (by Groom Dancer): dam, useful French 11.5f/1½m winner, half-sister to very smart 1½m performers Blue Stag and Oscar (both by Sadler's Wells): 8/1 and not wound up, weakened and eased in maiden at Newmarket: will be suited by 1¼m/1½m: should do better. *R. Hannon*

SPECIOSA (IRE) 4 b.f. Danehill Dancer (IRE) 117 – Specifically (USA) (Sky Classic **115** (CAN)) [2007 115: 9m² 8g 10s² 9.9m⁶ 8m 10d Oct 20] rangy filly: smart performer: successful in 2006 in 1000 Guineas at Newmarket: creditable second in 2007 in Earl of Sefton Stakes at Newmarket (4 lengths behind Manduro) and Pretty Polly Stakes at the Curragh (beaten 2 lengths by Peeping Fawn): below form otherwise: stayed 1¼m: had form on good to firm going, but easily best efforts on soft: got on edge in preliminaries when below form in Oaks at Epsom at 3 yrs: reportedly in season when well below form in Lockinge Stakes at Newbury on second outing and when forced to miss Falmouth Stakes at Newmarket intended fourth start: front runner: tended to hang left (did so throughout penultimate start), but was game: visits Oasis Dream. *Mrs P. Sly*

SPECKLED HEN (IRE) 4 b.f. Titus Livius (FR) 115 – Colouring (IRE) 79 (Catrail **–** (USA) 123) [2007 60: p6g p6g Jan 19] fair maiden at best: well held in Britain: stays 7f: tried blinkered. *D. Haydn Jones*

SPECTACULAR JOY (IRE) 3 b.g. Spectrum (IRE) 126 – Great Joy (IRE) (Grand **–** Lodge (USA) 125) [2007 60: p7.1g 8g 6g Jul 8] lightly-raced maiden: little form in 2007: tried in cheekpieces. *Mrs A. Duffield*

SPECTESTED (IRE) 6 ch.g. Spectrum (IRE) 126 – Nisibis (In The Wings 128) [2007 **§§** 55§: f14g 18g 21.6m Apr 23] tall gelding: fair performer at best: virtually refused to race second outing: one to avoid. *A. W. Carroll*

SPECTRANA 2 b.f. (Feb 21) Spectrum (IRE) 126 – Anapola (GER) (Polish Precedent **64** (USA) [2007 6m 7m⁵ 7g 8s 8d² p8m⁵ Nov 11] 15,000Y: second foal: dam German 7f/1m winner: modest maiden: second at Brighton: stays 1m: acts on good to soft going: tried blinkered. *Mrs A. J. Perrett*

SPEED DIAL HARRY (IRE) 5 b.g. General Monash (USA) 107 – Jacobina 71 **81 d** (Magic Ring (IRE) 115) [2007 86, a90: p12.2g⁴ p7g f8g³ f8g⁵ f8g p6g p6g 8g f8g⁵ Dec 27] smallish, sturdy gelding: fairly useful handicapper: left K. R. Burke after reappearance: on downgrade: stays 1½m: acts on all-weather and any turf going: wears headgear. *C. R. Dore*

SPEED DREAM (IRE) 3 ch.c. Pivotal 124 – Copper Creek 78 (Habitat 134) [2007 **102** 81: 9m* 6f⁴ 6m⁴ 5s 5s⁴ p5g 5g 5g Oct 7] €115,000Y: sturdy colt: half-brother to numerous winners, including 5f (including at 2 yrs)/6f winner Tipsy Creek (by Dayjur) and Irish 6f to 1m winner Abunawwas (7f winner at 2 yrs, by In The Wings), both smart: dam 6f winner: useful performer: won minor event at Tipperary in April: ran well after when fourth in listed race at Haydock (3¼ lengths behind Prime Defender) and handicap at Tipperary (to Senor Benny) third/fifth starts: effective at 5f/6f: acts on firm and soft ground: slowly away last 2 outings. *D. Wachman, Ireland*

SPEED GIFTED 3 b.c. Montjeu (IRE) 137 – Good Standing (USA) 93 (Distant View (USA) 126) [2007 12g* 12v⁵ 14g* Aug 23] 95,000Y: rather leggy colt: second foal: dam, 2-y-o 7f winner, out of useful 7f/1m performer Storm Dove: smart form: won maiden at Folkestone (ran green in rear long way) in June and Melrose Stakes (Handicap) at York (well-backed favourite, beat Celestial Halo by 2 lengths) in August: stays 1¾m: capable of better still. *L. M. Cumani* **114 p**

SPEED SONG 2 b.f. (Apr 3) Fasliyev (USA) 120 – Superstar Leo (IRE) 114 (College Chapel 122) [2007 5.1m³ 5.2g* 5m⁴ 6m Aug 28] rather leggy, lengthy filly: third foal: half-sister to 3-y-o Enticing: dam 2-y-o 5f winner (including Flying Childers Stakes): fair form: won maiden at Yarmouth in July: ran creditably in nurseries: will prove best kept to 5f/6f: acts on good to firm going. *W. J. Haggas* **77**

SPEED TICKET 3 b.c. Galileo (IRE) 134 – Kassiyra (IRE) (Kendor (FR) 122) [2007 p10m³ Oct 6] rather leggy colt: first foal: dam, French 1½m winner, half-sister to smart French stayer Kassani, out of half-sister to Derby winner Kahyasi: 9/1, green and looking well, caught the eye when 3½ lengths third to Prairie Tiger in maiden at Kempton, running on strongly under hands and heels: looks sure to improve. *L. M. Cumani* **77 p**

SPEED WINNER (AUS) 8 b.g. Danehill (USA) 126 – Think Twice (USA) (Alleged (USA) 138) [2007 p16g² p16g⁵ Jan 14] won 3 times up to 11f in Hong Kong prior to 2007: fit from hurdling (modest form), better effort on Flat in Britain when second in minor event at Kempton: stays easy 2m: raced on polytrack in Britain: often visored/blinkered. *G. L. Moore* **53**

SPEEDY DOLLAR (USA) 2 b.c. (Mar 4) Dixie Union (USA) 121 – Kelli's Ransom (USA) (Red Ransom (USA)) [2007 7m⁶ 7g⁶ Oct 26] $70,000Y, 60,000 2-y-o: medium-sized, good-bodied colt: second foal: dam, US maiden, half-sister to Breeders' Cup Juvenile runner-up Minister Eric, out of half-sister to smart performer up to 1¾m Salmon Ladder: fairly useful form in maidens, sixth to Fireside at Newmarket prior to winning at Doncaster (beat Tiger Dream by neck): will stay 1m: will continue to improve. *M. A. Jarvis* **93 p**

SPEEDY SAM 4 b.c. Medicean 128 – Warning Star 104 (Warning 136) [2007 103: f8g² a9f 10g³ p8.6g⁵ p10g 8.9s 10d⁴ 9.9g 10m² 10s p11g⁶ Dec 1] strong colt: useful handicapper: in-and-out form in 2007, best efforts when second at Southwell and Newbury (beaten 1¼ lengths by Monte Alto in John Smith's Stakes): effective at 1m/1¼m: acts on all-weather, unraced on firm ground but acts on any other turf: visored fourth outing. *K. R. Burke* **103**

SPEEDY SENORITA (IRE) 2 b.f. (Apr 11) Fayruz 116 – Sinora Wood (IRE) 70 (Shinko Forest (IRE)) [2007 5m² p5.1g² 5m² p5g⁵ 5m⁴ 5m³ 5g* p5.1g 5.3m* 5g⁵ 5g⁵ Nov 9] 5,200Y: sturdy filly: first foal: dam maiden: fair performer: won claimer at Hamilton in August and seller at Brighton in September: speedy, raced only at 5f: acts on polytrack and good to firm going: tried in cheekpieces. *K. R. Burke* **69**

SPELL CASTER 2 ch.f. (Jan 30) Bertolini (USA) 125 – Princess Claudia (IRE) 58 (Kahyasi 130) [2007 8.1f* 6.5d⁶ p8m⁶ Oct 11] 24,000Y: first foal: dam, staying maiden, half-sister to top-class miler Proclamation and smart stayer/hurdler No Refuge: fairly useful form: won maiden at Chepstow in August: didn't build on that, sixth in sales race at Ascot and nursery at Kempton: will be suited by 1¼m: acts on polytrack and firm going. *R. M. Beckett* **89**

SPELL CASTING (USA) 4 b.g. Kingmambo (USA) 125 – Copper Play (USA) (Fast Play (USA)) [2007 90: 10.4g 12m 10.1m² Aug 24] tall, quite good-topped gelding: fairly useful performer, lightly raced: won maiden at Newcastle in August: stays 1½m: acts on good to firm and good to soft going: not straightforward. *M. H. Tompkins* **90**

SPENT 2 b.c. (Mar 9) Averti (IRE) 117 – Top 74 (Shirley Heights 130) [2007 6g 6s⁶ 6g⁴ 8g⁵ 8.3d⁶ Oct 15] tall colt: fair maiden: stays 1m: raced only on good going or softer: sold 11,000 gns. *R. M. Beckett* **69**

SPHINX (FR) 9 b.g. Snurge 130 – Egyptale (Crystal Glitters (USA) 127) [2007 87: 14g² 14d³ 16d 14.1d* 13.1s² 13s³ 16s⁵ Oct 18] smallish, workmanlike gelding: useful handicapper: better than ever in 2007, winning at Nottingham (by 3 lengths from Olimpo) in August: good efforts when placed at Ayr and Hamilton within 3 days next 2 starts: stays 1¾m, not 2m: acts on polytrack, races mainly on good ground or softer on turf nowadays **96**

(acts on heavy): blinkered: has been bandaged behind: held up: consistent: sold 15,000 gns. *Jamie Poulton*

SPICE BAR 3 b.g. Barathea (IRE) 127 – Scottish Spice 92 (Selkirk (USA) 129) [2007 **61 +** 63: 8m⁶ 10.2f⁴ 11.7g 8m⁶ p10m⁵ p12m Oct 13] strong, close-coupled gelding: modest maiden: stays 1¼m: acts on all-weather and firm going: often in cheekpieces: reportedly finished lame third start: sold 10,000 gns. *A. M. Balding*

SPICE GARDENS (IRE) 3 ch.f. Indian Ridge 123 – Lime Gardens 113 (Sadler's **56** Wells (USA) 132) [2007 56p: 8.3d 6g³ p7g Oct 31] strong, lengthy filly: modest maiden, lightly raced: should stay 1m+: raced only on polytrack and good going or softer on turf: pulled too hard final outing. *W. Jarvis*

SPICE ROUTE 3 ch.g. King's Best (USA) 132 – Zanzibar (IRE) 113 (In The Wings **111** 128) [2007 10m 11.9g* 10.4g* 12d⁵ 13m⁴ 12d⁶ 10s⁶ Sep 22] small, well-made gelding: first foal: dam 11f (Oaks d'Italia) and 1½m winner: smart performer: won maiden at Haydock in April and handicap at York (beat Jeer by 1¾ lengths, hanging markedly right) in May: best efforts in listed race at Newmarket (length fourth to Tranquil Tiger) and Great Voltigeur Stakes at York (4¼ lengths sixth to Lucarno) fifth/sixth starts: stays 13f: acts on firm and good to soft going: gelded after final outing. *M. L. W. Bell*

SPICE TRADE 2 ch.c. (Feb 25) Medicean 128 – Nutmeg (IRE) 70 (Lake Coniston **79** (IRE) 131) [2007 6m 6d³ 8.2d⁴ p7.1s⁵ Dec 21] well-made colt: fair maiden: in frame at Haydock (third to Exclamation) and Nottingham: stays 1m: acts on good to soft going: visored (hung) final start. *J. Noseda*

SPIC 'N SPAN 2 b.g. (Apr 4) Piccolo 121 – Sally Slade 80 (Dowsing (USA) 124) [2007 **70** 6m p7g³ 6m p7.1g⁵ 6d² f7d Dec 14] good-topped gelding: fair maiden: left C. Cyzer 23,000 gns before final start: stays 7f: acts on polytrack and good to soft going. *R. A. Harris*

SPIDERBACK (IRE) 3 ch.g. Redback 116 – Geht Schnell (Fairy King (USA)) [2007 **88 §** 73: p10g⁶ 11.6m² p12g* 12g⁴ 11g⁶ 12m⁴ p11g⁵ 12f⁴ p12m⁴ p12.2g³ Oct 22] well-made gelding: fairly useful performer: won maiden at Kempton in May: better form in handicaps after when in frame: stays 1½m: acts on polytrack, soft and good to firm going: often blinkered: ungenuine: sold 24,000 gns, joined G. Lynch in Ireland, won on hurdling debut in December. *R. Hannon*

SPIFFING (IRE) 3 b.c. Indian Ridge 123 – Stunning (USA) 103 (Nureyev (USA) 131) **70** [2007 –: 6m⁵ 6d² 5.3s² 6s 6s⁶ p5.1g Oct 20] close-coupled colt: fair maiden: left K. Prendergast in Ireland after sole start at 2 yrs: ran poorly last 3 outings in 2007 (said to have had respiratory infection penultimate time): bred to stay at least 7f: acts on soft ground: tried blinkered: sold 6,000 gns, joined M. Hofer in Germany. *R. M. Beckett*

SPIN AGAIN (IRE) 2 b.c. (Apr 24) Intikhab (USA) 135 – Queen of The May (IRE) 80 **69 p** (Nicolotte 118) [2007 7s⁴ Oct 4] €9,000F, 28,000Y: third foal: half-brother to 4-y-o Radiator Rooney: dam, 5f/6f winner (including at 2 yrs), out of half-sister to smart 1m/9f performer Sign of Hope: 12/1, fourth to Blues Minor in maiden at Goodwood, needing experience: will do better. *R. M. Beckett*

SPINAIMANWIN (IRE) 3 ch.f. Spinning World (USA) 130 – Aiming Upwards **56** (Blushing Flame (USA) 109) [2007 58: 8d 10m 11.9g* 14d⁶ 16g 16g p16g⁴ p13.9g Oct 8] modest maiden handicapper: left Ms F. Crowley in Ireland after fourth start: stays 1¾m: raced mainly on good going or softer. *Ian Williams*

SPINAL TAP (IRE) 3 ch.g. Selkirk (USA) 129 – Glam Rock 102 (Nashwan (USA) **67** 135) [2007 7m⁴ p7g 8.1g⁶ p11g² 9.9s p11g⁶ p16g p16g Oct 4] tall gelding: fair maiden: stays 11f: acts on polytrack and good to firm going: blinkered/in cheekpieces last 4 starts: sold 5,000 gns. *C. R. Egerton*

SPINETAIL RUFOUS (IRE) 9 b.g. Prince of Birds (USA) 121 – Miss Kinabalu 50 **39** (Shirley Heights 130) [2007 54: p5g⁶ p6g 6g 5.2g 5g p5g 5.3d Aug 21] poor nowadays: effective at 5f to easy 7f: acts on all-weather, soft and firm going: often wears headgear: has been tongue tied. *Miss Z. C. Davison*

SPINNERET 3 ch.f. Pivotal 124 – Branston Jewel (IRE) 95 (Prince Sabo 123) [2007 **62** 7m p6g² 6s p8g Jul 10] 160,000Y: lengthy, angular filly: sixth foal: closely related to useful 5f/6f (including at 2 yrs) winner Falcon Hill (by Polar Falcon): dam, 2-y-o 5f winner, half-sister to Desert Deer (very smart at 1m/1¼m) and Branston Abby (smart at 6f/7f): modest maiden: best effort at 6f on polytrack: said to have bled final outing: sold 8,000 gns in December. *M. A. Jarvis*

SPINNING 4 ch.g. Pivotal 124 – Starring (FR) 74 (Ashkalani (IRE) 128) [2007 70: 8f⁵ **80** 8m³ 9.1g⁴ 8d² 7.9d 8s 8g 8m⁴ 10d⁶ 6m⁵ 7.2g² 7m 7.1d 7.1g* 7.2s* 8g⁴ p8.6g* Nov 16] leggy gelding: fairly useful handicapper: won at Musselburgh and Ayr in October and Wolverhampton in November: stays 8.6f: acts on polytrack, firm and soft going: usually blinkered. *T. D. Barron*

SPINNING COIN 5 b.m. Mujahid (USA) 125 – Cointosser (IRE) 66 (Nordico (USA)) **–** [2007 85: 14.1d Oct 3] quite good-topped, leggy mare: fairly useful handicapper: well below form in 2007, including over hurdles: in cheekpieces last 5 outings: has been reluctant to enter stall. *J. G. Portman*

SPINNING DANCER (IRE) 4 b.f. Spinning World (USA) 130 – Fair McLain (IRE) **–** 76 (Fairy King (USA)) [2007 –: f7g Jan 7] strong filly: no sign of ability: tried visored/blinkered. *J. R. Holt*

SPINNING DIXIE (IRE) 3 b.f. Spinning World (USA) 130 – Dixieline City (USA) **53** (Dixieland Band (USA)) [2007 p7g p7g p7f⁶ p8g 8g 11.6f Aug 6] leggy filly: third foal: dam unraced out of smart sprinter Central City: modest maiden at best: tongue tied. *J. A. Geake*

SPINNING GAME 3 b.f. Mind Games 121 – Spindara (IRE) 64 (Spinning World **53 §** (USA) 130) [2007 53§: f7s⁵ f5g³ f7g p5.1g f5g 6d 7g 7.5s 5m² 5m 5s² 5g⁴ 6d⁶ 5g 5m 5s Oct 4] leggy filly: modest performer: winner at 6f, probably best at 5f nowadays: acts on fibresand and any turf going: usually wears headgear: hung badly right/unseated rider fourth outing: often slowly away: quirky and inconsistent. *D. W. Chapman*

SPINNING GOLD 4 ch.f. Spinning World (USA) 130 – Blue Birds Fly 78 (Rainbow **–** Quest (USA) 134) [2007 –: p9.5g Sep 27] maiden: little form since 2005: tongue tied sole 4-y-o start. *Miss Gay Kelleway*

SPINNING LUCY (IRE) 2 ch.f. (Mar 29) Spinning World (USA) 130 – Dolara (IRE) **101** (Dolphin Street (FR) 125) [2007 5m³ 5m² 7m 6m³ 6g* 6g* Nov 2] €34,000F, €130,000Y: close-coupled, quite good-topped filly: has a quick, fluent action: fourth foal: half-sister to useful 2005 2-y-o 6f winner Midris (by Namid): dam unraced half-sister to smart 7f to 1¼m performer Idris: useful form: thrived in autumn, won maiden at Redcar and listed race at Newmarket (much improved, made all to beat Dubai Princess by length): seems best at 6f: raced only on good/good to firm going. *B. W. Hills*

SPINNING RIDGE (IRE) 2 ch.c. (Apr 15) Spinning World (USA) 130 – Summer **68** Style (IRE) 70 (Indian Ridge 123) [2007 6s p6g p6g⁶ p7.1g³ 7d p7g p6g* p6g⁵ Oct 17] fair performer: won maiden at Wolverhampton in October: stays 7f: acts on polytrack. *R. A. Harris*

SPINNING SOUND (IRE) 2 ch.c. (May 5) Spinning World (USA) 130 – Beryl 77 **89** (Bering 136) [2007 7s⁴ p7g* 8f⁴ 8f⁵ Dec 29] leggy, close-coupled colt: fifth foal: half-brother to 3 winners, including 4-y-o Glenmuir: dam 1½m winner: fairly useful form: won maiden at Lingfield in July (then left E. O'Neill): off 4 months, good efforts last 2 starts, in Grade 3 Generous Stakes at Hollywood (5¼ lengths fourth to The Leopard) and non-graded event at Santa Anita (4¼ lengths fifth to Yankee Bravo): stays 1m: acts on polytrack, firm and soft going. *P. Gallagher, USA*

SPIRITO DEL VENTO (FR) 4 b.g. Indian Lodge (IRE) 127 – Heavenly Song (FR) **122** (Machiavellian (USA) 123) [2007 a7.5g² 7s* 8g³ 8m* 8d³ 8d* 8g⁶ Dec 9] €28,000Y:

Prix Daniel Wildenstein Castel Marie-Louise de La Baule, Longchamp—Spirito del Vento quickens to take over from Racinger (left); both Blythe Knight (blaze) and Bertranicus catch the weakening Echo of Light (cheekpieces) to make the frame

good-topped gelding: second foal: dam, ran twice in France, half-sister to US Grade 3 8.5f winner Heaven's Command: very smart performer: improved in 2007, winning minor event at Longchamp in April, Prix du Chemin de Fer du Nord at Chantilly (by 2 lengths from Multiplex) in June and Prix Daniel Wildenstein Castel Marie-Louise de La Baule at Longchamp (finished strongly from rear to beat Racinger 2 lengths) in October: not discredited when running-on sixth to Good Ba Ba in Hong Kong Mile at Sha Tin final start: stays 1m: acts on all-weather at Deauville, soft and good to firm going: has worn cheekpieces/blinkers (not in 2007): held up. *J-M. Beguigne, France*

SPIRIT OF ADJISA (IRE) 3 b.g. Invincible Spirit (IRE) 121 – Adjisa (IRE) (Doyoun 124) [2007 66: 7.1m⁴ p8.6g⁵ 10.2m 10.2m⁶ 10d* p12g* p12.2g³ Nov 19] leggy gelding: fairly useful handicapper: won at Brighton and Kempton in October: effective at 1¼m/1½m: acts on polytrack, good to firm and good to soft going: blinkered last 3 starts: edgy sort, reared leaving stall second outing. *Pat Eddery* **84**

SPIRIT OF A NATION (IRE) 2 b.c. (Feb 20) Invincible Spirit (IRE) 121 – Fabulous Pet (Somethingfabulous (USA)) [2007 6d Oct 12] good-topped, quite attractive colt: half-brother to several winners, notably smart 1½m to 1¾m winner Murghem (by Common Grounds): dam Irish 1½m winner: 20/1, burly and green, eighth to Calming Influence in maiden at York, very slowly away: likely to stay 1m: will improve. *D. J. Murphy* **60 p**

SPIRIT OF AROSA (IRE) 4 b.f. Dansili 127 – Vettorina (IRE) (Vettori (IRE) 119) [2007 83: 7m 8f⁶ Oct 27] sturdy filly: fairly useful performer: said to have bled on reappearance, then left J. Akehurst: stays 1m: acts on firm and soft going: blinkered final start. *J. M. Cassidy, USA* **81**

SPIRIT OF CONISTON 4 b.g. Lake Coniston (IRE) 131 – Kigema (IRE) 58 (Case Law 113) [2007 66: f5g* p5.1g² p5g⁵ p5.1g f5g* f5g⁴ f5g⁶ p5.1g* p5.1g² 5m³ 5g⁵ 5d 5d⁵ 5m 6f p5.1g 5s² p5g* 5g* p5.1g² Nov 9] stocky gelding: fair performer: won claimers at Southwell in January and February (left Peter Grayson), and handicaps at Wolverhampton in May (left C. Teague after sixteenth outing) and Kempton and Catterick (24 hrs apart) in October: races mostly at 5f: acts on all-weather, firm and soft going: often wears headgear, though not for present stable: sometimes hangs left. *D. Nicholls* **76**

SPIRIT OF ECSTACY 3 b.f. Val Royal (FR) 127 – Isla Negra (IRE) (Last Tycoon 131) [2007 –: 9.8g³ 10.1d 9.2g 8m Sep 20] tall, leggy filly: modest maiden: stays 9.8f: said to have breathing problem second outing, and tongue tied last 2 starts. *G. M. Moore* **52**

SPIRIT OF SHARJAH (IRE) 2 b.c. (Mar 17) Invincible Spirit (IRE) 121 – Rathbawn Realm (Doulab (USA) 115) [2007 5m* 5g* 5m³ 6m 5g⁶ 5m² 5d Oct 13] 8,000F: tall, rather leggy, useful-looking colt: half-brother to several winners, including fairly useful 6f winner (including at 2 yrs) Blundell Lane (by Shalford) and fairly useful 1999 2-y-o 5f winner Lost In Hook (by Dancing Dissident): dam Irish 5f (at 2 yrs) and 7f winner: useful form: won minor event at Newmarket in April and listed race at Goodwood in May: placed in Norfolk Stakes at Royal Ascot (1¼ lengths third to Winker Watson) and, having left Miss J. Feilden, Flying Childers Stakes at Doncaster (best effort, 1¾ lengths second to Fleeting Spirit): best at 5f: acts on good to firm going: has run well when sweating. *P. W. Chapple-Hyam* **105**

SPIRIT OF THE MIST (IRE) 3 ch.g. Trans Island 119 – Exciting (Mill Reef (USA) 141) [2007 84: 8.2m³ 10.1g³ 10.4g p8m p10g f8d² Dec 20] rangy gelding: fairly useful performer: trained by T. Pitt first 3 starts: stays 1¼m: acts on polytrack, good to firm and good to soft ground: tried blinkered (below form). *D. J. Murphy* **86**

SPIRITOFTHESTORM (USA) 2 b.f. (Feb 3) Mizzen Mast (USA) 121 – Southern Issue (USA) (Southern Halo (USA)) [2007 p8g⁴ p8g² p8g⁴ p8m Nov 11] $25,000FT: first foal: dam, US maiden, half-sister to US Grade 2 7f winner Smooth Jazz: fair maiden: raced only at Kempton, in frame first 3 starts: may prove best up to 1m. *R. A. Teal* **72**

SPIRITOFTHETIGER (USA) 2 ch.f. (Feb 28) Hold That Tiger (USA) 117 – Royal Malt (IRE) (Royal Academy (USA) 130) [2007 p7g² 7f⁴ p8g⁴ p7g³ p7.1g² Nov 30] $12,000Y: rather leggy filly: fourth foal: half-sister to winner in US by In Excess: dam, maiden in US, half-sister to Japan Cup winner Horlicks, herself dam of Melbourne Cup winner Brew: fair maiden: in frame all starts: stays 1m: acts on polytrack, probably on firm going. *R. A. Teal* **68**

SPIRITONTHEMOUNT (USA) 2 b. or br.c. (Mar 22) Pulpit (USA) 117 – Stirling Bridge (USA) (Prized (USA)) [2007 7s⁵ 8g⁶ Oct 24] $80,000Y, resold $105,000Y, resold 62,000Y: fourth foal: half-brother to US 5f (at 2 yrs) to 8.5f winner Fire Path (by Tale of **68 p**

The Cat) and minor US winner around 1m (including at 2 yrs) Great Bridge (by Albert The Great): dam US 6.5f to 8.5f (minor stakes) winner: fair form in maidens at Folkestone and Bath (still green, sixth to Colony): stays 1m: capable of better. *B. W. Hills*

SPIRIT RISING 3 gr.g. Zilzal (USA) 137 – River's Rising (FR) 88 (Mendez (FR) 128) – [2007 46: 6.1m 8g 8f 6g⁶ 7f 8f 10.2m Sep 13] tall, close-coupled gelding: maiden: no form in 2007: tried in cheekpieces. *J. M. Bradley*

SPIRITUAL PEACE (IRE) 4 b.g. Cadeaux Genereux 131 – Emerald Peace (IRE) **83 d** 103 (Green Desert (USA) 127) [2007 91: 5g³ 5f 5d 6s³ 5s⁴ 6d* 5d⁴ 5d 7.1m Sep 30] lengthy, quite good-topped gelding: fairly useful performer: below form after reappearance, but still won claimer at Hamilton in July: stays 6f: acts on polytrack, good to firm and good to soft going: in cheekpieces/blinkers: sold 5,000 gns. *K. A. Ryan*

SPITFIRE 2 b.g. (Mar 30) Mujahid (USA) 125 – Fresh Fruit Daily 92 (Reprimand 122) **98** [2007 5.5d* 6d* 6m p6g⁴ 6m* 6g 6g⁴ Oct 27] 19,000Y: good-topped gelding: fifth foal: half-brother to several winners, including useful 5f to 1m winner Fruit of Glory (by Glory of Dancer) and 4-y-o Mr Cellophane: dam 1¼m/1½m winner: useful performer: won maiden at Warwick in May and minor events at Yarmouth later in May and Doncaster (beat Art Sale by neck) in September: fourth to Floristry in listed race at Doncaster final start: should prove best at 5f/6f: acts on good to firm and good to soft going: free-going type, suited by well-run race. *J. R. Jenkins*

SPITFIRE JANE (IRE) 2 b.f. (Mar 7) Xaar 132 – Hope of Pekan (IRE) (Sri Pekan **57** (USA) 117) [2007 p7g p7.1d⁴ Dec 7] €5,500F, €25,000Y: third foal: half-sister to winner in Italy by Docksider: dam won in Italy up to 11f: modest form in maidens at Lingfield and Wolverhampton. *K. R. Burke*

SPLASH THE CASH 2 b.g. (Mar 27) Lomitas 129 – Bandit Queen 90 (Desert Prince **64** (IRE) 130) [2007 5.7g⁶ 5s⁴ p5g² p5g 5m 5.1m⁶ p6g³ p7g² f7d Dec 18] modest maiden: claimed from P. Winkworth £5,000 seventh start: good second in nursery at Lingfield next time: stays easy 7f: acts on polytrack, soft and good to firm going. *K. A. Ryan*

SPLENDIDIO 3 b.f. Zamindar (USA) 116 – Diddymu (IRE) 66 (Revoque (IRE) 122) **58** [2007 52: p5g p6g³ p6g⁵ f5g⁶ p8g p8g f6g⁶ 6m⁴ 5d 5m⁴ 5s 6g⁵ 5f* 5.1g p6g Nov 20] unfurnished filly: modest performer: left D. Ivory after fifth start: won minor event at Folkestone in September (final outing for Mrs M. Fife): best at 5f: acts on all-weather and firm going: tried blinkered. *A. Crook*

SPLINTER GROUP 3 ch.c. Inchinor 119 – Haiyfoona (Zafonic (USA) 130) [2007 – 10m 10m May 25] sturdy, lengthy colt: well held in maidens. *N. A. Callaghan*

SPLIT BRIEFS (IRE) 3 b.f. Mull of Kintyre (USA) 114 – Jay Gee (IRE) 93 (Second **64** Set (IRE) 127) [2007 71: 8.2m p10g⁶ p8.6g⁴ p8g² p9.5g⁵ 8d⁴ 8d p7.1g Nov 9] good-bodied filly: modest maiden: left D. Daly after fifth start: stays 8.6f: acts on polytrack, good to firm and good to soft going. *C. A. Dwyer*

SPLITTHEDIFFERENCE 2 b.g. (May 1) Hunting Lion (IRE) 115 – Sky Light **68** Dreams (Dreams To Reality (USA) 113) [2007 p5g 5f* 6g May 20] leggy gelding: second foal: dam unraced: fair form: won claimer at Thirsk (left M. Channon £8,000) in April: form only at 5f: acts on firm going. *D. Carroll*

SPLIT THE WIND (USA) 3 ch.f. Just A Cat (USA) – Maple Hill Jill (USA) (Execu- **64** tive Pride 127) [2007 –: 8.2m⁵ p8g⁶ 9g² 9.7m 9.9g 9.9m⁴ p8g⁴ p8g⁵ Oct 10] sturdy, medium-sized filly: modest maiden: stays 1¼m: acts on polytrack and good to firm going. *Eve Johnson Houghton*

SPLODGER MAC (IRE) 8 b.g. Lahib (USA) 129 – Little Love (Warrshan (USA) – 117) [2007 58: 9.9g⁶ 9.9m 9m 8g 8.5g Aug 15] sturdy gelding: modest performer at best: no form in 2007: tried blinkered. *N. Bycroft*

SPOILSPORT 4 b.f. Muhtarram (USA) 125 – Spoilt Again 91 (Mummy's Pet 125) **47** [2007 57: p10g p8g 7s 8d⁶ Jun 16] maiden: poor at best in 2007, leaving P. D. Evans after second start: tried blinkered/in cheekpieces. *G. A. Butler*

SPOILT MADAME 2 b.f. (Apr 29) Bertolini (USA) 125 – Madame Jones (IRE) 79 – (Lycius (USA) 124) [2007 6m p7.1g p7.1g Oct 25] third foal: sister to 3-y-o Put It On The Card: dam 6f to 9.4f winner: no form. *P. D. Evans*

SPOOF MASTER (IRE) 3 b.g. Invincible Spirit (IRE) 121 – Talbiya (IRE) (Mujtahid **87** (USA) 118) [2007 86: p6g⁵ 6.1m 5g⁵ p6g f5d Dec 11] sturdy gelding: fairly useful handicapper: left W. Turner after third start: has form at 6f, but likely to prove best at 5f: acts on polytrack, firm and soft going. *N. A. Callaghan*

SPOOKY 2 br.g. (Mar 6) Vettori (IRE) 119 – Aneen Alkamanja (Last Tycoon 131) [2007   –
6m 7g 7g 7.2v Nov 3] lengthy, workmanlike gelding: no form. *W. Storey*

SPORTING ART (USA) 2 b.c. (Mar 2) Doneraile Court (USA) – Playful Run (USA)   **95**
(Run Softly (USA) 114) [2007 6m* 6m* p6g⁴ 8m⁴ Sep 15] $17,000F, $20,000Y, 45,000
2-y-o: robust colt: second foal: dam unraced half-sister to US Grade 1 1¼m/11f winner
Defensive Play: useful form: won maiden at Ascot in July and minor event at Ripon in
August: creditable fourth in Sirenia Stakes at Kempton (3 lengths behind Philario) and
listed race at Goodwood: stays 1m: acts on polytrack and good to firm going: sold
220,000 gns. *G. L. Moore*

SPORTING GESTURE 10 ch.g. Safawan 118 – Polly Packer 81 (Reform 132) [2007   **80**
85: 12.4m 12g³ 12d³ 12.1g² 13.8m² 12g² 12.3m⁵ 12f* 12d² 12d 13.8g³ Nov 6] rather
leggy, close-coupled gelding: has a round action: fairly useful handicapper: won amateur
event at York in September: stays 13.8f: acts on firm and good to soft going: tried blinkered in 2002. *M. W. Easterby*

SPOTONCON 6 b.g. Contract Law (USA) 108 – Emma Victoria (Dominion 123)   –
[2007 –: p10g⁶ p9.5g Jan 12] no form: tried blinkered. *A. J. Lidderdale*

SPOT THE SUBBIE (IRE) 4 b.g. Tagula (IRE) 116 – Agent Scully (IRE) 66 (Simply   **73**
Great (FR) 122) [2007 61: p8g* p8g* p10g² p8g⁶ p8g Apr 1] fair handicapper: won at
Kempton and Lingfield in January: stays 1¼m: acts on polytrack, firm and good to soft
going: tried in cheekpieces: joined F. Cottin in France. *Jamie Poulton*

SPRIGGAN 3 b.c. Ishiguru (USA) 114 – Hope Chest 70 (Kris 135) [2007 76p: 6g³ 7m²   **84**
8g² 7m² p7.1g* 8m p8m Oct 6] sturdy colt: fairly useful performer: landed odds in
maiden at Wolverhampton in August: has form at 1m, but may prove best at shorter: acts
on polytrack, raced only on good/good to firm ground on turf: sold 25,000 gns. *C. G. Cox*

SPRING CITY (GER) 3 ch.c. Monsun (GER) 124 – Spirit of Eagles (USA) (Beau's   **94**
Eagle (USA)) [2007 10d² 10d² 10d* Jul 23] big, angular colt: half-brother to several
winners in Germany, notably high-class 1¼m/11f winner Silvano (by Lomitas) and very
smart 1¼m to 1½m winner Sabiango (by Acatenango): dam, US 6f to 1m winner, sister
to US Grade 3 2-y-o 1m winner Best Pal: fairly useful form: won maiden at Windsor in
July by 4 lengths from Torba: better form when second to Black Rock at Sandown second
outing: will stay 1½m: unseated rider and bolted to post intended third outing. *Saeed bin
Suroor*

SPRING CREEK 3 b.f. Tipsy Creek (USA) 115 – Christening (IRE) (Lahib (USA)   **51**
129) [2007 8m⁶ 11.5d⁶ 12g p8.6g Nov 2] lengthy filly: sixth foal: half-sister to 6f and 9.5f
winner Star Fern (by Young Ern): dam unraced: form only when sixth to Distant Pleasure
in maiden at Redcar on debut: pulled too hard final outing. *M. W. Easterby*

SPRING DREAM (IRE) 4 gr.f. Kalanisi (IRE) 132 – Zest (USA) (Zilzal (USA) 137)   **73**
[2007 79: 12g⁵ 12f⁶ p16g 13.1m* 12.1g³ 16m⁴ 14.8d Jun 23] leggy filly: fair handicapper:
won at Bath in May: stays easy 2m: acts on polytrack and good to firm going: joined
A. King. *M. R. Channon*

SPRING GLORY 3 b. or gr.f. Dr Fong (USA) 128 – Doctor Bid (USA) (Spectacular   **73**
Bid (USA)) [2007 66p: f8g p10g² p12f* Feb 24] fair performer, lightly raced: won
maiden at Lingfield in February by 2½ lengths from Into Action: stays 1½m: acts on
polytrack (unraced on turf): sold 31,000 gns in July (reportedly in foal to Kyllachy). *Sir
Mark Prescott*

SPRING GODDESS (IRE) 6 b.m. Daggers Drawn (USA) 114 – Easter Girl (Efisio   **84**
120) [2007 79, a89: p7g⁶ p8g³ p8g* 8.2g² 7m 7s⁵ p8g⁵ 9g p11m p8g* Dec 1] good-topped
mare: fairly useful handicapper nowadays: won at Lingfield in April and Kempton
in December: stays 1¼m: acts on polytrack and good to firm going: has raced freely.
A. P. Jarvis

SPRING STYLE (IRE) 2 ch.f. (Mar 23) Pivotal 124 – Clear Spring (USA) (Irish   **66 p**
River (FR) 131) [2007 p8.6g³ Nov 17] second foal: dam, French maiden, closely related
to smart French 7.5f (at 2 yrs) and 10.5f winner Dark Nile, out of half-sister to very smart
1¼m performer Kefaah: 16/1, encouraging third to Wing Play in maiden at Wolverhampton: sold 42,000 gns, sent to USA: should improve. *E. J. O'Neill*

SPRING TIME GIRL 5 b.m. Timeless Times (USA) 99 – Daira 72 (Daring March   **51**
116) [2007 53: 7.9m³ 8.1d³ 8d⁵ Jun 25] modest performer: stays 1¼m: acts on polytrack,
firm and good to soft ground: usually wears headgear (not in 2007): sometimes slowly
away. *B. Ellison*

SPRITZA (IRE) 3 b.f. Spectrum (IRE) 126 – Starlight Smile (USA) (Green Dancer   **71**
(USA) 132) [2007 71: p8g² p10g³ 12.4m² 11m⁵ 10s³ 12m⁴ 11.1g* p12g⁵ p12g* p12m

Oct 3] angular filly: fair performer: won maiden at Hamilton in August and handicap at Kempton in September: folded as if amiss final outing: stays 1½m: acts on polytrack, firm and soft going: sold 50,000 gns. *M. L. W. Bell*

SPROUSTON (FR) 4 ch.g. Grand Lodge (USA) 125 – River Fantasy (USA) (Irish River (FR) 131) [2007 –: 10m Jul 11] tall gelding: fair maiden at 2 yrs: little form since: tried blinkered/in cheekpieces. *Karen George* —

SPUME (IRE) 3 b.g. Alhaarth (IRE) 126 – Sea Spray (IRE) 101 (Royal Academy (USA) 130) [2007 85p: 10g⁶ 10.4g 8.1s³ 8s⁶ 8m* 7.9g 9g 8.1g 8.1m 7.5d 7g 10g⁵ Oct 31] strong, lengthy gelding: fairly useful handicapper: left Sir Michael Stoute prior to winning at Thirsk in August: below form after: best around 1m: acts on soft and good to firm going: tried blinkered, usually tongue tied: seems none too genuine. *D. J. Murphy* — 85

SPUNGER 4 b.f. Fraam 114 – Complimentary Pass 80 (Danehill (USA) 126) [2007 –: 11.5m⁵ 12m⁵ 10d⁴ 10.2f³ 10.2m* p9.5g⁵ 10.2m 12d⁵ p11g p10m Dec 9] quite attractive filly: fair handicapper: won at Chepstow in September: stays 11.5f: acts on polytrack, firm and good to soft ground: visored. *H. J. L. Dunlop* — 73

SPURRON (IRE) 7 b.m. Flying Spur (AUS) – The Realtour 84 (Warning 136) [2007 54: p9.5g 9.5m³ 8g⁴ 10d 8s 9m p8g Dec 7] medium-sized mare: poor maiden handicapper: below form at Wolverhampton on reappearance: stays 9.5f: acts on heavy and good to firm ground: sometimes slowly away. *G. Keane, Ireland* — 48

SPY GAME (IRE) 7 b.g. Definite Article 121 – Postie (Sharpo 132) [2007 56: p12.2g Jul 16] ex-Irish gelding: fairly useful at 2/3 yrs, lightly raced and well held on Flat since: tried blinkered/visored. *Jennie Candlish* —

SPY GUN (USA) 7 ch.g. Mt Livermore (USA) – Takeover Target (USA) (Nodouble (USA)) [2007 –§, a55§: p8.6g⁶ p7.1g⁴ p7.1g³ p7.1g f7g⁴ p7.1g p9.5g f8g⁵ p8.6g⁵ f6g f8g³ f8g f7g⁵ 5.1s 7d p9.5g p6g⁴ p6g p6d⁵ f6d Dec 11] angular, useful-looking gelding: modest performer: stays 9.5f, effective at much shorter: acts on all-weather, soft and good to firm going: often wears headgear: has been slowly away: unreliable. *T. Wall* — 53 §

SQUADRON 3 b.g. Sakhee (USA) 136 – Machaera (Machiavellian (USA) 123) [2007 66: 11.6d⁵ 14g² 14g* 14.1s* 14g 14.1d⁴ 16d³ Oct 11] well-made gelding: fairly useful handicapper: won at Goodwood in June and Salisbury in July: stays 2m: raced only on polytrack and good ground or softer on turf: has carried head high: sold 65,000 gns, joined A. King. *Mrs A. J. Perrett* — 83

SQUARE DEALER 6 b.g. Vettori (IRE) 119 – Pussy Foot 83 (Red Sunset 120) [2007 12m⁶ 12m⁵ 12s 14.1m⁵ 15.8g⁴ 15.8g Sep 22] leggy gelding: modest maiden: stays 2m: acts on good to firm going: blinkered since debut. *J. R. Norton* — 59

SQUIFFY 4 b.g. Kylian (USA) – Cebwob 85 (Rock City 120) [2007 59: 11.7d f14g⁶ 16.2d* 16.2v³ p16g p12g Nov 19] leggy, close-coupled gelding: modest handicapper: won at Warwick in June: stays 2m: acts on polytrack and any turf going. *P. D. Cundell* — 62 a53 +

SQUIRREL TAIL 4 ch.g. Band On The Run 102 – Crees Sqaw (Cree Song 99) [2007 –: 10d 10f Aug 6] lengthy, workmanlike gelding: little form in maidens. *E. S. McMahon* —

SQUIRTLE (IRE) 4 ch.f. In The Wings 128 – Manilia (FR) (Kris 135) [2007 76: 12m⁵ 15d⁵ 13.1m⁴ 11.9s⁴ 17.2f⁶ 14.1d 15g³ p16.5g³ 14m² p13.9g 16.2m⁶ p16g 15.8s³ p12.2g⁴ p13.9g⁴ p16.5g² p13.9d³ p13.9g⁴ Dec 31] workmanlike filly: fair handicapper: stays 2m: acts on polytrack, firm and good going: has been visored: often slowly away: tends to run in snatches, and not one to trust. *W. M. Brisbourne* — 68 §

SRI DIAMOND 7 b.g. Sri Pekan (USA) 117 – Hana Marie 101§ (Formidable (USA) 125) [2007 114: p12g* p10m⁶ Apr 7] good-topped gelding: smart performer: won handicap at Lingfield in January by ½ length from Millville: off 3 months (had reportedly suffered from an infection in a hind leg), respectable fourth to Imperial Star in listed race at Kempton only other start at 7 yrs: stays easy 1½m: acts on polytrack, good to firm and good to soft ground: has run well sweating. *S. Kirk* — 112

SRI KUANTAN (IRE) 3 ch.c. Spinning World (USA) 130 – Miss Asia Quest 70 (Rainbow Quest (USA) 134) [2007 p12g² p10m⁶ p12g³ Oct 14] sturdy colt: fair form in maidens: stays 1½m: raced only on polytrack. *P. F. I. Cole* — 73

SRIOLOGY (IRE) 6 b.g. Sri Pekan (USA) 117 – Sinology (Rainbow Quest (USA) 134) [2007 58: p10g p11g Feb 4] modest in 2006: little form at 6 yrs: has worn visor/blinkers/tongue strap. *M. R. Hoad* —

SRI PEKAN TWO 3 b.g. Montjeu (IRE) 137 – Brigadiers Bird (IRE) (Mujadil (USA) 119) [2007 77, a87: p10g p8.6g p8g Dec 4] good-bodied gelding: just fair form at 3 yrs: — 74 well held after reappearance, pulled up second start (reportedly lame): should be suited by 1¼m/1½m: acts on polytrack and firm going. *P. F. I. Cole*

STACEYMAC (IRE) 4 ch.f. Elnadim (USA) 128 – Neat Shilling (IRE) (Bob Back (USA) 124) [2007 59: p6g⁵ Mar 16] modest performer: should stay 7f (raced freely when tried): raced only on polytrack. *W. R. Muir*   **52**

STAFFORD WILL (IRE) 3 b.g. Rossini (USA) 118 – Firstrusseofsummer (USA) (Summer Squall (USA)) [2007 10m 10.2m 12.1g 10.2m Sep 13] well held in maidens/handicap. *J. G. M. O'Shea*   **–**

STAGE ACCLAIM (IRE) 2 b.g. (Jan 13) Acclamation 118 – Open Stage (IRE) (Sadler's Wells (USA) 132) [2007 5m⁶ 5g* 5m⁶ 6g 7m 7.1m 6g⁶ p6g⁵ 6.1d Oct 18] lengthy gelding: fair performer: won maiden at Salisbury in May: lost his form, blinkered final start (gelded after): effective at 5f/6f: acts on good to firm going. *B. R. Millman*   **78**

STAGECOACH EMERALD 5 ch.g. Spectrum (IRE) 126 – Musician 104 (Shirley Heights 130) [2007 70: f14g² f16g² p13.9g p12.2g* p16.5g⁵ p13.9g⁶ Oct 30] close-coupled gelding: fair handicapper: won at Wolverhampton in October: stays 2m: acts on all-weather and good to soft ground: has been tongue tied, in cheekpieces of late. *R. W. Price*   **74**

STAGECOACH TOPAZ (USA) 2 b.g. (Mar 20) Stravinsky (USA) 133 – Indian Fashion (USA) 71 (General Holme (USA) 128) [2007 6.1m 6g⁶ 7g² Nov 6] €48,000Y: lengthy gelding: half-brother to several winners, including smart 7f (at 2 yrs) and 11.4f winner Solaia (by Miswaki): dam US 1m to 9f winner (second in Grade 2 1½m event): fair maiden: second at Catterick: gelded after: will be suited by 1m. *M. Johnston*   **71**

STAGE GIFT (IRE) 4 ch.g. Cadeaux Genereux 131 – Stage Struck (IRE) 83 (Sadler's Wells (USA) 132) [2007 116: a9f 9g 10g* 10.4s* 9.8d Oct 6] strong, well-made gelding: fluent mover: smart performer: left I. Mohammed in UAE after second outing: further   **119**

Godolphin's "Stage Gift"

progress when winning La Coupe at Longchamp (made all, by ¾ length from Willywell) in June and Sky Bet York Stakes (produced from off pace to beat Eagle Mountain by 1¼ lengths) at York in July: disappointing in Prix Dollar at Longchamp final start: stays 1¼m: acts on polytrack, good to firm and soft going. *Saeed bin Suroor*

STAGEHAND (IRE) 3 b.g. Lend A Hand 124 – Ridotto (Salse (USA) 128) [2007 76: **72** p8g⁵ 8.5g 8.1m⁵ 10.2m 9.9d³ 10m² p12g 10.2m² Sep 13] fair performer: stays 1¼m: acts on polytrack, firm and good to soft going: joined C. Down. *B. R. Millman*

STAGNITE 7 ch.g. Compton Place 125 – Superspring (Superlative 118) [2007 62: **54** p7.1g⁶ 7m 7g⁴ p7.1g 7.6s⁴ p7g p7.1g⁴ p8g Dec 5] lengthy gelding: modest performer: stays easy 7f: acts on polytrack, firm and good to soft going: sometimes wears headgear (not in 2007). *Karen George*

STAINLEY (IRE) 4 b.g. Elnadim (USA) 128 – Fizz Up 77 (Alzao (USA) 117) [2007 **–** 70: 12d Sep 17] rather leggy, close-coupled gelding: has a round action: fair handicapper: well held only Flat start at 4 yrs (winner over hurdles in January): stays 1¼m: acts on firm and soft going: usually races prominently. *Mrs S. C. Bradburne*

STAKED A CLAIM (IRE) 3 ch.g. Danehill Dancer (IRE) 117 – Twany Angel **65** (Double Form 130) [2007 72p: 5v⁴ 7g⁴ 5m⁴ 6v⁶ Oct 26] lengthy gelding: has scope: modest maiden: stays 7f: acts on heavy and good to firm going: tried blinkered: gelded after final start. *T. D. Barron*

STALKING TIGER (IRE) 3 b.g. King's Best (USA) 132 – Obsessed 80 (Storm Bird **74 p** (CAN) 134) [2007 10d 8.3d⁵ 8.3d³ Oct 15] 72,000F, 200,000Y: rangy, attractive gelding: fourth foal: half-brother to fairly useful 1m/1¼m winner Fasylitator (by Fasliyev) and winner in Greece by Pursuit of Love: dam, 2-y-o 6f winner, half-sister to dam of 3-y-o Excellent Art: fair form in maidens, third to Shadowy Figure at Windsor final start, dictating and not at all knocked about once headed: gelded after: stays 1¼m: raced only on good to soft going: likely to do better. *R. Charlton*

STALLONE 10 ch.g. Brief Truce (USA) 126 – Bering Honneur (USA) (Bering 136) **45** [2007 –: p12.2g⁶ f12g p12.2g⁶ Mar 27] good-bodied gelding: poor performer nowadays: effective at 1¼m to easy 1¾m: well beaten on heavy going, acts on any other turf and polytrack: tried tongue tied/in cheekpieces: tends to start slowly/usually held up. *N. Wilson*

STAMFORD BLUE 6 b.g. Bluegrass Prince (IRE) 110 – Fayre Holly (IRE) 57 (Fayruz **93** 116) [2007 71, a–: p6g 7.1m 7d* 6g* 6.1g* 7f⁶ 5.7g* 6g* 6v 6m⁴ 6g⁵ 6m 6d Oct 3] work-manlike gelding: fairly useful handicapper: much improved at 6 yrs, winning at Salisbury (2, apprentices/ladies) and Chepstow (apprentices) in May, Bath in June and Warwick (despite saddle slipping over 1f out) in July: has won over 1m, best at 5f/6f nowadays: acts on polytrack, firm and good to soft going: tried in cheekpieces, blinkered nowadays: has run well when sweating: sometimes slowly away: usually claimer ridden. *R. A. Harris*

STAND GUARD 3 b.g. Danehill (USA) 126 – Protectress 110 (Hector Protector (USA) **61** 124) [2007 8m Apr 21] lengthy gelding: first foal: dam, 2-y-o 7f winner (stayed 1¼m), out of useful sister to Racing Post Trophy winner/St Leger runner-up Armiger: 6/1 and in need of experience (coltish), 18 lengths ninth of 16 to Diamond Tycoon in maiden at Newbury, running green and not knocked about: sold 22,000 gns, and gelded. *Sir Michael Stoute*

STAND IN BLACK (NZ) 3 br.g. Istidaad (USA) 114 – Aprikot (NZ) (Iades (FR) **55 ?** 121) [2007 p10g⁴ p10g⁶ p8g 10m Jul 30] modest maiden: left B. Case after third start. *L. A. Dace*

STAND IN FLAMES 2 b.f. (Mar 16) Celtic Swing 138 – Maid of Arc (USA) 58 **60** (Patton (USA) 110) [2007 5m 6g 5.7m³ p7g 7.5g³ 7.1g Oct 2] first foal: dam 2-y-o 6f seller winner: modest maiden: stays 7.5f: acts on good to firm going. *Pat Eddery*

ST ANDREWS (IRE) 7 b.g. Celtic Swing 138 – Viola Royale (IRE) 90 (Royal Acad- **99** emy (USA) 130) [2007 114d: 8g⁶ 8m 8s³ 8m 9m 8.3m* 8.1s 8.3d³ Oct 29] lengthy, quite attractive gelding: useful handicapper nowadays: won at Windsor (beat Heroes by neck) in August: effective at 1m/1¼m: unraced on firm going, probably acts on any other: tried in cheekpieces: has run well when sweating. *M. A. Jarvis*

STANERRA'S STORY (IRE) 6 ch.g. Desert Story (IRE) 115 – Stanerra 128 (Guil- **72** laume Tell (USA) 121) [2007 p9.5g³ p12g⁴ p12.2g* Feb 5] fair form: won maiden at Wolverhampton in February by 3 lengths from Fringe: stays 1½m: raced on polytrack: tongue tied first 2 starts. *E. J. O'Neill*

STANLEY GEORGE (IRE) 3 b.g. Noverre (USA) 125 – Quinzey (JPN) (Carnegie **77** (IRE) 129) [2007 81: 8g 8.1m 8d 8m 8m p7.1g⁶ p8g⁴ p8.6d Dec 6] good-topped, quite attractive gelding: fair handicapper: should stay 1¼m: acts on all-weather: tried tongue tied. *M. A. Jarvis*

STANLEY WOLFE (IRE) 4 b.g. City On A Hill (USA) 114 – Quatredil (IRE) 67 **45** (Mujadil (USA) 119) [2007 50: 5.9g 5s 6g 5d⁵ 6m 6m 5g 5d⁶ 8v f6d⁵ Dec 11] poor performer: effective at 5f/6f: acts on good to firm and good to soft ground, probably on fibresand. *Garry Moss*

STAR BERRY 4 b.f. Mtoto 134 – Star Entry 67 (In The Wings 128) [2007 57: 11.7d⁵ **57** 11.5m³ p12g p12g 10m⁴ 10.5m p12.2g Oct 27] modest maiden: left B. Meehan 4,500 gns after fifth outing: should stay 1½m: acts on polytrack, good to firm and good to soft going: tried blinkered: has raced freely. *T. Wall*

STARBOUGG 3 b.f. Tobougg (IRE) 125 – Celestial Welcome 96 (Most Welcome 131) **–** [2007 72: 9m⁵ 10.1m 14.1f 16.1g Oct 3] good-topped filly: has scope: no form since debut at 2 yrs. *K. G. Reveley*

STARCREST 3 b.f. Soviet Star (USA) 128 – Singer On The Roof 62 (Chief Singer 131) **–** [2007 p7.1g p10g Feb 7] seventh foal: half-sister to several winners, including 5-y-o Pink Bay and 4-y-o Alto Vertigo: dam, 1m winner, half-sister to Prix Saint-Alary winner Air de Rien: little form in maidens. *Jean-Rene Auvray*

STARCROSS MAID 5 ch.m. Zaha (CAN) 106 – Maculatus (USA) (Sharpen Up 127) **64** [2007 59: f11g² f11g² 10m⁵ f12g f11g* f12g² f11g³ 10m 12g 12g⁶ f11d⁶ f12d⁵ Dec 20] modest handicapper: won at Southwell in May: stays 1½m: acts on all-weather and firm going: blinkered (raced freely) once: patiently ridden. *J. F. Coupland*

STARFALA 2 b.f. (Apr 12) Galileo (IRE) 134 – Farfala (FR) 106 (Linamix (FR) 127) **80** [2007 p7g 7g 7.5m³ Aug 25] fourth foal: half-sister to 4-y-o Under The Rainbow and 1m (at 2 yrs) to 1½m (in Spain) winner Speightstown (by Grand Lodge): dam, French 10.5f and 1½m winner, sister to very smart French middle-distance performer Fragrant Mix: fairly useful maiden: much improved when third to Jadaara at Beverley: will be suited by 1¼m/1½m. *P. F. I. Cole*

STARFINCH 2 b.f. (Feb 5) Fraam 114 – Mockingbird 64 (Sharpo 132) [2007 5s p6g 7.1d 6d Aug 18] compact filly: seventh foal: half-sister to 5-y-o Kempsey and 5f (at 2 yrs)/6f winner Ridicule (by Piccolo): dam, 6f seller winner, half-sister to useful stayer Anchor Clever: no form. *J. J. Bridger*

STARGAZER JIM (FR) 5 br.g. Fly To The Stars 124 – L'Americaine (USA) (Verbatim (USA)) [2007 89: 10f⁴ 10g⁶ 8g⁵ 8.3g* 8d 9.1g 8.2g* p8.6g p10g⁴ p9.5g³ p11g³ **87** p9.5g⁵ Dec 15] sturdy gelding: fairly useful handicapper: won at Hamilton in June and Nottingham in August: effective at 8.3f to 11f: acts on polytrack and any turf going: tried visored. *W. J. Haggas*

STARGAZY 3 b.g. Observatory (USA) 131 – Romantic Myth 105 (Mind Games 121) **–** [2007 71: p6g 6d 6.1m 5.7f p6g Dec 30] sturdy, well-made gelding: fair maiden at 2 yrs: well held at 3 yrs, leaving R. Charlton after second start: tried blinkered. *W. G. M. Turner*

STAR GRAZER 2 ch.f. (Apr 15) Observatory (USA) 131 – Oatey 68 (Master Willie **50** 129) [2007 6m 6m p7g⁶ Nov 7] 15,000Y: compact filly: sixth foal: half-sister to 6-y-o Jomus and fairly useful 5f (at 2 yrs) to 6.5f (in Spain) winner Alternative (by Dr Fong): dam, 5f winner, half-sister to 1½m to 2m performer Hateel and winner up to 11.5f Munwar, both smart: modest form in maidens: will stay 1m. *C. F. Wall*

STAR IN OUR EYES (IRE) 3 b.f. Daggers Drawn (USA) 114 – Mossy Maze (Zamindar (USA) 116) [2007 f8g Apr 22] first foal: dam, ran once, half-sister to useful 1m **–** winner Mossy Moor out of half-sister to St Leger winner Toulon: 100/1, slowly away and never dangerous in maiden at Southwell. *M. C. Chapman*

STAR IN THE EAST 2 ch.f. (May 2) Observatory (USA) 131 – Snipe Hall 93 (Croft- **59 d** hall 110) [2007 5.2g⁶ 5.7f⁵ p5g 7g⁵ p7.1g 5g p5.1g³ p6g 5g⁶ Sep 19] 13,000Y: close-coupled filly: sixth foal: half-sister to fairly useful 5f (at 2 yrs)/6f winner Spliff (by Royal Applause) and 5-y-o Ross Moor: dam 2-y-o 5f/6f winner: modest maiden: below form after second start (claimed from A. Balding £6,000 after fifth): best at 5f/6f: acts on firm going, probably on polytrack: blinkered last 3 outings. *Peter Grayson*

STARK CONTRAST (USA) 3 ch.g. Gulch (USA) – A Stark Is Born (USA) (Graus- **76** tark) [2007 79: 8.1m² 8.5m² 9g 11.5s 10.3m 9.7f³ 10d⁴ 11.6d p10m* p10g p10g⁵ Dec 22] tall, lengthy gelding: fair handicapper: left G. Butler after fifth start: won at Lingfield in

November: stays 1¼m: acts on polytrack and firm ground: tried blinkered/tongue tied. *J. Akehurst*

STARLIGHT GAZER 4 b.g. Observatory (USA) 131 – Dancing Fire (USA) (Dayjur **88** (USA) 137) [2007 77: 6d 7s* 7.1s² 7d* 7g 7d⁶ 7m Nov 10] tall, close-coupled gelding: fairly useful handicapper: won at Newbury and Leicester in July: will stay 1m: raced mainly on good ground or softer (well held on good to firm final start). *J. A. Geake*

STARLIGHT GIRL 2 ch.f. (Apr 9) Fantastic Light (USA) 134 – Intervene (Zafonic **65** (USA) 130) [2007 6m⁵ 5m⁵ 5d Jun 27] 26,000Y: strong filly: fifth foal: half-sister to 3-y-o Woqoodd: dam unraced half-sister to smart French performer up to 1¾m Short Pause and to dam of July Cup winner Continent: fair maiden: will be suited by 7f/1m. *T. D. Easterby*

STARLIGHT PRINCE 2 b.g. (Mar 25) Forzando 122 – Inchtina 85 (Inchinor 119) **63** [2007 8g 8.2g Nov 7] 100/1: modest form in maidens. *R. Hollinshead*

STARLIT SANDS 2 b.f. (Apr 5) Oasis Dream 129 – Shimmering Sea 89 (Slip Anchor **104** 136) [2007 5m* 5g* 5m² 5g⁴ 5.2m⁶ 5.5m* Sep 13] good-topped filly: half-sister to several winners, including 6f/7f winner Sheltering Sky (by Selkirk) and 5f/6f (latter including at 2 yrs) winner Sea Dane (by Danehill), both useful and later winners in Scandinavia: dam, 2-y-o 5f and 7f winner, half-sister to Petoski: useful performer: won maiden at Thirsk in May, minor event at Catterick in June and Prix d'Arenberg at Chantilly (beat Wilki by 2 lengths, in front from halfway) in September: also ran well in between in Queen Mary Stakes at Royal Ascot (½-length second to Elletelle) and Molecomb Stakes at Goodwood (fourth to Fleeting Spirit): will prove best at 5f/sharp 6f: raced only on good/good to firm going. *Sir Mark Prescott*

Miss K. Rausing's "Starlit Sands"

STAR MAGNITUDE (USA) 6 ch.g. Distant View (USA) 126 – Stellaria (USA) 98 – (Roberto (USA) 131) [2007 83, a87: p10g² p10g Mar 9] good-bodied gelding: fairly **a91** useful handicapper, better on all-weather: effective at 1m/1¼m: acts on polytrack and firm going, probably on soft: often held up. *S. Dow*

STAR OF ANGELS 3 b.g. Diktat 126 – City of Angels (Woodman (USA) 126) [2007 **80** p8.6g 12g 11.1d³ 11.1m⁴ 12.1d³ 10m⁴ 12d⁴ 11.1s 12m² 12.4d⁴ 12g* p12.2g² Nov 4] good-bodied gelding: fairly useful performer: won handicap at Catterick in October by 6 lengths: stays 1½m: acts on polytrack, good to firm and good to soft ground: tried blinkered: not straightforward: joined D. Pipe. *M. Johnston*

STAR OF CANTERBURY (IRE) 4 ch.g. Beckett (IRE) 116 – Villa Nova (IRE) 55 **76** (Petardia 113) [2007 80: p12g² p16g p12g⁶ 13.3m⁵ p10g³ 10g Aug 2] big, strong gelding: fair handicapper: stays 1½m: acts on all-weather and good to firm going: races up with pace: has looked wayward: joined D. Burchell 21,000 gns, winner over hurdles in October. *A. P. Jarvis*

STAR OF GIBRALTAR 2 b.f. (Mar 2) Rock of Gibraltar (IRE) 133 – Fallen Star 112 **70** (Brief Truce (USA) 126) [2007 7s 8m⁴ Sep 21] big, strong, good sort: second foal: dam, 7f (at 2 yrs)/1m winner, half-sister to very smart miler Fly To The Stars: fair form in maidens at Newmarket, fourth to Makaaseb latterly: stays 1m: type to make a better 3-y-o. *J. L. Dunlop*

STAR OF LIGHT 6 b.g. Mtoto 134 – Star Entry 67 (In The Wings 128) [2007 109: **103** 12s⁴ 10d⁶ 10d 10d 10m* 10.4d 10.3m 9m Oct 6] good-bodied gelding: useful handicapper: made all at Newmarket (beat Zaif by length) in August: stays 1½m: acts on polytrack and firm ground: sometimes goes freely, and has gone early to post (reluctant going down with main body final start): sold 20,000 gns, sent to Saudi Arabia. *B. J. Meehan*

STAR OF POMPEY 3 b.f. Hernando (FR) 127 – Discerning 96 (Darshaan 133) [2007 **70** 10.2d 9.9s⁶ p12g² Oct 24] 5,700 2-y-o: second foal: dam 11.5f winner (would have been suited by 2m+), half-sister to very smart performer up to 1½m Nowhere To Exit: easily best effort in maidens when length second to Garafena at Kempton: likely to be suited by 1¾m+: acts on polytrack. *A. B. Haynes*

STAR OF ROSANNA 2 b.f. (Feb 16) Bertolini (USA) 125 – Etma Rose (IRE) (Fairy **78** King (USA)) [2007 6s* 6.1s² a7f* Dec 27] fourth foal: half-sister to 5-y-o Pauline's Prince: dam maiden: fair form: won claimer at Leicester (left R. Hollinshead £12,000) in May and, having left K. Ryan 22,000 gns after second start, minor event at Nad Al Sheba in December: stays 7f: acts on dirt. *D. Watson, UAE*

STAR OF THE DESERT (IRE) 4 b. or br.g. Desert Story (IRE) 115 – Cindy's Star **64** (IRE) 68 (Dancing Dissident (USA) 119) [2007 76: 8m 8g p8.6g³ p9.5g⁵ f8d Dec 21] close-coupled, useful-looking gelding: modest maiden nowadays: stays easy 9.5f: acts on polytrack and firm ground: in cheekpieces last 4 starts. *Mrs K. Walton*

STAROFTHEMORNING (IRE) 6 ch.m. Foxhound (USA) 103 – Leggagh Lady **49** (IRE) 76 (Doubletour (USA)) [2007 39: p10g⁶ p16g⁴ Jan 10] poor maiden: stays easy 2m: acts on polytrack and good to firm going. *A. W. Carroll*

STARPARTY (USA) 3 gr.f. Cozzene (USA) – Cherie Yvonne (USA) (Vice Regent **76** (CAN)) [2007 70: 10g* p11g 12d⁵ 14m 11.7g Oct 24] lengthy, angular filly: fair handicapper: won at Sandown in June: stays 1½m: acts on good to soft going: in cheekpieces final outing. *Mrs A. J. Perrett*

STAR PATTERN (USA) 2 ch.c. (May 22) Seeking The Gold (USA) – Starlore (USA) **67 p** (Spectacular Bid (USA)) [2007 7g Nov 2] $650,000Y: fourth foal: brother to very smart US 1m/9f performer Quest: dam 1m/1¼m winner in US: 8/1, very green (but got in contention briefly) when tenth in maiden at Newmarket: will be suited by 1m/1¼m: bound to improve. *J. H. M. Gosden*

STARR FLYER 3 b.g. Star of Persia (IRE) 96 – Madame Butterfly 51 (Reprimand 122) **53** [2007 11g⁴ f11g 12d⁴ 14m Aug 11] neat gelding: modest maiden: stays 11f. *A. Bailey*

STARRY MESSENGER 3 b.f. Galileo (IRE) 134 – The Faraway Tree 113 (Suave **82** Dancer (USA) 136) [2007 74p: 11.9m² 12m* 12m 14m Oct 4] close-coupled filly: fairly useful form: won maiden at Ripon in August: should stay 1¾m: raced only on good to firm going: sold 24,000 gns. *M. P. Tregoning*

STARS ABOVE 3 b.f. Observatory (USA) 131 – Skimra 91 (Hernando (FR) 127) – [2007 48: f8g⁶ 8g 7.1s 6f Aug 4] sturdy, lengthy filly: poor maiden: well held at 3 yrs: trained by D. Keane on reappearance only. *M. S. Saunders*

STAR STRIDER 3 gr.g. Royal Applause 124 – Onefortheditch (USA) 79 (With **74**
Approval (CAN)) [2007 70: 5m³ 5d⁶ 5.7g 5m⁶ 6g⁵ 5.7f³ 6m Sep 17] leggy gelding: fair
maiden: effective at 5f (given test)/6f: acts on firm going: in cheekpieces last 4 starts: has
looked hard ride: joined Gay Kelleway. *A. M. Balding*

START OF AUTHORITY 6 ch.g. Muhtarram (USA) 125 – Heiden's Delight (USA) **50**
(Shadeed (USA) 135) [2007 56: 7d 7.6s 7d Oct 18] workmanlike gelding: modest performer: stays 1m: acts on all-weather, firm and good to soft ground. *J. Gallagher*

STARTORI 4 b.f. Vettori (IRE) 119 – Celestial Welcome 96 (Most Welcome 131) [2007 **–**
86, a75: f7g Jan 16] neat filly: fair handicapper: well held only start at 4 yrs: stays 8.6f:
acts on polytrack, good to firm and good to soft going: tried visored: sold 16,000 gns,
reportedly in foal to Ishiguru. *B. Smart*

STATE DILEMMA (IRE) 6 b.g. Green Desert (USA) 127 – Nuriva (USA) 100 **64**
(Woodman (USA) 126) [2007 67: p7g⁵ p8g p8g⁶ p7f Feb 24] good-bodied gelding: has a
quick, fluent action: modest handicapper: effective at 6f, and seemingly stays easy 1¼m:
acts on polytrack, soft and good to firm ground: wears headgear nowadays: usually
waited with: has shown signs of temperament. *D. Shaw*

STATEN (USA) 2 b.c. (Feb 11) Century City (IRE) 124 – Lever To Heaven (IRE) **61**
(Bluebird (USA) 125) [2007 7.2v⁵ Nov 3] 25/1, and green, never a threat but showed
ability when fifth in maiden at Ayr. *T. D. Barron*

STATESIDE (CAN) 2 b.f. (Mar 4) El Corredor (USA) 123 – Double Trick (USA) **49 +**
(Phone Trick (USA)) [2007 7d 7g⁶ 7.5g Aug 15] $50,000Y: workmanlike filly: second
foal: dam, US 7f to 8.5f winner, out of US Grade 3 1m winner Duo Disco: poor form in
maidens. *R. A. Fahey*

STATION PLACE 2 b.f. (Mar 28) Bahamian Bounty 116 – Twin Time 77 (Syrtos 106) **–**
[2007 p8m Dec 10] third foal: dam 7f to 1¼m winner: 33/1, well held in maiden at Lingfield. *A. B. Haynes*

STAY ACTIVE (USA) 3 gr.g. Johannesburg (USA) 127 – Mature Miss (USA) (Mi **60**
Cielo (USA)) [2007 65: 8.3g 8s 7.1m p12.2g⁶ 9.1s² p9.5g⁴ Nov 16] quite attractive gelding: fair maiden at 2 yrs, only modest in 2007: stays 9f: acts on soft and good to firm
going: visored last 2 outings. *I. Semple*

STAYING ON (IRE) 2 b.c. (Mar 29) Invincible Spirit (IRE) 121 – Lakatoi 82 (Sad- **89 p**
dlers' Hall (IRE) 126) [2007 p7.1g* Oct 21] second foal: dam, maiden (stayed 1¾m), out
of Oaks winner Bireme: 13/2, won maiden at Wolverhampton by 2 lengths from Counterclaim despite looking green (wandered in front): useful prospect. *W. R. Swinburn*

STEADY AS A ROCK (FR) 3 ch.c. Rock of Gibraltar (IRE) 133 – Metisse (USA) **84**
(Kingmambo (USA) 125) [2007 84p: 7d⁶ 8v³ 7.6s⁴ 7.6m Aug 5] good-topped colt: fluent
mover: fairly useful performer: below form after reappearance: should stay 1m: acts on
good to firm and good to soft ground: sold 3,000 gns in October. *M. Johnston*

STEAK N KIDNEY (USA) 4 br.g. Wild Again (USA) – Top Slipper (FR) (Top Ville **–**
129) [2007 10s Jun 4] tall gelding: well held both starts on Flat (20 months apart).
M. Wigham

STEAL MY FIRE (IRE) 2 b.c. (Mar 5) Iron Mask (USA) 117 – Lady of Pleasure **65**
(IRE) (Marju (IRE) 127) [2007 6m* p7g Sep 4] quite good-topped colt: modest form:
won seller at Redcar in August: favourite, better than bare result in nursery at Lingfield:
may prove best at 5f/6f: sold 8,500 gns. *E. J. O'Neill*

STEALTH PROJECT 2 b.c. (May 4) Elmaamul (USA) 125 – Guardee (Hector Pro- **61**
tector (USA) 124) [2007 7.5d 8d 8.2g⁶ Nov 7] compact colt: modest maiden: probably
stays 1m. *A. M. Hales*

STEAM CUISINE 3 ch.f. Mark of Esteem (IRE) 137 – Sauce Tartar 90 (Salse (USA) **104**
128) [2007 84: 8.2m 7g⁶ 7d* 7m⁴ 7m³ 7g⁴ 7d³ 7d* Oct 27] tall, close-coupled filly: useful
performer: won handicaps at Newmarket in June and Newbury (beat Ventura by 1¼
lengths despite tending to wander) in October: also good 1¼-length third to Miss Lucifer
in listed race at Ascot penultimate start, meeting trouble 2f out: will prove best up to 1m:
acts on polytrack, good to firm and good to soft going: held up. *M. G. Quinlan*

STEEL BLUE 7 b.g. Atraf 116 – Something Blue (Petong 126) [2007 92, a72: 5m 6m⁴ **81**
6m 6d 5v 6d 5.9m² 6m* 6m 6g 6m 6m 6.1d² 6.1s³ 6v Nov 3] leggy, quite good-topped
gelding: fairly useful handicapper on turf, fair on all-weather: won at Thirsk in August:
creditable efforts when placed after: stays easy 7f: acts on dirt, soft and good to firm
going: tried visored/in cheekpieces. *R. M. Whitaker*

STEEL CITY BOY (IRE) 4 b.g. Bold Fact (USA) 116 – Balgren (IRE) (Ballad Rock **67** 122) [2007 80: f5g* 5m 5.1d 5m⁶ 5m 5m 5g² 5d⁵ 6v p6g Nov 2] lengthy, good-bodied **a80** gelding: fairly useful handicapper: won at Southwell in May: best at 5f: acts on all-weather, good to firm and good to soft ground. *D. Carroll*

STEELCUT 3 b.g. Iron Mask (USA) 117 – Apple Sauce 70 (Prince Sabo 123) [2007 90: **88** 5f³ 5.1m 6m 5g 5d⁵ 5s 5g 5g 5m³ Sep 27] good-topped gelding: fairly useful handicapper: stays 6f: acts on firm going: tried blinkered: suspect attitude. *R. A. Fahey*

STEELE TANGO (USA) 2 ch.c. (Mar 3) Okawango (USA) 115 – Waltzing Around **69 p** (IRE) (Ela-Mana-Mou 132) [2007 p6g⁴ p7m⁶ Dec 9] $12,000F, $12,000Y, 30,000 2-y-o: fifth foal: half-brother to winner in Japan by Invincible Spirit: dam unraced half-sister to Poule d'Essai des Pouliches winner Valentine Waltz, out of half-sister to Last Tycoon: fair form in maidens at Lingfield, again late headway when sixth to Hold The Gold: will stay 1m: remains open to improvement. *R. A. Teal*

STEELEY FOX 4 b.g. Mind Games 121 – Foxie Lady 77 (Wolfhound (USA) 126) **63 d** [2007 6m³ 8.1m 6m⁶ 6m 6d p6g Aug 31] lengthy gelding: modest maiden, regressed after debut: will probably prove best at 5f/6f: acts on good to firm ground. *J. M. Bradley*

STEEL GREY 6 gr.g. Grey Desire 115 – Call Me Lucky 65 (Magic Ring (IRE) 115) **–** [2007 –: f8g³ f8g f7g* 7.5m 8s 8d p9.5g Sep 27] leggy gelding: modest performer on **a54** all-weather: won minor event at Southwell in March: stays 1m: acts on fibresand, no form on turf: sometimes very slowly away. *M. Brittain*

STEEL SILK (IRE) 3 b.g. Desert Style (IRE) 121 – Dear Catch (IRE) 69 (Bluebird **67** (USA) 125) [2007 –: 8.2g⁴ 8f³ 9.8g p12.2g Sep 21] sturdy gelding: fair maiden: stays 1m: acts on firm ground: tried visored. *B. Smart*

STEELY DAN 8 b.g. Danzig Connection (USA) – No Comebacks 70 (Last Tycoon **–** 131) [2007 –, a85: p7g p8g p8g Dec 28] strong gelding: fair performer nowadays: effec- **a76** tive at 7f to easy 1½m: acts on all-weather, firm and good to soft going: tried in cheek-pieces: best with waiting tactics: not straightforward. *Mrs L. C. Jewell*

STEENBERG (IRE) 8 ch.g. Flying Spur (AUS) – Kip's Sister (Cawston's Clown **–** 113) [2007 121: 6d⁶ 6g 7g 6d 7d Sep 29] big, lengthy gelding: very smart performer at 7 yrs: little form in 2007, in handicaps last 3 starts: blinkered (below form) twice. *M. H. Tompkins*

STEIG (IRE) 4 b.g. Xaar 132 – Ring of Kerry (IRE) 67 (Kenmare (FR) 125) [2007 81: **67** p8.6d² Dec 27] fairly useful maiden when trained by D. Wachman at 3 yrs, placed at Gowran and Leopardstown: only fair form when second at Wolverhampton sole Flat start in 2007: stays 1m: acts on firm ground, probably on polytrack. *Carl Llewellyn*

STELLAR ROSE (USA) 2 b.f. (Feb 17) Royal Academy (USA) 130 – Stellar Blush **–** (USA) (Blushing John (USA) 120) [2007 7d p6g p8.6g Oct 7] 5,000Y: unfurnished filly: half-sister to 3 US sprint winners: dam unraced half-sister to US Grade 1 1½m winner Both Ends Burning: little form. *B. J. Meehan*

STELLITE 7 ch.g. Pivotal 124 – Donation (Generous (IRE) 139) [2007 84: 7.1g 7.1m **74** 7d 5.9m³ 7.1g⁵ 6g 6s 7.2s 6v Nov 3] workmanlike gelding: fair handicapper: stays 8.6f, all 5 wins at 7f: acts on all-weather, soft and good to firm going. *J. S. Goldie*

STEPASIDE (IRE) 3 gr.g. Fasliyev (USA) 120 – Felicita (IRE) 97 (Catrail (USA) 123) **60** [2007 65: 7m⁵ 6g 7m 5d 8.3g 8.5g f6d Dec 21] maiden handicapper: below form after reappearance, leaving M. Johnston 5,000 gns following third start: best up to 7f: acts on good to firm and good to soft going: tried blinkered. *A. D. Brown*

STEPH THE REF 2 b. or br.f. (Jan 28) Rossini (USA) 118 – Fairy Ring (IRE) 69 **55** (Fairy King (USA)) [2007 5m 5m⁶ 6d 6g⁶ Oct 19] leggy filly: fifth foal: half-sister to 2003 2-y-o 5f winner Reidies Choice (by Royal Applause) and winner in Greece by Vettori: dam sprint maiden: modest maiden: should prove best at 5f/6f. *R. M. Whitaker*

STEP IN LINE (USA) 3 b.c. Giant's Causeway (USA) 132 – Quiet Weekend (USA) **81** (Quiet American (USA)) [2007 7f* p7g Oct 14] first foal: dam, French 2-y-o 5f winner, out of close relation to Preakness Stakes winner Summer Squall/half-sister to A P Indy: odds on, won maiden at Redcar in September by 1¼ lengths from Cassiara: ran as if amiss (virtually pulled up) in handicap at Lingfield next time: has left Godolphin. *Saeed bin Suroor*

STEPPE DANCER (IRE) 4 b.c. Fasliyev (USA) 120 – Exemina (USA) (Slip Anchor **117** 136) [2007 106: p12g* 13.4m³ 12g 12m p12g* 14m Sep 15] big, strong colt: impresses in appearance: smart performer: won listed race in March and totepool September Stakes (by 1½ lengths from Al Tharib) in September, both at Kempton: also good third to Ask

totepool September Stakes, Kempton—Steppe Dancer enhances his record on polytrack; Al Tharib (left), Lion Sands (hidden), Imperial Star (visor) and Grand Passion are next

in Ormonde Stakes at Chester: well below form in Irish St Leger at the Curragh final start: stays 13.4f: acts on polytrack, good to firm and good to soft going: usually held up. *D. J. Coakley*

STEP SOFTLY 2 b.f. (Mar 10) Golan (IRE) 129 – Step Aloft 87 (Shirley Heights 130) **95** [2007 7m* 6m* 8m⁶ 7m² Oct 6] neat filly: fifth foal: half-sister to 3 winners, including fairly useful 6f winner Free Lift (by Cadeaux Genereux) and useful 7f winner who stays 1¼m Chief Yeoman (by Machiavellian): dam, 1¼m winner, half-sister to smart performers up to 1¼m Starlet and Unknown Quantity: useful performer: won maiden at Folkestone in July and minor event at Haydock in August: further improvement when ½-length second to Raymi Coya in Oh So Sharp Stakes at Newmarket: should stay 1m: raced only on good to firm going: joined J-C. Rouget in France. *R. Hannon*

STEP THIS WAY (USA) 2 ch.f. (Apr 27) Giant's Causeway (USA) 132 – Lady In **87** Waiting (USA) (Woodman (USA) 126) [2007 7d 7m⁵ p8.6g* p8.6g² Oct 18] $150,000Y: tall, close-coupled filly: seventh foal: half-sister to 3 winners, including useful Irish 2003 2-y-o 6f winner Acciacatura (by Stravinsky) and US Grade 3 8.5f winner Kid Grindstone (by Grindstone): dam, US 8.5f/9f winner, out of Breeders' Cup Distaff winner Princess Rooney: fairly useful form: won maiden at Wolverhampton in September: more progress when second to Menadha in nursery there: stays 8.6f: acts on polytrack, promise on good to firm going. *M. Johnston*

STEP TO THE STARS (IRE) 3 ch.f. Galileo (IRE) 134 – Tudor Loom (Sallust 134) **73** [2007 55: 10d* Jun 22] leggy filly: fair form: won maiden at Redcar in June: stayed 1¼m: acted on good to soft ground: dead. *M. Johnston*

STERLING MOLL 4 gr.f. Lord of Men 116 – Princess Maud (USA) (Irish River (FR) **–** 131) [2007 –: p12g p16g 16m 13.3m p12g⁵ p12g 11.8g Oct 16] little form. *W. de Best-Turner*

STEROPE (FR) 2 b.f. (Jan 24) Hernando (FR) 127 – Sacred Song (USA) 116 (Diesis **– P** 133) [2007 7d Oct 9] well-made filly: second foal: half-sister to 4-y-o Multidimensional: dam, 6f (at 2 yrs) to 1½m (Lancashire Oaks) winner, half-sister to smart US performer up to 1½m Strut The Stage: 5/1, badly needed experience and considerably handled in maiden at Leicester (tenth behind Laughter): will be suited by 1¼m/1½m: type to improve considerably. *H. R. A. Cecil*

STEVE'S CHAMP (CHI) 7 b.h. Foxhound (USA) 103 – Emigracion (CHI) (Semen- **105** enko (USA) 111) [2007 a5.5g² 6g³ 5.8m* 6g⁴ 5.1d⁵ 6.8s 4.5g 5.8g a2g³ Nov 8] big, strong, close-coupled horse: useful performer at best nowadays: won listed race at Taby in May by 2½ lengths from Berri Chis: below form afterwards, including when last of 5 in similar event at Chester fifth start: stays 6.8f: acts on dirt, soft and good to firm going: blinkered: has worn tongue tie. *Rune Haugen, Norway*

STEVIE GEE (IRE) 3 b.g. Invincible Spirit (IRE) 121 – Margaree Mary (CAN) **–** (Seeking The Gold (USA)) [2007 101: p7g 10m⁶ May 5] leggy, quite good-topped geld- ing: useful performer at 2 yrs: well below form at Lingfield (listed race) and Newmarket (handicap) in 2007: should stay 7f: acts on fibresand and soft going. *G. A. Swinbank*

STEVIE SMURNOFF 2 b.g. (Apr 15) Mind Games 121 – Ladycake (IRE) 71 (Perugino (USA) 84) [2007 f5g 5m Apr 26] no form: dead. *M. W. Easterby* – –

STEVIE THUNDER 2 ch.g. (Mar 29) Storming Home 128 – Social Storm (USA) (Future Storm (USA)) [2007 7.1d* p7.1g³ Oct 25] fair form: won seller at Musselburgh in September: third in claimer at Wolverhampton: will stay 1m. *G. A. Swinbank* **66 +**

ST FRIS 4 gr.g. Silver Patriarch (IRE) 125 – Fragrance (Mtoto 134) [2007 56: p12g p16g 14.1d 16m Sep 16] little form: visored last 4 outings. *J. A. R. Toller* –

STICKY MINT (IRE) 4 b.f. Inchinor 119 – Creme de Menthe (IRE) (Green Desert (USA) 127) [2007 –: p8.6g Jan 19] little form. *M. Blanshard* –

STILL CALM 3 b.g. Zamindar (USA) 116 – Shining Water 111 (Kalaglow 132) [2007 59: 10.5g⁶ 8m Oct 8] close-coupled gelding: modest maiden: bred to be suited by 1½m: temperament under suspicion. *N. J. Vaughan* **58**

STILL CRAZY (IRE) 3 ch.f. Fath (USA) 116 – Miss Bagatelle 70 (Mummy's Pet 125) [2007 54: p8.6g* p8.6g³ p8.6g p7.1g p8g Jul 12] €40,000Y: half-sister/closely related to several winners, including fairly useful 5f/6f winner Alpaga Le Jomage (by Orpen): dam, Irish 6f winner, half-sister to Gold Cup winner Arcadian Heights: modest handicapper: trained by K. Prendergast in Ireland at 2 yrs: won at Wolverhampton (only start for W. M. Brisbourne) in February: stays 8.6f: acts on polytrack, best effort on turf on firm going: blinkered once: saddle slipped third 3-y-o start: sold 8,000 gns, sent to Bahrain. *E. F. Vaughan* **62**

STILL DREAMING 3 ch.f. Singspiel (IRE) 133 – Three Green Leaves (IRE) 97 (Environment Friend 128) [2007 10g 12m³ 10d³ 12s 14m 10.5s 9g⁶ 10d³ Oct 10] workmanlike filly: second living foal: dam 7f (at 2 yrs) to 1½m winner: modest maiden: stays 1½m: acts on good to firm and good to soft ground: blinkered last 3 starts. *M. Dods* **61**

STIMULATION (IRE) 2 b.c. (Feb 15) Choisir (AUS) 126 – Damiana (IRE) (Thatching 131) [2007 6m* 7d² 7d² Oct 27] **113 p**

Hughie Morrison's stable has had success with a wide variety of types, from champion sprinters and Group 1 stayers to championship-standard hurdlers and smart staying chasers, but the yard is still waiting for a classic runner. Morrison's father owned and bred the Oaks winners Scintillate and Juliette Marny, and Morrison junior was due to be represented by Pastoral Pursuits in the Two Thousand Guineas in 2003, but he didn't recover in time from a chipped bone in a knee sustained when winning the Sirenia Stakes at Kempton on his final outing at two. Morrison now has another possible for the Two Thousand Guineas in Stimulation who is available at a generous-looking 40/1 at the time of writing.

Stimulation justified support in a six-furlong maiden at Newbury on his debut in September, overcoming inexperience racing into a strong headwind and responding well to get in front in the final furlong before edging left and winning by a neck from Flowing Cape. Stimulation next ran in the Hyperion Stakes at Ascot—a race in which the stable's Sakhee's Secret had finished a disappointing fourth twelve months previously—and he showed considerable improvement in pulling well clear of the remainder with Confront, another very useful prospect. Had Stimulation been better placed early on, he might have given Confront more to do. That form—beaten a length—still gave Stimulation solid claims in the Horris Hill Stakes at Newbury a fortnight later when he looked most unlucky to be beaten a head by Beacon Lodge. Stimulation was trapped on the rail when the field merged just before halfway and had to work his way to the outer, starting off some three lengths behind the winner when finally in the clear around a furlong out and finishing so strongly that he would have won in another couple of strides.

	Choisir (AUS) (ch 1999)	Danehill Dancer (b 1993)	Danehill / Mira Adonde
Stimulation (IRE) (b.c. Feb 15, 2005)		Great Selection (ch 1990)	Lunchtime / Pensive Mood
	Damiana (IRE) (b 1996)	Thatching (b 1975)	Thatch / Abella
		Derena (ch 1984)	Crystal Palace / Dedra

Stimulation is from the first crop of Choisir, who enjoyed a pretty successful time of things with his first runners in both hemispheres. Choisir, a high-class sprinter in his homeland, became the first horse trained in Australia to win in Britain when landing the King's Stand Stakes and Golden Jubilee within five days at Royal Ascot in 2003. Choisir got better with age, something that will encourage connections of Choisir-sired three-year-olds in 2008, including those of Stimulation. Stimulation, who cost 92,000 guineas as a yearling, is the fourth foal out of the French maiden Damiana who stayed a mile and is a sister to the useful French mile winner Dirca. Stimulation is a half-brother to the fairly useful seven-furlong to mile-and-a-quarter winner Desert Cristal (by Desert King). The progressive Stimulation, who has yet to encounter extremes of going, certainly looks the part, being a well-made colt, and should have no problem stepping up to a mile at three. *H. Morrison*

STIR CRAZY (IRE) 3 b.g. Fath (USA) 116 – La Captive (IRE) 68 (Selkirk (USA) **69 §** 129) [2007 70: 6m p5.1g³ 6.1m 5.7d 5m p6g⁶ 5.3g² p6g 6d 5g* 5d 5m 5g 5.7f² p5g³ 6m 5m 6.1m 5.7g Oct 24] smallish gelding: fair handicapper: won at Folkestone in August: effective at 5f/6f: acts on polytrack and any turf going: none too consistent: sold 5,000 gns. *M. R. Channon*

ST JEAN CAP FERRAT 2 b. or br.c. (Feb 14) Domedriver (IRE) 128 – Miss Cap **79** Ferrat 53 (Darshaan 133) [2007 6m 7m⁴ 7m 8.2g² Oct 31] quite good-topped colt: fair maiden: upped in trip, improved when second to Doctor Fremantle at Nottingham: stays 1m: raced only on good/good to firm going. *G. Wragg*

ST MICHAEL'S MOUNT 2 b.g. (Feb 16) Mark of Esteem (IRE) 137 – Marithea **–** (IRE) (Barathea (IRE) 127) [2007 p8g Sep 7] 33/1, well held in maiden at Kempton. *M. P. Tregoning*

STOIC LEADER (IRE) 7 b.g. Danehill Dancer (IRE) 117 – Starlust 79 (Sallust 134) **87** [2007 87, a78: p8.6g³ p7g⁴ p7.1g p7.1g⁶ 7.1g* 7f p7.1g 7.1m 8m 7.1d³ 7.9d⁴ 6d⁴ 8m² **a75** 7.6m⁵ 7m p7.1g⁵ 6d 6m 7g 7g p7.1g Dec 4] sturdy gelding: fairly useful handicapper on turf, fair on all-weather: won at Musselburgh in April: effective at 6f to easy 8.6f: acts on all-weather, firm and soft going: tried in cheekpieces: has raced freely: tends to edge left: tough. *R. F. Fisher*

STOKESIES BOY 7 b.g. Key of Luck (USA) 126 – Lesley's Fashion 67 (Dominion **–** 123) [2007 p10m Oct 3] maiden: very lightly raced on Flat and well beaten sole outing since 2003. *C. Roberts*

STOKESIES LUCK (IRE) 4 gr.c. King Charlemagne (USA) 120 – Lesley's Fashion **–** 67 (Dominion 123) [2007 –: p10m Oct 3] big, leggy colt: little sign of ability. *C. Roberts*

STOLEN GLANCE 4 b.f. Mujahid (USA) 125 – Stolen Melody 74 (Robellino (USA) **84** 127) [2007 84: f11g f11g⁵ f8g⁵ f8g* 9.1g⁶ f8g² 9.2g³ 8d 8.3d* 8d 8.3g Aug 22] fairly useful handicapper: won at Southwell and Ayr in May, and Hamilton (by 5 lengths) in July: stays 1¼m: acts on fibresand, soft and good to firm ground: tried blinkered: has shown signs of temperament: reportedly in foal to Gentleman's Deal. *M. W. Easterby*

STOLEN HOURS (USA) 7 b. or br.h. Silver Deputy (CAN) – Fasta (USA) (Seattle **71** Song (USA) 130) [2007 79: p12g* 12m⁶ p12g p10g⁶ 11.6m⁶ Aug 13] good-topped horse: fair handicapper: won apprentice event at Kempton in June: was effective at 1½m/1¾m: acted on polytrack, firm and good to soft going: visored (carried head awkwardly) final 3-y-o start: dead. *J. Akehurst*

STOLEN SONG 7 b.g. Sheikh Albadou 128 – Sparky's Song 63 (Electric 126) [2007 **–** –: p16g Dec 4] good-topped gelding: poor performer in 2006: well held sole start at 7 yrs: often wears headgear. *J. Ryan*

STOLEN SUMMER (IRE) 4 ch.g. Spectrum (IRE) 126 – Touche-A-Tout (IRE) **59** (Royal Academy (USA) 130) [2007 88d: f8g f12g p12.2g⁴ f16s p12.2g a12g² a8.6g³ a12g⁶ 16d⁵ a12g⁵ a8.6g⁵ a8.6s³ 9g⁴ 8g 7g⁵ 8.5d⁴ a12g Oct 21] sturdy gelding: modest performer: sold from B. Rothwell 1,400 gns after fifth outing: stays easy 1½m: acts on polytrack/dirt and soft going: blinkered first 5 starts in 2007. *H-I. Larsen, Sweden*

STOLT (IRE) 3 b.g. Tagula (IRE) 116 – Cabcharge Princess (IRE) 64 (Rambo Dancer **86** (CAN) 107) [2007 86: 5d p5.1g 5m p6g p5.1d⁴ p5.1s* Dec 21] close-coupled gelding: fairly useful performer: won handicap at Wolverhampton in December: best at 5f: acts on polytrack, firm and good to soft going. *N. Wilson*

STONEACRE BABY (USA) 2 ch.f. (Apr 23) Stravinsky (USA) 133 – Katiba (USA) **–** 99 (Gulch (USA)) [2007 p6g p6g p5.1g⁶ Nov 5] €70,000Y: half-sister to several winners, including 1999 2-y-o 7f winner Meadaaar (by Diesis) and 1m/1¼m winner Badaayer (by

Silver Hawk), both useful: dam, 6f (at 2 yrs)/7f winner (stayed 1¼m), out of half-sister to Breeders' Cup Sprint winner Very Subtle: behind in maidens. *Peter Grayson*

STONEACRE BOY (IRE) 4 ch.g. City On A Hill (USA) 114 – Sans Ceriph (IRE) 75 **75** (Thatching 131) [2007 79: p5g⁵ p5g f5g² f5g² f5g f5g f5g p6g p5.1g⁶ p5m* p5.1g⁶ p5g⁶ Dec 12] strong gelding: fair handicapper: won at Kempton in October: effective at 5f/6f: acts on all-weather and good to firm ground: tried blinkered: unruly in stall fifth outing: sometimes slowly away/hangs right. *Peter Grayson*

STONEACRE DONNY (IRE) 3 br.c. Lend A Hand 124 – Election Special 78 (Chief **52** Singer 131) [2007 f5g p7g p5.1g p7g p5.1g 6d p6g p5.1g p5.1g⁴ Dec 31] modest maiden: raced mainly at 5f/6f: very slowly away fourth outing. *Peter Grayson*

STONEACRE FRED (IRE) 4 br.g. Lend A Hand 124 – Election Special 78 (Chief **57** Singer 131) [2007 55: p8g⁴ p8.6g⁵ p8.6g Feb 21] modest performer: was effective at 5f to 8.6f: acted on all-weather and good to soft going: tried in cheekpieces/blinkers: dead. *Peter Grayson*

STONEACRE GARETH (IRE) 3 b.g. Grand Lodge (USA) 125 – Tidal Reach **71 d** (USA) 68 (Kris S (USA)) [2007 75: p6g⁵ p5g² f5g⁶ p6g 5.2m⁶ 5g 6g p5g⁵ 5g⁴ 5m p6g⁵ p5.1g² p5g 5d⁴ 5m⁵ 5f p5g p5.1g Dec 31] rangy gelding: fair handicapper at best: effective at 5f to 7f: acts on polytrack, good to firm and good to soft ground: usually blinkered: suspect temperament. *Peter Grayson*

STONEACRE GIRL (IRE) 4 ch.f. Rossini (USA) 118 – Ring of Light (Auction Ring **–** (USA) 123) [2007 38: p5.1g Jan 28] smallish filly: poor maiden: effective at 5f/6f: acts on all-weather: tried blinkered. *Peter Grayson*

STONEACRE LAD (IRE) 4 b.c. Bluebird (USA) 125 – Jay And-A (IRE) 98 (Elbio **107 §** 125) [2007 94§: p5g⁴ p5g³ f5g³ 5.1d 5d 5d* 5m Oct 4] good-topped colt: useful handicapper: easily best effort when winning 24-runner Hong Kong Jockey Club Sprint at Ascot (by 2½ lengths from Hoh Hoh Hoh) in July: raced alone when below form in listed event at Newmarket final outing: best at 5f: acts on all-weather, firm and soft ground: blinkered: hangs left, often markedly so: quirky. *Peter Grayson*

STONEACRE MA 2 b.f. (Apr 21) Dubai Destination (USA) 127 – Silent Tribute **–** (IRE) 104 (Lion Cavern (USA) 117) [2007 p6g Oct 26] 26,000Y: fifth foal: dam, 2-y-o 6f to 1m winner, out of useful half-sister to Middle Park winner Balla Cove: tailed off in maiden. *Peter Grayson*

STONEACRE PAT (IRE) 2 b.c. (May 4) Iron Mask (USA) 117 – Sans Ceriph (IRE) **–** 75 (Thatching 131) [2007 p6d p6g⁵ Dec 22] €7,500F: half-brother to several winners, including 4-y-o Stoneacre Boy: dam Irish 7f winner: well held in maiden/seller. *Peter Grayson*

STONECRABSTOMORROW (IRE) 4 b.g. Fasliyev (USA) 120 – Tordasia (IRE) **80** (Dr Devious (IRE) 127) [2007 91: 5m 6m 6g 7f 6g³ 6v² 6d³ 6d⁴ p7g 5g⁶ p6g Oct 19] leggy gelding: fairly useful performer: stays 7f: acts on all-weather and heavy ground: tried in cheekpieces. *R. A. Fahey*

STONEHAUGH (IRE) 4 b.g. King Charlemagne (USA) 120 – Canary Bird (IRE) 59 **87** (Catrail (USA) 123) [2007 83: 7.1m² 8m⁶ 7.2s Sep 22] good-bodied gelding: fairly useful performer: good second in handicap at Musselburgh: below form after: best form at short of 1m: acts on firm ground: tongue tied. *J. Howard Johnson*

Hong Kong Jockey Club Sprint (Handicap), Ascot—everything clicks for Stoneacre Lad, who is clear of Hoh Hoh Hoh (halved sleeves, right), Dig Deep (stars, left of centre) and Tony The Tap (on Dig Deep's left)

STONES OF VENICE (IRE) 2 b.f. (Apr 4) Barathea (IRE) 127 – Midnight Fever   –
(IRE) (Sure Blade (USA) 130) [2007 p7g 8d Oct 23] 65,000Y: good-topped filly: seventh
foal: half-sister to several winners abroad, notably smart German winner up to 1¾m
Moonlady (by Platini): dam unraced half-sister to German Derby third Masterplayer: no
show in minor event/maiden: will benefit from 1¼m/1½m. *J. R. Fanshawe*

STOOP TO CONQUER 7 b.g. Polar Falcon (USA) 126 – Princess Genista 108 (Ile   **80**
de Bourbon (USA) 133) [2007 93: 16m 16g 14d⁶ Jul 6] big, leggy, lengthy gelding:
fairly useful handicapper: stays 2¼m: acts on any turf going: sometimes races freely.
A. W. Carroll

STOP ON 2 b.g. (Feb 6) Fraam 114 – Tourmalet 88 (Night Shift (USA)) [2007 7m³   **82**
8.5m³ 8.1m⁴ Sep 13] first foal: dam 2-y-o 5f winner (stayed 1m): fair form in frame in
maidens, close fourth to Black Jacari at Chepstow (hung left in front) final start: gelded
after: stays 8.5f: raced only on good to firm going. *M. R. Channon*

STOREY HILL (USA) 2 b. or br.g. (Mar 29) Richter Scale (USA) 119 – Crafty Nan   **75**
(USA) (Crafty Prospector (USA)) [2007 p6g⁴ p5.1g p6g* Nov 6] fair form: won maiden
at Lingfield (made all) final start: will prove best at 5f/6f: raced only on polytrack.
D. Shaw

STORMBEAM (USA) 2 b.c. (Mar 25) Tale of The Cat (USA) 113 – Broad Smile   **69 p**
(USA) (Broad Brush (USA)) [2007 p7m⁵ p7g⁵ Nov 17] $130,000Y: lengthy colt: has
scope: half-brother to several winners in US, including minor sprint stakes winners by
Mt Livermore and Coronado's Quest: dam US 6f (including at 2 yrs) to 1m winner: green,
encouraging fifth in maidens at Lingfield: will be suited by 1m: capable of better.
G. A. Butler

STORMBURST (IRE) 3 b.f. Mujadil (USA) 119 – Isca 66 (Caerleon (USA) 132)   **66**
[2007 64: 6m⁵ 6m⁶ 7g 6d 6g³ 5.9f⁵ p6g* 6d⁶ p6m⁵ p6m⁴ p6g² p6g² Dec 4] quite good-
topped filly: fair performer: left M. Dods, won handicap at Kempton in October: stays 6f:
acts on polytrack, firm and good to soft ground: tried visored: versatile regarding tactics:
sold 4,500 gns. *S. C. Williams*

STORM FORCE (IRE) 2 b.c. (Apr 6) Cape Cross (IRE) 129 – Aguinaga (IRE) 76   **105 p**
(Machiavellian (USA) 123) [2007 p7g* p7g* Nov 3] rather leggy colt: third foal: closely
related to 3-y-o Conquest: dam, Irish 12.5f winner, half-sister to very smart 6f/7f
performer Iktamal and smart French performer up to 12.5f First Magnitude: useful form:
impressive winner of both starts, namely maiden at Lingfield in October and minor event
at Kempton (beat Seasider by 2½ lengths, value extra): has plenty of speed, but likely to
stay 1m: will go on improving. *Saeed bin Suroor*

STORMINGMICHAELORI 4 b.g. Vettori (IRE) 119 – Stormswept (USA) 74   –
(Storm Bird (CAN) 134) [2007 46: 10.1m f8g May 14] maiden: well held in 2007: tried
in cheekpieces. *N. Wilson*

STORM LILY (USA) 3 b.f. Storm Cat (USA) – Crimplene (IRE) 120 (Lion Cavern   **55**
(USA) 117) [2007 8.3d 10.3g Sep 29] rather leggy filly: second foal: half-sister to useful
2004 2-y-o 6f winner Crimson Sun (by Danzig): dam 6f (at 2 yrs) to 1¼m (including Irish
1000 Guineas and Nassau Stakes) winner: well held in maidens at Windsor and Chester:
has left Godolphin. *Saeed bin Suroor*

STORM MISSION (USA) 3 b. or br.g. Storm Creek (USA) – Bemissed (USA)   **54**
(Nijinsky (CAN) 138) [2007 54: f7g³ 8.2g⁴ 10.1m f8g⁵ 8.1m⁶ 7s⁵ 8.3d⁶ 7.9f 7g Sep 18]
tall, close-coupled gelding: modest maiden: left Miss V. Haigh after sixth outing: stays
1m: acts on fibresand and good to firm going: tried blinkered/in cheekpieces/tongue tied:
inconsistent. *J. Mackie*

STORM OBSESSION (IRE) 3 b.f. Val Royal (FR) 127 – Myran (IRE) 53 (In The   –
Wings 128) [2007 66: 8.1m 10m May 22] €14,000Y: fifth foal: half-sister to winners
abroad by Dr Devious and Revoque: dam, Irish maiden (stayed 1½m), out of half-sister
to Middle Park Stakes winner Balla Cove: form only when fourth in maiden at Bellewstown in 2006: left Ms F. Crowley in Ireland after final start that year: stays 1m: acts on
good to firm ground: tried in cheekpieces. *P. J. Makin*

STORM OF ARABIA (IRE) 4 b.g. Intikhab (USA) 135 – Mauradell (IRE) (Mujadil   **67**
(USA) 119) [2007 73: p10g p12.2g⁶ Mar 5] well-made gelding: fair handicapper: stays
1½m: acts on polytrack, yet to race on extremes of going on turf. *W. R. Swinburn*

STORM PATH (IRE) 3 gr.c. Giant's Causeway (USA) 132 – Sianema 62 (Persian   **54**
Bold 123) [2007 –: 11m 7g² 10.2g p10g p10g p11g⁵ p12g Dec 16] close-coupled colt:
modest maiden: left Eve Johnson Houghton after third start: stays 11f: acts on polytrack.
D. R. C. Elsworth

STORM PETREL 3 b.f. Xaar 132 – Vitesse (IRE) 61 (Royal Academy (USA) 130) **61**
[2007 64p: 7g⁶ p8g 8.1m 6g⁶ 8d Oct 1] leggy filly: modest maiden handicapper: left
N. Littmoden after second start: likely to prove best at 7f/1m: acts on polytrack: tongue
tied last 2 starts. *R. M. Beckett*

STORM SHOWER (IRE) 9 b.g. Catrail (USA) 123 – Crimson Shower 61 (Dowsing **– §**
(USA) 124) [2007 f7g Feb 6] good-topped gelding: modest and ungenuine performer at
best: well held sole start since 2004: usually visored. *Mrs N. Macauley*

STORM SIR (USA) 2 ch.c. (Mar 2) Johannesburg (USA) 127 – Robust (USA) 55 **86**
(Conquistador Cielo (USA)) [2007 6m² p7g Oct 12] $270,000Y: lengthy colt: third foal:
half-brother to fairly useful 2005 2-y-o 7f winner Swan Maiden (by Swain): dam, ran 3
times in Ireland, half-sister to Belmont Stakes winner Danzig Connection and US Grade 2
9f winner Roi Danzig: fairly useful maiden: promising second to Paco Boy at Newbury:
longer trip, only seventh behind Storm Force at Lingfield: may prove best short of 7f.
J. Noseda

STORMY JOURNEY 2 b.g. (May 4) Mujahid (USA) 125 – Sabonis (USA) 68 (The **63**
Minstrel (CAN) 135) [2007 5m 6s⁶ 5d³ 5m² 6m 6m³ 5.5m 6d Oct 9] small, short-backed
gelding: modest maiden: will prove best kept to 5f/6f: acts on good to firm and good to
soft going. *Mrs K. Walton*

STORMY RIVER (FR) 4 gr.c. Verglas (IRE) 118 – Miss Bio (FR) (River Mist (USA) **119**
119) [2007 123: 8.9g 9.3s³ 8m* 8g⁵ 8d⁵ Sep 29] angular, heavy-topped colt: smart performer: returned to near best when winning Prix Messidor at Maisons-Laffitte in July by
1½ lengths from Satri: below-form fifth afterwards behind Manduro in Prix Jacques le
Marois at Deauville (didn't find much, reportedly coughed and gave dirty scope) and
Ramonti in Queen Elizabeth II Stakes at Ascot: stayed 1m: acted on heavy and good
to firm going: wore cheekpieces third/fourth starts in 2007: tended to be laid back in
preliminaries: carried head high/raced lazily, and seemed best produced late: wore
crossed noseband: to stand at Haras d'Etreham, France, fee €8,000. *N. Clement, France*

STORMY VIEW (USA) 2 b. or br.f. (Mar 16) Cozzene (USA) – Another Storm **66**
(USA) (Gone West (USA)) [2007 7m p8g⁴ Aug 29] useful-looking filly: second foal:
half-sister to 3-y-o Asperity: dam, US 2-y-o 8.5f winner, out of Breeders' Cup Juvenile
Fillies winner Storm Song: better effort in maidens when fourth to City of The Kings at
Kempton, possbily still needing run: stays 1m. *J. H. M. Gosden*

STORYBOOK (UAE) 3 ch.f. Halling (USA) 133 – Blixen (USA) 90 (Gone West **92 +**
(USA)) [2007 p8g* p8.6g* p8.5f 8g* Oct 19] first foal: dam, Irish 2-y-o 6f winner, out
of US Grade 1 9f winner Danish, herself sister to high-class performer up to 1½m Ace:
fairly useful form: won maiden at Lingfield in January, handicap at Wolverhampton
(dead-heated with Boscobel, making running and rallying, left M. Jarvis after) in February and allowance race at Keeneland in October: likely to stay 1¼m: acts on polytrack.
P. L. Biancone, USA

STORYLAND (USA) 2 b.f. (May 2) Menifee (USA) 124 – Auspice (USA) (Robellino **68 p**
(USA) 127) [2007 6m Oct 4] $10,000Y, 47,000 2-y-o: useful-looking filly: has a quick
action: second foal: dam, unraced half-sister to 3-y-o Strategic Prince, out of sister to
Ramruma: 33/1 and green, seventh to Shabiba in maiden at Newmarket: will be suited by
7f/1m: sure to improve. *W. J. Haggas*

STOTSFOLD 4 b.g. Barathea (IRE) 127 – Eliza Acton 70 (Shirley Heights 130) [2007 **114**
104: 10.3m² 10.1d 12g³ 9.9m* Sep 16] good-bodied gelding: smart performer: further
improvement in 2007, winning Select Racing UK On Sky 432 Stakes at Goodwood (by
½ length from Zaham, edging left) in September: also ran creditably when ¾-length
second to Temple Place in handicap at Chester and third to Purple Moon in listed race at
Goodwood (short of room 2f out): stays 1½m, at least as effective at 1¼m: acts on polytrack and good to soft going, goes particularly well on good or firmer: has been early to
post: usually held up. *W. R. Swinburn*

STOW 2 ch.g. (Feb 22) Selkirk (USA) 129 – Spry 84 (Suave Dancer (USA) 136) [2007 **71 p**
8d⁶ 8.2g⁴ p9.5g³ Nov 17] leggy, close-coupled gelding: fifth foal: brother to 3-y-o Bajan
Pride and half-brother to 6-y-o Serramanna: dam 1½m winner: fair form in maidens, in
frame at Nottingham (fourth to Doctor Fremantle) and Wolverhampton: gelded after: will
be suited by 1¼m/1½m: type to do well in handicaps. *H. Morrison*

ST PETERSBURG 7 ch.g. Polar Falcon (USA) 126 – First Law 57 (Primo Dominie **90**
121) [2007 107, a95: p8.6g p8g⁶ 8s p7g 8s³ p10m Nov 1] strong, lengthy gelding: fairly
useful handicapper nowadays: left M. Tompkins after third outing: stays 1m: acts on all-
weather, raced only on good going or softer (acts on heavy): tried tongue tied. *J. R. Boyle*

ST PHILIP (USA) 3 b.c. Dance Brightly (CAN) – Tender Moment (USA) (Torrential **106** (USA) 117) [2007 98: 7m⁴ 8m³ 6g Dec 9] tall, useful-looking colt: useful performer: best effort when ½-length third of 30 to Eddie Jock in Britannia Stakes (Handicap) at Royal Ascot, running on well after patient ride: sold privately, left R. Beckett and renamed Elite Champion before final outing: stays 1m: yet to race on extremes of going: refused to enter stall prior to intended return, and also looked temperamental on reappearance, hanging left. *D. J. Hall, Hong Kong*

STRABINIOS KING 3 b.g. King's Best (USA) 132 – Strawberry Morn (CAN) (Trav- **69** elling Victor (CAN)) [2007 63p: f8g⁴ 8g 7g* 7.1g 6.9f 6s² p7.1g p6g* p6g³ p6g⁴ p6d² Dec 28] workmanlike gelding: fair performer: won maiden at Catterick in June and claimer at Wolverhampton (left P. Haslam after) in December: effective at 6f to 1m: acts on all-weather and soft going. *R. A. Harris*

STRAIGHT AND LEVEL (CAN) 2 gr. or ro.c. (Mar 18) Buddha (USA) 122 – **77** Azusa (USA) (Flying Paster (USA)) [2007 p5g⁴ 5g 6f⁵ p6g³ 6d² p7g⁴ p8g³ p8g p8g* Dec 22] fair performer: claimed from J. Hills £15,000 fifth start (wore cheekpieces): won 4-runner minor event at Lingfield in December: stays 1m: acts on polytrack, firm and good to soft going: held up. *Miss Jo Crowley*

STRAIGHT FACE (IRE) 3 b.g. Princely Heir (IRE) 111 – Dakota Sioux (IRE) 90 **71 d** (College Chapel 122) [2007 73: p7.1g⁶ p8g² p7g p7.1g 5.2g 5d p8g 8.5g Sep 19] sturdy gelding: fair maiden: left W. Knight after second outing: well below form after: stays easy 1m: acts on polytrack, good to firm and good to soft going: effective visored or not: ungenuine. *M. Wigham*

STRAIGHT GAL (IRE) 4 br.f. Namid 128 – Kazimiera (IRE) 77 (Polish Patriot **48** (USA) 128) [2007 52: p5g⁶ p6g 7s⁴ 8d Jul 17] poor maiden on balance: best effort at 6f: reportedly bled second outing at 3 yrs. *Mrs N. Smith*

STRAIGHT (IRE) 2 b.c. (Apr 29) King Charlemagne (USA) 120 – Fun of The Fair **55 ?** (Mistertopogigo (IRE) 118) [2007 5g 6s⁶ 6d 7m⁵ 7g Oct 3] little impact in maidens, though seemingly modest form penultimate start. *M. Brittain*

STRATEGIC KNIGHT (USA) 2 b.c. (Apr 10) Johannesburg (USA) 127 – Western **71** Friend (USA) (Gone West (USA)) [2007 p8m³ f8d³ Dec 15] $275,000F, 270,000Y: half-brother to several winners, including smart 6f (including at 2 yrs)/7f winner Resplendent Cee (by Polar Falcon) and 6f/7f winner Rezzago (by Night Shift) and 5-y-o Jordan's Light, both fairly useful: dam ran once: fair form when third in maidens at Lingfield and Southwell. *P. F. I. Cole*

STRATEGIC MISSION (IRE) 2 b.c. (Jan 30) Red Ransom (USA) – North East Bay **91 p** (USA) (Prospect Bay (CAN) 117) [2007 7.1g³ 7m⁶ 8d* Oct 11] 74,000F, 120,000Y: tall, leggy colt: has scope: first foal: dam, ran once in US, half-sister to smart miler Hold To Ransom (by Red Ransom): fairly useful form: confirmed earlier promise (after 3-month break) when winning maiden at Newbury by 1¾ lengths from Saleima, making all: will probably stay 1¼m: sort to do better still at 3 yrs. *P. F. I. Cole*

STRATEGIC MOUNT 4 b.g. Montjeu (IRE) 137 – Danlu (USA) (Danzig (USA)) **102** [2007 99: 14g⁶ 12m* 14d 10m p12g Dec 1] big, strong gelding: useful handicapper: won at Ascot (by head from John Terry) in August: below form after, in listed event at Kempton final outing: gelded after: effective at 1½m/1¾m: acts on firm going, below form on softer than good: tried blinkered. *P. F. I. Cole*

STRATEGIC MOVER (USA) 2 ch.c. (Jan 13) Grand Slam (USA) 120 – Efficient **91** Frontier (USA) (Mt Livermore (USA)) [2007 7m³ 8m⁴ 8m⁴ Sep 15] $100,000Y, 65,000 2-y-o: useful-looking colt: second foal: dam, US 1m/8.5f winner (including minor stakes), half-sister to US Grade 2 9f winner Navesink: fairly useful maiden: seemingly best run when fourth to McCartney in listed event at Salisbury second start: stays 1m: raced only on good to firm going: tongue tied. *P. F. I. Cole*

STRATEGIC PRINCE 3 b.c. Dansili 127 – Ausherra (USA) 106 (Diesis 133) [2007 **111** 114: 8m 12g 7m Jun 20] tall, close-coupled, quite attractive colt: smart performer: won 3 times at 2 yrs, notably in July Stakes at Newmarket and Vintage Stakes at Goodwood: also third to Teofilo in Dewhurst Stakes at Newmarket on reappearance: respectable eighth to Cockney Rebel in 2000 Guineas at Newmarket, then tailed off in Derby at Epsom, then ran poorly in Jersey Stakes at Royal Ascot (shaped as if amiss) after: should have stayed at least 1m: acted on good to firm and good to soft going: had worn crossed noseband: sold privately, and to stand at Coolmore Stud, Ireland, fee €9,000. *P. F. I. Cole*

STRATHAIRD (IRE) 3 b.g. Medicean 128 – Heed My Warning (IRE) 102 (Second **44** Set (IRE) 127) [2007 47: f6g p7.1g³ 11.1f 13.8g p9.5g Oct 27] poor maiden: stays 7f: acts on polytrack. *P. C. Haslam*

STRATHMORE (IRE) 3 gr.g. Fath (USA) 116 – In The Highlands (Petong 126) **74**
[2007 70: p6g⁵ 5m⁴ 6m⁴ 6g* 6.1m⁵ 6d 5g 6.1s p6g³ p6g³ p6g² p6g⁶ p6g³ p6g⁶ Dec 29]
good-topped gelding: fair handicapper: won at Redcar in May: raced mainly at 6f, worth
another try at 7f: acts on polytrack and good to firm ground, well below form on softer
than good: tried in cheekpieces. *R. A. Fahey*

STRATN JACK 3 b.g. Rambling Bear 115 – Strat's Quest 65 (Nicholas (USA) 111) **–**
[2007 p10g⁵ p7g p8g Dec 28] first foal: dam 6f (including at 2 yrs)/7f winner: modest
form in 2 bumpers: well held in maidens/claimer. *B. G. Powell*

STRAVARA 4 b.g. Kayf Tara 130 – Stravsea 65 (Handsome Sailor 125) [2007 74: **77**
p13.9g⁴ p16.5g 10.9m 10d 10.2d³ 10.9d⁵ 10.5s 12.6s 10.3d³ 10.2d³ 10.5s⁴ Sep 28] good-
topped gelding: fair handicapper: probably stays 1½m: acts on all-weather and heavy
going: held up. *R. Hollinshead*

STRAVINSKY'S ART (USA) 3 b.c. Stravinsky (USA) 133 – Halo's Gleam (USA) **–**
(Halo (USA)) [2007 –: 7d 5.1m 5d 5.3g⁶ Jul 8] good-topped, useful-looking colt: little
sign of ability: has shown signs of temperament. *D. R. C. Elsworth*

STRAVITA 3 b.f. Weet-A-Minute (IRE) 106 – Stravsea 65 (Handsome Sailor 125) **70**
[2007 74: p8.6g⁵ 8.2s p9.5g p8.6g⁵ p9.5g Dec 26] compact filly: fair handicapper, lightly
raced: finished lame on reappearance and fell second outing: stays 8.6f: acts on polytrack.
R. Hollinshead

STRAVONIAN 7 b.g. Luso 124 – In The Evening (IRE) 73 (Distinctly North (USA) **– §**
115) [2007 9.2g 11.1m 12g⁵ Nov 8] little form: tried in cheekpieces: ungenuine.
D. A. Nolan

STRAWBERRY LOLLY 4 b.f. Lomitas 129 – Strawberry Morn (CAN) (Travelling **85**
Victor (CAN)) [2007 89: 10m 10f p8g⁶ p8.6g* p8g p8m Nov 24] long-backed filly: fairly
useful handicapper: won at Wolverhampton in October: stays 1¼m: acts on polytrack and
good to firm going: hung left third start. *M. Botti*

STRAWBERRY PATCH (IRE) 8 b.g. Woodborough (USA) 112 – Okino (USA) **60**
(Strawberry Road (AUS) 128) [2007 63: 5d 5f 5g 5g⁵ 6d⁵ 6s⁵ 5g 6d 5m 5m⁴ 5m 5d 5d 5m
Sep 30] strong, good-topped gelding: modest handicapper: best at 5f/6f: acts on firm and
soft ground: usually wears cheekpieces. *J. S. Goldie*

STRAW BOY 3 br.g. Hunting Lion (IRE) 115 – Sky Light Dreams (Dreams To Reality **–**
(USA) 113) [2007 57: 6d Aug 20] close-coupled gelding: modest maiden at 2 yrs: well
beaten in handicap sole start in 2007: should stay 1m: acts on soft and good to firm going.
R. Brotherton

STREET DEVIL (USA) 2 gr.c. (May 3) Street Cry (IRE) 130 – Math (USA) (Devil's **72 p**
Bag (USA)) [2007 7s³ Oct 9] $35,000Y, 40,000 2-y-o: half-brother to numerous winners,
notably 1m (at 2 yrs)/1¼m winner Art Trader (smart at 1m/9f in Hong Kong, by Arch):
dam, US 6f to 8.5f winner, out of half-sister to very smart miler Emperor Jones and
William Hill Futurity winner Bakharoff: 11/1, third in maiden at Folkestone, travelling
smoothly long way: will be suited by 1m: should progress. *P. A. Blockley*

STREET DIVA (USA) 2 ch.f. (Mar 19) Street Cry (IRE) 130 – Arctic Valley (USA) **69**
(Arctic Tern (USA) 126) [2007 p6g⁶ p7g⁵ p7g p6g⁴ Nov 8] 24,000 2-y-o: compact filly:
half-sister to several winners in US, notably 7f to 9f (Grade 2 event) winner Da Devil (by
Leo Castelli): dam US maiden: fair maiden: best effort when fifth at Kempton: likely to
stay 1m: raced only on polytrack. *P. A. Blockley*

STREET LIFE (IRE) 9 ch.g. Dolphin Street (FR) 125 – Wolf Cleugh (IRE) 65 (Last **78**
Tycoon 131) [2007 73: p12g* p12g p10g⁶ p10g p9.5g⁵ p10g 10g³ 10g* 10s* 11.6m 12d⁶
11s² 10g 10m 10g p12g 10d⁶ p9.5g⁶ p9.5g⁶ Nov 30] angular gelding: fair handicapper:
won at Kempton in January and Newmarket and Leicester in May: effective at 9.5f, barely stays 1¾m: acts on all-weather, heavy and good to firm going: held up. *W. J. Musson*

STREET POWER (USA) 2 b. or br.c. (Apr 29) Street Cry (IRE) 130 – Javana (USA) **67 p**
(Sandpit (BRZ) 129) [2007 p7m Dec 9] $70,000Y: second foal: dam, unraced, out of
sister to top-class miler Spinning World: 33/1, seventh to Hold The Gold in maiden at
Lingfield, not knocked about: should do better. *J. R. Gask*

STREET STAR (USA) 2 b.f. (Apr 19) Street Cry (IRE) 130 – Domludge (USA) (Lyp- **84 p**
hard (USA) 132) [2007 6f² 6d² 6g* Sep 19] lengthy filly: has scope: closely related to
useful French 6f/7f winner Vassia (by Machiavellian) and half-sister to several winners,
notably smart performers up to 1¾m Alva Glen (1m winner at 2 yrs, by Gulch) and
Shrewd Idea (by Alleged): dam once-raced half-sister to Cheveley Park and Prix Vermeille winner Mrs Penny: fairly useful form: twice runner-up, including behind Ancien

Regime at Yarmouth second start, before winning maiden there by short head from Applauded: free-going sort, may prove best at 5f/6f: acts on firm and good to soft going. *J. R. Fanshawe*

STREET WARRIOR (IRE) 4 b.g. Royal Applause 124 – Anne Bonny 105 (Ajdal (USA) 130) [2007 86: 8.2g⁵ 8.3f⁴ 8f* 9.1g⁴ 10f⁴ 10.2d 8g 8.2g⁵ Oct 31] rather leggy gelding: won at Bath in April: left M. Johnston 13,000 gns after fourth start, J. Unett after sixth: stays 1¼m: acts on polytrack and firm ground: sometimes slowly away. *G. H. Yardley* **81**

STRENGTH 'N HONOUR 7 b.g. Hernando (FR) 127 – Seasonal Splendour (IRE) 95 (Prince Rupert (FR) 121) [2007 p11g p10m Nov 11] strong, workmanlike gelding: fairly useful performer in 2005: unraced at 6 yrs, and only modest form in claimers on return: should stay beyond 1½m: acts on polytrack, raced only on good ground or firmer on turf (acts on firm). *Karen George* **64**

STRENSALL 10 b.g. Beveled (USA) – Payvashooz 78 (Ballacashtal (CAN)) [2007 76: 5m 5m² 5d 5d 5m* 5g 5m⁵ 5d² 5s⁵ 5g 5g p5.1g Dec 3] sturdy gelding: fair handicapper: won at Musselburgh in August: best at 5f: acts on fibresand, firm and soft ground: sometimes slowly away: often races prominently. *R. E. Barr* **78 a–**

STRETTON (IRE) 9 br.g. Doyoun 124 – Awayil (USA) 82 (Woodman (USA) 126) [2007 90, a65: 12.3g⁸ 14g³ 12v⁶ 12.3m 12.3m 12m⁶ 13.4g⁶ Sep 29] leggy, close-coupled gelding: fairly useful handicapper: won at Chester in May: stays 1½m: acts on polytrack, firm and soft going: wore cheekpieces once: held up. *J. D. Bethell* **89 a–**

STRICTLY ELSIE (IRE) 2 b.f. (Apr 24) No Excuse Needed 123 – Sophrana (IRE) (Polar Falcon (USA) 126) [2007 6s 7d⁵ 6g³ 7g Oct 6] €7,500F, 4,500Y: plain filly: fifth foal: half-sister to Irish 9.5f winner Jemmy's Flame (by Grand Lodge) and fairly useful 1m winner Altar (by Cape Cross): dam French 9.5f/10.5f winner: modest maiden: third at Thirsk: will stay 1m. *J. R. Norton* **57**

STRIFE (IRE) 4 b.g. Stravinsky (USA) 133 – Fife (IRE) 95 (Lomond (USA) 128) [2007 55: 9.1g 10.3d 8.3m⁴ 7m² 7.1m 8f² Sep 10] good-topped gelding: modest performer: stays 1m: acts on firm ground: tried in cheekpieces/visor: has been slowly away. *W. M. Brisbourne* **55**

STRIKEEN (IRE) 3 ch.g. Intikhab (USA) 135 – Sheen Falls (IRE) 56 (Prince Rupert (FR) 121) [2007 91: p8g 10d 9.9g 10m 12d Jul 29] good-bodied gelding: fairly useful handicapper: below best in 2007: stays 1¼m: acts on fibresand, unraced on extremes of going on turf: has shown signs of temperament: won juvenile hurdle in August. *T. G. Mills* **80**

STRIKE FORCE 3 b.g. Dansili 127 – Miswaki Belle (USA) 73 (Miswaki (USA) 124) [2007 71: p9.5g⁴ p8.6g⁴ p6g² p7g⁴ p6g* f6g⁵ 7g⁴ 6m³ p6g⁴ 6.1m⁴ 5.7d² p7.1g³ 6f p6g² 6s* 6d 7m⁶ p8.6d³ Dec 27] well-made gelding: fair performer: won sellers at Wolverhampton in March and Catterick in July: effective at 5.7f, probably stays easy 9.5f: acts on polytrack and soft going: tried blinkered, usually wears cheekpieces. *K. F. Clutterbuck* **65**

STRIKE THE DEAL (USA) 2 ch.c. (Feb 18) Van Nistelrooy (USA) 108 – Countess Gold (USA) (Mt Livermore (USA)) [2007 p6g* 5m⁵ 5.5m³ 6g* 7m 6m² 6m² 8d⁴ Oct 26] $40,000Y, 140,000 2-y-o: medium-sized, quite attractive colt: first foal: dam US sprint **111**

Richmond Stakes, Goodwood—Strike The Deal makes further progress to get the better of Fat Boy; Exhibition (left) and One Great Cat (third right) share third place

maiden: smart performer: won maiden at Lingfield in June and Richmond Stakes at Goodwood (beat Fat Boy by 1¼ lengths) in August: also ran well when second to Dark Angel twice, beaten a neck in Mill Reef Stakes at Newbury and ½ length in Middle Park Stakes at Newmarket: respectable 2¼ lengths fourth to Nownownow in Breeders' Cup Juvenile Turf at Monmouth final outing: probably stays 1m: acts on polytrack, good to firm and good to soft going: changed hands 480,000 gns in December. *J. Noseda*

STRIKE UP THE BAND 4 b.g. Cyrano de Bergerac 120 – Green Supreme (Primo Dominie 121) [2007 114: 6.5g a6f 6g p5g³ 5m 6d³ 6d 5g 5g5 5g Oct 27] strong, good-topped gelding: useful performer nowadays: creditable efforts in 2007 at Lingfield (listed race, third to King Orchisios), Longchamp (Prix de l'Abbaye, eighth to Benbaun) and Catterick (handicap, fifth to King Orchisios) fourth/eighth/ninth outings: best at 5f/6f: acts on polytrack, firm and good to soft going: races prominently. *D. Nicholls*   107

STRIKING SPIRIT 2 b.c. (Apr 8) Oasis Dream 129 – Aspiring Diva (USA) (Distant View (USA) 126) [2007 6m5 6g* 6d² Oct 12] good-topped colt: third foal: closely related to winner in Greece by Desert Prince and half-brother to useful French 2005 2-y-o 5f/5.5f winner Daring Diva (by Dansili): dam, fairly useful French 5f/6.5f winner (latter at 2 yrs), out of US Grade 2 8.5f winner Queen of Song: useful form: won maiden at Haydock (beat Beacon Lodge by 1½ lengths) in September: better still when neck second to Floristry in nursery at York, despite not settling fully: should prove best at 5f/6f: will continue to improve. *B. W. Hills*   98 p

STRINGSOFMYHEART 3 b.f. Halling (USA) 133 – Heart's Harmony (Blushing Groom (FR) 131) [2007 –: p10g p12.2g² p12g³ 12m* 12g5 11.1g* p12.2g f11d³ Dec 21] big, rangy filly: fair performer: won handicap at Pontefract in April and claimer at Hamilton (looked far from straightforward) in June: stays 1½m: acts on all-weather and good to firm going: tried in cheekpieces/blinkers: races prominently: temperamental. *Miss Gay Kelleway*   73 §

STRIVING (IRE) 2 b. or br.f. (Apr 4) Danehill Dancer (IRE) 117 – Wannabe 84 (Shirley Heights 130) [2007 7s 7.1g5 Oct 2] €300,000Y: big, lengthy, heavy-topped filly: eighth foal: closely related to Cheveley Park winner/1000 Guineas second Wannabe Grand (by Danehill) and half-sister to useful 2001 2-y-o 1m winner Assaaf (by Night Shift) and 4-y-o Wannabe Posh: dam 1m/1¼m (in France) winner: better effort in maidens when fifth to Swanky Lady at Warwick, still green: will stay at least 1m: type to progress at 3 yrs. *Sir Michael Stoute*   59 p

STRIVING STORM (USA) 3 b. or br.g. Stormin Fever (USA) 116 – Sugars For Nanny (USA) (Brocco (USA) 124) [2007 103: 8m5 10g² 12s 10m 8g Nov 3] big, lengthy gelding: has plenty of scope: has a short, choppy action: useful performer: good efforts in 2007 in Craven Stakes at Newmarket (sweating, 3¼ lengths fifth to Adagio) and Classic Trial at Sandown (2 lengths second to Regime, wandering): well held after: stays 1¼m: acts on heavy and good to firm going: gelded after final start. *P. W. Chapple-Hyam*   105

STROBE 3 ch.g. Fantastic Light (USA) 134 – Sadaka (USA) 77 (Kingmambo (USA) 125) [2007 59: 11.5m p12g* p12g4 p16g² 15.4m* 16.2m² 16m² p16g* 17.1m* 16m Oct 3] good-bodied gelding: fairly useful handicapper: won at Lingfield in June, Folkestone in August, and Kempton and Pontefract (dead-heated with Indonesia) in September: stays 17f: acts on polytrack and good to firm ground: usually makes running: tough and reliable: joined Mrs L. Normile. *J. A. Osborne*   87

STRONGHOLD 5 b.h. Danehill (USA) 126 – Insinuate (USA) 99 (Mr Prospector (USA)) [2007 120: 7d³ Aug 18] strong, lengthy, attractive horse: very smart performer in 2007: not disgraced when length third to Red Evie in Hungerford Stakes at Newbury only outing in 2007: was effective at 7f/1m: acted on good to firm and good to soft going (seemingly not on soft), probably on polytrack: retired. *J. H. M. Gosden*   113

STRONG MARKET 2 b.g. (Apr 4) Piccolo 121 – Bon Marche 89 (Definite Article 121) [2007 p7.1g Jul 10] 14/1, detached in maiden at Wolverhampton: withdrawn (upset in stall) intended second start. *H. J. L. Dunlop*   –

STRONG SURVIVOR (USA) 4 b.g. Kingmambo (USA) 125 – Summer Solstice (IRE) (Caerleon (USA) 132) [2007 64: 12d4 12m³ p12.2g5 Oct 19] big, rangy gelding: has scope: fair maiden handicapper: will stay 1¾m: acts on good to firm and good to soft ground. *P. R. Webber*   72

STRONG WILL 7 b.g. Primo Dominie 121 – Reine de Thebes (FR) 67 (Darshaan 133) [2007 f12g May 1] leggy gelding: shows knee action: modest maiden handicapper in 2003: well beaten in seller only Flat start since. *J. R. Holt*   –

STROPPI POPPI 3 b.f. Mtoto 134 – Capricious Lass (Corvaro (USA) 124) [2007 **48**
p10g p12m⁵ p12g Nov 15] third known foal: sister to fairly useful 1m winner King of
Diamonds: dam ran once in Ireland: form in maidens only when fifth to Top Tiger at
Kempton. *Jean-Rene Auvray*

STRUCTURA (USA) 2 b. or br.f. (Feb 10) Stormin Fever (USA) 116 – Sisterella **63 §**
(USA) (Diesis 133) [2007 5m⁴ 5.2g⁵ 5m 5m³ 5.7m p5g 5.1f p5.1g² p5g Oct 15]
$27,000Y: good-topped filly: sixth foal: dam, US 9f to 1½m winner, half-sister to US
Grade 3 1m winner Colonial Minstrel, out of Cheveley Park Stakes winner Minstrella:
modest maiden: best at 5f: acts on polytrack and firm going: tried in cheekpieces: ungenuine. *J. S. Moore*

STRUT THE STAGE (IRE) 3 b.g. Lil's Boy (USA) 109 – Eva Luna (IRE) 106 **72**
(Double Schwartz 128) [2007 79: 8d 6m⁴ 7m 8g⁵ 6d⁴ 6f⁶ 6f 6.1d³ p7g p6g³ 7g p7.1g p6g⁴
p7g² Dec 30] fair maiden: left J. Bolger in Ireland after third start: in-and-out form after:
stays 7f: acts on polytrack, firm and good to soft going: tried blinkered, in cheekpieces/
tongue tied last 3 outings. *B. W. Duke*

ST SAVARIN (FR) 6 ch.g. Highest Honor (FR) 124 – Sacara (GER) (Monsagem **101**
(USA) 117) [2007 96, a90: 12d⁶ 13.1s⁶ 13.1s* 12s² p12g⁶ f11d* Dec 18] sturdy gelding:
useful performer: won handicap at Ayr in October and claimer at Southwell in December:
best effort when short-head second to Buccellati in quite valuable handicap at Ascot
fourth outing: seems to stay 1¾m: acts on all-weather, firm and soft ground: sometimes
races freely: reliable: has joined B. Johnson. *R. A. Fahey*

STUART LITTLE (DEN) 3 b.c. Esprit du Nord (USA) 126 – Cocco Pio (IRE) (Turtle **91**
Island (IRE) 123) [2007 10m⁵ Apr 20] tall colt: third foal: dam unraced half-sister to
Norwegian 1000 Guineas and Oaks winner Turf Turtle: a leading 2-y-o in Scandinavia
when trained by F. Castro, unbeaten in maiden and 2 minor events (awarded first of them)
at Klampenborg: fairly useful form on British debut when fifth to Light Shift in minor
event at Newbury, fading: stays 1¼m. *P. W. Chapple-Hyam*

STUBBS ART (IRE) 2 ch.c. (Jan 28) Hawk Wing (USA) 136 – Rich Dancer 70 **94**
(Halling (USA) 133) [2007 5g 6m⁵ 7d³ 8m² 9m* 10g³ Nov 3] 30,000F, 30,000Y: rangy
colt: first foal: dam, maiden (stayed 7f), half-sister to 8-y-o Just James: fairly useful
performer: won nursery at Newmarket in September by 4 lengths despite idling: further
progress when 1¾ lengths third to Twice Over in minor event there, going freely: stays
1¼m: acts on good to firm and good to soft ground. *D. R. C. Elsworth*

STYLE AWARD 2 b.f. (Apr 3) Acclamation 118 – Elegant (IRE) (Marju (IRE) 127) **79**
[2007 5m³ 5m* 6s⁴ 5v* 5.1s⁶ 5m² 5d² 5m⁴ 5.5m⁴ 5.1g⁴ 6v³ 5g* Nov 9] leggy, lengthy
filly: fourth foal: half-sister to 3 winners, including 5-y-o Art Elegant: dam, Irish maiden,
half-sister to smart but irresolute performer up to 1½m Peking Opera: fair performer:
won maiden at Catterick in June, minor event at Beverley in July and nursery at Musselburgh in November: best at 5f/6f: acts on heavy and good to firm going: consistent.
W. J. H. Ratcliffe

STYLISTIC (IRE) 6 b.m. Daggers Drawn (USA) 114 – Treasure (IRE) 72 (Treasure **–**
Kay 114) [2007 67: p7.1g 9v 6.3d 5g Oct 20] fair maiden handicapper at her best: no form
in 2007, leaving J. Lambe after reappearance: tried in blinkers/cheekpieces/tongue tied.
K. F. O'Brien, Ireland

SUALDA (IRE) 8 b.g. Idris (IRE) 118 – Winning Heart 98 (Horage 124) [2007 85: **77**
11.7f 12m⁴ 11.9f p13.9g Dec 1] tall gelding: fair performer nowadays: left P. D. Evans
after third start: effective at 11.5f to 2m: acts on firm and good to soft going: tried in
blinkers/cheekpieces/tongue tied: often held up. *Ollie Pears*

SUBADAR 3 b.g. Zamindar (USA) 116 – Valencia 79 (Kenmare (FR) 125) [2007 73p: **65**
7m* p7g Sep 19] fair form: confirmed 2-y-o promise when landing odds in maiden at
Folkestone in April: gelded, ran poorly in handicap at Kempton final outing: should prove
as effective at 6f as 7f: acts on polytrack and good to firm ground: sold 12,000 gns, joined
M. Botti. *R. Charlton*

SUCCEED (IRE) 4 b.f. Elnadim (USA) 128 – Pico 71 (Piccolo 121) [2007 64: p5g⁶ **61**
p5g³ Jan 29] modest performer: will prove best at 5f/6f: acts on all-weather and firm
ground: has shown signs of temperament. *Mrs H. Sweeting*

SUDAN (IRE) 4 ch.c. Peintre Celebre (USA) 137 – Sarabande (USA) (Woodman **117**
(USA) 126) [2007 117: 12v⁶ 12g⁵ 12d* 12g Sep 9] leggy, close-coupled colt: smart
performer: changed ownership, back to best when winning Gran Premio di Milano at
Milan (by nose from Hattan) in June: left E. Lellouche in France, last of 10 in Stockholm
Cup at Taby final outing: ideally suited by 1½m: acts on good to firm and good to soft
ground. *M. A. Jarvis*

Tattersalls Ireland Sale Stakes, the Curragh—Sudden Impact takes this valuable prize back to Britain; Invincible Ash, Houston Dynimo (No.5) and Nikindi (left) are next

SUDDEN IMPACT (IRE) 2 b. or br.f. (Feb 3) Modigliani (USA) 106 – Suddenly 86 (Puissance 110) [2007 5m³ 5g 5m 5g* 6.1m⁶ 6d* 6m⁶ 6d 6g Nov 2] €21,000Y: lengthy filly: fourth foal: half-sister to 3 winners, including useful 2004 2-y-o 6f/7f winner Sudden Dismissal (by Inchinor) and Irish 1m winner Sudden Silence (by Kris): dam 2-y-o 7f winner: fairly useful on balance: won maiden at Thirsk in July and Tattersalls Ireland Sale Stakes at the Curragh (by 6 lengths, probably flattered) in August: well held in listed races subsequently: should prove best at 5f/6f: acts on good to soft going. *Paul Green* **100 ?**

SUDDEN IMPULSE 6 b.m. Silver Patriarch (IRE) 125 – Sanshang (FR) (Astronef 116) [2007 69: 9.9m 9.9m³ 12.4m* 12g 12m⁶ 12d* 12.1v⁴ 12s 10.1g² p9.5g p12g Dec 19] strong mare: fair handicapper: won at Newcastle in May and Musselburgh in June: effective at 1¼m/1½m: acts on polytrack, soft and good to firm ground: tried in cheekpieces. *A. D. Brown* **79**

SUDOOR 3 b.f. Fantastic Light (USA) 134 – Wissal (USA) (Woodman (USA) 126) [2007 98: 10m² 9.9g² 8d⁵ 8d⁴ 10.1g 8.3g* 10.3m³ Nov 10] small, useful-looking filly: useful performer: won minor event at Leicester (by ½ length from Lady Gloria) in October: also ran well when placed in listed races at Newmarket (6 lengths second to Dalvina), Goodwood (1½ lengths second to Cosmodrome) and Doncaster (2¼ lengths third behind Gower Song): stayed 1¼m: acted on good to firm going, probably on good to soft: consistent: visits Oasis Dream. *J. L. Dunlop* **100**

SUE'S HAWK (IRE) 2 ch.f. (Jan 25) Hawk Wing (USA) 136 – Desert Blues (IRE) (Desert Prince (IRE) 130) [2007 p7g Sep 11] 18,000F, 32,000Y: unfurnished filly: first foal: dam unraced half-sister to smart Irish/US performer up to 9f Rainbow Blues: 20/1, well beaten (looked a handful) in maiden at Lingfield. *A. P. Jarvis* **–**

SUES SURPRISE (IRE) 3 b.f. Montjeu (IRE) 137 – My Micheline (Lion Cavern (USA) 117) [2007 91p: 10.4g³ 12d 8d p9.5g² 10.3m* Aug 31] strong, lengthy filly: good mover: useful performer: in cheekpieces, won maiden at Chester (by 10 lengths from Demisemiquaver) in August: best effort when 2 lengths third to Passage of Time in Musidora Stakes at York on reappearance, dictating: stays 10.4f: acts on good to firm going: usually races prominently: reportedly finished distressed in Oaks at Epsom second outing: sold 60,000 gns. *B. W. Hills* **98**

SUFFOLK HOUSE 5 b.g. Paris House 123 – Suffolk Girl (Statoblest 120) [2007 46: f8g⁵ f8g p8.6g 7m 8s Jun 21] poor performer nowadays: stays 1m: acts on fibresand: tried in cheekpieces/blinkers. *M. Brittain* **46**

SUGARBUSH 3 b.f. Kingmambo (USA) 125 – Ive Gota Bad Liver (USA) (Mt Livermore (USA)) [2007 10m p11g⁶ Jul 4] big, lengthy filly: second foal: closely related to **72**

9.2f winner Otelcaliforni (by Gulch): dam, 6f/7f winner in USA, half-sister to 1000 Guineas winner Russian Rhythm (by Kingmambo) and 5-y-o Perfectperformance: better effort in maidens when seventh to Shirley A Star at Newbury on debut: better than bare result at Kempton next time, again plenty to do and not knocked about: suffered injury after. *J. R. Fanshawe*

SUGAR LAND 3 b.f. Dansili 127 – Time For Tea (IRE) 73 (Imperial Frontier (USA) **81** 112) [2007 p6g 7m³ p6g* Jun 29] sixth foal: half-sister to 3 winners, including 7f to 9f winner Frazzled (by Greensmith), later successful in Spain, and 6-y-o Trifti, both fairly useful: dam maiden who stayed 1¼m: fairly useful form: easily best effort when winning maiden at Wolverhampton in June: stays 6f: acts on polytrack: sold 4,500 gns in October. *C. A. Cyzer*

SUGAR MINT (IRE) 2 b.f. (Feb 28) High Chaparral (IRE) 132 – Anna Karenina **99 p** (USA) (Atticus (USA) 121) [2007 7m² 8m⁴ 8d⁶ Sep 29] tall, good-topped filly: has scope: second foal: half-sister to useful Irish winner around 7f (including at 2 yrs) Anna's Rock (by Rock of Gibraltar): dam unraced half-sister to Breeders' Cup Classic winner Arcangues and to dams of Aquarelliste and Cape Verdi: useful form: shaped well at Doncaster first 2 starts, runner-up in maiden then 2 lengths fourth to Spacious in May Hill Stakes, travelling strongly both times: again highly tried in Fillies' Mile at Ascot (sixth to Listen), no impression: will be suited by 1¼m/1½m: acts on good to firm going: type to make a better 3-y-o, and sure to win races. *B. W. Hills*

SUGAR RAY (IRE) 3 b.c. Danehill (USA) 126 – Akuna Bay (USA) 88 (Mr Prospector **96** (USA)) [2007 70p: 10m³ 10f* 10m² 11.8d³ Oct 9] good-topped colt: has plenty of scope: useful performer: won maiden at Windsor (by 6 lengths) in August: better form when placed in handicaps at Sandown and Leicester after: stays 1½m: acts on firm and good to soft going. *Sir Michael Stoute*

SUGGESTIVE 9 b.g. Reprimand 122 – Pleasuring 68 (Good Times (ITY)) [2007 114: **106** 7g⁵ 7s 7.1m⁵ a7.5g Jul 29] big gelding: smart performer at best, just useful in 2007: best effort when last of 5 to New Seeker in listed race at Leicester on reappearance: winner at 1m, best at 7f: acts on polytrack, firm and soft going: visored/blinkered: not straightforward. *W. J. Haggas*

SUGITANI (USA) 5 b.g. Kingmambo (USA) 125 – Lady Reiko (IRE) (Sadler's Wells **–** (USA) 132) [2007 81: f11g* May 1] sturdy gelding: fair handicapper: as good as ever **a79** when beaten short head by Apex at Southwell in May: stays easy 2m: acts on all-weather and good to firm going: tongue tied at 2 yrs: usually blinkered nowadays: held up: sold 19,000 gns, sent to Saudi Arabia. *N. B. King*

SUHAYL STAR (IRE) 3 b.g. Trans Island 119 – Miss Odlum (IRE) 81 (Mtoto 134) **59** [2007 72: p8.6g⁵ p7g⁶ p7.1g² 6m 7m 8.1m 5m p6g³ 7g p7g Oct 31] strong, close-coupled gelding: fair performer: joined S. Hall £6,000 after third start: rejoined former trainer following ninth outing: stays easy 8.6f: acts on polytrack and good to firm going: tried visored/in cheekpieces: has raced freely: reportedly suffered breathing problem seventh start. *M. Wigham*

SUHEZY (IRE) 4 b.f. Orpen (USA) 116 – Ervedya (IRE) (Doyoun 124) [2007 56: f7g **36** 6s 8d 7.1m Jul 24] plain, leggy filly: poor performer nowadays: effective at 5f to 7f: acts on fibresand, firm and soft going: tried in cheekpieces. *J. S. Wainwright*

SUITE FRANCAISE 2 gr.f. (Mar 19) Hernando (FR) 127 – Entente Cordiale (USA) **55 p** (Affirmed (USA)) [2007 6g 6g³ p7g² p7g 7.1g² 7.5g Aug 16] sister to several at least useful winners, notably 9-y-o Foreign Affairs, and half-sister to winner in Italy by Northern Park: dam ran once in France: modest maiden: second in nursery at Musselburgh: will be suited by 1¼m+: should do better at 3 yrs. *Sir Mark Prescott*

SUITS ME 4 ch.g. Bertolini (USA) 125 – Fancier Bit (Lion Cavern (USA) 117) [2007 **92** 73: p8.6g³ p8.6g⁶ p10g⁴ 10m² 10f⁶ 10.5s³ 9.8v* 9.8m⁹ 9.9m 10.5s³ 8.9d⁵ 10.3g* 9.1v* Nov 3] tall, close-coupled gelding: fairly useful handicapper: won at Ripon in July and August, Doncaster in October and Ayr in November: stays 10.5f: acts on polytrack and any turf going: races prominently: has raced freely. *T. P. Tate*

SUKI BEAR 3 br.f. Xaar 132 – Dominion Rose (USA) 65 (Spinning World (USA) 130) **67** [2007 73: 7.1g Jun 7] leggy, close-coupled filly: fair form, lightly raced: not discredited in handicap at Sandown only start in 2007: will be suited by 1m. *W. R. Muir*

SULARNO 3 ch.g. Medicean 128 – Star Precision 103 (Shavian 125) [2007 79p: 11.6d **–** f8g² 8.3g 10.3m p12.2g Sep 21] strong, good-bodied gelding: fair handicapper: well **a73** below form after second outing in 2007: stays 1m: acts on fibresand. *H. Morrison*

SULTAN OF THE SAND 2 b.g. (Feb 25) High Estate 127 – Desert Bloom (FR) (Last Tycoon 131) [2007 p6g⁶ 6.1v 6m Aug 1] poor form in maidens: shapes like a sprinter. *C. C. Bealby* **44 +**

SUMDANCER (NZ) 5 b.g. Summer Suspicion (JPN) – Epic Dancer (NZ) (Epidaurus (USA)) [2007 10g⁶ 10d³ 8g 10f 8v 10d p12m Dec 8] New Zealand-bred gelding: maiden in 11 starts in native country before showing nothing in minor event at Lingfield on final outing: stays 1¼m. *M. Madgwick* **53**

SUMI GIRL (IRE) 3 b.f. Tiger Hill (IRE) 127 – Allonia (GER) (Surumu (GER)) [2007 73: 9.9m³ 8.9d Oct 13] big filly: fairly useful form: much better effort in handicaps in 2007 when third at Beverley on reappearance: likely to stay 1½m: acts on soft and good to firm ground. *R. A. Fahey* **80**

SUMMER BOUNTY 11 b.g. Lugana Beach 116 – Tender Moment (IRE) 78 (Caerleon (USA) 132) [2007 71§, a50§: 12.6s 10d⁵ 12.1m 10.1d 10.2m³ 10.9g³ p12g⁵ p12.2g* p10g⁵ p11g* p11g⁴ p12g⁶ Dec 19] leggy, close-coupled gelding: modest performer nowadays: won minor event at Wolverhampton in October and handicap at Kempton in November: stays 12.3f: acts on any going: tried blinkered/tongue tied: held up: often starts slowly (has virtually refused to race) and one to treat with caution. *F. Jordan* **63 §**

SUMMER DANCER (IRE) 3 b.g. Fasliyev (USA) 120 – Summer Style (IRE) 70 (Indian Ridge 123) [2007 72p: 8g 7s² 7m* p8g⁶ 8m³ 7s³ 7m⁴ 7g³ p7g⁴ p10g⁵ Dec 19] tall gelding: fairly useful handicapper: won at Newbury in June: effective at 7f to easy 1¼m: acts on polytrack, soft and good to firm going: free-going sort: often held up: has been slowly away: consistent. *D. R. C. Elsworth* **86 +**

SUMMER GIFT 4 b.f. Cadeaux Genereux 131 – Summer Exhibition (Royal Academy (USA) 130) [2007 7.5m 6d 9.9m 8.5m⁶ 8.5g 7g⁵ p8.6g Oct 2] third foal: half-sister to useful French 1m/8.5f winner Bazart (by Highest Honor): dam, unraced, out of useful 2-y-o 6f winner Dangora, herself closely related to smart dam of Zafonic: modest maiden: ran twice at 3 yrs for D. Smaga in France (best efforts): stays 8.5f, may prove best at shorter: acts on good to firm going. *J. O'Reilly* **51**

SUMMER LODGE 4 b.g. Indian Lodge (IRE) 127 – Summer Siren (FR) (Saint Cyrien (FR) 128) [2007 76: 12.1m⁶ p9.5g⁵ p9.5g⁴ p8.6g⁴ p8.6g 10.1v 10g Jul 20] small, sturdy gelding: fair maiden handicapper: effective at 8.6f to 1½m: acts on all-weather, firm and soft going: blinkered/visored: fairly useful over hurdles, won in September/November. *A. J. McCabe* **70**

SUMMER OF LOVE (IRE) 3 b.f. Fasliyev (USA) 120 – Overboard (IRE) 73 (Rainbow Quest (USA) 134) [2007 67: 12.1m⁶ 11.6m⁶ 10m³ 10f⁴ 11.7d³ 10g⁶ Jul 8] big, rangy filly: fair maiden handicapper: stays 1½m: acts on polytrack and firm ground: often races prominently: wandered fourth outing: sold 14,000 gns and joined A. King: won juvenile hurdle in October. *P. F. I. Cole* **69**

SUMMEROFSIXTYNINE 4 b.c. Fruits of Love (USA) 127 – Scurrilous 56 (Sharpo 132) [2007 p10g⁵ p12g⁴ p12g⁵ p12g³ p12.2d* Dec 28] tall, leggy colt: modest performer: in cheekpieces, won maiden at Wolverhampton in December: stays 1½m: raced only on polytrack. *J. G. M. O'Shea* **64**

SUMMER RECLUSE (USA) 8 gr.g. Cozzene (USA) – Summer Retreat (USA) 78 (Gone West (USA)) [2007 78: 6g 5.7f 5.1g⁴ 6d² 6f 6g 5.7d⁵ 6g⁴ 5.7f 5.1m 6m³ 6d p7.1g⁴ p7.1g Oct 18] fair handicapper: effective at 5.5f to 1m: acts on polytrack, firm and soft going: tried in cheekpieces: tongue tied nowadays: often slowly away: tough. *J. M. Bradley* **70**

SUMMER'S EVE 4 gr.f. Singspiel (IRE) 133 – Early Rising (USA) (Grey Dawn II 132) [2007 104: 10.4g⁵ 12m⁴ 8.3s⁵ 8d 9.9g⁵ Aug 26] lengthy filly: useful performer: creditable effort in 2007 only when fifth of 12 to Samira Gold in listed handicap at Goodwood final outing: stays 1½m: acts on soft and good to firm going: has hung left. *H. Candy* **101**

SUMMERVILLE STAR (IRE) 3 b.f. Fruits of Love (USA) 127 – Alexandra Fair (USA) 104 (Green Dancer (USA) 132) [2007 –: 12.9g p9.5g Nov 12] lightly-raced maiden: little form, including in Britain. *Michael McElhone, Ireland* **–**

SUMMER WINDS 2 ch.c. (Apr 25) Where Or When (IRE) 124 – Jetbeeah (IRE) 95 (Lomond (USA) 128) [2007 7g Aug 24] 65,000Y: lengthy colt: has scope: half-brother to several winners, including 1997 2-y-o 6f winner Dazilyn Lady (by Zilzal) and 4-y-o Simondiun, both useful: dam 1m winner: 9/1, very green in maiden at Newbury: will stay 1m: should improve. *T. G. Mills* **– p**

SUMMIT SURGE (IRE) 3 b.g. Noverre (USA) 125 – Lady Peculiar (CAN) **114**
(Sunshine Forever (USA)) [2007 93: 8g³ 10m⁶ 7d 8m p7g* p7g² Dec 5] 30,000Y:
sturdy gelding: half-brother to several winners, including 4-y-o Vacation: dam Canadian
6f winner: smart performer: easily best effort when winning handicap at Dundalk in
November under 10-0 by 2½ lengths from Mojito Royale: odds on, neck second to Xinji
in minor event there final start: at least as effective at 7f as 1m: acts on polytrack and good
to firm going: tongue tied except debut. *G. M. Lyons, Ireland*

SUMMON UP THEBLOOD 2 b.g. (Mar 5) Red Ransom (USA) – Diddymu (IRE) **80**
66 (Revoque (IRE) 122) [2007 7m 8.1f⁴ 8.1m³ 8f⁶ Sep 27] tall, quite attractive gelding:
fairly useful maiden: third to Silver Regent at Sandown: should prove best up to 1m:
raced only on going firmer than good: gelded after final start. *M. R. Channon*

SUMNER (IRE) 3 b.c. Xaar 132 – Black Jack Girl (IRE) (Ridgewood Ben 113) [2007 **85**
65p: 12g* 12g⁶ 12f³ 10m* 10m⁴ Oct 5] big, workmanlike colt: fairly useful handicapper:
won at Salisbury in May and Pontefract in September: stays 1½m: acts on firm ground:
sold 70,000 gns. *M. H. Tompkins*

SUN 2 ch.c. (Feb 7) Medicean 128 – Radiant Bride (USA) (Blushing Groom (FR) 131) **67**
[2007 7m 7m Oct 5] good-topped colt: towards rear in maidens at Newmarket, seemingly fair form behind Fireside latterly (tongue tied): will stay 1m/1¼m: sold 7,500 gns.
P. W. Chapple-Hyam

SUN BIAN 5 b.g. Makbul 104 – Silken Dalliance 91 (Rambo Dancer (CAN) 107) [2007 **–**
–: p7g² p8g⁶ p8g⁵ p8.6g p8.6g³ 8.1d p8.6g p7g p8.6d⁴ Dec 27] tall gelding: modest **a59**
maiden nowadays: stays easy 8.6f: acts on polytrack: tried blinkered/in cheekpieces.
L. P. Grassick

SUNBURN (IRE) 3 b.g. Mark of Esteem (IRE) 137 – Sundrenched (IRE) 99 (Desert **63**
King (IRE) 129) [2007 –: 8.3m 8d⁵ p10g 10m Aug 10] good-bodied colt: modest
maiden: stays 8.3f: acts on good to firm ground. *Mrs A. J. Perrett*

SUN CATCHER (IRE) 4 b.g. Cape Cross (IRE) 129 – Taalluf (USA) 82 (Hansel **85**
(USA)) [2007 82: p7g² p6g* p7g⁶ p7g⁴ p8g² p8f⁴ p7g p7g³ p8g² 7.1d⁶ 7g p7g⁵ 7.1s⁶ 6g⁵
p7g p6g⁵ Oct 23] good-topped gelding: fairly useful handicapper: won at Lingfield in
January: creditable efforts when in frame after: effective at 6f to easy 1m: acts on polytrack, good to firm and good to soft going: usually blinkered nowadays: temperament
under suspicion: sold 12,000 gns. *R. Hannon*

SUNDAE 3 b.g. Bahamian Bounty 116 – Merry Rous 66 (Rousillon (USA) 133) [2007 **104 +**
65p: 6m² 6.1g* 5g* 5d* 6d* 6d³ Sep 21] useful-looking gelding: unfurnished at 3 yrs:
useful performer: won at Nottingham in May, and handicaps at Sandown and
Newmarket (by short head from Obstructive) in June and Newcastle (by 1½ lengths from
Barkass) in July: good 4 lengths third of 26 to Utmost Respect in Ayr Silver Cup final
outing: effective at 5f/6f: unraced on extremes of going: travels strongly. *C. F. Wall*

SUNDANCE (IRE) 5 ch.g. Namid 128 – Titchwell Lass 57 (Lead On Time (USA) **–**
123) [2007 81d: p10g p8.6g Feb 2] strong, lengthy gelding: has a round action: fairly
useful performer at best: on downgrade: best: visored. *H. J. Collingridge*

SUNDERLAND ECHO (IRE) 4 ch.f. Tagula (IRE) 116 – La Alla Wa Asa (IRE) 60 **–**
(Alzao (USA) 117) [2007 87: 6.1s⁵ 7.1m 6d 6v 6s Jul 2] strong, lengthy filly: fairly useful
performer at best: out of sorts in 2007 (reportedly finished lame final outing): tried tongue
tied: sold 20,000 gns in August. *B. Ellison*

SUNDOWNER (IRE) 2 b.c. (Apr 3) Galileo (IRE) 134 – Sunsetter (USA) 94 (Diesis **81 p**
133) [2007 7g³ Nov 2] 72,000Y: second foal: half-brother to 4-y-o Regal Sunset: dam
ninth in Cheveley Park Stakes and sixth in Nell Gwyn Stakes, only starts: 25/1, promising
third to Foolin Myself in maiden at Newmarket, running on strongly from rear: will be
suited by 1m/1¼m: should do better. *G. A. Butler*

SUNDRIED TOMATO 8 b.g. Lugana Beach 116 – Little Scarlett 54 (Mazilier (USA) **53**
107) [2007 50, a59: f6g⁵ p6g f6g³ f6g f5g f6g f6g 6g May 10] good-topped gelding:
modest performer nowadays: stays easy 7f: acts on all-weather, heavy and good to firm
going: tried blinkered, wears cheekpieces nowadays: reportedly bled second outing.
D. W. Chapman

SUN IN SPLENDOUR (USA) 2 ch.c. (Feb 7) Hold That Tiger (USA) 117 – Fit To **– p**
Win (USA) (Fit To Fight (USA)) [2007 6m Jun 9] $25,000Y, resold 30,000Y: rangy colt:
third foal: dam US 7f/1m winner: well-backed 4/1, needed experience (hung right) in
maiden at Goodwood: likely to improve. *A. P. Jarvis*

SUNISA (IRE) 6 b.m. Daggers Drawn (USA) 114 – Winged Victory (IRE) 93 (Dancing **86**
Brave (USA) 140) [2007 87: 9.9g³ 9.9g 9.9s² 10.4s⁴ 10.5s² 10d⁴ Oct 11] robust, close-
coupled mare: fairly useful handicapper: effective at 1¼m to 1½m: acts on all-weather,
soft and good to firm going: tongue tied in 2005. *J. Mackie*

SUNKEN RAGS 3 b.f. Superior Premium 122 – Mise En Scene 85 (Lugana Beach 116) **53**
[2007 64d: p5.1g³ f5g f5g⁶ Feb 20] good-quartered filly: modest performer: raced only at
5f: acts on polytrack: tried in cheekpieces. *K. R. Burke*

SUN LANE 3 ro.f. Daylami (IRE) 138 – Three Piece (Jaazeiro (USA) 127) [2007 9.8m **59**
9m 10m² p12g p16g Oct 4] lengthy filly: half-sister to several winners, including Poule
d'Essai des Poulains winner Victory Note (6f winner at 2 yrs, by Fairy King), useful
1¼m/1½m winner Dance So Suite (by Shareef Dancer) and 4-y-o Multicultural: dam
Irish maiden: left C. Laffon-Parias in France, modest form at best in 3 starts in Britain.
W. R. Swinburn

SUNLEY GIFT 3 b.f. Cadeaux Genereux 131 – Thracian 92 (Green Desert (USA) 127) **–**
[2007 70: 8m 5d 7g 7g Jul 26] quite attractive filly: fair winner at 2 yrs: well below form in
2007. *B. G. Powell*

SUNLEY PEACE 3 ch.g. Lomitas 129 – Messila Rose (Darshaan 133) [2007 80p: **106**
11.6d³ 9.9g⁵ 12m³ 16d⁵ 12s³ 12d⁴ 16.1m* 14g⁴ 14.1g³ 16g³ 18d Oct 20] strong, lengthy
gelding: has a quick action: useful performer: won handicap at Newmarket in August by
6 lengths from Cape Secret: ran well when in frame after, including in Melrose Stakes
(Handicap) at York (fourth to Speed Gifted) and listed race at Ascot (5 lengths third to
dead-heaters Distinction and Solent) on penultimate outing: should be suited by further
than 2m: acts on soft and good to firm ground. *D. R. C. Elsworth*

SUNLEY SMILES 2 ch.f. (Mar 11) Arkadian Hero (USA) 123 – Sunley Scent 85 **–**
(Wolfhound (USA) 126) [2007 p6g Nov 28] second foal: half-sister to 3-y-o Resplendent
Alpha: dam 6f/7f winner: 11/2, behind in maiden at Kempton, soon off bridle.
D. R. C. Elsworth

SUNLEY SONG 4 b.f. Fleetwood (IRE) 107 – Sunley Sinner 93 (Try My Best (USA) **–**
130) [2007 –: p16g Jan 10] little form on Flat. *B. G. Powell*

SUNLEY SOVEREIGN 3 b.g. Josr Algarhoud (IRE) 118 – Pharsical 80 (Pharly (FR) **64 d**
130) [2007 64: p7g³ p8.6g⁶ f7g* p5.1g⁵ 6g f5g 5m 5f 8.5m p6g Sep 14] big, leggy,
close-coupled gelding: modest performer: won seller at Southwell (left M. Channon) in
March: below form after: stays 7f: acts on all-weather and firm going: has given trouble
at stall (once withdrawn): has looked reluctant. *D. W. Chapman*

SUNLIGHT (IRE) 3 ch.f. Sinndar (IRE) 134 – Church Light 88 (Caerleon (USA) 132) **97**
[2007 92p: 11.5g p8g³ 8.1m* 9.7m⁶ 10.1g Sep 19] tall, attractive filly: useful performer:
won handicap at Haydock (by neck from Snaafy) in August: below form after: will be
suited by 1½m: acts on polytrack, raced only on good/good to firm ground on turf.
M. A. Jarvis

SUNNY AFTERNOON 7 ch.m. Atraf 116 – Pinup 44 (Risk Me (FR) 127) [2007 61: **43**
p10g 7m 9.7m⁵ p7m Aug 10] neat mare: only poor nowadays: stays 1m: acts on polytrack, raced mainly on good going or firmer on turf: tried visored: has carried head high.
R. Rowe

SUNNY PARKES 4 ch.f. Arkadian Hero (USA) 123 – Janette Parkes 39 (Pursuit of **–**
Love 124) [2007 48: p16.5g 12.3f Jun 12] tall filly: poor maiden handicapper: has wandered. *M. Mullineaux*

SUNNYSIDE TOM (IRE) 3 b.g. Danetime (IRE) 121 – So Kind 90 (Kind of Hush **78**
118) [2007 82p: 5g⁵ 6m⁵ 6m⁶ 7d 6d³ 6.9f⁵ 6g 7m 8.5d² 10m Oct 22] big, strong gelding:
has plenty of scope: fair handicapper: races freely, but stays 8.5f: acts on firm and good to
soft going: tried visored/in cheekpieces. *R. A. Fahey*

SUNNY SPRITE 2 b.g. (Mar 22) Lujain (USA) 119 – Dragon Star 54 (Rudimentary **77**
(USA) 118) [2007 p6g² 6m⁴ Sep 11] good-topped gelding: fair form in frame in maidens
at Lingfield, not knocked about when fourth to Missit: should prove best at 5f/6f.
J. M. P. Eustace

SUN OF THE SEA 3 b.g. Best of The Bests (IRE) 122 – Gem 58 (Most Welcome 131) **78**
[2007 58: 8d⁴ 9m* 10f 8g⁶ p9.5g Nov 30] leggy gelding: fair handicapper: won at
Lingfield in July: should stay 1¼m: acts on good to firm and good to soft going.
N. P. Littmoden

SUNOVERREGUN 3 b.c. Noverre (USA) 125 – Jumairah Sun (IRE) 98 (Scenic 128) **88**
[2007 81p: p6g³ p6g⁴ 6s³ 6m³ 6m⁶ p8m p6g* Nov 4] lengthy colt: fairly useful handi-

capper: won at Lingfield in November: stays 6f: acts on polytrack, good to firm and good to soft going. *J. R. Boyle*

SUNRISE SAFARI (IRE) 4 b.g. Mozart (IRE) 131 – Lady Scarlett (Woodman (USA) **113** 126) [2007 81: 5g 5d* 6g⁴ 6d 5d* 5m³ 6d⁴ 5g* 6m⁴ Nov 10] lengthy gelding: improved into smart performer in 2007: won handicaps at Ayr in May, Newcastle in July and Doncaster (beat Aegean Dancer by 1¼ lengths, easily best of those drawn high) in October: further improvement when fourth to Galeota in listed event at Doncaster final outing: stays 6f: acts on soft and good to firm going: visored. *I. Semple*

SUNSET BOULEVARD (IRE) 4 b.g. Montjeu (IRE) 137 – Lucy In The Sky (IRE) **77** 59 (Lycius (USA) 124) [2007 67: p12g* p10g p12g* 11.8m³ May 22] leggy, useful-looking gelding: fair performer: improved in 2007, winning maiden in January and handicap in May, both at Lingfield: stays 1½m: acts on polytrack, unraced on extremes of going on turf: tried visored. *Miss Tor Sturgis*

SUNSET RIDGE (IRE) 4 b.f. Indian Ridge 123 – Barbara Frietchie (IRE) (Try My **47 §** Best (USA) 130) [2007 56§: p8g Jan 28] lengthy filly: modest maiden at best: below form sole 4-y-o start: tried in cheekpieces: ungenuine. *Miss Gay Kelleway*

SUNSHINE KID (USA) 3 b.c. Lemon Drop Kid (USA) 131 – Nepenthe (USA) **110** (Broad Brush (USA)) [2007 94p: 8.1g² 10d³ 10.5g 10m⁴ 10s⁵ 10.4d² 9.5d⁶ Nov 10] rather leggy, useful-looking colt: smart performer: in frame in minor event at Sandown (beaten neck by Yeaman's Hall), Prix Greffulhe at Saint-Cloud (very close third to Quest For Honor), Winter Hill Stakes at Windsor and minor event at York (3 lengths second behind Fairmile): respectable sixth in Grade 2 Red Smith Handicap at Aqueduct final outing: likely to stay 1½m: acts on soft and good to firm ground: races prominently: consistent. *J. H. M. Gosden*

SUNSHINE LADY (IRE) 2 b.f. (Apr 16) Captain Rio 122 – Damezao (Alzao (USA) **60** 117) [2007 p6g p6g 6d p8.6g² p8.6g⁴ p8.6g² Dec 26] 17,000Y: sturdy filly: half-sister to several winners, including 4-y-o Damelza and 3-y-o Down The Brick: dam unraced: modest maiden: in frame both starts in nurseries: stays 8.6f: acts on polytrack. *D. Haydn Jones*

SUNTAN LADY (IRE) 3 b.f. Redback 116 – Scarletta (USA) 79 (Red Ransom **48** (USA)) [2007 46: p6g⁴ f6g⁶ 6g⁴ 6m p7.1g 6d 7.1g Aug 2] strong, close-coupled filly: poor maiden: probably best at 5f/6f: acts on all-weather and good to soft ground: usually in headgear. *Miss V. Haigh*

SUPA SAL 3 b.f. King's Best (USA) 132 – Supamova (USA) 88 (Seattle Slew (USA)) **80** [2007 73p: p7g* 7g 7.1g⁶ Jul 12] big, leggy filly: fairly useful performer, lightly raced: won handicap at Kempton in March: failed to settle both starts after: bred to be suited by 1m+: raced only on polytrack and good going. *P. F. I. Cole*

SUPASEUS 4 b.g. Spinning World (USA) 130 – Supamova (USA) 88 (Seattle Slew **106** (USA)) [2007 102: 9m* 8m⁴ 8g 9m Oct 6] big, good-bodied gelding: useful handicapper:

StanJamesUK.com Suffolk Stakes (Handicap), Newmarket—Supaseus makes a winning reappearance from Pinpoint (hooped sleeves), the latter putting up a noteworthy performance under top weight; Night Crescendo (No.11) and Instructor (rail) are next

won quite valuable event at Newmarket in May by short head from Pinpoint, making most: good 4¾ lengths fourth to Royal Oath in Hunt Cup at Royal Ascot next time, racing alone against far rail: below form in valuable events after: should stay 1¼m: acts on good to firm and good to soft going: signs of temperament: none too reliable. *H. Morrison*

SUPA TRAMP 4 b.g. Kayf Tara 130 – Shirley Superstar 94 (Shirley Heights 130) [2007 67: 12g⁴ Apr 2] well-made gelding: maiden, lightly raced: reportedly finished distressed sole Flat start in 2007: will stay beyond 1½m. *G. L. Moore* **58**

SUPERCAST (IRE) 4 b.g. Alhaarth (IRE) 126 – Al Euro (FR) 57 (Mujtahid (USA) 118) [2007 81: p7.1g p6g p6g² p6g⁵ p6g⁶ p7.1g 7.6m⁶ 7f p6g 6g Oct 2] lengthy gelding: fair handicapper: stays 7f: acts on polytrack, firm and good to soft going: tried in cheekpieces/blinkers/tongue tie: has reared leaving stall/shown signs of temperament. *W. M. Brisbourne* **71**

SUPERCRAFT (IRE) 3 ch.g. Indian Lodge (IRE) 127 – Between The Winds (USA) (Diesis 133) [2007 p9.5g 10d p12g 8d 8g Sep 18] no form, including in sellers: tried visored/blinkered: ungenuine (refused to race on debut). *M. Quinn* **– §**

SUPER CROSS (IRE) 3 b.g. Cape Cross (IRE) 129 – Super Trouper (FR) 64 (Nashwan (USA) 135) [2007 77: 11.8m⁵ 10.5g⁵ 9g² 8m 8d⁶ p9.5g⁴ Jun 30] good-topped colt: fair maiden: free-going sort, best short of 1½m: acts on polytrack, best turf efforts on good ground: bit slipped and eased fourth start: sold 22,000 gns, joined Ms Joanna Kunc in Ireland. *E. A. L. Dunlop* **78**

SUPER DOMINION 10 ch.g. Superpower 113 – Smartie Lee 66 (Dominion 123) [2007 –§, a53§: p9.5g⁵ Jan 19] sturdy gelding: poor nowadays: effective at 7f to 1¼m: acts on all-weather, firm and soft going: sometimes wears visor/cheekpieces: tongue tied earlier in career: unreliable. *R. Hollinshead* **44 §**

SUPERDUPER 2 b.f. (Feb 19) Erhaab (USA) 127 – I'm Magic 75 (First Trump 118) [2007 6m 6f³ 6m⁵ 6m⁴ 6d Oct 11] good-topped filly: first foal: dam 1m winner: fair maiden: in frame at Windsor and Newmarket: speedy and raced only at 6f, but bred to stay at least 1m. *R. Hannon* **72**

SUPER FRANK (IRE) 4 b.g. Cape Cross (IRE) 129 – Lady Joshua (IRE) 88 (Royal Academy (USA) 130) [2007 71: p7g* p7g* p7g* 8.3m³ 7m⁴ 8.1g⁶ p6g⁴ 7g p7g⁴ Dec 28] rather leggy gelding: fairly useful handicapper: won at Kempton and Lingfield in January and Lingfield in February: effective at 6f to 1m: acts on polytrack and good to firm ground: has been blinkered/tongue tied: races up with pace. *J. Akehurst* **80 a84**

SUPERIOR STAR 4 b.g. Superior Premium 122 – Lindfield Belle (IRE) 78 (Fairy King (USA)) [2007 73: 10.1s⁶ f8g⁴ 8v 8s² 8s² 8.5s⁴ 10d⁴ Sep 22] quite good-topped gelding: fairly useful handicapper: stays 1¼m: acts on firm and soft going: blinkered/visored: quirky. *R. A. Fahey* **80**

SUPERJAIN 3 b.f. Lujain (USA) 119 – Plie 75 (Superlative 118) [2007 60: 7m 5d 5m⁶ p6g⁶ 7.5s³ 7.5g 9.1s Oct 26] leggy, quite attractive filly: poor maiden: stays 7.5f: acts on soft ground. *J. M. Jefferson* **41**

SUPERMASSIVE MUSE (IRE) 2 br.c. (Mar 8) Captain Rio 122 – Cautionary (IRE) 78 (Warning 136) [2007 5.5d 5m² 5.1d* 6m 6m⁶ 6.1m⁵ Sep 1] strong colt: fair performer: won maiden at Bath in June: lost form after (tried in tongue tie/blinkers): should prove best at 5f/6f: acts on good to firm and good to soft going. *E. S. McMahon* **75**

SUPER NEBULA 3 b.g. Fantastic Light (USA) 134 – It Girl 60 (Robellino (USA) 127) [2007 –: 8g 10m 11.5s⁵ p12g Jun 30] small gelding: little form. *P. L. Gilligan* **–**

SUPER SENSATION (GER) 6 b.g. Platini (GER) 126 – Studford Girl 43 (Midyan (USA) 124) [2007 p12g⁴ p12g² p13g⁵ Jul 10] ex-German gelding: winner of 3 races, including handicap at Cologne in 2006: left C. Sprengel, modest form in handicaps in Britain in 2007: stays easy 1½m: acts on all-weather and soft going: tried blinkered: fair winning hurdler. *G. L. Moore* **61**

SUPER SIFTED (GER) 3 b.f. Saddlers' Hall (IRE) 126 – Sun Moon Stars (IRE) (Shahrastani (USA) 135) [2007 –: p12.2g² p12g⁵ 14.1s⁴ Jun 14] fair maiden: caught the eye at Wolverhampton on reappearance: marginally better effort in handicap on final start: likely to stay 2m: sold 13,000 gns, sent to Qatar. *H. R. A. Cecil* **66**

SUPERSONIC DAVE (USA) 3 b. or br.c. Swain (IRE) 134 – Vickey's Echo (CAN) (Clever Trick (USA)) [2007 89p: 10m² 8m⁴ 10g Jun 21] close-coupled colt: useful performer: best effort in listed races in 2007 when 3½ lengths second to Lucarno at Newmarket: likely to stay 1½m: said to have finished lame final outing. *B. J. Meehan* **107**

SUPER STARLET (IRE) 2 b.f. (Feb 11) Statue of Liberty (USA) 115 – Wings To — Soar (USA) 67 (Woodman (USA) 126) [2007 7g p7m p8m Dec 8] 13,000F, 30,000Y: lengthy filly: first foal: dam, maiden, out of Yorkshire Oaks winner Only Royale: little form in maidens. *M. Botti*

SUPER TUSCAN (IRE) 2 b.c. (Apr 20) Fath (USA) 116 – Ornellaia (IRE) 56 (Muja- **75 p** dil (USA) 119) [2007 7g 6m p6g³ p5.1d* Dec 17] 16,000Y: workmanlike colt: first foal: dam, maiden (stayed 1¼m), out of half-sister to very smart 1¼m performer Insatiable: fair form: won maiden at Wolverhampton final start: may prove best at 5f: acts on poly-track: should continue to progress. *J. G. Given*

SUPPORT FUND (IRE) 3 ch.f. Intikhab (USA) 135 – Almost A Lady (IRE) 70 **73** (Entitled 126) [2007 67p: 6m² 8.3g p8.6g p6g⁴ 6d* 6f 6.1m² 6m 6g⁶ 7d* 8g⁵ Oct 25] deep-girthed filly: fair performer: won maiden in July and handicap in October, both at Brighton: stays 1m: acts on good to firm and good to soft going: has run creditably when sweating. *Eve Johnson Houghton*

SUPPORTING ROLE (IRE) 2 b.c. (Feb 21) Marju (IRE) 127 – Intercession 90 **63** (Bluebird (USA) 125) [2007 7.2s 7g 8.2g Nov 7] lengthy, good-bodied colt: modest form in maidens: should be suited by 1m: suspect attitude. *E. S. McMahon*

SUPREME CHARTER 4 b.g. Diktat 126 – Alchi (USA) 112 (Alleged (USA) 138) — [2007 81, a71: p13.9g Feb 21] leggy gelding: fairly useful at 3 yrs: well below form sole 4-y-o outing: stays 1¼m: acts on polytrack, firm and good to soft going: tried blinkered: carries head high. *E. S. McMahon*

SUPREME KISS 4 b.f. Barathea Guest 117 – Kiss Me Again (IRE) 80 (Cyrano de **56 §** Bergerac 120) [2007 66: p7g⁴ 6m 6g⁶ 5m p5g⁶ p5g p6g⁵ Sep 15] good-topped filly: modest maiden handicapper: stays 6f: acts on polytrack and good to firm going: tried blinkered/tongue tied: often slowly away: best treated with caution. *Mrs N. Smith*

SURDOUE 7 b.g. Bishop of Cashel 122 – Chatter's Princess (Cadeaux Genereux 131) **45** [2007 60: p12g f11g² f12g⁶ f11g⁴ 10.1d⁵ 10d³ 10m p10g² p9.5m 10m p10g 8d p10g⁵ p10g **a60** Nov 7] leggy gelding: modest handicapper on all-weather, poor on turf: stays easy 1½m: acts on all-weather and good to firm ground: tried in cheekpieces: front runner: none too consistent. *D. Morris*

SURELY TRULY (IRE) 4 b.f. Trans Island 119 – Londubh (Tumble Wind) [2007 65: — p7.1g p6g Nov 7] rather leggy filly: generally regressive, and no form in 2007: tried in visor/cheekpieces. *A. E. Jones*

SURPRISE ACT 3 gr.g. Act One 124 – Surprise Surprise 91 (Robellino (USA) 127) **70** [2007 10d 10m 10.2g⁶ 8d* p8.6g f8d Dec 15] sturdy gelding: fair form: best effort when winning handicap at Brighton in October, making all: stays 1m: acts on good to soft ground. *P. R. Chamings*

SURPRISE PENSION (IRE) 3 b.g. Fruits of Love (USA) 127 – Sheryl Lynn (Mil- **58** ler's Mate 116) [2007 52: 8.3g* 8.3s⁶ 9.9g⁶ Aug 15] stocky gelding: modest performer: won handicap at Hamilton in June, racing freely and tending to carry head awkwardly: should be suited by further than 8.3f: acts on soft ground. *J. J. Quinn*

SURREY SPINNER 3 ch.c. Intikhab (USA) 135 – Markievicz (IRE) 73 (Doyoun 124) **86** [2007 53p: p8g³ p10g² 10g³ 11g 10s 12f⁵ 9.9d⁵ 10.3g³ Oct 26] strong, good-bodied colt: fairly useful performer: won maiden at Lingfield in March: better form though none too consistent after: probably stays 1½m: acts on polytrack, probably on firm going: tried blinkered: sold 40,000 gns. *Mrs A. J. Perrett*

SURWAKI (USA) 5 b.g. Miswaki (USA) 124 – Quinella (Generous (IRE) 139) [2007 **81** 84: f8g 7m⁶ 7f⁵ 7f 8g² 8d 8.1s* 8g 8.3d⁵ 9g⁴ Aug 26] close-coupled gelding: fairly useful performer: won claimer at Warwick in July: stays 1m: acts on firm and soft ground: tried in cheekpieces: has found little. *R. M. H. Cowell*

SUSANNA'S DANCE 3 b.f. Danehill (USA) 126 – Sonja's Faith (IRE) 116 (Sharp **60** Victor (USA) 114) [2007 8.3g p9.5g⁵ 10g p9.5g Sep 28] €150,000Y: well-made filly: fourth foal: half-sister to winner in USA by General Meeting: dam US 1m/9f (including Grade 2 event) winner: modest form in maidens (left Sir Michael Stoute after debut): tried visored/blinkered/tongue tied. *M. Botti*

SUSANNA'S PROSPECT (IRE) 3 ch.f. Namid 128 – Substantive (USA) (Distant **74** View (USA) 126) [2007 64: p8.6g² p8.6g p8.6g² 8s* 8.1d⁶ Jun 24] fair handicapper: won at Yarmouth in June: stays easy 8.6f: acts on polytrack and soft ground: tried blinkered: races freely: usually races prominently. *B. J. Meehan*

SUSIEDIL (IRE) 6 b.m. Mujadil (USA) 119 – Don't Take Me (IRE) (Don't Forget Me **53 d**
127) [2007 37§: f12g 12m³ p8.6g 10m 9.9s⁵ 10.1v 12s 12m p8.6d Dec 17] close-coupled
mare: modest performer: stays 1½m: acts on fibresand and firm ground: wears headgear
nowadays: sometimes hangs: unreliable. *S. T. Mason*

SUSIE MAY 3 ch.f. Hernando (FR) 127 – Mohican Girl 112 (Dancing Brave (USA) **76**
140) [2007 51: p10g⁶ p12g 16g⁴ 11.9m* 11.9m⁶ p16g² p16g⁴ Oct 17] fair performer:
won claimer at Brighton in August: stays 2m: acts on polytrack and good to firm ground.
C. A. Cyzer

SUSPENDER (IRE) 3 b.f. Distant Music (USA) 126 – Feather 'n Lace (IRE) 73 **44**
(Green Desert (USA) 127) [2007 7m⁴ 7.5m 5g p6g Dec 13] 10,000 2-y-o: second foal:
half-sister to Irish 1½m winner Proper Article (by Definite Article): dam 7f winner: poor
maiden: form only on debut: left D. Nicholls after second outing. *S. T. Mason*

SUZIEBLUE (IRE) 3 b.f. Redback 116 – Blue Holly (IRE) 83 (Blues Traveller (IRE) **–**
119) [2007 50: p7g p5g p7f Feb 27] handicapper: little form at 3 yrs: often wears
headgear. *D. C. O'Brien*

SUZI'S DECISION 2 b.f. (Mar 5) Act One 124 – Funny Girl (IRE) 78 (Darshaan 133) **72 p**
[2007 7m⁴ 7s³ 6m* Sep 17] 2,500Y: third foal: half-sister to 3-y-o Pippa Greene: dam
maiden (stayed 1¼m): fair form: progressive in maidens, won readily at Leicester final
start: effective at 6f, bred to be suited by 1m+: should do better still. *P. W. D'Arcy*

SUZI SPENDS (IRE) 2 b.f. (Mar 4) Royal Applause 124 – Clever Clogs 96 (Nashwan **76**
(USA) 135) [2007 6m³ p7.1g² 6m 7m⁴ 7m³ 8.3d* p8.6g Nov 9] 11,000Y: workmanlike
filly: first foal: dam 1½m winner: fair performer: won nursery at Windsor in October: will
stay 1¼m: acts on polytrack, good to firm and good to soft going. *M. Johnston*

SVEN (SWE) 3 b.g. Duty Time 104 – Last Romance (IRE) (Last Tycoon 131) [2007 –: **–**
f11g p12g May 23] strong, sturdy gelding: well held in maidens. *B. I. Case*

SWAINS BRIDGE (USA) 5 b.g. Swain (IRE) 134 – Saraa Ree (USA) 102 (Caro 133) **–**
[2007 79: 12d Oct 12] strong gelding: fair handicapper: well held sole 5-y-o start: stays
1¼m: acts on firm going. *Micky Hammond*

SWALLOW FOREST 2 b.f. (Apr 30) Averti (IRE) 117 – Sangra (USA) 69 (El Gran **55**
Senor (USA) 136) [2007 5g⁶ 5m Aug 13] good-topped filly: fourth foal: half-sister to
3-y-o Doctor Ned: dam maiden (stayed 7f): modest form in maidens at Thirsk: will stay
6f/7f. *T. D. Barron*

SWALLOW SENORA (IRE) 5 b.m. Entrepreneur 123 – Sangra (USA) 69 (El Gran **38**
Senor (USA) 136) [2007 46: 6g 6g⁴ 8d 5g⁵ Nov 6] lightly-made mare: poor maiden: tried
blinkered/tongue tied. *M. C. Chapman*

SWALLOW STAR 2 b.f. (Feb 21) Observatory (USA) 131 – Swift Baba (USA) **75**
(Deerhound (USA) 64) [2007 5m* 6m p6g⁴ a7f³ Dec 27] 15,500F, 12,000Y: second foal:
dam maiden: fair form: won maiden at Lingfield in June: left R. Beckett 8,000 gns
before final start: stays 6f (below form at 7f): acts on polytrack and good to firm going.
R. Bouresly, UAE

SWANKY LADY 2 b.f. (Feb 17) Cape Cross (IRE) 129 – Lady Links 100 (Bahamian **83**
Bounty 116) [2007 6g⁶ 6d 7.1g* Oct 2] 240,000Y: good-topped filly: second foal: half-
sister to 3-y-o Selinka: dam 6f winner (including at 2 yrs): fairly useful form: upped in
trip, won maiden at Warwick (beat Hieroglyph by ½ length) final start: will stay 1m.
R. Hannon

SWAN QUEEN 4 br.f. In The Wings 128 – Bronzewing 103 (Beldale Flutter (USA) **101**
130) [2007 85: 12d² 12g³ 14d* 14s² 14g Jul 31] lengthy, angular filly: useful handicapper: improved further in 2007, winning at Sandown in June by neck from Takafu,
idling: better effort after when good head second of 4 to Ogee at Goodwood: stays 1¾m:
acts on soft and good to firm going: looked none too keen final outing. *J. L. Dunlop*

SWAYZE (IRE) 4 b.g. Marju (IRE) 127 – Dance of Love (IRE) 99 (Pursuit of Love **57**
124) [2007 69: p8.6g 10.1d⁵ p9.5g Nov 12] good-topped gelding: just modest nowadays:
left C. Wall after reappearance: stays 1¼m: acts on polytrack and heavy going: said to
have bled final start. *M. Quinn*

SWAZILAND 2 b.c. (Mar 4) Green Desert (USA) 127 – Susu 122 (Machiavellian **–**
(USA) 123) [2007 7m Aug 10] angular, good-topped colt: has scope: 12/1, green and
burly when behind in maiden at Newmarket: sold 14,000 gns. *J. Noseda*

SWEENEY (IRE) 3 ch.g. Jade Robbery (USA) 121 – Arduine 79 (Diesis 133) [2007 **–**
95p: 7.5g 10m Apr 12] leggy gelding: useful at 2 yrs, winning both starts: tailed-off last
in 2007, taking strong hold (hung left latter outing): should stay 1¼m: loose in paddock
and troublesome at stall on debut: sold 12,000 gns in May. *M. A. Jarvis*

SWEEPSTAKE (IRE) 2 b.f. (Mar 10) Acclamation 118 – Dust Flicker 63 (Suave **98**
Dancer (USA) 136) [2007 5d* 5g* 5m 6d³ Jul 29] 22,000F, €65,000Y: good-quartered
filly: first foal: dam, maiden, sister to smart performer up to 1½m Dust Dancer and
half-sister to very smart performer up to 1½m Zimzalabim: useful form: won maiden at
Salisbury and listed race at Sandown in May: said to have pulled muscles in back in
Queen Mary Stakes at Royal Ascot: good 4 lengths third to Visit in Princess Margaret
Stakes at Ascot month later: likely to prove best at 5f/6f: acts on good to soft going: sent
to USA. *R. Hannon*

SWEET AFTON (IRE) 4 b.f. Mujadil (USA) 119 – Victory Peak (Shirley Heights **95**
130) [2007 98: 5.2m⁴ 5.1f 6m 5m⁶ 6f 6m Aug 11] lengthy filly: poor mover: useful performer: creditable effort in 2007 only on reappearance: effective at 5f/6f: raced on good
going or firmer. *M. S. Saunders*

SWEET ANDROMEDA 2 ch.f. (May 3) Observatory (USA) 131 – Smooth Princess **–**
(IRE) 63 (Roi Danzig (USA)) [2007 p6g 7g⁶ p7.1g p8g Dec 12] close-coupled filly: sixth
foal: half-sister to fairly useful 1m winner Fancy Foxtrot (by Danehill Dancer) and a
winner in Greece by Dansili: dam 2-y-o 7f seller winner: little form. *T. J. Fitzgerald*

SWEET CHEROKEE 4 b.f. Mind Games 121 – Sioux Lady (Petong 126) [2007 41: **–**
p7.1g Jan 26] smallish filly: poor maiden: well held in seller sole start at 4 yrs: tried
blinkered. *C. N. Kellett*

SWEET CLOVER 3 b.f. Rainbow Quest (USA) 134 – Trefoil 111 (Kris 135) [2007 **67**
8.2m⁶ 8.1m⁴ 7s* 8g Aug 17] 75,000 2-y-o: leggy filly: sister to useful French 1¼m to
1½m winner Trefula and half-sister to 3 winners, including smart 7f/1m winner Three
Graces (by Peintre Celebre) and useful 6.5f (in UAE)/7f (at 2 yrs) winner Subpoena (by
Diktat): dam, French 10.5f/11f winner, from very good family: fair performer: won
maiden at York in July by 2 lengths from Cow Girl: will be suited by 1¼m+: acts on soft
ground. *K. R. Burke*

SWEET DANE (IRE) 2 b.f. (Apr 13) Danetime (IRE) 121 – Griqualand (Connaught **–**
130) [2007 6g p6g p7g 7d Oct 30] €18,000Y: seventh foal: closely related to fairly useful 5f to 7f (latter including in France and at 2 yrs) winner Fort McHenry (by Danehill
Dancer) and half-sister to 2 winners, including useful 2003 2-y-o 5f winner Notable Lady
(by Victory Note): dam ran twice: no form: tried in cheekpieces. *V. Smith*

SWEET GALE (IRE) 3 b.f. Soviet Star (USA) 128 – Lady Moranbon (USA) (Trem- **88 +**
polino (USA) 135) [2007 7m p8g³ f7g* 7m* Jun 5] 42,000Y: half-sister to several
winners, including 6-y-o Diego Cao and fairly useful 1¼m winner Space Cowboy (by
Anabaa): dam French 9f/1¼m winner: progressive form: won maiden at Southwell in
May and handicap at Lingfield (did well to beat The Fifth Member by ½ length) in June:
not seen again: likely to stay 1¼m: acts on fibresand and good to firm going: tongue tied
last 3 starts. *J. Noseda*

SWEETHEART 3 b.f. Sinndar (IRE) 134 – Love And Adventure (USA) (Halling **79**
(USA) 133) [2007 62: p9.5g* 11.6m 9.9m⁵ 11g³ 14g⁵ 12d 14g⁶ p16g2³ 17.2d² 16d Oct
11] lengthy filly: fair performer: won maiden at Wolverhampton in January, then left
M. Jarvis: generally creditable efforts in handicaps after: stays 17f: acts on polytrack,
unraced on extremes of going on turf: won juvenile hurdle in December. *Jamie Poulton*

SWEET HOPE (USA) 2 b. or br.f. (Apr 30) Lemon Drop Kid (USA) 131 – High **83**
Heeled Hope (USA) (Salt Lake (USA)) [2007 5m 6.1m⁵ 7m³ p7g³ p8.6g⁴ p7g* Dec 19]
$75,000Y, $320,000 2-y-o: tall filly: sixth foal: half-sister to 2 winners in US, including
6f winner Highgate Park (by A P Indy): dam US 2-y-o 5.5f to 7f winner (later second in
Grade 1 1m event): fairly useful form: blinkered, improved to win maiden at Lingfield (by 5 lengths) final start: best up to 7f: acts on polytrack and good to firm going.
K. A. Ryan

SWEET INDULGENCE (IRE) 6 ch.g. Inchinor 119 – Silent Indulgence (USA) **92**
(Woodman (USA) 126) [2007 102: p12g³ Feb 3] lengthy gelding: useful handicapper at 5
yrs: below form sole 6-y-o outing: stayed 1¾m, seemed to find stamina stretched at 2¼m
(Cesarewitch): acted on polytrack, soft and good to firm going: tended to race freely/
carry head awkwardly: dead. *W. J. Musson*

SWEET KISS (USA) 2 gr.f. (Jan 28) Yes It's True (USA) 116 – Always Freezing **83**
(USA) (Robyn Dancer (USA)) [2007 6m³ 8m 6.1m⁵ Oct 3] $27,000F, $85,000Y, $80,000
2-y-o: rather leggy filly: second foal: dam US 5.5f to 6.5f winner: fairly useful maiden:
third to Laureldean Gale at Newmarket: below that form subsequently, but stiff task (May
Hill Stakes) second start: should stay 7f: raced on good to firm going. *B. J. Meehan*

SWEET LAVINIA 4 ch.f. Lomitas 129 – Latch Key Lady (USA) 48 (Tejano (USA)) **50**
[2007 51: 12m 16s⁶ 16g³ 16m 18m⁶ Oct 22] sparely-made filly: modest maiden
handicapper: stays 2m: acts on soft and good to firm going. *J. D. Bethell*

Variety Club Atalanta Stakes, Sandown—a drop in class works wonders for Sweet Lilly, who gains a deserved victory; Heaven Sent is second narrowly ahead of Basaata (No.7) and Bicoastal (cheekpieces)

SWEET LILLY 3 b.f. Tobougg (IRE) 125 – Maristax 74 (Reprimand 122) [2007 100: 8m 10.4g² 10.5m 8m⁵ 9.9m⁴ 10d⁶ 8.1m* 8m⁵ 10d³ Oct 19] big, rangy filly: useful performer: won listed race at Sandown in September by ¾ length from Heaven Sent, edging right: also ran well when neck second to Passage of Time in Musidora Stakes at York, fifth to Simply Perfect in Falmouth Stakes at Newmarket, fourth to Peeping Fawn in Nassau Stakes at Goodwood, fifth to Echelon in Matron Stakes at Leopardstown and ¾-length third to Short Skirt in listed event at Newmarket: stays 1¼m: acts on polytrack, firm and soft going: free-going sort: not straightforward (tail flasher). *M. R. Channon* **107**

SWEET MEDICINE 5 ch.m. Dr Devious (IRE) 127 – Crimley Crumb (Rainbow Quest (USA) 134) [2007 78d: p12.2g p9.5g Apr 21] regressive maiden on Flat. *P. Howling* **–**

SWEET MIND 2 b.f. (Mar 30) Mind Games 121 – Cape Charlotte (Mon Tresor 113) [2007 6g 6d p6g Oct 8] 4,000F, €26,000Y, 21,000 2-y-o: rather leggy, workmanlike filly: unfurnished at 2 yrs: first foal: dam unraced half-sister to useful dam of very smart sprinter Cape of Good Hope: modest form in maidens, more promise than bare result: likely to prove best at 5f/6f: capable of better. *R. A. Fahey* **59 p**

SWEET MISCHIEF (IRE) 3 b.f. Sadler's Wells (USA) 132 – Sneaky Quiet (USA) (Seeking The Gold (USA)) [2007 10.2g p12g³ p12.2g⁴ Nov 27] sixth foal: closely related to 2 winners in USA by Danzig: dam US 1m (at 2 yrs)/9f winner, including minor stakes: best effort in maidens when third at Lingfield, carrying head awkwardly: stays 1½m. *J. H. M. Gosden* **66**

SWEET NICOLE 2 ch.f. (Mar 8) Okawango (USA) 115 – Tatora (Selkirk (USA) 129) [2007 6f Aug 4] 22,000Y, 30,000 2-y-o: workmanlike filly: third foal: half-sister to 3-y-o Tariq: dam unraced: 11/1, clearly green in maiden at Windsor (seventh to In Honour): will do better. *J. R. Fanshawe* **54 p**

SWEET PEAK (IRE) 3 b.f. Desert Style (IRE) 121 – Victory Peak (Shirley Heights 130) [2007 80: 8d² p8.6g⁶ 7g 7g p10.7g⁶ 8.5g Oct 20] fairly useful maiden: stays 1m: acts on good to firm and good to soft ground: blinkered (below form) twice as 2-y-o. *E. Tyrrell, Ireland* **80**

SWEET PICKLE 6 b.m. Piccolo 121 – Sweet Wilhelmina 87 (Indian Ridge 123) [2007 74: f6g² p6g* f6g³ p6f* p6g⁵ f6g² p6g³ f6g³ 6g⁴ 7m 6m* 6g 6m p6g p6g* p6g⁴ Nov 27] leggy mare: fairly useful handicapper: won at Wolverhampton in January, Lingfield in February, Windsor in July and Wolverhampton in November: stays 7f: acts on all-weather and firm going: tried visored: sometimes slowly away: usually held up. *J. R. Boyle* **81**

SWEET REQUEST 3 ch.f. Best of The Bests (IRE) 122 – Sweet Revival 41 (Claude Monet (USA) 121) [2007 63p: 8m 8g 10m² 10g⁵ 11.5m 10.2s² 10f⁴ 10.2f² 11.7f³ p12.2g² p12.2g⁵ Nov 9] tall filly: fair maiden handicapper: stays 1½m: acts on polytrack, firm and soft ground: tried in cheekpieces: often held up: sold 14,000 gns. *R. M. Beckett* **76**

SWEET SARA 2 b.f. (Apr 9) Mark of Esteem (IRE) 137 – Mild Deception (IRE) (Glow (USA)) [2007 8.3m⁵ p8.6g⁵ Nov 2] 27,000Y: sturdy filly: half-sister to 5f winner (including at 2 yrs) Super Geil (by Superlative) and several winners abroad: dam unraced half-sister to Irish Oaks winner Margarula: fair maiden: better effort on debut (fifth to Nowaira at Leicester): stays 1m. *C. E. Brittain* **68**

SWEET SEVILLE (FR) 3 b.f. Agnes World (USA) 123 – Hispalis (IRE) (Barathea – (IRE) 127) [2007 55: f6g Dec 27] smallish filly: modest form in maiden at Haydock at 2 yrs: well held in similar event only outing in 2007. *Mrs G. S. Rees*

SWEETSFORMYSWEET (USA) 3 ch.f. Forest Wildcat (USA) 120 – Pent Up Kiss 63 (USA) (Pentelicus (USA)) [2007 p6g² 6f⁵ 5m⁴ p6g p5.1g⁶ p5m* Nov 11] $240,000Y, $450,000 2-y-o: fifth foal: sister to 2 minor winners in USA and half-sister to minor US winner by Delaware Township, all sprinters at/including at 2 yrs: dam US minor sprint stakes winner: modest performer: won handicap at Kempton in November: effective at 5f to easy 7f: acts on polytrack, probably on firm ground. *J. Noseda*

SWEET WORLD 3 b.g. Agnes World (USA) 123 – Douce Maison (IRE) 67 (Fools 73 Holme (USA)) [2007 63: p8.6g* p7.1g² p8g* p8g p10g* 10f³ p8g⁴ p11g 11.5m p8g³ 10d* 11.6d⁶ f11d⁴ Dec 18] lengthy gelding: fair performer: won claimers at Wolverhampton in January, Lingfield in February and Kempton in March, and seller at Ayr in September: stays 1¼m, not 11.6f: acts on all-weather, firm and good to soft going. *A. P. Jarvis*

SWIFT ACCLAIM (IRE) 2 b.f. (Apr 6) Acclamation 118 – Swift Chorus (Music 55 Boy 124) [2007 6s 6m 6d 5d⁵ Oct 9] €33,000Y: strong, angular filly: half-sister to several winners, notably 6-y-o Presto Shinko and 3-y-o Swift Princess: dam, Irish 2-y-o 6f winner, half-sister to smart 1¼m/1½m performer Talented: modest maiden: should prove best at 5f/6f. *K. R. Burke*

SWIFT CUT (IRE) 3 ch.g. Daggers Drawn (USA) 114 – Jugendliebe (IRE) (Persian 68 Bold 123) [2007 76: p8g⁵ 8m⁶ 7f⁶ 7m⁵ p8.6g³ p8g p7g f7d⁵ Dec 18] compact gelding: fair handicapper: stays 8.6f: acts on polytrack (probably on fibresand), raced only on good ground or firmer on turf: tried visored. *A. P. Jarvis*

SWIFT GIFT 2 b.c. (Apr 25) Cadeaux Genereux 131 – Got To Go 99 (Shareef Dancer 85 p (USA) 135) [2007 7m³ 7g⁴ p7.1g* Nov 30] 26,000Y: third foal: half-brother to 7f/1m winner Piano Player (by Mozart) and 3-y-o Morning Farewell: dam, 2-y-o 6f winner who stayed 1¼m, out of sister to very smart Japanese miler Zenno El Cid: fairly useful form: off 3 months, much improved to win maiden at Wolverhampton by 4 lengths: likely to stay 1m: should do better still. *B. J. Meehan*

SWIFTLY ADDICTED (IRE) 3 ch.f. King's Best (USA) 132 – Swiftly 73 (Cadeaux 53 Genereux 131) [2007 p6p: 6.1m⁶ 6.1g May 28] unfurnished filly: modest maiden: should stay 7f: sold 4,500 gns, sent to Greece. *A. King*

SWIFT PRINCESS (IRE) 3 b.f. Namid 128 – Swift Chorus (Music Boy 124) [2007 91 + –: 6m³ 6m³ 6d² 6v² 6m* 6d* 5d² Sep 21] good-bodied filly: fairly useful handicapper: won at Haydock and Leicester in August: excellent short-head second to Divine Spirit at Ayr final outing: effective at 5f/6f: acts on heavy and good to firm ground: usually visored. *K. R. Burke*

SWIMANDYOUWIN (IRE) 4 b.g. Xaar 132 – Mouette (FR) (Fabulous Dancer – (USA) 124) [2007 f11d Dec 20] €19,500Y: eighth foal: half-brother to winners in Germany by Mujtahid and Persian Heights: dam French 1m (including at 2 yrs) winner: 10/1, tailed off in maiden at Southwell. *Shaun Harley, Ireland*

SWINBROOK (USA) 6 ch.g. Stravinsky (USA) 133 – Dance Diane (USA) (Affirmed 90 (USA)) [2007 98: 6g⁵ 6g⁶ 6m⁴ 6g 6d³ p7g⁶ 6d⁶ p7.1g⁵ p6g Dec 4] workmanlike gelding: just fairly useful at 6 yrs: left J. Toller, said to have bled final outing: best at 6f/7f: acts on polytrack, firm and soft ground: usually visored: consistent. *R. A. Fahey*

SWINDON TOWN FLYER (IRE) 2 b.g. (Mar 4) Captain Rio 122 – Baltic Breeze 70 (USA) 70 (Labeeb 124) [2007 p5g⁶ 5.3m³ 6g² p6g 6m⁵ p7g 7m 5d³ 5.1g⁶ Oct 24] close-coupled gelding: fair maiden: placed 3 times, including at Catterick (wore blinkers) penultimate start: best at 5f/6f: acts on polytrack, good to firm and good to soft going. *A. B. Haynes*

SWING ON A STAR (IRE) 3 br.f. Celtic Swing 138 – Lady Stalker 57 (Primo Domi- 63 nie 121) [2007 64p: 8m 7.1s 6f³ p6g p5.1m⁵ 6g p6g⁵ p7.1g Nov 19] rather leggy filly: modest maiden: left W. Swinburn prior to final start: should stay 7f: acts on polytrack and firm ground. *Miss J. Feilden*

SWING THE RING (IRE) 4 b.c. Rossini (USA) 118 – Sharkiyah (IRE) 75 (Polish 85 Precedent (USA) 131) [2007 98: 8s 7d 6g 6m 6m p6g⁴ p7.1g Oct 22] close-coupled colt: useful performer at 3 yrs when trained in Germany by B. Hellier, just fairly useful in 2007: seems best around 6f: acts on good to firm going (some promise on polytrack): tried blinkered. *A. Berry*

SWIPER HILL (IRE) 4 b.g. City On A Hill (USA) 114 – Alkariyh (USA) 79 (Alydar **70 d**
(USA)) [2007 70: p7.1g⁶ 6v 6s p7.1m p7.1g⁵ p7m⁵ p8g p8.6g³ p8.6g p8.6g² p9.5g p12.2d
Dec 27] fair handicapper: has reportedly had a wind operation: stays 8.6f: acts on poly-
track, no form on turf: tried visored/tongue tied: sometimes hangs. *B. Ellison*

SWISS ACT 3 ch.g. Act One 124 – Dancing Mirage (IRE) 83 (Machiavellian (USA) **94**
123) [2007 81p: 12.3m* 12g 12g Jun 21] lengthy, good-topped gelding: useful performer:
won handicap at Chester in May, though tended to run in snatches: below form after in
Swiss Derby at Frauenfeld and handicap (never going well) at Royal Ascot: subsequently
gelded: should stay 1¾m: acts on good to firm and good to soft going. *M. Johnston*

SWISS FRANC 2 br.c. (Feb 6) Mr Greeley (USA) 122 – Swiss Lake (USA) 115 (Indian **106**
Ridge 121) [2007 5s³ 5d⁵ 5m² 6m² 6m³ 6g³ Aug 22] leggy, useful-looking colt: first foal:
dam, 5f winner (including at 2 yrs), out of useful 5f/6f winner Blue Iris: useful performer:
won maiden at Newmarket in May: improvement when ¾-length second to Henrythenavigator in Coventry Stakes at Royal Ascot and 1½ lengths third to Winker Watson in
July Stakes at Newmarket fourth/fifth starts: bit below best final one in Gimcrack Stakes
at York (3¾ lengths third to Sir Gerry), pulling hard and carrying head awkwardly: should
prove best at 5f/6f: acts on good to firm and good to soft going: quirky. *D. R. C. Elsworth*

SWOP (IRE) 4 b.g. Shinko Forest (IRE) – Changing Partners 58 (Rainbow Quest **95 p**
(USA) 134) [2007 p7g* Oct 29] 52,000Y: strong, attractive colt: half-brother to 3 winners, including 1m winner Love Affair (by Tagula): dam, 1½m winner, half-sister to
smart sprinter May Ball: 14/1 and carrying plenty of condition, won maiden at Lingfield
by length from Alpes Maritimes, despite clear signs of inexperience: sure to improve.
L. M. Cumani

SWORDS 5 b.g. Vettori (IRE) 119 – Pomorie (IRE) 67§ (Be My Guest (USA) 126) **64**
[2007 68: f14g 14.1g p12.2g⁶ p13.9g³ p12g Jul 4] sturdy gelding: modest handicapper:
effective at 1½m to 2m: acts on all-weather, unraced on extremes of going on turf.
Heather Dalton

SWORN IN (USA) 6 ch.h. Kingmambo (USA) 125 – Under Oath (USA) (Deputed **–**
Testamony (USA)) [2007 –: 16s 18g May 17] lengthy horse: bumper winner: little form
on Flat. *N. I. M. Rossiter*

SYDNEYROUGHDIAMOND 5 b.g. Whittingham (IRE) 104 – November Song **42**
(Scorpio (FR) 127) [2007 6.1g⁵ 6m 6.1s 7.1g² 6d p6g p8.6g Sep 28] big, workmanlike
gelding: poor maiden on balance: stays 7f: acts on all-weather and soft going: tried in
cheekpieces/blinkers. *M. Mullineaux*

SYLVAN (IRE) 3 b. or br.f. Shinko Forest (IRE) – Auriga 73 (Belmez (USA) 131) **–**
[2007 79: 7g 8.3d 8.1m Aug 7] angular filly: fair winner at 2 yrs: well held in handicaps
in 2007: should stay 7f: best effort on good ground. *S. Kirk*

SYLVIAS GROVE 2 b.f. (May 22) Royal Applause 124 – Branston Fizz 80 (Efisio **71**
120) [2007 6f 6d⁴ 6d Oct 12] 15,000Y, 36,000 2-y-o: medium-sized, well-made filly:
second foal: half-sister to German 5f to 7f winner Modovi (by Kyllachy): dam, 6f/7f
winner, half-sister to very smart miler Desert Deer and smart 6f/7f performer Branston
Abby: fair maiden: fourth to No Page at Haydock, only form: likely to prove best up to 7f.
D. Carroll

SYMBOL OF PEACE (IRE) 4 b.f. Desert Sun 120 – Rosy Lydgate 53 (Last Tycoon **85**
131) [2007 79: p12.2g² p12.2g⁴ p9.5g* p8.6g² p8.6g 8.2g* p8g⁵ p7g⁶ p8.6g 8m 9.8m
8.1m Sep 14] rangy filly: fairly useful handicapper: won at Wolverhampton (apprentices)
in February and Nottingham in April: effective at 1m to easy 1½m: acts on polytrack and
firm going, probably on soft: below form in blinkers final outing. *J. W. Unett*

SYMPATRIC FRIENDLY 3 b.f. Danehill Dancer (IRE) 117 – Intercede (Pursuit of **50**
Love 124) [2007 7m Apr 20] sturdy filly: fourth foal: half-sister to fairly useful 2002
2-y-o 7f winner Intercession (by Bluebird): dam unraced half-sister to Interval (very
smart at 6f to 1m) and Interim (smart up to 1½m): 40/1, seventh to Promising Lead in
maiden at Newbury, racing wide throughout, travelling strongly and threatening briefly:
sold 11,000 gns in December, reportedly in foal to Beat Hollow. *W. J. Haggas*

SYNERGISTIC (IRE) 2 b.c. (Feb 26) In The Wings 128 – Queens Wharf (IRE) 104 **78**
(Ela-Mana-Mou 132) [2007 8.5m² 7.5g⁴ 10.2d³ Oct 1] 30,000Y: first foal: dam Irish 11f
to 1¾m winner: fair maiden: in frame all starts, third to Inventor at Bath final one: will be
suited by 1½m+: sold 30,000 gns, sent to Austria. *M. Johnston*

SYNGE STREET 2 b.c. (Mar 5) Medicean 128 – Keep Quiet 54 (Reprimand 122) **67**
[2007 6m 6s⁴ 6m 7f⁶ p8g² p8m p6g⁴ Oct 24] 14,000F, 12,000Y: lengthy, unfurnished colt:
half-brother to several winners, including fairly useful 2003 2-y-o 5f winner Pivotal

Guest (by Pivotal): dam maiden (stayed 7f): fair maiden: second in nursery at Kempton: stays 1m: acts on polytrack, soft and firm going: sold 11,000 gns, sent to Serbia & Montenegro. *R. Hannon*

SYNONYMY 4 b.g. Sinndar (IRE) 134 – Peony 108 (Lion Cavern (USA) 117) [2007 77: p16g⁴ p16g⁴ p16.5g⁴ p16.5g* p16g³ 18g p16g⁵ 15d 11.8s⁶ p16g³ p16g 14m p16.5g³ 14.1m* p13.9g² p16g 14.1d² 16d p13.9g Oct 30] good-bodied gelding: fair handicapper: won at Wolverhampton in March and Salisbury in August: stays 17f: acts on polytrack, good to firm and good to soft going: usually blinkered: usually races prominently. *M. Blanshard* **65 a75**

SYNOPSIS (IRE) 3 ch.f. In The Wings 128 – Epitome (IRE) 71 (Nashwan (USA) 135) [2007 12d* 12g⁶ 12.5g* 14.6m⁴ 12.5d⁴ 10.5d³ Nov 10] leggy, close-coupled filly: first foal: dam, maiden (stayed 1½m), out of high-class 6f/7f performer Proskona: useful performer: won maiden at Longchamp in April and Prix Minerve Shadwell at Deauville (beat Darsha 1½ lengths) in August: creditable efforts last 3 starts when 2½ lengths fourth to Hi Calypso in Park Hill Stakes at Doncaster, 4 lengths fourth to Anna Pavlova in Prix de Royallieu at Longchamp and 2½ lengths third to Tashelka in Prix Fille de l'Air at Toulouse: stays 14.6f: acts on good to firm and good to soft ground. *A. Fabre, France* **107**

SYRIANA 2 b.f. (Apr 22) Dubai Destination (USA) 127 – Syrian Dancer (IRE) (Groom Dancer (USA) 128) [2007 7g Nov 3] big filly: second foal: dam, French maiden, out of half-sister to very smart sprinter/miler Rock City: last in maiden at Newmarket. *A. Bailey* **–**

SYVILLA 2 b.f. (May 9) Nayef (USA) 129 – Dance Steppe (Rambo Dancer (CAN) 107) [2007 7d⁵ Oct 9] sparely-made filly: sixth foal: half-sister to 3 winners, including useful performer up to 1m in Italy/US La Martina (by Atraf) and 2004 2-y-o 7f winner Icing (by Polar Falcon): dam maiden: 66/1 and green, fifth to Laughter in maiden at Leicester: open to improvement. *Rae Guest* **64 p**

T

TABADUL (IRE) 6 b.g. Cadeaux Genereux 131 – Amaniy (USA) 96 (Dayjur (USA) 137) [2007 97, a110: 10g* p11g⁵ 10.1g⁴ p10g* 10.1d⁴ 10d 9.9g Jul 31] leggy gelding: useful handicapper: won at Nad Al Sheba in January and Lingfield (beat Vacation by 1¼ lengths) in May: creditable fourth to Lake Poet in valuable event at Epsom next time: below form both outings after: free-going sort, but stays 1¼m: acts on polytrack, soft and good to firm ground: has looked none too genuine: joined M. Al Muhairi in UAE. *E. A. L. Dunlop* **107**

TABARET 4 ch.c. Bertolini (USA) 125 – Luanshya 78 (First Trump 118) [2007 105: 6f 5m⁶ 6g 5g² 5d 5m⁴ 5g 5m 5d⁵ Sep 25] small, good-bodied colt: fluent mover: useful performer: none too consistent in 2007, in frame in minor event at Newmarket (short-head second to Celtic Mill) and handicap at Haydock (fourth to Indian Trail) fourth/ninth starts: raced mainly at 5f: acts on firm and good to soft going. *R. M. Whitaker* **105**

TABOOR (IRE) 9 b.g. Mujadil (USA) 119 – Christoph's Girl 50 (Efisio 120) [2007 79: p5.1g⁶ p6g² f5g⁴ p6g⁶ p5g⁵ p6g 5.1d⁵ 5g 5m 5d 5.2m⁴ 5.2d p5.1g³ Dec 31] heavy-topped gelding: fair handicapper: below form after third start: best at 5f/easy 6f: acts on all-weather, firm and good to soft ground: has worn headgear/tongue tie: often slowly away. *R. M. H. Cowell* **69 d**

TABULATE 4 b.f. Dansili 127 – Let Alone 78 (Warning 136) [2007 64: f8g³ p9.5g f7g 10s f8g* p8g⁴ p8g³ 8d p10g p7m p10g p8.6g⁶ p12g p12g p12.2g Nov 1] close-coupled filly: fair handicapper: won at Southwell in May: left P. Gilligan after eighth outing: stays 9.5f: acts on all-weather: usually held up. *P. Howling* **69**

TACID 5 b.m. Diktat 126 – Defined Feature (IRE) 91 (Nabeel Dancer (USA) 120) [2007 59: p8g Jan 22] workmanlike mare: modest performer in 2006: stays 8.6f: acts on all-weather, soft and good to firm ground: below form in visor, including sole 5-y-o outing: has been slowly away. *Dr J. D. Scargill* **43**

TACKCOAT (IRE) 7 b.g. Sesaro (USA) 81 – Damaslin (Camden Town 125) [2007 61: p8.6g p8g⁵ f8s f8g⁵ Mar 13] modest performer: stays 1m: acts on all-weather, heavy and good to firm going: tried tongue tied, wears cheekpieces. *Eoin Doyle, Ireland* **58**

TACTICAL MOVE 2 b.c. (Apr 21) Diktat 126 – My Mariam 79 (Salse (USA) 128) [2007 6d⁵ 7m Aug 8] poor form in maidens: bred to stay 1m. *Miss V. Haigh* **46**

TADALAVIL 2 gr.g. (Mar 24) Clodovil (IRE) 116 – Blandish (USA) (Wild Again **89**
(USA)) [2007 6s² 6m³ 6m* 5m⁵ 6.5m 7m⁵ 6d³ 7g 6g⁴ 6m⁵ Nov 10] 8,000F, 16,000Y:
small, strong, close-coupled gelding: first foal: dam, US maiden, half-sister to smart
performer up to 9f Susurration out of high-class performer up to 1¼m Grease: fairly
useful performer: won maiden at Ripon in August: in frame in nursery at Newbury and
minor event at Newmarket (fourth to Paco Boy): should stay 7f: acts on soft and good to
firm going: gelded after final start. *M. R. Channon*

TAFIRA (IRE) 2 b.f. (Mar 17) Invincible Spirit (IRE) 121 – Sabayik (IRE) 93 (Unfu- **–**
wain (USA) 131) [2007 5m 5m⁵ 5d 5f Sep 17] €8,000Y, resold €6,500Y: leggy filly:
half-sister to several winners, including 1m/1¼m winner Khibrah (by Lahib) and 5f
(at 2 yrs) to 9f (in Hong Kong) winner Red Power (by Intikhab), both useful: dam, 1m
winner, half-sister to useful stayers Haitham and Libk: little form. *K. R. Burke*

TAFIYA 4 b.f. Bahri (USA) 125 – Fickle 95 (Danehill (USA) 126) [2007 74, a62: p9.5g⁶ **75**
11.5g² 11.6m p12g⁴ 11.5g² 11.9d⁵ p12.2g⁶ Oct 26] tall, leggy filly: fair maiden: stays **a65**
1½m: acts on polytrack and firm going. *J. W. Hills*

TAGHREED (IRE) 3 b.f. Zamindar (USA) 116 – Waafiah 57 (Anabaa (USA) 130) **72**
[2007 7s² 6s² 7.1d⁵ Jun 28] second foal: half-sister to 4-y-o Ragad: dam, second at 7f on
only start, out of Prix Morny winner First Waltz: fair maiden: best effort at 6f: hung right
second start, pulled hard final one. *W. Jarvis*

TAG TEAM (IRE) 6 ch.g. Tagula (IRE) 116 – Okay Baby (IRE) 67 (Treasure Kay 114) **52 +**
[2007 –, a75: f6g f6g f6g p6g 6d⁶ p6g⁴ 6m³ p6g* p6g⁵ p5.1g p6g² p6g³ p6g² p6g³ Dec 29] **a72**
tall gelding: fair handicapper on all-weather, modest on turf: won at Wolverhampton
in August: effective at 5f/6f: acts on all-weather, firm and good to soft going: tried blink-
ered/visored: races up with pace. *John A. Harris*

TAGULA KING (IRE) 2 b.c. (Apr 8) Tagula (IRE) 116 – Isla (IRE) (Turtle Island **–**
(IRE) 123) [2007 5m 7g Aug 24] workmanlike colt: well held in maiden and seller
(visored). *D. Carroll*

TAGULA SANDS (IRE) 3 b.g. Tagula (IRE) 116 – Pomme Pomme (USA) (Dayjur **44**
(USA) 137) [2007 p7m p8m p7g Dec 5] poor form in maidens. *J. C. Fox*

TAGULA SONG (IRE) 3 b.f. Tagula (IRE) 116 – Bouffant (High Top 131) [2007 7d **–**
8d 10f p10g Dec 19] 3,500F, 14,000Y: lengthy filly: sister to 2 winners, including fairly
useful 6f (at 2 yrs) to 1¼m winner Petrula, closely related to 2 winners by Taufan, including 1992 2-y-o 7f winner Fanfan, and half-sister to 2 winners: dam Irish maiden: little
sign of ability in maidens/claimer: tried visored. *J. A. Geake*

TAGULA SUNRISE (IRE) 5 ch.m. Tagula (IRE) 116 – Lady From Limerick (IRE) **96**
61 (Rainbows For Life (CAN)) [2007 101: 7v 7s⁴ 7m 6m³ Aug 11] good-topped mare:
fluent mover: useful handicapper: best effort in 2007 when third to Our Faye at Ascot:
probably needs good test at 6f nowadays, and stays 7f: acts on any going: usually held up.
R. A. Fahey

TAHAFUT 3 b.f. Marju (IRE) 127 – Farha (USA) 85 (Nureyev (USA) 131) [2007 52: **55**
6g 7g p7.1g p8.6g Nov 24] smallish, unfurnished filly: modest maiden: left E. Lynam in
Ireland after second start: probably stays 7f: acts on good to firm going: tried tongue tied.
R. A. Fahey

TAHAJJUM 2 b.f. (Apr 16) Diktat 126 – Bundle (Cadeaux Genereux 131) [2007 7d **–**
Oct 9] 7,000Y: lengthy, unfurnished filly: fourth foal: half-sister to 5-y-o Top Gear: dam
unraced out of useful half-sister to Japan Cup winner Jupiter Island and high-class 2-y-o
sprinter Precocious: 33/1 and burly, eighth to Laughter in maiden at Leicester, fading:
sold 2,200 gns. *C. E. Brittain*

TAHDEED 3 b.c. Green Desert (USA) 127 – Turn of A Century 85 (Halling (USA) 133) **72 §**
[2007 8m⁵ 10.9g 8.1d p6g 8.1m Sep 13] good-topped colt: easily best effort when fifth in
maiden at Newmarket on debut: stays 1m: acts on good to firm ground: tried blinkered/
tongue tied: reluctant to race penultimate outing: looks one to avoid: sold 7,000 gns. *Sir
Michael Stoute*

TAIKOO 2 b.c. (Apr 9) Dr Fong (USA) 128 – So True 116 (So Blessed 130) [2007 **70 p**
8.2g f8d⁴ Dec 19] workmanlike colt: half-brother to several winners, including smart 1m
winner Bomb Alaska and fairly useful 6f winner Sabrina Brown (both by Polar Falcon):
dam 5f (at 2 yrs) and 1m winner (stayed 1½m): better effort in maidens when fourth to
Pharaohs Justice at Southwell: open to further improvement. *H. Morrison*

TAILI 6 b.m. Taipan (IRE) 124 – Doubtfire 71 (Jalmood (USA) 126) [2007 –: 16m **–**
Apr 9] of no account. *D. A. Nolan*

TAINE (IRE) 2 b.c. (Apr 28) Invincible Spirit (IRE) 121 – Farjah (IRE) (Charnwood **75 p**
Forest (IRE) 125) [2007 p5.1g³ Dec 1] €45,000Y, 50,000 2-y-o: third foal: half-brother to
3-y-o Celtic Sultan: dam French 2-y-o 5.5f winner: 8/1, promising third to Fast Feet in
maiden at Wolverhampton, travelling strongly long way: likely to stay 6f: sure to do
better. *W. J. Haggas*

TAITA (GER) 3 ch.f. Big Shuffle (USA) 122 – Tamarita (GER) (Acatenango (GER) **94**
127) [2007 8g⁴ 8g 6g² 8s⁴ 7g 6d⁵ p7g Dec 19] first foal: dam useful German maiden
(stayed 1½m): fairly useful performer: won maiden at Hanover at 2 yrs: in frame in 2007
in listed races at Cologne and Baden-Baden (left H.-J. Groschel in Germany €70,000
after) and minor event at Deauville: left E. Danel in France, tailed off in listed race on
British debut at Kempton final start: stays 1m: acts on soft ground. *C. G. Cox*

TAJAAWEED (USA) 2 br.c. (Jan 25) Dynaformer (USA) – Uforia (USA) (Zilzal **91 p**
(USA) 137) [2007 8.2d* 8g Oct 27] $400,000Y: big, strong, close-coupled colt: fourth
foal: half-brother to useful 7f/1m winner Cat Ona High (by Tabasco Cat) and winning US
sprinter by Carson City: dam once-raced half-sister to very smart US sprinter Mr Greeley:
excellent impression when winning maiden at Nottingham (unextended to beat Hyde Lea
Flyer by 5 lengths) in October: 10/1, let down by relative inexperience when tenth to Ibn
Khaldun in Racing Post Trophy at Doncaster: will stay 1¼m, probably 1½m: should
make a smart 3-y-o. *Sir Michael Stoute*

TAJDEEF (USA) 2 gr.c. (Apr 13) Aljabr (USA) 125 – Tabheej (IRE) 100 (Mujtahid **110**
(USA) 118) [2007 6f* 7m⁴ 6m³ Oct 5] sturdy, compact colt: fourth foal: half-brother to
7f winner Tawaajud (by Dixieland Band): dam, 2-y-o 5f/6f winner, sister to useful 2-y-o
5f winner Mubhij: smart form: won maiden at Newbury in August: much improved
subsequently, 5 lengths fourth to McCartney in Champagne Stakes at Doncaster (stamina

Mr Hamdan Al Maktoum's "Tajdeef"

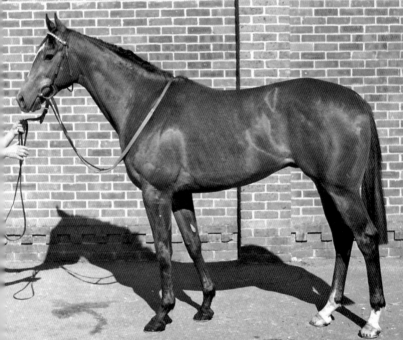

appeared stretched) and ¾-length third to Dark Angel in Middle Park Stakes at New-market: will prove best up to 7f: raced only on going firmer than good. *B. W. Hills*

TAJJREE 4 b.f. Lujain (USA) 119 – Rateeba (IRE) (Green Desert (USA) 127) [2007 **60** 59: p5.1g⁴ p5.1g* p5.1g 5d p5g⁴ p5.1g Nov 27] modest performer: won maiden at Wolverhampton in January: left Miss K. Boutflower after fourth outing: speedy, and will prove best at 5f: acts on polytrack: usually wears cheekpieces: tongue tied: gave trouble at start fifth outing. *H. J. Collingridge*

TAJWEED (IRE) 2 ch.c. (Feb 6) Pivotal 124 – Mannakea (USA) (Fairy King (USA)) **74 p** [2007 7m 8.2g³ Oct 31] 110,000F: good-bodied colt: has scope: fourth foal: half-brother to 4-y-o Revolving World: dam unraced close relative of Rodrigo de Triano: fair form: better for debut (green), promising third to Doctor Fremantle in maiden at Nottingham: will stay 1¼m: type to thrive at 3 yrs. *M. Johnston*

TAKAAMUL 4 ch.g. Almutawakel 126 – Mafaatin (IRE) (Royal Academy (USA) 130) **64** [2007 60: 7.1v 7.1d 5m p7g² p7g p7g² Dec 30] fairly useful maiden at best for K. Prendergast in Ireland: just modest in 2007: stays 7f: acts on polytrack and good to firm going: tried tongue tied/in cheekpieces. *K. A. Morgan*

TAKAFU (USA) 5 b.g. Lemon Drop Kid (USA) 131 – Proper Protocol (USA) (Deputy **90** Minister (CAN)) [2007 87: 11.7f⁵ 15d* 16g⁶ 14d² 14d* 14.1d⁶ 16.2g⁵ 18d Oct 20] tall, leggy, useful-looking gelding: fairly useful handicapper: won at Warwick in May and Sandown in July: barely stays 17f: acts on good to firm and good to soft going. *W. S. Kittow*

TAKANEWA (IRE) 4 b.f. Danetime (IRE) 121 – Lady Ingabelle (IRE) 71 (Catrail **58** (USA) 123) [2007 72d: 6g⁵ 5.9g⁵ 7.1g³ 6g² 6f Sep 17] tall filly: just modest maiden nowa-days: stays 9.8f: best efforts on good going: often front runner. *J. Howard Johnson*

TAKE A BOW 6 b.h. Royal Applause 124 – Giant Nipper (Nashwan (USA) 135) [2007 **117** 107: 8.1g³ 8.3d² 10g* 10.4s³ 10m Aug 25] medium-sized, quite good-topped horse: smart performer: better than ever in 2007, winning Betfair Brigadier Gerard Stakes at Sandown in May by short head from Mighty: also ran creditably when placed in Betfred Mile at Sandown (third to Jeremy), listed race at Windsor (neck second to Army of Angels) and York Stakes at York (1½ lengths third to Stage Gift): suffered fractures to near-hind 2f out in Winter Hill Stakes at Windsor final outing: stayed 1¼m: acted on firm and soft going: was game and consistent: dead. *P. R. Chamings*

TAKE A MILE (IRE) 5 ch.g. Inchinor 119 – Bu Hagab (IRE) (Royal Academy (USA) **–** 130) [2007 67: 14.1d Aug 16] tall gelding: fair handicapper at best: raced too freely sole start in 2007: stays 1¼m: acts on polytrack, firm and soft going: fair hurdler. *B. G. Powell*

TAKE IT THERE 5 ch.m. Cadeaux Genereux 131 – Feel Free (IRE) 86 (Generous **51** (IRE) 139) [2007 64: p8m Oct 13] lengthy mare: modest handicapper: stays 1m: acts on fibresand and firm ground: held up. *A. J. Lidderdale*

TAKEN (IRE) 2 b.g. (May 7) Red Ransom (USA) – Heart's Harmony (Blushing **75** Groom (FR) 131) [2007 7m⁶ 7m⁴ p7g² Dec 19] close-coupled gelding: half-brother to several winners, including smart 1m to 1¼m winner National Anthem (including in US, by Royal Academy) and 3-y-o Stringsofmyheart (by Halling): dam ran twice in France: fair form in maidens, off 5 months (and gelded) before neck second to Parisian Gift at Lingfield: will be suited by 1m. *J. R. Fanshawe*

TAKEOVER TARGET (AUS) 8 b.g. Celtic Swing 138 – Shady Stream (AUS) **126** (Archerack (CAN)) [2007 126: 7d⁵ 6g² 6.8g* 5m⁴ 6d² 6d* 6d* Dec 22] sturdy, good-bodied gelding: high-class performer: had another good year in 2007, successful at Doomben in Carlton Draught Doomben 10,000 in May and at Randwick in December in valuable event (by head from Dance Hero) and listed handicap (held on by nose from Alverta): creditable efforts at Royal Ascot fourth/fifth starts, 2½ lengths fourth to Miss Andretti in King's Stand Stakes (won race in 2006) and head second to Soldier's Tale in Golden Jubilee Stakes 4 days later (placed for second year running): effective at 5f, and has won at 7f: acts on firm and good to soft going, bit below form on heavy: races prominently: ridden on all bar one of his starts by J. Ford: tough, game and genuine. *Joe Janiak, Australia*

TAKES TUTU (USA) 8 b.g. Afternoon Deelites (USA) 122 – Lady Affirmed (USA) **63** (Affirmed (USA)) [2007 82d: p9.5g p9.5g f16s f12g f14g 10g p10g* 10m p10g² p12g* 14m Sep 9] tall, useful-looking gelding: just modest performer nowadays: won seller at Lingfield in July and handicap there (dead-heated) in August: effective at 7f to 1½m: acts on all-weather and firm going: sometimes wears headgear: can race freely/idle. *C. R. Dore*

TAKE THE GOLD (IRE) 3 ch.f. Grand Lodge (USA) 125 – River Missy (USA) **64**
(Riverman (USA) 131) [2007 10d² 12m⁵ p9.5g⁴ Aug 12] €19,000Y, resold 11,500Y,
€32,000 2-y-o: unfurnished filly: half-sister to numerous winners, including Irish 1¼m
winner Esperanto, 1½m winner Ticket To Dance (both useful by Sadler's Wells) and US
Grade 2 6f/7f winner Miss Golden Circle (by Crafty Prospector): dam, Irish 1¼m winner,
half-sister to Fillies' Mile winner Leap Lively: modest form in maidens: stays 1¼m: acts
on good to soft going: sold 14,000 gns. *M. A. Jarvis*

TAKE TO THE SKIES (IRE) 3 b.c. Lujain (USA) 119 – To The Skies (USA) 89 **63**
(Sky Classic (CAN)) [2007 –: p6g⁴ p6g p7g⁴ 8.1m p7g p7m Oct 11] tall colt: fair maiden:
ran creditably but failed to settle first 2 attempts at 7f: jinked right leaving stall and raced
wide second outing. *A. P. Jarvis*

TAKITWO 4 b.g. Delta Dancer – Tiama (IRE) 50 (Last Tycoon 131) [2007 74: p8g⁴ **73**
p7g⁵ p7g* p7.1g³ p7g⁵ 7m* 7g³ 7.6g⁵ p7g 7f³ 7g p7g p7.1g³ p7g Dec 16] fair handicapper: won at Kempton (apprentices) in March and Brighton in June: stays 7f: acts on
polytrack, firm and good to soft ground: unreliable. *P. D. Cundell*

TALAMAHANA 2 b.f. (May 9) Kyllachy 129 – Bahawir Pour (USA) (Green Dancer **58**
(USA) 132) [2007 6m⁵ 6s 6d 7m 6.5d p8m p6g p9.5g⁴ p7.1g⁴ Dec 29] 8,000F, 18,000Y:
close-coupled filly: seventh foal: half-sister to 3 winners, including useful 2002 2-y-o 7f
winner Captain Saif (by Compton Place) and 4-y-o Future's Dream: dam unraced: modest
maiden: seems to stay 1m: acts on polytrack, good to firm and good to soft going: tried
blinkered: none too consistent. *S. Kirk*

TALAYEB 2 b. or br.g. (Feb 14) Nayef (USA) 129 – Paper Chase (FR) 78 (Machia- **82**
vellian (USA) 123) [2007 7m 7m⁴ 8m⁴ Sep 21] 65,000F: big, rangy gelding: first foal:
dam, maiden (stayed 1½m), out of smart performer up to 1½m Papering: fairly useful
maiden: fourth to Latin Lad at Goodwood and to Centennial at Newbury (minor event,
looked none too keen in blinkers): gelded after: will stay 1¼m: raced only on good to firm
going. *M. P. Tregoning*

TALBOT AVENUE 9 b.g. Puissance 110 – Dancing Daughter 79 (Dance In Time **90**
(CAN)) [2007 105, a100: p6g⁶ p5g⁶ p5g² 5g⁵ 5d 5g 5.2f⁵ 5g 5m Sep 1] compact gelding:
fairly useful handicapper: hasn't won since 2003: effective at 5f/easy 6.5f: acts on polytrack, firm and soft going: blinkered (ran well) once in 2005: sometimes bandaged on
joints: has wandered. *M. Blanshard*

TALCEN GWYN (IRE) 5 b.g. Fayruz 116 – Cheerful Knight (IRE) (Mac's Imp **68**
(USA) 116) [2007 69: p5.1g 5.3d 5.3d* 5m³ 5m 6m³ 5.3d 5g⁶ 5.7f⁴ 5.1m³ 5d³ p5m 5.7g
Oct 24] workmanlike gelding: fair handicapper: won at Brighton in July: effective at 5f/
6f: acts on polytrack, firm and good to soft going: usually visored: sometimes hangs right:
said to have finished lame final outing. *M. F. Harris*

TALK MORE (USA) 3 b.f. More Than Ready (USA) 120 – Pomarola Talk (ARG) **66**
(Confidential Talk (USA)) [2007 7m⁴ 7m Aug 4] tall filly: third foal: dam won Argentinian 1000 Guineas: better effort in maidens when 6¾ lengths fourth to Promising Lead
at Newbury in April: sold 1,000 gns. *J. Noseda*

TALK OF SAAFEND (IRE) 2 b.f. (Mar 5) Barathea (IRE) 127 – Sopran Marida **81**
(IRE) (Darshaan 133) [2007 5m p5g⁵ p6g⁶ p7g 7m² 7m³ 7d² 8m 7m* Oct 6] 14,000Y:
unfurnished filly: half-sister to several winners, including useful 6f (at 2 yrs) to 8.5f (in
US) winner Millenium Princess (by Eagle Eyed): dam Italian 7f and 9f winner: fairly
useful performer: steady progress in nurseries, won at Newmarket final start: stays 1m:
acts on good to firm and good to soft going: tough. *R. Hannon*

TALLULAH SUNRISE 2 b.f. (Mar 7) Auction House (USA) 120 – Tallulah Belle 92 **68**
(Crowning Honors (CAN)) [2007 5m p6g⁵ p7m⁴ p6d³ Dec 28] good-topped filly: third
foal: dam 9f to 1½m winner: fair maiden: third in nursery at Wolverhampton: will stay
1m: acts on polytrack. *M. D. I. Usher*

TALON (IRE) 3 ch.g. (Apr 28) Indian Ridge 123 – Brief Lullaby (IRE) (Brief Truce **52**
(USA) 126) [2007 7.1g 7.5g 7.1m 8d Oct 23] lengthy, sturdy gelding: modest maiden:
stays 1m: sold 10,000 gns, then gelded. *W. J. Haggas*

TAMAGIN (USA) 4 b.c. Stravinsky (USA) 133 – Luia (USA) (Forty Niner (USA)) **109**
[2007 96: 6d* 6m* 6m² 6m² p5.1g² 6g* p6g* Nov 4] tall, close-coupled colt: smart handicapper: left P. D. Evans, dropped in trip and most progressive in 2007, winning at Redcar
in July, Newmarket in August, Doncaster (beat Commando Scott by 2 lengths) in October
and Lingfield (made all from wide draw, beat King's Caprice by ¾ length) in November:
has won at easy 1m, though will prove best at 5f/6f: acts on polytrack, firm and good to
soft going: usually wore cheekpieces in 2006: goes early to post: free-going front runner.
K. A. Ryan

TAMARACK (IRE) 3 b.g. Tamarisk (IRE) 127 – Sound Tap (IRE) (Warning 136) **66**
[2007 6m 6m⁴ 6g 7m Aug 1] good-bodied gelding: form in maidens only when 3¼
lengths fourth behind Shadow The Wind at Newbury: tailed off last 2 starts: should be
suited by 7f. *W. R. Muir*

TAMARA MOON (IRE) 2 b.f. (Jan 30) Acclamation 118 – Non Ultra (USA) 63 **75**
(Peintre Celebre (USA) 137) [2007 5m⁶ 6m 6s 7d* 7m 7m 8f* 7d p7g Nov 3] 12,000Y:
tall, lengthy filly, unfurnished at 2 yrs: first foal: dam 1m seller winner: fair performer:
won nurseries at Catterick in July and Bath in September: stays 1m: acts on firm and good
to soft ground. *M. R. Channon*

TAMASOU (IRE) 2 b.c. (Feb 18) Tamarisk (IRE) 127 – Soubresaut (IRE) (Danehill **71**
(USA) 126) [2007 7g² 8g⁴ 8g.6g² p8.6g³ Nov 10] compact colt: fair maiden: in frame all
starts: stays 8.6f. *S. Parr*

TAMATAVE (IRE) 5 b.g. Darshaan 133 – Manuetti (IRE) 86 (Sadler's Wells (USA) **53**
132) [2007 72: p8.6g f7g f8g 9.9s p7g Sep 12] quite attractive gelding: has a quick action:
maiden handicapper, modest at best in 2007: left K. Ryan after third start: stays 1m:
acts on all-weather and good to firm ground: tongue tied at 2 yrs: has looked ungenuine.
M. W. Easterby

TAMDIID (USA) 2 b.f. (Apr 18) Horse Chestnut (SAF) 119 – Ladue (USA) (Demons **67 +**
Begone (USA)) [2007 7m p8g⁴ Sep 26] $130,000Y: fourth foal: sister to smart US
performer up to 9f Lucifer's Stone and half-sister to 2 winners in US: dam US 6.5f to 9f
winner: better effort in maidens when fourth to Ballora at Kempton: stays 1m.
C. E. Brittain

TAMINO (IRE) 4 b.g. Mozart (IRE) 131 – Stop Out 89 (Rudimentary (USA) 118) **79**
[2007 72: 5m⁵ 5.1d 6g⁴ 7m³ 6m* 7d 6g* 6d³ 6g² p7g Dec 28] big gelding: fair handicapper: won at Salisbury (ladies) in July and Newbury (apprentices) in August: left
H. Morrison prior to final start: probably best at 6f: acts on good to firm and good to soft
ground: often tongue tied: races up with pace. *P. Howling*

TAM LIN 4 b.c. Selkirk (USA) 129 – La Nuit Rose (FR) 109 (Rainbow Quest (USA) **117 §**
134) [2007 120: 10g⁶ 10d² 8d³ 11.6m⁵ Aug 25] tall, attractive colt: has a fluent, round
action: smart performer: just about as good as ever when head second to Harland in listed
race at Sandown in July, clear entering straight: below form in similar events next 2 starts,
again refusing to settle: stays 1½m: unraced on extremes of going: doesn't impress with
attitude, tends to flash tail/carry head high (also hung markedly right final outing). *Saeed
bin Suroor*

TAMRAI DANCER 2 b.f. (Mar 21) Tamure (IRE) 125 – Rail Cat (Catrail (USA) 123) **66**
[2007 5m⁶ 5.1d 5d* 7.1s² 7f 8.3d⁶ Oct 1] rather leggy filly: first foal: dam unraced: fair
performer: won maiden at Warwick in June: stays 1m: acts on soft going. *R. M. Beckett*

TAMREEN (IRE) 6 b.g. Bahhare (USA) 122 – Na-Ayim (IRE) 68 (Shirley Heights **86**
130) [2007 p12g⁵ Mar 16] useful performer at 3 yrs, winning minor event at Longchamp:
left F. Head in France 5,000 gns and gelded after final 4-y-o outing: unraced on Flat in
2006: fairly useful form when fifth in handicap at Lingfield sole Flat start at 6 yrs:
probably stays 15f: acts on polytrack and good to soft ground: fair but temperamental
winning hurdler: sold £1,400 in November, joined C. Nenadich. *G. L. Moore*

TAMWORTH (IRE) 5 b.g. Perugino (USA) 84 – Faiblesse (Welsh Saint 126) [2007 **35**
61: p9.5g p8.6g p10g p8.6g⁵ Nov 24] poor at best in 2007: stays 1m: acts on sand/poly-
track, heavy and good to firm going: tried blinkered/visored/tongue tied. *E. J. Creighton*

TAN BONITA (USA) 2 b. or br.f. (Feb 15) More Than Ready (USA) 120 – Time For **76**
Hennessy (USA) (Hennessy (USA) 122) [2007 5m³ 5m* 5g 5m p6g³ 5m³ Dec 16]
$23,000F, 20,000Y: neat filly: first foal: dam unraced: fair performer: won maiden at
Catterick in May, best effort: left M. Wallace, third in minor event at Dos Hermanas final
start: best at 5f: acts on good to firm going, probably polytrack. *R. J. Smith, Spain*

TANCREDI (SWE) 5 b.g. Rossini (USA) 118 – Begine (IRE) (Germany (USA) 124) **79**
[2007 –: p11g* p10g⁶ p8.6g³ p10g p8.6g³ p9.5g⁵ f7g⁶ p7.1g* 8.1m² p8g⁶ p7.1g 6g 8d
p7.1g Dec 14] tall gelding: fair handicapper: won at Kempton in January and Wolverhampton in March: stays 11f: acts on polytrack and good to firm going: fly-jumped
leaving stall and unseated rider fourth outing: races prominently. *N. B. King*

TANFORAN 5 b.g. Mujahid (USA) 125 – Florentynna Bay 61 (Aragon 118) [2007 88: **62**
p6g⁵ 5f 6g⁵ p7.1m p8.6g p9.5g p8g p9.5g⁶ p7.1g* p7g² p7.1g² p7.1g⁵ Dec 14] quite **a73**
attractive gelding: fair handicapper on all-weather, modest on turf: left Ms J. Doyle after
reappearance: won at Wolverhampton in November: effective at 6f to 1m: acts on polytrack, firm and soft going: has worn blinkers/cheekpieces. *B. P. J. Baugh*

TANG 3 ch.f. Bahamian Bounty 116 – Hymne (FR) (Saumarez 132) [2007 63: p5g³ **54** p5.1g³ p6g⁵ 5.7d 5m p5.1g 5f⁶ p6g Oct 23] modest maiden: probably stays 6f: acts on polytrack and good to firm ground. *W. G. M. Turner*

TANGIBLE 5 b.m. Hernando (FR) 127 – Trinity Reef 80 (Bustino 136) [2007 79: 16m **66** 16m 13d 16g⁵ 12v* 12m⁶ 17.5s³ 14g⁵ Oct 29] leggy mare: fair handicapper: won at Tramore (awkward under pressure) in August: creditable third at Ayr penultimate outing: effective at 1½m to 2m: acts on any turf going: tried blinkered. *Liam McAteer, Ireland*

TANGO JACK (USA) 2 ch.c. (Mar 9) Stravinsky (USA) 133 – Life In Seattle (USA) **65** (Unbridled (USA) 128) [2007 6m Jun 14] strong colt: seventh in maiden at Newbury: dead. *Eve Johnson Houghton*

TANGO STEP (IRE) 7 b.g. Sesaro (USA) 81 – Leitrim Lodge (IRE) 64 (Classic **67** Music (USA)) [2007 78: p6g⁴ 5s 5m 6s p7g p7g⁶ p6m⁵ Nov 26] fair handicapper: credit-able efforts at Lingfield last 2 starts: best at 5f/6f: acts on polytrack, firm and soft going: tried blinkered/in cheekpieces. *Bernard Lawlor, Ireland*

TANLEY 2 gr.g. (Mar 30) Compton Admiral 121 – Schatzi 54§ (Chilibang 120) [2007 **57** 6m⁴ 5m⁵ 5m² 5m 5g² 5g 6g⁴ p6g Nov 12] close-coupled gelding: modest maiden: second in seller and claimer (wore cheekpieces, left James Moffatt £7,000): effective at 5f/6f: acts on polytrack and good to firm going: temperament under suspicion. *J. F. Coupland*

TANNING 5 b.m. Atraf 116 – Gerundive (USA) (Twilight Agenda (USA) 126) [2007 **–** 50: p12.2g Dec 15] modest performer: below form sole Flat start in 2007: tried in head-gear. *M. Appleby*

TANTIEN 5 b.m. Diktat 126 – Tahilla 112 (Moorestyle 137) [2007 44: f8g 7g p8.6g 6s⁴ **43** 6s⁶ 8v Jul 21] rather leggy mare: poor maiden: seems to stay 11f: acts on all-weather, soft and good to firm ground: wears cheekpieces/blinkers nowadays. *T. Keddy*

TANTRIS (IRE) 2 b.g. (Feb 10) High Chaparral (IRE) 132 – Emerald Cut (Rainbow **63 p** Quest (USA) 134) [2007 p7.1g⁵ Oct 21] 20,000F, €65,000Y: fifth foal: half-brother to Italian 1m to 11f winner Miss Emerald (by Kutub of Kintyre): dam unraced half-sister to smart Irish performer up to 12.5f Lime Gardens out of half-sister to Kooyonga: 20/1 and green, fifth to Staying On in maiden at Wolverhampton: will be suited by 1¼m/1½m: sure to improve. *J. A. Osborne*

TANWEER (USA) 2 ch.g. (Jan 18) Seeking The Gold (USA) – Fitted Crown (USA) **88 p** (Chief's Crown (USA)) [2007 7m* 8m⁵ Sep 15] $320,000Y: strong, sturdy gelding: half-brother to several US winners, notably multiple Grade 1 1m/9f (including at 2 yrs) winner Excellent Meeting (by General Meeting): dam, ran 3 times, half-sister to Grade 1-placed 2-y-o's Fair Advantage and Sophisticated Girl: fairly useful form: won maiden at Newmarket in August: favourite, unable to do himself justice (went freely held up off steady pace) when last of 5 to Meeriss in minor event at Goodwood: gelded after: stays 1m: will do better yet. *Sir Michael Stoute*

TANZANITE (IRE) 5 b.m. Revoque (IRE) 122 – Resume (IRE) 69 (Lahib (USA) **96** 129) [2007 100: p8.6g³ 8s p8g 10.4g 10d p8m p8m Nov 24] leggy, close-coupled mare: useful performer: below form after reappearance: effective at 1m to 10.5f: acts on polytrack and any turf going: sold 5,000 gns, sent to USA. *D. W. P. Arbuthnot*

TAPAS LAD (IRE) 2 b.c. (Apr 22) Modigliani (USA) 106 – Missish (Mummy's Pet **57 §** 125) [2007 6s 6s 6s 8.3d⁶ 7d³ p8m³ p10g³ p8.6g³ p8.6g³ f8d p8.6g⁵ Dec 31] 14,000Y: compact colt: half-brother to several winners, notably smart sprinter Andreyev (by Presidium): dam unraced: modest maiden: third 4 times in nurseries: stays 1¼m: acts on polytrack and soft going: tried tongue tied, often visored: temperamental. *V. Smith*

TAPSALTEERIE 4 b.f. Tipsy Creek (USA) 115 – Croft Sally (Crofthall 110) [2007 –: **–** f6g p6g 7g Apr 24] no sign of ability. *M. W. Easterby*

TARAN TREGARTH 3 b.f. Tobougg (IRE) 125 – Little Change 70 (Grundy 137) **48** [2007 41: 10.3m⁵ 10.3g p12.2g⁵ p12.2g p13.9g Nov 16] workmanlike filly: poor maiden: stays 1½m: acts on all-weather: tried in blinkers/cheekpieces: won over hurdles in November. *W. M. Brisbourne*

TARA'S FORCE (IRE) 2 b.f. (Apr 3) Acclamation 118 – Tara's Girl (IRE) 95 (Fayruz **56 p** 116) [2007 5g Apr 19] €40,000F, 20,000Y: tall, unfurnished filly: fourth foal: half-sister to fairly useful 6f/7f winner (including at 2 yrs) Triple Two (by Pivotal) and 3-y-o Blackat Blackitten: dam 2-y-o 5f winner: 10/1 and weak, seventh to Cristal Clear in maiden at Ripon: should do better. *J. J. Quinn*

TARA'S GARDEN 2 b.f. (Apr 9) Dr Fong (USA) 128 – Tremiere (FR) (Anabaa (USA) **57** 130) [2007 8d 8d Oct 27] lengthy filly: third foal: half-sister to 3-y-o Canongate: dam, French maiden (stayed 1m), sister to smart UAE/US miler Tsigane: modest form when mid-field in maidens. *M. Blanshard*

TARA TOO (IRE) 4 b.f. Danetime (IRE) 121 – Gone With The Wind (IRE) (Common **86** Grounds 118) [2007 97: 6m p6g⁴ 7s⁵ 7g p6g 7m⁵ 7d* 7m p8g Oct 14] leggy, close-coupled filly: fairly useful handicapper: won at Yarmouth in August: well below form after: stays 7f: acts on soft and good to firm going (probably on polytrack): blinkered last 5 starts: not straightforward. *J. G. Portman*

TARBOLTON (IRE) 2 b.c. (Mar 3) King's Best (USA) 132 – Golly Gosh (IRE) 103 **73** (Danehill (USA) 126) [2007 8.1d 7m 8f³ Sep 27] 40,000F, 48,000Y: lengthy, useful-looking colt: first foal: dam Irish 1½m winner (stayed 1¾m): fair maiden: third to Prince Desire at Pontefract: will be suited by 1¼m/1½m: acts on firm going: sold 17,000 gns. *M. Johnston*

TARELLIA 3 gr.f. Pivotal 124 – Amarella (FR) (Balleroy (USA) 115) [2007 58: 8s 10m **55** 11.9g p12.2g⁴ 10s Jun 26] modest maiden: below par after reappearance, including at Wolverhampton penultimate outing: probably stays 1½m: tried blinkered/in cheekpieces: pulled up third start: carried head awkwardly fourth 3-y-o outing. *E. M. D. Kelly, Ireland*

TARIQ 3 ch.c. Kyllachy 129 – Tatora (Selkirk (USA) 129) [2007 101: 7m⁵ 8g 7m* **124** 7m* 7g* 7d⁵ Oct 6]

Authorized wasn't the only Peter Chapple-Hyam-trained colt to carry the dark green and beige colours of Saleh Al Homeizi and Imad Al Sagar with distinction in 2007. Another three-year-old, Tariq, made a complete recovery from an injury sustained at two and rattled up a hat-trick of wins over seven furlongs during a period of just over two months in the summer, winning at listed, Group 3 then Group 2 level. Seven furlongs could well be Tariq's optimum trip, but it's too early to be adamant about that. Tariq seemed not to stay on his only attempt so far at a mile, in the Poule d'Essai des Poulains, already beaten when hampered over a furlong out, but he may well be given another chance at that distance, Chapple-Hyam having mentioned races such as the Breeders' Cup Mile and Hong Kong Mile as possible end-of-season targets. That said, a step back to six furlongs looks a better option for Tariq, something his trainer has already considered, Haydock's Sprint Cup coming into the reckoning after Tariq had completed his hat-trick.

Both of Tariq's runs at two were at six furlongs, his win in a maiden at Newmarket followed by third behind Hellvelyn and Major Cadeaux in the Coventry Stakes at Royal Ascot, Tariq reportedly fracturing his pelvis in the latter and subsequently being off the course for ten months. It wasn't until his third start back that Tariq began to fulfil that early promise, upsetting the odds laid on Mr Napper Tandy in a six-runner listed event at Newmarket. That race had been won twelve months earlier by Jeremy, who then followed up in the Jersey Stakes at Royal Ascot. The Jersey was also Tariq's next race. He faced fourteen rivals, one of them the very smart French challenger US Ranger, who on his previous start had finished seventh in the Two Thousand Guineas. US Ranger was heavily backed and went off favourite at 6/5, with Tariq next at 15/2. The pair filled the first two places but not in the order the betting suggested as Tariq, showing further improvement, emulated Jeremy. Held up in rear off a strong pace, Tariq was switched right at around the two-furlong marker, where US Ranger took it up. Tariq quickened to

Betfair Cup (Lennox), Goodwood—Tariq quickens away from Asset (second left), Dunelight (visor) and Thousand Words (second right)

collar him inside the last furlong and win by two and a half lengths. Similar tactics were employed in both of Tariq's subsequent races, the first of which was the Betfair Cup (registered as the Lennox) at Goodwood.

The Betfair looked a good renewal, with the three-year-olds well represented and most of the older horses in the thirteen-runner field proven at Group 2 level. The race itself wasn't without incident, several meeting trouble in the last two furlongs as the field bunched up in a race run at an uneven gallop. Both second favourite Tariq and the favourite Asset enjoyed a clear run as they made their efforts out wide, Tariq quickening the better to collar the leader Dunelight around half a furlong out and sustaining his effort to win by a length and a quarter from Asset. The race showed that Tariq was still progressing, and he started a short-priced favourite to complete a four-timer when stepped back up to Group 1 level in the Prix de la Foret at Longchamp. He failed to give his running, dropped right out and never a threat in fifth behind the enterprisingly-ridden outsider Toylsome. Though tactics played a part, it is also possible the good to soft going wasn't ideal for Tariq —apart from on his debut he had raced only on good and good to firm—but it

Tariq (ch.c. 2004)	Kyllachy (b 1998)	Pivotal (ch 1993)	Polar Falcon Fearless Revival
		Pretty Poppy (b 1988)	Song Moonlight Serenade
	Tatora (ch 1998)	Selkirk (ch 1988)	Sharpen Up Annie Edge
		Tatouma (ch 1986)	The Minstrel Sheer Fantasy

Saleh Al Homeizi and Imad Al Sagar's "Tariq"

couldn't be put any stronger than that, especially as Tariq hadn't seemed troubled by soft ground when winning easily on that first start.

Tariq was bred by David Botterill who picked up his dam Tatora very cheaply at the December Sales in 2000. 'That was in the days when the minimum bid at Tatts was 2,000 guineas, and I got her for the minimum price when she was a two-year-old, as a breeding prospect,' said Botterill. 'She was quite immature and I didn't have the money to put her into training at the time, so I thought "Well, a broodmare she's going to be"' Botterill has had no cause to regret that decision. At the latest December Sales he sold a brother to Tariq for 140,000 guineas as a foal, bought on behalf of Tariq's owners. Tariq himself was sold as a foal for 32,000 guineas, and fetched 65,000 guineas when resold as a yearling. He is the second foal produced by Tatora, whose third, Sweet Nicole (by Okawango), showed a bit of promise in a maiden at Windsor on her only start to date. The next dam Tatouma, successful over five and six furlongs at two, is also the grandam of smart sprinter Wi Dud, who is out of another Botterill-owned mare Hopesay. 'Handsome is as handsome does' is an adage which applies to Tariq as he is nothing much on looks, being small and leggy. A good walker, Tariq hasn't always impressed in his faster paces, but don't be put off him if he moves poorly to post, as he did so before both of his best performances. *P. W. Chapple-Hyam*

TARKAMARA (IRE) 3 ch.f. Medicean 128 – Tarakana (USA) 101 (Shahrastani (USA) 135) [2007 80: 8g p6g² p6g² 6m² 5m⁵ 6f Sep 25] big, useful-looking filly: has a round action: fair maiden: runner-up 3 times in 2007, but generally regressed: likely to prove best at 5f/6f: acts on polytrack and good to firm ground: tongue tied final outing: races prominently: found little fourth/fifth starts, and one to treat with caution. *P. F. I. Cole* — **76 d**

TARKHEENA PRINCE (USA) 2 b.g. (May 6) Aldebaran (USA) 126 – Tarkheena (USA) (Alleged (USA) 138) [2007 7d³ 7.5g Jul 31] $40,000Y, 20,000 2-y-o: tall gelding: half-brother to useful French 1m winner Clerical Error (by Kendor) and useful French 1m winner Coimbra (by Trempolino): dam unraced half-sister to US Grade 2 1½m winner Heron Cove: fairly useful maiden: encouraging third to Midnight Muse at Redcar: still green (slowly away), not clear run at Beverley week later: subsequently gelded: will stay 1m. *G. A. Swinbank* — **80**

TARRABURN 3 ch.g. Eltish (USA) 120 – Rahy's Wish (USA) (Rahy (USA) 115) [2007 75: 7m⁴ 8m 7g Aug 29] rather leggy, useful-looking gelding: fair handicapper: should stay 1m: acts on good to firm and good to soft ground. *J. Howard Johnson* — **77**

TARTAN BEARER (IRE) 2 ch.c. (Mar 29) Spectrum (IRE) 126 – Highland Gift (IRE) 95 (Generous (IRE) 139) [2007 7g² Nov 2] seventh foal: brother to 2000 Guineas/King George VI & Queen Elizabeth Stakes winner Golan, 7f winner at 2 yrs, and useful Irish 1m winner Gift Range, and half-brother to 3 winners, including fairly useful 1½m winner (stayed 2m) Highland Games (by Singspiel): dam, 1¼m winner, half-sister to smart middle-distance stayer Bonny Scot: 9/4, very promising second to Foolin Myself in maiden at Newmarket, badly hampered over 1f out and finishing strongly once switched: will be well suited by 1¼m/1½m: one to follow. *Sir Michael Stoute* — **87 p**

TARTAN SPECIAL 5 b.g. Fasliyev (USA) 120 – Colchica (Machiavellian (USA) 123) [2007 54: p8g p8.6g Feb 21] leggy gelding: modest performer at best: below form in handicaps both starts in 2007: stays 8.6f: acts on all-weather and good to firm ground: sometimes wears headgear. *K. R. Burke* — **–**

TARTAN TIE 3 b.c. Grand Lodge (USA) 125 – Trois Graces (USA) (Alysheba (USA)) [2007 69: 10g* May 29] tall colt: fairly useful form: improved effort when winning maiden at Redcar in May by 5 lengths from Murbek, making all: stays 1¼m. *M. Johnston* — **91**

TARTATARTUFATA 5 b.m. Tagula (IRE) 116 – It's So Easy 63 (Shaadi (USA) 126) [2007 87: f5g³ p5.1g⁴ p5f⁵ 5.1g 5d p6g p5.1g* p5.1g³ f5d² p5.1s³ Dec 21] strong mare: fairly useful handicapper: won at Wolverhampton in November: speedy and best at 5f: acts on all-weather, firm and soft going: usually visored: sometimes hangs: usually races prominently. *D. Shaw* — **a85**

TARTEEL (USA) 3 b.f. Bahri (USA) 125 – Elrehaan 96 (Sadler's Wells (USA) 132) [2007 91: 8d* 7m* 7g 8.1m Sep 1] tall, rather leggy filly: useful performer: improved in 2007, winning handicaps at Newmarket in June and July (beat Graduation 1½ lengths): well below form when hanging right last 2 starts, in Oak Tree Stakes at Goodwood and listed race at Sandown: would have stayed 1¼m: acted on good to firm and good to soft going: had been bandaged fore joints: to visit Lemon Drop Kid. *J. L. Dunlop* — **105**

TARTE TATIN (IRE) 3 b.f. Sakhee (USA) 136 – Femme Fatale 102 (Fairy King – (USA)) [2007 p9.5g p10g⁶ Nov 21] 65,000Y: third foal: half-sister to 2004 2-y-o 7f winner Sadie Thompson (by King's Best): dam, fair 4f winner (including at 2 yrs), half-sister to smart performer at up to 1¼m Foodbroker Fancy: well held in maidens at Wolverhampton and Lingfield. *J. L. Dunlop*

TASDEER (USA) 2 b.c. (Mar 25) Rahy (USA) 115 – Mehthaaf (USA) 121 (Nureyev **90 p** (USA) 131) [2007 7m⁴ 7g* 7m Oct 5] good-topped colt: closely related/half-brother to several winners, including 1¼m winners Najah (smart, by Nashwan) and Tanaghum (useful, by Darshaan): dam, 6f (at 2 yrs) to 1m (Irish 1000 Guineas) winner, closely related to July Cup winner Elnadim: fairly useful form: impressively won maiden at Yarmouth (beat City Stable by 4 lengths) in September: dropped away tamely in Somerville Tattersall Stakes at Newmarket final start: will stay 1m: should still do better. *M. A. Jarvis*

TASHEBA 2 ch.c. (Feb 6) Dubai Destination (USA) 127 – Tatanka (IRE) (Lear Fan **75 p** (USA) 130) [2007 8.1m 8m 7d* Oct 30] 72,000F: strong, well-made colt: third foal: dam unraced out of half-sister to Coronation Cup winner Be My Native: fair form: much improved to win maiden at Yarmouth final start, getting up cosily: should be suited by 1m: acts on good to soft going: will continue on the up. *P. W. Chapple-Hyam*

TASK COMPLETE 4 ch.f. Bahamian Bounty 116 – Taskone (Be My Chief (USA) **55** 122) [2007 55: p9.5g³ p6g p7g⁶ p7.1g 8f 6m 6d⁴ 7s³ p7g⁴ p7.1g p7g Nov 21] modest maiden: stays 7f: acts on polytrack and soft going: tried blinkered. *Jean-Rene Auvray*

TASLEYA 2 b.c. (Mar 26) Oasis Dream 129 – Princess Athena 119 (Ahonoora 122) – [2007 6m Jul 12] 180,000Y: big colt: eighth foal: half-brother to several sprint winners, notably smart Acclamation (by Royal Applause): dam 5f winner, including in Queen Mary Stakes: 9/1, burly and green, last in minor event at Newmarket. *B. W. Hills*

TASS HEEL (IRE) 8 b.g. Danehill (USA) 126 – Mamouna (USA) 113 (Vaguely Noble – 140) [2007 p16.5g Jan 5] strong, lengthy gelding: fair performer at best: lightly raced on Flat since 2003, and tailed off sole outing at 8 yrs: tried in cheekpieces. *B. J. Llewellyn*

TASTAHIL (IRE) 3 ch.c. Singspiel (IRE) 133 – Luana 101 (Shaadi (USA) 126) [2007 – 84: 10m Apr 19] strong, good sort: fairly useful performer at 2 yrs: tailed off in handicap at Newmarket only start in 2007 (said to have finished lame): should stay 1½m: acts on polytrack, raced only on good/good to firm going on turf. *B. W. Hills*

TASWEET (IRE) 3 b.g. Mujahid (USA) 125 – Injaad (Machiavellian (USA) 123) **74** [2007 71p: p8g* p10g p7g p8g p8m p8g Oct 29] deep-girthed gelding: fair handicapper: won maiden at Lingfield in January: stays 1m: acts on polytrack: often wears headgear: sold 6,000 gns. *T. G. Mills*

TATBEEQ (IRE) 2 b.f. (Feb 10) Invincible Spirit (IRE) 121 – Announcing Peace **74 +** (Danehill (USA) 126) [2007 5d⁴ 6s³ Jun 16] €72,000F, 275,000Y: compact, good-quartered filly: fifth foal: closely related to smart 6f (at 2 yrs) to 1½m winner Crosspeace and 3-y-o So Sweet (both by Cape Cross), and half-sister to Italian winner by College Chapel: dam Irish maiden: fair form in maidens at Sandown and Leicester (went freely, third to Highland Daughter): suffered injury after: should prove best at 5f/6f: raced on ground softer than good. *M. A. Jarvis*

TATHKAAR 2 ch.f. (May 1) Dr Fong (USA) 128 – Royal Patron 78 (Royal Academy **79** (USA) 130) [2007 7m⁴ 7g² Oct 6] 20,000Y: rather unfurnished filly: fourth foal: dam 1¾m winner out of Gold Cup winner Indian Queen: fair form in frame in maidens at Newbury and Redcar, likely insufficient test: will be suited by 1¼m/1½m. *C. E. Brittain*

TATILLIUS (IRE) 4 ch.g. King Charlemagne (USA) 120 – Aunty Eileen (Ahonoora – 122) [2007 –: 5m Aug 18] good-topped gelding: no form: tried tongue tied. *J. M. Bradley*

TAURIAN 2 b.g. (Apr 21) Zamindar (USA) 116 – Moon Carnival 94 (Be My Guest **94** (USA) 126) [2007 5m⁵ 5m* 5m⁴ 6m⁶ 6m* 6m* 6m³ 6m³ Sep 22] 4,000Y: big gelding: half-brother to 3 winners, including 7f (at 2 yrs) to 2m winner Carousing (by Selkirk): dam 1½m winner: fairly useful performer: won maiden and nursery at Hamilton and minor event at Newcastle: raced only at 5f/6f on good to firm going: dead. *Mrs L. Stubbs*

TAVALU (USA) 5 b.g. Kingmambo (USA) 125 – Larrocha (IRE) 116 (Sadler's Wells **69** (USA) 132) [2007 68: p16g p16g² p16g² 16m⁴ Jul 18] fair maiden handicapper: effective at 1½m to 17f: acts on polytrack, firm and soft going: tried blinkered. *G. L. Moore*

TAVARES (IRE) 4 b.g. King Charlemagne (USA) 120 – Tadkiyra (IRE) (Darshaan **64 d** 133) [2007 8.2g 7.1d⁶ 8.1d 10.5m 10d p8.6g p10m 16d Oct 11] tall gelding: regressive maiden: left P. McEntee after second start: stays 1m: tried blinkered. *J. Jay*

TAWAASH (USA) 2 b. or br.c. (Apr 25) Storm Cat (USA) – Victory Ride (USA) 119 **90 p**
(Seeking The Gold (USA)) [2007 6d² Oct 19] $1,550,000Y: leggy, quite good-topped
colt: second foal: brother to US 5f winner: dam US Grade 1 7f winner: 33/1, shaped well
when second to Insaaf in maiden at Newmarket, impressing with speed: may prove best
at 5f/6f: will progress and win races. *M. A. Jarvis*

TAWAASSOL (USA) 4 b.c. War Chant (USA) 126 – Montecito (USA) (Seeking The **109**
Gold (USA)) [2007 111: 5g 5m 7m 5m⁴ 6d Oct 13] strong, close-coupled colt: useful
performer: best efforts in 2007 in Supreme Stakes at Goodwood (eighth to Lovelace) and
listed race at Newmarket (fourth to Judd Street) third/fourth outings: probably stays 7f:
acts on good to firm going: usually tongue tied (not last 2 starts when visored): joined
E. Charpy in UAE. *Sir Michael Stoute*

TAWNYBRACK (IRE) 3 b.g. Rossini (USA) 118 – Ceannanas (IRE) 77 (Magical **63**
Wonder (USA) 125) [2007 68: 6g 5g* 5f³ 6.5m⁴ 5g² 5g* 5f* 6g a4.8g² a7.5g Dec 26]
modest performer: left Jane Chapple-Hyam after reappearance: successful at Ostend in
minor events in July and August and handicap in September: best at 5f: acts on firm
ground. *L. Braem, Belgium*

TAWZEEA (IRE) 2 ch.c. (Feb 24) Cadeaux Genereux 131 – Kismah 111 (Machiavel- **76 +**
lian (USA) 123) [2007 6g³ 6m² Sep 22] big, useful-looking colt: fifth foal: half-brother
to 3 winners, including useful 7f/1m winner Tahirah and 6-y-o Eijaaz (both by Green
Desert): dam, 1m winner on both starts, from excellent family of Singspiel and Rahy:
fair form in maidens: promising third behind Striking Spirit and Beacon Lodge at
Haydock: beaten 10 lengths when second to Hammadi at Catterick: will be suited by 7f/
1m. *M. Johnston*

TAX FREE (IRE) 5 b.g. Tagula (IRE) 116 – Grandel (Owington 123) [2007 117: a6f⁴ **117**
a6f 6f* 5m* 5d* 5m 5s² 5g³ 5m* 5m³ Oct 4] strong gelding: smart performer: won minor
event at Thirsk in April, Stan James Palace House Stakes at Newmarket (by short head
from Peace Offering) in May, listed event at Naas (beat Dandy Man by length) in June
and Prix du Petit Couvert Casino Barriere de Dinard at Longchamp (gamely by short neck
from Derison) in September: also good third in King George Stakes at Goodwood (beaten
2¼ lengths by Moorhouse Lad) and listed race at Newmarket (went down by ¾ length to

Naas Sprint Stakes, Naas—Tax Free completes a hat-trick;
Dandy Man and Desert Lord fill the minor placings

Judd Street): effective at 5f/6f: yet to race on heavy ground, acts on any other turf: consistent. *D. Nicholls*

TAYARAT (IRE) 2 b.g. (Feb 1) Noverre (USA) 125 – Sincere (IRE) 80 (Bahhare (USA) 122) [2007 5d 7.1d⁴ 7.1g p7g 8g* Sep 20] 21,000F, 110,000Y: attractive gelding: has a fluent action: first foal: dam, Irish 1½m winner, half-sister to dam of Sinndar: fairly useful form: longer trip, progressed to win nursery at Yarmouth (made all) final start: gelded after: will stay 1¼m: acts on polytrack, raced only on good/good to soft going on turf. *M. P. Tregoning* **83 +**

TAY BRIDGE (IRE) 4 ch.g. Tagula (IRE) 116 – Wild Liffey (USA) (Irish River (FR) 131) [2007 –: 7.1d⁶ Jun 28] lengthy gelding: little form since 2005: tried blinkered/tongue tied. *G. F. Bridgwater* **–**

TAYMAN (IRE) 5 b. or br.g. Sinndar (IRE) 134 – Sweet Emotion (IRE) 97 (Bering 136) [2007 71: 15.4m⁴ Aug 9] quite good-topped gelding: fair handicapper: stays 15.4f: acts on polytrack, good to firm and good to soft going: tried blinkered. *Carl Llewellyn* **72**

TAZAWUD 2 ch.g. (Feb 10) Noverre (USA) 125 – Alhufoof (USA) 100 (Dayjur (USA) 137) [2007 5.1g⁵ 5g Apr 19] strong-quartered, sturdy gelding: modest form in minor event/maiden: sold 8,000 gns and gelded. *M. Johnston* **54**

TAZEEZ (USA) 3 b. or br.g. Silver Hawk (USA) 123 – Soiree Russe (USA) (Nureyev (USA) 131) [2007 8.2m² 8.2g² Oct 31] €200,000Y: good-topped gelding: second foal: half-brother to winner in US by Deputy Commander: dam, French 1m winner, half-sister to smart middle-distance performer Ionio: better effort in maidens at Nottingham when ½-length second to Northern Spy on debut: still green, beaten neck by Hint of Spring next time, looking ungainly: bred to stay middle distances. *J. H. M. Gosden* **83**

TCHERINA (IRE) 5 b.m. Danehill Dancer (IRE) 117 – Forget Paris (IRE) (Broken Hearted 124) [2007 88d: 9.9m² 12g* 12g³ 12m³ 11.5d⁵ 12f 10.5s⁵ 12d 12g Nov 2] leggy, useful-looking mare: fairly useful handicapper: won at York in May: below form last 4 outings: stays 1½m: acts on soft and good to firm ground. *T. D. Easterby* **85**

TEA CAKE (IRE) 2 b.f. (Feb 26) Compton Place 125 – Griddle Cake (IRE) 62 (Be My Guest (USA) 126) [2007 6d 6.5d p6g⁶ Oct 15] 34,000F, 42,000Y: leggy filly: half-sister to 3 winners, including 1m winner Our Jaffa (by Bin Ajwaad) and 1m/1¼m winner Strudel (by Spectrum), both fairly useful: dam, maiden (stayed 1½m), half-sister to smart middle-distance performers Bonny Scot and Mary Stuart, and to dam of Golan: modest maiden: stiff tasks at Ascot first 2 starts, then encouraging sixth to Meydan Princess at Lingfield (finished fast): will be suited by 7f/1m: capable of better. *H. J. L. Dunlop* **59 p**

TEADANCER (IRE) 2 b.f. (Apr 16) Traditionally (USA) 117 – Dance Up A Storm (USA) (Storm Bird (CAN) 134) [2007 7s p7g p8g Oct 4] €3,000Y: workmanlike filly: fifth foal: half-sister to fairly useful Irish 1½m winner Bahrain Storm (by Bahhare) and French 13f winner Danse Imperiale (by Dernier Empereur): dam French 8.5f to 1¼m winner: well held in maidens. *J. G. Portman* **–**

TEARS OF A CLOWN 4 b.g. Galileo (IRE) 134 – Mood Swings (IRE) 77 (Shirley Heights 130) [2007 91: 9.7m² 10d* 11.9m 10d³ Sep 28] tall, good-bodied gelding: useful performer: reportedly fractured pelvis after final 3-y-o outing: won handicap at Ascot (by neck from Familiar Territory) in July: good 2¼ lengths third to King Charles in minor event there final start: stays 1¼m: acts on polytrack, good to firm and good to soft going: held up: restless at start when below form third 4-y-o outing. *J. A. Osborne* **101**

TEASING 3 b.f. Lujain (USA) 119 – Movieland (USA) 109 (Nureyev (USA) 131) [2007 76: 6m⁴ 7.1m⁶ 7m 8m p7.1g³ p7g* p7.1g² p7g² p7.1d² p7.1g* p7.1g Dec 31] close-coupled filly: fairly useful performer: won handicaps at Lingfield in October and Wolverhampton in December: stays 7f: acts on polytrack and good to firm going: tried in cheekpieces (ran poorly): held up. *J. Pearce* **90**

TEATIME LADY (USA) 2 b. or br.f. (Feb 13) Stormin Fever (USA) 116 – Tea Service (USA) (Atticus (USA) 121) [2007 5m Apr 23] $25,000Y, resold $77,000Y: first foal: dam, ran twice in US, half-sister to US Grade 2 winners Mio Robertino (11f) and Star of Manila (1½m): 7/1, outpaced in maiden at Pontefract: will be suited by 1m+. *T. D. Barron* **–**

TEBEE 3 ch.f. Selkirk (USA) 129 – Massarra 99 (Danehill (USA) 126) [2007 76P: 10m p10g⁶ 10g* 11.6f² p12g⁴ 10.5s⁴ Sep 29] lengthy filly: fairly useful handicapper on turf, fair on all-weather: won at Pontefract in July: further progress when second at Windsor next time: should stay 1½m: acts on polytrack and firm going: races up with pace. *J. H. M. Gosden* **89 a75 +**

TEDDY MONTY (IRE) 4 b.g. Bold Fact (USA) 116 – Mount Soufriere (IRE) – (Maledetto (IRE) 103) [2007 50: f7g f8g 7g 7m May 7] leggy gelding: little form since early-2006. *R. E. Barr*

TEDSTALE (USA) 9 ch.g. Irish River (FR) 131 – Carefree Kate (USA) (Lyphard **63** (USA) 132) [2007 78: f12g³ 12g⁶ 12m⁴ f12g² 12m³ May 8] smallish, sturdy, close-coupled gelding: unimpressive mover: just modest performer nowadays: barely stays 2m: acts on all-weather, firm and good to soft going: blinkered: usually waited with: sometimes finds little. *K. A. Ryan*

TEE JAY KASSIDY 7 b.g. Petong 126 – Priceless Fantasy (Dunbeath (USA) 127) – [2007 62: f8g Jan 1] smallish gelding: modest performer at 6 yrs, well held sole outing in 2007: sometimes wears headgear. *P. S. McEntee*

TEEN AGER (FR) 3 b.g. Invincible Spirit (IRE) 121 – Tarwiya (IRE) 103 (Dominion **68** 123) [2007 –: p8g³ p7g* p7g⁴ 7m 6g p6m² p6g p6g⁶ 7g Oct 27] strong, compact gelding: **a83** fairly useful performer on all-weather, fair on turf: won maiden at Lingfield in April: in-and-out form after: winner at 7f, but may prove best at 5f/6f: acts on polytrack: races freely: sold 13,000 gns. *J. S. Moore*

TEEN SPIRIT (IRE) 2 b.g. (Mar 7) Sinndar (IRE) 134 – Whitefoot 103 (Be My Chief – (USA) 122) [2007 8d Oct 11] good-bodied gelding: 50/1 and backward, last in maiden at Newbury: gelded after: bred for stamina. *J. W. Hills*

TEJAREB (IRE) 4 b.f. Sadler's Wells (USA) 132 – La Pepite (USA) (Mr Prospector – (USA)) [2007 –: 12s p12g 11.9m Sep 25] leggy, close-coupled filly: little form. *C. E. Brittain*

TELEGONUS 4 b.g. Fantastic Light (USA) 134 – Circe's Isle (Be My Guest (USA) **73** 126) [2007 73: p12g⁴ p12.2g³ 10.3d⁵ 10.5s Sep 28] leggy, close-coupled gelding: fair maiden: left C. Longsdon after second start: stays 1½m: acts on polytrack and good to soft going: tried blinkered: successful over hurdles in October. *D. McCain Jnr*

TELEPATHIC (IRE) 7 b.g. Mind Games 121 – Madrina 70 (Waajib 121) [2007 56: **57** p5.1g 7m⁶ 7m⁶ 5g 6d 6.9m³ 6d Aug 15] big, good-bodied gelding: modest performer: stays 7f: acts on firm and soft ground: tried tongue tied/blinkered: has reared leaving stall/been slowly away. *A. Berry*

TELL 4 b.c. Green Desert (USA) 127 – Cephalonie (USA) (Kris S (USA)) [2007 106: **115** 8g⁶ 10g 8.3s⁶ 8.1g 8f* 8m² 9d⁴ 8g² Nov 3] well-made colt: smart performer: trained by E. Charpy in UAE first 2 starts in 2007 before rejoining former trainer: won 4-runner minor event at Bath (by short head from Kilworth) in September: good efforts at Newmarket after, in Joel Stakes (3 lengths second to Creachadoir), Darley Stakes (fourth to Windsor Knot) and listed race (neck second to Jalmira): best form at 1m/9f: acts on firm and good to soft going: has worn blinkers (including last 4 starts). *J. L. Dunlop*

TELLING 3 b.g. Josr Algarhoud (IRE) 118 – Crystal Canyon 59 (Efisio 120) [2007 55: **53** p7.1g 9.9g 12g⁵ p9.5g⁵ Dec 13] leggy gelding: modest maiden: may prove best around 1m: acts on polytrack. *Mrs A. Duffield*

TELL ME WHAT (FR) 2 b.f. (Feb 10) Diktat 126 – Galgarina (FR) (Double Bed **50** (FR) 121) [2007 p6g 5d Jul 26] €45,000Y: small, angular filly: first foal: dam ran 3 times in France: modest form in maidens, early speed. *R. Hannon*

TELLTIME (IRE) 3 b.f. Danetime (IRE) 121 – Tesla (IRE) 42 (Fayruz 116) [2007 **83** 66p: p5g² p6g* p6g⁵ 5.3s* 6g² 7m⁵ 7m⁵ 7m⁵ p7.1g⁶ Sep 8] neat filly: fairly useful performer: won maiden at Lingfield in January and handicap at Brighton in May: good efforts in handicaps next 3 starts: effective at 5f to 7f: acts on polytrack, soft and good to firm ground. *A. M. Balding*

TEMPELSTERN (GER) 3 gr.c. Sternkoenig (IRE) 122 – Temple Esprit (Esprit du **104** Nord (USA) 126) [2007 78: 11m² 12m 14g⁴ 11.5d⁴ 14d* 14g Aug 23] neat colt: useful performer: 8-length winner of maiden at Yarmouth in June and handicap at Sandown (beat Dansant under enterprising ride) in July: well below form in Melrose Handicap at York final outing, weakening quickly: stays 1¾m: acts on good to firm and good to soft going: blinkered last 3 outings: bit slipped through mouth second outing. *H. R. A. Cecil*

TEMPLE OF THEBES (IRE) 2 b.f. (Mar 4) Bahri (USA) 125 – Franglais (GER) **77 p** (Lion Cavern (USA) 117) [2007 p6g³ p6g² Jul 11] second foal: dam, German 6f to 1m winner, half-sister to smart 1¼m performer Fraulein: placed in maidens at Kempton, second to Reel Gift: will stay 7f/1m: should improve further. *E. A. L. Dunlop*

TEMPLE PLACE (IRE) 6 b.g. Sadler's Wells (USA) 132 – Puzzled Look (USA) **101** (Gulch (USA)) [2007 93: 10.3m* 10.4g May 16] good-topped gelding: useful handicapper: 50/1, won at Chester (by ¾ length from Stotsfold) in May: well beaten at York only other Flat start in 2007: effective at 1m to 1½m: acts on good to firm and good to soft going: tried blinkered, tongue tied last 4 starts: none too consistent. *D. McCain Jnr*

TEMPLETUOHY MAX (IRE) 2 b.g. (May 4) Orpen (USA) 116 – Eladawn (IRE) – 57 (Ela-Mana-Mou 132) [2007 6m Aug 8] 33/1, pulled up in maiden. *J. D. Bethell*

TEMPLET (USA) 7 b.g. Souvenir Copy (USA) 113 – Two Step Trudy (USA) (Capote **63 §** (USA)) [2007 57§: p8.6g⁶ Feb 23] stocky gelding: modest performer: effective at 8.6f, seemingly at 2m: acts on all-weather and any turf going: wears headgear: reluctant to race third 6-y-o start: ungenuine. *W. G. Harrison*

TEMPSFORD FLYER (IRE) 4 b.g. Fasliyev (USA) 120 – Castellane (FR) (Dane-**83** hill (USA) 126) [2007 88: p8.6g⁴ 8m p8g p8g p8.6g 7d⁶ 8d⁵ Oct 23] neat gelding: fairly useful handicapper: below form after reappearance: stays 8.6f: acts on polytrack and good to firm ground: saddle slipped third 4-y-o start: sold 8,000 gns. *J. W. Hills*

TEMTATION (IRE) 3 b.f. Trans Island 119 – Ish (IRE) (Danehill (USA) 126) [2007 **58** 68: p5g⁴ p5.1g² p5g 5m⁴ 5m⁵ 5g² 6d 5.1g⁴ 5m⁶ 5g³ p5.1g p5.1g 5m f6d⁴ Dec 11] modest maiden: left J. Boyle after fourth outing, Peter Grayson prior to final one: best at 5f: acts on all-weather, good to firm and good to soft going: tried in cheekpieces/blinkers. *J. A. Pickering*

TENANCY (IRE) 3 b.g. Rock of Gibraltar (IRE) 133 – Brush Strokes (Cadeaux **67 d** Genereux 131) [2007 69: 8.3g⁶ 7m⁴ 6g⁵ 6f 5m³ 5m³ p6g p8.6g p6g 5g 5.1g f5d³ Dec 14] close-coupled gelding: has a round action: fair maiden: below form after second start, leaving J. Osborne after third: bred to stay 1m+, but free-going sort and may prove best at shorter: acts on polytrack (probably on fibresand), soft and good to firm ground: tried in cheekpieces/blinkers. *A. J. McCabe*

TEN A PENNY (USA) 3 b.c. Gulch (USA) – Dramatical (USA) (Theatrical 128) **105** [2007 p7.1g* p8g* p8g* 9.9m* 10m⁴ 8f* 8.5f³ 8.5f² 9f² 10f⁶ Nov 25] $70,000F, 54,000Y, 65,000 2-y-o: lengthy, medium-sized colt: half-brother/closely related to several winners, including smart Canadian 1m winner Numerous Times (by Numerous): dam ran twice in Ireland: useful performer: successful in maiden at Wolverhampton in January and handicaps at Lingfield and Kempton in March, and Beverley in April, and (having left J. Osborne after fifth start) non-graded stakes at Del Mar in July: good efforts last 4 starts, including in Grade 2 La Jolla Handicap at Del Mar (1½ lengths fourth, promoted to third, behind disqualified Medici Code), non-graded Bay Meadows Derby (head second to Unusual Suspect) and Grade 2 Oak Tree Derby (4½ lengths second to Daytona): stays 1¼m: raced only on polytrack and firm/good to firm going. *C. Dollase, USA*

TEN BLACK 3 ch.g. Dr Fong (USA) 128 – Pulau Pinang (IRE) 101 (Dolphin Street **47** (FR) 125) [2007 55: p7g⁶ p8.6g f7g⁵ p8.6g⁵ f7g 8.1m p12.2g 10.2m⁶ 10g p9.5g Dec 13] stocky gelding: just poor maiden in 2007: stays 1m: acts on polytrack: tried in cheek-pieces/visored. *R. Brotherton*

TENCENDUR (IRE) 3 ch.g. King Charlemagne (USA) 120 – Jallaissine (IRE) **81** (College Chapel 122) [2007 81: p7g⁴ 8g³ 8s 7g 6.9f* 8m² 8g 9.8m⁶ Sep 1] good-topped gelding: fairly useful handicapper: won at Carlisle in August: stays 1m: acts on polytrack, firm and soft going: usually front runner. *D. Nicholls*

TENDALAY (USA) 3 b. or br.g. Red Ransom (USA) – Mandalay Point (USA) (Gilded **80** Time (USA)) [2007 p6g* p7g* Mar 1] $20,000F, 38,000Y: third foal: dam, US 7f winner, half-sister to US Grade 2 1½m winner Abigailthewife: fairly useful form: won both starts, namely maiden at Kempton in January and claimer at Lingfield (claimed £20,000, then gelded) in March: should stay 1m. *J. A. Osborne*

TENDER FALCON 7 br.g. Polar Falcon (USA) 126 – Tendresse (IRE) 60 (Tender **79** King 123) [2007 87: 10g 12.3g 16g 11.6g⁶ Jul 9] tall, good-topped gelding: one-time useful handicapper, just fair in 2007: effective at 1¼m/1½m: acts on firm and good to soft going. *R. J. Hodges*

TENDER MOMENTS 3 br.f. Tomba 119 – Cherish Me 88 (Polar Falcon (USA) 126) – [2007 77: 7g May 19] tall, workmanlike filly: fair form at 2 yrs: below form only start in 2007: should stay 7f/1m: acts on soft and good to firm ground. *C. F. Wall*

TENDER PROCESS (IRE) 4 b.g. Monashee Mountain (USA) 115 – Appledorn 99 **82** (Doulab (USA) 115) [2007 83: f5g³ 5m 6d 5m Sep 27] big, strong gelding: fairly useful handicapper: below form after reappearance, though reportedly finished lame on penultimate outing: should prove as effective at 6f as 5f: acts on fibresand and heavy going: slowly away first 3 outings at 3 yrs. *E. S. McMahon*

TENDER THE GREAT (IRE) 4 br.f. Indian Lodge (IRE) 127 – Tender Guest (IRE) **94**
(Be My Guest (USA) 126) [2007 75: p8g³ p8g⁴ 7.1m* 7s⁴ 8f* 8d 8.3m³ 8m² 8.3m³ p8g⁴
p7g* 8m p8g² p7.1g² p7m³ p7g⁶ p6g⁴ p8g Dec 16] big, close-coupled filly: fairly useful
handicapper: won at Warwick in May, Bath in June and Kempton in September: creditable efforts when in frame after: stays 9.5f: acts on polytrack, firm and soft going: tried in
cheekpieces/visor: has pulled hard/flashed tail: held up. *B. G. Powell*

TENDER TRAP (IRE) 9 b.g. Sadler's Wells (USA) 132 – Shamiyda (USA) 83 (Sir   **–**
Ivor (USA) 135) [2007 88: p13.9g Jan 16] useful-looking gelding: fairly useful handicapper at 8 yrs, tailed off only Flat start in 2007: stays 2m: acts on all-weather, soft and
good to firm going: suspect temperament nowadays. *Miss J. E. Foster*

TEN DOWN 2 b.g. (Apr 28) Royal Applause 124 – Upstream 79 (Prince Sabo 123)   **79**
[2007 5.1g² 5f² 5m* 5g⁵ 5g⁴ p5g p6g 5.3f p5m⁶ p5.1g* p5m* Dec 8] close-coupled, quite
attractive gelding: fair performer: won maiden at Windsor in May, claimer at Wolverhampton in November and nursery at Lingfield in December: best at 5f: acts on polytrack
and firm going: blinkered (too free) once: forces pace. *J. A. Osborne*

TENDULKAR'S DIVA (IRE) 2 b.f. (Feb 22) Tendulkar (USA) 114 – Daring Con-   **–**
nection (Danzig Connection (USA)) [2007 6g Oct 19] first foal: dam, maiden, out of
smart 6f/7f winner Daring Destiny: tailed off in maiden at Redcar. *A. Berry*

TENEMENT (IRE) 3 b.g. Mull of Kintyre (USA) 114 – Afifah 66 (Nashwan (USA)   **60**
135) [2007 p7g p8g p8g² 7m⁴ 7m 11.5m Jun 6] strong gelding: modest maiden: left
J. Osborne after third outing: stays easy 1m: acts on polytrack. *Jamie Poulton*

TEN FOR TOSCA (IRE) 3 b.g. Distant Music (USA) 126 – Errazuriz (IRE) 94   **–**
(Classic Music (USA)) [2007 59: p6g p5.1g f6d Dec 21] modest maiden at 2 yrs: last all
starts in 2007: speedy, form only at 5f (bred to stay 1m): acts on firm going: tried tongue
tied. *R. A. Harris*

TENJACK KING 2 b.c. (Mar 26) Kyllachy 129 – Rash (Pursuit of Love 124) [2007   **80**
p7g³ 8.1m³ p8.6g³ Sep 22] 54,000Y: good-topped colt: seventh foal: closely related to
1m winner Somersault (by Pivotal) and half-brother to several winners, including
fairly useful 1m winner Loveleaves (by Polar Falcon): dam unraced: fairly useful maiden:
third all starts, 1¾ lengths behind Conduit at Wolverhampton final one: stays 8.6f.
J. A. Osborne

TENJACK QUEEN (IRE) 2 b.f. (Apr 21) Intikhab (USA) 135 – Kooyong (IRE) 88§   **63**
(College Chapel 122) [2007 6m p6g² p6g⁶ p6m⁶ p6g⁵ p6g Oct 24] €44,000Y: first
foal: dam Irish 2-y-o 6f winner: modest maiden: claimed from J. Osborne £6,000 fourth
start: raced mainly at 6f on polytrack. *Miss Tor Sturgis*

TEN MEROPA (USA) 2 b.c. (Feb 12) Johannesburg (USA) 127 – Tenderly (IRE)   **93**
(Danehill (USA) 126) [2007 5m³ p6g* 6m p6g³ p6g⁶ Sep 8] $67,000Y, 27,000 2-y-o:
leggy colt: first foal: dam, French/US maiden, half-sister to high-class French mare up to
1½m Pride and dam of 4-y-o Speciosa, out of half-sister to St Leger winner Touching
Wood: fairly useful form: won maiden at Wolverhampton in June: continued progress,
3½ lengths sixth to Philario in Sirenia Stakes at Kempton (did well from poor position)
final start: bred to stay 1m, but has plenty of speed: acts on polytrack, promise on turf on
debut (tongue tied): sold 70,000 gns, sent to USA. *J. A. Osborne*

TEN ON LINE (IRE) 2 ch.c. (Mar 27) Rossini (USA) 118 – Fastnet (Forzando 122)   **50**
[2007 5m⁵ p5g⁴ 6g p7.1g² 7d² 7d⁵ 7m p7.1g p8.6g Oct 30] smallish, close-coupled
colt: modest maiden: claimed from J. Osborne fourth start, J. O'Shea fifth and Miss
V. Haigh sixth (£6,000 each time): stays 7f: acts on polytrack and good to soft going.
J. G. M. O'Shea

TEN POLE TUDOR 2 b.g. (Apr 28) Royal Applause 124 – Amaniy (USA) 96 (Dayjur   **81**
(USA) 137) [2007 7f⁶ 7.1m 7m² 7m² 8g⁵ p8.6g⁵ p7.1g* p7.1g* p7m⁴ Dec 10] lengthy
gelding: fairly useful performer: claimed from J. Osborne £6,000 third start: won minor
event and nursery in November, both at Wolverhampton: barely stays 8.6f: acts on
polytrack and good to firm going: blinkered once. *R. A. Harris*

TEN PROPHETS (IRE) 4 b.g. Namid 128 – Mrs Evans (IRE) 97 (College Chapel   **51**
122) [2007 70: f6g⁶ p6g f6g p7g 6m Apr 29] modest performer on balance: left
D. Nicholls after second outing, H. Haynes after third: stays 6f: acts on polytrack and
sand. *J. J. Bridger*

TENRANINTHEMIST (IRE) 2 gr.f. (Apr 22) Tendulkar (USA) 114 – Saranyu   **–**
(IRE) (Rusticaro (FR) 124) [2007 p7g p8m p8m Nov 24] 5,000Y: eighth foal: half-sister
to several winners in Italy, including 1m/1¼m winner Per Noi (by Charnwood Forest):
dam Italian 7f to 9f winner: no form. *T. D. McCarthy*

TENSE (IRE) 2 b.f. (Apr 14) Invincible Spirit (IRE) 121 – Roses From Ridey (IRE) 78 **69** (Petorius 117) [2007 5.1f p6g⁴ 6m⁶ p7g⁶ p7g³ p7g³ Dec 19] €70,000Y: medium-sized filly: fifth foal: half-sister to winner in Austria by In The Wings: dam twice-raced half-sister to very smart 1¼m to 1½m performer Kutub: fair maiden: third at Lingfield last 2 starts (nursery former, blinkered latter): stays 7f: acts on polytrack and good to firm going. *J. A. Osborne*

TEN SHUN 4 ch.g. Pivotal 124 – Mint Royale (IRE) 44 (Cadeaux Genereux 131) [2007 **72** 83: 7g⁶ 6g 5g p6g Oct 5] fairly useful performer at 3 yrs, just fair in 2007: effective at 5f to 8.6f: acts on all-weather, heavy and good to firm going: tried in blinkers/visor (better without). *P. D. Evans*

TENSION MOUNTS (IRE) 2 b.g. (Apr 25) Daggers Drawn (USA) 114 – Dazzling **78** Maid (IRE) 64 (Tate Gallery (USA) 117) [2007 p7g² p7g³ p8.6g⁴ Sep 21] quite attractive gelding: fair maiden: in frame all starts, best effort when third to Kal Barg at Kempton: stays 8.6f: raced only on polytrack. *J. A. Osborne*

TENSION POINT 3 b.g. Hernando (FR) 127 – Blessed (IRE) (Jurado (USA)) [2007 **62** 71: p10g⁴ p8g³ p8g³ Jan 22] medium-sized, quite attractive gelding: just modest maiden at 3 yrs: will be suited by return to 1¼m: acts on polytrack and good to firm going: in cheekpieces last 2 starts: claimed £12,000 and joined D. L. Williams, won juvenile hurdles in July/September (2). *J. A. Osborne*

TEN SPOT (IRE) 2 b.f. (Jan 14) Intikhab (USA) 135 – Allergy 99 (Alzao (USA) 117) **57** [2007 7m⁶ p7.1g* p8m p8g p8m⁵ p7g p8g p7g p9.5s⁴ Dec 20] €45,000Y: first foal: dam 2-y-o 1m winner (stayed 1¾m): modest performer: won seller at Wolverhampton in September: left J. Osborne 5,000 gns after fourth start: stays 1m: acts on polytrack: tried blinkered/visored: slowly away first 2 outings: temperament under suspicion. *Stef Liddiard*

TENTERHOOKS (IRE) 3 b.f. Orpen (USA) 116 – Punta Gorda (IRE) (Roi Danzig **47** (USA)) [2007 55: f8g p8g⁴ p10f p7.1g 6m⁵ p7.1g 6m³ 5m⁵ 7s³ p7g 6d 7.5m 6m 10d Oct 9] workmanlike filly: poor maiden: left J. Osborne after second start: probably stays 1m: acts on polytrack and soft going, probably on good to firm: blinkered. *A. J. McCabe*

TENTH NIGHT (IRE) 2 b.c. (Mar 19) Mujadil (USA) 119 – Starlight Venture (IRE) **48** 95 (Hernando (FR) 127) [2007 5m⁶ 6g 6g⁵ 7m 7m 6s 7g⁴ Oct 19] tall, workmanlike colt: poor maiden: claimed from J. Osborne £6,000 third start: stays 7f: tried in cheekpieces. *P. T. Midgley*

TEN TO THE DOZEN 4 b. or ch.g. Royal Applause 124 – Almost Amber (USA) 88 **62** (Mt Livermore (USA)) [2007 70: 8.1d 8d⁶ 7.5g 8.1m 8m⁶ 7d* 7.1m⁴ 7.1m³ 8m² 8d⁶ 8g 7d* p7.1g Nov 9] strong, close-coupled gelding: modest performer: won seller at Brighton in August and claimer at Leicester in October: stays easy 1m: acts on firm and good to soft going: has twice been withdrawn at start (broke out of stall prior to intended reappearance in 2006). *P. W. Hiatt*

TEODORA ADIVINA 3 b.f. Fantastic Light (USA) 134 – Omara (USA) 87 (Storm **84** Cat (USA)) [2007 68p: p12.2g³ 10g³ 10m* 10s² 10g 10d* 10.3g Oct 26] tall, close-coupled filly: fairly useful performer: won maiden in September and handicap in October, both at Leicester: stays 1¼m: acts on soft and good to firm ground. *H. R. A. Cecil*

TEORBAN (POL) 8 b.g. Don Corleone 115 – Tabaka (POL) (Pyjama Hunt 126) [2007 **70** 62: p16g p16.5g² p16.5g p16.5g p16g³ p16g⁵ Oct 4] fair handicapper: stays 17f: acts on all-weather and good to firm going: tried in cheekpieces: makes running: has looked difficult ride. *Mrs N. S. Evans*

TEPEE 2 ch.f. (Mar 28) Halling (USA) 133 – Tentpole (USA) 85 (Rainbow Quest **67 p** (USA) 134) [2007 8.1m p7g⁴ p7m p8g⁶ Oct 29] tall filly: third foal: half-sister to French 2005 2-y-o 9f winner Playhouse (by Jade Robbery): dam, 1¾m winner, out of half-sister to Oaks winner Snow Bride, herself dam of Lammtarra: fair maiden: fourth to Albaraari at Kempton: should stay at least 1m: acts on polytrack: should do better at 3 yrs. *L. M. Cumani*

TEQUILA ROSE (IRE) 4 b.f. Danehill Dancer (IRE) 117 – Enthrone (USA) (Diesis **–** 133) [2007 47: p8g f7g⁶ f6g Apr 22] sparely-made filly: maiden: little form in 2007: tried visored. *M. A. Buckley*

TEQUILA SHEILA (IRE) 5 ch.m. Raise A Grand (IRE) 114 – Hever Rosina 63 **59** (Efisio 120) [2007 60: 7.9m 7.9g 7.6s* 6s p7.1g f7d Dec 15] quite attractive mare: modest performer nowadays: won seller at Lingfield in August: left K. Burke after fourth start: stays 1m: acts on polytrack, soft and good to firm going: has worn visor/cheekpieces: sometimes wanders. *M. A. Allen*

TERANDEIL 3 b.f. Auction House (USA) 120 – Frisson (Slip Anchor 136) [2007 6m 8.1g 6g Oct 8] 16,000Y: neat filly: sixth foal: half-sister to 7f and 9f winner Princes Theatre (by Prince Sabo) and 6-y-o Wanchai Lad: dam unraced: well beaten in maidens. *J. G. M. O'Shea* —

TERENTIA 4 br.f. Diktat 126 – Agrippina 99 (Timeless Times (USA) 99) [2007 103: 5.1g⁴ 5m³ 5g* 5g 5g Aug 2] strong, lengthy filly: useful performer: best effort when winning handicap at York (by ¾ length from Corridor Creeper) in May: below form otherwise in 2007: best at 5f: acts on firm and good to soft going. *E. S. McMahon* **108**

TERENZIUM (IRE) 5 b.g. Cape Cross (IRE) 129 – Tatanka (ITY) (Luge 113) [2007 62: 8f 8.5m³ 7.9m 10.5m 9.1g⁵ 7.9f 8.3m⁴ 8m Sep 18] leggy gelding: modest handicapper: should stay 1¼m: acts on polytrack, good to firm and good to soft ground: tried visored, in cheekpieces last 4 starts. *Micky Hammond* **56**

TERMINATE (GER) 5 ch.g. Acatenango (GER) 127 – Taghareed (USA) 93 (Shadeed (USA) 135) [2007 70: 10m 10d⁵ p8g⁶ p10g³ 10.9g* 10.2m⁴ p9.5g Oct 25] leggy gelding: fair performer nowadays: left N. Callaghan after fourth start: won handicap at Warwick in October: stays 11f: acts on polytrack, good to firm and good to soft going: tried in cheekpieces/blinkers: sometimes slowly away: often takes good hold. *Ian Williams* **65**

TERMSANDCONDITIONS (IRE) 3 b.f. Rock of Gibraltar (IRE) 133 – Council Rock 74 (General Assembly (USA)) [2007 p8g p8g Jan 27] half-sister to numerous winners, notably smart 2000 2-y-o 5f winner Superstar Leo (by College Chapel): dam, maiden, half-sister to dam of 2000 Guineas winner Footstepsinthesand: well beaten in maidens at Lingfield: blinkered second outing: sold 28,000 gns in July (reportedly in foal to Motivator). *W. J. Haggas* —

TERRACOS DO PINHAL 2 b.g. (Feb 24) Selkirk (USA) 129 – Sister Bluebird 94 (Bluebird (USA) 125) [2007 7s 7.2g 8m⁶ Sep 8] 42,000Y: big gelding: first foal: dam 2-y-o 7f winner: fair maiden: first encouragement when sixth to Dr Faustus at Thirsk, held up: gelded after: stays 1m. *M. Johnston* **67**

TERRASINI (FR) 2 gr.g. (Mar 29) Linamix (FR) 127 – Trazando (Forzando 122) [2007 5.9d⁶ 7s Jul 13] modest maiden, better effort on debut: bred to stay 1m. *J. Howard Johnson* **55 +**

TERRY MOLLOY (IRE) 3 b.g. Xaar 132 – Pile (USA) 62 (Shadeed (USA) 135) [2007 75: 10.5g 11.1g⁶ 10.1g 8.3m² 7.9f² 8.5g⁴ 7.1g⁵ p8g³ Oct 24] good-topped gelding: fair performer: stays 8.3f: acts on polytrack and firm (unraced on softer than good): visored last 5 starts: races up with pace: sold 6,000 gns. *K. R. Burke* **65**

TERRY'S TIP (IRE) 2 b.g. (Feb 20) Namid 128 – Kadarassa (IRE) (Warning 136) [2007 5m 5g² 6m⁴ 6.1d³ Oct 18] 17,000F, 10,000Y: tall gelding: fourth foal: half-brother to winner in Italy by Revoque: dam, French maiden, out of half-sister to Kahyasi: fairly useful maiden: standout performance when fourth of 28 to Exclamation in sales race at Newmarket: better at 6f than 5f: acts on good to firm going. *Mrs L. Stubbs* **91**

TESLIN (IRE) 3 b.g. In The Wings 128 – Yukon Hope (USA) 75 (Forty Niner (USA)) [2007 89: 8m 10m⁵ 11.1d⁴ 7g 9.9m* 10m* 9m³ Oct 6] strong, angular gelding: smart performer: left M. Johnston 65,000 gns and gelded after third start: much improved in handicaps after, winning at Beverley (quite valuable event, beat Monte Alto by ¾ length) in August and Newmarket (by ¾ length from Urban Spirit) in September: good 2½ lengths third to Pipedreamer in Cambridgeshire at Newmarket final outing, comfortably first home of smaller stand-side group: stays 1¼m: acts on good to firm going: held up nowadays: has joined Godolphin. *B. Ellison* **110**

TESSIE BEAR 2 b.f. (May 29) Red Ransom (USA) – Macaerleon (IRE) (Caerleon (USA) 132) [2007 p7g p8m p8g⁴ Dec 22] 11,000F: half-sister to several winners in Italy: dam, Italian maiden, half-sister to smart Italian 1¼m/1½m performer Masad: little form. *Andrew Reid* —

TETOUAN 3 b.c. Danehill Dancer (IRE) 117 – Souk (IRE) 98 (Ahonoora (122) [2007 61p: p7g² p7g⁶ 8.3g* 9m² 9.8m² 10g⁴ 11.9m² Aug 9] smallish, sturdy colt: fairly useful handicapper: won at Leicester in April: good efforts in frame after: stays 1½m: acts on polytrack and good to firm ground: often edgy in preliminaries: sold 62,000 gns. *R. Charlton* **89**

TETRODE (USA) 5 b.g. Quiet American (USA) – Mother Courage 67 (Busted 134) [2007 61d: p8.6g f5g p10g Mar 26] maiden: little form in 2007, leaving R. Cowell after second outing: tried in cheekpieces. *M. F. Harris* —

TEUTONIC (IRE) 6 b.m. Revoque (IRE) 122 – Classic Ring (IRE) 50 (Auction Ring – (USA) 123) [2007 50, a55: f14g Jan 25] tall, quite good-topped mare: modest maiden at 5 yrs: badly hampered sole outing on Flat in 2007: stays 2m: acts on all-weather, best turf effort on good going: often slowly away (has refused to race over hurdles). *R. F. Fisher*

TEVEZ 2 b.c. (Jan 29) Sakhee (USA) 136 – Sosumi 101 (Be My Chief (USA) 122) 71 [2007 6m 7m⁵ p8.6g³ p9.5s⁶ Dec 20] strong colt: fair maiden: third at Wolverhampton: stays 8.6f. *M. H. Tompkins*

TEWKESBURY (IRE) 3 b.g. King's Best (USA) 132 – Zeferina (IRE) 92 (Sadler's – Wells (USA) 132) [2007 p9.5d f6g Dec 27] well held in maidens at Wolverhampton (slowly away) and Southwell. *Mrs K. Waldron*

TEXAS GOLD 9 ch.g. Cadeaux Genereux 131 – Star Tulip 99 (Night Shift (USA)) 92 [2007 107: 5g 6m 5d 5m 5g⁴ 5m 6g 5m 5f² 5.7f³ 5g p5g³ p6g p5g² p6g² p6m⁴ Dec 9] sturdy, close-coupled gelding: smart performer at best, winner of 15 of his 102 races: just fairly useful in 2007: was effective at 5f/easy 6f: acted on polytrack, firm and good to soft going: usually waited with: reportedly retired. *W. R. Muir*

TEYAAR 11 b.g. Polar Falcon (USA) 126 – Music In My Life (IRE) 59 (Law Society – § (USA) 130) [2007 48§, a51§: p6g* p6g p7.1g⁶ p6g⁴ p7.1g p6g p6g p6g 6m Aug 10] a51 § strong gelding: fairly useful performer in his day, winning 8 of his 121 races: just modest on all-weather, poor on turf in recent years: successful in minor event at Kempton in January: stayed easy 7f: acted on all-weather, best turf form on good going or softer: had worn blinkers/visor: sometimes hung: was unreliable: reportedly retired. *M. Wellings*

THABAAT 3 ch.g. Pivotal 124 – Maraatib (IRE) 93 (Green Desert (USA) 127) [2007 94 89: 7g* 7.6m 7d 7g² 7d Oct 19] rather leggy, useful-looking gelding: fairly useful performer: landed odds in maiden at Folkestone in April: good second in handicap at Chester after: should stay 1m: unraced on extremes of ground: sold 17,000 gns. *B. W. Hills*

THANNAAN (USA) 2 gr.c. (Mar 17) Elusive Quality (USA) – Lady Aloma (CAN) 75 p (Cozzene (USA)) [2007 6m⁴ 6.5d² Oct 11] $575,000Y: big, rangy colt: sixth foal: half-brother to smart US miler Chopinina (by Lear Fan) and US 7f to 9f (including 1m minor stakes) winner Karra Kul (by Strawberry Road): dam Canadian 6f to 1m (minor stakes) winner: shaped well in maidens at Newbury, fourth to Paco Boy then second to Fateh Field: will be suited by 7f/1m: sure to go on improving. *B. W. Hills*

THANXFORTHAT (USA) 2 gr.g. (May 8) Alphabet Soup (USA) 126 – Paper Prin- 56 cess (USA) (Flying Paster (USA)) [2007 5m⁴ 6m 7.1d² Sep 17] sturdy, lengthy gelding: modest maiden: second in seller at Musselburgh: gelded after: stays 7f. *J. J. Quinn*

THARAWAAT (IRE) 2 b.c. (Mar 27) Alhaarth (IRE) 126 – Sevi's Choice (USA) (Sir 80 Ivor (USA) 135) [2007 7g 7m 7g³ Nov 2] 40,000F, €100,000Y: sturdy, lengthy colt: fifth foal: half-brother to 2003 2-y-o 5f winner Dontstopthemusic (by Night Shift): dam German 1¼m winner: fairly useful maiden: third to demoted Classic Descent at New-market: will be suited by 1m/1¼m. *B. W. Hills*

THARAYA 2 b.f. (Feb 15) Choisir (AUS) 126 – Karlaska (Lashkari 128) [2007 6d 6m 50 6s 7m Aug 8] 5,000F: tall filly: seventh foal: half-sister to 3-y-o Mason Ette and winners abroad by Linamix and Halling: dam useful French 1½m winner: modest maiden: form only at 6f. *T. D. Easterby*

THARUA (IRE) 5 b.m. Indian Danehill (IRE) 124 – Peig Sayers (IRE) 58 (Royal Aca- 51 demy (USA) 130) [2007 –, a56: p11g⁵ Feb 25] leggy, lengthy mare: modest performer: stays 16.5f: acts on all-weather, firm and good to soft ground: visored/in cheekpieces. *Ernst Oertel*

THAT LOOK 4 b.g. Compton Admiral 121 – Mudflap 82 (Slip Anchor 136) [2007 62: 62 p16g⁶ 16.4m⁵ Jul 12] modest maiden: stays 16.5f: raced on polytrack and good/good to firm going: won over fences in August/October. *D. E. Cantillon*

THAT'S BLUE CHIP 4 b.g. Namid 128 – Star Cast (IRE) 82 (In The Wings 128) – [2007 68: 5m p5g 5m 5.1d Aug 19] sturdy gelding: fair performer at 3 yrs: little impact in handicaps in 2007. *P. W. D'Arcy*

THAT'S HOT (IRE) 4 b.f. Namid 128 – Smoke Lady (IRE) (Barathea (IRE) 127) 111 [2007 99: 6g* 6f² 6g² 6m⁴ p6g 6m Sep 14] good-bodied filly: third foal: half-sister to a US winner by Flying Chevron: dam, ran once in US, half-sister to smart 7f/1m (includ-ing in US) performer Unanimous Vote: smart performer: won handicap at Cork in April: in frame after in listed race at same track, Ballyogan Stakes at Leopardstown (neck second to Liscanna) and Stewards' Cup at Goodwood (excellent close fourth to Zidane):

below form (things not run to suit) after: seems best at 6f: acts on firm ground: game.
G. M. Lyons, Ireland

THEA DI BISANZIO (IRE) 3 b.f. Dr Fong (USA) 128 – Tamnia 106 (Green Desert **57**
(USA) 127) [2007 7.1m⁵ p8g⁴ p5.1g p7g Nov 16] 23,000F, 115,000Y: close-coupled filly:
sixth foal: half-sister to smart French 1¼m/1½m winner Coroner (by Mtoto) and 8-y-o
Scurra: dam, 2-y-o 6f/7f winner, half-sister to smart middle-distance stayers Azzilfi and
Khamaseen: modest maiden: stays 1m: acts on polytrack: sold 6,500 gns. *G. A. Butler*

THE ALDBURY FLYER 4 b.g. Royal Applause 124 – Fantasy Ridge 92 (Indian **88**
Ridge 123) [2007 77: 10m⁴ 11m³ 10g² 10m May 25] angular gelding: fairly useful maid-
en handicapper: stays 11f: acts on good to firm and good to soft going. *W. R. Swinburn*

THEANN 3 b.f. Rock of Gibraltar (IRE) 133 – Cassandra Go (IRE) 119 (Indian Ridge **111**
123) [2007 101: 7g³ 8m 6m³ 6g⁵ 7m 6s* Jul 13] small, sturdy filly: smart performer:
easily best effort when winning Cuisine de France Summer Stakes at York (by 2½ lengths
from Gloved Hand, readily going clear) in July: was probably best at 6f/7f (shaped like
non-stayer in 1000 Guineas at Newmarket): acted on soft and good to firm going: visits
Galileo. *A. P. O'Brien, Ireland*

THEATRE GROOM (USA) 8 ch.g. Theatrical 128 – Model Bride (USA) (Blushing **–**
Groom (FR) 131) [2007 –: p12.2g* p13.9g⁵ p13.9g³ p16g 12d 13.3m Jun 9] fair **a76**
performer on Flat: won maiden at Wolverhampton in February: stayed 1¾m: acted on
polytrack: wore cheekpieces last 2 outings: dead. *M. R. Bosley*

THEATRE ROYAL 4 b.f. Royal Applause 124 – Rada's Daughter 107 (Robellino **67**
(USA) 127) [2007 67: 10g⁴ 11g⁶ 13.1m² 16m 11.9d 12m 8m 8m p7m p10g* p11m p10m
p10g p8.6g⁶ Dec 29] good-topped filly: fair handicapper: won at Kempton in October:
effective at 1¼m to 13f: acts on polytrack, firm and good to soft ground: in blinkers/
cheekpieces last 7 starts. *Mouse Hamilton-Fairley*

THE BEAR 4 ch.g. Rambling Bear 115 – Precious Girl 76 (Precious Metal 106) [2007 **–**
–: 6f f5g 5m May 26] angular gelding: fairly useful performer at 2 yrs: lightly raced and
well held since: tried visored. *J. S. Wainwright*

THE BETCHWORTH KID 2 b.c. (Mar 24) Tobougg (IRE) 125 – Runelia (Runnett **90**
125) [2007 7s⁵ 7g* 7g⁵ 8s³ 8m⁴ p8.6g⁴ 8g³ Oct 26] 31,000Y: rangy colt: has scope:
half-brother to several winners, including useful 1¼m/1½m winner (including in UAE)
Kumatour (by Batshoof): dam maiden: fairly useful performer: won maiden at Brighton
in July: better form in frame in nurseries last 4 starts, third to Jack Dawkins at Doncaster
final one: will be suited by 1¼m/1½m: acts on polytrack, soft and good to firm going: no
easy ride, especially so only try in visor. *M. L. W. Bell*

THE BLUE STACKS (USA) 3 b.g. Langfuhr (CAN) 124 – Touch of Honor (USA) **–**
(Devil's Bag (USA)) [2007 p7g⁵ 6f⁶ 6g a8.5g⁵ a9.8g Dec 23] no sign of ability: left
K. Ryan after third start and C. von der Recke after next outing. *P. Hirschberger, Germany*

THE BOGBERRY (USA) 2 ch.c. (Jan 17) Hawk Wing (USA) 136 – Lahinch (IRE) **81**
104 (Danehill Dancer (IRE) 117) [2007 7m⁶ 7.5m* 7g Jun 23] good-topped colt: second
foal: half-brother to useful Irish 6f (including at 2 yrs) winner Liscanna (by Sadler's
Wells): dam, Irish 5f (at 2 yrs) to 7f winner, half-sister to useful 2-y-o 5f winner (later
stayed 8.5f in US) Perugino Bay: fairly useful form: won minor event at Tipperary in
June: mid-division in listed race at Royal Ascot only subsequent start: will stay 1m: acts
on good to firm going. *A. P. O'Brien, Ireland*

THE BONUS KING 7 b.g. Royal Applause 124 – Selvi (Mummy's Pet 125) [2007 67: **46**
p8.6g* 8.1m 8d⁵ p8.6g p10g 9.7g 8m Sep 18] strong, angular, good-topped gelding: has a **a69**
fluent action: fair handicapper on all-weather, poor on turf: dead-heated with Gigs Magic
at Wolverhampton in April: best at 7f to 8.6f: acts on all-weather and any turf going: tried
blinkered: reportedly lost action second 7-y-o start: none too consistent. *J. Jay*

THE BORDERER 4 ch.g. Definite Article 121 – Far Clan (Clantime 101) [2007 10g **–**
Jul 10] strong, lengthy gelding: well beaten in maiden at Pontefract on Flat debut.
M. W. Easterby

THE BRAT 3 b.f. Perryston View 114 – Kalarram (Muhtarram (USA) 125) [2007 44: **42**
5m⁶ 5m³ 5g 5d 5m⁶ 5m 5g⁶ 5g 5g⁶ Nov 8] good-bodied filly: poor maiden: left
J. Wainwright after sixth start: best at 5f/6f: acts on good to firm going: tried visored, in
cheekpieces last 4 outings. *Miss Tracy Waggott*

THE BRONX 3 b.c. Dansili 127 – Carradale 73 (Pursuit of Love 124) [2007 66p: f5g **–**
9m p7.1s Dec 20] quite good-topped colt: modest maiden at 2 yrs: little impact in
handicaps in 2007: should stay 9f: tried in cheekpieces/visored. *M. J. Wallace*

THE CARLTON CANNES 3 b.c. Grand Lodge (USA) 125 – Miss Riviera Golf 106 **80 p**
(Hernando (FR) 127) [2007 73p: p10g* Dec 30] compact colt: fairly useful form: off 14
months, won maiden at Lingfield in December by ½ length from Emperor Court, not hard
driven: will stay 1½m: open to further improvement. *G. Wragg*

THE CARPET MAN 3 b.g. Iron Mask (USA) 117 – Yarrow Bridge 75 (Selkirk (USA) **57**
129) [2007 5.1f 6m 5.7d 5.1m 5.7f⁶ 5m⁶ 5.1g p6g p6g³ p6g⁴ p5g³ Dec 16] smallish
gelding: modest maiden: effective at 5f/6f: acts on polytrack and firm ground: sometimes
slowly away. *A. W. Carroll*

THE CAYTERERS 5 b.g. Cayman Kai (IRE) 114 – Silky Smooth (IRE) (Thatching **80**
131) [2007 81: 6g² 7g⁶ 5.7g 6m 6g 7m⁴ 6g⁶ 6m Sep 2] fairly useful handicapper: has won
over 7f, may prove best at 5f/6f: acts on firm and good to soft going: in cheekpieces last 4
starts: joined K. Prendergast. *J. M. Bradley*

THE CHIP CHOPMAN (IRE) 5 b.g. Sri Pekan (USA) 117 – Firstrusseofsummer **75**
(USA) (Summer Squall (USA)) [2007 –: 13m 16d* 12s* 12s* 12g³ p13.9g Sep 28] fair
handicapper: won at Ballinrobe, Limerick and Sligo within 9 days in June: ran as if amiss
at Wolverhampton final outing: effective at 1½m to 2m: acts on heavy and good to firm
ground: tongue tied nowadays: modest hurdler. *Seamus G. O'Donnell, Ireland*

THE CITY KID (IRE) 4 b.f. Danetime (IRE) 121 – Unfortunate 55§ (Komaite **71**
(USA)) [2007 66: p9.5g4 p8.6g² p9.5g² p9.5g p8.6g p9.5g* p8.6g² p9.5g 8.5m⁶ p8.6g
10m³ 10v⁴ p10g⁵ p12.2g³ p7.1g* p7.1g² p7.1g* p7.1g² Dec 4] leggy filly: fair performer:
won claimer (left P. D. Evans £8,000) in March and, having left S. Dow £6,000 after
seventh start and C. Dore £6,000 after fourteenth, handicaps in September and October,
all at Wolverhampton: stays easy 1¼m: acts on all-weather and heavy ground: often
wears headgear. *S. C. Williams*

THE COMPOSER 5 b.g. Royal Applause 124 – Superspring (Superlative 118) [2007 **66**
77: 10d p11g 12.6s⁵ 14.1s⁵ 14.1d⁶ 17.2d 12d Oct 27] good-bodied gelding: fair handicapper: stays 1¾m: acts on soft and good to firm ground. *M. Blanshard*

THE COOL SANDPIPER 3 ch.g. Piccolo 121 – The Dark Eider (Superlative 118) **70**
[2007 65p: 7s³ 7m p7g⁵ p8g⁶ Sep 26] fair maiden: stays 7f: acts on polytrack: tried in
cheekpieces. *P. Winkworth*

THE CROOKED RING 5 b.g. Magic Ring (IRE) 115 – My Bonus 79 (Cyrano de **60**
Bergerac 120) [2007 68: p7.1g 6g³ 7.1f 5.7d Oct 1] leggy, workmanlike gelding: fair
performer at 4 yrs, just modest in 2007: seems to stay 7f: acts on polytrack, firm and soft
ground: sometimes wears headgear. *A. G. Newcombe*

THE CUBE 3 b.g. Mind Games 121 – Nite-Owl Dancer 75 (Robellino (USA) 127) **59**
[2007 6.1g 6d⁶ 5v 5d⁴ 5d 5m² 5m³ 5m p6g⁴ 5.1g³ p6g Nov 20] good-bodied gelding:
modest maiden: stays easy 6f: acts on polytrack, heavy and good to firm going: tried
blinkered: sometimes slowly away. *J. Balding*

THE DAGGER 3 ch.g. Daggers Drawn (USA) 114 – Highland Blue 55 (Never So Bold **61**
135) [2007 –: p6g⁶ p7g⁴ p10g⁵ Mar 26] modest maiden: stays 1¼m: raced only on
polytrack. *J. R. Best*

THE DANDY FOX 3 b.f. Foxhound (USA) 103 – Classic Storm 73 (Belfort (FR) 89) **–**
[2007 52: 8.5m 7m May 28] well-grown, close-coupled filly: modest maiden at 2 yrs: no
form in 2007: tried blinkered. *R. Bastiman*

THE DIAMOND BOND 3 bl.g. Josr Algarhoud (IRE) 118 – Alsiba 68 (Northfields **54**
(USA)) [2007 50: p8.6g 8m⁶ 8m 8.5s p8.6g 12g⁴ 14.1m p13.9g⁶ p12.2g³ 15.8g 12g⁶
p13.9g³ p12m p12.2d³ Dec 28] tall gelding: modest maiden: stays 1½m: acts on polytrack, good to firm and good to soft ground. *G. R. Oldroyd*

THE DRAGON (IRE) 2 b.f. (Apr 12) Statue of Liberty (USA) 115 – Noble Rocket **–**
(Reprimand 122) [2007 5m Sep 13] €32,000Y: medium-sized filly: sixth foal: half-sister
to useful 5f (including at 2 yrs) winner Dragon Flyer (by Tagula): dam unraced sister to
useful 7f to 8.5f (in US) winner Royal Rebuke: last in maiden at Sandown. *M. Quinn*

THE DUNION 4 br.g. Beckett (IRE) 116 – Dacian (USA) (Diesis 133) [2007 47: 15d **53**
16.1m 13g 16g 14d 13g⁵ 16.1m Sep 10] good-bodied gelding: modest maiden handicapper: stays 1¾m: acts on good to firm ground: blinkered last 2 starts: usually held up.
Miss L. A. Perratt

THEEBAH 2 b.f. (Apr 27) Bahamian Bounty 116 – Shall We Run 59 (Hotfoot 126) **–**
[2007 5g 5s⁵ 5.7g Jun 1] 60,000Y: angular filly: half-sister to several winners, including
5f/6f (Gimcrack Stakes at 2 yrs) winner Bannister (by Inchinor) and useful 1999 2-y-o
5f/6f winner Roo (by Rudimentary): dam, maiden, half-sister to very smart but temp-

eramental sprinter Dead Certain: well held in maidens: sold 10,000 gns in December. *M. R. Channon*

THE FIFTH MEMBER (IRE) 3 b.c. Bishop of Cashel 122 – Palace Soy (IRE) **90** (Tagula (IRE) 116) [2007 66: 10m 7m² 8.3g 7.6f* 7g² p8g 7v* 7g Nov 3] fairly useful handicapper: left R. Flower after second start: much improved when winning at Lingfield in August and Folkestone (by 5 lengths) in October: stays 7.6f: acts on polytrack and any turf going. *J. R. Boyle*

THE FISIO 7 b.g. Efisio 120 – Misellina (FR) 57 (Polish Precedent (USA) 131) [2007 **72** 63: p5g³ p6g⁵ p5g* p6g* p6g³ f5g⁴ f5g⁵ 5m p5.1g³ p6g 6d p6g p6g³ Nov 14] smallish, strong gelding: fair performer: won handicaps at Lingfield (2) in March: best at 5f/6f: acts on all-weather, soft and good to firm going: visored: has refused to enter stall: sold 1,600 gns. *S. Gollings*

THE FLYING COWBOY (IRE) 3 b.g. Tagula (IRE) 116 – Sesame Heights (IRE) **76** 63 (High Estate 127) [2007 –: 8g 8.2g³ 10d* 11.9s⁴ 11.6d Oct 15] compact gelding: fair handicapper: won at Leicester (hung left) in August: stays 1½m: acts on soft ground. *Jane Chapple-Hyam*

THE FLYING PEACH 4 ch.f. Observatory (USA) 131 – Taffeta (IRE) 69 (Barathea **–** (IRE) 127) [2007 41: f11g p11g⁶ p13.9g Jan 27] strong filly: poor maiden: stays 8.3f: acts on good to firm going. *Miss Gay Kelleway*

THE FLYING PHENOM 4 gr.g. Paris House 123 – Miss Flossa (FR) (Big John (FR) **–** 125) [2007 p7f p11g Nov 14] poor form over hurdles: last in maidens on Flat. *J. D. Frost*

THEFLYINGSCOTTIE 5 gr.g. Paris House 123 – Miss Flossa (FR) (Big John (FR) **59** 125) [2007 p16.5g³ 14.1m⁶ p16g² 16.1m³ 14.1d⁵ 16s* 14.1m⁵ p13.9g⁴ p13.9g p13.9g² p16g p12g⁴ p12.2g Dec 29] modest handicapper: won at Thirsk in July: stays 2m: acts on polytrack, soft and good to firm ground: often visored: patiently ridden. *D. Shaw*

THE GAIKWAR (IRE) 8 b.g. Indian Ridge 123 – Broadmara (IRE) 91 (Thatching **76** 131) [2007 79, a63: p9.5g⁵ 8.1m 8m 8.1g* 9g 8f 8g 8.1s⁵ 8.1m⁵ 8.3m 9g³ 8.1m⁴ 8.1m **a55** 8.3g 8d⁶ Oct 3] lengthy gelding: fair handicapper on turf, modest on all-weather: won at Chepstow in May: stays easy 9.7f: acts on polytrack, firm and soft going: wears blinkers, tried in cheekpieces: sometimes slowly away: reportedly lost shoe third start at 8 yrs: none too consistent. *R. A. Harris*

THE GAME 2 b.g. (Mar 29) Compton Place 125 – Emanant (Emarati (USA) 74) [2007 **85** 5g⁵ 6d* p6g⁵ 5.1m p6g⁶ 6g p6m* p6g³ Dec 30] strong gelding: fairly useful performer: won maiden at Catterick in July and nursery at Lingfield in December: good third in nursery at Lingfield final start: will prove best kept to 5f/6f: acts on polytrack and good to soft going, probably good to firm: waited with. *J. R. Boyle*

THE GATEKEEPER 2 b.c. (Mar 13) Mujahid (USA) 125 – Tiempo 50 (King of **81** Spain 121) [2007 6m 6g² p7.1g* Nov 20] tall colt: fairly useful form: off 5 months after debut: second to Almoutaz at Newmarket prior to winning maiden at Wolverhampton: stays 7f. *M. H. Tompkins*

THE GEESTER 3 b.g. Rambling Bear 115 – Cledeschamps 46 (Doc Marten 104) **55** [2007 60: f5g 5.1g f5g³ 6.1g f5g⁵ p5.1g³ p5.1g⁵ 5d p5g 5s f5d² Dec 14] strong gelding: modest maiden handicapper: best at 5f/6f: acts on all-weather (below form on turf): tried in cheekpieces/tongue tie, blinkered nowadays. *S. R. Bowring*

THE GEEZER 5 ch.g. Halling (USA) 133 – Polygueza (FR) 78 (Be My Guest (USA) **109** 126) [2007 –: 12d² 16.4g⁴ 12m⁴ Jul 27] big, lengthy gelding: very smart performer at 3 yrs: just useful nowadays: easily best effort in 2007 when 1½ lengths second to Ivy Creek in listed race at Pontefract: below form in listed race at Sandown (found little) and minor event at Newmarket after: should stay 2m: acts on soft going, possibly unsuited by good to firm: sometimes hangs and has flashed tail/carried head awkwardly: left Godolphin, and gelded. *Saeed bin Suroor*

THE GRAIG 3 b.g. Josr Algarhoud (IRE) 118 – Souadah (USA) (General Holme **54** (USA) 128) [2007 –: p11g⁵ f11g p10g p12g 8.2g⁶ Aug 2] modest maiden: seems to stay 11f: acts on polytrack and firm ground. *C. Drew*

THE GREAT DELANEY 4 b.g. Inchinor 119 – Top 74 (Shirley Heights 130) [2007 **–** 64, a56: p9.5g Sep 13] modest handicapper at 3 yrs: well below form only outing in 2007: stays 1¼m: acts on polytrack and soft going: tried in cheekpieces/blinkers. *K. McAuliffe*

THE GREY BAM BAM 3 gr.f. Baryshnikov (AUS) – Leonie Samual 50 (Safawan **–** 118) [2007 –: 10.2f Apr 24] tall filly: little form. *R. J. Hodges*

National Bank of Dubai Cup (Handicap), Ascot—The Illies, despite being 5 lb out of the weights, wins in good style from Ea (striped sleeves) and Al Khaleej

THE GREY BERRY 3 gr.g. Observatory (USA) 131 – Elderberry (Bin Ajwaad (IRE) **107**
119) [2007 64: 8m* 8d* 8.5v* 8s⁶ 8d³ 10s* 10.4d² Oct 13] leggy, workmanlike gelding:
useful handicapper: progressed throughout 2007, winning at Newcastle in May, Newmarket in June, Beverley (barely off bridle) in July and Ayr in September: best effort
when neck second to Flying Clarets at York final start: stays 1¼m: unraced on firm going,
acts on any other: held up: a credit to connections: sold 340,000 gns, joined P. Hobbs.
T. D. Walford

THE GREY ONE (IRE) 4 gr.g. Dansili 127 – Marie Dora (FR) 86 (Kendor (FR) 122) **74**
[2007 64: f6g³ p6g⁵ f8g² f8g* 7m⁵ f7g⁴ 9.9m 9g² 8s² 8.1d* 8.1s⁶ 8.1d⁴ 7s⁵ 8.1m⁴ 8.1f²
p9.5m⁶ 9.7f 8d³ 10.2m 8g Oct 25] tall, close-coupled gelding: fair handicapper: won at
Southwell in April and Warwick in June: stays easy 9f: acts on all-weather and any turf
going: wears cheekpieces: has hung. *J. M. Bradley*

THE HISTORY MAN (IRE) 4 b.g. Titus Livius (FR) 115 – Handsome Anna (IRE) **79**
67 (Bigstone (IRE) 126) [2007 77§: p6g 5m 6g p5.1g 5g* 6m³ 5s* 5.4v⁵ 5f* 5g⁵ 5.1m 5d
5d Sep 21] workmanlike gelding: fair handicapper: won at Ayr (amateurs) and Beverley
in July and Pontefract in August: raced only at 5f/6f: acts on any turf going, well held
both starts on polytrack: usually blinkered: races prominently: quirky. *M. Mullineaux*

THE HOOFER (IRE) 2 b.f. (Apr 14) Vision of Night 115 – Dance In The Sun 94 **54**
(Halling (USA) 133) [2007 6s 6g⁶ 6m 7m 7d Oct 29] 9,000Y: sturdy filly: first foal: dam
1¼m winner: modest maiden: should be suited by 7f/1m. *J. L. Dunlop*

THE ILLIES (IRE) 3 b.c. Fasliyev (USA) 120 – Velvet Appeal (IRE) 101 (Petorius **108 +**
117) [2007 84: 8m⁶ 8.2g⁶ 8m 8m⁴ 8g* 8g* 8m* 9m⁵ Oct 6] strong, good sort: useful handicapper: much improved when winning at Ascot (quite valuable event, by 1½ lengths
from Ea) in July, York (by 1½ lengths from Docofthebay) in August and Doncaster (beat
Metropolitan Man by head) in September: good 2¾ lengths fifth of 34 to Pipedreamer in
Cambridgeshire at Newmarket final start, going on well after manoeuvered markedly for
run: should stay 1¼m: acts on good to firm going: sometimes races freely (pulled too hard
final 2-y-o outing), and usually ridden patiently: has joined Godolphin. *B. W. Hills*

THE IRON GIANT (IRE) 5 b.g. Giant's Causeway (USA) 132 – Shalimar (IRE) 95 **–**
(Indian Ridge 123) [2007 64: 10s p10g⁵ p13g p12m Dec 8] lengthy, good-topped gelding:
modest maiden at 4 yrs: below form in 2007: tried visored. *B. G. Powell*

THE JAILER 4 b.f. Mujahid (USA) 125 – Once Removed 65 (Distant Relative 128) **65**
[2007 47: 8f⁵ 10s⁴ 8m² 8d⁴ 8f* p8.6g⁵ 7g⁷* 8m⁵ p8g p7g² Nov 21] leggy filly: fair
performer: won seller at Bath in September and handicap at Kempton in October: stays
1m: acts on all-weather, firm and good to soft going: tried visored, often in cheekpieces:
has found little: front runner. *J. G. M. O'Shea*

THE JAY FACTOR (IRE) 3 b.c. Bold Fact (USA) 116 – Corn Futures 78 (Nomina- **72**
tion 125) [2007 61: 6.1m³ 7s p6g² p6g² p7g 6f² p6g 7.1m 6f⁵ p7m⁵ Oct 13] sturdy colt:
fair maiden handicapper: stays 6f: acts on polytrack and firm going: tried in cheekpieces:
sold 9,000 gns. *Pat Eddery*

THE JOBBER 6 b.g. Foxhound (USA) 103 – Clairification (IRE) 57 (Sher- **107**
nazar 131) [2007 108: 5m⁴ 5d⁵ 5g⁶ 5m⁴ 5g⁶ 5m² 5.2m Oct 4] big, strong gelding:
useful performer: several creditable efforts in 2007, including when fifth to Stoneacre
Lad in valuable handicap at Ascot, sixth to Moorhouse Lad in King George Stakes at
Goodwood and neck second to Siren's Gift in minor event at Leicester second/third/sixth

outings: effective at 5f/6f: acts on polytrack, firm and good to soft going: travels strongly. *M. Blanshard*

THE JOSTLER 2 b.f. (May 13) Dansili 127 – The Jotter 99 (Night Shift (USA)) [2007 **78** 6g 6d 6m* 6m Sep 22] robust, good-bodied filly: type to carry condition: half-sister to 3 winners, including useful US 5f to 1m winner Final Row (2-y-o 6f winner in Britain by Indian Ridge) and 8-y-o Out For A Stroll: dam 2-y-o 5f/6.5f winner: fair form: won maiden at Goodwood in September: will stay 7f/1m. *B. W. Hills*

THE KEEP 5 ch.m. Shinko Forest (IRE) – Poyle Amber 55 (Sharrood (USA) 124) **43** [2007 55: 6m 7m 8m 6s 7g 7m 5g⁶ Sep 3] leggy mare: poor maiden: stays 6f: acts on polytrack and any turf going: usually blinkered/visored. *R. E. Barr*

THE KIDDYKID (IRE) 7 b.g. Danetime (IRE) 121 – Mezzanine (Sadler's Wells **104** (USA) 132) [2007 113: 6d 6m 6m 7.6m 6d 6.1s⁵ 6s⁵ 6m⁵ 7d 7m³ 6m 7g⁵ p7g* p7m p7m⁶ Nov 24] tall, lengthy gelding: just useful handicapper nowadays: won at Lingfield (all-weather debut) in October: stays 7f: acts on polytrack and any turf going: tried visored: usually races up with pace. *P. D. Evans*

THE KING AND I (IRE) 3 b.g. Monashee Mountain (USA) 115 – Scrimshaw (Sel- **80** kirk (USA) 129) [2007 68: p7g⁶ 6d 8m³ 8.3g⁵ 11.7m⁶ p9.5g² p9.5g⁴ p12.2g* p12.2s² p12.2g³ Dec 26] quite attractive gelding: fairly useful handicapper: left J. S. Moore and returned to former trainer after fifth start: won at Wolverhampton in December: creditable placed efforts after: stays 1½m: acts on polytrack and good to firm going: tried visored, blinkered last 3 starts. *Miss E. C. Lavelle*

THE LADY GRANUAILE (USA) 2 b.f. (Apr 26) More Than Ready (USA) 120 – **71** Marlene (USA) (Theatrical 128) [2007 6m³ 6.1m Oct 3] $40,000F, $70,000Y: good-topped filly: fourth foal: half-sister to winners in US by Conquistador Cielo and Souvenir Copy: dam unraced: fair maiden: third to Fitzroy Crossing at Haydock: needed race at Nottingham 2 months later: likely to prove best at 5f/6f. *K. A. Ryan*

THE LADY LAPWING 2 b.f. (Jun 2) Mark of Esteem (IRE) 137 – Lonely Shore **– p** (Blakeney 126) [2007 p6g p6g Nov 28] half-sister to 2 winners, notably 11-y-o The Whistling Teal: dam Italian 13.5f winner: green and slowly away when behind in maidens at Kempton: should improve. *G. Wragg*

THE LAST BOTTLE (IRE) 2 ch.g. (Feb 24) Hawk Wing (USA) 136 – Mesmerist **68** (USA) 65 (Green Desert (USA) 127) [2007 6g⁵ 6m⁶ 7.5g⁶ 7m p7.1g² Nov 24] good-topped gelding: fair maiden: left T. Tate 5,000 gns, good second in nursery at Wolverhampton final start: stays 7f: acts on polytrack and good to firm going. *W. M. Brisbourne*

THE LAST DROP (IRE) 4 b.c. Galileo (IRE) 134 – Epping 81 (Charnwood Forest **109 ?** (IRE) 125) [2007 118: 14.1g² 16m³ 14g 20g 12g Aug 3] tall, good-bodied colt: smart at 3 yrs: useful at best in 2007: placed first 2 starts, neck second to Mount Kilimanjaro in listed race at Nottingham and 5 lengths third to Tungsten Strike in Sagaro Stakes at Ascot: pulled up in Yorkshire Cup third outing and well below form after: should stay 2m: has form on good to firm going, very best efforts on good or softer: tried tongue tied. *B. W. Hills*

THE LEATHER WEDGE (IRE) 8 b.g. Hamas (IRE) 125§ – Wallflower (Polar **54** Falcon (USA) 126) [2007 78: f5g⁵ f5g⁵ f5g f5g 5g Apr 19] good-topped gelding: just modest performer in 2007: was best at 5f: acted on all-weather, firm and good to soft going: tried blinkered/in cheekpieces/tongue tied: front runner: dead. *R. Johnson*

THE LIGHT FANDANGO 3 ch.f. Kyllachy 129 – Alifandango (IRE) 78 (Alzao **47** (USA) 117) [2007 50: f8g⁴ p8.6g⁵ p8g³ p7.1g p7f p8.6g f8g⁶ f8d Dec 20] poor maiden: stays 8.6f: acts on polytrack. *R. A. Harris*

THE LOAN EXPRESS (IRE) 2 b.f. (Feb 3) Choisir (AUS) 126 – Mamma's Too 104 **97** (Skyliner 117) [2007 5g* 5m² 6d⁵ 5m³ 6v⁴ 5m⁵ Sep 14] 14,000F, €47,000Y: tall, leggy, close-coupled filly: half-sister to several winners, including fairly useful 6f (at 2 yrs) and 1m winner Sandy Lady (by Desert King) and useful German 6.5f/7f winner Macina (by Platini): dam 5f/6f (including at 2 yrs) winner: useful performer: won minor event at Naas in April: ran well last 3 starts, including ½-length third to Elletelle in Queen Mary Stakes at Royal Ascot and 3½ lengths fifth to Fleeting Spirit in Flying Childers Stakes at Doncaster: should prove best kept to 5f/6f: acts on heavy and good to firm going. *T. Stack, Ireland*

THE LONDON GANG 4 b.g. Mind Games 121 – Nom Francais 39§ (First Trump **62 §** 118) [2007 70§: p6g³ p7g⁵ p7g p8.6g⁴ p10g⁴ p8.6g⁶ p6g p6g 7m p8.6g p5g 10.1m Jul 17] leggy, angular gelding: modest performer: claimed from P. D. Evans £6,000 after reappearance: stays easy 1¼m: acts on all-weather, heavy and good to firm going: wears headgear: usually soon off bridle: unreliable. *Miss D. A. McHale*

THE LOOSE SCREW (IRE) 9 b.g. Bigstone (IRE) 126 – Princess of Dance (IRE) – (Dancing Dissident (USA) 119) [2007 –: p16.5g p12.2g Mar 2] good-bodied gelding: little form since 2005. *C. W. Thornton*

THE LORD 7 b.g. Averti (IRE) 117 – Lady Longmead (Crimson Beau 124) [2007 108, **97** a94: p5g⁵ 5.2m 5.1m 5m⁴ 5g May 25] close-coupled, quite good-topped gelding: has a **a85 +** quick action: useful performer on turf, fairly useful on all-weather: best at 5f: acts on all-weather, firm and soft going: tried in cheekpieces/visor: often races prominently: sometimes slowly away. *W. G. M. Turner*

THE MAGIC BLANKET (IRE) 2 b.g. (Mar 20) Bahamian Bounty 116 – Zietun- **67** zeen (IRE) 99 (Zieten (USA) 118) [2007 5d 5.2d³ 5m 5m⁵ 5f⁴ 5m⁴ p6g³ Sep 7] lengthy gelding: fair maiden: left Mrs L. Stubbs 10,000 gns after fifth start: good third in nursery at Kempton: should prove best at 5f/6f: acts on polytrack, firm and good to soft going. *Stef Liddiard*

THE MIGHTY OGMORE 3 ch.f. Dr Fong (USA) 128 – Welsh Dawn (Zafonic **59 §** (USA) 130) [2007 63§: 8f 8m 9.3m³ 10m 8d² 9.2s³ 10g⁴ 9.1d⁵ 10.1d 10.1g 9.2s 12g 12.2g³ p11m⁵ p12.2g p12m⁶ p12g Dec 19] modest performer: stays 1½m: acts on poly- track, good to firm and good to soft going: tried visored, usually wears cheekpieces: temperamental. *R. C. Guest*

THE MIGHTY ONE 2 b.g. (Mar 14) Mujadil (USA) 119 – Presently 48 (Cadeaux **69** Genereux 131) [2007 7g³ p6d* p6d⁵ Dec 28] strong gelding: fair form: won maiden at Wolverhampton in December: below form in nursery there next time: will prove best at 5f/6f. *P. C. Haslam*

THE NAME IS FRANK 2 b.g. (Apr 28) Lujain (USA) 119 – Zaragossa 80 (Paris **72** House 123) [2007 5d 5.1g 6g³ 5m⁶ 6s* 7g Aug 15] tall gelding: fair performer: won maiden at Salisbury in July: seemed amiss in nursery final start: gelded after: best at 5f/ 6f: acts on soft going. *J. W. Mullins*

THE NAWAB (IRE) 5 ch.g. Almutawakel 126 – Eschasse (USA) (Zilzal (USA) 137) **88** [2007 99: 12m 10m 16.2m⁵ 16d⁵ 16s³ Jul 1] smallish, quite attractive gelding: just fairly useful handicapper at 5 yrs: respectable fifth to Colloquial at Haydock third start: stays 2½m: acts on polytrack, firm and good to soft going: has reportedly had breathing problem: tried tongue tied. *Barry Potts, Ireland*

THE NIFTY FOX 3 b.g. Foxhound (USA) 103 – Nifty Alice 80 (First Trump 118) **87** [2007 82: 5f⁵ 5g⁴ 5g* 6m 5m* 5.1s³ 5d 5g⁶ 5g 5m 5.1g⁶ 5g 5m⁵ 5g⁴ Nov 9] big, lengthy gelding: has a rather round action: fairly useful handicapper: won at Redcar in May and Ayr in June: best at 5f: acts on soft and good to firm going: tried visored, blinkered of late. *T. D. Easterby*

THEN 'N NOW 2 b.f. (Jan 24) Dansili 127 – Rise 'n Shine 67 (Night Shift (USA)) **71** [2007 6f 6d⁴ p6g* p6g² 7m Oct 6] strong, workmanlike filly: fifth foal: half-sister to 4-y-o Total Impact and 6f to 8.5f (in Spain) winner Scarlet Secret (by Piccolo): dam, 5f winner, half-sister to useful French sprinter Touch And Love: fair performer: won maiden at Lingfield in August: second in nursery there next time: flattered in Oh So Sharp Stakes at Newmarket (remote last of 8) final start: seems to stay 7f: acts on polytrack, good to firm and good to soft going: sold 26,000 gns. *C. A. Cyzer*

THE OIL MAGNATE 2 ch.g. (Mar 8) Dr Fong (USA) 128 – Bob's Princess 69 (Bob's **83 p** Return (IRE) 123) [2007 7d² Jul 22] 24,000Y: fifth foal: half-brother to 3 winners, including 3-y-o Ingleby Princess and 4-y-o Bob's Your Uncle: dam 2-y-o 7f winner (stayed 1½m): 20/1, neck second to Midnight Muse in maiden at Redcar: will stay at least 1m: open to improvement. *M. Dods*

THE OLD SOLDIER 9 b.g. Magic Ring (IRE) 115 – Grecian Belle 53 (Ilium 121) – [2007 61: 6m 5f Jun 7] tall gelding: modest performer: well held at 9 yrs: stays 7f: acts on polytrack, firm and good to soft going. *A. Dickman*

THEONEBOX (USA) 2 ch.g. (May 23) Johannesburg (USA) 127 – Khalifa of – Kushog (USA) (Air Forbes Won (USA)) [2007 6m Aug 13] big gelding: 100/1, no show in maiden at Windsor. *M. J. Wallace*

THEORETICAL 3 b.f. Marju (IRE) 127 – Relativity (IRE) (Distant Relative 128) **66** [2007 66: p6g 7g p6g p5.1g⁶ p5m⁶ p6g² Dec 22] smallish, workmanlike filly: fair handi- capper: probably stays 7f: acts on polytrack: tried in cheekpieces: free-going type. *A. J. McCabe*

THE OSTEOPATH (IRE) 4 ch.g. Danehill Dancer (IRE) 117 – Miss Margate (IRE) **81**
60 (Don't Forget Me 127) [2007 78: 8.2g³ 7g 7d⁶ 7m⁶ 7.1d* 7d⁵ 7s³ 8.2d³ 7d³ 8.2g⁵ 7g
Oct 20] leggy gelding: fairly useful handicapper: won at Warwick in June: best at 7f/1m:
acts on soft going: usually wears cheekpieces/blinkers: carries head awkwardly/tricky
ride. *M. Dods*

THE PEN 5 ch.m. Lake Coniston (IRE) 131 – Come To The Point (Pursuit of Love 124) **65**
[2007 65: p9.5g f12g⁶ 10g⁵ 9.9m 9.9m* 12.4m⁵ 10.1m 11.1d⁴ 11.1m⁵ 12.1g⁵ 14.1m **a–**
Sep 6] workmanlike mare: fair handicapper: won at Beverley in April: stays 1½m: acts
on firm and soft going: has raced freely. *C. W. Fairhurst*

THE PERFECT PLAN (IRE) 4 b.g. Kalanisi (IRE) 132 – Talbiya (IRE) (Mujtahid **54**
(USA) 118) [2007 –: f12g Jan 16] modest maiden: tried blinkered. *Tom Dascombe*

THE POWER OF PHIL 3 b.g. Komaite (USA) – Starboard Tack (FR) 76 (Saddlers' **52**
Hall (IRE) 126) [2007 –: p6g p6g⁶ p5g p6g p9.5g⁴ᵈ f8d² Dec 20] modest maiden: seems
to stay 9.5f: acts on all-weather: not easy ride. *Miss Joanne Priest*

THE QUANTUM KID 3 b.c. Desert Prince (IRE) 130 – Al Hasnaa (Zafonic (USA) **61**
130) [2007 –: 10g⁶ 9g⁴ 12g⁵ 9.8g Aug 27] good-topped colt: modest maiden: likely to
prove best short of 1½m: blinkered final start. *T. J. Etherington*

THE REAL GURU 2 b.c. (Jan 16) Ishiguru (USA) 114 – Aloma's Reality (USA) **73**
(Proper Reality (USA)) [2007 5g³ 5d* 5d⁴ 6g 5.1m 6g² p5.1g Nov 16] compact colt:
fair performer: won maiden at Pontefract in July: visored, second in nursery at Catterick
penultimate start: well held in cheekpieces final one (all-weather debut): should prove
best at 5f/6f: acts on good to soft going. *Mrs A. Duffield*

THE REBOUND KID 5 b.g. Royal Applause 124 – Hayhurst (Sandhurst Prince 128) **–**
[2007 66: 12g Nov 6] strong gelding: fair maiden in 2006: below form only Flat start at 5
yrs: stays 1¼m: acts on polytrack and good to soft going: tried blinkered. *J. R. Weymes*

THE RIDDLER (IRE) 2 b.c. (Feb 8) Daylami (IRE) 138 – Wimple (USA) 101 (King- **78**
mambo (USA) 125) [2007 7m⁵ 8.5m² 8.3g² Sep 23] good-bodied colt: fair maiden:
second at Beverley (beaten short head by Keenes Day) and Hamilton, hanging left both
times: stays 8.5f. *J. A. Osborne*

THE RIP 6 ch.g. Definite Article 121 – Polgwynne 48 (Forzando 122) [2007 –: p10g **–**
p16g p16g May 9] strong gelding: no form since 2005. *R. M. Stronge*

THERMIDORA 3 b.f. Theatrical 128 – Langoustine (AUS) 117 (Danehill (USA) 126) **55**
[2007 p10g 10g⁶ Aug 24] lightly-made filly: second foal: dam, Australian 2-y-o 5f
winner (including Group 2), out of half-sister to Royal Academy and the dam of Storm
Cat: modest form in maidens: sweating at Newbury second start. *J. R. Fanshawe*

THERMIDOR (USA) 4 ch.g. Giant's Causeway (USA) 132 – Langoustine (AUS) 117 **68**
(Danehill (USA) 126) [2007 6m⁵ 6f⁴ Sep 25] strong gelding: better effort in maidens
when fourth to Salsa Steps at Folkestone, not knocked about: will stay further than 6f:
sold 8,000 gns: should progress further. *R. Charlton*

THE SALWICK FLYER (IRE) 4 b.g. Tagula (IRE) 116 – Shimla (IRE) 55 (Rudi- **60**
mentary (USA) 118) [2007 60: f6g 6m⁶ 8d 6d³ 6d* p6g⁶ 5d³ 6s 6v⁴ p6g f7d* Dec 15]
small, leggy gelding: fair handicapper: left A. Berry after second start: won at
Hamilton (apprentice event) in August and Southwell in December: stays 7f: acts on
all-weather, soft and good to firm going: often races prominently. *I. Semple*

THE SKERRET 3 ch.g. Loup Sauvage (USA) 125 – Cosmic Star 58 (Siberian Express **60**
(USA) 125) [2007 57: 8.1m 8f 6s² 6s 7f⁴ 7.6f 6s³ Aug 22] leggy, lengthy gelding: modest
maiden: will prove best short of 1m: acts on firm and soft going: tried in cheekpieces: has
looked none too genuine: sold 4,200 gns. *P. Winkworth*

THE SLIDER 3 b.f. Erhaab (USA) 127 – Cottage Maid (Inchinor 119) [2007 54: p8.6g³ **52**
p10g⁵ p8g p7g p8g p10g p11g⁵ p12m⁴ Dec 8] quite good-topped filly: modest performer:
left P. Blockley after second outing: stays 1½m: acts on polytrack and firm going: tried in
cheekpieces: signs of temperament. *Mrs L. C. Jewell*

THE SNATCHER (IRE) 4 b.c. Indian Danehill (IRE) 124 – Saninka (IRE) 82 (Doy- **96 d**
oun 124) [2007 98: 8m p7g⁵ 6g⁶ 8.1g 7.1d 6g 8g p8g³ 10m 10d⁶ p8g⁵ p8g p8g³ Nov 3]
rather leggy, attractive colt: useful handicapper: not at best after second start: barely stays
1¼m: acts on polytrack, heavy and good to firm going: tried visored. *R. Hannon*

THE SOCIAL DRINKER 5 b.g. Tipsy Creek (USA) 115 – Sanshang (FR) (Astronef **–**
116) [2007 7m May 3] tailed off in bumpers: tongue tied, well held in seller at Catterick
on Flat debut. *F. P. Murtagh*

THE STAFFORD (IRE) 6 b.g. Selkirk (USA) 129 – Bint Zamayem (IRE) 95 (Rainbow Quest (USA) 134) [2007 –: p11g Nov 21] little form. *L. Wells* —

THETA 3 b.f. Rainbow Quest (USA) 134 – Self Esteem (Suave Dancer (USA) 136) [2007 –p: 10.3m⁴ p12g 12.1m* Sep 13] rather leggy, quite good-topped filly: fair performer: made all in maiden at Chepstow in September: stays 1½m: acts on good to firm ground: sold 14,000 gns. *H. R. A. Cecil* **71**

THE TATLING (IRE) 10 b.g. Perugino (USA) 84 – Aunty Eileen (Ahonoora 122) [2007 118d: 5.2m³ 5m* 5g⁵ 5m 5g⁴ 5g 6m 6m⁵ 5g 5m⁵ 6m 5.1m 5g Oct 27] strong, lengthy gelding: very smart performer at best: just useful nowadays: won minor event at Musselburgh in May by head from River Falcon: seemingly best effort at 10 yrs when fourth to Hoh Mike in Sprint Stakes at Sandown fifth outing (probably flattered): has won at 6f, probably best at 5f: acts on firm and soft going: tried tongue tied earlier in career: held up, and best in strongly-run race: sometimes early to post. *J. M. Bradley* **106**

THE TERMINATOR (IRE) 5 b.g. Night Shift (USA) – Surmise (USA) 75 (Alleged (USA) 138) [2007 –: p8.6g Jan 5] good-topped gelding: little form since 2005. *M. Mullineaux* —

THE THRIFTY BEAR 4 ch.g. Rambling Bear 115 – Prudent Pet 65 (Distant Relative 128) [2007 68d: 9.8g 7.1g 5v 6m 6g 5m 5s 5s Oct 4] big, workmanlike gelding: just poor performer nowadays: best at 5f/6f: acts on good to firm going, probably on good to soft: sometimes blinkered. *C. W. Fairhurst* **48**

THE TINKER MAN 3 b.c. Killer Instinct 111 – Sporting Affair (IRE) 59 (Ashkalani (IRE) 128) [2007 p6g f6g⁵ f6g⁵ f5g² f5g⁶ p5g 8.1m 8f⁶ 8m⁵ 11.7g⁴ 10.2g 7.6g 8m Aug 9] modest maiden handicapper: stays 11.7f: acts on fibresand and good to firm ground: tends to hang left. *M. D. I. Usher* **62**

THE TOKOLOSHE 5 ch.g. Zaha (CAN) 106 – Hay Danzig (IRE) (Roi Danzig (USA)) [2007 7g 15.8m Aug 7] tailed off in bumper: no form on Flat, pulled up latter start: dead. *M. A. Barnes* —

THE TRADER (IRE) 9 ch.g. Selkirk (USA) 129 – Snowing 88 (Tate Gallery (USA) 117) [2007 115: 5g⁴ 6m⁶ 5g 5g⁴ 5g² 6d⁵ 5d⁶ Sep 25] sturdy, close-coupled gelding: usually impresses in appearance: poor mover: smart performer at best: reportedly finished distressed final start in 2006, and just useful form at 9 yrs: best efforts at Deauville fifth/sixth starts, head second to Only Answer in listed race and 3 lengths fifth to Garnica in Prix de Meautry: effective at 5f to 6.5f: acts on firm and soft going: blinkered: often slowly into stride: held up, and usually travels strongly: tough. *M. Blanshard* **107**

THE TWELVE STEPS 2 b.c. (Jan 26) Diktat 126 – Polygueza (FR) 78 (Be My Guest (USA) 126) [2007 8d p8m f6d* Dec 14] 55,000 2-y-o: seventh foal: half-brother to several winners, notably 5-y-o The Geezer: dam Irish 7f winner: fair form: much improved to win maiden at Southwell (by 3 lengths) final start: should be suited by 1m+: will do better still. *P. F. I. Cole* **75 p**

THE TYKE 4 gr.g. Cloudings (IRE) 112 – Vonispet (Cotation) [2007 67: p7.1g⁶ 5.7g Oct 24] just modest maiden in 2007: should stay 1m: acts on polytrack. *C. G. Cox* **56**

THEWAYYOUARE (USA) 2 b.c. (Feb 9) Kingmambo (USA) 125 – Maryinsky (IRE) 107 (Sadler's Wells (USA) 132) [2007 7d 7.5g* 8d* 8d* 8s* Nov 1] **117 p**

The Criterium International, run over a mile at Saint-Cloud in early-November, was created as recently as 2001 to fill the gap left by the Grand Criterium when the latter had its distance reduced from a mile to seven furlongs. The new race was an immediate success judged on the three-year-old careers of its first three winners. Inaugural winner Act One went on to further Group 1 success in the Prix Lupin before finishing second in the Prix du Jockey Club. Injury curtailed Act One's career after that but the next two winners, Dalakhani and Bago, enjoyed full campaigns at three which culminated in wins in the Prix de l'Arc de Triomphe. Act One, Dalakhani and Bago have, however, proved hard acts to follow, Helios Quercus' two wins at three coming only at listed level, Carlotamix failing to win at all in four starts in his classic season and the 2006 winner Mount Nelson seen out only once in the latest season, when tailed off in the Champion Stakes.

The latest Criterium International winner, Thewayyouare, looks much more likely to take after the race's first three winners than the last three. His achievements at two prompted some to look even further ahead, beyond what Thewayyouare might achieve on the track as a three-year-old, to his potential as a stallion. That might seem premature in the case of a horse whose racing career has only just begun, but with competition between the bloodstock superpowers to secure the best stallion prospects particularly fierce, there seemed an urgency to strike while the iron was hot. In the event, Thewayyouare could not have been much hotter as a stallion prospect by the autumn, particularly in the eyes of Coolmore, who announced the purchase of his stud rights immediately after the Criterium International. As well as being a son of top sire Kingmambo and from a sire-producing family, his half-sister Peeping Fawn had developed into Europe's top three-year-old middle-distance filly for Ballydoyle, while another close family member Rags To Riches, also in the colours of Michael Tabor, had done the same in the States, emulating her own year-older half-brother Jazil by winning the Belmont Stakes.

There are potential rewards for the new stakeholders in Thewayyouare in the shorter term. In a year when Ballydoyle seemed unusually short of obvious classic contenders among its two-year-old colts, Thewayyouare (who will remain in training with Fabre) is a significant boost to the Coolmore team. In fact, for only the second time, Aidan O'Brien sent no representative over for the Criterium International—which either reflected a lack of suitable candidates at Ballydoyle (though the stable ran a couple of maidens in the Criterium de Saint-Cloud ten days later) or perhaps that Thewayyouare was effectively already a 'done deal' for Coolmore.

Thewayyouare, who started favourite, may not have faced any rivals from Ballydoyle in the Criterium International, but he was taken on by three other progressive French colts and a couple from Britain with pattern-race form. His French rivals—in betting order—comprised the Longchamp listed winner Sceptre Rouge, the Prix des Chenes winner Blue Chagall and Hello Morning, who had won his last two starts in maiden/minor company; the British-trained pair Redolent and Yankadi started as outsiders despite last-time-out placings in the Autumn Stakes (second to Ibn Khaldun) and Somerville Tattersall Stakes respectively. None of these had impressed quite so much as Thewayyouare on his previous start in the Prix Thomas Bryon, over the Criterium International course and distance in October. On that occasion, Thewayyouare made short work of his five rivals to win by two and a half lengths, needing just pushing out to join issue before going on to win impressively from Centennial. On that performance, Thewayyouare looked the one to beat in the Criterium International. In his three earlier races, Thewayyouare had finished seventh in a newcomers event at Deauville (which also saw the debut of both the other colts who went on to be placed in the Criterium de Saint-Cloud, Hannouma and Putney Bridge) in July, then improved to win a maiden at the same course just over a month later, and progressed again to beat the filly Luna Royale, already a listed winner, in a listed race at Lyon-Parilly in September.

Criterium International, Saint-Cloud—Thewayyouare, completing a four-timer,
and the grey Hello Morning show smart form in pulling clear of Redolent (hooped cap), Yankadi (left),
Blue Chagall and Sceptre Rouge (rail)

Redolent set a sound pace at Saint-Cloud, with Thewayyouare held up in touch. With the runners keeping to the far rail but fanning out off the home turn, Thewayyouare was forced to switch to make his challenge one off the rail, all six runners being virtually in line passing the two-furlong marker. Despite having four previous outings under his belt, Thewayyouare still looked inexperienced when asked for his effort, carrying his head slightly to one side and then tending to come off a true line when the whip was pulled. Although leaving most of his rivals behind, Thewayyouare's effort was matched by Hello Morning running on widest of all, and looking all set to assert inside the last furlong when going a neck up. To his credit, though, Thewayyouare responded to pressure and rallied to lead again and pass the post half a length in front, with a gap of six lengths behind Hello Morning to Redolent in third, just ahead of Yankadi, Blue Chagall and Sceptre Rouge.

As far as the classics are concerned, a run in the Two Thousand Guineas seems to have been ruled out for Thewayyouare, though he is reportedly to tackle the Poule d'Essai des Poulains, with the Prix du Jockey Club and Irish Derby his most likely objectives after that. Peeping Fawn's successes over a mile and a half in the Irish and Yorkshire Oaks gives considerably more encouragement for Thewayyouare's staying a mile and a half than might have been derived from the record of their dam Maryinsky over middle-distances; despite being by Sadler's Wells and finishing second in the Fillies' Mile at two, she was tailed off in the Oaks and beat only one home in the ten-furlong Blandford Stakes on her only attempts beyond a mile at three. Further encouragement for Thewayyouare's staying a mile and a half comes from his sire Kingmambo, in general a stronger influence for stamina than Peeping Fawn's sire Danehill. Further details of Thewayyouare's outstanding family can be found in the essay on Peeping Fawn. Suffice to say here that, in addition to two Belmont winners, the Group 1-winning descendants of his great-grandam Best In Show also include three winners of the Dewhurst (El Gran Senor, Try My Best and Xaar) and two winners of the Breeders' Cup Mile (Spinning World and Domedriver), while, so far as versatility of distances goes, they range from a Nunthorpe winner (Bahamian Pirate) to a Prix du Cadran winner (Chief Contender). As well as Thewayyouare, Peeping Fawn and Rags To Riches, a fourth direct descendant of Best In Show to win at Group/Grade 1 level in 2007 was Germany's Arc challenger Saddex, a Group 1 winner at Cologne in August, while Arc third Sagara was yet another who traces back directly to Best In Show. Thewayyouare was catalogued in the Tattersalls October Yearling Sales but seemingly changed hands privately without going through the ring.

	Kingmambo (USA) (b 1990)	Mr Prospector (b 1970)	Raise A Native
Thewayyouare (USA) (b.c. Feb 9, 2005)			Gold Digger
		Miesque (b 1984)	Nureyev
			Pasadoble
	Maryinsky (IRE) (b 1999)	Sadler's Wells (b 1981)	Northern Dancer
			Fairy Bridge
		Blush With Pride (ch 1979)	Blushing Groom
			Best In Show

Whether or not Thewayyouare, generally third favourite at around 16/1 in most ante-post lists, lines up at Epsom instead of Chantilly might depend to some extent on whether any (or how many) Derby contenders emerge from Ballydoyle during the spring. Andre Fabre has a poor record in the Derby and has said some uncomplimentary things about the race in the past. He saddled the favourite Visindar, who finished fifth, and Linda's Lad, also among the market leaders, who was ninth, in the 2006 renewal, his most recent raid on the race. The latter, incidentally, gave Thewayyouare's owner, Irish property developer Sean Mulryan, his first Group 1 success on the Flat when winning the Criterium de Saint-Cloud in 2005 and earned his place in the Derby field with a win in the Lingfield Derby Trial. Mulryan is much better known as an owner of jumpers, particularly at Auteuil where his horses have cleaned up in most of the top races in recent years. Thewayyouare has raced only on ground softer than good so far. *A. Fabre, France*

THE WHICH DOCTOR 2 b.g. (Mar 12) Medicean 128 – Oomph 83 (Shareef Dancer (USA) 135) [2007 7m² p7g* Oct 12] 28,000Y: strong, close-coupled gelding: third foal: half-brother to 4-y-o Very Agreeable: dam, 7f winner, half-sister to smart 7f/1m **85 p**

performer Swiss Law: fairly useful form: confirmed Newmarket promise (neck second to Tanweer) when winning maiden at Lingfield with plenty in hand, quickening well: gelded after: will stay 1m: will go on improving. *J. Noseda*

THEWHIRLINGDERVISH (IRE) 9 ch.g. Definite Article 121 – Nomadic Dancer **84** (IRE) 52 (Nabeel Dancer (USA) 120) [2007 74: 16m² 18d* 15.8m³ 16.2s* 16d² 18m 16.1m⁵ Aug 27] lengthy, good-topped gelding: fairly useful handicapper: won at Pontefract in June and Beverley in July: stays 2¼m: acts on firm and soft going. *T. D. Easterby*

THE WHISTLING TEAL 11 b.g. Rudimentary (USA) 118 – Lonely Shore (Blake- **108 d** ney 126) [2007 116: 12m⁶ 13.4m⁵ 13.3g⁴ 14s⁴ 13.3d⁴ 14m Sep 15] strong gelding: carries condition: smart performer at best, on downgrade: best efforts in 2007 in John Porter at Newbury (sixth to Maraahel) and Ormonde Stakes at Chester (fifth to Ask): best at 1½m to 2m: acts on fibresand, firm and soft going: usually held up. *G. Wragg*

THE WICKED WIZARD 4 br.g. Wizard King 122 – Sallyoreally (IRE) 57 (Com- **–** mon Grounds 118) [2007 f8g⁶ f7g Jan 7] tailed off in bumpers: no show in sellers. *W. Storey*

THE WILLOWY WIGEON 2 b.f. (Mar 12) Josr Algarhoud (IRE) 118 – The Dark **53** Eider (Superlative 118) [2007 6g⁴ 7.1m 7m⁴ 8.3d³ Oct 1] leggy filly: second foal: dam unraced out of half-sister to 11-y-o The Whistling Teal: modest maiden: stays 1m. *P. Winkworth*

THE WILY WOODCOCK 3 b.c. Mark of Esteem (IRE) 137 – Lonely Shore (Blake- **72** ney 126) [2007 60p: p8g⁴ 8.3m 10g⁴ 12m Aug 4] useful-looking colt: fair maiden: said to have finished lame final start: stays 1¼m: signs of temperament. *G. Wragg*

THEY ALL LAUGHED 4 ch.g. Zafonic (USA) 130 – Royal Future (IRE) (Royal **77** Academy (USA) 130) [2007 60: p8g p8.6g⁴ f8g⁶ p9.5g⁵ p10g f11g⁵ f12g² f14g² f14g² f12g* 15d³ 12d* 13f² 11.9d* 13d⁵ 14m²ᵈ f12d³ Dec 20] tall, useful-looking gelding: fair handicapper: won at Southwell in April, Newmarket (ladies event) in May and Brighton in July: stays 15f: acts on all-weather, firm and good to soft ground: tried blinkered/in cheekpieces: waited with: reliable. *P. W. Hiatt*

THIELLA (USA) 3 b. or br.f. Kingmambo (USA) 125 – Theoretically (USA) 114 **88** (Theatrical 128) [2007 103p: 8m 10d³ 10m 8g 9f⁴ 8.5f⁴ Nov 7] leggy filly: second foal: dam, Irish 2-y-o 7f winner (should have stayed 1½m), half-sister to smart French winner up to 10.5f Cudas: fairly useful performer: won maiden at Gowran at 2 yrs: stiff tasks, not discredited on third/fourth starts, in listed race at Newbury (seventh of 8 to Darrfonah) and Ontario Colleen Stakes at Woodbine (eighth behind Speak Wisely, left D. Weld, Ireland after): stays 1¼m: best efforts on soft/good to soft going. *C. Clement, USA*

THINKING POSITIVE 3 ch.f. Rainbow Quest (USA) 134 – Midnight Air (USA) **80** 111 (Green Dancer (USA) 132) [2007 76p: 8.2g² p11g⁴ p11g⁴ p12g² 11.7f* Sep 10] tall, leggy, quite attractive filly: fairly useful performer: won maiden at Bath in September: stays 1½m: acts on polytrack and firm ground. *J. H. M. Gosden*

THIRD SET (IRE) 4 b.g. Royal Applause 124 – Khamseh 85 (Thatching 131) [2007 **112** 92: 6s 6g² 7g 8m* 7g* 8g* Aug 3] tall, good-topped gelding: smart handicapper: much improved last 3 starts, winning at Newmarket (despite hanging left) and Ascot (27-runner totesport.com International Stakes, beat Racer Forever by 1¼ lengths), both in July, and

totesport.com International Stakes (Handicap), Ascot—Third Set is in control as Racer Forever finishes well to take second, ahead of Binanti (No.15) and Giganticus

totesport Mile at Goodwood (by 3 lengths from Humungous, in command from 2f out) in August: will stay 9f: acts on soft and good to firm ground: tried tongue tied: has good turn of foot: joined Godolphin. *R. Charlton*

THISTLE 6 ch.g. Selkirk (USA) 129 – Ardisia (USA) 87 (Affirmed (USA)) [2007 66: **60** 8.3m 8m⁵ May 21] good-topped gelding: one-time fairly useful winner: just modest nowadays: stays 11f: acts on good to firm ground. *J. Howard Johnson*

THIS WAY THAT WAY 6 b.g. Dr Devious (IRE) 127 – Ellway Dancer (IRE) 56 **61** (Mujadil (USA) 119) [2007 p12.2g⁶ p12.2g⁵ p16g³ Aug 1] modest maiden, lightly raced on Flat: stays 2m: acts on polytrack. *Ian Williams*

THOMAS A BECKETT (IRE) 4 b.g. Beckett (IRE) 116 – Kenema (IRE) 88 (Petar- **43** dia 113) [2007 55: p8g⁶ p11g Feb 4] unfurnished gelding: poor maiden nowadays: barely stays 1¼m: acts on good to firm and soft going. *P. R. Chamings*

THOMAS LAWRENCE (USA) 6 ch.g. Horse Chestnut (SAF) 119 – Olatha (USA) **58** (Miswaki (USA) 124) [2007 p8g p6g f7g 7g³ p7.1g 7s 7.6f p8.6g⁶ 7m³ Sep 2] well-made gelding: modest maiden: unraced in 2005/6: left G. Ham after second start, M. Saunders after third: stays 7f: acts on good to firm going: tried blinkered/visored. *P. A. Blockley*

THOMAS MALORY (IRE) 2 b.c. (Apr 2) Mujadil (USA) 119 – Isca 66 (Caerleon **65** (USA) 132) [2007 5f 6g 5m⁵ 6m 6.1s⁴ 6s⁵ 6m 6.1m 5m* 6m³ 6g p6g 5f⁴ 6d⁵ p7.1g Oct 25] tall, good-topped colt: fair performer: won seller at Musselburgh (dead-heated) in August: best at 5f/6f: acts on soft and firm going: tried blinkered/visored. *Miss V. Haigh*

THOMPSONS WALLS (IRE) 2 b.g. (May 7) Trans Island 119 – Nordic Living **80** (IRE) 53 (Nordico (USA)) [2007 6s⁴ 6m* 7m² 6m p7.1g p7g⁴ Nov 21] strong gelding: fairly useful performer: won maiden at Newcastle in August: 11 lengths second to Screen Star in minor event at Redcar, only sound run subsequently (clipped heels/unseated fifth start): stays 7f: acts on soft and good to firm going: tried tongue tied. *P. C. Haslam*

THORAX 3 br.c. Machiavellian (USA) 123 – Mezzogiorno 108 (Unfuwain (USA) 131) **66** [2007 12d³ 10g Jul 10] 48,000Y: sixth foal: brother to useful 6f/7f winner Monnavanna and half-brother to 2 winners, including smart 1m/1¼m Monturani (by Indian Ridge): dam, 7f (at 2 yrs) and 1¼m winner, third in Oaks: better effort in maidens when third to Flavius at Pontefract, tiring late on (clear of rest): eased next time. *M. Johnston*

THORNABY GREEN 6 ch.g. Whittingham (IRE) 104 – Dona Filipa 51 (Precocious **71** 126) [2007 61: 10.1m 10g² 9.9s⁴ 10.1v* 9.1d³ 10.1d⁶ 9.1s² 10.1g* 10m⁵ 10m⁶ 10.1d 10g p9.5g⁴ p9.5d³ p9.5s⁵ Dec 21] tall, quite good-topped gelding: fair handicapper: won at Newcastle in June and August: stays 1¼m: acts on all-weather and any turf going: tried in cheekpieces/visor: often makes running. *T. D. Barron*

THORNBILL 4 ch.g. Gorse 116 – Red Hot Dancer (USA) (Seattle Dancer (USA) 119) **51** [2007 –: 8.1g p7g Jun 14] big, strong gelding: modest form at best in maidens. *H. Candy*

THORNY MANDATE 5 b.g. Diktat 126 – Rosa Canina 91 (Bustino 136) [2007 68: **71** p12.2g 10m 10.5m⁴ p12.2g* p12g⁶ p12g2 12.3s⁵ p12.2g* 13m³ 12.1g³ 12.3m⁴ 12.6m p13.9g p12.2g p12.2g Oct 8] strong, close-coupled gelding: fair handicapper: won at Wolverhampton in June and July: stays 13f: acts on polytrack, firm and good to soft going (below best on soft): sometimes races freely: has been slowly away: usually held up. *W. M. Brisbourne*

THOUGHT IS FREE 2 b.f. (Mar 2) Cadeaux Genereux 131 – Dayville (USA) 86 **88** (Dayjur (USA) 137) [2007 6g 6s² 6m 6g p7g² 6m Oct 5] 60,000Y: lengthy filly: has scope: half-sister to several winners, including 3-y-o Day By Day, Irish 5f winner Alexander Ballet (by Mind Games) and 1¼m/1½m winner My Daisychain (by Hector Protector), all fairly useful: dam, 6f winner (including at 2 yrs), half-sister to US Grade 1 1¼m winner Spanish Fern: fairly useful maiden: mostly highly tried, best efforts in listed race at Newmarket (neck second to Polar Circle) and Lowther Stakes at York (eighth to Nahoodh) second/fourth starts: should stay 7f: acts on soft going. *J. S. Moore*

THOUGHTSOFSTARDOM 4 b.g. Mind Games 121 – Alustar 71 (Emarati (USA) **69** 74) [2007 63: p5.1g p5.1g* p5g⁶ f5g² p6g³ p5.1g³ f5g p5.1g⁶ 5.3m² 5g* 5g² p5.1g p5.1g **a65** p5g⁶ p6m² p6g³ p5m Dec 9] lengthy gelding: fair performer: won handicap at Wolverhampton in January and claimer at Hamilton in June: left P. McEntee after eleventh start: stays 6f: acts on all-weather, firm and soft going: usually wears headgear nowadays. *G. C. Bravery*

THOUSAND WORDS 3 b.c. Dansili 127 – Verbose (USA) 97 (Storm Bird (CAN) **113** 134) [2007 112: 8m³ 8g⁵ 7m 7g⁴ 8d⁵ 7.1m⁵ Sep 13] big, rather leggy, good-topped colt: has a quick action: smart performer: good efforts when fifth behind Astronomer Royal in Poule d'Essai des Poulains at Longchamp and 2 lengths fourth to Tariq in Betfair Cup (Lennox) at Goodwood second/fourth starts: failed to settle last 2 outings, getting going too late from impossible position when fifth to Eisteddfod in listed race at Sandown final outing: stays easy 1m: acts on good to firm and good to soft going: often sweats and gets on edge: joined R. Frankel in USA. *B. W. Hills*

THOU SHALT NOT 4 b. or br.g. Commands (AUS) – Soyalang (FR) (Alydeed – (CAN) 120) [2007 –: f14g p12.2g Jun 11] strong gelding: little form. *P. S. Felgate*

THREE BOARS 5 ch.g. Most Welcome 131 – Precious Poppy 70 (Polish Precedent **79** (USA) 131) [2007 69: f12g* f14g* f11g³ 12g 14.8d⁶ p13.9g p13.9g f14d* f12d² f16d² Dec 18] quite good-topped gelding: fair handicapper: won at Southwell in March (2) and December: effective at 1¼m to 16.5f: acts on all-weather, firm and good to soft ground: usually blinkered: travels strongly. *S. Gollings*

THREE COUNTIES (IRE) 6 b.h. Danehill (USA) 126 – Royal Show (IRE) 63 **63** (Sadler's Wells (USA) 132) [2007 –: 11.9m 8.1g⁵ 7m 7m⁴ 7.1f⁵ Aug 27] close-coupled horse: modest maiden: stays 1m: acts on firm going: tried blinkered: tended to hang final start. *N. I. M. Rossiter*

THREE GOLD LEAVES 2 ch.c. (Feb 11) Zaha (CAN) 106 – Tab's Gift (Bijou d'Inde – 127) [2007 8g Oct 19] big colt: 25/1, behind in maiden at Redcar. *J. G. Given*

THREE HALF CROWNS (IRE) 3 b.c. Barathea (IRE) 127 – My-Lorraine (IRE) – 77 (Mac's Imp (USA) 116) [2007 –: p8.6g 8m 8.5s 10.1d Jul 5] leggy, close-coupled colt: little sign of ability. *P. Howling*

THREE MATES 3 b.f. Auction House (USA) 120 – Great Aim (Great Nephew 126) **35** [2007 –: p5.1g⁶ Jan 12] poor maiden. *W. G. M. Turner*

THREE NO TRUMPS 3 ch.f. First Trump 118 – Renaissance Lady (IRE) 65 (Imp **45** Society (USA)) [2007 45: f8g³ p8.6g⁵ 9m 10.1d⁵ 8m Aug 9] good-topped filly: poor maiden: left D. Morris after second outing: stays 1m: acts on all-weather and firm ground: tried visored/tongue tied: sometimes slowly away. *P. S. Felgate*

THREE SHIPS 6 ch.g. Dr Fong (USA) 128 – River Lullaby (USA) (Riverman (USA) **54** 131) [2007 60: p11g 8s Jul 2] leggy, quite good-topped gelding: modest performer: stays 11f: acts on all-weather, raced mostly on good ground or firmer on turf: tried in blinkers/cheekpieces: often races up with pace. *Miss J. Feilden*

THREESTONEBURN (USA) 2 b.f. (Feb 20) Johannesburg (USA) 127 – White **68**
Bridle (IRE) 81 (Singspiel (IRE) 133) [2007 6m³ 6d⁵ 7.5m 8f⁴ p7m Dec 9] $35,000F,
68,000 2-y-o: well-made filly: second foal: dam, ran twice (third at 7f), out of half-sister
to Princess Royal Stakes winner Cunning: fair maiden: fourth in nursery at Pontefract,
then left P. Haslam 6,000 gns: will stay 1¼m: acts on firm and good to soft going.
J. R. Boyle

THREE THIEVES (UAE) 4 ch.g. Jade Robbery (USA) 121 – Melisendra (FR) **77**
(Highest Honor (FR) 124) [2007 70: p12g p13.9g² p12.2g* p12.2g² p13.9g* p13.9g²
p12g⁵ p16g f14g³ 12g⁶ p12.2d Dec 6] tall gelding: fair handicapper: won amateur events
at Wolverhampton in February and March (hanging left): said to have finished lame tenth
start (off nearly 6 months after): stays 1¾m: acts on all-weather, best turf efforts on good
going. *M. S. Saunders*

THROW THE DICE 5 b.g. Lujain (USA) 119 – Euridice (IRE) 66 (Woodman (USA) **64**
126) [2007 77d: f5g 6g 6m² 6g² 5d⁴ 6f⁴ 5g 6s 6d⁴ 5m⁵ 5m 5g* 5m⁶ 5d⁵ 5d⁴ 5s³ 5g⁵ 5g 5g⁴
Nov 6] strong, lengthy gelding: modest handicapper: claimed from D. Barker £15,000
after ninth start: won at Hamilton in September: free-going sort, best at 5f/6f: acts on firm
and soft going: often in cheekpieces in 2006, visored of late: sometimes slowly away:
often races prominently. *A. Berry*

THUMPERS DREAM 4 b.f. Cape Cross (IRE) 129 – Perfect Peach 100 (Lycius **84 d**
(USA) 124) [2007 86: 9.1g⁶ 9.8g 10d 7g 10m p8.6g⁶ p9.5g Nov 16] neat filly: fairly
useful performer at best: regressed in 2007: likely to prove best up to 1¼m: acts on firm
and soft going: blinkered last 3 starts: has found little. *I. W. McInnes*

THUNDER BAY 2 b.g. (Apr 13) Hunting Lion (IRE) 115 – Floral Spark 69 (Forzando **88**
122) [2007 p5g* 5m² 5f* 5m⁵ 5g 6.1m³ 5g⁵ 5m* 6.5m 5d² 5.1g² 5g⁵ 5d Oct 13] good-
quartered gelding: fairly useful performer: won maiden at Lingfield and minor event at
Thirsk in April and nursery at Sandown in August: best at 5f: acts on polytrack, firm and
good to soft going: sold 25,000 gns. *M. R. Channon*

THUNDERBOLT JAXON 3 ch.g. Dr Fong (USA) 128 – Composition 82 (Wolf- **63**
hound (USA) 126) [2007 p7g³ 7g² f8g⁴ p7.1g 6d Jun 19] modest maiden: stays 1m: acts
on all-weather: blinkered fourth start. *P. W. Chapple-Hyam*

THUNDERCLAP 8 b. or br.g. Royal Applause 124 – Gloriana 78 (Formidable (USA) **–**
125) [2007 10.1d Jul 28] quite good-topped gelding: fair handicapper at best: lightly
raced and little form on Flat since 2004: often wears headgear. *P. D. Niven*

THUNDER GORGE (USA) 2 b.c. (Apr 12) Thunder Gulch (USA) 129 – Renais- **75**
sance Fair (USA) (Theatrical 128) [2007 6m 6m⁴ 7m 6s² 6d p7g⁶ Nov 3] good-topped
colt: fair maiden: second in nursery at Goodwood: free-going sort, best up to 7f: acts on
polytrack, soft and good to firm going: often slowly away. *Mouse Hamilton-Fairley*

THUNDEROUSAPPLAUSE 3 b.f. Royal Applause 124 – Trustthunder 87 (Selkirk **94**
(USA) 129) [2007 81: 7m⁵ 6m⁴ 7.6s* 7.1d⁴ 6d p8m 6d Oct 19] lengthy filly: fairly useful
performer: improved when winning handicap at Chester in July by 8 lengths: stays 7.6f:
acts on soft going, probably on good to firm. *K. A. Ryan*

THUNDER STORM CAT (USA) 3 b.c. Storm Cat (USA) – Tenga (USA) (Mr Pros- **96**
pector (USA)) [2007 95p: 7m⁶ 8m³ 8.1m 8m 8s⁶ a9.5g* a9.5g Dec 12] strong, compact
colt: useful performer: left P. Cole, won minor event at Neuss in November by 31 lengths:
well held in listed race at Deauville final start: will stay 1¼m: acts on polytrack/sand and
good to firm ground: blinkered last 2 starts: edgy sort. *M. Rulec, Germany*

THUNDERSTRUCK 2 b.g. (Mar 27) Bertolini (USA) 125 – Trustthunder 87 (Selkirk **79**
(USA) 129) [2007 7d⁵ 7f⁴ 7.5g* Sep 19] workmanlike gelding: fair form: won maiden
at Beverley (beat Celtic Strand by 1½ lengths) final start, rallying despite hanging left:
subsequently gelded: stays 7.5f. *K. A. Ryan*

THUNDERWING (IRE) 5 b. or br.g. Indian Danehill (IRE) 124 – Scandisk (IRE) 88 **68 §**
(Kenmare (FR) 125) [2007 75: f8g² 12m⁵ 8m⁶ 10.5m 10s⁴ 8s 8d⁵ 11.1s⁶ 9.1v² Nov 3]
good-topped gelding: fair performer: left K. R. Burke after seventh start: barely stays
1½m: acts on fibresand, good to firm and heavy going: tried in visor/cheekpieces:
ungenuine. *James Moffatt*

THYOLO (IRE) 6 ch.g. Bering 136 – Topline (GER) (Acatenango (GER) 127) [2007 **–**
90: 7g 12g 12.6m p12m⁴ Dec 7] big, useful-looking gelding: one-time useful handicapper: left C. Cox after third start: broke shoulder in void race in December: stayed
1½m: acted on firm ground: tried in headgear: was edgy sort: dead. *B. G. Powell*

TI ADORA (IRE) 5 b.m. Montjeu (IRE) 137 – Wavy Up (IRE) (Brustolon 117) [2007 **96** 98: 12g Apr 25] leggy mare: useful performer: creditable eighth to Lake Poet in handicap at Epsom sole run in 2007: effective at 1½m to 2m: acts on polytrack and any turf going: has worn crossed noseband: tends to go freely: tough and consistent. *P. W. D'Arcy*

TIA JADE 3 gr.f. Imperial Ballet (IRE) 110 – Sunningdale (IRE) 68 (Indian Ridge 123) – [2007 p8g p8g 8.2m p10g p6g Nov 8] 3,500F, 4,500Y, 1,000 2-y-o: close-coupled filly: first foal: dam, 1m winner, closely related to very smart 1¼m (Nassau Stakes) winner Ruby Tiger: little form: left M. Gingell after third start. *G. Prodromou*

TIA MIA 2 ch.f. (Jan 27) Dr Fong (USA) 128 – Giusina Mia (USA) (Diesis 133) [2007 **88** 5g⁵ 5g² 5m 5g 6m⁴ Aug 18] 20,000Y: smallish, strong, sturdy filly: second foal: dam, 1¼m winner in Italy, out of half-sister to Grand Prix de Paris winner Swink: fairly useful performer: won maiden at Ripon in April: ran well in listed race at York (second to Janina) and Queen Mary Stakes at Royal Ascot (tenth to Elletelle) next 2 starts, but below form last 2: probably best at 5f: raced only on good/good to firm going. *J. G. Given*

TIANA 4 b.f. Diktat 126 – Hill Welcome 52 (Most Welcome 131) [2007 94: 8d 9.9g 8.1m **99** 7.1m⁶ 8d⁴ p8m⁴ Nov 1] strong filly: useful performer, lightly raced: seemed best efforts in 2007 when sixth to Eisteddfod in steadily-run listed race at Sandown fourth start and fourth to Sesmen in similar event at Lingfield final outing: stays 1m: acts on polytrack, yet to race on extremes of going on turf: blinkered last 3 starts: tongue tied twice at 2 yrs (including for win). *Mrs A. J. Perrett*

TIANA BLEU (IRE) 5 ch.m. Pistolet Bleu (IRE) 133 – Bobby Hays (IRE) (Bob Back – (USA) 124) [2007 p8.6g Mar 30] 33/1, showed nothing in claimer at Wolverhampton. *P. S. Felgate*

TIARA PRINCESS (IRE) 2 b.f. (May 2) Monashee Mountain (USA) 115 – All Our – Blessings (IRE) (Statoblest 120) [2007 5d⁵ 5.2m⁴ Aug 15] 2,500Y: good-bodied filly: fifth foal: dam maiden: well held in sellers (blinkered latterly). *Rae Guest*

TIBINTA 3 b.f. Averti (IRE) 117 – Bint Albadou (IRE) 91 (Green Desert (USA) 127) **56** [2007 57: 6.1m² 6d 5.1g³ 6m³ 6m 5m 6m 5.7m⁴ 7.1m⁶ p6g⁵ p5g⁴ p5.1g p6g Dec 19] close-coupled filly: modest maiden: effective at 5f/6f: acts on polytrack and good to firm ground: tried visored/blinkered: sometimes slowly away: none too consistent. *P. D. Evans*

TIBOUCHINA (IRE) 4 gr.f. Daylami (IRE) 138 – Kalimar (IRE) (Bigstone (IRE) **77** 126) [2007 69: p10g⁶ p10g 11.7f* 11.9d* 11.9d² 12m⁴ Jul 14] lengthy filly: fair handicapper: won at Bath and Brighton in June: would probably have stayed 1¾m: acted on polytrack, firm and good to soft going: had shown signs of temperament: reportedly in foal to Compton Place. *R. M. Beckett*

TICKING 4 ch.g. Barathea (IRE) 127 – Tuning 114 (Rainbow Quest (USA) 134) [2007 – –: 10.1f p8g Nov 28] little form. *T. Keddy*

TIDY (IRE) 7 b.g. Mujadil (USA) – Neat Shilling (IRE) (Bob Back (USA) 124) **67 §** [2007 74: 8m⁶ 9.1g⁵ 8s⁵ 10.1v⁴ 10g 8s 9.1v⁴ f8d Dec 15] smallish gelding: fair handicapper: stays 1¼m: acts on all-weather and heavy going: visored/in cheekpieces in 2007: temperamental. *Micky Hammond*

TIEGAN AN JOSH 2 b.f. (Apr 19) Lahib (USA) 129 – Poungada (FR) (Tropular) – [2007 f8d Dec 21] third foal: dam unraced: 50/1, well held in maiden at Southwell, slowly away. *A. Crook*

TIEGS (IRE) 5 ch.m. Desert Prince (IRE) 130 – Helianthus (Groom Dancer (USA) **53 §** 128) [2007 55: f12g* f12g p13g³ f12g f14g⁴ f12g 11.6d⁴ 12m 12.1g² p12g⁴ 12.1m⁴ Sep 7] angular mare: modest performer: won seller at Southwell in January: seems to stay 13f: acts on all-weather, good to firm and good to soft ground: tried in cheekpieces: races prominently: untrustworthy. *P. W. Hiatt*

TIEPIE 2 ch.c. (May 9) Tomba 119 – Contrary Mary 85 (Mujadil (USA) 119) [2007 6m – p5g Sep 29] lengthy colt: last in maidens. *J. Akehurst*

TIFERNATI 3 b.g. Dansili 127 – Pain Perdu (IRE) (Waajib 121) [2007 66p: p6g* 7.1d⁵ **89** 7s⁵ 8m⁵ 8d 10d⁴ 11.5s⁴ 10m⁴ 12m* 12g* 12f³ Sep 5] good-topped gelding: fairly useful performer: won maiden at Kempton in March and handicaps at Newmarket and Newbury (lady amateurs, by 5 lengths) in August: stays 1½m: acts on polytrack, firm and soft going: tried blinkered/in cheekpieces. *W. J. Haggas*

TIGER DREAM 2 b.c. (May 4) Oasis Dream 129 – Grey Way (USA) 109 (Cozzene **92** (USA)) [2007 8m² 7s² 7g² Oct 26] €195,000Y, 150,000 2-y-o: leggy, angular colt: has round action: fourth foal: half-brother to 5-y-o Distant Way: dam Italian 1¼m to 11f winner: fairly useful maiden: runner-up all starts, at Doncaster on first (behind Kandahar Run) and third (beaten neck by Speedy Dollar): not sure to stay beyond 1m. *K. A. Ryan*

TIGER KING (GER) 6 b.g. Tiger Hill (IRE) 127 – Tennessee Girl (GER) (Big Shuffle 67 (USA) 122) [2007 –: 9.1g⁶ 9.1g 11.1s² Sep 24] fair handicapper: likely to stay 1½m: acts on soft and good to firm ground: fair winning hurdler. *P. Monteith*

TIGER SPICE 2 b.f. (Mar 20) Royal Applause 124 – Up And About 77 (Barathea 68 (IRE) 127) [2007 6m⁵ 7g³ p7.1g⁴ p8.6g⁴ p8.6d³ p9.5g* Dec 15] 55,000Y: rather leggy, lengthy filly: fifth foal: half-sister to useful 1m (at 2 yrs)/9f (in UAE) winner Tamarillo (by Daylami): dam, 15f winner, out of very smart 1¼m/1½m winner Upend: fair performer: in frame 4 times, including in nursery, prior to winning claimer at Wolverhampton (blinkered): stays 9.5f: acts on polytrack. *W. J. Haggas*

TIGER'S ROCKET (IRE) 2 b.c. (Apr 3) Monashee Mountain (USA) 115 – Brown 65 Foam (Horage 124) [2007 5d 6g 7g 6m p6g⁶ p7g³ 8d p8g⁴ p8.6g⁵ p8g⁵ p7.1d* Dec 27] fair performer: won nursery at Wolverhampton in December: stays 1m: acts on polytrack and good to soft going. *R. Hannon*

TIGER TIGER (FR) 6 b.g. Tiger Hill (IRE) 127 – Adorable Emilie (FR) (Iron Duke 89 (FR) 122) [2007 100: p10g⁶ p10g 10.4g May 16] close-coupled gelding: just fairly useful handicapper in 2007: stays easy 1½m: acts on polytrack, heavy and good to firm ground: usually held up: none too consistent: sold 1,500 gns in November. *Jamie Poulton*

TIGER TRAIL (GER) 3 b.g. Tagula (IRE) 116 – Tweed Mill 88 (Selkirk (USA) 129) 54 [2007 7d p7g Sep 5] strong gelding: better effort in maidens when 7 lengths seventh of 11 to Gilded Youth at Kempton second start. *Mrs N. Smith*

TIGGERS TOUCH 5 b.m. Fraam 114 – Beacon Silver 75 (Belmez (USA) 131) [2007 – p10g f12g Mar 22] neat mare: little form since 2004. *A. W. Carroll*

TIGHNABRUAICH (IRE) 2 b.c. (Mar 24) Rainbow Quest (USA) 134 – Miss 80 p Mistletoes (IRE) 89 (The Minstrel (CAN) 135) [2007 8d⁶ 8g² Nov 9] 80,000Y: rangy colt: half-brother to several winners, including smart 7f (at 2 yrs) to 1¼m winner Hataab (by Woodman) and useful 7f (at 2 yrs) to 9.5f (in US) winner Governor Brown (by Kingmambo): dam, Irish 7f and 9f winner, out of useful sister to Le Moss and Levmoss: fairly useful form: promise in maidens at York and Musselburgh (second to Endless Luck): will be suited by 1¼m/1½m: should make a better 3-y-o. *M. A. Jarvis*

TIKINHEART (IRE) 2 ch.g. (Mar 29) Intikhab (USA) 135 – Inourhearts (IRE) 111 67 (Pips Pride 117) [2007 5m⁶ 5g⁶ 6v 5m 6g 6s 7m 5f³ Sep 17] smallish, sturdy gelding: fair maiden: best effort when sixth to New Jersey in minor event at York second start: third in nursery at Redcar final one (gelded after): should prove best at 5f: acts on firm going. *T. D. Easterby*

TILAPIA (IRE) 3 ch.g. Daggers Drawn (USA) 114 – Mrs Fisher (IRE) 94 (Salmon 93 Leap (USA) 131) [2007 64p: p8g* p7.1g f8g* f8g* p8g³ Jun 6] fairly useful performer: much improved in 2007, winning handicaps at Lingfield in January and Southwell (2) in May: ran well final outing: gelded after: stays 1m: raced only on all-weather: has carried head awkwardly, and tends to hang right. *Sir Mark Prescott*

TILEN (IRE) 4 ch.g. Bluebird (USA) 125 – New Sensitive (Wattlefield 117) [2007 50d: – f8g p9.5g p8.6g f12g Mar 22] strong gelding: modest performer at best: little form since early-2006: often blinkered/visored. *S. Parr*

TILLY ANN (IRE) 2 b.f. (Mar 29) Turtle Island (IRE) 123 – Buckland Filleigh (IRE) – (Buckskin (FR) 133) [2007 p6s Dec 21] sixth foal: dam hurdles winner: 40/1, well held in maiden at Wolverhampton. *Peter Grayson*

TILLY'S DREAM 4 ch.f. Arkadian Hero (USA) 123 – Dunloe (IRE) 54 (Shaadi 82 (USA) 126) [2007 75: f6g 5.2g⁵ 6s³ 5s³ 5d* 5g⁴ 5g 5.4v⁶ 5d⁴ 6d p6g⁶ p6g* p6d Dec 10] big, strong filly: fairly useful handicapper: won at Musselburgh (final start for P. McEntee) in June and (having left Miss K. Boutflower after eighth start) Wolverhampton in November: best at 5f/6f: acts on all-weather, soft and good to firm ground. *G. C. Bravery*

TILLY SHILLING (IRE) 3 b.f. Montjeu (IRE) 137 – Antiguan Jane 71 (Shirley 52 Heights 130) [2007 10f⁵ 10f⁵ 11.7d Aug 19] €180,000Y: well-made filly: half-sister to winner in USA by Crafty Prospector: dam, maiden (stayed 1¼m), sister to useful performer up to 1¾m (also US Grade 3 11f winner) Party Season: not unduly knocked about in maidens at Windsor and Bath: will stay at least 1½m. *C. R. Egerton*

TILSWORTH CHARLIE 4 bl.f. Dansili 127 – Glossary (Reference Point 139) 64 [2007 54: 6.1m⁶ 6m³ 5m 7d³ 7f⁶ 6d⁵ 7d² 7.1m³ 7g² 6d 7d p7g⁴ p7g p7m⁴ p8m⁶ p6g²

Dec 12] modest handicapper: stays 1m: acts on polytrack, firm and good to soft ground: wears headgear: has shown signs of temperament. *J. R. Jenkins*

TILT 5 b.g. Daylami (IRE) 138 – Tromond 94 (Lomond (USA) 128) [2007 95: 12g⁴ 12.1g³ 12g 13.1m³ 16.1v³ 16d 14g³ 14g⁴ 13s⁴ Sep 24] useful-looking gelding: useful handicapper: in frame 7 of 9 starts in 2007: effective at 1½m to 2m: acts on polytrack, heavy and good to firm going: held up: signs of temperament final 2 starts. *B. Ellison* **95**

TILTILI (IRE) 4 ch.f. Spectrum (IRE) 126 – Alexander Confranc (IRE) 73 (Magical Wonder (USA) 125) [2007 51: 12m⁴ 13.8m² 12s⁵ Jul 18] strong filly: modest maiden: seems to stay 2m: acts on good to firm going: blinkered final start. *P. C. Haslam* **50**

TIMARWA (IRE) 3 b.f. Daylami (IRE) 138 – Timarida (IRE) 125 (Kalaglow 132) [2007 79p: 10g⁸ 10s⁴ 12v⁴ 9d 9g⁴ 9.5g* 11s⁶ Oct 27] lengthy, useful-looking filly: fifth foal: half-sister to useful Irish 1m to 1½m winner Timawari (by Sadler's Wells): dam, Irish 7f to 1¼m (including Irish Champion Stakes) winner, successful in 5 countries: useful performer: won maiden at the Curragh in May and Denny Cordell & Lanwades Stud Fillies Stakes at Gowran (beat Many Colours by ½ length, settling better and asserting close home) in October: also ran well when 8½ lengths fourth to Peeping Fawn in Irish Oaks at the Curragh and 5¾ lengths sixth to Lahudood in Breeders' Cup Filly & Mare Turf at Monmouth on third/final outings: effective at 9.5f to 1½m: acted on heavy going: refused to enter stall on intended reappearance: reportedly amiss fourth start: stud. *John M. Oxx, Ireland* **108**

TIMBALIER (USA) 2 ch.c. (May 8) Dixieland Band (USA) – Gabacha (USA) (Woodman (USA) 126) [2007 p8g⁶ p8.6g⁵ Nov 10] modest form in maidens, held up both times: stays 8.6f. *D. M. Simcock* **62**

TIMBER CREEK 2 b.g. (Apr 10) Tobougg (IRE) 125 – Proserpine 95 (Robellino (USA) 127) [2007 6.5d 8.2d Oct 18] good-topped gelding: well held in maidens: bred to stay 1¼m/1½m: gelded after final start. *H. Candy* **–**

TIMBER TREASURE (USA) 3 b. or br.g. Forest Wildcat (USA) 120 – Lady Ilsley (USA) (Trempolino (USA) 135) [2007 65p: 7m 7.1m⁵ 8g² 10m³ 8.2m⁵ Oct 3] sturdy, close-coupled gelding: fair maiden: stays 1¼m: raced only on good/good to firm going: visored last 3 starts: difficult ride (veered right once held final start): sold 16,000 gns later in October, and gelded. *H. R. A. Cecil* **73 §**

TIME CONTROL 2 b.f. (Apr 23) Sadler's Wells (USA) 132 – Time Away (IRE) 114 (Darshaan 133) [2007 7g Jul 20] 1,200,000Y: well-made, attractive filly: third foal: sister to smart 9.7f to 1½m winner Time On: dam, 1m (at 2 yrs)/10.4f (Musidora Stakes) winner, granddaughter of Time Charter: 10/1, no threat (dropped out/ran green) in maiden at Newmarket: will be suited by 1¼m/1½m: bound to improve. *L. M. Cumani* **57 p**

TIME FOR CHANGE (IRE) 3 ch.g. Elnadim (USA) 128 – Dance Lesson 47 (In The Wings 128) [2007 50: p7g⁵ p7.1g² f7g* f8g² p7.1g p8g 11.6f p10g p10g p7g⁶ p8g p8m p6g p10g f7d⁴ f8d⁶ p7.1g Dec 26] leggy gelding: modest performer: won handicap at Southwell in April: left B. Hills after sixth start: stays 1m: acts on all-weather: tried in headgear: signs of temperament. *P. G. Murphy* **63 d**

TIME FOR YOU 5 b.m. Vettori (IRE) 119 – La Fija (USA) 49 (Dixieland Band (USA)) [2007 –: p10g Jan 3] workmanlike mare: one-time modest performer: lightly raced and no form in 2006/7: tried in blinkers/cheekpieces. *J. M. Bradley* **–**

TIME MARCHES ON 9 b.g. Timeless Times (USA) 99 – Tees Gazette Girl 42 (Kalaglow 132) [2007 45: 7m 8d 16m 16.1m⁶ 14.1m³ 12s⁴ Jul 18] leggy gelding: poor performer: stays 2m: acts on firm and soft going: tried tongue tied. *K. G. Reveley* **45**

TIME OVER 3 ch.f. Mark of Esteem (IRE) 137 – Not Before Time (IRE) (Polish Precedent (USA) 131) [2007 8g³ 8.2g* 10g Aug 15] has a quick action: closely related to smart 1m/1¼m winner Time Away (by Darshaan) and half-sister to several winners, notably smart 1¼m winner Time Ahead (by Spectrum): dam unraced daughter of top-class 1¼m/1½m performer Time Charter: fair form: third at Newmarket on debut prior to landing odds in maiden at Nottingham in August: ran as if amiss in handicap at Sandown final start: should be suited by 1¼m: raced only on good ground. *J. L. Dunlop* **76**

TIME SHARE (IRE) 3 b.f. Danetime (IRE) 121 – Clochette (IRE) 83 (Namaqualand (USA)) [2007 p6g⁴ p5g² p5g³ p6g 6m⁴ 5.7d p6g⁴ p6g* 5m⁵ 5d 6m⁵ 6s⁴ p6g⁶ p5g p5.1g⁶ p5g² p6m⁵ p6g p6g⁶ Dec 19] €3,000Y, resold €17,000Y: first foal: dam, Irish sprint maiden, half-sister to smart Irish sprinter Capricciosa: modest performer: won claimer at Wolverhampton (left J. Osborne £5,000) in June: left J. Ryan after twelfth start and Miss **63**

K. Boutflower after fourteenth: raced only at 5f/6f: acts on polytrack and good to firm going: tried in cheekpieces/tongue tied, often blinkered. *G. C. Bravery*

TIMETABLE 2 b.c. (Jan 29) Observatory (USA) 131 – Clepsydra 78 (Sadler's Wells **88 p** (USA) 132) [2007 7g² Aug 17] fourth foal: half-brother to 3-y-o Passage of Time and useful 1¼m winner Sandglass (by Zafonic): dam, 1½m winner, out of half-sister to very smart 1m to 1½m filly All At Sea: 3/1, promising neck second to Redesignation in maiden at Newmarket, going smoothly: will stay at least 1¼m: sure to progress and win races. *H. R. A. Cecil*

TIME TO REGRET 7 b.g. Presidium 124 – Scoffera 63 (Scottish Reel 123) [2007 60: **66** p8g* p8g* p8.6g* f8g³ p8g p8.6g 8m 8m⁵ 7s 8g 8s⁵ 7.5g⁶ 8.5g p7g⁵ 8m⁴ p8.6g* p8.6g* p8g⁴ p8.6g p8.6g f8d⁶ Dec 12] tall gelding: fair performer: won minor events at Kempton (2) in January and handicaps at Wolverhampton later in January, October and November: stays 9.3f: acts on all-weather and any turf going: tends to hang: usually races up with pace: wears cheekpieces nowadays. *I. W. McInnes*

TIME UPON TIME 3 b.f. Groom Dancer (USA) 128 – Watchkeeper (IRE) 86 (Rudi- **–** mentary (USA) 118) [2007 –: 10d 10d p12g Jun 21] compact filly: little form: signs of temperament (refused to enter stall intended debut): sold 1,000 gns, sent to Greece. *W. J. Knight*

TIMEWATCH 2 b.c. (Mar 12) Fantastic Light (USA) 134 – Maybe Forever 109 **63** (Zafonic (USA) 130) [2007 5m⁵ 5m⁴ 6m⁵ 7m 8g Sep 20] medium-sized, workmanlike colt: second foal: dam, French 5f/5.5f winner (including at 2 yrs), sister to useful 7f/1m performer Easy Air and half-sister to 7-y-o Court Masterpiece: modest maiden: best form at 5f/6f: raced only on good/good to firm going: sold 7,000 gns. *M. Johnston*

TIMOCRACY 2 br.c. (Feb 20) Cape Cross (IRE) 129 – Tithcar 67 (Cadeaux Genereux **64** 131) [2007 7d Jun 23] medium-sized colt: 8/1 and green, modest form (seventh of 8) in maiden at Newmarket. *M. Johnston*

TINA'S BEST (IRE) 2 b.f. (Apr 16) King's Best (USA) 132 – Phantom Waters 79 **68** (Pharly (FR) 130) [2007 6s⁵ 6m 7g⁵ 5.3f 6m³ 5.7d⁴ 6d p7g⁵ Oct 23] €35,000Y: close-coupled filly: fourth foal: half-sister to fairly useful Irish 9f winner Phantom Lad (by Desert Prince) and 3-y-o Tina's Ridge: dam, 1½m winner, half-sister to dam of winner Tenby: fair maiden: seemingly best effort when close third in minor event at the Curragh: stays easy 7f: acts on polytrack, firm and good to soft going. *R. Hannon*

TINA'S RIDGE (IRE) 3 ch.g. Indian Ridge 123 – Phantom Waters 79 (Pharly (FR) **69** 130) [2007 p7.1g f8g p9.5g⁵ 8.2g 10g 8.1m 8g⁴ 10d 8.3s* 8.3d* 8m 8s p9.5d⁵ Dec 28] unfurnished gelding: fairly useful performer: claimed from E. Alston after seventh start: won seller in July and handicap in August, both at Leicester: left R. Hollinshead prior to final start: stays 9.5f: acts on soft ground: blinkered once, wears cheekpieces nowadays. *Miss J. S. Davis*

TINSY 3 b.f. Groom Dancer (USA) 128 – Arkadia Park (IRE) (Polish Precedent (USA) **–** 131) [2007 7m Sep 11] 2,800Y: lengthy filly: second foal: dam unraced: 14/1 and better for race, last of 11 in maiden at Lingfield. *J. L. Spearing*

TINTED VIEW (USA) 3 ch.f. Distant View (USA) 126 – Gombeen (USA) (Private **–** Account (USA)) [2007 55: 8d 7.6s Aug 18] sturdy filly: modest form at 2 yrs: well held both starts in 2007: should stay 1m. *Mrs H. Sweeting*

TINTORERO 2 b.c. (Feb 7) Kyllachy 129 – Lady Hibernia (Anabaa (USA) 130) [2007 **49 §** 6d 7g p6g⁴ 6m⁵ 5.2m³ 5m⁶ 7s³ 8g³ 6g³ Dec 23] close-coupled colt: poor maiden: left M. Wallace after sixth start: probably stays 1m: acts on polytrack, soft and good to firm going: visored (none too keen) last 2 starts in Britain. *R. J. Smith, Spain*

TINY TIM (IRE) 9 b.g. Brief Truce (USA) 126 – Nonnita 71 (Welsh Saint 126) [2007 **45** 47: p7g p6g⁴ Mar 9] leggy, sparely-made gelding: poor performer: effective at 6f to 1m: acts on all-weather, firm and good to soft going: tried tongue tied: usually blinkered: claimer ridden. *A. M. Balding*

TIOGA GOLD (IRE) 8 b.g. Goldmark (USA) 113 – Coffee Bean (Doulab (USA) 115) **56** [2007 –: f14g* f16g⁵ f12g⁶ f14g³ f14g⁶ Apr 13] leggy gelding: modest performer: won handicap at Southwell (125/1) in January: stays 1¾m: acts on fibresand, very lightly raced on turf in recent years: tried blinkered/tongue tied/in cheekpieces. *L. R. James*

TIPSY LAD 5 b.g. Tipsy Creek (USA) 115 – Perfidy (FR) (Persian Bold 123) [2007 49: **61** f8g² f7g 7m⁵ 7g 8.1s⁵ p7g* 7.6g 8m p8g p8g p7.1g p7g p7g⁴ p7g p8.6g⁴ p7g p8g p7.1g⁶ Nov 22] modest performer: trained by H. Manners first 2 starts in 2007, then returned to former trainer: won handicap at Kempton in July: probably stays 8.6f: acts on all-weather and soft ground: usually in headgear: wears tongue tie: sometimes slowly away. *D. J. S. ffrench Davis*

TIPSY LILLIE 5 ch.m. Tipsy Creek (USA) 115 – Belle de Nuit (IRE) 85 (Statoblest 120) [2007 54: p8g Jan 22] modest performer in 2006: well held sole start at 5 yrs: tried blinkered/visored. *P. S. McEntee* —

TIPSY ME 4 b.f. Selkirk (USA) 129 – Time Saved 89 (Green Desert (USA) 127) [2007 70: p8g⁶ Jan 10] leggy filly: fair maiden: effective at 7f, likely to stay 1¼m: acts on poly-track, best effort on turf on good going: sometimes finds little. *M. L. W. Bell* **68**

TIPSY PRINCE 3 b.g. Tipsy Creek (USA) 115 – Princess of Garda 79 (Komaite (USA)) [2007 75: p6g⁴ p6g⁵ 7m⁶ 7m⁵ 7m⁶ 6s* p7g 7g⁶ p7.1g 6d 6.1d⁶ Oct 15] sturdy gelding: fair handicapper: won at Newbury in July: effective at 6f/7f: acts on polytrack, heavy and good to firm going. *David Pinder* **75**

TIP TOES (IRE) 5 b.m. Bianconi (USA) 123 – Tip Tap Toe (USA) (Pleasant Tap (USA)) [2007 55: p16g p16.5g⁴ p16.5g* p16f p16g⁴ 11.5m⁶ p16.5g² p16g⁵ 16m³ May 22] plain, close-coupled mare: modest handicapper: won selling event at Wolverhampton in February: stays 2m: acts on polytrack and firm ground: has carried head high. *P. Howling* **54**

TIP TOP STYLE 4 b.g. Tipsy Creek (USA) 115 – Eliza Jane (Mistertopogigo (IRE) 118) [2007 62: f8g⁴ f8g Jan 25] modest maiden: best efforts at 1m: acts on fibresand: tongue tied/in cheekpieces last 5 starts. *J. Mackie* **53**

TIRAILLEUR (IRE) 7 b.m. Eagle Eyed (USA) 111 – Tiralle (IRE) 71 (Tirol 127) [2007 48: f14g Jan 25] sturdy mare: poor performer: well held sole 7-y-o start: tried in headgear/tongue tie. *M. J. Gingell* —

TITAN TRIUMPH 3 b.c. Zamindar (USA) 116 – Triple Green 69 (Green Desert (USA) 127) [2007 81: 6s³ p7g³ 7m 7g* 8m³ 8s p7g* p8m³ p6m³ Dec 9] well-made colt: useful handicapper: won at Goodwood in August and Lingfield in November: good placed efforts after: effective at 6f to 1m: acts on polytrack and good to firm ground: tongue tied last 6 outings: travels strongly, and will prove best served by well-run race. *W. J. Knight* **95**

TITFER (IRE) 2 ch.c. (Apr 26) Fath (USA) 116 – Fur Hat (Habitat 134) [2007 5.1d 7d⁵ 5.1g 7m p8g p10g³ p8.6g Nov 9] compact colt: modest maiden on balance: left P. Blockley after debut: third in nursery at Kempton: stays 1¼m: acts on polytrack and good to soft going. *A. W. Carroll* **59**

TITIAN SAGA (IRE) 4 ch.f. Titus Livius (FR) 115 – Nordic Living (IRE) 53 (Nordico (USA)) [2007 59: f5g⁵ p5.1g 5m f6g f6g³ f7g 6m p6g p6g p5g⁵ Oct 29] smallish, sturdy filly: modest performer nowadays: left D. Nicholls after sixth start: stays 6f: acts on all-weather and good to firm ground: tried blinkered/visored/tongue tied: not straightforward. *C. N. Allen* **50**

TITINIUS (IRE) 7 ch.g. Titus Livius (FR) 115 – Maiyria (IRE) 68 (Shernazar 131) [2007 78: 7m 7m 5.9m 8m⁵ 7.9g³ 8m⁴ 8m² 8g 10m⁴ 10g² Nov 7] good-bodied gelding: fair handicapper: stays 1¼m: acts on any turf going: wore cheekpieces final start at 6 yrs. *Micky Hammond* **72**

TITLE DEED (USA) 3 b.g. Belong To Me (USA) – Said Privately (USA) (Private Account (USA)) [2007 p8g⁶ p8g⁴ f8g² p10g p11g³ p10g 11.9g p11g⁵ 14g p10g Nov 17] lengthy gelding: fair maiden: stays 11f: acts on all-weather: tried visored: has flashed tail: races prominently. *A. P. Jarvis* **74**

TITLE ROLE 2 b.g. (Apr 29) Mark of Esteem (IRE) 137 – No Comebacks 70 (Last Tycoon 131) [2007 6s 6m p7g³ p8.6g³ Nov 9] tall gelding: fair maiden: third in nursery at Wolverhampton: gelded after: stays 8.6f: acts on polytrack. *P. F. I. Cole* **74 +**

TITO (IRE) 2 b.c. (Feb 21) Diktat 126 – T G'S Girl 57 (Selkirk (USA) 129) [2007 6d 6m² Oct 22] tall, good-topped colt: fair maiden: better for debut, second to Kashimin at Pontefract (hung right): will prove at least as effective at 5f as 6f. *T. D. Barron* **69**

TITTLE 2 b.f. (Apr 13) Tobougg (IRE) 125 – Poppy's Song 76 (Owington 123) [2007 5d⁴ 5.1d⁴ Oct 10] neat filly: third foal: dam, 5f winner (including at 2 yrs), half-sister to high-class sprinter Kyllachy: fourth in minor event at Beverley and maiden at Nottingham (modest form behind Quiet Elegance): may prove best at 5f/6f. *H. Candy* **63**

TITUS LUMPUS (IRE) 4 b.g. Titus Livius (FR) 115 – Carabosse 52 (Salse (USA) 128) [2007 68: p8g p8g³ p8g p10g p8g 9.7s 7.6f⁵ p10g⁶ Aug 18] just modest handicapper in 2007: stayed 8.3f: raced mostly on polytrack, also acted on firm going: tried in blinkers/cheekpieces: raced prominently: dead. *R. M. Flower* **62**

TITUS WONDER (IRE) 4 ch.f. Titus Livius (FR) 115 – Morcote (IRE) 109 (Magical –
Wonder (USA) 125) [2007 54: p8.6g p8g Feb 4] modest performer at 3 yrs: well held in
2007: tried in cheekpieces. *J. W. Mullins*

TIVERS JEWEL (USA) 3 b. or br.g. Tiznow (USA) 133 – Box of Jewels (USA) (Half –
A Year (USA) 130) [2007 68: p8g Jul 12] very big gelding: fair form in maiden at Newbury on debut at 2 yrs: well held in similar events both starts since (9 months apart): sold
2,000 gns in August. *Mrs A. J. Perrett*

TIVERS SONG (USA) 3 gr.c. Buddha (USA) 122 – Rousing (USA) (Alydar (USA)) **64**
[2007 74: 11m⁶ p13g⁴ 14m 16m p13.9g⁴ Sep 27] close-coupled, workmanlike gelding:
maiden: only modest maiden in 2007: should be suited by 1¼m+: acts on polytrack: tried
tongue tied/in cheekpieces: gelded after final start. *Mrs A. J. Perrett*

TIZA (SAF) 5 b.g. Goldkeeper (USA) – Mamuska (SAF) (Elliodor (FR) 114) [2007 **117**
6.5g 6.5g² 6g³ a6f 6d* 6.5m 6d³ 5g⁶ 6d* 6g Dec 9] ex-South African gelding: smart performer: won twice in 2006, including Group 2 Post Merchants Handicap at Clairwood:
ran at Nad Al Sheba first 4 starts in 2007 before leaving H. Brown: won Prix de
Ris-Orangis at Deauville (by length from Garnica) in July and Prix de Seine-et-Oise at
Maisons-Laffitte (by 3 lengths from Advanced) in November: ran creditably in between
when 2¼ lengths third to Garnica in Prix de Meautry at Deauville and not discredited (trip
on short side) when sixth to Benbaun in Prix de l'Abbaye at Longchamp: below form in
Hong Kong Sprint at Sha Tin final start: suited by further than 5f and stays 1m: acts on
soft going, below form on dirt: effective blinkered or not: has had tongue tied: held up.
A. de Royer Dupre, France

TIZZYDORE (IRE) 3 b.f. Shinko Forest (IRE) – Shannon Dore (IRE) 81 (Turtle **47**
Island (IRE) 123) [2007 –: p8g⁶ p7g f8g f5g 7d 6d 8g 10.2s Jul 26] sturdy filly:
poor maiden: left A. Balding after second start: seems to stay 1m: tried in cheekpieces.
A. G. Newcombe

TIZZY MAY (FR) 7 ch.g. Highest Honor (FR) 124 – Forentia 89 (Formidable (USA) **82**
125) [2007 8m⁴ 10s² 10m² 12.3f⁵ 10.1v⁴ 9.1g* 8.5s² 8.3g⁶ p9.5m 10d⁴ 9m Sep 30]
close-coupled gelding: has a quick action: unraced on Flat in 2005/2006: fairly useful
handicapper nowadays: won at Ayr in July: effective at 9f to 1½m: probably acts on any
turf going: wore cheekpieces last 2 starts: tends to sweat: races prominently nowadays.
B. Ellison

TO ARMS 5 b.g. Mujahid (USA) 125 – Toffee 66 (Midyan (USA) 124) [2007 64: 16.2d² **71**
16s² p16.5g⁶ Dec 3] tall gelding: fair maiden handicapper: stays 2m: acts on soft and good
to firm going: fair winning hurdler. *K. J. Burke*

TOASTED SPECIAL (USA) 2 ch.f. (Feb 24) Johannesburg (USA) 127 – Sajjaya **62**
(USA) 97 (Blushing Groom (FR) 131) [2007 5.7f² 6m p7g p7g Nov 4] $95,000Y, resold
165,000Y: half-sister to several winners, including useful 1997 2-y-o 6f winner Shuhrah
(by Danzig): dam, 1m winner, half-sister to high-class 1m/1¼m performer Lahib: modest
maiden: runner-up at Bath on debut: should stay 7f/1m: acts on firm going, well beaten
on polytrack. *B. J. Meehan*

TOBAGO BAY 2 b.c. (Apr 24) Tobougg (IRE) 125 – Perfect Dream 72 (Emperor Jones –
(USA) 119) [2007 7g 7m⁵ 7f p7g p7g 6d⁶ Oct 1] neat colt: little form: tried visored.
M. R. Channon

TOBAGO REEF 3 b.g. Tobougg (IRE) 125 – Silly Mid-On (Midyan (USA) 124) [2007 **73 d**
75: p7.1g³ p8.6g⁵ p7.1g p7.1g p7.1g³ Dec 3] good-topped gelding: fair performer
at best: stays 7f: acts on polytrack, raced only on good/good to firm going on turf: tried
blinkered, in cheekpieces nowadays: often makes running. *Mrs L. Stubbs*

TOBALLA 2 b.f. (Apr 3) Tobougg (IRE) 125 – Ball Gown 98 (Jalmood (USA) 126) –
[2007 p8g⁶ Dec 19] fifth foal: half-sister to useful 7f winner Leoballero (by Lion Cavern)
and 1¼m winner Singlet (by Singspiel): dam 1m to 1½m winner: 20/1 and tongue tied,
well held in maiden at Kempton, slowly away. *H. J. Collingridge*

TOBARO (GER) 6 gr.g. Acambaro (GER) 118 – Top Girl (GER) (Park Romeo 121) –
[2007 16d Oct 20] 100/1, tailed off in Jockey Club Cup at Newmarket on belated debut.
T. T. Clement

TOBAR SUIL LADY (IRE) 2 b.f. (Apr 7) Statue of Liberty (USA) 115 – Stellarette **73**
(IRE) 73 (Lycius (USA) 124) [2007 5m³ 6f² p6g* 6v⁶ Nov 3] tall, good-topped filly: first
foal: dam, maiden, out of half-sister to US Grade 2 9f winner Dawn of The Condor: fair
form: placed at Ripon and Redcar (second to Maramba) prior to winning maiden at
Wolverhampton in October: will stay 7f: acts on polytrack and firm going, below form on
heavy final start (favourite for nursery): carries head awkwardly. *K. A. Ryan*

TO BE OR NOT TO BE 2 b.f. (Apr 24) Tobougg (IRE) 125 – Lady Mayor (Kris 135) **55 p**
[2007 p7g⁶ Dec 19] second foal: dam unraced sister to smart 1½m performer Little Rock
and half-sister to smart middle-distance stayer Whitewater Affair: 40/1 and green, sixth
to Sweet Hope in maiden at Lingfield: should improve. *W. Jarvis*

TOBERMORY (IRE) 3 b.f. Green Desert (USA) 127 – Kerrera 115 (Diesis 133) **79**
[2007 86: p5g⁵ 5g⁵ May 29] small, compact filly: just fair form in 2 handicaps in 2007:
should prove best at 5f/6f: sold 80,000 gns in July. *M. A. Jarvis*

TOBEROGAN (IRE) 6 b.g. Docksider (USA) 124 – Beltisaal (FR) (Belmez (USA) **56**
131) [2007 63: 5.8f 7s 6d 6s³ 6g³ 6s 6d f6d⁶ Dec 11] modest handicapper: ran 4 times in
Britain in 2007: best at 6f: acts on firm and soft going: said to have sustained injury to
hind leg third outing. *W. A. Murphy, Ireland*

TOBOGGANIST 2 b.c. (Mar 11) Tobougg (IRE) 125 – Seeking Utopia 76 (Wolfhound **74**
(USA) 126) [2007 6d 6g⁵ p7g⁴ 7m 7.1g* 8.3d Oct 15] good-topped colt: has a moderate,
quick action: fair performer: won nursery at Warwick in October: best at short of 1m: sold
35,000 gns. *W. Jarvis*

TOBOGGAN LADY 3 b.f. Tobougg (IRE) 125 – Northbend (Shirley Heights 130) **75**
[2007 –: 10g 9.9g 12m² 12.1s* 12s* 16g² 14.1m 16.1g² 18m⁶ Oct 22] close-coupled
filly: fair handicapper: won at Hamilton and Catterick in July, and Pontefract in October:
effective at 1½m to 2¼m: acts on soft and good to firm ground: tried in cheekpieces: often
races lazily. *Mrs A. Duffield*

TOBOSA 3 b.c. Tobougg (IRE) 125 – Sovereign Abbey (IRE) 68 (Royal Academy **112**
(USA) 130) [2007 107: 7m² 8m 8.1m* 8s⁵ 8m³ 8m* 8m⁴ Oct 6] lengthy, good-bodied,
attractive colt: impresses in appearance: smart performer: won totesport.com Silver Bowl
(Handicap) at Haydock in May by 2½ lengths from Annemasse and 4-runner minor event
at Doncaster (landed odds) in September by 7 lengths from Rock of Veio: unlucky short-
head second to Prime Defender in listed Free Handicap at Newmarket on reappearance:
creditable fourth to Creachadoir in Joel Stakes on same course final outing, edging right:
stays 1m: acts on firm and good to soft ground, well below form both starts on soft:
swishes tail in preliminaries, and has seemed lazy when racing: joined P. F. Yiu in Hong
Kong, where renamed Gem of Chiu Ton. *W. Jarvis*

TOBOUGGORNOTOBOUGG 2 ch.g. (Apr 4) Tobougg (IRE) 125 – Douce Maison **48**
(IRE) 67 (Fools Holme (USA)) [2007 p8.6g p6g⁵ p8.6g f7d⁶ p7.1d Dec 27] poor maiden:
best effort at 6f: raced only on all-weather. *D. Shaw*

TOBOUGG WELCOME (IRE) 3 ch.g. Tobougg (IRE) 125 – Three White Sox 73 **52**
(Most Welcome 131) [2007 –: p7.1g p7g p9.5g 14.1s⁵ 16.2s² 18d 16.2f⁴ p16g Sep 19]
modest maiden handicapper: stays 2¼m: acts on polytrack, firm and soft going: gelded,
then sold 15,000 gns, and joined B. Pollock. *S. C. Williams*

TO BUBBLES 2 b.f. (May 4) Tobougg (IRE) 125 – Effervescent 89 (Efisio 120) [2007 **–**
6.1d Oct 18] 17,000Y: compact filly: second foal: half-sister to fairly useful 2006 2-y-o
5f winner Supreme Speedster (by Superior Premium): dam 6f winner: 50/1 and poorly to
post, last in maiden at Nottingham. *T. D. Barron*

TOCCATA (IRE) 3 b.f. Cape Cross (IRE) 129 – Sopran Marida (IRE) (Darshaan 133) **80**
[2007 74: 10.9d* 10.1g 10s 10.5s Sep 29] leggy, close-coupled filly: fairly useful performer: won maiden at Warwick in May: well held in handicaps after: stays 10.9f: acts on
soft ground: sold 13,000 gns, joined Jim Best. *D. M. Simcock*

*totesport.com Silver Bowl (Handicap), Haydock—the patiently-ridden Tobosa storms clear
under top weight; it's close for second between Annemasse (hooped cap) and Billy Dane*

TODBER 2 b.f. (Feb 11) Cape Cross (IRE) 129 – Dominica 115 (Alhaarth (IRE) 126) **52 p**
[2007 p6g 5.7d Oct 1] first foal: dam 5f winner, including Cornwallis and King's Stand
Stakes: modest form in maidens 3 months apart, not knocked about: should do better.
M. P. Tregoning

TODLEA (IRE) 7 b.g. Desert Prince (IRE) 130 – Imelda (USA) (Manila (USA)) [2007 **75**
77: p7.1g⁶ p7g 8.1m⁴ 8f 9m 8.3m 8g Jul 8] smallish, quite good-topped gelding: has
reportedly had wind operation: fair handicapper: effective at 1m/1¼m: acts on polytrack,
firm and good to soft going: tried blinkered, usually tongue tied. *Jean-Rene Auvray*

TODWICK OWL 3 b.g. Namid 128 – Blinding Mission (IRE) 70 (Marju (IRE) 127) **53**
[2007 63: p8.6g p8.6g⁴ Dec 14] good-topped gelding: modest maiden: not at best in 2007:
should stay 8.6f: acts on polytrack and good to soft going. *J. G. Given*

TOGA PARTY (IRE) 5 b.g. Turtle Island (IRE) 123 – Fun Fashion (IRE) 64 (Polish **–**
Patriot (USA) 128) [2007 10d Jul 3] no form in bumpers/over hurdles: 66/1, well held in
Brighton maiden. *Miss S. West*

TOKYO JO (IRE) 3 b.f. Raise A Grand (IRE) 114 – Wakayi 87 (Persian Bold 123) **52**
[2007 57: p8.6g p7g 8g p7m 7.6s p8g³ 8.3g⁶ 8d p7g p7.1g Nov 22] modest performer: stays 8.3f: acts on polytrack and any turf going: often visored/in cheekpieces.
T. T. Clement

TOLEDO SUN 7 b.g. Zamindar (USA) 116 – Shafir (IRE) 68 (Shaadi (USA) 126) **47**
[2007 f12g⁵ f14g³ Jun 5] compact gelding: unraced in 2005/6: just poor nowadays: stays
easy 14.8f: acts on all-weather, soft and good to firm going: tried visored/blinkered.
S. Curran

TOLL GATE (IRE) 2 ch.f. (Feb 4) Dr Fong (USA) 128 – Knell (IRE) (Unfuwain **–**
(USA) 131) [2007 8g p8.6g⁶ Nov 8] attractive filly: second foal: dam unraced half-sister
to smart 1¼m/1½m performers Aldwych, Dombey and Spout: well held in maidens: once
refused at stall. *R. Charlton*

TOMBALINA 4 ch.f. Tomba 119 – Ashkernazy (IRE) 60 (Salt Dome (USA)) [2007 54: **33**
5g 5m 5v 5d Jul 25] smallish, close-coupled filly: just poor form in 2007. *J. Teague*

TOMBA MAESTRO 2 ch.g. (Apr 6) Tomba 119 – Ashkernazy (IRE) 60 (Salt Dome **– §**
(USA)) [2007 5m 6f 5.2m⁶ Aug 15] stocky gelding: temperamental maiden. *J. L. Spearing*

TOMBAS LEGACY 2 ch.c. (Apr 10) Tomba 119 – Regal Academy (IRE) 66 (Royal **–**
Academy (USA) 130) [2007 5.1g 7d Jul 25] last in sellers. *Mark Gillard*

TOM BELL (IRE) 7 b.g. King's Theatre (IRE) 128 – Nordic Display (IRE) 77 **53**
(Nordico (USA)) [2007 –: 10.2f⁶ Apr 11] leggy gelding: modest handicapper on Flat
(fair hurdler): stayed 17.2f: acted on heavy and good to firm ground: tried visored: dead.
J. G. M. O'Shea

TOMBI (USA) 3 b.g. Johannesburg (USA) 127 – Tune In To The Cat (USA) (Tunerup **98**
(USA)) [2007 90: 6.1m* 5g² 7g⁴ 6g* 6g⁴ Oct 26] rangy gelding: useful performer: won
maiden at Nottingham in May and handicap at Ripon (beat Avertuoso by 2½ lengths) in
August: best at 6f: acts on good to firm going: tried tongue tied. *J. Howard Johnson*

TOMINTOUL FLYER 2 br.c. (Apr 19) Dr Fong (USA) 128 – Miller's Melody 86 **90 p**
(Chief Singer 131) [2007 8m³ 8m* 10d* Oct 19] 34,000Y: good-topped colt: half-brother
to several winners, including 9-y-o Top Dirham and German 1¼m/1½m winner Metaxas
(by Midyan), both useful: dam maiden: fairly useful form: won maiden at Newmarket in
September and minor event at Leicester (overcame steady pace to beat Palmerin by 1¼
lengths) in October: stays 1¼m: has scope, and will go on improving. *H. R. A. Cecil*

TOMMY TOBOUGG 3 ch.g. Tobougg (IRE) 125 – Celebrate (IRE) 77 (Generous **65**
(IRE) 139) [2007 61p: 11.9g 9.2d 7.1g* 8m⁶ 6.9g 8m⁶ p8.6g Nov 5] sturdy gelding: fair
performer: won maiden at Musselburgh in July: effective at 7f, seemingly at 1½m: yet to
race on extremes of going. *I. Semple*

TOMMY TOOGOOD (IRE) 4 b.c. Danehill (USA) 126 – On The Nile (IRE) 103 **93**
(Sadler's Wells (USA) 132) [2007 89: 8m 10d p11g⁴ 10d p10g² Oct 24] strong colt: fairly
useful handicapper: will stay 1½m: acts on polytrack and good to firm going: waited
with: sold 10,000 gns. *B. W. Hills*

TOMMYTUSH (IRE) 2 b.c. (Feb 19) Mujadil (USA) 119 – Zilayah (USA) 79 (Zilzal **58**
(USA) 137) [2007 5f 6m 6g⁴ 5f⁵ p6g 6m p5.1g⁶ p6g³ p6d² f5g⁴ Dec 27] modest maiden:
placed in sellers at Wolverhampton: effective at 5f/6f: acts on polytrack and firm going:
sometimes tongue tied: often races prominently. *E. J. Alston*

TOMORROW'S DANCER 3 b.g. Danehill Dancer (IRE) 117 – Today (IRE) (Royal **55** Academy (USA) 130) [2007 64p: 6g p7.1g⁶ 8m⁴ 8g 5.9m 8.3s⁴ 8.3d⁵ Jul 14] rangy, angular gelding: modest performer: stays 8.3f: acts on soft and good to firm ground: has been slowly away: carries head high: inconsistent. *K. A. Ryan*

TOMORROW'S WORLD (IRE) 2 b.f. (Mar 11) Machiavellian (USA) 123 – **72** Follow That Dream 90 (Darshaan 133) [2007 7g⁵ p8g⁴ 8d⁶ Oct 23] fourth foal: half-sister to 6-y-o Desert Dreamer and German winner by Grand Lodge: dam, 1½m winner, half-sister to high-class 1¼m/1½m winner Storming Home (by Machiavellian): fair maiden: regressed after debut at Newmarket (fifth to Queen Scarlet): should be suited to 1m/1¼m. *Sir Michael Stoute*

TOM PARIS 3 b.g. Bertolini (USA) 125 – Nom Francais 39§ (First Trump 118) [2007 **76** 78: 8m 8.1m 8m⁴ 8m⁶ p7.1g³ 8.3m³ p8g p8.6g⁵ p8g p8.6d³ Dec 6] good-topped gelding: fair handicapper: stays 8.6f: acts on polytrack and firm going: tried blinkered/in cheekpieces: held up. *W. R. Muir*

TOMS LAUGHTER 3 ch.g. Mamalik (USA) 115 – Time Clash 67 (Timeless Times **66** (USA) 99) [2007 p7.1g⁴ f8g⁵ p7g 7s p7.1g² 7g 6.1s* 7m⁵ 7.1s³ 7.6g³ p6g⁶ p6g⁵ Dec 29] fair handicapper: won maiden event at Chepstow (flashed tail) in June: left B. Palling after tenth start: effective at 6f to easy 1m: acts on all-weather, soft and good to firm going: not straightforward. *R. A. Harris*

TOM TOWER (IRE) 3 b.g. Cape Cross (IRE) 129 – La Belle Katherine (USA) (Lyp- **–** hard (USA) 132) [2007 72: 6g⁵ 6d⁶ May 18] tall, good-topped gelding: fair performer at 2 yrs for M. Channon: no form in 2007. *A. C. Whillans*

TONI ALCALA 8 b.g. Ezzoud (IRE) 126 – Etourdie (USA) (Arctic Tern (USA) 126) **56** [2007 53: p13.9g³ p16g 15.8m² 21.6m³ 14m⁶ 16.1d⁴ 15.8g⁶ Jun 1] close-coupled gelding: modest handicapper: effective at 13f to 17f: acts on all-weather and any turf going: usually wears cheekpieces: edgy sort: sometimes held up: none too resolute. *R. F. Fisher*

TONNANTE 3 b.f. Hernando (FR) 127 – Thunder Queen (USA) (Thunder Gulch **82** (USA) 129) [2007 63p: 11.5g³ 11.5m⁵ 12f* 14d³ 14m* p13.9g⁵ Oct 21] good-topped filly: fairly useful handicapper: won at Folkestone and Musselburgh in September: stays 1¾m: acts on firm and good to soft going. *Sir Mark Prescott*

TONY JAMES (IRE) 5 b.h. Xaar 132 – Sunset Ridge (FR) (Green Tune (USA) 125) **104** [2007 p6g p8g p8g⁵ p7f p6g² 6g 6s⁴ 6.1s² 6f⁵ 6g⁶ 7d p6m p6g⁵ p7m Nov 24] tall, leggy, close-coupled horse: has a quick action: smart performer at best for C. Brittain: off 15 months, only useful on return: best efforts in 2007 when second in minor event at Kempton (beaten length by Eisteddfod) and handicap at Chepstow (3 lengths behind Viking Spirit), and when length fourth to Aahayson in handicap at Windsor: effective from 6f to 1m: acts on polytrack, firm and soft going: tried blinkered/tongue tied. *K. O. Cunningham-Brown*

TONY THE TAP 6 b.g. Most Welcome 131 – Laleston 73 (Junius (USA) 124) [2007 **94** 91: p6g⁵ 5m² 5d⁴ 6g 5m⁶ 5.7f⁶ 5.2g³ p5.1g³ p5g⁶ p6g⁵ p5g² p6g* p6g Nov 30] smallish gelding: fairly useful handicapper: won at Wolverhampton in November: stays 7f: acts on polytrack, firm and soft going: effective visored/blinkered or not: held up. *W. R. Muir*

TOO GRAND 2 ch.f. (Mar 28) Zaha (CAN) 106 – Gold Linnet 69 (Nashwan (USA) **58** 135) [2007 5m 5.7s⁵ 5.7m⁵ p7g 8f⁶ p7g⁵ p5g* p5.1g p6g² p6g p7g⁴ p7g Dec 19] modest performer: won nursery at Kempton in October: left A. Balding after ninth start: stays 7f: acts on polytrack, soft and good to firm going: usually visored. *J. J. Bridger*

TOO HOT TO HANDLE (IRE) 2 br.f. (Apr 24) Elnadim (USA) 128 – Tropical **52 p** Zone (Machiavellian (USA) 123) [2007 6d Oct 23] €24,000F: fifth foal: half-sister to French 2003 2-y-o 1m winner Tropical Mark (by Mark of Esteem): dam, unraced half-sister to smart French winner up to 1¼m The Scout, out of Prix Marcel Boussac winner Tropicaro: 33/1, green and not clear run when ninth to Wingbeat in maiden at Yarmouth: capable of better. *J. M. P. Eustace*

TOOLITTLEYOURLATE (USA) 2 b. or br.c. (Feb 16) Harlan's Holiday (USA) **91** 124 – Spirit In The Sky (USA) (Gulch (USA)) [2007 6d⁶ p5m* 5g⁵ Aug 22] $40,000Y: big, lengthy colt: second foal: half-brother to winner in Spain by Stravinsky: dam unraced close relative to useful performer up to 1¼m Gold History: fairly useful form: won minor event at Lingfield in August: much improved when 4 lengths fifth to Captain Gerrard in listed race at York: likely to prove best at 5f/6f: joined S. Seemar in UAE. *K. A. Ryan*

TO PARTY (IRE) 3 ch.f. Elusive Quality (USA) – Magongo 103 (Be My Chief (USA) **45**
122) [2007 76: 7m 6g p7.1g 5d Jul 22] close-coupled filly: just poor maiden in 2007:
should stay 1m: acts on polytrack and good to firm ground. *P. D. Evans*

TOPARUDI 6 b.g. Rudimentary (USA) 118 – Topatori (IRE) 89 (Topanoora 118) [2007 **88**
–: 8.2g 10m 16.1d² 15.8g² 14m* 14.1g³ 14.8d 14d* 14d⁵ 14d* Sep 17] big, good-topped
gelding: fairly useful handicapper: won at Musselburgh in June, Sandown in July and
Musselburgh in September: stays 2m: acts on heavy and good to firm ground: raced freely
sixth/seventh starts. *M. H. Tompkins*

TOPATOO 5 ch.m. Bahamian Bounty 115 – Topatori (IRE) 89 (Topanoora 118) [2007 **109**
108: 9m² 10.4g* 10d⁴ 10m Aug 25] leggy, angular mare: useful performer: easily best
efforts in 2007 when neck second to Echelon in Dahlia Stakes at Newmarket and winning
totepool Middleton Stakes at York (all 4 wins there) in May by neck from Anna Pavlova:
stays 10.4f: acts on soft and good to firm ground: held up: reliable. *M. H. Tompkins*

TOPAZES 2 ch.c. (Feb 27) Cadeaux Genereux 131 – Topkamp 104 (Pennekamp (USA) **–**
130) [2007 6g 6.1m Oct 3] strong colt: in rear in maidens. *M. L. W. Bell*

TOPAZLEO (IRE) 3 ch.g. Peintre Celebre (USA) 137 – Mer Noire (IRE) (Marju **54**
(IRE) 127) [2007 69p: 9g 8s⁶ 10.1m⁶ Aug 8] strong, angular gelding: has a quick action:
regressive maiden, leaving J. Howard Johnson after reappearance. *J. Wade*

TOP BID 3 b.g. Auction House (USA) 120 – Trump Street 77 (First Trump 118) [2007 **84**
84: 6g⁵ 5g 5d⁶ 6s² 6d³ 8g 7d 7g Oct 20] smallish, lengthy gelding: has a quick action:
fairly useful handicapper: likely to prove best at testing 5f/6f: acts on soft and good to
firm ground: tried blinkered: gelded after final start. *T. D. Easterby*

TOP DIRHAM 9 ch.g. Night Shift (USA) – Miller's Melody 86 (Chief Singer 131) **63**
[2007 44d: 8.2s f7g 7m⁴ 7.9g 8s* 8.1v³ 8v⁴ 6.9g⁵ 8.5g⁵ Sep 19] good-topped gelding: just
modest handicapper nowadays: won at Thirsk in July: stays 1m: acts on any turf going:
tried blinkered/tongue tied/in cheekpieces: waited with. *M. W. Easterby*

TOP DRAW (USA) 2 b. or br.f. (Feb 5) Elusive Quality (USA) – Cala (FR) 98 (Desert **67**
Prince (IRE) 130) [2007 7.1g⁴ p7g⁴ Oct 24] first foal: dam, 6f/7f winner, half-sister to
several useful 7f/1m performers: fair form when fourth in maidens at Warwick (behind
Love of Dubai) and Lingfield, fading: may prove best short of 7f. *M. L. W. Bell*

TOPFLIGHTCOOLRACER 3 b.f. Lujain (USA) 119 – Jamarj 113 (Tyrnavos 129) **89**
[2007 f5g⁵ p6g⁴ p8.6g p6g² p5.1g* p6g⁵ 5.1g⁶ 5d p5.1g⁶ p5.1g Nov 19] half-sister to 3
winners, notably useful 5.5f/6f (latter at 2 yrs) winner in Britain/France Madame Top-
flight (by Komaite): dam 5f (at 2 yrs) to 9f winner: fairly useful handicapper: won at
Wolverhampton (wandered and flashing tail) in August and Chester in September: best at
5f: acts on polytrack. *Mrs G. S. Rees*

TOPFLIGHTREBELLION 2 b.f. (Apr 22) Mark of Esteem (IRE) 137 – Jamarj 113 **60 p**
(Tyrnavos 129) [2007 p6g p6s³ Dec 21] 5,500Y: half-sister to several winners, notably
useful 5.5f/6f (latter at 2 yrs) winner in Britain/France Madame Topflight (by Komaite)
and 3-y-o Topflightcoolracer: dam 5f (at 2 yrs) to 9f winner: better effort in maidens at
Wolverhampton when third to Wise Melody: will stay 7f/1m: likely to progress.
Mrs G. S. Rees

TOPFLIGHT WILDBIRD 4 br.f. Diktat 126 – Jamarj 113 (Tyrnavos 129) [2007 67: **69**
p9.5g f12g 9.2g³ 9.2s⁴ 9.2d² 10.1d³ 10.5m³ 12.1d⁴ 12.1g 11.9s⁶ 10.1d Oct 16] big, strong **a59 +**
filly: fair handicapper on turf, modest on all-weather: stays 1¼m, not 1½m: acts on good
to firm and good to soft going: tried blinkered. *Mrs G. S. Rees*

TOP GEAR 5 b.g. Robellino (USA) 127 – Bundle (Cadeaux Genereux 131) [2007 10m **–**
11.6m p10m p8g Nov 7] good-topped gelding: fairly useful maiden winner for
D. Elsworth (reportedly returned with bone chips in a hind leg) in 2005: unraced in 2006,
and well held in 2007, including in blinkers/cheekpieces. *Mrs L. J. Mongan*

TOPIARY TED 5 ch.g. Zafonic (USA) 130 – Lovely Lyca 76 (Night Shift (USA)) **82**
[2007 70§: p8.6g* p10g p8.6g⁴ p8.6g p10g* p10g⁵ Nov 17] useful-looking gelding: fairly
useful handicapper: won at Wolverhampton in January and Lingfield (ladies) in March:
left H. Morrison and off 8 months prior to final start: stays easy 1¼m: acts on polytrack,
good to firm and good to soft ground: tried tongue tied/blinkered: sometimes wanders:
signs of temperament. *Tom Dascombe*

TOP JARO (FR) 4 b.g. Marathon (USA) 116 – Shahmy (USA) (Lear Fan (USA) 130) **77**
[2007 85: f14g p12.2g f12g p8.6g⁴ 8m² 7m f8g⁵ 10.5m 7.9m* 9.3g³ 8.1s⁴ 8m* 8m³ 8.3g
10d³ 8g⁶ Oct 3] sturdy gelding: fair performer: won claimers at Carlisle in June and

Redcar (left Jennie Candlish after) in August: stays 1¼m: acts on all-weather, heavy and good to firm going: sometimes slowly away/races freely: sold 11,000 gns. *D. W. Barker*

TOPJEU (IRE) 4 b.g. Montjeu (IRE) 137 – Arabian Lass (SAF) (Al Mufti (USA) 112) **96** [2007 95: 12m⁵ 13.1m² Jun 23] big, strong, close-coupled gelding: useful performer, lightly raced: good efforts in handicaps both starts in 2007, second to Misty Dancer at Ayr: will stay 1¾m: acts on good to firm ground: sweating (below form) final 3-y-o start: sold 160,000 gns in July, and gelded. *L. M. Cumani*

TOP MAN DAN (IRE) 2 b.g. (Jan 23) Danetime (IRE) 121 – Aphra Benn (IRE) 67 **74** (In The Wings 128) [2007 8d⁵ Oct 13] lengthy gelding: 14/1, fifth to Bright Falcon in maiden at York, soon well placed. *D. Carroll*

TOP MARK 5 b.g. Mark of Esteem (IRE) 137 – Red White And Blue (Zafonic (USA) **87** 130) [2007 83: p8.6g² p8g² p8g* p9.5g² p8g⁵ 8m p10g* p8g² 8.1d² 10g² 10d* Aug 14] **a94** tall, short-backed gelding: fairly useful handicapper: won at Lingfield in January, and apprentice events at Kempton in June and Nottingham in August: effective at 7f to 1¼m: acts on polytrack, good to firm and good to soft ground: tried visored: makes running: game and consistent: sold 40,000 gns, joined Miss Lucinda Russell. *J. R. Boyle*

TOP ROCKER 3 b.g. Rock City 120 – Top Hand 77 (First Trump 118) [2007 11g **56** 11.1m⁵ 12.4m⁶ 11.1f 12s³ 12d⁵ Jul 25] modest maiden: stays 1½m: acts on soft and good to firm ground. *E. W. Tuer*

TOP SEED (IRE) 6 b.g. Cadeaux Genereux 131 – Midnight Heights 104 (Persian **–** Heights 129) [2007 93d: p12g 10.3f p12.2g Jul 10] quite good-topped gelding: smart performer earlier in career: well held in 2007: tried visored/tongue tied: has looked ungenuine. *A. J. Chamberlain*

TOP SPEC (IRE) 6 b.g. Spectrum (IRE) 126 – Pearl Marine (IRE) (Bluebird (USA) **78** 125) [2007 81: p12.2g⁶ p12.2g³ 12m 12m 12f p12.2g Nov 19] small gelding: has a quick action: fair handicapper: stays 1½m: acts on polytrack, firm and soft ground: tried visored (looked unwilling): quirky, usually slowly away. *J. Pearce*

TOP TENOR (IRE) 7 b.g. Sadler's Wells (USA) 132 – Posta Vecchia (USA) (Rain- **52 §** bow Quest (USA) 134) [2007 f14g 12d 16m⁴ 15.8g Sep 22] strong, compact gelding: unraced on Flat in 2005/2006, and only modest nowadays: stays 2m: acts on firm going: tried blinkered/tongue tied: has shown reluctance at stall: hung left throughout third outing: one to treat with caution. *W. Storey*

TOP TICKET (IRE) 2 ch.c. (Apr 27) Alhaarth (IRE) 126 – Tathkara (USA) (Alydar **86** (USA)) [2007 8g³ 8.3g³ Oct 16] €52,000F, 36,000 2-y-o: compact colt: fifth foal: half-brother to 4-y-o Tumbleweed Glory: dam unraced sister to US Grade 1 9f winner Tali-num: fairly useful maiden: third at Yarmouth and Leicester (3 lengths behind Mountain Pride): not sure to stay much beyond 1m. *D. M. Simcock*

TOP TIGER 3 b.g. Mtoto 134 – Topatori (IRE) 89 (Topanoora 118) [2007 76p: 10.1s⁵ **81** 10g³ p12m* 12d p13g⁵ Nov 4] small, angular gelding: fairly useful performer: won maiden at Kempton in October: well held in handicaps after, pulling too hard final outing: gelded after: stays 1½m: acts on polytrack and soft going. *M. H. Tompkins*

TOP TREES 9 b.g. Charnwood Forest (IRE) 125 – Low Line 66 (High Line 125) [2007 **59 §** 61§, a–§: 17.2m⁶ 17.2f 14.1d⁵ 16m⁴ 16m³ Sep 16] modest handicapper: stays 16.5f: acts on any going: sometimes slowly away/reluctant to race: untrustworthy. *W. S. Kittow*

TOP VISION 2 ch.f. (Feb 22) Medicean 128 – Perfect Partner (Be My Chief (USA) **72 +** 122) [2007 6m 7g⁵ 7m Aug 17] 30,000F: big, strong, useful-looking filly: has plenty of scope: has a moderate, quick action: third foal: half-sister to 6f seller winner Molly Dancer (by Emarati): dam unraced half-sister to one-time smart 8-y-o Funfair Wane: fair form in maidens, fifth to Celtic Slipper at Goodwood: will stay 1m. *M. R. Channon*

TOPWELL 6 b.g. Most Welcome 131 – Miss Top Ville (FR) (Top Ville 129) [2007 12g **–** Nov 6] workmanlike gelding: bumper winner/modest maiden hurdler: 13/2, well held in maiden at Catterick on Flat debut. *R. C. Guest*

TORA WARNING 3 b.g. Warningford 119 – Torrecilla 68 (General Monash (USA) **–** 107) [2007 –: f7g 6s p8.6g Jul 10] lengthy gelding: little form, including in sellers: gelded after final start. *John A. Harris*

TORBA (IRE) 3 b.f. Daylami (IRE) 138 – Beeper The Great (USA) (Whadjathink **74** (USA)) [2007 10.2m³ 10.2g 10d² 8.1m⁶ Aug 7] €13,000Y: lengthy filly: sixth foal: half-sister to 3 winners, including useful 1m to 1¼m winner Corran Ard and fairly useful 11f winner Phamedic, both by Imperial Ballet: dam unraced half-sister to Prix Marcel

Boussac winner Tropicaro: fair maiden: will stay 1½m: acts on good to firm and good to soft ground: won juvenile hurdle in October. *Evan Williams*

TORCH OF FREEDOM (IRE) 2 b.g. (Mar 6) Statue of Liberty (USA) 115 – Danse **82 +** Royale (IRE) 112 (Caerleon (USA) 132) [2007 6g⁴ p6g* p7.1g² Nov 12] €16,000F, €47,000Y: big gelding: half-brother to several winners, including 10.5f to 1½m winner Mobasher (by Spectrum) and 1½m/1¾m winner Twickenham (by Woodman), both useful in Ireland: dam, Irish 7f to 1¼m winner, half-sister to Salsabil and Marju: fairly useful form: won maiden at Kempton in November: odds on, upset in/slow from stall and pulled hard when second in minor event at Wolverhampton: will be suited by 1m+. *Sir Mark Prescott*

TORNADODANCER (IRE) 4 b.g. Princely Heir (IRE) 111 – Purty Dancer (IRE) 71 **67** (Foxhound (USA) 103) [2007 67: 5s 5g 5.8f⁵ 5g⁴ 5d² 5v 5s 7g 5m p5g 6s Oct 22] fair maiden handicapper: best form at 5f/6f: acts on polytrack, firm and soft ground: often up with pace. *T. G. McCourt, Ireland*

TORQUEMADA (IRE) 6 ch.g. Desert Sun 120 – Gaelic's Fantasy (IRE) (Statoblest **77 §** 120) [2007 73: p7g³ p7g 7m³ 7m 7m* 7g 7d p8g² p8g p8m Dec 10] compact gelding: fair handicapper: left W. Jarvis, won at Leicester (for third time in 4 years) in September: stays 1m: acts on polytrack and good to firm going: tried in cheekpieces: races freely: temperamental. *J. Akehurst*

TORRENS (IRE) 5 b.g. Royal Anthem (USA) 135 – Azure Lake (USA) (Lac Ouimet **87** (USA)) [2007 88: p9.5g⁶ f11g⁴ f11g⁵ 9.9m³ 10m* 9.7m² 10m⁶ 10.3f* 10.1v 10.3d⁶ 12s⁶ 10m³ 12g 12f⁴ 9.2g⁵ p12g² 12g⁵ p12.2g² Oct 27] good-bodied gelding: fairly useful handicapper: won at Pontefract (apprentices) in April and Chester in June: left R. Fahey after seventeenth outing: stays 1½m: acts on polytrack, firm and soft ground: tried tongue tied: often held up. *J. Hetherton*

TORRENT 12 ch.g. Prince Sabo 123 – Maiden Pool 85 (Sharpen Up 127) [2007 36§: **42 §** p5.1g⁶ Jan 15] strong, lengthy gelding: poor performer: best at 5f/6f: acts on all-weather and any turf going: wears headgear: tried tongue tied: has bled, and reportedly can't be subjected to strong pressure: carries head high: unreliable. *J. M. Saville*

TORRID KENTAVR (USA) 10 b.g. Trempolino (USA) 135 – Torrid Tango (USA) **72** (Green Dancer (USA) 132) [2007 81: p13.9g⁴ 8d Jul 7] close-coupled gelding: fairly useful handicapper at best: respectable effort at Wolverhampton on reappearance: effective at 1m to 1½m: acts on all-weather and any turf ground: tried blinkered: free-going sort, usually held up: has hung: fair hurdler/fairly useful chaser. *J. J. Lambe, Ireland*

TORTOLA (IRE) 2 ch.c. (Apr 19) Cadeaux Genereux 131 – Suave Dancer **–** (USA) 136) [2007 p7g Nov 17] 33/1, well held in maiden at Lingfield. *M. H. Tompkins*

TORVER 3 br.f. Lake Coniston (IRE) 131 – Billie Blue 63 (Ballad Rock 122) [2007 58: **50** p7.1g⁵ p7g Oct 10] good-topped filly: modest maiden: stays 7f: acts on polytrack and good to firm going: hung right on reappearance. *Dr J. D. Scargill*

TORY BRAE (IRE) 3 b.g. In The Wings 128 – Solar Crystal (IRE) 110 (Alzao (USA) **–** 117) [2007 p10g p12g Mar 17] well beaten in maidens at Lingfield, blinkered in latter. *R. M. Beckett*

TORYT (POL) 8 b.g. Beaconsfield – Torana (POL) (Dixieland (POL)) [2007 p16g **50** May 7] successful 7 times up to 1½m in Poland: barely modest form when mid-field in handicap at Kempton on British debut. *Carl Llewellyn*

TOSHI (USA) 5 b.g. Kingmambo (USA) 125 – Majestic Role (FR) 107 (Theatrical 128) **72** [2007 88, a–: 9.2g 12m* 14m 13f⁵ 10g⁵ Aug 29] close-coupled gelding: fair handicapper: won at Musselburgh in May: stays 1½m: acts on polytrack, firm and good to soft going: tried in cheekpieces/visor: pulled hard third outing: has hinted at temperament. *P. Monteith*

TO SIR WITH LOVE (NZ) 6 b.g. Turbulent Dancer (USA) – Kudos (NZ) (Kreisler) **–** [2007 8.5m f8g May 14] placed once in 15 starts in Hong Kong for Y. Wong: well beaten both starts in Britain: tried visored/blinkered. *J. S. Wainwright*

TOTAL IMPACT 4 ch.g. Pivotal 124 – Rise 'n Shine 67 (Night Shift (USA)) [2007 96: **84** p5g p6g p5g⁴ p5.1g 5.1d p6g p6g Sep 4] close-coupled gelding: has a short, scratchy action: fairly useful handicapper nowadays: has won at 6f, well beaten at 5f: raced on polytrack and mainly good going or firmer on turf: blinkered last 2 starts. *C. A. Cyzer*

TOTALLY FOCUSSED (IRE) 2 gr. or ro.g. (Apr 1) Trans Island 119 – Premier **63** Place (USA) (Out of Place (USA)) [2007 7s 5m⁵ 6m⁵ Aug 9] modest form in maidens: should prove best at 5f/6f: acts on good to firm going: gelded after final start, and sent to France. *S. Dow*

TOTALLY FREE 3 ch.g. Woodborough (USA) 112 – Barefooted Flyer (USA) 67 (Fly **60** So Free (USA) 122) [2007 55: p6g⁴ p6g p6g f7g² p7g 7g³ f5g* 6m⁶ 5.7d f6g* p7.1g⁶ p6g⁴ **a68** 6.1v 5.1s⁵ 7d⁶ Aug 1] good-topped gelding: fair performer: won handicap at Southwell in April and claimer there in May: stays 7f: acts on all-weather and firm going: visored: inconsistent. *M. D. I. Usher*

TOTEM FLOWER (IRE) 2 ch.f. (Feb 6) Indian Ridge 123 – Tree Peony 79 (Wood- **72 p** man (USA) 126) [2007 6d 7m⁶ Sep 2] lengthy, useful-looking filly: has scope: first foal: dam, 7f winner, half-sister to smart performer up to 1¼m Evening World out of half-sister to dam of Peintre Celebre: fair maiden: eye-catching ninth to Albabilia at Ascot on debut: favourite, never moving freely when only sixth at Folkestone: should be suited by 7f/1m: remains open to improvement. *R. Charlton*

TO THE DANCE (IRE) 2 b.c. (Apr 12) Fasliyev (USA) 120 – Jules (IRE) 76 (Dane- – hill (USA) 126) [2007 p6g Sep 5] 7/4, very green when well held in seller at Lingfield: sold 5,000 gns. *E. J. O'Neill*

TO THE MAX (IRE) 3 b.c. Spectrum (IRE) 126 – Pray (IRE) (Priolo (USA) 127) – [2007 93+: 9m 10d⁵ 7.1d 8m⁶ Sep 22] angular colt: fairly useful winner at 2 yrs: tailed off in 2007, leaving R. Hannon after third outing. *Mrs C. A. Dunnett*

TOTOMAN 2 b.c. (Feb 22) Mtoto 134 – Norcroft Lady 85 (Mujtahid (USA) 118) [2007 **67 p** 7m⁵ Aug 9] second foal: dam 2-y-o 6f winner: 6/1, fifth to Flight Plan in maiden at Folkestone, meeting trouble: will stay 1m: open to improvement. *G. G. Margarson*

TOTO SKYLLACHY 2 b.c. (Mar 11) Kyllachy 129 – Little Tramp (Trempolino **78 p** (USA) 135) [2007 6g 5.9g⁴ 7.1s* Jul 5] 14,000F, 19,000Y: sixth foal: half-brother to 3 winners, including 5f winner Red China (by Inchinor): dam unraced out of smart winner up to 1m Chipaya: fair maiden: refused to race on debut, but progressed well after and won maiden at Warwick by 4 lengths from Billion Dollar Kid: will stay 1m: acts on soft going: should do better still. *T. P. Tate*

TOUCANTINI 3 b.f. Inchinor 119 – French Quartet (IRE) (Lycius (USA) 124) [2007 **65** 65: p6g⁴ p7g p7.1g⁵ p6g Nov 14] fair maiden: will stay 1m+: raced only on polytrack. *R. Charlton*

TOUCH OF IVORY (IRE) 4 b.f. Rossini (USA) 118 – Windomen (IRE) (Forest **58** Wind (USA) 111) [2007 69: 14g 8.3m 12m⁶ 13m 9.1s⁴ 10d Sep 20] leggy filly: modest performer: effective at 7.5f to 1¼m: acts on firm and good to soft going, probably on soft: tried blinkered, usually wears cheekpieces: often held up. *P. Monteith*

TOUCH OF PEP (IRE) 2 b.c. (Feb 19) Lando (GER) 128 – Touch of Class (GER) **64 p** (Be My Guest (USA) 126) [2007 8d⁶ Oct 11] 50,000Y: workmanlike colt: seventh foal: brother to very smart French performer up to 1½m Touch of Land and half-brother to winner in Spain by Grape Tree Road: dam German maiden: 40/1 and backward, sixth to Robby Bobby in maiden at Newbury, not knocked about: will be suited by 1¼m/1½m: should progress. *Jamie Poulton*

TOUCH OF STYLE (IRE) 3 b.g. Desert Style (IRE) 121 – No Hard Feelings (IRE) **83** 86 (Alzao (USA) 117) [2007 82: p8g⁵ 7d p7g² p7g p8g* p8g⁶ p8m p10g p9.5g² Dec 15] good-bodied gelding: fairly useful handicapper: won at Kempton in September: stays 9.5f: acts on polytrack and good to firm going: wore cheekpieces final start. *J. R. Boyle*

TOUGH LOVE 8 ch.g. Pursuit of Love 124 – Food of Love 109 (Music Boy 124) **80** [2007 79: 8f³ 7m³ 8m⁴ 7d* 7.1d 7.5s⁶ 7m⁴ 7m 8m⁶ 8m Sep 20] strong, lengthy gelding: fair handicapper: won at Thirsk in June: effective at 7f to 8.5f: acts on firm and soft going: often wears cheekpieces: tried tongue tied: waited with: has looked none too resolute. *T. D. Easterby*

TOUR D'AMOUR (IRE) 4 b.f. Fruits of Love (USA) 127 – Touraneena (Robellino **68** (USA) 127) [2007 74, a59: f8g² p8.6g⁶ f7g⁴ f8g² 8.3g⁴ 10.1m 9.8m 8m² 8f 7m² 7g⁵ 7g⁵ Oct 3] sparely-made filly: fair handicapper: stays 1m: acts on all-weather and any turf going: tried blinkered. *R. Craggs*

TOURIST 2 b.c. (Mar 7) Oasis Dream 129 – West Devon (USA) (Gone West (USA)) **79 p** [2007 7m 7g³ Oct 26] big, well-made, attractive colt: seventh foal: half-brother to several winners, including smart 6f (at 2 yrs) to 8.5f (in US) winner Salcombe (by Elmaamul) and 5-y-o Sparkwell: dam unraced sister to smart 5f performer Western Approach and half-sister to very smart US performer up to 1¼m Tinners Way: shaped well in maidens at Newbury and Doncaster, in latter upset in stall (reared and reportedly lost a shoe) but travelled strongly long way when ½-length third to Naval Review: likely to prove best up to 7f: will make a useful 3-y-o. *B. W. Hills*

TOURNEDOS (IRE) 5 b.g. Rossini (USA) 118 – Don't Care (IRE) 93 (Nordico **104** (USA)) [2007 114: a6f 6g a5f 5m 5.1m⁴ 5g 6g 5g⁶ 5v 5d 5d⁴ 5d* 6d Oct 13] sturdy gelding: good walker: has a quick action: just useful handicapper nowadays: awarded race at the Curragh (short of room final 1f when short-headed by Inourthoughts) in September: best effort otherwise in 2007 when fourth to Caribbean Coral in handicap at Chester fifth start: best at 5f: acts on any turf going: wore cheekpieces (well beaten) once: sometimes sweats: none too consistent. *D. Nicholls*

TOURNEVR (IRE) 2 b.f. (May 1) Danetime (IRE) 121 – Tuft Hill 92 (Grundy 137) **67** [2007 p6g 5g⁴ p5g⁶ Sep 29] €10,000Y, £12,000 2-y-o: leggy filly: sister to 7-y-o Danehill Stroller and half-sister to several winners, including Irish 6f (at 2 yrs)/9f winner Cnoc Rua (by Redback): dam 2-y-o 6f winner: fair maiden: fourth to Sudden Impact at Thirsk, only turf start: should prove best at 5f/6f. *Jane Chapple-Hyam*

TOUS LES DEUX 4 b.g. Efisio 120 – Caerosa 70 (Caerleon (USA) 132) [2007 80: **75** p10g p10g⁶ p10g* p10g⁴ p10f⁶ p10g³ p10g p10g⁵ 10.5g 10m p8.6g³ 8.1s 10.3d⁶ p5g⁴ **a87** p6g³ p7.1g² p6g³ p6g p8.6g p5g⁵ p6g⁴ p6g⁵ p5g⁵ Dec 22] strong gelding: fairly useful handicapper on all-weather, fair on turf: awarded race at Lingfield in January: stays easy 1¼m, but effective at much shorter: acts on polytrack, firm and good to soft going: sometimes slowly away: often held up: tends to race freely. *Peter Grayson*

TOWN AND GOWN 2 br.f. (Apr 12) Oasis Dream 129 – Degree 81 (Warning 136) **72** [2007 6d 6.5d p6g² p6g⁴ p5m³ Nov 24] 75,000Y: useful-looking filly: seventh foal: half-sister to 3 winners by Royal Applause, notably 2003 2-y-o 6f winner Auditorium and 5f (at 2 yrs) to 9f (including in US) winner Mister Cosmi, both smart: dam, 1m winner, sister to useful German sprinter Dark Marble: fair maiden: in frame last 3 starts: should prove best at 5f/6f: acts on polytrack, raced on good to soft going on turf. *J. H. M. Gosden*

TOWN HOUSE 5 gr.m. Paris House 123 – Avondale Girl (IRE) 73 (Case Law 113) **54** [2007 54: p5.1g² p5.1g⁶ p5.1g³ f5g f5g 5m 5.1f 5d 5d Sep 24] close-coupled mare: modest handicapper: best at 5f: acts on all-weather, good to firm and good to soft going: races prominently. *B. P. J. Baugh*

TOWNKAB (IRE) 2 b.g. (May 7) Intikhab (USA) 135 – Town Girl (IRE) 70 (Lamm- **70** tarra (USA) 134) [2007 p7.1g⁶ p7g 7m 7.5g⁴ 8s² 8m* 7m 9m² 10m Oct 3] €18,500Y, resold €36,000Y, 40,000 2-y-o: stocky gelding: fourth foal: half-brother to Irish 1½m winner Love City (by Spectrum): dam twice-raced half-sister to very smart performer up to 1¾m Gamut out of half-sister to dam of Derby winner North Light: fair performer: won nursery at Goodwood (dead heat) in September: gelded after final start: stays 9f: acts on soft and good to firm going. *N. P. Littmoden*

TOWY BOY (IRE) 2 b.c. (Apr 3) King Charlemagne (USA) 120 – Solar Flare (IRE) **65** (Danehill (USA) 126) [2007 5d³ 6f 5.1d⁵ p6g p7g² p8g p7g Nov 30] lengthy colt: fair maiden: runner-up at Lingfield: stays 7f: acts on polytrack, firm and good to soft going. *I. A. Wood*

TOWY GIRL (IRE) 3 b.f. Second Empire (IRE) 124 – Solar Flare (IRE) (Danehill **76 §** (USA) 126) [2007 77: 7s⁶ 8.1m p7g³ p7g³ p7.1g² p6g⁵ p7g² Dec 5] fair maiden: stays 1m: acts on polytrack: said to have bled second outing: ungenuine. *A. W. Carroll*

TOYLSOME 8 ch.h. Cadeaux Genereux 131 – Treasure Trove (USA) 62 (The **124** Minstrel (CAN) 135) [2007 111: 8g* 7g* 6.5g² 8g⁴ 6.5d* 6.5g* 7d* 7d³ Oct 20]

The creation of myths and legends tends to owe as much to accident as design—all that's required to sow the seed is some exaggeration of the facts. Take Toylsome's victory in the Prix de la Foret Casino Barriere de Biarritz at Longchamp, for example. Many, probably most, racing followers in Britain are likely to be labouring under the misapprehension that his starting price was 100/1—or even 112/1 on the pari-mutuel, as one Sunday newspaper reported. The BBC and the *Racing Post* both gave 100/1 as the odds, as did *The Blood-Horse*, *The Thoroughbred Times* and the Breeders' Cup website in the United States. Toylsome's starting price was not 100/1; those odds were the ones returned by bookmakers in Britain, the so-called industry prices. On the pari-mutuel, the only genuine measure of an SP in France, he started at 503/10. A Group 1 winner at 100/1 makes a much better headline and story than one at odds of just over 50/1, the widespread dissemination of the story perpetuating the 100/1 myth. In any event, long-odds winners of Group 1 events are not so rare as the status of the races suggests they ought to be. In the last thirty years there have been three long-odds British classic winners (Mon Fils, Snow Knight and Jet Ski Lady all at 50/1), plus winning rank outsiders in the

Queen Elizabeth II Stakes (Maroof at 66/1), Dewhurst Stakes (Generous at 50/1) and Falmouth Stakes (Rajeem at 50/1). In the same vein, overseas—before Toylsome—there had been two Arc winners (Star Appeal at 119/1 and Gold River at 53/1), a filly successful in the Prix de l'Opera (Kinnaird at 695/10), a Hong Kong Cup winner (Precision at 65/1) and three winners at the Breeders' Cup (Arcangues at 1336/10, Spain at 559/10 and Lashkari at 534/10).

In truth, the consistent Toylsome was in the form of his life. His record before the Foret stood at fifteen wins from thirty-four starts, including the Group 3 Grosser Preis von Berlin as a three-year-old and ten listed events (one a national listed), all at the Foret trip of seven furlongs or at six and a half furlongs. On his most recent appearance he had won the listed German Tote – Europa-Sprint at Cologne by six lengths, a performance, which, in hindsight, was on a par with that of just about any of his rivals at Longchamp, and one which led to his rider suggesting to connections that he should take his chance there. Perhaps German listed form was regarded with suspicion by the French (and by those in Britain judged on his industry odds). Perhaps they were influenced by the fact that Toylsome had acted as a pacemaker for the same owner's Manduro in the Prix Jacques le Marois at Deauville in August. Perhaps, despite the successes of such as eight-year-old My Best Valentine and ten-year-old Alcazar in French Group 1 events over the previous decade, Toylsome was thought to be too old. Whatever the reason, Toylsome duly started at longer odds than all but two of his twelve opponents, one of whom, eight-year-old Welsh Emperor, was at 91/1 despite running Red Evie to a short head in the Hungerford Stakes two outings before. On the industry prices Toylsome was the rank outsider of the party. The favourite on the pari-mutuel was Betfair Cup (Lennox) winner Tariq ahead of Marchand d'Or, first in the Prix Maurice de Gheest and runner-up in the Sprint Cup at Haydock. The winner of the latter race, Red Clubs, was also in the field, as were Lockinge Stakes winner Red Evie and four who had finished second in Group 1 races—Dutch Art, Jeremy, Linngari and Vital Equine. A strong field, in which in all probability the jockeys on the more fancied contenders fell into one or more of the traps that caught out the betting public. The habitual front runner Toylsome was given altogether too much rope for a horse of his ability. After breaking fast from his outside draw, Toylsome was able to get to the rail at the first bend and was allowed a lead of around four lengths. Instead of coming back to his field, Toylsome sailed along in front, galloping with great zest. By the time the jockeys on the other runners realised their mistake—making ground quickly on softish ground is far from easy—Toylsome was in an unassailable position. Welsh Emperor, Marchand d'Or and US Ranger kept on but never looked like catching the leader who passed the post two and half lengths in front of Welsh Emperor; Marchand d'Or was three quarters of a length further back in third.

Toylsome's win was a feather in the cap of his trainer Jens Hirschberger, the former assistant to Andreas Schutz who had taken over as private trainer to the von Ullmann family's Gestut Schlenderhan in a new facility near Cologne at the start of the year. Adlerflug's seven-length victory in the Deutsches Derby was another highlight of his first season. Up to the end of 2006, Toylsome had been trained by

Prix de la Foret Casino Barriere de Biarritz, Longchamp—
Toylsome is allowed to dictate and wins unchallenged from Welsh Emperor and the grey Marchand d'Or

Peter Schiergen. His only attempts in Group 2 races suggested he was unlikely to make a mark in such company as he was soundly beaten in Germany's top sprint, the Goldene Peitsche, at both three and four. After his success in the listed Reimer Sprint-Pokal in June 2006, Toylsome suffered an injury that kept him off the track for a year, but he made up for lost time on his comeback, landing four of his six outings before the Prix de la Foret. After a successful pipeopener in a minor event at Bremen over a mile, he picked up two listed races at Munich (winning them for the second and fourth time respectively) and, as mentioned in passing above, the Europa-Sprint at Cologne. The last-named was a good run, as Toylsome triumphed unchallenged by six lengths from Bahama Mama who had shown useful form in Britain as a juvenile before her transfer to Germany, where she had landed a six-and-a-half-furlong listed event at Hanover decisively and finished third in the Goldene Peitsche before taking on Toylsome. Bahama Mama won another listed race later. On his other starts, Toylsome went down by half a length to Lucky Strike in the Group 3 Silberne Peitsche at Cologne and did a first-class job of pacemaking on behalf of Manduro in the Prix Jacques le Marois, leading to over a furlong out and coming home fourth of six. On his only appearance after the Prix de la Foret, Toylsome did not quite confirm his new-found status but still ran respectably, under a penalty (which he was belatedly given only after the original entries for the race were published) for his Group 1 win, in the Challenge Stakes at Newmarket, losing the lead a furlong out and finishing three and a quarter lengths third of fifteen to Miss Lucifer.

		Young Generation (b 1976)	Balidar
	Cadeaux Genereux		Brig O'Doon
	(ch 1985)	Smarten Up (ch 1975)	Sharpen Up
Toylsome			L'Anguissola
(ch.h. 1999)		The Minstrel (ch 1974)	Northern Dancer
	Treasure Trove (USA)		Fleur
	(ch 1989)	River Jig (b 1984)	Irish River
			Baronova

Toylsome, a heavy-topped horse who won over a mile but was better at shorter distances and acted on soft going, cost 92,000 guineas as a foal at the Newmarket December Sales and 320,000 guineas as a yearling at Newmarket the following October. He was one of the more expensive of his sire Cadeaux Genereux's progeny sold that year—the twenty-two-year-old has had seven Group 1 winners, all of whom gained their major successes at up to a mile, with Bijou d'Inde the only one effective over further. Toylsome's dam Treasure Trove, who raced solely at two when twice second in maiden races over five furlongs, would not have done much better at stud without Toylsome. The tough nine-year-old Zhitomir (by Lion Cavern), successful nine times at up to almost nine furlongs from eighty starts, and Toylsome's three-year-old sister What A Treasure, who won two seven-furlong handicaps at Leicester in the summer, are her two other winners. The next dam River Jig won at nine furlongs as a two-year-old when also placed in the Criterium Femminile. She foaled four winners headed by Dance Parade, successful in the Queen Mary Stakes, the Fred Darling Stakes and the Grade 2 Buena Vista Stakes at Santa Anita. River Jig is a half-sister to the dam of Always Aloof, a stayer in Europe, where his tally included the Prix Gladiateur, but later successful in the Group 1 Underwood Stakes over nine furlongs in Australia. Toylsome has been retired to stand at the Gestut Erftmuhle at a fee of €5,000. *J. Hirschberger, Germany*

TOY TOP (USA) 4 gr. or ro.f. Tactical Cat (USA) 116 – I'll Flutter By (USA) (Concorde's Tune (USA)) [2007 86: 7.1g 6m 5m 5m 5m 5d⁴ 5g 5d³ 5m⁴ 5m² 5g⁶ 5g* 5g* 5m 5m 5s⁴ 5g Oct 3] leggy, angular filly: just fair handicapper nowadays: won at Thirsk (apprentices) and Catterick in August: best at 5f/easy 6f: acts on firm and good to soft going: blinkered nowadays. *M. Dods*   72

TRACE CLIP 9 b.g. Zafonic (USA) 130 – Illusory 81 (Kings Lake (USA) 133) [2007 58: 5.7d Oct 1] neat, quite attractive gelding: just modest in 2006, and well held sole start at 9 yrs: tongue tied earlier in career. *N. I. M. Rossiter*   –

TRACER 3 b.g. Kyllachy 129 – Western Sal 75 (Salse (USA) 128) [2007 72: p6g² p6g⁴ 7s 8.3m 9.9d⁶ 7.5d⁵ 7g 9.1v Nov 3] tall, close-coupled gelding: fair maiden handicapper: left R. Hannon after fifth outing: probably stays 1m: acts on polytrack, probably on good to firm going: tends to hang left. *M. W. Easterby*   69

TRACKATTACK 5 ch.g. Atraf 116 – Verbena (IRE) (Don't Forget Me 127) [2007 –: **54** 12.6m⁴ p12.2d⁵ p12.2g² p9.5s⁶ p12.2g Dec 29] modest performer: stays 1½m: acts on all-weather, good to firm and good to soft going: tried blinkered/in cheekpieces: races up with pace. *M. Appleby*

TRADITIONALIST (IRE) 3 ch.c. Traditionally (USA) 117 – Rouberia (IRE) 64 **58** (Alhaarth (IRE) 126) [2007 75: p8.6g 12.1g⁵ May 30] quite good-topped colt: lightly-raced maiden: only modest in 2007: bred to stay at least 1m: tried tongue tied: edgy sort, tends to sweat. *G. A. Butler*

TRAFALGAR BAY (IRE) 4 b.g. Fruits of Love (USA) 127 – Chatsworth Bay (IRE) **98** (Fairy King (USA)) [2007 100: 6s⁵ 6d² 7g 7s 7g Jul 28] compact gelding: useful handi-capper: ran creditably in 2007 only when length second to Commando Scott at New-market: best at 6f/7f: acts on firm and good to soft going: edgy sort, often early to post. *K. R. Burke*

TRAFALGAR DAY 4 b.g. Mark of Esteem (IRE) 137 – Rosy Sunset (IRE) (Red **79** Sunset 120) [2007 65: 16g* 15d⁴ 14m³ 13.1g² 12.6d* 12.6s³ 12d⁵ Sep 28] tall, attractive gelding: has a quick action: fair handicapper: won at Southwell (hung left) in April and Warwick (amateurs) in June: effective at 12.6f to 2m: acts on soft and good to firm ground: held up: sold 37,000 gns, joined Eric McNamara in Ireland. *W. M. Brisbourne*

TRAFALGAR SQUARE 5 b.g. King's Best (USA) 132 – Pat Or Else 72 (Alzao **97** (USA) 117) [2007 96: 7g* 8m 8m Oct 4] strong, compact gelding: useful handicapper: form in 2007 only when winning at Newmarket in May by head from Fajr: effective at 7f/1m: acts on heavy and good to firm going: sometimes hangs left: held up: gelded after final start. *J. Akehurst*

TRAFFIC GUARD (USA) 3 b.c. More Than Ready (USA) 120 – Street Scene (IRE) **106** (Zafonic (USA) 130) [2007 100: a7f² a8f² a9f⁶ 8m 7m⁴ 8m* 8m² 8d Sep 9] big, strong, lengthy colt: has scope: useful performer: won minor event at Newmarket in July by 1½ lengths from Drumfire: good efforts when in frame otherwise in 2007, second in minor event and UAE 2000 Guineas (beaten 4½ lengths by Asiatic Boy), both at Nad Al Sheba, 4 lengths fourth to Tariq in Jersey Stakes at Royal Ascot (hampered 1f out) and short-head second to Dubai's Touch in listed race at Goodwood: stays 1m (below form in UAE Derby at 9f): acts on dirt and good to firm going: in cheekpieces last 4 starts: has been attended by 2 handlers: often races prominently: tough and genuine. *J. S. Moore*

TRAITOR'S GATE 2 b.g. (Feb 4) Machiavellian (USA) 123 – Wilayif (USA) 75 **–** (Danzig (USA)) [2007 p6m 8.2g 7g Nov 6] deep-girthed gelding: little form in maidens: unseated leaving stall final start: gelded after: should be suited by 1m. *M. Johnston*

TRALANZA (IRE) 3 ch.f. Traditionally (USA) 117 – Alegranza (IRE) 106 (Lake **77** Coniston (IRE) 131) [2007 74: 7m⁵ 7g 10m² 10g⁵ p10.7g⁴ 8.5g⁵ 8f p12g⁴ p10.7g⁶ Dec 5] lengthy filly: fair maiden: mostly creditable efforts in 2007: stays 10.7f (stamina stretch-ed over 1½m at Kempton penultimate start): acts on polytrack, soft and good to firm going: wore cheekpieces final outing. *P. J. Prendergast, Ireland*

TRAMMON VENTRE (IRE) 3 b.f. Mujadil (USA) 119 – Classic Line 71 (Last **57** Tycoon 131) [2007 7m 6.5g⁵ 7f p6m p7.1g Dec 4] €8,000Y: good-topped filly: fifth foal: half-sister to 13f winner Vitelucy (by Vettori): dam 1¾m winner: modest maiden: blink-ered, little impact in handicaps in Britain last 2 starts: best effort at 6.5f on good going. *E. Tyrrell, Ireland*

TRANCE (IRE) 7 ch.g. Bahhare (USA) 122 – Lady of Dreams (IRE) 84 (Prince Rupert **88 §** (FR) 121) [2007 88§: 14g 16m⁴ 16g 16m⁴ 18g³ 15g* 16.1m³ 16g⁴ 14d 18d 14.6g 16g⁶ 14g⁵ Nov 9] strong, lengthy gelding: fairly useful handicapper: won at Ayr in May: stays 2¼m: acts on all-weather, firm and soft going: blinkered (well held) twice at 3 yrs, often wears cheekpieces: usually held up: moody. *T. D. Barron*

TRANOS (USA) 4 b.g. Bahri (USA) 125 – Balancoire (USA) (Diesis 133) [2007 68: **61** 12.4m 12.4m⁶ 10.1m Jun 2] good-topped gelding: just modest maiden handicapper on Flat nowadays: stays easy 1¼m: acts on polytrack and good to firm ground: tried visored. *Micky Hammond*

TRANQUILITY 3 b.f. Barathea (IRE) 127 – Immortelle (Arazi (USA) 135) [2007 –: **43** p7.1g f8g p10g 10m p12g Jun 9] poor maiden: stays 1¼m: acts on polytrack: tongue tied final outing (has reportedly had a breathing problem). *J. Pearce*

TRANQUILIZER 5 b.m. Dr Fong (USA) 128 – Tranquillity 70 (Night Shift (USA)) **81** [2007 –, a83: p13.9g⁵ p12.2g³ 12g 12d⁴ 13.3m³ 10.9d 11.5m* Jul 11] big, good-bodied **a88** mare: fairly useful handicapper: won at Lingfield in July: stays 2m: acts on polytrack, good to firm and good to soft going: tongue tied: consistent: sold 13,000 gns, sent to Saudi Arabia. *D. J. Coakley*

TRANQUIL TIGER 3 ch.c. Selkirk (USA) 129 – Serene View (USA) 105 (Distant **114** View (USA) 126) [2007 72p: 10m² 10m* 10g⁵ 13m* 12g 14d 14.1g* 14m⁴ Oct 4] big, strong colt: smart performer: won maiden in May and listed race in July (beat Wing Express by ¾ length), both at Newmarket, and minor event at Salisbury (beat Munsef by 2 lengths) in September: creditable fourth to Lion Sands in listed event at Newmarket final outing: should stay 2m: acts on good to firm ground: stirred up in preliminaries fifth start. *H. R. A. Cecil*

TRANSCEND 3 ch.g. Beat Hollow 126 – Pleasuring 68 (Good Times (ITY)) [2007 85: **95** 8.2m² 8g³ 7d* 7.1d p8g⁶ 7d² 6d 6g* Oct 25] sturdy colt: useful performer: won maiden at Newmarket in May and handicap at Brighton (beat Tamino readily by 1½ lengths) in October: effective at 6f to 8.2f: acts on polytrack, good to firm and good to soft ground: tried blinkered, in cheekpieces last 3 outings. *J. H. M. Gosden*

TRANSCENDENT (IRE) 2 b.c. (Mar 12) Trans Island 119 – Shannon Dore (IRE) 81 **50** (Turtle Island (IRE) 123) [2007 5g 6s 5m 6m p8.6g⁵ p7.1g Nov 20] good-topped colt: modest maiden: seems to stay 7f: has raced freely. *J. D. Bethell*

TRANSFER 2 b.g. (Mar 16) Trans Island 119 – Sankaty Light (USA) 55 (Summer **83 p** Squall (USA)) [2007 p7m³ p7g⁴ Nov 3] brother to 4-y-o Trans Sonic and half-brother to 7f winner Oceancookie (by Dashing Blade): dam maiden: fairly useful form: in frame in maiden and minor event (went freely, fourth to Storm Force) at Kempton: will stay 1m: should improve further. *A. M. Balding*

TRANSMISSION (IRE) 2 b.g. (Feb 24) Galileo (IRE) 134 – Individual (USA) 83 **75** (Gulch (USA)) [2007 6g⁶ 7d³ 7s² 7s³ 7m⁵ 8m Sep 13] workmanlike gelding: fair maiden: placed 3 times: gelded after final start: should stay 1m: acts on soft going. *B. Smart*

TRANS SIBERIAN 3 b.c. Soviet Star (USA) 128 – Dina Line (USA) 60 (Diesis 133) **81** [2007 10g p8.6g* Jun 25] 60,000Y: tall, good-topped colt: half-brother to fairly useful 2002 2-y-o 6f winner Pinkerton (by Alzao) and 6-y-o Bobby Charles: dam, 1m winner, half-sister to smart US 6f/7f performer Gold Land: better effort in maidens when winning at Wolverhampton in June by 3½ lengths from View From The Top, still green and veering both ways under whip: slowly away/raced freely on debut. *P. F. I. Cole*

TRANS SONIC 4 ch.g. Trans Island 119 – Sankaty Light (USA) 55 (Summer Squall **73** (USA)) [2007 74, a86: 11m 10d² 10g⁶ 10d p8g Dec 4] big, workmanlike gelding: only fair handicapper in 2007: stays 1½m: acts on polytrack and soft going: effective visored or not. *A. P. Jarvis*

TRANSVESTITE (IRE) 5 b.g. Trans Island 119 – Christoph's Girl 50 (Efisio 120) **86** [2007 92: 12g 12g 12g⁵ p10g⁵ 10v⁵ p11g* 11.9f⁵ 10m⁴ 10m p12m Oct 6] quite good-topped gelding: fairly useful handicapper: won at Kempton in July: stays 1½m: acts on polytrack, firm and good to soft going: has been visored (including last 5 starts). *J. W. Hills*

TRAPHALGAR (IRE) 2 br.c. (Mar 30) Cape Cross (IRE) 129 – Conquestadora 98 **92 +** (Hernando (FR) 127) [2007 6m 7d p7m* p8g² a7.5g* Dec 4] good-topped colt: second foal: half-brother to 3-y-o Converti: dam, 13f to 2m winner, half-sister to smart performer up to 1½m Saddler's Quest: fairly useful form: off 3 months, much improved in winter, won maiden and nursery at Lingfield and minor event at Deauville (beat Surething by 1½ lengths): will stay 1¼m: acts on polytrack. *P. F. I. Cole*

TRAPRAIN (IRE) 5 b.g. Mark of Esteem (IRE) 137 – Nassma (IRE) 95 (Sadler's **86** Wells (USA) 132) [2007 14d³ 14.6g Oct 26] good-bodied gelding: fairly useful handicapper: stays 14.6f: acts on good to firm and good to soft going: tried in cheekpieces: has found little: fairly useful hurdler. *D. Carroll*

TRAVELLING BAND (IRE) 9 b.g. Blues Traveller (IRE) 119 – Kind of Cute 52 **44** (Prince Sabo 123) [2007 –: 10v³ 8.1m Aug 7] leggy, quite attractive gelding: lightly raced and just poor nowadays: stays 1¼m: acts on heavy ground: tried in headgear. *J. Mackie*

TRAVELLING FOX 4 b.g. Slip Anchor 136 – Lola Mora (Nearly A Hand 115) [2007 – –: p10g⁴ f14g Apr 13] little form. *Jane Chapple-Hyam*

TRAWLERMAN (IRE) 2 b.c. (May 5) High Chaparral (IRE) 132 – Forest Lair (Hab- – itat 134) [2007 7m Sep 21] €190,000F: workmanlike colt: half-brother to numerous winners, including Irish 1½m winner Muakaad (by Muhtarram) and 1¼m/1½m winner Suhaad (by Unfuwain), both smart: dam Irish 2-y-o 1m winner: 50/1, needed experience in maiden at Newmarket: will benefit from 1¼m/1½m. *M. H. Tompkins*

TREACLE NOIR (IRE) 2 b.f. (Mar 29) Raise A Grand (IRE) 114 – Exponent (USA) **53**
(Exbourne (USA) 125) [2007 5m 6d 5.7s 5.1d p8g⁶ Sep 19] 17,000Y: fifth foal: half-sister
to 3-y-o Drayton and 5-y-o Exponential: dam unraced: modest maiden: barely stays 1m:
best effort on polytrack. *Tom Dascombe*

TREASON TRIAL 6 b.g. Peintre Celebre (USA) 137 – Pampabella (IRE) (High Est- **65**
ate 127) [2007 –: p13.9g⁶ p16.5g³ p12.2g⁵ 14.1g* 14.1m⁴ 14m 15.4g⁴ 16.2d⁵ 14.1s⁴ 14m²
14.1d* 16m⁶ 14d Oct 13] good-bodied gelding: fair handicapper: left W. M. Brisbourne
after third start: won at Nottingham in April and Yarmouth in August: stays 2m: acts on
polytrack, soft and good to firm going: often held up. *Stef Liddiard*

TREASURE HOUSE (IRE) 6 b.g. Grand Lodge (USA) 125 – Royal Wolff (Prince **69**
Tenderfoot (USA) 126) [2007 80: p8g⁵ 8m p8g⁴ p8g⁴ 8m⁵ 7m 8m 8.1m 7.5m⁴ p7g⁴ Sep 4]
well-made gelding: fair handicapper: stays 8.6f: acts on polytrack and firm ground: has
looked none too keen. *M. Blanshard*

TREASURE ISLANDS (IRE) 2 b.f. (Feb 14) Trans Island 119 – Gold Prospector **54**
(IRE) 78 (Spectrum (IRE) 126) [2007 7d p8m⁶ Nov 11] third foal: half-sister to 6f winner
Eden Star (by Soviet Star): dam, Irish maiden, half-sister to useful performer up to 1½m
Gypsy Passion: modest form in maidens. *S. W. Hall*

TREASURE ISLE 3 ch.f. Bahamian Bounty 116 – South Rock 102 (Rock City 120) **51**
[2007 7d 8s⁴ 7g⁴ 12m⁶ p12.2g⁵ p13.9g Oct 8] angular filly: sixth foal: half-sister to 7-y-o
Cold Turkey and Italian winner up to 9.5f Halling Rock (by Halling): dam, 7f/1m winner,
out of half-sister to very smart miler Soviet Line: modest maiden handicapper: seems
effective at 7f to 1½m. *R. A. Fahey*

TREAT 3 b.f. Barathea (IRE) 127 – Cream Tease 99 (Pursuit of Love 124) [2007 108p: **108**
8m⁴ 8g⁶ 10m⁴ 8.1g³ 8d Jul 27] tall filly: useful performer: good 5¼ lengths fourth to
Finsceal Beo in 1000 Guineas at Newmarket on reappearance: below form after in Irish
equivalent and in listed races: stays 1m: acts on good to firm and good to soft ground:
sweating penultimate outing: sometimes finds little. *M. R. Channon*

TREDEGAR 3 ch.c. Inchinor 119 – Ffestiniog (IRE) 96 (Efisio 120) [2007 99p: 8.1g⁵ **88**
7g 8m May 26] strong, good-bodied colt: just fairly useful at best in 2007: will prove best
up to 1m: acts on polytrack and good to firm going: raced too freely/hung left last 2 starts,
on toes and early to post final one. *P. F. I. Cole*

TREES OF GREEN (USA) 3 b.c. Elusive Quality (USA) – Grazia 111 (Sharpo 132) **79**
[2007 7d² 7.1s² 8g⁴ 8m² p7.1g 6g⁶ Oct 19] tall, attractive colt: fair maiden: well below
form last 2 outings: stays 1m: acts on soft and good to firm ground: tried visored: sold
8,500 gns, joined M. Wigham. *Saeed bin Suroor*

TREETOPS HOTEL (IRE) 8 ch.g. Grand Lodge (USA) 125 – Rousinette (Rousil- **71**
lon (USA) 133) [2007 74: p16g⁶ p12g 12m 11.9m⁵ 16m⁵ 11.6m² p12g⁴ 9g* p12g*
p12g⁵ p12.2d³ p12.2d Dec 27] quite attractive gelding: fair performer: won sellers at
Lingfield in June and August and handicap at Kempton in September: left B. Johnson
prior to final start: effective at 9f to easy 2m: acts on polytrack, firm and good to soft
going: tried in headgear/tongue tie: held up: has carried head awkwardly. *R. Hollinshead*

TREMELO POINTE (IRE) 3 b.f. Trempolino (USA) 135 – Kapria (FR) 103 (Simon **73**
du Desert (FR) 116) [2007 f8g* 9.7g⁵ p8g² 8s p8g⁴ Oct 29] €38,000Y: angular filly:
first foal: dam French 1¼m/10.5f winner: fair performer: impressive winner of maiden at
Southwell in March: bred to be suited by 1¼m+: acts on all-weather. *H. Morrison*

TRENCHANT 2 b.g. (Apr 15) Medicean 128 – Tromond 94 (Lomond (USA) 128) **– p**
[2007 8d Oct 30] closely related to 6-y-o Cesare and half-brother to several winners,
including very smart 1m (at 2 yrs) to 1½m winner Nowhere To Exit (by Exit To Nowhere)
and 5-y-o Tilt: dam, 9f winner (stayed 1½m), half-sister to 4-y-o Mont Etoile: 8/1,
immature and behind in maiden at Yarmouth won by First Avenue: subsequently gelded:
will do better. *J. R. Fanshawe*

TRENCHTOWN (IRE) 2 b.c. (Feb 23) King's Best (USA) 132 – Barbuda (Rainbow **94 p**
Quest (USA) 134) [2007 7.1g⁶ 8g² 8.1m* Sep 7] 20,000 2-y-o: well-made colt: second
foal: dam unraced sister to high-class winner (including in US) up to 1½m Fiji and
half-sister to smart 1½m performer Capri: fairly useful form: head second to Dauberval
(pair clear) at Goodwood prior to winning maiden at Chepstow readily by 2 lengths: will
be suited by 1¼m/1½m: should continue progressing. *R. Charlton*

TREPA (USA) 2 ch.g. Hennessy (USA) 122 – Ball Gown (USA) (Silver Hawk (USA) **71**
123) [2007 76p: 7.5m 6g 8m 9.9m Sep 16] sturdy, close-coupled gelding: fair performer:
lightly raced: should be suited by 1m+: sold 800 gns, sent to Spain. *W. Jarvis*

*Princess Royal Willmott Dixon Stakes, Ascot—a game front-running display from Trick Or Treat;
Queen's Best challenges strongly ahead of Samira Gold and Brisk Breeze (No.6)*

TRES BIEN 5 b.g. Bien Bien (USA) 125 – Zielana Gora (Polish Precedent (USA) 131) – [2007 p12.2g p12g p12g p16g Mar 25] little form on Flat or over hurdles: tried visored. *P. R. Webber*

TRES HOMBRES 3 ch.g. Tobougg (IRE) 125 – Duena (Grand Lodge (USA) 125) ? [2007 59d: p9.5g a6g³ a8g³ a8g⁵ a8g³ 8d⁴ a6g³ a6g⁵ a6.8g⁵ 8g a10g⁴ a10g a12g⁵ Dec 2] close-coupled, deep-girthed gelding: modest maiden: sold from Tom Dascombe 4,200 gns after well held (blinkered) on reappearance: stays 1½m: acts on dirt. *D. Persson, Sweden*

TRESOR SECRET (FR) 7 b.g. Green Desert (USA) 127 – Tresor (USA) (Pleasant 66 § Tap (USA)) [2007 –§: p12g² p12g⁴ p12.2g² f14g⁴ p12g² 12m⁴ p12g⁴ p12.2g³ p13.9g³ Jun 1] close-coupled gelding: fair performer: should stay easy 1¾m: acts on polytrack (probably on fibresand), good to firm and good to soft ground: tried blinkered (ran poorly): reportedly resents whip: tail flasher: sold £700 in July. *J. Gallagher*

TREVIAN 6 ch.g. Atraf 116 – Ascend (IRE) (Glint of Gold 128) [2007 61: 8.1m⁶ 8.5m⁶ 64 7m⁵ 8f³ p8.6g⁴ 8g³ p8.6g⁴ 10.1g⁶ p10g* 10.1m 10.2f⁴ 10.2m⁶ p8m p12g p8g⁴ Nov 12] big gelding: modest handicapper: won at Lingfield in August: stays 1¼m: acts on polytrack and firm going. *J. M. Bradley*

TREW STYLE 5 ch.g. Desert King (IRE) 129 – Southern Psychic (USA) (Alwasmi 67 (USA) 115) [2007 89: 12g 16g p13.9g⁴ Nov 27] big, workmanlike gelding: fairly useful handicapper at 4 yrs, fair at best in 2007: stays 15.4f: acts on polytrack, good to firm and good to soft going. *M. H. Tompkins*

TREZENE (USA) 5 b.g. Atticus (USA) 121 – Trevilla (USA) (Lyphard (USA) 132) 96 [2007 15d 15v⁶ 12d* a12g* 12d Aug 21] tall gelding: useful performer: won minor events at Maisons-Laffitte, Compiegne and Saint-Cloud in 2006, and claimers at Chantilly in June and Deauville (beat The Devil by 5 lengths) in July: left D. Smaga in France, last in handicap at York on British debut: stays 15.5f: raced only on all-weather and good ground or softer (acts on soft): has been successful in blinkers: races up with pace: has flashed tail. *G. L. Moore*

TRIANON 2 ch.f. (Mar 28) Nayef (USA) 129 – Trying For Gold (USA) 103 (Northern 79 p Baby (CAN) 127) [2007 8.1s 8d* Oct 27] big, rangy, rather raw-boned filly: half-sister to several winners, including smart 1m (at 2 yrs) to 13f winner Phantom Gold (dam of Oaks runner-up Flight of Fancy) and useful 1¼m winner Fictitious (later successful in US), both by Machiavellian: dam 1½m winner: fair form: better for debut, won maiden at Newbury by head from Nemo Spirit, still green (idled in front): will be suited by 1¼m/ 1½m: sure to improve further. *R. Charlton*

TRIBE 5 b.g. Danehill (USA) 126 – Leo Girl (USA) 100 (Seattle Slew (USA)) [2007 77: 86 18g* 18d 14.8m 16.1m Aug 11] very big gelding: fairly useful handicapper, lightly raced: won at Pontefract in April: twice ran as if amiss after: stays 2¼m: acts on good to firm and good to soft ground. *P. R. Webber*

TRIBUTE (IRE) 6 b.g. Green Desert (USA) 127 – Zooming (IRE) (Indian Ridge 123) 51 [2007 69d: f5g⁶ f6g f7g f8g⁶ p7.1g Mar 27] quite attractive gelding: just modest at best nowadays: best at 5f/6f: acts on firm going, probably on fibresand: tried in headgear: has worn tongue tie: sometimes early to post. *John A. Harris*

TRI CHARA (IRE) 3 ch.c. Grand Slam (USA) 120 – Lamzena (IRE) 92 (Fairy King **69** (USA)) [2007 10.3m⁶ 11.9m 10d 8m² 8m⁵ 8.5d p9.5g² p8.6g³ Nov 5] tall colt: fair maiden: should stay 1¼m: acts on polytrack and good to firm going: ran creditably in cheekpieces final outing. *R. Hollinshead*

TRICKLE (USA) 3 ch.f. Rahy (USA) 115 – Avitrix (USA) (Storm Bird (CAN) 134) **50** [2007 69: 8m 7d p7.1g p8g p7.1g p8g³ Dec 16] neat filly: just modest maiden handicapper in 2007: stays 7f: acts on polytrack: tried tongue tied. *Miss D. Mountain*

TRICK OR TREAT 4 b.f. Lomitas 129 – Trick of Ace (USA) (Clever Trick (USA)) **108** [2007 100: 11.9m* 12g 12m 14g³ 12d³ 14.6m 12s* Oct 13] lengthy filly: useful performer: improved again in 2007, winning listed race at Haydock (by ¾ length from Wannabe Posh) in May and Princess Royal Willmott Dixon Stakes at Ascot (beat Queen's Best by ½ length) in October: also made frame in Lillie Langtry Stakes at Goodwood (third to Hi Calypso) and Yorkshire Oaks at York (third to Peeping Fawn): stays 1¾m: acts on all-weather, firm and soft going: makes running nowadays: genuine and consistent. *J. G. Given*

TRIEL 4 b.c. Tout Ensemble – Winter Greeting (Hello Gorgeous (USA) 128) [2007 **–** p12.2g Feb 23] 50/1, tailed off in maiden at Wolverhampton. *D. Nicholls*

TRIFTI 6 b.g. Vettori (IRE) 119 – Time For Tea (IRE) 73 (Imperial Frontier (USA) 112) **53** [2007 62, a92: p10g⁴ p8g³ p8.6g⁴ p10g⁴ p8g⁶ p8g 8g⁴ 8.1m p16g⁴ 11.5m³ p12g⁶ p12g⁴ **a81** p8g² p8.6g² p10g⁵ Oct 12] medium-sized gelding: fairly useful on all-weather, modest on turf: best at 1m/1¼m: acts on polytrack and good to firm going: tried blinkered: has hung: often held up: sold 16,000 gns, joined Miss Jo Crowley. *C. A. Cyzer*

TRIGGER'S FRIEND 3 b.f. Double Trigger (IRE) 123 – Four-Legged Friend 101 **–** (Aragon 118) [2007 7d p12g Aug 29] smallish, sturdy filly: closely related to Irish 1½m winner Cupla Cairde (by Double Eclipse) and half-sister to several winners: dam, sprinter, half-sister to dam of Goodricke and Pastoral Pursuits: slowly away and well held in maidens at Salisbury and Kempton. *Jamie Poulton*

TRIMLESTOWN (IRE) 4 b.g. Orpen (USA) 116 – Courtier (Saddlers' Hall (IRE) **87** 126) [2007 94: 7s 7g 7d 7m⁵ 7.1d² 7m p7g Oct 14] strong, good-topped gelding: fairly useful handicapper: stays 7f: acts on good to firm and good to soft going: usually races prominently: blinkered (below form) final outing: sold 38,000 gns, joined K. Ryan. *H. Candy*

TRINCULO (IRE) 10 b.g. Anita's Prince 126 – Fandangerina (USA) (Grey Dawn II **75** 132) [2007 95: f6g³ p5.1g p5.1g⁴ f5g⁵ f5g⁶ p5.1g 5.1d 5g 5.1g² 5f⁴ 6s 5.1g 6f 7.1m* p6g 7g⁶ 6d⁶ 5.7g p7.1g p5.1g² f6d* p7.1s p6g Dec 22] good-bodied gelding: has a long, round action: fair handicapper nowadays: left D. Nicholls after reappearance: won at Chepstow in September and Southwell in December: stays 7f: acts on all-weather and any turf going: usually wears cheekpieces/blinkers: often forces pace: sometimes finds little: hung badly left seventeenth start: none too consistent. *R. A. Harris*

TRINITY COLLEGE (USA) 3 ch.c. Giant's Causeway (USA) 132 – City College **109** (USA) (Carson City (USA)) [2007 100: 7m⁶ 8m 10m² 10g 9v⁴ 9v* 10s⁴ 8g Aug 1] big, good-topped colt: has plenty of scope: useful performer: won minor event at Fairyhouse in July by neck from Fleeting Shadow: ran well otherwise in 2007 when 2 lengths second to Fracas in listed race at the Curragh and 2¼ lengths fourth of 6 to same horse in Meld Stakes at Leopardstown third/seventh outings: stays 1¼m: acts on heavy and good to firm going: ran as if amiss (at Royal Ascot) fourth start, acted as pacemaker in Sussex Stakes at Goodwood final outing. *A. P. O'Brien, Ireland*

TRINKILA (USA) 2 b.f. (Mar 29) Cat Thief (USA) 126 – Que Belle (CAN) 120 (Seat- **74** tle Dancer (USA) 119) [2007 6g 8.1f⁴ 8.3m³ p8.6g* Sep 21] $42,000Y, 50,000 2-y-o: tall, leggy filly: fourth foal: closely related to useful 5f (in France at 2 yrs) to 1m (US Grade 3 event) winner Osidy (by Storm Cat): dam, German 1m (including at 2 yrs) to 11f (Preis der Diana) winner, stayed 1½m and later successful in US: fair form: won maiden at Wolverhampton (made all) final start: stays 8.6f: acts on polytrack and good to firm going. *P. F. I. Cole*

TRIPLE BEAT 3 b.g. Beat Hollow 126 – Three More (USA) (Sanglamore (USA) 126) **80** [2007 8m⁵ 9g³ 8v³ a7.5g³ Nov 27] good-bodied gelding, type to carry condition: fifth foal: half-brother to useful 7f (at 2 yrs)/1m (in US) winner Trilogy (by Grand Lodge): dam unraced half-sister to very smart performer up to 1¼m Kefaah: fairly useful maiden: sold from H. Cecil 17,000 gns after second start: creditable third in France both starts for new stable, including in claimer: stays 9f. *H. Hofer, Germany*

TRIPLE SHADOW 3 ch.g. Compton Place 125 – Arctic High 62 (Polar Falcon (USA) **67**
126) [2007 74: 6g³ 5v 6d³ 5d⁶ 5m⁵ 5f⁵ 6f 6g 5m⁴ 7g p6g⁴ p5.1g Dec 3] fair handicapper:
left T. D. Barron after ninth outing: free-going sort, likely to prove best at 5f/6f: acts on
good to firm and good to soft ground: sometimes slowly away. *M. A. Peill*

TRIP THE LIGHT 2 b.g. (Mar 31) Fantastic Light (USA) 134 – Jumaireyah 91 (Fairy **47**
King (USA)) [2007 6s 6f⁵ 7.1g Sep 12] neat gelding: poor form in maidens, reluctant/
unseated to post final start (gelded after): bred to be suited by 1¼m+. *R. A. Fahey*

TRISKAIDEKAPHOBIA 4 b.g. Bertolini (USA) 125 – Seren Teg 80 (Timeless –
Times (USA) 99) [2007 81d: p5g p5.1g⁴ p5.1g⁶ p5g³ p5.1g* f5g³ 5m 5.1m 5.7m p5g **a67**
p5.1g² p5.1g⁵ p5g³ p5.1g p5g p5.1g* p5.1g* Dec 31] small, sturdy gelding: fair handicapper nowadays: won at Wolverhampton in March and December (2): best at 5f: acts on
all-weather and good to firm going: tried visored/blinkered, usually tongue tied: often
forces pace. *Miss J. R. Tooth*

TRITONVILLE LODGE (IRE) 5 b.g. Grand Lodge (USA) 125 – Olean (Sadler's **85**
Wells (USA) 132) [2007 p16g² Jan 20] fairly useful maiden, lightly raced: stays easy
2m: acts on polytrack and good to soft ground: fairly useful hurdler, successful in April.
Miss E. C. Lavelle

TRIVIA (IRE) 3 br.f. Marju (IRE) 127 – Lehua (IRE) (Linamix (FR) 127) [2007 7m **81**
8g³ 7.5m* 8m 8g² p8.6g* 7g Nov 3] €75,000Y: leggy filly: second foal: dam, French
10.5f/11f winner, half-sister to smart French/US performer up to 9f Bouccaneer: fairly
useful performer: won maiden at Beverley in June and handicap at Wolverhampton in
October: stays easy 8.6f: acts on polytrack and good to firm going: reared at start fourth
outing: sold 7,000 gns, joined Ms J. Doyle. *N. A. Callaghan*

TROIALINI 3 b.g. Bertolini (USA) 125 – Troia (IRE) 54 (Last Tycoon 131) [2007 89: **81**
p10g⁵ 11g⁵ 14g⁶ 11.9m 10g p12.2g⁶ 16.1g 11.8g* Oct 16] tall, rather leggy gelding: fairly
useful performer: won claimer at Leicester (joined D. Pipe) in October: seems to stay
1¾m: acts on polytrack, raced mainly on good ground on turf. *S. W. Hall*

TROJAN FLIGHT 6 ch.g. Hector Protector (USA) 124 – Fairywings 85 (Kris 135) **90**
[2007 82: 6m* 6m⁴ 6g² 6m³ 5g⁵ 7m² 6m Sep 13] good-topped gelding: fairly useful
handicapper: won at Thirsk in May: effective at 5f to easy 7f: acts on any going: effective
in cheekpieces: said to have bled final start: held up. *R. A. Fahey*

TROJAN HERO (IRE) 2 b.g. (Mar 13) Royal Applause 124 – Anne Boleyn (Rain- –
bow Quest (USA) 134) [2007 7d 6g Aug 24] no form in maidens. *A. Dickman*

TROMBONE TOM 4 b.g. Superior Premium 122 – Nine To Five 64 (Imp Society **53**
(USA)) [2007 65: p5.1g⁴ 5s 5g 5g³ Aug 29] modest performer nowadays: likely to prove
best at 5f: acts on polytrack, firm and good to soft going. *J. R. Norton*

TROMP 6 ch.g. Zilzal (USA) 137 – Sulitelma (USA) 63 (The Minstrel (CAN) 135) **82**
[2007 80: p12.2g³ p12g* p12g p12g 11.9f p12.2g p12g p16g p13.9g Oct 30] fairly useful
handicapper: won at Kempton in March: below form after: stays 13f: acts on polytrack
and good to soft ground: reportedly had breathing problem third start. *D. J. Coakley*

TROODOS JET 6 b.g. Atraf 116 – Costa Verde 77 (King of Spain 121) [2007 –: 10.1d –
Jul 28] big, good-topped gelding: modest performer at 3 yrs: no form on Flat since.
K. W. Hogg, Isle of Man

TROPICAL STRAIT (IRE) 4 b.g. Intikhab (USA) 135 – Tropical Dance (USA) 93 **95**
(Thorn Dance (USA) 107) [2007 10d⁴ p10g² p12g² p12g* p12.2g* 12m⁴ Nov 10] sturdy
gelding: useful performer: won maiden at Kempton (by 12 lengths) in September and
handicap at Wolverhampton in October: creditable fourth to Malt Or Mash in November
Handicap at Doncaster final start: stays 1½m: acts on polytrack and good to firm ground.
D. W. P. Arbuthnot

TROUBADOUR (IRE) 6 b.g. Danehill (USA) 126 – Taking Liberties (IRE) 57 **105**
(Royal Academy (USA) 130) [2007 8m⁴ 8m 8g 10s p8g* p8g² p10g⁵ Dec 22] big, rangy
gelding: has badly scarred near hip/quarter/knee: smart performer for A. O'Brien in
Ireland at 2/3 yrs: useful since: renamed Stable Mail, won 3 races for C. Fownes in Hong
Kong in 2005/6: back to form when winning handicap on all-weather debut at Lingfield
(by head from Jalil) in October: seems best around 1m: acts on polytrack and firm going,
all wins in Hong Kong on dirt: tried blinkered/visored. *W. Jarvis*

TROUBLE MAKER 6 b.g. Green Desert (USA) 127 – River Abouali (Bluebird –
(USA) 125) [2007 61: p8g May 31] well-made gelding: modest performer: well held only
start at 6 yrs: tried blinkered/visored. *A. M. Balding*

TROUBLE MOUNTAIN (USA) 10 br.g. Mt Livermore (USA) – Trouble Free **75**
(USA) (Nodouble (USA)) [2007 82: 9.1g⁵ 10m 10.1v 10.5v 10.1g⁶ 10.1m⁴ 10d³ 10s³
10g⁴ 10.1d⁴ 10g² Nov 7] small, sparely-made gelding: fair handicapper: best around
1¼m: acts on fibresand and any turf going: tried blinkered: tongue tied: tends to race in
snatches. *M. W. Easterby*

TROYS STEPS 3 b.f. Cloudings (IRE) 112 – Troys Guest (IRE) 66 (Be My Guest –
(USA) 126) [2007 10d 12g p12.2g⁶ Nov 27] strong filly: second foal: sister to Swedish
1m winner Head Above Clouds: dam maiden: little form: said to have had breathing
problem final outing. *E. J. Alston*

TRUCKLE 5 b.g. Vettori (IRE) 119 – Proud Titania (IRE) 103 (Fairy King (USA)) –
[2007 –: f8g⁵ Jan 1] lengthy, angular gelding: lightly raced and no form since 2005.
C. W. Fairhurst

TRUDDER (USA) 2 br.c. (May 2) Zavata (USA) 111 – Blue Talent (USA) (Local –
Talent (USA) 122) [2007 8m 7s Oct 9] stocky colt: behind in maidens (reportedly
finished lame latterly). *P. W. Chapple-Hyam*

TRUE COMPANION 8 b.g. Brief Truce (USA) 126 – Comanche Companion 88 **83**
(Commanche Run 133) [2007 84: 12d³ 11.6m Jun 4] angular gelding: fairly useful handicapper: stays 1½m: acts on polytrack, firm and soft going: usually held up: sometimes
races freely/wanders. *Miss E. C. Lavelle*

TRUE (IRE) 6 ch.m. Barathea (IRE) 127 – Bibliotheque (USA) 79 (Woodman (USA) **51**
126) [2007 55: 15.8m⁵ 21.6m⁵ 15.8m³ 15.8g³ 14.1m² 16d⁵ 18m⁶ 13.8g 15.8g Oct 30]
lengthy mare: modest performer: probably stays 21.6f: acts on fibresand, firm and good
to soft going: tried in cheekpieces: has carried head awkwardly. *Mrs S. Lamyman*

TRUE MAGIC 6 b.m. Magic Ring (IRE) 115 – True Precision 84 (Presidium 124) –
[2007 77: p7g Jan 20] compact mare: fair handicapper in 2006: well below form sole start
at 6 yrs: ran poorly in blinkers: sold 21,000 gns in July (reportedly in foal to Monsieur
Bond). *J. D. Bethell*

TRUE RUBY 4 b.f. Josr Algarhoud (IRE) 118 – St James's Antigua (IRE) 79 (Law –
Society (USA) 130) [2007 –: p12g p12g Nov 16] little form: tried blinkered.
Dr J. R. J. Naylor

TRUE TIME 2 ch.f. (Apr 25) Rahy (USA) 115 – True Fantasy (USA) (Seeking The **64**
Gold (USA)) [2007 6.1g 6.1g Oct 9] compact filly: second foal: dam once-raced
half-sister to Fantastic Light (by Rahy): modest maiden: third in nursery at Catterick: will
stay 1m: sold 21,000 gns. *E. A. L. Dunlop*

TRUE VISION (IRE) 3 b.f. Pulpit (USA) 117 – Mot Juste 115 (Mtoto 134) [2007 –
10.2g Oct 24] first foal: dam, 1m (at 2 yrs)/1¼m winner, half-sister to 1½m
performer Parasol: 4/1, well held in maiden at Bath: has left Godolphin. *Saeed bin Suroor*

TRUE WEST (USA) 4 b.f. Gulch (USA) – True Life (USA) 66 (El Gran Senor (USA) –
136) [2007 64: f8g p12.2g Feb 5] quite good-topped filly: maiden: little form in
2007: tried visored/blinkered: trained by N. King sole start over hurdles: dead. *Miss Gay
Kelleway*

TRULY ENCHANTING (IRE) 3 ch.f. Danehill Dancer (IRE) 117 – Truly Bewit- **90**
ched (USA) 81 (Affirmed (USA)) [2007 8.3m² 8.2g² 7g* 8.2m* 8m⁶ 7m 9d* 8g Nov 18]
€85,000F, €130,000Y: quite attractive filly: third foal: half-sister to 2003 2-y-o 5f winner
Red Trance (by Soviet Star) and useful 1m winner Arabian Spell (by Desert Prince): dam,
2-y-o 6f winner, granddaughter of 1000 Guineas winner Fairy Footsteps: fairly useful
form: won maiden at Goodwood in May, handicap at Nottingham in June and, having left
J. Noseda, allowance optional claimer at Aqueduct in October: stays 9f: acts on good to
firm and good to soft going: hung markedly left on debut. *J. A. Jerkens, USA*

TRULY ROYAL 3 b.c. Noverre (USA) 125 – Her Ladyship 119 (Polish Precedent **102**
(USA) 131) [2007 96P: 7.5g² 8m May 5] well-made colt: useful form in just 3 races: best
effort when neck second to Mount Hadley in minor event at Nad Al Sheba on reappearance: tongue tied, well held in 2000 Guineas at Newmarket next time (sustained ankle
chip and operated on): should stay 1m+. *Saeed bin Suroor*

TRUMP CALL (IRE) 3 b.g. Mull of Kintyre (USA) 114 – Trumped (IRE) 50 (Last **75**
Tycoon 131) [2007 70: p7g 10.5g 8g³ 10g² 9.9d⁵ 10d⁶ 10m⁵ 9.9g³ p12m² Oct 3] leggy
gelding: fair maiden: barely stays easy 1½m: acts on polytrack, probably on good to firm
going: visored fifth start (raced freely): held up: sold 45,000 gns, joined Venetia Williams.
R. M. Beckett

TRUMPET LILY 2 b.f. (Mar 20) Acclamation 118 – Periwinkle (FR) (Perrault 130) **72**
[2007 7s⁶ p7g⁴ 6.5d Oct 11] heavy-bodied filly: half-sister to winners around 1¼m in
France by Turgeon and Distant Relative: dam French maiden (stayed 11f): fair maiden:
encouragement first 2 starts, sixth to Kotsi at Newmarket on debut: will stay 1m.
J. G. Portman

TRUST RULE 7 b.g. Selkirk (USA) 129 – Hagwah (USA) 109 (Dancing Brave (USA) –
140) [2007 p13.9g Mar 10] tall gelding: fairly useful in 2005: well held only start on Flat
since: tried in cheekpieces/tongue tie: joined Miss L. Davis. *M. W. Easterby*

TRY ME (UAE) 2 b. or br.f. (Feb 12) Singspiel (IRE) 133 – Cunas (USA) 86 (Irish **63 p**
River (FR) 131) [2007 7m³ Sep 15] 40,000Y: second foal: dam, 1m winner, out of 1000
Guineas winner Sayyedati, from good family: 16/1, green (hung round bend) when third
to Bellomi in maiden at Chester: will stay at least 1m: likely to improve. *C. E. Brittain*

TRYSTING GROVE (IRE) 6 b.m. Cape Cross (IRE) 129 – Elton Grove (IRE) (Ast- **55**
ronef 116) [2007 50: p12.2g² f14g⁴ f12g⁶ p12.2g* p12g f11g May 8] leggy, unfurnished
mare: modest performer: won minor event at Wolverhampton in March: stays 1½m: acts
on all-weather and good to soft going: none too consistent. *E. G. Bevan*

TSAROXY (IRE) 5 b.g. Xaar 132 – Belsay 68 (Belmez (USA) 131) [2007 81: 10.1s **83**
9.2g* 11.5d 9.2d³ Aug 15] quite good-topped gelding: fairly useful handicapper: won at
Hamilton in May: stays 1¼m: acts on good to firm and good to soft going: blinkered (well
held) once: held up. *J. Howard Johnson*

TUANKU (IRE) 2 b.g. (Mar 4) Tagula (IRE) 116 – Be My Lover (Pursuit of Love 124) **68**
[2007 5.5d⁴ 7d 7m* 8m* 7g⁴ 8.3d Oct 15] leggy gelding: fair performer: won seller at
Newmarket and nursery at Newcastle in August: stays 1m: acts on good to firm going:
edgy sort: sold 23,000 gns. *M. R. Channon*

TUBBY ISAACS 3 b.g. Cyrano de Bergerac 120 – Opuntia (Rousillon (USA) 133) **68 p**
[2007 6m⁶ p6g² p6g* Nov 19] tall gelding: brother to useful 6f (including at 2 yrs)/7f
winner Point of Dispute and half-brother to several winners, including useful 5f/6f (latter
at 2 yrs) winner Boomerang Blade (by Sure Blade) and 6-y-o Pick A Nice Name: dam
unraced: fair form: won maiden at Wolverhampton in November: bred to prove best at 5f/
6f: acts on polytrack: open to further improvement. *P. J. Makin*

TUCKER 5 b.g. Inchinor 119 – Tender Moment (IRE) 78 (Caerleon (USA) 132) [2007 **110 §**
109: 8.5d⁴ 10d 10d² 8m⁴ Oct 14] big, close-coupled gelding: has a round action: smart
performer: good fourth to Unshakable in handicap at Epsom on reappearance: respectable
efforts at best after: stays 1¼m: acts on good to firm and good to soft going (won on soft at
2 yrs): visored (well below form) fourth outing 2006, often wears cheekpieces nowadays:
ungenuine: sold 25,000 gns, joined Micky Hammond. *W. R. Swinburn*

TUCKERMAN 6 b.g. Gulch (USA) – Remuria (USA) 93 (Theatrical 128) [2007 –: –
p9.5g⁵ p8.6g Jan 16] little form since 2005: tried blinkered/tongue tied. *Frederick John
Bowles, Ireland*

TUCKER'S TOWN (IRE) 2 ch.c. (May 15) Kingmambo (USA) 125 – Bermuda Girl –
(USA) (Danzig (USA)) [2007 p7.1g Oct 21] 11/4, apparent problem (tailed off) in maiden
at Wolverhampton: sold 11,000 gns. *Sir Michael Stoute*

TUDOR COURT (IRE) 2 b.f. (May 23) Cape Cross (IRE) 129 – Rise And Fall (Mill **74**
Reef (USA) 141) [2007 6d³ 6m⁶ 6f³ Sep 17] 110,000Y: small, quite attractive filly: half-
sister to several winners, including very smart miler Fly To The Stars (by Bluebird) and
smart 7f (at 2 yrs)/1m winner Fallen Star (by Brief Truce): dam, maiden, out of sister to
outstanding broodmare Highclere: fair form in maidens: placed at Pontefract and Redcar
either side of sixth to Laureldean Gale at Newmarket, not seeing races out thoroughly:
likely to prove best at 5f/6f. *M. Johnston*

TUDOR PRINCE (IRE) 3 b. or br.g. Cape Cross (IRE) 129 – Savona (IRE) 70 **93**
(Cyrano de Bergerac 120) [2007 94: 8m 7d⁵ 6s³ 7.1d⁵ p6m 8s⁶ 6d* Oct 30] well-made
gelding: fairly useful handicapper: left B. Meehan after fifth start: won at Yarmouth in
October: effective at 6f/7f: acts on polytrack, soft and good to firm going: tried blinkered
(well held). *A. W. Carroll*

TUFTON 4 b.g. King's Best (USA) 132 – Mythical Magic (Green Desert (USA) 127) **97 d**
[2007 p7f p10g² 8m⁴ p10g⁴ p10g 8m⁶ 10g² 10m² 10.5s p10m⁴ Oct 13] useful performer:
off nearly 17 months before reappearance: not at best in claimers/seller in second half of
2007 (claimed from M. Botti £8,000 after eighth outing): stays 1¼m: acts on polytrack
and firm going (ran poorly only start on ground softer than good): tongue tied in 2007:
front runner: gelded. *Ian Williams*

TUGALU (IRE) 2 b.c. (May 15) Tagula (IRE) 116 – Merci (IRE) (Cadeaux Genereux 131) [2007 5m⁴ p6g² 6g² 5.4m² 6s⁵ Oct 4] fairly useful maiden: runner-up 3 times: should prove best at 5f/6f: acts on polytrack and good to firm going: irresolute, hangs under pressure. *K. A. Ryan*   **77 §**

TULLYORIOR GLORY (IRE) 3 b.f. Desert Style (IRE) 121 – Cutlers Corner 111 (Sharpen Up 127) [2007 7.5m 5f 7m 6v 7v 5g² 5.1g p5g⁶ Nov 30] sturdy filly: modest maiden: mid-field at Nottingham seventh start: best effort at 5f: acts on firm going: tongue tied last 3 starts. *Emmanuel Hughes, Ireland*   **61**

TULLYTHERED (IRE) 3 ch.g. Docksider (USA) 124 – Marjie (IRE) (Desert Style (IRE) 121) [2007 –: 7m³ 8.1m 10.9d 10.2m p10m⁴ Oct 3] modest maiden: stays easy 1¼m: acts on polytrack and good to firm ground: sold 3,200 gns. *K. R. Burke*   **55**

TUMBELINI 3 b.f. Pivotal 124 – Kundalini (USA) (El Gran Senor 136) [2007 –: 6m⁴ p6g⁴ p7.1g⁶ Sep 3] modest maiden: best effort on reappearance: should stay 7f: acts on good to firm ground, probably on polytrack. *C. F. Wall*   **62**

TUMBLE JILL (IRE) 3 b.f. Dilshaan 119 – Jack-N-Jilly (IRE) 43 (Anita's Prince 126) [2007 50: p8g⁵ p10g⁵ p10g 10.2f 10m³ p11g⁵ 11m p10g⁵ 11.7f⁶ Aug 24] good-bodied filly: modest maiden: stays 1¼m: acts on polytrack and firm going: tried in cheekpieces: has looked difficult ride. *J. J. Bridger*   **50**

TUMBLEWEED DI 3 ro.f. Tumbleweed Ridge 117 – Peggotty 50 (Capricorn Line 111) [2007 5m⁴ 5m p7.1g⁶ p5g⁶ p6g p5.1g⁶ Dec 4] 1,200Y: third foal: dam, maiden, stayed 1m: modest maiden: in cheekpieces final start (best effort). *G. R. Oldroyd*   **54**

TUMBLEWEED GLORY (IRE) 4 b.g. Marju (IRE) 127 – Tathkara (USA) (Alydar (USA)) [2007 90: 8g 8.1g⁴ 8m 8d p8g² Sep 24] rangy gelding: useful handicapper on all-weather, fairly useful on turf: best effort when second to Blackat Blackitten at Kempton final start: stays 1¼m: acts on polytrack and good to firm going: blinkered (tailed off and dismounted after line) third 3-y-o start: sold 32,000 gns. *B. J. Meehan*   **81 a96**

TUMBLIN ROSIE 3 ch.f. Tumbleweed Ridge 117 – Myhat 71 (Factual (USA) 108) [2007 52: p7g p7.1g p8g⁶ Feb 10] poor maiden: best form at 6f. *M. Blanshard*   **42**

TUNGSTEN STRIKE (USA) 6 ch.g. Smart Strike (CAN) 121 – Bathilde (IRE) 102 (Generous (IRE) 139) [2007 118: 16m* 16.4d⁵ 20g 16g⁶ 14g* 16g Nov 6] good-bodied gelding: smart performer: won Woodcote Stud Sagaro Stakes at Ascot (by 1½ lengths from Baddam) in May and listed race at Goodwood (beat Samuel by 6 lengths, dictating) in August: below form otherwise, tailed off in Melbourne Cup at Flemington final start: stays 2m (seemingly not 2½m): acts on firm and soft going: seems best when allowed to dominate. *Mrs A. J. Perrett*   **118**

Woodcote Stud Sagaro Stakes, Ascot—Tungsten Strike (left) makes just about all; Baddam is his only serious challenger

HBLB Lancashire Oaks, Newmarket—
a race transferred from an abandoned Haydock meeting is won impressively by Turbo Linn;
Under The Rainbow (striped sleeves), Portal and Brisk Breeze (hooped cap) are her nearest pursuers

TUNING FORK 7 b.g. Alzao (USA) 117 – Tuning 114 (Rainbow Quest (USA) 134) **53**
[2007 61: p10m p7g³ Dec 30] strong, lengthy, attractive gelding: modest handicapper: effective at 1m/1¼m: acts on polytrack, good to firm and good to soft ground:
tried visored/in cheekpieces/tongue tied: makes running: sometimes looks ungenuine.
M. J. Attwater

TURBAN HEIGHTS (IRE) 3 ch.f. Golan (IRE) 129 – Turban 80 (Glint of Gold 128) **73**
[2007 8.2g 8.3d* 8.3g⁵ Oct 16] half-sister to numerous winners, including 1m/8.5f
winner Barboukh (by Night Shift) and 1½m winner Old California (by Sadler's Wells),
both useful: dam, 1¼m winner, half-sister to Old Vic: fair form: best effort when winning
maiden at Leicester in August: stays 8.3f: acts on good to soft ground: veered badly left at
start final outing. *E. J. O'Neill*

TURBO (IRE) 8 b.g. Piccolo 121 – By Arrangement (IRE) 60 (Bold Arrangement 127) **75**
[2007 15g⁵ 12.3f⁴ 18d 10s Jul 2] close-coupled gelding: fair handicapper nowadays:
effective at 1¼m/1½m: acts on any going: has worn visor/cheekpieces: tongue tied at 8
yrs: fair winning hurdler: sold 4,100 gns. *M. W. Easterby*

TURBO LINN 4 b.f. Turbo Speed 99 – Linns Heir (Leading Counsel (USA) 122) [2007 **116**
12m* 12m* 12m* 14.6m Sep 13] close-coupled filly: second foal: dam bumper winner:
smart form in bumpers, unbeaten in 5 starts: quickly progressed to similar level on Flat,
winning first 3 starts, namely maiden at Catterick in June, and HBLB Lancashire Oaks
(vastly improved, beat Under The Rainbow by 4 lengths) and listed race (beat Green
Room by 1¾ lengths), both at Newmarket in July: disappointing tenth of 14 to Hi Calypso
in Park Hill Stakes at Doncaster final outing: should stay beyond 1½m: raced only on
good to firm ground. *G. A. Swinbank*

TURFANI (IRE) 2 b.f. (Mar 22) Danetime (IRE) 121 – Tuhfah (Cadeaux Genereux
131) [2007 8d Oct 23] 14,500Y: third foal: half-sister to winner abroad by Nashwan: dam
unraced half-sister to useful Irish performer up to 1½m Rahn: 100/1, well held in maiden
at Yarmouth. *W. J. Knight*

TURFROSE (GER) 3 b.f. Big Shuffle (USA) 122 – Turfquelle (IRE) (Shaadi (USA) **116**
126) [2007 7.5d* 7.5m² 9g* 9m* 8m³ 10d³ 11d⁴ 10d 8g² 10g* 10g* Oct 28] €15,000Y:
fifth foal: sister to German 1m/9f winner Turfshuffle: dam twice-raced half-sister to very
smart German middle-distance performer Turfkonig: smart performer: won newcomers
race at Pisa in April, minor events at Rome and Milan in April, listed race at Rome in
September and Premio Lydia Tesio Shadwell at Rome (improved effort to beat Fair
Breeze a short neck, leading over 2f out and just holding on) in October: stays 1¼m: acts
on good to firm and good to soft ground: tough and consistent: sold privately, and has
joined A. Fabre. *P. Giannotti, Italy*

TURIBIUS 8 b.g. Puissance 110 – Compact Disc (IRE) 48 (Royal Academy (USA) 130) **–**
[2007 66: p6g Jan 17] compact gelding: fair handicapper: well held only start at 8 yrs:
effective at 5f/easy 6f: acts on polytrack, firm and good to soft ground: sometimes wears
headgear. *T. E. Powell*

TURKISH SULTAN (IRE) 4 b.g. Anabaa (USA) 130 – Odalisque (IRE) (Machia- **66**
vellian (USA) 123) [2007 66: 7.1m 6.1s⁵ p6g⁵ 6s⁴ 6d³ 5.1s 6f 7f³ 7.1d² 7.6m 7g Aug 25]
good-topped gelding: fair maiden: should stay 1m: seemingly acts on any turf going: in
cheekpieces/visored of late: joined Evan Williams. *J. M. Bradley*

TURN AND RIVER (IRE) 2 b.f. (May 2) Viking Ruler (AUS) – Scatter Brain (Risk **51**
Me (FR) 127) [2007 5d⁶ 5m⁵ 5g⁵ 6g⁴ 5s⁴ 5s³ 5g⁵ Jul 31] €8,000Y: workmanlike filly:

seventh foal: half-sister to 5f (at 2 yrs) to 11f (in Italy) winner Rinkie Dinkie Doo (by Key of Luck) and winner in Greece by College Chapel: dam German 6f winner: modest maiden: best at 5f: acts on soft and good to firm going. *M. Brittain*

TURNER'S TOUCH 5 ch.g. Compton Place 125 – Chairmans Daughter 68 (Unfuwain (USA) 131) [2007 80§: p12g⁴ f11g⁶ p12g p12g³ p12g* p12g² 11m 11.9d⁵ 11.5d³ p12g³ p10g p11g⁴ 11.6m³ p12g⁴ p11g⁴ p12g² p11g³ Oct 17] deep-girthed gelding: fair performer: won apprentice handicap at Lingfield in March: stays 1½m: acts on polytrack and good to firm ground, probably on good to soft: usually wears headgear: held up: ungenuine. *G. L. Moore*   **70 §**
a79 §

TURNKEY 5 br.g. Pivotal 124 – Persian Air (Persian Bold 123) [2007 104: 5.1g 6m 6g 6g⁵ 6d² 6v 6g* 6d⁶ 6s² 7g 6m 6d 6d 6d Oct 13] strong, close-coupled gelding: has a quick action: useful handicapper: won at Pontefract in July: creditable ¾-length second to Zomerlust in quite valuable event at York ninth start: not at best after: stays 7f: seems to act on any going: effective blinkered or not: usually carries ridden nowadays. *D. Nicholls*   **102**

TURN LEFT (IRE) 2 b.c. (May 2) Xaar 132 – Stamatina (Warning 136) [2007 p7g³ 8.2g* Oct 31] 11,000Y, 38,000 2-y-o: angular colt: half-brother to fairly useful 1m winner Just A Martian and 4-y-o Bolckow (both by Marju): dam Italian 7f to 9f winner: fair form: third to Storm Force at Lingfield, then won maiden at Nottingham (all out to get up by ½ length): will stay 1¼m. *R. M. Beckett*   **79**

TURN ME ON (IRE) 4 b.g. Tagula (IRE) 116 – Jacobina 71 (Magic Ring (IRE) 115) [2007 57: 6.1g 7m² 6m² p8.6g* 6.9m 6m 7m 7.1d p8g² p8.6g⁴ p8.6g⁶ Nov 27] tall gelding: fair handicapper: won amateur event at Wolverhampton in June: stays easy 8.6f: acts on polytrack and good to firm going: tried blinkered/tongue tied. *T. D. Walford*   **70**

TURN 'N BURN 6 b.g. Unfuwain (USA) 131 – Seasonal Splendour (IRE) 95 (Prince Rupert (FR) 121) [2007 77§: p13g p13.9g 16.2d⁴ 11g⁶ Aug 5] sturdy gelding: fair performer: left C. Cyzer 6,000 gns prior to final start: stays 2m: acts on polytrack, good to firm and good to soft ground: tried blinkered: ungenuine. *J. A. Borrego, Spain*   **65 §**

TURN OF PHRASE (IRE) 8 b.g. Cadeaux Genereux 131 – Token Gesture (IRE) 113 (Alzao (USA) 117) [2007 68: 10.1m 10.1v² 12d⁴ 10g* 12v² 12s* 12d 12m Nov 10] fairly useful handicapper: won at Catterick, Pontefract (apprentices, despite hanging left) and York (left B. Ellison after) in July: effective at 1¼m to 1¾m: acts on polytrack and any turf ground: usually wears headgear. *N. Wilson*   **84**

TURN ON THE STYLE 5 ch.g. Pivotal 124 – Elegant Rose 72 (Noalto 120) [2007 79: f6g* p5g* p5g* 5.1m⁵ 5v 5m² 5d⁴ 5g p5.1g² p6g³ p6m* p6g² Dec 28] good-topped gelding: smart handicapper: better than ever at 5 yrs, winning at Southwell and Lingfield (2) in January/February and Lingfield again (beat Lucayos by head) in December: very good ½-length second to Ebraam at Lingfield final start: stays 6f: acts on all-weather, soft and good to firm going: blinkered: served ban for failing 2 stall tests prior to 2006 reappearance: has been very early to post: races prominently/leads. *J. Balding*   **113**

TURTLE BOWL (IRE) 5 b.h. Dyhim Diamond (IRE) 117 – Clara Bow (FR) (Top Ville 129) [2007 115: a9.5g* 8s* 8s² 8g² 9.3s² 8m³ 8g³ 8g Sep 9] tall, good-topped horse: very smart performer: lightly raced in 2006, but back to best in 2007: won minor events at Pau (ladies) in February and Bordeaux in March: good efforts next 4 starts when neck second to Racinger in Prix Edmond Blanc and Prix du Muguet at Saint-Cloud, 5 lengths second to Manduro in Prix d'Ispahan at Longchamp and very close third to Ramonti in Queen Anne Stakes at Royal Ascot: only respectable third to Manduro in Prix Jacques le Marois at Deauville before below form in Prix du Moulin at Longchamp final outing: stayed 9.5f: acted on soft and good to firm going, and on all-weather: waited with: had worn tongue tie: to stand at Haras de la Reboursiere et de Montaigu, France, fee €5,000, Oct 1st, special live foal. *Francois Rohaut, France*   **121**

TURTLE SOUP (IRE) 11 b.g. Turtle Island (IRE) 123 – Lisa's Favourite (Gorytus (USA) 132) [2007 78: 9g 12d Sep 28] sturdy gelding: fairly useful handicapper, very lightly raced on Flat in recent years: well beaten both starts at 11 yrs. *J. J. Bridger*   **–**

TUSCAN EVENING (IRE) 2 b.f. (Apr 22) Oasis Dream 129 – The Faraway Tree 113 (Suave Dancer (USA) 136) [2007 6g 5m³ 5m 6s² 6.3v² 7v³ 6.3g³ Sep 17] 4,500Y: medium-sized, good-topped filly: fifth foal: half-sister to 3-y-o Starry Messenger: dam, 6f (at 2 yrs) and 1¾m winner, half-sister to very smart 9f/1¼m performer Sasuru: useful maiden: mostly kept listed/pattern company, including in Queen Mary Stakes at Royal Ascot (mid-division): placed in Anglesey Stakes (2 lengths second to Myboycharlie) and Debutante Stakes (1½ lengths third to Campfire Glow) at the Curragh fifth/sixth starts: stays 7f: acts on heavy and good to firm going. *John Joseph Murphy, Ireland*   **95**

TUSCAN FLYER 9 b.g. Clantime 101 – Excavator Lady 65 (Most Secret 119) [2007 **50** 52: f6g p6g f7g⁶ f6g p6g³ p6g⁵ 6m³ 6g 5s⁴ 6m 6f* Sep 10] deep-bodied gelding: modest performer: won minor event at Folkestone in September: effective at 5f/6f: acts on poly-track, firm and soft going: blinkered: usually races prominently. *R. Bastiman*

TUSCANY ROSE 4 ch.f. Medicean 128 – Rosewood Belle (USA) 70 (Woodman **–** (USA) 126) [2007 53: 16m Apr 9] modest performer: well held only start on Flat at 4 yrs. *M. Todhunter*

TUSCARORA (IRE) 8 b.m. Revoque (IRE) 122 – Fresh Look (IRE) 64 (Alzao (USA) **63** 117) [2007 70: p7.1g p8g p9.5g³ Jan 29] smallish mare: modest handicapper nowadays: effective at 7f to 9.5f: acts on polytrack (seemingly not fibresand) and firm going: some-times takes keen hold. *A. W. Carroll*

TUTOR (IRE) 3 ch.g. Dr Fong (USA) 128 – Glandore (IRE) 95 (Persian Bold 123) **79** [2007 p8.6g* p8.6g⁵ 8.1s⁶ 10m 9.9g Aug 15] fairly useful performer: won maiden at Wolverhampton in February: should stay 1¼m: acts on polytrack: tried blinkered/in cheekpieces/tongue strap: signs of temperament: sold 10,500 gns. *W. J. Haggas*

TWEED RIVER (USA) 3 b.c. Royal Academy (USA) 130 – Gotablush (Nashwan **59** (USA) 135) [2007 10.2g 14s Oct 4] modest form in maidens at Bath (left A. Balding 18,000 gns) and Goodwood (said to have finished lame) almost 3 months apart. *Miss E. C. Lavelle*

TWENTYFIRST DANSAR 4 b.g. Zahran (IRE) 77 – Jokers Luck (Desert Splendour **–** 97) [2007 –: p10g Sep 15] little form since 2005. *A. D. Smith*

TWENTY PERCENT 3 ch.g. Auction House (USA) 120 – Truly Madly Deeply (Most **58** Welcome 131) [2007 –: p7g 9m p8g Jul 17] smallish, sturdy gelding: modest maiden: sold £1,000. *P. R. Chamings*

TWICE OVER 2 b.c. (Mar 16) Observatory (USA) 131 – Double Crossed 102 **104 P** (Caerleon (USA) 132) [2007 8m* 10g* Nov 3]
　　　　The essay on Double Trigger in *Racehorses of 1993* reported that New-market's Zetland Stakes was thriving, with some calling for the race to be upgraded from listed to pattern status. Hardly surprising for a race that had, in the previous two runnings, been won by subsequent St Leger winner Bob's Return and by Bonny Scot, third in the Doncaster showpiece. Double Trigger also went on to finish third in the St Leger, before going on to enjoy one of the finest careers by a stayer in recent memory. The 1996 Zetland went to another subsequent St Leger winner in Silver Patriarch, but thereafter things went from bad to worse for the race; none of the ten winners afterwards went on to make much of a name for himself, though 2006 winner Empire Day (subsequently in training with Godolphin) has not been seen since a fine third to Passage of Time in the Criterium de Saint-Cloud on his next outing. As a result, the latest edition of the Zetland Stakes was run without special status, simply as a minor event. The field was still useful, Twice Over heading the market at 5/4-on, ahead of Planetarium at 11/4 and Stubbs Art at 11/2. Twice Over and Planetarium had recorded useful form (and timefigures) when winning maidens (Twice Over at Newmarket, where he beat Austintatious by two lengths, despite looking very green beforehand), Stubbs Art had won a nursery on the course by four lengths on his latest outing, and another runner, Donegal, repre-sented pattern form, having come third to Rio de La Plata in the Vintage Stakes at Goodwood. The betting proved an accurate guide to the race. Twice Over was always travelling strongly, and, patiently ridden and letting his rivals make first run, he did well to beat Planetarium by a length and a half, with Stubbs Art a neck back in third.

	Observatory (USA) (ch 1997)	Distant View (ch 1991)	Mr Prospector
Twice Over			Seven Springs
(b.c. Mar 16, 2005)		Stellaria (ch 1986)	Roberto
			Victoria Star
	Double Crossed (b 1998)	Caerleon (b 1980)	Nijinsky
			Foreseer
		Quandary (b 1991)	Blushing Groom
			Lost Virtue

　　　　Twice Over is an apt name considering the furore over his dam's finest hour. Double Crossed ran only four times, but by far her biggest day came when taking the Lingfield Oaks Trial by a neck from Silver Grey Lady. The stewards on the day demoted Double Crossed, who had hung across Silver Grey Lady, but Double

Crossed's connections felt Silver Grey Lady had brought about her own misfortune when shying away from a loop in the rail, an argument convincing enough to get Double Crossed reinstated on appeal. Double Crossed had two foals before Twice Over, the unraced fillies Deceived (by Selkirk) and Tricked (by Beat Hollow), and she also had a filly by King's Best in 2006. Double Crossed comes from a good family, one trainer Henry Cecil knows well. Double Crossed is the best racehorse produced by mile-and-a-quarter listed winner Quandary, while Double Crossed's half-sister Clepsydra is the dam of three-year-old Passage of Time. Quandary is a half-sister to the very smart All At Sea, who, while a fine second in the Oaks, was probably at her best short of that trip, winner of the Prix Moulin. Twice Over is by the Juddmonte stallion Observatory who, it is fair to say, has become a disappointment at stud after what looked a promising first crop. Observatory was a top class miler and, given the record of some of Twice Over's relatives and the way in which he travelled so strongly through his races, Twice Over's stamina for the Derby trip cannot be taken for granted. His form at the moment falls far short of classic standard anyway, and hardly justifies the odds of around 8/1 (clear second favourite behind New Approach) being offered for him for Epsom at the time of writing. That said, the big, heavy-topped Twice Over has looked a league above his rivals in his two starts so far, and he has considerable potential for improvement. His participation in the Derby depends on connections supplementing him (something they did not do for his dam for the Oaks), and it makes most sense, at this stage, to wait until he has contested one of the trials before going overboard about the Derby. *H. R. A. Cecil*

TWIGLET (IRE) 2 b.f. (Feb 22) Choisir (AUS) 126 – Regal Opinion (USA) (Gone **69 p** West (USA)) [2007 6g Aug 1] 12,000Y: leggy, close-coupled filly: has a round action: fifth foal: half-sister to fairly useful 1m winner Pearl King (by Daylami) and French 6f to 1¼m winner (including 1m at 2 yrs) Blushing Mary (by Nashwan): dam unraced half-sister to smart French performer up to 9f Campsie Fells: 50/1, green and considerably handled when eighth to Fashion Rocks in maiden at Goodwood: will do better. *B. W. Hills*

TWILIGHT AVENGER (IRE) 4 b.g. Dr Fong (USA) 128 – Asterita 103 (Rainbow **53 d** Quest (USA) 134) [2007 55: p8.6g⁶ p9.5g³ f11g³ f12g³ f11g p12.2g³ f11g 10.1m p12.2g³ f11g⁵ 10s⁵ 12.1g 12s 12.6s 11.1d⁶ 13g Sep 3] strong, compact gelding: modest maiden handicapper: in decline: stays 1½m: acts on all-weather and firm going: tried in headgear/ tongue tie. *W. M. Brisbourne*

TWILIGHT BELLE (IRE) 2 b.f. (Mar 5) Fasliyev (USA) 120 – Pretty Sharp 64 **53** (Interrex (CAN)) [2007 5g 6g⁶ f6g² 8m p8.6g p8.6g f7d⁴ Dec 18] 87,000Y: strong filly: half-sister to several winners, notably smart 5f (at 2 yrs) to 7f winner Twilight Blues (by Bluebird): dam maiden (stayed 7f): modest maiden: runner-up at Southwell third start (then late B. Meehan 19,000 gns): should prove best short of 1m: acts on all-weather: tried in blinkers/cheekpieces. *K. R. Burke*

TWILIGHT STAR (IRE) 3 b.g. Green Desert (USA) 127 – Heavenly Whisper (IRE) **77** 105 (Halling (USA) 133) [2007 7m⁴ 8d* Jul 29] 280,000Y: second foal: closely related to 4-y-o River Tiber: dam, 1m winner (including at 2 yrs) who stayed 1¼m, out of half-sister to very smart performer up to 1m Rock City: fair form: won maiden at Pontefract in July: will probably stay 1¼m: tongue tied: sold 18,000 gns in October. *Saeed bin Suroor*

TWILL (IRE) 4 ch.g. Barathea (IRE) 127 – Khafaya 68 (Unfuwain (USA) 131) [2007 **74** 87: p16g⁵ p16g Feb 4] big, good-bodied gelding: just fair handicapper in 2007: stays easy 2m: acts on all-weather, good to firm and good to soft going (ran poorly on soft): tried blinkered/visored: wandered (probably would have won otherwise) fourth start at 3 yrs: none too resolute. *G. L. Moore*

TWINNED (IRE) 4 ch.g. Soviet Star (USA) 128 – Identical (IRE) (Machiavellian **56** (USA) 123) [2007 63: p6g⁶ p5.1g⁵ p10g 5g p5.1g³ p5.1g² p5.1g Oct 20] leggy, well-grown gelding: modest performer: claimed from Karen George £5,000 after second start: raced handily at 5f: acts on polytrack, firm and good to soft going: tried blinkered/in cheekpieces: races prominently. *M. J. Wilkinson*

TWIST BOOKIE (IRE) 7 b. or br.g. Perugino (USA) 84 – Twist Scarlett (GER) (Lag- **65** unas) [2007 60: p13.9g³ p12.2s² Dec 21] fair performer: stays 1¾m: acts on polytrack and soft going: tried blinkered: fair over jumps. *S. Lycett*

TWITCH HILL 3 ch.f. Piccolo 121 – Whittle Woods Girl 80 (Emarati (USA) 74) **67** [2007 64: 6m³ 6m* 6.1g³ May 28] strong filly: fair performer: landed odds in handicap at Folkestone in May: may prove best kept to 5f/6f: acts on good to firm going. *H. Candy*

TWO ACRES (IRE) 4 b.g. Danetime (IRE) 121 – Raise-A-Secret (IRE) (Classic **61** Secret (USA) 91) [2007 57: p5g 6.1m 5g 5s³ 5.7g⁵ p6g² p6g⁴ f5d² p6g Dec 19] sturdy gelding: modest handicapper: effective at 5f/6f: acts on all-weather, firm and soft ground. *A. G. Newcombe*

TWO DREAMERS 3 ch.f. Best of The Bests (IRE) 122 – Mossy Rose 78 (King of – Spain 121) [2007 –: 8m May 12] good-topped filly: little form. *A. Crook*

TWO IMPOSTERS (USA) 2 b. or br.g. (Mar 15) Gulch (USA) – Queen of Women **55 p** (USA) (Sharpen Up 127) [2007 5m 7.1g 6m Aug 9] close-coupled gelding: best effort in maidens when seventh to Hitchens at Folkestone final start (gelded after): will be well suited by 1m+: open to further improvement. *J. R. Best*

TWO LEFT FEET 2 b.g. (Jan 27) Groom Dancer (USA) 128 – Sardegna 111 (Pharly **72 p** (FR) 130) [2007 p8g² Nov 14] 10,000Y: closely related to smart 1¼m winner Samoa (by Rainbow Quest) and half-brother to useful 1¼m winner Sardonic (by Kris): dam, 7f (at 2 yrs) and 1¼m winner, out of Lancashire Oaks winner Sandy Island, herself closely related to Slip Anchor: 16/1, encouraging length second to Howdigo in maiden at Kempton, always prominent: will stay 1¼m+: capable of better. *W. R. Swinburn*

TWOSHEETSTOTHEWIND 3 ch.f. Bahamian Bounty 116 – Flag (Selkirk (USA) **73** 129) [2007 6.1g³ 5g* 5m⁵ 5m³ 5d² 5.3d⁵ p6g Nov 4] 24,000Y: lengthy filly: second foal: half-sister to 4-y-o Azygous (by Foxhound): dam unraced out of half-sister to Kentucky Derby runner-up Bold Arrangement: fair performer: won maiden at Musselburgh in May: left M. Dods after fifth start: stays 6f: unraced on extremes of ground on turf. *C. R. Dore*

TWO STEP KID (USA) 6 ch.h. Gone West (USA) – Marsha's Dancer (USA) (Northern Dancer) [2007 p6g p7f 6g Jul 23] smallish, strong, stocky horse: useful performer at 3 yrs: lightly raced for T. Pletcher in USA after: well held on return to former trainer in 2007. *J. Noseda*

TWO TIMER (IRE) 3 ch.g. Selkirk (USA) 129 – Adultress (IRE) (Ela-Mana-Mou **75 §** 132) [2007 10m 10d 11.5s³ 12m⁴ 12m p10g Oct 24] rangy, good-topped colt: fair maiden: stays 1½m: acts on soft going: tends to carry head high: temperamental (ran out through rail fifth outing): sold 12,000 gns. *D. R. C. Elsworth*

TYBALT (USA) 3 b.c. Storm Cat (USA) – Tuzla (FR) 121 (Panoramic 120) [2007 97p: **107** p8g² 8.1g⁶ 8.1m 8m* 8m Aug 4] smallish, good-topped colt: useful performer: improved when winning handicap at Newmarket in July by 1¾ lengths from Artimino, quickening impressively: bit below form in listed race at Goodwood final start: stays 1m: acts on polytrack and good to firm going: has been blanketed for stall entry: sent to USA. *J. H. M. Gosden*

TYFOS 2 b.g. (Apr 30) Bertolini (USA) 125 – Warminghamsharpish (Nalchik (USA)) **71** [2007 7.1g 7g p6g* p7.1g Nov 24] fair form: won maiden at Wolverhampton in November: stiff task in nursery there final start: effective at 6f, bred to stay at least 1m. *W. M. Brisbourne*

TYKIE TWO 3 ch.f. Primo Valentino (IRE) 116 – Tycoon's Last 64 (Nalchik (USA)) **58** [2007 –: p8.6g 8m⁴ 10g 11.5g Jul 24] smallish filly: modest maiden: stays 1m: acts on good to firm going. *E. J. O'Neill*

TYPHOON GINGER (IRE) 12 ch.m. Archway (IRE) 115 – Pallas Viking (Viking **58** (USA)) [2007 68: 10.4m 8s 8g 10d Oct 16] close-coupled mare: modest handicapper nowadays: stays 1¼m: probably acts on any going: sometimes slowly away: held up. *G. Woodward*

TYRANNOSAURUS REX (IRE) 3 b.c. Bold Fact (USA) 116 – Dungeon Princess **70** (IRE) 62 (Danehill (USA) 126) [2007 6m⁶ p7.1g³ 6g p7.1g⁶ p6g² p7.1s Dec 20] fair maiden: should stay 1m: acts on polytrack, probably on good to firm ground: visored last 2 starts. *K. R. Burke*

TYRONE LADY (IRE) 4 b.f. Key of Luck (USA) 126 – Kutaisi (IRE) (Soviet Star – (USA) 128) [2007 –: f6g 9m Sep 6] rather leggy filly: no sign of ability. *M. C. Chapman*

TYRONE SAM 5 b.g. Mind Games 121 – Crystal Sand (GER) (Forzando 122) [2007 **64** 67: p7g* p7g³ p7g² p7.1g f7g 7m f8g Apr 13] modest performer: won handicap at Kempton in January: stays 7f: acts on all-weather and good to firm going: wears blinkers/cheekpieces: sometimes looks difficult ride. *K. A. Ryan*

TYRRELLS WOOD (IRE) 2 b.c. (Mar 30) Sinndar (IRE) 134 – Diner de Lune (IRE) **77** (Be My Guest (USA) 126) [2007 7.1g 8.1d⁴ 8.1m⁵ p9.5g⁵ Nov 17] sturdy colt: fair maiden: fourth to Jedediah at Sandown: should be suited by 1¼m: acts on good to firm and good to soft going. *T. G. Mills*

TYZACK (IRE) 6 b.g. Fasliyev (USA) 120 – Rabea (USA) 61 (Devil's Bag (USA)) **82**
[2007 91: p7.1g p7.1g f8g⁶ f7g f8g⁶ f8g 8g* 8.3g⁴ 8.1g 8g p8g Nov 3] good-topped
gelding: fairly useful handicapper: left W. M. Brisbourne and rejoined former trainer,
won at Salisbury in September: stays 1m: acts on fibresand and firm going, seemingly not
on soft: has been troublesome to post: held up. *Stef Liddiard*

U

UACE MAC 3 b.f. Compton Place 125 – Umbrian Gold (IRE) 83 (Perugino (USA) 84) **61**
[2007 –: 6m³ 6m 6g May 29] leggy, plain filly: modest maiden: fell final start. *N. Bycroft*

UBENKOR (IRE) 2 b.c. (Feb 17) Diktat 126 – Lucky Dancer (FR) (Groom Dancer **–**
(USA) 128) [2007 p7g Dec 19] 66/1, well beaten in maiden at Lingfield. *Christian Wroe*

UBIQUITOUS BOUNTY 2 b.g. (Mar 31) Bahamian Bounty 116 – In A Twinkling **–**
(IRE) 74 (Brief Truce (USA) 126) [2007 5m 5.3m Sep 25] looked temperamental in
maiden and seller (blinkered). *G. L. Moore*

UCETEK (IRE) 2 b.f. (Apr 27) Kalanisi (IRE) 132 – Dragnet (IRE) 72 (Rainbow Quest **53 p**
(USA) 134) [2007 p8m Nov 11] second foal: half-sister to 3-y-o Lang Shining: dam, 1¼m
winner, sister to Irish 2000 Guineas/Champion Stakes winner Spectrum and half-sister to
dam of high-class 1¼m/1½m performer Petrushka: 8/1, seventh to Burriscarra in maiden
at Kempton, taking good hold out wide and unable to quicken: should improve. *Sir
Michael Stoute*

UGENIUS 3 b.g. Killer Instinct 111 – I'm Sophie (IRE) 64 (Shalford (IRE) 124§) [2007 **40**
–: p6g⁵ f6g⁶ p8.6g⁶ p8g Dec 5] poor maiden. *R. A. Harris*

UGLY BETTY 2 b.f. (Feb 8) Where Or When (IRE) 124 – Dancing Steps (Zafonic **–**
(USA) 130) [2007 7.1g 6s Oct 4] 6,500F, 11,000Y: strong, long-backed filly: first foal:
dam unraced sister to useful performer up to 1¼m in UAE Seeking The Prize: last in
maidens. *Garry Moss*

UHOOMAGOO 9 b.g. Namaqualand (USA) – Point of Law (Law Society (USA) 130) **94**
[2007 109, a94: f8g³ 8g 7.5g p7.1g p7g 8.5d⁶ 7g 7g 8g Aug 3] leggy gelding: just fairly
useful handicapper at 9 yrs: brought down final start: effective at 7f to 8.5f: acts on all-
weather and any turf going: has worn cheekpieces/visor, blinkered nowadays: sometimes
takes long time to warm up/wanders, and best in strongly-run race. *K. A. Ryan*

UHURU PEAK 6 ch.g. Bal Harbour 113 – Catherines Well 99 (Junius (USA) 124) **62**
[2007 65: p9.5g p8.6g 8d 7.9f⁴ 7m⁵ 8.5g³ p8.6g p8.6g p8.6g⁵ Nov 2] lengthy gelding:
modest handicapper: stays 1¼m: acts on all-weather, firm and good to soft going: usually
blinkered: tongue tied. *M. W. Easterby*

UIG 6 ch.m. Bien Bien (USA) 125 – Madam Zando 51 (Forzando 122) [2007 69: p10g⁶ **77**
p10g² 10.2g* 10m⁵ 9.9g⁶ 10m 9g* 9d² 10m 10d p10m Nov 1] compact mare: fair handi- **a65**
capper, better on turf: won at Chepstow in May and Sandown in August: stays 1¼m: acts
on polytrack, soft and good to firm going: races freely. *H. S. Howe*

ULTIMATE AKDOV (USA) 3 ch.c. Two Punch (USA) – Pithy (USA) (Quiet Ameri- **–**
can (USA)) [2007 p6g 9g 8.8g Oct 31] well beaten all starts, leaving P. Cole after debut.
T. Vana, Czech Republic

ULYSEES (IRE) 8 b.g. Turtle Island (IRE) 123 – Tamasriya (IRE) (Doyoun 124) [2007 **58**
76, a53: 6d 7.1m 8.3d 8.3m 11.1s 6s⁵ Oct 4] quite good-topped gelding: modest handicapper: stays 1¼m: acts on heavy and good to firm going: tried in cheekpieces/visor: has
looked none too keen/carried head high. *J. Barclay*

UMPA LOOMPA (IRE) 3 ch.g. Indian Lodge (IRE) 127 – Bold Fashion (FR) (Nash- **68**
wan (USA) 135) [2007 57: f7g 8g 6d⁴ 5m 7g³ 6d* 5.7g 6g⁶ Oct 30] close-coupled
gelding: fair handicapper: won at Newcastle in October: will prove best at 5f/6f: acts on
good to soft going: visored nowadays: races prominently: has shown signs of temperament. *D. Nicholls*

UMVERTI 2 b.f. (Mar 10) Averti (IRE) 117 – Umbrian Gold (IRE) 83 (Perugino (USA) **47**
84) [2007 7s 6d 8g⁵ Oct 19] 4,000Y: leggy filly: fourth foal: half-sister to 2 winners,
including 5-y-o Kudbeme: dam 7f winner: poor form in maidens: probably stays 1m.
N. Bycroft

UNA AURORABOREALIS 2 br.f. (Mar 24) Fantastic Light (USA) 134 – Aly McBe **50 d**
(USA) (Alydeed (CAN) 120) [2007 5m 5m 6s⁴ 6g 6.1s p7.1g 8s 6m Sep 3] 2,000Y: leggy,

lengthy filly: second foal: half-sister to 3-y-o Music Box Express: dam unraced: modest maiden: no form after third start. *J. Ryan*

UNASUMING (IRE) 4 b.f. Orpen (USA) 116 – Untold 124 (Final Straw 127) [2007 **47** 59: 12m 10m⁶ 9.7g Aug 16] strong filly: poor performer: should stay 1½m: acts on fibre-sand and good to firm going: tried in cheekpieces/blinkers/tongue tie. *J. Pearce*

UNBREAK MY HEART (IRE) 2 ch.c. (Jan 29) Bahamian Bounty 116 – Golden **93 +** Heart 77 (Salse (USA) 128) [2007 6m 6m³ 6d* 7s* Oct 14] €160,000Y: useful-looking colt: first foal: dam, 7f winner, half-sister to smart winner up to 1m Leitrim House: fairly useful form: progressed well, won maiden at Windsor and nursery at Goodwood in October: will stay 1m: acts on soft going, promise on good to firm. *R. Charlton*

UNCLE HARRY 2 b.g. (Jan 27) Mind Games 121 – Lapadar (IRE) 82 (Woodborough **–** (USA) 112) [2007 7d Jun 19] rangy gelding: 18/1, very green in maiden at Thirsk: subsequently gelded. *J. J. Quinn*

UNCLE MAX (IRE) 7 b.g. Victory Note (USA) 120 – Sunset Park (IRE) 61 (Red **–** Sunset 120) [2007 –: 17.2m May 21] fair maiden in 2003, very lightly raced and no recent form, including over jumps. *R. A. Harris*

UNDER FIRE (IRE) 4 b.g. Lear Spear (USA) 124 – Kahyasi Moll (IRE) 35 (Brief **63** Truce (USA) 126) [2007 62: p9.5g⁴ p7g² p8.6g p8.6g⁵ 10d p8.6g 7.1m p7g p7g p8g* p8.6g Dec 8] sturdy gelding: modest handicapper: won at Kempton in November: effective at 7f to easy 9.5f: acts on all-weather and good to firm ground. *A. W. Carroll*

UNDERTHEMISTLETOE (IRE) 5 b.m. Lujain (USA) 119 – Christmas Kiss 82 **48 §** (Taufan (USA) 119) [2007 43§: 7g 7m 5d 7m 6g Sep 3] compact mare: poor maiden: best efforts at 6f: acts on fibresand and firm ground: tried in headgear: unreliable. *R. E. Barr*

UNDER THE RAINBOW 4 gr.f. Fantastic Light (USA) 134 – Farfala (FR) 106 **107** (Linamix (FR) 127) [2007 107: 14.1g³ 18.7m⁴ 16.4d⁶ 12s⁴ 12m² 12m³ 12d⁴ 14.6m⁵ 12d³ 16d⁵ Oct 20] big, good-bodied filly: useful performer: ran well in maiden without winning in 2007, including when 4 lengths second to Turbo Linn in Lancashire Oaks at Newmarket, 2½ lengths fifth to Hi Calypso in Park Hill Stakes at Doncaster on eighth outing, and 2¼ lengths third to Brisk Breeze in listed event at Ascot next time: effective at 1½m, and stays easy 18.7f: acts on soft and good to firm going: tried in cheekpieces. *B. W. Hills*

UNDETERRED 11 ch.g. Zafonic (USA) 130 – Mint Crisp (IRE) 108 (Green Desert **77 d** (USA) 127) [2007 80: p12.2g³ p12.2g p13.9g p12g f8g⁵ 10.2f⁵ 10g⁵ 10m p8g p12.2g Jun 25] lengthy, deep-girthed gelding: has a quick action: fair performer at best: regressed after reappearance: effective at 1m to easy 1½m: acts on polytrack, firm and soft going: tried visored/blinkered: edgy sort. *K. J. Burke*

UNILATERAL (IRE) 2 ch.f. (May 16) Rock of Gibraltar (IRE) 133 – Mira Adonde **103** (USA) (Sharpen Up 127) [2007 5.1m² 6m* 6m³ 6g³ 6d* 6m Oct 5] 85,000Y: quite good-topped filly: closely related to several winners, including Irish 2003 2-y-o 5f/6f winner Colossus and 6f/7f (including at 2 yrs) winner Danehill Dancer (both smart by Danehill), and half-sister to 2 winners, including useful Irish 9f/1¼m winner Adonesque (by Sadler's Wells): dam once-raced close relation of useful miler Swordsmith: useful performer: won maiden in June and 11-runner Laundry Cottage Stud Firth of Clyde Stakes (beat Broken Applause by ¾ length) in September, both at Ayr: ran well in between when 1¼ lengths fourth (promoted to third) to Nahoodh in Lowther Stakes at York: respectable ninth of 14 to Natagora in Cheveley Park Stakes at Newmarket final start: will stay 7f: acts on good to firm and good to soft going. *B. Smart*

UNION JACK JACKSON (IRE) 5 b.g. Daggers Drawn (USA) 114 – Beechwood **64** Quest (IRE) 65 (River Falls 113) [2007 63: f6g f6g⁵ f6g p7.1g* p6g* p6g² f6g* p7g⁵ f7g⁴ 6g⁵ 6s² p6g Jul 10] good-topped gelding: fair handicapper: left J. Harris after second outing: won at Wolverhampton in March, Lingfield in April and Southwell in May: best at 6f/7f: acts on all-weather and good to soft ground: tried in cheekpieces, usually blinkered. *John A. Harris*

UNITED NATIONS 6 ch.g. Halling (USA) 133 – Congress (IRE) 86 (Dancing Brave **83** (USA) 140) [2007 81: p8.6g² 10.5m⁴ 7.9d p8.6g 8m 8.5g* 8m⁴ 11.9g⁶ p8.6d f8d⁵ Dec 20] sturdy, lengthy gelding: fairly useful performer: easily won claimer at Beverley (left N. Wilson £10,000) in August: left M. Easterby after eighth start: effective at 1m to 10.5f: acts on polytrack, good to firm and good to soft going (possibly unsuited by soft). *N. Wilson*

UNLEASHED (IRE) 2 br.c. (Apr 19) Storming Home 128 – Uriah (GER) 109 (Acate- **85 p** nango (GER) 127) [2007 8.3g⁵ Oct 16] 40,000Y: tall, close-coupled colt: first foal: dam

10.5f (in Germany) to 1½m (US Grade 2) winner: 8/1, fairly useful form when never-nearer fifth to Mountain Pride in maiden at Leicester: will be suited by 1¼m/1½m: should improve. *H. R. A. Cecil*

UNLICENSED 2 ch.g. (Feb 12) Hawk Wing (USA) 136 – Multicolour 64 (Rainbow **70** Quest (USA) 134) [2007 6g p7g⁴ p8m⁵ Nov 26] fair maiden: fourth to Wasan at Lingfield: should stay 1m. *R. Hannon*

UNLIMITED 5 b.g. Bold Edge 123 – Cabcharge Blue 81 (Midyan (USA) 124) [2007 **59** 68: 6g³ 6d 6.1m p8g Dec 28] big, leggy gelding: modest performer: effective at 5f to 7f: acts on all-weather, soft and good to firm going: sometimes wears headgear: races freely. *R. Simpson*

UNNEFER (FR) 2 b.c. (Feb 5) Danehill Dancer (IRE) 117 – Mimalia (USA) (Silver **90** Hawk (USA) 123) [2007 6m 7d* 7g² 8.2d² 8g² Sep 6] useful-looking colt: first foal: dam, French maiden (stayed 1¼m), closely related to Derby winner Kris Kin: fairly useful performer: won maiden at Newmarket in June: runner-up after in listed race (beaten 5 lengths by Raven's Pass at Ascot) and minor events: will stay 1¼m: acts on good to soft going. *H. R. A. Cecil*

UNO DOS TRES 2 ch.c. (Apr 13) Night Shift (USA) – Sartigila 67 (Efisio 120) [2007 **51** p7.1g⁵ p8g Nov 19] modest form in maidens: likely to stay middle distances (half-brother to 8-y-o Montosari). *Jane Chapple-Hyam*

UNREACHABLE STAR 3 ch.f. Halling (USA) 133 – Spinning The Yarn 70 (Bara- **81** thea (IRE) 127) [2007 70p: 10m⁵ 10.9g² 11m² 11s⁶ 10.2g⁴ p12.2g⁴ Dec 8] quite good-topped filly: fairly useful maiden: reportedly lame final start: should stay 1½m: acts on good to firm going. *Mrs A. J. Perrett*

UNSHAKABLE (IRE) 8 b.g. Eagle Eyed (USA) 111 – Pepper And Salt (IRE) **100** (Double Schwartz 128) [2007 97: p8g² 8.5d* 8.1g³ 8g⁶ 9m Oct 6] good-bodied gelding: useful handicapper: won at Epsom in June by 1¼ lengths from Montpellier: mainly creditable efforts after, including when third to Ordnance Row in totescoop6 Stakes at Sandown: well below form in Cambridgeshire at Newmarket final start (forced wide): effective at 1m/9f: acts on polytrack, soft and good to firm going: has been bandaged behind: genuine. *Bob Jones*

UNTIL WHEN (USA) 3 b.g. Grand Slam (USA) 120 – Chez Cherie 108 (Wolfhound **75** (USA) 126) [2007 75: 6g⁴ 7.1g⁵ Nov 8] good-topped gelding: fair maiden: will be suited by 1m+: acts on firm going. *B. Smart*

UP IN ARMS (IRE) 3 b.g. Daggers Drawn (USA) 114 – Queenliness (Exit To No- **79** where (USA) 122) [2007 74: 8.1m 10.2m² p10g 10g 11.7g 11.6m⁵ 11.6m 10g* 12f⁵ 11d² p16g* p16.5g² Dec 3] strong gelding: fair performer: won claimer at Newbury in August and handicap at Kempton in November: stays 16.5f: acts on polytrack, firm and good to soft going: tried blinkered: held up. *P. Winkworth*

UPPER CLASS (IRE) 2 b.c. (May 8) Fantastic Light (USA) 134 – Her Ladyship 119 **77 p** (Polish Precedent (USA) 131) [2007 6s* Jun 21] closely related to 3-y-o Truly Royal and half-brother to several winners, including French 1999 2-y-o 7f/1m winner Dignify and useful Irish performer up to 1¾m House of Bourbon (both by Rainbow Quest): dam, French 10.5f winner, half-sister to smart middle-distance performer Lord of Men: 9/2, won maiden at Ripon in smooth style (by 2½ lengths), despite looking green in front: will be suited by 1m+: useful prospect all being well. *M. Johnston*

UPSTAIRS 3 ch.g. Sugarfoot 118 – Laena 72 (Roman Warrior 132) [2007 7d May 27] **–** 30,000Y: rangy gelding: half-brother to 3 winning sprinters by Clantime, notably useful Cape Merino, herself dam of very smart sprinter Cape of Good Hope: dam maiden: 33/1, far too green when well-held ninth of 12 in maiden at Newmarket, losing all chance at start. *D. R. C. Elsworth*

UPSTANDING 2 b.f. (Mar 15) Acclamation 118 – Uplifting 77 (Magic Ring (IRE) 115) **65** [2007 5g 5g⁵ 5g⁵ 5m⁵ 5m² 5m³ 5m⁴ 5m² 5.4m⁶ 6d⁴ Oct 9] 1,500Y: smallish filly: fourth foal: half-sister to fairly useful French 6.5f/7.5f winner Up And Coming (by Compton Place): dam 5f/6f winner: fair maiden: placed 3 times, twice in nurseries: best at 5f: acts on good to firm going. *M. Brittain*

UP TEMPO (IRE) 9 b.g. Flying Spur (AUS) – Musical Essence 65 (Song 132) [2007 **55** 79: f8g⁶ p6g p7g Apr 1] useful-looking gelding: modest performer nowadays: effective at 6f to 1m: acts on all-weather and any turf going, though goes particularly well on softer than good: wears headgear: sometimes soon off bridle: reportedly bled final start: unseated rider and bolted to post prior to intended second outing. *C. R. Dore*

UP THE CHIMNEY 3 gr.g. Kyllachy 129 – Simply Sooty 78 (Absalom 128) [2007 **64**
p7g⁵ 7g⁶ p6g p8g 10s Sep 26] lengthy gelding: modest maiden: stays 7f: acts on polytrack. *A. P. Jarvis*

UP THE WYCOMBE 2 b.g. (May 1) Diktat 126 – Mistitled (USA) 54 (Miswaki –
(USA) 124) [2007 p7g p7g p7g p7g Dec 19] rather leggy gelding: little form: tried blinkered. *S. Dow*

UPTON GREY (IRE) 2 b. or gr.c. (May 10) Dalakhani (IRE) 133 – Rosse 100 (Kris **96**
135) [2007 7m 7m 6d* 6d³ 6d⁴ 7g³ Oct 27] 66,000Y: smallish, workmanlike colt:
half-brother to 7f winner Lasso (by Indian Ridge) and 3-y-o Fidelia: dam, 7f winner, half-
sister to Coronation Stakes winner Rebecca Sharp: useful performer: won maiden at
Newmarket in August: in frame in nurseries after, third to Kal Barg at Doncaster final
start: stays 7f: acts on good to soft going. *J. H. M. Gosden*

URBAN SPIRIT 3 b.c. Dansili 127 – Tenuous 111 (Generous (IRE) 139) [2007 90p: **97**
10m⁵ 10.3m⁵ 10m* 9.9g 10m² 10m⁶ Oct 5] strong, angular colt: has a round action: useful
performer: won maiden at Newmarket in July by neck from Jack Junior, despite hanging
markedly left: best effort when second to Teslin in handicap there penultimate start: stays
1¼m, likely to prove at least as effective at 1m: acts on good to firm and good to soft
going: nervy sort (tends to sweat): sold 50,000 gns. *B. W. Hills*

URBAN TIGER (GER) 4 b.g. Marju (IRE) 127 – Ukraine Venture 96 (Slip Anchor –
136) [2007 87: 10m May 22] tall, useful-looking gelding: fluent mover: fairly useful
performer at best: tailed off only start on Flat at 4 yrs. *Carl Llewellyn*

URBAN WARRIOR 3 b.g. Zilzal (USA) 137 – Perfect Poppy 73 (Shareef Dancer **77**
(USA) 135) [2007 73d: p7g⁵ 9.7g⁴ p10g³ 10.5g* 11.6d⁶ 10d³ 10g⁶ 7.6g⁶ 10g⁵ 10.9m
Aug 27] leggy gelding: has a markedly round action: fair handicapper: won at Haydock
in April: stays 11.6f: acts on all-weather and heavy going (below form on good to firm):
tried visored. *Mrs Norma Pook*

URSIS (FR) 6 b.g. Trempolino (USA) 135 – Bold Virgin (USA) (Sadler's Wells (USA) –
132) [2007 –: 10.4d Oct 12] sturdy gelding: useful form in France at 2/3 yrs, well held
both starts on Flat since: tried blinkered: useful chaser. *S. Gollings*

URSUS 2 ch.g. (Feb 6) Rambling Bear 115 – Adar Jane (Ardar 87) [2007 7.5d Sep 25] –
tailed off in maiden at Beverley. *C. R. Wilson*

USEFUL 4 ch.f. Nashwan (USA) 135 – Tarf (USA) 92 (Diesis 133) [2007 52: p12g p8g – §
7g Jun 12] sparely-made filly: temperamental maiden: sold £900. *A. B. Haynes*

USETHEFORCE (IRE) 2 ch.g. (Apr 29) Black Minnaloushe (USA) 123 – Polyne- – p
sian Goddess (IRE) (Salmon Leap (USA) 131) [2007 p7g Dec 29] €18,000F, 32,000Y:
half-brother to several winners, including fairly useful 1997 2-y-o 6f winner Jay Gee (by
Second Set): dam Irish maiden: 16/1 and green, signs of ability when ninth to Whitcombe
Minister in maiden at Lingfield: sure to improve. *M. J. Wallace*

USK MELODY 3 ch.f. Singspiel (IRE) 133 – One of The Family 73 (Alzao (USA) 117) **74**
[2007 74: 11.4m 9.9d⁵ 6s⁶ 7m⁵ Jul 21] strong, workmanlike filly: fair maiden: flattered
when eighth in listed Cheshire Oaks at Chester on reappearance: bred to be suited by
1¼m+: acts on good to firm going: tried blinkered: has been bandaged behind: has hung:
sent to USA. *G. A. Huffer*

US RANGER (USA) 3 b.c. Danzig (USA) – My Annette (USA) 78 (Red Ransom **123**
(USA)) [2007 97P: 7g* 8m 7m² 6d* 7d⁴ Oct 6]
     Both the French two-year-olds awarded the large P symbol in *Racehorses
of 2006*, denoting that they were considered capable of much better form, raced
exclusively at a mile in their first season, but as three-year-olds they turned out to
be very different racehorses in terms of their distance requirements. US Ranger ran
his best races when dropped back in trip to distances short of a mile, while the best
of Royal And Regal was not seen until he was put over staying trips. Both colts
were seen out in Britain in the course of the season, the Andre Fabre-trained Royal
And Regal winning the Jockey Club Cup at Newmarket on Champions Day, the
pair improving considerably on their two-year-old form (both were rated 97P).
Royal And Regal showed himself to be smart, and US Ranger showed even better
form and made the more dramatic progress, leaping from the relative obscurity of
the French Provinces to starting second favourite for the Two Thousand Guineas in
what amounted to one bound. US Ranger had won all three of his races at two, none
of them of any great standing, but he was clearly in a different league to the opposi-

Waterford Testimonial Stakes, the Curragh—an easy win for US Ranger on his first start for his new trainer; Senor Benny is runner-up

tion he faced as a youngster. He trounced seven rivals by upwards of eight lengths in a newcomers race at Bordeaux in September and then won minor events at Toulouse in November and December, the first by a length and a half before stretching his advantage to five lengths in most impressive fashion against the same runner-up on the second occasion. Although, at that stage, he had yet to make much of a name for himself in his own country, let alone outside it, he had evidently already impressed the decision-makers at Coolmore. Before US Ranger made his reappearance, his breeder Joseph Allen had sold a half share, resulting in US Ranger's carrying Michael Tabor's colours from then on. The sale was to have a considerable bearing on US Ranger's future, in the shorter term leading to his participation in the Two Thousand Guineas, and in the longer term to a change of stables.

US Ranger did not even hold a Guineas entry when he changed hands, though in March William Hill had reported laying a substantial bet on the horse for the classic. US Ranger made his reappearance in the traditional trial used by French contenders for the Two Thousand Guineas, the listed Prix Djebel at Maisons-Laffitte in April. The Djebel was used as a preparatory race by the two most recent French-trained Guineas winners, the Andre Fabre-trained pair Zafonic and Pennekamp in the 'nineties, though Zafonic had lost his unbeaten record (narrowly, to Kingmambo) in the Djebel and Pennekamp had been less than convincing in his win two years later when the race was run at Evry. Like US Ranger, both Zafonic and Pennekamp were unbeaten at two but both were already established as leading members of their generation after winning the Dewhurst Stakes. The last Djebel winner to contest the Two Thousand Guineas was the 2004 winner Whipper who won by eight lengths at Maisons-Laffitte before finishing fifth behind Haafhd at Newmarket, having already established himself at two as being among the best of his generation. Officially at least, US Ranger won the Djebel by only half as far as Whipper (though US Ranger's margin of victory looked more like five lengths than four) but he could hardly have been more impressive, making all and responding

1129

immediately when ridden to draw clear. There was substance to go with the style of his win because the placed horses Prior Warning and Stoneside were already winners in listed company, while the runner-up went on to win another listed race a few days before the Guineas.

Duly supplemented for Newmarket at a cost of £25,000, US Ranger briefly, around a furlong out, looked like justifying the outlay in the Two Thousand Guineas. Patiently ridden in the far-side group (he seemed to be carried that way early on, rather than being there by design), US Ranger quickened to lead his group and narrowly held the overall advantage before eventually passing the post a respectable seventh behind Cockney Rebel, second home on his side of the course behind Dutch Art. Despite his record over a mile at two, when his last win had been in heavy ground, the overriding impression US Ranger had given in the Guineas was that speed was his forte. The return to seven furlongs for the Jersey Stakes (rather than the St James's Palace) at Royal Ascot therefore promised to suit him ideally, and he was sent off a short-priced favourite, part of a four-strong raiding party from his stable which had its first runners at the meeting. A big, strong, good-topped colt, US Ranger was turned out in magnificent shape (dwarfing the eventual winner Tariq who went on to beat him readily by two and a half lengths) but the way he finished his race, carrying his head awkwardly and edging left under pressure after looming up to challenge, suggested something might have been amiss. Whether it was or not, races like the July Cup and Prix Maurice de Gheest went by without US Ranger and it was three months before he was seen out again. By that time he had been switched from Rouget's stable to Ballydoyle. The reason given was that there were more opportunities for a horse of his type outside France.

US Ranger made his debut for Aidan O'Brien in a listed race at the Curragh and made an excellent impression on his first start over six furlongs. Coming off a strong pace, US Ranger forged clear (after an accidental blow on the head from a rival's whip) after hitting the front over a furlong out to beat Senor Benny by three and a half lengths, though value for more. Ironically, US Ranger made his final appearance of the season back in France, just a week later in the Prix de la Foret at Longchamp. On paper at least, the Foret was the strongest seven-furlong race of the season in Europe all year, the majority of the field at least very smart performers, but US Ranger was among several who failed to give their running behind one of the outsiders Toylsome. US Ranger was better placed than most to mount a challenge to the front-running winner, but could only keep on at the one pace, perhaps finding the race coming too soon after the Curragh. At any rate, in finishing just over three lengths behind the winner in fourth, US Ranger didn't disappoint as badly as some, and turned the tables on both Tariq (who started favourite) and Dutch Art who were the next two home. In short, the Foret form needs treating with caution, and US Ranger's performance at Longchamp doesn't make him any less of a high-class sprinting prospect for his four-year-old season.

As a prospective stallion, it was easy to see why US Ranger appealed to Coolmore, just on pedigree alone. He comes from the penultimate crop of Danzig and is out of a close relative of another excellent sire Dynaformer, responsible for the ill-fated 2006 Kentucky Derby winner Barbaro and the latest season's St Leger winner Lucarno. Dynaformer's biggest wins came on dirt in the Jersey Derby over a mile and a quarter and the Discovery Handicap over nine furlongs, both of them Grade 2 contests, but he also won at up to a mile and a half on turf. Dynaformer's dam and US Ranger's grandam Andover Way won nine races in the States, notably the Grade 1 Top Flight Handicap over nine furlongs. Dynaformer was Andover Way's first foal and none of her numerous subsequent offspring was anything like so successful on the racecourse. US Ranger's dam, My Annette (by Red Ransom, a son of Dynaformer's sire Roberto), for example, ran her best race in four starts for James Fanshawe at a mile and a quarter when third in a maiden at Windsor. US Ranger is her third foal and second to race after the North American six-furlong winner Our Bea (by Hennessy). US Ranger's two-year-old half-brother Forge (by Tale of The Cat) was also in training with Rouget but has yet to race. My Annette's close relative and stable-companion Publisher (by another son of Roberto, Kris S) looked a most promising colt (rated 92P) when winning a maiden at Yarmouth as a two-year-old but ran only once afterwards, albeit showing useful form. My Annette was a big filly and Publisher was reported to be over seventeen hands as a two-year-old, so in terms of physique US Ranger would seem to be typical of the family. My Annette is not alone among Andover Way's daughters in making her mark at stud. Black Speck (by yet another son of Roberto, Arch) is the dam of Battle Paint who was the Rouget stable's best two-year-old of 2006, finishing second in the Prix Jean-Luc Lagardere, though he disappointed in the Poule d'Essai des Poulains in the spring. Interestingly, Black Speck's two-year-old Blue Exit has made an almost identical start to his career for Rouget as US Ranger did, making a winning debut at Bordeaux and following up at Toulouse. The other daughter of Andover Way worth mentioning is Alvear, the dam of the Grade 1 Suburban Handicap winner Offlee Wild and the grandam of the Champagne Stakes dead-heater Silent Times and the useful Irish two-year-old in the latest season Rock of Rochelle.

US Ranger (USA) (b.c. 2004)	Danzig (USA) (b 1977)	Northern Dancer (b 1961)	Nearctic Natalma
		Pas de Nom (b or br 1968)	Admiral's Voyage Petitioner
	My Annette (USA) (b 1996)	Red Ransom (b 1987)	Roberto Arabia
		Andover Way (b or br 1978)	His Majesty On The Trail

It seems unlikely that US Ranger will be asked to race at a mile again, and he remains very much unexposed as a sprinter. He coped well with heavy ground as a two-year-old and is probably effective on good to firm. With form already good enough to win a Group 1 but not yet successful above listed level, US Ranger will have no shortage of options for his connections to aim at in 2008. With his prospective stallion career and his American pedigree in mind, connections will no doubt be keen to advertise US Ranger to an American audience at some stage. Until now at the Breeders' Cup, European sprinters have either had to take their chance on an unfamiliar surface in the Sprint on dirt or try the Mile on turf. The new sprint race on turf being added to the Breeders' Cup programme at Santa Anita in 2008 could not have come along at a better time for US Ranger. *A. P. O'Brien, Ireland*

UTMOST RESPECT 3 b.g. Danetime (IRE) 121 – Utmost (IRE) 30 (Most Welcome 131) [2007 104p: 6m 6m³ 6d* 7d Sep 29] good-bodied gelding: quickly developed into a smart handicapper: better than bare result first 2 starts at 3 yrs prior to winning 26-runner Ayr Silver Cup impressively by 1½ lengths from Northern Dare, pushed out final 1f having travelled extremely strongly long way: not discredited when eighth of 23 to

115 +

totesport.com Ayr Silver Cup (Handicap), Ayr—the stand-side runners dominate, in particular the progressive three-year-olds Utmost Respect, Northern Dare and Sundae

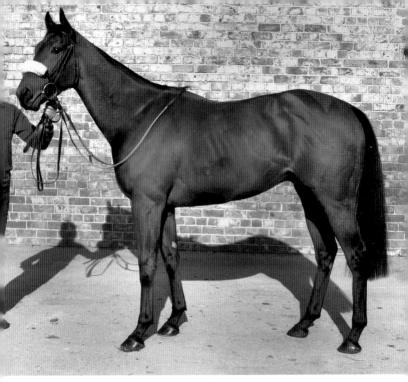

The Rumpole Partnership's "Utmost Respect"

Candidato Roy in valuable handicap at Ascot final start, stamina stretched: best form at 6f: acts on soft and good to firm going: sort to do well at 4 yrs. *R. A. Fahey*

UTRILLO'S ART (IRE) 2 ch.f. (Mar 24) Medecis 119 – Theory of Law (Generous (IRE) 139) [2007 6m 6s 7d 7d Jul 4] €14,000F, 20,000Y: fifth foal: half-sister to 3 winners, including French 6f winner Celtibero (by Celtic Swing): dam, French 11f winner, half-sister to Prix Morny winner Charge d'Affaires: no form. *M. W. Easterby* —

V

VACATION (IRE) 4 b.c. King Charlemagne (USA) 120 – Lady Peculiar (CAN) (Sunshine Forever (USA)) [2007 97: p7.1g⁶ 8s⁶ f8g⁵ p10g² 10.4g 8.1s² 8.1g 8.9s⁶ p8g p11g Aug 27] lengthy, good-topped colt: useful handicapper: good second to Moody Tunes at Haydock sixth start, tending to hang: stays 1¼m: raced on polytrack and good going or softer: held up. *V. Smith* **97**

VADAPOLINA (FR) 3 ch.f. Trempolino (USA) 135 – Vadaza (FR) (Zafonic (USA) 130) [2007 101: 11m* 10.5g* 10.5m 10d* 12m 10g Oct 7] medium-sized, well-made filly: third foal: half-sister to smart French 1¼m (Prix Saint-Alary) to 1½m winner Vadawina (by Unfuwain) and French 1m winner Vadazing (by Spinning World): dam, useful French 1¼m winner, half-sister to high-class miler Valixir (by Trempolino): smart performer on her day: won minor event at Longchamp in April, then impressive winner **116**

of Prix Cleopatre at Saint-Cloud (by 2½ lengths from Chill) in May and Prix de Psyche at Deauville (by 2 lengths from Believe Me) in July, quickening clear powerfully both times: disappointing in Prix de Diane at Chantilly and Prix Vermeille and Prix de l'Opera at Longchamp other 3 starts, favourite for first 2: stays 11f: acts on good to soft ground: needs treating with some caution. *A. Fabre, France*

VADINKA 3 b.g. Averti (IRE) 117 – Inchalong 80 (Inchinor 119) [2007 73: p6g² f6g 6g 6m⁵ 6g³ p6g 6g p6g Oct 15] fair maiden: well below form after reappearance: effective at 6f/7f: acts on all-weather, firm and good to soft going: tried in cheekpieces/tongue tied. *N. Tinkler* **70 d**

VAINGLORY (USA) 3 ch.c. Swain (IRE) 134 – Infinite Spirit (USA) 108 (Maria's Mon (USA) 121) [2007 p6g³ 6s* 7d³ p8g 8s³ 8s⁴ p9.5g* p10m Nov 24] 5,000 3-y-o: smallish colt: first foal: dam 6f (at 2 yrs) to 1m (in UAE) winner: useful form: won maiden at Yarmouth in June and handicap at Wolverhampton in November: stiff task, far from discredited when eighth of 9 in listed race at Lingfield final start: stays 9.5f: acts on polytrack and soft ground. *D. M. Simcock* **97**

VALANCE (IRE) 7 br.g. Bahhare (USA) 122 – Glowlamp (IRE) 93 (Glow (USA)) [2007 90: p16g p12g⁵ p16g⁶ p12g p12g p13.9g p12g p16g² 16m 14.1m⁴ 17.2d⁶ Oct 1] lengthy gelding: fairly useful handicapper on all-weather, fair on turf: stays 2m: acts on polytrack and firm going: tried blinkered/in cheekpieces: tongue tied nowadays: sometimes looks difficult ride. *C. R. Egerton* **73 a90**

VALART 4 ch.f. Bien Bien (USA) 125 – Riverine (Risk Me (FR) 127) [2007 72: p13.9g 12m⁴ p10g 11.5m⁴ 10m 8g p10g 8.1d 9.9m Aug 25] smallish filly: modest maiden, left T. Pitt after reluctant to race on reappearance: should stay beyond 1½m: acts on polytrack and good to firm going: in cheekpieces/tongue tied of late: one to treat with caution. *A. J. Lidderdale* **63 d**

VALASSINI 7 b.m. Dr Massini (IRE) 117 – Running Valley (Buckskin (FR) 133) [2007 11.5m⁵ 10.2m 8.3d Oct 15] lengthy mare: little sign of ability. *B. G. Powell* **–**

VALATRIX (IRE) 2 b.f. (Feb 6) Acclamation 118 – Dramatic Entry (IRE) 68 (Persian Bold 123) [2007 6d Oct 23] €30,000F, 24,000Y: sixth foal: half-sister to fairly useful 1m winner Bold Alaska (by Cape Cross) and winning sprinters in Norway by Emarati and Perugino: dam, Swedish 6f winner (including at 2 yrs), half-sister to very smart sprinter Royal Millennium: 40/1, good speed in maiden at Yarmouth (faded into eleventh): should prove best at 5f/6f: will do better. *C. F. Wall* **48 p**

VALDAN (IRE) 3 b.g. Val Royal (FR) 127 – Danedrop (IRE) (Danehill (USA) 126) [2007 95p: p7g p8g 8.1m 8m 8.1m⁶ 6g 8g 8g Oct 3] leggy, close-coupled gelding: fairly useful performer: well below form after third outing, leaving P. D. Evans after sixth start: probably stays 1m: raced only on good going or firmer on turf: tried tongue tied. *M. A. Barnes* **84 d**

VAL DE MAAL (IRE) 7 ch.g. Eagle Eyed (USA) 111 – Miss Bojangles (Gay Fandango (USA) 132) [2007 68: f6g f7g* p7.1g⁵ 8s a7g² 6g⁶ 6g² 5f⁴ 5g 5g³ 7s* 7d Oct 11] quite good-topped gelding: modest performer: won handicap at Southwell in January (sold from Miss J. Camacho 6,200 gns after next start) and claimer at Dieppe in September: stays 7f: acts on all-weather, soft and good to firm going: often wore headgear in Britain: usually races up with pace: has hung left. *Stal Lannoo, Belgium* **59**

VALE DE LOBO 5 b.m. Loup Sauvage (USA) 125 – Frog 84 (Akarad (FR) 130) [2007 82: f11g⁴ 12.1g* 10m⁴ 12m⁵ 10.5m⁴ 9.7m² 10d 12g² p9.5g³ p12.2g Dec 26] sturdy, close-coupled mare: fairly useful handicapper: won 4-runner event at Chepstow in May: pulled up amiss final start: effective at 1¼m/1½m: acts on all-weather, good to firm and good to soft going: effective held up or ridden prominently. *B. R. Millman* **84**

VALEESHA 3 b.f. Erhaab (USA) 127 – Miss Laetitia (IRE) (Entitled 126) [2007 47: 7m 5m³ 6s³ p6g 6m 8f 7g 10d Oct 9] quite good-topped filly: poor maiden: best effort at 6f on soft ground. *W. G. M. Turner* **49**

VALENTINE BLUE 2 ch.g. (Jan 26) Tobougg (IRE) 125 – Blue Topaz (IRE) (Bluebird (USA) 125) [2007 5g 7d 9s p7g Nov 7] workmanlike gelding: modest maiden: should stay 1m. *A. B. Haynes* **58**

VALENTINO SKY (USA) 2 b.c. (Jan 28) Stravinsky (USA) 133 – Lucky Lune (FR) (Priolo (USA) 127) [2007 6m 6m⁶ 6m p7.1g⁴ 8.3d p6g³ 7d⁶ Oct 29] well-made colt: fair maiden: in frame in nurseries at Wolverhampton and Kempton (third to High Standing): stays 7f: acts on polytrack and good to firm going: blinkered last 2 starts: sold 19,000 gns. *N. P. Littmoden* **66**

VALENTINO SWING (IRE) 4 ch.g. Titus Livius (FR) 115 – Farmers Swing (IRE) (River Falls 113) [2007 80: 7.1d² Jun 18] sturdy gelding: fair handicapper: good second **75**

at Warwick only outing at 4 yrs: stays 1m: acts on polytrack and good to soft going, probably on firm: tried in headgear. *Miss T. Spearing*

VALENTO 2 ch.g. (Apr 8) Noverre (USA) 125 – My Valentina 84 (Royal Academy 47 (USA) 130) [2007 7d 6.5d Oct 11] sturdy gelding: poor form in maidens: bred to stay 1m: gelded after final start. *Eve Johnson Houghton*

VALE OF BELVOIR (IRE) 3 b.f. Mull of Kintyre (USA) 114 – Sunrise (IRE) 58 (Sri 78 Pekan (USA) 117) [2007 96: 5g Jul 20] sturdy filly: useful performer at 2 yrs, winning 3 times: below form in minor event at Newmarket only outing in 2007: speedy, raced only at 5f: acts on firm and good to soft going: sold 18,000 gns in October. *K. R. Burke*

VALERY BORZOV (IRE) 3 b.g. Iron Mask (USA) 117 – Fay's Song (IRE) 84 89 p (Fayruz 116) [2007 76p: 5g* 6g 5s 5g³ 5g 5m² Sep 18] lengthy gelding: fairly useful handicapper: won at Musselburgh in April: good placed efforts after at Goodwood and Thirsk (second to Ishetoo, running on strongly near finish after racing freely): may prove best at 5f: acts on soft and good to firm ground: type to improve further, and win good races at 4 yrs. *D. Nicholls*

VALEUREUX 9 ch.g. Cadeaux Genereux 131 – La Strada (Niniski (USA) 125) [2007 – 60: p12.2g Oct 18] big gelding: modest performer: well held only start at 9 yrs: tried visored/in cheekpieces/tongue tied. *J. Hetherton*

VALHILLEN 2 ch.g. (Feb 27) Bertolini (USA) 125 – Dancing Nelly 52 (Shareef 67 Dancer (USA) 135) [2007 p5g² f5g⁵ 5m p7.1g⁴ p8g p6g³ p6g⁶ p5.1g* p6g⁴ p6d* Dec 17] has a high knee action: fair performer: won maiden in November and seller in December, both at Wolverhampton: best at 5f/6f: acts on polytrack. *M. J. Wallace*

VALIANCE (USA) 3 ch.c. Horse Chestnut (SAF) 119 – Victoria Cross (IRE) 101 – (Mark of Esteem (IRE) 137) [2007 94: 6g³ May 11] compact, well-made colt: fairly useful performer in 2006: well below form in minor event at Hamilton only start at 3 yrs: should be suited by 1m+: raced only on polytrack and good going on turf: raced freely final 2-y-o outing: sold 35,000 gns in July, joined M. de Kock in UAE. *J. H. M. Gosden*

VALIANT ROMEO 7 b.g. Primo Dominie 121 – Desert Lynx (IRE) 79 (Green Desert 53 (USA) 127) [2007 46: 5m⁶ 5m⁶ 5s⁶ 5.2d⁵ 6f 5m² 5s⁶ 5s⁵ 5g⁵ Nov 8] sturdy gelding: modest performer: raced mainly at 5f: acts on firm and good to soft ground, probably on soft: sometimes wears headgear. *R. Bastiman*

VALIANT VICAR (USA) 2 ch.g. (Feb 8) Hold That Tiger (USA) 117 – Lets Knock – On Wood (USA) (Woodman (USA) 126) [2007 7s 7m⁶ p7g 10m Oct 3] useful-looking gelding: little form: tried in cheekpieces. *B. J. Meehan*

VALIDITY 2 ch.f. (Feb 13) Forzando 122 – Wittily 69 (Whittingham (IRE) 104) [2007 – 5.1g 5s 7g p7.1g⁵ Dec 31] 16,000Y: sturdy filly: first foal: dam, 2-y-o 5f winner, half-sister to useful 2-y-o 5f winner Fortunately (by Forzando): well held in maidens: has been tongue tied. *A. J. McCabe*

VALLANI (IRE) 2 b.f. (Feb 19) Vettori (IRE) 119 – Hecuba 93 (Hector Protector 67 (USA) 124) [2007 p7g⁵ p8g⁴ Oct 4] €32,000Y: workmanlike filly: first foal: dam, 1¼m winner, half-sister to smart performers Prolix (up to 1½m) and Bangalore (stayer): fair form in maidens: will be suited by 1¼m+. *W. R. Swinburn*

VALLEMELDEE (IRE) 3 b.f. Bering 136 – Vassiana (FR) (Anabaa (USA) 130) 73 [2007 68: 8.2g⁶ 10m⁴ p10g* p11g⁴ 10m p12.2g² 14g³ p12m⁵ 14.1g p12.2g* p12.2s⁴ Dec a81 20] workmanlike filly: fairly useful performer on all-weather, fair on turf: won maiden at Lingfield in June and handicap at Wolverhampton in November: stays 1¾m: acts on polytrack and good to firm going. *P. W. D'Arcy*

VALLEY OBSERVER (FR) 3 ch.g. Observatory (USA) 131 – Valleyrose (IRE) 74 (Royal Academy (USA) 130) [2007 –: 8f⁴ p8g⁴ 9m⁵ 10.3f 8.3v² p8g⁶ 8.1m 8m f8d⁴ Dec 15] lengthy gelding: fair maiden: stays 8.3f: acts on polytrack and heavy ground: tried blinkered: has awkward head carriage. *W. R. Swinburn*

VALLEY OF THE MOON (IRE) 3 b.f. Monashee Mountain (USA) 115 – Unaria 80 (Prince Tenderfoot (USA) 126) [2007 75: 6f² 6d² 6m² 5s³ 5s 6m 6f⁴ 5f² 5m 5d² 5g p5.1g⁴ Nov 22] useful-looking filly: fairly useful handicapper: runner-up 5 times in 2007: effective at 5f/6f: acts on firm and good to soft going: sometimes takes strong hold. *R. A. Fahey*

VALRHONA (IRE) 3 b. or br.f. Spectrum (IRE) 126 – Minerva (IRE) (Caerleon 93 p (USA) 132) [2007 72p: p10g p12g* Sep 11] leggy filly: fairly useful form: easily best effort when winning maiden at Lingfield in September by 5 lengths from Gordonsville: stays 1½m: acts on polytrack: capable of further improvement. *J. Noseda*

VALTAT 2 b.g. (Jan 25) Fasliyev (USA) 120 – Wooden Doll (USA) 98 (Woodman – (USA) 126) [2007 p7g p7g p10g Nov 19] no form: tried visored. *B. R. Johnson*

VALUTA (USA) 4 gr. or ro.c. Silver Charm (USA) 132 – Misleadingmiss (USA) (Miswaki 124) [2007 76, a71: p16g a8d⁶ Dec 22] fair maiden: below form both starts at 4 yrs, leaving R. Kvisla after reappearance: stays 1½m: acts on polytrack and good to firm ground: usually tongue tied: visored (sweated up badly) once: none too consistent. *Yvonne Durant, Sweden* **?**

VALVIGNERES (IRE) 2 gr.g. (Mar 26) Dalakhani (IRE) 133 – Albacora (IRE) 98 (Fairy King (USA)) [2007 p9.5g p8m³ Nov 26] 20,000Y: sixth foal: closely related to useful 8.5f and 11.4f winner Hammiya (by Darshaan) and half-brother to 2 winners, including useful 2005 2-y-o 1m winner Achill Bay (by Peintre Celebre): dam, French 2-y-o 7.5f winner, closely related to smart French sprinter Pont Aven, herself dam of smart French performers Josr Algarhoud (7f/1m) and Sainte Marine (5f): dropped in trip, much better effort in maidens when third to Magical Fantasy at Lingfield, making running: subsequently gelded. *E. A. L. Dunlop* **68**

VAMPYRUS 4 ch.g. Dracula (AUS) 121 – Anna Karietta 82 (Precocious 126) [2007 73d: 8m 8.2g⁵ 7d p8.6g Jul 30] tall gelding: maiden: well held since debut: tried visored: sold 1,000 gns, sent to Sweden. *H. Candy* **–**

VANADIUM 5 b.g. Dansili 127 – Musianica 92 (Music Boy 124) [2007 84: p7g 10g 6s 5d 5m p7.1g* p7g⁴ p7g⁶ p7g Nov 19] tall, good-topped gelding: fair handicapper nowadays: left J. Given 11,000 gns after fourth start: won at Wolverhampton in October: effective at 6f to 1m: acts on polytrack, soft and good to firm going: tried in cheekpieces: races freely. *G. L. Moore* **71**

VANATINA (IRE) 3 b.f. Tagula (IRE) 116 – Final Trick (Primo Dominie 121) [2007 55: 8.1s⁶ 6g Aug 22] modest maiden: well held in 2007. *Heather Dalton* **–**

VAN BOSSED (CAN) 2 ch.g. (Mar 10) Van Nistelrooy (USA) 108 – Embossed (CAN) (Silver Deputy (CAN)) [2007 6d⁴ 6m³ 7g 5g* Aug 29] $60,000F, 48,000Y: good-bodied gelding: second foal: dam US sprint winner: fairly useful form: tongue tied, won maiden at Catterick final start by 2½ lengths, tending to idle: gelded after: should prove best at 5f/6f: type to go on improving. *D. Nicholls* **82 p**

VANCOUVER GOLD (IRE) 5 b.m. Monashee Mountain (USA) 115 – Forest Berries (IRE) (Thatching 131) [2007 72: f7g³ f8g f7g⁵ f8g² f8g⁶ Mar 13] sparely-made mare: modest performer nowadays: stays 8.6f: acts on all-weather, heavy and good to firm going: tried in cheekpieces. *K. R. Burke* **53**

VANDERLIN 8 ch.g. Halling (USA) 133 – Massorah (FR) 108 (Habitat 134) [2007 118: 7.1g⁴ 7g 8.3s³ 7d³ 7.6m* 7d Oct 21] strong gelding: usually impresses in appearance: just useful performer in 2007: won handicap at Chester in September by short head from Laa Rayb: below form in Badener Sprint-Cup at Baden-Baden final start: best at 7f/1m: acts on polytrack, firm and soft going: tried visored earlier in career. *A. M. Balding* **107**

VANILLA DELIGHT (IRE) 4 b.f. Orpen (USA) 116 – Fantastic Bid (USA) (Auction Ring (USA) 123) [2007 74: 8.3g⁵ 7d³ 6.9m² 6.9g Aug 22] workmanlike filly: fair handicapper: stays 1m: acts on soft and good to firm ground: races prominently. *J. Howard Johnson* **76**

VANISHING DANCER (SWI) 10 ch.g. Llandaff (USA) – Vanishing Prairie (USA) 93 (Alysheba (USA)) [2007 61: p11g* p13.9g* p13.9g p12g 21.7s p13.9g Dec 31] lengthy, workmanlike gelding: fair performer: won handicaps at Kempton (amateurs) in January and Wolverhampton (hung right) in February: left K. J. Burke before final start: effective at 11f to easy 2m: acts on all-weather and firm going, not on soft: tried visored/tongue tied/blinkered. *Mrs D. Thomas* **72**

VANQUISHER (IRE) 3 b.g. Xaar 132 – Naziriya (FR) (Darshaan 133) [2007 84+: p8.6g² f8g² f11g⁴ 9.9g⁵ 11.7g 12g⁴ 11.5m² 12m* Sep 22] leggy, useful-looking gelding: fair performer: won maiden at Newmarket in September: stays 1½m: acts on all-weather, soft and good to firm going: in visor/cheekpieces last 5 starts: consistent: sold 35,000 gns, joined Ian Williams. *W. J. Haggas* **79**

VAN RUYMBEKE (IRE) 3 ch.g. Indian Ridge 123 – Badrah (USA) 69 (Private Account (USA)) [2007 10.3m 6g⁴ 6m⁶ 7p.1g p12.2g f7d f6g* Dec 27] modest performer: trained by T. Pitt debut only: won maiden at Southwell in December: should stay at least 1m: acts on fibresand: tried blinkered: usually tongue tied (not for win). *D. J. Murphy* **54**

VARADOURO (BRZ) 5 b.g. A Good Reason (BRZ) – Orquidea Vermelha (BRZ) (Lucence (USA)) [2007 a6f 6g 6g 5.6m 6d 5.1g 6v Nov 3] successful 3 times in Brazil, including in 2 Grade 3s: little impact in handicaps at Nad Al Sheba (left A. Selvaratnam after second start), and in Britain: best form at 5f: acts on soft going: tried in visor/cheekpieces/tongue strap. *D. Nicholls* **–**

VARINIA (IRE) 2 b.f. (Apr 2) Spartacus (IRE) 107 – Bucaramanga (IRE) (Distinctly North (USA) 115) [2007 5.1g⁶ 5m³ 5m 6g⁵ 7.1g⁵ 5f⁵ p6g Sep 27] €12,000F, €15,000Y: well-grown, quite good-topped filly: third foal: dam Italian 7f (at 2 yrs) to 1¼m winner: modest maiden: best efforts at 5f: acts on firm going. *M. Brittain* **62**

VARYA 3 b.f. Diktat 126 – Regent's Folly (IRE) 101 (Touching Wood (USA) 127) [2007 p6g p7.1g⁶ p7g Jan 22] half-sister to several winners, including 1m (at 2 yrs) to 1½m winners Spree Vision (by Suave Dancer) and Summer Charm (by Dansili), both fairly useful: dam, 2-y-o 7f winner (stayed 14.6f), out of close relative to high-class 1¼m winner Ascot Knight: little impact in maidens: sold 1,800 gns, sent to Qatar. *Sir Mark Prescott* **–**

VEBA (USA) 4 ch.g. Black Minnaloushe (USA) 123 – Make Over (USA) (Time For A Change (USA)) [2007 –: p7g p10g⁶ p8.6g p10g p9.5g 10.1m² p9.5g² 10d p9.5g⁴ p12g⁶ p12.2g³ p10g⁴ 10.1g 8m 9m 6g p10g Sep 11] leggy gelding: modest maiden handicapper: stays easy 1½m: acts on polytrack and firm ground: held up: takes keen hold. *M. D. I. Usher* **52**

VEENWOUDEN 3 b.f. Desert Prince (IRE) 130 – Delauncy (Machiavellian (USA) 123) [2007 80: 8g 7m⁵ 8d⁶ 10f⁵ 12d* p12.2g⁴ 14m³ 16d³ Oct 20] neat filly: useful performer: left J. Fanshawe after third outing: won handicap at Salisbury in August: upped in trip, much improved when third last 2 starts, in listed race at Newmarket (to Lion Sands) and Jockey Club Cup there (beaten 2¼ lengths by Royal And Regal): stays 2m: acts on polytrack, firm and good to soft going: held up. *E. F. Vaughan* **107**

VEGAS BOYS 4 b.g. Royal Applause 124 – Brief Glimpse (IRE) 108 (Taufan (USA) 119) [2007 77: p6g³ 6g³ p6g² 7s* 6g² 6m* 6d³ 7s⁶ Jun 30] angular gelding: has a markedly round action: fair handicapper: won at Brighton in May and Lingfield in June: stays 7f: acts on polytrack, firm and good to soft going: carried head awkwardly second start: consistent: sold 22,000 gns, sent to Qatar. *M. Wigham* **82**

VEHARI 4 ch.g. Tomba 119 – Nannie Annie 60 (Persian Bold 123) [2007 77: 10s⁶ 11.8m 10.2m 12m Oct 8] sturdy gelding: fair maiden at 3 yrs, no form in 2007. *G. F. Bridgwater* **–**

VEILED APPLAUSE 4 b.g. Royal Applause 124 – Scarlet Veil 75 (Tyrnavos 129) [2007 77: 8f² 8m² 8.3m² 8.3g* 7.9d⁵ 10d² 10m² p9.5g* 10.9m p10g Oct 12] good-topped gelding: fairly useful handicapper: won at Windsor in June and Wolverhampton in September: stays 1¼m: acts on polytrack, firm and good to soft going: tends to hang, and no easy ride: sold 25,000 gns, joined J. Quinn. *R. M. Beckett* **87**

VELMA KELLY 3 b.f. Vettori (IRE) 119 – Possessive Artiste 73 (Shareef Dancer (USA) 135) [2007 p9.5g* Sep 3] sixth foal: half-sister to useful 1m to 1¼m winner in Hong Kong Blue Stitch (by Selkirk): dam, 11.5f winner, sister to smart Irish/Italian Oaks winner Possessive Dancer: 16/1, won maiden at Wolverhampton in September by short head from Auntie Mame, slowly away before leading line: should improve. *W. R. Swinburn* **63 p**

VELOCITYS GIFT 3 b.c. Kyllachy 129 – La Piaf (FR) (Fabulous Dancer (USA) 124) [2007 7m 7g² 8.3m⁵ 7g⁵ Jul 28] strong, sturdy colt: fair maiden: stayed 1m: dead. *Pat Eddery* **67**

VELOSO (FR) 5 gr.g. Kaldounevees (FR) 118 – Miss Recif (IRE) (Exit To Nowhere (USA) 122) [2007 p12.2g* Nov 14] fairly useful winner in 2005 when trained by J. Hammond in France: first outing for over 2 years and heavily backed, fair form when winning seller at Wolverhampton in November: stays 1½m: raced only on polytrack and good going or firmer. *Ronald O'Leary, Ireland* **66**

VELVET HEIGHTS (IRE) 5 b.h. Barathea (IRE) 127 – Height of Fantasy (IRE) 101 (Shirley Heights 130) [2007 104: 14g 14d⁴ 14.8m² 14.8s⁴ 16d⁶ 12s⁵ Oct 19] sturdy, close-coupled horse: useful handicapper on all-weather at 4 yrs, fairly useful on turf, best effort in 2007 when second at Newmarket: effective at 1½m to 2m: acts on all-weather, soft and good to firm going. *J. L. Dunlop* **93 +**

VELVET VALLEY (USA) 4 ch.g. Gone West (USA) – Velvet Morning (USA) (Broad Brush (USA)) [2007 73: p12.2g⁴ f11g* p12g⁶ f11g⁶ 11g May 10] rangy, good-topped gelding: fairly useful handicapper: won at Southwell in March: barely stays 1½m: acts on fibresand and firm going: tried blinkered (raced freely): held up: sold 6,200 gns. *C. E. Longsdon* **81**

VENEER (IRE) 5 b.g. Woodborough (USA) 112 – Sweet Lass (Belmez (USA) 131) [2007 59: p9.5g³ Dec 13] lengthy gelding: just modest performer nowadays: stays 9.7f: acts on all-weather and good to soft going: tried blinkered/in cheekpieces. *Mrs N. S. Evans* **52**

VENERABLE 3 b.g. Danehill (USA) 126 – Fragrant View (USA) 99 (Distant View **94** (USA) 126) [2007 56p: 10.2m* 11g 10m* 11.6g⁴ Oct 8] well-made gelding: fairly useful performer: won maiden at Chepstow in May and handicap at Sandown in September: stays 11.6f: acts on good to firm ground: races prominently: sold privately after final start, sent to Saudi Arabia. *J. H. M. Gosden*

VENIR ROUGE 3 ch.c. Dancing Spree (USA) – Al Awaalah 52 (Mukaddamah (USA) **85** 125) [2007 73: 10d 8.1g² 7m 10f* 10g² 10m⁵ 12m⁵ 12m 11.7g⁵ p12g² Nov 6] big, lengthy colt: fairly useful handicapper: won ladies event at Newbury in August: stays 1½m: acts on polytrack and firm going: tried blinkered: has run well sweating: hung badly left fifth start: usually held up. *M. Salaman*

VENTURA (USA) 3 b. or br.f. Chester House (USA) 123 – Estala (Be My Guest **115 +** (USA) 126) [2007 74p: 7s* 8.3m² 7s² 8.1g* 8d⁶ 7d² p8g* Nov 28] lengthy filly: smart performer: won maiden at Folkestone (by 8 lengths) in June, handicap at Sandown in September and listed race at Kempton (much improved when beating Wise Dennis by 2½ lengths, showing impressive turn of foot) in November: raced only at 7f/1m: acts on polytrack, soft and good to firm going: usually races prominently: joined R. Frankel in USA. *Mrs A. J. Perrett*

VERACITY 3 ch.c. Lomitas 129 – Vituisa (Bering 136) [2007 69p: 10m² p12.2g* 12g* **117** 16d² 16g² 14.6m⁵ Sep 15] lengthy, good-quartered colt: smart performer: won maiden at Wolverhampton in April and handicap at Newmarket in May: best form on last 2 starts, ½-length second to Allegretto in Goodwood Cup and 2 lengths fifth to Lucarno in St Leger at Doncaster: stays 2m: acts on polytrack, good to firm and good to soft going: has joined Godolphin. *M. A. Jarvis*

VERAS JOY 2 b.f. (Apr 1) Piccolo 121 – Fly South (Polar Falcon (USA) 126) [2007 6d **–** 8d 6d Oct 15] 5,500Y: rather unfurnished filly: sixth foal: sister to 7f (at 2 yrs)/1m winner Whitgift Rock and closely related to 3-y-o Just Joey (by Averti): dam unraced: no form. *T. D. McCarthy*

VERBAL KINT 3 b.g. Lake Coniston (IRE) 131 – Kintara (Cyrano de Bergerac 120) **–** [2007 5.1m Jun 6] 20/1, well held in maiden at Nottingham, hanging badly left leaving stall. *E. S. McMahon*

VERBATIM 3 b.f. Vettori (IRE) 119 – Brand (Shareef Dancer (USA) 135) [2007 –p: **70 d** 10m p10g³ p12g 10.3g⁴ p12.2g⁴ p12g⁵ p11g² Dec 19] leggy filly: fair maiden: below form after second start: should stay 1½m: acts on polytrack: tried visored. *A. M. Balding*

VERIFICATION 4 ch.g. Medicean 128 – Viewfinder (USA) (Boundary (USA) 117) **–** [2007 12f⁴ 9.1g May 31] tall, good-bodied gelding: maiden: unraced in 2006: well held at 4 yrs. *J. Howard Johnson*

VERITE 4 b.g. Foxhound (USA) 103 – Blushing Victoria 74 (Weldnaas (USA) 112) **58 d** [2007 f6g f5g p7g p6g 5.1m 7.5m Apr 26] good-topped gelding: fair performer at 2 yrs: missed 2006 and modest form at best at 4 yrs: will prove best at 5f/6f: acts on good to firm going: sometimes blinkered: often slowly away. *A. J. McCabe*

VERONE (USA) 3 b.f. Dixie Union (USA) 121 – Etheldreda (USA) 64 (Diesis 133) **67 d** [2007 f7g³ p8.6g 7.5g 8s p8g Jul 10] $60,000Y: close-coupled filly: half-sister to several winners, notably very smart 1m (at 2 yrs) to 10.5f (Prix Lupin) winner Flemensfirth (by Alleged) and fairly useful 1¼m winner Dan Dare (by Dynaformer): dam, maiden (stayed 1m), half-sister to US 2-y-o Grade 1 1m winner Bundler: form only on debut: stays 7f: acts on fibresand: tried tongue tied/visored: covered by Librettist, sent to France. *M. Botti*

VERONICAS WAY 2 b.f. (May 11) High Estate 127 – Mimining 83 (Tower Walk **62** 130) [2007 6f 6m⁴ 7m* 7d 7d Oct 29] good-bodied filly: eighth foal: half-sister to 4-y-o Mormeatmic and 9.4f and 1½m winner Wellcome Inn (by Most Welcome): dam 5f (at 2 yrs)/6f winner: modest performer: won maiden at Thirsk in September: will stay 1m: acts on good to firm going, well held in nurseries on good to soft. *G. M. Moore*

VERSATILE 4 b.g. Vettori (IRE) 119 – Direcvil (Top Ville 129) [2007 ?: p12g⁶ p10g **66 d** p16g p16g p12m⁶ Oct 3] good-topped gelding: fair form in Britain only on reappearance: stays easy 1½m: raced on polytrack and good ground or softer: tried blinkered/tongue tied: has reportedly had breathing problem. *G. A. Ham*

VERSTONE (IRE) 5 b.m. Brave Act 119 – Golden Charm (IRE) 63 (Common **–** Grounds 118) [2007 –: 12s Jul 18] leggy mare: lightly raced and no recent form on Flat. *R. F. Fisher*

VERTIGO BLUE 4 b.g. Averti (IRE) 117 – Soft Colours (Presidium 124) [2007 16m⁵ **–** Apr 9] lengthy gelding: poor maiden: stays 8.6f: acts on polytrack. *A. C. Whillans*

William Hill Lincoln (Handicap), Newcastle—another change of venue,
and they are well strung out at the finish behind all-the-way winner Very Wise;
Rio Riva comes from behind to take second, clear of Mutawaffer (rail) and Raptor

VERY AGREEABLE 4 b.f. Pursuit of Love 124 – Oomph 83 (Shareef Dancer (USA) **89**
135) [2007 87: 10m⁵ 12m⁶ 11.6m⁴ Jun 9] quite good-topped filly: fairly useful performer,
lightly raced: stays 1½m: acts on polytrack and good to firm going. *W. R. Swinburn*

VERY GREEN (FR) 5 b.g. Barathea (IRE) 127 – Green Bend (USA) (Riverman **70 d**
(USA) 131) [2007 14g⁴ 12v 16g p12g Nov 21] lengthy, rather leggy gelding: fair maiden:
below form after reappearance, left D. Hughes in Ireland 6,800 gns before final start
(pulled up, said to have bled): stays 1¾m: acts on good to firm ground. *Mrs A. L. M. King*

VERY WELL RED 4 b.f. First Trump 118 – Little Scarlett 54 (Mazilier (USA) 107) **78**
[2007 p8g p8g⁴ p8g⁶ p7.1g⁵ f7g² p8.6g* 8.2s* 8.5m* 8.3f⁵ 8.1d 8s⁴ 8.3g p8g 8g* **a72**
p8.6g⁵ p9.5g⁶ p8.6d f8d⁵ f8d⁴ Dec 21] compact filly: fourth foal: half-sister to 8-y-o
Sundried Tomato: dam 8.5f winner: fair handicapper: won at Wolverhampton (hung
right), Nottingham and Beverley, all in May, and Bath in October: stays easy 8.6f: acts on
all-weather, firm and soft going. *P. W. Hiatt*

VERY WISE 5 b.g. Pursuit of Love 124 – With Care 78 (Warning 136) [2007 92: f8g⁴ **107**
p10g³ p10g* p8.6g p10g² 8s* 8g⁶ 8g 10s³ 9m 8g* p8g p8g p8g Nov 28] tall, good sort: useful
handicapper: thrived at 5 yrs, winning at Lingfield in January, William Hill Lincoln at
Newcastle (by length from Rio Riva) in March and at Newmarket (beat Kinsya by 1¼
lengths) in November: ran poorly last 2 starts: stays 1¼m: acts on polytrack, best turf
form on good going or softer: has worn crossed noseband/bandages: tactically versatile.
W. J. Haggas

VERY WISE KID 4 b.f. Cloudings (IRE) 112 – Fantasy Flight (Forzando 122) [2007 **–**
6d 7s⁵ 7m Aug 4] good-topped filly: no form in maidens. *P. T. Midgley*

VESUVIO 3 br.g. Efisio 120 – Polo 83 (Warning 136) [2007 70: 5v⁴ 6v⁶ 7.1s⁵ 8s⁶ p9.5g **68**
p8.6g p8.6g Nov 30] heavy-topped gelding: fair on turf, poor on all-weather: won maiden **a49**
at Beverley in July: best form at 5f/6f: acts on polytrack and heavy going. *C. W. Thornton*

VETTORI DANCER 4 b.f. Vettori (IRE) 119 – Assertive Dancer (USA) (Assert 134) **–**
[2007 –: p10g p10m 11.9g Oct 25] little form: tried blinkered. *G. G. Margarson*

VEVERKA 6 b.m. King's Theatre (IRE) 128 – Once Smitten (IRE) 58 (Caerleon (USA) **–**
132) [2007 –: p16g May 7] small mare: fair maiden at 2 yrs: no form on Flat since.
J. C. Fox

VHUJON (IRE) 2 b.c. (Jan 17) Mujadil (USA) 119 – Livius Lady (IRE) (Titus Livius **93**
(FR) 115) [2007 5.1f* 5m 5d 6m* 6m 6d 6g⁴ 7m 6m⁶ 6g² 6d 6g Oct 27] 5,000F,
€23,000Y: neat colt: first foal: dam unraced: fairly useful performer: won maiden at
Bath in April and minor event at Salisbury in July: made frame only twice after, including
second of 23 to Dubai Dynamo in listed Two-Year-Old Trophy at Redcar: best at 5f/6f:
acts on firm going: effective tongue tied or not: pulled up (said to have had breathing
problem) eighth outing: none too reliable. *P. D. Evans*

VIABLE 5 b.g. Vettori (IRE) 119 – Danseuse Davis (FR) (Glow (USA)) [2007 69§: **67 §**
p10g⁴ p10g 10s⁶ 10v⁵ 8m* 7g⁵ p8g² p8g⁵ Nov 21] fair performer: won selling handicap
at Yarmouth in August: barely stays 11.8f: acts on polytrack, good to firm and good to
soft going: races prominently: ungenuine. *Mrs P. Sly*

VIAMI (IRE) 3 br.f. Daylami (IRE) 138 – Via Splendida (IRE) 80 (Project Manager **79**
111) [2007 76: f7g* 8.5g⁶ 10m⁵ 10d⁶ 12s Jun 22] fair performer: won maiden at Southwell in April: stays 1¼m: acts on fibresand, soft and good to firm going: blinkered final
start. *James G. Burns, Ireland*

1138

VIBRATO (USA) 5 b.g. Stravinsky (USA) 133 – She's Fine (USA) (Private Account **62 d**
(USA)) [2007 62: f8g³ f8g⁵ f8g⁵ f8g 7m 6d 7.5g Jul 31] tall gelding: modest handicapper:
no form after third start: stays 1m: acts on fibresand and heavy ground: in cheekpieces/
visor nowadays: tried tongue tied. *C. J. Teague*

VICE ADMIRAL 4 ch.g. Vettori (IRE) 119 – Queen of Scotland (IRE) 75 (Mujadil **68**
(USA) 119) [2007 70: 12.4m 15.8m* 16.2m* 12.3f⁶ 14.1d 16f² 16.1m³ 17.1d⁴ 14m⁶
15.8g 15.8s Oct 9] workmanlike gelding: fair handicapper: won at Catterick and
Beverley in May: stays 17f: acts on firm and soft going: tried blinkered: front runner.
M. W. Easterby

VICIOUS PRINCE (IRE) 8 b.g. Sadler's Wells (USA) 132 – Sunny Flower (FR) **–**
(Dom Racine (FR) 121) [2007 –: 13.1g 17.5s Sep 21] strong, lengthy gelding: no form
since 2005: trained by Mrs J. McGregor on reappearance. *R. M. Whitaker*

VICIOUS WARRIOR 8 b.g. Elmaamul (USA) 125 – Ling Lane (Slip Anchor 136) **93**
[2007 95, a–: 8.1m⁵ 8m 8.1s³ 8s* 8g 8m 9.8m 8s 8.9d³ 9.1v* 8v³ p9.5g Dec 1] big, strong **a74 +**
gelding: fairly useful handicapper: won at York in July and Ayr in October: stays 1¼m:
acts on polytrack, heavy and good to firm going: free-going sort: usually races prominently: reliable. *R. M. Whitaker*

VIC'S CHARM (IRE) 6 ch.g. Old Vic 136 – Sapien Dame (IRE) (Homo Sapien 121) **–**
[2007 f12g Jan 30] well held in bumpers, and in claimer at Southwell. *D. Carroll*

VICTORIAN BOUNTY 2 b.c. (Feb 9) Bahamian Bounty 116 – Baby Bunting 63 **85**
(Wolfhound (USA) 126) [2007 6m⁴ 5g* p5g² p6g² 6.1m² 6g* 6g⁵ 6m Sep 16] strong colt:
fairly useful performer: won maiden at Musselburgh in June and nursery at Catterick in
August: seemed to run well when seventh of 8 to Rock of Rochelle in listed race at the
Curragh final start: will prove best kept to 5f/6f: acts on polytrack and good to firm going:
front runner: sold 22,000 gns. *E. J. O'Neill*

VICTORIAN CAPE (IRE) 2 b.c. (Apr 3) Cape Cross (IRE) 129 – Inchoate (Machia- **52**
vellian (USA) 123) [2007 7.1g 7f⁶ 7m⁵ 7m Sep 11] strong colt: modest maiden: may
prove best up to 7f: acts on firm going: tried blinkered. *E. J. O'Neill*

VICTORIAN PRINCESS (IRE) 2 ch.f. (Mar 19) Giant's Causeway (USA) 132 – **53**
Red Zinger (USA) (Red Ransom (USA)) [2007 6g p7g 5.2f⁴ 6m 5m⁶ Aug 30] 15,000Y:
stocky filly: first foal: dam, US 8.5f/9f winner, out of close relative to high-class performer up to 1½m Ace: maiden: form (modest) only when fourth at Yarmouth: likely to
prove best at 5f: acts on firm going. *E. J. O'Neill*

VICTORIA REEL 2 ch.f. (Mar 13) Danehill Dancer (IRE) 117 – New Assembly **54**
(IRE) 99 (Machiavellian (USA) 123) [2007 7g Nov 3] tall, angular filly: third foal:
half-sister to fairly useful 1¼m winner Regent's Park (by Green Desert) and 3-y-o Small
Fortune: dam, 9f (in US) to 1¼m winner, sister to very smart 1m/1¼m performer Right
Approach: 20/1, always behind in maiden at Newmarket. *R. Hannon*

VICTORIA VALENTINE 2 b.f. (Feb 7) Royal Applause 124 – Denice 106 (Night **70 d**
Shift (USA)) [2007 6d 7g 6d 5.5m 5.1g Oct 24] €125,000Y: sturdy, deep-girthed filly:
third foal: dam German 2-y-o 5f winner and second in German 1000 Guineas: fair form
in maidens first 2 starts: well held after final start: sold 3,000 gns. *B. W. Hills*

VICTORS PRIZE (IRE) 5 b.m. Dr Devious (IRE) 127 – Spoken Word (IRE) (Peru- **–**
gino (USA) 84) [2007 –: p10g p10g⁶ Mar 5] lightly-raced maiden: no form since 2005:
tried in cheekpieces/blinkers. *S. Curran*

VICTOR TRUMPER 3 b.g. First Trump 118 – Not So Generous (IRE) 68 (Fayruz **–**
116) [2007 83: p10m⁶ Dec 8] close-coupled gelding: fairly useful performer at 2 yrs: well
held in handicap at Lingfield on sole 3-y-o start: stays 1m: acts on all-weather and good
to soft ground: tried blinkered: has failed to impress with attitude. *P. W. Chapple-Hyam*

VICTORY MILE (USA) 3 b.c. Victory Gallop (CAN) 130 – Viva Girl (USA) (Dep- **67**
uty Minister (CAN)) [2007 p8.6g 8.3m p10g 14m 11.7f* Aug 24] tall colt: fair performer:
won seller at Bath (sold 11,200 gns, joined M. Harris) in August: stays 11.7f: acts on firm
ground. *B. J. Meehan*

VICTORY QUEST (IRE) 7 b.g. Victory Note (USA) 120 – Marade (USA) (Dahar **77**
(USA) 125) [2007 71§: f16g* f16s* f16g³ 18g f14g 18m⁵ p16.5g p13.9g³ f14d² f14d*
f16d* Dec 18] fair handicapper: won at Southwell in January, February and twice in December for eighth career success there: stays 2m: acts on fibresand, unraced on extremes
of going on turf: visored: often races up with pace. *Mrs S. Lamyman*

VICTORY SHOUT (USA) 2 b.g. (Apr 13) Victory Gallop (CAN) 130 – Lu Lu's Lul- **–**
laby (USA) (Palace Music (USA) 129) [2007 5s 5m p6g p7g Oct 31] little form. *J. R. Best*

VICTORY SIGN (IRE) 7 b.g. Forzando 122 – Mo Ceri 63 (Kampala 120) [2007 –
11.6d p10g p16.5g Aug 13] big gelding: fair handicapper in 2003, well held all 3 starts
since: tried visored/tongue strap/cheekpieces. *P. Butler*

VICTORY SPIRIT 3 b.c. Invincible Spirit (IRE) 121 – Tanouma (USA) 114 (Miswaki 55
(USA) 124) [2007 75: 7.1m 7m 6g p6g p6g Sep 28] just modest performer in 2007: will
prove best at 5f/6f: acts on good to firm going: blinkered last 2 starts: sold 3,000 gns.
H. J. L. Dunlop

VIETNAM 3 ch.g. Compton Place 125 – Mosca 83 (Most Welcome 131) [2007 57: 68
11.7d p12g 7.1g 8.1d* 8d p8g6 10d* 11.5d5 Oct 23] compact gelding: fair performer: won
claimer at Sandown (claimed from S. Kirk £5,000) in August and seller at Nottingham in
October: stays 1¼m: acts on good to soft ground: often blinkered nowadays, including
for wins: races freely: said to have bled fifth outing: joined Michael J. McDonagh in
Ireland. *G. A. Huffer*

VIEWFORTH 9 b.g. Emarati (USA) 74 – Miriam 59 (Forzando 122) [2007 70, a63: 63
f5g p7.1g p7g 5g 6g3 5m4 5s 5.2d5 5d3 5.2d3 6m* 5m* 6g 6g Oct 2] good-bodied gelding:
modest handicapper: won at Lingfield and Beverley in September: best at 5f/6f: acts on
all-weather and any turf going: tried visored/in cheekpieces, usually blinkered: makes
running. *M. A. Buckley*

VIEW FROM THE TOP 3 b.c. Mujahid (USA) 125 – Aethra (USA) 89 (Trempolino 74
(USA) 135) [2007 69: 9.2g p8.6g2 8.3s p8.6g 10d4 p9.5g* 10.2m 11.9m2 12g6 Oct 5] fair
performer: won maiden at Wolverhampton in August: stays 1½m: acts on polytrack and
good to firm going, possibly not on soft: inconsistent: sold 14,000 gns. *Sir Mark Prescott*

VIGANO (IRE) 2 b.g. (Apr 7) Noverre (USA) 125 – Perugia (IRE) 94 (Perugino 68
(USA) 84) [2007 6g 6g 5g2 7m p6g p7g4 p8g p8.6g5 p8g4 Dec 12] smallish, sturdy gelding: fair maiden: stays 8.6f: acts on polytrack, best turf form (runner-up at Sandown) on
good going. *S. Kirk*

VIGO BRIDGE 3 ch.f. Bandmaster (USA) 97 – Peapod (Krayyan 117) [2007 7d Oct 9] –
good-topped filly: second foal: dam unraced: 40/1, little sign of ability in maiden at
Leicester. *B. R. Millman*

VIKING SPIRIT 5 b.g. Mind Games 121 – Dane Dancing (IRE) 68 (Danehill (USA) 111
126) [2007 108: 6m4 6m 6.1s* 6m p6g2 7d 6d Oct 13] tall, quite attractive gelding: smart
handicapper, quite lightly raced: confirmed promise of first 2 starts when winning at
Chepstow (by 3 lengths from Tony James) in July: creditable neck second to Diane's
Choice at Kempton: effective at 6f/7f: acts on polytrack, soft and good to firm going,
probably on firm: tried in cheekpieces/visor. *W. R. Swinburn*

VILA VELHA (IRE) 4 b.g. Bahhare (USA) 122 – Silver Union (IRE) (Bering 136) 53
[2007 p9.5g 9g 12g 12s 14d 9v6 12m 12g Oct 11] modest maiden: little impact at Wolverhampton on debut: tried tongue tied/in cheekpieces/blinkered. *Ms Caroline Hutchinson,
Ireland*

VILLA BIANCA'S (IRE) 4 ch.f. Priolo (USA) 127 – Ostrusa (AUT) (Rustan (HUN)) 45
[2007 52: f6g4 p7g4 p8g5 Jan 28] poor maiden: may prove best at 5f/6f: acts on polytrack:
tried blinkered: has flashed tail. *J. A. Osborne*

VILLAGE STORM (IRE) 4 b.g. Mujadil (USA) 119 – First Nadia (Auction Ring –
(USA) 123) [2007 –: f7g f6g5 8.5s6 5m p8.6g Nov 17] little form: tried blinkered.
C. J. Teague

VILNA (USA) 2 b.g. (Mar 30) Hold That Tiger (USA) 117 – Not To Be Outdone (USA) 68
(Smile (USA)) [2007 8m 7s 6f6 p7g5 p10g2 Oct 24] useful-looking gelding: fair maiden:
improved for longer trip when second in nursery at Kempton: gelded after: stays 1¼m:
acts on polytrack and firm going. *N. A. Callaghan*

VINANDO (FR) 6 ch.g. Hernando 127 – Sirena (GER) (Tejano (USA)) [2007 109: – §
21.7s5 14g 16m Aug 11] leggy, close-coupled gelding: useful performer in 2006: little
form at 6 yrs, looking temperamental: blinkered/tongue tied, tried in cheekpieces: one to
treat with caution. *C. R. Egerton*

VINCENNES 3 b. or br.f. King's Best (USA) 132 – Park Appeal 122 (Ahonoora 122) 109
[2007 74: p8g 8g* 8g2 8d3 8d3 8d 7g3 7d* 8s* Nov 4] useful performer: left M. Jarvis
after reappearance: won minor event at Royan in April and much improved last 2 starts,
winning listed race at Chantilly (beat Brofalya by 6 lengths) in October and Kolner
Herbst-Stuten-Meile at Cologne (held on gamely by ¾ length from Contentious) in
November, making virtually all both times: raced only at 7f/1m: acted on polytrack and
soft ground: raced freely: stud. *H-A. Pantall, France*

VINCENZIO (IRE) 3 b.g. Galileo (IRE) 134 – Mystic Lure 70 (Green Desert (USA) **77** 127) [2007 p7.1g⁴ 8.3s⁴ 10.2g⁶ 10d⁴ Aug 20] tall, lengthy gelding: fair maiden: not sure to stay beyond 1¼m: acts on soft going: gelded after final start. *C. R. Egerton*

VINEYARD 2 b.g. (Mar 17) Alhaarth (IRE) 126 – Abime (USA) (Woodman (USA) **76** 126) [2007 7m 6d³ 6d⁶ Oct 15] good-topped gelding: good mover: fair maiden: third to Seasider at Windsor: should stay 7f/1m: gelded after final start. *W. J. Haggas*

VINTAGE (IRE) 3 b.g. Danetime (IRE) 121 – Katherine Gorge (USA) (Hansel (USA)) **67** [2007 67: p6g 7d 5m p5g p6g* p7g⁵ Oct 10] lengthy, unfurnished gelding: fair performer: won minor event at Wolverhampton in October: stays easy 7f: acts on polytrack: tried tongue tied. *P. Mitchell*

VIOLA ROSA (IRE) 2 b.f. (Feb 1) Fraam 114 – Bleu Cerise (Sadler's Wells (USA) **41** 132) [2007 p7.1g 7d 7m p7g⁶ Dec 19] 22,000F, 30,000Y: half-sister to useful French 1¼m/1½m performer Billy The Kid (by Danehill) and French 11f/1½m winner Blue Lightning (by Alzao): dam maiden half-sister to high-class French 7f to 1¼m performer Bigstone: poor maiden: will stay at least 1m. *D. Shaw*

VIOLENT VELOCITY (IRE) 4 b.g. Namid 128 – Lear's Crown (USA) 82 (Lear **74** Fan (USA) 130) [2007 77: p7.1g⁴ p7.1g⁶ p7.1g² f7g 6g³ 6m* 7.1m* 5.9m 6m⁴ 7.1d⁵ 6.9m³ 8m⁴ 7m² 7.9g² 10g⁶ 10.1d Oct 16] neat gelding: fair handicapper: won at Catterick (apprentices) in April and Musselburgh in May: effective at 6f to 1m (below form at 1¼m): acts on polytrack (well below form on fibresand) and good to firm ground: tried visored: held up: has raced freely: consistent. *J. J. Quinn*

VIOLET'S PRIDE 3 b.f. Kyllachy 129 – Majalis 79 (Mujadil (USA) 119) [2007 62: **59** 5.1g⁶ 5m 5m 5d⁵ 5g 5m⁵ 5m* p5.1g⁵ 5m 5g³ p5.1g Oct 30] compact filly: modest maiden: left S. Parr after ninth start: best at 5f: acts on firm ground: tends to hang right, and crashed through rail second 2-y-o start: tried visored: tricky ride. *N. Tinkler*

VIRGILIA (IRE) 3 b.f. Barathea (IRE) 127 – Lanelle (USA) 79 (Trempolino (USA) **45** 135) [2007 p6g p7g⁵ p10g Nov 30] €80,000Y: second foal: dam, French 15f winner, closely related to smart stayer Landowner: poor form in maidens. *R. Hannon*

VIRTUAL 2 b.c. (May 10) Pivotal 124 – Virtuous 92 (Exit To Nowhere (USA) 122) **89** [2007 7m² 7m² Oct 5] big, good-topped colt: has plenty of scope: has a moderate, quick action: sixth foal: brother to fairly useful 1¼m winner Virtuosity, closely related to smart 2004 Coventry Stakes winner Iceman (by Polar Falcon) and half-brother to 2 winners, including fairly useful 1¼m winner Peace (by Sadler's Wells): dam, 2-y-o 1m winner who stayed 11.5f, out of half-sister to 2000 Guineas winner Entrepreneur: fairly useful form: second in maidens at Newmarket, beaten 1¼ lengths by Almajd in latter: will stay 1m. *J. H. M. Gosden*

VIRTUAL PADDY 2 br.g. (May 9) Averti (IRE) 117 – Petrovna (IRE) 78 (Petardia **–** 113) [2007 5.1f 6g 6m 6.1s 8.1m p8g Sep 24] close-coupled gelding: little form. *M. Blanshard*

VISCAYA (IRE) 2 b.f. (Feb 10) Xaar 132 – Fearfully Grand (Grand Lodge (USA) 125) **61** [2007 6g 6f⁶ 6m⁵ 6d Oct 9] 20,000Y: rather leggy filly: second foal: half-sister to 3-y-o Mandurah: dam unraced half-sister to useful performer up to 1m Himiko: maiden: form (modest) only on reappearance: tried in cheekpieces. *Mrs A. Duffield*

VISCONTI (IRE) 2 ch.c. (Mar 6) Medicean 128 – Now And Forever (IRE) (Kris 135) [2007 **65** 7m 6g Aug 24] angular, quite attractive colt: has a fluent action: towards rear in maidens, apparently fair form at Newmarket (behind Rio de La Plata) on debut: sold 4,000 gns. *P. W. Chapple-Hyam*

VISCOUNTESS (IRE) 2 b.f. (May 1) Green Desert (USA) 127 – Maria Isabella **67 p** (USA) 96 (Kris 135) [2007 7d⁴ Oct 30] fifth foal: half-sister to smart French 9f/9.5f winner Utrecht (by Rock of Gibraltar): dam, 2-y-o 1m winner, half-sister to Bosra Sham, Hector Protector and Shanghai: 6/1, always prominent (but clearly green) when fourth to Tasheba in maiden at Yarmouth: will stay 1m: sure to improve. *M. Johnston*

VISCOUNT MONTY 2 b.g. (Feb 28) Sugarfoot 118 – Desert Loch (IRE) 56 (Desert **–** King (IRE) 129) [2007 6s 6v⁶ 7m 7.5g 8g Oct 19] close-coupled, compact gelding: little form: tried visored. *N. Tinkler*

VISIT 2 b.f. (May 8) Oasis Dream 129 – Arrive 109 (Kahyasi 130) [2007 6d² 6d* 6g²ᵈ **110 +** 6m Oct 5] good-bodied, useful-looking filly: third foal: half-sister to 3-y-o Promising Lead: dam, 1¼m to 15f winner, sister to outstanding broodmare Hasili and half-sister to dam of high-class US miler Leroidesanimaux: smart performer: better for debut, successful in Princess Margaret Independent Newspaper Stakes at Ascot in July by 1½ lengths from Reel Gift, plenty to do 2f out but showing good turn of foot to win going away:

½-length second to Nahoodh in Lowther Stakes at York next time, held in as winner asserted, closing at finish (disqualified after failing dope test): favourite, only eighth behind Natagora in Cheveley Park Stakes at Newmarket final start, first off bridle: races lazily, and will be suited by 7f/1m: raced only on good/good to soft going prior to Newmarket. *Sir Michael Stoute*

VISON CELEBRE (IRE) 4 gr.c. Peintre Celebre (USA) 137 – Visionnaire (FR) 112 **118** (Linamix (FR) 127) [2007 12g* 12g² Jun 3] second foal: dam, French 1m winner who stayed 10.5f, half-sister to smart French performer up to 1½m Visindar: beat subsequent Prix du Jockey Club winner Darsi 1½ lengths in minor event at Longchamp on debut at 3 yrs: won similar event there after more than year's absence in April, comfortably beating Royal Commander by 2 lengths: smart form when 1½ lengths second to Saddex in Grand Prix de Chantilly only other start, finishing best of all from rear: stays 1½m: looked potentially high-class but evidently very hard to train. *A. Fabre, France*

VISTARIA (USA) 3 ch.f. Distant View (USA) 126 – Stellaria (USA) 98 (Roberto **–** (USA) 131) [2007 p8g Oct 15] sister to top-class 6f (at 2 yrs) to 9f winner Observatory and fairly useful 7f to 1¼m winner Star Magnitude and half-sister to several winners, including smart 7f (at 2 yrs) to 1½m winner High Praise (by Quest For Fame): dam 5f (at 2 yrs) to 8.5f (in US) winner: 7/2, struggling by halfway when last in maiden at Lingfield: sold 90,000 gns. *J. H. M. Gosden*

VITAL EQUINE (IRE) 3 b.c. Danetime (IRE) 121 – Bayalika (IRE) (Selkirk **121** (USA) 129) [2007 113: 8m² 8m⁶ 7d Oct 6]
The 2006 Champagne Stakes run at York, in which Vital Equine came out best in a very close finish with Eagle Mountain and Cockney Rebel, with Kirklees fourth, turned out to be a far hotter contest than it appeared at the time. Remarkably, Vital Equine never won again, but he certainly went on to play his part in boosting the form of the Group 2 Champagne Stakes. Successful in a maiden at Newcastle and minor event at Yarmouth before winning at York, Vital Equine raced only in Group 1 events subsequently. Third to Holy Roman Emperor in the Prix Jean-Luc Lagardere and fifth to Teofilo in the Dewhurst Stakes on the first two occasions, Vital Equine ran below form when stepped up to a mile in the Criterium International on his final juvenile start and then wasn't seen out again until May. The Two Thousand Guineas at Newmarket was Vital Equine's comeback race, and it's fair to say he wouldn't have appeared on many shortlists as a likely winner. Physically, though, the strapping Vital Equine had always looked the sort to make an even better three-year-old, and he belied odds of 33/1 in running a cracker to finish a length and a half second to Cockney Rebel, three places and just over a length ahead of Eagle Mountain. A strong-galloping sort, inclined to pull when waited with, Vital Equine was given his head from the start at Newmarket and managed to shake off all bar the winner with a decisive move into the Dip, collared inside the last furlong. The first two met again in the Irish Two Thousand Guineas at the Curragh, but Vital Equine could finish only sixth behind Cockney Rebel there, beaten three lengths. It's possible he hadn't quite got over his exertions at Newmarket and he certainly didn't go with quite the same zest as he helped force the pace until after two furlongs out. In what turned out to be the mistaken belief that the ground would probably ride too fast for him during the summer months, Vital Equine was kept for an autumn campaign. Unfortunately, in the end, that consisted of just one appearance, in the Prix de la Foret at Longchamp. Bumped on the first bend, Vital Equine was never going well after that and beat only one home, reportedly returning injured. Vital Equine was retired and will be standing at the Bearstone Stud, Shropshire in 2008, his fee set at £6,000.

Vital Equine (IRE) (b.c. 2004)	Danetime (IRE) (b 1994)	Danehill (b 1986)	Danzig
			Razyana
		Allegheny River (b 1987)	Lear Fan
			Allesheny
	Bayalika (IRE) (b 1998)	Selkirk (ch 1988)	Sharpen Up
			Annie Edge
		Bayrika (b 1991)	Kahyasi
			Behera

An 18,000-guinea foal who fetched 24,000 guineas when resold as a year-ling, Vital Equine is the second foal of the unraced Bayalika. Bred by the Aga Khan,

Bayalika is a daughter of Bayrika, a useful stayer in France and winner of the Prix Berteux at Maisons-Laffitte. Bayalika is a granddaughter of the Prix de l'Arc de Triomphe runner-up Behera, whose numerous winners include the very smart hurdler and top-class chaser Behrajan. There's stamina aplenty in the family but Vital Equine, by the sprinter Danetime, looked to find a mile far enough for him. A big, strong individual who acted on good to firm and good to soft going, Vital Equine sometimes wore a crossed noseband and he was tongue tied three times at two, including at York. *E. J. O'Neill*

VITAL STATISTICS 3 br.f. Indian Ridge 123 – Emerald Peace (IRE) 103 (Green **102** Desert (USA) 127) [2007 102: 7m⁶ 8m 7m⁵ 7g 7m 7d 6d⁵ Oct 19] good-bodied filly: useful performer: mainly stiff tasks in 2007, best efforts when sixth in listed European Free Handicap at Newmarket (behind Prime Defender) and fifth in Jersey Stakes at Royal Ascot (beaten 4 lengths by Tariq) first/third outings: stays 7f: acts on good to firm going: nervy sort, often sweats/on toes: held up. *D. R. C. Elsworth*

VITAL TRYST 3 ch.g. Pivotal 124 – Splicing 82 (Sharpo 132) [2007 –: p6g p9.5g 6m **–** Apr 12] good-quartered gelding: well held all starts, including in seller. *J. G. Given*

VITZNAU (IRE) 3 b.c. Val Royal (FR) 127 – Neat Dish (CAN) 90 (Stalwart (USA)) **110** [2007 79+: p7g² p7g² 7d* 7d* 6m⁶ 7g² 7g⁴ 7m⁴ 7d² Oct 19] tall, useful-looking colt: smart handicapper: progressed very well in 2007, winning at Epsom and Chester (beat White Deer by head) in June: good efforts in frame last 4 starts, particularly when ½-length second of 26 to Damika at Newmarket final outing, again finishing strongly: should stay 1m: acts on polytrack, firm and good to soft going: usually held up. *R. Hannon*

VIVACITA 3 b.f. Medicean 128 – Sandrella (IRE) (Darshaan 133) [2007 12.1m² **72** p13.9g² p12g p12.2g* p13.9g Nov 14] 25,000F: fourth foal: half-sister to 1½m/2m winner San Hernando (by Hernando): dam unraced half-sister to high-class 1¼m/1½m performer Storming Home: fair performer: won maiden at Wolverhampton in November: stays easy 1¾m: acts on polytrack and good to firm going: free-going sort: sent to France. *E. J. O'Neill*

VIVA LA FLAG (USA) 3 ch.f. Rahy (USA) 115 – On Parade (USA) (Storm Cat **104** (USA)) [2007 7g⁴ 8g³ 8.1d* 10s⁶ 10m* 10m⁴ 10g⁴ Nov 3] quite good-topped filly: second foal: dam, stakes-placed 2-y-o winner in USA, sister to Breeders' Cup Juvenile Fillies' winner Storm Flag Flying (also US Grade 1 1¼m winner at 4 yrs): useful form: won maiden at Sandown in July and handicap at Newbury (beat Ronaldsay by neck) in September: best effort when 3¾ lengths fourth to Mashaahed in listed race at Newmarket final outing, fading: stays 1¼m: acts on good to firm and good to soft going: tongue tied last 3 starts: sent to USA. *J. L. Dunlop*

VIVALDI (IRE) 2 b.c. (Jan 20) Montjeu (IRE) 137 – Parvenue (FR) 79 (Ezzoud (IRE) **86 p** 126) [2007 7g 8d* Jul 8] €140,000F: well-made colt: third foal: half-brother to fairly useful 2006 2-y-o 6f winner Three Decades (by Invincible Spirit) and Italian 2005 2-y-o 5f winner Golden Fasly (by Fasliyev): dam, 2-y-o 6f winner, out of sister to Middle Park Stakes winner/2000 Guineas runner-up Lycius: much better effort in maidens (fairly useful form) when beating Brazilian Star by a neck at Gowran in July: stays 1m: acts on good to soft going: capable of better still, provided all is well. *A. P. O'Brien, Ireland*

VIVA VETTORI 3 ch.c. Vettori (IRE) 119 – Cruinn A Bhord 107 (Inchinor 119) [2007 **89 p** 8d³ 10m⁵ p10g* Sep 29] 6,000Y: big, leggy, lengthy colt: fourth foal: brother to 1½m winner Chess Board and half-brother to 5-y-o Zantero: dam, 7f winner, half-sister to Ouija Board: fairly useful form: best effort in maidens when winning at Kempton (by 2 lengths from Comma, making all) in September: should stay 1½m: acts on polytrack: remains likely to do better. *D. R. C. Elsworth*

VIVA VOLTA 4 b.g. Superior Premium 122 – La Volta 86 (Komaite (USA)) [2007 77: **85** 7f 7m⁶ 7d⁴ 7m* 7.1g² 7s 7s⁶ 7m⁵ 6m⁵ p7m⁶ p7.1g⁴ 7g Oct 30] strong, lengthy gelding: fairly useful handicapper: won at Newcastle in June and August: stays 7.5f: acts on polytrack, good to firm and good to soft going, below form on soft: often blinkered: usually front runner. *T. D. Easterby*

VIVE LA CHASSE (IRE) 4 b.f. Mull of Kintyre (USA) 114 – Erne Project (IRE) 80 **–** (Project Manager 111) [2007 p8g 8.3g 7s Jun 29] €22,000Y: sturdy filly: fourth foal: half-sister to 5-y-o Beaver Patrol and to winner up to 1m in Italy, both by Tagula: dam Irish 13f winner: well held in maidens: tried blinkered. *Eve Johnson Houghton*

VIVE LES ROUGES 2 b.f. (Feb 14) Acclamation 118 – Bible Box (IRE) 93 (Bin **91** Ajwaad (IRE) 119) [2007 6d⁶ 6d* 6g² 6g Oct 6] lengthy filly: has scope: first foal: dam 7f to 9f winner: fairly useful form: won maiden at Lingfield in August: improved again when neck second to Fashion Rocks (Raymi Coya third) in listed race at Salisbury, impressing with speed: possibly amiss in Two-Year-Old Trophy at Redcar final start: will prove best at 5f/6f: raced only on good/good to soft going. *C. F. Wall*

VIVI BELLE 3 b.f. Cadeaux Genereux 131 – Locharia 91 (Wolfhound (USA) 126) **63**
[2007 –: p5.1g p6g 6d* 6d 6d⁵ p7m⁵ Nov 1] smallish filly: modest handicapper: won at Salisbury in June: stays 7f: raced only on polytrack and good to soft going: sold 2,500 gns, sent to Sweden. *M. L. W. Bell*

VIXENS DAUGHTER 2 b.f. (Jan 12) Foxhound (USA) 103 – Classy Relation (Puis- **49 d** sance 110) [2007 5m² 5g 6m p5.1g p6g 5.1g Nov 7] leggy filly: poor mover: sister to 4-y-o William John and half-sister to useful Italian sprinter Golden Pivotal (by Pivotal): dam unraced out of half-sister to 2000 Guineas winner King of Kings: maiden: form only when second in claimer at Thirsk on debut (left K. Ryan £10,000): tried tongue tied: sold £450. *R. T. Phillips*

VIXEN VIRAGO 4 ch.f. Foxhound (USA) 103 – Le Pin 59 (Persian Bold 123) [2007 **–** –: p8g⁶ Jan 3] quite good-topped filly: little form: tried in cheekpieces. *Jane Southcombe*

VLASTA WEINER 7 b.g. Magic Ring (IRE) 115 – Armaiti 78 (Sayf El Arab (USA) **a60** 127) [2007 –, a60: p5g² p5.1g* p6g f5g f6g⁵ p6g Mar 16] modest handicapper: won amateur event at Wolverhampton in January: clipped heels and unseated jockey final outing: stays 7f: acts on all-weather, raced mainly on good ground or firmer on turf: blinkered. *J. M. Bradley*

VOGARTH 3 ch.g. Arkadian Hero (USA) 123 – Skara Brae 49 (Inchinor 119) [2007 6s **62** 6s³ 6f⁴ 7.1m⁵ 5.7d³ 6g Oct 8] medium-sized gelding: modest maiden: may prove best at 6f: acts on good ground. *B. R. Millman*

VOICE 3 b.f. Zamindar (USA) 116 – Seven Sing (USA) 83 (Machiavellian (USA) 123) **79** [2007 57p: 7m p9.5g⁴ 8.3m² Jun 4] close-coupled filly: fair maiden: good second on handicap debut at Windsor final outing: stays 8.3f: acts on good to firm ground: sold 14,000 gns in December. *H. R. A. Cecil*

VOICE MAIL 8 b.g. So Factual (USA) 120 – Wizardry 83 (Shirley Heights 130) [2007 **59** 80, a63: p10g⁶ p10g² p10g³ p8g³ p10g p10g³ p8g⁵ 8m 10m 10.2d 10d⁴ 11.9m⁶ 10d 10g⁶ 10.2m⁴ p9.5g Sep 21] useful-looking gelding: just modest performer nowadays: rejoined former trainer from P. Howling after second outing: seems to stay 11.7f: acts on polytrack and firm going, probably on soft: tried in headgear: held up. *A. M. Balding*

VOIR DIRE 5 b.g. Vettori (IRE) 119 – Bobbie Dee 93 (Blakeney 126) [2007 p16g⁴ **57** 17.2m² p16g Aug 1] tall gelding: modest maiden on Flat, lightly raced: stays at least 1¾m: acts on heavy going, probably on polytrack: fair hurdler. *Mrs P. N. Dutfield*

VOLATICUS (IRE) 6 b.g. Desert Story (IRE) 115 – Haysel (IRE) (Petorius 117) **66** [2007 p9.5g⁴ f7g² p8.6g p10g⁵ 8.5m 9.1g⁴ 8s⁵ 12.1s⁴ 12m⁴ 11.1m 8.5g Sep 19] close-coupled gelding: fair performer: won 3 races at Mijas in 2005/6: left R. Smith after second start: barely stays testing 1½m: acts on sand/all-weather, soft and good to firm ground: tried visored/blinkered (ran freely). *A. D. Brown*

VOLIERE 4 b.f. Zafonic (USA) 130 – Warbler 110 (Warning 136) [2007 87: 8.1g 7d **102** 8m⁶ 8d⁵ 8m³ 8.3d⁵ 10m³ 10.1g² p8.6g* p8g³ 8g p10m⁴ p12g⁵ p10g³ Dec 22] 10,000Y: good-bodied filly: fifth foal: closely related to 1m winner Reed Minder (by Zamindar) and half-sister to 1¼m winner Trill (by Highest Honor), both useful in France: dam French 10.5f/11.5f winner (stayed 15f): useful performer: left G. Lyons in Ireland 16,000 gns after 3 yrs: won handicap at Wolverhampton in October: good efforts in frame in listed races at Lingfield 2 of last 3 starts, including third to Gentleman's Deal: effective at 1m/1¼m: acts on polytrack, firm and soft ground: often held up. *S. C. Williams*

VOLVORETAS RAINBOW 2 ch.f. (Feb 9) Rainbow Quest (USA) 134 – Volvoreta **56 p** 121 (Suave Dancer (USA) 136) [2007 7.5g⁵ Sep 19] second foal: dam, French 1m (at 2 yrs) to 1½m (Prix Vermeille) winner, also third in Arc: 18/1, needed experience when fifth in maiden at Beverley: will do better at 1¼m/1½m. *P. C. Haslam*

VONDOVA 5 b.m. Efisio 120 – Well Proud (IRE) (Sadler's Wells (USA) 132) [2007 –: **45** 6s 5g 6d 6d 5m 5m⁵ 6s 5d 5g⁶ 6m 5d⁶ 5g 6d 5m Sep 30] tall, leggy mare: poor performer nowadays: probably best at 5f/6f: acts on good to firm and good to soft ground: tried in cheekpieces. *D. A. Nolan*

VON WESSEX 5 b.g. Wizard King 122 – Gay Da Cheen (IRE) (Tenby 125) [2007 51§: **44 §** p5.1g 6g⁶ 6m p6g Aug 23] compact gelding: poor performer nowadays: effective at 5f/ easy 6f: acts on good to firm and good to soft going: tried in cheekpieces/tongue tied: tends to hang: unreliable. *W. G. M. Turner*

VOODOO MOON 3 b.f. Efisio 120 – Lunasa (IRE) 82 (Don't Forget Me 127) [2007 **92** 89: 7.5m* 8m⁵ 8.1m⁴ 9.1m 7m 8m⁶ 7g 7m⁵ 8g⁵ 8m⁶ Sep 6] tall, close-coupled, quite good-topped filly: fairly useful handicapper: won at Beverley in April: well below form final outing: stays 1m: acts on good to firm and good to soft going, below form on soft/ heavy: races prominently: has looked none too keen. *M. Johnston*

VORTEEVA (USA) 3 b.g. Bahri (USA) 125 Super Supreme (IND) (Zafonic (USA) – 130) [2007 91: 8g⁵ 10m 9.9m Aug 25] smallish, close-coupled gelding: fairly useful performer at 2 yrs, winning maiden at Tipperary (by 7 lengths) prior to sixth (behind Teofilo) in Futurity Stakes at the Curragh: left J. Oxx in Ireland 65,000 gns, well held in 2007: stays 7.5f: raced only on good ground or firmer (acts on firm): tried in cheekpieces: said to have finished distressed last 2 outings: sent to USA. *K. R. Burke*

VORTEX 8 b.g. Danehill (USA) 126 – Roupala (USA) 75 (Vaguely Noble 140) [2007 **114** 114: p8g³ 7.5g* 8g a8f² a8f p7g² 7g³ a8.7f 8m³ 7m 7g 8g 8m⁵ 7m⁶ p7g* Dec 28] big, good-bodied gelding: smart performer: won handicaps at Nad Al Sheba (beat Ans Bach by neck) in February and Lingfield (by ½ length from Ektimaal) in December: also ran well when ¾-length second to Boston Lodge in Burj Nahaar Stakes at Nad Al Sheba and third of 26 to Royal Oath in Hunt Cup at Royal Ascot fourth/ninth outings: stays 1m: acts on all-weather/dirt and good to firm going (possibly not firm): usually tongue tied: tried blinkered/visored: often wears bandages: travels strongly, and tends to idle: reportedly lost action penultimate start. *Miss Gay Kelleway*

VOSS 3 b.f. Halling (USA) 133 – Valdara (Darshaan 133) [2007 –: p10g² p9.5g p10g⁵ **55** Feb 14] leggy filly: should stay 1½m: acts on polytrack: sold 8,000 gns in July (reportedly in foal to Whipper). *M. Johnston*

W

WABBRAAN (USA) 2 b.c. (Jan 26) Aldebaran (USA) 126 – Madame Modjeska **68** (USA) (Danzig (USA)) [2007 7d p8g⁶ p7g Oct 24] rather leggy colt: fair maiden: best effort when sixth to Ordinance at Kempton: stays 1m. *D. M. Simcock*

WADI RAIDER 2 b.c. (Feb 9) Tobougg (IRE) 125 – Dowhatjen 86 (Desert Style (IRE) – 121) [2007 8m 8m Sep 21] tall colt: behind in maidens. *M. R. Channon*

WADLIA (USA) 2 ch.f. (Feb 19) Lemon Drop Kid (USA) 131 – Brusque (USA) **– p** (Canaveral (USA)) [2007 8d Sep 29] $75,000Y: lengthy filly: first foal: dam Canadian 2-y-o 6f to 8.5f (Grade 2) winner: unrealistic debut in Fillies' Mile at Ascot, green and detached: should do better down in grade. *C. E. Brittain*

WADNAGIN (IRE) 3 b.f. Princely Heir (IRE) 111 – Band of Colour (IRE) (Spectrum **72** (IRE) 126) [2007 59: p6g⁵ 7m 5.1g³ 6m² 6d⁴ p6g⁶ 6d 6.1d⁵ 6g* p7.1g* p7.1g⁶ p7g⁵ Nov 7] leggy filly: fair handicapper: won at Yarmouth in September and Wolverhampton in October: effective from 5f to 7f: acts on polytrack, good to firm and good to soft ground: held up. *I. A. Wood*

WAGTAIL 4 b.f. Cape Cross (IRE) 129 – Dancing Feather 72 (Suave Dancer (USA) **101** 136) [2007 101: 8d⁴ 8d³ 10d p8m³ Nov 1] leggy, attractive filly: useful performer: creditable efforts in frame in listed races in 2007, notably when 2¾ lengths third to Pintle at Bath second outing: stays 8.5f, probably not 1¼m: acts on polytrack, good to firm and good to soft going: usually tongue tied: tends to hang left. *E. A. L. Dunlop*

WAHHAJ 3 b.c. Muhtarram (USA) 125 – Scottish Royal (IRE) (Night Shift (USA)) – [2007 7g 10.1m⁶ 10.1m Aug 15] well held in maiden/claimers. *G. Prodromou*

WAHOO SAM (USA) 7 ch.g. Sandpit (BRZ) 129 – Good Reputation (USA) (Gran **79** Zar (MEX)) [2007 86: p7.1g* p9.5g³ f8g* p8.6g⁶ 8.1m 8.3g 9g³ 7.1m⁶ p8.6g⁶ 8m⁴ 8.1m 8s* 8m 8.1g 7.2s 7.2s 8g⁵ p8.6g Nov 20] lengthy, good-topped gelding: fair performer: won claimer at Wolverhampton and handicap at Southwell in January and, having left K. Ryan after tenth start, handicap at Musselburgh in August: effective at 7f to 9.8f: acts on all-weather, firm and soft going: tried blinkered, usually wears cheekpieces: front runner: inconsistent. *D. W. Barker*

WAIHEKE ISLAND 3 b.f. Winged Love (IRE) 121 – West of Warsaw (Danzig Con- **37** nection (USA)) [2007 69?: 5.9m 6.9g 7v⁵ 8.3d Jul 14] close-coupled filly: just poor maiden in 2007: should stay 1m+. *B. Mactaggart*

WAINWRIGHT (IRE) 7 b.g. Victory Note (USA) 120 – Double Opus (IRE) (Petorius **a62** 117) [2007 71: f6g⁵ p7g f6g² f6g⁴ f7g⁶ 6s 6m 6d 6d Oct 1] quite attractive gelding: modest handicapper nowadays, better on all-weather than turf: stays 7f: acts on all-weather, firm and soft going: tried tongue tied/in cheekpieces/blinkered. *P. A. Blockley*

WAIT FOR THE LIGHT 3 b.g. Fantastic Light (USA) 134 – Lady In Waiting 113 **86** (Kylian (USA)) [2007 80p: 11.6g⁴ 11.9m 12f³ 11.6g⁵ p12.2g Oct 21] rangy gelding, somewhat unfurnished at present: fairly useful performer: creditable efforts when in frame in handicaps in 2007: should stay 1¾m: acts on polytrack and firm ground: in cheekpieces/blinkered last 3 starts: not entirely straightforward: sold 15,000 gns. *E. A. L. Dunlop*

WAIT FOR THE WILL (USA) 11 ch.g. Seeking The Gold (USA) – You'd Be Sur- **79** prised (USA) 117 (Blushing Groom (FR) 131) [2007 –, a72: p13g p12g* p12.2g⁴ p12g⁵ 10m³ 11.6f* 12g⁶ p13g³ p12g Nov 21] tall gelding: fair handicapper: won at Lingfield in January and Windsor (amateur event) in August: effective at 1½m to easy 2m: acts on polytrack, firm and good to soft going: tongue tied/visored once, usually blinkered: held up: sometimes finds little. *G. L. Moore*

WAIT WATCHER (IRE) 3 b.f. Fath (USA) 116 – Campestral (USA) 97 (Alleged – (USA) 138) [2007 96: 7m 10m 10s Sep 22] tall filly: useful performer at 2 yrs: stiff tasks, little impact in 2007: should stay 1m: best effort on good to soft going. *P. A. Blockley*

WAKE UP MAGGIE (IRE) 4 b.f. Xaar 132 – Kalagold (IRE) 81 (Magical Strike **117** (USA) 114) [2007 110: 7g* 7s⁴ 7g* 7d⁴ 7m³ 8m Oct 6] strong, close-coupled filly: smart performer: better than ever in 2007, winning Chartwell Fillies' Stakes at Lingfield (by 3½ lengths from Leopoldine) in May and Oak Tree Stakes at Goodwood (best effort, beat Costume by ½ length) in August: respectable efforts in frame in Hungerford Stakes at Newbury and Park Stakes at Doncaster (2¾ lengths third to Arabian Gleam, plenty to do) next 2 starts: ran poorly in Sun Chariot Stakes at Newmarket final outing: stays 7f: acts on soft and good to firm going: waited with, and has sharp turn of foot: possibly not straightforward: sold 300,000 gns, joined C. Wall. *C. F. Wall*

WALKER (CZE) 3 ch.g. Signe Divin (USA) 117 – Wanateluthspilgrim (USA) (Pil- – grim (USA) 108) [2007 7.9m a8g Oct 7] second on debut in Czech Republic at 2 yrs but little form otherwise: tailed off in claimer (blinkered) only outing in Britain on reappearance, then sent to Belgium. *A. Berry*

WALKING TALKING 3 b.c. Rainbow Quest (USA) 134 – Wooden Doll (USA) 98 **99** (Woodman (USA) 126) [2007 83p: 8m 10g* 12g³ Jun 21] big, well-made colt: useful form: confirmed promise of reappearance when winning maiden at Sandown in June: upped in trip, further improvement when 4¼ lengths third to Heron Bay in King George V Handicap at Royal Ascot final start: stays 1½m. *H. R. A. Cecil*

WALK IN THE PARK (IRE) 5 b.h. Montjeu (IRE) 137 – Classic Park 115 (Robel- **110** lino (USA) 127) [2007 107: 12g 15d⁶ Aug 19] huge, rather leggy, good-topped horse: very smart form when 5 lengths second to Motivator in Derby at Epsom in 2005, but reportedly jarred up in Irish Derby at the Curragh next time: lightly raced and just smart form after, seventh of 8 to Saddex in Grand Prix de Chantilly and sixth of 9 to Getaway in Prix Kergorlay at Deauville only Flat outings in 2007 (held well only start over hurdles in September): best effort at 1½m: acted on soft going: had had tongue tied: tended to pull hard: sold €195,000, and to stand at Haras du Val Raquet, nr Lisieux, France, fee €2,500. *J. E. Hammond, France*

WALLY BARGE 4 b.g. Reprimand 122 – Linda's Schoolgirl (IRE) (Grand Lodge **59 d** (USA) 125) [2007 61: p10g⁵ p8.6g⁵ 10s p9.5g 11.5s p10g Aug 4] lengthy, good-topped gelding: modest maiden handicapper, on downgrade: stays 8.6f: acts on polytrack: joined John J. Walsh in Ireland. *D. K. Ivory*

WALNUT GROVE 4 b.f. Forzando 122 – Final Rush 66 (Final Straw 127) [2007 65: **67** 7.1m 7m 5.9m* 6f 6m Jun 8] strong, workmanlike filly: has a moderate, round action: fair handicapper: won at Carlisle in May: effective at 6f, should stay 1m: acts on firm going. *T. D. Barron*

WALTON HOUSE (USA) 2 ch.g. (Apr 8) Mutakddim (USA) 112 – Dominant Dancer – 97 (Primo Dominie 121) [2007 p8g⁵ Dec 19] 12/1, well held in maiden at Kempton, slowly away. *A. M. Balding*

WANCHAI LAD 6 b.g. Danzero (AUS) – Frisson (Slip Anchor 136) [2007 88: 5g* 6d **91** 5v⁶ Jul 7] good-topped gelding: fairly useful handicapper: won at Beverley in May: below form after: effective at 5f/6f: acts on firm and soft going: tried tongue tied. *T. D. Easterby*

WANDLE 3 b.c. Galileo (IRE) 134 – Artistic Blue (USA) 109 (Diesis 133) [2007 79p: **98** p12g* 10m³ 12g Jun 21] good-topped colt: useful form: won 4-runner maiden at Lingfield (by 5 lengths) in March: further improvement when third to Metaphoric in handicap at Newmarket next time: pulled too hard when well below form in King George V Handicap at Royal Ascot final outing: stays easy 1½m: acts on polytrack and good to firm ground. *T. G. Mills*

WANESSA TIGER (IRE) 3 ch.f. Titus Livius (FR) 115 – Lominda (IRE) 80 **54** (Lomond (USA) 128) [2007 58: p8.6g⁵ p8.6g May 14] modest maiden: may prove best short of 8.6f: sold 18,000 gns in July. *M. R. Channon*

WANNABE FREE 2 b.f. (Mar 16) Red Ransom (USA) – Wannabe Grand (IRE) 116 **71** (Danehill (USA) 126) [2007 6g⁶ p7g⁶ 7g³ p7g⁴ Dec 19] close-coupled filly: fifth foal: half-sister to several winners, including 4-y-o King of Argos, 2003 2-y-o 5f winner Bachelor of Arts (by Stravinsky) and 7f winner (including at 2 yrs) Walkonthewildside (by Giant's Causeway), latter 2 useful: dam Cherry Hinton/Cheveley Park winner and runner-up in 1000 Guineas: fair maiden: third to La Coveta at Newmarket: will be suited by 1m. *J. Noseda*

WANNABE POSH (IRE) 4 b.f. Grand Lodge (USA) 125 – Wannabe 84 (Shirley **107** Heights 130) [2007 94: 12m* 11.9m² 12g³ 14g² 12g* 14.6m Sep 13] well-made filly: useful performer: won handicap at Newmarket in May and listed race at York (beat Brisk Breeze by 1¾ lengths) in August: also ran well when third in Noblesse Stakes at Cork (behind Nick's Nikita) and second in Lillie Langtry Stakes at Goodwood (½ length behind Hi Calypso) third/fourth outings: stayed 1¾m: acted on soft and good to firm going: genuine and consistent: stud. *J. L. Dunlop*

WANNAROCK (IRE) 2 b. or br.g. (Apr 10) Rock of Gibraltar (IRE) 133 – Propensity **74** 93 (Habitat 134) [2007 6m⁶ 7m⁵ 8.2g³ Nov 7] compact gelding: fair maiden: third to Laterly at Nottingham: gelded after: stays 1m. *E. A. L. Dunlop*

WANNA SHOUT 9 b.m. Missed Flight 123 – Lulu (Polar Falcon (USA) 126) [2007 **–** 60d: p12g⁵ Jun 6] modest performer at 8 yrs: well held only start in 2007: stays 1¼m: acts on all-weather, firm and soft ground: tried in headgear/tongue tied: sometimes slowly away/wayward. *R. Dickin*

WAQAARR 3 b.g. Tobougg (IRE) 125 – Seeking Utopia 76 (Wolfhound (USA) 126) **63** [2007 p6g p7f³ 7.1m Apr 9] fair form in maidens: should stay 1m: sold 14,000 gns, gelded, joined Lady Herries. *M. R. Channon*

WAR ANTHEM 3 br.g. Vettori (IRE) 119 – Lucy Boo (Singspiel (IRE) 133) [2007 7m⁵ **73** 6.9m³ 7d² 9.8g⁴ p8.6g³ Sep 20] good-topped gelding: fair maiden: stays 9.8f: acts on polytrack, good to firm and good to soft ground: blinkered last 3 starts: gelded after final outing. *C. R. Egerton*

WAR AT SEA (IRE) 5 b.g. Bering 136 – Naval Affair (IRE) 101 (Last Tycoon 131) **75** [2007 67: p16g² p12g³ Jan 10] well-made gelding: fair handicapper: stays easy 2m: acts on polytrack, good to firm and good to soft going: tried visored (raced freely)/tongue tied: has found little: sold 10,000 gns in May. *A. W. Carroll*

WARDEN FIZZ 2 b.g. (Feb 12) Efisio 120 – Miss Rimex (IRE) 84 (Ezzoud (IRE) 126) **–** [2007 5m Sep 14] 33/1, very slowly away in maiden at Sandown: gelded after. *D. R. C. Elsworth*

WARDEN WARREN 9 b.g. Petong 126 – Silver Spell 54 (Aragon 118) [2007 55§: **– §** p7g p8g f7g Mar 6] sparely-made gelding: fairly useful performer at best: no form in 2007: wears headgear, tried tongue tied: sometimes races alone (reportedly unsuited by being crowded): unreliable. *Mrs C. A. Dunnett*

WAR FEATHER 5 b.g. Selkirk (USA) 129 – Sit Alkul (USA) 73 (Mr Prospector **54** (USA)) [2007 52: p10g⁵ p12g⁴ p11g² p12g⁶ p11g 16m p12g³ 15.4g p12g⁵ p12m Dec 8] tall gelding: modest maiden: stays 2m: raced mainly on polytrack: tried in cheekpieces: none too consistent. *T. D. McCarthy*

WARM EMBRACES (IRE) 3 ch.c. Halling (USA) 133 – Zapping (IRE) (Lycius **90** (USA) 124) [2007 p7f² p8g* p10g³ 9.9g² 10m⁴ 9.9m 10m² 10.9m* 10m⁵ Sep 22] third foal: dam, ran twice in France, out of half-sister to top-class sprinter/miler Last Tycoon: fairly useful performer: won maiden at Lingfield in March and handicap at Warwick in September: stays 10.9f: acts on polytrack and good to firm ground: joined T. K. Ng in Hong Kong. *D. R. C. Elsworth*

WARMING UP (IRE) 2 b.c. (Feb 22) Kalanisi (IRE) 132 – Sound Asleep (USA) **68** (Woodman (USA) 126) [2007 7f⁵ 7.1g 7.5g⁶ 10m³ p8.6g³ Oct 12] lengthy colt: fair maiden: third in nurseries last 2 starts: stays 1¼m: acts on polytrack and good to firm going: normally misses break. *C. E. Brittain*

WARM TRIBUTE (USA) 3 ch.g. Royal Anthem (USA) 135 – Gentle Mind (USA)   –
(Seattle Slew (USA)) [2007 58?: 7.1g 6g 5m 5g Aug 29] maiden: little form at 3 yrs,
leaving W. Harrison after reappearance: bred to stay 1m+. *J. S. Goldie*

WARNERS BAY (IRE) 2 b.c. (Mar 7) Iron Mask (USA) 117 – Romangoddess (IRE)   **62 ?**
(Rhoman Rule (USA)) [2007 6m³ 5.1g p5.1g Nov 14] good-topped colt: modest maiden:
third to Kashimin at Pontefract: inadequate trip subsequent starts: will be suited by 7f/
1m. *R. Bastiman*

WARNINGCAMP (GER) 6 b.g. Lando (GER) 128 – Wilette (GER) (Top Ville 129)   –
[2007 p12g Nov 17] leggy gelding: fair maiden in 2004, well held only outing on Flat
since: fairly useful hurdler. *Lady Herries*

WAR OF THE ROSES (IRE) 4 b.g. Singspiel (IRE) 133 – Calvia Rose (Sharpo 132)   **76**
[2007 –: p7.1g p6g p8g* p10g* p8g 10g 10d p10g⁶ p12g² p12.2g p12g p12g* p13g*
Dec 28] lengthy, angular gelding: fair performer: won 2 minor events at Kempton in
March and handicaps at Lingfield in November and December: stays 13f: acts on polytrack. *R. Brotherton*

WARREN BANK 2 b.g. (Apr 30) Nayef (USA) 129 – Neptunalia 70 (Slip Anchor 136)   –
[2007 p8g Sep 24] lengthy gelding: tailed off in maiden at Kempton. *Mrs Mary Hambro*

WARRINGAH 2 ch.c. (Feb 20) Galileo (IRE) 134 – Threefold (USA) 99 (Gulch   **64 p**
(USA)) [2007 p8m⁶ Nov 26] second foal: closely related to 3-y-o Hi Calypso: dam, 1m
winner, out of half-sister to Prix Saint-Alary winner Treble and to dam of high-class
sprinter Tamarisk: 5/1, 2¾ lengths sixth to Jaser in maiden at Lingfield, never nearer
under considerate ride: bred to be suited by middle distances: sure to do better. *Sir
Michael Stoute*

WARSAW (IRE) 2 ch.c. (Feb 15) Danehill Dancer (IRE) 117 – For Evva Silca 60   **95**
(Piccolo 121) [2007 6m* 5m* 5m 6v⁵ 7d⁴ 5m⁶ Sep 14] 250,000Y: sturdy colt: good
walker: first foal: dam, sprint maiden, half-sister to Prix Morny winner Silca's Sister and
smart performer up to 9f Golden Silca: useful performer: won maiden at Leopardstown in
April and listed race at the Curragh (by The Loan Express by 1½ lengths) in May: little
impact in pattern events after, including Norfolk Stakes at Royal Ascot and Flying
Childers Stakes at Doncaster (not discredited) third/final starts: best at 5f/6f: acts on good
to firm going. *A. P. O'Brien, Ireland*

WARSAW WALTZ 2 b.f. (Mar 16) Polish Precedent (USA) 131 – Generous Diana 90   **56**
(Generous (IRE) 139) [2007 7g 7.1g⁵ 8.1s Sep 29] strong, close-coupled filly: third foal:
dam 9f/1¼m winner who stayed 1½m: modest maiden: form only when fifth at Haydock:
should stay 1m. *J. G. Given*

WASALAT (USA) 5 b.m. Bahri (USA) 125 – Saabga (USA) 83 (Woodman (USA) 126)   **79**
[2007 79: 9.9m⁵ 10f⁵ 9.8m* 7.9d 8m 8m 10g p8.6g Oct 20] smallish, strong mare: fair
handicapper: won at Ripon in June: stays 10.3f: acts on polytrack and firm going: tried
blinkered/in cheekpieces: often starts slowly: inconsistent. *D. W. Barker*

WASAN 2 ch.c. (Mar 16) Pivotal 124 – Solaia (USA) 110 (Miswaki (USA) 124) [2007   **73 p**
p7g* Nov 17] 525,000Y: fourth foal: half-brother to smart 1m (at 2 yrs in France) to 1½m
(US Grade 2) winner Olaya (by Theatrical) and 3-y-o Fifty Cents: dam 7f (at 2 yrs) and
11.4f (Cheshire Oaks) winner: 7/2 favourite and green, won maiden at Lingfield in
November by neck from Segal, leading final 1f: likely to improve. *E. A. L. Dunlop*

WASHINGTON IRVING (IRE) 2 b.c. (Jan 14) Montjeu (IRE) 137 – Shouk 94   **75 P**
(Shirley Heights 130) [2007 7s⁴ Oct 22] tall, good sort: fifth foal: closely related to 3 at
least useful winners, including very smart 1m (at 2 yrs) to 1½m (Oaks and Irish/Yorkshire
Oaks) winner Alexandrova (by Sadler's Wells) and smart 2004 2-y-o 6f (including
Cheveley Park Stakes) winner Magical Romance (by Barathea) and half-brother to 1¼m
winner Grand Wizard (by Grand Lodge): dam, 10.5f winner, closely related to smart
performer up to 1¾m Puce and half-sister to very smart performer up to 2½m Golden
Quest: 2/1 favourite, 3¾ lengths fourth to Teacht An Earraig in maiden at the Curragh:
will be well suited by 1¼m/1½m: likely to do a lot better as 3-y-o. *A. P. O'Brien, Ireland*

WASSEEMA (USA) 4 br.f. Danzig (USA) – Vantive (USA) (Mr Prospector (USA))   **102**
[2007 111: 7g⁴ 8m Jun 20] tall filly: smart performer at 3 yrs, winning 3 times: only useful
form in 2007, better effort when seventh to Nannina in Windsor Forest Stakes at Royal
Ascot: was effective at 7f/1m: raced only on good/good to firm going: edgy sort: exuberant front runner: visits Shamardal. *Sir Michael Stoute*

WASSENDALE 3 b.f. Erhaab (USA) 127 – Megdale (IRE) 74 (Waajib 121) [2007 p7g⁴   **59**
p7g 10.1m² 11g⁵ 9g May 25] half-sister to several winners, including smart 7f (at 2 yrs)
to 1¾m winner Frank Sonata (by Opening Verse), useful 2000 2-y-o 7f winner Peaceful

Paradise (by Turtle Island) and 5-y-o Coup d'Etat: dam, maiden who stayed 1½m, half-sister to very smart miler Alhijaz: modest maiden: stays 1¼m: acts on good to firm going: withdrawn after unruly in stall intended final outing in June: joined D. Carroll. *J. W. Hills*

WASSFA 4 b.f. Mark of Esteem (IRE) 137 – Mistle Song 112 (Nashwan (USA) 135) **93 ?** [2007 76: p8g p8g 9.7m f7g⁵ 10d² 10m* 10.9d⁶ 12m 12f² 14.6m 10.3m Nov 10] tall, leggy filly: fairly useful performer: won handicap at Lingfield in June: seemingly best effort when 4 lengths second to Queen's Best in listed race at Newbury ninth start: effective at 1m, stays 1½m when emphasis is on speed: acts on polytrack, firm and good to soft ground: tried blinkered/tongue tied: none too consistent. *C. E. Brittain*

WATAMU (IRE) 6 b.g. Groom Dancer (USA) 128 – Miss Golden Sands 80 (Kris 135) **102 +** [2007 91: p12g² p12.2g⁵ p10g* Mar 17] strong, lengthy gelding: useful handicapper: much improved when winning at Lingfield (by 3 lengths from Very Wise, having plenty to spare) in March: stays 1½m, but not short of speed: acts on polytrack and good to firm going: tried visored (including last 2 starts): has run in snatches/flashed tail: said to be hard to train. *P. J. Makin*

WATCHFUL (IRE) 3 b.f. Galileo (IRE) 134 – Sharakawa (IRE) (Darshaan 133) [2007 **94 p** 11m* 11.6g² 12g⁴ p12g* Nov 17] €50,000F, 70,000Y: sturdy filly: half-sister to 3 winners, including smart 7f (at 2 yrs)/1m (including in US) winner Rabi (by Alzao) and fairly useful 1998 2-y-o 1m winner Ebinzayd (by Tenby): dam unraced out of Prix Vermeille winner Sharaya: fairly useful form: won maiden at Goodwood in September and handicap at Lingfield (beat Polish Power by length, idling) in November: will be suited by 1¾m+: acts on polytrack and good to firm ground: likely to do better still. *L. M. Cumani*

WATCHMAKER 4 b.g. Bering 136 – Watchkeeper (IRE) 86 (Rudimentary (USA) **73** 118) [2007 –: p11g⁵ p12g² p10g* p10g⁵ 10.1d p12g⁵ p12g p16g⁶ p11m² p10g² p10g Dec 22] fair handicapper: won at Lingfield in February: left W. Knight 13,500 gns after fifth start: stays 1½m: acts on polytrack. *Miss Tor Sturgis*

WATCH OUT 3 b.g. Observatory (USA) 131 – Ballet Fame (USA) 79 (Quest For Fame **49** 127) [2007 46?: 11.5s⁴ 12.1s 16.2s⁶ 12.1g⁶ Jul 31] neat gelding: poor maiden handicapper: stays 2m: acts on soft ground: blinkered last 2 starts. *M. W. Easterby*

WATCH THIS PLACE 2 b.g. (Jan 21) Compton Place 125 – Swissmatic 54 (Petong **–** 126) [2007 5d⁵ Jun 24] 9/2, outpaced in maiden at Warwick (gelded after). *K. R. Burke*

WATEERA (IRE) 3 b.f. Sakhee (USA) 136 – Azdihaar (USA) 81 (Mr Prospector **–** (USA)) [2007 74: 8d 10d⁵ Oct 11] lengthy filly: fair form in maidens at 2 yrs: little impact in handicaps in 2007: should stay 1¼m: quirky: visits Green Desert. *J. L. Dunlop*

WATERLINE TWENTY (IRE) 4 b.f. Indian Danehill (IRE) 124 – Taisho (IRE) 96 **82** (Namaqualand (USA)) [2007 89: p8g⁶ p8.6g⁶ p9.5g⁶ p10g⁶ 8m 7m 7.6m 8.3m⁶ 8m³ 8m 8.1m³ 8.1g 8g³ p8.6g⁴ p8g* p8g³ p10g p8g³ p10g⁴ p8g⁶ Dec 30] leggy filly: fairly useful handicapper: won at Kempton in November: stays 1¼m: acts on polytrack and firm going: held up. *P. D. Evans*

WATERLOO CORNER 5 b.g. Cayman Kai (IRE) 114 – Rasin Luck (Primitive Ris- **66** ing (USA) 113) [2007 73: p9.5g⁶ f11g⁵ f12g 12d 10s 8m³ 10f³ 7.9g⁶ 10.1m 10g² p9.5g* p9.5g⁴ f8d³ Dec 21] smallish, close-coupled gelding: fair handicapper: won at Wolverhampton in November: likely to prove best up to 1¼m: acts on all-weather and firm going: tried blinkered/visored. *R. Craggs*

WATERLOO DOCK 2 b.c. (Apr 13) Hunting Lion (IRE) 115 – Scenic Air (Hadeer **51** 118) [2007 5m⁵ 7m⁵ p7.1g⁵ Nov 12] modest maiden: will prove best up to 1m. *M. Quinn*

WATER MARGIN (IRE) 3 b.g. Shinko Forest (IRE) – Tribal Rite 95 (Be My Native **61** (USA) 122) [2007 –: 6s 5s² 5m³ Jul 19] modest maiden: will prove as effective at 6f as 5f: acts on soft and good to firm going: sold 1,000 gns in October. *T. G. Mills*

WATERMILL (IRE) 4 b.g. Daylami (IRE) 138 – Brogan's Well (IRE) (Caerleon **–** (USA) 132) [2007 –: p12.2g 16g 15d May 23] well held in bumpers: no form on Flat: tried blinkered. *D. W. Chapman*

WATER MILL (USA) 3 gr.c. Unbridled's Song (USA) 125 – Capote Miss (USA) **76** (Capote (USA)) [2007 88p: p8g⁶ Mar 31] leggy, close-coupled colt: fairly useful winner of only race at 2 yrs: shaped as if in need of run when below form in listed race at Kempton on sole start in 2007: should stay 1m: sent to USA. *A. M. Balding*

WATER PISTOL 5 b.g. Double Trigger (IRE) 123 – Water Flower 79 (Environment **–** Friend 128) [2007 –: 15.8m 21.6m 14.1m May 2] leggy gelding: maiden on Flat, no form since 2005: poor hurdler. *M. C. Chapman*

WATERSIDE (IRE) 8 b.g. Lake Coniston (IRE) 131 – Classic Ring (IRE) 50 (Auction **98**
Ring (USA) 123) [2007 97: p6g⁵ f7g² f6g* f7s² p7f³ p8.6g⁶ p7g* p7g 8g 8.5d 8m⁶ 8m² **a108**
8s² 8g³ 8m⁵ 7g³ p8g p7m⁴ p8g⁶ p8m Dec 8] strong, heavy-topped gelding: has a round
action: useful performer, better on all-weather than turf: won minor event at Southwell in
January and handicap at Kempton (by length from Cross The Line) in March: creditable
efforts in frame in handicaps after, including fourth to Capricorn Run at Lingfield eighteenth start: stays 1m, but very best efforts at 7f: acts on all-weather and any turf going:
tried tongue tied: sometimes slowly away: usually races up with pace: tough and reliable.
G. L. Moore

WATT A WILL 4 ch.f. Karinga Bay 116 – Wilming 35 (Komaite (USA)) [2007 8.2g 6s –
Jun 30] lengthy filly: first foal: dam sprint maiden: no form in maidens. *J. M. Bradley*

WATTYS THE CRAIC 3 ch.g. Erhaab (USA) 127 – La Puce Volante (Grand Lodge **52**
(USA) 125) [2007 p7.1g p8.6g p7m⁶ 6d Oct 23] modest maiden: gelded after final start.
G. Prodromou

WAVE HILL (IRE) 2 b.g. (Apr 27) Mujadil (USA) 119 – Bryna (IRE) (Ezzoud (IRE) **58**
126) [2007 6m 6.5d 5.1g Oct 24] big, lengthy gelding: modest form in maidens (off 4
months after debut). *B. J. Meehan*

WAVELINE (USA) 2 b.f. (Jan 11) Stravinsky (USA) 133 – Teresa Ann (USA) (Boston **87**
Harbor (USA) 122) [2007 p5g³ 5.1m* 6g 6m 6m³ 8f a6.5f⁴ Dec 2] €140,000Y: rather
leggy, angular filly: first foal: dam, US 2-y-o 6f winner, half-sister to very smart sprinter
Crystal Castle: fairly useful performer: won minor event at Bath in May: good third in
nursery at Goodwood final appearance in Britain: better effort in North America last 2
starts (left B. Meehan before final outing) when fourth of 5 in allowance optional claimer
at Hollywood: stays 6.5f: acts on polytrack and good to firm going: blinkered last 2
appearances. *B. D. A. Cecil, USA*

WAVERTREE ONE OFF 5 b.g. Diktat 126 – Miss Clarinet (Pharly (FR) 130) [2007 **54**
–: 17.2m f14g 14.1d 11.5d⁴ 14.1d⁴ 16g p13.9s² Dec 20] quite good-topped gelding:
modest maiden: stays 1¾m: acts on polytrack and soft ground: usually in cheekpieces/
blinkers. *J. Ryan*

WAVERTREE PRINCESS (IRE) 2 gr.f. (Feb 12) Invincible Spirit (IRE) 121 – **74**
Blushing Queen (IRE) 75 (Desert King (IRE) 129) [2007 5g⁶ 5.7f⁶ 5m² p7g⁵ 6m⁶ p5m*
p5m⁵ Dec 8] 20,000Y: good-topped filly: second foal: dam, maiden who stayed 7f, half-
sister to dam of Breeders' Cup Juvenile winner Wilko: fair performer: won maiden at
Lingfield in November: effective at 5f to easy 7f: acts on polytrack and good to firm
going. *N. P. Littmoden*

WAVERTREE WARRIOR (IRE) 5 br.g. Indian Lodge (IRE) 127 – Karamana **98**
(Habitat 134) [2007 99: p8g p7f* p7g 7s 8.5d⁵ 8.3m 7.1d⁶ 7d² p8g 8g 7.1d⁴ 8.3m⁵ 8s p8g⁴
p10g⁶ p7g³ p8m³ p8g⁴ Dec 29] leggy gelding: useful handicapper: won at Lingfield (by
neck from Bomber Command) in February: mainly creditable efforts after: best at 7f/1m:
acts on polytrack, soft and good to firm going: tried in cheekpieces, blinkered nowadays.
N. P. Littmoden

WAYMARK (IRE) 3 ch.c. Halling (USA) 133 – Uncharted Haven (Turtle Island (IRE) **80**
123) [2007 71p: p8g² 10m 8.1m 8.3m⁵ 8d Aug 25] strong, medium-sized colt: fairly
useful maiden: below form after second start: worth another try at 1¼m: acts on polytrack
and good to firm ground: sold 11,000 gns in October. *M. A. Jarvis*

WAYWARD SHOT (IRE) 5 b.g. Desert Prince (IRE) 130 – Style Parade (USA) 78 **57**
(Diesis 133) [2007 63: p9.5g p7.1g* f7g f7g Mar 6] lengthy gelding: modest handicapper:
won at Wolverhampton in February: stays 8.5f: acts on polytrack, soft and good to firm
going: effective blinkered or not: front runner. *M. W. Easterby*

WEBBOW (IRE) 5 b.g. Dr Devious (IRE) 127 – Ower (IRE) 71 (Lomond (USA) 128) **97**
[2007 77: 8m² 7.9d* 8s⁴ 8m* 8m* Aug 17] useful handicapper, lightly raced: won at
Carlisle in June, and Thirsk and Doncaster (by neck from Ekhtiaar) in August: stays 1m:
acts on all-weather, soft and good to firm going: versatile regarding tactics. *T. D. Easterby*

WEBBSWOOD LAD (IRE) 6 b.g. Robellino (USA) 127 – Poleaxe (Selkirk (USA) –
129) [2007 65: p12.2g⁵ Feb 5] fair maiden at 5 yrs: well below best only start in 2007:
seems to stay 16.5f: acts on polytrack, best turf run on good going: tried in cheekpieces.
M. R. Bosley

WEE BUNS 2 b.g. (Apr 24) Piccolo 121 – Gigetta (IRE) (Brief Truce (USA) 126) [2007 **66**
5m p6g⁵ 5.1d⁴ p6g* p6g p7g³ p7.1d⁴ p7.1g⁴ p6g³ Dec 22] rather leggy gelding: fair
performer: won nursery at Wolverhampton in September: best form at 6f: acts on polytrack and good to soft going. *S. Kirk*

WEE CHARLIE CASTLE (IRE) 4 b.g. Sinndar (IRE) 134 – Seasonal Blossom **58** (IRE) (Fairy King (USA)) [2007 74, a71: p12g f11g³ f11g³ 10g 10.1d p12g⁵ p8g⁴ 10.1m⁴ **a71** p10g⁵ p10g⁵ p11g³ Dec 19] rangy gelding: fair handicapper on all-weather, modest on turf: effective at 1m to 1½m: acts on all-weather, firm and good to soft going: tried visored/blinkered: has been slowly away, and of suspect temperament. *G. C. H. Chung*

WEE ELLIE COBURN 3 ch.f. Bold Edge 123 – Wathbat Mtoto 88 (Mtoto 134) **52** [2007 57: 6g 7.9f⁶ 8.5g 8.3g Sep 3] sparely-made filly: modest maiden handicapper: left I. Semple after reappearance: barely stays 8.5f: acts on all-weather: quirky. *M. Mullineaux*

WEEKEND FLING (USA) 3 b. or br.f. Forest Wildcat (USA) 120 – Woodman's **68** Dancer (USA) (Woodman (USA) 126) [2007 67: 6m* 6m f8g⁴ 8d⁶ Jun 19] leggy filly: won maiden at Catterick in April: stays 1m: acts on fibresand and good to firm going: sold 57,000 gns in July. *M. Johnston*

WEET A SURPRISE 2 b.f. (Mar 11) Bertolini (USA) 125 – Ticcatoo (IRE) 60 **76** (Dolphin Street (FR) 125) [2007 p5.1g⁶ 5d* 5.1s p6g⁵ 5m⁵ p5.1g³ p6g⁵ p5.1g* 5g p5.1g* f5d* f5g* Dec 27] sparely-made filly: second foal: closely related to 3-y-o Ishetoo: dam 2-y-o 5f winner: fair performer: won maiden at Warwick in June and nurseries at Wolverhampton in October and November, and Southwell (2) in December: best at 5f: acts on all-weather, good to soft and good to firm going. *R. Hollinshead*

WEET BY FAR 2 b.f. (May 9) Bertolini (USA) 125 – Shaiybara (IRE) 111 (Kahyasi **62** 130) [2007 7.1g⁴ 7.1m⁵ p6g p6g p8.6g⁶ p7.1g⁴ p7.1g³ p7.1g⁴ f7d² p7.1d⁵ Dec 28] 800Y: small filly: ninth foal: closely related to fairly useful 1m winner Shaiyzima (by Polish Precedent) and half-sister to Irish 1½m winner Shaiyran (by Darshaan): dam, Irish stayer, also won Prix de Lutece: modest maiden: made frame 5 times (once in nursery): should stay 1m: acts on all-weather. *R. Hollinshead*

WEET FOR EVER (USA) 4 br. or b.g. High Yield (USA) 121 – Wild Classy Lady **59** (USA) (Wild Again (USA)) [2007 59: f8g f8g² f8g f8g³ f7g Mar 22] modest maiden: stays 1½m: acts on all-weather and good to firm going. *P. A. Blockley*

WEETFROMTHECHAFF 2 gr.g. (May 5) Weet-A-Minute (IRE) 106 – Weet Ees **60** Girl (IRE) 75 (Common Grounds 118) [2007 6s 7.5g 7m⁵ 6m p7.1g⁴ p7.1g⁴ Dec 26] leggy, close-coupled gelding: modest maiden: will stay 1m: acts on good to firm going, probably polytrack. *R. Hollinshead*

WEET INTOLERANCE 2 b.f. (Jan 15) Polar Prince (IRE) 117 – Priorite (IRE) 85 **–** (Kenmare (FR) 125) [2007 f5g⁶ Apr 13] fifth foal: half-sister to 7f winner Cross Ash (by Ashkalani): dam Irish 2-y-o 7f winner: well held in maiden: dead. *B. D. Leavy*

WEET YER TERN (IRE) 5 b.g. Brave Act 119 – Maxime (IRE) 60 (Mac's Imp **–** (USA) 116) [2007 58: p8.6g² p8g* p8.6g⁶ p8.6g 8f 8.5g⁴ p10g³ p9.5m* p10g² p8.6g **a60** p9.5g⁴ p9.5g³ p9.5g⁴ p12.2g⁴ p9.5g Dec 3] tall gelding: modest performer on all-weather, little form on turf since 2004: won minor event at Kempton in February and handicap at Wolverhampton in September: stays easy 1½m: acts on all-weather and good to firm ground: sometimes wears headgear: tried tongue tied. *W. M. Brisbourne*

WEE ZIGGY 4 b.g. Ziggy's Dancer (USA) 97 – Midnight Arrow 81 (Robellino (USA) **–** 127) [2007 –: p8.6g p8.6g 6.1g 7.6d 12m 14m 12.1d Aug 15] compact gelding: little form. *M. Mullineaux*

WE HAVE A DREAM 2 b. or br.c. (Feb 18) Oasis Dream 129 – Final Shot 91 (Dal- **72** saan 125) [2007 6m 6s p6g 6v* 6.1m³ 6.1d² 6g p6g* 6.1d* Oct 18] good-bodied colt: fair performer: won nurseries at Lingfield in July, Kempton in September and Nottingham in October: should prove best at 5f/6f: acts on polytrack, heavy and good to firm ground: races prominently. *W. R. Muir*

WEIGHT IN GOLD 2 b.f. (Feb 2) Mujahid (USA) 125 – Golden Ciel (USA) **–** (Septieme Ciel (USA) 123) [2007 6d 6d p7g 7m 8g Sep 20] 3,000Y: smallish filly: fifth foal: half-sister to 3 winners, including 1m (at 2 yrs) and 1½m winner Bold Blade (by Sure Blade): dam 2-y-o 7f winner in Italy: little form. *P. J. McBride*

WEIGHTLESS 7 ch.g. In The Wings 128 – Orford Ness 107 (Selkirk (USA) 129) **99 §** [2007 109d: p8g p10g* p11g³ 16m⁶ p10g 12s 10d² 10d Aug 25] sturdy, lengthy gelding: useful performer nowadays: won handicap at Kempton in March: creditable second in similar event at Sandown: stays 11f: acts on polytrack, good to firm and good to soft going: usually free-going front runner: not one to trust: joined Mike Murphy. *N. P. Litt-moden*

WELCOME APPROACH 4 b.g. Most Welcome 131 – Lucky Thing (Green Desert **79** (USA) 127) [2007 75: 5m 5d⁶ 5m² 5.9m⁵ 5.7f 5m³ 5d³ 5.2m⁵ 5d⁵ 5.9m⁴ 5f² 5g³ 5m² 5m² 5d³ 5g³ 5m⁵ 5g Oct 6] sturdy, angular gelding: fair handicapper: best at 5f: acts on firm and good to soft ground: tried blinkered (ran poorly): consistent. *J. R. Weymes*

WELCOME CAT (USA) 3 b.c. Tale of The Cat (USA) 113 – Mangano (USA) (Quiet **68** American (USA)) [2007 12s 10g⁵ 10d 10.5g⁴ 12s a9.5g⁴ a12g² a12g⁶ 15s* a12g⁵ 12d² a12g³ p12g f14d p12.2g³ p13.9g Dec 31] fair performer: won claimer at Deauville in August: left P. Demercastel in France after twelfth start: third in claimer at Wolverhampton penultimate outing: stays 15f: acts on polytrack and soft going: blinkered last 2 starts. *A. D. Brown*

WELCOME INN 2 ch.f. (May 15) Zaha (CAN) 106 – Lambeth Belle (USA) (Arazi – (USA) 135) [2007 6g 6g 6m⁶ 7d 7.5v⁶ Jul 7] close-coupled filly: third foal: sister to winner in Italy: dam unraced out of smart Irish 1¼m performer Cockney Lass: of no account. *M. E. Sowersby*

WELCOME RETURN (IRE) 2 b.f. (Jan 18) Mull of Kintyre (USA) 114 – Aiaie **74** (Zafonic (USA) 130) [2007 5g 6m² 6m⁶ 7v⁶ 7m* 8m² 8m 8s Sep 22] €12,500Y: big, strong, lengthy filly: second foal: dam unraced half-sister to smart performer up to 1½m Don Micheletto: fair performer: won nursery at Newcastle in August: stays 1m: acts on good to firm going: blinkered last 4 starts: suspect temperament. *T. D. Easterby*

WELCOME SPIRIT 4 b.g. Most Welcome 131 – Valadon 72 (High Line 125) [2007 – –: 16g 11.1d Jul 14] quite good-topped gelding: no sign of ability: dead. *J. S. Haldane*

WE'LL COME 3 b.g. Elnadim (USA) 128 – Off The Blocks 55 (Salse (USA) 128) **103** [2007 93p: 8m² 8d* 8m³ 7g³ 8g³ Aug 23] big, heavy-bodied gelding: has a quick action: useful performer: landed odds in maiden at Yarmouth (by short head from Gongidas) in May: good third in handicaps at Newmarket and York (1¾ lengths behind The Illies) third/final starts: stays 1m: acts on soft and good to firm going: has swished tail/carried head high. *M. A. Jarvis*

WELL DEFINED 4 b.f. Barathea (IRE) 127 – Serene View (USA) 105 (Distant View – (USA) 126) [2007 8.1m May 25] 3,500 3-y-o: good-bodied filly: second foal: dam, French 1m winner, out of half-sister to dam of 1000 Guineas winner Wince: well held in bumpers, and in maiden at Haydock. *T. H. Caldwell*

WELL INFORMED 2 b.f. (Mar 10) Averti (IRE) 117 – May Light 62 (Midyan (USA) **75** 124) [2007 f5g* Apr 13] 16,000Y: half-sister to 6-y-o Bygone Days and fairly useful 1998 2-y-o 1m winner Trio (by Cyrano de Bergerac): dam maiden (stayed 7f): 6/4, won maiden at Southwell easily by 4 lengths: will prove best at 5f/6f: looked sure to improve. *K. A. Ryan*

WELLINGTON HALL (GER) 9 b.g. Halling (USA) 133 – Wells Whisper (FR) 71 – (Sadler's Wells (USA) 132) [2007 87: p12.2g p12.2g p12.2g p12g p12.2g Jul 30] leggy gelding: fairly useful handicapper at 8 yrs, little form in 2007: tried in headgear: has run well sweating. *M. Wigham*

WELL PLACED 3 b.g. Compton Place 125 – Pudding Lane (IRE) 64 (College Chapel – 122) [2007 6m May 7] 7/2 and green, well held in maiden at Windsor: sold 2,000 gns, sent to Greece. *W. J. Haggas*

WELLS LYRICAL (IRE) 2 b.c. (Feb 26) Sadler's Wells (USA) 132 – Lyrical 65 **71 p** (Shirley Heights 130) [2007 8.2g⁵ 8g⁶ Nov 9] quite good-topped colt: second foal: half-brother to winner in Italy by Grand Lodge: dam, maiden (likely to have stayed 1¾m+), half-sister to Oaks winner Love Divine, herself dam of 4-y-o Sixties Icon: fair form in maidens at Nottingham and Musselburgh, staying on: will be suited by 1¼m+: capable of better. *B. Smart*

WELLS OF BADR (IRE) 3 b.f. Fasliyev (USA) 120 – Tamburello (IRE) (Roi Danzig **58** (USA)) [2007 7m 8.1m² 7v⁴ 6g⁵ 7.6m 8m 8g Oct 25] 35,000F, 46,000Y: sturdy, lengthy filly: fifth foal: half-sister to 7f to 1¼m winner My Lilli (by Marju) and winner in France/ Spain by Second Empire: dam, sprint maiden, half-sister to useful performer up to 9.4f Reported: modest maiden: stays 1m: acts on good to firm ground: tried blinkered: sold 800 gns. *P. W. Chapple-Hyam*

WELSH AUCTION 3 gr.g. Auction House (USA) 120 – Anneli Rose 56 (Superlative **76 d** 118) [2007 –: 6g² 6.1m² 7m² 6.1g⁴ p6g⁵ 6d⁵ 6m 6m⁴ p8g⁶ p8g Oct 4] sturdy gelding: fair maiden: lost form after second outing, leaving G. Huffer after eighth start: stays 6f: acts on good to firm ground: tried blinkered. *K. J. Burke*

WELSH CAKE 4 b.f. Fantastic Light (USA) 134 – Khubza 86 (Green Desert (USA) – 127) [2007 76: 7.1m 7m Jun 9] close-coupled filly: fair performer at 3 yrs: well beaten in handicaps in 2007: stays 8.6f: acts on polytrack and firm ground: blinkered/tongue tied nowadays. *Mrs A. J. Perrett*

WELSH EMPEROR (IRE) 8 b.g. Emperor Jones (USA) 119 – Simply Times (USA) **116** 64 (Dodge (USA)) [2007 120: 6g 8.5g³ 7s⁴ 7d² 6d⁶ 7d² 7d* Oct 29] tall gelding: smart performer: won minor event at Leicester (by ¾ length from Babodana) in October: better efforts earlier in 2007 when second behind Red Evie in Hungerford Stakes at Newbury (caught on line and beaten short head) and Toylsome in Prix de la Foret at Longchamp (also runner-up in 2006): effective at 6f/7f: acts on heavy and good to firm going: formerly blinkered: front runner, best when able to dominate. *T. P. Tate*

WELSH GUARD (USA) 4 ch.g. Silver Hawk (USA) 123 – Royal Devotion (USA) – (His Majesty (USA)) [2007 12s 14m⁶ 10m Sep 14] sturdy gelding: little form. *G. P. Enright*

WELSH OPERA 2 b.f. (Jan 23) Noverre (USA) 125 – Welsh Diva 112 (Selkirk (USA) **72** 129) [2007 6d p7m³ p8m⁴ Dec 10] compact filly: first foal: dam, 1m winner, sister to smart 6f (at 2 yrs) to 8.5f winner Trans Island: fair maiden: twice in frame at Lingfield: should be suited by 1m. *Mrs A. J. Perrett*

WELSH WHISPER 8 b.m. Overbury (IRE) 116 – Grugiar (Red Sunset 120) [2007 50: **49** p8.6g p8.6g p9.5g⁴ p12.2g p8.6d p8.6d Dec 17] poor performer nowadays: seems to stay 9.5f: acts on all-weather and soft going: sometimes slowly away. *S. A. Brookshaw*

WENDY'S BOY 3 b.c. Elnadim (USA) 128 – Tatouma (USA) 79 (The Minstrel (CAN) **46** 135) [2007 –: p6g⁵ p5g p5g Apr 25] poor maiden: likely to prove best at 5f/6f. *R. Hannon*

WE'RE DELIGHTED 2 b.c. (Feb 16) Tobougg (IRE) 125 – Samadilla (IRE) 83 **68** (Mujadil (USA) 119) [2007 6f³ 7g⁵ 7.1m⁵ p8.6g 6d³ Oct 1] close-coupled colt: fair maiden: often better than bare result: should prove best at 5f/6f: acts on firm going: sold 10,000 gns. *M. R. Channon*

WESSEX (USA) 7 ch.g. Gone West (USA) – Satin Velvet (USA) 103 (El Gran Senor **99** (USA) 136) [2007 100: f8g⁵ f7g f7s³ p8.6g p7g f7g² p6g Aug 27] big, rather leggy gelding: useful handicapper: good efforts when placed at Southwell in 2007: effective at 6f to 1m: acts on all-weather, firm and good to soft ground: tried visored/tongue tied: sometimes slowly away: usually held up. *P. A. Blockley*

WESTBROOK BLUE 5 b.h. Kingsinger (IRE) 94 – Gold And Blue (IRE) (Bluebird **65** (USA) 125) [2007 87: 5m 5m 5s 5d⁶ 5.1s Jul 26] big, good-topped horse: just fair performer in 2007: should stay 6f: acts on all-weather, heavy and good to firm going: tried in cheekpieces: tongue tied nowadays: inconsistent. *W. G. M. Turner*

WEST END LAD 4 b.g. Tomba 119 – Cliburnel News (IRE) 76 (Horage 124) [2007 **61** p8.6g 8.3d⁵ p7.1g 10.9g 10g p13.9g f11d² Dec 12] modest maiden: stays 11f: acts on fibresand: in cheekpieces last 2 starts. *S. R. Bowring*

WESTERING HOME (IRE) 4 b.f. Mull of Kintyre (USA) 114 – Glympse (IRE) 59 **67** (Spectrum (IRE) 126) [2007 69: p12.2g³ p9.5g Jan 29] good-topped filly: fair handi-capper: stays 1½m: acts on polytrack and firm going: tried blinkered/in cheekpieces. *J. Mackie*

WESTERN ADVENTURE (USA) 3 b.c. Gone West (USA) – Larrocha (IRE) 116 **95** (Sadler's Wells (USA) 132) [2007 83p: 11m* 11.1d³ 12g⁵ Jun 21] sturdy, good-bodied colt: useful form: won maiden at Newbury in April: similar form after when third to Boscobel in listed race at Hamilton and fifth to Heron Bay in King George V Handicap at Royal Ascot (blinkered): stays 1½m: acts on good to firm and good to soft going: sent to UAE. *E. A. L. Dunlop*

WESTERN ART (USA) 2 b. or br.c. (Apr 8) Hennessy (USA) 122 – Madam West **100 p** (USA) (Gone West (USA)) [2007 5m² 5d* Jul 6] $40,000Y, 62,000 2-y-o: good-bodied colt: third foal: half-brother to US winner by Capote: dam, US 6f winner, closely related to US Grade 3 7f winner Mineral Wells: useful form: much improved from debut to win listed event at Sandown (beat New Jersey by length), coming from well off strong pace and quickening in good style: suffered pulled muscles after: will be suited by 6f/7f: smart prospect all being well. *P. W. Chapple-Hyam*

WESTERN LAND 3 ch.g. Zamindar (USA) 116 – Landowska (USA) (Langfuhr **63** (CAN) 124) [2007 f7g 7.5m 6d p7.1g² Sep 3] first foal: dam, US 6f winner, half-sister to useful French performer up to 1m Savannah's Honor: modest maiden: stays 7f: acts on polytrack. *B. Smart*

WESTERN POINT (IRE) 3 ch.g. Pivotal 124 – Hesperia (Slip Anchor 136) [2007 **76** 6d⁵ 6m p6g 8.3g p12g⁴ p10g² 12g⁵ 11.5m* 11.9d* 14m² p12.2g³ Sep 21] strong gelding:

fair handicapper: won at Yarmouth and Brighton in August: stays 1¾m: acts on polytrack, good to firm and good to soft ground: tends to edge left: raced up with pace: sold 35,000 gns. *Sir Mark Prescott*

WESTERN ROOTS 6 ch.g. Dr Fong (USA) 128 – Chrysalis 66 (Soviet Star (USA) **58** 128) [2007 58, a76: p8.6g⁴ p8.6g⁶ 10.9m p8.6g³ p8g³ p9.5g* p8g p8.6g⁴ p8.6g p8.6g **a70** 10d⁶ 10g p8.6g⁴ p12.2g⁵ p9.5g Dec 29] lengthy gelding: fair handicapper on all-weather, modest on turf: won at Wolverhampton in June: barely stays 10.8f: acts on polytrack and soft ground: effective with/without cheekpieces: has run well when sweating. *M. Appleby*

WESTER ROSS (IRE) 3 b.c. Fruits of Love (USA) 127 – Diabaig 76 (Precocious **79** 126) [2007 77: 10m⁶ 10d* 10d⁶ 12d Jun 29] compact colt: fair performer: won maiden at Windsor in May: barely stays 1½m: acts on good to soft going: races prominently. *J. M. P. Eustace*

WESTPORT 4 b.g. Xaar 132 – Connemara (IRE) 100 (Mujadil (USA) 119) [2007 85: **92** p5.1g⁵ 6g⁵ 6s⁶ 6d p6g* 5m² p6g³ f6d⁴ Dec 12] strong gelding: fairly useful handicapper: won at Wolverhampton in June: effective at 5f/6f: acts on all-weather, soft and good to firm going. *K. A. Ryan*

WEST WIND 3 ch.f. Machiavellian (USA) 123 – Red Slippers (USA) 111 (Nure- **118** yev (USA) 131) [2007 8s³ 9.8g² 10g* 10.5m* 10s³ 12m² Sep 16]

A French classic in which the winner, still less the first three home, were all trained in the Provinces would have been unthinkable until quite recently. But the result of the latest Prix de Diane Hermes, where the big Chantilly stables played only a minor role, was indicative of the strength of France's provincial trainers these days. The phenomenon is not just a Flat one either. The current leading jumps trainers, Arnaud Chaille-Chaille and Guillaume Macaire, are neighbours at Royan, in the south-west of the country, well away from Maisons-Laffitte in the Paris region where France's principal training centre for jumpers is located. On the Flat, Chantilly-based Andre Fabre may be France's perennial champion trainer, but his closest pursuers in the latest season were Jean-Claude Rouget at Pau and Henri-Alex Pantall, based near Cholet in the west of France.

With nearly two hundred individual runners, Pantall sent out more horses than any other Flat trainer in France in 2007. As well as striking a blow for the Provinces in general, West Wind's victory in the Prix de Diane had personal significance for Pantall as she was his first Group 1 winner in almost thirty years of training which have yielded more than three thousand winners. His first runner in a Group 1 was Harvest Time (also his first pattern-race winner in the Prix du Lys) in the 1989 Prix de l'Arc de Triomphe. Pantall had previously come closest to a success at the top level when Maiden Tower (also runner-up in the Poule d'Essai des Pouliches) was beaten a nose in the Queen Elizabeth II Challenge Cup at Keeneland in 2003. Appropriately, West Wind, like Maiden Tower, carried the colours of Pantall's principal owner Sheikh Mohammed. Pantall's first winner for Sheikh Mohammed was Bequeath in 1989 who had been sent by Andre Fabre to Pantall so that she could win a small race in the Provinces. The stable continues to receive 'cast-offs' (all fillies incidentally) from Sheikh Mohammed's other trainers, including British yards, which would otherwise struggle to win in more competitive environments. A notable example in the latest season was Vincennes, who failed to win in three all-weather maidens for Michael Jarvis in the winter but thrived for Pantall, duly winning in the Provinces but also going on to success in a listed race at Chantilly and a Group 3 event at Cologne. Incidentally, another of the lesser lights owned by Sheikh Mohammed to have passed through Pantall's hands is Katday, whose racing career was nothing out of the ordinary—she won three small races in the Provinces—but who subsequently gained fame as the dam of triple Cheltenham Gold Cup winner Best Mate.

Five years after Bequeath's success, Pantall received his first batch of Sheikh Mohammed yearling fillies. As for West Wind, she reportedly did not go into training until August as a two-year-old and was too big and backward to race that year. Consequently, she was not put in the Prix de Diane at the original entry stage but earned her supplementary place in the line-up when making rapid progress in the spring. She began with a third place in a newcomers race at Saint-Cloud in late-March, had the winner of that race behind her when second in a minor event at Longchamp the following month, and improved again to win a similar event at

Chantilly over a mile and a quarter a month before the Diane. Although progressing really well, West Wind still had about a stone's improvement to find to win just an average renewal. However, she started fourth favourite at just over 7/1 on the pari-mutuel, a factor in her odds perhaps the form of her rider Frankie Dettori who had completed the Epsom-Chantilly Derby double the previous weekend. The impressive Prix Cleopatre winner Vadapolina was sent off favourite in the fourteen-strong field ahead of the fillies who had finished first and second in the Prix Saint-Alary, the unbeaten Jean-Claude Rouget-trained Coquerelle (who had beaten West Wind at Longchamp) and Believe Me. But with the first three in the betting all disappointing to varying degrees, West Wind's task was made a lot easier. Held up in mid-division, she was eased towards the outside of the field early in the straight and quickened to take the lead from Vadapolina over a furlong out as the favourite hung left. West Wind kept on well to win by a length and a half from the Francois Rohaut-trained Mrs Lindsay, who had made much of the running, while the provincial one, two, three was completed by outsider Diyakalanie, a neck back in third, trained by Pantall's former stable jockey Joel Boisnard. Believe Me was only sixth, Vadapolina eighth (by the end of the season it was clear she had two very different ways of running), while Coquerelle was last of all, reported to have bled badly. The only British-trained runner, Musidora Stakes runner-up Sweet Lilly, was also well held.

West Wind's victory in the Prix de Diane came twenty years after Sheikh Mohammed's first win in the race with the top-class Indian Skimmer, also a supplementary entry incidentally. Dettori's feat of winning the Prix du Jockey Club and Prix de Diane in the same year had last been accomplished in 1956 by Serge Boullenger on Marcel Boussac's three-year-olds Philius and Apollonia. Dettori's partnership with West Wind could not be maintained for her two subsequent starts, though her transfer to Godolphin at the end of the year should mean they are reunited at some stage. West Wind was next seen out in the Pretty Polly Stakes at the Curragh, running a bit below her Chantilly form under much softer conditions, but finishing third, beaten two lengths and the same behind Oaks runner-up Peeping Fawn and the previous season's One Thousand Guineas winner Speciosa. With three more Group 1 wins to her name later in the summer, Peeping Fawn established herself as Europe's best middle-distance filly, so West Wind needed no excuses for her defeat at the Curragh.

With Peeping Fawn an absentee from the Prix Vermeille at Longchamp in September, West Wind's notable rivals included the two fillies who had chased her home at Chantilly, though once again it was Vadapolina who started favourite to beat them all. West Wind's performance at the Curragh had not really reinforced earlier impressions that she would stay a mile and a half, though the way she finished in the Vermeille left no doubt that she saw the trip out, even if not all of her connections were convinced. In fact, West Wind, back on good to firm ground, looked unlucky not to confirm superiority over Mrs Lindsay from the Prix de Diane. While Mrs Lindsay stole a lead turning into the straight at Longchamp, West Wind had to wait for room on the rail much further back in the field, finally obtaining a clear run under a furlong and a half out and closing strongly to be beaten only three quarters of a length by Mrs Lindsay at the line. West Wind had been expected to end her campaign in the Prix de l'Opera but the Vermeille proved to be her final start before joining Godolphin.

In his early days as jockey to the Luca Cumani stable, Dettori had also part-nered West Wind's dam Red Slippers to her biggest successes as a three-year-old, a

Prix de Diane Hermes, Chantilly—West Wind justifies the decision to supplement her and gives Frankie Dettori his third classic winner in nine days; she pulls away from Mrs Lindsay, Diyakalanie (rail) and Anabaa's Creation

Sheikh Mohammed's "West Wind"

listed race at Newcastle and the Sun Chariot Stakes (then run over a mile and a quarter) at Newmarket. By then she was carrying Sheikh Mohammed's colours, though she had begun her career in the ownership of Robert Sangster, for whom she had won a minor event at Ascot as a two-year-old. Red Slippers produced five other winners before West Wind, the best of them her first foal Redbridge (by Alleged), a smart performer at up to a mile and a half. The others were all successful abroad, Redones (by Seeking The Gold) winning at up to a mile in the UAE, Ammunition (by Zafonic), a six-furlong winner there, Hunt The Slipper (also by Seeking The Gold), a two-year-old mile winner for Pantall, and Wizard of Oz (by Singspiel) a nine-furlong winner in France for Fabre at the same age. West Wind's grandam Morning Devotion won a Newmarket maiden and finished third in the Fillies' Mile on her two outings as a two-year-old, but didn't fulfil that promise at three, though her fourth in the Lancashire Oaks showed she stayed a mile and a half. Red Slippers was smart but Morning Devotion produced an even better filly two years later in Balanchine. Like Red Slippers, she too was sold by Sangster to Maktoum interests (as part of a four-horse package reportedly valued at £1,500,000), forming an important part of what was then the experimental phase of the developing Godolphin operation. After wintering in Dubai, Balanchine carried joint-owner Maktoum Al Maktoum's colours as a three-year-old but gave Godolphin its first major success when winning the 1994 Oaks (also Dettori's first win in a British classic) and showed top-class form when beating the colts in the Irish Derby. Serious attacks of colic kept Balanchine off the track for the rest of the year and she failed to recapture her best form the following season.

Sangster sold another quartet of his best youngsters to Godolphin in 1997, that batch including the following season's One Thousand Guineas winner Cape

Verdi and Derby runner-up City Honours. A less publicised private transaction between Robert Sangster and Sheikh Mohammed in pre-Godolphin days saw subsequent Arc winner Carnegie change hands as a yearling for a reported 1,600,000 dollars. Morning Devotion's other winner of note was a smart brother to Red Slippers, Romanov, who remained in Sangster ownership, finishing third in the Derby and gaining his biggest win in the following season's Jockey Club Stakes. Big things were apparently also expected in some quarters from Morning Devotion's 2003 Storm Cat colt Pescatorio, who was well supported for the Guineas before he had ever run but proved no better than a fair maiden in six starts for Aidan O'Brien. Coming right up to date, Morning Devotion's latest offspring of racing age, Giant Love, won a two-year-old maiden for Mark Johnston at York in September.

West Wind (ch.f. 2004)	Machiavellian (USA) (b or br 1987)	Mr Prospector (b 1970)	Raise A Native
			Gold Digger
		Coup de Folie (b 1982)	Halo
			Raise The Standard
	Red Slippers (USA) (ch 1989)	Nureyev (b 1977)	Northern Dancer
			Special
		Morning Devotion (ch 1982)	Affirmed
			Morning Has Broken

Robert Sangster died in the spring of 2004 but products of his Swettenham Stud continued to race in his blue and green colours after his death in the name of the Sangster Family. Pescatorio proved to be the last of his dam's runners to carry those colours. Morning Devotion's unraced three-year-old Danzig filly, Morning Cry, featured in the British dispersal of the Swettenham Stud's breeding interests that took place at Tattersalls in December. The mares sold at Newmarket made a total of more than 8,500,000 guineas. Morning Cry was sold for 485,000 guineas, the most expensive pair being the Yorkshire Oaks runner-up Ocean Silk (3,200,000 guineas) and the last Group or Grade 1 winner to carry the Sangster colours, Angara (3,000,000 guineas), winner of the 2006 Diana Handicap. Ocean Silk, who is out of a sister to Divine Proportions and was in foal to Pivotal, became Sheikh Mohammed's latest acquisition from the Sangster empire when bought on his behalf by John Ferguson. At Keeneland the month before, where more of the Sangster bloodstock was sold, the 2004 Fillies' Mile winner Playful Act set a new record for a broodmare when falling to Ferguson for 10,500,000 dollars. An account of Robert Sangster's legacy as an owner-breeder can be found in the essay on Playful Act in *Racehorses of 2004*. Suffice to say here that the brochure produced for Swettenham Stud's dispersal at Tattersalls listed one hundred and fifty-six worldwide Group or Grade 1 wins in the Sangster colours, beginning in 1976 with the victories of Durtal and The Minstrel in the Cheveley Park Stakes and Dewhurst Stakes respectively and ending with Angara's win at Saratoga thirty years later. Sangster's greatest legacy was his part in the founding of Coolmore based on the success of top-class sires, but the Sangster bloodlines are also going to provide plenty of ammunition for rival empire Darley in years to come. When West Wind, a lengthy filly in appearance, eventually retires to the paddocks, as well as joining her own dam Red Slippers, she will be alongside Balanchine, Ocean Silk, Playful Act and Echoes In Eternity (Playful Act's half-sister who won a Newmarket maiden for Sangster before winning the Sun Chariot and Park Hill Stakes for Godolphin) in the Maktoum band of broodmares. Details of West Wind's wider family can be found in the essay on another of its notable members from the latest season, Saoirse Abu. *H-A. Pantall, France*

WEST WITH THE WIND 2 b.c. (Jan 14) Fasliyev (USA) 120 – Midnight Angel **84 p** (GER) 108 (Acatenango (GER) 127) [2007 7g 8.2g² Nov 17] 42,000Y: big, angular, good-topped colt: has long stride: first foal: dam, 8.5f (in US) to 10.5f (in Germany) winner, placed in German/Italian Oaks: fairly useful form, shaping well, in maidens at Doncaster and Nottingham (second to Wintercast): will be suited by 1¼m/1½m: type to thrive at 3 yrs. *T. P. Tate*

WESTWOOD 2 ch.g. (Feb 15) Captain Rio 122 – Consignia (IRE) 67 (Definite Article **91** 121) [2007 6g 6m² 6m³ 5.7f 6d* 6g Oct 27] rather leggy gelding: fairly useful performer: won nursery at Haydock in September by 4 lengths, standout effort (only start on going softer than good): should prove best at 5f/6f: front runner. *D. Haydn Jones*

WESTWOOD DAWN 2 gr.g. (Apr 10) Clodovil (IRE) 116 – Ivory Dawn 85 (Bats-   –
hoof 122) [2007 6d 6.1m p6g p7g p7.1g p5.1d⁴ Dec 17] leggy gelding: little form: tried
visored. *Mrs N. Macauley*

WHASTON (IRE) 2 b.g. (Feb 15) Hawk Wing (USA) 136 – Sharafanya (IRE) (Zafo-   **53**
nic (USA) 130) [2007 8m 7s p7.1g Oct 21] modest form in maidens: subsequently gelded.
J. D. Bethell

WHAT-A-DANCER (IRE) 10 b.g. Dancing Dissident (USA) 119 – Cool Gales 85   **53 §**
(Lord Gayle (USA) 124) [2007 77§: 7.1s 8.1m⁵ 8.1d 7.6s Aug 18] sparely-made gelding:
only modest performer in 2007: stays 1m: acts on polytrack, seems best on good going or
firmer on turf: wears blinkers/cheekpieces: sometimes slowly away: held up: sometimes
finds little, and not one to trust. *R. A. Harris*

WHATALOTOFBUTS 2 ch.c. (Apr 6) Kirkwall 118 – Wontcostalotbut 63 (Nicholas   –
Bill 125) [2007 6.1s⁵ 7s Jun 29] well held in minor event/maiden: bred for stamina. *B. De
Haan*

WHAT A TREASURE (IRE) 3 ch.f. Cadeaux Genereux 131 – Treasure Trove   **78**
(USA) 62 (The Minstrel (CAN) 135) [2007 73: 7s* 7m⁶ 7d² 7s* 7d Aug 26] unfurnished
filly: fair handicapper: won at Leicester in June and July: stays 7f: acts on soft and good
to firm ground. *L. M. Cumani*

WHAT DO YOU KNOW 4 b.g. Compton Place 125 – How Do I Know 91 (Petong   **81**
126) [2007 76: p7g⁶ p7f² p6g³ p6g³ p7g² p7.1g² 7g³ 5g² p5g* 5.3f⁵ 5.7d 6d⁵ p6g p5g* 5.7f
Sep 16] sturdy gelding: fairly useful handicapper: won at Kempton in June and August:
effective from 5f to 7f: acts on polytrack and firm going: tried tongue tied/in cheekpieces/
blinkered: front runner. *A. M. Hales*

WHATIZZIT 4 b.f. Galileo (IRE) 134 – Wosaita 70 (Generous (IRE) 139) [2007 88:   **88**
11.6m³ 10.3f⁴ Jun 12] fairly useful handicapper: stays 1½m: acts on polytrack and firm
going: consistent. *E. A. L. Dunlop*

WHAT KATIE DID (IRE) 2 b.c. (Mar 24) Invincible Spirit (IRE) 121 – Chatterberry   **70**
67 (Aragon 118) [2007 5d⁶ 5g 5g⁶ p6g* p7.1g² p6g* 7.1m 7m p7.1g⁶ p6g* p6m²   **a75**
Dec 7] rather leggy colt: fair performer: won nurseries at Kempton and Wolverhampton
in August and 2 claimers at Wolverhampton (left J. Osborne £16,000 after second) in
October: stays 7f: acts on polytrack, promise on turf (good to firm going). *P. F. I. Cole*

WHAT'S FOR TEA 2 b.f. (Apr 20) Beat All (USA) 120 – Come To Tea (IRE) (Be My   **64**
Guest (USA) 126) [2007 7d⁶ 7s⁶ 7d³ 7m³ 8.3d⁴ p8.6g⁴ p7g* p7.1g² p8.6g⁴ p7g³ p6g⁴ p7g²
p7.1d³ f6d² Dec 21] €1,000Y, resold €12,000Y, resold 7,200Y: good-bodied filly: ninth
foal: dam, Irish 2-y-o 7f winner, half-sister to high-class performer up to 1½m Ace, very
smart 1¼m performer Hawkeye and US Grade 1 9f winner Danish: modest performer:
claimed from T. Easterby £6,000 third start: won claimer at Kempton in October: held her
form very well: effective at 6f to 8.6f: acts on all-weather, good to firm and good to soft
going: tough. *Tom Dascombe*

WHATS YOUR GAME (IRE) 3 ch.g. Namid 128 – Tahlil 46 (Cadeaux Genereux   **54**
131) [2007 –: 6d 5d 5m 5s 5g 5m⁵ p5.1g² 5g⁶ p5.1g 5g⁶ p5.1g⁶ Dec 4] neat gelding:
modest maiden: raced mainly at 5f: acted on polytrack and good to firm ground: blinkered
last 5 starts: dead. *A. Berry*

WHAXAAR (IRE) 3 b.g. Xaar 132 – Sheriyna (FR) (Darshaan 133) [2007 –: p8g⁵   **64**
p8g⁵ 8m p12g⁴ p12g² Dec 19] modest maiden: left S. Kirk after third start: stays 1½m:
acts on polytrack. *R. Ingram*

WHAZZIS 3 br.f. Desert Prince (IRE) 130 – Wosaita 70 (Generous (IRE) 139) [2007   **109**
78: 7m 7g² 7d³ 7.1d⁴ 7m 8d* 8d⁶ 8m* 10g Oct 28] sturdy, useful-looking filly: useful
performer: won listed race at Ascot (by 6 lengths from Fann) in July and Premio Sergio
Cumani at Milan (by 1½ lengths from Mimetico) in October: best at 1m (always behind
in 1¼m Premio Lydia Tesio at Rome): acts on polytrack, soft and good to firm going:
visored last 5 starts: joined D. Selvaratnam in UAE. *W. J. Haggas*

WHEELAVIT (IRE) 4 b.g. Elnadim (USA) 128 – Storm River (USA) 81 (Riverman   **74**
(USA) 131) [2007 75: p10g⁶ p7g p7g p8g⁵ p8g 10g⁵ 12.6m³ Aug 27] close-coupled gelding: fair handicapper: stays 12.6f: acts on polytrack and firm ground: tried in cheekpieces:
fair hurdler. *B. G. Powell*

WHEELS IN MOTION (IRE) 3 b.c. Daylami (IRE) 138 – Tarziyana (USA) 76   **83**
(Danzig (USA)) [2007 83+: 10.4g⁵ 8.1s 8f² 8.2d⁴ 6d 8.1g⁴ 8.1s Sep 28] strong colt: fairly
useful handicapper: free-going sort, may prove best short of 1¼m: raced only on good
ground or softer (acts on heavy): sold 22,000 gns. *T. P. Tate*

WHENEVER 3 ch.c. Medicean 128 – Alessandra 101 (Generous (IRE) 139) [2007 **94 p**
9.9m³ 14s* 14.6g* Oct 26] strong colt: fifth foal: half-brother to 5-y-o Alessano and fairly
useful 5f to 1m winner Kryssa (by Kris): dam, 1½m winner, half-sister to dam of very
smart sprinters Avonbridge and Patavellian: fairly useful and progressive form: won
maiden at Goodwood and 19-runner handicap at Doncaster (beating Kahara by 1¼
lengths), both in October: will stay beyond 1¾m: acts on soft ground: should improve
again at 4 yrs. *R. T. Phillips*

WHENINEEDYOU 2 ch.f. (Apr 3) Best of The Bests (IRE) 122 – Party Turn 60 **–**
(Pivotal 124) [2007 p7g Oct 23] 6,000Y: first foal: dam, 7f winner, out of half-sister to
5-y-o Party Boss: 16/1, last in maiden at Lingfield. *I. A. Wood*

WHEN YER READY (IRE) 2 b.g. (Mar 12) Val Royal (FR) 127 – Rachel Green **59**
(IRE) 46 (Case Law 113) [2007 6v⁶ 6m⁶ 6m Sep 1] strong, good-topped gelding: modest
maiden: gelded after final start: will be suited by 7f/1m: best effort (debut) on heavy
going. *T. D. Easterby*

WHERE'S BROUGHTON 4 ch.f. Cadeaux Genereux 131 – Tuxford Hideaway 102 **73 d**
(Cawston's Clown 113) [2007 77: 10g p10g 9g⁵ 12g p9.5m p8g p10m p9.5s Dec 21]
useful-looking filly: fair handicapper, lightly raced: on downgrade: should stay 1¼m:
acts on polytrack, best turf effort on good ground. *W. J. Musson*

WHERE'S KILLORAN 2 b.f. (Apr 28) Iron Mask (USA) 117 – Calypso Lady (IRE) **46**
88 (Priolo (USA) 127) [2007 p6g p6g⁵ p5m p5m⁵ Dec 8] 3,500F, 30,000Y: fifth foal:
half-sister to 4-y-o Egyptian Lord and winner in Greece by Robellino: dam 2-y-o 6f
winner: poor maiden: raced only at 5f/6f on polytrack. *Peter Grayson*

WHERE'S SUSIE 2 ch.f. (Mar 4) Where Or When (IRE) 124 – Linda's Schoolgirl **66 +**
(IRE) (Grand Lodge (USA) 125) [2007 p7g p7m⁶ Oct 11] workmanlike filly: third foal:
dam unraced: mid-division in maidens at Kempton, not knocked about: will stay 1m.
D. K. Ivory

WHERE TO NOW 2 b.f. (Mar 18) Where Or When (IRE) 124 – Starminda 50 (Zamin- **–**
dar (USA) 116) [2007 8g 8d Oct 23] workmanlike filly: first foal: dam sprint maiden:
tailed off in maidens. *Mrs C. A. Dunnett*

WHINHILL HOUSE 7 ch.g. Paris House 123 – Darussalam 78 (Tina's Pet 121) [2007 **69**
77d: f5g f5g* f6g³ f6g 5m⁴ 5g³ 5m* 5m 5g 5d⁶ 5d⁴ 5g* 6m⁴ Aug 1] strong gelding: fair
performer: won handicap and seller at Southwell in April, claimer at Musselburgh in May
and apprentice handicap at Thirsk in July: best at 5f/6f: acts on all-weather, firm and good
to soft ground: sometimes in cheekpieces, usually visored: races up with pace: none too
consistent. *D. W. Barker*

WHIPCHORD (IRE) 3 ch.f. Distant Music (USA) 126 – Spanker 71§ (Suave Dancer **62**
(USA) 136) [2007 64: p7g² 7m 7g 7m 6d 8d Oct 18] lightly-made filly: modest maiden
handicapper: should stay 1m: acts on polytrack and firm ground: tried blinkered: sold 800
gns, sent to Spain. *R. Hannon*

WHISKEY CREEK 2 ch.g. (Mar 22) Tipsy Creek (USA) 115 – Judiam 74 (Primo **58**
Dominie 121) [2007 5m⁴ 5m 5d 6m 5.5m⁶ p6g³ Sep 19] stocky gelding: modest maiden:
left R. Fahey after third start: third in nursery at Kempton: should prove best at 6f/7f: acts
on polytrack and good to firm going. *Miss Tor Sturgis*

WHISKEY JUNCTION 3 b.g. Bold Edge 123 – Victoria Mill 59 (Free State 125) **74**
[2007 72: p5g² May 7] fair maiden: stays 6f: acts on polytrack: tried in cheekpieces: has
raced freely. *A. M. Balding*

WHISPERED DREAMS (GER) 2 ch.f. (Feb 26) Platini (GER) 126 – Waconda **87 p**
(GER) (Pursuit of Love 124) [2007 p7g* Oct 17] €28,000F, €110,000Y: third foal: sister
to useful Italian 7.5f/1m winner Windhuk: dam German 1m winner: odds on, won maiden
at Lingfield in good style by 2 lengths from Our Chairman: will be suited by at least 1m:
useful prospect. *Saeed bin Suroor*

WHISPERING DEATH 5 br.g. Pivotal 124 – Lucky Arrow 60 (Indian Ridge 123) **96**
[2007 91+: 14.1m² 18.7m⁶ p16g² 21g 18m² 14g⁶ 14.6m⁵ Sep 14] tall, good-topped gelding: useful handicapper: further improvement in 2007, placed 4 times, notably when third
to Dansant in Mallard Stakes at Doncaster: should stay beyond 2¼m: acts on polytrack,
firm and good to soft going: wears headgear: held up: quirky: sold 145,000 gns, joined
J. Howard Johnson. *W. J. Haggas*

WHISPERING DESERT 2 b.f. (Feb 6) Distant Music (USA) 126 – Nullarbor (Green **62**
Desert (USA) 127) [2007 5d⁴ 5v⁴ 5s² 5m⁵ 5g* 5m⁵ p6g Sep 19] €9,500Y: lengthy filly:
fifth living foal: half-sister to 7-y-o Desert Opal and 6f winner Disguise (by Pursuit of
Love): dam French 2-y-o 5.5f winner: modest performer: won maiden at Carlisle in
August: best at 5f: acts on heavy and good to firm going. *P. T. Midgley*

WHISTFUL MISS 2 b.f. (Mar 1) First Trump 118 – Mise En Scene 85 (Lugana Beach 116) [2007 5m 7m p7.1g⁶ p6m⁴ 5m p6g Nov 19] 3,500Y: good-bodied filly: third foal: sister to 4-y-o Ace Baby and half-sister to 3-y-o Sunken Rags: dam 2-y-o 5f winner: poor maiden: seems to stay 7f: form only on polytrack. *P. Howling* **a42**

WHISTLEDOWNWIND 2 b.c. (Mar 15) Danehill Dancer (IRE) 117 – Mountain Ash 107 (Dominion 123) [2007 7m 8d* Oct 27] 55,000F, 75,000Y: big, good-bodied colt: closely related to winner in Greece by Danehill and half-brother to several winners, including useful 7f/1m winners Analyser and Musical Treat (both by Royal Academy, latter also successful in Canada and dam of 3-y-o Finsceal Beo): dam, 7f/1m winner, out of Cheveley Park second Red Berry: fairly useful form: fitter for debut, won maiden at Newbury by 1¾ lengths from Andaman Sunset, quickening through from last and idling in front: stays 1m: will continue to progress. *P. W. Chapple-Hyam* **93 p**

WHISTLER 10 ch.g. Selkirk (USA) 129 – French Gift 99 (Cadeaux Genereux 131) [2007 68: 5.1m 5.3d 5.1g 5.1s⁶ 5.1d 5.3d⁵ 5.1f 5.1m 5.1g Nov 7] angular, workmanlike gelding: has a quick action: modest handicapper nowadays: best at 5f: acts on any turf going: wears headgear: sometimes hangs left: often gets behind: none too consistent. *Miss J. R. Tooth* **53**

WHISTLEUPTHEWIND 4 b.f. Piccolo 121 – The Frog Queen 64 (Bin Ajwaad (IRE) 119) [2007 64: p6g³ p6g³ p6g p7g p6f⁶ 6m 7s³ 8.1s 7f⁴ 7m 7d³ 7f* 7g Sep 19] neat filly: modest handicapper: won at Folkestone in September: effective at 6f to 1m: acts on polytrack, firm and soft ground: often blinkered, has run well in cheekpieces: often races prominently. *J. M. P. Eustace* **64**

WHISTLING FRED 8 b.g. Overbury (IRE) 116 – Megabucks (Buckskin (FR) 133) [2007 p12g Apr 30] maiden hurdler: well beaten in claimer at Lingfield. *B. De Haan* **–**

WHITBARROW (IRE) 8 b.g. Royal Abjar (USA) 121 – Danccini (IRE) 78 (Dancing Dissident (USA) 119) [2007 76: 6g f6g* p6g* f6g* f6g* p6g⁴ 5.9m* 6m⁵ 6m 5g p6g* p6g⁵ f6d Dec 12] strong, good sort: fairly useful performer: thrived in 2007, winning claimer at Southwell in April, handicaps at Wolverhampton and Southwell (2) in May and Carlisle in July, and claimer at Wolverhampton in October: best at 6f nowadays: acts on all-weather, firm and soft going: wears headgear (blinkered nowadays): front runner. *B. R. Millman* **90**

WHITCOMBE FLYER (USA) 2 b. or br.c. (Mar 22) Fusaichi Pegasus (USA) 130 – Bakewell Tart (IRE) 92 (Tagula (IRE) 116) [2007 p5g⁶ 6m p5m⁶ p6g⁶ p6g⁴ Dec 22] 14,000 2-y-o: first foal: dam, 2-y-o 7f/7.5f (latter in Italy) winner, sister to useful 7f performer Macaroon: modest maiden: will stay at least 7f: in cheekpieces/blinkered last 3 starts: tried tongue tied. *Jamie Poulton* **56**

WHITCOMBE MINISTER (USA) 2 b.c. (Mar 30) Deputy Minister (CAN) – Pronghorn (USA) (Gulch (USA)) [2007 7m⁴ p7g* Dec 29] $50,000Y, 15,000 2-y-o: rather leggy, useful-looking colt: second foal: dam, US sprint winner, half-sister to high-class 1¼m/1½m performer Muhtarram: fairly useful form: promising debut when fourth to Fireside in maiden at Newmarket: won weaker similar event at Lingfield by length, making all: will stay 1m: useful prospect. *Jamie Poulton* **87 p**

WHITCOMBE SPIRIT 2 b.c. (Feb 2) Diktat 126 – L'Evangile 105 (Danehill (USA) 126) [2007 8d p8g p10g⁴ Dec 12] lengthy colt: fair maiden: will stay 1½m: acts on polytrack. *Jamie Poulton* **65**

WHITE BEAR (FR) 5 ch.g. Gold Away (IRE) 125 – Danaide (FR) (Polish Precedent (USA) 131) [2007 76: p8g* 8.1g p7.1g p7g p7m Nov 26] leggy gelding: fair handicapper: won at Lingfield in April: stays 1m: acts on all-weather and good to firm going: tried visored, usually blinkered: bled once at 4 yrs: signs of temperament. *C. R. Dore* **73**

WHITE COCKADE 4 gr.g. Compton Place 125 – Swissmatic 54 (Petong 126) [2007 p11g Jan 10] 20/1, showed nothing in maiden at Kempton. *Ms J. S. Doyle* **–**

WHITE DEER (USA) 3 b.g. Stravinsky (USA) 133 – Brookshield Baby (IRE) (Sadler's Wells (USA) 132) [2007 85: 7.5m³ 10.4g⁶ 7m* 7d² 7s 7g² 7m⁵ 7m 8s Sep 22] lengthy, good-topped gelding: useful handicapper: won at Thirsk in June by a length from Hazzard County: good second after at Chester and Goodwood (beaten ½ length by King of Argos): best form at 7f, should be as effective at 1m: acts on firm and good to soft going: sold 16,500 gns. *M. Johnston* **104**

WHITE LEDGER (IRE) 8 ch.g. Ali-Royal (IRE) 127 – Boranwood (IRE) (Exhibitioner 111) [2007 54: p5.1g 5d Jul 29] useful-looking gelding: modest performer in 2006, little form in 2007: best at 5f/6f: acts on all-weather, firm and soft going: tried in headgear: sometimes slowly away. *R. E. Peacock* **–**

WHITE LIGHTENING (IRE) 4 ch.g. Indian Ridge 123 – Mille Miglia (IRE) 96 **78** (Caerleon (USA) 132) [2007 79: 12m⁴ 13d⁴ 16m Aug 4] fair maiden: left J. Howard Johnson after reappearance: stays 13f: acts on firm and good to soft ground. *J. Wade*

WHITE MOSS (IRE) 3 b.f. Peintre Celebre (USA) 137 – Saint Ann (USA) 66 (Geiger **68** Counter (USA)) [2007 p9.5g 12g³ 10.1m 9m 11.5g³ 10.5m² 10.1g 8m³ 8g⁴ 8d Oct 18] lengthy filly: fifth foal: sister to 4-y-o Sienna Storm and half-sister to fairly useful 1m winner Heversham (by Octagonal): dam, temperamental maiden, out of half-sister to very smart sprinter Primo Dominie: fair maiden: may prove best up to 1¼m: acts on good to firm going: sometimes hangs. *M. H. Tompkins*

WHITEOAK LADY (IRE) 2 ch.f. (May 22) Medecis 119 – French Toast (IRE) (Last **70** Tycoon 131) [2007 6d⁴ 6.1s* 6g⁶ Sep 23] €8,000Y: second foal: dam won up to 9.5f in Italy: fair form: won maiden at Chepstow in July: will stay 7f/1m: raced only on good ground or softer. *J. L. Spearing*

WHITE'S RUBY 3 gr.f. Iron Mask (USA) 117 – Negligee 94 (Night Shift (USA)) **53** [2007 5v 6m p6m³ p6m Oct 3] 50,000Y: smallish filly: first foal: dam 2-y-o 6f winner: modest maiden: stays 6f: blinkered (below form, wandered) final outing. *B. Smart*

WHITHORN 4 ch.g. Primo Valentino (IRE) 116 – Polar Refrain 59 (Polar Falcon **53 d** (USA) 126) [2007 6m⁵ f7g 7m 5m 5d 8s Jul 9] small gelding: form only in apprentice claimer at Catterick on debut: withdrawn after bolting prior to intended debut. *J. Balding*

WHITTINGHAMVILLAGE 6 b.m. Whittingham (IRE) 104 – Shaa Spin 63 **59** (Shaadi (USA) 126) [2007 65: 9.1g* 8.3d* 7m 5.6g⁵ 6.9g 10.1m 8g⁶ Oct 5] leggy, workman-like mare: modest handicapper: left D. Whillans after fourth start: stays 9f: acts on firm and good to soft going: tried in cheekpieces. *J. P. L. Ewart*

WHODOUTHINKUR (IRE) 2 b.g. (Feb 22) Beckett (IRE) 116 – Scarletta (USA) 79 **–** (Red Ransom (USA)) [2007 7m 6m p8.6g Sep 21] small, close-coupled gelding: well beaten in maidens: tried in cheekpieces. *Mrs C. A. Dunnett*

WHODUNIT (UAE) 3 b.g. Mark of Esteem (IRE) 137 – Mystery Play (IRE) 104 **56** (Sadler's Wells (USA) 132) [2007 p8g p8.6g⁵ 8.1m p8g 12.1g² p12g 12s 11.6m 9.9m⁵ Aug 26] good-topped gelding: modest maiden: left M. Johnston 4,000 gns after second outing: well held last 4 starts: stays 1½m: acts on polytrack: tried blinkered. *P. W. Hiatt*

WHOS COUNTING 3 ch.f. Woodborough (USA) 112 – Hard To Follow (Dilum **44** (USA) 115) [2007 44: p6g⁶ p8g Oct 29] poor maiden: stays 6f: raced only on polytrack. *R. J. Hodges*

WHO'S THIS (IRE) 3 b.g. Xaar 132 – Tarafiya (USA) (Trempolino (USA) 135) **55** [2007 p10g Jun 9] 16/1, tenth to Come April in maiden at Lingfield, weakening quickly. *W. R. Swinburn*

WHO'S WINNING (IRE) 6 ch.g. Docksider (USA) 124 – Quintellina 83 (Robellino **84** (USA) 127) [2007 87: p6g⁴ 5.1f³ 6f⁵ 6m* 6g* 6g⁴ 6s⁵ 5.7f² 5.7d⁴ 6d 6m 6g 6f² 6m² 5g⁶ 6m⁶ 6d p5g 6g⁵ p6m p7m Dec 10] sturdy gelding: fairly useful handicapper: won at Folkestone and Goodwood in May: seems best around 6f nowadays: acts on polytrack, firm and good to soft going: tried in headgear/tongue tied: free-going sort, often races prominently: has reportedly bled. *B. G. Powell*

WHOZART (IRE) 4 b.g. Mozart (IRE) 131 – Hertford Castle (Reference Point 139) **59** [2007 –: 6m 5g³ 6g* 6g² 5g⁶ 5d 5g 5g³ p6g Nov 8] good-topped gelding: modest performer: won amateur maiden handicap at Redcar in May: likely to prove best at 5f/6f: best efforts on good ground. *A. Dickman*

WIBBADUNE (IRE) 3 ch.f. Daggers Drawn (USA) 114 – Becada (GER) (Cadeaux **58** Genereux 131) [2007 58: p5.1g p5.1g² p5g* p5.1g⁵ Dec 31] modest performer: won maiden at Kempton in December: speedy, best at 5f: acts on polytrack. *Peter Grayson*

WICKED DAZE (IRE) 4 ch.g. Generous (IRE) 139 – Thrilling Day 112 (Groom **87** Dancer (USA) 128) [2007 p10g² 12d² p12g² Jul 17] tall gelding: fairly useful maiden: stays 1½m: acts on polytrack and good to soft ground. *Sir Mark Prescott*

WICKEDISH 3 b.f. Medicean 128 – Sleave Silk (IRE) 58 (Unfuwain (USA) 131) **54** [2007 –: 8m p10g⁵ 8m* 7g 10.1d Oct 30] sturdy, good-bodied filly: modest performer: won selling handicap at Yarmouth in August (left C. Wall later in month): bred to stay 1¼m+: tongue tied. *M. J. Gingell*

WICKED LADY (UAE) 4 b.f. Jade Robbery (USA) 121 – Kinsfolk (Distant Relative **–** 128) [2007 59: p12g p7g p12.2g Jul 16] lightly-raced maiden: left B. Johnson after second outing (visored): stays 1¼m: raced only on polytrack. *J. M. Bradley*

WICKED UNCLE 8 b.g. Distant Relative 128 – The Kings Daughter 79 (Indian King (USA) 128) [2007 68, a89: p6g⁵ 5m p6g p6g⁴ p6g⁶ p5.1g² p6d³ p5.1s⁶ Dec 20] smallish, sturdy gelding: impresses in appearance: just fair handicapper in 2007: best at 5f/6f: acts on all-weather and firm going: wears headgear. *S. Gollings* — **a72**

WICKSY CREEK 2 b.c. (Jun 1) Tipsy Creek (USA) 115 – Bridal White 66 (Robellino (USA) 127) [2007 6d⁴ 6g² Jul 23] modest form in frame in sellers at Yarmouth: should prove best at 5f/6f. *M. G. Quinlan* — **50**

WI DUD 3 b.c. Elnadim (USA) 128 – Hopesay 84 (Warning 136) [2007 116: 5g⁵ 6d 5g² 5g⁴ 5g⁵ 6g Sep 8] small, sturdy colt: carries plenty of condition: smart performer: best effort when 3 lengths fifth to Kingsgate Native in Nunthorpe Stakes at York on fifth start: ½-length second to Hoh Mike in Sprint Stakes at Sandown on third appearance: respectable seventh to Red Clubs in Sprint Cup at Haydock final outing: effective at 5f/6f: acts on good to firm and good to soft going, yet to race on extremes. *K. A. Ryan* — **118**

WID (USA) 3 gr.f. Elusive Quality (USA) – Alshadiyah (USA) 102 (Danzig (USA)) [2007 100: 7m 7m 6d² 6g² 6m Nov 10] lengthy, good-bodied filly: useful performer: best effort in 2007 when ½-length second to Lady Grace in listed race at Newmarket third outing: stirred up beforehand, tailed off in listed race at Doncaster final start: best form at 6f: acted on good to firm and good to soft going (unraced on extremes): sometimes raced freely: visits Nayef. *J. L. Dunlop* — **96**

WIESENPFAD (FR) 4 ch.c. Waky Nao 122 – Waldbeere (GER) (Mark of Esteem (IRE) 137) [2007 114: 8s 8g⁵ 8.5g* 10m* 10m³ 8.5s⁴ Oct 7] first foal: dam unraced sister to useful 1m/1¼m performer Waldmark out of smart German performer up to 1¾m Wurftaube: smart performer: won 4 times in 2006, notably Grosser Preis der Landeshauptstadt Dusseldorf and Hessen-Pokal at Frankfurt: back to form in August, winning listed race at Dusseldorf and Preis der Sparkassen-Finanzgruppe at Baden-Baden (by 2½ lengths from Kiton): ran creditably when close third to Shrek in Euro-Cup at Frankfurt next start: stays 1¼m: acts on soft and good to firm ground. *W. Hickst, Germany* — **117**

WIGHTGAR 3 b.c. Carisbrooke 99 – Main Brand 63 (Main Reef 126) [2007 p12g 10.1d⁶ 10.9g⁶ 16.2s 11.5m Aug 15] lengthy colt: little sign of ability: tried in cheekpieces, wears tongue tie. *R. A. Kvisla* — **–**

WIGRAM'S TURN (USA) 2 ch.c. (Apr 14) Hussonet (USA) – Stacey's Relic (USA) (Houston (USA)) [2007 5m* 6m³ 7g Jul 28] $25,000F, $25,000Y: leggy colt: third foal: half-brother to winner in US by Tactical Cat: dam US 2-y-o 1m winner: fairly useful form: won minor event at Redcar in May: third to Vhujon in similar race at Salisbury, again soon off bridle: stiff task final start: should be suited by 7f/1m. *A. M. Balding* — **82**

WIGWAM WILLIE (IRE) 5 b.g. Indian Rocket 115 – Sweet Nature (IRE) 71 (Classic Secret (USA) 91) [2007 89: 8m 8v* 8m 8m⁴ 8.3m 8s* 8d Oct 12] quite good-topped gelding: useful handicapper: won at Newcastle in June and Ayr (beat Mezuzah by 1¾ lengths) in September: best at 1m: acts on heavy and good to firm going (all 4 wins on softer than good): tried blinkered, wears cheekpieces. *K. A. Ryan* — **96**

WIKAALA (USA) 2 ch.g. (Feb 16) Diesis 133 – Roseate Tern 123 (Blakeney 126) [2007 p8g Aug 11] brother to useful 7f (at 2 yrs) to 1¼m winner Esloob and fairly useful 1¼m winner Majaales, and half-brother to 2 winners, including useful 1¼m winner Siyadah (by Mr Prospector): dam, won Yorkshire Oaks and third in Oaks/St Leger, half-sister to high-class performer up to 1¾m Ibn Bey: 12/1, behind in maiden at Lingfield: subsequently gelded. *M. P. Tregoning* — **–**

WILD BILL TRACEY 2 b.g. (May 26) Bahamian Bounty 116 – Travel Secret (Blakeney 126) [2007 5g 5g⁴ 5m⁵ p5m⁵ p5.1g² p6g³ p5.1g f5g³ Dec 27] rather unfurnished gelding: fair maiden: runner-up at Wolverhampton, below form after, including in cheekpieces/visor: best at 5f: acts on polytrack: carries head awkwardly. *M. J. Wallace* — **75 d**

WILD FELL HALL (IRE) 4 ch.g. Grand Lodge (USA) 125 – Genoa 96 (Zafonic (USA) 130) [2007 –: p8g 10f³ 11.8m² 12g* p12g* Jun 27] smallish, workmanlike gelding: fairly useful handicapper: won at Salisbury and Kempton in June, making all: stays 1½m: acts on polytrack and firm ground: has been early to post: sold 20,000 gns, joined A. Brown. *W. R. Swinburn* — **90**

WILD GARDENIA 3 b.f. Alhaarth (IRE) 126 – Frappe (IRE) 93 (Inchinor 119) [2007 57p: 12g² 11.8s Jun 4] angular filly: modest maiden: stays 1½m: acts on polytrack. *J. H. M. Gosden* — **58**

WILD LASS 6 ch.m. Bluegrass Prince (IRE) 110 – Pink Pumpkin 52 (Tickled Pink 114) [2007 52: 7g⁵ Jun 12] modest performer: respectable effort in claimer sole start in 2007: stays 7f: best effort on good going: blinkered/in cheekpieces nowadays. *J. C. Fox* — **42**

WILD PITCH 6 ch.g. Piccolo 121 – Western Horizon (USA) 58 (Gone West (USA)) **80**
[2007 66, a77: p10g* p11g p9.5g* p13.9g* p13.9g p12.2g6 p12g* 12g p12g 14d6 **a88**
p11g3 Aug 8] leggy, close-coupled gelding: fairly useful handicapper: improved in 2007,
winning at Kempton in January, Wolverhampton (2, first one apprentices) in February
and Lingfield in May: stays 1¾m: acts on polytrack, good to firm and good to soft going:
blinkered: has been slowly away, and usually held up. *P. Mitchell*

WILFORD MAVERICK (IRE) 5 b.g. Fasliyev (USA) 120 – Lioness 74 (Lion **–**
Cavern (USA) 117) [2007 56: p8g p9.5g p6g Mar 9] close-coupled gelding: modest
performer in 2006: little form in 2007, leaving M. Attwater after reappearance: tried
visored. *K. J. Burke*

WILLHEGO 6 ch.g. Pivotal 124 – Woodrising 64 (Nomination 125) [2007 93: 9d 10g **82 §**
p10g p12m3 Dec 7] plain gelding: fairly useful handicapper: effective at 1m to 1½m: acts
on polytrack, good to firm and good to soft going: refused to race second outing: one to
treat with caution. *J. R. Best*

WILL HE WISH 11 b.g. Winning Gallery 94 – More To Life (Northern Tempest **93**
(USA) 120) [2007 95: p7g4 p7g2 p7g5 8.1m* 8m6 8.1m 8.1m p8g5 8g p7.1g* p9.5g3
Dec 31] good-bodied gelding: fairly useful handicapper: won at Haydock in June and
Wolverhampton in October: stays 1m: acts on polytrack, firm and good to soft going:
sometimes blinkered, including for latest win. *S. Gollings*

WILLHEWIZ 7 b.g. Wizard King 122 – Leave It To Lib 66 (Tender King 123) [2007 **72**
86: 5.1f2 5m4 p6g4 5.7m2 p5g2 5d 5.7g 5.7f 5.7g6 p6g* p6g5 p5g4 p6g2 p6g Dec 19]
good-topped gelding: fair handicapper: won at Kempton in October: best at 5f/6f: acts
on all-weather, firm and soft going: effective with/without headgear: races prominently.
M. S. Saunders

WILLIAM JOHN 4 b.g. Foxhound (USA) 103 – Classy Relation (Puissance 110) **66**
[2007 66: 9.9g3 7.9m5 14.1g4 12d2 7.5g5 10m2 12.1m Sep 11] tall, workmanlike gelding:
fair handicapper: left P. Haslam and rejoined former trainer after fourth outing: stayed
1½m: acted on polytrack, firm and good to soft going: sometimes wore cheekpieces:
usually tongue tied: dead. *B. Ellison*

WILLIAM'S WAY 5 b.g. Fraam 114 – Silk Daisy 74 (Barathea (IRE) 127) [2007 80: **96**
f11g* p9.5g* p10g 10d 10d3 p11g p9.5g4 p11g Dec 1] quite good-topped gelding: useful **a90**
handicapper on turf, fairly useful on all-weather: won at Southwell in April and Wolverhampton in May: good third to Night Cru at Newmarket: effective at 9.5f to 1½m: acts on
all-weather, firm and good to soft going: usually held up. *I. A. Wood*

WILLIE EVER 3 b.g. Agnes World (USA) 123 – Miss Meltemi (IRE) 100 (Miswaki **53**
Tern (USA) 120) [2007 8g 8.3m p8.6d6 Dec 27] lengthy gelding: modest maiden: stays
1m. *W. J. Musson*

WILLIT (IRE) 2 ch.f. (Jan 25) Compton Place 125 – Fingal Nights (IRE) 81 (Night **56**
Shift (USA)) [2007 5.1d 5m 5.7f5 Sep 16] €25,000Y: sturdy filly: first foal: dam Irish 6f
and (at 2 yrs) 7f winner: modest maiden: dead. *M. R. Channon*

WILLKANDOO (USA) 2 b. or br.c. (Apr 15) Unbridled's Song (USA) 125 – Shann- **50 p**
kara (IRE) (Akarad (FR) 130) [2007 p8.6g Nov 10] $200,000Y, 24,000 2-y-o: eighth foal:
half-brother to several winners, including minor US stakes winner (also second in
Grade 2 8.5f event) Tekken (by Nureyev) and useful 1m winner Swan Knight (by Sadler's
Wells): dam, 1m winner (including at 2 yrs in France and Grade 3 event in US), half-sister
to Prix Vermeille winner Sharaya: 7/1, better than bare result (seventh to Mystery Star) in
maiden at Wolverhampton, making much of running: will do better. *K. A. Ryan*

WILLOFCOURSE 6 b.g. Aragon 118 – Willyet (Nicholas Bill 125) [2007 55: 7s 6.1s4 **65**
p5g 6m3 p6g2 6g4 6m4 p6g* p6g6 p6g Oct 14] fair handicapper: won at Kempton in
September: reportedly finished lame final outing: should have proved as effective at 5f as
6f: acted on polytrack and good to firm ground: tried visored: dead. *H. Candy*

WILLOW DANCER (IRE) 3 ch.g. Danehill Dancer (IRE) 117 – Willowbridge **78**
(IRE) (Entrepreneur 123) [2007 8.2m5 10.2m6 8.1d6 p8.6g3 10g5 p12.2g Sep 21] leggy,
lengthy gelding: fair maiden: stays 1¼m: acts on polytrack: signs of temperament.
W. R. Swinburn

WILLYN (IRE) 2 b.f. (Apr 13) Lujain (USA) 119 – Lamasat (USA) (Silver Hawk **64**
(USA) 123) [2007 5m6 5m4 6g4 7d 6g p7.1g2 7m* 7m 7m2 6d 7.1m3 7g 6s Oct 26]
2,200Y: compact filly: third foal: dam unraced out of useful performer up to 9f Awaamir:
modest performer: won claimer at Thirsk (left J. Weymes £10,000) in August: twice
placed in nurseries: stays 7f: acts on good to firm going: reluctant only try in cheekpieces.
J. S. Goldie

WILLY (SWE) 5 ch.g. Heart of Oak (USA) 103 – Kawa-Ib (IRE) 78 (Nashwan (USA) **53**
135) [2007 52: p12.2g⁶ p12.2g f12g⁶ Mar 22] modest performer: stays 1½m: acts on dirt
and all-weather: has worn blinkers/cheekpieces: usually tongue tied: winning hurdler.
R. Brotherton

WILMINGTON 3 ch.g. Compton Place 125 – Bahawir Pour (USA) (Green Dancer **70**
(USA) 132) [2007 72: p6g³ p7g⁶ p5g⁵ p8.6g 8m⁵ 8s Sep 20] strong, useful-looking
gelding: fair maiden: left N. Littmoden after fourth start: stays 1m: acts on polytrack and
good to firm ground: sometimes blinkered. *Mrs J. C. McGregor*

WILTSHIRE (IRE) 5 br.g. Spectrum (IRE) 126 – Mary Magdalene 78 (Night Shift **63**
(USA)) [2007 66, a62: p6g* p6g² 7m 7g* 7.1m⁵ 6g³ p7g³ 7.1m 6f p7.1g⁶ Dec 4] leggy
gelding: modest performer: won handicap at Kempton in February and seller at Southwell
in April: effective at 6f to easy 8.6f: acts on polytrack and firm ground: has worn headgear. *P. T. Midgley*

WIMOWEH (IRE) 2 b.g. (Feb 7) Intikhab (USA) 135 – Evening Serenade (IRE) 75 **–**
(Night Shift (USA)) [2007 6f 9f⁶ 8g Oct 19] lengthy, good-bodied gelding: no form: has
been tongue tied. *T. D. Easterby*

WINDBENEATHMYWINGS (IRE) 3 b.f. In The Wings 128 – Moneefa 73 (Dars- **78**
haan 133) [2007 65: 10g⁴ p10g 10.2m⁵ 12.1s⁵ 11.6v* 11.5m⁴ 12v* 12d² p9.5g Nov 30]
sturdy filly: fair handicapper: won at Windsor in July and, having left J. Hills 36,000 gns,
Tramore in August: stays 1½m: acts on heavy and good to firm ground. *M. J. Grassick,
Ireland*

WIND CHIME (IRE) 10 ch.h. Arazi (USA) 135 – Shamisen 86 (Diesis 133) [2007 **61**
61, a51: 8.1m³ 8f 10.1f 8.1m p11g Oct 17] smallish horse: modest performer, better on **a–**
turf than all-weather: effective at 1m/1¼m: acts on all-weather, firm and good to soft
going: tried in cheekpieces. *A. G. Newcombe*

WIND FLOW 3 b.g. Dr Fong (USA) 128 – Spring 112 (Sadler's Wells (USA) 132) **65 +**
[2007 72p: p8m⁶ p10m³ p10g² Dec 12] fair maiden: will be suited by 1½m: raced only on
polytrack and good to soft going: tried blinkered. *C. A. Dwyer*

WINDJAMMER 3 b.g. Kyllachy 129 – Absolve (USA) (Diesis 133) [2007 48: 5.1g³ **78**
5m* 5m* 5g 5m² 5d² 5v⁴ 5g² 5.1m 5d 5g 6d Oct 16] strong gelding: fair handicapper:
won at Catterick in April and Musselburgh in May: best at 5f: acts on good to firm and
good to soft going: makes running/races prominently. *T. D. Easterby*

WIND SHUFFLE (GER) 4 b.g. Big Shuffle (USA) 122 – Wiesensturmerin (GER) **70**
(Lagunas) [2007 66: 8g 6s 7.1g³ 7.2s Oct 26] big, leggy gelding: fair maiden handicapper,
lightly raced: stays 7f: has got upset in stall. *J. S. Goldie*

WINDS OF KILDARE (IRE) 4 b.g. Shaddad (USA) 75 – Asturiana (Julio Mariner **48**
127) [2007 p8g 8m f11g 7g 8m p8g³ p8g 9g p7g p8g Oct 17] poor maiden: stays 1m: acts
on polytrack: often tongue tied: pulled up lame fifth start. *C. N. Allen*

WINDSOR KNOT (IRE) 5 ch.h. Pivotal 124 – Triple Tie (USA) 81 (The Minstrel **118**
(CAN) 135) [2007 115: 9.9d³ 9d* Oct 19] big, rangy horse: good walker: fluent mover:
had been fired on near-hock: smart performer: trained by J. Gosden as 2-y-o, winning

*Georgia House Stud Darley Stakes, Newmarket—Windsor Knot comes off best
in a close finish with Mashaahed (left), Blue Ksar and Tell (blinkers)*

Solario Stakes at Sandown: shaped encouragingly on reappearance prior to best effort to win Georgia House Stud Darley Stakes at Newmarket in October by ¾ length from Mashaahed: stayed 11.6f: acted on good to firm and good to soft going: was genuine and reliable: to stand at Rossenarra Stud, Co Kilkenny, Ireland, fee €4,000. *Saeed bin Suroor*[2]

WIND STAR 4 ch.g. Piccolo 121 – Starfleet 66 (Inchinor 119) [2007 95: 8m³ 8f 10m² 8m 10m³ 11.9m 12d⁶ 10m 10.1g⁵ 10.4d Oct 13] leggy, lengthy gelding: useful handicapper: good placed efforts at Redcar (Zetland Gold Cup, beaten neck by Flipando) and Newmarket (beaten 2 lengths by Sahrati) third/fifth starts: barely stays 1½m: acts on firm and good to soft going. *G. A. Swinburn* **96**

WINDY PROSPECT 5 ch.g. Intikhab (USA) 135 – Yellow Ribbon (IRE) 72 (Hamas (IRE) 125§) [2007 54, a71: f8g⁶ p8.6g f6g² p6g p8.6g³ f8g* p8.6g³ 7d² p10g 8m 7d p7g p8g p10g Nov 7] rather leggy gelding: fair performer: won amateur handicap at Southwell in April: left P. Blockley after eighth outing: was effective at 6f to 1m: acted on fibresand, firm and good to soft going: often blinkered/in cheekpieces: dead. *Mrs L. J. Mongan* **67**

WINE 'N DINE 2 b.c. (May 19) Rainbow Quest (USA) 134 – Seasonal Splendour (IRE) 95 (Prince Rupert (FR) 121) [2007 8d⁴ Oct 19] deep-girthed colt: half-brother to several winners, including smart 1¾m winner When In Rome (by Saddlers' Hall), 7-y-o Strength 'n Honour and 3-y-o Restless Soul: dam 1½m and hurdles winner: 80/1, fourth to General Eliott in maiden at Newmarket, never far away: will be suited by 1¼m/1½m: has joined W. Haggas: open to improvement. *C. A. Cyzer* **75 p**

WINFORJOE (IRE) 3 b.f. Anzillero (GER) 120 – Run Or Bust (IRE) 53 (Commanche Run 133) [2007 p7g p10g p11g 11.5m⁶ 11.6d³ 11.5m⁴ p10g 11.9d Oct 18] leggy filly: third foal: dam maiden: third in seller at Windsor, only worthwhile form: stays 11.6f: acts on good to soft ground. *J. J. Bridger* **54 ?**

WINGBEAT (USA) 2 b.c. (Feb 25) Elusive Quality (USA) – Infinite Spirit (USA) 108 (Maria's Mon (USA) 121) [2007 6d* Oct 23] second foal: half-brother to 3-y-o Vainglory: dam 6f (at 2 yrs) to 1m (in UAE) winner: 11/4, won maiden at Yarmouth by 2½ lengths from Barbary Boy (pair clear), not hard pressed to assert: will probably stay 1m: should go on to better things. *Saeed bin Suroor* **86 p**

WING COLLAR 6 b.g. In The Wings 128 – Riyoom (USA) 83 (Vaguely Noble 140) [2007 94: 12v² 14s* 14d⁵ Aug 22] tall, quite good-topped gelding: useful handicapper: better than ever in 2007, winning 5-runner listed handicap at York in July by ¾ length from Macorville: creditable fifth to Purple Moon in Ebor on same course final outing: effective from 1½m to 2m: acts on any going: usually wears cheekpieces: sometimes races freely: usually held up: consistent. *T. D. Easterby* **103**

WINGED CUPID (IRE) 4 b.c. In The Wings 128 – Sweet Emotion (IRE) 97 (Bering 136) [2007 8.3s* 10.4s⁴ 10m² 8.1g Sep 8] smallish, attractive colt: not the best of walkers: smart performer: left M. Johnston and off 20 months due to leg problem, improved when winning listed event at Windsor in June by 4 lengths from Babodana: creditable ½-length second to Queen's Best in Winter Hill Stakes at same course in August: disappointing in listed race at Haydock final outing: stays 1¼m: acts on firm and soft going: has left Godolphin. *Saeed bin Suroor* **112**

WINGED D'ARGENT (IRE) 6 b.g. In The Wings 128 – Petite-D-Argent 91 (Noalto 120) [2007 115d: 18.7m 16.2m 20m 16.1v⁶ 14.1d* 18s 14s⁶ 16s⁴ Oct 18] sturdy gelding: just fairly useful handicapper nowadays: won jump jockeys event at Nottingham in July: stays 2½m: acts on heavy and good to firm going: often wears headgear: tends to race lazily: ungenuine. *B. J. Llewellyn* **86 §**

WINGED FARASI 3 b.c. Desert Style (IRE) 121 – Clara Vale (IRE) (In The Wings 128) [2007 68: p8.6g³ f7g⁴ f8g³ 8g 10g² 8m* p8g 8.1d⁴ 10m 8d⁶ p7.1g p8g³ f8d⁴ p8.6g² Dec 29] angular, rangy colt: fair performer: left Miss J. Feilden, won apprentice handicap at Salisbury in June: stays 8.6f: acts on polytrack, good to firm and good to soft going: tried in cheekpieces. *R. A. Harris* **70**

WINGED FLIGHT (USA) 3 b.g. Fusaichi Pegasus (USA) 130 – Tobaranama (IRE) 94 (Sadler's Wells (USA) 132) [2007 88: 10d 8d 7g p9.5g Nov 10] rangy, good-topped gelding: just fair form in handicaps in 2007: bred to be suited by 7f+: acts on good to firm ground. *M. Johnston* **76**

WINGED LEGACY (USA) 2 ch.c. (Jan 26) Diesis 133 – Fairy Glade (USA) (Gone West (USA)) [2007 7.1m Aug 31] strong colt: first foal: dam unraced half-sister to very smart US performer up to 1¼m Skimming: 8/1 and not wound up, tenth to Ridge Dance in maiden at Sandown, tiring and eased: to improve. *H. R. A. Cecil* **68 p**

WIN

WING EXPRESS (IRE) 3 b.c. Montjeu (IRE) 137 – Eurobird 118 (Ela-Mana-Mou 132) [2007 10g⁴ 11.8s* 13m² Jul 12] 290,000Y: good-topped, attractive colt: half-brother to several winners, most useful, including middle-distance stayers Garden Society (by Caerleon), Tamiami Trail (by Indian Ridge) and Bowmore (by Desert King): dam, won Irish St Leger, half-sister to Prix du Jockey Club winners Bikala and Assert: progressed well and smart form after just 3 races: won maiden at Leicester in June by 2 lengths from Dawn Sky: further significant improvement when ¾-length second to Tranquil Tiger in listed race at Newmarket next time: will stay 1¾m: acts on soft and good to firm ground. *L. M. Cumani* **112**

WING PLAY (IRE) 2 b.c. (Mar 15) Hawk Wing (USA) 136 – Toy Show (IRE) 86 (Danehill (USA) 126) [2007 8g 8.2g⁵ p8.6g* Nov 17] 36,000F: quite good-topped colt: first foal: dam 1¼m winner, including at 2 yrs: fairly useful form: progressive in maidens, won at Wolverhampton (beat Martyr by 1¾ lengths) despite still looking green: will stay 1¼m. *H. Morrison* **84 p**

WINGSINMOTION (IRE) 3 b.f. Indian Lodge (IRE) 127 – Coulisse (IRE) (In The Wings 128) [2007 –: 10.1s 11g 14.1m 10.9s⁴ 12g⁶ 12.1g Jul 31] lengthy filly: poor maiden: wore cheekpieces last 4 starts. *Miss Tracy Waggott* **44**

WINGS OF MORNING (IRE) 6 ch.g. Fumo di Londra (IRE) 108 – Hay Knot (Main Reef 126) [2007 58: f7g Jan 7] sturdy gelding: modest performer: well held in seller sole 6-y-o start: tried blinkered, usually visored: sometimes slowly away: none too consistent. *D. Carroll* **–**

WIN IN GOLD 6 b.g. Pivotal 124 – Sylvan Dancer (IRE) 64 (Dancing Dissident (USA) 119) [2007 f11g⁵ f12g Jan 30] well held in bumper/maiden/claimer. *John A. Harris* **–**

WINKER WATSON 2 ch.c. (Feb 19) Piccolo 121 – Bonica 56 (Rousillon (USA) 133) [2007 5.2m* 5m* 6m* Jul 12] **117 p**
    'The world's wiliest wangler' Winker Watson made his first appearance in *The Dandy* in April 1961. His equine counterpart also made his debut in April—forty-six years later—when he got his career off to a successful start in a Newbury maiden. Winker Watson had to show all the wiles of his namesake when going on to become the first horse since Noverre to win the July Stakes at Newmarket under a penalty. Starting slowly and left with seven lengths to make up at halfway, Winker Watson quickened well from a most unpromising position to catch River Proud

Norfolk Stakes, Royal Ascot—
Winker Watson has taken the measure of Art Advisor and Spirit of Sharjah (right)

virtually on the line, recording the best performance by a juvenile in the first half of the season. The Coventry runner-up Swiss Franc finished third and the thirteen-runner race looked to represent strong form, the winner's performance backed up by a good timefigure. The victory gave Winker Watson three wins from three starts after following up his Newbury win in the Norfolk Stakes at Royal Ascot where he accelerated in good style to beat Art Advisor with something in hand by a length and a quarter, a tardy start meaning he found himself with a bit to do at halfway. Winker Watson missed intended appearances in the Prix Morny (overnight rain), the Champagne Stakes (missed work due to infection) and the National Stakes (trainer's horses under a cloud). October came and his trainer dubbed Winker Watson the season's 'forgotten horse' and revealed plans for a tilt at both the Middle Park and the Dewhurst, a double last achieved by Diesis in 1982. Seemingly no sooner had the plans been announced than yet more misfortune befell Winker Watson. Three days before the Middle Park he was found to have stiffness in his near-fore knee. An x-ray revealed no chips or fractures, but it was decided to rest Winker Watson until 2008.

		⎧Warning	⎧Known Fact
	⎧Piccolo	⎪(b 1985)	⎨Slightly Dangerous
	⎪(b 1991)	⎨Woodwind	⎧Whistling Wind
Winker Watson	⎨	⎩(ch 1973)	⎨Garden Green
(ch.c. Feb 19, 2005)	⎪	⎧Rousillon	⎧Riverman
	⎪Bonica	⎪(b 1981)	⎨Belle Dorine
	⎩(b 1989)	⎨Flaming Rose	⎧Upper Nile
		⎩(b 1982)	⎩Papamiento

Winker Watson is the second July Stakes winner for his owners the Comic Strip Heroes, Captain Hurricane ('The mighty marine' Captain Hercules Hurricane was a character in *Valiant*) taking the race for them in 2004. Captain Hurricane never won again, and it must be hoped that a similar fate does not befall Winker Watson. Winker Watson is the tenth foal of his dam Bonica, and the sixth to win. Of the winners, he is by some way the best, though first foal Bacchus (by Prince Sabo) was a fairly useful winner at up to ten furlongs and Winker Watson's two-years-older half-sister Choysia (by Pivotal) is a similar standard to Bacchus at up to seven furlongs. Winker Watson's pedigree is very much that of a sprinter. His sire Piccolo was a King's Stand and Nunthorpe winner (the latter on the controversial disqualification of Blue Siren). Of Piccolo's progeny to achieve a Timeform rating of over 100 in Britain, only the enigmatic Turbo has proven himself beyond seven furlongs, that horse out of a mare who won at up to two miles. The distaff side of Winker

The Comic Strip Heroes and Mrs J. D. Trotter's "Winker Watson"

Watson's pedigree is equally speedy. Bonica ran only four times, showing her best form at six furlongs as a juvenile and is a half-sister to the smart juvenile sprinter Chipaya and out of a half-sister to Gwydion, a smart sprinting filly in the mid-'eighties. Both those relatives were smart at two, Chipaya a sales-race winner and Gwydion a Queen Mary winner. Both suffered setbacks after their juvenile seasons and Chipaya essentially failed to train on after suffering with a knee complaint, attributed to arthritis. Gwydion got over a setback that kept her out of action after the Queen Mary and came back to thrive as a three-year-old, winning two listed races and finishing in the frame in several important sprints. The well-grown, useful-looking Winker Watson, who is a good mover, cost 56,000 guineas as a yearling. He has been raced only on good to firm ground. He should stay seven furlongs at three but is not certain to get any further. *P. W. Chapple-Hyam*

WINNING PLEASURE (IRE) 9 b.g. Ashkalani (IRE) 128 – Karamana (Habitat 134) [2007 –, a82: f7g f6g f6s⁴ Feb 8] leggy, sparely-made gelding: just fair performer in 2007: probably best at 6f: acts on fibresand, best runs on turf on good/good to firm ground: tried in headgear. *J. Balding* — a68

WINNING SHOW 3 b.g. Muhtarram (USA) 125 – Rose Show (Belmez (USA) 131) [2007 p6g³ 7m⁶ 7.1m⁶ p8g 5.7f⁵ 6f p12.2g Oct 8] stocky gelding: fair maiden: best effort when sixth at Newmarket second start: should stay 1m+: acts on polytrack and good to firm going: has raced freely. *R. A. Harris* — 74 d

WINNING SMILE (USA) 3 ch.f. With Approval (CAN) – Acquiesce (Generous (IRE) 139) [2007 –: p7g p8g Mar 24] close-coupled, quite attractive filly: poor form in maidens. *P. W. Chapple-Hyam* — 49

WINNING SPIRIT (IRE) 3 b.g. Invincible Spirit (IRE) 121 – Taisho (IRE) 96 (Nam- – §
aqualand (USA)) [2007 82§: 5f 6.1m 5s 5m p5m p5g Oct 29] strong, good-quartered
gelding: fairly useful performer at 2 yrs for J. Noseda: last all starts in 2007, leaving
D. Nicholls after fourth outing, and dropping rapidly in the handicap: tried in cheekpieces: one to treat with caution. *Miss Z. C. Davison*

WINTER BLOOM (USA) 2 b.f. (Mar 31) Aptitude (USA) 128 – Bionic 105 (Zafonic 82
(USA) 130) [2007 7g² 7f* 7m⁴ 7m Oct 6] tall filly: fifth foal: half-sister to 3 winners,
including 3-y-o Phoenix Tower and fairly useful 2004 2-y-o 6f winner Krynica (by
Danzig): dam, impressive 2-y-o 7f winner on only start, half-sister to 6-y-o Day Flight:
fairly useful form: won maiden at Redcar (barely off bridle) in August: favourite in
nurseries, better effort when fourth to Dubai Dynamo at Doncaster: will stay 1m: acts on
firm going. *H. R. A. Cecil*

WINTERCAST 2 ch.c. (Feb 23) Spinning World (USA) 130 – Bright Hope (IRE) 84 86 p
(Danehill (USA) 126) [2007 8.2g* Nov 7] sturdy, attractive colt: second foal: brother
to 4-y-o Birkside: dam 1¼m winner out of half-sister to Sprint Cup winner Iktamal:
6/1, smooth win in maiden at Nottingham (beat West With The Wind by length), going
strongly long way: will stay 1¼m: one to follow. *W. R. Swinburn*

WINTER CRUISE (IRE) 3 b.g. Lil's Boy (USA) 109 – Arundhati (IRE) (Royal 62
Academy (USA) 130) [2007 66: p9.5g p9.5g p9.5g⁶ p8.6g p13.9d² p12.2g* Dec 29]
ex-Irish-trained gelding: modest handicapper nowadays: won at Wolverhampton in
December: stays easy 13.9f: acts on polytrack. *Ian Williams*

WINTER LANE 3 b.g. Hernando (FR) 127 – Winding (USA) (Irish River (FR) 131) 59 d
[2007 p10g⁶ 11m 10d 15.8g f14d⁶ Dec 11] tall gelding: maiden: form only on debut at
Lingfield: left A. Balding after second outing: visored final start. *J. R. Norton*

WINTER SUNRISE 3 b.f. Pivotal 124 – Winter Solstice 104 (Unfuwain (USA) 131) 103
[2007 10d* 10g* 12g⁵ 12s⁵ Oct 13] strong, lengthy filly: carried plenty of condition: had
powerful, round action: second foal: half-sister to useful 8.3f (at 2 yrs) and 1¼m winner
Shortest Day (by Zafonic): dam, French 2-y-o 1m winner, half-sister to very smart French
performer up to 13f Polish Summer out of sister to very smart middle-distance stayers
Sunshack and Raintrap: useful performer: won maiden at Sandown in May and handicap
at Newmarket (by short head from Pathos) in July: good fifth after in listed race at York
(to Wannabe Posh) and Princess Royal Stakes at Ascot (beaten 3½ lengths by Trick Or
Treat): stayed 1½m: stud. *Sir Michael Stoute*

WINTHORPE (IRE) 7 b.g. Tagula (IRE) 116 – Zazu 58 (Cure The Blues (USA)) 71
[2007 75: f6g⁶ f6g p6g⁶ f6g⁴ 6g⁶ p6g* p6g⁵ 5.5d⁴ 5m 6m* 6g⁴ 6d⁵ p6g⁶ 6m⁵ 5g⁵ 5m 6v
p6g p7.1g² f6d* p6g³ Dec 22] leggy gelding: fair handicapper: won at Wolverhampton
in April, Catterick in June and Southwell in December: effective at 5f to easy 7f: acts on
all-weather and any turf going: tried in cheekpieces/visor (raced freely): sometimes
carries head high. *J. J. Quinn*

WISDOM'S KISS 3 b.g. Ocean of Wisdom (USA) 106 – April Magic (Magic Ring 65
(IRE) 115) [2007 –: 8g 7f⁴ p8.6g 8.5s 6.9f² 7.2g p7m Oct 3] leggy gelding: fair maiden a–
handicapper: stays 7f: acts on firm ground, well held on polytrack: twice blinkered (raced
freely). *J. D. Bethell*

WISE CHOICE 4 b.g. Green Desert (USA) 127 – Ballykett Lady (USA) 105 (Sir Ivor –
(USA) 135) [2007 63: p12g p13.9g 12d Sep 17] angular, good-topped gelding: modest
handicapper: well held in 2007 (left N. Littmoden after second outing). *Mrs L. B. Normile*

WISE DENNIS 5 b.g. Polar Falcon (USA) 126 – Bowden Rose 100 (Dashing Blade 113
117) [2007 101: f7g* 7s* 8g² 7g⁴ 7g 7d⁶ 9d p8g² Nov 28] rather leggy, quite good-topped
gelding: smart handicapper: improved form in 2007, winning at Southwell in April and
28-runner totesport.com Victoria Cup at Ascot (by 4 lengths from Skhilling Spirit) in
May: creditable second to Ventura in listed race at Kempton final start: stays 1m: acts on
all-weather, soft and good to firm going: sometimes races freely: held up. *A. P. Jarvis*

WISE HAWK 2 b.c. (Jan 27) Hawk Wing (USA) 136 – Dombeya (IRE) 66 (Danehill 64 p
(USA) 126) [2007 6m⁵ p7.1g⁵ Nov 30] 12,000Y, 24,000 2-y-o: big, rangy colt: first foal:
dam, maiden (stayed 1½m), out of smart performer up to 1¾m The Faraway Tree, herself
half-sister to very smart 9f/1¼m performer Sasuru: green, encouraging fifth in maidens
at Doncaster and Wolverhampton: will be suited by 1¼m/1½m: sort to progress at 3 yrs.
W. J. Haggas

WISE LITTLE GIRL 3 b.f. Singspiel (IRE) 133 – Gretel 100 (Hansel (USA)) [2007 88
p8.6g² 10m* 9.7g⁶ 10g⁶ 10.3m* p12g p10g⁵ Nov 4] rangy filly: sixth foal: half-sister to
8.6f winner Farnborough (by Lear Fan) and 1m winner in USA by Saint Ballado: dam

2-y-o 7f winner: fairly useful performer: won maiden at Lingfield in June and handicap at Chester in September: stays 1¼m, possibly not 1½m: acts on polytrack and good to firm ground. *M. A. Jarvis*

WISEMAN'S DIAMOND (USA) 2 b.f. (Feb 28) Wiseman's Ferry (USA) 102 – Aswhatilldois (IRE) 84 (Blues Traveller (IRE) 119) [2007 p5.1m⁴ 5m⁵ p7.1g² 7d* p6g² p8.6g* Dec 3] sturdy filly: third foal: dam 7f (at 2 yrs) to 8.5f (US minor stakes) winner: fair performer: won nurseries at Leicester in October and Wolverhampton in December: stays 8.6f: acts on polytrack and good to soft going: tried in cheekpieces. *K. A. Ryan* **72**

WISE MELODY 2 b.f. (Feb 27) Zamindar (USA) 116 – Swellegant 84 (Midyan (USA) 124) [2007 p6g⁴ p6s* Dec 21] half-sister to several winners, including 5f/6f winner Dil (by Primo Dominie) and 2000 2-y-o 5f winner Racina (by Bluebird), both useful: dam, 2-y-o 5f winner, half-sister to very smart sprinter Prince Sabo: confirmed debut promise when winning maiden at Wolverhampton by 6 lengths, bursting clear: sort to make up into a useful sprinter. *W. J. Haggas* **82 p**

WISE SON 2 b.g. (Feb 20) Royal Applause 124 – Racina 103 (Bluebird (USA) 125) [2007 5m⁶ 5m* 6m² p6g 6m Oct 5] 24,000Y: small gelding: first foal: dam, 2-y-o 5f winner, out of half-sister to very smart sprinter Prince Sabo: fairly useful form: won maiden at Windsor in July: continued progress when second in nursery at Redcar and mid-division in sales race at Newmarket (hampered/lost action in between): gelded after: should prove best at 5f/6f: raced only on good to firm going on turf. *W. J. Haggas* **87**

WISETON DANCER (IRE) 3 b.c. Danehill Dancer (IRE) 117 – Your Village (IRE) 64 (Be My Guest (USA) 126) [2007 –: p6g⁵ p6g⁶ 6g Apr 24] leggy colt: lightly-raced maiden, modest form only on reappearance. *Miss V. Haigh* **53**

WISHES OR WATCHES (IRE) 7 br.g. Bravefoot 98 – Shadya's Amal (Shaadi (USA) 126) [2007 52: p12.2g² p13.9g⁴ p12g Dec 16] modest performer nowadays: in frame at Wolverhampton first 2 starts: appears to stay 1¾m: acts on polytrack, heavy and good to firm going: tried blinkered/in cheekpieces. *John A. Quinn, Ireland* **52**

WISHING ON A STAR 3 b.f. Fantastic Light (USA) 134 – Sephala (USA) (Mr Prospector (USA)) [2007 78: 10d⁶ p11g 8f Aug 24] close-coupled filly: maiden: no form since debut (at 2 yrs): tried in cheekpieces/tongue tie/blinkers. *E. J. O'Neill* **–**

WITCHINGHAM 3 b.g. Polish Precedent (USA) 131 – Assertive Dancer (USA) (Assert 134) [2007 p8g p9.5g⁴ p7g⁶ p8g⁶ p9.5g p9.5g⁴ p8g Nov 12] modest maiden: stays 9.5f: raced only on polytrack: sold 4,500 gns, sent to Holland. *R. Hannon* **63**

WITCHRY 5 gr.g. Green Desert (USA) 127 – Indian Skimmer (USA) 133 (Storm Bird (CAN) 134) [2007 80: f5g⁵ f5g⁶ 5m⁵ Apr 17] compact gelding: just fair handicapper in 2007: effective at 5f/6f: acts on polytrack and any turf going. *A. G. Newcombe* **75**

WITH CONFIDENCE 3 ch.f. Polish Precedent (USA) 131 – Farhana 109 (Fayruz 116) [2007 8d 7d⁴ 8.1m 6d³ p7g p6g⁶ Dec 4] 10,000Y: good-topped filly, type to carry condition: fourth foal: half-sister to fairly useful 2002 2-y-o 5f winner Free Wheelin (by Polar Falcon): dam 5.5f/6f (latter including at 2 yrs) winner: fair maiden: stays 7f: acts on polytrack and good to soft ground: signs of temperament. *D. R. C. Elsworth* **66**

WITH EASE (IRE) 3 br.g. Grand Lodge (USA) 125 – Twice The Ease 46 (Green Desert (USA) 127) [2007 6s 8d Jun 23] workmanlike gelding: well held in maidens at Yarmouth and Newmarket (poorly to post). *P. W. D'Arcy* **–**

WITHOUT A PRAYER (IRE) 2 ch.c. (Mar 20) Intikhab (USA) 135 – Prayer (IRE) 83 (Rainbow Quest (USA) 134) [2007 p7.1g² p7g⁸* 7g³ Aug 21] 10,500Y: well-made colt: first foal: dam ran twice in Ireland: useful form: won maiden at Lingfield in July by 4 lengths: much improved when 3½ lengths third to Fast Company in Acomb Stakes at York, finishing well: will be suited by 1m+: should do better still. *R. M. Beckett* **98 p**

WITHOUT EXCUSE (USA) 3 ch.g. Woodman (USA) 126 – Dixie Jewel (USA) (Dixieland Band (USA)) [2007 10m 9.9m⁶ 10s p9.5g⁴ p9.5g* p10g Dec 19] well-made gelding: trained by A. & G. Botti in Italy at 2 yrs, better effort at Rome when winning minor event: fairly useful form in Britain, off 6 months and gelded before winning claimer at Wolverhampton in November: will stay 1½m: acts on polytrack: tried in cheek-pieces, blinkered last 3 starts. *M. Botti* **83**

WITHYWOOD (USA) 3 b. or br.f. Woodman (USA) 126 – Castellina (USA) (Danzig Connection (USA)) [2007 5s p6g p8g⁴ 10m⁴ 10d Oct 1] angular filly: sister to useful 8.3f (at 2 yrs) to 1¼m winner Blaise Hollow and half-sister to 3 winners, including useful 2002 2-y-o 1m winner Blaise Castle and fairly useful 1¼m winner Castle River (both by **46**

Irish River): dam, US 8.5f winner, half-sister to US Grade 1 1¼m winner Chelsey Flower: poor maiden: probably stays 1¼m: acts on polytrack. *G. L. Moore*

WIZARDMICKTEE (IRE) 5 b.g. Monashee Mountain (USA) 115 – Epsilon 62 – (Environment Friend 128) [2007 –: p12.2g f8g Mar 13] leggy gelding: maiden: lightly raced and no form since 2005: tried blinkered/in cheekpieces. *D. G. Bridgwater*

WIZBY 4 b.f. Wizard King 122 – Diamond Vanessa (IRE) (Distinctly North (USA) 115) **55** [2007 57: 8.1m 8f 7.1m 9g 8d 8.1s 11.8g 8d p8g⁵ p10g p8.6d⁴ p8.6s⁶ Dec 21] compact filly: has a quick action: modest performer: stays 9f: acts on polytrack and any turf going: tried visored/tongue tied. *P. D. Evans*

WIZZY IZZY (IRE) 2 gr.f. (Feb 16) Shinko Forest (IRE) – Strelitzia (IRE) (Bluebird – (USA) 125) [2007 5d 5s⁶ 5g 5m Aug 28] €9,000F, 17,000Y: workmanlike filly: second foal: half-sister to 6f winner Imprimis Tagula (by Tagula): dam Irish maiden: no form: tried blinkered. *N. Wilson*

WODHILL BE 7 b.m. Danzig Connection (USA) – Muarij (Star Appeal 133) [2007 53: – f7g* f7g³ f7g³ p7.1g⁶ 7m⁶ f7g³ f7g⁵ p7g 8g 7f 7d p6g² p7m p6g p8g Dec 5] modest **a57** performer: won handicap at Southwell in January: best at 7f/1m nowadays: acts on all-weather, good to firm and good to soft going: has taken strong hold: usually held up: inconsistent. *D. Morris*

WODHILL GOLD 6 ch.g. Dancing Spree (USA) – Golden Filigree 48 (Faustus – (USA) 118) [2007 59: f8g² f8g* f8g² p8g⁵ f8g⁴ f8g⁴ p6g p8g p8.6g³ p8.6g p8.6g **a63** p8.6g⁴ p8.6g p8.6g⁵ Nov 27] sturdy gelding: modest handicapper on all-weather: won at Southwell in January: probably stays 1¼m: acts on all-weather, little form on turf: usually visored/blinkered. *D. Morris*

WODHILL SCHNAPS 6 b.g. Danzig Connection (USA) – Muarij (Star Appeal 133) **59** [2007 58: f8g p9.5g⁴ f8s³ p8.6g² 8m f8g³ f8g⁶ 8d f7g* 8d p7.1g* 7d⁵ 7.6f p7.1g⁴ p7.1g p7g p8.6g Oct 26] lengthy, deep-girthed gelding: modest performer: won minor event at Southwell in June and handicap at Wolverhampton in July: stays easy 1m: acts on all-weather, firm and good to soft ground: usually wears headgear: has looked far from keen: inconsistent. *D. Morris*

WOGAN'S SISTER 2 b.f. (Mar 4) Lahib (USA) 129 – Dublivia (Midyan (USA) 124) – [2007 6f p7g p7g Nov 7] €20,000Y: fifth foal: half-sister to Irish 7f winner Tashadelek (by Victory Note) and 1m/1¼m winner Princelywallywogan (by Princely Heir): dam sprint maiden: well held in maidens. *I. A. Wood*

WOLDS WAY 5 b.g. Mujahid (USA) 125 – Off Camera (Efisio 120) [2007 p12.2g **58** f12g⁴ 10m⁶ 12.4m 10.1m 10g Jun 13] tall gelding: bumper winner/poor maiden hurdler: modest maiden on Flat: tried blinkered. *T. D. Easterby*

WOLFMAN 5 ch.g. Wolfhound (USA) 126 – Madam Millie 99 (Milford 119) [2007 54: **54** f6g f6g² 6m⁴ 5g⁶ 5d³ 6m 8f³ 6.9g³ Aug 22] leggy, workmanlike gelding: modest maiden handicapper: stays 1m: acts on all-weather, firm and good to soft going: usually wears cheekpieces. *D. W. Barker*

WOLF PACK 5 b.g. Green Desert (USA) 127 – Warning Shadows (IRE) 113 (Cadeaux – Genereux 131) [2007 –: p8.6g 12.1d 6g 6s Oct 4] good-bodied gelding: left R. Price after reappearance: of no account. *D. A. Nolan*

WOLF RIVER (USA) 3 b.c. Mr Greeley (USA) 122 – Beal Street Blues (USA) **82** (Dixieland Band (USA)) [2007 76: 7m² p6g³ 7m³ 6f² 6g* p6g* p6g Oct 15] big, good-topped colt: fairly useful performer: won maiden at Catterick in August and apprentice handicap at Lingfield in September: raced only at 6f/7f: acts on polytrack and firm ground: makes running/races prominently: said to have hit head on stall final outing: sold 42,000 gns. *D. M. Simcock*

WOLGAN VALLEY (USA) 2 ch.c. (Mar 20) Mr Greeley (USA) 122 – Dancing **87** Naturally (USA) (Fred Astaire (USA)) [2007 5d² 5m² 6g² Jul 9] $300,000Y, $1,450,000 2-y-o: good-topped colt: seventh foal: half-brother to 3 winners in USA, including 6f (at 2 yrs) to 8.5f (including a minor stakes) Indian War Dance (by Cherokee Run): dam US 6f and 1m winner: fairly useful maiden: runner-up all starts, including behind Swiss Franc at Newmarket and Sharp Nephew at Windsor first/third starts: speedy, will prove best at 5f/6f. *Saeed bin Suroor*

WOMANISER (IRE) 3 b.g. Rock of Gibraltar (IRE) 133 – Top Table 65 (Shirley – Heights 130) [2007 p7.1g p8g May 7] 160,000Y: half-brother to several winners, including 4-y-o Zato, 1½m winner Manama Rose and 6f (at 2 yrs) and 1m winner Krispy Knight (both useful, by Kris): dam, second at 1½m, half-sister to smart miler Centre Stalls: green, well held in maidens at Wolverhampton and Kempton: subsequently gelded. *L. M. Cumani*

WOOD CHORUS 2 b.f. (Mar 23) Singspiel (IRE) 133 – Woodbeck 90 (Terimon 124) **76 p**
[2007 8d³ Oct 23] sixth foal: half-sister to 7f (at 2 yrs) to 1¾m (Yorkshire Cup) winner
Franklins Gardens (by Halling) and 7f (at 2 yrs) and 1m winner Polar Ben (by Polar
Falcon), both smart: dam, 7f winner, out of half-sister to Prix de Diane winner Madam
Gay: 20/1, encouraging third to Miss Emma May in maiden at Yarmouth, plenty to do:
will be suited by 1¼m/1½m: sure to improve. *M. L. W. Bell*

WOODCOTE (IRE) 5 b.g. Monashee Mountain (USA) 115 – Tootle (Main Reef 126) **96**
[2007 102: 5.2m 6m 5g 5m 5d 6g 5.6m p6g³ Aug 27] strong, lengthy gelding: useful
handicapper: only placing in 2007 when close third to Diane's Choice at Kempton: effective at 5f/6f: acts on polytrack, firm and good to soft going: wears cheekpieces/blinkers
nowadays: usually races prominently: formerly headstrong: sold 30,000 gns. *C. G. Cox*

WOODCOTE PLACE 4 b.c. Lujain (USA) 119 – Giant Nipper (Nashwan (USA) **92**
135) [2007 99: 7g 8.3m³ 8m 7.1s⁵ 8g⁴ 7m⁶ 7.1d Aug 16] small, well-made, attractive colt:
fairly useful handicapper: creditable efforts when in frame: stays 8.3f: acts on polytrack,
firm and good to soft going: held up. *P. R. Chamings*

WOODCOTE WILDCAT (USA) 2 b. or br.f. (May 8) High Yield (USA) 121 – **–**
Zappeuse (USA) (Kingmambo (USA) 125) [2007 7g 5m p6g Aug 30] close-coupled
filly: fourth foal: sister to useful French 1m winner (including at 2 yrs) La Reine Mambo
and half-sister to 2 winners abroad, including smart French/US 9f performer Danzon
(by Royal Academy): dam French 1½m winner: no form in maidens: sold 30,000 gns.
N. A. Callaghan

WOODCRAFT 3 ch.c. Observatory (USA) 131 – Woodwardia (USA) 93 (El Gran **83**
Senor (USA) 136) [2007 8.1m* 10.4g⁴ 9.9g⁶ 10g⁶ 10d⁵ 10m⁶ 10d³ Oct 1] good-bodied
colt: has scope: eighth foal: half-brother to several winners, including 1¼m/1½m winner
Edwardian (by Sanglamore) and French 6f winner Kirkwood (by Selkirk), both useful:
dam, 1m winner (stayed 11.4f), sister to smart US Grade 1 1¼m winner Spanish Fern:
fairly useful performer: won maiden at Warwick in April: mostly creditable efforts in
handicaps after: stays 1¼m: acts on good to firm and good to soft ground: free-going
sort, races prominently: hung right first 2 starts: sold 19,000 gns, joined D. McCain Jnr.
B. W. Hills

WOODCUTTER (IRE) 2 gr.c. (Mar 5) Daylami (IRE) 138 – Cinnamon Rose (USA) **– p**
96 (Trempolino (USA) 135) [2007 7m Aug 10] €170,000Y: lengthy, attractive colt: fifth
foal: half-brother to several winners, notably very smart Irish 7f (Moyglare Stud Stakes)
to 1½m winner Chelsea Rose (by Desert King), and useful 6f (at 2 yrs in Ireland) to 9f
(in US) winner European (by Great Commotion): dam, Irish 1¼m winner, half-sister to
smart French performer around 1¼m River Warden: 7/2, faded into rear in maiden at
Newmarket: will do better. *J. H. M. Gosden*

WOODEN KING (IRE) 2 b.g. (Apr 24) Danetime (IRE) 121 – Olympic Rock (IRE) **51**
(Ballad Rock 122) [2007 6d⁶ 5m 7.1d 6d p7g⁶ Sep 26] unfurnished gelding: modest
maiden: should stay 6f/7f. *P. D. Evans*

WOOD FERN (UAE) 7 b.g. Green Desert (USA) 127 – Woodsia 97 (Woodman **–**
(USA) 126) [2007 60: p12.2g Jan 8] strong, close-coupled gelding: modest performer:
ran poorly sole 7-y-o start: tried visored. *W. M. Brisbourne*

WOODFORD 2 b.g. (Feb 27) Mull of Kintyre (USA) 114 – Ice House 89 (Northfields **–**
(USA)) [2007 6m 6s 7d 5g Jul 9] behind in maidens. *M. W. Easterby*

WOODFORD CONSULT 5 b.m. Benny The Dip (USA) 127 – Chicodove 91 (In **–**
The Wings 128) [2007 52: 16.1m Jun 2] big, workmanlike mare: modest handicapper:
mid-field sole 5-y-o start: stays 2m: acts on fibresand, firm and good to soft going:
reluctant to enter/leave stall once at 3 yrs: modest/untrustworthy hurdler. *M. W. Easterby*

WOODFORD REGEN 2 b.f. (Feb 22) Hunting Lion (IRE) 115 – Katie's Kitty 42 **56**
(Noble Patriarch 115) [2007 f5g⁶ f5g³ 6d³ 5m⁶ 7m⁵ 6s Oct 4] 8,000Y: sixth foal: half-
sister to 1¼m winner Westcourt Dream (by Bal Harbour): dam, maiden, out of useful
sprinter Catherines Well: modest maiden: should stay 7f/1m: acts on fibresand, good to
soft and good to firm going. *M. W. Easterby*

WOODINS WAY 3 ch.g. Danehill Dancer (IRE) 117 – Lady Storm (IRE) 100 (Mujadil **65**
(USA) 119) [2007 7g 7g⁵ 8.1d 8f 8d 6g p10g³ p9.5g⁵ Dec 3] strong, useful-looking
gelding: fair maiden: seems to stay easy 1¼m: acts on polytrack: blinkered (tended to
hang left) sixth start: sold 10,500 gns, and gelded. *P. J. Makin*

WOODLAND MIST 2 b.f. (Mar 2) Tobougg (IRE) 125 – Aker Wood 86 (Bin Ajwaad **48**
(IRE) 119) [2007 p6g Sep 13] 1,000Y: workmanlike filly: has had shins fired: second

foal: dam 1¼m/1½m winner: 40/1, mid-field in maiden at Wolverhampton 5 months after intended debut (went lame going to post): will be suited by at least 1m. *M. Dods*

WOODLAND TRAVELLER (USA) 3 b.g. Gone West (USA) – Iftiraas 114 (Distant Relative 128) [2007 64: 8.2m 8g* 7.8m² 7.8g² 9.3m⁴ 8g 9d⁴ 7g a9.5g² a8.5g* Dec 9] tall, close-coupled gelding: modest performer: left N. Tinkler 3,600 gns after reappearance: won maiden at Munich in June and minor event at Dortmund in December: stays 8.5f: acts on sand, soft and good to firm ground: tongue tied last 3 starts in Britain. *C. von der Recke, Germany* **64**

WOODNOOK 4 b.f. Cadeaux Genereux 131 – Corndavon (USA) 95 (Sheikh Albadou 128) [2007 96: p6g* p6f² p7.1g p5g⁶ 5.1f⁴ 6m 6m p6m p6m Dec 7] rather leggy, lengthy filly: useful on all-weather, fairly useful on turf: won handicap at Lingfield in February: also ran well when head second to King Orchisios in listed event on same course: raced mainly at 5f/6f: acts on polytrack and good to firm going. *J. A. R. Toller* **84 + a101**

WOODWEE 4 ch.g. Woodborough (USA) 112 – Evaporate 51 (Insan (USA) 119) [2007 61: 7m 7m 6m Aug 24] big, plain gelding: just poor performer in 2007: effective at 6f/7f, probably at 1m: acts on fibresand, firm and good to soft going: tried in cheekpieces/blinkers. *R. E. Barr* **43**

WOODYGO 3 ch.g. Tobougg (IRE) 125 – Woodrising 64 (Nomination 125) [2007 p8g p8g p7g p8g⁵ 9.7g 11.6m 12.1m Jun 13] modest maiden: stays 1m: acts on polytrack (well held in handicaps all 3 starts on turf): tried visored: gelded after final outing. *J. R. Best* **– a59**

WOOLFALL BLUE (IRE) 4 gr.c. Bluebird (USA) 125 – Diamond Waltz (IRE) (Linamix (FR) 127) [2007 87: p11g² p11g² 10m* 10m⁴ 10.4g May 16] leggy colt: fairly useful handicapper: won at Windsor in April: stays 11f: acts on polytrack, soft and good to firm going. *G. G. Margarson* **87**

WOOLFALL KING (IRE) 4 b.g. King Charlemagne (USA) 120 – Bazaar Promise 58 (Native Bazaar 122) [2007 –: f8g Apr 30] useful-looking gelding: little form: tried visored. *G. G. Margarson* **–**

WOOLFALL ROSE 3 b.f. Generous (IRE) 139 – Rose Noble (USA) 62 (Vaguely Noble 140) [2007 10m⁴ 11.5d³ 9m 12m p12m Oct 3] 31,000F: half-sister to several winners, including 6f/7f (including at 2 yrs) winner Dowager (by Groom Dancer) and 12-y-o Dower House (both useful): dam, 11.5f winner, half-sister to Grand Lodge: fair maiden: stays 1½m: acts on polytrack and good to firm ground. *G. G. Margarson* **66**

WOOLFALL TREASURE 2 gr.c. (Mar 12) Daylami (IRE) 138 – Treasure Trove (USA) 62 (The Minstrel (CAN) 135) [2007 7s⁶ 7m 7m² 8m 7m⁵ Sep 12] 36,000F: close-coupled colt: eighth foal: half-brother to 3 winners, including 8-y-o Toylsome: dam, maiden who stayed 7f, half-sister to useful 5f (Queen Mary Stakes) to 1m (US Grade 2 event) winner Dance Parade: fairly useful maiden: second to Fifteen Love at Newmarket: stiff tasks after in listed race at Deauville and minor event at Doncaster (fifth to Newly Elected): seems to stay 1m: acts on good to firm going, probably on soft. *G. G. Margarson* **80**

WOOLSTONE BOY (USA) 6 ch.g. Will's Way (USA) 125 – My Pleasure (USA) (Marfa (USA)) [2007 –: f14g⁶ p12g f14g⁵ Feb 28] modest in 2005: lightly raced and no form subsequently: tongue tied: has carried head high/hung left. *A. M. Hales* **–**

WOQOODD 3 b.g. Royal Applause 124 – Intervene (Zafonic (USA) 130) [2007 72: 5g 6g 6f* 5m p6g⁴ p6g p6g⁶ Nov 2] well-made gelding: fair handicapper: won at Pontefract in August: stays 6f: acts on polytrack and firm ground. *R. A. Fahey* **73**

WORD GAMES 2 b.g. (Mar 18) Mind Games 121 – Salacious (Sallust 134) [2007 p7m⁶ p7g Oct 10] modest maiden: better effort on debut: sold 1,000 gns, sent to Sweden. *A. M. Balding* **62**

WORD OF WARNING 3 gr.g. War Chant (USA) 126 – Frosty Welcome (USA) 105 (With Approval (CAN)) [2007 7d 7.1d 7.1m⁴ Aug 27] 110,000Y: leggy, useful-looking gelding: first foal: dam 9f and 1½m winner (stayed 14.6f): clearly best effort in maidens when 7 lengths fourth to Own Boss at Warwick: sold 10,000 gns in October. *G. Wragg* **67**

WORD PERFECT 5 b.m. Diktat 126 – Better Still (IRE) (Glenstal (USA) 118) [2007 79: f6g³ f6g 6m 6s* 6.1s⁶ f6g⁶ 6d⁶ 6s² 6g* 5d Sep 21] tall, useful-looking mare: fairly useful handicapper: won at Hamilton in July and August: stays 6f/7f: acts on fibresand, heavy and good to firm going: blinkered. *M. W. Easterby* **80**

WORDY'S GIRL 4 b.f. Little Jim – Wordy's Wonder (Welsh Captain 113) [2007 f11d Dec 20] third foal: dam hurdles winner: well held in bumper/maiden (blinkered). *M. J. Gingell* **–**

WORLD AT MY FEET 5 b.m. Wolfhound (USA) 126 – Rehaab 72 (Mtoto 134) **58** [2007 48: 7m 10m 7d² 8s Jul 2] small, close-coupled mare: has a short action: modest performer at best: has form at 1¼m, effective at much shorter: acts on firm and good to soft going: tried blinkered/tongue tied. *N. Bycroft*

WORLD BEAT (GER) 3 b.f. Tiger Hill (IRE) 127 – World's Vision (GER) (Platini (GER) 126) [2007 12m³ Sep 22] lengthy filly: fourth foal: half-sister to 2 winners in Germany, including 2005 2-y-o 6.5f/7f winner World's Mission (by Fasliyev): dam, German 7.5f (including at 2 yrs) and 9f winner, half-sister to useful German performer up to 8.5f Wild Seed: 6/1 and green, well held in maiden at Newmarket. *M. Johnston*

WORLDLY WISE 4 b.g. Namid 128 – Tina Heights 79 (Shirley Heights 130) [2007 **99** 101: 8g 8m 8m 10d 7s p10.7g⁵ 7m 10m³ 9.5g* 8.5g 7m Nov 4] good-topped gelding: useful performer: won handicap at Gowran in October by 1¼ lengths from Migmatite: not discredited in listed events at Royal Ascot (Wolferton Handicap) and Cork (behind Jalmira) on fourth/penultimate starts: best at 1m/1¼m: acts on firm going, probably on polytrack: blinkered (raced too freely) fifth outing: gelded after final start. *Paul Flynn, Ireland*

WORLD OF CHOICE (USA) 2 b.c. (Feb 11) Distorted Humor (USA) 117 – Palace **72** Weekend (USA) (Seattle Dancer (USA) 119) [2007 8.1m 8g³ Oct 24] $700,000Y: lengthy, angular colt: sixth foal: half-brother to several winners, notably smart 6f (at 2 yrs) to 1m (including in US and Racing Post Trophy at 2 yrs) winner Palace Episode (by Machiavellian): dam unraced half-sister to Kentucky Derby runner-up Tejano Run and US Grade 2 8.5f winner More Royal: fair maiden: sharper for debut, third to Colony at Bath: likely to stay 1m. *Saeed bin Suroor*

WORLD'S HEROINE (IRE) 3 ch.f. Spinning World (USA) 130 – Metaphor (USA) **90** (Woodman (USA) 126) [2007 83: 7m² 7m⁶ 8.1g³ p8m² p8g p10g⁶ Nov 15] good-topped filly: fairly useful maiden: stays 1m: acts on polytrack, firm and good to soft ground: sold 55,000 gns. *G. A. Butler*

WORLD SPIRIT 3 b.f. Agnes World (USA) 123 – Belle Esprit (Warning 136) [2007 **97** 73p: 8.3d³ 8d* 8s⁴ 10d³ 8.3m² p8g* p10m⁶ Nov 24] smallish, close-coupled filly: fairly useful performer: won handicaps at Bath in June and Lingfield in October: far from discredited, though said to have finished lame, in listed race at Lingfield final start: probably stays 1¼m: acts on polytrack, soft and good to firm ground. *Rae Guest*

WORLD SUPREMACY (IRE) 4 b.g. Spinning World (USA) 130 – Cream Jug (IRE) (Spectrum (IRE) 126) [2007 –: 10.2d Jun 16] modest maiden at 2 yrs: little subsequent form. *G. A. Ham*

WORLD TOUR 2 b.g. (Apr 13) Spinning World (USA) 130 – Seven Wonders (USA) **67** (Rahy (USA) 115) [2007 8.3d⁵ 8.3g³ 8g Nov 9] fair maiden: regressed from debut, in minor event at Hamilton (fifth to McCartney): raced only at 1m. *I. Semple*

WORLD VIEW (IRE) 2 br.f. (Feb 17) Golan (IRE) 129 – Athene (IRE) 83 (Rousillon **47 p** (USA) 133) [2007 p6g⁵ Oct 8] half-sister to several winners, including 4-y-o Greek Renaissance, 7-y-o Machinist and useful French performer up to 13.5f Side Saddle (by Saddlers' Hall): dam, 1¼m winner, half-sister to smart stayer/very smart hurdler Landing Light, out of smart 1¼m/1½m performer Gay Hellene: 14/1, never-nearer fifth in maiden at Wolverhampton: will progress. *M. P. Tregoning*

WORLDWIND 4 b.f. Agnes World (USA) 123 – Reach The Wind (USA) (Relaunch – (USA)) [2007 p8g 10s May 28] 23,000F: half-sister to 3 winners, including 6f winner Thundergod (by Torrential): dam, Irish 6f winner (including at 2 yrs), half-sister to useful sprinter Ozone Friendly: tailed off in maiden/seller: sold £500 in December. *Mrs L. J. Mongan*

WOTASHIRTFULL (IRE) 2 ch.g. (Mar 20) Namid 128 – Madrina 70 (Waajib 121) **79** [2007 6m³ 6m³ 5d² 5m² 5g³ Aug 29] strong, lengthy gelding: fair maiden: placed all starts, neck second to Sophie's Girl at Thirsk on penultimate: gelded after final one (seemed not to handle Catterick): best at 5f: acts on good to firm and good to soft going. *K. A. Ryan*

WOTAVADUN (IRE) 4 ch.g. King of Kings (IRE) 125 – Blush With Love (USA) (Mt – Livermore (USA)) [2007 39: 5m Aug 25] strong, workmanlike gelding: poor maiden: well held sole 4-y-o outing: often blinkered: has hung badly left/bled. *B. P. J. Baugh*

WOTCHALIKE (IRE) 5 ch.g. Spectrum (IRE) 126 – Juno Madonna (IRE) (Sadler's **59** Wells (USA) 132) [2007 53, a67: p11g f11g⁶ Mar 22] strong, good-topped gelding: handicapper, only modest in 2007: seems to stay easy 2m: acts on polytrack, soft and good to firm ground: sometimes visored: usually races up with pace: gelded, sold £6,000 and joined Jim Best. *R. J. Price*

WOVOKA (IRE) 4 b.g. Mujadil (USA) 119 – Common Cause 87 (Polish Patriot (USA) 128) [2007 100: 10.1g 9.8g 10.1d² 10g 8d 8.5v⁴ 8m² 8d* 8g 8m⁶ 8g 8.1g Sep 7] workmanlike gelding: fairly useful handicapper: won at Ascot in July: stays 1¼m: acts on dirt, heavy and good to firm going: tried visored at 2 yrs: has run well when sweating: tricky ride: sold 16,000 gns. *M. R. Channon* **92**

WRAITH 3 b.c. Maria's Mon (USA) 121 – Really Polish (USA) (Polish Numbers (USA)) [2007 58p: 10m⁴ 10d⁴ 10d p13g² p12g² Nov 15] big colt: fairly useful maiden: runner-up last 2 starts, in handicap on first occasion: stays easy 13f: acts on polytrack and good to firm going. *H. R. A. Cecil* **85**

WRENINGHAM 2 br.g. (Feb 23) Diktat 126 – Slave To The Rythm (IRE) 63 (Hamas (IRE) 125§) [2007 p6g⁴ 6m 6.1d⁴ p6g² 6m p6g⁵ p5.1g² p5m⁶ p5.1g⁴ Dec 29] angular gelding: fair maiden: runner-up in nurseries at Kempton and Wolverhampton: should prove best at 5f/6f: acts on polytrack and good to soft going. *T. Keddy* **70**

WRIGHTY ALMIGHTY (IRE) 5 b.g. Danehill Dancer (IRE) 117 – Persian Empress (IRE) 51 (Persian Bold 123) [2007 79d: 7.1m 8m² 8f² 7m p6g⁵ 8d² 8f* 7d² 8.1m* p8.6g³ 8d⁵ p8g p8m* Dec 9] tall, useful-looking gelding: fair handicapper: won at Brighton in August, Chepstow in September and Lingfield in December: stays 1m: acts on polytrack, firm and good to soft going: tried in cheekpieces/blinkers: sometimes slowly away. *P. R. Chamings* **74**

WRITINGONTHEWALL (IRE) 2 b.c. (Jan 27) Danetime (IRE) 121 – Badee'a (IRE) (Marju (IRE) 127) [2007 5g⁵ 6m* 6d Oct 12] well-made colt: has a quick action: fair form: won maiden at Thirsk in September: softer ground, well held in nursery at York (free early): will stay 7f. *M. L. W. Bell* **72 +**

WRIT (IRE) 5 ch.g. Indian Lodge (IRE) 127 – Carnelly (IRE) 101 (Priolo (USA) 127) [2007 –, a82: p7.1g³ p7.1g* p7.1g p8g* 7.1m 7m⁶ p8.6g May 21] quite good-topped gelding: fairly useful on all-weather, modest on turf: won handicap at Wolverhampton in January and claimer at Lingfield in March: effective at 7f, barely stays easy 1¼m: acts on polytrack and good to firm going. *I. Semple* **62 + a84**

WROOT DANIELLE (IRE) 7 b.g. Fayruz 116 – Pounding Beat (Ya Zaman (USA) 122) [2007 12g⁶ Nov 8] leggy gelding: modest handicapper in 2005: well held only outing since: has worn cheekpieces. *D. W. Whillans* **–**

WROUGHTON (USA) 3 b.g. Royal Academy (USA) 130 – Lady Liberty (NZ) (Noble Bijou (USA)) [2007 9.9m 12.1m p12g Sep 24] tall gelding: form in maidens only when seventh to Demolition at Salisbury on debut, slowly away: should stay 1½m: sold privately after final start. *B. J. Meehan* **59**

WRYNOES PASS (IRE) 3 b.g. Bold Fact (USA) 116 – Home To Reality (IRE) (Imperial Frontier (USA) 112) [2007 –: f7g Jan 23] last all 3 starts, including in sellers. *R. F. Fisher* **–**

WULIMASTER (USA) 4 b. or br.g. Silver Hawk (USA) 123 – Kamaina (USA) (Mr Prospector (USA)) [2007 75: f8g⁵ p9.5g³ 12g² f12g 12.3g⁴ 12m 10.1m⁵ 14.1g 11.5d 10g⁶ 10s 11.1s³ 12s 10g⁵ 10g⁴ p12.2g⁴ Nov 20] close-coupled gelding: fair maiden handicapper: below form after fifth start: stays 1½m: acts on soft and good to firm ground, probably on all-weather: tried in cheekpieces/visor: has looked moody. *D. W. Barker* **79 d**

WUSUUL 2 br.f. (Apr 8) Kyllachy 129 – Cartuccia (IRE) (Doyoun 124) [2007 7.5g⁴ Sep 19] 20,000gns: sixth foal: half-sister to 6.5f (at 2 yrs) to 10.5f winner in Holland/Germany by Abou Zouz: dam unraced half-sister to Derby/Irish Derby second City Honours: 20/1, staying-on fourth in maiden at Beverley: open to improvement. *C. E. Brittain* **74 p**

WYATT EARP (IRE) 6 b.g. Piccolo 121 – Tribal Lady 80 (Absalom 128) [2007 100: 5m⁶ 6m 6g* 5g⁶ 7g 6d 6m 6g⁴ 6m³ 6g³ p6g Nov 4] smallish, sturdy gelding: useful handicapper: best effort in 2007 when winning at York (third course success, beat Zomerlust by ½ length) in May: barely stays 7f: acts on polytrack, firm and soft going: tried blinkered (ran poorly). *R. A. Fahey* **104**

WYETH 3 ch.g. Grand Lodge (USA) 125 – Bordighera (USA) 104 (Alysheba (USA)) [2007 58p: p10m 10d Oct 18] good-topped gelding: lightly-raced maiden: best effort when seventh at Kempton on reappearance: looked none too keen subsequent outing (gelded after). *J. R. Fanshawe* **69**

WYNBERG (IRE) 2 b.g. (Mar 11) Danetime (IRE) 121 – Jayzdoll (IRE) (Stravinsky **57**
(USA) 133) [2007 5d 6m 6f 6m p5g⁵ f6d Dec 14] good-quartered gelding: modest
maiden: will prove best at 5f/6f: acts on polytrack. *N. A. Callaghan*

X

XAARAWISE 2 b.f. (Jan 22) Xaar 132 – Spain 62 (Polar Falcon (USA) 126) [2007 7m –
Aug 8] third foal: half-sister to winner in Spain by Dr Fong: dam twice-raced half-sister
to smart 2-y-o sprinter Magic Ring: tailed off in maiden at Brighton. *M. Botti*

XAAR TOO BUSY 3 b.f. Xaar 132 – Desert Serenade (USA) (Green Desert (USA) **44**
127) [2007 54: 8m 10m⁶ 6.9g 9.8s Jul 9] just poor maiden in 2007: best effort at 6f:
visored/in cheekpieces. *Mrs A. Duffield*

XALTED 3 b.f. Xaar 132 – Joonayh 81 (Warning 136) [2007 –p: p6g³ p6g* 7m³ 6m 6g **57**
7g⁵ p7g p10g p6g p8g Oct 29] good-bodied filly: modest performer: won handicap at
Lingfield in February: stays 7f: acts on polytrack and good to firm ground. *S. C. Williams*

XALUNA BAY (IRE) 4 br.f. Xaar 132 – Lunadine (FR) (Bering 136) [2007 87: p5.1g **78**
6m 5m⁴ 6g p5g⁵ 5m Jul 12] tall, rather leggy filly: just fair handicapper in 2007: probably
needs good test at 5f, barely stays 7f: acts on polytrack and firm going: said to have bled
several times, including on second and final outings at 4 yrs. *W. R. Muir*

XARAVELLA (IRE) 2 b.f. (Apr 13) Xaar 132 – Walnut Lady 91 (Forzando 122) [2007 **59**
6d 7.1m³ p8g Oct 4] €38,000F: medium-sized filly: third foal: half-sister to 4-y-o
Alfie Tupper and 3-y-o Expensive Art: dam 5f to 7f winner, including at 2 yrs and in
France: modest maiden: beaten 9½ lengths when third at Musselburgh: should stay 1m.
J. G. M. O'Shea

XOCOLATL 4 b.f. Elnadim (USA) 128 – Chocolate (IRE) 77 (Brief Truce (USA) 126) –
[2007 –: p5.1g p5.1g p7g p6g Jan 29] little form: tried blinkered. *Peter Grayson*

XPRES BOY (IRE) 4 b.g. Tagula (IRE) 116 – Highly Motivated 84 (Midyan (USA) –
124) [2007 –, a58: f6g f8s f6g Feb 15] modest performer at best: no form in 2007: tried
blinkered/tongue tied. *S. R. Bowring*

XPRES MAITE 4 b.g. Komaite (USA) – Antonias Melody 86 (Rambo Dancer (CAN) **68**
107) [2007 77: f11g⁴ f7g⁶ 10g 8.5m³ 7.5m³ p7.1g⁵ 5s 6d⁴ p8.6g⁶ f8d⁶ Dec 15] sturdy, **a76**
compact gelding: fair handicapper, better on all-weather than turf: effective at 6f to 11f
(with emphasis on speed): acts on all-weather and firm ground: tried in cheekpieces/
blinkers. *S. R. Bowring*

XTRA TORRENTIAL (USA) 5 b.g. Torrential (USA) 117 – Offering (USA) (Maj- **100**
estic Light (USA)) [2007 105, a98: p8.6g* Jan 26] tall, leggy gelding: useful performer,
lightly raced: won minor event at Wolverhampton in January by ½ length from Blythe
Knight, only start at 5 yrs: stays 8.6f: acts on polytrack and good to soft going.
D. M. Simcock

XTRAVAGANZA (IRE) 2 b.f. (Mar 5) Xaar 132 – Royal Jubilee (IRE) 81 (King's **58**
Theatre (IRE) 128) [2007 5g⁵ 6m⁶ 6f p8g p8m⁵ p10g Oct 24] 11,000Y: rather leggy filly:
has a round action: third foal: half-sister to 3-y-o Bogside Theatre: dam, Irish 9f winner
(stayed 1½m), out of half-sister to high-class 1m/1¼m performer Kooyonga: modest
maiden: seems to stay 1¼m: best form on polytrack/good going. *J. W. Hills*

Y

YAB ADEE 3 b.g. Mark of Esteem (IRE) 137 – Kotdiji (Mtoto 134) [2007 p10g³ p9.5g³ **73 ?**
p8.6g⁵ p12m³ p13.9g Oct 25] fair maiden: best effort on debut: probably stays 1½m:
raced only on polytrack: gelded after final start. *M. P. Tregoning*

YADDREE 2 ch.c. (Feb 28) Singspiel (IRE) 133 – Jathaabeh 99 (Nashwan (USA) 135) **86**
[2007 7m p8g² 8.1g² 8g* Oct 25] strong, medium-sized colt: fourth foal: half-brother
to 3-y-o Sky More: dam, 1m winner, half-sister to high-class 6f/7f performer Iffraaj
out of half-sister to high-class miler Cape Cross: fairly useful form: progressive in
maidens, won at Brighton (gamely by short head from Downhiller) final start: stays 1m.
M. A. Jarvis

YAHRAB (IRE) 2 gr.c. (Jan 27) Dalakhani (IRE) 133 – Loire Valley (IRE) (Sadler's **104**
Wells (USA) 132) [2007 7m² 7f* 8m³ 8d⁶ 8s³ Oct 13] 55,000Y: close-coupled colt:
second foal: half-brother to 4-y-o Cabourg: dam unraced sister to Arc winner Carnegie,
closely related to very smart French middle-distance performer Antisaar, out of Arc
winner Detroit: useful performer: won minor event at Newbury in August: improved
form at Ascot last 2 starts, 1¾ lengths sixth to City Leader in Royal Lodge Stakes and 2½
lengths third to Ibn Khaldun in Autumn Stakes: will be suited by 1¼m/1½m: acts on firm
and soft going. *C. E. Brittain*

YAKAMA (IRE) 2 b.c. (Apr 17) Indian Danehill (IRE) 124 – Working Progress (IRE) **–**
(Marju (IRE) 127) [2007 7d⁴ 8d p7g Oct 29] angular colt: little form. *D. J. S. ffrench
Davis*

YAKIMOV (USA) 8 ch.g. Affirmed (USA) – Ballet Troupe (USA) (Nureyev (USA) **82**
131) [2007 91: f8g⁴ f8g* 10.3d² 8.1m⁶ 10g p7.1g f11d² Dec 18] strong, lengthy gelding: **a94**
fairly useful performer, better on all-weather than turf: won handicap at Southwell in
June: effective at 1m to 1½m: acts on fibresand, soft and good to firm going: hung right
on reappearance. *D. J. Wintle*

YA LATE MAITE 4 ch.f. Komaite (USA) – Plentitude (FR) (Ela-Mana-Mou 132) **60**
[2007 55: p8g p9.5g p8.6g* 8v⁵ Nov 10] good-bodied filly: modest performer: won handicap at Wolverhampton in October: sold from E. McMahon 2,500 gns before final start:
stays 8.6f: acts on polytrack, best turf form on good ground. *C. von der Recke, Germany*

YAMANMICKMCCANN 2 b.c. (Apr 5) Desert Style (IRE) 121 – Cashel Kiss **74**
(Bishop of Cashel 122) [2007 6d p6g p5g² p6g* Dec 1] strong colt: fair form: won maiden
at Kempton (made all) final start: stays 6f: acts on polytrack. *R. Hannon*

YANDINA (IRE) 4 b.f. Danehill (USA) 126 – Lughz (USA) (Housebuster (USA)) **89**
[2007 74: 7s² 7g* 7m² 7m² 7m 7f⁴ p7m Nov 1] sturdy filly: fairly useful handicapper:
won at Folkestone in June: good second next 2 starts: should prove as effective at 6f as 7f:
acts on firm and soft going: temperament under suspicion. *B. W. Hills*

YANKADI (USA) 2 b.c. (May 4) Johannesburg (USA) 127 – Clog Dance 103 (Pursuit **104**
of Love 124) [2007 7s²* 7m³ 8s⁴ Nov 1] big, close-coupled colt: has a round action: fourth
foal: closely related to useful 6f (at 2 yrs) and 1m winner Short Dance (by Hennessy):
dam, maiden (stayed 1¼m), half-sister to smart Ebor winner Tuning: useful form: won
maiden at Newmarket in August: improvement when length third to River Proud in
Somerville Tattersall Stakes there and 2 lengths fourth to Thewayyouare in Criterium
International at Saint-Cloud: will stay 1¼m: acts on soft and good to firm going: looks
highly strung, tends to get on edge (reluctant/unseated behind stalls in France), and takes
strong hold (wears crossed noseband). *B. W. Hills*

YANKEE BRAVO (USA) 2 b. or br.c. (Mar 12) Yankee Gentleman (USA) – Vickey **98 p**
Jane (USA) (Royal Academy (USA) 130) [2007 5m* 8f* Dec 29] $17,000Y, £5,000
2-y-o, resold 16,500 2-y-o: lengthy colt: has scope: first foal: dam unraced out of half-
sister to top-class US performer up to 1¼m Siphon: useful form: won maiden at Redcar
(by 6 lengths) in September and, having left Mrs A. Duffield, non-graded event at Santa
Anita (by ½ length from Sky Cape) in December: stays 1m: will improve further.
P. Gallagher, USA

YANKEE STORM 2 b.c. (Apr 8) Yankee Gentleman (USA) – Yes Virginia (USA) **62**
(Roanoke (USA)) [2007 p7.1g⁵ 7m 6f p5.1g⁴ p6g² p6d² Dec 21] quite attractive colt:
modest form: won nursery at Southwell final start: should stay 7f/1m: acts on all-weather
and good to firm going: races prominently. *M. J. Wallace*

YAQEEN 3 b.f. Green Desert (USA) 127 – Lady Elgar (IRE) (Sadler's Wells (USA) **107**
132) [2007 90p: 7m* 8m⁶ 8d 10.1m* 9.9m Aug 4] good-topped filly: had a quick, fluent
action: reportedly suffered ankle problem after only 2-y-o start: won maiden at Newmarket in April and listed race at Yarmouth (by 1¼ lengths from Samira Gold) in July:
not discredited on other starts, in 1000 Guineas at Newmarket (6½ lengths sixth to
Finsceal Beo), Coronation Stakes at Royal Ascot (forced to check when ninth to Indian
Ink) and Nassau Stakes at Goodwood (looked rather light in condition when seventh
behind Peeping Fawn, said by jockey afterwards not to be moving right in closing stages):
stayed 1¼m: acted on good to firm going: visits Nayef. *M. A. Jarvis*

YAROSLAV (USA) 3 b.c. Danzig (USA) – Always Loyal (USA) 113 (Zilzal (USA) **90**
137) [2007 8m⁴ p7g* 8m 8m 7g 7d p7g³ p7g Oct 14] close-coupled, useful-looking colt:
fifth foal: brother to fairly useful 2004 2-y-o 6f winner Loyal Love and winner in US:
dam, won Poule d'Essai des Pouliches and stayed 10.5f, half-sister to top-class French
sprinter Anabaa (by Danzig) and to high-class 1m/1¼m winner in USA/Dubai Key of

Luck: fairly useful performer: won maiden at Lingfield in May: respectable efforts at best in handicaps after: stays 7f: acts on polytrack, best turf effort on good ground: blinkered last 5 starts: sold 42,000 gns, sent to USA. *R. Charlton*

YARQUS 4 b.g. Diktat 126 – Will You Dance 83 (Shareef Dancer (USA) 135) [2007 **101** 101: f8g⁶ 8g 8g³ a8f p7g² 8s 8.1g 9m 7g⁵ 8m⁵ 8g 10.4d⁴ 10m² 10.1g⁶ 9m⁴ Oct 6] good-topped gelding: useful handicapper: without a win since April 2006 but generally ran well at 4 yrs, 2½ lengths fourth of 34 to Pipedreamer in Cambridgeshire at Newmarket final start: probably stays 1½m, races mostly at 7f to 1¼m: acts on polytrack, firm and good to soft going: sometimes tongue tied: has sweated: usually held up. *C. E. Brittain*

YASINISI (IRE) 2 br.f. (Apr 19) Kalanisi (IRE) 132 – Yazmin (IRE) 94 (Green Desert **91** (USA) 127) [2007 6g⁴ 6s⁴ 7.1d⁶ 8f⁴ Dec 30] leggy filly: third foal: half-sister to Italian 5f/6f winner Ibiscus (by Zafonic): dam 2-y-o 6f winner: fairly useful performer: won maiden at Redcar in May: better form after when fourth in listed race at Newmarket (to Polar Circle), and having left E. O'Neill after third outing, non-graded event at Santa Anita (3 lengths behind Gorgeous Goose): stays 1m: acts on firm and soft going. *P. Gallagher, USA*

YATHREB (USA) 2 b. or br.c. (Mar 8) Kingmambo (USA) 125 – Thawakib (IRE) 108 **75** (Sadler's Wells (USA) 132) [2007 7d 8.1m 8d Oct 3] sturdy colt: closely related to 4-y-o Haasem and half-brother to several winners, notably top-class 1m (at 2 yrs) to 1½m (Prix de l'Arc de Triomphe) winner Sakhee (by Bahri): dam, 7f (at 2 yrs) and 1½m (Ribblesdale Stakes) winner, half-sister to top-class middle-distance performer Celestial Storm: fair form in maidens, but also signs of temperament: will stay 1¼m/1½m. *J. L. Dunlop*

YATTENDON 2 ch.g. (Mar 25) Compton Place 125 – Arian Da 81 (Superlative 118) **61** [2007 6d p6g p6d³ p7.1d Dec 27] sturdy gelding: modest maiden: third at Wolverhampton: likely to prove best at 5f/6f. *S. Kirk*

YAZAMAAN 3 b.c. Galileo (IRE) 134 – Moon's Whisper (USA) (Storm Cat (USA)) **98** [2007 107p: 10.3m⁵ 8g⁴ 8g Oct 31] close-coupled, useful-looking colt: useful performer: won both starts at 2 yrs: failed to progress as expected in 2007, fifth of 6 behind Admiral-ofthefleet in listed race at Chester on reappearance: left J. Gosden prior to final outing: free-going sort, may prove best up to 1m: acts on good to firm and good to soft ground: has been bandaged hind joints. *K. P. McLaughlin, USA*

YEAMAN'S HALL 3 b.g. Galileo (IRE) 134 – Rimba (USA) 82 (Dayjur (USA) 137) **107** [2007 89p: 8.1g* 10g⁵ 8.1g Jul 7] big, strong gelding: useful performer: won minor event at Sandown in April by neck from Sunshine Kid: creditable efforts next 2 starts, 3 lengths fifth to Alexander of Hales in Gallinule Stakes at the Curragh and seventh of 17 to Ordnance Row in valuable handicap at Sandown (reportedly injured after, and gelded): probably stays 1¼m: acts on soft going. *A. M. Balding*

YEARNING (IRE) 3 b.f. Danetime (IRE) 121 – Hiraeth 76 (Petong 126) [2007 53: f5g **–** 7s Aug 24] leggy, close-coupled filly: little worthwhile form: bred to prove best at 5f/6f: has been slowly away/flashed tail. *J. G. Portman*

YEATS (IRE) 6 b.h. Sadler's Wells (USA) 132 – Lyndonville (IRE) (Top Ville **126** 129) [2007 128: 13f* 14m* 20g* 14m* 20g³ Oct 7]

The writing was on the wall, or to be more precise on the page, for Yeats four years ago. After he gained an emphatic four-length victory in a maiden race at the Curragh on his only appearance as a two-year-old, *Racehorses of 2003* concluded: 'This is a very stout family, and it is worth underlining just how much Yeats is going to improve when he gets the opportunity to tackle distances that are more in keeping with his pedigree.' With his record of ten wins from seventeen starts now including two Gold Cups, a Goodwood Cup, an Irish St Leger and a Coronation Cup, Yeats can fairly be said to have lived up to expectations in the grand manner. Since he stays in training, with the Gold Cup reportedly once again the principal objective, there may well be more to come.

In the sense that he did not maintain top form through the whole season, losing a race he ought to have won in the Prix du Cadran on his final appearance, Yeats's campaign as a six-year-old mirrored that of the two previous years. But first things first. The longest odds at which he started in five outings in the latest season was 13/8-on at Royal Ascot, and judged on his crushing victories by an aggregate of eleven lengths in the Vintage Crop Stakes at Navan and the Seamus & Rosemary McGrath Memorial Saval Beg Stakes at Leopardstown in May he was just about as good as ever in the run up to the Gold Cup. The opposition in these

Gold Cup, Royal Ascot—the margin is not so wide but Yeats wins with just as much authority as in 2006;
Geordieland (left) is second and Le Miracle third, while Finalmente (right)
and Montare (cheekpieces) are next

two races was not particularly testing for a horse of Yeats's ability but the way in which he accelerated must have worried the connections of the thirteen who lined up against him at the Royal meeting. The Gold Cup drew a representative field, including, from Britain, the 2006 Prix du Cadran winner Sergeant Cecil, fresh from a win in the Yorkshire Cup, Henry II Stakes winner Allegretto, Sagaro Stakes winner Tungsten Strike, former high-class middle-distance performer Cherry Mix trying a new trip, and Geordieland, runner-up to Sergeant Cecil at York. There were three challengers from mainland Europe—Lord du Sud, successful in the Prix Vicomtesse Vigier in the spring, Montare, whose tally included the Prix Royal-Oak, and Le Miracle, a five-length winner of the Prix Gladiateur and third in the Prix du Cadran the previous autumn. Yeats did not win by so wide a margin as a year earlier, when he had Reefscape four lengths adrift, but his victory was just as authoritative. Held up in the middle of the field as Lord du Sud took them along, Yeats moved through easily to join issue soon after turning for home and used his characteristic turn of foot to take command in no time. Unlike in 2006, Yeats tended to idle in front and wander around a bit but, despite Geordieland's launching a challenge a furlong out, the favourite never looked as if he would pull out all the stops. He passed the post a length and a half to the good with Le Miracle keeping on at one pace in third, three and half lengths further away. Sergeant Cecil ran way below form and finished tailed-off last. Yeats became the tenth horse to achieve two victories in the Gold Cup in the last forty years or so, the others being Fighting Charlie, Sagaro (who went on to make it three), Le Moss, Ardross, Gildoran, Sadeem, Drum Taps, Kayf Tara and Royal Rebel.

As a five-year-old Yeats had put up his best performance on his next start after the Gold Cup, when carrying a penalty to a five-length triumph in the Goodwood Cup. This time he missed Goodwood, and when he lined up for the Irish Field St Leger at the Curragh in mid-September it had just become clear—the day before, in fact—that Aidan O'Brien's stable housed a challenger for the title of champion stayer in the shape of easy Doncaster Cup winner Septimus. Yeats was again odds on, though he was taking on another high-class stablemate, Coronation Cup winner Scorpion. The Irish St Leger looked to concern just those two horses—the seven other contenders included only one three-year-old, Ballyroan Stakes winner Mores Wells being stepped up in distance, while the British-trained hopes were Mighty, Steppe Dancer, 2005 runner-up The Whistling Teal, seemingly a light of other days, and Macorville. Scorpion made the running and appeared to have Yeats in trouble when pushed clear over three furlongs out. However, with Scorpion not looking entirely comfortable on the good to firm going, Yeats gradually began to make ground and by the furlong pole he was fully opened out. Catching Scorpion fifty yards from home, and edging into him as he did so, Yeats forged ahead to win by half a length, the pair clear of Mores Wells. O'Brien had saddled ten runners in the Irish St Leger previously, gaining places with Ballingarry in 2002, Powerscourt in 2003 and Brian Boru in 2004, as well as with Yeats himself, beaten favourite when runner-up in 2006 and fourth in 2005. Yeats's victory completed a full set of British

Irish Field St Leger, the Curragh—Aidan O'Brien completes a full house of all the classics in England and Ireland as Yeats (right) wears down stable-companion Scorpion

and Irish classic victories for a trainer who got off the mark in such races with Classic Park in the Irish One Thousand Guineas in 1997. O'Brien has some way to go in France, having won only two of the five races, the Poule d'Essai des Poulains three times and Poule d'Essai des Pouliches once. O'Brien followed Vincent O'Brien and Dick Hern as the third to train winners of all ten races, and he achieved it in considerably less time then either, with O'Brien taking fifteen years from 1953 to 1968 and Hern eighteen years from 1962 to 1980. The only change in conditions in the intervening period was the opening of the Irish St Leger to horses above the age of three in 1983, so O'Brien's achievement, allowing for the fact that he has a much larger string than either of his predecessors, is remarkable. Vincent O'Brien was fifty-one when he reached the target and Hern fifty-nine but Aidan O'Brien is only thirty-eight. O'Brien's current total of Group 1 and Grade 1 victories by country are: Britain fifty, Ireland forty-one, France twenty-five, North America eight and Italy three, making a total of one hundred and twenty-seven. O'Brien is now ahead of Sir Michael Stoute and Henry Cecil, both of whom have also passed the hundred mark in much longer careers. However, O'Brien is still behind one trainer who has held a licence for only slightly longer, Saeed bin Suroor on one hundred and thirty-four, and another who trained his first Group 1 winner in 1982, Andre Fabre who is now on one hundred and thirty.

One Group 1 race that Aidan O'Brien has not yet won is the Prix du Cadran, and that is because Yeats was beaten at long odds on in the latest renewal. Yeats was attempting to become only the eighth horse to win the Gold Cup and the Cadran, and only the sixth to win them both in the same season, following Boiard, who landed the double in 1874, Arbar, who did so in 1948, Elpenor, Gold Cup in 1954 and Cadran 1955, Levmoss in 1969, Lassalle in 1973, Sagaro in 1976 and Westerner, Cadran in 2004 and Gold Cup in 2005. Westerner also won the Prix du Cadran in 2003 and finished runner-up in the Gold Cup in 2004. Yeats had already shown his superiority over second favourite Le Miracle, recently third in the Prix Gladiateur to another Cadran runner, the filly Varevees. Form counted for nothing in the race, though, as Yeats was never going particularly well and found little when asked to make ground in the straight, eventually finishing third to Le Miracle, three lengths behind short-head runner-up Varevees. An anti-climactic end to a fine campaign, and one which, given Yeats's failure now to run to his best in three starts in October over the last three years, may encourage O'Brien not to persevere with him that late as a seven-year-old. Only one horse, Sagaro, has managed to land a hat-trick of victories in the Gold Cup. Yeats is unlikely to be improving as a seven-year-old—only four horses of that age have won the Gold Cup in the last century or so, Bachelor's Button in 1906, Happy Man in 1923, Invershin in 1929 and Drum Taps in 1993—but with just seventeen starts to his name he has not exactly been overraced, and provided he remains fit and in good heart, he will be in with a good chance of emulating Sagaro, though his chances of success will be improved if stablemate Septimus is not aimed at the Gold Cup—the latter's form is marginally better, and he would be a very formidable opponent.

Yeats (IRE) (b.h. 2001)	Sadler's Wells (USA) (b 1981)	Northern Dancer (b 1961)	Nearctic
			Natalma
		Fairy Bridge (b 1975)	Bold Reason
			Special
	Lyndonville (IRE) (b 1988)	Top Ville (b 1976)	High Top
			Sega Ville
		Diamond Land (br 1978)	Sparkler
			Canaan

Sadler's Wells is no longer the perennial champion sire, and although Danehill, who died in 2003, will not be able to win the title again in 2008, Sadler's Wells will have a tough time regaining the crown in the face of fierce and numerically superior competition from his sons Montjeu and Galileo in particular. Sadler's Wells has been covering progressively smaller books as he has got older—his latest tally of sixty-four covered as a twenty-three-year-old, given in the *Return of Mares* published in November, down from ninety in 2006 and less than a third of the number of mares covered in 2000. If either Yeats or Septimus manages to win the Gold Cup, they will place their sire ahead of any other in the race's history—Son-In-Law was responsible for the winners of four, the same as Sadler's Wells at the moment thanks to the two successes each of Kayf Tara and Yeats. It is worth recapping some details of Yeats's pedigree on the distaff side, if only to point out the stamina there. His dam Lyndonville, who won once over a mile and three quarters, foaled two other stakes winners, notably Solskjaer (by Danehill), successful in the Royal Whip Stakes. Yeats's grandam Diamond Land won over thirteen and a half furlongs, produced Fillies' Mile winner Ivanka and was grandam of the good stayer Alcazar. A generation further back, Canaan was a half-sister to Cantelo (St Leger) and to fillies who featured in the bottom line of the pedigrees of Biskrah (Doncaster Cup), Bracey Bridge (Park Hill Stakes), Connaught Bridge (Yorkshire Oaks), Eric (Chester Cup) and Tug of War (Goodwood Cup).

In the modern era, the racing record of Yeats is hardly a commercial one for a Flat stallion and when he is retired he will surely follow another outstanding recent stayer, Westerner, as a Coolmore jump sire. Yeats has the looks to succeed in that department—he is tall and good-topped and a good walker with a powerful, round action who looked magnificent at Royal Ascot. Yeats, who has worn a crossed noseband, acts on any going and is effective at thirteen furlongs to two and a half miles; in a strongly-run race he may still, as it proved with Westerner, be capable of making his presence felt over a mile and a half, a trip at which Yeats hasn't been tried since October 2005. *A. P. O'Brien, Ireland*

YELDHAM LADY 5 b.m. Mujahid (USA) 125 – Future Options 71 (Lomond (USA) 128) [2007 –: p9.5g p9.5g Jan 19] quite attractive mare: no form since 2005. *A. J. Chamberlain*

YELLOW MANE (IRE) 4 ch.c. On The Ridge (IRE) 115 – Mother Nellie (USA) (Al **36** Nasr (FR) 126) [2007 –: p7g Jan 22] poor maiden: seventh in minor event at Kempton only start at 4 yrs. *Luke Comer, Ireland*

YELLOW RIDGE (IRE) 4 ch.c. On The Ridge (IRE) 115 – Jonathan's Rose (IRE) **59** (Law Society (USA) 130) [2007 73: p8g 10m 12m 8m 12m 7f 14s⁶ Jul 18] compact colt: modest performer: ran creditably at Lingfield on reappearance: seems effective at 7f to 1½m: acts on good to firm and good to soft going: tried blinkered/tongue tied. *Luke Comer, Ireland*

YELLOWSTONE (IRE) 3 b.c. Rock of Gibraltar (IRE) 133 – Love And Affection **119** (USA) (Exclusive Era (USA)) [2007 110: 8g⁵ 8m 10m² 12g 12d³ 10g⁴ 12g* 12d² 11f⁶ 12g Oct 7] big, good-bodied colt: smart performer: won Gordon Stakes at Goodwood in July by neck from Aqaleem (gave 3 lb), despite hanging right when first under pressure: also ran other good races in pattern company in 2007, including when 3 lengths fourth to Notnowcato in Eclipse Stakes at Sandown and length second to Lucarno in Great Voltigeur Stakes at York: acted as pacemaker when well held in Prix de l'Arc de Triomphe at Longchamp final start: stays 1½m: acts on firm and good to soft going: sold 520,000 gns, initially joined J. S. Moore and taken to UAE, then joined A. Manuel there. *A. P. O'Brien, Ireland*

YEM KINN 2 b.c. (Feb 5) Dubai Destination (USA) 127 – Nova Cyngi (USA) (Kris S **90** (USA)) [2007 5s* 6m 7m 7f² 7.1m 7.1g⁶ Sep 19] 55,000Y: close-coupled colt: second foal: half-brother to winner in Japan by Singspiel: dam unraced half-sister to dam of 3-y-o Light Shift: fairly useful performer: won maiden at Ascot (by ½ length from Fitzroy Crossing) in May: mainly stiff tasks subsequently, seemingly best effort when second to Yahrab in minor event at Newbury (dictated): will be suited by 1m: acts on firm and soft going: sold 40,000 gns, joined S. Seemar in UAE. *M. R. Channon*

YENALED 10 gr.g. Rambo Dancer (CAN) 107 – Fancy Flight (FR) 74 (Arctic Tern **–** (USA) 126) [2007 61, a67: 10.2g 10.2f 10.2d p12.2g p12g 10.2s 11.9m⁵ 10.2m 10g **a49** Oct 25] leggy, sparely-made gelding: poor performer nowadays: stays 13f: acts on all-weather and any turf going: tried in visor/cheekpieces: held up: sometimes races freely: quirky. *J. M. Bradley*

YEOMAN LEAP 3 b.g. Val Royal (FR) 127 – Chandni (IRE) (Ahonoora 122) [2007 **–** 58p: 8m p8g Apr 30] short-backed gelding: maiden: well held in 2007, then gelded. *A. M. Balding*

Gordon Stakes, Goodwood—Yellowstone holds on from Aqaleem (striped cap), Raincoat (right) and Champery (star on cap)

YEOMAN SPIRIT (IRE) 4 ch.g. Soviet Star (USA) 128 – Hollywood Pearl (USA) **85**
(Phone Trick (USA)) [2007 76: 10d⁶ p12g* Sep 19] big gelding: fairly useful performer,
lightly raced: made all in maiden at Kempton in September: stays 1½m: acts on polytrack
and good to soft ground: sold 25,000 gns. *A. M. Balding*

YEREVAN 3 b.f. Iron Mask (USA) 117 – Unfuwaanah 74 (Unfuwain (USA) 131) [2007 **79**
73: 6.1m⁶ 6s* 5m⁵ 6s⁴ 7s p6g 7m Nov 10] unfurnished filly: fair handicapper: won at
Leicester (dictated) in May: best at 5f/6f: acts on soft and good to firm going: races
prominently. *R. T. Phillips*

YES EIGHTEEN (IRE) 2 b.c. (Mar 5) Diktat 126 – Siskin (IRE) (Royal Academy **–**
(USA) 130) [2007 6m Aug 17] sturdy colt: 100/1 and backward, last in maiden at Newbury: bred to stay 1m. *J. W. Hills*

YES MEG 2 b.f. (Mar 31) Sagamix (FR) 129 – Segsbury Belle (Petoski 135) [2007 **61**
6.1g⁴ 6m* p7g p7.1g 8f⁴ Sep 10] leggy, lengthy filly: second foal: dam maiden: modest
form: won seller at Thirsk in June: fourth in nursery at Bath final start: will stay at least
1½m: acts on firm going. *P. F. I. Cole*

YES MR PRESIDENT (IRE) 2 b.c. (May 9) Montjeu (IRE) 137 – Royals Special **66 p**
(IRE) 72 (Caerleon (USA) 132) [2007 f8d⁵ Dec 21] third foal: dam, Irish maiden, half-
sister to high-class performers Distant Relative (miler) and Ezzoud (at 1¼m/1½m): 7/2
and green, fifth to Pharaohs Justice in maiden at Southwell, slowly away: should
improve. *M. Johnston*

YES ONE (IRE) 3 ch.c. Peintre Celebre (USA) 137 – Copious (IRE) (Generous (IRE) **78**
139) [2007 p7f p10g 10g⁵ 10m² 10.3f* 9.9d⁴ 12d p10g⁶ p12.2g⁶ Oct 19] small, sturdy **a72**
colt: fifth foal: half-brother to fairly useful Irish 2002 2-y-o 7f winner Fluirseach (stayed
1½m by In The Wings): dam unraced half-sister to dam of high-class miler Landseer and
very smart 1¼m performer Ikhtyar: fair handicapper: won at Chester in June: stays 1½m:
acts on firm and good to soft ground: sold 20,000 gns. *J. W. Hills*

YIPPYIAYIPPYIO 2 ch.f. (Feb 8) Fraam 114 – Sandy Lady (IRE) 91 (Desert King **–**
(IRE) 129) [2007 p7.1g p7.1g p7g Dec 29] first foal: dam, 6f (at 2 yrs) and 1m winner, out
of useful sprinter Mamma's Too: well beaten in maidens/seller. *Mrs C. A. Dunnett*

YO PEDRO (IRE) 5 b.g. Mark of Esteem (IRE) 137 – Morina (USA) (Lyphard (USA) **64**
132) [2007 85d: 5m 7g 8.5m 7m² p8g 8m 8m² 9d 10s⁴ Sep 26] leggy gelding: modest
performer nowadays: claimed from Barry Potts in Ireland £6,000 after fourth start: stays
1¼m: acts on polytrack and firm going: tried visored/blinkered/tongue tied. *D. Carroll*

YORK CLIFF 9 b.g. Marju (IRE) 127 – Azm (Unfuwain (USA) 131) [2007 64: f12g⁴ **66**
p12.2g⁴ 15d* 16.1m⁴ 16g² 16.2d 15.9d² 14d⁴ p13.9g 15.9m 13.4g p13.9g³ 12g⁴ p13.9g⁵
p13.9g Nov 5] good-bodied gelding: fair handicapper: won at Ayr in May: stays 2m: acts
on all-weather and any turf going: tried in cheekpieces/visor. *W. M. Brisbourne*

YORKE'S FOLLY (USA) 6 b.m. Stravinsky (USA) 133 – Tommelise (USA) (Dayjur **48**
(USA) 137) [2007 54: 5v 6m 5g⁵ 5g 5m⁴ 5.7d Oct 1] big, lengthy mare: poor maiden
handicapper: stays 6f: acts on fibresand and firm going: tried visored, usually blinkered
nowadays. *C. W. Fairhurst*

YORKIE 8 b.g. Aragon 118 – Light The Way 72 (Nicholas Bill 125) [2007 59, a41: 7d **–**
8m Aug 8] tall, quite good-topped gelding: modest performer: well held both starts at
8 yrs: tried blinkered/visored: formerly tongue tied. *J. Pearce*

YORKSHIRE BLUE 8 b.g. Atraf 116 – Something Blue (Petong 126) [2007 90: 6s **85**
6m² 6g 7v 6d⁵ 7d 6m⁴ 7g⁵ 6m⁶ 6m⁴ 6g* p7.1g 6v⁵ 7m Nov 10] close-coupled gelding:
fairly useful performer: won claimer at Hamilton in September: effective at 6f/7f: acts on
all-weather and any turf going: twice blinkered (below form) early in career: often gets
behind. *J. S. Goldie*

YOSSI (IRE) 3 b.g. Montjeu (IRE) 137 – Raindancing (IRE) 94 (Tirol 127) [2007 81: **88**
11.9g² 12g⁶ 12.3d² 12g² 11.5s⁴ 12g* 11.9g³ 13.1s 10.4d⁴ 10.1d⁵ Oct 30] good-bodied
gelding: fairly useful performer: won maiden at Catterick in August: stays 1½m: raced
only on good ground or softer: blinkered last 3 starts: has looked quirky: gelded after final
outing. *M. H. Tompkins*

YOU LIVE AND LEARN 4 ch.f. Galileo (IRE) 134 – Anniversary 101 (Salse (USA) **62**
128) [2007 64: 10d p12g 14.1g Oct 19] modest maiden: best form at 1¼m: yet to race on
extremes of going on turf. *H. Morrison*

YOUMZAIN (IRE) 4 b.c. Sinndar (IRE) 134 – Sadima (IRE) 103 (Sadler's Wells **127** (USA) 132) [2007 125: 12g^3 10.5g^3 12g^5 12g^2 12g^4 12g^2 Oct 7]

'Winning is a habit, unfortunately so is losing.' Youmzain's record in Group 1 company in the latest season included seconds in Europe's two most important all-aged middle-distance championship events, the King George VI and Queen Elizabeth Stakes and the Prix de l'Arc de Triomphe, in the last-named putting up a career-best performance when going down by a head to Dylan Thomas. Youmzain was also a clear second to Dylan Thomas at Ascot but, unfortunately, he failed to produce that form when facing more straightforward tasks and ended the campaign without a win.

Youmzain is a Group 1 winner, having landed the odds in the Preis von Europa at Cologne on his last start as a three-year-old after establishing himself as a high-class performer when winning the Great Voltigeur at York and finishing second to the subsequent winner of the Arc, Rail Link, in the Prix Niel. The Preis von Europa was chosen instead of the Arc for Youmzain, after his owner had also decided against a tilt at the St Leger, for which Youmzain had been second favourite after winning the Voltigeur. He was out early as a four-year-old and wasn't far below his best when threading his way through on the rail from the rear to finish just under two lengths third to Vengeance of Rain (pipping Derby winner Sir Percy) in the richly endowed Dubai Sheema Classic at Nad Al Sheba at the end of March. Not quite 'mission accomplished' but an encouraging reappearance nonetheless. It was back to Europe for the Tattersalls Gold Cup over a mile and a quarter at the Curragh in May and Youmzain was far from discredited when third to Notnowcato and Dylan Thomas in a race which turned into too much of a test of speed for him

Mr Jaber Abdullah's "Youmzain"

over a distance short of his best. Youmzain should have been suited by the return to a mile and a half at the end of June in the Grand Prix de Saint-Cloud, in which he had a good chance on his best form. Starting second favourite to the French filly Mandesha, Youmzain couldn't even reach the frame behind Mountain High, unable to make much impression after having plenty to do when the pace quickened turning for home. Youmzain hadn't looked a straightforward ride when winning the Great Voltigeur, carrying his head high and soon starting to pull himself up once he hit the front, and he never looked like getting into it at Saint-Cloud, though his jockey (Jamie Spencer on this occasion) reported that Youmzain slipped on the first bend and was never travelling thereafter.

Youmzain made his first appearance in Britain since the Great Voltigeur when beaten four lengths by Dylan Thomas in the King George VI and Queen Elizabeth Stakes in July, on what turned out to be Youmzain's only outing as a four-year-old in Britain. The latest King George was far from a vintage edition but strictly on that form—he looked like running Dylan Thomas closer after following him through in the straight—Youmzain should have given a much better account of himself than he did in Germany's 'King George', the Grosser Preis von Baden, in early-September. Starting third favourite behind the Deutsches Derby winner Adlerflug and Mountain High, and held up as usual, Youmzain stayed on after having to challenge wide but could finish no nearer than fourth, beaten just under four lengths by the winner Quijano (Adlerflug came second). Youmzain started at 80/1 for the Prix de l'Arc de Triomphe on his final start and, in a very strongly-run race that suited him down to the ground, he showed just what he is capable of when things go his way. The first four all came from off the pace at Longchamp, Youmzain—like the winner drifting right in the closing stages—almost pegging back Dylan Thomas (jockey Richard Hughes reporting that Youmzain 'changed his legs at a crucial moment' near the finish). Dylan Thomas hampered both Zambezi Sun and Soldier of Fortune in the closing stages, but neither would have finished in front of Youmzain on the day with a clear passage and he deserves full credit for his performance. Youmzain has won at thirteen furlongs and will stay further, and he will do best when the emphasis is firmly on stamina if he is campaigned again at a mile and a half as a five-year-old.

		Grand Lodge (ch 1991)	Chief's Crown
	Sinndar (IRE) (b 1997)		La Papagena
		Sinntara (b 1989)	Lashkari
Youmzain (IRE) (b.c. 2003)			Sidama
		Sadler's Wells (b 1981)	Northern Dancer
	Sadima (IRE) (b 1998)		Fairy Bridge
		Anima (b 1989)	Ajdal
			Cocotte

Youmzain is a strong colt by the 2000 Prix de l'Arc winner Sinndar, who is an influence for stamina at stud, out of the useful Sadler's Wells mare Sadima who gained her only win over a mile and a quarter. Youmzain is Sadima's first foal and her second is the very smart miler Creachadoir (by King's Best) in whose essay more details of the family can be found. Grandam Anima is a half-sister to the top-class Pilsudski, who, coincidentally, also finished runner-up in the King George and Arc in the same year (1997). Youmzain cost 30,000 guineas as a yearling and Creachadoir made €83,000, and Sadima's own fortunes in the sale-ring are worth recounting. She made IR 30,000 guineas at Goffs as a yearling and 125,000 guineas at the Tattersalls Breeze-Up six months later. As a six-year-old, she was sent up to Tattersalls again, to the December Sales in foal to Dalakhani (the filly foal she was carrying, her third foal, is now called Shreyas and was unraced at two). Sadima was bought back for 65,000 guineas and returned to Hamwood Stud in County Meath (owned by Frank Dunne, best known as the owner-trainer of that admirably tough racemare of the 'eighties Stanerra). Since then, the performances of Youmzain and Creachadoir have made Sadima worth a fortune, the market for well-bred race-mares with form, and well-connected broodmares, having reached record levels at the latest December Sales. Two more fillies out of Sadima—the first by Bahri and the second by Dalakhani—are following on after Shreyas, and Sadima is due to foal to Sinndar in 2008. Youmzain acts on good to firm and good to soft going and has run well when sweating (he was attended by two handlers at Ascot). *M. R. Channon*

1185

Swordlestown Stud Sprint Stakes, Naas—You'resothrilling, a full sister to Giant's Causeway, gets off the mark; Saoirse Abu and May Day Queen take the minor placings

YOUNG BERTIE 4 ch.g. Bertolini (USA) 125 – Urania 66 (Most Welcome 131) [2007 **81** 74: 6m p7g p6g⁴ p7g⁴ 6f² 6g³ 7f² 8m* 8d* 8.3g* 8g⁶ Oct 24] strong gelding: fairly useful handicapper: won at Pontefract in September, and Brighton (apprentices) and Windsor in October: stays 1m: acts on polytrack, firm and good to soft going: tried in cheekpieces, visored nowadays. *H. Morrison*

YOUNG EMMA 4 b.f. Vettori (IRE) 119 – Just Warning (Warning 136) [2007 –: 12m **–** 11.5d 11.6m Jul 16] angular filly: no sign of ability. *G. G. Margarson*

YOUNG IVANHOE 2 b.c. (Mar 7) Oasis Dream 129 – Cybinka 107 (Selkirk (USA) **69** 129) [2007 6g p6g³ p6g² Nov 8] 35,000Y, 11,000 2-y-o: fourth foal: dam, 7f winner (including at 2 yrs), out of half-sister to Kris and Diesis: fair maiden: runner-up at Wolverhampton: will be suited by 7f: tongue tied. *P. J. McBride*

YOUNG MICK 5 br.g. King's Theatre (IRE) 128 – Just Warning (Warning 136) [2007 **115** 118+: 12g 12m 11.8d² p12g⁵ Nov 3] sturdy, lengthy gelding: smart performer: easily best effort at 5 yrs when creditable ¾-length second to New Guinea in minor event at Leicester, hanging right: possibly found race coming too soon when only fifth in listed race at Kempton final start: stays 1¾m: acts on polytrack, soft and good to firm going: tried blinkered, usually wears visor: tried tongue tied: patiently ridden. *G. G. Margarson*

YOUNG PRETENDER (FR) 2 b.c. (Feb 25) Oasis Dream 129 – Silent Heir (AUS) **110** 82 (Sunday Silence (USA)) [2007 6g* 7g* 7g⁵ Oct 7] 175,000Y: first foal: dam, 1¼m winner, out of close relation to 2-y-o New Approach: smart form: won maiden at Newmarket in August and Qatar Prix La Rochette at Longchamp (got up close home to beat Shediak ½ length) in September: unsuited by false pace when 5 lengths fifth to Rio de La Plata in Prix Jean-Luc Lagardere back at Longchamp: will be suited by 1m: has joined Godolphin. *J. H. M. Gosden*

YOUNG SCOTTON 7 b.g. Cadeaux Genereux 131 – Broken Wave 103 (Bustino 136) **69** [2007 50: 8d 10.5m⁵ 15.8g² 16.1m 15.8g⁶ 13.8g⁴ p13.9g* p13.9g² f14d⁵ p13.9g* Dec 31] lengthy gelding: useful form in bumpers (for K. Ryan) prior to losing way over hurdles: fair handicapper: won at Wolverhampton in November and December: stays 2m: acts on polytrack and good to firm going. *J. D. Bethell*

YOUNG VALENTINO 5 ch.g. Komaite (USA) – Caprice (Mystiko (USA) 124) **–** [2007 –: p11g p8.6g 12.6m Sep 15] workmanlike gelding: little form since 2005: left A. Carroll after second start. *M. Appleby*

YOUR AMOUNT (IRE) 4 b.g. Beckett (IRE) 116 – Sin Lucha (USA) (Northfields **74** (USA)) [2007 73: p16.5g⁵ Mar 2] smallish, useful-looking gelding: has a quick action: fair handicapper: stays easy 2m: acts on polytrack, soft and good to firm going. *W. J. Musson*

YOU'RE MY SON 5 b.g. Bold Edge 123 – Sheer Nectar 72 (Piaffer (USA) 113) [2007 **–** 60: p8g p12g p12g Nov 30] workmanlike gelding: modest maiden at 4 yrs, no form in 2007: left A. Haynes after reappearance (blinkered). *K. O. Cunningham-Brown*

YOU'RESOTHRILLING (USA) 2 b. or br.f. (Feb 5) Storm Cat (USA) – Mariah's **103 p** Storm (USA) 116 (Rahy (USA) 115) [2007 5m² 6d* 6g² 6m* 6g Aug 23] well-made filly: good walker: sister to several at least useful winners, notably top-class 1m/1¼m performer Giant's Causeway and smart 6f/7f performer Freud: dam, won several Grade 2/ 3 events at 1m/9f in US, closely related to very smart French middle-distance performer Panoramic: useful form: won Swordlestown Stud Sprint Stakes at Naas (by length from Saoirse Abu) in June and Irish Thoroughbred Marketing Cherry Hinton Stakes at Newmarket in July, in latter beating Festoso by length despite racing in least-favoured group: met trouble after awkward start when unlucky second to Nijoom Dubai in Albany Stakes at Royal Ascot in between and badly hampered in Lowther Stakes at York final outing: will stay 7f/1m: acts on good to firm and good to soft going: should still do better. *A. P. O'Brien, Ireland*

YOUR PLEASURE (USA) 2 ch.f. (May 2) Forest Wildcat (USA) 120 – Pleasure **72 +** Center (USA) 97 (Diesis 133) [2007 5m³ 5.7d* Oct 1] third foal: half-sister to winner in US by Royal Academy: dam, 1m winner, half-sister to smart US performer up to 11f Crowd Pleaser, out of US Grade 1 2-y-o 8.5f winner Creaking Board: fair form: improved from debut (wayward) when winning maiden at Bath, always finding enough in front despite again flashing tail: likely to prove best at 5f/6f. *A. M. Balding*

YUNGABURRA (IRE) 3 b.g. Fath (USA) 116 – Nordic Living (IRE) 53 (Nordico **96** (USA)) [2007 100p: 5.1m 5m 5g 5m 5g³ 5m² 5d 5d 5g p5.1g f5d³ Dec 11] quite good-topped gelding: useful performer: trained by T. Pitt until after reappearance: best at 5f: acts on all-weather and good to firm ground (below form on good to soft): tried blinkered: sometimes tongue tied. *D. J. Murphy*

YURCHENKO 3 b.f. Mamalik (USA) 115 – Rajmata (IRE) 66 (Prince Sabo 123) **43** [2007 p7.1g⁶ 6m p5g⁴ p5.1g Dec 31] lengthy, workmanlike filly: first foal: dam, sprint maiden, half-sister to useful sprinters King of Russia and Fast Heart: poor maiden. *M. Wellings*

Z

ZAAFIRA (SPA) 3 b.f. Limpid 119 – Hot Doris (IRE) (Fayruz 116) [2007 48: p8.6g² **63** f7g⁵ p7g* p7.1g p8g p8g p8g⁶ p6g p8.6g* p8.6g⁴ p8g Dec 28] modest performer: won claimer at Lingfield in January and seller at Wolverhampton in November: stays 8.6f: acts on polytrack: tongue tied last 3 starts. *E. J. Creighton*

ZAAHID (IRE) 3 ch.c. Sakhee (USA) 136 – Murjana (IRE) 80 (Pleasant Colony **103 p** (USA)) [2007 53: 7g* 7.1g* 7d² 8m⁶ 8m 8.1s* 8d³ Oct 12] strong, deep-girthed colt: type to carry condition: progressed into a useful performer: won maiden at Newbury in May, and handicaps at Sandown in June and Haydock (beat Observatory Star a head) in September: best effort when ¾-length third to Amarna in similar event at York 2 weeks later, travelling smoothly: likely to prove best up to 1m: acts on soft going: held up last 2 starts: likely to improve further. *B. W. Hills*

ZABEEL HOUSE 4 b.g. Anabaa (USA) 130 – Divine Quest 81 (Kris 135) [2007 83: **69** p7g 8.1m p7g p7g⁶ p8.6g⁵ p12.2g p7g p8.6g* Dec 29] strong, well-made gelding: just fair performer nowadays: left J. Toller and in cheekpieces, won minor event at Wolverhampton in December: stays 8.6f: acts on polytrack and firm ground: tried visored: held up. *John A. Harris*

ZABEEL PALACE 5 b.g. Grand Lodge (USA) 125 – Applecross 117 (Glint of Gold **81** 128) [2007 88: p11g 14.1m 14.1d⁵ 12d Sep 26] useful-looking gelding: fairly useful handicapper, lightly raced: best effort at 5 yrs when fifth at Nottingham, looking very awkward under pressure (trainer fined £3,000, jockey suspended for 28 days and horse banned for 40 days under non-triers rule): best form at 1¼m: acts on polytrack and good to firm going, probably on good to soft: tongue tied at 4 yrs. *B. J. Curley*

ZAB

ZABEEL TIGER 2 b.c. (Feb 16) Cadeaux Genereux 131 – Odette 72 (Pursuit of Love **56**
124) [2007 6m 6g 7.1m 5f Sep 25] leggy colt: modest maiden: should prove best at 5f/6f:
raced only on good going or firmer: sold 6,500 gns. *M. R. Channon*

ZABEEL TOWER 4 b.g. Anabaa (USA) 130 – Bint Kaldoun (IRE) 82 (Kaldoun (FR) **59**
122) [2007 57: 12m 13f 9.1g* 9.1g³ 8m⁵ 11.1m 8m³ 6m⁴ 7.1d⁵ 10g³ p8.6g³ p9.5g p7.1d
Dec 27] leggy, useful-looking gelding: modest handicapper: won at Ayr in June: effective
at 6f to 1¼m: acts on polytrack, good to firm and good to soft going: tried in cheekpieces.
R. Allan

ZABOUGG 2 b.g. (Apr 4) Tobougg (IRE) 125 – Double Fault (IRE) 54 (Zieten (USA) **65**
118) [2007 6m⁵ 7d⁴ 6m Aug 18] useful-looking gelding: type to carry condition: fair
maiden: failed to confirm initial encouragement, looking awkward (gelded after final
start): will stay 1m: sold 5,000 gns. *G. A. Swinbank*

ZACATECAS (GER) 7 b.g. Grand Lodge (USA) 125 – Zephyrine (IRE) (Highest **–**
Honor (FR) 124) [2007 –: p12g p13.9g⁶ p16g f11g Feb 20] little form in Britain.
A. J. Chamberlain

ZACHARY SCOTT 3 br.c. Inchinor 119 – Wardeh (Zafonic (USA) 130) [2007 8m 10f **59**
8g May 19] tall, lengthy, unfurnished colt: modest form in maidens. *C. E. Brittain*

ZACH'S HARMONEY (USA) 3 ch.c. Diesis 133 – Cool Ashlee (USA) (Mister **73 d**
Baileys 123) [2007 p7g⁴ p7.1g² 8d p8.6g p8g⁶ Aug 18] rather leggy, quite attractive colt:
fair form in maidens first 2 starts: claimed £7,000 final outing: tried in cheekpieces.
B. J. Meehan

ZADALLA 3 b.f. Zaha (CAN) 106 – Inishdalla (IRE) 103 (Green Desert (USA) 127) **66**
[2007 68: f6g⁶ f5g³ 5m 5g 6.7s⁴ 5s Aug 5] fair handicapper: creditable third at Southwell
second outing: stays 6.7f: acts on fibresand and soft going: sold €10,000. *Andrew Oliver,
Ireland*

ZAFFEU 6 ch.g. Zafonic (USA) 130 – Leaping Flame (USA) (Trempolino (USA) 135) **61**
[2007 65: f12g⁴ p13.9g² p16.5g⁵ p12.2g p12.2g p13.9g⁶ p13.9g⁵ Dec 1] leggy, useful-
looking gelding: has only one eye: modest performer: stays easy 2m: acts on all-weather,
firm and soft ground: blinkered (well held) twice: sometimes slowly away: tends to hang.
A. G. Juckes

ZAFONICAL STORM (USA) 3 ch.c. Aljabr (USA) 125 – Fonage (Zafonic (USA) **82**
130) [2007 94: 8m 8d 7m 8g p7g Dec 28] tall, leggy colt: fairly useful performer: little
impact at 3 yrs, though not discredited final outing: stays 1m: acts on heavy ground: tried
tongue tied: often leads: said to have bled final outing: none too consistent. *B. W. Duke*

ZAHAM (USA) 3 ch.g. Silver Hawk (USA) 123 – Guerre Et Paix (USA) (Soviet Star **120**
(USA) 128) [2007 p8g² p8g* p8g* 8.1g³ 10g* 10.1g* 10g* 10.5m³ 9.9m² 12g² Sep 30]
$50,000Y: lengthy, good-topped gelding: has scope: fourth foal: brother to fairly useful
1¼m winner Alqaab and half-brother to winner in USA by Quiet American: dam, useful
1m (at 2 yrs in France)/8.5f (in US) winner, half-sister to useful 1¼m winner Freedom
Flame: very smart performer: progressed rapidly, winning maiden at Lingfield in March,
handicaps at Kempton in April, Newbury in May and Epsom in June, and listed Hampton
Court Stakes at Royal Ascot (beat Al Shemali by head) later in June: placed after in Rose
of Lancaster Stakes at Haydock, Select Stakes at Goodwood (½-length second to Stotsfold) and Cumberland Lodge Stakes at Ascot (upped in trip, best effort when 2 lengths
second to Ask, rallying): subsequently gelded: stays 1½m: raced only on polytrack and
good/good to firm going: front runner/races prominently: game. *M. Johnston*

*Hampton Court Stakes, Ascot—Zaham, Al Shemali (right), Desert Dew (star on cap)
and Kid Mambo (rail) provide a thrilling finish to this listed event*

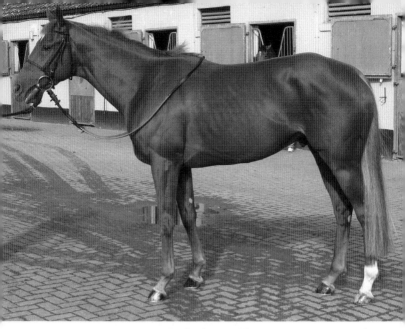

Mr Hamdan Al Maktoum's "Zaham"

ZAHOUR AL YASMEEN 3 b.f. Cadeaux Genereux 131 – Bareilly (USA) (Lyphard **93** (USA) 132) [2007 76p: 8.2m 7.1m⁵ 6d⁵ 6f 6m³ 5f* 5m* 5m³ 5.1m⁵ 5g Nov 9] leggy filly: fairly useful handicapper: won at York and Sandown, both in September: best form at 5f: acts on polytrack and firm going: races prominently. *M. R. Channon*

ZAHWAH 2 ch.f. (Apr 17) Zaha (CAN) 106 – Inishdalla (IRE) 103 (Green Desert **60 d** (USA) 127) [2007 5m 5m⁴ p5.1g³ 5g 5.7f p6g p6g 5.1g p6g⁵ p6m Dec 10] 7,000Y: smallish, sturdy filly: sister to 3-y-o Zadalla and half-sister to 3 winners, including useful 6f (at 2 yrs) to 13f winner Hearthstead Wings (by In The Wings): dam, 6f (at 2 yrs in Ireland) to 8.5f (in US) winner: modest maiden: below form after third start, in blinkers last 3: best efforts at 5f: acts on polytrack and good to firm going: difficult ride. *J. G. Portman*

ZAIF (IRE) 4 b.g. Almutawakel 126 – Colourful (FR) 97 (Gay Mecene (USA) 128) **90** [2007 96: 10.1g 11.6m 9.9m* 10d⁶ 10d 10m² 10d⁶ 10m⁵ 12m⁵ 12s⁶ Oct 13] close-coupled, quite good-topped gelding: fairly useful handicapper: won at Beverley in June: stays 1½m: acts on soft and good to firm going: has been blanketed for stall entry (once refused to go in): joined S. Earle. *D. R. C. Elsworth*

ZAIN (IRE) 3 b.g. Alhaarth (IRE) 126 – Karenaragon (Aragon 118) [2007 50: 8g⁶ 11.1f **64** 8d² 10g* 8.3m⁵ p11g 9.1s² 9.1v³ Nov 3] good-topped gelding: modest handicapper: won at Ayr in August: stays 1¼m: acts on polytrack and heavy ground: usually tongue tied. *J. G. Given*

ZAKHAAREF 2 gr.c. (Feb 10) Daylami (IRE) 138 – Shahaamah (IRE) (Red Ransom **93 p** (USA)) [2007 7d⁶ 7s* 8m² Oct 14] tall colt: first foal: dam unraced half-sister to useful 6f (in UAE) to 1m winner Thajja (by Daylami), out of close relation to Elnadim: useful form: won maiden at Redcar in September by 7 lengths: improved again when second to Meer Kat in minor event at Bath: stays 1m: type to make even better 3-y-o. *M. Johnston*

ZALKANI (IRE) 7 ch.g. Cadeaux Genereux 131 – Zallaka (IRE) (Shardari 134) [2007 **68** –, a79: p12.2g p16.5g⁶ p12g* p12.2g p12g³ p12g⁶ p12g⁴ p12.2g p12g² p13.9g² p13.9g⁵ p13.9g⁵ p12.2g⁶ p12.2g Dec 29] fair performer: won claimer at Lingfield in March: has

1189

form at 2m, best at shorter: acts on polytrack, firm and soft going: has hung left: held up.
J. Pearce

ZALZAAR (IRE) 5 b.g. Xaar 132 – Zalamalec (USA) (Septieme Ciel (USA) 123) –
[2007 60: p13.9g Nov 12] modest maiden: showed nothing on sole Flat start in 2007.
R. T. Phillips

ZAMALIK (USA) 4 b. or br.g. Machiavellian (USA) 123 – Ashbilya (USA) (Nureyev **76**
(USA) 131) [2007 8.1m 7s² 7.1v³ 7m 7.9g 6g* 6f⁶ Sep 17] strong gelding: fair performer:
missed 2006: won maiden at Hamilton in September by 7 lengths: effective at 7f, may
prove best at shorter: acts on heavy and good to firm going. *E. J. Alston*

ZAMAYA 3 b.g. Zamindar (USA) 116 – Hiwaayati (Shadeed (USA) 135) [2007 f8g –
Jan 16] 25/1, folded tamely after early speed in maiden at Southwell: sent to Germany.
K. R. Burke

ZAMBEZI SUN 3 b.c. Dansili 127 – Imbabala (Zafonic (USA) 130) [2007 10d* **117 +**
10.5m* 10.5g⁴ 12g* 12m³ 12g Oct 7]
Connections and racegoers at the course, not to mention an international
television audience, were all kept in suspense as the stewards deliberated at length
over the outcome of the Prix de l'Arc de Triomphe. However, it was far from being
the only important decision the Longchamp stewards had to make during the year.
The aftermath of Longchamp's summer highlight, the Juddmonte Grand Prix de
Paris, may not have had as much international exposure but it created just as much
suspense for those concerned, the race producing even more incident than the
Arc and the ensuing inquiry lasting even longer. Zambezi Sun was involved in the
inquiries in both races, though the part he played in the two contests was very
different. In the Arc, Zambezi Sun was an innocent victim of interference, the
consequences of which could have altered the result of the race, although not
enough to have more than academic consequences for Zambezi Sun himself. In
the Grand Prix de Paris, on the other hand, the stakes were higher as it was Zambezi
Sun's own position as winner that was in the balance. In a further twist of fate,
Stephane Pasquier, Zambezi Sun's rider, and Kieren Fallon were the principal
jockeys involved in the inquiries that followed both races.
Zambezi Sun started favourite for the Grand Prix de Paris in July, on just the
fourth start of his career. He won his first two at the course in April, a newcomers
race by a head from Airmail Special and a minor event by two lengths from Shamdinan. But it was his fourth-of-twenty finish in the Prix du Jockey Club which
advertised his claims for the Grand Prix de Paris. Forced to race wide throughout in
the big field at Chantilly, Zambezi Sun was well in rear on the home turn but made
eye-catching progress down the outside in the straight to be beaten around two
lengths by the winner Lawman and only a short neck by third-placed Shamdinan.
The step up to a mile and a half in the Grand Prix de Paris looked sure to suit
Zambezi Sun, though in Eagle Mountain, second to Authorized in the Derby and
third to his Ballydoyle stable-companion Soldier of Fortune in the Irish equivalent,
he had a rival already proven at the trip at the highest level. The remainder of the
seven-runner field looked to have plenty to find, though Airmail Special had won
twice, including the Prix du Lys over course and distance, since his first meeting
with Zambezi Sun. Sagara had finished three places behind Zambezi Sun at
Chantilly, Ashkazar had come only sixth in the King Edward VII Stakes at Royal
Ascot last time out, while the German-trained pair Axxos and Prinz had shown just
useful form.
With a small field and no dedicated pacemaker in the line-up, a steady pace
soon caused problems. Axxos, with Sagara on his outside, was the first to show,
with Eagle Mountain and Zambezi Sun tracking the leading pair. Initially the whole
field kept away from the inside, but, after a couple of furlongs, Axxos edged across
to race against the rail with the rest following. Seemingly trying to avoid the danger
of being boxed in, Fallon angled Eagle Mountain out from behind the leading pair
in an attempt to race three wide, perhaps with the intention of making the running
himself but, in so doing, he risked taking Zambezi Sun's ground and forcing him
wider. Pasquier reacted by trying to head off Fallon's manoeuvre with the result that
Eagle Mountain was short of room and appeared to clip the heels of Sagara in front
of him. Fallon became unbalanced and was unseated, falling heavily between his

own mount and Zambezi Sun. The race continued with the loose Eagle Mountain proving something of a nuisance to each of his rivals at one stage or another. Once into the straight, though, Zambezi Sun was clear of Eagle Mountain's attentions and settled matters decisively by drawing five lengths clear of nearest pursuer Axxos. Fallon suffered no serious injury, though the stewards took the somewhat unsympathetic view that he had been the cause of his own problems by provoking Pasquier into the manoeuvre which prompted their mounts to come together. No action was taken against Pasquier, and Fallon himself later readily accepted blame for the incident. Both riders have what might be termed an uncompromising style (Pasquier was involved in a couple of other controversial incidents during the season, on Manduro in the Prix Foy and Proviso in the Fillies' Mile) but there was certainly no hint of ill-feeling between the pair, something which was to prove crucial given what was to happen in the Arc. The inquiry into the Grand Prix de Paris also investigated a separate incident in the home straight involving the placed horses Axxos and Sagara, but their placings were left as they had passed the post. Sagara looked unlucky not take second after the runner-up denied him a run up the rail, and he also had to wait for the loose horse to pass him before finishing well. In addition, Sagara's rider Thierry Gillet launched an objection to the runner-up, aware that there was the possibility that, if Zambezi Sun were disqualified and Axxos demoted, Sagara would be awarded the race.

Zambezi Sun was the second successive winner of the Grand Prix de Paris to carry the colours of race sponsor Khalid Abdulla, after Rail Link's win in 2006. Christophe Soumillon had been in the saddle on Rail Link on that occasion, though, with Soumillon on stable-companion Shirocco, the winning ride on Rail Link in that year's Arc went to Pasquier instead. During the latest season, which he ended with his first French jockeys' title, Pasquier accepted a contract to ride all of Abdulla's French-trained horses. Zambezi Sun was an impressive winner of the Grand Prix de Paris but there appeared to be nothing of the quality of subsequent Breeders' Cup Turf winner Red Rocks (second to Rail Link the year before) in the field, at least not among the horses who completed the race. Even so, Zambezi Sun's odds were cut substantially for the Arc afterwards, which had him challenging Rail Link for second in the betting behind Derby winner Authorized. Zambezi Sun took the same route to the Arc as Rail Link had taken the year before, with just the one run beforehand in the Prix Niel back at Longchamp in September. Whereas Rail Link had landed the odds with a rather workmanlike win, Zambezi Sun could finish only third behind Soldier of Fortune, essentially repeating the form he had shown in the Grand Prix de Paris, though denied second by an improved Sagara. Trainer Pascal Bary reported that Zambezi Sun would improve a good deal for the run, though, to the Timeform representative, he looked in fine shape for the trial. What wasn't in dispute was that Zambezi Sun had not been subjected to a hard race by Pasquier. Zambezi Sun therefore lined up for the Arc with just smart form to his name against some top-class rivals but he was still sent off at 6/1 on the pari-mutuel. In the circumstances, Zambezi Sun didn't run at all badly but was beginning to struggle in a battle for second with eventual sixth Saddex when Dylan Thomas drifted across him as he made his winning run over a furlong out. Whilst Zambezi Sun would have finished closer than an eventual eased-down eighth without the interference, he would not have made the frame. Zambezi Sun's rider had

Juddmonte Grand Prix de Paris, Longchamp—Zambezi Sun is impressive;
Axxos (rail), Sagara and Airmail Special (right) are preceded by the riderless Eagle Mountain

apparently been of the same opinion and Fallon generously acknowledged that Pasquier's evidence at the inquiry had been a 'big factor' in Dylan Thomas keeping the race.

Zambezi Sun (b.c. 2004)	Dansili (b 1996)	Danehill (b 1986)	Danzig
			Razyana
		Hasili (b 1991)	Kahyasi
			Kerali
	Imbabala (ch 1995)	Zafonic (b 1990)	Gone West
			Zaizafon
		Interval (ch 1984)	Habitat
			Intermission

As well as providing his owner (who was also successful with Beat Hollow in 2001) with a third win in the Grand Prix de Paris, Zambezi Sun provided his sire Dansili with a second successive winner of the race. Dansili stood his first season at a fee of £8,000 but, after another successful year all round, his fee will be £75,000 in 2008 (up from £30,000), putting him second among British-based sires by fee only to Pivotal (whose rise to the top from a fairly unheralded start Dansili is close to emulating). The distaff side of Zambezi Sun's pedigree is one that his trainer Pascal Bary knows well. Bary trained the dam Imbabala, winner of a mile maiden at Fontainebleau from just four starts, and her first foal Kalabar (by Kahyasi), who was just as good as Zambezi Sun. Kalabar's most important win came in the Group 2 Prix Guillaume d'Ornano over a mile and a quarter, but he stayed a mile and a half, and also ended up winning over hurdles in Ireland for Tony Mullins, though had the misfortune to break a leg in the shadow of the post when doing so. The dam's next two foals, Landela (by Alhaarth) and Musango (by Night Shift)

Mr K. Abdulla's "Zambezi Sun"

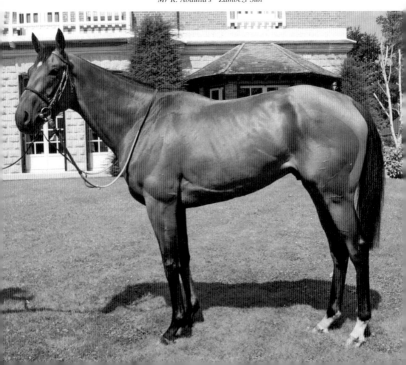

were sold to British yards without ever running for Bary, the latter successful three times at a mile and a half on the polytrack at Lingfield in the latest season. Zambezi Sun's two-year-old half-sister by Oasis Dream, Africana, is yet to race and the dam had another colt by Kahyasi in 2006. Bary was also the original trainer of the immediate family's best-known member Continent, who was out of a half-sister to Imbabala. The former July Cup and Prix de l'Abbaye winner was still capable of fairly useful form for David Nicholls at the age of ten in the latest season, winning twice in handicap company. Although the best of Imbabala's siblings was another smart French middle-distance performer Short Pause (later sold to contest the Melbourne Cup), there is by no means a lack of speed in the family, as Continent's presence suggests. Grandam Interval won the Prix Maurice de Gheest on her return to sprinting, after finishing third in the One Thousand Guineas. Interval was out of the Cambridgeshire winner Intermission who joined the Juddmonte broodmare band for 410,000 guineas at the December Sales in 1982. A half-sister to the Coronation Cup winner Quiet Fling out of the Blue Seal Stakes winner Peace, Intermission has two more half-sisters De Stael and Balabina who have founded their own successful branches of this family for Juddmonte. Details of Balabina's descendants can be found in the essay on her great-granddaughter Proviso, who is also by Dansili. Rail Link was denied the chance as a four-year-old to confirm his top-class effort in the Arc. Hopefully, the big, strong, good-topped Zambezi Sun, who has a round action, will at least have the opportunity to add to his success in the Grand Prix de Paris. Although already a Group 1 winner, Zambezi Sun is likely to need to improve to win more races at the top level. He stays a mile and a half and has raced mainly on good or good to firm ground, though he made his winning debut on good to soft. *P. Bary, France*

ZAMBOOZLE (IRE) 5 ch.g. Halling (USA) 133 – Blue Sirocco (Bluebird (USA) 125) [2007 86: 8.1g 10g 12d Jun 22] strong gelding: fair handicapper: stays easy 13f: acts on polytrack and good to firm going: held up: joined A. King, won over hurdles in October. *D. R. C. Elsworth*   **77**

ZAMELIANA 3 ch.f. Zaha (CAN) 106 – Amelia's Field 56 (Distant Relative 128) [2007 –: p7.1g⁵ 7d 8f 9.7m⁶ 11.7m p12g⁵ Nov 21] no sign of ability. *Dr J. R. J. Naylor*   **–**

ZAMHREAR 4 b.f. Singspiel (IRE) 133 – Lunda (IRE) 60 (Soviet Star (USA) 128) [2007 73: f8g⁴ Jan 7] fair handicapper: creditable effort only start at 4 yrs: stays 8.6f: acts on all-weather. *C. E. Brittain*   **69**

ZAM ZAMMAH 4 b.c. Agnes World (USA) 123 – Krisalya 98 (Kris 135) [2007 p8g* p8f³ 7g May 18] 160,000Y: closely related to smart 6f (at 2 yrs)/1m (Poule d'Essai des Pouliches) winner Rose Gypsy (by Green Desert) and 6f winner Day Star (by Dayjur) and half-brother to 3 winners: dam, 10.4f winner, half-sister to very smart 1¼m performer Sasuru: fairly useful form: reportedly suffered stress fracture to near-hind at 2 yrs: impressive when winning maiden at Lingfield in January: best effort when third to Gallantry in handicap there (again missed break and took strong hold): well held at Newmarket on turf debut final start: joined S. Woods in Hong Kong. *Sir Michael Stoute*   **93**

ZANDERIDO 5 b.g. Forzando 122 – Triple Concerto (Grand Lodge (USA) 125) [2007 f6g Jan 30] sturdy gelding: unreliable maiden: well held in seller only outing since 2005. *B. S. Rothwell*   **– §**

ZANDO 5 b.g. Forzando 122 – Rockin' Rosie 59 (Song 132) [2007 63: p9.5g³ p9.5g p9.5g f8g⁴ p10g Mar 26] big, good-topped gelding: modest performer: stays 9.5f: acts on all-weather, raced only on good going or firmer on turf: tried in cheekpieces/visor. *E. G. Bevan*   **52**

ZANIDA (IRE) 3 b.f. Mujadil (USA) 119 – Haraabah (USA) 99 (Topsider (USA)) [2007 91: 7.1d 7m 5g 6m Sep 13] tall, useful-looking filly: fairly useful performer: best effort at 3 yrs on second start: speedy, and likely to prove best at 5f/6f: acts on good to firm and good to soft going: blinkered last 2 starts. *K. R. Burke*   **86**

ZANJEER 7 b.g. Averti (IRE) 117 – Cloudslea (USA) (Chief's Crown (USA)) [2007 f7g 7m May 22] good-topped gelding: fair performer in 2005: unraced in 2006 and well held at 7 yrs: reportedly bled once in 2005. *N. Wilson*   **–**

ZANTERO 4 b.g. Danzero (AUS) – Cruinn A Bhord 107 (Inchinor 119) [2007 46: p7g p6g 7g 7.1s*ᵈⁱˢ p9.5g p8.6g Nov 27] modest performer: left W. M. Brisbourne after second outing: first past post in claimer at Chepstow in June, later disqualified after failing dope test: left M. Doyle after: stays 7f: acts on all-weather and firm going, best run on soft: tried blinkered: in cheekpieces/tongue tie last 2 starts. *K. M. Prendergast*   **62**

ZAP ATTACK 7 b.g. Zafonic (USA) 130 – Rappa Tap Tap (FR) 111 (Tap On Wood **56**
130) [2007 46: 6s⁶ 6m* 6f 6.9g Aug 22] close-coupled gelding: modest handicapper: won
at Thirsk (apprentices) in August: seemingly stays 8.6f: acts on fibresand and firm going:
tried in cheekpieces/tongue tie. *M. Brittain*

ZAPLAMATION (IRE) 2 b.c. (Apr 22) Acclamation 118 – Zapatista (Rainbow Quest **49**
(USA) 134) [2007 5f 6g 6f⁴ 6g 7.5m 6s⁵ 6s Oct 26] leggy colt: poor maiden: best at 5f/6f:
acts on firm and soft going. *D. W. Barker*

ZARABAD (IRE) 5 b.g. King's Best (USA) 132 – Zarannda (IRE) 112 (Last Tycoon **78**
131) [2007 77d: p7.1g* p7.1g³ p8.5f Apr 6] good-topped gelding: fair performer: won
handicap at Wolverhampton in February: stays 1m: acts on polytrack and firm going.
K. R. Burke

ZAREES 2 b.c. (Mar 11) Vettori (IRE) 119 – Night Mist (IRE) 82 (Alzao (USA) 117) **46**
[2007 6d 6g 8.1m p8m p6g⁶ Dec 4] poor maiden: left J. S. Moore after third start: should
stay 1m: tried visored. *Miss Gay Kelleway*

ZARENE 2 b.f. (Apr 8) Zaha (CAN) 106 – Polish Sprite (Danzig Connection (USA)) **–**
[2007 7s p8g Sep 19] good-bodied filly: second foal: dam unraced half-sister to Middle
Park Stakes winner Mon Tresor and smart sprinter Montendre: well held in maidens:
visored final start. *P. W. D'Arcy*

ZARKAVA (IRE) 2 b.f. (Mar 31) Zamindar (USA) 116 – Zarkasha (IRE) (Kahyasi **117 p**
130) [2007 8g* 8g* Oct 7]
    The Aga Khan isn't in the habit of pursuing lost causes but, from her retire-
ment in 1962 until her death in 1978, Petite Etoile, one of the best fillies to race in
Europe in the twentieth century, seemingly did little to justify her presence at stud
(though her brilliant racing career must have done more than enough to earn her life
membership of the Aga Khan's studs). From thirteen coverings she produced a
single minor winner from three surviving progeny including one unraced daughter
named (like the Aga Khan's own daughter) Zahra. Petite Etoile's broodmare career
has been described in print as 'a dismal failure' and 'a sad disappointment', but
such assessments are unlikely to be echoed by the Aga Khan. The mare is now in
the bottom line of the pedigrees of two fine fillies to have carried his colours, the
1998 Prix de Diane winner Zainta and Zarkava, whose striking success in the Prix
Marcel Boussac Royal Barriere de Deauville at Longchamp marked her down as
one of the leaders of her generation and a filly likely to develop into a formidable
opponent in the classics.
    Given her owner's claim after the Prix Marcel Boussac that 'We have
always held (Zarkava) in very high esteem' one is entitled to wonder why she was
not originally entered in the race. She was supplemented at a cost of €30,000, a
decision reportedly based not so much on her ready two-length, odds-on victory in
a nine-runner newcomers event on the same course early in September, but on a
piece of work at Chantilly racecourse fifteen days before the Marcel Boussac.
Trainer Alain de Royer Dupre described this as 'somptueux', which can be taken to
mean magnificent, a word which is equally applicable to Zarkava's performance on
Arc day. This was not one of the strongest renewals of France's top event for juvenile fillies. There were no pattern winners among the ten runners, Prestige Stakes
winner Sense of Joy having been pulled out earlier in the week due to injury and
unbeaten listed scorer Gipson Dessert withdrawn at the start after bursting out of
the stalls. Zarkava was second favourite behind Laureldean Gale, a creditable
second in the Prix du Calvados to Proviso, who had run in the Fillies' Mile at Ascot
in preference to Longchamp. The only other contenders with form in pattern
company were fourth favourite Mad About You, third in the Moyglare Stud Stakes
last time, and Sweet Solera Stakes runner-up Don't Forget Faith, who had been
soundly beaten subsequently in the May Hill Stakes. Runners with form in maiden
and/or minor events included Conference Call and Gagnoa from France, Queen
of Naples from Britain, Savethisdanceforme from Ireland and Peace Royale from
Germany.
    Gipson Dessert's antics at the start reportedly affected the favourite, who
was never going well, but this could not detract from the style of Zarkava's victory.
After waiting with her, Christophe Soumillon had to sit and suffer in seventh place
early in the straight, his mount on the rail with no sign of a gap, while Conference
Call made the best of her way home pursued by Mad About You. Eventually

Prix Marcel Boussac - Criterium des Pouliches Royal Barriere de Deauville, Longchamp—
Zarkava, on only her second start, quickens impressively once in the clear and wins going away
from Conference Call, Mad About You and Savethisdanceforme

extricated a furlong and a half out, Zarkava was switched outside and quickly responded. Producing a sparkling turn of foot, though she did flash her tail once under the whip, she made up five lengths on the leader, hit the front with eighty yards to go and won going away by two and a half lengths. Mad About You was a length and a half away third with the staying-on Savethisdanceforme, wide-margin winner of a listed race next time, fourth. Just after crossing the line Zarkava jumped a shadow, Soumillon taking the momentary problem in his stride. The post-race reaction of Zarkava's team was to say she would be put by for the season and trained for the Poule d'Essai des Pouliches—no mention was made of the One Thousand Guineas, though by the end of the year the filly was still being quoted at 7/1 joint favourite with Listen for that race by some British bookmakers. Rather surprisingly, in view of what had been said, Zarkava was entered for the Criterium International at Saint-Cloud almost a month after her big win, but she did not line up.

In terms of Zarkava's genetic make-up, Petite Etoile has exactly the same significance as any of the thirty-one other antecedents in the fifth generation of the pedigree. What counts principally with Zarkava is her sire and dam. She followed Darjina as the second Group 1 scorer of the year for the Aga Khan's family sired by Zamindar, who was also represented by Coquerelle, successful in the Prix Saint-Alary. Speed was Zamindar's defining characteristic and he used it to finish runner-up in the Prix Morny, though he showed he stayed a mile when fifth in the Two Thousand Guineas. He has had a slightly chequered career at stud, starting off at Banstead Manor but missing most of his third season there due to health problems, then spending two years in Florida standing at 5,000 dollars before being returned to his original base when his brother Zafonic died in 2002. Zamindar has now sired the same number of Group 1 winners as Zafonic, four, but from fewer than half the number of foals; Zafonic covered better mares in his seven seasons at stud at a fee of up to £30,000. Success as a stallion does not always correspond with the level of form shown on the racecourse, Zamindar being around a stone inferior to his brother. Zamindar's fee has now jumped from £7,000 to £15,000. Zamindar imparts more speed than stamina but a number of his better progeny have stayed further than a mile, including Coquerelle and Poule d'Essai des Pouliches winner Zenda, plus Corriolanus, Jubilation, Minds Locked and Victorian Order, all of whom won over at least a mile and a quarter.

			Gone West		Mr Prospector
		Zamindar (USA)	(b 1984)		Secrettame
		(b 1994)	Zaizafon		The Minstrel
Zarkava (IRE)			(ch 1982)		Mofida
(b.f. Mar 31, 2005)			Kahyasi		Ile de Bourbon
		Zarkasha (IRE)	(b 1985)		Kadissya
		(b 2000)	Zarkana		Doyoun
			(b 1992)		Zarna

Zarkava's dam Zarkasha did not race. By one of the Aga Khan's Derby winners, Kahyasi, a noted influence for stamina, she is also responsible for the unraced three-year-old Zarakiysha (by Kendor) and a yearling filly by Soviet Star and a colt foal by Azamour. Zarkasha's dam Zarkana won two small races at around a mile. Her other offspring include Zarkiya, successful in the Prix de Sandringham and now dead, and the listed-placed seven furlong/mile winner Zariyan, also succ-essful over jumps. Zarkana was sold for €75,000 at Deauville in December 2006, a bargain with the benefit of hindsight. The next dam Zarna was also a minor winner, dam of Prix d'Astarte runner-up Zarannda and a half-sister to the dam of the smart colt Zayyani, winner of the Greenham Stakes, and to the dam of Zainta. A colt by Sadler's Wells out of another daughter of Zarna was knocked down to Demi O'Byrne for 170,000 guineas at the Newmarket December Sales. Besides the Prix de Diane, Zainta, also a daughter of Kahyasi, won the Prix Saint-Alary and finished third in the Prix Vermeille. Zaiyad, Zainta's half-brother by Sadler's Wells, was in the news in the season under review as winner of two Grade 1 hurdle races including the Grande Course de Haies d'Auteuil. With or without opposition from Natagora and Proviso, Zarkava is likely to take some beating in the Poule d'Essai des Pouliches. There is sufficient stamina on the distaff side of the pedigree to suggest she should stay a mile and a quarter, the distance of the Prix de Diane, in which case she will be a tough opponent there as well. Perhaps the only question mark concerns Zarkava's apparently highly-strung temperament, seen in the Marcel Boussac and commented on by her connections. Provided her tendency to get on edge remains under control she looks set for a cracking three-year-old career. *A. de Royer Dupre, France*

ZAR SOLITARIO 3 b.c. Singspiel (IRE) 133 – Ginevra di Camelot (FR) (Alzao (USA) 117) [2007 69p: f8g² p8g* p10g* 10m* 10.5g* 12m May 20] sturdy colt: useful performer: progressed well in first half of 2007, winning maiden at Lingfield in February, handicaps at Kempton in March and Leicester (dead-heated with New Beginning but looked unlucky not to win outright after rider briefly took things easy) in April and listed race at Rome (made most, beat Rob's Love 2 lengths) later in month: failed to stay in Derby Italiano at Rome final start: stays 1¼m: raced only on all-weather and good to firm ground: sent to UAE. *M. Johnston*   **104**

ZARZU 8 b.g. Magic Ring (IRE) 115 – Rivers Rhapsody 104 (Dominion 123) [2007 83, a91: f6g² p6g p6g⁶ p6f² p6g⁶ p7g³ 6f f6g² f6g³ p6g Nov 2] close-coupled, good-topped gelding: fairly useful handicapper: effective at 5f/6f: acts on all-weather, firm and good to soft ground: tried in visor/cheekpieces: sometimes slowly away: held up. *C. R. Dore*   **–**   **a88**

ZASKAR 2 b.f. (May 6) Anabaa (USA) 130 – Bezzaaf 97 (Machiavellian (USA) 123) [2007 p6g* 7g⁶ 8d* Oct 23] €10,000Y: well-made filly: closely related to useful 6f (at 2 yrs)/7f winner Ans Bach (by Green Desert) and half-sister to 2 winners, including 3-y-o Zefooha: dam 1¼m winner: fair form: won maiden at Wolverhampton in September and nursery at Yarmouth (had bit in hand) in October: stays 1m: will progress further. *Tom Dascombe*   **75 p**

ZATO (IRE) 4 ch.g. Zafonic (USA) 130 – Top Table 65 (Shirley Heights 130) [2007 100: 10g⁵ 10g 8g⁶ p7g 8m 8f⁶ 8g 8.1m² 8.5d Jun 1] lengthy, useful-looking gelding: useful handicapper: stayed 1¼m: acted on polytrack, firm and soft going: held up: joined Venetia Williams: dead. *M. R. Channon*   **96**

ZAVILLE 5 gr.m. Zafonic (USA) 130 – Colleville 97 (Pharly (FR) 130) [2007 72: p13.9g f16s f14g⁵ 14.1m 16m 14.1m p13.9g⁶ p13.9g Oct 15] leggy mare: fair handi-capper in 2006: little form at 5 yrs: stays 1¾m: acts on polytrack and good to firm ground: in cheekpieces/blinkers. *J. O'Reilly*   **–**

ZAWARIQ (IRE) 3 b.f. Marju (IRE) 127 – Alikhlas 81 (Lahib (USA) 129) [2007 62p: 9.2s Sep 24] modest form in maiden at Lingfield at 2 yrs: well held in similar event at Hamilton only outing in 2007: sold 5,000 gns. *E. J. O'Neill*   **–**

ZAZOUS 6 b.g. Zafonic (USA) 130 – Confidentiality (USA) (Lyphard (USA) 132) [2007 68: p6g⁶ p7g⁶ p7g p7g⁴ p6g p6g⁴ p7g⁴ p7g 7m* p7g⁵ p7g² p6m⁵ p8m p7g Dec 29] well-made gelding: fair handicapper: won at Salisbury (ladies event) in May: stays 7f: acts on polytrack, soft and good to firm going: none too reliable. *J. J. Bridger*   **65**

ZED CANDY 8 b.g. Medicean 128 – Intrum Morshaan (IRE) 95 (Darshaan 133) [2007 71: f11g⁶ p11m⁶ Nov 11] leggy, angular gelding: fair form at 3 yrs, only modest in handicaps in 2007: stays 1½m: acts on fibresand and heavy going. *J. T. Stimpson*   **57**

ZEEUW (IRE) 3 b.g. Xaar 132 – Lucky Bet (IRE) 69 (Lucky Guest 109) [2007 70: 6m³ May 6] angular gelding: fair maiden, lightly raced: bred to be suited by 7f+. *D. J. Coakley*   **65**

ZEFOOHA (FR) 3 ch.f. Lomitas 129 – Bezzaaf 97 (Machiavellian (USA) 123) [2007 80p: 9.9g 8m 12.1m 14.1f³ 14.1g⁵ p12.2g² Nov 4] fair handicapper: left M. Channon 9,000 gns after second start: stays easy 1¾m: acts on polytrack and firm ground (unraced on going softer than good). *T. D. Walford*   **75**

ZELL (IRE) 4 b.f. Lend A Hand 124 – Skisette (Malinowski (USA) 123) [2007 65: 7.1m 9.1d² 9.2g Jun 20] modest maiden: stays 9f, at least when emphasis is on speed: acts on soft going: sometimes slowly away. *E. J. Alston* **57**

ZELOS (IRE) 3 b.g. Mujadil (USA) 119 – First Degree 50 (Sabrehill (USA) 120) [2007 66: p10g³ f8g⁴ p10g 10f⁶ 11.7d⁶ 8.1d 7d² 9m⁶ p8g* p8.6g³ 7d⁴ 8f² p8g⁵ 8m p8.6g² 10g* Oct 31] strong gelding: fairly useful performer: won claimer at Lingfield in July and, having been claimed from J. Osborne £10,000 after eleventh start, handicap at Nottingham (lady amateurs) in October: stays 1¼m: acts on polytrack and firm ground: usually wears blinkers: tongue tied for final win: held up: has shown signs of temperament: joined D. Bridgwater. *D. J. S. ffrench Davis* **80**

ZENDARO 5 b.g. Danzero (AUS) – Countess Maud (Mtoto 134) [2007 72, a63: p8.6g Aug 12] tall gelding: modest performer nowadays: stays 8.6f: acts on polytrack, firm and good to soft ground. *C. C. Bealby* **–**

ZEN FACTOR 2 b.g. (Apr 12) Josr Algarhoud (IRE) 118 – Zabelina (USA) 57 (Diesis 133) [2007 7s 7.6f⁴ 8d Oct 3] tall gelding: modest maiden: stays 7.6f: acts on firm going, well held on softer than good other starts. *J. G. Portman* **60**

ZEN GARDEN 6 b.m. Alzao (USA) 117 – Maze Garden (USA) (Riverman (USA) 131) [2007 11.9m 11.9m 10.3d 11.6m 14.1d Aug 26] stocky mare: little form. *W. M. Brisbourne* **–**

ZENNERMAN (IRE) 4 b.g. Observatory (USA) 131 – Precocious Miss (USA) 88 (Diesis 133) [2007 87: 7.1m⁵ 7g⁴ 7.9d p7.1g* 7.1m⁶ p8.6g 7.5m³ 7m p8g⁶ p7.1g² f8d⁶ Dec 14] smallish, strong gelding: fairly useful handicapper: won at Wolverhampton in July: left K. Ryan prior to final outing: stays 1m: acts on polytrack, firm and good to soft going: often in cheekpieces/blinkered: held up. *Miss J. E. Foster* **82**

ZERKY (USA) 2 b.f. (Jan 30) Kingmambo (USA) 125 – Penny's Valentine (USA) (Storm Cat (USA)) [2007 7g 7m 8.1s³ Sep 29] $300,000Y: good-topped filly: type to carry condition: sister to 2 winners, including smart 1m/8.5f (including in France and 2 US Grade 3 events) winner Penny's Gold, and half-sister to 2 US winners: dam, 6.5f (in France at 2 yrs) to 8.5f (in US) winner, out of Cheveley Park, Prix de Diane and Prix Vermeille winner Mrs Penny: modest form in maidens, third to Badalona at Haydock: stays 1m: acts on soft and good to firm going. *E. A. L. Dunlop* **64**

ZERO COOL (USA) 3 b. or br.c. Forestry (USA) 121 – Fabulous (USA) (Seeking The Gold (USA)) [2007 8d⁶ p8g² 8.3d* 10d³ p8g Dec 30] $700,000Y: big, close-coupled, good-topped colt: third foal: half-brother to winner in USA by Wild Again: dam, ran once in USA, out of US Grade 1 8.5f/9f winner and Breeders' Cup Distaff runner-up Gorgeous: fairly useful form: won maiden at Windsor in October: good third on handicap debut there next time: left J. Gosden 37,000 gns prior to final start: stays 1¼m: raced only on polytrack and good to soft going. *G. L. Moore* **90**

ZERO TOLERANCE (IRE) 7 ch.g. Nashwan (USA) 135 – Place de L'Opera 98 (Sadler's Wells (USA) 132) [2007 113: 8s 8m 8g⁴ 8s⁵ 9.9g 9m 10s⁶ 8g Nov 3] lengthy, workmanlike gelding: useful performer nowadays: standout effort at 7 yrs when fourth to Blythe Knight in listed handicap at York: pulled up amiss in Cambridgeshire at Newmarket on sixth start: stays 1¼m: has form on fibresand and good to firm going, best efforts (including 7 of 8 wins) on softer than good: tends to carry head awkwardly: freegoing sort, usually front runner. *T. D. Barron* **108 d**

ZEU TIN TIN (IRE) 2 b.f. (Feb 14) Where Or When (IRE) 124 – Littleton Arwen (USA) 94 (Bahri (USA) 125) [2007 7m³ 7m³ 7m⁴ a6g³ Nov 18] €80,000Y: sparely-made filly: first foal: dam, 2-y-o 7f winner, out of close relation to Irish 1000 Guineas winner Ensconse: fairly useful maiden: in frame all starts, best effort when fourth of 22 to Lush Lashes in very valuable sales race at the Curragh (final outing for R. Kvisla): will stay 1m. *Yvonne Durant, Sweden* **89**

ZEYDNAA (IRE) 7 b.g. Bahhare (USA) 122 – Hadawah (USA) 68 (Riverman (USA) 131) [2007 57: 15.8m May 8] close-coupled gelding: modest handicapper: below form only start at 7 yrs: stays 2m: acts on firm and good to soft going. *C. R. Wilson* **–**

ZHEBE 2 br.c. (Feb 7) Dr Fong (USA) 128 – Krajina (FR) 109 (Holst (USA) 119) [2007 7g p8.6g³ Nov 27] 14,000Y: seventh foal: half-brother to French 1¼m/11f winner Sobinka (by Sadler's Wells) and winner in US by Kaldoun: dam, French 1¼m winner, half-sister to US Grade 1 9f winner Tuzla: better effort when third to Hilbre Court in minor event at Wolverhampton (tongue tied): will be suited by 1¼m: should improve further. *P. J. McBride* **69 p**

Bluesquare.com Stewards' Cup (Handicap), Goodwood—the action unfolds down the middle of the track and Zidane (stripes) comes from well back to collar the previous year's winner Borderlescott (No.3), Knot In Wood (blaze) and That's Hot

ZHITOMIR 9 ch.g. Lion Cavern (USA) 117 – Treasure Trove (USA) 62 (The Minstrel **59** (CAN) 135) [2007 70: 7m² 7m 7d⁵ 8s⁴ 7m 7g 8m³ p9.5g Sep 27] strong gelding: modest handicapper nowadays: effective at 7f to easy 8.6f: acts on polytrack, heavy and good to firm going: has run well when edgy/sweating: sold 800 gns. *M. Dods*

ZIA ZABEL (IRE) 2 b.f. (Apr 23) Rock of Gibraltar (IRE) 133 – Blu Meltemi (ITY) **60** 103 (Star Shareef 105) [2007 8g Oct 26] leggy filly: half-sister to 3 winners in Italy, including useful performer up to 11f Miss Meltemi (by Miswaki Tern), 7.5f/1m winner at 2 yrs: dam Italian 9f (at 2 yrs) to 10.5f winner and second in Oaks d'Italia: 25/1 and burly, mid-field in maiden at Doncaster won by Cruel Sea. *J. L. Dunlop*

ZIBELINE (IRE) 10 b.g. Cadeaux Genereux 131 – Zia (USA) 88 (Shareef Dancer **60** (USA) 135) [2007 79: p16g² 10s 12.9g⁶ Sep 1] tall gelding: just modest performer in 2007, leaving B. Ellison after reappearance: stays 2¼m, effective at 1½m: acts on firm going, probably not on softer than good: often wears cheekpieces/blinkers, also tongue tied on reappearance: held up: sometimes pulls hard. *J. J. Lambe, Ireland*

ZIDANE 5 b.g. Danzero (AUS) – Juliet Bravo 61 (Glow (USA)) [2007 99p: p7g⁴ 6s* 6d **112** 6m* 6g⁴ 6d 6m Nov 10] lengthy gelding: smart performer: much improved again at 5 yrs, winning handicaps at Ascot in May and Goodwood (beat Borderlescott a short head in Bluesquare.com Stewards' Cup, quickening smartly to lead on line) in August: good fourth to Haatef in Diadem Stakes at Ascot next time: better than bare result in Bentinck Stakes at Newmarket (raced on wrong side) and listed race at Doncaster (denied clear run when eighth of 13 to Galeota) last 2 starts: likely to prove best around 6f: acts on polytrack, soft and good to firm going: waited with, and best in well-run race. *J. R. Fanshawe*

ZIFAAF (USA) 3 b.f. Silver Hawk (USA) 123 – Muklah (IRE) 101 (Singspiel (IRE) **77** 133) [2007 8m² p8g⁵ 9g² 10m⁴ 9s² 8f² 8d* Aug 19] small filly: first foal: dam, 2-y-o 7f winner, half-sister to useful sprinter Khasayl: fair performer: runner-up 4 times prior to winning maiden at Pontefract in August: stayed 1¼m: acted on firm and good to soft going: visits Dubai Destination. *B. W. Hills*

ZILLI 3 ch.f. Zilzal (USA) 137 – Zizi (IRE) 87 (Imp Society (USA)) [2007 45: p5.1g **48** p7f⁴ p10g⁴ 10d 8d Oct 30] poor maiden: stays 7f: raced only on polytrack and good to soft going: sold 3,200 gns. *N. P. Littmoden*

1198

ZIL UP 3 ch.c. Zilzal (USA) 137 – Sharpthorne (USA) 91 (Sharpen Up 127) [2007 f8g **49** p6g⁴ f7g⁵ p6g Jun 25] poor maiden: tongue tied: blinkered since debut. *S. R. Bowring*

ZIMBALI 5 ch.m. Lahib (USA) 129 – Dawn 70 (Owington 54: 5g 5.1g **52** 5.3m³ 5.5s⁵ 5.1m Aug 9] small mare: modest performer: effective at 5f/6f: acts on firm and soft going, little form on all-weather: tried in cheekpieces: races up with pace. *J. M. Bradley*

ZINGING 8 b.g. Fraam 114 – Hi Hoh (IRE) (Fayruz 116) [2007 51§, a54§: 10d⁶ 10s 9m **40 §** 7g 10f³ Aug 5] small gelding: poor performer: stays 1¼m: acts on all-weather, firm and soft going: usually blinkered/visored: has been tongue tied: ungenuine. *J. J. Bridger*

ZIPPI JAZZMAN (USA) 2 ch.c. (Mar 12) Dixieland Band (USA) – Redeem (USA) **80** (Devil's Bag (USA)) [2007 5g³ 5m² p5.1g* p5g⁴ 6m 5.1m³ Oct 14] well-made colt: fairly useful performer: won maiden at Wolverhampton in July: in frame in nurseries at Lingfield (blinkered) and Bath: best at 5f: acts on polytrack and good to firm going. *R. M. Beckett*

ZIRKEL (IRE) 4 br.g. Highest Honor (FR) 124 – Mythical Creek (USA) (Pleasant Tap **65** (USA)) [2007 73: p12g 10s⁵ 11.5m⁴ Aug 10] workmanlike gelding: fair maiden: stays 1½m: acts on good to firm ground, probably not on soft: joined A. King, won over hurdles in December. *Mrs A. L. M. King*

ZIZOU (IRE) 4 b.g. Fantastic Light (USA) 134 – Search Committee (USA) (Roberto **–** (USA) 131) [2007 61d: p10g f11g Mar 6] neat gelding: maiden: well held at 4 yrs: tried in visor/cheekpieces/tongue tie: won over hurdles in April. *J. J. Bridger*

ZOMERLUST 5 b.g. Josr Algarhoud (IRE) 118 – Passiflora 75 (Night Shift (USA)) **105** [2007 105: 7m⁶ 6m⁵ 7s 6g² 7m² 6v² 7m 6s* 6m⁶ 6d 6d 6g Oct 26] good-topped gelding: useful handicapper: won quite valuable event at York (by ¾ length from Turnkey) in July: respectable efforts at best after: best at 6f/7f: acts on heavy and good to firm going: visored last 5 starts: usually held up: tough. *J. J. Quinn*

ZONERGEM 9 ch.g. Zafonic (USA) 130 – Anasazi (IRE) (Sadler's Wells (USA) 132) **99** [2007 97: 9.9g² 10m Sep 13] good-topped gelding: useful handicapper: hasn't won since 2002: good second to Ravarino at Beverley: below form only other start at 9 yrs: stays easy 1½m: acts on polytrack and firm going: tried blinkered, often wears cheekpieces: has been slowly away/carried head high/found little: usually held up: quirky. *Lady Herries*

ZONIC BOOM (FR) 7 ch.g. Zafonic (USA) 130 – Rosi Zambotti (IRE) 104 (Law **58** Society (USA) 130) [2007 –: 9.9m 14.1m p16.5g* p13.9g 16.2m Aug 27] modest handicapper nowadays: won apprentice event at Wolverhampton in July: stays easy 2m: acts on polytrack, firm and good to soft going: tried blinkered/in cheekpieces/tongue tied. *Heather Dalton*

ZONTA ZITKALA 3 gr.f. Daylami (IRE) 138 – Sioux Chef 78 (Be My Chief (USA) **76** 122) [2007 76: 6m* 8m 7m⁶ 7g 8.3m⁴ 8.1g Oct 2] lengthy filly: fair handicapper: reportedly sustained slight fracture to knee after final 2-y-o start: won maiden at Pontefract in May: stays 1m: raced only on good ground or firmer: sent to Spain. *R. M. Beckett*

ZOOM ONE 3 ch.c. In The Wings 128 – Seyooll (IRE) 78 (Danehill (USA) 126) [2007 **89** 82p: 9.9m³ 12d 11m 9g a5f Dec 21] sturdy colt: type to carry condition: has a round action: fairly useful performer: left M. Tregoning before final start: had given impression he'd be suited by 1½m (refused to settle when tried): acts on good to firm and good to soft ground. *D. J. Selvaratnam, UAE*

ZOWINGTON 5 gr.g. Zafonic (USA) 130 – Carmela Owen (Owington 123) [2007 **93** 104: 6g 5m⁴ 5m⁴ 5d Jul 6] quite good-topped gelding: just fairly useful handicapper at 5 yrs: raced only at 5f/6f: acts on polytrack and good to soft going, probably on good to firm: blinkered final start: has started slowly/hung left: none too reliable: gelded. *C. F. Wall*

The following unraced horses appeared in ante-post lists for 2008 classics or had a Group 1 entry at two years, and are included for information purposes.

AL BARIZ (USA) 2 b.c. (Mar 12) Johannesburg (USA) 127 – Circuit City (IRE) (Exit To Nowhere (USA) 122) $270,000Y: second foal: half-brother to French 2006 2-y-o 7.5f winner Flash Ram (by Langfuhr): dam, French 1¼m winner, half-sister to Poule d'Essai des Pouliches runner-up Karmifira and French performer up to 15f Karmousil, both smart. *P. W. Chapple-Hyam*

AMAAKIN (USA) 2 b.c. (Apr 12) Gone West (USA) – Pink Coral (IRE) 104 (Sadler's Wells (USA) 132) $375,000Y: third foal: dam, Irish 2-y-o 1m winner (stayed 1½m), out of half-sister to Teenoso. *P. W. Chapple-Hyam*

CHARISMATIC (IRE) 2 b.f. (Jan 28) Galileo (IRE) 134 – Darling (Darshaan 133) €300,000Y: second foal: dam unraced close relation of useful 1½m performer Shemozzle. *J. Noseda*

CROP OVER (USA) 2 b.c. (Apr 22) Danzig (USA) – Vantive (USA) (Mr Prospector (USA)) $180,000Y, 245,000 2-y-o: fifth foal: brother to 4-y-o Waseema and US 8.5f minor stakes winner Pitamakan and half-brother to a winning US sprinter by Deputy Minister: dam, French 1m winner, closely related to useful 1¼m performers Island of Silver and Lord Charmer, from family of Green Desert (by Danzig). *M. Johnston*

DECREE (IRE) 2 b.c. (Feb 21) Pivotal 124 – Truly A Dream (IRE) 116 (Darshaan 133) 130,000Y: half-brother to several winners, including smart Irish 1m winner Catcher In The Rye (by Danehill), fairly useful 5.5f (in UAE) and 7f (in Britain at 2 yrs) winner Indian Dreamer (by Indian Ridge) and 3-y-o Envisage: dam, French/Canadian 1m (at 2 yrs) to winner, half-sister to smart 15f winner Wareed and to dam of Prix Saint-Alary winner Cerulean Sky. *A. P. O'Brien, Ireland*

EGYPTIAN HERO (USA) 2 b.c. (Jan 24) Danzig (USA) – Al Theraab (USA) 81 (Roberto (USA) 131) $5,200,000Y: closely related to several winners, including smart Irish 2004 2-y-o 1m winner Albert Hall (later successful in South Africa) and useful French 6f/7f winner Algallarens (both by Danehill) and half-brother to 2 useful winners, including 7f (at 2 yrs) to 8.5f winner Flightly Fellow (by Flying Spur): dam 1m winner (best at 1¼m). *A. P. O'Brien, Ireland*

EMIRATES HOLIDAYS (USA) 2 br.c. (May 3) Forestry (USA) 121 – Prospinsky (USA) (Mr Prospector (USA)) $475,000Y: eighth foal: brother to US 6f winner Tongass and half-brother to several winners in USA, including 8.5f/9f stakes winner Spin Control (by A P Indy): dam, ran 3 times in US, out of US Grade 2 9f winner Nikishka, herself half-sister to US Grade 1 winner Ida Delia. *Saeed bin Suroor*

EMPOWERED (IRE) 2 b.c. (Feb 8) Hawk Wing (USA) 120 – Funsie (FR) (Saumarez 132) 30,000F, 110,000Y: second foal: half-brother to 3-y-o Authorized: dam unraced half-sister to smart French performer up to 12.5f Brooklyn's Dance, herself dam of Prix du Jockey Club runner-up Prospect Park. *P. W. Chapple-Hyam*

GENTLE ON MY MIND (IRE) 2 b.f. (Mar 12) Sadler's Wells (USA) 132 – Ezilla (IRE) (Darshaan 133) €265,000F, 380,000Y: fifth foal: sister to smart Irish 1m to 1½m winner Ezima: dam unraced sister to smart Irish performer up to 1½m Ebaziya, herself dam of Gold Cup winner Enzeli, Irish Oaks/Prix Royal-Oak winner Ebadiyla and Moyglare Stud Stakes winner Edabiya. *A. P. O'Brien, Ireland*

HONORIA (IRE) 2 b.f. (Apr 8) Sadler's Wells (USA) 132 – Tedarshana (Darshaan 133) fourth foal: dam, useful French 1½m winner, sister to smart US 1¼m/1½m performer The Key Rainbow, out of half-sister to US Grade 1 7f (at 2 yrs) to 9f winner Ogyian. *A. P. O'Brien, Ireland*

ICY COOL (IRE) 2 b.c. (Jan 23) Galileo (IRE) 134 – Epping 81 (Charnwood Forest (IRE) 125) €380,000Y: second foal: brother to 4-y-o The Last Drop: dam, 7f winner from 3 starts, closely related to smart performer up to 1¾m Self Defense, out of half-sister to Irish Oaks winner Princess Pati and high-class 1½m performer Seymour Hicks. *J. Noseda*

MYANMAR (IRE) 2 ch.c. (Mar 13) Rock of Gibraltar (IRE) 133 – Bold As Love (Lomond (USA) 128) €290,000F: half-brother to 3 winners, including smart 2000 2-y-o 5f winner Misty Eyed (by Paris House) and fairly useful 1999 2-y-o 5f winner Travesty of Law (by Case Law): dam unraced. *J. Noseda*

MY DARK ROSALEEN 2 b.f. (Mar 17) Sadler's Wells (USA) 132 – Danilova (USA) (Lyphard (USA) 132) sister to useful Irish 2004 2-y-o 6f/7f winner (stayed 1½m) Silk And Scarlet and half-sister to 3 winners, notably smart 6f/7f performer Danger Over (by Warning): dam unraced half-sister to Prix du Jockey Club winner Sanglamore, out of Ribblesdale Stakes winner Ballinderry. *A. P. O'Brien, Ireland*

NATIONAL HERITAGE 2 b.c. (Apr 29) High Chaparral (IRE) 132 – French Quartet (IRE) (Lycius (USA) 124) 130,000Y: fifth foal: closely related to 1¼m winner Thebestis-yettocome (by Montjeu) and 1¼m winner Silver Palace (by Night Shift): dam, Irish maiden, half-sister to smart dam of Luso, Warrsan and Needle Gun. *A. P. O'Brien, Ireland*

OPTIMO MAXIMO (USA) 2 b.c. (Apr 5) Kingmambo (USA) 125 – Legend Maker (IRE) 111 (Sadler's Wells (USA) 132) seventh foal: brother to 1000 Guineas winner Virginia Waters (also Irish 2-y-o 7f winner) and half-brother to Irish 2002 2-y-o 1m winner Chevalier and 3-y-o Alexander of Hales, latter 2 smart by Danehill: dam French 10.5f and 1½m winner. *A. P. O'Brien, Ireland*

PURE SONG 2 b.f. (Feb 27) Singspiel (IRE) 133 – Pure Grain 121 (Polish Precedent (USA) 131) seventh foal: half-sister to several winners, including smart 7f (at 2 yrs) and 10.5f winner Goncharova (by Gone West) and useful 1¼m winner Grain of Truth (by Gulch), later successful in USA: dam 7f (Prestige Stakes at 2 yrs) to 1½m (Irish/Yorkshire Oaks) winner. *J. L. Dunlop*

ROYAL DESTINATION (IRE) 2 b.c. (Apr 7) Dubai Destination (USA) 127 – Royale (IRE) 102 (Royal Academy (USA) 130) 190,000Y: fifth foal: half-brother to 3 winners, including fairly useful 1¼m winner Love Appeal (by Singspiel) and 6f winner Maysarah (by Green Desert): dam Irish 7f/1m winner. *J. Noseda*

SEMAPHORE 2 b.f. (May 5) Zamindar (USA) 116 – Blue Duster (USA) 118 (Danzig (USA)) half-sister to 1¼m winners Blue Leader (fairly useful, by Cadeaux Genereux) and Blue Symphony (by Darshaan): dam, 5f (at 2 yrs) to 7f winner, including Cheveley Park Stakes, sister to Middle Park winner Zieten. *M. A. Jarvis*

ZULU CHIEF (USA) 2 b.c. (Apr 7) Fusaichi Pegasus (USA) 130 – La Lorgnette (CAN) (Val de L'Orne (FR) 133) brother to smart 7f (at 2 yrs) to 9.5f winner Race For The Stars, closely related to 3 winners, notably top-class 7f (at 2 yrs) to 1¼m (Eclipse Stakes) winner Hawk Wing (by Woodman) and half-brother to 2 US winners: dam champion 3-y-o filly in Canada. *A. P. O'Brien, Ireland*

ERRATA & ADDENDA
'Racehorses of 2005'

Mystical Ayr	Sobriety is by **Namaqualand**

'Racehorses of 2006'

Introduction	p5 line 40 – The Government effectively nationalised the Tote in **2003**
Dylan Thomas	p323 line 11 – had been the **longest**-priced favourite in the period since 1962
Foursquare Flyer	reinstated as winner at Wolverhampton after an appeal
Hurricane Run	p491 2nd paragraph Kris Kin won the Derby in **2003**
Island Prince	was **not** dead
Kilgary	put back to second at Wolverhampton after an appeal
p14	Trainers (1,2,3 earnings): J. Noseda **33** indiv winners, **46** races won, **18.5%** Stakes **£1,209,333**
Red Clubs	extended pedigree – sire of Miss Cindy is Mansingh
Rising Cross	p892 line 2: Prestige Stakes at **Goodwood**
Speciosa	p1012 line 8: earned her trainer Pam Sly the distinction of becoming the first **British** woman officially credited with training a classic winner in Britain. Also in Introduction p10 line 2: officially trained by a **British** woman (Criquette Head was the first woman officially to train a British classic winner)
Yeats	p1172 2 lines from bottom: since Solario **eighty** years before

PROMISING HORSES

Selected British-trained horses (plus those trained by Aidan O'Brien) with either a p or P in *Racehorses of 2007* are listed under their trainers for 2008.

R. M. BECKETT
Fr Dominic (USA) 2 b.c   90p
Look Here 2 b.f   84p
Without A Prayer (IRE) 2 ch.c   98p

M. L. W. BELL
Redford (IRE) 2 b.c   88p
Highland Legacy 3 ch.c   99p

J. R. BEST
Hucking Heist 3 b.g   80p

H. CANDY
Corrybrough 2 ch.c   94p

H. R. A. CECIL
Crystany (IRE) 2 b.f   98p
Jack Dawkins (USA) 2 b.c   97p
Kandahar Run 2 gr.c   106p
Rattan (USA) 2 ch.c   85p
Sterope (FR) 2 b.f   —P
Timetable 2 b.c   88p
Tomintoul Flyer 2 br.c   90p
Twice Over 2 b.c   104P
Unleashed (IRE) 2 br.c   85p
Multidimensional (IRE) 4 b.c   118p

M. R. CHANNON
Atlantic Sport (USA) 2 b.c   98p
Better Hand (IRE) 2 b.c   94p
Missit (IRE) 2 b.f   101p
Nahoodh (IRE) 2 gr.f   116p
Nijoom Dubai 2 b.f   104p

P. W. CHAPPLE-HYAM
Cape Amber (IRE) 2 b.f   95p
Fireside 2 b.c   97p
Glorious Gift (IRE) 2 b.c   86p
Orientalist Art 2 b.c   85p
Shallal 2 b.c   101p
Western Art (USA) 2 b.c   100p
Whistledownwind 2 b.c   93p
Winker Watson 2 ch.c   117p

R. CHARLTON
Bencoolen (IRE) 2 b.c   88p
Colorado Blue (IRE) 2 ch.g   85p
Cuban Missile 2 b.g   87p
Melodramatic (IRE) 2 b.f   92p
Oarsman 2 ch.c   80p
Prime Exhibit 2 b.c   94P
Scuffle 2 gr.f   77P
Trenchtown (IRE) 2 b.c   94p

P. F. I. COLE
General Eliott (IRE) 2 b.c   87p
James Dean (IRE) 2 b.c   83p
Moynahan (USA) 2 ch.c   104p
Strategic Mission (IRE) 2 b.c   91p

C. G. COX
Beacon Lodge (IRE) 2 b.c   107p
Jimmy Styles 3 ch.g   102p

L. M. CUMANI
Savarain 2 b.c   87p
Sky Dive 2 ch.c   92p
Bankable (IRE) 3 b.c   97p
Boz 3 gr.c   92p
Mad Rush (USA) 3 b.c   103p
Speed Gifted 3 b.c   114p
Watchful (IRE) 3 b.f   94p
Swop (IRE) 4 b.g   95p

TOM DASCOMBE
Max One Two Three (IRE) 2 b.f   102p

E. A. L. DUNLOP
Last Three Minutes (IRE) 2 b.c   88p
Malibu Girl (USA) 2 b.f   81p
Pinkindie (USA) 2 ch.c   87p
Broomielaw 3 ch.c   98p
Royal Jasra 3 b.c   87p

J. L. DUNLOP
Dona Alba (IRE) 2 b.f   91p
Festivale (IRE) 2 b.f   90p
Mountain Pride (IRE) 2 b.c   93p
Muthabara (IRE) 2 b.f   104p
Presbyterian Nun (IRE) 2 b.f   86p

D. R. C. ELSWORTH
Classic Fortune (IRE) 2 b.c   87p
French Art 2 ch.c   89p
Lazy Days 2 ch.c   82P
Pathos (GER) 3 b.g   101p
Silver Suitor (IRE) 3 b.g   97p
Viva Vettori 3 ch.c   89p

J. R. FANSHAWE
Prevailing Wind 2 b.c   81P
Spacious 2 b.f   106p
Street Star (USA) 2 b.f   84p

J. H. M. GOSDEN
Bronze Cannon (USA) 2 b.c   93p
Dar Re Mi 2 b.f   73P
Infallible 2 b.f   81P
Made To Ransom 2 b.c   93p
Michita (USA) 2 b.f   84p
Mukhber 2 br.g   92p
Queen of Naples 2 b.f   94p
Raven's Pass (USA) 2 ch.c   125p
Sense of Joy 2 b.f   108P
Pipedreamer 3 b.c   120p

W. J. HAGGAS
Alfathaa 2 b.c   104p
Aqlaam 2 b.c   93p
Collection (IRE) 2 b.c   87p
Majeen 2 ch.c   83p
Roaring Forte (IRE) 2 b.c   89P
Wise Melody 2 b.f   82p
Eco Centrism 3 ch.c   81p
Musaalem (USA) 3 gr.g   80P

R. HANNON
Chartist 2 ch.c 86p
Paco Boy (IRE) 2 b.c 98p
Redesignation (IRE) 2 b.c 89p
Grande Caiman (IRE) 3 ch.c 100p
Malt Or Mash (USA) 3 gr.c 114p

P. C. HASLAM
Choose Your Moment 2 b.c 99p
River Ardeche 2 b.g 82p

B. W. HILLS
Cigalas 2 ch.g 82p
Cruel Sea (USA) 2 gr.f 86P
Foolin Myself 2 b.c 87p
Hawaana (IRE) 2 b.c 87p
Mookhlesa 2 b.f 94p
Moville (IRE) 2 b.g 84p
Porthole (USA) 2 gr.c 84p
Striking Spirit 2 b.c 98p
Sugar Mint (IRE) 2 b.f 99p
Zaahid (IRE) 3 ch.c 103p

P. HOWLING
Generous Thought 2 b.c 92p

M. A. JARVIS
Al Cobra (IRE) 2 b.f 70P
All The Aces (IRE) 2 b.c 86p
Ancien Regime (IRE) 2 b.c 98p
Cool Judgement (IRE) 2 b.c 81p
Elysee Palace (IRE) 2 b.f 80p
First Avenue 2 b.c 88p
Kal Barg 2 b.c 98p
Makaaseb (USA) 2 b.f 96p
Royalist (IRE) 2 b.c 85p
Sortita (GER) 2 b.f 81p
Speedy Dollar (USA) 2 b.c 93p
Tasdeer (USA) 2 b.c 90p
Tawaash (USA) 2 b.c 90p
Tighnabruaich (IRE) 2 b.c 80p
Black Rock (IRE) 3 ch.c 102p
Rose Street (IRE) 3 b.f 94p

M. JOHNSTON
Age of Reason (UAE) 2 b.g 90p
Arctic Cape 2 b.c 89p
Call of Duty (IRE) 2 br.c 81p
Captain Webb 2 br.c 83p
Detonator (IRE) 2 b.g 85p
Endless Luck (USA) 2 b.c 93p
Flight To Quality 2 ch.c 84p
Grand Fleet 2 b.g 84p
Harlem Shuffle (UAE) 2 br.f 80p
Hawaass (USA) 2 b.c 89p
Jadaara 2 b.f 90p
Love Galore (IRE) 2 b.c 92p
Mafioso 2 b.c 88p
Missioner (USA) 2 b.c 85p
Planetarium 2 gr.c 99p
Red And White (IRE) 2 b.f 91p
Robby Bobby 2 ch.c 92p
Zakhaaref 2 gr.c 93p
Colorado Rapid (IRE) 3 b.c 105p
Greyfriars Abbey 3 b.g 81p

A. KING
Manyriverstocross (IRE) 2 b.c 58P

P. J. MCBRIDE
Jeninsky (USA) 2 ch.f 90p

B. J. MEEHAN
Cat Junior (USA) 2 b.c 100P
Classic Legend 2 b.f 92p
Exclamation 2 br.c 107p
Film Maker (IRE) 2 b.c 87p
Hilbre Court (USA) 2 b.c 85p
Hurricane Hymnbook (USA) 2 b.c 96p
Inventor (IRE) 2 b.c 83p
Masada (IRE) 2 br.f 85p
North Parade 2 b.c 94p
Skadrak (USA) 2 ch.c 96p
Swift Gift 2 b.c 85p

H. MORRISON
Rock Peak (IRE) 2 b.c 79P
Stimulation (IRE) 2 b.c 113p
Wing Play (IRE) 2 b.c 84p

D. J. MURPHY
Bright Falcon 2 ch.c 88p
Internationaldebut (IRE) 2 b.c 89p

D. NICHOLLS
Cape Vale (IRE) 2 b.c 88p
Inxile (IRE) 2 b.g 94p
Northern Bolt 2 b.c 92p
Van Bossed (CAN) 2 ch.g 82p
Valery Borzov (IRE) 3 b.g 89p

J. NOSEDA
Captain Brilliance (USA) 2 ch.c 96p
Forgotten Voice (IRE) 2 b.c 89p
Lemon N Sugar (USA) 2 b.f 82p
Messias Da Silva (USA) 2 b.f 89p
Meydan Princess (IRE) 2 b.f 80p
The Which Doctor 2 b.g 85p
Kafuu (IRE) 3 b.c 91p
Milne Graden 3 b.g 97p
Valrhona (IRE) 3 b.f 93p

A. P. O'BRIEN, IRELAND
Alessandro Volta 2 b.c 101p
Frozen Fire (GER) 2 b.c 90p
Halfway To Heaven (IRE) 2 gr.f 94p
Jupiter Pluvius (USA) 2 b.c 105p
Kingdom of Naples (USA) 2 b.c 95p
King of Rome (IRE) 2 b.c 95p
Kitty Matcham (IRE) 2 b.f 102p
Listen (IRE) 2 b.f 117p
One Great Cat (USA) 2 br.c 108p
Plan (USA) 2 ch.c 97p
Psalm (IRE) 2 b.f 83P
Savethisdanceforme (IRE) 2 b.f 108p
Vivaldi (IRE) 2 b.c 86p
Washington Irving (IRE) 2 b.c 75P
You'resothrilling (USA) 2 b.f 103p

E. J. O'NEILL
Haybrook 2 b.c 88p

MRS A. J. PERRETT
Foresight 2 ch.c 81p
Mystery Sail (USA) 2 b.f 80p
Sharp Dresser (USA) 3 ch.f 80p

1203

R. T. PHILLIPS
Whenever 3 ch.c 94p

JAMIE POULTON
Whitcombe Minister (USA) 2 b.c 87p

SIR MARK PRESCOTT
Fandangerina 2 b.f 81p
Points of View 2 b.g 89p
Caravel (IRE) 3 ch.g 97p
Alma Mater 4 b.f 102p

K. A. RYAN
Alexander Castle (USA) 2 b.c 108p
Errigal Lad 2 ch.g 86p

SIR MICHAEL STOUTE
Adversity 2 b.c 89p
Albaraari 2 b.f 79p
Almajd (IRE) 2 b.c 99p
Ascot Lime 2 ch.c 77P
Autocue 2 b.c 90p
Colony (IRE) 2 b.c 79p
Conduit (IRE) 2 ch.c 86p
Confidence Trick (USA) 2 ch.c 90p
Confront 2 b.c 116p
Doctor Fremantle 2 b.c 91p
Dr Faustus (IRE) 2 gr.c 98p
French Riviera 2 b.c 85p
Institute 2 ch.c 84p
Laughter (IRE) 2 b.f 87P
Lindelaan (USA) 2 ch.f 80p
Maramba (USA) 2 ch.f 97p
Mistress Greeley (USA) 2 ch.f 83p
Naval Review (USA) 2 b.c 87p
Patkai (IRE) 2 ch.c 79p
Perfect Stride 2 b.c 97p
Quotation 2 b.f 83p
Seasider 2 b.c 95p
Tajaaweed (USA) 2 br.c 91p
Tanweer (USA) 2 ch.g 88p
Tartan Bearer (IRE) 2 ch.c 87p
Hi Calypso (IRE) 3 b.f 114p
King's Event (USA) 3 b.c 98p
Lang Shining (IRE) 3 ch.c 103p
Praxiteles (IRE) 3 b.c 90P
Spanish Moon (USA) 3 b.c 104p

SAEED BIN SUROOR
Calming Influence (IRE) 2 b.c 100P
Etosha (IRE) 2 b.c 69p
Floristry 2 b.f 106p
Gothenburg (UAE) 2 b.c 111p
Ibis (USA) 2 b.f —p
Iguazu Falls (USA) 2 ch.c 106p
Majestic Marauder (USA) 2 b.c 80p
Plavius (USA) 2 b.c —p
Pont Des Soupirs (USA) 2 b.c 65p
Screen Star (IRE) 2 gr.f 110p
Siyabona (USA) 2 b.f 77p
Siyasa (USA) 2 ch.f —p
Storm Force (IRE) 2 b.c 105p
Whispered Dreams (GER) 2 ch.f 87p
Wingbeat (USA) 2 b.c 86p
Amarna (USA) 3 b.c 105p
Blackat Blackitten (IRE) 3 ch.c 107p
Envisage (IRE) 3 b.g 93p
Filios (IRE) 3 b.c 107p
Gold Sovereign (IRE) 3 b.g 97p

Jalil (USA) 3 b.c 102p
Kirklees (IRE) 3 b.c 121p
Poet Laureate 3 gr.c 120p
Shadowy Figure 3 b.c 82p

G. A. SWINBANK
Kashimin (IRE) 2 b.c 79p
Louis Seffens (USA) 2 b.c 80p

W. R. SWINBURN
Lytton 2 b.c 92p
Staying On (IRE) 2 b.c 89p
Wintercast 2 ch.c 86p
Bee Sting 3 b.g 89p
Pendulum Star 3 gr.f 89p

T. P. TATE
West With The Wind 2 b.c 84p
Greek Envoy 3 br.g 113p

M. P. TREGONING
Il Warrd (IRE) 2 b.c 94p
Shabiba (USA) 2 b.f 89p
Aajel (USA) 3 gr.c 104p
Ezdiyaad (IRE) 3 b.c 92p

E. F. VAUGHAN
Kotsi (IRE) 2 b.f 103p

SELECTED BIG RACES 2007

Prize money for racing abroad has been converted to £ sterling at the exchange rate current at the time of the race. The figures are correct to the nearest £. The Timeform ratings (TR) recorded by the principals in each race appear on the last line.

NAD AL SHEBA Saturday, Mar 31   Turf course: GOOD, Dirt course: FAST

1   **Dubai Sheema Classic Sponsored By Nakheel (Gr 1) (4yo+)**   1½m (Turf)
£1,530,612

VENGEANCE OF RAIN (NZ) DEFerraris,HongKong 7-8-11 (t) ADelpech (4)	9/1	1
ORACLE WEST (SAF) MFdeKock,SouthAfrica 6-8-11 WCMarwing (2) ...	33/1	1¼ 2
YOUMZAIN (IRE) MRChannon,GB 4-8-11 RichardHughes (13)	13/2	½ 3
Sir Percy MPTregoning,GB 4-8-11 MartinDwyer (7)	4/1f	sh 4
Sushisan (AUS) HBrown,SouthAfrica 5-8-11 KShea (9)	25/1	1¼ 5
Pop Rock (JPN) KSumii,Japan 6-8-11 OPeslier (10)	9/2	sh 6
Quijano (GER) PSchiergen,Germany 5-8-11 AStarke (12)	9/1	¾ 7
Bellamy Cay AFabre,France 5-8-11 SPasquier (1)	33/1	nk 8
Red Rocks (IRE) BJMeehan,GB 4-8-12 CNakatani (5)	9/2	1 9
Best Alibi (IRE) SaeedbinSuroor,UAE 4-8-11 LDettori (6)	14/1	2¼ 10
Honey Ryder (USA) TAPletcher,USA 6-8-7 (b) GGomez (14)	20/1	2¾ 11
Host (CHI) TAPletcher,USA 7-8-11 JVelazquez (15)	33/1	¾ 12
Obrigado (FR) NDDrysdale,USA 4-8-11 (v+t) DFlores (8)	25/1	sh 13
Laverock (IRE) SaeedbinSuroor,UAE 5-8-11 KerrinMcEvoy (3)	14/1	4¾ 14

Raymond Gianco & Chow Hon Man 14ran 2m31.03   TR: 124/122/123+/122/118/118

2   **Dubai Duty Free Sponsored By Dubai Duty Free (Gr 1) (3yo+)**   1m195y (Turf)
£1,530,612

ADMIRE MOON (JPN) HMatsuda,Japan 4-9-0 (t) YTake (10)	11/2jf	1
LINNGARI (IRE) HBrown,SouthAfrica 5-9-0 KShea (16)	20/1	½ 2
DAIWA MAJOR (JPN) HUehara,Japan 6-9-0 (b) KAndo (13)	11/2jf	4¼ 3
Seihali (IRE) DJSelvaratnam,UAE 8-9-0 (b) JMurtagh (1)	20/1	2 4
Kapil (SAF) MFdeKock,SouthAfrica 5-9-0 RFradd (7)	16/1	ns 5
Flashy Wings MRChannon,GB 4-8-10 RichardHughes (9)	20/1	2¼ 6
Formal Decree (GER) SaeedbinSuroor,UAE 4-9-0 KerrinMcEvoy (14)	16/1	½ 7
Pompeii Ruler (AUS) MPrice,Australia 5-9-0 CNewitt (8)	8/1	2¼ 8
Stormy River (FR) NClement,France 4-9-0 OPeslier (3)	10/1	¾ 9
Irridescence (SAF) MFdeKock,SouthAfrica 6-8-10 WCMarwing (4)	14/1	hd 10
Best Name SaeedbinSuroor,UAE 4-9-0 LDettori (2)	12/1	¾ 11
English Channel (USA) TAPletcher,USA 5-9-0 JVelazquez (11)	10/1	1 12
Bad Girl Runs (SAF) MFdeKock,SouthAfrica 5-8-10 MJKinane (15)	40/1	3¼ 13
Mystical (IND) SGanapathy,India 5-9-0 MartinDwyer (6)	20/1	1½ 14
Miesque's Approval (USA) MDWolfson,USA 8-9-0 (t) ECastro (12)	14/1	2 15
Lava Man (USA) DFO'Neill,USA 6-9-0 (v+t) CNakatani (5)	7/1	8¼ 16

Mr Riichi Kondo 16ran 1m47.94   TR: 126+/124/112/107/107

3   **Dubai World Cup Sponsored By Emirates Airline (Gr 1) (3yo+)**   1¼m (Dirt)
£1,836,735

INVASOR (ARG) KPMcLaughlin,USA 5-9-0 FJara (7)	5/4f	1
PREMIUM TAP (USA) JCKimmel,USA 5-9-0 (t) KDesormeaux (5)	7/1	1¾ 2
BULLISH LUCK (USA) ASCruz,HongKong 8-9-0 (b) BPrebble (3)	40/1	8 3
Vermilion (JPN) SIshizaka,Japan 5-9-0 OPLemaire (2)	33/1	5¼ 4
Forty Licks (ARG) IPDJory,SaudiArabia 5-9-0 (t) MJKinane (6)	18/1	2½ 5
Kandidate CEBrittain,GB 5-9-0 (t) SebSanders (4)	22/1	2¾ 6
Discreet Cat (USA) SaeedbinSuroor,UAE 4-9-0 LDettori (1)	11/8	2¾ 7

Mr Hamdan Al Maktoum 7ran 1m59.97   TR: 132/129/115/106/102

NEWMARKET Thursday, Apr 19   GOOD to FIRM (Rowley Mile Course)

4   **Weatherbys Earl of Sefton Stks (Gr 3) (4yo+)** £28,390   1m1f

MANDURO (GER) AFabre,France 5-8-12 SPasquier (5)	6/4f	1
SPECIOSA (IRE) MrsPSly 4-8-9 MickyFenton (1)	12/1	4 2
FINAL VERSE SirMichaelStoute 4-8-12 KerrinMcEvoy (8)	14/1	1¾ 3
Illustrious Blue WJKnight 4-8-12 PaulDoe (9)	12/1	hd 4
Snoqualmie Boy DRCElsworth 4-8-12 JohnEgan (2)	9/1	1½ 5
Ivy Creek (USA) GWragg 4-8-12 SteveDrowne (7)	9/1	1¼ 6
Secret World (IRE) JNoseda 4-8-12 LDettori (4)	11/2	½ 7
Dunelight (IRE) CGCox 4-8-12 (b) PhilipRobinson (3)	20/1	2½ 8
Imperial Star (IRE) JHMGosden 4-8-12 JimmyFortune (6)	13/2	25 9

Baron G. von Ullmann 9ran 1m47.26   TR: 125+/111/110/109/105/102

SANDOWN Friday, Apr 27   GOOD

5   **Betfred Gordon Richards Stks (Gr 3) (4yo+)** £28,390   1¼m7y

  1 RED ROCKS (IRE) *BJMeehan* 4-9-7 LDettori (2)...11/4   1
     MASHAAHED *BWHills* 4-9-0 RHills (6)...10/1   2 2
  3 KANDIDATE *CEBrittain* 5-9-3 (t) SebSanders (3).............................13/2   ½ 3
     Notnowcato *SirMichaelStoute* 5-9-7 JamieSpencer (5)......................7/2   1¼ 4
     Mountain High (IRE) *SirMichaelStoute* 5-9-0 JimmyFortune (4)...........5/2f   1 5
     Art Deco (IRE) *CREgerton* 4-9-0 JohnEgan (1)...............................7/1 17 6

Mr J. Paul Reddam 6ran 2m09.16   TR: 124/113/114/115+/106

LONGCHAMP Sunday, Apr 29   GOOD to FIRM

6   **Prix Ganay (Gr 1) (4yo+)** £102,041   1¼m110y

     DYLAN THOMAS (IRE) *APO'Brien,Ireland* 4-9-2 CSoumillon.................4/10f   1
     IRISH WELLS (FR) *FrancoisRohaut,France* 4-9-2 DBoeuf...................6/1   2 2
     DOCTOR DINO (FR) *RGibson,France* 5-9-2 OPeslier..........................20/1   ¾ 3
     Boris de Deauville (IRE) *SWattel,France* 4-9-2 YBarberot...............11/1   hd 4
     Egerton (GER) *PRau,Germany* 6-9-2 CPLemaire...............................11/1   6 5
     Pearl Sky (FR) *YdeNicolay,France* 4-8-13 ACrastus........................13/1   hd 6
     Blushing King (FR) *J-LGuillochon,France* 5-9-2 FVeron...................61/1   nk 7
     Sign of The Wolf *FrancoisRohaut,France* 7-9-2 (s) F-XBertras...........47/1   8 8

Mrs John Magnier 8ran 2m07.90   TR: 127+/122/119/120/105

NEWMARKET Saturday, May 5   GOOD to FIRM (Rowley Mile course)

7   **Stan James 2000 Guineas Stks (Gr 1) (3yo c+f)** £211,352   1m

     COCKNEY REBEL (IRE) *GAHuffer* 3-9-0 OPeslier (15)......................25/1   1
     VITAL EQUINE (IRE) *EJO'Neill* 3-9-0 ChrisCatlin (6).....................33/1   1½ 2
     DUTCH ART *PWChapple-Hyam* 3-9-0 JimmyFortune (18)..................14/1   ¾ 3
     Duke of Marmalade (IRE) *APO'Brien,Ireland* 3-9-0 MJKinane (11)...........14/1   sh 4
     Eagle Mountain *APO'Brien,Ireland* 3-9-0 CSoumillon (13)..................14/1   ½ 5
     Major Cadeaux *RHannon* 3-9-0 RichardHughes (7)..........................10/1   hd 6
     US Ranger (USA) *J-CRouget,France* 3-9-0 CPLemaire (16)..................5/1   ½ 7
     Strategic Prince *PFICole* 3-9-0 EddieAhern (4).............................8/1   1¼ 8
     Diamond Tycoon (USA) *BJMeehan* 3-9-0 JamieSpencer (2).................15/2   1 9
     Haatef (USA) *KevinPrendergast,Ireland* 3-9-0 DPMcDonogh (17)..........7/1   ¾ 10
     Yellowstone (IRE) *APO'Brien,Ireland* 3-9-0 JMurtagh (24).................50/1   hd 11
     Adagio *SirMichaelStoute* 3-9-0 KerrinMcEvoy (3)..........................4/1f   hd 12
     Al Shemali *SirMichaelStoute* 3-9-0 RHills (12)...........................200/1   2 13
     Tobosa *WJarvis* 3-9-0 PhilipRobinson (22)..................................28/1   nk 14
     Sonny Red (IRE) *RHannon* 3-9-0 SteveDrowne (10)........................66/1   1 15
     Jo'burg (USA) *MrsAJPerrett* 3-9-0 KDarley (1).............................200/1   nk 16
     Halicarnassus (IRE) *MRChannon* 3-9-0 DarrylHolland (9)...................66/1   ½ 17
     Fishforcompliments *RAFahey* 3-9-0 PaulHanagan (5).....................200/1   ½ 18
     Truly Royal *SaeedbinSuroor* 3-9-0 (t) LDettori (20).......................33/1   3½ 19
     Prime Defender *BWHills* 3-9-0 MichaelHills (23)...........................66/1   1½ 20
     Drayton (IRE) *MFdeKock,SouthAfrica* 3-9-0 WCMarwing (21)............100/1   nk 21
     Danum Dancer *NBycroft* 3-9-0 (b) SilvestreDeSousa (19)................250/1   nk 22
     Evens And Odds (IRE) *KARyan* 3-9-0 NCallan (8)...........................33/1   ½ 23
     Hurricane Spirit (IRE) *JRBest* 3-9-0 GeorgeBaker (4).....................100/1   2½ 24

Mr Phil Cunningham 24ran 1m35.28   TR: 125+/121/118+/118+/117+/116/115+

NEWMARKET Sunday, May 6   GOOD to FIRM (Rowley Mile Course)

8   **stanjamesuk.com Jockey Club Stks (Gr 2) (4yo+)** £51,102   1½m

     SIXTIES ICON *JNoseda* 4-9-3 LDettori (2)................................5/2   1
     ADMIRAL'S CRUISE (USA) *BJMeehan* 5-8-12 (b) JimmyFortune (4)........4/1   3 2
     MIGHTY *JaneChapple-Hyam* 4-8-12 JohnEgan (1)............................9/1   nk 3
     Papal Bull *SirMichaelStoute* 4-9-1 KerrinMcEvoy (5)......................9/4f   2½ 4
     Linda's Lad *AFabre,France* 4-8-12 SPasquier (3)...........................7/2   nk 5

Mrs Susan Roy 5ran 2m33.52   TR: 125/113/114/112/109

9   **Stan James 1000 Guineas Stks (Gr 1) (3yo f)** £198,730   1m

     FINSCEAL BEO (IRE) *JSBolger,Ireland* 3-9-0 KJManning (8)...............5/4f   1
     ARCH SWING (USA) *JohnMOxx,Ireland* 3-9-0 MJKinane (19)...............10/1   2½ 2
     SIMPLY PERFECT *JNoseda* 3-9-0 JMurtagh (10)............................9/1   1¼ 3
     Treat *MRChannon* 3-9-0 JamieSpencer (14)...............................14/1   1½ 4
     Indian Ink (IRE) *RHannon* 3-9-0 RichardHughes (13).....................17/2   nk 5
     Yaqeen *MAJarvis* 3-9-0 RHills (3)...12/1   1 6
     Scarlet Runner *JLDunlop* 3-9-0 KerrinMcEvoy (9)........................14/1   ½ 7
     Puggy (IRE) *RAKvisla* 3-9-0 (t) SPasquier (5)...........................150/1   1 8
     Satulagi (USA) *JSMoore* 3-9-0 StephenDonohoe (1).......................200/1   ¾ 9
     Theann *APO'Brien,Ireland* 3-9-0 CSoumillon (12)...........................20/1   1 10
     Cartimandua *ESMcMahon* 3-9-0 JimmyFortune (2)..........................200/1   1¾ 11

Sweet Lilly *MRChannon* 3-9-0 DarryllHolland (21)...................................... 33/1 3½ 12
Vital Statistics *DRCElsworth* 3-9-0 KDarley (22).. 100/1 2½ 13
Princess Valerina *BWHills* 3-9-0 MichaelHills (18)..................................... 250/1 2½ 14
Barshiba (IRE) *DRCElsworth* 3-9-0 JohnEgan (15)...................................... 40/1 1½ 15
Darrfonah (IRE) *CEBrittain* 3-9-0 (b) CPLemaire (23) .... 100/1 nk 16
Fantasy Parkes *KARyan* 3-9-0 NCallan (4)... 150/1 2½ 17
Miss Beatrix (IRE) *KevinPrendergast,Ireland* 3-9-0 DPMcDonogh (7)........ 12/1 ½ 18
Kaseema (USA) *SirMichaelStoute* 3-9-0 MartinDwyer (17) 20/1 2½ 19
Blue Rocket (IRE) *TJPitt* 3-9-0 OPeslier (11)... 33/1 nk 20
Selinka *RHannon* 3-9-0 EddieAhern (16).. 100/1 1¼ 21

M. A. Ryan 21ran 1m34.94   TR: 123/116/112/108/107+/104+

LONGCHAMP Sunday, May 13   GOOD

10 **Poule d'Essai des Pouliches (Gr 1) (3yo f)** £155,483   1m

DARJINA (FR) *AdeRoyerDupre,France* 3-9-0 CSoumillon (5)..................... 4/1   1
    9 FINSCEAL BEO (IRE) *JSBolger,Ireland* 3-9-0 KJManning (4) .... 4/5f   hd 2
RAHIYAH (USA) *JNoseda,GB* 3-9-0 TedDurcan (11)................................. 30/1   1½ 3
Costume *JHMGosden,GB* 3-9-0 RichardHughes (3)................................... 31/1   2½ 4
Peace Dream (FR) *J-CRouget,France* 3-9-0 IMendizabal (8) 11/2   1½ 5
Sesmen *MBotti,GB* 3-9-0 TJarnet (6)... 97/1   ¾ 6
Bicoastal (USA) *BJMeehan,GB* 3-9-0 (b) JimmyFortune (7)...................... 89/1   ns 7
Sander Camillo (USA) *JNoseda,GB* 3-9-0 LDettori (12) 81/10 10 8
Fairy Dress (USA) *RCollet,France* 3-9-0 JAuge (2).................................. 120/1 ½ 9
Zut Alors (IRE) *RCollet,France* 3-9-0 TThulliez (13)................................ 102/1 1 10
Iron Lips *CLaffon-Parias,France* 3-9-0 OPeslier (1)................................. 39/1   ½ 11
I Should Care (FR) *FRodriguez,Spain* 3-9-0 SPasquier (10) 104/1 2 12
Galaxie Des Sables (FR) *MmeNRossio,France* 3-9-0 RonanThomas (9)...... 74/1 6 13

Princess Zahra Aga Khan 13ran 1m37.20   TR: 117+/117/113/108/104/102/101

11 **Poule d'Essai des Poulains (Gr 1) (3yo c)** £155,483   1m

ASTRONOMER ROYAL (USA) *APO'Brien,Ireland* 3-9-2
    CO'Donoghue (9).. 34/10cp 1
CREACHADOIR (IRE) *JSBolger,Ireland* 3-9-2 KJManning (4)................... 7/1   ½ 2
HONOURED GUEST (IRE) *APO'Brien,Ireland* 3-9-2 GMosse (3)........ 34/10cp 1½ 3
Excellent Art *APO'Brien,Ireland* 3-9-2 JamieSpencer (13)...................... 34/10cp ¾ 4
Thousand Words *BWHills,GB* 3-9-2 RichardHughes (14) .... 16/1   ½ 5
Followmyfootsteps (USA) *DWachman,Ireland* 3-9-2 SPasquier (2)......... 34/10cp sn 6
Spirit One (FR) *PHDemercastel,France* 3-9-2 DBoeuf (12) 72/10 1½ 7
Visionario (IRE) *AFabre,France* 3-9-2 CSoumillon (4) 38/10 1½ 8
Battle Paint (USA) *J-CRouget,France* 3-9-2 OPeslier (5) 26/10f 1½ 9
Stoneside (IRE) *RodolpheCollet,France* 3-9-2 TGillet (6) 54/1   1 10
Dijeerr (USA) *SaeedbinSuroor,GB* 3-9-2 LDettori (8)............................. 79/10 sn 11
Brave Tin Soldier (USA) *APO'Brien,Ireland* 3-9-2 TThulliez (7) 34/10cp 2½ 12
Tariq *PWChapple-Hyam,GB* 3-9-2 JimmyFortune (10) 18/1   1½ 13
Mastership (IRE) *CEBrittain,GB* 3-9-2 (b) EddieAhern (11) 98/1   6 14

Mr D. Smith, Mrs J. Magnier, Mr M. Tabor 14ran 1m37.10
                                                            TR: 121/120/116/113+/112/112

YORK Thursday, May 17   GOOD

12 **totesport.com Dante Stks (Gr 2) (3yo)** £85,170   1¼m88y

AUTHORIZED (IRE) *PWChapple-Hyam* 3-9-0 LDettori (3) 10/11f 1
RAINCOAT *JHMGosden* 3-9-0 RichardHughes (1)................................... 8/1   4 2
    7 AL SHEMALI *SirMichaelStoute* 3-9-0 MJKinane (2)................................ 18/1   1 3
    7 Adagio *SirMichaelStoute* 3-9-0 KerrinMcEvoy (4)................................ 5/2   2½ 4
Proponent (IRE) *RCharlton* 3-9-0 JimmyFortune (6) 7/1   16 5
Prince Golan (IRE) *KARyan* 3-9-0 NCallan (5) 100/1 20 6

Saleh Al Homeizi & Imad Al Sagar 6ran 2m11.54   TR: 123+/115/113/108

NEWBURY Saturday, May 19   GOOD

13 **Juddmonte Lockinge Stks (Gr 1) (4yo+)** £113,560   1m

RED EVIE (IRE) *MLWBell* 4-8-11 JamieSpencer (7)................................ 8/1   1
RAMONTI (FR) *SaeedbinSuroor* 5-9-0 (t) LDettori (8)............................. 4/1   hd 2
PASSAGER (FR) *MmeCHead-Maarek,France* 4-9-0 RichardHughes (2) .... 20/1 hd 3
    4 Secret World (IRE) *JNoseda* 4-9-0 EddieAhern (5).................................. 40/1   2½ 4
Jeremy (USA) *SirMichaelStoute* 4-9-0 MJKinane (1)............................... 4/1   ¾ 5
Peeress *SirMichaelStoute* 6-8-11 KerrinMcEvoy (6)............................... 11/8f 1½ 6
    4 Speciosa (IRE) *MrsPSly* 4-8-11 MickyFenton (4)................................... 10/1   2½ 7
Marcus Andronicus (USA) *APO'Brien,Ireland* 4-9-0 RHills (3)................ 16/1   20 8

Mr Terry Neill 8ran 1m40.43   TR: 115/118/117/111/109/102

14 Prix d'Ispahan (Gr 1) (4yo+) £97,177   1m1f55y

4	MANDURO (GER) *AFabre,France* 5-9-2 SPasquier	9/10f	1
	TURTLE BOWL (IRE) *FrancoisRohaut,France* 5-9-2 OPeslier	7/2	5 2
2	STORMY RIVER (FR) *NClement,France* 4-9-2 TThulliez	7/2	5 3
	Willywell (FR) *J-PGauvin,France* 5-9-2 CSoumillon	23/4	3 4
	Palafamix (FR) *NClement,France* 4-9-2 J-MBreux	17/1	4 5

Baron G. von Ullmann 5ran 1m58.00   TR: 132/121/111/105

15 Boylesports Irish 2000 Guineas (Gr 1) (3yo c+f) £153,767   1m

7	COCKNEY REBEL (IRE) *GAHuffer,GB* 3-9-0 OPeslier (7)	6/4f	1
11	CREACHADOIR (IRE) *JSBolger* 3-9-0 KJManning (8)	7/1	1 2
	HE'S A DECOY (IRE) *DWachman* 3-9-0 MJKinane (3)	40/1	1 3
7	Duke of Marmalade (IRE) *APO'Brien* 3-9-0 JAHeffernan (12)	9/4	hd 4
11	Followmyfootsteps (USA) *DWachman* 3-9-0 WMLordan (5)	33/1	¾ 5
7	Vital Equine (IRE) *EJO'Neill,GB* 3-9-0 ChrisCatlin (1)	8/1	hd 6
	Confuchias (IRE) *FrancisEnnis* 3-9-0 DPMcDonogh (4)	50/1	5½ 7
	Kingsdale Orion (IRE) *MsFlorenceMills* 3-9-0 PShanahan (2)	500/1	½ 8
	Traffic Guard (USA) *JSMoore,GB* 3-9-0 JohnEgan (13)	50/1	1¼ 9
	Fleeting Shadow (IRE) *DKWeld* 3-9-0 PJSmullen (11)	33/1	3 10
	Ferneley (IRE) *FrancisEnnis* 3-9-0 WilliamSupple (9)	22/1	¾ 11
	Trinity College (USA) *APO'Brien* 3-9-0 DavidMcCabe (10)	100/1	½ 12

Mr Phil Cunningham 12ran 1m36.10   TR: 120+/117/114/114/112/111

16 Tattersalls Gold Cup (Gr 1) (4yo+) £127,397   1¼m110y

5	NOTNOWCATO *SirMichaelStoute,GB* 5-9-0 JMurtagh (9)	7/1	1
6	DYLAN THOMAS (IRE) *APO'Brien* 4-9-0 JAHeffernan (3)	1/2f	hd 2
1	YOUMZAIN (IRE) *MRChannon,GB* 4-9-0 RichardHughes (8)	7/1	4 3
	Danak (IRE) *JohnMOxx* 4-9-0 MJKinane (7)	10/1	1¼ 4
	Fracas (IRE) *DWachman* 5-9-0 WMLordan (2)	20/1	¾ 5
	Mustameet (USA) *KevinPrendergast* 6-9-0 DPMcDonogh (6)	16/1	2 6
	Arch Rebel (USA) *NMeade* 6-9-0 FMBerry (5)	66/1	3 7
	Nightime (IRE) *DKWeld* 4-8-11 PJSmullen (1)	25/1	hd 8
	Heliostatic (IRE) *JSBolger* 4-9-0 KJManning (4)	40/1	5½ 9

Anthony & David De Rothschild 9ran 2m16.20   TR: 128/129/121/118/115/111

17 Boylesports Irish 1000 Guineas (Gr 1) (3yo f) £153,767   1m

10	FINSCEAL BEO (IRE) *JSBolger* 3-9-0 KJManning (8)	9/10f	1
	DIMENTICATA (IRE) *KevinPrendergast* 3-9-0 CDHayes (11)	66/1	nk 2
	PEEPING FAWN (USA) *APO'Brien* 3-9-0 JAHeffernan (5)	12/1	2 3
	Alexander Tango (IRE) *TStack* 3-9-0 WMLordan (7)	10/1	sh 4
	Truly Mine (IRE) *DKWeld* 3-9-0 PShanahan (6)	20/1	2½ 5
9	Treat *MRChannon,GB* 3-9-0 JMurtagh (9)	9/1	½ 6
	Diamond Necklace (USA) *APO'Brien* 3-9-0 CO'Donoghue (3)	66/1	1¼ 7
	Gaudeamus (USA) *JSBolger* 3-9-0 DJMoran (1)	100/1	2½ 8
	Silk Dress (IRE) *JohnJosephMurphy* 3-9-0 DMGrant (10)	150/1	4½ 9
	Offbeat Fashion (IRE) *DKWeld* 3-9-0 PJSmullen (4)	25/1	½ 10
9	Arch Swing (USA) *JohnMOxx* 3-9-0 MJKinane (2)	10/3	7 11

Mr M. A. Ryan 11ran 1m39.30   TR: 110+/109/104/104/97/96

18 Vodafone Coronation Cup (Gr 1) (4yo+) £141,950   1½m10y

	SCORPION (IRE) *APO'Brien,Ireland* 4-9-0 MJKinane (2)	8/1	1
	SEPTIMUS (IRE) *APO'Brien,Ireland* 4-9-0 JMurtagh (3)	3/1	1¼ 2
	MARAAHEL (IRE) *SirMichaelStoute* 6-9-0 (b) RHills (7)	7/1	½ 3
	Rising Cross (IRE) *JRBest* 4-8-11 TedDurcan (6)	33/1	3½ 4
	Hattan (IRE) *CEBrittain* 5-9-0 SebSanders (5)	66/1	½ 5
1	Sir Percy *MPTregoning* 4-9-0 MartinDwyer (1)	7/2	hd 6
8	Sixties Icon *JNoseda* 4-9-0 LDettori (4)	11/8f	3½ 7

Mrs John Magnier & Mr M. Tabor 7ran 2m40.82   TR: 124/123/121/113/115/115

19 Vodafone Oaks (Gr 1) (3yo f) £222,350   1½m10y

	LIGHT SHIFT (USA) *HRACecil* 3-9-0 TedDurcan (11)	13/2	1
17	PEEPING FAWN (USA) *APO'Brien,Ireland* 3-9-0 MartinDwyer (9)	20/1	½ 2
	ALL MY LOVING (IRE) *APO'Brien,Ireland* 3-9-0 CSoumillon (6)	5/1	4 3
	Four Sins (GER) *JohnMOxx,Ireland* 3-9-0 MJKinane (13)	5/1	5 4
	Cherry Hinton (IRE) *APO'Brien,Ireland* 3-9-0 JAHeffernan (7)	66/1	1½ 5
9	Simply Perfect *JNoseda* 3-9-0 JMurtagh (5)	8/1	8 6
	Dance of Light (USA) *SirMichaelStoute* 3-9-0 KerrinMcEvoy (10)	33/1	2 7

Passage of Time *HRACecil* 3-9-0 RichardHughes (8)................................ 9/4f nk 8
Kayah *RMBeckett* 3-9-0 SebSanders (12).. 16/1 ½ 9
9 Darrfonah (IRE) *CEBrittain* 3-9-0 (t) EddieAhern (3)......................... 66/1 2 10
Dalvina *EALDunlop* 3-9-0 OPeslier (4).. 11/1 sh 11
Nell Gwyn (IRE) *APO'Brien,Ireland* 3-9-0 NCallan (2) 66/1 1¾ 12
Measured Tempo *SaeedbinSuroor* 3-9-0 LDettori (14)......................... 9/1 nk 13
Sues Surprise (IRE) *BWHills* 3-9-0 MichaelHills (1)......................... 66/1 dist 14

Niarchos Family 14ran 2m40.38   TR: 121/120/113/105/103

EPSOM DOWNS Saturday, Jun 2   GOOD

20   **Vodafone Derby Stks (Gr 1) (3yo c+f)** £709,750   1½m10y
12 AUTHORIZED (IRE) *PWChapple-Hyam* 3-9-0 LDettori (14) 5/4f 1
7 EAGLE MOUNTAIN *APO'Brien,Ireland* 3-9-0 JMurtagh (8)................ 6/1 5 2
AQALEEM *MPTregoning* 3-9-0 RHills (2) 9/1 2½ 3
Lucarno (USA) *JHMGosden* 3-9-0 SteveDrowne (17) .... 16/1 hd 4
Soldier of Fortune (IRE) *APO'Brien,Ireland* 3-9-0 WMLordan (9)........... 14/1 ½ 5
Salford Mill (IRE) *DRCElsworth* 3-9-0 TedDurcan (11) .... 20/1 ¾ 6
Kid Mambo (USA) *TGMills* 3-9-0 JoeFanning (19) 50/1 1¾ 7
7 Yellowstone (IRE) *APO'Brien,Ireland* 3-9-0 CO'Donoghue (16) .... 28/1 nk 8
Acapulco (IRE) *APO'Brien,Ireland* 3-9-0 FMBerry (5) 66/1 3½ 9
Admiralofthefleet (USA) *APO'Brien,Ireland* 3-9-0 JAHeffernan (15)...... 14/1 sh 10
Mahler *APO'Brien,Ireland* 3-9-0 PJSmullen (6) 20/1 6 11
Anton Chekhov *APO'Brien,Ireland* 3-9-0 DPMcDonogh (4)............ 50/1 2 12
Regime (IRE) *MLWBell* 3-9-0 MartinDwyer (7).......................... 20/1 8 13
Leander *BRJohnson* 3-9-0 MGallagher (3)................................ 100/1 2½ 14
Petara Bay (IRE) *TGMills* 3-9-0 DaneO'Neill (12) 100/1 1 15
7 Strategic Prince *PFICole* 3-9-0 EddieAhern (18)........................... 20/1 13 16
Archipenko (USA) *APO'Brien,Ireland* 3-9-0 MJKinane (10) 13/2 4 17

Saleh Al Homeizi & Imad Al Sagar 17ran 2m34.77 TR: 132+/123+/118+/118+/117/116

CHANTILLY Sunday, Jun 3   GOOD

21   **Grand Prix de Chantilly Mitsubishi Motors (Gr 2) (4yo+)** £50,068   1½m
SADDEX *PRau,Germany* 4-9-2 TMundry 96/10 1
VISON CELEBRE (IRE) *AFabre,France* 4-9-2 OPeslier 10/1 1½ 2
5 MOUNTAIN HIGH (IRE) *SirMichaelStoute,GB* 5-8-12 KerrinMcEvoy ...... 19/4 ns 3
6 Irish Wells (IRE) *FrancoisRohaut,France* 4-9-2 DBoeuf 2/1f 1½ 4
Champs Elysees *AFabre,France* 4-8-12 SPasquier 3/1 2 5
Daramsar (FR) *AdeRoyerDupre,France* 4-9-2 CSoumillon .... 29/4 sn 6
Walk In The Park (IRE) *JEHammond,France* 5-8-12 TGillet .... 10/1 sn 7
6 Sign of The Wolf *FrancoisRohaut,France* 7-8-12 F-XBertras 55/1 15 8

Stall Avena 8ran 2m28.70   TR: 124/118/117/119/111/115

22   **Prix du Jockey Club Mitsubishi Motors (Gr 1) (3yo c+f)** £579,122   1¼m110y
LAWMAN (FR) *J-MBeguigne,France* 3-9-2 LDettori 7/2f 1
LITERATO (FR) *J-CRouget,France* 3-9-2 CPLemaire...................... 13/2 1½ 2
SHAMDINAN (FR) *AdeRoyerDupre,France* 3-9-2 CSoumillon .... 13/1 sn 3
Zambezi Sun *PBary,France* 3-9-2 SPasquier .... 11/1 sn 4
Castlereagh (UAE) *AFabre,France* 3-9-2 KerrinMcEvoy 35/1 2½ 5
No Dream (USA) *CLaffon-Parias,France* 3-9-2 OPeslier .... 11/1 ½ 6
Sagara (USA) *JEPease,France* 3-9-2 (s) TGillet .... 19/1 ns 7
Loup Breton (IRE) *ELellouche,France* 3-9-2 TThulliez .... 23/1 sn 8
Brooklyn Boy (IRE) *J-CRouget,France* 3-9-2 IMendizabal............ 17/1 1½ 9
Indian Spring (IRE) *DSmaga,France* 3-9-2 GBenoist .... 80/1 ½ 10
12 Raincoat *JHMGosden,GB* 3-9-2 RichardHughes.......................... 6/1 sh 11
Sunshine Kid (USA) *JHMGosden,GB* 3-9-2 JimmyFortune............ 92/1 nk 12
Quest For Honor *AFabre,France* 3-9-2 JVictoire 28/1 5 13
11 Spirit One (FR) *PHDemercastel,France* 3-9-2 DBoeuf.................... 15/1 ½ 14
7 Halicarnassus (IRE) *MRChannon,GB* 3-9-2 DarryllHolland............ 59/1 hd 15
Alexander of Hales (USA) *APO'Brien,Ireland* 3-9-2 JAHeffernan ...... 39/1 ¾ 16
Beltanus (GER) *FrauIFerentschak,Germany* 3-9-2 TMundry .... 128/1 nk 17
11 Visionario (IRE) *AFabre,France* 3-9-2 MSautjeau .... 57/1 sh 18
Chinese Whisper (IRE) *APO'Brien,Ireland* 3-9-2 JMurtagh .... 21/1 nk 19
Medicine Path *EJO'Neill,GB* 3-9-2 RichardMullen 58/1 1½ 20

Mr C. Marzocco 20ran 2m05.90   TR: 118+/116+/115+/114+/108/107

CHANTILLY Sunday, Jun 10   GOOD to FIRM

23   **Prix de Diane Hermes (Gr 1) (3yo f)** £310,966   1¼m110y
WEST WIND *H-APantall,France* 3-9-0 LDettori........................... 71/10 1
MRS LINDSAY (USA) *FrancoisRohaut,France* 3-9-0 JMurtagh.............. 17/1 1½ 2
DIYAKALANIE (FR) *JBoisnard,France* 3-9-0 TThulliez .... 54/1 nk 3
Anabaa's Creation (IRE) *AdeRoyerDupre,France* 3-9-0 GMosse .... 19/1 ½ 4

1209

Beatrix Kiddo (FR) *RCollet,France* 3-9-0 ODoleuze 31/1 ¾ 5

Believe Me (IRE) *J-MBeguigne,France* 3-9-0 OPeslier 13/2 1½ 6

Marie Rossa *PHDemercastel,France* 3-9-0 ACrastus 31/1 nk 7

Vadapolina (FR) *AFabre,France* 3-9-0 CSoumillon 7/4f 2 8

Fontcia (FR) *DSepulchre,France* 3-9-0 DBoeuf 59/1 2 9

Cinnamon Bay *AFabre,France* 3-9-0 SPasquier 14/1 2½ 10

Sequoia (SLO) *J-PLopez,Slovakia* 3-9-0 WMongil 56/1 sh 11

9 Sweet Lilly *MRChannon,GB* 3-9-0 DarryllHolland 34/1 ½ 12

Topka (FR) *FDoumen,France* 3-9-0 TJarnet 61/1 1½ 13

Coquerelle (IRE) *J-CRouget,France* 3-9-0 CPLemaire 7/2 10 14

Sheikh Mohammed 14ran 2m06.30 TR: 112+/108/108/107/105/101

ASCOT Tuesday, Jun 19 GOOD to FIRM

24 King's Stand Stks (Gr 2) (3yo+) £121,259 5f

MISS ANDRETTI (AUS) *LeeFreedman,Australia* 6-9-1 CNewitt (19) 3/1f 1

DANDY MAN (IRE) *MissTAMCollins,Ireland* 4-9-4 PShanahan (1) 15/2 1¾ 2

MAGNUS (AUS) *PeterGMoody,Australia* 5-9-4 (b) DMOliver (17) 14/1 nk 3

Takeover Target (AUS) *JoeJaniak,Australia* 8-9-4 JFord (14) 11/2 ½ 4

Enticing (IRE) *WJHaggas* 3-8-9 JamieSpencer (12) 8/1 1½ 5

Desert Lord *KARyan* 7-9-4 (b) NCallan (20) 25/1 1¾ 6

Beauty Is Truth (IRE) *RCollet,France* 3-8-9 (b) TThulliez (10) 14/1 hd 7

The Tatling (IRE) *JMBradley* 10-9-4 DarryllHolland (15) 66/1 ½ 8

Green Manalishi *KARyan* 6-9-4 TedDurcan (21) 66/1 ½ 9

Moorhouse Lad *BSmart* 4-9-4 TomEaves (18) 100/1 1¼ 10

Tax Free (IRE) *DNicholls* 5-9-4 AdrianTNicholls (7) 14/1 hd 11

Benbaun (IRE) *MJWallace* 6-9-4 (v) PJSmullen (5) 10/1 sh 12

Pivotal Point *PJMakin* 7-9-4 SebSanders (4) 40/1 ½ 13

Moss Vale (IRE) *DNicholls* 6-9-4 LDettori (11) 25/1 hd 14

Conquest (IRE) *WJHaggas* 3-8-12 (b) JHBowman (9) 50/1 sh 15

Manzila (FR) *FHead,France* 4-9-1 OPeslier (2) 150/1 1 16

King Orchisios (IRE) *KARyan* 4-9-4 (s) DO'Donohoe (6) 66/1 1 17

Matsunosuke *ABCoogan* 5-9-4 JMurtagh (8) 200/1 nk 18

Dazed And Amazed *RHannon* 3-8-12 RichardHughes (16) 100/1 5 19

Bentley Biscuit (AUS) *GaiWaterhouse,Australia* 6-9-4 NashRawiller (3) 9/1 ½ 20

P.S. Buckley, D.B. Mueller, Ms G. Guenzi 20ran 57.44secs
TR: 127/123/122/120/109/108

25 St James's Palace Stks (Gr 1) (3yo c) £141,950 1m (Rnd)

11 EXCELLENT ART *APO'Brien,Ireland* 3-9-0 JamieSpencer (1) 8/1 1

15 DUKE OF MARMALADE (IRE) *APO'Brien,Ireland* 3-9-0 MJKinane (7) 11/1 nk 2

11 ASTRONOMER ROYAL (USA) *APO'Brien,Ireland* 3-9-0 CO'Donoghue (6) 14/1 1¼ 3

7 Dutch Art *PWChapple-Hyam* 3-9-0 JimmyFortune (4) 10/3 hd 4

15 Cockney Rebel (IRE) *GAHuffer* 3-9-0 OPeslier (3) 1/1f sh 5

15 Creachadoir (IRE) *JSBolger,Ireland* 3-9-0 KJManning (8) 12/1 1 6

Jack Junior (USA) *BJMeehan* 3-9-0 LDettori (2) 33/1 2½ 7

15 He's A Decoy (IRE) *DWachman,Ireland* 3-9-0 KerrinMcEvoy (5) 12/1 ¾ 8

MrsJohnMagnierMichaelTaborDSmithMGreen 8ran 1m39.33
TR: 125/124/121/120/120+/117

26 Queen Anne Stks (Gr 1) (4yo+) £152,170 1m (Str.)

13 RAMONTI (FR) *SaeedbinSuroor* 5-9-0 (t) LDettori (2) 5/1 1

13 JEREMY (USA) *SirMichaelStoute* 4-9-0 RyanMoore (6) 14/1 sh 2

14 TURTLE BOWL (IRE) *FrancoisRohaut,France* 5-9-0 (t) OPeslier (3) 33/1 sh 3

George Washington (IRE) *APO'Brien,Ireland* 4-9-0 MJKinane (8) 10/11f hd 4

Cesare *JRFanshawe* 6-9-0 JMurtagh (4) 9/2 ¾ 5

Racinger (FR) *FHead,France* 4-9-0 CSoumillon (5) 16/1 1¾ 6

13 Red Evie (IRE) *MLWBell* 4-8-11 JamieSpencer (7) 15/2 ½ 7

Notability (IRE) *SaeedbinSuroor* 5-9-0 KerrinMcEvoy (1) 50/1 10 8

Godolphin 8ran 1m37.21 TR: 122/122/121/121/119/114

ASCOT Wednesday, Jun 20 GOOD to FIRM

27 Windsor Forest Stks (Gr 2) (4yo+ f+m) £73,814 1m (Str.)

NANNINA *JHMGosden* 4-8-12 JimmyFortune (7) 3/1cf 1

SATWA QUEEN (FR) *JdeRoualle,France* 5-8-12 LDettori (5) 3/1cf 3 2

SABANA PERDIDA (IRE) *AdeRoyerDupre,France* 4-8-12 CPLemaire (2) 50/1 ¾ 3

Fann (USA) *CEBrittain* 4-8-12 RyanMoore (8) 100/1 ¾ 4

Echelon *SirMichaelStoute* 5-8-12 KerrinMcEvoy (9) 3/1cf 1 5

2 Flashy Wings *MRChannon* 4-8-12 JamieSpencer (10) 13/2 2 6

Wasseema (USA) *SirMichaelStoute* 4-8-12 RHills (6) 7/1 sh 7

Gwenseb (FR) *CLaffon-Parias,France* 4-8-12 OPeslier (4) 14/1 4 8

Expensive *CFWall* 4-8-12 EddieAhern (1) 20/1   23 9
Cheveley Park Stud 9ran 1m40.97   TR: 121/113/112/110?/107/102

28   **Prince of Wales's Stks (Gr 1) (4yo+)** £211,207   1¼m

    14 MANDURO (GER) *AFabre,France* 5-9-0 SPasquier (4) 15/8f   1
    16 DYLAN THOMAS (IRE) *APO'Brien,Ireland* 4-9-0 CSoumillon (1) 2/1   1¼ 2
    16 NOTNOWCATO *SirMichaelStoute* 5-9-0 JMurtagh (7) 13/2   4 3
     5 Red Rocks (IRE) *BJMeehan* 4-9-0 LDettori (5).. 4/1   ¾ 4
        Pressing (IRE) *MAJarvis* 4-9-0 OPeslier (2) 25/1   1½ 5
    18 Sir Percy *MPTregoning* 4-9-0 MartinDwyer (3)..................................... 11/1   ¾ 6

Baron G. von Ullmann 6ran 2m05.91   TR: 135/132/123/121/118/116

ASCOT Thursday, Jun 21   GOOD

29   **Gold Cup (Gr 1) (4yo+)** £127,755   2½m

        YEATS (IRE) *APO'Brien,Ireland* 6-9-2 MJKinane (2) 8/13f   1
        GEORDIELAND (FR) *JAOsborne* 6-9-2 JamieSpencer (5)........................ 12/1   1½ 2
        LE MIRACLE (GER) *WernerBaltromei,Germany* 6-9-2 DBoeuf (7) 50/1   3½ 3
        Finalmente *NACallaghan* 5-9-2 JMurtagh (3) 66/1   3½ 4
        Montare (IRE) *JEPease,France* 5-8-13 (s) OPeslier (4) 12/1   1¼ 5
        Lord du Sud (FR) *J-CRouget,France* 6-9-2 CPLemaire (8) 25/1   7 6
        Baddam *MRChannon* 5-9-2 IanMongan (6) 20/1   2½ 7
        Cherry Mix (FR) *SaeedbinSuroor* 6-9-2 (t) LDettori (9) 14/1   1½ 8
        Allegretto (IRE) *SirMichaelStoute* 4-9-0 (v) SebSanders (13).................. 14/1   nk 9
        Bulwark (IRE) *MrsAJPerrett* 5-9-2 (b+es) JimCrowley (1)....................... 66/1   5 10
        The Last Drop (IRE) *BWHills* 4-9-0 KerrinMcEvoy (4)............................ 66/1   2½ 11
    18 Rising Cross *JRBest* 4-8-11 TedDurcan (10).. 66/1   5 12
        Tungsten Strike (USA) *MrsAJPerrett* 6-9-2 RyanMoore (11) 50/1   1½ 13
        Sergeant Cecil *BRMillman* 8-9-2 JimmyFortune (12) 13/2   25 14

Mrs John Magnier & Mrs David Nagle 14ran 4m20.78   TR: 121+/119/115/112/107+/103

ASCOT Friday, Jun 22   GOOD to SOFT

30   **Coronation Stks (Gr 1) (3yo f)** £141,950   1m (Rnd)

     9 INDIAN INK (IRE) *RHannon* 3-9-0 RichardHughes (2)........................... 8/1   1
        MI EMMA (GER) *AWohler,Germany* 3-9-0 EPedroza (1)...................... 10/3jf   6 2
    10 DARJINA (FR) *AdeRoyerDupre,France* 3-9-0 CSoumillon (7)................... 7/2   hd 3
    17 Arch Swing (USA) *JohnMOxx,Ireland* 3-9-0 MJKinane (11) 10/1   1 4
        Missvinski (USA) *J-CRouget,France* 3-9-0 CPLemaire (5) .... 25/1   ½ 5
     9 Scarlet Runner *JLDunlop* 3-9-0 KerrinMcEvoy (6) .... 50/1   nk 6
        Majestic Roi (USA) *MRChannon* 3-9-0 JamieSpencer (8) .... 25/1   sh 7
    17 Finsceal Beo (IRE) *JSBolger,Ireland* 3-9-0 KJManning (3) .... 10/3jf   ½ 8
     9 Yaqeen *MAJarvis* 3-9-0 RHills (9).. 14/1   2 9
    10 Rahiyah (USA) *JNoseda* 3-9-0 TedDurcan (4)... 10/1   1½ 10
     9 Puggy (IRE) *RAKvisla* 3-9-0 (t) LDettori (10)... 22/1   5 11
    19 Cherry Hinton *APO'Brien,Ireland* 3-9-0 JMurtagh (13) 33/1   1 12
        Silk Blossom (IRE) *BWHills* 3-9-0 MichaelHills (12)............................... 50/1   8 13

Mr Raymond Tooth 13ran 1m42.26   TR: 122/107/107/104+/103/102

ASCOT Saturday, Jun 23   GOOD to SOFT

31   **Hardwicke Stks (Gr 2) (4yo+)** £79,492   1½m

    18 MARAAHEL (IRE) *SirMichaelStoute* 6-9-0 (b) RHills (4) 10/3   1
    18 SCORPION (IRE) *APO'Brien,Ireland* 5-9-5 MJKinane (5) .... 4/5f   ½ 2
     8 MIGHTY *JaneChapple-Hyam* 4-9-0 JohnEgan (2)................................... 10/1   2½ 3
     8 Admiral's Cruise (USA) *BJMeehan* 5-9-0 (b) JimmyFortune (8).................. 9/1   ½ 4
        Blue Bajan (IRE) *AndrewTurnell* 5-9-0 MichaelHills (7) .... 11/1   ½ 5
        Diamond Quest (SAF) *AMBalding* 6-9-0 JHBowman (6) .... 20/1   ¾ 6
        Akarem *KRBurke* 6-9-0 (v) NCallan (3)... 33/1   5 7

Mr Hamdan Al Maktoum 7ran 2m35.47   TR: 121/125/117/115/114/112

32   **Golden Jubilee Stks (Gr 1) (3yo+)** £198,730   6f

        SOLDIER'S TALE (USA) *JNoseda* 6-9-4 (v) JMurtagh (11) 9/1   1
    24 TAKEOVER TARGET (AUS) *JoeJaniak,Australia* 8-9-4 JFord (10) .... 8/1   hd 2
        ASSET (IRE) *RHannon* 4-9-4 RichardHughes (2)..................................... 14/1   ½ 3
        Red Clubs (IRE) *BWHills* 4-9-4 MichaelHills (22).................................. 25/1   ½ 4
     7 Drayton (IRE) *MFdeKock,SouthAfrica* 3-8-11 WMLordan (20) 100/1   2 5
        Bygone Days *SaeedbinSuroor* 6-9-4 LDettori (8)..................................... 18/1   1¼ 6
        Baltic King *HMorrison* 7-9-4 (t) JimmyFortune (13) .... 50/1   nk 7
        Borderlescott *RBastiman* 5-9-4 RoystonFfrench (17)................................ 20/1   sh 8
        Firenze *JRFanshawe* 6-9-1 JamieSpencer (4)... 25/1   ¾ 9
        Al Qasi (IRE) *PWChapple-Hyam* 4-9-4 KerrinMcEvoy (15) .... 8/1   ½ 10
        Amadeus Wolf *KARyan* 4-9-4 NCallan (7)... 13/2   2 11
        Presto Shinko (IRE) *RHannon* 6-9-4 (s) JHBowman (9)........................... 100/1   ½ 12

Wi Dud *KAR*yan 3-8-11 MJKinane (19).. 40/1 ¾ 13
24 Magnus (AUS) *PeterGMoody,Australia* 5-9-4 (b) DMOliver (21)................ 15/2 ¾ 14
24 Miss Andretti (AUS) *LeeFreedman,Australia* 6-9-1 CNewitt (16)................ 2/1f ½ 15
Assertive *RHannon* 4-9-4 RyanMoore (14)... 66/1 2 16
Quito (IRE) *DWChapman* 10-9-4 (b) KDarley (18)................................. 66/1 1¾ 17
Appalachian Trail (IRE) *ISemple* 6-9-4 (b) TomEaves (2)....................... 100/1 2½ 18
Rising Shadow (IRE) *TDBarron* 6-9-4 JimmyQuinn (1)........................ 25/1 ¾ 19
Fayr Jag (IRE) *TDEasterby* 8-9-4 JohnEgan (5)..................................... 100/1 1 20
Hamoody (USA) *PWChapple-Hyam* 3-8-11 OPeslier (6).......................... 100/1 nk 21

Budget Stable 21ran 1m14.51   TR: 126/125/123/121/113/112+

SAINT-CLOUD Sunday, Jun 24   GOOD

33 **Grand Prix de Saint-Cloud (Gr 1) (4yo+)** £154,432   1½m

21 MOUNTAIN HIGH (IRE) *SirMichaelStoute,GB* 5-9-2 KFallon 13/1   1
MANDESHA (FR) *AdeRoyerDupre,France* 4-8-13 CSoumillon 4/5f 1½ 2
PRINCE FLORI (GER) *SSmrczek,Germany* 4-9-2 JVictoire .... 21/4 ½ 3
21 Irish Wells (FR) *FrancoisRohaut,France* 4-9-2 DBoeuf 10/1 2 4
16 Youmzain (IRE) *MRChannon,GB* 4-9-2 JamieSpencer...................... 7/2 1 5
Ponte Tresa (FR) *YdeNicolay,France* 4-8-13 OPeslier 13/1 3 6

Mrs John Magnier & Mr M. Tabor 6ran 2m29.70   TR: 123/118/120/116/114/104

CURRAGH Sunday, Jul 1   SOFT

34 **Budweiser Irish Derby (Gr 1) (3yo c+f)** £568,792   1½m

20 SOLDIER OF FORTUNE (IRE) *APO'Brien* 3-9-0 JAHeffernan (11) 5/1   1
22 ALEXANDER OF HALES (USA) *APO'Brien* 3-9-0 MJKinane (9) 33/1 9 2
20 EAGLE MOUNTAIN (IRE) *APO'Brien* 3-9-0 KFallon (6)...................... 6/4f 18 3
Boscobel *MJohnston,GB* 3-9-0 JoeFanning (2).............................. 8/1 3½ 4
Mores Wells *KevinPrendergast* 3-9-0 (t) DPMcDonogh (3)............ 14/1 ½ 5
Prince Erik *DKWeld* 3-9-0 PJSmullen (7).................................... 33/1 2½ 6
12 Al Shemali *SirMichaelStoute,GB* 3-9-0 (t) RyanMoore (8) 12/1 1½ 7
Royal And Regal (IRE) *AFabre,France* 3-9-0 JMurtagh (4)............. 7/1 18 8
22 Shamdinan (FR) *AdeRoyerDupre,France* 3-9-0 CSoumillon (5)........ 15/2 ¾ 9
Spanish Harlem (IRE) *APO'Brien* 3-9-0 FMBerry (1)................... 50/1 ½ 10
Striving Storm (USA) *PWChapple-Hyam* 3-9-0 EddieAhern (10)......... 28/1 17 11

Mrs John Magnier 11ran 2m36.02   TR: 131/115/115/108/107/103

SANDOWN Saturday, Jul 7   GOOD

35 **Coral-Eclipse Stks (Gr 1) (3yo+)** £259,314   1¼m7y

28 NOTNOWCATO *SirMichaelStoute* 5-9-7 RyanMoore (1)...................... 7/1   1
20 AUTHORIZED (IRE) *PWChapple-Hyam* 3-8-10 LDettori (6) 4/7f 1½ 2
26 GEORGE WASHINGTON (IRE) *APO'Brien,Ireland* 4-9-7 JAHeffernan (8) 4/1 hd 3
20 Yellowstone (IRE) *APO'Brien,Ireland* 3-8-10 FMBerry (4)............ 50/1 1¼ 4
20 Admiralofthefleet (USA) *APO'Brien,Ireland* 3-8-10 MJKinane (2)......... 12/1 4 5
5 Kandidate *CEBrittain* 5-9-7 (t) EddieAhern (7)........................ 50/1 1¼ 6
20 Archipenko (USA) *APO'Brien,Ireland* 3-8-10 CO'Donoghue (3).......... 16/1 5 7
Champery (USA) *MJohnston* 3-8-10 JoeFanning (5)................... 150/1 sh 8

Anthony & David De Rothschild 8ran 2m05.85   TR: 128/123+/124/119/110/109

CHANTILLY Sunday, Jul 8   SOFT

36 **Prix Jean Prat (Gr 1) (3yo c+f)** £153,396   1m

22 LAWMAN (FR) *J-MBeguigne,France* 3-9-2 OPeslier 13/10f   1
11 STONESIDE (IRE) *RodolpheCollet,France* 3-9-2 (s) TGillet....... 10/1 3 2
GOLDEN TITUS (IRE) *ARenzoni,Italy* 3-9-2 CSoumillon 9/1 1½ 3
25 Astronomer Royal (USA) *APO'Brien,Ireland* 3-9-2 KFallon 11/4 4 4
7 Tobosa *WJarvis,GB* 3-9-2 MichaelHills .... 17/1 sn 5
Asperity (USA) *JHMGosden,GB* 3-9-2 JimmyFortune 25/4 1 6
Grand Vista *AFabre,France* 3-9-2 SPasquier .... 11/1 sn 7

Mr C. Marzocco 7ran 1m41.20   TR: 120+/112/109/100

NEWMARKET Friday, Jul 13   GOOD to FIRM (July Course)

37 **Darley July Cup (Gr 1) (3yo+)** £212,925   6f

SAKHEE'S SECRET *HMorrison* 3-8-13 SteveDrowne (16) 9/2   1
25 DUTCH ART *PWChapple-Hyam* 3-8-13 JimmyFortune (11) .... 5/1 ½ 2
32 RED CLUBS (IRE) *BWHills* 4-9-5 MichaelHills (7).............. 16/1 1¼ 3
Marchand (FR) *FHead,France* 4-9-5 DBonilla (1) .... 25/1 nk 4
24 Dandy Man (IRE) *MissTAMCollins,Ireland* 4-9-5 PShanahan (9)......... 8/1 ½ 5
32 Asset (IRE) *RHannon* 4-9-5 RichardHughes (5)................... 4/1f sh 6
32 Borderlescott *RBastiman* 5-9-5 RoystonFfrench (18).......... 50/1 1 7
Hellvelyn *BSmart* 3-8-13 TedDurcan (4)........................... 33/1 ½ 8
Mutawaajid (AUS) *MRChannon* 4-9-5 JHBowman (3) .... 16/1 sh 9

24	Bentley Biscuit (AUS) *GaiWaterhouse,Australia* 6-9-5 RyanMoore (8)	10/1	sh 10
32	Drayton (IRE) *MFdeKock,SouthAfrica* 3-8-13 WCMarwing (13)	33/1	½ 11
32	Amadeus Wolf *KARyan* 4-9-5 NCallan (20)	17/2	sh 12
7	Prime Defender *BWHills* 3-8-13 RHills (19)	33/1	1¾ 13
	Electric Beat *AndreasLowe,Germany* 4-9-5 AHelfenbein (14)	100/1	1¾ 14
32	Rising Shadow (IRE) *TDBarron* 6-9-5 JimmyQuinn (10)	100/1	2 15
32	Quito (IRE) *DWChapman* 10-9-5 (b) PhilipRobinson (6)	100/1	¾ 16
	Balthazaar's Gift (IRE) *LMCumani* 4-9-5 MJKinane (2)	33/1	¾ 17
10	Sander Camillo (USA) *JNoseda* 3-8-10 (v) SebSanders (17)	20/1	10 18

Miss B. Swire 18ran 1m10.77   TR: 128/126/124/123/121/121

CURRAGH Sunday, Jul 15   HEAVY

38   **Darley Irish Oaks (Gr 1) (3yo f) £189,527**   1½m

19	PEEPING FAWN (USA) *APO'Brien* 3-9-0 JMurtagh (4)	3/1	1
19	LIGHT SHIFT (USA) *HRACecil,GB* 3-9-0 TedDurcan (5)	9/4f	3½ 2
19	ALL MY LOVING (IRE) *APO'Brien* 3-9-0 JAHeffernan (2)	5/1	2 3
	Timarwa (IRE) *JohnMOxx* 3-9-0 MJKinane (6)	7/1	3 4
	Profound Beauty (IRE) *DKWeld* 3-9-0 PJSmullen (1)	10/1	2 5
	Uimhir A Haon (IRE) *APO'Brien* 3-9-0 CO'Donoghue (10)	20/1	4 6
19	Four Sins (GER) *JohnMOxx* 3-9-0 FMBerry (12)	10/1	4½ 7
	Vonne Owen (IRE) *JohnJosephMurphy* 3-9-0 DMGrant (11)	300/1	16 8
	Maid of Lorn (USA) *MissTAMCollins* 3-9-0 PShanahan (9)	200/1	3½ 9
	Athenian Way (IRE) *JohnMOxx* 3-9-0 NGMcCullagh (8)	40/1	8 10
	Aqraan *KevinPrendergast* 3-9-0 DPMcDonogh (7)	33/1	8 11
17	Gaudeamus (USA) *JSBolger* 3-9-0 KJManning (3)	80/1	dist 12

Mr Michael Tabor 12ran 2m39.12   TR: 122+/116/113/107/104

ASCOT Saturday, Jul 28   GOOD

39   **King George VI and Queen Elizabeth Stks (Gr 1) (3yo+) £425,850**   1½m

28	DYLAN THOMAS (IRE) *APO'Brien,Ireland* 4-9-7 JMurtagh (5)	5/4f	1
33	YOUMZAIN (IRE) *MRChannon* 4-9-7 RichardHughes (1)	12/1	4 2
31	MARAAHEL (IRE) *SirMichaelStoute* 6-9-7 (v) RHills (3)	6/1	3½ 3
1	Laverock (IRE) *SaeedbinSuroor* 5-9-7 LDettori (7)	11/1	½ 4
31	Scorpion (IRE) *APO'Brien,Ireland* 5-9-7 MJKinane (2)	3/1	3 5
29	Sergeant Cecil *BRMillman* 8-9-7 RyanMoore (4)	33/1	5 6
33	Prince Flori (GER) *SSmrczek,Germany* 4-9-7 JimmyFortune (6)	10/1	3½ 7

Mrs John Magnier & Mr M. Tabor 7ran 2m31.11   TR: 132/124/117/116/111/101

GOODWOOD Wednesday, Aug 1   GOOD

40   **BGC Sussex Stks (Gr 1) (3yo+) £170,340**   1m

26	RAMONTI (FR) *SaeedbinSuroor* 5-9-7 (t) LDettori (8)	9/2	1
25	EXCELLENT ART *APO'Brien,Ireland* 3-9-0 JamieSpencer (7)	15/8f	hd 2
26	JEREMY (USA) *SirMichaelStoute* 4-9-7 RyanMoore (4)	7/2	1¾ 3
	Asiatic Boy (ARG) *MFdeKock,SouthAfrica* 4-9-7 WCMarwing (2)	3/1	sh 4
35	Archipenko (USA) *APO'Brien,Ireland* 3-9-0 DavidMcCabe (6)	25/1	5 5
	Decado (IRE) *KevinPrendergast,Ireland* 4-9-7 DPMcDonogh (3)	50/1	1 6
	Munaddam (USA) *EALDunlop* 5-9-7 RHills (5)	14/1	6 7
15	Trinity College (USA) *APO'Brien,Ireland* 3-9-0 JMurtagh (1)	66/1	1 8

Godolphin 8ran 1m37.62   TR: 126/125/121/121/107/105

GOODWOOD Saturday, Aug 4   GOOD to FIRM

41   **Blue Square Nassau Stks (Gr 1) (3yo+ f+m) £113,560**   1m1f192y

38	PEEPING FAWN (USA) *APO'Brien,Ireland* 3-8-10 JMurtagh (8)	2/1f	1
33	MANDESHA (FR) *AdeRoyerDupre,France* 4-9-5 CSoumillon (7)	7/2	1½ 2
38	LIGHT SHIFT (USA) *HRACecil* 3-8-10 TedDurcan (4)	3/1	3½ 3
23	Sweet Lilly *MRChannon* 3-8-10 JHBowman (5)	22/1	½ 4
	Dont Dili Dali *JSMoore* 4-9-5 (s) JohnEgan (4)	80/1	2½ 5
13	Speciosa (IRE) *MrsPSly* 4-9-5 JamieSpencer (1)	14/1	nk 6
30	Yaqeen *MAJarvis* 3-8-10 RHills (2)	14/1	1¼ 7
27	Nannina *JHMGosden* 4-9-5 JimmyFortune (6)	6/1	10 8

Mr M. Tabor & Mrs John Magnier 8ran 2m04.53   TR: 120+/118+/108+/107/102/102

DEAUVILLE Sunday, Aug 5   GOOD to FIRM

42   **Prix Maurice de Gheest (Gr 1) (3yo+) £95,872**   6f110y

37	MARCHAND D'OR (FR) *FHead,France* 4-9-2 DBonilla	36/10	1
37	DUTCH ART *PWChapple-Hyam,GB* 3-8-12 JimmyFortune	6/4f	1 2
	SILVER TOUCH (IRE) *MRChannon,GB* 4-8-13 TPO'Shea	57/1	½ 3
	Garnica (FR) *J-CRouget,France* 4-9-2 CPLemaire	12/1	nk 4
7	Major Cadeaux *RHannon,GB* 3-8-12 RichardHughes	15/1	1½ 5
	Satri (IRE) *J-MBeguigne,France* 5-9-2 OPeslier	9/1	½ 6

	37	Bentley Biscuit (AUS) *GaiWaterhouse,Australia* 6-9-2 JamieSpencer	16/1	¾ 7
	24	Moss Vale (IRE) *DNicholls,GB* 6-9-2 KFallon	44/1	sn 8
		New Girlfriend (IRE) *RCollet,France* 4-8-13 YTake	52/1	½ 9
		Tiza (SAF) *AdeRoyerDupre,France* 5-9-2 CSoumillon	15/2	hd 10
	32	Bygone Days *SaeedbinSuroor,GB* 6-9-2 LDettori	13/1	nk 11
		Val Jaro (FR) *SMorineau,France* 4-9-2 TJarnet	77/1	½ 12
		Tycoon's Hill (IRE) *RCollet,France* 8-9-2 J-BHamel	72/1	13

Mme J. L Giral 13ran 1m14.90　　　　　　　　　TR: 123/120/115/117/112/111

ARLINGTON Saturday, Aug 11　GOOD to SOFT

43　Arlington Million Stks (Gr 1) (3yo+) £291,176　　　　　　1¼m

		JAMBALAYA (CAN) *CatherineDayPhillips,Canada* 5-9-0 RAlbarado	76/10	1
		THE TIN MAN (USA) *REMandella,USA* 9-9-0 VEspinoza	2/1f	¾ 2
	6	DOCTOR DINO (FR) *RGibson,France* 5-9-0 JMurtagh	49/10	ns 3
		Sunriver (USA) *TAPletcher,USA* 4-9-0 GGomez	149/10	nk 4
		Stream Cat (USA) *PLBiancone,USA* 4-9-0 (b) JLeparoux	27/10	dh 4
	16	Danak (IRE) *JohnMOxx,Ireland* 4-9-0 MJKinane	41/10	½ 6
	28	Pressing (IRE) *MAJarvis,GB* 4-9-0 DFlores	144/10	2 7

Kingfield Farms 7ran 2m04.76　　　　　　　TR: 121/119/119/118/118/117/113

DEAUVILLE Sunday, Aug 12　GOOD

44　Prix du Haras de Fresnay-le-Buffard-Jacques Le Marois (Gr 1) (3yo+)　1m
£231,649

	28	MANDURO (GER) *AFabre,France* 5-9-4 SPasquier	9/10	1
		HOLOCENE (USA) *PBary,France* 3-8-11 CPLemaire	26/1	3 2
	26	TURTLE BOWL (IRE) *FrancoisRohaut,France* 5-9-4 CSoumillon	17/2	½ 3
		Toylsome *JHirschberger,Germany* 3-8-11 JVictoire	35/1	4 4
	14	Stormy River (FR) *NClement,France* 4-9-4 (s) TThulliez	25/4	½ 5
	36	Lawman (FR) *J-MBeguigne,France* 3-8-11 OPeslier	9/4	5 6

Baron G. von Ullmann 6ran 1m37.40　　　　　　TR: 124+/115?/114/103/102

DEAUVILLE Sunday, Aug 19　GOOD to SOFT

45　Darley Prix Morny (Gr 1) (2yo c+f) £135,128　　　　　　6f

		MYBOYCHARLIE (IRE) *TStack,Ireland* 2-9-0 KFallon	6/4f	1
		NATAGORA (FR) *PBary,France* 2-8-11 CPLemaire	9/5	2 2
		ALEXANDROS *AFabre,France* 2-9-0 SPasquier	23/10	½ 3
		Etenia (USA) *SWattel,France* 2-8-11 YBarberot	24/1	6 4
		Flying Blue (FR) *RMartin-Sanchez,Spain* 2-9-0 TThulliez	23/1	1 5
		Ensis (SPA) *ORodriguez-Alguacil,Spain* 2-8-11 J-CJarcovsky	19/1	nk 6

Mrs John Magnier,Mr M.Tabor & Mr D.Smith 6ran 1m13.10　　　TR: 118/109/110

YORK Tuesday, Aug 21　GOOD to SOFT

46　Ladbrokes Great Voltigeur Stks (Gr 2) (3yo c+g) £76,653　　1½m

	20	LUCARNO (USA) *JHMGosden* 3-8-12 JimmyFortune (7)	7/2	1
	35	YELLOWSTONE (IRE) *APO'Brien,Ireland* 3-8-12 JMurtagh (9)	9/4f	1 2
		MACARTHUR *APO'Brien,Ireland* 3-8-12 RyanMoore (8)	12/1	½ 3
	20	Acapulco (IRE) *APO'Brien,Ireland* 3-8-12 JAHeffernan (6)	15/2	1¼ 4
	20	Mahler *APO'Brien,Ireland* 3-8-12 MJKinane (3)	6/1	sh 5
		Spice Route *MLWBell* 3-8-12 EddieAhern (5)	20/1	1½ 6
		Hearthstead Maison (IRE) *MJohnston* 3-8-12 GregFairley (4)	20/1	8 7
		Heron Bay *GWragg* 3-8-12 SteveDrowne (1)	18/1	18 8
	34	Boscobel *MJohnston* 3-9-1 LDettori (2)	9/2	20 9

Mr George Strawbridge 9ran 2m33.07　　　　　TR: 119+/117+/116/114/114/111

47　Juddmonte International Stks (Gr 1) (3yo+) £298,095　　　1¼m88y

	35	AUTHORIZED (IRE) *PWChapple-Hyam* 3-8-11 LDettori (1)	6/4f	1
	39	DYLAN THOMAS (IRE) *APO'Brien,Ireland* 4-9-5 JMurtagh (7)	2/1	1 2
	35	NOTNOWCATO *SirMichaelStoute* 5-9-5 RyanMoore (4)	7/2	3 3
	25	Duke of Marmalade (IRE) *APO'Brien,Ireland* 3-8-11 MJKinane (2)	12/1	nk 4
	40	Asiatic Boy (ARG) *MFdeKock,SouthAfrica* 4-9-4 JamieSpencer (6)	12/1	3 5
	18	Hattan (IRE) *CEBrittain* 5-9-5 SebSanders (5)	100/1	1½ 6
		Song of Hiawatha *APO'Brien,Ireland* 3-8-11 JAHeffernan (3)	200/1	1¾ 7

Saleh Al Homeizi & Imad Al Sagar 7ran 2m11.82　　　TR: 133/132/125/124/118/115

YORK Wednesday, Aug 22　GOOD to SOFT

48　Darley Yorkshire Oaks (Gr 1) (3yo+ f+m) £164,662　　　1½m

	41	PEEPING FAWN (USA) *APO'Brien,Ireland* 3-8-11 JMurtagh (8)	4/9f	1
	29	ALLEGRETTO (IRE) *SirMichaelStoute* 4-9-7 (v) RyanMoore (7)	9/1	4 2
		TRICK OR TREAT *JGGiven* 4-9-7 TPQueally (2)	66/1	5 3
		Under The Rainbow *BWHills* 4-9-7 NCallan (6)	100/1	1¼ 4
	19	Dalvina *EALDunlop* 3-8-11 JamieSpencer (3)	25/1	½ 5

19 Darrfonah (IRE) *CEBrittain* 3-8-11 (t) KerrinMcEvoy (4) .... 80/1 ½ 6
   Silkwood *MAJarvis* 3-8-11 PhilipRobinson (1) .... 10/3 ½ 7
   Mr M. Tabor & Mrs John Magnier 7ran 2m32.70   TR: 121+/113+/104/102/101/100

YORK Thursday, Aug 23   GOOD

49   Coolmore Nunthorpe Stks (Gr 1) (2yo+) £136,158   5f

   KINGSGATE NATIVE (IRE) *JRBest* 2-8-1 JimmyQuinn (13) 12/1   1
24 DESERT LORD *KARyan* 7-9-11 (b) DarryllHolland (7) 20/1   1¾ 2
37 DANDY MAN (IRE) *MissTAMCollins,Ireland* 4-9-11 PShanahan (16) .... 9/4f   hd 3
37 Red Clubs (IRE) *BWHills* 4-9-11 MichaelHills (2) .... 7/1   ¾ 4
32 Wi Dud *KARyan* 3-9-9 TedDurcan (12) .... 25/1 nk 5
   Hoh Mike (IRE) *MLWBell* 3-9-9 JamieSpencer (8) .... 10/1 sh 6
37 Amadeus Wolf *KARyan* 4-9-11 NCallan (5) .... 10/1 sh 7
   Sierra Vista *DWBarker* 7-9-8 PaulHanagan (10) .... 40/1   ½ 8
32 Magnus (AUS) *PeterGMoody,Australia* 5-9-11 (b) KerrinMcEvoy (15) ..... 6/1 hd 9
24 Beauty Is Truth (IRE) *RCollet,France* 3-9-6 (b) TThulliez (14) 16/1 1 10
24 Moorhouse Lad *BSmart* 4-9-11 RyanMoore (4) .... 7/1   ½ 11
   Celtic Mill *DWBarker* 9-9-11 PatCosgrave (3) .... 100/1 ¾ 12
24 Green Manalishi *KARyan* 6-9-11 RichardHughes (1) 100/1 1½ 13
   Mecca's Mate *DWBarker* 6-9-8 TonyHamilton (6) 100/1 3½ 14
24 The Tatling (IRE) *JMBradley* 10-9-11 KevinGhunowa (17) 80/1 1¾ 15
   Reverence *EJAlston* 6-9-11 KDarley (9) 14/1 1¾ 16
   Mr John Mayne 16ran 58.14secs   TR: 122/123/122/119+//118/118

GOODWOOD Saturday, Aug 25   GOOD

50   totesport.com Celebration Mile (Gr 2) (3yo+) £62,117   1m

   ECHELON *SirMichaelStoute* 5-8-12 RyanMoore (3) 7/1   1
26 CESARE *JRFanshawe* 6-9-4 JamieSpencer (1) 11/10f 1¼ 2
   BLUE KSAR (FR) *SaeedbinSuroor* 4-9-1 (t) LDettori (6) 4/1 1½ 3
 4 Dunelight (IRE) *CGCox* 4-9-1 (v) DaneO'Neill (8) 9/2   2 4
 9 Selinka *RHannon* 3-8-6 EddieAhern (7) .... 20/1 dh 4
   Charlie Cool *WJHaggas* 4-9-1 (v) DarryllHolland (2) 25/1 1½ 6
   Blythe Knight (IRE) *JJQuinn* 7-9-1 GrahamGibbons (4) 14/1   2 7
   Finicius (USA) *EoinGriffin,Ireland* 3-8-9 RichardHughes (5) 20/1   7 8
   Cheveley Park Stud 8ran 1m38.97   TR: 120/123/116/110/106/106

CURRAGH Saturday, Aug 25   SOFT

51   Galileo European Breeders Fund Futurity Stks (Gr 2) (2yo) £52,721   7f

   NEW APPROACH (IRE) *JSBolger* 2-9-1 KJManning (3) 8/11f   1
   CURTAIN CALL (FR) *MrsJHarrington* 2-9-1 FMBerry (5) 40/1   3 2
   HENRYTHENAVIGATOR (USA) *APO'Brien* 2-9-4 KFallon (4) .... 11/10 nk 3
   Warsaw (IRE) *APO'Brien* 2-9-1 JAHeffernan (2) 25/1 11 4
   Pretty Ballerina (IRE) *JohnJosephMurphy* 2-8-12 JMurtagh (1) 66/1 30 5
   Mrs J. S. Bolger 5ran 1m29.00   TR: 121+/113/115

SANDOWN Saturday, Sep 1   GOOD to FIRM

52   Iveco Solario Stks (Gr 3) (2yo) £21,009   7f16y

   RAVEN'S PASS (USA) *JHMGosden* 2-9-0 JimmyFortune (1) 11/8f   1
   CITY LEADER (IRE) *BJMeehan* 2-9-0 KDarley (8) 8/1   7 2
   GASPAR VAN WITTEL (USA) *NACallaghan* 2-9-0 DaneO'Neill (4) .... 12/1 sh 3
   Belgrave Square (USA) *APO'Brien,Ireland* 2-9-0 JMurtagh (9) .... 6/1   ¾ 4
   Pegasus Again (USA) *TGMills* 2-9-0 LDettori (5) 6/1   1 5
   Maze (IRE) *BSmart* 2-9-0 RoystonFfrench (7) 4/1   6 6
   Yem Kinn *MRChannon* 2-9-0 TPO'Shea (6) .... 25/1 hd 7
   Lindoro *WRSwinburn* 2-9-0 AdamKirby (3) .... 66/1   ½ 8
   Ernie Owl (USA) *BJMeehan* 2-9-0 KerrinMcEvoy (10) 22/1 10 9
   Stonerside Stable LLC 9ran 1m26.56   TR: 122//102/101/99/96

CURRAGH Sunday, Sep 2   GOOD

53   Moyglare Stud Stks (Gr 1) (2yo f) £114,694   7f

   SAOIRSE ABU (USA) *JSBolger* 2-8-12 (b) KJManning (3) 13/2   1
   LISTEN (IRE) *APO'Brien* 2-8-12 KFallon (2) 4/5f 1½ 2
   MAD ABOUT YOU (IRE) *DKWeld* 2-8-12 PJSmullen (8) .... 7/1 ½ 3
   Albabilia (IRE) *CEBrittain,GB* 2-8-12 KerrinMcEvoy (5) 7/2   1 4
   Allicansayis Wow (USA) *JSBolger* 2-8-12 FMBerry (7) 40/1   2 5
   Solas Na Greine (IRE) *JSBolger* 2-8-12 DJMoran (4) 16/1 2½ 6
   Queen Jock (USA) *MissTAMCollins* 2-8-12 PShanahan (1) .... 25/1 hd 7
   Juniper Berry (IRE) *JohnJosephMurphy* 2-8-12 WMLordan (6) 66/1   2 8
   Miss Red Eye (IRE) *LukeComer* 2-8-12 FFDaSilva (9) 200/1   6 9
   Ennistown Stud 9ran 1m25.01   TR: 108/103+/102//99/93

54   **Nolan & Brophy Auctioneers Flying Five Stks (Gr 3) (3yo+)** £33,163   5f

24	BENBAUN (IRE) *MJWallace,GB* 6-9-5 (v) PJSmullen (8)	10/3	1
49	DANDY MAN (IRE) *MissTAMCollins* 4-9-2 PShanahan (5)	11/10f	hd 2
42	MOSS VALE (IRE) *DNicholls,GB* 8-9-2 KFallon (10)	4/1	1¾ 3
	Senor Benny (USA) *MMcDonagh* 8-9-2 DPMcDonogh (1)	16/1	2 4
	Snaefell (IRE) *MHalford* 3-9-1 JMurtagh (9)	10/1	1 5
	Moone Cross (IRE) *MrsJHarrington* 4-8-13 NGMcCullagh (6)	50/1	nk 6
	Peak District (IRE) *DWachman* 3-9-1 WMLordan (11)	14/1	4½ 7
	Osterhase (IRE) *JEMulhern* 8-9-2 (b) FMBerry (3)	16/1	1½ 8
	Leitra (IRE) *MHalford* 4-8-13 RPCleary (4)	33/1	1 9

Ransley, Birks, Hillen 9ran 58.79secs   TR: 127/123/117/110/106+/102

BADEN-BADEN Sunday, Sep 2   GOOD

55   **Grosser Preis von Baden (Gr 1) (3yo+)** £102,041   1½m

1	QUIJANO (GER) *PSchiergen,Germany* 5-9-6 AStarke	59/10	1
	ADLERFLUG (GER) *JHirschberger,Germany* 3-8-9 FJohansson (2)	22/10f	nk 2
6	EGERTON (GER) *PRau,Germany* 6-9-6 TMundry	26/1	3½ 3
39	Youmzain (IRE) *MRChannon,GB* 4-9-6 RichardHughes	37/10	hd 4
	Axxos (GER) *PSchiergen,Germany* 3-8-9 EPedroza	88/10	1½ 5
	First Stream (GER) *MHofer,Germany* 3-8-9 CPLemaire	16/1	¾ 6
39	Prince Flori (GER) *SSmrczek,Germany* 4-9-6 AdeVries	65/10	1¼ 7
33	Mountain High (IRE) *SirMichaelStoute,GB* 5-9-6 RMoore	28/10	1¼ 8
	Sommertag (GER) *JHirschberger,Germany* 4-9-6 THellier	27/1	15 9

Stiftung Gestut Fahrhof 9ran 2m28.19   TR: 122/120/115/114/109/108

HAYDOCK Saturday, Sep 8   GOOD

56   **Betfred Sprint Cup (Gr 1) (3yo+)** £179,027   6f

49	RED CLUBS (IRE) *BWHills* 4-9-3 MichaelHills (6)	9/1	1
42	MARCHAND D'OR (FR) *FHead,France* 4-9-3 DBonilla (1)	13/2	¾ 2
37	BALTHAZAAR'S GIFT (IRE) *LMCumani* 4-9-3 JimmyFortune (7)	11/1	½ 3
37	Mutawaajid (AUS) *MRChannon* 4-9-3 DarryllHolland (14)	33/1	1¼ 4
37	Sakhee's Secret *HMorrison* 3-9-1 SteveDrowne (2)	11/8f	nk 5
37	Asset (IRE) *RHannon* 4-9-3 (b) LDettori (12)	6/1	1 6
49	Wi Dud *KARyan* 3-9-1 DO'Donohoe (9)	33/1	nk 7
30	Scarlet Runner *JLDunlop* 3-8-12 SebSanders (10)	66/1	2½ 8
	Somnus *TDEasterby* 7-9-3 RichardMullen (15)	100/1	2½ 9
	Advanced *KARyan* 4-9-3 PatCosgrave (3)	100/1	nk 10
49	Sierra Vista *DWBarker* 7-9-0 PaulHanagan (11)	50/1	2½ 11
49	Amadeus Wolf *KARyan* 4-9-3 NCallan (4)	16/1	1½ 12
	Per Incanto (USA) *JLDunlop* 3-9-1 MartinDwyer (13)	20/1	nk 13
37	Hellvelyn *BSmart* 3-9-1 TedDurcan (16)	15/2	½ 14

Mr R. J. Arculli 14ran 1m13.11   TR: 125/123/121/117/116/113

LEOPARDSTOWN Saturday, Sep 8   GOOD to FIRM

57   **Coolmore Fusaichi Pegasus Matron Stks (Gr 1) (3yo+ f+m)** £109,797   1m

Order as they passed the post: third and fourth placings were reversed

50	ECHELON *SirMichaelStoute,GB* 5-9-3 RyanMoore (2)	9/4f	1
26	RED EVIE (IRE) *MLWBell,GB* 4-9-3 JamieSpencer (3)	7/2	1½ 2
	EASTERN APPEAL (IRE) *MHalford* 4-9-3 RPCleary (7)	40/1	nk 3
30	Arch Swing (USA) *JohnMOxx* 3-8-12 MJKinane (1)	11/4	nk 4
41	Sweet Lilly *MRChannon,GB* 3-8-12 KFallon (4)	10/1	2½ 5
	Modeeroch (IRE) *JSBolger* 4-9-3 (t) KJManning (6)	20/1	hd 6
	She's Our Mark *PaulFlynn* 3-8-12 DMGrant (9)	25/1	1¼ 7
	Evening Time (IRE) *KevinPrendergast* 3-8-12 DPMcDonogh (8)	12/1	nk 8
9	Barshiba (IRE) *DRCElsworth,GB* 3-8-12 TQuinn (5)	14/1	1 9

Cheveley Park Stud 9ran 1m39.52   TR: 119/115+/114?/113+/107/106

58   **Tattersalls Millions Irish Champion Stks (Gr 1) (3yo+)** £404,730   1¼m

47	DYLAN THOMAS (IRE) *APO'Brien* 4-9-7 KFallon (5)	8/15f	1
47	DUKE OF MARMALADE (IRE) *APO'Brien* 3-9-0 JAHeffernan (3)	15/2	1½ 2
	RED ROCK CANYON (IRE) *APO'Brien* 3-9-0 CO'Donoghue (1)	100/1	2 3
28	Red Rocks (IRE) *BJMeehan,GB* 4-9-7 RichardHughes (4)	10/1	2½ 4
39	Maraahel (IRE) *SirMichaelStoute,GB* 6-9-7 (b) RHills (2)	14/1	3½ 5
30	Finsceal Beo (IRE) *JSBolger* 3-8-11 KJManning (6)	5/1	1¾ 6

Mrs John Magnier 6ran 2m02.27   TR: 121+/117+/113/107

LONGCHAMP Sunday, Sep 9   GOOD

59   **Qatar Prix du Moulin de Longchamp (Gr 1) (3yo+)** £154,432   1m

30	DARJINA (FR) *AdeRoyerDupre,France* 3-8-8 CSoumillon	39/10	1
40	RAMONTI (FR) *SaeedbinSuroor,GB* 5-9-2 LDettori	7/4f	2 2

```
   35  GEORGE WASHINGTON (IRE) APO'Brien,Ireland 4-9-2 KFallon ............. 9/4      1  3
    2  Linngari (IRE) AdeRoyerDupre,France 5-9-2 RyanMoore ........................... 29/1      1  4
   40  Archipenko (USA) APO'Brien,Ireland 3-8-11 JAHeffernan ........................ 39/1    2½  5
   44  Holocene (USA) PBary,France 3-8-11 CPLemaire ..................................... 12/1      2  6
   36  Astronomer Royal (USA) APO'Brien,Ireland 3-8-11 CO'Donoghue............ 40/1    nk  7
   44  Turtle Bowl (IRE) FrancoisRohaut,France 5-9-2 OPeslier ......................... 10/1    sn  8
   36  Golden Titus (IRE) ARenzoni,Italy 3-8-11 SPasquier ................................. 21/1      1  9
```

Princess Zahra Aga Khan 9ran 1m36.80   TR: 128/126/123+/120/113/108

DONCASTER Friday, Sep 14   GOOD to FIRM

60 GNER Doncaster Cup (Gr 2) (3yo+) £56,780   2¼m

```
   18  SEPTIMUS (IRE) APO'Brien,Ireland 4-9-4 JMurtagh (8)........................ 11/10f     1
   29  GEORDIELAND (FR) JAOsborne 6-9-1 TPQueally (5)............................... 7/1     5  2
   48  ALLEGRETTO (IRE) SirMichaelStoute 4-9-1 LDettori (6)........................ 7/2    ½  3
       Distinction (IRE) SirMichaelStoute 8-9-1 OPeslier (4)............................ 8/1   1¾  4
   29  Finalmente NACallaghan 5-9-1 (s) RichardHughes (2) ............................ 14/1     5  5
       Balkan Knight DRCElsworth 7-9-1 TedDurcan (1)................................... 12/1     6  6
       Land 'n Stars RAFahey 7-9-1 PaulHanagan (7) ..................................... 50/1   1¼  7
   29  Baddam MRChannon 5-9-1 IanMongan (3) ............................................ 33/1   dist 8
```

Mr D. Smith, Mrs J. Magnier, Mr M. Tabor 8ran 3m48.41

TR: 126+/117/118/115/111/106

DONCASTER Saturday, Sep 15   GOOD to FIRM

61 Ladbrokes St Leger Stks (Gr 1) (3yo c+f) £303,915   1¾m132y

```
   46  LUCARNO (USA) JHMGosden 3-9-0 JimmyFortune (8)............................ 7/2      1
   46  MAHLER (IRE) APO'Brien,Ireland 3-9-0 MJKinane (3) ........................... 13/2     1  2
       HONOLULU (IRE) APO'Brien,Ireland 3-9-0 JMurtagh (7) ..................... 13/8f    ¾  3
       Regal Flush SirMichaelStoute 3-9-0 RyanMoore (5) ............................... 13/2   nk  4
       Veracity MAJarvis 3-9-0 PhilipRobinson (1)......................................... 16/1   sh  5
   46  Macarthur APO'Brien,Ireland 3-9-0 CSoumillon (2).............................. 17/2   nk  6
       Celestial Halo (IRE) BWHills 3-9-0 RHills (4).................................... 66/1   ¾  7
   46  Acapulco (IRE) APO'Brien,Ireland 3-9-0 CO'Donoghue (9)..................... 25/1   1¼  8
       Samuel JLDunlop 3-9-0 TQuinn (6)...................................................... 40/1   12  9
   22  Raincoat JHMGosden 3-9-0 RichardHughes (10)................................... 12/1   16 10
```

Mr George Strawbridge 10ran 3m01.81   TR: 120+/118+/117/117/117/116+

CURRAGH Saturday, Sep 15   GOOD to FIRM

62 St Jovite Renaissance Stks (Gr 3) (3yo+) £33,163   6f

```
   54  BENBAUN (IRE) MJWallace,GB 6-9-8 (b) PJSmullen (2)........................... 5/4f      1
   54  MOSS VALE (IRE) DNicholls,GB 6-9-1 JohnEgan (6).............................. 10/3   ¾  2
   37  PRIME DEFENDER BWHills,GB 3-9-1 MichaelHills (1) .......................... 10/3  2½  3
       Absolutelyfabulous (IRE) DWachman 4-9-0 KFallon (5)......................... 14/1  1½  4
   54  Senor Benny (USA) MMcDonagh 8-9-3 DPMcDonogh (4) ...................... 16/1     1  5
   54  Snaefell (IRE) MHalford 3-9-1 RPCleary (3)......................................... 16/1   nk  6
   54  Moone Cross (IRE) MrsJHarrington 4-9-0 NGMcCullagh (7)................... 33/1   11  7
```

Ransley, Birks, Hillen 7ran 1m09.97   TR: 125/117/109+/101/104

63 Irish Field St Leger (Gr 1) (3yo+) £116,735   1¾m

```
   29  YEATS (IRE) APO'Brien 6-9-11 KFallon (4)........................................... 4/7f      1
   39  SCORPION (IRE) APO'Brien 5-9-11 JAHeffernan (3)................................ 7/2   ½  2
   34  MORES WELLS KevinPrendergast 3-9-0 (t) DPMcDonogh (4).................. 8/1  4½  3
       Macorville (USA) GMMoore,GB 4-9-11 FMBerry (5) ............................. 100/1  1½  4
   31  Mighty JaneChapple-Hyam,GB 4-9-11 JohnEgan (1)............................... 20/1   ¾  5
       Galistic (IRE) PaulFlynn 4-9-8 DMGrant (6) ...................................... 50/1     6  6
       Steppe Dancer (IRE) DJCoakley,GB 4-9-11 KJManning (2)..................... 25/1  2½  7
       The Whistling Teal GWragg,GB 11-9-11 WilliamSupple (8)..................... 66/1  2½  8
    1  Bellamy Cay DKWeld 5-9-11 PJSmullen (7)........................................ 16/1  5½  9
```

Mrs John Magnier 9ran 3m03.40   TR: 123+/122+/115/113/112

CURRAGH Sunday, Sep 16   GOOD to FIRM

64 Bank of Scotland (Ireland) National Stks (Gr 1) (2yo c+f) £116,599   7f

```
   51  NEW APPROACH (IRE) JSBolger 2-9-1 KJManning (7)............................ 9/4f      1
       RIO DE LA PLATA (USA) SaeedbinSuroor,GB 2-9-1 LDettori (5).............. 5/2  1¾  2
   45  MYBOYCHARLIE (IRE) TStack 2-9-1 KFallon (8)................................. 5/2  1¾  3
       Lizard Island (USA) APO'Brien 2-9-1 JAHeffernan (9).......................... 25/1  1½  4
       Great Barrier Reef (USA) APO'Brien 2-9-1 CO'Donoghue (3)................... 25/1     3  5
       Famous Name DKWeld 2-9-1 PJSmullen (1)......................................... 8/1     2  6
       Minneapolis APO'Brien 2-9-1 DPMcDonogh (2) .................................. 100/1  1¾  7
       Magna Cum Laude (IRE) APO'Brien 2-9-1 FMBerry (4)......................... 100/1     5  8
       Via Galilei (IRE) JSBolger 2-9-1 DJMoran (6)...................................... 33/1   sh  9
```

Mrs J. S. Bolger 9ran 1m23.51   TR: 125+/120/114/110/100

65   **Prix Vermeille Lucien Barriere (Gr 1) (3yo+ f+m)** £116,612   1½m

23	MRS LINDSAY (USA) *FrancoisRohaut,France* 3-8-9 JMurtagh (2)	183/10	1
23	WEST WIND *H-APantall,France* 3-8-8 JVictoire (9)	23/10	¾ 2
19	PASSAGE OF TIME *HRACecil,GB* 3-8-8 RichardHughes (11)	62/10	¾ 3
	Legerete (USA) *AFabre,France* 3-8-8 OPeslier (6)	15/1	1 4
	Macleya (FR) *AFabre,France* 3-8-9 JAuge (1)	16/1	nk 5
29	Montare (IRE) *JEPease,France* 5-9-2 (s) CPLemaire (10)	11/1	1½ 6
23	Diyakalanie (FR) *JBoisnard,France* 3-8-8 TThulliez (4)	15/1	2 7
	Tashelka (FR) *AFabre,France* 3-8-8 SPasquier (7)	23/10	2 8
23	Vadapolina (FR) *AFabre,France* 3-8-8 CSoumillon (8)	14/10cpf	sn 9
	Takaniya (IRE) *AFabre,France* 3-8-8 MSautjeau (3)	14/10cpf	dist 10

Mrs B. Jenney 10ran 2m27.00   TR: 117/114+/113/111/109/106

66   **Prix Niel Casino Barriere d'Enghien Les Bains (Gr 2) (3yo c+f)** £50,408   1½m

34	SOLDIER OF FORTUNE (IRE) *APO'Brien,Ireland* 3-9-2 JMurtagh (5)	23/10	1
22	SAGARA (USA) *JEPease,France* 3-9-2 TGillet (4)	23/1	1½ 2
22	ZAMBEZI SUN (FR) *PBary,France* 3-9-2 SPasquier (2)	11/10f	¾ 3
	Sageburg (IRE) *AFabre,France* 3-9-2 CSoumillon (1)	5/2	6 4
22	Spirit One (FR) *PHDemercastel,France* 3-9-2 DBoeuf (3)	15/1	8 5
47	Song of Hiawatha *APO'Brien,Ireland* 3-9-2 DavidMcCabe (4)	23/10	5 6

Mrs John Magnier,Mr M.Tabor & Mr D.Smith 6ran 2m25.60   TR: 122+/119/117/104

67   **Prix Foy Gray d'Albion Barriere (Gr 2) (4yo+ c+f)** £50,408   1½m

44	MANDURO (GER) *AFabre,France* 5-9-2 SPasquier (4)	2/5cpf	1
41	MANDESHA (FR) *AdeRoyerDupre,France* 4-8-13 CSoumillon (1)	22/10	2½ 2
	DRAGON DANCER *GWragg,GB* 4-9-2 DarrylHolland (5)	22/1	3 3
55	Sommertag (GER) *JHirschberger,Germany* 4-9-2 JVictoire (3)	2/5cpf	½ 4
	Distant Way (USA) *LBrogi,Italy* 6-9-2 MDemuro (2)	86/10	4 5

Baron G. von Ullmann 5ran 2m28.80   TR: 126+/118/115/114?/105+

ASCOT Saturday, Sep 29   GOOD to SOFT

68   **Meon Valley Stud Fillies' Mile (Gr 1) (2yo f)** £123,942   1m (Rnd)

53	LISTEN (IRE) *APO'Brien,Ireland* 2-8-12 JMurtagh (6)	10/3	1
	PROVISO *AFabre,France* 2-8-12 SPasquier (5)	11/10f	1 2
53	SAOIRSE ABU (USA) *JSBolger,Ireland* 2-8-12 (v) KJManning (3)	5/1	2½ 3
	Kotsi (IRE) *EFVaughan,GB* 2-8-12 LDettori (8)	11/2	5 4
	Kay Es Jay (FR) *BWHills* 2-8-12 RyanMoore (4)	66/1	2 5
	Sugar Mint (IRE) *BWHills* 2-8-12 MichaelHills (1)	16/1	4 6
	Wadlia (USA) *CEBrittain* 2-8-12 SebSanders (5)	100/1	9 7

Mr D. Smith, Mrs J. Magnier, Mr M. Tabor 7ran 1m43.30   TR: 117/115+/108/96/91

69   **Queen Elizabeth II Stks (Gr 1) (3yo+)** £123,783   1m (Rnd)

59	RAMONTI (FR) *SaeedbinSuroor* 5-9-3 (t) LDettori (4)	2/1	1
40	EXCELLENT ART *APO'Brien,Ireland* 3-8-13 JamieSpencer (1)	15/8f	½ 2
58	DUKE OF MARMALADE (IRE) *APO'Brien,Ireland* 3-8-13 MJKinane (6)	13/2	½ 3
50	Cesare *JRFanshawe* 6-9-3 JMurtagh (4)	6/1	hd 4
44	Stormy River (FR) *NClement,France* 4-9-3 TThulliez (9)	18/1	4 5
50	Blue Ksar (FR) *SaeedbinSuroor* 4-9-3 (t) KerrinMcEvoy (10)	25/1	sh 6
59	Darjina (FR) *AdeRoyerDupre,France* 3-8-10 CSoumillon (3)	11/4	sh 7

Godolphin 7ran 1m42.45   TR: 126/125/124/123/112/112

ASCOT Sunday, Sep 30   GOOD

70   **Grosvenor Casinos Cumberland Lodge Stks (Gr 3) (3yo+)** £28,390   1½m

	ASK *SirMichaelStoute* 4-9-3 RyanMoore (1)	11/4	1
	ZAHAM (USA) *MJohnston* 3-8-6 RHills (2)	8/1	2 2
61	HONOLULU (IRE) *APO'Brien,Ireland* 3-8-6 DarrylHolland (7)	6/4f	¾ 3
47	Hattan (IRE) *CEBrittain* 5-9-0 JimmyFortune (4)	20/1	1 4
39	Laverock (IRE) *SaeedbinSuroor* 5-9-0 LDettori (6)	5/1	1¼ 5
61	Acapulco (IRE) *APO'Brien,Ireland* 3-8-6 DavidMcCabe (10)	20/1	3½ 6
	Classic Punch (IRE) *DRCElsworth* 3-8-6 TQuinn (9)	33/1	28 7
	Young Mick *GGMargarson* 5-9-0 (v) GeorgeBaker (8)	14/1	6 8

Mr Patrick J. Fahey 8ran 2m34.47   TR: 126/120/119/116/114/108

NEWMARKET Friday, Oct 5   GOOD to FIRM (Rowley Mile Course)

71   **skybet.com Cheveley Park Stks (Gr 1) (2yo f)** £102,601   6f

45	NATAGORA (FR) *PBary,France* 2-8-12 CPLemaire (11)	7/2	1
	FLEETING SPIRIT (IRE) *JNoseda* 2-8-12 LDettori (8)	7/2	nk 2
	FESTOSO (IRE) *HJLDunlop* 2-8-12 EddieAhern (13)	33/1	4 3
	Perfect Polly *AndrewOliver,Ireland* 2-8-12 TedDurcan (6)	20/1	1 4
	Missit (IRE) *MRChannon* 2-8-12 DarrylHolland (9)	12/1	sh 5

Elletelle (IRE) *GMLyons,Ireland* 2-8-12 JMurtagh (7) .... 6/1   ¾ 6
Lady Aquitaine (USA) *BJMeehan* 2-8-12 KDarley (1)................................. 25/1   ½ 7
Visit *SirMichaelStoute* 2-8-12 RyanMoore (5) .... 11/4f   nk 8
Unilateral (IRE) *BSmart* 2-8-12 TomEaves (12) .... 20/1   hd 9
Dubai Princess (IRE) *JAOsborne* 2-8-12 TPQueally (3) .... 20/1   ½ 10
Polar Circle (USA) *PWChapple-Hyam* 2-8-12 JimmyFortune (4)................. 50/1   nk 11
Gone Fast (USA) *JRFanshawe* 2-8-12 OscarUrbina (14)............................ 100/1   1 12
Lady Avenger (IRE) *JMPEustace* 2-8-12 KerrinMcEvoy (2)....................... 66/1   1½ 13
Falcolnry (IRE) *JRFanshawe* 2-8-12 JamieSpencer (10) 22/1   2 14

Mr Stefan Friborg 14ran 1m11.55   TR: 116/115/102/99/98+/96

72   **Shadwell Middle Park Stks (Gr 1) (2yo c)** £102,601   6f

DARK ANGEL (IRE) *BWHills* 2-8-12 MichaelHills (1)............................. 8/1   1
STRIKE THE DEAL (USA) *JNoseda* 2-8-12 EddieAhern (10)..................... 9/1   ½ 2
TAJDEEF (USA) *BWHills* 2-8-12 RHills (5).. 9/2   nk 3
Red Alert Day *NACallaghan* 2-8-12 LDettori (7)..................................... 9/1   1½ 4
Achilles of Troy (IRE) *APO'Brien,Ireland* 2-8-12 JMurtagh (2) 7/1   1¼ 5
Dream Eater (IRE) *AMBalding* 2-8-12 FrancisNorton (8)......................... 7/1   sh 6
Rock of Rochelle (USA) *AndrewKinsella,Ireland* 2-8-12 (t)
   VRDeSouza (9).. 14/1   3½ 7
Sir Gerry (USA) *JRFanshawe* 2-8-12 JamieSpencer (4) 2/1f   3 8
Proud Linus (USA) *DCarroll* 2-8-12 StephenDonohoe (6) 25/1   3 9

The Hon Mrs J. M. Corbett & Mr C. Wright 9ran 1m12.08
                           TR: 113/111/110/106/101/101

NEWMARKET Saturday, Oct 6   GOOD to FIRM (Rowley Mile Course)

73   **Kingdom of Bahrain Sun Chariot Stks (Gr 1) (3yo+ f+m)** £105,043   1m

30   MAJESTIC ROI (USA) *MRChannon* 3-8-13 DarryllHolland (7) 16/1   1
41   NANNINA *JHMGosden* 4-9-2 JimmyFortune (3) .... 5/1   ¾ 2
57   ECHELON *SirMichaelStoute* 5-9-2 RyanMoore (6) 11/8f   1 3
19   Simply Perfect *JNoseda* 3-8-13 JMurtagh (4) .... 7/2   nk 4
      Harvest Queen (IRE) *PJMakin* 4-9-2 EddieAhern (2) .... 16/1   nk 5
57   Barshiba (IRE) *DRCElsworth* 3-8-13 TQuinn (1)..................................... 40/1   2 6
41   Speciosa (IRE) *MrsPSly* 4-9-2 MickyFenton (5)...................................... 15/2   6 7
48   Darrfonah (IRE) *CEBrittain* 3-8-13 (t) RichardHughes (5) 66/1   3 8
      Wake Up Maggie (IRE) *CFWall* 4-9-2 GeorgeBaker (8) .... 14/1   hd 9

Mr Jaber Abdullah 9ran 1m37.83   TR: 122/119/116+/116/115/110

LONGCHAMP Saturday, Oct 6   GOOD to SOFT

74   **Prix de la Foret Casino Barriere de Biarritz (Gr 1) (3yo+)** £99,895   7f

44   TOYLSOME *JHirschberger,Germany* 8-9-2 SPasquier (13) 503/10   1
      WELSH EMPEROR (IRE) *TPTate,GB* 8-9-2 IMendizabal (9) 91/1   2½ 2
56   MARCHAND D'OR (FR) *FHead,France* 4-9-2 DBonilla (4)...................... 36/10   ¾ 3
7   US Ranger (USA) *APO'Brien,Ireland* 3-9-0 KFallon (11)........................ 62/10   ns 4
11   Tariq *PWChapple-Hyam,GB* 3-9-0 LDettori (1)...................................... 17/10f   1½ 5
42   Dutch Art *PWChapple-Hyam,GB* 3-9-0 TThulliez (10)............................. 14/1   2½ 6
40   Jeremy (USA) *SirMichaelStoute,GB* 4-9-2 JVictoire (5) .... 14/1   ½ 7
42   Garnica (FR) *J-CRouget,France* 4-9-2 CPLemaire (1)............................. 14/1   sn 8
59   Linngari (IRE) *AdeRoyerDupre,France* 5-9-2 CSoumillon (12).................. 16/1   3 9
57   Red Evie (IRE) *MLWBell,GB* 4-8-13 JamieSpencer (8) 14/1   1 10
      Impressionnante *CLaffon-Parias,France* 4-8-13 OPeslier (6)..................... 81/1   ¾ 11
15   Vital Equine (IRE) *EJO'Neill,GB* 3-9-0 ChrisCatlin (2)............................. 26/1   2½ 12
56   Red Clubs (IRE) *BWHills,GB* 4-9-2 MichaelHills (7) 24/1   2½ 13

Baron G. von Ullmann 13ran 1m22.50   TR: 124/116/114/115/111/104

LONGCHAMP Sunday, Oct 7   GOOD

75   **Prix de l'Abbaye de Longchamp Majestic Barriere de Cannes (Gr 1) (2yo+)**
    £99,895   5f

62   BENBAUN (IRE) *MJWallace,GB* 6-9-11 (v) PJSmullen (8)...................... 58/10   1
49   KINGSGATE NATIVE (IRE) *JRBest,GB* 2-8-7 JimmyQuinn (9)................ 2/1f   2 2
49   DESERT LORD *KARyan,GB* 7-9-11 (b) NCallan (10)................................ 19/1   2 3
62   Moss Vale (IRE) *DNicholls,GB* 6-9-11 KFallon (17)............................... 61/10cp   sh 4
      Patavellian (IRE) *RCharlton,GB* 9-9-11 (b) SteveDrowne (3)..................... 33/1   nk 5
42   Tiza (SAF) *AdeRoyerDupre,France* 5-9-11 CSoumillon (14)..................... 23/1   nk 6
      Derison (USA) *PVandePoele,France* 5-9-11 (b) TJarnet (7) .... 13/1   ¾ 7
      Strike Up The Band *DNicholls,GB* 4-9-11 LDettori (6)........................... 61/10cp   1 8
      Peace Offering (IRE) *DNicholls,GB* 7-9-11 AdrianTNicholls (1) .... 61/10cp   nk 9
42   New Girlfriend (IRE) *RCollet,France* 4-9-8 OPeslier (12)........................ 73/10cp   hd 10
54   Dandy Man (IRE) *MissTAMCollins,Ireland* 4-9-11 PShanahan (11).......... 77/10   ¾ 11
      Kocooning (IRE) *RCollet,France* 4-9-8 CPLemaire (4)........................... 73/10cp   hd 12
49   Hoh Mike (IRE) *MLWBell,GB* 3-9-11 JamieSpencer (13)......................... 12/1   1 13

42 Tycoon's Hill (IRE) *RCollet,France* 8-9-11 J-BHamel (5) 73/10cp dh 13
7 Sonny Red (IRE) *RHannon,GB* 3-9-11 RyanMoore (15) 46/1 1½ 15
49 Beauty Is Truth (IRE) *RCollet,France* 3-9-8 (b) TThulliez (4) 73/10cp 3 16
Hogmaneigh (IRE) *SCWilliams,GB* 4-9-11 JimmyFortune (16) 38/1 2 17
Ransley, Birks, Hillen 17ran 56.70secs TR: 127/117/116/116/115/113

76 Prix Marcel Boussac - Criterium Des Pouliches Royal Barriere de Deauville (Gr 1) (2yo f) £119,874 1m

ZARKAVA (IRE) *AdeRoyerDupre,France* 2-8-11 CSoumillon (3) 9/2 1
CONFERENCE CALL *PBary,France* 2-8-11 SPasquier (8) 46/10 2½ 2
53 MAD ABOUT YOU (IRE) *DKWeld,Ireland* 2-8-11 PJSmullen (4) 62/10 1½ 3
Savethisdanceforme (IRE) *APO'Brien,Ireland* 2-8-11 KFallon (2) 19/1 2½ 4
Don't Forget Faith (USA) *CGCox,GB* 2-8-11 PhilipRobinson (5) 73/1 1 5
Peace Royale (GER) *AWohler,Germany* 2-8-11 EPedroza (10) 22/1 sh 6
Queen of Naples *JHMGosden,GB* 2-8-11 JimmyFortune (9) 17/1 ns 7
Laureldean Gale (USA) *SaeedbinSuroor,GB* 2-8-11 LDettori (11) 14/10f sn 8
Belle Allure (IRE) *RupertPritchard-Gordon,France* 2-8-11 DBonilla (1) 50/1 sh 9
Gagnoa (IRE) *YdeNicolay,France* 2-8-11 OPeslier (6) 14/1 1½ 10
H.H. Aga Khan 10ran 1m37.18 TR: 115+/107/103/97/94/94

77 Prix Jean-Luc Lagardere (Grand Criterium) (Gr 1) (2yo c+f) £139,853 7f

64 RIO DE LA PLATA (USA) *SaeedbinSuroor,GB* 2-9-0 LDettori (2) 4/5f 1
DECLARATION OF WAR (IRE) *PWChapple-Hyam,GB* 2-9-0 RyanMoore (4) 22/1 2½ 2
SHEDIAK (FR) *AFabre,France* 2-9-0 CSoumillon (3) 47/10 sh 3
Hatta Fort *MRChannon,GB* 2-9-0 DarryllHolland (8) 18/1 1 4
Young Pretender (FR) *JHMGosden,GB* 2-9-0 JimmyFortune (7) 38/10 1½ 5
Greatwallofchina (USA) *APO'Brien,Ireland* 2-9-0 KFallon (1) 78/10cp sn 6
Manassas (IRE) *BJMeehan,GB* 2-9-0 RichardHughes (6) 49/1 2½ 7
64 Minneapolis *APO'Brien,Ireland* 2-9-0 JMurtagh (5) 78/10cp ½ 8
Godolphin 8ran 1m21.50 TR: 116+/108/108/105/101/100

78 Prix de l'Opera Casino Barriere d'Enghien Les Bains (Gr 1) (3yo+ f+m) £99,895 1¼m

27 SATWA QUEEN (FR) *JdeRoualle,France* 5-9-2 TThulliez (7) 3/1 1
PROMISING LEAD *SirMichaelStoute,GB* 3-8-12 RyanMoore (4) 15/1 hd 2
65 LEGERETE (USA) *AFabre,France* 3-8-12 OPeslier (9) 18/1 hd 3
Mystic Lips (GER) *AndreasLowe,Germany* 3-8-12 SPasquier (1) 17/1 1½ 4
58 Finsceal Beo (IRE) *JSBolger,Ireland* 3-8-12 KJManning (8) 9/1 ¾ 5
41 Light Shift (USA) *HRACecil,GB* 3-8-12 TedDurcan (5) 17/10f ½ 6
65 Diyakalanie (FR) *JBoisnard,France* 3-8-12 TJarnet (3) 36/1 ¾ 7
Dominante (GER) *AWohler,Germany* 3-8-12 EPedroza (6) 26/1 3 8
65 Vadapolina (FR) *AFabre,France* 3-8-12 CSoumillon (11) 13/2 6 9
Majounes Song *MJohnston,GB* 3-8-12 KDarley (10) 56/1 6 10
Mahara (USA) *JEHammond,France* 3-8-12 LDettori (2) 15/1 3 11
Mr S. Lamprell 11ran 2m03.80 TR: 115/117/116/113/111/110

79 Prix de l'Arc de Triomphe Lucien Barriere (Gr 1) (3yo+ c+f) £799,160 1½m

58 DYLAN THOMAS (IRE) *APO'Brien,Ireland* 4-9-5 KFallon (6) 5/2cp 1
55 YOUMZAIN (IRE) *MRChannon,GB* 4-9-5 RichardHughes (4) 80/1 hd 2
66 SAGARA (USA) *JEPease,France* 3-8-11 TGillet (11) 32/1 1½ 3
Getaway (GER) *AFabre,France* 4-9-5 OPeslier (10) 27/1 sh 4
66 Soldier of Fortune (IRE) *APO'Brien,Ireland* 3-8-11 JMurtagh (5) 5/2cp ½ 5
21 Saddex *PRau,Germany* 4-9-5 TMundry (2) 20/1 4 6
67 Mandesha (FR) *AdeRoyerDupre,France* 4-9-2 (s) CSoumillon (3) 66/10 ¾ 7
66 Zambezi Sun *PBary,France* 3-8-11 SPasquier (8) 6/1 2½ 8
67 Dragon Dancer *GWragg,GB* 4-9-5 DarryllHolland (1) 108/1 1½ 9
47 Authorized (IRE) *PWChapple-Hyam,GB* 3-8-11 LDettori (12) 11/10f sn 10
46 Yellowstone (IRE) *APO'Brien,Ireland* 3-8-11 PJSmullen (9) 5/2cp 15 11
66 Song of Hiawatha *APO'Brien,Ireland* 3-8-11 DavidMcCabe (7) 5/2cp 15 12
Mrs John Magnier & Mr M. Tabor 12ran 2m28.31 TR: 127+/127/124/124/123+/116

80 Prix du Cadran Casino-Theatre Barriere de Toulouse (Gr 1) (4yo+) £99,895 2½m

29 LE MIRACLE (GER) *WernerBaltromei,Germany* 6-9-2 DBoeuf (2) 67/10 1
VAREVEES *JBoisnard,France* 4-8-13 TJarnet (7) 49/10 sh 2
63 YEATS (IRE) *APO'Brien,Ireland* 6-9-2 KFallon (4) 2/5f 3 3
60 Balkan Knight *DRCElsworth,GB* 7-9-2 JimmyFortune (5) 14/1 1½ 4
Juniper Girl (IRE) *MLWBell,GB* 4-8-13 JamieSpencer (6) 15/1 2½ 5
Belle Epine (FR) *J-JChavarrias,France* 5-8-13 ACrastus (1) 38/1 20 6
Rennstall Gestut Hachtsee 6ran 4m29.80 TR: 115/113/112/110/105

MILAN Sunday, Oct 14 GOOD to FIRM

81 Gran Premio del Jockey Club (Gr 1) (3yo) £75,000 1½m

SCHIAPARELLI (GER) *PSchiergen,Germany* 4-9-5 AStarke 14/10f 1

	21	CHAMPS ELYSEES *AFabre,France* 4-9-5 SPasquier	24/10	1¾ 2
	70	LAVEROCK (IRE) *SaeedbinSuroor,GB* 5-9-5 LDettori	38/10	1¼ 3
		Bussoni (GER) *HBlume,Germany* 6-9-5 ASuborics	28/10	1¾ 4
		Gimmy (IRE) *BGrizzetti,Italy* 3-8-12 DVargiu	32/1	¾ 5
		Sopran Promo (ITY) *BGrizzetti,Italy* 3-8-12 FBranca	55/1	2 6
		Estejo (GER) *RRohne,Germany* 3-8-12 DPorcu	47/1	2 7
	67	Distant Way (USA) *LBrogi,Italy* 6-9-5 MDemuro	118/10	2¾ 8

Stall Blankenese 8ran 2m28.50 TR: 120/117/115/111/111/107

NEWMARKET Saturday, Oct 20   GOOD to SOFT (Rowley Mile Course)

82   VC Bet Challenge Stks (Gr 2) (3yo+) £54,963 7f

		MISS LUCIFER (FR) *BWHills* 3-8-12 MichaelHills (4)	20/1	1
	32	AL QASI (IRE) *PWChapple-Hyam* 4-9-3 TedDurcan (3)	9/1	1¼ 2
	74	TOYLSOME *JHirschberger,Germany* 8-9-7 SPasquier (2)	6/1	2 3
	56	Balthazaar's Gift (IRE) *LMCumani* 4-9-3 JimmyFortune (9)	10/1	1½ 4
	56	Asset (IRE) *RHannon* 4-9-3 (b) RyanMoore (10)	10/1	nk 5
		Arabian Gleam *JNoseda* 3-9-5 JMurtagh (14)	8/1	¾ 6
		Candidato Roy (ARG) *WJHaggas* 6-9-3 LDettori (8)	10/1	½ 7
		Captain Marvelous (IRE) *BWHills* 3-9-1 DarrylHolland (1)	66/1	½ 8
		Duff (IRE) *EdwardLynam,Ireland* 4-9-3 DPMcDonogh (12)	16/1	nk 9
		Eisteddfod *PFICole* 6-9-3 NelsonDeSouza (15)	25/1	1½ 10
		Lovelace *MJohnston* 3-9-1 RoystonFfrench (5)	16/1	½ 11
		Caldra (IRE) *SKirk* 3-9-1 KJManning (13)	33/1	½ 12
		Pride of Nation (IRE) *LMCumani* 5-9-3 CPLemaire (7)	9/1	10 13
		Mac Love *JNoseda* 6-9-3 EddieAhern (6)	66/1	4 14
	69	Cesare *JRFanshawe* 6-9-7 JamieSpencer (11)	11/4f	¾ 15

Gainsborough 15ran 1m25.56 TR: 119/118/+/116/108/107/109+

83   Darley Dewhurst Stks (Gr 1) (2yo c+f) £149,559 7f

	64	NEW APPROACH (IRE) *JSBolger,Ireland* 2-9-1 KJManning (5)	6/4f	1
		FAST COMPANY (IRE) *BJMeehan* 2-9-1 TedDurcan (3)	14/1	½ 2
	52	RAVEN'S PASS (USA) *JHMGosden* 2-9-1 JimmyFortune (4)	3/1	2½ 3
	77	Rio de La Plata (USA) *SaeedbinSuroor* 2-9-1 LDettori (9)	9/2	2½ 4
		Luck Money (IRE) *PFICole* 2-9-1 TQuinn (6)	14/1	1¾ 5
	77	Hatta Fort *MRChannon* 2-9-1 DarrylHolland (1)	50/1	hd 6
		McCartney (GER) *MJohnston* 2-9-1 RyanMoore (8)	15/2	nk 7
	77	Greatwallofchina (USA) *APO'Brien,Ireland* 2-9-1 JMurtagh (10)	100/1	2½ 8
	72	Dark Angel (IRE) *BWHills* 2-9-1 MichaelHills (7)	25/1	½ 9
		Dubai Meydan (IRE) *MissGayKelleway* 2-9-1 JimmyQuinn (2)	100/1	17 10

Mrs J. S. Bolger 10ran 1m25.29 TR: 127/126/118+/111+/105/105

84   Emirates Airline Champion Stks (Gr 1) (3yo+) £222,350 1¼m

	22	LITERATO (FR) *J-CRouget,France* 3-8-12 CPLemaire (5)	7/2	1
	34	EAGLE MOUNTAIN *APO'Brien,Ireland* 3-8-12 JMurtagh (10)	5/1	sh 2
	43	DOCTOR DINO (FR) *RGibson,France* 5-9-3 OPeslier (4)	12/1	3 3
	25	Creachadoir (IRE) *SaeedbinSuroor* 3-8-12 LDettori (7)	9/1	3 4
		Multidimensional (IRE) *HRACecil* 4-9-3 TedDurcan (1)	7/1	½ 5
	47	Notnowcato *SirMichaelStoute* 5-9-3 RyanMoore (9)	9/4f	2½ 6
	73	Speciosa (IRE) *MrsPSly* 4-9-0 MickyFenton (4)	22/1	½ 7
		Mullins Bay *MFdeKock,SouthAfrica* 6-9-3 (t) JamieSpencer (11)	25/1	hd 8
		Championship Point (IRE) *MRChannon* 4-9-3 DarrylHolland (3)	50/1	7 9
	58	Maraahel (IRE) *SirMichaelStoute* 6-9-3 (b) RHills (6)	16/1	7 10
		Mount Nelson *APO'Brien,Ireland* 3-8-12 JimmyFortune (12)	16/1	16 11
		Pinot Noir (GER) *LOttofulling,Germany* 4-9-3 MDemuro (2)	100/1	dist 12

Mr H. Morin 12ran 2m04.24 TR: 126+/126/119+/112/111+/105

MILAN Sunday, Oct 21   GOOD to FIRM

85   Premio Vittorio di Capua (Gr 1) (3yo+) £75,000 1m

	74	LINNGARI (IRE) *AdeRoyerDupre,France* 5-8-12 JimmyFortune	103/100f	1
	59	GOLDEN TITUS (IRE) *ARenzoni,Italy* 3-8-10 DVargiu	61/10	¾ 2
		ECHO OF LIGHT *SaeedbinSuroor,GB* 5-8-12 (s) LDettori	18/10	4½ 3
		Dubai's Touch *MJohnston,GB* 3-8-10 RoystonFfrench	24/1	½ 4
		Aspectus (IRE) *HBlume,Germany* 4-8-12 MDemuro	15/1	sn 5
		Miles Gloriosus (USA) *RMenichetti,Italy* 4-8-12 LManiezzi	50/1	1¾ 6
		Apollo Star (GER) *MHofer,Germany* 5-8-12 AHelfenbein	6/1	2½ 7

Mr Peter Walichnowski 7ran 1m37.50 TR: 121/120/107/106/105/100

WOODBINE Sunday, Oct 21   FIRM

86   Pattison Canadian International Stks (Gr 1) (3yo+) £606,060 1½m

| | | CLOUDY'S KNIGHT (USA) *FJKirby,USA* 7-9-0 RamseyZimmerman | 184/10 | 1 |
| | 70 | ASK *SirMichaelStoute,GB* 4-9-0 RyanMoore | 265/100f | ns 2 |

1221

```
 55  QUIJANO (GER) PSchiergen,Germany 5-9-0 AStarke ..............................  39/10    1  3
     Stream of Gold (IRE) KPMcLaughlin,USA 6-9-0 ECastro .......................  166/10   nk  4
  1  Oracle West (SAF) MFdeKock,SouthAfrica 6-9-0 JMurtagh ....................  147/10   ½  5
 43  Sunriver (USA) TAPletcher,USA 4-9-0 GGomez ...............................  72/10    ¾  6
     Sky Conqueror (USA) DDBanach,Canada 5-9-0 JCastellano........................  5/1   nk  7
 70  Honolulu (IRE) APO'Brien,Ireland 3-8-7 MJKinane.............................  9/1    1  8
     Windhulu Islands (USA) MRFrostad,Canada 3-8-7 (b) TKabel ..............  38/10   ns  9
 33  Irish Wells (FR) FrancoisRohaut,France 4-9-0 OPeslier.......................  98/10  1¼ 10
  8  Linda's Lad EKenneally,USA 4-9-0 JVelazquez ...............................  34/1   1¾ 11
     Marsh Side (USA) MWDickinson,USA 4-9-0 Emma-JayneWilson ..............  45/1  3¾ 12
     S J Stables LLC 12ran 2m27.71                          TR: 124/124+/122/121/120/119
```

DONCASTER Saturday, Oct 27   GOOD

87   Racing Post Trophy (Gr 1) (2yo c+f) £113,560   1m (Str.)

```
     IBN KHALDUN (USA) SaeedbinSuroor 2-9-0 KerrinMcEvoy (6)............. 11/4f       1
 52  CITY LEADER (IRE) BJMeehan 2-9-0 KDarley (9)........................................ 8/1    3  2
     FEARED IN FLIGHT (IRE) BWHills 2-9-0 PhilipRobinson (11) ............... 66/1   sh  3
     Art Master SKirk 2-9-0 FrancisNorton (4)................................................ 66/1   2  4
 51  Curtain Call (FR) MrsJHarrington,Ireland 2-9-0 FMBerry (5)..................... 4/1  2½  5
 77  Declaration of War (IRE) PWChapple-Hyam 2-9-0 RobertHavlin (2) ...... 14/1  1½  6
     River Proud (USA) PFICole 2-9-0 TQuinn (7)......................................... 10/1   sh  7
     Frozen Fire (GER) APO'Brien,Ireland 2-9-0 JamieSpencer (12)............... 5/1  1¼  8
     Internationaldebut (IRE) DJMurphy 2-9-0 NCallan (3) .......................... 100/1  ½  9
     Tajaaweed (USA) SirMichaelStoute 2-9-0 MartinDwyer (10)................... 10/1  hd 10
     King of Rome (IRE) APO'Brien,Ireland 2-9-0 JAHeffernan (8)................. 9/1  nk 11
     Ridge Dance JHMGosden 2-9-0 JimmyFortune (1)................................. 14/1   8 12
     Godolphin 12ran 1m37.62                              TR: 119/111/111/105/98
```

MONMOUTH PARK Saturday, Oct 27   Turf course: SOFT, Dirt course: SLOPPY

**88   Emirates Airline Breeders' Cup Filly & Mare Turf (Gr 1) (3yo+ f+m)   1m3f (Turf)
£526,829**

```
     LAHUDOOD KPMcLaughlin,USA 4-8-11 AGarcia (6) ........................... 117/10       1
  1  HONEY RYDER (USA) TAPletcher,USA 6-8-11 JVelazquez (2) ............... 61/10   ¾  2
 65  PASSAGE OF TIME HRACecil,GB 3-8-6 RADominguez (4)................... 28/10f  nk  3
     Nashoba's Key (USA) CarlaGaines,USA 4-8-11 JTalamo (3)................... 33/10   1  4
 38  All My Loving (IRE) APO'Brien,Ireland 3-8-7 (v) PJSmullen (1)........... 178/10  ½  5
 38  Timarwa (IRE) JohnMOxx,Ireland 3-8-6 MJKinane (8) ......................... 25/1  3¼  6
     Arravale (USA) MBenson,Canada 4-8-11 JValdivia (10).......................... 27/1  2¼  7
     Precious Kitten (USA) RJFrankel,USA 4-8-11 RBejarano (12) ............... 10/1  3¼  8
     Argentina (IRE) RJFrankel,USA 5-8-11 KDesormeaux (7)........................ 79/10  2  9
     Danzon (USA) FParisel,USA 4-8-11 ELaparoux (9) .......................... 109/10  1¾ 10
 73  Simply Perfect JNoseda,GB 3-8-8 JMurtagh (11)................................. 107/10  pu
     Shadwell Stable 11ran 2m22.75                        TR: 116+/115/115/112/113/106
```

89   NetJets Breeders' Cup Mile (Gr 1) (3yo+) £692,780   1m (Turf)

```
     KIP DEVILLE (USA) REDutrow,jnr,USA 4-9-0 (b) CVelasquez (8)........ 82/10       1
 69  EXCELLENT ART APO'Brien,Ireland 3-8-10 JMurtagh (13) ................. 21/10f   1  3
     COSMONAUT (USA) FParisel,USA 3-8-10 JLeparoux (7)...................... 142/10   1  3
     Nobiz Like Shobiz (USA) BTagg,USA 3-8-10 JVelazquez (9) ............... 39/10  nk  4
  1  Host (CHI) TAPletcher,USA 7-9-0 GGomez (4).................................... 156/10   ½  5
     Trippi's Storm (USA) SMHough,USA 3-9-0 JCastellano (6) .................... 93/10  ¾  6
     Remarkable Karma (VEN) APennajnr,USA 5-9-0 RADominguez (14) ...... 162/10  3½  7
     Rebellion HGMotion,USA 4-9-0 ECoa (1) ........................................... 45/1   nk  8
     Icy Atlantic (USA) TAPletcher,USA 6-9-0 CDeCarlo (2) ...................... 39/1  1¾  9
 74  Jeremy (USA) SirMichaelStoute,GB 4-9-0 LDettori (5) ........................ 73/10  1 10
     Purim (USA) TFProctor,USA 5-9-0 JTheriot (12)................................... 208/10  1½ 11
     Silent Name (JPN) RJFrankel,USA 5-9-0 KDesormeaux (11)................. 182/10  6 12
     My Typhoon (IRE) WIMott,USA 5-8-11 ECastro (10)............................. 30/1  3¾ 13
     IEAH Stables/A. & J. Cohen/S.Cobb et al 13ran 1m39.78
                                                          TR: 126/123+/120/119/118/117
```

90   John Deere Breeders' Cup Turf (Gr 1) (3yo+) £790,244   1½m (Turf)

```
  2  ENGLISH CHANNEL (USA) TAPletcher,USA 5-9-0 JVelazquez (6) ........... 3/1       1
 34  SHAMDINAN (FR) APennajnr,USA 3-8-9 JLeparoux (4) ..................... 256/10   7  2
 58  RED ROCKS (IRE) BJMeehan,GB 4-9-0 LDettori (2) ............................ 56/10   ¾  3
     Better Talk Now (USA) HGMotion,USA 8-9-0 (b) RADominguez (3)....... 81/10   ¾  4
 79  Dylan Thomas (IRE) APO'Brien,Ireland 4-9-0 JMurtagh (7) ................... 9/10f  hd  5
     Grand Couturier RRibaudo,USA 4-9-0 KBorel (5)................................. 89/10  1¼  6
     Fri Guy (USA) DLRomans,USA 4-9-0 KDesormeaux (1) ...................... 291/10  1¼  7
     Transduction Gold (USA) JGlenney,USA 4-9-0 JDGraham (8)................ 581/10  24  8
     Mr James T. Scatuorchio 8ran 2m36.96                  TR: 126/118/115/113/113/111
```

91   **Breeders' Cup Classic - Powered By Dodge (Gr 1) (3yo+)** £1,317,073   1¼m (Dirt)

     CURLIN (USA) *SMAsmussen,USA* 3-8-9 RAlbarado (4)............................ 44/10   1
     HARD SPUN (USA) *JLJones,USA* 3-8-9 MPino (8) 81/10   4½ 2
     AWESOME GEM (USA) *CDollase,USA* 4-9-0 (b) DFlores (6) 283/10   4¾ 3
     Street Sense (USA) *CANafzger,USA* 3-8-9 CBorel (2) 25/10f   1 4
     Tiago (USA) *JAShirreffs,USA* 3-8-9 MikeESmith (9)................................ 128/10   8¼ 5
     Any Given Saturday (USA) *TAPletcher,USA* 3-8-9 GGomez (3) 39/10   10 6
     Lawyer Ron (USA) *TAPletcher,USA* 4-9-0 JVelazquez (1)........................ 39/10   hd 7
     Diamond Stripes (USA) *REDutrow,jnr,USA* 4-9-0 (b) CVelasquez (7) 39/1   8¼ 8
   59   George Washington (IRE) *APO'Brien,Ireland* 4-9-0 MJKinane (5)............ 9/1   pu

     George Bolton/Stonestreet/Padua et al 9ran 2m00.59   TR: 131/124/116/114/100

     LONGCHAMP Sunday, Oct 28   GOOD to FIRM

92   **Prix Royal-Oak - Principaute de Monaco (Gr 1) (3yo+)** £99,201   1m7f110y

   60   ALLEGRETTO (IRE) *SirMichaelStoute,GB* 4-9-1 RyanMoore 52/10   1
   65   MACLEYA (GER) *AFabre,France* 5-9-1 SPasquier .... 10/1   sn 2
   33   PONTE TRESA (FR) *YdeNicolay,France* 4-9-1 CSoumillon........................ 11/1   1 3
   80   Le Miracle (GER) *WernerBaltromei,Germany* 6-9-4 DBoeuf.................... 54/10   hd 4
     Brisant (GER) *MTrybuhl,Germany* 5-9-4 WMongil................................... 48/1   nk 5
     Anna Pavlova *RAFahey,GB* 4-9-1 PaulHanagan .... 66/10   ½ 6
   80   Varevees *JBoisnard,France* 4-9-1 TJarnet 7/2f   1½ 7
     Soapy Danger *MJohnston,GB* 4-9-4 KDarley .... 11/1   ¾ 8
     Latin Mood (FR) *PHDemercastel,France* 4-9-4 (s) TThulliez 33/1   10 9
   29   Lord du Sud (FR) *J-CRouget,France* 6-9-4 (s) CPLemaire 41/10   4 10
     Loup de Mer (GER) *WernerBaltromei,Germany* 5-9-4 JVictoire 54/10   11

     Cheveley Park Stud 11ran 3m15.50   TR: 116/115/114/117/116/112

     SAINT-CLOUD Thursday, Nov 1   SOFT

93   **Criterium International (Gr 1) (2yo c+f)** £99,895   1m

     THEWAYYOUARE (USA) *AFabre,France* 2-9-0 SPasquier.................... 14/10f   1
     HELLO MORNING (FR) *MmeCHead-Maarek,France* 2-9-0 CPLemaire . 58/10   ½ 2
     REDOLENT (IRE) *RHannon,GB* 2-9-0 JMurtagh 82/10   6 3
     Yankadi (USA) *BWHills,GB* 2-9-0 RichardHughes..................................... 12/1   ½ 4
     Blue Chagall (FR) *H-APantall,France* 2-9-0 JVictoire .... 4/1   ½ 5
     Sceptre Rouge (IRE) *AdeRoyerDupre,France* 2-9-0 CSoumillon............... 34/10   ½ 6

     Mr S. Mulryan 6ran 1m45.30   TR: 117/116/102/101/100

     ROME Sunday, Nov 4   GOOD to SOFT

94   **Premio Roma At The Races (Gr 1) (3yo+)** £75,525   1¼m

   43   PRESSING (IRE) *MAJarvis,GB* 4-9-2 NCallan 24/10   1
     MONACHESI (IRE) *F&LCamici,Italy* 4-9-2 OFancera 735/10   1½ 2
   6   BORIS DE DEAUVILLE (IRE) *SWattel,France* 4-9-2 TThulliez .... 19/10f   ns 3
   29   Cherry Mix (FR) *SaeedbinSuroor,GB* 6-9-2 (t) EddieAhern.................... 253/100   1½ 4
     Vol de Nuit *F&LBrogi,Italy* 6-9-2 (s) MPasquale .... 75/10   ½ 5
   55   First Stream (GER) *MHofer,Germany* 3-9-0 THellier.................................. 56/10   1½ 6
   81   Distant Way (USA) *LBrogi,Italy* 4-9-2 MDemuro 75/10   3 7
     Speciano *EmilioBorromeo,Italy* 4-9-2 SLandi 684/10   1½ 8
   81   Laverock (IRE) *SaeedbinSuroor,GB* 5-9-2 TedDurcan............................ 253/100   3 9
   70   Hattan (IRE) *CEBrittain,GB* 5-9-2 JohnEgan.. 756/100   1½ 10

     Mr Gary A. Tanaka 10ran 2m02.10   TR: 120/116/116/113/112/111

     FLEMINGTON Tuesday, Nov 6   GOOD

95   **Emirates Melbourne Cup (Hcap) (Gr 1) (3yo+)** £1,365,639   2m

     EFFICIENT (NZ) *GARogerson,Australia* 4-8-8 MRodd 16/1   1
     PURPLE MOON (IRE) *LMCumani,GB* 4-8-6 DMOliver .... 9/2   ½ 2
   61   MAHLER (IRE) *APO'Brien,Ireland* 3-7-13 SBaster 9/1   2½ 3
     ZIPPING (AUS) *GARogerson,Australia* 4-8-7 DNikolic............................ 13/2   nk 4
     Dolphin Jo (AUS) *T&KO'Sullivan,Australia* 5-8-2 ClareLindop 60/1   1 5
     On A Jeune (AUS) *APayne,Australia* 7-8-4 KerrinMcEvoy...................... 30/1   sn 6
     Blue Monday *DAHayes,Australia* 6-8-11 NashRawiller.......................... 30/1   1¾ 7
     Master O'Reilly (NZ) *DO'Brien,Australia* 5-8-9 VDuric 28/10f   2 8
     Sculptor (NZ) *PLMcKenzie,NewZealand* 5-8-3 LCropp 30/1   1¼ 9
     Lazer Sharp (AUS) *DAHayes,Australia* 4-8-4 BShinn............................... 50/1   ¾ 10
     Douro Valley (AUS) *DTO'Brien,Australia* 6-8-2 (b) JWinks...................... 40/1   sh 11
     Sirmione (AUS) *JBCummings,Australia* 4-8-2 (b) PMertens .... 12/1   sh 12
     Princess Coup (AUS) *MWalker,NewZealand* 4-8-0 NGHarris 12/1   1½ 13
     Tawqeet (AUS) *DAHayes,Australia* 5-9-0 (b) DDunn.............................. 60/1   3½ 14
     Eskimo Queen (NZ) *MMoroney,NewZealand* 4-8-6 (b) CNewitt 25/1   2¾ 15
     Scenic Shot (AUS) *DLMorton,Australia* 5-8-4 CraigAWilliams .... 100/1   hd 16
     Black Tom (AUS) *DAHayes,Australia* 7-8-6 (b) PeterHall 200/1   2½ 17

Sarrera (AUS) *MMoroney,NewZealand* 7-8-3 SebastianMurphy 100/1   1½ 18
Blutigeroo (AUS) *CLittle,Australia* 6-8-10 LNolen .... 60/1   sn 19
Railings (AUS) *RJames,NewZealand* 6-8-10 SArnold 200/1   6 20

29   Tungsten Strike (AUS) *MrsAJPerrett,GB* 6-8-7 DarryllHolland 30/1   25 21

Mr & Mrs L. J. Williams et al 21ran 3m23.34   TR: 123/118/119/115/109/111/115

TOKYO Sunday, Nov 25   FIRM

96   **Japan Cup (Gr 1) (3yo+)** £1,121,333   1½m

2   ADMIRE MOON (JPN) *HMatsuda,Japan* 4-9-0 YIwata 99/10   1
1   POP ROCK (JPN) *KSumii,Japan* 6-9-0 OPeslier... 95/10   hd 2
   MEISHO SAMSON (JPN) *STakahashi,Japan* 4-9-0 YTake...................... 8/10f   nk 3
   Vodka (JPN) *KSumii,Japan* 3-8-5 HShii.. 51/10   1 4
   Delta Blues (JPN) *KSumii,Japan* 5-9-0 YKawada 146/1   1¼ 5
   Chosan (JPN) *TShimizu,Japan* 5-9-0 NYokoyama .... 62/1   nk 6
8   Papal Bull *SirMichaelStoute,GB* 4-9-0 RyanMoore 51/1   2 7
   Artiste Royal (IRE) *NDDrysdale,USA* 6-9-0 JTalamo .... 36/1   ¾ 8
   Fusaichi Pandora (JPN) *TShirai,Japan* 4-8-10 SFujita.............................. 74/1   nk 9
   Inti Raimi (JPN) *SSasaki,Japan* 5-9-0 TSato 64/10   1½ 10
79   Saddex *PRau,Germany* 4-9-0 TMundry .... 72/1   hd 11
   Erimo Harrier (JPN) *HTadokoro,Japan* 7-9-0 KTake.............................. 204/1   ½ 12
   Cosmo Bulk (JPN) *KTabe,Japan* 6-9-0 MMatsuoka................................. 109/1   ¾ 13
   Dream Passport (JPN) *HMatsuda,Japan* 4-9-0 KAndo............................. 15/1   ½ 14
   Rosenkreuz (JPN) *KHashiguchi,Japan* 5-9-0 YFujioka.......................... 224/1   1 15
   Hiraboku Royal (JPN) *ROkubo,Japan* 3-8-10 HGoto............................... 258/1   5 16
22   Halicarnassus (IRE) *MRChannon,GB* 3-8-10 DarryllHolland................ 165/1   3 17
   Victory (JPN) *HOtonashi,Japan* 3-8-10 CPLemaire 47/1   7 18

Darley Japan Farm Co.Ltd 18ran 2m24.70   TR: 127/126/125/120/120/120

SHA TIN Sunday, Dec 9   GOOD

97   **Cathay Pacific Hong Kong Sprint (Gr 1) (3yo+)** £432,364   6f

   SACRED KINGDOM (AUS) *PFYiu,HongKong* 4-9-0 (t) GMosse ... 9/20f   1
   ABSOLUTE CHAMPION (AUS) *DJHall,HongKong* 6-9-0 BPrebble........... 9/1   2¼ 2
   ROYAL DELIGHT (AUS) *CFownes,HongKong* 5-9-0 (b) SDye .... 18/1   nk 3
   Scintillation (AUS) *CSShum,HongKong* 7-9-0 (h) ESaint-Martin 37/1   1¾ 4
   Sunny Power (AUS) *KWLui,HongKong* 5-9-0 YTCheng .... 25/1   ns 5
74   Marchand d'Or (FR) *FHead,France* 4-9-0 DBonilla .... 100/1   hd 6
   Green Birdie (NZ) *CFownes,HongKong* 4-9-0 (b) LDettori 30/1   1¾ 7
75   Tiza (SAF) *AdeRoyerDupre,France* 5-9-0 CSoumillon 100/1   1¾ 8
75   Desert Lord *KARyan,GB* 7-9-0 (b) NCallan 100/1   3½ 9
32   Miss Andretti (AUS) *LeeFreedman,Australia* 6-8-10 (t) CNewitt.............. 37/10   ¾ 10
   Why Be (AUS) *LLaxon,Singapore* 5-9-0 (t) NCallow 100/1   2¼ 11
   Sunny Sing (IRE) *JMoore,HongKong* 5-9-0 (s+t) DBeadman .... 71/1   hd 12
75   Benbaun (IRE) *MJWallace,GB* 6-9-0 (v) PJSmullen...................................... 40/1   1½ 13

Mr Sin Kang Yuk 13ran 1m08.40   TR: 131/123/122/116/115/115

98   **Cathay Pacific Hong Kong Vase (Gr 1) (3yo+)** £504,425   1½m

84   DOCTOR DINO (FR) *RGibson,France* 5-9-0 OPeslier................................. 31/4   1
86   QUIJANO (GER) *PSchiergen,Germany* 5-9-0 AStarke 87/10   1½ 2
81   BUSSONI (GER) *HBlume,Germany* 6-9-0 (t) CSoumillon .... 29/1   nk 3
16   Arch Rebel (USA) *NMeade,Ireland* 6-9-0 (s) FBerry 88/1   1 4
   Kocab *AFabre,France* 5-9-0 SPasquier .... 96/1   nk 5
55   Egerton (GER) *PRau,Germany* 6-9-0 TMundry .... 100/1   ½ 6
90   Dylan Thomas (IRE) *APO'Brien,Ireland* 4-9-0 JMurtagh 7/10f   1 7
   Ever Bright (NZ) *PO'Sullivan,HongKong* 5-9-0 ODoleuze....................... 40/1   sh 8
90   Red Rocks (IRE) *BJMeehan,GB* 4-9-0 LDettori .... 58/10   ns 9
   Hawkes Bay *DJHall,HongKong* 5-9-0 GMosse .... 48/1   ½ 10
92   Macleya (GER) *AFabre,France* 5-8-10 RyanMoore 23/1   3¾ 11
   Viva Macau (NZ) *JMoore,HongKong* 4-9-0 (s+t) DBeadman 22/1   1 12
   Vital King (NZ) *PO'Sullivan,HongKong* 5-9-0 (b) BPrebble 100/1   14 13

Mr J. Martinez Salmean 13ran 2m28.20   TR: 120+/117+/116/114+/114/113

99   **Cathay Pacific Hong Kong Mile (Gr 1) (3yo+)** £576,486   1m

   GOOD BA BA (USA) *ASchutz,HongKong* 5-9-0 (t) ODoleuze 57/20f   1
84   CREACHADOIR (IRE) *SaeedbinSuroor,GB* 3-8-13 LDettori...................... 18/1   sh 2
69   DARJINA (FR) *AdeRoyerDupre,France* 3-8-9 CSoumillon................... 39/10   1¼ 3
   Floral Pegasus (AUS) *ASCruz,HongKong* 5-9-0 (t) GMosse .... 79/10   ½ 4
   Joyful Winner (AUS) *JMoore,HongKong* 7-9-0 (t) DBeadman.................. 28/1   ¾ 5
   Spirito Del Vento (FR) *J-MBeguigne,France* 4-9-0 OPeslier .... 30/1   nk 6
   The Duke (AUS) *CFownes,HongKong* 8-9-0 GBoss .... 60/1   ¾ 7
89   Excellent Art *APO'Brien,Ireland* 3-8-13 JMurtagh .... 33/10   ½ 8
   Kongo Rikishio (IRE) *KYamauchi,Japan* 5-9-0 SFujita........................... 66/10   2½ 9
   Able One (NZ) *JMoore,HongKong* 5-9-0 MJKinane 21/1   1¾ 10

Mr John Yuen Se Kit 13ran 1m34.50   TR: 125/126/118+/120/117/116

Godolphin 7ran 2m02.80   TR: 123+/122+/112/115/114/113

INDEX TO SELECTED BIG RACES

THE TIMEFORM 'TOP HORSES ABROAD'

This review of the year covers the major racing countries outside Britain. It includes Timeform Ratings for the top two-year-olds, three-year-olds and older horses. Horses not rated highly enough to be included in the main lists, but which finished in the first three in a European pattern race, or, in the sections on Japan and North America, won a Grade 1 during the season are included below the cut-off line. Fillies and mares are denoted by (f); * denotes the horse was trained for only a part of the season in the country concerned; † against a horse in the sections outside Europe and the UAE indicates the horse has a commentary in the main section of *Racehorses*. Overseas customers wishing to keep in touch with Timeform's expanding coverage of racing through the year can subscribe to Timeform-i (see www.timeform-i.com for details), Timeform Perspective or our internet site (www.timeform.com) for reports on all the important races. It is also possible to obtain up-to-date Timeform commentaries (including many not published in the weekly Timeform Black Book), undertake progeny research and access daily form guides on the internet site. Race Cards for all meetings in Ireland, for many Group 1 races in France and for major races in several other countries, including the Dubai World Cup and the Breeders' Cup, are also available.

IRELAND   Racing in Ireland continues to thrive, in no small part due to a level of government subsidy that makes it the envy of most other racing nations, to a rich pool of talented horsemen and to the private investment made by Coolmore in particular. There were several clear signs of health in 2007, including an increase in fixtures (333 compared to 319 the previous year), prize money (€59.6m compared to €55m) and on-course betting (€282m from €261.9m), though racecourse attendances were all but static and the average slightly down on 2006 due to the bigger programme book. There was also a new racecourse on show, Ireland's first all-weather venue. The Dundalk track, mid-way between Dublin and Belfast, opened rather later than planned but established its popularity from the outset. The opening fixture on the left-handed, oval, polytrack surface on 26th August was sold out a long time in advance. Later meetings were run under floodlights, which meant that the Friday evening fixtures could continue after the customary end of the Irish Flat season. The majority of races had the maximum number of runners, and horses of the calibre of **Ezima**, **Red Moloney**, **Cheyenne Star** and **Savethisdanceforme** put in appearances. There have been official indications already that another all-weather track is likely to be built shortly, somewhere within fifty miles of Dublin, though against that it was announced in August that the south-western course of Tralee is being sold for development, with Thurles also reportedly under threat.

If the well-being of Irish racing were to be judged solely by events on the track then it could be described as another good year. **Dylan Thomas** was the chief standard-bearer, winning the Prix Ganay and Prix de l'Arc de Triomphe in France and the King George VI and Queen Elizabeth Stakes in Britain, in addition to a listed race at the Curragh and the Irish Champion Stakes at Leopardstown on home soil. Defeat late in the year in the Breeders' Cup Turf and Hong Kong Vase took little of the shine off an outstanding year and a tremendous career. Dylan Thomas is to stand at Coolmore. Coolmore had been the location for **George Washington**'s brief stud career, but the 2006 Horse of The Year was sensationally returned to training after suffering from fertility problems. He managed only four appearances, showing that he had retained a lot of his ability with thirds in the Eclipse Stakes at Sandown and the Prix du Moulin de Longchamp, but suffering a fatal injury on the same Breeders' Cup card that had earlier seen the defeat of Dylan Thomas. George Washington's return to the track led to the premature retirement of one of the previous season's best juveniles, Holy Roman Emperor, who took his older stable-companion's place at stud. An even more notable absentee was the champion two-year-old of 2006, Teofilo, who was beset by training problems and finally retired (to Kildangan Stud) in the summer. Alexandrova was also missing from action, after reports of her progress in training had suggested she would be back in the late-summer.

Jim Bolger, trainer of Teofilo, coped with the absence of his stable star better than even he might have hoped for. **Finsceal Beo** flew the flag early in the season with successes in the One Thousand Guineas at both Newmarket and the Curragh, whereas **New Approach** had a juvenile campaign of remarkable similarity to Teofilo's, culminating in wins in the National Stakes at the Curragh and the Dewhurst Stakes at Newmarket, to head the rankings for two-year-olds with a rating 1 lb higher than Teofilo had achieved. Finsceal Beo was one of four home-trained winners of the five Irish classics run at the Curragh (the exception being Cockney Rebel, who, like Finsceal Beo, doubled up in the Guineas). **Soldier of Fortune** was a runaway winner of the Irish Derby, **Peeping Fawn** took the Irish Oaks and **Yeats** the Irish St Leger, all of them trained by Aidan O'Brien. Soldier of Fortune also won the Prix Niel at Longchamp before finishing fifth to Dylan Thomas in the Arc, while Yeats—who had another good O'Brien horse **Scorpion** close behind in the Irish St Leger—had previously won the Gold Cup at Ascot. Peeping Fawn was even more of a success story, however, going from debutante to maiden winner to classic winner and then to four-on-the-trot Group 1 winner in less than five months.

The other foreign-trained Group 1 winners in 2007 were the Sir Michael Stoute pair Notnowcato (who claimed the scalp of Dylan Thomas in the Tattersalls Gold Cup at the Curragh) and Echelon (who landed Leopardstown's Matron Stakes). There was a healthy amount of trade in the opposite direction as well, with the O'Brien-trained pair **Excellent Art** (St James's Palace Stakes at Royal Ascot) and **Astronomer Royal** (Poule d'Essai des Poulains at Longchamp) gaining Group 1 success without even racing in their own country. Yeats lost out narrowly in the Timeform Best Stayer division to his stable-companion **Septimus**, who ran only once in Ireland in 2007 (winning the Mooresbridge Stakes at the Curragh) but was most impressive in landing the Lonsdale and Doncaster Cups in Britain when stepped up in trip on his last two appearances. Yeats and Septimus (as well as Peeping Fawn and Soldier of Fortune) reportedly remain in training for 2008, when O'Brien may have his work cut out keeping the pair and **Mahler** and **Honolulu** (second and third in the St Leger at Doncaster) apart in staying races.

At the other end of the distance spectrum, **Dandy Man** was the best sprinter trained in Ireland but managed to win just once in a listed race at Naas, despite running well more often than not. His status could be under threat in 2008 from **US Ranger**, who joined O'Brien in the second half of the year from France before winning a six-furlong listed race at the Curragh most impressively. One who won't be seen on the racecourse in 2008 is **Redstone Dancer**, who just got the palm in the older fillies/mares division ahead of Cheyenne Star, **Jalmira** and **Deauville Vision** on account of mid-summer Group 3 wins in the Brownstown Stakes at Leopardstown and Minstrel Stakes at the Curragh while in foal. The O'Brien-trained three-year-old colts **Eagle Mountain** (second in the Derby at Epsom and third in the Irish Derby) and **Yellowstone** (winner of the Gordon Stakes at Goodwood and a regular in top races through the year) left the yard late in the year, but the very smart **Duke of Marmalade** remains in training at Ballydoyle and must have sound prospects of getting his head in front in a good race at least once in 2008.

New Approach was the best Irish two-year-old and the best in Europe, but there were also noteworthy performances by **Myboycharlie** (winner of the Prix Morny but third behind New Approach in the National Stakes), **Listen** (the joint-best European two-year-old filly with Zarkava on Timeform ratings after her Fillies' Mile win at Ascot), **Curtain Call** and **Henrythenavigator**, the last two filling the minor placings behind New Approach in the Futurity Stakes at the Curragh. Curtain Call went on to win the Beresford Stakes at the Curragh by four lengths before disappointing on his final start and has joined Luca Cumani in Britain. Listen lost both the pattern races she contested at the Curragh—the Debutante Stakes won by **Campfire Glow** and the Moyglare Stud Stakes won by **Saoirse Abu**—but was possibly unlucky in both and proved much better suited by the longer trip at Ascot, having Saoirse Abu back in third. Saoirse Abu was another moneyspinner for Jim Bolger, being the only other horse (along with Peeping Fawn) to win two Group 1s in Ireland during the year, her other notable victory coming at the chief expense of a below-par Henrythenavigator in the Phoenix Stakes, also at the Curragh.

Not everything was rosy in the Irish garden, however, and the trial and tribulations of Kieren Fallon—discussed in the introduction to the main part of *Racehorses of 2007*—often dominated the headlines for the wrong reasons. It could also be argued that racing in

Ireland, for all its many positives, has an image problem with many punters which the authorities should be making much more of an effort to address. Irish racing is not alone in being plagued by inaccurate distances, and times for races, and other punter-friendly information, but the pusillanimous attitude of officialdom towards horses appearing to be given easy rides at the beginning of their careers and/or against more fancied stablemates is much more of a domestic problem and should not be excused. This issue is touched upon in the essay on **Kitty Matcham**, winner of the Rockfel Stakes at Newmarket, in *Racehorses of 2007*. Timeform's commitment to racing in Ireland became even stronger during the year, culminating in the production of an Irish companion to *Racehorses of 2007*. The coming year will see race cards, ratings and reports—from Timeform's Irish course representative and in-house analysts and handicappers—produced on a daily basis (as they already are for jump racing in Ireland) and available from www.timeform.com, Computer Timeform and Timeform-i.

Two-Year-Olds

127	New Approach
118	Myboycharlie
117p	Listen (f)
115	Henrythenavigator
114	Lizard Island
113	Curtain Call
110	Achill Island
110	Great Barrier Reef
108p	One Great Cat
108p	Savethisdanceforme (f)
108	Saoirse Abu (f)
106	Bruges
105p	Jupiter Pluvius
105	Domingues
104	Domestic Fund
104	New Zealand
103P	Lush Lashes (f)
103p	Famous Name
103p	You'resothrilling (f)
103	Mad About You (f)
103	Pencil Hill
102p	Katiyra (f)
102p	Kitty Matcham (f)
102	Rock of Rochelle
101p	Alessandro Volta
101	Achilles of Troy
101	Brazilian Star
101	Elletelle (f)
101	Going Public
101	Great War Eagle
101	Norman Invader
101	Triskel (f)
100	Billyford
100	Greatwallofchina
100	Lisvale
100	Minneapolis
99p	Dahindar
99p	Forthefirstime (f)
99	Belgrave Square
99	Campfire Glow (f)
99	Deal Breaker
99	Great Rumpuscat
99	Lucifer Sam
99	Perfect Polly (f)
98	Capt Chaos
98	Longing To Dance (f)
98	Slam Dunk
97p	Age of Chivalry (f)
97p	Plan
97	Bett's Spirit (f)
97	Dohasa
97	Mr Medici
97	South Dakota
97	Tale of Two Cities
97	The Loan Express (f)
96	Irish Jig
95p	Kingdom of Naples
95p	King of Rome
95p	Toirneach (f)
95	Bunsen Burner
95	Shining Armour
95	Tuscan Evening (f)
95	Warsaw
93p	Kyniska (f)
86	Indiana Gal (f)
73	Chun Tosaigh

Three-Year-Olds

131	Soldier of Fortune
126	Eagle Mountain
126	Peeping Fawn (f)
125	Excellent Art
124	Duke of Marmalade
124	Honolulu
123	Finsceal Beo (f)
123	*US Ranger
121	Astronomer Royal
119	Confuchias
119	Mahler
119	Yellowstone
117	Admiralofthefleet
117	Evening Time (f)
117	Ezima (f)
117	Haatef
117	Macarthur
117	Red Moloney
116	Arch Swing (f)
116	Honoured Guest
116	Mores Wells
115	Alexander of Hales
115	Finicius
114	Acapulco
114	Alexander Tango (f)
114	Archipenko
114	He's A Decoy
114	Summit Surge
113	All My Loving (f)
113	Red Rock Canyon
112+	Hasanka (f)
112	Followmyfootsteps
111	*Spanish Harlem
111	Theann (f)
110	Four Sins (f)
110	Song of Hiawatha
110	Vision of Grandeur
109	Abraham Lincoln
109	Chariots of Fire
109	Chinese Whisper
109	Consul General
109	Dimenticata (f)
109	Ferneley
109	Snaefell
109	Trinity College
108	*Anton Chekhov
108	Mojito Royale
108	Timarwa (f)
107	Eyshal
107	Many Colours (f)
107	Tamimi's History
107	Taralaya (f)
106	Anna's Rock (f)
106	Consulate
106	Inourthoughts (f)
106	She's Our Mark (f)
105	Downtown (f)
105	Liscanna (f)
105	Navajo Moon (f)
105	Temlett
105	Uimhir A Haon (f)
104	*Athenian Way (f)
104	Celtic Dane
104	Magic Carpet (f)
104	Peak District
104	Profound Beauty (f)
104	Saga Celebre (f)
103p	Mourilyan
103	Cherry Hinton (f)
103	Flash McGahon
103	*Howya Now Kid
103	Little White Lie
103	Prince Erik
103	*Supposition (f)
102	City of Tribes
102	Fleeting Shadow
102	Sorolla
102	Speed Dream
102	Thoughtless Moment (f)
101	Brave Tin Soldier
101	Dal Cais
101	Don Pedro Mendoza
101	Lucky Kyllachy

101	*Perfect Casting	113	Lord Admiral	102	Princess Nala (f)
100+	Westlake	112	*Decado	101	Baron De'l
100	Alarazi	112	Jalmira (f)	101	Power Elite
100	Aqraan (f)	112	Mutakarrim	101	Rekaab
100	Contest	112	Quinmaster	100	Baggio
100	Miss Gorica (f)	111	An Tadh	100	Belle Artiste (f)
100	Vincenzio Galilei	111	Deauville Vision (f)	100	Eagle's Pass
100	Warriors Key	111	Namaya	100	King of Tory
99	*Angelonmyshoulder	111	Rainbow Rising	100	King Rama
99	Belle of The Lodge (f)	111	Senor Benny	100	Kyles Bay
99	Extraterrestrial	111	That's Hot (f)	100	Lidanski (f)
99§	Diamond Necklace (f)	110	Attercliffe	100	Monteriggioni
98+	Zafarwal	110	*Cougar Bay	100	Orpailleur
98	Aleagueoftheirown (f)	110	Eastern Appeal (f)	100§	Absolute Image
98	Potion (f)	110	Incline	100§	Mooretown Lady (f)
98	Top Class	110	King Jock	99	Kestrel Cross
98	Truly Mine (f)	110d	Cool Touch	99	Sedna (f)
97	Fly Free (f)	109	Benwilt Breeze	99	Tis Mighty (f)
97	Impetious (f)	109	Dynamo Dancer	99	Worldly Wise
97	Kingsdale Orion	109	Excelerate	99§	King In Waiting
97	Mull On The Run	109	Hitchcock	98	Chained Emotion
97	Nell Gwyn (f)	109	Leg Spinner	98	Fit The Cove
96	Akua'ba (f)	109	Nick's Nikita (f)	98	Sina Cova (f)
96	Alpine Eagle	108	Modeeroch (f)	97	Bahrain Storm
96	*Blackberry Boy	107	Kempes	97	Dani's Girl (f)
96	Lake Pontchartrain (f)	107	Marcus Andronicus	97	Harchibald
96	Once Upon A Grace (f)	107	The God of Love	97	Menwaal
95	Copper Bell	106	Baby Blue Eyes (f)	97	Sandymount Earl
95	Divine Night (f)	106	Bawaader	97	Settigano
95	Gaudeamus (f)	106	Danehill Music (f)	97	Virginia Woolf (f)
95	In A Rush (f)	106	Mutamared	97d	Tajneed
95	La Conquistadora (f)	105	Absolutelyfabulous (f)	96	Caheerloch
95	Shibina (f)	105	Tartouche (f)	96	Do The Trick
		104	Ardbrae Lady (f)	96	Grafton Street
Older Horses		104	Common World	96	Ireland's Call
132	Dylan Thomas	104	Farinelli	96	Jalwada (f)
128	Septimus	104	Galistic (f)	96	Larkwing
126	Yeats	104	Grecian Dancer (f)	96	Mist And Stone (f)
125	Scorpion	104	Majestic Times	96	Orbit O'Gold
124	George Washington	103	Anna Karenina (f)	95	Arc Bleu
123	Dandy Man	103	Blessyourpinksox (f)	95	Forthright
120	Duff	103	Bush Maiden (f)	95	High Reef (f)
118	Danak	103	Crooked Throw	95	Hoffman
116	Arch Rebel	103	Latino Magic	95	Kasimali
116	Mustameet	103	Nightime (f)	95	Majestic Concorde
115	Fracas	102	Bon Nuit (f)	95	Mombassa
115	Jumbajukiba	102	Crossing (f)	95	Osterhase
115	Redstone Dancer (f)	102	Emmpat	95	Peculiar Prince
114	Cheyenne Star (f)	102	Empirical Power	95	Rain Rush
114	Hard Rock City	102	Moone Cross (f)	95	Royal Island
113	Heliostatic			95	Streets of Gold

FRANCE   After a frustrating run of placed efforts as a four-year-old, few would have picked **Manduro** to prove France's outstanding performer of 2007, let alone to develop into the world's best racehorse. But his improvement was such that he was unbeaten for the year in five races, making into a top-class horse. Manduro's wins included victories at a mile in the Prix Jacques le Marois and at a mile and a half in the Prix Foy, though his win at Deauville was gained against largely below-form opponents, while a career-ending injury sustained when winning his Arc trial meant that he never got to prove himself fully over the Arc trip. There was no quibbling about his wins at intermediate distances though, as he put up top-class efforts in the Prix d'Ispahan and Prince of Wales's Stakes, the latter gained at the chief expense of subsequent Arc winner Dylan Thomas. Manduro's place in the Arc was taken instead by the same connections' (Baron von Ullmann and Andre Fabre) stayer **Getaway**, who put up a career-best effort at long odds to take fourth place. Previously successful in the Prix Kergorlay and an unlucky second in the Prix Gladiateur, Getaway looks one to follow again as a five-year-old, though a middle-distance rather than a staying campaign is likely to be mapped out for him.

Doctor Dino was another improved five-year-old, and after he had finished third to Dylan Thomas in the Prix Ganay on his reappearance, connections found him lucrative opportunities abroad in the Man o' War Stakes at Belmont and the Hong Kong Vase at Sha Tin. He ran well in defeat in all his other races, finishing third in the Singapore International Cup, the Arlington Million and the Champion Stakes, and looks set for another good year abroad. A largely domestic campaign for the Ganay runner-up **Irish Wells** brought him a second successive win in the Grand Prix de Deauville. The Ganay also saw a good run from fourth-placed **Boris de Deauville**, who had Irish Wells behind him in third when winning the Prix d'Harcourt earlier in April. Injury prevented the previous season's Arc winner Rail Link from returning to action as a four-year-old, though his connections (Khalid Abdulla and Andre Fabre) were represented instead by the brother of that horse's sire Dansili, **Champs Elysees**. Although not as good as Rail Link, he improved when stepped up to a mile and a half or more, winning the Prix d'Hedouville and finishing placed in the Prix Maurice de Nieuil, Grand Prix de Deauville, Gran Premio del Jockey Club and (when sent to Bobby Frankel in the USA), the Hollywood Turf Cup. **Atlantic Air** showed improved form in the summer, winning the Grand Prix de Vichy before being narrowly denied a second successive win in the Prix Gontaut-Biron at Deauville when giving weight to Godolphin's Echo of Light. The Aga Khan's **Vison Celebre** would almost certainly have taken higher rank among the older middle-distance horses but has evidently proved very hard to train; the winner of his only start at three (when he beat the subsequent Prix du Jockey Club winner Darsi), he finished second in the Grand Prix de Chantilly on the second of only two appearances in 2007.

France's older milers were headed by **Linngari**, whose European campaign was handled this time by Alain de Royer Dupre. After another successful Dubai Carnival, Linngari gained his first Group 1 win in the Premio Vittorio di Capua at Milan after finishing a creditable fourth in what proved Europe's hottest mile race, the Prix du Moulin. Below-par performances from both **Turtle Bowl** (third) and **Stormy River** (fifth), contributed to the Prix Jacques le Marois taking less winning in comparison. The same pair had also finished behind Manduro in the Prix d'Ispahan but Stormy River struggled for form all year, returning to near his best only when winning the Prix Messidor from **Satri** and **Multiplex**. Although without a pattern win to show for it, the 2005 Prix Jean Prat winner Turtle Bowl was back to form earlier in the year, going down narrowly to **Racinger** in both the Prix Edmond Blanc and Prix du Muguet at Saint-Cloud, but having that rival behind him when a good third in the Queen Anne Stakes at Royal Ascot. **Passager** was third in both those races at Saint-Cloud and filled the same position when narrowly beaten in the Lockinge Stakes at Newbury. A new addition to the ranks of older milers was **Spirito del Vento** who beat Multiplex and Passager in the Prix du Chemin de Fer du Nord at Chantilly and had a back-to-form Racinger behind him in second in the Prix Daniel Wildenstein in the autumn.

Marchand d'Or was again France's best sprinter and repeated his previous season's successes in both the Prix de la Porte Maillot and the Prix Maurice de Gheest. In addition, he acquitted himself well on two visits to Britain, finishing fourth in the July Cup and second in the Sprint Cup at Haydock. **Garnica** was fourth in the Maurice de Gheest before winning the Prix de Meautry later at Deauville's August meeting, his second pattern win of the year after the Prix du Palais-Royal at Longchamp. Garnica ran another good race at Deauville in the summer when second to **Tiza** in the Prix de Ris-Orangis. Previously trained in South Africa and Dubai, Tiza finished behind Garnica in two more encounters at Deauville and found the five furlongs of the Prix de l'Abbaye too sharp (though still fared best of the French sprinters in sixth) before winning the Prix de Seine-et-Oise at Maisons-Laffitte in November. Speedy filly **Beauty Is Truth** proved the best three-year-old sprinter but failed to build on her win in the Prix du Gros-Chene at Chantilly in June.

At least until he came up against Getaway in the Prix Kergorlay in August, **Lord du Sud** again looked the best French stayer, winning the Prix Vicomtesse Vigier on his favoured soft ground at Longchamp in May. Conditions weren't soft enough for him in the Gold Cup though and were plainly too firm in the Prix Royal-Oak. A feature of the good staying races was that fillies and mares featured prominently in most of them.

Varevees was something of a fortunate winner of the Prix Gladiateur over Getaway, but ran well when narrowly beaten by German gelding Le Miracle in the Prix du Cadran, while the Prix de Pomone winner **Macleya** and **Ponte Tresa** completed an all-female first three in the Prix Royal-Oak behind British-trained filly Allegretto. Ponte Tresa had earlier been placed in the Prix Vicomtesse Vigier and Prix Kergorlay, and **Montare** (third in the Vicomtesse Vigier and Pomone) hit winning form as usual in the autumn, taking the Prix du Conseil de Paris.

The best older filly or mare to remain in training was **Mandesha**, though she failed to recapture quite the sort of form that had made her the best of her age and sex in Europe the year before. She made a winning reappearance in the Prix Corrida at Saint-Cloud against Macleya before second places in the Grand Prix de Saint-Cloud, Nassau Stakes and Prix Foy, and ended her career on rather a downbeat note when only seventh in the Arc, wearing cheekpieces. Runner-up to Mandesha in the Prix de l'Opera the year before, **Satwa Queen** was able to go one better in that event after winning the Prix Jean Romanet at Deauville for the second year running. Also runner-up in the Prix Allez France (to Macleya) and Windsor Forest Stakes, Satwa Queen was sold for 3.4 million guineas (a new European record for a filly or mare in training) at Newmarket in December. **Pearl Sky** won the opening pattern race of the season, the Prix Exbury, before finishing second in the Prix d'Harcourt and Prix de Pomone. **Musical Way** was a bit behind the best fillies or mares but she was in fine heart at the end of the year, winning La Coupe de Maisons-Laffitte for the second time, following up in the Prix Dollar at Longchamp, and then finishing third in the Premio Lydia Tesio at Rome and the Hong Kong Cup.

As expected, the lack of success of French two-year-olds at a high level in 2006 was not an indictment on a substandard crop but simply indicated that the best horses of the generation were to prove later developers. Indeed, nine of the top ten French-trained three-year-olds had had one run at most as juveniles and three of them had not run at all. The exception was **Literato**, who had been unbeaten in five races as a two-year-old. He trained on tremendously well, winning four pattern races as a three-year-old, including the Prix Guillaume d'Ornano at Deauville, and ending his year with a high-class effort to win the Champion Stakes, thereby giving his trainer Jean-Claude Rouget a first win in Britain. Literato found only one too good for him on the two occasions he was beaten, having excuses on his reappearance, and beaten a length and a half by **Lawman** in the Prix du Jockey Club. After making all at Chantilly, Lawman dropped back to a mile for his remaining starts, winning the Prix Jean Prat but disappointing badly on his final outing in the Prix Jacques le Marois. The third and fourth in what turned out to be a well-contested Prix du Jockey Club, **Shamdinan** and **Zambezi Sun**, went on to do well. Shamdinan was sold in mid-season to race in the USA, where he won the Secretariat Stakes and finished second in the Breeders' Cup Turf. Zambezi Sun stepped up to a mile and a half and gave his owner Khalid Abdulla a second successive win in the Grand Prix de Paris, which he took in good style but that was as far as he went in emulating Rail Link, as he finished only third in the Prix Niel and eighth in the Arc subsequently. Both the Niel and the Arc saw much-improved performances from **Sagara**, who had finished only seventh in the Prix du Jockey Club and third in the Grand Prix de Paris. He was runner-up in the Niel and came out best of the three-year-olds when staying for third in the Arc. Both Literato and Sagara have joined Godolphin, as has another of the leading French three-year-olds **Poet Laureate**. Very lightly raced in Sheikh Mohammed's colours for Andre Fabre, he could prove best of the trio as a four-year-old if maintaining the progress which saw him finish second in the Grand Prix de Deauville after winning a listed race at the same track. Fabre had a particularly strong hand among the staying three-year-olds and trained the first four home in the Prix Chaudenay. Best of them was **Coastal Path**, who is unbeaten in four starts and looks set to progress further as a four-year-old. **Royal And Regal** was third to Coastal Path in both the Prix de Lutece and Prix Chaudenay after having his limitations exposed at shorter trips, but he was another French-trained winner on Champions Day at Newmarket when successful in the Jockey Club Cup. Prix Daphnis winner **Loup Breton** (later promoted second in the Prix Dollar) proved to be the final pattern winner for leading owner/breeder Alec Wildenstein, who died early in 2008, little more than six years after inheriting the bloodstock of his father Daniel.

There were fewer performances of note from three-year-old colts over shorter trips. French colts cut little ice in the Poule d'Essai des Poulains, a race which Lawman had missed after his defeat by **Chichi Creasy** (not seen out again afterwards) in the main trial, the Prix de Fontainebleau. **US Ranger** kept his unbeaten record in impressive style when winning the Prix Djebel on his reappearance but failed to justify support in the Two Thousand Guineas (seventh) and Jersey Stakes (second) on his two remaining starts for Jean-Claude Rouget before joining Aidan O'Brien. **Holocene**'s second place to Manduro in the Prix Jacques le Marois possibly flatters him somewhat, though he had filled the same position behind Lawman in the Prix de Guiche before that. Much the best performance by a French-trained three-year-old over a mile came from the filly **Darjina** when beating older rivals in the Qatar-sponsored Prix du Moulin. Incidentally, the same sponsors are to back the Prix de l'Arc de Triomphe from 2008, making it the world's richest turf race. Darjina's defeat of Ramonti and George Washington in the Moulin reads a lot better than the rest of her form, but she remained unbeaten on home soil, also winning the Prix de la Grotte, the Poule d'Essai des Pouliches and the Prix d'Astarte, in the last-named race again outbattling the Grotte runner-up **Missvinski**. Darjina was a long way below her best in two visits to Ascot for the Coronation Stakes and Queen Elizabeth II Stakes, but fared better abroad when third in the Hong Kong Mile. She stays in training and looks set to be stepped up in trip.

France's best three-year-old middle-distance fillies were no better than smart but **West Wind** and **Mrs Lindsay** dominated both the Prix de Diane and Prix Vermeille, the pair representing provincial stables (Alex Pantall and Francois Rohaut respectively) which have long owed much of their success to fillies. They finished in that order at Chantilly but Mrs Lindsay turned the tables at Longchamp where West Wind looked unlucky after her rival had got first run. Mrs Lindsay went on to win the E. P. Taylor Stakes in Canada and stays in training, as does West Wind who was another Godolphin recruit. The Andre Fabre-trained **Vadapolina** started a short-priced favourite for both the Prix de Diane and the Prix Vermeille but disappointed badly both times (and finished well held again in the Prix de l'Opera) but she had impressed on a couple of occasions in lesser pattern company when winning the Prix Cleopatre and Prix de Psyche either side of the Diane. Her stable-companion **Legerete** proved more reliable, winning the Prix de Royaumont and Prix de Malleret before making the frame in the Vermeille and Opera. Another Fabre filly **Tashelka** finished down the field in the Vermeille (the stable fielded five of the ten runners) but had earlier won the Prix de la Nonette at Deauville from the Diane third **Diyakalanie** and late in the season led home a Sheikh Mohammed-owned one-two-three in the Prix Fille de l'Air at Toulouse.

There was more strength in depth in the latest crop of French two-year-olds. Peeping Fawn's half-brother **Thewayyouare** looks a particularly good prospect for 2008 after winning his last four starts. His last two wins came at Saint-Cloud, following an impressive win in the Prix Thomas Bryon with a more hard-won half-length defeat of **Hello Morning** in the Criterium International in which the first two pulled well clear of a field which included the Prix des Chenes winner **Blue Chagall** back in fifth. Criquette Head-Maarek gained compensation for Hello Morning's defeat when **Full of Gold** landed Saint-Cloud's other Group 1 contest for two-year-olds, the Criterium de Saint-Cloud. The form of that race is some way short of that shown by the first two in the Criterium International, but Full of Gold, from a family of hurdlers, should progress further at three given a sufficient test. His two-length defeat of **Hannouma** gives a line of form to the Prix de Conde winner **High Rock**, who beat the same runner-up by a length at Longchamp. **Alexandros** (like Thewayyouare, another Andre Fabre-trained son of Kingmambo) was not seen out after Deauville in August and subsequently joined Godolphin, but showed plenty of ability, winning a listed race over seven furlongs at Longchamp and the Prix de Cabourg over six furlongs at Deauville but shaping as though in need of a return to further when third in the Prix Morny on his final start. Another Fabre colt, **Shediak**, was placed in the Prix La Rochette and Prix Jean-Luc Lagardere at Longchamp but has been sold to race in the USA as a three-year-old. Andre Fabre's brief association with Shediak's owner the Aga Khan (dating from the transfer of Jean-Luc Lagardere's bloodstock in the spring of 2005) was terminated ahead of the 2008 season.

There was at least as much strength among the two-year-old fillies. **Natagora** was the first to show her hand, completing a four-timer in the Prix Robert Papin at the end of July. She looked to be more than just an early-season type however, and proved it when stepped up to six furlongs, finishing second in the Prix Morny before winning the Cheveley Park Stakes, making Pascal Bary another leading French trainer to register his first win in Britain. Natagora is no certainty to stay the trip in the Guineas but the other leading French fillies are all proven already at a mile. **Zarkava** won both her starts at Longchamp, showing plenty of improvement to beat **Conference Call** decisively in the Prix Marcel Boussac, and looks likely to stay at home for the Poule d'Essai des Pouliches rather than contest the Guineas. Conference Call was among a strong hand of two-year-old fillies owned by Khalid Abdulla. **Proviso** won her first two starts at Deauville, notably the Prix du Calvados, before not having the run of the race as much as the winner when second to Listen in the Fillies' Mile. Another progressive Abdulla filly was **Modern Look**, who completed a hat-trick when successful in the Prix Miesque at Maisons-Laffitte in November. The Yves de Nicolay stable-companions **Top Toss** and **Gagnoa** ended their seasons with Group 3 wins in the Prix d'Aumale and Prix des Reservoirs respectively.

Two-Year-Olds

117p	Thewayyouare
117p	Zarkava (f)
116p	Proviso (f)
116	Hello Morning
116	Natagora (f)
111	Blue Chagall
110	Alexandros
109p	Full of Gold
109p	Modern Look (f)
108p	High Rock
108	Shediak
107	Conference Call (f)
107	Ossun (f)
106p	Alnadana (f)
105	Hannouma
105	Putney Bridge
104p	Tamayuz
104	Stern Opinion
103p	Brillantissimo
103p	Top Toss (f)
103	Gagnoa (f)
103	Salut L'Africain
103	Sceptre Rouge
102	Beret Rouge
102	Mousse Au Chocolat (f)
102	Wilki (f)
101p	Goldikova (f)
101	Sanjida (f)
101	Verba (f)
101	War Officer
101	Water View
100p	Indian Daffodil
100	African Rose (f)
100	Gipson Dessert (f)
100	Salsalavie
96	Macellya (f)
94	Galaktea (f)
92	Faslen (f)

Three-Year-Olds

128	Darjina (f)
127	Literato
124	Sagara
123	*US Ranger
121	Lawman

120p	Poet Laureate
118	*Shamdinan
118	West Wind (f)
117p	Coastal Path
117+	Zambezi Sun
117	Mrs Lindsay (f)
116	Legerete (f)
116	*Missvinski (f)
116	Royal And Regal
116	Vadapolina (f)
115	Chichi Creasy
115?	Holocene
114	All Is Vanity (f)
114	Beauty Is Truth (f)
114	Loup Breton
114	Tashelka (f)
113	Kaloura (f)
113	Spirit One
112	Battle Paint
112	Indian Choice
112	Magic America (f)
112	*Stoneside
111	Coquerelle (f)
111	Shujoon
111	Utrecht (f)
111	*Visionario
110	Bal de La Rose (f)
110	Believe Me (f)
110	*Bleu Intense
110	Cicerole (f)
110	Cristobal
110	Russian Desert
109	Prior Warning
109	Sageburg
109	*Vincennes (f)
108	Castlereagh
108	Darsha (f)
108	Diyakalanie (f)
108	Friston Forest
108	Grand Vista
108	Hurricane Fly
108	Just Little (f)
108	La Hernanda (f)
108	Noble Prince
108	Tian Shan
108	Vertigineux
108	Winter Fashion (f)

107p	Salden Licht
107	Anabaa's Creation (f)
107	Cinnamon Bay (f)
107	Concentric (f)
107	Elva (f)
107	Law Lord
107	*No Dream
107	Quest For Honor
107	Synopsis (f)
107	Vespucci
106	Airmail Special
106	Chill (f)
106	Criticism (f)
106	Dancing Lady (f)
106	El Comodin
106	Maria Gabriella (f)
106	Never Green (f)
106	Not Just Swing
106	Spycrawler
106	*Testama (f)
105	Air Bag (f)
105	Ashkazar
105	Beatrix Kiddo (f)
105	Chinandega (f)
105	Fontcia (f)
105	Golden Life (f)
105	Gris de Gris
105	Makaan
105	Only Answer (f)
105	Party Girl (f)
105	Peace Dream (f)
105	Serabad
105	Zibimix
105	Zut Alors (f)
104	Doe Ray Me (f)
104	Sismix (f)
103	Noble Ginger (f)
102	Terra Incognita (f)
101	Toque de Queda (f)
100	Topka (f)
99	Garda
99	Le Paradis
98	Artistica (f)

Older Horses

135	Manduro

124	Getaway	114	Multiplex	109	Musketier
124	*Linngari	114	Ponte Tresa (f)	109	Princesse Dansante (f)
123	Doctor Dino	114?	Rhenus	109	Ricine (f)
123	Marchand d'Or	114§	Numide	108	Athanor
122	Garnica	113	Balius	108	Bedaly
122	Irish Wells	113	Bertranicus	108	Blushing King
122	Mandesha (f)	113	Echoes Rock	108	*Green Girl (f)
122	Spirito del Vento	113	Elasos	108	La Boum (f)
121	Turtle Bowl	113	Kentucky Dynamite	108	Marend
120	Boris de Deauville	113	Kilometre Neuf	108	Rageman
119	Lord du Sud	113	Varevees (f)	108	Touch of Land
119	Racinger	112	Alix Road (f)	108	Val Jaro
119	Stormy River	112	Derison	107	*Gold Sound
118	*Atlantic Air	112	Musical Way (f)	107	Gwenseb (f)
118	Vison Celebre	112	Sabana Perdida (f)	107	Luisant
117	*Champs Elysees	111	Chopastair	107	Ridaar
117	Passager	111	Freedonia (f)	106	Krataios
117	*Sudan	111	Host Nation	106	Major Grace
117	*Tiza	111	Kavafi	106	Mariol
116	*Bellamy Cay	111	Mister Conway	106	Mister Fasliyev
115	Daramsar	111	Soledad	106	Nickelle (f)
115	Macleya (f)	111	Trip To The Moon (f)	106	Young Tiger
115	Montare (f)	111	Willywell	105	Dynaforce (f)
115	Pearl Sky (f)	110	*Linda's Lad	105	King Luna (f)
115	Sanaya (f)	110	Merlerault	105	Solsiste
115	Satri	110	Runaway	105	Stop Making Sense
115	Satwa Queen (f)	110	Walk In The Park	105	Tirwanako
115	Spectaculaire	109	Latin Mood		
114	Kocab	109	*Mary Louhana (f)	103	Kourka (f)

GERMANY   A solid quartet of older mile-and-a-half performers ensured that Germany's top middle-distance prizes remained at home, while the continued pursuit of big international races by German stables brought success abroad as well. **Saddex** had reached the frame in the Deutsches Derby and Grosser Preis von Baden as a three-year-old but he improved into the leading older middle-distance horse in the latest season. Between wins at Cologne in the Gerling-Preis and the Rheinland-Pokal, he put up his best effort when successful in the Grand Prix de Chantilly. His season ended with defeats in the Prix de l'Arc de Triomphe and Japan Cup, though he wasn't discredited when sixth at Longchamp and was encountering firm conditions for the first time in Japan. Gelding **Quijano** was more successful abroad, completing a hat-trick at the Dubai Carnival early in the year in the Dubai City of Gold and then running well later in the year to be placed in the Canadian International and Hong Kong Vase. Quijano had made constant improvement in handicap company in 2006 and further progress in Dubai extended his winning sequence to ten races. He also won both his starts at home, becoming the first gelding to win Germany's most prestigious race, the Grosser Preis von Baden. Quijano's stable-companion **Schiaparelli** missed the Grosser Preis von Baden but the 2006 Deutsches Derby winner enjoyed another fine season, winning his last four starts, including three more Group 1 successes in the Deutschlandpreis at Dusseldorf, the Preis von Europa at Cologne and the Gran Premio del Jockey Club at Milan. It was no doubt as much his future stallion potential (he's a son of Monsun whose recent successes have made him continental Europe's most expensive sire) as what he might yet achieve on the track which made him one of Godolphin's most high-profile acquisitions late in the year. The fourth member of the quartet was the previous season's Grosser Preis von Baden winner **Prince Flori**. He was below form when attempting a repeat win at Baden-Baden and had finished last in the King George VI and Queen Elizabeth Stakes prior to that but he had been as good as ever earlier in the year, giving weight to Saddex when a close third in the Gerling-Preis, having Schiaparelli back in third when winning the Grosser Mercedes-Benz-Preis at Baden-Baden and running a good third in the Grand Prix de Saint-Cloud.

Six-year-old **Bussoni** enjoyed his best season yet, winning the Betty Barclay-Rennen at Baden-Baden over two miles for the second year running but proving at least as good over shorter trips with wins abroad in the Prix Maurice de Nieuil at Longchamp and the valuable Bosphorus Cup in Turkey. He was also placed behind Saddex at Cologne in the

Henkel Preis der Diana, Dusseldorf—
Mystic Lips loses her maiden tag by making all for a five-length win in the German Oaks

Gerling-Preis and Rheinland Pokal and finished just behind Quijano when third in the Hong Kong Vase. **Egerton** also ran creditably to take sixth place in the Vase for the second year running. He had a good season at home, particularly at Baden-Baden, where he finished third in the Grosser Preis (making the frame for the third time) before winning the Baden-Wurttemburg Trophy there later in the autumn, his second Group 3 win of the year after a successful reappearance at Cologne in the spring. **Poseidon Adventure**, who began his career with Aidan O'Brien, found only Schiaparelli too strong in both the Hansa-Preis and the Preis von Europa.

A fine career came to an end when the reliable seven-year-old **Soldier Hollow** was retired to stud towards the end of the latest season. Two more pattern wins during 2007 took his career total of such races to ten, the last of them coming in the Grosser Dallmayr-Preis at Munich, a Group 1 he had also won in 2005. Another of the best performances over a mile and a quarter came from **Wiesenpfad** when winning the Preis der Sparkassen-Finanzgruppe at Baden-Baden in August. There was little to choose between **Apollo Star**, **Aspectus**, **Konig Turf** and **Santiago** among Germany's leading older milers. All of them won at least once in pattern company as their paths crossed on several occasions. The front-running Apollo Star gained Group 2 wins at Milan and Hanover (from Konig Turf and Aspectus) during the summer and was just denied a third such victory in the Europa Meile at Cologne in September when coming off second-best in a three-way photo with Konig Turf and Santiago, giving weight to both. Former German Guineas winner Santiago ended the season with a Group 2 win of his own in the Premio Ribot at Rome, while his stable-companion Aspectus joined Andre Fabre from Hans Blume at the end of the year.

Germany's sprints were weak affairs on the whole and it says much for their standard that two of them went to the nine-year-old **Lucky Strike** who had seemed on the downgrade in 2006 but bounced back to win Group 3 contests at Baden-Baden (the Benazet-Rennen for the third time) and Cologne. However, he could finish only sixth to **Electric Beat** (well beaten at 100/1 in the July Cup the time before) in Germany's top sprint, the Goldene Peitsche at Baden-Baden. Among Germany's performers over shorter distances though, the revelation was the eight-year-old **Toylsome**. A prolific winner in listed company, his sole pattern win prior to the latest season had been as a three-year-old and he was only a pacemaker on Manduro's behalf when making a belated Group 1 debut in the Prix Jacques le Marois in the summer. Successful in two more listed races on his next two starts, he then caused the year's biggest upset in Group 1 company when making all to beat a strong field in the Prix de la Foret at Longchamp and wasn't discredited under a penalty when third in the Challenge Stakes at Newmarket on his final start. Germany's second Group 1 win on Arc weekend came courtesy of **Le Miracle** in the Prix du Cadran. Raced entirely outside Germany since early in 2005, Le Miracle ran well in defeat in several other top staying races in France and belied odds of 50/1 when third in the Gold Cup at Ascot.

The three-year-old crop had clear leaders among both the colts and fillies. **Adlerflug** ran out a seven-length winner of the Deutsches Derby, clearly handling the soft conditions better than most, though showed he didn't need the mud when an excellent second against older rivals in the Grosser Preis von Baden on his only subsequent start. He looks sure to be a threat to the established older horses over a mile and a half in 2008 and reportedly could make his reappearance in the Jockey Club Stakes at Newmarket. Adlerflug contributed to an excellent start to the career of Jens Hirschberger who was set up as private trainer of horses running in the colours of Baron Georg von Ullmann and his Gestut Schlenderhan. Others included the aforementioned Toylsome, the Mehl-Mulhens-Rennen (2000 Guineas) winner **Aviso,** and **Persian Storm,** who made all for Group 3 successes over a mile and a quarter at Munich and Baden-Baden but failed to last home in testing conditions over further in the Deutsches Derby. Like Shirocco and Manduro before him, a couple of other sons of Monsun owned by Baron von Ullmann, Persian Storm has been sent to continue his career with Andre Fabre. **Shrek** was another to underperform in the Deutsches Derby but he was second in the Derby Italiano prior to that and won a couple of Group 3 events at Frankfurt over a mile and a quarter, putting up a smart effort to beat Persian Storm on the second occasion. Neither **First Stream** nor **Conillon** contested the Deutsches Derby but both ran well against older rivals in Group 1 company when second in the Rheinland-Pokal and Deutschlandpreis respectively.

    Mi Emma proved much the best three-year-old filly, winning the German 1000 Guineas by a wide margin (officially nine lengths) from **Mystic Lips,** who was subsequently a five-length winner of the Preis der Diana. Mi Emma started joint-favourite for the Coronation Stakes but was below her best at Royal Ascot, even though finishing second. She remained unbeaten at home however when making all to beat Soldier Hollow and Konig Turf in the Oettingen-Rennen at Baden-Baden and remains in training. In a bid to boost the standard of the Preis der Diana and thereby maintain its Group 1 status, Germany's Oaks has been moved to an early-August date (from early-June) which it is hoped will also encourage foreign participants.

    Pomellato struck a blow for German two-year-olds abroad when dropping back in trip to run out a clear-cut winner of the Criterium de Maisons-Laffitte. He also won the Maurice-Lacroix Trophy at Baden-Baden and wasn't discredited when fourth in the Gran Criterium. A similar level of form was shown by the first two in Germany's top two-year-old race, the Preis der Winterfavoriten, in which **Precious Boy** (unbeaten in three starts) and **Liang Kay** finished five lengths clear. The equivalent race for fillies, the Preis der Winterkonigin, went to **Love Academy,** who comes from a top German middle-distance family and looks sure to progress at three.

Two-Year-Olds			
111p	Precious Boy	109	Axxos
110	Pomellato	109	Molly Max
110	Liang Kay	109	Scatina (f)
103p	Love Academy (f)	109	*Touch My Soul (f)
100p	Idonea (f)	108	Andorn
99	Diamantgottin (f)	107	Davidoff
97	Peace Royale (f)	107	Dominante (f)
97	Themelie Island (f)	107	Lord Hill
96	Manipura (f)	107	Rolling Home
96	Sehrezad	106	Sommersturm
96	Briseida (f)	105	Laeya Star (f)
96	Abbashiva		
95	Something Stupid		

94	Goose Bay (f)	104	Forthe Millionkiss
		104	Smokejumper
		104	Waldvogel

Three-Year-Olds			
120	Adlerflug	103	Bahama Mama (f)
118	Mi Emma (f)	102	Avanti Polonia (f)
115	Conillon	102	Global Dream
115	First Stream	102	Neele (f)
115	Shrek	102	Scoubidou (f)
114	Persian Storm	101	Red Diva (f)
113	Mystic Lips (f)	101	Waky Love (f)
110	Alaska River	99	Allanit
110	Belmundo	99	Foreign Music (f)
109	Antek	98	Meridia (f)
109	Aviso	96	Kaleo

Older Horses

124	Saddex	124	Toylsome
		122	Quijano
		121	Soldier Hollow
		120	Prince Flori
		120	Schiaparelli
		117	Bussoni
		117	Le Miracle
		117	Wiesenpfad
		116	Egerton
		116	Poseidon Adventure
		116?	Brisant
		115	Apollo Star
		115	Lucky Strike
		114	Aspectus
		114	Donaldson
		114	Fair Breeze (f)
		114	Konig Turf
		114	Santiago
		112	Donatello
		112	Electric Beat
		112	Key To Pleasure
		111	Ioannina (f)
		111	Matrix
		111	Mharadono
		110	Arcadio
		110	La Dancia (f)
		110	Lateral
		110	Lauro
		110	Sacho

110	Shinko's Best	107	Bergo	105	N'Oubliez Jamais
109	Dickens	107	Idealist	105	Willingly
109	El Tango	107	Madresal		
109	Kiton	106	Gandolfino	101	Soudaine (f)
109	Santiago Atitlan	106	Konig Speed	101	Stephenson
109	Waleria (f)	106	Mohandas	92	The Spring Flower (f)
108	Dragon Fly	105	Arc de Triomphe		
108	Oriental Tiger	105	Caudillo		

ITALY Just useful as a three-year-old when down the field in the Derby Italiano, it was the much-improved **Pressing** who emerged as Italy's best older horse, though as is the norm for horses who rise to the top in Italy, he soon attracted interest from abroad. He completed an early-season hat-trick at Milan in the Premio Ambrosiano before finishing second to **Distant Way** in the Premio Presidente della Repubblica, though by the time he won the Premio Federico Tesio and Premio Roma in the autumn, he had joined Michael Jarvis. Distant Way was repeating his 2006 success in the Presidente della Repubblica, though for the second year running he lost his form in the autumn and finished well behind Pressing in the Premio Roma in which rank outsider **Monachesi** showed improved form to finish second. **Vol de Nuit**, who had a disappointing spell with Luca Cumani in 2006, showed he retained his ability back with his former stable when finishing fifth in the Premio Roma. Miler **Miles Gloriosus**, who won three listed races during the season, and **Place In Line**, successful four times in similar company up to a mile and three quarters, will be among those with pattern-race aspirations in 2008. Sprinter **Dream Impact** completes the list of leading older horses. He returned to form to win the Premio Carlo & Franco Aloisi (formerly the Premio Umbria) at Rome in November, upsetting hot favourite **Le Cadre Noir**. The runner-up, a three-year-old, won seven races during the year, notably the Premio Omenoni at Milan, and finished a good second in the Prix de Meautry at Deauville. Another three-year-old sprinter, **Per Incanto**, joined John Dunlop after winning the Premio Tudini at Rome in May but was below form in his two starts in Britain.

A substandard renewal of the Derby Italiano went to **Awelmarduk** who joined Marco Botti in Britain afterwards but was not seen out again. The Derby is clinging on to Group 1 status (albeit shortened to eleven furlongs and to be run at an earlier date in 2008) but the rest of Italy's classics were belatedly downgraded in 2007, the two Guineas now Group

Premio Presidente della Repubblica At The Races, Rome—a second successive win in the race for Distant Way (right); German challenger Soldier Hollow (centre) loses second to Pressing, who joins Michael Jarvis after the race

Premio Lydia Tesio Shadwell, Rome—Turfrose (check sleeves) makes it five wins for the year ahead of German filly Fair Breeze (right) and French mare Musical Way (second left)

3 events and the Oaks a Group 2. **Golden Titus**, the top two-year-old of 2006, trained on well to win the Premio Parioli (2000 Guineas) from **Freemusic** and finished third in the Prix Jean Prat and excelled himself in the autumn when second against older horses in the Premio Vittorio di Capua. The only other three-year-old colt to show smart form was **Gimmy** who ran well in good company in the autumn, finishing second in the Premio Federico Tesio and fifth in the Gran Premio del Jockey Club. Much the best three-year-old filly was the German-bred **Turfrose** who has now joined Andre Fabre. She made the frame in both fillies' classics and proved tough and consistent, much the best of her five wins coming in the Premio Lydia Tesio at Rome in October.

Yet another export was leading two-year-old **Gladiatorus**, a winner of four listed races who joined Godolphin after finishing second to British-trained Scintillo in the Gran Criterium, with **Farrel** third. **Magritte** was a speedy filly early on, winning her first three starts, including the Premio Primi Passi, before finishing a good second to Natagora in the Prix Robert Papin.

Two-Year-Olds
108	Gladiatorus
106	Magritte (f)
105	Gran Zamir
103	Farrel
102	Amaldi
99	Black Mambazo
99	L'Indiscreta (f)
98p	Papetti
98	Eldest
98	Dematil
96p	Fathayer
96	Magico Marco
95	Rastignano
95	Sampeyre

93	Permesso
92	Cima On Fly
90	Mia Diletta (f)
90	Short Affair (f)

Three-Year-Olds
120	Golden Titus
116	Turfrose (f)

112	Gimmy
111	Le Cadre Noir
111	*Per Incanto
110	Freemusic
109	Alamanni (f)
109	Awelmarduk
107	Lokaloka (f)
107	Moi Non Plus (f)
107	Rob's Love
107	Sopran Promo
106	Docksil (f)
106	Titus Shadow
106	Zenone
105	Mimetico (f)
105	Riario

104	Amante Latino
104	Donoma (f)
103	Shot Bless (f)
102	Miss Annaleo (f)
102	Sakhee's Song (f)
101	Il Cadetto

Older Horses
120	*Pressing
119	Distant Way

116	Monachesi
112	Dream Impact
112	Vol de Nuit
111	Miles Gloriosus
111	Place In Line
110	Exhibit One (f)
110	Icelandic
108	Jack Aubrey
108	Joaquin
107	Speciano
106	Cocodrail
106	Magic Box
106	Mister Fasliyev
106	Patapan
105	Biff Tannen
105	Montalegre
105	Rattle And Hum

104	Solzah (f)
103	My Sea of Love (f)
101	Velvet Revolver (f)
101	Wickwing (f)
99	Irene Watts (f)

SCANDINAVIA   The mile and a half division was unusually weak in 2006, but was back up to strength in 2007 with three of the top Scandinavian horses all best at that trip. The improved five-year-old Swedish-bred gelding **Equip Hill** completed a four-timer when winning the Scandinavian Open Championship by five lengths, following up a win in a valuable and well-contested listed race over eleven furlongs at Ovrevoll from the mare **Miss The Boat**, a winner of three listed races at the same track during the year. Unusually for Scandinavia, a couple of three-year-old colts figured among the leading performers. **Appel Au Maitre** contested three pattern races in Germany in the first half of the season, finishing a good fourth in the Deutsches Derby before winning both the Swedish and Norwegian equivalents by five lengths. He had even more to spare against older rivals when winning the Stockholm Cup International (by eight and a half lengths) from **Peas And Carrots**, with both Equip Hill and Miss The Boat well below form. The other leading three-year-old was **Luca Brasi**, who was no match for Appel Au Maitre in either the Swedish or Norwegian Derby (runner-up in the former) but gained his own win over Peas And Carrots in a listed race on dirt at Jagersro in September. Appel Au Maitre is in a good position to dominate the middle-distance contests in Scandinavia in 2008 and hopefully his defeat in the Prix du Conseil du Paris on his final start won't dissuade connections from trying him abroad again. Scandinavian horses have generally found competition at the Dubai Carnival too strong, though **Binary File**'s close fifth place in the Group 3 Burj Nahaar over a mile was a good effort.

In contrast to the young profile of the leading middle-distance performers, veterans won both Scandinavia's Group 3 sprints, neither of which took much winning. Both eight-year-old **Hovman** and nine-year-old **Francis** were outsiders when winning the Polar Cup and Taby Open Sprint Championship respectively. Hovman had won up to a mile and a half in listed company earlier in his career but showed no other form in 2007, while Francis hadn't contested so much as a listed race prior to the latest season. **Muskateer Steel** finished only sixth in the two Group 3 sprints (starting favourite at Taby) but was better than that judged on his defeat of the Taby Open Sprint runner-up **Solvana** and Francis in a listed race at Ovrevoll in June. **Steve's Champ** was another to disappoint in the two Group 3 sprints (as well as in a listed race at Chester), having beaten **Berri Chis** (third in the Taby Open Sprint), Muskateer Steel and Solvana in a listed race at Taby in May.

Although not the best performer in Scandinavia and practically unknown further afield, the six-year-old mare **Funny Legend** has compiled a tremendous record in recent years which was enhanced in 2007 in particular. Another six wins took her tally to twenty-four wins from thirty-five starts, and they included both of Scandinavia's two Group 3 events over intermediate trips, the Stockholms Stora Pris (from **Angel de Madrid**) and the Marit Sveaas Minnelop (from the subsequently disqualified **Maybach**). Funny Legend's two listed wins included a third consecutive victory in the Coolmore Matchmaker Stakes at Taby in September.

Three-Year-Olds				
114	Appel Au Maitre	108	Muskateer Steel	105	Angel de Madrid
111	Luca Brasi	107	Mambo King	105	Maybach
		107	*Tiberius Caesar		
		106	Ecology	103	Calistoga
Older Horses		106	Jubilation	102	Berri Chis
113	Equip Hill	106	Moltas	102	Solvana (f)
113	Binary File	106	Novasky (f)	101	The Pirate
109	Hovman	106	Peas And Carrots	100	Steelwolf
108	Francis	106	Salt Track	94	Jagodin
108	Funny Legend (f)	106	Wazir		
108	Miss The Boat (f)	105	Steve's Champ		

The following European-trained horses also achieved significant ratings in major races

Two-Year-Olds		Older Horses		106	Simple Exchange
100	Ensis (f) (Spain)	118	Sabirli (Turkey)		(Slovakia)
97	Equiano (Spain)	112	Ribella (f) (Turkey)	106	Tiramisu (f) (Turkey)
		109	Fairson (Turkey)	106	Tunduru (Spain)

UNITED ARAB EMIRATES   The Dubai International Racing Carnival, held for the fourth time in 2007, consists of just seventy-five races (excluding the Dubai World Cup card), but its impact on racing around the world has been huge. The most significant and fascinating aspect of the Carnival has been that the international competition it has generated enables direct comparisons to be made between the strength of racing nations from different parts of the world. Some of the results have been eye-opening. In particular, South Africa and South America have been the two regions to have benefited most from international exposure afforded by the Carnival. Largely unknown quantities in the past due to the lack of form-lines with other countries, both South Africa (mainly due to the Carnival's most successful trainer Mike de Kock) and South America now have a much higher profile internationally. The knock-on effect on South American bloodstock in particular has been great, particularly in the wake of the Dubai World Cup success of Invasor who was bred in Argentina and began his career in Uruguay. Godolphin will have around a dozen South American-bred acquisitions to choose from for the 2008 Carnival, among them **Imperialista** and **Eu Tambem** who were Brazilian-bred winners of two rounds of the Maktoum Challenge series in 2007. Mile handicap winner **Nelore Pora** and **Impossible Ski**, runner-up to Imperialista in the first round of the Maktoum Challenge, were other Brazilian horses to do well at the 2007 Carnival. South American-breds (four-year-olds foaled to Southern Hemisphere time and treated accordingly on the weight-for-age scale) also figured prominently in the Carnival's classics. The Mike de Kock-trained but Argentinian-bred **Asiatic Boy** won all four of his starts by wide margins, including the UAE 2000 Guineas and Derby, while two more ex-South Americans, **Greetings** and Samba Reggae (rated 102) were placed in both the UAE fillies' classics behind Godolphin's US-bred **Folk**.

It is not just South American bloodstock that has received a boost from the Carnival. Closer to home, a new market has been created at the Autumn Horses In Training Sale for potential Carnival contenders. The quality of horse needed to compete there is rising steadily judging from the minimum rating level required to qualify for the Carnival's handicaps, which began at 85, but will be 95 in the turf races in 2008. Nine British stables were successful at the 2007 Carnival, with wins in a dozen races. Ed Dunlop (three wins, two of them with sprinter Munaddam) and Mick Channon were the trainers with more than one win apiece, while Clive Brittain's Kandidate, winner of Round 2 of the Maktoum Challenge, was the only British-trained winner outside handicap company.

Among visiting trainers, Mike de Kock again had the strongest stable, some of whom (including the aforementioned Asiatic Boy) also formed a team based at Newmarket later in the year. Six-furlong handicap winner **Bad Girl Runs** and listed mile winner **Kapil** joined former Carnival winners **Oracle West** (runner up to Germany's Quijano in the Dubai City of Gold and to Hong Kong's Vengeance of Rain in the Dubai Sheema Classic) and the mare **Irridescence**, third in the Jebel Hatta, as the stable's leading performers. Herman Brown was another South African with a strong Carnival team, headed by **Linngari** who won the Al Fahidi Fort for the second year and finished an excellent second to Japan's Admire Moon in the Dubai Duty Free before enjoying another successful

Dubai Sheema Classic Sponsored By Nakheel, Nad Al Sheba—Hong Kong and South Africa take the first two places in the world's joint-richest race on turf, as Vengeance of Rain keeps on to beat Oracle West; Youmzain and Sir Percy come next for Britain

Dubai Golden Shaheen Sponsored By Gulf News, Nad Al Sheba—
American-trained sprinters take four of the first five places as Frankie Dettori gets Kelly's Landing home
ahead of Friendly Island and locally-trained outsider Salaam Dubai

campaign in Europe. His stable-companions **Great Rhythm** and **Sushisan** were both smart winners of handicaps, the latter going on to finish a good fifth in the Sheema Classic, while South Africa's former champion sprinter **National Colour**, trained by Sean Tarry, made a good impression when winning a five-furlong minor event before reportedly chipping a bone when last in the Dubai Golden Shaheen, that race dominated as usual by American sprinters, headed by Kelly's Landing. Invasor was the sixth American-trained winner in twelve runnings of the World Cup, while Spring At Last made it three wins on the night for US stables in the Godolphin Mile. Australia has had success at Nad Al Sheba before with Elvstroem in the 2005 Dubai Duty Free but had its first successes at the Carnival outside World Cup night when stable-companions Smart And Mighty (rated 107) and Benedetti won handicaps, the latter winning twice from three starts. Another dual winner was **Mystical** who became India's first Carnival winner, bringing the number of countries successful over the four years of the meeting to twenty-three.

The focus of the Carnival may be on international competition but almost half of the races prior to World Cup night still went to UAE stables. Ismail Mohammed had a particularly successful Carnival (featuring a five-timer on one card at the end of February) and several of his winners were subsequently transferred to Godolphin. As well as Eu Tambem, already mentioned, they included the Al Rashidiya winner and Jebel Hatta runner-up **Formal Decree**, **Olympian Odyssey**, who was fourth and fifth respectively in the same races, mile and a half handicap winners **Book of Music** and **Crime Scene**, and **Laverock**, who was short-headed by Quijano in a similar event. Among other UAE-trained winners, eight-year-old **Seihali** maintained his record of winning at each of the Carnivals so far. Previously successful in handicaps, he gained the biggest win of his career in a well-contested renewal of the Jebel Hatta, with Godolphin's **Best Name** fourth. Sadly, another Carnival regular, dirt sprinter **Tropical Star**, had to be put down after a parade ring accident, but he was a Group 3 winner of his previous start, the Al Shindagha Sprint. Among the leading local horses on dirt, sprinter **Salaam Dubai** finished third in the Dubai Golden Shaheen, **Parole Board** was second in the Godolphin Mile after wins in a listed race at Jebel Ali and a Carnival handicap, and **Boston Lodge** won twice at a mile, including the Group 3 Burj Nahaar. The last-named race should have seen the return of Godolphin's main Carnival hope Discreet Cat, but he missed that contest with a temperature and disappointed badly in the Dubai World Cup when found to be suffering from a throat abscess. Godolphin's most successful performer at the Carnival was turf sprinter **Great Britain**, short-headed by Bad Girl Runs in a handicap before winning a listed race by a head from Munaddam. The UAE season is already well under way by the time the Carnival begins in mid-January, and an innovation for the 2006/7 season was the Winter Racing Challenge, a competition decided by points based on finishing position in certain races over three different distances. Mile and a quarter performer **Dynamic Saint** was the best horse to emerge from this series, going on to success in a handicap at the Carnival.

'We do not wait for things to happen, we make them happen' is one of Sheikh Mohammed's maxims, one which is being put into practice in a spectacular way with the construction of a successor to Dubai's Nad Al Sheba racecourse. Plans for the residential and business complex of Meydan City, of which the Meydan (roughly translated as 'meeting place') racecourse will be only a part, were unexpectedly unveiled on the eve of the 2007 Dubai World Cup, with work beginning within weeks for completion by November 2009 for the start of the 2009/10 UAE racing season. The scope of the project, which will include the construction of a canal and marina to enable access to the racecourse from Dubai Creek, is best appreciated by referring to the website www.meydan.ae. Unlike Nad Al Sheba, the new track will have its turf course outside the dirt circuit, with the track's configuration allowing the start for the World Cup (due to be worth ten million US dollars for the first running at Meydan in 2010) to take place in front of the stands.

The performances reviewed here are those that took place in the calendar year 2007. Horses which were trained and raced in the UAE but showed significantly better form elsewhere are not included in the list below.

Three-Year-Olds

114	*Folk (f)	113	Blatant	108	Jaffal
105	*Rallying Cry	113	*Diamond Quest	108	Killybegs
		113	*Impossible Ski	108	Mutasallil
		113	National Colour (f)	108	Pearly King
Older Horses		113	Polar Magic	108	Zeeno
124	*Linngari	113	Senor Dali	107	Bennie Blue
122	*Oracle West	112	Imperialista	107	*Bounty Quest
122	*Asiatic Boy	112	*Nelore Pora	107	Etihaad
120	*Laverock	112	Sir Gerard	107	Golden Arrow
120	Seihali	111	*Count Trevisio	107	*Key of Destiny
119	Bad Girl Runs (f)	111	Mezel	107	Lascaux
119	*Formal Decree	111	Wild Savannah	107	*National Captain
119	*Irridescence (f)	110	*Arabian Prince	107	Singing Poet
118	*Gravitas	110	Blue On Blues	107	Thor's Echo
118	Great Britain	110	Dubai Honor	107	Visionist
118	*Shakis	110	Dynamic Saint	106	Almaram
118	Sushisan	110	Mosaic	106	Doctor Hilary
117	Ace	110	Remaadd	106	Emirates Gold
117	Best Name	110	Sea Hunter	106	*Greetings (f)
117	*Kapil	110	Terrific Challenge	106	Jet Express
117	*Mystical	109	Ans Bach	106	Mutafanen
117	*Olympian Odyssey	109	Consular	106	*Paper Talk
117	Parole Board	109	*Fairson	106	So Will I
116	*Book of Music	109	Mooner	106	Subpoena
116	Boston Lodge	109	Rosberg	105	*Alpacco
116	Yasoodd	109	*Royal Alchemist	105	Evil Knievel
115	*Crime Scene	109	Taqseem	105	*Indochine
115	Great Rhythm	109	Thajja	105	Looking Good
115	Mulaqat	109	Tropical Star	105	Money Bags
114	*Mullins Bay	109§	*Candy Critic (f)	105	Naipe Marcado
114	Salaam Dubai	108	Anani	105	Opportunist
113	*Arenti	108	Eu Tambem	105	Red Duster
113	*Best Alibi	108	Express Way	105	Shanty Star
		108	Gharir		
		108	Great Plains		

NORTH AMERICA   Due to injury, all too often the colts which dominate America's classics are nowhere to be seen come the autumn and the Breeders' Cup. Prior to the latest season, none of the three previous Kentucky Derby winners for example made it beyond the triple crown series. Barbaro broke a leg in the Preakness, Smarty Jones was retired with bruised joints after the Belmont and Giacomo missed the rest of his three-year-old campaign after the latter race, requiring surgery for bone chips in his forelegs. The last three-year-old to win the Breeders' Cup Classic had been Tiznow in 2000, tellingly a late-developing three-year-old (unraced at two) who had missed the rigours of the triple crown races. It was back in 1992 that the Breeders' Cup Classic had last been won by a winner of a triple crown race when that year's Belmont Stakes winner A P Indy was successful. It was remarkable therefore that not just the top American three-year-old of 2007, but all five of the leading colts in the latest season enjoyed full

Breeders' Cup Classic - Powered by Dodge, Monmouth Park—the first three in the Kentucky Derby meet again but the order is reversed this time; Preakness winner Curlin draws clear of Hard Spun to secure Horse of The Year honours, while Kentucky Derby winner Street Sense (left) will lose third to Awesome Gem, the only four-year-old in the first six home

campaigns (each had between eight and ten races) incorporating the Kentucky Derby (two of them contested all three triple crown races) and concluding with the Breeders' Cup Classic. In a year when it was the ranks of the older horses which were depleted, the three-year-olds in question took five of the first six places in the Breeders' Cup. All five enhanced their reputations with wins between the triple crown and Breeders' Cup.

With **Street Sense** and **Curlin** dominating the Kentucky Derby betting, a long-standing record looked set to fall whichever of the pair won. Street Sense was bidding to become the first ever Breeders' Cup Juvenile winner to win the Kentucky Derby, while Curlin had even more history to defy as no horse unraced as a two-year-old had won the Derby since 1882. The rapidly-improving Curlin was unbeaten in three starts, including the Grade 2 Arkansas Derby by more than ten lengths, but on the day Street Sense's experience probably proved decisive, and certainly the way he found a clear run through from the rear on the inside rounding the home turn at Churchill Downs was reminiscent of his win on the same track in the Breeders' Cup Juvenile. Curlin was beaten eight lengths into third, but that proved the only time he finished behind Street Sense. A fortnight later in the Preakness Stakes, Curlin rallied to a game head victory over Street Sense as the pair pulled four lengths clear of the Kentucky Derby runner-up **Hard Spun**, with **C P West** fourth. Both colts gained another Grade 1 apiece before they met again in the Breeders' Cup Classic. Curlin defeated older horses in the Jockey Club Gold Cup, while Street Sense followed a Grade 2 win in the Jim Dandy Stakes over C P West with a hard-fought defeat of **Grasshopper** in the Travers Stakes. Street Sense was favourite for his third meeting with Curlin in the Breeders' Cup Classic but finished a well-held fourth as Curlin ran out a four-and-a-half length winner over Hard Spun.

As well as toughness, Hard Spun showed his versatility when dropping back to seven furlongs to gain a deserved Grade 1 success in the King's Bishop Stakes (from **First Defence**) and inflicted a defeat on Street Cry when making all in the Grade 2 Kentucky Cup Classic at Turfway Park prior to the Breeders' Cup. Hard Spun also finished ahead of Curlin (who was conceding 4 lb) when both colts were placed in the Haskell Invitational Stakes at Monmouth in August, that race seeing the emergence of another high-class three-year-old, **Any Given Saturday**. Narrowly beaten by Street Cry in a Grade 3 at Tampa Bay early in the year but only eighth in the Kentucky Derby (reportedly bruised a foot), Any Given Saturday beat the Wood Memorial winner Nobiz Like Shobiz in the Grade 2 Dwyer Stakes and followed his win in the Haskell with another Grade 2 success in the Brooklyn Handicap. Looking a serious challenger to Curlin for the title of top three-year-old going into the Breeders' Cup, Any Given Saturday seemingly failed to handle the wet conditions at Monmouth and was beaten before the home turn to finish only sixth. The quintet of leading three-year-old colts was completed by Giacomo's half-brother **Tiago**. He too failed to fire in the Breeders' Cup Classic (fifth) and wasn't at his best either in the Kentucky Derby (seventh) after winning one of the main trials, the Santa Anita Derby. The Belmont Stakes, in which he finished third, saw him in a better light though, and he went into the Breeders' Cup on the back of wins in the Grade 2 Swaps Stakes at Hollywood and a defeat of older rivals in the Goodwood Stakes at Santa Anita. Of the five leading colts, Tiago and Curlin both stay in training, the latter a leading contender for the Dubai World Cup. The other three, Any Given Saturday, Hard Spun and Street Sense, all begin stud careers in 2008 at Jonabell Farm as part of Sheikh Mohammed's concerted drive to recruit stallion prospects in the latest season.

Over shorter distances, **Daaher** emerged in the autumn as a good prospect for his four-year-old season with wins in the Grade 2 Jerome Handicap at Belmont and then the Cigar Mile at Aqueduct, inflicting a defeat on the Breeders' Cup Sprint winner Midnight Lute in the latter race. **Idiot Proof** was the best three-year-old sprinter, chasing home Midnight Lute at the Breeders' Cup but better judged on his win in the Ancient Title Stakes at Santa Anita.

Whilst Peeping Fawn was carrying all before her among the three-year-old fillies in Europe, her near relative **Rags To Riches** (their dams are half-sisters) was doing the same in the USA. She ran up a Grade 1 hat-trick against her own sex early on, overcoming a wide draw to win the Las Virgenes Stakes, beating the principals from that race with much more authority in the Santa Anita Oaks and then running out a clear-cut winner of the Kentucky Oaks from a representative field. But it was Rags To Riches' win in the Belmont Stakes which was her most important win, emulating her half-brother Jazil who had won the same race the year before. In running out a game head winner from Curlin in a thrilling finish (the pair clear of Tiago and Hard Spun), Rags To Riches became the first filly to win the Belmont since Tanya in 1905 and was a first classic winner for her trainer Todd Pletcher who had saddled five runners without success in the Kentucky Derby. However, unlike the colts she beat at Belmont, Rags To Riches was less fortunate in avoiding injury. She suffered a hairline fracture when trying to give 7 lb to **Lear's Princess** in the Gazelle Stakes back at Belmont in the autumn on her next start but is due to stay in training.

Rags To Riches may have missed the Breeders' Cup, but her genuine and consistent stable-companion **Octave** rounded off a fine campaign when beaten two necks into third in the Distaff. Her second place behind Rags To Riches in the Kentucky Oaks was the fourth time she'd filled the runner-up spot in a Grade 1 (she'd looked unlucky in the Ashland Stakes the time before) but her turn at the top level finally came at Belmont in the summer when successful in the Mother Goose Stakes, from **Lady Joanne**, and the Coaching Club American Oaks from Lear's Princess. Octave finished behind both those rivals when Lady Joanne and Lear's Princess took the first two places in the Alabama

Belmont Stakes, Belmont Park—Rags To Riches, a half-sister to the previous year's winner Jazil, comes out on top in a thrilling duel with Curlin to become the first filly in more than a hundred years to win the Belmont; Tiago keeps on for third

Stakes at Saratoga next time, but finished ahead of them again in the Distaff, in which Lady Joanne dead-heated for fourth and Lear's Princess was well beaten. Octave had competition from **Panty Raid** to be considered the Pletcher stable's second-best filly. Her wins included the American Oaks at Hollywood on her only turf start but she put up her best effort when successful on the polytrack at Keeneland in the Spinster Stakes, bouncing back from a disappointing effort in the Alabama with a gritty defeat of Lady Joanne and some older rivals. **Tough Tiz's Sis**, third to Lear's Princess in the Gazelle, earned a supplementary entry into the Distaff after a tenacious defeat of the year-older Hystericalady in the Lady's Secret Stakes and bounced back from a poor effort at Monmouth to finish a good second to Romance Is Diane (rated 115) in the Grade 2 Bayakoa Handicap at Hollywood in December. In the less competitive environment of shorter-distance races, **Dearest Trickski** progressed from claimers to win the La Brea Stakes at Santa Anita at the end of the year, while **Dream Rush** gained a Grade 1 double in the summer in the Prioress Stakes and Test Stakes.

The top three-year-old on turf, **Nobiz Like Shobiz**, started the year on dirt and showed plenty of ability on that surface, winning the Wood Memorial Stakes prior to finishing down the field in the Kentucky Derby and then running a good second to Any Given Saturday in the Grade 2 Dwyer Stakes. He proved better on turf though, winning three graded events, notably the Grade 2 Jamaica Handicap at Belmont (impressively from **Red Giant**), before finishing a respectable fourth in the Breeders' Cup Mile. Red Giant's best effort came when finishing second to **Shamdinan**, giving the winner weight, in the Secretariat Stakes at Arlington. The Secretariat marked a successful US debut for the Prix du Jockey Club third, and while the nine furlongs of the Jamaica Handicap was too sharp, Shamdinan proved well suited to the stiffer test provided by the Breeders' Cup Turf in which he finished second. **Daytona**, winner of a maiden at Lingfield for Mark Johnston early in the year, proved another successful European import, ending the year with three graded wins in California, notably the Hollywood Derby (from the Grade 2 Del Mar Derby winner Medici Code, rated 116, another all-weather winner in Britain early in the year), in which Nobiz Like Shobiz disappointed, and the Grade 2 San Gabriel Handicap at Santa Anita (Medici Code third). As well as the top three-year-old colt on turf, Barclay Tagg also trained the leading filly, **Bit of Whimsy**, whose most important win came in the Queen Elizabeth II Challenge Cup at Keeneland against the previous season's Breeders' Cup Juvenile Fillies winner Dreaming of Anna (rated 114). Canada's Horse of The Year Sealy Hill (rated 116) finished second to the French-trained **Mrs Lindsay** in the E. P. Taylor Stakes at Woodbine.

The 2006 Breeders' Cup Classic winner **Invasor** was again the top older horse on dirt but a leg injury sustained when preparing for the Suburban Handicap in June signalled the end of his racing career. He retired with a record of only one defeat in twelve starts, reappearing with a win in the Donn Handicap at Gulfstream before giving the US its sixth win in twelve runnings of the world's richest race, the Dubai World Cup. The Saudi-based **Premium Tap** (prepared by US trainer John Kimmel for the World Cup) chased him home but the anticipated rematch with Godolphin's Discreet Cat, the only horse to have beaten Invasor, was a non-event, with that rival finishing last. Discreet Cat had looked a most exciting prospect but he was seen out only twice more after Dubai, well below his best in the autumn both times.

Another to underperform at Nad Al Sheba was **Lava Man**, who finished last in the Dubai Duty Free on turf, though he again saved his best for top races in California. Less dominant in that state than he had been in 2006, Lava Man nonetheless gave plenty of weight away all round to win the Santa Anita Handicap (from **Molengao**) for the second year running and took his earnings past the five million dollar mark when gaining a third successive win in the Hollywood Gold Cup. Repeat wins eluded him in two more events, the Charles Whittingham Memorial Handicap and the Pacific Classic, but his effort in the former contest, on turf, when second to After Market, who was receiving 6lb, was on a par with the best of his dirt form and by our reckoning was actually the best effort by a horse on turf in North America in 2007. With Lava Man bypassing the Breeders' Cup, **Lawyer Ron** was the best older horse in the Breeders' Cup Classic field but finished well held in the race for the second year running. Prior to that, he put up a couple of high-class efforts at Saratoga to win the Whitney Handicap in track-record time before trouncing many of the same rivals by upwards of eight lengths in the Woodward Stakes just over a month later, with **Wanderin Boy** and then **Sun King** the runners-up in the two races. In a much closer encounter with Curlin than was to ensue at Monmouth, Lawyer Ron (odds on) went down by just a neck to his younger rival when they first met in the Jockey Club Gold Cup, the pair finishing clear of the Suburban Handicap winner **Political Force**. The only horse to prevent the three-year-olds completely dominating the finish of the Breeders' Cup Classic was four-year-old **Awesome Gem** who took third place to Curlin at long odds. A Grade 2 winner at Santa Anita early in the year and generally progressive, he was second to surprise winner **Student Council** in the Pacific Classic and beaten a nose by Tiago in the Goodwood Stakes at Santa Anita prior to the Breeders' Cup.

Unusually, there was a bit more strength in depth among the sprinters and milers on dirt than over longer distances. There was a new opportunity for such horses at the Breeders' Cup with the introduction of a Dirt Mile, one of three new races on the Breeders' Cup programme, the others being the Filly & Mare Sprint and the Juvenile Turf. The three new events were run on the eve of the main Breeders' Cup card and, as brand new contests, had to be run without graded status. The 2008 Breeders' Cup programme at Santa Anita will be expanded still further to fourteen races with the creation of a Turf Sprint, which ought to be well supported by European horses, a Juvenile Fillies Turf, a likely candidate to prove the meeting's weakest race, though another with potential for European success, and a Dirt Marathon, which, to be run over just a mile and a half, is something of a misnomer from a European standpoint and falls short of giving true stayers an opportunity at the meeting. Nor will it even be run on dirt. The other innovation for the 2008 Breeders' Cup is that it will be the first to be held on a 'synthetic' surface. Santa Anita was among several more racecourses in 2007 to continue the move towards replacing their dirt tracks (Arlington and Del Mar, both now polytrack, were others that host Grade 1 races), though Santa Anita was not alone in experiencing teething troubles with its new surface, in its case cushion track, which failed to cope with heavy rain during the winter.

None of the three new Breeders' Cup races detracted from the quality of the existing events and the Metropolitan Handicap winner **Corinthian** ran out a wide-margin winner of the Dirt Mile from **Gottcha Gold** (who'd beaten Lawyer Ron in a Grade 3 at Monmouth in the summer) and Discreet Cat. **Spring At Last**, fifth behind Lava Man in the Santa

TVG Breeders' Cup Sprint, Monmouth Park—eventual winner Midnight Lute (left) braves the sloppy kickback on the home turn before running out a near five-length winner, a record margin for the race

Anita Handicap, also put up a very smart performance when winning the Godolphin Mile on Dubai World Cup night. On the same card, American sprinters maintained their dominance in the Dubai Golden Shaheen, in which **Kelly's Landing** became the seventh US-trained winner in eight years. Only fifth in the Breeders' Cup Sprint, Kelly's Landing was among several who failed to give their running at Monmouth behind favourite **Midnight Lute**, who came off a blistering pace to win by nearly five lengths, a record margin for the race. Earlier successful in the Forego Stakes over seven furlongs from **Benny The Bull** (fourth in the Breeders' Cup Sprint before winning the Frank J. de Francis Memorial Dash), Midnight Lute was stepped back up in trip for the Cigar Mile on his final start, finishing second to Daaher. **Smokey Stover** and **Greg's Gold**, first and second in the Grade 2 Potrero Grande Handicap at Santa Anita in April, had some of the best form in the Breeders' Cup Sprint field but both finished well beaten. In between, Greg's Gold gained a Grade 2 win of his own in the Pat O'Brien Handicap at Del Mar and looked unlucky when beaten by Idiot Proof in the Ancient Title Stakes at Santa Anita. The Pat O'Brien runner-up **Surf Cat** had previously gone close in a Grade 1, giving the winner plenty of weight when touched off by **Bilo** in the Triple Bend Invitational Handicap at Hollywood. A lung infection ruled **Fabulous Strike** out of the Breeders' Cup Sprint, but he would have been a leading contender judged on his fine display of speed to beat the subsequent Monmouth third Talent Search (rated 114) by nearly six lengths in the Vosburgh Stakes. Six-year-old mare **Maryfield** beat a field of younger rivals to win the inaugural Breeders' Cup Filly & Mare Sprint, adding to her Grade 1 success in the Ballerina Stakes at Saratoga.

Over longer distances, the older fillies and mares on dirt contested a very open division in which the leading contenders took turns in beating each other, though in being supplemented to take her third Grade 1 race of the year, the Breeders' Cup Distaff winner **Ginger Punch** was a worthy leader. Her neck defeat of the Humana Distaff Stakes winner **Hystericalady** wasn't her best performance as she had previously been a decisive winner of the Go For Wand Handicap at Saratoga and the Ruffian Handicap at Belmont. **Miss Shop**, winner of the Personal Ensign Handicap, was runner-up on both occasions (beaten six lengths at Saratoga) and finished behind Ginger Punch for a third time when a well-held sixth in the Beldame Stakes, in which Ginger Punch finished only third. The first two in the Beldame, the Todd Pletcher-trained pair **Unbridled Belle** and **Indian Vale**, had earlier been placed behind Miss Shop in the Personal Ensign, though neither of the Pletcher stable-companions were at their best in the Distaff, Unbridled Belle faring the better in dead-heating for fourth. **Balance** was fourth in the Beldame and sixth in the Distaff, though for the second year running she was at her best at Santa Anita much earlier in the year, winning the Santa Margarita Invitational Handicap from the subsequent Apple Blossom Handicap winner **Ermine**. Apart from Miss Shop, the main absentees among the older fillies and mares from the Breeders' Cup Distaff were the Apple Blossom runner-up **Take d'Tour**, who went on to take the Ogden Phipps Handicap (gave weight and a neck beating to Ginger Punch) for the second year running, and the 2006 Distaff fourth **Asi Siempre**, who was a good second to Indian Vale in the Grade 2 Fleur de Lis Handicap at Churchill Downs in June.

Emirates Airline Breeders' Cup Distaff, Monmouth Park—Ginger Punch (blaze on rail) gets the better of a good tussle with Hystericalady as most of their rivals toil at the wettest Breeders' Cup meeting to date; scenes like this at a Breeders' Cup are unlikely to be repeated as more US tracks replace dirt with synthetic surfaces

NetJets Breeders' Cup Mile, Monmouth Park—
Kip Deville is one of three supplementary entries to prove successful on the Breeders' Cup card;
favourite Excellent Art overcomes a wide draw to take second from Cosmonaut

For the first time since the addition of the Filly & Mare Turf to the Breeders' Cup programme in 1999, all three turf races were won by US-trained horses and it was the first time since 1998 that there were no European-trained winners at the meeting as a whole. That was partly down to a weaker than usual European raiding party (unusually lacking any French horses) which in turn maybe reflects a growing feeling from European trainers that the Breeders' Cup is losing its lustre. Particularly from a European point of view, events at Monmouth did little to restore the meeting's appeal. The weather had much to do with that, with persistent rain resulting in sloppy going on the dirt track and soft on the turf. Only once before in twenty-three previous Breeders' Cup meetings had the going been given as soft on the turf (at Belmont in 1995), while on the dirt it had been muddy at Churchill Downs in 1988 (drying out from sloppy) and Belmont in 1995, though on neither occasion was it anything like as wet as the slop at Monmouth. George Washington's accident in the Classic will, unfairly perhaps, be what most will remember the 2007 Breeders' Cup for, though to blame the conditions for his breakdown, as some did, made little sense. Breeders' Cup meetings have had more than their fare share of fatalities over the years, among the high-profile ones being Go For Wand in the 1990 Distaff, Mr Brooks in the 1992 Sprint, and Landseer (another Aidan O'Brien-trained colt) in the 2002 Mile, while a grim statistic which was widely overlooked was that the last three Breeders' Cups have now all been marred by fatalities; Funfair broke a leg in the 2005 Mile and Pine Island an ankle in the 2006 Distaff. Even if the weather and George Washington's accident are dismissed as bad luck, the latest Breeders' Cup will go down as one of the least successful, with the average field size the smallest ever for the meeting, the attendance the second-lowest ever, and the all-important 'handle' or betting turnover down as well.

Kip Deville was another successful supplementary Breeders' Cup entry when putting up a career-best effort to win the Mile from Irish-trained three-year-old **Excellent Art** and the consistent **Cosmonaut**. Kip Deville gained his first Grade 1 win in the Frank E. Kilroe Mile Handicap at Santa Anita in April (with **Silent Name** best at the weights in a close third) and followed up in the Grade 2 Makers Mark Mile at Keeneland from the subsequently injured **Showing Up**. In his final start before the Breeders' Cup, Kip Deville ran a sound trial when second, trying to give 7 lb to the winner **Shakespeare**, in the Woodbine Mile. Shakespeare had lost his unbeaten record in the 2005 Breeders' Cup Turf and was having only his second start since at Woodbine, but he was retired when injury struck again before the Breeders' Cup. **After Market** was another absentee from the Breeders' Cup Mile, taken out on the day of the race due to the soft ground. A mile was a bare minimum for him in any case and he completed a four-timer in graded stakes at up to eleven furlongs. Those wins included a defeat of Lava Man in the Charles Whittingham Handicap and a taking performance to win the Eddie Read Handicap under top weight from dual Grade 2 winner **Out of Control**. Like Kip Deville, After Market ran a good trial in defeat on what would have been his final start before the Breeders' Cup, going down by half a length to the subsequent Mile sixth **Trippi's Storm** in the

John Deere Breeders' Cup Turf, Monmouth Park—English Channel makes it third time lucky in the race with a wide-margin win; three-year-old Shamdinan (noseband) takes second as Dylan Thomas (No.7) fails to halt the poor record of Arc winners in the Turf

Grade 2 Kelso Handicap at Belmont, giving the winner 9 lb. The 2005 Shadwell Turf Mile winner **Host** was a creditable fifth at Monmouth, but **Purim**, who beat Cosmonaut in the latest renewal of the Keeneland race, finished well held in the Breeders' Cup Mile.

As well as the Breeders' Cup Mile, After Market had also missed the Arlington Million earlier in the season due to softish ground. In a tight finish, Canadian gelding **Jambalaya**, also winner of the Gulfstream Park Breeders' Cup Turf Stakes early in the year, got up to beat the previous year's winner **The Tin Man,** who retained plenty of ability as a nine-year-old, winning the Shoemaker Breeders' Cup Mile at Hollywood in another slowly-run race. French-trained **Doctor Dino** took third at Arlington ahead of dead-heaters **Stream Cat** and **Sunriver**, the latter going on to finish second to Doctor Dino in the Man o'War Stakes before winning the Hollywood Turf Cup.

The first three from the Breeders' Cup Turf in 2006 met again in the latest renewal, though the result was very different this time, with **English Channel**, third the year before, turning the tables on former winners **Red Rocks** and **Better Talk Now** who were a well-held third and fourth respectively, though ahead of the odds-on favourite Dylan Thomas, who failed to improve the record of Arc winners running at the same year's Breeders' Cup. English Channel's win (officially by seven lengths, but it looked a little less) was a record margin for a Breeders' Cup race on turf and marked the highlight of his career (he was retired to stud afterwards) which has seen him near the top of the turf division for the last three seasons. Prior to the Breeders' Cup, English Channel repeated his 2006 victories in the United Nations Stakes and the Joe Hirsch Turf Classic. He was contesting his third Breeders' Cup Turf, but the eight-year-old Better Talk Now, winner in 2004 and runner-up in 2006, was back for a fourth time having narrowly beaten English Channel (who was giving him a couple of pounds) and **Shakis** in the Manhattan Handicap at Belmont in June. Despite coming just a week before the Breeders' Cup Turf, the Canadian International lacked nothing in competitiveness and was certainly a more closely-fought affair, with just four lengths covering the first nine home. Outsider **Cloudy's Knight** received a good ride to hold off European challengers **Ask** and **Quijano**, with the Joe Hirsch Turf Classic runner-up (and former Lincoln winner) **Stream of Gold** fourth,

Sunriver sixth and Canada's top horse **Sky Conqueror** (winner of the Woodford Reserve Turf Classic in May) seventh.

Like Ginger Punch and Kip Deville, the Breeders' Cup Filly & Mare Turf winner **Lahudood** was a supplementary entry for what proved the weakest renewal of the race in its eight-year history. The ex-French Lahudood stayed on to beat the six-year-old mare **Honey Ryder** (third to Ouija Board the year before) and the Henry Cecil-trained three-year-old Passage of Time, who started favourite. Honey Ryder was also a good second against male rivals earlier in the year in the Gulfstream Park Breeders' Cup Turf Stakes and the United Nations Stakes. The Flower Bowl Invitational at Belmont a month before the Breeders' Cup had taken a bit more winning on Lahudood's part when defeating fellow four-year-olds Rosinka (rated 116, an ex-John Dunlop filly) and the previous season's top three-year-old filly **Wait A While**. Although twice successful in lesser graded stakes in the latest season, Wait A While failed to match her three-year-old form, missing the Breeders' Cup because of the soft ground and then finishing second to the John C. Mabee Handicap winner **Precious Kitten** (badly hampered by the antics of Simply Perfect in the Filly & Mare Turf) over a mile in the Matriarch Stakes at Hollywood. Much the most progressive filly on turf was the four-year-old **Nashoba's Key**, who didn't make her debut until the latest season but won all seven of her races before finishing fourth in the Filly & Mare Turf. Nashoba's Key's biggest wins came in the Vanity Invitational Handicap on Hollywood's cushion track and the Yellow Ribbon Stakes back on turf from the Gamely Handicap winner **Citronnade**, who ended the year with a defeat of the Yellow Ribbon third **Black Mamba** in the Grade 2 Dahlia Handicap at Hollywood. In a wide-open division, **Royal Highness** and **Irridescence**, separated by just a head in the Beverly D Stakes, also had claims to being the best older females on turf, with Citronnade, Honey Ryder and Lahudood among those behind them at Arlington. The Beverly D proved to be the only US start for the well-travelled South African mare Irridescence, while Royal Highness was only sixth in the Flower Bowl next time. **My Typhoon** (a Giant's Causeway half-sister to Galileo) was well held in the Flower Bowl and Breeders' Cup Mile in the autumn, but earlier in the year she had beaten Precious Kitten and Wait A While in lesser graded events before a Grade 1 success in the Diana Stakes at Saratoga.

Despite the conditions at the Breeders' Cup, most races went to the form horses, and that was certainly the case in the two Juvenile races on dirt, which each went to the

Emirates Airline Breeders' Cup Filly & Mare Turf, Monmouth Park—Lahudood stays on well while Honey Ryder (not in picture) comes wide and late to deprive British-trained favourite Passage of Time (left) of the runner-up spot; Nashoba's Key (behind winner) is fourth

Bessemer Trust Breeders' Cup Juvenile, Monmouth Park—
unbeaten War Pass makes all for an authoritative win as runner-up Pyro (second right among pursuers)
stays on strongly to finish a dozen lengths clear of the rest

favourites, who in both cases were preserving unbeaten records. **War Pass** was never seriously challenged in making all for a near five-length win in the Breeders' Cup Juvenile over the staying-on **Pyro**. The margin had been tighter but the result the same when the pair met in the Champagne Stakes beforehand which had unfolded in similar fashion. Although the colt with much the best two-year-old form, stamina doubts temper enthusiasm for War Pass's prospects at three, at least as a Kentucky Derby contender. Pyro, on the other hand, looks to be crying out for longer trips. With another dozen lengths back to the third at Monmouth, nothing else came close to giving its running, though a couple with the best form beforehand completed the frame, with **Kodiak Kowboy** taking third from **Tale of Ekati**, who had beaten him into second in the Grade 2 Futurity Stakes at Belmont the time before. Apart from War Pass, the only other Grade 1 winner in the Breeders' Cup Juvenile field was **Wicked Style**, whose win in the Breeders' Futurity at Keeneland kept his unbeaten record on polytrack, but he finished well beaten on his dirt

Grey Goose Breeders' Cup Juvenile Fillies, Monmouth Park—Garrett Gomez's clean silks
bear witness to Indian Blessing's making all the running to remain unbeaten; eventual placed horses
Proud Spell (second left) and Backseat Rhythm (on rail) give chase round the final turn

debut at Monmouth. **Majestic Warrior** came off a strong pace to win the Hopeful Stakes at Saratoga but disappointed badly when hot favourite to beat War Pass and Pyro in the Champagne and missed a second crack at that pair when a hoof injury ruled him out of the Breeders' Cup. Another Grade 1 winner missing from the Juvenile line-up was Norfolk Stakes winner **Dixie Chatter**, who reversed form with **Salute The Sarge** at Santa Anita after the pair had finished fifth and second respectively behind **Georgie Boy** in the Del Mar Futurity.

Hollywood's CashCall Futurity, just before Christmas, looks the other key two-year-old colts' race of the season, and while the principals finished close together, they are all lightly-raced types who could develop into leading three-year-olds. **Into Mischief** was a workmanlike winner but turned earlier form round with third-placed **Massive Drama**, while runner-up **Colonel John** and **Monba**, who finished best of all from the rear to take fourth, shaped with particular promise. Other colts to make a good impression were the Grade 3 Nashua Stakes winner **Etched**, who has joined Godolphin after his six-and-a-half-length defeat of subsequent Grade 2 winner Anak Nakal (rated 107) at Aqueduct, and **Court Vision**, who shapes as though he'll relish the step up to a mile and a quarter after strong finishes from poor positions to win both the Grade 3 Iroquois Stakes at Churchill Downs and the Grade 2 Remsen Stakes at Aqueduct. **Cowboy Cal**'s win by more than six lengths in the non-graded Laurel Futurity was on turf but puts him among the leading youngsters and the formerly low profile of two-year-old racing on turf looks set to be raised from now on by the introduction of Juvenile Turf races at the Breeders' Cup. The inaugural running of the Breeders' Cup Juvenile Turf went to **Nownownow** from the Royal Lodge runner-up **Achill Island**, who fared best of the three British/Irish-trained runners. Incidentally, Nownownow (set to join David Wachman in Ireland) had to run in the name of Francois Parisel, assistant to the colt's actual trainer Patrick Biancone, who was about to start a ban for a drugs infringement. He wasn't the only leading trainer to be 'punished' in this way during the year; a similar six-month ban on Steve Asmussen ran its course early in January, while Todd Pletcher (who nonetheless broke his own prize-money record by the end of 2007) served a shorter ban early in the year.

Like the Juvenile, the Breeders' Cup Juvenile Fillies was also won with a fine display of front-running, **Indian Blessing** initiating a double on the card for trainer Bob Baffert which was completed by Midnight Lute in the Sprint. Indian Blessing gave a similar beating to **Backseat Rhythm** as she had in the Frizette Stakes at Belmont the time before, though at Monmouth the pair were split by the Grade 2 Matron Stakes winner **Proud Spell**, who was unbeaten until then. Baffert's other contender for the Juvenile Fillies, **Cry And Catch Me**, missed the Breeders' Cup with a high temperature, though the fillies she beat in the Oak Leaf Stakes at Santa Anita did little for the form afterwards, including runner-up **Izarra**, who was well beaten in the Juvenile Fillies. The chief rival to Indian Blessing for top spot among the two-year-old fillies was **Country Star**. Her win in the Alcibiades Stakes at Keeneland was another race where those she beat hardly upheld the form (placed horses **A To The Croft** and **Grace Anatomy** both well beaten at the Breeders' Cup next time) but that was only Country Star's second start and she still didn't look the finished article when following up in track-record time in the Hollywood Starlet Stakes in December from **Grace And Power**. Likely to stay further than Indian Blessing at three, Country Star has a fine future and is even being talked of as a Kentucky Derby prospect. From the first crop of Empire Maker, like Country Star, **Mushka** looks another with a good future after coming from last place to win the Grade 2 Demoiselle Stakes at Aqueduct in fine style. **Irish Smoke** had looked impressive when beating A To The Croft in the Spinaway Stakes at Saratoga but followed that with poor efforts in both the Alcibiades and the Juvenile Fillies.

European-trained horses who	116	Majestic Warrior	113p	Cowboy Cal
showed or reproduced their	116	Tale of Ekati	113	Backseat Rhythm (f)
best form in North America	116	Wicked Style	113	Irish Smoke (f)
are included in this list	115p	Into Mischief	113	Kodiak Kowboy
	115p	Pyro	113	Rated Feisty (f)
Two-Year-Olds	114p	Etched	112p	By The Light (f)
124 War Pass	114	Dixie Chatter	112p	Court Vision
120 Indian Blessing (f)	114	Proud Spell (f)	112p	Cry And Catch Me (f)
116p Country Star (f)	113p	Colonel John	112	Izarra (f)

112 Massive Drama
112 Mythical Pegasus
111p Monba
111 A To The Croft (f)
111 Grace And Power (f)
111 Lantana Mob
111 Nownownow
111 Paint
111 Ready's Image
111 Salute The Sarge
111 Tasha's Miracle (f)
111 Z Humor
110p Mushka (f)
110 †Achill Island
110 Georgie Boy
110 Grace Anatomy (f)
110 Set Play (f)

DIRT/ARTIFICIAL SURFACES

Three-Year-Olds
131 Curlin
128 Any Given Saturday
128 Street Sense
127 Rags To Riches (f)
124 Hard Spun
121 Tiago
120 Daaher
120 Grasshopper
120 Panty Raid (f)
120 Scat Daddy
119 Circular Quay
119 C P West
119 First Defence
119 Lady Joanne (f)
119 Octave (f)
119 Tough Tiz's Sis (f)
118 Chelokee
118 Idiot Proof
118 Johnny Eves
118 Lear's Princess (f)
118 Notional
117 Dearest Trickski (f)
117 Going Ballistic
117 Great Hunter
117 Stormello

116 Dream Rush (f)
115 Cotton Blossom (f)
114 Christmas Kid (f)
114 Dominican

Older Horses
132 †Invasor
129 *Premium Tap
128 Lava Man
128 Lawyer Ron
125 Midnight Lute

123 Corinthian
123 Fabulous Strike
123 Surf Cat
122 Ginger Punch (f)
122 Molengao
122 Smokey Stover
122 Spring At Last
121 Greg's Gold
121 Take d'Tour (f)
120 Asi Siempre (f)
120 Indian Vale (f)
120 Student Council
120 Unbridled Belle (f)
119 Arson Squad
119 Awesome Gem
119 Balance (f)
119 Brother Derek
119 Gottcha Gold
119 Hystericalady (f)
119 Magna Graduate
119 Miss Shop (f)
119 Proud Tower Too
119 Silent Name
119 Utopia
118 Diabolical
118 Ermine (f)
118 Flashy Bull
118 Kelly's Landing
118 Latent Heat
118 Political Force
118 Pussycat Doll (f)
118 Silver Wagon
118 Songster
118 Sun King
118 Wanderin Boy
117 Benny The Bull
117 Big Booster
117 Brass Hat
117 Friendly Island
117 In Summation
117 Master Command

116 Sugar Shake (f)
114 Bilo
114 Maryfield (f)
113 River's Prayer (f)

TURF

Three-Year-Olds
125 †Excellent Art
123 Nobiz Like Shobiz
121 †Daytona
119 Bit of Whimsy (f)
118 Red Giant
118 †Shamdinan
117 †Mrs Lindsay (f)

115 Rutherienne (f)

114 †Alexander Tango (f)

Older Horses
128 Lava Man
126 After Market
126 †Ask
126 English Channel
126 Kip Deville
124 Cloudy's Knight
124 Shakespeare
123 Better Talk Now
123 †Doctor Dino
122 †Quijano
122 Showing Up
122 Sky Conqueror
121 Jambalaya
121 *Stream of Gold
120 Cosmonaut
120 The Tin Man
119 Einstein
119 †Irridescence (f)
119 Lahudood (f)
119 Nashoba's Key (f)
119 Precious Kitten (f)
119 Royal Highness (f)
119 Sunriver
118 Cassydora (f)
118 Citronnade (f)
118 Criminologist (f)
118 †Danak
118 Go Between
118 Honey Ryder (f)
118 Host
118 Icy Atlantic
118 Lang Field
118 Out of Control
118 Prospect Park
118 Purim
118 Remarkable News
118 *Shakis
118 Silver Tree
118 Stream Cat
118 Trippi's Storm
118 Wait A While (f)
118 Zann
117 Black Mamba (f)
117 Brilliant
117 El Roblar
117 Fourty Niners Son
117 Get Funky
117 Grand Couturier
117 My Typhoon (f)
117 Naissance Royale (f)
117 Obrigado
117 Presious Passion
117 Red Fort
117 Spring House
117 Willow O Wisp

115 Artiste Royal

JAPAN With the retirement of top-class champion colt Deep Impact at the end of 2006, Japan's best middle-distance races had a more open look in the latest season. Two of those who came to the fore, **Admire Moon** and **Meisho Samson**, had already been two of the leading three-year-old colts from the year before. Admire Moon's narrow defeat in the Hong Kong Cup on his final three-year-old start had marked him down as a challenger for top honours in 2007 and he didn't disappoint, winning two of the world's richest turf races, the Dubai Duty Free and the Japan Cup, and in between beating Meisho Samson half a length in another contest worth more than a million pounds, the Takarazuka Kinen. Meisho Samson was odds on to turn the tables on Admire Moon in the Japan Cup but finished a narrowly-beaten third at Tokyo, with Admire Moon only just lasting home over the mile and a half trip. By then, Admire Moon was racing in the colours of Darley Japan after his purchase for a reported £16 million by Sheikh Mohammed during the summer. Darley's license to contest JRA races had taken several years to acquire due to the stringent rules governing ownership in Japan, but by the end of 2007 the license had been withdrawn following the retirement of Darley Japan's chairman Riki Takahashi; one condition of the license was that it had to be held by a Japanese resident. Meisho Samson may have failed narrowly in the Japan Cup but he did have a verdict over Admire Moon when winning the Tenno Sho (Autumn) a month earlier from **Agnes Ark** (Admire Moon sixth), becoming only the fourth horse to complete the double in the two Tenno Sho races in the same year; he had won the Spring version over two miles by a nose from **Erimo Expire**. Meisho Samson was favourite to win the Arima Kinen at Nakayama which, barring Admire Moon (by then already retired to stud), featured most of Japan's best middle-distance performers. However, all were eclipsed by 51/1-shot **Matsurida Gogh**, who had a good record at the track but had finished down the field in the two Tenno Sho races on his only previous starts in Group 1 company.

Meisho Samson had been an intended runner in the Prix de l'Arc de Triomphe until an outbreak of equine influenza in Japan in August. The effects of EI in Japan were nothing like as prolonged or as serious as the outbreak which took hold in Australia shortly afterwards, but other foreign ventures by Japanese horses in the autumn had to be cancelled as a result. The previous year's Melbourne Cup one-two, **Delta Blues** and **Pop Rock**, were denied another trip to Flemington but both put up their best performances of the year in the Japan Cup, Delta Blues finishing fifth and Pop Rock failing by just a head to collar Admire Moon. Pop Rock and Delta Blues had filled the positions behind **Inti Raimi** in a Group 2 at Kyoto prior to the Japan Cup. **Daiwa Major** was again the top older miler, winning the Yasuda Kinen from **Kongo Rikishio** and the Mile Championship (for the second year running) from **Super Hornet**. Daiwa Major began the year with third place behind Admire Moon in the Dubai Duty Free and maintained his position among the leading middle-distance performers as well by finishing third in the Arima Kinen for the second year running, his final start before retiring to stud. Japan Cup sixth **Chosan** gained his biggest win with a defeat of Agnes Ark and Daiwa Major in a Group 2 over nine furlongs at Tokyo in October. In addition to Admire Moon's win in Dubai, further Japanese success abroad came from **Shadow Gate**, who beat the previous year's winner **Cosmo Bulk** into second in the Singapore Airlines International Cup in May. Japan's dirt horses have so far struggled in the Dubai World Cup, and the latest to try, **Vermilion**, fared little better, finishing a well-held fourth at Nad Al Sheba. On home soil, though, Vermilion was seen to far better effect in the Japan Cup Dirt, which he won in track-record time from **Field Rouge** and the February Stakes winner **Sunrise Bacchus**. Vermilion's win was one of the domestic highlights of the year for jockey Yutaka Take,

Japan Cup, Tokyo—another huge prize goes to Japanese Horse of The Year Admire Moon (right) but he only just holds on from Pop Rock (left) as pacesetter Chosan (second right) fades to finish sixth

Japan Cup Dirt, Tokyo—a smooth win in track-record time for Vermilion ahead of Field Rouge; winning rider Yutaka Take became the JRA's most successful jockey by career wins during the year and the first to ride three thousand winners

who earlier in the season set a new record for number of career wins under JRA auspices and subsequently became the first Japanese rider to record three thousand wins in JRA races. For the second year running, Japan's sprinters lacked a performer of real note. **Suzuka Phoenix** had the strongest claims to being the best over sprint trips with his win in the Takamatsunomiya Kinen, but he was just as effective at a mile as he proved with third place behind Daiwa Major in the Mile Championship.

The three-year-olds also lacked an outstanding performer, and unusually, a pair of fillies headed the classic generation. **Vodka** beat **Daiwa Scarlet** by a neck in a Group 3 trial for the Oka Sho (1000 Guineas) but in three subsequent meetings at Group 1 level, it was Daiwa Scarlet who came out on top. Vodka was runner-up to Daiwa Scarlet in the 1000 Guineas itself and finished third to her in the Shuka Sho in their next clash in the autumn, while in the Arima Kinen at the end of the year, Daiwa Scarlet fared much the better of the pair, beating her half-brother Daiwa Major to the runner-up spot with Vodka down the field. Daiwa Scarlet's third Group 1 win came against older fillies and mares in the Queen Elizabeth II Commemorative Cup in which she beat the previous year's winner **Fusaichi Pandora**. Vodka was not quite the best of her sex but she did become only the third filly ever (and the first since 1943) to win the Tokyo Yushun (Derby) and ran her best race afterwards when finishing strongly to be beaten just over a length into fourth in the Japan Cup. Vodka had been another intended challenger for the Arc but she was already ruled out of the race with an injury when EI struck. In the absence of the two leading fillies, a substandard Yushun Himba (Oaks) fell to the American-bred **Robe Decollete** who made little impact afterwards but nonetheless made her own piece of history as the first foreign-bred winner of a Japanese classic. Another three-year-old filly to make her mark was sprinter **Aston Machan**, though as has been noted, that wasn't a strong division and she won a substandard running of the Sprinters Stakes which was a wholly domestic affair due to the EI outbreak.

Derby runner-up **Asakusa Kings** was the leading three-year-old colt though he was no better than smart and had only a head to spare when beating **Al Nasrain** in the Kikuka Sho (St Leger) in the autumn. With neither of that pair running again, it was up to the St Leger third **Roc de Cambes** to represent the three-year-old colts in the Arima Kinen in which he finished a good fourth. The only three-year-old colts to contest the Japan Cup were well beaten, including the Satsuki Sho (2000 Guineas) winner **Victory**. **Dream Journey** contested all three colts' classics, his best placings coming when fifth in the Derby and St Leger, but in between he had Asakusa Kings and Victory placed behind him in a Group 2 St Leger trial at Hanshin over a mile and a half.

Three-Year-Olds

121	Daiwa Scarlet (f)	126	Pop Rock	117	Fast Tateyama
120	Vodka (f)	123	Daiwa Major	117	I'll Love Again
118	Asakusa Kings	122	Erimo Expire	117	King's Trail
117	Al Nasrain	122	Kongo Rikishio	117	Precise Machine
116	Dream Journey	122	Shadow Gate	117	Tokai Trick
116	Furioso	122	Vermilion	116	Blue Concorde
116	Roc de Cambes	120	Chosan	116	Bonneville Record
		120	Delta Blues	116	Company
114	Aston Machan (f)	120	Field Rouge	116	Daring Heart (f)
114	Victory	119	Cosmo Bulk	116	Koiuta (f)
110	Robe Decollete (f)	119	Sunrise Bacchus	116	Meiner Scherzi
107	Pink Cameo (f)	119	Super Hornet	116	Silk Nexus
		118	Admire Fuji	115	Asahi Rising (f)
		118	Dream Passport	115	Erimo Harrier
Older Horses		118	Inti Raimi	115	Fusaichi Pandora (f)
127	Admire Moon	118	Suzuka Phoenix	115	Fusaichi Richard
127	Matsurida Gogh	117	Agnes Ark	115	Tosho Knight
126	Meisho Samson	117	Eye Popper	115	Wild Wonder

HONG KONG   For the second year running, Hong Kong was home to the world's best sprinter, **Sacred Kingdom** taking that accolade from the previous year's winner **Absolute Champion** when beating him into second in the Hong Kong Sprint in December. Like all the other winners of the Hong Kong Sprint, which was first run in 1999 with listed status, Sacred Kingdom is an Australian-bred gelding. Unraced in his native country, he has been beaten only once in nine starts in Hong Kong and made constant progress before developing into a top-class sprinter late in the year. Prior to the Hong Kong Sprint,

Cathay Pacific Hong Kong Sprint, Sha Tin—Sacred Kingdom takes over the mantle of world's best sprinter from previous year's winner Absolute Champion (cheekpieces); Royal Delight (blinkers) is third after setting the pace

Audemars Piguet Queen Elizabeth II Cup, Sha Tin—Hong Kong's top middle-distance performers Viva Pataca and Vengeance of Rain clashed several times during the year, on this occasion the pair proving too good for an international field

he broke the track record in the International Sprint Trial from Absolute Champion and **Scintillation**. Both placed horses were successful in the big sprints early in the year. Absolute Champion gained his only success in 2007 in the Chairman's Sprint Prize, while Scintillation won the Bauhinia Sprint Trophy and the Centenary Sprint Cup (the latter from Absolute Champion) before ending the year with fourth place in the Hong Kong Sprint. Third place in the Hong Kong Sprint went to **Royal Delight** who had Absolute Champion and Scintillation (both giving plenty of weight) among those behind him in the Premier Bowl, a Group 3 handicap, earlier in the autumn. Progressive as he was, Sacred Kingdom lost out to another up-and-coming sprinter **Medic Power** for the title of Most Improved Horse at the end of the 2006/7 Hong Kong season in July. Medic Power was unbeaten in six starts for the year by then, lowering the six-furlong track record in the Group 3 Sha Tin Vase Handicap in the last of them, the race in which Sacred Kingdom met with his only defeat when fourth. However, Medic Power was beaten in both his starts in the autumn, finishing third in the Premier Bowl and only eighth in the International Sprint Trial.

Hong Kong's other success among the four Group 1 International Races in December (now subtitled the 'Turf World Championships') was Mile winner **Good Ba Ba**, the biggest success so far for his trainer Andreas Schutz since moving from Germany in 2006. Better than ever in what was his third year in Hong Kong, Good Ba Ba took the International Mile Trial beforehand from **Floral Pegasus** and the Queen's Silver Jubilee Cup winner **Joyful Winner**, who were also the next Hong Kong-trained horses home in the Hong Kong Mile itself, finishing fourth and fifth. Good Ba Ba had taken his first scalp among the leading milers when beating Stewards' Cup winner **Armada** (runner-up in the 2006 Hong Kong Mile) in the Chairman's Trophy in March. Good Ba Ba was also among four Hong Kong-trained horses to contest the Yasuda Kinen (part of the Asian Mile Challenge) in Japan in June, and while finishing only seventh, fared best of the quartet. Also in the raiding party was **Able One**, who benefited from an enterprising ride to win the Hong Kong leg of the Asian Mile Challenge, the Champions Mile in April, from Joyful Winner, with Floral Pegasus and Good Ba Ba fourth and fifth, but failed to repeat the form. Floral

Pegasus won his first three starts in pattern races early in the year, including the Hong Kong Classic Mile and the Derby Trial over nine furlongs, but defeat in the Derby itself over another furlong, albeit by just a nose to **Vital King**, persuaded connections to return him to a mile for the rest of the year.

Over middle-distances, two horses dominated proceedings, with **Viva Pataca** and **Vengeance of Rain** clashing no fewer than six times during 2007. All bar one of their encounters went the way of Viva Pataca, but when the 2006/7 season awards were given out early in July, it was Vengeance of Rain who took the honours both as Horse of The Year and as Most Popular Horse of The Year. Vengeance of Rain had been the final winner of the World Racing Championship in 2005 when wins in the Queen Elizabeth II Cup and Hong Kong Cup enabled him to win the series without setting foot outside Hong Kong. A troubled 2006 campaign followed, though third place in the Hong Kong Cup (with Viva Pataca fourth) at the end of that year showed he retained plenty of ability. In 2007, Vengeance of Rain was right back to form, getting first run on Viva Pataca when beating him a neck in the Hong Kong Gold Cup in March and later in the month belatedly proving himself abroad with a win in the Dubai Sheema Classic which must have gone a long way to securing his Horse of The Year title. From then on though, Viva Pataca was securely on top, beating Vengeance of Rain into second in their next two meetings in the Queen Elizabeth II Cup and the mile and a half Champions & Chater Cup, which Viva Pataca took for the second year. Whilst Vengeance of Rain struggled for form in the new season later in the year, Viva Pataca remained in good heart, winning the International Cup Trial and finding only Ramonti too good in the Hong Kong Cup itself, in which Vengeance of Rain finished only sixth of the seven runners. Vengeance of Rain was not the only Hong Kong horse to run with distinction in Dubai. Eight-year-old **Bullish Luck** was the outsider of the field in the Dubai World Cup but was not at all discredited in being beaten just under ten lengths into third after filling the same position, but beaten only two necks, behind Vengeance of Rain and Viva Pataca in the Hong Kong Gold Cup.

2007 saw the retirement of two popular horses which have figured prominently among Hong Kong's best performers in recent years. Silent Witness, whose seventeen-race winning sequence included the 2003 and 2004 Hong Kong Sprints, was retired after two runs early in the year, while **The Duke** bowed out after contesting his fourth consecutive Hong Kong Mile in December, a race he won in 2006. Although only seventh on his final start, The Duke retained plenty of ability as he showed with third place in the Champions Mile.

131	†Sacred Kingdom	122?	Royal Delight	117	Sir Ernesto
126	Absolute Champion	121	Able One	116	Packing Winner
125	Good Ba Ba	120	Bullish Luck	116	Syllabus
125	Viva Pataca	119	Hello Pretty	115	Art Trader
124	Vengeance of Rain	119	The Duke	115	Medic Power
123	Armada	118	Vital King	115	Sunny Power
123	Scintillation	117	Down Town		
122	Floral Pegasus	117	Joyful Winner		

AUSTRALIA AND NEW ZEALAND   The biggest event which overshadowed all racing in Australia in 2007 was the detection of Equine Influenza at the Eastern Creek Quarantine Centre outside Sydney and the subsequent outbreak of the disease across most of New South Wales and south-east Queensland, bringing racing to a standstill in those major centres for almost a hundred days. August 25th was a defining day in Australian racing, with officials across the country agreeing to cancel all race meetings set for that day when it was learned that EI had spread to the Centennial Park Horse Centre in close proximity to Sydney's Randwick racecourse. A range of protocols banning horse movements across Australia was immediately implemented which put a stop to racing in all States while the Department of Primary Industries and officials tried to determine the extent of the outbreak. The immediate impact on the racing industry as a whole was severe, but fortunately the protocols put in place prevented EI from spreading any further. Slowly, racing returned to normal in the non-affected States, while 'closed' meetings (defined as those at which only horses trained on a particular course could compete) were held in some EI-free zones in New South Wales and Queensland.

The Sydney Spring Carnival was abandoned, resulting in the loss of several Group 1 events, but since Victoria had remained free of EI, the Victorian Spring Carnival and Melbourne Cup Carnival progressed as normal, except that horses from New South Wales and Queensland were prevented from travelling to compete, thereby depriving the meeting of several smart performers. In addition, the Melbourne Carnival lost several possible overseas runners. Hong Kong's Viva Pataca, for example, missed the Cox Plate amid fears that he could become stranded in Victoria if EI was to break out there as well. The impact of EI on the quality of racing in Victoria and elsewhere was quite severe; the better contests for two- and three-year-olds in Melbourne in general took less winning than in a normal year and most pattern races lacked their usual strength. Following the implementation of a successful inoculation programme for all horses in the affected areas which did not contract EI, racing resumed at Sydney and Brisbane tracks, as well as at major provincial centres, on December 1st, though with alterations to race programmes to cater for the horses available to compete. The impact of EI will continue to be felt for at least the first half of 2008, with several feature race dates being pushed back to allow trainers more time to prepare their best horses, among them the traditional AJC Easter Carnival and Golden Slipper Carnivals which have been postponed by up to a month.

The 2007 racing year saw one of the most successful owner-trainer partnerships draw to a close when John Hawkes relinquished his role as head trainer to major owners the Ingham family. The Hawkes/Ingham era will be best remembered for their champions Octagonal and Lonhro, while in total the partnership won almost five hundred pattern races, including 82 Group 1 successes, and more than A\$165 million in stakes earnings.

The ratings are jointly headed by the Gai Waterhouse-trained **Desert War** and the Lee Freedman-trained sprinter **Miss Andretti**. Desert War suffered a leg injury in August which ruled him out for the rest of the year, but the free-going eight-year-old gained decisive Group 1 wins over ten furlongs in the Ranvet Stakes at Rosehill and the Queen Elizabeth Stakes at Randwick. Miss Andretti raced with distinction in both Australia and Britain, remaining undefeated at home. Her only defeats in eight starts came on rain-affected going in the Golden Jubilee Stakes at Royal Ascot, and in the Hong Kong Sprint. Otherwise, she was successful four times at Group 1 level in Australia in the Lightning Stakes, Newmarket Handicap, Australia Stakes and The Age Classic, while her

Emirates Melbourne Cup (Handicap), Flemington—the grey Efficient returns to form with a bang to deny a couple of Europe's challengers; Ebor winner Purple Moon (right) is beaten only half a length ahead of another son of Galileo, St Leger runner-up Mahler

King's Stand victory made her the third Australian sprinter to enjoy success at Royal Ascot in five years.

Cox Plate winner **El Segundo** atoned for his narrow second in the 2006 renewal by sweeping to a convincing victory at Moonee Valley. The lightly-raced six-year-old was better than ever in 2007 and performed consistently throughout the year, winning four pattern races in all including the C F Orr Stakes. The best male sprinter was **Takeover Target** who returned to Group 1-winning form on home soil in May in the Doomben 10,000. After a narrow defeat in the Golden Jubilee Stakes at Royal Ascot, Takeover Target's campaign later in the year was curtailed by EI, with the gelding prevented from travelling to Melbourne for further clashes with Miss Andretti and Gold Edition. However, he resumed with two wins under top weight at Randwick when the track re-opened in December, the smart **Dance Hero** among his rivals on both occasions.

The four-year-old category was jointly headed by **Haradasun** and **Mentality**. Before the start of his four-year-old season Coolmore purchased a half-share in Haradasun (a half-brother to the 2005 Dubai Duty Free winner Elvstroem) for a reported A$22 million. Early in the year, Haradasun suffered from hoof problems, but, back at full fitness, he gained Group 1 wins in the George Ryder Stakes and Doncaster Handicap and finished out of the prize money just once in thirteen starts. Haradasun has joined Aidan O'Brien for a European campaign in 2008 when he is likely to contest top mile races. Mentality raced with distinction throughout 2007, winning the Randwick Guineas before finishing a close second to Haradasun in both the George Ryder Stakes and the Doncaster Handicap. **Gold Edition** earned the tag of 'iron filly' as she raced for almost the full year without a break, notching seven wins from sixteen starts. Her only Group 1 win came in the Manikato Stakes at Moonee Valley, but she was runner-up to crack sprinter Takeover Target in the Doomben 10,000, second to **Sniper's Bullet** in the Stradbroke Handicap at Eagle Farm and went down twice to Miss Andretti in close finishes to the Newmarket Handicap and The Age Classic. 2006 Victoria Derby winner **Efficient** shrugged off some indifferent form over much shorter trips to win the Melbourne Cup with a strong late run to defeat the European-trained pair Purple Moon and Mahler. Efficient became only the second VRC Derby winner to win the following year's Melbourne Cup after the mighty Phar Lap in 1929/30. The AJC Australian Derby was won by **Fiumicino**, who ploughed through the mud to win easily. He was another Caulfield/Melbourne Cup contender denied the opportunity of competing in Melbourne due to EI. Another highly rated four-year-old filly was the multiple Group 1 winner and 2006 VRC Oaks winner **Miss Finland**, who beat male rivals in the Australian Guineas and Group 2 Memsie Stakes, in the latter defeating Haradasun in a tight finish.

Weekend Hussler led the three-year-old age-group. A late starter to racing who did not make his debut until mid-August, Weekend Hussler raced seven times for five wins, including two at Group 1 level, the Caulfield Guineas (the third-highest rated winner of that event in the last twenty years) and the six-furlong Ascot Vale Stakes. The Gai Waterhouse-trained **Meurice**, winner of the Champagne Stakes in April, did not race in the last half of the year due to EI in New South Wales and subsequently he had to be put down after breaking a shoulder early in 2008. AJC Sires' Produce Stakes winner **Camarilla** was the best three-year-old filly ahead of **Forensics**, who had **Zizou** and Meurice placed behind her in the Golden Slipper.

Juvenile racing was significantly curtailed due to EI, with only a handful of pattern races being held. However, the Lee Freedman-trained Exceed And Excel colt **Exceedingly Good** made it two wins from as many starts when beating the best field of juveniles assembled in 2007 in the Maribyrnong Plate over the straight five furlongs at Flemington. The highest-rated juvenile filly **Hips Don't Lie** was also the winner of both her starts, while another filly to emerge late in the year was **De Lightning Ridge**, who scored effortlessly by six and a half lengths (with a further nine lengths to the third) in the Black Opal Qualifier at Canberra late in the season.

As well as the total of five Australian sprinters who ran in Europe in the latest season (those not already mentioned were **Bentley Biscuit**, **Magnus** and **Mutawaajid**), other Australian runners of note overseas were the Dubai Carnival winners **Benedetti** and Smart And Mighty (rated 107), and the David Hayes-trained **Anamato** who was third in the American Oaks at Hollywood.

Ratings and text for Australia and New Zealand are supplied courtesy of Gary Crispe (www.racingandsports.com.au) The ages listed below are as at 31st December 2007

Two-Year-Olds

116p	Exceedingly Good
113	Nato
113	Reaan
112p	Hips Don't Lie (f)
111	Sugar Babe (f)
109+	De Lightning Ridge (f)
109	Marveen (f)
109	Pachanga (f)
109	Starfish (f)
107	Ballerina Girl (f)
107	Kalash
107	Percussive (f)
106	Emma Princess (f)
106	San Bernardino
106	Woppitt (f)

Three-Year-Olds

125p	Weekend Hussler
123	Meurice
122?	Zizou
121	Camarilla (f)
120	Forensics (f)
120	Murtajill
119	Shaft
119	Solo Flyer
118p	Kibbutz
118	Deferential
118	Marching
118?	Husson Lightning
117p	Danehill Smile (f)
117	Arapaho Miss (f)
117	Royal Asscher (f)
117	Sleek Chassis (f)
116p	Sliding Cube (f)
116	Chinchilla Rose (f)
116	Gabbidon (f)
116	Gamble Me (f)
116	Mimi Lebrock (f)
116	Scenic Blast
116	Serious Speed (f)
116	Shrewd Rhythm

116	Tan Tat de Lago (f)
116	Warhead
116?	Press The Button (f)
115	Masked Assassin
115?	I Have No Fear (f)
115?	Schilling
115?	Wind Shear

Four-Year-Olds

126	Haradasun
126	Mentality
125	Gold Edition (f)
123	Efficient
123	He's No Pie Eater
122	Casino Prince
122	Fiumicino
122	Miss Finland (f)
121	Jokers Wild
121	†Mutawaajid
121	Sniper's Bullet
121	Teranaba
120	Tipungwuti
119	Sirmione
119	Tuesday Joy (f)
119	Wonderful World
118	Ambitious General
118	Gorky Park
117	Reigning To Win
116	Danleigh
116	Devil Moon (f)
116	Here de Angels
116	Raheeb
116	Universal Queen (f)
116?	Banc de Fortune (f)
116?	Our Maharaja
115	Anamato (f)
115	Cheeky Choice (f)
115	Dorabella (f)
115	Lucky Secret
115	Magic Cape
115	Princess Coup (f)
115	Vormista (f)
115	Zupaone

Older Horses

127	Desert War
127	†Miss Andretti (f)
126	Marasco
126	†Takeover Target
125	Apache Cat
125	El Segundo
125	Maldivian

125	Pompeii Ruler
122	†Bentley Biscuit
122	Blutigeroo
122	†Magnus
122	Mitanni
122	Natural Destiny
122	Rubiscent
122?	Black Ink
122?	Tawqeet
120	Aqua d'Amore (f)
120	Divine Madonna (f)
120	Niconero
120	Spark of Life
120	Undue
119	Zipping
119?	Casual Pass
119d	Confectioner
118	Dance Hero
118	Eremein
118	German Chocolate
118d	Railings
117	Honor In War
117	Let Go Thommo
117	Master O'Reilly
117	Sir Slick
117	Sonic Quest
117?	Lad of The Manor
116	Benedetti
116	Bon Hoffa
116	Cog Hill
116	Mandela
116	Maybe Better
116	Regal Cheer (f)
116	Seachange (f)
116	Tesbury Jack
116	Xcellent
116?	Blue Monday
116?	Coalesce
116?	Scenic Shot
115	Beauty Watch (f)
115	Cinque Cento (f)
115	County Tyrone
115	Daunting Lad
115	Fast 'n' Famous
115	Gallic
115	Shadoways
115	Stanzout
115	Valedictum
115?	Annenkov

Timeform Horse of the Year

Timeform's 'Racehorses' series stretches back to 1948 when the first prototype Annual—the 'Timeform Supplement'—was produced covering the 1947 season. The selecting of a 'horse of the year' began in the 'sixties. The title has usually been awarded to the highest rated horse, except in 1969 (when Habitat was rated higher at 134), 1984 (El Gran Senor 136), 1985 (Slip Anchor 136) and 2003 (Hawk Wing 136).

1960	Charlottesville	135	1983	Habibti	136
	Floribunda	135	1984	Provideo	112
1961	Molvedo	137	1985	Pebbles	135
1962	Match	135	1986	Dancing Brave	140
1963	Exbury	138	1987	Reference Point	139
1964	Relko	136	1988	Warning	136
1965	Sea Bird	145	1989	Zilzal	137
1966	Danseur	134	1990	Dayjur	137
1967	Petingo	135	1991	Generous	139
1968	Vaguely Noble	140	1992	St Jovite	135
1969	Levmoss	133	1993	Opera House	131
1970	Nijinsky	138	1994	Celtic Swing	138
1971	Brigadier Gerard	141	1995	Lammtarra	134
	Mill Reef	141	1996	Mark of Esteem	137
1972	Brigadier Gerard	144	1997	Peintre Celebre	137
1973	Apalachee	137	1998	Intikhab	135
	Rheingold	137	1999	Daylami	138
1974	Allez France	136	2000	Dubai Millennium	140
1975	Grundy	137	2001	Sakhee	136
1976	Youth	135	2002	Rock of Gibraltar	133
1977	Alleged	137	2003	Falbrav	133
1978	Alleged	138	2004	Doyen	132
1979	Troy	137	2005	Hurricane Run	134
1980	Moorestyle	137	2006	George Washington	133
1981	Shergar	140	2007	Manduro	135
1982	Ardross	134			

INDEX TO PHOTOGRAPHS

PORTRAITS & SNAPSHOTS

RACE PHOTOGRAPHS

Darley Prix Morny (Deauville)	*Bill Selwyn*	731
Darley Yorkshire Oaks (York)	*Alec Russell*	807
Deloitte Autumn Stakes (Ascot)	*John Crofts*	491
Derrinstown Stud Derby Trial Stakes (Leopardstown)	*Caroline Norris*	70
Deutschlandpreis (Dusseldorf)	*Frank Sorge*	952
Dimitrova 1000 Guineas Trial Stakes (Leopardstown)	*Peter Mooney*	71
Doncaster Audi Stakes (Handicap) (Doncaster)	*Ed Byrne*	409
Dubai Duty Free Arc Trial (Newbury)	*John Crofts*	451
Dubai Duty Free Mill Reef Stakes (Newbury)	*John Crofts*	266
Dubai International Airport World Trophy (Newbury)	*John Crofts*	918
Dubai World Cup Sponsored By Emirates Airline (Nad Al Sheba)	*Bill Selwyn*	509
Duke of Edinburgh Stakes (Handicap) (Royal Ascot)	*Bill Selwyn*	818
Duke of York Hearthstead Homes Stakes (York)	*Alec Russell*	53
EBF Pricewaterhousecoopers Harvest Stakes (Ascot)	*George Selwyn*	162
Emirates Airline Champion Stakes (Newmarket)	*John Crofts*	608
Emirates Airline Yorkshire Cup (York)	*Bill Selwyn*	968
Empire Property Group On The House Stakes (Goodwood)	*Bill Selwyn*	311
European Breeders' Fund Lansdown Fillies' Stakes (Bath)	*Bill Selwyn*	345
Floodlit Stakes (Kempton)	*George Selwyn*	256
Frenchgate First For Fashion May Hill Stakes (Doncaster)	*George Selwyn*	1020
Galileo EBF Futurity Stakes (the Curragh)	*Caroline Norris*	749
Georgia House Stud Darley Stakes (Newmarket)	*John Crofts*	1164
GNER Doncaster Cup (Doncaster)	*Alec Russell*	966
GNER Park Stakes (Doncaster)	*Ed Byrne*	68
Goffs/DBS Park Hill Stakes (Doncaster)	*John Crofts*	471
Golden Jubilee Stakes (Royal Ascot)	*George Selwyn*	1012
Gold Cup (Royal Ascot)	*John Crofts*	1179
Goldring Security Services Pembroke Cup (Handicap) (Salisbury)	*Bill Selwyn*	792
Gordon Stakes (Goodwood)	*George Selwyn*	1182
Gran Criterium (Milan)	*Stefano Grasso*	954
Grand Prix de Deauville Lucien Barriere (Deauville)	*Frank Sorge*	513
Grand Prix de Saint-Cloud (Saint-Cloud)	*Ed Byrne*	712
Grosser Dallmayr-Preis - Bayerisches Zuchtrennen (Munich)	*Frank Sorge*	1006
Grosser Preis von Baden (Baden-Baden)	*Frank Sorge*	862
Grosvenor Casinos Cumberland Lodge Stakes (Ascot)	*Ed Byrne*	80
Hampton Court Stakes (Ascot)	*John Crofts*	1188
Hardwicke Stakes (Royal Ascot)	*John Crofts*	658
HBLB Lancashire Oaks (Newmarket)	*John Crofts*	1120
Hong Kong Jockey Club Sprint (Handicap) (Ascot)	*Bill Selwyn*	1041
IG Index EBF Maiden Stakes (York)	*Alec Russell*	173
Igloos Bentinck Stakes (Newmarket)	*Ed Byrne*	442
Independent Waterford Wedgwood Phoenix Stakes (the Curragh)	*Caroline Norris*	942
intercasino.co.uk Easter Stakes (Kempton)	*John Crofts*	306
intercasino.co.uk Magnolia Stakes (Kempton)	*John Crofts*	498
intercasino.co.uk Rosebery Stakes (Handicap) (Kempton)	*John Crofts*	622
Invesco Perpetual Goodwood Stakes (Handicap) (Goodwood)	*John Crofts*	960
Ireland Gimcrack Stakes (York)	*Alec Russell*	991
Irish Field St Leger (the Curragh)	*Caroline Norris*	1180
Irish National Stud Blandford Stakes (the Curragh)	*Peter Mooney*	397
Irish Stallion Farms EBF Brownstown Stakes (Leopardstown)	*Caroline Norris*	889
Irish Stallion Farms EBF Fillies Maiden (Leopardstown)	*Peter Mooney*	47
Iveco Solario Stakes (Sandown)	*John Crofts*	877
IVG - Preis von Europa (Cologne)	*Frank Sorge*	953
Jaguar Cars Lowther Stakes (York)	*Ed Byrne*	738
Jockey Club Cup (Newmarket)	*Alec Russell*	919
John Guest Diadem Stakes (Ascot)	*John Crofts*	449
John Roarty Memorial Scurry Handicap (the Curragh)	*Caroline Norris*	632
John Smith's Cup (Handicap) (York)	*Alec Russell*	199
John Smith's Northumberland Plate (Newcastle)	*Alec Russell*	532
John Smith's Stakes (Handicap) (Newbury)	*John Crofts*	704
Juddmonte Grand Prix de Paris (Longchamp)	*Bertrand*	1191
Juddmonte International Stakes (York)	*Alec Russell*	96
Juddmonte Lockinge Stakes (Newbury)	*George Selwyn*	885
Juddmonte Royal Lodge Stakes (Ascot)	*Ed Byrne*	208
Killavullan Stakes (Leopardstown)	*Caroline Norris*	534
Kingdom of Bahrain Sun Chariot Stakes (Newmarket)	*Ed Byrne*	641
King Edward VII Stakes (Royal Ascot)	*George Selwyn*	156

King George V Stakes (Handicap) (Royal Ascot)	*John Crofts*	470
King George VI and Queen Elizabeth Stakes (Ascot)	*John Crofts*	316
King's Stand Stakes (Royal Ascot)	*Caroline Norris*	688
Kleinwort Benson Stakes (Handicap) (Newmarket)	*John Crofts*	462
Ladbrokes Bunbury Cup (Newmarket)	*John Crofts*	423
ladbrokes.com Stakes (Handicap) (Ascot)	*John Crofts*	165
Ladbrokes Fred Archer Stakes (Newmarket)	*John Crofts*	210
Ladbrokes Great Voltigeur Stakes (York)	*Ed Byrne*	622
Ladbrokes Portland (Handicap) (Doncaster)	*Ed Byrne*	402
Ladbrokes St Leger Stakes (Doncaster)	*John Crofts*	623
Lanwades & Staffordstown Studs Stakes (the Curragh)	*Caroline Norris*	949
Laurent-Perrier Champagne Sprint Stakes (Sandown)	*George Selwyn*	479
Man o'War Stakes (Belmont)	*International Racing Photos*	290
Meon Valley Stud Fillies' Mile (Ascot)	*John Crofts*	605
Mountgrange Stud Stakes (Horris Hill) (Newbury)	*John Crofts*	118
Moyglare Stud Stakes (the Curragh)	*Caroline Norris*	943
Naas Sprint Stakes (Naas)	*Caroline Norris*	1073
National Bank of Dubai Cup (Handicap) (Ascot)	*John Crofts*	1084
Nolan & Brophy Auctioneers Flying Five Stakes (the Curragh)	*Caroline Norris*	126
Norfolk Stakes (Royal Ascot)	*George Selwyn*	1166
paddypower.com Sprint Trophy (Handicap) (York)	*Alec Russell*	392
Parknasilla Hotel Goffs (C&G) Million (the Curragh)	*Caroline Norris*	626
Parknasilla Hotel Goffs Fillies Million (the Curragh)	*Caroline Norris*	629
Patrick P. O'Leary Memorial Phoenix Sprint Stakes (the Curragh)	*Peter Mooney*	51
Play Casino At ladbrokes.com Stakes (Golden Rose) (Lingfield)	*David Williams*	646
Polypipe Flying Childers Stakes (Doncaster)	*Ed Byrne*	385
Pomfret Stakes (Pontefract)	*Alec Russell*	144
Poule d'Essai des Poulains (Longchamp)	*Bertrand*	84
Poule d'Essai des Pouliches (Longchamp)	*Bertrand*	261
Premio Roma At The Races (Rome)	*Stefano Grasso*	840
Prince of Wales's Stakes (Royal Ascot)	*Ed Byrne*	651
Princess of Wales's wbx.com Stakes (Newmarket)	*George Selwyn*	794
Princess Royal Willmott Dixon Stakes (Ascot)	*John Crofts*	1114
Prix Chaudenay Casino Barriere de Menton (Longchamp)	*Bertrand*	213
Prix Daniel Wildenstein Castel Marie-Louise de La Baule (Longchamp)	*Bertrand*	1026
Prix d'Astarte (Deauville)	*Bertrand*	262
Prix de Diane Hermes (Chantilly)	*Bertrand*	1155
Prix de l'Abbaye de Longchamp Majestic Barriere de Cannes (Longchamp)	*Ed Byrne*	127
Prix de la Foret Casino Barriere de Biarritz (Longchamp)	*Bertrand*	1109
Prix de l'Arc de Triomphe Lucien Barriere (Longchamp)	*Bertrand*	319
Prix de l'Opera Casino Barriere d'Enghien Les Bains (Longchamp)	*Bertrand*	947
Prix de Royallieu Hotel Hermitage Barriere de La Baule (Longchamp)	*George Selwyn*	60
Prix de Saint-Georges (Longchamp)	*Bertrand*	802
Prix d'Ispahan (Longchamp)	*Bertrand*	650
Prix du Cadran Casino-Theatre Barriere de Toulouse (Longchamp)	*Bertrand*	590
Prix du Calvados - Haras des Capucines (Deauville)	*George Selwyn*	852
Prix du Gros-Chene Mitsubishi Motors (Chantilly)	*Ed Byrne*	120
Prix du Haras de Fresnay-le-Buffard-Jacques le Marois (Deauville)	*Bertrand*	652
Prix du Jockey Club Mitsubishi Motors (Chantilly)	*Bertrand*	583
Prix Eugene Adam (Maisons-Laffitte)	*Bertrand*	455
Prix Foy Gray d'Albion Barriere (Longchamp)	*Bertrand*	653
Prix Ganay (Longchamp)	*Bertrand*	315
Prix Jean-Luc Lagardere (Grand Criterium) (Longchamp)	*Frank Sorge*	902
Prix Jean Prat (Chantilly)	*Bertrand*	584
Prix Marcel Boussac - Criterium des Pouliches Royal Barriere de Deauville (Longchamp)	*Bill Selwyn*	1195
Prix Maurice de Gheest (Deauville)	*Bertrand*	659
Prix Niel Casino Barriere d'Enghien Les Bains (Longchamp)	*Ed Byrne*	1009
Prix Royal-Oak - Principaute de Monaco (Longchamp)	*Bertrand*	45
Prix Vermeille Lucien Barriere (Longchamp)	*Frank Sorge*	718

Qatar Prix du Moulin de Longchamp (Longchamp)	*Bill Selwyn*	263
Queen Alexandra Stakes (Royal Ascot)	*Bill Selwyn*	344
Queen Anne Stakes (Royal Ascot)	*Frank Sorge*	869
Queen Elizabeth II Stakes (Ascot)	*John Crofts*	871
Queen Mary Stakes (Royal Ascot)	*John Crofts*	337
Queen's Vase (Royal Ascot)	*John Crofts*	638
Racing Post Trophy (Doncaster)	*Alec Russell*	492
Rheinland-Pokal der Sparkasse KolnBonn (Cologne)	*Frank Sorge*	929
Ribblesdale Stakes (Royal Ascot)	*John Crofts*	984
Richmond Stakes (Goodwood)	*Bill Selwyn*	1046
Ridgewood Pearl Stakes (the Curragh)	*Bill Selwyn*	203
Royal Hunt Cup (Handicap) (Royal Ascot)	*John Crofts*	922
Sandringham Handicap (Royal Ascot)	*Bill Selwyn*	114
Seriousquitters.co.uk Rockfel Stakes (Newmarket)	*Ed Byrne*	560
Shadwell Middle Park Stakes (Newmarket)	*Alec Russell*	267
Sixty Years of Timeform Stakes (Handicap) (York)	*John Crofts*	341
SKF City of York Stakes (York)	*Alec Russell*	308
skybet.com Cheveley Park Stakes (Newmarket)	*Ed Byrne*	742
Sodexho Prestige Shergar Cup Mile (Handicap) (Ascot)	*Bill Selwyn*	124
Somerville Tattersall Stakes (Newmarket)	*Ed Byrne*	908
Space Property Rosemary Stakes (Handicap) (Ascot)	*John Crofts*	815
Stan James 1000 Guineas Stakes (Newmarket)	*Ed Byrne*	376
Stan James 2000 Guineas Stakes (Newmarket)	*Frank Sorge*	214
Stan James 2000 Guineas Stakes (Newmarket)	*George Selwyn*	216
StanJamesUK.com Jockey Club Stakes (Newmarket)	*John Crofts*	995
StanJamesUK.com Stakes (Handicap) (Newmarket)	*Ed Byrne*	121
StanJamesUK.com Suffolk Stakes (Handicap) (Newmarket)	*John Crofts*	1054
Starair Kilternan Stakes (Leopardstown)	*Ed Byrne*	463
St James's Palace Stakes (Royal Ascot)	*Alec Russell*	353
Swordlestown Stud Sprint Stakes (Naas)	*Caroline Norris*	1186
Tattersalls Gold Cup (the Curragh)	*Peter Mooney*	769
Tattersalls Ireland Sale Stakes (the Curragh)	*Caroline Norris*	1049
Tattersalls Millions Acomb Stakes (York)	*Alec Russell*	366
Tattersalls Millions Irish Champion Stakes (Leopardstown)	*Ed Byrne*	317
Tattersalls Musidora Stakes (York)	*George Selwyn*	799
The Age Classic (Flemington)	*Bronwen Healy*	689
£300000 St Leger Yearling Stakes (York)	*Bill Selwyn*	265
Timeform Silver Salver (Cecil Frail) (Haydock)	*Alec Russell*	186
TNT July Stakes (Newmarket)	*George Selwyn*	1167
totepool August Stakes (Windsor)	*John Crofts*	299
totepool Beverley Bullet Sprint Stakes (Beverley)	*Alec Russell*	466
totepool September Stakes (Kempton)	*John Crofts*	1038
totescoop6 Prestige Stakes (Goodwood)	*John Crofts*	964
totescoop6 Sirenia Stakes (Kempton)	*John Crofts*	819
totescoop6 Stakes (Handicap) (Sandown)	*John Crofts*	784
totescoop6 Two-Year-Old Trophy (Redcar)	*Alec Russell*	305
totesport Chester Cup (Handicap) (Chester)	*Alec Russell*	444
totesport.com Ayr Gold Cup (Handicap) (Ayr)	*Alec Russell*	32
totesport.com Ayr Silver Cup (Handicap) (Ayr)	*Alec Russell*	1131
totesport.com Cambridgeshire (Handicap) (Newmarket)	*Ed Byrne*	826
totesport.com Celebration Mile (Goodwood)	*John Crofts*	327
totesport.com Challenge Cup (Handicap) (Ascot)	*Ed Byrne*	176
totesport.com Dante Stakes (York)	*John Crofts*	90
totesport.com International Stakes (Handicap) (Ascot)	*John Crofts*	1091
totesport.com London Mile Handicap (Series Final) (Kempton)	*John Crofts*	636
totesport.com November Stakes (Handicap) (Doncaster)	*Alec Russell*	647
totesport.com Old Newton Cup Stakes (Handicap) (Haydock)	*Alec Russell*	257
totesport.com Silver Bowl (Handicap) (Haydock)	*Alec Russell*	1101
totesport.com Sovereign Stakes (Salisbury)	*Bill Selwyn*	843
totesport.com Stakes (Handicap) (Newmarket)	*John Crofts*	979
totesport.com Winter Hill Stakes (Windsor)	*John Crofts*	858
totesport Derby Trial Stakes (Lingfield)	*John Crofts*	66
totesport Ebor (Handicap) (York)	*John Crofts*	855
totesport Mile (Handicap) (Goodwood)	*George Selwyn*	1092
totesport Pontefract Castle Stakes (Pontefract)	*Alec Russell*	518
TurfTV Strensall Stakes (York)	*Alec Russell*	330
£2.5 Million totescoop6 Cesarewitch (Handicap) (Newmarket)	*Bill Selwyn*	588

ADDITIONAL PHOTOGRAPHS

The following photographs appear in the Introduction:– The Old Bailey (photo taken by George Selwyn), the Coolmore triumvirate (Peter Mooney), Prix de l'Arc de Triomphe (Bill Selwyn), Prince of Wales's Stakes (John Crofts), Henry Cecil and Aidan O'Brien (Bill Selwyn), Frankie Dettori (Bill Selwyn), Seb Sanders and Jamie Spencer (George Selwyn), Greg Fairley (Bill Selwyn), Kevin Darley (George Selwyn).

Credits for the photographs in 'Top Horses Abroad' are as follows:– Preis der Diana (Frank Sorge), Premio Presidente della Repubblica and Premio Lydia Tesio (Stefano Grasso), Dubai Sheema Classic (Frank Sorge), Dubai Golden Shaheen (Bill Selwyn), Belmont Stakes (International Racing Photos), Breeders' Cup Classic, Breeders' Cup Mile and Breeders' Cup Juvenile Fillies' (all Bill Selwyn), Breeders' Cup Distaff and Breeders' Cup Juvenile (Frank Sorge), Breeders' Cup Sprint, Breeders' Cup Turf, Breeders' Cup Filly & Mare Turf (all George Selwyn), Japan Cup (Bill Selwyn), Japan Cup Dirt (Keibabook), Hong Kong Sprint (George Selwyn), Melbourne Cup (Bronwen Healy).

By INDIAN RIDGE - NOSEY
by Nebbiolo

By INCHINOR -
RAMBLING ROSE
by Cadeaux Genereux

NOTNOWCATO

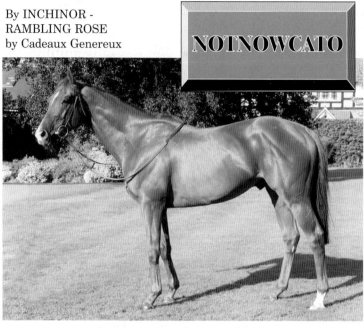

TRIPLE GROUP 1 WINNER

Won Gr.1 Coral Eclipse Stakes, 1m 2f, Sandown,
beating **AUTHORIZED** and **GEORGE WASHINGTON**

Won Gr.1 Tattersalls Gold Cup, 1m 2½f, The Curragh,
beating **DYLAN THOMAS**

Won Gr.1 Juddmonte International Stakes, 1m 2f, York,
beating **DYLAN THOMAS**

"Inchinor's premature death was keenly felt but he left some good ones
behind, and Notnowcato was the best of them...*As game as they come, he
is well bred on both sides of his pedigree*" *Thoroughbred Owner & Breeder*

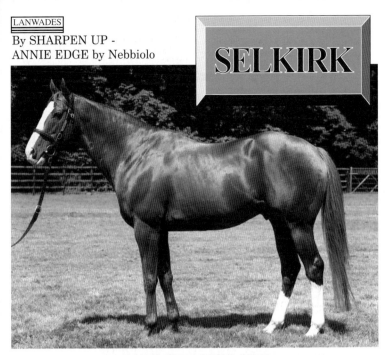

By FORZANDO -
DEVIL'S DIRGE by Song

THE RIGHT PLACE AT THE RIGHT TIME.

In-running place betting for ALL British and Irish racing – flat and jumps – now available at Betfair.

Try it today with your **FREE £20** bet.

Please gamble responsibly. Visit www.gambleaware.co.uk.

£20 FREE BET*

↟↟ betfair
sports casino poker

BETTING AS IT SHOULD BE.

AGE, WEIGHT & DISTANCE TABLE

Timeform's scale of weight-for-age for the flat

Dist	Age	July 1-16	July 17-31	Aug 1-16	Aug 17-31	Sept 1-16	Sept 17-30	Oct 1-16	Oct 17-31	Nov 1-16	Nov 17-30	Dec 1-16	Dec 17-31
5f	4	10-0	10-0	10-0	10-0	10-0	10-0	10-0	10-0	10-0	10-0	10-0	10-0
	3	9-11	9-12	9-12	9-12	9-13	9-13	9-13	9-13	10-0	10-0	10-0	10-0
	2	8-8	8-9	8-10	8-11	8-12	8-13	9-0	9-1	9-2	9-2	9-3	9-4
6f	4	10-0	10-0	10-0	10-0	10-0	10-0	10-0	10-0	10-0	10-0	10-0	10-0
	3	9-10	9-10	9-11	9-11	9-12	9-12	9-12	9-13	9-13	9-13	9-13	10-0
	2	8-5	8-6	8-7	8-8	8-9	8-10	8-11	8-12	8-13	9-0	9-1	9-2
7f	4	10-0	10-0	10-0	10-0	10-0	10-0	10-0	10-0	10-0	10-0	10-0	10-0
	3	9-9	9-9	9-10	9-10	9-11	9-11	9-11	9-12	9-12	9-12	9-13	9-13
	2	8-2	8-3	8-4	8-5	8-6	8-7	8-9	8-10	8-11	8-12	8-13	9-0
1m	4	10-0	10-0	10-0	10-0	10-0	10-0	10-0	10-0	10-0	10-0	10-0	10-0
	3	9-7	9-8	9-8	9-9	9-9	9-10	9-10	9-11	9-11	9-12	9-12	9-12
	2			8-2	8-3	8-4	8-5	8-6	8-7	8-8	8-9	8-10	8-11
9f	4	10-0	10-0	10-0	10-0	10-0	10-0	10-0	10-0	10-0	10-0	10-0	10-0
	3	9-6	9-7	9-7	9-8	9-8	9-9	9-9	9-10	9-10	9-11	9-11	9-12
	2					8-1	8-3	8-4	8-5	8-6	8-7	8-8	8-9
1¼m	4	10-0	10-0	10-0	10-0	10-0	10-0	10-0	10-0	10-0	10-0	10-0	10-0
	3	9-5	9-5	9-6	9-7	9-7	9-8	9-8	9-9	9-9	9-10	9-10	9-11
	2						8-0	8-1	8-2	8-4	8-5	8-6	8-7
11f	4	10-0	10-0	10-0	10-0	10-0	10-0	10-0	10-0	10-0	10-0	10-0	10-0
	3	9-3	9-4	9-5	9-5	9-6	9-7	9-7	9-8	9-8	9-9	9-9	9-10
1½m	4	10-0	10-0	10-0	10-0	10-0	10-0	10-0	10-0	10-0	10-0	10-0	10-0
	3	9-2	9-2	9-3	9-4	9-5	9-5	9-6	9-7	9-7	9-8	9-9	9-9
13f	4	9-13	9-13	10-0	10-0	10-0	10-0	10-0	10-0	10-0	10-0	10-0	10-0
	3	9-0	9-1	9-2	9-3	9-4	9-4	9-5	9-6	9-6	9-7	9-8	9-8
1¾m	4	9-13	9-13	9-13	10-0	10-0	10-0	10-0	10-0	10-0	10-0	10-0	10-0
	3	8-13	9-0	9-1	9-2	9-3	9-3	9-4	9-5	9-5	9-6	9-7	9-7
15f	4	9-12	9-13	9-13	9-13	9-13	10-0	10-0	10-0	10-0	10-0	10-0	10-0
	3	8-12	8-13	9-0	9-1	9-1	9-2	9-3	9-4	9-4	9-5	9-6	9-6
2m	4	9-12	9-12	9-13	9-13	9-13	9-13	10-0	10-0	10-0	10-0	10-0	10-0
	3	8-10	8-11	8-12	8-13	9-0	9-1	9-2	9-3	9-3	9-4	9-5	9-5
2¼m	4	9-11	9-12	9-12	9-12	9-13	9-13	9-13	9-13	10-0	10-0	10-0	10-0
	3	8-8	8-9	8-10	8-11	8-12	8-13	9-0	9-1	9-2	9-2	9-3	9-4
2½m	4	9-10	9-11	9-11	9-12	9-12	9-12	9-13	9-13	9-13	9-13	10-0	10-0
	3	8-6	8-7	8-8	8-9	8-10	8-11	8-12	8-13	9-0	9-1	9-2	9-3

For 5-y-o's and older, use 10-0 in all cases
Race distances in the above tables are shown only at 1 furlong intervals.
For races over odd distances, the nearest distance shown in the table should be used:
thus for races of 1m to 1m 109 yards, use the table weights for 1m;
for 1m 110 yards to 1m 219 yards use the 9f table

**The age, weight and distance table covering January to June
appears on the end paper at the front of the book**